Dictionary
OF THE Old Testament:
Historical Books

Editors:

Bill T. Arnold

H. G. M. Williamson

IVP Academic

An imprint of InterVarsity Press
Downers Grove, Illinois

Inter-Varsity Press
Nottingham, England

InterVarsity Press
P.O. Box 1400, Downers Grove, IL 60515-1426
ivpress.com
email@ivpress.com

Inter-Varsity Press, England
Norton Street, Nottingham NG7 3HR, England
ivpbooks.com
ivp@ivpbooks.com

InterVarsity Press® is the book-publishing division of InterVarsity Christian Fellowship/USA®, a movement of students and faculty active on campus at hundreds of universities, colleges, and schools of nursing in the United States of America, and a member movement of the International Fellowship of Evangelical Students. For information about local and regional activities, visit intervarsity.org.

Inter-Varsity Press, England, is closely linked with the Universities and Colleges Christian Fellowship (formerly the Inter-Varsity Fellowship), a student movement linking Christian Unions in universities and colleges throughout Great Britain, and a member movement of the International Fellowship of Evangelical Students. For information about local and national activities write to UCCF, 38 De Montfort Street, Leicester LE1 7GP, email them at email@uccf.org.uk, or visit the UCCF website at www.uccf.org.uk.

All Scripture quotations, unless otherwise indicated, are the authors' own translations.

The publisher cannot verify the accuracy or functionality of website URLs used in this book beyond the date of publication.

Cover design: David Fassett
Design: Cindy Kiple
Image: King David and musicians painting © De Agostini Picture Library / Bridgeman Images

USA ISBN 978-0-8308-1782-5
UK ISBN 978-1-84474-094-9

Printed in the United States of America ∞

InterVarsity Press is committed to ecological stewardship and to the conservation of natural resources in all our operations. This book was printed using sustainably sourced paper.

Library of Congress Cataloging-in-Publication Data

Dictionary of the Old Testament: hisorical books/editors, Bill T.
Arnold, H. G. M. Williamson
      p. cm.
   Includes bibliographical references and indexes.
   ISBN 0-8308-1782-4 (cloth: alk. paper)
   1. Bible. O.T. Historical books—Dictionaries. I. Arnold, Bill T.
   II Williamson, H. G. M. (Hugh Godfrey Maturin), 1947-
   BS1205.55.D53 2005
   222'.03—dc22

                                                            2005026648

British Library Cataloguing in Publication Data

A catalogue record for this book is available from the British Library.

P 36 35 34 33 32 31 30 29 28 27 26 25 24 23 22 21 20 19 18 17 16 15 14 13 12 11

Y 46 45 44 43 42 41 40 39 38 37 36 35 34 33 32 31 30 29 28 27 26 25 24 23 22 21

InterVarsity Press

Project Staff

Reference Book Editor/Project Editor
Daniel G. Reid

Managing Editor
Allison Rieck

Copyeditor
Robert G. Maccini

Editorial Assistant
Kristie Berglund

Design
Cindy Kiple

Design Assistant
Mark Eddy Smith

Typesetters
Gail Munroe
Maureen Tobey

Proofreaders
Drew Blankman
Bill Kerschbaum
Lisa Rieck
Elaina Whittenhall
David Zimmerman

Technical Support
Tricia Koning

InterVarsity Press

Publisher
Robert A. Fryling

Editorial Director
Andrew T. Le Peau

Associate Editorial Director
James Hoover

Production Manager
Anne Gerth

Print Coordinator
Jim Erhart

Contents

Preface

This volume takes its place in the well-established series of IVP dictionaries which have been proving to be so helpful to students of the Bible at all levels. It is our hope that the present volume will be found equally valuable.

There are, however, some particular problems that arise in treating the Historical Books of the Old Testament, so we should make our position on these clear to prospective readers.

First, here probably to a greater extent than elsewhere in the Bible it is necessary to be clear that *history* is a multifaceted word and that different people hear it to mean different things. The most obvious distinction is between history as what actually happened in the past and history as a written record of that past. While the two meanings naturally overlap, they are equally clearly not the same thing. No record of the past could hope to be fully comprehensive, for instance, so any written account is bound to be heavily selective in what it chooses to include. Furthermore, the record may be written with one or more of many possible purposes in view, and this too will affect the presentation.

In this dictionary we have tried to keep both points in view, and we hope that our readers will do the same as they approach each entry. On the one hand, for example, there are substantial articles that offer the best approximation the authors can achieve at a scholarly reconstruction of the past history of Israel in the various phases of its existence from Joshua to Nehemiah. For this, many sources besides the Bible need to be used, so often, as might be expected, the reconstruction may have a very different feel from the biblical account taken on its own. On the other hand, the entries on the books themselves generally tend to focus more on literary and theological issues and less on the historical events that they refer to in order to convey their message. Both approaches are legitimate and necessary for a full understanding of this part of the Bible, and we hope that the right balance has been struck in order for readers to have all the resources they need for answering the different questions that they will be bringing to the text.

Second, however, it is no secret that in some cases (particularly regarding the premonarchic period and the time of the united monarchy) there is at present a fierce scholarly debate about whether the gulf between history as a record of the past and the biblical material which relates to it is not so great as to be unbridgeable. On this we have had to take a clear and firm editorial line which will be fair both to our authors and to the texts. Clearly on the one hand it would not have been right to ask our scholarly colleagues to change their minds on issues they have pondered deeply and on which they have come to a decision after weighing all the relevant evidence. Equally, however, we have been sensitive all along to the unavoidable fact that not all our readers will agree on these matters. As a result, we have naturally allowed our contributors complete freedom to express their own point of view, but at the same time we have insisted (often requesting significant revision of preliminary drafts) that all other major points of view, whether more conservative or more radical, be summarized in an even-handed manner. In this way, we hope that readers (and students in particular) will have material at hand that will guide them in their own thinking on these difficult issues.

Finally, the Historical Books of the Old Testament contain so many names of people and places that a Bible dictionary faces the danger of becoming little more than a list of entries which add little, if anything, to what could already be known by a straightforward reading of the text. To overcome this, and in line with the policy adopted for previous dictionaries in this series, we have limited our choice of entries to those topics that require more extended evaluation. At the same time, we have sought to group many of the sorts of subject that might otherwise claim a short entry on their own into coherent topics (e.g., David's family; Omri dynasty), and we have been pleasurably surprised to find how often this policy has resulted in fresh insights which would not have emerged had each family member or each king in a dynasty been treated separately. Similarly, the substantial entry for "God," which brings into a single article treatment of the many divine names, appellatives and attributes, results in a much richer theological discussion than would each of these if taken in isolation. This policy made the initial listing of entries into a challenging and thought-provoking task in itself, and we can only hope that our readers will not disagree too much with the choice of topics that were eventually selected for inclusion and exclusion.

We were saddened to learn during the preparation of this dictionary of the untimely death of one of our contributors, Martin J. Selman. Martin undertook distinguished research under the guidance of Professor D. J. Wiseman on the social and legal background of the patriarchal period as known to us from Mesopotamian sources. He then gave himself untiringly to his teaching ministry at Spurgeon's College, London. He will be best remembered in the wider church for his valuable two-volume commentary on Chronicles in the Tyndale Old Testament Commentary series. His entry on the "Chronicler's History" in the present volume, one of the last pieces he wrote, thus serves as a fitting memorial.

As we conclude our editorial task, we should be remiss if we did not offer our personal thanks to all who have contributed to this work: our contributors, of course, who patiently endured our constant requests for sometimes substantial revision as we sought to bring all into conformity with our vision for this volume; our patient copyeditor, Robert Maccini, who coaxed diverse material into a pleasing unity of presentation; and above all Dan Reid, who has overseen the whole project at the administrative level but also, much more, as an Old Testament scholar in his own right, has always been quick with sound guidance and advice on all sorts of issues. Working relationships between publishers and authors do not always run smoothly, but with Dan at the helm the voyage has been not only trouble free but a richly rewarding experience, and we are grateful.

It is said of Ezra that he "set his heart to study the law of the Lord, to do it, and to teach" (Ezra 7:10). Those three ambitions seem to us to be listed in the right order, and we hope that this volume will be found helpful to many as they in turn seek to follow Ezra's example.

Bill T. Arnold
H. G. M. Williamson

How to Use This Dictionary

Abbreviations
Comprehensive tables of abbreviations for general matters as well as for scholarly, biblical and ancient literature may be found on pages xiv-xix.

Authorship of Articles
The authors of articles are indicated by their first initials and last name at the end of each article. A full list of contributors may be found on pages xxi-xxiii, in alphabetical order by their last name. The contribution of each author is listed following their identification.

Bibliographies
A bibliography will be found at the end of each article. The bibliographies include works cited in the articles and other significant related works. Bibliographical entries are listed in alphabetical order by the author's name, and where an author has more than one work cited, they are listed alphabetically by title. In articles focused on the Historical Books, the bibliographies are divided into the categories "Commentaries" and "Studies."

Cross-References
This dictionary has been extensively cross-referenced in order to aid readers in making the most of material appearing throughout the volume. Five types of cross-referencing will be found:

1. One-line entries appearing in alphabetical order throughout the dictionary direct readers to articles where a topic is discussed, often as a subdivision of an article:

ANAT. *See* CANAANITE GODS AND RELIGION.

2. An asterisk before a word in the body of an article indicates that an article by that title (or closely worded title) appears in the dictionary. For example, "*David" directs the reader to an article titled "David." Asterisks typically are found only at the first occurrence of a word in an article.

3. A cross-reference appearing within parentheses in the body of an article directs the reader to an article by that title. For example, (*see* God) directs the reader to an article by that title.

4. Cross-references have been appended to the end of articles, immediately preceding the bibliography, to direct readers to articles significantly related to the subject:

See also HISTORY OF ISRAEL 5: ASSYRIAN PERIOD; OMRI DYNASTY.

5. Occasionally references are made to articles in the companion volumes, primarily the *Dictionary of the Old Testament: Pentateuch (DOTP)*. Others include *Dictionary of Jesus and the Gospels (DJG)*, *Dictionary of Paul and His Letters (DPL)*, *Dictionary of the Later New Testament and Its Developments (DLNTD)* and *Dictionary of New Testament Background (DNTB)*. These references are found within the body of the text of articles. For example, a reference such as (*see DOTP*, Law) refers to the article on "Law" in the *Dictionary of the Old Testament: Pentateuch*.

Indexes
Since most of the dictionary articles cover broad topics in some depth, the *subject index* is intended to assist readers in finding relevant information on narrower topics that might, for instance, appear in a standard Bible dictionary. For example, while there is no article titled "Calendar," the subject index might direct the reader to pages where calendrical issues are discussed in the articles on "Agriculture," "Chronology" or elsewhere.

A *Scripture index* is provided to assist readers in gaining quick access to the numerous Scripture texts referred to throughout the dictionary.

An *articles index* found at the end of the dictionary allows readers to review quickly the breadth of topics covered and select the ones most apt to serve their interests or needs. Those who wish to identify the articles written by specific contributors should consult the list of contributors, where the articles are listed under the name of each contributor.

Maps and Figures

A map of Arabia appears in the article "Arabia, Arabians." Small maps sketching the geographical boundaries of Israel may be found in the article "Geographical Extent of Israel." General maps of Palestine and the ancient Near East appear on pages 1027-28.

Transliteration

Hebrew has been transliterated according to the system set out on page xx.

Abbreviations

General Abbreviations

/	parallel text (e.g., 2 Kings 18—19/Is 36—37)
§ or §§	section or paragraph number(s)
Akk	Akkadian
augm.	augmented
BCE	Before the Common Era
c.	circa
CE	Common Era
cf.	*confer*, compare
chap(s).	chapter(s)
col(s).	column(s)
DSS	Dead Sea Scrolls
Egyp	Egyptian
Eng	English
e.g.	*exempli gratia*, for example
esp.	especially
ET	English translation
fem.	feminine
fig.	figure
Gk	Greek
Heb	Hebrew
i.e.	*id est*, that is
lit.	literally
masc.	masculine
mg.	margin
M.R.	Map Reference
no(s).	number(s)
NT	New Testament
obv.	obverse (front) of a tablet
OT	Old Testament
pers. comm.	personal communication
pl.	plural
p(p).	page(s)
repr.	reprint
rev.	reverse (back) of a tablet
rev. ed.	revised edition
sg.	singular
Sum	Sumerian
Ugar	Ugaritic
v(v).	verse(s)
vol(s).	volume(s)
x	times (e.g., 2x = two times)

Texts and Translations of the Bible

ESV	English Standard Version
JB	Jerusalem Bible

LXX	Septuagint
MT	Masoretic Text
NAB	New American Bible
NIV	New International Version
NJB	New Jerusalem Bible
NKJV	New King James Version
NRSV	New Revised Standard Version
REB	Revised English Bible

Books of the Bible

Old Testament	1-2 Kings	Is	Mic	Mk	1-2 Thess
Gen	1-2 Chron	Jer	Nahum	Lk	1-2 Tim
Ex	Ezra	Lam	Hab	Jn	Tit
Lev	Neh	Ezek	Zeph	Acts	Philem
Num	Esther	Dan	Hag	Rom	Heb
Deut	Job	Hos	Zech	1-2 Cor	Jas
Josh	Ps	Joel	Mal	Gal	1-2 Pet
Judg	Prov	Amos		Eph	1-2-3 Jn
Ruth	Eccles	Obad	*New Testament*	Phil	Jude
1-2 Sam	Song	Jon	Mt	Col	Rev

Ancient Near Eastern and Later Jewish Literature

1 En.	*1 Enoch (Ethiopic Apocalypse)*	*Meg.*	*Megillah*
1-2 Esdr	1-2 Esdras	*Mos.* 1, 2	Philo, *De vita Mosis* I, II
1-4 Kgdms	1-4 Kingdoms	P.Oxy.	Oxyrhyncus Papyrus
1-4 Macc	1-4 Maccabees	*Rab.*	*Rabbah*
2 Bar.	*2 Baruch (Syriac Apocalypse)*	*Roš Haš.*	*Roš Haššanah*
Ag. Ap.	Josephus, *Against Apion*	RS	Ras Shamra tablet (Field identification
Ant.	Josephus, *Jewish Antiquities*		of tablets excavated at Ras Shamra
B. Bat.	*Baba Batra*		[Ugarit] are identified by RS followed
b.	Babylonian Talmud		by number.)
CD	Cairo Genizah copy of the *Damascus*	*Sanh.*	*Sanhedrin*
	Document	Sir	Sirach
Contemp.	Philo, De *vita contemplativa*	*t.*	*Tosefta*
J.W.	Josephus, *Jewish War*	*y.*	*Jerusalem Talmud*
Jdt	Judith	*Yad.*	*Yadayim*
L.A.B.	*Liber antiquitatum biblicarum* (Pseudo-Philo)		

Classical and Early Christian Literature

Arrian		Plato	
Anab.	*Anabasis*	*Phaedr.*	*Phaedrus*
Diodorus Siculus		Plutarch	
Bib. Hist.	*Bibliotheca Historica*	*Art.*	*Artaxerxes*
Eusebius		Strabo	
Hist. eccl.	*Historia ecclesiastica*	*Geogr.*	*Geographica*
Praep. ev.	*Praeparatio evangelica*	Tacitus	
Herodotus		*Hist.*	*Historiae*
Hist.	*Historiae*	Xenophon	
Irenaeus		*Anab.*	*Anabasis*
Frag.	*Fragmenta*	*Cyr.*	*Cyropaedia*
Justin		*Hell.*	*Hellenica*
Dial.	*Dialogue with Trypho*		

Periodicals, Reference Works and Serials

AASF	Annales Academiae scientiarum fennicae		BAMA	British Academy Monographs in Archaeology
AASOR	Annual of the American Schools of Oriental Research		*BAR*	*Biblical Archaeology Review*
			BARIS	Biblical Archaeology Review International Series
ÄAT	Ägypten und Altes Testament			
AB	Anchor Bible		*BASOR*	*Bulletin of the American Schools of Oriental Research*
ABD	*Anchor Bible Dictionary*, ed. D. N. Freeman (6 vols.; New York: Doubleday, 1992)			
			BBB	Bonner biblische Beiträge
			BCC	Believers Church Commentary
ABG	Arbeiten zur Bibel und ihrer Geschichte		BDB	F. Brown, S. R. Driver and C. A. Briggs, *A Hebrew and English Lexicon of the Old Testament* (Oxford: Oxford University Press, 1907)
ABRL	Anchor Bible Reference Library			
ABS	Archaeology and Biblical Studies			
ADAJ	*Annual of the Department of Antiquities of Jordan*			
			BE	Biblische Enzyklopädie
ADP	Abhandlungen des Deutschen Palästinavereins		BEAM	Beiträge zur Erforschung der antiken Moabitis
AfO	*Archiv für Orientforschung*		BEATAJ	Beiträge zur Erforschung des Alten Testaments und des antiken Judentum
AfOB	Archiv für Orientforschung: Beiheft			
AJA	*American Journal of Archaeology*			
AJSL	*American Journal of Semitic Languages and Literature*		BETL	Bibliotheca ephemeridum theologicarum lovaniensium
ALASP	Abhandlungen zur Literatur Alt-Syrien-Palästinas und Mesopotamiens		BEvT	Beiträge zur evangelischen Theologie
			BHT	Beiträge zur historischen Theologie
ANEP	*The Ancient Near East in Pictures Relating to the Old Testament*, ed. J. B. Pritchard (Princeton, NJ: Princeton University Press, 1954)		BI	Beiträge zur Iranistik
			Bib	*Biblica*
			BibInt	*Biblical Interpretation*
			BibJS	Biblical and Judaic Studies
ANESSup	Ancient Near Eastern Studies Supplements		BibOr	Biblica et orientalia
			BibSem	Biblical Seminar
ANET	*Ancient Near Eastern Texts Relating to the Old Testament*, ed. J. B. Pritchard (3d ed.; Princeton, NJ: Princeton University Press, 1969)		BIFAO	Bulletin de l'Institut français d'archélogie orientale
			BIOSCS	*Bulletin of the International Organization for Septuagint and Cognate Studies*
AnOr	Analecta orientalia		BIS	Biblical Interpretation Series
ANRW	*Aufstieg und Niedergang der römischen Welt: Geschichte und Kultur Roms im Spiegel der neueren Forschung*, ed. H. Temporini and W. Haase (Berlin: de Gruyter, 1972-)		*BJRL*	*Bulletin of the John Rylands University Library of Manchester*
			BJS	Brown Judaic Studies
			BLS	Bible and Literature Series
			BN	*Biblische Notizen*
AOAT	Alter Orient und Altes Testament		*BO*	*Bibliotheca orientalis*
AOS	American Oriental Series		*BRev*	*Bible Review*
AOTC	Abingdon Old Testament Commentaries		*BSac*	*Bibliotheca sacra*
ArOr	*Archiv Orientální*		*BSFE*	*Bulletin de la Société française en Égypte*
AS	Assyriological Studies		*BSOAS*	*Bulletin of the School of Oriental and African Studies*
ASORAR	American Schools of Oriental Research Archaeological Reports			
			BTAVO	Beihefte zum Tübinger Atlas des Vorderen *Orients*
ASORDS	American Schools of Oriental Research Dissertation Series		*BTB*	*Biblical Theology Bulletin*
ASTI	*Annual of the Swedish Theological Institute*		BUS	Brown University Studies
AsTJ	*Asbury Theological Journal*		BWA(N)T	Beiträge zur Wissenschaft vom Alten (und Neuen) Testament
AT	*The Alalakh Texts*, ed. D. J. Wiseman (London: British Institute of Archaeology, 1953)		*BZ*	*Biblische Zeitschrift*
			BZAW	Beihefte zur Zeitschrift für die alttestamentliche Wissenschaft
ATANT	Abhandlungen zur Theologie des Alten und Neuen Testaments		*CAD*	*The Assyrian Dictionary of the Oriental Institute of the University of Chicago*, ed. A. L. Oppenheim et al. (Chicago: University of Chicago Press, 1956-)
AUSS	*Andrews University Seminary Studies*			
BA	*Biblical Archaeologist*			
BAIAS	*Bulletin of the Anglo-Israel Archaeological Society*		*CAH*	*Cambridge Ancient History*

CahRB	Cahiers de la Revue biblique	FCB	Feminist Companion to the Bible
CANE	Civilizations of the Ancient Near East, ed. J. Sasson (4 vols.; New York: Scribner, 1995)	FCI	Foundations of Contemporary Interpretation
CBET	Contributions to Biblical Exegesis and Theology	FGrH	F. Jacoby, Die Fragmente der Griechische Historiker (Berlin 1923-)
CBQ	Catholic Biblical Quarterly	FOTL	Forms of Old Testament Literature
CBQMS	Catholic Biblical Quarterly Monograph Series	FRLANT	Forschungen zur Religion und Literatur des Alten und Neuen Testaments
CBW	Cities of the Biblical World	GBSNT	Guides to Biblical Scholarship: New Testament
CDAFI	Cahiers de la Délégation archéologique française en Iran	GBSOT	Guides to Biblical Scholarship: Old Testament
CHANE	Culture and History of the Ancient Near East	GO	Göttinger Orientforschungen
ChrEg	Chronique d'Égypte	GTA	Göttinger theologischer Arbeiten
CIA	Corpus inscriptionum iranicarum	GTS	Gettysburg Theological Studies
ConBOT	Coniectanea biblica: Old Testament Series	HALOT	The Hebrew and Aramaic Lexicon of the Old Testament, L. Koehler, W. Baumgartner and J. J. Stamm (4 vols.; Leiden: E. J. Brill, 1994-99)
COS	The Context of Scripture, ed. W. W. Hallo (3 vols.; Leiden: E. J. Brill, 1997-)	HAT	Handkommentar zum Alten Testament
CSHJ	Chicago Studies in the History of Judaism	HBT	Horizons in Biblical Theology
CTAT-1	Critique textuelle de l'Ancien Testament. 1. Josué, Juges, Ruth, Samuel, Rois, Chroniques, Esdras, Néhémie, Esther, D. Barthélemy. (OBO 50/1; Fribourg/Suisse: Éditions Universitaires, and Göttingen: Vandenhoeck & Ruprecht, 1982)	HCOT	Historical Commentary on the Old Testament
		Hen	Henoch
		HO	Handbuch der Orientalistik
		HS	Hebrew Studies
		HSAO	Heidelberger Studien zum alten Orient
		HSCPRT	Heythrop Studies in Contemporary Philosophy, Religion and Theology
CTM	Calwer Theologische Monographien	HSM	Harvard Semitic Monographs
CurBS	Currents in Research: Biblical Studies	HSS	Harvard Semitic Studies
DANE	Dictionary of the Ancient Near East, ed. P. Bienkowski and A. Millard (Philadelphia: University of Pennsylvania Press, 2000)	HTIBS	Historic Texts and Interpreters in Biblical Scholarship
		HTR	Harvard Theological Review
		HUCA	Hebrew Union College Annual
DDD	Dictionary of Deities and Demons in the Bible, ed. K. van der Toorn, B. Becking and P. W. van der Horst (Leiden: E. J. Brill, 1995)	HUCM	Monographs of the Hebrew Union College
		HvTSt	Hervormde teologiese studies
DJD	Discoveries in the Judaean Desert	IA	Iranica Antiqua
DNWSI	Dictionary of the North-West Semitic Inscriptions, J. Hoftijzer and K. Jongeling (2 vols.; Leiden: E. J. Brill, 1995)	IASup	Iranica Antiqua Supplément
		IBC	Interpretation: A Bible Commentary for Teaching and Preaching
DOTP	Dictionary of the Old Testament: Pentateuch, ed. T. D. Alexander and D. W. Baker (Downers Grove, IL: InterVarsity Press, 2003)	IBHS	An Introduction to Biblical Hebrew Syntax, B. K. Waltke and M. O'Connor (Winona Lake, IN: Eisenbrauns, 1990)
		IBT	Interpreting Biblical Texts
DSD	Dead Sea Discoveries	ICC	International Critical Commentary
EAEHL	Encyclopedia of Archaeological Excavations in the Holy Land, ed. M. Avi-Yonah (4 vols.; Jerusalem: Israel Exploration Society, 1975-1978)	IDB	The Interpreter's Dictionary of the Bible, ed. G. A. Buttrick (4 vols.; Nashville: Abingdon, 1962)
		IEJ	Israel Exploration Journal
EBib	Etudes bibliques	ILBS	Indiana Literary Biblical Series
ER	The Encyclopedia of Religion, ed. M. Eliade (16 vols.; New York: Macmillan, 1987)	Int	Interpretation
		IntC	Interpretation Commentary
		IOS	Israel Oriental Studies
ErIsr	Eretz-Israel	ISBE	International Standard Bible Encyclopedia, ed. G. W. Bromiley (rev. ed.; 4 vols.; Grand Rapids: Eerdmans, 1979-1988)
ETL	Ephemerides theologicae lovanienses		
EvQ	Evangelical Quarterly		
EvT	Evangelische Theologie	ISBL	Indiana Studies in Biblical Literature
FAS	Freiburger altorientalische Studien	ITC	International Theological Commentary
FAT	Forschungen zum Alten Testament		

ITQ	*Irish Theological Quarterly*	NCBC	New Century Bible Commentary
JA	*Journal asiatique*	NDBT	*New Dictionary of Biblical Theology*, ed. T. D. Alexander and B. S. Rosner (Downers Grove, IL: InterVarsity Press, 2000)
JANESCU	*Journal of the Ancient Near Eastern Society of Columbia University*		
JAOS	*Journal of the American Oriental Society*	NEA	*Near Eastern Archaeology*
JBL	*Journal of Biblical Literature*	NEAEHL	*The New Encyclopedia of Archaeological Excavations in the Holy Land*, ed. E. Stern (4 vols.; Jerusalem: Israel Exploration Society & Carta; New York: Simon & Schuster, 1993)
JBQ	*Jewish Bible Quarterly*		
JBS	*Jerusalem Biblical Studies*		
JCS	*Journal of Cuneiform Studies*		
JDS	Judean Desert Studies		
JEA	*Journal of Egyptian Archaeology*	NEASB	*Near East Archaeology Society Bulletin*
JESHO	*Journal of the Economic and Social History of the Orient*	NES	*Near Eastern Studies*
		NIB	*The New Interpreter's Bible*, ed. L. E. Keck et al. (12 vols.; Nashville: Abingdon, 1994-2002)
JJS	*Journal of Jewish Studies*		
JNES	*Journal of Near Eastern Studies*		
JNSL	*Journal of Northwest Semitic Languages*	NIBC	New International Bible Commentary
JPOS	*Journal of the Palestine Oriental Society*	NIBCOT	New International Biblical Commentary: Old Testament
JPSTC	Jewish Publication Society Torah Commentary	NICOT	New International Commentary on the Old Testament
JQR	*Jewish Quarterly Review*		
JSJ	*Journal for the Study of Judaism in the Persian, Hellenistic, and Roman Periods*	NIDOTTE	*New International Dictionary of Old Testament Theology and Exegesis*, ed. W. A. VanGemeren (5 vols.; Grand Rapids: Zondervan, 1997)
JSJSup	Supplements to the Journal for the Study of Judaism		
JSOT	*Journal for the Study of the Old Testament*	NIVAC	NIV Application Commentary
JSOTSup	Journal for the Study of the Old Testament: Supplement Series	NVBS	New Voices in Biblical Studies
		OBO	Orbis biblicus et orientalis
JSS	*Journal of Semitic Studies*	OBOSA	Orbis biblicus et orientalis: Series archaeologica
JSSEA	*Journal of the Society for the Study of Egyptian Antiquities*		
		OBS	Oxford Bible Series
JSSSup	Journal of Semitic Studies Supplements	OBT	Overtures to Biblical Theology
JTS	*Journal of Theological Studies*	OEANE	*The Oxford Encyclopedia of Archaeology in the Near East*, ed. E. M. Meyers (5 vols.; Oxford: Oxford University Press, 1997)
JTSA	*Journal of Theology for Southern Africa*		
KAI	*Kanaanäische und aramäische Inschriften*, ed. H. Donner and W. Röllig (2d ed.; 3 vols. in 1; Wiesbaden: Otto Harrasowitz, 1966-1969)		
		OIC	Oriental Institute Communications
		OIE	Oriental Institute Essays
KAT	Kommentar zum Alten Testament	OIP	Oriental Institute Publications
KTU	*Die keilalphabetischen Texte aus Ugarit*, ed. M. Dietrich, O. Loretz and J. Sanmartín (AOAT 24/1; Neukirchen-Vluyn: Neukirchener Verlag, 1976)	OLA	Orientalia lovaniensa analecta
		OLZ	*Orientalistische Literaturzeitung*
		OPSNKF	Occasional Publications of the Samuel Noah Kramer Fund
LA	Levantine Archaeology	*Or*	*Orientalia*
LAI	Library of Ancient Israel	OTE	*Old Testament Essays*
LAPO	Littératures Anciennes du Proche-Orient	OTG	Old Testament Guides
		OTL	Old Testament Library
LCBI	Literary Currents in Biblical Interpretation	OTM	Oxford Theological Monographs
		OTR	Old Testament Readings
LD	Lectio divina	OTS	Old Testament Studies
LevAr	Levantine Archaeology	*OtSt*	*Oudtestamentische Studiën*
LJLE	Library of Jewish Law and Ethics	PA	Palaestina Antiqua
LSTS	Library of Second Temple Studies	*PEQ*	*Palestine Exploration Quarterly*
MDOG	*Mitteilungen der Deutschen Orient-Gesellschaft*	PIASH	Proceedings of the Israel Academy of Sciences and Humanities
MHEOP	Mesopotamian History and Environment Occasional Publications	POS	Pretoria Oriental Series
		PTMS	Pittsburgh Theological Monograph Series
MLBS	Mercer Library of Biblical Studies		
MSIA	Monograph Series of the Institute of Archaeology	QD	Quaestiones disputatae
		RA	*Revue d'assyriologie et d'archélogie orientale*
NAC	New American Commentary	RB	*Revue biblique*
NCB	New Century Bible	REA	*Revue des etudes anciennes*

RelSRev	Religious Studies Review	SOTBT	Studies in Old Testament Biblical Theology
RevQ	Revue de Qumran		
RGW	Religions in the Graeco-Roman World	SOTSMS	Society for Old Testament Studies Monograph Series
RIMA	The Royal Inscriptions of Mesopotamia, Assyrian Periods	SSN	Studia semitica neerlandica
RIMB	The Royal Inscriptions of Mesopotamia, Babylonian Periods	*ST*	Studia theologica
		SWBA	Social World of Biblical Antiquity
RlA	Reallexikon der Assyriologie, ed. E. Ebeling et al. (Berlin: de Gruyter, 1928-)	SWR	Studies in Women and Religion
		TA	Tel Aviv
SAA	State Archives of Assyria	TAD	B. Porten and A. Yardeni, *Textbook of Aramaic Documents from Egypt* (4 vols.; Jerusalem: Hebrew University, 1986-1999)
SAAB	State Archives of Assyria Studies Bulletin		
SAAS	State Archives of Assyria Studies		
SAHL	Studies in the Archaeology and History of the Levant		
SAM	Sheffield Archaeological Monographs	TB	Theologische Bücherei: Neudrucke und Berichte aus dem 20. Jahrhundert
SANE	Sources from the Ancient Near East	TBC	Torch Bible Commentaries
SAOC	Studies in Ancient Oriental Civilization	TCS	Texts from Cuneiform Sources
SBLAB	Society of Biblical Literature Academia Biblica	*TDOT*	Theological Dictionary of the Old Testament, ed. G. J. Botterweck and H. Ringgren (Grand Rapids: Eerdmans, 1974-)
SBLABS	Society of Biblical Literature Archaeology and Biblical Studies		
SBLDS	Society of Biblical Literature Dissertation Series	*THAT*	Theologisches Handwörterbuch zum Alten Testament, ed. E. Jenni, with C. Westermann (2 vols.; Munich: Kaiser; Zurich: Theologischer Verlag, 1971-1976)
SBLEJL	Society of Biblical Literature Early Judaism and Its Literature		
SBLMS	Society of Biblical Literature Monograph Series	*ThWAT*	Theologisches Wörterbuch zum Alten Testament, ed. G. J. Botterweck and H. Ringgren (Stuttgart: Kohlhammer, 1970-)
SBLSBL	Society of Biblical Literature Studies in Biblical Literature		
		TJ	Trinity Journal
SBLSCS	Society of Biblical Literature Septuagint and Cognate Studies	*TLOT*	Theological Lexicon of the Old Testament, ed. E. Jenni, with C. Westermann (3 vols.; Peabody, MA: Hendrickson, 1997)
SBLSymS	Society of Biblical Literature Symposium Series		
SBLWAW	Society of Biblical Literature Writings from the Ancient World	*TLZ*	Theologische Literaturzeitung
		TOTC	Tyndale Old Testament Commentaries
SBT	Studies in Biblical Theology	TSAJ	Texte und Studien zum antiken Judentum
SBTS	Sources for Biblical and Theological Study		
		TSK	Theologische Studien und Kritiken
ScrHier	Scripta hierosolymitana	*TWOT*	Theological Wordbook of the Old Testament, ed. R. L. Harris, G. L. Archer Jr and B. K. Waltke (2 vols.; Chicago: Moody)
SCSS	Septuagint and Cognate Studies Series		
SdO	Seminari di orientalistica		
SEÅ	Svensk exegetisk årsbok	*TynBul*	Tyndale Bulletin
SEL	Studi epigrafici e linguistici	TZB	Theologische Zeitschrift Sonderbände
SemeiaSt	Semeia Studies	UBL	Ugaritisch-biblische Literatur
SFSHJ	South Florida Studies in the History of Judaism	UCOP	University of Cambridge Oriental Publications
		UF	Ugarit-Forschungen
SFSMD	Studia Francisci Scholten memoriae dicata	*USQR*	Union Seminary Quarterly Review
		VE	Vox evangelica
SH	Scripture and Hermeneutics	*VT*	Vetus Testamentum
SHANE	Studies in the History of the Ancient Near East	VTSup	Vetus Testamentum Supplements
		WBC	Word Biblical Commentary
SHBC	Smith & Helwys Bible Commentary	WMANT	Wissenschaftliche Monographien zum Alten und Neuen Testament
SHCANE	Studies in the History and Culture of the Ancient Near East		
		WTJ	Westminster Theological Journal
SHR	Studies in the History of Religions (supplement to Numen)	YNER	Yale Near Eastern Researches
		ZA	Zeitschrift für Assyriologie
SJLA	Studies in Judaism in Late Antiquity	*ZABR*	Zeitschrift für altorientalische und biblische Rechtsgeschichte
SJOT	Scandinavian Journal of the Old Testament		
SJSJ	Supplements to the Journal for the Study of Judaism	*ZAH*	Zeitschrift für Althebräistik
		ZAW	Zeitschrift für die alttestamentliche Wissenschaft
SO	Symbolae osloenses	*ZDPV*	Zeitschrift des deutschen Palästina-Vereins

Transliteration of Hebrew

Consonants		
א	=	ʾ
ב	=	b
ג	=	g
ד	=	d
ה	=	h
ו	=	w
ז	=	z
ח	=	ḥ
ט	=	ṭ
י	=	y
כ, ך	=	k

ל	=	l
מ, ם	=	m
נ, ן	=	n
ס	=	s
ע	=	ʿ
פ, ף	=	p
צ, ץ	=	ṣ
ק	=	q
ר	=	r
שׂ	=	ś
שׁ	=	š
ת	=	t

Short Vowels

ַ	=	a
ֶ	=	e
ִ	=	i
ָ	=	o
ֻ	=	u

Very Short Vowels

ֲ	=	ă
ֱ	=	ĕ
ְ	=	ĕ (if vocal)
ֳ	=	ŏ

Long Vowels

(ה)ָ	=	â
ֵי	=	ê
ִי	=	î
וֹ	=	ô
וּ	=	û
ָ	=	ā
ֵ	=	ē
ֹ	=	ō

Contributors

Amit, Yairah, PhD. Professor, Tel Aviv University, Tel Aviv, Israel: **Narrative Art of Israel's Historians.**

Arnold, Bill T., PhD. Director of Postgraduate Studies and Professor of Old Testament and Semitic Languages, Asbury Theological Seminary, Wilmore, Kentucky: **Hezekiah; Samuel, Books of; Word of God.**

Auld, A. Graeme, DLitt. Professor of Hebrew Bible, University of Edinburgh, Edinburgh, Scotland, United Kingdom: **Amphictyony, Question of.**

Baker, David W., PhD. Professor of Old Testament and Semitic Languages, Ashland Theological Seminary, Ashland, Ohio: **Scribes and Schools.**

Bartholomew, Craig, PhD. H. Evan Runner Chair in Philosophy, Redeemer University College, Ancaster, Ontario, Canada: **Hermeneutics.**

Beaulieu, Paul-Alain, PhD. Visiting Associate Professor, University of Notre Dame, South Bend, Indiana: **Babylonia, Babylonians; History of Israel 6: Babylonian Period.**

Bedford, Peter R., PhD. Associate Professor in History and Religious Studies; Associate Dean, Research and Higher Degrees, Edith Cowan University, Perth, Western Australia, Australia: **History of Israel 8: Postexilic Community; Postexilic Temple.**

Block, Daniel I., DPhil. Professor of Old Testament, Graduate Biblical and Theological Studies, Wheaton College, Wheaton, Illinois: **God.**

Boda, Mark J., PhD. Professor of Old Testament, McMaster Divinity College, McMaster University, Hamilton, Ontario, Canada: **Ezra; Nehemiah; Prayer.**

Borowski, Oded, PhD. Professor, Biblical Archaeology & Hebrew, Emory University, Atlanta, Georgia: **Water & Water Systems.**

Butler, Trent, PhD. Vice President and Editorial Director, Chalice Press, Gallatin, Tennessee: **Bethel.**

Carter, Charles E., PhD. Associate Professor and Chair of Department of Religious Studies, Seton Hall University, South Orange, New Jersey: **Social-Scientific Approaches.**

Chavalas, Mark W., PhD. Professor of History, University of Wisconsin-La Crosse, La Crosse, Wisconsin: **History of Israel 2: Premonarchic Israel.**

Cook, Paul M., MDiv. Hebrew Teaching Fellow, Asbury Theological Seminary, Wilmore, Kentucky: **Word of God.**

Curtis, Adrian H. W., PhD. Senior Lecturer in Hebrew Bible, University of Manchester, Manchester, England, United Kingdom: **Canaanite Gods and Religion.**

Dearman, J. Andrew, PhD. Professor of Old Testament, Austin Presbyterian Theological Seminary, Austin, Texas: **Moab, Moabites.**

Depuydt, Leo, PhD. Associate Professor of Egyptology, Brown University, Providence, Rhode Island: **Egypt, Egyptians.**

Dever, William G., PhD. Professor of Near Eastern Archaeology and Anthropology, University of Arizona, Tucson, Arizona: **Gezer.**

Drinkard, Joel F., Jr., PhD. Professor of Old Testament Interpretation, Southern Baptist Theological Seminary, Louisville, Kentucky: **Omri Dynasty.**

Duke, Rodney K., PhD. Professor of Philosophy & Religion, Appalachian State University, Boone, North Carolina: **Chronicles, Books of.**

Ehrlich, Carl S., PhD. Professor of Humanities, York University, Toronto, Ontario, Canada: **Philistines.**

Enns, Peter, PhD. Professor of Old Testament and Biblical Hermeneutics, Westminster Theological Seminary, Philadelphia, Pennsylvania: **Faith.**

Evans, Mary J., MPhil. Vice Principal, London School of Theology, London, England, United Kingdom: **Samuel; Women.**

Fleming, Daniel E., PhD. Associate Professor of Hebrew Bible and Assyriology, New York University, New York, New York: **Anointing; Hebrews.**

Fouts, David M., ThD. Professor of Old Testament and Biblical Hebrew, Bryan College, Dayton, Tennessee: **Numbers, Large Numbers.**

Fox, Nili S., PhD. Associate Professor of Bible, Hebrew Union College, Cincinnati, Ohio: **State Officials.**

Fritz, Volkmar, Dr. Theol. Habil. Professor Emeritus of Old Testament and Biblical Archaeology, University of Giessen, Germany: **Architecture.**

Gilmour, Garth H., DPhil. Research Associate, Institute of Archaeology, University of Oxford, Oxford, United Kingdom and Senior Fellow, W. F. Albright Institute of Archaeological Research, Jerusalem: **Dan; Hazor; Meggido; Shechem; Shiloh.**

Grayson, A. Kirk, PhD. Professor, Department of Near and Middle Eastern Civilizations, University of Toronto, Toronto, Ontario, Canada: **Assyria, Assyrians; Non-Israelite Written Sources: Assyrian.**

Greenwood, Kyle R., PhD (cand.). Hebrew Union College–Jewish Institute of Religion, Cincinnati, Ohio: **Census.**

Groves, J. Alan, PhD (cand.). Professor of Old Testament and Vice President for Academic Affairs, Westminster Theological Seminary, Philadelphia, Pennsylvania: **Zion Traditions.**

Hadley, Judith M., PhD. Associate Professor, Villanova University, Villanova, Pennsylvania: **Hebrew Inscriptions.**

Hagedorn, Anselm C., DPhil. Wissenschaftlicher Assistant, Humboldt Universität zu Berlin, Berlin, Germany: **Honor and Shame.**

Handy, Lowell K., PhD. Indexer/Analyst, American Theological Library Association, Chicago, Illinois: **Solomon.**

Hartley, John E., PhD. Professor of Old Testament, Haggard School of Theology, Azusa Pacific University, Azusa, California: **Levitical Cities.**

Hawk, L. Daniel, PhD. Professor of Old Testament and Hebrew, Ashland Theological Seminary, Ashland, Ohio: **Joshua, Book of.**

Heim, Knut, PhD. Tutor in Biblical Studies, Queen's Foundation for Ecumenical Theological Education, Birmingham, England, United Kingdom: **Kings & Kingship.**

Heller, Roy L., PhD. Assistant Professor of Old Testament, Perkins School of Theology, Southern Methodist University, Dallas, Texas: **Hebrew Language.**

Hess, Richard S., PhD. Professor of Old Testament and Semitic Languages, Denver Seminary, Denver, Colorado: **Oral Tradition & Written Tradition; Taxes, Taxation; Tribes of Israel & Land Allotment/Borders.**

Hill, Andrew E., PhD. Professor of Old Testament, Wheaton College, Wheaton, Illinois: **History of Israel 3: United Monarchy.**

Hobbs, Raymond T., PhD. Professor Emeritus, McMaster University, Hamilton, Ontario, Canada: **War & Peace.**

Hostetter, Edwin C., PhD. Professorial Lecturer, American University, Washington, DC: **Beersheba.**

Hubbard, Robert L., Jr., PhD. Professor of Biblical Literature, North Park Theological Seminary, Chicago, Illinois: **Ai; Caleb, Calebites; Gilgal.**

Irwin, Brian P., PhD. Assistant Professor of Old Testament/Hebrew Scriptures, Knox College, Toronto School of Theology, University of Toronto, Toronto, Ontario, Canada: **Ekron.**

Jeffers, Ann, PhD. Lecturer in Biblical Studies, Heythrop College, University of London, London, England, United Kingdom: **Magic & Divination.**

Jenson, Philip P., PhD. Lecturer in Old Testament Theology, Ridley Hall, Cambridge, England, United Kingdom: **Sin.**

Johnston, Philip S., PhD. Director of Studies, Wycliffe Hall, Oxford, England, United Kingdom: **Death & Afterlife.**

Kelle, Brad E., PhD. Assistant Professor of Biblical Literature, Point Loma Nazarene University, San Diego, California: **History of Israel 5: Assyrian Period.**

Kitchen, Kenneth A., PhD. Professor Emeritus of Egyptology, University of Liverpool, Liverpool, England, United Kingdom: **Arabia, Arabians; Chronology.**

Klingbeil, Gerald A., DLitt. Professor of Old Testament and Ancient Near Eastern Studies; Editor *DavarLogos*; Director of Research Institute, Theology Faculty, River Plate Adventist University, Libertador San Martín, Entre Ríos, Argentina: **Agriculture & Animal Husbandry; Priests & Levites.**

Klingbeil, Martin G., DLitt. Professor of Old Testament and Ancient Near Eastern Studies, River Plate Adventist University, Libertador San Martín, Entre Ríos, Argentina: **Trade & Travel.**

Knauth, Robin J. DeWitt, ThD. Assistant Professor, Lycoming College, Williamsport, Pennsylvania: **Israel.**

Kugler, Robert A., PhD. Paul S. Wright Professor of Christian Studies, Lewis & Clark College, Portland, Oregon: **Canon.**

Kuhrt, Amelie, ThL. Professor of Ancient Near Eastern History; Fellow of the British Academy, University College London, London, England, United Kingdom: **Persia, Persians.**

Lamb, David T., DPhil. Tutor, University of Oxford, Oxford, England, United Kingdom: **Jehu Dynasty.**

Li, Tarsee, PhD. Assistant Professor, Oakwood College, Huntsville, Alabama: **Goliath.**

Linton, Gregory L., PhD. Vice President of Academic Affairs and Professor of New Testament, Great Lakes Christian College, Lansing, Michigan: **Roads & Highways.**

Longman, Tremper, III, PhD. Robert H. Gundry Professor of Biblical Studies, Westmont College, Santa Barbara, California: **History of Israel 7: Persian Period.**

Lucas, Ernest C., PhD. Vice-Principal and Tutor in Biblical Studies, Bristol Baptist College, Bristol, England, United Kingdom: **Miracles.**

Lund, Jerome A., PhD. Senior Research Associate, Comprehensive Aramaic Lexicon, Hebrew Union College, Cincinnati, Ohio: **Aramaic Language; Aram, Damascus and Syria.**

Mabie, Frederick J., PhD. Associate Professor, Talbot School of Theology, Biola University, La Mirada, California: **Geographical Extent of Israel.**

MacDonald, Burton, PhD. Professor, St. Francis Xavier University, Antigonish, Nova Scotia, Canada: **Edom, Edomites.**

Master, Daniel M., PhD. Associate Professor of Archaeology, Wheaton College, Wheaton, Illinois: **Ashkelon.**

Matthews, Victor H., PhD. Professor of Religious Studies and Associate Dean of the College of Humanities and Public Affairs, Southwest Missouri State University, Springfield, Missouri: **Israelite Society.**

McConville, J. Gordon, PhD. Professor of Old Testament Theology, University of Gloucestershire, Cheltenham, England, United Kingdom: **Jericho; Kings, Books of.**

McKenzie, Steven L., ThD. Professor of Hebrew Bible/Old Testament, Rhodes College, Memphis, Tennessee: **David's Family; Historiography, Old Testament; History of Israel 4: Division of the Monarchy.**

McKeown, James, PhD. Vice Principal, Belfast Bible College, Belfast, Northern Ireland, United Kingdom: **Nathan.**

McKnight, Scot, PhD. Karl A. Olsson Professor, North Park University, Chicago, Illinois: **Rehoboam.**

Mead, James K., PhD. Assistant Professor of Religion, Northwestern College, Orange City, Iowa: **Elijah; Elisha.**

Meier, Sam A., PhD. Associate Professor, Near Eastern Languages and Cultures, Ohio State University, Columbus, Ohio: **History of Israel 1: Settlement Period.**

Meyers, Carol, PhD. Mary Grace Wilson Professor, Duke University, Durham, North Carolina: **Jerusalem.**

Millard, Alan R., MPhil. Rankin Professor Emeritus of Hebrew & Ancient Semitic Languages, The University of Liverpool, Liverpool, England, United Kingdom: **Writing, Writing Materials and Literacy in the Ancient Near East.**

Miller, Cynthia L., PhD. Associate Professor, Department of Hebrew & Semitic Studies, University of Wisconsin-Madison, Madison, Wisconsin: **Linguistics.**

Miller, Robert D., II, PhD. Associate Professor of Sacred Scripture, Mount St. Mary's Seminary, Emmitsburg, Maryland: **Cities & Villages; Quest of the Historical Israel.**

Möller, Karl, PhD. Lecturer in Theology & Religious Studies, St. Martin's College, Lancaster, England, United Kingdom: **Prophets & Prophecy.**

Monson, John, PhD. Associate Professor of Archaeology, Wheaton College, Wheaton, Illinois: **Solomon's Temple.**

Nelson, Richard D., PhD. Professor of Biblical Hebrew and Old Testament Interpretation, Perkins School of Theology, Southern Methodist University, Dallas, Texas: **Joshua.**

Noegel, Scott B., PhD. Associate Professor, University of Washington, Seattle, Washington: **Phoenicia, Phoenicians.**

O'Mathúna, Dónal P., PhD. Lecturer in Health Care Ethics, Dublin City University, Dublin, Ireland: **Sickness & Disease.**

Olley, John W., PhD. Principal (retired), Baptist Theological College of Western Australia, Perth, Western Australia, Australia: **Isaiah.**

Ortiz, Steven M., PhD. Assistant Professor of Archaeology, New Orleans Baptist Theological Seminary, New Orleans, Louisiana: **Archaeology, Syro-Palestinian; Gath; Gaza; Hebron.**

Oswalt, John N., PhD. Research Professor of Old Testament, Wesley Biblical Seminary, Jackson, Mississippi: **Forgiveness; Justice & Righteousness.**

Overland, Paul B., PhD. Associate Professor of Old Testament and Semitic Languages, Ashland Theological Seminary, Ashland, Ohio: **Wisdom.**

Parker, Simon B., PhD. Professor of Hebrew Bible and Harrell F. Beck Scholar of Hebrew Scripture, Boston University, Boston, Massachusetts: **Non-Israelite Written Sources: Syro-Palestinian.**

Petter, Donna L., PhD (cand.). Instructor in Old Testament, Biblical Theological Seminary, Hatfield, Pennsylvania: **High Places.**

Petter, Thomas D., PhD. Assistant Professor of Old Testament, Biblical Theological Seminary, Hatfield, Pennsylvania: **Arad.**

Richter, Sandra L., PhD. Associate Professor of Old Testament, Asbury Theological Seminary, Wilmore, Kentucky: **Deuteronomistic History.**

Roberts, J. J. M., PhD. William Henry Green Professor of Old Testament Literature Emeritus, Princeton Theological Seminary, Princeton, New Jersey: **Davidic Covenant.**

Rooke, Deborah W., DPhil. Lecturer in Old Testament Studies, King's College, London, England, United Kingdom: **Zadok, Zadokites.**

Rose, Wolter H., DPhil. University Lecturer in Semitic Studies, Theologische Universiteit van de Gereformeerde Kerken, Kampen, The Netherlands: **Zerubbabel.**

Salvesen, Alison G., DPhil. University Research Lecturer, Oriental Institute, University of Oxford, Oxford, England, United Kingdom: **Royal Family.**

Satterthwaite, Philip E., PhD. Lecturer in Old Testament and Hebrew, Biblical Graduate School of Theology, Singapore: **David; Judges.**

Scalise, Pamela J., PhD. Associate Professor of Old Testament, Fuller Theological Seminary, Seattle, Washington: **Jeremiah.**

Schniedewind, William M., PhD. Professor of Biblical Studies & NWS Languages, UCLA, Los Angeles, California: **Innerbiblical Exegesis.**

Seibert, Eric A., PhD. Associate Professor of Old Testament, Messiah College, Grantham, Pennsylvania: **Salvation & Deliverance.**

Selman, Martin J., PhD. Formerly Deputy Principal, Spurgeon's College, London, England, United Kingdom: **Chronicler's History.**

Shalom Brooks, Simcha, PhD. Independent scholar, London, England, United Kingdom: **Gibeah, Geba; Gibeon; Saul & Saul's Family.**

Soza, Joel R., PhD. Assistant Professor of Old Testament, Malone College, Canton, Ohio: **Jeroboam.**

Sparks, Kenton L., PhD. Associate Professor of Biblical Studies, Eastern University, St. Davids, Pennsylvania: **Ark of the Covenant; Ethnicity; Propaganda.**

Spawn, Kevin L., D.Phil. Associate Professor of Old Testament, Simpson University, Redding, California: **Sources, References to.**

Sprinkle, Joe M., PhD. Professor of Old Testament, Crossroads College, Rochester, Minnesota: **Carmel; Law.**

Stone, Lawson G., PhD. Professor of Old Testament, Asbury Theological Seminary, Wilmore, Kentucky: **Judges, Book of.**

Strawn, Brent A., PhD. Assistant Professor of Old Testament, Candler School of Theology, Emory University, Atlanta, Georgia: **History of Israel 5: Assyrian Period.**

Sweeney, Marvin A., PhD. Professor of Hebrew Bible, Claremont School of Theology, and Professor of Religion, Claremont Graduate University, Claremont, California: **Josiah.**

Tappy, Ron E., PhD. G. Albert Shoemaker Professor of Bible and Archaeology, Pittsburgh Theological Seminary, Pittsburgh, Pennsylvania: **Samaria.**

Tiemeyer, Lena-Sofia, DPhil. Lecturer in Old Testament, University of Aberdeen, Aberdeen, Scotland, United Kingdom: **Lebanon; Manasseh; Sanballat.**

Tsumura, D. T., PhD. Professor of Old Testament and Acting Dean, Japan Bible Seminary, Hamura, Tokyo, Japan: **Canaan, Canaanites.**

Tull, Patricia K., PhD. A. B. Rhodes Professor of Old Testament, Louisville Presbyterian Theological Seminary, Louisville, Kentucky: **Methods of Interpretation.**

Turkanik, Andrzej, PhD. Lecturer in Old Testament, Schloss Mittersill Study Centre, Schloss Mittersill, Austria: **Tirzah.**

Walls, Jerry L., PhD. Professor of Philosophy of Religion, Asbury Theological Seminary, Wilmore, Kentucky: **Evil.**

Walton, John H., PhD. Professor of Old Testament, Wheaton College, Wheaton, Illinois: **Genealogies.**

Watts, James W., PhD. Associate Professor of Religion, Syracuse University, Syracuse, New York: **Poetry.**

Way, Kenneth C., PhD (cand.). Hebrew Union College, Cincinnati, Ohio: **Jehoshaphat.**

Weisberg, David B., PhD. Professor of Bible and Semitic Languages, Hebrew Union College-Jewish Institute of Religion, Cincinnati, Ohio: **Non-Israelite Written Sources: Babylonian.**

Williamson, H. G. M., PhD, DD. Regius Professor of Hebrew and Student of Christ Church, University of Oxford, Oxford, England, United Kingdom: **Jezreel; Lachish; Non-Israelite Written Sources: Egyptian Aramaic Papyri; Non-Israelite Written Sources: Old Persian & Elamite.**

Williamson, Paul R., PhD. Lecturer in Old Testament, Moore Theological College, Sydney, New South Wales, Australia: **Land.**

Wolters, Al, PhD. Professor of Religion & Theology, Redeemer University College, Ancaster, Ontario, Canada: **Text & Textual Criticism.**

Wright, Christopher J. H., PhD. International Ministries Director, Langham Partnership International, London, England, United Kingdom: **Ethics.**

Wright, Paul H., PhD. Executive Director, Jerusalem University College, Jerusalem, Israel: **Ashdod; Ezion-geber.**

Yamauchi, Edwin M., PhD. Professor of History Emeritus, Miami University, Oxford, Ohio: **Ezra & Nehemiah, Books of.**

Younker, Randall, PhD. Professor of Old Testament and Biblical Archaeology and Director of the Institute of Archaeology, Andrews University, Berrien Springs, Michigan: **Ammon, Ammonites.**

Zorn, Jeffrey R., PhD. Visiting Associate Professor, Department of Near Eastern Studies, Cornell University, Ithaca, New York: **Mizpah.**

A

ABIMELECH. *See* HISTORY OF ISRAEL 2: PRE-MONARCHIC ISRAEL.

ABSALOM. *See* DAVID'S FAMILY.

ACHAEMENID EMPIRE. *See* PERSIA, PERSIANS.

ADMINISTRATIVE BUILDINGS. *See* ARCHITECTURE.

ADONAY. *See* GOD.

AFTERLIFE. *See* DEATH AND AFTERLIFE.

AGRICULTURE AND ANIMAL HUSBANDRY

Ancient Israelite society was predominantly a nonurban, agriculturally based society whose economy was mostly pastoral or agrarian oriented (Borowski 2003, 25-26) and whose foundational elements were the extended family (*bêt ʾāb*) and the village (Blenkinsopp, 49-57; Tsumura, 60-62). In order to systematize the present article, a basic threefold division has been adopted: First, the available sources and the methodology for a discussion of agriculture and animal husbandry in the period depicted in the Historical Books of the OT are briefly discussed. Second, following these important methodological prolegomena, the relevant biblical data pertaining to the discussion of agriculture and animal husbandry in the Historical Books are presented in two sections and seek to interact with other data from auxiliary disciplines such as archaeology or iconography. Third, a succinct conclusion sketches the broader picture of this important facet of ancient Israelite life.

1. Sources and Methodology
2. Agriculture in the Historical Books
3. Animal Husbandry in the Historical Books
4. Conclusions

1. Sources and Methodology.
The reconstruction of crucial human activities connected to animal husbandry and agriculture in a particular portion of the OT faces several methodological issues. First, in a book such as the Bible, which has a strong theological agenda and seeks to describe the interaction of the covenant deity Yahweh with his people Israel, what kind of information about mundane and commonplace activities such as the tilling of soil or the care of animals can be found? Second, how does this information gleaned from the biblical text compare with data originating outside the Bible? Third, is it possible to develop a valid methodology that helps to reconstruct their daily life adequately?

In order to find convincing answers to these three crucial issues, recent scholarship has advocated a multidisciplinary approach by looking at textual (both biblical and extrabiblical), archaeological (including paleobotanical and paleozoological), iconographical and, sometimes, ethnographical data (Klingbeil 2003c, 401-3; King and Stager, 1-4). It must be stated from the outset that most scholars have a preferred angle, which in itself is not a bad thing if duly recognized. For example, some focus predominantly on one particular element, as can be seen in D. C. Snell, who argues that social and economic factors represent the most important influences in ancient daily life. Unfortunately, many volumes dealing with agriculture or animal husbandry or, in the larger context, daily life are more illustrative than interpretive and lack an important section dealing with crucial methodological questions.

Textual data (biblical and extrabiblical) have always played an important role in the reconstruction of history or cultural realities. Work with textual sources requires genre recognition, such as the broad distinction between "official" and "private" texts (Klingbeil 2003c, 406). However, over the past decades the biblical textual data often have been characterized as "fictitious" or "ideological" (for a review of the present discussion about the Solomonic period, see Knoppers; for the patriarchal period, Lemche, 19-47; more generally, Halpern, 68) and in consequence has been relegated to the status of unhistorical. In this sense, is it feasible to draw information concerning mundane efforts such as agriculture and animal husbandry from this text? And furthermore, does the literary artistry and nature of the biblical text preclude per se its historical reliability? The situation does not change particularly when one includes extrabiblical epigraphical material from the same historic stream and area. Although most of these texts are easily datable by their archaeological context, their content often is fragmentary and does not go beyond the odd list, simple accounts or incidental messages that on their own provide insufficient information to reconstruct satisfactorily economic, cultural and religious realities from a time long past. Relevant information from epigraphical sources includes the Samaria ostraca dating to the later part of the eighth century BCE (Kaufman, 923), the Arad ostraca (both in Hebrew and Aramaic) from the eighth and fifth/fourth centuries BCE respectively (Aharoni and Naveh, 9), the Lachish ostraca dated to the early part of the sixth century BCE (Davies, 282; J. C. L. Gibson, 32-49), the Gezer calendar thought to be one of the earliest Hebrew inscriptions and dated to the tenth century BCE (Jaroš, 37-38; Davies, 273), the Siloam inscription found in Hezekiah's tunnel in Jerusalem dated to the eighth century BCE (J. C. L. Gibson, 21; Davies, 279) and some funerary inscriptions from the Silwan tomb in Jerusalem (J. C. L. Gibson, 23-24). Smaller *Hebrew inscriptions include the important stamp seal corpus from Palestine (Avigad and Sass) and graffiti inscribed on jar handles whose presence suggests an intricate system of royal tariffs and regional organization for the later part of the Israelite and Judean monarchies (Kletter). Other important epigraphical data pertaining to the historical period depicted in the Historical Books of the OT (roughly equated with Iron Age I and II, the Neo-Babylonian period and

the early Persian period) come from the other side of the Jordan River, generally known as Transjordan, and include Ammonite, Moabite and Edomite inscriptions (Lemaire). The most significant for our present interest are undoubtedly the Mesha inscription, dated to the ninth century BCE (Davies, 274-75; J. C. L. Gibson, 71-83), and to a lesser degree the Heshbon ostraca IV and XI, dated to around 600 and 525 BCE respectively, which contain important agricultural references (Cross 1975, 1-14; 1976).

While epigraphical material is often very fragmentary or simply irrelevant, the biblical material was not necessarily intended as a manual on agriculture and animal husbandry, but includes relevant snippets of information in the larger context of historical reports and theological constructs that focus upon the visible interaction of the covenant deity Yahweh with his people Israel. There are, however, other important sources of information that need to be tapped if a more complete picture is to emerge. The study of the material culture is one of these, and archaeological research focusing upon paleoethnobotany or paleozoology provides helpful additional data. Paleoethnobotany studies the interaction between humans and plants through time and examines material unearthed in archaeological excavations of ancient tells such as carbonized plant remains, seeds, wood, roots, fibers, starches, oils and juices (Warnock, 27; Rosen, 203; Hansen). The resulting data provide a welcome window on the environment of Iron Age Palestine, including diet, disease, cultural practices, domestication and trade. Another useful source of information on ancient animal husbandry comes from paleozoology, which is the systematic recovery and study of faunal remains from archaeological sites. The majority of these involve bone, dental or skin remains and provide important data concerning the process of domestication, food production, and economic, social and religious realities (Wapnish; Hesse and Wapnish; Wapnish and Hesse). Unfortunately, both paleoethnobotany and paleozoology are relatively recent methodological advances, and the systematic collection of the relevant data has been undertaken only during the past few decades. None of the major sites of Palestine (such as *Hazor, *Megiddo, Beth Shean, *Samaria) that were excavated before that period of time included this research strategy, and thus there exist significant lacunae in our knowledge of ancient faunal and floral realities. One should also remember the often limited surface area unearthed by modern excavations, which obviously results in the partial recovery of the relevant data. In many instances the paleozoologist can assign a specific bone fragment only to a general taxonomic category, such as *equid,* and is unable to identify it further as "horse" or "donkey" or "hinney" or "mule" (Hesse 1995, 216).

Another important source of information for the reconstruction of animal husbandry and agriculture in ancient Israel during the period of Iron Age I-II (including the Neo-Babylonian and the Persian periods, which corresponds roughly to the internal chronology of the Historical Books, c. 1250-450 BCE) is the iconographical data gleaned from ancient images. While ancient Near Eastern iconography is not always a useful tool to pinpoint the individual person or the particular historical event, it is quite suitable to illustrate the typical and the institutional (Keel, *ABD* 3.361). Iconographical research has been integrated into studies illustrating the biblical text (Keel 1996), into historical research (Pitard; Uehlinger; Rainey), as well as into the study of the religious cosmos of the ancients (Keel and Uehlinger; van der Toorn; Ornan). Recent iconographical research (often combined with archaeological and historical data) has also focused on more general sociocultural elements such as the function of seals in ancient societies (Collon), the importance of technological innovation in cultural process of the ancient Near East (Wilde), and the interaction of animals in daily life (Klingbeil 2003b; 2003c). The iconographical study of the *Lachish relief has yielded invaluable information concerning the agricultural realia of Palestine during the late eighth century BCE (Amar). In addition, the publication of the first two volumes of the stamp seal corpus from Palestine by O. Keel (1995; 1997) has also opened a window upon the "worldview" of ancient miniature art, which was used predominantly in private contexts, as contrasted to the more ideologically tinted monumental art. In this sense, the naive illustrative use of iconography, so characteristic of earlier studies, has been replaced by a more systematic and critical analysis of the ancient art in its particular context of presentation. Furthermore, it should be remembered that the very act of producing an image in ancient times was a laborious and costly process that involved specialized artists and required a certain socioeconomic level (Klingbeil 2003c, 411), thus limiting to a certain degree its value for the reconstruction of mundane aspects of daily life such as agriculture and animal husbandry.

2. Agriculture in the Historical Books.

Agriculture involves the varied array of activities and knowledge employed by humans to exploit plants to produce food and other crops (Hopkins, 22). Crop cultivation (together with animal domestication) marked an important advance in human society and was connected to social organization. Geography and climate influenced the development of agriculture and often determined the particular type of specialization. For example, dry semidesert conditions prompted inhabitants to opt for a mix of sedentary and nomadic lifestyles, a feature still observable in modern Arabic societies such as Jordan, where entire clans move around with their livestock during six to eight months of the year, returning to their fully constructed houses for the colder and wetter winter months (Baird). This social phenomenon has been described as "subsistence pastoralism," involving the adaptation of people groups to changing climatic or sociopolitical conditions (LaBianca). By the time during which the Historical Books of the OT originated (c. 1250-450 BCE), the major elements of the Mediterranean mixed economy, involving the interaction of urbanized centers, subsistence pastoralists, nomads and small villages, had already been in place for several millennia (Hopkins, 25-28). In fact, "the Iron Age in Palestine marks a particularly sharp and well-documented spike in the course of Levantine and Near Eastern agricultural history" (Hopkins, 28) and is characterized by changes in regional settlement patterns that in turn influence agricultural strategies. Geographical realities as well as sociopolitical changes played an important role in this regard, particularly considering the fall or decline of many international major players, such as the Hittites, the influence of the Mitanni kingdoms, the Middle Assyrian Empire and the Egyptian Empire at the end of the Late Bronze Age (Strange; Leonard; Akkermans and Schwartz, 358-59). Some of these international ups and downs can be seen in the sociohistorical realities reflected in the biblical books of Joshua, Judges and the first part of 1 Samuel.

Geographically, Palestine is marked by seven geomorphological regions: (1) the coastal plain, (2) the hill country, (3) the Dead Sea rift, (4) the Transjordanian Plateau, (5) the semiarid Negev steppe, (6) the Sinai Peninsula, and (7) the Jezreel Valley to the north of Palestine. Each of these regions has its own set of particular soil types, climate patterns, and *water resources and systems that in turn require distinct strategies for human survival and utilization of the ground (Raphael). For example, someone living in the semiarid Negev would be required to adopt a mixed farming strategy, including as many different products/animal types as possible in order to absorb and compensate for climate changes (such as droughts). Subsistence pastoralism would be an adequate response to this geographic and climatic challenge. Interestingly, land use innovations during the Iron Age included runoff farming, which provided another way to cope with the particular climatic conditions of the Negev (Borowski 1987, 6).

Some of the agricultural products mentioned in the Historical Books include flax (*pēšet*), different types of grain, figs, grapes (or in dried form, raisins), dates, olives and, without particulars, vegetables. The two Israelite spies who visit Jericho prior to its destruction are hidden beneath a bunch of flax stalks by Rahab on the roof of her house (Josh 2:6). The messenger for King *David on his way to report on the movement of the rebel Absalom is hidden under some improvised grain-drying design over an empty cistern (2 Sam 17:19). Flax *(Linum usitatissimum)* is a winter crop, a fact that interestingly coincides with the particular historical description of the settlement of Palestine by the Israelites contained in the book of Joshua involving the celebration of the Passover (Josh 5:10-12), as well as the description of the high water level of the Jordan typical for the period at the end of the winter (Josh 4:18). It was used to produce oil or as the basis for weaving and is considered one of the world's oldest textiles (Jacob and Jacob, 815). Flax seeds have been found at Tell el-ʿAreini in the Early Bronze Age Stratum IV (Borowski 1987, 98).

Different types of grains played a major role in the life of Israel. The author of the book of Joshua connects the eating of the produce of the land (*ʿābûr hāʾāreṣ),* including roasted grains and unleavened bread (Josh 5:11-12), with the significant cultic event of the first cele-

bration of the Passover ritual on Canaanite soil. Although the MT reads only *wĕqālûy,* "and roasted" or "and parched," most versions add for clarification the noun *grain* (NRSV, NASB, NKJV).

Gideon threshes wheat *(ḥiṭṭâ [Triticum durum])* in a wine press in order to save it from the Midianites (Judg 6:11). Wheat was the major field crop in Israel throughout the biblical period (Miller, 296), and Gideon's clandestine action underlines the desperate need of Gideon's clan to assure sufficient supplies of the most important staple food. After all, threshing inside the village compounds—as suggested by the use of Hebrew *gat,* "wine press," instead of *yeqeb,* "wine vat/press," which appears more in rural settings and is generally hewn from rock outside of a city (Is 5:2; 16:10) (see Borowski 1987, 63)—produced lots of irritating stalks and husks, which are unpleasant for the thresher. Together with the earlier mentioned "flax," the term *wheat* also appears in the Gezer calendar (J. C. L. Gibson, 2). The important Arad ostraca contain additional relevant references to this staple (Arad 3:7; 31:1; 33:1-4, 6-8), indicating its importance in the Israelite economy.

The destruction of harvests has always been a strategic weapon in warfare, as can be seen in the conflict between Samson (representing Israel) and the *Philistines (Judg 15:4-5) as well as in the destruction of trees and orchards during the time of Jehoshaphat (2 Kings 3:19). This later line of attack was also employed by the Israelites in their war against the Moabites. Additionally, the earth was to be burned, every spring of water was to be stopped, and every good piece of arable land was to be impoverished by adding stones. Similar strategies have also been observed in Egyptian military activity of the Late Bronze Age (Hasel 1998, 75-83, 251-52; 2002). In other instances, particularly in the context of the conquest/settlement, the tribes are admonished to secure arable land by felling trees and clearing woods (Josh 17:15-18).

Both wheat and barley *(śĕʿōrâ [Hordeum vulgare])* are used to pay tribute, as can be seen in the case of the Ammonites who paid ten thousand cors of wheat and ten thousand cors of barley every year to King Jotham of Judah (2 Chron 27:5). There is no unanimous consensus position for the metrical value of the Hebrew unit "cor," with estimates ranging from about 150 liters (King and Stager, 200) to about 360 liters (Powell, 904). In both cases, the amount is significant and demonstrates the economic incentives for an overlord in the ancient Near East.

Technology played (and still plays) an important role in the evolution of society. The traditional chronological system employed in archaeological research is primarily based on technological advances, particularly the dominion of metals (e.g., Stone Age, Bronze Age, Iron Age) (see Wilde, 1-6). The absolute validity of this system has been questioned (Finkelstein 1996), but the overall importance of technology per se in agriculture is undeniable. The knowledge and mastery of certain techniques also enabled people to dominate others, as can be seen in 1 Samuel 13:19-21, detailing the fact that in the time of the last judge, *Samuel, there were no blacksmiths (ḥārāš; lit., "engraver, artificer") in Israel, which affected not only the military arsenal, but also the agricultural tools, such as plows (mahărēšâ). The apparent technological monopoly of the Philistine artisans enabled them not only to dominate Israel militarily, but also to determine the market value of the job, which cost two-thirds of a shekel (pîm) (see Powell, 906-7), a price that is quite high, particularly when one considers that the legislated yearly contribution of an Israelite to the sanctuary was to be half a shekel (Ex 30:13, 30). The ancient plow consisted of a pole made from hard wood, a stick for the handle, a blade with a metal tip and a horizontal yoke (King and Stager, 92). The basic technology of the scratch plow had not changed from biblical times until the beginning of the twentieth century, as can be seen in pictorial representations or archaeological finds (Borowski 1987, 48). *Elijah calls *Elisha while the latter was plowing the fields of his father (1 Kings 19:19-20) together with a significant number of workers totaling twelve plow units pulled by double-yoked oxen. After Elijah covered him with his mantle, a legal act indicating election and transference of power (Viberg, 127-35), Elisha likewise reacted in a ritual way when he sacrificed the pair of oxen that he had worked with, utilizing the wood of his plow as the necessary elements for the fire. After giving the boiled meat to his coworkers, Elisha follows Elijah and ministers (šārat) to him, thus beginning his prophetic apprenticeship. The symbolic act of Elijah together with the ritual response of Elisha, resulting in the complete destruction and transformation of his prior tools of trade and livelihood, mark Elisha's complete separation from his previous life.

Other agricultural products mentioned in the Historical Books include the fruits of figs, grapes (and raisins) and dates. The common fig (tĕʾēnâ [Ficus carica]) is indigenous to the region and has been documented from Neolithic, Chalcolithic and Bronze Age Jericho (Borowski 1987, 114) as well as on pictorial remains of the ancient Near East such as the Lachish relief of Sennacherib in the palace of Nineveh (Amar, 1). Figs were dried and made into cakes, constituting an extremely effective energy booster that could be carried during military expeditions. When David and his four hundred men pursue the marauding Amalekites who had plundered Ziklag, they give dried fig and raisin cakes to revive a left-behind Egyptian slave who helps them find the enemy (1 Sam 30:12). King Hezekiah's malignant swelling is treated by a poultice of pounded figs (2 Kings 20:7). The fig tree also appears in Jotham's parable (Judg 9:10-11) as one of the trees (albeit not the first!) asked to reign over the others. For the biblical authors, the scenario of a carefree, safe and blessed environment is depicted by "each man living under his own vine and fig tree," as during the time of *Solomon's reign (1 Kings 4:25). Interestingly, the Assyrian Rabshakeh (chief butler [Cogan and Tadmor, 230]) employs the same imagery when he seeks to entice the listening Jerusalemites to surrender (2 Kings 18:31/Is 36:16). The tree motif also appears in the context of special divine blessings. After all, the Israelites settled in a land, lived in cities, and ate from trees that they did not plant (Josh 24:13; Neh 9:25). On the other hand, rampant idolatry—mostly described in terms of licentious marital infidelity—is also connected to trees. Ritual behavior deviant from the Jerusalem-centered worship of Yahweh takes place on the "high places" and "under every green tree" (2 Kings 16:4; 17:10; 2 Chron 28:4), and thus is closely related to nature.

Vineyards and their fruits are also mentioned many times in the Historical Books. The vineyard (kerem) of Naboth the Jezreelite, right next to the royal palace of King Ahab, becomes an object of desire for the king, who wants to acquire it from its owner in order to make a conveniently located vegetable garden (lĕgan yārāq; lit., "for a garden of herbs") for the royal household (1 Kings 21:1-2). Although Ahab offers financial benefits or a more ideally located vineyard, he does not reckon with the strong land-inheritance concept (*see* Land), which considers the preservation of the patrimonial property *(naḥălat ʾăbōtay)*, one of the most important duties to the ancestors as well as to the future generations of a family (2 Kings 21:3) (see Habel, 33-35; Brueggemann, 90-106). In this sense, the narrative depicts not just a greedy king, a cunning wife and a helpless peasant, but rather the confrontation of two land ideologies. Ahab and Jezebel represent the idea of royal control over the land, a concept that is also reflected in the short narrative of 2 Kings 8:1-6, where the Shunammite woman, after a prolonged absence from her land due to a severe drought, receives back her land (as well as all of the benefits from the produce of the land) after a special intervention of Gehazi, the former servant of the prophet Elijah. On the other side, Naboth is faithful to the principle of the ancestral household concept based upon the divinely designated tribal allotments (Num 36:7-9). The violent resolution of this conflict, resulting in the death of Naboth, the taking over of the property by the royal household and the subsequent condemnation of the royal house of Ahab by the prophet Elisha (1 Kings 21:18-26), illustrates the importance of this principle in ancient Israel. It is this conflict over land and divinely established legal principles that Samuel describes in his passionate plea to the people of Israel to reconsider their request for a king in 1 Samuel 8:10-18 (also 1 Sam 12:3). "A king," admonishes Samuel, "will affect all aspects of your life: your land, your time [as visible later in the institution of the *mas,* "tribute, tax, compulsory labor" (see Klingbeil 1997, 992-95)], your crops and also your animals."

Grapes *(ʿēnāb),* both in their fresh and dried forms, appear several times. In Nehemiah 13:15 they are among the fresh produce offered—to the dismay of Nehemiah—to the inhabitants of Jerusalem during the sabbath day. Due to their particular vow, Nazirites are not to eat any produce connected to the vine (Judg 13:14), and in 1 Kings 4:25 the idyllic depiction of peace and safety involves Israelites sitting under their vines and fig trees. Raisin cakes often are connected to festal occasions. When David successfully brings the ark of the covenant to Jerusalem, the celebrations involve the distribution of free bread, date and raisin cakes to the Israelites (2 Sam 6:19/1 Chron 16:3). The earliest remains of the grapevine *(gepen [Vitis vinifera])* in Palestine date to the beginning of the third millennium BCE and were found in Early Bronze Jericho and Arad, as well as Lachish, Taʿanach, Bab edh-Dhraʿ and Numeiri (Borowski 1987, 102). It is also present in the Lachish relief of the palace of Sennacherib (Amar, 1), and is mentioned in the Gezer calendar (J. C. L. Gibson, 1) as well as in the Samaria ostraca. The data gleaned from these important epigraphical finds suggest small farm production of wine and oil and emphasize the domestic locus of agricultural production as opposed to centrally administered production (Walsh, 51-59).

There is only one tentative mention of dates, the fruit of the date palm *(Phoenix dactylifera),* in the Historical Books: 2 Samuel 6:19, during the celebration of the arrival of the ark of the covenant. The existence of date palms has been documented archaeologically from the Chalcolithic site of Teleilat Ghassul in Transjordan and from the Cave of the Treasure at Nahal Mishmar (Borowski 1987, 127). The date palm grew in Palestine along the northern seacoast, south of Jaffa and around Gaza and in the Jordan Valley. It also is depicted on the Lachish relief and is easily identified by its straight, rugged trunk, the characteristic shapes of the palm leaves and the clusters of dates (Amar, 2). Branches of the date palm, together with branches from olive trees, myrtle trees and other leafy trees, are used to build the temporary shelters for the Feast of Tabernacles (Neh 8:15).

Another important element of Israelite agricultural economy is the olive tree. The olive *(zayit [Olea europaea])* is one of the most important fruit trees in the economy of the ancient Near East. It is native to the eastern Mediterranean basin, and its domesticated version has been found from the Chalcolithic period onward (Borowski 1987, 117; Jacob and Jacob, 807-8). In Judges 15:5 the destruction of the livelihood of the Philistines is marked when Samson burns the grain fields and the vineyards and olive groves. Samuel admonishes the Israelites that a future king will take from the best fields, vineyards and olive groves and will give them to his courtiers (1 Sam 8:14). To own an olive grove was considered a sign of prosperity (2 Kings 5:26). In Jotham's parable in Judges 9:8-15 it was the olive tree that was first asked to be the king of the trees, a fact that underlines its status in Israelite economy and folklore.

During the early part of the united monarchy David initiates an administrative structure that includes supervision of royal fieldworkers, field supplies, vineyards, wine supplies, olive trees, mulberry trees (which thrive in the Shephelah region) and oil supplies (1 Chron 27:25-28), a fact challenged by recent historical and archaeological studies on the size and reach of the united monarchy of David and Solomon (Lehmann, 156-62; Finkelstein 2003). Some of these assertions are based upon survey data, which generally represent an incomplete and thus tendentious data set (Klingbeil 2003a). Others center upon historical notions that appear to be slightly out of date (Kitchen; Millard) or base themselves upon the tentative interpretation of archaeological data that is at best questionable or at least open to different interpretations (see Mazar, and references there).

Interestingly, a couple of centuries later King Uzziah of Judah is said to have been a champion of agriculture, excavating many cisterns, organizing his workers supervising his livestock, both in the Shephelah and in the plains, as well as the farmers and vinedressers in the hill country, because "he loved the soil" (2 Chron 26:10). From the perspective of the biblical author, this organizational work does not appear to have been innovative but may be a conscious reflex to mold Uzziah after the ideal king, David, and his administrative work, as described in 1 Chronicles 27:25-28.

In ancient Israel agriculture is not the mere interaction between technology, geography and human being but rather is embedded in the larger context of human-divine interaction. Yahweh is responsible for sufficient rain and growth, and lack of rain is mostly understood in terms of divine wrath or human guilt. Hunger, pest, drought—everything affecting the land—can be remedied by God (2 Chron 6:26-31; 20:9); and these are always caused by idolatry—the illegitimate relationship of the people (or individuals) with other gods—as can be seen in the conflict between Elijah and the priests and prophets of Baal on Mount Carmel (1 Kings 18). Another area of interaction between agriculture and religion involved the festival calendar of Israel, which is closely connected to the agricultural calendar (Weisman, 253-57). Spring is connected to the Feast of Unleavened Bread and the Passover (Ex 12), which is the first feast celebrated when Israel enters the Promised

Land (Josh 5:10-12). A harvest festival is celebrated in the narrative of Abimelech during the time of the judges (Judg 9:27), and in the time of *Hezekiah the tithing and offering system involving wheat, new wine, oil, honey and produce of the field is reintroduced (2 Chron 31:5), as can be seen during the time of *Nehemiah's reform some 250 years later (Neh 10:36-38; 13:5, 12). It appears that revival in Israel is always connected with a renewal of the pentateuchal offering and tithing system that seems to have been forgotten or neglected with the passing of time. Another interesting transformation of Israelite cult can be seen in the metamorphosis from a nomadic God who dwells in a tent to a settled deity whose temple is the central focal point of religious activity (Weisman, 260). This transformation represents an echo of the change in socioeconomic realities from a nomadic ideal to fixed settlements with predominant agricultural activities. This growing focus upon agricultural activities is reflected also in the metaphors indicating the relationship between Yahweh and his people, generally known as the covenant. In 2 Samuel 7:10 Yahweh not only has appointed a place for Israel but also has planted *(nāṭaʿ)* them so that they can truly take roots. The verbal form employed here clearly belongs to the semantic field of agricultural terminology (Abegg, 94-96).

3. Animal Husbandry in the Historical Books.
The integration of living animals into human society, generally known as domestication, has had tremendous effects upon human society and is part and parcel of a major cultural process (Clutton-Brock, 28-35). Six main reasons for the domestication of animals should be considered: (1) the need for reliable meat provision, (2) the need for significant cultic offerings, (3) as social indicators, (4) as beasts of burden, (5) as draft animals, (6) as provider of secondary (recyclable) benefits such as fiber, wool, milk and dung [Klingbeil 2003c, 411-12; Ryder 1993]). Particularly the last factor, also known as "secondary products revolution" (Hesse, *OEANE* 1.142; Firmage, 1115-16), needs to be considered in our present context since it represents one of the most significant motivators for animal husbandry, given its recyclable nature. Animal husbandry, like agriculture, is highly dependent upon geographical and climatic factors. Vegetation and climatic cycles determined the grazing

7

patterns, the type of animals and the quantity of stock that a particular region could support. Areas that depended highly upon animal husbandry included the desert fringe (steppe) and the highland valleys (Miller, 298). Another factor determining the ecological realities of a particular location concerns the human intervention. The Mediterranean climate of Palestine is characterized by two seasons: a dry summer (May through October) and a wet winter (November through April); and the normal annual rainfall may be as much as 1,000 mm or more (Firmage, 1110; Frick, 119-26). The flora of this zone originally were dominated by oak forests. However, increasing human intervention, beginning during the Early Bronze Age, has changed tremendously the natural flora and fauna of Palestine. Forests were cleared for cultivation (see Josh 17:15-18), and new flora (such as the vine and olive) were introduced. Although it is methodologically rather difficult to estimate accurately the level of deforestation, the results involving washed off soil, subtle climatic changes and a changing distribution of undomesticated animals can be gleaned from archaeology (particularly paleozoology and paleobotany).

In the following section a closer look at the predominant domesticated species, such as sheep, goat, cattle, pigs and equids, is undertaken, always in relation to the textual evidence found in the Historical Books of the OT. At the outset one must note the close relationship between animal and human being in the worldview of the biblical authors (Simkins, 15-40; Stipp 1999; Riede 2002). Animals are created similar to humanity (Gen 1—2), and both are *nepeš ḥayyâ*, "living being" (Gen 2:7, 19), sharing common physiological and environmental elements. When Yahweh decides to destroy humanity, animals are destroyed as well (Gen 6:7). When Yahweh makes a plan to preserve humanity, the plan also includes the preservation of animals (Gen 6:14-20). However, sometimes animals are also included in the execution of the ban *(ḥērem)*, and they, together with the human inhabitants of cities or members of a particular clan, are destroyed (Josh 6:21; 7:24; 1 Sam 15:3; 22:19). In other cases the animals are taken over by the Israelites while the inhabitants of the particular city are executed (Josh 8:27; 11:14).

The most common domesticated animal species in Israel is the sheep *(Ovis aries)*—more precisely, the fat-tailed Awassi (Borowski 1998, 66-71). The central place of sheep in the life of the Israelites can be demonstrated by reviewing the different Hebrew terms for them employed in the OT (Firmage, 1152-53; Riede, 291-305) that appear in the Historical Books, including ʾayil, "ram" (1 Sam 15:22; 1 Chron 15:26); kebeś, "lamb" (1 Chron 29:21; Ezra 8:35); kibśâ, "ewe lamb" (2 Sam 12:3, 4, 6); ṭāleh, "suckling lamb" (1 Sam 7:9); kār, "lamb" (1 Sam 15:9; 2 Kings 3:4); ṣōʾn, "sheep/goats" (collective term) (Josh 7:24; 1 Sam 8:17); śeh, "sheep" (Josh 6:21; Judg 6:4). Individual references or combinations of these seven terms appear in eighty verses in the Historical Books. In 1 Samuel, 24 verses of the 811 (2.95%) refer to sheep, while at the other end of the spectrum the book of Judges includes in only one of its 611 verses (0.16%) a reference to sheep. These ratios suggest that the authors of the Historical Books did not pay particular attention to issues of animal husbandry. In contrast to typical administrative cuneiform tablets that appear so often in the archives of the surrounding cultures (Syria, Mesopotamia), the biblical material pays only marginal attention to these issues. The biblical texts are not administrative ledgers that contain detailed accounts of animal ownership or copies of sale documents or animal transfers, but rather are predominantly concerned with Israel's political and religious history, focusing upon crucial events and personalities, and evaluating their particular relevance from Yahweh's perspective. A discussion of the specific textual data illustrates this point: due to the evil practices of Israel, Yahweh gives his people for seven years into the hand of the Midianites, who raid Israel repeatedly, leaving no foodstuff, no sheep, no oxen and no donkeys (Judg 6:1-4). It seems that the biblical author has employed the technique of exaggeration (or hyperbole) to communicate the complete lack of perspective and hope for Israel.

Another member of the caprine family of domesticated animals involves the goat family *(Capra hircus)*. In the Historical Books there are five Hebrew terms indicating goats, including ʿēz, "goat" (Judg 6:19; 13:15); śāʿir, "he-goat" (2 Chron 11:15; 29:23); tayiš, "he-goat" (once in 2 Chron 17:11); ṣāpir, "he-goat" (2 Chron 29:21; Ezra 8:35); gĕdi, "young he-goat" (Judg 6:19; 13:15; 14:6). Gideon offers a young he-goat to the divine visitor (Judg 6:19), as does Manoah, the father of Samson (Judg 13:15). Rich man Nabal owns three thousand sheep and one thousand goats (1 Sam 25:2), while the daily rations of the court of Solomon include one hundred sheep, together with ten fat oxen and twenty pasture-fed oxen (1 Kings 4:23). Often, the collective term $ṣō'n$ seems to have included both sheep and goats (1 Chron 27:31), as can be deduced from the description of David's royal administrative organization of the natural resources of his kingdom, including supervisors over the grazing cattle in the Sharon plain, the cattle in the valleys, the camels, the donkeys and the flocks (1 Chron 27:29-31). Again, geographical and climatic realities are reflected in the type of animals associated with a particular region. Interestingly, the tribute of the Arabs $(hā'arbî'îm)$—most probably nomadic tribes living in the desert border regions adjoining Palestine, which should not be confused with the modern ethnic marker "Arab" (Staubli, 156-58)—pay King Jehoshaphat 7,700 rams and 7,700 goats (2 Chron 17:11). The lack of cattle in this list perfectly reflects the living conditions of nomads during Iron Age II and their preferred stock (Staubli, 177-78).

Another important domesticated animal includes the bovine family. While not exhibiting the same variety of terminology as do the caprines, bovines played an increasingly important role in Israelite economy and animal husbandry. In the Historical Books the following Hebrew terms are employed to indicate bovines: the collective $bāqār$, "cattle" (1 Sam 11:5; 14:32); $šôr$, "a head of cattle" (Josh 6:21; 7:24; 1 Sam 22:19); par, "bull" (Judg 6:25; 1 Sam 1:24); $'egel$, "calf" (1 Sam 28:24; 1 Kings 7:23). Cattle *(Bos taurus)* initially were domesticated for milk, meat, hide, bone and dung, and only later did they become draft animals (Borowski 1998, 73-74). During the Iron Age cattle were raised primarily for traction and for their milk and dung, since their use as a source of meat represented a major investment in terms of monetary value and replacement costs. Thus, offerings involving a large number of cattle should be considered highly significant in terms of the value of the sacrifice. The Philistines, desperate to get rid of the Israelite ark of the covenant, use two milk cows to transport it back to Israel (1 Sam 6:7-12). When the transport arrives in Beth-Shemesh, its inhabitants offer the cows in sacrifice to Yahweh (1 Sam 6:14). When David imitates this means of transportation in his misguided attempt to bring the ark to his newly established capital Jerusalem, Uzzah dies in front of Yahweh when he attempts to safeguard the cart and its precious cargo (2 Sam 6:6/1 Chron 13:9). Clearly, whereas the Philistines cannot be supposed to know the correct procedure to move the ark of the covenant, Israel should know better (see Ex 25:12-15; Num 4:15; 7:9; Deut 10:8) and transport the ark by authorized personnel and in the proper way (Gordon, 231), a point already made by the later Chronicler (1 Chron 15:13). Another interesting reference to cattle or, more precisely, to calves is seen in the narrative of Jeroboam I's founding of two major cult centers in Bethel and Dan, where two golden calves (reminiscent for every reader of Scripture of the famous episode of the golden calf during the desert journey [Ex 32]) were erected in representation of Yahweh himself or Yahweh in the guise of the Canaanite deity El (1 Kings 12:28/2 Chron 13:8). It is widely known in the iconography of the ancient Near East that animals often functioned as cult stands for the deity, who was not always shown. At times, the deity appears in human form astride the back of its animal servants (Cogan, 358; for images see *ANEP*, 470-74, 486, 599-501, 522, 531, 534, 537). However, in light of the close connection to the Exodus tradition in terms of time (a cult-founding moment) and type of animal (a calf instead of a bull), it is highly probable that Jeroboam I recognized this crucial founding moment of Israelite religion, while at the same time avoiding direct identification of Yahweh with the calves (Fleming).

Numerous times caprines and bovines appear in religious contexts, predominantly in the context of sacrifices (1 Sam 7:9-10; 14:34; 1 Kings 1:9, 19, 25; 8:5, 63). The huge amount of sacrifices offered during the dedication of the temple include 120,000 sheep and 22,000 oxen (1 Kings 8:63/2 Chron 7:5); meanwhile, the sacrifice of thanksgiving that King Asa of Judah offers during a covenant-renewal ceremony (Dillard, 212) some time after his victory over Ethiopian invaders includes 700 oxen and 7,000 sheep (2 Chron 15:11). The renovation of the temple during the time of King Hezekiah is celebrated with the offering of 7 bulls, 7 rams, 7 sheep and 7 goats as sin offerings for the king and the sanctuary (2 Chron 29:21); meanwhile the congregation gives as burnt offerings 70 bulls, 100 rams and 200 lambs (2 Chron 29:32), and 600 bulls and 3,000 sheep as gifts—most probably for the

Table 1. Ratio of Caprines/Bovines in Religious Contexts in the Historical Books

Reference	Event	Caprines	Bovines	Ratio
Judg 6:19	Gideon offers a sacrifice for Yahweh.	1	—	1:0
Judg 6:25-28	Gideon pulls down altar of Baal and offers a bull on new altar.	—	1	0:1
Judg 13:19	Manoah offers a goat to Yahweh.	1	—	1:0
1 Sam 1:24-25	Samuel's family offer a bull before Yahweh in Shiloh.	—	1	0:1
1 Sam 6:14	People of Beth-Shemesh offer sacrifice to Yahweh after the return of the ark of the covenant.	—	2	0:2
2 Sam 24:22-24/ 1 Chron 21:18-26	David buys threshing floor and oxen from Araunah and offers sacrifices.	—	2 (?)	0:2
1 Kings 1:9, 19, 25	Adonijah prepares a great feast with cultic undertones.	Not specified	Not specified	—
1 Kings 8:63/ 2 Chron 7:5	Solomon's peace offerings during dedication of temple.	120,000	22,000	5.45:1
1 Kings 18:23	Conflict between prophets of Baal and Yahweh: two altars.	—	2	0:2
2 Chron 15:11	Thanksgiving sacrifice of Asa after victory over Ethiopians.	7,000	700	10:1
2 Chron 29:21	Temple renovation during time of Hezekiah.	21	7	3:1
2 Chron 29:32	Thank offerings of people during rededication ceremony.	300	70	4.28:1
2 Chron 29:33	Offerings for temple (no further explanation).	3,000	600	5:1
2 Chron 30:23	Hezekiah's Passover celebrations: king's offering.	7,000	1,000	7:1
2 Chron 30:24	Hezekiah's Passover celebrations: nobility's offering.	10,000	1,000	10:1
2 Chron 35:7	Josiah's Passover celebrations: king's offering.	30,000	3,000	10:1
2 Chron 35:8	Josiah's Passover celebrations: nobility's offering.	2,600	300	8.66:1
2 Chron 35:9	Josiah's Passover celebrations: offering from Levitical leaders.	5,000	500	10:1
Ezra 8:35	Sin offering of returnees.	185	12	15.4:1

sanctuary, although the biblical text provides no further indications (2 Chron 29:33). During the Passover celebrations in the time of King Hezekiah the king donates 1,000 bulls and 7,000 sheep, while the nobility gives 1,000 bulls and 10,000 sheep (2 Chron 30:23-24). The figures for the same event during the reign of King Josiah are similar: the king offered 30,000 lambs and goats and 3,000 bulls, the nobility donated 2,600 lambs and goats together with 300 bulls, while the Levitical leadership gave 5,000 lambs and goats and 500 bulls (2 Chron 35:7-9). After the return from the exile the returnees offered 12 bulls, 96 rams, 77 lambs and 12 goats (Ezra 8:35), and a simple comparison of these figures with the earlier ones found in Chronicles gives one an appreciation of the postexilic decline and may represent a conscious theological strategy of the author of Ezra-Nehemiah.

Space limitations here do not permit a discussion of some of the large numbers in Chronicles (*see* Numbers, Large Numbers), but the difference in numbers between the preexilic and postexilic periods is quite marked, as can be seen in Table 1.

Table 1 provides some interesting clues in terms of socioeconomic developments as well as hierarchical considerations. During the premonarchical period there are no recorded major sacrificial communal events. Most offerings are presented to the deity by individuals (e.g., Gideon, Manoah) whose socioeconomic resources clearly are limited. This emphasizes the more private nature of Israelite worship (Albertz 1978; 2002, 91-92) during this particular period and reflects the tribal and clan sociopolitical structure. The biblical authors describing this period often emphasize the unorthodox nature of worship ("All the people did what was right in their own eyes" [Judg 17:6; 21:25]). Due to the lack of a central administrative force, the economy involving animal husbandry and agriculture is primarily geared toward survival. Frequent wars, droughts and uncertain political conditions did not allow for surplus production, and thus subsistence farming prevailed. Breeding technologies and agricultural techniques (including iron implements and water management) were not yet highly developed. Agricultural terracing, though not necessarily an Israelite innovation, was done, but it became a widespread practice only during the later Iron Age II period, including also climatically marginal lands in the Judean desert and the Negev (S. Gibson, 137-38). Most probably this was due to the lack of economic stability and the lack of strong organizational authority. Beginning in the united monarchy there are instances of offerings that affect the community, as can be seen in the case of the bringing of the ark of the covenant to the newly chosen capital Jerusalem. Interestingly, there are two instances (to be repeated

also in the conflict between Yahweh and Baal on Mount Carmel) where the ratio involves exclusively cattle instead of the more economical caprines. Beginning with the dedication of the temple during the reign of Solomon, the absolute numbers of offerings increase dramatically and the ratio changes. While Solomon's offerings involve roughly five caprines to one head of cattle, in later contexts this number increases to a ratio of 10:1, and reaches approximately 15:1 after the exile. Again this seems to be an indication of the impoverished state of the returnees, in terms of both absolute numbers and ratios.

Table 2 presents a sample of the paleozoological data concerning both caprines and bovines in Palestine during the Iron Age. It should be noted that the data are given in terms of the percentages of the bone fragments.

The average ratio between caprines and bovines is approximately 4.5:1, not considering the extremely small sample from the Hebrew Union College excavation of Tel 'Ira. It is also interesting to note the high ratio from Ḥorvat Qitmit (13.2:1), which should be explained in terms of the particular nature of the site: an Edomite cult site involving sacrifices that apparently did not include a high percentage of cattle. The extremely high bovine percentage at Tel Nov, resulting in a 1.1:1 ratio, should be explained in terms of the limited data sample of the site as well as its geographical location in the fertile Golan Heights, where the raising of cattle is much more feasible than in the less fertile central highlands. It is also interesting to note the development in some sites where data exist from both Iron Age I and Iron Age II of increasing the percentage of bovines during Iron Age II (e.g., Jerusalem), while other sites (e.g., Tel Masos or Lachish in the border region of the Negev) show a decrease in bovines in Iron Age II as compared to Iron Age I. This may be due to changing climatic conditions.

Another important subgroup of domesticated animals, generally known as equids, includes the horse (*sûs* or *sûsâ* [fem.]; *pārāš*, "chariot horse"), donkey (*ḥămôr*; also *ʿayir*, "stallion of ass"; *ʾātôn*, "she-ass"), mule/hinny (*pered*, or *pirdâ* [fem.]) and the special-purpose horse (*rekeš*) that may have indicated a fast express service during the Persian period (Klingbeil 1995). As shown in a detailed study of the textual data

Table 2. Faunal Remains of Caprines and Bovines from Palestine during Iron Age I-II

Location	Caprines (%)	Bovines (%)	Ratio C:B	Source
Beersheba	77.5%	12.5%	6.2:1	Firmage, 1122
Dan	52.0%	33.0%	1.6:1	Firmage, 1122
Heshbon	82.3%	7.7%	10.7:1	Firmage, 1122
Ḥorvat Qitmit	93.0%	7.0%	13.2:1	Kolska Horwitz and Raphael, 298
ʿIzbet Ṣarṭah	52.7%	34.4%	1.5:1	Firmage, 1122
Jerusalem (city of David excavations 1978-1985) (IA I)	88.0%	10.0%	8.8:1	Kolska Horwitz 1996, 313
Jerusalem (City of David excavations 1978-1985) (IA II)	77.4%	19.6%	3.9:1	Kolska Horwitz 1996, 313
Lachish (IA I)	46.9%	48.3%	1:1	Firmage, 1122
Lachish (IA II)	67.5%	17.5%	3.9:1	Firmage, 1122
Mount Ebal (IA I)	68.0%	22.0%	3:1	Kolska Horwitz 1986-1987, 185
Shiloh (IA I)	75%	22.9%	3.3:1	Firmage, 1122
Shiloh (IA II)	66.8%	27.7%	2.4:1	Firmage, 1122
Tel ʿIra (Tel Aviv excavations)	83.0%	12.0%	6.9:1	Kolska Horwitz 1999, 491
Tel ʿIra (HUC excavations)	94.0%	1.0%	94:1	Kolska Horwitz 1999, 491
Tel Masos (IA I)	65.8%	25.8%	2.6:1	Firmage, 1122
Tel Masos (IA II)	42.8%	7.3%	5.9:1	Firmage, 1122
Tel Michal (IA II)	58.8%	30.2%	1.9:1	Firmage, 1122
Tel Nov (IA II)	35.0%	30.0%	1.1:1	Kolska Horwitz 2000, 123
Tel Qiri	81.6%	14.6%	5.6:1	Firmage, 1122
Tel es-Saʿidiyeh (IA II)	50.0%	24.0%	2.1:1	Firmage, 1122

from 1-2 Kings (Klingbeil 2003b), a functional analysis of equids in Israelite society provides some interesting data. Approximately 50 percent of the references to equids in 1-2 Kings involve the military use of the animals, mostly referring to chariot or cavalry warfare (e.g., 1 Kings 4:26, 28; 20:21; 2 Kings 3:7), while some 28.5 percent indicate transportation use (e.g., 1 Kings 2:40; 13:13; 2 Kings 4:22), and in 20.6 percent of the cases equids functioned as social-status marker, involving the use of donkeys (2 Kings 6:25), mules/hinnies (1 Kings 1:33, 38, 44; 10:25; 18:5; 2 Kings 5:17), horses (1 Kings 10:25, 28, 29; 18:5; 2 Kings 5:9) and chariot horses (1 Kings 1:5).

The social-status function in particular requires further comment, especially when viewed from a diachronic perspective. More than 60 percent of the social-status references are to be dated to the tenth century BCE, which generally is viewed as the formative period of the monarchy in Israel. Socially, this was a time of great change, with the monarchy still trying to establish itself (Tadmor). Interestingly, and far removed from our present perception, the hybrid mule represented in the tenth century BCE a highly prized commodity indicating social status (Klingbeil 2003c, 413-21). Absalom, in his unsuccessful bid for the crown, is caught on a mule (2 Sam 18:9). King David's sons all use mules as their preferred means of transportation (2 Sam 13:29), and Solomon is led to the place of coronation on the hinny of his father, David (1 Kings 1:33, 38, 44). Later on, when the entire world is paying homage to the wisdom of King Solomon, they bring mules among the choicest presents (1 Kings 10:25/Chron 9:24). A century later, during the ninth century BCE, Ahab demands that his captain Obadiah water the royal horses and mules during a time of extreme drought (1 Kings 18:5). Also outside the realm of Palestine the mule was understood as a royal means of transportation at Mari (Sasson; Kupper, 191). At Ebla mules were the highest-priced animals, their average selling price being 60 shekels; the highest bid ever found is 300 shekels (Zarins, 185-87), a staggering figure in light of the fact that a sheep could be had for 1 shekel, while an oxen cost 10 shekels, and a horse 20 shekels. Similar prices have been documented in Hittite sources (Dent, 62). Later usage of the mule suggests a change, inasmuch as it was used more for transportation purposes, which is reflected also in the biblical data (Ezek 27:14; Ezra 2:66; Neh 7:68) and in Neo-Assyrian sources (Klingbeil 2003c, 420-21). The elevated status of the mule most probably was due to the fact that as a hybrid it was among the costliest animals to breed, was unable to reproduce (and thus was dead capital) and had to be imported because of the prohibition of breeding hybrids found in Leviticus 19:19.

1 Kings 10:25-29 describes Solomon's tremendous riches, the gifts he received from other royalty and his trade in chariots and horses. This international trade in status animals with important military connotations constituted an important element in the "internationalization"

of tastes and affairs of the Israelite monarchy (Ikeda). However, by far the highest use of equids should be related to their military function. When one analyzes the time distribution (in rough divisions according the centuries) of the military use of equids, an interesting pattern arises: only 19 percent should be attributed to the tenth century BCE, followed by 13 percent connected to the ninth century BCE, compared to 68 percent appearing in the context of the eighth century BCE (Klingbeil 2003b). The usage seems to correlate with the general historical picture of the tenth to eighth centuries BCE: a tenth century (which begins in 1 Kings at the end of David's reign) with little challenge or interference from outside powers, followed by a ninth century with even less large-scale military activity but plenty of small-scale state problems, and an eighth century that testifies to a tremendous surge in the military use of equids (at least from the angle of the author[s] of Kings), most probably connected to the reawakened Neo-Assyrian Empire and its hunger for land, resources, people and power (Kuhrt, 2.416, 473).

Another relevant function of equids involves general transportation, often employing donkeys (1 Sam 25:18-19, 23, 42; 2 Sam 16:1-2; 17:23; 1 Kings 2:40; 13:13, 23, 24, 28, 29) or horses (2 Kings 5:9; 9:17-20). During the late premonarchical period it seems that in some cases the biblical text hints at a seminomadic lifestyle. When Saul and a servant look for lost family donkeys, they pass through fairly extensive terrain, which may suggest that the donkeys were grazing semi-independently (1 Sam 9:1-4). Perhaps this involved communal herds that were managed by several families or clans together. The indication of sheepfolds along the way in 1 Samuel 24:3 (*gĕdērâ*, "wall, hedge" [MT 1 Sam 24:4]) may suggest this, at least for caprines. The job of shepherd often was assigned to the youngest family member, as can be seen in the case of David before his anointing by Samuel (1 Sam 16:11). A flock without a shepherd is lost and will be scattered. The same pastoral imagery is applied to Israel, which after the death of Ahab will be scattered without a shepherd (i.e., a king) (1 Kings 22:17/2 Chron 18:16).

Numbers play an important role in the communication strategy of the Historical Books. Solomon has 1,400 chariots and 12,000 horsemen that were stationed in the chariot cities (1 Kings 10:26/2 Chron 1:14). In 1 Kings 4:26 (MT 5:6) Solo-

Table 3. Faunal Remains of Equids from Palestine During Iron Age I-II

Location	Strata/Period	Equids (%)	Source
Khirbet Seilun	Stratum IV (8th-7th centuries BCE)	—	Hellwing, Sade and Kishon
Tel Michal	Strata XIV-XII (10th-8th centuries BCE)	0.49%	Hellwing and Feig
Tel Dan	Area B (1974 season) (Israelite period)	0.65%	Wapnish, Hesse and Ogilvy
Tel Nov	Only one stratum	2.50%	Kolska Horwitz 2000
Tel Qiri, Yokneʿam Regional Project	1975-1977 seasons	0.20%	Davis
ʿIzbet Ṣarṭah	Stratum I (early 10th century BCE)	—	Hellwing and Adjeman
Tel Masos	IA II	0.26%	Tchernov and Drori
Ḥorvat Qitmit	IA II	—	Kolska Horwitz and Raphael
Jerusalem (city of David excavations 1978-1985)	Area D1, Stratum XIV Area D2, Stratum XII	0.25%	Kolska Horwitz 1996
Hesban	Strata XVIII-XVI (12th-6th centuries BCE)	1.57%	LaBianca and von den Driesch, 35-44

omon is said to have had 40,000 stalls for horses and 12,000 horsemen. The first number may represent a scribal error, seeing that LXXB and also the parallel verse in 2 Chronicles 9:25 mention only 4,000 horse stalls, a figure also more in harmony with the number of chariots referred to in 1 Kings 10:26 (Mulder, 193-94). These numbers are purposefully high and rounded in order to express the military prowess of Solomon. A similar tendency has already been shown in regard to the immense number of sacrifices offered during the dedication of the temple (22,000 oxen and 120,000 sheep/goats), which underlines Solomon's loyalty to Yahweh. Great victories are highlighted by great numbers: David subdues the king of Zoba in Syria and takes 1,000 chariots and 7,000 horsemen, leaving the king only sufficient chariot horses to run 100 chariots (1 Chron 18:4). The Ammonites contract 32,000 chariots to fight David and are defeated. An Aramaean force of 7,000 chariots and 40,000 infantry is destroyed by David (1 Chron 19:18). By means of these high numbers the Chronicler emphasizes David's victories and underlines the tendency to take David as the model of all later monarchs (Fouts, 387; Japhet, 48-49).

Ascertaining the presence or absence of equids in Palestine during the period covering the Historical Books is difficult, particularly in view of the fact that systematic recovery of paleozoological data was not common practice during the first sixty to seventy years of twentieth-century archaeological fieldwork in Palestine, when most major sites (such as Hazor, Megiddo, Lachish, Beth-Shean) were being excavated. Table 3 provides some raw data, although it should be noted that most major (i.e., royal) cities are not included in the list due to lack of data.

The paleozoological data from selected (and published) Iron Age II sites suggest that the standard ratio of equids to total identifiable faunal remains generally is way below the 1 percent mark and thus should be considered fairly insignificant. Most sites (including the published data from Jerusalem) exhibit the typical Iron Age II paleozoological profile of a high percentage (generally in the region of 70 to 80 percent) of sheep/goats with a decreasing number of cattle (exception: Tel Nov) and a few other nondomesticated species (deer, gazelle, etc.). Equids are way down the line, which probably indicates their costliness and may point to their status function.

In the published data (which does not claim completeness) there is no evidence for the use of equids in military contexts. In addition to the previously mentioned limitation of the lack of systematic recovery of faunal data in the major digs during the first part of the twentieth century, this perhaps is due to the fact that only a limited percentage of each site has been uncovered, and only a limited percentage of the faunal remains have survived and can be interpreted.

The iconographical data concerning equids provide another interesting angle from which to understand the function and use of these animals in Israelite society. In many instances it is not entirely clear whether the ancient artist intended to describe a donkey, a mule or a horse, although general trends are perceivable. The iconographical data include also representational art, or figurines, including the more recently published horse/rider figurines from Jerusalem (Gilbert-Peretz). Of the over 1,300 ceramic figurines belonging to Iron Age II, 73 percent correspond to animal representations, and of these, 82 percent are horse figurines (Gilbert-Peretz, 39). It should be noted that the majority of these figurines date between the eighth and the sixth centuries BCE, although the figurine type developed earlier, during the first part of Iron Age II. Among the stamp seals published in the first volume of Keel's (1997) catalog, eleven stamp seals contain equids and should be dated to Iron Age II (Klingbeil 2003b).

Before this section is drawn to a close, some other domesticated species need to be mentioned. Although generally these species did not play a major role in Israelite animal husbandry (or at least did not leave a significant impression in the OT text), they were present, and they include camels, pigs, chicken, dogs and cats.

Camels *(gāmāl)* are not frequently mentioned in the Historical Books, although they had been domesticated and are documented in the paleozoological data from Syro-Palestinian sites. Camel bones have been found in three different levels at Kadesh-Barnea, at ʿIzbet Ṣarṭah, and also in large quantities at Tel Jemmeh, as well as numerous Nabatean sites in the Negeb (Firmage, 1139-40). In the OT camels are associated predominantly with nomadic people or groups living outside Palestine, and often they are associated with exotic products (Staubli, 199-202). When the Aramean king Ben-hadad, who is ill, sends Hazael to inquire

from the prophet Elisha whether he will recover from his sickness, he sends along forty camel loads of goods to repay the prophet for his trouble (2 Kings 8:9). The Midianites oppressing Israel, together with the Amalekites and "sons of the East," come to Israel on their camels in numbers so great as to be compared to a swarm of locusts (Judg 6:5; 7:12). David's raids into neighboring regions result in the destruction of settlements, while at the same time taking livestock as spoil of war (1 Sam 27:9). When David recovers his loved ones from the Amalekites, only four hundred young men of the enemy can flee on their camels (1 Sam 30:17). The Queen of Sheba comes to Solomon's court with a long train of camels, carrying spices, gold and precious stones (1 Kings 10:2/2 Chron 9:1). During the initial conquest the Gadites make war against the Hagrites and acquire 50,000 camels, 250,000 sheep and 2,000 donkeys (1 Chron 5:21). Camels, together with donkeys, were mainly used for transportation purposes (1 Chron 12:40). The returnees from the Babylonian exile bring 435 camels with them (Ezra 2:67/Neh 7:68), which again represents a small number compared to the earlier figures, and which underlines the sorry state of the returnees.

The pig *(ḥăzîr)* appears only seven times in the OT (Lev 11:7; Deut 14:8; Ps 80:14; Prov 11:22; Is 65:4; 66:3, 17), none of which are in the Historical Books. Its absence is to be explained by the categorical prohibition against Israelites eating the meat of pigs (Lev 11:7; Deut 14:8), which obviously would not encourage its breeding. Pigs are by nature omnivorous and thrive on foraging in forests. They are not well adapted to cellulose diets (e.g., grass), and they do not provide important secondary products such as milk, wool or dung. For these reasons pigs generally are not found in communities where pastoral nomadism is the dominant way of life (Firmage, 1130). Many different explanations for the stringent prohibition of pig meat consumption in the OT have been offered (Borowski 1998, 142), including (1) the political/cultural need to preserve a specific group identity, (2) a religious response to cultic practices of another group (e.g., the Hittite practice of pig sacrifice [Moyer, 29-33]), (3) particular environmental and social conditions favoring or discouraging the raising of pigs, (4) health considerations, especially the fear of trichinosis, (5) economic and political conditions that encourage or discourage the raising of pigs. Faunal pig remains are rare in Iron Age sites in the hill country and the Negev (Borowski 1998, 143). While pig remains generally represent less than 1 percent of the faunal remains in sites from these regions (e.g., Hazorea, 2.0%; Tel Dan, 2.0%; Beersheba, 0.02%; Tel Masos, 0.2%; Tel Michal, 0.7%; Shiloh, 0.7%; ʿIzbet Ṣarṭah, 0.4% [see Kolska Horwitz 1986-1987, 185]), larger percentages have been found at sites generally associated with the Philistines or other ethnic groups (e.g., Tel Miqne/Ekron, 18.0% [Firmage, 1134]; Tel Qasile, 1.0% [Kolska Horwitz 1986-1987, 185]; Tel Nov, 25.0% [Kolska Horwitz 2000, 123]; Tel es-Saʿidiyeh, 13.0% [Firmage, 1134]).

Biblical Hebrew has no term denoting "chicken" or "rooster," although the species must have been known in ancient Israel, as iconographical depictions on stamp seals dating to Iron Age II demonstrate. During the excavation of Tel en-Naṣbeh in 1932 a stamp seal including the Hebrew inscription "Belonging to Yaʾazanyahu, servant of the king" as well as the image of an aggressive fighting cock walking toward the left (or right in the impression) was found in tomb 19 (seal 8 in Avigad and Sass, 52). Another seal with a similar image, bought on the antiquity market in Jerusalem, contains the inscription "Belonging to Yehoʾaḥaz, son of the king" (seal 13 in Avigad and Sass, 54), although its authenticity has been questioned. Another unprovenanced seal, possibly of Phoenician origin and dating to the eighth century BCE, depicts two roosters facing each other and ready to fight (Aufrecht). The earliest attestation in Palestine comes from the Late Bronze Age at Tel Michal, where it represented 1.8 percent of the total faunal remains. During the following periods this figure was more or less stable (e.g., Iron Age, 1.2%; Persian period, 1.5%; Hellenistic period, 3.6% [Hellwing and Feig, 245]). Other sites including faunal remains of chicken during the Iron Age and later include Lachish and Tel Hesban (Borowski 1998, 158).

Dogs *(keleb)* appear mostly in negative contexts in the Historical Books. Goliath's mocking of David when David faces him with a stick hints at the bad treatment of dogs in society (1 Sam 17:43). David compares himself to a dead dog or an insignificant flea when he laments Saul's persecution of him (1 Sam 24:14). A similar sentiment is expressed by Jonathan's descendant Mephibosheth when he faces David (2 Sam 9:8), and it is also echoed in Hazael's response to Elisha (2 Kings 8:13). Abishai compares the cursing Shimei, who needs to be silenced, with a "dead dog" (2 Sam 16:9). Complete annihilation of an enemy often involves the licking of blood and the eating of the carcass by dogs, resulting in no future for the deceased (1 Kings 14:11; 16:4; 21:19, 23; 22:38; 2 Kings 9:10, 36). It is possible that this involved bands of unmanaged dogs, which apparently were common (Borowski 1998, 135).

The cat is not mentioned in the OT, although it was highly important in Egyptian culture, where it was a sacred animal (Osborn and Osbornová, 108-10). It is also mentioned in the Mishnah. Faunal remains of cats have been discovered in Ashdod and Vered Jericho (Borowski 1998, 145). More recently, a rare Persian-period mold of a terra-cotta cat from Beth Gan has been discovered, and the analysis of the materials from which it was made, as well as a similar cat figurine from Akziv, suggests that the figurine was produced at a site along the coastal plain of Palestine (Liebowitz and Dehnisch 1998).

4. Conclusions.

Agriculture and animal husbandry played a central role in Israelite society and religion. After all, it was Yahweh who had given the land as ancestral property to his chosen people Israel. It was also Yahweh who supplied the precipitation and sun necessary to raise crops and maintain herds of domesticated animals. The OT sacrificial system depended heavily upon offerings of sheep, goats, bulls or oxen (and to a lesser degree on doves or pigeons) and distinguished between "clean" animals and "unclean" animals that were unfit for consumption or sacrifice. In many instances loyalty to Yahweh is expressed by means of great numbers of sacrifices. An interesting exercise is to compare the ratios of these sacrificial lists with the ratios of excavated faunal remains from different sites. In some instances the ratios reflect accurately the typical mix of caprines and bovines during the Iron Age and Persian periods. However, in some cases, particularly concerning offerings by individuals, the ratio suggests a very significant sacrifice (e.g., when a bull/oxen was offered) that corresponded to a high economic value. Other important elements connecting religious practice and agricultural activities (including animal husbandry) involve the festal calendar of the OT, which connects particular events in the salvation history of Israel with agricultural realities. Throughout the entire period depicted in the Historical Books of the OT there exists a recognizable tension between the true worship of Yahweh, based upon sound theology, and the idolatrous Baal worship prevalent in Syria-Palestine.

Geographical realities also played an important role in the shaping of Israelite agricultural and sociocultural patterns. In many instances the interaction between plains and highlands, as well as the adaptation to particular seasonal climatic changes, led to highly adapted lifestyles, such as subsistence pastoralism. The introduction of the monarchy marks a turning point in Israelite agriculture and animal husbandry. Besides the technological advances of the particular period at the beginning of Iron Age II, the organizational and also ideological changes brought on by a centralized administration based upon dynastic rule tremendously affected the production and distribution of foodstuffs. The biblical text provides interesting glimpses into these changes. During the formative period of the monarchy one can note an increase in status animals (such as mules and chariot horses), which did not appear earlier in the more tribal reality of premonarchical times. These elements are not always easily perceivable, and disciplines such as iconography, paleozoology and paleobotany provide welcome insights to help the exegete understand the biblical text in its true cultural, historical and religious dimensions. After all, while the biblical writers thought in theological patterns involving Yahweh in all the components of their lives, they lived in actual human history, with genuine links to their neighbors and in concrete places, climates and material cultures. The study of their agricultural realities and their practices of animal husbandry has illuminated these material realities, which in turn shed light upon their important theological perceptions.

See also ARCHAEOLOGY, SYRO-PALESTINIAN; CITIES AND VILLAGES; ISRAELITE SOCIETY; TRADE AND TRAVEL; WATER AND WATER SYSTEMS.

BIBLIOGRAPHY. **M. G. Abegg Jr.,** "נטע," *NIDOTTE* 3.94-96; **Y. Aharoni and J. Naveh,** *Arad Inscriptions* (JDS; Jerusalem: Israel Explora-tion Society, 1981); **P. M. M. G. Akkermans and G. M. Schwartz,** *The Archaeology of Syria: From Complex Hunter-Gatherers to Early Urban Societies (c. 16,000-300 BC)* (Cambridge: Cambridge University Press, 2003); **R. Albertz,** *Persönliche Frömmigkeit und offizielle Religion: Religionsinterner Pluralismus in Israel und Babylon* (CTM A/9; Stuttgart: Calwer, 1978); idem, "Religion in Preexilic Israel," in *The Biblical World,* ed. J. Barton (2 vols.; London: Routledge, 2002) 2.90-100; **Z. Amar,** "Agricultural Realia in Light of the Lachish Relief," *UF* 31 (1999) 1-11; **W. E. Aufrecht,** "A Phoenician Seal," in *Solving Riddles and Untying Knots: Biblical, Epigraphical, and Semitic Studies in Honor of Jonas C. Greenfield,* ed. Z. Zevit, S. Gitin and M. Sokoloff (Winona Lake, IN: Eisenbrauns, 1995) 385-87; **N. Avigad and B. Sass,** *Corpus of West Semitic Stamp Seals* (Jerusalem: Israel Academy of Sciences and Humanities; Israel Exploration Society; Institute of Archaeology, Hebrew University Jerusalem, 1997); **D. Baird,** "Agriculture," *DANE* 6; **J. Blenkinsopp,** "The Family in First Temple Israel," in *Families in Ancient Israel,* ed. L. G. Perdue et al. (Louisville: Westminster/John Knox, 1997) 48-103; **O. Borowski,** *Agriculture in Iron Age Israel* (Winona Lake, IN: Eisenbrauns, 1987); idem, *Daily Life in Biblical Times* (SBLABS 5; Atlanta: Scholars Press, 2003); idem, *Every Living Thing: Daily Use of Animals in Ancient Israel* (Walnut Creek, CA: AltaMira, 1998); **W. Brueggemann,** *The Land: Place as Gift, Promise, and Challenge in Biblical Faith* (OBT; Philadelphia: Fortress, 1977); **J. Clutton-Brock,** "The Unnatural World: Behavioural Aspects of Humans and Animals in the Process of Domestication," in *Animals and Human Society: Changing Perspectives,* ed. A. Manning and A. Serpell (London: Routledge, 1994) 23-35; **M. Cogan,** *I Kings* (AB 10; New York: Doubleday, 2001); **M. Cogan and H. Tadmor,** *II Kings* (AB 11; New York: Doubleday, 1988); **D. Collon,** "How Seals Were Worn and Carried. The Archaeological and Iconographic Evidence," in *Proceedings of the XLVe Rencontre Assyriologique Internationale: Historiography in the Cuneiform World,* 2: *Seals and Seal Impressions,* ed. W. W. Hallo and I. J. Winter (Bethesda, MD: CDL Press, 2001) 15-30; **F. M. Cross Jr.,** "Ammonite Ostraca from Heshbon: Heshbon Ostraca IV-VIII," *AUSS* 13 (1975) 1-20; idem, "Heshbon Ostracon XI," *AUSS* 14 (1976) 145-48; **G. Davies,** "Hebrew Inscriptions," in *The Biblical World,* ed. J. Barton (2 vols.; London: Routledge, 2002) 1.270-86; **S. Davis,** "The Faunal Remains from Tell Qiri," in *Tell Qiri: A Village in the Jezreel Valley; Report of the Archaeological Excavations 1975-1977*, ed. A. Ben-Tor and Y. Portugali (Qedem 24; Jerusalem: Institute of Archaeology, Hebrew University, 1987) 249-51; **A. Dent**, *Donkey: The Story of the Ass from East to West* (London: Harrap, 1972); **R. B. Dillard**, "The Reign of Asa (2 Chronicles 14-16): An Example of the Chronicler's Theological Method," *JETS* 23 (1980) 207-18; **I. Finkelstein**, "The Rise of Jerusalem and Judah: The Missing Link," in *Jerusalem in Bible and Archaeology: The First Temple Period*, ed. A. E. Killebrew and A. G. Vaughn (SBLSymS 18; Atlanta: Society of Biblical Literature, 2003) 81-101; idem, "Toward a New Periodization and Nomenclature of the Archaeology of the Southern Levant," in *The Study of the Ancient Near East in the Twenty-First Century: The William Foxwell Albright Centennial Conference*, ed. J. S. Cooper and G. M. Schwartz (Winona Lake, IN: Eisenbrauns, 1996) 103-23; **E. Firmage**, "Zoology," *ABD* 6.1109-65; **D. E. Fleming**, "If El Is a Bull, Who Is a Calf? Reflections on Religion in Second-Millennium Syria-Palestine," in *Frank Moore Cross Volume*, ed. B. A. Levine et al. (Eretz-Israel 26; Jerusalem: Israel Exploration Society, 1999) 23*-27*; **D. M. Fouts**, "A Defense of the Hyperbolic Interpretation of Large Numbers in the Old Testament," *JETS* 40 (1997) 377-87; **F. S. Frick**, "Palestine, Climate of," *ABD* 5.119-26; **J. C. L. Gibson**, *Textbook of Syrian Semitic Inscriptions*, 1: *Hebrew and Moabite Inscriptions* (Oxford: Clarendon, 1971); **S. Gibson**, "Agricultural Terraces and Settlement Expansions in the Highlands of Early Iron Age Palestine: Is There Any Correlation Between the Two?" in *Studies in the Archaeology of the Iron Age in Israel and Jordan*, ed. A. Mazar (JSOTSup 331; Sheffield: Sheffield Academic Press, 2001) 113-46; **D. Gilbert-Peretz**, "Ceramic Figurines," in *Excavations at the City of David (1978-1985), Directed by Yigal Shiloh*, 4: *Various Reports*, ed. D. T. Ariel and A. de Groot (Qedem 35; Jerusalem: Institute of Archaeology, Hebrew University of Jerusalem, 1996) 29-41; **R. P. Gordon**, *I & II Samuel* (Grand Rapids: Zondervan, 1986); **N. C. Habel**, *The Land Is Mine. Six Biblical Land Ideologies* (OBT; Minneapolis: Fortress, 1995); **B. Halpern**, *The First Historians. The Hebrew Bible and History* (San Francisco: Harper & Row, 1988); **J. Hansen**, "Paleobotany," *OEANE* 4.200-201; **M. G. Hasel**, "The Destruction of Trees in the Moabite Campaign of 2 Kings 3:4-27: A Study in the Laws of Warfare," *AUSS* 40 (2002) 197-206; idem, *Domination and Resistance: Egyptian Military Activity in the Southern Levant, ca. 1300-1185 BC* (Probleme der Ägyptologie 10; Leiden: E. J. Brill, 1998); **S. Hellwing and Y. Adjeman**, "Animal Bones," in ʿ*Izbet Ṣarṭah: An Early Iron Age Site Near Rosh Haʿayin, Israel*, ed. I. Finkelstein (BAR International Series 299; Oxford: John and Erica Hedges/Archaeopress, 1986) 141-52; **S. Hellwing and N. Feig**, "Animal Bones," in *Excavations at Tel Michal, Israel*, ed. Z. Herzog et al. (Publications of the Institute of Archaeology 8; Minneapolis: University of Minnesota Press; Tel Aviv: Sonia and Marco Nadler Institute of Archaeology, Tel Aviv University, 1989) 236-47; **S. Hellwing, M. Sade and V. Kishon**, "Faunal Remains," in *Shiloh: The Archaeology of a Biblical Site*, ed. I. Finkelstein et al. (Institute of Archaeology Monograph Series 10; Tel Aviv: Institute of Archaeology, Tel Aviv University, 1993) 309-50; **B. Hesse**, "Animal Husbandry," *OEANE* 1.140-43; idem, "Animal Husbandry and Human Diet in the Ancient Near East," in *Civilizations of the Ancient Near East*, ed. J. M. Sasson (4 vols.; New York: Scribner, 1995) 1:203-22; **B. Hesse and P. Wapnish**, "Palaeozoology," *OEANE* 4.206-7; **D. C. Hopkins**, "Agriculture," *OEANE* 1.22-30; **Y. Ikeda**, "Solomon's Trade in Horses and Chariots in Its International Setting," in *Studies in the Period of David and Solomon and Other Essays*, ed. T. Ishida (Winona Lake, IN: Eisenbrauns, 1982) 215-38; **I. Jacob and W. Jacob**, "Flora," *ABD* 2.803-17; **S. Japhet**, *I & II Chronicles. A Commentary* (OTL; Louisville: Westminster/John Knox, 1993) **K. Jaroš**, *Hundert Inschriften aus Kanaan und Israel* (Fribourg: Katholisches Bibelwerk, 1982); **I. T. Kaufman**, "Samaria (Ostraca)," *ABD* 5.921-26; **O. Keel**, *Corpus der Stempelsiegel-Amulette aus Palästina/Israel: Von den Anfängen bis zur Perserzeit; Einleitung* (OBOSA 10; Göttingen: Vandenhoeck & Ruprecht; Freiburg: Universitätsverlag, 1995); idem, *Corpus der Stempelsiegel-Amulette aus Palästina/Israel: Von den Anfängen bis zur Perserzeit; Katalog Band I, Von Tell Abu Farag bis ʾAtlit* (OBOSA 13; Göttingen: Vandenhoeck & Ruprecht; Freiberg: Universitätsverlag, 1997); idem, *Die Welt der altorientalischen Bildsymbolik und das Alte Testament* (5th ed.; Göttingen: Vandenhoeck & Ruprecht, 1996); idem, "Iconography and the Bible," *ABD* 3.358-74; **O. Keel and C. Uehlinger**, *Gods, Godesses, and Images of God in Ancient Israel* (Minneapolis: Augsburg, Fortress, 1998); **P. J. King and L. E. Stager**, *Life in Biblical*

Israel (LAI; Louisville: Westminster/John Knox, 2001); **K. A. Kitchen,** "The Controlling Role of External Evidence in Assessing the Historical Status of the Israelite United Monarchy," in *Windows into Old Testament History: Evidence, Argument, and the Crisis of "Biblical Israel,"* ed. V. P. Long, D. W. Baker and G. J. Wenham (Grand Rapids: Eerdmans, 2002) 111-30; **R. Kletter,** "Temptation to Identify: Jerusalem, *mmšt,* and the *lmlk* Jar Stamps," *ZDPV* 118 (2002) 136-49; **G. A. Klingbeil,** "Getting the Big Picture: History, Method, Potential and Possible Pitfalls of Archaeological Survey Work," in *Wort und Stein: Studien zur Theologie und Archäologie; Festschrift für Udo Worschech,* ed. F. Ninow (BEAM [Ard el-Kerak] 4; Frankfurt: Peter Lang, 2003a), 145-78; idem, "'Man's Other Best Friend': The Interaction of Equids and Man in Daily Life in Iron Age II Palestine as Seen in Texts, Artifacts, and Images," *UF* 35 (2003b [2004]) 259-90; idem, "Methods and Daily Life: Understanding the Use of Animals in Daily Life in a Multi-Disciplinary Framework," in *Life and Culture in the Ancient Near East,* ed. R. Averbeck, D. B. Weisberg and M. W. Chavalas (Bethesda, MD: CDL Press, 2003c), 401-33; idem, "בקר," *NIDOTTE* (1997) 2.992-95; idem, "*rkš* and Esther 8,10.14: A Semantic Note," *ZAW* 107 (1995) 301-3; **G. N. Knoppers,** "The Vanishing Solomon: The Disappearance of the United Monarchy from Recent Histories of Ancient Israel," *JBL* 116 (1997) 19-44; **L. Kolska Horwitz,** "Animal Remains from Tel Nov, Golan Heights," ʿ*Atiqot* 39 (2000) 121-34; idem, "Areas L and M," in *Tel ʿIra: A Stronghold in the Biblical Negev,* ed. I. Beit-Arieh (Tel Aviv: Emery and Claire Yass Publications in Archaeology, 1999) 488-94; idem, "Faunal Remains from Areas A, B, D, H and K," in *Excavations at the City of David 1978-1985, Directed by Yigal Shiloh, 4: Various Reports,* ed. D. T. Ariel and A. de Groot (Qedem 35; Jerusalem: Institute of Archaeology, Hebrew University of Jerusalem, 1996) 302-17; idem, "Faunal Remains from the Early Iron Age Site on Mount Ebal," *TA* 13-14.2 (1986-1987) 173-89; **L. Kolska Horwitz and O. Raphael,** "Faunal Remains," in *Horvat Qitmit: An Edomite Shrine in the Biblical Negev,* ed. I. Beit-Arieh (Institute of Archaeology Monograph Series 11; Tel Aviv: Institute of Archaeology, Tel Aviv University, 1995) 287-302; **A. Kuhrt,** *The Ancient Near East c. 3000-330 BC* (2 vols.; Routledge History of the Ancient World; London: Routledge, 1995); **J. R. Kupper,** "L'opinion publique

a Mari," *Iraq* 25 (1963) 190-91; **Ø. S. LaBianca,** "Subsistence Pastoralism," in *Near Eastern Archaeology: A Reader,* ed. S. Richard (Winona Lake, IN: Eisenbrauns, 2003) 116-23; **Ø. S. LaBianca and A. von den Driesch,** eds., *Faunal Remains: Taphonomical and Zooarchaeological Studies of the Animal Remains from Tell Hesban and Vicinity* (Hesban 13; Berrien Springs, MI: Andrews University Press and Institute of Archaeology of Andrews University, 1995); **G. Lehmann,** "The United Monarchy in the Countryside: Jerusalem, Judah, and the Shephelah During the Tenth Century B.C.E.," in *Jerusalem in Bible and Archaeology: The First Temple Period,* ed. A. E. Killebrew and A. G. Vaughn (SBLSymS 18; Atlanta: Society of Biblical Literature, 2003) 117-62; **A. Lemaire,** "Epigraphy, Transjordanian," *ABD* 2.561-68; **N. P. Lemche,** *Die Vorgeschichte Israels: Von den Anfängen bis zum Ausgang des 13. Jahrhunderts v. Chr.* (BE 1; Stuttgart: Kohlhammer, 1996); **A. Leonard Jr.,** "The Late Bronze Age," in *Near Eastern Archaeology: A Reader.* ed. S. Richard (Winona Lake, IN: Eisenbrauns, 2003) 349-56; **H. Liebowitz and A. M. Dehnisch,** "A Mould-Made Seated Terra-cotta Cat from Beth Gan," *IEJ* 48 (1998) 174-82; **A. Mazar,** "Remarks on Biblical Traditions and Archaeological Evidence Concerning Early Israel," in *Symbiosis, Symbolism, and the Power of the Past: Canaan, Ancient Israel, and Their Neighbors from the Late Bronze Age through Roman Palestina,* ed. W. G. Dever and S. Gitin (Winona Lake, IN: Eisenbrauns, 2003) 85-98; **A. R. Millard,** "King Solomon in His Ancient Context," in *The Age of Solomon: Scholarship at the Turn of the Millennium,* ed. L. K. Handy (SHCANE 11; Leiden: E. J. Brill, 1997) 30-53; **R. D. Miller II,** "Modeling the Farm Community in Iron Israel," in *Life and Culture in the Ancient Near East,* ed. R. E. Averbeck, M. W. Chavalas and D. B. Weisberg (Bethesda, MD: CDL Press, 2003) 289-309; **J. C. Moyer,** "Hittite and Israelite Cultic Practices: A Selected Comparison," in *Scripture in Context II: More Essays on the Comparative Method,* ed. W. W. Hallo, J. C. Moyer and L. G. Perdue (Winona Lake, IN: Eisenbrauns, 1983) 19-38; **M. J. Mulder,** *1 Kings 1-11* (HCOT; Leuven: Peeters, 1998); **T. Ornan,** "The Bull and Its Two Masters: Moon and Storm Deities in Relation to the Bull in Ancient Near Eastern Art," *IEJ* 51 (2001) 1-26; **D. J. Osborn and J. Osbornová,** *The Mammals of Ancient Egypt* (Natural History of Egypt 4; Warminster: Aris & Phillips, 1998); **W. T. Pitard,** "The Identity of

19

Bir-Hadad of the Melqart Stela," *BASOR* 272 (1988) 3-21; **M. A. Powell,** "Weights and Measures," *ABD* 6.897-908; **A. F. Rainey,** "Israel in Merneptah's Inscription and Reliefs," *IEJ* 51 (2001) 57-75; **C. N. Raphael,** "Geography and the Bible (Palestine)," *ABD* 2.964-77; **P. Riede,** *Im Spiegel der Tiere: Studien zum Verhältnis von Mensch und Tier im alten Israel* (OBO 187; Göttingen: Vandenhoeck & Ruprecht; Freiburg: Universitätsverlag, 2002); **A. M. Rosen,** "Paleoenvironmental Reconstruction," *OEANE* 4.201-4; **M. L. Ryder,** "Sheep and Goat Husbandry with Particular Reference to Textile Fiber and Milk Production," in *Domestic Animals of Mesopotamia, Part I,* ed. J. N. Postgate and M. A. Powell (Bulletin on Sumerian Agriculture 7; Cambridge, MA: Sumerian Agriculture Group, 1993) 9-32; **J. M. Sasson,** "Official Correspondence from the Mari Archives," in *Civilizations of the Ancient Near East,* ed. J. M. Sasson (4 vols.; New York: Scribner, 1995) 2.1204; **R. A. Simkins,** *Creator and Creation: Nature in the Worldview of Ancient Israel* (Peabody, MA: Hendrickson, 1994); **D. C. Snell,** *Life in the Ancient Near East, 3100-332 B.C.E.* (New Haven: Yale University Press, 1997); **T. Staubli,** *Das Image der Nomaden im Alten Israel und in der Ikonographie seiner sesshaften Nachbarn* (OBO 107; Göttingen: Vandenhoeck & Ruprecht; Freiburg: Universitätsverlag, 1991); **H.-J. Stipp,** "'Alles Fleisch hatte seinen Wandel auf der Erde verdorben' (Gen 6,12): Die Mitverantwortung der Tierwelt an der Sintflut nach der Priesterschrift," *ZAW* 111 (1999) 167-86; **J. Strange,** "The Late Bronze Age," in *The Archaeology of Jordan,* ed. B. MacDonald, R. Adams and P. Bienkowski (LevAr 1; Sheffield: Sheffield Academic Press, 2001) 291-321; **H. Tadmor,** "Traditional Institutions and the Monarchy: Social and Political Tensions in the Time of David and Solomon," in *Studies in the Period of David and Solomon and Other Essays,* ed. T. Ishida (Winona Lake, IN: Eisenbrauns, 1982) 239-57; **E. Tchernov and I. Drori,** "Economic Patterns and Environmental Conditions at Hirbet el-Msas during the Early Iron Age," in *Ergebnisse der Ausgrabungen auf der Hirbet el-Msas (Tel Masos) 1972-1975,* ed. V. Fritz and A. Kempinski (3 vols.; ADP; Wiesbaden: Harrassowitz, 1983) 1.213-22; **D. T. Tsumura,** "Family in the Historical Books," in *Family in the Bible,* ed. R. S. Hess and M. D. Carroll R. (Grand Rapids: Baker, 2003) 59-79; **C. Uehlinger,** "Bildquellen und 'Geschichte Israels': Grundsätzliche Überlegungen

und Fallbeispiele," in *Steine, Bilder, Texte: Historische Evidenz ausserbiblischer und biblischer Quellen,* ed. C. Hardmeier (ABG 5; Leipzig: Evangelische Verlagsanstalt, 2001); 25-77; **K. van der Toorn,** "Currents in the Study of Israelite Religion," *CurBS* 6 (1998) 9-30; **Å. Viberg,** *Symbols of Law: A Contextual Analysis of Legal Symbolic Acts in the Old Testament* (ConBOT 34; Stockholm: Almqvist & Wiksell, 1992); **C. E. Walsh,** *The Fruit of the Vine: Viticulture in Ancient Israel* (HSM 60; Winona Lake, IN: Eisenbrauns, 2000); **P. Wapnish,** "Archaeozoology: The Integration of Faunal Data with Biblical Archaeology," in *Biblical Archaeology Today, 1990: Proceedings of the Second International Congress on Biblical Archaeology, Jerusalem, June-July 1990,* ed. A. Biran and J. Aviram (Jerusalem: Israel Exploration Society, 1993) 426-42; **P. Wapnish and B. Hesse,** "Archaeozoology," in *Near Eastern Archaeology: A Reader,* ed. S. Richard (Winona Lake, IN: Eisenbrauns, 2003) 17-26; **P. Wapnish, B. Hesse and A. Ogilvy,** "1974 Collection of Faunal Remains from Tell Dan," *BASOR* 227 (1977) 35-62; **P. Warnock,** "Paleoethnobotany," in *Near Eastern Archaeology: A Reader,* ed. S. Richard (Winona Lake, IN: Eisenbrauns, 2003) 27-32; **Z. Weisman,** "Reflection of the Transition to Agriculture in Israelite Religion and Cult," in *Studies in Historical Geography and Biblical Historiography Presented to Zecharia Kallai,* ed. G. Galil and M. Weinfeld (VTSup 81; Leiden: E. J. Brill, 2000) 251-61; **H. Wilde,** *Technologische Innovationen im zweiten Jahrtausend vor Christus: Zur Verwendung und Verbreitung neuer Werkstoffe im ostmediterranen Bereich* (GO 4, Reihe Ägypten 44; Wiesbaden: Harrassowitz, 2003); **J. Zarins,** "Equids Associated with Human Burials in Third Millennium B. C. Mesopotamia: Two Complementary Facets," in *Equids in the Ancient World,* ed. R. H. Meadow and H.-P. Uerpmann (2 vols.; BTAVO A19/1-2; Wiesbaden: Dr. Ludwig Reichert Verlag, 1986) 1.164-93.   G. A. Klingbeil

AHAB. *See* HISTORY OF ISRAEL 5: ASSYRIAN PERIOD; OMRI DYNASTY.

AHAZIAH. *See* HISTORY OF ISRAEL 5: ASSYRIAN PERIOD; JEHOSHAPHAT; OMRI DYNASTY.

AI

A city in the central hill country associated with Abram's early years in *Canaan (Gen 12—13) and with the later conquest under *Joshua (Josh 7—8).

1. Biblical Data
2. Location and History

1. Biblical Data.

Both the city's name (*hāʿay*, "the ruin") and biblical comments regard Ai as a prominent landmark east of *Bethel. Just west of Ai Abram camped, built an altar (Gen 12:8), and later returned (Gen 13:3). The Historical Books know it as the site of the disastrous defeat that exposed Achan's hidden sin (Josh 7) and of the still visible "heap of ruins" left by Joshua after its capture (Josh 8:28; cf. Josh 12:9). The only other mention of Ai occurs in postexilic lists of reoccupied towns (Ezra 2:28; Neh 7:32; cf. Is 10:28 ["Aiath" is a variant of "Ai"]). Jeremiah 49:3 laments an Ammonite city named Ai (ʿay, "ruin").

1.1. Joshua 7—8: Victory Follows Defeat. After victory at *Jericho, Joshua sends spies to reconnoiter Ai, presumably as Israel's next conquest (Josh 7:2). Their report advises against sending the whole army against Ai (some thirteen miles uphill); they deem a small attack force of two or three units (here *ʾelep* means "unit" not "thousand") sufficient to take the city because its defenders "are so few" (Josh 7:3). Joshua concurs, but Ai's defenders deal Israel a disastrous defeat, leaving about thirty-six dead (Josh 7:4-5). The defeat shatters Israel's courage, and a grieving Joshua accuses God of treachery (Josh 7:6-9). What Joshua does not know (but the reader does) is the root of the disaster: Yahweh is angry at Israel because Achan had sinned by secretly keeping booty from Jericho (Josh 7:1). The casting of lots publicly identifies him (Josh 7:10-18); he confesses and is executed, and God's anger ends (Josh 7:19-26).

Yahweh takes charge of the second assault on Ai. He reassures Joshua of victory, commands the entire army (thirty units) to go, permits Israel to keep any booty taken, and orders a tactical ambush from behind the city (Josh 8:1-2). Joshua obeys, hiding the ambush force of five units west of the city and positioning his main force to its north (Josh 8:3-8, 12-13). The next morning, when the king of Ai and his army attack Israel east of the city, Israel feigns a hurried retreat, thus drawing out the city's remaining defenders and also troops from nearby Bethel (Josh 8:14-17). At Yahweh's command, Joshua raises his scimitar, symbol of his authority, toward Ai. The ambushers enter

and burn it (Josh 8:18-19), then head east to trap and slaughter Ai's forces in open country between them and Joshua's force (Josh 8:20-22). Ai's casualties total twelve units (Josh 8:24-26), including the king, whom Joshua hangs and has buried under a symbolic pile of rocks at the city gate still visible in the writer's day (cf. Josh 12:9). Israel reduces the city to ruins but keeps its livestock and booty (Josh 8:27-29). Strategically, the city's fall gives Israel access to central Canaan and sends shockwaves of fear among the Hivites of nearby *Gibeon (Josh 9:3). Pretending to be foreign visitors, they trick Israel into making a nonaggression treaty (Josh 9:15). More important, the twin shocks of Ai's fall and the treaty with Gibeon caused King Adoni-zedek of Jerusalem to rally four other southern Canaanite kings to attack Gibeon (Josh 10:1-5). Joshua honors the treaty with Gibeon, leads Israel to save the city, and ends up conquering southern Canaan (Josh 10:6-43).

1.2. Postexilic Ai. Ezra and Nehemiah list Ai with Bethel among the hometowns to which Judah returned after the exile (Ezra 2:28; Neh 7:32). Scholars believe that the list in Ezra 2 probably draws on that of Nehemiah 7, so its tally of 223 (LXX: 423) returnees— exactly one hundred more than in Nehemiah 7—probably reflects a textual corruption. The list marks the only biblical evidence of Ai's possible occupation after its fall to Joshua.

2. Location and History.

Biblical data place Ai just east of Bethel ("next to Bethel" [Josh 12:9]) and near Beth-aven (Josh 7:2). That soldiers from Bethel joined Ai's defenders in chasing Joshua's main force suggests close proximity between the two cities (Josh 8:17; but LXX omits "and Bethel"). The location of Beth-aven remains uncertain, although it may lie somewhere west of Michmash (1 Sam 13:5; 14:23) and north or northeast of Bethel (Josh 18:12-13). But two indicators suggest that its mention may even be a superfluous gloss. The LXX of Joshua 7:2 omits it completely, but most modern translations follow MT in retaining the reference to Beth-aven. (In Hosea, Beth-aven marks a derogatory name for Bethel [Hos 4:15; 5:8; 10:5, 6].) A strong scholarly consensus regards the identification of Bethel with modern Beitin as certain (but see below), and three sites around modern Deir Dibwan (two miles east of Beitin) commend consideration as biblical Ai: Khirbet Haiyan (south), Khirbet Khudriya (east), and et-Tell (southeast). Excavations reveal the first two to be Byzantine settlements, perhaps monasteries (323-636 CE), but extensive excavations at et-Tell led most recently by J. A. Callaway yielded evidence of four Early Bronze Age settlements (c. 3100-2400 BCE) and one in Iron Age I (1200-1050 BCE).

2.1. Et-Tell as Ai. Most scholars accept the identification of et-Tell (a huge site covering 27.5 acres) as biblical Ai. Its Arabic name ("ruin heap") may render the ancient Hebrew one ("the ruin"), and its location on the southern ridge of the Wadi el-Jaya that runs east to Jericho comports well with biblical details that a ravine lay between the city and Joshua's camp north of it (Josh 8:11, 13; but cf. LXX). The Iron Age settlement stood just east of the ruin's acropolis and accommodated a small population (perhaps 150-300). It had no fortifications, but its streets were paved with cobblestones. Two technological innovations sustained its residents: the digging of cisterns to store captured rainwater, and the terracing of hillsides for farming. Material remains (e.g., stone saddles, mortars, sheep and goat bones) imply that they were both shepherds and farmers. According to Callaway, two phases of occupation are evident: one c. 1200 BCE by settlers (perhaps extended families) fleeing the Sea Peoples' arrival along the Canaanite coast; and a second c. 1125 BCE that saw an increase in population, less orderly designs of houses and streets, and the use of underground silos (not large clay jars) for grain storage. Callaway interprets the latter settlers as "proto-Israelites," the people portrayed in the book of Judges and from whom (in his view) Israel emerges. Sling stones found on residence floors suggest that an attack may have ended their small settlement at "the Ruin" (c. 1050 BCE).

2.2. The Difficulty and Proposed Alternate Sites. The identification of biblical Ai with et-Tell creates a historical problem. This is especially true for those who hold an "early" date for the exodus and conquest (e.g., c. 1450-1400 BCE), but it also would trouble holders of a "late" date (e.g., c. 1280-1230 BCE). The city shows no evidence of occupation from 2700 BCE to 1200 BCE, the very time when the events of Joshua 7—8 would have occurred. For that reason, some scholars reckon the narrative as an unhistori-

cal, etiological legend told to explain the ruins of Ai. Alternatively, W. F. Albright suggested that the biblical writer confused an original account about the fall of Bethel (which was destroyed) as being about Ai instead. But this seems unlikely because the topographical details of Joshua 7—8 seem to fit the terrain of et-Tell better than that of Bethel. Some also argue that the text's mention of Bethel is a later expansion (LXX omits it). On the other hand, biblical references to Ai commonly pair it with Bethel, so the latter's mention may in fact imply the conquest of both cities. (Note that Josh 12:16 celebrates the conquest of Bethel, but Joshua nowhere details it.) Another approach is to propose an alternative location for Ai (e.g., Khirbet Nisya or Khirbet el-Maqatir) and even for Bethel (e.g., el-Bireh), but three decades of vigorous discussion apparently have not weakened the consensus favoring the traditional identifications of both cities. Finally, some scholars who accept et-Tell as Ai argue that details in Joshua 7—8 suggest that the then extant ruins of Ai may actually have served as a temporary defensive outpost for Bethel. This view is consistent with the fact that the spies initially found "so few" at Ai (Josh 7:3), that defenders from Bethel joined Ai's forces against Israel, and that only twelve "units" of Ai perished. Such an ad hoc defensive force probably would leave few, if any, archaeological traces. One must also concede that two millennia of erosion may have washed away some evidence of occupations at Ai.

See also JERICHO.

BIBLIOGRAPHY. **R. G. Boling and G. E. Wright,** *Joshua* (AB 6; Garden City, NY: Doubleday, 1982); **J. A. Callaway,** "Ai," *ABD* 1.125-30; idem, "Ai," *NEAEHL* 1.39-45; **R. E. Cooley,** "Ai," *OEANE* 1.32-33; **R. K. Harrison,** "Ai," *ISBE* 1.81-84; **R. S. Hess,** *Joshua* (TOTC; Downers Grove, IL: InterVarsity Press, 1996); **D. Livingston,** "Location of Biblical Bethel and Ai Reconsidered," *WTJ* 33 (1970) 20-44; idem, "Further Considerations on the Location of Bethel at El-Bireh," *PEQ* 126 (1994) 154-59; **H. G. M. Williamson,** *Ezra, Nehemiah* (WBC 16; Waco, TX: Word, 1985); **K. L. Younger Jr.,** "Early Israel In Recent Biblical Scholarship," in *The Face of Old Testament Studies,* ed. D. W. Baker and B. T. Arnold (Grand Rapids, MI: Baker, 1999) 176-206; **Z. Zevit,** "The Problem of Ai," *BAR* 11 (1985) 58-69.

R. L. Hubbard Jr.

AKKADIAN. *See* BABYLONIA, BABYLONIANS.

"ALL ISRAEL." *See* CHRONICLER'S HISTORY; CHRONICLES, BOOKS OF; ISRAEL.

ALLOTMENTS, TRIBAL. *See* TRIBES OF ISRAEL AND LAND ALLOTMENTS/BORDERS.

AMMAN CITADEL INSCRIPTION. *See* NON-ISRAELITE WRITTEN SOURCES: SYRO-PALESTINIAN.

AMMON, AMMONITES

The Ammonites, known from both biblical and ancient Mesopotamian sources, were an ancient people who inhabited the central Transjordanian Plateau from about the middle of the second millennium until the middle of the first millennium BCE. Their country was known as Ammon, and their capital was called Rabbah-ammon or Amman. They are best known for their numerous encounters with the biblical Israelites.

1. Ammonites in Biblical Tradition
2. Recent Archaeology in Ammon
3. Biblical Ammon and Ammonites in Archaeological Perspective

1. Ammonites in Biblical Tradition.

According to Genesis 19:36-38, the ancestor of the Ammonites was Ben-ammi, the son of an incestuous relationship between Lot and his younger daughter. Many scholars assume that the name *Ben-ammi*, which means "son of my people" or "son of my paternal father," was a popular etymology that developed in support of a tradition of a kindred relationship between Ammon and Israel. However, G. M. Landes (1956, 4-6) shows from Ugaritic texts that "Ben-ammi" was a genuine clan name as well as a personal name. D. I. Block (1984) further shows that *běnê ʿammôn* (the Hebrew expression for the Ammonite people) cannot be interpreted in the same way as *běnê yiśrāʾēl* ("sons of Israel"), even though they appear to be analogous. Rather, the prefixed element *bn* or *bny* was an integral part of the full name, similar to the well-known Semitic name "Benjamin." Thus the proper designation for the land of the Ammonites was not "Ammon," but "Bene-ammon." Similarly, the full and proper form of the name for the eponymous ancestor of the Ammonites is "Ben-ammi." Therefore, while it is highly unlikely that the existence of Lot's son could be

historically established apart from the biblical record, the idea that the Ammonites had an ancestor with such a name is not at all impossible.

The biblical tradition views the Ammonites as an indigenous people who descended directly from Lot. According to Deuteronomy 2:20-21, the Ammonites eventually grew strong enough to displace an ancient people known as the Rephaim (called the Zamzummim by the Ammonites) from the headwaters of the Jabbok. There the Ammonites established their capital, Rabbah-ammon (2 Sam 12:27). Thus the biblical record indicates that the Ammonites occupied the central Transjordanian Plateau for some time before the Israelites arrived on the scene (Gen 19:38; Num 21:24; Deut 2:19). From a purely scientific perspective, it is presently impossible either to prove or to disprove the Bible's view of Ammonite origins. Critical scholarship tends to view the biblical account of Ammonite origins as an Israelite attempt to disparage their long-time enemies, and it generally prefers to look for an exogenous origin for the Ammonites (Younker 2003).

2. Recent Archaeology in Ammon.

Recent archaeological survey and excavation within the territory of Ammon as described in biblical sources indicate a Late Bronze Age population that was more pastoral and less sedentary as compared with the earlier Middle Bronze Age and later Iron Age populations (see Younker 1999; 2003). It is possible that the Late Bronze population, for which we have no indigenous written sources at present, was included among the people whom the Egyptians called the Shasu. Their social organization had not reached the level that could be called a "state" in sociopolitical terms; rather, they were organized along kin-based or tribal lines (in some classification schemes they would be called a chiefdom). At the time of the transition from the Late Bronze Age to Iron Age I, this same population appears to undergo a significant increase in sedentarization and intensifies its agricultural production—numerous villages and farmsteads "sprout up" throughout Ammon during this time. The number of farms, villages and urban centers continues to increase and grow throughout Iron Ages I-II. By the peak of Iron Age II (seventh century BCE) there is enough evidence to suggest that the social organizational complexity had increased to the level of a small, secondary "state," although the kin-based elements remained strong enough throughout society to suggest that the term "tribal state" might be more appropriate. The evidence for this increased complexity includes a three-tiered settlement hierarchy, as well as a variety of substantial public works (fortifications, water systems, etc.). These technical sociopolitical designations should not be understood to contradict the designations that contemporary or later biblical writers would have assigned, such as "king" and "kingdom," although we need to be careful not to retroject our contemporary ideas of what those terms mean onto ancient times.

There is some change within the material culture of this population between the latter part of the Late Bronze Age and Iron Age II, but there is no evidence at present of any significant intrusive elements in the population—that is, they appear to be the same basic people group that occupies this region throughout this entire period. Since we have in situ indigenous epigraphical evidence as well as textual sources from Assyria that these people were identified as Ammonites, it seems reasonable to suggest that the Late Bronze Age people are indeed the ancestors of the Iron Age II Ammonites, regardless of how they were identified by the Egyptians or how they identified themselves in the Late Bronze Age.

3. Biblical Ammon and Ammonites in Archaeological Perspective.

In regard to the historical background of the Late Bronze Age and Iron Age I settlement process in Ammon, it is interesting to note that according to the biblical tradition, Ammon was settled prior to Israel (see Gen 19:38; Num 21:24-26; Deut 2:19). At present, it appears that the initial phase of early Israelite settlement coincided with the diminishment of Egyptian control in Canaan that occurred during the twenty-five year period following the reign of Merneptah (c. 1213-1203 BCE), but prior to the initial arrival of the *Philistines along the southwest coast of Canaan around 1180 BCE (Younker 2003, 168). Ammon, which was more distant from the harassment by Egyptian and Canaanite city-state authorities to the west, appears to have begun settling a little earlier. Indeed, recent work at ʿUmayri (south of the capital city, Amman) suggests that the Iron Age I

site indeed was settled prior to sites west of the Jordan, based on the ceramic assemblage that includes the earliest Iron Age I forms and a higher percentage of Late Bronze Age forms than is typical of parallel sites in the west. Whether this has anything to do with the Israelite tradition is hard to say at present. However, the currently available archaeological data do not contradict this possibility.

According to Judges 3:12-14, the Ammonites' initial hostile action against Israel occurred when the former joined a coalition of *Moabites and Amalekites. As a result of the conflict, Israel became subject to King Eglon of Moab for eighteen years. The domination was broken when Ehud, the son of Gera the Benjamite, assassinated Eglon at Jericho and led Israel in a successful campaign against Moab that resulted in Moab's subjection for some eighty years (see Judges). How Ammon benefited from its initial alliance with Moab against Israel is uncertain, but present archaeological evidence for this period suggests a time of growth and stability for Ammon.

Judges 11 records a confrontation between the Israelite judge Jephthah and an unnamed Ammonite king. The first Ammonite king whose name is recorded is Nahash, noted for his conquest of Israelite territories bordering Ammon, especially his invasion across the Jabbok and the siege of Jabesh-gilead (1 Sam 11:1-11), only to be pushed back by Israel's king *Saul. Although there is no direct archaeological evidence for these events, there is a distinct increase in the number of Ammonite sites during Iron Ages IA-IB.

When David's envoys were humiliated by Nahash's successor, Hanun, war broke out between Israel and Ammon. In spite of help from several Aramaean city states, the Ammonites were defeated by David's generals, Joab and Abishai (2 Sam 10; 1 Chron 19). The Ammonites eventually became tributary to *David when he captured their capital city, Rabbah (2 Sam 11:12; 1 Chron 20:1-3). David is said to have placed the Ammonite crown upon his head. Samples of such a crown have been found on numerous stone busts of Ammonite kings found in the Ammon area.

During the reign of *Solomon (tenth century BCE), the Ammonites relationship with Israel seems to have improved, with Solomon taking wives from the princesses of the Ammonites

(1 Kings 11:1). However, they attempted another invasion of Judah in the time of *Jehoshaphat (2 Chron 20: 1-30) and were again forced to pay tribute. Tribute continued to be paid by Ammon to Israel during the times of Uzziah (Azariah) (2 Chron 26:8) and Jotham (2 Chron 27:5).

During Iron Age II (ninth through sixth centuries BCE) the Ammonites appear to have reached the zenith of their power, in spite of the fact that they were mostly under *Assyrian domination during that time. Indeed, it was at this time, some scholars suggest, that Ammon truly reached the sociopolitical level of a small-scale secondary (tribal) state (Younker 2003, 168-70). When Ammon was conquered by the Assyrians, the tribute that the former had paid to Judah was now redirected to Assyria. Assyrian texts first mention the Ammonites during the reign of Shalmaneser III (Battle of Qarqar in 853 BCE). Tiglath-pileser III's (745-727 BCE) records claim that he received tribute from Sanipu of the house of Ammon. Similarly, Esarhaddon (681-669 BCE) received payments from Pusuil and Ashurbanipal (c. 669-627 BCE) from Amminadbi. The relatively high amount of tribute paid by the Ammonites has led some scholars to conclude that Ammon was among the wealthy kingdoms of Syria-Palestine during the time of Assyrian domination. Archaeological survey work confirms the presence of many well-planned agricultural farmsteads throughout Ammon during this time, which would have provided the foundation for Ammon's wealth during Iron Age II.

After the fall of the Assyrian Empire, the Ammonites became vassals of the *Babylonians. When Jehoiakim of Judah rebelled against Nebuchadnezzar, the Ammonites took up their overlord's cause by harassing Judah (2 Kings 24:2). After Jerusalem fell, the Ammonite king Baalis hired Ishmael, a former general of Judah, to assassinate Gedaliah, the Babylonian appointed governor of Judah (2 Kings 25:23; Jer 40:14; 41:1, 2). Baalis's name recently has been found on both a seal and a bulla; the latter was found at Tall al-ʿUmayri (sometimes spelled "Tell el-ʿUmeiri"), a major Ammonite site south of Amman (see Herr 1998). It appears that the prosperity that Ammon enjoyed under the Assyrians continued under the Babylonians. This success may be reflected in Jeremiah 49:4, where the prophet rebukes the Ammonites for taking advantage of Judah's misfortunes by moving into the territory of Gad: "Why do you boast of your valleys, boast of your valleys so fruitful? O unfaithful daughter, you trust in your riches and say, 'Who will attack me?'" Again, survey work by the Madaba Plains Project throughout the Ammonite hinterland has uncovered numerous farmsteads and agricultural installations providing the economic foundation that Jeremiah describes (Younker 1994, 312-13).

The transition from the period of Babylonian dominance to that of the *Persians (sixth century BCE) is difficult to discern archaeologically. Although it is possible that some sites exhibit some destruction from the Babylonian period, it now seems clear that general occupation throughout Ammon was unbroken and the region continued as a province during the Persian period and even into Hellenistic times. Jar handles with the name "ʾAmmon" stamped on them parallel the "Yehud" (Judah) stamps found in Cis-Jordan and represent Persian provincial seals (Herr 1993). Important biblical references for later Ammon are found in Nehemiah 2:10, 19; 4:3, 7; 6:1, 12, 14; 13:4-8, where the activities of a certain Ammonite, Tobiah, are described. Tobiah was seen as attempting to resist Nehemiah's restoration work in Jerusalem. Evidence for the later Tobiads in Ammon has been found in Jordan at Iraq el-Amir, a large Hellenistic palace west of Ammon. The name "Tobiah" is actually carved in Old Hebrew characters on the entrances to two caves, not far from the palace, on the north side of the wadi.

See also EDOM, EDOMITES; MOAB, MOABITES.

BIBLIOGRAPHY. **D. I. Block,** *"Bny ʿamwn*: The Sons of Ammon," *AUSS* 22 (1984) 197-212; **L. G. Herr,** "Tell el-ʿUmayri and the Madaba Plains Region," in *Mediterranean Peoples in Transition: Thirteenth to Early Tenth Centuries BCE,* ed. S. Gitin, A. Mazar and E. Stern (Jerusalem: Israel Exploration Society, 1998) 251-64; idem, "Whatever Happened to the Ammonites?" *BAR* 19.6 (1993) 26-35, 68; **G. M. Landes,** "A History of the Ammonites" (Ph.D. diss.; Johns Hopkins University, 1956); idem, "The Material Civilization of the Ammonites," *BA* 24 (1961) 66-86; **R. W. Younker,** "Ammonites," in *Peoples of the Old Testament World,* ed. A. J. Hoerth, G. L. Mattingly and E. M. Yamauchi (Grand Rapids: Baker, 1994) 293-316; idem, "The Emergence of Ammon: A View of the Rise of Iron Age Polities from the Other Side of the Jordan," in *The Near East in the South-*

west: Essays in Honor of William G. Dever, ed. B. A. Nakhai (Boston: American Schools of Oriental Research, 2003) 153-76; idem; "Review of Archaeological Research in Ammon," in *Ancient Ammon,* ed. B. MacDonald and R. W. Younker (SHCANE 17; Leiden: E. J. Brill, 1999) 1-18.

R. W. Younker

AMNON. *See* DAVID'S FAMILY.

AMON. *See* HISTORY OF ISRAEL 5: ASSYRIAN PERIOD.

AMORITES. *See* BABYLONIA, BABYLONIANS.

AMPHICTYONY, QUESTION OF

Amphictyony was not always a question. Over much of the twentieth century *amphictyony* and *covenant* were two parts of a shared answer widely given to two key questions: How should historians describe the structure of ancient Israel before the monarchy? What was the nature of Israel's twelve-tribe system? The story of this classic answer, itself now become question, can be told as part of the account of a remarkable German academic succession, almost a family: A. Alt (1883-1956), M. Noth (1902-1968), R. Smend (1932-), C. Levin (1950-), each at some stage the student or assistant of the one before.

1. M. Noth's Early Israelite Amphictyony
2. R. Smend and Criticisms of the Amphictyony Hypothesis
3. C. Levin: A Postmonarchical Origin of Twelve Tribes?

1. M. Noth's Early Israelite Amphictyony.

M. Noth was far from the first scholar to compare aspects of early Israel with amphictyonies in classical Greece and similar leagues in early Italy before Roman dominion. H. Ewald's history of the people Israel (1864) had already noted links with Greek and Italian groupings; then E. Szanto, in his treatment of the Greek tribes (1901), moved in the opposite direction and mentioned the Israelite system as analogous. H. Gunkel's commentary on Genesis used Szanto in his discussion of Genesis 29:31—30:24. O. Weber had also made the link in the second edition of *Die Religion in Geschichte und Gegenwart* (vol. 3 [1929], col. 438). Alt's own use of the term *amphictyony* in connection with early Israel appears to have started in the same period. However, it is Noth's 1930 monograph on Israel's twelve-tribe system, at the same time both cautious and bold, that is rightly recognized as fundamental to subsequent discussion. Smend (1969, 146) recalls Alt commending it in 1952 as the most important publication of recent times in the field.

To clarify his method, Noth insisted that the task of exploring the history of Israel's traditions is not at an end when the written sources of the biblical books have been critically analyzed. Some elements of the biblical tradition had their own traceable history before they were adopted into the written sources used in the composition of the books. Tradition history should seek to identify the historical time and place from which the origin of any element of tradition could be satisfactorily explained in whole and in part. Noth starts by probing the two systems found in the OT for listing Israel's twelve tribes. Three texts—the blessing of Jacob (Gen 49), the census after the plague (Num 26) and the list of tribal heads (Num 1:5-15)—provide the only evidence of once-independent traditions about a complete people of Israel in twelve tribes. All other references result from written developments of one or the other.

The lists in Numbers 1 and Numbers 26 are close to each other: neither includes Levi, and both list Ephraim and Manasseh rather than Joseph. But Noth holds Genesis 49 to be older than either. Landless Levi could not have achieved third place among the twelve (as Gad did in the later form) had it not been an original member of the twelve. It is only the earlier form that is used to list both tribes and their eponymous leaders (Jacob's sons); the later is used only in connection with the tribes. Noth insists that the origins of the system can be properly understood only in a period in which the tribes could still claim for themselves an interest, while they did still form the historically given individual members of the Israelite people. The second form must reflect a change in historical circumstances. Another early text, the Song of Deborah (Judg 5), illustrates a stage intermediate between the two more familiar listings of the twelve, for it still knows of Machir (and not yet the classical Manasseh) as paired with Ephraim.

The origin of the tradition could be understood only from the historical situation of the so-called period of the *judges; and its continuance, after the formation of the state had made it less relevant, had depended on written memories. Classical Greece and Italy knew several sacral leagues of twelve (or six) members responsible for the care of a common sanctuary, of which the best known was the amphictyony (from a Greek term meaning "next neighbours") centered on Delphi. And Noth set himself to explore whether such an institution was at all conceivable in the judges period. Shared religion must have meant more than each tribe worshiping Yahweh in its own way at its own local sanctuary. He drew on E. Sellin's work depicting the *Shechem "covenant" (Josh 24) as the occasion when the Rachel tribes, which recently had entered the land with Joshua, united with the Leah tribes already there: that group of six had preceded the full group of twelve. "Israel" was the name of this union, and Yahweh was its common god.

Noth ventured the claim that the title "Yahweh, the god of Israel" belonged with the *ark of the covenant: in the cult of the twelve-tribe amphictyony, it was the ark (though movable) that served as central sanctuary. Yet he admitted that this combination could not be proved; it only had a certain likelihood. Then there was so much legal material in the OT that it would hardly be surprising if it still contained remnants of the early Israelite amphictyonic law: perhaps the *mišpaṭim* (ordinances) of the book of the covenant. Its Hebrew name may have been *ʿēdâ* (gathering) or *qāhāl* (assembly), and *nāśîʾ* had been the title of each tribe's delegate. It should cause no surprise, he claimed, that words such as these, which had an intimate connection with a sacral institution, should appear in only two OT contexts: first the few passages that had an immediate connection with the early tradition of the amphictyony (such as Judg 19—21), and then the extended but much later priestly corpus. Noth found the thesis helpful in explaining the unity under the first king: *Saul (1 Sam 11) was able to base himself on a unity already demonstrated in the call-up in Judges 19. The ark had a very special meaning for the history of the cult of Yahweh in Israel: *David used it to give the sanctuary in his new residence the status, or at least the aura, of the amphictyonic central sanctuary.

Noth added four substantial appendices to his main discussion. The first concerned Numbers 26, which he placed between the Song of Deborah and the rise of David. He argued that both Joshua 17:1-3 and Genesis 46:8-25 were ex

tracts from it—this against both B. Baentsch and O. Procksch, who surprisingly had reversed the link between Genesis 46 and Numbers 26. The second offered a literary analysis of a group of related passages: Joshua 24; Deuteronomy 11:29, 30; 27:1-13; Joshua 8:30-35. The third discussed the usage and meaning of *nāśîʾ*. The fourth, on Judges 19—21, argued that these chapters must be either (1) illustrated by the amphictyony, transmitted at the central shrine, and even a report of an actual amphictyonic event, or (2) a late invention without historical basis. If the latter, then they would display a bias or intention, and they lack such; and so they do illustrate the early amphictyony, in which they have their origin.

In 1930 Noth held that the *nĕśîʾîm* corresponded to the Greek *hieromnēmonēs,* the representatives sent by the individual states to the amphictyonic council. Twenty years later he was to observe that it was the "minor judges" listed in Judges 10:1-5 and Judges 12:7-15 who were the only officials reported in that book as having an Israel-wide responsibility. He now found it significant—perhaps in light of his major study of the laws in the Pentateuch (1940)—that this unique early leadership had a legal not a cultic role. And it was with this important supplement that his twelve-tribe thesis became much more familiar through his own *Geschichte Israels* (1950). In 1960 this *History of Israel* was issued in a reliable English translation (see esp. pp. 85-109).

In that same year, J. Bright's widely used *History of Israel* was published. He had already (1956) offered a respectful but critical review of the work of Alt and Noth, and now he was able to draw on G. Mendenhall's work (1955), which offered Near Eastern and not just classical Mediterranean parallels for elements in Israel's traditions. Bright adopted with great enthusiasm, but with much less nuance, what had remained for Noth simply an analogy from classical history for the tribal system of early Israel. He described early Israel variously, repeatedly and promiscuously, as "tribal league," "confederation," "amphictyony" and "covenant society." Put briefly: "Yahwism and covenant are coterminous!" (Bright 1960, 146).

2. R. Smend and Criticisms of the Amphictyony Hypothesis.
R. Smend's 1963 study of Yahweh-war and tribal covenant sought to link together the contribution of Alt and his two best-known students,

Noth and G. von Rad, while insisting on the hypothetical nature of the enterprise. Alt's work on the formation of Israelite states (1930) had drawn attention to some institutional continuities between monarchy and what had gone before; Noth's study of the twelve-tribe system (1930) had described one of these in some detail, and von Rad's account of holy war in ancient Israel another (1951). Smend began by reviewing the evidence for "tribal activity and a league of twelve" in the Song of Deborah, widely reckoned the most authentic, even the only authentic, source for the period of the judges; then he moved to consider "warlike event and cultic institution." "Major and minor judges," "ark and central sanctuary," "Rachel tribes and Leah tribes" and "Exodus from Egypt and covenant-making at Sinai" continued the series of paired topics through which he sought to probe Israel's earliest traditions; and the seventh and last was "Moses at Exodus and Sinai." He concluded that the decisive expressions of the relationship between Yahweh and Israel may have been the wars conducted neither by the amphictyonic institution nor by the totality of the tribes. Yet, without the institution, perhaps there would never have been the statement "Yahweh the god of Israel, Israel the people of Yahweh." The book was reprinted in 1966 with some supplements, and Smend returned to the theme in a short article (1971) responding to criticism of an early Israelite amphictyony from three sides: (1) that the twelve-tribe system had not yet come into existence by the judges period (Herrmann and Mowinckel); (2) that the twelve-tribe system had nothing to do with an amphictyony (Fohrer); (3) that no proofs existed of the amphictyony's arrangements or actions (Eissfeldt).

2.1. G. Anderson. G. Anderson commented on many of the key issues in an essay probing "the nature of Israel's self-understanding" (1970). He recalled Fohrer's reminder (1966) of five different forms of the amphictyony hypothesis—(1) the duodecimal parallels adduced by H. G. A. Ewald and H. Gunkel, (2) J. Wellhausen's "warlike confederacy," (3) Noth's system, (4) ten-member versions of the thesis, (5) theories of smaller amphictyonies earlier than or even contemporaneous with the twelve-tribe confederacy—and he went on to discuss four points. He accepted Noth's argument that the twelve-tribe system was pre-Davidic: "it includes tribes which had ceased to exist as such by David's reign." He

was less persuaded that the historical happening that had brought the confederacy into existence was the invasion of Canaan by the house of Joseph leading to the formation of a twelve-tribe system at Shechem. He was sympathetic to the observation by B. D. Rahtjen that the five-city structure of the Philistines, Israel's closest neighbors of all, offered a closer analogy to the leagues of classical Greece and Italy than Israel's twelve tribes (which could have seven, ten, and eleven members as well as twelve). And he found that H. Orlinsky, in his "vigorous assault" (1962), had misunderstood Noth's position on the ark as central sanctuary but had rightly noted the absence of evidence in the judges period that tribal representatives had met regularly at the center. Anderson concluded with the suggestion that the Hebrew terms *ʿam, qāhāl* and *ʿēdâ*, while having "no necessary reference to an amphictyony," did "merit much fuller discussion as expressions of Israel's self-understanding as the people of Yahweh." Given "the divisive influence of the period of the judges," he preferred to locate the ideal in an earlier Sinaitic covenant.

Anderson's essay drew with approval on the Edinburgh doctoral dissertation of A. Mayes, "Amphictyony and Covenant." This was reworked for publication as *Israel in the Period of the Judges*. Several features of Israel's early activities could readily fit an amphictyonic hypothesis, but could be interpreted quite as well without it. To explain the link between Judah and the rest of Israel, Mayes looked to the traditions underlying Numbers 13—14 of all parts of the later Israel together at Kadesh, before Judah and Simeon moved due north to southern Palestine and the rest entered the center and north via Transjordan and a Jordan crossing. In a volume of essays celebrating H. G. May, Anderson's contribution immediately followed one by R. de Vaux anticipating his own *Early History of Israel* (vol. 2 [1973]). He was equally doubtful about the theory of a twelve-tribe amphictyony at the time of the judges ("seriously questioned today") and of a six-tribe amphictyony in the south that had included Judah. His conclusion was that "the constituted tribe of Judah is to be identified with the first kingdom of David at Hebron."

2.2. N. Gottwald. N. Gottwald's massive study of *The Tribes of Yahweh* (916 pages) has enjoyed even greater popularity outside than inside biblical studies. One explanation he offered himself: "It is not easy to shift from thinking of cultural and social realities deriving from beliefs about God to thinking of cultural and social realities as the matrices for spawning correlative beliefs about God" (Gottwald 1979, 912). Yet it is also true that while Gottwald was wrestling with that methodological shift, several biblical scholars were departing from Noth's basic source-analysis of the texts, to which Gottwald remained very broadly committed. His socioliterary introduction to the Hebrew Bible (1985, 280-81) continues to present a literary history of the Pentateuch and Former Prophets almost indistinguishable from Noth's, down to his common basis G before the familiar sources J and E, and respect for E. Sellin's 1926 discussion of the crucial assembly at Shechem. Gottwald located the origins of the familiar twelve-tribe structure in the administrative units created by David and *Solomon for their united kingdom, and he rejected the amphictyony model. But he rejected it as providing too weak an analogy for what had existed before the monarchy: in Greece, such leagues provided simply "a limited way for autonomous city-states to achieve certain specific purposes." In fact, the Israelite confederacy in the (same) period of premonarchical "liberated Israel" (1250-1050 BCE) "was a consciously contrived 'substitute state' for its peoples, indeed a veritable anti-state" (Gottwald 1985, 282).

2.3. N. P. Lemche. If Noth's model was not strong enough for the historical reality pictured by Gottwald, it was being criticized in Danish from the opposite direction by N. P. Lemche (as early as 1968 according to T. L. Thompson [1993]). However, it was not until 1984 that Lemche provided in English a summary and updating of his 1972 Danish monograph on Israel in the time of the judges. Noth should not be blamed for the use (or abuse) of his thesis by Bright and H.-J. Kraus; yet the term "amphictyony" should be given up because the classical analogy was imperfect. The absence of clear evidence for a center (not just a central sanctuary) removed a vital element, not just of a sacral league, but of a political league as well. Neither Levites nor judges nor the *nāśî'* provided credible personnel for a league. Even Smend's separation of "holy war" from the institution of the amphictyony, where von Rad had located it, could not save the amphictyony. As for the two forms of the tribal list, Lemche argued that neither should be detached from its Pentateuch set-

ting: the form with Levi is found only before the report in Exodus 32 of that tribe's priestly "ordination," and the form without Levi only after. Neither list was premonarchical; list B (without Levi) might derive from Solomon's economic district division. "Now, the amphictyony gone, the basis of the formation of the historical tradition at such an early date has also disappeared" (Lemche 1984, 22).

2.4. G. Ahlström. G. Ahlström's *History of Ancient Palestine* (1993) is crisply dismissive of the amphictyonic hypothesis, and he rightly notes that those who have preferred to talk of a "tribal league" have neither spelled out the difference nor proved the existence of the latter. The Song of Deborah is a poet's celebration of a past, not a present, event and need imply no more than a temporary association of tribes. The same J. Bright as wrote of Samuel that he "more than any other labored to keep the amphictyonic tradition alive" also maintained that "we know almost nothing of what occurred during the years of Philistine occupation"! Ahlström is scathing about the proposal to describe as amphictyonic the Late Bronze Age temple found in Transjordan, at the airport in Amman. Indeed, one wonders (*pace* Dever 2003, 130) exactly what would constitute archaeological support for an amphictyony.

In his 1992 overview article in the *Anchor Bible Dictionary*, A. D. H. Mayes noted how attention had shifted away from amphictyony, "both towards other possible analyses for understanding the totality 'Israel' and toward the study of the basic social units of which any possible Israelite federation was composed." This shift was nicely illustrated in the volume that he himself edited for the Society for Old Testament Study in 2000: it was not mentioned at all in K. Whitelam's essay on the "Foundations of Israel," and there was only a passing comment in J. Day's discussion of "The Religion of Israel" (in Mayes 2000, 430).

Both of the studies by Smend noted above were reprinted in the second volume of his collected studies (1987). Although the dust jacket insisted that the author wanted thereby to indicate his adherence to the now vigorously disputed twelve-tribe theory, his own brief introduction made particularly warm mention of the critique by de Vaux and by Lemche. He even declared himself skeptically interested in any attempt, provided it were open-eyed, to locate the origins of the system in the post- rather than premonarchical period (but certainly not monarchical). It was precisely this challenge that his former student and assistant took up.

3. C. Levin: A Postmonarchical Origin of Twelve Tribes?

C. Levin has done the debate great service by questioning a large number of Noth's (often tentative) answers in three linked papers delivered first in 1992, 1996 and 2001, and republished in 2003. The first of them closes with an explicit citation of Smend's challenge. He quotes C. H. J. de Geus (1976) with approval: "really relevant criticism must . . . begin with Noth's own argumentation." If the witnesses on which Noth supported himself cannot be made probable as early tradition, then the debate on whether the extra-Israelite analogies may or may not be adduced for a hypothetical early Israelite amphictyony ends before it has begun (Bächli 1977). The same reservation holds for the question of the institutions of the tribal league from the social-historical point of view (where Levin presumably has Gottwald in mind).

It was not for nothing that Noth, like his teacher Alt, bestowed the greatest attention on the weighing of the sources. The history of "the amphictyony question" has also been since 1930 the history of the interpretation of a few key texts. Levin finds Noth's placing of Numbers 26:5-51 firmly in the second half of the judges period a particular surprise, in that it did not belong to the basic stock of P, and so could better be part of the final redaction of the Pentateuch. Its links with Genesis 46:8-25 do imply literary dependence. Levin argues, against Noth's detailed excursus in critique of Baentsch and Procksch (see 1 above), that the heading in Numbers 26:4b depends on Genesis 46:8b; that mention in Numbers 26 of Er and Onan is secondary, down to their replacement by sons of Perez; and that Noth's third pillar, Genesis 49, is not old in its entirety—parts of the blessing of Jacob depend on late elements in Genesis. In the documentary analysis of the Pentateuch, its principal source (Gen 35:22b-26) is attributed to P; and so, since it synthesizes P style and JE material, Genesis 49 also presupposes the final redaction. Despite the late dating implied, Levin insists that this is the earliest text to comprehend the twelve sons of Jacob in the sense of a "system." The analysis of Genesis 29—30 confirms

that the tradition of Genesis right into the latest period knew only six sons of Jacob: Reuben, Simeon, Levi, Judah, Benjamin and Joseph. It is only the presentation of the settlement that is aligned with the tribes, and the fact that the number "twelve" must be explained at the few places that add this symbolism into the historical presentation says enough. Levin concludes that the system of the twelve tribes of Israel belongs, pretty much from the beginning, in the genealogical entrance hall of Chronicles.

Beside the system of the twelve tribes, it is the Song of Deborah that has helped make pre-state Israel pass for an institutional entity. Yet this poem takes over postexilic overworkings and glosses from Psalm 68, down to the very letter. Like other poems in Deuteronomy through 2 Kings, it may belong to the most recent texts of the narrative books (see Poetry). Wellhausen had described the Song of Deborah as the earliest monument of Hebrew literature, belonging clearly to an early stage in a people's history, over against the prose report in Judges 4 that had stripped the deity of mystery. Levin cites a letter of von Rad, when Smend had sent him a copy of his 1963 study, stating that von Rad and Noth were not so sure about early dating of the Song of Deborah, but kept their doubts quiet. The view was widespread, from classical antiquity down to Herder, that poetry is older than prose. Yet a study by Vernes, too early for its time (1892), had dated the Song of Deborah to the postexilic restoration, and not to the earlier years of that period, but rather to the fourth or even the third century BCE. His main ground was linguistic: the song contained lexical, morphological and syntactical Aramaisms in considerable number and had contacts with the vocabulary of the late psalms and Chronicles.

Levin complements Vernes's case, arguing that the narrative main part of the Song of Deborah (Judg 5:6-30) is a poetic variant to the Deborah-Barak narrative in Judges 4, which reckons at every point on the reader or hearer knowing the prose model. It is not firmly anchored in the book of Judges, but is one of the biblical "songs for the text" (Diebner): psalms included in the text at particular places, composed on the texts of the Torah and the Prophets read in the cult. Judges 5:16-17 is intrusive in the song: the supplementer had recourse to the blessing of Jacob because it was important to comprehend the twelve-tribe-people in its totality. The ballad in Judges 5:6-27(-30) is framed by a kind of psalm in Judges 5:3-5 and 5:31a. Freed from the assumption that Judges 5 is from the earliest Israelite period, everything speaks for Psalm 68 being the older of the linked texts (Judg 5:4-5 is from the start a double citation of Ps 68:8-9 and Is 64:1 (MT 63:19).

Introducing the English translation of Noth's collected essays, N. Porteous repeated the ancient claim that not "the monarchical system of government," but rather "the continuing religious confederation of the tribes" corresponded "to the abiding reality of Israel." Levin insists that kingship did not run counter to Israel's nature: "Israel" in fact followed the Iron Age kingdom onto the stage of history. That is shown by evidence gathered outside of the OT that does, however, on closer examination tally with OT sources. Hypotheses concerning an Israel prior to the rise of the nation-state, which hitherto have shaped our view of Israel's history, will not stand up to critical scrutiny. The biblical depiction of Israel prior to its becoming a nation-state reflects the situation and the hopes of postexilic Judaism. In a discussion of "Globalization in Biblical Studies," D. Jobling observed that "while the great German tradition appears to have receded in importance, the *terms* developed in that tradition . . . tend to remain alive and well in recent discussion" (Jobling 1993, 107). Levin's three studies demonstrate that "that tradition"—including that part of the tradition in which he himself stands—remains able to be radically self-critical.

Levin's results converge with G. Auld's work, although he seems prepared to allow greater historicity than does the latter (Auld 2004) to the traditions in Samuel of the beginnings of monarchy. Comparing the different ancient texts of Joshua (Hebrew and Greek) led Auld (1987) to conclude that interest in tribes increased in the later stages of the development of that book. Gottwald's use of the traditional rendering of Psalm 122 in the title of his large-scale study had been unfortunate: the double mention of "thrones" in Psalm 122:5 suggests that "scepters" may be more appropriate a rendering of *šbṭym* in Psalm 122:4 than "tribes" (Auld 1998, 72). Indeed, the development in the sense of *šbṭ* (or *mṭh*) from "scepter" or "staff" to "tribe" is symbolic of the shift in later biblical texts from monarchy to a tribal perception of the reality of Israel. The tribal system, especially as presented

in Joshua, finds many echoes in Chronicles; however, it is in (the Pentateuch and) Joshua that twelveness is made an explicit issue, and never in Chronicles, where both the number "twelve" and lists of exactly twelve names remain resolutely elusive (Auld 1998, 115-16). Thus in Auld's view, either the Chronicler is surprisingly careless with a conclusion so recently achieved, or he was not aware of it. It may have been his assemblage of the tribal traditions that led to their "systematization" within (later strata of) Joshua and the Pentateuch.

See also HISTORY OF ISRAEL 1: SETTLEMENT PERIOD; HISTORY OF ISRAEL 2: PREMONARCHIC PERIOD; ISRAEL; TRIBES OF ISRAEL AND LAND ALLOTMENTS/BORDERS.

BIBLIOGRAPHY. **G. W. Ahlström,** *The History of Ancient Palestine* (Minneapolis: Fortress, 1993); **A. Alt,** "Der Gott der Väter" (1929); ET: "The God of the Fathers," in *Essays on Old Testament History and Religion* (Oxford: Blackwell, 1966) 1-77; idem, "Die Staatenbildung der Israeliten in Palästina" (1930); ET: "The Formation of the Israelite State in Palestine," in *Essays on Old Testament History and Religion* (Oxford: Blackwell, 1966) 171-237; idem, "Die Ursprünge des israelitischen Rechts" (1934); ET: "The Origins of Israelite Law," in *Essays on Old Testament History and Religion* (Oxford: Blackwell, 1966) 79-132; idem, "Israel: Politische Geschichte," in *Die Religion in Geschichte und Gegenwart: Handwörterbuch für Theologie und Religionswissenschaft,* vol. 3, ed. H. Gunkel et al. (2d ed.; Tübingen: Mohr, 1929) cols. 437-42; **G. W. Anderson,** "Israel: Amphictyony: 'AM; KAHAL; 'EDAH," in *Translating and Understanding the Old Testament: Essays in Honor of Herbert Gordon May,* ed. H. T. Frank and W. L. Reed (Nashville: Abingdon, 1970) 135-51; **A. G. Auld,** *Joshua Retold: Synoptic Perspectives* (OTS; Edinburgh: T & T Clark, 1998); idem, *Samuel at the Threshold: Selected Works of Graeme Auld* (SOTSMS; Aldershot: Ashgate, 2004); **O. Bächli,** *Amphiktyonie im Alten Testament: Forschungsgeschichtliche Studie zur Hypothese von Martin Noth* (TZS 6; Basel: Reinhardt, 1997); **J. Bright,** *Early Israel in Recent History Writing* (SBT 19; London: SCM, 1956); idem, *A History of Israel* (OTL; London: SCM, 1960); **W. G. Dever,** *Who Were the Early Israelites and Where Did They Come From?* (Grand Rapids: Eerdmans, 2003); **G. Fohrer,** "Altes Testament—'Amphiktyonie' und 'Bund,'" *ThLZ* 91 (1966) 801-16, 893-904; **C. H. J. de Geus,** *The Tribes of Israel: An Investigation into*

Some of the Presuppositions of Martin Noth's Am-phictyony Hypothesis (SSN 18; Assen: Van Gor-cum, 1976); **N. K. Gottwald,** *The Hebrew Bi-ble: A Socio-Literary Introduction* (Philadelphia: Fortress, 1985); idem, *The Tribes of Yahweh: A Soci-ology of the Religion of Liberated Israel 1250-1050 B.C.E.* (London: SCM, 1979); **D. Jobling,** "Global-ization in Biblical Studies," *BibInt* 1 (1993) 96-110; **N. P. Lemche,** *Israel i dommertiden: En over-sigt over diskussionen om Martin Noths "Das System der zwölf Stämme Israels"* (Tekst og tolkning 4; Copenhagen: Institut for Bibelsk Eksgese: i kom-mission hos Gad, 1972); idem, "'Israel in the Pe-riod of the Judges'—The Tribal League in Re-cent Research," *ST* 38 (1984) 1-28; **C. Levin,** *Fortschreibungen: Gesammelte Studien zum Alten Testament* (BZAW 316; Berlin: de Gruyter, 2003); **A. D. H. Mayes,** "Amphictyony," *ABD* 1.212-16; idem, *Israel in the Period of the Judges* (SBT 29; London: SCM, 1974); idem, ed., *Text in Context: Essays by Members of the Society for Old Testament Study* (Oxford: Oxford University Press, 2000); **G. E. Mendenhall,** *Law and Covenant in Israel and the Ancient Near East* (Pittsburgh: Biblical Colloquium, 1955); **M. Noth,** "Das Amt des 'Richters Israels'" (1950) (= Noth 1969, 71-85); idem, *Das System der zwölf Stämme Israels* (BWANT 4/1; Stuttgart: Kohlhammer, 1930); idem, *Gesam-melte Studien zum Alten Testament II* (TB 39; Mu-nich: Kaiser, 1969); idem, *Geschichte Israels* (Göttingen: Vandenhoeck & Ruprecht, 1950); ET: *The History of Israel* (2d ed.; London: Black, 1960); **H. Orlinsky,** "The Tribal System of Israel and Related Groups in the Period of the Judges," in *Studies and Essays in Honor of Abra-ham A. Neuman, President, Dropsie College for He-brew and Cognate Learning,* ed. M. Ben-Horin, B. D. Weinryb and S. Zeitlin (Leiden: E. J. Brill, 1962) 375-87; **N. W. Porteous,** introduction to M. Noth, *The Laws in the Pentateuch and Other Es-says* (Edinburgh: Oliver & Boyd, 1966) v-vi; **G. von Rad,** *Der Heilige Krieg im alten Israel* (ATANT 20; Zürich: Zwingli, 1951); **R. Smend,** *Jahwekrieg und Stämmebund: Erwägungen zur ältes-ten Geschichte Israels* (FRLANT 84; Göttingen: Vandenhoeck & Ruprecht 1963) (2d ed. [1966] repr. in Smend, 1987, 116-99); idem, "Nachruf auf Martin Noth," in M. Noth, *Gesammelte Studien zum Alten Testament II,* ed. H. W. Wolff (TB 39; Munich: Kaiser, 1969) 139-65; idem, *Zur ältesten Geschichte Israels* (BEvT 100; Munich: Kaiser, 1987); idem, "Zur Frage der altisraelitischen Amphiktyonie," *EvT* 31 (1971) 623-30 (repr. in Smend 1987, 210-16); **T. L. Thompson,** "Martin Noth and the History of Israel," in *The History of Israel's Traditions: The Heritage of Martin Noth,* ed. S. L. McKenzie and M. P. Graham (JSOTSup 182; Sheffield: Sheffield Academic Press, 1994) 81-90; **R. de Vaux,** *Histoire Ancienne d'Israël,* 2: *La période des juges* (Paris: Lecoffre, 1973); ET: *The Early History of Israel,* vol. 2 (London: Darton, Longman & Todd, 1978); idem, "The Settlement of the Is-raelites in Southern Palestine and the Origins of the Tribe of Judah," in *Translating and Under-standing the Old Testament: Essays in Honor of Her-bert Gordon May,* ed. H. T. Frank and W. L. Reed (Nashville: Abingdon, 1970) 108-34.

A. G. Auld

ANAT. *See* CANAANITE GODS AND RELIGION.

ANCESTOR CULT. *See* DEATH AND AFTERLIFE.

ANIMAL HUSBANDRY. *See* AGRICULTURE AND ANIMAL HUSBANDRY

ANOINTING

In the Historical Books of the Hebrew Bible anointing is almost entirely a matter of choosing and legitimizing kings. The texts have a story to tell about the fortunes of the people whom Yah-weh chose to be identified with himself, and anointing appears only when it serves that story. We have no systematic record of who was anointed and for what purpose, nor do we find any attempt to establish universal definitions. Exodus and Leviticus recount the anointing of Aaron and his sons as *priests with what might be understood as a model for future practice, if not as legislation. There is no such pentateuchal tradition for anointing *kings, who were not es-sential for the leadership of Yahweh's people. In our exploration of the biblical evidence general-ization is unavoidable, but it must be under-taken cautiously. Royal anointing tends to be treated as essentially a single phenomenon, al-beit with varied expressions. In fact, the Bible shows two separate anointing customs, one by *prophets before the people have even consid-ered the man a potential monarch, and the other in the company of cheering crowds at ac-tual coronation. This distinction has important historical implications, and prophetic anointing was a particular adaptation of the political col-lective called *"Israel" (see 2 below) to new lead-ership by kings. By its very nature, the practice was not appropriate to the dynastic legitimation of kings in Judah, where it was sufficient to be descended from *David.

1. Applying Oil to People or Objects.

The act usually translated as "anointing" involves the application of oil to people or objects. This oil could consist of any variety of greasy substances, from vegetable, animal or even mineral origin. In Israel olive oils were particularly common, and Exodus 30:22-25 describes the anointing oil for the priests and the tabernacle as a blend of olive oil with four fragrant spices: myrrh, cinnamon, fragrant cane or grass, and cassia, all of which would had to have been imported at considerable cost. The idea in Exodus is that the recipe is unique, so that everything and everyone belonging to Yahweh will share the same distinctive scent, but this offers a rough notion of the oil for anointing kings. The effect of anointing oil was not just symbolic. Anointing oil was a pungent and durable perfume. Its fragrance persisted, and its oil produced a permanent stain on clothes, as when Aaron and his sons were sprinkled with oil and blood at their installation (Ex 29:21; Lev 8:30). Oil could be applied in different ways, including sprinkling, rubbing with hands and pouring over the head. Among the priests, only Aaron has oil poured over his head as high priest, and this rite also marks him permanently by saturating his official turban (Ex 29:6-7; Lev 8:9, 12). Both *Saul and *Jehu are anointed to be future kings by prophets who pour an entire bottle of oil over their heads (1 Sam 10:1; 2 Kings 9:3, 6). No headdress is mentioned, but given the importance of the lasting stain and scent, perhaps we should imagine that both men were wearing some kind of cloth headgear that carried the mark and fragrance of their anointing for a long time to come.

Anointing was such a specialized act that it merited a verb of its own (mšh), although accounts of anointing do not require its use. Both the anointing of priests and of kings was associated with the beginning of their work, and both priests and kings were set apart by being doused with perfumed oil. Just as much as priests, kings were considered to perform a special service for God, and their anointing marked them for this divine service. Nevertheless, the two rites were conceived to have different impacts, however much the nature of the difference eludes us. The priests, the tabernacle and all its sacred contents were marked by anointing to live with God at his sacred shrine. Both the anointing and its oil were bound to the idea of "holiness" (verbal root qdš [Ex 30:29-33]). Kings, by contrast, were not "consecrated" (made holy), neither by their anointing nor otherwise. They were chosen by Yahweh for a special office, but this did not somehow involve direct divine contact as understood in the circles of priests. So far as kings were set apart by their anointing, they were not made "holy." A provocative fable about trees choosing a king offers another terminology. The olive tree is made first choice because of its oil, by which "they honor gods and men" (verb kbd [Judg 9:9]), where some may be distinguished for special "honor," not defined by "holiness."

2. The Israelite Tradition of Anointing by Prophets.

Two separate customs for anointing kings are found in the Historical Books, distinguished above all by their times of performance. Saul, David and Jehu are anointed before they actually become kings (1 Sam 9:15-16; 10:1; 16:1-13; 2 Kings 9:1-6). Long after his initial anointing by *Samuel, however, David is anointed king, first by the people of Judah (2 Sam 2:4) and then seven years later by the leadership of a separate "Israel" (2 Sam 5:3). These events represent the public proclamation of a new king, whose reign begins with the anointing ceremony. The reign of *Solomon likewise begins when he is publicly anointed (1 Kings 1:34, 39), as do those of Joash and Jehoahaz, two later rulers of Judah (2 Kings 11:12; 23:30). Other features distinguish these two anointing customs, and they must be understood to reflect two sharply different political and ritual traditions.

All three anointings that take place before accession to the throne are performed by prophets in the context of the political entity called Israel. Yahweh instructs the prophet Samuel to anoint Saul to lead "my people Israel" (1 Sam 9:16), using the title nāgîd to define this designated ruler, rather than the word "king" (melek). Samuel's mission to anoint David begins only after Yahweh has rejected Saul as king "over Israel" (1 Sam 15:35; 16:1). By the time Jehu comes on the scene, about 150 years later, the tribe of Judah has broken away from "Israel" in order to keep a king from David's line on a much diminished throne at Jerusalem. Jehu is anointed by an unnamed prophet from the company of *Elisha, likewise as king "over the people of Yahweh, over Israel" (2 Kings 9:6).

In political terms, "Israel" is not simply the name of a people to be passed from king to king, eventually to be claimed by a renegade northern state. "Israel" represents the collective identity of a coalition of tribes that appears to have functioned without kings through most of Iron Age I (c. 1200-1000 BCE). The biblical books of Moses certainly portray Israel as a coalition, but it is difficult to demonstrate an early date for this tradition. While no one tribe is attested outside the Bible before the ninth century BCE, Israel appears in a monument celebrating the accomplishments of Egypt's king Merneptah (c. 1207 BCE). In the Bible itself, the Song of Deborah (Judg 5) offers a view of Israel as a loose coalition having obligations for mutual defense and sharing worship of Yahweh, the god who goes to war on their behalf. The list of tribes in Judges 5 overlaps with the standard pentateuchal lists, but certain names do not match these, so that the Song of Deborah is shown to represent an independent text, remembering Israel directly from its existence without kings.

The entire tradition of prophets anointing kings before they take the throne comes from this framework of tribal Israel. The books of Samuel and Kings show that until the reign of Jehu, "Israel" still represented a collective political entity having the ability to offer or refuse its support. Kings had to persuade Israel to go to war, as in the days of Deborah, and Israel could set up or depose its rulers. According to the biblical story, the separate decision-making power of collective Israel could bestow surprising influence on religious leaders called "prophets," who could operate outside the institutions of temples or palaces, and whose claims to speak directly for Yahweh could be granted real authority. It seems that this authority had a special role in collective Israel that never applied to the dynastic monarchy of David's line in Judah.

At least in the cases of Saul, David and Jehu, Israel attributed the authority of a new royal house to explicit selection by its god, Yahweh,

communicated through a prophet. Anointing by the prophet gave the designated man the very mark of divine choice, as if Yahweh himself had set him apart, and no one could assassinate "Yahweh's anointed" in order to replace him (1 Sam 24:6, 10; 26:9-10, 16, 23; cf. 2 Sam 1:14). None of the three Israelite kings who is said to have been anointed this way dies at Israelite hands. We cannot assume that such advance anointing by prophets was standard for all Israelite kings. In fact, there is no reason to suppose that it was associated with the other founders of Israelite royal houses: *Jeroboam, Baasha and Omri (see Omri Dynasty). According to the books of Kings, Jeroboam did receive prophetic authorization to rule (1 Kings 11:29-40), and both Jeroboam and Baasha are warned by prophets that Yahweh has decreed their removal (1 Kings 14:6-11; 16:1-4). Of all the northern kings who founded new Israelite royal houses before Jehu (see Jehu Dynasty), only Omri has no association with prophets. Somehow, Omri is overshadowed in the books of Kings by his son Ahab, who is remembered to have endured a persistent conflict with the prophet *Elijah.

This tradition of prophetic involvement with the selection and rejection of kings, including special instances of divine designation by anointing, is central to the whole political framework of an Israelite tribal kingdom that survived until the arrival of Jehu. This king began a centralization of decision making into the palace administration that the book of 2 Kings treats as a success. In this record, collective Israel, represented by regional and tribal leaders, is removed from major activities such as choosing a king or going to war. Before Jehu, prophetic legitimation, including anointing, served as one part of a nondynastic monarchy. Israelite royal houses were not assumed to rule by simple right of paternity. An effective individual leader would be acknowledged by collective Israel as king. His son would have first right to rule in his place, but without a strong dynastic obligation. For over 150 years, from Saul to Jehu, only two royal houses ruled Israel with two successful monarchs, David and Solomon, and Omri and Ahab. Israel was set up for frequent turnover of kings, not because it was unstable, but because this tradition preserved the power of broad-based, decentralized leadership that reflected old tribal and local categories. One essential feature of royal legitimation in this political setting was the need to persuade all to follow. Before kings, Israelite leadership is presented as depending on "the spirit of Yahweh," which would fill the person in question with unstoppable power (Othniel [Judg 3:10]; Gideon [Judg 6:34]; Jephthah [Judg 11:29]; Samson [Judg 13:25; 14:6-19; 15:14]) (*see* Judges). Both Saul and David are anointed by prophets with the expectation that Yahweh's Spirit will come over them to demonstrate his power in them (1 Sam 10:6; 16:13). The effect of the Spirit is a sign of divine selection that will persuade the people to follow, when the king has no automatic institutional authority.

The custom of special anointing by prophets is never joined to the language of "covenant" that comes to be associated with David and his heirs (*see* Davidic Covenant). David's anointing by Samuel (1 Sam 16:1-13) has nothing to do with Yahweh's covenant, which does not emerge until David has become king (see 2 Sam 7, which makes no reference to anointing). When two psalms recall the covenant of David's dynasty and identify a royal "anointed one," this language should derive not from the Israelite anointing by prophets but from Judah's anointing at coronation (e.g., Ps 89:3, 20; 132:10-12). The entire idea of a lasting royal covenant pertains only to the dynastic legitimation that characterized the southern kingdom of Judah.

3. Israelite and Judahite Anointing at Coronation.

According to the Bible, King David was anointed three times. Besides his designation by the prophet Samuel, David was anointed by the collective leadership of the tribe called Judah to rule them separately after the death of Saul (2 Sam 2:4). This willingness to stand apart from the main body of Israel anticipates the later secession of Judah from Israel after Solomon. Meanwhile, Israel acknowledged a son of Saul named Ishbosheth, but his leadership was weak, and Israel was ready to accept a new royal house by the time David had proven his strength. The tribes of Israel come to David at his southern base in Hebron and declare kinship with David, and their senior leadership anoints him their king (2 Sam 5:3). In the cases of both Judah and Israel, David is anointed at the moment of coronation in a grand public event by collective leadership that agrees to support a new royal house.

It is not clear what happened to the practice of anointing at coronation in the kingdom of Israel after David. The tribes of Israel, as distinct from Judah, are said to have anointed Absalom as their king, much as they had done with his father, David (2 Sam 19:9-10). Solomon does not receive any advance prophetic anointing, which is mentioned only for new royal houses. Instead, the public anointing of Solomon by *Zadok the priest marks his secure taking of the throne after Adonijah's abortive attempt (1 Kings 1:39). The prophet Nathan is said to join Zadok, perhaps to lend some of the authority of the Israelite tradition (1 Kings 1:34). Solomon's anointing anticipates what seems to become a particularly Judahite custom, as seen in the accession to the throne of the boy Joash in the ninth century BCE. The high priest Jehoiada brings out Joash, puts a crown on his head, gives him a copy of "the covenant" *(hā^cēdût)*, evidently associated with David, and the people acclaim him by shouting, "Long live the king!" (2 Kings 11:12). This combination of rites, including the supervising priest, is much like the anointing of Solomon, also at the moment of enthronement. In the end, prophets have nothing to do with the ceremony and they need not, because selection of the king is based on dynastic succession within David's house, not on fresh divine choice. Anointing is associated with covenant only in this restricted framework. Jehoahaz, son of Josiah, is anointed in what appears to be the same Davidic and Judahite tradition (2 Kings 23:30). We cannot tell whether the biblical stories reflect a practice integrated into every coronation. All the preserved accounts include the anointing as an indication of legitimacy, where the circumstances required affirmation of this. It seems likely that anointing at coronation was a regular event, and that the selective references reflect this literary focus.

The language of "the anointed one," or "messiah," seems to have become attached to the dynasty of David in a way that transferred its ritual point of reference, at least in the biblical writings. David called Saul "the anointed of Yahweh" (1 Sam 24:6, 10; 26:9, 10, 16, 23), based on his anointing by Samuel, who speaks of "Yahweh and his anointed one" (1 Sam 12:3, 5). Especially in confrontations between David and Saul, the phrase seems to recall the notion that through the prophet, Yahweh himself has anointed the king as a sign of divine choice (cf.

1 Sam 10:1). The references to "the anointed one" in Psalms 89 and 132, however, have translated the title into a blanket legitimation for every king from David's line (see also 2 Chron 6:42, quoting Ps 132:8-10). The anointing has then become the rite at coronation, from a strikingly different royal ideology, with an entirely different idea of how kings are chosen. After the demise of the Judahite state, with its Davidic dynasty, the idea of restoration under a future "anointed" king naturally inherited the coronation and covenant framework of the dynastic tradition. At the same time, however, this anticipated messiah became more and more removed from selection directly from an active royal house. In the end, any messiah would have to be identified by something more like the Israelite anointing by prophets, even if with eventual reference to the covenant with David.

See also KINGS AND KINGSHIP; PRIESTS AND LEVITES; PROPHETS AND PROPHECY.

BIBLIOGRAPHY. **A. Alt,** "The Monarchy in Israel and Judah," in *Essays on Old Testament History and Religion* (Oxford: Blackwell, 1966) 239-59 (= *VT* 1 [1951] 2-22); **A. Campbell,** *Of Prophets and Kings: A Late Ninth-Century Document (1 Samuel-2 Kings 10)* (Washington, DC: Catholic Biblical Association of America, 1986); **D. E. Fleming,** "The Biblical Tradition of Anointing Priests," *JBL* 117 (1998) 401-14; **C. Houtman,** *Exodus* (4 vols.; Kampen: Kok Pharos; Leuven: Peeters, 1993-2002); **E. Kutsch,** *Salbung als Rechtsakt im Alten Testament und im Alten Orient* (BZAW 87; Berlin: Töpelmann, 1963); **P. K. McCarter,** *1 Samuel* (AB 8; Garden City, NY: Doubleday, 1980); **T. N. D. Mettinger,** *King and Messiah: The Civil and Sacral Legitimation of the Israelite Kings* (ConBOT 8; Lund: Gleerup, 1976). **K. R. Veenhof,** review of *Salbung als Rechtsakt im Alten Testament und im Alten Orient,* by E. Kutsch, *BO* 23 (1966) 308-13.   D. E. Fleming

APOLOGY OF DAVID. *See* DAVID; PROPAGANDA.

ARABIA, ARABIANS

Arabia is the large peninsula (and Arabians its peoples) between the Red Sea and Arabo-Persian Gulf on west and east, its south washed by the Arabian Sea, while northward it merges into the deserts of Jordan, Syria and also Mesopotamia along the Euphrates. Most of it is sandy desert with scattered oases; in the southwest and along to the southeast, mountainous terrain collects rainfall of the annual monsoons that courses down the watercourses (wadis), enabling good vegetation at higher levels and irrigation agriculture from prehistoric times on-ward lower down and along the desert margins. Major land routes ran from the ancient kingdoms in the southwest: one, northward (parallel to the Red Sea) through Midian, with one branch north to Damascus, and the other across southern Canaan to Gaza. From this long route, but nearer its southern end, a side route crossed eastward via Qaryat al-Faw to the gulf near Bahrain. Further north, from Yathrib (now Medina) via Hail, and from Tema via Dumah, two roughly parallel routes thrust northeastward to reach Mesopotamia at various points along the Euphrates, from Ur up to Hindanu (just southeast from Mari). Camel caravans from the south brought various products northward, including aromatics, gold and gems, which added to the wealth of the basically agricultural/pastoral southern kingdoms of Sheba and its neighbors.

1. Ancient Arabia: Historical Background
2. Ancient Arabia and the Bible (First Millennium BCE)

1. Ancient Arabia: Historical Background.
The vast central deserts divide ancient Arabia into eastern and western zones. In the east, along the gulf from Kuwait to Oman, arose the kingdoms of Dilmun (in east Arabia and Bahrain island) and of Magan (in much of the United Arab Emirates and Oman), the latter becoming Qade by the seventh century BCE, with an archaeology extending from the eighth millennium BCE to the sixth century CE (for a detailed account see Potts; for a wider, well-illustrated account, especially on Dilmun, see Crawford and Rice).

In the west, oasis-based chiefdoms and kingdoms arose in the northwest oases. Assyrian and local records mention Qedar from the eighth to fifth centuries BCE; it probably covered the area east of Edom, down the Wadi Sirhan to Dumah (Dumat al-Jandal), south to Tema (Tayma), and west and north back up to Tabuk and Maan (on the south of Edom). South from Qedar, Dedan was based in the lush Wadi al-Ula, between Tabuk and Medina; local inscriptions exist from the sixth century BCE. The prehistoric archaeology runs from the eighth millennium to c. 1000 CE.

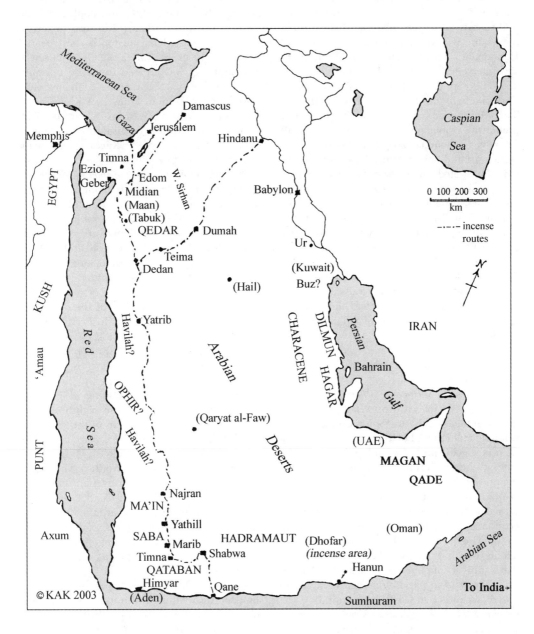

Figure 1. Ancient Arabia and environs

After an equally long prehistory, there arose in southwest Arabia four major kingdoms (and some minor ones) during at least the tenth through the seventh centuries BCE. Preeminent was Saba (biblical Sheba), whose kings early on adopted the title *mukarrib,* or "paramount ruler," marking ascendancy over all the southwest kingdoms. In the fifth century BCE, just eastward, Qataban's kings broke away and took that title briefly, as did fleetingly the kings of Hadramaut (biblical Hazermaveth) still further east, who ruled over the incense-producing terrain in Dhofar. North of Saba, from the Madhabian princedoms, arose the merchant kingdom of

Main. Main and Qataban were taken over by Saba by the second/first centuries BCE and second century CE respectively. After Saba became the realm of Himyar, it finally took over the Hadramaut kingdom c. 280 CE, lasting until outside intervention by the sixth/seventh centuries BCE. The period c. 1000 BCE to 570 CE has left some six thousand local inscriptions in the Old South Arabian alphabet and dialects (for a comprehensive bibliography see Kitchen 2000). There is a rich archaeology of towns, forts, cemeteries, art and objects of daily life (for a splendidly illustrated survey see Simpson). Major monuments include the huge end piers of the fabled Marib Dam, which served the irrigation system of the Sabean capital, Marib, for over a thousand years prior to its final fall in the sixth century CE, and the great temples Bar'an and Awwam in Marib's south zone. Further north in Main still stands the buried city of Yathill (now Baraqish), with its encircling walls and towers still intact in places, some fifty feet high, with the temple of Naqrah excavated within, intact up to roof level.

2. Ancient Arabia and the Bible (First Millennium BCE).

2.1. Solomon, Sheba and Others. The text of 1 Kings 10:1-13 (cf. 2 Chron 9:1-12) narrates a queen of Sheba's visit to *Solomon at the time when he and Hiram I of Tyre opened up exploration for gold and timber in Ophir by sea. The latter was most likely in western Arabia (centering on the great gold-bearing zone of Madhab al-Dhahab), directly athwart the incense caravan route from Sheba to the Levant. So, urgent economic issues may have engaged the two royals. The queen's gift to Solomon of only 120 talents of gold is not out of line by ancient standards; only a couple of centuries later, Metten II of Tyre had to pay 150 talents in tribute to Assyria (see Kitchen 1997). It was not the practice for ancient Near Eastern kings to carry on diplomacy face to face; only vassals usually came in person to their overlords. Thus, despite a common assumption to the contrary, it is most likely that the queen came as the highest-level emissary from her husband, the ruling *mukarrib* of Saba; during the period c. 970-930 BCE, he could have been any one of three or four such rulers. Long-distance travel by rulers and their relatives in *war and peace was commonplace in antiquity (*see* Trade and Travel).

Assyrian sources document the caravan trade explicitly from the eighth, and implicitly from the ninth, centuries BCE (Liverani); hence, it most likely existed in the tenth—and beginning from the twelfth, when the Old South Arabian alphabet was created for trade reasons, based on the Late Canaanite alphabet. Solomon's other Arabian kings in 1 Kings 10:14 probably were the more "local" northern rulers of Qedar and Dedan (for lists of all the main rulers in early Arabia see Kitchen 1994, with updates in Kitchen 2000).

2.2. Ancient Arabia and the Divided Monarchy. During the ninth to seventh centuries BCE, the Assyrian royal annals preserve mentions of at least eight rulers of northwest Arabia, and specifically of Qedar; from them were taken camels and other livestock, spices, gold and so on; a text of one Kabaril son of Mati-il, king of Dedan is known, probably sixth century BCE. Both kingdoms recur in the oracles of the Hebrew prophets, including mention of their caravan trade, livestock and other products and possessions: so with Isaiah (Is 21:13-17 [along with Tema oasis; and Dumah in 21:11-12]; 42:11 [settlements]; 60:7 [flocks]); later also by Jeremiah (Jer 2:10; 25:23-24; 49:8, 28); and finally by Ezekiel (Ezek 27:20-24 [as trading with Tyre]). An Assyrian document of the eighth century BCE tells of a Sabaean caravan of two hundred camels that (with their cargoes) was confiscated for not paying dues to the ruler of Hindanu on the Middle Euphrates (see Liverani). The Assyrian kings Sargon II and Sennacherib mention two Sabean rulers in 705 and 685 BCE, as Itamru and Karibil, who most likely are the Yitha'amar Bayyin I and Karibil Watar I of the Sabean monumental inscriptions; the latter was a noted warrior who led eight campaigns against neighboring peoples. The land of Buz, whence hailed Elihu, disputant with Job (Job 32:2, 6), sometimes is identified with the Bazu of cuneiform sources (disputed in Eph'al 1982, but compare how Apum becomes Upi, for *a/u* interchange), but its location is uncertain (near the head of the gulf?). Sheba, too, continues to appear as a trading land (cf. the preceding references to Isaiah, Jeremiah and Ezekiel, plus Ps 72:10, 15; Job 6:19).

2.3. Arabia and Postexilic Judea. Alongside *Sanballat of *Samaria and Tobiah from *Ammon, there stood against *Nehemiah the shadowy figure of Geshem (or Gashmu) the Arab

(Neh 2:19; 6:1-2, 6). It is highly likely that he was the father of Qaynu, son of Geshem king of Qedar, who dedicated a silver bowl in an east delta shrine in Egypt, about the mid-fifth century BCE, and quite probably he is named in a graffito in Dedan as Gashm or Jasm (for these see Porten). The objection that there were many Gashmus is invalid; none but he of the silver bowl was a ruler, as in Nehemiah 2 and 6. It appears that Qedar had extended its rule into southern *Edom and across Sinai, such that its rulers could dedicate precious objects in the Egyptian delta and exercise power in what had been southern Judah as far as Lachish (for references see Kitchen 2000, 722).

See also AMMON, AMMONITES; ARAM, DAMASCUS AND SYRIA; EDOM, EDOMITES; MOAB, MOABITES.

BIBLIOGRAPHY. **H. Crawford and M. Rice,** eds., *Traces of Paradise: The Archaeology of Bahrain 2500 B.C.-300 A.D.* (London: Dilmun Committee; Manama: Bahrain National Museum, 2000); **I. Eph'al,** *The Ancient Arabs: Nomads on the Borders of the Fertile Crescent, 9th-5th Centuries B.C.* (Jerusalem: Magnes; Leiden: E. J. Brill, 1982); **K. A. Kitchen,** *Documentation for Ancient Arabia, 1: Chronological Framework and Historical Sources* (Liverpool: Liverpool University Press, 1994); idem, *Documentation for Ancient Arabia, 2: Bibliographical Catalogue of Texts* (Liverpool: Liverpool University Press, 2000); idem, "Sheba and Arabia," in *The Age of Solomon: Scholarship at the Turn of the Millennium,* ed. L. K. Handy (SHANE 11; Leiden: E. J. Brill, 1997) 126-53; **M. Liverani,** "Early Caravan Trade Between South-Arabia and Mesopotamia," *Yemen* 1 (1992) 111-15; **B. Porten,** "Tell el-Maskhuta Libation Bowls," *COS* 2.51:175-76; **D. T. Potts,** *The Arabian Gulf in Antiquity* (2 vols.; Oxford: Clarendon Press, 1990); **St J. Simpson,** ed., *Queen of Sheba: Treasures from Ancient Yemen* (London: British Museum Press, 2002). K. A. Kitchen

ARAD

Situated at the eastern edge of the Beersheba Valley (22 mi. east-northeast of Beersheba), Arad (*'ărād*) sits prominently in the rolling hills of the northeastern Negev. According to Numbers 21:1-3, a *Canaanite "king of Arad" (who remains anonymous) ambushed the Israelites as they began their journey toward Transjordan. The Israelites retaliated, and the Canaanites suffered a crushing defeat (cf. Num 33:40). As first fruit of the conquest, the place was named Hormah (cf. *ḥērem,* "devoted to destruction"). Thus in the Numbers narrative the victory of the second generation stands in contrast to the defeat of the first generation (Num 14:44-45; Deut 1:44). In the tribal list of Joshua, Arad comes under the jurisdiction of Simeon (Josh 12:14; 15:21 [LXX]; cf. Josh 19:2-6; 1 Chron 4:28-31). However, Judges 1:16 indicates that Kenites (a tribal group related to the Midianites) also settled the "Negev of Arad." Shishak's campaign in Palestine (925 BCE [see 1 Kings 14:25-26]) lists "Great Arad" and "Arad of Jehoram" among the seventy settlements conquered in the Negev (Kitchen, 440). During the divided monarchy, as a gateway to *Edom and the lucrative *Arabian trade, Arad gained military, economic and religious importance in this contested region. Famous finds at the site include a temple and an archive of preexilic Hebrew letters. Questions of relevance to the OT Historical Books include whether the biblical conquest narratives can be reconciled with the archaeology of Arad, the nature of the settlement during the time of Solomon and how the Arad sanctuary fits into the chronology of the kings of Judah.

1. Arad in the Conquest Narratives
2. Arad during the Iron Age

1. Arad in the Conquest Narratives.
Excavations at Tel Arad and other sites in the eastern Negev have failed to uncover Late Bronze Age levels, which, according to biblical chronology, would correspond to the events of the conquest. Y. Aharoni, aware of the problem, looked instead to the Middle Bronze Age fortified settlements of Tel Masos (Hormah?) and Tel Malhata (Arad of Jehoram?), both of which are located in the region of Arad (Aharoni, 71-74). This view has the advantage of supplying evidence of permanent settlements in the region. However, many questions remain as to how Middle Bronze Age sites could relate to events situated in the Late Bronze Age in the biblical text. Another, more radical, solution to this problem is to dismiss the biblical story as legendary (Mazar, 329-30). No actual battle took place when the Israelites came through the region. In this perspective, the value of the account is limited to providing a literary explanation for the origins of the town Hormah/"devoted to destruction" (see Noth, 154).

Although no solution is likely to solve all the problems involved, another look at the ecology of the region provides some helpful context. In transitional frontier zones, settlement patterns among tribal populations vary according to their shifting subsistence strategies (Labianca and Younker, 403-4). The Beersheba Valley, with long gaps in its settlement history, clearly belongs to the ecological margins (Herzog, 8). Thus the lack of permanent settlements during the Late Bronze Age may indicate a switch to pastoral nomadism among the local populations (see LaBianca and Younker, 406). This fluid setting would explain why the king of Arad (probably a tribal head [Glueck, 114]) dwelt "in the Negev" as opposed to a permanent town (Num 21:1; Judg 1:17; 1 Sam 30:29). In this context the mention of destroyed "cities" ('ārîm [Num 21:3; cf. Josh 15:21]) perhaps alludes to encampments (Num 13:19) rather than fortified settlements.

2. Arad During the Iron Age.

Since the excavations of Iron Age Arad in the 1960s, the stratigraphy and the history of the fortress complex have been the subject of several reappraisals (see Herzog et al.; Mazar and Netzer; Herzog). These have resulted in significant changes in our understanding of the site during the monarchy.

2.1. The Solomonic Enclosure. After the end of the Early Bronze Age II city, Tel Arad went into a long hiatus until the Iron Age. The first Iron Age settlers established a small enclosure on the upper mound. They apparently reused Early Bronze Age domestic houses and dug new storage pits and stone-lined granaries. Y. Aharoni, the original excavator, dated the village to the period of the Judges (Iron Age I) and identified a small paved area inside the enclosure as a Kenite shrine (Herzog et al., 2-6; cf. Judg 1:16). Following this village, a fortress with casemate walls (parallel walls with cross sections) was built. Aharoni attributed this development to the building program of *Solomon in the tenth century BCE. The destruction of the fortress was linked to Shishak's campaign of 925 BCE (Herzog et al., 6-8).

However, on account of the pottery assemblage (red-slipped hand-burnished ware), it is the enclosure, not the casemate fortress, that should be dated to the tenth century BCE (Singer-Avitz, 111-17). As for the alleged Kenite installation, it now has been identified as a curved wall belonging to a subsequent and unrelated phase (Herzog, 20). Thus the Solomonic southward ex-

pansion was more modest than initially thought and stands in contrast to his building projects elsewhere in the country (cf. 1 Kings 9:15-19) (*see* History of Israel 3: United Monarchy). The date of the end of the Solomonic enclosure is still a matter of debate, but probably it was phased out shortly after Shishak's campaign of 925 BCE (Singer-Avitz, 114).

2.2. The Judean Fortress. Tel Arad's depositional history clearly reflects the vicissitudes of life on the frontier. In the course of the Iron Age II the square fortress was destroyed six times. Although it is difficult to pinpoint when the transition from village to fortress took place, the casemate structure (see 2.1 above) usually is dated to the ninth century BCE (Mazar and Netzer). Perhaps Edomite threats motivated the Judean royal administration to maintain this strong outpost (2 Chron 20; 2 Kings 8:16-24).

After the destruction of the casemate fort (the earthquake of c. 760 BCE? [Herzog, 97]), a solid wall fortress was built (52 x 52 m). A sanctuary was erected inside the fortress (see 2.3 below), along with a new gate and an earthen glacis around the walls. With other eighth-century fortified settlements in the Beersheba Valley (*see* Beersheba), Arad became part of a major effort to build a strong line of defense in that contested region (Herzog, 99). Water storage inside the fort consisted of three underground plastered cisterns hewn into the bedrock. The spring was situated in the Early Bronze II city on the lower part of the tel. In peace time, inhabitants carried water into the fortress from the well. During a siege, water supplies were provided by a concealed channel that passed under the city wall.

In the course of the eighth century BCE the fortress was destroyed on three occasions. As background to these unstable times, the biblical record mentions persistent problems with Edom, particularly during the reigns of Amaziah (c. 796-767 BCE [2 Chron 25:5-13]) and Ahaz (c. 735-716 BCE [2 Kings 16:6]). Sennacherib's campaign of 701 BCE probably claimed Arad as well. Rapidly rebuilt in the seventh century BCE, but now without a temple (see 2.3 below), the fortress continued its role as trade and distribution center. Arad's final demise came as a result of the Babylonian conquest in 586 BCE. The Arad inscriptions open the possibility that it was perhaps the Edomites who took advantage of the Babylonian crisis and destroyed the fortress

(Herzog et al., 29; cf. Obad 10-14).

2.3. The Sanctuary. Tel Arad's outstanding and unique contribution comes in the form of a Yahwistic temple excavated in the northwestern quadrant of the fort. Erected when the first solid-wall fortress was built, the temple's lifespan is connected to two consecutive stratigraphic phases. This view stands in contrast to Y. Aharoni's initial idea that the Arad temple lasted throughout the Judean monarchy (cf. Herzog). Significant features include a tripartite layout with a rectangular courtyard, a central hall ("the holy place") and a square cultic niche, "the holy of holies" (1.2 m x 1.2. m). In contrast to the Solomonic North Syrian long-room plan, the Arad temple was quite small and followed a local broad-room layout. The main altar (2.2 m x 2.4 m) was located in the courtyard. In its second phase, the altar was constructed with unhewn stones (cf. Ex 27:1). Excavators discovered several artifacts related to the cult, among which were an incense burner, priestly vessels and a stela (*maṣṣēbâ*, "standing-stone" [cf. Ex 24:4]) inside the holy of holies. Epigraphic data also suggest that Arad's temple officials were related to Jerusalem priestly families (Herzog et al., 32).

Pottery analysis seems to favor an eighth-century context for both phases of the temple (Singer-Avitz, 159-76). In this general historical context the identity of the Judean king(s) responsible for the two consecutive sanctuaries cannot be established with certainty. Possibilities include Amaziah (796-767 BCE), Uzziah (792-740 BCE), Jotham (750-732 BCE) and Ahaz (735-716 BCE). Perhaps the kingdom of Judah felt the need to establish a counterpart to its border temple in Jerusalem on its southern border (also perhaps at Beersheba). In this respect, Judah might have emulated Israel's practice of setting up centers of worship at both ends of its territory (cf. 1 Kings 12) (*see* Dan).

After two building phases, evidence points to an intentional cancellation of the temple. The stratigraphic layer in which the second phase of the temple was found ended in destruction. The temple itself, however, did not show signs of destruction. Instead, it was deliberately hidden (with the hope of future use?). Two incense altars at the entrance of the holy of holies were laid on their sides and covered with a protective earth layer. Also in the cultic niche the standing-stone was found on the floor, lying on its flat side. To complete the process, after the disman-

tling of the top of the walls, both the hall and the niche also were covered with a protective layer of earth (Herzog, 39-40).

The cessation of the temple has been interpreted in light of the religious reforms of *Hezekiah (c. 714 BCE [2 Kings 18]). In his effort to eradicate competing cult structures, Hezekiah ordered the termination of religious rituals at Arad, along with the dismantling of a horned altar at nearby Beersheba (cf. 2 Chron 31:1). Whether this scenario is correct or not cannot be established with certainty. Ultimately, Arad's real contribution may lie in its telling picture of Judah's wayward commitment to orthodox worship (cf. the book of Amos).

See also HISTORY OF ISRAEL 1: SETTLEMENT PERIOD.

BIBLIOGRAPHY. **Y. Aharoni,** "Nothing Early and Nothing Late," *BA* 39 (1976) 55-76; **N. Glueck,** *Rivers in the Desert: A History of the Negeb* (New York: Farrar, Straus and Cudahy, 1959); **Z. Herzog,** "The Fortress Mound at Tel Arad: An Interim Report," *TA* 29 (2002) 3-109; **Z. Herzog et al.,** "The Israelite Fortress at Arad," *BASOR* 254 (1984) 1-34; **K. A. Kitchen,** *The Third Intermediate Period in Egypt (1100-650 BC)* (rev. ed.; Warminster: Aris & Phillips, 1996); **O. S. LaBianca and R. W. Younker,** "The Kingdoms of Ammon, Moab and Edom: The Archaeology of Society in Late Bronze/Iron Age Transjordan (ca. 1400-500 BCE)," in *The Archaeology of Society in the Holy Land,* ed. T. E. Levy (New York: Facts on File, 1995) 399-415; **A. Mazar,** *Archaeology of the Land of the Bible, 10,000-586 B.C.E.* (ABRL; New York: Doubleday, 1990); **A. Mazar and E. Netzer,** "On the Israelite Fortress at Arad," *BASOR* 263 (1986) 87-91; **M. Noth,** *Numbers* (OTL; Philadelphia: Westminster, 1968); **L. Singer-Avitz,** "Arad: The Iron Age Pottery Assemblages," *TA* 29 (2002) 110-214.   T. D. Petter

ARAD OSTRACA. *See* HEBREW INSCRIPTIONS.

ARAM, DAMASCUS AND SYRIA

"Aram" designates a territory or city-state ruled by an Aramaean king or kings in Syria, Lebanon and upper Mesopotamia. It often was joined to another name in compound, such as "Aram-naharayim," whence came the oppressor of Israel Cushan-Rishathayim and later Aramaean auxiliaries who fought against Israel, and Aram-Zobah, the most powerful Aramaean city-state during the time of King *David. Damascus was the most prominent Aramaean city-state in the ninth and eighth centuries BCE, the full name of which was "Aram-Damascus." The translators of the Old Greek version of the OT rendered Hebrew *Aram* as "Syria" and Hebrew *Aramaean* as "Syrian," reflecting a contemporary Greek designation for the area. This essay focuses on the Aramaean kingdoms of Lebanon and Syria during the Iron Age.

1. Meaning of the Words *Aram*, *Damascus* and *Syria*
2. Aram, Damascus and Syria in the Bible
3. Aram, Damascus and Syria in Extrabiblical Literary Sources
4. Archaeology
5. Economy
6. Religion
7. Script and Language

1. Meaning of the Words *Aram*, *Damascus* and *Syria*.

1.1. Aram. There is no consensus on the meaning of the noun *Aram* (*'ărām*). Some have suggested an etymology on the basis of the root *r-w-m*, "to be high," explicating the form as "highland." Lipiński (2000, 51-54) explains the form as a broken plural, the existence of which is dubious in *Aramaic (one could argue that internal plurals are attested at Sikan [see Kaufman, 148-49]), from the noun *raym*, "wild bull, buffalo," and believes the term describes the people as "wild bulls."

1.2. Damascus. Inasmuch as no convincing Semitic etymology has been offered for "Damascus," the name is probably non-Semitic in origin (Pitard 1987, 7-10).

Three spellings of *Damascus* appear in the Hebrew Bible: *dammeśeq* (Gen, 2 Sam, 1 Kings, 2 Kings, Is, Jer, Ezek, Amos, Zech, Song), *darmeśeq* (only in Chronicles: 1 Chron 18:5, 6; 2 Chron 16:2; 24:23; 28:5, 23), *dummeśeq* (only 2 Kings 16:10).

1.3. Syria. The word *Syria* comes from Greek. Probably, the Greeks took the term from *Assyria itself as defined by the boundaries of the neo-Assyrian Empire, which included Syria and northern Mesopotamia. The normal form for "Assyria" in Neo-Assyrian was *Aššūr*, but the shorter form *Sūr* [Neo-Assyrian regularly dropped unstressed vowels at the beginning of words] also was used. By the seventh century BCE Aram had become part of Assyria, and Assyrians spoke and wrote Aramaic. At the time of the translation of the Old Greek version of the

OT the Seleucids ruled Syria and northern Mesopotamia, roughly the territory of the northern and western parts of the Neo-Assyrian Empire. The use of *Syria* for "Aram" may have entered Greek via Demotic as early as the Persian period (Steiner, 82 n. 15).

2. Aram, Damascus and Syria in the Bible.
The Bible sheds light on the origins of the Aramaeans of Damascus, on the territories of various Aramaean states, on the histories of these states and on individual Aramaeans, especially Damascenes.

2.1. Origins. With the collapse of the Hittite Empire, Aramaeans took control of much of Lebanon and Syria beginning sometime around 1200 BCE The place of their origin is unknown. What is clear, however, is that their entrance into Syria and Lebanon came from the upper and middle Euphrates.

The prophet Amos announced that God would reverse the history of the Aramaeans of Damascus by sending them back to Kir *(Qir)*, whence they emigrated (Amos 1:5; 9:7). Tiglath-pileser III, the king of Assyria, carried this out (2 Kings 16:9). The location of Kir is unknown, although Lipiński (2000, 40-45) makes a good case for its being located in the middle Euphrates area.

2.2. Territory. The OT Historical Books mention several Aramaean states, the two most prominent of which, Aram-Zobah and Aram-Damascus, will be presented here in chronological order, followed by the others in alphabetical order.

2.2.1. Aram-Zobah = Zobah. Aram-Zobah (*'ăram şôbā'* and *'ărām şôbāh*) or Zobah (*şôbāh*) was located in the central part of the Lebanon Valley (the modern Beqa Valley) lying between the Lebanon and Anti-Lebanon mountain ranges, although its exact location is not known (Lipiński 2000, 319-20). Since it had the Hittite city of Hamath as an adversary (2 Sam 8:9-10; 1 Chron 18:9-10), it certainly was located south of Lebo-Hamath, which is located on the southernmost part of the Orontes River. The locations of the two cities belonging to Zobah that David plundered are unknown (called *bĕţah* and *bērotay* in 2 Sam 8:8, but *ţibḥat* and *kûn* in 1 Chron 18:8), but probably they were on the Litanni River in the central part of the Lebanon Valley (Lipiński 2000, 322-26). Lipiński (2000, 333-34) believes that Zobah and Beth-Rehob are one and the same place, arguing that "Rehob" was the name of a tribal chieftain from Zobah and that his dynasty was called Beth-Rehob, "the house of Rehob," and that the terms were made into two place names by a process of textual conflation.

2.2.2. Aram-Damascus = Damascus. The Abana or Amana River (2 Kings 5:12: Kethib ʾăbānâ, Qere ʾămānâ [the modern Barada River]) and the Pharpar River (2 Kings 5:12: *parpar* [probably the modern Awaj River, south of Damascus) made Damascus a fertile oasis on the edge of the Syrian Desert, just east of the Anti-Lebanon mountain range. The extent of the kingdom of Aram-Damascus is uncertain, but the Anti-Lebanon Mountains may have limited it on its west; certainly the Lebanon Mountains did. Northward, it probably extended to the oasis of Tadmor, on the trade route to Mesopotamia. Its dominion extended southward toward the northern kingdom of Israel at the time of the divided monarchy. Because of its location, Damascus served as a hub for trade routes leading north-south and east-west.

2.2.3. Aram-naharayim. Aram-naharayim (Heb ʾăram năhărayim [Judg 3:8]) means "Aram of the Two Rivers"—that is, the Euphrates and probably the Habur, in northern Mesopotamia. Traditionally, the two rivers have been identified with the Tigris and the Euphrates. By contrast, Lipiński (2000, 252) proposes that Naharayim means "river-land," not "two rivers," arguing (Lipiński 1997, 228 §29.54) that the afformative-*ayim* is an archaic locative morpheme rather than a dual morpheme. According to Lipiński (1997, 573 §67.16), "Aram of the River-land" refers to the region of the middle Euphrates.

Aram-naharayim was also called "Aram which is across the (Euphrates) river" (ʾărām ʾăšer mēʿēber hannāhār [2 Sam 10:16]). On the basis of later Assyrian terminology, Lipiński (2000, 374) suggests that the term "beyond the river" (ʿēber hannāhār) refers only to lands west of the Euphrates and thus that the text of 2 Samuel 10 describes a war waged by Hadadezer of Damascus against Israel during the reign of Omri, not one waged by Hadadezer of Zobah against Israel during the reign of David. However, elsewhere in the Historical Books "beyond" (ʿēber) refers to that opposite the standpoint of the speaker/narrator and can refer to lands east of the Euphrates. For example, the Lord says that

he took Abraham "from beyond the river" (mēʿēber hannāhār [Josh 24:3]), a clear reference to lands east of the Euphrates (Josh 24:2; cf. 1 Kings 14:15). In describing the extent of the rule of *Solomon, the narrator uses "beyond the river" (ʿēber hannāhār [1 Kings 4:24 = 5:4 MT]) to refer to lands west of the Euphrates.

Outside the Historical Books this area was also called Paddan-Aram (*paddan ʾărām* [Gen 25:20]) or "the field of Aram" (śĕdēh ʾărām [Hos 12:12]).

2.2.4. Beth-Rehob = Rehob. Beth-Rehob or Rehob was situated in the southern Beqa Valley, north of Laish (*Dan). Under the rule of Hadadezer it was united with its northern neighbor Zobah. The NRSV emends the MT ʾādām, " man," to ʾărām, "Aram," in Judges 18:7, 28, making the term *Aram* refer to the Aramaean kingdom of Beth Rehob. According to Numbers 13:21, Rehob marked the northern limits of *Canaan, being situated near Lebo-hamath. Lipiński (2000, 234) believes that "Rehob" was not a place name but rather a dynastic name.

2.2.5. Geshur. Geshur was located in the Golan Heights south of Maacah.

2.2.6. Maacah = Aram-Maacah. Maacah was a small Aramaean city-state located in the Golan Heights (Josh 12:5; 13:11), south of Mount Hermon, north of Geshur, west of the Bashan.

2.2.7. Tob. Tob was a small Aramaean city-state located in the north of the Transjordan, apparently east of Gilead (Judg 11:3, 5).

2.3. History of Aramaean Kingdoms. The presentation of the history here corresponds to the sequence of the presentation of the territory: Aram-Zobah, Aram-Damascus, Aram-naharayim, Beth-Rehob, Geshur, Maacah, Tob.

2.3.1. Aram-Zobah = Zobah. Prominent among the Aramaean city-states in the eleventh and tenth centuries BCE was Aram-Zobah, listed among the enemies of Saul (1 Sam 14:47). King Hadadezer brought Aram-Zobah to the pinnacle of its power, subjugating many vassal states even to the east of the Euphrates (2 Sam 10:16) and strong enough to wage war with the Hittite city-state of Hamath over a long period of time (2 Sam 8:10). King David eventually defeated him in battle (2 Sam 8:3).

The Historical Books do not present the material about Zobah in chronological order, but rather subordinate the presentation to their telling the story of David; that is, 2 Samuel 8:3-8/ 1 Chronicles 18:3-8 and 2 Samuel 10/1 Chronicles 19 do not appear in chronological order, but rather are included as they shed light on King David. The story contained in 2 Samuel 8:3-8/1 Chronicles 18:3-8 belongs to a summary of David's victories over Israel's enemies, which demonstrate the Lord's blessing on David as king. The material in 2 Samuel 10/1 Chronicles 19 provides background to the story of Bathsheba and Uriah, part of the court history of David.

Zobah's conflict with Israel can be divided into three episodes: military conflict in the wake of the Ammonite war, the battle of Helam and the battle near Hamath.

The Ammonites brought the Aramaeans of Zobah and Beth-Rehob, probably united under Hadadezer, into their conflict with David. The Bible says that the Ammonites "hired" them (2 Sam 10:6). While *hire* could refer to the hiring of mercenaries, it may refer to the payment of a vassal to his overlord for protection. In other words, it may be that Hadadezer was in fact the overlord of his vassal Ammon and welcomed the opportunity to put upstart Israel in its place (Pitard 1987, 92). As David's general Joab marched against Ammon, he encountered an Aramaean army as well as an Ammonite army (2 Sam 10:8). Joab routed the Aramaeans (2 Sam 10:13), while his brother Abishai forced the Ammonites to retreat to their city.

Hadadezer regrouped his forces at Helam under the command of Shobach (= Shophach), adding soldiers from his vassal states beyond the Euphrates (2 Sam 10:16). David engaged them in battle, defeating them and killing Shobach. Minor Aramaean kings, who had been subject to Hadadezer, now made peace with Israel (2 Sam 10:19).

Hadadezer apparently still held on to Zobah. On an expedition to the Euphrates, near Hamath (1 Chron 18:3), David struck down Hadadezer, taking many cavalry and infantry captive, hamstringing most of the chariot horses, and carrying away gold and bronze. At this time the Aramaeans of Damascus came as an auxiliary force to Hadadezer's aid, only to be defeated too (2 Sam 8:5-6). In celebration, the neo-Hittite king of Hamath presented David with many gifts.

Others consider the episode in 2 Samuel 10 to be a retelling of that in 2 Samuel 8, but the details differ considerably.

2.3.2. Aram-Damascus = Damascus. Damascus provided soldiers to help Aram-Zobah against Israel. Whether Damascus was a vassal state of

Zobah or an ally at that time remains unclear. However, it did not gain dominance among the Aramaean kingdoms until the mid-ninth century BCE, after the death of Solomon.

King David took control of Damascus after he defeated Zobah. In the days of King Solomon, Rezon son of Eliada wrested Damascus from the control of Israel and founded the kingdom of Aram-Damascus (1 Kings 11:23-25). This must have occurred toward the end of Solomon's reign because he apparently controlled central Syria up to Tadmor in his twentieth year (2 Chron 8:4). Aram-Damascus would remain a powerful kingdom throughout the ninth and eighth centuries BCE.

Hazyan (Heb *Hezion*) and Tabramman (Heb *Tabrimmon*) followed Rezon as kings of Damascus.

Bar-Hadad I (Heb *Ben-Hadad*), after receiving a large sum from Asa of Judah, broke his treaty with Baasha of Israel and captured some northern Israelite towns (1 Kings 15:16-20).

Assyrian annals record that Hadadezer (Assyrian *Adad-idri*) of Damascus led a twelve-state coalition, which included Ahab of Israel, against Shalmaneser III at Qarqar in 853 BCE. This Hadadezer is never mentioned in the Bible, though Lipiński (2000, 337-38, 374-75) thinks differently. Shalmaneser led three subsequent campaigns against Hadadezer in 849, 848 and 845 BCE.

The identity of the Bar-Hadad of 1 Kings 20 and 22 remains a matter of debate. Some believe that he was the grandson or son of Bar-Hadad I and so label him Bar-Hadad II. Others claim that "Bar-Hadad" served as a throne name for the Hadadezer of the Assyrian annals. Still others maintain that the author of 1 Kings uses this reference anachronistically, identifying the Israelite king incorrectly as Ahab of the house of Omri. Instead, in this view, the Israelite king should have been from the *Jehu dynasty, of a later period, probably Joash (798-782/781 BCE) or possibly his father, Joahaz (814/813-798 BCE) (Pitard 1987, 118-25; Lipiński 2000, 397).

At the death of Bar-Hadad II, Hazael usurped the throne of Damascus about 843 BCE. Joram (= Jehoram) son of Ahaz, king of Israel (852-841 BCE), in confederation with Ahaziah son of Jehoram, king of Judah (841 BCE), waged war against Hazael at Ramoth-Gilead. Joram was wounded (2 Kings 8:28-29; 2 Chron 22:5). The Tel Dan stela apparently recounts this victory of Hazael over "the king of Israel" and "the king of the house of David"—that is, Judah (Lipiński 2000, 378). Upon ascending the throne in Israel in 841 BCE, Jehu (Yamada, 192) brought tribute to Shalmaneser III, who then moved against Hazael. Hazael was forced to defend himself against the Assyrian king and to retreat from northern Israel.

Bar-Hadad III (others: Bar-Hadad II) ruled Damascus after the death of his father, Hazael. He ceded territory to Jehoash (798-782/781 BCE) of Israel (2 Kings 13:25), had Zakkur of Hamath and Luash as an enemy, and was attacked by the Assyrian king Adad-nirari III (810-783 BCE), to whom he paid tribute, if *Marʾi* ("my lord") of the Assyrian inscriptions refers to him.

A certain Ḥadyān, known only from Assyrian sources, followed Bar-Hadad III. During his reign Damascus was subject to Jeroboam II (782/781-753 BCE; co-regent from 793/792 BCE) of Israel.

In the days of the prophet *Isaiah, King Rezin of Aram-Damascus and King Pekah son of Remaliah of Israel (740/739-732/731 BCE) attempted to coerce King Ahaz of Judah (732/731-716/715 BCE; co-regent from 744/743 BCE; senior partner from 735 BCE) into an anti-Assyrian alliance (2 Kings 16:5), even trying to replace him with their puppet Ben Tabeal (son of a "good for nothing," a deformation from "Tabeel," "God is good" [*HALOT*, 367]) (Isa 7:6). Tiglath-Pileser III of Assyria (744-727 BCE) crushed Aram-Damascus in his campaigns of 733 and 732 BCE, breaking the kingdom up into a number of Assyrian provinces.

Damascus existed as a city before its domination by the Aramaeans (cf. Gen 14:15; 15:2).

2.3.3. Aram-naharayim. Cushan-rishathayim from Aram-naharayim oppressed Israel in the days of the *judges (Judg 3:8). In the days of King David Aramaeans from Aram-naharayim came to fight with Aram-Zobah against Israel (1 Chron 19:6; cf. heading to Ps 60).

According to the Bible, kinfolk of Abraham, Isaac and Jacob lived in Aram-naharayim, whence came the wives of Isaac and Jacob. The sons of Jacob, except for Benjamin, were born there. The profiteering prophet Balaam came from Pethor in Aram-naharayim (Deut 23:5).

2.3.4. Beth-Rehob = Rehob. United with Zobah under the rule of Hadadezer, Beth-Rehob provided auxiliaries to aid the *Ammonites in their war against King David (Judg 18:28; 2 Sam 10:6).

2.3.5. Geshur. Geshur seems to have been a non-Aramaean city (contra *HALOT*, 205), probably Hurrian to judge by the royal name "Talmai" (*HALOT*, 1740), the father-in-law of David and grandfather of Absalom through his daughter Maacah (2 Sam 3:3; 13:37; 1 Chron 3:2). However, it was closely allied with the Aramaean city-state of Maacah (Josh 13:13; 1 Chron 2:23) and in fact may have been annexed by an Aramaean state, as it is called "Geshur in Aram" (2 Sam 15:8).

2.3.6. Maacah = Aram-Maacah. The Aramaean city-state of Maacah or Aram-Maacah, as the Chronicler calls it, provided auxiliaries for the Ammonites in their war against David (2 Sam 10:6; 1 Chron 19:6).

2.3.7. Tob. Jephthah fled to Tob to escape his brothers who lived in Gilead (Judg 11:3, 5). Men of Tob and Maacah, along with Aramaeans from Beth-Rehob and Zobah, served as auxiliaries for the Ammonites in their war against King David (2 Sam 10:6, 8).

2.4. Individuals. The Historical Books mention several Aramaeans and Damascenes (listed in alphabetical order here).

2.4.1. Ben-Hadad. The Historical Books mention two or three kings having the name *Ben-Hadad*, which is the equivalent of *Bar-Hadad* in Aramaic. Aramaic *Bar-Hadad* means "the son of (the god) Hadad," the chief deity in the Aramaean pantheon.

2.4.1.1. Bar-Hadad I. Bar-Hadad I was the son of Tabrimmon and king of Damascus (1 Kings 15:18), who ruled at the time of Asa of Judah (911/910-870/869 BCE) and Baasha of Israel (909/908-886/885 BCE). Asa sent tribute to Bar-Hadad to break his treaty with Baasha and pressure Baasha to ease up on Judah (1 Kings 15:16-22/2 Chron 16:1-6). Some believe that Bar-Hadad I had a reign of close to fifty years, being the king who engaged Ahab of Israel in 1 Kings 20 and 22.

2.4.1.2. Bar-Hadad II (?). The identity of the Bar-Hadad of 1 Kings 20 and 22 is enigmatic. He could be a son or grandson of Bar-Hadad I and so is referred to as Bar-Hadad II instead of being the same person as Bar-Hadad I. Alternatively, "Bar-Hadad" could be the throne name for Hadadezer of Damascus, known from Assyrian sources.

This Bar-Hadad was the king of Damascus who attacked King Ahab of Israel (874/873-853 BCE) at his capital of *Samaria with a coalition of thirty-two kings. He was fond of drinking (1 Kings 20 [contrast the wisdom taught to King Lemuel by his mother in Prov 31:4-5]) and rode a horse. A year later he made a treaty with Ahab after another defeat.

At a time of critical illness the prophet *Elisha went to visit him (2 Kings 6:24; 8:7, 9). Hazael was his servant, who would usurp the throne of Damascus.

2.4.1.3. Bar-Hadad III. Bar-Hadad III was the son of the usurper Hazael (2 Kings 13:25; cf. Amos 1:4), who took towns from Jehoahaz of Israel (814/813-798 BCE). Jehoash of Israel (798-782/781 BCE), son of Jehoahaz, defeated Bar-Hadad three times and so recovered the towns for the northern kingdom Israel (2 Kings 13:25). Scholars who do not accept the existence of Bar-Hadad II as described here (see 2.4.1.2 above) identify this Bar-Hadad as Bar-Hadad II.

2.4.2. Cushan-rishathayim. Cushan-rishathayim (*kûšan rišʿātayim,* "Cushan of double wickedness"), a pun that deliberately disfigures the name of a king of Aram-naharayim, was the first oppressor of Israel mentioned in the book of Judges (Judg 3:8).

2.4.3. Eliada. Eliada (*ʾelyādāʿ,* "God knows") was the father of Rezon (1 Kings 11:23).

2.4.4. Hadadezer.

2.4.4.1. Hadadezer of Zobah. Hadadezer (Heb *hădadʿezer,* retroverted to Aramaic as *hadad-ʿidr,* "[the god] Hadad is help") was the king of the united Aramaean kingdom of Zobah and Beth-Rehob, whom David defeated (2 Sam 8:5-6). His epithet "son of Rehob" may refer to his place of origin and so be rendered "Rehobite," rather than refer to his father.

2.4.4.2. Hadadezer of Damascus. The Assyrian annals of Shalmaneser III mention Hadadezer of Damascus as the adversary of the Assyrian king. According to the annals, he was a contemporary of Ahab of Israel. This Hadadezer does not appear in the Bible, at least under this name. Some think that "Bar-Hadad II" is the throne name of this Hadadezer.

2.4.5. Hazael. Hazael (*hăzāʾēl,* "God has seen," explicated as "God has looked [at the misery]" in *HALOT,* 300) was a usurper who brought Damascus to its zenith politically.

2.4.6. Hezion. Hezion (MT *hezyôn,* a short form from the Aramaic root *hzy,* "to see," probably to be retroverted as *hazyān* in Aramaic) was the father of Tabrimmon and grandfather of Ben-Hadad I (1 Kings 15:18). He probably was a king of Damascus. Pitard (1987, 104-7) properly rejects the Arabic etymology "lop-eared" (*HALOT,* 302) and the theory that Hezion is equivalent to Rezon. *Hazyān* appears to be a hypocorism of the type *hzy* + divine name.

2.4.7. Naaman. Naaman (*naʿāmān,* "delightful") was an Aramaean general, who in the days of the prophet Elisha came from Aram-Damascus to Israel for healing (2 Kings 5:20).

2.4.8. Rehob. Rehob (*rĕhôb*) was the father of Hadadezer, unless the epithet "son of Rehob" (2 Sam 8:3) refers to the land of Hadadezer's origin rather than to his father. In the latter case, Rehob would refer to the city Beth-Rehob in the southern Beqa Valley.

2.4.9. Rezon. Rezon (Heb *rĕzôn*), son of Eliada and servant of King Hadadezer of Zobah, seized Damascus after the demise of his master Hadadezer (1 Kings 11:23-24). There is no compelling reason to equate Rezon and Hezion as has been done in the past (Pitard 1987, 100-104).

2.4.10. Rezin. Rezin (Heb *rĕṣîn,* probably to be retroverted as *raʿyān* in Aramaic, from the Semitic root *rʿy,* meaning "pleasure, delight") was the king of Damascus, who pressed Judah to join its anti-Assyrian coalition in the days of Isaiah the prophet.

The king of Assyria, Tiglath-Pileser III (744-727 BCE), killed Rezin for his insurrection (2 Kings 16:9).

2.4.11. Shobach = Shophach. Shobach (*šôbak* 2 Sam 10:16, 18) = Shophach (*šôpak,* 1 Chron 19:16, 18) commanded the army of King Hadadezer of Aram-Zobah and was killed at the battle of Helam against Israel. The *beth/pe* interchange is insignificant, being merely phonological.

2.4.12. Tabrimmon. Tabrimmon (MT *ṭabrimmôn,* to be retroverted in Aramaic as *ṭābrammān,* "Ramman ['the thunderer' = the god Hadad] is good") was the father of Ben-Hadad and son of Hezion (1 Kings 15:18). In all likelihood he was king of Damascus before his son.

3. Aram, Damascus and Syria in Extrabiblical Literary Sources.

3.1. Old Aramaic Sources.

3.1.1. From Syria. Aramaic commemorative stelae and inscriptions recording international treaties have been found in Syria, some referring to Aramaean kingdoms found in the Historical Books, and others to Aramaean kingdoms not found in the Historical Books.

3.1.1.1. Sefire. Three texts found at modern Sefire pertain to treaties made by the ancient Aramaean kingdom of Arpad, located in northern Syria. Arpad was better known as Bet Gush or Bet Agush (Lipiński 2000, 199). Stela I contains the geographical terms "Aram all of it" or "all Aram" (*'rm klh* [I.A.5]) and "all the upper part of Aram and its lower part," commonly rendered "all upper and lower Aram" (*kl 'ly 'rm wtḥth* [I.A.6]). Aram in this context probably refers to Arpad, not to Damascus.

3.1.1.2. The Melqart Stela. A certain Bar-Hadad, "king of Aram," offered this stela to the god Melqart, the patron deity of the *Phoenician city of Tyre and apparently of this king. Based on the script, scholars date the inscription to late ninth or early eighth century BCE. The Bar-Hadad in this stela apparently refers to a king of Arpad, not to a king of Damascus.

3.1.1.3. Zakkur Memorial Stela. In his memorial stela set up before the weather god Elwer in Apish, Zakkur, king of Hamath and Luʿash, mentions "Bar-Hadad, son of Hazael, king of Aram," who organized a coalition against him. The mention of Bar-Hadad, son of Hazael, places the inscription firmly into the early eighth century BCE. The use of *Aram* to refer to Aram-Damascus is the same use as in the books of 1 and 2 Kings, where *Aram* always refers to the Aramaean kingdom of Damascus. Largely on the basis of this inscription, Lipiński (2000, 254) posits an Aramaean kingdom of Hammath from about 807 BCE.

Zakkur also mentions another Aramaean king by name: Bar-Gush. Gush or Agush had founded the Aramaean dynasty Bet Agush based at Arpad and had fought against the Assyrian king Ashurbanipal about 877 BCE.

3.1.1.4. Hamath Bricks. Danish archaeologists unearthed bricks inscribed with Semitic personal names, presumably from the ninth or eighth century BCE. Some interpret the form *ṣbh*, appearing on a number of bricks, as the geographic term "Zobah."

3.1.1.5. Nerab Funerary Texts. An early seventh-century BCE funerary relief of a priest named *Š'gbr*, vocalized as *Se'gabbar* on the basis of Assyrian *Se'gabbāri* (Parpola, 149, text no. 189), meaning "Sehr (Sin) is a warrior," found at Nerab southeast of Aleppo, honors the god Sehr, the Aramaic equivalent of the Assyrian deity Sin. The relief depicts the priest *Se'gabbar* sitting and offering a libation to Sehr before an altar. In addition to Sehr, this relief mentions two other deities: Nikkal (= Assyrian Ningal, the consort of Sin) and Nusk.

The other funerary relief found at Nerab depicts Sin-zer-ibni (*šnzrbn*, "Sin has created a seed"), priest of Sehr (*šhr* = Sin) at Nerab, lifting his hands in prayer. The inscription mentions the deity Shamash (the sun god) in addition to Sehr, Nikkal and Nusk.

3.1.2. From Israel.

3.1.2.1. Tel Dan Stela. This stela commemorates the victory that the god Hadad gave the Aramaean king, probably Hazael, over "the king of Israel" and "the house of David," a reference to the southern kingdom of Judah. The king states that Hadad had made him king and had given him booty in war. Apparently, it is a memorial stela in which the king is remembered before the god. Lacunae make the exact historical reference a matter of debate, with "[Je-ho]ram son of [Ahab] king of Israel" and "[Ahaza]yah" (of Judah) being the most appealing restorations.

3.1.3. From Jordan.

3.1.3.1. Deir Alla Plaster Text. At modern Deir Alla (biblical Sukkoth) an inscription on wall plaster recounts a vision of "Balaam, son of Beor," known from Numbers 22—24. The plaster is broken in pieces, and different reconstructions have been offered. The inscription demonstrates that a legendary figure Balaam was known in literature of the eighth and seventh centuries BCE, the probable time of the text. It seems probable that the legendary Balaam of Deir Alla lived centuries before the use of his name here.

3.1.4. From Turkey.

3.1.4.1. Sam'al. Two dynasties, one Aramaean and the other Neo-Hittite, can be identified as rulers of Sam'al ("North"; modern Zincirli). Kilamuwa, who received an Anatolian name from his father, Hayya, in deference to the largely Neo-Hittite population, descended from the Aramaean dynasty of Gabbar but wrote in Phoenician.

The Neo-Hittite dynasty of Qrl, on the other hand, produced two inscriptions in a highly idiosyncratic form of Aramaic and one in Standard Old Syrian. Panamu I not only wrote in Aramaic, but also gave his son the Aramaic name *Barsur* (*brṣr*, "son of the rock"), testifying to the importance of Aramaeans in his realm. Barrakkab erected a monument to his father,

Panamu II, in the guise of a votive gift to the god Hadad. In a relief depicting Barrakkab in Assyrian dress, the scribe, on behalf of Barrakkab, writes in Standard Old Syrian. Barrakkab calls himself "the servant of Tiglathpileser [III]."

The alternative name of Sam'al, *Y'dy*, may be a Semitic tribal name, as no known Anatolian language can explain its meaning (Lipiński 2000, 235).

3.1.5. From Upper Mesopotamia.

3.1.5.1. Sikan Statue.
A bilingual inscription (Aramaic and Neo-Assyrian) was found on a statue of the Assyrian vassal Had-yith'i (spelled in Aramaic *hdys'y*, "Had[ad] is my salvation"; Assyrian *adad-id'ī*), "king" (Aramaic *mlk;* Assyrian *šakin*, "governor") of Guzan (biblical Gozan, modern Tell Halaf), Sikan (Tell Fekheriye) and Azran (unknown location), on the upper Habur River, set up before the god Hadad of Sikan. Had-yith'i was the son of Sas-nuri ("Sas [= Shamash] is my light"; Assyrian *sassu-nūrī*), who was the eponym of the year 866 BCE (Millard, 105), which indicates a date in the mid-ninth century BCE for the inscription.

3.2. Assyrian Sources.

3.2.1. Middle-Assyrian Sources.
Inscriptions of the Middle Assyrian rulers Tiglath-pileser I (1114-1076 BCE) and Ashur-bel-kala (1073-1056 BCE) refer to "the Aramaeans" encountered along the middle Euphrates and west of the Euphrates as the arch enemies of Assyria (see Grayson 1991, 43, A.0.87.4, lines 34-36, 101-3, A.0.89.7).

3.2.2. Neo-Assyrian Sources.
Annals of Ashurnasirpal II (883-859 BCE), Shalmaneser III (859-824 BCE) and Adad-nirari III (811-783 BCE) record campaigns into the Aramaean territories west of the Euphrates reaching even to the Mediterranean Sea (see Grayson 1991; 1996; Yamada). These rulers established and maintained an Assyrian corridor via the Aramaean kingdom of Arpad to the Mediterranean. In 856 BCE Shalmaneser III captured the Aramaean kingdom of Bit-Adini (= Heb *bêt 'eden* [Amos 1:5]), the capital of which was Til-Barsip on the Euphrates, and made it a province of Assyria (Grayson 1996, 35). The Aramaean kingdom of Damascus checked the Assyrian expansion westward in the eighth century BCE until the ascendancy of Tiglath-pileser III.

After merging Assyria and *Babylonia, Tiglath-pileser III (744-727 BCE), whose Babylonian throne name was "Pul" (2 Kings 15:19), subjugated Syria, beginning with the annexation of Arpad, followed by the conquest of the north Syrian states of Unqi, Hadrach and Simirra. At the end of the campaigns of 734-732 BCE Assyria subjugated Damascus and made it an Assyrian province. His annals refer to Aram-Damascus by its dynastic name, *bit haza'ili*, "the house of Hazael," and Israel by the dynastic name *bit humria*, "the house of Omri."

By the time of Sargon II (722-705 BCE) Assyria had thoroughly integrated the western Syrian states of Damascus, Hamath and Zobah, as is attested by correspondence of their Assyrian governors (Parpola, 133-43).

4. Archaeology.
No large-scale excavations of Damascus have yet been carried out (Lipiński 2000, 348). Zobah remains unexcavated, as its location is unknown. In short, much archaeological work remains to be done in Syria and Lebanon. Of course, all the inscriptions are archaeological finds, some of which had been reused as building materials of later periods (e.g., the Melqart stela).

5. Economy.
In the north Syrian kingdom of Sam'al in the eighth century BCE the economy was based on agriculture, including grains (wheat and barley), vineyards, cattle and sheep (see Sam'al inscriptions).

The area of Damascus is suitable for agriculture. Its location brought caravans through it, which provided income to the Damascenes.

6. Religion.
The Aramaeans were polytheists, while holding to belief in personal deities, dynastic deities and deities that patronized certain cities.

The patron deity of the city of Damascus and the head of the Aramaean pantheon was Hadad, the storm god, also called by the epithet *rammān*, "the thunderer." Hadad Ramman had a temple in Damascus (2 Kings 5:18). The Hebrew Bible vocalizes the epithet *rammān* incorrectly as *rimmôn* ("pomegranate" [2 Kings 5:18; Zech 12:11]). Whether or not this was deliberate on the part of the Masoretes is a moot point. As the storm god, Hadad brought fertility and prosperity to the land (cf. Sikan stela). The Aramaean kings believed that Hadad had installed them in their position as king and that he gave them victory in war. Some kings were called "Bar-

Hadad" (Heb "Ben-Hadad"), "son of Hadad" (see 2.4.1 above).

As exemplified by Naaman, worship of Hadad involved prostration and prayer (2 Kings 5:18; cf. Sikan stela). Later, King Ahaz had the priest Uriah copy the altar found at Damascus, probably in the temple of Hadad, and build a model of it in the temple in Jerusalem. Ahaz used that altar to offer a burnt offering with its grain and drink offerings and to sprinkle blood from his peace offering on it, which probably indicates that the original was used for expiatory sacrifices in the temple of Hadad (2 Kings 16:10-15).

In earlier times Hadad had another epithet, *Baal* ("lord"), which by the ninth century BCE had become a separate deity worshiped by the Canaanites.

According to the inscription found at ancient Sikan on the Habur River, there was a localized Hadad revered there called "Hadad of Sikan," who was "lord of the Habur (River)" (Aramaic *mrˀ ḥbwr;* Assyrian *bēl ḥabur*). Perhaps, Hadad manifested himself in different ways at different locations and was known variously as "Hadad of [place name]," much like Baal of the Canaanites. At Sikan, Hadad had a consort, the lady Sul (Aramaic, instead of *wsl* [error by metathesis], read *swl;* Assyrian *šala*). The Aramaean king had the name Had-yithˁi ("Had[ad] is my salvation"), while his father bore a name containing that of the sun-god Shamash: "Sas-nuri" (Assyrian *sassu-nūrī,* "Sassu [= Shamash] is my light").

Zakkur credits the god Bˁelshamayin, "Lord of Heaven," with establishing him as king over Hazrach (Heb *ḥadrāk* [Zech 9:1]). Zakkur "raised" his "hands" in prayer to Bˁelshamayin, and Bˁelshamayin answered him through seers (*ḥzyn*) and diviners (*ˁddn*). Zakkur mentions the divine pairs Bˁelshamayin and Elwer, and Shamash and Sehr.

7. Script and Language.

Aramaic has an alphabetic script, which led to its being used alongside Akkadian as a language of communication in the Neo-Assyrian and Neo-Babylonian Empires. The *Persian Empire adopted Aramaic as its official language of communication within its empire after it conquered Babylon. Long after the Aramaeans assimilated into the surrounding cultures, their language lived on.

Aramaic belongs to the Northwest Semitic subgroup of the Semitic languages. The further back one goes, the closer Aramaic is to Hebrew. This is evident from the *waw*-consecutive (*wˀšˀ ydy,* "and I lifted my hands [in prayer]" [Zakkur A.11]; *wyškb ˀby,* "and my father lay down [died]" [Tel Dan Stela, line 3]) and in the use of the infinitive absolute (*rqh trqhm,* "you must in fact placate them" [Sefire III.6]; *nkh tkwh,* "you must in fact strike it" [Sefire III.12-13]). Although later Aramaic dialects continue the use of the infinitive absolute, they do not continue the use of the *waw*-consecutive. The narrative tense in subsequent dialects is either the active participle or the perfect (suffix conjugation).

See also ARAMAIC LANGUAGE; ASSYRIA, ASSYRIANS; LEBANON; NON-ISRAELITE WRITTEN SOURCES: SYRO-PALESTINIAN.

BIBLIOGRAPHY. C.-J. Axskjöld, *Aram as the Enemy Friend: The Ideological Role of Aram in the Composition of Genesis-2 Kings* (ConBOT 45; Stockholm: Almquist & Wiksell, 1998); J. J. Bimson and J. P. Kane, *New Bible Atlas* (Leicester: InterVarsity Press, 1985); A. Biran and J. Naveh, "The Tell Dan Inscription: A New Fragment," *IEJ* 45 (1995) 1-18; G. Bunnens, ed., *Essays on Syria in the Iron Age* (ANESSup 7; Louvain: Peeters, 2000); J. A. Fitzmyer, *The Aramaic Inscriptions of Sefire* (rev. ed.; BibOr 19A; Roma: Editrice Pontificio Istituto Biblico, 1995); J. C. L. Gibson, *Textbook of Syrian Semitic Inscriptions,* 2: *Aramaic Inscriptions* (Oxford: Clarendon Press, 1975); idem, *Textbook of Syrian Semitic Inscriptions,* 3: *Phoenician Inscriptions* (Oxford: Clarendon Press, 1982); A. K. Grayson, *Assyrian Rulers of the Early First Millennium BC I (1114-859 BC)* (RIMA 2; Toronto: University of Toronto Press, 1991); idem, *Assyrian Rulers of the Early First Millennium BC II (858-745 BC)* (RIMA 3; Toronto: University of Toronto Press, 1996); J. C. Greenfield, "Hadad," *DDD* 377-82; W. W. Hallo, ed., *The Context of Scripture,* 2: *Monumental Inscriptions from the Biblical World* (Leiden: E. J. Brill, 2000); S. Kaufman, "Reflections on the Assyrian-Aramaic Bilingual from Tell Fakhariyeh," *Maarav* 3 (1982) 137-75; E. Lipiński, *The Aramaeans: Their Ancient History, Culture, and Religion* (OLA 100; Leuven: Peeters, 2000); idem, *Semitic Languages: Outline of a Comparative Grammar* (OLA 80; Leuven: Peeters, 1997); A. R. Millard, "Assyrians and Arameans," *Iraq* 45 (1983) 101-8; R. T. O'Callaghan, *Aram Naharaim: A Contribution to the History of Upper Mesopotamia in the Second Millenium B.C.* (AnOr 26; Roma: Pontificium Institutum Biblicum, 1948); **B. Otzen,** "The Aramaic Inscriptions," in *Hama: Fouilles et recherches de la Fondation Carlsberg, 1931-1938, 2.2: Les objets de la période dite syro-hittite (Âge du Fer),* ed. P. J. Riis and M.-L. Buhl (Nationalmuseets skrifter, Større beretninger 12; Copenhagen: Fondation Carlsberg, 1990) 267-318; **S. Parpola,** ed., *The Correspondence of Sargon II,* 1: *Letters from Assyria and the West* (SAA 1; Helsinki: Helsinki University Press, 1987); **W. T. Pitard,** *Ancient Damascus: A Historical Study of the Syrian City-State from Earliest Times Until Its Fall to the Assyrians in 732 B.C.E.* (Winona Lake, IN: Eisenbrauns, 1987); idem, "Arameans," in *Peoples of the Old Testament World,* ed. A. J. Hoerth, G. L. Mattingly and E. M. Yamauchi (Grand Rapids: Baker, 1994) 207-30; **R. C. Steiner,** "Why the Aramaic Script Was Called 'Assyrian' in Hebrew, Greek, and Demotic," *Or* 62 (1993) 80-82; **H. Tadmor,** ed., *The Inscriptions of Tiglath-Pileser III, King of Assyria* (Jerusalem: Israel Academy of Sciences and Humanities, 1994); **S. Yamada,** *The Construction of the Assyrian Empire: A Historical Study of the Inscriptions of Shalmaneser III (859-824 BC) Relating to His Campaigns in the West* (CHANE 3; Leiden: E. J. Brill, 2000). J. A. Lund

ARAMAIC LANGUAGE

The Aramaic language of *Ezra, contained in copies of official letters, memoranda and narrative, represents the literary Aramaic of the Achaemenid period. While the official letters preserved in Ezra came from a Persian chancellery, the author of Ezra rewrote them in a literary dialect of the same period as he incorporated them into his composition. The Aramaic language of Ezra dates close to the time that it purports to reflect, the fifth century BCE.

1. An Overview of Aramaic
2. The Importance of Aramaic in the World of Ancient Israel
3. The Aramaic of Ezra

1. An Overview of Aramaic.

1.1. Aramaic Is a Semitic Language. Aramaic is a Semitic language. Traditionally, scholars divide the Semitic languages geographically into East Semitic and West Semitic. Scholars further divide the West Semitic group into Northwest Semitic and South Semitic. Geographically, Aramaic belongs to the Northwest Semitic subgroup, which includes Hebrew (*see* Hebrew Language), Phoenician, Moabite, Ammonite

and Ugaritic. Other Semitic languages include the East Semitic language Akkadian, an umbrella term covering both Babylonian and Assyrian, and the South Semitic languages Arabic, Ancient South Arabian and Geez (classical Ethiopic).

1.2. History of Aramaic. Aramaic has an almost three-thousand-year datable history, with the earliest texts dating to the mid-ninth century BCE and with dialects spoken yet today. S. A. Kaufman (1997) divides the history of Aramaic into periods: Old Aramaic (c. 850-612 BCE, that is, to the end of the Neo-Assyrian Empire), Imperial or Official Aramaic (c. 600-200 BCE, used throughout the Neo-Babylonian and Persian Empires), Middle Aramaic (c. 200 BCE-250 CE, during the Hellenistic and Roman periods), Classical Aramaic (c. 200-1200 CE), Modern Aramaic. The dates are approximate, with overlap.

The Aramaic of Ezra belongs to Official Aramaic. According to Kaufman (1997, 115), Official Aramaic gave birth to a Standard Literary Aramaic, which continued in use throughout the Ancient Near East after the Greek conquest. Literary texts produced in Greek and Roman times, then, were written in this literary dialect, with any given text coming under the influence of local languages or local coloring. Thus the Aramaic texts from Qumran were written in a Jewish form of this literary standard, called Jewish Literary Aramaic, and not in the Jewish Palestinian spoken dialect, though they may contain Hebraisms.

In his study of the Northwest Semitic form of the letter, D. Schwiderski argues that the first four Aramaic letters contained in the book of Ezra (Ezra 4:11-16; 4:17-22; 5:7-17; 6:6-12) are not authentic Achaemenid period letters, but are forgeries from the Hellenistic-Roman times. He is less dogmatic about the fifth Aramaic letter (Ezra 7:12-26). His argument focuses largely on the "prescript" of the letters. A letter prescript contains the name of the sender, the name of the recipient and a greeting, and it precedes the body of a letter. He alleges that the omission of part (Ezra 4:11-16 lacks the greeting) or all (Ezra 6:6-12) of the prescript points to a fabrication by the author of Ezra. Furthermore, he contends, this forgery belongs to the Hellenistic period, based on his evaluation of the greetings found, šělām ("peace" [Ezra 4:17]) and šělāmāʾ kollāʾ ("all peace" [Ezra 5:7]), and the use of *lamad* to mark the recipient (lědāryāweš, "To Darius" [Ezra 5:7]) instead of the expected ʿal ("to") or

ʾel ("to"). He regards the use of the transition markers ûkeʿĕnet ("and now" [Ezra 4:11; cf. 7:12]) and ûkĕʿet ("and now" [Ezra 4:17]), both attested in Official Aramaic but not in Middle Aramaic, as the result of the fabricator being historically accurate in using Aramaic.

Besides rejecting the authentic transition markers, Schwiderski suppresses other evidence from Achaemenid Aramaic texts that is contrary to his thesis. Thus a letter in which the preposition lamad introduces the addressee he dismisses as "unproductive" or "no longer unambiguously recognizable as a letter" (Schwiderski, 98)—lqly ʾhy kʿnt . . . , "To Qallay, my brother. Now . . . " (TAD D 7.33)—which letter Yardeni dates to the fifth century BCE. He also rejects the relevance of following text that contradicts his thesis: [sn]yʾ šdr lrmn[ʾ]lm snyʾ lrmnʾ, "The bramble dispatched to the pomegranate as follows: 'The bramble to the pomegranate'" (TAD C 1.1:101). He also ignores the use of lamad with the verb šlḥ ("to send"), which though commonly governing the preposition ʿl ("to"), also governs the preposition lamad in letters: hʾ šlḥt lnbwntn, "here I sent (word) to Nabûnĕtan" (TAD A 3.1 R2-3); šlḥw lnbwntn, "send (word) to Nabûnĕtan" (TAD A 3.1 V6); wšlḥ ʾgrh ʿldbrkn lṣʾ, "and he sent a letter regarding this matter to Djeo" (TAD 3.6 R4). The introductory formula "PN [= Personal Name] to PN" must be short for "PN sends a letter to PN," so that these examples are relevant to the discussion. Furthermore, he deems as irrelevant evidence of the greeting šĕlām ("peace") in fifth-century BCE letters found on ostraca, such as [š]lm ʾḥwṭb wkʿnt . . . , "Peace, ʾAḥuṭab. And now . . . " (TAD D 7.3); šlm ʾwryh kʿn . . . , "Peace, ʾUriyah. Now . . . " (TAD D 7.8); šlm yslḥ kʿnt . . . , "Peace, Yislaḥ. Now . . . " (TAD D 7.16). More importantly, the bodies of the letters themselves contain Persian words, which are telltale markers of Achaemenid composition, especially the adverbs ʾaptōm ("surely" [Ezra 4:13]) and ʾosparnāʾ ("exactly" [Ezra 5:8; 6:8, 12, 13; cf. 7:17, 21, 26]) and the adjective ʾărîk ("fitting" [Ezra 4:14]), which are not found in Middle Aramaic. Compare the adverb ʾadrazdāʾ ("correctly" [Ezra 7:23]).

2. The Importance of Aramaic in the World of Ancient Israel.

2.1. The Patriarchs of Israel. The book of Genesis connects the patriarchs of Israel with an Aramean tribe of Aram-naharayim (ʾăram naḥărayim, "Aram of the Two Rivers," probably Aram situated between the Euphrates and Habur Rivers in northern Mesopotamia rather than between the Euphrates and Tigris Rivers, that is, all of Mesopotamia). Abraham sent his servant to Aram-naharayim to fetch a wife for his son Isaac from the clan of Nahor his brother. Isaac married Rebekah the daughter of Bethuel "the Aramean" from Paddan Aram (Gen 25:20; paddan ʾărām, "Field of Aram," so correctly Hos 12:13: śĕdēh ʾărām), who was the son of Nahor (Gen 22:20-23). Isaac also sent his son Jacob to Paddan Aram to find a wife (Gen 28:1-5). There, Jacob married Leah and Rachel, daughters of Laban "the Aramean" (Gen 25:20; 31:20, 24). All the sons of Jacob, except Benjamin (Gen 35:16-18), were born in Paddan Aram (Gen 29:31—30:24; 46:15; 48:7). When Jacob and Laban make an agreement after Jacob's unannounced departure, they heap up a pile of stones as a witness to that agreement. This "heap of witness" Jacob calls galʿēd, which is Hebrew, while Laban calls it yĕgar sāhădûtāʾ, which is Aramaic (Gen 31:47). Aramaic phraseology also colors the Hebrew that comes from Laban's mouth when he says, "You did not let me kiss my sons and daughters goodbye" (Gen 31:28). The verb "to let," nāṭaš, which normally means "to leave, abandon, forsake" in Hebrew, is a calque of the Aramaic verb šĕbaq in the meaning "to let, allow." When Jacob speaks with his "Aramean" wives, he says, "God has taken your father's possessions and given them to me" (Gen 31:9). The sequence of verbs, hnṣl (hipʿil of nṣl, "to take") + ntn ("to give") echoes Aramaic; the normal Hebrew verb "to take" would be lāqaḥ. The narration, too, contains an Aramaism. When Laban pursues Jacob and overtakes him, the narration uses the Aramaic calque wayyadbēq, "to overtake" (Gen 31:23), in place of the expected Hebrew wayaśśēg, which is used later in the same narrative (Gen 31:25). An alert hearer or reader would not miss this local Aramaic coloring. It is no wonder that Deuteronomy describes Jacob as ʾărammî ʾōbēd, "a wandering Aramean" (Deut 26:5). The Chronicler records that Manasseh had an Aramean concubine who bore him Machir (1 Chron 7:14), from whom would emerge the strongest clan of the Menassite tribe.

2.2. Arameans and Aramean Kingdoms in the History of Biblical Israel.

2.2.1. Balaam the Son of Beor. As Israel

camped on the plains of Moab before entering Canaan, Balak, the king of Moab, brought the seer Balaam from Pethor in Aram-naharaim to curse Israel, but instead he blessed Israel (Num 23:7; Deut 23:5).

2.2.2. Cushan-rishathayim, Oppressor of Israel. Cushan-rishathayim ("Cushan of Double Wickedness"), king of Aram-naharayim, was the first oppressor of Israel mentioned in the book of Judges (Judg 3:8).

2.2.3. The Aramean Kingdom of Aram-Zobah. Prominent among the Aramean city-states in the eleventh-tenth centuries BCE was Aram-Zobah (*ʾăram ṣôbāh*), listed among the enemies of Saul (1 Sam 14:47). King Hadadezer brought Aram-Zobah to its zenith of power, but King *David defeated him (2 Sam 8:3). The Arameans of Damascus came as an auxiliary force to Hada-dezer's aid, only to be defeated too (2 Sam 8:5-6).

Some time later, the *Ammonites hired the Arameans of Bet-Rehob, of Zobah, and of Maacah as mercenaries to fight against David (2 Sam 10:6). David's general Joab routed the Arameans. Hadadezer regrouped the troops and fought another and decisive battle against David, which he lost (2 Sam 10:18). Minor Aramean kings, who had been subject to Hadadezer, now made peace with Israel (2 Sam 10:19).

2.2.4. The Aramean Kingdom of Aram-Damascus. In the latter days of King *Solomon, Rezon son of Eliada wrested Damascus from the control of Israel and founded the kingdom of Aram-Damascus (*ʾăram dammeśeq* [1 Kings 11:23-25]). Aram-Damascus would remain a powerful kingdom throughout the ninth-eighth centuries BCE.

In the days of the prophet *Elisha, Naaman "the Aramean" came from Aram-Damascus to Israel for healing (2 Kings 5:20).

Joram (= Jehoram) son of Ahaz, king of Israel, in confederation with Ahaziah son of Jehoram, king of Judah, waged war against Hazael, king of Aram-Damascus, at Ramoth-Gilead. Joram was wounded (2 Kings 8:28-29; 2 Chron 22:5). The Tel Dan stela apparently recounts the victory of Hazael over "the king of Israel" and "the king of the house of David," namely, Judah.

In the days of the prophet Isaiah, King Rezin of Aram-Damascus and King Pekah son of Remaliah of Israel attempted to coerce King Ahaz of Judah into an anti-Assyrian alliance (2 Kings 16:5), even trying to replace him with their puppet Ben Tabeal (Is 7:6). Tiglath-Pileser III of As-

syria crushed Aram-Damascus in his campaigns of 733 and 732 BCE, breaking the kingdom up into a number of Assyrian provinces. He later did the same to Israel, capturing *Samaria in 722 BCE.

2.2.5. A Word to the Nations from Jeremiah the Prophet. In denouncing the nations for their idolatry, *Jeremiah instructs his fellow Judeans in Aramaic ("Thus you shall say to them") to declare to their foreign neighbors in Aramaic, "The gods . . . will perish!" (Jer 10:11).

2.3. Aramaic as the Lingua Franca of the Empires of Assyria, Babylon and Persia.

2.3.1. Neo-Assyrian Empire (746-609 BCE). As the *Assyrian Empire expanded westward, so did its use of Aramaic as a language of diplomatic correspondence and communication. From the time of Tiglath Pileser III (746-727 BCE), the founder of the Neo-Assyrian Empire, Aramean scribes are mentioned in texts and depicted in art along with Assyrian scribes. During a campaign by Sennacherib (705-681 BCE) against Judah in 701 BCE, the Bible records the diplomatic use of Aramaic (2 Kings 18:26).

2.3.2. Neo-Babylonian Empire (625-539 BCE). In 625 BCE the Chaldean prince Nabopolassar founded the Neo-Babylonian Empire, which continued the use of Aramaic as a lingua franca. By this period Aramaic had replaced Babylonian as the most widely spoken language in Babylonia itself. Nebuchadnezzar II (605-562 BCE), while still a general, put Judah under vassalage after defeating Pharaoh Neco II of Egypt at the battle of Carchemish in 605 BCE (Jer 46:2; 2 Kings 24:1). In the same year he carried off members of the royal family and nobility from Jerusalem, including Daniel, Hananiah, Mishael and Azariah, to *Babylon (Dan 1:1-3, 6). After Judah rebelled, Nebuchadnezzar laid siege to Jerusalem, captured it in 597 BCE, and led away Jehoiachin and other leading Jerusalemites, including the prophet Ezekiel (Ezek 1:1-2), while installing Zedekiah as king (2 Kings 24:10-17). When Zedekiah rebelled, Nebuchadnezzar once more marched against Jerusalem, capturing and destroying it in 586 BCE. This marks the beginning of the Babylonian exile (2 Kings 25:11, 21), during which time the Judean exiles apparently adopted Aramaic as the language of everyday use.

2.3.3. Persian Empire (539-330 BCE). The *Persian Empire likewise adopted Aramaic as the "official" language of communication from one end of the empire to the other. In 538 BCE Cyrus the Great issued a decree to rebuild the temple in Jerusalem (Ezra 1:1-4). Within a year the Judeans began rebuilding the temple, but soon they stopped. In 520 BCE, during the reign of Darius I, at the urging of the prophets Haggai and Zechariah, and under the leadership of Zerubbabel the Persian-appointed governor of Yehud (Judah) and Yeshua the high priest, they resumed the work of rebuilding the temple, which they completed in 515 BCE (*see* Postexilic Temple). Later, under the rule of Xerxes (485-465 BCE), called Ahasuerus in Ezra 4:6, and Artaxerxes I (464-424 BCE) (Ezra 7:7), opposition arose against the refortification of the city of Jerusalem (Ezra 4:6-7). This is the setting of the book of Ezra.

The Assyrian form *egurru*, "temple," appears in Achaemenid (Persian) period texts found in Egypt, spelled *ˀgwrˀ*, and not the Babylonian form *ekurru*. This suggests that the neo-Assyrian, Aramean scribes and scribal schools were taken over without change by the neo-Babylonians and subsequently by the Persians.

3. The Aramaic of Ezra.

In this section distinctive features that characterize the Aramaic of Ezra (Ezra 4:8—6:18; 7:12-26) are described with respect to vocabulary, orthography and phonology, morphology, syntax and other issues.

3.1. Bilingualism in Ezra. The author of Ezra used both Hebrew and Aramaic in his composition to express point of view (Arnold). After the Lord rouses King Cyrus of Persia to issue a decree to rebuild the Lord's temple in Jerusalem and the builders subsequently lay its foundation, opposition is raised. At this point of transition and change in point of view from that of an ideologue (Ezra 1:1-4:7) to one of detached observer (Ezra 4:8-6:18), the author switches from Hebrew to Aramaic. He continues his use of Aramaic until he switches back to being an ideologue, with focus on the Passover (Ezra 6:19-7:10). The author switches back to Aramaic to record the Persian king's support of Ezra's mission by quoting an official letter written in Aramaic (Ezra 7:11-26). Immediately following the letter, the author inserts a psalm of praise to God for his intervention (Ezra 7:27). This marks a return to ideological concerns and so also to Hebrew (Ezra 7:27—10:44). Both the author and his audience were bilingual, at

home in both Hebrew and Aramaic.

3.2. Vocabulary of the Aramaic of Ezra.

3.2.1. Persian Words. The Aramaic of Ezra contains a number of Persian loanwords, primarily to do with administration and official correspondence: *ginzayyāˀ* ("treasures") in the collocation *bêt ginzayyāˀ* ("treasury" [Ezra 5:1]), *gizzabrayyāˀ* ("treasurers" [Ezra 7:21]; written *gedāběrayyāˀ* in Dan 3:2-3, i.e., with *dalath* instead of *zayin*), *ˀăparsatkāyē* ("messengers" [Ezra 4:9]), *dātāˀ* ("law" [Ezra 7:12]), *ništěwānāˀ* ("written order" [Ezra 4:18]), *paršegen* ("copy" [Ezra 4:11]), *pitgāmāˀ* ("message" [Ezra 4:17]), *ˀosparnāˀ* ("exactly" [Ezra 5:8]), *ˀadrazdāˀ* ("diligently" [Ezra 7:23]), *ˀaptōm* ("surely" [Ezra 4:13]). The *hapax legomenon* *ˀărîk* ("fitting" [Ezra 4:14]) has an Old Persian etymology, not a Semitic one (i.e., it is not a passive participle from the Semitic root *ˀrk*, "to be long"). The geographic terms *yěhûd* ("Yehud" [Ezra 7:14]) and *ˁăbar nahărāh* ("Across-the-River [Euphrates]" [Ezra 4:10]) reflect Persian administration.

3.2.2. Akkadian Words. The Aramaic of Ezra contains Akkadian words: *běˁēl ṭěˁēm* ("commander" [Ezra 4:8, 9, 17]); *bîrtāˀ* ("citadel" [Ezra 6:2]); three types of taxes: *hălāk* (Ezra 4:13, 20, 24), *bělô* (Ezra 4:13, 20, 24) and *mindāh* (Ezra 4:13, 24) = *middāh* (Ezra 4:20; 6:8); *ˀuššayyāˀ* ("foundations" [Ezra 5:16]). The month name *ˀădār* ("Adar" [Ezra 6:15]) is Babylonian.

3.2.3. Possible Updated Vocabulary. In contrast to the Elephantine documents, which use both *baytāˀ* and the Assyrian *egurru* (Aramaic *ˀgwrˀ*) for "temple," Ezra uses only *baytāˀ*. It is possible that the author of Ezra rewrote the official Aramaic *ˀēgûrāˀ zēk* ("this temple," as found in the official letter of the Yedanyah archive *TAD* 4.7:13 = *TAD* 4.8:12) as *bêt ˀělāhāˀ dēk* ("this house of God" [Ezra 6:7-8]). The *zayin/dalath* interchange in the (masculine) deictic pronoun—*zēk* over against *dēk*—could also reflect rewriting.

Yet the scribe *Peṭeese bar Nabûnětan*, whose first name is Egyptian and whose patronymic is Aramaic, uses the (feminine) deictic pronouns *dkˀ* and *dky* spelled with *dalath*: *bmwmˀh dkˀ* ("with that oath" [*TAD* B 2.8:6]) and *bšm mwmˀh dky* ("regarding that oath" [*TAD* 2.8:9]) in a document found in Egypt and dated 440 BCE. This stands in contrast to the more widely attested form *zky* in the Aramaic documents found in Egypt. (On this issue see 3.3.1 below.)

3.2.4. Other Words. The collocation *ˀeben gělāl*

(Ezra 5:8; 6:4) means either "large stone block," which was moved on rollers because it was too heavy to transport by other means (traditional view), or "specially selected stone" (Williamson), but not "round stones"—that is, cobble or rubble fill.

The *paʿel* infinitive *lĕbaqqārāʾ* means "to investigate a situation," not "to exercise the office of overseer" (Ezra 7:14). Elsewhere in Ezra the verb means "to make an investigation" (Ezra 4:15, 19; 5:17; 6:1). In a customs account from Egypt (*TAD* C 3.7), an Achaemenid Aramaic text dating to about 475 BCE, the verb appears often, meaning "to inspect" (the cargo of a ship).

The form *yaḥiṭû* (Ezra 4:12) is a *paʿel* suffix conjugation from the root *yḥṭ,* which is related to the middle weak root *ḥwṭ.* The meaning may be "to examine" (the foundations) based on an Akkadian cognate rather than "to repair" (the foundations) based on the regular meaning "to sew."

The phrase *mĕlaḥ hêklāʾ mĕlaḥnāʾ,* "we have salted (eaten?) the salt of the palace" (Ezra 4:14), refers to a covenant of salt, whereby one puts oneself under obligation to the king.

The participle *mĕpāraš* means "simultaneously translated" (Ezra 4:18) and reflects the Persian practice of reading in one language with simultaneous translation into another language. Thus the phrase *ništĕwānāʾ . . . mĕpāraš qĕrî qādāmāy* means "the document . . . was read before me (in Aramaic) while being simultaneously translated (to Persian)."

The verb *ntn* ("to give") appears in the *peʿal* imperfect and infinitive (Ezra 4:13; 7:20), while the verb *yhb* appears in the *peʿal* perfect, both active and passive (Ezra 5:12, 14, 16), and in the *hitpeʿel* (Ezra 4:20; 6:4, 8, 9; 7:19). This pairing is common throughout the various Aramaic dialects.

3.3. Orthography and Phonology of the Aramaic of Ezra.

3.3.1. The Consonant d *Represents* */ḏ /. Extrabiblical fifth- and fourth-century BCE corpora, namely the Achaemenid Aramaic documents found in Egypt, the Samaritan Aramaic legal documents from Wadi Daliyeh and the Idumean Ostraca, have *zî* ("of, who, which, that") with few exceptions. This fact has led many to conclude that *dî* in Ezra reflects a later updating of the language, perhaps dating to the third century BCE. Nevertheless, there is some extrabiblical attestation of *dî,* along with *zî,* in the Egyptian cor-

pus, which fact prevents one from being overly dogmatic on the issue. The scribe Haggai bar Shemayah used *dî* alongside of *zî* in two letters dated 437 BCE (*TAD* B 3.4) and 402 BCE (*TAD* B 3.12). In two personal letters to family members (*TAD* A 2.3 and A 2.4), Makkibanit uses *kdy* ("as") instead of the widely attested *kzy*. It is possible that the official correspondence cited in Ezra originally had the spelling *zî* and that the author himself altered the language for inclusion in his literary work.

3.3.2. The Consonant ʿ *Represents* */ḍ/. The Aramaic of Ezra reads *ʾarʿāʾ* ("the earth" [Ezra 5:11]), not the chronologically earlier form *ʾarqāʾ* (Jer 10:11) < */ʾarḍ. The Aramaic of Ezra attests *ʾāʿ* ("beam" [Ezra 5:8; 6:4, 11; cf. "wood" [Dan 5:4, 23]) over against the spelling *ʿq* ("wood"), appearing consistently in the Aramaic documents found in Egypt and the Samaritan papyri from Wadi Daliyeh.

3.3.3. The Consonant ś *Does Not Change to* s *as in Later Dialects.* The Aramaic of Ezra retains the spelling with /ś/, whereas later Aramaic dialects replace it with /s/: *śābê* ("the elders of" [Ezra 5:5]), *śaggîʾān* ("many [years]" [Ezra 5:11]).

3.3.4. Nondissimilation of Emphatic Consonants. Initial /q/, preceding /ṣ/, is not dissimilated, as in *qṣp,* "rage" (Ezra 7:23). This agrees with the form *qṣt* ("part") found in a letter of Makkibanit from Hermopolis (*TAD* A 2.2), a draft petition from the communal archive of Yedanyah (*TAD* A 4.5), a bequest from the Anani Archive (*TAD* B 3.10) and documents of obligation (*TAD* B 4.5, 4.6). Contrast the forms *kṣph* ("his rage"), *hkṣr* ("reap") and *kṣyr* ("harvest") found in the proverbs of Ahiqar (*TAD* C 1.1), the form *krṣy* ("slander of") in the Carpentras funerary stela (*TAD* D 20.5) and the form *kṣt* ("part" [*TAD* C 3.11, D 4.15], in which initial */q/ followed by /ṣ/ dissimilates to /k/.

3.3.5. Dissimilation by Nun. The progressively assimilated form from the root *ydʿ* ("know") producing gemination is dissimilated by *nun:* *tiddaʿ > *tindaʿ* (Ezra 4:15). The Aramaic of Daniel does the same: *maddaʿ > *mandaʿ* ("intelligence," Dan 5:12).

3.3.6. Representation of Final Long /ā/. Final long /ā/ can be indicated by an *alaf* or a *he,* as demonstrated by *ʾănaḥnāʾ* ("we" [Ezra 5:11]) = *ʾănaḥnāh* (Ezra 4:16), *lĕmāʾ* ("why" [Ezra 6:8]) = *lĕmāh* (Ezra 4:22), *kāhănāʾ* ("the priest" [Ezra 7:12]) = *kāhănāh* (Ezra 7:21). Nevertheless, there is a strong preference for use of *alaf*.

Final long /ā/ is not closed with a *nun* as in later Aramaic dialects: *tammā* ("there"), not *tammān;* *ʾănaḥnā* or *ʾănaḥnāh* ("we"), not *ʾănaḥnān; šěʾēlnāʾ* ("we asked" [Ezra 6:10]), not *šěʾēlnān.* As in the last example, the suffix *-nāʾ* denotes "we" in verbs in the suffix conjugation; later Aramaic dialects have *-nān.*

3.3.7. Vocalization of the Noun šm *("Name").* The word *šum* ("name") has the vowel /u/ (Ezra 5:1, 10), not /e/ as in the later dialect of Jewish Palestinian Aramaic.

3.3.8. Spelling of the Causative Conjugation with and without /h/. Within Aramaic the *hapʿel* conjugation predates the *apʿel* conjugation, in which the primitive *h* has been elided. In Ezra forms of the verb in which *h* is initial—the suffix conjugation (as in *haglî,* "he exiled" [Ezra 4:10]) and the infinitive (e.g., *lěhôdāʿûtāk,* "to make you known to you" [Ezra 5:10])—retain the primitive *h.* Where *h* is intervocalic, forms with *h* are preferred, although forms without *h* also appear. Ezra contains six cases of the prefix conjugation spelled with *h* (*těhôděʿûn,* "you should inform" [Ezra 7:25]; *těhanziq,* "it will damage" [Ezra 4:13]; *těhaškaḥ,* "you will find" [Ezra 4:15, 7:16]; *yěhašnēʾ,* "[who] should alter" [Ezra 6:11]; *yahătîbûn,* "they should return" [Ezra 6:5]) over against two cases spelled without *h* (*taḥēt,* "you shall deposit" [Ezra 6:5]; *yětîbûn,* "they should return [the letter]" [Ezra 5:5]), and five cases of the participle spelled with *h* (*měhôděʿin,* "make known" [Ezra 4:16, 7:24]; *měhanzěqat,* "harmful" [Ezra 4:15]; *měhaḥătin,* "deposited" [Ezra 6:1]; *měhaqrěbin,* "offer" [Ezra 6:10]) over against two cases spelled without *h* (*maṣlaḥ,* "prospers" [Ezra 5:8]; *maṣlěḥin,* "prospering" [Ezra 6:14]). Forms of the imperative also present a mixed result: *hašlêm* ("deliver" [Ezra 7:19]) and *ʾăḥēt* ("deposit" [Ezra 5:15]).

3.3.9. Hapʿel *Conjugation of Initial Yod Verbs.* The diphthong *ay* contracts to *ê* in the *hapʿel* conjugation of the verb *ybl:* *wěhêbēl* ("and he brought" [Ezra 6:5]), *ûlěhêbālāh* ("and to bring" [Ezra 6:5]). Where the initial *yod* represents historical *waw,* the *waw* appears, as in the verbs *ydʿ* (e.g., *měhôděʿin,* "make known" [Ezra 4:16]) and *ytb* (*wěhôtēb,* "and he made settle" [Ezra 4:10]).

3.3.10. Phonology of Initial Nun Verbs. With the verbs *nzq* ("to damage"), *npq* ("to go out") and *ntn* ("to give"), the *nun* remains, as in *měhanzěqat* ("harmful" [Ezra 4:15]), *hanpēq* ("[Nebuchadnezzar] took out" [Ezra 5:14]) and *tintēn* ("you shall give" [Ezra 7:20]). In the only case of the

verb *npl* ("to fall"), assimilation occurs: **yinpel >* *yippel* ("[whatever] is required" [Ezra 7:20]). With regard to the verb *nḥt* ("to go down"), in the causative conjugation the *nun* disappears: imperative *ʾăḥēt* ("deposit" [Ezra 5:15]), participle *měhaḥătin* ("deposited" [Ezra 6:1]) and prefix conjugation *wětaḥēt* ("and you shall deposit" [Ezra 6:5]). In the imperative of *nśʾ* ("to go away") the *nun* is elided: *śēʾ* ("take" [Ezra 5:15]).

3.3.11. The Forms yittěśām *and* mittěśām. The forms *yittěśām* (Ezra 4:21) and *mittěśām* (Ezra 5:8) are in the *hitpeʿel* conjugation (passive of the *peʿal*), not the *hittapʿel* (passive of the *hapʿel*).

3.4. Morphology of the Aramaic of Ezra.

3.4.1. Pronouns.

3.4.1.1. Independent Personal Pronouns. *ʾănāh* ("I" [Ezra 6:12]), *ʾant* (masc. sg., "you" [Ezra 7:25]), *hûʾ* ("he" [Ezra 5:8]), *hîʾ* ("she" [Ezra 6:15]), *ʾănaḥnā* = *ʾănaḥnāh* ("we" [Ezra 5:11 and 4:16 respectively]), *ʾinnûn* ("they" [Ezra 5:4]), *himmô* ("they, them" [Ezra 4:10]; by contrast, Daniel has *himmôn,* where *nun* closes a final long syllable).

3.4.1.2. Suffixed Personal Pronominal Elements. Both the more primitive forms *-km* (second person masc. pl.) and *-hm* (third person masc. pl.) and the chronologically later form *-hwn* (third person masc. pl.) are attested, as is the case in other Achaemenid texts. Attestations of *-km:* *lěkom* ("to you" [Ezra 5:3, 9; 7:24]), *ʾēlāhăkom* ("your God" [Ezra 7:17-18]). Examples of *-hm:* *lěhom* ("to them" [Ezra 5:3]), *běyedhom* ("in their hand" [Ezra 5:8]), *ʾălêhôm* ("upon them" [Ezra 7:24]), *ʾēlāhăhom* ("their God" [Ezra 7:16]), *běrāʾšehom* ("at their head" [Ezra 5:10]), *šemāhāthom* ("their names" [Ezra 5:10]). Examples of *-hwn:* *lěhôn* ("to them" [Ezra 4:20; 5:2]), *ʾălêhôn* ("to them" [Ezra 5:1, 3]), *wěʾiměhôn* ("and with them" [Ezra 5:2]), *kěnāwāthôn* ("their colleagues" [Ezra 4:9]), *bipělugāthôn* ("in their divisions" [Ezra 6:18]), *běmaḥlěqāthôn* ("in their courses" [Ezra 6:18]), *ûminḥāthôn* ("and their grain offerings" [Ezra 7:17]), *wěniskêhôn* ("and their libations" [Ezra 7:17]).

3.4.1.3. Demonstrative Pronouns. *děnāh* (masc. sg., "this" [Ezra 4:11]), *dēk* (masc. sg., "that" [Ezra 5:16]), *dāk* (fem. sg., "that" [Ezra 4:13]), *ʾēl* = *ʾēlleh* ("these" [Ezra 5:15]), *ʾillēk* ("those" [Ezra 4:21]).

3.4.1.4. Interrogative Pronouns: *māh* ("what" [Ezra 6:9]), *man* ("who" [Ezra 5:3]).

3.4.2. Morphology of the Noun.

3.4.2.1. The masculine plural emphatic phoneme is *-ayyā’*, as in *kāhănayyā’* ("the priests" [Ezra 6:9]), *tārā‘ayyā’* ("the gatekeepers" [Ezra 7:24]).

3.4.2.2. The plural construct of *yôm*, "day," is *yômat*, not *yômê* (Ezra 4:15, 19).

3.4.3. Morphology of the Verb.

3.4.3.1. Infinitive. While the infinitive of the *pe‘al* has a *mem* preformans, as in *lĕmibnē’* ("to build" [Ezra 5:2, 17; 6:8]), the infinitives of the derived stems do not have a *mem* preformans, as in the *pa‘el lĕbaṭṭālā* ("to make cease" [Ezra 4:21]) and in the *hap‘el ulĕhêbālāh* ("and to bring" [Ezra 7:15]). The form *libbĕnē’* ("to build" [Ezra 5:3, 13]) reflects a more primitive form.

The infinitive of the derived conjugations appears with both *-at* and *-ût* endings: *lĕhanzāqat malēkin* ("to cause harm to kings" [Ezra 4:22]), *hitnaddābût ‘ammā’* ("contributing of the people" [Ezra 7:16]), *lĕhôdā‘ûtāk* ("to inform you" [Ezra 5:10]).

3.4.3.2. Internal Passive. As in the Achaemenid Aramaic texts found in Egypt, which date to the fifth and fourth centuries BCE, so also the Aramaic of Ezra attests an internal passive.

3.4.3.2.1. pe‘il: śîm ("[an order] was given" [Ezra 4:19; cf. 5:17; 6:8, 11; 7:13, 21]).

3.4.3.2.2. hop‘al: hohorbat ("[this city] was destroyed" [Ezra 4:15]).

3.4.3.3. Prefix Conjugation of the Verb hĕwāh. The prefix conjugation of the verb *hĕwāh* takes a *lamad* preformative to indicate third person masculine, whether subjunctive or jussive in function: *di lehĕwôn mĕhaqrĕbîn nîhôhîn* ("so that they might offer pleasing sacrifices" [Ezra 6:10]), *šāpĕṭin wĕdayyānin di lehĕwôn dā’nîn* ("magistrates and judges who might judge" [Ezra 7:25]), *yĕdîa‘ lehĕwē’ lĕmalkā’* ("may it be known to the king" [Ezra 4:12]), *lehĕwē’ mityĕhēb lĕhom* ("let it be given to them" [Ezra 6:9]). In the Aramaic of Daniel this form also functions indicatively: *ûmin niṣbĕtā’ di parzĕlā’ lehĕwē’ bah* ("and some of the hardness of iron will be in it [the kingdom]" [Dan 2:41]).

3.4.4. Morphology of the Adjective. The adjectival pattern *kattîb* is well represented: *yaqqîr* ("noble" [Ezra 4:10]), *raḥîq* ("distant" [Ezra 6:6]), *śaggî’* (pl., "many" [Ezra 5:11]), *šallîṭ* ("lawful" [Ezra 7:24]), and *taqqîp* ("mighty" [Ezra 4:20]). The form *mārād* ("rebellious" [Ezra 4:12, 15]) apparently derives from the agentive pattern *kattāb*, that is, *marrād. Some adjectives are *pe‘al*

passive participles: *gĕmîr* ("perfect" [Ezra 7:12]) and *zĕhîr* ("cautious" [Ezra 4:22]). The following adjectives also appear: *b’îš* ("evil" [Ezra 4:12]), *ṭāb* ("good" [Ezra 5:17]), *ḥădat* ("new" [Ezra 6:4], but perhaps emend to *ḥad*, "one").

3.5. Syntax of the Aramaic of Ezra.

3.5.1. Function of the Definite Article. In general, the definite article (/ā/ suffixed to the base form of the noun) expresses definiteness, as in *sāprā’* ("the scribe" [Ezra 4:9]) and *’iggartā’* ("the letter" [Ezra 4:11, 5:6]). By contrast, the absolute state expresses indefiniteness, as in *ûmĕrad* ("and rebellion" [Ezra 4:19]) and *šālû* ("negligence" [Ezra 4:22]). Some foreign words do not take determination when they are definite, like *bĕ‘el ṭĕ‘ēm* ("the commander" [Ezra 4:8]). The numeral one at times functions as the indefinite article with the head noun in the absolute state, as in *’iggĕrâ ḥădâ* ("a letter" [Ezra 4:8]).

3.5.2. Expressions of the Genitive Relationship.

3.5.2.1. Simple Construct. The nouns *bar* ("son") and *bêt* ("house") always appear in simple construct in Ezra: PN *bar* PN (Ezra 5:1-2; 6:14), *bĕnê gālûtā’* ("exiles" [Ezra 6:16]), *bêt ’ĕlāhā’* ("temple" [Ezra 4:24]), *bêt ginzayyā’* ("treasury" [Ezra 5:17]), *bêt malkā’* ("royal treasury" [Ezra 6:4]), *bêt siprayyā’* ("archive" [Ezra 6:1]). The simple construct also functions to express ordinals with the nominal head "year" followed by a cardinal number: *bišĕnat ḥădāh* ("in the first year" [Ezra 5:13, 6:3]), *šĕnat tartēn* ("the second year" [Ezra 4:24]), *šĕnat šēt* ("the sixth year" [Ezra 6:15]). Other simple construct chains with a geographic name as the genitive noun include *melek bābel* ("king of Babylon" [Ezra 5:12]), *bĕkōl mĕdînat bābel* ("in the whole province of Babylon" [Ezra 7:16]). The geographic name also appears as genitive noun in constructions with *di*. Other examples of simple construct include *kĕmē’mar kāhănayyā’* ("according to the request of the priests" [Ezra 6:9]), *ḥănukkat bêt ’ĕlāhā’* ("the dedication of the temple" [Ezra 6:16]), *sāpar dātā’* ("the scribe of the law" [Ezra 7:21]), *malkût malkā’ ûbĕnôhî* ("the realm of the king and his descendants" [Ezra 7:23]). In simple construct chains the genitive noun appears in the absolute state when the chain is indefinite: *bĕnê tôrin* ("bulls" [Ezra 6:9]), *ṣĕpîrê ‘izzîn* ("male goats" [Ezra 6:17]).

3.5.2.2. Constructions with di. The use of *di* as genitive ("of"), which does not appear in the Old Aramaic texts of the tenth through eighth centuries BCE, reflects the influence of Akkadian on Official Aramaic.

3.5.2.2.1. The syntagm noun determined by definite article + *dî* + geographic name: *malkāʾ dî bābel* ("king of Babylon" [Ezra 5:13]), *hêklāʾ dî bābel* ("temple of Babylon" [Ezra 5:14]).

3.5.2.2.2. The syntagm noun determined by definite article + *dî* + noun determined by definite article: *wĕdātāʾ dî malkāʾ* ("and the law of the king" [Ezra 7:26]).

3.5.2.2.3. The syntagm noun determined by proleptic pronominal suffix + *dî* + noun determined by definite article: *ʿabdôhî dî ʾĕlāh šĕmayyāʾ* ("servants of the God of heaven" [Ezra 5:11]).

3.5.2.2.4. The syntagm noun in absolute form + *dî* + noun in absolute form: *nidbākîn dî ʾeben gĕlāl . . . wĕnidbāk dî ʾāʿ* ("courses of dressed stone . . . a course of wood" [Ezra 6:4]); cf. *ṣĕlēm dî dĕhab* ("a statue of gold" [Dan 3:1]), *nĕhar dî nûr* ("a river of fire" [Dan 7:10]). The genitive noun in this syntagm expresses the substance out of which the head noun is made.

3.5.2.3. Constructions with Lamad. Lamad can introduce the genitive noun: *šĕnat tartēn lĕmalkût dāryāweš* ("the second year of the rule of Darius" [Ezra 4:24]); *ûmelek lĕyiśrāʾēl rab* ("and a great king of Israel" [Ezra 5:11]).

3.5.3. Quantification of "Hundreds." In expressions of counting by hundreds the word *hundred* follows the "digit" and is in the singular, as in *ʾarbaʿ mĕʾāh* ("four hundred" [Ezra 6:17]). By contrast, the word *hundred* is in plural in Hebrew: *ʾarbaʿ mĕʾôt.* The later Palestinian Aramaic dialects—Jewish Palestinian Aramaic, Christian Palestinian Aramaic and Samaritan Aramaic—have the syntagm *ʾarbaʿ māʾwān*, under the influence of Hebrew.

3.5.4. Order of the Constituents Subject (= S), Verb (= V), Direct Object (= O).

3.5.4.1. Verb = Suffix Conjugation. When only S and V are present, the order SV appears in main clauses where V is in the passive voice: *ništĕwānāʾ . . . qĕrî* ("the letter . . . has been read" [Ezra 4:18]); *paršegen ništĕwānāʾ . . . qĕrî* ("the copy of the letter . . . was read" [Ezra 4:23]). The order SV also appears in relative clauses: *dî nĕbûkadneṣṣar hanpēq* ("which Nebuchadnezzar took out" [Ezra 5:14; 6:5]). The order VS appears both in main clauses: *bĕṭēlat ʿăbîdat* ("the work stopped" [Ezra 4:24]); *wĕhitnabbî ḥaggay* ("and Haggai prophesied" [Ezra 5:1]); *qāmû zĕrubbābel . . . wĕyēšûaʿ* ("Zerubabel and Yeshua arose"

[Ezra 5:2]); *śim ṭĕʿēm* ("a decree was made" [Ezra 4:19; 5:17; 7:13]); *wĕhištĕkaḥ . . . mĕgillāh ḥădāh* ("and a scroll was found" [Ezra 6:2]); and in relative clauses: *dî šĕlaḥ tatnay* ("that Tatnai sent" [Ezra 5:6]); *dî šĕlaḥ dāryāweš* ("that Darius sent" [Ezra 6:13]).

When only V and O are present, the order VO always appears when O = a personal pronoun: *wĕhôtêb himmô* ("and settled them" [Ezra 4:10; cf. 4:23; 5:5, 12, 14]); or when O = a *dî* clause: *wĕhaškaḥû dî . . .* ("and they found that . . ." [Ezra 4:19]). The order VO also appears in narrative after a *waw*: *wĕhaqribû . . . tôrîn* ("and they offered . . . bulls" [Ezra 6:17; cf. 6:15, 18]); and in the relative clause: *dî šakkin šĕmēh* ("who made his name dwell" [Ezra 6:12]).

The order OV appears in narrative clauses: *wĕʿammāh haglî* ("and the people he exiled" [Ezra 5:12; cf. 4:12]); *pitgāmāʾ hătîbûnāʾ* ("they returned us the word," i.e., "they replied to us" [Ezra 5:11; cf. 5:7]); *wĕʾap šĕmāthom šĕʾēlnāʾ* ("and also their names we asked" [Ezra 5:10]); and in a causal clause introduced by *kol qŏbēl dî*: *kol qŏbēl dî mĕlaḥ hêklāʾ mĕlaḥnāʾ* ("because the salt of the palace we salted" [Ezra 4:14]).

With all three constituents the order SVO appears in main clauses: *rĕḥûm bĕʿēl ṭĕʿēm wĕšimšay sāprāʾ kĕtābû ʾiggĕrāh ḥădāh* ("Rehum the commander and Shimshai the scribe wrote a letter" [Ezra 4:8]); *kôreš malkāʾ śām ṭĕʿēm* ("Cyrus the king gave a command" [Ezra 5:13; 6:3]), *ʾănāh dāryāweš śāmet ṭĕʿēm* ("I, Darius, gave a command" [Ezra 6:12]); *ûmelek . . . bĕnāhî wĕšaklĕlēh* ("and a king . . . built it and completed it" [Ezra 5:11]).

When both S and O follow V, the order VSO appears when O = a substantive, but the order VOS appears when O = a personal pronoun. Contrast *min dî hargizû ʾăbāhātanāʾ leʾĕlāh šĕmayyāʾ* ("after our fathers had angered the God of heaven" [Ezra 5:12]) and *waʿăbadû bĕnê yiśrāʾēl kāhănayyāʾ wĕlēwāyēʾ ûšĕʾār bĕnê gālûtāʾ ḥănukkat bêt ʾĕlāhāʾ* ("and the children of Israel, the priests, the Levites, and the rest of the exiles made a dedication of the temple" [Ezra 6:16]) with *hanpēq himmô kôreš malkāʾ* ("Cyrus the king brought them out" [Ezra 5:14]).

The order OVS appears only when O = the word *pitgāmāʾ* and when the constituents constitute a main clause: *pitgāmāʾ šĕlaḥ malkāʾ* ("the king sent the report" [Ezra 4:17; cf. Ezra 5:7, 11]).

3.5.4.2. Verb = Prefix Conjugation. When only

S and V appear, the sequence SV appears when V is passive or active in statements: *hēn qiryĕtā᾽ dāk titbĕnē᾽* ("if that city is built" [Ezra 4:13]); *nipqĕtā᾽ tehĕwē᾽ mityahābā᾽* ("the expense shall be given" [Ezra 6:8]); *kol mitnaddab . . . yĕhāk* ("every volunteer . . . should go" [Ezra 7:13]). By contrast, the order VS appears in a question: *lĕmāh yiśgē᾽ ḥăbālā᾽* ("why should damage increase?" [Ezra 4:22]).

When only V and O are present, the order OV appears in direct discourse: *mindāh bĕlô wahălāk lā᾽ yintĕnûn* ("they will not pay taxes" [Ezra 4:13]); *ûr῾ût malkā᾽ . . . yišlaḥ* ("and may he send the will of the king" [Ezra 5:17]); *mā᾽nê bêt ᾽ĕlāhā᾽ . . . yahătîbûn* ("and may they return the vessels of the temple" [Ezra 6:5]). By contrast, the order VO appears in *dî* clauses: *dî niktub šum gubrayyā᾽* ("that we might write the names of the men" [Ezra 5:10]); *kol ᾽ĕnāš dî yĕhaśnē᾽ pitgāmā᾽ dĕnāh* ("everyone who shall alter this word" [Ezra 6:11]). The order VO also appears when O = a *dî* clause: *wĕtinda῾ dî . . .* ("and you know that . . . " [Ezra 4:15]). The order VO also appears in this sentence: *tiqnē᾽ . . . tôrin . . . ûtĕqārēb himmô* ("you should buy . . . bulls . . . and you should offer them" [Ezra 7:17]).

The order SVO appears in a main clause: *wē᾽lāhā᾽ . . . yĕmaggar kol melek wĕ῾am* ("and may the God . . . destroy any king or people" [Ezra 6:12]). The order VOS appears in a relative clause with the object being a personal pronoun: *kol dî yiš᾽ălenkôn ῾ezrā᾽* ("everything that Ezra asks you" [Ezra 7:21]). The sequence SOV is also attested: *paḥat yĕhûdāyē᾽ [ûl] < wĕ > śābê yĕhûdāyē᾽ bêt ᾽ĕlāhā᾽ dēk yibnôn* ("and the governor of the Jews and the elders of the Jews should build this temple" [Ezra 6:7]).

3.5.4.3. Verb = Imperative. When O = a substantive, both the orders VO and OV are attested. VO: *śîmû ṭĕ῾ēm* ("give an order" [Ezra 4:21]); *mennî šāpĕtin wĕdayyānin* ("appoint magistrates and judges" [Ezra 7:25]); *šĕbuqû la῾ăbidat bêt ᾽ĕlāhā᾽ dēk* ("leave the work on this temple alone" [Ezra 6:7]). OV: *᾽elleh mā᾽nayyā᾽ śē᾽* ("these vessels take" [Ezra 5:15]); *ûmā᾽nayyā᾽ . . . hašlēm* ("and the vessels . . . deliver" [Ezra 7:19]).

But when O = a personal pronoun, only the order VO is attested: *᾽ăḥēt himmô* ("deposit them" [Ezra 5:15]).

3.5.4.4. Verb = Active Participle. The order VO appears in the continuation of a narrative: *᾽ănaḥnā᾽ himmô ῾abdôhî . . . ûbānayin baytā᾽* ("we are servants [of the God of heaven and earth]

and are building the temple" [Ezra 5:11]). This order also appears when the O = *dî* clause: *ûlĕkom mĕhôdĕ῾în dî . . .* ("and to you [we] make known that . . . " [Ezra 7:24]). It also appears in relative and purpose clauses introduced by *dî*: *᾽ătar dî dābĕḥin dibḥin* ("the place where they could offer sacrifices" [Ezra 6:3]); *dî lehĕwôn mĕhaqrĕbin nihôḥin* ("that they may offer sweet aromas" [Ezra 6:10]); *dî lehĕwôn dā᾽ănin lĕkol ῾ammāh* ("that they might judge all the people" [Ezra 7:25]); *wĕkol dî lā᾽ lehĕwē᾽ ῾ābēd dātā᾽* ("and whoever will not do the law" [Ezra 7:26]).

The order OV appears in main and relative clauses where the focus is on O: *qiryĕtā᾽ mārādtā᾽ ûb᾽ištā᾽ bānayin* ("that rebellious and evil city they are building" [Ezra 4:12]); *wĕ᾽ eštaddûr ῾ābĕdin bĕgawwah* ("and sedition they were making in her midst" [Ezra 4:15]); *dî dĕnāh binyānā᾽ bānayin* ("who this building are building" [Ezra 5:4]).

When S = an independent personal pronoun and O = a sentence introduced by *dî*, the order VSO is attested: *mĕhôdĕ῾în ᾽ănaḥnāh lĕmalkā᾽ dî . . .* ("we make known to the king that . . . " [Ezra 4:16]).

3.5.4.5. Verb with the Infinitive as Its Complement. With the infinitive (= I), the Aramaic of Ezra attests three sequences: VIO (seven cases), VOI (five cases), OVI (one case). Example of VIO: *wĕšāriyw lĕmibnē᾽ bêt ᾽ĕlāhā᾽* ("and they began building the temple" [Ezra 5:2]). Example of VOI: *man śām lĕkom ṭĕ῾ēm baytā᾽ dĕnāh libbĕnē᾽ wĕ᾽uššarnā᾽ dĕnāh lĕšaklālāh* ("who gave you the order this temple to build and this carpentry work to complete?" [Ezra 5:3]). The case of OVI: *wĕ῾arwat malkā᾽ lā᾽ ᾽ārik lanā᾽ lĕmeḥĕzē᾽* ("and the shame of the king it is not proper for us to see" [Ezra 4:14]). The fronting of the object before infinitive reflects the syntax of Old Persian.

3.5.5. Government of the Verb.

3.5.5.1. Marking of the Direct Object. The direct object does not need a marker: *wahăqîmû kāhănayyā᾽ . . . wĕlēwāyē᾽* ("and they installed the priests . . . and the Levites" [Ezra 6:18]). However, *lamad* can mark the direct object: *hargizû ᾽ăbāhātanā᾽ le᾽ĕlāh šĕmayyā᾽* ("our fathers angered the God of heaven" [Ezra 5:12]); *šĕbuqû la῾ăbidat bêt ᾽ĕlāhā᾽ dēk* ("leave the work on this temple alone" [Ezra 6:7]); *mennî šāpĕtin wĕdayyānin dî lehĕwôn dā᾽nin lĕkol ῾ammā᾽* ("appoint magistrates and judges who should judge all the people" [Ezra 7:25]).

3.5.5.2. "Send to (a Person)." The verb *šĕlah* ("to send") governs the preposition *ʿal* ("to") + person (Ezra 4:17-18; 5:7, 17).

3.5.6. The Position of the Verb hĕwāh *in Relation to Its Participial or Adjectival Complement.* When a *peʿal* passive participle or an adjective appears with the verb *hĕwāh*, the verb *hĕwāh* comes after that *peʿal* passive participle or adjective, except in a relative clause. Contrast *yĕdîaʿ lehĕwē* ... *dî* ... ("may it be known ... that ... " [Ezra 4:12, 13; 5:8]); *ûzĕhîrîn hĕwô* ("and be cautious" [Ezra 4:22]); and *rāhîqîn hāwô* ("be far" [Ezra 6:6]) with *baytāʾ dî hăwāʾ bĕnēh* ("the temple which was built" [Ezra 5:11]). The active participle and participles of the *hitpeʿel* conjugation appear after the verb *hĕwāh: wahăwāt bāṭelāʾ* ("and it ceased" [Ezra 4:24]); *nipqĕtaʾ tehĕwēʾ mityahăbāʾ* ("the expense shall be given" [Ezra 6:8]); *dî lehĕwôn mĕhaqrĕbîn nihôḥîn* ("that they may offer appeasing smells" [Ezra 6:10]).

3.6. Functions of the Qĕrê *in Relation to the* Kĕtîb.

3.6.1. To Correct Faulty Word Division. The *qĕrê, wĕšûrayyāʾ šaklilû* ("and the walls they have completed"), corrects the faulty word division of the *kĕtîb, wšwry ʾškllw,* in Ezra 4:12.

3.6.2. To Record Alternate Phonology.

3.6.2.1. The Historical Alaf. The *qĕrê* preserves the historical *alaf,* while the *kĕtîb* updates the language: *nĕbîʾāh* and *nĕbîʾayyāh* are written, *nĕbîyāʾ* and *nĕbîyayyāʾ* are read ("the prophet" and "the prophets" respectively [Ezra 5:1]).

3.6.2.2. The Masculine Plural Morpheme with Attached Second Person Singular Pronoun. The *kĕtîb* preserves the ending *-ayik,* while the *qĕrê* reads *-āk: ʿabdayik* is written, *ʿadbāk* is read ("your servants" [Ezra 4:11]).

3.6.2.3. Gentilic. The *kĕtîb* reads *kaśdāyāʾ,* while the *qĕrê* reads *kaśdāʾāh* ("the Chaldean" [Ezra 5:12]).

3.6.2.4. Middle Weak Participle with Medial Yod in the Root. The *kĕtîb* reads *dāʾănîn,* while the *qĕrê* reads *dāyĕnîn* (Ezra 7:25).

3.6.3. To Record a Different Word.

3.6.3.1. In a list of different peoples found in Ezra 4:9, *dihû* ("that is") is written, *dehāyēʾ* ("the Dehites") is read. The problem with the reading *dihû* ("that is") is that the conjunctive *dî* is always written separately from the word that follows in all Achaemenid period Aramaic texts, including biblical Aramaic; it is never conjoined. The closest parallel example in Ezra is found in Ezra 6:15: *dî hîʾ* ("which is"), using the feminine pronoun. The problem with the reading *dehāyēʾ* ("the Dehites") is that such a people group is difficult to identify.

3.6.3.2. Two words with the same meaning, "banishment" ("rooting out"), and from the same root *(šrš),* appear: *šĕrôšû* is written, *šĕrôšî* is read (Ezra 7:26).

3.7. Suggested Emendations for Critical Evaluation. Readers should critically evaluate for themselves the following emendations adopted in some Bible translations.

3.7.1. Emend *dînāyēʾ* ("the Dinites") to *dayyānayyāʾ* ("judges") in Ezra 4:9. Some have suggested emending the gentilic *dînāyēʾ* ("the Dinites") to *dayyānayyāʾ* ("the judges") on the basis of 3 Esdras 2:13, the Greek of which reads *hoi kritai,* "the judges."

3.7.2. Emend *ʾămarnā* ("we asked") to *ʾămarû* ("they asked") in Ezra 5:4. The context requires a change of person in the verb.

3.7.3. Emend *yĕbaqqar* (paʿel, "let one investigate") to *yitbaqqar* (hitpaʿal, "let it be investigated") in Ezra 4:15 in light of Ezra 5:17. Left as written, the form *yĕbaqqar,* third person masculine singular, should be interpreted as an indefinite subject, where the active *(paʿel)* takes place of the passive *(hitpaʿal).*

3.7.4. Emend *ʾuššôhî* ("its foundations") to *ʾiššayyāʾ* ("burnt offerings") in Ezra 6:3. The NRSV reads "and burnt offerings are brought," emending the MT from *ʾuššôhî* ("its foundations") to *ʾiššayyāʾ* ("burnt offerings") and interpreting the verbal form *mĕsôbĕlîn* as a *sapʿel* from the root *ybl.* Nowhere else in Achaemenid Aramaic texts is a *sapʿel* of this verb attested, nor is the verb ever used of offering sacrifices. The only support for *ʾeššāʾ* meaning "offering by fire" comes from Hebrew *ʾeššāh* (see Lev 2:3), not from Aramaic. The NIV retains the MT by reading "and let its foundations be laid," interpreting the verbal *mĕsôbĕlîn* as a *poʿel* passive participle from the root *sbl.* Support for retaining the MT may be found in Ezra 3:10.

3.7.5. Emend the measurements of the second temple in Ezra 6:3 to correspond to those of the first temple (1 Kings 6:2). According to a memorandum *(dikrōnāh)* of Cyrus recorded in Ezra 6:3, the height *(rûmēh)* of the second temple was to be sixty cubits, and its width *(pĕtāyēh)* sixty cubits; the length is omitted. A comparison of these measurements with those of the first temple—length *(ʾorkô)* sixty cubits, width *(roḥbô)* twenty cubits, height *(qômātô)* thirty cubits (1 Kings 6:2)—together with the fact that the second temple presumably was to be built on the site of the first temple, leads some to suggest that the Ezra text was corrupted in transmission and that it too originally had identical measurements with the first temple. If so, emend the height from sixty to thirty, the width from sixty to twenty, and possibly add the length sixty.

3.7.6. Emend *ḥădat* ("new") to *ḥad* ("one") in Ezra 6:4. Two parallel phrases describe materials used in rebuilding the temple in Jerusalem: *nidbākîn dî ʾeben gĕlāl tĕlātāʾ wĕnidbāk dî ʾāʿ ḥădat*, "courses of dressed stone—three; a course of wood—new." In light of the first phrase and typical scribal practice in lists of commodities in other Achaemenid Aramaic texts, some suggest emending *ḥădat* ("new") to *ḥad* ("one").

3.7.7. Delete the preposition *lamad* in the form *ûlĕsābê* ("and the elders") in Ezra 6:7, thus making *sābê* part of the subject of the sentence. The context dictates this small change.

3.7.8. Emend the singular *wĕšêṣîʾ (kĕtib)/wĕšêṣî (qĕrê)* to the plural *wĕšêṣîʾû* ("and they finished") in Ezra 6:15 with the Greek. Against the proposed emendation, the singular may function as an indefinite plural.

3.7.9. Emend *gĕmîr* ("perfect") to *šĕlām* ("peace") in Ezra 7:12. This unusual use of *gĕmîr* ("perfect") should not be easily dismissed, as there is no graphic similarity between it and *šĕlām* ("peace").

See also ARAM, DAMASCUS AND SYRIA; EZRA AND NEHEMIAH, BOOKS OF; HEBREW LANGUAGE; LINGUISTICS; NON-ISRAELITE WRITTEN SOURCES: EGYPTIAN ARAMAIC PAPYRI.

BIBLIOGRAPHY. **B. T. Arnold,** "The Use of Aramaic in the Hebrew Bible: Another Look at Bilingualism in Ezra and Daniel," *JNSL* 22.2 (1996) 1-16; **Comprehensive Aramaic Lexicon:** <http://call.cn.huc.edu>; **E. M. Cook,** "Word Order in the Aramaic of Daniel," *Afroasiatic Linguistics* 9.3 (1986) 1-16; **I. Ephʾal and J. Naveh,** *Aramaic Ostraca of the Fourth Century BCE from Idumaea* (Jerusalem: Magnes, 1996); **S. E. Fassberg,** "The Origin of the *Ketib/Qere* in the Aramaic Portions of Ezra and Daniel," *VT* 29 (1989) 1-12; **J. A. Fitzmyer and S. A. Kaufman,** *An Aramaic Bibliography, Part I: Old, Official, and Biblical Aramaic* (Baltimore: Johns Hopkins University Press, 1992); **M. L. Folmer,** *Aramaic Language in the Achaemenid Period* (OLA 68; Leuven: Peeters, 1995); **J. C. Greenfield,** *ʿAl Kanfei Yonah: Col-* *lected Studies of Jonas C. Greenfield on Semitic Philology,* ed. S. M. Paul, M. E. Stone and A. Pinnick (2 vols.; Leiden: E. J. Brill; Jerusalem: Magnes, 2001); **D. M. Gropp,** "The Samaria Papyri from Wadi Daliyeh," in *Wadi Daliyeh* (DJD 28; Oxford: Clarendon Press, 2001) 1-116; **S. A. Kaufman,** *The Akkadian Influences on Aramaic* (AS 19; Chicago: University of Chicago Press, 1974); idem, "Aramaic," in *The Semitic Languages*, ed. R. Hetzron (Routledge Family Language Descriptions; New York: Routledge, 1997) 114-30; **L. Koehler, W. Baumgartner and J. J. Stamm,** *The Hebrew and Aramaic Lexicon of the Old Testament, 5: Aramaic* (Leiden: E. J. Brill, 2000); **E. Lipiński,** *The Aramaeans: Their Ancient History, Culture, Religion* (OLA 100; Leuven: Peeters, 2000); **T. Muraoka and B. Porten,** *A Grammar of Egyptian Aramaic* (HO 32; Leiden: E. J. Brill, 1998); **B. Porten and J. A. Lund,** *Aramaic Documents from Egypt: A Key-Word-in-Context Concordance* (Winona Lake, IN: Eisenbrauns, 2002); **B. Porten and A. Yardeni,** *Textbook of Aramaic Documents from Ancient Egypt* (4 vols.; Jerusalem: Hebrew University, 1986-1999); **E. Qimron,** *Biblical Aramaic* [in Hebrew] (2d ed.; Jerusalem: Bialik, 2002 [1993]); **D. Schwiderski,** *Handbuch des nordwestsemitischen Briefformulars: Ein Beitrag zur Echtheitsfrage der aramäischen Briefe des Esrabuches* (BZAW 295; Berlin and New York: de Gruyter, 2000); **M. Sokoloff,** "Review of *Hebräisches und aramäisches Lexikon zum Alten Testament*, by L. Koehler and W. Baumgartner, neu bearbeitet von W. Baumgartner, I. J. Stamm, und B. Hartman, unter Mitarbeit von Z. Ben-Hayyim, E. Y. Kutscher, und P. Reymond, 2 vols. Leiden: Brill, 1995 [= HALAT]," *DSD* 7 (2000) 74-109; **R. Steiner,** "The *mbqr* at Qumran, the *Episkopos* in the Athenian Empire, and the Meaning of *lbqrʾ* in Ezra 7:14: On the Relation of Ezra's Mission to the Persian Legal Project," *JBL* 120 (2001) 623-46; **E. Vogt,** *Lexicon Linguae Aramaicae Veteris Testamenti* (Rome: Pontifical Biblical Institute, 1971); **H. G. M. Williamson,** "*ʾeben gĕlāl* (Ezra 5:8, 6:4) Again," *BASOR* 280 (1990) 83-88. J. A. Lund

ARAMEANS. *See* ARAMAIC LANGUAGE.

ARAM-NAHARAYIM. *See* ARAM, DAMASCUS AND SYRIA.

ARCHAEOLOGY, SYRO-PALESTINIAN

The Iron Age period in Syro-Palestinian archaeology has perhaps been the most extensively studied period in the discipline of biblical archaeology. This pattern of research interest is due to the use of archaeology to support the historicity of the biblical text and the establishment of the modern state of Israel. Various trends and issues have dominated the research of the Iron Age, specifically the use of archaeology as a means to validate or invalidate the biblical record. The biblical narrative has influenced archaeological research in that scholars have overemphasized the search for ethnic markers such as the identification of Israelite material culture.

This article surveys the issues and trends within Iron Age research of Syria-Palestine and provides an overview of the reconstruction of the history and archaeology of the southern Levant associated with the events described in the narratives of the Historical Books. The article may be viewed as having two parts. The first part (1-3) addresses theoretical trends and provides an overview of the history of the discipline focusing on archaeological research as it relates to biblical history. The second part (4-5) presents a synthesis of the archaeological material culture of the Iron Age and Persian periods.

1. History of Research
2. Current Issues
3. Archaeological Method and Theory
4. Overview of Iron Age (I and II) Archaeological Data
5. Overview of Later Iron Age (III) and Persian Period Archaeological Data

1. History of Research.
The history of Iron Age research corresponds to developments within biblical archaeology. Based on recent histories of the discipline (Silberman 1982; Moorey; King; Davis), generally, three major periods can be isolated within the history of research.

1.1. Early Period. The development of biblical archaeology finds its roots in the exploration of the Holy Land. The exploration of the Holy Land has a long history. Western fascination with the ancient world, popular interest in the antiquity of humankind, and the various ancient monuments fueled popular interest in the ancient Near East during the nineteenth century. This fascination led explorers to bring new treasures back to national museums. The decipherment of cuneiform texts and Egyptian hiero-

glyphs enhanced the scholarly pursuit of the biblical world. There were no comprehensive attempts to write a history of the area based on archaeological discoveries until the middle of this century. The archaeology of the southern Levant, and more specifically of ancient Israel, was not initiated until the following period. As with the broader discipline of anthropology developing in academia, the emphasis was on a cultural-historical approach to classifying and reconstructing society in the ancient Near Eastern world.

1.2. Biblical Archaeology as an Academic Discipline. The synthesis of the archaeology of Israelite history, the cornerstone of biblical archaeology, is to be attributed to W. F. Albright. Albright and his contemporaries inaugurated the current paradigm of the coalescing of the archaeological record and the biblical text. Albright's excavations of Tell Beit Mirsim were a watershed for the discipline of biblical archaeology. It was these excavations that set the template for the correlation of ceramic analysis with biblical periods and the integration of archaeology, history of the ancient Near East and biblical studies. Albright wrote the first comprehensive and synthetic work that incorporated the archaeological and biblical data, *The Archaeology of Palestine* (1949). Albright's work and breadth of knowledge led him to construct the conquest model of Israelite settlement, which basically proposed that the cities recorded in the campaign of *Joshua were destroyed in the singular event of a new ethnic group's migration into and conquest of the western highlands.

This paradigm was adopted by Albright's Israeli contemporary Y. Yadin. Yadin excavated at *Hazor and associated a destruction level with the battle of Joshua (Josh 11:11, 13). However, it was the excavation of a monumental gate system and its correlation with gates at *Megiddo and *Gezer that became the classic case study and impetus for associating actual archaeological remains with a historical figure and event in the biblical text. Yadin postulated that these gates represent the Solomonic building projects recorded in 1 Kings 9:15. Yadin was instrumental in the establishment of the Israeli school, but also he was influential during this period as he inaugurated the archaeology of the united monarchy. During this period biblical archaeology was seen as one of many methods within biblical studies. This was the paradigm for most of biblical archaeology in the 1950s and 1960s, and it is still a dominant enterprise among biblical archaeologists today. The paradigm continued under Albright's student G. E. Wright, who attempted to unite archaeology with theology in the biblical theology movement. This trend was short-lived and was strictly an American phenomenon. Concurrent with the development of the Albrightian paradigm of archaeology and biblical studies, K. Kenyon, of the British school, was introducing new field methodologies with her excavations at *Jericho, *Jerusalem and *Samaria.

This period in biblical archaeology is considered the heyday, when it appeared that archaeological research was continuously supporting the accounts found in the biblical text. Thus Iron Age archaeological research focused on documenting the destructions left in Joshua's wake as he conquered the Promised Land. In addition, the archaeology of *David and *Solomon also dominated Iron Age research. This initial euphoria regarding the verification of the biblical text as an accurate historical document was short-lived as the archaeological record grew and the earlier confirmations were not supported. Albright and Yadin's conquest model was brought into question.

1.3. Processual Approaches. The next major period of Syro-Palestinian archaeology can be characterized by the adoption and utilization of methodologies from other disciplines. Perhaps the two most dominant approaches were landscape archaeology, in terms of research focus, and the adoption of the processual paradigm, in relation to research strategy. In Israel the publication and translation into English of Y. Aharoni's *The Land of the Bible* (1967) represents the shift and emphasis on studying settlement patterns and survey work in addition to the excavation of major tells. This coincided with the creation of the Institute of Archaeology at Tel Aviv University in 1969. Also during this period the Department of Antiquities (now the Israel Antiquities Authority) carried out extensive survey and reconaissance work throughout the country. In Jordan survey work was also being conducted by many national schools working cooperatively with the Jordanian Department of Antiquities. This emphasis on regional patterns also led to consideration of settlement and demographic shifts, adaptations to the environment over long periods of time (e.g., *longue duree*) from the prehistoric to the modern period, rather than documenting historical events or political history.

In addition to the emphasis on landscape archaeology and the explosion of settlement studies, W. G. Dever was introducing the paradigm shift of the "New Archaeology" within biblical archaeology. New Archaeology, better defined as processual archaeology, was becoming the dominant paradigm in New World archaeology, while in biblical archaeology it remained a unique emphasis among North American biblical archaeologists. Dever was the dominant voice in the incorporation of processual approaches into Syro-Palestinian archaeology. Dever did not fully adopt the paradigm of the new archaeology in terms of developing general laws of human behavior; his programmatic goal was to differentiate the research aims of biblical studies and archaeology, producing a separation between the two disciplines. This was valuable in that it expanded biblical archaeology's focus beyond correlating the archaeological record with the biblical textual account to a larger framework of the historical and social processes of the ancient world. For example, research shifted from finding Joshua's conquest cities to documenting the process of sedentarization and tribalism. Hence, research designs emphasized anthropological models rather than historical correlations between the texts and artifacts. One of the major changes in terms of field methodology was a multidisciplinary emphasis. The result was an incorporation of various specialists (geologists, osteologists, archaeobotanists, etc.) to excavate and interpret the data. This led to research designs focused on all aspects of human culture—rural settlements and the common people were as valuable as royal cities and kings.

Concurrent with these theoretical trends has been the reevaluation of the Israelite conquest and settlement as recorded in the book of Joshua. Initially, it was assumed that discrepancies between the archaeological data and the biblical account would disappear with further archaeological research. As the conquest model was tested and new data were accumulated, it became apparent that the hypothesis produced more problems than it solved in the coalescing of the archaeological and biblical data. This led to the search for new models of Israelite settlement and the adoption of anthropological theory and model building to address questions of the origin of ancient Israel.

This shift from historical to anthropological models has set the foundation for the current paradigm for understanding the archaeological and textual data. Perhaps the most noteworthy change in terms of scholarship is the realization that just as biblical historians are attempting to reconstruct the past, archaeologists are attempting to reconstruct it using different data sets. Biblical archaeologists did not stop asking the questions of biblical scholarship, but they more clearly defined the differences between archaeological data and textual data and the different hermeneutical methods used for each data set. Today there is a more complex and refined approach to the use of the archaeological and textual data in reconstructing ancient society.

2. Current Issues.

With the growth of archaeological excavations and research paradigm shifts, archaeologists are now proposing models to explain the archaeological record based primarily on the archaeological data and secondarily on the biblical text and ancillary ancient Near Eastern texts and inscriptions. There are currently four main research focuses in Iron Age archaeological research in the southern Levant: the Israelite settlement/conquest, *ethnicity, the rise of the state and, most recently, postprocessual critiques.

2.1. Israelite Settlement/Conquest. The period of the settlement/conquest is one of the major research emphases of Iron Age archaeological investigations, just as it was one of the major emphases of the discipline of biblical archaeology. The understanding of the Iron Age has greatly increased, with various regional studies allowing for a variety of syntheses of data and regional analyses. Initially the two dominant models were the conquest model and the peaceful-infiltration model. These early models were influenced by current trends that viewed social change as outward. The next phase of model development was influenced by Marxist social theory, and the peasant-revolt model was proposed. These three models and their many variations became the major models for explaining the nature of the Israelite settlement. They continued to be supported as the major historical reconstructions in biblical studies, while archaeologists were focusing on processual archaeological

theory and models with a more complex approach to synthesizing the archaeological and textual data. These latter models place an emphasis on defining social processes and developing general laws of culture. Processual models that have been introduced to explain the cultural change between the Late Bronze Age and Iron Age I have focused on different processes: collapse and center-and-periphery theory, sedentarization (ruralization, retribalization, resedentarization) theory, techno-functionalist theory, ecological determinist theory, economic theory and paleodemographic theory. The most prominent and influential model is the sedentarization model proposed by I. Finkelstein (1988) that suggested a gradual migration over time from east to west as nomadic tribes settled into agricultural communities and slowly moved from Transjordan to the western highlands. Finkelstein later developed his model into an ecological-determinist approach that postulated a long history of cyclical periods of growth and degeneration, with the Iron Age I being one of these periods of abatement between the Early Bronze Age and the later Iron Age II period. This group of processual models has a common denominator: they reconstruct the Iron Age settlement pattern from indigenous people of the Late Bronze Age.

A developing trend is to view the Israelite settlement and rise of the state as a convergence of various trajectories. This development is influenced by postprocessual trends. The present paradigm for the Israelite settlement can best be summarized as a complex, or synthesis, model. The general consensus is that there was not a single trajectory or event (e.g., revolution, ecological adaptation) that caused the settlement patterns, but that the process of Israelite settlement, as well as settlement patterns throughout the Levant during Iron Age I, consisted of a multitude of events and processes. It is apparent that the Israelite settlement did not consist of only a singular mass migration and conquest from without. Dever proposed a symbiotic model that uses state-collapse theory to explain the social processes and defines the Iron Age I settlers of the hill country as "proto-Israelites." The issue in terms of reconstructing ancient Israel is when and if the Iron Age I settlers defined themselves as Israelite. The question now has focused on the ethnic identity of the Israelites instead of on their origin.

Scholars who view the biblical text as historical have approached the issue of Israelite settlement and conquest in a variety of ways. Most fall under one of two research approaches. The first approach is taken by those who propose that the Albright model misdated the Israelite conquest to the thirteenth century BCE. Their solution is to search for the Israelite conquest in the fifteenth century BCE, and their research has emphasized reevaluating stratigraphical sequences. This approach is illustrated by the work of J. Bimson and B. Wood.

The second approach employs the symbiotic model. This can be termed a Neo-Albrightian approach using linguistic, textual and archaeological data to reconstruct biblical history. These scholars view the accounts in the books of *Joshua and *Judges as reflecting a particular period in Israelite history, from the exodus event to the rise of the Israelite state. Each account focuses on various aspects of the Israelite conquest and settlement. One account, that in Joshua, records major campaigns or regional battles, while the book of Judges recounts the settlement of Israelites among *Canaanites in the tribal allotments and the commingling of the Israelite tribal groups with the local Canaanite population. The emphasis of research has been to isolate the structure of the books and reconstruct the historical events as reflected in both accounts. The approach takes the biblical accounts at face value as a collection of historical accounts that has been placed into a literary structure. This approach to biblical history—reading the texts alongside the archaeological record—provides a more accurate synthesis of the biblical text in relation to the archaeological data. The conquest and settlement of the Israelite tribes as recorded in the books of Joshua and Judges reflects the archaeological data that show destructions and gradual settlement processes occurring concurrently.

2.2. Ethnicity in the Archaeological Record. During the 1990s the debate shifted from the origin of ancient Israel and the nature of the Israelite settlement to ethnicity. Biblical archaeologists were trying to determine how to distinguish Israelite material culture from Canaanite material culture. If the Israelite conquest and settlement was a complex process and represents a transition between Canaanite and Israelite settlement processes, then archaeologists needed to be able to differentiate and define the material cor-

relates of ethnicity. The question of whether ethnicity can be distinguished in the archaeological record became important at this time.

One of the difficult yet common classification systems in archaeology is the definition of ethnic and national groups. Archaeologists working on the Iron Age Period have attempted to define these distinctions. Many Near Eastern texts of the Late Bronze Age and the Iron Age document the presence of several ethnocultural groups in Palestine, such as *Egyptians, Hurrians, Canaanites, *Philistines, and Israelites. The name "Israel" in the Merneptah Stela has been debated as to whether it is a national or tribal reference. In the early stages of biblical archaeology it was common to distinguish between Canaanite, Israelite and Philistine material culture. Problems arose when these patterns were not as clear or easily definable in the archaeological record. If a Canaanite storage jar is found in an Israelite settlement, does it reflect evidence of trade, or is the site a Canaanite one? Is there a mixed ethnic population at the site, or is the jar actually an Israelite storage jar? These distinctions are particularly important in the attempt to define the process of Israelite settlement. When did a Canaanite settlement become an Israelite settlement? How did the inhabitants of that site define themselves: as a tribal entity, such as Ephraimite, or by a national identity, such as Israelite? The biblical and ancient texts demonstrate that people differentiated and defined themselves and others using ethnic and national terms. Biblical archaeologists shifted their research to address the theoretical and methodological issues of distinguishing ethnicity in the archaeological record.

Archaeologists and biblical historians have realized that connecting ethnic and national terms found in the biblical text with the archaeological data is not a simple process, because ethnicity and identity are fluid within human society. One of the research shifts resulting from this factor is the study of the processes of ethnicity. An illustration of this research trend is the model that Dever has proposed, labeling the Iron Age I settlements in the western highlands as "proto-Israelite." He proposes a term to reflect the process of multiethnic tribal groups coalescing into the ancient Israelite state because the material culture of these settlements reflects Late Bronze Age Canaanite affinities that become part of the Israelite state in the later Iron Age II.

In spite of the paradigm shift that views ethnicity as a process, there have been major advances in defining the various people groups in the Iron Age archaeological record. Biblical archaeologists recognize the methodological and theoretical pitfalls of associating pots with people and that any definition of classification or ethnic association of material culture will be debated. Most agree that these boundaries and borders are definable in the material culture. The Philistine material culture has been studied and refined by T. Dothan and M. Dothan. In addition, Jordanian archaeology has advanced, and experts have now defined geo-ethnic variations in the material culture such as *Ammonite, *Edomite and *Moabite material culture and regional boundaries. In addition, archaeologists are able to isolate ethnic and national material correlates that can be associated with the *Phoenicians and Arameans as well as the *Assyrians, Egyptians, and the Aegean world.

2.3. State Formation. During the 1990s two trends dominated the research of the united monarchy. The first was an attempt to define the Israelite state in the archaeological record, and the second was a shift in the theoretical framework to view state formation as part of a long historical process.

The first trend focused on isolating the archaeological evidence for David and Solomon dated to the tenth century BCE. Although this date was originally determined by syncretism between the biblical and other ancient Near Eastern texts, most archaeologists find collaborative evidence for this date based on ceramic seriation, stratigraphy and carbon dating. The archaeological strata associated with the tenth century BCE demonstrate a drastic shift in settlement and *architecture suggesting a state level of society. To a majority of biblical archaeologists this coincides with the united monarchy and centralized authority, and this view and interpretation have become dominant. Research has emphasized the association of the archaeological data with David and Solomon—for example, the Solomonic monumental gate systems, red-slip burnished pottery and proto-aeolic capitals.

The second trend was to view the rise of the Israelite state as part of the sociopolitical process in the Levant rather than finding archaeological data that match the account of David and Solomon in the Hebrew Bible. Archaeologists realized that while the development of any state will have common elements (e.g., complexity, centralization), it will look different in each region of the world. This trend of adopting anthropological models to explain cultural change rather than the documentation of historical events is evident in the essay collection *From Nomadism to Monarchy* (Finkelstein and Naʾaman 1994). This volume of essays documents the shift in research to examine the rise of the Israelite state within a larger social development. Most scholars have adapted models from anthropological theory, particularly the neo-evolutionary model of the growth of social organization from band to tribe to chiefdom to state. Other issues include the application of modern concepts or terms to ancient society. Archaeologists have attempted to develop trait lists for definitions of social complexity based on material culture (e.g., monumental architecture, writing/court records), but also they acknowledge that even modern states are complex and do not fit into easy definitions.

Recently, some have challenged the traditional date of the rise of the Israelite state, shifting it from the tenth century to the ninth century BCE (see 2.4 below) because of the limited archaeological evidence for traits of statehood (e.g., writing and monumental inscriptions). The question is whether the evidence for state development suggests that it occurred in the Davidic and Solomonic period or in the divided kingdom of Israel and Judah. This has led some scholars to debate whether the united monarchy was a chiefdom, a polity, a nation, a kingdom or a state in transition, such as client state, a dimorphic chiefdom or a mature state.

Although these revisionist trends are popular in biblical studies and have influenced the archaeological reconstructions and interpretations, the majority of archaeologists postulate that there was an entity of centralized authority in the tenth century BCE that can be attributed to the Davidic kingdom in the biblical texts. The debate is not on the existence but on the nature of this kingdom, and most research in the past decade has focused on the process of state formation.

2.4. Postprocessual Critiques. Another trend in current Iron Age research is the adoption of postprocessual trends common within the larger discipline of archaeology. Postprocessual archaeology is difficult to define because all critiques of the processual paradigm (e.g., functionalist and materialist approach, linear evolution, positivism) are considered part of this trend. One dominant theme is that there is no metanarrative, and so there needs to be multivocality in the interpretation of data. This self-evaluation was necessary to correct the positivism of the processual paradigm, but it also brought critical and revisionist trends along with new approaches (e.g., world archaeology, gender and ethnic archaeology, cognitive studies). Within biblical archaeology, N. Silberman's work on the history of archaeology and the Bible and the use of archaeology for the modern political nation-building policies within the region is an example of this trend (Silberman 1982; 1989). Silberman has pointed out how archaeology has been used to support national agendas. This is particularly relevant with regard to the use of the archaeology of David and Solomon to support the territorial integrity and expansion of the modern state of Israel. An extreme example of the use of archaeology as political practice is seen in K. Whitelam's 1996 monograph *The Invention of Ancient Israel: The Silencing of Palestinian History.*

While the aforementioned trends focused on method and theory within the practice of biblical archaeology, the postprocessual critique of the interpretation of the archaeological record is perhaps best illustrated by the "low chronology" proposal of I. Finkelstein, who defined it in several articles in the mid 1990s. His first article postulated that sites with locally made monochrome pottery should be redated nearly one hundred years to the end of the twelfth century BCE or beginning of the eleventh century BCE. This redating creates a domino effect, lowering all Iron Age strata of the Philistine countryside. A second article, written a year later, postulated that all evidence of a state level of society currently dated to the tenth century BCE should be lowered to the ninth century BCE. Thus all the archaeological evidence of a state level of society (monumental architecture, gate systems, palaces, etc.) that was associated with David and Solomon now gets placed in the ninth century BCE. The proposal of a low chronology by Finkelstein is based on the *Lachish and *Jezreel ceramic corpuses and a ceramic-distribution model that states that contemporaneous sites must exhibit the same ceramic patterning. Most archaeologists have not adopted this revi-

sionist model, although it has been influential, and the model of the low chronology is slowly gaining adherents, particularly within biblical studies.

3. Archaeological Method and Theory.
Originally, biblical archaeology was defined as one method within the field of biblical studies. Now that biblical archaeology stands alone as a separate discipline, there is a need to articulate its own method and theory apart from biblical studies. Although the endeavor of biblical archaeology to coalesce archaeological data with the textual data is still dominant, there is a nuanced difference in the paradigm shift. This is apparent in the research goals and methodologies of archaeological research. There are two basic types of biblical archaeologists: those who consider themselves archaeologists who specialize in the southern Levant, and those who consider themselves biblical historians who use textual and archaeological data to reconstruct the biblical world. Each uses the same data; however, their methodologies are different because they are addressing different questions.

3.1. The Archaeological Record. Inherent to archaeological method and theory is the nature of the archaeological record. There are many data sets used to study human behavior. The material record of a society represents only a fragment of human behavior; that is, the archaeological record is only a fragment of the data available to study the past. Of this data set, the archaeological record is a small subset of the material correlates. For example, examination of a temple and the objects found within it might help determine the components of religious practice and to some extent provide information on religious beliefs. But this alone, without texts or information gathered from those who used the temple, will inform the scholar little about the users' complex theology. This information is available to historians and anthropologists; thus they focus more on the analysis of writings and ethnographic research.

The archaeological record is fragmentary; it does not represent the complete record of the material correlates of society. This is due to forces that transform the archaeological record. In the past the archaeological record was changed and acted upon by people and by natural processes such as erosion and deterioration. These same forces act upon the archaeological record today. The archaeological record is also fragmentary in the sense that only a small percentage is actually excavated. Rarely are most major tells of the biblical world excavated more than five to ten percent. This is a small percentage of a site on which to make inferences about the past.

In addition, archaeologists realize that research and model building are not based solely on objective data but on data that are usually interpreted with many levels of reconstruction. Archaeologists do not find Solomonic gate systems; rather, they find contemporary monumental gate houses that are evidence of centralized authority. Based on a historical correlation with a text found in the Hebrew Bible, the structures are identified as Solomonic.

3.2. The Nature of Archaeological Research: Domains of Archaeological Inquiry. Archaeological inquiry is unique because it is a subset of many disciplines (e.g., classics, anthropology, history, economics, material science, art history, biblical studies), which has led many to debate whether archaeology is a hard science or part of the humanities. This debate has never affected the archaeology of the southern Levant, as most archaeologists working in this field continue to view the material data and textual data as equally important in their work. They realize that with the growth of the field, they must specialize in the archaeological data but still be conversant within another discipline.

The domains of archaeological inquiry correspond to three major arenas of inquiry within a multidisciplinary context: material culture studies, history and anthropology. These arenas also correspond to the debates concerning the nature of archaeology. Does archaeology belong to the hard sciences? Is it a subdiscipline of anthropology? Or of history? The domains of inquiry are the types of questions asked and answered by the archaeological enterprise. Although most disciplines are now fully integrated, and it is getting more difficult to draw research boundary lines, there are some generalizations that can be offered to illustrate the complexity of the archaeological enterprise.

The first arena is material culture studies. Since the data of the archaeologist are the material correlates of society, it makes sense that archaeologists emphasize the study of the material culture. The central material correlate of bibli-

cal archaeology is the potsherd, but other material remnants of society are also studied. Hence, the archaeological enterprise is focused on researching and comparing the material culture. A major research focus is the development of classification systems and typology. Correlating disciplines are art history, museum studies and material science. Iron Age archaeology has emphasized defining chronological and geographical classification systems of ceramics. A cultural-historical framework has dominated material culture studies as Iron Age archaeologists focus on defining what is Israelite material culture versus Philistine or Canaanite.

The second arena of inquiry is historical reconstruction, and this is perhaps where Iron Age archaeology has spent most of its research. The questions of the historian are addressed using the archaeological data. The main emphasis has been on correlating the history of ancient Israel with its broader context (e.g., Egypt and Assyria) and on writing a history of ancient Israel. Besides placing an emphasis on political history, biblical archaeologists have attempted to address and write a history of those elements of society that do not survive the historical record: peasants and women. Archaeological research has attempted to go beyond a rewriting or support of the history of ancient Israel as found in the biblical text to studying the history of the southern Levant. Questions are now asked by archaeologists that deal with the hinterland and the daily life of the people.

The third arena is the study of processes, particularly questions of anthropology. This research domain asks broader questions about human society. Such inquiries focus on the rise and collapse of states, plant and animal domestication, social stratification, and the nature of ruralism and urbanism. This is the current domain of inquiry among Syro-Palestinian archaeologists working in the Iron Age period. No longer are archaeologists focusing on proving or defining the conquest and settlement, but rather on defining processes of the Iron Age period.

3.3. Archaeological Dating. In addition to major domains of inquiry, at the core of any archaeological interpretation is how archaeologists date the material culture. This is the basic methodology or building block for archaeological inquiry. Reconstructions and interpretations cannot be correct if the dates do not correspond. There are four controlling factors in the dating of archaeological data: material culture (specifically, pottery sequencing), relative stratigraphy, historical collaboration and, more recently, the use of scientific dating methods (i.e., carbon 14). Ceramic analysis is the basic mode of inquiry of biblical archaeology because it is central to all reconstructions, interpretations and study. This is especially true of the Bronze and Iron Ages. Although other material correlates of ancient society also are key to documenting chronological change (e.g., metal artifacts, figurines, architecture), none is as plentiful and durable in the archaeological record as pottery. Thus the most basic analysis of the archaeological data is the development of ceramic typologies. This is the most common dating technique of the majority of archaeological strata in the Iron Age. Ceramic typologies were the main goal of archaeologists during the early stage of the development of the discipline.

An inherent assumption of the development of ceramic typologies is that chronological patterning is consistent throughout Syria-Palestine. Archaeologists realized that there is regional as well as chronological patterning in the ceramic record; also, changes in material culture do not neatly correspond to historical events. In addition, each site and region experienced different processes and influences on the change of the material correlates; therefore, relative chronology becomes a defining framework for intrasite stratigraphical correlations. Hence, there is a level of interpretive process in the development of ceramic typologies. Another factor is that relative chronology only documents chronological changes and patterning among the material culture; it does not provide absolute dates.

Historical correlations provide the absolute datum points for the material culture. Most historical correlations in biblical archaeology are military campaigns. The most important historical correlations for the Iron Age period are the collapse of the Late Bronze Age and Aegean migrations; Shishak's campaign in 925 BCE; Assyrian campaigns of the eighth century BCE; the Babylonian campaigns of the early sixth century BCE. But even these correlations are debated within the archaeological record. A site might have multiple destruction layers, thus making it difficult to assign each one to a foreign campaign. While military campaigns might provide absolute dates, other historical correlations use

events and descriptions in the biblical text (e.g., battles between the Israelites and their neighbors, such as the Philistines and the Transjordanian kingdoms; boundary lists; specific deeds of Israelite and Judean kings). This type of research, usually the domain of historical geography, offers useful reconstructions from the archaeological and textual records, but it does not provide absolute dates, only approximations.

Other attempts at historical correlations are artifacts that can be associated with a person, usually a ruler. Examples are the hundreds of Egyptian cartouches, scarabs and seals. One of the best examples is the *lmlk* stamped jars associated with *Hezekiah. These types of artifacts, although associated with absolute dates, do not allow for precision in dating stratigraphy because of the reuse or the long time span of use for the artifact. These usually only provide *terminus a quo* or *terminus ad quem* dates.

Recently, archaeologists working on the Iron Age period have attempted to use carbon 14 as a means to obtain absolute dates without relying on biblical or extrabiblical texts. This focus on carbon 14 dates is associated with the debate over the low chronology; most of the carbon 14 dates come from sites currently being excavated in the north of Israel. The use of scientific dating provides a range of absolute dates. Its contribution to Iron Age archaeology will serve as a corrective or help date isolated strata.

4. Overview of Iron Age (I and II) Archaeological Data.

Although there have been numerous research trends and issues, a consensus of the historical and cultural development in the southern Levant has developed within the past decade. This is evidenced A. Mazar and E. Stern's two-volume *Archaeology of the Land of the Bible;* A. Ben Tor, ed., *The Archaeology of Ancient Israel;* T. Levy, *The Archaeology of Society in the Holy Land;* and by two major multivolume encyclopedias: E. Stern, ed., *The New Encyclopedia of Archaeological Excavations in the Holy Land (NEAEHL)* and E. Meyers, ed., *The Oxford Encyclopedia of Archaeology in the Near East (OEANE).* In addition to these works there are some that specifically deal with the Iron Age: I. Finkelstein, *The Archaeology of the Israelite Settlement;* I. Finkelstein and N. Naʾaman, *From Nomadism to Monarchy;* S. Gitin, A. Mazar and E. Stern (eds.) *Mediterranean Peoples in Transition.*

4.1. Iron Age I (1200-1000 BCE). Iron Age I is a period in which the Late Bronze Age balance of power between Egypt and the Hittites ended with the decline and collapse of the eastern Mediterranean. There are many theories as to why this collapse happened. Whichever collapse model is proposed, the outcome was the same. The geopolitical nature of the Levant changed with the disruption of societies across the eastern Mediterranean. With the dissolution of Hittite and Egyptian hegemony and the migration of displaced peoples from the east, the Levant becomes a staging ground for smaller states to develop (e.g., Phoenicia, Philistia, Israel/Judah, Edom, Moab, Ammon, Aramean states). Along with the disruption of the geopolitical situation, international trade is disrupted, as evidenced by the complete cessation of imports.

The southern Levant is characterized by the collapse and destruction of the major city-states (Egyptian controlled) and a shift in settlement patterns. The coastal plain is developed by the arrival of the Sea Peoples, and new settlements are exploiting the hill country. The first half of the twelfth century BCE demonstrates the Egyptian Twentieth Dynasty's attempt to establish control in its Canaanite urban centers of the previous period, but these are destroyed again.

In spite of the drastic changes in geopolitics and international trade, the ethnic composition and the material culture of the period reflect strong affinities with the previous Late Bronze period. Iron Age I is characterized by remnants of Canaanite Bronze Age cultures that are overlapped by new cultures. Toward the end of the period, as new states are created and formed in the Levant, the material culture begins to reflect this regionalization. This period is associated with the biblical period of Joshua and Judges and the interactions between the developing Davidic monarchy and the Philistines. The economic subsistence consisted of herding and a gradual transformation into *agriculture in the hill country. Along the coast, the fertile valleys were exploited. There appears to have been little trade internationally or regionally.

4.1.1. Chronology. The Albright/Wright chronological framework, commonly called American, designates the dates 1200-950 BCE as the Iron Age I Period. This is based on Egyptian and biblical chronology associating this period with the Twentieth and Twenty-first Dynasties and the period of the *judges and the united

monarchy. Albright divided the Iron Age I period into three subdivisions: IA (1200-1150 BCE), IB (1150-1000 BCE), IC (1000-950 BCE). R. Amiran and Y. Aharoni dated the Iron Age I period between 1200 and 1000 BCE based on the material culture rather than the historical reconstruction of the Albright division. The Hazor excavations played a major role in the Israeli chronology scheme. They maintained the twofold division of Albright, dividing the period at 1150 BCE but ending at 1000 BCE. This division is used in the *New Encyclopedia of Archaeological Excavations in the Holy Land* and has been adopted by most archaeologists. D. Ussishkin, using the results of his excavations at Lachish and evidence in the south of ancient Israel, concludes that the Egyptian Twentieth Dynasty's influence and dominance continued into the twelfth century BCE. Thus he designates the period 1200-1150 BCE as part of the Late Bronze Age; Iron Age IA does not start until the mid-twelfth century BCE.

4.1.2. History/People. Although archaeologists have begun to delineate cultural diversity in the Bronze Age, it is in the Iron Age I period that clear demarcations between sociopolitical and ethnic identities begin to emerge. Ancient Palestine was divided into three major sociopolitical groups: (1) the Philistines (Sea Peoples) along the coast, (2) Canaanite cities in the central, northern and inland valleys that still retained some Egyptian dominance or influence, and (3) sedentary tribal polities in the hills of Cisjordan and Transjordan—Israelites, Ammonites, Moabites, Edomites. Current archaeological research has also focused on defining socioeconomic groups such as pastoralists and agriculturalists, and social transformations between the regions.

4.1.3. Settlement Patterning/Architecture. There are two major patterns in settlement planning and architecture during the Iron Age I period. The first is the start of regional variation between the coastal plain and inland valleys, and the western highlands. Palestine enters a phase of regionalism that will eventually develop into the small states of the Iron Age II period. These regions are western highlands (hill country), southern coastal plain (Philistine), Jezreel Valley, Phoenician coast and Transjordan. The Philistine coast and major Canaanite centers contain public architecture (e.g., city walls, monumental temples, fortifications, defenses, gates), while the settlements in the hill country are small towns and villages. The second pattern is the last attempt by Egypt in the first half of the twelfth century BCE (Iron Age IA) to retain control of the region. This is particularly evident in Canaanite centers that were reoccupied after the thirteenth-century BCE collapse.

4.1.3.1. Canaan. Most sites along the coast and the inland valleys (e.g., Jezreel Valley, Shephelah) continue from the Late Bronze Age II period, although there are destructions at many sites (c. 1200 BCE), such as Hazor XIII, Beth-Shan VII, Megiddo VIIB, Aphek, Beth Shemesh IV, Gezer XV, Lachish VII, *Ashdod XIV, *Ekron VIII and Tell Beit Mirsim C. These destructions are associated with the collapse of the eastern Mediterranean. The most striking phenomenon in the material culture is the absence of the Aegean imported pottery common in the earlier Late Bronze Age. In spite of these destructions and cessation of trade, it appears that Egypt regained some regional pockets of control until the mid-twelfth century BCE (Iron Age IIB). The continuation of Canaanite culture and the strong Egyptian presence in the country during this time are evident at several key sites (Beth Shan, Megiddo, Lachish, Tel Mor, Tel Seraʿ, Shechem, Gezer, Tell el-Farʿah [S]).

4.1.3.2. Philistia. Along the southern coastal plain, Philistine occupation is evident by the destruction of Ashdod and Ekron, Late Bronze Age cities. The next occupational levels contain Mycenaean IIIC:1b pottery, identical with forms found at Cyprus, implying settlements of Aegean migrants. There are two major stages of Philistine settlement patterns. The first stage is the establishment of a beachhead with key cities built on destroyed Late Bronze Age Canaanite sites. This phase is congruent with the reestablished Egyptian control in the Iron Age IB and is characterized by Mycenaean IIIC:1b pottery, locally made but with forms and decoration of the Aegean. The second phase dates from the mid-twelfth century BCE until the mid-eleventh century BCE and is a period of growth and expansion. This period is characterized by the hallmark Philistine bichrome pottery. A third stage of development is defined in the archaeological record but does not represent any major settlement shifts. It is a period defined by a continued acculturation process of red-slip burnished pottery replacing the Philistine bichrome ware.

The city plans for Iron Age I Philistine sites

(Ashdod, Ekron) show well-defined and organized zones (acropolis, temple, domestic, industrial zones, etc.) as well as perimeter city walls for defense and gates. At Ekron the initial settlement of the Philistines witnessed the expansion of the city from ten acres to over fifty acres in Iron Age IA. Unique features of the Philistine material culture include large circular hearths in the middle of main rooms in public buildings (a Megaron temple was built at Ekron).

4.1.3.3. Hill Country. Several extensive surface surveys have revealed a new settlement pattern in the mountains of Cisjordan and Galilee. Over 250 sites have been identified in the hill country of Judah and Samaria. Most of these sites range from two to five acres, while the largest are ten to twenty acres. There is no monumental public architecture and city planning. Most of the sites in the western highlands were newly founded, with only a few having earlier Late Bronze Age occupation (e.g., Tell Beit Mirsim, Beth Shemesh, *Bethel, Tell el-Farah [N]). The typical Iron Age I settlements are hamlets or small villages laid out in oval-shaped plans with a large open space in the center and a ring of buildings around the settlement. These settlements reflect social units based on groups of extended families (tribal) that were self-sustaining agricultural and pastoral economies. The typical hill-country residence was the "pillared" or "four-room" house (*see* Architecture). This is a rectangular structure with a rear broadroom and a front courtyard with one or two side rooms separated from the courtyard by rows of pillars. There is evidence of a partial second story for living and sleeping space. This house type supports an agricultural/pastoral family-centered subsistence. The sites that contain an earlier Late Bronze Age occupation and were rebuilt in Iron Age I tend to have buildings twice the size of typical highland sites. Most sites contain cisterns, storage pits and silos, and agricultural terracing. No major city planning or public architecture is evident. One of the settlement patterns is that in the hill country of Ephraim and Manasseh there is a 4 to 1 density of settlements over against the Judean hills to the south.

During the eleventh century BCE several fortresses were constructed that hint at the developing social organization of the hill-country settlers (e.g., Giloh, Tel el-Ful, Har Adir, several sites in the Benjamin plateau). These were square fortresses surrounded by casemate walls in the midst of a group of small villages. The Giloh fortress consisted of a solid square foundation (11.2 x 11.2 m) for a tower with inner rooms (see Judg 9:46-49, 50-52).

4.1.4. Ceramics. The pottery of the Iron Age I period, unlike the earlier Late Bronze Age corpus, is a poor repertoire limited to types essential for basic subsistence. In terms of general forms, the Late Bronze repertoire continues into the twelfth century BCE (especially pithoi, kraters, bowls [degenerate platter, carinated, simple], flasks, cooking pots, pyxides, etc.). The Early Iron I wares are also in the Late Bronze Age tradition, but they lack the decorative elements, with the exception of red-banded monochrome paint with geometric and animal motifs. New features that appear in the twelfth century BCE include storejars with single-grooved rim and four handles, cooking pots with longer-flanged rim, simple-footed chalices, and "collar-rim" storejars. Cypriot and Mycenaean imported pottery ceases during the Iron Age I period. Toward the end of the eleventh century BCE, red-slipped burnished pottery appears in the assemblages, initially on the coast and in the Negev.

New regional and ethnic ceramic corpuses that are evident in the Iron Age I period are the Philistine pottery and Midianite pottery (southern Arabah). Common Philistine forms are the pyxides, cooking jugs and jugs with strainer spouts. The pyxis (a small, usually cylindrical container), originally an Aegean form, becomes popular in the following Iron Age II period. The Philistine pottery has a distinct chronological development from the Mycenaean IIIC:1b pottery from their initial settlement, to the hallmark bichrome pottery in Iron Age IB, to degenerate forms and the replacement of bichrome decoration with red-slip burnished pottery that becomes common in Iron Age II.

4.1.5. Metallurgy. The term *Iron Age* evokes a transition from bronze to iron, but iron usage does not become the dominant metal until the tenth century BCE (iron first appears in the twelfth century BCE). Bronze is still the main metal in Iron Age I. The transition from bronze to iron may have been motivated by a shortage of tin (required for bronze), perhaps due to the disruption of the Late Bronze Age trade network. Iron can be produced from readily available ore. Earliest iron implements found in ancient Palestine are a sword from Tell el-Farʿah and a knife and from Tell Qasile.

The Bronze weapons of the Iron Age I period continue the Canaanite traditions from the Late Bronze Age. This continuity is illustrated in the axes, arrowheads and javelin heads. There are also Aegean and Cypriot influences in the repertoire: double axes, hammer axes, long socketed javelin heads. Weapons are found at Megiddo, Tell Qasile, Tel Zeror and Akhziv. Bronze tableware sets have been found in Iron Age I contexts, perhaps a remnant of the international nature of the Late Bronze Age. The basic set, commonly called "wine sets," consists of a bowl, jug and strainer. Bronze tableware has been found mainly at northern sites: Megiddo, Beth Shean and Tell es Saʿidiyeh in the Jordan Valley. Other metal artifacts are bronze tripods (Tell es-Saʿidiyeh, Megiddo). Metal workshops were found at Tel Dan, Tel Harashim, Tell Deir ʿAlla, Tell Qasile, *Ai, Beth Shemesh, Tel Mor and Tel Masos. Raw materials probably came from Cyprus or the Timna Valley.

4.1.6. Burials. Iron Age I burials continue Late Bronze Age traditions, and some scholars suggest that all the elements of Iron Age II bench-type tombs were already present in Iron Age I. One of the unique patterns of Iron Age I archaeology is that no burials have been found in the western highlands. This pattern probably is due to the use of simple, shallow graves outside of settlements or the use of natural caves lacking grave goods, indicating a relatively poor society with simple stratification.

4.1.7. Religion (Belief and Practice). The material correlates of religious belief and practice can be found in architecture and religious artifacts. There will always be debates on the inferences and interpretations of artifacts, but there is widespread consensus on the religious nature of several finds such as cult vessels used for libations (chalices, zoomorphic vessels) and anthropomorphic and zoomorphic figurines. One unique find is an 18 cm bronze bull statuette associated with an open-air cult site. This is the only evidence of religious iconography. Major temples/cultic sites are the Bull site and Mount Ebal in the western highlands; the Philistine temples found at Ekron and Tel Qasile; and Canaanite-Egyptian temples found at Megiddo, Bethshean and Lachish.

There are several temples that date to the Iron Age I period. There is a distinctive pattern in regard to settlement. Most are located in major Canaanite centers in the Jezreel Valley.

These temples are Megiddo VIIIA, Beth Shean (VIB, lower V/VIA), Tell Abu-Hawam Temple 30, Tell es-Sa'idiyeh XIA and Tell Qasile (XII-VIII).

There are secondary shrines that are either public cult rooms associated with other buildings (Hazor XI, Ai, Tel Miqne Field I, Lachish Room 49, perhaps Taanach), and domestic cult corners (Tel Qiri Area D, possibly Megiddo 2081 and Tell Irbid). Other cult structures are associated with industry (*Dan, Tell el-Hammah, Tell Amal, possibly Tell Mazar). In addition to cultic structures found in settlements there are open-air, outdoor cult places, such as the bull site and the structure on Mount Ebal, and extramural shrines (Tel Michal-Makmish, Tel Michal Area C).

4.2. Iron Age II (1000-586 BCE). This period can be characterized by secondary state formation found throughout the southern Levant. This period corresponds to the development and creation of the Israelite monarchy: from the regionalism of the Iron Age I (tribal and chiefdoms) to the territorial state. This state level of society is seen in the monumental buildings and evidence of centralization. In the eighth century BCE we see extensive literary activity in Syria-Palestine.

4.2.1. Chronology/Periodization. The Iron Age II period has been subdivided in various schemes by archaeologists. Most have subdivided the system based on historical events and persons: united and divided monarchy, campaign of Shishak (925 BCE), fall of Samaria (721 BCE) and the fall of Jerusalem (586 BCE). Although these events can be defined in the archaeological record, they reflect political and biblical history and not necessarily cultural history. Although military campaigns assist in the comparison of intrasite stratigraphy, changes in material culture over time are influenced by many more variables than political events (e.g., trade patterns, technological innovations). The first scheme was proposed by G. E. Wright, who divided Iron Ages I and II at the divided monarchy, designating the period of the united monarchy as part of the Iron Age I period. The ninth century BCE was assigned to Iron Age IIA, and the period from 800-586 BCE was the Iron Age IIB period. Aharoni (1978) associated the Iron Age II period with the united monarchy (tenth century BCE)—Iron Age IIA. The period from Shishak's campaign to the fall of Samaria was

Iron Age IIB (925-721 BCE), and the Iron Age IIC was 720-586 BCE. This has been the dominant subdivision among biblical archaeologists, but recently scholars are dividing the period based on the changes in material culture. G. Barkay subdivides the Iron Age into IIA (tenth to ninth centuries BCE), IIB (eighth century BCE), IIIA (seventh to early sixth centuries BCE), IIIB (sixth century BCE); L. Herr subdivides the Iron Age into IA (tenth century BCE), IIB (ninth to late eighth centuries BCE), IIC (late eighth to mid-sixth centuries BCE).

Periodization is based on variations in the continuity and discontinuity of the material culture, and therefore the adoption of subdivisions is subjective among archaeologists. There is general agreement on relative chronology of the material culture of the Iron Age, but biblical scholars need to be mindful of the scheme used by each individual archaeologist.

4.2.2. Written Sources. Perhaps one of the most dramatic differences between the Iron Age I and II periods in the archaeological record is the dramatic increase in the amount of written sources. This phenomenon is twofold. First, with the resumption of the expansion and resource acquisition by Egypt and Assyria, the mention of sites and persons in the southern Levant are documented since these nations mount several campaigns. These events naturally allow for chronological synchronization, particularly eighth- and seventh-century BCE destructions. Second, in addition to sources from without, the southern Levant sees an increase in written materials (*see* Hebrew Inscriptions). There are monumental inscriptions—for example, Tel Dan, Mesha, Siloam Tunnel, Royal Steward and Ekron. Other written artifacts include ostraca, religious texts and amulets, seals, arrowheads, and bullae. The texts of the Hebrew Bible also correspond to this expansion in writing, since most were arguably written during this period, but those key to the reconstruction of the history of ancient Israel are the Prophets.

There are also several groups of ostraca, as well as hundreds of isolated ostraca. Some of the best caches of ostraca are from the sites of Samaria, Horvat Uza, *Arad and Lachish. Several key single-find ostraca are from 'Izbet Sartah, Mezad Hashavyahu, Kadesh Barnea, Tel Beersheba and Tel 'Ira.

For Iron Age II, evidence of religious texts is

found. The silver amulet from Ketef Hinnom is the earliest biblical text discovered (Num 6:24-26). The Kuntillet ʿAjrud inscription mentioning Yaweh and "his asherah" along with graffiti, Deir ʿAlla, and perhaps the unprovenanced and suspect pomegranate scepter inscription.

This period contains hundreds of seal and seal impressions, bullae, and arrowheads providing biblical scholars with a large corpus of onomastic evidence. From the eighth century BCE, hundreds of *lmlk* jar handles bearing the statement "belonging to the king" provide evidence of a thriving administrative system (*see* Hebrew Inscriptions).

4.2.3. History and People. The identification of people groups, nations and ethnicity in the archaeological record is a debated topic. Nevertheless, archaeologists and historians acknowledge that at some level these distinctions are encoded on the material correlates of society. For the Iron Age II period, archaeologists have started to define these distinctions in the archaeological record, and while archaeologists acknowledge that there can be no simple equation "pots = people," most are comfortable with the postulate that although an Assyrian bowl found in an eighth-century BCE site can represent any reconstruction—from an Assyrian presence to merely trade—the average Israelite would know that it is an Assyrian bowl, not an Israelite one. Archaeologists must always be cautious of connecting ethnic or national markers to the archaeological record in the Iron Age II period, but there are some generally accepted patterns in the association of the material correlates of society with broader types of definitions such as nations, ethnicity and geographical regions. Hence, for this period, archaeologists are defining the boundaries and making inferences based on material-culture studies of Egyptians, Assyrians, Aramean states of southern and central Syria, national states of Transjordan (Ammonites, Moabites, Edomites), Neo-Hittite states of northern Syria and eastern Anatolia, the Phoenician state in the Syrian-Lebanese littoral, and the united and divided monarchies of Israel.

For the Iron Age II period, the archaeological data allow for the reconstruction and assignment of political events and social developments. The key social developments are the formation of nations (secondary states)—particularly the Israelite united monarchy—Aramean states and the Transjordan tribal states. Other dynamics defined in the archaeological record are the expansion of trade and dominance of the Phoenicians as intermediaries in the renewed trade in the eastern Mediterranean. In addition to associating the archaeological record with historical developments, there are some events that can be defined, such as Shishak's invasion (c. 925 BCE), the Assyrian campaigns of the eighth century BCE (Tiglath-pileser, Shalmaneser, Sargon II, Sennacherib, Esharhaddon) and the Babylonian campaigns (c. 605, 587/6 BCE).

4.2.4. Settlement Patterning and Architecture. Generally, the Iron Age II settlement patterns, compared to those of Iron Age I, are characterized by hierarchy of settlements, greater population growth, considerable increase in settlements and size, and centralization and urbanization. The pattern of Iron Age II settlements is defined by emerging nations and ethnic groups. The archaeological record reflects small national entities developing in geopolitical spheres: the Israelite state in the hill country, Philistines and Phoenicians along the coast, Arameans in the Syrian desert, and the Transjordanian states of Edom, Moab and Ammon.

In addition to social hierarchical systems in settlement patterns, variation and stratification are now evidenced in architecture. Domestic architecture continues to be the four-room house, but there are various zones of occupation in the western highland sites. Public architecture consists of fortifications such as casemate and offset-inset city walls, multichambered gate systems (four to six chambers) that open to large plazas, and double-ringed city-wall systems with glacis between the outer and inner lines and double gate systems with outer gate houses. Several palaces and administrative structures are built, as well as elaborate water systems (*see* Water and Water Systems).

The beginnings of centralized authority and monumental architecture in the western highlands occurs in Iron Age IIA (tenth century BCE). The first elaborate gate systems were utilized; the most well-known is the six-chamber, four-entry gate found at Hazor, Megiddo and Gezer. Initially, these were associated only with Solomonic administrative activity. They have been found in later periods and at non-Israelite sites. Although no longer singularly a reference to the Israelite united monarchy, the correlation with the aforementioned gates still reflects a unified administrative policy of a central authority that can be postulated as the reign of Solomon. Two administrative structures appear in the archaeological record: the palace and the pillared building. The palace is adapted from Syrian *bit hilani* palaces comprised of a central court surrounded by rectangular rooms, stairwell and a pillared entryway. These palaces have been found at northern sites: Megiddo (Buildings 1723, 6000) and Bethsaida. Pillared storage buildings (also identified as stables by some archaeologists) were found at Tell Abu Hawam, Tel Hadar, Tel Qasile, Tell el-Hesi, Tel Malhata and Tel Masos. In the central Negev highlands there are several fortified enclosures and many additional small settlements and isolated farmsteads that were close to water sources that could support some agriculture. They were located on hills within sight of each other; most were 25-70 m in diameter and circular, oval, rectangular or amorphic in shape with rows of casemate rooms surrounding a large central courtyard with a narrow entrance. There are several theories regarding the context of these settlements, but most archaeologists associate them with the Israelites, although some think that they could be Amalekite in origin.

Perhaps the greatest change in Iron Age IIB (ninth and eighth centuries BCE) is the discernable settlement hierarchy. Naturally, the two capitals of the kingdoms, Samaria and Jerusalem, were at the top of the hierarchy, but there were "royal" cities such as at Megiddo IV and Lachish IV-III. Tripartite pillared buildings were constructed throughout the kingdoms as part of tertiary provincial distribution centers. Multichambered city gates continue in use: the earlier four-chambered gate from the tenth century BCE and now a new two-chambered type.

Defensive systems now include monumental water systems (e.g., Megiddo, Hazor, Jerusalem), and a double city-wall system consisting of two parallel walls. The lower wall was further down the slope of the city, and usually there was a stone-covered glacis between the lower and upper walls. Several cities had an additional gate house associated with the second wall. The seventh century BCE was influenced by the Assyrian conquest. Assyrian palaces were constructed at Hazor V, Megiddo III-II, Gezer, Buseireh, Tel Jemmeh, Tel Sera and Sheikh Zuweid. Fortresses were built throughout Judah in the Judean hills and wilderness and in the Negev (e.g.,

Vered Jericho, Khirbet Abu et-Twein).

4.2.5. Ceramics. Iron Age pottery continues to exhibit regional variations due to production centers, trade and geopolitical variables, but the overall corpus becomes standardized. During the tenth century BCE imports begin to appear, especially Cypro-Phoenician ware and forms such as the black-on-red ware. Most forms continue from the Iron Age I period with few major additions, except for the adoption of coastal forms such as strainer jugs and decanters.

4.2.6. Burials. There are a variety of burial practices in the Iron Age II period. The most common forms are the simple graves, the cave and the bench/arcosolia tombs. Simple graves dug into the ground, sometimes with stones covering the grave, have been found at Tell el-Ajjul, Akhzib, Tel Amal, Azor, Tel Bira, Dhiban, Tell el-Farah, Joya, Khalde, Lachish, Tell er-Ruqeish and Khirbet Silm. Cave, shaft and chamber tomb types have been excavated in the western highlands, Transjordan and the Jezreel Valley. Bench and arcosolia tombs have been found at Aitun, Akhzib, Amman [Jebel Jofeh], Tell Beit Mirsim, Beth Shemesh, Tel Bira, Dhiban, Gezer, Haifa, Halif, Tel Ira, Irbed, Lachish, Tell en-Nasbeh, Ramot, Sahab, Samaria, Tubas, Khirbet Za'aq and Jerusalem (old city walls, Silwan, and St. Ettiene). In addition to these types there are cist graves and simple interments.

Other, less common burial practices include jar burials (Amman [Jebel el-Qusur and the royal palace], Azor, Dhiban, Dothan, Megiddo, Mount Nebo, Sahab); anthropoid, wooden or stone coffin burials (Amman [Jebel el-Qusur and the royal palace], Dhiban, Jerusalem [Old City walls and Silwan], Mount Nebo, Sahab); bathtub coffin burials (Tell el-Fa'rah [N], Tell en Nasbeh); above-ground monolithic tombs in the Kidron Valley of Jerusalem; and cremation burials (Tell el-'Ajjul, Akhzib, 'Atlit, Tel el-Fa'rah [S], Joya, Khalde, Lachish, Megiddo, Mount Nebo, Qasmieh, Tell er-Ruqeish, Khirbet Silm).

4.2.7. Religion (Belief and Practice). In the Iron Age II period a plethora of archaeological evidence associated with cultic practice has been defined. As with other aspects of the Iron Age II material culture, ethnic/national markers are distinguished in the archaeological record of cultic activity. A major Philistine temple complex has been excavated at Tel Miqne-Ekron, an Edomite cult complex at Horvat Qitmit, and an Aramean cult corner has been found in the gate complex at Bethsaida. Although there are no remains of the Jerusalem temple, several Israelite cult places have been found at Ai, Arad, *Beersheba, Lachish, Ein Gev, Samaria, Taanach, Tirzeh and Tel Dan.

In addition to regional and national cultic practices, public cultic practices, particularly associated with urban centers, are well documented in the Iron Age II archaeological record. Tel Dan was the site of major cultic activity, as evidenced by a large cult center found there dating from the tenth century BCE (Stratum IV) to the ninth/eighth century BCE (Stratum III). This room has a large altar with horns. In addition to this cult center in the heart of the city, at the lower gate of the city there was a cult corner with pillars (*maṣṣēbôt*), and a standing stone or altar. In the environs west of Jerusalem several tumuli have been surveyed. These served as cult complexes and probably represent the funeral fires and rituals associated with the deaths of the Judean kings.

In addition to temples, several artifacts can be associated with religious practice, such as figurines, large and small altars, ceramic stands (fenestrated and plain) and model shrines, amulets, scarabs and seals. The large altars provide evidence for public religious centers outside of the capital cities. Large altars have been found at Arad, Beersheba, Dan and Megiddo. There are also several sites with inscriptions that refer to religious belief, such as the Judean desert cave (near En-Gedi), Khirbet El-Qom, Kuntillet ʿAjrud, an inscribed tomb at Khirbet Beit Lei and the Ketef Hinnom inscriptions.

5. Overview of Later Iron Age (III) and Persian Period Archaeological Data.

The archaeology of the Babylonian and Persian periods in the southern Levant has been neglected by archaeologists of Syria-Palestine. This period has not been important for the historiographical issues associated with the development of biblical archaeology, nor is it a period that has been studied to address issues in Iron Age archaeology. In addition to this period not being on the radar of many scholars, it is difficult to isolate and define material culture that belongs to this period. Most archaeologists acknowledge that this period exists, but in most reports or surveys it is common to refer to material culture as Iron Age II-Persian or Persian-Hellenistic. Unfortunately, there is a paucity of ar-

chaeological data in comparison to that of other periods, and in regard to the data that have been excavated there is a bias among archaeologists to focus research and analysis on the earlier periods. Another problem is that it is difficult to isolate sixth-century material culture from that of the seventh century, and fourth-century material culture from that of the third century. Most sites do not have well-stratified material culture to define the archaeology of this period. Recent trends in biblical studies and archaeology have brought a renewed interest in this neglected period.

5.1. History of Research, Chronology and Nomenclature. The first comprehensive study of material culture of Syria-Palestine from the Persian period came in the early 1980s with the publication of E. Stern's *Material Culture of the Land of the Bible in the Persian Period, 538-332 B.C.* Ironically, the next major publication of Persian-period archaeology was Stern's *The Assyrian, Babylonian, and Persian Periods (732-332 B.C.E.),* published in 2001, which is the second volume of the two-volume *Archaeology of the Land of the Bible* in the Anchor Bible Reference Library. The interest in the archaeology of the Persian period is starting to pick up as several scholars are now addressing broader sociocultural developments during the Persian Empire (see Carter; Edelmen; Lipschits and Blenkinsopp).

In addition to the scholarly interest in the Persian period, another trend in the archaeology of Syria-Palestine is to question the historically arbitrary end of the Iron Age period with the Babylonian conquest of Jerusalem (586 BCE). Most scholars acknowledge that this date is based solely on a historical event, not any changes in the material culture. The archaeological material of the sixth century BCE is similar to the seventh-century BCE Iron Age material data, and therefore there is a tacit understanding that based on the archaeological data, the Iron Age should continue into the sixth century BCE.

Research designs of the archaeology of the Persian period have focused on addressing the question of the nature of the settlement and demographics associated with the nature of the Babylonian deportations and the Jewish migrations as recorded in the biblical text. This debate has commonly been referred to as the "myth of the empty land." In addition, research has focused on the nature of the administrative policies of the Babylonian and Persian Empires, specifically on the administrative districts in Syria-Palestine (e.g., the borders of Yehud and Idumea) and international trade, particularly with the Phoenicians.

For the first time we see an emphasis on placing the material culture within a historical framework; no longer are the periodizations based dominantly on material culture, but now the archaeological periods match with historical periodization (e.g., Persian, Hellenistic, Roman, Byzantine). Hence, only recently have archaeologists attempted to create subdivisions incorporating changes in the archaeological record. Several archaeologists who specialize in the Iron Age are proposing that the Iron Age should extend to the end of the sixth century BCE—for example, 539 BCE with the title "Iron Age III" or "Iron Age IIC" (Barkay; Herr; Zertal). A. Zertal proposes that the fall of Samaria in 722/723 BCE should be the start of the Iron Age III period. This timeframe is still divided by historical periods such as the Babylonian (604-539 BCE) and the Persian (539-332 BCE) (Stern 2001). Recently, C. Carter has suggested dividing up the period as Iron Age IIC (605-539 BCE), Persian I (539-450 BCE) and Persian II (450-332 BCE).

5.2. Settlement Patterns and Architecture. One of the questions in the archaeology of the Babylonian period (sixth century BCE) is whether or not the archaeological data support the notion that there was complete devastation and abandonment of Palestine. This is the view among most archaeologists because of the evidence of widespread Babylonian destructions at major sites and the archaeological vacuum found at all sites, especially when compared to the previous Assyrian period in Palestine. Unfortunately, this has created a caricature in historical reconstructions of complete abandonment and depopulation. Recent reevaluations of the data suggest that although this was a period of collapse in the historical cycles of this region, there was not a complete abandonment by the local population.

There is no clearly defined period that can be associated with the sixth century BCE, but two clearly defined regions can be identified in the archaeological record: north of Jerusalem in the Benjamin territory, with Tell en-Nasbeh as the main center, and the Ammonite territory. The sixth-century BCE strata are elusive, but what is clear is the total destruction of Iron Age

IIB sites throughout Palestine. The Babylonian destruction is well documented in the archaeological record of major tells such as Lachish II, Jerusalem, Hazor IV, Megiddo III, Acco, Tell Keisan Stratum 4, Ashdod VI, Ekron IB, Timnah II, *Ashkelon, Tell el-Hesi, Tel Seraʿ, Tel Haror, Tell Jemmeh, Ruqeish, Dothan I, Samaria VIIA, Shechem VI, Tell el-Farʿah [N], Gezer V, Bethel, *Gibeon, Tell el-Ful, Jericho, En-Gedi and Ramat Rahel. At some of these sites there is evidence of a small occupation immediately after this destruction (e.g., Hazor, Megiddo, Ekron), but at other sites there is evidence that settlement was not renewed until the Persian period.

During the Persian period the settlement pattern is very similar to that of the Neo-Babylonian Period, although denser. The main sites are along the major highways and road systems (see Roads and Highways). In the coastal area the main cities were settled, particularly the Acco Plain, which was influenced by Tyre and the Carmel Coast and the Sharon Plain. In these regions were densely built settlements such as Achzib, Kabri, Nahariya, Acco, Khirbet Usa, Tell Bireh, Tell Keisan, Gilʿam, Tell Abu Hawam, Dor and Shiqmona. In the north settlements are found at Hazor, Megiddo, Tel Abu Shusha, Tel Qiri, Jokneam, Beth Shan and Taanach, as well as several other sites. In the southern coastal Plain sites are Ashdod, Nebi Yunis, Tel Zippor, Tel ʿErani, Ashkelon, Tel el Hesi, Gaza, Tell Jemmeh, Tel el-Farʿah (S), Tel Haro and Tel Seraʿ.

The western highlands (provinces of Samaria and Yehud) in the Persian period have been studied by Zertal and by Carter (2003b). Zertal analyzed the settlement as part of a larger study on the territory of Manasseh, and Carter's research has focused on a sociocultural study of Yehud based on historical and archaeological data. Carter's study notes that twenty-two sites have been excavated within the province of Yehud and date to the Babylonian and Persian periods; eighteen of these sites are settlements. Adding survey data, Carter (2004) estimates that there were 86 settlements that date to the Persian I period, and 125 sites to the Persian II period. The most densely populated area is along the central spur from Bethel to *Hebron. Zertal's study is based on survey data where he defined the Iron Age III period as 722-535 BCE. He has delineated a pattern where there is a stark demographic shift due to Assyrian deportation policies. Comparing sites during the Iron Age II-

III periods, Zertal notes a 53 percent decline in the Shechem syncline, 71 percent in the eastern valleys, and 85 percent in the Iron-Shechem subregion. Parts of eastern Samaria were emptied and replaced by Cutheans, who brought a new wedge-shaped decoration of local Iron Age III bowls originating from Mesopotamia. In addition, several new forts and administrative centers were built. For the following Persian period, strata are found at Samaria VIII and Shechem V.

5.3. Ceramics. There are no diagnostic Babylonian (Iron III) pottery types. Most are either continuations of Iron II forms or vessel types that also appear in the Persian period. Thus it is difficult to date a corpus or stratum unless both types are found demonstrating that the pottery group exhibits this transitional nature between the earlier Iron II period and the later Persian period. Vessel types typical of the sixth century BCE are "carrot-shaped" bottles, clay alabastra, round black pyxides and "sack-shaped shoulder" decanters. A type that illustrates the transitional nature is the lamp. Three types are common: the Judean high-footed lamp of the late Iron Age II, the rare closed Babylonian lamp with a long nozzle, and a large, flat open lamp that becomes common in the Persian period.

The pottery corpus of the Persian period tends to be local, with very few imports from Persia. Most ceramic forms continue the Iron Age II tradition, particularly the cooking pots, storage jars, bowls, flasks, oil lamps, jugs/juglets and kraters. Several Greek and Cypriot imports are found, such as lekythoi (flasks for perfumed oil), bowls, jars, lamps and Attic black-and-red ware. Decorative motifs include painted bands and geometric designs on burnished and glaze vessels. Other local decorative techniques are the "wedge-shaped and reed impression" combination.

5.4. Other Material Culture. Most of the artifacts attributed to the Babylonian period were found in tombs. As with the ceramic vessels, a majority also occur in the early Iron Age and the later Persian Period. One pattern is that in the Babylonian period many new metal vessels begin to appear quite suddenly, some originating in Mesopotamia, but the majority being local imitations (Stern 2001, 345). Metal artifacts include bowls, some with leaf decoration, strainers and dippers, mirrors, jewelry, toggle pins, toilet vessels, and kohl sticks. Weapons include both local and Babylonian arrowheads (Irano-Scythian

type). Glass and bronze bottles as well as alabaster vessels are found. Other finds include Babylonian seals and seal impressions, the majority being nonepigraphical. Most are conical chalcedony stamp seals with octagonal base, while a couple of the seals are cylinder seals.

The archaeological data of the Persian period contains large assemblages of metalware, alabaster, bone and glass, evidence of an increase in the standard of living and the commercial stimulus of luxury articles. Household metalware items are common, such as bowls, dishes, jugs, chalices and ladles. Several alabaster vessels have been discovered in Persian-period strata, as well as chalk vessels discovered in Jerusalem, apparently local imitations of the alabaster vessel forms. Metal objects include jewelry and weapons. Arrowheads consist of Irano-Scythian, Greek and local types.

5.5. Burial and Burial Practices. One of the most important sites for the Babylonian period is Ketef Hinnom. This is a series of Iron Age rock-cut tombs on the western slope of the Hinnom Valley just outside the city of Jerusalem. Tomb 25 contained over 250 vessels dating to the late Iron Age II-Hellenistic period. This illustrates that this family tomb was in use throughout the Babylonian period, implying that there was cultural continuity between the seventh and sixth centuries BCE. Tombs attributed to the sixth century BCE are Horvat ʿAlmit, Tell en-Nasbeh, Tell el-Ful, Ketef Hinnom, Abu Ghosh and Tomb 14 at Beth Shemesh. Tombs in the Ammonite territory were found at Meqabelein, Umm Uthainah, Khilda and Tell Mazar. All these tombs have similar ceramic vessels, and all are part of larger cemeteries.

Burials from the Persian period have been found in all regions of ancient Palestine: in Galilee and the Jezreel Valley (Hazor, Khirbet Ibsan, ʿEn ha-Naziv, Mishmar ha-ʿEmeq); along the coast (Achzib, Shavei Zion, Acco, Beth ha-Emeq, Lohamei ha-Getaʾot, Yasʿour, ʿAtlit, Dor, Tel Michal, Azor, Bat-Yam, Ashkelon, Tell el-Hesi, Tell el-Farʿah [S], Gaza); in the western highlands (Shechem, Nahshonim, Tell el-Ful, Abu Ghosh, Beth Shemesh, Gezer, Lachish, Horvat Beth Loyah, Eshtemoa, ʿAin ʿArrub); and in Transjordan and the Jordan Valley (Meqabelein, Umm Uthainah, Khilda, Tell el-Mazar, ʿIraq el-Emir, Yafit). Persian-period tombs belong to three distinct types: cist graves, shaft tombs and pit graves. Mesopotamian influence is evident by the sarcophagi-style clay coffins (originating in Palestine in the Assyrian period), and two Phoenician stone anthropoid sarcophagi were found in shaft tombs at Gaza and in the Acco region. These are common farther up the coast in Phoenicia.

5.6. Trade and Economics. The growth of international trade resumed in the Persian period. Coins were used in Palestine in the Babylonian period, but they do not become common until the end of the fifth century BCE and especially the fourth century BCE. It is apparent from papyri documents that the Persian period was in a transition from weighted precious metal to the use of coins. The coins in circulation in Palestine include Greek coins, Phoenician city coins, royal Persian coins (daric gold coin and a silver coin) and Palestinian coins. Of the Palestinian coins, there are city coins from the southern coastal strip: Ashdod, Ashkelon and Gaza. Other Palestinian coins are the *yehud* coins of the province of Judah and the Samaritan coins.

Ostraca from the Persian period provide evidence that there were two units of liquid measure, the *kur* and the *bat,* and two units of dry measure, the *seah* and the *qav.* These names are similar to those of earlier periods. It appears that by the Persian period there was a different uniform standard of weights that differed from the Judean standard of the late Iron Age. Evidence of weights from Palestine is lacking in the excavated archaeological record.

5.7. Religion. No cultic buildings or objects can stratigraphically be attributed to the Babylonian period. One pattern is the disappearance of the typical Iron Age II clay figurines. Perhaps the only structure is at Bethel, where an earlier sanctuary continued in use. This pattern changes in the Persian period, from which several cultic buildings and artifacts have been excavated. There are three types of cultic buildings: large city temples, medium-sized sanctuaries and small cultic niches.

Cultic buildings in the Persian period correlate in plan and dimensions to previous periods—evidence of close connections with older traditions. Two patterns emerge from the archaeological data: close homogeneity among the contents of each building, and the lack of pagan cult temples in the western highlands. Only one large city temple has been discovered—the so-called solar shrine at Lachish. This building (27 x 17 m) consists of a square court-

yard with a row of small chambers to the east and a rectangular antechamber in the back containing incense altars and other cultic vessels. This building was plastered with a vaulted roof. Medium-sized sanctuaries were uncovered at Sarepta, Tel Michal (Makmish and another eastern shrine) and Mizpe Yammim. Other structures have been partially excavated at Dan and Acco. Although these are the only cult structures excavated, there are more temples represented in the archaeological record by various dedicatory inscriptions, temple statuettes and several *favissae* (repositories of discarded cult objects) all hinting at the existence of Persian-period temples. A unique cultic practice dating to the Persian period is sacred dog burials. The largest and most well-known cemetery was found at Ashkelon, but others have been found at Berytus, Dor and Ashdod.

Perhaps the most ubiquitous find of the Persian period are the figurines. Several hundred have been found in *favissae,* temples and graves distributed throughout Galilee, the coast, the Shephelah and Idumaea. Most are either hollow mold-made or solid handmade figurines, plaques and masks. These figurines contain features of Phoenician, Persian, Egyptian, Canaanite, Cypriot and Greek influences. Other cultic artifacts are bronze figurines, bronze incense stands and the cuboid limestone or clay incense altars.

See also AI; AMMON, AMMONITES; ARAD; ASHDOD; ASHKELON; BEERSHEBA; BETHEL; DAN; EDOM, EDOMITES; EKRON; ETHNICITY; EZION-GEBER; GATH; GAZA; GIBEAH, GEBA; GIBEON; GILGAL; HAZOR; HEBREW INSCRIPTIONS; HEBRON; HIGH PLACES; HISTORY OF ISRAEL 1-8; ISRAEL; JERICHO; JEZREEL; LACHISH; MEGIDDO; MIZPAH; MOAB, MOABITES; PHILISTINES; PHOENICIA, PHOENICIANS; SAMARIA; SHECHEM; SHILOH; SOCIAL-SCIENTIFIC APPROACHES; TIRZAH.

BIBLIOGRAPHY. **Y. Aharoni,** *The Land of the Bible: A Historical Geography* (Philadelphia: Westminster, 1967); **Y. Aharoni and R. Amiran,** "A New Scheme for the Sub-division of the Iron Age in Palestine," *IEJ* 8 (1958) 171-84; **W. F. Albright,** *The Archaeology of Palestine* (Harmondsworth: Penguin, 1949); **G. Barkay,** "The Iron Age II-III," in *The Archaeology of Ancient Israel,* ed. A. Ben-Tor (New Haven: Yale University Press, 1992) 302-73; **A. Ben Tor,** ed., *The Archaeology of Ancient Israel* (New Haven, CT: Yale University Press, 1992); **E. Bloch-Smith and B. A. Nakhai,**

"A Landscape Comes to Life: The Iron Age I," *NEA* 62 (1999) 62-92, 101-27; **C. E. Carter,** *The Emergence of Yehud in the Persian Period: A Social and Demographic Study* (JSOTSup 294; Sheffield: Sheffield Academic Press, 1999); idem, "Ideology and Archaeology in the Neo-Babylonian Period: Excavating Text and Tell," in *Judah and the Judeans in the Neo-Babylonian Period,* ed. O. Lipschits and J. Blenkinsopp (Winona Lake, IN: Eisenbrauns, 2003a) 301-22; idem, "Syria-Palestine in the Persian Period," in *Near Eastern Archaeology,* ed. S. Richard (Winona Lake, IN: Eisenbrauns, 2003b) 398-412; **T. Davis,** *Shifting Sands: The Rise and Fall of Biblical Archaeology* (Oxford: Oxford University Press, 2004); **W. Dever,** "Archaeology and the 'Age of Solomon': A Case Study in Archaeology and Historiography," in *The Age of Solomon: Scholarship at the Turn of the Millennium,* ed. L. K. Handy (SHCANE 11; Leiden: E. J. Brill, 1997) 217-51; idem, "Ceramics, Ethnicity, and the Question of Israel's Origins," *BA* 58 (1995) 200-213; idem, "From Tribe to Nation: State Formation Processes in Ancient Israel," in *Nouve Fondazioni nel Vicino Oriente Antico: Realtà e ideologia,* ed. S. Mazzoni (Seminari di orientalistica 4; Pisa: Giardini, 1994) 213-19; idem, *Who Were the Israelites and Where Did They Come From?* (Grand Rapids: Eerdmans, 2003); **D. Edelman,** *The Origins of the 'Second' Temple: Persian Imperial Policy and the Rebuilding of Jerusalem* (London: Equinox, 2005); **I. Finkelstein,** *The Archaeology of the Israelite Settlement* (Jerusalem: Israel Exploration Society, 1988); idem, "The Archaeology of the United Monarchy: An Alternative View," *Levant* 28 (1996) 177-87; idem, "The Date of the Settlement of the Philistines in Canaan," *TA* 22 (1995) 213-39; **I. Finkelstein and N. Na'aman,** eds., *From Nomadism to Monarchy: Archaeological and Historical Aspects of Early Israel* (Jerusalem: Israel Exploration Society, 1994); **S. Gitin, A. Mazar and E. Stern,** eds., *Mediterranean Peoples in Transition: Thirteenth to Early Tenth Centuries BCE* (Jerusalem: Israel Exploration Society, 1998); **L. Herr,** "The Iron Age Period: Emerging Nations," *BA* 60 (1997) 114-83; **P. King,** *American Archaeology in the Mideast: A History of the American Schools of Oriental Research* (Philadelphia: American Schools of Oriental Research, 1983); **P. King and L. Stager,** *Life in Biblical Israel* (Louisville: Westminster/John Knox, 2001); **T. Levy,** ed., *The Archaeology of Society in the Holy Land* (New York: Facts on File, 1995); **O. Lipschits,** "The History of the Benjamin Region Under Babylonian Rule," *TA* 26 (1999) 155-90; **O. Lipschits and J. Blenkinsopp,** eds., *Judah and the Judeans in the Neo-Babylonian Period* (Winona Lake, IN: Eisenbrauns, 2003); **A. Mazar,** *Archaeology of the Land of the Bible, 10,000-586 B.C.E.* (New York: Doubleday, 1990); idem, ed., *Studies in the Archaeology of the Iron Age in Israel and Jordan* (JSOTSup 331 Sheffield: Sheffield Academic Press, 2001); **E. Meyers,** ed., *The Oxford Encyclopedia of Archaeology in the Near East* (5 vols.; New York: Oxford University Press, 1997); **R. D. Miller II,** *Chieftains of the Highland Clans: A History of Israel in the Twelfth and Eleventh Centuries B.C.* (Grand Rapids: Eerdmans, 2005); **P. R. S. Moorey,** *A Century of Biblical Archaeology* (Louisville: Westminster/John Knox, 1991); **N. Silberman,** *Between Past and Present: Archaeology, Ideology, and Nationalism in the Modern Middle East* (New York: Doubleday, 1989); idem, *Digging for God and Country: Exploration, Archeology, and the Secret Struggle for the Holy Land, 1799-1917* (New York: Knopf, 1982); **N. Silberman and D. Small,** *The Archaeology of Israel: Constructing the Past, Interpreting the Present* (JSOTSup 237; Sheffield: Sheffield Academic Press, 1997); **E. Stern,** *Archaeology of the Land of the Bible, 2: The Assyrian, Babylonian, and Persian Periods (732-332 BCE)* (ABRL; New York: Doubleday, 2001); idem, *Material Culture of the Land of the Bible in the Persian Period, 538-332 B.C.* (Jerusalem: Israel Exploration Society; Warminster: Aris & Phillips, 1982); idem, ed., *The New Encyclopedia of Archaeological Excavations in the Holy Land* (4 vols.; Jerusalem: Israel Exploration Society & Carta; New York: Simon & Schuster, 1993); **D. Ussishkin,** "Levels VII and VI at Tel Lachish and the End of the Late Bronze Age in Canaan," in *Palestine in the Bronze and Iron Ages: Papers in Honour of Olga Tufnell,* ed. J. N. Tubb (Occasional Publication, University of London Institute of Archaeology 11; London: Institute of Archaeology) 213-30; **K. Whitelam,** *The Invention of Ancient Israel: The Silencing of Palestinian History* (New York: Routledge, 1996); **A. Zertal,** "The Province of Samaria (Assyrian Samerina) in the Late Iron Age (Iron Age III)," in *Judah and the Judeans in the Neo-Babylonian Period,* ed. O. Lipschits and J. Blenkinsopp (Winona Lake, IN: Eisenbrauns, 2003) 377-412.

S. M. Ortiz

ARCHITECTURE

As long as people were able to live in natural caves, there was no need to engage in building activity. Only with the transition to permanent settlement did there arise the necessity of constructing a permanent habitation. The development of architecture thus coincided with the transition from a hunter-gatherer culture to one of *agriculture; the first buildings constructed derive from the final phase of the Mesolithic Period. With the Neolithic Period (8000-4000 BCE), building activity began on a large scale. Architecture belongs among the achievements of the Neolithic revolution, during which the rectangular building form soon developed and replaced the round style of building. A decisive contribution here was the production of special bricks for the various forms of building. Although there are no great differences in the building materials used in the Holy Land from the beginnings of architecture onward, the building forms show a marked development over the course of the millennia. The time span covered by the Historical Books of the OT corresponds more or less to the so-called Iron Age, which divides into three periods: Iron Age I (1200-1000 BCE), Iron Age II (1000-587 BCE) and Iron Age III (587-337 BCE). The greatest break occurs between Iron Ages I and II because the transition to the monarchy from the community of tribes was completed c. 1000 BCE.

    1. Building Materials
    2. Construction Method
    3. Building Forms

1. Building Materials.
During the whole of the Iron Age the use of hitherto favored materials continued; these include stones, mud-brick, wood and plaster. In the case of stone, differentiation can be made between the various types and the method of working; in addition to the varieties of local limestone, basalt occasionally was used. Since the latter differs markedly from limestone in its hardness and durability, it was used mainly in locations where particular wear was indicated— for instance, thresholds, doorjambs and stairways. In the case of limestone, a differentiation is to be made between fieldstone and quarry stone. Fieldstones were used in building exactly as they had been found in the fields, whereas quarry stones were obtained in rectangular blocks from quarries. They were further hewn and worked with hammer and chisel. The use of such worked stones increased during Iron Age II.

For millennia, mud-bricks had been made from a mixture of mud, chopped straw and water, and air dried. Although originally formed by hand, they were made in wooden molds from Early Bronze Age II (3000-2650 BCE) onward; hence their rectangular shape. In the hill country, where stones were available, they usually were put on stone foundations. The wood needed for building was obtained from the forests with which the country was once extensively covered. Various types of wood were used from trees that are still found in the land: cypress, tamarisk and acacia. Since air-dried mud-brick is strongly affected by water, it had to be protected by a layer of plaster. The latter was made from a mixture of calcined lime (obtained from limestone) and water; it could be applied directly onto the mud-brick in a thin layer to afford protection.

2. Construction Method.
The method of building with the aforementioned materials also underwent little change during the course of the various periods down into the Iron Age. A stone foundation was laid, and the wall above it built of mud-brick. The roof consisted of beams laid horizontally on top of the walls or several supports, with a filling in between them that was also sealed with a layer of plaster. Accordingly, only flat roofs existed, which had to be repaired after every period of rain. As a rule, the fabric of the wall consisted of two parallel rows of stones and a core, the so-called *Schalenmauerwerk*. Walls built with only one row of stones and no core are rare. For the upper courses of mud-bricks, the binder technique of headers and stretchers was employed. Pillars (used as roof supports) consisted of stones laid on top of each other, or they were monoliths specially produced in the stone quarries. The pillared house as a building form is typical for Israel during the Iron Age.

3. Building Forms.
Since in archaeological excavations only lower walls or foundations are uncovered, little can be said about the upper courses of the walls. Accordingly, the differentiation between (open) courts and (covered) rooms is often subject to an uncertainty that itself gives rise to differences in the reconstruction of buildings. Various types of buildings can be discerned for the Iron Age according to their uses.

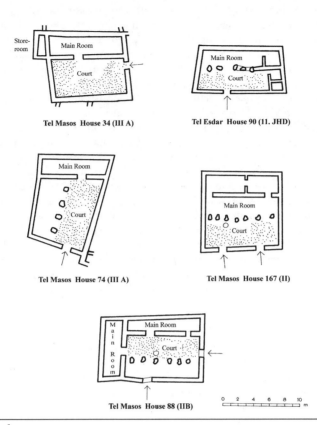

Figure 1. Four-room house

3.1. The Residential House. During the Iron Age, one building type predominates, which differs in a characteristic way from the widely distributed courtyard house of the second millennium BCE. In accordance with its layout, it is designated the four-room house (fig. 1). Along both of the long sides of a rectangular unit, two further units are separated off, often through supporting pillars. On the short side there is another (fourth) unit, which extends over the whole width of the building. The entrance, situated on the other short side, where no additional unit has been added, usually leads into the middle unit. In the three-room type of house, one of the units on the long sides is missing. As a rule, the central unit is somewhat wider and has a floor of compacted earth, while the two units along the long sides normally have a floor of paving stones.

The origin of this type of building is as disputed as its construction. On the one hand, the presence of ovens in the central unit indicates that this part was not roofed over but left open, and therefore can be designated a court; on the other hand, stairways indicate the existence of an upper story above the ground floor. It is probable in the case of this type, which was already widely distributed in Iron Age I, that a differentiation is to be made between one- and two-story houses. In the one-story house the central unit was not roofed over, and thus served as a court; the stone pillars guaranteed the light and ventilation of the rooms on the long side. In the case of the two-story house the whole of the ground floor was roofed over, including the central space, which, in the upper story, simply constituted an open court with adjacent rooms. All the rooms on the ground floor served as stalls for animals. The living space for the human inhabitants was on the upper floor, or on the ground floor in a one-story house. In neither case can it be assumed that light and ventilation were provided by windows. Although no walls are preserved to window height, the construction of this type of building in rows excludes the presence of windows, since the individual houses abutted each other along their long sides. Light and ventilation could have been provided only through the door or via the inner court. In addition, where a stairway is absent, an upper floor could have been reached by means of a wooden ladder. Nevertheless, it seems that in the settlements this type of building usually had only one floor.

As open as the question of the construction of the house is that of its origin. The four-room house is not found so far during the periods of the Middle and Late Bronze Ages, which preceded Iron Age I in the second millennium BCE. It was rather the courtyard house that constituted the predominant building form here: rooms bordered a courtyard, often nearly square, on two, three or four sides. Thus the question of whether the four-room house is an "invention" of the newly arrived Israelites (Shiloh 1970) or follows the Canaanite building tradition (Ahlström) must remain open.

3.2. Palaces. The residences of the rulers are designated as palaces, although individual rooms of this type of building could also be used for administrative purposes. Palaces normally are differentiated from residential houses through their particular size, which necessitated the layout of the rooms around several courts. It is evidenced from the Early Bronze Age onward that the palaces could reach a size of 60 x 40 m.

During Iron Age I, Building 2072 was constructed to the west of the gate in Stratum VI A at *Megiddo (fig. 2). In Stratum VI B there had been residential houses in this location, while in the Late Bronze Age from Stratum VII A to Stratum VIII the area was occupied by a palatial building (2041). The external walls of Building 2072 in Megiddo had suffered great destruction; however, the remaining sections permit a reconstruction of the complete building. In the northern part there is a rectangular court; its western, short side is abutted by a stairwell, of which a few steps have been preserved, and two more small rooms. The rooms in the southern part of Building 2072 are arranged in a way that three rooms, each adjacent to the other, can be reached via a rectangular court. A door connects the north and west courts, while the east court could be reached only through the external wall. The point of access could not be established. At any

rate, the two-story building permits recognition of a clear arrangement into courts, stairwell and rooms. The adjacent position of various courts is noteworthy. A similar arrangement is observed in the case of Building 1482 in Megiddo Stratum V A. Both building complexes demonstrate the enlargement of simple courtyard houses with the addition of an external court. Building 2072 thus may be attributed to the Canaanite building tradition, but in this context the question of whether Megiddo Stratum VI A was (still) a Canaanite or (already) an Israelite city can be left open.

The Early Iron Age Building 906 on Tell eš-Šeriʿa Stratum IX was rightly interpreted by E. Oren as the residence of an Egyptian governor. It finds its parallels in Building 480 on Ḥirbet el-Mšāš, the "residency" on Tell el-Fārʿa (South), and House 1500 in Bet-Shean. All four buildings exhibit a strong Egyptian influence; apparently,

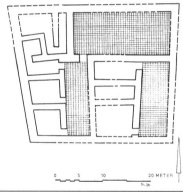

Figure 2. Palace (Building 2072, Megiddo, Stratum VI A)

houses of the Egyptian residential type occasionally were built in Canaan during the time of the New Kingdom. Even if this type of building does not exactly correspond in all details to the Egyptian residential house with its central living space, a strong Egyptian influence can be discerned for the twelfth century BCE, which is due to Egyptian hegemony.

No new type of palace was developed during Iron Age I. On the one hand, Canaanite building tradition was perpetuated during this period, and on the other hand, Egyptian influence is discernible. This is not surprising, given the Egyptian domination that lasted until the second half of the twelfth century BCE.

Three types of palace can be differentiated

in Iron Age II: (1) the palace with a central court, (2) the palace without a court, and (3) the Bit Hilani (a style originating in Syria).

A new type of palace appears under Assyrian influence in Iron Age II, in the form of the Assyrian open-court building (Amiran and Duna-yevsky). This primarily served the administration of the country during Iron Age III in the area of the former states of Israel and Judah.

Palaces 1723 and 6000 in Megiddo Stratum V A, and the palace situated in the south of the acropolis of *Samaria, dated to the ninth century BCE, are counted among the examples with a central court. Palace 1723 at Megiddo (fig. 3) measures 23 x 26.5 m, thus being almost square. The rooms are arranged around the central court (A), whereby Room G probably served as a corridor. Palace 1723 in no way belongs to the type of building designated as a Bit Hilani, as D. Ussishkin assumed. The entrance to the building probably was on the eastern side. Palace

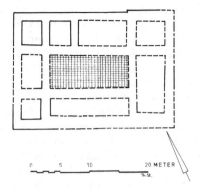

Figure 4. Palace (Building 6000, Megiddo, Stratum V A)

rooms are grouped around a court is located on the acropolis of Samaria (Sebastia). The acropolis was surrounded by an enclosing wall, and in addition to the palace it contained other buildings that had been built to serve the administration of the kingdom. The palace probably was laid out under the direction of *Omri after the purchase of the city hill of Samaria (1 Kings 16:24). It is situated on the southern side of the acropolis and is in a bad state of preservation.

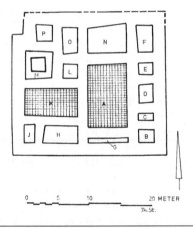

Figure 3. Palace (Building 1723, Megiddo, Stratum V A)

6000 in Megiddo (fig. 4) is situated at the northern edge of the city of Stratum V A. It was discovered only in 1960 by Y. Yadin and was not completely excavated. All the rooms are located around a central courtyard. The central unit could have served only as a court, since it is too wide to be roofed over. But Yadin interpreted this building as a Bit Hilani. Against this interpretation the understanding of the building as a palace with an inner court seems more probable, since at a Bit Hilani the entrance hall never has the same length as the main room (see Fritz 1983). Another palace in which the

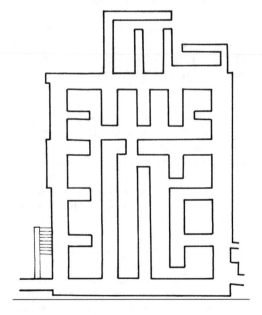

Figure 5. "Citadel" at Hazor

Remains of the southwestern part have mainly been uncovered, but it may be assumed that it extended further northward and eastward. Another court can be reconstructed in the north. This building probably served all the kings of the northern kingdom from Omri onward until the conquest of the city by the Assyrians in 722 BCE. Given its layout, it most likely follows the Canaanite tradition.

The "citadel" of *Hazor (fig. 5) and Palace 338 in Megiddo exhibit no trace of a central court. Only the lower floor of the "citadel" of Hazor is preserved. Nothing can be said about the function of the individual rooms. The "citadel" is a structure measuring 25 x 21.5 m, situated on the western tip of the Tell. The external walls and some of the partition walls inside the building are between 1.9 and 2 m thick, with corners and doorways of hewn stone set in position with particular care. The excavated parts represent the lower floor, but the same ground plan can be assumed for the upper floor. The assumption that the two long rooms in the middle of the upper floor formed a court is a highly unlikely one, given the impossibility of making such a court both waterproof and accessible at the same time. The building has a quite regular layout. Smaller rooms are arranged around the two long rooms on three sides. Y. Yadin was the first to point out that the passageways demarcated an inner area; the latter is accessible only via a door, and otherwise constitutes a closed entity, while the rooms situated on two sides around this block are all accessible from one another. Since no court is discernible, the question of the light and ventilation of the individual rooms remains unsolved, unless the existence of windows on the outer walls is assumed. In the east a four-cornered projecting structure, subdivided by a wall, was added to the building. The relatively thin walls argue against the identification of the projecting structure as a tower, since they exclude the possibility that it may have reached any great height. It is probable that the entrance into the corridor that ran along the northern wall was especially constructed with pillars, on top of which the volute capitals found in the vicinity had been placed. Since one of the two capitals had been worked on each side, it can be assumed that there was a pillar arrangement in the middle of the entrance. Both the lower and upper floors were accessible via the corridor on the northern side. An entrance led through the northeastern corner room into the lower floor. The upper floor was reached by a stairway, of

which nine steps were preserved, at the western end of the north wall. It can also be assumed that there was a staircase inside the building made of wood, although no signs of its location have been found.

The building was constructed in Stratum VIII during the ninth century BCE, and it existed without modifications through Strata VII, VI and V B until the middle of the eighth century BCE. In Stratum V A the whole area was altered inasmuch as the city wall was continued around the building, to the detriment of other buildings, in order to give greater protection to this part of the city. In addition, as a substitute for the partial loss of the adjacent buildings, two large houses of the four-room type (3169 and 3148) were newly constructed. The "citadel" is surrounded by an open space. To date, a typological assignment of the building has not been possible; its form, apart from the similarity with Building 338 in Megiddo, has until now been designated as singular for Iron Age II.

Building 338 in Megiddo clearly consists of two parts. In the southern part a further room (340) lies at an oblique angle to two elongated rooms, 338 and 339. There is greater differentiation in the arrangement in the northern part, inasmuch as to the north of two elongated rooms (333 and 337) there are three square rooms (334-336); the room situated in an oblique position to the latter is subdivided by a wall (331 and 332). None of these rooms is clearly identifiable as a court, since their dimensions would have allowed them to be roofed over without difficulty. From its position, Room 340 could possibly have been a court. Whether there was interconnection between the rooms is also unknown, except for an entry found between Rooms 333 and 337. Access to Rooms 333 and 337 was via Room 332 and into Rooms 338 and 339 via Room 340. The building is partly built with hewn stones.

The extension to the building includes the projecting structure adjoining Room 332 in the east with Rooms 346-348, while further rooms (342-344) that abut the substructure of the external stairway project out at the northeastern corner. The stairway, of which three steps are preserved, leads through Room 342 either into Room 331 or into the projecting structure and from there into Room 332. The exact relationship cannot be established from what has been found. Another court adjoined the building to the west and north and was separated by a wall from the streets that ran past it. The volute capitals found in this area of the building probably originated from it, as did those pieces that had been incorporated into building works in the later strata. The circumstances of the finds permit no conclusions as to their original location, but indicate the particular embellishment of the building. Although the building is not particularly large, the organization of the rooms, additional buildings with the external stairway and the special way in which it was constructed suggest that it served an official function that justifies its classification as a palace. The purpose of the individual rooms cannot be more closely discerned in view of the lack of criteria. A certain analogy with the Iron Age "citadel" of Hazor is suggested by the ground plan. Despite the differences in detail, a broad correspondence regarding the organization of the rooms in the northern part can be discerned: next to two elongated rooms, which are interconnected, there are three square units. More rooms adjoin on the short side of the complex thus formed. There is a possibility that this section was located at the heart of the palace of Megiddo and of the "citadel" at Hazor, with various extensions added. A further point of correspondence is the construction of an additional square building that was used in Megiddo as a stairway, although in Hazor the external stairway leading to the upper floor is located at a different point and not in the area of the additional structure.

It is probable that the palace of *Lachish also had no inner court, but this building belongs together with a large external court, which extends in the east along the whole long side of the building. In accordance with the stratigraphy of the Iron Age city in Strata V to III, the palace exhibited three building phases, designated A, B, C. The state of preservation is extremely bad, since the whole platform once constructed for the palace was cleared for the building of the so-called residency in the Persian period; accordingly, it is impossible to establish even a roughly comprehensive plan of the palace complex.

Palace A in Stratum V forms almost a square with a side of about 32 m. The positioning of the rooms exhibits a clear arrangement. On both of the long sides there are three smaller rooms; the remaining rooms are arranged along the external walls. Nothing can be said about their individual function. D. Ussishkin presumed that the entrance led through the almost square room on the eastern side; therefore a stairway or ramp must also have existed at this location. Palace B in Stratum IV is an extension of Palace A, which continued to be in use. To begin with, a platform was also laid down for the new part and filled in with rubble from the surrounding Iron Age and Late Bronze Age levels. Both parts certainly were interconnected with one another. The arrangement of the rooms is not discernible, and their closer differentiation is impossible. The palace was extended in the north by means of three elongated storerooms, and on the southwestern corner by two pillared houses.

For Palace C in Stratum III the existing platform was extended by means of a new wall on the eastern side. A new stairway and a large external court were added on this side. In addition, modifications were made during the last phase to the division of rooms.

Excavations on the mound et-Tell, identified as Bet Zaida to the north of Lake Gennesaret, revealed a building that on the basis of its layout is clearly a Bit Hilani (Arav and Bernett). Excluding later intrusions, it consisted of an entrance hall, main room and eight other rooms, each of which was accessible from the main room. The building most probably belonged only to the last Iron Age II Stratum of the city and was destroyed by Tiglath-Pileser III between 734 and 732 BCE. Arav and Bernett cite only Building 6000 in Megiddo and the so-called Bit Hilani in *Jericho as parallels. Of these, Building 6000 in Megiddo has already been interpreted as a palace with a central court, while the building in Jericho (Tell es-Sulṭān) has already been designated a Bit Hilani by the excavators. Given its layout, the building in Jericho certainly could have been a Bit Hilani.

Thus the building form of the Bit Hilani is known only from two places west of the Jordan for Iron Age II: et-Tell and Jericho (Tell es-Sulṭān). This foreign type of building had its origins in Syria and was widely distributed there during the Late Bronze Age and the Iron Age (Fritz 1983). At any rate, the Bit Hilani constitutes a type of building that was developed elsewhere and permeated into Israel only in Iron Age II.

With the conquest of the northern kingdom of Israel by the *Assyrians in the second half of the eighth century BCE, a new type of palace building evolved that clearly bears the stamp of the Assyrian overlords. To date, no complete palace in Assyrian style has been excavated in Palestine, but parts of such buildings have been uncovered at Hazor, on Tell Ğemme and also at Šēḫ Zuwēyid (Sinai) (Kempinski and Reich, 214-22).

The presence of a governor charged with the administration of the Assyrian provinces brought about the adoption of the building form of the Assyrian open-court building in Iron Age III (Amiran and Dunayevsky). Buildings 1052 and 1369 in Megiddo Stratum III (fig. 6) constitute the first examples of this new type of palace; later on they were interconnected. Characteristic of these types of building is a central inner court, the arrangement of the rooms along the external wall, access near to a corner, and the location of the main room in the south, so that their entrances open toward the north (Fritz 1979). This type of palace is clearly attributable to Assyrian influence, which in turn draws on southern Mesopotamian building tradition.

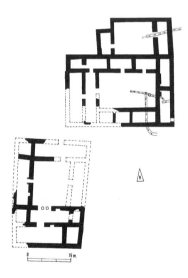

Figure 6. Palaces showing Assyrian influence (Buildings 1052 and 1369, Megiddo, Stratum III)

Even after the Assyrian conquest, when Palestine was a part of the new *Babylonian and *Persian Empires, the Assyrian open-court-building type served high officials as a seat of authority. This presupposes that the administration of this province and its subdistricts was taken over and further carried on each time. A series of buildings of the same type exists from Iron Age III, although their exact dating is not always certain due to the lack of finds: (1) the buildings in Stratum III in Hazor, (2) Building 737 on the slope at Kinneret, (3) the so-called residence on Tell ed-Duwēr, (4) Building A on Tell Ğemme, and (5) Building A in Buṣērā

Since the classification of these buildings is clear (see Fritz 1979), an individual description is unnecessary here. It is probable that southern Mesopotamian building tradition was adopted for this type of palace. At any rate, the dissemination of the building form can be traced to the foreign powers that ruled in the country after the end of the kingdom of Israel in 722 BCE and Judah in 587 BCE.

3.3. Cultic Buildings. Apart from the temple at *Jerusalem, which is known only through the biblical tradition (see 1 Kings 6), only one sanctuary has been found for Iron Age II: the temple of *Arad (fig. 7). The latter was built in the northwestern corner of the fortress. In contrast to former opinions (see Aharoni 1968), a new investigation of the stratigraphy had the result that the temple existed only in Strata X and IX. Z. Herzog (2001) dates these two strata to the eighth century BCE. Thus the temple of Arad was erected and destroyed in the eighth century BCE and had nothing to do with the cultic reforms of *Hezekiah and *Josiah mentioned in the Bible. The temple comprises a broad room with a court in front of it in which the altar is situated. It therefore is clear that the building plan differs from that of the temple at Jerusalem, which, according to its description, can be reconstructed as consisting of a long room. Whereas the long-room temple goes back to Canaanite tradition, the broad-room temple at Arad may represent a genuine Israelite tradition. It is apparent that at least two different traditions of cultic building are to be reckoned within Israel: the long-room and the broad-room. That the broad-room temple at Arad followed a genuine tradition of temple building in Israel is also shown by the two sanctuaries dating from the Hellenistic period on Tell ed-Duwēr (see Aharoni 1968) and Tell es-Seba'. The origin of this building tradition has not yet been clarified, but by no means can it be derived from the broad-room temple of the Early Bronze Age, since the interval of time between the two of more than a millennium is too great. Although originally in the third millennium BCE there was a correspondence between the temple and the residential house, temple and house construction had drifted far apart since the second millennium BCE; each had gone a separate way. There were no temple buildings at any of the other cultic sites. The so-called sanctuary discovered on Mount Ebal probably was a farmstead; the so-called bull-site on Mount Ephraim, with its round structure, can just possibly be interpreted as a *bāmâh* (*"high place"). The temples in Strata XII to X on *Tell Qasīle* evidently are of Philistine type, and the cultic sites at Qitmit and Havzeba are just as clearly *Edomite; each follows its own traditions.

3.4. Administrative Buildings. Buildings that had an evident official function are represented by the so-called pillared house. They take their name from the subdivision of a large rectangular construction through two rows of supporting pillars along its length. This type of building is found in rows as well as in individual instances. To date, they have been identified in both Iron Age I and II at the following places (see Kochavi): Hazor, Kinneret, Šeḫ Ḫoḍor (Tel Hadar), Ḫirbet el-Āšeq Megiddo, Tell Abū Ḫuwām, Tell Qasīle, Bet Shemesh, Tell el-Ḥesi, Tell es-Sebaʿ, Tell el-Milḥ. The origin of this building form is as unclear as its purpose. Suggestions for the latter have included its use as a stall, a storehouse, a barracks, a market hall. It may be the case that the pillared house was employed as a standard building form for various purposes; the determination of the use to which each building was put follows from the position of the building within the city and from the related finds. On grounds

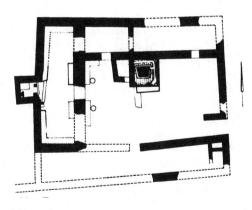

Figure 7. Temple at Arad

of building form and the finds, the interpretations as a stall or a storehouse can be eliminated. The fact that in a society of self-providers there was no need to sell or store produce in a central place argues against the designation as a market hall. The designation as a barracks is a possibility. At any rate, this was a building constructed on military or administrative grounds within the city, at the behest of the central government.

The existence of other public buildings during the Iron Age is attested by the construction of storehouses. These took the form of one-room long-houses, as those built north of the palace in Lachish. I recognize more storerooms in the building that has been identified as the palace of the governor on Tell es-Sebaʿ. Otherwise, the number of public buildings in the Israelite cities is strongly reduced compared with the period of the Bronze Age. Above all, these afforded the inhabitants behind the walls protection from attack. The building of the city walls certainly was carried out by the central government. The city wall meant that the country would not have to face an attacker without any protection. Entrance to a city surrounded by a wall was via the city gate, which was developed only during the course of the second millennium BCE and taken from the Canaanite tradition into the Iron Age (see Herzog 1986). It consisted of six, four or two chambers, which were situated opposite one another and formed through pincer walls. In addition to its defensive role, the city gate also served civil purposes; thus it was an important structure for each city. As a rule, the gateway building was situated inside the city, with an open space behind it. This area was not built upon and probably served traders as a market place. Apart from the gate construction, pillared houses and palaces, the Israelite city in general contained only residential houses. Thus it should be designated a residential city, although administrative measures could also be implemented by the authorities.

See also ARCHAEOLOGY, SYRO-PALESTINIAN; CITIES AND VILLAGES; SOLOMON'S TEMPLE.

BIBLIOGRAPHY. **Y. Aharoni,** "Trial Excavation in the 'Solar Shrine' at Lachish," *IEJ* 18 (1968a) 157-69; idem, "Arad: Its Inscriptions and Temple," *BA* 31 (1968b) 2-32; idem, "The Stratification of Israelite Megiddo," *JNES* 31 (1972) 302-11; **W. G. Alström,** "The Early Iron Age Settlers at Ḫirbet el-Mšāš (Tēl Maśoś)," *ZDPV* 100 (1984) 35-52; **R. Amiran and I. Dunayevsky,** "The Assyrian Open Court Building and Its Palestinian

Derivatives," *BASOR* 149 (1958) 25-32; **R. Arav and M. Bernett,** "The *bīt ḫilāni* at Bethsaida: Its Place in Aramaean/Neo-Hittite and Israelite Architecture in the Iron Age II," *IEJ* 50 (2000) 47-81; **E. Bloch-Smith and B. A. Nakhai,** "A Landscape Comes to Life: The Iron Age I," *NEA* 62 (1999) 62-127; **S. Bunimowitz and A. Faust,** "Ideology in Stone: Understanding the Four-Room House," *BAR* 28.4 (2000) 33-41; **W. G. Dever,** "Solomonic and Assyrian Period 'Palaces' at Gezer," *IEJ* 35 (1985) 217-30; **V. Fritz,** "Bestimmung und Herkunft des Pfeilerhauses in Israel," *ZDPV* 93 (1977) 30-45; idem, "Die Paläste während der assyrischen, babylonischen und persischen Vorherrschaft in Palästina," *MDOG* 111 (1979) 63-74; idem, "Paläste während der Bronze- und Eisenzeit in Palästina," *ZDPV* 99 (1983) 1-42; idem, "Die syrische Bauform des Hilani und die Frage seiner Verbreitung," *Damaszener Mitteilungen* 1 (1983) 43-58; **L. Herr,** "Tripartite Buildings and the Marketplace in Iron Age Israel," *BASOR* 272 (1988) 47-67; **Z. Herzog,** *Das Stadttor in Israel und in den Nachbarländern* (Mainz: Zabern, 1986); idem, *Archaeology of the City: Urban Planning in Ancient Israel and Its Social Implications* (Sonia and Marco Nadler Institute of Archaeology Monograph Series 13; Tel Aviv: Emery and Claire Yass Archaeology Press, 1997); idem, "The Date of the Temple at Arad: Reassessment of the Stratigraphy and the Implications for the History of Religion in Judah," in *Studies in the Archaeology of the Iron Age in Israel and Jordan,* ed. A. Mazar and G. Mathias (JSOTSup 331; Sheffield: Sheffield Academic Press, 2001) 156-78; **J. S. Holladay Jr.,** "The Stables of Ancient Israel: Functional Determinants of Stable Construction and the Interpretation of Pillared Buildings Remains of the Palestinian Iron Age," in *The Archaeology of Jordan and Other Studies Presented to Siegfried H. Horn,* ed. L. T. Geraty and L. G. Herr (Berrien Springs, MI: Andrews University Press, 1986) 103-65; **A. Kempinski and R. Reich,** eds., *The Architecture of Ancient Israel from the Prehistoric to the Persian Periods* (Jerusalem: Israel Exploration Society, 1992); **P. J. King and L. E. Stager,** *Life in Biblical Israel* (LAI; Louisville: Westminster/John Knox, 2001); **M. Kochavi,** "The Eleventh Century BCE Tripartite Pillar Building at Tel Hadar," in *Mediterranean Peoples in Transition: Thirteenth to Early Tenth Centuries BCE,* ed. S. Gitin, A. Mazar and E. Stern (Jerusalem: Israel Exploration Society, 1998) 468-78; **R. Naumann,** *Architektur Kleinasiens von ihren Anfängen bis zum Ende der hethitischen Zeit* (2d ed.; Tübingen: Wasmuth, 1971); **E. D. Oren,** "Governors 'Residencies' in Canaan under the New Kingdom: A Case Study of Egyptian Administration," *JSSEA* 14.2 (1985) 37-56; **R. Reich,** "The Persian Building at Ayyelet ha-Shahar: The Assyrian Palace at Hazor," *IEJ* 25 (1975) 233-37; **Y. Shiloh,** "The Four-Room House: Its Situation and Function in the Israelite City," *IEJ* 20 (1970) 180-90; idem, *The Proto-Aeolic Capital and Israelite Ashlar Masonry* (Qedem 11; Jerusalem: Institute of Archaeology, Hebrew University of Jerusalem, 1979); **E. Stern,** *Archaeology of the Land of the Bible,* 2: *The Assyrian, Babylonian, and Persian Periods, 732-332 BCE* (ABRL; New York: Doubleday, 2001); **D. Ussishkin,** "King Solomon's Palace and Building 1723 in Megiddo," *IEJ* 16 (1966) 174-86; **Y. Yadin,** *Hazor: The Head of All Those Kingdoms; Joshua 11:10, with a Chapter on Israelite Megiddo* (Schweich Lectures of the British Academy, 1970; London: Oxford University Press, 1972).

V. Fritz

ARK NARRATIVE. *See* ARK OF THE COVENANT; SAMUEL, BOOKS OF.

ARK OF THE COVENANT

The fullest depiction of the ark of the covenant is found in the Pentateuch, where it is described as a portable gold-plated wooden chest containing holy objects and covered with a lid adorned with two cherubim. Placed within the most holy place of the tabernacle, it represented the throne of Yahweh. By contrast, in the Historical Books the ark is not described in such elaborate terms. The diversity of images and traditions regarding the ark has intrigued interpreters and inspired attempts to reconstruct the historical development of the ark and its significance.

1. Priestly Images of the Ark
2. History of the Ark
3. The Ark in the Deuteronomistic History and in Chronicles
4. The Ark at War
5. Conclusions

1. Priestly Images of the Ark.
The Hebrew Scriptures rarely use the term "box" or "chest" (*ʾărôn*) in a casual sense, but more often with reference to a holy cult object that contained Israel's law from God: the ark of the covenant. Our images of the ark generally mirror the Bible's most detailed descriptions of

it, which are found in the priestly lore of the Pentateuch (see Ex 25:10-22; 26:33-34). According to these texts, the ark was a small, gold-plated wooden chest measuring 2.5 x 1.5 x 1 cubits (i.e., about 1.25 x .75 x .5 m). Attached to the ark were four gold rings, one on each foot, through which two staves could be placed to allow for easy transportation without human contact. The ark's lid, often called a "mercy seat," was yet more elaborate, being entirely of gold and adorned by two winged cherubim. Iconographical evidence from the Near East suggests that cherubim signaled the throne of a king or god, which conforms well to the Israelite notion that God was "enthroned on/above the cherubim" (e.g., 1 Sam 4:4; Ps 80:1; cf. Ex 25:22). Within the ark was a copy of God's *ʿēdût* with Israel, a term that translates best as "covenant" even though most translations render it as "testimony." The primary reason for this substitution has been to leave room for *bĕrît*, another Hebrew term that denotes Israel's "covenant" with Yahweh.

According to priestly tradition, the ark was placed within the holy precinct of the tabernacle, a mobile tent shrine (also known as the "tent of meeting") that accompanied the Israelites on their postexodus journeys through the wilderness and into Palestine. Tent shrines of this sort were familiar in the ancient world (Fleming), as was the practice of housing deities in the holy celas of temples. The primary distinction of the tabernacle in comparison with other ancient shrines was that its cela contained God's "throne" (the ark) but no divine statue. This reflected Israel's strong aniconic tradition, so vividly expressed in the Decalogue: "You shall not make for yourself a graven image" (Ex 20:4; Deut 5:8). During its desert travels, Israel frequently would have disassembled the tabernacle and removed the ark for transport, but this could be done only after God's glory (*kābôd*) had departed from the holy precinct. The exception to this rule was Israel's Day of Atonement.

According to priestly tradition, once each year, on the tenth day of the first civil month, rites were performed to cleanse Yahweh's cela of its uncleanness (see Lev 16). The primary rituals included the scapegoat rite, which transferred uncleanness from the temple via an animal, and the *kipper* ritual, from which Yom Kippur ("Day of Atonement") took its name. During the *kipper,* the blood of sacrificial animals was applied to the temple and sprinkled on the ark's "mercy seat" *(kappōret)* as a kind of holy detergent, whose purpose was to remove pollution in God's dwelling place. It is commonly assumed that the *kipper* was designed to mimic a very similar Mesopotamian expiation rite known as the *kuppuru* (see *ANET,* 331-34), which was also observed during the New Year season. A primary difference between the two rites was that Mesopotamian *kuppuru* removed demonic pollution from the temple, while the Israelite *kipper* removed impurities caused by human sin. This reflects the more general preoccupation of Israel's priestly legislation, which was to protect Yahweh's temple from the uncleanness generated by cultic and moral failures of human beings.

Apart from the *kipper* ritual, the ark's use and function as understood in priestly tradition is not easy to discern. Some postexilic texts may suggest that it was publicly displayed during certain festivals and on other special occasions (e.g., Ps 132), but little is known about these ritual processions. If we may judge from other biblical depictions of the ark, it is also possible that the priestly tradition conceived of the ark accompanying the Israelites during military campaigns (see 2 below).

Like all religious institutions, the nature and role of Israel's ark underwent various changes during the course of its history. Although our portrait of the priestly ark is presently nested in the old Mosaic tradition, there is a widely held scholarly opinion that this portrait actually represents an overlay of postexilic interpretation of the ark's development. For this reason, it is valuable to consider earlier conceptions of the ark that may have influenced the writers of Israel's histories.

2. History of the Ark.

The biblical sources that scholars use to reconstruct the ark's history are difficult to date with confidence. For this reason, a critical construal of the ark's chronological development can proceed only cautiously and in the most general terms, focusing on the preexilic, exilic and postexilic notions of the institution.

In its preexilic form the ark appears to have been a simple wooden chest that contained Israel's written covenant *(bĕrît)* with Yahweh (Deut 10:1-8). Because Yahweh's presence was believed to accompany this ark, the chest was highly valued in times of war and accompanied the

Israelites during military campaigns (Josh 6; 1 Sam 4—6). This unadorned ark contrasted sharply with the more elaborate priestly ark described above, and the two institutions also differed in other respects. In the preexilic traditions the tent that housed the ark and the "tent of meeting" were two different institutions (Haran 1960). Later priestly conceptions fused these two traditions into one, so that the ark became the deity's dwelling place and throne. By what historical process could this change have arisen?

Tradition connects the early ark with various sites, but especially with a tent shrine at *Shiloh, where Israel's northern tribes apparently worshiped Yahweh before the rise of the Judean monarchy (Josh 18:1; 1 Sam 1—3). The ark eventually was taken from Shiloh and was moved from one place to another until King *David took an interest in it after defeating Saul's regime (cf. 1 Sam 4—6; 2 Sam 6). David attempted to consolidate his support among those living north of Judah by bringing their ark to his new capital in *Jerusalem. His son *Solomon in turn placed the ark in his newly constructed Yahweh temple (1 Kings 6—9). Because of Israel's aniconic tendencies, it was natural for this wooden cult object to be regarded as a kind of divine footstool for the invisible God dwelling in Jerusalem; perhaps this idea already had taken hold at Shiloh. At any rate, the fact that Solomon stationed large wooden cherubim in the temple cela, and carved them into its walls (1 Kings 6), would have reinforced the iconographic image that the ark marked the dwelling place of God. The power of this ark-throne imagery undoubtedly strengthened during the course of the monarchy.

A decisive moment in the conceptual development of the ark appears in the theology of Ezekiel. Ezekiel, a priestly prophet sensitive to matters of ritual purity, faced the imminent destruction of the Jerusalem temple. How could he maintain that the desecration and destruction of Yahweh's temple by Babylonian hordes would not occasion the defeat of his deity? Ezekiel's answer was to disassociate Yahweh from the physical temple itself by averring that Yahweh would abandon his temple in Jerusalem before it was destroyed (Ezek 10). Ezekiel's vision fused together images of the ark, cherubim and divine throne to render a movable ark that followed Yahweh's glory wherever it traveled (cf. Ezek 1; 10; 43). Because this mobile, spiritual ark represented the genuine presence of Yahweh, it was much more elaborate than the physical wooden chest still lying in the temple.

Ezekiel's theology and imagery bring us very close to the priestly ark, and often it is conjectured that the prophet's ideas inspired it. However, while Ezekiel's vision came during the early exile, scholars surmise that the priestly ark was conceived somewhat later, toward the end of the exile or during the postexilic period. As a result, the priestly ark is thought to reflect greater influences from the Jewish stay in Babylon. Rather than containing a copy of the Deuteronomic běrît ("covenant"), the priestly ark contained the ʿēdût, a term for "covenant" that reflects Aramaic influences from the exile. Mesopotamian influence is also suggested by the priestly ark's kappōret ("mercy seat") and kipper cleansing ritual, which find their parallels in the annual kuppuru rites of Babylon (de Tarragon). Consequently, a simplified critical history of the ark's imagery and significance can be divided into three periods: the simple preexilic ark, the elaborate ark vision of Ezekiel and the exilic/postexilic priestly ark.

We should be cautious about assuming that these conceptions of the ark reflected concrete realities in every case. The ark seems to have disappeared toward the end of the Judean monarchy, and there is little evidence that it was either returned to the temple or rebuilt by postexilic Jews (note, in this connection, Jeremiah's vision of an Israel without the ark in Jer 3:16). It is therefore possible that the very elaborate priestly ark existed, like Ezekiel's ark, only in the minds of its creators.

3. The Ark in the Deuteronomistic History and in Chronicles.

Generally speaking, the simple preexilic ark was the one featured in the *Deuteronomistic History, but a close reading will easily discern a complexity in the institution as understood by the Deuteronomistic History. Prior to the construction of Yahweh's temple, the Deuteronomistic History demanded no inflexible connection between the ark, Yahweh's house and sacrifices to Yahweh. For this reason, Solomon could offer almost simultaneous sacrifices at a *"high place" in *Gibeon (1 Kings 3:4-14) and at the ark's location in Jerusalem (1 Kings 3:15) without occasioning theological difficulties. However, from the construction of

*Solomon's temple onward, the Deuteronomistic History demanded that sacrifices be observed only at the temple site where the ark stood. In fact, according to the Deuteronomistic History, Israel's propensity to sacrifice elsewhere was an important reason for its punishment in the Babylonian exile. (Readers should note, however, that a few postexilic additions to the history reflect the later and more ornate priestly ark [e.g., 1 Kings 8:1-13].)

By way of contrast, the *Chronicler's History presumed the priestly institutions of the postexilic era, wherein the ark, the tent of meeting and all sacrifices had been inseparably linked since the tabernacle of the Mosaic era. For this reason, the Chronicler made no allowances for legitimate sacrifices at various sites. Whereas the Deuteronomistic History countenanced Solomon's sacrifices at both Gibeon and at the ark in Jerusalem, the Chronicler seems to have assumed that this was impossible. He corrected the problem by rendering Gibeon's "high place" as the tent of meeting and by removing all references to Solomon's sacrifice at the ark in Jerusalem (2 Chron 1:3-13). The Chronicler's terminology reflects influences from both priestly and nonpriestly traditions. Its "tent of meeting" reflects priestly influence (used seven times), but the Chronicler's terminology for the covenant favored the term bĕrît ("covenant") over the priestly ʿēdût. In sum, the ark's history as depicted in the Deuteronomistic History and in the Chronicler's History was shaped by the theologies of the respective historians.

4. The Ark at War.

During the twentieth century the theory emerged that early Israel was an *amphictyony, akin to the Greek sacral leagues, in which various tribes were united in a military alliance around a common cultic shrine, of which the centerpiece would have been the ark of the covenant (Alt; Noth; Smend). The tribes would rally together to protect the shrine or to protect each other, and in the resulting battles the ark would have accompanied the tribes because its mere presence guaranteed divine assistance. This modern sketch of Israel and its ark is not very different from the biblical portrait of early Israel. However, in recent years the amphictyonic theory has fallen into disfavor because it is based largely on what have come to be regarded as late and tenuous sources, especially the Deuteronomistic narrative of Joshua (de Geus). We should be cautious with our sources in such cases, but it is important to note that the association of the Israelite tribes with the ark at Shiloh appears to have been very early, and the so-called Song of Deborah (Judg 5), another early source, clearly presupposes an Israelite military league composed of various tribal groups. Hence, although many of our sources may be late, there are reasons to regard positively the basic reliability of the amphictyonic portrait of early Israel and its ark.

Israel's theological perspective on the ark and war is well illustrated by the "Ark Narrative" in 1 Sam 4—6 and 2 Sam 6. According to this section of 1 Samuel, Israel removed the ark from its shrine in Shiloh so that it could accompany them into battle against the *Philistines. Unfortunately, the Philistines subsequently captured the ark, which was returned to Israelite hands only because of Yahweh's miraculous intervention. Many scholars believe that this story reflects an old source that eventually was incorporated into the story of David's rise or into the later Deuteronomistic History. On this reading, although the original focus of the Ark Narrative would have been on the cult object itself and would have paralleled other Near Eastern tales about the capture and return of divine images, in its present literary context the cult legend serves the somewhat different purpose of explaining why the ark was removed from Shiloh and how the priestly family of Shiloh—the house of Eli—came to be disqualified from temple service (cf. 1 Sam 2; 1 Kings 2:26-27) (see McCarter; Hertzberg).

There is an ongoing debate about whether the Ark Narrative reflects actual historical events or whether it was composed for theological purposes, either to illustrate the consequences of a naive confidence in the ark, or to provide the basis for rejecting the Shiloh priesthood, or for some other purpose (e.g., Gitay; Ahlström; Davies). Some scholars view the story as a late composition by the Deuteronomistic Historian, for whom the ark served as the conceptual link between his history of Moses/Joshua and the story of David/Solomon (Van Seters). The compositional questions posed by the Ark Narrative have made it difficult for many scholars to employ the story as a source for reconstructing the ark's history.

5. Conclusions.

Despite the ambiguities that continue to envelop the early history, development and eventual disappearance of the ark, most critical scholars have concluded that the ark underwent a pattern of development from the simple to complex. Generally, this trajectory is described as moving from an unadorned wooden chest to an elaborate gold icon, and from an object associated with the divine presence to the very throne of God. Because the biblical historians, notably the Deuteronomistic Historian and the Chronicler, wrote at different times and to different audiences, the particular conceptions of the ark that influenced them varied considerably. In neither case, however, were these historians merely purveyors of tradition. Each writer provided theological insights by shaping his portrait of the ark's history, and the results in turn shaped Israel's memory of the ark of the covenant.

See also PRIESTS AND LEVITES; SOLOMON'S TEMPLE; WAR AND PEACE.

BIBLIOGRAPHY. **A. Ahlström**, "The Travels of the Ark: A Religio-Political Composition," *JNES* 43 (1984) 141-49; **A. Alt**, *Der Gott der Väter: Ein Beitrag zur Vorgeschichte der israelitischen Religion* (BWANT 3/12; Stuttgart: Kohlhammer, 1929); ET: "The God of the Fathers," in *Essays on Old Testament History and Religion* (BibSem 9; Oxford: Blackwell, 1966) 3-77; **J. Blenkinsopp**, "Kiriath-Jearim and the Ark," *JBL* 88 (1969) 143-56; **A. F. Campbell**, *The Ark Narrative, 1 Sam 4-6, 2 Sam 6: A Form-Critical and Traditio-Historical Study* (SBLDS 16; Missoula, MT: Scholars Press, 1975); **P. R. Davies**, "The History of the Ark in the Books of Samuel," *JNSL* 5 (1977) 9-18; **C. H. J. de Geus**, *The Tribes of Israel: An Investigation into Some of the Presuppositions of Martin Noth's Amphictyony Hypothesis* (SSN 18; Assen: Van Gorcum, 1976); **D. E. Fleming**, "Mari's Large Public Tent and the Priestly Tent Sanctuary," *VT* 50 (2000) 484-98; **T. E. Freitheim**, "The Ark in Deuteronomy," *CBQ* 30 (1968) 1-14; **V. Fritz**, *Tempel und Zelt: Studien zum Tempelbau in Israel und zu dem Zeltheiligtum der Priesterschrift* (WMANT 47; Neukirchen-Vluyn: Neukirchener Verlag, 1977); **Y. Gitay**, "Reflections on the Poetics of the Samuel Narrative: The Question of the Ark Narrative," *CBQ* 54 (1992) 221-30; **J. Gutman**, "The History of the Ark," *ZAW* 87 (1971) 22-30; **M. Haran**, "The Ark and the Cherubim," *IEJ* 9 (1959) 30-38, 89-94; idem, "The Disappearance of the Ark," *IEJ* 13 (1963) 46-58; idem, "The Nature of the 'Ohel Mo'edh' in Pentateuchal Sources," *JSS* 5 (1960) 50-65; idem, "Shiloh and Jerusalem: The Origin of the Priestly Tradition in the Pentateuch," *JBL* 81 (1962) 14-24; **H. W. Hertzberg**, *1 & 2 Samuel* (OTL; Philadelphia: Westminster, 1964) 45-63; **P. K. McCarter Jr.**, *1 Samuel* (AB 8; New York: Doubleday, 1980) 23-26; **P. D. Miller and J. J. M. Roberts**, *The Hand of the Lord: A Reassessment of the "Ark Narrative" of 1 Samuel* (Baltimore: Johns Hopkins University Press, 1977); **E. Nielsen**, "Some Reflections on the History of the Ark," in *Congress Volume: Oxford, 1959*, ed. G. W. Anderson (VTSup 7; Leiden: Brill, 1960) 61-74; **M. Noth**, *Geschichte Israels* (Göttingen: Vandenhoeck & Ruprecht, 1950); ET: *The History of Israel* (New York: Harper, 1958); **R. Smend**, *Jahwekrieg und Stammebund: Erwägungen zur ältesten Geschichte Israels* (FRLANT 84; Göttingen: Vandenhoeck & Ruprecht, 1963); ET: *Yahweh War and Tribal Confederation: Reflections upon Israel's Earliest History* (Nashville: Abingdon, 1970); **J. M. de Tarragon**, "Le Kapporet est-elle une fiction ou un element du cult tardiff?" *RB* 88 (1981) 5-12; **J. Van Seters**, *In Search of History: Historiography in the Ancient World and the Origins of Biblical History* (New Haven: Yale University Press, 1983) 346-53.

K. L. Sparks

ARSAMES ARCHIVE. *See* NON-ISRAELITE WRITTEN SOURCES: EGYPTIAN ARAMAIC PAPYRI.

ARTAXERXES. *See* EZRA AND NEHEMIAH, BOOKS OF; HISTORY OF ISRAEL 7: PERSIAN PERIOD; PERSIA, PERSIANS.

ASHDOD

Throughout biblical history Ashdod was an important commercial city on the international coastal highway. Although the city is best known as one of the five primary Philistine cities (Josh 13:3), Ashdod played an important role in each era of Israel's history in Palestine.

1. Site Identification
2. Geography
3. History

1. Site Identification.

The location of Ashdod (Tel Ashdod) has never been in doubt, as the site has maintained its name in various forms (e.g., Gk *Azōtos*, "Azotus" [see Acts 8:40]) throughout history. Eusebius *(Onomasticon)*, Jerome and the Crusaders all made the proper identification, as did Condor, who, visiting the site on behalf of the Survey of Western Palestine in 1875, noted that the Arab village of Esdud, adjacent to the tel, preserved the ancient name. Tel Ashdod was excavated by M. Dothan from 1962 to 1972.

2. Geography.
Tel Ashdod is located three miles from the Mediterranean shore between *Ashkelon and Joppa on the route of the historic international highway that connected Egypt with Mesopotamia. As this route crossed the *Philistine coastal plain in the southern Levant, it, like the modern coastal highway today, tracked just behind a wide sheet of sand dunes that extend three to five miles inland. Ashdod, together with Ashkelon and *Gaza to the south, was situated where this coastal route crossed the international route connecting *Arabia to the Mediterranean. Clearly, any power seeking to control the economy of the southeastern Mediterranean basin had to maintain a strong presence in this region.

The strategic importance of Ashdod can also be described locally in terms of its proximity to Nahal Lachish. Ashdod's control of the western end of the Nahal Lachish drainage system (which includes the Nahal Guvrin and the Nahal Elah) gave it access into the valleys of the mid-Shephelah and hence the all-important western approaches to Judah.

Ashdod, although inland, maintained an anchorage on the coast. The unsheltered, straight-line sandy shore of the southern Levant makes landing and launching boats difficult, and no artificial breakwaters are known to have existed in the area prior to the end of the Judean monarchy. For this reason, Ashdod's earliest harbor apparently was located at Tel Mor, a site six miles northwest of the ancient city in the estuary of Nahal Lachish (now adjacent to Ashdod's busy modern seaport). The archaeological profile of Tel Mor parallels that of early Ashdod (Middle Bronze II through the Iron Age). By the late eighth century BCE, Tel Mor's role as Ashdod's anchorage appears to have been eclipsed by Ashdod-Yam (Minet Esdud, today part of an Ashdod municipal beach), just three miles from the ancient city. Ashdod-Yam grew in importance from the Persian through Byzantine periods, and it served as the port of NT Azotus.

Ancient Ashdod, on the edge of the dune sheet, faced the fertile alluvial coastal plain to

the east, and a number of wells in the vicinity gave access to the high water table below. This mix of arable soil and plentiful water provided the inhabitants of the Philistine coastal plain a real advantage in agriculture, and hence a relatively stable local economic base, compared to the Judeans living in the hill country farther east (see 2 Kings 8:1-6).

Today the ancient site of Ashdod is tightly enclosed on three sides by a major north-south highway and on the fourth by a railroad, and is overshadowed on the northwest by a large industrial zone that lies on the outskirts of the modern city of Ashdod. This situation fittingly preserves the role of Ashdod as a center of commerce and trade in antiquity.

3. History.
3.1. Middle and Late Bronze Ages. There is scant archaeological evidence for settlement on Tel Ashdod prior to Middle Bronze IIC (c. 1650-1600 BCE), when the acropolis of the tel was first fortified. Ashdod first appears in written documents from Late Bronze Age Ugarit, indicating that by that time the city was a center of export for dyed woolen purple fabric and garments. Ashdod apparently played an important role in Levantine maritime trade during the Late Bronze Age along with cities such as Ugarit, Arvad, Byblos, Tyre, Acco, Dor, Joppa and Ashkelon. Archaeological remains from the Late Bronze Age include strong walls (either fortifications or buildings), one complex of which resembles the so-called Egyptian residencies common to the plains and large valleys of the southern Levant at this time. The presence of Cypriot and Mycenaean ware found in Late Bronze contexts at Ashdod also suggests cultural and commercial ties with the larger eastern Mediterranean world.

3.2. Philistine Ashdod. A thick conflagration layer attests to the destruction of Late Bronze Age Ashdod in the late thirteenth century BCE, and *Philistine remains abound from when the city was rebuilt in the early twelfth century BCE after a short transitional phase. The archaeological record generally coincides with the historical account of Rameses III's battle against the Sea Peoples in the eighth year of his reign, although it must no longer be supposed that Rameses allowed the Philistines to settle the south Levantine coast after the battle to serve Egyptian military interests. Rather, the archaeological record and historical common sense point to a gradual incursion of Sea Peoples (including the Philistines) in the region throughout the late thirteenth and early twelfth centuries BCE, resulting in a clear Philistine dominance at Ashdod by the middle of the twelfth century BCE. Archaeological evidence includes locally decorated Philistine pottery as well as imported pottery (primarily Mycenaean IIIC).

The biblical record makes much of the Philistine presence on the coastal plain, including Ashdod, at this time. The book of Joshua indicates that even though the Philistine coastal plain was apportioned to lie within the tribal inheritance of Judah (Josh 15:45-47), Israel was not able to occupy the region (Josh 11:22; 13:1; cf. Judg 1:18 LXX: "Judah did *not* capture . . . "). The Philistines were governed by a confederation of five "tyrants" (Heb *seren*, related to Gk *tyrannos*), each ruling a separate city: Gaza, Ashkelon, Ashdod, *Ekron and *Gath (Josh 13:3; 1 Sam 6:16-18). Archaeological evidence suggests that the Philistine presence in the region was more extensive than just these five cities together with their outlying territories, and it is likely that the emphasis placed on them in the Bible reflects the importance of their role in Judean history.

After defeating Israel on the battlefield at Ebenezer in the waning days of the priesthood of Eli, the Philistines took their trophy of war, the *ark of the covenant, to the temple of Dagan at Ashdod (1 Sam 5:1-6). From Ashdod the ark was moved to Gath and then Ekron, each progressively closer to Judah (1 Sam 5:7—6:16). This narrative is part of a larger sequence that reflects the uneasy military, religious, economic and social dynamic that existed between the Philistines and Israel in the days leading up to the establishment of the Israelite monarchy.

3.3. Ashdod during the Judean Monarchy. Although having some success against the Philistines militarily (see 2 Sam 5:17-25; 8:1), *David apparently was unable to fully incorporate Philistia into his realm. The region largely lay outside immediate Judean control until the mid-eighth century BCE when, for a brief time, Uzziah was able to exert his influence over Ashdod, Gath and Jabneh (2 Chron 26:6-8). It is possible that the Judean administrative district that includes Ekron, Ashdod and Gaza that is preserved in Joshua 15:45-47 dates to this time. Archaeological evidence shows that by the early

part of Iron II, Ashdod had expanded off the acropolis of the tel to include a large lower city and become a wealthy and influential urban center, and as such it provides an adequate indicator of the success of Uzziah's achievements on the coast. The prophetic invectives hurled against Ashdod and the other Philistine cities (Amos 1:6-8; 3:9; Jer 25:20; Zeph 2:4-7; Zech 9:5-7) reflect the hostility that continued to fester between Philistia and Judah throughout the time of the monarchy.

Because of its importance and location on the international highway, Ashdod became a target for the *Assyrian imperial advance into the southern Levant in the late eighth century BCE. A rebellion against Assyria led by Azuri, king of Ashdod, which was inspired by the Egyptian pharaoh Shabako, prompted Sargon II to campaign against the city in 713 BCE; Ashdod was defeated, and its king was deposed. The next year the city revolted again, this time under the popular leadership of Iamani (a Cypriot Greek?) and in league with Judah (against the advice of Isaiah [see Is 20:1-6]), *Edom and *Moab. Sargon II responded quickly by sacking Ashdod and capturing Gath and Ashdod-Yam, cities within its territorial influence. He then reorganized the territory of Ashdod into an Assyrian province. Because Sennacherib's annals report that land conquered from *Hezekiah was turned over to Ashdod's king Mitinti and the kings of Ekron and Gaza, we can assume that these cities remained loyal to the Assyrians in the face of the Judean revolt of 701 BCE. The region remained securely in the hands of Assyria until the mid-seventh century BCE.

Judean territorial expansion under *Josiah in the wake of the collapse of the Assyrian Empire in the late seventh century BCE reached the international coastal highway (see 2 Kings 23:29). An ostracon containing a letter found at Mezad Hashavyahu, a Judean fortress between Ashdod and Jabneh, indicates that Josiah posted a military garrison in the region. Judean nationalistic aspirations were dealt a blow with Josiah's death at Megiddo, and by the end of the seventh century (probably 604 BCE) Nebuchadnezzar had incorporated the Philistine plain, including the region of Ashdod, into the *Babylonian Empire.

3.4. Ashdod after the Return from Exile. The residents of Ashdod, together with *Sanballat, Tobiah, the Arabs and the Ammonites, opposed the return of Judean control in Jerusalem under *Nehemiah (Neh 4:7). In the end, everyday cultural assimilation proved to be even stronger than political force, as Jewish men married women from Ashdod and raised their children in the local language (Neh 13:23-24). Indeed, for the next four centuries, until Jonathan the Maccabee pushed the limit of Judaean political control to Ashkelon, Ekron and Ashdod (now Azotus [1 Macc 10:77-84]), Ashdod remained firmly within the political and cultural sphere of foreigners: Persia, the Ptolemies and the Seleucid Greeks.

See also ASHKELON; EKRON; GATH; GAZA; PHILISTINES.

BIBLIOGRAPHY. **Y. Aharoni,** *The Land of the Bible* (Philadelphia: Westminster, 1979); **D. Baly,** *The Geography of the Bible* (rev. ed.; New York: Harper & Row, 1974); **M. Dothan,** "Ashdod," *NEAEHL* 1.93-102; idem, "The Foundation of Tel Mor and of Ashdod," *IEJ* 23 (1973) 1-17; **M. Dothan and T. Dothan,** *People of the Sea: The Search for the Philistines* (New York: Macmillan, 1992); **T. Dothan,** *The Philistines and Their Material Culture* (Jerusalem: Israel Exploration Society, 1982); **S. Gitin, A. Mazar and E. Stern,** *Mediterranean Peoples in Transition: Thirteenth to Early Tenth Centuries BCE* (Jerusalem: Israel Exploration Society, 1998); **J. Kaplan,** "The Stronghold of Yamani at Ashdod-Yam," *IEJ* 19 (1969) 137-49; **A. Mazar,** "A Note on Canaanite Jars from Enkomi," *IEJ* 38 (1988) 224-26; **J. Monson,** *Regions on the Run: Introductory Map Studies in the Land of the Bible* (Rockford, IL: Biblical Backgrounds, 1998); **J. Naveh,** "A Hebrew Letter from the Seventh Century BC," *IEJ* 10 (1960) 129-39; **N. Na'aman,** "The Kingdom of Judah under Josiah," *TA* 18 (1991) 3-71.

P. H. Wright

ASHDOD REVOLT. See HISTORY OF ISRAEL 5: ASSYRIAN PERIOD.

ASHERAH. See CANAAN, CANAANITES; CANAANITE GODS AND RELIGION.

ASHKELON

The ancient mound of Ashkelon is located on the southern coast of Israel about 63 km (39 mi) south of Tel Aviv and 16 km (10 mi) north of Gaza. The site is adjacent to the sea and sits above an underground fresh water river. This rare geological confluence allowed Ashkelon to become an important oasis on the ancient maritime route between Egypt and the ports of Lebanon and Syria. Ashkelon became a major city in the Early Bronze Age and continued as a port until Salidin destroyed the fortifications and filled the harbor in 1191 CE.

1. Ashkelon in the Bible
2. Excavations

1. Ashkelon in the Bible.

The biblical writers refer to Ashkelon in two ways. The books of Joshua, Judges and Samuel mention Ashkelon in conjunction with other Philistine cities and emphasize the territorial conflict between the *Philistines and Israelites. The book of Joshua notes that neither Ashkelon nor any other Philistine city was conquered by the Israelites (Josh 13:3); in Judges, Samson kills thirty Philistines at Ashkelon to pay off Philistines elsewhere (Judg 14:19); in Samuel, *David laments Ashkelon's exultation over the death of *Saul at Philistine hands (2 Sam 1:20). Jeremiah and Amos, however, have a very different focus. These writers portray Ashkelon as part of the "remnant" of the Philistines; to them, the power of Ashkelon rests not in its territorial ambition but in its connection with the merchants of *Phoenicia (Jer 47:1-7; Amos 1:6-8). Recent excavations at Ashkelon illustrate both the Deuteronomistic and prophetic perspectives.

2. Excavations.

Small-scale excavations were conducted at Ashkelon beginning in 1815 under H. Stanhope, and more digging was done in the early twentieth century by D. Mackenzie, J. Garstang and W. J. Phythian-Adams for the Palestine Exploration Fund. Unfortunately, none of these efforts were able to excavate to the depth necessary to reach substantial remains from any of the biblical periods. The only excavation to explore the period of the OT writers with any breadth is the Leon Levy Expedition to Ashkelon (1985 to the present), directed by L. E. Stager of Harvard University.

2.1. Iron Age I. In the early twelfth century BCE Ramesses III described devastation around the Mediterranean caused by the arrival of "Sea Peoples" from the west. At the same time, new inhabitants arrived at Ashkelon. In Ashkelon these new arrivals constructed houses with Aegean-style hearths in the center of every room. They practiced weaving on looms with Aegean-style loom weights. They ate sheep, goats and cattle but, distinct from their highland neighbors, also ate pigs and dogs. They worshiped Aegean-style deities in the shape of a woman with her hands clasped to her head as if in mourning or of a woman seated in a chair (often called Ashdoda). Their pottery brought Aegean-style forms and designs into the local repertoire of the Levant. When they pictured themselves or were pictured by others, the men had long, spiked hair in the Aegean tradition. Because of all of these distinctive cultural traits, excavators at Ashkelon link the new inhabitants to the Mycenaeans of the Aegean Late Bronze Age, to the Sea Peoples who attacked the Egyptians, and to the group referred to in the Bible as the *Philistines.

The Philistines retained Aegean cultural traits for some time, but in the eleventh and tenth centuries BCE they also began to absorb ways of life that mirrored the groups among whom they were now living. Their pottery forms, for instance, lost their vibrant emblematic decoration. Aegean- and Cypriot-style hearths were increasingly replaced by Levantine tabuns (ovens). The historical irony is that this acculturation, visible in the excavations at Ashkelon, came at a time when the Philistines and surrounding groups such as the Israelites were, according the biblical writers, mortal enemies.

2.2. Iron Age II. In the late eleventh or the early tenth century BCE the inhabitants at Ashkelon refortified the abandoned Middle Bronze Age ramparts and built substantial mud-brick houses to line their city streets. They adopted pottery similar to the red slipped pottery found throughout the region and appeared to be thriving. At some point in the tenth century BCE, however, much of the city was abandoned. In some areas the ninth- and eighth-century remains are entirely absent, and in the areas where they have been found, the artifacts are poorly preserved. Among the finds, eighth-century Phoenician storage jars demonstrate that Ashkelon's inhabitants were beginning to participate again in the commerce of the Mediterranean.

Ashkelon did not reemerge as a power in the region until the end of the eighth century BCE. The conquest of the region by Tiglath Pileser III in 734 BCE changed the geopolitical balance, and the new order provided the opportunity for Ashkelon to establish some economic power in the region. In 701 BCE the *Assyrians took away

several tributaries of Ashkelon along the coast to the north, but, at least as far as the economy of Ashkelon was concerned, this economic loss was more than offset by new freedom from Judahite power and the destruction of competitors in the Judahite lowlands.

The rulers of seventh-century Ashkelon were confident enough to build new large-scale production facilities. One excavation area revealed a beautiful winery, complete with extensive ashlar masonry and a regular layout that placed winepresses in every room. The quality and organization of the construction make it unlikely to be merely an example of household production. Rather, the people of Ashkelon were using new methods to meet a new demand from new markets. The Assyrian conquest had eliminated all competitors in the immediate area, and the merchants of Phoenicia served as willing buyers for anything that could be efficiently produced. For Tel Miqne/*Ekron this development encouraged the increased production of olive oil; at Ashkelon it involved the increased production of wine.

Even when the *Phoenicians were not buying all of Ashkelon's produce and production diminished, the commercial die had been cast. As the seventh century BCE progressed, the inhabitants of Ashkelon built a marketplace by the sea. The market contained shops of all varieties, including a wine shop, a butcher shop and a counting house for transactions. Ashkelon was now part of the commercial Mediterranean world. Now new merchants arrived from the Aegean, the very area from which the Philistines had originally emigrated. These Greeks came not to settle, but to sell delicate drinking cups and finely made crockery. The market at Ashkelon had become an international trading center, and Ashkelon itself was developing into a cosmopolitan city. The finds suggest that even a contingent of *Egyptians made their home in the city.

This thriving port, so focused on the west, could not escape the powerful military machines farther to the east. While the Assyrians left Ashkelon unscathed, the triumphant *Babylonians did not pass by this independent port. The Babylonian Chronicle records that in December of 604 BCE Nebuchadnezzar made Ashkelon into a "ruin forever" (Grayson, 100, chronicle 5, obverse 18-19; Glassner, 229). Every house was completely burned to the ground; even the soil itself was vitrified by the heat of the blaze. People had no time to stop and retrieve even the most precious objects. Instead, many of the inhabitants were trapped and killed where they stood, witness to the power of Babylon.

See also ASHDOD; EKRON; GATH; GAZA; PHILISTINES.

BIBLIOGRAPHY. **J.-J. Glassner,** *Mesopotamian Chronicles* (SBLWAW 19; Atlanta: Society of Biblical Literature, 2004); **A. K. Grayson,** *Assyrian and Babylonian Chronicles* (TCS 5; Winona Lake, IN: Eisenbrauns, 2000); **D. M. Master,** "Trade and Politics: Ashkelon's Balancing Act in the Seventh Century B.C.E.," *BASOR* 330 (2003) 47-64; **J. D. Schloen,** "Ashkelon," *OEANE* 1.220-23; **L. E. Stager,** "Ashkelon," *NEAEHL* 1.102-12; idem, *Ashkelon Discovered: From Canaanites and Philistines to Romans and Moslems* (Washington: Biblical Archaeology Society, 1991); idem, "Forging an Identity: The Emergence of Ancient Israel," in *The Oxford History of the Biblical World,* ed. M. Coogan (Oxford: Oxford University Press, 1998) 122-218; idem, "The Fury of Babylon: Ashkelon and the Archaeology of Destruction," *BAR* 22 (1996) 54-77; idem, "The Impact of the Sea Peoples (1185-1050)," in *The Archaeology of Society in the Holy Land,* ed. T. Levy (London: Leicester University Press, 1995) 332-48; **B. J. Stone,** "The Philistines and Acculturation: Culture Change and Ethnic Continuity in the Iron Age," *BASOR* 298 (1995) 7-32.

D. M. Master

ASHTORETH/ASTARTE. *See* CANAANITE GODS AND RELIGION.

ASHURBANIPAL. *See* ASSYRIA, ASSYRIANS; HISTORY OF ISRAEL 5: ASSYRIAN PERIOD.

ASSYRIA, ASSYRIANS

Assyria and Assyrians are frequently referred to in the Historical Books of the OT, and often these references can be fitted into the larger context of Assyrian history. In the Bible there are several references to Asshur, and these are always to the land, people and kings of Assyria, as well as to their patronymic, Asshur. In Genesis 10:22 and 1 Chronicles 1:17 Asshur is said to have been a son of Shem. The god Asshur is never mentioned in the Bible.

1. Geography and Ethnicity
2. The Discovery of Ancient Assyria
3. Economic and Social Patterns
4. Political and Military History
5. Culture
6. Religion and Magic
7. Monarchy

1. Geography and Ethnicity.
Assyria, in geographical terms, encompasses the northern part of Mesopotamia, "the land between two rivers" (Tigris and Euphrates), principally modern day Iraq. The geopolitical shape of Assyria is roughly a triangle, with the city Asshur on the Tigris its southern point, Nineveh, also on the Tigris, its northwestern point, and Arbela, near the upper Zab River, its northeastern point. As to the people in this region and their history before 2000 BCE, little is known apart from occasional political and military contacts with southern Mesopotamia, Sumer and Babylonia. However, trading caravans certainly were traveling to and fro across Assyria long before that time and continued to do so afterward.

The ethnic identity of the people in this area in early times, before 2000 BCE, is hard to define, but certainly there were people who could speak, and some who could read and write, Sumerian and Akkadian, the latter being a Semitic language. The "Assyrians," as they came to be called, spoke one of the two major dialects of Akkadian, the other main dialect being Babylonian. Both dialects were written in the cuneiform script, the first *writing system invented in world history.

2. The Discovery of Ancient Assyria.
Virtually all that is described in this section has been discovered only within the last century and a half. The great breakthrough in the nineteenth century was the decipherment of a trilingual inscription, written in Old Persian, Akkadian and Elamite (all in the cuneiform script), that Darius I (521-486 BCE) of Persia had had carved on the side of the cliff at Bisitun in western Iran. H. Rawlinson, a colonel in the British army, with the aid of a Kurdish boy and at the risk of both their lives on the precipitous rocks, studied and deciphered this monumental text. Rawlinson began with the Old Persian version, which, since it was an Indo-European language, he deciphered in a reasonable length of time. With this momentous step forward he turned his attention to the Akkadian version. The decipherment of this language (c. 1850 CE) was the key that the study of ancient Mesopotamian, including Assyrian, civilization needed,

for it immediately opened up the secrets of thousands of Assyrian documents found in the sands of Mesopotamia. Rawlinson was by no means the only person who tried to decipher cuneiform. G. F. Grotefend of Germany, with whom Rawlinson exchanged information, and E. Hincks of Ireland were just two more of several contemporaries who worked on the decipherment of cuneiform. The third version of the Bisitun inscription, which was in Elamite, was deciphered some years later.

Rawlinson was not an isolated discoverer. H. Layard, another Briton, began excavations in Assyria, chiefly at Calah (Nimrud) at approximately the same time as Rawlinson was working on decipherment (c. 1850 CE). Layard discovered palaces and temples containing monumental human-headed bulls, walls lined with stone reliefs bearing scenes of Assyrian soldiers in action, and inscriptions describing Assyrian military conquests and building projects. The work of these two pioneers of Assyriology was contemporary with the work of many others of various nationalities, and that work, finding and deciphering ancient Assyrian inscriptions and unearthing numerous artifacts and buildings at ancient Assyrian sites, continues today.

3. Economic and Social Patterns.
Unlike Egypt, Mesopotamia, including Assyria, is not an easily defined area in terms of historical culture. While Egypt presents a rather unilateral development throughout ancient history, with foreign invasions and influences being more the exception than the rule, Assyria's development is a kaleidoscope of peoples, languages and cultures. We can divide the history of Assyria into chronological units (see 4 below), but first let us look at the broad pattern. It was relatively easy for migrant peoples to move long distances into Assyria because physical geography provided few natural barriers that could easily be defended. Cultural, economic and social interchanges of both a warlike and peaceful sort were commonplace in Assyria.

The peaceful interchanges had to do with *trade because from prehistoric times well-established trade routes crossed Assyria. These routes stretched eastward as far as India and possibly China, south as far as southern Arabia, west to Israel, Egypt and Europe, and north to the steppes of central Asia. The trade often was intensive. Assyria, for example, established a

colony of merchants in Anatolia (in present-day Turkey) at Kanesh (modern Kultepe) to trade in tin c. 2000 BCE.

The most dramatic of these interchanges was the mass movement of peoples—a characteristic of the history of the region. Throughout the ancient period there were peoples on the fringes of Assyria watching and waiting for an opportunity to penetrate the richer area of Assyria. Whenever there was any sign of political weakness in the fertile area, large groups began to push in, sometimes peacefully and other times forcefully, and to settle down.

The most important of these migrations were the four penetrations by Semitic-speaking peoples from *Arabia: the Akkadians in the early third millennium BCE, the Amorites about 2000 BCE, the Arameans toward the end of the second millennium BCE, and the Arabs at the beginning of the first millennium BCE. In addition, Indo-European-speaking people from the east pushed into the neighborhood of Assyria in the first half of the second millennium BCE, as well as the Hurrians and Kassites, who came probably from central Asia.

The migrations of peoples and the conduct of trade across the extent of Assyria involved cultural exchanges of all kinds. Thus the ethnic composition and language of Assyria were altered from time to time—mainly Akkadian to Amorite to Aramaic. Over the centuries the steady incursions and alterations gave rise to an Assyrian militaristic state ruled by an absolute monarch.

One social phenomenon that remained constant throughout Assyria's long history was loyalty to the family and the tribe. Trade was, as far as we can tell, never seriously disrupted for any long period of time, nor did the other economic patterns, *agriculture and animal husbandry, change. These two ways of life were the basic elements in the socioeconomic structure of Assyria. Agriculture involved grain (mainly barley), vegetable oil, and vines for grapes and wine. Animal husbandry was concerned largely with sheep and goats, which supported a large and profitable textile industry. Cattle were also bred. But very early on, just after 2000 BCE, booty from military conquests also became a major economic factor in Assyria.

The urbanization of Assyria began in prehistoric times and was a natural development from the agricultural economy of the area, which required a central authority to control irrigation. From this development arose the most important city-states of Assyria: Asshur, Nineveh and Arbela. Calah became a major city only early in the first millennium BCE. Gradually this urbanized and militaristic state under an absolute sovereign became the dominant political power, not only in Mesopotamia, but also throughout western Asia.

4. Political and Military History.

4.1. The Rise of Assyria (to 1076 BCE).

Assyrian history traditionally is divided into three periods: Old Assyrian (to c. 1365 BCE), Middle Assyrian (1364-935 BCE), and Neo-Assyrian (934-612 BCE). Little is known of the Old Assyrian period. As mentioned earlier, an Assyrian merchant colony was established at Kanesh in Anatolia about 2000 BCE, and tens of thousands of cuneiform tablets concerning the trading that went on there have been recovered, and still more are being excavated. The preeminent king of this period was Shamshi-Adad I (c. 1813-1781 BCE), who ruled first from Asshur on the Tigris, later from Shubat-Enlil, and created a proto-empire in northern Mesopotamia that included the great city Mari on the Euphrates. Shamshi-Adad was able to fend off attacks from the south by Hammurabi (c. 1792-1750 BCE), king of Babylonia, until the Assyrian's death and the decline of Assyria until the Middle Assyrian period.

The first great Middle Assyrian king, after a long dark period, was Asshur-uballit I (1364-1329 BCE). He not only assured Assyrian independence from Mitanni, a state west of Assyria, but also ruled Babylonia to the south as a vassal state. During the three-quarters of a century after his death, his successors capitalized on his successes in that they gained control of Mitanni. But they were considerably troubled by the Babylonians, who were ruled by vigorous kings of the Kassite dynasty. This was the situation that Tukulti-Ninurta I (1243-1207 BCE) inherited. With Tukulti-Ninurta I we encounter the most ambitious imperial expansion yet of any Assyrian monarch.

Tukulti-Ninurta campaigned in every possible direction with considerable success. To the west his armies defeated a Hittite bid to seize Mitanni from the Assyrians. The Hittites presumably were emboldened to attempt this because a few decades earlier they had checked the Egyptians at Kadesh (1286 BCE), and now a peace treaty existed between them and Egypt. To the north and east Tukulti-Ninurta marched into the mountains and successfully subdued numerous groups of people that had been a threat to the civilized areas. But his most important military achievement was his conquest of Babylonia to the south. The history of Assyria is permeated with the influence of Babylonia, and whenever Babylonia was independent and hostile, Assyria's military ambitions were seriously inhibited. Tukulti-Ninurta, in conquering Babylonia, gave great impetus to Assyria's rise to power. It also, incidentally, made Babylonian influence on Assyrian culture much more pronounced. His success was short-lived, however. A palace revolt, led by his son, brought an untimely end to his life and was followed by a brief decline of Assyrian power.

The decline was prompted by the mass movements of a variety of people in considerable numbers (c. 1200 BCE): the Dorians' and Ionians' movement into the Greek peninsula and Anatolia, the latter pushing the Hittites into Syria; the Sea Peoples traveling down the Syrian coast, where they troubled the Egyptians in the delta, and some of them, the Philistines, settled on the Palestinian coast; the appearance of the Phrygians (the Mushku, as the Assyrians called them) in Anatolia; the entrance of the Medes and Persians in western Iran; and the spread of the Aramaeans from the Arabian peninsula all over the Fertile Crescent.

Toward the end of the twelfth century BCE, under Tiglath-pileser I (1114-1076 BCE), Assyria again strode confidently forth and became a power of unrivaled strength and size in the Near East. In the military sphere there were three pressing problems with which Tiglath-pileser dealt successfully. These problems were the Mushku (Phrygians), the Aramaeans and the Babylonians. Tiglath-pileser campaigned against the Mushku early in his reign. By conquering and plundering their cities, he effectively reduced this potential danger. The Aramaeans were a large body of Semitic-speaking peoples that, like the Amorites before them, had established themselves in Syria and were now trying to penetrate Mesopotamia. In Syria Tiglath-pileser boasts of having defeated them, and then, according to his account, he proceeded at the head of his army to the coast of the Mediterranean.

The third dangerous opponent was Babylonia. The Kassite dynasty had come to an end a few years before (c. 1156 BCE), and the young and energetic line now in control of the Babylonian throne renewed rivalry with its Assyrian neighbor. Tiglath-pileser emerged the winner from this conflict, and emulating his forefather, Tukulti-Ninurta I, he marched into Babylonia and captured the city Babylon. The Assyrian Empire under this mighty king stretched from the Mediterranean Sea and Anatolia in the west to the Zagros Mountains and the Arabian Gulf in the east. No Asiatic power had ever controlled so much or been so prosperous. Yet Assyria was to rise to even greater heights in the first millennium BCE.

4.2. The Neo-Assyrian Empire (1075-612 BCE).
After the death of Tiglath-pileser I, internal difficulties, coupled with increasing pressure from the Aramaeans, had brought a period of darkness. The Aramaeans remained a thorn in the Assyrian side in the first millennium BCE, and they left an indelible stamp not only on Assyria, but also on all of western Asia. Their language and alphabetic writing system, which was written on papyrus, gradually became the means of international communication, replacing most of the indigenous tongues and modes of writing, including Akkadian and the cuneiform script. This is unfortunate from the point of view of the modern historian, for their chosen writing material, papyrus, disintegrates in the Assyrian climate, unlike cuneiform on clay, which is durable.

A fact that made the Aramaean problem pressing for Assyria at the beginning of the first millennium BCE was that these people were on both sides of Assyria. They were established not only in Syria, but also in Babylonia. In the latter area a curious mixture of native Babylonians and freshly arrived Aramaeans managed, on occasion, to unite and present a formidable front to their northern neighbors, the Assyrians. Successive Assyrian kings in the tenth century BCE came face to face with the task of defeating these people. At times their task was made easier by new incursions of Aramaeans, as well as of other nomadic groups, into Babylonia, which resulted in internecine warfare with the dread results of plague and famine. If Assyria had a hard struggle in the tenth century BCE to reassert itself, Babylonia had an even harder one simply trying to remain a state in its own right.

The fortunes of Assyria improved in the ninth century BCE, and the Neo-Assyrian Empire became a reality. There are in fact two phases in the history of the Neo-Assyrian Empire, separated by a brief period of eclipse. The first phase can be conveniently called the Calah period, named after the new capital of the Assyrian Empire; it covers one century (883-783 BCE). The two most important monarchs of this period were Ashurnasirpal II (883-859 BCE) and his son Shalmaneser III (858-824 BCE).

Shalmaneser III was the first Assyrian king to concentrate an exceptional amount of energy on the west, and this brought him into contact with Israel. Beginning in 853 BCE, he crossed the Euphrates and marched south along the Levantine coast. On this occasion he encountered the Damascus Coalition. This alliance consisted of Adad-idri (called Hadad-ezer in the Bible) of Damascus, Irhuleni of Hamath (these two cities being the leaders), Ahab of Israel, Gindibu the Arab, Byblos, Egypt, Matinu-ba'al of Arvad, Irqantu, Usanatu, Adunu-ba'al of Shianu, Ba'asa of Bit-Ruhubi and "the Ammonite." The coalition made its stand at Qarqar on the Orontes. Shalmaneser claims to have beaten them and to have slaughtered and plundered as the enemy fled the scene of battle. One must always be skeptical of Assyrian claims, and the real outcome of the battle at Qarqar is debatable. Unfortunately, we have no other source for this event. It is not mentioned in the Bible, despite the Assyrian record that Ahab of Israel was there. Whatever the outcome, the Damascus Coalition again made a stand against Shalmaneser in the following years of 849, 848 and 845 BCE. On all of these occasions the Assyrian claimed a victory, but if that had been so, why did Shalmaneser have to return to fight the coalition again and again? It is known, however, that Israel volunteered submission to Shalmaneser III, presumably in 841 BCE; on the Black Obelisk, Jehu (called Yaua in the Assyrian inscription) is portrayed kneeling before the king.

Superficially, the military conquests of Ashurnasirpal II and Shalmaneser III appear to be the same as those of their eminent forefather, Tiglath-pileser I, for the Assyrian Empire in both periods stretched from Anatolia and Syria to the Zagros Mountains and the Arabian Gulf. But there was significant difference in that beginning with Ashurnasirpal, the military was more systematically organized and therefore more effective. Campaigns were conducted annually rather than sporadically, and archery, chariots and siege engines were used with devastating effect. The cruelty for which the Assyrians were to become notorious, especially in the Bible, was also more pronounced, with the calculated result that numerous small states were intimidated into voluntary submission. The Assyrian army combined efficiency with bloodthirsty methods to gain for itself the doubtful honor of being the best military machine the world had yet seen.

Scarcely had Assyria regained its former preeminence, however, when it almost lost it. The reasons were internal and external. An endemic weakness in the Assyrian state was the absolute position of the monarch, whose office was hereditary. As long as there was a forceful character on the Assyrian throne, Assyria could assert itself, but as soon as the royal arm was weak, Assyria was in serious trouble. This happened in the latter part of the reign of Shalmaneser III (858-824 BCE). As time went by, the aging monarch entrusted more and more of his powers to subordinates. This led to friction, rivalry and eventually civil war. Out of the chaos emerged Shamshi-Adad V (823-811 BCE), but in the process of gaining the throne he had been forced to make an ignominious treaty with the Babylonians, and Babylonian influence on Assyrian monarchs was to prevail for some decades. But even more disturbing for Assyria, the period of confusion had allowed an entirely new power, Urartu, to flex its muscles and, from its base in the Armenian mountains to the north of Assyria, make serious inroads into the Assyrian heartland. For over a century (c. 823-714 BCE) Urartu remained poised on the borders of Assyria, and for a portion of that time the extent of its control, from Syria and the Taurus range east as far as Lake Urmia, exceeded that of Assyria. The Urartian Empire spread like an umbrella over the Neo-Assyrian Empire.

The final phase of the Neo-Assyrian Empire is the one that won it eternal fame, and is the one in which it was most in contact with biblical lands. The period encompassed a little over a century (744-612 BCE), but during this time the five most important Assyrian monarchs, Tiglath-pileser III (744-727), Shalmaneser V (726-722), Sargon II (721-705), Sennacherib (704-681), Esarhaddon (680-669) and Ashurbanipal (668-631), conquered western Iran, Urartu, Babylonia, Syria, Israel and Judah, eastern Anatolia, and Egypt (*see* History of Israel 5: Assyrian Period).

There is a theory (see Cogan) that Assyrian expansion went through various phases, with exile being the final resort. Before the land was actually incorporated into Assyria proper, it went from vassaldom to an intermediate sort of client kingdom, and finally to provincial annexation. For some, this hypothesis explains events of the Syro-Ephraimite crisis (735-732 BCE) quite well, when the northern kingdom of Israel went into the second level of imperial control, and Judah went at the same time into the first level, vassaldom.

It was Shalmaneser V who laid siege to *Samaria, capital of Israel, as narrated in 2 Kings 17:1-41; 18:1-12 (cf. 2 Esdr 13:40). The Israelites were carried off to live in exile in Assyria and Media. In their place the king of Assyria settled in Israel people from various cities such as Hamat in Syria, and Babylon and Cutha in Babylonia. Samaria fell in 722 BCE, the year of Shalmaneser V's death and the accession of Sargon II. Thus the leading of the Israelites into exile by the Assyrians was carried out probably during the reign of Sargon.

Another deed noteworthy for its biblical connection is the third campaign (701 BCE) of Sennacherib, which was directed against Syria and Palestine. One of the most important events on this campaign was the battle of Eltekeh, in which the Assyrian fought against a coalition including *Ekron (called Amqarruna by Sennacherib), Egypt and Nubia. The Assyrians, naturally, claimed a victory. The Assyrians then went on to lay siege to *Jerusalem, which was ruled by *Hezekiah. This much is clear from Assyrian and biblical sources (2 Kings 18:13—19:37; 2 Chron 32:1-21). The Bible adds that while the Assyrian army was besieging Jerusalem, Sennacherib, who was at Libnah, sent his *rab-shākeh* ("chief cupbearer," a senior officer in the Assyrian army) to harangue the people of Jerusalem who were sitting on the wall, urging them to abandon their reliance on Egypt and surrender. But Hezekiah refused to give in. The biblical narrative continues: "That night the angel of the Lord went forth and slew a hundred and eighty-five thousand in the camp of the Assyrians." It goes on to say that Sennacherib returned to Nineveh, where he was slain by his sons. Sennacherib's account, however, has none of this; after saying that he laid siege to Jerusalem, he abruptly states that he received extensive booty from Hezekiah in Nineveh. Surprisingly, he says nothing about the outcome of the siege. This great disparity between the biblical and Assyrian accounts has been a conundrum in Assyrian history for a long time. Some scholars try to resolve it by attempting to blend the accounts together, while other scholars argue that there must have been a second campaign late in Sennacherib's reign. The latter scholars assign the successful siege of Lachish, known from the famous reliefs found at Nineveh, to this second campaign.

The political success of these Neo-Assyrian kings is to be attributed mainly to further improvement of the military machine and a serious concern with the administration of the empire. Moreover, to eliminate the possibility of revolt in their conquered territories, the Assyrians resorted to extensive transportation of conquered peoples. This practice had been known before, but it was used sparingly, as, for example, by Tukulti-Ninurta I, Tiglath-pileser I and Ashurnasirpal II. The later Neo-Assyrian kings regularly removed refractory groups from their homelands and settled them in undeveloped regions where they were put to work farming or near cities where they performed forced labor on great building projects. The most famous example of this practice is known from the later period of the Neo-Babylonian Empire when Nebuchadnezzar II (604-562 BCE), following the example of the Assyrians, transported large numbers of Judeans to Babylonia. In administration the Neo-Assyrians were responsible for forming provinces with governors and resident garrisons. Such organization was far superior to the previous custom of annual razzias (raids) to collect tribute. Although the Assyrian provincial administration was fairly rudimentary, it provided the foundation for the later Persian, Hellenistic and Roman systems.

As the power of Assyria grew during the seventh century BCE, and as it more and more victimized its neighbors, the more these suppressed people began to draw together to form a united front against the giant. Such alliances usually were tenuous and short-lived, but occasionally they were sufficient to check Assyrian expansion, and one alliance (Babylonians, Medes and probably the Scythians) finally brought about Assyria's downfall. In the west,

Egypt, before it was conquered by Assyria, stirred up trouble in Palestine to try to keep Assyria occupied there. The disastrous results of this policy for the Judeans, who were caught in the middle, led the prophet Isaiah to warn his compatriots, "Egypt's help is worthless and empty" (Is 30:7). Nevertheless, the policy saved the Egyptians for a time, and it was only with Esarhaddon (680-669 BCE) that the first Assyrian inroads into Egypt were made. In the east the Elamites and the Medes at various times allied themselves with the Babylonians, to the great distress of the Assyrians. Indeed, the Assyrians never did devise a satisfactory method of administering Babylonia, and the Assyrian military presence in southern Mesopotamia was generally high during the seventh century BCE. It is interesting to note that at one point the Babylonians, led by a certain Merodach-baladan II, actually attempted to weld a grand alliance between east and west that included making overtures to the Judeans to join them against the Assyrians (2 Kings 20:12-19; Is 39:1-8). This maneuver caused Sennacherib (704-681 BCE), Assyria's king at the time, no end of trouble. Toward the end of the seventh century BCE, Assyria, weakened by the mounting resistance and drain on its resources, finally succumbed to a coalition with amazing rapidity. The forces of Babylonia, Media and the Scythians combined and destroyed the Assyrian Empire within less than two decades. The highlight of this swift downfall was the capture and sack of Nineveh, the Assyrian capital, in 612 BCE. The ancient world, which had suffered under the might of Assyria for so long, reverberated with the joyous news. The prophet Nahum proclaimed, "And all who look on you will shrink from you and say, 'Wasted is Nineveh; who will bemoan her?'" (Nahum 3:7). But their cause for celebration was to be short-lived; Babylonia soon moved in and took over the former territories of the Neo-Assyrian Empire and created the Neo-Babylonian Empire.

5. Culture.

Assyrian culture was, apart from a few distinctive features, intertwined with Babylonian culture. The most distinctive characteristic of the Assyrians was their attitude about *war. For the Assyrians, war was a way of life, and their whole state, from the monarch down to the lowest peasant, was molded along military lines. For the Babylonians war was a necessity of survival but not a subject to dwell on. While the Assyrians boast constantly in their inscriptions of military accomplishments, the Babylonians rarely mention them and instead describe in detail their religious and building activities. Since the Assyrians devoted the majority of their time and energy to war and building, they had little opportunity to develop themselves culturally in the narrower sense of that word. Instead, the Assyrians were prone to borrow from the Babylonians, particularly in the realm of literature. The term *literature* is used here in a broad sense to include scientific, religious and other written treatises. Thus, as curious as it may be, the greatest repository of Babylonian literature was not in Babylonia but in Assyria. The last great Assyrian monarch, Ashurbanipal (668-631 BCE), sent emissaries throughout Babylonia to collect every scrap of Babylonian literary material that they could find. These tablets, or copies of them, were brought back to the capital at Nineveh, where they were carefully kept as a library. Here they remained until c. 1850 CE, when they were discovered by the English and gradually removed to the British Museum. This collection, created by Assyrians, is, ironically, still the major source for our knowledge of Babylonian culture.

A brief description of the contents of Ashurbanipal's library will provide an excellent survey of the most important aspects of Assyro-Babylonian culture. The largest group of texts concerns divination. The Assyrians and Babylonians believed that signs of coming events surrounded them, and to predict the future one needed to learn how to read these signs. The signs could take innumerable forms, and so the diviners looked for them in the movement of the stars, the activities of animals, dreams, cloud formations, unusual births, etc. The most popular forms of divination were extispicy (the examination of a sheep's entrails, especially the liver) and astrology. Extispicy spread from Assyria and Babylonia throughout the Near East, and its influence is found even among the ancient Etruscans in Italy. Astrology went even farther, for, by means of the Greeks, it found its way into the mainstream of Western civilization, and its popularity today is evident from the horoscopes published in daily newspapers. A voluminous amount of inscribed tablets in Ashurbanipal's library are treatises drawn up to serve as reference works for those who practiced divination.

The next most important group in Ashurbanipal's magnificent collection is lexical material. From the earliest days of cuneiform writing, scribes compiled lists of words. These lists were in fact dictionaries written to aid the scribe in his everyday work. There are lists of names of professions, plants, stones, animals, legal terms, grammatical terms, divine names, etc. There are also dictionaries giving the meanings of Sumerian words in Akkadian, as well as lists of cuneiform signs with possible readings. These lists, drawn up for the use of the ancient scribes, are invaluable tools for the modern scholar.

In Ashurbanipal's library, after omen and lexical texts, there is no single group that is particularly large. The remaining texts fall into many different categories: literary, historical, scientific, religious, magical, etc. Assyrian literary compositions—literary in the narrow sense of the word—are rare, but there are many types of Babylonian literary compositions: myths (such as the creation of the world), legends (such as the flood stories), epics (such as the Gilgamesh Epic), hymns, prayers, etc.

Only limited quantities of historical works are known from Ashurbanipal's library, but many texts of a historical nature are known outside of the confines of his library. The Assyrians wrote a vast number of royal inscriptions that were essentially commemorative inscriptions composed in connection with military and building (temples and palaces) activities. Also the Assyrians compiled a few chronicles, but the Babylonians were responsible for writing many more important chronicles.

6. Religion and Magic.

Assyrian religion, like Assyrian culture, was strongly influenced by Babylonian religion. An outstanding feature is polytheism: the Assyrians, like the Babylonians, had numerous gods, but not all were identical between the two civilizations. Lists of gods in hierarchical order were compiled, and some of them provide the Assyrian equivalent of Babylonian or Sumerian deities. The religion was cultic, and the temple was the focal point. The chief Assyrian god was Asshur, and his main temple was at the city of Asshur. Under him there were a number of important deities, such as Ishtar, Nergal, Ninurta, Shamash and Adad. Assyrian religion also embraced some Babylonian deities, such as Marduk and Nabu. The most important religious festival in Assyria was the *Tākultu* (lit., "banquet"), which included the New Year's celebration *(Akītu)* and the gods' granting the power to rule for another year to the reigning monarch. The god Asshur, the national god of Assyria, is never mentioned in the Bible, although there are a few rare references to Assyrian religion.

Witchcraft and *magic were endemic, and although much of such lore would have been oral rather than written, a considerable amount of textual material has been recovered. This is because there was a strong element of magic and ritual in the great state cults, where there were scribes to record these things. There was a variety of priests and incantation experts, their activities ranging from performing rituals in the temples to casting out evil spirits from an afflicted individual. Regular offerings of food and drink to the gods in their shrines were an essential part of the cult.

7. Monarchy.

The monarch in Assyria had absolute power, and this institution was an indigenous development in the early years of Assyrian history; there were no foreign influences that brought this about. The only authority to whom the Assyrian sovereign was responsible was the god Asshur, and this is evident already in the early period, when a major title of the king is "viceregent of the god Asshur." There were, nevertheless, some natural checks to his power. Under no circumstances could he do anything that appeared to go against the god Asshur's will, and thus a common phrase in Assyrian royal inscriptions is "By the command of the god Asshur I did . . ." Another natural check was the Assyrian nobility; the king had to be careful not to offend the ancient influential and wealthy families and tribes of Assyria. Indeed, during one period in Assyrian history (c. 782-745 BCE) a few leading members of the nobility achieved extensive power and had only a tenuous respect for the Assyrian king. For example, Shamshi-ilu, the "field marshal" *(turtannu;* called *tartān* in the Bible), gained such influence in the state that he personally led Assyrian military campaigns, including the capture of Damascus, while paying only lip service to the king, Adad-nirari III (810-783 BCE). Yet another check was legal precedent, such as the traditional rights of individuals, property ownership, and traditional tax exemptions granted to privileged cities.

The Assyrian monarch was not regarded as a god, although the theory of a divine monarch had had some vogue in earlier cultures in southern Mesopotamia among the Sumerians and Babylonians. There is some evidence that in the last centuries of Assyrian history an attempt was being made to deify the king, but it never came to fruition. Under the absolute monarch were a number of levels, in diminishing authority, of state officials who usually held both a civil role and a military role, as Assyria was a militaristic state. An important feature of Assyrian thought about the monarchy is that the sovereignty passed on from father to eldest son, and that there was never a break in this descent. It is well known, however, from recovered records, that this was not always the case. There were rebellions from time to time that put someone on the throne who was not the eldest son of the king, and occasionally only distantly related to him.

The Assyrian king was commander-in-chief of the armed forces and often led them in person on campaign. He lived the life of a soldier and ruled his people with the might of his weapon. He was supreme legislator, legislation being issued by royal decree, and he was the high priest. In theory he also owned all the land of Assyria, although, as mentioned before, he had to respect traditional land ownership by individuals and institutions such as temples.

Today there is a large population group living in the area of ancient Assyria that speaks *Aramaic, the language spoken by the ancient Assyrians sometime before the fall of Nineveh. The modern group believes that they are the descendants of the ancient Assyrians, and they call themselves *Assyrians*. They are Christians with ancient churches and monasteries, and they revere Thomas as their patron saint.

In conclusion, a dominant characteristic of Assyrian civilization, in addition to militarism, is conservatism. Some new ideas, some innovations, appear throughout Assyria's long history, but these are all the more noteworthy because of their rarity. In general, the Assyrians preferred to preserve, even if in a modified form, the traditions and practices of the past. The modern world owes a great debt to the Assyrians for preserving this heritage, some important parts of which have been passed on through subsequent civilizations to the present day.

See also BABYLONIA, BABYLONIANS; HISTORY

OF ISRAEL 5: ASSYRIAN PERIOD; NON-ISRAELITE WRITTEN SOURCES: ASSYRIAN; PERSIA, PERSIANS.

BIBLIOGRAPHY. **W. Andrae,** *Die wiedererstandene Assur* (2d ed.; Munich: Beck, 1977); **R. D. Barnett,** *Sculptures from the North Palace of Ashurbanipal at Nineveh* (London: British Museum Publications, 1976); **R. D. Barnett and M. Falkner,** *The Sculptures of Assur-nasir-apli II (883-859 BC), Tiglath-pileser III (745-727 BC), Esarhaddon (681-669 BC), from the Central and South-West Palaces at Nimrud* (London: Trustees of the British Museum, 1962); **R. D. Barnett and A. Lorenzini,** *Assyrian Sculpture in the British Museum* (Toronto: McClelland and Stewart, 1975); **R. D. Barnett et al.,** *Sculptures from the Southwest Palace of Sennacherib at Nineveh* (2 vols.; London: British Museum Press, 1998); *CAH²ᐟ³* 1/2-3/2; **M. Cogan,** *Imperialism and Religion: Assyria, Judah, and Israel in the Eighth and Seventh Centuries B.C.E.* (SBLMS 19; Missoula, MT: Scholars Press, 1974); **D. Collon,** *First Impressions: Cylinder Seals in the Ancient Near East* (London: British Museum Press, 1987); **S. Dalley and J. N. Postgate,** *The Tablets from Fort Shalmaneser* (Cuneiform Texts from Nimrud 3; Oxford: British School of Archaeology in Iraq, 1984); **A. K. Grayson,** *Assyrian Royal Inscriptions* (2 vols.; Wiesbaden: Harrassowitz, 1972-1976); **A. K. Grayson et al.,** ed., *Royal Inscriptions of Mesopotamia: Assyrian Periods* (3 vols.; Toronto: University of Toronto Press, 1987-1996); **M. T. Larsen,** *The Old Assyrian City-State and Its Colonies* (Copenhagen Studies in Assyriology 4; Copenhagen: Akademisk Forlag, 1976); **D. D. Luckenbill,** *Ancient Records of Assyria and Babylonia* (2 vols.; Chicago: University of Chicago Press, 1926-1927); **M. E. L. Mallowan,** *Nimrud and Its Remains,* vols. 1-2 (London: Collins, 1966); **D. Oates,** *Studies in the Ancient History of Northern Iraq* (London: University of Oxford Press, 1968); **A. T. Olmstead,** *History of Assyria* (Chicago: University of Chicago Press, 1923); **S. M. Paley,** *King of the World: Ashur-nasir-pal II of Assyria 883-859 B.C.* (New York: Brooklyn Museum, 1976); **S. Parpola et al.,** ed., *State Archives of Assyria* (Helsinki: University of Helsinki Press, 1987-); **J. N. Postgate,** *Taxation and Conscription in the Assyrian Empire* (Studia Pohl, Series Maior 3; Rome: Pontifical Biblical Institute Press, 1974); **J. M. Russell,** *Sennacherib's Palace Without Rival at Nineveh* (Chicago: University of Chicago Press, 1991); **S. Yamada,** *The Construction of the Assyrian Empire: A Historical Study of the Inscriptions of Shalmanesar III (859-824 B.C.) Relating to His Campaigns to the West* (CHANE 3; Leiden: E. J. Brill, 2000).

A. K. Grayson

ASSYRIAN EPONYM CHRONICLES. See NON-ISRAELITE WRITTEN SOURCES: ASSYRIAN.

ASSYRIAN EPONYM LISTS. See NON-ISRAELITE WRITTEN SOURCES: ASSYRIAN.

ASSYRIAN KING LISTS. See NON-ISRAELITE WRITTEN SOURCES: ASSYRIAN.

ATHALIAH. See HISTORY OF ISRAEL 5: ASSYRIAN PERIOD; OMRI DYNASTY.

ATHIRAT. See CANAANITE GODS AND RELIGION.

ATONEMENT. See FORGIVENESS.

AZATIWADA. See NON-ISRAELITE WRITTEN SOURCES: SYRO-PALESTINIAN.

B

BAAL. *See* CANAAN, CANAANITES; CANAANITE GODS AND RELIGION; GOD.

BABYLONIA, BABYLONIANS

The term *Babylonia* refers to the region lying in the center and south of Iraq in antiquity, and the term *Babylonians* indicates the people who inhabited it and shared its culture, language and religion. Although these two terms derive from the ancient native name of the city of Babylon (*bābilu*), concepts such as "Babylonia" and "Babylonians," in the sense we understand them in modern scholarship, were not coined by the Babylonians. They find no exact equivalents in Akkadian, the Semitic language spoken in Iraq and parts of Syria from the third to the first millennia BCE. In Akkadian the adjective *Babylonian* (attested in the forms *bābilû* and *bābilayu*) referred only to things and people originating from the city of Babylon. Therefore a "Babylonian" was a resident of Babylon. Residents of Nippur or Uruk would not have called themselves "Babylonians," although both cities were located in Babylonia. They would have considered themselves "Nippurians" and "Urukeans." Moreover, the word *Babylonia* did not exist in the Akkadian language. The geographic reality "Babylonia" usually was expressed in Akkadian by the pair "Sumer and Akkad," "Sumer" referring to the southernmost part of Iraq, between Nippur and the Persian Gulf, and "Akkad" to central Iraq north of Nippur, where the city of Babylon was located. The term *Akkad* sometimes was used alone to refer to all of Babylonia, and starting in the late Bronze Age the term *Karduniash*, which first appeared under the Kassite rulers of Babylon, appears to have had a similar meaning. After Babylonia fell under foreign rule with the conquest of the Neo-Babylonian Empire by Cyrus the Great in 539

BCE, the Persian rulers of Babylonia began to refer to all of Babylonia by the term *Babirus*. This was the first instance of a term based on the name of the city Babylon being used as a general name for southern and central Iraq. Later on, under the Greco-Macedonian rulers of the Seleucid dynasty, the Greeks coined the terms *Babylonia* and *Babylonian* to refer to the region and its people, which they perceived as a distinct nation within their empire. Therefore *Babylonia* and *Babylonians* were largely concepts created by outsiders. Yet it is clear that the Babylonians fully realized that they shared a common civilization. Babylonian identity gradually took shape over a very long period of time to become one of the last two manifestations of the civilization of ancient Mesopotamia, the other being Assyria.

1. Origins of Babylon
2. The Amorites and the First Dynasty of Babylon
3. Emergence of a Babylonian Identity
4. The Kassites
5. The Second Dynasty of Isin and the Triumph of the God Marduk
6. Classical Babylonian Civilization
7. Aramaeans and Chaldeans
8. Assyrian Interlude
9. The Neo-Babylonian Empire
10. Late Babylonian Civilization
11. Defining Babylonian Identity

1. Origins of Babylon.

During the third millennium BCE Mesopotamian civilization flourished mainly in central and southern Iraq, with its main geographic area divided along linguistic lines: Sumer in the south, Akkad in the north. Sumerian city-states prevailed for a long time, but hegemony passed to Akkad in the second half of the twenty-fourth century BCE when Sargon (reigned 2334-2279 BCE) established the seat of his power in the city of Agade and founded a dynasty that was to rule for two centuries. The earliest mention of Babylon occurs in the name of a regnal year of the fifth ruler of that dynasty, Šar-kali-šarri (2217-2193 BCE): "The year when [Šar-k]ali-šarri laid [the foundations] of the temple of the goddess Anunītum and of the temple of the god Ilaba in Babylon, and captured Šarlak, king of Gutium." The Gutians, who inhabited the mountainous regions east of Akkad, eventually played a decisive role in the demise of the Sargonic dynasty. Hegemony went back south with the third dynasty of Ur (2112-2004 BCE), which reaffirmed the primacy of Sumerian culture. Its sovereigns ruled an empire with Sumer and Akkad as its core area. Their influence also extended over additional territories in the mountainous areas east of Mesopotamia that formed a more loosely controlled network of tributaries and vassal states. The core area was divided into some twenty provinces, each headed by a governor (*ensi*). The fact that Babylon was the seat of an *ensi* indicates its growing significance at that time.

2. The Amorites and the First Dynasty of Babylon.

At the end of the third millennium BCE the empire of the third dynasty of Ur crumbled under the conjugated assault of hostile powers located on the Iranian plateau and of the Amorites, a new wave of Semitic invaders who poured massively into Mesopotamia and settled important areas of Sumer and Akkad. During the century that followed the fall of Ur, a new dynasty ruling from Isin south of Nippur tried to maintain the administrative and cultural heritage of the Ur III empire. Yet its power soon began to wane, and by the beginning of the nineteenth century BCE the old pattern of competing city-states had re-emerged in Sumer and Akkad, except that this time most of the new dynasties were of Amorite origin. One such dynasty was founded by Sumula-el, who seized power at Babylon in 1880 BCE and reigned until 1845 BCE. His successors Sabium (1844-1831 BCE), *Apil-Sîn* (1830-1813 BCE) and *Sîn-muballiṭ* (1812-1793 BCE) carefully consolidated their power in the vicinity of Babylon and central Akkad, making strategic alliances with other dynasts. By the time of the accession of Hammurabi (1792-1750 BCE) the

mosaic of small city-states had been replaced by significantly larger territorial states vying with each other for hegemony over Sumer and Akkad, and even beyond. The spirit of this new era is encapsulated in an oft-quoted letter from a high official of the city of Mari in the Middle Euphrates region: "No king is truly powerful just by himself. Ten or fifteen kings follow Hammurabi, lord of Babylon; as many follow Rim-Sîn, lord of Larsa; as many Ibal-pi-el, lord of Eshnunna; as many Amut-pi-el, lord of Qatna. Twenty kings follow Yarim-Lim, lord of Yamhad (Aleppo)." Eventually it was Hammurabi who emerged triumphant from this international contest of military strength and diplomatic skill. With the conquest of Larsa, Eshnunna and Mari in the last part of his reign he brought under his dominion a larger portion of Mesopotamia than the third dynasty of Ur had controlled. The First Dynasty of Babylon had reached its apex. Levantine states such as Yamhad and Qatna, however, did not fall under Babylonian control.

The kingdom assembled by Hammurabi could not be maintained very long. Already under Samsu-iluna (1749-1712 BCE) the edifice began to crack. His ninth regnal year commemorates armed incursions by a new enemy, the Kassites. Soon secessionist movements arose in the south, first at Larsa under a king named Rim-Sîn (II), then under a new dynasty that claimed control of Sumer and was remembered in later chronicles as the First Dynasty of the Sealand. The south also experienced at the same time a severe economic collapse that forced evacuation of part of its population to Akkad. For the remainder of its existence the First Dynasty of Babylon ruled essentially over Akkad, with a northern extension in the middle Euphrates region. The four successors of Samsu-iluna—Abi-ešuh (1711-1684 BCE), Ammi-ditana (1683-1647 BCE), Ammi-ṣaduqa (1646-1626 BCE), and Samsu-ditana (1625-1595 BCE)—almost exclusively commemorate pious foundations and public works in their year names. A Hittite raid on Babylon in 1595 BCE brought their rule to a close.

3. Emergence of a Babylonian Identity.

The three centuries of Amorite rule in Babylon were a momentous period culturally, during which the old Sumero-Akkadian traditions gradually were transformed into a new phase of Mesopotamian civilization that can truly be called

Babylonian. One important change occurred in the linguistic area. The influx of Semitic-speaking Amorites in the south after the fall of Ur accelerated the demise of Sumerian as spoken language. In spite of this, Sumerian retained its position as the language of scribal schools, literature and royal inscriptions for a period of two more centuries. But all this ended when Babylon became the sole power under Hammurabi. He and his successors favored the rise of Akkadian as the dominant literary and administrative language of Sumer and Akkad. The cuneiform script was reformed and better adapted to the Old Babylonian dialect of Akkadian. Schools sponsored a new literature written in a high poetic form of Akkadian, the so-called Hymnic-Epic Dialect, and gradually discarded much of the traditional corpus of Sumerian literature. Legal and administrative texts and letters now were cast exclusively in the Old Babylonian dialect, and even royal inscriptions began to use primarily Akkadian, while bilingual editions of them were made in which the Sumerian version was clearly translated from the Semitic original.

Above all, the First Dynasty laid the foundations for the political primacy of Babylon. The time-honored pattern of competing city-states was definitively over. This political shift had a considerable impact on religion and ideology. Like all ancient civilizations, Mesopotamia was a cosmological civilization. The state was believed to be coextensive with the cosmos. The capital city or the main religious metropolis was viewed as world center and cosmic axis. Standing at the apex of the social pyramid, the king was considered to be a reflection of the demiurge, divine hero and king of the gods, and in that role he was responsible for preserving the cosmic and political order. In Sumer and Akkad, Nippur was viewed as cosmic axis, and its main god, Enlil, assisted by his son Ninurta, acted as king of the gods and divine hero. Marduk, the city-god of Babylon, was for a long time a deity of no significance except locally. However, the ascent of Babylon to hegemony suddenly propelled him to the summit of the pantheon. Already in the prologue of the famous Law Code of Hammurabi he is given the same powers as the god Enlil, the *Enlilūtu* ("Enlilship"), and a hymn to Marduk with prayer for king Abi-ešuḫ states that Enlil gave Marduk the kingship of heaven and earth. This was the starting point of an ideological shift from Nippur to Babylon as cosmic center

that was fully achieved only in the latter part of the second millennium BCE and was an essential component in the creation of a new Babylonian identity.

4. The Kassites.
After the demise of the First Dynasty, an obscure period followed, during which the political vacuum was filled by a new dynasty of Kassite origin. The Kassites came from the Zagros Mountains east of the Tigris and had already clashed with the Babylonian armies on a couple of occasions in the preceding two centuries. Kassite workers and mercenaries often are mentioned in documents from the Old Babylonian period. Their language is known only from bilingual vocabularies, personal names and occasional Kassite words appearing in Akkadian texts, mostly related to horse training and chariot warfare. They did not settle massively in Babylonia, which kept more or less the same ethnolinguistic composition that it had during the Old Babylonian period. The Kassite Dynasty provided Babylonia with remarkable stability and prosperity until its demise in 1157 BCE, four hundred years after its rise to power, making it the longest-lived dynasty in the history of Babylon.

The rise of Marduk continued under the Kassites. He is one of the most frequently encountered gods in personal names, and also the main deity invoked in prayers inscribed on cylinder seals from that period. The ruling dynasty, however, appears to have espoused a conservative policy favoring Nippur and the god Enlil, even adopting an artificial form of Sumerian for its official inscriptions. Although Babylon remained the capital during the entire duration of their rule, the Kassite kings created a second capital at Dur-Kurigalzu in central Akkad, about twenty miles west of modern Baghdad. There they built palaces as well as temples dedicated to the gods of Nippur, mainly Enlil and Ninlil, their son Ninurta, and his wife Gula. Devotion to the Nippur pantheon is also evidenced by the fact that some Kassite kings bear names honoring the god Enlil (Kadašman-Enlil, Kudur-Enlil, Enlil-nādin-šumi), while only one king bears a Marduk name. The city of Nippur enjoyed a prominent status. Its governor, the *šandabakku*, acted almost as second-in-rank after the king. Clearly the official policy of the Kassite Dynasty was to recognize the preeminence of Enlil as leader of the pantheon and the role of Nippur as cosmological center, while recognizing at the same time the preeminence of Marduk as main god of Babylon.

5. The Second Dynasty of Isin and the Triumph of the God Marduk.

All this was to change under the Second Dynasty of Isin (1157-1026 BCE). Although probably they originated from Isin, just south of Nippur, those kings ruled from Babylon. Of the eleven members of that dynasty, no fewer than six bear names honoring Marduk, and two honoring his son, the god Nabû, against one Enlil name and one Ninurta name. The shift from an Enlil-Ninurta to a Marduk-Nabû theology is clear. The reign of Nebuchadnezzar I (Nabû-kudurri-uṣur [reigned 1125-1104 BCE]) was a major turning point in this process. On the occasion of a victorious military campaign to the neighboring kingdom of Elam, he triumphantly brought back to Babylon the statue of Marduk that the Elamites had previously carried off to their capital, Susa. On this occasion he sponsored the redaction of compositions exalting the god Marduk, who is attributed for the first time the epithet "king of the gods." It is also generally believed that *Enuma Elish,* the Babylonian creation epic, was composed during his reign. The Epic is truly a foundational document of Babylonian identity. It tells how Marduk was selected by the ancestral gods to battle Tiamat, the personification of the primeval chaos. After his victory he creates cosmic order out of her dismembered body and selects Babylon as cosmological center and axis of the world. The gods elevate Marduk to the status of king over them, and the epic ends with a long hymn of glorification celebrating his universal power and his fifty names. One of the main theological points of the epic is that Marduk usurps the position of Enlil as king of the gods, and that of his son Ninurta as conqueror of the primeval chaos. Marduk's elevation to the position of Enlil was completed by the reign of Simbar-Shipak (1025-1008 BCE), the first king who reigned after the Second Dynasty of Isin. An inscription of that king recording the rededication of the throne of the god Enlil in the Ekurigigal temple at Nippur ends with a clear statement that it is the god Marduk who sits on that throne, not the god Enlil. More than a simple syncretism, this inscription proposes an outright usurpation of Enlil's identity by the chief god of Babylon. The status of Babylon as world center and cosmic axis was now enshrined in the Mesopotamian tradition.

6. Classical Babylonian Civilization.

The Kassite and Isin II period was one of consolidation for Babylonian civilization. Much of the scholarship and literature found in official and private cuneiform libraries of the first millennium BCE finds its roots in developments that took place during the latter part of the second millennium BCE. The schools of the Kassite period created a literary form of Akkadian, the Standard Babylonian dialect, which was largely modeled on the Hymnic Epic and Old Babylonian dialects. Standard Babylonian became the language of literature, scholarly texts and royal inscriptions in both Babylonia and Assyria for the next one thousand years, and it was instrumental in enhancing the prestige of Babylonian scholarship and belles lettres. Classical Babylonian literature reached new heights with compositions such as *Ludlul bēl nēmeqi,* "I will praise the Lord of Wisdom," often compared to the book of Job in its illustration of the problem of theodicy. Its opening hymn to Marduk proclaims the inscrutability of the divine will and the dual nature of the god as savior and chastiser. This was also a creative period in the domain of science and scholarship. The later tradition especially remembered the figure of Esagil-kīn-apli, an exorcist and scholar who lived during the reign of king Adad-apla-iddina (1068-1047 BCE). A catalog known from several manuscripts attributes to him the organization of the curriculum of the *ašiputu,* or "craft of the exorcist," one of the main intellectual and scientific disciplines of late Babylonian scholarship. He may have been identical with Esagil-kīna-ubbib, author of the *Babylonian Theodicy,* a classical piece of wisdom literature reflecting on the problem of evil and divine abandonment (*see* Non-Israelite Written Sources: Babylonian).

7. Aramaeans and Chaldeans.

The equilibrium reached by Babylonian civilization under the Second Dynasty of Isin and its sense of cosmological centrality were soon to be severely disrupted during the long period of turmoil and economic regression that accompanied the transition from the late Bronze Age to the Iron Age at the end of the second millennium BCE. The near collapse of the Assyrian and Babylonian states facilitated incursions from the outside as new waves of Semitic invaders poured into Mesopotamia. The two principal groups that settled in Babylonia were the Aramaeans and the Chaldeans. However, documentation is so sparse between around 1100 and 750 BCE that almost nothing is known of the early history of their settlement. Inscriptions dated to the middle of the eighth century BCE discovered in the Middle Euphrates region mention that groups of Aramaean nomads still posed a serious threat at that time. Inscriptions of the Assyrian king Tiglath-pileser III (744-727 BCE) mention no fewer than thirty-six Aramaean tribes settled in Babylonia, mostly along the Tigris River from the south to the area north of present-day Baghdad, and along the Euphrates River near Sippar. The relations between Aramaeans and native Babylonians sometimes were adversarial. Contrary to their Amorite predecessors a thousand years earlier, the Aramaeans did not adopt the Akkadian language but rather maintained their own. Further spread of the *Aramaic language was encouraged by the policy of mass deportations practiced by the Assyrian Empire in the eighth and seventh centuries BCE, which brought additional contingents of Aramaic speakers into Mesopotamia. Aramaic eventually became the lingua franca of the entire Near East, inducing the Achaemenid Persians who made it one of the official languages of their empire. Akkadian probably was already a dead language by the time Alexander the Great entered Babylon. The extent and nature of the influence of Aramaic is difficult to trace, however, because most of the writings have perished.

The Chaldeans, the other major group that settled in Babylonia, established residence mostly along the Euphrates and in the region between the two rivers from Babylon to the Persian Gulf. They were organized into three large territorial clans: the Bit Dakkuri south of Borsippa, the Bit Amukani between Nippur and Uruk, the Bit Yakin in the "Sealand Province" bordering on the Persian Gulf. Generally speaking, Chaldeans had better relations with the native population and the city elites than the Aramaeans, and during the time of Assyrian expansion they even became the champions of Babylonian independence. The best-known of these Chaldean leaders is Marduk-apla-iddina II, the Merodach-Baladan of the Bible, sheikh

of Bit-Yakin and king of Babylon from 721 to 710 BCE and again in 703 BCE. The Bit Yakin eventually formed the spearhead of resistance to Assyrian occupation until Assurbanipal (668-630 BCE) decimated it almost completely. The Chaldeans became so closely identified with Babylonia that the Bible consistently labels the Babylonian king Nebuchadnezzar II as leader of the Chaldeans *(Kasdim)*. Later during the Hellenistic period the word *Chaldean* acquired the meaning of astrologer and soothsayer versed in Babylonian lore. It seems dubious that these labels closely corresponded to ethnolinguistic reality, but they may reflect a perception of how completely the Chaldeans embraced Babylonian civilization.

Other ethnic groups appear in Iron Age documents. The identity of the Suteans is uncertain, and in many cases the name may just have been a generic term for bands of marauders. From the ninth century BCE onward Arabs are mentioned with increasing frequency, and during the period of the Neo-Babylonian Empire a large number of foreigners from all parts of the Near East and the eastern Mediterranean appear to have settled in Babylonia. Although Babylonia during the Iron Age was linguistically and ethnically diverse and became even increasingly so during the Persian and Hellenistic periods, Babylonian culture and institutions continued to flourish and prevail in an astonishingly resilient manner. It is only in the second and first centuries BCE, when the Parthians had included all of Mesopotamia in their empire, that we see clear evidence of the massive demise of Babylonian institutions, of temples being abandoned, cuneiform writing disappearing.

8. Assyrian Interlude.

The political history of Babylonia during the Iron Age is confused. Some kind of revival occurred in the ninth century BCE under kings Nabû-apla-iddina and his successor Marduk-zakir-šumi I, who was even in a position to pose as equal to his Assyrian counterpart. But soon afterward the country was plunged in turmoil for a protracted period until the Assyrian Empire embarked on a policy of forced integration of Babylonia into its system of political and economic control (*see* Assyria, Assyrians). This culminated in the dramatic campaigns of Sennacherib (704-681 BCE), who sacked Babylon, desecrated its shrines and carried off the statue of Marduk to Assyria. Sennacherib's intentions were far-reaching. He wanted to usurp the role of Babylon as cosmological center and transfer it to the Assyrian capital, Nineveh, and he even favored the redaction of a new version of the Babylonian creation epic in which Marduk was replaced by Ashur (Anshar), the chief god of Assyria. His son and successor Esarhaddon (680-669 BCE) returned to more conciliatory policies and encouraged restoration of the temples and monuments of Babylon. This eventually led to the return of Marduk's statue to its rightful abode. Upon Esarhaddon's death, his son Ashurbanipal ascended the throne of Assyria, while his other son Šamaš-šum-ukin was crowned as king of Babylon. In 652 BCE, however, Šamaš-šum-ukin rebelled against his brother and led a Babylonian war of independence that was suppressed at great cost in 648 BCE. Still, Ashurbanipal maintained the fiction of dual kingship by placing a puppet ruler named Kandalanu (647-627 BCE) on the Babylonian throne. The last decades of the seventh century BCE saw the gradual weakening of Assyria and the disintegration of its empire. After the death of Ashurbanipal, which occurred probably in 630 BCE, fierce competition erupted for the throne that by 626 BCE had degenerated into civil war. This was the year when an usurper named Nabopolassar (626-605 BCE) proclaimed himself king in Babylon and founded a new dynasty that was to establish forever the fame of Babylon in the collective memory of humankind.

9. The Neo-Babylonian Empire.

In 620 BCE Nabopolassar finally expelled the Assyrians from Babylonia. He then took the offensive and made an alliance with the Medes in order to strike a mortal blow to Assyria, now at bay. The results were dramatic. Nineveh was taken and sacked in 612 BCE, and the last Assyrian king, Ashur-uballit II, capitulated at Harran in 609 BCE. The Assyrian Empire had vanished, and now Babylon was in a position to claim most of its inheritance. Nebuchadnezzar II (605-562 BCE), the son and successor of Nabopolassar, destroyed Egypt's pretensions in the Levant at the battle of Carchemish in 605 BCE. The second capture of Jerusalem in 586 BCE sealed off the Syro-Palestinian corridor, and Babylon now fully assumed its imperial ambitions. The riches of the conquered regions flowed through Babylonia and allowed Nebuchadnezzar to embellish his capital with spectacular architecture. The empire even expanded under the usurper Nabonidus (556-539 BCE), the last king of Babylon, to include northern Arabia down to modern Medina. Nabonidus tried to impose the cult of the moon-god Sîn at the expense of Marduk, but his efforts found little echo among the population. His ten-year residence in the Arabian oasis of Teima, during which he entrusted effective power to his son Belshazzar, may have endangered the Babylonian Empire, now threatened on its eastern and northern borders by the growing power of the Persians. The conflict between the two states erupted in 539 BCE when Cyrus the Great led the Persian armies on a swift conquest of the Neo-Babylonian Empire. His capture of Babylon put an end to the last independent political manifestation of Mesopotamian civilization.

10. Late Babylonian Civilization.

In spite of two series of rebellions against Persian rule in the years 522-521 and 482 BCE, Babylonia accommodated itself to its new role as satrapy in a far-flung multinational empire. It is probably this new circumscribed and provincial status, combined with the highly distinctive character of Babylonia as heir to an old civilization, that gradually led to the characterization by outsiders of the entire region as one nation with a unified culture. This is the background that explains the creation of concepts such as Babylonia and Babylonians. Indeed, Babylonian civilization did not vanish with the loss of independence; it continued to flourish for a few more centuries under the rule of the Achaemenid Persians (*see* Persia, Persians) and then of the Greco-Macedonian dynasty of the Seleucids that seized power in Babylon in the year 311 BCE. Babylonian science and scholarship reached unprecedented heights in that period, especially in the fields of astronomy and astrology, which became emblematic of Babylonian, or "Chaldean," learning. The invention of mathematical astronomy by the schools of Babylon and Uruk between the fifth and third centuries BCE ranks as one of the great achievements of the human intellect and may be considered the first exact science in history.

Which factors preserved Babylonian civilization in the face of increasing ethnolinguistic diversity and permanent foreign occupation?

Babylonia was, above all, a land of cities, and the city elites played a leading role in this process. Organized into tightly knit clans claiming descent from a common ancestor, they controlled the temples and civic institutions of the old cities of Sumer and Akkad: Sippar, Babylon, Borsippa, Nippur, Uruk, Ur and several others spread along a narrow strip in the western part of the alluvial plain of Babylonia. These are the members of the *mār-bani* class often mentioned in documents from that period. They were the main factor of continuity and stability throughout the difficult times that their country traversed between the ninth and seventh centuries BCE, and they even succeeded in wresting from their Assyrian overlords significant privileges for their cities in the form of tax exemptions (*kidinnūtu*). Their power and influence rested on a substantial economic power base in the form of temple land and revenues. After the fall of Assyria they had to accommodate themselves to a new national monarchy with centralizing policies. In spite of this, they controlled enough wealth to assert their influence in all sectors of civic life and to promote their role as preservers of Babylonian identity and culture. The leading members of these city elites were the heirs to a millennial tradition of cuneiform scholarship, which they jealously guarded and cultivated. Although the late temple and scholarly libraries of Babylonia have been found in a very fragmentary state, there is no doubt that some of them, especially in Babylon, approached in size and scope the famed library of Ashurbanipal in Nineveh, which was still remembered in Hellenistic Babylonia as a paramount cultural achievement.

One of the most striking facts about late Babylonia is the resilience of cuneiform and Akkadian for record keeping. Some temple and private archives span the entire spectrum of the late Assyrian, Neo-Babylonian and early Achaemenid Empires, showing little change in the course of centuries. The religion of the great temple complexes of Sippar and Uruk, for example, is documented by thousands of administrative cuneiform tablets that allow us to peer into the minutest aspects of the cult and the temple economy. These texts detail the abundant offerings presented to the gods, the sumptuousness of their clothing and jewelry, and the complex daily rituals in their temples. They reveal a religion centered on temple ceremonial and the encounter with anthropomorphic divine images

that flourished at least until the end of Seleucid rule in Babylonia, and in some places even into the Parthian period. That religion played a central role in shaping Babylonian identity and defining it in the eyes of outsiders, and it became vilified in Judeo-Christian consciousness as immoral worship of idols.

11. Defining Babylonian Identity.

At the beginning of the third century BCE a cleric of the god Bēl (Marduk) in Babylon named Berossus wrote a book on the history and culture of the Babylonians for Antiochus I, the Seleucid ruler of Mesopotamia. Although the *Babyloniaka* has survived only in fragments, it is possible to reconstruct the original plan and intent of the work. The first book is a primeval history that presents Babylonia as a land of extremely remote antiquity to which civilization originally was brought by primeval sages. Berossus follows the plot of *Enuma Elish* in ascribing the creation of the world to the god Bēl, "the Lord" (Marduk), and in assigning to Babylon the status of first city and center of the world. Books 2 and 3, which are devoted to antediluvian and postdiluvian kings, are also primarily centered on Babylon and detail its history down to the Persian conquest. Like Manetho in Egypt, Berossus assumed the role of recorder and interpreter of his own culture and identity for the Greek rulers. Writing in Greek, he fully assimilated and accepted the Greek concepts of a land of Babylonia and of a Babylonian people. Although he also employs the terms *Chaldean* and *Chaldea* several times, one can hardly determine which kind of distinction he makes between Babylonian and Chaldean, or between the lands of Babylonia and Chaldea. But this question probably is secondary. For Berossus, Babylonian identity did not rest on ethnicity, language or territory. Indeed, when describing the primeval state of his country in remotest times, Berossus claims that "in Babylonia there was a large number of people of different ethnic origins who had settled in Chaldea," thus projecting the ethnolinguistic diversity of Hellenistic Babylonia back into mythical time. Nor did Berossus propose that the Babylonians possessed the sense of a singular common destiny as a nation, as was the case for Israel. For Berossus, Babylonian identity ultimately rested on the role of Babylon as cosmological center. Such ideas were not new, yet their Greek reformulation by

Berossus in his *Babyloniaka* represents an ultimate attempt to give Babylonia its credentials as sacred land in a world dominated by Hellenism. In the final analysis, Babylonian identity rested on the remote antiquity of Babylonia—the place where civilization began—and on its mythical role as center of the world.

See also ASSYRIA, ASSYRIANS; HISTORY OF ISRAEL 6: BABYLONIAN PERIOD; NON-ISRAELITE WRITTEN SOURCES: BABYLONIAN.

BIBLIOGRAPHY. **B. T. Arnold,** *Who Were the Babylonians?* (SBLABS 10; Atlanta: Society of Biblical Literature, 2004); **P.-A. Beaulieu,** "King Nabonidus and the Neo-Babylonian Empire," in *Civilizations of the Ancient Near East,* vol. 2, ed. J. M. Sasson et al. (New York: Scribner, 1995) 969-79; idem, "Nabopolassar and the Antiquity of Babylon," *ErIsr* 27 (2003) 1-9; **J. A. Brinkman,** *A Political History of Post-Kassite Babylonia (1158-722 B.C.)* (AnOr 43; Rome: Pontifical Biblical Institute, 1968); idem, *Prelude to Empire: Babylonian Society and Politics, 747-626 B.C.* (Occasional Publications of the Babylonian Fund 7; Philadelphia: University Museum Publications, 1984); **S. M. Burstein,** ed., *The Babyloniaca of Berossus* (SANE 1/5; Malibu, CA: Undena, 1978); **D. Charpin,** *Hammu-rabi de Babylone* (Paris: Presses Universitaires de France, 2003); **I. L. Finkel,** "Adad-apla-iddina, Esagil-kīn-apli, and the Series SA.GIG," in *A Scientific Humanist: Studies in Memory of Abraham Sachs,* ed. E. Leichty et al. (Occasional Publications of the Samuel Noah Kramer Fund 9; Philadelphia: University Museum Publications, 1988) 143-59; **G. Frame,** *Rulers of Babylonia: From the Second Dynasty of Isin to the End of Assyrian Domination (1157-612 BC)* (RIMB 2; Toronto: University of Toronto Press, 1995); **A. R. George,** *Babylonian Topographical Texts* (OLA 40; Leuven: Peeters, 1992); **W. G. Lambert,** "The Assyrian Recension of Enuma Elish," in *Assyrien im Wandel der Zeiten: XXXIXe Rencontre Assyriologique Internationale, Heidelberg, 6.-10. Juli 1992,* ed. H. Waetzoldt and H. Hauptmann (HSAO 6; Heidelberg: Heidelberger Orientverlag, 1996) 77-79; idem, *Babylonian Wisdom Literature* (Oxford; Clarendon Press, 1960); idem, "The Reign of Nebuchadnezzar I: A Turning Point in the History of Ancient Mesopotamian Religion," in *The Seed of Wisdom: Essays in Honor of T. J. Meek,* ed. W. S. McCullough (Toronto: University of Toronto Press, 1964) 3-13; idem, "Studies in Marduk," *BSOAS* (1984) 1-9; **J. Oates,** *Babylon* (London: Thames & Hudson, 1979); **J. M. Sasson,** "King Hammurabi of Babylon," in *Civilizations of the Ancient Near East,* vol. 2, ed. J. M. Sasson et al. (New York: Scribner, 1995) 901-15; **W. Sommerfeld,** "The Kassites of Ancient Mesopotamia: Origins, Politics, and Culture," in *Civilizations of the Ancient Near East,* vol. 2, ed. J. M. Sasson et al. (New York: Scribner, 1995) 917-30; **G. P. Verbrugghe and J. M. Wickersham,** *Berossos and Manetho, Introduced and Translated: Native Traditions in Ancient Mesopotamia and Egypt* (Ann Arbor: University of Michigan Press, 1996); **D. J. Wiseman,** *Nebuchadnezzar and Babylon* (Schweich Lectures 1983; Oxford: Oxford University Press, 1985).   P.-A. Beaulieu

BABYLONIAN CHRONICLES. *See* NON-ISRAELITE WRITTEN SOURCES: BABYLONIAN.

BABYLONIAN KING LISTS. *See* NON-ISRAELITE WRITTEN SOURCES: BABYLONIAN.

BARAK. *See* JUDGES.

BARLEY. *See* AGRICULTURE AND ANIMAL HUSBANDRY.

BATHSHEBA. *See* DAVID'S FAMILY; WOMEN.

BEERSHEBA

The ancient town of Beersheba, located in the Negev, plays an occasional role in the Historical Books. It is perhaps best known to Bible readers today as the southern extremity of Israel's territory in the formulaic expression "from Dan to Beersheba."

    1. Setting and Ruins
    2. Beersheba in Israelite History
    3. Archaeological Strata

1. Setting and Ruins.
Ancient Beersheba was a town located about midway between the Mediterranean Sea and the southern end of the Dead Sea. It was situated in the heart of a basinlike tract called the Beersheba Valley, whose rich soil was suitable for cultivation despite a location on a desert's periphery with little precipitation. The settlement itself was built on a hill at the fork of the Beersheba and Hebron riverbeds—that is, Wadi es-Saba and Nahal Hebron (or Wadi el-Khalil) respectively. After converging at Beersheba, the brook continued westward, forming the Wadi Besor, which eventually moved in a northwest-

erly direction to the Mediterranean Sea. The hill provided the site with natural protection, while the beds of the streams were used during the dry season as highways by merchants and caravans. This gave ready access to the Judean Desert and the Dead Sea on the east and the coastal plain on the west. Additionally, a major north-south route of the central hill country passed through Beersheba (*see* Roads and Highways). That made it an important crossroad, including service as a road station for Arabian international trade (Singer-Avitz, 55).

The small mound of ruins measures about three acres in area. It is now known as Tell es-Saba, or more commonly, Tel Beersheba. The modern city of Beersheba, however, lies near a bend of Wadi es-Saba approximately three miles to the west of its junction with Nahal Hebron. And it is at the industrial center of this modern Beersheba that the ancient name is most closely preserved in the Arabic Bir es-Saba. Thus some scholars seek biblical Beersheba there while placing biblical Sheba/Shema (Josh 15:26; 19:2) at Tel Beersheba. Other scholars propose that Beersheba was a dual site comprising a royal city at the tell along with a civilian settlement further west on the banks of the wadi. On the one hand, the central location of the mound and the absence of any other fortified city in the vicinity that could have served as an administrative center support its identification with ancient Beersheba. Yet excavations at the modern town have also revealed an Iron Age occupation. A letter from around the seventh century BCE found at *Arad and referring to Beersheba probably signifies the Bir es-Saba settlement rather than the Tell es-Saba fortress, because the latter lay in ruins then.

2. Beersheba in Israelite History.
Beersheba heads the list of Simeon's tribal cities (Josh 19:2; 1 Chron 4:28), but it also appears among those of Judah (Josh 15:28). It was under the label "Beersheba, which belongs to Judah" (1 Kings 19:3) that it served as a way station for the prophet *Elijah on his journey from *Jezreel southward to Mount Horeb. Beersheba early on came to be known as the southern extremity of Israelite territory, even as *Dan was in the north—delineated in the formula "from Dan to Beersheba" (Judg 20:1). The Chronicler reverses the order: "from Beersheba to Dan" (e.g., 1 Chron 21:2). Beersheba is likewise mentioned as the southern boundary of the kingdom of

Judah alone: "from Geba to Beersheba" (2 Kings 23:8) or "from Beersheba to the hill country of Ephraim" (2 Chron 19:4). In the late premonarchical period *Samuel's sons Joel and Abijah judged over Israel at Beersheba (1 Sam 8:1-2). Afterward, the census that King *David had his general Joab conduct ended there (2 Sam 24:7). A subsequent monarch, *Josiah, targeted the town's worship center in his effort to root out *high places during the seventh century BCE (2 Kings 23:8).

Presumably Beersheba's Hebrew name, *bĕʾēr šebaʿ*, stems from either *šābaʿ* ("to swear") or *šibʿâ* ("seven"). In the former case, "well of oath," it might allude to the oaths exchanged between Abraham or Isaac and Abimelech (Gen 21:31; 26:31). In the latter case, "well of seven," it might allude to the seven lambs that Abraham gave Abimelech as a token of ownership (Gen 21:28-30; cf. Isaac at Gen 26:33). Thanks to the presence of such freshwater springs there, Tel Beersheba was settled soon in the Iron Age. Already during the tenth century BCE various rulers started to turn the site into an administrative capital, a religious center and a border fortress, complete with rampart, walls and gateway necessary for military functions. Several strata span mainly the twelfth through the eighth centuries BCE. The remainder of this article explores those nine layers.

3. Archaeological Strata.
Stratum IX dates to the second half of the twelfth and the first half of the eleventh centuries BCE. We may estimate a community of around twenty families to have inhabited tents or huts alongside pits hewn into the hill's bedrock. The population's subsistence was based on raising sheep and cattle.

The first houses at the site were erected in Stratum VIII, dated to the third quarter of the eleventh century BCE. In that century the Beersheba Valley witnessed the densest occupation in its premodern history. Although citizens at Tel Beersheba did raise more substantial structures on stone foundations, most of the remains show a continued use of the pits and caves from the prior period.

The Stratum VII settlement, dating to the late eleventh and early tenth centuries BCE, was built over abandoned pits and houses of the previous layer. The pattern exhibits the beginning of organized town planning here. The houses were built encircling the perimeter of the mound, with their connected rear walls facing outward to form a basic defensive system. The entrances of these houses opened inward toward a central courtyard, where inhabitants could pen flocks and herds at night.

The remains in Stratum VI, dating to the first half of the tenth century BCE, are interpreted as belonging to a short-lived interim stage during which a new fortified town of the next stratum was being constructed. Houses of the previous settlement on the summit were dismantled, and the area was leveled off and filled for reconstruction. A type of work camp containing poorly built and randomly arranged quarters apparently was established then. Those remains too eventually were razed toward the final stage of constructing the city's fortifications.

Stratum V dates to the Davidic and Solomonic period, that of the united or dual monarchy, the second half of the tenth century BCE. From this phase onward the settlement became a small fortified city, as just noted. A solid wall some four to five yards thick surrounded the entire three acres of the summit, which amounted to an artificially constructed base approximately twenty-three feet high. Major destruction by fire occurred at the town later in the tenth century BCE, probably at the hands of Egyptian Pharaoh Shoshenq I (Shishak in the OT [1 Kings 14:25; 2 Chron 12:2]), who invaded Judah around 926 BCE.

Soon, around the end of the tenth century BCE, a new city was built on the ruins of the prior stratum, reusing the solid fortification walls. However, little time elapsed before this Stratum IV itself was destroyed at the beginning of the subsequent century.

Stratum III's pottery indicates the extended occupation enjoyed by the city from the middle ninth to the middle eighth centuries BCE. Starting in this layer, drain channels beneath paved streets collected rainwater from the town's interior and directed it outside through the gate to a well, seventy-five yards deep, that had existed since earlier layers for residents and passersby. Stratum III also suffered a destruction, possibly under the Assyrian king Tiglathpileser III in 734 BCE (Blakely and Hardin, 54), but one caused by a conflagration clearly less violent and widespread than those that terminated Strata V and II.

Isolated areas were repaired and rebuilt during Stratum II. For instance, integrated into a wall of the main storehouse near the city gate were well-dressed stones clearly in secondary use. Peculiar rounded projections at the top of these sandstone blocks identified them as originally part of a large four-horned altar. Additional stones gave evidence of fire on their surfaces, likely an indication that the altar had been used for sacrifices. Another of the stones bore the image of a deeply incised serpent. The dismantling of the altar at Beersheba is viewed as coming from the cultic reform that Judah's King *Hezekiah carried out in the late eighth century BCE (2 Kings 18:22). Indeed, through biting criticism the Israelite prophet Amos does imply some sort of worship significance connected with Beersheba in the decades leading up to Hezekiah (Amos 5:4-5; 8:14). Besides public buildings, the town had roughly seventy-five dwellings holding an estimated three or four hundred people. The sections of the city exposed attest that the domestic units were not uniform; their sizes differed, and their internal divisions varied. It seems to have been conquered and demolished during the campaign against Judah in 701 BCE by Assyria's King Sennacherib.

Following this destruction the ruins of the city evidently were used temporarily as a squatters' site. The last occupational phase, Stratum I, was an ultimately halted attempt to rebuild the city. The meagerness of the repairs indicates that they were the result not of royal policy, but rather of local effort. The site became deserted for almost three hundred years; the village's repopulation may be what Nehemiah 11:27, 30 refer to. Perhaps the main elements of the Tel Beersheba settlement in the seventh century BCE had moved west to Bir es-Saba, as hinted above.

See also DAN; WATER AND WATER SYSTEMS.

BIBLIOGRAPHY. **Y. Aharoni**, ed., *Beer-Sheba I: Excavations at Tel Beer-Sheba, 1969-1971 Seasons* (Publications of the Institute of Archaeology 2; Tel Aviv: Tel Aviv University, Institute of Archaeology, 1973); **J. A. Blakely and J. W. Hardin**, "Southwestern Judah in the Late Eighth Century B.C.E.," *BASOR* 326 (2002) 11-64; **L. F. De Vries**, "Beersheba: Traditional Southern Boundary of Ancient Israel," in *Cities of the Biblical World* (Peabody, MA: Hendrickson, 1997) 150-55; **Z. Herzog**, "Beersheba," *OEANE* 1.287-91; idem, *Beer-Sheba II: The Early Iron Age Settlements* (Publications of the Institute of Archaeology 7; Tel Aviv:

Tel Aviv University, Institute of Archaeology; Ramot, 1984); idem, "Tel Beersheba," *NEAEHL* 1.167-73; **D. W. Manor,** "Beer-sheba," *ABD* 1.641-45; **L. Singer-Avitz,** "Beersheba—A Gateway Community in Southern Arabian Long-distance Trade in the Eighth Century B.C.E.," *"TA* 26 (1999) 3-74; **H. F. Vos,** "Beersheba," *NIDOTTE* 4.439-40.   E. C. Hostetter

BEITIN. *See* BETHEL.

BETHEL

This city, located ten and a half miles north of Jerusalem on the border of the northern and southern kingdoms, served as one of two major worship places for the northern kingdom. Its previous name was "Luz" (Gen 28:19; 35:6; 48:3; Josh 16:2; 18:13; Judg 1:23, 26).

    1. Biblical Data
    2. Location and History

1. Biblical Data.

The name *Bethel* ("house of God") carries the expectation that it will play an important role in Israel's religious history. Patriarchal ties with Abraham (Gen 12:8; 13:3) and Jacob (Gen 28:19; 31:13; 35:1-16) enhance this expectation. The expectation is fulfilled in the Historical Books. Bethel serves to locate *Ai in Joshua's conquest (Josh 7:2; 8:9, 12), and its citizens join the battle, suffering the disastrous consequences (Josh 8:17; cf. 12:9, 16). It served as a border point for the territorial allotment to the Joseph tribes (Josh 16:1-2) but belonged to Benjamin (Josh 18:13, 22; Neh 11:31; but cf. 1 Chron 7:28). Still, the house of Joseph, not Benjamin, completed the conquest of the city (Judg 1:22-26), and Bethel served as a gathering place for Israel's troops when they gained revenge against Benjamin (Judg 20:18-48; cf. 21:2, 19). Bethel helps locate Deborah's work as a *judge (Judg 4:5) as well as Samuel's (1 Sam 7:16). It plays a subsidiary role in the early *Saul and *David stories (1 Sam 10:3; 13:2; 30:27).

Bethel reaches its greatest biblical importance when *Jeroboam I rebels against the southern kingdom and sets up Bethel and *Dan as worship places with golden calves, supplanting the southern *Jerusalem (1 Kings 12:29-33; cf. 2 Kings 10:29). Building Dan and Bethel became the sin of Jeroboam that led to Israel's downfall (1 Kings 12:30; 13:34; 14:16; 15:30; 16:31; 2 Kings 3:3; 10:29, 31; 13:2, 11; 14:24; 15:9,

18, 24, 28). God sent a *prophet to predict Bethel's destruction (1 Kings 13:1-10), resulting in a prophetic debate with serious consequences (1 Kings 13:11-32). Abijah of Judah took Bethel from Jeroboam (2 Chron 13:19). Hiel of Bethel lost his two sons when he violated God's command and rebuilt *Jericho (1 Kings 13:34), and some Bethel lads paid the penalty for mocking Elisha's bald head (2 Kings 2:23-25). A prophetic company lived in Bethel (2 Kings 2:2).

*Assyria finally conquered Israel, but the situation there grew so bad that the Assyrians had to send back a priest of Bethel to teach the people the local religion (2 Kings 17:28). Finally, in his religious reform in the south, *Josiah sought to bring the northern remnant to worship in Jerusalem. He defiled the sanctuary at Bethel and destroyed its altar (2 Kings 23:4-20).

Exiles returning from Babylon under *Zerubbabel included citizens of Bethel and Ai (Ezra 2:28; Neh 7:32).

1.1. Joshua 7:1—8:29; 12:9, 16: Mysterious History. Bethel's place in the conquest narrative remains open to debate. The sudden appearance of its army (Josh 8:17) is neither prepared for nor followed up in the narrative. The narrative focuses on Ai, not Bethel, and the traditional site of Ai faces archaeological problems at this period of history, so that scholars often ask if Bethel, not Ai, is the narrative's original center. But this appears more of a scholarly escape hatch than a real solution to the problem. Bethel is first called "Beth-aven," meaning "house of iniquity" (Josh 7:2; cf. Josh 18:12; 1 Sam 13:5; 14:23; Hos 4:15; 5:8; 10:5), which may be a separate city or, more likely, a derogatory name that Judah used for Bethel. The Albright school contended that Israel conquered Bethel, but its ongoing history as an occupied city led to the narrative being transferred to the ruin of Ai. J. A. Soggin points to the Samaritan tradition locating Beth-el on Mount Gerizim near *Shechem. Hess (cf. Gray) argues that Bethel is central to the narrative, its soldiers using the remains of Ai's walls as a "strategic fortress." Ai then was featured in the narrative to make a wordplay on its name and because it was the site of the battle though the soldiers came from Bethel. R. B. Coote dismisses this and sees Ai as a symbol for the hated Bethel and its cult. Coote views the Ai story as pure etiology. The narrative in the book of *Joshua thus adds mystery to Bethel's history.

Was the city actually involved with the battles against Joshua? Did it suffer destruction at this point, or only serious defeat? How is the narrative of Joshua 7—8 related to that of Judges 1:23-26? Why do the narratives mentioning Ai relate it so closely to Bethel?

At least the narrative structure in Joshua focuses all its geographical description on Ai. The battle must have occurred there. The narrative structure likewise requires action from Bethel prior to the moment when the Israelite tribes spring their ambush. Otherwise, the citizens of Bethel would easily spy the Israelite troops rising to fight and would attack them. Thus the solution to the Bethel-Ai mystery lies not in changing the participants or the location of the battle. The onus of solving the mystery lies on historical geographers and archaeologists to correctly locate and recreate the history of the two cities or to prove beyond doubt that one or both of the cities did not exist at the time, leading to the conclusion that the narrator created materials from traditions of various ages. Until further evidence appears, we must lay historical and geographical questions aside to concentrate on the literary structure of the narratives and their literary/theological intentions and meanings.

1.2. Joshua 16:1; 18:13, 22: Tribal Allotments. The land allotment narratives in Joshua 13—21 clearly place Bethel in the territory of Benjamin, but as a town marking the southern border of Ephraim. Thus it stood as a counterpart to Dan on the northern edge of Israel, Jeroboam placing his worship places not in the capital city or at centrally located places, but on the country's extreme borders. Thus Bethel served as a gathering place of the army of Saul, from the tribe of Benjamin, and figured in border wars between Judah and Israel (2 Chron 13:19).

1.3. Judges 20—21: Intertribal War. Bethel's border status gains another perspective in the closing chapters of Judges. The men of *Gibeah, a major city in Benjamin, viciously raped a Levite's concubine. The other tribes from Dan to *Beersheba, including Gilead east of the Jordan, declared holy war on Benjamin. Israel gathered at Bethel to determine God's will for the battle (Judg 20:18) and again after their defeats to lament before God (Judg 20:26; 21:2). Thus Bethel was a sacred site for all-Israel in the period of the judges. It also served as a transportation center, being located on the main road

going north from *Hebron to Jerusalem to Shechem (Judg 20:31; 21:19) and a main road going from the Mediterranean coast at Joppa above the Aijalon Valley through Bethel down to Jericho and the Jordan River.

1.4. 1 Kings 12:29-33: The Sin of Jeroboam. The sins of *Solomon led God to remove the blessing of David from his lineage and leave his son *Rehoboam only one tribe (or two [1 Kings 11:13, 36; cf. 12:21]) to govern, giving the others to Jeroboam (1 Kings 11:9—12:24). But this event became a sin (1 Kings 12:30) with drastic consequences, as Ahijah the prophet outlined: "the result being he (Yahweh) will give Israel away on account of the sins of Jeroboam that he sinned and that he caused Israel to sin" (1 Kings 14:16), a prophecy that quickly came true for Jeroboam (1 Kings 15:30) and eventually for the entire nation (2 Kings 17:1-18).

1.5. 2 Kings 23:1-20: Josiah and Bethel. A new discovery of God's law book led Josiah to reform Judah's idol-infested worship (2 Kings 22). The reform had political as well as religious ramifications, as Josiah tried to reclaim at least part of the northern kingdom. One strategy for doing this involved Bethel. The king had the idols in the Jerusalem temple burned, but he did not bury them in Jerusalem. Instead, they were taken to Bethel and buried. Bethel's altar also came tumbling down. The entire worship place experienced destruction. All this made the city as impure as the idols and as the normal burial places or garbage dumps outside Jerusalem. Thus the "House of God" city no longer met anyone's requirements as a worship place. Josiah could incorporate it into his southern kingdom with the expectation that the people would come ten miles further south to Jerusalem to worship. Josiah's political aspirations also sent him to *Megiddo, where Pharaoh Neco quickly ended Judean dreams for a renewal of the Davidic kingdom (2 Kings 23:29).

2. Location and History.

Although Bethel is mentioned in the OT more often than any Palestinian city except for Jerusalem, we still know very little about it. Bethel is located "in the hill country" (Gen 12:8) near Ai (Gen 12:8; 13:3; Josh 7:2; 8:9, 12, 17; 12:9; Ezra 2:28; Neh 7:32) in the tribe of Ephraim (Judg 4:5). Naaran lies to the east, and *Gezer to the west (1 Chron 7:28). It is south of *Shiloh (Judg

21:19) on the road from Jericho (2 Kings 2:15-23) to the hill country (Josh 16:1) that proceeds from Bethel westward to Ataroth and lower Beth-horon (Josh 16:2-3). The northern border of Benjamin fits the same description (Josh 18:13-14), so that Bethel is a border town in Benjamin (Judg 18:21-22; Neh 11:31), but bordering Ephraim. Somewhere south of Bethel a road forks, one line going to Bethel, the other to Gibeah (Judg 20:31; cf. 1 Sam 13:2). Bethel is also on the highway going north to Shechem (Judg 21:19). Michmash is nearby (1 Sam 13:2). All this means that it also straddles the border between the two kingdoms, Judah and Israel. This location sets it on the water divide, with waterways to its east flowing into the Jordan, and those to the west going into the Mediterranean. This has led archaeologists and historical geographers to locate Bethel at Beitin, and Ai at Et-tell. Archaeological findings at Beitin have been highly propagated as proof of the Bible, but recent assessment of the findings emphasizes the poor quality of both the archaeological work there and of the publication of that work (Dever). J. Kelso, the leader of the most recent excavations, offers a brief history of Bethel, as-suming that Beitin can be equated with Bethel and admitting that the modern city leaves little room for archaeological exploration. Kelso traces the city's origins to about 3200 BCE. It was soon abandoned, to be occupied again between 2400 and 2200 BCE. Shortly after 2000 BCE continuous occupation began, with a massive wall surrounding the city only about 1700 BCE in the Middle Bronze Age 2B. Kelso finds a fine stone temple in this period, along with a layer of ashes pointing to destruction. Between 1550 and 1400 BCE the city lay in ruins, with Late Bronze Age occupation showing a deterioration in quality from the early period to the later.

Kelso describes two early Iron Age conquests, one by Canaanites, with the other recorded in Judges 1:22-26. The Iron Age village apparently did not have a protective wall, and its pottery repertoire is early Israelite, with a noticeable absence of Philistine ware. One unique quality of the city is that the *Babylonians did not destroy it in 586 BCE when they razed Jerusalem.

The paucity of evidence at Beitin and the total lack of occupation apparent at et-Tell have led several scholars to search for new locations for Bethel, a step applauded by several conservative scholars but lightly rejected or ignored by more critical scholars. Until both sides are heard and particularly until further evidence appears, the question of the location and occupation dates of Bethel (and Ai) must remain open. Fortunately, the inability to answer such questions does not deter Bible students from understanding God's message through the texts. That message sees a city chosen at the beginning of God's interaction with the patriarchs gone bad as an ongoing representation of a nation's violence and false worship.

See also AI.

BIBLIOGRAPHY. **R. G. Boling and G. E. Wright,** *Joshua* (AB6; Garden City, NY: Doubleday, 1982); **R. B. Coote,** "Joshua," *NIB* 2.553-719; **W. G. Dever,** "Beitin, Tell," *ABD* 1.651-52; **J. Gray,** *Joshua, Judges, and Ruth* (NCB; London: Nelson, 1967); **J. M. Grintz,** "'Ai Which Is Beside Beth Aven: A Reexamination of the Identity of ʿAi," *Bib* 42 (1961) 201-16; **R. S. Hess,** *Joshua* (TOTC; Downers Grove, IL: Intervarsity Press, 1996); **D. M. Howard,** *Joshua* (NAC 5; Nashville: Broadman & Holman, 1998); **J. L. Kelso,** "Bethel," *NEAEHL* 1.192-94; **J. L. Kelso and W. F. Albright,** *The Excavation of Bethel (1934-1960)* (AASOR 39; Cambridge, MA: American Schools of Oriental Research, 1968); **K. Koenen,** *Bethel: Geschichte, Kult und Theologie* (OBO 192; Freiburg: Universitätsverlag; Göttingen: Vandenhoeck & Ruprecht, 2003). **D. Livingston,** "Further Considerations on the Location of Bethel at El-Bireh," *PEQ* 126 (1994) 154-59; idem, "Location of Biblical Bethel and Ai Reconsidered," *WTJ* 33 (1970) 20-44; **I. Provan, V. P. Long and T. Longman III,** *A Biblical History of Israel* (Louisville: Westminster/John Knox, 2003) 173-92; **A. F. Rainey,** "Bethel Is Still *Beitîn*," *WTJ* 33 (1971) 175-88; **J. A. Soggin,** *Joshua* (OTL; Philadelphia: Westminster, 1972). T. C. Butler

BIBLICAL ARCHAEOLOGY. *See* ARCHAEOLOGY, SYRO-PALESTINIAN.

BIR HADAD. *See* NON-ISRAELITE WRITTEN SOURCES: SYRO-PALESTINIAN.

BIR-RAKIB. *See* NON-ISRAELITE WRITTEN SOURCES: SYRO-PALESTINIAN.

BOOKS. *See* WRITING, WRITING MATERIALS AND LITERACY IN THE ANCIENT NEAR EAST.

BORDERS, TRIBAL. *See* TRIBES OF ISRAEL AND
LAND ALLOTMENTS/BORDERS.

BUILDING. *See* ARCHITECTURE.

BUREAUCRACY, ISRAELITE. *See* STATE OFFI-
CIALS.

BURIAL. *See* DEATH AND AFTERLIFE.

C

CALEB, CALEBITES

The name of two individuals (and their descendants) from Israel's early history genealogically and geographically associated with the tribe of Judah. The Pentateuch and the Historical Books portray Caleb I as an ancestral hero, while Caleb II is known only from genealogical lists.

1. Name
2. Caleb I: The Son of Jephunneh
3. Caleb II: The Son of Hezron
4. One Caleb or Two?

1. Name.

Traditionally, one regards "Caleb" (Heb *kālēb*) as a form of the common Semitic word *klb* ("dog"; Heb *keleb*), with its connotations of self-deprecation (e.g., 2 Kings 8:13) or insult (e.g., 2 Sam 16:9). The Mari letters attest an Amorite proper name *ka-al-ba-an* ("dog"), while the proper names *klb* and *klby* occur in Ugaritic, Aramaic, Phoencian and Punic, probably connoting "servant." Mesopotamian names combine the root *kalb-* ("dog of" . . .) with theophoric names (e.g., Akk *kalbi-ᶦᶦmarduk*, "dog [i.e., servant] of Marduk"), so the biblical name "Caleb" may represent an abbreviated form of such examples (i.e., *kalb-* > *kālēb*), connoting self-abasement and perhaps "faithful servant." The phrase "my servant Caleb" (Num 14:24) might even pun on the name. "Chelubai" (Heb *kĕlûbāy*) probably represents a variation on the name analogous to the above West Semitic cognates (1 Chron 2:9).

2. Caleb I: The Son of Jephunneh.

This individual is the wilderness hero whose "different spirit" as Judah's representative among the twelve spies God rewarded with a special inheritance in *Canaan (Num 13:6, 30; 14:6, 24, 30, 38; cf. Num 26:65; 32:12; Deut 1:36).

2.1. Family Background. The Bible identifies Caleb's father, Jephunneh, as "the Kenizzite" (Num 32:12; Josh 14:6, 14), a gentilic tracing his ancestry either to a pre-Israelite people in southern Canaan (Gen 15:19) or to a prominent western Edomite clan (cf. Gen 36:11, 15, 42; cf. Kenaz, Caleb's youngest brother [Josh 15:17; Judg 1:13]). Caleb I represents a non-Israelite clan incorporated into the tribe of Judah and larger Israel. Its ancestry may help explain its later settlement areas within Judah.

2.2. Special Inheritance: Joshua 14—15. Caleb I reappears as Judah's spokesman as *Joshua begins to distribute land west of the Jordan. At his request, Joshua fulfills Moses' oath (actually, Yahweh's oath; cf. Deut 1:36), allotting Caleb I his inheritance within Judah's boundaries, the city of *Hebron (previously, Kiriath-Arba), home to the terrifying Anakim. At age eighty-five, Caleb expels Anak's three sons from Hebron (Josh 14:6-14; 15:13-14; Judg 1:20; cf. Sir 46:9-10) and also takes Debir (previously, Kiriath Sepher; probably Khirbet er-Rabud, c. 15 mi southwest of Hebron) through his nephew Othniel, whose victory Caleb rewards with marriage to his daughter (Josh 15:15-17). As a wedding gift, he presents the newlywed Achsah with the upper and lower springs in the Negev, presumably to irrigate her semiarid land, itself a gift from Caleb (Josh 15:18-19). Later, Israelite leaders give Hebron to the priestly family of Kohath, but Caleb still holds the city's surrounding farmland and villages (Josh 21:11-12; cf. 1 Chron 6:41). Thus the book of Joshua singles out Caleb I for singular honor as the first person to receive inherited land west of the Jordan because he "followed the LORD . . . wholeheartedly" (Josh 14:14; cf. 1 Macc 2:56).

2.3. Caleb I and Judah: Judges 1. Judges 1 reports the same events as Joshua 14—15, but with striking differences. Here Joshua is dead (Judg 1:1), the conquest remains unfinished, and the enemy is broadly called "Canaanites" ("the sons of Anak" in Hebron's case). Also, the collective tribe of Judah, not an individual, leads the fight as Joshua's divinely appointed successor (Judg 1:1-2), and the picture of events differs significantly. Judges 1 credits Judah, not Caleb, with first "defeating" (Heb *nkh* Hiphil) the sons of Anak at Hebron and with first attacking Debir (Judg 1:10-11), although Judges 1:12-15 reports verbatim Othniel's capture of Debir and Caleb's wedding gift from Joshua 15. Contextually, Othniel's literary reprise anticipates his later exploits as judge (Judg 3:9-11), but two things are striking: short reports of other Judahite victories (Judg 1:17-19) take precedence over the report of Caleb's "dispossession" (Heb *yrš* Hiphil) of Hebron (Judg 1:20b; cf. Josh 15:14); and Judah, not Joshua, authorizes it ("they gave" [Judg 1:20a]). Obviously, Judges 1 accords Judah pride of place, perhaps literarily foreshadowing the tribe's important future and David's rise later. It also portrays the Calebites as a distinct clan yet already incorporated into Judah. Apparently aware of Joshua 15's contents, Judges 1 fleshes out details of timing and means absent in the former.

2.4. Genealogy. A simple list of his sons (Iru, Elah and Naam) and one grandson (Kenaz, Elah's son) marks Caleb I's final biblical appearance (1 Chron 4:15, reading "the son of Elah: Kenaz" [NRSV, NIV]). Despite the vague, fragmentary context (1 Chron 4:1-23), it reckons Caleb I genealogically to Judah's son Perez (1 Chron 4:1), the line from which David descends (cf. Gen 38; Ruth 4:12, 18). The lack of correspondence between these traditions and the data on Judah in *Ezra and Nehemiah (Ezra 2:3-35/Neh 7:8-33; 11:4-9, 25-30) suggest that they at least reflect Judah's preexilic, if not early, tribal situation. The Chronicler signals the Calebites' unique prominence in and full incorporation within Judah.

2.5. Caleb I and Calebites: Geography. Presence around Hebron and possession of Debir suggest Calebite holdings southwest of Hebron, and Caleb I's gift of land and springs assumes his control of territory into the southern hill country of Judah and the Negev. The term "Negev of Caleb" (1 Sam 30:14) might also locate some Calebites in the northeastern Negev, south of the Wadi Besor. The sketchy data deny us precise conclusion concerning the extent of Calebite territory within southern Judah and the northern Negev, but Caleb I's association with Hebron and inclusion in David's genealogy imply that Calebites enjoyed high social stature in Judah.

3. Caleb II: The Son of Hezron.
This individual is the grandson of Perez (cf. Gen 46:16; Ruth 4:18) and brother of Jerahmeel and Ram (1 Chron 2:9), known only from his genealogy. That his great-grandson Bezalel is a contemporary of Moses places Caleb II chronologically among the early Israelite generations sojourning in Egypt.

3.1. Genealogy. Though fragmentary and textually corrupt at points, Caleb II's genealogy (1 Chron 2:18-20, 24, 42-50a) is more extensive than that of Caleb I. His identification as "brother of Jerahmeel" (1 Chron 2:42) places him genealogically parallel to the Davidic royal line of Ram (1 Chron 2:9-15) and probably presumes close ties between Calebites and Jerahmeelites (Japhet). Given the Chronicler's special concern for the temple cult, Caleb II's main importance is probably as great-grandfather of the craftsman Bezalel, designer and builder of the tabernacle (1 Chron 2:18-20; cf. Ex 31:2-5; 38:22). But besides fathers and sons, the genealogy also mentions wives and concubines, and many of its "sons" are actually town names (e.g., 1 Chron 2:46, 48-49). The metaphor pictures family geographical expansion as the "fathering" (i.e., the founding or occupying) of newborn "sons" (i.e., towns). Thus the family branches offer an intriguing geographical glimpse of Calebite II clan locations (see 3.2 below). Behind it probably stands an ancient tradition about Calebite settlements from the united monarchy or shortly thereafter (Williamson)—sources probably older than those for Caleb I. But one wonders whether the association of two distinct Calebite clans with Hebron, each with a daughter of Caleb named Achsah (see 2.2 above and 1 Chron 2:49b), might imply some relationship (see 4 below).

3.2. Geography. Though details are sketchy, the identifiable place names in Caleb II's genealogy (Hebron, Ziph, Maon, Jorkeam, Beth-zur, Tappuah and Tekoa) locate the Calebites in the hill country of Judah within a ten-mile radius of Hebron. The most far-flung cities are Tekoa (c. 16 mi northeast) and Madmannah (c. 25 mi southwest; 12 mi southwest of Debir [1 Chron

2:49; cf. Josh 15:31]). The general impression is of an early fanning out of Calebites to other son-cities. Since Maon was his hometown, Nabal, the only biblical person called a "Calebite," probably belonged to Caleb II's family (1 Sam 25:1-3). Also, that Hur, son of Caleb II and Ephrath, "fathered" Bethlehem (also called "Ephrath/Ephrathah" [Gen 35:16, 19; Mic 5:2]) suggests that Ephrathites—for example, David's ancestors (Ruth 1:2; 1 Sam 17:12)—comprised a Calebite subgroup centered there (1 Chron 2:19-20, 50; 4:4). The genealogy singles out the Calebite Mareshah as the founder or first clan occupant of Hebron and credits it with founding and/or occupying four "sons" (1 Chron 2:42-43). This falls short of the strong claims to possession of Hebron that Joshua 14—15 assert for the Caleb I group, but it clearly affirms a clan connection of some sort with the city. A Calebite-Bethlehem connection, plus David's fugitive days in Calebite territory (1 Sam 23 and 26), might explain his choice of Hebron as his first royal capital and imply positive relations between his family and the Calebites.

4. One Caleb or Two?

Many scholars believe that "Caleb" originally was a clan name adopted by a single clan, the Calebites, whose traditions underlie the Bible's supposed Caleb the son of Hezron and Caleb the spy. Their prima facie case argues that everything Calebite descends from a common ancestor (Perez), concerns the same central city (Hebron), inhabits the same region (southern Judah), and shares the same inclusion in Judah. That the genealogies imply two different individuals, living at different times, poses no problem because, as R. R. Wilson has shown, biblical *genealogies often represent social and political relationships between groups rather than actual physical descent. But a contrary case can also be made. The Chronicler clearly seems to know two individuals named Caleb. His terminology consistently distinguishes between Caleb II (son of Hezron) and "Caleb son of Jephunneh" (1 Chron 4:15; 6:56 [MT 6:41]), and the wide use of *klb* in ancient proper names certainly means that two individuals might share the name *Caleb*, even in the same area. Also, although the evidence is minimal, a slight difference in location for each of the Calebite groups is perceptible: the Calebites of Caleb I are associated with Debir and the Negev, while several Caleb II towns

(e.g., Bethlehem, Tekoa, Maon, Ziph) lie near the wilderness east of Hebron. As for Hebron, the Bible incorporates ancient sources from the two Calebite groups and hence offers only brief snapshots of scattered historical moments. How they all fit together remains speculative.

See also JOSHUA.

BIBLIOGRAPHY. **W. Beltz,** *Die Caleb-Traditionen im Alten Testament* (BWANT 5/18; Stuttgart: Kohlhammer, 1974); **G. J. Botterweck,** "כָּלֵב," *TDOT* 7.146-57; **M. J. Fretz and R. I. Panitz,** "Caleb," *ABD* 1.808-10; **G. F. Hasel,** "Caleb, Calebite," *ISBE* 1.573-74; **S. Japhet,** *I & II Chronicles* (OTL; Louisville: Westminster/John Knox, 1993); **R. de Vaux,** "The Settlement of the Israelites in Southern Palestine and the Origins of the Tribe of Judah," in *Understanding and Translating the Old Testament*, ed. H. T. Frank and W. L. Reed (Nashville: Abingdon, 1970) 108-34; **H. G. M. Williamson,** *1 and 2 Chronicles* (NCB; Grand Rapids, MI: Eerdmans, 1982); **R. R. Wilson,** *Genealogy and History in the Biblical World* (New Haven: Yale University Press, 1977). R. L. Hubbard Jr.

CALENDARS. *See* CHRONOLOGY.

CANAAN, CANAANITES

Study of the land of Canaan and its culture is crucial for understanding the message of the Historical Books of the OT because these books take place in the context of Canaan. Furthermore, *Hebrew is linguistically a branch of the Canaanite languages, and literary forms in the Bible have strong affinities with the "Canaanite" literatures of both the Late Bronze Age and the Iron Age. Also, the Israelites early on adopted the Canaanite-Phoenician alphabetic scripts for writing.

1. Sources
2. The Name *Canaan*
3. Geographical Area
4. Ethnic Group
5. Language
6. Writing
7. Culture
8. Religion

1. Sources.

Information about Canaan and the Canaanites comes from three different sources: documentary or inscriptional, archaeological and traditional.

Unfortunately, inscriptional data from Canaan

(i.e., Syria-Palestine) during the Late Bronze Age (1550-1200 BCE) is scarce, and virtually all linguistic data concerning the Canaanites come from outside Canaan (i.e., el-Amarna and Ugarit) through cuneiform texts on clay tablets, except for a few Akkadian clay tablets found at Late Bronze *Hazor, Aphek and other sites.

The Amarna tablets are a direct source of information. Among the large number of fourteenth-century documents (some four hundred texts) found in the Middle-Nile city of Amarna written in Akkadian (the lingua franca of the ancient Near East at the time), the majority were letters sent to the pharaohs by vassal kings of Syria-Palestine and the rulers of Cyprus and Ugarit (see Moran). The city of Ugarit was located north of Canaan, but its culture and religion seem to have been similar to that of Canaan. Egyptian and Mesopotamian records also shed indirect light on various aspects of the life of the Canaanites.

From the first millennium BCE about three hundred alphabetic inscriptions are known from southern Canaan, but most are very short, often with only one word or name (see Renz and Röllig). However, remains of several hundred bullae (small clay lumps with traces of stamp seals), sometimes with short inscriptions, and with traces of papyrus on the back, show that in southern Canaan perishable papyrus was used for writing materials, presumably due to Egyptian influence (see Deutsch).

Knowledge about Canaan is provided also by artifacts such as pottery, weapons, figurines, reliefs and buildings and city structures excavated in Syria-Palestine. Some reliefs found in *Assyrian royal palaces in Nimrod, Nineveh and other places also depict life in Canaan.

Authors from the Greco-Roman era recorded some traditions about ancient Canaan. For example, according to Eusebius (d. 340 CE), Philo of Byblos (d. 160 CE) preserved a Phoenician tradition by Sanchuniathon about the creation of the world. However, Philo's understanding of Phoenician cosmogony was highly Hellenized. By far the richest data about Canaan and the Canaanites come from the OT.

2. The Name *Canaan*.

The earliest attestation of Canaan is in an Akkadian document c. 1800 BCE from Mari on the Mid-Euphrates: *Canaanite* (^{lú}ki-na-aḫnum). Next, in a fifteenth-century Akkadian text, Idrimi's autobiography from Alalakh, the expression "the land of Canaan" appears. A fifteenth-century Egyptian text mentions the Canaanites in a list of booty from the Asian campaign of Amenhotep (Amenophis) II, and Merneptah's famous "Israel stela" of the thirteenth century BCE refers to Canaanites as one of the vanquished peoples (see Naʾaman).

The name *Canaan* is written as *knʿn* (Phoenician, Hebrew), *ki-na-aḫ-num* (Akkadian), *ki-na-ḫi* (Ugaritic, written syllabically) and so on, but its etymology is obscure. Formerly, it was explained on the basis of Hurrian *kinaḫḫu*, "blue-dyed cloth," but now it is thought to be more likely related to *knʿ*, "to bend, to bow," although there is not much basis for that view either.

3. Geographical Area.

Canaan was never a political unity, and no single city dominated. What, then, was its geographical area? Commonly, it is accepted as the area between the Mediterranean seacoast and the river Jordan; it includes the southern coast of Syria and Lebanon and Israel (Palestine) on the modern map. If used to refer to the area where the Canaanite-speaking peoples (*Phoenicians, *Hebrews, *Moabites, *Ammonites, *Edomites, but not Aramaeans) lived, Canaan includes the area east of the Jordan. In Ugarit the "Canaanites," *knʿny* (see Olmo Lete and Sanmartín, 449), are listed as foreigners. Thus *Canaan* refers politically and ethnically to the area to the south of Ugarit. The Amarna letters view Canaan as an Egyptian province that included Tyre and Byblos but not Ugarit. N. P. Lemche (1991) disputes the historical reality of a Canaanite land or people, and he thinks that Canaan was simply "a geographical entity of some sort" and that *Canaanites* was a social term in the second millennium BCE. However, his views are based on a lack of adequate control of the primary sources of Late Bronze Age (1550-1200 BCE) data, in particular of the Armarna letters (see Naʾaman; Rainey).

In the early Late Bronze Age *Egypt administered Canaan as one of the three provinces (the others were Amurru and Upi) in Syria-Palestine. Later, after the battle at Kadesh in the thirteenth century BCE, Amurru, the northernmost province, came under Hittite rule. After the invasion of the Sea Peoples in the reign of Ramesses III (1184-1153 BCE), *Canaan* sometimes specifically referred to southern Palestine.

Still later, the Greeks called Canaan "Phoenicia."

The document that mentions *Canaan* most frequently is the OT, where the name appears eighty times, sixty-four times as the "land of Canaan" (*'ereṣ kĕnaʿan*). According to Numbers 34:3-12 (cf. Ezek 47:15-20), the southern boundary of "the promised land" ran from the wilderness of Zin to the southern end of the Dead Sea, and down to the south of Kadesh-barnea (Num 34:3-5); the northern boundary was Lebo-hamath (Num 34:7-9) (*see* Geographical Extent of Israel). However, sometimes *Canaan* in the Bible refers only to Phoenicia (see Num 13:29; Josh 5:1), which includes the Phoenician cities in Canaan but excludes the Lebanon Mountains. Occasionally, it refers only to Philistia (e.g., Zeph 2:5). Such different uses of the term mirror changes of its use in other ancient Near Eastern documents (see Tammuz).

4. Ethnic Group.

It is difficult to determine who the "Canaanites" of the OT were (*see* Ethnicity). Sometimes the word is a general designation of the pre-Israelite inhabitants of the land (e.g., Gen 50:11; Deut 11:30). Sometimes it refers to one of the seven nations that lived in pre-Israelite Canaan: Hittites, Girgashites, Amorites, Canaanites, Perizzites, Hivites, Jebusites (Deut 7:1; cf. 20:17). Canaanites were among the nations that Yahweh told Moses to drive out (Deut 33:2) or exterminate (Deut 20:17). The Canaanites and the Amorites often are mentioned side by side; the former resided near the coast, while the latter lived in the hill country (Deut 1:7).

5. Language.

The Canaanite languages belong to the Northwest Semitic family (see Huehnergard). All are characterized by a phonetic change, called the "Canaanite shift," in which an accented long *a* changed to an accented long *o*, as attested in Phoenician, Punic, Hebrew and so on. Ugaritic and *Aramaic, which lack this shift, are classified as a separate branch of Northwest Semitic, although some scholars do consider Ugaritic to be Canaanite.

The Akkadian of the fourteenth-century Amarna letters from Byblos, *Gezer, *Jerusalem and *Shechem exhibits characteristics of Canaanite grammar. Phoenician is attested at Byblos, Tyre, Sidon and other places from the tenth century BCE onward. Punic was a Phoenician dialect spoken at Carthage and its colonies from the fifth century BCE; after the fall of Carthage it was called Neo-Punic.

Hebrew is by far the best-known Canaanite language; the earliest inscriptional evidence is the Gezer Calendar of the tenth century BCE (*see* Hebrew Inscriptions). The OT preserves Archaic and Classical Hebrew as well as Late Classical Hebrew (*see* Hebrew Language). There are differences between the Judean (southern) dialect and the Israelian (northern) dialect. Moabite, Ammonite and Edomite differ from Hebrew only dialectally.

6. Writing.

There were basically two types of writing in Canaan. One, used in the Amarna letters, was reasonably standard Akkadian script, written with a mixture of syllabic and logographic cuneiform ("wedge-shaped") characters on clay tablets. The other was the alphabet (see Naveh).

The earliest known example of the Canaanite alphabetic script is that found on a rock in *Wadi el-Hol* of the Upper Nile near Thebes, dated as early as c. 1900 BCE. Probably some forced laborers from Palestine inscribed their language by simplifying Egyptian hieroglyphic writings. The slightly later Proto-Sinaitic inscriptions seem to use a similar system. Some of the letters resemble the Proto-Canaanite scripts of the seventeenth to sixteenth centuries BCE from Gezer, Shechem and *Lachish. Presumably, these alphabetic texts normally were written on perishable materials such as papyrus, following Egyptian practices.

The alphabet that developed during the Late Bronze Age consisted of twenty-some letters, usually written with a linear script, although in some places (as Ugarit) the letters were written in cuneiform on clay tablets. A few cuneiform alphabetic texts were found in southern Palestine—for example, Beth-shemesh (*KTU* 5.24), east of Mount Tabor (*KTU* 6.1), Taanach (*KTU* 4.767). Several Ugaritic tablets ("mirror texts" [*KTU* 4.31; 4.710]) were written from right to left using the "shorter" alphabet of twenty-two letters like later Phoenician and Hebrew, instead of being written left to right with the thirty letters usual in Ugaritic. All linguistic data found in Canaan itself from the Iron Age was written using the Phoenician linear alphabet in Canaanite languages such as Phoenician, Hebrew, Moabite and Ammonite, as well as in Aramaic (*see* Writing, Writing Materials and Literacy in the Ancient Near East).

7. Culture.

The Bible seems to suggest that a common Canaanite culture existed from at least patriarchal times. Abraham, from the *Aramaic-speaking district of Haran, could talk with the native Canaanites. In Genesis 31:47-48 Laban used an Aramaic term, *Yegar-Sahadutha,* for the heap of stones, while Jacob gave it a Hebrew (i.e., Canaanite) name, *Gal-ed.* So the ancestors of the Israelites had been linguistically Canaanized. The Aegean Philistines in the district of Gerar were Semitized during the patriarchal era; note that the king had a Semitic name, *Abimelech* (e.g., Hebrew, Ugaritic), while the army commander kept his Philistine (i.e., non-Semitic) name, *Phicol* (Gen 26:26). Later, during the times of Samson, Samuel and Saul, the Philistines were thoroughly Canaanized, even adopting Dagon, the traditional god of Syria-Palestine (e.g., Judg 16:23; 1 Sam 5:2), although preserving their ability in metal works (Judg 13:19-22) and pottery, notably bichrome wares.

However, extrabiblical Canaanite sources for Canaanite culture are extremely limited; therefore the Ugaritic evidence is very important (see Watson and Wyatt). Ugarit is located outside Canaan, its language is not, strictly speaking, Canaanite, the Ugaritians considered the Canaanites foreigners, and Ugarit was destroyed around 1200 BCE, before the Israelites had established themselves in Canaan. Nevertheless, its culture probably was quite similar to the later Canaanite culture.

Ugarit was not isolated; as a port linking the Aegean, especially Cyprus, and even Egypt with inland states, it was located on a crossroad of Near Eastern culture. It bought ships from Egypt to use in trade with the Hittites, Cyprus and Aegean peoples. The southern Palestine ports of *Ashdod and Acco are mentioned in Ugaritic texts. The Cypriot wares found in *Jericho and widely imitated there may have come via Ugarit and Ashdod.

The Amarna letters include letters from Ugarit to an Egyptian pharaoh, and a letter from the governor of Ugarit to the Egyptian high commissioner of Canaan was found at the southern Palestine city of Aphek. All these were written in the lingua franca, Akkadian. Certainly, the "Amarna Age" of the fourteenth century BCE was international, and the entire area, which included both Canaan and Ugarit, enjoyed cultural contact with other parts of the ancient Near East, promoted particularly by the activities of merchants and technicians. They certainly could communicate easily either in Akkadian or in their own languages, either orally or in writing. Presumably much day-to-day communication used the simple Semitic alphabet.

How intercultural the Ugaritic culture was is illustrated by the existence of several quadralingual vocabulary lists, in Sumerian, Akkadian, Hurrian and Ugaritic, as well as other texts written in Egyptian, Cypro-Minoan and Hittite languages, besides thirteen hundred Ugaritic and Akkadian documents.

Inscriptions written in Ugaritic using the cuneiform alphabet have been found not only at the nearby sites of Ras Ibn Hani, Sultan Tekke of eastern Cyprus, and Tell Sukas, but also in southern Palestine—for example, Beth-shemesh, Mount Tabor, Taanach. In Ugarit the second-largest element of the population was the non-Semitic Hurrians, who were not organized as a political body after the destruction of Mitanni in the thirteenth century BCE, yet contributed greatly to cultural contact among various people in Syria and Palestine. The Egyptians even called the Syria-Palestine area the land of *Hurru.*

Although Ugarit probably was destroyed by Aegeans around 1200 BCE and was never rebuilt, the culture that it represented probably continued on in the area as well as in Canaan. The traditions about Phoenician religion have obvious affinities with Ugaritic religion. In Canaan, as in Syria, the main political unit was the city-state ruled by a king and controlling a small area of its own, as illustrated by biblical references to the kings of Canaan or the Canaanites (Judg 5:19; Josh 5:1). No king unified the entire area politically or militarily. The Canaanites who had "iron chariots" (Josh 17:16, 18) are heirs of the Late Bronze Age *maryannu* ("charioteer"), attested in Ugaritic society.

Our knowledge of the ancient Canaanites is limited, and we should not generalize. However, it certainly is true that the Canaanite cultures, especially those of the Late Bronze Age (1550-1200 BCE) and the Iron Age (1200 BCE onward) were highly developed and intermingled. Thus the entire land of Canaan had essentially become one common culture, with a common Canaanite language, very similar to that of Ugarit. Therefore, until substantial literary evidence is discovered in Palestine, the Ugaritic documents will remain important evidence for the study of Canaan. In the section that follows, Ugaritic myths and liturgical texts are used to concentrate on the religious aspect of the Canaanite culture.

8. Religion.

8.1. Data. Until the discovery of the mythico-religious Ugaritic texts in 1929, almost the only sources for Canaanite religion outside of the OT were the much later traditions of Philo of Byblos, Lucian of Samosata and others. Contemporary data from Canaan itself provides little information about its religious practices, since Phoenician and Punic inscriptions are limited in literary genre, and virtually no mythological or liturgical texts are available for comparison. Hebrew inscriptions are mostly very short, and no substantial literary or religious texts are known.

Pre-Israelite Canaanite *high places (Heb *bāmôt;* cf. Ugar *bmt*) have been excavated in *Meggido, Hazor and other sites. Even in the Israelite period, a Baalized Yahweh cult was practiced at these local sanctuaries "on every high hill and under every green tree" (e.g., 2 Kings 17:10) until *Josiah abolished them in 621 BCE. Stone pillars (*maṣṣēbôt*)—symbolic of the male deity—altars and incense altars are among the characteristic items found at these sites. However, interpreting those artifacts is often very difficult, and without inscriptional support it is virtually impossible to decide what kind of religious practices were performed. Even the identification of divine images can be elusive; scholars argue endlessly whether bull images in Syria-Palestine symbolize El or Baal.

However, Ugarit and some neighboring cities provide both textual and archaeological information about the religious life in Syria-Palestine. For example, Dagan worship was an ancient Syrian practice dating back to the third millennium BCE, as can be seen in the Ebla texts. The Hittite-Canaanite "Elkunirsha and Ashertu" myth (*COS* 1.55:149) of the second millennium BCE is informative. Egyptian texts show that Canaanite gods were worshiped from the earliest times also in the Nile Delta area.

8.2. Ugaritic Religion. The study of religious texts is not the study of the religion itself. Never-

theless, without a careful analysis of texts, religious studies are subjective. Ugarit is exceptional in providing abundantly both textual and nontextual data about its religious life (see Watson and Wyatt, chap. 13). Still, those texts usually were found in royal or temple archives; popular religious traditions were not necessarily reflected. There were differences in the national cult practiced in the temples, the royal family's cultic practices in the palace and the popular religious practices in the ordinary family life.

The deities involved in these various cults and in the myths often were different. Ugarit had one temple dedicated to Dagan, and another to Baal. Significantly, Dagan does not appear as a character in the extant mythological texts. However, Baal, said to be his son, is a major figure. Some deities in the official pantheon list, such as the "Divine Ancestor" *(Ilib)* (Olmo Lete and Sanmartín, 52) and Rashpu, are not active figures in the myths; many of those appearing in the ritual texts, such as Horon and the "Lady-of-the-Palace" *(Bʿlt bhtm),* do not appear either. On the other hand, chthonic (underworld) deities such as Mot ("Death"), often active in myths, normally were abhorred and do not appear in the pantheon. There were also many minor yet popular deities whose names are found only in magical incantations.

8.3. The Ugaritic Pantheon. The "official" pantheon list from Ugarit (*KTU* 1.47; 1.118 [= RS 24.264 + 24.280] // RS 20.24), which is known from several copies and in several languages (Ugaritic, Akkadian, Hurrian), lists some thirty gods and goddesses in fixed order. The most important are the following.

First in the list is *Ilib,* the "Divine Ancestor" (not the "God of the Ancestor"). This indicates the importance of ancestor worship or the cult of the dead in Ugarit.

The next, El, is the main character in the myth of the "Birth of the Good Gods *[ilm nʿmm]*" (*KTU* 1.23), while in the Baal myths he is rather an authority making decisions and giving advice to younger deities. He is the creator of "creatures," the progenitor of the gods, and the "father of mankind" *(ab adm)*. He has the epithet "Bull" *(tr);* but whether the bull images found in Syria-Palestine symbolize him or Baal is in doubt. However, when Aaron (Ex 32:4) and later *Jeroboam (1 Kings 12:28) used the golden calf/bull to symbolize Yahweh, the Israelites were following this religious tradition of El. For one thing, neither of these leaders was conscious of introducing a foreign deity, Baal. Due to the linguistic sameness of "God" (*'ēl*) and the Canaanite god El, they unconsciously introduced the bull image for Yahweh.

The god Dagan is third in the pantheon, and one of the two temples in Ugarit was dedicated to him. He is known from Early Bronze Age Mesopotamia and northern Syria, especially Mari and Ebla. The Philistines apparently adopted this god as their national deity soon after they arrived in Palestine early in the Iron Age (Judg 16:23; 1 Sam 5:2), which illustrates the continuing role of Dagan among the religions of Syria-Palestine.

Baal, the most popular god among the Canaanites, is next in order. The other Ugaritic temple is dedicated to him. As storm god, he became king among the deities after defeating the chaotic Sea (Yam). However, he was not a creator. He was the "Lord of the Earth" (*b'lars*), who brought about fertility in the earth. As the god of life, he was defeated by Mot, the god of death, and remained dead for seven years, but eventually he conquered death. This tradition of a "sabbatical" cycle of severe famine is reflected in the Joseph story (Gen 41:30).

Baal is listed seven times in the list, with *Baal Ṣapānu* on the top. He is also mentioned in various texts under local names—for example, "Baal of Ugarit," "Baal of Aleppo" and the Phoenician "Baal of Sidon." The biblical Baal-peor, one of the leading gods of the Moabites, Midianites and Ammonites, probably is the locally manifested Canaanite Baal (Num 25). The names of Jezebel and her father, Ethbaal (1 Kings 16:31), mean "Where is the prince?" and "There is Baal," referring to the story of Baal, the "prince" (*zbl*), who disappeared from this world and was revived. Baal worship was a real temptation to the Israelites throughout their life in Canaan.

There are fertility goddesses paired with gods, but who is paired with whom varies in different sources. In Ugaritic myths El's wife is Asherah, the mother of seventy divine children. In Ugarit Baal is paired with Anath, called the "virgin," goddess of war and love like Ishtar of Mesopotamia and the "Queen of Heaven" (Jer 44:15). However, during Ahab's time Baal is associated with Asherah (1 Kings 18), and in other biblical passages with Astarte (= Ugaritic fertility goddess *ttrt* [see 1 Sam. 7:4; 12:10]), as he was in

the Syrian city of Emar.

Besides the ordinary deities, there are the god *Ṣapānu,* who is the deified Mount Ṣapānu, Baal's residence; the god *utḫt,* the deified incense burner; and the god *kināru,* the deified harp (see Olmo Lete and Sanmartín, 450-51). These three well illustrate the animistic nature of "Canaanite" religion.

8.4. Phoenician Religion. The Phoenicians retained earlier "Canaanite" traditional gods such as Baal, El, Baalat, Astarte and Resheph, but they added other gods such as Melqart, Baal-shamen, Eshmun and Adonis. In Punic religion Baal-hammon and Tinnit were worshiped together with Melqart, Eshmun, Resheph and others.

In the cosmogony of Philo of Byblos (summarizing Sanchuniathon), Hellenistic influence can be seen in the names of divine figures such as Elos (El), Zeus Belos (Baal), Adodos (Hadad) Dagon, and Elioun, father of Ouranos (Heaven) and Ge (Earth).

8.5. Religious Practices. Religious festivals in Canaan were basically agricultural; the new year festival was at the time of the autumn harvest. Unfortunately, not much information is available about the nature of these festivals.

Sacrifices were important. Their purpose was to provide food for the gods, as seen in the Aqht epic (*KTU* 1.17:I:2-13), where Daniel feeds them and eats and drinks with them. Ugaritic and Hebrew have many ritual terms in common—for example, *dbḥ,* "sacrifice, feast"; *šrp,* "burnt offering"; *šlm(m),* "communion victim/sacrifice, peace-offering" (Olmo Lete and Sanmartín, 819); *ndr,* "oath." However, there are many conceptual differences.

Divination of many types was prevalent throughout the ancient Near East, such as hepatoscopy (Ezek 21:21), in which priests divined by analyzing lines on the organs, such as livers and lungs, of slaughtered animals. Clay models of organs with messages recorded on them have been discovered at Mari, Ugarit, Hazor and Meggido. Unnatural births were also considered a bad omen.

Hymns and prayers are basic features in any religion; many have been found in Mesopotamia, dedicated to, for example, Marduk and Shamash. A Ugaritic example is a prayer for deliverance from enemy attack. A unique clay tablet preserves a Hurrian hymn to Nikkal, along with Akkadian musical notation and a colophon.

The fertility cult was central in Canaan. In one Ugaritic tablet El is depicted as having sexual relationships with two women who bore the seven "Good Gods" *(ilm n'mm)*, who would bring fertility to the land. However, before their birth, *Mt w Šr* ("Death-and-Evil"), the god of death and futility, had to be destroyed by sympathetic magic. It is possible that a *hieros gamos* (sacred marriage) was acted out at some stage in the ritual for inducing fertility (Tsumura 1999).

Sacred prostitution presumably was a form of sympathetic magic practiced to encourage fertility. In Ugarit, besides the regular priests *(khnm)*, there was a class called *qdšm*, who possibly were cult prostitutes associated with Asherah, who had the epithet "Holiness" *(qdš)* (Tarragon, 138-41; cf. Olmo Lete and Sanmartín, 696). The male prostitutes *(qĕdēšim)* in the Bible seem associated with Asherah (see 1 Kings 14:23-24; 15:12-13; 2 Kings 23:4, 6-7). The Phoenicians inherited this practice of sacred prostitution. Deuteronomy 23:17 forbids temple prostitution, either male *(qādēš)* or female *(qĕdēšāh)*.

The cult of the dead was well established in Ugarit. Many rituals required sacrifices to *ilib*, the "Divine Ancestor," the first god in the pantheon list. One text *(KTU* 1.17:I:26-33) states that the eldest son must "set up the stele of his [father's] divine ancestor *[ilib]* in the shrine" as well as "send out his incense from the dust." He must also eat a ceremonial meal in the house of Baal. Many Ugaritic houses had pipes leading into basement tombs, evidently to provide the deceased with water, probably daily (see Margueron).

A Ugaritic text *(KTU* 1.113:13-26) lists royal ancestors with the title *il*, as, for example, "god Niqmaddu" *(il nqmd)* and "god Yaqaru" *(il yqr)*, so postmortem deification of kings existed. Not only *il*, but also *rpim-ilnym* and *ilm-mtm (KTU* 1.6:VI:46-48), refer to the deceased in Ugaritic. In the Bible the term *'ĕlōhim* sometimes (see 1 Sam 28:13) refers to the dead *(mētim)*, as in Isaiah 8:19, and these terms appear in Psalm 106:28 *(mētim)* and Numbers 25:2 *('ĕlōhim)*, where the daughters of the Moabites invited the people of Israel to eat the sacrifices to dead ancestors.

The royal funerary ritual *(KTU* 1.161; see Tsumura 1993) sends the recently deceased king to join his royal ancestors in the underworld and prays for the welfare of Ugarit and the new king. The ancestral line of dead heroes and kings *(rpum;* OT: *rĕpā'im*, e.g., Is 14:9 [see Smith, *ABD* 5.674-76; also *COS* 2.56-57:181-83; Olmo Lete and Sanmartín, 742-43]) and the spirits of recent kings *(mlkm)* are invoked. There is no mention of such a practice or belief in the official Yahwistic religion in Israel. The prophet Ezekiel denounces what seems to be the practice of putting royal tombs or mortuary stelae defilingly near the temple (Ezek 43:8) (see Lewis, 139).

The *marzēaḥ*, a drinking festival sometimes associated with funerary feasts (Olmo Lete and Sanmartín, 581), was widely practiced from Syria to North Africa, from Ugarit in the Late Bronze Age to Palmyra in the third century CE (see Greenfield, 71). Jeremiah 16:5-8 implies that it was widely practiced among the Israelites also. The "revelry" *(mizraḥ)* of Amos 6:7 too seems related. The very need to prohibit offerings to the dead (Deut 26:14; Ps 106:28) and self-laceration rituals (Lev 19:28; Deut 14:1; Jer 16:6) is an indication that the problem of "pagan" cults of the dead was persistent on a popular level in Israel.

Necromancy (see Finkel; Lewis) seems to have been widespread in Canaan, even in Israel, despite the commands against the abominations *(tô'ēbôt)* of mediums, wizards and necromancers, who consult the spirits of the dead (Deut 18:11; Lev 19:31; 20:6, 27). 1 Samuel 28:3 reports that "Saul had put the mediums and the wizards out of the land," and necromancy is denounced in Isaiah 8:19, so it was a continuing problem.

"Molech," which appears in Leviticus 18:21; 20:2-5; 1 Kings 11:7; 2 Kings 23:10; Jeremiah 32:35, usually is taken as a Canaanite divine name, whose Ugaritic counterpart is *mlk* (Olmo Lete and Sanmartín, 554). The cult has been interpreted as a kind of (child?) sacrifice related to the cult of the dead ancestors. It usually appears in contexts suggesting divination, along with the underworld connections of the god Malik (Milku/i). Some scholars claim that it is a sacrificial term rather than a divine name, cognate with Punic *molk*, but others hold that it is simply a dedication in fire. As yet, its exact nature is unknown (see Day 1989).

8.6. Kings and Cults. In Ugarit the king played a sacral role in royal court rituals such as full moon or new moon festivals, purifying himself with a bath (e.g., *KTU* 1.119:5; 1.41) and officiating during part of the liturgy (see Miller, 60-63). He sacrificed to the "Divine Ancestor" *(ilib)*, the

"Lady of the Palace" *(b'lt bhtm)* and deities such as Baal and Anath so that he, his family, the city and the people might receive blessings from the ancestors. However, in national rituals a priest, not the king, officiated (see Tsumura 1999). In Phoenicia two kings of Sidon, Tabnit and Eshmunazar, served as priests of Astarte *(KAI* 13:1, 2). In Canaan kingship was "sacral" rather than "divine" (see Gen 14:18).

*Saul, as head of the royal family, seems to have presided over the new moon festival meal, in which males of the royal family and perhaps others were expected to take part (1 Sam 20:5).

8.7. Solar Worship. The solar deity Shapshu (Ugar *špš* = Akk ^{d}*šamaš* [Sum UTU]), was a popular Ugaritic deity, often appearing in myths, the cult and incantations (e.g., *KTU* 1.100), and in personal names (see Miller, 57; Lipiński). The place name "Beth-shemesh" ("House of the Sun" [see 1 Sam 6:9-15]), as well as the feminine gender of the sun in Hebrew (see, e.g., 1 Sam 20:19; Jer 15:9; Mic 3:6; Nahum 3:17; Ps 104:22) probably reflect the pre-Israelite worship of the solar goddess in Canaan (see Taylor; Tsumura, *NIDOTTE* 4.185-90). She may have also been considered a guide of the dead *(psychopompē)* like the Mesopotamian solar god Shamash, who is called "the lord of the spirits of the dead" *(bel etemmi)*; the necromancer *('ēšet ba'ălat 'ôb)* in 1 Samuel 28:7 was literally "a woman who serves the Lady of the *'ôb*-spirits," "the Lady" probably referring to the sun goddess (see Tsumura 1993).

Not surprisingly, sun worship was practiced somewhat among the Israelites, as is shown by the polemical references in Deuteronomy 4:19; 17:3; Jeremiah 8:2; Job 31:26-28. The sun cult flourished especially in the time of *Manasseh, and even after (2 Kings 23:5, 11; Ezek 8:16). As K. van der Toorn observes, given the long history of the sun cult in Syria and Palestine, "there is no need to assume that it was a 7th-century innovation on the part of the Assyrian overlords" (van der Toorn, 238).

8.8. Canaanite Religious "Influences" on Israel.

8.8.1. Methodology. When discussing the influences of Canaanite religion on Israel, we can, following R. S. Hess, distinguish at least four levels of religion in Israel: (1) the prophetic religion, which taught belief in Yahweh alone; (2) the state religion, which sometimes adapted Canaanite traditions or foreign state deities; (3) popular religion, which accepted Canaanite customs such as divination, necromancy and ancestor worship; (4) foreign religion, which was officially adopted in the national cult. Usually these various levels appeared as a mixture.

When we compare the Bible and Canaanite religion, we must be careful and thorough. We must compare the biblical text with that in another culture according to its literary genre. In particular, finding similarities in linguistic and literary expressions is not enough; we must make a thorough study of differences in these similarities as well (Tsumura 1988). Although Israel inherited many Canaanite religious practices, prophetic Yahwism was consistent in rejecting foreign polytheistic elements, although sometimes expressions originating in Canaanite myths and legends were adopted for metaphorical purposes (see 8.8.3 below).

8.8.2. Yahweh and the Canaanite Gods. It often is asserted that Canaanite religious elements were appropriated into the Bible "in a form compatible with Israel's own distinctive faith" (Day, *ABD* 1.831-37). In particular, it often is claimed that biblical writers identified Yahweh with the Canaanite Baal or El, not just linguistically but conceptually (see Smith 2002).

According to J. Day *(ABD* 1.831-37), "the chief god of the Canaanites, El, is equated in the OT with Yahweh." It often is claimed that names such as "El-Shaddai," "El-Bethel," "El-Olam," "El Elohei Israel," "El-Roi" and "El-Elyon" are manifestations of the Canaanite "El" that became identified with Yahweh (e.g., Ex 6:2-3), probably the Midianite god of Mount Sinai. However, there is no reason to think that the component "El" in these titles was a proper name. In Ugaritic *il*, though it certainly could refer to the god El, was primarily a common noun referring to the deity par excellence, "god," like the Akkadian *ilu*. The element *il* is used as a common noun, "god" (Olmo Lete and Sanmartín, 48-50), in personal names such as *ilb'l* (DINGIR.^{d}U), *ilršp* (DINGIR.^{d}MA∑.MA∑), *ilšpš* (DINGIR. ^{d}UTU^{ðu}), *ildgn*—"Balu is god," "Rashpu is god," "Shapshu is god," "Daganu is god"— as well as phrases such as *il bldn*, "gods of the country"; *ily ugrt*, "the gods of Ugarit"; *il mṣrm*, "gods of Egypt"; *il bt*, "the god of the house"; *ilm w ilht*, "gods and goddesses"; *nhr il rbm*, "Naharu, the great god"; *bn ilm mt*, "the divine Motu." Furthermore, although many place names contain "Baal"—for example, Baal-hazor and Baal-hermon—there are no indisputably "El" names, which suggests that the cult of "El" was not widespread in Canaan. Thus the name "El-Bethel" may simply mean "God of Bethel," and "El-Elyon" (see Gen 14:18, 19, 22) simply be an epithet ("God Most High") of Yahweh.

On the other hand, there does seem to be some amalgamation of Yahweh and Baal on the popular level and the level of foreign imports. "Yahweh of Samaria" and "Yahweh of Teman" in the eighth-century inscriptions from Kuntillet Ajrud (see Hadley; Hess) compare with Baal's manifestations such as "Baal of Ṣapānu," "Baal of Ugarit" and "Baal of Aleppo" (Olmo Lete and Sanmartín, 209). In the Bible we find Baal-plus-toponym formulations such as "Baal-Peor," "Baal-Gad," "Baal-Hazor" and "Baal-Hermon."

"Yahweh of Samaria/Teman . . . and his Asherah" should be compared with Baal and Asherah in the eras of Ahab (1 Kings 18:19) and Manasseh (2 Kings 23:4) rather than with the Ugaritic divine pair El and Asherah. Also, the frequent references to "Baals" and "Asherahs" in association (e.g., Judg 3:7; 6:25; 2 Kings 17:16; 2 Kings 21:3) support this association of Yahweh with Baal on a level of popular and foreign religion.

However, in the prophetic religion, which taught belief in Yahweh alone, there is no place for monolatry, a system that worships one deity while admitting the existence of others. Expressions such as "Who is like you among the gods, O Yahweh?" (Ex 15:11) and "There is none like you among the gods, O Yahweh" (Ps 86:8a) are not signs of monolatry; they simply express the incomparability of Yahweh (Labuschagne) and point to the true monotheism, as in "There is no one like you, and there is no God but you" (2 Sam 7:22).

8.8.3. Chaoskampf in the Bible. It often is asserted that creation in the Bible is associated with a *Chaoskampf* (divine battle against chaos) between Yahweh and the sea, following older religious traditions. Certainly, there are many references to fights between gods and monsters in myths. However, it is only in the rather late and syncretistic Babylonian *Enuma Elish* that battle is associated with creation. Baal's battle with the sea Yam (note: not the *těhôm* of Gen 1:2) has nothing to do with creation (see Tsumura 1989); there is no reason to think that creation in the Bible was ever associated with battle. In Psalm 46 the chaotic sea waters bring about not creation, but destruction. In poetic passages, such as Habakkuk 3, storm and war imageries express Yahweh's victorious acts. There is no reason to associate them with creation or with Baal. Storm and war imageries often are used interchangeably in ancient Near Eastern literature. Furthermore, the Ugaritic myth does not associate storm imagery with the battle between Baal and Yam. Yahweh's kingship in Psalm 29 is unrelated to Baal's kingship after his victory over Yam, the chaos water, for the water *mabbûl* (Ps 29:10) refers to the Deluge, like the Akkadian *abūbu* (*CAD* A/1.77-81)—that is, to Yahweh's weapon, not his enemy.

There are expressions referring to Yahweh fighting creatures similar to Baal's enemies, such as Leviathan (Ps 74:14; 104:26; Is 27:1), Rahab (Ps 89:10; Is 51:9) and a monster (Ps 74:13). However, these almost always occur in isolated phrases in poetic texts, and should be treated as imagery, metaphors and idioms rather than as religious statements. It should be noted that even in the Ugaritic myth the victory over *Ltn* (i.e., Leviathan) and the dragon *tnn* were described as past events, and it is reasonable to assume that such traditions had already become widely known in Canaan in the Late Bronze Age. The biblical authors used them metaphorically (see Tsumura 2005).

8.8.4. Cult of the Dead. The paucity of the biblical references to the spirits of the dead or to life after death probably was a conscious reaction against the pagan practices of neighboring peoples.

There is no practice of postmortem deification in the prophetic religion of Israel. Even King *David and great figures such as Abraham and *Samuel were not deified after death. When the people buried Samuel "in his house" in Ramah (1 Sam 25:1), there was no hint of the Ugaritic practices of worshiping his spirit or holding a *marzēaḥ*, although they did lament his death and have a burial service (1 Sam 28:3). It was an abomination for the Israelites to eat the "sacrifices for the dead," for to do so was to identify with the Canaanite god Baal-peor (Ps 106:28).

The biblical expression "slept with his ancestors," which means "died and was buried," used for David (1 Kings 2:10), *Solomon (1 Kings 11:43), *Jeroboam (1 Kings 14:20), *Rehoboam (1 Kings 14:31) and others, has nothing to do with ancestor worship. In the biblical religion it is Yahweh who holds authority over life and death of humans (see Yamauchi), for, as Hannah said, "The Lord kills and makes alive; he brings down to Sheol and raises up" (1 Sam 2:6).

8.8.5. Summary and Conclusions. In various ways, therefore, it is apparent that Canaanite religion exerted an influence on the religious life of the Israelites. On the other hand, those Canaanite religious practices were completely rejected by the prophetic religion, although the biblical authors sometimes adopted Canaanite expressions and divine names for metaphorical purposes. We should carefully distinguish between literary metaphors and religious syncretism. These Canaanite expressions were used by biblical writers metaphorically or apologetically.

See also CANAANITE GODS AND RELIGION; GOD; NON-ISRAELITE WRITTEN SOURCES: SYRO-PALESTINIAN.

BIBLIOGRAPHY. **J. Day,** *Molech: A God of Human Sacrifice in the Old Testament* (UCOP 41; Cambridge: Cambridge University Press, 1989); idem, "Religion of Canaan," *ABD* 1.831-37; **R. Deutsch,** *Biblical Period Hebrew Bullae: The Josef Chaim Kaufman Collection* (Tel Aviv: Archaeological Center Publication, 2003); **L. Finkel,** "Necromancy in Ancient Mesopotamia," *AfO* 29/30 (1983-1984) 1-17; **J. C. Greenfield,** "Aspects of Aramaean Religion," in *Ancient Israelite Religion: Essays in Honor of Frank Moore Cross,* ed. P. D. Miller Jr., P. D. Hanson and S. D. McBride (Philadelphia: Fortress, 1987) 67-78; **J. Hadley,** *The Cult of Asherah in Ancient Israel and Judah: Evidence for a Hebrew Goddess* (Cambridge: Cambridge University Press, 2000); **R. S. Hess,** "Yahweh and His Asherah? Epigraphic Evidence for Religious Pluralism in Old Testament Times," in *One God, One Lord in a World of Religious Pluralism,* ed. A. D. Clarke and B. W. Winter (Cambridge: Tyndale House, 1991) 5-33; **J. Huehnergard,** "Languages," *ABD* 4.155-70; **C. J. Labuschagne,** *The Incomparability of Yahweh in the Old Testament* (POS 5; Leiden: E. J. Brill, 1966); **N. P. Lemche,** *The Canaanites and Their Land: The Tradition of the Canaanites* (JSOTSup 110; Sheffield: Sheffield Academic Press, 1991); idem, "City-dwellers or Administrators: Further Light on the Canaanites," in *History and Traditions of Early Israel: Studies Presented to Eduard Nielsen, May 8, 1993,* ed. A. Lemaire and B. Otzen (VTSup 50; Leiden: E. J. Brill, 1993) 76-89; **T. J. Lewis,** *Cults of the Dead in Ancient Israel and Ugarit* (HSM 39; Atlanta: Scholars Press, 1989); **E. Lipiński,** "Shemesh," *DDD* 1445-52; **J. Margueron,** "Quelques réflexions sur certaines pratiques funéraires d'Ugarit (fig. 1-17)," *Akkadica* 32 (1983) 5-31; **A. R. Millard,** "The Canaanites," in *People of Old Testament Times,* ed. D. J. Wiseman (Oxford: Clarendon Press, 1973) 29-52; **P. D. Miller Jr.,** "Aspects of the Religion of Ugarit," in *Ancient Israelite Religion: Essays in Honor of Frank Moore Cross,* ed. P. D. Miller Jr., P. D. Hanson and S.D. McBride (Philadelphia: Fortress, 1987) 53-66; **W. L. Moran,** *The Amarna Letters* (Baltimore: Johns Hopkins University Press, 1992); **N. Na'aman,** "The Canaanites and Their Land: A Rejoinder," *UF* 26 (1994) 397-418; **J. Naveh,** *Early History of the Alphabet: An Introduction to West Semitic Epigraphy and Palaeography* (rev. ed.; Jerusalem: Magnes; Leiden: E. J. Brill, 1987); **G. del Olmo Lete and J. Sanmartín,** *A Dictionary of the Ugaritic Language in the Alphabetic Tradition* (2 vols.; HO 67; Boston and Leiden: E. J. Brill, 2003); **D. Pardee,** "Ugaritic Myths," *COS* 1.241-83; **A. F. Rainey,** "Who Is a Canaanite? A Review of the Textual Evidence," *BASOR* 304 (1996) 1-15; **J. Renz and W. Röllig,** *Handbuch der Althebräischen Epigraphik, Band 2/2: Johannes Renz: Materialien zur Althebräischen Morphologie; Wolfgang Röllig: Siegel und Gewichte* (Darmstadt: Wissenschaftliche Buchgesellschaft, 2003); **P. C. Schmitz,** "Canaan," *ABD* 1.828-31; **K. N. Schoville,** "Canaanites and Amorites," in *Peoples of the Old Testament World,* ed. A. J. Hoerth, G. L. Mattingly and E. M. Yamauchi (Grand Rapids: Baker, 1994) 157-82; **M. S. Smith,** "Rephaim," *ABD* 5.674-76; idem, *The Early History of God: Yahweh and the Other Deities in Ancient Israel* (2d ed.; Grand Rapids: Eerdmans, 2002); **O. Tammuz,** "Canaan—A Land without Limits," *UF* 33 (2001) 501-43; **J.-M. de Tarragon,** *Le culte à Ugarit: D'après les textes de la pratique en cunéiformes alphabétiques* (CahRB 19; Paris: Gabalda, 1980); **J. G. Taylor,** *Yahweh and the Sun: Biblical and Archaeological Evidence for Sun Worship in Ancient Israel* (JSOTSup 111; Sheffield: Sheffield Academic Press, 1993); **K. van der Toorn,** "Sun," *ABD* 6.237-39; **D. T. Tsumura,** *Creation and Destruction: A Reappraisal of the Chaoskampf Theory in the Old Testament* (Winona Lake, IN: Eisenbrauns, 2005); idem, *The Earth and the Waters in Genesis 1 and 2: A Linguistic Investigation* (JSOTSup 83; Sheffield: Sheffield Academic Press, 1989); idem, "The Interpretation of the Ugaritic Funerary Text *KTU* 1.161," in *Official Cult and Popular Religion in the Ancient Near East: Papers of the First Colloquium on the Ancient Near East—the*

City and Its Life, Held at the Middle Eastern Culture Center in Japan (Mitaka, Tokyo), March 20-22, 1992, ed. E. Matsushima (Heidelberg: Winter, 1993) 40-55; idem, "Kings and Cults in Ancient Ugarit," in *Priests and Officials in the Ancient Near East: Papers of the Second Colloquium on the Ancient Near East—the City and Its Life, Held at the Middle Eastern Culture Center in Japan (Mitaka, Tokyo), March 22-24, 1996,* ed. K. Watanabe (Heidelberg: Winter, 1999) 215-38; idem, "שמש, Sun," *NIDOTTE* 4.185-90; idem, "Ugaritic Poetry and Habakkuk 3," *TynBul* 40 (1988) 24-48; **G. E. Watson and N. Wyatt,** eds., *Handbook of Ugaritic Studies* (HO 39; Boston and Leiden: E. J. Brill, 1999); **E. Yamauchi,** "Life, Death, and the Afterlife in the Ancient Near East," in *Life in the Face of Death: The Resurrection Message of the New Testament,* ed. R. N. Longenecker (Grand Rapids: Eerdmans, 1998) 21-50.   D. T. Tsumura

CANAANITE GODS AND RELIGION

The Historical Books of the Hebrew Bible present the Israelites as taking over the land of the Canaanites, and Israelite religion as continuing to be in tension with the worship of Canaanite deities, in particular that of the god Baal. Not surprisingly, therefore, Canaanite gods and religion receive a very critical and negative treatment at the hands of the biblical writers. However, it is important that readers of the Bible should know how the Canaanites themselves thought of their gods and described their own religious practices. This is now possible, thanks in particular to the discoveries made at Ras Shamra, ancient Ugarit.

1. *Canaan* and *Canaanites* in the Hebrew Bible
2. The City of Ugarit
3. The Religious Beliefs and Practices of Ugarit
4. Canaanite Deities and Religion in the Hebrew Bible
5. Conclusion

1. *Canaan* and *Canaanites* in the Hebrew Bible.

1.1. The Canaanites. In the Hebrew Bible the term *Canaanites* often seems to be used rather loosely to refer to those who were in the land before the arrival of the Israelites. The statement "At that time the Canaanites were in the land" (Gen 12:6; cf. 13:7) suggests that this was not the case when those traditions were committed to writing. It occurs sometimes on its own

(e.g., Judg 1:1, 3), but at other times alongside the names of other ancient peoples in what appear to have become stylized lists of the former inhabitants of the land (e.g., Josh 3:10). The listing of the numerous ancient peoples reputed to have been defeated may have enhanced the achievement of Israel and, more importantly, of Israel's God. There are, however, some references to Canaanites continuing to live alongside Israelites (e.g., Josh 17:12; Judg 1:29, 33).

A difficulty lies in the extent to which it is possible to distinguish the Canaanites from other groups, such as the Amorites. In Joshua 7:7-9 both these names seem to be used to refer to the pre-Israelite inhabitants of the land into which the Israelites were entering rather than to distinct groups. It is not always easy to differentiate Canaanites from *Phoenicians, and it is possible that the Phoenician culture is to be understood as a continuation of that of the Canaanites. A. R. Millard (36) has described the Phoenicians as "latter-day Canaanites," so, as with the Israelites, the difference may be primarily temporal. And indeed the Israelites themselves have been regarded as Canaanites (see Lemche). However, the writers of the Hebrew Bible seem to have regarded the Israelites as distinct from the Canaanites.

Predominantly, then, the Canaanites are the pre-Israelite inhabitants, and in the light of this usage it will be appropriate to look for evidence of Canaanite religion in sources that predate the time when Israelites were living in the southern Levant.

1.2. The Land of Canaan. Mention must also be made of the extent of the area occupied by the Canaanites, in particular of its northern extent, in view of issues regarding the appropriateness of using the discoveries from ancient Ugarit as evidence for describing Canaanite religion (see 2.1 below). The biblical "Table of Nations" (Gen 10:15-19) suggests that its compiler understood Canaan to stretch from Gaza in the south, beyond Sidon, as far north as Hamath. Such a northerly extent would reach almost as far as Ugarit. But another description of the boundaries of Canaan (Num 34:2-12) places its northern limit at Lebo-hamath (Lebweh), considerably further south. Numbers 33:51 suggests that Canaan covered the whole area west of the Jordan, whereas Numbers 13:29 suggests that the Canaanites inhabited the coastal area and land along the Jordan only. Evidence from

Egyptian sources (see Millard, 30-33) suggests that the Egyptian province of Canaan comprised the territory north of Gaza, between the Mediterranean to the west and the Jordan valley to the east. Unfortunately, the northern limits are less clear.

2. The City of Ugarit.

2.1. The Discovery of Ugarit. Knowledge of the Canaanites initially was derived largely from the Hebrew Bible. However, in 1929 what was deemed to be an important advance came about with the discovery on the site of Ras Shamra in Syria of the remains of the ancient city of Ugarit. Excavations have revealed a cosmopolitan city with a huge royal palace and other impressive buildings. Many artifacts have been found, including some (e.g., statuettes, altars) that may provide clues to religious practices (for a general description see Curtis 1999). Texts in several languages were discovered, but particularly important were those inscribed using the cuneiform method of writing but in a hitherto unknown language. This language was surmised to be the local language, and it has come to be known as Ugaritic. Excavations demonstrate that Ugarit was a very ancient city, dating back to the Neolithic period, but whose golden age was in the Late Bronze Age (c. 1550-1200 BCE), the period during which the texts were produced.

But was Ugarit a Canaanite city? According to some definitions (see 1.2 above), it was too far north to be so. D. Pardee (236) has suggested that some of the archaic features of Israelite religion may reflect a southern Canaanite tradition, whereas Ugarit reflects "older 'Amorite' connections." Millard (44) warns against the danger of regarding Ugarit as typically Canaanite. But it is important to note that texts in the Ugaritic language have been found in other locations, some near Ras Shamra, but others much further afield, including Israel; tablets were found at Taanach and Beth-shemesh, and an inscribed dagger near Mount Tabor. This suggests that the beliefs and practices reflected in the texts from Ugarit may represent a more widespread phenomenon. J. N. Tubb comments, with reference to Ugarit, "It is clear from the material remains that this northernmost part of the Syrian coast lay within the same cultural continuum as the rest of Canaan" (Tubb, 73). Thus the discussion that follows here centers on the evidence from Ugarit on the grounds that it offers the nearest thing available to a picture of Canaanite religion.

2.2. Temples. Prominently located on the city's acropolis was the temple dedicated to the god Baal. It was identified as such thanks to the discovery of a dedicatory stela that had been presented by an Egyptian ambassador and, nearby, another stela bearing what has become the most familiar of the representations of Baal. He is depicted in a striding pose, wearing a helmet decorated with horns, probably symbolizing his divinity (though there may also be a fertility connection), a skirt and a scabbard. In his right hand, raised above his head, is a club, and in his left hand he holds out in front of him an object that is pointed like a spear. These have been interpreted as symbols of thunder and lightning, respectively. Thus Baal appears as a warrior, armed with the weapons associated with the storm god.

The temple building was surrounded by a walled enclosure, creating a sacred precinct within which the base of a stepped stone altar was found. The sanctuary proper comprised an outer room, and also an inner sanctum within which was a structure made of large blocks of stone that may have been an altar or platform. It is likely that an image of the god was placed here. This tripartite pattern of inner room, outer room and courtyard often is a feature of Semitic sanctuaries, and it recalls the pattern of *Solomon's temple (1 Kings 6). The temple had a staircase that led to an upper area, perhaps a roof chapel and altar (of the type mentioned in 2 Kings 23:12) and/or a tower. There may be a reference to the "tower of Baal of Ugarit" in text *KTU* 1.119 12 (on the problem with this reading see Wyatt, 419).

In view of Baal's importance, it is not surprising that there was a temple of Baal on the city's acropolis. Perhaps more surprising is the presence there of a temple apparently dedicated, based on the evidence of two dedicatory stelae found outside its southern façade, to Dagan. Dagan plays little part in the mythological texts, other than being named as Baal's father, although that in itself might be a reason for him to have a temple in close proximity to that of his son. But in what may have been an official pantheon list, Dagan's name appears very near the top of the list between El and Baal. (On the relationship between El, Dagan and Baal, see 3.4 below; if, as has been suggested, Dagan was equated with El, then any apparent difficulty might be removed.)

Between the temples of Baal and Dagan was an impressive building that was identified as the house of the high priest, thanks to the discovery there of a cache of bronze objects—weapons, tools and a decorated tripod—some of which bore the inscription "chief of the priests" and probably were the offering of a metalworker. Within this house were found several groups of texts, including some containing myths about Baal, and some that have been thought to be writing exercises. This suggests that the building had several functions, being not only the residence of the high priest, but also a school for scribes and a place where texts were copied and stored. Whether the discovery of such tablets in the vicinity of the temples means that the texts were used within the cult practiced there is uncertain, but some of the texts do include hints that they may have been read aloud, perhaps during worship.

During excavations in the center of the city, another sanctuary was discovered. It came to be known as the "Rhyton Temple" because some conical drinking vessels were found in its vicinity, and it was thought that these might be associated with the sanctuary. The building comprised an entrance porch giving access to a large room in which was a structure identified as an altar, and also another small room. Another discovery led to the possible identification of the deity to whom this temple was dedicated. This was a stone statue representing a bearded and helmeted figure seated on a throne, thought to be the god El, the head of the pantheon and therefore a deity to whom it might be expected that there would be a temple at Ugarit. But whether the temple was in fact dedicated to El is uncertain, and another suggestion is that it was a private sanctuary.

Other structures have been identified as sanctuaries. One to the north of the royal palace has become known as the "Hurrian Sanctuary," while an area within the royal palace has also been thought to have been a sanctuary.

2.3. Tombs. Many of the houses had tombs beneath their floors or courtyards. These often were approached by a flight of steps leading down into a carefully built vaulted chamber with a paved floor. Within the walls of the tomb were niches. There is no evidence that bodies were placed in coffins, so probably they were placed directly on the floor, wrapped in shrouds. The presence of items of funerary equipment suggests that it was believed to be appropriate to make provision for the deceased, and in particular the fact that cups were provided raises the question as to whether the people of Ugarit believed in some form of post mortem existence. In the story of Aqhat (see 3.9.2-3 below) there is an episode that may shed light on this issue.

3. The Religious Beliefs and Practices of Ugarit. Information about the religion of Ugarit comes partly from literary sources, including myths and legends, ritual and cultic texts, and lists of sacrifices, and partly from buildings, artifacts and iconography, some of which have already been mentioned. Brief outlines of some of the major myths and epics are included at appropriate points in what follows.

3.1. The Ugaritic Pantheon. The texts from Ugarit bear witness to numerous deities. It has been calculated that the total is about 240, although there may be some overlap of titles and epithets. Many of these gods are known only from lists of deities and sacrifices. However, the mythological and epic texts provide insight into the activities and attributes of some of the major gods and goddesses by describing their doings and by the use of a number of stock epithets that presumably indicate something of what was understood to be the nature of the particular deity. In what follows, particular reference is made to those deities who may be mentioned in the Historical Books of the Hebrew Bible. It should be noted that the names of the deities are Anglicized in differing ways in various publications. For some, what might be termed "standard" English forms of the name have emerged, but some treatments use a form that is judged to approximate more closely to the likely original vocalization (compare, e.g., "El" and "Ilu," "Baal" and "Ba'lu"). Generally, in the discussion that follows the forms found in Wyatt are used.

3.2. El. The head of the pantheon was El. His principal epithets in the mythological texts were "king" *(mlk)*, probably reflecting his position as the chief deity and the one who presided over the assembly of the gods (although he is not the only god given this title); "bull" *(tr)*, a title thought to have some connection with fertility but that may be an indication of power and strength; "compassionate/gentle one, god of mercy" *(ltpn il dpid)*. Other titles are "creator of creatures" *(bny bnwt)* and "father of human-kind" *(ab adm)*, perhaps suggesting that El was a creator-god (although no creation myth as such has yet been found at Ugarit). A title whose meaning is unclear is *ab šnm;* it has been understood as meaning "father of years," suggesting longevity or perhaps control of the seasons, but this interpretation has been questioned. Partly in the light of this epithet, and partly because El was relatively inactive in some of the mythological texts, it has been suggested that he was a senile figure who had been supplanted by the warrior god Baal. Iconography, insofar as it is possible to be sure who is being depicted in a statue or on a stela, shows El as a bearded and seated figure, and this again has been taken to point to an aged or otiose figure. However, it is more appropriate to describe El as a figure of seniority. The mythological texts describe him as presiding over the divine assembly, so it is not inappropriate that he should have been depicted as enthroned. He was the one from whom permission was required for major undertakings such as the building of Baal's palace. In the stories of Keret and of Aqhat, El tends to be in the foreground, with Baal playing a subsidiary role—for example, interceding with El on behalf of the heroes of the epics. This has led to the suggestion that they are earlier than the versions of the myths about Baal that have been preserved. There is also a text (*KTU* 1.23) that combines a myth with various liturgical instructions and depicts a far-from-senile El. The myth describes El becoming aroused and having intercourse with two wives, Athirat and Rahmay, and the resultant birth of the gods Shahar and Shalem, who possibly represent the morning and evening stars.

3.3. Athirat. El's principal consort was Athirat. She was described as *rbt aṯrt ym*, which could be understood as meaning "great lady Athirat of the sea" or "great lady Athirat of the day." N. Wyatt (83) has suggested that it should be understood as "the Great Lady-who-tramples-Yam." Another important epithet was *qnyt ilm* ("creatress/mother of the gods"), suggesting that she and El were regarded as the mother and father of other deities. The texts in fact refer to them as parents of "seventy" offspring—certainly not to be taken as a precise number but as an indication that they were believed to have many children—including some of the deities who played a prominent role in the mythologi-cal texts. Notable among these were Yam ("Sea," also known as Nahar ["River"]), and Mot ("Death"), both of whom Baal engaged in conflict.

3.4. Dagan. Although there is one possible reference in the mythological texts to Baal as a son of El, he was much more frequently designated as son of Dagan. Dagan is well known from ancient Near Eastern sources, and it is likely that he was an Amorite deity; in the Hebrew Bible he was associated with the *Philistines. He plays no role in the longer mythological texts hitherto discovered, but his name features prominently in sacrifice lists, and there was a temple dedicated to him at Ugarit. A possible explanation for this is that Baal was not thought to be a member of El's family, and it is noteworthy that it was with two prominent members of El's family that Baal came into conflict. Some have suggested that there was a conflict between Baal and El for supremacy among the gods, but this goes beyond the evidence of the available texts. It may be preferable to see the texts as reflecting how Baal, a member of a different family of gods perhaps brought to Ugarit by the influx of a new and powerful population group (Amorites?), came to prominence among the gods revered at Ugarit without completely ousting the old order. An alternative possibility is that El and Dagan came to be identified as a result of the merging of the two pantheons (on this issue, see Smith, 87-96).

3.5. Baal.

3.5.1. The "Baal Cycle" of Myths. Particularly important among the texts in Ugaritic are those which describe the activities of the god Baal. These often are called the "Baal Cycle," and sometimes they are regarded as a unitary composition. However, a note of caution is needed because it is not absolutely clear in what sequence the tablets are to be read, and there are other longer and shorter mythic fragments that may be associated with those that have come to be seen as a Baal Cycle (on this issue see Smith, 2-19). Nevertheless, there seem to be three major episodes described in the texts, and a case can be made for what has become the customary sequence in which to read them. That sequence is followed here. Another caveat is needed. The texts often are fragmentary, and there are frequent gaps, so reconstruction of the stories is tentative.

3.5.2. Baal and Yam (KTU 1.1 and 1.2). These

tablets are very incompletely preserved, so there are some significant gaps. However, they appear to describe the arrival of messengers from El to Baal's sister, Anat, and then the sending of messengers to Kothar-and-Hasis, the craftsman of the gods, to summon him to attend upon El. There follows a declaration by El that his son Yam ("Sea") is his regent, and a feast follows, perhaps in celebration of Yam's coronation. Then Kothar-and-Hasis is instructed to build a palace for Yam. A complaint by the god Athtar that he has no palace apparently is dismissed. Subsequently, Yam sends an embassy to the assembly of the gods to demand the surrender of Baal. Baal is enraged and attacks the messengers of Yam, but he is restrained by Anat. After a lacuna in the text, Kothar-and-Hasis appears to be encouraging Baal to take action against Yam. He fashions two clubs or maces for Baal with which he subdues and kills Yam. Thereupon Kothar-and-Hasis declares that Baal will be king.

3.5.3. The Building of Baal's Palace (KTU *1.3* and *1.4*). There does seem to be a prima facie case for suggesting that the building of a palace for Baal was seen as the setting of the seal upon his kingly status, achieved as a result of his defeat of Yam. The tablets describe a feast in Baal's honor and then depict Anat engaging in warlike activity. Envoys from Baal approach Anat, and she goes to Baal and undertakes to demand of El that a palace should be provided for Baal. She appears to threaten El and then to make her request. This apparently is not yet successful, and the help of El's consort, Athirat, is sought. Kothar-and-Hasis is summoned to make presents for Athirat, and Baal and Anat take them to Athirat, who initially is disturbed at their arrival but then sees the gifts. They beg her to intercede with El, and she goes to El to plead that Baal, as a king, should have a palace. El grants the request, the news is conveyed to Baal, and Kothar-and-Hasis begins work on the palace on Baal's holy mountain, Saphon. After a discussion as to whether there is to be a window in the palace, the building is brought to completion, and a banquet is held. Baal then seems to undertake a tour of his kingdom, apparently seizing numerous cities, before settling in his palace and finally agreeing that a window be constructed (the window perhaps was understood to be the means whereby Baal was able to manifest himself in the form of his voice—i.e., the thun-

der). Baal then announces his resolve to send a message to Mot ("Death"), apparently to inform him of the building of his palace.

3.5.4. Baal and Mot (KTU *1.5* and *1.6*). In view of the message, just noted above, that Baal sends to Mot, this episode perhaps is to be seen as next in the sequence. Mot speaks threatening words to the effect that despite Baal's victories, Mot will devour him. Messengers are dispatched to Baal, who apparently does not resist and accepts that he must go to Mot's underworld abode. After a break, Baal is seen being instructed to go into the underworld, accompanied by his attendants and his daughters, taking with him the phenomena associated with his characteristics as a storm-god, including the rains. On the way, he apparently is described as copulating with a heifer, which bears him a son. This puzzling episode has been variously understood as Baal somehow guaranteeing the continuance of fertility, or perhaps providing an heir, or a substitute to be devoured by Mot, or a gift for Mot. When the text again becomes legible, it is being reported to El that Baal's body has been found, and El enters into mourning. Anat goes to retrieve the corpse and succeeds with the help of Shapsh, the sun-goddess. Baal is buried, accompanied by the slaughter of many animals as a funeral offering. El then instructs Athirat to propose one of her sons to be king, and Athtar is nominated, a deity whose stock epithet has been understood to mean "the terrible," "the tyrant" or "the brilliant." Athtar is described as mounting Baal's throne, but his feet do not reach the footstool, nor his head its top, so he descends and becomes ruler of the earth. The precise significance of this episode has been differently interpreted. Some have felt that it shows Athtar's inadequacy to take Baal's place, and that therefore he was given some less prominent role—for example, as god of irrigation. But Wyatt (132-33) has suggested that the incident parallels the notion of the royal ascent wherein the earthly king would gain authority from the gods before "returning" to earth to exercise that authority. The text continues with an account of Anat encountering Mot and destroying him. The description of the destruction has been seen as reflecting the harvesting of grain, but not all the elements easily fit such an understanding, and it is perhaps more likely that some ritual lies behind the terminology. Then, in a dream, El learns that Baal is alive. Rejoicing, he calls upon Anat to instruct Shapsh to search for Baal. After a lacuna, Baal is seen fighting against the sons of Athirat and then taking his throne. Seven years pass, then Mot, presumably also restored to life, confronts Baal, and the two engage in conflict. Baal appears to be gaining the upper hand when Shapsh calls upon Mot to accept that he cannot prevail, whereupon Mot appears to acknowledge Baal's kingship.

3.5.5. A Seasonal Myth? The myth of Baal and Mot has widely been thought to reflect the annual seasonal pattern, Baal and Mot reflecting the fertile rainy season and the arid dry season, respectively. But this view has not been universally accepted, and there are problems with this interpretation. There are details of the story that are difficult to integrate, in particular the clear reference to the passage of seven years before Mot becomes a threat to Baal once again. Although it could be argued that, in the context of myth, such time statements should not be taken literally, it nevertheless seems strange that a myth intended to provide the rationale for the annual seasonal cycle would include reference to the passage of a much longer period. It is likely that the story of Baal's victory over Yam provided for his worshipers the assurance that he had control over the waters, underlining his status as the god of rain and storm. That episode then might offer the guarantee that Baal would send his rains after the dry summer months. But from time to time the rains may not have come, and periods of drought would disrupt the regular pattern of the seasons. Perhaps the story of Baal and Mot was intended to reassure the worshiper that if occasionally Mot appeared to have the upper hand over Baal, nevertheless Baal would indeed return, and Mot would not prevail forever.

3.5.6. Baal's Epithets. Baal's epithets reflect his prominence among the gods, achieved as a result of demonstrations of his might in conflict, and may also allude to his powers to send fertility. He was "victor" or "valiant" *(aliyn),* "king" *(mlk),* "prince" *(zbl),* "judge" *(tpt,* a virtual equivalent of the title "ruler"), "most high" *('ly),* "lord of the earth" *(b'l arṣ).* He was also described as *rkb 'rpt,* a title that has usually been understood to mean "rider/charioteer of the clouds." Baal is also given the name "Haddu," probably the Ugaritic equivalent of "Hadad," the name of a well-known ancient Near Eastern storm-god. This perhaps was the real name of the god

whose title was *b'l,* "lord."

3.6. Anat. In the Ugaritic mythological texts Baal was closely associated with the goddess Anat, who perhaps was regarded as his sister. She was a warlike goddess and seems to have been associated with Baal in some of his conflicts. Her epithets, however, may present a somewhat different picture. She is described as "virgin" *(btlt)* and perhaps as "damsel" *(rhm).* Some have seen an epithet of Anat in the phrase *mšnqt ilm,* understood as meaning "wet-nurse of the gods." Another description, *ybmt limm,* has been interpreted as "sister-in-law of peoples" or "beloved of the powerful one."

3.7. Athtart. In the Hebrew Bible Baal tends to be associated not with Anat, but with Athirat/Asherah or with another goddess, Ashtoreth/Astarte. The latter also appears in the Ugaritic texts as Athtart, but she does not figure prominently in the myths. But that she too was associated with Baal is suggested by her epithet *šm b'l,* which means "name of Baal."

3.8. Ugaritic Cult and Ritual. In addition to the mythological and epic texts from Ugarit, numerous texts have been found that shed light on religious practices. Of particular interest has been the discovery of what are often described as "pantheon lists," although Pardee (11) has rightly pointed out that such lists are in fact connected with sacrificial practice. However, there may have been what amounted to an "official" deity list with carefully arranged groupings of deities. Two copies of this list, plus an Akkadian translation, have been found. G. del Olmo Lete has described this "pantheon" as reflecting "a special synthesis, different from those known in other parts of the ancient Near East and determined by specific geographic and social factors: a coastal location, a dependence on rain, and the monarchic and feudal organization of the state" (del Olmo Lete, 53-54). Other texts are associated with the sacrificial cult, describing or prescribing the rituals for various regular or special sacrifices or series of sacrificial rites, sometimes lasting over days and indeed months. Especially noteworthy is what Wyatt (342-47) entitles "A Liturgy for a Rite of Atonement for the People of Ugarit." Several copies of this ritual have survived, the most complete being *KTU* 1.40.

Perhaps sometimes closely associated with sacrifices is the evidence of the practice of divination. Models of livers and lungs probably reflect the practice of consulting the entrails of sacrificial animals for omens. Divinatory "manuals" suggest the taking of omens from malformed human and animal fetuses, as well as divination by means of the heavenly bodies. *KTU* 1.124 may reflect the consultation of some sort of divine oracle for the purposes of a healing; del Olmo Lete (312) sees an analogy with the incident described in 2 Kings 1:2-3.

Evidence also has been found relating to funerary practices, as well as nonsacrificial liturgies, oaths, incantations and prayers. *KTU* 1.119 includes what may be the only example yet known of a prayer directed to Baal. It begins, "O Baal! If you will drive the strong one from our gates, the warrior from our walls, a bull, O Baal, we shall dedicate, a vow, Baal, we shall fulfil, a male animal, Baal, we shall dedicate, a propitiation we shall fulfil, a feast, Baal, we shall prepare" (Wyatt, 421-22). Where Wyatt translates "male animal," it is possible that "firstborn" should be read, and an allusion to child sacrifice has been seen. But even if that is the correct reading, the reference need not be to a child (see Pardee, 233). In fact, there is no clear evidence of the practice of child sacrifice in the Ugaritic texts. There are also a number of what D. Pardee (167) has described as "historiolae," where mythological and more practical or magical elements are juxtaposed—for example, in two stories involving the gods Shapsh and Horon that involve spells against snakebite and perhaps the ridding of the land of serpents (*KTU* 1.100 and 1.107). Another of these (*KTU* 1.114) describes El at a banquet, and it may include a recipe for hangover; El is described as being in his *mrzḥ*, a term that has been understood as referring to a feasting house (so Wyatt, 410) or drinking club (so Pardee, 169). The Hebrew prophets criticized the behavior associated with such institutions (Jer 16:5; Amos 6:7).

3.9. The Religious Status and Role of the King. Among the longer texts in Ugaritic are two groups that tell the stories of two figures, Keret and Danel, who probably were thought of as kings, although this is not explicitly stated of the latter. They seem to have been envisaged as human beings, although there is constant interplay between the divine and human participants. But these stories perhaps are better described as epics or legends rather than myths. Nevertheless, they may offer some clues as to what was believed about the status and religious significance

of the king in Ugaritic society.

3.9.1. The Story of Keret (KTU *1.14, 1.15 and 1.16).* The story begins with a description of how Keret's entire family has been destroyed as a result of various misfortunes and disasters. As Keret weeps in his bedchamber, El appears to him in a vision, and when Keret tells the god that the cause of his distress is his desire for descendants, he is told to offer sacrifices and then gather an army to undertake a military campaign against Pabil, king of Udum, to gain his daughter Hurriy as a bride. Keret follows El's instructions and departs for Udum. On the way, he stops at a sanctuary of Athirat and makes a vow to give the goddess twice his bride's weight in silver and three times her weight in gold if he succeeds in his quest. The journey is completed, Udum is besieged and, as foretold by El, Pabil sends messengers to offer Keret wealth if he will withdraw. But Keret demands Hurriy, and Pabil presumably accedes because, when it next becomes possible to follow the story, Keret is holding a banquet for the gods and inviting El to bless him. El does so, assuring Keret that offspring will be born to him, which proves to be the case. Keret, however, seems to have forgotten his vow. He appears to order the preparation of a feast for his commanders, but when they arrive, they are told to weep for Keret, who apparently has succumbed to illness, probably brought upon him by Athirat. One of Keret's sons, Ilhu, comes to lament for his father, asking, "How can it be said that Keret is the son of El, the offspring of the Wise and Holy One? Or do the gods die, the offspring of the Wise One not live?" (*KTU* 1.16 i 20-23). He is told to summon his sister, who is angry that she has not been told of Keret's illness. After a break, there appears to be a description of a ritual being performed to counteract the effects of famine and drought, perhaps thought to be the result of Keret's illness. Subsequently, a herald is sent to summon the gods to see who will cure Keret, but when none volunteers, El creates a goddess, Shatiqat, from clay and sends her to cure him. She succeeds, a feast is held, and Keret returns to his throne. But another son, Yasib, comes to challenge Keret, perhaps unaware that he has been healed. He taunts Keret, "You have not tried the case of the widow; you have not judged the cause of the powerless" (*KTU* 1.16 vi 33-34), and urges him to vacate the kingship. Keret, however, curses his son.

3.9.2. The Story of Aqhat (KTU *1.17, 1.18 and 1.19*). The background of the story is that Danel, probably a king, has no son. He offers sacrifices over several days, until on the seventh day Baal intercedes on his behalf with El that he should have a son who will perform the duties expected of a son. El blesses Danel and, after a gap in the text that presumably must have described the birth of Aqhat, Danel holds a feast for the Kotharat, goddesses of childbirth. There is a lengthy break before it becomes possible to follow the story again. Danel, who, we are told at this point, "tried the case of the widow, he judged the cause of the orphan" (*KTU* 1.17 v 7-8), sees Kothar-and-Hasis approaching, bringing a remarkable composite bow, a gift for Aqhat. While a feast is being held, the goddess Anat arrives and covets the bow, offering silver and gold for it. When Aqhat refuses, she offers him immortality in return for the bow, but he accuses her of lying, stressing that he must share the fate of all humans; he also taunts her that bows are for warriors, not for women! Enraged, Anat goes to El to complain of Aqhat's insolence. Subsequently, Anat invites Aqhat to go hunting, and then she instructs a certain Yatipan to take the form of a raptor, swoop upon Aqhat and kill him. This he does, and Aqhat's bow falls into a river, shattered, whereupon Anat appears to regret what has happened. Danel is dispensing justice when he is approached by Pughat, his daughter, who sees that plants are withering, perhaps understood to be a result of what has happened. She tears Danel's cloak, at which he either utters a curse upon the land or prays that rain will return. Thereafter he goes around his land, apparently looking for healthy plants, wishing that Aqhat might be there to harvest the grain. Messengers arrive to tell him that Aqhat is dead and of Anat's involvement. Danel sees raptors overhead. He curses them, and as they fall at his feet, he examines the contents of their stomachs and eventually finds the remains of his son and buries him. He then visits various nearby towns and curses them. Mourning lasts for seven years, after which Danel sacrifices to the gods, and Pughat puts on the garb and weapons of a warrior to go in search of Yatipan, who killed her brother. She finds him and gives him wine to drink. Here the tablet ends, but presumably the story is not over.

3.9.3. The King's Special Status. These stories suggest certain beliefs about the king and his role. Both stress the importance of the continuance of the royal dynasty; they suggest a possible belief in the potential negative effects of a king's or heir's sickness. Both show the king in the role of judge and as the protector of vulnerable members of society. The king is also seen offering sacrifices. The encounter between Aqhat and Anat has been seen as suggesting that the people of Ugarit believed in some sort of afterlife, a suggestion perhaps supported by possible evidence of the making of provision for the dead (see 2.3 above). But in fact the episode might seem to argue against this, with Aqhat insisting that the offer of immortality is a lie, and that death is the fate of all humans. The story perhaps points to a belief that it was possible for the gods to grant immortality in special circumstances (cf. in the Hebrew Bible *Elijah, who apparently was allowed to escape death [2 Kings 2:11]).

In this context it is noteworthy that there is a text (*KTU* 1.113) that appears to contain on the obverse fragments of a liturgy and on the reverse a list of the kings of Ugarit, each preceded by the word *il* ("god"), pointing to the likelihood that the dead kings were regarded as gods. There are also fragments of a myth (*KTU* 1.20, 1.21 and 1.22) that describe the activities of the *rpum*, who perhaps are to be understood as dead and deified kings or heroes, and who journey to take part in a ritual. This story may provide the mythology lying behind such rituals as the royal funerary liturgy preserved in *KTU* 1.161 (so Wyatt, 314; del Olmo Lete, 168). A number of other rituals are thought to be associated with the royal funerary cult (see del Olmo Lete, 213-53). Yet others confirm the picture given in the stories of Keret and Aqhat that the king played his part in the sacrificial cult—for example, *KTU* 1.115, which opens with a specific instruction that the king is to make a sacrifice (Pardee, 66).

4. Canaanite Deities and Religion in the Hebrew Bible.

A number of the deities mentioned in the discussion above are referred to in the Historical Books of the Hebrew Bible. One somewhat puzzling feature is that in some cases the names appear in the plural—for example, "Baals" (Judg 2:11; 3:7; 8:33; 10:6, 10; 1 Sam 7:4; 12:10; 1 Kings 18:18; 2 Chron 17:3; 24:7; 28:2; 33:3; 34:4). A possible explanation of this phenomenon is that the reference is to local manifestations of the single deity. In the Ugaritic pantheon lists (see 3.8 above), after a reference to Baal of Saphon, Baal's name recurs six times; the form is *b*ʿ*lm*, a plural, but the Akkadian version suggests that it is to be understood as singular. It is also possible that the plural forms are deliberately used to stress the multiplicity of such deities. In what follows here, brief mention is made of those deities and of some other elements of Canaanite religion that may be of relevance to understanding the Historical Books of the Hebrew Bible.

4.1. El. In the Hebrew Bible the noun ʾ*ēl* ("God") is used with reference to Israel's God, in addition to the more common ʾ*ĕlōhîm* and the divine name *yhwh* ("Yahweh"). This, along with the fact that there is little if any polemic against El in the Hebrew Bible, raises the possibility that Yahweh and El were connected or perhaps even one and the same. This may be further supported by the evidence for links between Yahweh and Asherah (see 4.3 below). The element ʾ*ēl* frequently is found in theophoric names, although in such instances it could be understood simply as the generic term "God" and in fact to refer to Yahweh.

4.2. Baal. The Hebrew Bible presents Baal as the principal threat to Yahweh and suggests that this threat persisted down to the fall of Judah to Babylon. In the Historical Books Baal worship is attested in the book of Judges, where it is mentioned in a summary statement (Judg 2:13) and again in the context of the story of Gideon (Judg 6:25, 31). Then, in the time of Ahab, a temple and altar to Baal were built (1 Kings 16:31-33), the background to *Elijah's contest with the prophets of Baal (and Asherah) on Mount Carmel (1 Kings 18:20-40; cf. 1 Kings 19:18). It has been suggested that the deity mentioned in this episode is more properly thought of as Melqart, the chief god of the Phoenician city of Tyre. J. Day (2000, 73-76), however, has argued convincingly that the deity referred to is the Canaanite storm-god Baal. Yahweh, by sending lightning and ending drought, is shown here as being capable of the very things for which Baal was renowned. Other references to Baal worship are found in the context of *Jehu's purge (2 Kings 10:18-28), in the subsequent tearing down of Baal's temple (2 Kings 11:18), and then in a summary description of the evils that had brought the Assyrian invasion upon the Israelites (2 Kings 17:16). Altars for Baal were erected

in the time of *Manasseh (2 Kings 21:3), but the trappings of Baal worship were removed in the context of the reforms instituted by *Josiah (2 Kings 23:4-5). The element *baʿal* sometimes is found as a theophoric element in personal names, but it is possible that in such instances it is an epithet, "lord," and refers to Yahweh.

4.3. Asherah. The goddess known from the Ugaritic texts as Athirat is called Asherah in the Hebrew Bible. The plural forms "Asherim" and (less frequently) "Asheroth" also occur. With one exception (Deut 16:21), all occurrences of the form in the singular are found in the Historical Books (Judg 6:25, 26, 28, 30; 1 Kings 15:13; 16:33; 18:19; 2 Kings 13:6; 17:16; 18:4; 21:3, 7; 23:4, 6, 7, 15; 2 Chron 15:16). The three occurrences of the plural form "Asheroth" occur in the Historical Books (Judg 3:7; 2 Chron 19:3; 33:3), as do a number of the plural form "Asherim" (1 Kings 14:15, 23; 2 Kings 17:10; 23:14; 2 Chron 14:3 [MT 14:2]; 17:6; 24:18; 31:1; 33:19; 34:3, 4, 7). The precise significance of these usages has long been a source of debate. In a number of instances the reference seemed to be to some sort of cult object symbolizing a goddess, perhaps a wooden pole or a tree, or an image or even (though difficult to equate with the idea of a goddess) a phallic symbol. Other references seemed to be to a goddess, but prior to the discovery of the texts from Ugarit, some thought that the allusion was to the goddess Ashtoreth/Astarte (see 4.5 below), whereas others thought that it was to some other deity. Since the discovery of the Ugaritic texts, most have been prepared to accept that a number of the references (including some of the plural forms) are to the goddess Athirat/Asherah, not to Ashtoreth/Astarte (Judg 3:7; 1 Kings 15:13; 18:19; 2 Kings 21:7; 23:4; 2 Chron 15:16). Debate has continued about the nature of the cult objects alluded to by the other occurrences, with the most likely understanding being that the references are to some sort of symbol of the goddess, perhaps a wooden pole.

Another issue of debate has been the relationship, if any, between Yahweh and Asherah. If Yahweh was equated with El, is it possible that Asherah was regarded as Yahweh's consort? This speculation was fueled by the discovery of inscriptions at Kuntillet Ajrud, in the northern part of the Sinai Peninsula, dating from about 800 BCE, apparently linking Yahweh and Asherah. One of these inscriptions was on a pithos and included the statement "I bless you by Yahweh of Samaria and by his A/asherah" and was close to a picture showing a number of figures, two of which were thought possibly to represent the divine pair Yahweh and Asherah. However, it is now thought unlikely that the picture and the inscription are directly related. Another inscription reads "I bless you by Yahweh of Teman and by his A/asherah." There is also an inscription from Khirbet el-Qom, west of Hebron, probably dating from the eighth century BCE, that mentions Yahweh and also refers to "his Asherah," the antecedent of "his" probably being Yahweh. Such inscriptions have been thought to point to religious syncretism, but the possibility has to be considered that they reflect a form of Yahwism (perhaps relatively early) in which Yahweh indeed was thought to have a female counterpart or consort. With the emergence of monotheism, such notions may have been rejected in some circles but perhaps lived on in popular religion.

4.4. Anat. Possible references to Anat in the Hebrew Bible are quite limited. In Judges 3:31 brief mention is made of a judge called "Shamgar, son of Anath," but in phrases of the type "X son of Y," Y usually is the father of X, and it is unlikely that the father would be given the name of a goddess, unless the name was hypocoristic. The name of the goddess probably does occur in the place name *Beth-anath* (e.g., Josh 19:38) and possibly also in the name of Jeremiah's ancestral home, *Anathoth* (e.g., Jer 1:1). However, the texts from the Jewish colony that became established at Elephantine in Egypt may point to a tradition in which Yahweh and Anat were connected (see Day 2000, 143-44).

4.5. Ashtoreth/Astarte. The goddess Athtart (Astarte) appears in the Hebrew Bible with the name *Ashtoreth*, the form of the name doubtless being a deliberate distortion of the name of the Canaanite goddess by the substitution in the latter part of the name of the vowels of the Hebrew word *bōšet* ("shameful thing"), thereby not simply naming her, but making a judgment on her. She is mentioned three times in the singular: 1 Kings 11:5, 33 speak of Solomon following and worshiping Ashtoreth, and 2 Kings 23:13 refers to Josiah defiling the *high places that Solomon had made for various deities, including Ashtoreth. Other references use the plural form of the name, and the context is often general statements about Canaanite deities. One of the plural

usages (1 Sam 31:10) is frequently emended to the singular and taken to be a reference to a temple of Ashtoreth. It is possible that the name of the goddess is preserved in the name of a city in Manasseh, *Beeshterah* (Josh 21:27). This may be an abbreviation of *Beth-ashtoreth*, "house/temple of Ashtoreth," suggesting that perhaps it was originally a sanctuary of the goddess. This may be the same town mentioned in 1 Chronicles 6:71 (MT 6:56) as "Ashtaroth."

4.6. Dagan. In the Hebrew Bible Dagan appears as Dagon and is particularly associated with the Philistines (Judg 16:23; 1 Sam 5:2-7; 1 Chron 10:10), who perhaps adopted this Canaanite deity. Two places named "Beth-dagon" ("house/temple of Dagon") are attested in Joshua 15:41; 19:27, suggesting the presence at one time of sanctuaries to this god.

4.7. Shalem. The name of the city of Jerusalem may contain the name of a deity, perhaps the god mentioned in the Ugaritic texts—for example, *KTU* 1.23.

4.8. The Sun. In the Ugaritic texts the word *špš* can refer to the sun or specifically to the sun-goddess Shapsh. The Hebrew equivalent, *šemeš*, sometimes is treated as masculine in Hebrew, but sometimes it is feminine, and usually it refers to the heavenly body. However, there are place names that include this element presumably because they had been associated with the solar cult, *Beth-shemesh* ("House/temple of Shemesh" [e.g., Josh 15:10]) and *Ir-shemesh* ("City of Shemesh" [Josh 19:41]; there is some textual evidence for the readings *En-shemesh* or *Beth-shemesh* here, but in any case the *šemeš* element is present). It is possible that the personal names *Shamsherai* (1 Chron 8:26), *Shimshai* (e.g., Ezra 4:8, 9) and even *Samson* (e.g., Judg 13:24) preserve this as a theophoric element.

4.9. Rĕpā'îm. In the Hebrew Bible the term *rĕpā'îm* refers to the shades of the dead (e.g., Is 14:9), but also to former inhabitants of the land (e.g., Josh 17:15), sometimes with an indication that they were renowned for their gigantic stature (e.g., Deut 2:10-11; 3:11; see also, e.g., Josh 12:4; 13:12). There are several references to a Valley of Rephaim (2 Sam 5:18, 22; 23:13; 1 Chron 11:15; 14:9). The term may have associations with the *rpum* of the Ugaritic texts, who appear to have been dead kings or heroes who achieved divinized status.

4.10. The King. Israelite *kingship may have shared certain features of Canaanite kingship.

There are several instances of a king offering sacrifice (e.g., 1 Sam 13:9; 2 Sam 6:17; 24:25; 1 Kings 3:15). It is also possible that the Israelites shared some of the views of the king's elevated status. In the Ugaritic texts Keret was regarded as El's "son" and "servant," and these terms are used also of the Israelite monarch, who is Yahweh's servant (e.g., 2 Sam 3:18; 7:5, 8) and son (Ps 2:7). On the whole, however, suggestions that the Israelites believed in some form of sacral or even divine kingship have not been widely accepted (see, e.g., Johnson). It is clear that the Israelite king, like Keret and Danel, was expected to protect vulnerable members of society (e.g., Ps 72:1-4; see also 2 Sam 14:4-8).

4.11. Sacrificial Practice and Terminology. Although not principally relevant to the study of the Historical Books, there are a number of Hebrew terms for types of sacrifice or offering that are etymologically related to terms found in the Ugaritic texts, and others that seem to describe similar sacrificial practices (see Curtis 1985, 94). The similarities may not be the result of borrowing, but rather reflect a common stock of vocabulary and practice, and it must be remembered that the meaning and usage may not have been precisely the same in both cultures. As noted previously (see 3.8 above), there is no evidence for child sacrifice in the Ugaritic texts, although the Hebrew Bible suggests that it was practiced by previous inhabitants of the land (2 Kings 16:3), and that the practice continued as an act of apostasy (e.g., 2 Kings 17:17; 21:6; 23:10).

5. Conclusion.
The Canaanites may have predated much if not all of the period covered by the Historical Books. However, some of them may have lived on, some of their beliefs may have lived on and some of their gods may have lived on. The evidence from Ugarit in particular provides the student of the Hebrew Bible with a wealth of material against which to study the references to these people and their gods.

See also CANAAN, CANAANITES.

BIBLIOGRAPHY. **A. H. W. Curtis,** "Canaanite Goddesses in the Old Testament," in *Women in the Biblical Tradition,* ed. G. J. Brooke (SWR 31; Lewiston, NY: Mellen, 1992) 1-15; idem, "Ras Shamra, Minet el-Beida and Ras Ibn Hani: the Material Sources," in *Handbook of Ugaritic Studies,* ed. W. G. E. Watson and N. Wyatt (HO 39; Leiden: E. J. Brill, 1999) 5-27; idem, *Ugarit (Ras Shamra)* (CBW; Cambridge: Lutterworth, 1985); **J. Day,** "Asherah in the Hebrew Bible and Northwest Semitic Literature," *JBL* 105 (1986) 385-408; idem, *Yahweh and the Gods and Goddesses of Canaan* (JSOTSup 265; Sheffield: Sheffield Academic Press, 2000); **M. Dietrich, O. Loretz and J. Sanmartín,** *The Cuneiform Alphabetic Texts from Ugarit, Ras Ibn Hani and Other Places* (ALASP 8; Münster: Ugarit Verlag, 1995); **J. C. L. Gibson,** *Canaanite Myths and Legends* (Edinburgh: T & T Clark, 1978); **J. M. Hadley,** *The Cult of Asherah in Ancient Israel and Judah: Evidence of a Hebrew Goddess* (UCOP 57; Cambridge: Cambridge University Press, 2000); **A. R. Johnson,** *Sacral Kingship in Ancient Israel* (2d ed.; Cardiff: University of Wales Press, 1967); **N. P. Lemche,** *The Canaanites and Their Land: The Tradition of the Canaanites* (JSOTSup 110; Sheffield: JSOT, 1991); **A. R. Millard,** "The Canaanites," in *Peoples of Old Testament Times,* ed. D. J. Wiseman (Oxford: Clarendon Press, 1973) 29-52; **G. del Olmo Lete,** *Canaanite Religion According to the Liturgical Texts of Ugarit* (Winona Lake, IN: Eisenbrauns, 2004); **D. Pardee,** *Ritual and Cult at Ugarit* (SBLWAW 10; Atlanta: Society for Biblical Literature, 2002); **M. S. Smith,** *The Ugaritic Baal Cycle Volume 1: Introduction with Text, Translation & Commentary of KTU 1.1-1.2* (VTSup 55; Leiden: E. J. Brill, 1994); **J. N. Tubb,** *Canaanites* (London: British Museum Press, 1998); **N. Wyatt,** *Religious Texts from Ugarit* (2d ed.; BibSem 53; London: Sheffield Academic Press, 2002).   A. H. W. Curtis

CANAANITE LANGUAGE. *See* CANAAN, CANAANITES.

CANON
The Historical Books differ in their arrangement in the canonical collections of Jews and of Christians. In the Jewish Scriptures *Joshua, *Judges, 1-2 *Samuel and 1-2 *Kings earned the designation "Former Prophets," and *Ezra-Nehemiah and 1-2 *Chronicles were relegated to the "Writings," appearing in that order as the final four books of the Hebrew Bible. The Christian OT, by contrast, does not classify these books as "prophetic." Instead, tradition designates them as "Historical Books" and places them after Deuteronomy in the following order: Joshua, Judges, 1-2 Samuel, 1-2 Kings, 1-2 Chronicles, Ezra and Nehemiah. The books of Ruth and Esther are integrated with the Historical

Books of the Christian OT after Judges and Nehemiah, respectively.

Any attempt to address the canon(ization) of the Historical Books of the Hebrew Bible must begin by defining *canon*. Once that issue has been addressed, the present article surveys the primary evidence from the fifth century BCE to the sixth century CE for the canonization of the Historical Books. Then follows a review of the most significant of the recent views on the matter in light of the definition and survey of the primary evidence, and finally a modest proposal regarding how the Historical Books achieved full canonical status.

1. Defining *Canon*
2. The Evidence for the Canonization of the Historical Books of the Hebrew Bible
3. Recent Studies of the Canonization of the Hebrew Bible
4. The Historical Books from Composition to Canon 1 to Canon 2: A Tentative Hypothesis

1. Defining *Canon*.

Comparativists who treat the topic of canon among a variety of religions help us in this endeavor. This approach has suggested that the meaning of *canon* ranges between two poles (Sheppard, 65-67). At one end of the spectrum, "canon 1" can signal "a rule, standard, ideal, norm or authoritative office or literature, whether oral or written"; at the other end of the spectrum, "canon 2" refers to a "temporary or perpetual fixation, standardization, enumeration, listing, chronology, register, or catalog of exemplary or normative persons, places, or things" (including books) (Sheppard, 64; for other historians of religion who have contributed to this two-part definition of canon see J. Z. Smith; W. C. Smith; Graham). G. T. Sheppard (65-66) observes that the former type of canon is exemplified in diverse phenomena such as Taoism's "posthumous deification of Lao-tzu" and the "Sayings of the Lord" that Justin Martyr set in authority over written texts (Eusebius *Hist. Eccl.* 3.39). Closed collections such as the Samaritan Pentateuch epitomize the second type of canon, and the Masoretic Text of the Hebrew Bible might be taken as an extreme expression of this type, exhibiting not only a closed collection, but also a standardized text.

These two notions of canon provide a minimum threshold for identifying something as canon (canon 1), as well as a maximalist definition of it (canon 2). Perhaps more importantly, they also establish the field of "canon" possibilities between them (not unlike the spectrum between "Scripture" and "canon" defined by Barton, 55-75). The two types may also be taken to demarcate the beginning and end of what some biblical scholars have called the "canonical process" or "canonization" (Sanders). Together, canon 1 and canon 2 offer a convenient framework for assessing the evidence for the emergence of a canon of the Historical Books, for judging the conflicting scholarly perspectives on the question, and for constructing a fresh hypothesis on the topic.

2. The Evidence for the Canonization of the Historical Books of the Hebrew Bible.

The oft-cited passages in which ancient authors hint at the existence of an emerging tripartite canon are, for our purposes, of little significance (Prologue to Sirach; 4QMMT C 9-12; 2 Macc 2:13-14; Philo *Contempl.* 3.25-28; *Mos.* 2.37-40; Luke 24:44; Josephus *Ag. Ap.* 1.37-43; *4 Ezra* 14:22-48; *b. B. Bat.* 14b-15a). Even if one accepts the view that such references prove a tripartite canon as early as the third or second century BCE, repeated occurrences of the phrase "the prophets" (or similar language) prove nothing regarding the inclusion or exclusion of the Historical Books. References to numbers of books in each supposed division are equally unhelpful (e.g., without naming them, Josephus says that there are thirteen books by the prophets who wrote from "the death of Moses to Artaxeres" [*Ag. Ap.* 1.37-43]; for competing attempts to name those books see VanderKam and Flint, 166-67). Indeed, inasmuch as J. Barton (35-55) has demonstrated that the moniker "prophets" may have included everything that was not Torah, we are compelled to look for less blunt tools to assess the status of the Historical Books. To attain greater clarity regarding their journey to canon 2 status, we turn to more subtle evidence for the canonization of the Historical Books: the testimony of various Jewish and Christian texts that bear traces of the canonical process.

2.1. The Evidence of Primary Texts. The following survey of primary evidence assumes that authors cite, retell or interpret an earlier text because they deem it at least in some degree to be a "rule, standard, ideal, norm" or "authoritative . . . literature" (canon 1). Otherwise, we must assume that authors would simply ignore the texts that they call on, not bothering either to cite them for support or to dispute their claims. The primary texts that offer evidence of this sort regarding the emergence of a canon of the Historical Books include the Hebrew Bible itself, the Septuagint, the Dead Sea Scrolls, the NT, the rabbinic canon and the writings of early Christian authors.

2.1.1. The Hebrew Bible. The Hebrew Bible provides slim yet significant evidence for the emergence of a canon of the Historical Books. First, 1-2 Chronicles proves that as early as the fourth century BCE Samuel through Kings had become influential enough to serve as a provocateur and source for an author and the readers (on the idea that the history narrated in Samuel and Kings was the *Bezugspunkt* for the Chronicler, see especially Willi; see also Steins). Few question the Chronicler's reliance on Samuel and Kings, or that the repeated references to "the Book of the Kings of Israel (and Judah)" (1 Chron 9:1; 2 Chron 16:11; 20:34; 25:26; 27:7; 28:26; 32:32; 35:27; 36:8) are to the same biblical books (*see* Chronicler's History). Thus we see that even as the contents of the Hebrew Bible were still taking form, Samuel and Kings already had begun to function as canon 1, at least inasmuch as they were sufficiently normative to provoke their own renewal for a new age in 1-2 Chronicles. Indeed, one hardly need go so far as G. Steins (507-17) does in asserting that 1-2 Chronicles was a "canon-closing" composition meant to put the exclamation mark on the Hebrew Bible's story from creation to the exile to appreciate the Chronicler's testimony to the emergence of Samuel and Kings as canon 1 material.

The relationship between Ezra-Nehemiah and 1-2 Chronicles, whatever its precise nature, may also be cited as evidence within the Hebrew Bible for the early canon 1 nature of some Historical Books. Even if we accept the currently dominant view that the author(s) of 1-2 Chronicles and Ezra-Nehemiah were not one and the same, there remains the matter of the close thematic association between the two pairs of books (and the overlap between 2 Chron 36:22-23 and Ezra 1:1-3a) that prompted an earlier generation to posit a single author for all four and has encouraged at least one commentator to speak of a Chronicler school of thought that produced both sets of books. However, it is not necessary to posit an enduring school of thought to explain the strong thematic linkages between 1-2 Chronicles and Ezra-Nehemiah. Instead, we may see in the relationship between the two sets of books something like what we see in the connection between Samuel-Kings and 1-2 Chronicles: the author of the second set, whichever one it was, had sufficient respect for its predecessor to emulate it, to give it authority by extending its story backward (Chronicles) or forward (Ezra-Nehemiah) in time. Thus we may have evidence within the Hebrew Bible not only for the emerging canon 1 status of Samuel and Kings, but also for 1-2 Chronicles and Ezra-Nehemiah.

Thus far we have left aside the books of Joshua and Judges, chiefly because there is little within the Hebrew Bible to suggest that they had even the sort of influence just now posited for 1-2 Chronicles or Ezra-Nehemiah, let alone that of Samuel and Kings. There are echoes of Joshua and Judges in later books of the Hebrew Bible (e.g., 2 Chron 15:1-7 may invoke a military exhortation in the same way a similar catchphrase is invoked in Josh 1:7-9), but these hardly denote the authority of the earlier work over the author of the later work; such echoes are too faint to lift Joshua and Judges to the same canon 1 status that we attribute to Samuel and Kings and, with lesser conviction, to 1-2 Chronicles or Ezra-Nehemiah.

2.1.2. The Septuagint. The Septuagint provides further support for the supposition that the Historical Books developed early on as canon 1 material, but their transition to canon 2 status took longer.

That the Historical Books continued to qualify as "authoritative," "normative" or "ideal" is apparent from the words of a second-century BCE Jewish historian named Eupolemus, part of whose work was preserved verbatim in Eusebius's record of Alexander Polyhistor's history (Eusebius *Praep. ev.* 9.34). Although some find reason to dispute this, Eupolemus seems to have quoted 2 Chronicles 2:11 LXX in writing an apologetic account of the letter exchange between Solomon and Hiram. Although he also knew and used the Hebrew text of Chronicles, he apparently sought to borrow also on authority assigned to the Chronicler's account of Solomon in Greek translation, repeating on at least one occasion word for word the Septuagint's modestly different version of Chronicles. This suggests that in a few short centuries the Chronicler's portion of the Historical Books had developed from a new composition to one that had cachet not only in its original version, but also in its first translation. If this was true for Chronicles, one can imagine that it was all the more so true for the older portions of the Historical Books, Joshua through 2 Kings.

That said, the extensive evidence of textual fluidity among the Greek texts of the Historical Books proves that they did not quickly move from canon 1 to canon 2 status. One indication is the widely varying disposition of the books of Ezra and Nehemiah in Greek translations (see 1-2 Esdras). Furthermore, Joshua LXX is sometimes shorter and sometimes longer than the Hebrew text, suggesting textual fluidity (that may have existed even earlier among Hebrew editions of the book). Among the most significant pluses in Joshua LXX is a passage following Joshua 24:33 that explains how Israel, even after affirming the covenant with God, "worshiped Astarte and Ashteroth, and the gods of the nations round about them," and that as a result God "gave them into the hands of Eglon, king of Moab." Drawing from elements in Joshua 24:33; Judges 2:6, 9, 11-14; 3:12, 14, this passage efficiently sets out the pattern established more elaborately by Judges 2:11-23 and leads into the Ehud story that begins in Judges 3:12. For some this plus is secondary, a creation of the Septuagint translator; for others it is a fragment of a form of Joshua-Judges that treated the two books as one and continued after the plus with the Ehud story. In another significant difference in Joshua, the Greek translation, reflecting either the efforts of the Greek translator or a non-Masoretic Hebrew manuscript tradition, places Joshua's construction of the altar at Ebal (Josh 8:30-35) after Josh 9:1-2, so that the defensive action of the kings in the latter two verses follows more naturally on the defeat of Ai and its implications regarding the Israelites' military prowess.

Also suggesting either Greek translators' efforts or alternative Hebrew textual traditions are the major differences between the Masoretic and Septuagint editions of the Samuel and Kings books. We note in particular the addition of a paragraph (shared in large part with Josephus) between 1 Samuel 10 and 11 that clarifies the events narrated in 1 Samuel 11 as well as the substantial differences between the two ac-

counts of the David and Goliath story (1 Sam 16—18). As for 1-2 Kings (3-4 Kgdms LXX), the major variation between the Greek and Hebrew texts lies in the *chronology of the kings. All of these instances of textual variation indicate two things about the "canonical" status of the Historical Books at the turn of the eras: they were held in high enough regard to merit recopying, translation and adjustment for varying sensibilities (canon 1), but they had not yet become so firmly established among users that their form was unchangeably fixed (canon 2).

2.1.3. The Dead Sea Scrolls. In innumerable ways the discovery of the Dead Sea Scrolls revolutionized study of the Hebrew Bible, not the least of which is their impact on the canon question. It is not surprising, then, that the scrolls add important insights on the canonization of the Historical Books. In a study of the evidence from Qumran for the development of the canon J. Trebolle suggests that Joshua, Judges, 1-2 Samuel and 1-2 Kings belong to a group of books that were "differently copied and preserved, transmitted, composed and edited, translated, quoted, ordered, interpreted and authorized" from the "books of the Pentateuch, Isaiah, Minor Prophets and Psalms plus Job" (Trebolle, 383). These differences signal that at least Joshua through 2 Kings, though carrying some weight among the people of the scrolls and the wider Jewish (and eventually Christian) communities, wielded far less authority over readers than did the Pentateuch and the other texts listed with it above, and certainly they had not achieved canon 2 status at Qumran.

Indeed, among the Dead Sea Scrolls we find only two copies of Joshua, three of Judges, four of Samuel, three of Kings, one of Ezra, none of Nehemiah and one of Chronicles. Moreover, there are striking textual variations among the copies of Joshua and of Samuel at Qumran, further indicating that these books remained fluid in the group's appreciation of them. And apart from a quotation of Nathan's prophecy for David (2 Sam 7:11) in 4Q174 3:7, they were never cited with any of the typical quotation formulas (e.g., "as it is written," "the scripture says"). As for interpretive uses of these books at Qumran, while the Pentateuch, Isaiah, some Minor Prophets and some psalms were taken up in the unique Qumranic pesharim, and Genesis received full-scale commentary (4Q252), the Historical Books were reworked only in the form of paraphrases and "rewritten" Scriptures (4QPsalms of Joshua [4Q378-379]; 4QVision of Samuel [4Q160]; 6QApocryphon of Samuel-Kings [6Q9]), genres at Qumran that, in the absence of pesharim or commentaries on the same works, could signal the community's abiding sense that the "original" books were not yet so sacrosanct as to merit commentary instead of revision for the sake of interpretation. (Note that the "*Reworked Pentateuch*" texts from Qumran [4Q158; 4Q364-367] are so different in character from the "rewritten" forms of the Historical Books listed above as to negate any comparison that may undercut the point just made.) So the evidence from Qumran also indicates that by late in the first century CE Joshua through 2 Kings, 1-2 Chronicles and Ezra and Nehemiah had only crept forward slightly in their canon 1 status and remained far removed from canon 2.

2.1.4. The New Testament. If we measure the authority of OT books by their use in the NT, the Historical Books earn little credit. Apart from allusions to the Historical Books that are often difficult to discern (e.g., cf. 2 Sam 22:3 with Heb 2:13) or are better explained as quotations of the "primary" occurrences of the Hebrew Bible phrase (e.g., cf. Josh 22:5 and Deut 6:5 with Mt 22:37; Mk 12:30, 33; Lk 10:27), there are only two direct quotations of the Historical Books in the NT. Hebrews 1:5 uses 2 Samuel 7:14 (see also Ps 2:7), Nathan's prophecy to David regarding Solomon's dynastic succession, to confirm the uniqueness of Jesus. And in Romans 11:1-6 Paul recalls Elijah's plaintive claim to be the only faithful soul left and God's reply that he had preserved a remnant (1 Kings 19:10, 14, 18) to argue that through Jesus, God had not abandoned Israel, but had saved a remainder of the people by grace.

Another NT reference to the Historical Books is even thought to provide early evidence for the order of the books in the Jewish Scriptures. In Matthew 23:35 Jesus condemns the scribes and the Pharisees, charging them with "all the innocent blood shed on earth, from the blood of righteous Abel to the blood of Zechariah son of Berachiah, whom you murdered between the sanctuary and the altar." The last clause is likely a reference to 2 Chronicles 24:21, and the verse often is taken to be an indication of Jesus' (or Matthew's) awareness of a canon that stretched from Genesis to 2 Chronicles, although this can hardly be proved.

Quotations aside, more telling is the dependence of Luke-Acts on elements from the *Deuteronomistic History. For instance, the frequent use of speeches to mark turning points in Luke-Acts is likened to the orations that hold the Deuteronomistic History together. Likewise, Jesus' healings occasionally are aligned with some performed in the Deuteronomistic History (e.g., cf. 1 Kings 17:17-24 with Lk 7:11-17; cf. Lk 4:24-25). These and other symmetries suggest that Luke attempted to echo and thus borrow on the authority of the historiographical traditions in the Deuteronomistic History. So for one NT author, one portion of the Historical Books held significant authority, a characteristic of canon 1. However, echoes of Joshua and Judges are not so apparent in any part of the NT, and traces of influence from 1-2 Chronicles and Ezra and Nehemiah are virtually absent.

2.1.5. The Rabbis. The rabbinic witness further expands the evidence that the Historical Books long possessed the characteristics of canon 1 material before they ever became canon 2. Starting with the youngest testimony, *b. B. Bat.* 14b-15a reports, "Our Rabbis taught that the order of the prophets is Joshua and Judges, Samuel and Kings, Jeremiah and Ezekiel and the Twelve." The *baraita* also gives an order for the books of the Writings that places Chronicles last, after Ezra and Nehemiah. Inasmuch as this passage is at pains to address the Prophets and the Writings, but assumes the Torah's order to be known, there is reason to believe that the first two collections were only then, as late as the late sixth century CE, attaining canon 2 status.

J. Lightstone observes, however, that earlier rabbinic texts do seem to presume a tripartite collection. In the Mishnah, *m. Roš Haš.* 4:6 prescribes the Scriptures to be read at an extra New Year liturgy in such a way as to assume awareness of a tripartite collection. The Tosefta passage, by its nature explicatory of the Mishnah text, also assumes the tripartite collection (*t. Roš Haš.* 2:12-14), as does the corresponding passage in the Jerusalem Talmud (*y. Roš Haš.* 4:7, 59c) (Lightstone, 180). Yet like texts such as the prologue to Sirach, none of these passages specify the books in each division, leaving us only to assume that the middle division contained Joshua, Judges, Samuel and Kings, and quite uncertain that the third division already included 1-2 Chronicles.

At the same time, the disputes within the

Mishnah regarding the capacity of Ecclesiastes and Song of Songs to "make the hands unclean" indicate that some decisions were being made about what was authoritative (*m. Yad.* 3:5b). However, the very fact that there were disputes indicates as well that the matter was not settled, and that the conversation that eventually produced canon 2 material was still underway. Thus the rabbinic testimony on the whole suggests that between the time of the Mishnah and the Babylonian Talmud the Historical Books continued to linger between canon 1 and canon 2 status, attaining the latter only late in that period.

2.1.6. The Early Christians. The evidence for the canonization of the Historical Books from Christian writers beyond the NT adds further evidence that they only gradually made the transition from canon 1 to canon 2. We focus here on just two texts, one each from the second and fourth centuries CE.

The first passage is from Melito, a second-century bishop of Sardis. In a fragment preserved by Eusebius (*Hist. eccl.* 4.26.12-14), Melito provided his list of "the books of the Old Testament." After the Pentateuch he lists "Joshua [son of Nun], Judges, Ruth, four of the Kings, [and] two of the Chronicles." Esdras (Ezra and Nehemiah of the Hebrew Bible) came last in his list, after "Isaiah, Jeremiah, the twelve in one book, Daniel [and], Ezekiel." So while Melito undeniably counts all of the Historical Books as part of his OT, he orders Ezra and Nehemiah oddly, and (not surprisingly) follows the tradition among some Greek translations of treating them as a single book. Thus Melito's inclusion of the Historical Books in his list suggests that he found them not only to be authoritative, but also to belong to a defined collection. Notably, however, Melito does not denounce additions to the collection, nor does he concern himself with a fixed text. Thus we find in Melito a strong, though incomplete move toward canon 2.

Athanasius's Festal Letter of 367 CE offers a later perspective. After giving the order of the Pentateuch, Athanasius adds, "Then comes Joshua, Judges, and Ruth; the four books of the Kings, counted as two; then Chronicles, the two counted as one; and then 1 and 2 Esdras" (here, 1 and 2 Esdras are Ezra and Nehemiah). Athanasius's listing leaves no doubt that by this time the order of the Historical Books was established as we have them in the Christian canon, but just as in the case of Melito's testimony,

Athanasius's list gives no hint of the fixedness of the text of those books in Alexandria. So we may say from this evidence that at least in Alexandria, and perhaps more widely among Christian communities, the Historical Books had attained a degree of canon 2 status.

2.2. Summary of the Primary Evidence. It hardly bears repeating that this survey of the primary evidence demonstrates a long journey for the Historical Books of the OT to canon 1 and finally canon 2 status. The Hebrew Bible itself testifies that as early as the Persian period some of the Historical Books held enough sway over audiences to provoke the composition of still other Historical Books (from Samuel-Kings to 1-2 Chronicles). We also see evidence from sources that chronicle the Bible's development between the Persian period and the sixth century CE that the Historical Books remained canon 1 material for a long time. There seemed to be little impulse to fix their text, set unchangeably their order, or decree them closed *and* binding.

3. Recent Studies of the Canonization of the Hebrew Bible.
Unfortunately, with some notable exceptions (e.g., Steins), recent studies addressing the canonization of the OT have not dwelt specifically on the Historical Books, so we rely instead on approaches to the general question. There are two basic perspectives on this matter. Some, defining canon as canon 1 and relying in large part on the early references to a (supposedly) tripartite canon, argue for an early determination of the collection. Others, defining canon as canon 2 and depending on much of the evidence surveyed above, argue that the collection remained open and fluid well into the early Common Era. Both perspectives offer little regarding *how* the Historical Books achieved type 2 canon status.

Representatives of the first approach include S. Leiman, R. Beckwith, A. van der Kooij and, with special reference to 1-2 Chronicles, G. Steins. The first two assert that the *baraita* in *b. B. Bat.* 14b-15a reflects the division and ordering of the biblical books implied by the reference to "the law, the prophets, and the other books of our ancestors" in the prologue to Sirach. Additionally, Leiman takes 2 Maccabees 2:13-14 as evidence that while Nehemiah canonized the Law and the Prophets, Judas closed the Writings collection. Beckwith is more modest, assigning the closure of the Prophets as well to Judas around 150 BCE. Adding Josephus (*Ag. Ap.* 1.37-43) and 4QMMT C 9-12 to the mix, van der Kooij agrees in great part with Leiman and Beckwith but modifies them on three key counts. First, although he accepts that there was a "defined" tripartite collection of texts by 150 BCE, it was not "definitive." Second, the text of any collection was not yet standardized. Third, the arrangement of such a tripartite collection was not that of later Judaism so much as what we find in Josephus with its large collection of prophetic books. Steins simply accepts the early dating for a tripartite canon proposed by Leiman and Beckwith and argues that 1-2 Chronicles served as an *Abschlußphänomen* for the canon as a whole.

There are difficulties with this position. Although van der Kooij's resistance to the term *definitive* is to be applauded, one searches in vain for sound indicators between the second century BCE and the second century CE that the collection was even "defined," let alone "definitive." Indeed, the terms *Prophets, Writings* or *other books* hardly establish a defined collection, and Barton (55-75) has credibly argued instead for a bipartite division between Torah (Scripture) and "the prophets" (ancillary texts). Moreover, this approach fails to define *canon* as broadly as the comparativists do. Indeed, if Leiman, Beckwith and van der Kooij entertained the notion of canon 1, their argument might be more persuasive. However, that would also entail greater respect for the evidence surveyed above, as well as less reliance on the tripartite canon passages as proof that a "defined" collection existed as early as the second century BCE. As for Steins, when the early date for canon formation proposed by Leiman, Beckwith and van der Kooij falls, so also do his claims for 1-2 Chronicles as *Abschlußphänomen.*

The second approach to canon is exemplified in the work of J. Trebolle, E. Ulrich and J. VanderKam. This approach is typified by a fondness for the canon 2 standard, and by attention to most, if not all, of the evidence elicited above. For instance, Ulrich holds the view that the fluid notion of canon entailed in Sheppard's canon 1 and 2 unnecessarily confuses the conversation. Instead, he pleads that discussion begin with agreement that canon entails books (not specific textual forms) that have been included in a closed list as a result of the reflective

judgment of users of the book. Likewise, Trebolle and VanderKam seem to construe canon in a canon 2 manner. In addressing the signs of canon in the Qumran corpus, VanderKam signals his view by writing, "Before 70 CE no authoritative body of which we know drew up a list of books that alone were regarded as supremely authoritative, *a list from which none could be subtracted and to which none could be added*" (VanderKam, 91 [italics added]). Trebolle surveys the copying and preservation, transmission, composition and editing, translation, quotation, ordering, interpretation, and authorization of the books that became the Hebrew Scriptures to conclude that the Pentateuch, Isaiah, the Minor Prophets and Psalms formed what he calls a "canon within the canon" at least up to the end of the first century CE. Others, including the majority of the Historical Books, were also known and used, but not in the same way that the "canon within the canon" was used. Although Trebolle's use of the term *canon* is regrettably imprecise, the thrust of his assessment is that the first collection of books that he cites was authoritative in the manner of Sheppard's canon 1 early on, while the second set of works (that includes most of the Historical Books) lagged far behind in influence; indeed, Trebolle's evidence suggests that they were barely to the stage of canon 1 by the end of the period that he surveys.

Although the approach of Trebolle, Ulrich and VanderKam is more attentive to the evidence than that of Leiman, Beckwith and van der Kooij in addressing the question of when the Historical Books achieved canonical status, it fails to explain how those books transitioned to canon 1 and then canon 2 status. Because Ulrich and VanderKam hew so closely to Sheppard's canon 2 as their idea of canon, they are little occupied with the transition from canon 1 to canon 2 status, and Trebolle's imprecise use of the term and his principal interest in the earlier period preclude concern for sketching the transition.

4. The Historical Books from Composition to Canon 1 to Canon 2: A Tentative Hypothesis.
Trebolle's observation regarding the early authority enjoyed by the Pentateuch, Isaiah, the Minor Prophets and Psalms seem sound. He records compelling evidence for the canon 1 status of these books around the turn of the

eras. Yet he also reports that at least some of the Historical Books likewise were known and trusted in that period, though not to the same degree as the first group of books. So one wonders what first drew the Historical Books into the orbit of the more authoritative works, and how they eventually came to possess canon 1 and, finally, canon 2 status. The views of Barton (35-95) on the relationship between Torah and "the prophets" bear some resemblance to what follows here, although, under the influence of Trebolle's research, I part ways on the scope of the primary collection of texts.

I offer a simple hypothesis suggested by the evidence surveyed above. Initially, the Historical Books functioned in two roles ancillary to the central collection (the Pentateuch, Isaiah, the Minor Prophets and Psalms) to provide support for the canon 1 status of the central collection. First, they completed the national history begun in the book of Exodus (and in any case, Joshua through 2 Kings likely were already linked to Deuteronomy as the history illustrative of its theological claims). Second, they provided the historical and narrative "background" for Isaiah, the Minor Prophets and Psalms: the oracles in Isaiah and in many of the Minor Prophets are better understood against the backdrop of the kingdoms' histories and the narratives of 1-2 Chronicles and Ezra-Nehemiah (e.g., cf. Is 36—39 with 2 Kings 18:13; 18:17—20:19; Haggai and Zech 1—8 with Ezra 5:1; 6:14); and many psalms assigned to David (and others associated with him or with other figures and moments from Israel's history in the land) are best read in conjunction with the stories related in the Historical Books (see, e.g., Ps 51 and 2 Sam 11—12). As for 1-2 Chronicles in particular, apart from his insistence regarding its canon closure significance, there may even be something to Steins's argument that the Chronicler's work aims to embrace and evoke the Hebrew Bible's entire narrative sweep.

The evidence indicates that Trebolle's central collection quickly achieved canon 1 status and soon thereafter began to move toward canon 2 status, perhaps under pressure from additional works and interpretive traditions that both affirmed and challenged their central value. For example, *Jubilees* and the *Temple Scroll* may have been read not only as appreciative interpretive rewritings of major portions of the Pentateuch (or even as the "secrets" that God re-

vealed only to the initiated [on this see Barton, 72-75]), but also as challenges to its normative status. Similarly, the multiple psalm collections at Qumran hint at an equally interpretive-competitive relationship among such collections. This sort of competition with and development of the elements present in Trebolle's "canon within a canon" surely not only hastened their transition to canon 2 status but also intensified the importance of the Historical Books as ancillary works that could offer additional legitimacy to the Pentateuch, Isaiah, the Minor Prophets and Psalms. And whereas the latter books faced competitors, for the most part the Historical Books did not. Thus the impetus that moved the central collection toward canon 2 status was largely absent for the Historical Books. The last stage in the Historical Books' journey from book to canon 2 status was perhaps just the natural conclusion to the establishment of the central collection's claim to canon 2 status: when they achieved that, their ancillary, supporting books likewise were granted this crowning eminence—they were "definitive" by default.

See also HERMENEUTICS; INNERBIBLICAL EXEGESIS; ORAL TRADITION AND WRITTEN TRADITION; TEXT AND TEXTUAL CRITICISM.

BIBLIOGRAPHY. **J. Barton,** *Oracles of God: Perceptions of Ancient Prophecy after the Exile* (New York: Oxford University Press, 1986); **R. Beckwith,** *The Old Testament Canon of the New Testament Church* (Grand Rapids: Eerdmans, 1985); **W. A. Graham,** *Beyond the Written Word: Oral Aspects of Scripture in the History of Religion* (Cambridge: Cambridge University Press, 1987); **A. van der Kooij,** "The Canonization of Ancient Books Kept in the Temple of Jerusalem," in *Canonization and Decanonization,* ed. A. van der Kooij and K. van der Toorn (SHR 82; Leiden: Brill, 1998) 17-40; **S. Z. Leiman,** *The Canonization of the Hebrew Scripture: The Talmudic and Midrashic Evidence* (Hamden, CT: Archon, 1976); **J. Lightstone,** "The Rabbis' Bible: The Canon of the Hebrew Bible and the Early Rabbinic Guild," in *The Canon Debate,* ed. L. M. McDonald and J. A. Sanders (Peabody, MA: Hendrickson, 2002) 163-84; **J. Sanders,** *Torah and Canon* (Philadelphia: Fortress, 1972); **G. T. Sheppard,** "Canon," *ER* 3/4.62-69; **J. Z. Smith,** "Sacred Persistence: Toward a Redescription of Canon," in *Imagining Religion: From Babylon to Jonestown* (CSHJ; Chicago: University of Chicago Press, 1987) 36-52; **W. C. Smith,** *What Is Scripture? A Comparative Ap-*

proach (Minneapolis: Fortress, 1993); **G. Steins,** *Die Chronik as kanonisches Abschlußphänomen: Studien zur Entstehung und Theologie von 1/2 Chronik* (BBB 93; Weinheim: Beltz Athenäum, 1995); **E. Tov,** *Textual Criticism of the Hebrew Bible* (Minneapolis: Fortress, 1992); **J. Trebolle,** "A 'Canon Within a Canon': Two Series of Old Testament Books Differently Transmitted, Interpreted and Authorized," *RevQ* 19 (2000) 383-99; **E. Ulrich,** "The Notion and Definition of Canon," in *The Canon Debate,* ed. L. M. McDonald and J. A. Sanders (Peabody, MA: Hendrickson, 2002) 21-35; **J. VanderKam,** "Authoritative Literature in the Dead Sea Scrolls," *DSD* 5 (1998) 382-402; **J. VanderKam and P. Flint,** *The Meaning of the Dead Sea Scrolls: Their Significance for Understanding the Bible, Judaism, Jesus, and Christianity* (San Francisco: HarperSanFrancisco, 2003); **T. Willi,** *Die Chronik als Auslegung: Untersuchungen zur literarishcen Gestaltung der historischen Überlieferung Israels* (FRLANT 106; Göttingen: Vandenhoeck & Ruprecht, 1972).   R. A. Kugler

CANONICAL CRITICISM/INTERPRETATION. *See* HERMENEUTICS; METHODS OF INTERPRETATION.

CANONIZATION. *See* CANON.

CARMEL

"Carmel" (Heb *karmel*) is used in the Bible as a proper name for two places: Mount Carmel, which juts into the Mediterranean south of modern Haifa, and a city, Carmel, southeast of *Hebron.

    1. Etymology
    2. Mount Carmel
    3. Carmel (City in Judah)

1. Etymology.

The Hebrew term *karmel* is used both as a geographic name and as a common noun. *Karmel* often denotes an "orchard" (parallel with "forest" at Is 10:18; 29:17; 32:15; Mic 7:14), though the term can also refer to grape vines (Is 16:10; Jer 48:33) and fresh ears of grain (Lev 2:14; 23:14; 2 Kings 4:42).

    HALOT (2.499, 481) discerns two lexemes: *karmel* IV, "new corn," which it derives from Arabic *kamala*, "to become complete, ready" (though lack of a *rêš* is a problem for this view), and *karmel* I, "orchard," which it derives from Heb *kerem*, "vineyard." However, a good case can be made that all the terms *karmel* are etymologically related to *kerem*, "vineyard," to which was added a postformative *nûn* for an adjective/noun formation that then dissimilated into *lāmed*, thus: *kerem + n > karmen > karmel* (Mulder, 326). W. Pick (201) suggests that the etymology is "vineyard of God" *[kerem + ʾel > karmel],* though the lack of an ʾalep before the *lāmed* seems fatal to that view. If related to *kerem + n*, it also shows that the original sense of *karmel* probably would have been "vineyard-like," and hence "fruitful," "fertile [field]," "lush," "newly grown [of grain]," or the like. In that case, *karmel* as a geographic name presumably was chosen for places such as the forested Mount Carmel with luxuriant vegetation. Mount Carmel remains a center of wine production in modern Israel, and though less developed, so is the region south of Hebron in the vicinity of Carmel the city.

    This derivation of *karmel* from *kerem*, though likely, falls short of certainty. The existence of afformative *lāmed* as a noun formation type is recognized by Gesenius's grammar (GKC §85s), but is questioned by Joüon's grammar (*Joüon* §88M m). *Karmel* and other forms ending in supposed afformative *lāmed* might instead be non-Semitic loanwords, in which case *karmel* would relate to *kerem* only on the level of folk etymology.

2. Mount Carmel.

"Mount Carmel" denotes a range of limestone hills between the Jezreel Valley/Plain of Esdraelon to the northwest and the coastal plain/Sharon Valley to the south. Carmel rises from the Mediterranean coast immediately south of the modern port of Haifa and south of the Kishon river (cf. 1 Kings 18:40) to a maximum height of 546 m (1790 ft), and runs inland about 25 km (15.5 mi) to the southeast (Carta, 327-28) at least as far as Jokneam, which "belongs to Carmel" (Josh 12:22). The biblical term *Carmel* possibly at times applies also to the lower foothills (the Shephelah of Carmel) that continue a similar distance further inland. Hills also run south along the coast, forming a triangular wedge. "The heights of Dor" (NIV mg.; Heb *nāpôt dôr* [Josh 11:2; 12:23]) may be a reference to this southern extension of Carmel toward this Canaanite port city (Woudstra, 189); however, "heights" as the translation of Heb *nāpôt* is uncertain (Hess, 210; NJPS renders "district of Dor").

    Mount Carmel has been inhabited from

prehistoric times. During the Epi-paleolithic period (c. 10500-8500 BCE), evidence of what has been labeled Natufian culture was found on Carmel 20 km south of Haifa at el-Wad Cave, and evidence of Pre-Pottery Neolithic (8500-6000 BCE) is seen on Carmel at Nahal Oren 10 km south of Haifa (Mazar, 37, 40). *Megiddo was a major town on the northern edge of the less steep Shephelah of Carmel, as were Jokneam to its northwest and Taanach to its southeast. Carmel itself, however, was sparsely populated, making it a place appropriate for hiding (Amos 9:3).

Mount Carmel, along with upper Galilee, receives the most rain in present-day (and presumably ancient) Israel (Beitzel, 50). Mount Carmel receives an average of 700-900 mm (28-36 in) of rain per year. This rainfall allowed it to support forests and thickets renowned for their splendor (Is 35:2), as well as rich grasslands for grazing on the lower slopes (Jer 50:19). Although these forests are much reduced today, the remains of fallow deer, roe deer, wild pig and the forest-dwelling broad-toothed field mouse from Roman-Byzantine and medieval sites at Khirbet Sumaqa and at Sefunim Cave confirm the existence of these natural thickets and forests up to the Ottoman period (Horwitz, Tchernov and Dar, 303-4). Song of Songs 7:5 compares this dense, beautiful forest with a woman's thick, lovely hair. Its forests, along with its height, made Carmel a fitting analogy of a king's majesty and strength (Jer 46:18). A 273/272 BCE Phoenician worshiper's votive offering discovered at Lapethos in Cyprus refers to the worshiper "Yatan-baal, . . . [great-grand]son of ŠLM" as the "fruit of Carmel," perhaps to stress the beauty and majesty of his lineage (Beyerlin, 233; Gibson, 3.36:134-41, esp. 135, 138-39). Conversely, when even Carmel withers and drops its leaves (Amos 1:2; Nahum 1:4; Is 33:9), then a drought must be especially severe. This seems an undertone in the choice of Carmel as the locale of the contest between *Elijah and the prophets of Baal during the great drought (1 Kings 18:19; cf. 17:1), for it is there where the effects of the drought would be seen last, where the power of the storm-god Baal would be expected to be strongest, and where the end of the drought would be expected to begin, as was in fact the case (1 Kings 18:41-45).

Mount Carmel formed a landmark and barrier to north-south traffic along the Levant, and so it received mention in Egyptian texts, although under other names. An inscription of the tomb of Uni, commander, army of Pepe I, Abydos, refers to the campaign of Pepi I (c. 2350 BCE) in which "Nose of the Antelope's Head" possibly refers to the Mount Carmel headland (Aharoni et al., 25, map 21; ANET, 228). An inscription of Thutmose III (c. 1482 BCE) possibly refers to Carmel as "Rosh Kedesh" or "Holy head" (Aharoni et al., 33, map 30; ANET, 243a), which would fit its later association with worship. In any case, Thutmose III faced a military dilemma as to which road to take through the Shephelah of Carmel (ANET, 235-36; COS 2.2A:8-13, esp. 9). One choice was to march his army on the Via Maris highway to Megiddo, a road only moderate in slope, though it became so narrow due to forests and thickets in addition to gullies (Baly and Tushingham, 95) that it required his army to march single file, thus vulnerable to attack. His generals suggested either a broader pass to the east to Taanach, or to take a road to the northwest to Djefty, probably one of several roads to Jokneam (see Dorsey, 82-83). He chose the narrow, central path, and was victorious. A satirical letter written about the time of Ramses II (thirteenth century BCE) seems to label Carmel "Mount User" (wśr), or "strong/mighty mountain," listed between Acre and *Shechem (Aharoni et al., 41, map 41; Aharoni, 111, 183; ANET, 477).

Among those whom *Joshua defeated were "the king of Jokneam in Carmel," along with the kings of Achshaph, Megiddo and Taanach along Carmel's north and east, and the king of Dor to its south (Josh 12:20-23). The regions Dor, Taanach and Megiddo were allotted by Joshua to the tribe of Manasseh, but Manasseh was unable to drive out the Canaanites in those cities, only reduce them to servitude (Josh 17:11-13). Achshaph, along with the rest of Carmel westward, defined the southern extent of the tribe of Asher (Josh 19:24-26).

An Assyrian text of Shalmaneser III (858-824 BCE), found in the wall of the city of Assur, mentions that in his eighteenth year he set up a stela of his own image on the mountains of Ba'ali ra'ši ("Baal of the head[lands]") at the side of the sea in conjunction with actions against Damascus, Tyre and Sidon, and *Jehu of Israel (ANET, 280; COS 2.113C:266-67). Although it is debated (COS 2.113C:267 n. 4), this term may refer to the Carmel range, which formed the border between Israel and Tyre from the time of *Solomon, who according to 1 Kings 9:11-14 ceded to Hiram the territory of Cabul to pay for his building projects (Aharoni, 341). If the *Baʾali raʾši* does refer to Carmel, it also shows the importance of Baal worship at Carmel in the ninth century BCE.

The Bible indicates that in the ninth century BCE there was an altar of Yahweh in addition to an altar of Baal on Mount Carmel, though the altar of Yahweh had been damaged (1 Kings 18:30). It was repaired by Elijah in conjunction with his famous contest with 450 prophets of Baal (1 Kings 18:20-40). The site is traditionally identified with el-Muhraqa, at the southeastern edge of the mountain facing Jezreel and overlooking Tell el-Qasis (Cogan, 439).

Mount Carmel continued to be an important locale in the travels of Elijah's successor, *Elisha. The Shunammite woman whose son had died knew to seek Elisha's help there (2 Kings 2:25; 4:25). Her husband was surprised that she would seek Elisha when it was not a new moon or sabbath (2 Kings 4:23), suggesting that Carmel was a holy site frequented by the prophet and worshipers on those specific occasions (Mulder, 334).

Carmel is mentioned once in the Apocrypha as a region along with Gilead, upper Galilee, and the Plain of Esdraelon (Jdt 1:8). It continued to be a place of pagan worship after OT times: Pseudo-Skylax (c. fifth century BCE) refers to a temple of Zeus on Mount Carmel (Aharoni, 414). Tacitus (*Hist.* 2.78.3) and Suetonius (*Vesp* 5.6) record that the Roman emperor Vespasian, under whom Jerusalem was captured, around 69 CE, went to Mount Carmel, which once belonged to Galilee (until Solomon [see above]) but at that time belonged to Phoenician Tyre (Josephus *J.W.* 3.35), to seek a sign from "Carmel," which was both the name of the mountain and the name of a god. Finding no image or temple but only an open altar for sacrifice there, Vespasian received a favorable oracle by lots from the priest of Carmel to do whatever he planned to do. Pythagoras was said by the neoplatonist Iamblichus (c. 300 CE) to have been brought to a shrine at Mount Carmel, "the most sacred of all mountains," by Egyptian sailors (Mulder, 332). M. Avi-Jonah (118-19) reported finding a roughly second-century CE Roman-period Greek inscription at the museum of the Monastery of Elijah that refers to the god Carmel. This inscription is on the foot of a statue dedicated to "Heliopolitan Zeus Carmel" (Thompson, 875) that evidently identifies the god Carmel with Heliopolitan Zeus (Mulder, 332). Some scholars (e.g., Avi-Jonah, 124; Cogan, 439) believe that this later Carmel/Heliopolitan Zeus worship is really a continuation under a different name of the worship of the storm-god Baal-Shamem (also known as Baal Hadad and Hadad-Rimmon), whose prophets Elijah confronted.

Mount Carmel remained an important religious site subsequently. From the fourth century CE it became a place of Christian pilgrimage. The Carmelite order began as a monastery on Mount Carmel during the Crusader period (twelfth century CE), which was expelled from the mountain in the thirteenth century CE but reestablished there in the 1600s (see Zimmerman). Carmel is home to a shrine for worship by the Druze (an offshoot of Islam), and there is a major Bahai shrine there as well.

3. Carmel (City in Judah).

The city of Carmel is now the Arab village of Khirbet el-Kirmil, about 12 km (7.5 mi) southeast of Hebron. Occupied as early as the Middle Bronze Age (see Dever), this Carmel is first mentioned in the Bible along with Maon and Ziph, all southeast of Hebron, as cities allotted to Judah (Josh 15:55). After defeating the Amalekites, *Saul set up a victory stela there, oblivious to God's displeasure with his conduct of the war (1 Sam 15:11-12).

When *David was on the run from Saul, he confronted the surly Nabal, a Calebite citizen of Carmel, who insulted him. Nabal was saved from attack by David's men through the intervention of his beautiful and levelheaded wife, Abigail, whom David married after Nabal's death (1 Sam 25:2-42; 27:3). Abigail bore to David a son, Chileab/Daniel (2 Sam 3:3; 1 Chron 3:1). Hazrai/Hezro the Carmelite ("Hazrai" is the Qere in 2 Sam 23:35; "Hezro" is its Kethib and the pronunciation of 1 Chron 11:37) was one of David's notable warriors.

Carmel became a large town during Roman and Byzantine periods, being fortified to protect routes to the Negev. Remains of a cemetery and storage pool from the Roman-Byzantine period exist, and various tombs from Roman periods. There are also remains of two churches and a fort from Crusader periods. Its population in the early 1980s was estimated at one hundred (Carta, 270).

See also ELIJAH.

BIBLIOGRAPHY. **Y. Aharoni,** *The Land of the Bible: A Historical Geography* (2d ed.; Philadelphia: Westminster, 1979); **Y. Aharoni et al.,** *The Macmillan Bible Atlas* (3d ed.; New York: Macmillan, 1993); **M. Avi-Jonah,** "Mount Carmel and the God of Baalbek," *IEJ* 2 (1952) 118-24; **D. Baly and A. D. Tushingham,** *Atlas of the Biblical World* (New York: World Publishing, 1971); **B. J. Beitzel,** *The Moody Atlas of the Bible* (Chicago: Moody, 1985); **W. Beyerlin,** ed., *Near Eastern Religious Texts Relating to the Old Testament* (Philadelphia: Westminster, 1975); **Carta,** *Carta's Official Guide to Israel and Complete Gazetteer to All Sites in the Holy Land* (Jerusalem: State of Israel, Ministry of Defense Publishing House; Carta, 1983); **M. Cogan,** *1 Kings* (AB 10; New York: Doubleday, 2001); **W. Dever,** "A Middle Bronze I Cemetery at Khirbet el-Kirmil," *ErIsr* 12 (1975) 18*-33*; **D. A. Dorsey,** *The Roads and Highways of Ancient Israel* (ASOR Library of Biblical and Near Eastern Archaeology; Baltimore: Johns Hopkins University Press, 1991); **J. C. L. Gibson,** *Textbook of Syrian Semitic Inscriptions* (3 vols.; Oxford: Clarendon, 1971-1982); **R. S. Hess,** *Joshua* (TOTC; Downers Grove, IL: InterVarsity Press, 1996); **L. K. Horwitz, E. Tchernov and S. Dar,** "Subsistence and Environment on Mount Carmel in the Roman-Byzantine and Medieval Periods: The Evidence from Kh. Sumaqa," *IEJ* 40 (1990) 287-304; **A. Mazar,** *Archaeology of the Land of the Bible: 10,000-586 BCE* (ABRL; New York: Doubleday, 1990); **M. J. Mulder,** "בַּרְמֶל," *TDOT* 7.325-36; **P. W. Pick,** "On the Cognomen 'Tishbite' of the Prophet Elijah," *HS* 26.2 (1985) 197-202; **H. O. Thompson,** "Carmel, Mount," *ABD* 1.874-75; **M. H. Woudstra,** *The Book of Joshua* (NICOT; Grand Rapids: Eerdmans, 1981); **B. Zimmerman,** "The Carmelite Order," in *The Catholic Encyclopedia,* ed. C. G. Herbermann et al. (London: Caxton, 1907-1922). J. M. Sprinkle

CATTLE. *See* AGRICULTURE AND ANIMAL HUSBANDRY.

CEDARS OF LEBANON. *See* LEBANON.

CENSUS

The word *census* is a Latin term meaning "assessing" or "taxing." The verb form *censeo* was the act of registering Roman citizens, their property and wealth for the purposes of *taxation. The census has always been associated with a central government, serving specific purposes. In addition to taxation, the census may be used to determine the available labor force, both civil and military. Thus a census is not simply any enumeration of people, livestock or property; it is an official, sanctioned registry of people used to assess the number of citizens available for taxation or enlistment.

1. Old Testament Definition
2. United Monarchy
3. Divided Monarchy
4. Ezra-Nehemiah
5. Conclusions

1. Old Testament Definition.
There is no one Hebrew or Aramaic word or phrase used to depict the act of census-taking. Furthermore, those that are used in this capacity have other connotations, not related to the census, as well. Thus a simple search for these terms will not provide a concise listing of passages dealing with the subject. The most common nouns used for authorized enumeration in the Hebrew Bible are *mispār, mipqād* and *pĕquddâ.* Verbs used in this capacity include *sāpar, mānâ, pāqad* and *yāhaś.*

In addition to the individual words employed to describe census activity, the expression *nāśā' et-rō'š,* though limited to the Pentateuch, sheds important light on defining census in the Hebrew Bible. Literally meaning "lift the head," it is an idiom for taking a head count and is restricted to the divine commissioning of the task (Sanders). Furthermore, its use appears to be relegated to cultic purposes. In Exodus 30:11-16 the purpose of the census was to impose a poll tax of a half-shekel ransom *(kōper),* which was necessary for the upcoming construction of the tabernacle (Ex 38:24-26). The cultic function of the census is also evident in the case of the Kohathites (Num 4:2) and Gershonites (Num 4:22) aged thirty to fifty, whose conscription was for service in the tent of the presence. Moreover, the cultic function seems to be evident with the military censuses. Numbers 31:48-50 provides the raison d'être for the censuses of Numbers 1 and 26. These two censuses provided the number of soldiers available for the ensuing battles in the quest for Canaan. Due to this administrative foresight, the officers and commanders were able to determine that no soldier had been lost during the battle of Midian. Since God had spared them in battle, the soldiers offered a *kōper* for their lives (Levine, 68).

Although Exodus 30 and Numbers 31 have the common theme of *kōper* resulting from census, a significant distinction should be made. The 16,750-shekel *kōper* of Numbers 31 does not correspond with the required *kōper* of a half shekel per man of Exodus 30. Furthermore, in the Numbers 31 account it is only the commanders who bring the offering to the priests, not every male aged twenty and upward. This suggests two separate *kōper*-census types. One was designated for the poll tax, in which the half-shekel *kōper* served to remind God not to strike the people with a plague. Another was designated for military purposes, in which soldiers returning unscathed from the battlefield gave an offering in gratitude.

The data from the *nāśā' et-rō'š* passages underscore what has already been stated about how census is defined. Applying that definition to the Hebrew Bible, the following generalities may be made. First, a biblical census involves authoritative mandate, from either God, priest or king. Second, the purpose of the census must obligate the subjects of the census to one of two duties: taxation or enlistment, whether that be military, cultic or corvée (Mendenhall, 54). Third, demographics are an important feature of the census, since the nature of the mandate requires only individual males of certain ages to be registered. The minimum age for service in the cult varied: three years (2 Chron 31:16), twenty years (2 Chron 31:17; Ezra 3:8), twenty-five years (Num 8:24), thirty years (Num 4:3; 1 Chron 23:3). For all other functions the age requirement stood at those twenty years old and older.

It follows, then, that certain enrollment categories fall outside the technical definition of census. The three main types are genealogies, inventories and population aggregates. Each of these lacks at least one of the three necessary criteria. Although genealogies and inventories may be mandated, they lack pertinent demographic features such as age or gender. More importantly, they do not place any obligatory service on the subject of the census. Likewise, population aggregates may provide demographic data, but they fail to demonstrate the compulsory responsibilities of those numbered.

2. United Monarchy.

2.1. David. The most comprehensive account of census taking in the Historical Books is the enigmatic episode found in 2 Samuel 24 and its parallel, 1 Chronicles 21. In the Deuteronomistic recounting, *David has been incited by the Lord to "go, number Israel and Judah." Despite Joab's protests, David ordered him to register the number of soldiers. On completion of the census, David is struck with remorse for having "sinned egregiously" *(ḥāṭā'tî mĕ'ōd)*. David is left to ponder the fate of his people, electing to choose punishment by the hand of God rather than that of humans. The impending plague delivered by an angel of the Lord strikes seventy thousand people, according to the biblical record, before the Lord intervenes at the brink of Jerusalem's gates. Whereas in Samuel the Lord is both the instigator and the punisher, the Chronicler distances the Lord from involvement by attributing the provocation to Satan. Even more clever is the Aramaic Targum of 1 Chronicles 21, which states, "Satan incited God to incite David." Hence, surrounding the events of David's census is a tension regarding where to place blame for the plague.

Also at issue is the degree to which Joab was culpable. The Deuteronomist indicates that after nearly ten months of traversing the entire landscape of Israel, Joab had reached a final tally. By contrast, 1 Chronicles 21 reports that Joab is so troubled by David's orders that he leaves the Levites and Benjaminites unnumbered. However, the implication in 1 Chronicles 27:24 is that it was this very insubordination that caused the plague.

The fact that the census plague elicited internal debate is interesting, but not as intriguing as why the plague occurred in the first place. In light of the Exodus 30 passage (see 1 above), the prevailing thought, dating back to Josephus (*Ant.* 7.318), is that the plague is a direct result of David's neglect in collecting the appropriate half-shekel *kōper* (Speiser, 21-22; Fishbane, 107) and the corresponding violation of purity laws by enlisted men (McCarter 1984, 513-14). At least three problems are evident with this solution, however. First, as previously noted, the *kōper* received in Exodus 30 was a direct result of a poll tax intended for the construction of the tabernacle. It had a specific function in a specific milieu. Second, the plague that is threatened in Exodus 30 applied only to males twenty years of age and older. Although the Chronicler's account of the census plague of David might imply this demographic *(ʾîš)*, the Deuteronomist indicates the plague was indiscriminate of age or gender *(hāʿām)*. Third, there are no other cited incidents in the Hebrew Bible in which a plague resulted from failing to assess the half-shekel *kōper*.

Another common argument with respect to the plague is that census-taking in the ancient Near East was fraught with danger in that it was believed to have placed the life of the enrollee in jeopardy (Sanders, 547; Levine, 67). In support of this position E. A. Speiser (24) cites the Epic of Gilgamesh (VII iv 49-52; X vi 36-39) as evidence that deities sometimes determined the fate of humans with the simple act of enrollment, giving rise to the taboo of counting heads. According to this argument, it was the act of census-taking itself that was deemed deserving of divine fury.

More recently, J. J. Adler (95) has posited that David's sin was not in taking the census, but in failing to take the Jebusite-occupied Mount Moriah, which would become the future site of *Solomon's temple. Adler observes that the plague subsides only after the purchase of Araunah/Ornan's threshing floor. Regardless of the various scholarly positions on the cause of the plague, there is virtual consensus that the episode does serve the etiological purpose of describing how the threshing floor became the sacred temple location.

2.2. Solomon. Adler's observation regarding the plague's relationship to the future site of the temple leads to another possible explanation. 2 Chronicles 2:17 states, "Then Solomon took a census of all the resident aliens of Israel, similar to the census which David his father had taken." The explicit purpose of this census was for the enlistment of corvée labor for the construction of the temple (1 Kings 5:13-18). In both the Chronicler's account and that of the Deuteronomist, David had been told unequivocally that he was not to be the builder of God's house (2 Sam 7; 1 Chron 17). This juxtaposition of the censuses of *Solomon and David strongly suggests an interconnectedness between the census itself and the construction of the temple. The implication, then, is that the plague associated with David's census was a result of premature organization and planning for the construction of the temple, an act that was reserved for Solomon. This solution assumes that the narration of David's preparations for the temple in 1 Chronicles 22—27 is

the particularization of the census act of 1 Chronicles 21/2 Samuel 24 (Ackroyd, 78), following the same structural pattern of Solomon's census in 2 Chronicles 2.

3. Divided Monarchy.

There were two by-products of Solomon's census. The intended benefit was that it would determine the available labor force for the construction of the temple. The unintended consequence, however, was the dissolution of the united kingdom of Israel (1 Kings 12:1-20/ 2 Chron 10:1-19). The kings discussed below who conducted censuses during the period of the divided monarchy have two commonalities: first, each was a Judean monarch; second, each "acted rightly in the eyes of the Lord." This is consistent with the Chronicler's assertion that one of the hallmarks of a good king was the strength of his army (see Dillard, 76-81), thereby necessitating the census to maintain military forces.

3.1. Jehoshaphat. Some uncertainty exists concerning whether the enrollment conducted by *Jehoshaphat in 2 Chronicles 17:12-19 is a legitimate census. In some respects the soldier tallies recorded in 2 Chronicles 17 resemble those of other kings, which do not fall under the rubric of census (1 Chron 13:3; 14:8; 2 Chron 11:1/ 1 Kings 12:21). What separates this enrollment from the others, however, is the fact that the enrollment, *pĕquddâ*, was done systematically according to family, thus meeting the requirements of mandate and demographic interest. With Judah on the rise as a military power in Syro-Palestine, the census allowed Jehoshaphat to determine his available troops, enabling him to make strategic assignments for fortification.

3.2. Joash. In 2 Kings 12 and its parallel, 2 Chronicles 24, Joash has resolved to make repairs to the temple, so he orders an annual fund drive to raise the necessary capital. M. Fishbane (107-9) has argued for the connection between this collection and the poll tax of Exodus 30:14. In his assessment the word *ʿōbēr* is an ellipsis of the phrase *hāʿōbēr ʿal happĕqûdîm*, "those enrolled in the census." The link between the two is even more apparent in the Chronicler's account: "Why have you not required the Levites to bring from Judah and Jerusalem the tax of Moses . . . for the tabernacle of testimony?" (2 Chron 24:6). Although it is unclear whether this neglect of priestly duty was an isolated incident or standard practice, there is no indication that a plague resulted from it.

3.3. Amaziah. Of all the censuses taken in the Historical Books, Amaziah's census in 2 Chronicles 25:5-10 most closely mirrors the calamity associated with David's. The conflict portrayed in Amaziah's incident is not that he merely took a census, but that he enrolled excessive troops. In response to a warning issued by a certain "man of God," Amaziah released the Israelite conscripts, thereby staying the hand of God against his army. In contrast to David's census, however, there can be no dispute as to the nature and purpose of Amaziah's census, which was to enlist soldiers for the ensuing battle with Edom.

3.4. Azariah/Uzziah. Similar to that of Jehoshaphat, Uzziah's enrollment in 2 Chronicles 26:11-13 meets the necessary qualifications to be considered a census. First, it was mandated by Uzziah's royal commander, Hananiah, and conducted by two officials, Jeiel and Maaseiah. Second, it provided the king with a standing army of veteran soldiers. Third, like the census of Jehosphaphat, Uzziah's enrollment involved the heads of families, meeting the requirement of demographic interest.

4. Ezra-Nehemiah.

4.1. Repatriation Lists. The repatriation list of the Babylonian exiles returning to Judah is repeated in Ezra 2:1-67 and Nehemiah 7:6-69, with minor variations, which can be attributed mostly to textual corruption (Williamson 2004, 245). It is introduced with the same Hebrew phrase, *ʾēlleh běnê*, as the genealogies of 1-2 Chronicles. However, contrary to the lists in Chronicles, the repatriation list of *Ezra-Nehemiah was officially sanctioned and implied civic duty.

First, both accounts (Ezra 2:62-63; Neh 7:64-65) make clear that as a result of the census certain individuals were excluded from service in the priesthood. Second, the intent of the census was to ensure adequate financial (Ezra 2:69; Neh 7:69-71) and labor (Ezra 2:68) resources. For *Ezra, the data were necessary for the construction of the second temple in Jerusalem (Ezra 3:8-11), whereas *Nehemiah required it for the repopulation of Jerusalem (Neh 11:1-36). Furthermore, the account in Nehemiah unequivocally attributes the impetus for this census to God (Neh 7:5), which, at the very least, meets the qualifications for mandate, and perhaps intentionally contrasts Nehemiah

with David (1 Chron 21:1).

4.2. Ezra's Second Census. According to the biblical record, three days after the exiles' departure from Babylonia, Ezra conducted a second census (Ezra 8:15), the details of which are reported in the preceding verses (Ezra 8:1-14). Unlike the census in Ezra 2, this census is interested only in the heads of households, introduced by the phrase *ʾēlleh rāʾšê ʾăbōtêhem*. In addition, the list is conspicuously artificial with its pervasive use of round *numbers (see Williamson 1985, 111). However, the text makes explicit that the list in Ezra 8 was not intended for military enlistment (Ezra 8:21-23), but rather had ramifications for priestly obligations. In particular, the census enabled Ezra to ascertain the deficiency of Levites and temple servants (Ezra 8:15-20), who were critical for the mission (Williamson 1985, 116).

5. Conclusions.

Three general conclusions may be drawn from the data. First, the term *census* has a specific technical definition that does not apply to every text involving the numbering of individuals. A census must be officially decreed, carried out with the purpose of collecting taxes or conscripting labor, and concerned with demographics. Second, the census plague of David is the most enigmatic account in the Historical Books, giving rise to multiple explanations for its occurrence. Among the candidates are (1) failure to collect the half-shekel *kōper* payment of Exodus 30; (2) breaching the taboo of counting heads; (3) failure to occupy Mount Moriah; (4) premature planning for the construction of the temple. Finally, with the exception of the anomalous case of 2 Samuel 24, census narratives in the Historical Books are absent from the *Deuteronomistic History.

See also TAXES, TAXATION.

BIBLIOGRAPHY. **P. R. Ackroyd,** *I & II Chronicles, Ezra, Nehemiah* (TBC; London: SCM, 1973); **J. J. Adler,** "David's Last Sin: Was It the Census?" *JBQ* 23 (1995) 91-95; **R. B. Dillard,** *2 Chronicles* (WBC 15; Waco, TX: Word, 1987); **M. Fishbane,** "Census and Intercession in a Priestly Text (Exodus 30:11-16) and in Its Midrashic Transformation," in *Pomegranates and Golden Bells: Studies in Biblical, Jewish, and Near Eastern Ritual, Law, and Literature in Honor of Jacob Milgrom,* ed. D. P. Wright and D. N. Freedman (Winona Lake, IN: Eisenbrauns, 1995) 103-11; **B. A. Levine,** *In the*

Presence of the Lord: A Study of Cult and Some Cultic Terms in Ancient Israel (SJLA 5; Leiden: E. J. Brill, 1974); **P. K. McCarter Jr.,** *II Samuel* (AB 9; Garden City, NY: Doubleday, 1984); **G. E. Mendenhall,** "The Census Lists of Numbers 1 and 26," *JBL* 77 (1958) 52-66; **J. A. Sanders,** "Census," *IDB* 1.547; **E. A. Speiser,** "Census and Ritual Expiation in Mari and Israel," *BASOR* 149 (1958) 17-25; **J. R. Weeks,** *Population: An Introduction to Concepts and Issues* (8th ed.; Belmont, CA: Wadsworth/Thomson Learning, 2002) 41-77; **H. G. M. Williamson,** *Ezra, Nehemiah* (WBC 16; Waco, TX: Word, 1985); idem, *Studies in Persian Period History and Historiography* (FAT 38; Tubingen: Mohr Siebeck, 2004).   K. R. Greenwood

CERAMICS. *See* ARCHAEOLOGY, SYRO-PALESTINIAN.

CHALDEANS. *See* BABYLONIA, BABYLONIANS.

**CHAOS, *CHAOSKAMPF. See* CANAAN, CANAANITES.

CHRONICLER'S HISTORY

The term *Chronicler's History* refers to the theory that the books of 1 and 2 *Chronicles, Ezra and Nehemiah originally constituted a single work. Since ancient witnesses make it clear that 1 and 2 Chronicles originally were one book, as were the books of Ezra and Nehemiah, the theory is concerned with the combination of the two books of Chronicles and *Ezra-Nehemiah. The traditions of both rabbinic Judaism and medieval Christianity attributed both works to *Ezra, but modern scholarship often has regarded them as the work of an anonymous writer known simply as the Chronicler, hence the description "the Chronicler's History."

The modern theory of the Chronicler's History was set out originally by L. Zunz (1832) and F. C. Movers (1834), and it became widely accepted in biblical scholarship until the latter half of the twentieth century. Demurring voices were few, limited to A. C. Welch (1935) and M. H. Segal (1943, in Hebrew). M. Noth's major work on the Chronicler's History, for example, continued to accept Chronicles, Ezra and Nehemiah as a single work, affirming that "there is no need to start with a demonstration of the work's literary unity" (Noth 1987, 29).

It was not until S. Japhet (1968) and H. G. M. Williamson (1977) raised substantial objections

to the theory that the situation began to change. Their arguments have proved so persuasive, however, that the situation is now almost completely reversed, and the dominant view among scholars is that Chronicles and Ezra-Nehemiah were separate works. The theory of the Chronicler's History is still being defended, however, by scholars such as J. Blenkinsopp (1988) and Z. Talshir (1999). The current consensus has also been questioned by some who previously supported the idea of separate works, on the grounds of various kinds of structural links between Chronicles and Ezra-Nehemiah (see, e.g., the essays by Wright, Schniedewind and Kartveit in Graham and McKenzie).

1. Key Arguments for the Chronicler's History
2. Key Arguments Against the Chronicler's History
3. Conclusions

1. Key Arguments for the Chronicler's History.
There are five key arguments that have been put forward to support the idea of the Chronicler's History.

1.1. Textual Links Between Chronicles and Ezra-Nehemiah. This argument concerns two sets of passages: the apparent repetition of 2 Chronicles 36:22-23 in Ezra 1:1-3a, and the close association between 1 Chronicles 9:2-17 and Nehemiah 11:3-19. The former connection is particularly significant because it often is assumed that because Ezra 1:1-3a follows 2 Chronicles 36:22-23 in English Bibles, and because the events described in Ezra and Nehemiah follow those in Chronicles, the two books form a continuous story.

However, it is much more likely that the writer of Chronicles has adapted material from the existing text of Ezra-Nehemiah in both instances. The most persuasive indication is that the quotation from Cyrus's edict in 2 Chronicles 36:22-23 seems to be a brief and truncated version of the fuller text in Ezra, since Chronicles effectively ends in the middle of a sentence: "may he go up" (cf. Ezra 1:3). Several minor differences in wording also point in the same direction. For example, the inclusion of God's name in 2 Chronicles 36:23 in the phrase *yhwh ʾĕlōhāyw ʿimmô* ("may Yahweh his God be with him") is likely to be later than the simpler *yĕhî ʾĕlōhāyw ʿimmô* ("may his God be with him") in Ezra 1:3, and the use of *bĕpî* ("by the mouth of") in 2 Chronicles 36:22 seems to have been conformed with v. 21, in contrast with *mippî* ("from the mouth of") in Ezra 1:1.

Although the relationship between 1 Chronicles 9:2-17 and Nehemiah 11:3-19 is less clear, three factors suggest that Chronicles is later. First, the numbers for comparable groups of people are consistently higher in Chronicles (cf. the figures for Judah, Benjamin, the priests and the gatekeepers in 1 Chron 9:6, 9, 13, 22 with Neh 11:6, 8, 12, 13, 14, 19). Second, since Nehemiah 11:1-2 describes the initiation of the policy to repopulate *Jerusalem, it is likely that 1 Chronicles 9 represents the continuation of that policy. Third, the unique reference to the term "temple servants" *(nětînîm)* in 1 Chronicles 9:2 in contrast with its frequent appearance in Ezra-Nehemiah (e.g., Ezra 7:7; 8:20; Neh 11:3, 21) indicates that Chronicles probably is quoting from Ezra-Nehemiah.

1.2. Evidence of the Greek Work 1 Esdras. This book, preserved in the LXX and in some collections of the Apocrypha, comprises 2 Chronicles 35—36, Ezra 1—10 and Nehemiah 7:72—8:13a, though the material sometimes occurs in a different order, and it contains some sections that are not in the canonical books. The crucial point is that it makes no break between the end of 2 Chronicles 36 and the start of Ezra 1, linking these two works by a single version of Cyrus's edict—that is, the longer account from Ezra 1. This, however, is probably of little consequence for the original relationship of Chronicles and Ezra-Nehemiah, since 1 Esdras is almost certainly a secondary work dependent on the biblical material. For example, the setting of Artaxerxes' correspondence in 1 Esdras 2:15-25 in a context that makes little sense in comparison with its literary function in Ezra 4:6-24 (see McKenzie in Graham and McKenzie), and the indication in 1 Esdras 9:37 that the compiler knew that the equivalent passage in Nehemiah 7:72—8:13a originally was preceded by Nehemiah 7 (see Williamson), argue strongly for the priority of the biblical material. Even if 1 Esdras is based on an existing tradition in which 2 Chronicles 36 and Ezra 1 were already joined together, as Talshir argues, that does not necessarily mean that the join was original.

1.3. The Presence of Common Distinctive Words and Phrases. This argument is complicated by two factors. First, the limited extent of our knowledge of late biblical *Hebrew means that the amount of comparable material is also limited—a problem compounded by the fact that both Chronicles and Ezra-Nehemiah contain a significant amount of material from other sources, perhaps as much as 70 percent in the case of Ezra-Nehemiah. Second, two different sets of criteria have been applied to this argument, making it more difficult to evaluate. The easier criterion is to identify terms that are distinctive to Chronicles and Ezra-Nehemiah (Blenkinsopp), such as *hityaḥēś* ("to enroll in a genealogy") or *māʿal* ("to act unfaithfully; unfaithfulness"). This criterion, however, establishes only that the two books share common interests. Clear evidence for common authorship of a single work requires a more demanding second criterion: such distinctive terms should be expressed in different ways in other literature of the period (Williamson). Application of this criterion, however, has resulted in a very brief list of common items, with examples being confined either to idiomatic expressions such as *yôm bĕyôm* ("day by day"; seven occurrences in 1-2 Chronicles and Ezra-Nehemiah) or to technical terms such as *mĕṣiltayim* ("cymbals"; thirteen occurrences; cf. the earlier term *ṣelṣĕlîm*, which occurs twice). In light of the limited extent of postexilic Hebrew literature, this latter criterion seems rather unrealistic. Under the circumstances, it is impossible to do more than acknowledge that although the two works do share some distinctive vocabulary, this can be only a contributory rather than a decisive argument.

1.4. The Presence of Common Ideas. This would involve ideas such as the building and worship of the temple, the Levites and musical instruments, and the role of *Zerubbabel. Blenkinsopp has also argued that the two books present some of these in parallel patterns. These include, for example, the preparations for *Solomon's temple and the second temple (1 Chron 22:2, 4, 15; 2 Chron 2:9, 15-16; Ezra 3:7), the common refrain "he is good, his love endures for ever" (2 Chron 7:3; 20:21; Ezra 3:11), and the pattern of religious infidelity followed by renewal and reform and climaxing in a Passover celebration (cf. 2 Chron 30; 35:1-19; Ezra 6:19-22). These features do demonstrate thematic connections between the two books, though they fall short of evidence for common authorship. It is not too surprising that parallels exist in the accounts of temple building, given the special significance of the temple, or that the refrain from the psalms "he is good, his love endures for ever" was popular in postexilic worship. As with the issue of common vocabulary, this argument tends to illustrate that the two books share common interests rather than demonstrate the existence of a closer connection.

1.5. The Analogy of the Deuteronomistic History. According to Noth, "The real pattern for his [the Chronicler's] composition was the work of Dtr" (Noth 1987, 97). Both were composite works in which the final editors traced the history of God's dealings with his people by bringing together shorter works. The analogy depends, of course, to some extent on the validity of the theory of the Deuteronomistic History, but it does at least account for one possible objection to the Chronicler's History, which is that it combines two works of a somewhat different character, format and purpose (see Talshir). It certainly is possible on this basis to acknowledge that although Chronicles was written about the distant past and Ezra-Nehemiah written about the present or recent past, they could have been combined in a single work. On the other hand, the analogy is not exact, as Noth himself recognized, since in contrast to the Deuteronomic editors who brought together several different works, the Chronicler presumably compiled one of the two major works as well as bringing them both together.

2. Key Arguments Against the Chronicler's History.

In contrast to the above points, counterarguments have been made in an attempt to show that Chronicles and Ezra-Nehemiah are more likely to have been conceived as separate works.

2.1. Lack of Overlap of Key Ideas. In each of the two works several key ideas are either dealt with briefly or not at all in the other. Five of these ideas are the most important.

2.1.1. The Davidic Covenant and Monarchy. The *Davidic covenant and the Davidic monarchy are central to Chronicles' understanding of the relationship between the temple and the monarchy, but they are hardly present in Ezra-Nehemiah. Whereas the tribe of Judah, the reigns of *David and *Solomon, and the subsequent history of the Davidic monarchy are structural features in Chronicles, David's role in Ezra-Nehemiah is limited primarily to his connection with the Levites and musical worship (Ezra 3:10; Neh 12:36, 45-46). Even the Davidic

ancestry of the governor Zerubbabel, who plays an important role in Ezra-Nehemiah, is of no interest to the author of Ezra-Nehemiah, though it is mentioned in Chronicles (1 Chron 3:19).

2.1.2. The Theme "All Israel." The theme "all Israel" is important throughout Chronicles, whereas Ezra-Nehemiah usually refers to the postexilic community as "Judah and Benjamin" or "Judah and Jerusalem." Although Ezra-Nehemiah does refer to *Israel as the twelve tribes (Ezra 6:17; 8:35), the rarity of this usage stands in sharp contrast to the emphasis on all Israel throughout Chronicles, especially in the period after the fall of Israel (2 Chron 30:1-20; 34:9, 21). Chronicles' use of a phrase such as "all Israel in Judah and Benjamin" (2 Chron 11:3; added to 1 Kings 12:23) seems to indicate a concern that "Judah and Benjamin" was an insufficient description. The relationship between north and south also has been a key issue, since it was assumed for a long time that the anti-Samarian tendency in Ezra-Nehemiah was also applicable to Chronicles (especially Noth). In fact, this has now been shown not to be the case. Furthermore, a distinction should be made in Ezra-Nehemiah between the problem of people from *Samaria who opposed God's purposes (Neh 2:10) and the positive emphasis on the postexilic community's descent from the twelve *tribes (Ezra 6:17; 8:35).

2.1.3. The Exodus. The exodus plays a key role in Ezra-Nehemiah (e.g., Ezra 9; Neh 9) but hardly appears in Chronicles. While Chronicles assumes the foundational significance of God's revelation to Moses, it prefers to emphasize God's purposes for David. On the other hand, the different perspectives on the exodus should not divert attention from the fact that the *law of Moses is of fundamental importance in both books.

2.1.4. Prophecy. *Prophecy is prominent in Chronicles but is hardly mentioned in Ezra-Nehemiah. Although this argument has been countered by the observation that prophecy underwent a fundamental change after the exile (Blenkinsopp), this overlooks the fact that it is Chronicles that draws attention to this change by highlighting the prophetic nature of the Levites' ministry (1 Chron 25:1-8).

2.1.5. Theology of Retribution. The theology of immediate retribution—God deals directly with people according to their attitude toward him—is important in Chronicles but not in Ezra-

Nehemiah. Although God's response to human behavior in Chronicles is considerably more nuanced than this understanding traditionally has allowed (see Selman; Kelly), it remains true that the consequences of faith or disobedience in Ezra-Nehemiah do not fit the kinds of patterns evident in Chronicles.

2.2. Strong Difference in Some of the Literary Characteristics. Two examples must suffice. First, whereas most of Chronicles indicates the activity of a single author, Ezra-Nehemiah is primarily a compilation of sources such as the *Aramaic material, the lists, and the Ezra and Nehemiah memoirs. According to Talshir, this is "perhaps the main difference between Chr and Ezr-Neh" (Talshir, 25). Second, the literary architecture of the two works is different. Although both works use techniques such as periodization of history and concentric patterns, Chronicles makes extensive use of models and paradigms to connect both persons and events, and also of speeches of various kinds, such as prayers and prophecies. Ezra-Nehemiah, on the other hand, uses parallel panels and repetitive resumptions, and is constructed around a repeated pattern of implementation, conflict and resolution (Throntveit; Eskenazi).

3. Conclusions.

We may draw three conclusions. First, consideration of these various factors has led to widely differing views about the possible existence of a Chronicler's History. The main options are these: (1) the Chronicler's History is a single work by a single author; (2) Chronicles and Ezra-Nehemiah are separate works by the same author (Welten; Willi); (3) Chronicles and Ezra-Nehemiah were brought together by a redactor (Talshir; Steins); (4) Chronicles and Ezra-Nehemiah are separate works.

Second, The fact that an author or editor of Chronicles brought the two works together at some point by using parts of Ezra 1 and Nehemiah 11 in 2 Chronicles 36 and 1 Chronicles 9 respectively is a clear indication that a formal relationship existed between them before they reached their final scriptural form. The key issue, therefore, is not whether such a relationship existed, but what the nature of that relationship was. The aforementioned arguments suggest that the strongest connections between the two works exist at the redactional level rather than at the linguistic or ideological level.

The analogy of the Deuteronomistic History remains helpful in that historical works of probably different origins have been brought together to form a connected story. Although the two works share a common ideology in their focus on the restoration of Israel (cf. 2 Chron 7:12-16; Neh 8—10) and the importance of temple worship, and they also use some common terminology, these features are supportive rather than decisive factors in determining the character of their relationship.

However, the overall evidence seems to fall short of being able to regard Chronicles and Ezra-Nehemiah as a single work for two main reasons: (1) The two works originally were conceived for distinct purposes, as is indicated by their ideological and structural differences. Chronicles' focus on the Davidic covenant as well as the temple, and its setting of Israel's history in a context of the whole world as well as all twelve tribes, set it apart from the more circumscribed account of Ezra-Nehemiah. The latter is concerned to tell the story of Israel's restoration under God's providence and the authority of *Persian emperors (Ezra 6:14) and its reconstitution as a covenant people based on the law of Moses (Neh 8—10). The endings of the two works provide a good example of their differing purposes. The rather disappointing story of continuing problems in Nehemiah 13 contrasts with the optimistic invitation of the last two verses of 2 Chronicles. (2) The indications that Chronicles is later than Ezra-Nehemiah suggest that it is unlikely that such an extensive work was composed primarily as a prelude to the much briefer account of the postexilic restoration in Ezra-Nehemiah. In any case, Chronicles' adaptation of parts of Ezra-Nehemiah is not an indication of its special dependence on the latter, but rather a typical example of the way in which Chronicles interprets many parts of the Hebrew Bible.

Third, the most likely conclusion, therefore, is that Ezra-Nehemiah does not simply continue the Chronicler's history of Israel, contrary to what is implied by the order of the two works in English Bibles and the LXX. Rather, as their reverse order in the MT indicates, they originally were two distinct works, both of which dealt with the restoration of Israel, but from quite different perspectives. They then were brought together by an editor, perhaps by the Chronicler personally, to demonstrate that the work of restoration in the sixth and fifth centuries BCE had its origins in God's purposes for the whole human race and his promises to the Davidic line.

See also CHRONICLES, BOOKS OF; DEUTERONO-MISTIC HISTORY; EZRA AND NEHEMIAH, BOOKS OF.

BIBLIOGRAPHY. J. Blenkinsopp, *Ezra-Nehemiah* (OTL; London: SCM, 1988); T. C. Eskenazi, *In an Age of Prose: A Literary Approach to Ezra-Nehemiah* (SBLMS 36; Atlanta: Scholars Press, 1988); M. P. Graham and S. L. McKenzie, eds., *The Chronicler as Author: Studies in Text and Texture* (JSOTSup 263; Sheffield: Sheffield Academic Press, 1999); S. Japhet, "The Supposed Common Authorship of Chronicles and Ezra-Nehemiah Investigated Anew," *VT* 18 (1968) 330-71; B. E. Kelly, *Retribution and Eschatology in Chronicles* (JSOTSup 211; Sheffield: Sheffield Academic Press, 1996); F. K. Movers, *Kritische Untersuchungen über die biblische Chronik: Ein Beitrag zur Einleitung in das alte Testament* (Bonn: Habicht, 1834); M. Noth, *Überlieferungsgeschichtliche Studien*, 1: *Die sammelnden und bearbeitenden geschichtswerke im Alten Testament* (Halle: Niemeyer, 1943); ET, *The Chronicler's History* (JSOTSup 50; Sheffield: JSOT, 1987); K. H. Richards, "Reshaping Chronicles and Ezra-Nehemiah Interpretation," in *Old Testament Interpretation: Past, Present and Future*, ed. J. L. Mays, D. L. Petersen and K. H. Richards (Nashville: Abingdon, 1995) 211-24; M. H. Segal, "The Books of Ezra-Nehemiah" [Hebrew], *Tarbiz* 14 (1943) 81-103; M. J. Selman, *1 and 2 Chronicles* (TOTC; Downers Grove, IL: InterVarsity Press, 1994); G. Steins, *Die Chronik als kanonisches Abschlussphänomen: Studien zur Entstehung und Theologie von 1/2 Chronik* (BBB 93; Weinheim: Beltz Athenäum, 1995 [cf. *VT* 48 (1998) 285-86]); Z. Talshir, *1 Esdras: From Origin to Translation* (SBLSCS 47; Atlanta: Society of Biblical Literature, 1999); M. Throntveit, *Ezra-Nehemiah* (IntC; Louisville: John Knox, 1992); A. C. Welch, *Post-exilic Judaism* (Edinburgh and London: Blackwood, 1935); P. Welten, *Geschichte und Geschichtsdarstellung in den Chronikbüchern* (WMANT 42; Neukirchen-Vluyn: Neukirchener Verlag, 1973); T. Willi, *Die Chronik als Auslegung: Untersuchungen zur literarischen Gestaltung der historischen Überlieferung Israels* (FRLANT 106; Göttingen: Vandenhoeck & Ruprecht, 1972); H. G. M. Williamson, *Israel in the Books of Chronicles* (Cambridge: Cambridge University Press, 1977); L. Zunz, "Dibre Hajamim oder die Bücher der Chronik," in *Die gottesdienstlichen Vorträge der Juden historisch entwickelt: Ein Beitrag zur Altertumskunde und biblischen Kritik, zur Literatur- und Religionsgeschichte* (Berlin: Asher, 1832) 12-34. M. J. Selman

CHRONICLES, BOOKS OF

The books of Chronicles are a historical narrative that tells the story of Israel to the community of faith that was reconstituted after the Babylonian exile and living under Persian control in the province of Judea (Yehud). The author(s), in a prophet-like manner, re-presents the community's past story from a postexilic perspective with a focus on the role of *David and the Davidic kings, the establishment of the proper temple cultus, and the need for kings and people to seek God. The author(s) apparently sought to establish for the postexilic community an identity of continuity with the past and to encourage them to actualize the traditions and lessons from their past in their current lives.

1. The Role of Chronicles for the Postexilic Community of Faith and Subsequent Communities
2. Historical Value
3. Setting the Stage for Reading Chronicles
4. The Message of the Chronicler

1. The Role of Chronicles for the Postexilic Community of Faith and Subsequent Communities.

1.1. A Second History of Israel. The books of Chronicles (Hebrew title: "The Events/Words of Days") make up one of two sweeping accounts of the history of Israel found in the OT. Covering the generations from Adam to *Saul, primarily through *genealogies and lists, and then relating the history of Israel from *David to the Babylonian exile, Chronicles retells much of the story found in the books of *Samuel and *Kings. Often viewed as a supplementary work to those books, it received the title "The Things Left Out" *(Paraleipomenōn)* in the Septuagint, a Greek translation of the Hebrew Bible. The Christian scholar Jerome used the title "Chronicles" ("Chronicle of the Entire Divine History") in the fourth century CE. However, Chronicles is neither merely a supplement nor a chronicle of events; it retells Israelite history from a unique perspective with its own themes and emphases.

1.2. A Formative Work from a Formative Time. Chronicles, although often neglected by current Bible readers, is a formative work that stands at a formative stage of the history of Judaism. It comes from and spoke to an era when the character of Judaism proper was being formed. Before this work was composed, the nation of Judah had, for all practical purposes, come to an end. By 586 BCE the Babylonian Empire had besieged Judah's major cities, killed many people, crushed its capital city of *Jerusalem, destroyed its temple of Yahweh, and carried off many upperclass survivors to Babylonia (see History of Israel 6: Babylonian Period). Although living in a foreign land of foreign gods, some of these deportees retained a strong sense of identity, ethnically, nationalistically and religiously. Their strong sense of nationalistic identity was enabled perhaps by the recitation of a nationalistic historical narrative, the *Deuteronomistic History. The deportees' strong sense of religious identity as worshipers of Yahweh was preserved perhaps through the dissemination of the words of the prophet *Jeremiah and the presence and messages of the prophet Ezekiel. Whatever the contributing factors were, a deported community of faithful worshipers of Yahweh remained alive to the hope of restoration. When the winds of power shifted from the Babylonians to the Persians, the offer was extended to captives of Babylonian warfare to return to their homelands. A remnant of this people and their offspring were willing to return and start life anew in the Promised Land in the face of many challenges. This return began a new formative period, one to which the books of Chronicles belong and that it indirectly addresses (see History of Israel 7: Persian Period). Those who returned, through their acts of preservation, compilation and composition, have given the world the Hebrew Bible (Old Testament), a Yahwistic account of their history, their culture, worship, spokespersons and stories. Their descendants became the "People of the Book," the Jews. Chronicles stands at the heart of this transition. Reading Chronicles can show the reader some of the major themes of the returnees' rehearsal of their past that were important to this transitional era.

1.3. An Instructive Work for a Postmodern Time. Current readers of Chronicles, who belong to the so-called postmodern period of the Western world, have the advantage of being able in one respect to hear the messages of Chronicles more like the ancient Jewish audiences than did the previous modern generation. To explain this point about hearing the message, some background information is necessary. The OT contains two major blocks of historical narrative that both rehearse much of the same period of history. Both works were formed, however, from different perspectives, for different audiences, and highlight different lessons of the past. The first block of narrative is referred to as the Former Prophets in the Hebrew Bible, but it is designated as the Deuteronomistic History by contemporary scholars. It consists of Joshua, Judges, 1-2 Samuel and 1-2 Kings. The second block is the *Chronicler's History, which consists of Chronicles, Ezra and Nehemiah. The presence of two histories of Israel in the Hebrew canon runs against the modern notion of historiography in the Western world. For the modern historian, there could be only one, true, factual history. A task of the modern historian was to conclude which one, if either, of the two histories preserved the true account, or to choose selectively the true facts from one or the other source. To be sure, it is still the goal of contemporary historians, who wish to reconstruct the history of Israel as accurately as possible, to work with these two histories in much the same manner. However, with the shift to postmodernity there has grown an increasing appreciation of the process of history-telling through which different people, or even the same person at different times, can look back at the same historical field of the past and draw out different but equally valid story lines. An analogy to this process is how two skilled painters can paint two different but equally accurate portraits of the same person. The result of such postmodern insight into the nature of history-telling is that the study of Chronicles no longer is limited to an assessment of its value as a source for reconstructing *the* story of Israel. Instead, the current reader can study how history-telling in Chronicles communicated its messages to its audience. Ironically, since both the Deuteronomistic History and the Chronicler's History were accepted as canonical by ancient Judaism, that community of faith must have accepted the concept that both histories could communicate valid messages—a very postmodern conclusion! Thus the current readers of the community of faith can share with the ancient audiences the goal of reading Chronicles as a historical story that communicates abiding messages of truth. (For support of this position, a discussion of the history of biblical historiography and a critique of the current state of affairs see Provan, Long and Longman, 3-74.)

2. Historical Value.

All historical narratives involve creativity not only on the perceptual and conceptual levels of "reality" and of "events" and their relationships in the historical field of the past, but also in the employment of the structures of narrative used to present the "stories" of the past (Duke 1990, 31-35; Provan, Long and Longman, 75-97). Modern historians often lost sight of the tendentiousness of all history-telling and the biases behind their own critical reconstructions. Indeed, for the community of faith, a canonical reading of historical narrative does not observe the text as an artifact for the goal of reconstructing *the* history of Israel within the constraints of a modern, secular worldview. On the contrary, a canonical reader seeks to become a participant in the narrative world of the text, with the goals of being addressed by the divine perspective on the life of Israel and having one's own worldview shaped and informed. Nonetheless, since the implicit claim behind the biblical historical narratives is that they are interpretations of that which happened in real time and space, the issue of historical accuracy arises. In the history of the critical scholarship of Chronicles, the dominant questions have revolved around its value as a historical record (for a comprehensive survey see Peltonen).

2.1. Trends in Chronicles Scholarship.
The nineteenth century presented the major turning point in Chronicles studies. Prior to the nineteenth century, Christian and Jewish scholars generally highly appraised the historical worth of Chronicles. The Christian Fathers assumed its historical reliability, and medieval commentators tended to harmonize differences between Chronicles and Samuel-Kings. The change in historical perspective of the Renaissance began to lay a foundation for the reversal of this assessment as some scholars began to see Chronicles as a late "interpretation" rather than as a "real history." Still, moving into the nineteenth century, the scholarly consensus, as represented by J. G. Eichhorn in 1803, was that the author of Chronicles had drawn on canonical works and other historical sources preserved by temple personnel. Differences between Chronicles and Samuel-Kings were accounted for primarily as scribal inaccuracies in the source materials.

However, W. M. L. de Wette, in a very significant work for OT studies in 1806, sharply criticized Eichhorn and soundly rejected the reliability of Chronicles. Intimately connected to this thesis was his rejection of the authenticity of the Pentateuch, since both Chronicles and the Pentateuch supported the early existence of Mosaic laws and cultic institutions that de Wette did not find supported in the Former Prophets. De Wette argued that where the Chronicler's material paralleled Samuel-Kings, he had used that source; however, where the material was different, the Chronicler had worked in alterations, additions and fabrications. Vigorous debate ensued throughout the century. Although there was a conservative response to argue for the reliability of the Pentateuch and Chronicles, with J. Wellhausen's *Prolegomena* of 1878, the late date of the Pentateuch source P and the historical unreliability of Chronicles became widely accepted in critical biblical scholarship.

During the twentieth century the connection of Chronicles to Pentateuchal issues lessened, and Chronicles was studied more in its own right. In general, the majority of scholars began building on the rise of archaeological studies and on the development of a historico-geographical approach to biblical studies (e.g., Noth's work of 1943). Chronicles was recognized as a source that should be examined critically at each point for reliable data on topography, place names, genealogies and incidental military and political details, but examined also with the acknowledgment that at all points the data still was cast within the Chronicler's theological agenda. Still, discussion over the historical reliability of Chronicles and its sources covered the spectrum from total rejection as a source for the preexilic period (Torrey 1910; Welten) to holding Chronicles in higher regard (Williamson 1982; Japhet 1993). Although the close of the twentieth century still revealed the debate to continue between "minimalist" and "maximalist" historians, one might say that there was a growing skepticism on two levels. The first is a modern skepticism about the ability ever to prove the validity of records for which there is so little outside corroborative data. The second is a postmodern skepticism about the viability of taking any historical story out of the context of its worldview and projecting it into the historian's worldview in order to get at the "real history."

2.2. The Sources of Chronicles. Tied intimately with the discussion of the historicity of Chronicles has been debate about the sources behind the work (see Peltonen; for a summary see Japhet 1993, 14-23). First, the Chronicler has material that is also known to us from the OT (for parallel text see Endres, Millar and Burns; comparative list, Myers 2.227-31). From pentateuchal material in some form he has drawn genealogical materials and legal traditions associated with the Israelite cult (on the Chronicler's use of legal traditions see Shaver). Parallel to the Deuteronomistic History, he has some genealogies found in Joshua, but then has very little parallel material until he presents the reign of David, from which point on he relies heavily on material found in Samuel-Kings, but with the omission of the material in Kings that deals exclusively with the northern kingdom. Due to the verbatim material that is shared, the consensus opinion is that the Chronicler was heavily dependent on some edition of the Deuteronomistic History. Others have argued that the two works shared the same source material but used it differently (recently Auld 1994). In either case, the arguments become circular and unprovable because we have no other such source material to compare. Chronicles also has some overlap with the books of *Ezra and Nehemiah, the edict of Cyrus (2 Chron 36:22-23 = Ezra 1:1-3) and a list of the inhabitants of Jerusalem (1 Chron 9:2-17 = Neh 11:3-19), and it cites from Psalms 96, 105, 106 (1 Chron 16). Moreover, there are some allusions to prophetic sayings, particularly in the speeches of prophet-like characters (von Rad 1966; Schniedewind, 108-22).

Second, Chronicles has source citations found in the accounts of some of the kings (e.g., 1 Chron 29:29; 2 Chron 9:29; 12:15). Although it seems probable that these refer to sources that the Chronicler used in his account, it is also possible to understand them only as sources to which the Chronicler directed his audience for additional information (*see* Sources, References to). Scholars have taken various positions: (1) these are references to real noncanonical works (Eichhorn, 2.579-601; Rainey: possibly in one greater work); (2) they are various titles for the same outside source (Curtis and Madsen, 22-24); (3) they are various terms for the Deuteronomistic History (Schniedewind, 215-17); (4) they are paraphrases of the source references in the Deuteronomistic History (Klein, 996); (5) they

are made-up references intended to produce the aura of credibility (Torrey 1909, 172-73; Willi, 54; Welten, 191-94). The last position, although possible, seems to ignore the existence of royal and temple *scribes who would have served as a check against such fabrication.

Third, there is evidence of noncanonical sources that are used but not attributed. This includes things such as genealogical material that has no parallel and various references to building projects and military events that seem to be historically accurate (e.g., the reference to Hezekiah's tunnel in 2 Chron 32:30; see Noth, 51-61; Williamson 1982, 19-21). Still, such material might have come from the cited noncanonical sources (Rainey, 30-72).

3. Setting the Stage for Reading Chronicles.
The precise setting, date and authorship of Chronicles are widely debated among scholars. However, it is necessary to explore these issues in order to help the contemporary reader understand Chronicles' original communicative context.

3.1. Historical Setting. Chronicles is situated in the time in which the ancient Yahwistic religious core of the community of Israel was reconstituted in the form that became the foundation for modern Judaism and Christianity. Roughly speaking, Chronicles belongs to the Persian period (538-c. 330 BCE), the early Second Temple period (see 3.2 below.) Little is known about this period. The books of Haggai, Zechariah, Malachi and Ezra-Nehemiah directly provide contemporary perspectives on conditions during this period; Isaiah 40—66 perhaps provides information less directly; Esther reflects knowledge of the Persian court; Chronicles provides insight by inference. Currently, material remains in the area of Judea provide only a skeletal background of the probable social conditions. Still, what is known shows that this time period was one of great cultural change in which competing ideologies were in play. One would suspect that such a historical context played a role in the way in which the author of Chronicles retold the history of Israel.

3.1.1. The Aftermath of the Babylonian Invasions. From the perspective of the OT writers, the exile appeared to ring the death knell of the nation of Judah (for the view that the biblical texts present a mythic, ideologically controlled perspective exaggerating the impact of the deportations see Carroll). The Babylonian control of the region, beginning with its victory at Carchemish (605 BCE), eventually led to the devastation of major cities of Judah, the destruction of Jerusalem and the temple of Yahweh (586 BCE), the end of the economic and governmental state of Judah, and deportations of many of its people who were resettled in a community near Babylon. Deported people included nobility, government officials, leading men, fighting men, craftsmen and artisans, priests and prophets, and residents of the coastal plain and Negeb (2 Kings 24:14-16; Jer 13:18-19; 24:1; 29:1-2). Some of the poorest people deliberately were left to work the lands (2 Kings 25:12), presumably to be joined by others who had successfully fled for refuge and returned, as well as by foreigners who seized the opportunity.

3.1.2. Early Persian Period (538-c. 450 BCE). A second chance on life for Israel came with the rise of the *Persian Empire. The neo-Babylonian Empire soon came to an end under the Persian ruler Cyrus II with his relatively peaceful conquest of Babylon in 539 BCE. Subsequently, the new Persian overlords allowed many of the people-groups that had been deported and resettled by Babylonian kings the opportunity to return to their homelands and to reestablish their national and religious identities, albeit under Persian governance. Under this policy Cyrus permitted groups of former inhabitants of Judah to return to Jerusalem and rebuild the city and the temple as the old kingdom of Judah became the province of Judea under his rule. From the biblical records, it appears that not all exiles of Judah wanted to return, and from external records, it appears that some of the deported community had become assimilated into the Babylonian culture (Beer). However, others, many being government and religious officials or their descendants, had maintained their sense of identity and were willing to return. Although the nation of Judah had the opportunity to be reconstituted as the province of Judea, the loss of their Davidic king threatened their sense of political identity, while they sought to retain their sense of religious and ethnic identity.

The restoration of the formal worship of Yahweh and the (re)shaping of the religious community of Judea did not take place without difficulties (*see* History of Israel 8: Postexilic Community). In 538 BCE a leading Babylonian Jew, Sheshbazzar, was commissioned by the Per-

sians to return to Jerusalem and serve as the first governor (Ezra 1:8-11). He sought to rebuild the temple. Apparently, that work was stopped and begun again under the diarchic rule of another governor, *Zerubbabel, and the high priest, Joshua. From the book of Haggai we learn that the general population, which was suffering from a streak of famine, a poor economic situation and low morale, had to be encouraged to make worshiping Yahweh a priority and to rebuild the temple. We also learn from Ezra that some Israelites who had remained in the land, as well as people who had moved in during the exile, came into an ideological conflict with the returning "people of the exile" and sought to prevent construction of the temple (Ezra 3:1—6:18; Hag 1:1-2:9). It appears that the rural indigenous population was not altogether receptive of the influx of the more aristocratic elite and the new social and economic structures that would accompany the temple. Still, the problems were resolved, and the temple was completed in 515 BCE (*see* Postexilic Temple). Those who had remained in the land, who had remained faithful Yahwists and had kept themselves pure from Gentile neighbors, apparently were accepted into the restored religious community of Judea (Ezra 6:21).

Another formative influence on Judaism during this period was the impetus to codify religious laws. Under the Persian ruler Darius I (reigned 521-486 BCE), a commission was appointed to codify traditional law in Egypt as a means of promoting peace in that troublesome area. On the basis of that knowledge, it seems reasonable to suppose that such Persian policy might have promoted the codification of Jewish law as is found more fully developed in Ezra-Nehemiah (Blenkinsopp, 64-66, 151-57).

More social and religious changes took place with the arrival of another group of exiles about 458 BCE under the leadership of *Ezra, a Jewish priest and scribe (for a discussion of dating issues, with some scholars dating Ezra after Nehemiah, see Clines, 14-24; Williamson 1987, 55-69). Ezra was, according to Ezra 7:11-26, commissioned by the Persian king Artaxerxes to appoint magistrates and bring the people and the temple functions into compliance with the civil and religious laws of the Torah, although the actual extent of Ezra's authority is uncertain (see Williamson 1987, 69-76). However, to this end he made sure to bring many temple functionaries with him (Ezra 8:1-21), as well as, apparently, some form of the Torah, which he later "published" through public readings (Neh 8—9). According to the book of Ezra, by this time the current Judean community had taken on unacceptable religious practices. The reestablished community had been assimilating the practices of the people around them. They, and even *priests and Levites, had married foreign women to the endangerment of the Yahwistic distinctiveness of the reestablished community (Ezra 9). With the arrival of Ezra's group it is possible that not only a more focused religious structure arose, including a redefining of the roles of priests, Levites and scribes, but also a growing class system.

3.1.3. Late Persian Period (c. 450-c. 330 BCE). A turning point for the status of Jerusalem began with the return of another group of exiles in 445 BCE. Prior to this time Jerusalem probably was, to the Persians, a rather inconsequential town whose value lay in the taxation of its rural produce (Matthews, 112-18). One would expect a rather rural culture, with whatever centralized economy and social structure existed being focused around the growing role of the Jerusalem temple. This group came under the leadership of *Nehemiah, a Jew who had risen to a high-ranking position in the Persian court (that of cupbearer), and who had been appointed as governor of the province. He undertook the task of rebuilding the walls of Jerusalem. This task likewise met with opposition from non-Jewish people living in the area. To Jews it probably meant the strengthening and rededication of Jerusalem as their sacred city. Those outside the religious community probably saw it as a divisive threat to their way of life. With its walls rebuilt, Jerusalem became an inland urban center with an increasingly urban culture under the control of an elite class.

Chronicles, then, most probably belongs to this formative period when Judea was under Persian rule. On the surface, the author of Chronicles is retelling the history of Israel, primarily up through the time when it appeared that Israel had ceased to exist as a nation, with its capital city and temple destroyed. Beneath this surface is a historical setting in which the culture is in flux, power struggles are underway, ideologies are competing, and modified religious and political identities are being formed. The burning issues that the author faced were

(1) the physical reconstitution of *"Israel" within a "promised *land" that was under Persian control and had been settled by a mixed population; (2) the (re)establishment of its identity as the people of Yahweh, whose temple had been rebuilt and put back into operation within the holy city of Jerusalem. The author was faced with questions such as these: Could Yahweh's people start a new life? What would it take for them to succeed and not experience disaster again? It is likely that such a historical context, then, influenced the author's telling of the history of Israel as he chose material, emphasized features and structured the narrative.

3.2. Date and Extent of the Chronicler's Work. The search for a precise date of composition is not only elusive, but also somewhat misguided. The contemporary reader should dispense with the modern notion of a single author having a "copyright" to one's work and recognize that Chronicles, like much of the biblical literature, probably was transmitted in a context of communal editing, so that the traditions would make sense to each current audience. Even if there was one primary composer, until the work became a "frozen" work of canonical Scripture, later scribes bent on preserving the intent of the original work might at least have updated place names, genealogies and technical terms. Still, there are certain factors that can give us some guidance for narrowing down the time of origin.

3.2.1. Relationship of Chronicles to Ezra-Nehemiah. Although prior to the nineteenth century Ezra traditionally had been identified as the author of the book of Ezra and most of Chronicles, the work of L. Zunz (13-36) and F. K. Movers (11-14) led nineteenth-century scholarship to the virtually axiomatic conclusion that 1-2 Chronicles, Ezra and Nehemiah were the work of one major hand, the Chronicler, who composed the Chronicler's History (Japhet 1968, 330-33). The date and authorship of these works were tied together until D. N. Freedman noted that the Chronicler's interest in the house of David was a significant concern only in the first couple of chapters of Ezra. Subsequent work by S. Japhet (1968), T. Willi (176-81) and H. G. M. Williamson (1977, 5-70) accumulated evidence supporting the current consensus that 1-2 Chronicles was basically separate from Ezra-Nehemiah (against this position see Blenkinsopp, 47-54), although these scholars disagreed on the relative dating and authorship of these two bodies of work. (See

2.1 above and 3.2.2 below.)

3.2.2. Date. The scholarly consensus on the relative distinction between Chronicles and Ezra-Nehemiah still does not lead to a consensus on the date, since scholars weight various factors differently. In general, Chronicles usually is dated in the Persian period, 539-333 BCE. The internal reference to the Persian kingdom in 539 BCE (2 Chron 36:20) gives the earliest possible date; whereas the external second-century references to Chronicles set the latest possible date around 200 BCE. These parameters are narrowed further by other considerations. Incidental details, such as a corresponding phrase between 2 Chronicles 16:9 and Zechariah 4:10 (Zechariah was active in 520-518 BCE), and the mention of a Persian coin, a "daric" (1 Chron 29:7; but possibly a later updating), which was not minted before 515 BCE, lead some scholars to the inference that the date was no earlier than 515 BCE. Also, a general consensus that Chronicles shows no evidence of Greek thought allows the latest date to be moved to about 333 BCE (although some find stylistic parallels to Greek historiography [Hoglund 1997; Knoppers]).

Evidence from the genealogies and lists also plays an important role in the discussion but is assessed differently. The genealogy of Jeconiah/Jehoiachin of the Davidic lineage (1 Chron 3:17-24) extends for six generations in the MT and eleven in the LXX, suggesting even later dates of about 350 or 250 BCE respectively. So too Y. Levin (242-43) supports a date in the mid-fourth century BCE based on the genealogies in 1 Chronicles 1—9, and J. Jarick (10) even later. Levin argues, first, that these genealogies display the kind of depth, segmentation and fluidity that one associates with oral genealogies in a living tribal society, and although used in a literary context were contemporary with the author. Second, he argues that these genealogies show no tension between the returnees and the people remaining in the land, a tension seen in Ezra-Nehemiah, and therefore reflect a social setting in the late Persian period. Drawing on lists of cultic personnel, L. C. Allen (*NIB* 3.299-301) also dates Chronicles in the late Persian period and after Ezra-Nehemiah, partly due to finding different stages of development in the roles of cultic singers and gatekeepers. However, dating Chronicles on the latest state of these lists could be misleading. Updating genealogies, particularly

of the lineage of David, would likely be the kind of modification that later scribes would make. Contra Levin, it could be argued that the tribal character of the genealogies and the lack of tension between people groups come from the period prior to Ezra (458 BCE) or from a different authorial perspective. And, contra Allen, one could argue that the discrepancies within various lists give evidence to divergent traditions or redactions but do not necessarily support a linear development that would put the creation of the bulk of Chronicles at the last stage.

On linguistic grounds Japhet (1968), supported by Williamson (1977), separated the authorship of the works and dated Chronicles later than Ezra-Nehemiah. Such fine linguistic dating within the corpus of late biblical *Hebrew is doubtful, and some of Japhet's arguments (e.g., the lack of Persian loanwords and the use of the short form of the imperfect "consecutive") could point to the opposite conclusion. (An analysis of the various linguistic arguments led Throntveit [1982, 215] to conclude that such arguments conclusively support neither unity nor diversity of authorship, but support only that these works belong to the same language of late biblical Hebrew.)

Other dating arguments seek to relate ideological themes to a given historical period. For instance, Allen (*NIB* 3.300) sees a theme in the account of David's appeal for temple contributions followed by a generous response in 1 Chronicles 29, as well as the lavish temple building described in 2 Chronicles 3, a theme that corresponds to the greater prosperity of the Jerusalem community in the second Persian period. Levin (237-41), finding no disharmony in the genealogies among the returnees and the people who remained, suggests that the rift found in Ezra-Nehemiah had already been healed. Other themes, however, fit better earlier in the Persian period rather than later: (1) Chronicles' continuation of a royal ideology and the importance of the king's behavior for the fate of the nation, which fits well close to the era of Zerubbabel, whom the prophets Haggai and Zechariah apparently thought of as a Davidic ruler (Hag 2:20-23; Zech 4:6-7); (2) the Chronicler's doctrine of moral responsibility, which seems to get replaced by Ezra's focus on the law; (3) the Chronicler's more favorable presentation of the northern tribes and Samaritans, over which there is increasing tension in the later periods;

and (4) the Chronicler's close thematic links with Zechariah 1—8 (Throntveit [1987, 97-107], which would place the original work around 527-517 BCE).

3.2.3. Versions and End of Chronicles. Dating Chronicles becomes quite complicated if it has undergone different redactions or lesser editorial emendations, as has been variously proposed. For example, A. C. Welch (5-6, 146-60) found an early originator of about 515 BCE and a later contributor; W. Rudolph (402) found one main work with several additions; F. M. Cross found three major editions. In connection with dating and the relative order of Chronicles to Ezra-Nehemiah, there is some debate about where Chronicles proper ended, in part due to the duplicate material ending Chronicles and beginning Ezra (2 Chron 36:22-23 = Ezra 1:1-3). For instance, D. N. Freedman proposed that the original ending of Chronicles continued on into what is now the beginning of Ezra. Because of the interest in the house of David only in the first part of Ezra, and because of the parallels between the accounts of the building of the first temple in Chronicles and the second temple in Ezra, Freedman suggested that the Chronicler's narrative originally contained the building of the second temple under Zerubbabel. He suggested that the account of the Chronicler was supplanted by an Aramaic record, and that later material was added until the need for a new ending point was created at the current break between Chronicles and what became Ezra-Nehemiah (for a contrary conclusion see Williamson 1977, 5-35). Cross's three-stage theory finds basic agreement with Freedman in the thesis that the original work of the Chronicler required an early Persian period setting. Indeed, the first six chapters of Ezra describe events in the early Persian period (538-515 BCE), and they seem to be based on a combination of documents rather than a continuous source; whereas Ezra 7 picks up over fifty years later (458 BCE) (however, for the thesis that Ezra 1—6 was a late addition to Ezra-Nehemiah see Williamson 1987, 42-46). Some observations still appear to support Freedman's thesis: (1) the continuation of royal ideology into the first section of Ezra; (2) the continuing theme of establishing the cult versus the later theme of rebuilding the walls and political position of Jerusalem; (3) the Chronicler's theme of seeking God, illustrated in Ezra 3; 6:13-22 and mentioned in Ezra 4:2;

6:21, which is not mentioned again in Ezra-Nehemiah; (4) an increasing reliance on textual authority: although cultic matters are carried out according to the Torah, in Chronicles and early Ezra there is an appeal to the stimulus of prophets (only Ezra 5:1; 6:14) that is replaced by motivating the people through an appeal to the written law; (5) a similar dominance of the use of *Yahweh* over *Elohim* in Chronicles (ratio 1.42:1), which becomes reversed as one moves further into Ezra-Nehemiah (ratio 1.22:1 for Ezra 1—6, but .31:1 for Ezra 7—Neh 13); (6) a positive presentation of the Levites that later becomes rather negative in the second half of Ezra (note also their celebratory phrase "his love endures forever," found in Chronicles and at Ezra 3:11 but not later); (7) not only a celebration of the Passover, but also, like Hezekiah's and Josiah's celebrations in Chronicles, one that included all who sought God (2 Chron 30:1; 35:1-3; Ezra 6:19-21).

3.3. Author and Audience.

3.3.1. Author. Depending on one's view of the relationship of Chronicles to Ezra-Nehemiah, Chronicles has been associated variously with the early postexilic prophets Haggai, Malachi and Zechariah, with the later Ezra, and with the unnamed "Chronicler." First, today's reader should realize that the origin of Chronicles probably does not fit the modern model of composition of one author sitting down and writing creatively from the first word to the last. A more likely model is that a person or group of people in authority (Jarick [2] calls such a putative group the "Annalists"), probably having scribal training, gathered a variety of archival records that had been produced and collected over time (see 2.2 above). This person, or persons, then creatively arranged, shaped and supplemented it with material by dictating to a scribe, who did the actual writing, in order to form an initial work. This work too might have been supplemented as it was copied and transmitted, until it became canonical.

Second, even if there was one major author-editor or a group in authority (still called the "Chronicler" for convenience), as is the case with many of the biblical works, the text provides no direct identification of that author. As a result, scholars make attributions of authorship by inference. One would first suppose that such a work could be composed only by one of an "academic" scribal class who also had access to royal court and temple records. Again, because of the thematic emphases in the book on the tribe of Judah and on the Davidic kings, as well as on the priestly tribe of Levi and the need to establish and maintain the temple cultus, evidence points to a court or temple authority, with the weight falling more toward one of the temple personnel with scribal training. Since such a person or persons of this upper class would have been among those deported into Babylonian exile, it is likely that the author of Chronicles had been exiled or came from one of the families that were exiled and returned. Still, for the community of faith, the text's authority was not based on identifying the specific human author.

3.3.2. Audience. Knowledge of the original intended audience and the means of "publication" of Chronicles would give contemporary readers a better understanding of the intended communicative purpose of this work. Again, the text of Chronicles is silent on this point, and one has to proceed by inference. We cannot assume that Chronicles was written to be read by the "average Judean," because the average Judean would have been unable to afford a copy of the scrolls of the text and probably unable to read much of it. The evidence of an increasing number of incidental textual artifacts that come from the eighth century BCE down to the time of the Babylonian destruction of the temple raises the possibility that minimal literacy, at least the ability to read one's name and minor texts, might have been relatively widespread and not limited to a particular social class (Hess, 92-94). Still, most writing of significance would have come from the vocational class of scribes who generally were employed at court or temple. An important cultural trend to note in the background of Chronicles, and exemplified in the function of the written law in Ezra-Nehemiah, is that this was a period of increasing "textuality," when greater authority was being ascribed to written texts as opposed to oral proclamations (*see* Writing, Writing Materials and Literacy in the Ancient Near East).

Who, then, was the intended audience? Since it is probable that an authoritative person with academic scribal training composed Chronicles, one might argue that only persons with similar scribal training could have fully understood it and appreciated its full literary skill. It is possible, then, that Chronicles was intended to be a private "library" work for scholars. However, if the intended audience was other temple scribal personnel, then the author would have been "preaching" his message to those who presumably already shared the same ideology. Moreover, it is unnecessary to expect that the intended audience appreciate the full literary artistry of a work, but rather only be able to gain the general communicative intent. A second possibility is that the audience was a hoped-for Davidic ruler who might resume the throne after Persian dominance, and who would need to know the history of the people. In one biblical tradition kings were expected to write a copy of statutes for themselves to read periodically (Deut 17:18-19). Perhaps, then, Chronicles was to be stored for royal instruction. A third possibility is that the work was composed with "average Judeans" in mind as the perceived audience, whether or not they would have learned of the work. Indeed, it is possible that the work was "published" for the people of Judea by reading it section by section in public gatherings.

There is both suggestive internal and external evidence for such a means of "publication." Internal to the composition of Chronicles is the number of speeches that are found. Although lists and genealogies make up over half of the material that is unique to Chronicles, of the remaining material over three-fourths is speech material (Duke 1990, 119). Although the uniformity of the style and content of these speeches had long been observed, it was G. von Rad (1966) who suggested that some of them reflected Levitical sermons. R. Mason (2), though disagreeing with von Rad's form-critical assessment and attribution of the speeches, concluded that such speeches reflect the preaching that must have taken place in the temple. It is also important to note that direct speech in narrative not only depicts what was said to the narrative audience, but also has the rhetorical impact of directly addressing the immediate audience, so that instructions "preached" to the narrative audience become instructions preached to the Chronicler's audience (on use of speeches see Duke 1990, 119-35). Moreover, Allen (1988), examining various rhetorical structuring devices in Chronicles, came to the conclusion that the whole of Chronicles had been composed on homiletic lines as a series of self-contained messages. There is also external evidence for such a text being "preached." A Persian-period account of the people of Judea being gathered together for a public hearing of "the law" is found in Nehemiah 8. According to this tradition, Ezra not only read from the law from daybreak to noon on the first day, but also read some for seven days (Neh 8:2-3, 18; and on other occasions [Neh 9:3; 13:1]). Moreover, there are other biblical antecedents of public readings to gatherings of Israelites (Ex 24:7, reading the book of the covenant; Deut 31:11; Josh 8:32-35; 2 Kings 23:1-3; Jer 36:8-10; and perhaps Jer 51:59-64 was to be a public reading). Although some of these texts may be anachronistic for their settings, such texts would at least witness to a late tradition of public readings that would fit with a practice of the Persian period. In conclusion, it appears that one should read Chronicles with the conjecture that all audiences are in mind: academic temple personnel, future possible royal audience and general populace.

3.4. Reading Chronicles as Midrash, History and Scripture. Chronicles is, in a sense, midrash, history and Scripture. *Midrash* is a slippery term used by scholars in different senses, but in a loose sense it is an appropriate term for the form and purposes of Chronicles. In general usage "midrash" refers to the interpretation of authoritative tradition, which, among other forms, can be in the form of narrative. Chronicles does that in part. It works with known traditions, although perhaps not yet fully viewed as canonical in authority, and reconstructs them within new story lines to interpret them for contemporary application. Chronicles represents part of a long process through which the Israelite and Jewish communities of faith told and retold their stories of the past, rephrasing them for new audiences, applying them to new situations, and drawing out new insights—all, as the community of faith believes, within the process of divine inspiration, with the result that the Scriptures communicate God's intentions.

However, to identify Chronicles as history as well as midrash might appear to some readers to create a conflict. Scholars who assumed the historical positivism of modernity once made a firm distinction between history and interpretative story. For them, history was the one, true, scientifically uncovered account of the past, while interpretive story was "midrash" (Welch, 54). From this perspective, to call Chronicles "midrash" would impugn its historicity. However, a proper understanding of what people do when they create historical narratives reveals that there is no such thing as objective history, and no sharp dichotomy between history and interpretive story. Throughout the twentieth century philosophers of history have recognized that all history telling is a subjective and philosophically laden enterprise: historians (all people) perceive segments of our time/space continuum as "events" with a beginning and ending; they selectively choose certain such events from the historical field of the known past; they plot them within the structures of narrative as if they have a teleology and natural story line; they implicitly or explicitly convey how one event relates to another according to their own values and understanding of the "laws" of reality. The consequential observation is that all historical narrative is interpretive story, even when based on "factual" data. Historical stories do not simply present subjectively interpreted data and observations, but also, and more importantly, they capture and reveal a worldview, a presentation of the nature of reality. Given this understanding of history telling, the distinction between "midrash" and "history" blurs (Duke 1993; Provan, Long and Longman, 75-97).

Finally, the work of Chronicles is Scripture. That is to say that the messages of Chronicles have not been viewed by the community of faith as applicable only to one generation; rather, its stories were recognized as imbued with divine authority and as having an abiding value for later Jewish and Christian believers. Scriptural historical narratives reveal the nature of reality with divinely guided insight, with the result that the biblical worldview teaches its audience how life really works. The reader of Chronicles, therefore, is invited not only to read the work as a retelling of Israel's history that presented and interpreted stories of the past for application to the Chronicler's generation, but also to ask what the work means today.

3.5. Reading Chronicles Synchronically and Diachronically. General readers of Chronicles as Scripture tend to read it synchronically ("with time") as a single unit without regard for historical antecedents. However, biblical scholars are prone to read Chronicles diachronically ("through time") in a couple of senses. One sense is based on an analysis of how Chronicles reached its final stage of composition through time, and seeks to understand the messages that it might have had at different stages of composition. However, recreating the history of composition without the presence of datable editions of composition is quite speculative. Also, the community of faith, not knowing what other editions might have existed previously, will be more interested in understanding the canonical version that we now possess.

A second kind of diachronic reading is based on examining Chronicles in close association with the books of Samuel-Kings to see how these two histories interpret the same historical field of the past differently. This is a more difficult issue to address. Some scholars in the past have tried to compare the Hebrew texts of Samuel-Kings to Chronicles to note every difference in detail in parallel sections and to draw conclusions about how the Chronicler "changed" the text. Of first concern is the fact that we do not know in what form the Chronicler knew the material of Samuel-Kings. It is not unlikely that someone privy to court and temple archives had such material in written form. However, our current knowledge of the manuscript evidence suggests that the Chronicler did not have the same text of Samuel that has come down to us in the canon of the Hebrew Bible (Lemke). As a result, differences on the level of words and phrases probably should not be used as indications of intentional changes on the part of the Chronicler. Second, and more important, is the consideration of what kind of comparative reading the Chronicler envisioned for the audience. Since there are instances in Chronicles where the author appears to assume an audience that already knows some of the traditions of Samuel-Kings, we can infer that at least some general comparisons to Samuel-Kings were expected (e.g., 1 Chron 11:3 refers to how David became king according to the word of Samuel, which is found in 1 Sam 16; and 2 Chron 10:15 refers to the fulfillment of the prophecy of Ahijah, which is recorded at 1 Kings 11:29-39). However, if the Chronicler's audience was to extend beyond a limited number of academic scribes who had access to traditions of Samuel-Kings in written form, then we would have to assume that a detailed comparative reading was not intended. Based on the assumption that the intended audience was broader than academic scribes, it seems best to read Chronicles synchronically for its unique message, with an understanding of the traditions of Samuel-Kings in mind, but without making detailed comparisons.

4. The Message of the Chronicler.

4.1. A New Beginning, a New Story. The Chronicler stood at some point in time after the Babylonian exile. From his perspective, God, in continuing faithfulness, had restored the people to the Promised Land in 538 BCE. The sights and sounds of sacrificial worship did, or would, once again fill the temple at Jerusalem. The Chronicler looked back over the historical panorama of his people and arrived at new insights into God's ways of interacting with Israel—a coherent and comprehensive system. He saw new lessons for the continuing community of faith in the patterns of the past. He also saw ways in which to encourage them to form a communal identity with a common perspective and goal. In the Chronicler's presentation he provides an explanation of the exile as well as other disasters, an explanation of the return from exile and other blessings, a defense of his religious and political institutions, and an implicit call for his community to identify with their past and to respond in faithfulness to Yahweh. Along with J. E. Dyck, one might also agree that the ideological aspects of the Chronicler's presentation not only helped to create an identity for his people by connecting them to their past, and not only legitimated the social structures connected to the religious system, but also might have sought to bridge a gap between the demands of the temple system and those who felt alienated from it. (Much of what follows here has been adapted from Duke 1996.)

As a result of the Chronicler's new perspective and agenda for his community, his re-presentation of the past differs from that of the Deuteronomistic History in some key respects. First, the Chronicler illustrates more fully how Israel's times of prosperity and success were the results of Yahweh's blessing. As Japhet (1997, 150-65) notes, his goal was not just to explain the negative consequence of the exile, but to present a more comprehensive system that accounted for both good and evil events.

Second, although the Chronicler too sees Israel's disasters as the results of God's judgment for Israel's unfaithfulness, he describes that unfaithfulness differently. The former history explained Israel's unfaithfulness as acts of idolatry and the failure to keep God's statutes (cf. 2 Kings 17:7-18). The Chronicler's explanation probes more deeply and clarifies Israel's unfaithfulness. For the Chronicler, Israel's unfaithfulness is identified as "forsaking Yah-weh," or not properly "seeking Yahweh." In his usage, "seeking Yahweh" implies a total response of the Israelite king and people to God. In order to "seek Yahweh," one turns to, prays to, inquires of, trusts, praises and worships Yahweh and no other god. Most importantly, one does so through the proper religious means and in the proper place: in the presence of the ark of Yahweh or the temple. On the other hand, "forsaking Yahweh" entails the opposite. It was more than idolatry. It was an unfaithfulness demonstrated by failing to turn to Yahweh, by neglecting God's temple, and by ignoring God's ordained religious and political institutions: the Levitical priesthood and the Davidic king. For some current readers, the Chronicler's emphasis on proper religious structures might seem foreign and even "legalistic." However, for him the immediacy of Israel's relationship to Yahweh, and therefore Israel's fate, was directly linked to Israel's exclusive and wholehearted worship service of Yahweh (see Japhet [1997, 199-265], who states, "Temple worship represents the practical side of Israel's relationship with its God; by establishing and maintaining Temple ritual, the continuity and constancy of the bond between YHWH and the people was expressed" [Japhet, 222]). Indeed, one could say that the whole ritual system symbolized the maintenance of the creational distinction between that which was holy and that which was unholy for the purpose of sustaining an unpolluted relationship with God.

Third, unlike in the Deuteronomistic History, in which sin was cumulative and the results could be poured out on succeeding generations (Japhet 1997, 160), the Chronicler illustrates a characteristic of Yahweh's relationship with Israel in which Israel's fate never was sealed. Reversals in Israel's state of blessing or ruin could and did take place from generation to generation. If the king and people were suffering the consequences of forsaking God, and they humbled themselves and sought God, then they could be restored. But if they were experiencing the blessings of God and they forsook God, then they would face disaster.

4.2. The Structure of the Chronicler's Account.
The Chronicler narrates his story with his agenda and vision of how life works, using a communicative strategy that appears to be well thought out in order to be effectively persuasive. In brief, he is careful not to depend on his own authority as author/narrator and overtly explain why things happened until he has first established his case through implication by examples. Also, rather than appealing to his personal authority—presumably the first audience knew what person(s) had crafted this history—he relies on other sources of authority: known traditions, genealogical records, the citing of sources, and speeches from the mouths of authoritative characters (for a summary of the Chronicler's communicative/rhetorical strategies see Duke 1999). To serve his communicative purposes, the Chronicler arranged his work in three discrete sections, which have different structures and narrative styles. The first section of the book (1 Chron 1—9) gives a "collapsed history" of Israel, presented in the form of genealogies and lists. Still, in this material the Chronicler subtly identifies his main subject concerns and reveals his theological worldview, a view in which Yahweh is active in history. The second section covers the reigns of Saul, David and Solomon (1 Chron 10—2 Chron 9). Here the Chronicler advances his main thesis about how the nation prospers under God. He creates this argument not by coming to the fore of the story through obtrusive narrator comments, but inductively, by giving numerous examples that depict David and Solomon as the model kings. The third section tells the stories of the remaining Davidic kings (2 Chron 10—36). Now the Chronicler as narrator comes to the fore in obtrusive comments that readily explain why events happened the way they did, often comparing them explicitly or implicitly to the model of David and Solomon.

4.2.1. 1 Chronicles 1—9. The Chronicler's work opens with genealogical materials and lists (1 Chron 1—9) that lead the audience into the subject matter and worldview of the main narrative. Beginning with creation (Adam), the focus quickly narrows down temporally, geographically and nationally to the tribes of Israel (1 Chron 2—8). Emphasis is placed on (1) the tribe of Levi and the Levitical priesthood; (2) the tribe of Judah and the Davidic monarchy; (3) the tribe of Benjamin, a key part of "all Israel," and from which came the first Israelite king, with whom the narrative proper begins in 1 Chronicles 10. In 1 Chronicles 9:2-21 genealogical lists record the first exiles to resettle the land, an event alluded to at the close of Chronicles (2 Chron 36:2-23). Brief narrative comments are interspersed among these lists. These comments reveal to the audience a recognized Israelite principle that Yahweh rewards those who trust him (1 Chron 4:10; 5:20-22) and punishes those who are unfaithful (1 Chron 2:3; 5:25-26; 9:1).

Such genealogical material not only collapses the historical recital to the essential points, but also reveals the postexilic concern to reestablish a "pure" and identifiable community of people who can legitimate their status through their ancestry. Levin has argued that the genealogies of the central tribes were so complex, segmented, deep and fluid that the Chronicler was drawing not just on ancient records, but on "living" traditions. Levin (244-45) also notes that the Chronicler did not make a genetic difference between those of the southern kingdom and those of the northern kingdom who had remained in the land, and draws the conclusion that the Chronicler's audience included "people of the land," who were part of an alive and functioning tribal village society of the hill country of Judah and Benjamin, as well as Ephraim and Manasseh. Moreover, the Chronicler continues to appeal to such an inclusive audience of "all Israel" in his accounts of Hezekiah's Passover celebration (2 Chron 30:1-12) and Josiah's reforms (2 Chron 34:1-11).

4.2.2. 1 Chronicles 10—2 Chronicles 9. The Chronicler's narrative proper begins at 1 Chronicles 10. In the body of Chronicles (1 Chron 10—2 Chron 9) the Chronicler, as narrator, establishes his main historical argument "inductively," while presenting examples from the reigns of the first three kings: Saul, David and Solomon. The Chronicler works from an accepted Israelite maxim found in the Deuteronomistic History as well as in the Israelite prophetic tradition: proper responses to Yahweh lead to blessing, and improper responses to Yahweh lead to curse. The Chronicler works with that maxim and refines the proper response ("seeking" Yahweh) primarily in terms of the temple system. When a king seeks Yahweh through establishing the proper temple rituals, as well as sincerely and prayerfully, then king and nation are blessed through victory, peace, building projects, unity and so on. However, when a king forsakes properly seeking Yahweh, he comes to calamity (for a chart of these events see Duke

1990, 78-79). As the narrative proper begins, King Saul is briefly sketched in a negative portrayal, which stands in contrast to the following positive portrayals of David and Solomon. Saul died, and his kingdom was turned over to David because Saul sought (on "seek," *drš*, see Throntveit 1987, 116-20) advice through a medium, the witch of Endor (1 Sam 28), and not through Yahweh (1 Chron 10:13-14). The history then devotes much material to David. However, in stark contrast to the portrait depicted in Samuel, the audience learns little about David the man, his shortcomings, his thoughts, his feelings. Rather, one hears almost exclusively about David's positive interactions with Yahweh. Through the juxtaposition of contrasting scenes, the narrator presents a reciprocal relationship between David (with all Israel) and Yahweh. This relationship demonstrates the principle of seeking Yahweh: David establishes the proper worship of Yahweh in regard to the ark, the appointment of religious officials, preparations for the building of the temple (1 Chron 13; 15—16; 21—29), and so on, and Yahweh establishes the kingdom of David, granting popular support, military victory and a lasting dynasty (1 Chron 11—12; 14; 17—20). In David's closing speeches the Chronicler clearly spells out the principle of seeking: "If you seek him [the LORD], he will let you find him; but if you forsake him, he will reject you forever" (1 Chron 28:9; see 1 Chron 22:6-16, 17-19; 28:1-8, 9-10). Next, the Chronicler shows Solomon as one who completes the program initiated by David. Solomon established the proper worship of Yahweh, carrying out the construction of the temple. Yahweh established him, granting him wisdom, peace and prosperity (2 Chron 1—9).

In this section, again in stark contrast to Samuel-Kings, the audience hears about a fully articulated cultic system. Levites clearly are subordinate to priests, and they are divided into various roles as musicians and gatekeepers. The temple cultus is of primary concern, even though David himself is not allowed by Yahweh to build the actual structure. In fact, the one incident in which the Chronicler portrays David in a negative light—David's sin of taking a census (1 Chron 21:1—22:1)—must be included in the narrative, for it was the resolution of this event that determined the location of the temple and initiated David's preparation of the building material (1 Chron 22:2-4).

Table 1. Implicit Comparisons: "Signs" of Blessing and Cursing

Reigns	Military Success (1)	Building Projects	Large Army/ Fortifications	Popular Support (2)	Peace/Rest
Genealogies I 1-9	5:20-22				
Saul I 10					
David & Solomon I 11—II 9	I 14:8-16 I 18:1—20:8	I 14:1; I 15:1; II 2:1; II 8:1-6	I 11—12; I 18:6, 13; II 1:14	I 11—12; I 29:23-24	I 22:18; I 23:25
Rehoboam I 10-12	12:7-8[5]	11:5-12	11:1, 11-12	11:13-17	
Abijah II 13	13:13-18			13:10, 12	
Asa II 14-16	14:9-15	14:6-7	14:8	14:4-11; 15:9-15	14:4-7; 15:15, 19
Jehoshaphat II 17-20	18:31; 20:2-30	17:12	17:2, 12-19	17:5; 19:4; 20:3-4	17:10; 20:3
Jehoram II 21					
Ahaziah II 22:1-9					
Athaliah II 22:9-23:21					
Joash II 24		24:13			
Amaziah II 25	25:11-13		25:2-6		
Uzziah II 26	26:4-8	26:2, 6, 9-10	26:11-15	26:1	
Jotham II 27	27:5-7	27:2-4			
Ahaz II 28					
Hezekiah II 29-32	32:20-22	32:5, 29-30	32:5	29:36; 30:1-27	32:22[7]
Mannaseh II 33:1-20		33:14	33:14		
Amon II 33:1-20					
Josiah II 34-35				34:29-33	
Jehoahaz II 36:1-4					
Jehoiakim II 36:5-9					
Jehoiachin II 36:9-10					
Zedekiah II 36:11-20					

Prosperity/ Might (3)	Point of Reversal Forsook	Humbled	Military Failure	Lost Support	Illness/ Death (4)
			5:25-26; 9:1		2:3
			10:1-6		10:6, 13-14
I 14:2; 29:2-5, 23, 28, 30; II 1:1, 15; II 9:13-14, 22	I 21:1	I 21:16-17			I 21:14
12:1, 13	12:1	12:6	12:2-4; 12:9[5]		
13:21					
14:7	16:7		16:7-9	16:10	16:12
17:5, 12; 18:1					
	21:6		21:8-11; 21:16-17	21:19-20	21:12-15, 18-19
					22:4, 7-9
				23:1-7	23:14-15
	27:17-24		24:23-24	24:25-26	24:25
	25:14-15		25:17-24	25:27-28	25:27
26:8, 13, 15	26:16				26:16-23
27:6					
			28:1-9, 16-21		
31:21; 32:23, 27-29	32:25	32:26			
		33:12	33:10-11		
					33:24
	35:20-22	34:27-28	35:20-24		35:23-24
			36:5-7		
			36:9-10		
			36:12-20		

4.2.3. 2 Chronicles 10—36. The third section (2 Chronicles 10—36) presents the subsequent Davidic kings in quick succession, but in a different style of narration. Having demonstrated his argument "inductively" through narrative examples in the previous section while staying in the background of the narrative, the Chronicler now comes to the foreground and presents his argument "deductively" as he tells stories of the Davidic kings with more blatant interpretive comments. In so doing, he illustrates the pattern of "seeking Yahweh" further as he uses it to characterize their reigns. *Jehoshaphat, Ahaz, *Hezekiah and *Josiah are explicitly compared to David and/or Solomon (2 Chron 17:3; 28:1; 29:2; 34:2, 3). Other comparisons are implicit. If the king (usually with the people) engages in some form of seeking Yahweh, then Yahweh blesses him with military success, wealth, the ability to execute building projects, and so forth. If the king forsakes Yahweh, then he and the people meet with a reversal of fate. This pattern continues down to the time of Zedekiah, when king, priests and people forsake God, defiling the temple and rejecting all prophetic warnings. As a result, the Babylonians, used by Yahweh, destroy the temple and carry the people off into exile (2 Chron 36:11-21). Chronicles then closes with an allusion to the return from exile allowed under the rule of Cyrus (2 Chron 36:22-23).

In terms of subject matter and focus, the Chronicler's account differs from that of the Deuteronomistic History. During the period of the divided monarchy the Chronicler, unlike the historian behind Samuel-Kings, does not alternate between recording the accounts of the kings of the northern kingdom of Israel and the kings of the southern kingdom of Judah. For the Chronicler, the people who followed the Davidic king and worshiped Yahweh at the temple in Jerusalem were the real "Israel," wherever they resided. Thus his focus remains on "all Israel." He mentions the north only when its story overlaps with that of the south. From his perspective, the people of the north were still potentially among the people of God. However, he presents them as having forsaken Yahweh by rejecting the institutions of the Davidic monarchy, the Levitical priesthood and the Jerusalem temple (2 Chron 10:19; 11:13-15; and particularly Abijah's homiletical speech in 2 Chron 13:4-12). The south was not to attack the north, for they still were God's people (2 Chron 11:1-4). Nor was it to ally with the north (e.g., 2 Chron 18), for the northern kingdom was not legitimate (2 Chron 19:2). However, when the northern kingdom fell to the Assyrians (722 BCE), the south could welcome its people to return and worship Yahweh (2 Chron 30:1, 6-9). Again, in this section, the Chronicler has reinforced the argument that the fate of the people of God depends on properly seeking Yahweh through the Jerusalem temple system.

This third section of Chronicles also differs structurally from what has preceded. Indeed, this section does not appear to have one main plot line running through it, but rather is composed of several stories. The communicative impact is important. In the Deuteronomistic History the various stories tend to make up a larger story line that tells about how and why the Babylonian exile came about. Particularly from the time of King *Manasseh onward, the fate of the nation seemed to be sealed (2 Kings 23:26). No matter how good a king Josiah was, the nation could not recover. In contrast, the Chronicler portrays the generation of each Davidic king as a separate vignette (von Rad 1962, 347-54). Each king and his people have their own story, whether it be to rise by seeking Yahweh or to fall by forsaking Yahweh. As a result, the message that is communicated is that each generation stood in immediacy to Yahweh. Ja-phet (1997, 160-64) points out that there was no accumulation of sin, as in the Deuteronomistic History; rather, similar to the principle of divine justice for individuals found in Ezekiel (Ezek 18; 33:10-20), in Chronicles each generation was accountable for its own righteousness and sin. Each generation determined its own fate. Such a message would also address the Chronicler's audience (Duke 1990, 66-74). The exile was not the end of the story. Repentance and seeking Yahweh could result in a reversal of one's situation. Seeking Yahweh properly meant the proper maintenance of the temple system. They, his immediate audience, had to determine whether they would be ones who would seek Yahweh or forsake Yahweh.

4.3. The Chronicler's Foci.

4.3.1. The Davidic Monarchy. The main characters around whom the Chronicler tells the story of Israel are the Davidic monarchs. For the sake of the people of Israel, Yahweh established the rule of David (1 Chron 14:2), a king who sought God and who, along with Solomon, established the proper institutions of worship. God promised David that a dynastic successor would sit on the throne of Yahweh's kingdom forever (1 Chron 17:11-14), although it was required that the successor faithfully seek Yahweh (1 Chron 28:6-9). The Davidic monarchs held the primary responsibility for establishing and maintaining the proper worship of Yahweh. They could abandon the forms of Yahweh worship (e.g., Ahaz and Manasseh) or they could restore them (e.g., Hezekiah and Josiah). They sat on Yahweh's throne (1 Chron 17:14; 28:5; 29:23; 2.9:8). They represented the people in corporate petition before Yahweh (2 Chron 6:18-42; 14:11; 20:5-12). Their positive or negative spiritual leadership influenced the response of the people of Israel (2 Chron 14:4; 15:9-15; 19:4; 20:4, 20-21; 21:11; 28:19; 32:6-8; 33:9, 16; 34:33). When the people of the northern kingdom rejected the Davidic monarchy, they forsook Yahweh (2 Chron 13:4-12). The Chronicler, by holding this perspective of the Davidic monarchy at a time when Israel was under foreign dominion, projected a hope in the return of a Davidic king to the throne of Yahweh.

4.3.2. The Temple Cultus and the Levitical Priesthood. Even though the Chronicler's account is structured around the Davidic monarchs, the main story line is about Israel's relationship to Yahweh. The Chronicler's history focuses on how this relationship rose and fell in connection with the establishment and maintenance of the institutions that represented the presence of Yahweh: the *ark of the covenant, Jerusalem, the temple, the sacrificial system, the officiating priests, their levitical assistants and musicians, and the Davidic king, who sat on Yahweh's throne. These institutions were the means by which Israel demonstrated their exclusive and wholehearted relationship with God. It must be remembered that for the Chronicler, the destruction of the temple and the exile constituted a near-death experience for his people. Never again did he want Israel to stand on such a brink of extermination. The Chronicler saw Israel's failure to seek Yahweh humbly and in accord with the proper means of worship as the cause of the exile. Accordingly, his attention was focused on its religious institutions as he re-presented Israel's past: as these institutions fared, so fared the well-being of the nation.

For the Chronicler, the Levitical priesthood operated jointly with the Davidic monarchy in preserving the correct forms of seeking Yahweh, of maintaining the proper relationship with God.

The king's civil power extended over these officials, but they ruled a domain of divinely given responsibility that the king could not usurp (2 Chron 26:16-21). Moreover, when the Davidic lineage instituted by Yahweh was threatened, they stepped in to preserve it (2 Chron 22:10—23:21). According to the Chronicler, the northern kingdom forsook Yahweh by rejecting the institution of the Levitical priesthood as they rejected the Davidic monarchy (2 Chron 11:13-15; 13:8-12). Such an emphasis on the Davidic lineage and role of the priesthood fits the dyarchic form of government under which the people of Judea were ruled when they returned to their land under Persian rule.

4.3.3. "All Israel." Another major character for the Chronicler is "all Israel." He uses the expression in various ways to refer to all of the Israelites (1 Chron 11:1), to those just of the south (2 Chron 11:3) or to those of the north (2 Chron 13:4, 15). One point to note is that to whichever group the phrase refers in any one context, that group stands as an entity responsible before Yahweh. The kings and religious leaders alone are not accountable for the destiny of the nation; the people of all Israel as a whole are held accountable (2 Chron 11:3-4, 16-17; 13:14; 15:9-15; 20:18; 23:16; 24:17-21, 24; 28:6; 36:14-16). Official prophets address the kings, while other messengers speak prophetically to the people as well (2 Chron 11:3-4; 15:1-2; 20:14-15; 24:20; 36:23) (for the distinction between prophets and messengers see 4.3.4 below); and sometimes the people are deemed guilty when the king is innocent (2 Chron 27:2; 34:24-28). The people act responsibly when in unity they support the chosen king (1 Chron 11:1-2) and the proper worship of Yahweh (1 Chron 13:5). When the division between the north and south occurs, those who comprise all Israel must decide whether or not to seek Yahweh (2 Chron 11:13-17). Thus each generation of the people, although tending to follow the model of their leaders, shared in the responsibility for their state of affairs. So too the message of accountability would apply to the people of the Chronicler's generation, presumably some of whom were an intended audience of the narrative.

A second point to note about the "all Israel" motif is that from the genealogies onward, the Chronicler is willing to receive any of the descendants of the Israelite tribes into the "fellowship" of the community of faith if they were committed to Yahweh and the Jerusalem cult.

One does not sense a background situation of antagonism between the people of Judah who returned from exile and the people who remained in the land, as is found in the period of Ezra-Nehemiah. Rather, one finds the kind of acceptance that was found in Ezra 6:21, when the first Passover after the rebuilding of the temple was celebrated, and both returnees and the faithful in the land came together.

4.3.4. Prophets and Messengers. *Prophets and prophecy play a major role in Chronicles, and one that is transitional for the postexilic community. In citations that refer the audience to additional source material, the Chronicler often refers to writings of prophets (e.g., 2 Chron 20:24; 32:32). When examined closely and in parallel to the references to source material in Kings, it appears likely that the Chronicler understood a greater work of annals of the kings of Israel and Judah to be composed of annals kept by various prophets (Rainey). Whether or not such records existed independently or at all, as is debated by scholars, it is apparent that the Chronicler understood a major role of prophets to be that of interpreting the hand of God in history. Indeed, in Chronicles prophets tend to interpret past or future events to kings in such a way that at least implicitly warns them and calls them to repentance (cf. 2 Chron 20:20; 24:19). Such warnings, as pointed out by Japhet (1997, 176-91), display the retributive process of seeking/forsaking as less mechanical than it might first appear (although Japhet possibly overstresses the necessity of warning through her reliance on rabbinic tradition). Although the kings and people are responsible for their own fate in the retributive process, the element of God's mercy is present to break that chain when the king and people respond to warnings in humility and repentance (see 2 Chron 12).

Having examined the terminology and roles of prophetic figures closely, W. M. Schniedewind has made significant further observations. He has noted that there are two types of prophetic figures in Chronicles: those who receive the traditional designations of the "classical" prophet (such as "prophet," *nābiʾ*, and "seer," *ḥōzeh*), and those upon whom the spirit comes ad hoc and speak a prophetic word. The first figures, the traditional prophets, are interpreters of history and primarily address kings. Indeed, their function as prophets corresponds to the existence of the monarchy, which had ceased in the Chronicler's postexilic time. The second group appears as inspired messengers, validated by the Spirit of God coming on them. They speak primarily to the people, and they interpret not history, but previous prophetic tradition, and apply it to new situations. Moreover, the Chronicler takes traditional phrases that applied solely to oral prophecy (e.g., "the word of the LORD") and applies them to the written tradition of Mosaic law (see 2 Chron 34:21, where "obey the word of the LORD" replaces "listen to the words of this book" in 2 Kings 22:13). What can be observed here is a beginning of two transitions. The first transition is from authority being based on inspired speech to authority being based on written tradition—a growing "textuality." The second transition is from the role of prophet as interpreter of history to the prophetic messenger who interprets sacred tradition. It becomes quite likely, then, that the Chronicler saw himself as an inspired messenger, reinterpreting the prophetic interpretations of history (the prophetic annals of kings) to communicate their significance to his generation (Schniedewind).

4.4. Conclusion.

4.4.1. The Chronicler's Worldview. The Chronicler, like all historians, approached his task with an understanding of how the world operates, or better, how God operates in relationship with the world, and with Israel in particular. Thus his historical narrative presents to his audience a worldview, a picture of reality, an ideology. Even through the few narrative comments in the genealogical material of the first nine chapters he depicted a world in which Yahweh is the primary agent of history. The existence of Yahweh and his supreme sovereignty were foregone conclusions. The Chronicler did not seek to prove them; rather, he sought to show how Yahweh interacted in the life of Israel and why.

In the Chronicler's world God is sovereign, but God does not dictate the course that people take. To be sure, Yahweh may choose to speak prophetically through a foreign king (2 Chron 35:21; 36:22-23), or he might even choose to manipulate nations such as Egypt or Babylon to achieve his ends. Still, the Chronicler demonstrated quite clearly that all Israel, the kings and the people were responsible for their actions. They were responsible for maintaining a proper relationship with God. They chose whether they would seek or forsake Yahweh, whether they would listen to words of warning and repent or not. It is they who set into motion the divine principles that order the world.

The Chronicler's attitude about the way the world operates is more positive than that of the historian behind Samuel-Kings. One might draw from Samuel-Kings a pessimistic and rather fatalistic attitude. At least from Manasseh onward, the fate of Israel appears to be sealed (2 Kings 21:10-15). However, the manner in which the Chronicler portrayed each king and his own generation as self-contained units displays a different perspective. The course of history was not so tightly determined. In the Chronicler's representation of reality, reversals of negative or positive situations could take place within a given reign or generation, even more than once. The potential for change always existed. Access to the mercy of Yahweh and to restoration was always present for Israel, even after the people of Israel had brought themselves to near extinction.

4.4.2. The Chronicler's Message. The Chronicler's presentation of the past implores a response in the present. Through his selection and arrangement of Israel's traditions, his stereotypical portrayal of characters, his presentation of David and Solomon as model kings, and more he invites his audience to evaluate each of his portraits of the generations of their past and to understand why things happened as they did. However, the audience is not to stop there. Their identity is connected to the "all Israel" of the past. They are called to exclusive and heartfelt worship of Yahweh. Thus they are implicitly invited to evaluate their current situation and to respond appropriately. Relationship to Yahweh is still of ultimate importance. The divine system operative in the world of the past was still operative. The Chronicler's audience now knows what brings blessing and what brings ruin. They know that one's situation may be reversed, depending on whether or not one seeks or forsakes Yahweh. Through his re-presentation of their past, the Chronicler calls his community to a proper relationship with Yahweh and offers them the hope of blessing.

See also CHRONICLER'S HISTORY; DAVIDIC COVENANT; DEUTERONOMISTIC HISTORY; EZRA AND NEHEMIAH, BOOKS OF; HISTORIOGRAPHY, OLD TESTAMENT; ISRAEL; KINGS AND KINGSHIP; NARRATIVE ART OF ISRAEL'S HISTORIANS; POST-EXILIC TEMPLE; SOLOMON'S TEMPLE.

BIBLIOGRAPHY. *Commentaries*: L. C. Allen, "The First and Second Books of Chronicles," *NIB* 3.299-659; **R. L. Braun,** *1 Chronicles* (WBC; Waco, TX: Word, 1986); **E. L. Curtis and A. A. Madsen,** *A Critical and Exegetical Commentary on the Books of Chronicles* (ICC; Edinburgh: T & T Clark, 1910); **S. J. De Vries,** *1 and 2 Chronicles* (FOTL; Grand Rapids: Eerdmans, 1989); **R. B. Dillard,** *2 Chronicles* (WBC; Waco, TX: Word, 1987); **P. K. Hooker,** *First and Second Chronicles* (WBCom; Louisville: Westminster/John Knox, 2001); **S. Japhet,** *I & II Chronicles* (OTL; Louisville: Westminster/John Knox, 1993); **J. Jarick,** *1 Chronicles* (Readings; London: Sheffield Academic Press, 2002); **W. Johnstone,** *1 and 2 Chronicles, Volume 1: 1 Chronicles 1 through 2 Chronicles 9: Israel's Place among the Nations* (JSOTSup, 253; Sheffield: Sheffield Academic Press, 1997); idem, *1 and 2 Chronicles, Volume 2: 2 Chronicles 10-36: Guilt and Atonement* (JSOTSup, 254; Sheffield: Sheffield Academic Press, 1997); **G. N. Knoppers,** *1 Chronicles 1-9* (AB; New York: Doubleday, 2004); idem, *1 Chronicles 10-29* (AB; New York: Doubleday, 2004); **J. G. McConville,** *1 and 2 Chronicles* (DSB: Philadelphia: Westminster, 1984); **J. M. Myers,** *I-II Chronicles* (2 vols.; AB 12, 13; Garden City, NY: Doubleday, 1965); **M. J. Selman,** *1 Chronicles* (TOTC; Downers Grove, IL: InterVarsity Press, 1994); idem, *2 Chronicles* (TOTC; Downers Grove, IL: InterVarsity Press, 1994); **J. A. Thompson,** *1 and 2 Chronicles* (New American Commentary; Nashville: Broadman & Holman, 1994); **S. S. Tuell,** *First and Second Chronicles* (IntC; Louisville: John Knox, 2001); **H. G. M. Williamson,** *1 and 2 Chronicles* (NCB; Grand Rapids: Eerdmans, 1982). *Studies:* **L. C. Allen,** "Kerygmatic Units in 1 & 2 Chronicles," *JSOT* 41 (1988) 21-36; **A. G. Auld,** *Kings Without Privilege: David and Moses in the Story of the Bible's Kings* (Edinburgh: T & T Clark, 1994); **M. Beer,** "Judaism (Babylonian)," *ABD* 3.1076-83; **J. Blenkinsopp,** *Ezra-Nehemiah* (OTL; Philadelphia: Westminster, 1988); **R. P. Carroll,** "Israel, History of (Post-Monarchic Period)," *ABD* 3.567-76; **D. J. A. Clines,** *Ezra, Nehemiah, Esther* (NCB; Grand Rapids: Eerdmans, 1984); **F. M. Cross,** "A Reconstruction of the Judean Restoration," *JBL* 94 (1975) 4-18; **R. K. Duke,** "Chronicles, Theology of," in *Evangelical Dictionary of Biblical Theology,* ed. W. A. Elwell (Grand Rapids: Baker, 1996) 92-95; idem, "A Model for a Theology of Biblical Historical Narratives: Proposed and Demonstrated with the Books of Chronicles," in *History and Interpretation: Essays in Honour of John H. Hayes,* ed. M. P. Graham, W. P. Brown and

K. Kuan (JSOTSup 173; Sheffield: JSOT, 1993) 65-77; idem, *The Persuasive Appeal of the Chronicler: A Rhetorical Analysis* (JSOTSup 88; Sheffield: Almond, 1990); idem, "A Rhetorical Approach to Appreciating the Books of Chronicles," in *The Chronicler as Author: Studies in Text and Texture,* ed. M. P. Graham and S. L. McKenzie (JSOTSup 263; Sheffield: Sheffield Academic Press, 1999) 100-135; **J. E. Dyck,** *The Theocratic Ideology of the Chronicler* (BIS 33; Leiden: E. J. Brill, 1998); **G. J. Eichhorn,** *Einleitung in das Alte Testament* (3d ed.; 3 vols.; Leipzig: Weidman, 1803); **S. J. Endres, W. R. Millar and J. B. Burns,** eds., *Chronicles and Its Synoptic Parallels in Samuel, Kings, and Related Biblical Texts* (Collegeville, MN: Liturgical Press, 1998); **D. N. Freedman,** "The Chronicler's Purpose," *CBQ* 23 (1961) 436-42; **M. P. Graham and S. L. McKenzie,** eds., *The Chronicler as Author: Studies in Text and Texture* (JSOTSup 263; Sheffield: Sheffield Academic Press, 1999); **M. P. Graham, S. L. McKenzie and G. N. Knoppers,** eds., *The Chronicler as Theologian: Essays in Honor of Ralph W. Klein* (JSOTSup 371; London: T & T Clark, 2003); **M. P. Graham, K. G. Hoglund and S. L. McKenzie,** eds., *The Chronicler as Historian* (JSOTSup 238; Sheffield: Sheffield Academic Press, 1997); **R. S. Hess,** "Literacy in Iron Age Israel," in *Windows into Old Testament History: Evidence, Argument, and the Crisis of "Biblical Israel,"* ed. V. P. Long, D. W. Baker and G. J. Wenham (Grand Rapids: Eerdmans, 2002) 82-102; **K. G. Hoglund,** *Achaemenid Imperial Administration in Syria-Palestine and the Missions of Ezra and Nehemiah* (SBLDS 125; Atlanta: Scholars Press, 1992); idem, "The Chronicler as Historian: A Comparativist Perspective," in *The Chronicler As Historian,* ed. M. P. Graham, K. G. Hoglund and S. L. McKenzie (JSOTSup 238; Sheffield: Sheffield Academic Press, 1997) 19-29; **S. Japhet,** *The Ideology of the Book of Chronicles and Its Place in Biblical Thought* (2d ed.; BEATAJ 9; Frankfurt: Peter Lang, 1997); idem, "The Supposed Common Authorship of Chronicles and Ezra-Nehemiah Investigated Anew," *VT* 18 (1968) 330-71; **I. Kalimi,** *Books of Chronicles: A Classified Bibliography* (Simor Bible Bibliographies; Jerusalem: Simor, 1990); **R. W. Klein,** "Chronicles, Book of 1-2," *ABD* 1.992-1002; **J. W. Kleinig,** "Recent Research in Chronicles," *CurBS* 2 (1994) 43-76; **G. N. Knoppers,** "Greek Historiography and the Chronicler's History: A Reexamination," *JBL* 122 (2003) 627-50; **W. Lemke,** "The Synoptic Problem in the Chronicler's History,"

HTR 58 (1965) 627-50; **Y. Levin,** "Who Was the Chronicler's Audience? A Hint from His Genealogies," *JBL* 122 (2003) 229-45; **R. Mason,** *Preaching the Tradition: Homily and Hermeneutics after the Exile* (Cambridge: Cambridge University Press, 1990); **V. H. Matthews,** *A Brief History of Ancient Israel* (Louisville: Westminster/John Knox, 2002); **F. K. Movers,** *Kritische Untersuchungen über die biblische Chronik: Ein Beitrag zur Einleitung in das Alte Testament* (Bonn: Habicht, 1834); **M. Noth,** *The Chronicler's History* (JSOTSup 50; Sheffield: Sheffield Academic Press, 2001 [1943]); **K. Peltonen,** *History Debated: The Historical Reliability of Chronicles in Pre-Critical and Critical Research* (2 vols.; Publications of the Finnish Exegetical Society 64; Helsinki: Finnish Exegetical Society; Göttingen: Vandenhoeck & Ruprecht, 1996); **I. Provan, V. P. Long and T. Longman III,** *A Biblical History of Israel* (Louisville: Westminster/John Knox, 2003); **G. von Rad,** "The Levitical Sermon in I and II Chronicles," in *The Problem of the Hexateuch and Other Essays* (New York: McGraw-Hill, 1966) 267-80; idem, *Old Testament Theology,* 1: *The Theology of Israel's Historical Traditions* (New York: Harper & Row, 1962 [1957]); **A. F. Rainey,** "The Chronicler and His Sources—Historical and Geographical," in *The Chronicler As Historian,* ed. M. P. Graham, K. G. Hoglund and S. L McKenzie (JSOTSup 238; Sheffield: Sheffield Academic Press, 1997) 30-72; **W. Rudolph,** "Problems of the Books of Chronicles," *VT* 4 (1954) 401-9; **W. M. Schniedewind,** *The Word of God in Transition: From Prophet to Exegete in the Second Temple Period* (JSOTSup 197; Sheffield: Sheffield Academic Press, 1995); **J. R. Shaver,** *Torah and the Chronicler's History Work: An Inquiry into the Chronicler's References to Laws, Festivals, and Cultic Institutions in Relationship to Pentateuchal Legislation* (BJS 196; Atlanta: Scholars Press, 1989); **M. A. Throntveit,** "Linguistic Analysis and the Question of Authorship in Chronicles, Ezra and Nehemiah," *VT* 32 (1982) 201-16; idem, *When Kings Speak: Royal Speech and Royal Prayer in Chronicles* (SBLDS 93; Atlanta: Scholars Press, 1987); **C. C. Torrey,** "The Chronicler as Editor and as Independent Narrator," *AJSL* 25.2 (1909) 157-73; idem, *Ezra Studies* (Chicago: University of Chicago Press, 1910); **A. C. Welch,** *The Work of the Chronicler: Its Purpose and Its Date* (London: Oxford University Press, 1939); **J. Wellhausen,** *Prolegomena to the History of Ancient Israel* (Edinburgh: A. & C. Black, 1885; repr., Cleveland:

World, 1957 [1878; 2d ed., 1883]); **P. Welten,** *Geschichte und Geschichtsdarstellung in den Chronikbüchern* (WMANT 42; Neukirchen-Vluyn: Neukirchener Verlag, 1973); **W. M. L. de Wette,** *Beiträge zur Einleitung in das Alte Testament* (2 vols.; Halle: Schimmelpfennig, 1806); **T. Willi,** *Die Chronik als Auslegung: Untersuchungen zur literarischen Gestaltung der historischen Überlieferung Israels* (FRLANT 106; Göttingen: Vandenhoeck & Ruprecht, 1972); **H. G. M. Williamson,** *Ezra and Nehemiah* (OTG; Sheffield: JSOT, 1987); idem, *Israel in the Books of Chronicles* (Cambridge: Cambridge University Press, 1977); **L. Zunz,** *Die gottesdienstlichen Vorträge der Juden historisch entwickelt: Ein Beitrag zur Altertumskunde und biblischen Kritik, zur Literatur- und Religionsgeschichte* (repr., Hildesheim: Olms, 1966 [1832]).

R. K. Duke

CHRONOLOGY

In the Historical Books may be distinguished four distinct periods: (1) from the entry of *Joshua into Canaan down to the beginnings of kingship (reign of *Saul); (2) the relatively brief span of the main united monarchy (*David and *Solomon); (3) the almost 350 years of the divided monarchy and Judah; (4) the exilic and postexilic period. Of these four periods, only for the last three do the total data suffice to establish reasonably accurate dates, covering the history of the *Hebrews from the tenth to fifth centuries BCE, utilizing the full range of chronological information presently available both from the biblical writings and from the neighboring civilizations, especially Egypt and Mesopotamia.

    1. From Joshua to the Death of Saul
    2. The Monarchy of David and Solomon
    3. The Divided and Judean Monarchies
    4. The Exile and After

1. From Joshua to the Death of Saul.
At the death of Moses (Deut 34:9; Josh 1:1-3), and traditionally forty years after the exodus from Egypt (Deut 1:3, cf. 2:14), Joshua became unitary leader of tribal Israel, led them into Canaan, and established a foothold in the highlands during his leadership and likewise that of a committee of "elders" (Josh 24:31; Judg 2:7); for him and them, no figures are given. A considerable time later, Solomon's founding of his Jerusalem temple in his fourth year is synchronized with "the four hundred eightieth year

since the Israelites came from Egypt" (1 Kings 6:1), which was then also the four hundred fortieth year since Joshua took over from Moses, covering everyone from Joshua to Solomon's fourth year. If Kings were a modern Western book, and this datum our sole evidence, one might proceed (as some still do) simply to add this 480/440 years to the date for the fourth year of Solomon to obtain dates BCE for the exodus and Joshua respectively. That fourth year is c. 967 BCE (see 2 below), hence the temptation to set the exodus at 1447 BCE and Joshua from 1407 BCE respectively.

However, 1 Kings 6:1 is not our sole datum, either biblical or external, and it cannot be mechanically privileged over all other evidence; nor are the OT writings modern, Western-type books. These writings were composed in the biblical world of the ancient Near East and by its norms, not ours. Also the main weight of other biblical and related data suggests solutions other than a simplistic reading of the four hundred eightieth year.

If we take account of all the other biblical figures for individuals Hebrew and otherwise (when available), then we have a total of $554 + x + y + z$ years from the exodus (see listings in Rowley, 87-88), or $514 + x + y + z$ years from Joshua's appointment down to Solomon's fourth year, and not 480. The $x + y + z$ years represent the unstated years' rule by Joshua and then by the elders, plus any period over 20 years by Samuel, plus the period over 2 years by Saul. If x is an outright minimum of a mere $5 + 5$ years, y a 0, and if for z Saul is given 30 years plus the attested 2, then this further 42 years would give 596 years since the exodus and 556 years from Joshua to Solomon's fourth year, not 480. Naturally, the reply has been that the excess (116 years or whatever) above 480 can be met by overlapping the periods of rulers and oppressions between the elders and the accession of Saul. This is valid (see below), but it is inadequate just to meet a figure of 480. In sharp contrast to both the 480 figure and even more the 556 years listable from Joshua downwards, we have the succession and generations of the priests from Aaron's son Eleazar down to Zadok I under Solomon, some ten or so generations (see 1 Chron 6:1-10). At 25 or so years to a generation, this represents about 250/300 years, not 480 or 556. So, we would require to overlap a figure more like 230 and 180 years (= 480-250, and

181

480-300) than 116 years (a difference of between 64 and 114 years respectively). This is quite feasible if one looks carefully at the data in the book of *Judges. Only in some eight cases does it give explicit successions of *judges, in three groups: Judges 3:31; 4:1-4; separately, Judges 8:30-31 with 9:1-2; 10:1; 10:3; separately, Judges 12:8; 12:11; 12:13. There is no directly expressed link of succession between any of these three groups. The common phrase "Again the Israelites did evil" has no direct or exclusively chronological reference; it simply means "Here is yet another example of Israel's religious infidelity," in order to multiply evidence, not to give dates. Many of these judges had only local rule, not over all Israel, and they can be readily distributed according to region (see below). As a close-to-absolute bottom date for Israel's presence in Canaan, we can place them there already by the fifth year of Merenptah of Egypt (c. 1209/1208 BCE), on his victory stela of that date; Joshua would have died by c. 1220/1215 BCE at the very latest, and Merenptah's reign (c. 1213-1203 BCE) could have seen the start of the judges' period at the very latest.

Thus, using the biblical data on geographical distribution of judges and for oppressions and periods of rule, we can outline a "minimal date" list of people, places and theoretical dates as follows below. It should be borne in mind that during c. 1200 BCE (or earlier) down to before Saul, there originally would have been more local leaders than are recorded in the biblical selection in Judges and 1 Samuel.

1. Southwest: (a) Some Danites went off to Laish (c. 1190-1180 BCE); (b) Shamgar (c. 1170 BCE [after arrival of the Philistines, c. 1180-1177 BCE, from year eight, Ramesses III]); (c) no more news in the southwest until the Philistine oppression (c. 1100-1060 BCE), opposed by Samson (c. 1080-1060 BCE).

2. South Judah and Negev: (a) Kushan-Rishathaim (c. 1200-1192 BCE), and Othniel (c. 1192-1152 BCE); (b) much later, Ibzan (c. 1067-1060 BCE) and sons of Samuel (c. 1045 BCE).

3. East Center/Benjamin: (a) Eglon (c. 1200-1182 BCE) and Ehud (c.1182-x BCE); (b) "eighty years of peace" (c. *1182-1102 BCE); (c) Samuel (c. 1062-1042 BCE).

4. Center/Ephraim: (a) Jabin II (c. 1180-1160 BCE) and Deborah (c. 1165-1150? BCE); (b) "forty years of peace" (c. *1160-1120 BCE); (c) Tola (c. 1136-1113 BCE); (d) Abdon (c. 1050-1042 BCE),

Eli (c. 1102-1062 BCE), Samuel.

5. North Center/Manasseh: Midian (c. 1186-1179 BCE), Gideon, (c. 1179-1139 BCE), Abimelech (1139-1136 BCE).

6. Galilee and North: (a) Barak, time of Deborah (c. 1165-1150 BCE); long interval, then (b) Elon (c. 1060-1050 BCE).

7. East of Jordan: (a) Jair (1113-1091 BCE); (b) Ammon (1091-1073 BCE) and Jephthah (1073-1067 BCE).

Then there is a unitary reign of Saul of probably thirty-two years (c. 1042-1010 BCE) (for a fuller statement of the data, with diagrams, see Kitchen 2003, chap. 5).

Thus, a much shorter span of about 240 years from Joshua/elders to Solomon (rather than 440 years, from the 480 for the exodus) is quite feasible. The 480 years sometimes is taken as 12 x 40 years as ten "long" generations (cf. above on ten generations of the Aaronide priestly line). More likely is the suggestion that it represents the aggregate of Hebrew rulers from Moses through to the fourth year of Solomon, omitting all oppressions, which (with *thirty-two years for Saul) would come to 475 years, plus *five for Joshua and elders (see the tabulation in Kitchen 2003, chap. 6). Thus it would include figures for the regimes of judges who indeed occur in overlaps, and would have been a formal "era" to bridge a complex epoch, as people did with such "intermediate" periods in Egypt and Mesopotamia also. And what of the 300 years spoken of by Jephthah (Judg 11:26)? He came from an extremely poor and deprived background, with plenty of bravery but no known education. His boast to the king of Ammon is simply a round figure, a bluster—"We've been here donkey's years!"—and not a learned calculation.

A fair body of external factors also favors a Joshua active c. 1220 BCE rather than almost two centuries before. The long list of towns that he defeated in Joshua 12 fits very well with known Late Bronze II remains at locatable sites in nearly all cases. Many of these were defeated, some damaged, but none totally destroyed except *Jericho (Late Bronze II levels all but totally eroded!), *Ai (location not fully agreed) and *Hazor (final Canaanite city and citadel, spectacularly destroyed c. 1230/1220 BCE [see Kitchen 2002; 2003b]). So, outside of these three places, it is Canaanite occupation that counts, not destructions (Kitchen 2003a, chap. 5).

When Ramesses II raided through Canaan and/or the Negev c. 1273 BCE to invade Moab and Seir/Edom, he found no Israelites either west or east of the Jordan, whereas some sixty years later Merenptah did; thus it is simplest to bring the Israelites through Transjordan and into Canaan within that interval (c. 1270-1210 BCE). In the thirteenth century BCE the city of Raamses (Ex 1:11)—the Pi-Ramesse of Ramesses II—was a huge metropolis some four by two miles in extent, unequaled by any previous occupation there. The Hyksos town of Avaris was destroyed c. 1540 or 1530 BCE at the latest; the following Eighteenth Dynasty built no vast city there, only a fortified headquarters for the later royal expeditions; no metropolis in 1447 or 1407 BCE. The format of the covenant between Israel and their God in Joshua 24 is an abbreviated form of what occurs in Exodus-Leviticus and most clearly of all in Deuteronomy; it is the format of c. 1350-1190 BCE exclusively, as attested in almost forty Hittite, Anatolian and northern Syrian documents and with Egypt in that period, which firmly excludes all other epochs, including both 621 BCE and 1447/1407 BCE, when entirely different formulations dominated, equally exclusively (cf. Kitchen 2003, chap. 6). Thus the later date (thirteenth century BCE) for Joshua's lifetime would fit in well with almost all of the relevant external evidence and with the biblical data when understood in line with the practices of their own world.

2. The Monarchy of David and Solomon.

In our sole source, David and Solomon are each assigned forty years of reign (1 Kings 2:11 and 1 Kings 11:42 respectively). It should be noted that these are not just round-figure approximations, nor is there any necessary problem in having two successive long reigns. David's reign clearly falls into two phases: seven and a half years as local king in *Hebron, then thirty-three years over all Israel and Judah (1 Kings 2:11). Most of Solomon's reign can also be accounted for from his recorded history. He began building the Jerusalem temple in his fourth year, taking seven years up to his eleventh year (1 Kings 6:37-38), and then he worked on his extensive palace complex for thirteen years (1 Kings 7:1), for a total of twenty years (1 Kings 9:10), which should be taken as consecutive to the temple (i.e., during his years eleven through twenty-four). His last sixteen years would be needed for

his other building works, both at Jerusalem (*millô*, "terraces" [?], after the palace [see 1 Kings 9:24]; and walling) and then further out around his kingdom: *Gezer, *Megiddo and Hazor; lower Beth-Horon, Baalath Tamar/Ta(d)mor and various other places (see 1 Kings 9:15-19). Work was going on at the Jerusalem *millô* and walls when young *Jeroboam fled to Egypt, to the court of Shishak (i.e., Shoshenq I) (1 Kings 11:27, 40); that could occur only after the accession of Shoshenq I in c. 945 BCE, hence Jeroboam's flight from his work at the *millô* etc. could not be earlier than that date, and probably was a little later, or (from 945 BCE) year twenty-five onward of Solomon. So, Solomon's last sixteen years would not be empty of activity. As for successive long reigns, it must be remembered that Solomon was not David's firstborn son, but rather came along in David's international war years, in the midst of his reign—a young king succeeded an old father. This is paralleled elsewhere in the ancient Near East. From about 1330 BCE down to c. 1180 BCE, just five Hittite kings ruled in Carchemish from father to son throughout, which is an average of thirty years for each of these five kings; in fact, after a first short reign, three kings reigned about fifty-three, forty and thirty years in succession, being tied by synchronisms to kings of the Hittite Empire, Ugarit and elsewhere (Kitchen, forthcoming, table IX). Back in Egypt in the twentieth and nineteenth centuries BCE, in the Twelfth Dynasty, Sesostris I and Amenemhat II (father and son) reigned for forty-five and thirty-five years, with only a brief three-year co-regency. Thus we have no valid a priori grounds for doubting the reign lengths of David or Solomon.

As for actual working dates for these rulers, it is most likely that Solomon died in 931/930 BCE (see 3.2 below), and hence reigned c. 971/970 to 931/930 BCE. David appointed him king before his own death (by several months?) in order to ward off any more threats to the succession (see 1 Kings 1:32—2:12). Thus David's forty years would have covered c. 1010-970 BCE at the latest. That included seven and a half years in Hebron (1010-1003 BCE) and then thirty-three years as overall ruler (1003-970 BCE). In his first seven years the ill-starred Ishbaal/Ishbosheth son of Saul reigned as an Israelite puppet king in Gilead under Abner's tutelage (2 Sam 2:8-10). It would take a year or so of negotiation after Ishbaal's death before the tribes of Israel finally consented to accept David's rule, and after Saul's death they had been so scattered and routed by the Philistines that they would need three or four years to regroup in their own territories under such as Abner. Thus Ishbaal's brief reign might provisionally be put at roughly 1006-1004 BCE. External synchronisms for David and Solomon remain rather indirect at present. Solomon's pharaoh who sacked Gezer and gave him a daughter in marriage alliance within Solomon's first four years (c. 971-967 BCE) is not named (1 Kings 3:1; 9:16). However, there is only one pharaoh at this time in Egypt's Twenty-First Dynasty who shows any trace of military involvement abroad: Siamun (datable to c. 979-960 BCE), an exact contemporary, who left a triumph scene, now fragmentary, but showing him smiting foes who hold a peculiar axe possibly of Aegean derivation (Philistine?). For David, we have a highly probable topographical mention of him in a place name, "Heights of David," in the name list of Shoshenq I (c. 925 BCE), less than fifty years after David's death (c. 970 BCE) (see Kitchen 1997, 39-42), while his opponent Hadadezer of Aram-Zobah probably was the "king of Aram" who held control of the west Euphrates fords and beyond (2 Sam 10:16), reported for the time of Assur-rabi II of Assyria, c. 990 BCE (a date well inside David's reign), by his later descendant Shalmaneser III (see *COS* 2.113A:261-64).

3. The Divided and Judean Monarchies.

3.1. The Question of Calendars. Throughout the books of *Kings and *Chronicles we encounter a long series of kings of Israel and Judah to whom are attributed an equally long series of detailed figures for the lengths of their reigns, and a large number of synchronisms between regnal years of rulers in the two kingdoms. As anyone who has tried to work out these dates by modern methods soon finds out, it is impossible to arrive at any overall sensible solution that way, any more than for earlier periods. Only when these regnal data are understood in terms of their own world, the ancient Near East, do they make any sense, and then the vast majority of them do fall neatly into place as a coherent whole. The breakthrough on this subject was achieved by E. R. Thiele (1951 and later editions), whose work is still by far the best in the field, with only minor corrections. Preference for LXX variants was long

since thoroughly refuted by Thiele (1951 and later editions) and by Gooding (1965; 1967). The work of Galil (1996) in large measure concurs with Thiele but fails to account for synchronisms, among other weaknesses. There are several factors involved. One is how reigns were reckoned against the calendar; another is what calendar or calendars were current, and (for Israel and Judah) whether neighboring kingdoms used the same or different calendars. No king is ever known to have conveniently died at the stroke of midnight on the last day of the year in any calendar, such that his successor might begin to reign in the first few seconds of the new year! A ruler could, of course, die at any time during a given calendar year, but to whose reign should that otherwise divided year be attributed? The biblical world used two options. In the first option, the whole year in which the change of ruler occurred was credited to the recently deceased ruler; the portion in which the new ruler reigned was an "accession year," not beginning year one until next new year's day of the calendar in force. This "accession" system was customary in Mesopotamia. In the second option, the year in which the former ruler died simply became year one of the new incumbent, so that next new year began year two of the reign. This, in effect a "nonaccession" system, was the usage in Egypt (except that New Kingdom pharaohs simply kept every year as a full year from their accession, disregarding calendrical new year).

Calculation shows that during the Hebrew divided monarchy, the two kingdoms did not normally use the same kind of regnal year. Thanks to a pair of synchronisms between Shalmaneser III of Assyria and the Israelite kings Ahab in 853 BCE and Jehu in 841 BCE, twelve actual years apart, we begin to see how their reigns were calculated. In that time span between Ahab and Jehu reigned Ahaziah I and J(eh)oram I, for two and twelve years respectively (1 Kings 22:51; 2 Kings 3:1)—a total of fourteen years at first sight, not twelve. But, if Israel used the nonaccession system, then these kings reigned only one and eleven full years respectively, for a total of twelve, fitting the case precisely. It should be recalled that Jeroboam I came to power after a sojourn in Egypt; thus it would appear that he brought this usage thence to Israel. In turn, the six successive rulers reigning a year or more, from Jeroboam I to Ahab inclusive, total nominally eighty-four years; but subtracting one year from each of the six rulers leaves seventy-eight full years, setting the accession of Jeroboam I in 931/930 BCE, also setting the death of Solomon then. One may compare dating for Judah and Israel, going back from 841 BCE, when Jehu murdered two kings in one year: Ahaziah II of Judah and J(eh)oram I in Israel (2 Kings 9:14-29). Back to 931/930 BCE is 89/90 years, into which the nonaccession years of Israel fit directly. For Judah, the assumption of nonaccession years also would give 89 years; but except for the last two kings (under Israel's thumb), Judean kings otherwise used accession years. The last two (J[eh]oram II and Ahaziah II) would then have a full year less (a total of two less years); before that, Jehoshaphat's 25 years seemingly included a co-regency with the ill and elderly Asa of some three or four years, a time when interference from Israel was possible. Thus the formal 95 years for Judean kings from Rehoboam to Ahaziah II would in fact be 89/90 years (= $95\frac{5}{6}$ years), from 931/930 BCE, again, for Solomon's death. From the eighth century BCE onward not only Judah, but also Israel, under Assyrian influence, used accession-year dating. Under these circumstances the dates for Israel run down to 722 BCE, and for Judah to 587/586 BCE, with relatively few problems, and showing good correlations with external foreign powers. Thus there is good reason, on an independent Egyptian chronology, to date Shoshenq I (biblical Shishak) to c. 945-924 BCE, with his invasion in the fifth year of Rehoboam falling in 926/925 BCE, just 5 years after Solomon's death, as suggested by the joint Hebrew/Assyrian chronology outlined just above. The independence of the Egyptian dates should be noted; we have ten successive kings of the Twenty-Second Dynasty who ruled for 230 years (945-715 BCE), followed directly by the three Kushite kings who ruled Egypt for just 51 years, during 715 BCE (second year of Shabako) to 664 BCE (death of Tirhakah) with the rise of the Twenty-Sixth Dynasty. The Egyptian King So (725 BCE) has to be Osorkon IV, attested from the time of Piye (Piankhy) in 728 BCE, again as Shilkanni with Sargon II of Assyria in 716 BCE, until Shabako's conquest in 715 BCE (for these Egyptian dates see Kitchen 1996). Assyrian correlations with Ahab (853 BCE), Jehu (841 BCE onward), Jehoash (796 BCE), Menahem (738 BCE), Pekah, (733 BCE), Ahaz (734 BCE), Hoshea (732 BCE), fall of *Samaria (722 BCE),

*Hezekiah (701 BCE) and *Manasseh (676, and again c. 666 BCE) form a close series, meshing in well with the Hebrew dates.

On top of all this, what calendars were used? Not our winter-to-winter calendar (January to December), and not the Egyptian summer-to-summer agricultural calendar (based on the annual Nile flood in July/August). The only relevant West Semitic inscription, the late tenth-century Gezer agricultural calendar, runs through the year from autumn/fall to the following summer; it is the equivalent of the later fall calendar that began with the month of Tishri (September/October) through to Elul (August/September). But a spring-to-spring calendar was also widely known. From the third millennium BCE onward it is attested in Syria and Mesopotamia, and in the late second millennium BCE at Ugarit (for Near Eastern calendars see Cohen); and in the spring Abib is the first of months in Exodus 12:2 and 13:4. Calculation shows that the two sets of kings in Israel and Judah did not use the same calendar (either spring or fall); they differed from each other. But which used a spring calendar and which a fall one is not so easily settled. The regnal years and synchronisms work regardless of which pairing is adopted. In the OT the common usage is to number the months of the year, not name them—a custom perhaps based on Egyptian usage. The month names Ziv, Bul and Ethanim were Phoenician (see Cohen, 385), owed to Solomon's Phoenician artisans who worked on his temple and palace (1 Kings 6:1, 38; 8:2), and which the Hebrew annalist glossed with the Hebrew numerical terms "second," "eighth" and "seventh" respectively. The standard Mesopotamian calendar (beginning with Nisannu in the spring) came into full use by about 1500 BCE as far west as Alalakh in North Syria, and was known also in thirteenth-century Ugarit (Cohen, 381). However, in biblical usage it was not until Neo-Babylonian and Persian times—the exile and after—that the standard Mesopotamian calendar gained use, along with numeration, as appears in Esther (e.g., Esther 2:16; 3:7, 13) and elsewhere (e.g., Hag 1:1, 15; Zech 1:1, 7) (for a handy summation of the Mesopotamian, Hebrew and Arabic calendar and month names see Bienkowski and Millard, 63).

3.2. Dates for the Divided and Judean Monarchies. On the basis of the foregoing considera-

Table 1. Dates for the Divided and Judean Monarchies

BCE	Kings of Judah
931/930-915/914	Rehoboam
915/914-912/911	Abijam
912/911-871/870	Asa
871/870-848/847	Jehoshaphat (cr. 871)
848/847-842	J(eh)oram I (cr. 853)
842-841	Ahaziah II
841-835	Queen Athaliah [and Joash]
841/835-797/796	J(eh)oash I
797/796-768/767	Amaziah
767/766-736/735	Uzziah (cr. 787ff.; not active 750ff.)
752/751-732/731	J(eh)otham
732/731-716	Ahaz (cr. 736/735ff.)
716-687/686	Hezekiah (cr. 729ff.)
687/686-643	Manasseh (cr. 698/697ff.)
643-641	Amon
641-609	Josiah
609	Jehoahaz II
609-598	Jehoiakim
598/597	Jehoiachin
597-586	Zedekiah; fall of Jerusalem

BCE	Kings of Israel
931/930-910/909	Jeroboam I
910/909-909/908	Nadab
909/908-886-885	Baasha
886/885-885/884	Elah
885; 885/884-880	Zimri (7 days); Tibni (rival, Omri)
885/884-874/873	Omri
874/873-853/852	Ahab
853/852-852/851	Ahaziah I
852/851-841	J(eh)oram II
841-814/813	Jehu
814/813-798/797	Jehoahaz I (cr. 822/821ff.)
798/797-782/781	J(eh)oash II
782/781-749	Jeroboam II (cr. 793/792ff.)
749/748; 748	Zachariah; Shallum
748/747-738/737	Menahem
738/737-736/735	Pekahiah
752-736/735 736/735-732/731	Pekah (rival ruler) (full ruler)
732/731-723/722	Hoshea; fall of Samaria (722)

tions, one may tabulate reasonable basic dates as follows below for the kings of Israel and Judah. Alternate dates here reflect the complexities of coordinating the new year's options in ancient calendars (see 3.1 above) with the modern Julian calendar. In Table 1 "cr." signifies coregency with previous ruler. These associations of royal father and son tend to cluster in times of real or potential political threats to the Judean monarchy, from either Assyria or the Arameans or both; they are of political importance, not just a chronological convenience.

4. The Exile and After.

4.1. Exile in Babylon. The reduction of Judah from kingdom to a tiny province in serfdom to the Neo-Babylonian Empire, with loss of some segments of its population into captivity in Mesopotamia, was not an instant process. From 605 BCE at the battle of Carchemish, when Nebuchadrezzar II (as crown prince) ousted Egypt from the Levant, down to 586 BCE, when he as king destroyed Jerusalem and its kingdom, several deportations of Judeans occurred. In Nabopolassar's twenty-first (last) year, 606/605 BCE, Nebuchadrezzar explicitly took over the Levant as far as Hamath (Grayson, 99 and note), but on news of his father's death (Ab, in July-August), he sped back to Babylon to take the throne on the first of Elul (August). Thereafter, still in his accession year (605 BCE), he promptly returned to the Levant to reduce everybody to order, and he took all his loot and captives back to Babylon (month of Shebat) about January 604 BCE, in time to celebrate the beginning of his official year one in Nisan (March) 604 BCE. His first year was the fourth of Jehoiakim of Judah (Jer 25:1), and thus the Babylonian's accession year was the third year of Jehoiakim, when that loot (and captives) was collected, including Daniel and his companions (see Dan 1:1). Thus in 605/604 BCE Jerusalem had been besieged, had submitted, and had to pay tribute in goods and captives, along with other centers. There is no clash here with any other record or event. The next *Babylonian invasions were in later 604, 603 (?), 602 and 601 BCE, and in this last year the Egyptian forces ground the Babylonian war machine to a halt. After an interval (600 BCE) Babylon was again in Syria, but not sufficiently to prevent Jehoiakim from rebelling, ending in the siege of Jerusalem and its capture under his hapless son Jehoiachin (March 597 BCE), replaced by Zede-

kiah (see 2 Kings 24:8-17), when a second batch of Judeans (over 8,000; 3,023 specified in Jer 52:28) was sent off to Babylon. A third batch (832 people) went off captive to Babylon at the final fall of Jerusalem in 586 BCE (cf. 2 Kings 25:1-21; Jer 52:29), and a fourth lot of 745 people in 582 BCE, after the murder of the Babylonian nominee Gedaliah (2 Kings 25:22-26; cf. Jer 52:30). While some of "the poor people of the land" were exiled thus (Jer 52:15), we are also told explicitly that "the rest of the poor of the land" were left in Judah to cultivate the land (Jer 52:16)—empires were economic organisms, and had to pay their way. These goings-on are paralleled by other datelines given by the prophet Ezekiel, as a contemporary of these events (e.g., Ezek 1:1-2; 8:1; 29:1; 33:21). Then time passed until the last decades of the Neo-Babylonian Empire, when in 562 BCE the king Awel-Marduk ("Evil-Merodach") released the long-captive Jehioachin from prison into the royal court (2 Kings 25:27-30), and finally the city and kingship of Babylon fell to Cyrus of Medo-Persia in 539 BCE.

4.2. Under the Persian Empire. Here the books of *Ezra, Esther and *Nehemiah are our biblical sources, plus mentions in Daniel. Ezra 1—6 gives an outline of the first return of Jewish exiles under Sheshbazzar and Zerubbabel, and the leading priests from the first year of Cyrus; from the second year (538 BCE) they sought to rebuild the Jerusalem temple under Persian license (Ezra 1:2-4), but not without opposition from others around (Ezra 4:1-5). After sundry delays the task was completed (Ezra 6:15) in the sixth year of Darius I (516 BCE).

Not surprisingly, the Jews thereafter sought to enclose Jerusalem with a defense wall to protect themselves and the new temple, but this aroused further opposition (with some success) under Xerxes (under whom Esther is placed) and Artaxerxes I—a situation appended in Ezra 4:6-23 to the account of opposition to the temple's rebuilding. Although this procedure probably was a logical placement to a Hebrew writer, it sometimes has confused modern writers who have not realized that the author's aim was to follow the account of the dedication of the temple with his account of the mission of *Ezra to reinforce the role of the law and cult at the temple in the seventh year (458 BCE) of Artaxerxes I (Ezra 7:7-8). A dozen years later the emperor's cupbearer *Nehemiah heard disquieting news about the state of Jerusalem and its (uncompleted) walls, and so he was sent to remedy affairs in the twentieth year (445 BCE) of Artaxerxes I (Neh 1:1—6:15), when the work was finished and dedicated, along with the assistance of Ezra. Nehemiah then served as governor for twelve years until Artaxerxes I's thirty-second year, 433 BCE (Neh 5:14), when he returned east to the emperor (Neh 13:6). But without his strong executive hand, morals and law observance slipped, necessitating a renewal of Ezra's and his earlier reforms (Neh 13). How long after 432 BCE Nehemiah continued as governor of Judea is unknown (on Judean governors see Williamson). At various times biblical scholars have experimented with theories of dating Ezra and his mission after Nehemiah (e.g., under a later Artaxerxes), but none of these ingenious suggestions can offer any improvement on a straight reading of the texts (see Cross, 151-64). The latest datable reference in these memoirs is a mention of a king Darius in Nehemiah 12:22 that, in its context of priestly families, is most likely Darius II (424-404 BCE), into whose early years Nehemiah might well have lived.

See also HISTORY OF ISRAEL 1-8.

BIBLIOGRAPHY. **P. Bienkowski and A. R. Millard,** eds., *Dictionary of the Ancient Near East* (London: British Museum Press, 2000); **M. E. Cohen,** *The Cultic Calendars of the Ancient Near East* (Bethesda, MD: CDL Press, 1993); **F. M. Cross,** *From Epic to Canon: History and Literature in Ancient Israel* (Baltimore: Johns Hopkins University Press, 1998); **G. Galil,** *The Chronology of the Kings of Israel and Judah* (SHCANE 9; Leiden: E. J. Brill, 1996); **D. W. Gooding,** "Pedantic Timetabling in 3rd Book of Reigns," *VT* 15 (1965) 153-66; idem, "The Septuagint's Rival Versions of Jeroboam's Rise to Power," *VT* 17 (1967) 173-89; **A. K. Grayson,** *Assyrian and Babylonian Chronicles* (TCS 5; Locust Valley, NY: J. J. Augustin, 1975; repr., Winona Lake, IN: Eisenbrauns, 2000); **W. W. Hallo and K. L. Younger Jr.,** *The Context of Scripture,* 2 (Leiden: Brill, 2000); **K. A. Kitchen,** "An Egyptian Inscribed Fragment from Late-Bronze Hazor," and "Addendum: A Further Egyptian Item bearing on Late-Bronze Hazor," in *IEJ* 53 (2003) 20-28; idem, "Hazor and Egypt: An Egyptological and Ancient Near-Eastern Perspective," *SJOT* 16 (2002) 309-13; idem, *Hittite Hieroglyphs, Arameans and Hebrew Tradition* (forthcoming); idem, *On the Reliability of the Old Testament* (Grand Rapids: Eerdmans, 2003); idem, "A Possible Mention of David in the Late Tenth Century BCE, and Deity *Dod as Dead as the Dodo?" JSOT* 76 (1997) 29-44; idem, *The Third Intermediate Period in Egypt (1100-650 BC)* (2d ed.; Warminster: Aris & Phillips, 1996); **H. H. Rowley,** *From Joseph to Joshua: Biblical Traditions in the Light of Archaeology* (Schweich Lectures of the British Academy, 1948; London: Oxford University Press, 1950); **E. R. Thiele,** *The Mysterious Numbers of the Hebrew Kings: A Reconstruction of the Chronology of the Kingdoms of Israel and Judah* (1st ed., Chicago: University of Chicago Press, 1951; 2d and 3d eds., Grand Rapids: Eerdmans, 1965, 1983); **H. G. M. Williamson,** "The Governors of Judah under the Persians," *TynBul* 39 (1988) 59-82. K. A. Kitchen

CISTERNS. *See* WATER AND WATER SYSTEMS.

CITADEL. *See* ARCHITECTURE.

CITIES AND VILLAGES

The OT Historical Books deal extensively with settled life in the ancient Near East. Human settlements in the biblical world ranged from small hamlets to large, complexly organized cities. Although the term *town* occurs frequently in English translations of the Bible (e.g., Josh 10:37 NRSV), it is better to distinguish only between simple villages, usually unwalled, and cities, usually walled (1 Sam 6:18).

    1. Cities
    2. Villages

1. Cities.

1.1. Definition. For much of the time period covered by the Historical Books, it is almost a misnomer to speak of Israelite "cities." During the pre-state period especially—the duration of Joshua, Judges, and 1 Samuel—Israel never produced anything like Tel Miqne/*Ekron, whose twelfth-century Levels VIIIa-VII reveal a fifty-acre site with fortifications more than 3 m thick (Dothan, 9). Even the largest contemporary Israelite towns did not exceed twenty-five acres.

Most scholars would agree, however, that size alone does not constitute what it means to be a city (Willis, 15). Multiple factors, including *trade, *warfare, *writing, art, mass production, settlement patterns and *architecture all enter into this designation (Beaudry, 32). And not all of these elements are needed to make a city. There are many different kinds of cities (Griffeth and Thomas). Anomalous city-states-type polities are, oxymoronically, quite common: Angkor Wat in Cambodia is a prime example, but also Neolithic *Jericho, Mohenjo Daro in the Indus Valley, and others. The *Canaanite cities of the Late Bronze Age (Joshua-Judges), for example, were without professional guilds, merchant groups, royal retainers or any state bureaucracy beyond a small urban elite, yet engaged in geopolitics and extensive international trade (Marfoe, 15-16).

It is also clear that "the modern concepts of a city (as opposed to a town or village), do not necessarily correspond to the 'city' (עיר)" of the Bible (Willis, 16). T. M. Willis illustrates the fluidity of the latter term in references to the "city" of *Hebron (Willis, 17-18). The biblical term merely designates "a site ideologically apart from its environs" (Willis, 14), and thus it includes almost any kind of settlement (see Levitical Cities).

Given these caveats, the period of time covered by the Historical Books constitutes what has been called the "Third Urban Phase" in the *archaeology of Syria-Palestine (Herzog) (the first phase was the Early Bronze Age I-II, and the second was Middle Bronze IIA). This Third Urban Phase can be further divided, for Israelite society, into the pre-state and the state phases.

1.2. Pre-state Period. Before the rise of monarchy in Israel, the cities of ancient Palestine are those of the non-Israelite groups that surrounded Israel's highland settlement. These cities were occupied variously by Canaanites, Philistines and other Sea Peoples (Negbi; see Judg 1:27-36). Twelfth-century Beth Shean Levels VIIB-A were Egyptian, but Canaanite or Sea Peoples are evidenced in the eleventh-century Strata S2 and S1 (Weinstein, 143). Twelfth-century *Megiddo VIB similarly reverted from Egyptian to local control in the eleventh century BCE as Levels VIA-VB (Singer, 319). *Jerusalem was already post-Egyptian by the twelfth century BCE, and it continued as a ten-acre Canaanite city into the eleventh century BCE (Redford, 32). Other important non-Israelite cities of this period include Taanach (Tell Taanek), for the twelfth-century Levels IA-IB, an eleven-acre city, and *Gezer, a seventeen-acre city in twelfth-century Level XIV and eleventh-century Levels XIII-XI (Dever, 100); most assuredly Philistine are *Ashdod (Strata XIII through XA), 20 acres (Mazar 1990, 532), *Ekron (see above) and *Ashkelon, which dwarfs all the

other Philistine cities, extending to 150 acres in the twelfth century BCE (Stager, *NEAEHL* 1.107).

Israelite cities of this period are few (for all of which see Miller 2003a). Dothan (Levels 6 and 5) was a city of twenty-five acres; *Tirzah (Level VI-IA) was the same size. *Shechem (Level XI) covered six acres, however, and *Shiloh was only a three-acre site. Other Israelite cities include *Bethel (Levels 1-3), *Ai (Phases II-III), *Gibeah (Levels I-II), Khirbet Raddanah (biblical identification unknown; Phases 2-3), *Gibeon (Period I), Beth Shemesh (Level III), Tel Masos (Level II) and *Beersheba (Levels VIII-VI). Most of these cities were somewhat fortified—for example, Gibeah, Gibeon, Bethel, Khirbet Raddanah, Shiloh (which also shows evidence of regional storage) and probably Shechem, but not Ai, Tirzah or Dothan (Miller, 2005).

1.3. Monarchic Period. With the rise of monarchy in Israel it is possible to categorize cities systematically (see Herzog, 211-59; Fritz, 234-36). This systemization is based on both the biblical text and archaeology; the text provides the framework to interpret the archaeological data, while not dictating the specifics of that data. Thus for both the united monarchy and for the kingdoms of Israel and Judah, one may speak of major cities, administrative centers, industrial cities and forts.

Major cities would be characterized primarily by large population. For Israel this would include *Samaria (Periods I-II), Tirzah (Levels VIIB-D), Gezer (Levels VII-VI), and from the seventh century BCE, Dor (Herzog, 221-24). In Judah, such cities were Jerusalem and Timnah (Herzog, 235-41). The Israelite cities are by far larger: Samaria is 100-125 acres, while Timnah is only 6.4. All of the capitals of the two kingdoms fall into this category. While the northern kingdom saw several capitals, including also Penuel and *Jezreel, it seems that only Samaria and Jerusalem combined the roles of unifying political and administrative center and ideological religious focus as well (Niemann, 92-96).

Administrative centers are cities not dominated by residences, but having extensive water systems, regional storage, caravan courtyards, temples and palaces. In Israel these include Dan (Levels IVA-II), *Hazor (Levels XB-VI) and Megiddo (Levels IVB-A) (Herzog, 226-29). In Judah the example is *Lachish (Levels IV-III). Although not properly a city, the Judahite palace complex at Ramat Rahel (late seventh century BCE) is a similar situation (King and Stager, 206-7).

Industrial cities are those that are also not heavily residential, but that are dominated by industrial installations and craft workshops rather than by public architecture. Examples of these are only from Judah: *Mizpah, En Gedi and Tel Beit Mirsim (Debir?) Level A (Herzog, 237-44; Niemann, 171).

Forts are small in size but heavily fortified. In Israel such places include Kinneret (Niemann, 134-47). In Judah, Beersheba (Levels V-II) is an example known from archaeology (Herzog, 247, 276), as are Arad (Levels X-VI), *Ezion-Geber/ Eilat, Kadesh-Barnea and, from the seventh century BCE, Aroer (Niemann, 105-8). The biblical text suggests also that Solomon's gate cities would fall into this class (1 Kings 9:19).

All these cities shared characteristics such as paved roads (Tirzah, Megiddo, Hazor, Beersheba) and water systems (Gibeon, Jerusalem, Megiddo, Hazor, Gezer), and all were fortified (Beaudry, 41-43).

1.4. Later Periods. As the independence of the Israelite and Judean kingdoms ended, non-Israelite cities were again found in Palestine. The Assyrian conquest of the northern kingdom and of most of the southern led to the establishment of Assyrian administrative centers near Hazor (Ayelet ha-Shahar) and at Megiddo (Level III) and Yurza (Tell Jemmeh) (King and Stager, 208-10). Under Persian rule, in the time of *Ezra and *Nehemiah, cities largely disappear, as the economy was essentially agrarian, and Jerusalem certainly is the only site that can be considered urban (Grabbe, 20, 23). There were a number of fortresses founded, and ostraca "mention individuals with non-Hebrew names in connection with the Persian garrisons" (Hoglund, 68).

1.5. City Life. Though an integral part of the larger administrative structures (*see* State Officials), these cities maintained their own leadership. These were known variously as the "elders" (e.g., 1 Sam 16:4) or "men of the city" (*'anšê hā'îr* [Judg 19:22]). Schäfer-Lichtenberger (290-96) has examined both terms in an extensive study and identifies the elder as a judiciary office and the "men of the city" as executive. Others remain unconvinced that such a distinction can be made (Neu, 208-9). Certainly administration of justice fell to city officials in many

cases; the charges fabricated against Naboth in 1 Kings 21:5-14 are tried by the elders of Jezreel. The city gate was the primary location for such judiciary proceedings, as can be seen in 2 Samuel 15:2-5.

2. Villages.

2.1. Definitions. While the Hebrew word for city, *'îr*, could designate villages as well, there are several terms that apply to open villages only: *ḥāṣēr, kāpār, pĕrāzôt* (King and Stager, 231). Unlike cities, village life in ancient Israel remained largely unchanged throughout the period covered by the Historical Books. Small villages of four hundred people or less remained in occupation for long periods of time with little change (see below on the period of Ezra and Nehemiah). Although villages in both the pre-state and monarchic periods existed "from Dan to Beersheba" and farther, regional variation was likewise minimal (Bloch-Smith and Nakhai, 116). These little villages were partly self-sufficient, but never entirely so; there was a sharing of risk and responsibilities to cope with local environmental constraints and labor needs (Matthews and Benjamin, 43).

2.2. Housing and Families. Villagers lived in nuclear families, but often in clusters of houses around a common courtyard with their relatives. Census records, household archives and marriage contracts from late third-millennium through early seventh-century Babylon and Assyria suggest that complex families were a rare phenomenon, which even when they did occur would have taken the form of joint multiple families rather than stem extended families (Routledge, forthcoming). In an extensive study, J. D. Schloen argues that these Mesopotamian analogies are irrelevant because Roman Egypt and Islamic villages show complex families to be common (Schloen, 108-17), but he shows no basis for choosing these analogies as preferential. A nuclear family averaged 4.5 to 5.5 individuals, based on gross reproductive rate and life expectancy of premodern Middle Eastern populations (Zorn, 33; Bloch-Smith and Nakhai, 75). Schloen (122-26) uses other theoretical models and arrives at nuclear families of 2.4 to 4.2 members, which is much lower. But since Schloen's argument is for extended families, he actually arrives at 8.8 to 10.3 people per house, which clearly is far larger (see Schloen, 135-36, 147-48). In any case, his construction of gross reproductive rates from *both* mortality and fertility levels is questionable; J. Smith and J. Oeppen offer viable alternatives. We may conclude that the average nuclear family had two or three children that survived infancy.

Many scholars have followed an influential article by L. Stager (1985) in seeing housing units configured to create shared central courtyards for extended family use, and in identifying these house clusters with the biblical *bêt 'āb* (e.g., 2 Sam 3:29), a socially and economically integrated extended family of three to four generations (Bloch-Smith and Nakhai, 75; Schloen, 150-55). Some caution should be exercised, however. Aside from a perhaps too straightforward reading of the biblical text (particularly of Lev 18—20) into the archaeology, it is questionable whether all these house clusters really exist; the supposed clustered houses at Khirbet Raddanah Phase 2, Site S, can just as easily be interpreted as a three-room house with a typical noncommunicating side room that was cut by later construction (King and Stager, 11).

A hierarchy of construction materials existed for dwellings (*see* Architecture). Rubble stone houses would have been doomed to collapse in the earthquake-ridden regions of the north central Palestinian highlands. Historically, only the poorest dwellings have been of rubble and clay constructions (Canaan, 31). Most intermediate quality houses were therefore of mud-bricks, using a few courses of stones to keep water from washing away the mud and to keep osmosis from bringing water up (Canaan, 31). Additionally, the prevailing winds come from the northwest, making a house in the northwest quarter of a site the ideal, and most expensive, location. Most village houses had three or four rooms, and likely often had sleeping quarters on the roof or a covered roof loft (see Judg 3:23). The house of a moderately prosperous family might have had a second story of wood—tamarisk or poplar or palm (1 Kings 4:10).

2.3. Economy. Grazing animals often were kept in the house courtyard (Crist, 47), inside the house on the first floor (Canaan, 35), or in small buildings that once were houses but then abandoned (Kana'an and McQuitty). Most villagers raised animals—caprovids (sheep and goats), primarily, rather than cattle—and did so for dairy products, not meat. The herders took the animals out in the morning up to 10-15 km away from the village (Grant, 142; cf. 1 Sam 16:11); one shepherd could tend about eighty-five caprovids (Killen). Wheat was the dominant field crop wherever possible, grown on terraced hillsides within an hour's walk of the village. These terraces also served for olive and grape cultivation, and for lesser crops, including lentils, chick peas, broad beans, barley and millet (*see* Agriculture and Animal Husbandry). Villages of the Sharon Plain and Haifa Bay participated in a more maritime-based economy (Bloch-Smith and Nakhai, 117).

There has yet to be a full study modeling the village communities of ancient Israel. The closest are works by G. Stanhill and by U. Zwingenberger that incorporate not only productivity of the environmental zone, but also human energy expenditure, percentages of men to women, manure from animals working in the fields as it impacts on fertilization, harvest-seed ratios, percentage of food coming from difficult-to-quantify sources such as eggs and milk, and much more (see Miller 2003b; *see* Israelite Society).

2.4. Changes in Village Life. Only in the period of *Persian rule in Palestine does village life change substantially. Archaeologically, K. Hoglund notes that "there was a pervasive and dramatic drop in the number of settlements from the Iron II period to the Persian period, reflective of a process of urbanization or depopulation. The Judean territory is the only exception to this pattern, showing a 25% increase in the number of settlements" (Hoglund, 60). Thus Judea was anomalous, and it experienced ruralization rather that urbanization. Hoglund argues that this probably was the result of intentional Persian policy, because most of these sites were not re-occupations of Iron II sites, and because most of these sites were settled simultaneously in the late sixth century BCE rather than over the course of the entire Persian period. In light of Persian and Hellenistic sources, Hoglund (61) explains this ruralization as part of the Persian imposition of a tributary mode of production, supplying a continual flow of tribute to Persia (cf. Neh 5:15). Hoglund concludes that Persian imperial land policy apparent from the forced settlement pattern would have nullified "land claims by any group rooted in the notion of familial or tribal possessions" (Hoglund, 62).

See also ARCHITECTURE; ISRAELITE SOCIETY; JERUSALEM; LEVITICAL CITIES; SAMARIA; WATER AND WATER SYSTEMS.

BIBLIOGRAPHY. **R. Bagnall and B. Frier,** *The Demography of Roman Egypt* (Cambridge: Cambridge University Press, 1994); **M. Beaudry,** "L'urbanisation à l'Époque du Fer," in *"Où demeures-tu?" (Jn 1,38): La maison depuis le monde biblique,* ed. J.-C. Petit (Montreal: Fides, 1994) 31-52; **E. Bloch-Smith and A. Nakhai,** "A Landscape Comes to Life: The Iron I Period," *NEA* 62 (1999) 62-92, 101-27; **J. Bocquet-Appel and C. Masset,** "Farewell to Paleodemography," *Journal of Human Evolution* 11 (1982) 321-33; **T. Canaan,** "The Palestinian Arab House," *JPOS* 13 (1933) 1-83; **A. J. Cole and P. Demeny,** *Regional Model Life Tables and Stable Populations* (Princeton, NJ: Princeton University Press, 1966); **R. E. Crist,** *Land for the Fellahin: Land Tenure and Land Use in the Near East* (New York: Robert Schalkenbach Foundation, 1961); **W. G. Dever,** "The Late Bronze-Early Iron I Horizon in Syria-Palestine," in *The Crisis Years: The Twelfth Century B.C. from Beyond the Danube to the Tigris,* ed. W. A. Ward and M. S. Joukowsky (Dubuque, IA: Kendall/Hunt, 1992) 99-110; **T. Dothan,** "The Arrival of the Sea Peoples," in *Recent Excavations in Israel: Studies in Iron Age Archaeology,* ed. S. Gitin and W. G. Dever (AASOR 49; Winona Lake, IN: Eisenbrauns, 1989) 1-14; **V. Fritz,** "The Character of Urbanization in Palestine at the Beginning of the Iron Age," in *Nuove fondazioni nel vicino Oriente antico: Realtà e ideologia,* ed. S. Mazzoni (Seminari di orientalistica 4; Pisa: Giardini, 1994) 231-52; **L. L. Grabbe,** *Judaism From Cyrus to Hadrian,* 1: *The Persian and Greek Periods* (Minneapolis: Fortress, 1992); **E. Grant,** *The People of Palestine* (Philadelphia: Lippincott, 1921; repr., Westport, CT: Hyperion, 1976); **D. L. Green, D. P. Van Gerven and G. J. Armelagos,** "Life and Death in Ancient Population: Bones of Contention in Paleodemography," *Human Evolution* 1 (1986) 193-207; **R. Griffeth and C. G. Thomas,** eds., *The City-State in Five Cultures* (Santa Barbara, CA: ABC-CLIO, 1981); **M. I. Gruber,** "Social Institutions: Private Life in Canaan and Ancient Israel," *CANE* 1.633-50; **Z. Herzog,** *The Archaeology of the City: Urban Planning in Ancient Israel and Its Social Implications* (Monograph Series of the Sonia and Marco Nadler Institute of Archaeology 13; Tel Aviv: Emery and Claire Yass Archaeology Press, 1997); **K. Hoglund,** "The Achaemenid Context," in *Second Temple Studies,* 1: *Persian Period,* ed. P. R. Davies (JSOTSup 117; Sheffield: JSOT, 1991) 54-72; **R. Kana'an and A. McQuitty,** "The Architecture of Al-Qasr on the Kerak Plateau," *PEQ* 126 (1994) 127-51; **J. Killen,** "Records of Sheep and Goats at Mycenaean Knossos and Pylos," *Bulletin of Sumerian Agriculture* 7 (1993) 209-18; **P. J. King and L. E. Stager,** *Life in Biblical Israel* (LAI 8; Louisville: Westminster/John Knox, 2001); **L. Marfoe,** "The Integrative Transformation," *BASOR* 234 (1979) 1-42; **V. H. Matthews and D. C. Benjamin,** *Social World of Ancient Israel, 1250-587 BCE* (Peabody, MA: Hendrickson, 1993); **A. Mazar,** *Archaeology of the Land of the Bible, 10,000-586 B.C.E.* (ABRL; New York: Doubleday, 1990); idem, "The Iron Age I," in *The Archaeology of Ancient Israel,* ed. A. Ben-Tor (New Haven: Yale University Press, 1992) 258-301; **R. D. Miller II,** "A Gazetteer of Iron I Sites in the North-Central Highlands of Palestine," in *Preliminary Excavation Reports and Other Archaeological Investigations: Tell Qarqur, Iron I Sites in the North-Central Highlands of Palestine,* ed. N. Lapp (AASOR 56; Boston: American Schools of Oriental Research, 2003a) 143-218; idem, "Modeling the Farm in Early Iron Age Israel," in *Life and Culture in the Ancient Near East,* ed. R. E. Averbeck, M. W. Chavalas and D. B. Weisberg (Bethesda, MD: CDL Press, 2003b) 289-310; idem, *Chieftains of the Highland Clans: A History of Israel in the 12th and 11th Centuries B.C.* (The Bible in Its World; Grand Rapids: Eerdmans, 2005); **O. Negbi,** "Were There Sea People in the Central Jordan Valley at the Transition from Bronze Age to the Iron Age?" *TA* 18 (1991) 205-43; **R. Neu,** *Von der Anarchie zum Staat: Entwicklungsgeschichte Israels vom Nomadtum zur Monarchie im Speigel der Ethnosoziologie* (Neukirchen-Vlyun: Neukirchener Verlag, 1992); **H. M. Niemann,** *Herrschaft, Königtum und Staat: Skizzen zur soziokulturellen Entwicklung im monarchischen Israel* (FAT 6; Tubingen: Mohr Siebeck, 1993); **D. B. Redford,** *Egypt and Canaan in the New Kingdom* (Beer-Sheva 4; Beer-Sheva: Ben-Gurion University of the Negev Press, 1990); **B. Routledge,** "More Equal Than Others? Big Houses and Small Towns in the Southern Levantine Iron Age," *NEA* 66 (forthcoming); **C. Schäfer-Lichtenberger,** *Stadt und Eidgenossenschaft im Alten Testament: Eine Auseinandersetzung mit Max Webers Studie "Das antike Judentum"* (BZAW 156; Berlin: de Gruyter, 1983); **J. D. Schloen,** *The House of the Father as Fact and Symbol: Patrimonialism in Ugarit and the Ancient Near East* (Studies in the Archaeology and History of the Levant 2; Winona Lake, IN: Eisenbrauns,

2001); **I. Singer,** "Egyptians, Canaanites, and Philistines in the Period of the Emergence of Israel," in *From Nomadism to Monarchy: Archaeological and Historical Aspects of Early Israel,* ed. I. Finkelstein and N. Naᵓaman (Washington: Biblical Archaeology Society, 1994) 282-338; **J. Smith and J. Oeppen,** "Estimating Numbers of Kin in Historical England Using Demographic Microsimulation," in *Old and New Methods in Historical Demography,* ed. D. Reher and R. Schofield (Oxford: Clarendon Press, 1993) 280-317; **L. E. Stager,** "The Archaeology of the Family in Ancient Israel," *BASOR* 260 (1985) 1-35; idem, "Ashkelon," *NEAEHL* 1.103-12; **G. Stanhill,** "The Fellah's Farm," *Agro-Ecosystems* 4 (1978) 433-48; **J. Weinstein,** "The Collapse of the Egyptian Empire in the Twelfth Century B.C.," in *The Crisis Years: The Twelfth Century B.C. from Beyond the Danube to the Tigris,* ed. W. A. Ward and M. S. Joukowsky (Dubuque, IA: Kendall/Hunt, 1992) 142-50; **T. M. Willis,** *The Elders of the City: A Study of the Elders-Laws in Deuteronomy* (SBLMS 55; Atlanta: Scholars Press, 2001); **J. Zorn,** "Estimating the Population Size of Ancient Settlements," *BASOR* 295 (1994) 31-48; **U. Zwingenberger,** *Dorfkultur der frühen Eisenzeit in Mittelpalästina* (OBO 180; Göttingen: Vandenhoeck & Ruprecht, 2001). R. D. Miller II

CIVIL OFFICIALS. *See* STATE OFFICIALS.

CLAN. *See* ISRAELITE SOCIETY.

CONCUBINES, ROYAL. *See* ROYAL FAMILY.

CONQUEST. *See* HISTORY OF ISRAEL 1: SETTLEMENT PERIOD; LAND.

CORVÉE. *See* TAXES, TAXATION.

COURT HISTORY OF DAVID. *See* SAMUEL, BOOKS OF.

CREATOR. *See* GOD; MIRACLES.

CULTIC BUILDINGS. *See* ARCHITECTURE.

CUPBEARER. *See* NEHEMIAH.

CURRENCY. *See* TRADE AND TRAVEL.

CYRUS. *See* EZRA AND NEHEMIAH, BOOKS OF; HISTORY OF ISRAEL 7: PERSIAN PERIOD; PERSIA, PERSIANS.

CYRUS DECREE. *See* HISTORY OF ISRAEL 7: PERSIAN PERIOD; PERSIA, PERSIANS.

D

DAGAN/DAGON. *See* CANAAN, CANAANITES; CANAANITE GODS AND RELIGION.

DAMASCUS. *See* ARAM, DAMASCUS AND SYRIA.

DAN

Biblical Dan, also known as Laish or Leshem before it was appropriated by the Israelites in the early Iron Age, is identified with Tell el-Qadi at the foot of Mount Hermon in the north of Israel. The location of the largest spring in the Middle East and one of the sources of the River Jordan, Dan has been occupied since the Neolithic period in the fifth millennium BCE and features prominently in the Bible. It defines the northern border of Israel throughout the Iron Age (*see* Geographical Extent of Israel), when it served as a prominent religious and political center in the period of the monarchy, and both the biblical and archaeological records testify to Dan's complex relationship with Israel's neighbors to the north, particularly Aram-Damascus. Israelite Dan was destroyed by the *Assyrians in the late eighth century BCE, and after a brief renascence as an Assyrian town it endured a long decline in size and significance until it was finally abandoned in the fourth century CE.

1. Biblical References
2. Excavations
3. Middle Bronze Age (c. 2000-1550 BCE)
4. Late Bronze Age (c. 1550-1200 BCE)
5. Iron Age I (c. 1200-1000 BCE)
6. Iron Age II (c. 1000-732 BCE)
7. From the Assyrian Occupation to the Roman Period (Seventh Century BCE to Fourth Century CE)

1. Biblical References.

Early references in Genesis 14:14 and Deuteronomy 34:1 refer to Dan as a distant place, but earlier references come in Joshua and Judges where the town's Canaanite identity as Laish or Leshem is revealed. In Joshua 19:47 we are told of the migration of the tribe of Dan from the coastal plain north to Leshem, which they attacked and conquered, naming it after Dan their forefather. The story is repeated in greater detail in Judges 18. Soon the name became synonymous with the northern extent of the country, as in the phrase "from Dan to Beersheba" (Judg 20:1; 1 Sam 3:20; 2 Sam 3:10 etc.) or later, in Chronicles, "from Beersheba to Dan" (1 Chron 21:2; 2 Chron 30:5). Dan as metaphoric north is reflected in the prophets too, as Jeremiah, Ezekiel and Amos imply that Dan defines the northern border of Israel (Jer 4:15; 8:16; Ezek 48:1-2, 32; Amos 8:14).

During the united monarchy the Danites declared loyalty to *David in his civil war against the house of *Saul (1 Chron 12:35). The town is mentioned again during the reign of *Solomon, when a metal craftsman named Huram-Abi was sent by Hiram of Tyre to Jerusalem to work on Solomon's royal buildings. His mother was from Dan, his father from Tyre (2 Chron 2:13-14). In 1 Kings 15:18-20 (also 2 Chron 16:4) Ben Hadad I of Aram was encouraged by Asa king of Judah to attack the northern kingdom of Israel, and he conquered Dan and other nearby towns.

Dan's position as a religious center in the northern kingdom of Israel is first noted in 1 Kings 12:29-30, where Jeroboam son of Nebat erected two shrines with golden calves at Dan and *Bethel. During the reign of Jehu the shrines are referred to again, (2 Kings 10:29) and their presence is alluded to throughout the period of the monarchy in Israel as successive kings are condemned for following the sins of Jeroboam son of Nebat (e.g., 2 Kings 13:2, 11; 14:24; 15:9, 18).

2. Excavations.

A short test excavation at Tell el-Qadi in 1963 by Z. Yeivin of the Israel Department of Antiquities and Museums was followed from 1966 to 1999 by excavations directed by A. Biran, initially under the auspices of the Israel Department of Antiquities and, from 1974 onward, on behalf of the Nelson Glueck School of Biblical Archaeology of the Hebrew Union College in Jerusalem. Excavations resumed in 2005 under the direction of D. Ilan, also of the Hebrew Union College in Jerusalem. Sixteen major strata dating from the Neolithic to the Roman periods have been exposed, and the excavations have confirmed the identification of the site with biblical Dan that was first made by E. Robinson in 1838.

3. Middle Bronze Age (c. 2000-1550 BCE).

Following a period of urban decline that affected the entire region at the end of the third millennium BCE, Dan/Laish became an important urban center during the Middle Bronze Age and is mentioned in the later Egyptian Execration Texts. In stratum XI, dated to the nineteenth to eighteenth centuries BCE, a large earthen rampart was thrown up around the entire tell. It covered and sloped down on both sides of a solid stone core 10.5 m high, so that at its base the rampart was some 50 m wide.

A triple-arched mud-brick gate uncovered in Area K in the east of the site was built into the rampart. The gate, preserved almost to its original height, stood about 7 m high, with a passageway of 10.5 m. Flanked by four towers, two inside the town and two outside, the gate was built of sun-baked mud-bricks on a stone foundation. The walls were originally covered with a white plaster. It was approached from both sides by several stone steps. The gate went out of use after a generation or two, and was deliberately buried in the rampart, thereby preserving it almost completely.

There is no evidence of a wall on top of the rampart. Inside the ramparts domestic structures and several tombs were excavated. The latter included chamber tombs built with basalt slabs for containing adult remains, stone-built cist tombs for older children, and jar burials beneath the floors of houses that contained infant and even fetal remains.

The Middle Bronze Age settlement was destroyed violently by fire in the sixteenth century BCE.

4. Late Bronze Age (c. 1550-1200 BCE).

The city was rebuilt on the ruins of the destroyed Middle Bronze Age town, and although Dan is listed by Tutmoses III as one of the cities defeated in his Canaanite campaign of c. 1468 BCE, it appears not to have suffered the gradual decline throughout this period that beset settlements further south.

One notable industry that arises during the Late Bronze Age is metallurgy, and evidence particularly of the resmelting of scrap copper and bronze was found in the south and northeast of the mound. Metalworking at Dan continues into the Iron Age, providing an element of continuity between the Canaanite and Israelite settlements there.

The wealth of at least a section of Laish society was observed in a large stone-built tomb excavated in the south of the site that became known as the "Mycenaean" tomb. It was in use from the late fourteenth to the early thirteenth century BCE, and contained the remains of some forty men, women and children who were buried there over two generations. The rich assemblage of artifacts from the tomb included a large number of local and imported vessels, and was distinguished by twenty-eight Mycenaean vessels. Other items included bronze tools and weapons, gold and silver jewelry, alabaster objects, carved ivories and beads.

5. Iron Age I (c. 1200-1000 BCE).

The transition from Bronze to Iron Age at Dan is characterized by a thin destruction layer discerned in several parts of the site that is followed by a transformation in character and material culture. The most striking feature of the new level, stratum VI, is a large number of deep storage pits, some stone-lined, that contained a variety of ceramic vessels, particularly cooking pots and storage jars. These included both local "Galilean" pithoi and the collared-rim type that is so predominant in the central hill country to the south, and typical of the Israelite settlement there and at such sites as *Hazor and *Megiddo in the Iron Age I. The destruction of Late Bronze Age Laish at the start of the twelfth century BCE and its resettlement by people using pits and collared-rim jars may reflect archaeologically the migration to the site and its conquest by elements of the tribe of Dan described in Joshua 19:47 and Judges 18.

The metallurgy industry continued in this

early phase of the Iron Age I in the south of the tell, where it was characterized by a small shrine that contained several ritual artifacts, including a cylindrical model with cultic connotations similar to others from Kamid el-Loz to the north in the Lebanese Beqaa and Tell Deir ʿAlla in the Jordan Valley.

The pits of the first settlement of the Israelite period gave way later in the twelfth century BCE to a better developed town with stone-built houses that lasted well into the eleventh century BCE before it was destroyed violently by fire.

6. Iron Age II (c. 1000-732 BCE).

Although the destruction debris was found in all areas of the site, and in some places was a meter or more deep, the site was not abandoned. Rather, the late eleventh and tenth centuries BCE represent a period of rebuilding and consolidation at the site. The occupants reused many walls from the destroyed stratum V buildings, and the material culture displays significant continuity from before, together with indications of renewed influence from the Phoenician world.

A new phase of construction toward the end of the tenth century BCE signals a change in the administration of the town. Three major building levels, strata IVA, III and II, define the period of the Divided Monarchy and the northern kingdom of Israel. These Israelite levels at Dan are characterised by growth and prosperity that is most dramatically illustrated by the high place in the north and the city gate complex in the south of the site.

6.1. The High Place at Dan. The high place was built into the inner slope of the Middle Bronze Age rampart and looking north toward Mount Hermon. The three successive levels uncovered there were labelled by the excavator "Bamah" A to C, and attributed by him to three prominent kings of Israel in the late tenth, ninth and eighth centuries BCE respectively (Biran 1994).

6.1.1. Bamah A. The earliest level of the cult center is dominated by a platform measuring at least 18 x 7 m that is built of large semi-dressed travertine blocks. To its south was a complex of storerooms and other structures that included an ashlar-paved altar platform and a libation installation or olive press. A rich assemblage of pottery and other finds dated the complex to the tenth and early ninth centuries. The construction of Bamah A is credited to King Jeroboam I,

who built shrines at Dan and Bethel following his rebellion against Jerusalem and his establishment of the northern kingdom (1 Kings 12:29). This level at the cult site, as elsewhere on the mound, was destroyed by fire, perhaps by the Aramean king Ben Hadad I (1 Kings 15:20, 2 Chron 6:14).

6.1.2. Bamah B. The reconstruction of the high place to a new design in the ninth century BCE has been ascribed to King Ahab, again due to the dating of the pottery assemblage from this phase. The platform in the north was rebuilt on a larger scale with bossed limestone ashlar headers and stretchers with wooden beams at regular intervals. This style is characteristic of Israelite royal buildings of the ninth and eighth centuries BCE at such sites as Megiddo and *Samaria, and is reminiscent of the biblical description of the construction of royal buildings in Jerusalem during the reign of Solomon (1 Kings 7:9-12). The podium of Bamah B measured 18.7 x 18.3 m, and was raised at least 3 m above the surrounding courtyard. Wall stubs on its rear half indicated that at least part of the podium served as the foundation of a building.

The altar platform in front of the podium was also rebuilt on a larger scale, and the whole cultic precinct was enclosed on three sides by a series of narrow chambers. The courtyard that surrounded the altar and podium was defined by a thick yellow travertine floor created by on-site work by stonemasons during the reconstruction of the complex.

6.1.3. Bamah C. The final phase of the Israelite cult center is dated to the early eighth century BCE and reflects the renewed influence and prosperity of the northern kingdom during the reign of Jeroboam II. The large podium that dominated the precinct was augmented by the construction of a monumental staircase 8 m wide on its south side, offering direct access from the courtyard. The altar platform at the foot of the staircase was transformed. A new massive four-horned altar 3 m high, with steps in the southwest and northeast corners, was built over the earlier level and was surrounded by an ashlar enclosure wall 14 x 12.5 m with entrances in the south and east. Further important finds were made in one of the long rooms defining the west side of the cultic enclosure, including a low altar 1.03 x 1.03 m built into the floor, three iron shovels, two small incense altars, an incised bronze bowl and a bronze sceptre head.

6.2. The Israelite City Gate. The ninth-century city gate and fortifications of stratum III in the south of the mound were built over the earlier stratum IV remains, which were not recovered in any detail. The well-preserved stratum III gate complex is a monumental structure that had at its heart a four-chambered gate measuring 29.5 x 17.8 m. The road into the city passed through the gate before turning north and climbing steeply into the town. The road continued all the way across the tell to the high place. Later in stratum II, in the eighth century BCE, a smaller inner gate was added at the top of the slope.

Outside the main gate was an impressive courtyard enclosed by the city wall and a single-entrance outer gate. Inside this courtyard, facing the outer gate, was an ashlar "canopy structure," perhaps the platform for a throne, with three associated decorated stone column bases. Nearby were a bench built against an inner wall and a small shrine of five standing stones with an offering table in front of them. Their significance was not determined. However, some 40 m beyond the outer gate another set of five standing stones against the outer face of the city wall echoed the set in the courtyard of the gate. These too dated to stratum III. Later, in stratum II of the eighth century BCE, a third set of five standing stones was added at the top of the slope outside the small inner gate leading into the city.

Beyond the outer gate was a large paved plaza that separated the gate complex from a block of extramural buildings identified by the excavator as *ḥûṣṣôt*, or a market place, such as those referred to in 1 Kings 20:34. Among the many significant finds from these buildings are two bronze plaques incised with Assyrian cultic imagery. They are indicative of the complex cultural and religious relationship between Dan and its northern neighbours throughout the Iron Age II period.

6.3. The "House of David" Inscription. In 1993 and 1994 fragments of a stela inscribed in Aramaic were discovered in the area of the outer plaza and *ḥûṣṣôt*. The text, which is incomplete, describes the conquests of a king and mentions the king of Israel and the (king) of the House of David. Although the stela has been the subject of controversy, there is broad scholarly agreement (Schniedewind 1996) with the conclusions of the excavator that the carving of the inscrip-

tion dates to the mid- to late-ninth century BCE, that its author was Hazael of Damascus, and that the kings of Israel and Judah should be identified as Jehoram and Ahaziah respectively. The events described in the stela refer to *Jehu's rebellion in Israel detailed in 2 Kings 9.

The stela is significant for several reasons, not least for its reference to the "House of David" and its alternative perspective on the nature of Jehu's *coup d'état*.

The final Israelite level at Dan, stratum II, was destroyed by fire in the second half of the eighth century BCE. This destruction should probably be attributed to the violent campaign of Tiglath-Pileser III (also known as Pul; 2 Kings 15:19, 29; 1 Chron 5:26) in 732 BCE that saw the conquest and annexation of the northern part of the kingdom of Israel.

7. From the Assyrian Occupation to the Roman Period (Seventh Century BCE to Fourth Century CE).

Following the Assyrian destruction Dan was resettled. New buildings, an orthogonal street pattern, evidence of widespread trade relations, and the ongoing use of the cult center in the north of the site all testify to a period of relative prosperity under *Assyrian rule.

In the south of the mound, the gate area was not redeveloped, but above the destruction debris that lay over the plaza and *ḥûṣṣôt*, a small shrine was excavated from this phase that consisted of three basalt standing stones behind a flagstone pavement. In front of one of the stones was a basalt bowl lying on a decorated capital that served as an offering table.

Sporadic settlement followed the decline of the Assyrian empire in the seventh century BCE. During the Hellenistic period the cult center was again redeveloped, and a bilingual dedicatory inscription in Greek and *Aramaic dated to the third to second centuries BCE was found there, which stated, "To the god who is in Dan."

Later, in the Roman period, Dan was supplanted in importance as a cult center by nearby Baneas, and the site was finally abandoned in the fourth century CE.

See also BEERSHEBA; GEOGRAPHICAL EXTENT OF ISRAEL; NON-ISRAELITE WRITTEN SOURCES: SYRO-PALESTINIAN.

BIBLIOGRAPHY. **A. Biran,** *Biblical Dan* (Jerusalem: Israel Exploration Society and the Hebrew Union College—Jewish Institute of Religion,

1994); idem, "Dan," *NEAEHL* 1:323-32; idem, "Sacred Spaces: of Standing Stones, High Places and Cult Objects at Tel Dan," *BAR* 24:5 (1998) 39-45, 70-72; idem, "Two Bronze Plaques and the *Hussot* of Dan," *IEJ* 49.1-2 (1999) 43-54; **A. Biran and R. Ben-Dov,** *Dan II: A Chronicle of the Excavations and the Late Bronze Age "Mycenaean" Tomb* (Jerusalem: Nelson Glueck School of Biblical Archaeology, Hebrew Union College-Jewish Institute of Religion, 2002); **A. Biran, D. Ilan and R. Greenberg,** *Dan I: A Chronicle of the Excavations, the Pottery Neolithic, the Early Bronze Age and the Middle Bronze Age Tombs* (Jerusalem: Nelson Glueck School of Biblical Archaeology, Hebrew Union College-Jewish Institute of Religion, 1996); **A. Biran and J. Naveh,** "An Aramaic Stele Fragment from Tel Dan," *IEJ* 43.2-3 (1993) 81-98; idem, "The Tel Dan Inscription: A New Fragment," *IEJ* 45 (1993) 1-18; **D. Ilan,** "Dan," *OEANE* 2:107-12; idem, "Mortuary Practices at Tel Dan in the Middle Bronze Age: a Reflection of Canaanite Society and Ideology," in *The Archaeology of Death in the Ancient Near East,* ed. S. Campbell and A. Green (Oxbow Monograph 51; Oxford: Oxbow, 1995) 117-37; **W. Schniedewind,** "Tel Dan Stela: New Light on Aramaic and Jehu's Revolt," *BASOR* 302 (1996) 75-90.

G. Gilmour

DARIUS. *See* EZRA AND NEHEMIAH, BOOKS OF; HISTORY OF ISRAEL 7: PERSIAN PERIOD; PERSIA, PERSIANS.

DATES. *See* AGRICULTURE AND ANIMAL HUSBANDRY.

DAUGHTERS, ROYAL. *See* ROYAL FAMILY.

DAVID

David son of Jesse (reigned c. 1010-970 BCE) was Israel's second king, who succeeded *Saul and founded a royal dynasty that lasted until the Babylonian exile (586 BCE). David's son *Solomon ruled over all Israel, and David's descendants after Solomon ruled over the southern kingdom of Judah.

This article surveys and evaluates the accounts of David in the OT Historical Books, along with relevant extrabiblical data.

1. David in the Historical Books
2. David in Extrabiblical Sources
3. Was the Biblical David a Historical Figure?
4. Conclusion

1. David in the Historical Books.
The main accounts of David are found in 1-2 Samuel, 1 Kings and 1 Chronicles. There are also brief references in Ruth, Ezra and Nehemiah.

1.1. The Books of Samuel.
1.1.1. Summary. David is introduced in 1 Samuel 16 as the man chosen by God to replace Saul as king (see 1 Sam 15:28). 1 Samuel 17—31 describes David's rise to prominence in Israel during Saul's lifetime. 2 Samuel 1—7 tells how he became king over Judah and then all Israel, capturing *Jerusalem, which became his royal city (2 Sam 5:6-16), and receiving divine promises about the dynasty that he would found (2 Sam 7). He defeated the Philistines (2 Sam 5:17-25), breaking their previous hold over Israel (2 Sam 8:1), and he won victories over other neighboring peoples (2 Sam 8:2-8; 10; 1 Kings 11:14-18), making some of them his subjects. He was on friendly terms with Hiram of Tyre (2 Sam 5:11). Royal administration, already found under Saul (1 Sam 14:50-52), developed under David (2 Sam 8:15-18; 20:23-26; it would develop further under Solomon [1 Kings 4]). The later years of David's reign were marred by family conflict and civil war (2 Sam 13—18), though peace of a sort was restored (2 Sam 19—20). 2 Samuel 21—24 is a coda to the account of David as king that brings together varied material, some of it relating to earlier periods of David's reign.

1.1.2. What Kind of Account and Sources? What kind of text is the account of David in 1-2 Samuel? How are we to interpret it?

It is, first, a literary masterpiece, "probably the greatest single narrative representation in antiquity of a human life evolving by slow stages through time, shaped and altered by the pressures of political life, public institutions, family, the impulses of body and spirit, the eventual sad decay of the flesh," a brilliant example of "the Bible's astringent narrative economy, its ability to define characters and etch revelatory dialogue in a few telling strokes" (Alter, ix).

Second, it is a complex account. It handles topics (the Israelite monarchy, the character and acts of David) about which the writer apparently was ambivalent, so that no simple evaluation was possible.

Third, the account of David in 1-2 Samuel is a literary unity. Whether or not it is in fact the work of one person, it is sufficiently coherent that it could be (hence the references to "the writer" of this account in what follows).

Many would dispute this last statement. Until recently it was widely held that the books of Samuel are composite, fashioned from different sources that can be at least partially reconstructed today on the basis of their divergent viewpoints. Scholars accordingly spoke of an "Ark Narrative" (1 Sam 4—6; 2 Sam 6), describing the fortunes of the ark in the days of *Samuel, Saul and David; of a "History of David's Rise" (1 Sam 16:14—2 Sam 5:25); of a "Succession Narrative" (2 Sam 9—20; 1 Kings 1—2), whose theme is the question of who will succeed David. Many still hold these views, but others argue that the different sections of 1-2 Samuel are better integrated with each other than such views would imply (Gordon 1984; Alter, ix-xiv). Even the common argument that 1 Samuel contains two accounts of how Saul first came to meet David (1 Sam 16:18-23; 17:12, 55-58) has been questioned (Provan, Long and Longman, 222-24).

Space does not permit an argument of these issues here. This article assumes the view that the narrative of David in 1-2 Samuel is a single, complex account, and that whatever sources may underlie this narrative, and however many people were involved in its composition, the earlier stages of its literary history are no longer accessible to us.

We can, of course, speculate about the traditions available to the writer. Accounts of David's military campaigns (2 Sam 8; 10) and lists of his officials and soldiers (2 Sam 20:23-26; 23:8-39) may have existed in official records. But this explanation hardly applies to many other incidents—for instance, the many apparently private dialogues (e.g., 1 Sam 20:1-23; 26:14-25; 2 Sam 6:20-22). Are we to imagine the writer as a contemporary or near contemporary of David, collecting traditions relating to David, perhaps interviewing those who had been associated with David, or even David himself? This is not impossible. If David was such as he is described in 1-2 Samuel, then his contemporaries and later generations may well have wanted to preserve traditions about him. But the books of Samuel, in common with other OT Historical Books, contain no statement of historical method. And even allowing that the writer had extensive traditions available, how did he use them? Did he sometimes produce what Gordon (1994, 297) terms "faction"—artful reconstructions (with possibly only a slender basis in tradition) of the

"kind of thing" that must have been said or done on particular occasions? We cannot answer these questions. The writer or writers have effaced themselves entirely, leaving not even their names behind, still less any description of sources and method.

1.1.3. Propaganda? If we can say little about the sources for the account in 1-2 Samuel, are there other grounds for accepting it as reliable? To answer this question we must examine in more detail how David is portrayed.

At many points David is presented favorably—for example, in the accounts of his battle with *Goliath (1 Sam 17) and of his flight from Saul. The account of his early years as king (2 Sam 5—10) shows how his rule brought great blessing to Israel (see 2 Sam 5:12). 2 Samuel 7, the climax of the account of David's rise, suggests the theological and historical significance of what David accomplished: he gave Israel the "rest" (security) in Canaan that Moses had foretold, succeeding where earlier leaders had failed (2 Sam 7:1, 10-11; cf. Deut 12:10). The narrator notes that David was widely accepted as the only suitable successor to Saul (2 Sam 5:1-2; cf. 1 Sam 18:16). Even Jonathan and Saul acknowledged this (1 Sam 23:17; 24:20).

Taken together, these features suggest that the account is partly intended as pro-Davidic apologetic. David, after all, could be described as a usurper, for he was not Saul's son; it is not surprising that the account explains why he was justified in assuming power and defends the steps by which he did so.

A comparison can be drawn with the Apology of Hattushili, a Hittite text dating from the thirteenth century BCE, in which Hattushili describes how he became king of the Hittites, deposing his nephew Urhiteshub. The Apology throughout emphasizes the rightness of Hattushili's actions, and how the goddess Ishtar guided and blessed his life (*COS* 1.77:199-204). In a similar way, the account of David's rise does all it can to vindicate him: God clearly was with him from the beginning (1 Sam 16—17); David was loyal to Saul, and fled from him only in self-preservation (1 Sam 18—20); he gathered about him a group that could have been described as rebels (1 Sam 22:2), but he never led them against Saul, even though he had opportunity (1 Sam 24; 26); he served a Philistine king for a while (1 Sam 27—29), but that was only to escape Saul (1 Sam 27:1-4), and while in Philistine service he never attacked Israelites (1 Sam 27:5-12); he was not at Gilboa when Saul died (1 Sam 29—31); he did not order the deaths of Abner and Ishbosheth, and he was displeased when he learned of them (2 Sam 3:6—4:12). In these and other ways the account defends David against possible charges of wrongdoing (McKenzie, 32-34).

Some are suspicious of this apologetic intent: why such strenuous assertions of David's innocence unless the underlying reality was less acceptable? Thus B. Halpern (73-93) speaks of the "ten little indians," people whom David probably killed or had killed, the contrary claims of the account notwithstanding: Nabal (1 Sam 25); Saul and his sons at Gilboa (1 Sam 31); Abner (2 Sam 3); Ishbosheth (2 Sam 4); Saul's other descendants (2 Sam 21); Amnon (2 Sam 13); Absalom (2 Sam 18); Amasa (2 Sam 20); Uriah (2 Sam 11).

S. L. McKenzie (89-127) follows a similar approach. McKenzie (44-45) bases his argument on two principles. The first is a "principle of skepticism": "when some aspect of the biblical story fits a literary or ideological theme we should be skeptical about its historical value" (McKenzie, 44). To this he adds a "principle of analogy": "the past was basically analogous to the present"; in particular, "people of all time have the same basic ambitions and instincts" (McKenzie, 44). Following these principles, he reads the biblical narrative "against the grain," applying the rule *cui bono?* (Who stood to benefit?). If the narrative wants us to believe that David bore no responsibility for an individual's death, even though he benefited from that death, then we should "counter-read" the narrative and conclude that David was after all responsible (McKenzie, 45).

This approach fails to convince partly because it seems overly suspicious. If the biblical account is suspect whenever it attempts to defend David (which is what Halpern's and McKenzie's approaches amount to), then no defense is possible. The account itself tells us that David was accused or at least suspected of wrongdoing during his lifetime (2 Sam 3:37; 16:5-8), and in this situation we might expect some kind of defense of David. To hold David guilty simply because the defense was in fact attempted is to press the "principle of skepticism" too far. Provan, Long and Longman (217-21) note that the "principle of analogy" tends to be

reductionist, casting doubt on any report of unusual (in this context, principled or altruistic) behavior.

This approach, moreover, does not do justice to other parts of the account. Apologetic elements certainly are present in 1-2 Samuel, but some parts of the account cannot easily be explained along these lines. The character of Saul in 1 Samuel is one example. Saul is not a caricature of the type that we might expect in a purely apologetic text, but rather is a complex character for whom the narrator seems to have some sympathy.

Above all, 2 Samuel 9—20 contain much negative characterization of David himself, beginning with the incident with Bathsheba and Uriah (2 Sam 11—12) and continuing with a tale of rape and murder within David's family (2 Sam 13—14). The account of the civil war between David and his son Absalom (2 Sam 15—18) puts him in a better light: he submits to God's will (2 Sam 15:26; 16:11-12) and avoids unnecessary destruction (2 Sam 15:14). But this section ends with David prostrated by grief for Absalom and humiliated by Joab's rebuke (2 Sam 18:33—19:7). His return to Jerusalem is marred by tribal discontent (2 Sam 19:41-43), and this section of narrative closes with Amasa's murder and the sordid compromise that ended Sheba's rebellion (2 Sam 20). In these chapters David clearly is under God's judgment (see 2 Sam 12:10).

So obviously does 2 Samuel 9—20 highlight David's shortcomings that J. Van Seters (277-91) regards them (along with 1 Kings 1—2) as a later interpolation designed to undermine the positive presentation of David elsewhere in 1-2 Samuel. But this does not necessarily follow. More plausibly, the writer had a nuanced view of David, wanting to give due weight both to David's achievements and to his shortcomings (Gordon [1994, 288-95] notes other problems with Van Seters's approach).

In any case, negative portrayal of David is not restricted to 2 Samuel 9—20. In the "coda" of 2 Samuel 21—24 David is presented both at his best (2 Sam 22: David's vindication as God's chosen king; 2 Sam 23:1-7: David as righteous ruler) and at close to his worst (2 Sam 24: the account of David's pride and its consequences; note also the pointed reference to Uriah at the end of the list of David's warriors in 2 Sam 23:39). (For further discussion of the portrayal of David in 1—2 Samuel, and particularly in

2 Samuel 21—24, see Satterthwaite.)

1.1.4. A Theological History. It seems unlikely, then, that the "literary or ideological theme" (McKenzie's term) of this account can simply be identified as the vindication of David. The books of Samuel are best seen as a subtle theological reflection on the implications of the coming of the monarchy to Israel, which acknowledges both gains (e.g., greater political stability) and drawbacks (e.g., scope for abuse of power). The portrayal of David fits with this: he is zealous for God's honor, talented and brave, and at his best represents an ideal of Israelite kingship, but he does not always live up to that ideal, and the disappointments of his later years point up some of the problems that later come to haunt the monarchy. The very ambivalence of the account toward David is an argument for its historical reliability. The account cannot simply be treated as heavily biased *propaganda.

1.2. The Books of Kings. 1 Kings 1—2 describes David's last years and Solomon's succession to the throne. They clearly reflect the same misgivings about the monarchy that we noted in the second half of 2 Samuel. The David of 1 Kings 1—2 is a weak old man, whose hesitancy in publicly naming Solomon as his successor gives rise to intrigues (1 Kings 1), and whose last words, a terrible mixture of piety and vindictiveness (1 Kings 2:1-9), lead to Solomon executing Adonijah, Joab and Shimei under dubious circumstances (1 Kings 2:13-46).

Later references to David in the books of Kings are, by contrast, generally positive. 1 Kings 11:14-18 gives further details of David's subjugation of Edom. Other texts mention God's promise to David (1 Kings 6:12; 8:15-26; 9:4-5), cite David as a model of religious faithfulness (1 Kings 11:4-6; 15:4-5; 2 Kings 14:3; 18:3; 22:2) and describe how God spared later kings of Judah "because of David" (1 Kings 11:12-13; 2 Kings 8:19; 19:34).

1.3. The Books of Chronicles.

1.3.1. Comparison with the Books of Samuel and Kings. Many incidents found in 1-2 Samuel are related in similar or nearly identical form in 1 Chronicles 11—29 (e.g., compare 1 Chron 11:1-9 with 2 Sam 5:1-10; 1 Chron 17 with 2 Sam 7). Overall, however, the account of David in 1 Chronicles differs considerably from that in Samuel and Kings.

Large blocks of material in Samuel and Kings are not paralleled in Chronicles. There is almost nothing in 1 Chronicles corresponding to 1 Samuel 16—30 (David's career during Saul's lifetime), 2 Samuel 2—4 (the war between David's and Saul's houses after Saul's death), 2 Samuel 9 (David's kindness to Mephibosheth), 2 Samuel 11 (David's affair with Bathsheba), 2 Samuel 12 (Nathan's prophecy of judgment on David's house), 2 Samuel 13—14 (Tamar's rape and Amnon's murder), 2 Samuel 15—20 (Absalom's revolt and the civil war that followed), 2 Samuel 21:1-14 (the execution of seven of Saul's sons), 2 Samuel 22:1—23:7 (David's song and last words), and 1 Kings 1—2 (the intrigues concerning the succession).

Conversely, there is hardly anything in Samuel and Kings corresponding to 1 Chronicles 12 (the list of those who sided with David during his rise), 1 Chronicles 16:7-43 (David's thanksgiving when the ark came up to Jerusalem; arrangements for the ark and the tabernacle), 1 Chronicles 22 (David's charge to Solomon), 1 Chronicles 23—26 (David's organization of temple staff and duties), 1 Chronicles 27 (army divisions and tribal officers), 1 Chronicles 28:1—29:9 (David's plans for the temple, the collection of materials and money), and 1 Chronicles 29:10-25 (David's prayer; Solomon's anointment as king at a gathering of tribal leaders).

The accounts of David in 1 Chronicles and in Samuel and Kings are to some extent complementary, each filling in gaps left by the other. But in general, David's reign and Solomon's accession read very differently in 1 Chronicles compared to Samuel and Kings. For example, it is an interesting question how to harmonize the accounts of the transition from David to Solomon in Kings and Chronicles: the weak, indecisive and vengeful David of 1 Kings 1—2 seems far removed from the authoritative figure in 1 Chronicles 22 and 28—29 who makes preparations for Solomon's temple, instructs Solomon in his duties, and secures the people's allegiance for him (see Williamson, 151-89; Selman, 210-63).

There are other references to David in Chronicles. The genealogies of 1 Chronicles 1—9 trace David's line down to the postexilic period (1 Chron 3:1-24). Like Kings, Chronicles contains references to David in its accounts of later kings. These references are consistent with the account in 1 Chronicles 11—29, focusing on David's arrangements for the temple and temple worship (2 Chron 2:7; 8:14; 23:18), on God's promise to him (2 Chron 1:9; 6:4-17; 23:3), according to which his descendants are the rightful kings of all Israel (2 Chron 10:19; 13:5-8) and on his religious faithfulness (2 Chron 28:1; 34:2).

1.3.2. Sources and Method. Chronicles dates from after the exile (1 Chron 3:17-24; 9:1-44), and it is a retelling of earlier traditions for a postexilic audience (Jones, 92-94). The Chronicler was offering his contemporaries a clear vision of what Israel should be. Central to this vision were the claims that the only viable kingship for the twelve tribes of Israel was that provided by David's line, that the only legitimate place of worship was the Jerusalem temple and that both these points had always been true, even during the time of the divided monarchy, when rival kings and worship sites had been available (see 2 Chron 13; 30). The Chronicler regards the promise to David's line as still in force (the small alterations in 1 Chron 17 compared to 2 Sam 7 bring out this point [see Williamson, 132-37]) and sees what God accomplished through David and Solomon as a pledge for his future acts on Israel's behalf (Kelly, 262-64).

In pursuit of his aims the Chronicler produces an account of David that, by comparison with Samuel and Kings, seems extremely one-sided. The books of Samuel present David's rise to power as messy and protracted, and 1 Kings brings out the moral ambiguities of Solomon's succession. 1 Chronicles, by contrast, presents David as the faithful successor to the unfaithful Saul, his leadership being swiftly recognized by the twelve tribes after Saul's death (1 Chron 10—11), and in many cases before that (1 Chron 12:1-22; note verse 22). Solomon's succession is similarly treated as unproblematic, an event for which David made careful preparations (1 Chron 22:2-19; 28:1—29:9) and that was ordained by God (1 Chron 28:5; 29:1).

However, the label "pro-Davidic apologetic" does not fit the account of David in 1 Chronicles any better than it does that in Samuel and Kings, although for different reasons. First, one should distinguish between apologetic for David himself produced at most shortly after his death (see 3.2.3 below) and claims made for the Davidic dynasty several centuries later. Second, and more important, it seems likely that the Chronicler presupposed in his audience knowledge of the traditions in Samuel and Kings (Williamson, 17-23). For example, 1 Chronicles 11:3 describes David being anointed king of Israel "according to the word of the LORD through Samuel," when there has been no previous reference to Samuel (but cf. 1 Sam 13:14). Similarly, the accounts of 1 Chronicles 12:19-22 (David's supporters while on the run) and 1 Chronicles 20:1-3 (the capture of Rabbah) seem hardly coherent to the reader who does not know the fuller story in Samuel. It seems, indeed, that part of the effect of Chronicles depends on the audience's noting what is missing, and thus realizing that the presentation of David is deliberately selective and positive. (But note the view of Auld [34-39], according to whom the accounts of Samuel-Kings and of Chronicles are based on a common text recounting the history of the kings of Judah from David to the fall of Jerusalem, which they have each supplemented independently of the other. If accepted, his view would undermine the last argument. He does not, however, discuss the passages cited above in detail.)

Chronicles' presentation of David might better be described as a theological account designed to make postexilic Israelites reflect on the continuing significance for them of God's choice of David and Jerusalem several centuries before.

1.4. Ezra, Nehemiah, Ruth. The books Ezra and Nehemiah contain only brief references to David. Some of them trace aspects of temple worship back to him (Ezra 3:10; 8:20; Neh 12:24, 36, 45-46; cf. 1 Chronicles). There are also references to Jerusalem as the "city of David" (Neh 3:15; 12:37). The book of Ruth is a narrative about David's ancestors Boaz and Ruth, as the closing verses make clear (Ruth 4:18-22). But David in Ruth 4 is a mere name, and any significance that the reader sees in the references to him depends on knowledge derived elsewhere.

In short, the references to David in Ezra, Nehemiah and Ruth underscore his significance in Israel's history but tell us nothing not already told at greater length in Samuel, Kings and Chronicles.

2. David in Extrabiblical Sources.

We now consider other data relating to David.

2.1. Archaeological Data. Various archaeological findings have been linked to the time of David.

2.1.1. Destruction Levels. A. Mazar (374) notes that *Megiddo (a Canaanite settlement) and Tel Qasile (a Philistine site not referred to in the Bible) apparently were destroyed by fire around 1000 BCE, and suggests that this destruction "can perhaps be attributed to David." To this list K. A. Kitchen (98, 100) adds *Ekron (Tel Miqne), apparently abandoned at the end of the eleventh century BCE, and Beth-Shan, destroyed around 1000 BCE and perhaps resettled by Israelites (see the entries on these sites in *NEAEHL*). That David captured or destroyed these sites would fit with the biblical accounts (e.g., 2 Sam 5:12, 25; 8:1), although the OT does not ascribe such actions to him.

2.1.2. Settlements, Urbanization. Megiddo and Tel Qasile continued to be inhabited after this destruction, although on a more modest scale than previously. These and other settlements, such as those found at Khirbet Dawara (near Michmash) and at Tel *Beersheba, may be dated to the period of David's reign (Mazar, 374).

A series of about fifty small fortified settlements in the central Negev, which follow on a long period in which the region saw no settlement, may date from the period of David and Solomon (Mazar, 390-96). They perhaps were established to secure trade routes through the Negev toward the Red Sea. The dating of the settlements to the time of David and Solomon is, however, disputed (Barkay, 324). More secure perhaps is the dating of a series of fortifications in the Beersheba Valley to the early tenth century BCE. These may plausibly be linked to initiatives of the united monarchy (Herzog).

The period of David and Solomon also saw expanding settlement along the Palestinian coast (Mazar, 389), possibly as a result of the friendly relations between both kings and Phoenicia (2 Sam 5:11; 1 Kings 5:1).

In general, Mazar (387-89) characterizes the period of David and Solomon as one of greater urbanization: many of the small villages of the period of the judges either were abandoned or became towns (see also Kitchen, 154-56). W. G. Dever, drawing on state formation theory, argues that the tenth century BCE saw the emergence of an Israelite state in Palestine. Dever cites the following criteria for state formation: (1) population size; (2) a "hierarchical, urban settlement pattern . . . characterized by regional centers" (Dever, 249); (3) king, bureaucracy, standing army and defense works; (4) evidence of social stratification and trade specialization; (5) the presence of palaces and temples; (6) a "redistributive economic system, based on taxes

and tribute" (Dever, 249); (7) a system of writing. Even taken by itself, the archaeological evidence for tenth-century BCE Palestine meets these criteria, apart from the third, for which the evidence is largely biblical. Note, however, that the chronology on which the approach of Mazar and others is based has been challenged (see 3.1.1 below).

2.1.3. Jerusalem. Many of the preceding findings relate either to developments not specifically described in the OT or apply as much to the period of Solomon as to that of David. One site where we might expect a clear correlation between the biblical accounts and the archaeological record is *Jerusalem. David is said to have captured Jerusalem (previously Jebusite), made it his royal city, and undertaken building works there (2 Sam 5:6-10). However, even on the most optimistic assessment, Jerusalem has yielded few finds that can securely be dated to the early tenth century BCE (Cahill, especially 54-72).

2.2. Inscriptions. Three inscriptions refer, or may refer, to David by name.

2.2.1. Tel Dan Stela. The Tel Dan stela, a fragmentary inscription in Aramaic from Tel Dan, was discovered and published only in the 1990s (for translation, brief discussion and further references see Kitchen, 36-37). In this inscription an Aramean king describes his victory over a "[xxx]ram son of [xxxx] king of Israel" and "[xxx]iah son of [xxxx.xx] ? the house of David" (lines 8 and 9 [missing characters represented by "x" and uncertain character by "?"]). The names of the kings can plausibly be reconstructed with the aid of 2 Kings 8—9 as "Jehoram son of Ahab" and "Ahaziah son of Joram," kings of Israel and Judah respectively, whose deaths after a battle with Hazael of Aram are described in 2 Kings 9. The author of this inscription would then be Hazael, and the inscription would date from 841 BCE or shortly afterwards. The relevant point is the reference to David as the founder of the dynasty of Judah, such that kings of Judah are referred to by a foreign king as belonging to "the house of David."

2.2.2. Mesha Inscription. Part of the damaged line 31 of the inscription of King Mesha of Moab, dating also from the mid-ninth century BCE, has been restored to read "and the house of [Da]vid dwelt in Horonem" (Lemaire, 30-37 [Horonem is in southern Moab]). If this restoration is correct, the text would refer to David as the founder of a royal dynasty.

2.2.3. Shoshenq's Topographical List. An inscription of Pharaoh Shoshenq I commemorating an invasion of Israel in 926/925 BCE lists the places that his army passed through. The section of this list covering southern Judah and the Negev contains a reference to "the heights of *Dwt*." Kitchen (93) suggests that *Dwt* may be the Egyptian equivalent of "David." David is said to have been active in the Negev for some years before he became king (1 Sam 24:1; 27; 30), and this inscription, dating from about fifty years after David's death, may echo that historical connection.

No inscriptions have been found in Israel that mention David. This is not hard to explain. Inscriptions promulgated by David, Solomon or later kings of Judah are unlikely to have survived the invasions and occupations of later centuries, particularly in Jerusalem, the site where such inscriptions are most likely to have stood at one time. Other comparable first-millennium kingdoms have left similarly scanty remains: Aram-Damascus, Aleppo, Moab, Ammon, Edom, Tyre and Sidon (Kitchen, 90-91).

3. Was the Biblical David a Historical Figure?

The archaeological and inscriptional evidence is interesting, but by itself it would tell us nothing about David beyond his name and the fact that he founded a royal house. For this reason, modern accounts of David's reign until recently tended more or less to follow the books of Samuel (supplemented with details from Chronicles), and accommodated the extrabiblical data within the framework of the biblical accounts (e.g., Bright, 195-211; Herrmann, 145-73). Even J. M. Miller and J. H. Hayes (149-88), who suspect the presence of legendary elements in the biblical accounts, still largely followed them in their presentation. But recently questions have been raised against this procedure: can the biblical accounts of David be used in this way?

3.1. Arguments Against.

3.1.1. Archaeology. We have noted the paucity of archaeological evidence relating to tenth-century BCE Jerusalem. This may seem to undermine the claims of the biblical accounts. Thus M. Steiner's survey essay concludes, "It seems unlikely that [tenth-century BCE Jerusalem] was the centre of a large state, the capital of the united monarchy of the biblical texts. It was too small and unimpressive to conform to biblical

descriptions of the city under David and Solomon" (Steiner, 363; cf. Killebrew, 345).

I. Finkelstein (cf. Finkelstein and Silberman, 340-44) has proposed a revised chronology for Palestinian archaeology in the twelfth to the eighth centuries BCE, which would mean that many of the findings previously linked to the period of the united monarchy (see 2.1.2 above) are to be dated to the ninth century BCE, thus removing a substantial support for the biblical picture of the kingdoms of David and Solomon. Finkelstein and Silberman (153-59) argue that there never was a united monarchy: the kingdoms of Israel and Judah were always separate, and they developed along independent lines. The proposal for a revised chronology has, however, been strongly contested (Kitchen, 139-46; Halpern, 451-78).

3.1.2. Literary/Historical Arguments. Archaeologically based arguments of this sort are combined with arguments concerning the nature of the biblical accounts of David, according to which they are tendentious creations of a later period, variously the seventh century BCE (Finkelstein and Silberman, 144), the Persian period (Davies, 72-89) or even the Hellenistic period (Thompson, 207-10), invented in support of political/religious aims relating to the writers' own day, and are better viewed as evidence not for the tenth century BCE, but for the period when they were actually composed. Thus T. L. Thompson links the accounts of David and Solomon with the aims of the Hasmonean rulers of the mid-second century BCE and argues that "the Bible's stories of Saul, David and Solomon aren't about history at all . . . to treat them as if they were history is to misunderstand them" (Thompson, 206).

A full discussion of the issues raised by this approach is not possible here (see the extensive treatment by Provan, Long and Longman, 3-104). We simply note some arguments that have been advanced in support of the biblical account.

3.2. Counterarguments.

3.2.1. Jerusalem. The lack of substantial tenth-century BCE remains at Jerusalem may not be a good argument against the site having functioned as David's capital. Many parts of the ancient city have been built over by modern dwellings or are otherwise inaccessible to excavation (e.g., the Temple Mount). Jerusalem has suffered much destruction and rebuilding during its long history, so perhaps we should not expect much of tenth-century BCE Jerusalem to have survived down to modern times. Few remains of Bronze Age Jerusalem (1550-1200 BCE) have been discovered, and yet the Amarna letters from Jerusalem (nos. 285-90 [Moran]) indicate that it was a regional center for Egyptian rule in the fourteenth century BCE. This being so, the absence of remains relating to the tenth century BCE need not rule out the possibility of Jerusalem having acted as the center of David's administration (Kitchen, 150-54; but note the divergent views of Steiner, 349-51).

3.2.2. Parallels to David's Empire. David's "empire" as depicted in 2 Samuel 8 and 10 is not impossible in the tenth-century BCE Levant (Kitchen, 98-104). It is said to have consisted of a heartland (Israel), conquered territories under Israel's control (Edom, Moab, Aram-Damascus and perhaps Zobah) and subject allies (Hamath, Ammon and perhaps Geshur)—a substantial territory, but not so huge as to place it in the realm of legend. Kitchen notes evidence for other empires of a similar size and structure in the Levant in the twelfth to ninth centuries BCE: Tarhuntassa, Carchemish, Aram-Zobah. This was, after all, the period when the great powers of the Late Bronze Age (Egypt, Assyria and Babylon) were in decline (the Hittite kingdom in Anatolia had come to an end entirely), and when smaller states for a while had a chance to flourish. Furthermore, against the argument that tenth-century BCE Jerusalem was too small to have served as the center of a Davidic empire, it can be maintained that it would not be unprecedented for an empire in its early stages to be governed from a relatively small city (Kitchen, 154).

3.2.3. Retrojection from a Later Period? Lastly, against the view that the biblical David is an invention dating a number of centuries after the time he is supposed to have lived, a number of scholars argue that the accounts in 1-2 Samuel are not what we might have expected from a Persian- or Hellenistic-period writing. Halpern (57-72) lists a number of historical and linguistic details that suggest the sources for 1-2 Samuel date from no later than the ninth century BCE. McKenzie sees the apologetic elements in 1-2 Samuel, concerning which he is skeptical, as nonetheless showing that the accounts "contain genuine historical information about David. . . . Who would invent such allegations against Da-

vid just to try to explain them away?" (McKenzie, 35-36). Alter comments, "Were David an invention of much later national tradition, he would be the most peculiar of legendary founding kings," and he cites David's service as a vassal of the Philistines, the Bathsheba incident and the way in which he "is repeatedly seen in his weakness, and oscillates from nobility of sentiment and act to harsh vindictiveness on his very deathbed" (Alter, xvii).

4. Conclusion.
This can form our conclusion. David as depicted in the OT Historical Books is seen from many angles: as an Israelite leader zealous for God who united his people and brought them a peace that they had not known before; as a man whose personal failings undermined many of his earlier achievements; and (in Chronicles) as a symbol of hope for the postexilic generations, a sign that God would yet restore Israel's fortunes. The depth, complexity and (at times) ambivalence of these portrayals of David suggest that they are rooted in historical facts.

See also DAVIDIC COVENANT; DAVID'S FAMILY; HISTORY OF ISRAEL 3: UNITED MONARCHY; PROPAGANDA.

BIBLIOGRAPHY. **R. Alter,** *The David Story: A Translation with Commentary on 1 and 2 Samuel* (New York: Norton, 1999); **A. G. Auld,** *Kings Without Privilege: David and Moses in the Story of the Bible's Kings* (Edinburgh: T & T Clark, 1994); **G. Barkay,** "The Iron Age II-III," in *The Archaeology of Ancient Israel,* ed. A. Ben-Tor (New Haven: Yale University Press, 1992) 302-73; **J. Bright,** *A History of Israel* (4th ed.; Louisville: Westminster/John Knox, 2000); **J. M. Cahill,** "Jerusalem at the Time of the United Monarchy: The Archaeological Evidence," in *Jerusalem in Bible and Archaeology: The First Temple Period,* ed. A. G. Vaughn and A. E. Killebrew (SBLSymS 18; Atlanta: Society of Biblical Literature, 2003) 13-80; **P. R. Davies,** *In Search of "Ancient Israel"* (2d ed.; JSOTSup 148; Sheffield: Sheffield Academic Press, 1995); **W. G. Dever,** "Archaeology and the 'Age of Solomon': A Case Study in Archaeology and Historiography," in *The Age of Solomon: Scholarship at the Turn of the Millennium,* ed. L. K. Handy (SHCANE 11; Leiden: E. J. Brill, 1997) 217-51; **I. Finkelstein,** "The Archaeology of the United Monarchy: An Alternative View," *Levant* 28 (1996) 177-87; **I. Finkelstein and N. A. Silberman,** *The Bible Unearthed: Archaeology's Own Vi-*

sion of Ancient Israel and the Origin of Its Sacred Texts (New York: Touchstone, 2002); **R. P. Gordon,** *1 & 2 Samuel* (OTG; Sheffield: JSOT, 1984); idem, "In Search of David: The David Tradition in Recent Study," in *Faith, Tradition, and History: Old Testament Historiography in Its Near Eastern Context,* ed. A. R. Millard, J. K. Hoffmeier and D. W. Baker (Winona Lake, IN: Eisenbrauns, 1994) 285-98; **B. Halpern,** *David's Secret Demons: Messiah, Murderer, Traitor, King* (Grand Rapids: Eerdmans, 2001); **S. Herrmann,** *A History of Israel in Old Testament Times* (rev. ed.; London: SCM, 1981); **Z. Herzog,** "The Beer-Sheba Valley: From Nomadism to Monarchy," in *From Nomadism to Monarchy: Archaeological and Historical Aspects of Early Israel,* ed. I. Finkelstein and N. Na'aman (Jerusalem: Yad Izhak Ben-Zvi; Israel Exploration Society; Washington, D.C.: Biblical Archaeology Society, 1994) 122-49; **G. H. Jones,** *1 & 2 Chronicles* (OTG; Sheffield: JSOT, 1993); **B. Kelly,** "Messianic Elements in the Chronicler's Work," in *The Lord's Anointed: Interpretation of Old Testament Messianic Texts,* ed. P. E. Satterthwaite, R. S. Hess and G. J. Wenham (Tyndale House Studies; Carlisle: Paternoster; Grand Rapids: Baker, 1995) 249-64; **A. E. Killebrew,** "Biblical Jerusalem: An Archaeological Assessment," in *Jerusalem in Bible and Archaeology: The First Temple Period,* ed. A. G. Vaughn and A. E. Killebrew (SBLSymS 18; Atlanta: Society of Biblical Literature, 2003) 329-45; **K. A. Kitchen,** *On the Reliability of the Old Testament* (Grand Rapids: Eerdmans, 2003); **A. Lemaire,** "'House of David' Restored in Moabite Inscription," *BAR* 20.3 (1994) 30-37; **A. Mazar,** *Archaeology of the Land of the Bible, 10,000-596 B.C.E.* (New York: Doubleday, 1992); **S. L. McKenzie,** *King David: A Biography* (New York: Oxford University Press, 2000); **J. M. Miller and J. H. Hayes,** *A History of Ancient Israel and Judah* (Philadelphia: Westminster, 1986); **W. L. Moran,** *The Amarna Letters* (Baltimore: Johns Hopkins University Press, 1992); **I. W. Provan, V. P. Long and T. Longman III,** *A Biblical History of Israel* (Louisville: Westminster/John Knox, 2003); **P. E. Satterthwaite,** "David in the Books of Samuel: A Messianic Expectation?," in *The Lord's Anointed: Interpretation of Old Testament Messianic Texts,* ed. P. E. Satterthwaite, R. S. Hess and G. J. Wenham (Tyndale House Studies; Carlisle: Paternoster; Grand Rapids: Baker, 1995) 41-65; **M. J. Selman,** *1 Chronicles* (TOTC; Leicester: Inter-Varsity Press, 1994); **M. Steiner,** "The Evidence from Kenyon's Excavations in Jerusalem: A Response Essay," in *Jerusalem in Bible and Archaeology: The First Temple Period,* ed. A. G. Vaughn and A. E. Killebrew (SBLSymS 18; Atlanta: Society of Biblical Literature, 2003) 347-63; **T. L. Thompson,** *The Mythic Past: Biblical Archaeology and the Myth of Israel* (New York: Basic Books, 1999); **J. Van Seters,** *In Search of History: Historiography in the Ancient World and the Origins of Biblical History* (New Haven: Yale University Press, 1983); **H. G. M. Williamson,** *1 and 2 Chronicles* (NCBC; London: Marshall, Morgan & Scott; Grand Rapids: Eerdmans, 1982).   P. E. Satterthwaite

DAVIDIC COVENANT

The Historical Books explicitly mention a *bĕrît*, "covenant," between God and *David only a few times: three times in Chronicles (2 Chron 13:5; 21:7; 23:3) and once in Samuel (2 Sam 23:5). Nonetheless, a comparison of these passages with the prophet Nathan's well-known oracle to David (2 Sam 7:11-16) indicates that this passage, though it does not use the term *bĕrît*, reflects the same idea as well as the same general content of such an agreement between God and David. Moreover, references to such an agreement between God and David outside the Historical Books, in the prophets and the psalms, demonstrate that this tradition was not a late creation of the Deuteronomistic Historian, much less the Chronicler, but rather, though influential in the postexilic period, goes back much earlier and helped shape both theology and politics during the monarchical period in the areas controlled by David's successors. Attempts to delineate the genre and structure of the Davidic covenant based on Near Eastern models have been less than successful, and the appropriate solution to the apparent conflict within the sources as to the conditional or unconditional nature of the divine promises contained in this covenant remains hotly disputed. Nonetheless, recourse to a plurality of Davidic covenants seems ill-conceived; at best, one can speak of a plurality of interpretations of the tradition of the Davidic covenant. Finally, the influence of this tradition lives on in the later Jewish and Christian expectations of a Davidic messiah.

1. Texts
2. Near Eastern Models
3. Conditionality
4. Afterlife

1. Texts.

1.1. The Chronicler. According to the Chronicler, Yahweh, the God of Israel, gave to David and to his descendants the rule *(mamlākâ)* over Israel *(ʿal-yiśrāʾēl)* forever *(lěʿôlām)* by a covenant of salt *(běrît melaḥ)* (2 Chron 13:5). The significance of salt in this locution is unclear, since the expression occurs only this one time, but the nature of God's commitment in this contract is clear enough. The giving of the rule *(mamlākâ)* to David and his descendants meant that the members of the Davidic dynasty were the legitimate human regents through which God's rule on earth was administered. 2 Chronicles 13:8 speaks of the rule of Yahweh in the hand of the descendants of David *(mamleket yhwh běyad běnê dāwîd)*. For the Chronicler, the expression "over Israel" *(ʿal-yiśrāʾēl)* meant that ideally even the northern tribes, which had split off from the Davidic state and formed their own independent kingdom in the time of David's grandson, should continue to be subject to the Davidic dynasty. He judges their rebellion as tantamount to a rebellion against God's rule, as withstanding the rule of Yahweh in the hands of the descendants of David (2 Chron 13:8). The term "forever" *(lěʿôlām)* indicates that the covenant committed God to permanently maintaining the Davidic line. Even when the ruling Davidide was as evil as the illegitimate northern kings, God was unwilling to destroy the dynasty of David *(bêt dāwîd)*, because of the covenant God had made with David to preserve for him and his descendants *(ûlěbānāyw)* a lamp *(nîr)* for all the days *(kol-hayyāmîm)* (2 Chron 21:6-7). God's commitment to the Davidic line meant that a Davidide should always sit on the throne of David in *Jerusalem. Thus the interregnum of Athaliah, the *Omride widow of the legitimate Davidide, was unacceptable, and it was important to replace her with the surviving son of the dead king so that a legitimate Davidide could continue the rule of the Davidic house "just as Yahweh had spoken concerning the descendants of David" (2 Chron 23:3). One can only guess at the Chronicler's resolution of the obvious discrepancy between God's promise to the Davidic dynasty and the absence of any Davidic ruler at the end of his history, but the concluding mention of Cyrus's edict permitting the Jews to return to Jerusalem (2 Chron 36:22-23) suggests, however obliquely, that the Chronicler was unwilling to give up on God's commitment to David.

1.2. The Deuteronomic History. As is generally acknowledged today, the primary source for the *Chronicler's History was the material found in Deuteronomy, Joshua, Judges, 1-2 Samuel and 1-2 Kings—material preserved, edited and arranged by a series of Deuteronomistic editors. Within this collection there is one quite explicit reference to a covenant between God and David in the poem known as "the last words of David" (2 Sam 23:1-7). Despite an ongoing debate about its date, this poem contains archaic features similar to the oracles of Balaam, presupposes a monarchy that is still alive and functioning, and shows no trace of later Deuteronomistic editing (*see* Poetry). It is clearly monarchic, probably pre-Deuteronomistic, and perhaps even Davidic as its designation claims. In it David, "the man whom God exalted, the anointed of the God of Jacob, the favorite of the Strong One of Israel" (2 Sam 23:1 NRSV), cites God's commendation of one who rules over people righteously and in the fear of God (2 Sam 23:3-4), and then he claims, "Surely my house *[bêtî]* is like this with God, for he has given to me *[śām lî]* an eternal covenant *[běrît ʿôlām]*, ordered in every detail *[ʿărûkâ bakkōl]* and legally recorded *[ûšěmūrâ]*" (2 Sam 23:5). The text pays less attention to the content of the contract between God and David than to the claim that the contract was legally binding because it was thoroughly executed and officially filed, but the reference to David's house and the characterization of the covenant as being eternal suggests that the covenant formalized the elevation of David as the anointed king of the God of Jacob as an enduring appointment that would be passed on in perpetuity to David's descendants.

Though not explicitly designated as a covenant *(běrît)*, God's promises to David in *Nathan's oracle (2 Sam 7:11-16) as well as David's references back to them in his following prayer (2 Sam 7:18-29)—passages preserved with only very slight, primarily stylistic variations in 2 Chronicles 17—clearly are the narrative traditions underlying the Chronicler's explicit references to God's covenant with David. The numerous points of contact between the promises in 2 Samuel 7 and the language of Psalm 89, which repeatedly refers to such promises as a covenant *(běrît* [Ps 89:3, 28, 34, 39]) that God swore to David (Ps 89:3, 35, 49), also suggest that a narrative tradition like that found in 2 Samuel 7 lay behind the work of this psalmist. In 2 Samuel 7, when David asked permission to build

God a *bayit,* a house or temple, for God to dwell in, God refused and, playing on the ambiguity of the Hebrew word *bayit,* promised instead to build David a *bayit,* a dynasty. The text then elaborates in detail what that means, but here a number of difficulties emerge.

The debate over the literary analysis of this material, including the question of the extent and number of levels of Deuteronomistic editing, is sharp, extensive and complicated, far too complicated to unravel in a short dictionary article, but a few comments are necessary. There is undoubtedly significant Deuteronomistic editing in the passage, but there is no warrant to dismiss it as merely a late, ad hoc creation of the Deuteronomistic Historian. Apart from other early, non-Deuteronomistic texts that point to the existence of a very similar tradition of God's commitment to the Davidic dynasty (2 Sam 23:1-7; Ps 132), there are too many inconsistencies in the narrative of 2 Samuel 7 to regard it as the unified creation of a single author. It is curious, for example, that a promise being given to David focuses so clearly in 2 Sam 7:13-15 on David's immediate successor, *Solomon, who, in the typical Deuteronomistic phraseology also found in 1 Kings 8, would build the house for God's name (2 Sam 7:13). It is striking that what is said in 2 Samuel 7 of God being Solomon's father, and of God not removing his covenant faithfulness *(ḥesed)* from him, is said of David in Psalm 89 (cf. 2 Sam 7:14 with Ps 89:26-27; 2 Sam 7:15 with Ps 89:24, 28). It is also noteworthy that while 2 Samuel speaks specifically of the possible sins of this immediate successor of David—"If he commits iniquity, I will discipline him with the rod humans use, and with the blows of mortals" (2 Sam 7:14)—similar passages in the psalms speak more generally of David's descendants in the plural: (1) "If his descendants *[bānāyw]* forsake my law and do not walk in my statutes, if my ordinances they profane and my commandments they do not keep, I will punish their transgression with a rod and their sins with blows, but I will not abrogate from him *[mēʿimmô* (David)] my covenant faithfulness *[ḥasdî]*" (Ps 89:30-33); (2) "If your descendants *[bānêkā]* keep my covenant and my ordinance which I shall teach them, their descendants *[běnêhem]* shall also sit on your throne forever" (Ps 132:12). Moreover, after 2 Samuel 7:13-15, the text shifts its attention away from Solomon and back to David: "And your dynasty *[bêtěkā]* and your kingdom

[ûmamlaktěkā] shall be firm forever before me [reading *lěpānay* with LXX] and your throne shall be established forever" (2 Sam 7:16; cf. 7:18-19, 25-27, 29, all of which speak of David or his dynasty, not of his immediate successor, Solomon). In light of these observations, it is hard to avoid the conclusion that a Deuteronomistic editor has intentionally altered an older narrative that spoke merely of David and his descendants, inserting a specific reference to Solomon, the builder of the temple (2 Sam 7:13-15), in order to prepare the reader for the Deuteronomistic treatment of Solomon's dedication of the temple (1 Kings 8) and his eventual apostasy and punishment (1 Kings 11:1-13).

Psalm 132 links God's election of David and his dynasty with God's equally perduring election (*ʿădê-ʿad,* "forever" [Ps 132:12, 14]) of Jerusalem, and similar ideas are found in Psalm 2. Moreover, a number of passages in the eighth-century prophets indicate that such views were already widely held and provided a common theological basis from which a Judean prophet could appeal to an audience. Although some of the passages are of disputed date, some of them are not. *Isaiah's oracles of reassurance to the Judean king Ahaz that the Syro-Ephraimite plan to depose him would fail (Is 7:1-17; 8:1-4) clearly are no later than the period of the Syro-Ephraimitic war (735-732 BCE). Rezin of Damascus and Pekah of Samaria wanted to replace the Davidide Ahaz with a certain, presumably non-Davidide, son of Tabal, perhaps a garbled form of "Ittobaal," the king of Tyre. In both the narrative introduction to this material and in Isaiah's second oracle to Ahaz, Ahaz and his court are specifically referred to as "the house/dynasty of David" (*bêt dāwîd* [Is 7:2, 13]), and the logic of Isaiah's argument in his first oracle is that Yahweh chose David and Jerusalem, not Rezin and Damascus, much less the son of Remaliah and Samaria (Is 7:7-9). Moreover, the conclusion of the first oracle, "If you do not believe *[taʾămînû]*, you will not be established *[tēʾāmēnû]*" (Is 7:9), with its play on the root *ʾmn,* probably is alluding to the divine promise that David's dynasty and kingdom would be made firm *(wěneʾěman)* forever (2 Sam 7:16).

2. Near Eastern Models.

In several influential articles written in the early 1970s, M. Weinfeld attempted to show that the Davidic covenant was modeled on the royal land grants known from the Hittite and Mesopotamian realms. In contrast to the Mosaic covenant, based on the suzerainty treaties, in which the primary obligation is placed on the vassal and his descendants to obey the stipulations of the treaty, in the royal grants the primary obligation is on the suzerain to guarantee his grant to his vassal and his descendants. The royal grant focuses on the past loyalty of the vassal, for which the grant is a reward, whereas the suzerainty treaty focuses on the future loyalty of the vassal, regulated by stipulations, the acceptance of which is sealed by the oath of the vassal. Weinfeld's analysis highlighted obvious differences of emphasis between the Mosaic covenant and the Davidic covenant, appeared to root those differences in different genres inherited from Israel's ancient Near Eastern background, and, because of this apparent fit, was widely accepted. Recently, however, G. Knoppers has challenged Weinfeld's analysis on three grounds: (1) the problematic and changing structure of land grants; (2) the multiple sources possible for the assumed parallels in language; (3) the question as to how unconditional such royal commitments actually were. It is difficult to isolate a fixed and consistent land grant genre, much less show that it corresponds to a single genre in the different biblical references to God's promises to David. The assumed parallels in language are found in all sorts of ancient Near Eastern texts, not just or even primarily in land grants. And, finally, the unconditionality of the land grants has been vastly overstated. In administering grants, monarchs do not characteristically swear a self-imprecatory oath, and it is clear that in most cases, whether explicitly stated or not, the crown preserved the right to redistribute the land, depending on the continuing loyalty of the vassal and his descendants. In contrast to the suzerainty treaty model, which does help explain numerous features in the Mosaic covenant, the land grant model simply highlights elements already obvious in the promises to David without explaining them, and given the weaknesses pointed out by Knoppers, the model probably should be abandoned.

3. Conditionality.

The different biblical formulations of God's promises to or covenant with David differ in their expression of the conditionality or unconditionality with which God's commitments are made, and the appropriate resolution of this apparent conflict has been a source of continuing debate among scholars. According to 2 Samuel 7:14-16, even if David's successor sins, although God will punish him, the punishment will be measured and will not involve turning aside God's steadfast commitment to him (ḥesed) as God turned it aside from *Saul. As mentioned previously, the formulation seems a bit awkward in its focus on Solomon, and this momentary focus may be secondary, since the text soon returns to David when it promises that David's dynasty, kingdom and throne will be firmly established forever (2 Sam 7:15-16). Psalm 89:30-37 contains a similar formulation without any such awkwardness. It mentions the possible rebellion of a plurality of David's descendants, but while such rebellion may provoke God's measured punishment of the guilty parties, such punishment will not result in the end of the Davidic dynasty. God has bound himself by oath that despite the sins of David's successors, the dynastic line will continue. In the words of Psalm 89:36, "His seed will endure forever, his throne like the sun before me." The question of conditionality is not explicitly addressed in the poem in 2 Samuel 23:1-7, although the speaker does seem to stress the righteousness of David's rule. In contrast, however, Psalm 132:11-12 does seem to introduce an explicit condition: "Yahweh swore to David a reliable oath from which he will not turn back, 'One of the offspring of your body I will place on your throne. If your descendants keep my covenant and the decrees which I teach them, then also their descendants forevermore will sit on your throne.'" The contrast between this formulation and the basically unconditional formulations in 2 Samuel 7:14-16 and Psalm 89:30-37 have led scholars to explain the distinction in terms of a diachronic development. Some scholars argue that the promise originally was unconditional, but in the course of time, particularly under Deuteronomistic influence, a conditional element was introduced. Others argue the opposite scenario. An originally conditional commitment to the Davidic dynasty was elaborated and shaped by Judean court theologians into an unconditional divine commitment. Neither of these positions seems compelling. As Knoppers astutely observes, such differences need not be explained chronologically; they could just as easily be contemporary yet conflicting points of view. The closest parallel to the unconditional language of 2 Samuel 7 and Psalm 89 actually is found in the Hittite suzerainty treaty with Ulmi-Teshshup. In it the Hittite suzerain commits himself to maintaining Ulmi-Teshshup's dynastic line even if some of his successors sin against the great king and must be removed from the throne:

> I, My Majesty, will [not depose] your son. [I will accept] neither your brother nor anyone else. Later your son and grandson will hold [the land] which I have given [to you]. It may not be taken away from him. If any son or grandson of yours commits an offense, then the king of Hatti shall question him. And if an offense is proven against him, then the King of Hatti shall treat him as he pleases. If he is deserving of death, he shall perish, but his household and land shall not be taken from him and given to the progeny of another. Only someone of the progeny of Ulmi-Teshshup shall take them. Someone of the male line shall take them; those of the female line shall not take them. But if there is no male line of descent, and it is extinguished, then only someone of the female line of Ulmi-Teshshup shall be sought out. Even if he is in a foreign land, he shall be brought back from there and installed in authority in the land of Tarhuntassa (Beckman, 104).

In light of that analogy, one could posit an original formulation of the Davidic covenant similar to the formulation found in 2 Samuel 7 and Psalm 89, in which God makes a commitment to maintaining the Davidic dynasty while preserving the divine freedom to punish individual members of the dynasty who rebel against the divine suzerain's rule. Such a formulation would allow us to situate the covenant with David within the overarching context of God's prior Mosaic covenant with Israel. Moreover, if one posits such a formulation of God's original promise to David, it is easy to see how different parties in the theological debate over the legitimacy of continuing Davidic rule could focus on different aspects of the promise. The critics of the Davidic monarch could point to the current ruler's sins that called for divine punishment and, stretching a little, could even suggest that they were so flagrant as to threaten the dynasty itself, while the defenders of the monarch could point to God's commitment to the dynasty despite a particular ruler's sins, and, stretching a

little, could even suggest that the ruler's transgressions were not so flagrant as to demand more than a light disciplinary rebuke—a punishment analogous to human discipline of errant children. We should also note that Psalm 132 gives no indication that its composer felt that the descendants of David had failed to keep the covenant. As long as there was no general sense that David's descendants had failed to live up to the conditions of the covenant, the conditional formulation of Psalm 132 would present no theological problem. On the other hand, when the dynasty was in very serious trouble, as is obviously the case in Psalm 89, trouble that could be explained as punishment due to the Davidic king's breach of covenant, it was important in theological argumentation with the deity to stress God's unconditional commitment to the dynasty.

4. Afterlife.

Despite the psalmist's insistent appeal to God's irrevocable oath in Psalm 89, and despite the Chronicler's somewhat later reaffirmation of God's commitment to the Davidic dynasty, it is clear from Jeremiah 33:21 that the end of the monarchy and the difficulties of the exilic and postexilic periods led many to believe that God's covenant with David had been abrogated. Yet other voices from the exilic and postexilic periods continued to find hope for themselves and their people in God's promise to the Davidic line. According to the exilic prophet Second Isaiah, God invites those dead and despairing in exile to a divine banquet of new life, and God promises that he will make an everlasting covenant (*běrît ʿôlām*) with them, his steadfast commitment to David (*ḥasdê dāwīd hanneʾĕmānîm*) (Is 55:1-3). The move seems to suggest that the prophet was answering a theological problem by reapplying the Davidic covenant to the nation as a whole. In contrast, the author of Jeremiah 33:14-26 has God proclaim that days are coming when God would fulfill his good word and raise up a shoot (*ṣemaḥ*) for David, so that there would never again lack a Davidide to sit on the throne of David. Contrary to the skeptics, one could no more abrogate God's covenant with David to always have one of his descendants ruling on his throne than one could abrogate God's covenant with night and day. To insure that, God promises to make the descendants of David as numerous as the stars of heaven or the sand of the seashore. Such expectations of the renewal of the Davidic dynasty and the Levitical priesthood, which the Jeremiah passage also mentions, probably explain the messianic fervor that seems to have been attached to *Zerubbabel, the Davidic governor of Judea, who received the epithet "shoot" *(semah),* and Joshua, the high priest, during the rebuilding of the temple in the early postexilic period (Hag 2:21-23; Zech 3:8; 4:3-14; 6:11-14). The Jeremiah-Zechariah trajectory probably is the source for the Qumran expectation for messiahs of Aaron and Israel (CD 12:23-13:1; 14:19; 19:10-11, 19:21-20:1; 1QS 9:9b-11; 1QSa 2:11b-22), while the more common and more restricted emphasis on God's eternal commitment to the Davidic dynasty lies behind the expectation of a Davidic messiah known from late Judaism (4QDimHam A [4Q504]; 4QpGen^a [4Q252] 5:1-7; 4QFlor [4Q174] 1:10-13; 4QpIsa^a [4Q161]; 4Q285 5:3; 4 Ezra 12:32-34; *Pss. Sol.* 17:5, 23) and the NT (Mt 12:23; Mk 11:10; Lk 1:32; Jn 7:42; Acts 13:34; 2 Tim 2:8; Rev 5:5; 22:16).

See also DAVID; KINGS AND KINGSHIP; SAMUEL, BOOKS OF.

BIBLIOGRAPHY. **G. M. Beckman,** *Hittite Diplomatic Texts,* ed. H. A. Hoffner (Writings from the Ancient World 7; Atlanta: Scholars Press, 1996); **J. H. Charlesworth,** ed., *The Messiah: Developments in Earliest Judaism and Christianity* (Minneapolis: Fortress, 1992); **G. N. Knoppers,** "Ancient Near Eastern Royal Grants and the Davidic Covenant: A Parallel?" *JAOS* 116 (1996) 670-97; **K. E. Pomykala,** *The Davidic Dynasty Tradition in Early Judaism: Its History and Significance for Messianism* (SBLEJL 7; Atlanta: Scholars Press, 1995); **J. J. M. Roberts,** "Solomon's Jerusalem and the Zion Tradition," in *Jerusalem in Bible and Archaeology: The First Temple Period,* ed. A. G. Vaughn and A. E. Killebrew (SBLSymS 18; Atlanta: Society of Biblical Literature, 2003) 163-70; **M. Weinfeld,** "The Covenant of Grant in the Old Testament and in the Ancient Near East," *JAOS* 90 (1970) 184-203; idem, "Addenda to JAOS 90 (1970), pp. 184ff.: The Covenant of Grant in the Old Testament and in the Ancient Near East," *JAOS* 92 (1972) 468-69; idem, "Covenant Terminology in the Ancient Near East and Its Influence on the West," *JAOS* 93 (1973) 190-99. J. J. M. Roberts

DAVID'S FAMILY

The complex and varied references to the family of *David in the Bible may be treated in regard to his origins, wives and children.

1. David's Origins
2. David's Wives
3. David's Children

1. David's Origins.

David's ancestry is given in two OT passages, Ruth 4:18-22 and 1 Chronicles 2:4-15, and once in the NT (Mt 1:3-5). The genealogy is similar, though not identical, in all three, and is striking for its frank admission of David's non-Israelite roots, from Ruth the *Moabite, as well as the *Canaanites Tamar and Rahab:

Judah (through Tamar [Gen 38])
Perez
Hezron
Ram
Amminadab
Nahshon
Salma or Salmon (through Rahab
  [according to, uniquely, Mt 1:5])
Boaz (through Ruth)
Obed
Jesse
David

The purpose of this genealogy (*see* Genealogies), evident in 1 Chronicles 2, was to provide a clear descent from Judah to David—something not extant elsewhere in the OT. This was accomplished through Ram and Salma, both of whom are unknown outside of this chapter and the genealogies in Ruth and Matthew. The genealogy for Ram in 1 Chronicles 2:10-17 is different in form from the ones for Jerahmeel and Caleb that follow, indicating that Ram's was originally independent. It is linear up to Jesse, inclusive, in 1 Chronicles 2:12. Then Jesse's family—David and his siblings—is listed in 1 Chronicles 2:13-17 (the Bible never names David's mother). Ram, who is otherwise the son of Jerahmeel (1 Chron 2:25, 27), here bridges Hezron and Amminadab (1 Chron 2:10). The reference to Amminadab and his son Nahshon, "the prince of the sons of Judah," is borrowed from Numbers 2:3. Then Salma (the father of Bethlehem in 1 Chron 2:51) connects Nahshon to Boaz (1 Chron 2:11). The manufacture of the genealogy resembles the Chronicler's work elsewhere, and it is integral to Chronicles but may be an appendix to Ruth. Still, both authors may have made use of a previously constructed genealogy.

The Bible hints that David's family was affluent and socially prominent. The expression *gibbôr ḥayil* (NRSV: "rich man") used for Boaz, David's great-grandfather, in Ruth 2:1 and for Kish, Saul's father, in 1 Samuel 9:1 (NRSV: "man of wealth") also occurs for David in 1 Samuel 16:18, where the NRSV "man of valor" makes the next descriptor, "man of war," redundant. It may also be inferred from 1 Samuel 16:5, in which Samuel sanctifies Jesse and his sons after commanding the elders of Bethlehem to sanctify themselves, that Jesse was one of those elders and thus a leading citizen of the city.

These hints evoke an image of David different from the traditional one of a lowly shepherd. As the son of a prosperous owner of land and livestock, perhaps a "sheep breeder" like the king of Moab in 2 Kings 3:4, the young David may have tended sheep, but this was not his profession. The few references in the David story to him as a shepherd come mainly at the beginning (1 Sam 16:11, 19; 17:15, 28, 34, 40; 2 Sam 7:8), and they may be intended to foreshadow his future by drawing on the common ancient Near Eastern metaphor of a king as shepherd of his people (cf. 2 Sam 5:2).

1 Chronicles 2:13-15 lists seven sons of Jesse from oldest to youngest: Eliab, Abinadab, Shimea, Nethanel, Raddai, Ozem and David. The source of this list is unknown. 1 Chronicles 27:18 mentions David's brother Elihu, presumably a variant of "Eliab." 1 Samuel 16:6-10 and 17:12-15 name only Eliab, Abinadab and Shammah (a variant of "Shimea," also called Shimeah [2 Sam 13:3] and Shimei [2 Sam 21:21]). The other three names in the list—Nethanel, Raddai and Ozem—are otherwise unknown.

1 Samuel 16:10 says that Jesse presented his seven sons (or "seven of his sons") to Samuel before David was summoned, and 1 Samuel 17:12 says explicitly that Jesse had eight sons. Some scholars suggest that David was the seventh son in accord with the favored status of that position in traditional literature, and that the statement in 1 Samuel 16:10 is misplaced or proleptic. Others assert that David's designation as the eighth son emphasizes his anonymity so that his future greatness was the result of divine blessing rather than of birth order. Still others propose that Jesse's sons numbered only four—David and the three brothers who are named in Samuel—and that the number grew to seven because of the traditional motif that the seventh son is special.

These texts agree in depicting David as the youngest in accord with a literary and theological theme found elsewhere in the Bible. Thus in Genesis God consistently favors younger siblings such as Isaac, Jacob, Rachel and Joseph. L. E. Stager argues that David's status as the youngest son makes sense in light of environmental and economic conditions in Palestine in the early Iron Age, when a population increase in the central highlands strained natural resources and the agricultural economy. As the last in the line of inheritance, youngest sons would have needed to seek out other means of support, such as the military or freebooting.

Aside from 1 Chronicles 2:16-17, David's two sisters, Abigail and Zeruiah, are mentioned together only in 2 Samuel 17:25, which calls Abigail the daughter of Nahash, not of Jesse. If this is not a textual error—a misplacement of the name "Nahash," which occurs two verses later—Abigail may have been David's half-sister. The only other Abigail in the OT is Nabal's former wife, who married David (1 Sam 25); the two may have been the same woman (Levenson; Levenson and Halpern).

Zeruiah's name occurs often in the David story in the expression "the sons of Zeruiah," referring to Joab, Abishai and Asahel. J. Van Seters (25) proposed that Zeruiah was actually a man, since sons in ancient Israel typically were designated by their father's name. The family tie of the sons of Zeruiah with David's also has been questioned, since they play virtually no role in David's rise until he becomes king; perhaps their status in his army eventuated in their identification as his blood relatives (McKenzie 2000, 55).

2. David's Wives.

The harem was a feature of Near Eastern monarchy that David introduced into Israel. It also represented David's political alliances and maneuverings. The Bible attributes at least nineteen wives and concubines to David:

Michal (1 Sam 18:20-29; 25:44; 2 Sam 6:20-23; 1 Chron 15:29)

Ahinoam (1 Sam 25:43; 2 Sam 2:2; 3:2; 1 Chron 3:1)

Abigail (1 Sam 25; 2 Sam 2:2; 3:3; 1 Chron 3:1)

Maacah (2 Sam 3:3; 1 Chron 3:2)

Haggith (2 Sam 3:4; 1 Chron 3:2)

Abital (2 Sam 3:4; 1 Chron 3:3)

Eglah (2 Sam 3:5; 1 Chron 3:3)
unnamed (2 Sam 5:13-16; 1 Chron 14:3-7)
ten concubines (2 Sam 15:16; 16:21-22; 20:3)
Bathsheba (2 Sam 11—12; 1 Kings 1—2;
    called Bathshua in 1 Chron 3:5)
Abishag (1 Kings 1—2)

Michal's political value to David is apparent in 1 Samuel 18:20-29, where the exchange between him and *Saul is consistently about becoming "the king's son-in-law," a position that would place David, indirectly, in line for the throne. David is never said to love Michal and is cast as unambitious, but he is willing to risk his life to become Saul's son-in-law. Although he never attempts to see Michal all the time that he is fleeing from Saul, he demands her return as a condition for negotiating with Abner (2 Sam 3:13), and it is Saul's heir, Ishbaal, of all people who sends her back. These peculiarities raise the possibility that this "marriage" was contrived for political purposes: to solidify David's claim to the throne of Israel *after* he had become king (McKenzie 2000, 118, 137-38). Michal's childlessness (2 Sam 6:23) would then have been a strategy on David's part to ensure that she produced no heirs to Saul.

Ahinoam's hometown, Jezreel, presumably was a village (location unknown) in the Judean wilderness rather than the famous northern valley, as indicated by her consistent appearance in tandem with Abigail as David moves to rule Judah (1 Sam 25:43; 27:3; 30:5; and especially 2 Sam 2:2). More importantly, she may have been identical to Saul's wife of the same name (1 Sam 14:50), as there is no other Ahinoam in the Bible. This would explain Nathan's statement in 2 Samuel 12:8 that Yahweh had given Saul's ("your master's") wives to David.

The story of David's marriage to Abigail in 1 Samuel 25 is a literary masterpiece, which also contains intriguing clues about history (see Levenson; Levenson and Halpern; McKenzie 2000, 95-101). Abigail prevents a bloodbath after her former husband, Nabal (meaning "fool" and likely symbolic rather than his real name), incites David's wrath with insults. Nonetheless, Nabal dies providentially, and Abigail brings to David Nabal's wealth, social prominence and political status, making this episode a crucial step in David's rise to the throne of Judah.

Like Michal, Maacah was a princess, the daughter of King Talmai of Geshur (the Golan Heights). Her marriage to David probably

sealed a treaty between the two kings.

The marriage to Bathsheba was motivated, exceptionally, by passion rather than by politics. 2 Samuel 11—12 stands out from the surrounding material in its lack of apologetic tone for David and probably is a later insertion (McKenzie 2000, 155-61). Bathsheba is called the daughter of Eliam (2 Sam 11:3; daughter of Ammiel in 1 Chron 3:5), the name of the son of David's exceedingly wise adviser Ahithophel (2 Sam 15:12; 16:23; 23:34). Thus Ahithophel's change of allegiance from David to Absalom may have been in response to the execution of Uriah and the humiliation of Bathsheba.

The politics surrounding the story of Abishag differed from those of David's other marriages. She served as a test of the aged king's virility and hence his suitability for the throne. Thus Adonijah's exaltation of himself as king (1 Kings 1:5) follows directly upon the statement "the king did not know [Abishag] sexually" (1 Kings 1:4), despite her beauty and accessibility (1 Kings 1:2-3). Knowledge that the marriage was not consummated may have emboldened Adonijah later to solicit Bathsheba's agency before *Solomon in requesting marriage to Abishag. Still, it is difficult to see why Adonijah would be so foolish as to ignore the political implications of his request or to trust Bathsheba's advocacy. The story has thus been viewed as a literary construct designed to provide some pretense for Solomon's execution of his brother.

Similar explanations occur in 1 Kings 2 for the deaths (or banishment in the case of the priest Abiathar) of others of Solomon's political opponents, including David's "nephew" Joab. David's deathbed condemnation of Joab for the murders of Abner and Amasa, crimes now decades past, especially in the case of Abner, hardly obscures the real reason for Joab's execution: his support of Adonijah (1 Kings 1:7). Solomon's true motive is so obvious that some scholars read 1 Kings 1—2 as a kind of parody of royal apology illustrating the bloodshed that inevitably tarnished the Davidic line or the institution of monarchy in general.

3. David's Children.
2 Samuel contains two lists of David's sons—those born in *Hebron (2 Sam 3:2-5) and those born in *Jerusalem (2 Sam 5:13-16)—which are combined in 1 Chronicles 3:1-9, albeit with some important differences.

2 Samuel 3:2-5	2 Samuel 5:13-16	1 Chronicles 3:1-9
Amnon (by Ahinoam)		Amnon (by Ahinoam)
Chileab (by Abigail)		Daniel (by Abigail)
Absalom (by Maacah)		Absalom (by Maacah)
Adonijah (by Haggith)		Adonijah (by Haggith)
Shephatiah (by Abital)		Shephatiah (by Abital)
Ithream (by Eglah)		Ithream (by Eglah)
	Shammua	Shimea
	Shobab	Shobab
	Nathan	Nathan
	Solomon	Solomon
	Ibhar	Ibhar
	Elishua	Elishama
		Eliphelet
		Nogah
	Nepheg	Nepheg
	Japhia	Japhia
	Elishama	Elishama
	Eliada	Eliada
	Eliphelet	Eliphelet

Figure 1. Lists of David's sons

The differences between *Shimea* and *Shammua* and between *Elishama* and *Elishua* are minor matters of spelling or textual corruption. The name *Bathshua* instead of *Bathsheba*, though possibly a spelling variation, is more likely an allusion to Judah's wife (Gen 38). Chronicles' ascription of the first four sons in the list, with Solomon as the fourth, to Bathshua contradicts 2 Samuel 12:24, where Solomon is the first surviving son of David and Bathsheba. Apparently, the Chronicler sought to continue the pattern in 1 Chronicles 3:1-3 of naming the mothers. Since Bathsheba was the only Jerusalem mother mentioned in 2 Samuel, and since Solomon clearly was her son, the Chronicler assigned the first four names in the list to her. *Eliphelet* and *Nogah* are dittographs of *Nepheg*

and the later *Eliphelet* in the Chronicles list.

Amnon raped his half-sister Tamar (the only daughter of David's named in the Bible) and was murdered by her full brother Absalom at the instigation of David's wily nephew Jonadab (2 Sam 13). Amnon's status as firstborn and the son of Ahinoam, perhaps Saul's former wife, raises the possibility of political intrigue in his assassination.

The name of the second son is corrupt in the MT of both Samuel and Chronicles. Based on other textual witnesses for both books the best reading seems to be *dlwyh* = Daluiah (McCarter 1984, 101-2). Nothing more is known about this son, and generally it is assumed that he died in infancy.

Absalom stood as the next in line to succeed

David, and this may have been a factor behind his revolt in 2 Samuel 15—19.

The story of turmoil in the kingdom and royal family in 2 Samuel 13—20 typically is read at face value as the result of David's personal weaknesses and as punishment for his sin with Bathsheba. But some scholars conclude that it likely was written to deflect suspicion of David's involvement in his sons' deaths (McCarter 1981; McKenzie 2000, 165-72), and the Bathsheba story was added later. This view may be set out as follows: Amnon and Absalom were each the oldest son and heir to the throne at the time of their respective deaths, and Absalom obviously was in revolt, so each represented a threat to David. Although the story presents Amnon's murder as Absalom's doing for personal reasons, David may have been behind it. Absalom hid for three years with his grandfather Talmai, while David sought to capture him (2 Sam 13:37-39; following the McCarter [1984, 344] translation of 2 Sam 13:39: "the king's spirit was spent for going out against Absalom"). Since Talmai was David's treaty partner, one wonders why David did not compel him to return Absalom. Perhaps David sent Absalom to Geshur for safekeeping. Similarly, the story presents Absalom's death as Joab's doing, contravening David's order (2 Sam 18). Yet despite David's display of grief, Joab never was punished for disobedience. Was he perhaps actually following orders? Indeed, David's gentleness in these chapters, especially where his sons are concerned, in contrast to the ruthlessness of the "sons of Zeruiah" is a recurring motif.

Following Absalom's demise, Adonijah was next in line for the throne, hence his self-proclamation in 1 Kings 1:5 after David was deemed unfit to rule by reason of flaccidity. The story in 1 Kings 1:11-40 is necessary in order to explain why Solomon was the eventual successor rather than the rightful heir. Yet some have noted the artificiality of the story as suggested by the fact that there is no record of a promise by David to Bathsheba that Solomon would succeed him. The name "Solomon" means "his replacement," and although it probably referred originally to "replacing" David and Bathsheba's first child, who died in infancy (2 Sam 12:15b-25), the possible allusions to Uriah and to David are hard to ignore. Curiously, the name chosen by Yahweh, "Jedidiah" (2 Sam 12:25), is not used again.

See also DAVID; GENEALOGIES; KINGS AND KINGSHIP; ROYAL FAMILY; SOLOMON.

BIBLIOGRAPHY. **B. Halpern,** *David's Secret Demons: Messiah, Murderer, Traitor, King* (Grand Rapids: Eerdmans, 2001); **J. D. Levenson,** "1 Samuel 25 as Literature and History," *CBQ* 40 (1978) 11-28; **J. D. Levenson and B. Halpern,** "The Political Import of David's Marriages," *JBL* 99 (1980) 507-18; **P. K. McCarter,** "The Apology of David," *JBL* 99 (1980) 489-504; idem, "'Plots, True or False': The Succession Narrative as Court Apologetic," *Int* 35 (1981) 355-67; idem, *I Samuel* (AB 8; Garden City, NY: Doubleday, 1980); idem, *II Samuel* (AB 9; Garden City, NY: Doubleday, 1984); **S. L. McKenzie,** *King David: A Biography* (New York: Oxford University Press, 2000); idem, *1-2 Chronicles* (AOTC; Nashville: Abingdon, 2004); **L. E. Stager,** "The Archaeology of the Family in Ancient Israel," *BASOR* 260 (1985) 1-29; **J. Van Seters,** "Problems in the Literary Analysis of the Court History of David," *JSOT* 1 (1976) 22-29. S. L. McKenzie

DEAD SEA SCROLLS. *See* CANON; TEXT AND TEXTUAL CRITICISM.

DEATH AND AFTERLIFE

The Historical Books record numerous deaths over many centuries, mostly as the natural end of life and without further elaboration. There is very little of the anguish of the psalms, where death is emotionally resisted, or of the invective of the prophets, where death is forcefully pronounced. Burial is often recorded, but not always, with kings given fuller treatment. There is very little reference to the underworld or interest in the afterlife, with the partial exception of 1 Samuel 28. Some critical scholars argue that the Historical Books occasionally betray the existence of widespread preexilic ancestor cults. However, the texts adduced in support of this are unclear. For the most part, death was simply the end of life. (For a fuller treatment of all points see Johnston; for other recent surveys see Avery-Peck and Neusner; Gittlen.)

1. Death
2. Mourning
3. Burial
4. Afterlife
5. Ancestor Cult

1. Death.

In death one would "go the way of all the earth" (Josh 23:14; 1 Kings 2:2). *David died "in a good old age, full of days, riches and honor" (1 Chron

29:28), whereas Abner died violently and prematurely "as a fool" (2 Sam 3:33). Death clearly was irreversible: David asserted of his dead son, "I shall go to him, but he will not return to me" (2 Sam 12:23); Joab's wise woman echoed this sentiment: "We are like water spilled on the ground, which cannot be gathered up" (2 Sam 14:14). The death penalty often occurred in individual punishment, but death is never associated with human sinfulness in general (unlike Gen 2—3). For Israel's historians, death was simply a fact of life.

There are a few exceptions. Human sacrifices occur occasionally: Jephthah's daughter (Judg 11:31, 39); Hiel's sons at Jericho (1 Kings 16:34; cf. Josh 6:26); and the heirs of Mesha (2 Kings 3:27), Ahaz (2 Kings 16:3) and *Manasseh (2 Kings 21:6). These sacrifices are implicitly censured by the Israelite historians, except perhaps the first. Here some interpreters (e.g., Marcus) argue that Jephthah's vow was fulfilled in his daughter's perpetual virginity, but most see it as fulfilled in her death. Despite some ambiguity, the latter is the more obvious reading.

Suicides also feature rarely: Abimelech (Judg 9:53), Samson (Judg 16:29f.), *Saul and his armor-bearer (1 Sam 31:3-5), Ahitophel (2 Sam 17:23), and Zimri (1 Kings 16:18). A. J. Droge (228) suggests that suicide was "natural and perhaps heroic." But several factors indicate that it was highly abnormal: the small number of suicides, their occurrence in contexts of strife, and their complete absence in other circumstances. Life was not to be scorned without exceptional reason.

2. Mourning.

In ancient Israel as elsewhere, mourners would weep, tear clothes, wear sackcloth or "mourning garments," uncover or dishevel their hair, cover themselves with dust, sit and sleep on the ground, walk barefoot, and fast (e.g., 2 Sam 1:11-12; 13:31; 14:2). David fasted for one day over Abner (2 Sam 3:35), and the Jabesh-Gileadites for seven days over Saul (1 Sam 31:13). This last text suggests a one-week period of intense mourning, which became normal in postbiblical Judaism.

Laments were common, whether a simple "alas" (hôy, 1 Kings 13:30), or dirges by male and female singers (2 Chron 35:25), or special compositions—for example, by David for Saul (2 Sam 1) and *Jeremiah for *Josiah (2 Chron 35:25).

However, the Historical Books give no information on mourning rituals and very little on funerals. A funeral procession for Abner is mentioned (2 Sam 3:31), but no funerary rites or religious ceremonies. *Kings were normally buried surrounded by expensive spices, with great bonfires lit in their honor (2 Chron 16:14; 21:19; 32:33; see also Jer 34:5).

3. Burial.

Burial clearly was as important in Israel as elsewhere, and most accounts of death also mention burial. However, notice of burial is occasionally omitted—for example, for five judges (including Eli), several kings and some minor figures whose death is recorded (e.g., Amnon, Adonijah, Athaliah). Public exposure of corpses before or instead of burial was a sign of great opprobrium (Josh 8:29; 10:26-27; 1 Sam 4:12; 2 Sam 21:9-14).

Burial normally occurred in the family tomb on family land, as is sometimes explicitly mentioned (e.g., Gideon, Samson, Barzillai) and frequently implied (e.g., *Joshua, Eleazar and most judges). The remains of Saul and his sons, buried hurriedly at Jabesh-Gilead, were later reinterred at their home. Indeed, there are only rare and explicable exceptions, like the disobedient man of God (1 Kings 13:22). *Samuel and Joab were each buried "in his house" (1 Sam 25:1; 1 Kings 2:34). This could indicate burial directly beneath the house, as was common before the Iron Age, but it probably refers to the family tomb, given archaeological evidence, other OT texts and the parallel notices of Manasseh's burial "in his house" (2 Chron 33:20) and "in the garden of his house" (2 Kings 21:18). There was also a communal burial ground for ordinary Jerusalemites in the late monarchy, if not earlier (2 Kings 23:6; cf. Jer 26:23).

E. Bloch-Smith (111) suggests that the burial place of key figures was recorded because they "were thought to possess special powers and to maintain intimate contact with Yahweh." However, this is unlikely: (1) burial location is not always noted; (2) the biblical consensus is that death separates one from Yahweh; (3) the only recorded consultation of such a figure (Samuel) occurred away from his tomb; and (4) there is scant evidence of petitioning the dead at their graves (possibly Is 57:6; 65:4).

The books of *Kings note several royal burial locations: David's descendants to Ahaz were interred in the city of David; Manasseh and Amon in the garden of Uzza; Josiah in his own tomb in Jerusalem. Presumably after Ahaz there was no further space in the city of David's royal tombs. There is no specific burial record for *Hezekiah or Jehoiakim (though see 2 Kings 20:21; 24:6).

*Chronicles mostly records the same kings as buried in the city of David (also exceptionally the high priest Jehoiada; 2 Chron 24:16), with several minor variations: Jehoram and Joash were buried there, but not in the royal tombs (2 Chron 21:20, 24:25); Amaziah was buried in the "city of Judah" (2 Chron 25:28; most MSS); Uzziah "with his fathers in the kings' burial field" (2 Chron 26:23); Ahaz "in the city, in Jerusalem," but not in the royal tombs (2 Chron 28:27). Of the kings after Ahaz, Hezekiah was buried "on the ascent to the tombs of the sons of David" (2 Chron 32:33), Manasseh "in his house" (2 Chron 33:20) and Josiah "in the tombs of his fathers" (2 Chron 35:24). There is no burial record for Ahaziah, Amon or Jehoiakim (who presumably died in Babylon). The only significant difference concerns Josiah, but this may be more apparent than real if he was buried in his own tomb alongside Manasseh and Amon.

Many a king of Israel and Judah "slept with his fathers." This phrase does not indicate burial, since usually it is followed by mention of burial. Nor does it refer specifically to the family tomb, since it occurs for David, Ahaz and Manasseh, who were not buried in such a location, yet is omitted for Ahaziah and Joash, who were. Nor does the phrase indicate a literal reunion with the ancestors, since it occurs for only about half the kings. Nor indeed does it relate to theological assessment, since it applies to kings both "good" and "bad." Rather, with few exceptions, it indicates kings who died peacefully (so Alfrink; Driver; see Johnston, 34-35). Conversely, the starker term "died" normally is used of those who died violently. It is interesting to note a similar distinction in the Code of Hammurabi, where the terms "went to his fate" and "died" convey natural and unnatural death respectively.

Joshua's generation was "gathered to its fathers" (Judg 2:10), while Josiah was told that he would be "gathered to his fathers" (2 Kings 22:20/2 Chron 34:28). This expression is a hybrid of two phrases, "slept with his fathers" and "gathered to his peoples," which occurs in the

Pentateuch for patriarchs, Moses and Aaron. It seems likely that these various expressions reflect an early belief in joining one's family after death. But in the Hebrew Bible their use is restricted specifically to national leaders who die peacefully. This suggests that they developed an idiomatic use distinct from their probable origin.

4. Afterlife.
The Hebrew underworld, often called Sheol *(šĕʾôl)*, was an unwelcome, gloomy, distant place of somnolent inactivity whose denizens were irretrievably separated from Yahweh. While many English versions leave *Sheol* untranslated, the NIV usually renders it as "the grave," following R. L. Harris. However, this overlooks many indications that Sheol is more than the grave, as the NIV itself acknowledges in certain texts (e.g., Amos 9:2; Deut 32:22).

The term *Sheol* occurs only in literary contexts of personal emotional involvement, not those of dispassionate narrative record. The Historical Books almost never mention Sheol, and never its synonyms ("pit," "destruction": *bôr, bĕʾēr, šaḥat, ʾăbaddôn*) or its inhabitants ("shades": *rĕpāʾîm*). The few exceptions, all in poetry or direct speech, illustrate various aspects of Sheol: it was a place of entrapment (2 Sam 22:6), suitable for the early consignment of enemies (1 Kings 2:6, 9), and ultimately within Yahweh's power (1 Sam 2:6). On the whole, Hebrew historiography concentrates on the present life and has scant interest in what follows it.

Hannah's song affirms that Yahweh "kills and brings to life" (1 Sam 2:6). But as with a similar claim in Moses' song (Deut 32:29), this is neither the song's climax nor evidenced in its immediate context. *Elijah apparently escaped death by ascending in a whirlwind to heaven (2 Kings 2:11). However, as with Enoch (Gen 5:24), his fate never becomes an aspiration for the canonical Israelite writers. Two dead boys are resuscitated by Elijah and *Elisha (1 Kings 17:22; 2 Kings 4:34), as is a dead man through contact with Elisha's bones (2 Kings 13:20-21). But these are isolated incidents, evoking an immediate recognition of prophetic power but no later theological development. Apparently, death could be transcended in exceptional cases, but this had no obvious bearing on Israel's life and faith.

Consulting the dead through necromancy is

occasionally mentioned. It was practiced by Saul (1 Sam 28) and Manasseh (2 Kings 21:6; 2 Chron 33:6), but proscribed by Josiah (2 Kings 23:24). Its efficacy is undenied in the first passage, while its condemnation is clear in the second two. The relevant terms (*ʾôb, yiddĕʿōnî*) can indicate both the practitioners ("mediums, wizards") and the spirits consulted (see 1 Sam 28:7-9), indicating their near identity. The only historical narrative with an explicit afterlife element is that of Saul's necromancy (1 Sam 28), and this reveals several aspects of the practice: one could consult a named individual; only the medium saw the spirit; the spirits (pl.; note the verb *ʿōlîm* in 1 Sam 28:13) were called *ʾĕlōhîm;* Samuel's spirit was "disturbed" (*rgz;* cf. Is 14:9 and Phoenician tomb curses). However, the story's main interest is in the prophetic denunciation of Saul, who was about to join the defunct Samuel. This implies that the same fate awaited all, though it is not called Sheol here. Only a few, nonhistorical texts glimpse an alternative fate.

J. Tropper argues that necromancy was widespread until the seventh century BCE, and that its proscription was retrojected into the Saul narratives. Conversely, B. B. Schmidt argues that interest in the dead developed only in the late monarchy. However, necromancy's illegality and therefore its existence are affirmed elsewhere in early narrative (e.g., 1 Sam 6:2; 15:23) and implied throughout 1 Samuel 28: the last recourse, the nocturnal secrecy, the absence of local necromancers, the medium's initial caution, Saul's oath, her reaction, his excuse to Samuel, the meal's justification. These many factors clearly imply that necromancy's illegality was part of the ancient story, and part of early monarchic Yahwism.

5. Ancestor Cult.

Many scholars argue that domestic veneration of the ancestors was part of a preexilic heterodox Yahwism (with solar imagery, Asherah, necromancy, etc.); the Deuteronomists then vigorously attacked this and expunged most references to it from their rewritten history, but a few texts still give glimpses of these earlier practices. However, P. S. Johnston (chap. 8) argues in response that the textual evidence remains elusive, particularly in the Historical Books.

Ruth's first child, Obed, was declared Naomi's *gōʾēl* (Ruth 4:14-15). For H. C. Brichto, Obed would guarantee her afterlife by perform-

ing the appropriate rites. But the use of *gōʾēl* in Ruth for Boaz and the nearer kinsman and its use elsewhere hardly indicate an afterlife concern. After his séance, Saul ate a meal (1 Sam 28:22-25). Tropper (221-22) sees this as venerating the summoned ancestors, but this requires substantial reinterpretation of the text. Before he died, Absalom set up a memorial pillar (2 Sam 18:18). Several scholars see a parallel with the pillar to be attended by Danel's son in the Ugaritic Aqhat epic (KTU 1.17.i.27, 45). But the latter case required a son to perform the necessary ritual, whereas Absalom's pillar testified to his childlessness. On Jezebel's death, *Jehu ordered his attendants to "see to [p-q-d] that accursed woman" (2 Kings 9:34). T. J. Lewis (121) links this to the "caretaker" (*pāqidu*) in Akkadian ancestor cults, but the immediate textual context and the wide semantic field of *pqd* in both Hebrew and Akkadian make this link tenuous.

Elkanah sacrificed at Shiloh (1 Sam 1:21, 2:19), Samuel at Ramah (1 Sam 9:12), David at Bethlehem (1 Sam 20:5-6). Some scholars interpret these occasions as ancestor veneration, either monthly, like the Akkadian *kispum*, or annually at a new moon (e.g., van der Toorn 1996a, 211-18). This is most unlikely for Elkanah, since he sacrificed at the central shrine. It is possible for the other two, but direct evidence is lacking. W. F. Albright considered *"high places" (*bāmôt;* better, "cultic places") as burial sites and ancestor cult centers, but others have discounted his archaeological, etymological, and textual evidence, and this view is not now accepted (see Lewis, 140-41).

Teraphim have long been identified as local deities. The Danites stole Micah's teraphim (Judg 18:14, 18, 20); Michal dressed one as David (1 Sam 19:13, 16; note sg. of "*its* head"); Josiah destroyed them (2 Kings 23:24). These figures varied from saddlebag-size (Laban's; Gen 31:19, 34-35) to life-size (Michal's), and are associated with other images and divination. K. van der Toorn (1990) and others argue that teraphim were ancestor figures, as follows. They were called *ʾĕlōhîm* (Gen 31:30, 32; possibly Judg 18:24), a term used for spirits (1 Sam 28:13); they were consulted in divination and necromancy; Josiah's banishment of mediums and teraphim (2 Kings 23:24) mirrors prohibition of mediums and the dead (Deut 18:11); and elsewhere household gods and ancestors receive veneration together. However, these arguments are not decisive: *'ĕlōhîm* normally means "gods," not "spirits"; consultation of teraphim hardly proves that they were ancestor figures; the supposed parallel between Josiah's reform and Deuteronomy is deceptive because both texts include several other terms; and the non-Israelite texts distinguish between household gods and *eṭemmu* ("spirits"; Assyria, Nuzi) or *mētē* ("dead"; Emar). Nevertheless, the biblical teraphim sometimes may have represented ancestors. But their cameo role in narrative and their general absence from prophetic condemnation suggest that they were not seen as a major threat to Yahwism.

Kinship names (e.g., "Absalom," "Ahab") usually have been seen as theophoric, with "father" (*'āb*), "brother" (*'āḥ*), etc., referring to a tribal or national god. For van der Toorn (1996b), they refer rather to deceased family members and indicate ancestor worship. This is a stronger argument than many, but caution is still needed: (1) only a minority of Hebrew names have kinship terms; (2) other explanations for these terms are still feasible, such as "substitute names"; (3) reference to ancestors need not imply their continued cult, just as names such as "Christine" and "Christopher" today do not necessarily imply Christian faith.

To conclude, some Israelites may well have venerated their dead as other ancient peoples did. However, the arguments adduced from historical (and other) biblical texts to support this as a widespread and acceptable practice are mostly unconvincing.

See also CANAANITE GODS AND RELIGION.

BIBLIOGRAPHY. **W. F. Albright**, "The High Place in Ancient Palestine," in *Volume du Congres Strasbourg 1956,* (VTSup 4; Leiden: Brill, 1957) 242-58; **B. Alfrink**, "L'expression שָׁכַב עִם אֲבֹתָיו," *OtSt* 2 (1943) 106-18; **A. J. Avery-Peck and J. Neusner**, eds., *Judaism in Late Antiquity, 4: Death, Life-After-Death, Resurrection and the World-to-Come in the Judaisms of Antiquity* (HO 1/49; Leiden: E. J. Brill, 2000) sect. 1; **E. Bloch-Smith**, *Judahite Burial Practices and Beliefs About the Dead* (JSOTSup 123; Sheffield: JSOT, 1992); **H. C. Brichto**, "Kin, Cult, Land and Afterlife—A Biblical Complex," *HUCA* 44 (1973) 1-54; **G. R. Driver**, "Plurima Mortis Imago," in *Studies and Essays in Honor of Abraham A. Neuman*, ed. M. Ben-Horin, B. D. Weinryb and S. Zeitlin (Leiden: E. J. Brill, 1962) 129-43; **A. J. Droge**, "Suicide," *ABD* 6.225-31; **B. M. Gittlen**, ed., *Sa-*

cred Time, Sacred Place: Archaeology and the Religion of Israel (Winona Lake, IN: Eisenbrauns, 2002) part 4; **R. L. Harris**, "Why Hebrew She'ol Was Translated 'Grave,'" in *The Making of a Contemporary Translation: New International Version*, ed. K. L. Barker (London: Hodder & Stoughton, 1987) 75-92; **P. S. Johnston**, *Shades of Sheol: Death and Afterlife in the Old Testament* (Downers Grove, IL: InterVarsity Press; Leicester: Apollos, 2002); **T. J. Lewis**, *Cults of the Dead in Ancient Israel and Ugarit* (HSM 39; Atlanta: Scholars Press, 1989); **D. Marcus**, *Jephthah and His Vow* (Lubbock: Texas Tech Press, 1986); **B. B. Schmidt**, *Israel's Beneficent Dead: Ancestor Cult and Necromancy in Ancient Israelite Religion and Tradition* (FAT 11; Tübingen: Mohr Siebeck, 1994; repr., Winona Lake, IN: Eisenbrauns, 1996); **K. Spronk**, *Beatific Afterlife in Ancient Israel and in the Ancient Near East* (AOAT 219; Neukirchen-Vluyn: Neukirchener Verlag, 1986); **K. van der Toorn**, "The Nature of the Biblical Teraphim in the Light of the Cuneiform Evidence," *CBQ* 52 (1990) 203-22; idem, *Family Religion in Babylonia, Syria, and Israel: Continuity and Changes in the Forms of Religious Life* (SHCANE 7; Leiden: E. J. Brill, 1996a); idem, "Ancestors and Anthroponyms: Kinship Terms as Theophoric Elements in Hebrew Names," *ZAW* 108 (1996b) 1-11; **J. Tropper**, *Nekromantie: Totenbefragung im Alten Orient und im Alten Testament* (AOAT 223; Kevelaer: Butzon & Bercker; Neukirchen-Vluyn: Neukirchener Verlag, 1989).

P. S. Johnston

DEBORAH. *See* JUDGES; HISTORY OF ISRAEL 2: PREMONARCHIC ISRAEL.

DECALOGUE. *See* ETHICS.

DECONSTRUCTION. *See* METHODS OF INTERPRETATION.

DEIR ALLA TEXT. *See* ARAM, DAMASCUS AND SYRIA; NON-ISRAELITE WRITTEN SOURCES: SYRO-PALESTINIAN.

DELIVERANCE. *See* SALVATION AND DELIVERANCE.

DEUTERONOMISTIC HISTORY

The Deuteronomistic History is defined as the historical work encompassing the biblical books of Deuteronomy through 2 Kings. The term itself was coined by M. Noth in 1943 in his brilliant treatment of the Deuteronomist and the Chronicler in *Überlieferungsgeschichtliche Studien*. Noth changed the face of biblical studies by proposing that Deuteronomy—2 Kings was a single literary complex: the composition of an editor/writer who had compiled and rewritten an extensive collection of older source material with a singular theology and intent. It is this individual, the Deuteronomistic Historian, for whom the history is named. With his hypothesis, Noth identified Deuteronomy—2 Kings as one of the three great historical corpora of the Hebrew Bible: the Pentateuch, the Deuteronomistic History and the *Chronicler's History.

The content of the Deuteronomistic History is the story of Israel's emergence, success and ultimate failure as an independent political entity in the land of Canaan. It is a *theological* history. Inspired and shaped by the tenets articulated in the book of Deuteronomy, and narrated from the platform of a covenantal understanding of Yahweh's relationship with *Israel, this epic work accounts for Israel's successes and failures as the predictable outworkings of Israel's faithfulness to the *bĕrît* articulated at Sinai. Hence, from the Plains of Moab to the Plains of Jericho (2 Kings 25:5), from Moses to Jehoiakin, the history's overarching agenda is to explain Israel's covenant relationship with God, and how the failure of this relationship eventually leads to the nation's demise at the hands of the Neo-Babylonian Empire in 586 BCE.

As the student of the Deuteronomistic History quickly discovers, the terminology used to describe the Deuteronomistic History and its sources and influence can be quite confusing. In this article, the terms *Deuteronomic* and *Deuteronomist* will be reserved for things pertaining to Deuteronomy (most specifically the proposed "D-source" of the Pentateuch), and *Deuteronomistic* will be used for material influenced by Deuteronomy, in particular the history that it inspired.

1. The Early Development of the Theory
2. Martin Noth
3. The Deuteronomistic History After Noth
4. The Deuteronomistic History in Current Scholarship
5. Conclusions

1. The Early Development of the Theory.
Although traditionally the Pentateuch and the Former Prophets have been understood as separate corpora within the canon, as early as B. Spinoza's *Tractatus Theologico-politicus* (1670), distinctive connections between Deuteronomy and the books of Joshua through 2 Kings were recognized. In response to these connections and his own groundbreaking studies of the Deuteronomic Code, W. M. L. de Wette was the first to suggest that Deuteronomy was more closely associated with the book of *Joshua than it was with the Tetrateuch. De Wette (233) went so far as to characterize the book of Joshua as "Deuteronomic" in style and theology (see Römer and de Pury, 31-35). Following J. Wellhausen's publication of *Prolegomena zur Geschichte Israels* in 1878, and the establishment of K. H. Graf's hypothesis of the fourfold source division of the Pentateuch (JEDP), the distinctive link between Joshua and Deuteronomy was reconfigured such that the academy began to speak of a Hexateuch. Thus, by the late 1800s, the book of Joshua was understood as a continuation of the pentateuchal sources, and the compositional unity of the Hexateuch was assumed. In this same era detailed arguments were presented claiming that pentateuchal sources (specifically J and E) extended through the Hexateuch and could be located as far as the books of *Kings (Cornill; Budde; see Nicholson 1981, vii). Meanwhile, the Deuteronomic flavor of the books of *Judges, *Samuel and Kings was reassessed as the result of several "Deuteronomic" redactions. Wellhausen maintained that these redactions synthesized literary sources associated with those of the Tetrateuch; S. R. Driver (103-203), G. Fohrer (193-95) and R. H. Pfeiffer (293-412) would argue later that the books of Joshua, Judges, Samuel and Kings originated as individual units, but multiple Deuteronomic redactions had brought them to their present state. In 1859 and 1885, respectively, H. Ewald and A. Kuenen argued for a pre- and postexilic redaction of this corpus (see Römer and de Pury, 35-39; Nelson, 14-28). By the 1920s these theories regarding the formation of the books of Joshua through 2 Kings were expanded and championed by scholars such as I. Benzinger, O. Eissfeldt and G. Hölscher. The books of the Former Prophets were well on their way to a source-critical treatment reminiscent of pentateuchal studies.

With the rise of form criticism, opposition to the application of pentateuchal methodologies to the Former Prophets was voiced. Scholars from this newly emerging discipline claimed that the sources behind Joshua—2 Kings should be understood as multiple, independent literary units and complexes that were not related to the biblical divisions of the books but were employed by the biblical authors in the composition of Israel's preexilic history. And although scholars such as R. Kittel admitted some association between these original units and the sources of the Tetrateuch, scholars such as L. Rost did not (a famous example of one of Rost's sources is his "Succession Narrative" in 2 Sam 9—20 and 1 Kings 1—2). It was this sort of form-critical methodology—particularly the work of Noth's teacher A. Alt on the book of Joshua—that laid the groundwork for Noth's groundbreaking assessment (see Römer and de Pury, 35-46; Nicholson 1981, vii-ix, 13-22; McKenzie, *ABD* 2.160-61; Mayes, 1-21).

2. Martin Noth.

Into this cacophony of critical methodology stepped Noth. In opposition to those of the source-critical bent, Noth argued that none of the tetrateuchal sources extended beyond Numbers. Rather, Noth accounted for the source material underlying the Deuteronomistic History as an assortment of preexilic traditional material of varying genres and lengths that had been selected and arranged by a highly discriminating (and extremely respectful) historian in order to support and develop his thesis. "In general Dtr. [the Deuteronomistic Historian] simply reproduced the literary sources available to him and merely provided a connecting narrative for isolated passages" (Noth, 10). In contrast to the hypothesis that the books of Joshua through Kings originated as discrete compositions that subsequently were subjected to multiple Deuteronomic redactions, Noth argued that the history found in the books of Deuteronomy through 2 Kings was simply too unified, and its transitions too smooth, to be anything other than the work of a single editor/author. Rather, Noth accounted for the present division of the biblical books as the Deuteronomistic Historian's partition of Israel's history into five eras, which were organized around the great figures associated with those eras: the review and reiteration of the Moses era; the occupation of *Canaan under *Joshua; the period of the *judges; the rise of the monarchy under *Samuel; the era of the monarchy. Hence, in agreement with his form-critical predecessors and in anticipation of the

then burgeoning discipline of redaction criticism, Noth made a case for a single historian, with true antiquarian intent, who had employed a range of existing written source material in order to compose an account of his people's national history in Palestine. "Dtr. is wholly responsible for the coherence of this complex of material and hence the unity of the whole history in Joshua-Kings which is clearly *intentional* as is shown by the form of these books as we have it" (Noth, 10)

In Noth's reconstruction of the Deuteronomistic History, the "first large-scale complex of tradition" employed by the historian was the Deuteronomic Law (Noth, 17). He identified this original law code as Deut 4:44—30:20 (minus additions) and Deuteronomy 1—3 (possibly parts of Deut 4) (Noth, 14, 26-34) as the Deuteronomistic Historian's introduction to the larger history. Similarly, Noth labeled Deuteronomy 31—34 as selected materials and original composition used by the Deuteronomistic Historian to conclude Deuteronomy and transition to the book of Joshua (Noth, 34-35). According to Noth, this first section of the Deuteronomistic History was critical to the Deuteronomistic Historian's composition for two reasons: (1) the theology of Deuteronomy dictated his entire treatment of Israel's history; (2) the speech of Moses that begins the history served as the first of many speeches employed to structure the larger composition; "At all important points in the course of the history, Dtr. brings forward the leading personages with a speech, long or short, which looks forward and backward in an attempt to interpret the course of events, and draws the relevant practical conclusions about what people should do" (Noth, 5). These speeches include Joshua's monologues in Joshua 1:11-15 and 23:2-30, which initiate and conclude the era of the settlement; Samuel's speech in 1 Samuel 12:1-24, which serves as a segue between the era of the judges and that of the monarchy; and Solomon's prayer in 1 Kings 8:12-51, which summarizes the era of the united monarchy, introduces the temple era, and foreshadows the divided monarchy. Noth also proposed that Joshua 12 (the summary of the conquest battles), Judges 2:11-23 (our narrator's discussion of the sin of Israel and its consequences in the era of the judges) and 2 Kings 17:7-18, 20-23 (the peroration of *Samaria) served the same purpose, although appearing as the narrator's own reflections as opposed to an actual monologue (Noth, 5-6). Although Noth himself was a bit puzzled by this historiographic method ("this practice of inserting general retrospective and anticipatory reflections at certain important points in the history has no exact parallels in the Old Testament outside Dtr." [Noth, 6]), thirty years after Noth the work of J. van Seters in ancient Near Eastern historiography would resolve the quandary by associating this exact method with that of Herodotus and Thucydides. According to Noth, in addition to the old Deuteronomic Law, the Deuteronomistic Historian's source material included a "self-contained and detailed account, already existing in a fixed literary form" of Joshua 1—12; two collections of stories regarding various tribal heroes and "minor" judges, respectively; an extensive collection of the Saul-David traditions; and the historiographic texts cited throughout the books of Kings: "the Books of the Chronicles of the Kings of Israel," "the Books of the Chronicles of the Kings of Judah," and "the Book of the Acts of Solomon" (Noth, 36, 42, 54, 63).

Noth's evidence for his singular tradent included the repetition of similar phraseology apparent throughout the Deuteronomistic History (see Weinfeld, 320-65); the prophecy/fulfillment schema of the history; the strategic appearance and function of unifying speeches and narratives by the leading characters; the Deuteronomistic Historian's integrated and stylized chronology; and the overarching Deuteronomic ideology that permeates the entire work. But for Noth, it was the singularity of thesis evidenced throughout the corpus that marked the work as a discrete literary complex. Identifying the Deuteronomistic Historian as an exile who wrote shortly after Jehoiachin's release from prison in 562 BCE (2 Kings 25:27-30), Noth argued, "Dtr. did not write his history to provide entertainment in hours of leisure or to satisfy a curiosity about national history, but intended it to teach the true meaning of the history of Israel from the occupation to the destruction of the old order. The meaning which he discovered was that God was recognisably at work in this history, continuously meeting the accelerating moral decline with warnings and punishments and, finally, when these proved fruitless, with total annihilation. Dtr., then, perceives a just divine retribution in the history of the people. . . . He sees this as the great unifying factor in the course of events, and speaks of it not in general terms but in relation to the countless specific details reported in the extant traditions" (Noth, 89). This identification and articulation of the Deuteronomistic Historian as a single historian with a singular thesis is the essence of Noth's contribution to the field.

3. The Deuteronomistic History After Noth.

Noth's theories regarding the Deuteronomistic History were quickly embraced, and for many years they remained, for the most part, unchallenged. One exception was Noth's "singular thesis"—his assessment of the Deuteronomistic History as a composition focused solely on the well-deserved outpouring of divine retribution on the covenant-breaking nation of Israel. Shortly after the release of *Überlieferungsgeschichtliche Studien*, G. von Rad countered that Noth had failed to account for the equally powerful messages of hope and grace within the Deuteronomistic History. He argued that the Deuteronomistic Historian's emphasis on the promise of hope to the Davidides is a significant theme within the history and must somehow be incorporated into the evaluation of the Deuteronomistic Historian's agenda. Moreover, he proposed that the historian's chosen conclusion for his epic—the release of Jehoiachin from a Babylonian prison (2 Kings 25:27-30)—was intended to communicate the hope of the restoration of the Davidic line (von Rad, 74-79). In 1961 H. W. Wolff similarly criticized Noth's thesis, highlighting a number of texts in which Israel's return and Yahweh's mercy were expressed, and arguing, with von Rad, that the last four verses of Kings, although not an explicit hope, certainly allowed for the possibility of hope in repentance. Moreover, Wolff proposed the existence of redactional activity within the history *after* Noth's Deuteronomistic Historian. The criticisms made by von Rad and Wolff triggered two of the most significant expansions of Noth's thesis: (1) the "Harvard school" begun by F. M. Cross, which proposes a pre- and postexilic redaction of the Deuteronomistic History, and (2) the "Göttingen school" begun by R. Smend Jr., which proposes three postexilic redactions of the Deuteronomistic History, each contributing a distinct perspective to the history. Both schools have had tremendous influence on the field, the first primarily in America, the second primarily

in Europe (see Römer and de Pury, 62-74; Mc-
Kenzie, *ABD* 2.163-65; O'Brien, 3-23; Provan, 2-
31).

**3.1. The Double Redaction of the Deuteronomistic
History.** Although birthed among the nineteenth-century critics, this theory gained its
place in the field through the work of F. M.
Cross. It has been furthered by his students J. D.
Levenson, R. E. Friedman and B. Halpern (144-
240), as well as by R. Nelson (13-22). As articulated by Cross in *Canaanite Myth and Hebrew Epic*
(274-89), the thesis is that the Deuteronomistic
History underwent a double redaction: (1) the
primary compilation of the history by Dtr^1,
which dates to the days of *Josiah, and (2) a redaction by Dtr^2 in the early exilic period. In the
second redaction the main corpus of Dtr^1 was
modified and updated in order to complete the
history and to better suit it to an exilic audience.

Cross's critique of Noth's hypothesis focused
on the conspicuous absence of Nathan's oracle
(2 Sam 7:1-17) and David's speech (2 Sam 7:18-
29) among Noth's transitional speeches. Although these momentous interactions appear to
be crucial to the Deuteronomistic History, Noth
chose to attribute them to sources other than the
Deuteronomistic Historian himself: "We cannot
possibly claim that the latter section [speaking of
Nathan's prophecy] is Deuteronomistic, since
neither the prohibition of temple-building nor
the strong emphasis on the value of the monarchy are in the spirit of Dtr" (Noth, 55). Cross
(274-89) pointed out that Noth's strictly "negative" view of the Deuteronomistic Historian's
agenda had compelled him to expel this positive
report regarding the monarchy on presupposi-
tional rather than empirical evidence. Building
on the work of D. J. McCarthy, who argued that
2 Samuel 7 not only belongs within the core materials of the Deuteronomistic History, but is in
fact essential to it as a transitional speech like
those of Deuteronomy 31 and Joshua 23, Cross
demonstrated that the texts of the *Davidic covenant do indeed bring a theme of grace to the
Deuteronomistic History—a theme embodied in
the divine promise of a never-ending kingdom.

According to Cross (275), this theme of grace,
in apparent contradistinction to Noth's "unre-
lieved and irreversible doom," should be understood as the second of Dtr^1's two great themes.
Cross maintains that Dtr^1 interacts throughout
his history with two themes: (1) the sin of *Jeroboam I and its consequences; (2) the faithful-

ness of *David and its consequences. Here the
bulls of Bethel and Dan are juxtaposed with the
ark and the Jerusalem temple, the peroration of
Samaria (2 Kings 17) with the reform of Josiah
(2 Kings 22). In this manner Dtr^1 accommodated the themes of judgment and grace in that
judgment was the ultimate fate of Jeroboam I
and his kingdom, while a future and a hope
were the ultimate fate of the Davidides and their
kingdom. This paralleling of judgment and
hope was not merely an engaging narrative
strategy; it was the vehicle by which Dtr^1 communicated the central concerns of the Josianic
reform. As for the ultimate demise of the Davidides at the hands of Nebuchadnezzar, and the
message of inevitable doom that it conveyed, according to Cross, Dtr^1 knew nothing of that demise. Rather, he concluded his history with the
climactic tale of Josiah's reforms in the south,
which, from his perspective, forever purged
Judah of *ʾĕlōhîm ʾăḥērîm*, brought some level of
political unity between the ravaged north and
Judah, and vindicated "the man of God who
came from Judah" (1 Kings 13:1-3; 2 Kings 23:17,
18). In this scheme the conclusion of the Deuteronomistic History (2 Kings 23:26—25:30) was
written by the exilic Dtr^2, who "retouched or
overwrote the Deuteronomistic work to bring it
up to date in the Exile, to record the fall of Jerusalem, and to reshape the history, with a minimum of reworking, into a document relevant to
exiles for whom the bright expectations of the
Josianic era were hopelessly past" (Cross, 285).
Thus it was Dtr^2 who was responsible for what
Cross names the subtheme of inevitable rejection, which appears periodically in the Deuteronomistic History. What is common to all of
Cross's Dtr^2 passages is that they speak of an exile for Judah, real or potential, as the result of
covenant breaking (for a list of Dtr^2 passages see
Cross, 285-87; Friedman, 25). Cross holds that
this theme is epitomized in the paradigmatic
Dtr^2 pericope regarding the evils of *Manasseh
and the consequences that his irresponsibility
brought on Judah (2 Kings 21:2-15).

Subsequent treatments of the double-redaction
theory have added a welcome nuance to Cross's
theory by challenging his demarcation of Dtr^1
and Dtr^2 passages according to their assessment
of the Davidic covenant. The work of Nelson
and Halpern is of particular significance in that
they have refuted the assumption that Dtr^2 is responsible for "reinterpreting" the originally un-

conditional Davidic covenant in 2 Samuel 7 as now conditional (Nelson, 104-18; Halpern, 157-75). Arguing with Friedman and Levenson, Nelson and Halpern demonstrate that the preexilic perception of David's covenant was in reality both conditional and unconditional (Levenson 1979; Friedman, 10-13).

A frequent criticism of the Harvard school is that it has dramatically altered Noth's original thesis by postulating that the primary historian of the Deuteronomistic History is a preexilic figure. The great strength of this reconstruction, however, is its ability to account for the disproportionate emphasis that the history places on the righteousness of Josiah, as well as the optimistic preexilic perspective that governs so much of the Deuteronomistic History. Moreover, if a Josianic redaction is adopted, the social location of the historian assists in explaining both the content and the impetus for the Deuteronomistic History. We are left with a Judahite court personality commissioned during the reign of Josiah to compose a history garnered from the official documents of Israel's monarchy, a history that climaxes with reforms galvanized by the discovery of the *běrît* in Josiah's temple.

3.2. The Göttingen School. R. Smend Jr. is credited with the birth of the Göttingen school. This school of thought postulates that the core composition of the Deuteronomistic History is postexilic, and that this core has been modified by as many as two further postexilic redactions. The assumption underlying the identification of these various literary layers is that some sort of Deuteronomistic school continued to operate well into the exilic period. In his 1971 essay "Das Gesetz und die Völker" (see Knoppers and McConville, 95-110), Smend focused on the diachronic testimony of selected passages from the books of Joshua and Judges. Here Smend embraced Noth's Deuteronomistic Historian (whom he designated DtrG, later DtrH) as the individual responsible for the core history compiled in the early exile, but he proposed in addition to this primary compiler a later nomistic redactor, DtrN. DtrN might be recognized by two related themes: (1) the law and (2) foreign peoples remaining in the land. According to Smend, DtrN adapted DtrH's core history in accordance with his perspective that obedience to the law was crucial to the successful conquest of the land, and that the ongoing presence of foreign

peoples within the land demonstrated that the law had not been observed (see Provan, 16-18). (In a subsequent publication Smend also suggested that his DtrN may have been responsible for the insertion of Deut 4—30 into the Deuteronomistic History [see Smend 1978, 73; cf. Levenson 1975]). Smend's reconstruction has often been criticized in that it was based on such a small sampling of the Deuteronomistic History. Hence, in 1972 Smend's student W. Dietrich expanded the theory by studies in the books of Kings. Dietrich's attempt to address the complex ideology of this segment of the Deuteronomistic History resulted in a third redactor: DtrP (prophetic). Dietrich proposed that DtrP had augmented the core history of DtrH with a significant number of prophetic narratives and oracles and was the one responsible for the prophecy/fulfillment schema within the Deuteronomistic History. Dietrich affirmed Smend's DtrN as the final redactor of the Deuteronomistic History, but he significantly expanded the texts that Smend had assigned to him, crediting DtrN with the last four verses of Kings as well as a variety of pro-Davidic passages. Dietrich was initially criticized for failing to address the relationship between 2 Samuel 7 and the DtrP redaction. But in a later article, "David in Überlieferung und Geschichte" (61), Dietrich analyzed 2 Samuel 7, concluding that 2 Samuel 7:8-10, 11b, 13, 15b, 16 are DtrH (whom he dates to 580 BCE, twenty years earlier than Smend's DtrH). Even within the Göttingen school, however, it has been noted that the theology, language and ideology of DtrH and DtrP are extremely similar, and therefore the existence and the delineation of DtrP remain in question (see Provan, 24-25). Another persuasive criticism regarding Dietrich's DtrP hypothesis is the silence of the Deuteronomistic History regarding the writing prophets. K. Koch has pointed out that not one of these, outside of Isaiah in 2 Kings 18—20, is mentioned within the history (see Albertz, 4-6). Moreover, there is growing concern regarding the assumption of the existence of a Deuteronomistic school. R. Coggins has synthesized this concern, stating that the theory "becomes 'more tenuous and vague' as its implications are examined in greater detail" (Coggins, 33). Dietrich's current views of DtrP can be located in "Prophetie im Deuteronomistischen Geschichtswerk." Here he suggests the existence of a pre-DtrH prophetic narrative work dating to the era of Manasseh, and speaks of his postexilic DtrP as "'an honest broker' between the prophetic and the historiographic traditions" (Dietrich 2000, 64).

A third voice within the Göttingen school is T. Veijola. Also a student of Smend, his major focus has been the contrasting views of kingship present in the Deuteronomistic History. In pursuit of this topic Veijola has addressed the majority of the Deuteronomistic History through the Smend/Dietrich lens. Although he has, in part, countered Dietrich (considerably reducing the portion of 2 Sam 7 allotted to DtrH [Veijola 1975, 68, 79, 126, 42]), Veijola has done much to enhance the Smend/Dietrich paradigm by explaining the often complex portrayal of David and his offspring in terms of the three redactional levels identified by his predecessors. Veijola concludes that the apparently contradictory messages regarding the monarchy may be resolved by understanding DtrH as pro-David and promonarchy, DtrP as generally antimonarchy, and DtrN as pro-David but generally antimonarchy (see Provan, 18-20).

The major criticisms made of the Göttingen school include (1) a lack of clarity regarding the dates and locales of the redactions, (2) an unsatisfactory analysis of the nature and extent of the history that remains (DtrH) once the layers of later redaction are removed (O'Brien, 10), and (3) the tendency within this school toward the multiplication of redactors.

3.3. Additional Advances in Deuteronomistic Studies. Since the first publications of Cross and Smend, an enormous amount of work has been done in discussion with their theories regarding the formation of the Deuteronomistic History, far more than can be acknowledged here. However, a few distinctive movements that either lie outside this discussion or have served to augment it uniquely must at least be summarized. The first is most often associated with M. Weinfeld, *Deuteronomy and the Deuteronomic School,* and E. W. Nicholson, *Deuteronomy and Tradition.* Similar to Smend, these scholars postulate a "school" or "circle" of Deuteronomists who executed a series of redactions and compositions from the days of *Hezekiah through the early exile. It is understood that the agenda of this Deuteronomistic school was largely *propagandistic, and their agenda was focused on the centralization of the cult in *Jerusalem.

Another significant development is the "triple-redaction" modification of Cross's double-redaction hypothesis. For the most part this hypothesis is dependent on what B. Halpern and D. Vanderhooft (183) name the "skeletal formulary" around which the books of Kings have been constructed (i.e., formulas involving the evaluation of the king, his death and burial, the naming of the queen mother, etc.). Those who adhere to this model have found in these formulas evidence indicating a shift in the authorship of the Deuteronomistic History at the era of Hezekiah. First proposed by H. Weippert in 1972, this Hezekian redaction of the Deuteronomistic History has been embraced by scholars such as B. Peckham, S. L. McKenzie, I. Provan, B. Halpern, and D. Vanderhooft, but the debate continues within this circle as to whether Cross's Josianic redaction should be maintained in the reconstruction (see Provan, 22-55; Peckham; McKenzie 1985; Halpern and Vanderhooft). Provan's work is somewhat unique in this regard in that he recognizes only one preexilic redaction of the Deuteronomistic History, Hezekian in focus, but early Josianic in date. Peckham, on the other hand, affirms the Hezekian redaction but understands the Deuteronomistic History as part of a sweeping historiographic effort that encompasses all of the Pentateuch and the Former Prophets. Hence, he champions a Deuteronomistic redaction of the Pentateuch and two Deuteronomistic Historians, stating that "the Dtr^2 history is not an editorial compilation of materials but the culmination of an eminent Israelite literary and historiographic tradition" (Peckham, 73).

Another important movement in Deuteronomistic studies is that of the new literary approaches (*see* Narrative Art of Israel's Historians). As exemplified in the work of R. Polzin, this methodology seeks to address the Deuteronomistic History as a literary and theological piece as opposed to a historiographic one. Characterizing the quest for sources and redactors as unproductive and even deleterious to true interpretation, this group is quite critical of the historico-critical exegesis that has characterized past studies, and credits the Deuteronomistic Historian with virtually all of the text as we now have it.

A fourth movement of critical importance is historiographic in focus. This movement can be associated with J. van Seters and B. Halpern. The contribution of van Seters is his focus on the genre of ancient history writing in association with the Deuteronomistic History. Contesting many of the earlier theories regarding Israelite historiography by comparing the work of the Deuteronomistic Historian to the early Greek historians Herodotus and Thucydides, as well as many of the historiographic writings of the ancient Near East, Van Seters isolates the distinctions between modern and ancient history-writing and discusses Israel's unique position in the ancient Near East as a civilization that moved beyond historiographic texts into true history writing. Van Seters claims that the Deuteronomistic Historian is not only the first Israelite historian, but also the first historian of Western civilization. Based on his genre focus, Van Seters argues against the mainstream effort to identify source material and layers of redaction within the Deuteronomistic History: "A history is not merely the sum of its parts, and to analyze a history by taking it apart in order to discern the original functions of the various elements will never yield the meaning of the whole" (Van Seters, 3). The primary critique of Van Seters's work has to do with his failure to affirm any historiographic materials underlying the final form of the Deuteronomistic History. Van Seters seriously entertains the possibility that the sources that the Deuteronomistic Historian refers to within the history may be only a literary device—that these "sources," and therefore the Deuteronomistic History itself, may be completely fictional (Van Seters, 43-49). As a result, many have criticized Van Seters's view of the historicity of the Deuteronomistic History as "overly negative" (McKenzie, *ABD* 2.167).

B. Halpern's work also is focused on the form and function of the Deuteronomistic History as ancient history writing. Unlike Van Seters, however, Halpern is quite optimistic about the historiographic nature of the Deuteronomistic Historian's sources, and he is openly critical of Van Seters's historiographic skepticism. In his compelling treatment Halpern defines history writing partly by authorial intent, asking the question "Did the writer have authentic historical intent?" In regard to the Deuteronomistic Historian, Halpern answers yes: "Noth's historian fits the mold of a thinker emboldened by honest conviction to impose meaningful order on his nation's past" (Halpern, 31). Hence, Halpern recognizes historiographic source material behind the Deuteronomistic History and argues that the historian was both constrained

and shaped by his data. The contribution of Halpern's work is that it moves the discussion of the Deuteronomistic History out of the abstractions of modern analysis and back into the concrete context first envisioned by Noth: a historian working with his data, attempting to create an intellectual form through which to offer his people an account of their past.

A final contribution that has the potential of moving Deuteronomistic studies in a new direction is recent work that questions the existence of a "Name Theology" in the Deuteronomistic History. A broadly accepted paradigm, the Name Theology assumes that the Hebrew Bible demonstrates a three-stage, immanence-to-transcendence evolution regarding the mode of divine presence at the cult site. These stages are: (1) the anthropomorphic and immanent presence of the deity in the JE source(s), (2) the near-material presence of the deity in the Deuteronomistic History, and (3) the abstract, demythologized, and transcendent presence in the P source. According to the theory, the catalyst for the evolution between stages one and two was the "deuteronomistic correction," an intentional redefinition of the divine presence enacted by the Deuteronomists. The identifying feature of this "correction" is the use of the word *name* as a theological tag supposedly intended to communicate the near-material divine presence of stage two (see Richter 2002, 7-39). In recent years, however, G. J. Wenham, A. S. Van der Woude and I. Wilson have brought significant evidence to bear that seriously undermines several aspects of this hermeneutical paradigm. Moreover, Richter has demonstrated that a linchpin of the Name Theology, the Deuteronomic phrase *lĕšakkēn šĕmô šām* (which is usually translated "[the place where Yahweh] will cause his name to dwell"; cf. its synonymous reflex in the Deuteronomistic History, *lāśûm šĕmô šām* [1 Kgs 9:3; 11:36; 14:21; 2 Kgs 21:4, 7]), is actually a loan-adaptation of a cognate Akkadian phrase common to the royal monumental literary typology of Mesopotamia, Akk *šuma šakānu*. In its native context, Akk *šuma šakānu* (as with its NWS calque *lāśûm šĕmô šām*) means to place one's inscription on a monument; it can also mean to install an inscribed monument. Thus, Richter argues that *lĕšakkēn šĕmô šām* should be retranslated as "(the place where Yahweh) will place his name," and that Yahweh's "name" in these instances should be related to an inscribed monument, not a semi-hypostatic presence as long theorized by the Name Theology. As a result of these new studies, the existence of the Name Theology in the Deuteronomistic History will need to be reconsidered.

4. The Deuteronomistic History in Current Scholarship.
In 1992 S. McKenzie stated, "To the extent that any position in biblical studies can be regarded as the consensus viewpoint, the existence of the DH has achieved almost canonical status" (McKenzie, *ABD* 2.161). But as G. Knoppers observed in 2000, "This is no longer the case. One can no longer assume a widespread scholarly consensus on the existence of a Deuteronomistic History. In the last five years an increasing number of commentators have expressed grave doubts about fundamental tenets of Noth's classic study" (Knoppers, 120). The recognition of the existence of the Deuteronomistic History was the gift of redaction criticism, but in its expansion over recent decades the gift apparently has become a curse. As R. Person remarks, "The problem lies in the inability of redaction criticism to distinguish one Deuteronomic redactor from another Deuteronomic redactor, since all Deuteronomic redactors use similar Deuteronomic language and themes!" (Person, 4). Hence, in recent years the apparent contradictions of theme and perspective in the Deuteronomistic History, and the ever multiplying levels of source and redaction, have been dealt with by returning to *Formgeschichte* theories of the late nineteenth and early twentieth centuries that preceded Noth. As summarized by Knoppers, chief among these newer approaches are those of C. Westermann and J. G. McConville, both of whom prefer to emphasize distinct books within a larger and somewhat loosely edited corpus (Knoppers, 120-24; Westermann, 13-39; McConville, 3-13). E. A. Knauf's work is proving to be equally influential. Knauf not only considers the Deuteronomistic History to be composed of a series of independent works, but also regards these books themselves as the result of "fundamentally unrelated exilic and postexilic redactions" (Knoppers, 122). A. G. Auld recently has suggested a Q-type source behind both Kings and Chronicles, claiming that it is this shared source that influenced the message of Deuteronomy, not vice versa. There are also those who suggest a "block model"—the idea that larger

segments of the history, which incorporate separately authored books, were redacted fairly late in the editorial process (see Eynikel). And then there is the most recent, and in the mind of the present author, the most disturbing trend as articulated by T. Römer in his foreword to *The Future of the Deuteronomistic History*: "The debate is becoming quite confusing and in recent years more and more scholars are inclined to deny the existence of a Deuteronomistic History as elaborated by Noth . . . they argue against any editorial coherence" (Römer, viii). Along with the frustration voiced here is the rising specter of "pan-Deuteronomism." This is the thesis of a recent publication edited by L. S. Schearing and S. L. McKenzie, *Those Elusive Deuteronomists*. Herein is a series of articles that address the growing tendency to attribute "virtually every significant development within ancient Israel's religious practice" to a Deuteronomistic source or redactor (Coggins, 22). This critique is not meant to address scholarship done on the Deuteronomistic History itself, but aims to address the growing pool of scholarship identifying the "Deuteronomists" in nearly every other corpus of the Hebrew Bible. In this publication a call is issued for more precision in identifying "Deuteronomistic" vocabulary, concepts, literature, influence and literary process. What is the conclusion drawn from this "pan-Deuteronomic" trend? "Recent research may in fact have demonstrated, unwittingly, that the concept of Deuteronomism has become so amorphous that it no longer has any analytical precision and so ought to be abandoned" (R. Wilson, 82). In many ways, the disarray that is now confronting Deuteronomistic scholarship recalls the chaos that preceded Noth's original proposal.

5. Conclusions.
In the mind of the present author, the current state of confusion in Deuteronomistic studies ultimately is the result of an overly optimistic opinion of how much redactional activity might be isolated within a finished piece, augmented by the atomistic tendencies that seem to be inherent to the critical methodologies of OT exegesis. Too often this atomistic optimism has been further exacerbated by a lack of respect for the ancient historian—the apparent assumption that an *ancient* historian would be incapable of maintaining a complex perspective on the subject matter, or unable to hold

conflicting views in tension. In light of the present cacophony of voices regarding the Deuteronomistic History, it seems wise at this juncture to step back, to simplify, and to identify a few truths that we might hold to be self-evident.

For the present author, there are six such truths. The first is that there is a Deuteronomistic History, and that it is historiographic in nature. The second, as Noth proposed, is that the literary and theological foundation of the Deuteronomistic History is the "old Deuteronomic law." As George Mendenhall first recognized in 1954, the literary form of the book of Deuteronomy is an intentional echo of the international diplomatic texts of the ancient world. In other words, the *theological* foundation of Israel's self-understanding is structured as a *political* agreement that dictates the precepts by which Yahweh and Israel had agreed to govern their relationship. Hence, the land grant of Palestine, the laws of loyalty, tribute and war, the blessings that would result if this bilateral agreement were kept, and the curses that would be enacted if it were broken are all articulated in the opening chapter of the Deuteronomistic History. It is this opening chapter that lays the foundation, sets the tone, and predicts the outcome of Deuteronomistic Historian's history: Israel will rise and fall based on its ability to keep covenant. A third truth is that the Deuteronomistic History is structured by transitional speeches. Whether these speeches are source material or created out of whole cloth, clearly the historian is transitioning through his history by means of this literary device. A fourth truth is the existence of at least one pre- and one post-exilic redaction of the history. A fifth is that the historian(s) of the Deuteronomistic History made use of extensive source material, source material that was utilized in a highly deferential fashion and served both to constrain and to mold history and historian alike. A sixth truth involves the issue of "pan-Deuteronomism." I must agree with McKenzie that the presence of Deuteronomic vocabulary and ideology throughout the bulk of the *canon need not be interpreted as Deuteronomistic redaction; rather, in most cases it is probably best understood as Deuteronomic influence (Schearing and McKenzie, 262-71). Certainly, it would be difficult to overstate the influence of Deuteronomy's covenant on Israel's self-understanding. In concert with this reality, we should not be surprised that the content of this formational ideology is remembered and reiterated throughout the written record of Israel's ongoing national and religious experience.

See also CHRONICLER'S HISTORY; HISTORIOGRAPHY, OLD TESTAMENT; ORAL TRADITION AND WRITTEN TRADITION; SOURCES, REFERENCES TO.

BIBLIOGRAPHY. **R. Albertz,** "In Search of the Deuteronomists," in *The Future of the Deuteronomistic History,* ed. T. Römer (BETL 147; Leuven: Leuven University Press, 2000) 1-18; **A. Alt,** "Josua," in *Kleine Schriften zur Geschichte des Volkes Israel* (3 vols.; Munich: Beck, 1953-1959 [1936]) 1.176-92; **G. A. Auld,** *Kings Without Privilege: David and Moses in the Story of the Bible's Kings* (Edinburgh: T & T Clark, 1994); **I. Benzinger,** *Jahvist und Elohist in den Königsbüchern* (BWAT 2; Berlin: Kohlhammer, 1921); **K. Budde,** *Die Bücher Richter und Samuel: Ihre Quellen und ihr Aufbau* (Giessen: Ricker, 1890); **R. Coggins,** "What Does 'Deuteronomistic' Mean?" in *Those Elusive Deuteronomists: The Phenomenon of Pan-Deuteronomism,* ed. L. S. Schearing and S. L. McKenzie (JSOTSup 268; Sheffield: Sheffield Academic Press, 2000) 22-35; **C. H. Cornill,** "Ein Elohistischer Bericht über die Entstehung des israelitischen Konigthums in 1 Samuelis i-xv aufgezeigt," *Zeitschrift für kirkliche Wissenschaft und kirkliches Leben* 6 (1885) 113-28; idem, "Noch einmal Sauls Königswahl und Verwerfung," *ZAW* 10 (1890) 96-109; **F. M. Cross,** *Canaanite Myth and Hebrew Epic: Essays in the History of the Religion of Israel* (Cambridge, MA: Harvard University Press, 1973); **W. M. L. de Wette,** *Lehrbuch der historisch-kritischen Einleitung in die kanonischen und apokryphischen Bücher des Alten Testaments* (8th ed.; Berlin: Reimer, 1817); **W. Dietrich,** *Prophetie und Geschichte: Eine redaktionsgeschichtliche Untersuchung zum deuteronomistischen Geschichtswerk* (FRLANT 108; Göttingen: Vandenhoeck & Ruprecht, 1972; idem, *David, Saul und die Propheten: Das Verhältnis von Religion und Politik nach den prophetischen Überlieferungen vom frühesten Königtum in Israel* (BWANT 7/2; Stuttgart: Kohlhammer, 1987); idem, "Prophetie im deuteronomistischen Geschichtswerk," in *The Future of the Deuteronomistic History,* ed. T. Römer (BETL 147; Leuven: Leuven University Press, 2000) 47-65; **S. R. Driver,** *Introduction to the Literature of the Old Testament* (New York: Scribner, 1913 [1898]); **O. Eissfeldt,** *Hexateuch-Synopse: Die Erzählung der Fünf Bücher Mose und des Buches Josua mit dem An-*

fange des Richterbuches (Leipzig: Hinrichs, 1922); idem, *Die Quellen des Richterbuches* (Leipzig: Hinrichs, 1925); **H. Ewald,** *Geschichte des Volkes Israel bis Christus* (6 vols.; Göttingen: Dieterich, 1843-1859); **E. Eynikel,** *The Reform of King Josiah and the Composition of the Deuteronomistic History* (Oudtestamentische studiën 33; Leiden: Brill, 1996); **G. Fohrer,** *Introduction to the Old Testament* (Nashville: Abingdon, 1968 [1965]); **R. E. Friedman,** *The Exile and Biblical Narrative: The Formation of the Deuteronomistic and Priestly Works* (HSM 22; Chico, CA: Scholars Press, 1981); **B. Halpern,** *The First Historians: The Hebrew Bible and History* (San Francisco: Harper & Row, 1988); **B. Halpern and D. Vanderhooft,** "The Editions of Kings in the 7th-6th Centuries B.C.E.," *HUCA* 62 (1991) 179-244; **G. Hölscher,** "Das Buch der Könige, seine Quellen und seine Redaktion," in *Eucharisterion I: Studien zur Religion und Literatur des Alten und Neuen Testaments,* ed. H. Schmidt (FRLANT 36; Göttingen: Vandenhoeck & Ruprecht, 1923) 158-213; **G. N. Knoppers,** "Is There a Future for the Deuteronomistic History?" in *The Future of the Deuteronomistic History,* ed. T. Römer (BETL 147; Leuven: Leuven University Press, 2000) 119-34; **G. N. Knoppers and J. G. McConville,** eds., *Reconsidering Israel and Judah: Recent Studies on the Deuteronomistic History* (Winona Lake, IN: Eisenbrauns, 2000); **A. Kuenen,** *Historisch-kritische Einleitung in die Bücher des Alten Testaments* (Leipzig: Schulze, 1887 [1885]); **J. D. Levenson,** "Who Inserted the Book of the Torah?" *HTR* 68 (1975) 203-33; idem, "The Davidic Covenant and Its Modern Interpreters," *CBQ* 41 (1979) 205-19; idem, "From Temple to Synagogue: 1 Kings 8," in *Traditions in Transformation: Turning Points in Biblical Faith,* ed. B. Halpern and J. Levenson (Winona Lake, IN: Eisenbrauns, 1981) 143-66; idem, "The Last Four Verses in Kings," *JBL* 103 (1984) 353-61; **A. D. H. Mayes,** *The Story of Israel Between Settlement and Exile: A Redactional Study of the Deuteronomistic History* (London: SCM, 1983); **D. J. McCarthy,** "II Samuel 7 and the Structure of the Deuteronomic History," *JBL* 84 (1965) 131-38; **J. G. McConville,** "The Old Testament Historical Books in Modern Scholarship," *Themelios* 22.3 (1997) 3-13; **S. L. McKenzie,** *The Chronicler's Use of the Deuteronomistic History* (HSM 33; Atlanta: Scholars Press, 1985); idem, "Deuteronomistic History," *ABD* 2.160-68; **S. L. McKenzie and M. P. Graham,** *The History of Israel's Traditions: The Heritage of Martin Noth* (JSOTSup 182; Sheffield: Sheffield Academic Press, 1994); **R. D. Nelson,** *The Double Redaction of the Deuteronomistic History* (JSOTSup 18; Sheffield: JSOT, 1981); **E. W. Nicholson,** *Deuteronomy and Tradition* (Philadelphia: Fortress, 1967); idem, foreword to *The Deuteronomistic History,* by M. Noth (JSOTSup 15; Sheffield: JSOT, 1981); **M. Noth,** *The Deuteronomistic History* (JSOTSup 15; Sheffield: JSOT, 1981 [1943]); **M. A. O'Brien,** *The Deuteronomistic History Hypothesis: A Reassessment* (OBO 92; Göttingen: Vandenhoeck & Ruprecht, 1989); **B. Peckham,** *The Composition of the Deuteronomistic History* (HSM 35. Atlanta. Scholars Press, 1985); **R. F. Person Jr.,** *The Deuteronomic School: History, Social Setting, and Literature* (Studies in Biblical Literature 2; Atlanta: Society of Biblical Literature, 2002); **R. H. Pfeiffer,** *Introduction to the Old Testament* (2d ed.; New York: Harper, 1948); **R. Polzin,** *Moses and the Deuteronomist* (New York: Seabury, 1980); idem, *Samuel and the Deuteronomist* (San Francisco: Harper & Row, 1989); idem, *David and the Deuteronomist* (ISBL; Bloomington, IN: Indiana University Press, 1993); **I. W. Provan,** *Hezekiah and the Books of Kings: A Contribution to the Debate about the Composition of the Deuteronomistic History* (BZAW 172; New York and Berlin: de Gruyter, 1988); **G. von Rad,** *Studies in Deuteronomy* (SBT 9; London: SCM, 1953 [1947]); **S. Richter,** *The Deuteronomistic History and the Name Theology:* lĕšakkēn šĕmô šām *in the Bible and the Ancient Near East* (BZAW 318; New York and Berlin: de Gruyter, 2002); **T. Römer,** ed., *The Future of the Deuteronomistic History* (BETL 147; Leuven: Leuven University Press, 2000); **T. Römer and A. de Pury,** "Deuteronomistic Historiography (DH): History of Research and Debated Issues," in *Israel Constructs Its History: Deuteronomistic Historiography in Recent Research,* ed. A. de Pury, T. Römer and J.-D. Macchi (JSOTSup 306; Sheffield: Sheffield Academic Press, 2000) 24-143; **L. Rost,** *Die Überlieferung von der Thronnachfolge Davids* (BWANT 3/6; Stuttgart: Kohlhammer, 1926); ET, *The Succession to the Throne of David* (Historic Texts and Interpreters in Biblical Scholarship 1; Sheffield: Almond, 1982); **L. S. Schearing and S. L. McKenzie,** eds., *Those Elusive Deuteronomists: The Phenomenon of Pan-Deuteronomism* (JSOTSup 268; Sheffield: Sheffield Academic Press, 1999); **R. Smend Jr.,** "Das Gesetz und die Völker: Ein Beitrag zur deuteronomischen Redaktionsgeschichte," in *Probleme biblischer Theologie,* ed. H. W. Wolff (Munich: Kaiser, 1971) 494-509; idem, *Die Entstehung* *des Alten Testaments* (Theologische Wissenschaft 1; Stuttgart: Kohlhammer, 1978); **A. S. Van der Woude,** "םש," *TLOT* 3.1348-67; **J. Van Seters,** *In Search of History: Historiography in the Ancient World and the Origins of Biblical History* (New Haven: Yale University Press, 1983); **T. Veijola,** *Die ewige Dynastie: David und die Entstehung seiner Dynastie nach der deuteronomistischen Darstellung* (AASF B193; Helsinki: Suomalainen Tiedeakatemia, 1975); idem, *Das Königtum in der Beurteilung der deuteronomistischen Historiographie: Eine redaktionsgeschichtliche Untersuchung* (AASF B198. Helsinki: Suomalainen Tiedeakatemia, 1977); **M. Weinfeld,** *Deuteronomy and the Deuteronomic School* (Oxford: Clarendon Press, 1972; repr., Winona Lake, IN: Eisenbrauns, 1992); **H. Weippert,** "Die 'deuteronomistischen' Beurteilungen der Könige von Israel und Juda und das Problem der Redaktion der Königsbücher," *Bib* 53 (1972) 301-39; **J. Wellhausen,** *Die Composition des Hexateuchs und der historischen Bücher des Alten Testaments* (2d ed.; Berlin: Reimer, 1899); **G. J. Wenham,** "Deuteronomy and the Central Sanctuary," *TynBul* 22 (1971) 103-18; **C. Westermann,** *Die Geschichtsbücher des Alten Testament: Gab es ein deuteronomistisches Geschichtswerk?* (TB 87; Gütersloh: Kaiser, 1994); **I. Wilson,** *Out of the Midst of the Fire: Divine Presence in Deuteronomy* (SBLDS 151; Atlanta: Scholars Press, 1995); **R. R. Wilson,** "Who Was the Deuteronomist? (Who Was Not the Deuteronomist?): Reflections on Pan-Deuteronomism," in *Those Elusive Deuteronomists: The Phenomenon of Pan-Deuteronomism,* ed. L. S. Schearing and S. L. McKenzie (JSOTSup 268; Sheffield: Sheffield Academic Press, 2000) 67-82; **H. W. Wolff,** "Das Kerygma des deuteronomistischen Geschichtswerkes," *ZAW* 73 (1961) 171-86; ET, "The Kerygma of the Deuteronomic Historical Work," in *The Vitality of Old Testament Traditions,* ed. W. Brueggemann and H. W. Wolff (Atlanta: John Knox, 1972) 83-100.

S. L. Richter

DIASPORA. *See* HISTORY OF ISRAEL 7: PERSIAN PERIOD.

DISEASE. *See* SICKNESS AND DISEASE.

DIVINATION. *See* MAGIC AND DIVINATION.

DIVINE KINGSHIP. *See* GOD; SAMUEL, BOOKS OF.

DIVORCE. *See* EZRA.

DYNASTY. *See* ROYAL FAMILY.

E

ECONOMIC JUSTICE. *See* ETHICS.

EDOM, EDOMITES
According to the Bible, Edom and its inhabitants were closely related to the Israelites genealogically, territorially and religiously. However, for the most part, the biblical writers depict the Edomites as enemies of the Israelites. On the basis of extrabiblical texts, it is apparent that Edom was known to the *Egyptians, *Assyrians and *Babylonians. Biblical studies and archaeological excavations and surveys are continually adding to our knowledge of Edom's economy, script and language, occupational history, religion, and territory.

1. Meaning of the Words "Edom," "Esau" and "Seir"
2. Edom/Edomites in the Bible
3. Edom/Edomites in Extrabiblical Literary Sources
4. Archaeology
5. Economy
6. Religion
7. Script and Language

1. Meaning of the Words "Edom," "Esau" and "Seir."
The Hebrew word *ʾĕdôm* is based on the root *ʾdm,* meaning "be red" (*HALOT* 1.14). Thus the name probably was given to the area to the southeast of the Dead Sea because of the reddish color of the sandstone of the region.

Esau (*ʿēśaw* [see 2.1 below])—that is, Edom (Gen 36:1; 36:8; 36:19)—is the putative ancestor of the Edomites (Gen 36:9). He settled in the hill country of Mount Seir (Gen 36:9; Deut 2:4, 5, 8, 12; 22; 29), and the land of Seir is identified as the country of Edom (Gen 32:3; Judg 5:4).

The Hebrew word *śēʿîr* comes from the word *śāʿîr,* meaning "hairy," "made of hair," "the

hairy one" (*HALOT* 3.1341), "thicket, or small wooded region" (*HALOT* 3.1342).

2. Edom/Edomites in the Bible.
The Bible provides information on the origins, territory and history of Edom/Edomites.

2.1. Origins. Genesis 25:19-26 states that Abraham was the father of Isaac, and that Isaac, when he was forty years old, married Rebekah. She conceived and gave birth to twins. "The first came out red, all his body like a hairy mantle; so they named him Esau" (Gen 25:25 NRSV). "Afterward, his brother Jacob came out, with his hand gripping Esau's heel; so he was named Jacob" (Gen 25:26 NRSV). As noted above, Genesis 36 identifies Esau with Edom and sees Esau as the ancestor of the Edomites. Thus Esau and Jacob are seen as the ancestors of Edom and Israel respectively. Genesis, therefore, as well as other books of the Bible, posits a close relationship between Edom and Israel.

Throughout Genesis, Esau (i.e., Edom) is portrayed in a poor light: to satisfy his immediate hunger, he sells his birthright (Gen 25:29-34); to his parents' grief, he marries foreigners, Hittite women (Gen 26:34-35); and his future is one of subjugation to his brother Jacob—that is, Israel (Gen 27:40).

2.2. Territory. Egyptians knew of both Seir and Edom in the latter part of the second millennium BCE (see 3.1 below). Other than an indication that they were located to the east of the Nile Delta, it is not possible, on the basis of the Egyptian evidence, to pinpoint their location.

Biblical texts locate the territory of Edom both east and west of Wadi Arabah. However, the heartland of Edom is southeast of the Dead Sea in the territory between Wadi al-Hasa (biblical Wadi Zered [Num 21:12; Deut 2:13-14]) in the north and the Gulf of al-Aqaba, an arm of the Red Sea, in the south. Specifically, King *Solomon is said to have "built a fleet of ships at Ezion-geber, which is near Eloth on the shore of the Red Sea, in the land of Edom" (1 Kings 9:26 NRSV). Thus the territory of Edom extended southward to the northern end of the Gulf of al-Aqaba. The eastern boundary would have been the desert.

It is through this region that the group led by Moses is said to have traveled after leaving Kadesh and Elath and Ezion-geber (Deut 2:8). Moreover, the Bible also locates Seir (i.e., Edom) east of Wadi Arabah (Deut 2). However, the territory of Edom extended, at least in certain periods, west of Wadi Arabah. For example, Numbers 34:3-4 describes the southern border of Israel as extending "from the wilderness of Zin along the side of Edom" (NRSV), while Joshua 15:1-3 has the boundary of the tribe of Judah reaching "southward to the boundary of Edom, to the wilderness of Zin at the farthest south" (NRSV) (see Geographical Extent of Israel). Moreover, the Bible locates Seir partly in the Negev, to the west of Wadi Arabah (Josh 11:17; 12:7), and in relation to the territories of Judah (Josh 15:10) and Simeon (1 Chron 4:42). Thus the land of Edom included, at least in certain periods, territory both east and west of Wadi Arabah.

2.3. History. Genesis 36:31-39 presents a list of "the kings who reigned in the land of Edom, before any king reigned over the Israelites" (Gen 36:31 NRSV).

During the period of the desert wanderings the Israelites sent envoys to Edom requesting permission to cross through their land (Num 20:14-17). However, Edom refused the request (Num 20:18-21; Judg 11:17) and "came out against them with a large force, heavily armed" (Num 20:18-21 NRSV). This tradition indicates that Israel did not cross through Edomite territory. However, Deuteronomy 2:1-8 implies that the Israelites did indeed travel through Edomite territory (see especially Deut 2:4, 8).

When *David became king, he is said to have subdued Edom (2 Sam 8:11-12), among other nations. David put garrisons in Edom, and the Edomites became his servants (2 Sam 8:14). 1 Kings 11:15 claims that when "David was in Edom, and Joab the commander of the army went up to bury the dead, he killed every male in Edom" (NRSV) (see also 1 Kings 11:16). However, Hadad, a young boy at the time, fled to Egypt

with some Edomites and married into the Egyptian royal house (1 Kings 11:17-19). He later became an adversary of Solomon (1 Kings 11:14).

Solomon built a fleet of ships at *Ezion-geber, on the shore of the Red Sea, in the land of Edom (1 Kings 9:26). Also, Edomite women were among the foreigners that Solomon loved (1 Kings 11:1).

The king of Edom is said to have joined Jehoram, king of Israel, and *Jehoshaphat, king of Judah, in an unsuccessful attempt to restore Israelite sovereignty over *Moab (2 Kings 3:6-27).

Because there was no king in Edom (1 Kings 22:47), Jehoshaphat was able to build a fleet of ships. However, they were wrecked at Ezion-geber (1 Kings 22:48).

"Edom revolted against the rule of Judah, and set up a king of their own" (2 Kings 8:20 NRSV). This would have been during the reign of Jehoram. The king of Judah responded unsuccessfully, and Edom gained its independence (2 Kings 8:21-22).

2 Kings 14:7 relates a conflict between Edom and Judah when Amaziah "killed ten thousand Edomites in the Valley of Salt and took Sela by storm" (NRSV). Uzziah/Azariah "rebuilt Elath and restored it to Judah, after King Amaziah slept with his ancestors" (2 Kings 14:22 NRSV). However, during the reign of Ahaz of Judah, "the king of Edom recovered Elath for Edom, and drove the Judeans from Elath; and the Edomites came to Elath, where they live to this day" (2 Kings 16:6 NRSV; see also 2 Chron 28:16-17).

Edom was a member of a ten-nation coalition that threatened to invade Israel (Ps 83; see especially Ps 83:6). This event is not mentioned elsewhere in the Bible.

There is no extrabiblical evidence that the Edomites had kings before the Israelites (Gen 36:31). In fact, as will be pointed out (see 4 below), there is little archaeological evidence for sedentary occupation in Edom before the Iron II period. While J. R. Bartlett (1989, 94-102; 2002, 54) dates the list of Genesis 36:31-39 to the first half of the eighth century BCE, when Edom was a hostile neighbor on the border of Judah and thus of increased interest and concern to Judah, E. A. Knauf argues for a date for the list no earlier than the sixth century BCE, reasoning that it reflects a situation in the Persian period, when such places as Bozrah and Tell al-Khalayfi were main centers of government.

In keeping with the above, B. MacDonald (1994; 2000) concludes that the stories about Transjordanian events and places in the Historical Books best fit into the Iron II period and later. This is especially true for Edom, since there is little in the way of Late Bronze Age and a paucity of Iron I materials in the archaeological record. On the other hand, Iron II material is well represented in Edom (see 4 below). This leads MacDonald to the conclusion that the group led by Moses, on its way from Egypt to the land of *Canaan, would have encountered little if any opposition from Edomites. Similarly, David's subjection of Edomites would have involved, for the most part, tribal groups.

MacDonald does not deny that there are older traditions behind the biblical narratives in the Historical Books relative to Edom/Edomites. However, the texts in question most probably were written in light of the settlement conditions that prevailed in the Iron II period and toward the end of that period. Thus the assumption "is that although the biblical writer may have used material that predates his time, he set that material into a context, namely, the Iron II and later periods, that would be meaningful to his readers" (MacDonald 2000, 5).

3. Edom/Edomites in Extrabiblical Literary Sources.

There is reference to Seir and Edom in Egyptian literary sources. Moreover, Edom is referred to several times in Assyrian and Babylonian inscriptions. Finally, there is epigraphic evidence from Edom itself.

3.1. Egyptian. There is explicit reference to "the lands of Seir" in the Tell el-Amarna tablets (early fourteenth century BCE) (*ANET,* 488). Ramesses II (thirteenth century BCE) claims to have "plundered Mount Seir" (Bartlett 1989, 77), while Ramesses III (twelfth century BCE) claims to have "destroyed the people of Seir among the Bedouin tribes" (*ANET,* 262).

The term *Edom* appears for the first time in a group of letters that served as models for school children during the reign of Merneptah (late thirteenth century BCE). In this case, there is reference to granting permission to "the Bedouin tribes of Edom" to enter the east Nile Delta region of Egypt "to keep them alive and to keep their cattle alive" (*ANET,* 259; see also Bartlett 1989, 77). From the above, it is evident that Egypt knew of Seir and Edom as early as the last half of the second millennium BCE.

3.2. Assyrian. Edom is one of the states that paid tribute to the Assyrian king Adad-nirari III (810-783 BCE) (Luckenbill, 1.262-63; *ANET,* 281). Qosmalak, king of Edom, paid tribute to Tiglath-pileser III (744-727 BCE) (Luckenbill, 1.287-88; *ANET,* 282). Edom joined with Judah and several other states of the southern coastal plain of Palestine in a coalition against Sargon II (721-705 BCE). The coalition was unsuccessful, and Edom appears in lists of those states that paid tribute, between 720 and 715 BCE, to Sargon II (Luckenbill, 2.105) and later to Sennacherib (704-681 BCE) (Luckenbill, 2.118-19; *ANET,* 287) as a proof of its loyalty. Qosgabri of Edom is listed as a loyal vassal of both Esarhaddon (680-669 BCE) (*ANET,* 291) and Ashurbanipal (668-627 BCE) (*ANET,* 294, 298). Moreover, the king of Edom is said to have been among those who provided human resources for building Esarhaddon's armory in Nineveh (c. 673 BCE) (Luckenbill, 2.265-66). In addition, the king of Edom provided troops for Ashurbanipal's first campaign against Egypt in 669 or 667 BCE (*ANET,* 294), as well as paying tribute (Luckenbill, 2.340-41; *ANET,* 301). This same Assyrian king claims to have defeated the king of Arabia as far south as the land of Edom (*ANET,* 298).

3.3. Babylonian. Nabonidus (555-539 BCE), the last Babylonian king, laid siege to the "town of Edom" (*ANET,* 305), probably Bozrah, the Edomite capital (Bartlett 1989, 157-61; Bienkowski 2002, 477-78). He probably captured it in the second half of the third year of his reign.

3.4. Epigraphic Evidence from Edom. Explorations and excavations in the heartland of Edom have uncovered a number of seals (dated to late eighth [?] to early sixth centuries BCE), a seal-impression (bulla), fragments of pottery with inscriptions in ink (ostraca), a cuneiform tablet and a Babylonian stela. Moreover, a large number of Aramaic ostraca, dated to the fifth and fourth centuries BCE, attest to Edomite presence west of Wadi Arabah.

A bulla bearing the name "Qaws-g[abar], king of E[dom]" was found in the excavations of Umm al-Biyara, an Edomite site that overlooks Petra from the west (*COS* 2.73:201). This king is mentioned in the inscriptions of the Assyrian rulers Esarhaddon and Ashurbanipal.

Excavators have found three Edomite ostraca at Tell al-Khalayfi, just north of the Gulf of al-Aqaba in Wadi Arabah, one at Umm al-Biyara, and one, dated from the end of the seventh to the beginning of the sixth centuries BCE, at Horvat Uza in the eastern Negev. Arad Ostraca 40 indicates Edomite hostility toward Judah at the time of Sennacherib's invasion c. 701 BCE (*COS* 3.43L:85).

The cuneiform tablet found in the excavations at Tawilan, to the north of Petra, witnesses to the purchase of oxen and sheep from an *Aramaean by an Edomite, Qusu-shama (Dalley 1995, 67-68).

The Babylonian stela is located high in the cliffs as one begins the climb to the top of as-Selaʿ, an Edomite place of refuge to the northwest of Busayra. The person depicted on the relief appears to be Nabonidus, who is believed to have besieged Busayra and annexed Edom on his way to Tayma in Arabia (Dalley and Goguel; Zayadine; Bienkowski 2002).

The events of the book of Nehemiah, the last of the Historical Books, are dated to the second half of the fifth century BCE. Although the book does not mention Edom or the Edomites, this period was a time when Edomite presence is well documented, in the form of ostraca and other material remains, in the area of southern Judah that later, during the Hellenistic period, became known as Idumaea (Diodorus 19.25.2; 98.1).

It is believed that due to pressure from the Arabs, Edomites moved into southern Judah at the end of the sixth century BCE or possibly somewhat earlier. This movement was made possible by the collapse of Jewish settlements in the area and their final destruction by the Babylonians (Stern, 444).

Evidence of Edomite presence in the area comes especially in the form of Edomite names in ostraca, written in Aramaic, from *Arad and Tel Sheva, as well as from an unknown site or sites. The ostraca from Tel Arad number about one hundred and date to the late fifth century BCE (Naveh 1981; Ephʾal and Naveh, 9). They "are mainly short messages concerning specific amounts of barley supplied to horsemen and ass-drivers and their animals" (Ephʾal and Naveh, 9). The sixty-seven from Tel Beer-sheba date to the fourth century BCE (Naveh 1973; 1979; Ephʾal and Naveh, 9). In addition, Ephʾal and Naveh (16-18) and Lemaire (1.136; 2.199-201) have published hundreds more Aramaic ostraca, dated to the fourth century BCE, that are believed to have come from a site(s) in southern

Judah (Lemaire [1.138-42; 2.197-98] locates the site to the west of *Hebron, probably Khirbet al-Qom).

The majority of the people named on the ostraca are "Edomite Arabs" (Ephʾal and Naveh, 9). This conclusion is based on the fact that the names have the divine component Qaus/Qos, and in some instances this Edomite divine component is compounded with Arabic verbal elements (Stern, 446). Thus the ethnic identity of the population of the area is reflected (Lemaire 2.220).

4. Archaeology.

Archaeological survey work in the territory of northwest Edom, east of Wadi Arabah, has resulted in the identification of pottery from the Iron I and II periods (MacDonald et al. 1988; 1992; 2004). Comparatively speaking, however, the evidence for Iron II presence in the area is much greater than that for Iron I. Thus it appears that there was an increase in both settlement and population in the region in the Iron II period. However, none of the surveyed sites that have been excavated indicate sedentary occupation before the eighth century BCE (MacDonald 1994; Herr and Najjar, 331).

Edomite culture has been elucidated by excavations south of Wadi al-Hasa and east of Wadi Arabah at Iron Age II sites such as Busayra, Feifeh, Ghareh, Khirbat an-Nahas, Tell al-Khalayfi, Tawilan and Umm al-Biyara (MacDonald 2000, 185-87). West of Wadi Arabah, Edomite cultural material dating from the eighth to early sixth centuries BCE has been uncovered at many sites—for example, Tel Aroer, Tel Ira, Tel Malhata, Horvat Qitmit and En Hatzeva (Beit-Arieh 1995a; 1995b; Cohen and Yisrael; Dever, 48-49). Moreover, Edomite presence, as noted previously, is evident in southern Judah in the Persian period.

The results of archaeological excavations at Busayra, Tawilan, Umm al-Biyara and Tell al-Khalayfi, major Edomite sites to the east of Wadi Arabah, indicate that these sites were not established before the Iron II period. Some of them, however, continued in existence throughout the Persian period and into the Hellenistic period.

Busayra, on the basis of pottery analysis, "dates between the late eighth century and c. 300/200 BC" (Bienkowski 2002, 477). There certainly was later occupation at the site. However, in light of the present interest, settlement at the site terminated in the fourth/third centuries BCE.

Tawilan, to the north of Petra, was occupied probably "from the earlier seventh century BC, possibly as late as the fourth century BC" (Bennett and Bienkowski, 103).

Umm al-Biyara, located on a mountain within Petra, was occupied during the Iron II period, specifically the seventh to sixth centuries BCE, and Nabataean periods (Bienkowski, *OEANE* 5.275). Similarly, mountaintop Edomite sites located in the vicinity of Petra are dated to the Iron II period (Lindner; Linder, Vieweger and Bienert).

A reexamination by G. D. Pratico (1993) of the excavated pottery from Tell al-Khalayfi, possibly biblical Eloth/Elath (MacDonald 2000, 81-82), led him to posit that the site dates from the eighth to the sixth centuries BCE, with some material from the fifth and fourth centuries BCE.

Extensive explorations in the copper mining areas of Wadis Fidan and Faynan indicate that the area was exploited, probably by the Edomites, during the late Iron I (Fritz 1994; 1996), throughout the Iron II period and into the Persian period (Hauptmann, 310). In fact, the location of the Edomite capital of Bozrah, to the northeast, may be due to these copper resources (MacDonald 2000, 189).

As noted previously (see 3.4 above), there is evidence of Edomite settlement in southern Judah during the Persian and early Hellenistic periods.

5. Economy.

The basis of the economy of Edom was mixed farming. The main crops were barley and, to a lesser extent, wheat (for Idumaea see Eph'al and Naveh, 10; Lemaire, 1.142; 2.23-24), because it requires more water. Vegetable and fruit crops, especially olives and grapes (Eph'al and Naveh, 10-11; Lemaire, 1.142; 2.224), were grown where there was sufficient water for irrigation. The main animals raised were goats, sheep and, to a lesser extent, cattle (Köhler-Rollefson; Bienkowski and Reese, 471-72). Because the mining and smelting areas of Wadis Fidan and Faynan were in Edomite territory, and because of the location of the capital city on the plateau to the east, it is hard to believe that the Edomites were not involved in metallurgy (Bienkowski 2002, 480). Moreover, Edom apparently was engaged in the slave trade with the Philistine cities of the southeast coast of the Mediterranean (Amos 1:6). And because it controlled the main crossing points at the northern end of the Gulf of al-Aqaba and in Wadi Arabah, Edom also would have been involved in the Arabian trade in myrrh, frankincense and other luxury goods on their way westward toward Egypt, *Beersheba and the Mediterranean coast (Singer-Avitz 1999; Bienkowski and van der Steen, 36-37; Bienkowski 2002, 480-81).

6. Religion.

There appears to have been a close affinity between Yahweh and the Edomites, since it is Yahweh who has "given Mount Seir to Esau as a possession" (Deut 2:5 NRSV). Moreover, the Bible has Yahweh associated with, and coming from, the region of Seir/Edom/Teman (Deut 33:2; Judg 5:4-5; Hab 3:3).

Two of the Edomite kings mentioned in the Assyrian texts have names that preserve the name of a deity: Qaus/Qos. This same name is also found on seals, bullae and ostraca from southern Jordan and the eastern Negev (Bartlett 1989, 200-205; Beit-Arieh 1995b; Eph'al and Naveh; Lemaire). Thus it can be concluded that Qaus/Qos was the god of the Edomites during the Iron Age and the Persian period. The association between this god and Yahweh is a subject of debate (Bartlett 1989, 194-200; Dearman 1995).

From an archaeological perspective, P. Bienkowski (2002, 57, 94-95) tentatively identifies one of the major structures excavated at Busayra as a temple. Furthermore, C.-M. Bennett and P. Bienkowski (85, 303) have published incense altars from the Tawilan excavations.

I. Beit-Arieh's findings in the eastern Negev are important for an understanding of Edomite religion. At Horvat Qitmit, for example, he found cult objects at an Edomite shrine. Among the materials excavated were more than eight hundred figurines, anthropomorphic stands, reliefs, along with three incomplete inscriptions bearing the theophoric element Qaus/Qos (Beit-Arieh 1995b). To the southeast, at En Hazeva, R. Cohen and Y. Yisrael have excavated a hoard of religious artifacts at what probably is another Edomite shrine.

J. R. Bartlett concludes that Qaus/Qos was a weather god, and that his devotees "might hope for his help and support in various situations, personal and domestic as well as national" (Bartlett 1989, 204).

7. Script and Language.

As noted previously, a number of ostraca, bullae and seals have been identified as Edomite. On the basis of this material, it can be concluded that "the Edomites used a regional variant of the north-west Semitic script and language" (Bartlett 1989, 209; see also Beit-Arieh 1995a, 34).

See also MOAB, MOABITES.

BIBLIOGRAPHY. **J. R. Bartlett,** "Bozra in the Hebrew Scriptures," in *Busayra: Excavations by Crystal-M. Bennett 1971-1980,* ed. P. Bienkowski (BAMA 13; New York: Oxford University Press, 2002) 53-55; idem, *Edom and the Edomites* (JSOT-Sup 77; Sheffield: JSOT, 1989); **I. Beit-Arieh,** "The Edomites of Cisjordan," in *You Shall Not Abhor an Edomite for He Is Your Brother: Edom and Seir in History and Tradition,* ed. D. V. Edelman (ABS 3; Atlanta: Scholars Press, 1995a) 33-40; idem, ed., *Horvat Qitmit: An Edomite Shrine in the Biblical Negev* (MSIA 11; Tel Aviv: Institute of Archaeology of Tel Aviv University, 1995b); **C.-M. Bennett and P. Bienkowski,** *Excavations at Tawilan in Southern Jordan* (BAMA 8; New York: Oxford University Press, 1995); **P. Bienkowski,** ed., *Busayra: Excavations by Crystal-M. Bennett, 1971-1980* (BAMA 13; New York: Oxford University Press, 2002); idem, "Umm el-Biyara," *OEANE* 5.274-76; **P. Bienkowski and D. S. Reese,** "The Animal Bones," in *Busayra: Excavations by Crystal-M. Bennett, 1971-1980,* ed. P. Bienkowski (BAMA 13; New York: Oxford University Press, 2002) 471-74; **P. Bienkowski and E. van der Steen,** "Tribes, Trade, and Towns: A New Framework for the Late Iron Age in Southern Jordan and the Negev," *BASOR* 323 (2001) 21-47; **R. Cohen and Y. Yisrael,** "Smashing the Idols: Piecing Together an Edomite Shrine in Judah," *BAR* 22.4 (1996) 40-51, 65; **S. Dalley,** "The Cuneiform Tablet," in *Excavations at Tawilan in Southern Jordan,* ed. C.-M. Bennett and P. Bienkowski (BAMA 8; Oxford: Oxford University Press, 1995) 67-68; **S. Dalley and A. Goguel,** "The Sela Sculpture: A Neo-Babylonian Rock Relief in Southern Jordan," *ADAJ* 41 (1997) 169-76; **J. A. Dearman,** "Edomite Religion: A Survey and an Examination of Some Recent Contributions," in *You Shall Not Abhor an Edomite for He Is Your Brother: Edom and Seir in History and Tradition,* ed. D. V. Edelman (Archaeology and Biblical Studies 3; Atlanta: Scholars Press, 1995); **W. G. Dever,** "Archaeology, Ideology, and the Quest for an 'Ancient' or 'Biblical Israel,'" *NEA* 61.1 (1998) 39-52; **D. V. Edelman,** ed., *You Shall Not Abhor an Edomite for He Is Your Brother: Edom and Seir in History and Tradition* (ABS 3; Atlanta: Scholars Press, 1995); **I. Eph'al and J. Naveh,** *Aramaic Ostraca of the Fourth Century BC from Idumaea* (Jerusalem: Magnes Press, Hebrew University, Israel Exploration Society, 1996); **V. Fritz,** "Ergebnisse einer Sondage in *Hirbet en-Nahas, Wadi el-Arabah,*" *ZDPV* 112 (1996) 1-9; idem, "Vorbericht über die Grabungen in *Baraqa el-Hetiye* in Gebiet von *Fenan, Wadi el-Arabah* (Jordanien) 1990," *ZDPV* 110 (1994) 125-50; **A. Hauptmann,** "Feinan," *OEANE* 2.310-11; **L. G. Herr and M. Najjar,** "The Iron Age," in *The Archaeology of Jordan,* ed. B. MacDonald, R. Adams and P. Bienkowski (LA 1; Sheffield: Sheffield Academic Press, 2001) 323-45; **E. A. Knauf,** *Midian: Untersuchungen zur Geschichte Palästinas und Norarabiens am ende des 2. Jahrtausends v. Chr.* (ADP; Wiesbaden: Harrassowitz, 1988); **I. Köhler-Rollefson,** "The Animal Bones," in *Excavations at Tawilan in Southern Jordan,* ed. C.-M. Bennett and P. Bienkowski (BAMA 8; Oxford: Oxford University Press, 1995) 97-100; **A. Lemaire,** *Nouvelles inscriptions araméennes d'Idumée au Musée d'Israël* (2 vols.; Supplément à Transeuphratène 3, 9; Paris: Gabalda, 1996-2002); **M. Lindner,** "Edom Outside the Famous Excavations: Evidence from Surveys in the Greater Petra Area," in *Early Edom and Moab: The Beginning of the Iron Age in Southern Jordan,* ed. P. Bienkowski (SAM 7; Sheffield: Collis, 1992) 143-66; **M. Lindner, D. Vieweger and H.-D. Bienert,** *Über Petra hinaus: Archäologische Erkundungen im südlichen Jordanien* (Rahden: Leidorf, 2003); **D. D. Luckenbill,** *Ancient Records of Assyria and Babylonia* (2 vols.; Chicago: University of Chicago Press, 1926-1927); **B. MacDonald,** "Early Edom: The Relation between the Literary and Archaeological Evidence," in *Scripture and Other Artifacts: Essays on Archaeology and the Bible in Honor of Philip J. King,* ed. M. D. Coogan, J. C. Exum and L. E. Stager (Louisville: Westminister/John Knox, 1994) 230-46; idem, *East of the Jordan: Territories and Sites of the Hebrew Scriptures* (ASOR Books 6; Boston: American Schools of Oriental Research, 2000); **B. MacDonald et al.,** *The Southern Ghors and Northeast Arabah Archaeological Survey, 1985-1986, Southern Jordan* (SAM 5; Sheffield: Collis, 1992); idem, *The Tafila-Busayra Archaeological Survey, 1999-2001* (ASORAR 9; Boston: American Schools of Oriental Research, 2004); idem, *The Wadi el Hasa Archaeological Survey,*

1979-1983, West-Central Jordan (Waterloo, ON: Wilfrid Laurier University Press, 1988); **J. Naveh,** "The Aramaic Ostraca," in *Beer-sheba, 1: Excavations at Tel Beer-sheba, 1969-1971 Seasons,* ed. Y. Aharoni (Tel Aviv: Tel Aviv University, Institute of Archaeology, 1973) 79-82; idem, "The Aramaic Ostraca from Tel Arad," in *Arad Inscriptions,* ed. Y. Aharoni (Jerusalem: Israel Exploration Society, 1981) 153-74; idem, "The Aramaic Ostraca from Tel Beer-sheba (Seasons 1971-1976)," *TA* 6 (1979) 182-98; **G. D. Pratico,** *Nelson Glueck's 1938-40 Excavations at Tell el-Kheleifeh: A Reappraisal* (ASORAR 3; Atlanta: Scholars Press, 1993); **L. Singer-Avitz,** "Beersheba—A Gateway Community in Southern Arabian Long-Distant Trade in the Eighth Century B.C.E.," *TA* 26 (1999) 3-75; **E. Stern,** *Archaeology of the Land of the Bible,* 2: *The Assyrian, Babylonian, and Persian Periods 732-332 BCE* (ABRL; New York: Doubleday, 2001); **F. Zayadine,** "Le relief néo-babylonien à Sela᾽ près de Tafileh: Interprétation historique," *Syria* 76 (1999) 83-80.

B. MacDonald

EGYPT, EGYPTIANS

The present concern is with a relation between a nation and a text, between ancient Egypt and the OT Historical Books. The focus is on events and beliefs about Egypt reported in those books. Other facets of this relation will not be considered here. Among those other facets is the role of the books as texts of religious purport in Egyptian history. For example, Alexandrian Jews first translated the Hebrew original into Greek in the third century BCE. And by the fourth century CE, Egypt had become predominantly Christian, and the Bible its most important book.

The natural point of departure consists of the sparse references to Egypt found in the Historical Books. The following survey is an attempt to outline an answer to this question: What information do the Historical Books transmit about Egypt's history, and how reliable is that information in relation to everything else we know about Egypt? In principle, the following limitation will apply: Egyptian history will be considered only as far as is necessary to interpret as fully as possible the limited number of references to Egypt in the Historical Books of the OT.

Four references to Egypt are far more worthy of attention than all others. They have naturally produced the most discussion. Four properties make them especially interesting to historians. First, all four references are detailed and specific, not vague or general. Second, there is certain or possible confirmation of the persons and events mentioned in the references from native Egyptian sources. In other words, the references perhaps do not stand in complete isolation. Third, all four references describe events dating to the time period covered by the Historical Books, as opposed to being reminiscences of earlier times. Fourth, adding much to their importance, all four references are macropolitical. They pertain to the history of entire nations, not just to the lives of individuals. More specifically, all four concern interventions by rulers of Egypt in the history of Israel. In chronological order, the Egyptian rulers are (1) a King Shishak of the second half of the tenth century BCE (1 Kings 11:40; 14:25; 2 Chron 12:2, 5 [2x], 7, 9); (2) a King So of the second half of the seventh century BCE (2 Kings 17:4); (3) a King Tirhakah of around 700 BCE (2 Kings 19:9; see also Is 37:9); (4) a King Neco (Necho, Nekho) of around 600 BCE (2 Kings 23:29, 33, 34, 35; 2 Chron 35:20, 22; 36:4). Thus four case studies concerning Pharaohs Shishak, So, Tirhakah and Neco form the centerpiece of this survey. They are discussed in §4, while §§1, 2 and 3 provide context.

Two related kinds of data will not be systematically treated: (1) references to Egypt by the prophets, who are contemporary with the Historical Books, from sometime in the eighth century BCE onward, including the only other reference by name to a native Egyptian king in the entire Bible: Hophra (Jer 44:30), whom everyone equates with Apries (589-570 BCE); (2) references to Kush and Libya, two lands adjacent to Egypt, and any people originating there, such as Zerah the Kushite, who fought Asa (c. 910-870 BCE) (2 Chron 14:9-15; cf. 2 Chron 16:8; see Kitchen, 309 §268; Schipper, 133-39), and the Kushites accompanying King Shishak on a campaign (2 Chron 12:3). The ancient Kush of Hebrew is the ancient Ethiopia of Latin and Greek, or the modern nation of Sudan, just south of Egypt.

1. Historicity of the References to Egypt in the Historical Books
2. Egypt and Canaan from Joshua (c. 1200 BCE?) to Jeroboam I and Rehoboam (c. 930 BCE), and from Jeroboam I and Rehoboam to Ezra and Nehemiah (fifth-fourth centuries BCE)

1. Historicity of the References to Egypt in the Historical Books.

Only little that is said about Egypt in the Historical Books of the OT is positively verifiable by certain high standards, comparable to those required in court to prove guilt beyond reasonable doubt. Then again, by those same standards, there is also much that is not positively falsifiable. This no-man's land between certainty and falsehood—the vast expanse of the nonimpossible—is always a potential breeding ground for speculation, fed in the present case by the geographical contiguity of Egypt and Syro-Palestine, by abundant evidence of contact between the two nations, and by typological resemblances between events reported in the Bible and events known from Egyptian sources. There is a certain danger, however, that such speculation produces a body of opinions and theories of increasingly self-referential complexity that obscures to outsiders how little of what we could have known about ancient Egypt has survived, and how much less of it is preserved in the Bible. The evidence for most persons and events is so sparse that the old saying may be applied to them, mutatis mutandis, that the *Iliad* was written either by Homer or by another person with the same name. Much crucial information pertaining to the Bible's ancient Near Eastern context has come to light relatively recently. At the outset, the natural scholarly instinct is to make as many connections as possible, hypothetical or factual. But after this intellectual land rush, the time seems right for increased efforts to look back and discern what in all that has been proposed can withstand rigorous scrutiny. Much that has been done may need to be undone.

In terms of historicity, the most significant divide in the period covered by the Historical Books lies at the death of *Solomon (1 Kings 11:40, 43; 2 Chron 9:31) and the ensuing partition of the monarchy, when *Jeroboam I became king of Israel, and *Rehoboam king of Judah. For the long period before the divide, in which Egypt features prominently, historical authenticity is almost impossible to confirm or discredit positively. Episodes of great narrative power appear in the tracts of text pertaining to this period. This literary quality can be, and has been, interpreted variously as signifying anything from embellishment to total fabrication. For the period following the divide, some measure of positive confirmation from extrabiblical sources is possible in places. In fact, the latter period begins with one potential corroboration from outside sources involving Egypt. It pertains to the Egyptian king Shishak and his conquest of Palestine (see 4.1 below).

2. Egypt and Canaan from Joshua (c. 1200 BCE?) to Jeroboam I and Rehoboam (c. 930 BCE), and from Jeroboam I and Rehoboam to Ezra and Nehemiah (fifth-fourth centuries BCE).

2.1. Time Frame. The institution in 45 BCE of the Julian calendar, still in use today, renders chronology from 45 BCE onward and down to the present time reasonably transparent. Much less transparency characterizes the centuries before 45 BCE. Chronology therefore necessarily assumes a much more prominent role in any historical inquiry into events preceding 45 BCE, which obviously include the events related in the Historical Books of the OT. As a result, chronology and history are almost inseparable.

In relation to chronology, as we noted also in regard to historicity, the main divide is Solomon's death and the ensuing partition of the monarchy into Israel and Judah. Dates from that time onward exhibit a degree of firmness that dates of earlier events lack. The partition happened roughly around 930 BCE. There is general agreement on this approximate date. However, no consensus seems possible regarding the length of the period that stretches back from Solomon to Joshua, and even earlier to the sojourn in Egypt and the exodus—traditions that exhibit an Egyptian connection but fall outside the scope of this survey because they are narrated in the Pentateuch (*see DOTP*). In light of information from the Bible alone, about forty years each are traditionally assigned to Solomon's reign and *David's reign, and about twenty years to *Saul's reign back from about 930 BCE. About 1200 BCE is a conjectured date often cited for *Joshua's conquest of Canaan, which is the first major event in the period treated in the Historical Books, but the historicity of events in Joshua's time and in the time of the judges (ending with Samuel) and of the united monarchy under Saul, David and Solomon is impossible to verify positively. There has been no lack of trying, however (*see* History of Israel 1-3). In the view of many, absence of positive proof makes all these earlier events unhistorical in at least some sense of the word. What follows here on chronology focuses on the period from about 930 BCE onward.

*Chronology is a structure in which elements come in a necessary logical order, and one element comes first. The present focus is on Canaan in its relationship to Egypt in the period beginning in about 930 BCE and ending with the events narrated in Ezra and Nehemiah (*see* Ezra and Nehemiah, Books of). The date of the latter events is best described as the fifth to fourth centuries BCE. Artaxerxes is mentioned in both Ezra and Nehemiah, but it is not absolutely certain which and how many of the following Persian kings are meant: Artaxerxes I (465/64-424 BCE), Artaxerxes II (405/4-359/58 BCE) and Artaxerxes III (359/58-338/37 BCE) (for these dates see Depuydt 1995a; 1995c). As a result, Ezra could either precede or follow Nehemiah in time. Canaan's chronology and Egypt's chronology are intricately intertwined in the period at hand. A brief outline of their structure follows here.

The ultimate foundation of first-millennium BCE chronology is the longest sustained research project of all time: Babylonian astronomy. At Babylon, celestial events were recorded continuously in astronomical diaries from the eighth century BCE to the first century CE (Sachs and Hunger). Sophisticated theories rooted in these observations were formulated in the third and second centuries BCE (recently Brack-Bernsen). Babylonian astronomy first surfaced not in the original cuneiform tablets, but in Greek works on astronomy, especially those of Ptolemy of Alexandria (second century CE). Ptolemy's Royal Canon is antiquity's single most important chronological document (Depuydt 1995b). Manuscripts of the Royal Canon came to light in the early seventeenth century CE. The Royal Canon lists three types of data: (1) the successive rulers earlier of Babylon and later of Alexandria, including Assyrians, Babylonians, Chaldeans, Persians, Macedonians and Egyptians, beginning with the Babylonian king Nabonassar; (2) the lengths of their reigns converted into multiples of Egyptian 365-day years, with day 1 being February 26, 747 BCE; (3) the cumulative count of years from Nabonassar, the so-called Era of Nabonassar. The Royal

Canon's veracity has never been doubted, but neither has it ever been positively proven. Paradoxically, proving the Royal Canon will also render it superfluous. Thus a shift in the foundations of ancient chronology is to be expected in the years ahead (Depuydt, in press [b]; Jonsson). Proof of the Royal Canon is to be found in Babylonian astronomical texts. These sources emerged at the end of the nineteenth century CE. The decipherment of Babylonian astronomy soon followed. Some principal sources have become more easily accessible to historians only recently. Babylonian astronomy takes us back to 747 BCE. Then Assyrian limu lists take over. In Assyria, each year was named after an official called the limu. Lists of limus have survived (Millard). These lists make Near Eastern chronology reasonably solid back to about 910 BCE.

Three periods can be distinguished in the chronology of Israel, Judah and Egypt from 930 BCE onward.

2.1.1. From 930 BCE to 690 BCE. In this period Canaan's chronology is relatively firm compared to that of many nations. The evidence does exhibit contradictions and inconsistencies, but the order of the kings is generally clear. Firmness is owed mainly to a confluence of four factors: (1) synchronisms between Hebrew, Mesopotamian and Egyptian kings as reported in the Bible and cuneiform sources; (2) the lengths of the reigns of the Hebrew kings in number of years as reported in the Bible; (3) the overall match of sums of reigns in the two independent lines of kings of Israel and Judah; (4) notices in the Bible when in the reign of a king of one line a king of the other line died or began to rule.

The date of about 930 BCE is obtained by counting back about ninety years from synchronisms of the Bible with Assyrian sources of Shalmaneser III's reign in the mid-ninth century BCE (Kugler, 150). As for the reigns of the Hebrew kings, E. R. Thiele's dates have been influential; F. X. Kugler's are largely forgotten but deserve consideration; W. F. Albright's are still often cited; other treatments are by W. H. Barnes and by J. Finegan. The nature of the evidence precludes a definitive solution for the lengths of the reigns of the Hebrew kings. There are two problem areas. The first is whether the civil year began in Nisan in the spring or in Tishri in the fall. I suspect (with Kugler) that the civil year (as opposed to the religious or the agricultural year) mostly if not always began in Nisan (as it always did in Babylon). Presumably, it changed to Tishri sometime after Alexander the Great's conquests of 332-323 BCE, owing to the fact that the Macedonian lunar calendar began in the fall. The second problem is how regnal years relate to calendar years. Regnal year 1 can begin on the day of accession and last either until the first new year (predating) or until the first anniversary of the accession (accession dating); or its beginning can be postponed to the first new year of the reign (postdating).

For this same period, Egyptian chronology is quite uncertain. From the end of the second millennium BCE onward, two or more rulers typically reigned simultaneously in Egypt. The four centuries or so down to 690 BCE are a dark interlude between two periods of greater chronological transparency. Historians try to thread together the many reigns, all of uncertain length, to bridge the gap.

2.1.2. From 690 BCE to about 525 BCE. Canaan's chronology is equally firm as in the first period. Egyptian chronology now becomes fully fixed, definitely by 664 BCE, the beginning of the reign of the first ruler of the Saite period, or Dynasty 26, Psammetichus I (664/63-610 BCE), and possibly already by the reign of Taharqa (690-664/63 BCE, or perhaps 691-664/63 BCE), the last Nubian ruler of all of Egypt. Egyptian chronology is now day-exact (Depuydt, in press [a]): if an event's Egyptian date is known, then the event can be dated to the exact day. The year 664 BCE (or perhaps 690 BCE) is the beginning of earliest day-exact chronology of all of history. Day-exact chronology remains a monopoly of Egyptian history until the institution of the Julian calendar in 45 BCE. The day-exactness is owed mainly to the regularity of the Egyptian civil calendar. Its years always have twelve months of thirty days plus five added days, for a total of 365 days. Lunar calendars, used everywhere else, do not allow dating to the exact day.

2.1.3. From About 525 BCE Onward. Around 525 BCE the *Persian ruler Cambyses conquered Egypt. Egypt and postexilic Judah became part of the same vast Persian Empire. The temple in Jerusalem had been destroyed and the people of Judah deported to Babylonia about six decades earlier. The reigns of the last pre-Persian rulers of Babylon—the Chaldeans Nebuchadnezzar, Amel-Marduk, Neriglissar and Nabonidus—and the reigns of the Persian rulers themselves are year-exact. To the extent that dates in Ezra and Nehemiah can be related to Babylonian regnal years, the chronology of Canaan is year-exact. The Babylonian lunar calendar is well understood for this period (Parker and Dubberstein), but Babylonian chronology is not day-exact. It is not possible to know exactly where lunar day 1 fell in relation to new moon. All we know is that it was close. By contrast, in Egypt the structure of the civil calendar of 12 x 30 + 5 days guarantees day-exactness in the same period.

2.2. Egypt and Canaan in the Iron Age (c. 1200-300 BCE). The histories of Canaan and Egypt in the Iron Age form the wider context of the sparse references to Egypt in the Historical Books. The present focus is on Egypt (for surveys see Kitchen; Kienitz; Myśliwiec; Redford; Montet; Ash; Schipper; see also, in *CAH²*, Edwards; James; Lloyd; Ray).

A brief characterization of Egypt during the period covered by the Historical Books is as follows. After the highly centralized, very powerful and fabulously rich New Kingdom (Dynasties 18-20) of the second half of the second millennium BCE, culminating in the long reign of Ramesses II (thirteenth century BCE), Egypt's political landscape changed greatly in the first millennium BCE. The two principal distinctive macropolitical characteristics of the centuries up to Alexander's conquest of 332 BCE are fragmentation and foreign rule. Whether this constitutes a decline is open to interpretation. The division into dynasties is Manetho's (third century BCE). The northern kings of Dynasty 21 (around 1000 BCE) competed with the powerful priesthood of Amun, located in the vast and resplendent southern city of Thebes. Under Dynasties 22 to 24 (early tenth to late eighth centuries BCE), which probably partly overlapped, chieftains with names such as Sheshonq, Osorkon and Takelot, typically of Libyan origin, as the names attest, competed for power and territory, with several of them sometimes simultaneously claiming the Egyptian title of king. Dynasty 25 consisted of a line of Nubian kings (Piye, Shabaka, Shabataka and Taharqa) that conquered Egypt in the late eighth century BCE and ruled it until about the mid-seventh century BCE. Under Dynasty 26 a line of rulers originating in the northern city of Sais came to power. The dates of the reigns in the Saite period are fixed (see Table 1. All years are BCE).

Table 1. Dynasty 26 (Saite Period)

Dynasty 26	*664/3-c. 527-525*
Psammetichus I	664/3-610
Neco II	610-595
Psammetichus II	595-589
Apries	589-570
Amasis	570-527/6
Psammetichus III?	a few months (six?) in 527-525?

Around 525 BCE the Persian king Cambyses conquered Egypt. Egypt became part of the largest empire that the world had hitherto seen. Dynasty 27 consisted of Persian rulers. The dates of the reigns are fixed (see Table 2).

Table 2. Dynasty 27 (Persian Rulers)

Dynasty 27	*527/5-c. 400*
Cambyses (later reign)	527/5-522
Darius I	522-486
Xerxes I	486-465
Artaxerxes I	465-424/3
Darius II	424/3-405/4
Artaxerxes II (early reign)	405/4-c. 400

Around 400 BCE autonomy returned to Egypt for about sixty years under Dynasties 28, 29 and 30. A second Persian conquest occurred around 340 BCE, followed by less than a decade of Persian rule, known already in antiquity as Dynasty 31. The dates of the reigns in the fourth century BCE are probably a couple of years off at most (see Table 3).

Table 3. Dynasties 28, 29 and 30

Dynasty 28	
Amyrtaios	c. 404/3-398/7
Dynasty 29	
Nepherites I	c. 398/7-392/1
Achoris	c. 392/1-379/8
Psammuthis	brief reign
Nepherites II	brief reign
Dynasty 30	
Nectanebo I (Nectanebes)	c. 379/8-361/0
Teos/Tachos	c. 361/0-359/8
Nectanebo II (Nectanebos)	c. 359/8-341/0 or 340/39

Then, in 332 BCE, Alexander conquered Egypt. With Alexander's death in the late afternoon of June 11, 323 BCE, Ptolemaic rule over Egypt began. The Ptolemies ruled for about three centuries, until Cleopatra and Mark Anthony surrendered to Octavian in 30 BCE, and Egypt became a Roman province.

The present focus is on the relationship between Egypt and Canaan. Macropolitically, one phenomenon that commonly characterizes the commerce between nations is interference, be it peaceful or violent. It comes as no surprise that the four principal references to Egypt in the Historical Books (discussed in §4 below) concern warfare between Egypt and its neighbors in Asia.

3. References to Egypt in the Historical Books. For the sake of completeness, a brief but comprehensive survey of references to Egypt other than the four key references discussed in §4 below is in order. They include references to (1) Israel's sojourn in Egypt as well as the exodus; (2) Egypt as a land bordering Canaan; (3) Egyptians other than kings; (4) a variety of other aspects pertaining to the land of Egypt. No attempt is made here to calibrate the degree of historical veracity of these references.

3.1. Israel in Egypt. The milestone events relating to Egypt in Israel's history up to the conquest of Canaan are passed in review at Joshua 24:4-7. In regard to the sojourn in Egypt, there are references to "all that [the LORD] did in Egypt" (Josh 9:9), to how the ancestors worshiped Egyptian gods (Josh 24:14), to how the LORD revealed himself to Israel "when they were slaves to the house of Pharaoh" (1 Sam 2:27), and to how Pharaoh and the Egyptians hardened their hearts against Israel (1 Sam 6:6).

The exodus is a dominant theme. The event is dated explicitly to 480 years before year 4 of Solomon, when the building of the temple began in the second month, Ziv (1 Kings 6:1). The references are mostly generic. The exodus is at times no more than a point in time since when a certain practice has prevailed (Judg 19:30; 2 Kings 21:15). Often the LORD is credited for delivering Israel from Egyptian slavery and oppression, either speaking in the first person (= [1] in the list of references that follows), being addressed in the second person (= [2]), or being referred to in the third person (= [3]) (Josh 24:17 [3]; Judg 2:1 [1], 12 [3]; 6:8 [1], 9 [1], 13 [3]; 10:11 [1]; 1 Sam 8:8 [1]; 10:18 [1]; 2 Sam 7:6 [1], 23 [2]; 1 Kings 8:16 [1], 21 [3], 53 [2]; 9:9 [3]; 2 Kings 17:36 [3]; 2 Chron 6:5 [1], 7:22 [3]; Neh 9:18 [3]). More specific references pertain to how the Lord dried the water of the Red Sea (Josh 2:10) and divided the Red Sea when he heard of Israel's distress (Neh 9:9-11), to how Is-

241

rael came "through the wilderness to Kadesh" (Judg 11:16), to how it was Moses and Aaron who led them (1 Sam 12:6, 8), to how Israel spared Ammon, Moab and Mount Seir from attack on their journey to Canaan (2 Chron 20:10). Later Saul punishes the Amalekites and rewards the Kenites for their behavior toward the Israelites on their journey to the Promised Land (1 Sam 15:2, 6). Also later, the king of the Ammonites demands restitution of land that Israel took on their journey, "from the Arnon to the Jabbok and to the Jordan" (Judg 11:13). Moses and the tablets in the ark are mentioned (1 Kings 8:9; 2 Chron 5:10). At some point Jeroboam I has two golden calves made, referring to them as gods that led Israel from Egypt (1 Kings 12:28). On the occasion of an attack by the Israelites, *Philistines are said to fear their gods because they "smote the Egyptians with every sort of plague in the wilderness" (1 Sam 4:8).

3.2. Egypt as a Land Bordering Canaan. The principal references are to the border region between Canaan and Egypt. There are references to four geographical entities: (1) Shihor "east of Egypt" (Josh 13:3; 1 Chron 13:5) (Na'aman 1980); (2) the Brook or Wadi of Egypt (Josh 15:4; 15:47; 1 Kings 8:65; 2 Kings 24:7; 2 Chron 7:8) (Na'aman 1979); (3) Shur "east of Egypt" (1 Sam 15:7; 27:8) (Na'aman 1980); (4) the border of Egypt (1 Kings 4:21; 2 Chron 9:26; 26:8).

3.3. References to Egyptians Other Than Rulers. Six Egyptian individuals other than the four rulers discussed in §4 below are mentioned in the Historical Books. One is a king's sister-in-law. Two are princesses. The identity of their royal fathers is unknown. No outside evidence exists to corroborate the existence of any of these individuals. The six persons are (1) Tahpenes, Pharaoh's sister-in-law, who married Hadad the Edomite after he fled to Egypt to escape David's wrath and who bore him a son named Genubath (1 Kings 11:17-22); (2) a princess, wife of Solomon (1 Kings 3:1; 7:8; 9:24; 11:1; 2 Chron 8:11) alongside the many other women he loved (1 Kings 11:1), whom Pharaoh gave in marriage to Solomon after the capture and destruction of *Gezer (1 Kings 9:16-17), and for whom Solomon builds a house (1 Kings 7:8; 9:24; 2 Chron 8:11); (3) princess Bithiah, who is mentioned with her husband, Mered, in the long list of descendants of Judah and therefore presumably lived much later (1 Chron 4:17); (4) an Amalekite's young servant who collaborates with

David in his war against the Amalekites (1 Sam 30:11-15); (5) a handsome spear-bearing enemy combatant killed by the warrior Benaiah armed with only a staff (2 Sam 23:21; 1 Chron 11:23); (6) a slave named Jarha married to Sheshan's daughter, who bears him a son called Attai (1 Chron 2:34-35). A special case is the personified Egypt featuring in the genealogy of nations as son of Ham and father of Ludim, Anamim, Lehabim, Naphtuhim and so on (1 Chron 1:8, 11-12).

3.4. References of Various Kinds. A number of other events pertaining to Egypt receive mention: (1) the transfer of Joseph's bones from Egypt to Shechem (Josh 24:32); (2) the superiority of Solomon's wisdom over Egypt's (1 Kings 4:30); (3) the circumcision of Israelites in Egypt but not in the wilderness (Josh 5:2-7); (4) the importation of goods from Egypt, especially horses and chariots (1 Kings 10:28-29; 2 Chron 1:16-17; 9:28); (5) the deceiving of enemy Arameans into thinking that Egyptians were about to attack them (2 Kings 7:6); (6) the intermarriage of Israelites with Egyptians and other foreigners viewed as racial impurity (Ezra 9:1).

4. Israel and Pharaohs Shishak, So, Tirhakah and Neco.

The few references to Egypt in the Historical Books that transcend the generic or isolated kinds are those to four Pharaohs: Shishak, So, Tirhakah and Neco. They appear in three of the ten books: 1 Kings, 2 Kings and 2 Chronicles. Five of the other seven books—Joshua, Judges, 1 Samuel, 2 Samuel and 1 Chronicles—cover the epoch lasting from the exodus to the end of David's reign. Hardly any specific events in that period are positively verifiable. The remaining two—Ezra and Nehemiah—contain no references to Egypt. The reason for this may be that in Ezra's and Nehemiah's time Egypt and Canaan were united under the same strong Persian Empire and therefore less likely to enter into conflict; and conflict, as we will see, is what all the substantial references to Egypt in the Historical Books are about.

The only other Egyptian king mentioned by name in the Bible is Hophra—that is, Apries—at Jeremiah 44:30. Apries, who ruled Egypt in 589-570 BCE, is presumably also the unnamed king mentioned at Jeremiah 37:5, 7, 11 who causes the Babylonians to retreat from Jerusalem in the events leading up to the final fall of the city (587/586 BCE). Apries' predecessor, Psammetichus II, died on February 9, 589 BCE, not on February 8, 588 BCE as earlier accounts up to the 1950s and 1960s state (Depuydt, in press [a]). Apries is presumably also the pharaoh said to own a palace at Tahpanhes in Egypt (Jer 43:9) in a passage describing Jeremiah's flight to Egypt, where he would spend the rest of his days.

Each of the following four sections provides four types of information: (1) the verses in which the name of the Egyptian king is mentioned; (2) the events associated with the king in the biblical text; (3) references to discussions, most of them recent, chosen mainly because they should lead to most else that is relevant up to about the end of the twentieth century; (4) a few comments on the potential historicity of the reported events.

4.1. Shishak.

4.1.1. Verses. A King Shishak is mentioned exactly seven times in the Historical Books: 1 Kings 11:40; 14:25; 2 Chronicles 12:2, 5 (2x), 7, 9.

4.1.2. Events. Two sequences of events are associated with him. First, Jeroboam flees to Shishak because Solomon seeks to kill him, and he stays in Egypt until Solomon's death (1 Kings 11:40). Upon his return (1 Kings 12:2; 2 Chron 10:2), Jeroboam becomes king of Israel, while Rehoboam becomes king of Judah. Second, in Rehoboam's year 5, Shishak conquers Jerusalem and carries off the temple treasures, including Solomon's golden shields (1 Kings 14:25-26; 2 Chron 12:9). Twelve hundred chariots, sixty thousand cavalry, and Libyans, Sukkiim and Ethiopians (i.e., Nubians) accompany Shishak, who takes the fortified cities of Judah on the road to Jerusalem (2 Chron 12:3-4). After chastising Rehoboam and his officers for abandoning the Lord, Shemaiah prophecies that because they humbled themselves, Shishak would not destroy them, but only make them his servants (2 Chron 12:5-8).

4.1.3. Discussions. Recent discussions include Ash, 29-34, 50-56; Barnes, 57-71; Kitchen, 72-76 §§58-60, 293-300 §§252-58, 432-47 §§398-415; Montet, 41-44; Redford, 312-15; Schipper, 119-32.

4.1.4. Comments. In terms of historicity, two facts are certain from Egyptian sources. First, *Sh-sh-n-q* is the name of more than one ruler in the early first millennium BCE. The name has four consonants; *q* is close to *k*; hieroglyphic writing

does not represent vowels; the vowels in the modern forms "Sheshonq" and "Shoshenq" are speculative; Masoretic punctuation spells "Shishaq," with front vowel *i;* an alternative, and perhaps original, pronunciation "Shushak," with back vowel *u* (or *o*), is suggested by the spelling with Hebrew *mater lectionis waw* at 1 Kings 14:25 (Kitchen 73, n. 356). The second fact is that a Palestinian campaign is attributed to Shoshenq I, the founder of Dynasty 22, and described in detail in a large relief at the Bubastite Portal in Karnak; two other sources are an inscription at the temple of Amun at El Hibeh and a fragmentary stela found in hall K at Karnak (Ash, 50). No Palestinian campaign is documented for many years before and after Shoshenq I.

On the basis of these similarities, many if not most historians have equated Shishak with Shoshenq I. *Jerusalem is not mentioned, however, or at least not preserved, among the 180 or so names listed of conquered Palestinian cities in the Egyptian sources mentioned above. In regard to chronology, the reign of Shoshenq I is a unique case in which Egyptian chronology has been derived from biblical chronology, not the other way around. It was a priori clear that Shoshenq I and Rehoboam belong in the same general epoch, but 925 BCE as a rough date of Shoshenq I's Palestinian campaign in Rehoboam's year 5 is based entirely on the premise that Rehoboam's reign began roughly around 930 BCE, which is itself obtained by counting back about ninety years from synchronisms of Ahab of Israel and Jehu "son" of Omri of Israel with Shalmaneser III. It remains uncertain when Shoshenq I's reign began.

4.2. So.

4.2.1. Verses. A certain "So king of Egypt" is mentioned just once in the Historical Books: 2 Kings 17:4.

4.2.2. Events. King Hoshea of Israel secretly seeks an alliance with "So king of Egypt" against the Assyrian king Shalmaneser V (727-722 BCE), a maneuver prompting Assyria to invade Israel, besiege its capital *Samaria for three years, eventually conquer the city (in 721 BCE, under the Assyrian king Sargon II), and abolish forever the northern kingdom of Israel (1 Kings 17:1-6).

4.2.3. Discussions. Recent discussions include Barnes, 131-37; Christensen; Day; Kitchen, 372-74 §§333-34, 582-83 §526 in the supplement to the second edition, xxxiv-xxxix in the preface to the reprint edition; Redford, 346; Schipper, 151-52.

4.2.4. Comments. The identity of So is unknown. There have been many proposals and countless discussions. Suggestions for So's identity include King Osorkon IV of Dynasty 22 (Kitchen), King Tefnakht of Dynasty 24 (Christensen), the city of Sais (Goedicke) and a "Saite (king)" (Redford).

4.3. Tirhakah.

4.3.1. Verses. A King Tirhakah is mentioned just once in the Historical Books: 2 Kings 19:9. He is mentioned once more in Isaiah 37:9, in a parallel account of the same events.

4.3.2. Events. 2 Kings 18:13—19:36 describes hostilities between King Hezekiah of Judah and King Sennacherib of Assyria, beginning in year 14 of Hezekiah (2 Kings 18:13). At some point Sennacherib learns that a certain "king Tirhakah of Ethiopia [i.e., Nubia]" has set out to fight against him, and he promptly sends a message to Hezekiah (2 Kings 19:9). Tirhakah's role in the conflict is not further detailed.

4.2.3. Discussions. Recent discussions include Barnes, 73-130; Gallagher; Kitchen, 154-61 §§126-29, 552-53 §465 in the supplement to the second edition, xxxix-xlii in the preface to the reprint edition; Redford, 351-58; Schipper, 210-17.

4.2.4. Comments. A Nubian king named Taharqa (the vowels are hypothetical) did exist around the time in question. Consequently, the equation of Tirhakah with Taharqa has been universally accepted. However, there is a problem. Taharqa's reign begins in 690 BCE (or perhaps 691 BCE) (Depuydt, in press [a]). However, Sennacherib's only known Palestinian campaign took place in 701 BCE. Taharqa cannot have been king yet in 701 BCE, as 2 Kings 19:9 seems to imply. Three explanations have been proposed for this problem: (1) Tirhaqa was a general, not yet a king, in 701 BCE; (2) the text is plainly anachronistic—that is, in error; (3) Sennacherib undertook a second Palestinian campaign, not attested in the sources, after 690 BCE. Most have assumed that King Shabaka ruled in 701 BCE, but just when the debate was in danger of turning stale, a new piece of evidence became generally accessible: a cuneiform rock inscription at Tang-i Var in Iran dating to Sargon II (721-705 BCE) (Frame). At first sight, the inscription suggests that Shabaka's successor and Taharqa's predecessor, Shabataka, whom Taharqa may have killed (Depuydt 2001), ruled already as early as 706 BCE, five years before Sennacherib's campaign of 701 BCE. Until now, no regnal year higher than year 3 was known for Shabataka. Thus a length of reign for Shabataka of two to three years (c. 692-690 BCE) was not positively falsifiable (Depuydt 1993). The reading of the name "Shabataka" in the Tang-i Var inscription seems secure. The sign for *ta* in *šá-pa-ta-ku-u* is clearly visible on a photograph of the inscription. Still, some arguments can be adduced against the notion that Shabataka reigned as early as 706 BCE. First, in general, Sargon II's inscriptions are known for their many chronological problems. Second, parallel texts in Sargon II's palace do not name King Shabataka. The absence of the name in the original casts doubt on the reliability of the name's appearance in a copy high upon a rock in far-away Tang-i Var. Indeed, the Tang-i Var text may have been inscribed years after 706 BCE, when at a later time Shabataka had come to the throne. Third, the editor (Frame, 54) admits that in the Tang-i Var inscription the Assyrian scribe seems to assign events to Shabataka's reign that may belong in Shabaka's reign. Then why could the name "Shabataka" not have been inserted, or substituted for another name, in the later copy at Tang-i Var?

4.4. Neco.

4.4.1. Verses. An Egyptian King Neco is mentioned exactly seven times in the Historical Books: 2 Kings 23:29, 33, 34, 35; 2 Chronicles 35:20, 22; 36:4. Neco is also mentioned once more at Jeremiah 46:2.

4.4.2. Events. King Neco intervenes in the internal affairs of the kingdom of Judah around 609 BCE, under the three kings Josiah, Jehoahaz and Jehoiakim.

First, there are two accounts of an encounter between Neco and *Josiah at *Megiddo. Neco is on his way to the Euphrates to support the Assyrians (against the ascendant Neo-Babylonians). 2 Chronicles 35:20 specifies Charchemish as the ultimate destination. According to the shorter account at 2 Kings 23:28-30, Neco kills Josiah at Megiddo when the latter comes to meet him. The expanded account at 2 Chronicles 35:20-25 describes a battle between Neco and Josiah at Megiddo. Josiah is shot by Neco's archers and carried home to Jerusalem, where he dies. 2 Kings 23:28-30 could be interpreted as an abbreviated version of 2 Chronicles 35:20-25. A discrepancy exists, however, with regard to where Josiah dies.

Second, Neco deposes the people's choice as Josiah's successor, Jehoahaz, after only three months of reign, carrying him off to Egypt, where later he dies, appointing Jehoiakim as king instead and subsequently extracting heavy taxes from Judah (2 Kings 23:30-35; 2 Chron 36:1-4).

In addition, Jeremiah 46:2-12 speaks of Neco's defeat at the hands of the Babylonian king Nebuchadnezzar. This battle is presumably the one of Charchemish in 605 BCE, well documented in cuneiform sources (Finegan, 253-54). Furthermore, at 2 Kings 24:7, which belongs in the reigns of Jehoiakim of Judah (c. 609-598 BCE) and Nebuchadnezzar of Babylon (September 7, 605 BCE to the beginning of October of 562 BCE), the unnamed pharaoh who "did not again come out of his land" because "the king of Babylon had taken all that belonged to the king of Egypt from the Brook of Egypt to the river Euphrates" (presumably after the battle of Charchemish) would have to be Neco as well. And it was presumably also to Neco's Egypt that Judahites fled after the destruction of Jerusalem (2 Kings 25:26).

4.4.3. Discussions. Recent discussions include Finegan, 251-54; Kienitz, 20-29, 159-61; Montet, 47-48; Redford, 447-55, 464-69; Schipper, 234-46.

4.4.4. Comments. On the whole, the references to Neco exhibit fewer problems than those to Shishak, So and Tirhakah above. The king in question is with hardly a doubt Pharaoh Neco (610-595 BCE). There is also little cause to doubt the overall veracity of the references. It is true that no extant Egyptian sources corroborate the events related. However, a Babylonian chronicle describes how Egyptians and Assyrians together cross the Euphrates to move against the Babylonian king Nabopolassar, apparently early in the latter's year 17—that is, in the summer or early fall of 609 BCE. This troop movement may well be the one anticipated in 2 Kings 23:28-30 and 2 Chronicles 35:20-25. Both Egyptians and Assyrians are mentioned, as well as the river Euphrates (Kienitz, 159-60). At face value, about four years would seem to separate the hostilities at Megiddo around 609 BCE from the final battle at Charchemish in 605 BCE.

See also ASSYRIA, ASSYRIANS; BABYLONIA, BABYLONIANS; CHRONOLOGY; NON-ISRAELITE WRITTEN SOURCES: EGYPTIAN ARAMAIC PAPYRI; PERSIA, PERSIANS.

BIBLIOGRAPHY. W. F. Albright, "The Chronology of the Divided Monarchy of Israel," *BASOR* 100 (1945) 16-22; **P. S. Ash,** *David, Solomon and Egypt: A Reassessment* (JSOTSup 297; Sheffield: Sheffield Academic Press, 1999); **W. H. Barnes,** *Studies in the Chronology of the Divided Monarchy of Israel* (HSM 48; Atlanta: Scholars Press, 1991); **L. Brack-Bernsen,** *Zur Entstehung der babylonischen Mondtheorie: Beobachtung und theoretische Berechnung von Mondphasen* (Boethius 40; Stuttgart: Steiner, 1997); **D. L. Christensen,** "The Identity of 'King So' in Egypt (2 Kings XVII 4)," *VT* 39 (1989) 146-53; **J. Day,** "The Problem of 'So, King of Egypt' in 2 Kings XVII 4," *VT* 42 (1992) 291-310; **L. Depuydt,** "The Date of Death of Artaxerxes I," *Die Welt des Orients* 26 (1995) 86-96; idem, "The Date of Piye's Egyptian Campaign and the Chronology of the Twenty-fifth Dynasty," *JEA* 79 (1993) 269-74; idem, "Foundations of Day-exact Chronology," in *Handbook of Egyptian Chronology*, ed. R. Krauss and E. Hornung (Handbuch der Orientalistik; Leiden: E. J. Brill, in press [a]); idem, "Glosses to Jerome's Eusebios as a Source for Pharaonic History," *ChrEg* 76 (2001) 30-47; idem, "'More Valuable Than All Gold': Ptolemy's Royal Canon and Babylonian Chronology," *JCS* 47 (1995) 97-117; idem, "Regnal Years and Civil Calendar in Achaemenid Egypt," *JEA* 81 (1995) 151-73; idem, "Saite and Persian Egypt, 664-332 B.C.E. (Dynasties 26-31, Psammetichus I to Alexander's Conquest of Egypt)," in *Handbook of Egyptian Chronology*, ed. R. Krauss and E. Hornung (Handbuch der Orientalistik; Leiden: E. J. Brill, in press [a]); idem, "The Shifting Foundation of Ancient Chronology," in *Modern Trends in European Egyptology: Papers from a Session Held at the Ninth Meeting of European Association of Archaeologists Held at St. Petersburg, Russia*, ed. A.-A. Maravelia (Oxford: Archaeopress, in press [b]); **I. E. S. Edwards,** "From the Twenty-second to the Twenty-fourth Dynasty," *CAH²* 3/1.534-81, 966-74; **J. Finegan,** *Handbook of Biblical Chronology* (Princeton, NJ: Princeton University Press, 1964; rev. ed., Peabody, MA: Hendrickson, 1998); **G. Frame,** "The Inscription of Sargon II at Tang-i Var," *Or* 68 (1999) 31-57; **W. Gallagher,** *Sennacherib's Campaign to Judah: New Studies* (SHCANE 18; Leiden: E. J. Brill, 1999); **H. Goedicke,** "The End of 'So, King of Egypt,'" *BASOR* 171 (1963) 64-66; **T. G. H. James,** "Egypt: The Twenty-fifth and Twenty-sixth Dynasties," *CAH²* 3/2.677-750, 860-67; **C. O. Jonsson,** *The Gentile Times Reconsidered: Chronology and Christ's Return*

(3d ed.; Atlanta: Commentary Press, 1998); **F. K. Kienitz,** *Die politische Geschichte Ägyptens vom 7. bis zum 4. Jahrhundert vor der Zeitwende* (Berlin: Akademie-Verlag, 1953); **K. A. Kitchen,** *The Third Intermediate Period in Egypt (1100-650 BC)* (1st ed.; Warminster: Aris & Phillips, 1972; 2d ed. with supplement, 1986; repr. of 2d ed. with new preface, 1995]); **F. X. Kugler,** *Von Moses bis Paulus: Forschungen zur Geschichte Israels nach biblischen und profangeschichtlichen insbesondere neuen keilinschriftlichen Quellen* (Münster: Aschendorff, 1922); **A. B. Lloyd,** "Egypt 404-332 B.C.," *CAH²* 6.337-60, 981-87; **A. R. Millard,** *The Eponyms of the Assyrian Empire, 910-612 BC* (SAAS 2; Helsinki: Helsinki University Press, 1994); **K. Myśśliwiec,** *The Twilight of Ancient Egypt: First Millennium B.C.E.* (Ithaca, NY: Cornell University Press, 2000); **P. Montet,** *L'Égypte et la Bible* (Cahiers d'archéologie biblique 11; Neuchâtel: Delachaux & Niestlé, 1959); **N. Na'aman,** "The Brook of Egypt and Assyrian Policy on the Border of Egypt," *TA* 6 (1979) 68-90; idem, "The Shihor of Egypt and Shur That Is before Egypt," *TA* 7 (1980) 95-109; **R. A. Parker and W. H. Dubberstein,** *Babylonian Chronology 626 B.C.-A.D. 75* (BUS 19; Providence: Brown University Press, 1956); **J. D. Ray,** "Egypt 525-404 B.C.," *CAH²* 4/ 2.254-86, 833-39; **D. B. Redford,** *Egypt, Canaan, and Israel in Ancient Times* (Princeton, NJ: Princeton University Press, 1992); **A. Sachs and H. Hunger,** *Astronomical Diaries and Related Texts from Babylonia* (3 vols.; Österreichische Akademie der Wissenschaften, Philosophisch-historische Klasse, Denkschriften 195, 210, 247; Vienna: Verlag der Akademie, 1988-1996); **B. U. Schipper,** *Israel und Ägypten in der Königszeit: Die kulturellen Kontakte von Salomo bis zum Fall Jerusalems* (OBO 170; Freiburg: Universitätsverlag; Göttingen: Vandenhoeck & Ruprecht, 1999); **E. R. Thiele,** *The Mysterious Numbers of the Hebrew Kings: A Reconstruction of the Chronology of the Kingdoms of Israel and Judah* (1st ed.; Chicago: University of Chicago Press, 1951; 2d ed.; Grand Rapids: Eerdmans, 1965; 3d ed.; Grand Rapids: Zondervan, 1983). L. Depuydt.

EHUD. *See* HISTORY OF ISRAEL 2: PREMONARCHIC ISRAEL; JUDGES.

EKRON

A site at the eastern edge of the coastal plain best known as one of the five cities of the *Philistines and now to be identified with Khirbet el-Muqanna/Tel Miqne (M.R. 136 132). The name "Ekron" (*'eqrôn*) is Semitic and perhaps means "uprooted."

1. Identification
2. Archaeological Exploration
3. References in the Historical Books

1. Identification.

The first modern attempt to identify Ekron was made in the nineteenth century by E. Robinson (3.23), who placed it at the village of Akir (M.R. 133 141), basing his conclusion on linguistic similarity and the general location of the latter. In this he was followed by G. A. Smith (141). The absence of significant ancient remains at this site, however, prompted several alternate identifications. One such proposal was made by R. A. S. Macalister (74-78), who argued for the existence of two Ekrons, a northern one in Danite territory, and a southern one in Judah, identical with the Philistine city. Philistine Ekron he identified with Dhikhrin (M.R. 136 119), a site several miles southeast of Gath/Tell es-Safi (M.R. 135 123). In 1923 W. F. Albright (3-7) argued that Ekron should be located at Qatra (M.R. 129 136). While Albright considered Khirbet el-Muqanna as a possible candidate, he failed to recognize the presence of the forty-acre lower city and so thought the site too small to be the renowned Philistine stronghold. Later, J. Naveh (1958, 165-70) marshaled evidence from archaeological surveys, the biblical text and the *Onomasticon of Eusebius* to argue convincingly that ancient Ekron should be located at Khirbet el-Muqanna. This view was confirmed in 1996 by the discovery at the site of a royal dedicatory inscription mentioning "Ikausu, son of Padi . . . ruler of Ekron" (Gitin, Dothan and Naveh, 8-16; *COS* 2.42:164).

2. Archaeological Exploration.

In 1957 J. Naveh conducted an archaeological survey of Ekron (Khirbet el-Muqanna) and identified surface remains including Philistine pottery, portions of a city wall and a gate complex (Naveh 1958, 91-100). Archaeological excavations proper began in 1981 under the auspices of the Hebrew University of Jerusalem and the Albright Institute of Archaeological Research. Since that time, work at the fifty-acre site has revealed stratified remains stretching from the Late Bronze through the Iron II periods (c. 1500-586 BCE), including a period of significant

Philistine occupation in the twelfth to tenth centuries BCE (Strata VII-IV). Throughout the tenth to eighth centuries the site decreased in importance, with settlement restricted to the ten-acre upper city. During the period of *Assyrian domination in the seventh century BCE settlement once more extended to the lower tell. During this time Ekron became a significant center of olive oil production, with one conservative estimate setting output at 230 tons annually (Eitam, 183). The quantity of olives required for this level of production suggests that this period of Assyrian dominance was characterized by regional economic cooperation between Ekron and the territory of Judah further to the east, as is suggested also by the increased use at the site of hill country limestone in place of the local mud-brick (Gitin, 40-41).

3. References in the Historical Books.

Situated in a transitional zone where the Shephelah merges with the coastal plain, Ekron figured prominently in Israelite territorial ambitions. In Joshua 13:3 Ekron is given as the northern limit of a coastal swath of territory that remained under the control of the Philistines and the *Canaanites at the end of *Joshua's lifetime. Despite this, the city seems originally to have been allotted to the tribe of Dan (Josh 19:43). When the Danites were unable to establish a presence on the coastal plain, the city was subsumed under the territorial aspirations of Judah and was included in that tribe's territorial list (Josh 15:11). In that text Judah's northern border is said to pass along the "slope to the north of Ekron"—a feature likely to be identified with the low ridge that rises immediately to the northeast of Khirbet el-Muqanna.

In Judges 1:18 Judah is described as capturing the territory of Ekron along with the southern coastal cities of *Gaza and *Ashkelon. The LXX adds *Ashdod to the list and suggests that Judah did not take these cities. If the MT is accepted, the dating of this event is unclear. Although it is nestled among the old traditions of the capture of Debir by Othniel (Judg 1:11-13) and the failure of Benjamin to take Jebus (Judg 1:21), this verse may depict a later event placed here in order to continue the book's emphasis on Judah's achievements and primacy (see Judg 1:1-2, 8; 17:6; 18:1; 19:1; 20:18; 21:25). A later date for this verse is made more likely by the picture of Philistine regional dominance

depicted in the Samson cycle (Judg 13—16) and in 1 Samuel.

Ekron appears again in 1 Samuel 5—6 in the account of the movements of the *ark following the Israelite defeat at Aphek-Ebenezer. Taken initially to Ashdod where it is briefly housed in the temple of Dagon, the ark is moved east to *Gath (Tell es-Safi) (M.R. 135 123) and then north to Ekron, thus placing it nearer the border with Judah. In each city the ark brings plague and death. What the armies of Israel were unable to do on the battlefield, therefore, Yahweh's portable throne is able to achieve by its mere presence in three of the five Philistine cities. Loath to have further contact with this destructive trophy, the Philistines send the ark via unattended cart east into the Sorek Valley and Israelite territory.

Ekron figures also in the summary of *Samuel's achievements found in 1 Samuel 7:14. The text here describes Israelite territorial gains at the expense of Ekron and Gath and points to greater Israelite control over Philistine possessions in the Shephelah. Such advantage was short-lived, however, for by the reign of *Saul, the Philistines had advanced as far as Socoh (M.R. 147 121) at the eastern end of the Elah Valley. In the rout that followed *David's victory over Goliath, the Philistines fled west through the valley, scattering near its mouth to the safety of nearby Ekron and Gath.

A final reference to Ekron in the Historical Books occurs in 2 Kings 1, where it is the home of the god Baal-Zebub (or Baal-Zebul; cf. Mt 10:25; 12:24; Mk 3:22; Lk 11:15, 18-19), consulted by King Ahaziah (853-852 BCE) of Israel. In this narrative the prophet *Elijah twice calls down fire on the military contingent sent to arrest him. The fact that the prophet faces his foes from atop a hill and destroys them with heavenly fire (2 Kings 1:9-10, 12) invites comparison with the manner in which Elijah earlier dispatched the prophets of Baal in the days of Ahaziah's father, Ahab (1 Kings 18:16-46). The shape of the narrative seems a clear invitation to view Ahaziah's actions as a continuation of the apostasy of his mother and father.

Ekron likely came under Assyrian domination in 734 BCE, when Tiglath-pileser III (745-727 BCE) marched through Philistia on his way to Gaza (COS 2.117C:287-89; 2.117E-F:290-92; ANET, 283). Throughout the following three decades Ekron and the other cities of Philistia vacillated between submitting to Assyria and striving for independence—a tendency observable also in the neighboring kingdoms of Judah and Israel. In either 720 or 712 BCE, Sargon II (722-705 BCE) conquered the city as part of a punitive campaign through Philistia and memorialized the event in an undated relief in his palace at Khorsabad. During the confusion that accompanied the succession from Sargon II to Sennacherib (705-681 BCE), elements at Ekron deposed the king, Padi, and joined *Hezekiah of Judah in rebellion against Assyria. As a major fortified city that straddled the eastern branch of the coastal highway and guarded access to both the Sorek and Elah Valleys, Ekron was an important element in Judean defenses against Sennacherib. After Sennacherib's largely successful campaign of 701 BCE, Padi was restored, and territory formerly belonging to Judah was added to his realm (COS 2.119B:302-3; ANET, 287-88). In the time of Esarhaddon (681-669 BCE), Ikausu of Ekron was one source of forced labor required to transport building materials to Nineveh (ANET, 291). A recently discovered dedicatory inscription commissioned by Ikausu and mentioning a previously unknown non-Semitic goddess (Ptgyh) has been regarded by some as providing evidence of the Philistine's Aegean roots (Naveh 1998, 35-36; Schäfer-Lichtenberger, 86-91; COS 2.42:164). Even so, the West Canaanite dialect of the inscription and the occurrence elsewhere at Ekron of the divine names Baal, Asherat, Qudshu and Anat show that by this same time the Ekronites had largely assimilated to Canaanite culture. Later, during Ashurbanipal's (668-627 BCE) 667 BCE campaign against *Egypt, Ikausu was conscripted along with those of other coastal cities to provide funds and troops in support of the expedition (ANET, 294).

With the waning of Assyrian power toward the end of the seventh century BCE, the loyalty of Ekron appears to have shifted to Egypt. In 609 BCE, Pharaoh Necho passed unopposed through Philistia on his way north to do battle with the *Babylonians. Only *Josiah of Judah appears to have attempted to prevent the Egyptian advance. In a papyrus letter dated a short while later and recently attributed to the ruler of Ekron, a certain Adon appeals to the pharaoh for support against the approaching king of Babylon (COS 3.54:132-34; Porten, 36-52). Several more Babylonian campaigns followed, and by 598 BCE, Ek-

ron and the rest of the coastal plain were firmly under Babylonian control.

See also ASHDOD; ASHKELON; GATH; GAZA; PHILISTINES.

BIBLIOGRAPHY. W. F. Albright, "The Sites of Ekron, Gath, and Libnah," AASOR 2-3 (1921-1922) 1-17; T. Dothan and S. Gitin, "Tel Miqne (Ekron)," NEAEHL 3.1051-59; C. S. Ehrlich, The Philistines in Transition: A History from ca. 1000-730 B.C.E (SHCANE 10; (Leiden: E. J. Brill, 1996); D. Eitam, "The Olive Oil Industry at Tel Miqne-Ekron in the Late Iron Age," in Olive Oil in Antiquity: Israel and Neighbouring Countries from the Neolithic to the Early Arab Period, ed. D. Eitam and M. Heltzer (History of the Ancient Near East/Studies 7; Padova: Sargon, 1996) 167-96; S. Gitin, "Ekron of the Philistines, Part II: Olive-Oil Suppliers to the World," BAR 16.2 (1990) 32-42, 59; S. Gitin, T. Dothan and J. Naveh, "A Royal Dedicatory Inscription from Ekron," IEJ 47 (1997) 1-16; R. A. S. Macalister, The Philistines: Their History and Civilization (Schweich Lectures, 1911; London: Oxford University Press, 1913); N. Na'aman, "Ekron under the Assyrian and Egyptian Empires," BASOR 332 (2003) 81-91; J. Naveh, "Khirbat al-Muqanna'-Ekron: An Archaeological Survey," IEJ 8 (1958) 87-100, 165-70; idem, "Achish-Ikausu in the Light of the Ekron Dedication," BASOR 310 (1998) 35-37; B. Porten, "The Identity of King Adon," BA 44 (1981) 36-52; E. Robinson, Biblical Researches in Palestine, Mount Sinai and Arabia Petraea: A Journal of Travels in the Year 1838 (3 vols.; Boston: Crocker & Brewster, 1841); C. Schäfer-Lichtenberger, "The Goddess of Ekron and the Religious-Cultural Background of the Philistines," IEJ 50 (2000) 82-91; G. A. Smith, The Historical Geography of the Holy Land (repr., New York: Harper & Row, 1966 [1931]); H. Tadmor, "The Campaigns of Sargon II of Assur: A Chronological-Historical Study," JCS 12 (1958) 12-40, 77-100.

B. P. Irwin

EKRON INSCRIPTION. See NON-ISRAELITE WRITTEN SOURCES: SYRO-PALESTINIAN.

EL. See CANAAN, CANAANITES; CANAANITE GODS AND RELIGION; GOD

ELAMITE SOURCES. See NON-ISRAELITE WRITTEN SOURCES: OLD PERSIAN AND ELAMITE.

ELEPHANTINE JEWISH COMMUNITY. See

HISTORY OF ISRAEL 7: PERSIAN PERIOD.

ELEPHANTINE PAPYRI. *See* NON-ISRAELITE WRITTEN SOURCES: EGYPTIAN ARAMAIC PAPYRI; SANBALLAT.

ELI. *See* HISTORY OF ISRAEL 2: PREMONARCHIC ISRAEL; SAMUEL; SAMUEL, BOOKS OF.

ELIJAH

Elijah was a ninth-century *prophet in the northern kingdom (Israel) who challenged King Ahab's court-sponsored Baal worship, ultimately defeating the prophets of Baal in a dramatic encounter on Mount *Carmel and receiving a commission from Yahweh on Mount Horeb to set in motion the end of the *Omri dynasty. His role as a Yahwistic prophet, after the model of Moses, has strengthened Elijah's place in the biblical tradition. The narratives making up the Elijah cycle occur in 1 Kings 17—19, 1 Kings 21 and 2 Kings 1—2; apart from these, Elijah is mentioned only in 2 Chronicles 21:12 and Malachi 4:5. Three other OT characters are named Elijah, one among the descendants of Benjamin (1 Chron 8:27), and two among the returning exiles who had married foreign women (Ezra 10:21, 26). Recent scholarly study of Elijah may be explored from the perspective of the biblical materials themselves, the figure of the prophet in his context, and the religious and theological message of his ministry.

1. The Elijah Cycle as Biblical Narrative
2. Elijah's Historical and Literary Portrayal
3. Religious and Theological Implications of Elijah's Ministry Against Baal Worship

1. The Elijah Cycle as Biblical Narrative.
1.1. The Sources and Forms of the Elijah Stories.
1.1.1. The Sources Behind the Elijah Cycle. Stories about Elijah probably were transmitted in oral form at the earliest stage. Although the company of prophets, who could have passed on the stories about their master *Elisha (e.g., 2 Kings 4), are never associated directly with Elijah, their knowledge of and reverence for him is apparent in 2 Kings 2, making them potential bearers of traditions about Elijah. There is no way to be certain of the date of the earliest written accounts about the prophet, but several features of the Elijah cycle point to their independent formation—that is, outside of the authorship of the regnal histories that make up

the bulk of 1-2 Kings. Elijah's sudden introduction (1 Kings 17:1) into the opening account of Ahab's kingship (1 Kings 16:29-34) is awkward, perhaps indicating the loss of some preceding materials to explain his origin. Moreover, the lack of concern for the central sanctuary in *Jerusalem also seems to run counter to the narrator's rhetoric in the chapters preceding the appearance of Elijah (Robinson, 515), though it is debated as to whether the prophetic cycle was inserted before or after the completion of the primary history in 1-2 Kings (see 1.2.2 below). In the same vein, M. Cogan (457) believes that the Elijah narratives probably were independent of the Elisha narratives and set before those were written, given that a single author would not have had Elisha carry out the anointings that Yahweh commissioned Elijah to do.

1.1.2. Form-Critical Issues. The work of form-critical scholars has drawn attention to the individual stories within the Elijah cycle, describing them as "prophetic legends," though some stories, like that concerning the widow of Zarephath (1 Kings 17:8-24), do not focus strictly on miraculous elements but instead point to ethical features, such as the woman's faithful recognition of Elijah as a "man of God" (Rofé, 132-33). This use of "man of God" and similarities to some of Elisha's deeds have led some scholars to see this particular story as originating in the Elisha narratives. More recently, B. Britt has argued for a "type scene" relating Elijah to Moses and others where concealment of the prophet is part of a pattern elsewhere in Scripture. Moving beyond the individual stories, A. Rofé (183) classifies the entire Elijah cycle as an "epic," in part because of its overall portrayal of a "Battle of the Gods." Apart from the issue of the stories' purported legendary character, it has been cogently argued that 1 Kings 17:1—19:18 functions in its present form as a literary unity (Robinson; Simon), though the connection of these chapters to the stories in 1 Kings 21 and 2 Kings 1—2 remains unclear. The fact that the LXX offers a different arrangement of the end of 1 Kings, placing the Naboth story (chap. 21 in the MT) immediately after the selection of Elisha in 1 Kings 19:19-21, could indicate that at least some written versions of the Elijah cycle did unite these other narratives to the struggle against Baal worship in chapters 17—19.

1.2. The Elijah Cycle and Redaction Criticism.
1.2.1. The Question of the Deuteronomistic Histo-

ry. The issue of how and when the Elijah and Elisha cycles were written and incorporated into 1-2 Kings relates to the much larger debate over the compositional history of the *Deuteronomistic History, a debate that has fostered an enormous amount of literature since Martin Noth's 1943 proposal of a single, exilic Deuteronomistic author (*see* Deuteronomistic History). A majority of scholars now seem to hold to a theory of some kind of preexilic redaction of the historical narratives in 1-2 Kings, occurring during the reigns of *Hezekiah (c. 700 BCE) or *Josiah (c. 620 BCE). B. Halpern and D. S. Vanderhooft have presented a strong case for preexilic editions of the books of Kings during the reigns of Hezekiah and Josiah, based on changes in the formulaic introductions and burial notices of individual kings.

1.2.2. The Elijah Cycle Within the Books of Kings. Regardless of when one posits the redaction of the books of Kings, it remains an open question as to the relative time when the Elijah and Elisha cycles were included in the regnal history of the northern kingdom. While Halpern and Vanderhooft (234-35) would suggest that Deuteronomistic historians were responsible for this literary decision, S. L. McKenzie (98) has maintained that the Elijah and Elisha narratives were predominantly "post-Dtr additions." The arguments for both positions become quite complex and often turn on technical details in biblical vocabulary. McKenzie employs historical and tradition-historical arguments that seem to show the absence of any Deuteronomistic editing of the prophetic cycles. Halpern and Vanderhooft (230-35) argue that changes in regnal, death and burial formulas, and source formulas at the times of Hezekiah and Josiah point to a Deuteronomistic redaction in the time of Hezekiah that would include the Elisha and Elijah materials, though a unique problem is raised by Ahab's death and burial notice (1 Kings 22:37-40), possibly indicating a Josianic handling of the story in 1 Kings 22. Although the debate remains lively and complex, it seems reasonable to assume some kind of preexilic editing of the sources that stand behind the prophetic narratives. After the fall of *Samaria (c. 722 BCE), the Elijah narratives probably were brought to Judah and could have been incorporated into the royal history during a Hezekian redaction.

1.3. The Literary Structure of the Elijah Cycle.
1.3.1. The Content of the Stories. Over half of

the Elijah cycle is devoted to his interaction with Ahab during a three-year period of intense drought predicted by the prophet (1 Kings 17:1). The Lord provided food and water for Elijah east of the Jordan River (1 Kings 17:2-7), and then sent him to a widow in Zarephath, along the Phoenician coastline, where Elijah promised a continuous supply of food for her family until the drought ended (1 Kings 17:8-16). During his stay with the widow, her son became ill and died, but God miraculously restored the boy to life in answer to Elijah's prayer (1 Kings 17:17-24). After about three years, the Lord commanded Elijah to meet Ahab in preparation for drought-ending rains (1 Kings 18:1-2). Along the way, Elijah met Obadiah, one of Ahab's servants, who secretly had been protecting one hundred prophets of Yahweh from Jezebel's wrath (1 Kings 18:3-16). Elijah commanded Ahab to summon the prophets of Baal to Mount Carmel, where the Lord vindicated Elijah and demonstrated his exclusive and sovereign power over creation, precipitating the execution of the Baalistic prophets (1 Kings 18:17-40). Once the rains arrived (1 Kings 18:41-46), Elijah escaped the murderous threats of Jezebel by making his way through Judah and the wilderness to Mount Horeb, where Yahweh reveals himself to the prophet (1 Kings 19:1-14). To commence God's plan of judgment on Israel, Elijah is commanded to anoint Hazael as king of Aram, Jehu as king of Israel, and Elisha as his own prophetic successor (1 Kings 19:15-18), though it is only the latter commissioning that Elijah actually accomplishes (1 Kings 19:19-21). Two later stories have Elijah pronouncing judgment on Ahab for his murder and confiscation of Naboth's property (1 Kings 21), and on Ahab's son Ahaziah when that king seeks guidance from the *Canaanite god Baal-Ekron (2 Kings 1). In a concluding story that serves as a transition to Elisha's ministry, Elijah is miraculously taken in a whirlwind to heaven, leaving his mantle and prophetic office to Elisha (2 Kings 2).

1.3.2. The Structure of the Cycle in Its Canonical Order. Granting that the "final form" of the Elijah narratives is now embedded with various interludes in the accounts of Ahab and Ahaziah, there nevertheless appears to be some literary balance and organization of the material just described. The prophet's sudden entrance on and exit from the stage of Israelite history form a frame around the intervening stories (1 Kings

17:1; 2 Kings 2:11). Standing in the middle of the cycle are the two peaks, Carmel and Horeb, where the Lord's power and word are displayed (1 Kings 18:20—19:18). The scenes that surround the Carmel and Horeb accounts involve Elijah's contact with faithful followers of Yahweh (Obadiah and Elisha), as well as with Ahab himself for his sins against the Lord (1 Kings 18:1-19 and 1 Kings 19:19-21; 21:1-29). Creating an "inner frame" around the cycle are two accounts where Elijah offers life in the place of death (the widow's son [1 Kings 17:8-24]) or judgment in the threat of death (King Ahaziah [2 Kings 1]). Both stories locate the dead or dying on a bed in an "upper room" and have some connection to a Canaanite context, whether in Zarephath or by the king's appeal to a Canaanite deity at Ekron. The following structure modifies a similar outline by Y. T. Radday (59):

A Introduction: Elijah's sudden appearance near the Jordan River
  B To Zarephath: Miraculous provision for a Canaanite widow; restoration of her son
    C Ahab looks for water, is challenged by Elijah; Obadiah a faithful servant
      D The contest on Mount Carmel
      D' The revelation on Mount Horeb
    C' Ahab murders Naboth, is challenged by Elijah; Elisha a faithful servant
  B' To Ekron? Miraculous judgment on soldiers; the death of an Israelite king's son
A' Conclusion: Elijah's sudden departure near the Jordan River

2. Elijah's Historical and Literary Portrayal.

2.1. The Historical Background of Elijah's Ninth-Century Ministry.

2.1.1. Elijah as Historical Figure. It is impossible to reconstruct a historical portrait of the prophet, given the selective nature and theological purposes of the stories about him. Elijah is called "the Tishbite" (1 Kings 17:1), but this appellation offers little help in light of differences between the MT ("from the sojourners of Gilead") and the LXX ("from Tishbe of Gilead"). Moreover, the ambiguous reference to his place of refuge near the Jordan River (1 Kings 17:3) does not guarantee that he was from a trans-Jordanian tribe (Cogan, 426), though tradition has placed Tishbe north of the Jabbok River (Cogan, 425). If his name, meaning "My God is Yahweh," is a proper name, it could indicate a family background loyal to Yahweh worship in the northern kingdom. In spite of this lack of definite information, the narratives about him provide no reason to overstate the "legendary" character of the narratives, as M. C. White does by proposing that they are "literary creations" to legitimize Jehu's overthrow of the Omri dynasty. In White's view, the historical Elijah, on whom the legends were based, was a "holy man who lived during Ahab's time and was known for his rainmaking activities" (White, 77). Neither the religio-political intent of the Elijah narratives nor their miraculous deeds make them, a priori, fictional, insofar as they are narrated with much the same tone of voice as most of the Deuteronomistic History, and in many respects they are less "fanciful" than the stories about his successor, Elisha. T. Overholt believes that some aspects of Elijah's prophetic activity can be explained by the ancient Near Eastern phenomenon of shamanism. To be sure, not all behavior associated with shamans (e.g., trances) appears in the Elijah cycle, but his act of resuscitating the boy in 1 Kings 17 seems to "have analogies in shamanic activities" (Overholt, 109). There can be no precise parallels with this phenomenon, given the great span of time and space between ninth-century Israel and its expression in other cultures, but the notion may help to fill out the portrait of Elijah as a popular holy man among the people of Israel (Overholt, 111).

2.1.2. The Omri Dynasty. Elijah's ministry occurred in the middle of the ninth century BCE, during the reigns of Ahab (c. 869-850), Ahaziah (c. 850-849) and Jehoram (c. 849-842), all descendants of King Omri (c. 876-869), a former army commander who rose to power when Zimri murdered Elah (c. 877-876). The Deuteronomistic purpose of demonstrating the religious and moral shortcomings of Israelite kings explains the lack of interest in the political and historical contributions of the Omri dynasty. The book of 1 Kings devotes eight verses to Omri's twelve-year reign (1 Kings 16:21-28; contrast six verses for Zimri's seven-day reign), but archaeological and inscriptional evidence (e.g., the Mesha inscription and various Assyrian inscriptions) points to Israel's significant growth and military strength during this period of relative Assyrian weakness. The fortification of Samaria (1 Kings 16:24), alliances with *Phoenicians (1 Kings 16:31) and control over *Moab (2 Kings 3:4) are all alluded to but not developed in the biblical texts about Omri and his successors.

2.2. Elijah's Social Role as a Ninth-Century Prophet.

Unlike Elisha, Elijah is not associated with prophetic guilds, nor do the narratives place him in regular contact with the royal court. His laments about being a lone prophet (1 Kings 18:22; 19:10, 14), while spoken out of intense emotion, at least point to the general pattern of his ministry. The fact that he does not seem aware of the one hundred prophets whom Obadiah hid (1 Kings 18:13) or the seven thousand faithful Israelites whom Yahweh mentions (1 Kings 19:18) supports this perspective. Thus, D. L. Petersen's identification of Elijah as a "peripheral" prophet remains reasonable. Such prophets were not directly involved with the central powers of society, but neither did they function completely "outside the bounds of the social structure" (Petersen, 46-47). Elijah can live among and serve the poor (1 Kings 17:8-24), but he (and Elisha) can also be thought of as "archetypes of all the biblical prophets as rival figures to the kings" (Collins, 130). Beyond his critiques of Ahab and Ahaziah in 1-2 Kings, there is one reference to Elijah by the Chronicler (2 Chron 21:12), which mentions a letter that he wrote to King Jehoram of Judah, indicting him for idolatry and murder; but this brief detail is not attested in the books of Kings, nor does it easily fit with the most widely accepted chronology, according to which Elijah would have died before Jehoram's reign (Williamson, 306-7).

2.3. Literary Criticism of Elijah's Portrayal in 1-2 Kings.

It seems fair to say that for much of the twentieth century, scholars generally emphasized Elijah's role as the "quintessential hero" in "the long line of Yahweh's intermediaries in Israel" that began with Moses (Walsh, 465). However, recent literary interpretations have painted the character of Elijah in a more ambiguous, if not negative, light. Through the use of close readings that highlight the psychological dimensions of his character and apparent inconsistencies in his behavior, B. P. Robinson, for example, states that Elijah was "obsessed with his image of himself as a latter-day Moses," "devoured by egotism," and an "arrogant prima donna of a prophet" (Robinson, 520, 528, 535). J. W. Olley (41) argues that it is Elijah's own zeal, rather than "compassionate identification" with God's people, that motivates him in ministry. Whereas a traditional interpretation might understand the scene on Mount Horeb as the oc-

casion when Elijah most reflects Moses, Robinson (529) suggests that this is where Elijah's prophetic role ends, even though the canonical form of 1-2 Kings has Elijah continuing his activity beyond the Horeb episode.

What are we to make of these contrasting interpretations? In fairness to both positions, it should be said that the traditional view was cognizant of Elijah's personal shortcomings (Simon, 225) and the more recent interpretations admit that even his weaknesses encourage the exiles that God's grace extends to them (Olley, 49). If the traditional view tended primarily to view Elijah from the perspective of the Deuteronomistic narrators, then the literary critics perhaps have overemphasized the perceived intent of apparent literary inconsistencies. To contend that Elijah is not a "new Moses" is not to demonstrate that the allusions to the books of Exodus and Joshua serve the sole purpose of subverting the portrait of Elijah. Both leaders had moments of despondency as well as selfless service. For Elijah, his willingness to risk identification with the unclean corpse of the widow's son is evidence of such service (Kiuchi, 78-79). Close readings will continue to make us aware of the tensions and ambiguities in characterization, but the rhetorical impact of the current canonical shape of the cycle moves readers away from Elijah's psychological profile to his continued struggle against the house of Ahab and finally to his miraculous translation, after which Elisha carries on his work.

3. Religious and Theological Implications of Elijah's Ministry Against Baal Worship.

3.1. The Ninth-Century Israelite Religious Context.

The books of Kings indict all of the Omride rulers for following in the sins of *Jeroboam, involving syncretistic worship at various high places (see 1 Kings 12:25-33). Ahab himself is particularly held responsible for much of Israel's apostasy: "Ahab son of Omri did more evil in the eyes of Yahweh than all who were before him" (1 Kings 16:30). The text immediately links this judgment to Ahab's marriage to Jezebel and his subsequent Baal worship (1 Kings 16:31). Nevertheless, on this issue too, scholars have recently begun to suggest that Ahab was not as evil as he appears in the summaries written by the Deuteronomists, insofar as he works with prophets (1 Kings 20:13-15), gives his sons Yahwistic names (Walsh, 464) and repents after the

Naboth incident (1 Kings 21:27-29)—a point that even the Deuteronomistic historians admit (Roberts, 643). Furthermore, K. L. Roberts argues that Ahab is encouraged by Elijah to share in a covenant renewal meal after the Carmel incident (1 Kings 18:41), which may demonstrate "provisional prophetic acceptance of Ahab" (Roberts, 643). Finally, surely there is some truth to T. Overholt's contention that there is no "simple dichotomy between 'official' and 'popular' religion" (Overholt, 95)—a fact that makes it difficult to determine the relative strengths of Yahwism and Baalism in ninth-century Israel. Still, there is no denying that religious syncretism was roundly condemned by the authors of 1-2 Kings, even if the Yahwists were "an intransigent, not to say fanatical, minority" (Walsh, 464).

The narratives challenge the belief that Baal could be responsible for either rain or drought, demonstrating that Yahweh is the sole God of creation and life. This is not to say that the narratives were merely polemics against Baal worship, but they do show "that the people of the Northern Kingdom are left without excuse in electing to follow Baal" (Battenfield, 29). In this regard, recent study has raised the issue of what connections, if any, exist between the Baal invoked by his prophets in the Carmel episode (1 Kings 18:26) and the various deities of that name mentioned in Ugaritic literature from four to five hundred years earlier. Through the use of comparative literature before and after the ninth century BCE, J. R. Battenfield concludes, "There seems to be no reason why Jezebel's Tyrian version of Baal, that is, Baal-Melqart, cannot be shown to answer to the attributes of Baal generally, as the latter has been customarily identified throughout the ancient Near East" (Battenfield, 33).

3.2. The Elijah Cycle and Its Theological Message. There are a number of themes in the life and ministry of Elijah that illuminate Israel's relationship with God and the message of the Deuteronomistic History, but the following two concepts may be held up as among the most significant.

3.2.1. Prophetic Ministry in the Leadership of Israel. The Hebrew Bible presented the books of Joshua through 2 Kings within the portion of the canon known as the Former Prophets. The ministry of prophets such as Elijah no doubt was a contributing factor to this designation, but at a deeper level the canonical shape of the Hebrew Bible affirmed that Israel's national history should be seen from the perspective of God's active prophetic word. The books of 1-2 Kings are prophetic history, and the location of the Elijah narratives within the flow of this history suggests that their theological message be sought, at least partly, in the way that they challenge Israel and its leaders to heed Yahweh's commands and recognize the truthfulness of Yahweh's claims. The numerous echoes of motifs from Moses' ministry (e.g., wandering in the wilderness, challenging kings, building altars, meeting Yahweh on Mount Horeb, and the ending of their earthly life [see Walsh, 464-65]) reveal Elijah as "a prophet like Moses" (Deut 18:15) who prosecutes Israel's apostasy before Yahweh at the same place where Moses interceded for his rebellious people. Along with this strong support for prophetic ministry is God's willingness to use the political and military power of kings to achieve his desired ends. Ahab's house is judged through the prophetic word, but the judgment eventually is carried out by means of prophetic activity (Elisha) and military activity (Hazael and Jehu). When kings misuse their office, as Ahab did in the Naboth episode, they come under judgment. Israel of the eighth century BCE would be encouraged by these stories to heed the voice of prophets such as Hosea and Amos, just as the subjects of Hezekiah and Josiah would see how their leaders heeded the words of *Isaiah and *Jeremiah, respectively.

3.2.2. Yahweh and Baal. The Elijah cycle clearly reflects the conflict within Israelite religion during the divided monarchy. Scholars have proposed a variety of historical, religious, social and political dynamics as contributing to the eventual transcendence of Yahweh worship in Israel. M. Smith (80-91) and others have documented the complex connections between the portrait of Yahweh in the Bible and that of Baal in the Ugaritic literature (*see* Canaanite Gods and Religion). In light of such evidence, it is not always easy to distinguish between continuities and discontinuities when it comes to comparative religious traditions in the ancient Near East. Smith's rubric of "convergence" ("the coalescence of various deities and/or some of their features into the figure of Yahweh") and "differentiation" (when "numerous features of early Israelite cult were later rejected as 'Canaanite' and non-Yahwistic") is one possible way to explain the textual and archaeological data (Smith, 7-9).

Whatever the precise circumstances behind forms of religion in Israel, P. D. Miller's balanced study reminds us that the perspective of the biblical authors was to advocate "the centrality of the worship of Yahweh throughout the course of ancient Israel's history" (Miller, 1). The resounding and emphatic exclamation of 1 Kings 18:39—"Yahweh, he is God. Yahweh, he is God"—might well serve as a central message of Elijah's ministry. In historical terms, it seems that Elijah failed in the task of completely turning Israel to an exclusive worship of Yahweh, but the abiding theological message of his narratives reminded Israel that Yahweh has kept in every generation those who have not bowed to Baal but have gladly lifted up Elijah's mantle.

See also ELISHA; KINGS, BOOKS OF; OMRI DYNASTY; PROPHETS AND PROPHECY.

BIBLIOGRAPHY. **J. R. Battenfield,** "YHWH's Refutation of the Baal Myth Through the Actions of Elijah and Elisha," in *Israel's Apostasy and Restoration: Essays in Honor of Roland K. Harrison,* ed. A. Gileadi (Grand Rapids, MI: Baker, 1988) 19-37; **B. Britt,** "Prophetic Concealment in a Biblical Type Scene," *CBQ* 64 (2002) 37-58; **M. Cogan,** *1 Kings* (AB 10; New York: Doubleday, 2000); **T. Collins,** *The Mantle of Elijah: The Redaction Criticism of the Prophetical Books* (BibSem 20; Sheffield: JSOT, 1993); **B. Halpern and D. S. Vanderhooft,** "The Editions of Kings in the 7th-6th Centuries B.C.E.," *HUCA* 62 (1991) 179-244; **N. Kiuchi,** "Elijah's Self-Offering: I Kings 17,21," *Bib* 75 (1994) 74-79; **S. L. McKenzie,** *The Trouble with Kings: The Composition of the Book of Kings in the Deuteronomistic History* (VTSup 42; Leiden: E. J. Brill, 1991); **P. D. Miller,** *The Religion of Ancient Israel* (Louisville: Westminster/John Knox, 2000); **J. W. Olley,** "YHWH and His Zealous Prophet: The Presentation of Elijah in 1 and 2 Kings," *JSOT* 80 (1998) 25-51; **T. Overholt,** "Elijah and Elisha in the Context of Israelite Religion," in *Prophets and Paradigms: Essays in Honor of Gene M. Tucker,* ed. S. B. Reid (JSOTSup 229; Sheffield: Sheffield Academic Press, 1996) 94-111; **D. L. Petersen,** *The Roles of Israel's Prophets* (JSOTSup 17; Sheffield: JSOT, 1981); **Y. T. Radday,** "Chiasm in Kings," *Linguistica Biblica* 31 (1974) 52-67; **K. L. Roberts,** "God, Prophet, and King: Eating and Drinking on the Mountain in First Kings 18:41," *CBQ* 62 (2000) 632-44; **B. P. Robinson,** "Elijah at Horeb, 1 Kings 19:1-18: A Coherent Narrative?" *RB* 98 (1991) 513-36; **A. Rofé,** *The Prophetical Stories: The Narratives about the Prophets in the Hebrew Bible, Their Literary Types and History* (Jerusalem: Magnes, 1988); **U. Simon,** "Elijah's Fight Against Baal Worship: The Prophet's Role in Returning Israel to Its God," in *Reading Prophetic Narratives* (ISBL; Bloomington: Indiana University Press, 1997) 155-226; **M. S. Smith,** *The Early History of God: Yahweh and the Other Deities in Ancient Israel* (2d ed.; Grand Rapids, MI: Eerdmans, 2002); **J. T. Walsh,** "Elijah," *ABD* 2.463-66; **H. G. M. Williamson,** *1 & 2 Chronicles* (NCBC; Grand Rapids, MI: Eerdmans, 1982); **M. C. White,** *The Elijah Legends and Jehu's Coup* (BJS 311; Atlanta: Scholars Press, 1997). J. K. Mead

ELISHA

Elisha was a ninth-century *prophet in the northern kingdom (Israel) who succeeded his mentor, *Elijah, and ministered with a company of prophets and among Israelite and Aramean kings and their subjects. Except for references to Elisha's call (1 Kings 19:16-21) and his death (2 Kings 13:14-21), he is mentioned in the OT only in 2 Kings 2—9, a corpus generally referred to as the Elisha cycle or Elisha narratives. The prophet Elisha and the narratives about him have been studied from a variety of perspectives, highlighting their history of tradition, socio-historical background, literary features and theological message.

1. Elisha Narratives in Tradition History
2. Elisha's Historical and Social Context
3. Literary Interpretation of the Elisha Narratives
4. Theological Message of Elisha's Ministry

1. Elisha Narratives in Tradition History.
How did the Elisha narratives come to be in their present form and location in the Historical Books?

1.1. Oral Tradition About Elisha. There is evidence that stories about Elisha circulated in oral form even in his own time. For example, 2 Kings 3:11-12 demonstrates a public awareness of the prophet's deeds. He was the leader of a group of prophets (lit., "sons of prophets" [e.g., 2 Kings 4:1, 38; 6:1]), but whether they were the only initial tradents is unclear. At least two of the narratives (2 Kings 4:8-37; 5:1-27) recount Elisha's ministry as an individual working with his servant, Gehazi, who later tells the king about his master's mighty deeds (2 Kings 8:4-5). A. Rofé's form-critical studies of prophetical stories suggest that similar kinds of Elisha narratives may have been grouped as short legends, political legends, etc., but whatever role such groupings may have played in the compilation of the whole cycle, B. O. Long has shown the necessity of examining the literary structure, social setting and intention of each story.

1.2. The Narratives in the Deuteronomistic History.

1.2.1. Their Independent Formation. The Elisha narratives are found in *1-2 Kings and therefore are part of the larger *Deuteronomistic History. Nevertheless, in 2 Kings 2—9 the hand of the Deuteronomistic editor(s) interrupts the narrative flow in only two places, with information unrelated to Elisha himself (2 Kings 3:1-3; 8:16-29). The individual accounts of Elisha's ministry proceed with little transitional narration, as if they were part of an established corpus of stories needing little commentary. For example, the story of the widow's oil (2 Kings 4:1-7) begins abruptly on the heels of the unsuccessful Israelite campaign against *Moab (2 Kings 3:27) and offers very little background information to explain when and where the event occurred. These factors seem to indicate that the formation of the Elisha cycle was somehow independent of the Deuteronomistic editorial process— a conclusion reasonably supported by text-critical treatments, such as that by H.-J. Stipp.

1.2.2. Dating the Written Traditions. Although the scholarly consensus has been that "many of these stories achieved their form prior to their inclusion in the Deuteronomistic History" (Whitelam, 472), there has been no broad agreement on precisely when, how or why they were united with the other materials in 1-2 Kings. They may have been combined with the Elijah traditions, thus forming a larger prophetic cycle, but eventually these were separated from each other in order to place the intervening material about King Ahab's demise (1 Kings 20—22) in its proper chronological location. The myriad of theories that have been advanced to explain the history of redaction behind 1-2 Kings is beyond the scope of this discussion (*see* Deuteronomistic History; Elijah), but the basic choice seems to be between inclusion of the Elisha narratives by a Deuteronomistic editor (Hezekian or Josianic) or as a later, post-Deuteronomistic addition. S. L. McKenzie (95-98) argues that most of the Elisha stories, except perhaps for those involving *Jehu, entered 2 Kings after Deuteronomistic au-

thorship. Nevertheless, it is not entirely necessary to posit a much later entrance into 2 Kings because different titles were used for Elisha ("man of God" or "prophet") or the stories "represent late genres" (McKenzie, 96). As with the Elijah narratives, a reasonable reconstruction of the literary history of the Elisha narratives might see the written traditions being brought to Judah following the fall of *Samaria (c. 722 BCE) and being incorporated into the regnal histories during a redaction of these materials under the reign of *Hezekiah, or at least by the kingship of *Josiah (Halpern and Vanderhooft).

2. Elisha's Historical and Social Context.

2.1. Elisha's Historical Background.

2.1.1. The Man Elisha. It is difficult to describe the life and times of the "historical Elisha" based on the scant biblical references to his family background or the complete context of his public actions. B. Halpern has identified in the Elisha narratives the "heaviest concentration" of *miracles stories in the Deuteronomistic History, suggesting that these stories are something other than "mundane political history" (Halpern, 248). The name "Elisha" means something like "my God is salvation," a common name in light of its presence in Israelite inscriptions as early as the eighth century BCE. His father, Shaphat, is unknown except in relation to Elisha (e.g., 1 Kings 19:16). Their home town, Abelmeholah, probably was located just west of the Jordan River in the territory of Manasseh (Judg 7:22). Elisha's economic prosperity and religious sensitivity are both suggested by the call narrative in 1 Kings 19:19-21, where he plows with a large team of oxen and seems ready to follow Elijah after saying goodbye to his family. During his ministry, Elisha is known by two major titles found on the lips of characters in the stories or in the voice of the narrator. King *Jehoshaphat alludes to Elisha as a "prophet" (2 Kings 3:11-12), a title also used by an Israelite servant of Naaman's family (2 Kings 5:3) and by Aramean military officers (2 Kings 6:12). The Shunammite woman calls Elisha a "man of God" (2 Kings 4:9, 16, 22), as do members of his own prophetic company (2 Kings 4:40) and the Aramean king (2 Kings 8:8); but the greatest number of such references are made by the biblical narrator (e.g., 2 Kings 4:21, 25). H.-J. Stipp believes that this title points to God's presence by means of the prophet who does miracles in the midst of problems such as "death, hunger, illness, and war" (Stipp, 100). Although Elisha never refers to himself with this title, he does not dissuade others from using it. On the whole, the conclusion of K. W. Whitelam (472) that these two titles are virtually synonymous seems well-supported by the larger biblical evidence.

2.1.2. Elisha's Historical Setting. Elisha began his five decades of ministry near the end of the *Omri dynasty, around 850 BCE, and he lived well into the *Jehu dynasty, when J(eh)oash was on the throne of Israel (2 Kings 13:14), around 800 BCE. This era saw a lull in *Assyrian power, thus providing opportunity for Aramean expansion by the Ben-Hadad dynasty. Judah seems to have acted as something of a vassal to Israel, at least during the war with Moab (2 Kings 3), where Jehoshaphat readily serves as Jehoram's ally (2 Kings 3:7). Since J. M. Miller's important work forty years ago (see Miller 443-48), the scholarly consensus has been that the historical context of the Elisha narratives is actually that of the later Jehu dynasty, and the narratives were displaced decades earlier into the time of Jehoram. This reconstruction, however, takes into account only those narratives having political and military significance (2 Kings 3; 6—7). Moreover, it seems safe to assume that the transitional scenes in 2 Kings 2 and 9 are rightly placed. Given the fact that precise chronological data are lacking, the order and interrelationships of the stories in between may be driven by concerns other than historical ones (see 3.1.2 below).

2.2. Elisha and Prophetism in Israelite Society. Elisha represents something of a middle position between earlier prophets who associated mainly with specific kings (*Nathan), and later classical prophets whose ministry could focus on the monarchy, other national leaders or society at large (*Isaiah, *Jeremiah). Elisha worked as an individual and with a "company of prophets," a group almost exclusively related to him in the OT, but his influence on the larger society occurred primarily through the actions of kings. Scholarly treatments of Elisha's social location have focused on his leadership of the company of prophets, his political relationship with the kings of the Omri and Jehu dynasties, and his connections to various expressions of Yahwistic religion in Israel (Whitelam, 472-73). D. L. Petersen's (47) interpretation of Elisha (and Elijah)

as "peripheral" prophets remains helpful, as long as some distinction is maintained in their respective experience with kings. With Elisha, one finds a slightly more supportive role of Israelite kingship than in the Elijah stories, although the support that Elisha gives the king is mainly for the sake of the Israelite people rather than the royal institution or a particular king. Moreover, he could show disdain for the Israelite king Jehoram while expressing regard for the Judean monarch Jehoshaphat (2 Kings 3:13-14). More recently, W. J. Bergen (176-79) has argued that the portrayal of Elisha represents both a weakening of the prophet's connection with Yahweh and an increase in the monarchy's ability to carry out Yahweh's will without prophetic involvement. To be sure, differences between Elisha and previous Deuteronomistic prophets exist, but the similarities seem to be stronger than the differences (see 4.2 below). The social and political function of prophets may decline significantly in Israel following Elisha, but the biblical writers suggest that this decline owed more to Yahweh's judgment on a recalcitrant people than to the limitations of the prophets themselves (2 Kings 17:13-14).

3. Literary Interpretation of the Elisha Narratives.

3.1. The Literary Structure of the Cycle.

3.1.1. The Biblical Order of Events. Elisha's ministry proceeds from his call by Elijah (1 Kings 19:19-21) to his succession of Elijah when the latter was taken into heaven (2 Kings 2:1-18), a succession confirmed for good or ill by his healing of Jericho's waters (2 Kings 2:19-22) and the cursing of an impudent gang in *Bethel (2 Kings 2:23-25). He prophesied during an Israelite military campaign into Moab (2 Kings 3), instructed a widow whose children were about to be taken into debt servitude (2 Kings 4:1-7) and raised the dead son of a Shunammite woman (2 Kings 4:8-37), whom he later advised concerning a famine (2 Kings 8:1-6). He provided leadership for the company of prophets by transforming a deadly pot of stew into an edible one (2 Kings 4:38-41), miraculously fed one hundred people (2 Kings 4:42-44), and raised an iron axe head from a river (2 Kings 6:1-7). Elisha healed the Aramean general Naaman from leprosy (2 Kings 5) and also stayed the devastating effects of Aramean aggression, first at the city of Dothan (2 Kings 6:8-23) and then in the capital of Samaria

(2 Kings 6:24-7:20). Near the end of his ministry he carried out the remainder of the commission that Elijah received (1 Kings 19:15-16) by prophesying Hazael's rise to power in *Aram (2 Kings 8:7-15) and anointing Jehu, whose violent coup destroyed Ahab's family line (2 Kings 9:1-13). Just before his death he prophesied three Israelite victories over Aram (2 Kings 13:14-19). Sometime after his death and burial there was a resurrection of a corpse that came into contact with Elisha's bones (2 Kings 13:20-21).

3.1.2. The Organization of the Whole Cycle. The current order of the narratives listed above reflects a certain balance through repetitions, similarities in plot, and comparable or contrastive characterization. A case could be made for a loose chiastic structure, laid out as follows:

A Beginning: 1 Kings 19:16-21—being called by Elijah

B Succession: 2 Kings 2:1-25—succeeding Elijah

  C War Story: 2 Kings 3:1-27—prophesying during the war with Moab

   D^1 Prophetic Company: 2 Kings 4:1-7—instructing the needy widow

    E^1 Individual Ministry: 2 Kings 4:8-37—raising the Shunammite's son

   D^2 Prophetic Company: 2 Kings 4:38-44—transforming a deadly meal; feeding people

    E^2 Individual Ministry: 2 Kings 5:1-27—healing Naaman

   D^3 Prophetic Company: 2 Kings 6:1-7—raising an axe head

  C' War Story: 2 Kings 6:8-23; 6:24-7:20—delivering Dothan; prophesying Samaria's release

    E^3 Individual ministry: 2 Kings 8:1-6—epilogue to the Shunammite's story

 B' Succession: 2 Kings 8:7-15; 9:1-13—Hazael's succession over Aram; Jehu's succession in Israel

A' Conclusion: 2 Kings 13:14-21—prophesying victory over Aram; raising the dead to life

This balance points to several basic spheres in which Elisha worked as a prophet to all walks of life within and outside of Israel: rich and poor, male and female, royalty and commoner, military and civilian, Israelite and Aramean. Moreover, Elisha's service in these spheres confronts the ways that death, disease, war and poverty threaten life and prosperity.

3.2. Literary Artistry and Ideology.

3.2.1. The Rhetoric of External Design. The figure of Elisha is presented, from beginning to end, in such a way as to create a discernible impression. Just before Elisha appears on the stage of history, God reveals to Elijah that Elisha may have to wield the sword against Israel. Thus the first verb used in connection with Elisha is "to kill" (1 Kings 19:17). But when Elijah places his mantle on Elisha, the latter does not proceed to kill anyone but rather sacrifices some of his own animals in order to provide food. The very last verb connected with Elisha is "to live" (2 Kings 13:21), as a corpse that touches Elisha's bones is resurrected. The potential threat of death through Elisha's ministry is countered by the miracle of life, on which the narratives about him both begin and conclude. In between this outer frame the individual accounts present many circumstances in which people must trust Elisha's power to bring life, health, provision and peace. His prophetical sayings "witness to the care of God" for the neediest members of society (Thiel, 199).

3.2.2. Ideology and Reputation. The rise in literary and ideological criticism in biblical studies has been represented by several shorter studies on Elisha, particularly the story of the Shunammite woman (2 Kings 4:8-37). M. E. Shields's treatment, representative of many studies, argues that different literary features point to a role reversal over the course of the narrative, where the woman is exalted while the prophet is diminished, even though "the patriarchal perspective wins out in the end" (Shields, 66). U. Simon (235) recognizes the strength of the Shunammite woman while also reaffirming that Elisha alone has the power to work miracles. In light of this and other cases of literary ambiguity in the cycle, P. J. Kissling (199) argues that Elisha appears less reliable than Moses, Joshua and Elijah. In spite of this tension in Elisha's portrayal, surely he stands in the larger spectrum of Deuteronomistic prophecy. Numerous literary echoes clearly portray him as Elijah's rightful successor, although N. Levine (45) rightly notes the more "lateral" focus in Elisha's work on behalf of the people. His ministry overcomes the threat of death and, in the case of the Shunammite's son, overturns the power of death by giving life and blessing. Even when Elisha carries out Yahweh's initial plan of judgment on Israel, he prophesies such disaster only through tears

(2 Kings 8:11-12), and he has to send someone else to anoint Jehu as an instrument of judgment (2 Kings 9:1-13).

4. Theological Message of Elisha's Ministry.

4.1. As a Former Prophet. Elisha left no compilation of his prophetic messages, but he is no less an Israelite prophet. His words and deeds expressed Israel's fundamental understanding that prophetic ministry is the hinge on which the political and social history of the nation turns. What is unique about the Elisha narratives is the way they occasionally step out of the flow of national history to demonstrate that God was active even when Elisha was not challenging or guiding kings. Through him, God embraced the needs of the prophets and other faithful individuals who would otherwise never figure in a national history. Thus Israelites before and after the exile would see in these stories an affirmation that God still cares for a righteous remnant even while the nation itself suffers judgment for its disobedience.

4.2. As a Deuteronomistic Prophet. There can be little doubt that the persons responsible for including the Elisha narratives in 2 Kings believed that the prophet carried out the kind of ministry affirmed by Moses in Deuteronomy (Whitelam, 472). As Israelite kings were judged according to their sins against God's *law, so also prophets such as Samuel, Nathan, Elijah and Elisha declared God's intentions for both judgment and mercy. Kings and people needed to respond with *faith in the prophets' word if they were to enjoy mercy and avoid judgment. For this reason, it is accurate to understand Elisha as a prophet of both judgment and hope, although this is not carried out according to any simple formula. Elisha's complex personality only serves to confirm the reasonableness of his portrayal in 1-2 Kings. Judgment on Ahab's sinful house was postponed but never completely dismissed, and the stories that contain a cause for hope also describe the consequences of failing to trust the prophet (2 Kings 7:17-20). Thus, the thesis of R. D. Moore (147) that the theology of the Elisha narratives is revealed in his name, "God saves," accurately expresses the major theme of the stories of Aramean aggression (2 Kings 5—7); but the crucial factor in the entire Elisha cycle remains the kind of relationship that people had with the prophet. Since the time of Moses, the prophets invited

Israel to "choose life" (Deut 30:19). In Elisha's day, life's blessings were enjoyed when the people trusted in his prophetic word.

See also ELIJAH; JEHU DYNASTY; KINGS, BOOKS OF; MIRACLES; PROPHETS AND PROPHECY.

BIBLIOGRAPHY. **W. J. Bergen,** *Elisha and the End of Prophetism* (JSOTSup 286; Sheffield: Sheffield Academic Press, 1999); **R. B. Coote,** ed., *Elijah and Elisha in Socioliterary Perspective* (SemeiaSt; Atlanta: Scholars Press, 1992); **B. Halpern,** *The First Historians: The Hebrew Bible and History* (San Francisco: Harper & Row, 1988); **B. Halpern and D. S. Vanderhooft,** "The Editions of Kings in the 7th-6th Centuries B.C.E.," *HUCA* 62 (1991) 179-244; **P. J. Kissling,** *Reliable Characters in the Primary History: Profiles of Moses, Joshua, Elijah and Elisha* (JSOTSup 224; Sheffield: Sheffield Academic Press, 1996); **N. Levine,** "Twice as Much as Your Spirit: Pattern, Parallel and Paronomasia in the Miracles of Elijah and Elisha," *JSOT* 85 (1999) 25-46; **B. O. Long,** *2 Kings* (FOTL 10; Grand Rapids, MI: Eerdmans, 1991); **S. L. McKenzie,** *The Trouble with Kings: The Composition of the Book of Kings in the Deuteronomistic History* (VTSup 42; Leiden: E. J. Brill, 1991); **J. M. Miller,** "The Elisha Cycle and the Accounts of the Omride Wars," *JBL* 85 (1966) 441-54; **R. D. Moore,** *God Saves: Lessons from the Elisha Stories* (JSOTSup 95; Sheffield: Sheffield Academic Press, 1990); **D. L. Petersen,** *The Roles of Israel's Prophets* (JSOTSup 17; Sheffield: JSOT, 1981); **A. Rofé,** *The Prophetical Stories: The Narratives about the Prophets in the Hebrew Bible, Their Literary Types and History* (Jerusalem: Magnes, 1988); **M. E. Shields,** "Subverting a Man of God, Elevating a Woman: Role and Power Reversals in 2 Kings 4," *JSOT* 58 (1993) 59-69; **U. Simon,** "Elisha and the Woman of Shunem," in *Reading Prophetic Narratives* (ISBL; Bloomington: Indiana University Press, 1997) 227-62; **H.-J. Stipp,** *Elischa, Propheten, Gottesmänner: Die Kompositionsgeschichte des Elischazyklus und verwandter Texte, rekonstruiert auf der Basis von Text- und Literarkritik zu 1 Kön 20.22 und 2 Kön 2-7* (St. Ottilien: EOS Verlag, 1987); **W. Thiel,** "Character and Function of Divine Sayings in the Elijah and Elisha Traditions," in *Eschatology in the Bible and in Jewish and Christian Traditions,* ed. H. Reventlow (JSOTSup 243; Sheffield: Sheffield Academic Press, 1997) 189-99; **K. W. Whitelam,** "Elisha," *ABD* 2.472-73.   J. K. Mead

ELOHIM. *See* GOD.

ELON. *See* HISTORY OF ISRAEL 2: PREMONAR-CHIC ISRAEL; JUDGES.

ELYON. *See* GOD.

"EMPTY LAND." *See* EZRA AND NEHEMIAH, BOOKS OF.

ESARHADDON. *See* ASSYRIA, ASSYRIANS.

ESDRAS. *See* EZRA AND NEHEMIAH, BOOKS OF.

ETHICS

The word *ethics*, when used in connection with the OT, can mean one of three things. First, in a purely descriptive sense it can refer to the kinds of moral behavior, choices and values found within the historical culture called ancient Israel, for which these texts are our primary evidence. Second, in a more evaluative sense, it can refer to the way these historical texts assess such behavior and to the explicit or implicit ethical criteria and standards by which they do so. Third, in a normative or prescriptive sense it can refer to the ethical teaching authoritatively expressed through these texts for those who accept them as Scripture. Put simply, "the ethics of the Historical Books" could refer to how the Israelites *did* behave, or to how those who produced this literature thought the Israelites *should* have behaved (and why), or to how we think *we* should behave in the light of these texts being part of the canon of Scripture. This article focuses largely on the second of these three possibilities, which obviously in any case involves the first. The third must be left substantially as a task for the reader's own faith commitment in response to the Bible.

1. Theological Foundations Common to the Rest of the Old Testament
2. Ethical Values Particularly Important to the Historical Books
3. The Shaping of Ethical Life in Israel
4. Ethical Difficulties

1. Theological Foundations Common to the Rest of the Old Testament.
The Historical Books share the theological underpinnings of the other major sections of the OT canon, and these clearly provide the foundations, the shape and the motivation for ethics throughout the literature. These may be summarized under three headings.

1.1. Yahweh: Universal and Sovereign Creator.
Ethics in the Historical Books, as everywhere else in the OT, are theological. They flow from the identity, character and actions of Yahweh as *God. Yahweh is not merely the local god of the country (although it appeared so to external observers [2 Kings 17:26-28]). Just as is affirmed in the Torah (e.g., Deut 4:35, 39), in the Prophets (e.g., Jer 10:6-10; Is 40—55), and of course in Israel's worship (e.g., Ps 96:1-6), so also the Historical Books affirm that Yahweh is unique and universal (Josh 2:11); that he is beyond compare, for none is like Yahweh (1 Sam 2:2; 2 Sam 7:22 = 1 Chron 17:20; 1 Kings 8:23 = 2 Chron 6:14); that he is sovereign over all other kingdoms, not just in Israel (2 Kings 19:15; 2 Chron 20:5-6); that he owns and rules everything in the universe (1 Chron 29:11-12); and that he does all these things by right of being universal creator and sustainer of all things (Neh 9:6).

The effect of these convictions on ethics includes the awareness that Yahweh is inescapable as the God who knows the truth in spite of temporary circumstances (1 Sam 2:3) or external appearances (1 Sam 16:7), and who sees what hoped to be concealed (Josh 7:20-21; 2 Sam 11:27; 2 Kings 5:20-27). All people are morally accountable to him, including pagan emperors (2 Kings 19:20-28). As the psalmist declared, so the Chronicler agrees, "the eyes of the LORD range throughout the earth," weighing deeds, searching hearts, understanding motives (Ps 33:13-15; 1 Chron 28:9; 29:17; 2 Chron 6:30; 16:9).

On the larger canvas, Yahweh is the moral judge of human history and all its international affairs. Both major historical corpora, the *Deuteronomistic History and the books of *Chronicles, set out to demonstrate the justice of God's judgment on Israel in the exile. The ethical principle intrinsic to both accounts is that moral wickedness ultimately brings divine retribution, and God acts within history to bring it about. Thus Yahweh could use Israel to bring moral judgment upon the wickedness of the Canaanites (the moral dimension is more fully articulated in Lev 18:24-28; 20:23; Deut 9:4-5, but the same justification is mentioned in Ezra 9:11). Or, more commonly, Yahweh could use other nations to bring judgment upon the wickedness of the Israelites, who tragically imitated the ways of the nations from whom they were supposed to remain distinct (1 Kings 9:7 =

2 Chron 7:20-22; 2 Kings 17:8, 15—echoing Lev 18:3-5; cf. Ezek 5:6-17).

1.2. Israel: Elect People in Covenant Relationship with Yahweh. OT ethics are not only theological but also fundamentally social. Although clearly individuals are held morally accountable for their own choices and actions (as the Historical Books amply testify), the shape of OT ethics is governed not primarily by the individual, but by the nature of the community called *Israel. To belong to this people was to inherit an ethical agenda. It was an agenda that had been built into their genetic code, so to speak, in the loins of Abraham. In the context of a world going the way of Sodom and Gomorrah, Yahweh had declared that the reason for his election of Abraham was so that he would inaugurate a community that would "keep the way of the LORD" by "doing righteousness and justice"—two powerful and pervasive ethical expressions (Gen 18:19). Election, then, one of the central pillars of Israel's self-understanding and worldview, had an ethical dynamic from the start.

The great narrative of the Torah moves forward from Israel's election in Abraham to their redemption from Egypt and the covenant at Sinai, both of which are presupposed, of course, throughout the Historical Books. In the *law, the exodus is used as a positive motivation for Israel's social legislation (e.g., Ex 22:21; 23:9; Deut 15:15). In the Historical Books, the exodus sometimes is used, in the style of Deuteronomy, as a positive motivation for covenant commitment (e.g., Josh 24:5-7), but more often in the same way as in the Prophets: as a backdrop for accusations against Israel's covenant unfaithfulness manifested in moral decay (e.g., Judg 2:1-2; 6:7-10; 1 Sam 12:6-8), or in relation to prayers for forgiveness (1 Kings 8:51; Neh 9:9-12). The exodus figures in the catalog of the northern kingdom's covenant-breaking wickedness, in which the historian gives his explanation for the scattering of the northern tribes of Israel. That great event, which should have led them to exclusive worship of Yahweh alone, instead had been ignored (2 Kings 17:7, 35-39). The Chronicler, however, who begins his narrative with *Saul and *David and then focuses much of his moral evaluation on comparing other kings with David, does not make use of the Exodus-Sinai material in this way. He removes the reference to it in Solomon's prayer of dedication of the temple (2 Chron 6; cf. 1 Kings 8:51, 53), and he

explains the exile simply in terms of Israel's unfaithfulness and contempt for the word of God through the prophets (1 Chron 9:1; 2 Chron 36:13-16).

Thus covenant obedience is the prime ethical demand on Israel as a people, and thereby on individual Israelites, from the king down. In this the Historical Books are at one especially with the Prophets. And the prime focus of covenant obedience was the worship of Yahweh alone. Idolatry, therefore, is the prime *sin. The Historical Books bulge with this issue, and repeatedly we find kings being weighed up in terms of whether they led Israel either after other gods or back to the worship of the living God. We should not, however, conceive this as purely a theological or "religious" issue. There are profound ethical implications that the Historical Books demonstrate. If Ahab acquiesces in Jezebel's vandalizing Israel's covenant faith with the worship of Canaanite Baal, then Israel will no longer be a safe place for people such as Naboth to live in (1 Kings 21). Yahweh stood for equality and justice on the land; Baal permitted royal greed and unfettered aggression. The ethical fabric of society depended on which God Israel would choose, as *Elijah recognized. If *Manasseh reverses the reforms of his godly predecessor *Hezekiah and brings back the degraded practices of Canaanite religion, then innocents will suffer and blood will flow (2 Kings 21:6, 16). Idolatry goes hand in hand with cruelty, injustice and oppression. This too was a prophetic perception, and we recall that the books of Joshua to 2 Kings are known in the Hebrew canon as the Former Prophets.

1.3. The Land: Yahweh's Gift and Israel's Responsibility. Ethics in Israel are not only theological and social, but also deeply "earthy," rooted in the *land. Israel had a twin theology of land: it was theirs by Yahweh's promise and gift, and it still belonged to Yahweh as ultimate landlord. The first aspect generated a sense of security to Israelite families on their share of the land; the second aspect generated a wide range of economic responsibilities in the social realm, especially for those who were vulnerable from lack of family or land (e.g., widows, orphans, aliens). Both are reflected in the Historical Books. The land-gift tradition, as in the Prophets, mostly serves to challenge people to covenant obedience or to make their disobedience all the more culpable (Josh 2:9; 24:8-13; 1 Chron 28:8; Neh

9:8, 15, 22-25). Yahweh as landlord reserves the right to say how the land should be divided up, and his will was for it to be equitably distributed in multiple family lots (Josh 13—19; note the repeated "according to their clans") (*see* Tribes of Israel and Land Allotments/Borders). Then it should remain within those families to ensure their long-term economic viability (Lev 25). This is the theological background to the clash of cultures, religions and economic systems in the Naboth incident (1 Kings 21).

2. Ethical Values Particularly Important to the Historical Books.

Having observed those areas of ethical concern that the Historical Books share with the rest of the canon (especially the matter of covenant obedience to the sole sovereignty of Yahweh and its outworking in the social and economic realms), we may observe other ethical values that seem of particular interest to the Hebrew narrators.

2.1. Integrity in Public Affairs. The Historical Books by their very nature are dominated by the public affairs of Israel throughout the many centuries that they span. Personal narratives are embedded, of course, but the stage is usually public, social, political and increasingly international as well. The spotlight of Yahweh's ethical demands is trained by the narrators on the changing scenes, some of which are dark in the extreme.

2.1.1. Political (Especially Royal) Power. The essence of Israel's covenantal understanding of their relationship to Yahweh was that Yahweh was their "Great King." Israel, in that sense, was a theocracy, in which all the major functions of authority were claimed by Yahweh himself. Yahweh was the ultimate king, law-giver, judge, landlord and military commander. This had the effect, on the one hand, of relativizing and "flattening" all human authority structures, and, on the other hand, of holding all human incumbents of such public office morally accountable to Yahweh. Thus there was a for a long time steady resistance to the idea of having a human king at all because Yahweh was the real king (Judg 8:23), and the first attempt ended in fiasco (Abimelech [Judg 9]). When the pressure to have a human king could no longer be resisted, it was interpreted as a rejection of Yahweh's kingship (1 Sam 8:7; 12:12-15). *Samuel, on the one hand, held up before the people a prescient

portrait of how greedy and tyrannical monarchy would likely become (1 Sam 8:10-18), and, on the other hand, reinforced the Deuteronomic ideal of what a king in Israel should be like—a model of obedience to Yahweh's covenant law (1 Sam 12:14, 23-25).

The primary ethical duty of kings was to sustain justice in society (*see* Kings and Kingship). In this regard, the ideal of monarchy in Israel had the same ethical core as the rule of Yahweh himself, the foundations of whose throne are righteousness and justice (Ps 97:2) (*see* Justice and Righteousness). The prayer of Psalm 72 ("of Solomon"), that the king would do justice in defense of the poor and needy, is echoed in the Historical Books, particularly (and ironically, as it turned out), in relation to *Solomon. Solomon's celebrated prayer for wisdom was specifically that he could rule with justice (1 Kings 3:9-11), and an early example is given (the two prostitutes) to show that "he had wisdom from God to administer justice" (1 Kings 3:28). With noticeable irony (in view of what is to follow in the very next chapter—the account of oppressive nature of Solomon's later reign), the narrator has the Queen of Sheba reminding Solomon that Yahweh had made him king "to maintain justice and righteousness" (1 Kings 10:9 = 2 Chron 9:8)—the very thing that he and his sons and successors so lamentably failed to do. *Rehoboam, ignoring the model of mutual servanthood proposed by his elder statesmen (1 Kings 12:7), deliberately turned oppression into state policy (1 Kings 12:10-14). Although a few kings rose above this (e.g., Joash [2 Kings 11:12, 12:2] and Hezekiah [2 Kings 18:6]), the only one who receives an unqualified Deuteronomic accolade in the Historical Books is *Josiah (2 Kings 23:25)—and that, according to Jeremiah, was because he "did righteousness and justice . . . he defended the cause of the poor and needy, and so all went well. Is that not what it means to know me?" (Jer 22:15-16; cf. Deut 10:18-19).

2.1.2. Judicial Integrity. Maintaining social justice was not only the ethical duty of kings, it also was a matter of the judicial integrity of judges and courts. The administration of justice in Israel was a less formal matter than in modern societies, having a more local flavor. Decisions were made by elders functioning "at the gate"—that is, in the main public space of a town or village. Samuel's apologia sheds interesting light on the concern for honesty in those who stood in judgment on others. Samuel claims (and his claim is accepted) that he had neither made personal profit from extortion nor corrupted justice through bribery (1 Sam 12:1-5). Once monarchy was established, the integrity of the judicial system was part of the king's responsibility. The evidence of the prophets is that few of them prevented the slide into judicial chaos and corruption, and some callously abetted it (e.g., Jezebel [1 Kings 21:8-16]). One monarch stood against the trend: *Jehoshaphat (whose name appropriately means "Yahweh is judge") initiated a thorough judicial reform throughout his kingdom, with ethical exhortation to the different layers of judges that echoed Deuteronomy (2 Chron 19:4-11; Deut 16:18-20).

2.1.3. Economic Justice. Because of the theological importance of the land, as explained above, the economic sphere was a major touchstone of covenant faithfulness or otherwise. So there is an economic ethic also evident in the Historical Books. It is interesting that even though the desire for monarchy is presented as a rejection of Yahweh, Samuel's tirade against it focuses not primarily on its spiritual tendency to apostasy, but on the economic effects that it will impose on Israel's hitherto relatively free and equal society. Under kings, Israelites would suffer military conscription that would damage their production, confiscation of land and taxation—all for the king's benefit (1 Sam 8:10-18). The oppression of Solomon's later years that, under his arrogant son Rehoboam, finally split the kingdom was mainly economic and proved the accuracy of Samuel's predictions (1 Kings 12). There are indeed echoes of the exodus narrative in the way that *Jeroboam is initially presented as a liberator demanding freedom from an oppressive tyrant and being refused. But the northern kingdom, born in this struggle for economic justice, itself succumbs to the opposite in the following century, as the starkly narrated story of Naboth shows (1 Kings 21). Even in the postexilic period economic hardship caused by ruthless exploitation of people's need was exposed by the ethical outrage of *Nehemiah (Neh 5).

2.2. Qualities of Personal Ethics. While the ethics of the Historical Books are predominantly focused on such major social ethical issues, the smaller narratives are, of course, filled with individuals whose actions, words, decisions and motives are subject to ethical evaluation—

occasionally explicit, but more often implicit. Certainly, as readers, we are invited to enter into each narrative and engage ethically with the characters there, forming our own judgments on the basis of the clues in the text and the values that we extrapolate from the wider canonical context. A small selection of ethical values that emerge from such reading includes the following.

2.2.1. Integrity and Trustworthiness. David (whose own life did not always match up with this standard, or that so frequently claimed in the psalms attributed to him) echoes the high value that God himself places on this: "I know, my God, that you test the heart and are pleased with integrity" (1 Chron 29:17). Both historians are pleased to notice the trustworthiness and honesty of those who, on different occasions, worked on the restoration of the temple (2 Kings 12:13-15 = 2 Chron 24:13-14; 2 Chron 34:12). And Nehemiah, who was not too modest to remind God of his own integrity, comments favorably on those whom he trusted to handle substantial quantities of goods and money (Neh 13:13).

2.2.2. Kindness, Mercy and Generosity. Saul, in one of his better moments, sets the tone with his generous refusal to take revenge against those who despised him (1 Sam 11:12-13). David, of course, repeatedly declines to lift a hand against Saul, which even Saul recognizes as "righteous" (1 Sam 24:17-19; 26). David reflects Saul's generosity after the battle of Ziklag (1 Sam 30:21-25), but it is explicitly "God's kindness" that he chooses to emulate toward the crippled son of Saul, Mephibosheth—even if there was some self-interested political calculation in his action of bringing Mephibosheth within the confines of the palace (2 Sam 9:1, 3). Even more ambiguous is David's action toward Shimei. We are impressed with David's refusal to allow the cursing fellow to be summarily dispatched (2 Sam 16:5-14), and with his mercy on his cringing apology (2 Sam 19:16-23). But the ethical glow of this generosity is rather undone by David himself in his dying words to Solomon (1 Kings 2:8-9). David was a man of his word, but his word did not bind his son! Later, an interesting observation about the quality of kingship within Israel, for all its faults, is found in the mouth of foreign witnesses who say, "We have heard that the kings of the house of Israel are merciful" (1 Kings 20:31)— and the king in question, Ahab, proved them right, although he showed more mercy to a defeated pagan king than he did to an Israelite farmer in the following chapter. Generosity in the literal sense, which is highly commended in Deuteronomy (e.g., Deut 15), characterized the people's response to David's appeal for funds and materials to build the temple, but it is put in proper theological perspective by the Chronicler's account of David's response to it: such generosity was only a pale reflection of the boundless generosity of Yahweh himself (1 Chron 29:1-20).

2.2.3. Wholehearted Commitment and Faithfulness. For the Chronicler, almost all other ethical values seem to flow from wholehearted commitment and faithfulness to the Lord. His evaluation of many major characters in his epic hinges on whether or not they manifested these qualities. They are the core of David's charge to Solomon (1 Chron 28:9-10), although it must be said that the Chronicler downplays the extent to which Solomon failed to sustain them (e.g., he omits the reasons why Jeroboam rebelled against Solomon [1 Kings 11:26-40]). He affirms that Asa, Jehoshaphat and Hezekiah demonstrated these qualities (2 Chron 15:17; 17:6; 31:20-21), whereas Amaziah did not (2 Chron 25:2). Hezekiah even gave them a higher ethical priority than the technical details of ritual purity (2 Chron 30:19-20), in an interesting echo of the prophetic scale of values (Hos 6:6; cf. 1 Sam 15:22) and anticipation of that of Jesus (Mt 15:1-20; 23:23). The Chronicler even hints at a universalizing of such values through the words of Hanani the seer: "The eyes of the LORD range throughout the earth to strengthen those whose hearts are fully committed to him" (2 Chron 16:9).

2.3. Echoes of the Decalogue. Although the Ten Commandments are not mentioned in precise terms anywhere in the Historical Books, they may be implied in the frequent references to the law and commandments of Yahweh, or to the covenant itself.

- As we have seen, there is a preoccupation throughout the whole sweep of both major historical works with the exclusive worship of Yahweh and the problem of idolatry, and this reflects the first two commandments.
- Concern for the sabbath (fourth commandment) is seen in Nehemiah's attempts to protect it (Neh 13:15-22).
- Relationships between parents and children

(fifth commandment) generate some significant narratives. Samson's disregard of his parents' wishes launches his wild career (Judg 14:1-4). More explicitly, the sons of Eli and of Samuel both fail to honor either their fathers or the Lord (1 Sam 2:12-17; 8:1-5). The irony of this narrative is not merely in the sad tragedy that Samuel, whose career began by condemning the house of Eli, lived to hear the elders of Israel accusing him regarding his own sons' failure to do justice. There is also a surely deliberate play on the fact that the same Hebrew root *(kbd)* underlies the words "honor," "heavy" and "glory" (1 Sam 2:30; 4:18, 21-22), and may be an echo of the main verb in the fifth commandment, which Eli's sons had so grossly failed to observe.

- The sixth commandment, defending the sanctity of human life against murder, is well illustrated throughout the whole sordid narrative, sometimes in the observance (as in Abigail's timely intervention against David's rage [1 Sam 25:26-31], a speech that surely expresses the narrator's own theological ethic), but more often in the breach (as in David's constructive murder of Uriah [2 Sam 11], or the excessive shedding of innocent blood that characterized Manasseh [2 Kings 21:16]). Even the fact that David had shed much blood in battle, not in murder, is interpreted by the Chronicler as the reason he was not permitted to build the temple for Yahweh (1 Chron 22:7-8; 28:3).
- Sexual disorder and abuse (seventh commandment) invade David's life and family in uncontrolled ways (2 Sam 11—12; 13:1-22; 16:21-22).
- Theft (eighth commandment) is how Nathan interprets David's action with the wife of Uriah (2 Sam 12:1-6). Indeed, in that one terrible narrative David trampled on all five of the commandments in the second table: murder, adultery, theft, deceit and covetousness. Legalized theft is also how Ahab's acquisition of Naboth's vineyard is portrayed, in a narrative that possibly is intended to be illustrative of what many others suffered—certainly later prophets saw it that way also (1 Kings 21; cf. Amos 2:6; Mic 2:1-2; Is 5:8; 10:1-2).
- The ninth commandment may be extended to include all kinds of lying, and several narratives illustrate the nemesis that that may bring (2 Sam 1:1-16). More ambiguously, there are occasions where lying seems necessary to save

life, either the life of another (1 Sam 19:11-17) or one's own (1 Sam 27). In this last example, however, the narrator may be concealing an ethical critique behind the wonderfully ironic compliment that the pagan Achish pays to David for his reliability—David who has repeatedly lied to him (1 Sam 29:6-9; cf. 27:10-12)! But the original target of the ninth commandment is the integrity of the judicial system by forbidding false witness. The Naboth incident once again illustrates the breach of this commandment (1 Kings 21:13-14). Solomon's prayer at the dedication of the temple, more in line with his early endowment with wisdom for doing justice, indicates the importance of oaths being taken seriously and truthfully in court cases if the will of Yahweh was to be done (1 Kings 8:31-32 = 2 Chron 6:22-23).

• Covetousness (tenth commandment) is indicated in the narratives of Achan (Josh 7), of David's adultery (2 Sam 11—12), and of Gehazi (2 Kings 5:20-27). In all cases, the judgment of God falls.

By means of these varied narratives, then, the Historical Books bear out the assessment made by prophets of different centuries that the ten commandments were sadly and persistently broken within Israel (Hos 4:1-3; Jer 7:9; Ezek 22:6-12).

3. The Shaping of Ethical Life in Israel.
What do the Historical Books tell us about how the ethics of ancient Israel were shaped and transmitted?

3.1. Knowledge and Teaching of the Law. The view of Israel's historians is that Israel's ethics should have been governed by the laws and commandments of Yahweh, their covenant Lord. While the discovery of the book of the law in the temple during the reign of Josiah in the seventh century BCE gave a major boost to his reforms, there are abundant earlier references to the law in ways that assume that it was supposed to have been known and obeyed. Exactly how the terms "law" and "commands" in the Historical Books relate to what we now have in the different collections within the completed Pentateuch is, of course, a question probably forever beyond historical certitude (*see DOTP*, Law). There are only two clear references to specific pentateuchal laws: 1 Kings 11:1-6 (concerning foreign wives; cf. Ex 34:16; Deut 7:3-4; see also Judg 14:1-3; Ezra 9—10) and 2 Kings 14:5-6

(concerning sons of murderers; cf. Deut 24:16). Other allusions to laws perhaps are found in Joshua 10:27 (cf. Deut 21:22-23); 2 Kings 17:15-17 (cf. Lev 18:1-3; Deut 12:30-31); 2 Chronicles 19:6-7 (cf. Deut 1:16-17; 16:18-20). In any case, there seems no doubt that a tradition of law, understood in connection with Israel's covenant with Yahweh at Sinai through Moses, is presupposed throughout the historical narratives as we now have them.

As early as Joshua, the law of Moses is impressed upon the people (Josh 1:6-9; 8:30-35; 22:5). The historian's choice of Psalm 18 as part of David's epitaph stresses his observance of all God's laws (2 Sam 22:21-24)—the irony of which in view of the narrative of his life was not lost on the historian himself, who later adds the comment in 1 Kings 15:5 that "David had not failed to keep any of the LORD's commands—except in the case of Uriah the Hittite" (when, we might add, he broke half the Decalogue!). David passes on to Solomon the duty of obedience to the law of Moses, much as Moses had done to Joshua (1 Kings 2:2-4 = 1 Chron 28:8), and God himself repeats the lesson to Solomon in such a way as to subordinate the temple itself to the moral demands of the covenant law (1 Kings 6:11-13). Theologically and ethically, Sinai takes precedence over Zion (as Jeremiah later preached in the temple itself [Jer 7]). Our historian's sharp eye for irony exposes another jarring dissonance with Solomon. The king who urged his people that they should be fully committed to obeying all God's commands (1 Kings 8:61) signally failed to do so himself (1 Kings 11:10-11). The wisdom given to him to exercise justice—a prime concern of the covenant law (1 Kings 3:9, 11, 28)—became squandered as a tourist attraction and a nice little earner for the palace (1 Kings 10:24-25). In the later monarchy the historians regularly evaluate kings by whether they observed God's laws or not: Jehu did not (2 Kings 10:31); the northern kingdom collectively failed to do so (2 Kings 17:13); Manasseh in the south was the worst of all (2 Kings 21:7-9). A few southern kings get a better report card: Joash, who was given a "copy of the covenant" at his youthful coronation (2 Kings 11:12 [one wonders what happened to it]); Jehoshaphat, who tried to reform the whole judicial system around "the law of the LORD" (2 Chron 19:4-11); Hezekiah, who surpassed them all (2 Kings 18:5-6), until Josiah, of course, whose response to the discovery of the book of the law is legendary (2 Kings 22—23 = 2 Chron 34).

With such all-pervasive emphasis on the moral importance of the law, how was it supposed to be known by ordinary people? There seem to have been two major mechanisms for the dissemination of the law in Israel so that it could perform its task of ethical guidance.

3.1.1. The Teaching of the Priests. The teaching function of the *priests, though often overlooked by contemporary Bible readers in comparison with their sacrificial duties, was of vital importance. It was part of their ordination charge (Lev 10:10-11), is mentioned ahead of their sacrificial role in the blessing of Moses (Deut 33:10), and is the proverbial function attributed to them in Jeremiah 18:18. In the Historical Books we find a reforming king, Jehoshaphat, turning to the Levitical priests to assist in the dissemination and administration of the law under his new judicial arrangements (2 Chron 19:4-11). Similarly, *Ezra employs Levites in his mass program of "theological education by extension" in the restored postexilic community (Neh 8). Ezra, himself a priest in the line of Aaron, set an example to all those whom he used as teachers, since he himself "had set his heart to study and to do and to teach the law of the LORD" (Ezra 7:10). Thus it was through the priests that the people should have known the moral will of God. So important was this role that the Chronicler could make the remarkable comment that the lack of a teaching priest was tantamount to being without the law and even without the living God (2 Chron 15:3). The prophets' quarrel with the priests was precisely that they had failed in their teaching role, and thus the people, deprived of knowledge of the law (and thus lacking knowledge of God as well), were understandably living in disobedience to it (Hos 4:4-9; Mal 2:1-9).

3.1.2. Education in the Family. The first education that an Israelite should have had, however, in the ethical values of the law was within the family. The head of each household had a primary responsibility in this domestic moral education (Deut 6:7; 11:19; 32:46-47). Joshua 4:6-7, 21-23 may preserve elements of ancient Israelite catechesis, in which parents and children engage in question and answer, so that the historical memory that was the foundation of OT ethics was preserved (cf. Ex 12:26-27; 13:14-15; Deut 6:20-25). The expectation that the moral

ethos of Israel be handed on from father to children is thrown into relief by those two notable occasions when it was not met: Eli and Samuel. A more positive example is Ezra's use of the heads of households, alongside the Levites, to fulfill their traditional role of proper teaching of the law to their own families (Neh 8:13).

3.2. Instinctive Moral Reasoning. The historians recognize that not every situation fits some given law. Decisions sometimes have to be made in the heat of the moment, and ethical reasoning draws on various sources, including social custom and the instinctive awareness of what is right, or "not done in Israel."

The moral ambiguity of situations in and of themselves is also recognized. Had David slain Saul in the cave or the camp (1 Sam 24; 26), even Saul acknowledged that David could have felt morally justified in taking the life of someone who was intent on killing him. His men added to such instinctive situation ethics the theological argument that God himself had engineered the situation for that very purpose. But David (in a rare OT reference to the conscience: 1 Sam 24:5; cf. 25:31; 2 Sam 24:10) places a prior principle above the apparent demands of the situation: the sanctity of someone anointed by God. Then he chooses the still higher principle of entrusting just retribution to God himself (1 Sam 24:12), almost as if he had just read Romans 12:17-21 (which is, of course, based on OT texts). On that occasion David's moral reasoning triumphed over an instinctive and opportunist ethic. On another occasion it was the calm moral reasoning of a woman that prevented David carrying through a raging vengeful course of action against Nabal. Abigail's arguments (1 Sam 25:26-31) included a mixture of deontology (the sanctity of human life, the wrongness of innocent bloodshed and of taking personal vengeance) and consequentialism (the later effects on David's conscience, as king, of what he was now planning in hot blood). Such examples of ethical argument and decision in the Historical Books are an illuminating sidelight on the more didactic material of the law and wisdom traditions.

3.3. The Rhetorical Strategy of the Historical Books. We should keep in mind that the Historical Books themselves functioned strongly in the ethical shaping of the mind of Israel. It has been argued (e.g., Janzen; Birch) that this great narrative tradition in Israel was even more important than statute law in shaping OT ethics, for it inculcated in the Israelites who were steeped in these stories some fundamental ethical paradigms for what constituted appropriate behavior. Even if the completed form of the Deuteronomistic History was not achieved until the exile, the art of storytelling and the great Hebrew narrative tradition must have emerged centuries earlier. The *narrative art of Israel's historians engages the original hearers and generations of readers ever since in the ethical issues intrinsic to the stories they tell (see, e.g., Wenham's survey of the ethics of Judges from this rhetorical perspective). The skill built into the tensions and surprise of the plots; the subtle characterization of the participants; the economy of information that engages our imagination; the constant implied invitation to the reader to form his or her own moral judgments about the events, motives and behavior described; the "prophetic" perspective by which everything is weighed (sometimes explicitly, but more often by implicit rhetorical skill) in the balances of God's moral assessment—all of these are ingredients in the ethical power of these books. We scarcely notice the "omniscient narrator" (i.e., his claim to know the inner thoughts and motives of some characters), but we cannot fail to notice the "omnipresent deity"—for the main character throughout is the supreme Character—Yahweh, the covenant Lord of Israel.

And in the end, what matters most is not the ethical failure of all the characters—even the best of them—or the ethical mess and horror that many of the stories portray, but rather the sheer persistence of this God with this people, and the grace that endures beyond judgment (cf. 1 Kings 8:46-50 = 2 Chron 6:29-31, 36-40; 2 Chron 7:13-16; 33:10-13; Neh 9:17, 28, 31). Were it not for the patience and grace of Yahweh, the history of Israel never would have filled these books, let alone persisted beyond them. And it is in that redemptive grace that biblical ethics are founded on gratitude and freed from legalism.

4. Ethical Difficulties.

The phrase "the ethics of the Historical Books" must raise for many readers the question of certain aspects of these narratives that are, to us, ethically dubious or even repulsive. Here I mention but two.

4.1. The Conquest of Canaan. This is the event that is most troubling to sensitive readers, and rightly so. We cannot ignore its horror, although we should allow for the fact that Israel, like other nations of the ancient Near East whose documents we possess, had a rhetoric of war—an exaggerated language that often exceeded reality on the ground. A number of perspectives may be helpful, even if they do not entirely remove our ethical discomfort.

We should remember, first, that the conquest was a limited event. The conquest narratives in Joshua and Judges describe one particular period of Israel's long history. Many of the other wars that occur in OT narrative had no divine sanction, and some clearly were condemned as the actions of proud and greedy kings or military rivals.

Second, the OT itself puts an ethical framework around the conquest. The conquest of Canaan is consistently described as an act of God's justice and punishment on a morally degraded society. It is inappropriate to describe it as random genocide or ethnic cleansing. The wickedness of Canaanite society is anticipated even before it had reached the stage of calling forth judgment (Gen 15:16), and it is described in moral and social terms (Lev 18:24; 20:23; Deut 9:5; 12:29-31). This interpretation is accepted in the NT (e.g., Heb 11:31 speaks of the Canaanites as "the disobedient," implying that they were morally aware of their sin but chose to persist in it). There is a vital ethical distinction between arbitrary violence and violence inflicted within the moral framework of punishment, whether human or divine.

We should note, third, God's moral consistency. The OT argues that God used Israel as the agent of his punishment on the Canaanites. But the text also makes clear the warning to Israel that if they behaved in the same way the Canaanites did, then God would treat Israel as his enemy too and would inflict the same punishment on them using other nations (Lev 18:28; Deut 28:25-68). The Historical Books record exactly this. Israel's status as God's chosen people, far from bringing consistent favoritism, exposed them all the more to God's moral judgment and historical punishment— more in the long term than for the generation of Canaanites who experienced the conquest. The law, narratives and prophets agree that those who choose to live as enemies of God eventually face God's judgment.

And fourth, in the wider canonical context the conquest anticipated the final judgment. Like the stories of Sodom and Gomorrah and the flood, the story of the conquest of Canaan stands in the Bible as a "prototypical" narrative. The Bible affirms that ultimately, in the final judgment, the wicked will face the awful reality of the wrath of God in exclusion, punishment and destruction. That will constitute the final vindication of God's ethical justice. But at certain points in history, such as the conquest, God has demonstrated the power of his judgment. The story of Rahab, set in the midst of the conquest narrative, also demonstrates the power of repentance and faith, and God's willingness to spare his enemies when they choose to identify with God's people. Rahab thus enters the NT hall of fame—and faith (Heb 11:31; Jas 2:25).

4.2. Flawed Heroes. Rahab's inclusion in Hebrews 11, however, does not indicate ethical approval of her profession as a prostitute. The same must be said of the other characters. What is commended in Hebrews 11 is faith in the promises and power of God, not all the recorded actions of all the listed characters. All of them were flawed in some way (Noah got drunk; Abraham lied; Jacob cheated; Moses murdered; David committed adultery), and some of them were flawed in appalling ways, whether by utter lack of control (Samson) or out of possibly sincere ignorance (Jephthah). We do not have to try to excuse the morally outrageous behavior of OT characters, or worse, try to twist them into some kind of moral paragon to teach the children. OT saints were sinners like the rest of us.

The Historical Books describe what simply happened, not necessarily what was approved by the writers or by God. We easily make the mistake of thinking that just because a story is in the Bible, it must somehow be "what God wanted." But the biblical narrators deal with the real world, "telling it like it is," with all its corrupt and fallen ambiguity. We should not mistake the realism of biblical narrative for ethical approval. The Historical Books challenge us to wonder at the amazing grace and patience of the God who continues to work out his purpose through such morally compromised people, and to be discerning as we evaluate their conduct ethically according to standards that the OT itself provides. In all these respects we find that these historical texts were indeed, as Paul affirms, "written for our instruction" (1 Cor 10:6).

See also HERMENEUTICS; ISRAELITE SOCIETY; JUSTICE AND RIGHTEOUSNESS; LAND; LAW; SIN; WAR AND PEACE.

BIBLIOGRAPHY. **J. Barton,** *Ethics and the Old Testament* (London: SCM, 1998); **R. Bauckham,** *The Bible in Politics: How to Read the Bible Politically* (London: SPCK; Louisville: Westminster/John Knox, 1989); **B. C. Birch,** "Divine Character and the Formation of Moral Community in the Book of Exodus," in *The Bible in Ethics: The Second Sheffield Colloquium,* ed. J. W. Rogerson, M. Davies and M. D. Carroll R. (JSOTSup 207; Sheffield: Sheffield Academic Press, 1995) 119-35; idem, *Let Justice Roll Down: The Old Testament, Ethics, and Christian Life* (Louisville: Westminster/John Knox, 1991); idem, "Old Testament Narrative and Moral Address," in *Canon, Theology, and Old Testament Interpretation: Essays in Honor of Brevard S. Childs,* ed. G. M. Tucker, D. L. Petersen and R. R. Wilson (Philadelphia: Fortress, 1988) 75-91; **W. Brueggemann,** *The Prophetic Imagination* (Philadelphia: Fortress, 1978); **R. E. Clements,** ed., *The World of Ancient Israel: Sociological, Anthropological and Political Perspectives* (Cambridge: Cambridge University Press, 1989); **J. Goldingay,** *Approaches to Old Testament Interpretation* (rev. ed.; Leicester: Apollos, 1990); idem, "Justice and Salvation for Israel and Canaan," in *Reading the Hebrew Bible for a New Millennium: Form, Concept, and Theological Perspective,* ed. W. Kim et al. (Harrisburg, PA: Trinity Press International, 2000) 169-87; **S. Hauerwas,** *A Community of Character: Toward a Constructive Christian Social Ethic* (Notre Dame, IN: University of Notre Dame Press, 1981); **W. Janzen,** *Old Testament Ethics: A Paradigmatic Approach* (Louisville: Westminster/John Knox, 1994); **W. C. Kaiser Jr.,** *Toward Old Testament Ethics* (Grand Rapids: Zondervan, 1983); **D. A. Knight and C. Meyers,** eds., *Ethics and Politics in the Hebrew Bible* (Semeia 66; Atlanta: Scholars Press, 1994); **M. C. Lind,** "The Concept of Political Power in Ancient Israel," *ASTI* 7 (1968-1969) 4-24; **J. G. McConville,** *Grace in the End: A Study of Deuteronomic Theology* (SOTBT; Grand Rapids: Zondervan, 1993); **M. E. Mills,** *Biblical Morality: Moral Perspectives in Old Testament Narratives* (HSCPRT; Aldershot and Burlington, VT: Ashgate, 2001); **J. Muilenburg,** *The Way of Israel: Biblical Faith and Ethics* (New York: Harper, 1961); **O. M. T. O'Donovan,** *The Desire of the Nations: Rediscover-*

ing the Roots of Political Theology (Cambridge: Cambridge University Press, 1996); **T. Ogletree,** *The Use of the Bible in Christian Ethics: A Constructive Essay* (Philadelphia: Fortress, 1983); **D. J. Pleins,** *The Social Visions of the Hebrew Bible: A Theological Introduction* (Louisville: Westminster/ John Knox, 2001); **C. Rodd,** *Glimpses of a Strange Land: Studies in Old Testament Ethics* (Edinburgh: T & T Clark, 2001); **J. W. Rogerson, M. Davies and M. D. Carroll R.,** eds., *The Bible in Ethics: The Second Sheffield Colloquium* (JSOTSup 207; Sheffield: Sheffield Academic Press, 1995); **P. Trible,** *Texts of Terror: Literary-Feminist Readings of Biblical Narratives* (OBT 13; Philadelphia: Fortress, 1984); **G. J. Wenham,** *Story as Torah: Reading the Old Testament Ethically* (Edinburgh: T & T Clark, 2000); **C. J. H. Wright,** *Deuteronomy* (NIBCOT 4; Peabody, MA: Hendrickson; Carlisle: Paternoster, 1996); idem, *God's People in God's Land: Family, Land, and Property in the Old Testament* (Grand Rapids: Eerdmans; Exeter: Paternoster, 1990); idem, *Old Testament Ethics for the People of God* (Downers Grove, IL: InterVarsity Press, 2004).   C. J. H. Wright

ETHICS OF INTERPRETATION. *See* METHODS OF INTERPRETATION.

ETHNICITY

Even when done well, history writing presents its audience with a very finite cross-section of reality, a cross-section bounded finitely by the historian's choice of sources and temporally by the history's beginning and end. How do historians decide where to begin and end their histories, and what criteria do they employ to determine which sources to include and which to ignore? By what rationale do historians choose the moral and causative dynamics that will govern their portrait of the past? In the last few decades scholars have become increasingly aware of how deeply this historical process is influenced by the cultural perspectives of the historian. As a result, students of historiography now attend not only to the histories themselves, but also to the social identities of the men and women who wrote them, and often one of the most important elements in social identity is ethnicity.

1. Ethnic Theory
2. Ethnicity and Identity in the Ancient Near East
3. Ethnicity and Israelite History
4. Ethnicity in Israelite History Writing
5. Conclusions

1. Ethnic Theory.

Contemporary uses of the term *ethnicity* reflect two different but related concepts, one broad and one narrower. Many social scientists now define ethnicity so that it is essentially equivalent to "society" or "culture." These theorists are interested in helping small, persecuted social groups escape the oppression of larger core sociopolitical modalities. By adopting this broad definition, they insure that all repressed groups will fit the theoretical purview of ethnicity. In many respects this concept of ethnicity suits ancient Israel well, for as a nation it was frequently exploited by the larger civilizations to the east and the west: *Egypt and Mesopotamia.

The other concept of ethnicity—a more narrow definition that will be our primary focus in this article—refers to groups of individuals who view themselves as being alike by virtue of their common ancestry. For instance, the ancient Greeks believed that they were all children of a single forefather named Hellen (hence the term *Hellenism*), and the modern Tiv people of Africa believe that they are the offspring of a man named Tiv. Those familiar with the Hebrew Bible will recognize immediately the important role that ethnicity played in Israelite concepts of identity. Israel traced its origins back to a single person named Jacob/Israel, and each of its twelve tribes was the progeny of a forefather bearing the tribe's name (e.g., Reuben was the forefather of the tribe of Reuben). Ethnicity also served the Israelites as an organizing principle for describing the origins of other nations, so that the *Ammonites were the children of Ben-ammi, the *Moabites children of Moab, the *Edomites of Esau, the *Assyrians of Asshur, etc. Scholars refer to these ethnic forefathers whose name matches that of the people as "eponymous ancestors." Anthropological evidence suggests that such eponyms are usually traditional ascriptions rather than strictly facts of history.

Of course, social identities are always more complex than "we are the sons of Jacob," so there is more theoretical ground to cover before we focus on ethnicity as it relates to ancient Israel and its history-writing. In order to facilitate this discussion of ethnicity, we need to introduce several technical terms, beginning with the word pairs *emic/etic* and *endonym/exonym*. It is important when discussing identity to differentiate between emic and etic points of view. The emic point of view is the insider's perspective, while the etic view is that of an outsider. So, for instance, when the first Europeans in North America described the natives as "Indians," this was an etic rather than emic perspective. Emic perspectives would have produced a very different set of names, such as the Iroquois, the Dakota and the Cherokee peoples. Because the term *Indian* was placed upon Native Americans from without, scholars refer to this name as an exonym (coined by etic outsiders) rather than as an endonym (coined by emic insiders). In certain respects, however, distinctions such as this are difficult to preserve in practice. Although the "Indian" label was an exonym created from an etic point of view, eventually it was adopted by Native Americans and so became an emic description of their identity.

Another pair of terms important for students of ethnicity is *exogamy* and *endogamy*. Those cultures are exogamous that allow members of the group to marry outsiders, while endogamous societies forbid this. The distinction between exogamy and endogamy presumes, of course, some sense of boundary that separates the ethnic group from outsiders. Scholars refer to these socially constructed boundaries as "ethnic boundaries"—that is, social boundaries that partition population groups on the basis of one or more of the following criteria: (1) genealogical characteristics (required for our purposes); (2) cultural traits such as language, religion, customs, shared history; (3) geographical territoriality; (4) inherited phenotypical characteristics (physical appearance). Ethnic boundaries vary in intensity, with some societies allowing for easy assimilation of outsiders and others not so. Functioning ethnic boundaries obviously require that there be some convenient way to distinguish insiders from outsiders. For this reason, one or more of the criteria listed above, especially language, custom and phenotypical characteristics, serve as ethnic indicators—that is, features used to make ready judgments about group membership. A good example from biblical literature is found in the well known *shibboleth-sibboleth* episode, where Gileadites used linguistic dialect to exclude Ephraimites from their territory (Judg 12).

2. Ethnicity and Identity in the Ancient Near East.

Although there is some evidence of ethnic sentiment in the large core societies of the Near East, the national identities of *Egypt, *Assyria, *Babylon and *Persia were political and cultural rather than ethnic per se, and their imperial desires, when stirred, had the natural effect of producing empires with heterogeneous populations. More important for our purposes is the fact that Israel was most affected by these larger nations when it fell under their dominion, and ethnic theorists predict that oppression of this sort creates and intensifies ethnic sentiment. This may explain why ethnicity was a common component in the national identities of Israel and the other small states of Syria-Palestine.

Regarding the large civilizations in Israel's ancient context, only in Greece do we find that ethnicity played an important role in its notions of identity. Greek and Israelite expressions of ethnicity are at points very similar (eponyms, tribal lineages, migration traditions etc.), prompting some scholars to suppose that there was an exchange of ethnic ideas between the two societies. This was perhaps so, but the features that Greek and Israelite ethnicity share are so common in the anthropological evidence that the similarities alone cannot provide the adequate basis for such a conclusion. Ethnicity was also a prominent mode of identity in the smaller regional states of Syria-Palestine, like *Aram, *Philistia, *Ammon and *Edom, where not only eponymous ancestry but also migration traditions served as a basis for ethnic unity (Sparks 1998). The prophet Amos (Amos 9:7) seized upon this reality when he questioned whether Israel's migration from exodus could serve as an expression of its ethnic and religious uniqueness.

3. Ethnicity and Israelite History.

Israel's national histories—the *Deuteronomistic History and the *Chronicler's History—are, in their canonical form, products of the exilic and postexilic periods. This does not mean that these histories are useless as sources for exploring the history of the united and divided monarchies, but it does mean that these works are necessarily anachronistic at points. Just as medieval artists depicted their biblical characters wearing garments from the Middle Ages, so too do these histories present Israelite identity through the much later lenses of nascent Judaism. A good example is the book of *Judges. Although the book portrays the judges as military figures ruling over all of Israel, a careful reading of the material shows that the judges actually were local heroes whose exploits covered a rather narrow geographical range. In this case, it appears that the author of Judges (presumably the Deuteronomistic Historian or one of his sources) either intentionally or unconsciously presented Israel as more ethnically and politically united than did his sources. The implication is that here and elsewhere, our reconstruction of preexilic Israelite social history—and ethnicity—will need to sift out of the histories those older sources that provide a clearer window into earlier periods. Another implication is that our interest in Israelite ethnicity should be explored by considering other available sources that can be more securely dated, such as the archaeological evidence, Near Eastern texts and especially the Hebrew prophetic literature.

Let us begin with a brief history of Israel's ethnicity and identity. If one demands evidence outside of the Bible itself, there is little that can be said with confidence about early Israelite identity. Excepting the Egyptian Merneptah stela (c. 1200 BCE), which refers to the "people of Israel," there are no extrabiblical references to Israel in the early period. Some scholars have suggested that early Israel might be connected with the bellicose *hapiru* (= *"Hebrews"?) who ravaged Syria-Palestine during the second millennium BCE, but this remains a matter of conjecture (although we should note in passing that the term "Hebrew" is probably an exonym because in the Bible it almost invariably is used by non-Israelites). Archaeological evidence reflects settlement patterns in Iron Age Palestine that might be associated with the appearance of Israelites in the region, but this evidence can only isolate cultural entities; it cannot tell us much about the role that ethnicity (perceived common ancestry) played in shaping the culture's identity. Because the Pentateuch, like the other Hebrew histories, is increasingly viewed as a late composition, and as being based on even more opaque historical sources, one of the primary biblical sources for this early period is the "Song of Deborah" (Judg 5), widely believed to be one of the oldest portions of the Hebrew Bible (*see* Poetry). It depicts Israel as a group of loosely affiliated tribes, each ethnically and territorially distinct (*see* Tribes of Israel and Land Allotments/Borders), that shared a common devotion to the god Yahweh and who, together, stood in contrast to the *Canaanites. Although there is evidence here of ethnic sentiment within the tribes and perhaps also between them, it is important to observe that it was religious identity, not ethnicity, that was central to this author's concept of *Israel.

The period of the united monarchy (*Saul, then *David and *Solomon) saw the religious and ethnic affiliations between the Israelite tribes intensify, largely because of the common threat they faced from Philistia and other enemies (for a similar phenomenon note that diverse Greek tribes came together to fight Persia). Once these threats dissipated, northern portions of the kingdom quickly split away from the south, suggesting that the fundamental modes of identity in the north and south were actually somewhat different. This distinction appears especially in the earliest prophetic literature (Hosea, Amos, Isaiah), where we find that ethnicity played a significant role in the Israelite north while Judean identity was more firmly fixed to the Davidic dynasty and its divine patron, Yahweh (Sparks 1998). It is likely that the strong ethnic sentiments of the north were a response to the Assyrian oppression that preceded the nation's downfall in 722 BCE.

The fall of the north left Judah alone to experience the Babylonian exile in 587/586 BCE, an event that had profound influence on Jewish identity. Now thrust into a foreign context, Judaism's features (mono-Yahwism, sabbath-keeping, circumcision) became significant markers of ethnic and religious identity (Sparks 1998). Some of these distinctive practices, such as Sabbath keeping, provided ready indicia for recognizing who was Jewish and who was not. By the time Jews began to return to Palestine during the Persian era, they were foreign not only to the Mesopotamian context from which they came, but also to their new surroundings in Palestine. As a result, the ethnic identity of postexilic returnees was greatly intensified. Older laws that once excluded certain foreigners from the Israelite assembly were interpreted as a general rejection of foreigners (cf. Deut 23:4-8; Neh 13), and "Israel" came to refer mainly to Jews returning from Babylon, so that the natives of Palestine, however "Jewish," were excluded from the community. Endogamy replaced earlier laxity toward exogamy (Ezra 9—10; Neh 10) in one of many policies that drove a wedge between the returnees and "the people of the land" (Ezra 4:4). Some Jews apparently resisted these rigid ethnic and religious boundaries (e.g., Is 56:3-7), but it is worth noting that even the ethnically charged Ezra-Nehemiah community invited non-Jews to join the community of Israel (Ezra 6:19-22). In other words, although variations in the intensity of ethnic sentiment are visible in the biblical sources from beginning to end, these sentiments are consistently secondary to religious identity, which permitted outsiders to assimilate to Israel/Judaism. This historical overview provides a framework for discussing ethnicity in the Israelite histories, and we will begin with the Deuteronomistic History.

4. Ethnicity in Israelite History Writing.

It is possible that there were two editions of the *Deuteronomistic History, one preexilic and one exilic, but for our purposes we will assume only the text's final form, which dates no earlier than the exile. The Deuteronomistic History's concept of Israelite identity was based largely on the book of Deuteronomy, where "Israel" means an ethnic brotherhood covenanted to worship Yahweh in its homeland under the watchful eye of a Davidic king (Deut 6:1-15; 17:1-15). The central problem tackled by the Deuteronomistic History was to show why Yahweh exiled Israel from its land when this geographical setting, with its temple, capital and holy land, seemed essential to Israelite identity. According to the Deuteronomistic History, this outcome was the consequence of Israel's long and checkered history, a cyclical pattern of idolatry and polytheism that so taxed Yahweh's patience that he finally brought an end to all but the people itself. For the Hebrew historian, the ideal symbols of Israelite identity—land, temple and king—could be restored only when the exiles adhered again to the Deuteronomic law. By concluding his history with the release of Judah's king from Babylon's prison (2 Kings 25:27-30), the Deuteronomistic Historian implied that this restoration might one day come about. But, as in other biblical sources, it was religious identity rather than ethnicity per se that was central to the agenda of the Deuteronomistic History.

This brings us to the Hebrew Chronicler, who wrote during the postexilic period and imbibed of its ethnically charged religious spirit. This is expressed most vividly in the first nine chapters of his work, where Israel's history is presented as a series of segmented family *genealogies—an expression of ethnicity par excellence. But more important than ethnicity for the Chronicler was the purity of the temple and its cultic activities. If we compare the Chronicler to his Deuteronomistic History source, we can see where ethnic motivations were afoot in expressing this concern. The Chronicler presents Samuel the Ephraimite as a Levite because only Levites should offer sacrifices (1 Chron 6:16-28 [MT 1 Chron 6:1-13]), and the ethnicity of Solomon's temple artisans becomes Danite instead of Naphtalite, so that he paralleled the Danite artisans of the Mosaic tabernacle (cf. 2 Chron 2:13-14 [MT 2 Chron 2:12-13]; Ex 31:6). In these cases the Chronicler made ethnic distinctions within Judaism itself, but he was, of course, interested as well in distinguishing Jews from outsiders. In his description of the house that Solomon built for his Egyptian wife, the Chronicler adds, "My wife shall not live in the house of David . . . for the places to which the ark of the Lord has come are holy" (2 Chron 8:11).

5. Conclusions.

Generally speaking, the biblical writers viewed religious faith as a more appropriate and powerful basis for social integration than ethnicity. They envisioned a Yahwistic Israel whose ethnicity helped to exclude the foreignness of idolatry without splintering Israel into tribal factions. Because the chief end of this religio-ethnic agenda was theological rather than ethnic per se, foreigners were persistently invited to join the Israelite community, although we should note that the ethnic boundaries through which assimilating foreigners had to pass differed substantially in the various sources. In fact, the biblical sources make it clear that often there was strong resistance to the biblical vision of the proper relationship between the religious and ethnic dimensions of identity.

See also ISRAEL; ISRAELITE SOCIETY.

BIBLIOGRAPHY. **F. Barth,** *Ethnic Groups and Boundaries: The Social Organization of Culture Difference* (Boston: Little, Brown, 1969); **L. Bohannan,** "A Genealogical Charter," *Africa* 22 (1952) 301-15; **S. Grosby,** *Biblical Ideas of Nationality: Ancient and Modern* (Winona Lake, IN: Eisenbrauns, 2002); **E. T. Mullen Jr.,** *Ethnic Myths and Pentateuchal Foundations: A New Approach to the Formation of the Pentateuch* (SemeiaSt; Atlanta:

Scholars Press, 1997); idem, *Narrative History and Ethnic Boundaries: The Deuteronomistic Historian and the Creation of Israelite National Identity* (SemeiaSt; Atlanta: Scholars Press, 1993); **F. W. Riggs,** *Ethnicity: Concepts and Terms Used in Ethnicity Research* (Honolulu: COCTA, 1985); **K. L. Sparks,** *Ethnicity and Identity in Ancient Israel: Prolegomena to the Study of Ethnic Sentiments and Their Expression in the Hebrew Bible* (Winona Lake, IN: Eisenbrauns, 1998); idem, "Genesis 49 and the Tribal List Tradition in Ancient Israel," *ZAW* 115 (2003) 327-47. **R. H. Thompson,** *Theories of Ethnicity: A Critical Appraisal* (New York: Greenwood, 1989); **I. M. Wallerstein,** *The Capitalist World-Economy: Essays* (Studies in Modern Capitalism; Cambridge: Cambridge University Press, 1979).   K. L. Sparks

EVIL

Evil is a continuous thread that runs throughout the Historical Books and is an important key to discerning the theological coherence of the narrative. The bulk of this article will spell out the narrative from the standpoint of the pervasive theme of evil and will highlight some important theological implications.

1. The Broad Biblical Context
2. Lexical Summary
3. The Thread of Evil in the Narrative

1. The Broad Biblical Context.
In biblical thought the fundamental reality, *God, is perfectly good. Moreover, everything else that exists was created by God, and as such was also good as originally created. Evil, then, is secondary, and can be understood only in relation to the fundamental reality of goodness. It is a parasite and exists only by way of reacting against or distorting that which is good. It is not an eternal reality on par with God. As F. E. Deist puts it, evil "is not a transcendent or ontological reality. Neither is it a state of being"; rather, it is most fundamentally a matter of conscious and willful disobedience that "causes unhappiness, strife and death to enter God's creation" (Deist, 76).

Accordingly, the main Hebrew words translated "evil" refer to that which is opposed to the good and the right. Whereas the good and the right promote life and flourishing, any action or event or circumstance that is detrimental to life and flourishing is evil. While evil is fundamentally opposed to God, when it occurs, it is always permitted under his all-embracing sovereignty. Indeed, sometimes evil in the form of disaster is the result of God's acts of judgment in response to human evil.

2. Lexical Summary.
The word for "evil" *(ra^c)* occurs some 127 times in the Historical Books, in a variety of contexts and with numerous shades of meaning: Joshua (2x), Judges (14x), 1-2 Samuel (33x), 1-2 Kings (49x), 1-2 Chronicles (22x), Ezra (1x), Nehemiah (6x).

The large majority of these instances refers to human disobedience or unfaithfulness and can be translated straightforwardly as "evil," with clear moral connotations. Another significant portion of these refers to various misfortunes and are sometimes rendered as "calamity" or "disaster." These pertain to such events as plagues, untimely deaths, illnesses, military defeats and the like. Sometimes these are ascribed to God (1 Sam 12:11), sometimes to human beings (2 Sam 15:14), and sometimes their origin is unspecified (2 Sam 19:17). All this is in line with W. Eichrodt's observation, "The popular conception of evil as a blow from God, and a revelation of his wrath, was never systematized into a watertight entailment making every evil a punishment of sin" (Eichrodt, 483). Occasionally, the word refers to bad products, without any sort of moral connotations (2 Sam 19:35).

3. The Thread of Evil in the Narrative.
Both uses of the term *evil* in the book of *Joshua are somewhat ironic. In his farewell address Joshua reminds the people that none of God's good promises have failed, and then he goes on to assure them that just as certainly God will bring on them the evil he has threatened if they violate the covenant (Josh 23:15). The irony lies in the fact that the "evil" of punishment is a certain consequence of the fact that God is a good God, whose word can be absolutely trusted. Later in the discourse Joshua directs the people to choose whom they will serve if serving the Lord seems "evil" to them (Josh 24:15). This points out that what is considered evil is sometimes relative to the perspective of some person or group of persons. It also highlights that evil is a free choice that human beings make when they do not rightly trust in the goodness of God, just as Adam and Eve did not in committing the aboriginal sin. Of course, serving the Lord is in

reality the epitome of goodness, and it is only human evil that could distort one's perspective to such a degree that one would see serving the Lord as evil or undesirable—thus the irony again.

This irony continues in the book of *Judges, a period characterized as a time when there was no king in Israel, and "all the people did what was right in their own eyes" (Judg 17:6; 21:25). What is right in the eyes of sinful men and women is obviously evil in the eyes of God. Indeed, acts described in Judges as right in the eyes of the perpetrators often are acts of notorious depravity and degradation. The human bent to evil is also demonstrated by the recurring pattern throughout the book as the Israelites continually revert back to idolatry and other forms of disobedience after periods of renewal and reform led by the judges. The death of a judge invariably is followed by a new generation that does not know the Lord or what he has done for Israel. God then sends them "evil" in the form of oppression and defeat at the hands of their enemies, and only then do they cry out to him for deliverance, and God responds by raising up another judge.

The correlation of human evil in the form of disobedience followed by "evil" in the form of punishment appears elsewhere in the Historical Books besides the book of Judges (Judg 2:11, 15; 1 Kings 14:9-10; 21:20-21, 29; 2 Kings 21:9, 12, 15-16; 1 Chron 21:15, 17; Neh 13:17-18). This correlation paints a vivid picture of a deep theological and moral truth: when people do evil by failing to honor God with worship and obedience, they bring evil upon ourselves. As D. Baker points out, this is the context for reading Isaiah 45:7, which identifies God as the creator of all things, light as well as darkness, prosperity as well as disaster. To commit evil against God is in fact to act self-destructively, to thwart one's own flourishing.

On the other hand, the "evil" of punishment or adversity from God is actually a good insofar as it discloses the truth to people and the folly of their actions. Evil in this sense is a sort of mirror that God holds up to people for the sake of correcting them and drawing them back to him. "Evil" from God helps people to see the evil of their actions and to repent. Although it seems adverse to the immediate flourishing of humans, it can contribute to their flourishing at a deeper level and in the long run.

Evil is also central to the story of Israel as it unfolds in the books of *Samuel, *Kings and *Chronicles. The king who was lacking in the time of the judges, when people did what was right in their own eyes, is now supplied. The hope that things might change for the better under the reign of a human king is dimmed from the outset by the fact that the request for a king by the people is described as an evil that is added to their other sins (1 Sam 12:19). The early promise of *Saul, suggested by his initial humility, is quickly disappointed when he disobeys the command to destroy the Amalekites, including the plunder. At this point in the narrative he is no longer "small in his own eyes," and as a result he does that which is evil in the eyes of the Lord (1 Sam 15:17-19). After God rejects Saul as king, he plunges further into evil. This is accelerated when the Spirit of the Lord departs from Saul, and an evil spirit from the Lord begins to torment him (1 Sam 16:14-23; 18:10; 19:9). As a result, Saul is determined to do evil to *David (1 Sam 20:7, 9, 13).

By stark contrast, the narrative emphasizes that David resists the temptation to do evil, particularly the evil of revenge. Whereas Saul returns evil to David for good, David returns good for evil (1 Sam 24:11, 17-18; 26:18). The same is true of Nabal, who returns evil to David for good (1 Sam 25:3, 17). Although David was bent on harming Nabal, through the wise intervention of Nabal's wife, Abigail, he was prevented from bloodshed. Both Abigail and David see the hand of God in these events and recognize that God acted to keep him from committing evil (1 Sam 25:26, 39). Indeed, Abigail expresses the hope that evil will not be found in David as long as he lives (1 Sam 25:28). Her hope, of course, was not fulfilled. In his affair with Bathsheba and his subsequent murder of Uriah, David acted not unlike Saul in returning evil for good. Whereas he responded positively to the word of the Lord as delivered by Abigail, in the Bathsheba affair he despised the word of the Lord by doing what was evil in the Lord's eyes (2 Sam 12:9). The contrast between these two cases underscores the crucial role of human freedom in all evil choices. David could have respected and obeyed the word of the Lord in the latter case just as he did in the former.

After the time of David and his son *Solomon, it is increasingly clear that the problem of evil suggested by the book of Judges is not solved, for many of the kings themselves are evil and even lead the way in disobedience and idolatry. Each of the kings of Israel and Judah is given a moral report card, and frequently the kings fail miserably on the moral and spiritual scale. Once the kingdom is split after Solomon, every king of Israel does evil in the eyes of the Lord, and often this is true of the kings of Judah as well.

The fact that every king of Israel, without exception, is described as evil perhaps reflects the historian's literary point of view as much as it reflects the character of the kings in question. Jeroboam II, for instance, may not have particularly deserved this description on more objective grounds, but given the commitments of the southern historian, he was bound to categorize this king as evil. In view of this consideration, it is also possible that the word "evil" in these contexts does not have all the moral and ethical connotations that Christian readers normally associate with the term.

At any rate, the downward spiral reaches its nadir with *Manasseh, who leads the people astray to such an extent that they do even more evil than the people that the Lord had destroyed before the Israelites (2 Kings 21:9). The narrative emphasizes that had the Israelites been faithful to the covenant, they would have remained in the land. But now their idolatry has reached such a point that they must be expelled from the land. The importance of freedom in the choice of evil is also suggested by the fact that Manasseh's father was *Hezekiah. The sons of good kings may freely choose evil, just as *Josiah, son of a wicked king, chose good.

Josiah's reform could delay but not prevent the evil that God had decreed on Judah because of its unfaithfulness (2 Kings 22:16, 20). Because of persistent evil, God thrust Judah from the land and from his presence (2 Kings 24:19-20). The Historical Books conclude with the reforms of *Nehemiah after the Israelites have returned from exile but again have fallen into disobedience, recalling the evil that led to their exile in the first place (Neh 13:17-18, 27).

The problem of evil that pervades the Historical Books is never solved within their scope. No merely human king, not even one such as David, who is a man after God's own heart and usually resists evil, is up to the task. Nor is it the case that evil as divine discipline, even in the form of exile, altogether remedies the malady. The true so-

lution to human evil is yet to come.

See also ETHICS; SICKNESS AND DISEASE.

BIBLIOGRAPHY. **D. W. Baker,** "רעע," *NIDOTTE* 3.1154-58; **F. E. Deist,** "The Nature and Origin of Evil: Old Testament Perspectives and Their Theological Consequences," *JTSA* 76 (1991) 71-81; **W. Eichrodt,** *Theology of the Old Testament* (2 vols.; Philadelphia: Westminster, 1967) 2.483-95.   J. Walls

EXILE. *See* HISTORY OF ISRAEL 6: BABYLONIAN PERIOD; HISTORY OF ISRAEL 7: PERSIAN PERIOD; LAND.

EZION-GEBER

Ezion-geber is best known as the location of *Solomon's port on the Red Sea (1 Kings 9:26-28; 2 Chron 8:17-18) and for its subsequent role as the farthest possible terminus of Judean political and economic expansion into the southern wilderness. Of related interest is Elath (Eloth), a place that sometimes is mentioned in the Bible together with Ezion-geber (Deut 2:8; 1 Kings 9:26; 2 Chron 8:17) and other times appears alone but in similar contexts (2 Kings 14:22; 16:5-6; 2 Chron 26:2). The one must be considered in any analysis of the other.

1. Site Identification
2. Geography
3. History
4. Tell el-Khefeileh

1. Site Identification.

It is generally agreed that the best candidate for the site of Ezion-geber is Tell el-Kheleifeh. This suggestion, first made by F. Frank in 1934, was popularized by N. Glueck, who excavated the site from 1938 to 1940. G. D. Pratico reassessed Glueck's conclusions and found that the earliest remains at Tell el-Kheleifeh, rather than reaching into the tenth century BCE as Glueck had proposed, instead do not predate the ninth century BCE. This casts doubt on the identification of the site as the Ezion-geber of *Solomon and the wilderness wanderings. Some (e.g., *Tübinger Bibelatlas*) place Ezion-geber at Jezirat Faraun, an island with good anchorage just off the western shore of the Gulf of Eilat/Aqaba. Other suggestions consider that the remains of Ezion-geber were on a mountain above Aqaba or under the modern city itself, or have been totally washed away.

Glueck also assumed that Elath (Eloth) was a

late alternative name (perhaps Edomite?) for Ezion-geber. On the strength of Deuteronomy 2:8 and 1 Kings 9:26, however, it is preferable to follow Y. Aharoni, who held that Elath was a site in the vicinity of Ezion-geber, probably located under modern Aqaba, which wholly covers the ancient remains.

2. Geography.

2.1. Regional Dynamic.
The inverted triangle of land that comprises the southern half of the modern state of Israel is a large arid-to-hyperarid rocky wilderness that in biblical times functioned as a "land between" (Monson) the major kingdoms of the southern Levant: Israel and Judah to the north, *Edom to the east, and *Egypt, across the Sinai, to the west. In and of itself, this "great and terrible wilderness" (Deut 1:19 NASB) through which Moses led the Israelites had little to offer the outsider except for copper deposits at Timnah (mined by the Egyptians in the thirteenth and twelfth centuries BCE), and the lack of adequate rainfall even for shepherding greatly hindered settlement in the area. Rather, the value of this region for the biblical world lay in its twofold role as a "land between": first, it both separated and pulled together Egypt, Edom and Israel as each sought to check the advance of the others into the area in an ongoing attempt to control the routes that had to cross this barren expanse; second, it served as a gateway to the Red Sea and the exotic lands in northeastern Africa and the Arabian Peninsula beyond.

Ezion-geber (and Elath) functioned as the anchor point for the southern end of this wilderness, providing a hub for the land routes between the Arabian Peninsula, Egypt and Israel, as well as offering the region's only Red Sea port. Here the Darb el-Hajj ("the Pilgrim's Route," a name dating from the first millennium CE), which connected Egypt to *Arabia through the desolation of the mid-Sinai, joined two routes heading north. Of these, the more important climbed from the Red Sea via Ezion-geber into the high Transjordanian highlands, passing through Edom, *Moab and *Ammon (the "King's Highway" [Num 20:17]) on the way to Damascus, or, alternatively, headed south to the spice lands of southern Arabia. The Damascus-Alia (Aqaba) section of this natural route was improved and elevated to the status of a Roman road, the Via Nova Traiana, in the early second

century CE. Of lesser importance for the regional scene, but more so for the biblical story itself, was the longitudinal route that led from the Red Sea through Ezion-geber up the Rift Valley to the oasis of Tamar (the "Aravah Road" [Deut 2:8]), then climbed northwest to Beersheba in the heart of the biblical Negev, a 150-mile journey fraught with difficulty. It was this route that allowed Solomon to push south from *Beersheba, normally the southernmost point of permanent settlement in ancient Israel (see 1 Kings 4:25), into the deep southern wilderness, his eyes fixed on Ezion-geber and the economic opportunities of the Red Sea.

2.2. Specific Conditions.
Ezion-geber, if Tell el-Kheleifeh, was located halfway along the northern shore of the Red Sea's Gulf of Aqaba/Elat, at the last freshwater spring heading west from modern Aqaba (probably ancient Elath). Both sites today are in the Hashemite kingdom of Jordan. The ground all around is an expanse of wholly unproductive stony desert alluvium. Rainfall seldom exceeds one inch annually, and summer temperatures are often in excess of 110° F. Clearly, all resources necessary to maintain life in the biblical period, just as in the present, had to have been brought in from the outside.

The same harsh conditions hold for travel on the Red Sea. Consistently strong northerly winds, unpredictable currents, and the presence of shoals and sharp coral reefs, combined with the insufferable heat and scant fresh water along the shore, all taxed the skills of even the most experienced sailors in premodern times.

3. History.

3.1. Wilderness Wanderings.
Ezion-geber first appears in the detailed itinerary of Numbers 33:1-49, which reviews places that the Israelites camped on their journey from Egypt to the plains of Moab (Num 33:35-36). Because Ezion-geber and Kadesh-barnea (Num 32:8) are the only two places on this route of whose location scholars are reasonably certain, they provide important geographical pegs for Israel's journey. It may be surmised that the region of Ezion-geber was generally under the control of the Midianites at this time (cf. Ex 2:15-21; Num 31:1-9), although Deuteronomy 2:8 indicates that the Edomites were already present in the mountains to the northeast.

3.2. Israelite and Judean Monarchy.
Solomon's

economic control over the eastern Mediterranean seaboard in the late tenth century BCE took place in what was otherwise a power vacuum in the region. Access to the profitable markets of the Red Sea, rarely tapped by the small nation states of the Levant, was an important part of this trade network. Solomon relied on the shipbuilding and sailing expertise of the *Phoenicians for this endeavor (1 Kings 9:27; 2 Chron 8:17-18). By launching his ships into the Red Sea from Ezion-geber, Solomon not only was laying claim to a port that was "in the land of Edom" (1 Kings 9:26), but also was moving into markets that customarily had belonged to larger powers such as Egypt and Babylon. Solomon's ships brought him an immense quantity of gold (420 talents, approximately 31,500 pounds) from Ophir (1 Kings 9:28; cf. Job 22:24; 28:16; Ps 45:9; Is 13:12), a near-fabled land that probably was located in the southern Arabian Peninsula. The port of Ezion-geber also received almug trees (aromatic sandal wood) and precious stones from Ophir (1 Kings 10:11), as well as silver, ivory, apes and peacocks from expeditions launched every three years (1 Kings 10:22). Solomon's reputation as an international merchant reached the Queen of Sheba, who journeyed from her home, which was located either in southern Arabia or on the horn of Africa, to Jerusalem, possibly via the port of Ezion-geber (1 Kings 10:1-13).

Israelite control over Ezion-geber apparently was disrupted by the invasion of Shishak in the fifth year of *Rehoboam (see 1 Kings 14:25-28). It was not until the mid-ninth century BCE, when Edom again fell under Judean control, that a Judean king, *Jehoshaphat, tried to revive trade on the Red Sea (1 Kings 22:47-48). Jehoshaphat was unsuccessful; apparently lacking the assistance of skilled Phoenician sailors in spite of his political alliance with Israel, Phoenicia's main ally to the south, Jehoshaphat's ships broke apart under the hazardous sailing conditions of the sea (1 Kings 22:48; cf. 2 Chron 20:35-37).

In the mid-eighth century BCE Azariah (Uzziah) revived Judean control over the wilderness as far as Elath (2 Kings 14:22; 2 Chron 26:2, 7-8), pushing the Egyptians, Edomites and various Arabian tribes from the area. This was Judah's last successful venture to the Red Sea; within two decades Rezin, king of Syria, took advantage of local instability in the face of the first of the Assyrian invasions (during the so-called Syro-

Ephraimite War, c. 735 BCE) and captured Elath, thus exerting Syrian influence throughout Transjordan and cutting Judah's southern and eastern trade routes (2 Kings 16:5-6).

4. Tell el-Khefeileh.

The earliest revealed structures at Tell el-Khefeileh comprise a square casemate fortress with an open inner courtyard, in the middle of which was a large building of the "four-room house" plan. This building could be considered a citadel, although its specific use (military, commercial, industrial, etc.) is unknown. A lack of ceramic evidence precludes giving a firm date to this fortress, although subsequent building on the site makes a ninth century BCE date likely. The next phase, which probably dates to the eighth through sixth centuries BCE, was larger and more substantial. A solid inset-offset wall, rather thick, enclosed the square site, with a four-chambered gate opening on the seaward side. The area within this perimeter wall contained numerous buildings. Fragmentary evidence suggests some settlement at the site in the fifth and early fourth centuries BCE. The archaeological evidence at Tell el-Khefeileh, then, supports Judean and/or Edomite activity as a fortified mercantile caravanserai from the ninth century BCE (Jehoshaphat), but fails to corroborate the account of Ezion-geber in the wilderness wanderings narrative or as Solomon's port. Proper site identification, therefore, remains an open issue.

See also SOLOMON; TRADE AND TRAVEL.

BIBLIOGRAPHY. **Y. Aharoni,** *The Land of the Bible: A Historical Geography* (2d ed.; Philadelphia: Westminster, 1979); **D. Baly,** *The Geography of the Bible* (rev. ed.; New York: Harper & Row, 1974); **D. Dorsey,** *The Roads and Highways of Ancient Israel* (Baltimore: Johns Hopkins University Press, 1991); **F. Frank,** "Aus der 'Araba I: Reiseberichte," *ZDPV* 57 (1934) 191-280; **N. Glueck,** *The Other Side of the Jordan* (Cambridge, MA: American Schools of Oriental Research, 1970); idem, "The Topography and History of Ezion-Geber and Elath," *BASOR* 72 (1938) 2-13; **N. Glueck and G. D. Pratico,** "Kheleifeh, Tell el-," *NEAEHL* 3.867-70; **Z. Meshel,** "On the Problem of Tell el-Kheleifeh, Elath and Ezion-Geber," [in Hebrew] *ErIsr* 12 (1975): 49-56; **S. Mittmann and G. Schmitt,** eds., *Tübinger Bibelatlas* (Stuttgart: Deutsche Bibelgesellschaft, 2001); **J. Monson,** *Regions on the Run: Introductory Map Studies in the*

Land of the Bible (Rockford, IL: Biblical Backgrounds, 1998); **G. D. Pratico,** "Nelson Glueck's 1938-1940 Excavations at Tell el-Kheleifeh: A Reappraisal," *BASOR* 259 (1985) 1-32; idem, "Where is Ezion-Geber? A Reappraisal of the Site Archaeologist Nelson Glueck Identified as King Solomon's Red Sea Port," *BAR* 12.5 (1986) 24-35; **A. Raban,** "Near Eastern Harbors: Thirteenth-Seventh Centuries BCE," in *Mediterranean Peoples in Transition: Thirteenth to Early Tenth Centuries BCE,* ed. S. Gitin, A. Mazar and E. Stern (Jerusalem: Israel Exploration Society, 1998) 428-38. P. H. Wright

EZRA

The ministry of the postexilic priest and scribe named Ezra is primarily known to us through the books of Ezra and Nehemiah. Ezra was sent by the Persian emperor to Jerusalem to perform a legal administrative role in the province of Yehud. He was also to maintain the temple cult in Jerusalem, which gave him opportunity to strengthen the temple and its services as well as promulgate the law among the Jews.

1. Sources
2. The Time of Ezra's Tenure in Jerusalem
3. Yehud in Mid-Fifth Century BCE
4. The Role of Ezra Within Yehud and Abar Nahara (Beyond the River)
5. The Shape of the Law
6. The Divorces

1. Sources.

The earliest evidence for the man Ezra "priest and scribe" is the Hebrew canonical book of Ezra-Nehemiah (Ezra 7—10; Neh 8; 12 [and Neh 9 in LXX Esdras gamma]). The books of Esdras (alpha, beta, gamma) in the LXX appear to be early translated editions of this Hebrew work, beta and gamma following the storylines of the Hebrew Ezra 1—10 and Nehemiah 1—13 respectively, and alpha reproducing 2 Chronicles 35—36; Ezra 1—10; Nehemiah 8:1-13; and extra material at 1 Esdras 3:1—5:6. In later tradition Ezra will be either ignored (Sir 49:13; *1 En.* 89:72; 2 Macc 1:18-36; *2 Bar.* 53—74; Acts 7; Heb 11) or exalted (Josephus *Ant.* 11.120-158; 4 Ezra 14:21-48) (see Kraft; Bergren; Porton).

There have been varying levels of affirmation of the authenticity of the materials about Ezra in the earliest sources—that is, the canonical books of Ezra and Nehemiah. The result of this evaluation has led to a variety of views on the historicity of Ezra, ranging from thorough doubt of his existence to simplistic replications of the canonical text. Early on, the letter of Artaxerxes in Ezra 7:12-26 was affirmed as authentic, but in recent years this affirmation has been a matter of debate. Some have noted the appearance of strong Jewish elements and dissonance with Persian official letters (Janzen, 49-52). These arguments have been sufficiently answered by noting that such letters which grant authority would be written in consultation with the recipient, and thus it is not surprising to find Jewish religious or linguistic features in the text (Williamson 1987; 1999). Furthermore, uniqueness among Persian epistolary materials is not as pronounced as sometimes is argued (Fried, 63 n. 4). Others have argued that the letter betrays affinities with later Hellenistic rather than Persian epistolary style (Schwiderski) and royal ideology (Grätz), observations that have raised again the question of the authenticity of this letter as a product of Artaxerxes' court. However, one must carefully nuance these conclusions. In the case of D. Schwiderski's form-critical work, it is important to mention that there are enduring debates over what constitutes Hellenistic versus Imperial Aramaic epistolary usage and how much of the latter is found in the documents "cited" in Ezra (see Conklin). Furthermore, if the Ezra-Nehemiah corpus was assembled in the early Hellenistic period, the redactor may have shaped the documents to fit their new literary context without losing the basic historical evidence drawn from the original letter. In the case of S. Grätz, it is highly questionable that the euergetism that he highlights in Hellenistic royal ideology is absent from the Persian court. The approach implied by the letter in Ezra 7 is one that fits with the Persian balance between imperial order and local custom (see Briant, 584).

The Ezra material outside of the letter, however, has been attacked by many as inauthentic. At first this material was ascribed to the writer of Chronicles, but scholarship has demonstrated that such links are only features of Late Biblical Hebrew (Throntveit). The material has been labeled as a "midrash" on the letter of Artaxerxes, but the lack of clear literary connections between the letter and the narrative proper undermines this argument. The switch back and forth between first-person autobiography and third-person biography as one moves from Ezra 7 to 10 suggests that an editor is drawing on a first-person account and completing the story using lists from temple archives.

Many have found it odd that one important aspect of Ezra's commission (promulgation of law) is now separated from the main Ezra material (Ezra 7—10) and appears in Nehemiah 7:73b—8:18, leading many to argue that the account in Nehemiah originally was connected to Ezra 7—10, most favoring a place between Ezra 8 and 9 (following Torrey), with a minority, influenced by 1 Esdras, suggesting after Ezra 10. As we will see further below, there is evidence of Ezra's fulfillment of the entire commission of Artaxerxes in the present form of Ezra 7—10, including the promulgation of law and appointment of judges—a conclusion that alleviates the oddity mentioned above. Nevertheless, evidence noted long ago by Torrey supports the origin of at least a form of Nehemiah 8 between Ezra 8 and 9, in particular (1) the similarity between Nehemiah 8 and Ezra 7—10 and dissimilarity between Nehemiah 8 and Nehemiah 1—13 in the form of month name used (compare Ezra 7:8-9; 8:31; 10:9, 16-17 and contrast Neh 1:1; 2:1; 6:15 with Neh 7:73b and 8:2); (2) the lack of any mention of Ezra in Nehemiah 1—7, and the resultant smooth chronological sequence (Ezra 7—8: departure in first month [Ezra 8:31], arrival in fifth month [Ezra 8:31; cf. 7:8]; Neh 8: assembly in seventh month [Neh 7:73b; 8:2]; Ezra 9—10: assembly in ninth month [Ezra 10:9], enquiry from tenth month to first month [Ezra 10:16-17]). If this view is accepted, then, the reference to Nehemiah alongside Ezra in Neh 8:9-10 is credited to later scribal or editorial activity.

Although there is plenty of debate and unquestionably the Ezra of Ezra-Nehemiah is not the entire "historical Ezra," the materials found within these books contain much of worth for historical research, even if they do present a certain picture of Ezra motivated by theological interests. As we will see, there are ways of explaining Ezra's mission and purpose in light of broader imperial interests, but this does not discount the agenda displayed by Ezra as relayed through the canonical tradition.

Thus this article provides a snapshot of the figure of Ezra in his socio-historical context. It is based on historical reflection that incorporates literary, archaeological and sociological evidence.

2. The Time of Ezra's Tenure in Jerusalem.

We are told in Ezra 7 that Ezra's story begins "during the reign of Artaxerxes king of Persia" (Ezra 7:1), and more specifically, that he set out from Babylon on the first day of the first month in the seventh year of Artaxerxes and arrived in Jerusalem on the first day of the fifth month of the same year (Ezra 7:8-9). Much debate has circled around the identity of this Artaxerxes. It is almost universally assumed that the Artaxerxes of Nehemiah is Artaxerxes I, and since Ezra precedes Nehemiah in the books of Ezra and Nehemiah (which are considered a unity in ancient Hebrew tradition), many have concluded that the king here also was Artaxerxes I (465-424 BCE). This would make the starting date of Ezra's mission 458 BCE, and that of Nehemiah's mission 445 BCE. This view, however, has been challenged on several grounds, the three most prominent of which are rehearsed as follows.

First, the state of the city and population in the time of Ezra suggests a time after Nehemiah rather than before, because of the condition of the wall around Jerusalem (compare Ezra 9:9 with Neh 2:13) and the size of the population within Jerusalem (compare Ezra 10:1 with Neh 7:4). Second, Nehemiah faces the mixed-marriage problem that Ezra purportedly mastered during his mission (compare Neh 13:23-29 with Ezra 9—10). Third, the Ezra narrative refers to a certain Jehohanan son of Eliashib, who has a room in the temple precincts, as a contemporary of Ezra, while the book of Nehemiah names Eliashib as the high priest when Nehemiah arrived in Jerusalem (compare Ezra 10:6 with Neh 12:22-23). The Elephantine papyri tell us that a man with the name *Johanan* (a variant of *Jehohanan*) was high priest in Jerusalem in 408 BCE—that is, well after the time of Nehemiah.

This evidence led to the theory that while Nehemiah's patron was Artaxerxes I (465-424 BCE), the ruler during Ezra's time was Artaxerxes II (405-359 BCE), placing Ezra's arrival in Jerusalem in 398 BCE. However, neither the early theory nor the late theory offers strong evidence for the appearance of Ezra and Nehemiah together in passages such as Nehemiah 8:9 (reading of the law) and Nehemiah 12:36-38 (dedication of the wall). This has led to the suggestion of a textual emendation for the text citing the year of Ezra's mission in Ezra 7. The word *thirty* was accidentally dropped out of the text, and so "seven" should be read as "thirty-seven" (Pavlovsky 1957; Bright, 391-402). This would place the arrival of Ezra at 428 BCE, a time after Nehemiah's first arrival and during what is often considered his second governorship (Neh 13). This theory has enjoyed little success among scholars, especially because it introduces a textual change not attested in any tradition (see Emerton); however, other scholars have sought to deal with the synchronicity of the work of Ezra and Nehemiah by arguing that multiple dating systems are represented in the text of Ezra-Nehemiah (McFall; Demsky). These theories have failed to garner a following among scholars, especially because of their speculative and complicated argument.

It appears that the two strongest candidates remain as 458 BCE and 398 BCE. Each of the criticisms offered by proponents of a late date has been met. Either Ezra's reference to a wall is metaphorical (notice "in Judah and Jerusalem"), or it refers to a wall that was in existence prior to Nehemiah's program (compare Neh 1:3 with Ezra 4:12-13). Descriptions of the size of a population are relative, and no definition is given as to the composition of the crowd (whether Jerusalem or the broader area). The fact that two leaders face similar challenges such as mixed marriages in the same time period is not surprising in light of Israel's record of disobedience. And finally, it is interesting that Jehohanan/ Johanan is not called the high priest in Ezra 10:6, leaving open the possibility that as a junior member of a powerful priestly family, he had a room that was expendable for Ezra's use. Furthermore, it has been suggested that there are names missing from the list of high priests in the fifth century BCE, names that were lost because of the practice of naming one's son after his grandfather, and that possibly the Jehohanan/ Johanan of Ezra 10:6 is from a family responsible for the maintenance of the temple and not from the high priestly family at all (compare Ezra 10:6 with Neh 13:4).

Both dates would be appropriate in light of Persian concerns during their respective historical contexts, whether that is Persian attempts to contain revolts during the period in question (Egyptian revolts in both 460 and 401 BCE) or Persian policies on legal systems. However, recent work has shown that patterns of imperial rule favor the order of Ezra before Nehemiah because legal reforms usually preceded major changes in the socioeconomic structure of a territory (see Hoglund, 44). Additionally, Nehemi-ah's mixed-marriage crisis in Nehemiah 13 appears to be based on the innovative (and more substantively argued) exegesis of the law found in Ezra 9 and is a more localized phenomenon (Neh 13:23). In light of this evidence, there is no reason to overturn the order of events in Ezra-Nehemiah.

3. Yehud in Mid-Fifth Century BCE.

If Ezra did indeed come to Yehud in 458 BCE, he represents a later wave of Jews returning to the land after the rise of the *Persian Empire in 539 BCE. In 539 BCE Cyrus took control of the city of Babylon and with it inherited the holdings of the former empire led by its final king, Nabo-nidus. The former kingdom of Judah, referred to as the province of Yehud (by its Aramaic name), was within this *Babylonian Empire and was administrated as part of a larger political unit called the satrapy of Babylon/Abar Nahara (Babylon/Beyond the River). Jews were permitted to return to the land, and they did so under the leaders Sheshbazzar (c. 538 BCE [Ezra 1]) and *Zerubbabel and Jeshua (c. 520 BCE [Ezra 3—6]). However, no account is offered in Ezra-Nehemiah of the history between the stories in Ezra 6 and 7 (a span of fifty-seven years) except for a few letters that are included in Ezra 4:6-23. These letters reveal that there were considerable challenges to Jewish efforts to rebuild the infrastructure of their province. There appears to be a shift in Persian policy toward this community in the midfifth century BCE, most likely because of a serious challenge to Persian control over the western part of its empire (exemplified in the Greek-backed Egyptian revolt of 460 BCE), which consumed Persian interests from 460 to 450 BCE and resulted in the construction of imperial garrisons throughout the Levant. There is ample evidence and justification for Persian concern for their western territories, and the appearance of Ezra to promulgate a legal system that would promote both Yahwistic and imperial interests is not surprising (Ezra 7:26) (see Hoglund). No governor is mentioned in Ezra 7—10, but scholars have been able to reconstruct a list of governors for Yehud from the very beginning of Persian rule (see Avigad; Meyers; Meyers and Meyers, 14; Williamson 1988). In Nehemiah 8:9 and Nehemiah 12:36-38, however, Nehemiah is listed alongside Ezra, showing (unless this is a harmonistic scribal insertion or deliberate theologizing [see Shaver 1992]) either that Ezra remained in the land from

458 BCE until at least 445 BCE, when Nehemiah arrived, or that Ezra, after completing his initial commission from Artaxerxes, had returned to the Persian court and then later in 445 BCE returned to the land with Nehemiah (similar to Nehemiah's two stints in Jerusalem [see Neh 13:6]).

4. The Role of Ezra Within Yehud and Abar Nahara (Beyond the River).

Various views have been put forward for the role that Ezra played in the empire in relationship to the province of Yehud. The long *genealogy in Ezra 7 suggests to some that he was a high priest, while the sweeping powers afforded him by Artaxerxes suggest to others that he was appointed as part of the Persian satrapal structure, either as governor over Yehud or commissioner for Jewish affairs. Others have linked his role to similar roles or initiatives of the Persian court, whether displayed in Darius's use of the Egyptian Udjahorresnet to establish a temple cult and reorganize the legal system (indicative of a larger project of Darius throughout his empire), or in Artaxerxes' desire to secure Yehud on the fringes of its empire, concerned with the recent Greco-Egyptian rebellion. Finally, some connect Ezra with administrators (šatammu) in temple collectives (puḫru) common in Babylon in the Persian period. Such administrators presided over temple assemblies that had economic power within provinces. Their administrators functioned more as facilitators of the community than as leaders.

The suggestion of high priest is not surprising in light of the long genealogy in Ezra 7, which links Ezra through *Zadok to Aaron. However, he is never called "high priest" in the text, only "priest," and is not connected intimately with the temple. Similarly, he is not afforded the title of governor, neither in the letter of Artaxerxes nor in the surrounding narrative material, and does not appear to wield the power of a governor (cf. Neh 5). As for the role of commissioner for Jewish affairs, evidence of such a position for an official is not forthcoming for any other ethnic group in the Persian Empire. As for the link to a "citizen-temple community," the theory of such a community in Yehud has come under considerable critique in recent years, not least because the temple in Jerusalem does not appear to be an economic center. Should we then concur with L. L. Grabbe that the "closer one looks, the more enigmatic Ezra's

mission becomes" and conclude that "Ezra's mission is a puzzle" (Grabbe 1994, 297-98; cf. Grabbe 1991)? An investigation of the letter of Artaxerxes and Ezra's subsequent behavior suggests that Ezra's role was focused on a legal and judicial agenda, even though he was able to secure significant support from the crown for the temple and its services.

In the text of Ezra and Nehemiah, Ezra is described as both *priest* and *scribe*. The first of these two terms may merely be a reference to his sociological position within the Jewish community, explaining why he was chosen for the particular task. The second term is one that does appear in Persian period texts and can signify a particular office within the imperial administration, although it also can be a designation for someone involved in scribal activity. Whether or not these terms can be linked to a specific office within Jewish or Persian culture does not matter, for the letter of Artaxerxes reveals that Ezra has been commissioned by the king for specific tasks and thus functioned as representative of the emperor. Such appointments which circumvent the satrapal system are not uncommon in the Persian context—for instance, the appointment of both military and political leaders within a satrapy along with royal inspectors (see Briant, 66-67, 338-47).

According to the letter of Artaxerxes (Ezra 7:26), the legal role that Ezra was to play is connected both to the *law of God and to the law of the king. This link between divine and imperial law has prompted research on the role of the Persian Empire in establishing a legal foundation for the Jewish community. P. Frei argued that the Persians authorized some form of Jewish Torah as local law for the Persian province of Yehud beginning with Darius, and that this was the major impetus for the creation of the Torah. Frei highlights evidence in the early Persian period that imperial law was drawn from local legal traditions rather than imposed from Persia. Frei's theory has been challenged in recent years (see especially Watts), highlighting the difficulty of defining political and sociological realities in the period under discussion. In the end, however, one can say that there is evidence for the promulgation of law (whether in oral or written form, from imperial or divine authorities, over the entire satrapy or merely the province) in the early Persian period, and that Ezra's role is plausible in this context. One must, however, be careful in how this phenomenon is described. The role of a legal code in the ancient world is radically different from our Western models. It functioned symbolically to signal the authority of the king, but local oral traditions and precedents were used for deciding specific cases (Fried). Some have suggested that Ezra's agenda extended to the entire satrapy of Abar Nahara (Ezra 7:25), but this statement must be read in light of the introduction to the letter of Artaxerxes, which limits this to "Judah and Jerusalem" (Ezra 7:14). Therefore, Ezra came to fulfill some form of legal role for the Persian emperor. He also was used to transport significant resources from the crown for the maintenance of the temple cult in Jerusalem. The motivation on the part of the Persians most likely is linked to the control of a province that lay near a frontier of the empire and to the desire to continue the flow of taxation from this province through the temple to the crown. Although Ezra fulfilled his commission for the emperor, he takes this opportunity as priest and scribe to strengthen the temple and its services as well as to promulgate the law among the Jews of Yehud.

This promulgation is showcased both in Ezra 9—10 and in Nehemiah 8. In both cases the narrative depicts Ezra as taking a passive role, with the people as active agents, telling Ezra of violations (Ezra 9:1-2), instigating proceedings against offenders (Ezra 10:1-4), encouraging him to read the law to the people (Neh 8:1-2), gathering around him to read the law (Neh 8:13), and responding without exhortation (Neh 8:16). Clearly this is written to accentuate the eagerness of this community to obey the law, even if it reduces the narrative focus on Ezra's role as promoter of the law (see Eskenazi 1988). In Ezra 9—10 the focus is on the mixed-marriage issue, while in Nehemiah 8 the focus is on festal issues, possibly on the role of the law within a festal context, here the festival of the new moon (Neh 8:1-12), as well as on the role of the law as the basis for the festal calendar, here the Feast of Tabernacles (Neh 8:13-18). Here we see the use of law as direction for the social as well as liturgical dimensions of the Jewish community.

5. The Shape of the Law.

The pseudepigraphical book 4 Ezra relates the story of Ezra's role in the restoration of the Scriptures after their destruction by fire in the destruction of Jerusalem (4 Ezra 14). According to this account, God delivers afresh not only the Torah of Moses through Ezra and his five scribes, but also the other twenty-three books of the Hebrew Bible and seventy additional books that were to be reserved only for the "wise" among the people. This view supports the common assumption that the law that Ezra was to promulgate among the people was the Torah in the form that we possess today. This connection between Ezra and the completed book of the law appears to be supported by the descriptive phrases "the law of Moses" (Ezra 7:6); "the law of YHWH" (Ezra 7:10); "the book of the law (of God)" (Neh 8:3, 14); "law which YHWH had commanded through Moses" (Neh 8:14). This view, however, has not been universally accepted in modern scholarship.

Some scholars, based on their dating of the final form of the Torah and evidence of the actual laws cited in the Ezra material, have suggested that the law of Ezra is one of the more limited streams of Torah tradition such as the Priestly source, the Holiness Code or the book of Deuteronomy. Others see here a collection of laws based on Torah tradition. Still others make a distinction between the law (*tôrâ*) of Ezra found in Ezra 7:10 and Nehemiah 8 and the law (*dāt*) that Artaxerxes entrusted into his care in his commission (Ezra 7:12-26), with the latter being merely a civil code developed by Artaxerxes.

A definitive answer to this question is beyond our grasp, but a few points are in order. First, as already noted in relation to Frei's theory (see 4 above), there is evidence that in the early Persian period law codes from local traditions were affirmed within the Persian empire, a fact that reminds us to avoid drawing too strong a line between secular (Persian *dāt*) and sacred (Jewish Torah) legal codes. This point is bolstered by the reference to "the law(s) of your God" alongside a reference to the "law of the king" in Ezra 7:25-26. Second, there is evidence in the application of Torah to the issue of the foreign wives in Ezra 9—10 and the response of the people to the reading of the law in Nehemiah 8:13-18 that the law of Ezra contained legislation from both the Priestly and the Deuteronomic legal streams (compare: [1] Ezra 9:1 with Deut 7:1; 23:3; Lev 18; [2] Ezra 9:2 with Deut 7:3; Lev 19:19; [3] Ezra 9:11-12 with Deut 7:1-3; 11:8; 23:6; Lev 18:24-30; [4] Neh 8:14-15 with Lev 23; Deut 16:15; see Williamson 1987, 94-98; Boda, 69-70). Third, clearly the language used of the law in Nehemiah 8 alludes to a written form of the law that could be seen in an assembled group and that took a substantial period of the day to read (Ezra 8:3). This evidence shows that Ezra possessed a substantial written form of the Torah that incorporated both the Priestly and the Deuteronomic streams of legal tradition.

6. The Divorces.

The final glimpse of Ezra in the book that bears his name is one of a man leading the people through an exercise in which they put away "foreign" wives. Ezra is cast as a passive character (see Eskenazi 1988). He is approached by Jews who claim that their compatriots have taken foreign wives. Rather than directly attacking the people, he prays in their presence a prayer that echoes the style of a prophetic covenant lawsuit (see Boda). This prayer is contagious among the people, leading them to similar rites and ultimately prompting them to approach him to rectify their predicament. He calls for a tribunal to which the people are to come voluntarily and resolve their disobedience. The book ends with the record of those involved in the legal proceedings. There are many dimensions to this key event in Ezra's career, but here we investigate three issues: (1) the identity of the foreign women; (2) the interpretation of the Torah that justified the divorces; (3) the purpose of the divorces.

The precise identity of these "foreign women" has been a point of debate (Smith-Christopher; Eskenazi and Judd). They could have been Jewish females from a different community than those of the exiles who dominated Yehud, or foreign females from traditional neighbors of Israel (Ammon, Moab) or more distant nations (Persia, Greece, Egypt). Although it is true that Ezra 9—10 reveals a deep disagreement between those associated with Ezra and another group among whom were many priests (see Ezra 10:18-24), this does not necessarily mean that the "foreign" women were merely Jews who had not been in exile. Furthermore, although it is true that the list of nations in Ezra 9:1 is a stock list used throughout the Hebrew tradition, this does not mean that it loses its significance as metaphor for those who are ethnically not Jewish. Sociological analysis of the phenomenon of mixed marriages leads D. Smith-Christopher to conclude in the case of Nehemiah that the "guilty are males who are

presumably attempting to 'marry up' to exchange their low status of 'exiles' for participation in aristocratic society" (Smith-Christopher, 260). Smith-Christopher continues by showing from Persian and Greek sources that intermarriage was encouraged as imperial policy to consolidate the power of the ruling elite. This appears to be the case in the intermarriage between the families of the governor of Samaria and the high priest in Jerusalem (Neh 13:28) and would relate as well to the kind of community of Ezra's day that recently had experienced threat from imperial or intrasatrapal forces (see Ezra 4:7-23).

The issue of the "foreign women" provides some insight into the interpretation of the law by Ezra and his followers. In the prayer proper, which begins at Ezra 9:10, Ezra introduces the basis for his concern in Ezra 9:11 with the Hebrew formula *lēʾmōr* ("saying"). What follows is a citation of the Torah that J. Milgrom argues reveals that Ezra is using an interpretive technique called "halachic midrash": "D's limited prohibition on intermarriages (Deut 23:4; cf. Neh 13:1-3, 23-27) is extended to all exogamous union. Next, Ezra derives from D (Deut 7:6; 14:2, 21; 26:19; 28:9) that Israel is a sanctum and from P that trespass upon sancta merits divine punishment. . . . Ezra fuses them into a legal midrash directed against Israel itself which has allowed the 'enemy' to infiltrate by means of intermarriage. Thus, Israel, the 'holy seed,' has been adulterated" (Milgrom, 72-73). H. G. M. Williamson has noted a similar technique at work in the words of "the leaders" who approached Ezra with the intermarriage dilemma in Ezra 9:1-2, a technique in which "several originally quite separate laws (Deut 7:1, 3; 23:3; Lev 18:3; 19:19) are being brought into combination with each other in order to establish new guidelines for the life of the people" (Williamson 1987, 96). This technique thus employs a series of textual bites from both Deuteronomic and Priestly materials to create a collage (Blenkinsopp 1988, 184) or "mosaic" (Clines 1984, 124; Williamson 1985, 137), a technique that can be discerned also in Nehemiah 10 (see Clines 1981).

There has been much debate over the purpose behind Ezra's call to put away the foreign wives and their children (see Janzen). Some have traced this to religious reasons: the wives had to be removed in order to prevent apostasy through idolatry. Others have cited ethnic reasons: the wives threatened the preservation of ethnic identity, key to the continuance of the Jewish community, especially in light of the loss of control over their national affairs. Related to this are economic and political implications of such a loss, because of potential threat either to the inheritance of the land or to Persian structures for the control of the land. Finally, there is the possibility that the drastic measures in Ezra 9—10 are related to a ritualized act of purification that sought to purify the society of a perceived social evil that was seen (without proof) as the cause of social dissension in the community (similar to a witch hunt). Each of these suggestions appears to contain some kernel of truth. However, close attention to the evidence in the record of Ezra 9—10, especially the argument displayed in the prayer of Ezra in Ezra 9, reveals that the concern for ethnic purity is directly related to concern over idolatry, in particular because it was this sin that is linked to the stain that brought the exile in the first place. Ethnic purity is related to this, and surely the conclusion of the process leads to a cleansing using ritual purity language from the priestly stream in Israel. There most likely were economic and political reasons for this (especially as outlined by Hoglund), but this does not preclude the religious concern expressed in the one text that speaks of it specifically.

See also Ezra and Nehemiah, Books of; History of Israel 8: Postexilic Community; Law; Nehemiah; Postexilic Temple; Priests and Levites; State Officials.

Bibliography. N. Avigad, *Bullae and Seals from a Post-Exilic Judean Archive* (Qedem 4; Jerusalem: Hebrew University, 1976); T. A. Bergren, "Ezra and Nehemiah Square Off in the Apocrypha and Pseudepigrapha," in *Biblical Figures Outside the Bible*, ed. M. E. Stone and T. A. Bergren (Harrisburg, PA: Trinity Press International, 1998) 340-65; J. L. Berquist, *Judaism in Persia's Shadow: A Social and Cultural Approach* (Philadelphia: Fortress, 1995); J. Blenkinsopp, *Ezra-Nehemiah: A Commentary* (OTL; Philadelphia: Westminster, 1988); idem, "The Mission of Udjahorresnet and Those of Ezra and Nehemiah," *JBL* 106 (1987) 409-21; M. J. Boda, *Praying the Tradition: The Origin and Use of Tradition in Nehemiah 9* (BZAW 277; Berlin: de Gruyter, 1999); P. Briant, *From Cyrus to Alexander: A History of the Persian Empire* (Winona Lake, IN: Eisenbrauns, 2002); J. Bright, *A History of Israel* (4th ed.; Louisville: Westminster/John Knox, 2000); D. J. A. Clines, *Ezra, Nehemiah, Esther* (NCB; London: Marshall, Morgan & Scott, 1984); idem, "Nehemiah 10 as an Example of Early Jewish Biblical Exegesis," *JSOT* 21 (1981) 111-17; B. Conklin, review of *Handbuch des nordwestsemitischen Briefformulars*, by D. Schwiderski, *JSS* 48 (2003) 137-40; P. R. Davies, ed., *Second Temple Studies, 1: Persian Period* (JSOTSup 117; Sheffield: Sheffield Academic Press, 1991) (in Davies 1991 see esp. Hoglund, 54-72; Smith, 73-97; Grabbe, 98-106; Halligan, 146-53); A. Demsky, "Who Came First, Ezra or Nehemiah? The Synchronistic Approach," *HUCA* 65 (1994) 1-19; M. Duggan, *The Covenant Renewal in Ezra-Nehemiah (Neh 7:72b-10:40): An Exegetical, Literary, and Theological Study* (SBLDS 164; Atlanta: Society of Biblical Literature, 2001); J. A. Emerton, "Did Ezra Go to Jerusalem in 428 B.C.?" *JTS* n.s. 17 (1966) 1-10; T. C. Eskenazi, "Current Perspectives on Ezra-Nehemiah and the Persian Period," *CurBS* 1 (1993) 59-86; idem, *In an Age of Prose: A Literary Approach to Ezra-Nehemiah* (SBLMS 36; Atlanta: Scholars Press, 1988); T. C. Eskenazi and E. P. Judd, "Marriage to a Stranger in Ezra 9-10," in *Second Temple Studies, 2: Temple and Community in the Persian Period*, ed. T. C. Eskenazi and K. H. Richards (JSOTSup 175; Sheffield: JSOT, 1994) 266-85; T. C. Eskenazi and K. H. Richards, eds., *Second Temple Studies, 2: Temple and Community in the Persian Period* (JSOTSup 175; Sheffield: JSOT, 1994); P. Frei, "Zentralgewalt und Lokalautonomie im Achämenidenreich," in *Reichsidee und Reichsorganisation im Perserreich*, ed. P. Frei and K. Koch (OBO 55; Göttingen: Vandenhoeck & Ruprecht, 1996) 5-132; L. S. Fried, "'You Shall Appoint Judges': Ezra's Mission and the Rescript of Artaxerxes," in *Persia and Torah: The Theory of Imperial Authorization of the Pentateuch*, ed. J. W. Watts (SBLSymS 17; Atlanta: Society of Biblical Literature, 2001) 63-89; G. Garbini, *History and Ideology in Ancient Israel* (New York: Crossroad, 1988); L. L. Grabbe, "Reconstructing History from the Book of Ezra," in *Second Temple Studies, 1: Persian Period*, ed. P. R. Davies (JSOTSup 117; Sheffield: Sheffield Academic Press, 1991) 98-106; idem, "What Was Ezra's Mission?" in *Second Temple Studies, 2: Temple and Community in the Persian Period*, ed. T. C. Eskenazi and K. H. Richards (JSOTSup 175; Sheffield: JSOT, 1994) 286-99; S. Grätz, *Das Edikt des Artaxerxes: Eine Untersuchung zum religionspolitischen und historischen Umfeld von Esra 7,12-26*

(BZAW 337; Berlin: de Gruyter, 2004); **M. Heltzer,** "The Right of Ezra to Demand Obedience to 'The Laws of the King' from Gentiles of the V Satrapy (Ez 7:25-26)," *ZABR* 4 (1998) 192-96; **K. G. Hoglund,** *Achaemenid Imperial Administration in Syria-Palestine and the Mission of Ezra and Nehemiah* (SBLDS 125; Atlanta: Scholars Press, 1992); **D. Janzen,** *Witch-hunts, Purity and Social Boundaries: The Expulsion of the Foreign Women in Ezra 9-10* (JSOTSup 350; Sheffield: Sheffield Academic Press, 2002); **R. A. Kraft,** "'Ezra' Materials in Judaism and Christianity," *ANRW* II.19.1:119-36; **L. McFall,** "Was Nehemiah Contemporary with Ezra in 458 BC?" *WTJ* 53 (1991) 263-93; **C. L. Meyers and E. M. Meyers,** *Haggai, Zechariah 1-8* (AB 25B; Garden City, NY: Doubleday, 1987); **E. M. Meyers,** "The Shelomith Seal and Aspects of the Judean Restoration: Some Additional Reconsiderations," *ErIsr* 18 (1985) 33*-38*; **J. Milgrom,** *Cult and Conscience: The Asham and the Priestly Doctrine of Repentance* (SJLA 18; Leiden: E. J. Brill, 1976); **V. Pavlovský,** "Die Chronologie der Tätigkeit Esdras: Versuch einer neuen Lösung," *Bib* 38 (1957) 275-305, 428-56; **G. G. Porton,** "Ezra in Rabbinic Literature," in *Restoration: Old Testament, Jewish and Christian Conceptions,* ed. J. M. Scott (JSJSup 72; Leiden: E. J. Brill, 2001) 305-33; **D. Schwiderski,** *Handbuch des nordwestsemitischen Briefformulars: Ein Bei-trag zur Echtheitsfrage der aramäischen Briefe des Esrabuches* (BZAW 295; Berlin: de Gruyter, 2000); **J. R. Shaver,** "Ezra and Nehemiah: On the Theological Significance of Making Them Contemporaries," in *Priests, Prophets and Scribes: Essays on the Formation and Heritage of Second Temple Judaism in Honour of Joseph Blenkinsopp,* ed. E. Ulrich, J. W. Wright and R. P. Carroll (JSOTSup 149; Sheffield: JSOT Press, 1992) 76-86; **D. Smith-Christopher,** "The Mixed Marriage Crisis in Ezra 9-10 and Nehemiah 13: A Study of the Sociology of Post-Exilic Judaean Community," in *Second Temple Studies, 2: Temple and Community in the Persian Period,* ed. T. C. Eskenazi and K. H. Richards (JSOTSup 175; Sheffield: JSOT, 1994) 243-65; **M. A. Throntveit,** "Linguistic Analysis and the Question of Authorship in Chronicles, Ezra and Nehemiah," *VT* 32 (1982) 201-16; **C. C. Torrey,** *The Composition and Historical Value of Ezra-Nehemiah* (BZAW 2; Giessen: J. Ricker, 1896); **J. W. Watts,** ed., *Persia and Torah: The Theory of Imperial Authorization of the Pentateuch* (SBLSymS 17; Atlanta: Society of Biblical Literature, 2001); **J. P. Weinberg,** *The Citizen-Temple Community* (JSOTSup 151; Sheffield: Sheffield Academic Press, 1992); **H. G. M. Williamson,** "Exile and After: Historical Study," in *The Face of Old Testament Studies: A Survey of Contemporary Approaches,* ed. D. W. Baker and B. T. Arnold (Grand Rapids: Baker, 1999) 236-65; idem, *Ezra and Nehemiah* (OTG; Sheffield: JSOT, 1987); idem, "The Governors of Judah under the Persians," *TynBul* 39 (1988) 59-82.

M. J. Boda

EZRA AND NEHEMIAH, BOOKS OF

Ezra and Nehemiah are the most important sources for the history of the Jewish community after the return of exiles from their "Babylonian captivity." Under the leadership of *Zerubbabel, *Ezra and *Nehemiah, the Jewish community succeeded in rebuilding the temple (*see* Postexilic Temple), reviving allegiance to the Torah, rebuilding the city wall of *Jerusalem and repopulating the city. These accounts highlight the importance of the temple and its personnel (*see* Priests and Levites). Of vital importance were the attempts to keep the community pure from the syncretistic influence of the neighbors who surrounded it. The experience of *prayer, fasting, repentance and exposition of the Torah (Neh 8) set the pattern for the later development of synagogue services.

1. Historical Background
2. Text and Canon
3. Relation to Chronicles
4. The Order of Ezra and Nehemiah
5. Sources and Narrative Composition
6. The Ezra Memoirs
7. The Nehemiah Memoirs
8. Relation to Esdras
9. The Message of Ezra and Nehemiah

1. Historical Background.

1.1. Assyrian Invasions and Deportations. Tiglath-pileser III, who brought an end to the Aramaean kingdom of Damascus in 732 BCE, also attacked Galilee and Gilead and began the first deportations of Israelites (2 Kings 15:29), carrying off at least 13,520 people to *Assyria (*ANET,* 283-84). Ten years later Sargon II claimed the capture of *Samaria, the capital of the northern kingdom of Israel (2 Kings 17:6; 18:10). Sargon boasted that he carried off 27,290 persons from Israel, replacing them with other populations from Mesopotamia and Syria (*ANET,* 284-87). Some of those deportees can be identified from cuneiform texts, but since the Israelites had already departed from a strict devotion to Yahweh and had no compunction about intermarriage, they soon were assimilated and became the so-called lost tribes of Israel. Sennacherib, after his invasion of Judah, boasted that he deported 200,150 people, a problematic number (Yamauchi 2002, 357).

Ezra 4:2 reports that some of those whose offer to help was rejected were brought to the region by the Assyrian king Esarhaddon. Surveys by A. Zertal in the area of Samaria have identified the numerous new sites occupied by those people brought into the area by the Assyrians, and have found at a number of sites a particular type of bowl with decorations similar to cuneiform writing, which is the first archaeological evidence of these newcomers.

1.2. Babylonian Invasions. Although we have no extrabiblical evidence for Nebuchadnezzar's assault against Jerusalem in 605 BCE (Dan 1:1), we do have confirmation of his attack upon Jerusalem in 597 BCE from the Babylonian Chronicles. After the Jews rebelled again, Nebuchadnezzar attacked in 587 or 586 BCE, destroying the *Solomonic temple. The invasions wreaked havoc and left only small, poor villages in their wake. Excavations by N. Avigad, K. Kenyon, Y. Shiloh and E. Mazar in various parts of Jerusalem have uncovered evidence of the Babylonian attacks (Lipschits, 132).

On the other hand, archaeological evidence confirms the biblical record that the *Babylonians spared the cities of Benjamin to the north of Jerusalem, and made *Mizpah (Tell en-Nasbeh) their provincial capital. Archaeological evidence and inscriptions reveal that the *Phoenicians occupied the Philistine coast, and that the *Edomites occupied the area south of *Hebron.

1.2.1. Babylonian Deportations. One striking difference between the earlier Assyrian deportations and those of the Babylonians is that the former brought newcomers into the land of Israel, whereas the Babylonians did not do the same with the land of Judah. The biblical references to the numbers of people deported by the Babylonians are incomplete and have given rise to differing interpretations. In 597 BCE Nebuchadnezzar carried off a total of 10,000 fighting men, craftsmen and artisans (2 Kings 24:14); he also deported 7,000 fighting men and 1,000 craftsmen (2 Kings 24:16). On the other hand,

Jeremiah enumerates for 597 BCE only 3,023 captives (Jer 52:28), and for 586 BCE 832 from Jerusalem (Jer 52:29). In 582 BCE, after the murder of the governor Gedaliah, 745 were deported, for a grand total of 4,600 (Jer 52:30).

Population estimates for Judah have varied widely, from 250,000 to 80,000, as well as the proportion of those deported, from 50 percent to 10 percent. R. Albertz (88) recently calculated that 25 percent of a population of 80,000 were deported.

1.2.2. Jews in Exile. Light is shed on the Jews in Mesopotamia who did not return to their homeland by the archive of the Murashu family, wealthy bankers and brokers, dated to the reigns of Artaxerxes I, Darius II and Artaxerxes II (from 454 to 404 BCE), whose clients included many Jews (Yamauchi 2002). A remarkable cuneiform tablet from the reign of Darius I has shed new light on a number of Jews who lived in uru ia-a-hu-du, "the city of Judah" (Joannès and Lemaire). Aramaic letters from a Jewish military garrison on Elephantine Island in Upper Egypt, serving during the Persian occupation, provide information about another Jewish community, its social and legal practices, and its religious accommodations.

1.2.3. "The Empty Land." H. M. Barstad, in an influential monograph, has attempted to overturn the "myth of the empty land," the impression given by the hyperbolic language of Chronicles that the deportations had left Palestine essentially desolate. Barstad minimizes the effects of the Babylonian invasions, stresses the essential continuity of life in Judah, and characterizes Ezra and Nehemiah as giving a one-sided view that completely overlooks any possible contribution of those who remained in the land. Some have cited the discovery in Jerusalem at Ketef Hinnom of the tomb of a wealthy family as supporting an element of continuity even after the destruction of the temple. However, this may be an isolated rather than a representative case. Since it was the upper classes that were deported, leaving behind the poorest of the land (2 Kings 25:12; Jer 39:10; 52:16) to work the vineyards and the fields, it is not surprising that it was the returning exiles who provided the spiritual and political leadership that enabled Judaism to evolve. A. Faust refutes Barstad's view that there was continuity in rural Judah. B. Oded cites archaeological and textual evidence to show that Judah was bereft of leadership until the exiles returned.

1.3. The Persian Empire. The *Persian Empire, established by the Achaemenids, extended from India to Cush (Esther 1:1) and lasted from 550 BCE until Alexander's conquests (336-323 BCE).

1.3.1. Cyrus. Cyrus was the founder of the Persian Empire and was the greatest Achaemenid king. He reigned over the Persians from 559 to 530 BCE. He established Persian dominance over the Medes in 550 BCE, conquered Lydia and Ionia in 547-546 BCE, and captured Babylon in 539 BCE. It was Cyrus who permitted Jews who wished to do so to return to their homeland (Ezra 1:1; 6:3). In the book of Isaiah, Cyrus is spoken of as the Lord's "shepherd" (Is 44:28) and "anointed one" (Is 45:1).

1.3.2. Darius. After the death of Cambyses, who is not mentioned in the Hebrew Scriptures, and the seven month usurpation of a magos named Gaumata/Smerdis, Darius I (522-486 BCE) established himself as an effective ruler, but not before suppressing numerous revolts, an accomplishment memorialized in his famous Behistun Inscription. It was under Darius that the second temple finally was completed in 515 BCE (Ezra 6:15).

1.3.3. Xerxes. Xerxes (485-465 BCE), who is called Ahasuerus in the book of Esther, is best known for his war with Greece, as recounted by Herodotus. His massive army and navy invaded Greece in 480 BCE, but they were defeated in the famous battles at Salamis in 480 BCE and at Plataea in 479 BCE. During his reign a charge of disloyalty was brought against the Jews by their neighbors.

1.3.4. Artaxerxes I. Artaxerxes I (464-424 BCE) faced a major revolt in *Egypt upon his accession. The Athenians sent two hundred ships to aid the rebels. In 459 BCE they helped capture Memphis, the capital of Lower Egypt. If we assume the traditional order of Ezra and Nehemiah (see 4 below), Ezra's return in 458 BCE may have been facilitated by the Persian king to secure a loyal buffer state in Palestine. Nehemiah served as the king's cupbearer (Neh 2:1) before he was commissioned to serve as the Persian governor of Judah.

1.3.5. "Beyond the River." The Jewish territory of Yehud belonged to the satrapy called Abar Nahara, "Beyond the River" (Ezra 4:10, 11, 16, 17, 20). The governor of Beyond the River who came to investigate the conflict between the Jews and their neighbors was Tattenai (Ezra 5:3, 6; 6:6, 13), who appears in cuneiform sources as Tattannu and is known to have held this position between 520 and 502 BCE.

1.3.6. Persian Authorities and Their Subjects. Ezra-Nehemiah presents the Persian kings as bestowing numerous favors upon their Jewish subjects, from allowing those who wish to return to their homeland to do so, to returning the carefully inventoried vessels to their former temple, to offering financial assistance to them for the rebuilding of their new temple. This was in marked contrast to the harsh policies of deportation practiced by the Assyrians and the Babylonians. Some have ascribed this enlightened behavior to Cyrus's Zoroastrianism, but that monarch's allegiance to this religion is not certain, though there is no doubt that Darius I was a devoted follower of Ahura Mazda (Yamauchi 1990, 419-26).

In an influential monograph K. G. Hoglund has clarified the mission of Ezra and the refortification of Jerusalem by Nehemiah as part of the imperial Persian strategy against the dangers of Athenian imperialism, which included the coastal Palestinian city of Dor in its Delian League. Extrabiblical examples of local leaders who cooperated (collaborated, some would say) with Persian authorities may be cited, most notably an Egyptian priest named Udjahorresnet, who served both Cambyses and Darius I. Since Darius I authorized the codification of Egyptian laws, some scholars have argued that Artaxerxes I may have had a similar motive in sending Ezra back to establish the Torah.

2. Text and Canon.

2.1. Text. The Masoretic Text of Ezra-Nehemiah has been relatively well transmitted, with few corruptions. The differences between the identical lists of Ezra 2 and Nehemiah 7 can be explained by the difficulty of transmitting numbers and the confusion of certain letters. Only three small fragments (4QEzra) of the Hebrew and Aramaic text of Ezra 4:2-11; 5:17; 6:1-5 have been found among the Dead Sea Scrolls. On the assumption that Ezra-Nehemiah was one book, only Esther is unrepresented in the extant biblical scrolls from Qumran.

Apart from Daniel, which, like Ezra, contains significant Aramaic passages, Ezra-Nehemiah is the only book in the Hebrew canon lacking a Targum (Aramaic paraphrase). This is one factor, along with calques—Hebrew forms occurring in a manner expected of Aramaic morphology and syntax—that inclines D. Marcus to suggest that Nehemiah may originally have been composed in Aramaic (*see* Aramaic Language).

2.2. Ezra-Nehemiah. In the Hebrew Bible Ezra and Nehemiah were reckoned as one book. The division into two books dates to Origen; its division was followed by Jerome in the Vulgate and then adopted into the printed Hebrew Bibles. J. VanderKam expresses a minority view when he holds that both books took shape separately rather than as the result of a single author/editor.

3. Relation to Chronicles.

3.1. The Chronicler. Inasmuch as *Chronicles ends with verses (2 Chron 36:22-23) practically identical to Ezra 1:1-3a and has many words and themes similar to those found in Ezra-Nehemiah, it had been a scholarly consensus for a century and a half that a so-called Chronicler was the author of both Chronicles and of Ezra-Nehemiah (*see* Chronicler's History). Writing early in the twentieth century, C. C. Torrey regarded the Chronicler as manufacturing historical fiction. A few scholars today take the "minimalist" view that the exile is a fiction created by Jewish writers in the Hellenistic era.

Although not as dismissive of the Chronicler's accuracy as was Torrey, a number of important scholars (e.g., Blenkinsopp; D. Talshir) still defend the thesis of a common authorship by the "Chronicler" of Chronicles and Ezra-Nehemiah. For example, in both Chronicles and Ezra-Nehemiah the descriptions of the building of the first and second temples are done in parallel ways; both show great interest in sacred vessels and liturgical music.

3.2. Differences with Chronicles. Beginning with a seminal essay by S. Japhet in 1968, followed by additional arguments by Williamson in 1977, many scholars abandoned the theory of a common authorship because of the differences that have been noted by these scholars. For example, Chronicles is especially concerned to exalt the Davidic line, while Ezra-Nehemiah displays little interest in David. Ezra-Nehemiah denounces Solomon's foreign wives, whereas Chronicles simply omits this subject. On the other hand, Ezra-Nehemiah emphasizes Moses and the exodus, whereas

Chronicles does not.

4. The Order of Ezra and Nehemiah.

4.1. The Traditional and the Reverse Order. No one questions that Nehemiah came to Jerusalem in the twentieth year of Artaxerxes I in 445 BCE. The traditional order holds that Ezra preceded Nehemiah in the seventh year of this same king, 458 BCE. But for a variety of complex arguments, some scholars have opted for a reverse order, placing Ezra after Nehemiah in the seventh year of Artaxerxes II, 398 BCE. The placement of Ezra after Nehemiah once was a part of "critical orthodoxy" and included the arguments that follow here.

4.2. The List of Priests. (1) Ezra 10:6 mentions that Ezra went to the chamber of "Jehohanan the son of Eliashib." (2) Nehemiah 12:10-11 mentions Jonathan the son of Joiada, who was the son of Eliashib. (3) Nehemiah 12:22 mentions a Johanan after Joiada and before Jaddua, and Nehemiah 12:23 identifies Johanan as the son of Eliashib. (4) The Elephantine papyri (dated 411-410 BCE) refer to Johanan as high priest (*ANET,* 492). (5) Josephus (*Ant.* 11.297-301) refers to a Johanan who killed his brother Jesus.

Are all five persons the same individual? Scholars who believe so reason that in Nehemiah 12:11 "Jonathan" is an error for "Johanan" and that Nehemiah 12:23 indicates that Johanan was the descendant (i.e., grandson) of Eliashib. They argue that since the Elephantine papyri indicate that Johanan was high priest in 410 BCE, it is more likely that Ezra came twelve years later in the seventh year of Artaxerxes II (398 BCE) rather than forty-eight years earlier under Artaxerxes I (458 BCE). If these identifications are correct, this reasoning provides one of the strongest arguments for reversing the order of Ezra and Nehemiah.

There are, however, a number of strong objections to such a reconstruction. For example, would Ezra have consorted with a known murderer, as he would have if he had arrived in 398 BCE? This would have been the case if we identify Ezra's Jehohanan with the Jehohanan of Josephus. Such an identification would be undermined if Jehohanan was the son of Eliashib and the brother of Joiada rather than the grandson of Eliashib. The name *Jehohanan (Johanan),* after all, was a most common one; it was used by fourteen different individuals in the OT, five in Maccabees, and seventeen in Josephus. In Ezra 10:6, moreover, Jehohanan is not identified as a high priest.

A certain Jaddua, the son of Jonathan, is mentioned in Nehemiah 12:11, 22. Josephus (*Ant.* 11.302-307) identified this Jaddua with the high priest at the time of Alexander's invasion of Palestine, but Josephus probably was mistaken and wrongly identified the Hellenistic Jaddua with his grandfather.

4.3. The Contemporaneity of Ezra and Nehemiah. As the text stands, Nehemiah and Ezra are noted together in Nehemiah 8:9 at the reading of the law, and in Nehemiah 12:26, 36 at the dedication of the wall. Because Nehemiah's name is lacking in the 1 Esdras 9:49 parallel to Nehemiah 8:9, it has been argued that Nehemiah's name was inserted as a gloss. It has also been claimed that Nehemiah 12:26, 36 were added to the original text. Those who adopt the reverse order must of necessity excise these references to the contemporaneity of Ezra and Nehemiah, and even many scholars who accept the traditional order (e.g., Blenkinsopp) reject them.

But to excise the name of Ezra from Nehemiah 12:26, 36 would leave one procession without a leader. That references to the contemporaneity of Ezra and Nehemiah are few is readily explicable. We have other examples of contemporary OT figures who do not refer to each other—for example, Jeremiah and Ezekiel, Haggai and Zechariah.

4.4. Mixed Marriages and the Alleged Failure of Ezra. Both Ezra (Ezra 9—10) and Nehemiah (Neh 13:23-27) dealt with the problem of mixed marriages. Ezra adopted a more rigorous approach, demanding the dissolution of all such marriages. Apart from the expulsion of Joiada, Nehemiah simply forbade future mixed marriages. Some hold that Ezra's handling most naturally follows Nehemiah's attempt and regard this as the strongest argument for the reverse order. But the idea that a more rigorous handling of the problem should come later is purely subjective. Closely allied to the preceding argument is the often-expressed idea that if he had preceded Nehemiah, Ezra must have failed, since Nehemiah had to correct the same abuse. But the converse argument could be made: if Nehemiah preceded Ezra, the former must have failed. As a matter of note, Nehemiah deals with but isolated instances of mixed marriages with the women of Ashdod (Neh 13:23-27), who are characterized as being like the women of Am-

mon and Moab of old (cf. Deut 23:3).

4.5. The Current Consensus. Only a few recent scholars, such as R. Albertz, now support the reverse order of Ezra and Nehemiah. J. Bright, in his influential history of Israel, favored an intermediate position that maintains the contemporaneity of the two men but places Ezra later than the traditional order by a textual emendation of the seventh to the thirty-seventh year of Artaxerxes I, 428 BCE. The overwhelming majority of current scholars now support the traditional order of Ezra's priority over Nehemiah. These include J. Blenkinsopp, D. J. Clines, F. M. Cross, R. W. Klein and H. G. M. Williamson.

5. Sources and Narrative Composition.

5.1. The Book of Zerubbabel (Ezra 1—6). The introductory chapters relate the story of the initial return of the Jews after Cyrus's conquest of Babylon, the laying of the altar under Sheshbazzar, the completion of the temple under Zerubbabel, and conclude with the celebration of the Passover. Williamson (1985, xxxiv-xxxvi) has suggested that Ezra 1—6 was composed after Chronicles in about 300 BCE as a polemic against the building of the Samaritan temple on Mount Gerizim. Klein, however, believes that the collaborative attitude toward the Persians in this section is an argument against such a late date. Clines (14) dates the books of Chronicles and of Ezra-Nehemiah within a few decades after the activities of Ezra and Nehemiah.

5.1.1. The Decree of Cyrus (Ezra 1:1-4). Many scholars have questioned the Hebrew version of Cyrus's decree because of the biblical, even prophetic, expressions in the text. New evidence indicates that Assyrian royal scribes were familiar with Hebrew (Dalley, 394-95). It may also be argued from the analogy of the trilingual Xanthos inscription (Briant, 704-9, 995-99) that Jews could have aided the chancellery in adapting the king's proclamation for the intended audience as the Lycians did. It may also be argued that it differed from the Aramaic memorandum in Ezra 6:3-5, inasmuch as it was an oral proclamation. There can be no doubt but that Cyrus's general policy was one of benevolence toward conquered subjects. The famous Akkadian document known as the Cyrus Cylinder indicates that upon the capture of Babylon, one of Cyrus's first acts was to return the gods that had been removed from their local sanctuaries by Nabonidus. It states, "I gathered all their inhabitants and returned (to them) their dwellings" (*COS* 2.124:315). Some cuneiform tablets have been interpreted as evidence for a deportation of Aramaeans from Neirab in northern Syria to southern Mesopotamia early in the reign of Nebuchadnezzar and then their repatriation under Cyrus, providing a striking parallel to the experience of the Jews (Timm).

5.1.2. Inventory of Temple Vessels (Ezra 1:9-11). The inventory of booty taken was carefully tabulated by the Assyrians and Babylonians, and no doubt by the Persians also, though we lack similar records from them. 2 Kings 25:14-15 describes how the Babylonians carried off the temple vessels. Jeremiah (Jer 28:1-17) rebuked Hananiah, who prophesied that these would be returned within two years. It was also customary to seize the gods of captured temples, such as the statue of Marduk from Babylon. However, since there was no idol in the Jewish temple, the closest substitute would have been the *ark of the covenant, but this, evidently, was destroyed by Nebuchadnezzar, since we no longer hear of it.

5.1.3. List of Returnees (Ezra 2:2-64). Despite some minor differences in names and numbers (about 8 percent of the total), it is quite clear that the list in Ezra 2 is identical with the list in Nehemiah 7. The list in Ezra is ostensibly the list of those who returned in response to the decree of Cyrus. But the large total numbers (an assembly of 42,360, plus 7,337 slaves and 200 singers [Ezra 2:64-65]) have inclined most scholars to regard this as a cumulative total of the returnees. Ezra 8:1-20 records additional exiles who returned with Ezra.

5.1.4. Sheshbazzar and Zerubbabel. The proposal that Sheshbazzar is to be identified with Shenazzar (1 Chron 3:18), the fourth son of Jehoiachin, and therefore a royal descendant of David, should be abandoned. Sheshbazzar, who is called "prince" in Ezra 1:8 and "governor" in Ezra 5:14, was presented the temple vessels by Cyrus and laid the foundations of the temple (Ezra 5:16).

Zerubbabel, whose name reveals his birth in Babylon, came after Sheshbazzar and resumed the work begun by his predecessor, some eighteen years later under Darius (Ezra 3:1-6). Zerubbabel is called *governor* in Haggai (Hag 2:20-23), but not in Ezra. As the grandson of Jehoiachin (1 Chron 3:19), he was of the royal line of David. Some believe that his exalted background raised messianic expectations (Hag 2:20-23). Others have gone beyond the biblical text to suggest that Zerubbabel was regarded as a veritable vassal king. His disappearance from the scene after Zechariah 4:6-10 has prompted some to suggest that Darius removed him or even had him killed, but this is simply speculation.

5.1.5. Aramaic Documents (Ezra 4:8-16, 17-22; 5:6-17; 6:3-12). The Aramaic documents probably were cited to provide authenticity, inasmuch as *Aramaic was the official international language of the Persian Empire, as its alphabetic script was much easier to write than the cuneiform used for Old Persian, Akkadian and Elamite in the royal inscriptions. These documents include a letter to Artaxerxes I (Ezra 4:8-16), a letter from Artaxerxes I (Ezra 4:17-22), a letter to Darius I (Ezra 5:6-17) and a letter of Darius citing an Aramaic memorandum of a decree of Cyrus (Ezra 6:3-12). The authenticity of the official Persian documents has been supported by the citation of extrabiblical sources by L. V. Hensley. An important cuneiform text examined by M. Heltzer corroborates the officials mentioned in Ezra 4. Note should be taken of a study by D. Schwiderski, who argues for a Hellenistic date for the Aramaic documents in Ezra 4—6.

When opposition to the Jewish attempt to rebuild the temple reached the ears of Tattenai, the governor of the province, he sent a letter to Darius (Ezra 5:7-12) and received a response from the king himself (Ezra 6:6-12). Some have questioned whether the Persian kings would have been personally interested in the affairs of the Jews in far-off Palestine, and whether they would have intervened directly. That such inquiries were sent directly to the king himself has been vividly illustrated by the publication of Elamite texts from Persepolis.

According to Ezra 6:8, Cyrus not only permitted the Jews to return, but also gave them carte blanche authorization for funds from the imperial treasury. Because the accounts in Haggai and Zechariah do not speak of support from the Persian treasury, scholars have questioned the promises made in this verse. Extrabiblical evidence, however, makes it quite clear that it was a consistent policy of Persian kings to help restore sanctuaries in their empire. Cyrus repaired the Eanna temple at Uruk and the Enunmah at Ur. Cambyses gave funds for the temple of Sais in Egypt at the behest of Udjahorresnet. The temple of Amon at Hibis in the Khargah oasis in Egypt was rebuilt by order of Darius. Both Cyrus's original decree and Darius's renewal of the permission to rebuild the temple specify that it should be refounded in Jerusalem—that is, on its original site. This was a matter of special concern in the restoration or rebuilding of temples (Hurowitz).

Priests and other temple personnel were given exemptions from enforced labor or taxes (Ezra 7:24). The Gadatas Inscription of Darius I to a governor in Ionia in western Turkey reveals the king's concern for the priests of Apollo at a temple near Magnesia (Briant, 491-93).

5.1.6. Haggai and Zechariah and the Temple. Important sources on the project of the rebuilding of the temple (*see* Postexilic Temple) are provided by the prophets Haggai and Zechariah (Ezra 5:1; 6:14). Haggai's proclamation is dated to 520 BCE and Zechariah's to 520-518 BCE. Because the temple's completion in 515 BCE is not mentioned in these prophets, it has been proposed that Haggai and Zechariah 1—8 may have been published in anticipation of the temple's dedication.

P. R. Bedford suggests that Haggai and Zechariah held out expectations that were not fully realized. The completion of the temple did not solve the issue of political autonomy. He believes that it was in defense of the continuing eastern Diaspora that Ezra and Nehemiah came to be written. J. P. Weinberg has proposed that Judah developed a unique "citizen-temple community," which consisted of a union of temple personnel and landowners. According to Weinberg, the Jerusalem temple, unlike other Near Eastern temples, had no land of its own. Weinberg's assumption that the whole of this community was exempted from Persian taxes is contradicted by Nehemiah 5:4; only the temple personnel were exempt (Ezra 7:24).

6. The Ezra Memoirs (Ezra 7—10; Neh 8—9).
The Ezra Memoirs, which combine first-person and third-person accounts, evidently stems from an editor who had access to a source by Ezra. Williamson (1999, 259) argues that the Ezra Memoirs are based on a report written by Ezra to Artaxerxes I.

6.1. Ezra 7—10. Ezra, who was both a priest and a skilled *scribe (Ezra 7:1-6), led a further group of nearly two thousand Jews to their homeland in 458 BCE (see 4.1 above). He was entrusted

with considerable treasures and given extraordinary powers, according to a letter of Artaxerxes I (Ezra 7:12-26). In contrast to Nehemiah, Ezra's caravan proceeded without an armed escort. The journey took four months (Ezra 7:9). When the problem of mixed marriages was brought to his attention, Ezra tore out his hair (Ezra 9:3). Ezra then uttered a prayer confessing the sins of his people (Ezra 9:6-15). An extraordinary convocation then gathered in the rain (Ezra 10:13) to hear Ezra's rebuke of their failings, leading to a dismissal of the foreign wives.

6.2. Nehemiah 8. Because Nehemiah 8 deals primarily with Ezra, a number of scholars believe that this chapter has been displaced. Williamson (1985, 283) argues that the dating system used in this chapter is consistent with the Ezra materials, where months are numbered, whereas in the Nehemiah Memoirs months are always referred to by name (Neh 1:1; 2:1; 6:15). By a repositioning of Nehemiah 8 between Ezra 8 and 9, Ezra's work is accomplished in a single year. He leaves Mesopotamia in the first month and arrives in Judah in the fifth month (Ezra 7:9). He then reads the law in the seventh month (Neh 8:2) rather than thirteen years later after Nehemiah's arrival. He concludes by dealing with the problem of mixed marriages on the first day of the first month (Ezra 10:17). This rearrangement, however, assumes that the mention of Nehemiah (Neh 8:9) is a redactional addition because the verb is singular and that the list of the signatories to the covenant, including Nehemiah (Neh 10:1), was an invention. D. R. Daniels, who is unpersuaded by Williamson's arguments, prefers to consider Nehemiah 8—10 as an integrated unit.

6.3. Nehemiah 9. Clines, who assigns Nehemiah 9 to the Ezra Memoirs, would place Nehemiah 8—9 after Ezra 8. Nehemiah 9, which is attributed to Ezra in the LXX, betrays a critical attitude toward kings (Neh 9:36-37), which contrasts with the generally favorable attitude toward the Persian monarchs found in the Ezra Memoirs. Williamson (1985, 306-7) suggests that Nehemiah 9:5b-37 (along with Is 63:7—64:12 and Ps 106) may have arisen out of liturgies recited at the site of the ruined temple (cf. Jer 41:4-5).

7. The Nehemiah Memoirs (Neh 1—7; 10—13).
The Nehemiah Memoirs are accepted by L. L. Grabbe, who is quite skeptical about the Ezra

Memoirs (Grabbe, 1.98-99). Williamson (1985, xxviii) suggests that Nehemiah originally composed the memoirs in Aramaic as a report to Artaxerxes I after a year in office, and then he revised it later to claim due credit for certain achievements that had not been acknowledged. Although defensive and self-glorifying monuments from Egypt and elsewhere have been cited as parallels, the Nehemiah Memoirs are not addressed to posterity as those were, but to God himself (Neh 5:19; 6:14; 13:14, 22, 29, 31). Williamson (1985, xxxiii-vi) believes that the Nehemiah Memoirs and the Ezra Memoirs were combined about 400 BCE.

7.1. The King's Cupbearer. Nehemiah, the cupbearer of Artaxerxes I, heard about the ruinous condition of the walls of Jerusalem and successfully petitioned the king for leave to rectify the situation. Empowered as the king's representative, he was accompanied by royal troops and given authorization to requisition timber from the royal forest (*pardes*). Nehemiah arrived in the twentieth year of the king's reign, 445 BCE. After staying for twelve years, he returned to Persia and then came back a second time (Neh 13:6).

7.2. Previous Governors. Against an older view that Judah was only a subprovince of Samaria, proposed despite Nehemiah's reference to previous governors (Neh 5:15), we now have bullae (seal impressions) that provide evidence of a series of governors prior to Nehemiah (Williamson 2004, 46-63). One seal bears the impression "property of Shelomith, the maid of Elnathan the Governor." If this Shelomith can be identified with Zerubbabel's daughter (1 Chron 3:19), then a case can be made that her husband married her to secure his succession to the office.

7.3. Rebuilding the Walls (Neh 3:1-32). Because this account is in the third-person, and because there is a reference to Nehemiah as "their lord," Williamson (1985, 201) holds that this was not authored by Nehemiah, but that it was included in the original Nehemiah Memoirs. Archaeological evidence includes the discovery of rubble on the eastern slope, which would have blocked the progress of Nehemiah's donkey (Neh 2:14), and the "Broad Wall" mentioned in Nehemiah 3:8, a wall probably built by *Hezekiah to enclose the Mishneh, a quarter to house refugees from the north.

7.4. Sanballat of Samaria. The returning exiles had come back to a tiny enclave completely surrounded by hostile neighbors: the Samarians to the north, the *Ammonites to the east, the Arabs and the Edomites to the south, the Phoenicians to the west. Numerous Phoenician inscriptions have been found along the coast. There had been opposition to the rebuilding of the temple. There was even greater concern about the attempt to rebuild the walls as Judah's neighbors learned of Nehemiah's plans. The opposition of the Samarians was motivated not primarily by religious differences, but by political considerations. The appearance of a vigorous governor of Judah threatened the authority of the governor of Samaria.

Nehemiah's chief opponent was *Sanballat the Horonite (Neh 2:10, 19; 4:1, 7; 6:1-2, 5, 12, 14; 13:28). His name is derived from Akkadian *Sin-uballiṭ*, which means "Sin [the moon god] has given life." The epithet *Horonite* identifies him as coming from one of three areas: Hauran east of the Sea of Galilee, Horonaim in Moab (Jer 48:34) or, most probably, upper or lower Beth-Horon, two key cities located twelve miles northwest of Jerusalem (Josh 10:10; 16:3, 5). S. Mittmann makes the rather dubious suggestion that Nehemiah's opponents Tobiah and Sanballat were members of families that had been repatriated with other exiles and then placed respectively by the Persian authorities over Ammon and over Hauran, the latter on the basis of Sanballat's identification as a Horonite.

Although Sanballat is not called *governor* in the book of Nehemiah, an important Elephantine papyrus makes his position explicit. A letter to Bagoas, the governor of Judah, refers to "Delaiah and Shelemiah, the sons of Sanballat the governor (*peḥâ*) of Samaria" (*ANET,* 492). It is interesting that Sanballat's sons both bear Yahwistic names.

In 1962 Bedouins found a cave in Wadi ed-Daliyeh, northwest of Jericho, which contained fourth-century BCE papyri. They were found with the grim remains of about two hundred men, women and children from Samaria who tried unsuccessfully to flee from the troops of Alexander the Great. As an indication of the syncretistic nature of the Samarian religion, we have among the papyri divine names such as Qos (Edomite), SHR (Aramaic), Chemosh (Moabite), Baʿal (Canaanite) and Nebo (Babylonian). F. M. Cross (1988), however, notes that the majority of the names are Yahwistic.

7.5. Tobiah of Ammon. The name *Tobiah* (Neh

2:10, 19) means "Yahweh is Good." No doubt he was a Yahwist, as is indicated also by the name of his son, *Jehohanan* (Neh 6:18), "Yahweh is Gracious." Tobiah was descended from an aristocratic family that owned estates in Gilead and was influential in Transjordan as early as the eighth century BCE. Not only was he allied with Sanballat, but also he had strong ties with the nobles (Neh 6:17) and with Eliashib the priest (Neh 13:4).

The region of Ammon was located in Transjordan around the modern capital of Amman. Tobiah is called ʿ*ebed,* literally "slave" or "servant." However, ʿ*ebed,* often was used of high officials both in biblical and in extrabiblical texts. Tobiah probably was the governor of Ammon under the Persians. A later Tobiah is explicitly called "the governor of Ammon." The latter was a leader of the Jewish Hellenizers under Ptolemy II, a relationship illumined by the Zenon papyri.

The site of ʿAraq el-Emir, "Caverns of the Prince," about eleven miles west of Amman, was the center of the Tobiads. The visible remains of a large building on top of the hill, Qasr el-ʿAbd "Castle of the Slave," measuring 60 by 120 feet, have been identified as a structure built by a Tobiah. On two walls are inscriptions with the name *Tobiah* in Aramaic characters. The date of the inscriptions is much disputed, ranging from the sixth to the second centuries BCE.

7.6. Geshem the Arab. Arabs provided key support to the Persian expeditions to Egypt under both Cambyses and Darius. Geshem (Neh 2:19) is also called *Gashmu* (in the Hebrew) in Nehemiah 6:1, a variant that would have been closer to his original Arabic name, *Jasuma,* which means "bulky" or "stout." A Lihyanite inscription from Dedan (Modern al-Ulâ) in northwest Arabia that reads, "Jashm son of Shahr and ʿAbd, governor of Dedan," may refer to the biblical Geshem. A silver vessel from Tell el-Maskhuta near Ismaila, Egypt, bearing the inscription, "Qaynu the son of Gashmu, the king of Qedar," may also be cited, indicating that Geshem controlled vast areas from northeast Egypt to northern Arabia and southern Palestine. In 1979 a new Aramaic inscription was discovered at Tayma in Arabia bearing the name *Gashm ben Shahr,* perhaps the grandfather of Geshem (Cross 1986).

7.7. Economic Problems. Nehemiah faced a grave social and economic crisis (Neh 5)

brought on by heavy Persian taxation. It may be possible that the introduction of coinage aggravated the economic gap between the rich and the poor, as it did in Greece during the archonship of Solon. The Persians may have been tolerant about religious views, but they were quite stern about collecting taxes (Briant, 399, 406, 810). The collection of *taxes in Mesopotamia under the Persians is illustrated by the archive of the Egibi family, which extended over three generations (Abraham).

7.8. Repopulating Jerusalem (Neh 7; 11). The list in Nehemiah 7:7-69 is considered by some to be a census of the total Judean community in the time of Nehemiah. In contrast to other scholars, Williamson (1985, 267-69) has argued for the priority of Nehemiah 7 over Ezra 2. Some have suggested that the "father's houses" may have allowed the integration of the returnees with some of those who remained behind

On the basis of archaeological surveys C. E. Carter has proposed a radically reduced province of Yehud. He excludes the relatively fertile region of Ono (Neh 6:1-2), although he does note that some Jews lived outside the boundaries of the province. He estimates the size of Jerusalem in the Persian period as between 130 and 140 dunams, with 80 dunams occupied by the Temple Mount (1 dunam = 1,000 m^2). He estimates the population of Yehud as ranging from eleven thousand to seventeen thousand, and Jerusalem to have had about fifteen hundred inhabitants in the Persian era. Other scholars estimate Jerusalem's population as three to four times that number. In 1978 excavations for the first time found archaeological evidence for the resettlement of Jerusalem.

8. Relation to Esdras.

The relation of the Hebrew MT text of Ezra to its Greek translations is complicated by the presence of two rival Greek versions of Ezra, including one that differs considerably, now commonly called either 1 Esdras or simply Esdras, which is included among the OT apocryphal books considered deuterocanonical by the Catholic Church after the Council of Trent, though modern Catholic Bibles such as the JB and the NAB omit it.

8.1. Nomenclature. The confusing nomenclature of several books is clarified in Table 1.

8.2. The Contents of 1 Esdras. 1 Esdras contains the last two chapters of 2 Chronicles, all of Ezra, and Nehemiah 7:73—8:12, omitting entirely the narrative of Nehemiah. Its principal novelty is a long story (1 Esdr 3:1—5:6) about three young bodyguards of Darius who seek to answer the riddle of what is the strongest thing in the world. Zerubbabel, by giving "truth" as the answer, is allowed to lead the exiles back to their homes. Josephus followed 1 Esdras in constructing his history of this period. Although a few scholars have followed Torrey in believing that 1 Esdras has preserved a superior account to Ezra, most scholars conclude that it is a secondary and late adaptation that provides no independent historical information (Z. Talshir).

8.3. The Contents of 2 Esdras (= 4 Ezra). This pseudepigraphical work is preserved in its entirety only in Latin recensions of the seventh to thirteenth centuries CE. Most scholars believe that the original, central section, which is an apocalypse (2 Esdr 3—14), was composed in Hebrew or Aramaic by a Jewish author about 100 CE. We have but three verses of 2 Esdras 15 in Greek (P.Oxy. 1010). The work was translated into several languages, including an important Armenian version that goes back to a Greek original. 2 Esdras 3—14 relates seven visions by which the angel Uriel instructs Ezra about the problem of evil and the destiny of souls after death. 2 Esdras 14:1-48 describes how God commanded Ezra to dictate the Scriptures in forty days to five rapidly writing scribes who produced twenty-four canonical books and seventy secret books.

8.4. The Contents of 5 Ezra. The first two chapters now included in 4 Ezra sometimes are designated 5 Ezra. This clearly was a separate Christian composition from the middle of the second century CE. 5 Ezra is the source of a number of phrases in the Catholic liturgy: *Requiem aeternam dona eis, Domine,* "Give them eternal rest, Lord" (cf. 4 Ezra [= 2 Esdr] 2:34); *Lux perpetua luceat eis,* "May the eternal light shine upon them" (cf. 4 Ezra [= 2 Esdr] 2:35).

9. The Message of Ezra and Nehemiah.

Unlike those deported by the Assyrians from Israel, those deported by the Babylonians from Judah steadfastly retained their faith in Yahweh during the ordeal of their exile and maintained their identity as a distinct religious community. When the exiles returned, they revived an exclusive loyalty to Yahweh, which was no longer compromised by the worship of other gods. As E. Stern (479) reports, since the beginning of the Persian era not a single piece of evidence has been found for any pagan cults in Judah and Samaria.

9.1. The Message of Ezra. The book of Ezra reveals the providential intervention of the God of heaven on behalf of his people (Ezra 7:6, 9, 28; 8:18, 22, 31). In Ezra 1 the Lord is sovereign over all kingdoms (Ezra 1:2) and moves even the heart of a pagan ruler to fulfill his will (Ezra 1:1; cf. 6:22; 7:6, 27-28). God accomplishes the refining of his people through calamities such as the conquest and the exile. God stirs the hearts of his people to respond and raises people of God to lead his people (Ezra 1:5).

In Ezra 3 we see that the service of God requires a united effort (Ezra 3:1), leadership (Ezra 3:2a), obedience to God's word (Ezra 3:2b), courage in the face of opposition (Ezra 3:3), offerings and funds (Ezra 3:4-7), and an organized division of labor (Ezra 3:8-9). Meeting these requirements would result in a sound foundation for later work (Ezra 3:11), tears and joy (Ezra 3:11-12), and praise and thanksgiving to the Lord (Ezra 3:11).

Ezra 4 teaches that doing the work of God brings opposition: in the guise of proffered cooperation from those who do not share the exiles' basic theological convictions (Ezra 4:1-2) to complete work that they alone are responsible for (Ezra 4:3); from those who would discourage and intimidate (Ezra 4:4); from professional counselors who offer misleading advice (Ezra 4:5); from false accusers (Ezra 4:6, 13); from secular authorities (Ezra 4:7, 21-24). Far from being

Table 1. The Nomenclature of Ezra, Nehemiah and Apocryphal Literature

	OT Ezra	OT Nehemiah	A Paraphrase of Ezra	A Latin Apocalypse
Septuagint	Esdras beta	Esdras gamma	Esdras alpha	
Vulgate	1 Esdras	2 Esdras	3 Esdras	4 Esdras
Modern	Ezra	Nehemiah	3 Esdras	2 Esdras

discouraged, however, God's people need to be alert and vigorous, knowing that by God's grace they can triumph over all opposition and accomplish his will with rejoicing (Ezra 6:14-16).

Ezra experienced the good hand of God. As a scribe, he was more than a scholar; he was an expounder of the Scriptures (Ezra 7:6, 12). He believed that God could guide and protect from misfortune (Ezra 8:20-22). As an inspired leader, he enlisted others and assigned trustworthy persons to their tasks (Ezra 7:27-28; 8:15, 24). He regarded what he did as a sacred trust (Ezra 8:21-28). Ezra was, above all, a man of fervent prayer (Ezra 8:21; 10:1) and deep piety and humility (Ezra 7:10, 27-28; 9:3; 10:6).

9.2. The Message of Nehemiah. Perhaps more than any other book of the OT, the book of Nehemiah reflects the several facets of its author's character. (1) Nehemiah was a man of responsibility. That he served as the king's cupbearer (Neh 1:11 2:1) can only mean that he had proven himself trustworthy over a long period. (2) Nehemiah was clearly a man of vision. The walls of Jerusalem had been in ruins for 141 years when Nehemiah learned of an abortive attempt to rebuild them (Ezra 4:23). He had a great vision of who God was and what God could do through his servants. (3) As a man of prayer, Nehemiah's first resort was to prayer (Neh 1:4-11), and he prayed spontaneously even in the presence of the king (Neh 2:4-5). (4) Clearly Nehemiah was a man of action and of cooperation, one who would explain what needed to be done (Neh 2:16-17) and inspire others to join him (Neh 2:18). He knew how to organize the rebuilding work (Neh 3). In spite of opposition, the people responded so enthusiastically that they mended the wall in less than two months (Neh 6:15). He inspired the people with his own example (Neh 5:14 18). Nehemiah, a layman, was able to cooperate with his contemporary Ezra, the scribe and priest, in spite of the fact that these two leaders were of entirely different temperaments. In reaction to the problem of mixed marriages, Ezra plucked out his own hair (Ezra 9:3), whereas Nehemiah plucked out the hair of the offenders (Neh 13:25)! (5) As a man of compassion, Nehemiah renounced his own privileges (Neh 5:18) and denounced the wealthy who had exploited their poorer compatriots (Neh 5:8). He did this because of his reverence for God (Neh 5:9, 15), and models the need for leaders to be sensitive to issues of economic exploitation and

distress (Yamauchi 1980). (6) Nehemiah was a man who triumphed over opposition, despite his opponents' using every ruse to intimidate him. They started with ridicule (Neh 2:19; 4:2-3). They attempted slander (Neh 6:5-7). Hired prophets gave him misleading advice (Neh 6:10-14), yet Nehemiah responded with prayer (Neh 4:4), with redoubled efforts (Neh 4:6), with vigilance (Neh 4:9) and with trust in God (Neh 4:14). Finally (7), Nehemiah was a man with right motivation. Although he justified his ministry, his primary motive was not to be judged aright by others or to be remembered by posterity. The last words of Nehemiah—"Remember me with favor, O my God" (Neh 13:31)—recapitulate a frequently repeated theme (Neh 5:19; 13:14, 22). His motive throughout his career was to please and serve his divine Sovereign. His only reward would be God's approbation. He was in many ways a model leader (Yamauchi 1982).

See also EZRA; HISTORY OF ISRAEL 7: PERSIAN PERIOD; HISTORY OF ISRAEL 8: POSTEXILIC COMMUNITY; NEHEMIAH; POSTEXILIC TEMPLE; SANBALLAT; ZERUBBABEL.

BIBLIOGRAPHY. *Commentaries*: J. Blenkinsopp, *Ezra-Nehemiah* (OTL; Philadelphia: Westminster, 1988); D. J. Clines, *Ezra, Nehemiah, Esther* (NCB; Grand Rapids: Eerdmans; London: Marshall, Morgan & Scott, 1984); H. G. M. Williamson, *Ezra, Nehemiah* (WBC 16; Waco, TX: Word, 1985). *Studies*: K. Abraham, *Business and Politics under the Persian Empire: The Financial Dealings of Marduk-nasir-apli of the House of Egibi (521-487 B.C.E.)* (Bethesda, MD: CDL Press, 2004); R. Albertz, *Israel in Exile: The History and Literature of the Sixth Century B.C.E.* (SBLSBL 3; Atlanta: Society of Biblical Literature, 2003); H. M. Barstad, *The Myth of the Empty Land: A Study in the History and Archaeology of Judah during the "Exilic" Period* (SO 28; Oslo: Scandinavian University Press, 1996); P. R. Bedford, *Temple Restoration in Early Achaemenid Judah* (JSJSup 65; Leiden: E. J. Brill, 2001); P. Briant, *From Cyrus to Alexander: A History of the Persian Empire* (Winona Lake, IN: Eisenbrauns, 2002); C. E. Carter, *The Emergence of Yehud in the Persian Period* (JSOTSup 294; Sheffield: Sheffield Academic Press, 1999); M. Cogan, "Cyrus Cylinder," *COS* 2.314-16; F. M. Cross, "A New Aramaic Stele from Tayma," *CBQ* 48 (1986) 387-94; idem, "A Report on the Samaria Papyri," in *Congress Volume, Jerusalem, 1986,* ed. J. A. Emerton (VTSup 40; Leiden: E. J. Brill, 1988) 17-26; S. Dalley, "Recent Evidence from Assyrian Sources for Judaean History from Uzziah to Manasseh," *JSOT* 28 (2004) 387-401; **D. R. Daniels,** "The Composition of the Ezra-Nehemiah Narrative," in *Ernten, was man sät: Festschrift für Klaus Koch zu seinem 65. Geburtstag,* ed. D. R. Daniels, U. Glessmer and M. Rösel (Neukirchen-Vluyn: Neukirchener Verlag, 1991) 311-28; **A. Faust,** "Judah in the Sixth Century B.C.E.: A Rural Perspective," *PEQ* 135 (2003) 37-53; **L. L. Grabbe,** *Judaism from Cyrus to Hadrian* (2 vols.; Minneapolis: Fortress, 1992); **M. Heltzer,** "A Recently Published Babylonian Tablet and the Province of Judah after 516 B.C.E.," *Transeuphratène* 5 (1992) 57-61; **L. V. Hensley,** "The Official Persian Documents in the Book of Ezra" (Ph.D. diss., University of Liverpool, 1977); **K. G. Hoglund,** *Achaemenid Imperial Administration in Syria-Palestine and the Missions of Ezra and Nehemiah* (SBLDS 125; Atlanta: Scholars Press, 1992); **V. Hurowitz,** *I Have Built You an Exalted House: Temple Building in the Bible in the Light of Mesopotamian and North-West Semitic Writings* (JSOTSup115; Sheffield: JSOT, 1992); **S. Japhet,** "The Supposed Common Authorship of Chronicles and Ezra-Nehemiah Investigated Anew," *VT* 18 (1968) 330-71; **F. Joannès and A. Lemaire,** "Trois tablettes cuneiforms à onomastique ouest-sémitiques (collection Sh. Moussaïeff)," *Transeuphratène* 17 (1989) 17-34; **R. W. Klein,** "Ezra-Nehemiah, Books of," *ABD* 2.731-42; **O. Lipschits,** "Judah, Jerusalem and the Temple 586-539 B.C.," *Transeuphratène* 22 (2001) 129-42; **D. Marcus,** "Is the Book of Nehemiah a Translation from Aramaic?" in *Boundaries of the Ancient Near Eastern World: A Tribute to Cyrus Gordon,* ed. M. Lubetski, C. Gottlieb and S. Keller (JSOTSup 273; Sheffield: Sheffield Academic Press, 1998) 103-10; **S. Mittmann,** "Tobia, Sanballat und die persische Provinz Juda," *JNSL* 26 (2000) 1-50; **B. Oded,** "Where Is the 'Myth of the Empty Land' to Be Found?" in *Judah and the Judeans in the Neo-Babylonian Period,* ed. O. Lipschits and J. Blenkinsopp (Winona Lake, IN: Eisenbrauns, 2003) 55-74; **D. Schwiderksi,** *Handbuch des nordwestsemitischen Briefformulars: Ein Beitrag zur Echtheitsfrage der aramäischen Briefe des Esrabuches* (BZAW 295; Berlin: de Gruyter, 2000); **E. Stern,** *Archaeology of the Land of the Bible,* 2: *Assyrian, Babylonian, and Persian Periods (732-332 B.C.E.)* (New York: Doubleday, 2001); **D. Talshir,** "Linguistic Analysis and the Question of Authorship in Chronicles, Ezra and Nehemiah," *VT* 32 (1982) 201-16; **Z. Talshir,** "Ezra-Nehemiah and First Esdras: Diagnosis of a Relationship between Two Recensions," *Bib* 81 (2000) 566-73; **S. Timm,** "Die Bedeutung der spätbabylonischen Texte aus Nërab für die Rückkehr der Judäer aus dem Exil," in *Meilenstein: Festgabe für Herbert Donner zum 16. Februar 1995,* ed. M. Weippert and S. Timm (ÄAT 30: Wiesbaden: Harrassowitz, 1995) 276-88; **C. C. Torrey,** *Ezra Studies* (New York: KTAV Publishing, 1970 [1910]); **J. C. VanderKam,** "Ezra-Nehemiah or Ezra and Nehemiah?" in *Priests, Prophets and Scribes: Essays on the Formation and Heritage of Second Temple Judaism in Honour of Joseph Blenkinsopp,* ed. E. Ulrich et al. (JSOTSup 149; Sheffield: Sheffield Academic Press, 1992) 55-75; **J. P. Weinberg,** *The Citizen-Temple Community* (JSOTSup 151; Sheffield: Sheffield Academic Press, 1992); **H. G. M. Williamson,** "Exile and After: Historical Study," in *The Face of Old Testament Studies: A Survey of Contemporary Approaches,* ed. D. W. Baker and B. T. Arnold (Grand Rapids: Baker, 1999) 236-65; idem, *Israel in the Books of Chronicles* (London: Cambridge University Press, 1977); idem, *Studies in Persian Period History and Historiography* (FAT 38; Tübingen: Mohr Siebeck, 2004); **E. M. Yamauchi,** "The Eastern Jewish Diaspora under the Babylonians," in *Mesopotamia and the Bible: Comparative Explorations,* ed. M. W. Chavalas and K. L. Younger Jr. (Grand Rapids: Baker, 2002) 356-77; idem, "Nehemiah: A Model Leader," in *A Spectrum of Thought: Essays in Honor of Dennis F. Kinlaw,* ed. M. L. Peterson (Wilmore, KY: Asbury, 1982) 171-80; idem, *Persia and the Bible* (Grand Rapids: Baker, 1990); idem, "Two Reformers Compared: Solon of Athens and Nehemiah of Jerusalem," in *The Bible World: Essays in Honor of Cyrus H. Gordon,* ed. G. Rendsburg et al. (New York: KTAV, 1980) 269-92; **A. Zertal,** "The Pahwah of Samaria (Northern Israel) during the Persian Period: Types of Settlement, Economy, History and New Discoveries," *Transeuphratène* 3 (1990) 9-21.

E. M. Yamauchi

F

FAITH

Faith in the Historical Books must be understood as a covenantal concept that describes the dynamic, mutual relationship between *God and his people: an affirmation in word and deed of Israel's covenant obligation to God, who is faithful and loyal in his covenant with his people Israel.

1. Defining Faith
2. Hebrew Vocabulary for Faith
3. God's Faithfulness and Israel's Response

1. Defining Faith.

Faith in the Historical Books (and in the OT as a whole) is not to be equated with how the term "faith" is commonly used today. It does not refer primarily to a confession of a set of beliefs *about* God. It may imply such things, but certainly that is not the biblical focus. Also, there is little if anything in the Historical Books that one could turn to as examples of "saving faith." In other words, "faith" does not designate who is and who is not an Israelite (as an abstract notion of having "faith in God"). In the Historical Books Israel's attitude toward the nations largely concerns Israel's covenantal obligations to remain distinct from them, specifically to maintain its distinctiveness as a people who worship Yahweh, not the gods of Canaan. The role that the nations play is largely negative and oppositional. In fact, it is fair to say that the nations generally are considered a threat to Israel's identity and are there to be disposed of (conquest narratives in Joshua), subjugated (e.g., Ammonites [1 Sam 10]) or resisted (against intermarriage [Ezra 9]).

If pressed, one could appeal to the story of Rahab as an example of saving faith (Josh 2), but certainly this would be reading too much into a complex narrative. Rahab is not converted. She simply confesses how news of God's display of might in the exodus reached the ears of her people, causing their hearts to melt with fear (Josh 2:8-13). She is, in a word, afraid, which is a realization of passages such as Exodus 15:14: "The nations will hear and tremble." Joshua makes the same point at the end of the story: "all the people are melting in fear because of us" (Josh 2:24).

The point of the story of Rahab, therefore, is the spread of Yahweh's reputation (see, e.g., Josh 6:27) and the fear that Yahweh's reputation strikes in the hearts of foreigners. Furthermore, this story is meant to be seen in contrast to the story of Achan's sin in Joshua 7 (Hawk, 25-33). Rahab, a foreigner, and a prostitute at that, who did not witness God's works, nevertheless hears of them, fears God and acts accordingly (by hiding the spies). Achan, who as an Israelite should know better, disobeys God by keeping some of the plunder after the conquest of Jericho. This is described in Joshua 7:1 as an act of unfaithfulness (*m'l* [see 2.7 below]). As a result, the Israelites are routed by the people of Ai, which, ironically, causes the hearts of the Israelites to melt (Josh 7:5; cf. 2:11). Furthermore, Achan's behavior is itself an adumbration of what will occupy the remainder of the Historical Books: forgetfulness (i.e., faithlessness) on the part of God's own chosen people.

The fact that in the NT both Hebrews (Heb 11:31) and James (Jas 2:25-26) cite Rahab's act as an example of faith does not settle the issue of how the story functions in its original literary and historical context. The use of this story in these NT books clearly is a function of their specific rhetorical-theological contexts, which raises complex questions of its own, as does the whole matter of the NT's use of the OT. Appeal cannot be made to these NT texts to settle the issue of faith in the Historical Books (for a slightly contrasting view see Spina, 1125; Hess, 96-97). But, regardless of how we look at the story of Rahab, it is only one story in a specific literary and theological context, and it hardly points us toward a general understanding of the concept of faith in the Historical Books.

Faith in the Historical Books must be understood as a covenantal concept that describes the dynamic, mutual relationship between God and his people. First, it concerns Israel's collective and individual obedience/faithfulness/loyalty to God, primarily with respect to matters of worship (rejection of idolatry). It is not a matter of conversion, or a statement of beliefs, and not even primarily a comment on the disposition of the heart (although it does include such things). It is an affirming in word and deed of Israel's covenant obligation to God. To speak of faith, therefore, overlaps considerably with notions expressed in English words such as "faithfulness, integrity, trust, reliability, loyalty, fear, obedience, covenant" and others. At times such concepts are associated with the Hebrew roots ʾmn, ʾmt, ḥsd, ṣdq, yrʾ, ʾhb and bṭḥ (see 2 below), but these concepts are certainly neither defined by nor limited to these word groups. Also, in the Historical Books the role of the king must be highlighted as vital to Israel's faithfulness, as it falls upon him to lead Israel toward greater covenant obedience, thus highlighting the corporate covenantal dimension of Israel's faith, and not merely that of the individual.

Second, and equally important, faith in the Historical Books also includes God's faithfulness, his covenant loyalty, toward his people. In fact, it is fundamental to the theologies of these books that the very motive for Israel's faithfulness is to be reminded of God's faithfulness toward Israel. What is in view primarily is God's past action of redeeming the Israelites from Egypt, which includes not only the act of redemption itself, but also the giving of the law and the promise of land.

After a brief survey of Hebrew vocabulary that intersects the notion of faith, the organization of this article proceeds along the lines of the historical period covered by the books themselves: premonarchical (Joshua and Judges), monarchical (Samuel and Kings) and postexilic (Chronicles, Ezra and Nehemiah). This organization is not to imply, however, that the books themselves represent a historical unfolding of

the concept of faith. The books of Joshua and Judges likely have a complex historical relationship to each other, and, although reflecting older stories and events, are nevertheless essentially products of the monarchical period and so must be understood from that perspective. Likewise, the accounts of the united and divided monarchies in Samuel and Kings no doubt have their point of origin sometime during those periods, but both works underwent editing in the exilic period, if not afterward. Ezra and Nehemiah are postexilic works, and therefore they more clearly reflect some of the concerns of that period, as does the Chronicler's recounting of the southern kingdom's rise and fall. With these qualifications in mind, we proceed with an overview of the concept of faith in the Historical Books as they reflect the theologies of the biblical authors at various stages in Israel's history.

2. Hebrew Vocabulary for Faith.
The concept of faith in the Historical Books is not limited to the Hebrew roots below. Nor are these words used exclusively, or necessarily predominantly, in the contexts indicated below. Nevertheless, observing how these words are used will help bring clarity to how "faith" operates in the Historical Books. The English translations (NIV) of the respective Hebrew words are in italics.

2.1. ʾmn, ʾmt. This root is used both to describe Israel's covenant obligation to God as well as God's faithful behavior toward Israel. For example, in 1 Samuel 2:35 a *faithful* priest is one who obeys God. By contrast, Israel is chided in 2 Kings 17:14 for being stiff-necked, meaning that they did not *trust* God. As the immediate context makes clear, such lack of trust is a function of Israel's disobedience toward the *law. In 2 Samuel 7:28 it is God who is said to be *trustworthy*, meaning that God shows his faithfulness to *David by establishing his kingdom. In Nehemiah 9:8 Nehemiah praises God for making a covenant with Abraham, whose heart was *faithful* to God. Here Nehemiah certainly appeals to Abraham as an example not of "believing" in God, but of obeying God; his covenant faithfulness to God is contrasted to the sinfulness of Israel's confession of sin in the face of the reading of the law.

2.2. bṭḥ. Normally translated *trust,* this root may appear to have more of a psychological dimension, but on one level that is true of all of these roots. The point, however, is that trust is demonstrated by action, i.e., covenant obedience. Thus in 2 Kings 18:5 Hezekiah is said to have *trusted* in Yahweh by virtue of his having combated idolatry (2 Kings 18:4) and keeping the Mosaic law (2 Kings 18:6). Certainly there is a sense in which this root is used to describe more of an attitudinal disposition, as can be seen in, for example, 2 Kings 18:30 (with respect to *trusting* God for Israel's deliverance) and 1 Chronicles 5:20 (*trusting* God for victory refers to "crying out" in battle). But it must also be pointed out that such attitudes of trust are not baseless assertions; rather, they are founded on Israel's memory of God's past faithfulness toward them.

2.3. ḥsd. This root is commonly used to describe fidelity between human parties (e.g., Josh 2:12, 14; Judg 1:24; 1 Sam 15:6; 2 Sam 2:5; 9:3, 7). In these instances it is normally translated as showing *kindness* or dealing *faithfully* with someone. It is also used very often to describe God's covenant faithfulness toward his people—that is, treating them in a way befitting the covenant relationship. The term can refer to God's actions (1) toward individuals (*kindness* [Ruth 1:8; 2:20]); (2) very often toward kings as representatives of the people (*kindness* [2 Sam 22:51, 1 Kings 3:6, 2 Chron 1:8, Ezra 7:28 (concerning Ezra)]; *love* [2 Sam 7:15]); (3) toward Israel as a whole as expressed in, for example, military victory (*love* [1 Chron 16:34, 41]), more generally as a response to Israel's obedience (*love* [Neh 1:5]) or also despite Israel's rebelliousness (*love* [Neh 9:17]). In all these instances, God's ḥsd is an expression of his unwavering commitment, his faithfulness, to Israel as his people.

2.4. 'hb. In the Historical Books to *love* God is a function of obedience. In Joshua 22:5 to *love* God means "to walk in all his ways, to obey his commands." In Joshua 23:11 *love* of God is a response to military victory and likewise expressed in obedience to "all that is written in the book of the law of Moses" (Josh 23:6). Solomon shows his *love* for God "by walking according to the statutes of his father David" (1 Kings 3:3). The word is also used to express God's love for his people—for example, God expresses his *love* for Israel by making Solomon king (1 Kings 10:9).

2.5. yr'. Israel's covenant faithfulness to God is also commonly expressed as *fear*. The term should be understood not as an abstract emotional disposition or response, but as one that is

worked out in obedience to God (Josh 4:24, 24:14; 1 Sam 12:14, 24; 2 Chron 6:31; Ezra 10:3).

2.6. yšr, ṣdq, ṣdqh. Although these are two different roots, they often are translated in the sense of *acting justly* or *rightly,* which in the context of the present discussion would refer to the proper conduct of the covenant parties. The word ṣdqh is also often translated "righteousness," but there too it denotes not a quality or attribute of God, but right actions—that is, covenant faithfulness, either from God toward Israel or the reverse. On the many uses of yšr to denote Israel's (especially the king's) covenant obedience, see 1 Samuel 12:23; 29:6; 1 Kings 9:4; 11:33, 38; 2 Kings 12:3; 14:3; 15:3; 2 Chronicles 24:2; 25:2. God's righteous deeds (ṣdqh) toward Israel are mentioned in, for example, Joshua 5:11; 1 Samuel 12:7. Reference to Israel's (or the king's) ṣdqh is found in, for example, 2 Samuel 8:15; 22:21, 25; 1 Kings 3:6.

2.7. m'l. This word, often translated *unfaithful,* describes the opposite of the other words considered above. It refers to Israel's (or the king's) rebellion against God—that is, covenant disobedience, typically pertaining to false worship (Josh 22:16; 1 Chron 5:25; 9:1; 2 Chron 26:16, 18; 28:19, 22) or some other aspect of lawbreaking such as intermarriage (Ezra 9:2, 4, 6; 10:2, 6, 10; Neh 13:27).

3. God's Faithfulness and Israel's Response.

If we understand Israel's faith in God as describing much more than intellectual assent or verbal articulation *about* God, and rather as something demonstrated as covenant obedience, trust in God and behaving rightly in response to God's prior acts of faithfulness, then we can see that "faith" is really a subcurrent for all the Historical Books. To put it another way, what forms the backdrop to much of the historical narratives is the question "Whom will Israel trust?" which is to say, "How will the people of Israel demonstrate faith in God, who has acted faithfully toward them?"

3.1. Premonarchical Israel: Joshua and Judges. The Historical Books begin by announcing an important theme: "As I was with Moses, so I will be with you" (Josh 1:5). This is the motivation for why the Israelites are to be "strong and courageous" as they fight to take the land that God has promised to give them (Josh 1:6), and as they obey the law (Josh 1:7). Here in brief we have the thematic substructure to the Historical Books.

The most concrete manifestation of Israel's faith, and one that recurs throughout the Historical Books, concerns Israel's obedience to God's commands, especially as they are enumerated in Israel's legal corpus. We see this in Joshua's farewell address and the renewing of the covenant at Shechem (Josh 23—24), where Joshua commands Israel "to obey all that is written in the book of the law of Moses, without turning aside to the right or to the left" (Josh 23:6). The motive for Israel's faithfulness is God's faithfulness in driving the nations out of Canaan, and its purpose is that Israel remain separate from the nations and thus not be tempted to "invoke the names of their gods or swear by them" (Josh 23:7). It is because God gave the Israelites the land (Josh 24:13) that they are commanded to "fear [yr'] the Lord and serve him with all faithfulness ['mt]" (Josh 24:14).

To deal faithlessly with God (i.e., to disobey) had clear ramifications. In Judges it was Israel's "violation of the covenant" that prevented them from driving the nations out completely (Judg 2:20-23). This sentiment is repeated in Judges 6, where Israel's disobedience toward the God of the exodus, demonstrated as idolatry, is what puts them at the mercy of the Midianites. Gid-eon is called by God to deliver the Israelites. Like Moses before him, Gideon needs some convincing, but after testing God twice with the fleece (Judg 6:36-40), he obeyed God and defeated the Midianites (Judg 7). It is Israel's covenant unfaithfulness during this period that sets the stage for the subsequent narratives of Samuel and Kings. As we read in the last verse of Judges, "In those days there was no king in Israel; all the people did what was right in their own eyes" (Judg 21:25). Perhaps a king, one who truly follows the Lord, can lead Israel, by word and example, to greater covenant faithfulness, thus realizing the purpose for which God brought Israel out of Egypt: to make them a great nation.

3.2. Monarchical Israel: Samuel and Kings. 1 Samuel begins with two narratives that further explicate the degree of Israel's unfaithfulness: the stories of Eli (1 Sam 1—2) and of Saul's fall from favor (1 Sam 13—15). Eli is rebuked by a "man of God" for not fulfilling his priestly obligations properly (1 Sam 2:27-29), which also involved the behavior of his sons Hophni and Phinehas. Eli's punishment was the death of the sons and the discontinuation of their priestly line. Of course, there is much more to this episode in 1 Samuel than merely citing an example of an individual's lack of faith. It highlights the need for Israel to have a leader, a king, who will lead God's people into greater faithfulness, greater covenant obedience. The same can be said for *Saul. He fell from favor after he performed sacrifices on his own rather than waiting for Samuel to show up at Gilgal (1 Sam 13:7-14). Like Eli, Saul's cultic disobedience had dramatic consequences, and it serves to adumbrate what will occupy a fair amount of the *Deuteronomistic History: the lack of faith on the part of Israel's *kings. These stories also highlight the importance of the king's faith in God as it affects the well-being of the people in general. For the king to disobey had implications for the nation as a whole.

It is in this context that we can understand the role of *Samuel. Hannah's prayer (1 Sam 2:1-10), where much of the theology of 1-2 Samuel is anticipated (see also the similar themes in David's song [2 Sam 22:1-51], thus forming a theological frame to 1-2 Samuel), is recorded not simply to recount a mother's prayer of thanksgiving for a male child. This prayer serves a larger theological purpose: Hannah's child is the first phase in a series of acts by God to bring Israel back to covenant faithfulness. In the days when "the word of the LORD was rare; there were not many visions" (1 Sam 3:1), Samuel's role was to inaugurate kingship. It certainly is a complex matter within 1 Samuel whether kingship in general is portrayed as a divine institution or as further evidence of Israel's faithlessness. Regardless, one of the king's central tasks was to bear the responsibility of leading the people to follow God's law—that is, to respond faithfully to the God who had acted faithfully toward them. This is punctuated in Samuel's farewell speech in 1 Samuel 12. He reminds the people of Israel's covenant disobedience since the exodus and the consequences of such waywardness. If they continue in this pattern—neglecting God's past acts—then "both you and your king will be swept away" (1 Sam 12:25).

In 2 Samuel 7 we begin to see the realization of the role that kingship could play in Israel. Nathan's prophecy is a promise by God to establish David's kingship. God recounts his own faithful acts toward David (2 Sam 7:8-11). David's response (2 Sam 7:18-29) is a prayer of praise for God's faithfulness, ending with an exclamation of trust that he and his kingly line will be blessed forever (2 Sam 7:29). Of course, such an ideal state is short-lived. David's sin with Bathsheba (2 Sam 11) is not simply a private matter. The king has reneged on his obligation to lead Israel in covenant faithfulness. The immediate result was the death of their child (2 Sam 12:14), but the ramifications were long-term and national. Despite the efforts of *Hezekiah and *Josiah to remain faithful and turn Israel around, the national corruption was thorough, and so Israel earned the ultimate punishment. The very purpose for which God brought the Israelites out of Egypt—to be a holy nation, to be faithful to God through law and cult, to maintain an unbroken line of kings from David onwards (2 Sam 7:11-16)—was undone. Israel had broken faith.

In contrast to the kings' disobedience is the zeal of *Elijah for God and his law. His faith in God is also to be contrasted to the Israelites' lack of faith: they reject God's covenant by breaking down his altars and killing his prophets (1 Kings 19:10). To have faith in God means to "follow" him rather than "wavering between two opinions" (1 Kings 18:21). To fail to follow God's commands means to break faith with him.

Similar to the Rahab story, 1 Kings provides instances where foreigners are said to acknowledge God because of his deeds. In Solomon's prayer of dedication of the temple he asks God to hear the prayers of any foreigners who come to Jerusalem to worship, for in doing so, "all the peoples of the earth may know your name and fear you" (1 Kings 8:43). Likewise, the Queen of Sheba praises Solomon's God as one who has "eternal love" for Israel (1 Kings 10:9). But again, to argue that the foreigners come to what we might call today a "saving faith" in Israel's God is purely conjectural, and at best only peripheral. The focus is on how word of Israel's God is spreading, thus vindicating Israel's God as one who builds a mighty nation out of slaves. However, such praise was the exception rather than the rule.

3.3. Postexilic Israel: Chronicles, Ezra and Nehemiah. The faithlessness of Israel toward God is what led them into exile. The postexilic literature therefore shows a marked concern that Israel not continue that posture of disobedience. Thus in the book of Ezra we see two emphases: plans to rebuild the temple against opposition (Ezra 3—6)

and a ban on intermarriage (Ezra 9—10). Both are designed to recapture Israel's ideal as a covenant-keeping community, one that keeps faith with Yahweh. A similar emphasis can be seen in Nehemiah's prayer, particularly Nehemiah 1:8-9, which nicely sums up Israel's postexilic agenda: "Remember the instruction you gave your servant Moses, saying, 'If you are unfaithful [m'l], I will scatter you among the nations, but if you return to me and obey my commands, then even if your exiled people are at the farthest horizon, I will gather them from there and bring them to the place I have chosen as a dwelling for my Name.'" Like *Ezra, *Nehemiah had a building project (the walls of Jerusalem) (Neh 1—6) and a call to Israel to return to the ideal of complete covenant obedience (Neh 8—13), lest they repeat the faithlessness of their ancestors.

The Chronicler paints an idealized portrait of Israel's past as a means to motivate the postexilic community to work toward restoration and not repeat past mistakes. The Chronicler's emphasis on immediate retribution underscores this. David is portrayed in a much more positive light than in the Deuteronomistic History (e.g., the sin with Bathsheba is omitted). Also, David and Solomon's role in the building of the temple is elaborated and expanded, which speaks to the importance of the king's role in leading God's people in faithfulness. The Chronicler bridges the gap between Israel's past and present. The old way of life is gone, or at least very broken. He reminds the readers that the God who was faithful to their ancestors is their God as well and calls them back to a life of covenant faithfulness so that the ideal that was never reached may become real.

See also GOD.

BIBLIOGRAPHY. **D. A. Baer and R. P. Gordon,** "חסד," *NIDOTTE* 2.211-18; **R. M. Hals,** *Grace and Faith in the Old Testament* (Minneapolis: Augsburg, 1980); **L. D. Hawk,** *Joshua* (Berit Olam; Collegeville, MN: Liturgical Press, 2000); **R. S. Hess,** *Joshua* (TOTC; Leicester: InterVarsity Press, 1996); **R. W. L. Moberly,** "אמן," *NIDOTTE* 1.427-33; idem, "בטח," *NIDOTTE* 1.644-49; **D. T. Shannon,** *The Old Testament Experience of Faith* (Valley Forge, PA: Judson Press, 1977); **F. A. Spina,** "Rahab," *NIDOTTE* 4.1123-26; **S. S. Taylor,** "Faith, Faithfulness," *NDBT* 487-93; **G. J. Wenham,** *Faith in the Old Testament* (Leicester: Theological Students Fellowship, n.d.).

P. Enns

FAMILY. *See* ISRAELITE SOCIETY.

FARMING. *See* AGRICULTURE AND ANIMAL HUS-BANDRY.

FEMINIST INTERPRETATION. *See* METHODS OF INTERPRETATION.

FIGS. *See* AGRICULTURE AND ANIMAL HUS-BANDRY.

FORGIVENESS

There are three primary terms for forgiveness in the OT, and all three are represented in the Historical Books: *nāśāʾ*, "to bear, carry off"; *sālaḥ*, "to forgive"; *kāpar*, "to atone for, to pardon." A fourth term, the Hiphil of *ʿābar*, "to take away," occurs twice in the Historical Books (2 Sam 12:13; 24:10/1 Chron 21:8) and twice elsewhere (Job 7:21; Zech 3:4). Although the three primary terms all occur in these books, it is not with great frequency. *Nāśāʾ* occurs only three times with the sense of "forgiveness" (Josh 24:19; 1 Sam 15:25; 25:28), and *kāpar* occurs only once in the sense of "pardon" (2 Chron 30:18). *Sālaḥ* occurs fourteen times, but ten of these are found in Solomon's prayer dedicating the temple (1 Kings 8:22-53; 2 Chron 6:12-42). This article treats the occurrences of these four terms under the headings of forgiveness as a human act and as a divine act. It also gives attention to certain instances where it may be said that forgiveness has occurred although none of the terms is present.

1. Forgiveness as a Human Act
2. Forgiveness as a Divine Act
3. Narrative Expressions of Forgiveness

1. Forgiveness as a Human Act.

As elsewhere in the OT, *nāśāʾ* is the term used when a human is extending forgiveness. The word may also be used for the divine act, but neither of the other two words is used for the human act (see Stamm, *TLOT* 2.798). In the Historical Books it is used twice in such a way (1 Sam 15:25; 25:28). In the second of these Abigail, the wife of Nabal, asks *David for forgiveness for her "transgression" in having had the temerity to pursue him and ply him with gifts. She had violated the convention of the day in taking such precipitous action and speaking directly to another man instead of going through her husband. There is a certain irony in the request

because the reader knows that it was really her husband who needed David's forgiveness. Interestingly, her appeal was not that in any way Nabal (or she) deserved forgiveness, but that David should not take vengeance into his own hands; rather, he should leave it in God's hands, and thus be innocent of bloodshed. Thus the forgiveness that was being requested would be an expression of enlightened self-interest. David agreed, and as the story turned out, the divine vengeance fell on Nabal from his own body, as he fell down with an apparent stroke when he heard how foolish his rejection of David's request had been. He died ten days later (1 Sam 25:36-39).

The second example of human forgiveness is found in 1 Samuel 15:25. Here the issue is more profound, and the way in which the appeal is addressed seems highly significant. This is the encounter of *Saul with *Samuel after Saul's failure to carry out the Lord's command to exterminate the Amalekites. Saul was brought to an admission of sin only at length, having first announced that he had obeyed God (1 Sam 15:23), and then having claimed that he had at least obeyed the spirit of God's command (1 Sam 15:20-21). But finally, in the face of Samuel's continued insistence that Saul had not obeyed even the spirit of what God required, the king admitted his sin. But interestingly, he did not ask for forgiveness from God; rather, he asked that Samuel forgive him and return (where to is not specified) to worship God with Saul before the elders of the people (1 Sam 15:25-31). All this suggests that what was really important to Saul was not so much the restoration of God's favor but the avoidance of the appearance of any breach between him and the powerful priest-prophet Samuel. But it was not the forgiveness of Samuel that Saul really needed, and his failure to seek God's forgiveness says a great deal about the state of Saul's relationship with God at this point in his life.

2. Forgiveness as a Divine Act.

*2.1. Forgive (**nāśāʾ**).* The third occurrence of *nāśāʾ* is found in Joshua 24:9 in the valedictory address by *Joshua. As in 1 Samuel 15, the setting in which the term appears is fraught with theological significance. Joshua was confronting what he knew to be the persistently idolatrous spirit of his people. Before dying, he wished to make it as clear as possible to them that their covenant with Yahweh was an exclusive one that forever barred the inclusion of worship of the gods alongside the worship of the Lord (Josh 24:20). He recognized that their way of thinking was thoroughly pagan: they would do whatever they wanted, particularly in regard to worshiping idols, and then would seek to procure Yahweh's forgiveness through the magical manipulation of ritual. At the very moment they were piously asserting their exclusive choosing of the Lord, there were idols among them (Josh 24:23). So Joshua asserted with hyperbolic force that God would not forgive their transgressions. Of course, that is not absolutely true. The classic statement of 2 Chronicles 7:14 (see 2.4 below) makes it plain that God will forgive when the appropriate conditions are met. But Joshua was confronting a people whose attitude was the very opposite of the conditions set out there. The important point here is that forgiveness is a matter not of ritualistic precision, but of attitude. Forgiveness is available to those who intend to live exclusively for God but for various reasons fall short (as the Levitical rituals specify). It is not available for those who intend to live in sin and then expect to manipulate God into forgiving them.

2.2. "Take Away" ('ābar). As noted above, this usage of this verb is infrequent. The two occurrences in the Historical Books both refer to David. In 2 Samuel 12:13 the prophet told David in response to his admission of sin in the matter of Bathsheba that the Lord had "taken away" the sin, with the result that David would not die. In 2 Samuel 24:10/1 Chronicles 21:8 it is reported that David asked God to "take away the iniquity" of his having conducted the census of his people. In this latter case the prayer seems not to have been immediately granted. It was only after David had made the sacrifice on the threshing floor of Araunah that the ensuing plague was restrained.

2.3. "Make Atonement For" (kāpar). Kāpar normally stresses the idea of making atonement for, and it has sacrificial overtones. However, it is apparent that the connection with ritual is not essential, as such a usage as that found in Exodus 32:30 makes plain. There, Moses says that he will attempt to make atonement (*kāpar*) for the people's sin in making the golden calf. Clearly, no ritual was involved there. Moses simply interceded for the people and asked God to forgive (*nāśā'*) their sin (Ex 32:32). That understanding

of the term is reinforced in 2 Chronicles 30:18-19, where *Hezekiah is said to have prayed for the people of the north who had not had opportunity to purify themselves properly for participation in the Passover celebration that Hezekiah had sponsored. Hezekiah's prayer was, "May the Lord, who is good, pardon *[kāpar]* everyone who settles his heart to seek God, the Lord God of his fathers, even though not according to the purity of the sanctuary." Once again, the key issue is the attitude of the worshiper, and that attitude is so critical that it predominates even in spite of ritual incorrectness. It is not merely a matter of ritual plus correct attitude; it is a matter of attitude in spite of ritual. As with the previous example, forgiveness is available to those who are sincerely seeking to do the will of God and to experience his presence in their lives. If this attitude is present, ritual, though helpful (they *were* participating in the rituals of Passover!), is very much secondary. Without this attitude, ritual is not merely useless, but is positively disgusting to God, as was painfully apparent in Saul's case (1 Sam 15:22; see also Is 1:11-15).

2.4. "Forgive" (sālaḥ). It is often asserted that *sālaḥ* is closely associated with ritual activity (see Olivier, 3.260). Although that is undoubtedly true in other parts of the OT, the connection is not as apparent in the Historical Books. The parade example already mentioned is 2 Chronicles 7:14. Here, as in the cases of the other two terms already discussed, the emphasis is strictly upon the attitude of the supplicant. There are four conditions specified: humbling oneself (i.e., admission of need), turning away from one's sin (repentance), seeking God's "face" (doing whatever is necessary to experience his active presence in one's life) and prayer. If these conditions were met, then God would hear, forgive the people, and heal their land. Ritual performance is not one of the conditions. However, it must quickly be pointed out that this statement from God is made as a response to the dedicatory prayer of *Solomon for the temple (2 Chron 6 = 1 Kings 8). Furthermore, 2 Chronicles 7:12 has God explicitly saying that he has chosen the place for himself "as a house of sacrifice." Furthermore, ten of the fourteen occurrences of *sālaḥ* in the Historical Books are found in the two editions of Solomon's dedicatory prayer. So, is it warranted to say that the term is not directly connected to ritual activity in this part of the canon? It is, and in part because of this setting. Given the temple setting, and that Solomon had just sponsored thousands of sacrifices, one might very well expect that correct sacrifice, or at least ritualistically correct *prayer, might be one of the necessary conditions for forgiveness. But that is distinctly not the case. Solomon's prayer does not make a single reference to sacrifice. Instead, by its repeated mentions of prayer (some twenty times in twenty-five verses), the prayer goes far toward agreeing with Isaiah's definition of the temple as a "house of prayer" (see Is 56:7-8). The fact that forgiveness is not inextricably linked to ritual activity is especially apparent when Solomon mentions the possibility of exiles who pray in the direction of the temple being forgiven (1 Kings 8:46-51). It would be impossible for them to perform correct ritual away from the temple.

However, is it not significant that the prayer is to be made in the direction of the temple? Unquestionably it is. But it is important to note that it is never suggested that merely praying in that direction will effect forgiveness. The temple does not have magical powers as the residence of God. At the outset Solomon says that this is not the house of God (1 Kings 8:27). And he says repeatedly that God will hear *from heaven* (e.g., 1 Kings 8:30, 32, 34). But if these things are so, why is the prayer of repentance and *faith to be made in the direction of the temple? It is because this is the place on earth that represents the "name" of God (1 Kings 8:29)—that is, his character. To pray in that direction is to remember the character and nature of God, and to think and act accordingly. There is no forgiveness available except on the basis of God's character and nature (so Eichrodt, 2.257-58; see also below on Neh 9:17). At the same time, the person who demonstrates a cavalier attitude toward those physical means that God has ordained to represent the changed character of the worshiper shows that he or she does not indeed possess that changed character. Thus the person who refuses to recognize that God has uniquely revealed himself and his will in the context of the temple at Jerusalem is not a true candidate for forgiveness.

In this regard, Naaman is a most interesting case. The Syrian officer recognized that in healing him, God had demonstrated a uniqueness and a power that effectively de-deified all the so-called gods, including the god Rimmon, whom Naaman's master worshiped. Thus for Naaman to seem to worship that god would convey a wrong picture of his true attitude: exclusive devotion to the Lord (2 Kings 5:17). However, his position would demand that he accompany the king of Syria to the worship of Rimmon and to bow to the idol. Thus he asked *Elisha for forgiveness for ritual actions that would not reflect his true attitude. Although Elisha did not give him the specific absolution that he requested, he did give the benediction "Go in peace" (2 Kings 5:19), which, if it does not suggest approval, at least indicates understanding that attitude is the fundamental quality in relation to God.

A contrary example to that of Naaman is the Judean king *Manasseh. In 2 Kings 24:4 it says that God was unwilling to forgive Judah because Manasseh had filled Jerusalem with blood. This is an important point because 2 Chronicles 33:12-17 recounts how Manasseh, in prison in Assyria, turned to God and prayed and was restored to his kingdom in Jerusalem. Furthermore, *Josiah, Manasseh's grandson, had led the nation in a notable revival that included restoring correct ritual to the worship in the land (2 Chron 34:8-33). Nevertheless, God would not forgive the land. The attitudes and behaviors that had been inculcated in Manasseh's long first years had become too deeply ingrained. This says that although personal repentance and restoration are possible, and although correct ritual may be performed subsequently, it is also possible to set in place attitudes and behaviors that will prevail among one's followers irrespective of everything else. And if those attitudes and behaviors prevail, there is no magical manipulation that will produce forgiveness (see 2 Kings 21:10-15; 23:26-27).

But this refusal to forgive Judah because of the attitudes and behaviors that Manasseh set in motion does not in any way suggest a reluctance to forgive on God's part. The very opposite is true. The only reason forgiveness is possible at all is because of the character of the Creator of the universe. He is slow to get angry and quick to forgive, constantly looking for the slightest pretext to exercise abundant compassion, mercy and unfailing love. This understanding, which was first revealed to Moses in the experience recorded in Exodus 34:1-7, is found in every part of the OT canon. Among the Historical Books, Nehemiah 9:17 gives expression to it. *Nehemiah realizes that the only reason Israel continues to exist after the exile is because "You are a forgiving God, gracious and compassionate, slow to anger and abounding in love. Therefore you did not desert them." He is saying the same thing that the psalmist says when he cries out, "If you kept a record of sins, who could stand? But with you there is forgiveness of sins" (Ps 130:3-4). If God were merely the embodiment of implacable justice, there would be no humans left on the planet. But he is not that sort of God, and like the rest of the OT and, indeed, the Bible, the Historical Books celebrate that fact.

3. Narrative Expressions of Forgiveness.
Nowhere is this character of God more evident than in the book of *Judges, where time after time God responds to the pleadings of his sinful people by sending them a deliverer and deliverance (e.g., Judg 3:9, 15; 10:10-16). The same point continues to be made in the books of *Samuel (1 Sam 7:2-9; 12:19-25), where the Lord is said to have continued to be willing to be entreated by the people even though they had repeatedly broken his covenant. *Ezra and Nehemiah were devastated to discover that the exile had not produced any real change in the attitudes and behavior of the people, but they also hoped that on the basis of the unchanging character of God, national forgiveness was still possible (Ezra 9:6—10:4; Neh 9:16-38). On a personal level, there is God's forgiveness of David (2 Sam 12:13), and much more surprisingly, given his terrible record, Ahab (1 Kings 21:25-28). The books of *Chronicles, besides recording the forgiveness of Manasseh already mentioned, also record the repentance of *Rehoboam and his partial deliverance from Shishak as a result (2 Chron 12:7-8). The most dramatic expression of human forgiveness in the Historical Books is David's giving of a lifetime pension to Mephibosheth, the grandson of Saul and son of Jonathan, as an expression of covenant faithfulness to Jonathan (2 Sam 9:1-13). In many ways, David's actions toward the helpless scion of the enemy dynasty are a close reflection of God's actions toward the human race.

See also FAITH; SIN.

BIBLIOGRAPHY. **W. Eichrodt,** *Theology of the Old Testament* (2 vols.; OTL; Philadelphia: Westminster, 1967); **H. F. Fuhs,** "עבר," *TDOT* 10.421-22; **V. P. Hamilton,** *Handbook on the Historical Books* (Grand Rapids: Baker, 2001); **J. Hausmann,** "סלח," *TDOT* 10.258-65; **W. C. Kaiser,** "סלח," *TWOT* 2.626; **K. Koch,** "Sühne und Sündevergebung um die Wende von der exilischen zur nachexilischen Zeit," *EvT* 26 (1966) 217-39; **J. S. Kselman,** "Forgiveness (OT)," *ABD* 2.831-33; **J. P. J. Olivier,** "סלח," *NIDOTTE* 3.259-64; **G. von Rad,** *Old Testament Theology* (2 vols.; New York: Harper & Row, 1965); **J. J. Stamm,** *Erlösen und Vergeben im Alten Testament* (Bern: Francke, 1940); idem., "סלח," *TLOT* 2.797-803.

J. N. Oswalt

FORM CRITICISM. *See* METHODS OF INTERPRETATION.

FOUR-ROOM HOUSE. *See* ARCHITECTURE.

G

GAD. *See* PROPHETS AND PROPHECY.

GATH

Gath was one of the five cities of the *Philistines that sat on the border between Judah and Philistia (1 Sam 17:52). Gath is infamous in the biblical narrative as the hometown of Goliath and one of the Philistine cities where the *ark of the covenant resided. The word *Gath* usually is translated as "winepress," although it might have a wider meaning based on a comparison with Ugaritic texts in which the term refers to a processing center for agricultural goods (Schniedewind). This latter term might be more appropriate because other cities have the word *Gath* in their name (e.g., Gath-rimmon in the territory of Manasseh [Josh 21:25], Gath-hepher [Josh 19:13], Gath-rimmon [Josh 19:45]).

1. Site Identification
2. Historical Overview

1. Site Identification.
In spite of its importance as a biblical city, the location of the ancient site has been greatly debated. To date, five major sites have been suggested. In the nineteenth century J. R. Porter proposed Tell es-Safi as the ancient site of Gath as early as 1887. W. F. Albright challenged this proposal and suggested Tell Erani/el-ʿAreini in 1921. Albright's proposal so dominated scholarly opinion that the modern Israeli town next to the tell was named Kiryat Gat. Excavations demonstrated that there are no Iron Age I remains at this site. This led to various alternative proposals, such as Tell Seraʾ (G. E. Wright in 1966) and Tell Nagila (S. Bülow and R. Mitchell in 1961) in the western Negev. A. Rainey wrote several articles arguing for the identification with Tell es-Safi, and currently this is the dominant view among scholars. L. Stager recently

suggested Tel Haror in the western Negev as the site of Gath. Stager made a strong case for Tel Haror based on the Egyptian settlements of the Iron Age IA period (1200-1150 BCE) and the Iron Age I archaeological evidence (e.g., Philistine monochrome and bichrome pottery). Current excavations at Tell es-Safi and the geopolitical context of Gath in the biblical narrative still make Tell es-Safi the probable site of the ancient city, and this identification retains widespread support among most archaeologists and biblical scholars. The first excavations of the site were conducted by F. J. Bliss with the assistance of R. A. S. Macalister on behalf of the British Palestine Exploration Fund. Ongoing excavations of the site are currently under the direction of A. Maeir of Bar Ilan University.

Tell es-Safi (Heb Tel Zafit) is located on the southern side of the Elah Valley at the intersection between the Philistine coastal plain and the Shephelah (M.R. 1359 1237). The site is located just 8 km from Tel Miqne (biblical site of Ekron). Albright thought that this placed the cities too close together, but a closer reading of the biblical text (1 Sam 7:14; 17:52) suggests that the cities were in close proximity. The site is at the entrance to the Elah Valley, which provides an easy access from the coast through the foothills up to the hill country. The Israelite site of Azekah sits on the eastern edge of the valley guarding the hills. The tell is 232 m above sea level and about 100 m above the valley bed.

2. Historical Overview.
2.1. Bronze Age. The earliest remains from Gath date to the third millennium BCE (Early Bronze II-III). Based on the amount of material culture excavated, the current excavations postulate that the city was of relatively large size and probably was the main urban center in this area.

No Middle Bronze Age strata have been found, although surveys have found Middle Bronze Age pottery suggesting that there was a small settlement. The *Canaanite city of Gath is known for the first time in historical sources during the Late Bronze Age. In the fourteenth century BCE the city appears in several Amarna letters written by its ruler Shuwardata to Pharaoh of Egypt. The city was called Gimti or Ginti. Shuwardata's correspondence reveals the nature of the geopolitics of this region. In one letter he is aligned with the ruler of *Gezer against the ruler of *Jerusalem, and in another letter he has a dispute over Keilah (a site in the Elah Valley) and Bethlehem, which were aligned with Jerusalem. This border tension between the Canaanite cities on the coastal plain and the cities in the hill country continues in the biblical period, albeit between Philistines and Israelites. This geopolitical dynamic illustrates the strategic location of Gath. Excavations have revealed at least two occupational strata that date to the Late Bronze Age. The finds of the last Late Bronze Age stratum contain an assortment of Egyptian and Egyptianized objects. The Late Bronze Age Canaanite city was destroyed by fire around 1200 BCE. This destruction should be associated with the newly arriving Philistines. In the coalition of the five city-states that go up against the Gibeonites who form a treaty with the Israelites, Gath does not participate in the coalition that contains both Gezer and Jerusalem. Perhaps this story reflects the geopolitical shift in the hill country and Shephelah around 1200 BCE (Josh 10). For the biblical writers, tradition has the Anakim continuing to live in Gath, as well as Gaza and Ashdod (Josh 11:22).

2.2. Iron Age I. Archaeological evidence demonstrates that Gath was a major Philistine city during Iron Age I (1200-1000 BCE) and that the Philistines started to expand their boundaries during the middle of the twelfth century BCE. This expansion eastward is documented by the biblical writers. Gath has played an important role in the traditions of the Israelites. Two major stories of the wars between the Philistines and Israelites are preserved in the biblical text. The first is the battle at Ebenezer, when the ark of the covenant was captured (1 Sam 4). The ark of the covenant resided in Gath briefly after its capture and was moved to Ekron after an outbreak of tumors (1 Sam 5:8-10). After this incident Samuel gathered the Israelites at *Mizpah and fought

the Philistines and struck them down as far as Beth-car. The cities "that the Philistines had taken from Israel" were restored "from Ekron even to Gath." (1 Sam 7:14). The Philistines again campaigned against Israel in the Elah Valley (see 1 Sam 17), where the champions of each army, *David and Goliath, faced off. The text notes that Goliath came from a race of giants from Gath. While both of these stories contain theological overtones, the stories reflect the underlying border tensions between the Israelites and Philistines and the city of Gath.

2.3. Iron Age II. Gath was always a border town between Philistia and Judah, as is demonstrated by the archaeological data and the biblical accounts associated with the rise of David. David occasionally sought refuge from the king of Gath. The first time, David was at Nob and fled to Gath when the king's servants recounted how David was well known in Israel for his support and valor as a servant of *Saul (the Philistines' enemy). As a ruse, David feigned insanity by scribbling on the doors of the gate and drooling on his beard (1 Sam 21:10-15). David was allowed to depart, and he hid in the cave of Adullam (1 Sam 22:1). Later, David sought refuge from Saul by moving out of the hill country across the border to Gath, whereupon Saul stopped searching for him (1 Sam 27:2-4). The king of Gath, Achish son of Maoch, allowed David to reside in Ziklag, a town under the domain of Gath in the western Negev. David made this town his base of operations as he made many raids against the tribes in the Negev region. David won favor with the leaders and inhabitants of Judah as he protected them from attacks on the southwestern and southern borders while he tricked Achish into thinking that he was attacking Judahite tribes (1 Sam 27:5-12). The archaeological phase associated with this period contains "degenerate Philistine pottery" illustrative of the Philistine acculturation process that is evident in the eleventh century BCE and continues throughout their history.

When David became king of Israel, he defeated the Philistines and "took Gath and its towns" from the hand of the Philistines (1 Chron 18:1). Later, he apparently had support among inhabitants from Gath. When his son Absalom rebelled against him and he had to flee, six hundred men who were Gittites that came up with him from Gath were among David's supporters (2 Sam 15:18-22). The author of Samuel records, toward the end of David's reign, another battle at Gath against a man of great stature (2 Sam 21:20). After the campaign of Shishak, *Rehoboam fortified several sites in his territory, particularly in the Shephelah and Gath was one of these cities (2 Chron 11:8). Archaeological excavations at Tel es-Safi have shown that Gath continued to be occupied by the Philistines. The description by the Chronicler should not be interpreted as Israelite occupation of Gath but probably some form of influence or hegemony during this period, or perhaps the writer is referring to another Gath in Judahite territory.

Current excavations have shown that the city of Gath was at a zenith during the ninth century BCE (c. 50 ha) when it was destroyed by an all-consuming fire. To date, the excavators have dated this destruction to the very end of the ninth century BCE or the very beginning of the eighth century BCE. This destruction can be attributed to Hazael, king of Aram, who fought against Gath and captured it before he went up to Jerusalem, where Jehoash paid him tribute (2 Kings 12:17-18). One of the most interesting features excavated is a large trench, over 2 km long, surrounding the site on the eastern, southern, and western sides. This has been interpreted as a siege trench, tentatively dated to the conquest by Hazael.

The site has the remnants of an eighth-century BCE stratum. King Uzziah "broke down the wall of Gath" (2 Chron 26:6), and *lmlk* stamp jar handles have been found—evidence for Judahite activity and interest toward the end of the eighth century BCE. Sargon conquered the city in 712 BCE (see ANET, 286). This is the last city of Gath, with a possible limited Persian occupation. Gath's demise is hinted at in the prophetic literature, where lists of Philistine cities appear without Gath (e.g., Jer 25:20; Zeph 2:4). The city and its fate became a proverb among the Israelites, from David's lament over the death of Saul ("Tell it not in Gath" [2 Sam 1:20]) to later prophets (Amos 6:2; Mic 1:10).

See also GOLIATH; PHILISTINES.

BIBLIOGRAPHY. F. J. Bliss and R. A. S. Macalister, Excavations in Palestine During the Years 1898-1900 (London: Committee of the Palestine Exploration Fund, 1902); A. M. Maeir and C. S. Ehrlich, "Excavating Philistine Gath," BAR 27.6 (2001) 22-31; B. Mazar, "Gath and Gittaim." IEJ 4 (1954) 227-35; A. Rainey, "The Identification of Philistine Gath—A Problem in Source Analysis for Historical Geography, ErIsr 12 (1975) 63*-76*; W. Schniedewind, "The Geopolitical History of Philistine Gath," BASOR 309 (1998) 69-77; L. Stager, "The Impact of the Sea Peoples (1185-1050 BCE)," in The Archaeology of Society in the Holy Land, ed. T. Levy (New York: Facts on File, 1995), 332-48; E. Stern, "Tel Zafit," NE-AEHL 4.1522-24.   S. M. Ortiz

GAZA

The ancient city of Gaza is situated on the southern coastal plain of ancient Palestine. Its geographic importance lies in its proximity to the Mediterranean Sea, the western end of the Negev trade routes and the northern end of the route through northern Sinai. Because of its strategic importance on the major route between Africa and Asia, it has always played an important role in the economic and military history of this region and has had continuous occupation throughout the history of the region.

1. Site Identification
2. Historical Overview

1. Site Identification.

The site is identified with Tell Harube/Tell ʿAzza, about 55 hectares in the heart of the modern Palestinian city of Gaza. The present old city of Gaza sits on the tell. The ancient city was about three miles from the Mediterranean Sea. The ancient city of Gaza was partially excavated by three large trenches on the northern part of the tell. Excavations were conducted by W. J. Phythian-Adams in 1922 on behalf of the Palestine Exploration Fund. Phythian-Adams identified five brick city walls and a glacis made of field stones. He assigned relative dates to the walls from Alexander the Great to the middle of the second millennium. Ceramics found in the trenches dated to the Late Bronze Age, Iron Age I (Philistine pottery) and Iron Age II. The site has been continuously occupied until the modern period, as evidenced by Roman, Byzantine and Early Arab pottery.

2. Historical Overview.

The city is known in the biblical sources as one of the *Philistine Pentapolis cities (Jos 13:3; 1 Sam 6:17). It was first mentioned in the annals of Thutmose III, where it was under the property of the *Egyptian crown and became the capital of the Egyptian province of *Canaan. Gaza is mentioned in the Amarna and Tanaach tablets as an Egyptian administrative center, and in a relief of Seti I it is a well-fortified town. During the Late Bronze Age it functioned as Egypt's base of operations for military incursions up the coast and as a border between Egypt and Canaan. This is reflected in the hyperbole of summary descriptions of Joshua's conquests such as Joshua 10:40-41: "Thus Joshua struck all the land . . . from Kadesh-barnea even as far as Gaza."

2.1. Philistine Control and Occupation. At the end of the Nineteenth Dynasty Egypt lost control of this beachhead as the geopolitics of the ancient Mediterranean world shifted in what is commonly referred to as the "thirteenth-century collapse." Waves of Sea Peoples were fought off by Merneptah and Ramesses III. The Philistines were part of this Aegean migration and settlement along the coast of ancient Palestine, and, as surmised from excavations throughout the southern coastal plain, they destroyed major Canaanite cities and resettled them during the Late Bronze-Iron Age I transition. This period of settlement, migration and demographic shifts is reflected in the biblical text. Deuteronomy 2:23 states that the Caphtorim destroyed the villages of the Avvim in Gaza and lived in their place, and Joshua 11:22 mentions that no Anakim were left in the land except in Gaza, Gath and in Ashdod.

Although Gaza was part of Judah's tribal allotment (Josh 15:47; Judg 1:18), the biblical text points out that the city, as well as the larger region of the Philistine coastal plain, was not occupied or subdued (Josh 13:2-4; Judg 1:19). In spite of the lack of archaeological evidence, it can be surmised that Gaza was a well-planned and fortified city, as evidenced by other Pentapolis cities that have been extensively excavated. During the Iron Age I the southern coastal plain was transformed into the heartland of Philistia. The material culture, city-planning and architecture reveal a more complex and sophisticated culture compared to the villages and towns of the western highlands. Gaza's prominence is reflected in the Samson narratives (Judg 13—16). These stories describe the border tensions between Judah and the Philistines and depict the city as well fortified (Judg 16:1-3) and containing a prison (Judg 16:21). One of the central features of the city in the Judges narrative is the temple of Dagon (Judg 16:23-30), a multistoried pillared structure (Judg 16:26-27, 29), probably similar to

the Iron Age I Philistine temples excavated at Tell Qasile and *Ekron.

2.2. Philistine Expansion (Eleventh Century BCE). The shift in the biblical narrative to *Samuel and *Saul focuses on the Philistine dominance and the wars against Judah and the tribal confederation developing under Saul. This was a period of Philistine expansion during the eleventh century BCE. Gaza is not mentioned in the biblical narrative, but more than likely it played a part in the Philistine expansion, particularly in the Negev, as evidenced by several sites with Philistine degenerative pottery. During the reign of *David, the Philistine expansion was checked, and it appears that the Philistine city-states were relegated to a status of tributaries to the Davidic and Solomonic dynasty. This is evidenced by hyperbolic statements of the reign of *Solomon: "[Solomon] controlled the whole region west of the River from Tiphsah to Gaza" (1 Kings 4:24), and "from the entrance of Hamath to the Wadi of Egypt" (1 Kings 8:65).

2.3. Iron Age II (Tenth Century BCE). During the tenth century BCE the Egyptian pharaoh came up through Philistia via Gaza to capture *Gezer and give it as a dowry for a marriage alliance between Egypt and Solomon (1 Kings 9:16). Toward the end of the century, during the reign of *Rehoboam of Judah, Pharaoh Shishak raided Judah and Israel (c. 928-911 BCE). It is apparent that either Egypt took advantage of the weakness of Philistia or Philistia was in alliance with Egypt. According to Shishak's campaign place list on the temple of Amon at Karnak (Kitchen, 398-415), the apparent starting point of the campaign was Gaza. With the division of the Davidic kingdom into Israel and Judah, and the reestablishment of Egyptian military activity, the regional geopolitics shifted, and territorial and political tensions are evidenced by Rehoboam's fortifications (2 Chron 11:5-12).

2.4. Iron Age II (Ninth and Eighth Centuries BCE). During the end of the ninth century BCE and beginning of the eighth century BCE, alliances between Philistines, Arabs and the kingdom of *Edom cooperated to oppose Judah and control the trade to the south, mainly spices and incense. Although not mentioned by name in the texts, Gaza would have been the Philistine city integral to facilitating the trade routes from Edom to the coast and opposition to Judah. Hints of Gaza's role in the regional geopolitics of this period are mentioned in Amos's oracles delivered about 760 BCE against Gaza (Amos 1:6-7), as well as when Judah regained dominance under Amaziah and Uzziah (2 Kings 14:7, 22; 2 Chron 21:16-17; 26:2).

2.5. Assyrian Vassal. The next period of Gaza's history (second half of the eighth century BCE) found Gaza as part of the *Assyrian Empire's expansion policy with control of the international coastal route connecting Damascus to Egypt. The name of Hanno, king of Gaza, appears in a tribute list of Tiglath-pileser in 738 BCE (*ANET*, 282), and in 734 BCE Tiglath-pileser came "against Philistia" and established Gaza as a "custom station of Assyria" (*ANET*, 283; Wiseman, 121). Hanno fled at this time, the royal family was captured, and a huge tribute was imposed on the city. Hanno apparently was pardoned by Tiglath-pileser and restored to the throne, but he joined Hamath, with the backing of Egypt, in rebellion against Assyria when Sargon II came to power. Gaza became an Assyrian vassal city and remained loyal. *Hezekiah tried to force Philistia to join him in his rebellion against Sennacherib: he "overran Philistia as far as Gaza and its border areas, from watchtower to fortified town" (2 Kings 18:8). Sennacherib allocated some of the border cities of Judah to kings of Philistia (Sil-Bel of Gaza) after putting a stop to Hezekiah's rebellion (*ANET*, 288). Sil-Bel ruled Gaza for a long time during Assyria's dominance and is mentioned in the annals of Sennacherib in 701 BCE, Esarhaddon in 677 BCE, and Assurbanipal in 667 BCE.

2.6. Egyptian Influence and Babylonian Dominance. The Assyrian Empire rapidly declined toward the last quarter of the seventh century BCE, and Egypt reasserted and regained its hold in western Asia under the Egyptian pharaoh Psammetichus I. In 616 BCE Egypt was on the banks of the Euphrates, supporting the Assyrians against the rising *Babylonian Empire. Pharaoh Neco occupied Gaza briefly in 609 BCE. This period of Egyptian control over Philistia is reflected in Zephaniah's prophecy that lists woes for the four Philistine cities (Gaza, Ashkelon, Ashdod, Ekron) from south to north (Zeph 2:4; cf. 9:5).

Nebuchadnezzar's defeat of the Assyrians and Egyptians placed Gaza, along with the southern coastal plain, in Babylon's domain. This shift of international control of Gaza is reflected in 2 Kings 24:7, which states that the king of Babylon had taken all that belonged to the king of Egypt from "the Wadi of Egypt to the River Euphrates." It then changed hands between Neco and Nebuchadnezzar until Nebuchadnezzar's campaigns against Judah. Gaza apparently became a Babylonian garrison under Nebuchadnezzar, and Babylonian records show that the king of Gaza was held with other kings in Babylon (*ANET*, 308).

Gaza continued to be an important prize in the Persian and Hellenistic periods. It became known as a center of "Arab trade" during the Hellenistic period. Gaza, like all of Philistia, was prone to acculturation, and the ethnic-national identity of Philistines ended with the Babylonian deportations. Gaza was fully Hellenized under Seleucid rule.

See also PHILISTINES.

BIBLIOGRAPHY. **H. H. Katzenstein**, "Before Pharaoh Conquered Gaza (Jeremiah 47:1)," *VT* 33 (1983) 249-51; idem, "Gaza (Prehellenistic)," *ABD* 2.912-15; idem, "Gaza in the Egyptian Texts of the New Kingdom," *JAOS* 102 (1982) 111-13; **K. A. Kitchen**, *The Third Intermediate Period in Egypt (1100-650 B.C.)* (Warminster: Aris & Phillips, 1973); **A. Ovadiah**, "Gaza," *NEAHL* 2.464-67; **W. J. Phythian-Adams**, "Report on Soundings at Gaza," *PEQ* 55 (1923) 11-30; **H. Tadmor**, "Philistia Under Assyrian Rule," *BA* 29 (1966) 86-102; **D. J. Wiseman**, "A Fragmentary Inscription of Tiglath-pileser III from Nimrud," *Iraq* 18 (1956) 117-29.   S. M. Ortiz

GEBA. *See* GIBEAH, GEBA.

GEDALIAH. *See* HISTORY OF ISRAEL 6: BABYLONIAN PERIOD.

GENEALOGIES

A genealogy is defined as "a written or oral expression of the descent of a person or persons from an ancestor or ancestors" (Wilson 1977, 9). Genealogies of all sorts occur throughout biblical literature in various literary contexts. In addition to study based on internal criteria, they also may be studied in light of the external criteria supplied by anthropological research and ancient Near Eastern sources. Genealogies can take various forms, with the most common distinction being made between linear (one line of descent [e.g., Gen 5]) and segmented (more than one line of descent [e.g., Gen 10]). These two forms can occur together, as in 1 Chronicles 6, where we find a linear genealogy from Aaron to exiled Jehozadak (1 Chron 6:3b-15) embedded in a segmented genealogy from Levi to Aaron (1 Chron 6:1-3a) and for each of Levi's sons (1 Chron 6:16-19). The Chronicler returns to linear form in 1 Chronicles 6:20-29, interrupted by some segmenting (Samuel's two sons [1 Chron 6:28]). A second distinction is whether the genealogy is traced backward (ascending) or forward (descending). Both form-critical and literary-critical studies of genealogies are important and have been carried out in detail, but they cannot begin to be summarized adequately here. The goal of this article is to offer an up-to-date and carefully nuanced understanding of the approach to genealogy as Scripture.

1. History of Interpretation
2. Ancient Near Eastern Data
3. Anthropological Data
4. Biblical Data
5. Function of Genealogies

1. History of Interpretation.

R. R. Wilson, writing in the mid-1970s, summarized a scholarly impasse that had developed in the history of critical interpretation of genealogies:

> On the one hand, a large group of scholars, exemplified by M. Noth, claims that the biblical genealogies were primarily literary creations. A variant of this view holds that most of the genealogies were originally tribal genealogies that reflect the political and cultural situation of the time in which they were constructed. In either case the genealogies have little historiographical value. On the other hand, another group of scholars, exemplified by Albright, claims that many of the genealogies were based on old lists. If this is the case, then the genealogies may be regarded as reliable historiographic sources (Wilson 1977, 7).

Since that time, however, and due in large part to the careful work of Wilson, the consensus has shifted dramatically. Anthropological and literary research has thrown doubt on the idea that genealogies could simply be literary creations. Categories such as "tribal genealogies" and "old lists" are among the possible literary sources, but labels such as these cannot be applied arbitrarily. Study of genealogies must seek out the function served by the genealogy and seek to understand its tradition history. It is a given that a genealogy may exist as an oral

record for a long time before becoming a written record, and that, in addition, it may serve a different function as a written record than it served as an oral record.

Consequently, modern research into the Chronicler's genealogies, for instance, deals first with the literary shape, context and function of each genealogy in Chronicles, and then seeks out other information through the biblical text to explore the history of transmission. Whatever that complex path may have been by which a genealogy came into a written document, and whatever can or cannot be determined about it, the genealogies do carry some level of historiographic significance. The most progress has been made in the ability to nuance the possibilities that exist in understanding the historiographic significance, and that will be the main focus here.

2. Ancient Near Eastern Data.

Mesopotamian genealogies are mostly royal, mostly linear and rarely more than three or four generations deep. Study of fluidity is hampered by the absence of examples of overlapping genealogies in different sources. Fluidity occurs primarily in telescoping (i.e., eliminating names), though some rearrangement of the order of the ancestors may be detected in the king lists. Most notably, the genealogy of Ammisaduqa (a descendant of Hammurabi in the first dynasty of Babylon) evidences shuffling of the sequence of kings and garbling of some names when compared with the Assyrian king list (see Finkelstein; Malamat; Wilson 1977, 109-10).

Egyptian sources, mostly from the Persian and Hellenistic periods, preserve long linear genealogies, sometimes extending fifteen to twenty generations, and often connecting to priestly lines like the genealogies in Ezra-Nehemiah and Chronicles. Fluidity is also evident only in telescoping within these genealogies (Wilson 1977, 125-28).

Perhaps a word should be added concerning the Safaitic Inscriptions (earliest examples from the first century BCE), though these do not date to the OT period. Found in Syria and Jordan, these graffiti-type rock inscriptions often include extensive genealogical information (linear) that traces the writer's line six or seven generations back to an eponymous ancestor (Wilson 1977, 130).

Some additional ideas that the ancients had

about genealogies can be inferred from how they continually reorganize the genealogies of the gods. "Ever since the gods acquired their anthropomorphic character, the theologians have engaged in grouping them into generations and families whereby the rank and function of a given god was determined by his genetic relationship to another god in the pantheon" (Klein, 279). Since genealogies of the gods are manipulated in this way to serve a particular function, it would be logical to assume that human genealogies were treated in similar ways.

Wilson concludes that the data from the ancient Near Eastern genealogies argue for an increased recognition of the genealogies as historical sources in a qualified sense. "Even though the genealogies may be fluid and tendentious, they are still valuable historical sources provided their nature and functions are taken into account. In addition, in a number of cases, when we compared parallel genealogies, we found them to be identical, so until we have evidence to the contrary, we must consider them to be accurate and potentially valuable historical sources" (Wilson 1977, 133).

3. Anthropological Data.

What modern researchers refer to as fluidity in the form and function of genealogies was noted as far back as the writings of Josephus: "For such is the nature of the Samaritans. . . . When the Jews are in difficulties, they deny that they have any kinship with them, thereby indeed admitting the truth, but whenever they see some splendid bit of good fortune come to them, they suddenly grasp at the connection with them, saying that they are related to them and tracing their line back to Ephraim and Manasseh, the descendants of Joseph" (Josephus *Ant.* 11.341). Just like anthropological researchers today, Josephus is observing the way that genealogy functions among the Samaritans and how fluid the genealogies are as they feel free to weave themselves in or write themselves out. Anthropologists today likewise study the function of genealogies in cultures and observe the amount and nature of fluidity that is evidenced.

3.1. Function. Much of the anthropological research relates to oral genealogies in tribal contexts where kinship is the framework of society. On the individual level, the kinship ties of a person are found to serve as the foundation for rights and obligations. Linear genealogies offer

an understanding of an individual's kinship ties, and as such they function as the basis of claims to power, status, rank, office or inheritance (Wilson, *ABD* 2.931).

On the corporate tribal level, the current relationship of tribes and clans is expressed by means of genealogical connections between the tribes. Users would have recognized that such genealogies may or may not represent what we would consider the actual historical origin of the groups involved (Johnson, 6). The understood function of the genealogy was to express current realities.

3.2. Fluidity. As a result of these functions, fluidity is a common characteristic in oral genealogies and, to a lesser extent, in written genealogies. Fluidity can take the form of telescoping, changing the order of names in a linear genealogy, or reorganizing the relationships in a segmented genealogy. Such creative activity can be undertaken by individuals, corporate groups or institutions. Fluidity can represent shifting realities or polemical attempts to mold the present realities by people seeking to support their political, social or religious agendas (Wilson 1977, 29). Telescoping is often simply a convention related to limitations of memory or writing space. As names are continually added to the end of a list, other names will drop out or merge (Aufrecht, 216-17).

3.3. Genealogy and Historiography. On the one hand, Wilson's anthropological analysis of oral genealogies found no evidence of genealogies being either created or preserved for historiographical purposes only (Wilson 1977, 54). Despite this, he found that when genealogies were agreed upon, they could be used as historical evidence to support contemporary social configurations (Wilson 1977, 55). On the other hand, then, genealogies were usually accepted, for whatever reasons, as having historical validity and were found to contain a great deal of information that should be judged of historical value. Neither genealogies nor ancestors show evidence of being invented wholesale, and they do not change capriciously. If fictitious ancestries were going to be proffered, it makes the most sense that well-known or respected individuals would be incorporated, whether gods, heroes, or primeval founding fathers or mothers.

Oral genealogies were much more fluid than written genealogies, and once a genealogy was written down and assumed stability, it often was

Table 1. Major Genealogies of the Old Testament

Reference	Linear (L) or Segmented (S)	Ascending (A) or Descending (D)	Family Line	Number of Generations
Gen 4:17-22	L	D	Cain to 3 sons of Lamech	7
Gen 5:3-32	L	D	Adam to 3 sons of Noah	11
Gen 10:1-32	S	D	Sons of Noah to Joktan's sons	Japheth, Ham 3 Shem 6
Gen 11:10-30	L	D	Shem to Abram	10
Gen 22:20-24	S	D	Nahor to Rebekah	3
Gen 25:1-4	S	D	Abraham to descendants of Dedan	4
Gen 25:13-16	S	D	Ishmael and sons	2
Gen 36:9-14	S	D	Esau and grandsons	3
Gen 36:15-19	S	D	Esau and grandsons	3
Gen 36:20-29	S	D	Seir and grandsons	3
Ex 6:14-25	S	D	Levi to Phinehas	5
Ruth 4:18-21	L	D	Perez to David	10
1 Chron 1:1-37	L/S	D	Adam to Jacob	22
1 Chron 1:38-42	S	D	Seir and grandsons	3
1 Chron 2:1—4:21	S	D	Judah to postexilic	Max 34
1 Chron 4:24-37	S	D	Simeon's tribe	14
1 Chron 5:3-6	L	D	Reuben's tribe	10
1 Chron 5:11-15	S/L	A	Gad's tribe	9
1 Chron 6:1-15	L	D	Levi to exile	26
1 Chron 6:16-30	S	D	Levi to Shaul	7
1 Chron 6:50-51	L	D	High priests	12
1 Chron 7:1-3	S	D	Issachar's tribe	4
1 Chron 7:6-10	S	D	Benjamin's tribe	4
1 Chron 7:14-19	S	D	Manasseh's tribe	5?
1 Chron 7:20-26	L	D	Ephraim to Joshua	11
1 Chron 7:30-39	S	D	Asher's tribe	7?
1 Chron 8:1-28	S	D	Clans of Benjamin	4?
1 Chron 8:29-39	S	D	Family of Saul	10
1 Chron 9:3-21	L series	A	Jerusalem settlers	Most 3 or 4 Max 7
1 Chron 9:35-44	S	D	Family of Saul	15
Neh 11:4-17	L series	A	Leaders in Jerusalem	Most between 5 and 8

accorded a higher degree of historical reliability and was more likely to be treated as a historical record. To some extent, this reflects the reality that written genealogies served different functions than oral ones.

4. Biblical Data.

Most biblical genealogies are found in the material up to Moses and in the literature connected to the postexilic period. The major genealogical lists are detailed in table 1.

When we compare these genealogies to the ancient Near Eastern material, some contrasts become evident. The first observation is that in the ancient Near East most genealogies are linear, while in the OT most are segmented. Second, R. S. Hess (1989, 242) argues concerning Genesis 1—11 that the comparative genealogical material is not precisely parallel to the biblical material. For example, he notes, "A purpose of Ancient Near Eastern genealogies, as well as those from other cultures, is to give a certain status to a leader or official. This is not true within Genesis 1—11. There each genealogy seems to end with figures who perform acts which bring about condemnation not status" (Hess 1989, 248). A third difference is that biblical genealogies are consistently linked literarily to theological issues of election and promise (Satterthwaite, 656), which is largely absent from the ancient Near Eastern materials. Thus we find significant differences in form, function and literary context.

There is even less basis for comparison when we turn our attention to the postexilic literature. M. Johnson concludes that the purpose of the Chronicler is "to present a summary of the members of 'all Israel,' that is, of the true Davidic theocracy; in short, to give a picture of the complete kingdom of God" (Johnson, 57). S. De Vries calls 1 Chronicles 1—9 a "table of organization" listing individual positions or responsibilities, relating them to one another, and assigning individuals or groups to fill the positions or carry out the responsibilities. The criteria for assessment and organization extend beyond the genealogical to include territorial, military or cultic information (De Vries, 26-27). In the end, it must be admitted that there is nothing from the ancient world to compare to the scope and range of the biblical genealogies, or to offer a parallel to the theological function of these genealogical lists.

5. Function of Genealogies.

5.1. Form and Function. Genealogies are social and/or literary constructs, and as such operate differently from one culture to another depending on their purpose and function. We should therefore be wary of imposing our own expectations or constraints on the genre, lest we thereby misinterpret the texts. Form and function are driven by purpose, and the ancient purposes for formulating and recording genealogies may have been very different from our own. Our hermeneutical approach to the biblical literature must recognize this. Why was the genealogy important to the authors of Scripture and to the Israelites? We have seen that genealogies can at times be driven by political and/or apologetic purposes, but there are numerous other theoretical possibilities that interpreters must keep in mind. Some possible functions (known from anthropological and literary sources) to consider when approaching a biblical genealogy include the following (many of these are represented in the summary in Johnson, 77-82):

1. *Social Function* (when dealing with groups): Establishes community between groups (projecting the present into the past using segmented genealogy [Gen 10]?).
2. *Legitimizing Function* (when dealing with individuals): Establishes legitimacy for an individual's inclusion in a group for purposes of establishing rights and privileges connected with the group—for example, land ownership, succession to leadership or enhancing of status. In Ezra and Nehemiah, for example, lists are used to safeguard the purity of the nation and the *priesthood (Ezra 2:62-63; Neh 7:64-65). This function can use linear or segmented forms.
3. *Theological Function:* Establishes continuity of covenant people to give hope to postexilic people as they identify themselves as heirs to the promises. This function can use linear or segmented forms (1 Chron 2:1—4:21).
4. *Historical Function:* Orders the information of the past to understand the present.
5. *Literary Function* (when embedded in narrative): Joins narrative elements.
6. *Schematic Function* (when ages are given): Divides the history of world into cycles of epochs (Johnson, 32-36).
7. *Military Function:* Classifies people for purposes of clan involvement in conscription for government service.

5.2. Historiography. The next hermeneutical question that interpreters must address is to what extent "historiographic value" is the appropriate criterion by which to assess the genealogies (*see* Historiography, Old Testament). Historiographic value would be an appropriate criterion only when historiographic functions were intended. As an example of some of the complex issues, H. G. M. Williamson suggests that the genealogy of Judah (1 Chron 2:3—4:23) is arranged chiastically, with the sons of Hezron in the middle drawing particular attention to David. Thus, though it is a presentation of genealogical information, it is not intended to be understood in a linear way. The reality that genealogies are designed to express may not be transparent to us. Some may depend on or assume historical authenticity, while others may allow and even encourage creativity or artificiality as an artistic literary form, in which case legitimacy or credibility could not be judged by the criterion of authenticity. Alternatively, genealogies could be used (and manipulated) to communicate lines of power and prestige rather than as a means of preserving historical records. If it were determined that the biblical authors were using them in such a way, and that the audience would have understood them in that way, then we could not demand that such genealogies conform to our criteria of genealogy that are associated with a vastly different purpose. As W. E. Aufrecht observes, "It is inaccurate to say that these genealogies do not represent reliable facts. It is more accurate to say that the conception of history for and by which they were maintained caused them to develop in certain ways" (Aufrecht, 218). Therefore, to assess the historiographical role that any given genealogy can play, the interpreter must examine the purpose of the genealogy in its socio-literary context.

For the modern reader to grasp this expanded way of thinking about genealogies in the ancient world, it would be helpful to compare them to something more familiar to us. Employing De Vries's label "table of organization," we might consider the analogy of a corporation and its corporate structure. Linear structures would identify who my boss is, who his boss is, etc., all the way up to the CEO. Levels could be ignored in some contexts (telescoping)—for instance, when a low-level employee might point out the president and identify her as his boss. Segmented structures would be represented in the corporate organizational chart, which would show all the lines of communication and accountability beginning with the CEO, then all the senior vice presidents, and down through the management team and into the various departments. Every once in a while a corporate structure gets reorganized. An employee might still be doing the job that she or he was doing before, but now it is in a different department and under a different vice president. Alternatively, perhaps one vice president is elevated over the others, or a director is given direct access to the CEO. Some people get promoted while others get fired or marginalized. The corporate chart reflects present realities, not the history of the company or what it looked like when one was hired. The corporate chart is not intended as a historiographical document, though it could have historiographical value. It offers a way to determine the standing of each person within the corporation. Additional analogies can be drawn when we consider the circumstances of companies merging or departments being spun off into separate corporations. The organizational chart(s) must be adjusted to reflect the new realities. How could such a chart be wrong? It could be wrong if did not accurately reflect the current realities.

The strength of this analogy is that it provides an example of a genre that is similar to genealogies in format (linear or segmented) and in function (portraying relationship within a corporate group), and yet has no historiographic implications—it is merely a reflection of current realities. It provides an illustration that will help us to think of how it would be possible for genealogies to operate with integrity without being historiographic in nature. A nuanced understanding of the historiographic value of a genealogy recognizes that the reliability of a genealogy may relate more to the accuracy of its description of present reality than to whether it offers a precise or comprehensive record of ancestral history, though unquestionably some genealogies do intend to do the latter, in which case we have no reason to doubt their reliability. Even those that intend to describe present realities, however, cannot be considered to be worthless or fictional when it comes to historiographic value. There is a difference between historiographic purpose and historiographic value. This can best be explored in the biblical context as we consider the theology associated with the interpretation of genealogies.

5.3. Theology. It has become evident that the legitimacy of a genealogy cannot be measured only by assessing its historiographic reliability. Conversely, the historiographic value must be assessed on the basis of the intended purpose and function of the genealogy. This is simply good biblical hermeneutics: literature needs to be interpreted in light of its function as determined by its context and the characteristics of the genre. This nuancing is important in theory, but it cannot be used to override the overt claims that the text makes by means of the genealogy. Herein lies the tension for the theological interpreter. It is important for us to understand genealogies anthropologically and in their ancient Near Eastern context, but still we must allow the biblical text to depart from those models, just as we must allow it to depart from our own cultural models.

On an issue such as fluidity we cannot assume that since we know of anthropological examples of fluidity, therefore the biblical genealogies are fluid. Biblical genealogies offer little transparent evidence of fluidity beyond telescoping, though there may be a few examples (see the comparative analysis of overlapping genealogies in Chronicles and Nehemiah in Aufrecht, 218-22). Fluidity can be demonstrated only when there is more than one record of a genealogy. There are not many such instances in the OT, and often when they do occur, evidence of fluidity beyond telescoping is debatable. So, although there is no reason to rule out fluidity a priori, there is less reason to assume extensive fluidity if the existing evidence does not support it. Limited fluidity is also the norm for the ancient Near Eastern data, with its numerous examples of telescoping but only a few possible examples of switching the order within a genealogical line. Furthermore, even fluid genealogies do not typically fabricate fictional ancestors, so this should not be an activity imposed on the biblical genealogies. Anthropological and ancient Near Eastern data offer cases in which someone adopts a family line that is not his own, but there is very little suggestion of this in the OT genealogies. Perhaps the most likely candidate is the association of Samuel with the family of Levi (1 Chron 6:25-28), but even that has various possible explanations.

In conclusion, there is every reason to consider the biblical genealogies as having a signifi-cant level of historiographic value, even if historiography was not their main purpose. If we encounter cases where the historiographic reliability is open to question, we should not fear the theological implications. The ancient genre has a wider range of flexibility than we assume for modern genealogies. R. B. Dillard sums up the situation well:

> The doctrine of Scripture should not be used in such a way as to make the Chronicler a modern historian operating under the influence of historical positivism. The Chronicler was not a newspaper journalist. He was a teacher and theologian, a painter rather than a photographer. . . . The Chronicler wrote within the framework of culturally acceptable historiographic practices and genres. To impose on him canons for historiography that are derived from historical positivism would not only be an anachronism, but it would also strike in a fundamental way at the incarnational analogy by abstracting the Chronicler from his own time. We cannot deny to the Chronicler the liberties in the presentation of his data that his culture allowed (Dillard, xix).

See also CENSUS; CHRONICLER'S HISTORY; CHRONICLES, BOOKS OF; DAVID'S FAMILY; EZRA AND NEHEMIAH, BOOKS OF; HISTORIOGRAPHY, OLD TESTAMENT; ROYAL FAMILY; SAUL AND SAUL'S FAMILY.

BIBLIOGRAPHY. **W. E. Aufrecht,** "Genealogy and History in Ancient Israel," in *Ascribe to the Lord: Biblical and Other Essays in Memory of Peter C. Craigie,* ed. L. Eslinger and G. Taylor (JSOT-Sup 67; Sheffield: JSOT, 1988) 205-35; **R. Braun,** "1 Chronicles 1—9 and the Reconstruction of the History of Israel: Thoughts on the Use of Genealogical Data in Chronicles in the Reconstruction of the History of Israel," in *The Chronicler as Historian,* ed. M. Graham, K. Hoglund and S. McKenzie (Sheffield: Sheffield Academic Press, 1997) 92-105; **M. Chavalas,** "Genealogical History as 'Charter': A Study of Old Babylonian Period Historiography and the Old Testament," in *Faith, Tradition, and History: Old Testament Historiography in Its Near Eastern Context,* ed. A. R. Millard, J. K. Hoffmeier and D. W. Baker (Winona Lake, IN: Eisenbrauns, 1994) 103-28; **S. J. De Vries,** *1 and 2 Chronicles* (FOTL 11; Grand Rapids: Eerdmans, 1989); **R. B. Dillard,** *2 Chronicles* (WBC 15; Dallas: Word, 1987); **J. J. Finkelstein,** "The Genealogy of the Hammurabi

Dynasty," *JCS* 20 (1966) 95-118; **R. S. Hess,** "The Genealogies of Genesis 1—11 and Comparative Literature," *Bib* 70 (1989) 241-54; repr., in *I Studied Inscriptions from Before the Flood: Ancient Near Eastern, Literary, and Linguistic Approaches to Genesis 1—11,* ed. R. S. Hess and D. T. Tsumura (Winona Lake, IN: Eisenbrauns, 1994) 58-72; **S. Japhet,** *I & II Chronicles* (OTL; Louisville: Westminster/John Knox, 1993); **M. Johnson,** *The Purpose of Biblical Genealogies* (rev. ed.; Cambridge: Cambridge University Press, 1988); **J. Klein,** "The Genealogy of Nanna-Suen and Its Historical Background," in *Proceedings of the XLV Rencontre Assyriologique Internationale, 1: Historiography in the Cuneiform World,* ed. T. Abusch et al. (Bethesda, MD: CDL, 2001) 279-301; **G. Knoppers,** *1 Chronicles 1—9* (ABC; New York: Doubleday, 2003) 245-65; **Y. Levin,** "From Lists to History: Chronological Aspects of the Chronicler's Genealogies," *JBL* 123 (2004) 601-36; **A. Malamat,** "King Lists of the Old Babylonian Period and Biblical Genealogies," *JAOS* 88 (1968) 163-73; **N. Na'aman,** "Sources and Redaction in the Chronicler's Genealogies of Asher and Ephraim," *JSOT* 49 (1991) 99-111; **J. Sasson,** "A Genealogical 'Convention' in Biblical Chronography?" *ZAW* 90 (1978) 171-85; **P. E. Satterthwaite,** "Genealogy in the Old Testament," *NIDOTTE* 4.654-63; **H. G. M. Williamson,** "Sources and Redaction in the Chronicler's Genealogy of Judah," *JBL* 98 (1979) 351-59; idem, *1 and 2 Chronicles* (NCBC; Grand Rapids: Eerdmans, 1982); **R. R. Wilson,** "The Old Testament Genealogies in Recent Research," *JBL* 94 (1975) 169-89; idem, *Genealogy and History in the Biblical World* (New Haven: Yale University Press: 1977); idem, "Genealogy, Genealogies," *ABD* 2.929-32.   J. H. Walton

GEOGRAPHICAL EXTENT OF ISRAEL

The geographical extent of Israel should be considered against the backdrop of the natural divisions of the land of *Canaan. Although small, the geographical area of what would become Israel contains rather divergent topographical regions. These geographical regions tended to foster division and fragmentation, and impeded efforts toward social and political unification. In addition to this impact of topography, the geopolitical realities of various time periods facilitated expansion or reduction of Israel's geographical extent. Furthermore, it should be

stressed that the changing geographical extent of Israel is couched within the theological dynamics of covenant. The geographical extent of Israel ebbed and flowed throughout the different periods of Israel's history, and this fact gives shape to the present article. Finally, it should be noted that many details concerning the geographical extent of Israel connect one way or another to the biblical text, which is given due regard here; questions of historicity and the like are treated elsewhere.

1. Preconquest Anticipation of the Geographical Extent of Israel
2. Geographical Extent of Israel Prior to the Entry into Canaan
3. Geographical Extent of Israel During the Conquest Period
4. Geographical Extent of Israel During the Time Frame of the Judges
5. Geographical Extent of Israel During the United Monarchy (c. 1040/1030[?]-930 BCE)
6. Geographical Extent of Israel and Judah During the Divided Kingdom (c. 930-720 BCE)
7. Geographical Extent of Judah Following the Fall of the Northern Kingdom (c. 720-539 BCE)
8. Geographical Extent of Judah (Judea) During the Postexilic Time Frame (c. 539-430 BCE)

1. Preconquest Anticipation of the Geographical Extent of Israel.

The anticipation of the geographical extent of Israel is interwoven with the understanding of the geographical extent of the "land of Canaan" (cf. Gen 17:8; Lev 25:38), particularly with respect to the northern border of *Canaan.

From the perspective of *Egypt and various Mesopotamian states, the geographical area between Mesopotamia in the north and Egypt in the south was commonly considered to be one geopolitical unit, which did not preclude other geographical regions, such as Gilead to the east of the Jordan (Aharoni, 64-67). This one-unit understanding seems to have been utilized in the earliest definition of the geographical extent of the Promised Land: "from the river of Egypt as far as the great river, the Euphrates River" (Gen 15:18; cf. Ex 23:31; Deut 1:7-8; 11:24; Josh 1:4). That said, the Mari letters seem to imply a northern boundary of Canaan further south

(south of Qatna), while some Ugaritic texts imply that the northern extreme of Canaan was even further south (in the vicinity of the northern end of the Litani River adjacent to the high point [Mount Hor?] of the Lebanese range and Lebo Hamath) (Aharoni, 67-80; Mazar 1986b, 189-202). This latter understanding parallels the description of the border of Canaan in the Table of Nations (Gen 10:18-19), the route taken by the spies in Numbers 13 and the detailed delineation of Israel's land inheritance in Numbers 34. In the description of Numbers 34 Israel's northern border is marked out from the Great (Mediterranean) Sea to Mount Hor, and from Mount Hor to Lebo Hamath and onward to Hazar Enan (Num 34:7-9). A northern boundary in this region is also reflected in the tribal land allotments in Ezekiel's vision (Ezek 47:13-48:29). Finally, note that in Deuteronomy 11:24 the Euphrates may be functioning as an eastern border rather than the northern border (likewise, Gen 15:18 may be a southwest-northeast description of the Promised Land), a factor that might shed light on the question of the northern border.

2. Geographical Extent of Israel Prior to the Entry into Canaan.

Prior to its "official" entry into Canaan, Israel acquired land in the Transjordan area in conjunction with the defeat of Sihon and Og (cf. Num 21:21-35; Deut 2:24-3:10). The area taken from Sihon extended from the border of *Moab at the Arnon River/Canyon to the Jabbok River/Canyon and eastward to the border of the *Ammonites, including the agriculturally bountiful Medeba Plateau (the Mishor/Tableland). Afterward, Israelite control was extended north, ultimately including the eastern Jordan Valley from the Salt (Dead) Sea to the Sea of Chinnereth (Galilee). Israel then defeated Og and took possession of his landholdings, which extended north to the Yarmuk River/Canyon and eastward. The allure of this region, given its agricultural richness and prime grazing areas (cf. Lot in Gen 13), prompts Reuben and Gad to seek the "land of Gilead" as their inheritance (Num 32). Although not well received initially, the proposal is accepted, and this territory across the Jordan is allotted to Reuben, Gad and part of Manasseh. Although efforts are made to insure that the Jordan River did not divide the tribes of Israel (cf. Josh 22:21-34), it nevertheless func-

tioned as a barrier to east-west communication and hence tribal integration (Monson 1996, 55).

All told, by the time the Israelites were camped in the Plains of Moab opposite Jericho, they ostensibly controlled a sizable portion of the Transjordan region, although the extent of initial settlement is uncertain (Kallai, 241-59).

3. Geographical Extent of Israel During the Conquest Period.

Despite innumerable attempts to discredit much or all of the conquest accounts chronicled in the book of *Joshua, the political and territorial system implied in these accounts corresponds to what would be expected in the Late Bronze Age. That said, the book of Joshua is a selective (and theologically driven) summary of Israel's entry into the Promised Land. Thus certain events receive little detail (e.g., Josh 9:1-2), while others are unknown (e.g., Israel's relationship with and taking of *Shechem [cf. Josh 8:30-35; 24]).

Israel's entry into the land of Canaan begins with the divinely facilitated crossing of the Jordan and subsequent victory over *Jericho in the southern Jordan Valley and (eventually) *Ai in the hill country (Josh 6:1-8:29). Israel's success prompts the Gibeonites to seek a covenant with Israel (Josh 9:1-27), a treaty that gives Israel instant leverage over the central Benjamin Plateau (a prerequisite for controlling the central hill country). This advantage given to Israel by the Gibeonites prompts five nearby city-states to attack *Gibeon. Following a plea from the Gibeonites, this coalition is defeated by the Israelites (Josh 10:1-11), giving Israel a larger foothold in the hill country and part of the Shephelah. This string of victories sets up the first summary notice of Joshua conquering "all the land" (Josh 10:40-43), which is delineated via four geographical regions: the (central and southern) hill country, the Negev, the Shephelah and the wilderness slopes (between the hill country and the Jordan Rift Valley); and also by specific points in the land: Kadesh Barnea to *Gaza and all the land of Goshen as far as Gibeon. In light of this description, the expression "all the land" should be understood along the lines of "all *this* land, namely . . . " Also, in contrast to the anticipated "little by little" approach to attaining the Promised Land (cf. Deut 7:22), this summary specifies that this land was taken "at one time" (Josh 10:42). Nevertheless, it should be pointed out that the Israelites return to the camp at *Gilgal

(Josh 10:43), illustrating the reality that battles might be won over various cities without those cities being subsequently occupied by the Israelites.

Following these battles in the south, Israel is drawn into battle in the Galilee region against a multiethnic coalition of city-states led by *Hazor, "the head of all those kingdoms" (Josh 11:1-15; cf. the "Galilee of the nations" [Is 9:1]). Victory over this coalition enables Israel to obtain a foothold in this region, although once again immediate occupation does not seem to take place (Gal, 39-46). The outcome of this "northern campaign" sets up the second summary notice of Joshua taking "all the land" (Josh 11:16-23), a summary that overlaps with and expands that of Joshua 10:40-43. This summary stresses the geographical regions wherein military victory has been attained ("from Mount Halak and the ascent of Seir as far as Baal Gad in the valley of Lebanon below Mount Hermon" [Josh 11:17]) and sets up the list of defeated kings in Joshua 12.

The wide geographic swath of this second summary notwithstanding, this section also introduces the sometimes challenging notion that while "all the land" might be "taken" and have "rest from war" (Josh 11:16, 23), unconquered cities and peoples nevertheless remain (Josh 11:22)—parallel realities that will be returned to in the remaining chapters of Joshua and the opening chapters of Judges (Kallai, 102-11). Although it is commonly misconstrued that only the book of *Judges reflects the incomplete aspects of the conquest, both Joshua and Judges reflect the reality of unconquered peoples, cities and territories. Indeed, the chapter following the list of defeated kings articulates a daunting list of unconquered areas spanning from the far south to the far north, particularly on the Coastal Plain and in the Jezreel and Beth Shean Valleys (Josh 13:1-6, 13). Similarly, during the dividing of the land, other unconquered areas are noted (cf. Josh 15:63; 16:10; 17:11-16). Likewise, at the tent of meeting assembly at *Shiloh the Israelites are rebuked for "neglecting to possess" the land, since there are still seven tribes that have not received their inheritance (Josh 18:1-3).

Despite the reality of unconquered areas, the *entire* land is divided among the tribes by lot at the command of Yahweh (Josh 13:6); thus all the land is given as Yahweh promised (cf. Josh 21:43-45). This interplay between given and unconquered land is nicely reflected in Joshua's exhortation to the leadership of Israel in Joshua 23, which is situated "a long time after Yahweh had given rest to Israel from all their surrounding enemies." While this speech notes Israel's victories in the land and stresses that everything Yahweh promised had "come to pass," it also clarifies that some allotted land is still inhabited by unconquered nations (Josh 23:4, 9-10, 14). In addition, Joshua stresses that Yahweh will continue to drive out these remaining nations in line with Israel's faith and obedience (Josh 23:6), but that unfaithfulness and disobedience will put this in jeopardy (Josh 23:12-13, 15-16). In short, this speech helps to clarify the theological nuances surrounding the parallel realities of *completely given land* and *incomplete conquest* (cf. Num 33:53; Deut 8:1; 11:22-23).

Finally, the various factors impacting Israel's entry into the land of Canaan should also be considered vis-à-vis the hegemony of *Egypt. While this issue connects with the question of the date of the exodus (mid-fifteenth or mid-late thirteenth century BCE), it should be stressed that Egypt's interest in Canaan in either time period was focused on maintaining Egyptian oversight of lucrative *trade routes on the Coastal Highway as well as those passing from the Coastal Highway through the Jezreel Valley en route to locations such as Mari, Damascus and Hamath. Thus campaigns by Thutmose III and Amenhotep II (fifteenth century BCE) or Seti (Sethos) I, Ramesses II and Merneptah (thirteenth century BCE) primarily focus on asserting (or reasserting) Egyptian control over cities on these routes (ANET, 22-23, 199-203, 234-48, 253-58, 376-78). Conversely, the absence of cities located in interior regions listed in Egyptian campaign annals reflects the fact that these areas were of little importance to Egypt. Given that these remote areas are the very areas of early Israelite conquests and settlement, it is not surprising to witness the absence of Egyptian resistance to Israel's early conquests in Canaan.

In summary, in view of conquered and unconquered areas, Israel's geographical extent toward the end of the conquest period should be seen as concentrated in the hill country, parts of Transjordan, the Negev, the southern Jordan Valley and (perhaps) the Upper Galilee region (see Zertal, 47-69; Finkelstein 1988, 324-35; Mazar 1986a, 35-48).

4. Geographical Extent of Israel During the Time Frame of the Judges.

The opening chapters of the book of Judges (Judg 1:1—3:6) work to transition the reader from the generation entering the land to the eve of the monarchy. As such, they overlap aspects of Joshua and provide a theological backdrop for the accounts of the *judges that follow. In short, the time frame of the judges sheds light on the fragile foothold that Israel attained in the

Figure 1. Approximate geographical extent following the Conquest period

land of Canaan detailed above. Hence, we learn of ongoing battles and unconquered areas throughout the Promised Land (Judg 1:18-35 [following the LXX at Judg 1:18, which says that Judah did *not* dispossess Gaza, Ashkelon and Ekron]). Furthermore, the transition in Judges restates the consequences for unfaithfulness vis-à-vis possessing the land and makes it clear that unfaithfulness was the norm (Judg 2:1-19; recall Num 33:55-56; Josh 23:12-13).

Once again, it is useful to consider Egypt's interest in Canaan. Egypt's involvement can be appreciated in light of Amarna letters sent from city-states in *Aram and Canaan. These letters largely reflect the time frame of Amenhotep IV (Akhenaten [c. 1350-1334 BCE]) and illustrate nominal Egyptian control (if not neglect) over this region (Moran, xiii-xxxix). Following the Amarna period, Egypt's involvement in Canaan declines until the time frame of Seti I (c. 1294-

1279 BCE), who campaigns in Canaan in order to reestablish Egyptian control over the Coastal Highway as well as routes through the Jezreel Valley and beyond (note the Seti I inscription discovered at Beth Shean [*COS* 2.4B:25-26]). Following Seti I, his son Ramesses II (c. 1279-1213 BCE) campaigns extensively before entering a peace treaty with Hatti acknowledging Egyptian control of Canaan (*ANET*, 199-203, 255-58). Following this treaty, Egypt's involvement in Canaan once again declines until the reign of Merneptah (c. 1213-1203 BCE), whose famous stela mentions victories against cities in the Jezreel Valley, the Coastal Plain, the Shephelah, the northern Transjordan area and the ethnic-national entities of Hurru and Israel (*COS* 2.6:40-41; *ANET*, 376-78). After Merneptah, Egypt's involvement in Canaan again declines until Ramesses III (c. 1182-1151 BCE), who begins to reassert control until the arrival of the Sea Peoples.

During the era of the judges the geographical extent of Israel fluctuates in line with various episodes of oppression and relief. The first mention of oppression (from Aram Naharaim in the north [Judg 3:7-11]) aptly illustrates some of the challenges in chronology, as the time frame of this oppression is uncertain (in absolute or relative terms) (see Kitchen, 199-209). The next oppression comes from the east (Moabites aided by Ammonites and Amalekites), resulting in the loss of some Transjordanian territory and some of the Jordan Valley until the daring assassination of the Moabite king (Judg 3:12-30). The next period(s) of foreign oppression comes from both the north (Hazor) and the west (*Philistines). In the north the oppression by the king of Hazor is thwarted by a multitribal coalition initiated at the urging of Deborah (Judg 4:10-5:31). In the west, although the details of the Philistine oppression are lacking, the Song of Deborah notes that during this period, "roadways were deserted; travelers made their way via roundabout paths . . . normal life ceased in Israel" (Judg 5:6-7). This major change of life likely correlates with the major influx of the Sea Peoples (which included the Philistines) at the beginning of the twelfth century BCE. During the next period of oppression, Israel's border is encroached by the Midianites together with Amalekites and "people from the east," which causes some Israelites to take up residence in mountain caves and dens (Judg 6:2-5), until the invaders are pushed back by Gideon's northern tribal coalition (Judg 6:33-8:12).

The final two judge accounts (Jephthah and Samson) likely stem from a similar time frame and set up the territorial challenges that will figure prominently in the early days of the monarchy. At the time of Jephthah (Judg 10:6-12:7) the Ammonites are encroaching the Transjordan region as well as parts of the central hill country until the exiled Jephthah returns and successfully drives the Ammonites out (note the interesting interchange between Jephthah and the Ammonite king concerning ownership claims of Gilead [Judg 11:12-28]). Finally, the Samson account (Judg 13—16) stresses the extent of Philistine domination over Israel (cf. Judg 14:4; 15:11, 20) and makes it clear that the Philistines have expanded from their original confines on the southern Coastal Plain into the Shephelah and central hill country (Singer, 295-332).

5. Geographical Extent of Israel During the United Monarchy (c. 1040/1030[?]-930 BCE).

5.1. Time Frame of Saul. Israel's territorial conflicts with the Philistines and Ammonites stressed in Judges 10—16 are likely not far removed from the time frame of *Samuel and dovetail with the establishment of the monarchy. Indeed, the people's desire for a king is connected with Ammonite incursions (1 Sam 12:12), and Yahweh states that he will use *Saul to "bring my people deliverance from the power of the Philistines" (1 Sam 9:16).

Although the Philistine threat was tempered during the days of Samuel (1 Sam 7:13), it was not eradicated. In fact, the degree of Philistine dominance over Israel at this time is shown by the garrisons that they were able to establish in Judah and Benjamin (cf. 1 Sam 10:3-5; 13:3), as well by their prohibition of metal workers in Israel (1 Sam 13:19-22; cf. the dominance of the Sea Peoples reflected in the eleventh-century BCE story of Wenamon [COS 1.41:89-93]). Despite this dominance, Saul (with the able assistance of Jonathan) pushes the Philistines back to the Coastal Plain (cf. 1 Sam 13:3—14:46). In addition, Saul reasserts Israelite control over the Negev and keeps the Ammonite threat in check. Despite these successes, there was "fierce war against the Philistines all the days of Saul" (1 Sam 14:52). Indeed, although Saul was able to solidify his kingdom and deliver Israel from the hand of certain plunderers, he nevertheless had

ongoing battles on all sides—the kings of Zobah from the north, the *Edomites from the south, the Moabites and Ammonites from the east, the Philistines from the west (1 Sam 14:47-48).

The last extended battle narrative between Israel and the Philistines during Saul's reign ends in his demise (1 Sam 28—31). This particular conflict between the Israelites and the Philistines is unique in that it is centered in the Jezreel Valley rather than in the Shephelah or hill country, and may relate to control of trade routes through this region. This location also

Figure 2. Approximate geographical extent at the height of Saul's power

brings to mind the unconquered cities in this area and raises the possibility that these cities assisted the Philistines. In any event, the Israelites are routed, Saul is killed, and the fledgling nation is left in disarray (cf. 1 Sam 31:7). Moreover, this victory gives the Philistines control over the Jezreel-Harod-Beth Shean Valleys, effectively driving a wedge between Cisjordan tribes (Monson 1996, 57).

5.2. Time Frame of David (c. 1010-970 BCE). Following the death of Saul, *David begins an incremental journey toward reigning over "all Israel." In the interval before this happens, a divided kingdom results as Saul's son Ishbosheth

(Eshbaal) is anointed as king over "all Israel," while David is anointed king over Judah (2 Sam 2:1-11). This division of tribal fidelity culminates in a "long war between the house of Saul and the house of David" (2 Sam 3:1). In time, David prevails and is affirmed as king by "all the tribes of Israel" (2 Sam 5:1-3; 1 Chron 11:1-3). Afterward, David moves his capital from deep in the territory of Judah to the more centralized (and neutral) location of *Jerusalem, following his defeat of the long-entrenched Jebusites (2 Sam 5:6-10; 1 Chron 11:4-8). After realizing that David had reconsolidated the tribes of Israel, the Philistines attack twice, but they are driven back, removing the Philistine foothold in the hill country and part of the Shephelah (2 Sam 5:25).

The list of David's accomplishments in 2 Samuel 8 (cf. 1 Chron 18) provides a highly condensed summary of the political and military moves that effected a solidification and expansion of Israel's geographical extent during David's reign (as celebrated in Ps 60 and Ps 108). These victories take place in the east against the Ammonites and Moabites, in the west against the Philistines, in the south against Edom, and in the north against several Aramaean city-states (see Kitchen, 98-107). David's victories in the north, particularly in the Beqa Valley, prompt Toi (Tou) king of Hamath to seek peace and goodwill from David (2 Sam 8:9-10; 1 Chron 18:9-10). All told, this summary illustrates that Israel now controlled a significant portion of the Coastal Highway and the Transjordan King's Highway. It should be noted that despite the broad geographical control of Israel during this time, the expanse of Israel proper was understood as "from Dan to Beersheba" (cf. Joab's itinerary in his pursuit of Sheba and in conducting David's ill-advised census [2 Sam 24:2-8]). That said, these cities were not exact border points but rather principal cities in the vicinity of the northern and southern limits of the kingdom.

5.3. Time Frame of Solomon (c. 970-930 BCE). The transition from Davidic to Solomonic rule (c. 970 BCE) comes at a time when there is "rest on every side," as the land had been "subdued before Yahweh and his people" (1 Chron 22:18). The progress made by *Solomon in nation building and regional influence is seen in several ways, including his treaty via political marriage with Egypt (although note the curious issue of Pharaoh conquering Gezer [1 Kings 9:16]), blossoming relations with Tyre (although note Solomon cedes some of Asher's territory—Yahweh's land—to Tyre [1 Kings 9:10-14]) and visits from the *Arabian Queen of Sheba and other gift-bearing dignitaries (1 Kings 3:1; 5:1; 10—11; 2 Chron 9:1-12, 23-24).

The geographical extent of Solomon's empire can be gauged via his feast celebrating the dedication of the temple, which hosted attendees from Lebo Hamath in the north to the Brook of Egypt in the south (1 Kings 8:65; 2 Chron 7:8). In addition, Solomon is noted as having authority over the regions "across the river" (southwest of the Euphrates) and over kings from Tipsah on the Euphrates in the northeast to the border of Egypt in the southwest (1 Kings 4:24; cf. 2 Chron 9:26). This geographical expansion extends Israelite control over the Coastal Highway and the Transjordan King's Highway (which is now controlled from the maritime port of *Ezion Geber to Tipsah on the Euphrates), allowing Israel to profit from the lucrative trade activity flowing between Egypt, Arabia and Mesopotamia (1 Kings 9:26-27; 10:14-29) (Hoerth, 284-92). It should be noted, however, that the northern boundary of Israel on the coast did not extend north of Sidon, although clearly it extended north of this point in the interior. Nevertheless, Judah and Israel are described as dwelling safely "from Dan to Beersheba" during the days of Solomon, again reflecting the fact that this was the understood north-south expanse of Israel even when geographical control extended much farther. In addition, even at the zenith of Solomon's power and regional control there are still blocks of the original inhabitants of the land of Canaan within the confines of Israel (cf. 1 Kings 9:20-21; 2 Chron 8:7-8). As also periodically noted in Joshua and Judges, these groups were conscripted for the building needs of the kingdom.

6. Geographical Extent of Israel and Judah During the Divided Kingdom (c. 930-720 BCE).

6.1. Early Divided Kingdom (c. 930-885 BCE). Solomon's accomplishments noted above often came at the expense of fidelity to the precepts of Yahweh (cf. Deut 17:14-20). Indeed, in the closing years of Solomon's reign internal and external troubles begin to surface and multiply as Yahweh raises up adversaries against Solomon, including *Jeroboam, who is granted refuge in Egypt before returning after the death of Solomon and facilitating the division of the kingdom (by divine decree [1 Kings 11:1-40]). From this point forward (c. 930 BCE), the geographical extent of Israel is understood in two parts: the southern kingdom (Judah) and the northern kingdom (Israel).

In terms of landholdings, tribes, natural resources, trade routes and population, the northern kingdom comes out ahead of the southern kingdom (Finkelstein 1994b, 158-62). In short order both *Rehoboam of the southern kingdom and Jeroboam of the northern kingdom begin to fortify their respective "kingdoms." Jeroboam fortifies hill country and Transjordan

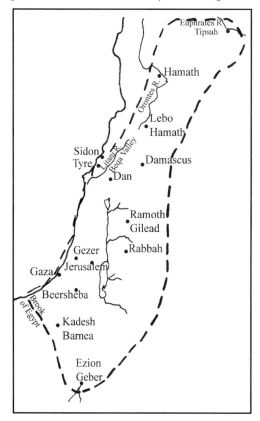

Figure 3. Height of Israelite hegemony under David and Solomon

cities and also establishes religious centers (to facilitate political separation) in the far north (*Dan) and far south (*Bethel) of the northern kingdom (1 Kings 12:25-33). In the southern kingdom Rehoboam fortifies several cities in the hill country of Judah and the Shephelah (2 Chron 11:5-12). All this fortification notwithstanding, Pharaoh Shishak (Shoshenq I [c. 945-924 BCE])

of Egypt (with whom Jeroboam found asylum) heads an African coalition in an invasion of the southern and northern kingdoms during the fifth year of Rehoboam (1 Kings 14:25-26; 2 Chron 12:2-4, 9). While the OT stresses the damage done in the southern kingdom, Shishak's inscription at Karnak (*ANET*, 242-43) shows that his invasion agenda went beyond Judah and included the Coastal Highway, numerous cities in the southern wilderness region (presumably to assert control over land and sea trade routes running to and from Arabia), and northern kingdom cities in the hill country, Jezreel Valley (note that a Shishak stela fragment was discovered at Megiddo) and the northern Transjordan region. Shishak's attack on the northern kingdom is surprising, given that Jeroboam was his former "houseguest" in Egypt, raising the possibility that Shishak's invasion in northern kingdom territories was punishment for an arrangement not lived up to by Jeroboam. In any event, Shishak's invasion markedly trims the geographical extent of both the northern and the southern kingdoms, facilitating the loss of control over trade routes. On top of the losses inflicted by Shishak there was constant war between Rehoboam and Jeroboam, primarily over control of the territory of Benjamin (cf. 1 Kings 14:30; 15:6). Such conflict continues with little abatement over the next several decades until the northern kingdom-southern kingdom border becomes fairly stable in the area between Bethel and *Mizpah (Rasmussen, 124-27).

6.2. The Omride and Jehu Dynasties of the Northern Kingdom (c. 885-750 BCE). Following several years of political division in the northern kingdom, Omri emerges victorious, inaugurating the impressive and much-maligned *Omride dynasty (c. 885-841 BCE). The era of the Omride dynasty was marked by political stability (including peace with the southern kingdom), expanded relations with *Phoenicia (note the marriage of Ahab and Jezebel) and military strength. These factors enabled the northern kingdom to reassert control over lucrative trade routes on both sides of the Jordan River. However, this prosperity and international contact also facilitated social and religious degeneration; note that the ministries of *Elijah and *Elisha are juxtaposed to the Omride dynasty. In addition, the northern kingdom's control over Transjordan trade routes did not go uncontested, as is reflected in the ongoing skirmishes between the northern kingdom and Aram (Syria), the northern kingdom's main threat during the ninth century BCE. Eventually, a combination of prophetic advice and divine deliverance enables Omri's son Ahab to prevail over Aram and secure an advantageous treaty that included the return of lost northern kingdom territory (1 Kings 20). During this time of peace several city-states of Canaan and Aram form an anti-Assyrian alliance that successfully stems the advance of Shalmaneser III (c. 853 BCE) (*COS* 2.113A:261-64).

After a few years of peace, Ahab attempts to retake Ramoth Gilead (on the King's Highway)

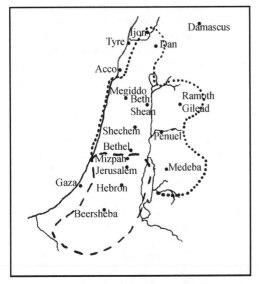

Figure 4. Approximate geographical extent of israel and judah during the early divided kingdom

from Aram with the help of *Jehoshaphat of the southern kingdom (who, incidentally, allied himself to Ahab via political marriage [2 Chron 18:1]). In line with an ominous prophecy, this assault ends in defeat as well as the death of Ahab (1 Kings 22:1-38; 2 Chron 18:28-34). Prior to this northern kingdom-southern kingdom coalition, Jehoshaphat had fortified cities in Judah and Ephraim (taken by his father, Asa) and was receiving tribute from the Philistines and Arabians (2 Chron 17:1-12). However, after this defeat Moab, Ammon and some Meunites join forces in rebellion against Jehoshaphat, until thwarted by Yahweh (2 Chron 20:1-30).

Following the death of Ahab, Mesha of Moab rebels against the northern kingdom and seizes areas to the north of the Arnon Canyon (2 Kings 1:1, 3:4-27). The Mesha Stela (Moabite Stone)

notes that Mesha fortified several cities north of the Arnon, presumably in preparation against invasion from the northern kingdom (*COS* 2.23:137-38). These fortifications may well be the reason that Joram (Jehoram) of the northern kingdom decides to attack Moab from the south via "the way of the wilderness of Edom" (2 Kings 3:8). Once again, Jehoshaphat of the southern kingdom assists the northern kingdom, together with his vassal Edomite king. Although the northern kingdom-southern kingdom coalition gains some initial victories, Moab's quest for independence and control of the Medeba Plateau ultimately succeeds (2 Kings 3:26-27; note Moab's expanded geographical control in later prophetic oracles [e.g. Is 15—16; Jer 48]). Following the unsuccessful battle against Moab, Joram returns to the northern kingdom to face a series of conflicts with Aramaean forces—narratives that are interwoven with stories of *Elisha. Indeed, the ministry of Elisha leads to a lull in aggression from Aram (2 Kings 6:8-23). Following this lull the Aramaeans once again invade the northern kingdom and besiege *Samaria, only to retreat when divine intervention causes the Aramaeans to believe that Israel had engaged Neo-Hittite and Egyptian military assistance (2 Kings 6:24-7:20).

In the southern kingdom the perceived weakness of Jehoshaphat's successor Jehoram (Joram) prompts Edom in the south and Libnah in the west to rebel against Judah (2 Kings 8:20-22; 2 Chron 21:8-10). In addition, Yahweh incites Philistines and Arabians to attack Judah, leading to the death of the older sons of Jehoram (2 Chron 21:16-17). The remaining son (Ahaziah) continues the spirit of northern kingdom-southern kingdom cooperation by assisting Joram in another battle at Ramoth Gilead (2 Kings 8:28-29). This battle sets the scene for the outworking of a divinely driven throne change in both Aram and the northern kingdom (2 Kings 9:1-10; cf. 1 Kings 19:15-17). This throne change (Jehu's revolt) not only brings an end to the Omride dynasty in the northern kingdom by the murder of Joram and Jezebel, but also entails the murder of Ahaziah, leading to the six-year reign of the Phoenician princess Athaliah (daughter of Ahab and Jezebel) in the southern kingdom (2 Kings 9—11).

Although Jehu was Yahweh's agent for the removal of the family of Ahab and Jezebel as well as the eradication of Baal worship from Israel, unfaithfulness on Jehu's part causes Yahweh to dramatically reduce the geographical extent of the northern kingdom (2 Kings 10:31-33). Moreover, the new leader (by assassination) of Aram (Hazael) invades the Shephelah and hill country of the southern kingdom and receives payment taken from the palace and the temple (2 Kings 12:17-18; 2 Chron 24:23-24). Although Aram continues to diminish the military potency and geographical extent of the northern kingdom during the days of Jehu and his son Jehoahaz (2 Kings 13:3-4), Yahweh responds to the plea of Jehoahaz and sends the northern kingdom a deliverer, perhaps Adad-nirari III of Assyria, who captured Damascus around 806 BCE (2 Kings 13:5; *COS* 2.114G:276-77; *ANET,* 281-82). This deliverance aside, Aramaean pressure on the north and Transjordan regions of the northern kingdom is described as perpetuating "all the days of Jehoahaz" (2 Kings 13:22). Afterward, Joash successfully recaptures cities lost to Hazael (2 Kings 13:25), while Amaziah in the southern kingdom retakes Edom, pushing southern kingdom control to the port city of Elath, adjacent to Ezion Geber (2 Kings 14:7, 22).

The successors of Joash in the northern kingdom (Jeroboam II) and Amaziah in the southern kingdom (Uzziah/Azariah) usher in a new era of northern kingdom-southern kingdom cooperation and regional influence during the first half of the eighth century BCE. In the northern kingdom Jeroboam II expands the geographical extent of Israel's control to Lebo Hamath and recaptures previously lost territory in the Transjordan region (2 Kings 14:25, 28), while in the southern kingdom Uzziah buttresses his military capability, fortifies the Negev and wilderness regions and prevails over Philistine cities in the west, Ammonites in the east and Arabians and Meunites in the south (2 Chron 26:6-10). As a result, the combined territories of the northern kingdom and southern kingdom (Elath in the south to Lebo Hamath in the north) nearly reach that seen at the height of the united monarchy under David and Solomon. However, all of this will change radically with the geopolitical upheaval that the Neo-Assyrian Empire will bring to the nations "Beyond the River."

6.3. The Neo-Assyrian Period (c. 745-720 BCE). The birth of the Neo-Assyrian Empire under Tiglath-pileser III (745-727 BCE) dramatically changes the political situation of the northern

and the southern kingdoms, as well as the ancient Near East as a whole. The expansionary efforts of Tiglath-pileser III (Pul) in Aram and Canaan coincide with a particularly unstable political situation in the northern kingdom following the death of Jeroboam II. By contrast, in the southern kingdom Uzziah's successor (Jotham) continues to fortify the southern kingdom and receives tribute from the Ammonites (2 Chron 27:3-5).

The large (and growing) *Assyrian threat prompts the nations and city-states of Aram and Canaan to put aside their border squabbles and attempt to form a united front against the Assyrian advance, as in earlier days. However, the successor to Jotham in the southern kingdom (Ahaz) refuses to join this anti-Assyrian coalition. This prompts an attack on Ahaz by the northern kingdom (Pekah) and Aram (Rezin) around 736 BCE with the goal of installing a more cooperative southern kingdom ruler—moves that coincide with Yahweh's displeasure toward Ahaz (Is 7; 2 Kings 15:37; 16:5-6; 2 Chron 28:5-8). This onslaught (the Syro-Ephraimite crisis), together with incursions by Edomites from the south and Philistines from the west, prompts Ahaz to turn to Tiglath-pileser III for help (2 Kings 16:7-8; 2 Chron 28:17-18). Tiglath-pileser III is happy to oblige and in (probably) two campaigns makes his way down the Coastal Highway and then inland, destroying Damascus around 732 BCE (cf. *COS* 2.117F:291-92). Tiglath-pileser III then turns his attention to the northern kingdom, taking cities (and captives) in the Huleh Valley, the Transjordan region and the Galilee region (2 Kings 15:29). With an attack on Samaria imminent, Hoshea assassinates Pekah and surrenders to the Assyrians (cf. *COS* 2.117C:287-89; *ANET,* 284). As a result, both the northern kingdom (by force) and the southern kingdom (willingly) lose their independence and become vassals of Assyria.

Following the surrender of Hoshea, Assyria markedly reduces the size of the northern kingdom and creates several provinces in what had been the northern kingdom. In short, by 732 BCE the northern kingdom is essentially confined to the hill country of Manasseh and Ephraim. In addition, the corresponding upheaval of this time frame prompts refugees from the northern kingdom to flee to the southern kingdom (Broshi, 21-26). About five years later (at the death of Tiglath-pileser III in 727 BCE) Hoshea attempts to regain northern kingdom independence, ultimately resulting in the destruction of the northern kingdom under Shalmaneser V (with further military operations by Sargon II [cf. *COS* 2.118A:293-94; *ANET,* 284]) and the deportation-repopulation of the northern kingdom (2 Kings 17:1-24 [cf. *COS* 2.118D:295-96, 2.118H:298]).

7. The Geographical Extent of Judah Following the Fall of the Northern Kingdom (c. 720-539 BCE).

7.1. Time Frame of Hezekiah. *Hezekiah was a teenager when his father, Ahaz, voluntarily placed Judah in subjection to Assyria, and he was in the sixth year of his reign when the northern kingdom was destroyed (2 Kings 18:1-10). Hezekiah's early years were focused on religious reforms in Judah and what had been the northern kingdom, including inviting those "from Beersheba to Dan" to come to Jerusalem to celebrate Passover (cf. 2 Chron 30). In addition, during Hezekiah's reign Judah expanded moderately by gains made in the south and southeast (against Amalekites and Meunites) as well as in the western Negev (1 Chron 4:39-43). Furthermore, Hezekiah reclaimed territory in the west taken by the Philistines during the days of his father, Ahaz, and subdued the Philistines "as far as Gaza" (2 Kings 18:8).

In time, Hezekiah's religious reforms likely contribute to a desire to throw off the Assyrian yoke inherited from his father, ultimately culminating in rebellion following the death of Sargon II (c. 705 BCE). This rebellion was marked by an impressive degree of preparation (cf. 2 Kings 20:20; 2 Chron 32:5), preparation likely stimulated by his witness of Hoshea's failed rebellion. During the time leading up to Sennacherib's invasion(s) (c. 701 BCE) Jerusalem's size and population increased dramatically (Vaughn, 19-79). In addition, significant growth was seen in the environs of Jerusalem as well as in the Negev (Aharoni, 387-401). Although Jerusalem is spared, Sennacherib's invasion(s) brings devastation to the balance of Judah (Finkelstein 1994a, 176-78). This devastation is especially felt in the Shephelah, where much of Sennacherib's destruction of "all the fortified cities of Judah" took place (forty-six cities and countless villages, according to Sennacherib [*COS* 2.119B:302-3; Finkelstein 1994a, 172-74; Rainey, 15-16]). Fol-

lowing Sennacherib's destruction the population in and around Jerusalem grows even further as more refugees flood into the area (Broshi, 21-26). The net effect of this population surge is a more centralized and urban society— a demographic shift reflected in several prophetic oracles of the time (e.g., Micah).

7.2. The Neo-Babylonian Period (c. 626-539 BCE). In the decades following Sennacherib's campaign the Assyrian Empire reaches its height of geographical expanse under Esarhaddon (681-669 BCE) and Ashurbanipal (669-627 BCE), even extending into Egypt for several years. However, during the second half of the seventh century BCE Assyria begins to lose control over various pockets of its empire. This disintegration of Assyrian hegemony picks up speed following the death of Ashurbanipal, most notably with the revolt of *Babylon under Nabopolassar in 626 BCE, father of Nebuchadnezzar and founder of the Neo-Babylonian (Chaldean) Empire. By 614 BCE Ass(h)ur had fallen to the Medes, and in 612 BCE Nineveh fell to a joint force of Medes and Babylonians. As a result of this geopolitical change Judah experienced what might be described as "pseudo-independence" during the reign of *Josiah (640-609 BCE), freedom that no doubt aided Josiah's religious reforms. In addition, the reduced Assyrian presence in what had been the northern kingdom enables Josiah's reforms (and his border) to stretch from his initial geographical confines ("from Geba to Beersheba") to cities "throughout all the land of Israel" (2 Kings 23:8-19; 2 Chron 34:4-32). Moreover, Josiah seems to have expanded westward to the coast in the area north of *Ashdod (cf. *COS* 3.41:77-78) and (most likely) to the east in the Transjordan region (see Aharoni, 403-4). This expansion of Judah's geographical extent (in what had been the Assyrian provinces of "Samaria," "Megiddo" and "Gilead") is also reflected in Josiah's ability to confront Pharaoh Nec(h)o II at Megiddo (2 Chron 35:20-24).

Josiah's unsuccessful confrontation of the Egyptian army en route to aid the Assyrians against the Babylonian army (a move seemingly connected with the covert relationship that Judah developed with Babylon during the days of Hezekiah [cf. Is 39]) not only ends in Josiah's death, but also triggers a rapid series of political changes in the southern kingdom as Judah goes from pseudo-independence to Egyptian vassalage (at Josiah's death, 609 BCE [2 Kings 23:33-

35]) to Babylonian vassalage (following Babylonia's defeat of Egypt at Carchemish, c. 605 BCE [cf. 2 Kings 24:7])—all within the span of five years.

The challenges of Babylonian vassalage are exacerbated by Judah's attempts to throw off the Babylonian yoke against the will of God (cf. the oracles of Jeremiah). This disobedience prompts Yahweh to send Babylonians, Aramae-

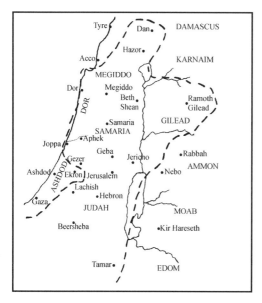

Figure 5. Approximate geographical extent of Josiah's kingdom

ans, Moabites and Ammonites against Judah "to destroy it" (2 Kings 24:2) and ultimately to cast Judah "out from his presence" in conjunction with the rebellion of Zedekiah (Mattaniah) around 588 BCE (2 Kings 24:17-20; Jer 52:1-3). This rebellion is crushed by Nebuchadnezzar, who moves city by city in the Shephelah (cf. Azekah and *Lachish in Jer 34:7, and Lachish letter no. 4 [COS 3.42C:80]) before destroying Jerusalem in 586 BCE (2 Kings 25:1-21; Jer 52:4-27). The resulting desolation in and around Jerusalem is poetically captured by Lamentations 1:4: "The roads to Zion mourn, empty of those traveling to the appointed feasts."

After the destruction of Jerusalem and further large-scale deportations to Babylonia, Nebuchadnezzar appoints Gedaliah as governor of Judah in Mizpah, just north of Jerusalem (2 Kings 25:22-24). The establishment of this new administration prompts those who had scattered to return to Judah (Jer 40:5-12). Yet before long, Gedaliah is murdered, triggering more deportations and flights abroad (especially to Egypt; e.g., Yeb/Elephantine [cf. COS 3.46-53:116-32]). Moreover, Edom takes advantage of Judah's weakness at this time by encroaching in southern parts of Judah's territory (cf. Ps 137; Obad 1—4; Arad letter no. 24 [COS 3.43K:84-85]; this area later is known as Idumea).

8. Geographical Extent of Judah (Judea) During the Postexilic Time Frame (c. 539-430 BCE).

All of what had been Israel and Judah fall under one of the large administrative units of the *Persian Empire (satrapies) known as "Beyond the [Euphrates] River." Within this region was the small province of Judea (Yehud), which seems to have been further divided into five or six districts (cf. Neh 3). Following the decree of Cyrus (539 BCE), those exiled to Babylonia begin to return with *Zerubbabel with the daunting task of rebuilding what was left of Judah (Ezra 2:1-35; Neh 7:5-73). Although still clearly under the hegemony of the Persian Empire, Judea was granted some degree of political autonomy under the governorship of Sheshbazzar and subsequent leaders. Beyond the challenges of rebuilding homes, infrastructure, the temple and the like, these returnees faced various episodes of opposition, including from those whose heritage traced back to the repopulation policies of the Assyrians.

The time frame of *Ezra and *Nehemiah falls in the range of 75-110 years after Cyrus's decree, during the reign of Artaxerxes I (c. 465-424 BCE). During the decades following the decree of Cyrus the challenges noted above made the overall situation in postexilic Judea somewhat bleak (cf. Neh 1:2-3), giving rise to Nehemiah's appointment as governor (Neh 5:14) and Ezra's appointment in the realm of civil and religious affairs (Ezra 7:24-26). The geographical extent of Judea at the onset of Ezra and Nehemiah's time in Judea seems to have been largely centered in the central hill country, the Jordan Valley (Jericho) and some cities in the Shephelah (Neh 3:1-25, 11:29-36) (see Aharoni, 413-23; Avi-Yonah, 13-31).

After the completion of the wall, some of the returnees settle in Jerusalem (leaders and those chosen by lot), while the rest of the people return to their respective inheritance (Neh 11). The list of cities inhabited by the "sons of

Judah" and the "sons of Benjamin" that follows the details of the Jerusalem resettlement (Neh 11:25-36) suggests that by the end of the Ezra-Nehemiah period the geographical extent of postexilic Judea had expanded modestly to the west and to the south.

Figure 6. Approximate geographical extent of Yehud (Judah)

This geographical extent of Judea remains more or less stable until NT times and factors into the political, social and religious dynamics at the time of Jesus (e.g., Samaritans, Essenes, Herod/Idumeans, the Galilee region and the like).

See also LAND; ROADS AND HIGHWAYS; TRIBES OF ISRAEL AND LAND ALLOTMENTS/BORDERS.

BIBLIOGRAPHY. **Y. Aharoni,** *The Land of the Bible* (rev. ed.; Philadelphia: Westminster, 1988); **Y. Aharoni et al.,** *The Carta Bible Atlas* (4th ed.; Jerusalem: Carta, 2002) [formerly *The Macmillan Bible Atlas*]; **M. Avi-Yonah,** *The Holy Land from the Persian to Arab Conquests (536 B.C. to A.D. 640): A Historical Geography* (rev. ed.; Grand Rapids: Baker, 1977); **D. Baly,** *The Geography of the Bible* (rev. ed.; New York: Harper & Row, 1974); **M. Broshi,** "The Expansion of Jerusalem in the Reigns of Hezekiah and Manasseh," *IEJ* (1974) 21-26; **C. E. Carter,** *The Emergence of Yehud in the Persian Period: A Social and Demographic Study* (JSOTSup 294; Sheffield: Sheffield Academic Press, 1999); **I. Finkelstein,** "The Archaeology of the Days of Manasseh," in *Scripture and Other Artifacts: Essays on the Bible and Archaeology in Honor*

of Philip J. King, ed. M. D. Coogan, J. C. Exum and L. E. Stager (Louisville: Westminster/John Knox, 1994a) 169-87; idem, *The Archaeology of the Israelite Settlement* (Jerusalem: Israel Exploration Society, 1988); idem, "The Emergence of Israel: A Phase in the Cyclic History of Canaan in the Third and Second Millennia BCE," in *From Nomadism to Monarchy: Archaeological and Historical Aspects of Early Israel,* ed. I. Finkelstein and N. Naʾaman (Jerusalem: Yad Izhak Ben-Zvi and Israel Exploration Society; Washington, DC: Biblical Archaeology Society, 1994b) 150-78; **R. Frankel,** "Upper Galilee in the Late Bronze-Iron I Transition," in *From Nomadism to Monarchy: Archaeological and Historical Aspects of Early Israel,* ed. I. Finkelstein and N. Naʾaman (Jerusalem: Yad Izhak Ben-Zvi and Israel Exploration Society; Washington, DC: Biblical Archaeology Society, 1994) 18-34; **Z. Gal,** "Iron I in Lower Galilee and the Margins of the Jezreel Valley," in *From Nomadism to Monarchy: Archaeological and Historical Aspects of Early Israel,* ed. I. Finkelstein and N. Naʾaman (Jerusalem: Yad Izhak Ben-Zvi and Israel Exploration Society; Washington, DC: Biblical Archaeology Society, 1994) 35-46; **A. Hoerth,** *Archaeology and the Old Testament* (Grand Rapids: Baker, 1998); **Z. Kallai,** *Historical Geography of the Bible: The Tribal Territories of Israel* (Jerusalem: Magnes; Leiden: E. J. Brill, 1986); **K. A. Kitchen,** *On the Reliability of the Old Testament* (Grand Rapids: Eerdmans, 2003); **B. Mazar,** "The Early Israelite Settlement in the Hill Country," in *The Early Biblical Period: Historical Studies,* ed. S. Ahituv and B. A. Levine (Jerusalem: Israel Exploration Society, 1986a) 35-48; idem, "Lebo-hamath and the Northern Border of Canaan," in *The Early Biblical Period: Historical Studies,* ed. S. Ahituv and B. A. Levine (Jerusalem: Israel Exploration Society, 1986b) 189-202; **J. M. Monson,** *The Land Between: A Regional Study Guide to the Land of the Bible* (Mountain Home, AR: Biblical Backgrounds, 1996); idem, ed., *Student Map Manual: Historical Geography of the Bible Lands* (Jerusalem: Pictorial Archive, 1983); **W. L. Moran,** ed., *The Amarna Letters* (Baltimore: Johns Hopkins University Press, 1992); **N. Naʾaman,** *Borders and Districts in Biblical Historiography: Seven Studies in Biblical Geographic Lists* (JBS 4; Jerusalem: Simor, 1986); **A. F. Rainey,** "The Biblical Shephelah of Judah," *BASOR* 251 (1983) 1-22; **C. G. Rasmussen,** *Zondervan NIV Atlas of the Bible* (Grand Rapids: Regency Reference Library, 1989); **I. Singer,** "Egyptians,

Canaanites, and Philistines in the Period of the Emergence of Israel," in *From Nomadism to Monarchy: Archaeological and Historical Aspects of Early Israel,* ed. I. Finkelstein and N. Na'aman (Jerusalem: Yad Izhak Ben-Zvi and Israel Exploration Society; Washington, DC: Biblical Archaeology Society, 1994) 282-338; **A. G. Vaughn,** *Theology, History, and Archaeology in the Chronicler's Account of Hezekiah* (ABS 4; Atlanta: Scholars Press, 1999); **A. Zertal,** "'To the Land of the Perizzites and the Giants': On the Israelite Settlement in the Hill Country of Manasseh," in *From Nomadism to Monarchy: Archaeological and Historical Aspects of Early Israel,* ed. I. Finkelstein and N. Na'aman (Jerusalem: Yad Izhak Ben-Zvi and Israel Exploration Society; Washington, DC: Biblical Archaeology Society, 1994) 47-69.   F. J. Mabie

GESHEM. *See* EZRA AND NEHEMIAH, BOOKS OF.

GEZER

The prominent thirty-three-acre mound of Tell el-Jezer near Ramleh, at the juncture of the Shephelah/central hills and central coastal plain, is to be identified with ancient Gezer. The site was excavated by British archaeologists in 1902-1909 (R. A. S. Macalister) and 1934, and again by an American team in 1964-1974, 1984 and 1990, directed by W. G. Dever, J. D. Seger and others. The combined excavations have revealed twenty-six strata, more than almost any other site in ancient Palestine (see Table 1).

1. Bronze Age Strata
2. Iron Age Strata
3. Persian, Hellenistic and Herodian Eras

1. Bronze Age Strata.

The Bronze Age strata, though confined to the prebiblical era (i.e., pre-Israelite), indicate that Gezer gradually became one of the most strategic sites in an increasingly urban Palestine. The Middle Bronze Age is particularly noteworthy, boasting massive city walls (the "Inner Wall"), a triple-entryway gate and a citadel, among the most impressive anywhere in the country. Also significant is the famous Field V "High Place" consisting of ten enormous aligned standing stones and a large basin, probably a Canaanite forerunner of the biblical *bāmôt* (*"high places"). A heavy destruction ends this era, no doubt part of the well-documented *Egyptian campaign of Thutmosis III in 1468 BCE.

Following a partial gap in occupation in the fifteenth century BCE, Gezer becomes one of the Palestinian city-states known from the fourteenth-century Amarna letters found in Egypt.

These texts, which include nearly a dozen letters from three successive kings of Gezer, illuminate socioeconomic conditions in Palestine during the beginning of New Kingdom pharaohs. The American excavations attributed the impressive "Outer Wall" to this period, although others disagree. Disruptions at the very end of the period may be the result of the campaign of Pharaoh Merneptah, whose "Victory Stela" of c. 1207 BCE mentions Gezer.

Gezer apparently was not taken during the early Israelite settlement in the thirteenth-twelfth centuries BCE, in keeping with biblical sources (Josh 10:33; 12:12;16:10; Judg 1:29). Strata XIII-XI represent a continued *Canaanite occupation, but with bichrome pottery and other elements that indicate some *Philistine presence. At least two destructions punctuate the twelfth to eleventh century levels. There follows a "post-Philistine/pre-Israelite" horizon (Strata X-IX: late eleventh to mid-tenth centuries BCE) characterized by red-slipped unburnished wares.

2. Iron Age Strata.

Stratum VIII is dated to the mid-to-late tenth century BCE and attributed by the American excavators to *Solomon and the united monarchy. Particularly significant is the rebuild of the "Outer Wall," with the addition of a series of Phoenician-style ashlar (dressed) masonry towers; and on the south side of the mound (Field III) a gatehouse, a four-entryway upper city gate, and a stretch of casemate or double city wall. These well-planned and constructed monumental structures are very similar to those of *Hazor X and *Megiddo VA/IVB, and thus they are taken by the majority of scholars to reflect Solomon's building activities described in 1 Kings 9:15-17. Red-slipped and hand-burnished pottery characterizes this horizon. Domestic structures are not well attested. Gezer may have served largely as a fortified outpost on the Judean-Israelite border, perhaps the capital of one of Solomon's twelve administrative centers (see 1 Kings 4:7-19). A few of Macalister's tombs belong to this horizon. A heavy destruction ends Stratum VIII, probably evidence of the well-known raid of the Egyptian Twenty-

Table 1. Archaeological Strata at Gezer

Stratum XXVI: Late Chalcolithic	3400-3300 BCE	Stratum XII: Iron I	
Stratum XXV: Early Bronze I	3300-3100 BCE	Stratum XI: Iron I	
Stratum XXIV: Early Bronze II		Stratum X: Iron I	1200-1000 BCE
Stratum XXIII: Early Bronze II	3100-2650 BCE	Stratum IX: Iron IIA	
Stratum XXII: Middle Bronze I	2000-1800 BCE	Stratum VIII: Iron IIA	
Stratum XXI: Middle Bronze II		Stratum VII: Iron IIB	
Stratum XX: Middle Bronze II	1800-1650 BCE	Stratum VI: Iron IIB	900-700 BCE
Stratum XIX: Middle Bronze III		Stratum V: Iron IIC	700-600 BCE
Stratum XVIII: Middle Bronze III	1650-1500 BCE	Stratum IV: Persian	fifth century BCE
Stratum XVII: Late Bronze I	1500-1400 BCE	Stratum III: Hellenistic	fourth century BCE
Stratum XVI: Late Bronze II		Stratum II: Late Hellenistic	third-second centuries BCE
Stratum XV: Late Bronze II			
Stratum XIV: Late Bronze II 1	1400-1200 BCE	Stratum I: Herodian	first century CE
Stratum XIII: Iron I			

second Dynasty pharaoh Sheshonq c. 925 BCE (the "Shishak" of 1 Kings 14:25). The Shishak stela apparently names Gezer in topographical order in listing campaigns in the Shepelah district, although the text is partially broken at this point.

Israelite occupation at Gezer in the ninth century BCE (Stratum VII) is not especially well attested. The upper city gate is now rebuilt, following its destruction, as a three-entryway gate, similar to that of Megiddo Stratum IVA. A series of well-constructed private houses was found northwest of the gate area (Field VII), many of them rebuilt and used until the destruction of the site in the Neo-Assyrian period (see below).

Stratum VI marks the eighth-century occupation, brought to a fiery end in a destruction that surely is to be attributed to Tiglath-pileser III in his campaigns of 734/733 BCE. A relief found long ago in the ruins of his palace at Nimrud (now lost) depicts an Assyrian battering ram drawn up against the tower of a city wall, its defenders on top surrendering. The accompanying cuneiform inscription specifies *gazru* (Gezer). Evidence of just such a breach was found immediately to the east of the Field III city gate. Iron arrowheads and pottery covered by calcined (burnt) limestone were found in one of the casemate chambers to the west of the gate.

Stratum V belongs to the post-Assyrian horizon, when Gezer was now reckoned as a Judean site. Evidence comes chiefly from Macalister's "royal stamped jar handles" and a few cuneiform tablets. The city gate is now converted into a rather flimsy two-entryway gate. In several places destruction debris witnesses the Neo-

Babylonian destruction of 587/586 BCE, after which Gezer sinks into decline.

3. Persian, Hellenistic and Herodian Eras.
There are few stratified levels of the Persian epoch (Stratum IV), although Macalister's rich "Philistine Tombs" belong here.

Strata III-II illustrate the Hellenistic era. The Field III gate is finally rebuilt in Stratum II, no doubt in connection with the efforts of the Maccabean insurgents, who came from nearby Modin. The "Outer Wall" was also reused for a final time, with the addition of semicircular ashlar bastions surrounding the towers. Coins of Demetrius II (c. 144 BCE) and Antiochus VII (c. 138-129 BCE) confirm the dates.

The scant remains of Stratum I are Herodian, but the site was largely deserted by this time. Nearly a dozen "boundary inscriptions," carved into the bedrock in an arc some distance away, read in archaizing Hebrew "boundary of Gezer," and in Greek *Alkiou*, the genitive of *Alkios*, probably the landowner of a large estate including the largely abandoned site. A few Byzantine tombs and traces of medieval activity in the vicinity attest to some lingering occupation in the general area. Then Tell el-Jezer was forgotten, and the location of Bronze Age and biblical Gezer lay unknown until Clermont-Ganneau's discovery of some of the boundary inscriptions in 1870. The name, however, was preserved in a corrupted version on the medieval *wêli* (tomb) of a Muslim holy man on the highest rise of the mound (as Tell ej-Jezairli, "Tomb of the Algerian").

BIBLIOGRAPHY. **W. G. Dever, H. D. Lance and G. E. Wright,** *Gezer I: Preliminary Report of the 1964-66 Seasons* (Jerusalem: Hebrew Union College Biblical and Archaeological School, 1970); **W. G. Dever et al.,** *Gezer II: Report of the 1967-70 Seasons in Fields I and II* (Jerusalem: Hebrew Union College/Nelson Glueck School of Biblical Archaeology, 1974); **W. G. Dever,** ed., *Gezer IV: The 1969-71 Seasons in Field VI, the "Acropolis"* (Jerusalem: Nelson Glueck School of Biblical Archaeology, 1986); idem, "Late Bronze Age and Solomonic Defenses at Gezer: New Evidence," *BASOR* 262 (1986) 9-34; idem, "Gezer," *ABD* 2.998-1003; idem, "Further Evidence on the Date of the Outer Wall at Gezer," *BASOR* 289 (1993) 33-54; **H. D. Lance,** "Gezer in the Land and in History," *BA* 30.1 (1967) 34-47; **R. A. S. Macalister,** *The Excavation of Gezer, 1902-1905 and 1907-1909* (3 vols.; London: Murray, 1912); **J. D. Seger,** *Gezer V: The Field I Caves* (Jerusalem: Nelson Glueck School of Biblical Archaeology, 1988). W. G. Dever

GEZER CALENDAR. *See* HEBREW INSCRIPTIONS.

GIBEAH, GEBA

Gibeah (Heb *gibʿâ* means "hill") was a central city in the territory of Benjamin and the royal capital at the time of *Saul.

    1. History
    2. Identifying Gibeah with Tell el-Ful
    3. The Archaeological Evidence
    4. Dating Tell el-Ful

1. History.
Gibeah was located on the main road from Judah to Mount Ephraim (Judg 19:11-13), near the Jerusalem-Shechem road. The territory of the tribe of Benjamin is characterized by a hilly terrain. The biblical sources relating to this territory contain a large number of place names based on the root *gbʿ*, the stem for the Hebrew word meaning "hill." These include *Gibeon, Geba (1 Sam 14:5) and Gibeah (Judg 19:12; 1 Sam 14:2), the latter thought to be Tell el-Ful. There are also longer terms such as "Geba of Benjamin" (1 Sam 13:16), "Gibeah of Benjamin" (1 Sam 13:2) and "Gibeath ha-Elohim" (1 Sam 10:5).

According to the story in Judges 19—21, the city was burned during the civil war that was caused by the atrocities committed by the people of Gibeah against the concubine from Judah. Later, Gibeah became a *Philistine stronghold in the highlands (1 Sam 10:5). According to 1 Samuel 10:26; 11:4, Saul came from Gibeah; however, the genealogical lists in 1 Chronicles 8:29; 9:35 suggest that Saul's ancestral home was at Gibeon. After the battle of Michmash (1 Sam 13—14), Gibeah became Saul's capital and was renamed after him as "Gibeah of Saul" (1 Sam 15:34).

After the schism Gibeah became an important strategic city on the northern border of Judah. It is also mentioned in Isaiah 10:29 in Sennacherib's journey through the region north of Jerusalem.

2. Identifying Gibeah with Tell el-Ful.
The modern site of Tell el-Ful is situated 5.5 km north of the Damascus Gate in Jerusalem. It is located on the crest of the watershed, with deep wadis extending east and west. The hill rises with steep terraces on the east, south and north, but on the west the slope is more gradual. The ancient road from Judah to Mount Ephraim ran along the base of the tell. This was the main north-south route of central Palestine, and the tell, 840 m above sea level, commanded it. The top was relatively flat, about 150 m (north-south) by 90 m (east-west).

E. Robinson (14-15) first identified Gibeah with modern Jaba, but later changed his mind and identified it with Tell el-Ful. Although the identification with Tell el-Ful is generally accepted, it continues to provoke debate; there were, and still are, scholars who challenge this view.

Thus, more recently, both J. M. Miller and P. M. Arnold have challenged this identification and proposed that Gibeah should be identified with Geba (modern Jaba). But this proposal has been rejected because Gibeah belongs to a group of sites whose precise location was already lost in ancient times. The name "Gibeah" was transferred as "Geba" to the place known today as Jaba. Moreover, there is no archaeological evidence to support the claims of Miller or Arnold. In a recent survey Jaba revealed ceramics from Iron Age II as well as Persian sherds, but none from Iron Age I. Yet Tell el-Ful produced ample evidence from Iron Age I. Tell el-Ful is also an extremely commanding and important site; the view from the summit covers a wide area. The strong fortress (or tower) at the summit is situated on the main trade route leading from Jerusalem to the north, and from the coast in the west to Moab and Ammon in the east. No other proposed site has these advantages.

3. The Archaeological Evidence.

Tell el-Ful was excavated by W. F. Albright (1922-1923 and 1933) and by P. Lapp (1964). Five phases of occupation were uncovered, from Iron Age I to the Roman period. However, the earliest occupation had been in the Middle Bronze Age (c. 2000-1550 BCE), as is indicated by potsherds and a mace head. No building remains dating from earlier than the Iron Age have been discovered. The most relevant to the present topic are from the first phase (Iron Age I). This phase is divided into three: (1) Period I: miscellaneous constructions antedating the foundation of the fortress (which do not belong to the fortress at all) were destroyed by fire; (2) Period II: Fortress I was destroyed by a massive fire; (3) Period II: Fortress II, a reconstruction of the first one, was abandoned.

Lapp's main objection to Albright's results was the suggestion that during Period II at Tell el-Ful an entire fortress was built. Albright also suggested that similar towers were built on the corners of the fortress, which, when reconstructed, measure 62 x 57 m. However, in actual fact the contour of the mound precludes such an extension of the fort eastward; and since the tower that Albright discovered stood at a height of 3 m and was well preserved, it is not clear why so few traces of the fort have been discovered elsewhere on the site.

The evidence so far indicates that there was only one massive tower, not a fortress, at Tell el-Ful Period II (the period of Saul). It is possible that at the time of Saul only the tower was necessary, and that the walls were added later.

4. Dating Tell el-Ful.

The main reason for the uncertainty in dating the early archaeological periods at Tell el-Ful stems from the attempts to correlate the archaeological finds with the biblical story in Judges 19—21. Albright (1924, 45) dated the foundation of Tell el-Ful to 1230 BCE and the fortress to 1200 BCE. Albright was convinced that the archaeological results supported the story as it appears in Judges, and he dated the destruction of Gibeah in this story to 1100 BCE. Albright based this on the assumption that the Benjaminites' war must have occurred long before Saul's accession to kingship, by which time the atrocities at Gibeah would have been forgotten. The second period Albright (1933, 8) assigned to the time of Saul on the evidence of potsherds attrib-

uted to the last phase of Iron Age I and before the transition to Iron Age II in the tenth century BCE.

However, the data from Tell el-Ful does not provide enough substantial evidence from which an accurate chronology can be deduced. Thus consideration must be made of A. Mazar's dating of Giloh. The settlement at Giloh (south of the Rephaim Valley, and a twin site of Tell el-Ful) started about the time *Lachish was destroyed in the reign of Ramesses III, c. 1184-1153 BCE—that is, in the first half of the twelfth century BCE. It is not possible to determine whether this was a few years before or after the destruction. Some of the vessels that appeared at Giloh have parallels at Lachish, but other types, especially the "collared rim" jars and some of the cooking pots, do not appear at Lachish. Taking this dating into consideration, one can assume that Period I at Tell el-Ful (like Giloh) was constructed c. 1153 BCE at the latest, even though there is no clear indication as to how long the Period I settlement survived or how many years elapsed between Period I and Period II at Tell el-Ful.

Lapp's excavation results allowed Period I to run fifty years, from 1200 to 1150 BCE, though a slight modification could be made. Thus fifty years should be allowed for Period I, from 1153 BCE, placing Period II (i.e., Saul's period) to roughly 1100 BCE. It is generally accepted that Saul reigned for a period of about twenty years. It has been argued (Shalom Brooks 1998) that there was a gap of at least seventeen years between Saul's death and David's accession to the throne. Hence, taking away about forty years from 1100 BCE brings us closer to the date of 1060-1050 BCE, the time that marks the end of the rule of the house of Saul, contrary to the generally accepted dates for Saul—that is, 1025-1005 BCE.

In light of this discussion it is possible to propose that the end of Period I at Tell el-Ful (most probably a Philistine post defeated by Saul, as described in 1 Sam 13—14) ended by a small fire some time before or around 1100 BCE. It is possible that Saul built the big tower (Period II, Fortress I), which ended with violent destruction after Saul's death. The second fortress (Period II, Fortress II) was built almost immediately after the destruction of the first fortress as a reconstruction. This second fortress, according to the archaeological finds, survived for a short period of about ten years. Because the fortress was built immediately after the first one was destroyed, and the building followed exactly the same plan, it might be suggested that the builder was closely connected with Saul. That person probably was Abner, Saul's uncle, or Ishbaal, Saul's son. Is it possible that they tried to rebuild Saul's tower in order to resettle in Saul's town? Abner was murdered a few years later (2 Sam 3:27), which would explain why Fortress II was abandoned.

The archaeological evidence shows that Gibeah stood in ruins until the eighth century BCE. No attempts were made to rebuild or inhabit the site. Perhaps it was during this period that the story in Judges was written to explain why Gibeah had been sacked.

See also SAUL AND SAUL'S FAMILY.

BIBLIOGRAPHY. **W. F. Albright,** *Excavations and Results at Tell el-Ful (Gibeah of Saul)* (AASOR 4; New Haven: American Schools of Oriental Research, 1924); idem, "A New Campaign of Excavation at Gibeah of Saul," *BASOR* 52 (1933) 6-12; **P. M. Arnold,** *Gibeah: The Search for a Biblical City* (JSOTSup 79; Sheffield, JSOT, 1990); **N. L. Lapp,** ed., *The Third Campaign at Tell el-Ful: Excavations of 1964* (AASOR 45; Cambridge, MA: American Schools of Oriental Research, 1981); **P. W. Lapp,** *The Tale of the Tell: Archaeological Studies* (PTMS 5; Pittsburgh: Pickwick, 1975); **A. Mazar,** "Giloh: An Early Israelite Site Near Jerusalem," *IEJ* 31 (1981) 1-36; **J. M. Miller,** "Geba/Gibeah of Benjamin," *VT* 25 (1975) 145-66; **E. Robinson,** *Biblical Researchers in Palestine, Mount Sinai and Arabia Petraea: A Journal of Travels in the Year 1838* (Boston: Cracker & Brewster, 1841); **S. Shalom Brooks,** "Was There a Concubine at Gibeah?" *BAIAS* 15 (1997) 31-40; idem, *Saul and the Monarchy: A New Look* (SOTS; Aldershot: Ashgate, 2005). S. Shalom Brooks

GIBEON

Gibeon (Heb *gibʿôn*) was the largest and best-known city in the territory of the tribe of Benjamin; it was "like one of the royal cities" (Josh 10:2).

1. Identification
2. History
3. Archaeological Excavations

1. Identification.
Biblical Gibeon has been identified with modern el-Jib, 9 km north of *Jerusalem. The first proper scientific identification with modern el-

Jib was in 1838 by E. Robinson. During the archaeological excavations of 1956, 1957 and 1959 directed by J. B. Pritchard (24-52), this identification was confirmed by the discovery of fifty-six jar handles inscribed with the name *gbʿn*.

2. History.
The first mention of Gibeon is in Joshua 9, which tells how the Hivite inhabitants of Gibeon deceived *Joshua into a peace covenant with them. When the deception was discovered, the Gibeonites were sentenced to become "hewers of wood and drawers of water" (Josh 9:21, 23). Later, when the Amorite king Adoni-Zedek attacked Gibeon for siding with the Israelites, Joshua was obliged to protect them and chased the Amorites down the pass of Beth-Horon, supported by hailstones and the sun standing still on Gibeon (Josh 10:1-14; cf. Is 28:21). However, the reference to this story in Joshua 9 presents a problem because there is no archaeo-logical evidence for a settlement at Gibeon during the Late Bronze Age, the period in which the conquest stories in Joshua are placed.

In Joshua 21:17 Gibeon is described as one of the *Levitical cities. 2 Samuel 2:12-17 describes the contest at the "pool of Gibeon" between two groups of opponents: that of Abner (Saul's supporters) and that of Joab (David's supporters). In that contest twelve men from each group were "thrust through" by the swords of their opponents. In 2 Samuel 20:8 Joab slew Amasa at Gibeon; in 2 Samuel 21:1-10 seven of Saul's sons were executed—that is, two sons of Saul from his concubine Rizpah, and five sons of Michal from her marriage to Paltiel (not Adriel as mentioned in 2 Samuel 21:8. Adriel is the Aramaic version of the Hebrew Paltiel [see Ben-Barak 1991:87]). According to the narrative, the execution had to be carried out to end the three-year famine during David's reign caused by Saul's violation of the covenant with the Gibeonites, not recorded anywhere else in the Bible.

It is noted in 1 Kings that the people were sacrificing at the *high place at Gibeon, that *Solomon offered one thousand burnt offerings on the altar there, and that Solomon's famous inaugural dream occurred at the high place at Gibeon (1 Kings 3:1-15). According to 1 Chronicles 16:39; 21:29, the "tabernacle" *(miškān)* also was there.

Based on the textual material, S. Shalom Brooks argues that Gibeon played an important role in Israelite cultic life before Solomon—that is, since the time of Saul. First, it is implausible that Gibeon was insignificant throughout the period between Samuel and Saul and David; its cultic popularity does not make sense unless the sanctuary had a long history behind it. Second, the description of worship at Gibeon makes sense and is convincing because Gibeon is also described as a Levitical city (Josh 21:17). This view may be supported by the work of J. Blenkinsopp (1974), who proposed that the sanctuary that *David visited (2 Sam 21:1) was at Gibeon, and that the first altar that Saul built to Yahweh (1 Sam 14:33) was in the Gibeonite region and must be the great stone *(hā'eben haggĕdôlâ)* at Gibeon (2 Sam 20:8). This story has cultic significance (Josh 24:26; 1 Sam 6:14-16) and may be identified with the altar on which Solomon offered sacrifices (1 Kings 3:4).

In the book of Jeremiah, Gibeon is mentioned as the home of the false prophet Hananiah (Jer 28:1), and the "great pool" of Gibeon is mentioned again as the site of a bloody combat when Johanan unsuccessfully attacked Ishmael, Gedaliah's assassin (Jer 41:12). A reference from the postexilic period is found in Nehemiah 3:7, which indicates that the men from Gibeon assisted in the rebuilding of the city wall of Jerusalem. The earliest extrabiblical reference to Gibeon is found at Karnak, in a list of cities either captured or visited during Sheshonk I's (biblical Shishak [1 Kings 14:25]) campaign in Canaan c. 924 BCE.

3. Archaeological Excavations.

Archaeological excavations indicate that there were no Late Bronze Age (c. 1550-1200 BCE) settlements at Gibeon—that is, prior to the settlement in the Iron Age I period (Pritchard 1976, 2.449-50). However, the site was occupied in Early Bronze Age I (c. 3300-3050 BCE) and Middle Bronze Age I (c. 2300-2000 BCE), but it is represented only by pottery and other artifacts that were discovered in tombs on the west side of the mound; Late Bronze Age pottery was found, but only in eight of the tombs. During the 1960s an additional eighteen burial caves were uncovered. They had been cut into the limestone of the west side of the hill and were used in Middle Bronze Age I and the Late Bronze Age.

Iron Age I (c. 1200-1000 BCE) produced a massive city wall, 3.2 to 3.4 m thick, which was built around the hill. Two water systems were discovered; they were constructed in the Iron Age to provide the inhabitants of the city with water in time of siege. The first system was a rock-hewn shaft 11.3 m in diameter and 10.8 m deep. A spiral staircase (seventy-nine steps) was cut along the north and east sides of the pool. At the bottom the stairs continued into a tunnel to provide access to the water chamber, which lies 13.6 m below the floor of the pool. Thus the inhabitants had access to water lying 24.4 m below the level of the city. It has been estimated that three thousand tons of limestone were quarried and removed to create the "pool of Gibeon" mentioned in 2 Samuel 2:13. The second system was the stepped tunnel that led from inside the city to the spring of the village. This system was constructed later in Iron Age II, possibly due to the flow of the water into the chamber, which was inadequate.

The winery at Gibeon indicates that it was a prosperous city; the flat land around was suitable for agricultural production and the slopes beyond were suitable for vineyards. The karstic character of the soil meant that there were many springs, and the largest of them was at Gibeon. This flourishing economy is evidenced by the large number of pots that were found and by the frequent occurrences of wine cellars. About forty such cellars have been discovered. These were cistern-like constructions, each 2 m deep and dug out of the rock. The jars inside each cellar held about forty-five liters of wine. In the same area wine presses also were found; they were carved from the rock with channels for conducting the grape juice into fermentation tanks. It is estimated that the cellars provided storage space for jars containing twenty-five thousand gallons of wine. There were smaller jars that had been used to export the wine produced at Gibeon. Stoppers and a funnel for filling the jars also were found.

Studies by A. Demsky and by S. Yeivin have demonstrated that there is a link between the names inscribed on the jar handles and Saul's genealogical lists in 1 Chronicles (1 Chron 8:29-40; 9:35-44). The studies of these genealogies provide some evidence relating to the Benjaminites' settlement in their territory. Demsky attests that these lists present at one and same time the history of the branch of the Ner family as well as the clans and villages that depended on Gibeon both culturally and administratively. These lists also illustrate the relationship of the clans to each other and to Gibeon, which would not have changed from the time of the initial Benjaminite settlement until the exile. Yeivin suggests that after the Benjaminites' penetration there must have been considerable integration with the local inhabitants, mainly through marriage, the results of which are reflected in the genealogical lists in Chronicles. These lists are concerned not with the Gibeonites at Gibeon but with the Benjaminite group that came to settle at Gibeon in the course of time. Their eponymous ancestor is called "the father of Gibeon" in 1 Chronicles 8:29-40 and its duplicate in 1 Chronicles 9:35-44. In the first list his personal name is not given, whereas in the second list he is named as Jeiel.

The most interesting aspect of these lists is the naming of the wife of "the father of Gibeon" as Maacah. This name does not appear as an Israelite name, but is the name of an Aramean principality in the Golan. When it appears as a personal name, it always represents a non-Israelite or someone of non-Israelite descent. This reference to the non-Israelite Maacah may express itself in intermarriage with the local women. Such intermarriages probably resulted in acquisition of rights of heritage and property. The "father of Gibeon" could indicate the head of a large family, quite wealthy and influential. Saul's ancestors are recorded as Kish, Ner and Benjamin—that is, in ascending order from the smaller to the larger unit (see Saul and Saul's Family). Also in 1 Samuel 9:1 Kish, Saul's father, is described as *gibbôr ḥayil*, which is also taken to mean a man of wealth.

See also SAUL AND SAUL'S FAMILY.

BIBLIOGRAPHY. **Z. Ben-Barak**, "The Legal Background to the Restoration of Michal to David," in *Telling Queen Michal's Story*, ed. D. J. A. Clines and T. C. Eskenaszi (JSOTSup 119; Sheffield: Sheffield Academic Press, 1991) 74-90; **J. Blenkinsopp**, *Gibeon and Israel: The Role of Gibeon and the Gibeonites in the Political and Religious History of Early Israel* (SOTSMS 2; Cambridge: Cambridge University Press, 1972); idem, "Did Saul Make Gibeon His Capital?" *VT* 24 (1974) 1-7; **A. Demsky**, "The Genealogy of Gibeon (1 Chronicles 9.35-44): Biblical and Epigraphic Considerations," *BASOR* 202 (1971) 16-23; **J. B. Pritchard**, *Gibeon, Where the Sun Stood Still: The Discovery of a Biblical City* (Princeton, NJ: Princeton University Press, 1962); idem, "Gibeon," *EAEHL*, ed. M. Avi-Yona and E. Stern (Oxford: Oxford University Press, 1976) 2:446-50; **S. Shalom Brooks**, *King Saul and the Emergence of Monarchy in Israel: A New Look* (SOTS; Aldershot: Ashgate, 2005); **S. Yeivin**, "The Benjaminite Settlement in the Western Part of Their Territory," *IEJ* 21 (1971) 141-54.

S. Shalom Brooks

GIDEON. *See* JUDGES; HISTORY OF ISRAEL 2: PREMONARCHIC ISRAEL.

GILGAL

A common place name in ancient Israel, the Historical Books report four identifiable places called Gilgal: one the site of several momentous narratives in Israel's national life, and three others in brief references (for a fifth site near *Shechem see Deut 11:30). The location (or locations) of the Gilgal mentioned in two other texts is uncertain.

1. The Name
2. Gilgal Near Jericho
3. Gilgal Near Bethel
4. The Border Marker
5. A Regional Term
6. Uncertain Locations

1. The Name.

The name *Gilgal* derives from the root *gālal*, "to roll, roll away," and Isaiah 28:28 attests a noun *gilgāl* ("wheel" [of a cart or chariot]; cf. the more common *galgāl*, "wheel" [Is 5:28; Ezek 10:2, 6]). With two exceptions (Josh 5:9; 12:23), the place name always has the definite article prefixed *(haggilgāl)*. Thus the form comprises a common noun (perhaps a "rolling" or "round" thing/place) made definite ("*the* rolling/round [place/thing]") that through usage became the toponym *Gilgal*. Though often stated, the definition of Gilgal as "circle of stones" is problematic. Joshua 4 says nothing about how the stones were configured (see 2.1.1 below), and the other Gilgals need not share the same meaning.

2. Gilgal Near Jericho.

2.1. Its Location. Brief biblical comments locate this Gilgal "on the east border of Jericho" (Josh 4:19) in "the plains of Jericho" (Josh 5:10). The latter is a small north-south plain along the Jordan's west bank near *Jericho (cf. "the plains of Moab" [Num 36:13; Josh 13:32]), while "east border" puts Gilgal on Jericho's eastern outskirts—that is, outside the city's control. That *David "went on to Gilgal" from the Jordan (2 Sam 19:40 [41]) places it inland a short distance from the river. Attempts to identify Gilgal with modern sites have proved inconclusive thus far. Tell en-Nitla lies 3.5 km northeast of Jericho but lacks evidence of occupation before the Byzantine period. Soundings at two small sites near Khirbet Mefjir (c. 3 km northeast of Jericho), a mound near a main Jordan ford, found typical Iron Age pottery (1200-600 BCE) at the northern one but nothing certain at the western one. An outcropping of flint rock lies near the latter, perhaps the source for Joshua's circumcision knives (Josh 5:2-3). On the other hand, the Bible portrays this Gilgal as an open campground or outdoor memorial shrine for pilgrims, not a city or place with many (if any) permanent residents. Its only likely remains would be altars and cultic objects. Gilgal probably lay in this general area with plentiful water available in the nearby Wadi en-Nuʾeima and elevated spots suitable for addressing large crowds or conducting cultic rites.

2.2. Its Narrative History. Several important narratives of Israel's early history are set at Gilgal and suggest something of its importance in that period.

2.2.1. Gilgal and Joshua. Gilgal was Israel's first campsite in their new homeland after crossing the Jordan (Josh 4:19). There *Joshua set up twelve stones taken from the dry Jordan riverbed to commemorate that miraculous event (Josh 4:20). The text implies that later Israelites would regularly visit them to remember the crossing (Josh 4:4-7, 21-24), but scholarly attempts to reconstruct the contours of such ceremonies from Joshua 3—6 have not won a consensus. At Gilgal Joshua also circumcised the generation born during the wilderness wanderings (Josh 5:2-9), an event given special significance by a word play on the place name. Henceforth "Gilgal" would recall Yahweh's declaration "I have rolled away [gallôtî] from you the disgrace of Egypt" (Josh 5:9)—that is, his welcome of this generation to a fresh start in its new land. At Gilgal Israel celebrated its first Passover in the land and ate its first homegrown food instead of manna (Josh 5:10-12). At Gilgal a delegation from *Gibeon, an important Hivite city in central Canaan, pretended to be foreigners and tricked Israel into accepting a nonaggression treaty (Josh 9:6). From Gilgal Joshua

led the rescue operation that broke the siege of Gibeon by a Canaanite coalition (Josh 10:6, 7, 9, 15), and to Gilgal he returned after his victorious blitzkrieg of southern Canaan (Josh 10:43). There he distributed the first inheritance land, awarding *Hebron to *Caleb for his steadfast faith in God when the ten other spies despaired (Josh 14:6; cf. Num 14:24). Presumably, at Gilgal he also allotted lands to other tribes (Josh 15—17), although *Shiloh is the site of several distributions (Josh 18:1; 21:2) and Shechem the place of covenant renewal (Josh 24:1).

2.2.2. Gilgal: Samuel and Saul. Once military conquest gave way to settlement and nation-building, Shiloh apparently became Israel's preeminent cultic center (see Judg 18:31; 21:19; 1 Sam 1:3; 3:21). But events involving *Samuel and *Saul at Gilgal may reflect its renaissance as a kind of national spiritual capital after the *Philistines destroyed Shiloh (1 Sam 4; Jer 7:12, 14). After anointing Saul, Samuel sent him down to Gilgal to await his arrival there in seven days (1 Sam 10:8). Samuel led Israel to Gilgal to reaffirm Saul as king, everyone capping off the ceremony with burnt offerings (1 Sam 11:14-15). There also Saul rallied Israel after Jonathan's capture of the Philistine outpost at Geba threatened Israel with reprisals (1 Sam 13:3-4). But with Israel scattering in fear and no sign of Samuel on day seven, Saul lost patience and offered burnt offerings at Gilgal (1 Sam 13:7-9). On his arrival, Samuel condemns Saul's presumption and announces that God had chosen someone else, not Saul's kin, as his successor (1 Sam 13:10-14). After Saul defeated the Amalekites, Samuel again condemned him at Gilgal, this time for not destroying the enemy's flocks (1 Sam 15:12-14, 22-30). Saul's excuse that he spared them "to sacrifice [them] to the Lord your God in Gilgal" (1 Sam 15:21) attests the site's religious importance at the time but failed to dissuade Samuel from announcing God's rejection of Saul as king (1 Sam 15:23, 26). Finally, Samuel hacked to death the Amalekite king Agag, whom Saul had captured (1 Sam 15:32-33).

2.2.3. David's Return. Some years later, Judah's leaders met at Gilgal to welcome David back from exile in *Moab after Absalom's coup attempt against his father failed (2 Sam 19:15, 40).

3. Gilgal Near Bethel.
According to 2 Kings 2:1, *Elijah and *Elisha left

Gilgal for *Bethel en route to Elijah's departure for heaven in a whirlwind. Since Jericho was their ultimate destination (2 Kings 2:4-5), this Gilgal probably lies somewhere near Bethel. Later, Elisha returns to rejoin a community of prophets there (2 Kings 4:38) for whom he performed two miracles to help them survive a famine.

4. The Border Marker.
Gilgal is a village marking the boundary line between the tribal territories of Judah and Benjamin (Josh 15:7; 18:17 ["Geliloth"]; Neh 12:29 ["Beth-gilgal"]). It sits between Debir (probably Khirbet er-Rabud, c. 25 km southwest of Hebron) and En-shemesh (probably Ein Haud, 3 km east of Jerusalem) along a ridge parallel to and north of the Ascent of Adummim, the northeast-southwest slope that bears the road between Jericho and *Jerusalem. Along with Geba and Azmaveth it apparently was close enough to Jerusalem for temple singers to reside there and still execute their duties (Neh 12:29), but attempts to identify it with modern sites are inconclusive.

5. A Regional Term.
The list of kings defeated by Joshua includes "the king of Goiim in Gilgal" (Josh 12:23b), but textual uncertainly haunts this statement. For "Gilgal" the LXX reads "Galilee" (haggālîl [so NRSV]), understanding "Goiim" to be the royal city—perhaps Harosheth-ha-goiim, home of Sisera (Judg 4:2)—and "Galilee" the larger region (cf. Is 9:1). Stylistically, this fits the context (see Josh 12:22, 23a) and commends the LXX reading, but linguistically "Gilgal" and "Galilee" may also represent variant forms of the same northern regional name (both derive from the root gālal). If so, rather than a city, the MT's "Gilgal" designates the region of Lower Galilee north of the Jezreel Valley. But if the MT refers to a Canaanite city, this Gilgal probably would lie between Dor and Tirzah on the eastern side of the Sharon Plain, perhaps the modern town of Jiljuliyeh, c. 5 km north of Aphek, whose name may preserve the biblical name.

6. Uncertain Locations.
Judges 2:1 reports that the angel of the Lord moved from Gilgal to Bochim ("weeping") to announce divine judgment against Israel, but the lack of contextual details hinders the identification of either site. The tribute to Joshua in the following pericope (Judg 2:6-10) might assume Gilgal near Jericho as the angel's departure point, and some suggest that Moabite occupation of the area around Jericho (Judg 3:13-14) may underlie the move with a resulting decline in Gilgal's importance. The LXX reads "to the Weeping Place and to Bethel," so another possibility identifies Bochim with Allon-bacuth ("Oak of Weeping") near Bethel (Gen 35:8), thus locating Gilgal in that vicinity as well. According to 1 Samuel 7:16-17, Bethel, Gilgal and *Mizpah formed the judicial circuit that Samuel visited annually to settle legal cases. Bethel and Mizpah were prominent cities in the central highlands on the main north-south highway, the latter not far from his hometown at Ramah (1 Sam 7:5-6; 10:3). Gilgal near the Jordan probably is not in view here, because it was not a population center and lay way east of the other stops. More likely, this Gilgal lay in the same general area as Bethel, Mizpah and Ramah. Indeed, it may be that both Judges 2:1 and 1 Samuel 7:16-17 refer to the same city near Bethel later associated with Elijah and Elisha (2 Kings 2:1; 4:38). It seems improbable that the Bethel area would have two separate towns named Gilgal, although confirming evidence is lacking.

See also JERICHO.

BIBLIOGRAPHY. **B. M. Bennett Jr.**, "The Search for Israelite Gilgal," *PEQ* 104 (1972) 111-22; **W. H. Brownlee**, "Gilgal," *ISBE* 1.470-72; **D. J. A. Clines**, ed., *Dictionary of Classical Hebrew* (5 vols.; Sheffield: Sheffield Academic Press, 1993-2001) 1.347-48; **W. R. Kotter**, "Gilgal (Place)," *ABD* 2.1022-24; **F. Langlamet**, *Gilgal et les récits de la traversée du Jourdain, Jos. III-IV* (CahRB 11; Paris: Gabalda, 1969); **E. Otto**, *Das Mazzotfest in Gilgal* (BWANT 6/7; Stuttgart: Kohlhammer, 1975); **J. R. Vannoy**, *Covenant Renewal at Gilgal: A Study of 1 Samuel 11:14—12:25* (Cherry Hill, NJ: Mack, 1978). R. L. Hubbard Jr.

GOATS. *See* AGRICULTURE AND ANIMAL HUSBANDRY.

GOD
The rise of literary approaches to the OT in recent decades has alerted students of the Historical Books to the extraordinary skill of Israelite historians in their portrayal of the characters in the narratives (*see* Narrative Art of Israel's Historians). Although the human characters, espe-

cially major players such as Joshua, Samuel, David, Elijah, Hezekiah and Josiah, fascinate modern readers, ultimately the Historical Books are primarily concerned with the character and role of God. This is apparent not only from the fact that the character of God represents the only thread that ties together all these books (with the notable exception of Esther), but also from the fact that God is referred to by name or title more frequently in these books than the top twenty human characters combined. The discussion that follows here seeks to describe how God is portrayed in the Historical Books of the OT (Joshua, Judges, 1-2 Samuel, 1-2 Kings, 1-2 Chronicles, Ezra and Nehemiah).

When we speak of "God" in the Historical Books, we must distinguish between "God" as perceived by ancient Israelites—these perceptions varied greatly from polytheism to poly-Yahwism to monotheism—and the images of "God" espoused by the narrators of the OT. Since the Historical Books of the OT were written from a monotheistic Yahwistic perspective, we expect their portrayals of God to be complementary rather than contradictory. However, this does not mean that they speak in unison or monotone. On the contrary, the distribution of names and titles for God in the books alone reflects differences in emphases if not perceptions. For example, the ratio of references to God by divine name (YHWH) versus divine title ("God," 'ĕlōhîm) varies significantly from c. 2.8:1 in the Deuteronomistic History (Joshua-2 Kings) to 1.7:1 in 1-2 Chronicles and 1:2.3 in Ezra-Nehemiah. This immediately raises questions regarding the historians' perceptions regarding God.

But these issues arise not only when we compare the various Historical Books. Within compositions we must always ask *whose* perspectives are being reflected in specific statements about God: Are they presented as God's own view of himself? Are they the views of a faithful Israelite? Are they the views of an apostate or compromising Israelite (e.g., Jephthah's comments about Chemosh in Judg 11:24, or Saul's challenge to David to go and serve other gods in 1 Sam 26:19)? Are they the views of a non-Israelite character (e.g., the Philistines in 1 Sam 5—6)? Do they represent the narrator's view of God? Sometimes one character's viewpoint differs from that of another, and sometimes it differs from that of the narrator. The issue is illustrated

by 1 Samuel 15, where in successive statements Yahweh says that he "rues" *(niḥam)* that he has made Saul king (1 Sam 15:11); Samuel declares that Yahweh is not human, and therefore never lies or "rues" *(niḥam)* anything (1 Sam 15:29); the narrator declares that Yahweh "rued" *(niḥam)* that he had made Saul king (1 Sam 15:35). The threefold repetition of the word *niḥam* adds depth and texture to the portrayal of God, and cautions the reader not to reduce his character to a simple formula.

Beyond asking whose perceptions of God are being expressed, we must also consider *how* God is being presented. As is the case with human personalities in biblical narratives, the character of God is presented through his own actions and interactions with others, through his own speeches, through others' speeches about him, and through the narrators' comments about him (see Bowman, 29-30). To illustrate the point, we may compare the ways in which God is referred to in the Davidic narratives concerning the time from his assumption of the throne of all Israel to his transgression with Bathsheba (2 Sam 5—12), on the one hand, and those revolving around his succession (2 Sam 13—20), on the other. Not only is the frequency of references to God greatly diminished (in the former, Yahweh is named 62 times, or once about every 48 words; in the latter, only 24 times, or once every 187 words), but also the way in which the name is used changes drastically. Whereas in the former, the narrator speaks freely of Yahweh's/God's involvement in human affairs, in the latter the name *Yahweh* appears only in direct speech; the narrator never mentions God by name outside human conversation. Furthermore, the narrator refers directly to God only four times in the latter, though never as a participant in events. God is mentioned only to qualify an object: the ark of the covenant of God (2 Sam 15:24); the ark of God (2 Sam 15:29); the hilltop where God was worshiped (2 Sam 15:32); the word of God (2 Sam 16:23). Although people will still invoke the name of Yahweh, one gets the impression that in the narrator's mind, God had withdrawn from David's life during his struggle to hold the throne.

All of this is to say that although (or perhaps because) God is the primary subject and object of so much of the OT historical narrative, when these factors are taken into consideration, we discover God to be the most complex character in the Bible. For this reason, any attempt to describe God in a short essay such as this one is, by definition, limited.

1. Names and Epithets for God
2. The Declared Characteristics of God
3. The Relational Actions of God
4. Conclusion

1. Names and Epithets for God.
Since most of the names and/or epithets for God that occur in the Historical Books are found in the Pentateuch, the reader should see the information provided in *Dictionary of the Old Testament: Pentateuch* (*see DOTP*, God, Names of). Rather than reproduce that information here, we will highlight the distinctive ways in which the various compositions employ these names and epithets.

1.1. The Personal Name "Yahweh" (YHWH).
The 2,019 occurrences of "Yahweh" in the Historical Books represent 30 percent of the OT total (6,828), which is slightly below the proportion of the OT taken up by these books (33 percent by word count; see Andersen and Forbes, 330; *TLOT* 3.1444-45 [= *THAT* 2.539-40]). But this should not detract from the fact that God is referred to by his name "Yahweh" more than twice as often as all other titles and epithets combined. This overwhelming preference for "Yahweh" reflects the perspective of these writings: since they were written by Israelites for Israelites, it is natural that they should refer to God by the name most familiar to all.

According to the narratives of Exodus, "Yahweh" was not only the personal name of the God of Israel's ancestors, but also his eternal name by which he invited Israel to address him (Ex 3:13-16). While the etymological meaning of the name remains disputed (see *DOTP* 362-64), its historical significance is demonstrated in God's deliverance of Israel from Egypt, his establishment of Israel as his covenant people, and his provision of the land of Canaan as their hereditary homeland in fulfillment of his covenant promises to the ancestors (Ex 6:2-8) (see Martens, 3-19). Because the Israelites seemed to be in constant danger of losing the memory of these gracious actions, in the Historical Books God continues to introduce himself by the formula "I am Yahweh your God" (e.g., Judg 6:10) (see Zimmerli, 1-28), and his spokespersons flesh out this formula with "who brought you out of the land of Egypt" and additional expressions

of his favors (Josh 24:17; 1 Sam 12:8; 1 Kings 9:9; 2 Kings 17:36; 2 Chron 7:22). Indeed, Yahweh's involvement in Israel's historical experiences continues to serve his revelatory agenda, as is reflected in the use of the divine recognition formula "Then you will know that I am Yahweh your God" (e.g., 1 Kings 20:13, 28), and other declarations of the demonstration of his person and presence (Josh 3:10; 4:24; 22:31; 1 Sam 17:46-47; 1 Kings 8:43, 60; 18:37; 20:13, 28; 2 Kings 5:15; 19:19). In all the Historical Books Yahweh is first and foremost the redeeming and covenant God of Israel (see further below).

1.2. The Generic Designation "God" (ʾĕlôah/ ʾĕlōhîm / ʾĕlāh). While only two of the 57 occurrences of the Hebrew ʾĕlôah are found in the Historical Books, Ezra contains 43 of the 95 occurrences of ʾĕlāh, its Aramaic cognate. Both Hebrew texts are late: 2 Chronicles 32:15, in a message from Sennacherib to the people of Judah; and Nehemiah 9:17, a poetic prayer of Levites. Although ʾĕlôah is used in the book of Job as a proper name (e.g., Job 4:17), scholars generally assume that the word is cognate to the common Semitic term for deity, ʾil-, and that this singular form underlies the plural ʾĕlōhîm (*HALOT* 1.52; Pardee). In Sennacherib's message (delivered in Hebrew translation, i.e., yĕhûddît, "Judaean" [2 Kings 18:26; Is 36:11]) ʾĕlôah obviously is used in a generic sense. In Nehemiah 9:17, where the reader hears echoes of Exodus 34:6-7, the expression functions as an alternative to yhwh ʾēl.

The 953 occurrences of the plural form ʾĕlōhîm in the historiographical narratives account for more than one-third (37 percent) of the 2,600 occurrences in the OT. Remarkably, the 264 occurrences of hāʾĕlōhîm (with the article) account for almost three-fourths of the total of 373 in the OT. That Hebrew historians recognized the plural form ʾĕlōhîm as a generic designation for deity is reflected in their use of the term as a common noun, specifically their frequent references to divinities of non-Israelites by this designation. Such divinities are identified by name (Ashtaroth/Ashtoreth [Judg 10:6; 1 Kings 11:33]; Baal [Judg 6:31; 8:33; 1 Kings 18:25]; Baal-zebub [2 Kings 1:2-3, 6, 16]; Chemosh [Judg 11:24; 1 Kings 11:33]; Dagon [Judg 16:23; 1 Sam 5:2, 7]; Milcom [1 Kings 11:33]; Succoth-benoth, Nergal, Ashima, Nibhaz, Tartak, Adrammelech and Anammelech [2 Kings 17:29-31]), by ethnicons/nationality (generally god/gods of the peoples/nations/kingdoms [Judg 2:12; 2 Kings 17:29; 18:33-35; 19:12; 1 Chron 5:25; 16:26; 2 Chron 25:15; 32:13-19]; god/gods of Ammonites [Judg 10:6; 1 Kings 11:33]; Amorites [Josh 24:15; Judg 6:10]; Philistines [Judg 10:6]; Sidonians [1 Kings 11:33]; Moab [Judg 10:6; 1 Kings 11:33]; Edom [2 Chron 25:20]; Damascus [2 Chron 28:23]; kings of Aram [2 Chron 28:23]), by place (generally god/gods of the land/lands [2 Kings 17:26-27]; god/gods of Ekron [2 Kings 1:2-3, 6, 16]; Seir [2 Chron 25:14]; Sidon [Judg 10:6]; Aram [Judg 10:6]; Hamath, Arpad, Sepharvaim, Hena, Ivvah [2 Kings 18:33-35]), or by topography (god of hills/valleys [1 Kings 20:23]). Despite the surrounding peoples' worship of a plurality of deities (*see* Canaanite Gods and Religion), expressions such as these reflect a common ancient Near Eastern conviction that each nation or people group, however defined (ethnically or territorially), enjoyed a special relationship with a patron (in a few instances, matron) deity (see Block 2000, 35-74). The Philistines' fivefold reference to "the ark of the God of Israel" in 1 Samuel 5:7—6:3 (plus the narrator's reference, 1 Sam 5:8) suggests that outsiders viewed Yahweh's relationship with Israel to be like their own to their gods (*'ĕlōhîm*).

Israelites occasionally speak of the gods of the nations in similar terms, as in Jephthah's comment that the Ammonites possess land that Chemosh their god has given them (Judg 11:24). And on the surface, Hebrew historians' free use of expressions such as "other gods" (*'ĕlōhîm 'ăhērîm* [e.g., Josh 23:16; Judg 2:12; 1 Sam 8:8; 1 Kings 9:6; 2 Chron 7:22]) and "foreign gods" (*'ĕlōhê [han]nēkār* [Josh 24:20, 23; Judg 10:16; 1 Sam 7:3; 2 Chron 33:15]) suggests concurrence with this perspective. This conclusion might find support in the fact that the narrators, like the characters in the narratives, often employ the expression "Yahweh, the God of Israel," (e.g., Josh 8:30; Judg 11:21; 1 Kings 15:30; 1 Chron 15:14; 2 Chron 30:1; Ezra 4:1; cf. 1 Sam 5:8). Characters with syncretistic religious viewpoints frequently express belief in a multiplicity of deities. This seems to be the case in, for example, *Jeroboam's declaration at the inauguration of the worship of the calves at Bethel and Dan: "See your gods [*'ĕlōhîm*], O Israel, who brought you up [*he'ĕlûkā*, pl. verb] from the land of Egypt" (1 Kings 12:28). However, since this statement adapts a form of the soteriological formula "I am Yahweh your God who brought you up/

out of the land of Egypt" (Ex 6:7; 20:2; Lev 19:36; 26:13; Num 15:41; Deut 5:6; 20:1; Josh 24:17; 2 Kings 17:7, 36; Jer 2:6; 16:14-15; 23:7-8; Ps 81:10), he may be expressing a poly-Yahwistic perspective, as if Yahweh manifests himself in different forms at different places (cf. the ninth/eighth-century inscriptions from Kuntillet 'Ajrud, which speak of Yahweh of Samaria and Yahweh of Teman [for discussion and bibliography on these texts see Keel and Uehlinger, 225-32; on poly-Yahwism in Israel see Donner, 48-49; Smith, 118-25; Albertz, 83, 206-9]).

But Israel's historians countenance no such notion. To be sure, the embedded "Song of Deborah" refers to "Yahweh, the One of Sinai" (*yhwh zeh śînay*), but this speaks less of a local manifestation of Yahweh than of Sinai as a place of theophanic revelation. For the narrators, Yahweh is the one and only God. Scholars rarely comment on the significance of *'ĕlōhîm* appearing so frequently with the article: *hā'ĕlōhîm* (lit., "the God"). In accordance with the general monotheistic thrust of the OT, when used as a title of God, this form suggests he is the one and only God deserving of the title *'ĕlōhîm*.

1.3. El ('ēl*).* Of the 238 occurrences of *'ēl* in the OT, only 14 occur in the Historical Books. Since the preponderance of references to El elsewhere are found in poetic texts, it is not surprising that of these fourteen occurrences more than one-half appear in metrical texts (1 Sam 2:3; 2 Sam 22:31, 32, 33, 48; 23:5; Neh 9:31, 32). Except for Judges 9:46, where the narrator refers to a Shechemite temple of El-berith (cf. the references to Baal-berith in Judg 8:33; 9:4), the remaining occurrences are found in passionate speeches (Josh 3:10 [*'ēl hay*, "the living El"]; 22:2 [2x]; 24:19) and prayers (Neh 1:5).

Although some see *'ĕlōhîm* as a plural form of *'ēl*, two considerations argue against this link. First, it is difficult to account for the *h* in *'ĕlōhîm*; a connection with *'ĕlôah* seems more likely. Second, biblical Hebrew has a more natural plural version of *'ēl*, which is *'ēlîm* (Ex 15:11; Ps 29:1; 89:7). Daniel 11:36 is especially instructive inasmuch as the superlative expression *'ēl 'ēlîm*, "God of gods," answers not only to the Aramaic *'ĕlāh 'ĕlāhîn* in Daniel 2:47, but also to the Hebrew *'ĕlōhê hā'ĕlōhîm* in Deuteronomy 10:17 and Psalm 136:2. In Northwest Semitic texts *'l* usually functions as an appellative, meaning "god, divinity" (see *DNWSI* 1.53-55), but there are numerous instances in which the word functions as a proper noun. An eighth-century BCE Aramaic text from Sam'al lists Hadad, El, Resheph, Rakkabel, Shamash and ʿRQRŠP (*KAI* 214:2, 11); another from Sefire, which lists more than a dozen divine names, places El next to Elyon (*KAI* 222A:6-12). In the Deir ʿAllah inscription from c. 700 BCE, El conveys a message to the prophet Balaam (*COS* 2.27:142). Another eighth-century BCE Phoenician inscription from Karatepe refers to *ʾl qn ʾrṣ*, "El—creator of the earth." This title recalls the late second-millennium mythological texts from Ugaritic in which El is fully developed as a "round" character (see Berlin, 23-24), not only as the head (*mlk*) of the pantheon and husband of Athirat (Asherah, who is mother of the gods), but also *bny bnwt*, "the builder of offspring," and *ʾab ʾadm*, "father of humankind" (for the text in translation see *COS* 1.86:256-58). The reference to the Shechemite temple of El-berith in Judges 9:46 apparently refers to this deity.

Israelite historiographers use "El" as a common designation for divinity and as a proper name for God. In cases of the former we should translate *ʾēl* generically as "a god," and *hāʾēl* specifically as "the God." The issue becomes significant where the character of Yahweh is described: (1) *ki ʾēl ḥay bĕqirbĕkem*, "for the living God is in your midst" (Josh 3:10); (2) *kî-ʾĕlōhîm qĕdōšîm hûʾ ʾēl qannôʾ hûʾ*, "for he is a holy God; he is an impassioned God" (Josh 24:19); (3) *ki ʾēl dēʿôt yhwh*, "for Yahweh is a God of knowledge" (1 Sam 2:3); (4) *ʾĕlōhê haššāmayim hāʾēl haggādôl wĕhannôrāʾ šōmēr habbĕrît wāḥesed*, "God of heaven, the great and awesome God, who keeps the covenant and faithful love" (Neh 1:5); (5) *kî ʾēl-ḥannûn wĕrāḥûm ʾattâ*, "for you are a gracious and compassionate God" (Neh 9:31). However, in Josh 22:22, where the two and one-half tribes invoke Yahweh by repeating *ʾēl ʾĕlōhîm yhwh ʾēl ʾĕlōhîm yhwh*, "El, God, Yahweh! El, God, Yahweh!" the common noun "God" is sandwiched between two proper designations, "El" and "Yahweh." The clearest instances of "El" as a proper noun occur in the embedded Davidic poems in 2 Samuel 22 and 23.

As for El *[hāʾēl]*, his way is perfect;
The word of Yahweh is tested.
For who is El *[ʾēl]*, other than Yahweh *[yhwh]*,
And who is Rock *[ṣûr]*, other than our God *[ʾĕlōhênû]*?

El *[hāʾēl]* is my strong fortress,
And he sets the blameless in his way.
(2 Sam 22:31-33)

Yahweh lives, and blessed be my Rock;
Let the God of the Rock of my salvation be exalted.
El *[hāʾēl]* executes strong vengeance for me,
And brings down peoples under me.
(2 Sam 22:47-48)

Is not my house so with El *[ʾēl]*?

For he has established an eternal covenant with me. (2 Sam 23:5)

In 2 Samuel 22:32, El is explicitly identified with Yahweh; in 2 Samuel 23:5, El identifies the God who made an eternal covenant with David, referred to earlier as "Yahweh" (2 Sam 23:2), "the God of Jacob" (*ʾĕlōhê yaʿăqōb* [2 Sam 23:1]), "the God of Israel" (*ʾĕlōhê yiśrāʾēl* [2 Sam 23:3]), and "the Rock of Israel" (*ṣûr yiśrāʾēl* [2 Sam 23:3]). As in the cases involving *hāʾĕlōhîm* mentioned above, the article on *ʾēl* in 2 Samuel 22:31, 33; 22:48 suggests that to the poet, Yahweh is the one and only El—that is, the only divinity worthy of the designation.

1.4. Lord (ʾĀdôn/ʾĂdōnāy). *ʾĀdôn* is a common noun denoting "lord, owner, master," which expresses the subordination of an inferior to a superior. Various forms of the noun are applied to God twenty-eight times in the Historical Books. The simple form *ʾādôn* is applied to Yahweh only twice, in Joshua 3:11, 13, where Joshua identifies the ark as *ʾărôn habbĕrît ʾădôn kol-hāʾāreṣ*, "the ark of the covenant of the Lord of all the earth," and *ʾărôn yhwh ʾădôn kol-hāʾāreṣ*, "the ark of Yahweh, the Lord of all the earth." In Joshua's mind, Yahweh is not only Lord of Israel, but also cosmic sovereign. Most other occurrences involve *ʾădōnāy*, which on the surface appears to involve the plural form plus a first-person suffix (lit., "my lords"; cf. sg., *ʾădōnî*, "my lord"), which then fossilized into a fixed form of direct address. However, the facts that Yahweh identifies himself as *ʾădōnāy yhwh* and that speakers (pl.) use the expression when *ʾădōnênû*, "our Lord," would be more natural (Ps 44:24, as in Neh 8:10; 10:29 [MT 10:30]; cf. *ʾădōnêhem*, "their Lord," in Neh 3:5) argue against this interpretation. It is preferable, therefore, to interpret the *-āy* ending as an emphatic sufformative, signifying something like

"Lord of all" (*TDOT* 1.62-72; *IBHS* 7.4.3f), a sense captured by Joshua when he refers to Yahweh as *ʾădôn kol-hāʾāreṣ*, "Lord of all the earth," in Joshua 3:15 (cf. Josh 3:11).

The Historical Books use the compound form *ʾădōnāy yhwh*, "O Lord Yahweh," as a vocative of direct address twelve times (Josh 7:7; Judg 6:22; 16:28; 2 Sam 7:18, 19a, 19b, 20, 22, 28, 29 [some MSS read *ʾădōnāy yhwh* in v. 25 as well]; Neh 1:11). In three additional cases *ʾădōnāy* functions vocatively alone (Judg 6:15; 13:8; Neh 1:11). The instances in which *ʾădōnāy* is used as a designation for God outside of these vocative cases are rare. Characters in the narrative do so in 1 Kings 2:26 (Solomon, referring to the ark as the ark of *ʾădōnāy yhwh*), 1 Kings 22:6 (false prophets), 2 Kings 19:23 (Isaiah), Ezra 10:3 (? Shecaniah), and Nehemiah 4:14 [MT 4:8] (Nehemiah). Narrators refer to Yahweh as *ʾădōnāy* only three times: 1 Kings 3:10 ("the matter was good in the eyes of *ʾădōnāy*"); 1 Kings 3:15 ("Solomon stood before the ark of the covenant of *ʾădōnāy*"); 2 Kings 7:6 ("*ʾădōnāy* caused the Aramaean camp to hear the sound of chariots"). However, the discomfort felt by Hebrew scribes with these readings is reflected in the fact that Hebrew manuscripts and/or early versions suggest alternate readings in every one of these nonvocative cases: deleting *ʾădōnāy* before *yhwh* in 1 Kings 2:26; replacing *ʾădōnāy* with *ʾĕlōhênû* in Nehemiah 4:14 [MT 4:8]; replacing *ʾădōnāy* with *yhwh* in 1 Kings 3:10, 15; 22:6; 2 Kings 7:6; 19:23; Ezra 10:3.

Although other peoples also expressed their subjection to their divinities by referring to them as *ʾdn* (fem., *ʾdt*) (for Northwest Semitic inscriptions see *DNWSI* 1.16), in Israel this title often served as a convenient way to express the special suzerain-vassal covenant relationship that Yahweh had established with his people. This relationship is reflected in suffixed forms of the title ("our Lord" [Neh 8:10; 10:29 (MT 10:30)]; "their Lord" [? Neh 3:5]) and in references to the ark as "the ark of the covenant of *ʾădōnāy*" (1 Kings 3:15; cf. "the ark of *ʾădōnāy yhwh*" in 1 Kings 2:26). Inasmuch as 2 Samuel 7 contains the only occurrences of *ʾădōnāy* as a title for Yahweh in the books of Samuel, this chapter represents a special case. David refers to God as *ʾădōnāy yhwh* seven times, thereby expressing his recognition of his personal vassal status vis-à-vis Yahweh. This status is reinforced by Yahweh's own identification of David as "my servant" (*ʿabdî* [2 Sam 7:5, 8]) and by David's tenfold reference to himself as "your servant" (*ʿabdĕkā* [2 Sam 7:19-29]).

1.5. Baal (ba**ʿ**al). Technically, like *ʾādôn/ʾădōnāy*, *baʿal* is not a divine name, but rather a title meaning "master, owner, lord." When used of a deity, it denotes the divine patron/owner of the city/land where he was venerated. This conclusion is reinforced by the frequent attachment of the article (*habbaʿal*) and the common use of the plural *habbĕʿālîm*, "the baals" (i.e., "divine masters"; see *HALOT* 1.143-44), not to mention the reference to "the name of the baal" in 1 Kings 18:26. The storm god referred to by the title *baʿal* was known by various names, depending on location: Hadad in Syria; Melqart in Tyre (cf. the inscriptional designation *mlqrt bʿl ṣr*, "Melqart, lord of Tyre" [*KAI* 47:1]); Chemosh in Moab; Milkom in Bene Ammon. Although various forms of *baʿal* are used as epithets of pagan deities more than seventy times in the Historical Books, Hebrew historians never ascribe this title to Yahweh in the way Hosea 2:16 [MT 2:18] suggests that syncretistic Israelites did. Nevertheless, the epithet surfaces as the theophore in several personal names: *Bĕʿalyâ*, "Yahweh is Baal" (one of David's warriors [1 Chron 12:5 (MT 12:6)]); *Bĕʿelyādāʿ*, "Baal knows" (one of David's sons [1 Chron 14:7], apparently also known as *ʾElyādāʿ*, "El knows" [2 Sam 5:16; 1 Chron 3:8]); *Yĕrubbaʿal*, "let Baal contend/give increase" (another name for Gideon [Judg 6:30-32], though Joash's etymology ascribes it an adversarial significance, "Let Baal contend against him," and 2 Sam 11:21 changes it to *Yĕrubbešet*); *ʾEšbaʿal*, "man of Baal" (1 Chron 8:33, which in 2 Sam 2:8 and elsewhere is changed to *ʾĪš-bōšet*, "man of shame"); *Mĕrîb-baʿal*, "Baal is my advocate (1 Chron 9:40; in 2 Sam 4:4 and elsewhere it is changed to *Mĕpîbōšet*, the meaning of which is uncertain).

The significance of these names is not clear. Interpreted most negatively, they testify to the veneration of Baal in the highest circles. This is obviously the case in Judges 6:25-32, where Jerubbaal, Gideon's father, is said to have had an altar of Baal and an Asherah image at his place. The other names are all associated with Saul or David. Apparently interpreting *baʿal* in each case to refer to the pagan deity, the Deuteronomistic narrator of 2 Samuel replaced the theophoric element with *bōšet*, "shame." Interpreted most positively, in these names *baʿal* serves as an epithet for Yahweh, in which case *baʿalyâ,* "Yahweh is lord," may represent a deliberate and polemical attribution to Yahweh of the storm and fertility functions generally associated with Baal (cf. Deut 6:12-14; 11:13-15).

1.6. Most High (ʿelyôn). Although *ʿelyôn* appears elsewhere in the OT as a divine title more than thirty times, in the Historical Books it occurs only in 2 Samuel 22:14. Deriving from the root *ʿālâ,* "to go up," the designation suggests something higher than something else, in this case a supreme deity, hence the common translation "Most High." Comparative evidence from Ugarit and Northwest Semitic inscriptions suggests that *ʿelyôn* or its cognate was a common epithet applied to any deity perceived to be supreme (Elnes and Miller, 295). In the OT compound titles such as *ʾēl-ʿelyôn,* "El-Elyon" (e.g., Gen 14:18, 19, 20, 22; cf. *ʾĕlāhāʾ ʿillāyʾā,* which occurs repeatedly in the Aramaic portions of Daniel) and the use of "El" and "Elyon" as parallel elements in Hebrew poetry (Num 24:16; Ps 73:11) suggest that El was perceived as the supreme deity. The use of the compound title *yhwh ʿelyôn* (Ps 7:17 [MT 7:18]; Ps 47:2 [MT 47:3]) and the juxtaposing of *yhwh* and *ʿelyôn* as parallel designations in poetry (2 Sam 22:14 = Ps 18:13 [MT 18:14]; Ps 21:7 [MT 21:8]; Ps 92:1 [MT 92:2]) identify Yahweh as this supreme deity. According to Psalm 97:9, Yahweh, as Elyon, not only is supreme over all the earth (*kî-ʾattâ yhwh ʿelyôn ʿal-kol-hāʾāreṣ*), but also is exalted above all gods (*mĕʾōd naʿălêtā ʿal-kol-ʾĕlōhîm*) (cf. Ps 83:18 [MT 83:19] and Ps 97:9). Remarkably, "Elyon" never occurs in the narrative texts under review, suggesting that this title was reserved for formal/liturgical compositions.

1.7. Rock (ṣûr). Of the forty-plus occurrences of *ṣûr* as a divine epithet in the OT, only six are found in the Historical Books. Consistent with the distribution elsewhere, all of these occur in poetic texts: once in Hannah's oracle (1 Sam 2:2) and five times in the Davidic poems at the end of 2 Samuel (2 Sam 22:2, 3, 32, 47; 23:3). Indeed, the four in 2 Samuel 22 recur in Psalm 18 (Ps 18:3a, 3b, 32, 47). Although *ṣûr* generally is rendered "Rock," based on an etymological connection with Ugaritic *ǵr,* "mountain," which occurs as a divine name in Ugaritic god lists (*KTU* 1.118; see Wyatt, 360-62), Amorite personal names (Huffmon, 258) and Aramaic *ṭwr,* "mountain," some prefer to translate the word "Mountain" (McCarter, 71-72; Klein, 16). In either case,

the epithet connotes strength, stability and permanence (see 2 Sam 22:2-3, 47). Although foreign gods may be referred to as "rocks" elsewhere (Deut 32:31, 37), several significant references to Yahweh as "Rock" occur in contexts emphasizing his incomparability (see Labuschagne, 70-71, 115-16). Note especially 1 Samuel 2:2:

> There is none holy like Yahweh *[yhwh];*
> there is none besides you;
> there is no Rock *[ṣûr]* like our God *[ʾĕlōhênû].*

And note the precise parallelism of 2 Samuel 22:32 (cf. Is 44:8):

> For who is God, but Yahweh? *kî mî-ʾēl mibbalʿădê yhwh*
> And who is Rock, except our God? *ûmî ṣûr mibbalʿădê ʾĕlōhênû*

Yahweh alone is Israel's basis of security. Indeed, Yahweh's role as protector is reflected in David's identification of him as *ṣûr yiśrāʾēl,* "Rock of Israel" (2 Sam 23:3; cf. Is 30:29).

1.8. Glory of Israel (nēṣaḥ yiśrāʾēl). This epithet occurs only in 1 Samuel 15:29. To emphasize how fixed is Yahweh's determination to remove Saul, Samuel coins a new title, *nēṣaḥ yiśrāʾēl,* "the Glory of Israel." The term *nēṣaḥ* communicates both splendor and duration, hence Stoebe's rendering "perpetual glory" (Stoebe, 291). In 1 Chronicles 29:11 David uses the expression for an attribute of Yahweh alongside "greatness" *(gĕdûllâ),* "power" *(gĕbûrâ),* "magnificence" *(tipʾeret),* "splendor" *(hôd),* demonstrated in his dominion *(mamlākâ)* over all.

1.9. God of Heaven (ʾĕlōhê haššāmayîm). This epithet occurs for the first time in Cyrus's decree in which the Persian emperor gives credit to "Yahweh, the God of Heaven" *(yhwh ʾĕlōhê haššāmayim)* for giving him all the kingdoms of the earth and appointing him to build him a house in Jerusalem (2 Chron 36:23; Ezra 1:2). Since the Jews became quite comfortable applying it to Yahweh after their experience with the Persians (2 Chron 36:23; Ezra 1:2; 5:11-12; 6:9-10; 7:12, 21, 23; Neh 1:4-5; 2:4, 20; Elephantine Papyri), some have speculated that they adopted it to gain acceptance with their overlords, who might have seen in the title a link with Ahura Mazda (see Williamson 1985, 12).

However, the absence of the title in the literature need not indicate the title "God of Heaven" was unknown earlier. And even if it was, the notion of Yahweh as the deity who ruled the universe from the heavens was ancient. Like most ancient Near Easterners and other Israelites, Hebrew narrators assumed a three-tiered universe with Yahweh and his court residing in heaven. This view is reflected especially in Solomon's prayer at the dedication of the temple, in which he recognizes that if heaven and the highest heaven cannot contain God, how much less so an earthly house (1 Kings 8:27; 2 Chron 6:18). Nevertheless, Solomon affirms that God does reside in heaven (1 Kings 8:23, 27; 2 Chron 6:18), and from there he hears the prayers of human beings who turn toward the temple at the place he has chosen to establish his name (1 Kings 8:30-49; 2 Chron 6:21—7:14). Elsewhere the cherubim above the ark of the covenant are understood to be the earthly throne above which Yahweh of hosts sits enthroned and from which he governs not only his people Israel (1 Sam 4:4; 2 Sam 6:2) (see Mettinger 1982, 80-115) but also the nations (2 Kings 19:15). Micaiah ben Imlah provides one of the most graphic pictures of the heavenly scene in 1 Kings 22:19: "I saw Yahweh sitting on his throne, and all the host of heaven standing beside him on his right hand and on his left." This understanding of Yahweh's sovereignty over heaven and earth certainly underlies the title "God of Heaven," which became common in postexilic Jerusalem.

2. The Declared Characteristics of God.
Although an examination of God as he is presented in the Historical Books may begin with an exploration of his names and epithets, this is only the beginning. It is instructive also to note how the historians characterize God. We begin by examining how the various voices in the narratives, including Yahweh's own, testify to his character in the absolute.

2.1. Yahweh's Self-characterization. In contrast to the extended divine speeches in the prophetic books, the direct speeches of God in the Historical Books tend to be short (Ezra and Nehemiah lack divine speeches altogether). Even more remarkable, apart from describing his actions, Yahweh says very little about himself, particularly his character. Employing a version of the self-introduction formula, in Judges 6:10 he introduces himself by name and relationship to Israel: "I am Yahweh your God." This special tie with Israel is reinforced more than a dozen times in citation formulas announcing many of his speeches:

"Thus says Yahweh the God of Israel" (e.g., Josh 7:13; 24:2; Judg 6:8; 1 Sam 10:18; 2 Sam 12:7; 1 Kings 11:31; 14:7; 17:14; 2 Kings 9:6; 19:20; 21:12; 22:15,18; 2 Chron 34:23, 26). In 2 Kings 19:22, in an embedded prophecy delivered by Isaiah, Yahweh identifies himself as "the Holy One of Israel," *qĕdôš yiśrāʾēl* (the epithet appears two dozen times in the book of Isaiah; see Motyer, 17-18). This remarkable conjunction of transcendent separation and relational immanence (see Brueggemann, 288-93) recalls Yahweh's own definition of his transcendent glory *(kābôd)* in Exodus 33:18-19 in immanental terms of goodness *(ṭôb),* grace *(ḥānan)* and compassion *(riḥam)* (cf. Ex 34:6-7). But it also captures in a single phrase the significance of the tabernacle (and later the temple), which, as his *miqdāš* ("sanctuary, holy place"), keeps him separate from the people, but as his *miškān* ("residence, dwelling place") provides for his residence in the midst of his people.

In the same context Yahweh speaks of his passion *(qinʾâ)* as the driving force behind his actions against the Assyrians and in defense of Israel (2 Kings 19:31). In the OT *qinʾâ* is aroused when a legitimate and wholesome relationship is threatened by interference from a third party. Thus the word expresses an entirely appropriate response by a husband or wife when another "lover" enters the picture (Prov 6:32-35; cf. Num 5:12-31). Since the marriage metaphor provides the basic image for understanding Yahweh's covenant with Israel, the description of his response to infidelity as *qinʾâ* is both logical and natural. Indeed, *qannāʾ* is not merely an attribute of God; it is an epithet (cf. the self-introduction formula in Ex 20:5 and Deut 5:9: *ʾānōkî yhwh ʾēl qannāʾ,* "I am Yahweh El Qanna"; cf. also Ex 34:14; Deut 4:24).

Another characteristic that Yahweh claims to exhibit is *ḥesed,* commonly rendered "steadfast love." Though with perhaps less emphasis on the emotion, *ḥesed* functions within the same semantic range as *qinʾâ,* speaking fundamentally of "tenacious fidelity in a relationship, readiness and resolve to continue to be loyal to those to whom one is bound" (Brueggemann, 217; see also Sakenfeld; Clark). In 2 Samuel 7:15 (= 1 Chron 17:13) *ḥesed* functions as a virtual synonym for *bĕrît,* "covenant," as Yahweh speaks of his commitment to be a father to David's son and his claiming him as his own son as his irrevocable *ḥesed* (cf. 2 Sam 23:5).

2.2. Israelites' Characterization of Yahweh. In

contrast to Yahweh's apparent reluctance in later narratives to reiterate his creedal-like declaration in Exodus 34:6-7, the human characters in the Historical Books freely cite and recite the attributes of God. Whereas the gods of other peoples are dead idols, he is the living God (ʾēl ḥay [Josh 3:10]; ʾĕlōhîm ḥayyîm [1 Sam 17:26, 36]; ʾĕlōhîm ḥay [2 Kings 19:4, 16]; cf. also the oath formula ḥay hāʾĕlōhîm, "by the life of God" [2 Samuel 2:27], or much more commonly ḥay yhwh, "by the life of Yahweh" [e.g., Judg 8:19; 1 Sam 14:39; 2 Sam 4:9; 1 Kings 1:29; 2 Kings 2:2]; on the formula see Greenberg).

Beyond this emphasis on Yahweh as the living God, the characteristics attributed to him may be divided into qualities that separate him from humanity (transcendent attributes) and those that express his relationship with humankind (immanent attributes). Reiterating Yahweh's self-characterization, the human characters speak of his holiness (qādōš [Josh 24:19; 1 Sam 2:2; 1 Sam 6:20]; cf. the references to his holy name in 1 Chron 16:10, 35), glory (kābôd [1 Chron 16:24, 28, 29]), perpetual glory (nēṣaḥ [1 Sam 15:29; 1 Chron 29:11]), awesomeness (nôrāʾ [Judg 13:6; Neh 1:5; 4:7; 9:32]), majesty (tipʾeret [1 Chron 29:11]), greatness (gādôl, gĕdullâ [2 Sam 7:22; Neh 8:6; 1 Chron 16:25; 29:11; 2 Chron 2:5]), might (gĕbûrâ [1 Chron 29:11; Neh 9:32]) and strength (ʿōz [1 Chron 16:28]). David provides the most eloquent expression of Yahweh's transcendent qualities in 1 Chronicles 29:11-13:

> Yours, O Yahweh, is the greatness and the power and the glory and the victory and the majesty, for all that is in the heavens and in the earth is yours. Yours is the kingdom, O Yahweh, and you are exalted as head above all. Both riches and honor come from you, and you rule over all. In your hand are power and might, and in your hand it is to make great and to give strength to all. And now we thank you, our God, and praise your glorious name.

The boundaries between Yahweh's transcendent and immanent attributes often are blurred. Inasmuch as an expression such as qinʾâ/qannôʾ, "passion, zeal, jealousy," expresses his intolerance of any compromise in Israel's commitment to him (Moberly, 429), one might classify this as a transcendent quality alongside his glory and awesomeness. At first sight this seems to be the way Joshua understands the term in

Joshua 24:19, when he declares, "He [Yahweh] is a holy God; he is a passionate God" (ʾĕlōhîm qĕdōšîm hûʾ ʾēl qannôʾ hûʾ). However, he makes these comments in the context of an exchange with the people concerning the latter's fidelity to Yahweh, a conversation that climaxes in the making of a covenant. If Yahweh is passionate about Israel's fidelity to him, he is steadfast in his commitment to Israel. This quality is expressed in declarations such as "he keeps his covenant" (1 Kings 8:23; 2 Chron 6:14; Neh 1:5; 9:32), and in a handful of related attributive expressions.

In 2 Chronicles 15:3 the narrator notes, "For a long time Israel was without the God of faithfulness, and without a teaching priest and without Torah." The expression ʾĕlōhê ʾĕmet generally is interpreted adjectivally: "true God." However, the concern of the present context is not the true God versus false gods, but the God who reveals himself in the Torah, a revelation often associated with truth/truthfulness (ʾĕmet) in the Psalter (Ps 19:9; 25:5; 43:3; 86:11; 119:43, 142, 151, 160). Furthermore, although the present construct occurs nowhere else, it finds a close analogue in ʾēl ʾĕmet in Psalm 31:6, which generally is translated either as "God of truth" or "faithful God." These expressions speak not only of God's moral integrity, but also of his reliability, truthfulness to his word, keeping his promises, especially his covenant promises to Israel. This is seen in the pairing of ʾĕmet with ḥesed, "loyal love," as in 2 Samuel 2:6; 15:20. Indeed, the latter term occurs more frequently as an attribute of Yahweh than any other in the Historical Books (e.g., 2 Sam 2:6; 15:20; 1 Kings 3:6; 2 Chron 7:3, 6; Ezra 3:10; Neh 9:17, 32), and is often associated with "keeping his covenant" (1 Kings 8:23 = 2 Chron 6:14; Neh 1:5; 9:32). Within this context we should also note those texts in which people describe Yahweh as righteous (ṣaddîq). In Nehemiah 9:8, 33 this word expresses Yahweh's demonstration of fidelity to his covenant and loyalty to his vassal (cf. 2 Chron 12:6).

Beyond these attributes, people speak of Yahweh's goodness (ṭôb [1 Kings 8:66; 1 Chron 16:34; 2 Chron 5:13; 6:41; 7:3; 30:18; Ezra 3:11; Neh 9:25, 35]), compassion/mercy (raḥămîm, riḥam, rāḥûm [1 Kings 8:50; 2 Kings 13:23; 2 Chron 30:9]) and graciousness (ḥannûn, ḥanan [2 Sam 12:22; 2 Kings 13:23; 2 Chron 30:9; Neh 9:17, 31]). In Nehemiah 9:17 we hear the clearest echo of Exodus 34:6-7. Looking back on Israel's history and reciting Yahweh's attributes of immanence, the Levites affirm Yahweh's self-description with "You are a God ready to forgive, gracious and merciful, slow to anger and abounding in steadfast love, and did not forsake them." Nehemiah overtly links the two sides of God: "And I said, 'O Yahweh God of heaven, the great and awesome God who keeps covenant and steadfast love with those who love him and keep his commandments'" (Neh 1:5).

3. The Relational Actions of God.

If the recitation of the attributes of God is rare in the OT as a whole, this is especially true of the Historical Books, which reveal his character primarily through his actions and the way he relates to second and third parties. We will explore several dimensions of these relationships.

3.1. Yahweh's Relationship to Other Gods. Although all Hebrew historians represent monotheistic Yahwism, their narratives involve other deities from three perspectives. First, non-Israelite characters naturally acknowledge other gods (as in oaths [1 Kings 19:2; 20:10]), but they also recognize Yahweh as the God of Israel, equivalent to their own patron deities (1 Sam 5—6; 1 Kings 10:9; 20:22-30; 2 Kings 19:10-13), though their opinions of him vary. The *Philistines recognized the gods (plural!) of Israel to have invaded Egypt and struck that land with all sorts of plagues (1 Sam 4:8). When the image of Dagon, their own deity, fell down before the ark of the God of Israel, they acknowledged Yahweh's superiority over him (1 Sam 5:7). The *Aramaeans misunderstood Yahweh as a territorial divinity, hypothesizing that since the gods (plural!) of the Israelites were gods of the mountains, they could defeat them by attacking them in the plain (1 Kings 20:23-28). The *Assyrians expressed the same contempt for Yahweh as they did for the gods of all the other peoples whom they had conquered; all these gods were impotent in the face of their military might (2 Kings 19:18-19). Accordingly, the Chronicler reports in 2 Chronicles 32:19 that the Assyrians spoke of the God of Jerusalem as if he were just like the gods of the peoples of the earth, in his words, "the work of human hands."

Using inscriptional and artifactual evidence, scholars are recognizing increasingly the diversity of religious affections within ancient Israel. Although the historiographical narratives were written from a thoroughly monotheistic and exclusivistically Yahwistic perspective, they recognize that many Israelites served other gods, either alongside Yahweh or in place of him (e.g., Judg 10:6; 1 Kings 11:2-8; 12:25-33). In fact, the Deuteronomistic Historian expressly attributes the demise of both the northern and the southern kingdoms to this spiritual disaffection (2 Kings 17:7-23; 24:20). This does not mean that the orthodox could not speak of other gods. For a contrary example, in 2 Samuel 7:23 David recognizes that Yahweh has redeemed Israel for himself from the nation and the gods of Egypt, as if the latter were actually a force with which to reckon (cf. Ex 12:12; Num 33:4). But the statement must be interpreted within its literary context. In the previous verse (2 Sam 7:22) he had declared not only the surpassing greatness of Yahweh ("You are great, O Lord Yahweh, for there is none like you [kî-ʾên kāmôkā])," but also the exclusive existence of Yahweh ("There is none besides you" [ʾên zûlātekā]). This statement on Yahweh's incomparability and autonomy recalls Hannah's poetic utterance in 1 Samuel 2:2:

There is none holy like	
Yahweh;	ʾên-qādôš kayhwh
there is none besides	
you;	kî ʾên biltekā
there is no rock like	
our God.	wĕʾên ṣûr kēʾlōhênû

This perspective is celebrated also by the Chronicler, particularly in the song that David assigned to Asaph and his relatives in 1 Chronicles 16, especially 1 Chronicles 16:25-26:

For great is Yahweh, and greatly to be praised,
and he is to be held in awe above all gods.
For all the gods of the peoples are worthless things [ʾĕlîlîm],
but Yahweh made the heavens.

Responding to the Rabshakeh's speech defying Yahweh to rescue Jerusalem, in 2 Kings 19:17-19, Hezekiah acknowledges that the kings of Assyria have cast the gods of conquered nations into the fire, a treatment that is possible because they were no gods at all (kî lōʾ ʾĕlōhîm hēmâ), but merely "the work of human hands" (maʿăśēh yĕdê ʾādām), made of wood and stone (2 Kings 19:18; cf. 2 Chron 32:19). Solomon recognizes Yahweh's supremacy over all imaginable deities in his prayer of dedication for the temple: "The house that I am to build will be great, for our God is greater than all gods" (2 Chron 2:5).

But the narrators' polemics against other gods are often more subtle. With irony and satire they expose other gods as futile and impotent figments of the human imagination. Joash's challenge to Baal to defend himself if he is a god (Judg 6:25-27) seems ridiculous, especially since he hosted the worship of this god in his own backyard. The villagers' subsequent demand that the person who had destroyed the altar of Baal and the Asherah image be killed is precisely the penalty that the Torah demanded for those who lead Israelites into idolatry (Deut 13). Elijah's contest with the prophets of Baal is explicitly cast as a challenge to Baal to prove that he is a god (1 Kings 18:21), but in the event he is exposed as a worthless deity. In fact, the entire *Elijah-*Elisha sequence of narratives may be interpreted as an extended polemic against Baalism (see Bronner). The ultimate outrage against idolatry is committed by *Josiah, whose treatment of pagan symbols recalls Moses' actions with respect to the golden calf (Ex 32:20): combustible items (such as the Asherah) he burned outside the city near the garbage dump (the Kidron), and incombustible items (such as the sacred pillars of Baal) he smashed. The remains of both he ground to dust and desecrated by carrying them off to Bethel, scattering them over the graves of the common people, or throwing them into the Kidron brook. He desecrated the sacred sites themselves by replacing the cult images with the bones of the victims of his purge (2 Kings 23:4-16).

3.2. Yahweh's Relationship to the Cosmos. We have noted the epithet "God of Heaven" for Yahweh (see 1.9 above). Although the epithet itself occurs for the first time in the Persian era, the concept is much older. As God of heaven, Yahweh rules over the entire universe, including the earth (as Cyrus acknowledges in Ezra 1:2). The latter notion is recognized both in the way in which Yahweh generally dominates the narratives, and in particular expressions, such as Joshua's epithetic references to Yahweh as "Sovereign over all the earth" (ʾădôn kolhāʾāreṣ [Josh 3:11, 13]), and Rahab's explicit statement "Yahweh your God, he is God in the heavens above and on the earth beneath" (Josh 2:11). David's declaration in 1 Chronicles 29:11 (see 2.2 above) declares this notion as eloquently as any. Hannah's embedded oracle celebrates Yahweh's control over all, both human and cosmological,

ending with the confident declaration "Yahweh will judge the ends of the earth" (1 Sam 2:10). This motif of Yahweh as judge of all the earth recurs in the poetry of 1 Chronicles 16:14, 33, where it is balanced by the celebration of his universal providential care for the righteous (1 Chron 16:9).

Perhaps because of their preoccupation with historical events, Hebrew historians and their characters have little to say about God's actions as creator of the universe. Hannah alludes to God's creative role poetically in 1 Samuel 2:8: "For the pillars of the earth are Yahweh's, and on them he has set the world." In Hiram's remarkable response to Solomon's request for aid in building the temple, this king of Tyre acknowledges "Yahweh, God of Israel, who made heaven and earth" as the one who loves Israel and has made him king (2 Chron 2:12). The most comprehensive expression of Yahweh's creative role is found in the Levites' recitation of his works on Israel's behalf, which places his election of Abram, his deliverance of Israel from Egypt, his revelation at Sinai, and his provision in the desert in the context of creation: "You are Yahweh, you alone. You have made heaven, the heaven of heavens, with all their host, the earth and all that is on it, the seas and all that are in them; and you preserve all of them; and the host of heaven prostrates before you" (Neh 9:6).

It is fascinating to explore how OT narrators describe the manner in which Yahweh exercises his authority over humankind. For the most part they portray him as directly involved in earthly events, often concretizing the image of divine control with metaphorical references to "the hand of Yahweh/God" (e.g., Josh 4:24; Judg 2:15; 1 Sam 5:6, 9, 11; 12:15; 24:14; 1 Kings 18:46; 2 Kings 3:15; Ezra 7:6; 2 Chron 30:12). Yahweh's involvement in otherwise seemingly purely human events is illustrated dramatically in the parallel accounts of Saul's death. Whereas the Deuteronomistic Historian presents the event as Saul committing suicide to avoid further humiliation from the Philistines following his injury in battle (1 Sam 31:3-6), the Chronicler expressly attributes his death to Yahweh: "Therefore he [Yahweh] killed him and turned the kingdom to David the son of Jesse" (1 Chron 10:13-14). Elsewhere, Yahweh is described as intervening in earthly affairs through intermediaries, including human prophets (as in the calling of Barak through Deborah [Judg 4:4-16]), natural and unnatural meteorological forces (Josh 10:12-14; Judg 5:20-21), the military forces of heaven (2 Kings 6:15-16), or heavenly envoys (*malʾākîm,* usually translated "angels" [Judg 13:3-21; 2 Sam 24:16-17; 1 Kings 19:5,7; 2 Kings 19:35; 1 Chron 21:12-30]). Within this last category we probably should include the *rûaḥ rāʿâ* (disaster-producing spirit, traditionally rendered "evil spirit") that Yahweh sends *(šālaḥ)* upon targets of his displeasure (Abimelech [Judg 9:23]; Saul [1 Sam 16:14-16, 23]), the *rûaḥ šeqer* ("spirit of delusion") through which Yahweh inspires false prophets (1 Kings 22:19-23), and the "adversary" *(śāṭān,* lit., "an adversary") who incites David to number the people (1 Chron 21:1; cf. 2 Sam 24:1, which attributes David's actions directly to Yahweh). As in the narratives of Job (Job 1:6-12; 2:3-7), this enigmatic figure obviously plays an adversarial role in relation to people, but it is less obvious that he is an adversary of God. Rather, he seems to be functioning as an agent of Yahweh (cf. Job 42:11), and like the "spirit of delusion" in 1 Kings 22:22-23 probably should be recognized as a member of the heavenly council (cf. Block, 2005).

3.3. Yahweh's Relationship to Non-Israelites. Since the Historical Books of the OT interpret the story of Israel within the context of international events, it is helpful to examine the perspective of the narrators toward the nations around Israel, more particularly their view of the relationships between Yahweh and the nations. Although the respective compositions have their own distinctive emphases, in general the historians agree that two primary threads characterize these relationships. On the one hand, as creator of the universe and sovereign over the world, Yahweh is also Lord of the nations. To be sure, the nations typically direct their religious affections toward other gods and assume that their welfare depends on the disposition and power of their own national deities (Judg 2:12; 11:24; 2 Kings 18:33; 19:12; 1 Chron 5:25; 16:26; 2 Chron 32:13, 17, 19), but to the narrators, as true Yahwists, only Yahweh determines the destinies of the nations. Accordingly, he chose Israel from all the peoples of the earth to be his own possession (*naḥălâ* [1 Kings 8:53]) and rescued them from the clutches of Egypt, the mightiest nation on earth (Josh 24:6,17; Judg 2:12; 1 Sam 8:8; 10:18; 12:6, 8; 1 Kings 8:16, 21, 51, 53; 9:9; 2 Kings 17:7, 36; 2 Chron 6:5; 7:22;

Neh 9:18). Then he drove out the Canaanite nations and delivered them and their land into the hands of the Israelites (Josh 3:10; 9:26; 10:30, 32; 11:8; 13:6; 15:14; 23:5, 13; 24:12, 18; Judg 2:3, 21, 23; 6:9; 2 Sam 7:23 = 1 Chron 17:21; 1 Kings 14:24; 2 Kings 16:3; 17:8; 21:2; 2 Chron 20:7; 28:3; 33:2).

But this did not end Yahweh's involvement with the nations. When the Israelites abandoned him and imitated the abominable ways of the nations (1 Kings 11:5, 7; 14:24; 2 Kings 21:11; 23:13; 2 Chron 28:3; 33:2; 36:14; Ezra 9:1, 11), in accordance with the covenant curses (Lev 26:17, 25; Deut 28:48-57) Yahweh delivered them over to the nations, using them as his agents of punishment (Josh 11:8; Judg 2:14-15; 3:8; 4:2; 6:1-2; 10:7; 13:1; 1 Sam 12:9; 2 Kings 13:3; 17:20; 2 Chron 28:5; Ezra 5:12; 9:7; Neh 9:27, 30). In the end, he brought in the armies of Assyria and Babylonia, who deported the populations of the northern and the southern kingdoms, respectively (2 Kings 17; 24). However, in accordance with the promises of Leviticus 26 and Deuteronomy 28—30, Israel's exile among the nations could not be the last word. According to the Chronicler, when the divinely appointed time for the return of the Israelites and the rebuilding of Jerusalem had arrived, Yahweh stirred the heart of Cyrus, the head of the new *Persian Empire, to authorize the exiles to return and rebuild Jerusalem (2 Chron 36:22-23; cf. Ezra 1:1-4). It is evident that throughout their history, Israel's own fate and fortune were determined by the way Yahweh dealt with the nations.

If Israel's place among the nations provides the context in which Yahweh's story with the Israelites is played out, the nations also represent the targets of his revelatory actions. According to the Exodus narratives, one of Yahweh's primary goals in sending the plagues on Egypt and in delivering Israel from slavery was that the Egyptians might know that he is Yahweh (Ex 7:5; 14:4, 18). It is evident from the Historical Books that the narrators considered this only the first phase of divine activity through which the goal of revealing himself to all the nations was to be achieved. Using explicit statements within the text, we may note at least four subsequent events that were interpreted in a similar light.

1. The crossing of the Jordan River (Josh 4:21-24). Joshua draws a direct link between Yahweh's revelatory goals through Israel's crossing the Jordan and their earlier crossing of the

Red Sea: "that all the peoples of the earth may know that the hand of Yahweh is mighty."

2. David's defeat of Goliath (1 Sam 17). On the surface, David's prediction that the whole earth will know that Yahweh is God in Israel after he has triumphed over Goliath (1 Sam 17:46) looks like hyperbolic, youthful bravado. However, in the mind of the narrator, who knows how the story of David ends, this was no flippant boast, but rather a remarkable declaration of the ultimate consequence of this event.

3. The construction of the temple (1 Kings 8; 2 Chron 6). The magnificence of the temple that Solomon built (*see* Solomon's Temple) might suggest that the splendor of the complex would be the primary means of impressing on the minds of the nations the person and character of Yahweh. However, in a remarkable turn in Solomon's dedicatory prayer, the king digresses momentarily from his concern with the significance of the temple as the dwelling place of God for his own people to consider the case of the foreigner. He pleads with Yahweh that when, in response to hearing of Yahweh's mighty deeds, a foreigner prays toward this house, he would answer this person's prayer from heaven fully in accordance with the request so that "all the peoples of the earth may know your name and fear you, as do your people Israel, and that they may know that this house that I have built is called by your name" (1 Kings 8:43). Later, in his benediction after this event, Solomon prays that Yahweh would maintain the cause of his servant and his people Israel so that "all the peoples of the earth may know that Yahweh is God; there is no other" (1 Kings 8:60).

4. Hezekiah's victory over the Assyrians (2 Kings 19:14-19). In the face of the Rabshakeh's defiance of Yahweh (2 Kings 19:8-13), Hezekiah recognizes that the significance of the present crisis extends far beyond his personal fate or even that of his people. He pleads with Yahweh that he would deliver Jerusalem from the enemy so that "all the kingdoms of the earth may know that you, O Yahweh, are God alone."

Given this international revelatory purpose behind Yahweh's actions on behalf of Israel, the historians' recounting of events that demonstrate that this goal was being achieved should not surprise. Four cases must suffice here.

1. Rahab, the prostitute of *Jericho. In the wake of Israel's dramatic passage through the Red Sea and Israel's victories over the trans-

jordanian kingdoms of Sihon and Og, Rahab declares, "I know that Yahweh has given you the land, and that the fear of you has fallen upon us, and that all the inhabitants of the land melt away before you. . . . Our hearts have melted, and no spirit was left in any one because of you, for Yahweh your God, he is God in the heavens above and on the earth beneath" (Josh 2:9a, 11).

2. Hiram/Huram of Tyre. Elaborating on Hiram of Tyre's blessing of Yahweh at the accession of Solomon (1 Kings 4:27), the Chronicler quotes him: "Because Yahweh loves [ʾāhab] his people, he has made you king over them. . . . Blessed be Yahweh, the God of Israel, who made heaven and earth, who has given King David a wise son, who has discretion and understanding, who will build a temple for Yahweh and a royal palace for himself" (2 Chron 2:11-12 [MT 2:10-11]). He recognizes not only that Yahweh is the creator of all, but also that as Israel's deity, he has maintained their cause by providing an excellent heir for David.

3. The Queen of Sheba. Amazed at the wealth and wisdom of Solomon, this foreign queen echoes the comments of Hiram: "Blessed be Yahweh your God, who has delighted in you and set you on the throne of Israel! Because Yahweh loved [ʾāhab] Israel forever, he has made you king, that you may execute justice and righteousness" (1 Kings 10:9). It seems that the historian perceives this as a fulfillment of Solomon's plea to Yahweh to maintain the cause of Israel in 1 Kings 8:60.

4. Naaman. We have noted that one of the overall themes of the Elijah-Elisha narratives is Yahweh's conflict with Baal for the allegiance of the Israelites (see 3.1 above; 1 Kings 18). In 2 Kings 5 Yahweh's revelatory actions target the Aramaean Naaman. Naaman's confession following his miraculous healing in the Jordan ("I know that there is no God in all the earth but in Israel; so accept now a present from your servant" (2 Kings 5:15) and his determination from now on to sacrifice to no god but Yahweh (2 Kings 5:17) demonstrate that this goal was achieved.

3.4. Yahweh's Relationship to Israel. Even a cursory reading of the historical narratives reveals that they are driven more by Yahweh's relationship with Israel than anything else. Since limitations of space preclude a detailed treatment of the subject, the observations that follow represent an attempt to highlight key elements in the Hebrew historians' portrayal of Yahweh in this relationship. This relationship is affirmed whenever the name Yahweh appears with ʾĕlōhê yiśrāʾēl (Hebrew) or ʾĕlāh yiśrāʾēl (Aramaic), "the God of Israel," in apposition (95x), when he is referred to simply as "the God of Israel," or as "Yahweh their/your/our God" (c. 120x), or simply "their/your/our God" (c. 80x), with the pronoun referring to Israel. But it is instructive to explore how that relationship was perceived.

The historical narratives agree with the pentateuchal traditions that Yahweh's relationship with Israel has its roots in his election of Abram/Abraham as his covenant partner. This is reflected in the identification of Abraham as the "covenant partner" (ʾōhēb) of God (2 Chron 20:7) on the one hand, and of the one who is God in Israel as "Yahweh, the God of Abraham, Isaac and Jacob" (1 Kings 18:36; 1 Chron 29:18; 2 Chron 30:6), on the other. The narratives also highlight this notion with explicit statements that recognize Yahweh's election of Abraham (Josh 24:2-3; Neh 9:7) and in his covenant with Abraham (2 Kings 13:23; 1 Chron 16:16), as well as by mentioning specific promises encompassed in God's covenant with Abraham: the issue of numerous progeny (Josh 24:23), and the *land of Canaan as the eternal possession of Abraham's descendants (2 Chron 20:7; Neh 9:7-8). The latter is found especially in contexts recalling Yahweh's oath to the ancestors to give them the land of Canaan. In fact, in the book of Joshua the thematic center of gravity is that Yahweh has fulfilled his promises to the ancestors by delivering the land of Canaan into the Israelites' hands (Josh 1:6; 5:6; 21:43; cf. Judg 2:1).

As in the book of Deuteronomy, the use of the term ʾābôt in these contexts is often ambiguous. Judging from the references to the oath sworn to the ancestors in Exodus-Numbers, which for chronological reasons can refer only to the patriarchs, one's immediate impulse is to interpret "ancestors" (ʾābôt) as the patriarchs Abraham, Isaac and Jacob, and to see here a reference to God's covenant with Abraham rather than his covenant with Israel at Sinai. However, the issues are not that simple. First, Leviticus 26:45 prepares the reader to interpret the people of the exodus generation, with whom Yahweh entered into covenant relationship, as the "ancestors" of future generations. Second, already in Deuteronomy "fathers" often refers to the generation that came out of Egypt (Deut 4:31; 8:18; 26:15; 28:11). Third, unlike Joshua

5:6, the patriarchal narratives never identify the land of Canaan as a land "flowing with milk and honey." This occurs for the first time in Yahweh's promise to Moses and the exodus generation (Ex 3:8, 17; 13:5; Lev 20:24). Fourth, in the prophets, Ezekiel speaks specifically of Yahweh's oath to the exodus generation to bring them to the land flowing with milk and honey. Fifth, Nehemiah 9:15 speaks explicitly of the land (of Canaan), which Yahweh swore to give the exodus generation (cf. 2 Kings 17:15, which also speaks of the exodus generation as "their fathers" with whom Yahweh made a covenant).

In the end, the ambiguity in the use of the term ʾābôt probably is intentional, in keeping with the historians' conviction that the covenants that God made with Abraham and with the Israelites at Sinai are not two different covenants, but the latter represents a fleshing out of the former (see DOTP, Covenant). The identification of Israel with the patriarchal ancestors is most evident in the embedded poem found in 1 Chronicles 16:12-18, which, when compared with its parallel in Psalm 105:5-11, highlights the nation as Yahweh's covenant partner (see Japhet, 318; Williamson 1977, 62):

Remember the wondrous works that
  he has done,
    his miracles and the judgments he uttered,
O offspring of Israel his servant,
    sons of Jacob, his chosen ones!
He is Yahweh our God;
    his judgments are in all the earth.
Remember his covenant forever,
    the word that he commanded, for a
  thousand generations,
the covenant that he made with Abraham,
    his sworn promise to Isaac,
which he confirmed as a statute to Jacob,
    as an everlasting covenant to Israel,
saying, "To you I will give the
  land of Canaan,
    as your portion for a special possession."

Not only is the nation of Israel the elect of Yahweh (2 Chron 16:13), the eternal covenant involving the land of Canaan as Yahweh's special grant that Yahweh made (kārat) with Abraham, and his oath (šĕbûʿâ) with Isaac, he also confirmed (heʿĕmîd) with Jacob as an ordinance (ḥōq) to him and an everlasting covenant (bĕrît ʿôlam) with Israel.

If Yahweh's relationship with Israel originates in his election of Abraham, it extends to

Abraham's descendants through two defining events: his rescue of Israel from slavery in Egypt in the exodus, and his establishment of Israel as his covenant people at Sinai. Allusions to the former are ubiquitous, especially in the frequent introduction of Yahweh as the God who brought Israel up from Egypt (Josh 24:5-6; Judg 2:1, 12; 6:8; 1 Sam 8:8; 10:18; 12:6, 8; 1 Kings 8:16, 21, 51, 53; 9:9; 12:28; 17:7; 2 Kings 17:36; 2 Chron 6:5; 7:22; Neh 9:18). Israel is the product of Yahweh's gracious saving action. References to the latter are also common, though Sinai is mentioned by name only twice (both in embedded poems: Judg 5:5; Neh 9:13), and Horeb only three times (1 Kings 8:9 [= 2 Chron 5:10]; 19:8). But allusions to the covenant relationship that Yahweh established with Abraham's descendants at this place are common. David grasps the essence of what happened at Sinai in his adaptation of the covenant formula in 2 Samuel 7:24: "And you established for yourself your people Israel to be your people forever. And you, O Yahweh, became their God" (on the covenant formula see Smend; Baltzer). This statement is significant on two counts. First, it affirms the divine initiative in establishing Israel as his people. Second, in accordance with Yahweh's promise to Abraham and his descendants (Gen 17:7), it affirms the eternality of Yahweh's covenant with Israel (cf. Ex 31:16-17; Lev 24:8; Judg 2:1; Ps 111:2-9; Is 24:4-5; 54:4-10; Jer 31:35-37). This covenant established Yahweh as the God of Israel, and Israel as his privileged vassal.

In accordance with the Deuteronomic perspective, fundamental to Israel's response to Yahweh's gracious salvation and the privilege of covenant relationship was the call to exclusive allegiance to him, expressed as fear (*yārē*ʾ [Josh 24:14; 1 Sam 12:14, 24; 2 Kings 17:28; 17:36, 39; cf. Deut 10:12-13]) and love (*ʾāhab* [Josh 22:5; 23:11]) for Yahweh alone. Joshua summarized what this meant in practical terms: "Only be very careful to observe the commandment and the law that Moses the servant of Yahweh commanded you, to love Yahweh your God, and to walk in all his ways and to keep his commandments and to cling to him and to serve him with all your heart and with all your being" (Josh 22:5). Nehemiah 9:13 characterizes the revealed will of Yahweh as "just laws" *(mišpāṭîm yĕšārîm)*, "true instructions" *(tôrôt ʾĕmet)*, and "good ordinances and commandments" *(huqqîm ûmiṣwōt ṭôbîm)*.

In the *ark of the covenant, Yahweh provided his people with a physical symbol of his covenant commitment to them. The Historical Books present a complex picture of the significance of the ark. First, in the conquest narratives of Joshua the ark functions as a palladium, a visible sign of Yahweh's presence going before the armies of Israel (Josh 3—4; 6). This image is fleshed out by the designation of the object as "the ark of the covenant of Yahweh of hosts" in 1 Samuel 4:4 and 2 Samuel 6:2. In the sequel to the former (1 Samuel 5) we learn, however, that Yahweh was not bound by the spiritual condition of the people. In their absence and in the presence of a pagan deity he used the ark to demonstrate his superiority over other gods. The title *yhwh ṣĕbāʾôt*, "Yahweh of hosts," highlights the military role of the ark. Both texts add the clause *yōšēb hakkĕrubîm* (ʿālāyw), "who sits (enthroned) above the cherubim," suggesting that the ark functioned as a visible throne pedestal above which sat the invisible God. In 1 Chronicles 28:2 it is referred to as the "footstool" *(hădōm raglê)* of the God of Israel. According to the narrative sequence of 2 Samuel 6—7, David's transportation of the ark to Jerusalem inspired him to seek to build a permanent residence for Yahweh in Jerusalem. The Chronicler highlights the sanctity of the ark of the covenant in its transfer to Jerusalem even more than does the Deuteronomistic Historian in the Samuel and David narratives (1 Chron 15:2, 12, 23-24; 16:4, 37). Recognizing the significance of the ark finally arriving at its permanent resting place in the temple, the Chronicler ends Solomon's prayer dedicating the temple with a highly significant addition:

And now arise, O Yahweh God, and go to
your resting place,
  you and the ark of your might.
Let your priests, O Yahweh God, be clothed
with salvation,
and let your saints rejoice in your goodness.
(2 Chron 6:42)

This poetic verse is taken from Psalm 132, which celebrates Yahweh's promise of eternal title to the throne to David, and Yahweh's election of Jerusalem as his permanent home.

However, as the designation "ark of the covenant" suggests, the primary significance of the ark lay in its association with the covenant that Yahweh had established with Israel. The expression *ʾărôn bĕrît* occurs thirty-five times in the

Historical Books, twenty-three times in the Deuteronomistic works, twelve times in Chronicles. To this we should add Joshua 4:16, which identifies it as *ʾărôn hāʿēdût,* "ark of the [covenant] stipulations." These designations derive from the primary function of the ark: it is a repository for the official covenant document, the Decalogue, as Solomon recognizes in 1 Kings 8:9 and 2 Chronicles 5:10. In accordance with ancient Near Eastern custom, stored in the presence of Yahweh in the holy of holies, the tablets served as a reminder to him of his obligations to the covenant and to the Israelites of his role as divine guarantor of their commitment.

Although the Chronicler's focus with reference to David and Solomon differs somewhat from the Deuteronomistic Historians' (see Kelly, 249-64), he agrees with them that Israel's history was a history of spiritual and moral failure. Despite Yahweh's repeated appeals to covenant fidelity through his prophets, instead of loving and serving only him, the nation abandoned him in favor of other gods. As a consequence, Yahweh imposed upon the northern kingdom in the eighth century BCE and then the southern kingdom in the sixth century BCE the covenant curses as spelled out in Leviticus 26 and Deuteronomy 28, bringing in the Assyrians and Babylonians, respectively, and driving their populations into exile (*see* History of Israel 5-6). The reader should not interpret these events as a termination of the covenant, nor even its suspension, but rather as the precise application of the fine print. 2 Kings ends not with the end of Israel, but with a future that remains open. A remnant of the population survives in Babylon, and a scion from the house of David enjoys relative favor in the Babylonian court. 2 Chronicles ends with the Persians as the only remaining world power, and Yahweh stirring the spirit of Cyrus in fulfillment of his own word to Jeremiah to authorize the return of the Judaean exiles to rebuild Jerusalem. With a heavy emphasis on God's involvement, Ezra and Nehemiah describe the reconstitution of the community of faith in Judah.

3.5 Yahweh's Relationship to the King. The amount of text devoted to *David and the frequency with which his name appears lead to the conclusion that he was the most important figure in Israel's history. However, his significance lay not primarily in his meteoric rise and in the brilliance of the empire that he left with his son

Solomon, but in his significance in the divine scheme. As Gideon recognized, albeit hypocritically (Judg 8:23), Israel was a constitutional theocracy. The narrator of Judges laments the fact that in the centuries following the conquest there were no kings in Israel (Judg 17:6; 18:1; 19:1; 21:25). This is generally interpreted as reflecting a promonarchic, specifically pro-Davidic, stance, anticipating the institution as the solution for the problems of the time (Brettler, 109-16). However, in the light of the monarchic paradigms represented by Gideon and Abimelech within the book, and the role of the monarchy (beginning with Solomon [1 Samuel 11]) in sponsoring the apostasy that led eventually to the demise of both the northern and the southern kingdoms, it is difficult to imagine a later author viewing the monarchy as the solution to the persistent evil recounted in the book of Judges (see Block 1999, 57-59). These refrains declare that in this time the Israelites needed no kings to lead them into evil. As Micah, and the Danites, and the people of Gibeah, and the rest of the Benjamites demonstrate (Judg 17—21), the people themselves found their own creative ways of violating the covenant and rejecting the kingship of Yahweh. According to Yahweh's own assessment in 1 Samuel 8:7-9 and 12:12, when the Israelites demanded a king, this represented a repudiation of his divine kingship and followed the paradigm of their persistent rejection of the one who had rescued them from Egypt.

But this does not mean that the biblical historians viewed human kingship in principle as antithetical to Yahweh's rule (*see* Kings and Kingship). On the contrary, the institution of the monarchy is anticipated in the traditions of the patriarchs (Gen 17:6, 16; 35:11; 49:8-10) and in the oracles of Balaam (Num 24:17). The books of Samuel open with an oracle that is concerned largely with Yahweh's cosmic rule, but ends with an explicit announcement concerning a king:

The adversaries of Yahweh shall be broken to pieces;
  against them he will thunder in heaven.
Yahweh will judge the ends of the earth;
  he will give strength to his king
  and exalt the horn of his anointed.
    (1 Sam 2:10)

This oracle creates anticipation, inviting the reader to conceive of a theocracy with a special human figure at the head representing Yahweh. The rest of 1 Samuel is devoted to introducing this anointed one, while 2 Samuel describes his reign and rule.

But the narrative does not move smoothly from promise to fulfillment. Instead it takes a by-way, introducing into the royal plot an "anti-messiah" king in *Saul. David and Samuel will freely refer to him as Yahweh's anointed (Samuel: 1 Sam 10:1; 12:3, 5; 15:17; David: 1 Sam 24:6, 10; 26:9, 11, 16, 23; 2 Sam 1:14, 16), and Yahweh himself will use the verb "anoint" in 1 Samuel 9:16, but the narrator never does. In his mind, Saul's kingship is fundamentally illegitimate. In the end Yahweh himself rues *(niham)* the fact that he has made Saul king (1 Sam 15:11,35) (on *niham*, "to grieve, rue," in this context see Van Dyke Parunak, 519). Contrary to many (see Willis, 161), this response has less to do with Saul's kingship turning out differently than God had hoped or expected than with his disposition toward Saul's kingship in the first place. Yahweh had expressed the latter poignantly in 1 Samuel 8:7-9; Israel's request for a king at this moment is of a piece with their long history of rebellion against Yahweh. Accordingly, Yahweh's grief is directed less at Saul as king than at the Saulide kingship and the Israelite disposition that demanded it.

But Saul's kingship was doomed from the beginning. Answering the people's request to be like the nations (1 Sam 8:5, 20), Yahweh gave them a man from the tribe of Benjamin. According to the last chapters of Judges, only a couple of generations earlier Saul's ancestors had engaged the rest of Israel in a civil war in defense of the actions of neo-Sodomites (Judg 19:22-25; cf. Gen 19:1-8). As the lot procedure described in 1 Samuel 10:20-24 demonstrates, Saul was Yahweh's concessionary choice to fulfill the people's demand. However, in accordance with Deuteronomy 17:14-20, and Yahweh's firm resolve as expressed by Samuel in 1 Samuel 15:29, from the outset Yahweh had only one legitimate person in mind. Jacob's oracle had anticipated that the king would be a Judahite (cf. Gen 49:10). In the event, he turns out to be the eighth son of Jesse from Bethlehem, David (1 Sam 13:14). All Israel acknowledged him as the legitimate king after the death of Saul and Ishbosheth (2 Sam 5:1-2).

No text in the Historical Books is as important for understanding the place of David and his descendants in Yahweh's plan as 2 Samuel 7 (1 Chronicles 17) (*see* Davidic Covenant). With

the settlement of the civil conflict over Saul's succession (2 Sam 5:1-5), the defeat of the Canaanite remnant of Jebusites in Jerusalem and the establishment of *Zion as David's capital (2 Sam 5:6-10/1 Chron 11:5), the friendship of Hiram of Tyre secured (2 Sam 5:11-12), and the Philistine menace eliminated (2 Sam 5:17-25), the rest promised by Deuteronomy 12:10-11 as the precondition of Yahweh's establishing a unitary place for his name had been established. Although neither 2 Samuel 6 nor 1 Chronicles 16 alludes to this text, the placement of the account of the transfer of the ark of the covenant to Jerusalem after these events suggests strongly that the narrator had Deuteronomy 12 in mind. This conviction is strengthened by 2 Samuel 7:1, in which the narrator explicitly links David's impulse to build a permanent residence for Yahweh with Yahweh's granting of rest to David. Nevertheless, whereas Deuteronomy 12 had associated the achievement of rest with the identification of Yahweh's central place of worship, 2 Samuel 7 takes an unexpected turn by subordinating the latter concern to the establishment of David's descendants as Yahweh's chosen line of vice-regents.

Although Yahweh's granting to David's house eternal title to the throne of Israel represents the central issue in 2 Samuel 7, this chapter has great significance for understanding the nature of Yahweh's relationship with Israel and with the Davidic kings.

First, both Nathan's oracle and David's response reiterate that Yahweh chose David and his descendants not for their own sakes, but for the sake of Israel. Yahweh explicitly places his election and appointment of David within the context of his care for the nation:

I took you from the pasture, from following the sheep, that you should be prince over my people Israel. And I have been with you wherever you went and have cut off all your enemies from before you. And I will make for you a great name, like the name of the great ones of the earth. And I will appoint a place for my people Israel and will plant them, so that they may dwell in their own place and be disturbed no more. And violent men shall afflict them no more, as formerly, from the time that I appointed judges over my people Israel. (2 Sam 7:8b-11a ESV; cf. 1 Chron 17:7b-10a)

To which David responds,

And who is like your people Israel, the one nation on earth whom God went to redeem to be his people, making himself a name and doing for them great and awesome things by driving out before your people, whom you redeemed for yourself from Egypt, a nation and its gods? And you established for yourself your people Israel to be your people forever. And you, O Yahweh, became their God. (2 Sam 7:23-24, adapted from ESV; cf. 1 Chron 17:21-22)

This accords with the narrator's observation of David's earlier realization "that Yahweh had established him king over Israel, and that he had exalted his kingdom *for the sake of his people Israel*" (2 Sam 5:12). It is also reinforced by two foreigners' comments with reference to Solomon's accession. Hiram of Tyre blesses Yahweh, saying, "Blessed be the LORD this day, who has given to David a wise son to be over this great people" (1 Kings 5:7). But the Chronicler's rendering of the blessing heightens Yahweh's concern for the nation in the election of David and the succession of his son: "Because of Yahweh's covenant commitment to [ʾāhab, usually rendered "loves"] his people, he has made you king over them" (2 Chron 2:11). This comment bears a close resemblance to the blessing of Yahweh that we hear from the lips of the Queen of Sheba in 1 Kings 10:9: "Blessed be Yahweh your God, who has delighted [ḥāpēṣ] in you and set you on the throne of Israel! Because Yahweh was covenantally committed [ʾāhab] to Israel forever, he has made you king, that you may execute justice and righteousness." Accordingly, it should be recognized that the *Davidic covenant does not supersede the covenant that God made with Israel at Sinai. Rather, it complements and builds on it, providing Israel with a divinely appointed ruler who not only embodies the ideals of the national covenant, but also serves as the agent through whom Yahweh's rule over Israel is established.

Second, when Yahweh chooses David as his viceregent, he adopts him and his descendants collectively as his own son (2 Sam 7:14; 1 Chron 17:13; cf. 1 Chron 22:10) (see Mettinger 1976, 254-93). This comment is remarkable, especially since the Historical Books lack any reference to Israel as Yahweh's son (cf. Ex 4:22-23; Deut 1:31; 8:5; 14:1) or his firstborn (cf. Jer 31:9), on the one hand, or Yahweh as Israel's father, on the other (cf. Jer 32:6, 18). This designation both highlights the personal relationship between Yahweh and the Davidic rulers and declares the kings' vassal status vis-à-vis Yahweh as divine suzerain (2 Sam 7:14) (see Kalluveettil, 129-30). The latter accounts for the twelve references to David as the servant of Yahweh (twice by Yahweh: "my servant" [2 Sam 7:5, 8], and ten times by David: "your servant" [2 Sam 7:19-21, 25-29]; for the conjunction of *ben* and *ʿebed* as terms of vassalage in a political sense see 2 Kings 16:7), and the sevenfold reference to Yahweh as ʾădōnāy in 2 Samuel 7. It is scarcely coincidental that these represent the only occurrences of this epithet for Yahweh in the books of Samuel.

Third, 2 Samuel 7 emphasizes that Yahweh's commitment to David is eternal (ʿad ʿôlām) and irrevocable (2 Sam 7:15). The eternality of the covenant is explicitly declared twice by Yahweh (2 Sam 7:13, 16) and recognized five times in David's response (2 Sam 7:24-26, 29). This feature of Yahweh's commitment to David and his descendants is a prominent theme in both the books of Kings (1 Kings 2:33, 45; 9:5; 2 Kings 8:19) (see Provan, 67-85) and Chronicles. The Chronicler's insistence on Yahweh's eternal commitment to the Davidic monarchy in post-Solomonic narratives (2 Chron 13:5; 21:7; and alluded to in 2 Chron 23:3) is particularly remarkable because this composition was written more than two centuries after its collapse.

Of course, a recognition of the declared unconditionality/irrevocability of Yahweh's promises to David and his descendants must be balanced by an acknowledgment of the bilateral nature of this relationship and the conditionality of the enjoyment of the benefits promised (see Knoppers, 1996, 686-96). Whereas Psalm 132:12 gives explicit expression to the contingent element in the covenant, the warning to David's sons that if they commit iniquity they will experience Yahweh's punishment (2 Sam 7:14) is as close as 2 Samuel 7 comes to declaring any contingency (the deletion of this note in 1 Chron 17:13 strengthens the unconditionality of the promise; cf. 2 Chron 21:7). In any case, Yahweh quickly adds that he will never retract his *hesed* from David's son as he retracted it from Saul. But the correlation of 2 Samuel 7:14 with the history of the dynasty as presented in both Samuel-Kings and Chronicles creates some tension. If the nation ultimately falls because of the failures of its kings (2 Kings 21:11-15; 23:26-27), and the kings themselves are removed from the throne because of their sin, the fates of individual kings do not necessarily conform to the expected pattern. Ironically, Manasseh, the king who sinned the most according to the historians' own testimony (2 Kings 21; 2 Chron 33), reigned the longest (fifty-five years [2 Kings 21:1]), while Josiah, who came the closest to embodying the ideals of Deuteronomy 17:14-20, was cut off by a "random" arrow (2 Chron 35:20-24). In 586 BCE the razing of Jerusalem and especially the death of Zedekiah signaled the suspension not only of Yahweh's covenant promises to Israel, but also of his covenant promises to David. Although the author of 2 Kings offers no theological reflection on the development, the book closes with a tantalizing report of Jehoiachin's elevation among the subject kings in Babylon (2 Kings 25:27-30). The survival of a scion of David provided the basis for the hopes of historians, prophets and psalmists that Yahweh one day would remember his covenant and reinstall a Davidide on Zion.

Fourth, 2 Samuel 7 lays the foundation for the universalization of God's reign through his Messiah in the psalms and the prophets. Critical scholars generally have stumbled over the clause *zōʾt tôrat hāʾādām,* "this is the revelation concerning humanity" (2 Sam 7:19), but the Hebrew is perfectly defensible and understandable (see Kaiser, 310-18). This phrase has been anticipated since Hannah's oracle, the final lines of which conjoin an announcement of Yahweh's universal reign with his exaltation of his anointed (1 Sam 2:10).

Although Solomon's worldwide fame may have been interpreted by some as a fulfillment of the oracle and David's words, the fact remains that the historians of Israel show little interest in Israel's kings as Yahweh's agents of universal rule. For the development of this notion we must look to the psalms (e.g., Ps 2; 89:24-29), which combine the motifs of divine sonship and universal rule through the Messiah (Ps 72:8-11; 110) and the prophets (Is 11:1-10; Mic 5:2-5; Zech 9:9-10).

Not only do the Historical Books present Hezekiah and Josiah as idealized heirs to the Davidic throne, but also the events that they describe lay the groundwork for later reflection on David as an idealized figure through whom Yahweh will administer his reign in the distant future (e.g., Is 9:2-7; 11:1-10; Jer 23:5-8; Ezek 34:23-29; 37:15-28). However, the narrative texts display little interest in Yahweh's eschatological rule through the Messiah, especially if by "Messiah" one understands "a future figure who will play an authoritative role in the end time, usually the eschatological king" (Collins, 11). For the most part they are concerned with Yahweh's relationship with historical Israel, and the role of the Davidic king in that relationship. If the Davidic kings were granted the high honor of governing Yahweh's flock on his behalf, they also were held largely responsible for the ultimate demise both of the dynasty and the nation. Nevertheless, the survival and elevation of Jehoiachin in Babylon (2 Kings 25:27-30) represented the key to the hope that Yahweh one day would reestablish his rule through a new David.

4. Conclusion.
Obviously, a complete analysis of the portrayal of God in the Historical Books requires a careful consideration of each literary composition, whether it be a complete book or smaller cycles within books, to see whether and what kinds of variations in perceptions are reflected in the texts. In particular we would need to examine how the perspectives grow and develop in time. This requires a careful and critical analysis of each book to establish the times and circumstances of their respective composition. Space limitations here preclude such an analysis in favor of a more synthetic canonical and thematic reading of the Historical Books. The present study has demonstrated the complexity of the divine character in ancient Israelite historiographic narratives. Neither God's personality nor his actions may be reduced to simple formulas. His responses in specific historical situations often catch the reader by surprise. Nevertheless, whether the historians of ancient Israel wrote from the Deuteronomistic perspective, as in Joshua-Kings, or the Priestly point of view, as in Chronicles and Ezra-Nehemiah, they all present Yahweh as a deity who is both sovereign over the universe and over history on the one hand, and gracious to all who will submit to him on the other. Herein lay the hope of Israel, and herein lies the hope of all.

See also CANAANITE GODS AND RELIGIONS; FAITH; ISRAEL; KINGS AND KINGSHIP; PRAYER; SOLOMON'S TEMPLE; WORD OF GOD.

BIBLIOGRAPHY. **R. Albertz,** *A History of Israelite Religion in the Old Testament Period* (2 vols.; OTL; Louisville: Westminster/John Knox, 1994); **F. I. Andersen and A. D. Forbes,** *The Vocabulary of the Old Testament* (Rome: Pontifical Biblical Institute, 1992); **K. Baltzer,** *The Covenant Formulary: In Old Testament, Jewish, and Early Christian Writings* (Philadelphia: Fortress, 1971); **A. Berlin,** *Poetics and Interpretation of Biblical Narrative* (Bible and Literature 9; Sheffield: Almond, 1983); **D. I. Block,** *Judges and Ruth* (NAC; Nashville: Broadman & Holman, 1999); idem, *The Gods of the Nations: Studies in Ancient Near Eastern National Theology* (2d ed.; Evangelical Theological Society Studies; Grand Rapids: Baker, 2000); idem, "What Has Delphi to Do with Samaria?: Ambiguity and Delusion in Israelite Prophecy," in A. R. Millard Feschrift (Oxford: Oxford University Press, 2005); **G. Bowman,** "Narrative Criticism: Human Purpose in Conflict with Divine Presence," in *Judges and Method: New Approaches in Biblical Studies,* ed. G. Yee (Minneapolis: Fortress, 1995) 17-44; **M. Z. Brettler,** *The Book of Judges* (OTR; New York: Routledge, 2002); **L. Bronner,** *The Stories of Elijah and Elisha as Polemics Against Baal Worship* (Pretoria Oriental Series 6; Leiden: Brill, 1968); **W. Brueggemann,** *Theology of the Old Testament: Testimony, Dispute, Advocacy* (Minneapolis: Fortress, 1997); **G. R. Clark,** *The Word Ḥesed in the Hebrew Bible* (JSOTSup 157; Sheffield: Sheffield Academic Press, 1992); **J. J. Collins,** *The Scepter and the Star: The Messiahs of the Dead Sea Scrolls and Other Ancient Literature* (New York: Doubleday, 1995); **J. Day,** *Yahweh and the Gods and Goddesses of Canaan* (JSOTSup 265; Sheffield: Sheffield Academic Press, 2000); **H. Donner,** "'Hier sind deine Götter, Israel!'" in *Wort und Geschichte: Festschrift für Karl Elliger zum 70. Geburtstag,* ed. H. Gese and H. P. Rüger (AOAT 18; Kevelaer: Butzon & Bercker, 1973) 45-50; **E. E. Elnes and P. D. Miller,** "Elyon," *DDD²* 293-99; **M. Greenberg,** "The Hebrew Oath Particle ḥay/ ḥē," *JBL* 76 (1957) 34-39; **H. B. Huffmon,** *Amorite Personal Names in the Mari Texts: A Structural and Lexical Study* (Baltimore: Johns Hopkins University Press, 1965); **S. Japhet,** *I & II Chronicles* (OTL; Louisville: Westminster/John Knox, 1993); **W. C. Kaiser,** "The Blessing of David: A Charter for Humanity," in *The Law and the Prophets: Old Testament Studies Prepared in Honor of Oswald Thompson Allis,* ed. J. Skilton (Philadelphia: Presbyterian & Reformed, 1974) 298-318; **P. Kalluveettil,** *Declaration and Covenant: A Comprehensive Review of Covenant Formulae from the Old Testament and the Ancient Near East* (AnBib 88; Rome: Biblical Institute Press, 1982); **O. Keel and C. Uehlinger,** *Gods, Goddesses, and Images of God in Ancient Israel* (Minneapolis: Fortress, 1998); **B. Kelly,** "Messianic Elements in the Chronicler's Work," in *The Lord's Anointed: Interpretation of Old Testament Messianic Texts* (Tyndale House Studies; Grand Rapids, MI: Baker, 1995) 249-64; **R. W. Klein,** *1 Samuel* (WBC 10; Waco, TX: Word, 1983); **G. Knoppers,** "Ancient Near Eastern Royal Grants and the Davidic Covenant," *JAOS* 116 (1996) 670-97; **C. J. Labuschagne,** *The Incomparability of Yahweh* (Pretoria Oriental Series 5; Leiden: E. J. Brill, 1966); **P. K. McCarter,** *I Samuel* (AB 8; Garden City, NY: Doubleday, 1980); **E. A. Martens,** *God's Design: A Focus on Old Testament Theology* (3d ed.; North Richland Hills, TX: Bibal Press, 1998); **T. Mettinger,** *King and Messiah: The Civil and Sacral Legitimation of the Israelite Kings* (ConBOT 8; Lund: Gleerup, 1976); idem, *The Dethronement of Sabaoth: Studies in the Shem and Kabod Theologies* (ConBOT 18; Lund: Gleerup, 1982); **R. W. L. Moberly,** "אמן," *NIDOTTE* 1.427-33; **J. A. Motyer,** *The Prophecy of Isaiah* (Downers Grove, IL: InterVarsity Press, 1993); **D. Pardee,** "Eloah," *DDD* 285-88; **H. Van Dyke Parunak,** "A Semantic Survey of *NHM,*" *Bib* 56 (1975) 512-32; **I. W. Provan,** "The Messiah in the Book of Kings," in *The Lord's Anointed: Interpretation of Old Testament Messianic Texts,* ed. P. E. Satterthwaite, R. S. Hess and G. J. Wenham (Tyndale House Studies; Grand Rapids, MI: Baker, 1995) 67-85; **K. D. Sakenfeld,** *Faithfulness in Action: Loyalty in Biblical Perspective* (Philadelphia: Fortress, 1985); **R. Smend,** *Die Bundesformel* (Theologische Studien 68; Zurich: EVG Verlag, 1963); **M. S. Smith,** *The Early History of God: Yahweh and the Other Deities in Ancient Israel* (2d ed.; Grand Rapids: Eerdmans, 2002); **H. J. Stoebe,** *Das erste Buch Samuelis* (KAT 8/1; Gütersloh: Mohn, 1973); **H. G. M. Williamson,** *Israel in the Books of Chronicles* (Cambridge: Cambridge University Press, 1977); idem, *Ezra, Nehemiah* (WBC 16; Waco, TX: Word, 1985); **J. T. Willis,** "The 'Repentance' of God in the Books of Samuel, Jeremiah, and Jonah," *HBT* 16 (1994) 156-75; **N. Wyatt,** *Religious Texts from Ugarit* (2d ed.; Biblical Seminar 53; Sheffield: Sheffield Academic Press, 2002); **W. Zimmerli,** *I Am Yahweh* (Atlanta: John Knox, 1982) 1-28. D. I. Block

GOLIATH

Goliath was a soldier in the *Philistine army from the city of *Gath. His name appears six times in the Historical Books, once in Sirach 47:4, and once in the superscription of Psalm 151 LXX and Syriac (the body of Ps 151 refers to the *David and Goliath story but does not mention Goliath by name). He is also alluded to in 1 Maccabees 4:30. The meaning of his name is uncertain. It is possible that the terminative element -*yat* points to a Luwian, Lydian or Hittite origin (see discussion in McCarter, 291; Görg, 17-18). More recently, M. Görg proposed that the name comes from the Egyptian root *qny*, "to be strong," and may have been a military title that eventually became a proper name. His view, however, involves an unstated assumption of phonetic correspondences between Egyptian *q* and Semitic *g*, and between Egyptian *n* and Semitic *l*, the latter being plausible, but the former problematic. Goliath is described in 1 Samuel 17:4, 23 as *ʾîš-habbēnayim*, which was interpreted by R. de Vaux as "champion," but by P. K. McCarter (290-91) as "infantryman." The LXX translates that expression as *anēr dynatos*, "a mighty man," similar to *ho dynatos*, "the mighty one" in 1 Sam 17:51, which translates the Heb *gibbôr*.

1. Text and/or Source-critical Issues
2. Brief Comments on 1 Samuel 17:1—18:5

1. Text and/or Source-critical Issues.

There are a number of textual and/or source-critical issues in biblical passages that mention Goliath.

1.1. How Tall Was Goliath? Goliath's height (1 Sam 17:4) is described in the MT as six cubits and a span (about 9 ft. 9 in.), but in some LXX MSS, 4QSam^a and Josephus (*Ant.* 6.171) as four cubits and a span (about 6 ft. 9 in.). At first sight, the lower height would appear to be the original, since it is easier to explain an exaggeration than an understatement. However, D. Kellermann suggests that Goliath's symptoms in 1 Samuel 17 match those of pathological gigantism (a pituitary condition known as acromegaly), including a tunnel-vision type of visual defect, which David presumably took advantage of in defeating him. If so, then the MT reading need not be considered an exaggeration.

1.2. Who Killed Goliath? According to 2 Samuel 21:19, Elhanan slew Goliath, but according to 1 Chronicles 20:5, he slew Goliath's brother Lahmi (this discrepancy is in both the MT and the LXX). It has been suggested that the tradition that Elhanan killed Goliath was the original, which later was transferred to David. Other scholars have tried in various ways to harmonize the two passages, including (1) identifying Elhanan with David and emending the proper name *yʿry* in 2 Samuel to *yšy*, "Jesse"; (2) reinterpreting the syntax so that Elhanan killed "Oregim the Bethlehemite," who was "with Goliath"; (3) interpreting "Goliath" as a title rather than a name (see Fouts 2000, 15-16). D. M. Fouts compares the two passages and concludes that both show signs of textual corruption. He suggests that both passages originally read, *wayyak ʾelḥānān ben-(dôdô) bêt hallaḥmî ʾet-(?)ʾăḥî golyat haggittî*, "and Elhanan, the son of (Dodo) the Bethlehemite slew (?) the brother of Goliath the Gittite" (Fouts, 23).

1.3. Which Is the Original Version of the David and Goliath Pericope? There are at least two versions of the story of David and Goliath (1 Sam 17:1—18:5): a longer one preserved in the MT, and a shorter one preserved in some manuscripts of the LXX, which are missing 1 Sam 17:12-31; 17:55—18:6a. Though shorter in overall length, the latter also contains material not found in the MT. For example, in 1 Sam 17:43 of Codex B, David responds to Goliath's question "Am I a dog?" by saying, "No, worse than a dog!" Since the secondary literature on this topic is quite extensive and goes back to the nineteenth century, here we will only briefly mention some recent works.

For some, the shorter version of the David and Goliath story is the earlier one. E. Tov, by studying translation technique, concludes that the shorter LXX version is a relatively literal translation of an older Hebrew version, whereas the MT is a later text that is longer due to editorial expansion (for the respective views of Barthélemy, Gooding, Lust and Tov see Barthélemy et al.). According to J. Lust, the shorter LXX version was a translation of an earlier Hebrew original, whereas the MT was an expanded version that conflated both the shorter version (in Hebrew) and another independent story (so also McCarter, 295-98, 306-9). A. G. Auld and C. Y. S. Ho, judging from stylistic similarities between the stories of *Saul and David, conclude likewise that 1 Samuel 17:12-31 is a later interpolation. However, although they agree that the shorter version is earlier, they do not see evidence for the existence of two separate conflated stories. Rather, the MT is simply an embellishment of the shorter version. J. Trebolle agrees that the shorter version is the earlier one but bases his study on the use of double readings and resumptive repetitions, which he considers traces of editorial activity, especially in light of the Lucianic text of the LXX. He concludes that the shorter LXX version was based on an earlier Hebrew original containing a number of unrelated episodes, whereas the MT version is later and contains allusions and parallels both to the story units attested in the shorter version and to other parts of the larger narrative, resulting in a highly elaborated text.

Among scholars who argue for the priority of the MT over the shorter LXX version there is disagreement over the originality of the MT version. For some, the MT represents the original. Thus, for example, H. Jason, using ethnopoetic tools, concludes that the MT version of the story of David and Goliath is a romantic epic work of oral tradition. By contrast, the shorter LXX version is missing some important elements of such literary works. D. W. Gooding (in Barthélemy et al.) explains apparent tensions in the MT of 1 Samuel 16—18 as a literary device of narrative suspense and concludes that the MT is the original, whereas the shorter Greek version resulted from an attempt to remove doublets and discrepancies.

On the other hand, there are those who hold that the MT version is earlier than the shorter LXX version, but not necessarily original. A. Rofé suggests that whereas the LXX employs the strategy of harmonization by removal, the MT occasionally employed the strategy of smoothing out difficulties by addition. Thus the original, written during the late Persian period, contained inconsistencies and contradictions, which the *Vorlage* of the LXX removed. Those parts within the MT that minimize the inconsistencies are also not original. D. Barthélemy argues that the MT of 1 Samuel 17:12-31 originally existed separately and was integrated later than 1 Samuel 16:14-23. 1 Samuel 17:32-54 is a continuation of 1 Samuel 17:12-31, and 1 Samuel 17:1-11 was later added as an introduction to 1 Samuel 17:12-31. After the final redaction of the books of *Samuel, motivated by the difficulties and inconsistencies in the story, a shortened Hebrew version was created, which is preserved in the LXX.

Likewise, A. van der Kooij argues that 1 Samuel 17:12-31 is an older independent story that formed the basis of the MT version, which was incorporated into the final redaction of that part of Samuel, and the shorter LXX version is the product of later literary activity. According to W. Dietrich, Goliath is killed by Elhanan in the original story (2 Sam 21:19), but by the soldier David in the second version of the story. The more extensive (and artistic) story of Goliath and the shepherd David as found in the MT is a later composite of many sources. Finally, the shorter LXX version attempted to eliminate problematic repetitions.

Thus there is no consensus on the relationship between the MT and the LXX versions of the David and Goliath pericope, notwithstanding the fact that progress has been made in recent years, especially in the understanding of LXX translation techniques and in the application of the tools of literary interpretation. Although no one can doubt that the books of *Samuel, *Kings and *Chronicles are compiled from previous sources, it does not follow that the textual differences in this pericope must be source-critical rather than text-critical in nature. Currently, the available evidence is insufficient to determine whether these differences are due to the history of the composition of the text or of the transmission of the text or both (*see* Text and Textual Criticism). In the final analysis, more evidence is needed before a definitive history of the composition and transmission of the Goliath story can be written.

2. Brief Comments on 1 Samuel 17:1—18:5.

Since Goliath is best known from the story of the contest between him and David, and since most of what we know about Goliath comes from that story, a few brief comments on that pericope are in order. These comments are based on the MT version because it is more complete and artistic. Although the fact that the MT version has more aesthetic and literary appeal does not prove it to be the original, it does show that this version is neither a mindless embellishment nor the product of an unskilled redactor.

The story of David and Goliath belongs to a genre that involves the battle of representatives in order to obviate the bloodshed of a full engagement of rival armies (Hoffner, 220). Parallels can be found both in the Bible (2 Sam 2:12-16) and in the ancient Near East (see Hoffner).

A novel idea concerning the details of the contest was proposed by A. Deem, who suggested that since Goliath's armor was that of a typical Aegean warrior, there was no native Hebrew word for such items as a "greave." Thus the Hebrew *hapax legomenon mishat*, "greave," in 1 Samuel 17:6 should be vocalized as *mishot* and understood as the plural of *mēsah* (as in Ezek 9:4), the same word translated "forehead" in 1 Samuel 17:49. Therefore, David's stone sank into Goliath's "greave," preventing his knee from bending, rather than into his "forehead." In other words, David first caused Goliath to fall, and then he killed him.

J. P. Fokkelman (143-45) insightfully includes 1 Samuel 18:1-5 in this pericope because of the parallels between this pericope and the one in 1 Samuel 13:2—14:46. Both episodes are rather long. In both instances the Philistines are advancing, all Israel trembles, and a youth provides "a surprising turn in the military confrontation." This results in the question of how Jonathan, the hero of 1 Samuel 14, will react to the new hero, David, a question answered in 1 Samuel 18:1-5. Here we subdivide the pericope into six parts, with slight differences from Fokkelman's divisions. The first section introduces Goliath (1 Sam 17:1-11). Next, David is introduced (1 Sam 17:12-22). The third section focuses on David's reaction to Goliath (1 Sam 17:23-30), including the contrast between Israel's fear and David's courage, as well as the interchange between David and Eliab. The next section is the conversation between David and Saul (1 Sam 17:31-40). The fifth section presents David's fight with and victory over Goliath (1 Sam 17:41-54). The last section of the pericope begins with Saul's question, "Whose son is this young man?" (1 Sam 17:55) and ends with David in the household of Saul, who did not let him go back to his father's house (1 Sam 18:2). Thus to the readers, who already know that David was anointed to succeed Saul (1 Sam 16:13), the fight with Goliath is presented as a step on his path toward the throne.

A distinction must be made between history and narrative (*see* Historiography, Old Testament; Narrative Art of Israel's Historians). That is, whereas historical events are objective and neutral, narratives can be told only from a specific point of view, like a two-dimensional picture of a three-dimensional object. Narrative, even if divinely inspired, is by necessity selective. Thus a literary interpretation of the passage fo-

cuses not on the events behind the narrative, but on how the narrative is told. In other words, in terms of literary analysis, *hermeneutics must pay attention to poetics. Central to the poetics of this pericope is the role of characterization. Whereas David is a "round," or full-fledged, character, Goliath is a "flat" character. That is, although the narrative reveals David's multifaceted personality, including his emotions and motives, it tells us almost nothing about Goliath beyond what is necessary for the plot. He is simply the villain on the occasion that introduced David to Israel as a national hero. In fact, he is more often referred to as "the Philistine" than by name. Goliath, Saul and Eliab stand as a backdrop against which David is contrasted and thus characterized.

Several examples can be given to show that the characterization of David is central to the pericope. Although Goliath mentioned Saul by name (1 Sam 17:8), Saul was afraid (1 Sam 17:11), and Saul's inability to respond serves as a backdrop for David's willingness to fight Goliath. David's courage, therefore, is highlighted in contrast with Saul's (and Israel's) fear. Even Eliab's questioning of David's motives (1 Sam 17:28-29) serves a function in the characterization of David. Since the narrator had already explained the reason why David left the flock (1 Sam 17:17-20), Eliab's accusation contrasts with the reader's prior knowledge and reinforces the purity of David's motives—that is, David was not seeking personal glory. In contrast to Goliath's height and awesome appearance, David is portrayed as young, ruddy and handsome (1 Sam 17:42), implying more than only outward appearance—that is, David was attractive and likeable, and he would become popular (see 1 Sam 18:6-8). The story also highlights David's piety. That is, although Goliath simply defied the armies of Israel (1 Sam 17:10), David interpreted it as against the Lord and his armies (1 Sam 17:26, 36, 45). It is not until Goliath later cursed David by his gods (1 Sam 17:43) that the religious and theological significance of the battle becomes prominent in the story (1 Sam 17:45-47). Therefore, although God's role in the battle is acknowledged, the narrative focuses on the characterization of David, rather than on God's role.

Finally, though not an example of characterization, the dialogue between David and Saul serves an important role in the narrative. David points to his shepherding experience as a qualification for the task (1 Sam 17:32-36). That is, as a shepherd, he fought against colossal enemies of the flock. Now the narrative uses another colossal enemy in anticipation of the fact that David will someday shepherd Israel.

Though brief, the foregoing observations lay out what may be considered to be the primary function of the pericope in its context: it is one of several episodes leading to David's rise to the throne. Thus Goliath is significant in the biblical narrative only as a backdrop, being one of several characters along David's path to the throne. Nevertheless, it is to a large extent Goliath's characterization that makes possible David's characterization in the pericope. Goliath is such a fitting character that the motif of "David vs. Goliath" in popular and proverbial settings owes perhaps more to Goliath than to David.

See also DAVID.

BIBLIOGRAPHY. **A. G. Auld and C. Y. S. Ho,** "The Making of David and Goliath," *JSOT* 56 (1992) 19-39; **D. Barthélemy et al.,** *The Story of David and Goliath: Textual and Literary Criticism* (OBO 73; Göttingen: Vandenhoeck & Ruprecht, 1986); **A. Deem,** "'. . . And the Stone Sank into His Forehead.' A Note on 1 Samuel XVII 49," *VT* 28 (1978) 349-51; **W. Dietrich,** "Die Erzählungen von David und Goliat in 1 Sam 17," *ZAW* 108 (1996) 172-91; **J. P. Fokkelman,** *Narrative Art and Poetry in the Books of Samuel: A Full Interpretation Based on Stylistic and Structural Analyses*, 2: *The Crossing Fates (I Sam. 12—23 & II Sam. 1)* (SSN 23; Assen: Van Gorcum, 1986); **D. M. Fouts,** "Who Really Killed Goliath? 2 Samuel 21:19 versus 1 Chronicles 20:5," *Journal of Translation and Textlinguistics* 13 (2000) 14-24; **M. Görg,** "Goliat aus Gat," *BN* 34 (1986) 17-21; **H. A. Hoffner Jr.,** "A Hittite Analogue to the David and Goliath Contest of Champions?" *CBQ* 30 (1968) 220-25; **H. Jason,** "The Story of David and Goliath: A Folk Epic? *Bib* 60 (1979) 36-70; **D. Kellermann,** "Die Geschichte von David und Goliath im Lichte der Endokrinologie," *ZAW* 102 (1990) 344-57; **A. van der Kooij,** "The Story of David and Goliath: The Early History of Its Text," *ETL* 68 (1992) 118-31; **P. K. McCarter Jr.,** *I Samuel* (AB 8; Garden City, NY: Doubleday, 1980); **A. Rofé,** "The Battle of David and Goliath: Folklore, Theology, Eschatology," in *Judaic Perspectives on Ancient Israel,* ed. J. Neusner, B. A. Levine and E. S. Frerichs (Philadelphia: Fortress, 1987) 117-51; **J. Trebolle,** "The Story of David and Goliath (1 Sam 17—18): Textual Variants and Literary Composition," *BIOSCS* 23 (1990) 16-30.

T. Li

GRAINS. *See* AGRICULTURE AND ANIMAL HUSBANDRY.

GRAPES. *See* AGRICULTURE AND ANIMAL HUSBANDRY.

GREAT TRUNK ROAD. *See* ROADS AND HIGHWAYS.

H

HADAD. *See* ARAM, DAMASCUS AND SYRIA.

HAD-YIŠʿI INSCRIPTION. *See* NON-ISRAELITE
WRITTEN SOURCES: SYRO-PALESTINIAN.

HAGGAI. *See* EZRA AND NEHEMIAH, BOOKS OF.

HAMATH BRICKS. *See* ARAM, DAMASCUS AND
SYRIA.

HAZOR

The biblical city of Hazor is strategically located some ten miles north of the Sea of Galilee at the foot of the eastern ridge of the Upper
Galilee mountains, overlooking one of the
main branches of the Via Maris route from
Egypt to Assyria. It was the largest and most important city in Canaan during the Bronze Age
and an important Israelite center in the Iron
Age. Mentioned in Egyptian texts and the Mari
documents in the first half of the second millennium, Hazor also plays a prominent role in
the conquest narratives in the Bible, where it is
referred to as the "head of all those kingdoms"
(Josh 11:10). Later, during the period of the Israelite monarchy, the city was rebuilt as a royal
citadel and then expanded to become an important administrative center in the north of
the northern kingdom. Its decline was rapid after it was destroyed by the Assyrians in the second half of the eighth century BCE, and in spite
of an Assyrian presence at the site it never recovered.

    1. Historical and Biblical References
    2. Excavations
    3. Middle Bronze Age (c. 1800/1750-1550 BCE)
    4. Late Bronze Age (c. 1550-1200 BCE)
    5. Iron Age I (c. 1200-1000 BCE)
    6. Iron Age II (c. 1000-732 BCE)
    7. Later Periods

1. Historical and Biblical References.

Canaanite Hazor's prominence in international
relations in the second millennium BCE is testified to by its appearance in several foreign documents. It first appears in the nineteenth century
BCE in the Egyptian Execration texts, and a century later it features in the documents from the
archive at Mari in present-day Syria. Hazor is
the only Canaanite city mentioned with some
frequency in the Mari documents (*Dan is mentioned as well), and they testify to the city's commercial importance, wealth and regional significance.

    Later, from the fourteenth century, three let-
ters from Abdi-Tirshi, king of Hazor, appear in
the Amarna archive in Egypt, and other references to the city occur in records of military
campaigns conducted by Egyptian pharaohs in
Canaan in the fifteenth and fourteenth centuries BCE.

    According to the biblical account in Joshua
11:1-15, a coalition of northern kings headed by
Jabin king of Hazor was defeated by Joshua at
the Waters of Merom. The account makes clear
that Hazor was singled out for special attention
by the victorious Israelites, who killed the king,
captured the city and burned it to the ground
(Josh 11:10-11). This victory opened the way for
the completion of the Israelite conquest of
Canaan, and Hazor was subsequently included
in the territory of Naphtali (Josh 19:36) (*see*
Joshua, Book of).

    A second account is found in Judges 4, where
the Israelites come under the influence of Jabin
of Hazor and his army commander Sisera (Judg
4:2). They were delivered from the oppression
by Deborah and Barak, and Jabin was subdued
and later destroyed (Judg 4:24; see also 1 Sam
12:9).

    Later, in the tenth century, Hazor was built

up by Solomon along with *Jerusalem, *Gezer and *Megiddo (1 Kings 9:15). The city is referred to only once more in the Bible, in 2 Kings 15:29, where it is listed as one of the cities conquered by Tiglath-Pileser in the year 732 BCE.

2. Excavations.

The archaeological site of Hazor consists of two parts, an upper and a lower city. The upper city, or acropolis, is a bottle-shaped tell with an area of 120 dunams/30 acres/12 hectares, and the large rectangular lower city which extends to the north measures about 700 dunams/175 acres/ 70 hectares. While the acropolis contains remains from all the periods of settlement at Hazor, excavations have revealed that the occupation of the lower city was confined to about 500 years in the second millennium, from the eighteenth to the thirteenth centuries BCE.

Following a small excavation by J. Garstang in 1928, Hazor has hosted two major projects. The first was the J. A. de Rothschild Expedition, which conducted excavations there from 1956 to 1959 and in 1968, and was directed by Y. Yadin on behalf of the Hebrew University of Jerusalem, the Palestine Jewish Colonization Association and the Anglo-Israel Exploration Society. It uncovered twenty-one strata dating from the Early Bronze Age in the third millennium to the Hellenistic Period of the second century BCE, and revealed for the first time the magnificence of the archaeological record of the site. The richness and excellent preservation of architecture and finds at Hazor complemented the historical and biblical record of the city's size, wealth and influence in the ancient Near East.

In 1990 the Selz Foundation Hazor Excavations in Memory of Yigael Yadin resumed excavations at the site under the direction of A. Ben-Tor on behalf of the Hebrew University of Jerusalem, Complutense University of Madrid and the Israel Exploration Society. The project, which is ongoing at the time of writing, has confined its excavations to the acropolis and has continued to reveal the splendor of both the Canaanite and Israelite cities.

3. Middle Bronze Age (c. 1800/1750-1550 BCE).

Following a period of decline that coincided with the First Intermediate Period in Egypt, a new city was built at Hazor in the eighteenth century BCE. The population quickly expanded from the acropolis to cover the entire lower city, ultimately rising to between 20,000 and 30,000 people.

The Canaanite city of the Middle Bronze Age is characterised by monumental architectural features that betray the northern influences from the Syro-Mesopotamian cultural sphere. The most prominent of these were the massive rampart and moat surrounding the lower city, particularly in the west and north, and two city gates. However, it is the number and variety of temples that most emphatically indicate the cosmopolitan character of the city. Their different designs and features suggest that a variety of ethnic and religious traditions existed side-by-side at Hazor throughout the Middle and Late Bronze Ages.

At the far northern edge of the lower city the first of a series of four successive temples was built in Area H. The earliest structure, dated to the last phase of the Middle Bronze Age in the late seventeenth and early sixteenth centuries, was a freestanding symmetrical building oriented to the northwest. Built on an artificial platform to raise its profile, the temple was entered from a spacious courtyard through a small lobby flanked by two rooms into a main hall with a small niche opposite the entrance. The building bears some resemblance to the tower temples of the same period at *Shechem and Megiddo, though at both of these the central hall was a long room, while at Hazor there was a broad room design. It bears rather more resemblance to the temples at Alalakh in Syria.

A rectangular double temple dating to the same period was found in Area F, also on the lower tell. The entrance on the long western side was reached via an enclosed porch room, and led to two nearly identical almost square shrines situated side by side. Yadin related the design to the Sin-Shamash double temple at Asshur, stressing again the influence from the north (Yadin 1972, 97).

On the acropolis, two separate temples were erected almost side by side in the area of the royal court in Area A. The first, slightly to the north of the second, was exposed below the Solomonic gate by Yadin in 1968. It consisted of a single long hall entered from the east through a narrow entrance lined and paved with basalt orthostats. Opposite the entrance, against the west wall, was a plastered brick platform. Close by was a second temple of similar design. Yadin exposed a corner of this building in the 1950s and suggested it was the Middle Bronze Age palace. Now excavated more completely by the current expedition, the building is also rectangular with a recessed niche in the center of the western wall. In the middle of the floor was a circular pit that served as a *favissa* and contained a large number of votive bowls, chalices and incense-burner fragments. Both temples were abandoned at the end of the first phase Late Bronze Age and filled in.

4. Late Bronze Age (c. 1550-1200 BCE).

The Middle Bronze Age city was destroyed by fire in the mid-sixteenth century BCE. After a short interlude characterized by several graves cut into the ashy destruction layer on the acropolis, urban life returned to Hazor. Once again the whole site, upper and lower, was settled, and many of the domestic buildings were constructed to new plans. However, the material culture shows continuity from before, as do several of the monumental features and buildings, such as the ramparts, city gates and the temples in Areas A and H. A more significant change occurred toward the end of the fifteenth century, when the temples on the acropolis were decommissioned and a massive new palace was built there in the fourteenth century. This stratum was again violently destroyed by fire at the end of the fourteenth century, perhaps in one of the campaigns of the Egyptian pharaoh Seti I. The Canaanite city was rebuilt for the last time, and although there are some signs of decline, Hazor remained by far the largest and most important city in Canaan until its destruction in the thirteenth century BCE.

4.1. Late Bronze Age Temples. The number and variety of Hazor's temples were maintained in the Late Bronze Age. The two temples on the acropolis continued into the fifteenth century, after which they were buried. A small open-air shrine with stelae and cultic installations was established over the entrance of the northern temple, indicating a continuing sacred regard for the location, and the area over the southern temple was not built on for the rest of the Bronze Age.

The temple in Area H also continued into the Late Bronze Age with some alterations, but the changes at the end of the fifteenth century were considerably more significant. The entire building was rebuilt on a revised, tripartite de-

sign, which was copied when it was rebuilt again in the thirteenth century. The entrance lobby was enlarged into a hall, and the rooms that flanked it were transformed into massive towers with staircases. The main hall was entered from the smaller hall by descending two steps, and a revised niche with a bench was set into the back wall. Outside, an entry porch, probably unroofed, was added to the front of the façade. Two pillars with no structural function stood at the entrance to the porch.

The orthostats found in the final phase of the temple can be assigned with certainty to this phase, although they probably originated even earlier, in the Middle Bronze Age. In addition to the finely worked rectangular basalt orthostats, two others shaped like crouching lions flanked the entrance. Their heads are carved in the round, while the bodies are in relief. One was found by Yadin in the ruins of the temple, the other by Ben-Tor on the acropolis, where it had been used as construction material in an Israelite building. Among the finds and cultic paraphernalia found in the temple were altars and figurines carved with the symbol of the Anatolian-north Syrian god Hadad.

In its design, the use of orthostats, the presence of lion orthostats, and in the artifacts representing the storm god Hadad, the temple in Area H shows strong influence from the Syro-Hittite regions to the north and suggests that a proportion of the people living there brought these traditions with them to Hazor.

The double temple in Area F was replaced in the first phase of the Late Bronze Age with a square building of unusual design. Its closest parallels are at Tananir on Mount Gerizim to the south, from the sixteenth century, and from Amman across the Jordan in the thirteenth century. It was replaced in the fourteenth and thirteenth centuries by an open cult area with a paved piazza dominated by a massive carved stone altar that was 2.4 m long, 0.85 m high and 1.2 m long, and weighed nearly five tons.

In Area C, a residential area in the southwest part of the lower city, just below the western acropolis, a small shrine was built in the fourteenth century against the inner slope of the rampart. In the niche opposite the entrance were ten basalt stelae, a small seated male figurine, a small crouching lion statuette and a small stone offering table. On the central stela was a carving in relief of two hands stretching upward to a crescent moon. Likewise, the figurine had a carved image of an inverted crescent moon on its chest. Both indicate that the deity of this shrine was the moon god Sin.

4.2. The Late Bronze Age Palace. A Late Bronze Age palace that dominates the acropolis has recently been uncovered just to the south of the decommissioned temples. An extensive pebbled courtyard to the east leads up a few steps onto a porch and into a large central hall twelve meters square. The porch is flanked by a room on each side, and other rooms lead off the north, south and west sides of the main hall.

The walls of the palace are built of mudbrick on stone foundations and are massive. The eastern façade is nearly 5 m wide, and the rest of the walls are 1.5 m wide. The porch, the outer walls on the north, south and west, and the inner walls of the main hall are all lined with carved basalt orthostats similar to those from the Area H and Area A temples. The main hall, identified by the excavator as a throne room (Ben-Tor and Rubiato 1999, 29), had a pebble surface, but charred plank fragments of cedar of Lebanon indicate that it was originally covered with a wooden floor. Cedar planks were also set into the mudbrick walls for support.

Once again, the closest parallel for the Hazor palace comes from the contemporary palace in stratum IV at Alalakh in Syria, although the Hazor structure is more than twice the size of its northern counterpart. The same Syro-Babylonian unit of measurement that divides every length into sixty centimeter multiples was used in both buildings. The wooden beams, the orthostats and indeed the plan itself are also indicative of a shared tradition.

Finds in the palace that reinforce its importance include a hoard of decorated ivories second only to one from Megiddo, also from the thirteenth century BCE, several cylinder seals, a large statue of a deity, two basalt statue heads and several Egyptian statue fragments. Near the entrance were the broken remains of a basalt human statue, originally nearly 1 m tall and the largest Canaanite statue ever found in Israel. It was decorated with images of the sun and the moon on its chest.

The palace is dated to the second half of the Late Bronze Age, at least from after the decommissioning of the Area A temples at the end of the fifteenth century BCE. It continued into the thirteenth century BCE, when it was destroyed

with the rest of the city. Beneath the eastern part of the courtyard, evidence has emerged of an earlier palace, less well preserved, dating to the Middle Bronze Age, with even larger walls.

4.3. Access from the Lower City to the Acropolis. A principal access point from the lower to the upper city in the Late Bronze Age was built on the north slope of the acropolis. A monumental entrance flanked by two small towers led from the lower city into an impressive basalt-paved plaza dominated by a square podium set into a niche in the rear wall. The podium, also of basalt slabs, was 1.5 m square. In the upper surface four small holes had been bored into the basalt slab, suggesting that it served as the foundation for the throne of a deity or king. To the west a few steps led up to a street that continued in the direction of the acropolis. An earlier staircase leading uphill was uncovered to the east of the plaza. The excavator has described the area as a cultic center within the gate of the city (Ben-Tor and Rubiato 1999, 32-33).

4.4. The Destruction of Canaanite Hazor. A massive and comprehensive destruction by fire brought an end to the last Bronze Age city at Hazor. The attackers not only burnt the city to the ground but also deliberately attacked and mutilated all statues, figurines and images of deities that they encountered. Following his excavations in the 1950s, Yadin dated this destruction to no later than 1230 BCE, and on the basis of the biblical account in Joshua 11, especially verses 10 to 13, attributed the destruction to the Israelites under Joshua (Yadin 1972, 108-9). Ben-Tor cautions that the pottery from the destruction can be dated to any stage in the thirteenth or even late in the fourteenth century BCE. However, the preponderance of evidence points to a thirteenth-century date for the destruction, and Ben-Tor agrees that the most likely perpetrators were the early Israelites who settled in the central hill country of Canaan shortly afterward, and who were mentioned in the Merneptah Stela in the late thirteenth century BCE (Ben-Tor 1998, 465-66; Ben-Tor and Rubiato 1999, 36-39).

5. Iron Age I (c. 1200-1000 BCE).

After the destruction of Canaanite Hazor, the site lay abandoned for up to 200 years until the eleventh century. The first Iron Age settlement was identified by the presence of more than thirty circular stone-lined storage pits that cut into the earlier strata all over the acropolis. Other features of this rudimentary settlement included cooking installations and foundations for tents or huts.

In the west of the acropolis, evidence was found of a subsequent smaller settlement, whose most important feature was a small building identified as a shrine. Remains of five broken incense stands were found nearby, and a pot containing metal objects, including a bronze deity figurine, was excavated below the floor. Yadin concluded that the jar and its contents were a foundation offering placed beneath the floor, and the building itself served as an Israelite *high place (Yadin 1972, 132-34). However, doubt has been cast on this identification, most notably by O. Negbi, who noted that the items in the jar were in poor condition and were probably collected from the ruins of the Canaanite city to be melted down as scrap (Negbi, 360-61). Ben-Tor has proposed that a basalt pillar that Yadin identified as a bench served instead as a standing stone in the building (Ben-Tor 1996, 267), and if so, then it rather than the metal hoard offers a more plausible reason for interpreting the building as a shrine.

6. Iron Age II (c. 1000-732 BCE).

The period of the monarchy at Hazor is divided into a further seven strata, X to IV, dated from the tenth to the end of the eighth century BCE. They represent three main periods in the life of the city: the united monarchy and its immediate aftermath in the tenth and early ninth centuries; the Omride dynasty in the ninth century, when Israelite Hazor reached its apex in size, importance and grandeur; and the gradual decline of the city that culminated in its destruction by the *Assyrians in 732 BCE.

6.1. Strata X-IX (Tenth to Early Ninth Centuries BCE). After another gap Hazor was occupied once again in the tenth century BCE, during the reign of *Solomon. The verse in 1 Kings 9:15 referring to Solomon building up Hazor, Megiddo and Gezer has been cited in support of this dating, notably by Yadin (1972, 11, 147). I. Finkelstein, among others, has sought to ascribe this level to a later period (Finkelstein 1999 and 2000), partly due to his attempts to lower the traditionally accepted dates of Iron Age levels by up to a century (*see* Megiddo). Ben-Tor rejects Finkelstein's arguments and continues to assign stratum X to the tenth century on the basis of

the ceramic record rather than the biblical account (Ben-Tor 2000a; Ben-Tor and Ben-Ami 1998).

The Solomonic city was built from scratch on the acropolis. A casemate wall encircled the settlement, which was entered through a monumental six-chambered gate. Gates similar in plan and size from the same period were excavated at Megiddo and Gezer, and the design continued to be appropriated at other cities in Israel in the ninth and eighth centuries BCE.

The Solomonic city only covered an area of some 40 dunams/10 acres/4 hectares in the western half of the acropolis. Few domestic remains were found, though a large building with an area of over 200 square meters was excavated just inside and across a pebbled street from the casemate wall, to the south of the six-chambered gate.

Hazor functioned as a royal citadel in this level. Its impressive and intimidating fortifications, large buildings and limited size, perhaps augmented by a garrison of soldiers, served to remind the population of the new political reality in the land, and that although power was centralized in the south, its influence extended as far north as Hazor.

Minor changes in stratum IX followed the death of Solomon, and the level ended in an early-ninth-century destruction attributed to Ben Hadad of Damascus (1 Kings 15:18-20; 2 Chron 16:4).

6.2. Strata VIII-VII (Ninth Century BCE). The size of the city doubled when it was rebuilt in the ninth century by *Omri or his son Ahab. A solid three-meter-wide city wall, preserved in places to a height of over three meters and with offsets and insets on its outer face, enclosed new buildings in the east of the city. Such massive fortifications are common at sites in northern Israel during the ninth century, and are indicative of the constant threat from the north, especially from Assyria.

Among the new buildings in this level was a massive citadel in the west of the acropolis. It was a rectangular building with an area of over five hundred square meters. Separated from the rest of the city and entered through an elaborate gate, its walls were between 1.4 and 2 meters thick, and it had at least two stories. Additional buildings constructed in the compound alongside the citadel are identical in plan to royal administrative buildings at Samaria.

Two more public buildings excavated just inside the casemate wall were characterized by two rows of monolithic pillars that divided the space into three long rooms. The design is well known from Iron Age Israel and appears to have had a number of different functions. At Hazor, however, the pottery and other finds found on the floors indicate they served as storerooms.

The most impressive new building project at Hazor during the ninth century was the water system. A wide shaft was cut from the surface through ten meters of earlier strata until it came to bedrock. The edges of the cut were supported with large holding walls to prevent them from collapsing. A further nineteen meters of bedrock was removed until the shaft was flattened out, and a staircase for access was carved around its wall. From the surface of the shaft a stepped tunnel with a vaulted ceiling extended down another twenty-five meters into the bedrock, to an additional depth of about ten meters. At the bottom of the tunnel was ground water.

The water system greatly increased security as it obviated the need to leave the city to obtain water in a time of siege. It is one of several similar systems that were constructed around the country during the ninth century BCE (*see* Water and Water Systems).

6.3. Strata VI, V and IV (Eighth Century BCE). The city was rebuilt again following another destruction in the second half of the ninth century BCE. Many of the earlier buildings were reused, and they were augmented by new buildings. However, some of the reused and restored buildings were subdivided, and the new buildings were of poorer quality than before. The general impression is of prosperity accompanied by encroaching decline.

Following an earthquake the city was quickly restored, but this level, stratum V, was destroyed by Tiglath-Pileser III in 732 BCE in the campaign that saw the conquest and annexation of the northern part of the kingdom of Israel by Assyria (2 Kings 15:29; 1 Chron 5:26). An indication of the pending doom is the military guardhouse built on the western slope of the acropolis, alongside the citadel. Following the destruction of the city, a squatter settlement arose in the ruins. The pottery used in this level, stratum IV, is identical to that from the destroyed stratum V, indicating that it was survivors that returned to the site soon after the Assyrian destruction.

Hazor's decline in importance was complete.

Following the destruction of *Samaria in 722/721 BCE, prosperity in the new Assyrian province shifted north to Dan, and Hazor never recovered.

7. Later Periods.
An Assyrian military fort was built in stratum III over the destroyed Israelite citadel and was reused with alterations in stratum II of the Persian period in the fourth century BCE. Other meager buildings and pits, as well as a cemetery, also testify to this period. Poorly preserved remains from stratum I show that the fort finally went out of use in the Hellenistic period, and the tell was abandoned.

See also HISTORY OF ISRAEL 1: SETTLEMENT PERIOD; JOSHUA, BOOK OF.

BIBLIOGRAPHY. **A. Ben-Tor,** "Notes and News: Tel Hazor, 1996," *IEJ* 46 (1996) 262-68; idem, "The Fall of Canaanite Hazor-The "Who" and "When" Questions," in *Mediterranean Peoples in Transition: Thirteenth to Early Tenth Centuries BCE,* ed. S. Gitin, A. Mazar and E. Stern (Jerusalem: Israel Exploration Society, 1998) 456-67; idem, "Notes and News: Tel Hazor, 1999," *IEJ* 49 (1999a) 269-74; idem, "Solomon's City Rises from the Ashes," *BAR* 25.2 (1999b) 26-37, 60; idem, "Hazor and the Chronology of Northern Israel: A Reply to Israel Finkelstein," *BASOR* 317 (2000a) 9-15; idem, "Notes and News: Tel Hazor, 2000," *IEJ* 50 (2000b) 243-9; idem, "Notes and News: Tel Hazor, 2003," *IEJ* 53 (2003) 218-23; idem, ed., *Hazor III-IV: Text* (Jerusalem: Israel Exploration Society, 1989); **A. Ben-Tor and D. Ben-Ami,** "Hazor and the Archaeology of the Tenth Century B.C.E.," *IEJ* 48 (1998) 1-37; **A. Ben-Tor and R. Bonfil,** eds., *Hazor V: An Account of the Fifth Season of Excavations, 1968* (Jerusalem: Israel Exploration Society, 1997); **A. Ben-Tor and M. T. Rubiato,** "Did the Israelites Destroy the Canaanite City?" *BAR* 25.3 (1999) 22-39; **I. Finkelstein,** "Hazor and the North in the Iron Age: A Low Chronology Perspective," *BASOR* 314 (1999) 55-70; idem, "Hazor XII-XI with an Addendum on Ben-Tor's Dating of Hazor X-VII," *TA* 27 (2000) 231-47; **A. Mazar,** "Temples of the Middle and Late Bronze Ages and the Iron Age," in *The Architecture of Ancient Israel from the Prehistoric to the Persian Periods,* ed. A. Kempinski and R. Reich (Jerusalem: Israel Exploration Society, 1992) 161-87; **O. Negbi,** "The Metal Figurines," in *Hazor III-IV: Text,* ed. A. Ben-Tor (Jerusalem: Israel Exploration Society, 1989)

348-62; **Y. Yadin,** *Hazor: The Schweich Lectures of the British Academy* (London: British Academy, 1972); idem, *Hazor: The Rediscovery of a Great Citadel of the Bible* (New York: Random House, 1975); **Y. Yadin, Y. Aharoni, R. Amiran, T. Dothan, I. Dunayevsky and J. Perrot,** *Hazor I* (Jerusalem: Magnes Press, 1958); idem, *Hazor II* (Jerusalem: Magnes Press, 1960); idem, *Hazor III-IV: Plates* (Jerusalem: Magnes Press, 1961).

G. Gilmour

HEALING. *See* SICKNESS AND DISEASE.

HEBREW INSCRIPTIONS

An inscription is generally considered to be Hebrew if it is written in the classic Hebrew script of the preexilic period (ninth to sixth centuries BCE) and is in the *Hebrew language. There are various types of Hebrew inscriptions, with different methods of writing and used for various purposes. Perhaps the most permanent method of writing is by making an incision. These could be chiseled in stone, scratched in metal or directly incised on pottery, either before or after firing. A second method was by using an incised seal to make impressions in clay (or wax). These impressions have been preserved as bullae (lumps of clay used to seal papyrus documents) and as seal impressions on pottery jar handles. A third method was by writing with ink, either on pottery pieces (known as ostraca, sg. ostracon), on plaster, on cave walls or on papyrus. The content of the inscriptions are of various types: narratives, letters, tomb inscriptions, prayers/poems, graffiti and nonliterary (names of people or places, receipts, weights, etc.). Of all of these various types of inscription, the major inscriptions incised in stone are no doubt the most impressive, and together with some of the longer ostraca (esp. letters) and prayers provide some of the most useful information for archaeologists and biblical scholars. And yet even the shortest inscriptions can add to our knowledge of the period. Ironically, it may be that some of the nonliterary inscriptions (such as seals) have the most potential overlap with the biblical text.

Since to date we have hundreds of Hebrew inscriptions, it is impossible to even list let alone discuss them all. (For more exhaustive lists see Davies; Gogel's "Introduction" and "Corpus"; Ahituv; and Renz.) For ease in immediate identification all inscriptions discussed here will be identified by the corpus number provided in G. I. Davies, *Ancient Hebrew Inscriptions: Corpus and Concordance*, which also gives a basic bibliography for each inscription.

1. Background
2. Incised Inscriptions
3. Inscriptions Written in Ink or Paint
4. Nonliterary Inscriptions

1. Background.

1.1. Dating and Authenticity. Cuneiform literature in Palestine ceases during the twelfth to eleventh centuries. Linear writing continues, and in the eleventh century is developed in Phoenicia. The distinctive Hebrew tradition does not appear until the end of the ninth century. It must also be remembered that dating by palaeographic criteria is fraught with many hazards and should only be attempted in the absence of good archaeological data (see Whitt, 2385). Only when we have clear stratigraphical evidence or explicit internal dating can we be at all confident of dates. The script of the so-called Gezer Calendar shows Phoenician influence, and many scholars now consider it to be non-Hebrew, whether Phoenician or South Canaanite (Renz, 12; Gogel, 9 n. 14). Although hints of the developed Hebrew script may be seen in inscriptions of the tenth to ninth centuries, the first inscription that exhibits the full style of script is not Hebrew, but the Moabite Stone—traditionally dated to the ninth century.

Much can be seen from the nature and distribution of inscriptions, quite apart from their content. Most inscriptions for Judah occur during the period of dominance of the state: the eighth and seventh centuries. Before the eighth century the amount of material is "negligible" (Parker, 8). The period of maximum activity is roughly 722-580. The inscriptions also vanish after the destruction of Jerusalem in 587 BCE (Halpern, 132 n. 26). In terms of the kings of Israel/Judah, the period is basically from the time of Jeroboam II/Azariah until the fall of Jerusalem.

We expect more inscriptions to survive in Judah—especially southern Judah—than in Israel, as the climate is dryer. Thus in principle inscriptions are best preserved the further south they are found, and best preserved in the strata just before a destruction (Millard, 305). This may partly explain the amount of material found at the end of the seventh century in Judah.

As every archaeology student is told, unless an item is found in a secure context, it has little value—except perhaps as a museum specimen. With the recent discovery of just how extensive forgery of artifacts of the monarchic period has been, even the value of unprovenanced artifacts as museum items is doubtful. As in all scams, the forger relies on the desire of the collector to be fooled, to believe in its genuineness. As always, if it appears too good to be true, it almost certainly is. This is particularly true for seals found in private collections. It is a great pity, as so much of our onomastic evidence comes from seals and bullae. Extra vigilance is required with all seal evidence.

1.2. Lack of "Royal" Inscriptions. What is immediately striking is the total absence of "royal" inscriptions, that is, inscriptions in the first person, purportedly dictated by the king. There are no decrees, building inscriptions, victory reports, autobiographies or dedications to the gods written in the name of the reigning king. All these are found not only as Assyrian, Babylonian and Egyptian inscriptions, but even in the surrounding nations comparable to Israel and Judah—Phoenicia, Moab, Samalia (Ya˒udi) (cf. Pardee, 57). There are none for Israel or Judah (with the possible exception of Arad ostracon 88; see 3.2.1.3). There are very few monumental inscriptions at all. We know more of the individual kings from royal inscriptions of Assyria and other nations than from indigenous writing. The major kind of documents we have preserved are secular documents, reflecting the ordinary, noncultic life of Israel and Judah.

The contrast between the inscriptions and the book of Kings could not be greater. The book of Kings is the book of kings. The basic structure is devoted to the role of the king. Whether for good or evil, the king sets the whole tone of the kingdom, and he is responsible for the health—not only moral but physical—of the realm (McKenzie, 81-100).

2. Incised Inscriptions.

The inscriptions discussed here represent "monumental" inscriptions, which are finely engraved and intended to be official and on public display. Three of these are from Jerusalem and the fourth from Samaria. Next follow tomb inscriptions (from Jerusalem, Khirbet-el Qom and Khirbet Beit Lei), two silver amulets discovered in a burial cave on the shoulder of the Hinnom valley in *Jerusalem, known as Ketef Hinnom, and lastly other inscriptions on stone and pottery. It will be noted that most of the longer in-

scriptions come from Jerusalem, and apart from the Samaria fragment of a monumental Inscription, all are from Judah.

2.1. Monumental Inscriptions.

2.1.1. The Siloam Tunnel Inscription (Davies 4.116). Underneath the City of David lies a rock-hewn tunnel that curves in a rough S-shape, extending from the Gihon Spring on the eastern side of the Ophel ridge, and exiting at the Byzantine-period Pool of Siloam on the southwest side of the Ophel ridge. An inscription was engraved directly into the side of the tunnel. The inscription seems to begin in the middle of the account. (Interestingly, the space above the inscription was smoothed to prepare for some type of carving, but has not been engraved.) It has been dated to the end of the eighth century BCE, partly based on the shape of the letters but also on the similarity of the events detailed in the inscription with the events occurring during the reign of Hezekiah. 2 Kings 20:20 talks about the deeds of Hezekiah and "how he made the pool and the conduit and brought water into the city" (NRSV), but a conduit is not necessarily a tunnel, nor does the text give any reason for Hezekiah's actions. 2 Chronicles 32:3-4 notes that Hezekiah "stopped all the springs and the wadi that flowed through the land" (NRSV). Quite a few water systems have been discovered, and presumably the Gihon Spring, the major water supply for the city of Jerusalem, would have been included in this reference. However, it is not until the Chronicler's closing remarks at the end of Hezekiah's reign, that the parallel account to the Kings' passage is given: "This same Hezekiah closed the upper outlet of the waters of Gihon and directed them down to the west side of the city of David" (2 Chron 32:30 NRSV) (*see* Water and Water Systems).

Nevertheless, it is this similarity between the biblical text and the background events of the inscription that has caused scholars to connect the two events and even call the Siloam tunnel "Hezekiah's tunnel." It does not appear to be an official inscription and almost certainly has nothing to do with any "annals of the kings of Judah." It is interesting that the biblical text does not mention the tunnel, and the tunnel does not mention the king or any invasion.

It is the sense of achievement plus the efforts of the tunnelers that is celebrated here. Only the climactic breakthrough is described. The inscription mentions that two groups, working from either end, met near the middle. The direction of the chisel marks and several "dead ends" near the joining support that claim. But there is no name of any person setting up the inscription or even mention of who planned the tunnel or why it was needed. The inscription ignores the name not only of the king but also of God. This is unlike any other ancient Near Eastern monumental inscription. It is a purely secular document, as are most of our inscriptions.

2.1.2. The Ophel Inscription (Davies 4.125). The Ophel monumental inscription was discovered in 1982, south of the Temple Mount in Jerusalem. It is a fragment of a larger seventh-century inscription that was chiseled on a limestone slab. The beginning of four lines of text remain, each consisting of six letters. It is tempting to read this inscription in the light of the Siloam tunnel inscription. The dates are roughly the same, and the occurrence of words such as "underneath," "the water" (pool, spring) and "in the innermost part or recesses" are very provocative. Unfortunately, this is all we have, and any reconstruction of a longer inscription on the basis of the extant text would be pure speculation.

2.1.3. The "City of David" Inscription (Davies 4.120). A third monumental inscription from Jerusalem was discovered in 1978 in the City of David excavations. It dates to the late eighth century BCE, and the script is so reminiscent of the Siloam inscription that F. M. Cross "is tempted" to argue that the same engraver produced both inscriptions (Cross 2001, 44). The inscription is very fragmentary, and only a few words have been preserved. Cross speculates that it refers to the seventh year of Hezekiah's reign, while he was preparing to revolt against Assyria as well as carrying out cultic reforms (Cross 2001, 46). Cross points to the account in 2 Chronicles 31:3-9, where Hezekiah commands the people to present their first fruits, tithes and offerings to the priests, as an interesting parallel to the type of collection referred to in the inscription (Cross 2001, 46-47). It is an intriguing suggestion, but any further reconstruction is pure speculation.

2.1.4. The Samaria Stela (Davies 3.312). From Samaria we have one small fragment (of about 4 in) of a beautifully engraved stone tablet from the eighth century BCE. On the fragment is preserved only one word, *'šr*, in large, finely chiseled letters. Ironically, this one word of a monumental inscription is of momentous importance. It is the only fragment we have from

Samaria, but it clearly shows that the northern kingdom, like Judah (and all the surrounding nations), had at least one monumental inscription—in Hebrew.

Thus we have very few monumental inscriptions from Judah and from Israel only one. The lack of such inscriptions, especially after so much intensive excavation and since they have been found in all the surrounding nations, may come as a surprise. Even with what monumental inscriptions we have discovered, none mention any king or God. As yet there is no evidence that Israel and Judah had royal or cultic inscriptions, though a few have speculated that some of the inscriptions we do have may have been based on them.

2.2. Tomb Inscriptions. Most of the tomb inscriptions that have been preserved are incised in stone, and so appear in this section. The tomb inscriptions can be found written outside the tomb itself (as is the case with the Silwan "Royal Steward" inscription), or else in the interior of the tomb, next to one of the chambers where the body would be laid out to decompose on one of the burial benches. The inscriptions are also of two types: in general, the "Royal Steward" inscription is finely engraved and is meant for public display; other tomb inscriptions are incised much more roughly and are considered graffiti. Even so, despite the many Iron Age necropoli excavated, we have relatively few tomb inscriptions, of which the main examples are discussed here.

2.2.1. The Silwan "Royal Steward" Inscriptions (Davies 4.401 and 4.402). Silwan is on the eastern slopes of the Kidron valley in Jerusalem, directly opposite the City of David. Above the door of the tomb was a sunken rectangular panel, 4.3 feet long, with a three-line inscription dating (on palaeographic grounds) to approximately 700 BCE. To the right of the door lay a second sunken panel with a one-line inscription of the same period (Avigad 1953, p. 137). Both inscriptions were badly damaged.

N. Avigad's reading of the three-line inscription remains virtually unchallenged to this day:

1. This is [the sepulchre of . . .]yahu who is over the house. There is no silver and no gold here
2. but [his bones] and the bones of his slave-wife with him. Cursed be the man
3. who will open this (Avigad 1953, 143).

The officer "who is over the house" seems to

be the highest officer in the kingdom. The term occurs twelve times in the Bible. 1 Kings 4:6 sees him as one of the small group of "highest officials" *(śārîm)* of the king. In 2 Kings 15:5 Jotham, the king's son, fulfills this role and "rules" *(śōpēt)* over the people of the land. In every instance but Genesis 44:1, "the house" refers to the royal palace, in Samaria or Jerusalem *(see* State Officials).

The tomb also contains the bones of his *'āmâ.* This in the Bible refers to a maidservant, a slave. It is often assumed to refer to a secondary wife (or "slave wife," a concubine in English translations); she is "sold" in Exodus 21:7-11 to be the "wife" of a man or his son; but in Genesis 35:25, 26 she is the maid of a man's wife, though he has sexual rights over her.

Although the name of the owner of the tomb has not been fully preserved, and even though none of the names of the royal stewards mentioned in the Bible end in -*yhw*, it is tempting to find a connection. Avigad has proposed to restore it as Shebanyahu, and thus connect the one interred here with the royal steward Shebna, known from Isaiah 22:15. The monumental nature and imposing placement of the tomb seems to fit the description in the biblical text. Unfortunately, we lack evidence.

The shorter tomb inscription (Davies 4.402) was translated by Avigad (1955, 166) as "(Tomb-) chamber in the side (or slope) of the rock (or mountain)." During his survey of burial caves in Silwan, D. Ussishkin determined that there was a second burial chamber quarried out of the rock to the side of the first. He therefore interprets the second inscription as referring to a third burial in the tomb, which would account for the second inscription in a different hand, albeit from approximately the same period. The inscription is in front of the second chamber. He therefore translates it as "a burial-chamber in the side of the rock-cut burial chamber" (if referring to the main chamber) or "in the side of the tomb" (if referring to the visible monolithic tomb) (Ussishkin, 21). The presence of the second burial chamber within the monument makes Ussishkin's argument quite compelling.

2.2.2. The Khirbet el-Qom Tomb Inscriptions (Davies 25.001; 25.002; 25.003). Khirbet el-Qom is located 6.5 miles east-southeast of Lachish and 8.5 miles west of Hebron. There are a total of three tomb inscriptions, two of which were scratched into the soft, chalky limestone, in the manner of graffiti. The first two, both dating to the mid-seventh century BCE, are from the same burial cave (Dever, 151, 156). Both inscriptions appear to refer to Ophay, son of Netanyahu (cf. Davies 25.001, 25.002). The second, shorter inscription was written in black paint or ink. By far the most interesting inscription is inscription number 3 (Davies 25.003). This was discovered in a second tomb and appears to date to the mid eighth century BCE.

The inscription consists of three lines above a deeply gouged hand image, with a fourth and shorter line to the left of the hand, and two fragmentary lines below and to the left of the hand. It is difficult to read for various reasons, but appears to state (Hadley, 86):

1. Uriyahu the rich wrote it.
2. Blessed be Uriyahu by Yahweh
3. for from his enemies by his (YHWH's) asherah he (YHWH) has saved him
4. by Oniyahu
5. by his asherah
6. and by his a[she]rah

The naming of Yahweh and asherah together here in a context that implies approval or acceptance is of considerable importance in the study of Israelite religion. Asherah was a northwest Semitic deity worshiped by the ancient Israelites *(see* Canaanite Gods and Religion). Forms of the word *asherah* appear forty times in the Hebrew Bible, where in most instances it refers to the wooden symbol of the goddess and only rarely to the goddess herself, and almost always in a negative fashion (Hadley, 54-83). It may be that the mention here refers to the symbol of the goddess, since in biblical Hebrew the possessive pronominal suffix is never attached to a name, as it would be here if it were the proper name of a goddess (Hadley, 99 and references there).

In either case, even if the word *asherah* here referred to the wooden symbol of the goddess, associations with the goddess herself would still remain. Therefore, Yahweh and "his asherah" are inextricably linked, and Yahweh alone appears to have been unable to effect the salvation of Uriyahu without the help of "his asherah."

The mention of Yahweh and Asherah together in an eighth-century inscription within a favorable context runs counter to the picture we have from the Bible that the worship of Asherah or the erection of asherah poles was to be condemned.

The engraved hand is reminiscent of other

funerary monuments and may have served as a memorial. Indeed, the word *hand* is sometimes used in the OT in the sense of a monument (1 Sam 15:12; 2 Sam 18:18; 1 Chron 18:3; Is 56:5). It may also serve an apotropaic function (Hadley, 102-4).

2.2.3. The Khirbet Beit Lei Inscriptions (Davies 15.001-15.008). Khirbet Beit Lei is located five miles east of Lachish and 10.5 miles west-north-west of Hebron, in the vicinity of Khirbet el-Qom just discussed. The tomb consists of two burial chambers. Inside the tomb on the walls were many engravings, including three human figures, two ships, several written inscriptions, and assorted other scratches in the shape of circles, lines, hash marks or crosses, reminiscent of the paleo-Hebrew letter *taw*. All of the inscriptions date to about 700 BCE. The word *cursed* can be noted in the shorter inscriptions, and very little else. We will therefore concentrate on the three main inscriptions.

Most scholars read Inscription A (Davies 15.005 and 15.006) as follows:

1. Yahweh, the God of all the earth; the moun-
2. tains of Judah belong to the God of Jerusalem (cf. Naveh 1963, 84; Gogel, 411; Davies 15.005 and the references there).

An alternative reading proposed by Cross and followed by Miller is:

1. [I am] Yahweh your God, I will accept
2. the cities of Judah; I will redeem Jerusalem (cf. Cross 1970, 301; Miller, 321-22; Gogel, 411; Davies 15.006 and references there).

Inscription B is equally contested, spawning such varied translations as:

The (Mount of) Moriah thou hast favoured the dwelling of Yah, Yahveh (Naveh 1963, 86)

or:

Be mindful, Yah Gracious God
Absolve, Yah Yahweh (Miller, 328; cf. Gogel, 411 and Davies 15.007).

The third inscription, Inscription C, is much shorter and easier to read. It simply states: Save (us), Yahweh (Davies 15.008).

It will be noted that none of the inscriptions refer to any burials in the tomb. They are all prayers for deliverance or expressions of faith in Yahweh. Indeed, one of the drawings is of a man with his arms raised as if in prayer (Naveh 1963, 77 and 78, fig. 5). It has been suggested that the engravings in the tomb are the work of later visitors, perhaps people hiding in the cave

at the time of the Assyrian invasion of Sennacherib in 701 BCE.

If the first reading of Inscription A (Davies 15.005) is to be accepted, we have an interesting poetic parallel between Yahweh and "the God of Jerusalem." The phrase does occur in 2 Chronicles 32:19, but as the expression of an "idolatrous" viewpoint: "They (or he) spoke to (or about) the God of Jerusalem as (if) about the gods of the peoples of the world, humanly made objects." Whichever reading is to be accepted, Inscription A contains the only sure preexilic reference to Jerusalem in an inscription.

2.3. Incised Inscriptions on Metal.

2.3.1. The Ketef Hinnom Silver Plaques (Davies 4.301 and 4.302). In 1979 during the course of excavations along the shoulder of the Hinnom valley (Ketef Hinnom) in Jerusalem, opposite the modern-day "Mount Zion," a series of Iron Age tombs was cleared. Among a rich collection of finds were two silver plaques. The most significant problem with these inscriptions is the dating. The excavator, G. Barkay, suggests a date in the late-seventh/early-sixth century—right at the end of the monarchy (Barkay et al., 170). J. Renz (Renz I.449-52) has argued for a date in the Hellenistic period, which would certainly present less of a challenge to current ideas. There can be no question of authenticity, as I found the larger amulet in situ, and the context had been sealed in late antiquity by rockfall from the roof. However, the tomb was in use for an extended period, as shown, for example, by the discovery of a well-used Greek coin. Yet Barkay et al. argue from the find spot and associated pottery for an earlier date. The writing, though little more than scratched into the metal and difficult to read, is compatible with the earlier date.

The larger scroll (3.82 in long, 1.06 in wide) reads (Barkay et al., 170):

1. . . .] YHW . . .
2. . . .
3. The grea[t who keeps]
4. the covenant and
5. [g]raciousness towards those who love [him] and (alt. Those who love [hi]m;)
6. those who keep [his commandments . . .
7. . . .].
8. The Eternal? [. . .].
9. [the?] blessing more than any
10. [sna]re and more than Evil.
11. For redemption is in him.

12. For YHWH
13. is our restorer [and]
14. rock. May YHWH bles[s]
15. you and
16. [may he] keep you.
17. YHWH make
18. [his] face [sh]ine . . .

The smaller scroll (1.54 in long, 0.43 in wide) reads:

[For PN, (the son/daughter of) xxxx]
1. h/hu. May h[e]/sh[e] be blessed
2. by Yahweh,
3. the warrior [or helper] and
4. the rebuker of
5.-6. [E]vil: May Yahweh bless you,
7. keep you.
8. May Yahweh make
9. his face shine
10. upon you and
11.-12. grant you p[ea]ce.

Two precise parallels to biblical texts have been found. The first to be recognized was a version of Numbers 6:24-26, the so-called priestly benediction. The context makes it clear that this was a traditional blessing to be recited on formal occasions by the priests. In Psalm 67:1 we have another form of this prayer: "May God be gracious to us and bless us and make his face to shine upon us" (NRSV), the occasion being a harvest festival (Ps 67:6-7), where God has blessed the people with the fruits of the earth. The scroll confirms that this was an old prayer.

The other verse restored by Barkay et al. (170) is: "who maintains covenant loyalty with those who love him and keep his commandments" (NRSV). This also seems to have been something very familiar, as it occurs over a wide series of circumstances. It occurs in a rhetorical "sermon" in Deuteronomy 7:9 and an even closer parallel in Daniel 9:4 and Nehemiah 1:9 (which have other phrases also in common).

The occurrence of the characteristic Deuteronomic word *covenant* in such an early context could be very significant. The smaller scroll has the phrase "rebuker of evil," which is echoed in Zechariah 3:2.

Since these amulets are over 300 years older than the Dead Sea Scrolls, they are the earliest fragments of a prayer identical in many words to a biblical prayer in Numbers. This part of the Pentateuch is often considered to have been written later than this, though dependent on an earlier priestly tradition. It shows the existence of personal devotion before the destruction of the temple. Such things as amulets had not been thought to be this early. This is the earliest mention of Yahweh in a text from Jerusalem. It is the first intact repository from Iron Age Jerusalem, providing the only assemblage of pottery and finds for this period in Jerusalem. As a family tomb it continued to be used after the destruction of Jerusalem, and it is the first evidence that Jerusalem was not totally evacuated even by the well-off, since these silver items from that time show they could afford very pure silver.

2.4. Miscellaneous Incised Pottery and Stone Objects. The final category of incised objects is composed of mainly short dedicatory inscriptions on pottery jars and bowls incised after firing, or on stone bowls. Since it is much more difficult to incise an inscription on pottery rather than to write in ink, this procedure was used mainly for quite short inscriptions. The content of the inscriptions is of three basic types: (1) a personal name (PN), often with a patronymic, to establish ownership of an item or a vessel's contents; (2) a description of the contents or volume of a vessel; (3) a dedication or designation of how the object or its contents is to be used. Examples of all three types of inscription are attested, especially that of ownership. The writing can be quite crude, and it is possible that the inscriber—whether owner or potter or craftsman—need not have been strictly literate, just able to reproduce a name as if it were a glyph.

3. Inscriptions Written in Ink or Paint.
Apart from seals and seal impressions, the greatest number of inscriptions are written in ink on pieces of broken pottery called ostraca. However, we also have ink or paint inscriptions on plaster or stone (especially as graffiti in tombs), as well as on papyrus. That the ancient Israelites wrote on papyrus is evidenced by the many bullae, or clay seal impressions, which have been discovered, some still bearing the impression of papyrus on the back. To date only one actual papyrus fragment from the monarchical period has been discovered, because the climate is not favorable to the survival of papyrus. Unfortunately, since papyrus was evidently a valuable commodity, most of the ink of the original text has been scraped off and the papyrus used again. Fortunately for archaeologists, pottery was much cheaper to produce and both fragile and durable. That is, if dropped, the chances

were good that the pottery would break. But once broken, the pieces of pottery were very durable and provided an abundant and cheap source of writing material. Thus most of the longer inscriptions we have are ostraca.

3.1. The Wadi Murabbaʿat Papyrus (Davies 33.001 and 33.002). The Wadi Murabbaʿat cuts through the cliffs on the western shore of the Dead Sea and contains many caves where papyrus scrolls have been found, but most of these date to the second century BCE or later. Both of the inscriptions on the Wadi Murabbaʿat palimpsest appear to date to the early seventh century BCE. The papyrus is included here not so much because the inscription is particularly relevant to this study but because it is the *only* inscription on papyrus from this period that has survived.

The original inscription (Davies 33.001) is in the form of a letter. Some time relatively soon after the letter was written, the ink was scraped off and the papyrus was used to record a list of names with a number following each name. One cannot generalize from one example, but it is interesting that both uses of the papyrus are identical to the examples for which elsewhere ostraca were used. So it seems that theories that ostraca and papyrus were used for very different purposes are not supported by this example.

3.2. Ostraca. Much of our information comes from documents in letter form. At the end of our period, the Assyrians—followed by the Persians—had an actual postal service (Herodotus *Hist.* 9.98). This was for official business, but the concept was pervasive, and though private letters depended upon the chance of "someone going that way," delivery of letters was anticipated. Standard letter forms were followed. The Lachish letters are well on the way to this standard form: the "To" address (lacking generally the "From"), the blessing by God or gods of a superior, the words "and now" introducing the content of the letter. The earlier "letters"—the forms found, for example, at Kuntillet ʿAjrud—may not yet be letters. In the earlier period most communication was by messenger; and often a messenger would carry an aide memoire to remind him of his message. The graffiti at Kuntillet ʿAjrud probably still belong to the messenger stage, but might also be practice in the use of the correct phrases (whether spoken or written). It is still a time when Israel was within the general Phoenician culture area.

3.2.1. Tell Arad Ostraca (Davies 2.001-2.088). The Iron Age citadel of Tell Arad is located in the Judaean Negev, about twenty miles east-northeast of Beersheba. It is thought that the site was a military outpost to defend the southern part of the Judaean kingdom, but the size of this site, complete with its own temple, shows that it must have also served as a regional administrative and perhaps religious center as well. Y. Aharoni's publication of the inscriptions included eighty-eight Hebrew ostraca, of which fifteen are whole (seven of which consist of only one name). Most of the Hebrew inscriptions date to the eighth to sixth centuries BCE, with some possibly extending back to the tenth century BCE. Indeed, Arad is unique among the sites such as Lachish and Samaria that have collections of ostraca in that the inscriptions do not all come from the last years of occupation of the site but are spread out over several centuries, from the tenth to sixth centuries BCE. This has been a considerable benefit to archaeologists and epigraphers, as it has thus been possible to trace the evolution of the Hebrew script at one site through the whole of the Iron Age. In addition to the ostraca, the Hebrew inscriptions include sixteen incised jar inscriptions and five seals. The ostraca inscriptions are of several types. Perhaps the most interesting are the letters. There are also lists of names and lists of various commodities, sometimes combining the two and sometimes separate, as well as brief jar inscriptions similar to those described above.

3.2.1.1. The Eliashib Archive. Eighteen of the ostraca were discovered together in one of the casemate rooms of the southern wall, in the destruction layer of stratum 6, dating to the end of the seventh/beginning of the sixth centuries BCE. It was this stratum that was destroyed by the Babylonians, around 595 BCE (Aharoni, 9). All of these ostraca are more or less in letter form and are written to the commander/administrator of the fortress, whose name was Eliashib. Therefore, this collection is often called the Eliashib collection. Most of these eighteen inscriptions deal with the distribution of various foodstuffs to a group of people called here "the Kittim." The inscriptions appear to be vouchers authorizing the distribution of the food. When completed, this was noted. There is even a receipt on the back of one of them (Davies 2.017). These vouchers were not meant to be saved for a long period of time, and they probably appear here only because the site was destroyed.

It is clear from the lack of a greeting and the tone of the letters that most of the ostraca in the Eliashib archive are written from a superior to an inferior, who is in charge of the distribution of the provisions, perhaps in a capacity similar to 1 Chronicles 26:24, 30, 32. The *kittim* are known from the Bible, where the word refers to people of Aegean origin, and especially from Kition in Cyprus. They are associated with Tarshish in Genesis 10:4, and mentioned in Numbers 24:24 and Daniel 11:30. Perhaps the word here refers to mercenaries in the Judaean army.

Perhaps the most interesting letter (Davies 2.018) is written by a subordinate to Eliashib, as is clear from the address. It reads:

To my lord, Eliashib, may Yahweh ask after your welfare.

And now: give Shemaryahu a *lethech* and to the Kerosite a *homer*. Now concerning the matter about which you commanded me, it is well. He is staying in the house (temple) of Yahweh.

The Kerosite is presumably a member of the Keros family mentioned in Ezra 2:44 and Nehemiah 7:47. Aharoni notes that "this is the first mention of one of the names of families of Nethinim in the First Temple Period, which strengthens the tradition in 1 Chronicles 9:1-2 regarding their ancient origins" (Aharoni, 36).

The interpretation of the mention of the "house," or "temple," of Yahweh (a temple was considered to be the "house" of a god) is fraught with many pitfalls (see Aharoni, 36-37 and references there). Whatever interpretation is to be accepted, whether the mention of the house of Yahweh here refers to the Yahweh temple in Arad or to "the" temple in Jerusalem, this Arad ostracon 18 remains the *only* genuine reference outside of the Bible to any preexilic temple dedicated to Yahweh *anywhere* (remembering that the Jerusalem pomegranate inscription and the Jehoash inscription have been shown to be forgeries).

3.2.1.2. Ostraca Referring to Edom. A few of the Arad ostraca refer to the *Edomites, apparently as enemies. They show the threat of the Edomites to the south, who no doubt took advantage of the Babylonian invasion in 597 BCE and the weakened state of Judah to take over the southern part of the country. Aharoni believes that ostracon 24 (Davies 2.024) shows that the Edomites are the ones who finally destroyed

Arad and the other remaining southern fortresses in about 595 BCE (Aharoni, 150).

3.2.1.3. Arad Ostracon 88 (Davies 2.088). This ostracon was assigned to stratum VII on account of the script (Aharoni, 103). Aharoni believes this city was destroyed by the Egyptians in 609 BCE (Aharoni, 149). This is perhaps the only inscription we have from Israel or Judah that can be classified as a "royal" inscription, and that only if it is a copy of a royal stela that has not been preserved (see, e.g., Halpern, 132 n. 25). The beginning of three lines have been preserved.

Aharoni reads the ostracon as follows:
1. I have come to reign in a[ll] . . .
2. Take strength and . . .
3. King of Egypt to . . .

If this reading is correct, it appears to be a letter sent out to all the military fortresses and administrative centers that a new king has come to power. If Aharoni's dating is correct, his suggestion that this new king is Jehoahaz, the successor to Josiah who was killed at Megiddo in 609 BCE (according to 2 Kings 23:31), is plausible. If so, the reference to the king of Egypt and the command to take strength would make sense on the heels of the death of the previous king at the hands of Pharaoh Neco.

This interpretation has not gone unchallenged. Nevertheless, whichever interpretation is to be accepted, this ostracon, if genuine, is unique. It is unfortunate that it was not excavated by the Arad team (it was a chance find by a visitor to the site), and so strictly speaking it should not be discussed here. It appears to be a communique from a newly established king, whether of Judah or elsewhere. It is therefore the *only* inscription that could possibly be classed as a "Royal Inscription."

3.2.2. Lachish Ostraca. *Lachish has been identified as the site of Tell ed-Duweir, about 45 miles southwest of Jerusalem in the foothills of the Judaean mountains known as the Shephelah. Its strategic location marked it as an important administrative center for the region and a first line of defense for Jerusalem. Davies lists twenty-three ostraca from Lachish, eighteen of which were discovered in 1935, all of them in a heavily burned gateroom that was destroyed in 587 BCE by Nebuchadnezzar. One of the ostraca seems to be an abecedary (Davies 1.023), five are name lists in which one of each name is followed by a number (Davies 1.019), and another is a list of owners or recipients with a prefixed *lamed* (Davies 1.022); the rest are letters, the so-called Lachish letters. Most of the letters appear to be written from an inferior (named Hoshayahu in letter 3, Davies 1.003.1) to a superior (named Yaush in letters 2, 3 [but broken] and 6; Davies 1.002.1, 1.003.2 and 1.006.1). Several of the letters contain an interesting phrase that compares the sender to a dog, for example, in letters 2 and 5 (Davies 1.002.3-4; 1.005.3-4) we find the phrase: "what is your servant but a dog . . . ?" This compares to 1 Samuel 17:43 ("am I a dog?") and 2 Samuel 3:8 ("Am I a dog's head?"). The indignant rejection in these words shows how objectionable the name-calling was, far below "slave." The words "What is your slave that you should regard (with favor) a dead dog like me" in Merib-baal(Mephibosheth)'s mouth (2 Sam 9:8) show that Hoshayahu was either *very* insecure or a sycophant.

Some of the letters are concerned with provisions—for example, Lachish 5 (Davies 1.005) with its wish for a good harvest—and several of them contain hopes for good news. This is especially poignant considering the letters were found in destruction debris and thus were written before very bad news indeed, the destruction of the city. Lachish 6 (Davies 1.006), although broken in several places, sounds especially heartwrenching as the writer tells about communications that are "not good" and discouraging. It includes a request to his superior to ask why they are doing this, and seems to close with the statement that "as Yahweh your God lives, ev[er sin]ce your servant read the letter[s] your servant has not had [peace of mind]." The oath of asseveration can be found, for example, in 1 Kings 17:12; 18:10.

Lachish letter 3 (Davies 1.003) is the only one in the Lachish collection that has both the names of the sender (Hoshayahu) and the recipient (Yaush, albeit broken in this letter). This makes it unique among all Hebrew letters of the monarchic period (cf. Pardee, no other letter has the sender).

Lachish letter 4 (Davies 1.004) is at the forefront of the discussion concerning the dating of the archive—either to just before the Babylonian destruction in 587 BCE or a year or two earlier.

Of the whole ostracon, the last few lines are the most intriguing:

10. And know that for the Lachish signals we
11. are watching, according to the code which my lord
12. gave, for we cannot see
13. Azekah.

The fire signals that are referred to were evidently some form of communication between cities in times of need. This type of signal is known from the Bible (Jer 6:1 uses this word in a general sense of any kind of signal; it can also be used of the rising of smoke, cf. Judg 20:38, 40. Could they be smoke signals?). Some sort of secret code is referred to, since the author refers to "signs" that his commander gave him to follow. They would not want their secret code to be witnessed by any outsiders.

The letter closes with the observation that they are looking for the "watch fires" (signals) of Lachish because they cannot see Azekah. The site of Azekah is about ten miles north of Lachish, and it cannot be seen from Lachish. Therefore it is thought that the writer was stationed somewhere a few miles away in the hill country, at a point where both Lachish and Azekah could be seen. It is assumed that as long as the site was under Judaean control, at a specified time, certain fire (or smoke) signals would be made. Since Azekah could no longer be seen, the conclusion would be that it had been destroyed. This juxtaposition of Lachish and Azekah during the final days of the Judaean monarchy is in startling agreement with Jeremiah 34:7, which talks about the words that Jeremiah the prophet spoke to Zedekiah, king of Judah, "when the army of the king of Babylon was fighting against Jerusalem and against all the cities of Judah that were left, Lachish and Azekah; for these were the only fortified cities of Jerusalem that remained" (NRSV). This parallel is perhaps the strongest argument for those who date the ostraca to the final days of Judah. In my opinion, we have in Lachish letter 4 a "snapshot" of an event from the last days of the kingdom of Judah, which was recorded perhaps just days after the corresponding picture from the biblical text.

3.2.3. The Samaria Ostraca. Samaria was, according to Kings, settled by *Omri, which would be in the early ninth century BCE, to be the capital of the northern kingdom of Israel. It was finally destroyed by the Assyrians in 722/21 BCE (*see* Samaria). It is located about forty-two miles north of Jerusalem. In 1910 a team of excavators from Harvard University discovered a large group of ostraca right next to the royal palace.

A. F. Rainey (69), however, says that Reiner's notebooks show that they actually come from the fill under that floor and are therefore older. They may be dated to the eighth century BCE and are the only major corpus of inscriptions preserved from the northern kingdom, apart from seals.

The ostraca appear to be receipts dealing with various foodstuffs, mostly wine and oil, judging by the names of the contents that have been preserved. There are four principal elements for each inscription when they have been fully preserved. These are the date; the origin (mostly place names); the owner, whether recipient or supplier; the commodity. For example, Samaria ostracon 6 (Davies 3.006) reads:

bšt . htšʿt .	In the ninth year
mqsh . lgd	from Qoseh, belonging to
	[or given to] Gaddi-
yw . nbl . yn .	-yaw, a jar of wine
yšn .	old(= a jar of old wine).

What is the meaning of these shipments of wine and oil? Various solutions have been proposed, including taxes paid to the central administration, gifts designated to be sent to supporters or other favorites of the crown (1 Sam 8:14-15), provisions sent to the palace (cf. 1 Kings 4:7-19, 22-28). For absent landlords the case would be similar to 2 Samuel 9:9-13, where Ziba, Saul's servant, was to run the estate for Saul's successor Mephibosheth (Merib-baal), who would remain in Jerusalem and eat at the king's table. However, since all of the ostraca were written in a similar, fine style of writing, and they all have such similar structure, it is more likely that they are receipts for goods sent to the central administration, presumably as payment of taxes.

3.2.4. The Inscriptions from Kuntillet ʿAjrud. Kuntillet ʿAjrud, "the solitary hill of the water wells," is located in northern Sinai approximately thirty miles south of Kadesh-barnea. The site is strategically located near several intersecting routes through the desert. The site dates to the end of the ninth century/beginning of the eighth century BCE, and from the nature of the finds it appears to have been a caravanserai, or way-station, used by a variety of people (see Hadley, 106-20).

The ostraca from Kuntillet ʿAjrud come mainly from two large pithoi that were intensively decorated with drawings, inscriptions, abecedaries, numerals and stray marks. Many of the drawings and inscriptions overlap one another, thereby making deciphering them difficult.

An indication that the site was used by a diversity of peoples is that some of the inscriptions appear to be in Phoenician script (Davies 8.014 and 8.015), which might indicate that Phoenicians visited the site. Furthermore, although Kuntillet ʿAjrud is in the extreme southern part of Judah, several of the names inscribed there have the *-yw (yaw)* suffix for the divine name, which is the northern Israelite form, as opposed to the Judaean *-yhw (yahu).*

The ostraca inscriptions come from two storage jars, one placed inside a small chamber in the entrance way (Pithos A), and the other from a corner of the inner courtyard just on the other side of the wall (Pithos B). They are therefore not truly ostraca but rather graffiti. However, since all the inscriptions on one jar were not necessarily meant to accompany any other inscription (or drawing) on the jar, they can be treated individually as if the jar had been already broken when they were made.

3.2.4.1. Kuntillet ʿAjrud Inscription 1 (Davies 8.017). The inscription is written on Pithos A, above the heads of two standing Bes figures (for a discussion of the drawings see Hadley, 136-52). The inscription reads:

> *ʾmr . ʾ . . . h . . . k. ʾmr . lyhl[lʾl] wlywʿšh. w . . . brkt . ʾtkm. lyhwh . šmrn . wlʾšrth .*

X says: say to Yehal[lelʾel] and to Yoʿasah and [to Z]: I bless you by Yahweh of Samaria and by his asherah. (Hadley, 121)

The mention of "Yahweh of Samaria" has an interesting parallel with the Khirbet Beit Lei inscription noted above, which may read: "God of Jerusalem." This reading brings up some interesting questions. Why would someone invoke the name of Yahweh of Samaria at a site so far south? Also, would a Judaean write Yahweh of Samaria? So is it more likely to be someone from the northern kingdom? It is unlikely that such a designation indicates a belief in multiple deities, all called Yahweh. It is more likely that the writer wanted to invoke the name of Yahweh as worshiped or manifested in Samaria.

But together with Yahweh the petitioner asks for the blessing of "his asherah." This is the same form of the name as found in the Khirbet el-Qom inscription. As discussed earlier (see 2.2.2), it may be that the wooden symbol of the goddess is indicated as the use of the third person masculine singular suffix for a personal name is unknown in biblical Hebrew. (If it is not a suffix, but part of the name Asherata, this does not hold.) However, usually only deities are agents of blessing. But here Asherah joins with Yahweh as a joint agent of blessing. But since "his asherah" appears with "Yahweh of Samaria," we have an interesting case that did not apply to the Khirbet el-Qom inscription. That is, it would be possible to interpret "I bless you by Yahweh of Samaria and *its* Asherah," that is, the Asherah of Samaria. 2 Kings 13:6 mentions that "the asherah also remained in Sa-maria." This may have been the asherah that Ahab erected (1 Kings 16:33), which would have then survived Jehu's reform. But this is an argument from silence. Nevertheless, the mention of the asherah in Samaria during the reign of Jehoahaz (815-801 BCE) fits in well with the chron-ology of the site of Kuntillet ʿAjrud and the inscription. It is therefore possible that this inscription refers to the asherah statue that stands in the temple of Yahweh in Samaria, perhaps representing Yahweh and Asherah as a divine pair.

3.2.4.2. Kuntillet ʿAjrud Inscription 2 (Davies 8.021). This inscription was written on Pithos B in a vertical format of about 8-10 characters wide.

This inscription (Hadley, 125) reads:

> ʾmr ʾmryw ʾmr l. ʾdny hšlm. ʾt brktk . lyhwh tmn
> wlʾšrth. ybrk. wyšmrk wyhy ʿm. ʾd[n]y . . . k

Amaryau says: say to my lord: Is it well with you? I bless you by Yahweh of Teman and by his asherah. May he bless you and keep you and be with my lord . . .

Like the inscription just discussed, this inscription appears to be a request for blessing and divine protection.

It will be noted that this inscription has Yahweh of Teman instead of Yahweh of Samaria. Teman evidently refers to the southern region, rather than a city like Samaria. Teman is known from Habakkuk 3:3, where it says "God came from Teman, the Holy One from Mount Paran" (NRSV). Teman is also mentioned in Zechariah 9:14, where it is translated "the south": "Yahweh Elohim will sound the trumpet, and march forth in the whirlwinds of the south (Teman)." Thus it

is clear that Yahweh has a special connection with Teman, or the southern regions, and perhaps even that Yahweh had originally come from there. It therefore appears that the blessing of Yahweh of Teman was seen to be propitious for travelers as they journeyed through the southern region. It is also interesting to note that we have the name of a northern Israelite, Amaryau, in an inscription which invokes a southern deity, Yahweh of Teman, or at least that invokes Yahweh as worshiped in the south.

The second part of this inscription is, "May he bless you and keep you and be with my lord." The prayer for Yahweh to "be with" someone is reminiscent of a number of biblical passages, including Genesis 28:15; 1 Kings 1:37; 2 Samuel 14:17; 1 Kings 8:57 and 1 Chronicles 22:11.

But an even closer parallel to the first two clauses of the blessing is Numbers 6:24, *ybrkk yhwh wyšmrk* ("May Yahweh bless you and keep you"). The language is virtually the same, except that the passage in Numbers has *ybrkk* whereas this inscription has *ybrk*. So the closest parallel is in the two Ketef Hinnom amulets discussed earlier (Hadley, 125-29) (see 2.3.1).

3.2.5. An Ostracon from Mesad Hashavyahu (Yavneh Yam) (Davies 7.001). This ostracon is one of three that were discovered inside the guard room near the fortress gate. It is very important not only for the society the text reveals but even more as it is one of only two narrative inscriptions we have from preexilic Israel (the other being the Siloam inscription). As S. B. Parker notes, since much of what is preserved in the biblical text is narrative, for comparison with biblical literary style these inscriptions represent the closest analogues. The Bible largely uses conversation to advance a story, while this ostracon has the words of only one person, directly quoted.

Palaeographically the ostracon is later than those of Samaria and earlier than those of Lachish. Because he considers the best fit to be the time when the sea coast was in the hands of Josiah, J. Naveh (1960, 139) dates the ostracon to the time of Josiah (640-609 BCE).

(1-2) Let my lord the officer hear the case of his servant.

(2-6) Your servant was reaping, was your servant, in Hasar-ʾasam. Your servant reaped and measured and stored as usual before stopping.

(6-9) When your [se]rvant had measured his harvest and stored it as usual, Hoshaʿyahu ben Shobay came and took your servant's garment. When I had measured my harvest as usual, he took your servant's garment.

(10-12) And all my comrades will testify for me, those who were reaping with me in the heat [of the sun], my comrades, will testify for me. Truly, I am innocent of any of[fence.

(12-14) Please restore] my garment. But if it is not your duty to resto[re your serv]ant's [garment], then sho[w him mer]cy and [resto]re your [ser]vant's [garment] and do not ignore [. . .]

(After Parker)

In the OT, petitions are made to kings, prophets or other influential persons orally and in person (2 Sam 12:1-7; 14:1-23; 1 Kings 3:16-17; 20:38-42; 2 Kings 4:1-7; 6:24-30). This petition is written. Overall it is rather vague. Why did Hoshayahu take the cloak? Why should the officer intervene?

Lines 1-2, "Let my lord hear the case of his servant," has parallels with 1 Samuel 26:19: "and now, please may my lord the king hear the words of his servant." The rules concerning the taking of a garment are seen in Exodus 22:26 and Deuteronomy 24:10-13, where a garment taken as a pledge is to be returned by nightfall (see also Amos 2:8; Prov 20:16; 27:13).

Perhaps the most interesting biblical parallels are to be found in the book of Ruth, which some think was written about the same time as the ostracon. But even if Ruth were written later, it refers to the organization of reaping that would have existed during the monarchy. In Ruth, the landowner Boaz leaves the reaping to "reapers," who are supervised by a member of his household, "the young man set over the reapers," quite possibly equivalent to the man Hoshayahu, who took this reaper's cloak. The word "stopping" in line 6 is equivalent to the end of Ruth 2:7, which is very obscure in the Hebrew but is now taken as meaning either "without resting even for a moment" (NRSV) or "before knocking-off time" (sunset).

4. Nonliterary Inscriptions.

Most of the inscriptions in this section are derived from incised stones used as seals. We do not merely have actual seals but also the impressions that were made in antiquity and which have survived, both on pottery (usually the handles of jars)—stamped onto the wet clay before firing—and on bullae, pieces of clay that were used to seal papyrus documents. Many of these bullae that have been discovered still bear traces of papyrus fibre and/or impressions of the cord used to tie the rolled-up papyrus. It is likely that a number of forgeries exist among these specimens, but we cannot be sure of detecting them. Because of this uncertainty no unprovenanced seals or seal impressions will be discussed here. It is better to have no information than false information.

4.1. Seals. Iron Age seals are usually relatively small (no larger than a quarter), ovoid, made of stone, often local limestone or much finer stone, but also semiprecious gems. Virtually no seals from this period were made of metal. The seals are almost universally stamp seals, which made their impression by pressing them into the wet clay, as opposed to cylinder seals, which were rolled across the clay. The seals were generally pierced through lengthwise so that they could be worn around the neck in a similar fashion to the Ketef Hinnom amulets. The engraving on the seals falls into three general categories: seals bearing only images, inscribed seals with images, and seals with only inscriptions. The engraving was done in mirror image so that the impression would be correctly oriented. One purpose of the seals was to indicate ownership. It could simply mark ownership of a vessel (and presumably of its contents), or it could be used to seal a vessel closed in preparation for shipping to ensure nothing was lost along the way (or added) and that the owner had sent the required amount (cf. Davies 2.004.2 and 2.017.6-7 noted above). Or it could be used to seal a document, to indicate the sender, to authorize any command in it. 1 Kings 21:8 illustrates all three significances: "So she [Jezebel] wrote letters in Ahab's name and sealed them with his seal" (NRSV).

The seals generally date from the eighth to sixth centuries BCE, with the decorated seals predominating in the eighth century and the seals without decoration in the seventh and sixth centuries. Most of the decorated seals belong to a different subcategory called *lmlk* seals ("belonging to the king"), and will be discussed separately below. Almost all of the seals from throughout this period, whether decorated or not, follow the same pattern of a prefixed *lamed* signifying "belonging to," then the name of the owner followed by the word *bn* ("son of") or more rarely *bt* ("daughter of"; Davies 100.412), then the father's name in a lower register. Between the two registers there may be two ruled lines or there may be some image. Rarely there is a third name: this may be a personal name or it may be an animal.

We do not have any provenanced personal seal of any king of Israel or Judah. We have some putative examples, but they have been proved to be forgeries. The provenanced seals we do have seem to be official seals, used by men and women in the discharge of their duties. We do not know whether or not we have seals of nobility, men of social class independent of their service to the king. Some of the seals with references to family names rather than, or in addition to, patronymics, may be of such a type.

Also on some of the seals certain titles or professions are indicated (cf. Hestrin for a list of these titles), for example, "servant of the king" (2 Kings 22:12; 2 Chron 24:20) and "governor of the city" (1 Kings 22:26). One seal (Davies 100.068) reads, "belonging to Shema, servant of Jeroboam." This seal most likely belonged to an official in the court of Jeroboam II of Israel (786-746 BCE), leaving Jeroboam II to be the only king mentioned on a provenanced seal.

Of the dozen or so seals belonging to *women that have been published in recent years, two are provenanced. The presence of seals and seal impressions bearing women's names is very significant for our understanding of the roles of women in ancient Israel. The fact that a woman had her own seal meant that she would be able to mark objects as belonging to her and would also be able to speak on her own authority. The presence of a jar stamp with the name of a woman is even more striking (Davies 100.733), as the jar stamps are from people with a certain degree of authority and are to be considered officials or military officers. A certain Hannah's seal was used not just to send a personal communication but to mark a jar of wine or oil or something similar with her seal, claiming her ownership. Could it be that she was responsible for paying taxes, as in the Samaria ostraca? Or that she was involved in overseeing the production of wine or oil? She could be a "noble," acting similarly to an official.

4.2. Bullae. Of the 276 bullae collected in Davies, only 45 are provenanced. Of the 231 that are unprovenanced, 212 came from a single collection. It is possible that many of these bullae are genuine, but we cannot take the risk of adding false information to the study of the seals and seal impressions. Therefore, gone is the

bulla referring to Berekyahu son of Neryahu the scribe, thought to be of Jeremiah's amanuensis (Jer 36:32), and gone too is the bulla referring to Gedaliah, servant of the king. Some real gems remain, however. Many of these bullae came from the City of David. This is a priceless resource, and collections such as this that come from a controlled excavation need to be the basis of scholarly discussion of the material.

Among particularly interesting examples are a bulla of "Gedaliah, who is over the house" (Davies 100.149; perhaps to be identified with the governor of 2 Kings 25:22), two with the title "son of the king," which occurs several times in the Bible, and another "belonging to Gemaryahu, son of Shaphan" (Davies 100.802), which precisely matches Jeremiah 36:10.

4.3. Seal Impressions on Jar Handles. There are two basic types of seal impressions on jars (mostly on the handles). The first is from a class of seal commonly called "private seals," and the second are known as "lammelek," or "belonging to the king," seal impressions, because they have *lmlk* on the top register (or are identical to those that have this inscribed, though it happens to be missing on these particular seals). These are obviously royal seals, though it is not clear whether at this time there was any distinction between the king's private estates ("privy purse") and the possessions of the state ("crown property"). They form the largest group of seal impressions we have. The private seals were originally thought to be owned by private citizens, as most of them have only the name and patronym. However, the types of jars on which they occur are the same types as those with "royal" seals, the same seal impression is found on widely distributed sites, and they come from the same time period as the royal seals. There are jars on which there is a *lmlk* seal on one handle and a "private" seal on the other. Furthermore, with the discovery of the three Eliashib seals (which would be considered private due to the general lack of any title or designation on the seals; Davies 100.231; 100.232; 100.282), and the knowledge that we have about Eliashib from the Arad archives, it is clear that many of these so-called private seals are also seals of officials of the king or military officers acting in their official roles. Therefore the designation "nonroyal" seal impressions will be used here.

4.3.1. Nonroyal Seal Impressions. These seal impressions are usually found on the handles of jars or other closed vessels and are often found alone or else with a number of other seal impressions, including *lmlk*. Some of these seal impressions have titles, but most do not. In fact, among the provenanced material to date, "servant of the king" spelled with ʿ*bd* (i.e., slave, or metaphorically for feudal dependent) occurs only on seals, whereas "servant of the king" with *n*ʿ*r* (member of household) occurs only on stamped jar handles. Whereas we would expect *n*ʿ*r* to be found on jars rather than bullae sealing documents (and would not expect ʿ*bd* on a jar, but would expect them on bullae), it is interesting to note that no bullae with ʿ*bd* and no seals with *n*ʿ*r* have been discovered in controlled excavations. Similarly, we only have "Royal Steward" and "son of the king" from bullae. Since the jar handle impressions have been made by seals it is merely a curious anomaly that will no doubt be eliminated with further controlled excavation of material.

4.3.2. lmlk Seal Impressions (Davies 105.001-105.020). Of all the Hebrew inscriptions from controlled excavations, by far the most common are the *lmlk* stamped jar handles. To date, well over 1,500 of these jar handles have been discovered in Judaean sites over the past 130 or so years. They all date to the late eighth century BCE, and lately they have been dated even more closely to the time of Hezekiah. The distribution of the seal impressions seems to bear out this identification. Amazingly enough, all of these seal impressions can be traced to only twenty-two seals. Davies classifies these seals according to the classification system established by A. Lemaire (*see* Lemaire). Generally the seals have three registers, with a decoration as the middle register. The seals fall into two general groups: those with the depiction of a four-winged scarab beetle in flight, and those with a two-winged flying sun disk (cf. Egyptian, Assyrian and, with AhuraMazda, Old Persian) or perhaps a flying scroll ("and behold, a flying scroll," Zech 5:1). Since the object here has a rectangular shape and traces of what could be string tying it, I prefer the designation of a scroll.

One of four place names are (predominantly) noted on the seals, *Hebron (e.g., 2 Sam 5:1, etc.); Socoh ("Socoh which is in Judah," 1 Sam 17:1); Ziph (Josh 15:24, 55; 1 Sam 23:14, 15, 24; 26:2, etc.); and *mmšt*, an unknown designation. In Lemaire's classification scheme, "I" repre-

sents those seals with the winged scarab beetle, "II" represents the two-winged scroll, "H" represents Hebron, "Z" represents Ziph, "S" represents Socoh and "M" represents *mmšt*. The full inscription reads *lmlk* [beetle] *ḥbrn* belonging to the king—Hebron; *lmlk* [] *z(y)p*, belonging to the king—Ziph; *lmlk* [] *śwkh*, belonging to the king—Socoh, *lmlk* [] *mmšt*, belonging to the king—*mmšt*. Furthermore, on some two-winged scroll seals there is only the place name, no *lmlk* (Type "IIc"), and others lack the place name, having only *lmlk* (referred to as "X"). A final style has no inscription, only the winged scroll, represented by "O." There are also two styles for each type of seal with both inscribed words.

The chemical analysis of the clay of the storage jars shows that all of the storage jars that bear these impressions were made at the same site, somewhere in the Shephelah. It also appears that the nonroyal stamps and the *lmlk* stamps are related. They both show up on the same vessels, and otherwise the types of vessels are the same, having the same area of distribution. Since all of these storage jars and seal impressions date to the late eighth century BCE, it can be assumed that the king is Hezekiah. The storage jars are probably connected in some way to the distribution of provisions to the various military garrisons and outposts that served to feed the military.

The picture we get from 2 Chronicles 32:1-8 is that Hezekiah made extensive preparations for his revolt against Assyria. The digging of the Siloam tunnel is just one example of those preparations, and here with the nearly 2,000 stamped jar handles spread throughout his kingdom is another.

See also ARCHAEOLOGY, SYRO-PALESTINIAN; HEBREW LANGUAGE; NON-ISRAELITE WRITTEN SOURCES: SYRO-PALESTINIAN; WRITING, WRITING MATERIALS AND LITERACY IN THE ANCIENT NEAR EAST.

BIBLIOGRAPHY. **Y. Aharoni,** *Arad Inscriptions* (JDS; Jerusalem: Israel Exploration Society, 1981); **S. Ahituv,** *Handbook of Ancient Hebrew Inscriptions from the Period of the First Commonwealth and the Beginning of the Second Commonwealth* (Jerusalem: Mosad Bialik, 1992) (Hebrew); **N. Avigad,** "The Epitaph of a Royal Steward from Siloam Village," *IEJ* 3 (1953) 137-52; idem, "The Second Tomb-Inscription of the Royal Steward," *IEJ* 5 (1955) 163-66; **G. Barkay, M. J. Lundberg, A. G. Vaughn, B. Zuckerman,**

K. Zuckerman, "The Challenges of Ketef Hinnom: Using Advanced Technologies to Reclaim the Earliest Biblical Texts and Their Context," *NEA* 66.4 (2003) 162-71; **F. M. Cross,** "The Cave Inscriptions from Khirbet Beit Lei," in *Near Eastern Archaeology in the Twentieth Century: Essays in Honor of Nelson Glueck,* ed. J. A. Sanders (Garden City, NY: Doubleday, 1970) 299-306; **G. I. Davies,** *Ancient Hebrew Inscriptions: Corpus and Concordance* (Cambridge: Cambridge University Press, 1991); **W. G. Dever,** "Iron Age Epigraphic Material from the Area of Khirbet el-Kôm," *HUCA* 40 (1970) 139-204; **S. L. Gogel,** *A Grammar of Epigraphic Hebrew,* ed. M. A. Sweeney (SBL Resources for Biblical Study 23; Atlanta: Scholars Press, 1998); **J. M. Hadley,** *The Cult of Asherah in Ancient Israel and Judah: Evidence for a Hebrew Goddess* (UCOP 57; Cambridge: Cambridge University Press, 2000); **B. Halpern,** "Biblical or Israelite History," in *The Future of Biblical Studies: The Hebrew Scriptures,* ed. R. E. Friedman and H. G. M. Williamson (Atlanta: Scholars Press, 1987) 103-39; **R. Hestrin,** "Hebrew Seals of Officials," in *Ancient Seals and the Bible,* ed. L. Gorelick and E. Williams-Forte (Malibu, CA: Undena Publications, 1983) 50-54; **A. Lemaire,** "Classification des Estampilles Royale Judéennes," *ErIsr* 15 (1981) 54*-60*, Plate VIII; **S. L. McKenzie,** *The Trouble with Kings* (VTSup 42; Leiden: E. J. Brill 1991); **A. R. Millard,** "An Assessment of the Evidence for Writing in Ancient Israel," in *Biblical Archaeology Today: Proceedings of the International Congress on Biblical Archaeology, Jerusalem, April 1984,* ed. J. Amitai (Jerusalem: Israel Exploration Society, 1985) 301-12; **P. D. Miller Jr.,** "Psalms and Inscriptions," in VTSup 32, *Congress Volume, Vienna 1980,* ed. J. Emerton (Leiden: E. J. Brill, 1981) 311-32; **J. Naveh,** "A Hebrew Letter from the Seventh Century B.C.," *IEJ* 10 (1960) 129-39; idem, "Old Hebrew Inscriptions in a Burial Cave," *IEJ* 13 (1963) 74-92; **D. Pardee,** "Literary Sources for the history of Palestine and Syria. II: Hebrew, Moabite, Ammonite, and Edomite Inscriptions," *AUSS* 17 (1979) 47-69; **S. B. Parker,** *Stories in Scripture and Inscriptions: Comparative Studies on Narratives in Northwest Semitic Inscriptions and the Hebrew Bible* (New York: Oxford University Press, 1997); **A. F. Rainey,** "Toward a Precise Date for the Samaria Ostraca," *BASOR* 272 (1988) 69-74; **J. Renz and W. Röllig,** eds., *Handbuch der Althebräischen Epigraphik* (3 vols.; Darmstadt: Wissenshaftliche Buchgesellschaft, 1995); **D. Ussishkin,** "On the Shorter Inscription from the 'Tomb of the Royal Steward,'" *BASOR* 196 (1969) 16-22; **W. Whitt,** "The Story of the Semitic Alphabet," *CANE* 4:2379-97.   J. M. Hadley

HEBREW LANGUAGE

With few exceptions, Hebrew was the original language in which the texts of the OT were written. Except for Ezra 4:8—6:18; 7:12-26, which were written in *Aramaic, the Historical Books were composed in the Hebrew language. This article provides a general overview of the characteristics of Hebrew, and then it notes some of the recent discussions about the distinctions in the Hebrew used in the Historical Books, particularly between the Hebrew of Joshua—2 Kings and that of Chronicles and Ezra-Nehemiah.

1. General Characteristics of Hebrew
2. Hebrew in the Historical Books

1. General Characteristics of Hebrew.

The term *Hebrew* as a name of a language originates in the Hellenistic period around 180 BCE, when it appears in the prologue to the book of Sirach. Within the Hebrew Bible, *Hebrew* never refers to the language itself, but rather is an ethnic designation of an individual person or group (*see* Hebrews), usually spoken from the perspective of a non-Hebrew person (e.g., 1 Sam 4:6, 9). When it is named, the Hebrew language is usually called *yĕhûdît,* "the language of Judah," or "Judahite" (2 Kings 18:26, 28; 2 Chron 32:18; Neh 13:24). This designation in these specific passages, however, refers only to the language spoken in and around Jerusalem in the fifth and sixth centuries BCE. The broader language spoken by the peoples who occupied the nations of Israel and Judah collectively during the first millennium BCE is never given a name within the Hebrew Bible itself, but is, rather, generally called *śēpat kĕnaʿan,* "the language of Canaan" (Is 19:18).

1.1. Context, Origin and Inscriptional Evidence. Hebrew belongs to the Semitic language family. The Semitic group comprises approximately seventy different languages and dialects, spoken in the general geographical area bounded by the Horn of Africa, the Mediterranean Sea, the Caspian Sea and the Tigris River Valley. Scholars usually differentiate three smaller groupings within the larger family: East Semitic (Eblaite and Akkadian, itself further composed of the dialects of Babylonian and Assyrian; attested from

2350 BCE), South Semitic (composed of Ethiopic, the South Arabian dialects and North Arabic, which includes classical Arabic) and Northwest Semitic (composed of Ugaritic, Phoenician-Punic, Ammonite, Edomite, Moabite, Aramaic and Hebrew). These various Semitic language groups share many grammatical features and lexical roots.

Hebrew as a distinct language probably had its origin in the latter part of the second millennium BCE. The earliest datable extrabiblical inscription written in Hebrew is the Gezer Calendar, usually assigned to the tenth century BCE. Various collections of Hebrew inscriptions have been discovered dating from the eighth century BCE: the pithoi inscriptions from Kuntillet-Ajrud, the Khirbet el-Qom tomb inscription, the Samaria ostraca and the Siloam tunnel inscription. The sixth century BCE, likewise, produced several collections that have been found, most importantly the Arad letters and the Lachish letters. These various writings are important for showing the character of the Hebrew language in the first half of the first millennium BCE (*see* Hebrew Inscriptions). Thus they have been used recently as evidence for dating various biblical writings (Davies; Ehrensvärd; Hurvitz 2001).

1.2. Alphabet and Orthography.

1.2.1. Consonants. Hebrew is written and read from right to left and employs a system of twenty-two signs in its alphabet, which represent twenty-three consonantal sounds. The discrepancy between the number of signs and sounds is due to the sign שׁ, which usually represented the /sh/ sound (later called a *shin*) but occasionally stood for another sibilant sound (later called a *sin*). Which sound the single sign represented in a particular context would have been as unambiguous for Hebrew speakers as the English consonant C is for English speakers: C = /k/ in "cow," but C = /s/ in "city." Vowel signs were not originally indicated in the written version of the biblical text. Thus the Hebrew alphabet consists only of consonants. In the same way that a literate English speaker can distinguish words without vowels—THS SNTNC S NT HRD T RD—likewise, when Hebrew was a living language, vowels were not seen as vital to the written form.

1.2.2. Matres Lectionis. Early in the development of the language three of the consonant signs began to represent basic, long vowel sounds, in addition to their usual consonantal sounds. These consonants are called *matres lectionis,* or "mothers of reading." The letters *yod, waw* and *hey* often represent, respectively, i-class vowel sounds (produced in the middle of the mouth), u-class vowel sounds (produced in the front of the mouth near the lips) and a-class vowel sounds (produced in the back of the mouth and in the throat). Since the consonantal sounds represented by these three consonants rarely appear on the end of words in Hebrew, these signs were employed to unambiguously represent final long /i/, /u/ or /a/ sounds. When these vowel sounds were appended to the end of a word, the corresponding consonant would represent the sounds. Thus the final *waw* on the written word *ymšlw* clearly represents the /u/ sound: *yimšĕlû,* "they will rule." If vowel sounds were not represented at all, one could not distinguish between, for example, *yimšĕlû,* "they will rule," and *yimšōl,* "he will rule"—both would be written *ymšl.*

Around the beginning of the eighth century BCE the *waw* and *yod* also occasionally began to represent long vowel sounds in the middle of words. Medial *matres lectionis,* however, do not consistently appear, even within the same text. Within the corpus of the Hebrew Bible the same word may appear with and without an internal *mater* even within a verse. In Jeremiah 3:12, for example, the negation *lōʾ,* "not," appears both with and without the internal *mater waw: lwʾ ʾpyl pny,* "I will not look," and *lʾ ʾṭwr,* "I will not be angry."

1.2.3. Masoretic Vowel Points. Between 600 and 1000 CE various schools were organized in Babylon and in Palestine, the most well-known of which was at Tiberias on the Sea of Galilee. The intention of these academies included protecting the biblical text and representing, by the use of diacritical marks, its pronunciation, particularly noting the vowel sounds that should be pronounced when reading the consonantal text aloud. Although the vocalization of the consonantal Hebrew text was done over a millennium after the final OT texts were written, there is significant evidence that the work of the Masoretes represents a reading of the text that dates at least to the early centuries of the Common Era (Waltke and O'Connor, 22-28).

1.3. Grammar and Morphology. On a rudimentary level the grammatical structure of Semitic languages in general, and Hebrew in particular, can be thought of as the intersection of "roots" and "affixes." Roots are the basic building blocks of the language and most often consist of a series of three consonants, which usually have a broad field of meanings. Onto these roots certain affixes—prefixes on the beginning of the root, infixes in the middle of the root, suffixes on the end of the root—are applied to define and delimit the particular meaning that a word may have.

1.3.1. Nouns and Adjectives. For example, the root *mem-lamed-kaf* has the broad field of meaning of "ruling" or "having dominion." Various particular nouns having to do with that broad concept have *mlk* as their basic foundation, each of which is defined by the particular affixes that appear: *melek,* "a king"; *malkâ,* "a queen"; *mamlākâ,* "dominion." The affixes that appear in these three words (*-e-e-* and *-â* and *m—â*) regularly appear on other roots, representing very similar types of nouns—for example, ʿ*br* = "passing over": ʿ*ēber,* "region beyond"; ʿ*ăbārâ,* "a ford in a river"; *maʿbārâ,* "a passage." This intersection of foundational roots and regularly applied affixes forms the morphological and grammatical basis upon which Hebrew rests.

1.3.2. Verbal System. The system of roots and affixes also applies for the verbal system, in which the triconsonantal root signals the broad meaning and regularly applied affixes signal the various verbal forms. It must be acknowledged that the Hebrew verbal system is the most debated area within the study of Hebrew, and the present discussion provides only the most introductory of remarks (see McFall).

Unlike English verbs, Hebrew verbs are not marked for tense. Thus one cannot read an isolated Hebrew verbal form and tell whether the action of the verb occurred in the past, occurs in the present or will occur in the future. This does not mean, however, that Hebrew has no sense of time or that tense is completely removed from the language. Hebrew verbs do not, of course, occur in isolation, and in the majority of cases the tense of a particular verbal form is clearly discernable from context. The purpose of the varying forms of finite verbs in Hebrew usually is attributed in grammars as marking the particular verb forms for aspect. A perfective verbal form describes a complete, completed or punctual action, while an imperfective verbal form describes an incomplete, durative or habitual action.

The verbal system, broadly speaking, is set up on a continuum of, on one extreme, the two finite verbal forms (variously called either perfect or *qatal,* and imperfect or *yiqtol*), which describe real actions done in real time (e.g., "he ran," "she will run"). Next on the continuum are the volitive forms (imperative, cohortative, jussive), which express real actions or attitudes desired by the speaker to be done or achieved (e.g., "run!" "let's run!" "would that they ran!"). Next on the continuum are the infinitive forms (infinitive absolute and infinitive construct). The infinitive absolute functions primarily as an adverb, emphasizing the force or duration of a complementary finite verb (e.g., "he really ran," "he kept running"). The infinitive construct describes verbal ideas independent of persons, often performing the role of nouns (e.g., "to run," "running"). Next, and at the other extreme of the continuum, are the participial forms, in which a person or thing is defined by the verbal idea (e.g., "a runner"). At this point in the continuum the participial verbal sense is very close to the sense of nouns.

The verbal system is also organized according to a series of seven "stems" or "themes," which describe various types of activity/passivity as well as types of causation. The seven stems are organized in three groupings. The first group, which includes the Qal and Nifal stems, provides the basic verbal meaning. The Qal is the basic, active verbal form (e.g., "it broke"). Nifal is the passive (or reflexive) form ("it was broken," "it broke itself"). The second grouping, which includes the Piel, Pual and Hitpael stems, is factitive and describes the causing or bringing about of a particular state of being. In these stems the significance of the verbal idea is in the state of being that is accomplished by the verb, rather than the verbal action itself. Piel is the active factitive form ("she made it [to be] broken"); Pual is the passive factitive form ("it was made [to be] broken"); Hitpael is the reflexive or iterative form ("he made himself [to be] broken"). The third grouping, which includes the Hifil and Hofal stems, represents an action that a subject causes a direct object to perform. In these stems the significance of the verbal idea is focused on the action that is caused. Hifil is the active causative form ("they made it [to] break"); Hofal is the passive causative form ("it was made [to] break") (Waltke and O'Connor, 343-61).

Since English does not mark verbs for causation, the same Hebrew verb present in multiple stems usually is translated into English using different verbs. For instance, in regard to the earlier example of the root ʿbr = "passing over," the Qal of the root usually is translated simply as "to pass through" or "to cross," as in 1 Samuel 9:4: "He [Saul] *passed through* the hill country of Ephraim and *passed through* the land of Shalishah, but they did not find them [his father's donkeys]. And they *passed through* the land of Shaalim, but they were not there. Then he *passed through* the land of Benjamin, but they did not find them." When the verb appears in Hifil (meaning "to cause something to pass through"), however, it is variously translated in the NRSV of the books of Samuel as "to spread" (1 Sam 2:24), "to bring" (2 Sam 2:8; 19:15, 19, 40, 41), "to transfer" (2 Sam 3:10), "to put away" (2 Sam 12:13), "to send" (2 Sam 12:31) and "to take away" (2 Sam 24:10). In each of these cases, of course, the basic meaning of "to cause something to pass through" is present, but translating each of the verbs in such a way would produce awkward English. Moreover, in 1 Kings 6:21 the verb ʿbr appears in Piel (meaning "to cause something to be passed" or, more clearly, "to cause something to be transfixed"). The NRSV translates the verb here as "to draw across": "And Solomon overlaid the inside of the house with pure gold, and he *drew* chains of gold *across* [it]." Yet the significance of the verb is not in explaining what Solomon actually did, but rather in showing what state of being Solomon brought about: "And Solomon made the inside of the house [to be] overlaid with pure gold, and he made chains of gold [to be] transfixed across it." Having an appreciation for the system of stems in Hebrew helps the exegete not only to recognize the nuances of meaning presented by verbs, but also to note different passages that might be parallel because they share vocabulary, although the same verb may be translated very differently because of the various stems in which the root may appear.

1.4. Syntax. It is generally acknowledged that all Semitic languages of the second millennium BCE, including perhaps archaic Hebrew, had a declension system for nouns. Thus certain suffix endings were attached to nouns to indicate their function in a sentence. The "subject noun" of a sentence would have had a *-u* suffix if singular, *-ū* if plural, and *-ā* if it regularly occurred in pairs. A noun that functioned as an adjective or was the object of a preposition was a "genitive

noun," and it would have had the corresponding suffixes *-i, -ī, -ay*. A noun that functioned as an adverb or was the direct object of a verb was an "accusative noun," and it would have had the suffixes *-a, -ī, -ay*. The system of singular and plural noun case endings, however, was lost in all first-millennium BCE Northwest Semitic languages, including almost all examples of inscriptional and biblical Hebrew. Although dual case endings appear in a few texts dated to the early first millennium BCE (e.g., the Gezer Calendar), they too seem to have soon faded thereafter from the syntax of Hebrew.

With the loss of the case system, Hebrew relied more heavily upon word order and syntactical relationships between words to express meaning. Thus it is the system of Hebrew syntax—the ways in which words are ordered and regularly combined into groups to form phrases, clauses and sentences—that contributes most directly to the expression of sense and meaning in the language. The study of Hebrew syntax is a complex field. Recent studies by Waltke and O'Connor and by Arnold and Choi are clear expositions of this area of study.

1.5. Metasyntactical Markers. The original texts of the OT not only had no representations for vowel sounds (with the exception of the few *matres lectionis*), but also they had no chapter divisions, punctuation or any formatting conventions to organize and designate the different larger and smaller blocks of material that constitute long narratives. For example, the books of Samuel and Kings clearly do not form one long undifferentiated story; rather, they are composed of a collection of individual stories, each having an internal coherence and integrity, and each having a (usually) clear beginning, middle and ending. Moreover, it is apparent that these stories are further composed of smaller blocks of material that we might term paragraphs, in which a narrative sequence moves, generally uninterrupted, from initiation to termination. Furthermore, it is plain that there are some clauses and sentences that do not cause the narrative of a paragraph to progress but rather provide parenthetical information, much like an actor in a play might speak an aside directly to the audience. Finally, it is clear that there are some extended blocks of material that do not provide a real narrative sequence at all but rather provide the setting of a following story or explain the summation or denouement of a preceding story. Without the use of indentation or parentheses or font changes, Hebrew relied upon the use of a relatively constant, regular set of syntactical constructions to signal for the reader these types of larger organizing elements.

The normal, default narrative sequence in biblical Hebrew narrative is accomplished by the *waw*-consecutive or *wayyiqtol* verbal form. Practically all biblical stories have as their backbone a series of clauses, each governed by an active *wayyiqtol* verbal form. These *wayyiqtol* chains are what propel the narratives from one action or incident to the next: "And he did A, and then he did B, and then she did C, and then they did D." Clauses that are not governed by active *wayyiqtol* verbal forms break the chain and cause the narrative to be shaped in any number of ways. Such clauses may mark initiations or terminations of paragraph blocks. The use of participial or verbless clauses often provides information apart from the narrative flow. Groups of non-*wayyiqtol* clauses often provide a detailed setting or denouement of a following or preceding narrative.

Examples of this type of metasyntactical structuring are found throughout the Historical Books. Perhaps one example may be helpful. In 2 Samuel 16:1-15 the story is told of David granting the inheritance of Saul to Ziba the servant of Saul's son Mephibosheth, and of Shimei cursing David for the violence supposedly incited by him against Saul. The initiation of the story is marked by an independent perfect verb form in the first clause of 2 Samuel 16:1. A parenthetical statement about the approach of Ziba with various wares is marked by a series of three verbless clauses in the rest of 2 Samuel 16:1. The narrative sequence proper begins in 2 Samuel 16:2 with a series of *wayyiqtol* clauses that continues uninterrupted through 2 Samuel 16:4. 2 Samuel 16:5-8 is set apart as an extended parenthetical comment by its assorted complex of perfects, participles, verbless clauses and nonsequential *wayyiqtol*s. 2 Samuel 16:9-13 again picks up the primary narrative sequence with its chain of sequential *wayyiqtol* clauses, which terminates in the final clause of 2 Samuel 16:13 with a perfect with a prefixed *waw*, a *weqatal*. 2 Samuel 16:14-15 provides another parenthetical statement about the goings of David and Absalom, being composed of nonsequential *wayyiqtol* clauses, a participle, a *qatal* and a verbless clause. Rather than simply being a series of independent clauses, the combination of particular clause types signals for the reader whether the information in the clause is part of the main narrative sequence of the plot (2 Sam 16:2-4, 9-13), begins or ends a narrative block (2 Sam 16:16aα, 13bβ), whether the information details a parenthetical bit of information (2 Sam 16:16b), or whether the information is an extended parenthetical description of supporting information (2 Sam 16:5-7, 14-15) (Heller, 316-27).

A growing number of scholars have recognized that limiting the study of Hebrew grammar and syntax to the level of clause and sentence does not adequately account for these larger narrative organizational functions that are played by particular syntactical constructions (*see* Linguistics, esp. §2, "Linguistic Approaches to Hebrew"). The study and exposition of these metasyntactical constructions is the work of discourse linguistics, also known as "discourse analysis" or "text linguistics." Several recent studies have been particularly helpful in explaining this burgeoning discipline (Bodine 1992; 1995; Bergen; Miller 1996; 1999; van der Merwe, Naude and Kroeze).

2. Hebrew in the Historical Books.

The preceding overview of the status of Hebrew generally applies for all the texts found throughout the Historical Books. There are, however, notable differences between the Hebrew of the *Deuteronomistic History (Joshua—2 Kings) and that found in *1-2 Chronicles and *Ezra-Nehemiah. These differences were first systematically discussed by W. Gesenius in 1815 in his *Geschichte der hebräischen Sprache und Schrift*. Furthermore, almost a century later, S. Driver forcefully argued that the differences between the two corpora are attributable to different chronological stages of the language. He noted that Chronicles and Ezra-Nehemiah (as well as Ecclesiastes, Esther and Daniel) were linguistically distinct from the rest of the Hebrew Bible and represented a late stage of the language, which he called "New Hebrew." This formulation and subsequent research continued apace throughout much of the twentieth century.

In the 1970s the diachronic study of Hebrew received two further refinements. A. Hurvitz has argued that the parallel texts in Samuel-Kings and Chronicles systematically reveal that the differences between them are based on linguistic differences between two languages rather than simple stylistic differences between two authors. His work focuses upon the morphological and lexical differences between the two texts and concentrates in particular upon Aramaic words that are found in the Chronicles and Ezra-Nehemiah corpus. He argues that the changes that occur in the later texts are due mainly to Aramaic influence (Hurvitz 1972; 1982). He is, however, quick to point out that Aramaisms in a biblical text are not de facto indications of late biblical Hebrew.

On the other hand, R. Polzin, in his analysis of the Hebrew of Chronicles, almost completely ignores the parallel texts with Samuel-Kings, believing that the independent Chronicles texts can give a clearer insight into the language of the Chronicler (see Chronicler's History). Moreover, he suggests that looking at the language from a broader grammatical/syntactical perspective provides a firmer basis for analysis. Polzin (11, 27-28) argues that the differences between the two sets of texts are due to the natural evolution of the language through time rather than to any particular Aramaic influence.

More recently, however, this straightforward diachronic schema has been revised on several fronts. On the one hand, I. Young has noted that such arguments are based upon the assumption that "the language of the text under consideration has a relationship with the language used at the time of the composition of that text" (Young, 312). Yet the biblical texts as we have them (both within the Historical Books and elsewhere) are products not just of authors but also of *scribes who were involved in preserving and explaining the text. It is clear that part of the scribal tradition involved the introduction of tendencies toward archaizing (in which older words or forms are used in place of newer words or forms), modernizing (in which newer words or forms supplant older ones) and smoothing (in which lexical, grammatical or syntactical characteristics of texts are carried throughout a text, making the text more or less standard) (Waltke and O'Connor, 11-13).

There has also been a great deal of work on dialectical differences within the Deuteronomistic History itself. G. Rendsburg has shown that texts connected to the north have characteristics that reflect a distinct dialect that he calls "Israelian Hebrew." The connection of these texts with the north occurs in specific settings: poetic passages, wisdom texts that may have circulated throughout the West Semitic world, narratives set in the northern kingdom (because Israelian Hebrew shares many features with Aramaic) and narratives in which Arameans play a major role (Rendsburg 1992; 2002). With texts such as these, in which scribal activity often has blurred or skewed linguistic differences and in which dialectical differences play a role in synchronically produced texts, analyzing and explaining the differences between the Hebrew of the Deuteronomistic History and of Chronicles/Ezra-Nehemiah become much more nuanced and difficult. A collection of essays published in 2003, edited by I. Young, provides a thorough review of the arguments and perspectives.

See also ARAMAIC; HEBREW INSCRIPTIONS; LINGUISTICS; SCRIBES AND SCHOOLS; WRITING, WRITING MATERIALS AND LITERACY IN THE ANCIENT NEAR EAST.

BIBLIOGRAPHY. **B. T. Arnold and J. H. Choi,** *A Guide to Biblical Hebrew Syntax* (New York: Cambridge University Press, 2003); **R. D. Bergen,** ed., *Biblical Hebrew and Discourse Linguistics* (Winona Lake, IN: Eisenbrauns, 1994); **W. R. Bodine,** ed., *Discourse Analysis of Biblical Literature: What It Is and What It Offers* (SemeiaSt; Atlanta: Scholars Press, 1995); idem, ed., *Linguistics and Biblical Hebrew* (Winona Lake, IN: Eisenbrauns, 1992); **P. R. Davies,** *In Search of "Ancient Israel"* (JSOTSup 148; Sheffield: JSOT, 1992); **S. R. Driver,** *An Introduction to the Literature of the Old Testament* (Oxford: Clarendon Press, 1913); **M. Ehrensvärd,** "Once Again: The Problem of Dating Hebrew," *SJOT* 11 (1997) 29-40; **R. L. Heller,** *Narrative Structure and Discourse Constellations: An Analysis of Clause Function in Biblical Hebrew Prose* (HSS 55; Winona Lake, IN: Eisenbrauns, 2004); **A. Hurvitz,** "The Archaeological-Historical Debate on the Antiquity of the Hebrew Bible in the Light of Linguistic Research of the Hebrew Language," in *The Controversy over the Historicity of the Bible,* ed. I. L. Levine and A. Mazar [Hebrew] (Jerusalem: Yad Yitshak Ben-Zvi; Merkaz Dinur, 2001) 34-46; idem, *A Linguistic Study of the Relationship Between the Priestly Source and the Book of Ezekiel: A New Approach to an Old Problem* (Paris: Gabalda, 1982); idem, *The Transition Period in Biblical Hebrew: A Study of Post-Exilic Hebrew and Its Implications for the Dating of Psalms* [Hebrew] (Jerusalem: Mosad Harev Kook, 1972); **C. L. Miller,** *The Representa-*

tion of Speech in Biblical Hebrew Narrative: A Linguistic Analysis (HSM 55; Atlanta: Scholars Press, 1996); idem, *The Verbless Clause in Biblical Hebrew: Linguistic Approaches* (Winona Lake, IN: Eisenbrauns, 1999); **C. H. J. van der Merwe, J. A. Naude and J. H. Kroeze,** *A Biblical Hebrew Reference Grammar* (Biblical Languages: Hebrew 3; Sheffield: Sheffield Academic Press, 1999); **L. McFall,** *The Enigma of the Hebrew Verbal System: Solutions from Ewald to the Present Day* (HTIBS 2; Sheffield: Almond, 1982); **R. Polzin,** *Late Biblical Hebrew: Toward an Historical Typology of Biblical Hebrew Prose* (HSM 12; Missoula, MT: Scholars Press, 1976); **G. Rendsburg,** *Israelian Hebrew in the Books of Kings* (Bethesda, MD: CDL Press, 2002); idem, "Morphological Evidence for Regional Dialects in Ancient Hebrew," in *Linguistics and Biblical Hebrew*, ed. W. R. Bodine (Winona Lake, IN: Eisenbrauns, 1992) 65-88; **B. K. Waltke and M. O'Connor,** *An Introduction to Biblical Hebrew Syntax* (Winona Lake, IN: Eisenbrauns, 1990); **I. Young,** ed., *Biblical Hebrew: Studies in Chronology and Typology* (JSOTSup 369; London: T & T Clark, 2003).

R. L. Heller

HEBREWS

In modern parlance, *Hebrew* is above all the language preserved among Jewish people through the ages from their origins in Israel and Judah (*see* Hebrew Language). As an adjective, the term may also describe people or traditions that are Jewish or of Israelite heritage. In the Bible itself, however, the term is relatively rare, clearly not a general word for Israelite or Judahite identity. *Hebrews* appear in two main clusters: (1) the Jacob people in the Joseph and Moses stories (Gen 37—50; Ex 1—15), set against the *Egyptians; (2) the Israelites during the emergence of the monarchy (1 Samuel), set against the *Philistines. Somehow, the word reflects the particular contact of Israelites with lands to the south and west, away from Israel's traditional kinship with the inland peoples of Jordan and Syria. Many have wondered whether the word *Hebrew* (*ʿibrî*) is related to the West Semitic *ʿapiru*, a class of social renegades found all over Syria-Palestine in the Late Bronze Age. In spite of the compelling arguments for some connection, however, neither the form nor the meaning of the word *ʿapiru* offers a direct, intelligible avenue for deriving the Bible's *ʿibrî*. The archives of early second-millennium Mari provide a better etymology from another noun with the same verbal root. In the Mari evidence the *ʿibrum* (written as *hibrum*) is the mobile community that travels in the back country with the flocks, especially among the Binu Yamina tribespeople.

1. The Social and Political Significance of the "Hebrew" Category.
2. Hebrews in 1 Samuel.
3. Hebrews and Mari's *ʿibrum*.

1. The Social and Political Significance of the "Hebrew" Category.

The most common biblical name for the people at its center is *"Israel," until the division that produced a separate kingdom of Judah, which took its name from a southern tribe. The Israelite category is ultimately rooted in a political entity, a loose coalition of tribes that shared this identity especially to fight in mutual defense (see Judg 5). Not all biblical terms for identifying people by group carry this political aspect. When Laban is called an "Aramaean" (e.g., Gen 31:20), no single group that acts under the Aramaean banner is intended. Most biblical references to *Canaanites have the same broad identifying force, not bound to a political unit.

When we encounter the word *Hebrew* in the Joseph story, a similar nonpolitical category seems to be in view. Potiphar's wife calls Joseph a "Hebrew" when he is still the only member of his family in Egypt (Gen 39:14, 17). While in prison, Joseph himself tells the pharaoh's cupbearer about how he had been plundered from "the land of the Hebrews" (Gen 40:15). Eventually, we learn that Egyptians consider it repugnant to share a meal with Hebrews (Gen 43:32). None of this terminology defines a group capable of acting as a unit. By the time the family of Jacob has grown into the people of Israel in the generation of Moses, the "Hebrew" label is applied more restrictively to Israelites. The Hebrew midwives and mothers (Ex 1:15-19; 2:7), the Hebrew children (Ex 2:6) and the Hebrew workers (Ex 2:11-13) all seem to belong to the suffering but prolific Israelites (Ex 1:7, 9, 12). This limitation of Hebrew identity to Israelites is complete by the time the narrative reaches the first book of Samuel.

Regardless of the exact dates of our texts, they present a chronological awareness whereby the Israelite Hebrews could at one time have been regarded as part of a broader group that occupied the land of Joseph's family in Canaan.

Both aspects of the Hebrew terminology should be taken seriously: the notion of origin in a broader social category, and the specific identification with the body of all Israelites, once Jacob's clan had grown into a large tribal alliance. In light of the Bible's own chronological sense that in the world before Israel "Hebrews" were a category of people in Palestine, a connection with a broad class known outside the Bible is attractive. Defense of this early framework requires more space than is available here, but it is significant that the Bible situates Hebrews almost entirely in the second millennium BCE. For years, a connection with a broader class has been offered by the ʿapiru, a widely used category for defining outsiders and derived from a tantalizingly similar verbal root. At Mari, the ʿabirū were simply any people uprooted from their settled homes, and the term had no inherent negative cast. Several instances are now known for the cognate verb, which means simply "to leave one's place of fixed residence." By the Late Bronze Age, the word had acquired a pejorative aspect and implied the renegade status of outcasts from settled communities who represented a threat to the towns they had left behind.

The proposed relationship is immediately alluring because it would provide an external basis for a term that is strongly associated in the Bible with how foreigners identify Israelites during the period before the states. Because the West Semitic word ʿapiru occurs so widely as a prominent social category, and one that applies to displaced people who are automatically outsiders, it seems to resemble the Hebrews of the Joseph story. The different labials (b/p) need not represent an insuperable obstacle. M. Weippert accounts for the variation as "oscillation of the labial plosive before the following voiceless consonant" (Weippert, 74-82). The common Hebrew verb ʿbr, "to pass over, through, or by," seems to derive from the same transitional movement expressed in the old Mari examples of the verb for leaving one's residence.

Even if only an indirect relationship between ʿibrî and ʿapiru is proposed, however, there remain problems of both form and meaning. In purely formal terms, the two words belong to different types, with contrasting ʿibr- and ʿapir- vowel patterns. Furthermore, the Hebrews of the Bible are not easily derived from the outcasts of the ʿapiru class. The problem with different meanings is particularly striking in the book of 1 Sam-

uel, where the Philistines identify the Israelites as "Hebrew."

2. Hebrews in 1 Samuel.

Use of the "Hebrew" category is surprisingly limited in the Historical Books. Although Joseph tells the Egyptians that he came from "the land of the Hebrews," the Israelites are never said to encounter any Hebrews when they return to conquer the land. There are hostile Canaanites, Amorites, Hittites and others to be displaced, and there are potentially friendly Kenites and Midianites, but not a "Hebrew" to be found, either in Joshua or in Judges, even in exchanges with the Philistines. After *David establishes his rule over Judah and Israel, the word is equally absent, applied neither to Israelites nor to any other population.

We find the Hebrews only in the book of 1 Samuel, in the context of full-scale war between Israel and the Philistines, unlike the single-handed assaults of Samson in Judges 14—16. Before the appearance of *Saul, the Philistines fight and defeat Israel, whom they call "the Hebrews," near Aphek (1 Sam 4:6, 9). When Saul is established as king, and he and his son Jonathan turn their attention to the Philistines, Saul himself calls his people "Hebrews" (1 Sam 13:3). Israel fails in its resistance, however, and the narrator identifies fugitive Israelites who cross into the Transjordan as Hebrews (1 Sam 13:7). Under Philistine domi-nance the ruling people voice their concern that "the Hebrews" may arm themselves with swords and spears (1 Sam 13:19). Only Jonathan is capable of facing the Philistine invaders, alone with his armor-bearer, and when they launch their attack, the Philistines comment arrogantly that the Hebrews have at last come out of their hiding places (1 Sam 14:11). Jonathan's courageous raid leads to a wider Israelite victory, and the narrator speaks of "Hebrews" who had joined the Philistines but who are inspired to side with Saul and Jonathan (1 Sam 14:21). As soon as David enters the story, the Hebrew terminology disappears. Israel confronts Goliath and the Philistines without reference to Hebrews (1 Sam 17), and David continues the fight with marvelous success (1 Sam 18). David even lives among the Philistines (1 Sam 27). The only time the category appears after 1 Samuel 14 is when the Philistine commanders refuse David's company in war against Saul by identifying them as Hebrews (1 Sam 29:3).

As a group, the 1 Samuel references share the chronological sense of Genesis and Exodus, where the "Hebrew" category narrows by the time of Moses to identify Israelites alone. In these texts the Hebrews are always found in the plural, always describing Israelites who are gathered in opposition to the Philistines, especially for battle. As "Hebrews," the Israelites never speak or act as an explicit unit, but the term cannot be assigned a broad ethnic definition, to be separated from political coherence. Before the battle near Aphek the Philistines identify their enemy as "the camp of the Hebrews," and they fear that they may be subjected to rule by "the Hebrews," just as the Philistines themselves had ruled the Hebrews (1 Sam 4:6, 9). Israel does not unite to fight under a "Hebrew" identity, but the Hebrew entity identified by the Philistines from outside is essentially Israel. When Saul sounds the call to muster "the Hebrews," this is no open invitation to some broad ethnic group, but rather is addressed specifically to "all Israel" (1 Sam 13:3-4). In their conflict with these coastal neighbors, Israel's Hebrew identity mirrors to some degree the collective identity of the plural "Philistines" themselves, who also unite as such only for mutual defense. Philistia consisted of at least five independent city-based states, and the biblical category of plural "Philistines" derives from shared background as a distinguishable group whose identity preceded their establishment in southern Canaan. Egyptian texts from the early twelfth century BCE identify one of several enemy invaders from the sea as the "Peleset."

The Hebrews in 1 Samuel cannot easily be equated with or derived from the ʿapiru of the Late Bronze Age. From a Philistine perspective, the Hebrews are the back-country population in the interior hinterlands of a territory that the Philistines would like to control from their urban lowland centers. These Israelite Hebrews show an emergent political coherence and certainly are not defined by their removal from recognized social networks. If there is one group portrayed in 1 Samuel that would fit the Late Bronze definition of the ʿapiru, it is David and his roaming band of malcontents (1 Sam 22:1-2), and they are not defined as Hebrews. David and his band are only called Hebrews when the Philistine commanders refuse to accept them as true free agents. The Philistines insist that in the end, the loyalties of this renegade group will remain with the settled Israelites whom they had left. The Hebrew identity links David to the Israelites, and he is perceived as a danger to the Philistine force because he retains this association with his social group as "Hebrew," not because he has abandoned it.

In broad terms, this usage of the word *Hebrew* is consistent with its occurrences elsewhere in the Bible. In both the Joseph and the Moses stories that link the books of Genesis and Exodus, Hebrews are regarded as foreign and eventually as a threat because of their numbers. The idea that the term itself is portrayed as derogatory, however, is overplayed. Hebrews are foreigners who do not even enjoy the status of citizenship from a recognized state, and Egyptians were famous for distancing themselves from foreigners. In the Amarna letters political marriages only brought the daughters of foreign kings to Egypt, never the reverse.

Three more texts define slaves who are Israelite kin as "Hebrew"(Ex 21:2; Deut 15:12; Jer 34:14). The special status of the Hebrew slaves seems to come not from classification as a type of slavery but simply as a definition of inclusion in the inside social group, "our people." This usage is consistent with that of 1 Samuel. The real conundrum is not what the word means here, but why it was preserved in slave law alone. In Deuteronomy 15 the law for freeing slaves (Deut 15:12-18) contrasts with the law for canceling debts (Deut 15:1-11), where the "brother Israelite" is opposed to the "foreigner."

3. Hebrews and Mari's ʿibrum.

In suggesting that the biblical word ʿibri finds its most closely attested cognate in a social category from the tribal peoples known to the Mari archives in the eighteenth century BCE, I am consciously extending my own larger exploration of how the Bible may preserve threads of Israelite heritage that go back to the Bronze Age. These lines of connection ground Israelite identity in social categories that are not originally or uniquely Israelite, and they are embedded in biblical traditions that present them as pre-Israelite, especially in the book of Genesis. I have suggested elsewhere that the Genesis tradition of ancestral roots in northern Syria finds no adequate explanation in Israelite interests of the first millennium BCE. Most striking is the choice of far northern Harran as the home of Abraham's and Jacob's closest kin. Although the co-incidence of the likeness of the tribal name "Bin-yamin" (Benjamin) to the Binu Yamina tribal confederacy has long been considered just that, we now know that these Binu Yamina represented the southwestern division of a tribal duality whose grazing ranges were understood to span all of modern Syria. It then turns out that these Binu Yamina had strong links with the *Balih* River region, where Harran was one of the urban centers of the Yaminites' closest allies, the confederacy of Zalmaqum. The Genesis tradition of north Syrian ancestral origins seems to have a particularly Yaminite cast, an affiliation that should not be surprising when we realize that in the Middle Bronze Age the Binu Yamina were not a local tribe but rather a far-flung coalition whose activities already reached far toward pre-Israelite Palestine.

In Mari evidence, the ʿibrum is the component of the Binu Yamina population that is based in the dry steppe, traveling with the flocks. All Yaminites were identified as either town dwellers or back-country ʿibrum. The ʿibrum is not known to us from anything like the number and range of documents that attest the ʿapiru, but surely this reflects its use for the mobile herders among a tribal confederacy that left us no urban archive of the Mari sort. In spite of its relative obscurity, the ʿibrum was no minor local phenomenon; it was the dominant social category for the mobile sheep-herding communities that ranged across southwestern Syria during the Mari period.

An etymology of ʿibri that is focused on the ancient ʿibrum retains many of the advantages of the ʿapiru etymology. The word ʿibrum comes from the same verbal root as ʿapiru, in documentation that attests both nouns, along with the verb from which they are derived. Like the ʿapiru, the ʿibrum defines a class of people that was intelligible to a world beyond Israel, a type that would have been regarded by both Egyptians and Philistines as fundamentally separate and foreign. The ʿibrum also consists of people who have left their settled residence, in this case without cutting ties with their settled communities. These ties are preserved by the ideology of tribal identity.

At the same time, the ʿibrum connection avoids some of the difficulties of the ʿapiru hypothesis. First, the noun form ʿibr- offers an exact match, so that we would truly be talking

about ʿibri as a later expression of the same substantive. Moreover, the ʿibrum offers a better social fit with the biblical traditions for "Hebrew" identity. The Hebrews of Joseph's family finally move into Egypt en masse as a coherent clan of shepherds. When Joseph coaches his brothers on what to tell the pharaoh about themselves, he tells them to say, "Your servants have been men of flocks, from our youth until now, ourselves just like our fathers." Pharaoh will then allow you to make your base in the land of Goshen, "because all shepherds are repugnant to Egyptians"(Gen 46:34). The identification of Jacob's sons as belonging to a herder type is indirectly linked to the word *Hebrew* itself when we recall the one other "repugnance" of the Egyptians in the Joseph story: eating with "Hebrews" (Gen 43:32). By the time the biblical narrative reaches the Hebrews who oppose the confederated Philistine state, they represent the gathered population of a whole territory that the Philistines regard as dangerous back country. The "Hebrew camp" that has assembled with its sacred ark against the Philistines at Ebenezer has no king or state, but represents the united population of the territory, not a band of social outcasts (1 Sam 4:6).

Both Joseph's shepherd clan and the hill-country Israelites of 1 Samuel would offer a natural extension of the pastoralist ʿibrum as encountered by the dominant states of southern Palestine. Intrusion of Syrian pastoralists into southern lands would have begun with their mobile communities. The Binu Yamina were not the only tribal peoples who called their permanent mobile herdsmen the ʿibrum, but the Mari evidence indicates a preference for this term among the groups most oriented toward the southwest. If a significant proportion of new herding peoples in Palestine and the vicinity called themselves part of an ʿibrum, the term then could have acquired a more generic, southern use for people of this type, especially as back-country herders. Unlike the word ʿapiru, the word ʿibrum does not appear to have gained wide currency among the urban centers of Egypt or Canaan in the Late Bronze period. It seems to have survived in Hebrew as a way of describing "how lowland urbanites view people like us." As the idea of "people like us" eventually lost its earlier points of reference, the adjective ʿibri could come to be applied exclusively to Israelites and finally to Jews and their language, though the Bible reflects only very limited application to the whole ethnicity. One wonders whether even the legal protection of "Hebrew slaves" originally was defined not by Israelite political affiliation but rather by a more inclusive social definition.

See also ETHNICITY; ISRAEL; SOCIAL-SCIENTIFIC APPROACHES.

BIBLIOGRAPHY. **M. Anbar**, "Le pays des Hébreux," *Or* 41 (1972) 383-86; **J. Bottéro**, *Le problème des Habiru à la 4e Rencontre assyriologique internationale* (Cahiers de la Société asiatique 13; Paris: Imprimérie Nationale, 1954); **D. E. Fleming**, *Democracy's Ancient Ancestors: Mari and Early Collective Governance* (Cambridge: Cambridge University Press, 2004); idem, "Genesis in History and Tradition: The Syrian Background of Israel's Ancestors, Reprise," in *The Future of Biblical Archaeology*, ed. J. K. Hoffmeier and A. R. Millard (Grand Rapids: Eerdmans, 2004) 193-232; idem, "Mari and the Possibility of Biblical Memory," *RA* 92 (1998) 41-78; **M. Greenberg**, *The Hab/piru* (AOS 39; New Haven: American Oriental Society, 1955); **O. Loretz**, *Hapiru-Hebräer: Eine sozio-linguistische Studie über die Herkunft des Gentiliziums 'ibrî vom Appellativum habiru* (BZAW 160; Berlin: de Gruyter, 1984); **S. A. Meier**, "Diplomacy and International Marriages," in *Amarna Diplomacy: The Beginnings of International Relations*, ed. R. Cohen and R. Westbrook (Baltimore: Johns Hopkins University Press, 2000) 165-73; **N. Na'aman**, "Habiru and Hebrews: The Transfer of a Social Term to the Literary Sphere," *JNES* 45 (1986) 271-88; **K. L. Sparks**, *Ethnicity and Identity in Ancient Israel* (Winona Lake, IN: Eisenbrauns, 1998); **M. Weippert**, *The Settlement of the Israelite Tribes in Palestine* (London: SCM, 1971).

D. E. Fleming

HEBRON

Hebron is an important city in the biblical narrative, mentioned over sixty times in the Hebrew Bible. It is associated with the activities of the patriarch Abraham and as the first capital of David's monarchy. The ancient city was located on an important plateau in the southern Judean hills, about eighteen miles south of *Jerusalem and twenty-three miles northeast of *Beersheba. The modern city of Hebron and its suburbs are spread over several hills and valleys, each with various archaeological remains providing evidence of the chronological and demographic shifts of the area.

1. Site Identification and Excavations
2. Toponomy
3. Historical Overview

1. Site Identification and Excavations.

Biblical Hebron (Bronze and Iron Age city) should be associated with Tell Hebron, which lies on a secondary spur of Jebel Remeida. It overlooks the modern Arab city El-Khalil in the Hebron Valley to the south. The ancient city occupied probably not more than twelve acres. On an opposite slope is Haram el-Khalil, a monumental structure built during the Roman period marking the traditional spot of the cave of Machpelah. Several shaft tombs dating to Middle Bronze Age I and some perhaps to the Iron Age are beneath the structure and on the slope. This structure is commonly attributed to Herod the Great, although there are no textual records to support this. Its construction techniques are contemporary with Herod's building projects in Jerusalem. There are several other sites in the greater Hebron area with archaeological evidence for later periods (Persian-Early Arab): Jebel Nimbra, Haram Ramet el-Khalil, Khirbet en-Nasara, and Jebel Batrak.

The ancient tell was first surveyed and identified as Hebron by W. F. Albright, A. E. Mader and F. M. Abel. Modern archaeological excavations were conducted by the American Expedition to Hebron, led by P. C. Hammond from 1964 to 1966 after a preliminary survey in 1963. Excavations were renewed from 1983 to 1986 by the Judean Hills Survey Expedition, under the direction of A. Ofer of Tel Aviv University. New excavations were conducted by E. Eisenberg in 1999 on the northern side of the mound. In total, about nine areas of the site have been excavated, most by the American Expedition. The earliest known occupation of the mound was the Early Bronze Age I. Ceramic evidence for Early Bronze Age II was found as well as evidence of settlement on the northern side of the mound dating to Early Bronze Age III. During the Early Bronze Age III period the site was surrounded by a fortification wall twenty feet thick. Shaft tombs across the way show that the cemetery was in use during the Early Bronze Age IV period, although there was no evidence of occupation on the tell.

During the Middle Bronze Age I a city six-to-seven acres in size was founded and surrounded by a cyclopean wall. Parts of the defenses and dwellings were found by all three excavations.

This was the main city in the Judean hills during the Middle Bronze Age. An Akkadian cuneiform tablet with a list of animals was found. The proper names on the tablet indicate a West Semitic (Amorite) population with a Hurrian minority. The city seems to have been abandoned during the Late Bronze Age, but tombs in the area hint that the area served a tribal population. Also, unpublished data from the American expedition suggest that the Late Bronze Age city might have been confined to the acropolis.

The tell was reoccupied during the Iron Age I, with the zenith of the city being between the eleventh century BCE and the end of the tenth century BCE. During the Iron Age IIB period Hebron was one of the four cities associated with the *lmlk* seal impressions on storage jars. This was part of the royal initiatives of *Hezekiah. The tell was abandoned during the Persian period when occupation shifted to the valley.

2. Toponomy.
The modern Arabic name *El-Khalil* ("the friend") refers to the patriarchal tradition from 2 Chronicles 20:7 in which Abraham is called the friend of God. The *Canaanite city was named Kiriath-arba, which was built seven years prior to the establishment of Zoan (Gk Tanis) in Egypt (Gen 23:2). Biblical tradition associates the name with an ancestor of the Anakim (Josh 14:15; 15:13). Another proposed origin is that the name suggests four villages or suburbs connected with the city—"city of four." The texts of Joshua 15:54 and 2 Samuel 2:3 hint that Hebron consisted of multiple villages. The numerical reference to four perhaps refers to clans or sons of a tribal patriarch (Num 3:19; 1 Chron 2:42-43; 23:12, 19, 23). The biblical narrative associates several geographical references to the Hebron area: oaks of Mamre, the Eshcol and Hebron Valleys, the cave (field) of Machpelah. Possibly sometime in the Late Bronze Age or Early Iron I Age the name of the city became Hebron (Num 13:22). The name switched back to Kiriath-Arba during the Persian period (Neh 11:25).

3. Historical Overview.
Hebron was a major city during the patriarchal period. Archaeological evidence demonstrates that there was a well-fortified city during the first half of the second millennium BCE. It might have been an early Canaanite royal and cultic center, with the oaks of Mamre functioning as an oracle center. According to the patriarchal traditions and accounts found in the book of Genesis, Hebron was where Abraham pitched his tent and built an altar to the Lord after separating from Lot (Gen 13:18). It is also the site where he entertained "angels" and pleaded with God over the inhabitants of Sodom (Gen 18). Hebron is the city of Sarah's death. Abraham went to the sons of Heth to purchase a burial place for Sarah (Gen 23:1-20), which became the family burial place for Abraham and Isaac (Gen 25:9-10; 35:27-29).

3.1. Hebron in Joshua and Judges. Hebron is a key city in the accounts of the settlement and conquest of the Promised Land. It was in the vicinity of Hebron, in the valley of the Wadi Eschol, that the twelve spies brought back grapes, pomegranates and figs from the land and recounted the fertility of the land and the fortified cities (Num 13:22-33). When the Israelites finally started the settlement and conquest of the land, Hebron was part of a coalition of Amorites against *Joshua. After the Gibeonites formed a treaty with the Israelites, a coalition of five Amorite cities from the Shephelah and southern hill country was headed by Adonizedek, king of Jerusalem. Hoham, king of Hebron, was one of the five kings. This southern battle provides a description of the natural geopolitical dynamic between the Judean hill country and the southern Shephelah. This natural dynamic will be repeated with the political fortunes and boundaries of the later Judean monarchy.

The conquest of Hebron is attributed to Israelites led by Joshua (Josh 10:36-37), to the tribe of Judah (Judg 1:10) and to *Caleb (Josh 14:13-15). While the Canaanites retained centers at Jerusalem and centers in the valleys of the Shephelah, it appears that the Hebron region, along with the southern Judean hills, became a region of Israelite settlement. Hebron and its region were given to the inheritance of Caleb (Josh 14:13). The city became a Levitical city (Josh 21:11-13) and a city of refuge (Josh 20:7; 21:13). Joshua 11:21 recounts that the Anakim were driven from the hill country, including Hebron; no Anakim were left in the "land of the sons of Israel" except for the Philistine coastal plain (Josh 11:22).

3.2. Hebron During the Monarchy. During the tumultuous reign of *Saul, *David won the hearts of the Israelites in the greater Hebron region from the east in the Judean wilderness

(Kenite territory) to the Negev, and in the southern Shephelah (1 Sam 30:26-31). It was during this period that David cultivated the support of the people in the southern Judean hill country, so that with the death of Saul, David easily established his capital in Hebron when he first reigned as king (2 Sam 2:1-11). David ruled from Hebron for seven and a half years, during which he was able to consolidate and establish his rule as he was anointed king over all twelve tribes (2 Sam 5:1-4; 1 Chron 11:1-3).

Even though the capital of the kingdom was moved north to Jerusalem, Hebron retained some political clout in the Israelite kingdom. When David's son Absalom attempted to overthrow his father, he went to Hebron and established a base from which to rebel against his father's rule and claim the throne (2 Sam 15).

With the division of the Israelite tribes into two kingdoms, Hebron's strategic position as the southern border and defense for the Judean hills became more important in the ninth century BCE. *Rehoboam fortified a number of cities in the Shephelah and hill country, and Hebron was one of these administrative centers (2 Chron 11:5-12). Although Hebron is not mentioned in the biblical narrative as such, archaeological evidence demonstrates that the city continued as an important administrative center, being one of four cities associated with the royal *lmlk* storage jars. It is still debated whether these four cities represent military districts in Hezekiah's kingdom or supply cities for military rations. Either interpretation is supported by Hebron's strategic military location for Hezekiah and its rich and fertile hinterland for supplying troops.

After the fall of Jerusalem in 586 BCE, the *Edomites controlled territory almost to Bethzur, which is five miles north of Hebron (1 Macc 14:33). After the exile, Jews moved back into many towns of Judah, which was a Persian province, and Hebron was one of these towns (Neh 11:25). Hebron belonged to Idumea in the second century BCE when it was conquered by the Hasmoneans, who converted the inhabitants to Judaism. Antipater, Herod the Great's grandfather, was made governor. Most scholars attribute the ashlar masonry enclosure that surrounds the cave of Machpelah and is similar to the Temple Mount in Jerusalem to one of Herod's building projects.

See also DAVID.

BIBLIOGRAPHY. **J. Chadwick,** "The Archaeol-

ogy of Biblical Hebron in the Bronze and Iron Ages: An Examination of the Discoveries of the American Expedition to Hebron" (Ph.D. diss.; University of Utah, 1992); **P. C. Hammond,** "Hebron," *OEANE* 3.13-14; **D. M. Jacobson,** "The Plan of the Ancient Haram el-Khalil in Hebron," *PEQ* 113 (1982) 73-80; **A. Ofer,** "Hebron," *NEAEHL* 2.606-9.   S. M. Ortiz

HERMENEUTICS

The overarching story line embodied in Joshua through Kings and Chronicles and Ezra-Nehemiah is clear. These books tell the story of what happened after Moses' death. They tell of the occupation of the Promised Land under Joshua's leadership, of the increasingly fragmented period of the judges that followed and that leads to the appointment of a king over Israel, of the establishment of the Davidic dynasty, and of the eventual demise of both the northern and the southern kingdoms followed by the return from exile and the reconstruction of Israel (see Bartholomew and Goheen 2004a, 79-112). However, if the story line is clear, much about these books is contested nowadays. Hermeneutics at its best helps us to know *how* to read biblical books so as to discern their distinctive voices in the context of the canon as a whole. In light of the changing paradigms shaping the interpretation of the Historical Books, this article explores ways in which these challenging books can best be read today.

1. The Deuteronomistic History
2. Chronicles and Ezra-Nehemiah
3. The Literary Turn
4. The Postmodern Turn
5. Reengaging Theology
6. Required: An Integrated Hermeneutic
7. Required: A Canonical, Kerygmatic Hermeneutic
8. History and the Historical Books
9. Conclusion

1. The Deuteronomistic History.
In Jewish tradition Joshua through Kings (excluding Ruth, which comes after Proverbs in the Hebrew Bible), are known as the Former Prophets. This recognizes that they fit together in terms of their prophetic telling of the story of Israel. These historical books cover a long, continuous period of Israel's history, but critical scholarship has struggled to articulate their relationship to one another and to the Pentateuch. Source-

critical approaches thought in terms of the pentateuchal sources extending into the Historical Books, but the dominant paradigm for reading the Historical Books that has emerged over the last fifty years is undoubtedly that of the *Deuteronomistic History. M. Noth formulated the view that Deuteronomy through 2 Kings is the work of the Deuteronomistic Historian, who wrote during the exilic period. Thus the corpus Deuteronomy through 2 Kings is a unified work, although some room is made for additions. The author had at his disposal numerous literary units and complexes, including the original form of Deuteronomy, which he edited to form the first chapter and introduction to his history.

From this perspective the Deuteronomistic History was published just before or in the Judean exile. Four arguments are given for its unity:

1. The language of the work is recognizable. According to A. D. H. Mayes, the Deuteronomistic History "shows a certain consistency pointing to unity of authorship: it is plain, lacking 'any particular artistry or refinement,' and it is notably repetitive" (Mayes 1985, 11).

2. At decisive points throughout the history there are speeches or narratives that share a Deuteronomistic style and aim at reviewing Israel's history and deriving lessons from it for the future. Examples of these are Joshua 1; 12; 23; Judges 2:11-23; 1 Samuel 12; 1 Kings 8:14-53; 2 Kings 17:7-41.

3. A consistent chronology holds the work together.

4. The work has a theological unity that is seen particularly in its maintenance of an overall theme: the history of Israel as something in the past. It was a history of disobedience to the covenant law—the old Deuteronomic law code is used as the standard by which to assess the key players in the history—thus bringing the covenant curse down on the Israelites. For Noth, the historian has no concern for a future of Israel, because such a future does not exist. This has been a matter of debate among subsequent proponents of the Deuteronomistic History. H. W. Wolff, for example, argues that at each stage God continues to work with his people, and that the Deuteronomistic History is an exhortation to repentance.

Thus Mayes maintains that these four arguments establish Noth's theory. The history, in Noth's view, was published some time after 587 BCE and is the creative and original work of one author.

The major development in this hypothesis since Noth is the question of whether there were one or more Deuteronomistic editors (see McConville, 66-90). For Mayes, as for most recent proponents of the Deuteronomistic History, there are two Deuteronomistic editors. The original Deuteronomistic History was a work composed initially in preexilic times in support of Josiah's reform. The work was particularly concerned to emphasize the unity of Israel under one leader—Moses, David and Josiah being the key figures. After the exile this work was edited to bring it up to date and to introduce new material emphasizing God's judgment. In Mayes's view, although there is a glimmer of hope, the work essentially became an address to the exiles, summoning them to recognize the reason for their plight—God's judgment—and calling them to repent (Mayes, 12-13).

Despite these developments, in the 1981 reprint of Noth's *The Deuteronomistic History* Nicholson was able to assert, "This is a classic work in the sense that it . . . still provides, as far as the majority of scholars are concerned, *the basis and framework for further investigation of the composition and nature of this corpus*" (Nicholson, ix, italics added). And writing in 2000, G. N. Knoppers is still able to say, "Over the past half century, research on Deuteronomy through Kings has been dominated by one model—Noth's Deuteronomistic History hypothesis" (Knoppers, 13).

The twists and turns in the debates about the Deuteronomistic History are well documented elsewhere, and so they will receive no further elaboration here (see Knoppers and McConville; Schearing and McKenzie). However, looking back on this approach to the Historical Books now, we do well to pause to reflect on two aspects of the hermeneutical dimension of this paradigm for reading the Historical Books.

First, the Deuteronomistic History approach exemplifies a historical-critical approach to the OT. The focus is not first on the Historical Books as we have received them, but rather on a reconstructed book, in this case the Deuteronomistic History. Inevitably this is somewhat speculative, demonstrated not least in making

Deuteronomy the opening salvo of this work. In terms of the developing story, Deuteronomy is positioned between the Pentateuch and the Historical Books, and not surprisingly, as historical criticism got going, debates developed over whether we ought to think of a Pentateuch, with Deuteronomy as the fifth and final book, or of a Hexateuch, because of the strong thematic links between Deuteronomy and Joshua, or of a Tetrateuch, because Deuteronomy seems to initiate the Deuteronomistic History. The reconstructive nature of this enterprise raises questions about precisely what constitutes "a work."

It is perhaps unrealistic to expect historical-critical scholars of an earlier generation to meet the standard of more recent understandings of the literary nature of the Bible. In retrospect, it appears that neither at the level of individual books nor at the level of the newly discovered Deuteronomistic History were views of the complex literary nature of a work terribly sophisticated, although contemporary scholars disagree about the implications of the literary turn (see 3 below) for earlier critical approaches to the Deuteronomistic History. In light of the four reasons that Mayes thinks establish the existence and unity of the Deuteronomistic History, it is hard to feel that they are convincing by themselves. This is not to deny the existence of the Deuteronomistic History, but rather to suggest that if we continue to work with this hypothesis, better reasons that take full account of the literary turn will be needed to establish its existence.

Second, the Deuteronomistic History approach takes seriously the broader shape of the narrative and the need to read the Historical Books of the OT with a sense of their ongoing story line. To a naive reader of the OT this would seem obvious, but often it has not been so to scholars. At the narrative level these books clearly presuppose each other, and their individual story lines cannot be understood without what precedes and follows. This resonates with the recognition by J. Barr (1999) and others in recent years that story has a significant role to play in appropriating the inner unity of the Bible, although it remains debatable to what extent a narrative or story approach is applicable across the whole of the OT (see Bartholomew and Goheen 2004a). Clearly, in this respect the Prophetic Books are not as strongly connected into a narrative framework as are the Historical Books. However, accessing this story line by dis-cerning a larger work behind the individual Historical Books raises again the question of what constitutes a work. It was the literary turn in biblical studies that focused this question for the Historical Books, as we will see.

2. Chronicles and Ezra-Nehemiah.
Although Chronicles extends its narrative back to Adam, after the extensive genealogies with which it begins, the story line focuses on the monarchy through to the exile and concludes with Cyrus's edict that allowed Israelites to return to Jerusalem. Thus much of the same ground is covered as in Samuel and Kings, albeit with significantly different emphases. Particularly noticeable is Chronicles' focus on the Davidic monarchy and the temple. Chronicles is the final book in the Hebrew Bible, and for a long time in the history of interpretation it was neglected as a supplement to Samuel and Kings. In the early nineteenth century, however, W. M. L. De Wette stimulated critical reflection by arguing that the Chronicler radically reworked his sources, including, of course, Samuel and Kings, in terms of his ideology and thereby rendered Chronicles of little historical value. Ever since, the relationship of Chronicles to the books of the Deuteronomistic History, and Samuel and Kings in particular, has been central to studies of Chronicles (see, e.g., Childs 1979, 643-53).

Also of hermeneutical significance is the question of Chronicles' relation to *Ezra-Nehemiah. Is Ezra-Nehemiah part of a *Chronicler's History or is it a distinct entity? One's view of the parameters of Chronicles "considerably influences interpretation as a whole, because this is bound up with the question whether the author of Chronicles also described and interpreted the postexilic continuation of the history of Israel" (Rendtorff, 287). Interpretation of Ezra-Nehemiah has also been complicated by seeing it as an extension of Chronicles and thus written by the same author. This view of a large Chronicler's history was proposed by L. Zunz in the nineteenth century and soon became an "assured result" of criticism. However, more recently it has been strongly contested so that it makes sense hermeneutically to focus on Chronicles and Ezra-Nehemiah as distinct literary entities and then to compare one with the other (see Eskenazi, 11-36).

The literary parameters of a work are important to determine if one is to focus on it as a whole. English Bibles continue to divide Ezra-Nehemiah into two distinct books, a separation first attested by Origen. However, the evidence as a whole strongly supports reading Ezra-Nehemiah as a single book (Williamson, xxi-xxii).

3. The Literary Turn.

We have noted the importance for reconsideration of the view of "a work" that underlies Noth's seminal analysis of the Deuteronomistic History. This sort of issue was to receive sustained attention with the literary turn in biblical hermeneutics.

At the end of the nineteenth century and the start of the twentieth, positivism was the dominant philosophy in Europe. In literary studies this manifested itself in a concern with questions of genesis, context and authorial intent. What such an approach neglected was the literary text itself, and this neglect is paralleled in historical criticism's concern with questions of origin and what lies behind the text, and consequent neglect of the literary shape of the text itself. R. Alter and F. Kermode perceptively say of historical criticism, "The effect of this practice was curious: one spoke of the existing books primarily as evidence of what must once have been available in an original closer to what actually happened. That was their real value—as substitutes for what had unfortunately been lost" (Alter and Kermode, 3). Although the discernment of the Deuteronomistic History is a significantly different type of analysis from that of source criticism, the common tendency is to construct an alternative literary work and to focus attention exegetically there rather than first on the books in their final form; Joshua through Kings thus becomes the means to recover the Deuteronomistic History.

In literary studies "new criticism" developed in response to this neglect of the literary text, and somewhat later the literary turn developed in biblical studies to fill the parallel gap. Alter and Kermode identify E. Auerbach's *Mimesis* (1946 [ET 1953]) as a landmark in this literary turn. The literary turn in OT studies has been traced from the growing awareness of the limitations of the historical-critical method through canon criticism and new criticism (including J. Muilenberg's rhetorical criticism) to the narratology of R. Alter, A. Berlin and M. Sternberg (Gunn, 65-68).

In 1981 Alter was able to write, "Over the last few years, there has been growing interest in literary approaches among the younger generation of biblical scholars . . . but, while useful explications of particular texts have begun to appear, there have been as yet no major works of criticism, and certainly no satisfying overview of the poetics of the Hebrew Bible" (Alter, 15). Alter's *The Art of Biblical Narrative* is such an overview, but M. Sternberg's *The Poetics of Biblical Narrative* is the major work on OT narrative. In 1987 D. M. Gunn rightly noted that "Sternberg's recent book on poetics moves such a narratology into a whole new dimension of discrimination and sophistication and will be fundamental to the emerging generation of narrative critics" (Gunn, 68).

The literary turn has radical implications for how we read the Historical Books. What was part of a larger source or clear evidence of the hand of the Deuteronomistic editor(s) now can be shown to be an integral part of the individual book as a literary entity. Quite naturally, the literary turn focused attention, at least to some extent, on the literary shape of the books in the final form received.

Intriguingly, the literary turn was initiated largely by literary scholars interested in the Bible rather than by biblical exegetes. Alter and Sternberg are the obvious examples. G. Josipovici is another. He articulates clearly the way in which what critics see as signs of sources and stitching can be read as literary artifice. Writing about Judges, he says,

To put it in terms we have been using so far, I would want to argue that in this book the underlying rhythm, which was established in the very first chapter of Genesis . . . here comes under such strain that it almost collapses. . . . It is important for the larger rhythm of the whole book that this should occur, and that it prepares us for a re-establishment of the rhythm, after a stutter under Saul, when David appears on the scene, and for its eventual disintegration under the Kings of Israel and Judah. In other words, I want to argue that the sense of fragmentation, sometimes of parody and absurdity, which recent scholars have detected in many of the episodes of the book of Judges, is not the result of confusion on the part of authors and redactors, but has to be taken seriously as the central feature of what the book is all about. (Josipovici 1988, 110)

Josipovici (114-15) argues that the best OT readings of Judges still fall short of articulating the nuanced literary nature of that book, especially in terms of their seeing Judges 17—21 as an appendix. The motif of the cutting up of a body occurs at the beginning of the book (Judg 1:5-7) and recurs at the end with the cutting up of the Levite's concubine (Judg 20:6), "as though to stress in a quite literal way the notion of fragmentation. . . . What begins as the triumphant entry of the Israelite tribes into the land which had been promised them, ends with twelve parcels of flesh and the monotonous repetition of the phrase: 'every man did what was right in his own eyes'" (Josipovici 1988, 130).

It is apparent how this sort of reading casts a significantly different light on the Deuteronomistic History theory, according to which the stitching of the books can be easily discerned. Similarly, L. R. Klein, in her work on irony in Judges, asserts that Judges is a structured entity in which the different elements are put together so as to contribute to the integrity and significance of the whole. Rather than reading Judges as part of the Deuteronomistic History, Klein focuses on it as a literary work, analyzing the different voices in the text in order to discern the perspective of the implied author. This is a far cry from the sort of treatment of Judges that we find in the older critical readings of Judges. Drawing on the work of Sternberg, among others, Klein asserts, "I regard the work as an entity and credit the work of perhaps many hands to a single author, whom I call just that" (Klein, 11).

Another example of how a literary approach alters one's reading of the sources discerned in the Deuteronomistic History is the Succession Narrative in Samuel and Kings, first presented as an independent narrative by L. Rost in 1926. In his 1968 monograph on the Succession Narrative, R. N. Whybray sums up his approach to this narrative: it comprises at least 2 Samuel 9—20 and 1 Kings 1—2; 2 Samuel 21—24 lies outside of it; and the beginning probably is missing, but it cannot easily be reconstructed. Whybray then focuses his analysis on this reconstructed narrative. The widespread influence of this kind of reconstruction on interpretation of Kings is apparent in, for example, G. H. Jones's 1984 commentary. At the outset of his exegesis of 1 Kings 1—2 Jones simply asserts, "For the reasons noted in the Introduction . . . these first two chapters are to be separated from the account of

Solomon's reign in 3:1—11:43. . . . But the common authorship of these two chapters cannot be disputed" (Jones, 1:88). Here it is apparent how confident reconstruction of the Succession Narrative dominates critical reading of Kings.

The recovery of Kings as a literary work in its own right raises acute questions about such an approach. As has been demonstrated in recent years, 1 Kings 1—2 is patent of being read logically as the introduction to Solomon's reign and as such is an integral part of Kings. In terms of story line, these chapters link back strongly into 2 Samuel, but that does not mean that they should be read as part of a separately reconstructed Succession Narrative. Jones's confidence about the authorship of 1 Kings 1—2 is redolent of a sort of historical criticism that lacks literary sensibilities. Thus in his narrative commentary on Kings, J. T. Walsh (373) argues convincingly that 1-2 Kings are a crafted literary unity. The overarching literary pattern reveals a carefully balanced interest in the affairs of the two kingdoms, so that the kingdom of Judah is the subject of nineteen chapters and so too is the kingdom of Israel. The movement of the whole suggests that a single kingdom ruled from Jerusalem is the central concern of Kings.

Recent scholarship has also brought other aspects of the Succession Narrative under critical scrutiny. H. Klement has shown that the misnamed "Appendix 2," 2 Samuel 21—24, is integral to Samuel. G. Keys contends that Rost's hypothesis is based on weak foundations; succession is not the theme of the narrative, and 1 Kings 1—2 does not belong with this narrative. Keys argues that the full extent of the narrative is 2 Samuel 10—20. This unit is the nucleus of 2 Samuel, and the rest of the book forms a framework around it. The framework was brought together by the author of 2 Samuel 10—20, who juxtaposed this work with the earlier Samuel-Saul-David material. This large work was used by the Deuteronomistic Historian to provide a record of the early monarchy and career of David. Deuteronomistic activity in 2 Samuel was limited.

Clearly, the literary turn has significant implications for how we read the Historical Books. Such literary readings do not necessarily obviate the Deuteronomistic History, but they rightly complicate such a theory. As Sternberg in particular has noted, we cannot dispense with a diachronic or a synchronic approach in reading

Hebrew narrative, but in terms of reading these narratives, there is a primacy to the synchronic in that we first encounter these books as books with a particular shape. Thus critical readings of the Historical Books in relation to the Deuteronomistic History could not avoid this, but as was typical of much historical criticism, the move from the books as we have them to the book beneath or above the books was relatively unsophisticated. The literary turn rightly fills in that gap and brings its energies to bear on all or parts of the texts as literary entities. In the process, the move from the Historical Books to the Deuteronomistic History is complicated, and it is fair to say that the verdict is still out on this issue, or perhaps to put it another way, a plurality of verdicts are in.

What are some of the different ways in which the literary turn has affected the Deuteronomistic History? On some scholars it seems to have had little effect. B. Lindars continues to work within the Deuteronomistic History paradigm. Despite his holistic work on the Psalter, J. C. McCann develops a theological reading of Judges firmly within the framework of the Deuteronomistic History. Others, by comparison, set themselves firmly against this tendency. Despite his strong historical concerns, P. Guillaume, for example, is adamant in wanting "to read the book [of Judges] outside the mental framework of Noth's Deuteronomistic History" (Guillaume, 1).

Others combine the Deuteronomistic History with the smorgasbord of methods that have emerged within biblical studies in recent decades. An example is T. Fretheim, who combines the Deuteronomistic History with a rhetorical strategy. Regarding the Deuteronomistic History, Fretheim insists that "it is necessary to understand how the entire history may have functioned in the exilic context" (Fretheim, 17). He acknowledges that one can discern the different sources that the Deuteronomistic Historian used, but the final shape is clearly exilic. The Deuteronomistic History is hortatory, and we need to listen to it in its exilic context. There is no one simple theme or exhortation, but crucial to an understanding of the work is the sense that it is written for Israelites in exile and not first for people living in the events described.

In regard to Ezra-Nehemiah, we noted above the importance of discerning its literary parameters as a unified work. However, even once one has identified Ezra-Nehemiah as the focus of attention, there remain difficult questions about its unity that have been raised by historical criticism. Critical scholars have devoted considerable attention to the sources identifiable in the book, and earlier critical scholarship focused attention on a reconstruction of these sources (see, e.g., Myers). More recent work on Ezra-Nehemiah has continued to focus on the diverse sources while also attending to the role of redactor(s) in placing material in its present context. The role and placement of Nehemiah 8—10 is at the heart of these critical concerns, and H. G. M. Williamson's combination of source and redactional analysis indicates well more recent critical approaches. He says of Nehemiah 8—10, "It will be argued in this commentary that each of chaps. 8, 9, and 10 has an independent literary and historical origin. The purpose of these introductory remarks is, however, to affirm emphatically that they have not come together by the random processes of chance or error in transmission, but rather that they have been carefully assembled and thoughtfully located by the editor responsible for combining the Ezra and Nehemiah material" (Williamson, 276). In this way Williamson is able to maintain earlier critical concerns while also attending to Ezra-Nehemiah as a narrative unity (for a reflection on Ezra-Nehemiah as narrative see Williamson, xlviii-lii).

Williamson's work makes genuine progress in terms of connecting historical criticism with literary analysis, but there remain significant methodological differences, especially in regard to the relationship between literary and other forms of critical analysis. T. C. Eskenazi's literary approach to Ezra-Nehemiah highlights these differences. Drawing on Sternberg (for discussion of his work see 6 below), among others, Eskenazi, while stressing the importance of keeping discourse and diachronic analysis in discussion with each other, privileges the final form of the work in its literary shape. Eskenazi asserts, "I consider Ezra-Nehemiah to be a single work. To interpret the text in the wholeness of its present canonical shape is not to ignore the fissures within the book. It is, however, to insist that the transmitted unity take precedence in the interpretation. From a literary perspective, the divisions and fissures cease to be occasions to sever limbs but become, instead, clues to the book's overall intention" (Eskenazi, 13). Eskenazi reads Ezra-Nehemiah as a story and analyzes it along narrative-structuralist lines. She argues that the basic story of Ezra-Nehemiah is straight-forward: it describes how God's people built God's house in accordance with the Torah. Es-kenazi (38) discerns three main sections in this narrative: (1) potentiality: decree to the com-munity to build the house of God (Ezra 1:1-4); (2) actualization: the community builds the house of God (Ezra 1:5—Neh 7:72); (3) success: the community celebrates the completion of the house of God (Neh 8:1—13:31). Methodologi-cally, Eskenazi notes that her conclusions "have emerged from an investigation . . . that focuses on literary markers rather than historical ones, on 'discourse-oriented' analysis rather than 'source-oriented' inquiry. . . . Literary concerns have overshadowed historical ones in order to sustain a methodological consistency and pro-vide an alternative vision for material that has received ample historical scrutiny" (Eskenazi 176). In accord with Sternberg, Eskenazi (176-78) notes that such an approach should not ig-nore historical and source-critical concerns; there needs to be a dialectic between them, and she notes their fruitful interaction.

Inevitably, a strong focus on the Historical Books as literature would raise the question of the extent to which they are indeed historical. Historical criticism has, of course, raised acute questions about the historicity of parts of the Historical Books and explores this rigorously within the limitations of source, form, tradition and redaction criticism. This tendency is contin-ued in the literary turn, but in very different ways. Indeed, some scholars have seized the op-portunities presented by the literary turn as an occasion to get on with creative readings of these books and simply ignore historical-critical issues and referential issues. Others have ar-gued that approaching these books as "histori-cal" books is simply unhelpful. Thus M. Z. Brettler finds it unhelpful to approach Judges as a history book. Similarly, M. Bal (1988), in her narrative-feminist reading of Judges, openly challenges the ideas that Judges is unified and that it is primarily a history and theology book. She proposes the countercoherence of gender-based violence in the context of a narrative ap-proach to Judges.

I will discuss the thorny issue of reference in the Historical Books below; suffice it here to note that the full implications of the literary turn for historical criticism have still to be absorbed.

The literary turn should compel us to revisit the whole notion of a work that undergirds Noth's hypothesis, and certainly any new version or de-fense of this theory should take a full detour through that approach favored by J. G. McCon-ville: "an interpretive model that underscores the distinctive nature and individual integrity of each of the books that make up the Deuterono-mistic History" (Knoppers, 11). Only via such a detour would a contemporary defense of the Deuteronomistic History have validity.

4. The Postmodern Turn.
So-called postmodernism began in literary stud-ies and then was extended to a critique of West-ern culture as a whole in the 1980s. The postmodern debate has questioned central as-sumptions of modernity, including its notions of history, and it was inevitable that such question-ing eventually would threaten the dominance of that quintessentially modern method in biblical studies, historical criticism. Interwoven with this is the fact that since the literary turn in biblical studies, biblical scholars have kept an eye on de-velopments in literary studies and the door open to importing their methods. Thus it is no sur-prise that literary theory's colonizing drive should find a receptive audience in biblical stud-ies. By the late 1960s the new criticism was being replaced by structuralism, and then came the poststructuralist developments, and it was only a matter of time before the work of S. Fish, R. Rorty, J. Derrida, R. Barthes, M. Foucault and others was being applied in OT studies.

The contours of the postmodern landscape are not always easily identifiable. Postmodern-ism is synonymous with diversity and pluralism, and one needs to take care not to impose unifor-mity on diverse positions. Thus Rorty is to be distinguished from Derrida, and Derrida from J. Baudrillard, and so on. Nevertheless, it is clear that in its more extreme forms postmodernism constitutes a radical challenge to biblical studies, whether historical or literary, and this at two main levels.

First, there is the surface level of method-ological pluralism. Postmodernism has chal-lenged the hegemony of historical criticism, and the effect has been an explosion of methodolo-gies. At conferences such as those of the Ameri-can Academy of Religion and Society of Biblical Literature a plethora of methodologies are ap-plied to the Historical Books, and this trend is visible in books such as *Judges and Method: New Approaches in Biblical Studies,* in which six interpretive approaches are applied to Judges: narrative, social-scientific, feminist, structuralist, deconstructive, ideological. Some, such as D. J. A. Clines, celebrate this pluralism and argue for a market-oriented approach to biblical interpretation in which we do what we desire and what will sell. This is deeply redolent of the consumerism of our age. Others are more critical of the wild pluralism of contemporary biblical studies. Either way, the critique of historical criticism and the development of a myriad ways of interpreting biblical texts are clear phenomena of the present situation. For the Historical Books this means a growing corpus of very diverse readings of these texts.

Second, there is the depth level of philosophical plurality. The methodological pluralism of contemporary biblical interpretation is bewildering until one starts to connect it with the various philosophical paradigms that underlie the surface. What are we to make of, for example, D. N. Fewell's deconstruction of Judges 1:11-15, in which Caleb offers his daughter Achsah to the man who takes Kiriath-sepher?

Fewell is concerned about how translations tame the text and cover over the traces in words. The first area of deconstruction Fewell locates is the place names. For example, Fewell turns to the name of the city. Kiriath-sepher is renamed Debir. The victors have the power to rename, but this is not absolute, as traces remain. "Kiriath-sepher" means "city of writing/books." "Though the predominant tone in Joshua and Judges 1:1-18 foregrounds triumphalism, remnants of meaning undermine that attitude, suggesting that the place to be destroyed is a centre of learning: a place where records are kept, where history and order are valued, a place where texts are produced. . . . A city of writing is simply erased" (Fewell, 132). For Fewell, this casts the conquest in a rather different light for a reader who respects learning and culture, and it deconstructs the triumphalist representation of the conquest in Judges. Debir also bears these traces, according to Fewell. Most scholars take it to mean "inner sanctuary," but the root letters *(dbr)* indicate other traces: the verb "speak" and the nouns "speech," "matter," "plague."

Fewell makes much of the indeterminacy and instability of texts. In terms of her strategy, first the text is read determinatively, or a determinative "along the grain" reading is assumed. Then places in the text are located that can be read in contradiction to this determinative reading. These are discerned to be in irreconcilable tension with the grain of the text, and thus the text is said to be deconstructed.

For mainstream biblical scholars it is hard to know what to make of such readings. Deconstruction is the approach to texts that emerges from the philosophy of J. Derrida. Central to Derrida's philosophy is a view of language that resists meaning being contained and that ensures that texts are chock full of aporia that make them vulnerable to deconstruction. Derrida's approach to language and texts has yielded an arsenal of interpretative strategies, some of which Fewell brings to bear on Judges. To understand and evaluate such unusual readings, one has to discern the connection between the reading strategy and the underlying philosophy.

Historical criticism always had its own philosophical underpinnings, although it conspired at points to conceal these (Bartholomew 2000). While historical criticism was the dominant method in biblical exegesis, it could be taken for granted as objective and scientific without there being any need for it to defend its foundations. As long as the standard narrative of modernity as rational progress was assumed, historical criticism did not have to worry much about its philosophical presuppositions. Indeed, to this day the myth continues to be entertained that historical criticism has no philosophical presuppositions. J. Barr still asserts, "The typical biblical scholarship of modern times has been rather little touched by philosophy—certainly much less than it has been touched by theology" (Barr 2000, 26-27). Postmodernism has, however, made us far more aware of the "prejudices" of historical criticism and indeed of the fact that all approaches have their prior commitments (see Levenson). Thus historical criticism invariably brings particular philosophies of history to bear on the biblical text, and as postmoderns remind us, they are not the only (legitimate?) ones.

With its wild pluralism, its view of texts as radically indeterminate and its suspicion of getting behind texts, much postmodernism renders the historical-critical enterprise deeply problematic. Says A. Munslow, "The past is not discovered or found. It is created and represented by the historian as a text, which in turn is consumed by the reader" (Munslow, 178); if so, where does this leave the enterprise of historical criticism? The depth of the postmodern challenge in this respect should be noted. Postmodernism questions the foundational assumptions of modernity, so that its challenge to an enterprise such as historical criticism is not always immediately obvious except at a deep, philosophical level. But postmodernism queries such objective neutrality and insists that particular epistemologies and views of history underlie the practice of historical criticism. If such views are to be maintained, then their basis must be argued for—it cannot simply be assumed.

It is particularly via postmodern views of history that historical criticism and any view of the biblical narratives as accurately representing what happened are challenged. Munslow discerns three current options in historiography: reconstructionism, constructionism, deconstructionism. Reconstructionism is the view that the more carefully we write history, the closer we will get to what actually happened. Constructionism refers to the approaches to history that invoke general laws, Marxism being the most well-known example. Munslow gathers postmodern approaches together under the category of deconstructionism, and this includes authors such as H. White and K. Jenkins. Such approaches stress the fact that history writing is always an example of literary production, with all the attendant complexities that this entails.

Central to postmodern debates about history is the question of the extent to which history can ever accurately represent the past through narrative. Scholars point to the unavoidable interpretative and hermeneutical element in all history writing, and many draw radical conclusions from this. This postmodern emphasis on the linguistic and narrative nature of history raises profound questions about historiography whether one agrees with the likes of White and Jenkins or not. What kind of knowledge production is history writing? History always brings a narrative grid to bear on its telling of the past, and Munslow suggests that "history is best viewed epistemologically as a form of literature producing knowledge as much by its aesthetic or narrative structure as by any other criteria" (Munslow, 5). History is a form of narrative, and as such, it is part of the historical process: "All such narratives make over events and explain why they happened, but are overlaid by the assumptions held by the historian about the forces influencing the nature of causality" (Munslow, 10).

In such ways the postmodern turn problematizes the literary and historical turn in biblical studies and focuses our attention below the surface on the implications of diverse philosophical foundations.

5. Reengaging Theology.
Ultimately, the depth or philosophical diversity underlying the wild methodological pluralism of postmodernism confronts us with issues of faith and religion. G. Steiner articulates this clearly in his assessment of deconstruction. He boldly asserts that deconstruction confronts us with a stark choice: "It is Derrida's strength to have seen so plainly that the issue is neither linguistic-aesthetic nor philosophical in any traditional, debatable sense—where such tradition and debate incorporate, perpetuate the very ghosts which are to be exorcized. The issue is, quite simply, that of the meaning of meaning as it is re-insured by the postulate of the existence of God. 'In the beginning was the Word.' There was no such beginning, says deconstruction; only the play of sounds and markers amid the mutations of time" (Steiner 1989, 120). From Steiner's perspective, the wager that real presences underlie language makes a tremendous difference to how we interpret texts, and not least the Bible. In reviewing Alter and Kermode's *The Literary Guide to the Bible,* Steiner (1988) lambastes them for a literary approach that fails to attend to the divine provocations in the Bible. In other words, he asserts strongly that a literary approach that does not take the theological dimension seriously is woefully inadequate.

N. T. Wright and J. Milbank make comparable points in their assessments of postmodernism. As Wright says, "Protests, then, against the postmodern readings of the Bible are likely to be ineffectual. Unless, that is, those who care about serious reading of the gospels set about exploring ways in which to articulate a better epistemology, leading to a better account of what happens when a text is being read, a better account of what happens when a *sacred* text is being read. . . . *There is a sense . . . in which this demands a full theory of language. We need to understand, better than we commonly do, how language works*" (latter italics added; Wright, 61, 63). And in response to Derrida and deconstruction Milbank asserts, "If Derrida can give a gnostic hermeneutic of the human text in the light of the gnostic logos, then we should have the confidence to give a Christian hermeneutic in the light of the real one" (Milbank, 79).

The foundational diversity in biblical studies means that scholars will have to make choices about the most appropriate hermeneutic for the Bible and the Historical Books. In my opinion, not only does postmodernism make Enlightenment-style objective neutrality difficult, but also this position is incongruent with (Christian) faith anyway. J. Barton notes the crisis of pluralism and diversity in OT studies and that an emerging response is to call for a *religious* hermeneutic. Barton is suspicious of this move and argues for a recovery of Enlightenment values as the center of OT studies. That, however, is only to argue for a particular foundation for biblical studies, and one that is deeply problematic from a theological perspective (see Buckley). The way forward, in my opinion, is to allow room in the academy for a genuine pluralism that would make space for the development of hermeneutical approaches that are congruent with Christian, Jewish, secular and other perspectives on the world, allowing faith to shape our critical work from the foundation up.

Such a perspective remains so alien to most biblical scholarship that it immediately gets read as a form of fundamentalism in which a doctrinal strait jacket gets imposed on the Bible, which it most decisively is not. As S. Neill (in Neill and Wright) notes, developments of such a (theological) hermeneutic will not solve all the problems, but they will create the ring within which solutions may be found.

In terms of taking (Christian) theology seriously in OT interpretation, there are, of course, major scholars already doing this. K. Barth's work, B. S. Childs's canonical approach and Yale's postliberal theology are major ingredients in this renewed interest in theological interpretation. Childs has long argued that the goal of the interpretation of Christian Scripture must be to understand both Testaments as witness to the self-same divine reality: the God and Father of Jesus Christ. Childs's extensive corpus has played a major role in laying the foundation for a theological, canonical hermeneutic in biblical studies. This theological turn is now gathering momentum in response to the pluralism and nihilistic direction of (some) postmodernism. In-

evitably, as with Childs, a theological turn will involve going back to premodern readings of OT texts and finding traditions that can be reappropriated and developed in our day (see Childs 2004).

There are at least two directions to this theological turn. One aspect is that of simply getting on with reading the Bible theologically. Scholars such as C. R. Seitz invoke in this respect the plain sense of Scripture, allow a limited role for historical criticism, and get on with interpretation in relation to the church and Christian doctrine. A somewhat different approach is to argue that we need a theology of history (and literature, etc.) to fund biblical interpretation. Thus Neill and Wright state, "It is an exciting idea . . . that 'An understanding of history which is incompatible with a Christian doctrine of revelation is bound to land the New Testament scholar in grave perplexities; a true theological understanding of history would not of itself solve any New Testament problems, but it would, so to speak, *hold the ring within which a solution can be found.*' But where are the scholars sufficiently familiar with actual history-writing, sufficiently at home in philosophy and the history of ideas, and sufficiently committed to the study of the New Testament, to undertake the task?" (italics added; Neill and Wright, 366). Wright himself makes considerable progress in this direction (see Wright), but little comparable work has been done in relation to the OT Historical Books.

6. Required: An Integrated Hermeneutic.

6.1. An Appropriate Hermeneutic for the Historical Books. Certainly, this complex issue cannot be resolved here, but we should note from the foregoing discussion that an urgent requirement is to develop a hermeneutic for the Historical Books that integrates their historical, literary and theological dimensions—all three. Too often, as with much historical criticism, these books have been read through a deeply reductionistic hermeneutic that zooms in on an aspect of the text to the neglect of the others, whether it be the historical, literary or theological dimension. But each of these is a vital part of the Historical Books, and we urgently need a hermeneutic that integrates these dimensions so that we can begin to see how they relate to each other in the production of the rich tapestry of meaning in these texts.

Fortunately, there are some promising models around in this respect. A. C. Thiselton has foregrounded the need for a hermeneutic that integrates the three dimensions referred to, and his highly sophisticated work on philosophical and biblical hermeneutics constantly seeks to guard against simplistic reductionism. In NT studies, precisely in order to get at the history of Jesus, N. T. Wright has proposed a hermeneutic informed by a critical realist perspective that integrates the historical, literary and theological dimensions of NT texts. A. Wolters similarly has proposed a creative, multifaceted and intentionally antireductionistic hermeneutic that has been well received by a diversity of biblical scholars. In terms of the sort of Hebrew narrative texts that we have in the Historical Books, the most remarkable work on an integrated hermeneutic has been done by Sternberg in *The Poetics of Biblical Narrative*. In view of the creativity and importance of his work for reading the Historical Books, here I will outline his hermeneutic in some detail.

6.2. Sternberg's Integrated Hermeneutic for Reading Hebrew Narrative: The Drama of Reading.

For Sternberg, biblical narrative is a work of literature, so that in a poetics such as his the discipline and its object come together: "Biblical narrative is oriented to an addressee and regulated by a purpose or set of purposes involving the addressee. Hence our primary business as readers is to make purposive sense of it" (Sternberg, 1). Sternberg argues for an embodied notion of textual intentionality. This discernment of *"objectified or embodied intention"* Sternberg regards as crucial: "Such intention fulfils a crucial role, for communication presupposes a speaker who resorts to certain linguistic and structural tools in order to produce certain effects on the addressee; the discourse accordingly supplies a network of clues to the speaker's intention" (Sternberg, 9)

Taking embodied intention seriously means that source criticism and narratology should not be set against each other. This is especially so in light of the gap in sociocultural context between our time and that of the origin of the biblical narratives. Of course, we can never fully bridge this gap, but this does not mean we cannot try. In fact, this is the only alternative: "Once the choice turns out to lie between reconstructing the author's intention and licensing the reader's invention, there is no doubt where most of us

stand" (Sternberg, 10). Of course, the nature of the source criticism that we engage in needs careful attention, and Sternberg is highly critical of much that has been called source criticism. There is an inevitable tension between source and discourse, but Sternberg appeals for a closer partnership between the two; indeed, he maintains that the two cannot but work together, and neither has the primacy over the other, although in our reading of a text the focus of our interpretive energies must be on the text as we have it.

Frequently it is falsely assumed that the Bible as a religious text is antithetical to the Bible as literature. For Sternberg, this is a false antithesis. In the ancient world highly poetic and literary material was regularly highly ideological and attended to for instruction. "The question is how rather than whether the literary coexists with the social, the doctrinal, the philosophical" (Sternberg, 35). Representation is never to be set against evaluation, although the extent to which these aspects dominate in any piece of literature will vary. Only if the Bible were ideological in an extreme form of didacticism would taking it seriously as literature be inadmissible. However, "if biblical narrative is didactic, then it has chosen the strangest way to go about its business. For the narrator breaks every law in the didacticist's decalogue. Anything like preaching from the narrative pulpit is conspicuous for its absence" (Sternberg, 37-38). Narrative is the means whereby the Bible presents its message, and the two, narrative technique and message, are not to be set against each other.

In this respect it is time we stopped seeing the techniques of narrative as literary techniques. Those in the literary field often have been in the forefront of examining these techniques, but that does not mean that they are confined to literary texts where art may be high and content and message low. "What determines literariness is not the mere presence but the dominance of the poetic function, the control it exerts over all the rest" (Sternberg, 40). Narrative techniques are as much the prerogative of the historical biblical narratives as of fictional texts, and the presence of these techniques must not be seen as compromising the texts' ideological nature.

How, then, does the aesthetic aspect relate to the ideological in biblical narrative? "Biblical narrative emerges as a complex, because multifunctional, discourse. Functionally speaking, it is regulated by a set of three principles: ideological, historiographic, and aesthetic" (Sternberg, 41). The ideological is particularly prominent in the law sections of the Pentateuch and in prophetic moralizing, for example. The historiographic is prominent in the names of places, people and etiologies; the aesthetic is in high profile in the narratives. The relation of these three principles is one of coordination and tense complementarity. Sternberg sums up the point at which the three merge as "the drama of reading": "They join forces to originate a strategy of telling that casts reading as a drama, interpretation as an ordeal that enacts and distinguishes the human predicament" (Sternberg, 46).

The sophistication of Sternberg's hermeneutic is apparent, and the rich exegetical yield that results from applying this to the OT is evident again and again in his *Poetics of Biblical Narrative*. His work is profoundly relevant to interpretation of the Historical Books, as V. P. Long (1994) and others have noted. An example of what taking Sternberg seriously for the Historical Books might produce is I. Provan's 1997 commentary on 1-2 Kings. He develops an approach to Kings that takes it seriously as narrative, as history-telling and as didactic. Such an integrated hermeneutic also bears on the thorny issue of the relationship between Samuel-Kings and Chronicles. Chronicles, like Samuel and Kings, is historiographic, but also it is narrative and kerygmatic/didactic. Although it attends in particular to the reigns of David and Solomon, as do Samuel and Kings, its historical sweep extends backward to Adam, and its audience is much later than that of Samuel and Kings. Writing probably around 400 BCE, the Chronicler tells his story with the postexilic community in mind, with a particular focus on the temple and temple worship. Evaluation of the historical and theological differences between Samuel-Kings and Chronicles must weigh carefully the intricate relationship of the historical to the literary and theological in these books.

7. Required: A Canonical, Kerygmatic Hermeneutic.

The Historical Books should be read and analyzed with the utmost critical rigor—an approach that the present volume exemplifies—but to what end? This, in my opinion, is a ques-

tion that too often has been lacking across the spectrum in interpretation of the Historical Books. In terms of commentaries on Judges, for example, it is instructive to compare A. E. Cundall's 1968 Tyndale Old Testament Commentary with R. G. Boling's 1975 Anchor Bible Commentary. They are distinctive in terms of their stance on historical issues and the composition of Judges, but neither helps us get at the communicative and canonical trajectory of Judges. J. C. McCann's 2002 Interpretation commentary is well informed critically but far more helpful in getting at the kerygma of the text. With regard to Kings, on historical issues the commentaries of J. Gray and D. J. Wiseman could not be further apart, but neither attends to the world in front of the text, the world that the text calls the reader to indwell. There are, of course, a thousand things one can do with a book, as postmodernism constantly reminds us. However, from a confessional perspective, a hermeneutic for the Historical Books will be deeply inadequate if its goal is not to discern the communicative, kerygmatic function of the text, and this ultimately as part of Scripture.

In this respect a rhetorical or communicative hermeneutic has proved particularly fertile. We know for certain that the Historical Books were not written for Israelites living in the events that they describe, but rather for Israelites for whom those events were in the past but instructive for the present. However difficult a precise dating of the Historical Books may be, such awareness opens up the kerygmatic, communicative trajectory of the Historical Books and alerts us to where we need to focus if we wish to hear the distinctive voice of each of these books.

It is, however, important to remember that the Historical Books must be read finally in the context of the canon as a whole. We noted above how a very positive aspect of the theory of the Deuteronomistic History is that it recognizes the need to read the Historical Books as part of a larger narrative. A danger with the Deuteronomistic History, though, is that this narrative may be unnecessarily limited. Interpretation of Joshua, for example, is profoundly affected by whether or not one reads its theology of the land in the context of Genesis 12 and God's promises to Abraham. This is rare in commentaries on Joshua, but it is highly illuminating when taken seriously. And of course, not only must the context be extended backward, but also, for Christians, forward into the NT.

In his commentary on 1 Kings J. T. Walsh is sensitive to the danger of limiting the narrative context of the Historical Books to the Deuteronomistic History. He notes that in the Hebrew Bible the books following Kings (Isaiah, Jeremiah, etc.) do not continue the narrative, so that 2 Kings brings us to the conclusion of a major block of OT narrative. However, the books preceding 1 Kings are in continuity with the narrative of Kings: "Although the first chapters of 1 Kings can be read as self-contained narratives (as we have done in this study), they nonetheless presume the entire complicated history of adultery and murder, rape and fratricide, rebellion and restoration that is the Succession Narrative" (Walsh, 374-75). However, as Walsh points out,

> On a still larger scale, however, the entire first part of the Hebrew Bible can be appreciated as a single continuous narrative. The first eleven books tell a multifarious story that begins with the chaos out of which God creates all things and ends with the chaos of exile into which the history of Israel's sin eventually leads. The grand scale of the story reveals its universal relevance. It is not simply the story of the Israelite monarchy . . . but of all the children of Adam and Eve (from Genesis 4), indeed of all creatures (from Genesis 2) and all creation itself (from Genesis 1). Most of all, it is the story of the God whose creative word brought forth the past and whose prophetic word, whether of blessing or punishment, anger or forgiveness, continues to generate the future. It is the story of the God who is faithfully and eternally present to all his works. (Walsh, 375)

Although Kings ends a block of narrative in the OT, the Christian reader will be well aware that the narrative does not end there, and that one needs to read the narrative explicated in the Historical Books as part of the story line of the entire Bible (see Bartholomew and Goheen 2004a). Indeed, from a Christian perspective what is urgently required is thick theological interpretation of the Historical Books, interpretation deeply informed by the canon as a whole in the context of the Christian tradition. The Historical Books deal with human life in all its dimensions and especially in relation to politics. Sadly, these dimensions are rarely mined theologically by exegetes. J. Ellul, for example, rightly says of 2 Kings that it "is probably the most political of all books of the Bible. For its reference is to Israel genuinely constituted as a political power and playing its part in the concert of empires. Furthermore its reference is also to an age of crisis. Above all we see politics in action and not just in principle" (Ellul, 13). Reading modern commentaries, one gets little sense of the rich yield these books have for political theology. However, reading a political theology such as the 1996 volume by O. O'Donovan, one starts to get a sense of the rich legacy of political interpretation of the Historical Books (see Bartholomew et al., 2002).

This is not to suggest that theological interpretation of the Historical Books is straightforward. For the commentator they present a smorgasbord of challenges: their use of force, the nationalistic focus on Israel and the land, and so on present real interpretive challenges. At the same time, they focus theologically on issues that are of vital importance today. For example, how we think about place and *land is a crucial concern today, and both W. Brueggemann and O. O'Donovan (1989) have demonstrated the theological fecundity of the Historical Books in this respect.

8. History and the Historical Books.

As is well known, the contemporary debate about OT history is highly polarized (see, e.g., Davies; Lemche; Provan, Long and Longman). Naturally, this debate bears heavily on the referential dimension of the Historical Books. Evangelical scholars continue to insist that the referential dimension of the Historical Books is vital and an integral part of their interpretation. As G. Fackre says, "Evangelical theology sharply opposes any understanding of narrative theology that does not require the correspondence of the chapters in the Christian story to 'the real order'" (Fackre, 198). However, even among evangelical OT scholars there is a considerable diversity on these issues, a diversity that is exemplified in the debate between (evangelical) maximalists and minimalists. Evangelical maximalists argue that for the Historical Books to be part of Scripture, it is crucial that most if not all of what they report as event actually happened. Even here the basis on which this position is argued varies. K. A. Kitchen (3) is adamant that his maximalist approach is based on history, literature and culture, not on theology, doctrine or dogma. Kitchen concludes, "In terms of general reliability . . . the Old Testament comes out remarkably well, so long as its writings and writers are treated fairly and evenhandedly, in line with independent data, open to all" (Kitchen, 500).

J. Goldingay acknowledges the theological imperative toward a maximalist position: "We do have important and precious theological grounds for believing that the scriptures provide us with fully adequate witness to the events they narrate" (Goldingay, 46). However, Goldingay (71) insists that we attend closely to the complex nature of the biblical tradition in which nearly all narrative is on a continuum between historiography and imaginative writing. In terms of Genesis to Kings, he argues that "the proportion of 'story' . . . as opposed to 'history' . . . is at its highest at the opening of the work. It is at its lowest at the end, where the events in focus had taken place not long before the work's writing. The story of Israel's exodus and their occupation of the land lies somewhere in between" (Goldingay, 56). The description of the slaughter of the Canaanites in Joshua may be "imaginative fictional expressions" rather than literal descriptions (Goldingay, 75).

In this way, Goldingay, while taking note of the theological constraint toward maximalism, opens the door for a range of positions between maximalism and minimalism. Others show considerable latitude in making room for diverse genres and types of narrative writing and argue that a minimum of historical actuality is necessary for these books to be a full part of sacred Scripture.

These complex issues cannot be fully dealt with here. Suffice it to note that our growing discovery of the awareness of the highly crafted literariness of the Historical Books does not by itself resolve the complex issue of their historicity. For Sternberg, seeing narrative technique as part of the text itself means taking the historical construction of the text seriously if one is going to come to grips with the functional purpose of biblical narrative. Sternberg is highly critical of the tendency to categorize OT narratives as fiction. Fiction and history cannot, in Sternberg's view, be distinguished by form, but crucially only in terms of the overall purpose of the communicator/author. And in Sternberg's opinion, when the OT narratives are assessed by this criterion, "the product is neither historicized fiction nor fictionalized history, but historiography pure and uncompromising" (Sternberg, 35). Everything, in Sternberg's view, points in this direc-

tion. The Israelite obsession with memory of the past and its significance for the present, and Israel's uniqueness in this respect in the ancient Near East—these factors confirm that the OT narratives are making a strong historical truth claim. "Were the narrative written or read as fiction, then God would turn from the lord of history into a creature of the imagination, with the most disastrous results" (Sternberg, 320).

Of course, Sternberg's approach is not uncontested, but, contra Kitchen and others, it indicates well the impossibility of keeping theological issues out of the debate about the historical dimension of the Historical Books. Indeed, a crucial question concerns the elements that shape the decision for or against the historicity of the Historical Books. A. Plantinga, in common with other Reformed epistemologists, has argued that belief in God is properly basic and may rationally be assumed without evidence that proves it to be true (Bartholomew 2003). An implication of this is that one would be warranted in taking the basic story line of the Bible to be historically accurate without depending on evidence that proves this to be so. In my opinion, this is the correct way to proceed. However, the important thing to note is that this provides the ring within which the real debates can begin. Granted that God has acted in Israel's history, and granted that we take seriously the notion that God speaks and acts, by no means are all the historical problems of the Historical Books solved. All the data surfaced by historical critics and literary scholars still have to be accounted for, albeit from a theistic perspective.

9. Conclusion.

Contemporary interpretation of the Historical Books takes place against a complex hermeneutical background. The legacy of historical criticism remains strong but has been complicated and challenged by the literary, postmodern and theological turns. Although attention to the text itself must ever be the prime concern of interpreters of the Historical Books, it is naive to think that one can escape an interpretive grid with which one approaches these books. As R. E. Palmer perceptively notes, and as this article has sought to show, "We see . . . how decisive is our underlying theory of knowledge and our theory of the ontological status of a work, for they determine in advance the shape of our theory and practice in literary interpretation" (Palmer, 80-81).

See also HISTORIOGRAPHY, OLD TESTAMENT; METHODS OF INTERPRETATION; NARRATIVE ART OF ISRAEL'S HISTORIANS; QUEST OF THE HISTORICAL ISRAEL; TEXT AND TEXTUAL CRITICISM.

BIBLIOGRAPHY. R. Alter, *The Art of Biblical Narrative* (New York: Basic Books, 1981); R. Alter and F. Kermode, eds., *The Literary Guide to the Bible* (London: Fontana, 1987); M. Bal, *Death and Dissymmetry: The Politics of Coherence in the Book of Judges* (CSHJ; Chicago: University of Chicago Press, 1988); J. Barr, *The Concept of Biblical Theology: An Old Testament Perspective* (Minneapolis: Fortress, 1999); idem, *History and Ideology in the Old Testament: Biblical Studies at the End of a Millennium* (Oxford: Oxford University Press, 2000); C. G. Bartholomew, "Uncharted Waters: Philosophy, Theology and the Crisis in Biblical Interpretation," in *Renewing Biblical Interpretation*, ed. C. G. Bartholomew, C. Greene and K. Möller (SH 1; Grand Rapids: Zondervan, 2000) 1-39; idem, "Warranted Biblical Interpretation: Alvin Plantinga's 'Two or More Kinds of Scripture Scholarship,'" in *"Behind" the Text: History and Biblical Interpretation*, ed. C. G. Bartholomew et al. (SH 4; Grand Rapids: Zondervan, 2003) 58-78; C. G. Bartholomew and M. Goheen, *The Drama of Scripture: Finding Our Place in the Biblical Story* (Grand Rapids: Baker, 2004a); idem, "Story and Biblical Theology," in C. G. Bartholomew et al., eds., *Out of Egypt: Biblical Theology and Biblical Interpretation* (SH5; Grand Rapids: Zondervan, 2004b) 144-71; C. G. Bartholomew et al., eds., *"Behind" the Text: History and Biblical Interpretation* (SH 4; Grand Rapids: Zondervan, 2003); idem, *A Royal Priesthood? The Use of the Bible Ethically and Politically: A Dialogue with Oliver O'Donovan* (SH 3; Grand Rapids: Zondervan, 2002); J. Barton, *The Future of Old Testament Study: An Inaugural Lecture Delivered Before the University of Oxford on 12 November 1992* (Oxford: Clarendon Press, 1993); R. C. Boling, *Judges* (AB 6A; Garden City, NY: Doubleday, 1975); M. Z. Brettler, *The Book of Judges* (OTR; London: Routledge, 2002); W. Brueggemann, *The Land* (Philadelphia: Fortress, 1977); M. J. Buckley, At the Origins of Modern Atheism (New Haven: Yale University Press, 1987); B. S. Childs, *Introduction to the Old Testament as Scripture* (Philadelphia: Fortress, 1979); idem, *The Struggle to Understand Isaiah as Christian Scripture* (Grand Rapids: Eerdmans, 2004); D. J. A. Clines, "Possibilities and Priorities of Biblical Interpretation in an International Perspective," BibInt 1 (1993) 67-87; A. E. Cundall and L. Morris, *Judges, Ruth* (TOTC; Downers Grove, IL: InterVarsity Press, 1968); P. R. Davies, *In Search of "Ancient Israel"* (JSOTSup 204; Sheffield: Sheffield Academic Press, 1992); J. Ellul, *The Politics of God and the Politics of Man* (Grand Rapids: Eerdmans, 1972); T. C. Eskenazi, *In an Age of Prose: A Literary Approach to Ezra-Nehemiah* (SBLMS 36; Atlanta: Scholars Press, 1988); G. Fackre, "Narrative Theology from an Evangelical Perspective," in *Faith and Narrative*, ed. K. E. Yandell (New York: Oxford University Press, 2001) 188-201; D. N. Fewell, "Deconstructive Criticism: Achsah and the (E)razed City of Writing," in *Judges and Method: New Approaches in Biblical Studies*, ed. G. A. Yee (Minneapolis: Fortress, 1995) 119-45; T. E. Fretheim, *Deuteronomic History* (IBT; Nashville: Abingdon, 1983); idem, *First and Second Kings* (Westminster Bible Companion; Louisville: Westminster/John Knox, 1999); J. Goldingay, *Models for Scripture* (Carlisle: Paternoster, 1994); J. Gray, *I and II Kings* (2nd ed.; OTL; Philadelphia: Westminster, 1970); P. Guillaume, *Waiting for Josiah: The Judges* (JSOTSup 385; Sheffield: Sheffield Academic Press, 2004); D. M. Gunn, "New Directions in the Study of Biblical Hebrew Narrative," *JSOT* 39 (1987) 65-75; G. H. Jones, *1 and 2 Kings* (2 vols.; NCB; Grand Rapids: Eerdmans, 1984); G. Josipovici, *The Book of God: A Response to the Bible* (New Haven: Yale University Press, 1988); G. Keys, *The Wages of Sin: A Reappraisal of the "Succession Narrative"* (JSOTSup 221; Sheffield: Sheffield Academic Press, 1996); K. A. Kitchen, *On the Reliability of the Old Testament* (Grand Rapids: Eerdmans, 2003); L. R. Klein, *The Triumph of Irony in the Book of Judges* (BLS 14; Sheffield: Almond, 1988); H. Klement, *II Samuel 21-24: Context, Structure and Meaning in the Samuel Conclusion* (European University Studies 32/682; Frankfurt: Lang, 2000); G. N. Knoppers, "Introduction," in *Reconsidering Israel and Judah: Recent Studies on the Deuteronomistic History*, ed. G. N. Knoppers and J. G. McConville (SBTS; Winona Lake, IN: Eisenbrauns, 2000) 1-18; G. N. Knoppers and J. G. McConville, eds., *Reconsidering Israel and Judah: Recent Studies on the Deuteronomistic History* (SBTS; Winona Lake, IN: Eisenbrauns, 2000); N. P. Lemche, *Prelude to Israel's Past: Background and Beginnings of Israelite History and Identity* (Peabody, MA: Hendrickson, 1998); J. D. Levenson, *The Hebrew Bible, the Old Testament, and the Historical Criticism: Jews and*

Christians in Biblical Studies (Louisville: Westminster/John Knox, 1993); **B. Lindars,** *Judges 1-5* (Edinburgh: T & T Clark, 1995); **V. P. Long,** *The Art of Biblical History* (FCI 5; Grand Rapids: Zondervan, 1994); idem, *The Reign and Rejection of King Saul: A Case for Literary and Theological Coherence* (SBLDS 118; Atlanta: Scholars Press, 1989); **V. P. Long, D. W. Baker and G. J. Wenham,** eds., *Windows into Old Testament History: Evidence, Argument and the Crisis of "Biblical Israel"* (Grand Rapids: Eerdmans, 2002); **A. D. H. Mayes,** *Judges* (OTG; Sheffield: JSOT, 1985); **J. C. McCann,** *Judges* (IBC; Louisville: John Knox, 2002); **J. G. McConville,** *Grace in the End: A Study in Deuteronomic Theology* (SOTBT; Grand Rapids: Zondervan, 1993); **J. Milbank,** *The Word Made Strange: Theology, Language, Culture* (Oxford: Blackwell, 1997); **A. Munslow,** *Deconstructing History* (London: Routledge, 1997); **J. M. Myers,** *Ezra, Nehemiah* (AB 14; Garden City, NY: Doubleday, 1965); **S. Neill and N. T. Wright,** *The Interpretation of the New Testament 1861-1986* (2nd ed.; Oxford: Oxford University Press, 1988); **E. W. Nicholson,** Foreword, in M. Noth, *The Deuteronomistic History* (JSOTSup 15; Sheffield: JSOT, 1981) vii-x; **M. Noth,** *Überlieferungsgeschichtliche Studien: Die sammelnden und bearbeitenden Geschichtswerke im Alten Testament* (Schriften der Königsberger Gelehrten Gesellschaft, geisteswissenschaftliche Klasse 18/2; Halle [Saale]: M. Niemeyer, 1943); **O. O'Donovan,** *The Desire of the Nations: Rediscovering the Roots of Political Theology* (Cambridge: Cambridge University Press, 1996); idem, "The Loss of a Sense of Place," *ITQ* 55 (1989) 39-58; **R. E. Palmer,** *Hermeneutics: Interpretation Theory in Schleiermacher, Dilthey, Heidegger, and Gadamer* (Evanston, IL: Northwestern University Press, 1969); **I. Provan,** *1 and 2 Kings* (OTG; Sheffield: Sheffield Academic Press, 1997); **I. Provan, V. P. Long and T. Longman,** *A Biblical History of Israel* (Louisville: Westminster/John Knox, 2003); **R. Rendtorff,** *The Old Testament: An Introduction* (Philadelphia: Fortress, 1986); **L. Rost,** "Die Überliefering von der Thronnachfolge Davids," in *Das kleine Credo und andere Studien zum alten Testament* (Heidelberg: Quelle & Meyer, 1965) 119-253; **L. S. Schearing and S. L. McKenzie,** eds., *Those Elusive Deuteronomists: The Phenomenon of Pan-Deuteronomism* (JSOTSup 268; Sheffield: Sheffield Academic Press, 1999); **C. R. Seitz,** *Word Without End: The Old Testament as Abiding Theological Witness* (Grand Rapids: Eerdmans, 1998); **G. Steiner,**

Real Presences: Is There Anything in What We Say? (London: Faber & Faber, 1989); idem, review of *The Literary Guide to the Bible,* by R. Alter and F. Kermode, *The New Yorker,* January 11, 1988, 94-98; **M. Sternberg,** *The Poetics of Biblical Narrative: Ideological Literature and the Drama of Reading* (ISBL; Bloomington: Indiana University Press, 1985); **A. C. Thiselton,** "On Models and Methods: A Conversation with Robert Morgan," in *The Bible in Three Dimensions: Essays in Celebration of Forty Years of Biblical Studies in the University of Sheffield,* ed. D. J. A. Clines, S. E. Fowl and S. E. Porter (JSOTSup 87; Sheffield: JSOT, 1990) 337-56; **J. Van Seters,** *In Search of History: Historiography in the Ancient World and the Origins of Biblical History* (New Haven: Yale University Press, 1983); **J. T. Walsh,** *1 Kings* (Berit Olam; Collegeville, MN: Liturgical Press, 1996); **R. N. Whybray,** *The Succession Narrative: A Study of II Samuel 9-20, 1 Kings 1 and 2* (SBT 9; London: SCM, 1968); **H. G. M. Williamson,** *Ezra, Nehemiah* (WBC 16; Waco, TX: Word, 1985); **D. J. Wiseman,** *1 & 2 Kings* (TOTC; Downers Grove, IL: InterVarsity Press, 1993); **H. W. Wolff,** "The Kerygma of the Deuteronomistic Historical Work," in *Reconsidering Israel and Judah: Recent Studies on the Deuteronomistic History,* ed. G. N. Knoppers and J. G. McConville, (SBTS; Winona Lake, IN: Eisenbrauns, 2000) 62-78; **A. Wolters,** "Confessional Criticism and the Night Visions of Zechariah," in *Renewing Biblical Interpretation,* ed. C. G. Bartholomew, C. Greene and K. Möller (SH 1; Grand Rapids: Zondervan, 2000) 90-117; **N. T. Wright,** *The New Testament and the People of God* (Minneapolis: Fortress, 1992).

C. G. Bartholomew

HERMOPOLIS PAPYRI. *See* Non-Israelite Written Sources: Egyptian Aramaic Papyri.

HEZEKIAH

Hezekiah son of Ahaz was king of Judah c. 715-686 BCE. His mother was Abijah, daughter of Zechariah (2 Chron 29:1, hypocoristically written "Abi" in 2 Kings 18:2). Hezekiah came to the throne at age twenty-five and ruled twenty-nine years (2 Kings 18:2; 2 Chron 29:1). His name is a theophoric compound using the root *ḥzq,* "Yahweh (is) my strength" or "Yahweh is strong," and has variant forms in the Old Testament (*ḥizqiyyâ/-yāhû, yĕḥizqiyyâ/-yāhû;* Layton, 122-25). He is most noted for his piety and religious reforms, and his involvement in international affairs culminating in a standoff with the Assyrian king Sennacherib in 701 BCE, a turning point in Judah's history. The large amount of biblical material devoted to Hezekiah's reign (2 Kings 18—20; 2 Chron 29—32; Is 36—39) and the numerous extrabiblical sources from this period illuminate Hezekiah politically and personally, perhaps more than any other king of Israel or Judah.

1. The Account of Hezekiah's Reign in the Deuteronomistic History
2. The Account of Hezekiah's Reign in the Chronicler's History
3. Extrabiblical sources
4. Hezekiah in Historical and Theological Perspective

1. The Account of Hezekiah's Reign in the Deuteronomistic History.

The account of Hezekiah's reign plays an important part in the narrative structure of 2 Kings and the Deuteronomistic History as a whole. He is identified in the "judgment formulae" as the king who removed the high places, and Hezekiah is therefore the worthy successor of King David and the pious king anticipated in the earlier judgment formulas in the books of Kings (2 Kings 18:3-4; see Provan, 57-131). It is precisely his devotion to Yahweh that is at stake in the conflict with Sennacherib (2 Kings 18:13—19:37), as the Rabshakeh's speech makes clear, when the Assyrian field commander links salvation to the legitimacy of Hezekiah's trust in Yahweh (2 Kings 18:22). Hezekiah is vindicated when the Assyrians are miraculously defeated (2 Kings 19:35-36). In the accounts of Hezekiah's illness (2 Kings 20:1-11) and the Babylonian envoy (2 Kings 20:12-19), his reign is placed within the broader framework of the Deuteronomistic History, so that even righteous King Hezekiah is incapable of saving the nation Judah from its ultimate fate.

The positive evaluation of Hezekiah in the books of Kings (especially in 2 Kings 18—19) may reflect a composition of the Deuteronomistic History that originally ended with an account of his reign. In a three-tiered redactional approach, the first edition of the Deuteronomistic History had Hezekiah as its goal, while subsequent Josianic and exilic redactions altered this first edition in light of subsequent events (*see* Deuteronomistic History). This redactional history is especially apparent in the various types of

formulas used in the books of Kings to introduce and conclude each king: death and burial, naming queen mothers, regnal evaluation and source citation (Halpern and Vanderhooft). A similar approach, also based primarily on various formulas in the books of Kings, proposes a two-tiered redactional approach, the first ending with an account of Hezekiah's reign, though composed during Josiah's day, and the second exilic (Provan). In this way the books of Kings interchange reformists kings (Asa, Jehoshaphat, Joash, Hezekiah and Josiah) with all the others in a crescendo of contrast between hope and despair, culminating in a scheme of five kings from Ahaz to Josiah: Ahaz (bad), Hezekiah (good), Manasseh and Amon (bad), Josiah (good). In the final form of the book Hezekiah becomes a foil for the sins of Manasseh, where the blame is ultimately placed for the destruction of Jerusalem (2 Kings 23:26; 24:3). For the final editors of 1-2 Kings, the sins of Manasseh could not be turned back, even by the incomparable trust of his father, Hezekiah, the second David, or by the incomparable reforms of his grandson, Josiah, the second Moses (Knoppers 1992, 418-31).

The same materials found in the Deuteronomistic History are included in Isaiah 36—39, with some variation, plus Hezekiah's prayer of thanksgiving after his recovery from illness (Is 38:9-20).

Scholarship on the book of Isaiah long considered these materials to be an adaptation of 2 Kings 18—20, which were simply appended to the prophetic collection of the eighth-century prophet. In recent decades, a new emphasis on the redactional intentionality of the book of Isaiah and literary connections between Isaiah 36—39 and earlier portions of the book have challenged this consensus without dislodging it completely. It is possible to argue that Isaiah 36—39 (or perhaps only 36—38) were written in close association first with the rest of the Isaianic corpus and then were incorporated into the Deuteronomistic History as a source (Seitz, 104, 141), or perhaps both canonical works drew on a common independent source devoted to Jerusalem, Isaiah and the Davidic kingship as it is represented by Hezekiah (Clements, 278). It seems more likely that these materials were composed in Isaianic circles and incorporated as a source in 2 Kings and subsequently borrowed from Kings by a later editor of the book of Isaiah (Williamson 1994, 189-211). In any case, the Hezekiah materials in Isaiah 36—39 serve as a literary counterpart for Isaiah 6:1—9:6, and Hezekiah as a theological foil for King Ahaz. Turned the other direction along a trajectory in the book of Isaiah, Hezekiah's role in 36—39 as a second David who fulfills the promises of God for Judah prepares for the salvation oracles of Isaiah 40—55. He bears all the marks of the promised king, whose reign nevertheless fails to bring all the promises to fulfillment and who therefore points beyond himself to another in the future.

2. The Account of Hezekiah's Reign in the Chronicler's History.

The Deuteronomistic History included little on noncultic reforms in its account of Hezekiah's reign (besides a passing reference to a *water works project in Jerusalem, 2 Kings 20:20). Even his religious reforms are described only briefly (2 Kings 18:4-6) because the historian was concerned more with the Assyrian crisis and Hezekiah's faithfulness in its resolution. However, extrabiblical evidence, such as the Siloam Tunnel Inscription and lmlk jar impressions, suggests a strong central administrative and military organization in Jerusalem during Heze-kiah's reign, and the Chronicler's history provides more detail on these points (2 Chron 29—32; Knoppers 1997, 189-202) (see Hebrew Inscriptions).

Scholarship tended to dismiss the historical value of the books of Chronicles generally until the early 1980s (Peltonen, 2:633-795). Although vigorous debate continues, many today hold Chronicles in higher regard, while admitting that it must be allowed to speak with its own tendentious voice (see Chronicles, Books of). With his particular interests in the temple, the priesthood and the festivals, it is not surprising that the Chronicler provides more extensive treatment of the religious reformers. Hezekiah in particular is the king who reunites the religious community of "all Israel," lost since the united kingdom of *David and *Solomon. The temple is a focus for that unity in the reform of Hezekiah, who is portrayed as a second Solomon in his care of the temple and his unification of the tribes of Israel (Williamson 1977, 119-25), or perhaps as a second David and Solomon combined (Throntveit, 121-24). Hezekiah is thus the model for winning back the allegiance of the northern tribes to adherence to the God of the Jerusalem temple (2 Chron 30). In his enthusiasm for and observance of Passover too, Hezekiah is matched only by Solomon (2 Chron 30:26). The Chronicler was interested in whether Hezekiah faithfully observed the feasts of the priestly calendar (2 Chron 31:3; and for Josiah, 2 Chron 35:1), which is not unlike the Babylonian Chronicle's interest in Nabonidus's neglect of the New Year Festival (Arnold and Michalowski, 416-18). For the Chronicler, Hezekiah is the paradigmatic king in whom the kingship of Israel is equated with the kingship of God (Williamson 1982, 26-28) (see Kings and Kingship).

Thus the biblical materials on Hezekiah reflect a progression of thought from the Deuteronomistic History and Isaiah to Chronicles, in which the figure of King Hezekiah assumes ever-increasing dimensions of theological, perhaps even eschatological, importance. This development is more distinct if certain oracles of eighth-century Isaiah critique Hezekiah's participation in a revolt of *Ashdod and other regional states against *Assyria in 712 BCE, which may be the case in Isaiah 20 and perhaps Isaiah 30—31 (but see Younger, 313-18). Regardless of the specifics of these oracles or of Hezekiah's involvement in the revolt of 712 BCE, the other passages surveyed here evince a growing appreciation of Hezekiah, creating a trajectory in the Old Testament that continues into the rabbinic literature, where he is occasionally considered the messiah (b. Sanh. 99a, and cf. b. Ber. 28b), as well as into the New Testament, where several parallels between Hezekiah and Jesus have been observed (Provan, NIDOTTE 4.706).

3. Extrabiblical Sources.

In addition to the biblical materials devoted to Hezekiah, we also have epigraphic evidence from Syria-Palestine and cuneiform texts from the Assyrian Empire related to his reign, as well as relatively abundant archaeological data from the late eighth century BCE.

3.1. lmlk Jar Impressions. Debate has surrounded the date and purpose of over 1,700 storage jars with lmlk, "belonging to the king," stamped on the handle, which have been discovered throughout Judah (see Hebrew Inscriptions). Seals were impressed into the wet clay of the jar handles, with lmlk inscribed in a top register and the name of a city (see Hebron, Ziph, etc.) in the bottom, with a depiction of typically a two-winged sun or four-winged scarab in the middle, which were mostly royal emblems. It now appears these *lmlk* jars came from the period of Hezekiah's preparations for the Assyrian invasion toward the end of the eighth century BCE, especially as many were discovered in the destroyed storerooms inside the gate area of Lachish level III (Na'aman 1979; 1986). A slightly different approach is to assume a broader use of the jars during a longer period of time in Hezekiah's reign, in which he issued commodities shipped in these jars as soon as he stopped paying tribute to Assyria in anticipation of an attack by Sennacherib (Vaughn, 81-167). At any rate, the distribution of these *lmlk* storage jars in the late eighth century BCE reflects the influence of a central administrative or military organization and the degree of royal involvement in the administration of Jerusalem and Judah during Hezekiah's reign (Rosenbaum 1979).

3.2. The Siloam Tunnel Inscription. Among evidence available for Hezekiah's public works projects, one of the most ambitious was a tunnel to bring water from Jerusalem's principal water source, the Gihon Spring in the Kidron Valley, inside the city walls to the Pool of Siloam at the lower end of the Tyropoeon Valley (2 Kings 20:20; 2 Chron 32:30). The successful completion of the project has been preserved and celebrated in six lines of classical Hebrew describing the dramatic final phases of the tunnel's construction, in which two crews worked from opposite ends and met in the middle (*COS* 2.28:145-46; Renz and Röllig, 1:178-89; 3:16-17, taf. XVIII, 3) (*see* Hebrew Inscriptions). This remarkable inscription, discovered in 1880, has been almost unanimously associated with Hezekiah's tunnel mentioned in the biblical sources, although an attempt has been made to date the inscription to the Hasmonean period instead on the basis of paleography and archaeology (Rogerson and Davies 1996). However, the overwhelming consensus continues to date the inscription to Hezekiah's reign, and to associate it with fortifications and other preparations he made throughout Judah for defending the country against Sennacherib's invasion (Hackett et al. 1997) (*see* Water and Water Systems).

3.3. Neo-Assyrian sources. A variety of written sources from the Assyrian empire make specific mention of Israelite kings (Omri, Ahab, Jehu, Menahem, Pekah and Hoshea) or Judahite kings (Ahaz, Hezekiah and Manasseh) (*see* Non-

Israelite Written Sources: Assyrian). In the case of Hezekiah, the military campaign of Sennacherib in southern Syria-Palestine in 701 BCE is richly documented, not only in the Bible (2 Kings 18:13—19:37; Is 36—37; 2 Chron 32:1-22), Herodotus (*Hist.* 2.141) and Josephus (*Ant.* 9.13; 10.1-3), but also in the annals of Sennacherib himself, composed a few months after the campaign and preserved in copies on large barrel-shaped cylinders, or prisms, several bull inscriptions, and a fragmentary letter to the god Assur, which also contains a report of the campaign. (For a complete treatment of copies of the text and related Assyrian sources, see Mayer, 186-200.) The fullest Assyrian account of the campaign is preserved in the so-called Oriental Institute Prism, which has recently been retranslated (Strawn et al., 344-48), and the most important early copy, the Rassam Cylinder, has also received full treatment (Frahm, 47-61; and see also *COS* 2.119B:302-3). Sennacherib marched against the western regions because of revolts among vassal states shortly after the death of his predecessor, Sargon II. After describing the destruction of much of Judah, including the plundering of forty-six fortified cities, Sennacherib claims to have encircled Jerusalem with watchtowers, and to have confined Hezekiah (*Ḥa-za-qi-a-ú KUR Ia-ú-da-a-a*, "Hezekiah, the Judean") in the capital city like "a caged bird." Additionally, sculptured reliefs at Nineveh were found in Sennacherib's palace depicting the siege of Lachish, including the siege ramp (*COS* 2.119C:304). The capital city itself was not taken, and the biblical account of a miraculous deliverance of Jerusalem itself (2 Kings 19:35), together with archaeological and iconographical data, make this event a particularly useful case study for the historical method (Grabbe).

3.4. Archaeological Evidence for Hezekiah's Reign. Archaeological data gathered in surface surveys from the Shephelah indicate greater settlement there than elsewhere in Judah during Hezekiah's reign. These settlement patterns reach a population peak in the late eighth century BCE and suggest that Hezekiah's reign witnessed significant economic buildup and civil strength in the Shephelah, more so than during the United Monarchy before or Josiah afterward (Vaughn, 22-27). Although many of these settlements were built without extensive fortification and may therefore indicate stability during Hezekiah's reign, it seems likely that the fifteen fortified cities of 2 Chronicles 11:5-10 attributed to Rehoboam reflect instead Hezekiah's emergency military-supplies buildup in preparation for the Assyrian campaign of 701 BCE (Naʾaman 1986). Other archaeological data portray Hezekiah's reign as one of significant economic buildup and centralized civil and administrative power, as suggested by data from sites not only in the Shephelah but also in the central hill country, the Negeb and Jerusalem itself (Vaughn, 32-79).

4. Hezekiah in Historical and Theological Perspective.

Despite all the archaeological, biblical and extrabiblical evidence, the historical Hezekiah remains elusive. Precise chronology, of course, is impossible for most of the Israelite and Judahite kings, but the dates of Hezekiah's reign are especially difficult because the biblical sources on his date of accession are inconsistent (see Chronology). Did he begin to rule six years prior to the fall of *Samaria (727/6 BCE, as at 2 Kings 18:10), or fourteen years prior to Sennacherib's conquest of Judah in 701 (716/5 BCE, as 2 Kings 18:13 has it)? This latter option seems to be preferred, if only because it matches the stated length of Hezekiah's reign at twenty-nine years (2 Kings 18:2; 2 Chron 29:1). But in general, to accept the first option of 727/6 BCE requires the historian to emend the text of 2 Kings 18:13 despite the lack of versional or manuscript evidence for the emendation, while the second option of 716/5 BCE requires a rejection of the other regnal synchronisms of 2 Kings 18 (Tadmor, 407; Becking, 47-61).

In addition to the chronological problems, there is the lack of archaeological evidence for the kind of iconoclasm described in Hezekiah's reforms, since there are no signs of a drastic change in the cult in the late eighth century BCE. A building at *Arad stratum IX is frequently alleged to be a temple that was systematically and deliberately dismantled and buried under a layer of soil, and this nonviolent destruction is sometimes attributed to Hezekiah's reforms (Herzog, 175; but see the objections of Naʾaman 1995, 184-85). In fact, the archaeological data suggest that private and domestic idolatry among the general populace was persistent from the eighth to sixth centuries BCE and was unaffected by both the Hezekian and Josianic reforms (Milgrom, 7-10). It is possible that the religious reforms were focused solely on the official cult of Yahweh, leaving no traces of evidence in the popular religion. Another approach has been to deny any comprehensive cultic reform took place in Hezekiah's time and to assume the biblical materials related to his reign intended to portray him as a prototype of Josiah (Naʾaman 1995, 184-95).

The biblical account of Sennacherib's campaign of 701 BCE also raises difficulties (especially 2 Kings 18). Assyrian sources have brought to light a military campaign in 712 BCE by Sennacherib's father, Sargon II, to put down a revolt in *Ashdod (see History of Israel 5: Assyrian Period). This event gave rise to the only biblical text to mention Sargon by name, who sent his commander-in-chief, the Tartan, to quell the revolt (Is 20:1). Since the biblical materials are quiet about Hezekiah's early years, and since the Assyrian sources specifically name Judah as part of the rebellion in 712 BCE (ANET 287; but see Younger, 313-14), it has been suggested that elements of the biblical narrative of the 701 BCE conflict are better suited to the earlier Ashdod revolt. In this approach the original Israelite account of Sargon's 712 BCE campaign was led by an anonymous Assyrian king, who was later identified as Sennacherib when that account was combined with the materials in 1 Kings 18 (Jenkins). Perhaps Sargon's campaign into Syria-Palestine was a "limited invasion," which was later reported as 2 Kings 18:13-16 and combined with the materials on Sennacherib (Goldberg). Alternatively, the view that 2 Kings 18:13-16 is generally accurate requires postulating a complicated and conflicting use of two different systems of dating the events recorded in the chapter (Gallagher, 160-62). The older view of a second western campaign by Sennacherib much later, around 688 BCE, has largely been abandoned (Becking, 59; and see History of Israel 5: Assyrian Period).

The biblical materials devoted to Hezekiah's reign are clearly less concerned with these historical specifics and more interested in his religious reforms and individual trust in Yahweh. Today's historians can only conclude that his foreign policies were disastrous for Judah, resulting in the loss of Judah's territories, mass deportations and the subjection of Judah to Assyrian rule. But the Bible's undaunted adulation of Hezekiah is related to the fact that he survived the most direct encounter Judah had with Assyrian might. Jerusalem was spared Sennacherib's sword, and regardless of the tribute it cost or the specifics of the Assyrian army's miraculous withdrawal (2 Kings 19:35-36; 2 Chron 32:21; Herodotus *Hist.* 2.141), the reign of Hezekiah is interpreted and evaluated in this light (2 Kings 18:3; 2 Chron 29:2). This heroic portrait emerges in the biblical materials, creating a trajectory from Isaiah and 2 Kings to 2 Chronicles, continuing into the early rabbinic and Christian literature, resulting in messianic dimensions for the figure of King Hezekiah. Contributing to this imagery of devout Hezekiah are traditions of his support of ancient Israel's wisdom literature (Prov 25:1), his reliance on prayer (2 Kings 19:14-19; 20:2-3; 2 Chron 32:20, 24) and certainly his religious reforms. But central to all of this is Hezekiah's unwavering trust in Yahweh to deliver. A reverberating theme of these texts is Hezekiah's reliance or "trust" in Yahweh. The verb *bāṭaḥ*, "trust," occurs eighteen times in the texts devoted to Hezekiah (2 Kings 18:5, 19, 20, 21 (2x), 22, 24, 30; 19:10; 2 Chron 32:10; Is 36:4, 5, 6 (2x), 7, 9, 15; 37:10), representing perhaps the greatest concentration of the theme of OT faith in any of its narrative compositions. Trust is at the root of Hezekiah's opposition to idolatry (2 Kings 18:4-5), his observance of Mosaic law (2 Kings 18:6) and his attitudinal disposition of dependence on Yahweh for deliverance (2 Kings 18:30).

See also HEBREW INSCRIPTIONS; HISTORY OF ISRAEL 5: ASSYRIAN PERIOD; ISAIAH.

BIBLIOGRAPHY **B. T. Arnold and P. Michalowski,** "Achaemenid Period Historical Texts Concerning Mesopotamia," in *The Ancient Near East: Historical Sources in Translation,* ed. M. W. Chavalas (Oxford: Blackwell, 2005) 405-28; **B. Becking,** "Chronology: A Skeleton Without Flesh? Sennacherib's Campaign as a Case-Study," in *"Like a Bird in a Cage": The Invasion of Sennacherib in 701 BCE,* ed. L. L. Grabbe (JSOTSup/European Seminar in Historical Methodology 363/4; London: Sheffield Academic Press, 2003) 46-72; **R. E. Clements,** *Isaiah 1-39* (NCB; Grand Rapids: Eerdmans, 1980); **E. Frahm,** *Einleitung in die Sanherib-Inschriften* (AfOB 26; Wien: Institut für Orientalistik der Universität, 1997); **W. R. Gallagher,** *Sennacherib's Campaign to Judah: New Studies* (SHCANE 18; Leiden: E. J. Brill, 1999); **J. Goldberg,** "Two Assyrian Campaigns Against Hezekiah and Later Eighth Century Biblical Chronology," *Biblica* 80 (1999) 360-90; **L. L. Grabbe,** ed., *"Like a Bird in a Cage": The Invasion of Sennacherib in 701 BCE* (JSOTSup/European Seminar in Historical Methodology 363/4; London: Sheffield Academic Press, 2003); **J. A. Hackett et al.,** "Defusing Pseudo-Scholarship: The Siloam Inscription Ain't Hasmonean," *BAR* 23/2 (1997) 41-50, 68-69; **W. W. Hallo,** "Jerusalem Under Hezekiah: An Assyriological Perspective," in *Jerusalem: Its Sanctity and Centrality to Judaism, Christianity, and Islam,* ed. L. I. Levine (New York: Continuum, 1999) 36-50; **B. Halpern and D. S. Vanderhooft,** "The Editions of Kings in the 7th-6th Centuries B.C.E.," *HUCA* 62 (1991) 179-244; **Z. Herzog,** "Arad: Iron Age Period," *OEANE* 1:174-76; **S. Japhet,** *I & II Chronicles: A Commentary* (OTL; Louisville: Westminster/John Knox Press, 1993); **A. K. Jenkins,** "Hezekiah's Fourteenth Year: A New Interpretation of 2 Kings xviii 13-xix 37," *VT* 26/3 (1976) 284-98; **G. N. Knoppers,** "'There Was None Like Him': Incomparability in the Books of Kings," *CBQ* 54 (1992) 411-31; idem, "History and Historiography: The Royal Reforms," in *The Chronicler as Historian,* ed. M. P. Graham, Kenneth G. Hoglund, and Steven L. McKenzie (JSOTSup 238; Sheffield: Sheffield Academic Press, 1997) 178-203; **S. C. Layton,** *Archaic Features of Canaanite Personal Names in the Hebrew Bible* (HSM 47; Atlanta: Scholars Press, 1990); **W. Mayer,** "Sennacherib's Campaign of 701 BCE: The Assyrian View," in *"Like a Bird in a Cage": The Invasion of Sennacherib in 701 BCE,* ed. L. L. Grabbe (JSOTSup/European Seminar in Historical Methodology 363/4; London: Sheffield Academic Press, 2003) 168-200; **J. Milgrom,** "The Nature and Extent of Idolatry in Eighth-Seventh Century Judah," *HUCA* 69 (1998) 1-13; **N. Na'aman,** "Sennacherib's Campaign to Judah and the Date of the *lmlk* Stamps," *VT* 29 (1979) 61-86; idem, "Hezekiah's Fortified Cities and the *LMLK* Stamps," *BASOR* 261 (1986) 5-21; idem, "The Debated Historicity of Hezekiah's Reform in the Light of Historical and Archaeological Research," *ZAW* 107 (1995) 105-17; idem, "New Light on Hezekiah's Second Prophetic Story (2 Kings 19, 9b-35)," *Bib* 81 (2000) 393-402; **K. Peltonen,** *History Debated: The Historical Reliability of Chronicles in Pre-Critical and Critical Research* (Publications of the Finnish Exegetical Society 64; Helsinki/Göttingen: Finnish Exegetical Society/Vandenhoeck & Ruprecht, 1996); **I. W. Provan,** *Hezekiah and the Books of Kings: A Contribution to the Debate About the Composition of* *the Deuteronomistic History* (BZAW 172; Berlin: de Gruyter, 1988); idem, "Hezekiah," *NIDOTTE* 4.703-7; **J. Renz and W. Röllig,** *Handbuch der althebräischen Epigraphik* (Darmstadt: Wissenschaftliche Buchgesellschaft, 1995-); **J. W. Rogerson and P. R. Davies,** "Was the Siloam Tunnel Built by Hezekiah?" *BA* 59/3 (1996) 138-49; **J. Rosenbaum,** "Hezekiah's Reform and Deuteronomistic Tradition," *HTR* 72 (1979) 23-43; **C. R. Seitz,** *Zion's Final Destiny: The Development of the Book of Isaiah: A Reassessment of Isaiah 36—39* (Minneapolis: Fortress Press, 1991); **B. A. Strawn et al.,** "Neo-Assyrian and Syro-Palestinian Texts II," in *The Ancient Near East: Historical Sources in Translation,* ed. M. W. Chavalas (Oxford: Blackwell, 2005) 329-79; **H. Tadmor,** "The Chronology of the First Temple Period: A Presentation and Evaluation of the Sources," in *An Introduction to the History of Israel and Judah,* ed. J. A. Soggin (2nd ed.; Valley Forge, Penn.: Trinity Press International, 1993) 394-417; **M. A. Throntveit,** *When Kings Speak: Royal Speech and Royal Prayer in Chronicles* (SBLDS 93; Atlanta: Scholars Press, 1987); **A. G. Vaughn,** *Theology, History, and Archaeology in the Chronicler's Account of Hezekiah* (ABS 4; Atlanta: Scholars Press, 1999); **H. G. M. Williamson,** *Israel in the Books of Chronicles* (Cambridge: Cambridge University Press, 1977); idem, *1 and 2 Chronicles* (NCB; Grand Rapids: Eerdmans, 1982); idem, *The Book Called Isaiah: Deutero-Isaiah's Role in Composition and Redaction* (Oxford: Clarendon Press; Oxford University Press, 1994); **K. L. Younger Jr.,** "Recent Study on Sargon II, King of Assyria: Implications for Biblical Studies," in *Mesopotamia and the Bible: Comparative Explorations,* ed. M. W. Chavalas and K. L. Younger (JSOTSup 341; London: Sheffield Academic Press, 2002) 288-329.

B. T. Arnold

HEZEKIAH'S TUNNEL. See WATER AND WATER SYSTEMS.

HIGH PLACES

"High places," or *bāmôt* (sg., *bāmâ*), were cultic installations found in a variety of locations in Israel and used by the population before and during the monarchy. Making sacrifices and burning incense were recurring activities held in or at *bāmôt*. *Bāmôt*, along with the tabernacle and the temple, were human-made structures where worshipers encountered Yahweh. Thus *bāmâ* is a generic term related to places where

sacrifices were offered.

1. Survey of *Bāmôt* in the Old Testament
2. Problems of Research
3. Etymology
4. Physical Considerations
5. Perceptions from Chronicles
6. Conclusions

1. Survey of *Bāmôt* in the Old Testament.
Prior to the monarchy, *bāmôt* were considered legitimate worship spaces and received no condemnation, neither for their existence nor for their use. *Bāmôt* met the religious needs of the fluid environment of the tribal confederacy along with the "temple" or "house" of Yahweh at *Shiloh, a semipermanent structure perhaps built around the ancient tabernacle (1 Sam 1:7, 24; 3:15; 1:9; 3:3). Even though a plurality of *bāmôt* existed, there is no hint in the narrative that the people were sacrificing indiscriminately.

During the monarchy, however, *bāmôt* were considered illegitimate worship spaces and received considerable condemnation for their existence and use. After the building of *Solomon's temple, their inadequacy should have been apparent. Yet people continued to sacrifice at and multiply *bāmôt* as if no temple existed. The text mentions four categories of *bāmôt*: (1) Yahweh's *bāmôt*; (2) foreign deity *bāmôt*; (3) "high places of the gates," *bāmôt haššĕ'ārîm*; (4) "houses of the high places," *bêt bāmôt*. All these construction projects received condemnation. This situation resulted in a heightened expectation for the kings to remove *bāmôt*, particularly in the Judean kingdom. Although *Hezekiah removed Yahweh's *bāmôt*, it was *Josiah who finally destroyed all foreign deity *bāmôt*, including those built by *Solomon, and Jeroboam's northern "houses of the high places," *bêt bāmôt*, with its associated personnel. The story line in Kings would not be complete until all the threats to centralized worship in *Jerusalem were eradicated from the entire land (see Provan).

2. Problems of Research.
Since the etymology of the term remains unknown, Hebrew *bāmâ* (sg.) or *bāmôt* (pl.) usually appears as "high place(s)" in English versions on the basis of the ancient witnesses (the LXX and the Vulgate). This is the first difficulty one encounters when trying to understand *bāmôt*.

The second problem arises due to the relatively silent archaeological record about physical descriptions of *bāmôt*. The third issue concerns the biblical texts themselves, in that they offer only limited details pertaining to *bāmâ* usage, activities, size, location and associated personnel. Thus, regardless of their importance, especially in the books of Kings, little evidence about *bāmôt* actually exists.

3. Etymology.

The root *bmh* is not attested in biblical Hebrew, although some have posited *bhm* or *bwm* as possibilities (Emerton, 117-18). Therefore, one must consider cognates in other Semitic languages for suggestions. Ugaritic (*bmt*) most likely refers to the back of the body. Akkadian (*bāmtu/ bamâtu*) carries the meaning of "high ground" or "hilly." Thus both indicate a notion of elevation but without any religious associations (Vaughan, 121). Moabite (*bmt*), however, speaks of a type of cultic structure(s) (*COS* 2.23:137-38), even though some read this reference as a geographical name (see 4.3 below). Some LXX recensions transliterated the lexeme without providing further interpretive nuances. *Bāmâ/ bāmôt* in the LXX also has the semantic range of "high" or "lofty" in either a physical or metaphorical sense, perhaps on the basis of poetic *bāmôtê*, "heights," found in 2 Samuel 1:19, 25; 22:34. In a few instances the LXX substituted *bāmâ* with terminology referring to cult objects (LaRocca-Pitts, 274-84). Largely based on context, the LXX equated *bāmôt* with "high places" and understood them as cultic installations positioned on an elevation. Thus the Vulgate and also modern translations take their cues from the LXX.

4. Physical Considerations.

4.1. Provenance of **bāmôt.** Before the building of *Solomon's temple, we do not know who the originators of these installations were. The texts simply mention the presence of *bāmôt* (e.g., 1 Sam 9:14, 19; 10:13; 1 Kings 3:4). The term is associated with the introduction of *Saul to *Samuel (1 Sam 9:11-27) and Saul's encounter with a band of prophets (1 Sam 10:5-8). 1 Kings 3:3-4 announces Solomon's preference for the Gibeon *bāmâ*, and 1 Kings 3:2 notes that *bāmôt* were used by the general population. These passages presuppose the existence of *bāmôt* without stating their origin.

In the narratives dealing with the period following the building of the temple, another picture emerges. Now the texts explicitly indicate who built *bāmôt* and detail their multiplication throughout the land. In the south, *bāmôt* were built or torn down—a reflection of their human-made nature (1 Kings 11:7, 14:23; 2 Kings 17:9). Besides building Yahweh's temple, Solomon engaged in the ad hoc project of building *bāmôt* for foreign gods, including Molech and Chemosh (1 Kings 11:7; 2 Kings 23:13). Under the leadership of *Rehoboam, however, it was the people (assuming the general public) who built *bāmôt*, presumably for Yahweh (1 Kings 14:23).

The narratives of the northern kingdom focus on structures that originated with *Jeroboam. Besides the sanctuaries at *Dan and *Bethel, Jeroboam constructed numerous "houses of the high places," *bêt bāmôt* (1 Kings 12:25-33). The fact that Jeroboam built *bêt bāmôt* and not merely *bāmôt* distinguishes northern from southern *bāmôt*. As was the case under Rehoboam of Judah, the people followed in Jeroboam's footsteps and built *bāmôt* for themselves (2 Kings 17:9). Thus, in contrast to the premonarchical period, the text clearly communicates that *bāmôt* originated with certain monarchs and people. And now two categories of *bāmôt* existed: foreign deity *bāmôt* and Yahweh's *bāmôt*.

4.2. Locations of **bāmôt.** The available linguistic data indicate that some *bāmôt* were built on elevations (1 Sam 9:11-14, 27; 10:5). The passages in Samuel show participants ascending to or descending from the *bāmâ* (1 Sam 9:13-14, 19; 1 Sam 10:5). By virtue of its lexical connections to *gibʿâ*, "hill," the *Gibeon *bāmâ* most likely was situated on an elevation (1 Kings 3:3; cf. 2 Sam 21:1-11). The *bāmôt* that Solomon dedicated to Molech and Chemosh were erected on the mountain east of Jerusalem (1 Kings 11:7). This geographical indicator highlights two things. Foreign deity *bāmôt*, like Yahweh's *bāmôt*, could be built on or at an elevation; but more pertinent to the plot in Kings, the notification of location signals their competition with Yahweh and his Jerusalem residence. In addition, the people under Rehoboam built not only *bāmôt*, but also *maṣṣēbôt*, "pillars," and *ʾăšērîm*, "sacred poles." The text pinpoints the location of all these items, "on every hill and under every green tree" (1 Kings 14:23). This latter phrase, while possibly alluding to two types of open-air or countryside cult locations (Zevit, 260), reveals more about the excessive multiplication of *bāmôt* as well as pillars and sacred poles.

The phrase, however, does not prove that *bāmôt* had to be on elevations, since many texts reveal otherwise. At the time of Josiah's reforms *bāmôt* dotted the land in "cities of Judah" (2 Kings 23:5, 9). Sanctuaries called "high places of the gates," *bāmôt haššĕʿārîm*, also appeared (2 Kings 23:8). This latter designation positions *bāmôt* specifically at the city gate—a reflection of their publicly accessible nature. Likewise in the north, Jeroboam's *bêt bāmôt* were located "in all the cities of Samaria" (1 Kings 13:32). And the *bāmôt* built by those of the northern kingdom were placed "at all their towns, from watchtower to fortified city" (2 Kings 17:9).

Thus *bāmâ* is not synonymous with "high place." Each situation must be examined in its context. Furthermore, no specific ethnic interpretation can be derived from the location of a *bāmâ*. Based upon Deuteronomic sources that link worship on high ground to practices of the nations (Deut 12:2-3), the conclusion is sometimes drawn that much of Israelite cultic activities performed on hilltops must represent an illegitimate form of Canaanite worship in Israel (Nakhai, 18-29). Or conversely, it is argued that an installation found on mid-slope should be identified as a legitimate form of Israelite worship (Elitzur and Nir-Zevi, 35; for a similar discussion concerning a Transjordan find see Rainey, 85). However, the mere location of a cultic item on mid-slope does not automatically make it a legitimate Israelite *bāmâ*. As Z. Zevit (262) has warned, *bāmâ* labels should be the exception when identifying cultic structures in the archaeological record because the lexical data remain unclear.

4.3. Descriptions and Perceived Stature of bāmôt. Based on limited descriptions in the OT, not all *bāmôt* are equal in size and importance. The Samuel *bāmôt* were sizable structures that accommodated a banquet of thirty or more in an accompanying "room," *liškâ* (1 Sam 9:22), and a band/company of prophets (1 Sam 10:5, 10). The *bāmâ* described in 1 Samuel 9:22 has architectural affinities to the later sanctuary, which reflects the substantial nature of the former. *Lĕšākôt* (pl.), "rooms" or "chambers," that served a variety of functions are also found connected to Solomon's temple (2 Kings 23:11;

1 Chron 9:33) and to the postexilic second temple (Ezra 8:29; Neh 10:38-39).

The *bāmâ* at Gibeon must have represented one of the largest in town either in size or reputation, since it is designated as *haggĕdôlâ*, "the great" or "the principal" *bāmâ* (1 Kings 3:4). It accommodated Solomon's lavish worship to Yahweh, which consisted of one thousand sacrifices (1 Kings 3:4). It also stood as a place of revelation. Yahweh spoke to Solomon in a dream at Gibeon (1 Kings 3:5-14). Chronicles reveals that by David's design, the *ark of the covenant and the tabernacle were in or at the *bāmâ* at Gibeon (1 Chron 16:39-40; 21:29; 2 Chron 1:3, 13). For this reason, Solomon sacrificed and sought God there. Thus the Gibeon *bāmâ* earned its reputation as "great" and stood apart from all others. Unfortunately, there is nothing in the archaeological record from the site to support these claims.

Solomon's Molech and Chemosh *bāmôt* should also be noted for implicit descriptions of them offered in the text. First, the passage highlights them by name, as opposed to the other *bāmôt* that he built "for all his foreign wives, who burned incense and offered sacrifices to their gods" (1 Kings 11:8). Second, they appear to have stood in close proximity to the Jerusalem temple. Perhaps both these announcements attest to the significance of their size.

Jeroboam's *bêt bāmôt*, "houses of the high places" (1 Kings 12:31-32; 13:2, 32-33), are found only in narratives concerning the northern kingdom. This designation (contra Judah's "house of Yahweh") probably boasts about the size of these installations. They seem to be sanctuary complexes rather than "utilitarian structures" along the lines of a *liškâ*, "room" or "chamber" (Barrick 1996, 623). Most likely they were more sophisticated than their southern *bāmâ* counterparts and stood in direct competition with the temple of Yahweh because they were part of a larger, illegitimate system of worship, one synonymous with the name of Jeroboam son of Nebat.

In the case of *bāmâ* descriptions from extrabiblical sources we know that King Mesha of *Moab built and dedicated a *bāmâ* to his god Chemosh at Qarhoh (*COS* 2.23:137, line 3b). This *bāmâ* was also human-made and used for religious purposes. Likewise, Mesha might have rebuilt a cultic installation at Aroer called a *bêt bāmôt* (lines 26-27). Most commentators assume that the latter phrase refers to a place name, but the structure of this section of the inscription argues against this reading. According to lines 22-30, Mesha rebuilt Qarhoh, Aroer and Beser. After mentioning Qarhoh and Aroer, a list of specific reparations to those places ensues. For example, in Qarhoh he repaired the walls, gates, towers, the royal palace and hewed ditches (lines 22-30). Then it says that he "rebuilt Aroer." His work there consisted of making a highway and rebuilding the *bêt bāmôt*. It is entirely possible that *bêt bāmôt* refers not to a rebuilt town, but to a sanctuary complex, not unlike Jeroboam's *bêt bāmôt* in 1 Kings 12:31 (so Barrick 1996, 623). Current excavations in *Moab are continuing to produce exciting material culture that begs to be interpreted with some of Mesha's projects in the area, but more analysis is needed.

Excavations at Tel *Dan purport to have features descriptive of a biblical *bāmâ* (see Biran). The first feature is a podium, or raised platform, built three meters high, whose south side contained a staircase ascending to the top. The second feature associated with a *bāmâ* installation is three sets of pillars within the gate chambers. A. Biran interprets the podium, the entire complex and the sets of pillars as examples of a *bāmâ*, *bêt bāmôt* and *bāmôt haššĕʿārîm* respectively. He likens them to Jeroboam's complexes in the north (1 Kings 12:28-31; 2 Kings 23:8b), even though the texts do not specifically mention Dan as possessing these buildings. Although we do have material cultural data relating to cult places such as the temple in Khirbet el-Mudeiyineh (Transjordan), the temple complexes in *Arad, *Megiddo (Early Bronze), the cult complex of Ebal and the Bull site (an early Iron Age cult site where a miniature bull statue was discovered), to equate these with *bāmôt* goes beyond the evidence at these sites.

4.4. Activities, Usages and Associated Personnel. Activities in or at *bāmôt* before the temple was built included sacrifices (1 Sam 9:12-13; 1 Kings 3:2-3), incense burning (1 Kings 3:3), ceremonial feasts (1 Sam 9:1-26), prophetic inspiration (1 Sam 10:5-8) and divine revelation (1 Kings 3:5-15). Other than Samuel, who blessed the sacrifice in 1 Samuel 9:13, and the cook in 1 Samuel 9:23-24, no specific *bāmâ* personnel are highlighted. Thus a common purpose for *bāmôt* was to provide adequate places of Yahweh worship for the people. However, 1 Kings 3:2 suggests that *bāmôt* usage was intended as a temporary measure.

Even with Solomon's temple at center stage, sacrificing at Yahweh's *bāmôt* continued (1 Kings 3:2; 2 Chron 33:15-17). In fact, each Judean king, starting with Asa through Jotham, was suspect because he did not remove or tear down the *bāmôt* (1 Kings 15:14; 22:43; 2 Kings 12:4; 14:4; 15:4, 35), and by association probably continued using them for sacrificial purposes. The text's emphasis on the kings and their inability to remove *bāmôt* reflects the expectations articulated in 1 Kings 3:2: *bāmôt* should have been discarded, presumably because they were obsolete and replaced by the Jerusalem temple. However, it was not until the arrival of Hezekiah that these hopes were met (2 Kings 18:4). He destroyed Yahweh's *bāmôt* and altars in order to ensure worship at the Jerusalem temple (2 Kings 18:22). Thus one sees the enduring nature of *bāmâ* usage as late as the eighth century BCE.

Bāmôt activities expanded, however, with certain monarchs. Some of Ahaz's and Manasseh's *bāmâ* rituals may have included human sacrifices—a practice of former occupants of the land (2 Kings 16:3; 21:6; 2 Chron 28:3; 33:6). The "high places of the gates," *bāmôt haššĕʿārîm*, built before Josiah's reign, probably were utilized by travelers desiring a blessing or by those wishing to consult or swear to the deity with respect to legal matters (Rainey, 85). In addition, *ʾăšērîm*, "sacred poles," and *maṣṣēbôt*, "pillars," were set up and used in conjunction with some *bāmâ* activities (1 Kings 14:23; 2 Kings 17:9-10; 18:4; 2 Chron 14:3; 31:1; 34:3)—customs that provoked the Lord to anger.

We learn of *bāmâ* personnel from the reigns of *Manasseh and Josiah. Manasseh's long reign included, among other things, the rebuilding of *bāmôt*. Attached to the rebuilt *bāmôt* was an establishment of priestly personnel. Josiah's reforms targeted both, but of note are his dealings with three varieties of *bāmâ* personnel. In the south he found and deposed "idolatrous priests," those whose job descriptions included burning incense to Baal in the high places built in the cities of Judah (2 Kings 23:5). He also encountered "the priests of the high places," those who were merely officiating sacrifices in places other than Jerusalem (2 Kings 23:8-9). Josiah evacuated this group from the premises and restricted them from future temple services, either as a disciplinary measure or because they did not come from Levitical stock. Finally, in his aggressive northern reforms he slayed priestly staff serving the *bêt bāmôt* in the cities of Samaria (2 Kings 23:19-20). Thus at the time of Josiah large numbers of personnel were associated with these sanctuaries.

5. Perceptions from Chronicles.
The perspective of the Chronicler concerning the attitudes and actions of various monarchs toward *bāmôt* testifies to the selective nature of the material in Chronicles. In general, the Chronicler adopts the negative views of *bāmôt* presented in Kings. However, for the purpose of highlighting the bright spots of the nation's past, in some regnal accounts he chooses not to emphasize the wrongness of *bāmôt*. This is achieved by making subtle distinctions between foreign *bāmôt* and Yahweh's *bāmôt*. Thus some of the Chronicler's adaptations appear as a justification of the monarch's association with *bāmôt*.

For example, in the reign of Solomon, Chronicles avoids a Deuteronomic condemnation (1 Kings 1:3; 11:6-13) by clarifying that the *bāmâ* used by Solomon at Gibeon was indeed Yahweh's (1 Chron 16:39-40; 21:29; 2 Chron 1:1-13). Likewise, in documenting Manasseh's repentance and resulting return to Yahweh worship (2 Chron 33:10-17), the Chronicler makes a substantial qualification about actions that clearly were negative in Kings (2 Kings 21:2-5): "The people still sacrificed at the *bāmôt*, but only to the LORD their God" (2 Chron 33:17). Although Chronicles and Kings agree that Asa failed to remove *bāmôt* from the land (1 Kings 15:14; 2 Chron 15:17), Asa receives merit from the Chronicler for the successful removal of "foreign" altars and *bāmôt* (2 Chron 14:2-4). In context, it is not inconceivable that both altars and *bāmôt* are viewed as foreign. Thus from these texts, it appears that the Chronicler is mirroring a premonarchical perspective of *bāmôt*, yet without denying the Deuteronomic prohibition reflected in Kings.

6. Conclusions.
In the biblical text *bāmâ* does not appear to have the status of a technical term, but serves instead as a generic designation for whatever is not the central place of worship, either tabernacle or temple. Because of the heterogeneous religious environment present during the monarchy, it is difficult to apply a generic term to specific and varied cultic installations. We cannot assign the label *bāmâ* to every cultic installation emerging from the archaeological record. To set up criteria, even in the cautious manner of Z. Zevit, is asking too much of the term. Zevit remarks that *bāmôt* are "publicly accessible places with *massebot* [pillars]" (Zevit, 262). Although *maṣṣēbôt* are associated with some *bāmâ* texts, they are not a standard feature. In fact, they are a part of a larger grouping of cultic items that may or may not be connected to *bāmôt* (LaRocca-Pitts, 148). The texts show that *bāmôt* are found in a variety of religious and geographical contexts without a fixed set of associated cultic items.

In this pluralistic milieu there may have been other names to characterize the variety of the material evidence that we possess. As indirect support, we have no epigraphical data linking a particular cultic installation or object to the biblical *bāmâ* (Emerton, 129). Thus we should be content to accept the biblical record, which takes a generic term to describe what the archaeological record reveals as a diversified and complex religious landscape.

See also CANAANITE GODS AND RELIGION; SOLOMON'S TEMPLE.

BIBLIOGRAPHY. **W. B. Barrick,** "The Funerary Character of High-places in Ancient Palestine: A Reassessment," *VT* 25 (1975) 565-95; idem, "High Place," *ABD* 3.196-200; idem, "On the Meaning of Beth-Ha/Bamoth and the Composition of the Kings History," *JBL* 115 (1996) 621-42; idem, "What Do We Really Know About High-places?" *SEÅ* 45 (1980) 50-57; **A. Biran,** "Sacred Spaces: Of Standing Stones, High Places, and Cult Objects at Dan," *BAR* 24.5 (1998) 38-45, 70; **Y. Elitzur and D. Nir-Zevi,** "A Rock-Hewn Altar Near Shiloh," *PEQ* 135 (2003) 30-36; **J. A. Emerton,** "The Biblical High Place in the Light of Recent Study," *PEQ* 129 (1997) 116-32; **P. J. King and L. Stager,** *Life in Biblical Israel* (Louisville: Westminster/John Knox, 2001); **E. C. LaRocca-Pitts,** *"Of Wood and Stone": The Significance of Israelite Cultic Items in the Bible and Its Early Interpreters* (HSM 61; Winona Lake, Ind.: Eisenbrauns, 2001); **B. A. Nakhai,** "What's a Bamah? How Sacred Space Functioned in Ancient Israel," *BAR* 20.3 (1994) 18-29, 77-78; **I. W. Provan,** *Hezekiah and the Books of Kings: A Contribution to the Debate about the Composition of the Deuteronomistic History* (BZAW 172; Berlin: de Grutyer, 1988); **A. F. Rainey,** "The New Inscription from Khirbet el-Mudeiyineh," *IEJ* 52 (2002) 81-86; **P. H. Vaughan,** *The Meaning of "bāmâ" in* *the Old Testament: A Study of Etymological, Textual and Archaeological Evidence* (SOTSMS 3: Cambridge: Cambridge University Press, 1974); **Z. Zevit,** *The Religions of Ancient Israel: A Synthesis of Parallactic Approaches* (New York: Continuum, 2001). D. L. Petter

HIGHWAYS. *See* ROADS AND HIGHWAYS.

HIRAM. *See* PHOENICIA, PHOENICIANS.

HISTORICAL-CRITICAL METHOD. *See* HERMENEUTICS; METHODS OF INTERPRETATION.

HISTORICAL CRITICISM. *See* METHODS OF INTERPRETATION.

HISTORICAL ISRAEL. *See* QUEST OF THE HISTORICAL ISRAEL.

HISTORIOGRAPHY, OLD TESTAMENT

Historiography and *history writing* are terms often applied to a number of OT books. The most complete list includes Genesis, Exodus, Leviticus, Numbers, Deuteronomy, Joshua, Judges, Ruth, 1-2 Samuel, 1-2 Kings, 1-2 Chronicles, Ezra-Nehemiah and Esther. The present article focuses on Joshua, Judges, Samuel, Kings, Chronicles and Ezra-Nehemiah in keeping with the parameters of this dictionary.

1. The Bible's Historical Literature as Ancient History Writing
2. The Writing of History in the Bible

1. The Bible's Historical Literature as Ancient History Writing.

1.1. Assumptions and Expectations. The designation *historical literature* for certain biblical books has elicited various assumptions about the nature of these books that biblical scholarship recently has called into question. The Hebrew Bible does not use the designation *historical books.* Genesis, Exodus, Leviticus, Numbers and Deuteronomy comprise the Torah, "law" or "instruction." Joshua, Judges, Samuel and Kings are classed as the Former Prophets. The rest of the books named above are in the Writings. None of these books refers to itself as history. Indeed, the word *history* is Greek in origin. Its definition as a literary genre and the extent to which its use for biblical material may be anachronistic are ques-

tions raised by recent scholarship.

Biblical and archaeological scholarship over the past two hundred years has called into question the historical reliability of some of the Bible's best-known narratives. In the past fifty years especially, historical investigation and scientific analysis have convinced the majority of scholars that events such as the flood, the exodus from Egypt, and the conquest of Canaan did not occur in the way the Bible describes them (*see DOTP,* Historical Criticism). Yet it has only been in the last two decades that the question of the nature of history writing in the Bible has been broached. Recent research into the genre of ancient historiography suggests that modern readers often approach the Bible with an incorrect set of assumptions and expectations. Thus the problem lies not with the Bible, but with the way in which it has been read (*see* Hermeneutics). A better understanding of biblical history writing in its ancient context may help to resolve tensions between the Bible's account and historical analyses.

History, for most modern Westerners, is what happened in the past, and history writing as a literary genre is an account of what happened in the past. The latter is judged by how accurately and objectively it recounts past events. There is some recognition that historians have their own biases, that no one is completely objective and that writing history involves interpretation. If pressed, most moderns probably will admit that it may be impossible to know for certain exactly what happened in the past. Nevertheless, telling exactly what happened remains the goal and the essential definition of the genre as it is generally envisioned. Thus there is a tendency to apply to history the same standards that apply to journalism. This same understanding is typically applied not only to modern history writing, but also to ancient history writing, including that found in the Bible. Recent biblical scholarship has called into question the assumption that ancient historians, and the biblical writers in particular, had the same definition of history and history writing as we do. The biblical writers may not have understood their task simply as relating what happened in the past.

1.2. In Search of History. The question of the definition of history writing in the Bible remained largely unexplored until J. Van Seters's 1983 study of historiography in the ancient world, which has had a considerable impact on biblical scholarship. Van Seters sought to describe the nature and origin of history writing in the Bible by comparison with historiographical works from other cultures, notably Greece, Mesopotamia, the Hittites and Egypt. He adopted the definition of history coined by the Dutch historian J. Huizinga: "History is the intellectual form in which a civilization renders account to itself of its past." This definition has three important parts, whose implications were pursued by Van Seters.

1.2.1. Historiography Versus History Writing. Following Huizinga's definition, Van Seters distinguished between *historiography* as a general term for all historical texts and *history writing* as the genre in which a civilization or nation tried to render an account of its collective past. Although historiographical materials are preserved from Egypt, Mesopotamia and the Hittites, Van Seters concluded that true history writing developed first in Israel and then in Greece, where its closest analogs are found.

1.2.2. Intellectual Form. Van Seters discerned a number of features of history writing in ancient Greece, especially in the work of Herodotus, who is widely called "the father of history," that illumine the nature of the Bible's history writing. Two facets of Herodotus's work constitute it as an intellectual form. First, Herodotus engaged in personal research or investigation. Indeed, the basic meaning of the Greek term *historia*, from which our word *history* is derived, is "investigations" or "researches." Herodotus gathered first-hand information, especially about geography and social customs, as well as traditions, legends and even myths of local peoples about whom he wrote.

Second, Herodotus recorded the traditions that he received in writing. Thus history writing was the deliberate product of a literate society rather than the result of the gradual accumulation of traditions. What sources Herodotus possessed came to him in both oral and written forms, but it was his crafting of them into a unified whole that set his work apart from that of individual storytellers (or "logographers") who preceded him. Ancient history writing was not journalism; it was closer to storytelling than to the objective reporting of past events.

Several features of ancient Greek history writing illustrate the freedom that historians exercised in their literary creations. First, Herodotus and his successors organized their histories "paratactically" by stringing together different stories and episodes, often with their own introductions and conclusions, but with little or no verbal connection between them. Some Greek historians used genealogies to frame their works. Ancient Greek historians also used speeches and narrative formulas as structuring devices. Such speeches typically were invented by the historian, in both wording and substance, according to what was deemed appropriate to the occasion (see Finley 1986, 13). After all, the historian usually was not present at the occasions when speeches were delivered, especially those in the distant past. These historians also invented stories and sources to fill in gaps in their work.

1.2.3. A Civilization Renders Account to Itself of Its Past. Of special significance for our purposes is Van Seters's observation that history writing in ancient Greece was not primarily concerned with relating past events "as they really happened." Rather, the primary objective of ancient history writing was to "render an account" of the past that explained the present.

"Rendering an account" carried two connotations. First, it entailed assessing responsibility for and passing judgment on a nation's past actions as a way of explaining consequences for the present. Ancient historians had axes to grind—theological or political points to make. Second, a civilization rendering an account of its past also entailed an expression of the corporate identity of the nation—what it was and what principles it stood for. Hence, the historian's primary concern was not detailing exactly what happened in the past as much as it was interpreting the meaning of the past for the present, showing how the "causes" of the past brought about the "effects" of the present.

These cause-effect explanations were not scientific in nature, but typically had to do with moral and religious matters. Thus Greek historians used myth or legend as causes of the past leading to the present. These were the only sources available for the distant past, which had not produced written records. Even historians who did not believe the myths were compelled to use them because they had no other sources. These historians often "rationalized" the myths they incorporated by offering more "scientific" interpretation for them.

Applying his observations from Huizinga's definition and from Greek history writing to the

Bible, Van Seters (4-5) isolated five criteria for identifying history writing in ancient Israel:

1. History writing was a specific form of tradition in its own right rather than the accidental accumulation of traditional material.
2. History writing considered the reason for recalling the past and the significance of past events and was not primarily the accurate reporting of the past.
3. History writing examined the (primarily moral) causes in the past of present conditions and circumstances.
4. History writing was national or corporate in nature.
5. History writing was literary and an important part of a people's corporate tradition.

1.3. History in the Bible as Etiology and Theology. The Bible's "historical literature" functions within the genre of ancient history writing in line with several of Van Seters's criteria. Its authors conducted "research" into traditional materials and collected stories and traditions, which they then fashioned into literary products whose interests were national in scope. Of particular significance are criteria 2 and 3. The Greek word for "cause," *aitia,* lends itself to the word *etiology* (also spelled "aetiology"). An etiology is a story that explains the cause or origin of a given phenomenon—a cultural practice or social custom, a biological circumstance, even a geological formation. It is not a scientific explanation, not historical in the modern sense of an event that actually took place in the past exactly as described; etiologies can be quite imaginative, even if not always constituted of fiction (Millard, 40-42). An etiology is, rather, a story that "renders an account"—that is, offers some explanation—of present conditions and circumstances based on past causes.

The Bible's historical literature is etiological in the sense that it seeks to "render an account" of the past—to provide an explanation *(aitia)* for circumstances or conditions in the historian's day. Whether the events that the Bible relates as past causes or explanations actually took place as described was not the ancient historian's primary concern. This does not mean that all of the traditions recorded as part of Israel's history writing are fictional. Many are no doubt based on actual events of the past. According to this view, a proper understanding of ancient history writing allows for the incorporation of non-

historical and even fictional narratives. Van Seters's definition of history writing implies that to attempt to read the account of Israel's history in the Bible from a modern perspective as strictly a record of actual events is to misconstrue its genre and force it to do something that it was not intended to do.

The historical literature in the Bible provides explanations from the past for prime elements of Israel's self-understanding. Key to that self-understanding is Israel's perception of its relationship to its God, Yahweh, in whom ancient Israelite historians found the ultimate explanation for their people's origin and present state. As for ancient Greek historians, so also in the Bible, history was written for an ideological purpose. History writing was theology.

2. The Writing of History in the Bible.

Biblical historiographers used the same techniques that ancient Greek historians used to render an account of their national past, including paratactic organization, the use of *genealogies to frame narratives, the composition of speeches, and the invention of stories and sources to fill gaps in the narrative. The following texts illustrate the freedom and creativity exercised by biblical historians in their literary creations.

2.1. The Book of Joshua and Israel's Emergence in Canaan. One of the most vexing problems faced by biblical scholars is that of Israel's historical origins. Archaeology has raised serious doubts about the historical veracity of the conquest as depicted in Joshua 1—12. Cities such as *Jericho and *Ai, which are at the heart of the Bible's conquest narrative (Josh 6—8), attest little or no occupation at the time that they were supposedly conquered by the invading Israelites. Moreover, Israelite culture seems to have its origins in central highland villages that were native to *Canaan rather than being introduced from the outside (Dever 2003; Finkelstein and Silberman 2001).

The difficulties involved in reconstructing actual events behind these episodes suggest that the narratives about them are ripe for a different kind of interpretation. Again, the problem may lie not with the Bible, but with the way it is interpreted. The conquest story seems to make the most sense when read in the light of the nature and techniques of ancient history writing. The story of the flight of the Hebrews from

Egypt and their defeat of Canaanite cities may contain genuine historical elements, as scholars from widely divergent perspectives have contended (Redford, esp. 408-22; Provan, Long and Longman, 129-56). But the primary intent of the story is to account for how Israel gained possession of the *land of Canaan. Its explanation is theological: God gave Israel the land of Canaan.

The etiological nature of these stories is most apparent in the case of Ai (Josh 8:1-2), whose very name means "ruin." Jericho was the oldest city in Canaan and a legendary symbol of Canaanite might. As such, it symbolized Canaan. Biblical historians saw the fact that Jericho had come to belong to Israel as representative of God's gift of the whole land to the Israelites (see History of Israel 1: Settlement Period).

2.2. The Book and Period of the Judges.

2.2.1. Composition of the Book of Judges. Biblical scholars have long surmised that the Deuteronomistic Historian had two kinds of sources for the book of Judges (see Judges, Book of): stories about the victories of military leaders (Ehud, Deborah, Gideon, Jephthah), and a list of local officials of some sort (Tola, Jair, Jephthah, Ibzan, Elon, Abdon) with their administrative centers and lengths of judgeship (Noth, 42-46) (see Judges). The presence of Jephthah's name in both sources led the Deuteronomistic Historian to combine them by placing the list of local officials immediately after the collection of war stories and incorporating Jephthah's story into the list at the point where he was mentioned as a local official.

The Deuteronomistic Historian then imposed a theological pattern on his sources. It is a cyclical pattern of *sin, punishment, repentance and *deliverance that is articulated in Judges 2:11-19. This pattern necessitated other changes. The traditions that the Deuteronomistic Historian inherited concerned local heroes from different tribes facing different adversaries. The Deuteronomistic Historian turned them into national figures in order to convey a message about the nation as a whole. As local heroes, the careers of the military leaders overlapped. The Deuteronomistic Historian's theological pattern required that they be sequential. Thus he employed a chronological pattern, using forty, the round number for a generation, as the base (see Numbers, Large Numbers).

The story of Othniel (Judg 3:7-11) was added at the beginning to serve as a model. Scholars typically have viewed it as an invention of the Deuteronomistic Historian. What few details it has beyond the theological pattern appear artificial and contrived. Hence, Othniel's foe, Cushan-rishathaim, has a name that means "dark, double wicked" and rhymes with Aram-naharaim, where he is from. The materials about Shamgar, Abimelech and Samson were independent and either were incorporated by the Deuteronomistic Historian or were interpolated later.

2.2.2. The Death of Sisera (Judges 4—5). The two versions of Sisera's assassination (Judg 4:17-22; 5:24-30) provide a more focused example of literary creativity. The historian, presumably the Deuteronomistic Historian, used the ancient poem in Judges 5 to formulate the prose account in Judges 4 (see Poetry). He did so by interpreting the poem literally. Thus Jael's gift of milk to Sisera after he had requested water (Judg 4:19) is based on the poetic pair in Judges 5:25a: "He asked for water / She gave him milk." Then in the poem, while Sisera drank, "[Jael] put her hand to the tent peg / Her right hand to a laborer's hammer" (Judg 5:26a). The threefold occurrence of the verbs "sank" and "fell" (Judg 5:27) in the poem envision Sisera as standing, enjoying his drink when Jael dealt the fatal blow.

In the prose version Sisera is already lying down when he requests drink (Judg 4:18). The historian retained the motif of Sisera drinking but altered the circumstances in order to allow Jael to use both implements, hammer and tent peg, to kill him by nailing his head to the floor (Judg 4:21). Ignoring the device of parallelism, the historian fashioned a prose account of Sisera's death that incorporated all the details of the poem—water, milk, tent peg, hammer. The other facets of the prose story are all logical deductions arising from its elaboration of the means of Sisera's death. He was lying in the tent, which must mean that he was hiding, which in turn means that he was forced to flee on foot (Halpern, 84-85).

2.3. The Election of Saul (1 Samuel 9—11).
Another focused example of the literary skill of a biblical historiographer is the series of stories in 1 Samuel 9—11 about how *Saul became Israel's first king. Scholars have long perceived that these chapters contain different versions of Saul's election. This view of the ancient historian's method may be sketched as follows.

2.3.1. The First Version: Saul's Private Anointing (1 Samuel 9:1—10:16).

The first version (1 Sam 9:1—10:16), in which Saul goes searching for his father's lost donkeys and finds kingship, exhibits clear signs of editorial revision. In 1 Samuel 9:9, for instance, the historian, again presumably the Deuteronomistic Historian, interrupts the story to define the term "seer" for his readers, showing that he is relating an older story.

Other revisions are only slightly more subtle. *Samuel is unknown by name to Saul's servant (1 Sam 9:6) despite being Israel's national leader, according to the previous two chapters. This suggests that a nameless seer or man of God in the older story was identified by the historian as Samuel. Then, in 1 Samuel 9:19 Samuel invites Saul to spend the night at his home, promising to tell him "all that is on your mind" the next morning. Yet in the very next verse he tells Saul that the lost donkeys have been found—the very thing on Saul's mind. This revision exhibits the historian's change of the story's original focus from Saul's search for lost donkeys to that of his election as king. Saul's overnight stay in the older story gave occasion for the seer to experience a dream revelation revealing the location of the lost animals.

These more apparent examples of revision suggest that the historian here took an older story from his sources about Saul's search for lost donkeys and rewrote it so as to relate Saul's anointing as king. Accordingly, those portions of the story that identify the seer as Samuel are the historian's revision, as is any part of the story that presumes Samuel's foreknowledge about Saul's coming or future as king (1 Sam 9:15-17, 20-21)—including his favored status at the banquet (1 Sam 9:22-24). Saul's anointing (1 Sam 9:27-10:1) is the focus of the revision.

Saul's interrogation by his uncle at the end of the story (1 Sam 10:14-16) is also editorial. The uncle plays no role in the story, but rather functions to make the single point that Saul's anointing was a private affair between him and Samuel (1 Sam 9:27-10:1). The historian added this scene to the story in order to pave the way for the second account of Saul's designation as king, this time publicly, which follows directly (1 Sam 10:17-27).

2.3.2. The Second Version: Saul's Designation by Lot in Public (1 Samuel 10:17-27).

In this second version Saul is chosen by lot. There is no contradiction between the two stories precisely be- cause the first has a private setting while the second is public. The second story is likely the Deuteronomistic Historian's composition drawn from traditional motifs. Again, the ending (1 Sam 10:27) is significant for its literary function. The fact that certain individuals question Saul's military leadership ("How can this man save us?") paves the way for yet a third story about how Saul was chosen king, one in which he demonstrates his military capability and silences his critics.

2.3.3. The Third Version: Saul Acclaimed King After Victory (1 Samuel 10:27b—11:15).

The third story about Saul's accession to kingship once was independent. Its original beginning was lost but can be restored on the basis of a Dead Sea Scroll fragment (cf. 1 Sam 10:27b NRSV). The story begins with a crisis: the Israelite city of Jabesh-Gilead, east of the Jordan, is being assailed by the Ammonite king Nahash. The city elders send messengers throughout Israel looking for someone to rescue them (1 Sam 11:3). The messengers go through all Israel rather than directly to Saul, indicating that originally the story did not presuppose that Saul was king. The messengers happen to come to *Gibeah, Saul's hometown (1 Sam 11:4), where he is engaged not in the affairs of state, but in plowing his field. He learns of the crisis only when he hears the people of Gibeah weeping at the news from Jabesh (1 Sam 11:5). He is then impelled by the divine spirit to lead Israel in victory.

After the victory there is a cry to execute those who doubted Saul's prowess (1 Sam 11:12-13). These latter two verses constitute another editorial addition by the Deuteronomistic Historian. He used this notice to bind this story with the previous one. Saul's victory answered all doubts about his capability as a military leader (1 Sam 10:27). The historian's hand is also apparent in 1 Samuel 11:14. The story once ended with the people making Saul king for the first time in *Gilgal (1 Sam 11:15). By inserting Samuel's call to renew the kingship in Gilgal (1 Sam 11:14), the historian connected this third story of Saul's designation as king with the previous two.

In composing the account of Saul's election to kingship, then, the Deuteronomistic Historian rewrote older sources and combined them with a story of his own composition in order to present an account of Saul's accession in stages: private anointing, public designation by lot, and proving himself militarily followed by kingship renewal (*see* Samuel, Books of).

2.4. The Royal Houses of Israel in the Book of Kings.

2.4.1. The Case of Omri (1 Kings 16:23-28). One of the best examples of the work of biblical historians being shaped by theological interests is the account of *Omri's reign (1 Kings 16:23-28). Omri's historical and political importance is indicated by the reference to Israel in Assyrian annals as "the house of Omri." Yet Omri receives little attention in the Bible—a mere six verses in Kings, most of which consist of standard formulas. In contrast, Kings spends six chapters on Omri's son Ahab (1 Kings 16:29—22:40), for theological reasons. The Deuteronomistic Historian portrays Ahab as the worst king of Israel because of the religious threat posed by his Phoenician wife, Jezebel, and their opposition by the prophet *Elijah. The wickedness of his wife and the religious significance of his prophetic opponent led to the prominence of Ahab's reign in the Deuteronomistic Historian's historical treatment. By contrast, Omri, for all his genuine historical importance, is all but ignored.

2.4.2. Prophets and Kings. Following the division of the kingdom after *Solomon, the book of Kings traces a series of royal houses or dynasties headed in turn by *Jeroboam, Baasha, Omri and *Jehu. Each is overthrown in a military coup, and each overthrow is predicted by a prophet who also forecasts the slaughter of all the males in the household.

The prophecies (1 Kings 14:7-11; 16:1-4; 21:20-24; 2 Kings 9:7-10a; 10:30) and their fulfillment notices (1 Kings 15:27-30; 16:11-13; 2 Kings 9:25-26, 36-37; 10:9-11; 15:12) share certain expressions, such as the reference to Yahweh cutting off every male, "bond or free," within the royal house and the threat of nonburial ("the dogs will eat those who die in the city; the birds will eat those who die in the open country"), indicating that they were written by the same author, the Deuteronomistic Historian (McKenzie, 61-80).

The Deuteronomistic Historian inserted these prophecies into older stories, as shown by the prediction of the end of the house of Omri on the lips of Elisha's disciple (2 Kings 9:1-10). *Elisha tells the young prophet to go to the army commander, Jehu, to anoint him king privately, and then to flee without lingering (2 Kings 9:1-

3). In the original story (2 Kings 9:4-6, 10b) this is exactly what the young man did. However, the Deuteronomistic Historian inserted his prophecy against the reigning house (2 Kings 9:7-10a), resulting, ironically, in the young prophet's disobedience of his master's order.

The Deuteronomistic Historian used this prophecy-and-fulfillment scheme to account etiologically and theologically for Israel's national history. It was common practice for a usurper to kill the males of the royal family that he overthrew in order to prevent them from leading a future uprising against him. Baasha, Omri and Jehu each followed this practice. The Deuteronomistic Historian explained their actions as the fulfillment of prophecies against sinful dynasties. He composed the prophecies himself, tailoring them to fit the historical circumstances that he narrated. In this way, he accounted for both the series of dynasties in Israel (in contrast to the single Davidic dynasty in Judah) and Jehu's being the lengthiest of the royal dynasties. It survived through four complete generations following Jehu because of his faithfulness in getting rid of the wicked Omri dynasty, with Jezebel and her legacy of Baal worship (2 Kings 10:30; 15:12).

2.5. Chronicles. Writing probably in the fourth century BCE, the Chronicler (the name given to the author of 1-2 Chronicles) used the earlier OT books, especially 1-2 Samuel and 1-2 Kings, as his main source. Chronicles is essentially a rewritten version of the history of Israel presented earlier in the Hebrew Bible. As such, it affords a unique opportunity for insight into how biblical historians worked with their sources (*see* Chronicler's History; Chronicles, Books of).

The revisions introduced by the Chronicler are mostly theological in nature and shaped by four main interests: (1) the idealization of the reigns of *David and *Solomon as the golden age of Israel, and the presentation of them, especially Solomon, as model kings; (2) the central importance of the temple, its worship and its personnel to the faith and life of Israel; (3) the unity of "all Israel" as Yahweh's chosen people; (4) the idea of immediate reward for righteousness or retribution for evildoing.

2.5.1. The Genealogies (1 Chronicles 1—9). The genealogies in 1 Chronicles 1—9 serve several functions. As with some Greek histories, they provide a frame and a prologue to the narrative history. The Chronicler borrowed most of his genealogies from other parts of the Bible, so that they furnish a kind of summary of Israel's previous history. Above all, they define Israel's identity and promote the unity of all twelve tribes. They also adumbrate the Chronicler's priorities. The genealogies of Judah, Levi and Benjamin are the longest by far, and they provide the structure of these chapters, with Judah coming first, Benjamin last, Levi in the middle. Judah and Benjamin comprised the bulk of exilic Israel; Levi was the priestly tribe.

2.5.2. The Reign of David (1 Chronicles 10—29). The Chronicler begins his narrative with the death of Saul, Israel's first king, borrowed from the final chapter of 1 Samuel. The Chronicler's reason for beginning at this point is to show how Yahweh "turned the kingdom over to David the son of Jesse" (1 Chron 10:14). Omitting all reference to the civil war between David and Saul's heir (2 Sam 1—4), the Chronicler describes "all Israel" coming to make David king (1 Chron 11:1). The parallel (2 Sam 5:1) refers only to the northern tribes, since he has been ruling over Judah for seven and one-half years. Chronicles paints an entirely different picture, albeit of the same event and using similar language.

1 Chronicles 11—16 combines David's coronation with the conquest of Jerusalem and transfer of the *ark of the covenant. Although these are separate events in Samuel, in Chronicles they are described as one enormous, joyful celebration involving all Israel. They turn the reader's focus to *Jerusalem and the building of the temple. David offers to build the temple (1 Chron 17), but he is told that this task will belong to his son. The Chronicler here borrows the text of 2 Samuel 7 with only minor changes. He later clarifies the reason that David was not allowed to build the temple: he had shed too much blood (1 Chron 22:8; 28:3). His role was to create a state of peace by doing away with Israel's enemies so that Solomon could build the temple (see Solomon's Temple).

The Chronicler rewrites history not just by what he includes, but also by what he omits. The story of David and Bathsheba (2 Sam 11:2—12:25) was unbefitting the portrait of a model king and is absent from Chronicles. So are the stories about the rape of Tamar and Absalom's revolt (2 Samuel 13-20). The Chronicler does include the story of David's sin in ordering a *census (1 Chron 21/2 Sam 24), because God's acceptance of the offering at its end lent divine

legitimacy to the site on which the temple, and particularly its sacrificial altar, were to stand (1 Chron 21:26—22:1). But the idea that Yahweh incited David to take the census (2 Sam 24:1) was theologically unacceptable, and the Chronicler changed it to read that one of Israel's enemies (*śāṭān*, often erroneously taken here as a proper name for the devil) led him to sin.

The remainder of 1 Chronicles deals with the transition from David's reign to Solomon's. Again the Chronicles version differs remarkably from that of Samuel-Kings. Chronicles never mentions Adonijah or the rivalry between him and Solomon (1 Kings 1—2). Its focus is on David's commissioning of Solomon as his replacement to build the temple. In a series of speeches (1 Chron 22; 28; 29) the Chronicler has David say that Solomon was chosen by Yahweh to build the temple because he is a man of peace (*šālôm*, a play on Solomon's name, *šĕlōmōh*).

2.5.3. The Reign of Solomon (2 Chronicles 1—9). Six of the nine chapters concerning Solomon's reign deal with the temple. The Chronicler's theology is well expressed in a letter from the Phoenician king Huram, who provides lumber and expertise for building the temple (2 Chron 2:11-16 [MT 2:10-17], based on 1 Kings 5:7, 8-12 [MT 5:21, 22-26]). Huram confesses that Yahweh, the maker of heaven and earth, has endowed Solomon with discretion and understanding for building the temple. This thought accords with David's wishes (1 Chron 22:12) and articulates the Chronicler's view that the temple manifests Solomon's wisdom. The letter attributes remarkable familiarity with Israelite theology and politics to a foreign king. Like David's speeches, it is the Chronicler's composition.

2.5.4. The Divided Kingdom (2 Chronicles 10—36). The Chronicler presents Solomon as a model king and thus could not blame the division of the kingdom on him as does Kings (1 Kings 11). Instead, the Chronicler places the bulk of the blame on Jeroboam and the people of the north for rejecting the divinely chosen Davidic dynasty and proper worship in Jerusalem. The Chronicler regards the kingdom of Israel as illegitimate and does not recount its history in 2 Chronicles, except when it overlaps with Judah's. This view is expressed in a speech by King Abijah of Judah (2 Chron 13). Though judged evil in Kings (1 Kings 15:1-8), Abijah is evaluated positively in Chronicles and credited with a speech admonishing Israel for apostasy (2 Chron 13:4-12).

A common technique in 2 Chronicles is "periodization"—the division of a king's reign into different parts. The account of Joash's reign is a good example (2 Chron 24). 2 Kings 12 depicts him as a good king who, despite restoring the temple, suffered foreign invasions and assassination. For the Chronicler, disaster was the inevitable retribution for sin, so that the calamities that befell Joash must have been brought on by sin. Thus in Chronicles Joash is righteous only in the first half of his reign, while his priestly mentor, Jehoiada, is living (2 Chron 24:1-14). During that time his reign prospers. Afterward, however, Joash allows his advisors to lead him into idolatry, and his misdeeds result in invasion and assassination.

Chronicles provides the clearest perspective on the nature of history writing in the Bible, for we have both the historian's final product and his main sources. The differences between Chronicles and Samuel-Kings show that the recounting of exactly what happened in the past was not the chief objective of biblical historiographers. Rather, history served ideological purposes. It was the forum for the presentation of theology. Biblical historians used history to draw and illustrate theological lessons. The composition of speeches was a principal tool for the Chronicler and other biblical historians to draw out the lessons that they found in history. Chronicles exemplifies the inventiveness of biblical historians and the freedom they exercised in shaping sources and filling in gaps left by them.

See also CHRONICLER'S HISTORY; DEUTERONOMISTIC HISTORY; NARRATIVE ART OF ISRAEL'S HISTORIANS; QUEST OF THE HISTORICAL ISRAEL.

BIBLIOGRAPHY. **W. G. Dever,** *Who Were the Early Israelites and Where Did They Come From?* (Grand Rapids: Eerdmans, 2003); **I. Finkelstein and N. A. Silberman,** *The Bible Unearthed: Archaeology's New Vision of Ancient Israel and the Origin of Its Sacred Texts* (New York: Free Press, 2001); **M. I. Finley,** *The Use and Abuse of History* (New York: Viking, 1975); idem, *Ancient History: Evidence and Models* (New York: Viking, 1986); **B. Halpern,** *The First Historians: The Hebrew Bible and History* (San Francisco: Harper & Row, 1988); **J. Huizinga,** "A Definition of the Concept of History," in *Philosophy and History: Essays Presented to Ernst Cassirer,* ed. R. Klibansky and H. J. Paton (Oxford: Clarendon Press, 1936) 1-10; **V. P. Long,** *The Art of Biblical History* (Grand Rapids: Zondervan, 1994); idem, *Israel's Past in Recent Research: Essays on Ancient Israelite Historiography* (SBTS 7; Winona Lake, IN: Eisenbrauns, 1999); **S. L. McKenzie,** *The Trouble with Kings: The Composition of the Book of Kings in the Deuteronomistic History* (VTSup 42; Leiden: E. J. Brill, 1991); **A. R. Millard,** "Story, History, and Theology," in *Faith, Tradition, and History: Old Testament Historiography in Its Near Eastern Context,* ed. A. R. Millard, J. K. Hoffmeier and D. W. Baker (Winona Lake, IN: Eisenbrauns, 1994) 37-64; **A. R. Millard, J. K. Hoffmeier and D. W. Baker,** eds., *Faith, Tradition and History: Old Testament Historiography in Its Near Eastern Context* (Winona Lake, IN: Eisenbrauns, 1994); **R. D. Nelson,** *The Historical Books* (IBT; Nashville: Abingdon, 1998); **M. Noth,** *The Deuteronomistic History* (JSOTSup 15; Sheffield: JSOT, 1981); **I. Provan, V. P. Long and T. Longman III,** *A Biblical History of Israel* (Louisville: Westminster/John Knox, 2003); **D. B. Redford,** *Egypt, Canaan, and Israel in Ancient Times* (Princeton, N.J.: Princeton University Press, 1992); **J. Van Seters,** *In Search of History: Historiography in the Ancient World and the Origins of Biblical History* (New Haven: Yale University Press, 1983).

S. L. McKenzie

HISTORY OF ISRAEL 1: SETTLEMENT PERIOD

The "settlement of Israel" is a contested phrase that is nevertheless used by many to refer to some period at the end of the second millennium BCE when the ancestors of the later kingdoms of Judah and Israel made their first distinctive appearance in the land of *Canaan. The book of *Joshua provides the primary yet often schematic literary presentation of this settlement. The degree to which researchers can employ the book of Joshua as a guide to the settlement results in a broad spectrum of responses, of which only distillations from an enormous body of literature can be presented here.

1. Integrity of the Literary Sources
2. Problem of Interpretation
3. History of Interpretation
4. Proposed Dating
5. Exclusively External Origin?
6. Archaeology of the Settlement
7. Conclusion

1. Integrity of the Literary Sources.
On the one hand, the book of Joshua preserves

exotic non-Semitic personal names suggestive of the second millennium BCE (Hess) and an appropriate political picture of second-millennium Canaan that is at odds with later periods. On the other hand, the book of Joshua also displays a checkered textual history, including duplicate accounts of the same story often told elsewhere in exactly the same words (Josh 15:14b-19/Judg 1:10b-15; Josh 15:13-14/Judg 1:20; Josh 15:63/Judg 1:21; Josh 17:11-13/Judg 1:27-28; Josh 16:10/Judg 1:29). In one of these parallels the same words are used to describe the same phenomenon even as one text applies it to Judah and the other to Benjamin (Josh 15:63/Judg 1:21). This is not the only case in which specific details are unstable. For example, the MT says that Judah captured *Gaza, *Ashkelon and *Ekron (Judg 1:18-19), but the LXX in these verses states that Judah did not capture these cities (Josephus [*Ant.* 5.128] records that Judah captured Ashkelon but not Gaza and Ekron). At the end of the book of Joshua the LXX adds an entire paragraph (not found in the MT) that seems to lead straight into the story of Ehud in Judges 3:12, suggesting to some that the conquest accounts in Judges 1 have been incorporated secondarily from elsewhere (Rofé 1982). Rearranged accounts can result in a significantly different sequence of events, as in the case of the account of the building of the Ebal altar (Josh 8:30-35), which is found in a different place in the LXX (after Josh 9:2), in yet another location after the conquest of the land according to Josephus (after Joshua 12 [*Ant.* 5.68-69]; cf. *L.A.B.* 21:7), and in yet a further position in a Hebrew text from Qumran (4QJosh[a] places the account before Josh 5). To add to the perplexity, Samaritan biblical texts consistently identify this mountain not as Ebal but as Gerizim. Nor can one always be sure where the tribes gather: does the meeting place move from Gilgal to Shiloh before the land allotments (i.e., after Josh 12, according to Josephus *Ant.* 5.68) or after the initial land allotments are made (Josh 18:1; cf. 14:6), or after the building of the altar by the Transjordanian tribes (*L.A.B.* 22:8)? Does the final gathering take place at *Shechem (Josh 24:1, 25 MT) or Shiloh (LXX; *L.A.B.* 23:1-2; note the LXX omission of references to *Gilgal in Josh 10:15, 43)? Elsewhere, the battle at *Ai is significantly modified by the presence of Joshua 8:11b, 12, 13a (not in the LXX), an entirely different account of the inheritance of Dan (which includes a refer-

ence to its southern neighbor, Judah) is preserved in Joshua 19:47-48 LXX, and a reference in Joshua 10:13 to the Book of Jashar is missing in the LXX. The fact that the book of Joshua in the LXX is some 4-5 percent shorter than in the MT indicates a substantially divergent recension and acutely raises the question of the consistent transmission of both major and minor details upon which one might erect historical reconstructions (see van der Meer) (*see* Text and Textual Criticism).

2. Problem of Interpretation.

Readers of the biblical text can be overzealous in seeing things that they wish to see. For example, the spies are said to report an exaggerated account of the fortifications of the land and the size of their inhabitants (Num 13:28, 30-33; Deut 1:28), and Moses is portrayed as repeating this intelligence (Deut 9:1-2). As the actual conquest narratives unfold, however, neither description is found to be an accurate representation of most of the population. Large foes appear in the area of *Hebron (Num 13:22; Josh 14:12) but not elsewhere in Canaan, where nothing exemplary is noted of Canaanite stature or cities (contrast Josephus *Ant.* 5.71-74). Indeed, other spies underestimate Ai's defenses (Josh 7:2-3), which are never said to consist of walls. It is not clear that a reader is supposed to trust the spies' hyperbole ("fortified to heaven") and expect archaeologists to find the remains of heavily fortified cities.

Nor does the text of Joshua presuppose an Israelite army of a half million men (e.g., thirty-six Israelites killed in battle in Josh 7:5 is considered a disaster), a number whose significance continues to be debated (Rendsburg 2001) (*see* Numbers, Large Numbers). And what are we to make of Israel's entrance into the land preceded by a ṣirʿâ, "hornet" (Ex 23:28; Deut 7:20; Josh 24:12), sent from God to afflict Israel's opponents? Is this literal biological warfare (Neufeld), or is it a metaphor? If a metaphor, are the referents mythological or royal (e.g., Egyptian titulary)? More importantly, is there a contradiction between a simultaneous presentation of a partial conquest and of a complete conquest (Weinfeld), or is this a rhetorical posture attested in other Near Eastern texts (Kitchen 1998, 110; Younger, 242-48)? Are there reading strategies to which readers have been blind (see Polzin, 127-28; Hawk)?

In the battle in defense of the Gibeonites

against a southern coalition of five city-states, Joshua 10:12-14 presents Joshua petitioning the sun at *Gibeon and the moon in the valley of Ayyalon to ʿmd ("to stand") and dmm ("to be silent"). The most stunning total eclipse of the sun observable in central Palestine between 1500 BCE and 1050 BCE occurred at midday on September 30, 1131 (Sawyer). On the other hand, an eclipse would not result if the moon and sun were positioned as widely apart as the verse indicates, which in fact implies an early morning conjunction (Margalit). The poetic lines that are said to be excerpted from a larger work that is no longer extant, the Book of Jashar, are susceptible to other interpretations: do they reflect the well-attested technical language of astral omens (Holladay), or is this a reference to the astral armies assisting God in battle (Miller, 123-28)?

Finally, the impression that one might receive from a quick read of the book of Joshua is that of a devastating incineration of the land and its inhabitants. However, the only cities singled out as specifically and exclusively destroyed from this period are *Jericho, *Ai, *Hazor, *Jerusalem and *Dan (Josh 6:24; 8:28; 11:11, 13; Judg 1:8; 18:27)—a perspective that corresponds with the repeated notion that the Israelites began to live in cities that they did not build (Deut 6:10-11; Josh 24:13). This raises the following question: What kind of physical evidence can the archaeologist expect to find that might point to a new presence of Israel in Canaan if there were few destructions?

3. History of Interpretation.

The earliest stage of confessional analysis of the canonical text by both Jews and Christians was characterized by scrutinizing the biblical texts with sophisticated reading strategies such as midrash and allegory, with an eye primarily to the dominant narrative of militant confrontation between Israel and inhabitants in Canaan. Thus early Christian and rabbinic interpreters recognized the implication that Joshua had to break the sabbath when encompassing Jericho over a period of seven days, but instead of this leading them to question the integrity of the text, the observation on the contrary provided a challenge to discover a deeper significance to the text. When early interpreters (e.g., Origen in *Homilies on Joshua*) asked questions of the text that differed from the questions posed in later stages,

there was a tendency to overlook the ramifications of less obtrusive biblical texts that might suggest different scenarios. For example, some texts seem to suggest a lengthy coexistence between Canaanites and Israelites unaccompanied by divine interventions, and others present the perspective that Israel (or portions of it) had never left the land at all (see Japhet). Where a conflict was observed between biblical texts, such as the Chronicler's presentation of Ephraim in the land of Canaan (1 Chron 7:20-24) in contrast to the Pentateuch, where Ephraim is attested only in Egypt, where he was born (Gen 48:5), rabbinic exegesis simply sought to harmonize the accounts by postulating two separate settlement attempts (*b. Sanh.* 92b). With little evidentiary material apart from the Bible itself, means were lacking to test or challenge hypotheses, conjectures or perspectives that often became enshrined as received wisdom with the passage of time.

A second stage is primarily a function of the European Renaissance and Age of Enlightenment, when some readers began to read the settlement accounts less from a confessional perspective and more with a consistently critical eye. No new data became available for the study of the beginning of Israel's presence in the southern Levant, but the European cultural revolution that purposefully questioned all authority and sought reasons for all claims began to apply regularly to the biblical text. Earlier readers had assumed the authority and integrity of the Bible, but this now became negotiable as the Bible and the readings of former centuries had to prove themselves if they were not to be jettisoned. Thus the biblical description of the arresting of the sun's movement for Joshua demonstrated for some that Joshua was quite misinformed about the true nature of the earth's movement around the sun (Spinoza, *Tractatus Theologico-Politicus,* chap. 2).

A third stage began when new epigraphical and literary data became available, providing insight into literary and cultural conventions of the ancient Near East that might affect the interpretation of the biblical text. The nineteenth century witnessed the beginning of a cascade of ancient Near Eastern texts that provided leverage for investigating biblical texts that were set in the contexts of second-millennium history and culture. As a result, the biblical description of the destruction of Jericho as a ḥērem, "ban," for example, could be read in the light of cognate usage in other Semitic texts. Pre-Islamic desert poets and religious institutions were especially explored at that time for their relevance in providing controls upon the reading of the Hebrew Bible as a text that was perceived as deriving from a similar cultural milieu.

A fourth stage in the treatment of the origins of Israel in Canaan began to flourish after World War 1 with the vigorous resumption of what had been but sporadic archaeological forays in Palestine (in the final days of the Ottoman Empire) that had begun with W. F. Petrie's work at Tell el-Hesi (1890). For the first time, controlled excavation of sites in the new British Mandate of Palestine provided fresh artifactual material that began to be used to interpret the biblical book of Joshua and matters related to it, and vice versa. The wealth of new information provided by archaeological work that began in the 1920s continues to this day and is the primary impetus now for changing perspectives and the multiplication of models for understanding earliest Israel in Canaan (*see* Archaeology, Syro-Palestinian). It is in this context of a rapidly increasing quantity of new data in conjunction with increasing application of other disciplines (anthropology, sociology, economics, literary theory) that rival theories began to emerge and compete—and were found increasingly inadequate—in their explanatory power over all the artifactual data, which included the Bible as an informative guide when critically read. W. F. Albright set the pattern for those who saw a close connection between the discoveries of archaeology and a military conquest by early Israel. A. Alt and M. Noth, focusing upon geographical and social contexts, led the way in countering this conquest model with mechanisms by which Israelite tribes, more peacefully than not, entered Canaan, settled and coalesced over an extended period of time. G. Mendenhall launched a third model in 1962 when he proposed that Israel crystallized largely in the wake of social upheavals caused by oppressed peoples within Canaan, analogous to the behavior of the fourteenth-century ʿapiru of the international correspondence found at Tell el-Amarna, Egypt. This perspective was developed in new directions by N. Gottwald's application of social science and Marxist economic theory (Boer; cf. Lemche 1985). Further modifications and redefining of these basic positions continue (e.g., a symbiotic

or more peaceful emergence of Israel from within Canaanite society).

A fifth stage can be traced back to the 1970s when some (associated notably, although not exclusively, with Scandinavian institutions) began to question the utility of the Bible, increasingly seen as a product of the Persian and even Hellenistic periods, as a helpful source for investigating any aspects of the end of the second millennium BCE. The rising tide of extrabiblical textual material and archaeological data that required sifting made possible an optimism that a new kind of history could be written with the Bible de-centered from its privileged position (cf. the simultaneous demise of "biblical archaeology"). Although many of the conclusions reached by other investigators could be endorsed or modified to varying degrees by these biblical scholars, their reluctance to employ the Bible to investigate the Israelite settlement has resulted in an often acrimonious debate. Thus to explain the evidence of the thirteenth to twelfth centuries BCE, N. P. Lemche (1998) proposed that a Late Bronze Age Egyptian absence and consequential power vacuum in the central highlands was followed by a thirteenth-century Egyptian resurgence and restructuring of power (*see* Egypt, Egyptians), including the deliberate resettlement of urbanites in the hill country, along with the induced settlement of less sedentary elements. Those who disagree with Lemche and with scholars sharing a similar method express frustration at their exclusion of the Bible as usable evidence at least at some level—a position that results in a reluctance to even speak of Israel in the thirteenth to twelfth centuries BCE.

In each of these five stages, distinct advantages provided by the method of inquiry were counterbalanced by problematic drawbacks. In the fourth stage, where archaeological investigation began to provide floods of new data, the establishment of relative and absolute dating, both for sites in general and for specific sites, has been a slow process with not always precise results. At present, for example, there is a proposal to readjust Iron Age chronology as Philistine pottery synchronisms become more refined (Bunimovitz and Faust 2001). Many premature statements by archaeologists about the dating of finds or the correlation of data with specific historical events have been overturned with the continuing refinement of investigative tools, with the result that much that has been written in the twentieth century is no longer reliable. Thus, as of this writing, A. Ben-Tor's reexcavation of Hazor has resulted in an even less certain date for its final destruction than was proposed by its first excavator, Y. Yadin. One must also distinguish between excavations and surveys, the latter initially valuable for heuristic panoramas of the past but often precarious and unreliable for specific sites. Finally, the very substantial contributions that archaeology can make must be balanced by an awareness of its limitations, evident in the equivocal nature of its evidence when it comes to answering questions that are beyond its purview. Physical remains generally permit deductions about social generalities and the most superficial aspects of human society. For a period where there is relatively little other evidence, such as the settlement of Israel in Canaan, archaeology is more valuable than it would be otherwise, but its latitude for abuse in licensing speculation is correspondingly higher—a fact that has characterized all sides of the debate over the settlement. The conclusion by McNutt (1999, 63) that all models are presently inadequate in the face of data that are ambiguous is probably the most defensible position at present. Informed hypotheses that by definition move beyond the data are essential and healthy for integrating the growing mass of new information available, but this brief survey of the history of interpretation demonstrates a myopia on this subject where one cannot often speak with confidence—a malady that also too easily afflicts (post)modern interpreters when they forget their own lack of immunity.

4. Proposed Dating.

4.1. The Iron Age. The designation "Iron Age," identifying the period beginning with the twelfth century BCE and following the Late Bronze Age (c. 1550-1200 BCE), can be a misleading relic from an earlier schematic view of human history. Iron was worked long before 1200 BCE, and there was no remarkable increase in its use at that time, its adoption occurring slowly over several centuries, while bronze continued for some time to be the main and most sophisticated tool. Carburization of iron, which seems to have been developed in the twelfth or eleventh century BCE in the eastern Mediterranean, began to be practiced with some consistency only by the tenth century BCE, and iron as a diagnostic technology is primarily associated

with the first millennium BCE (McNutt 1990). Nor for dating purposes is it entirely clear what meaning is intended by the lowland Canaanite "chariots of iron" that intimidated the Israelites in the hills (Josh 17:16, 18; Judg 1:19; 4:3, 13). In the late Neo-Assyrian Empire iron tires could be attached to a chariot, and even later the Persians employed iron-edged scythes. Chariots of gold and silver (thin sheets over a wooden frame) are attested in the second millennium BCE, but a chariot's tactical advantage, speed, is compromised proportionately to its increasing weight (Drews; Millard).

4.2. Alternatives. The militant expulsion of the Hyksos from Egypt and their subsequent settlement in Canaan in the sixteenth century BCE ranks among the earliest proposed contexts for Israel's settlement in Canaan (Manetho, in Josephus *Ag. Ap.* 1.85-105). Some contemporary scholars endorse this historical event as one of the elements around which Canaanite folktales crystallized, ultimately resulting in the biblical story of the conquest (Redford, 412-22). As the chronology of antiquity has been increasingly refined in the past century, there has been a tendency to focus on one of two other main options: a settlement either in the late fifteenth century BCE or in the late thirteenth century BCE.

Among the primary, although not exclusive, motivations for perceiving the entrance of Israel into the land of Canaan in the fifteenth century BCE is the chronological datum of 1 Kings 6:1: Solomon built the Jerusalem temple in the middle of the tenth century BCE "in the four hundred and eightieth year after the Israelites came out of the land of Egypt" (cf. Judg 11:26). Among other data used to buttress this date, one may include some type of correlation between early Israelites and the fourteenth-century ʿapiru of the Amarna letters, along with archaeological evidence for many urban destructions (Kaiser). J. Bimson has provided the most recent sustained defense of a fifteenth-century entry into the land by suggesting a complete overhaul of the chronology of late Middle Bronze and early Late Bronze remains (see Halpern) (*see DOTP,* Exodus, Date of).

The second main alternative of a thirteenth-century settlement responds primarily to, among other data, the archaeological record exhibiting major cultural transformations in the period that follows the thirteenth century BCE, or textual data such as the only pharaonic name mentioned in the Bible in connection with this period, "Ramesses" (cf. Ex 1:11), first borne by a pharaoh reigning at the beginning of the thirteenth century BCE.

A number of historical and archaeological realities prompt some to envision a settlement no earlier than the middle of the twelfth century BCE (Rendsburg 1992). Among the data that encourage proponents of this theory are the complete absence of Egypt from biblical settlement accounts (Egypt remained a significant presence in Canaan until at least the middle of the twelfth century BCE), the destruction of urban centers with a strong Egyptian presence only after the middle of the twelfth century BCE (e.g., *Lachish, Beth-shean, *Megiddo), and archaeological realia from places such as Heshbon that are said to be conquered by Israel (Num 21:21-26) but show no evidence of occupation until the twelfth century BCE (Tel Hisban).

None of these views prevents one from also subscribing to two other perspectives. First, many postulate not a single settlement that took place in a single generation, but rather a prolonged settlement that spanned as many as several centuries, accomplished either by numerous groups coming from Egypt to the south (e.g., Kelm), or by mobile populations from the east (Transjordan), the west (the Mediterranean; e.g., Dan) or the north (Aramean populations). Second, many argue that substantial elements of what would become known as Israel were already an indigenous population in the land of Canaan throughout the Late Bronze Age; they were already settled in the land until their identity was crystallized by revolutionary religious, social or economic upheavals.

4.3. The ʿapiru. The ʿapiru (sometimes transliterated *habiru*) often have figured in theories of Israel's origin, especially in light of their richly documented activities in fourteenth-century Canaan. The relationship of this noun to the term *Hebrew* is not without difficulties, however, and rendered less likely with the availability of other origins for the latter term (Fleming, 74-75) (*see* Hebrews). The absence of any remains of Late Bronze Age highland occupation in Canaan, which begins only around 1200 BCE, makes it also problematic to draw cultural or social connections between the fourteenth-century ʿapiru of the Amarna letters and the Israelites as depicted in the Bible. If we had an Amarna archive for the twelfth century BCE, would these highland dwellers be identified as ʿapiru? One may speculate, but the question underscores our ignorance of the most basic issues.

4.4. Egypt. The complete absence in biblical literature of any Egyptian presence after the exodus from Egypt supports the notion that Israel's presence in the land should correspond with a time when Egyptian influence had waned in Canaan. Since the northern border of the Egyptian empire extended well into Syria throughout most of the New Kingdom, and Egyptian influence extended even to significant portions of the central highlands, the conditions under which Israel would no more encounter an Egyptian presence in Canaan would come only with the withdrawal of New Kingdom imperial influence, which can be observed in the course of the twelfth century BCE (Weinstein).

At the same time that the Bible preserves no record of any encounter with Egypt after the exodus, it is a great irony that the only time when the word *Israel* appears in Egyptian sources comes precisely from the end of the New Kingdom when Merenptah records Israel's annihilation in a poetic passage on a victory stela (1209/1208 BCE) (see J. K. Hoffmeier, "The (Israel) Stela of Merenptah," *COS* 2.6:40-41). Israel in this text is described with, but distinguished from, conquered Canaanite cities in the same inscription and thus is presumably an unsettled, transient population. The determination of the geographical location of this Israel is not transparent and depends upon whether one stresses a poetic arrangement, a geographical sequence or a schematic presentation. If we correlate Merenptah's stela with some of the pictorial reliefs flanking Ramsses II's treaty at Medinet Habu, we may even have depictions of how individuals associated with this "Israel" dressed and were armed, which is in the fashion of Canaanites (Stager). Does this represent an Israel that is assimilating to Canaan, or is it in fact indigenous (Noll)? Or is "Israel" to be identified elsewhere on the relief with individuals who are dressed as Shasu (Rainey)?

There is general agreement that the Israel to which the Merenptah stela refers is in some fashion to be connected with the Israel that later becomes a well-attested kingdom in the early first millennium BCE. But without further details, many are reluctant to say much more than what the inscription says or implies. But how can Egypt be absent from biblical settlement accounts and yet confront Israel in Canaan in the late thirteenth century BCE (and be present in Canaan for at least another half century)? A thematic or chronological selectivity at work in the biblical texts should be considered, but this underscores how meager is the information that the Bible actually provides on the subject of the settlement.

5. Exclusively External Origin?

Biblical texts never endorse Israel's claim to their *land because they were there first. On the contrary, a vigorous affirmation reverberates throughout the Bible that Israel came to Canaan from elsewhere, and that this past included a nomadic component (Homan; Dever 1998). The patriarchs are depicted as coming to Canaan from the northeast, from Mesopotamia with Aramean connections (Gen 11:27-12:5; 24:2-59; 29:1-30; 31:17-18; Deut 26:5). An extended residence in Egypt to the southwest precedes the arrival of the tribes of Israel as a political force in Canaan (Ex 1—14). Yahweh and his armies are depicted coming from the south and east (Deut 33:2; Judg 5:4; Hab 3:3), corresponding to Israel's movement through Transjordan among their kin. The descendants of *Manasseh through an Aramean concubine (1 Chron 7:14) correspond with this—keeping in mind that *genealogies can portray both biological and social relationships (Wilson).

Nevertheless, there are significant ties to inhabitants already within the land, such as Judah's and Simeon's offspring through their Canaanite wives (Gen 38:2-5; 46:10; 1 Chron 4:21-23), Rahab's assimilation into Israel (Josh 6:25) along with Caleb the Kenizzite (Josh 14:6) and perhaps the Jerahmeelites (Weinfeld, 115-16; Galil). Such connections allow for the possibility of alternate accounts of how various components of Israel came to be in the land (Kallai, 114-17; Rofé 2000). Many have been persuaded over the past half century that the tribe of Dan has roots among the Sea Peoples, specifically the group known as the Danaoi/Danuna (Arbeitman and Rendsburg). Consequently, the notion that Israel ultimately derives from a variegated and ethnically diverse background (cf. Gen 41:45, 50-52; Ex 12:38; Num 11:4; Deut 29:11; Judg 1:16; 5:14), from elements both within Canaan and without, is hardly masked by biblical texts, although sometimes it is obscured by selective misreadings.

6. Archaeology of the Settlement.

6.1. Cultural Remains. Several features point to striking new cultural trends in Iron Age IA (c. 1200-1100 BCE), some of which will persist to varying degrees into the period when the Israelite monarchy comes into existence. These continuities with later Israelite remains, and discontinuities (along with some continuities) with former Canaanite remains, may provide useful indicators for the presence of Israel. For example, a lack of pig bones in excavated sites in the highlands, despite a plethora of other animal bones, contrasts significantly with the wide attestation of pig bones in lowland, coastal and Transjordanian sites. Does this distribution of pig bones correlate with the prohibition of pork in biblical texts, or is the distribution an effect of some other phenomenon—economic, social, environmental (see Knauf)?

Among other observable cultural discontinuities that demarcate Iron I from the preceding Late Bronze II culture, one may include the disappearance of virtually all Late Bronze II temples and the relocation of sacred sites elsewhere, indeed the extreme difficulty in even identifying sacred sites in Iron Age I (whether the remains on Mount Ebal or the so-called Bull Site in the Samaria hills are sacred sites, and the connection of the former with Josh 8:30-35, remains moot [see Zevit; Fritz]). A sharp break is also evident between Late Bronze and Iron Age burial customs, once again the former being well-documented and the latter difficult to find (Kletter). The very phenomenon of new settlements in Iron Age I is itself quite peculiar, usually comprising only a few houses and no more than two or three acres in size, located where no previous settlements are attested, and concentrated in the hills.

A phenomenon of the southern Levantine Iron Age, particularly in the hill country of southern Canaan and in Transjordan and associated with the settlements just noted, found neither before the twelfth century BCE nor after the sixth century BCE (with only exceptional examples outside this geographical area), is a house with a floor plan (with variations) of four rectangular rooms where three are parallel (often separated by pillars), on one end of which is a perpendicular fourth (*see* Architecture). It has been argued that the form evolves from a nomadic tent, that it has roots in Late Bronze Canaanite architecture, that it reflects a distinctive social (family or egalitarian) or economic (agricultural) system, or that it facilitated separation between pure and impure. Most important for present purposes is that some see a close connection between this architecture and the Israelites (e.g., Bunimovitz and Faust 2003), a connection that the plan's chronological and geographical distribution seem to endorse.

Although there is much in Iron I pottery that represents a continuation of Late Bronze traditions, a sudden proliferation begins in the early Iron Age of distinctive forms and decoration that are characteristic only of Iron Age I and only of specific regions, not found before or after. Along the coast a distinctive inventory (e.g., bowls, kraters, stirrup jars, strainer spouts) and decoration (e.g., birds, fish, spirals) correlate well with the presence of a new population from the Aegean (*Philistines). Similarly, in the central highlands and in northern Transjordan a large storage jar with a distinctive band encircling the jar's neck ("collared-rim jar") is characteristic of most sites, and it is in the highlands that the jar is most densely represented (Finkelstein, 275-85). Many argue that this form and its associated pottery assemblages are in some way to be associated with the early Israelite presence in the hills, even if there is not a one-to-one correlation between ethnicity and pottery.

We may also note that although one finds sporadic small pits for storing grain in the preceding Late Bronze and the following Iron II periods, the ubiquity and quantity of such pits in Iron I sites, from the Negev (*Beersheba) to the north (Dan), is striking (Finkelstein, 264-69). All of these cultural innovations, which begin to flourish in the twelfth century BCE, and some of which in varying degrees are continuous with clear later Israelite culture, lend credibility to the claim that a distinct group of which Israel was at least a part makes its appearance in the archaeological record for the first time in the twelfth century BCE.

6.2. Sites. There is no uniform archaeological picture that is characteristic for all sites in the thirteenth to twelfth centuries BCE, which is in accord with the larger picture of cultural upheavals at this time in the eastern Mediterranean. Some sites preserve remains of completely new foundations in the twelfth century BCE with no earlier history. Of these, some are along the Mediterranean coast and associated with Sea Peoples (Philistine; cf. Tel Qasile). Beersheba in

the Negev has no Late Bronze settlement, but in the twelfth century BCE it exhibits a small, one-acre oval-shaped village that shares several features with a twelfth-century proliferation of small, newly founded settlements in areas formerly uninhabited, especially in the hill country (cf. Josh 17:16-18; Judg 1:19, 34), a few of which have been excavated, exhibiting the new cultural features noted above (Raddana, Giloh).

Other thirteenth-century settlements indicate an uninterrupted transition into the twelfth century BCE with no sign of destruction in the northern hills in the Galilee (Tell el-Wawiyat), in the central hills (*Tirzah), and in the southern hills (Yarmuth). On the other hand, the destruction in the thirteenth century BCE of the largest and most prosperous site (*Hazor) is followed by its essential abandonment, while the thirteenth-century destruction of Tell Yinʿam in the Jezreel Valley has a succeeding twelfth-century settlement with high quality architecture and pottery. The destruction of sites along the coast in the thirteenth century BCE (or the early twelfth century BCE in the case of Tell Keisan) is followed by a twelfth-century new occupation with the evidence of a new and different culture, specifically Sea Peoples, and even more specifically Philistine (Ekron, Aphek). Other thirteenth-century coastal sites are destroyed in the early twelfth century BCE and abandoned (Tel Nami).

Rarely can a specific destruction be associated unequivocally with a specific event, as is true of the thirteenth-century destruction of Gezer by Merenptah. In addition, there are several sites mentioned in the book of Joshua that pose a problem in the light of their excavated remains (*Jericho, *Ai, *Arad, Heshbon). This schematic selection of some sites is designed here to underscore the variety of histories prompting the need to evaluate each site on its own terms. There are general trends, but exceptions abound, and new data often prompt major revisions of prior theories—a sign of a field still in its infancy.

7. Conclusion.

If there is a tendency to think of Jericho as the epitome of Israel's experience in the settlement in Canaan, there are on the contrary good reasons not to see that city as paradigmatic, but rather as a fixation that has prompted misreadings of the text. There are actually very few recorded miracles in the Bible that are associated with the Israelite settlement, for only three events provide prodigies of nature: the crossing of the Jordan River, the collapse of Jericho's walls, and the campaign on behalf of the Gibeonites where hailstones precede the immobilization of the sun and moon. Furthermore, the narratives as a whole vacillate between an intense microscopic analysis of some events and broadly schematic panoramas for others: a detailed military encounter is recounted for only two cities (Jericho, Ai); a detailed negotiation with only one city appears (Gibeon); a schematic summary refers to military activities in the south and north along with isolated tribal ventures (Josh 10—11; Judg 1). This dominant narrative of nonindigenous immigrants is also supplemented with narratives that make no attempt to cover up the fact that much of Israel's constituency derives from within the land of Canaan itself, amalgamated by considerable symbiosis. Precisely when and where "Israel" can be physically identified as a distinct entity remains a problem none of whose proposed solutions compel agreement, although the thirteenth to twelfth century hill country is the horizon in which most researchers look, in accord with the perspective of the book of Joshua (Josh 14:12; 17:16-18; Judg 1:19, 34). The biblical text preserves remarkable memories of second-millennium realities at the same time that it raises major questions on topics where archaeologists disagree with archaeologists, biblical scholars with biblical scholars, historians with historians, and Egyptologists with Egyptologists. The fissures of the discussion are neither easily predictable nor readily resolvable, and inevitably subject to revision in the near future if the history of the interpretation of this subject is any guide.

See also ARCHAEOLOGY, SYRO-PALESTINIAN; CHRONOLOGY; ETHNICITY; HISTORY OF ISRAEL 2: PREMONARCHIC ISRAEL; ISRAEL; JERICHO; JOSHUA; JOSHUA, BOOK OF; LAND; SOCIAL-SCIENTIFIC APPROACHES; TRIBES OF ISRAEL AND LAND ALLOTMENTS/BORDERS.

BIBLIOGRAPHY. **Y. Arbeitman and G. Rendsburg,** "Adana Revised: 30 Years Later," *ArOr* 49 (1981) 145-57; **R. Boer,** ed. *Tracking the Tribes of Yahweh: On the Trail of a Classic* (JSOTSup 351; Sheffield: Sheffield Academic Press, 2002); **S. Bunimovitz and A. Faust,** "Building Identity: The Four-Room House and the Israelite Mind,"

in *Symbiosis, Symbolism, and the Power of the Past: Canaan, Ancient Israel, and Their Neighbors from the Late Bronze Age through Roman Palaestina; Proceedings of the Centennial Symposium, W. F. Albright Institute of Archaeological Research and American Schools of Oriental Research, Jerusalem, May 29/31, 2000,* ed. W. G. Dever and S. Gitin (Winona Lake, IN: Eisenbrauns, 2003) 411-23; idem, "Chronological Separation, Geographical Segregation, or Ethnic Demarcation? Ethnography and the Iron Age Low Chronology," *BASOR* 322 (2001) 1-10; **W. G. Dever,** "Israelite Origins and the 'Nomadic Ideal': Can Archaeology Separate Fact from Fiction?" in *Mediterranean Peoples in Transition: Thirteenth to Early Tenth Centuries BCE,* ed. S. Gitin, A. Mazar and E. Stern, (Jerusalem: Israel Exploration Society, 1998) 220-37; idem, *Who Were the Early Israelites, and Where Did They Come From?* (Grand Rapids: Eerdmans, 2003); **R. Drews,** "The 'Chariots of Iron' of Joshua and Judges," *JSOT* 45 (1989) 15-23; **I. Finkelstein,** *The Archaeology of the Israelite Settlement* (Jerusalem: Israel Exploration Society, 1988); **I. Finkelstein and N. A. Silberman,** *The Bible Unearthed : Archaeology's New Vision of Ancient Israel and the Origin of Its Sacred Texts* (New York: Free Press, 2001); **D. E. Fleming,** "Mari and the Possibilities of Biblical Memory," *RA* 92 (1998) 41-78; **V. Fritz,** "The Character of the Urbanisation in Palestine at the Beginning of the Iron Age," in *Nuove fondazioni nel vicino oriente antico: Realtà e ideologia; Atti del colloquio 4-6 dicembre 1991, Dipartimento di scienze storiche del mondo antico, Sezione di egittologia e scienze storiche del vicino oriente, Università degli studi di Pisa,* ed. S. Mazzoni (SdO 4; Pisa: Giardini, 1994) 231-52; **G. Galil,** "The Jerahmeelites and the Negeb of Judah," *JANES* 28 (2001) 33-42; **B. Halpern,** "Radical Exodus Redating Fatally Flawed," *BAR* 13.6 (1987) 56-61; **D. L. Hawk,** *Every Promise Fulfilled: Contesting Plots in Joshua; Literary Currents in Biblical Interpretation* (Louisville: Westminster/John Knox, 1991); **R. S. Hess,** "Non-Israelite Personal Names in the Book of Joshua," *CBQ* 58 (1996) 205-14; **J. S. Holladay,** "The Day(s) the Moon Stood Still," *JBL* 87 (1968) 166-78; **M. M. Homan,** "To Your Tents, O Egypt, Canaan, and Israel: An Ancient Formula for Council Disbandment," *UF* 31 (1999) 237-40; **S. Japhet,** "Conquest and Settlement in Chronicles," *JBL* 98 (1979) 205-18; **W. C. Kaiser Jr.** A *History of Israel from the Bronze Age through the Jewish Wars* (Nashville: Broadman & Holman, 1998); **Z. Kallai,** "The Explicit and

Implicit in Biblical Narrative," in *Congress Volume: Paris, 1992*, ed. J. A. Emerton (VTSup 61; Leiden: E. J. Brill, 1995) 107-17; **G. Kelm,** *Escape to Conflict: A Biblical and Archaeological Approach to the Hebrew Exodus and Settlement in Canaan* (Fort Worth, TX: IAR Publications, 1991); **K. A. Kitchen,** "Egyptians and Hebrews, from Ra ͨamses to Jericho," in *The Origin of Early Israel—Current Debate: Biblical, Historical and Archaeological Perspectives; Irene Levi-Sala Seminar, 1997,* ed. S. Ahituv and E. D. Oren (Beer-Sheva 12; Beer-Sheva: Ben Gurion University of the Negev Press, 1998) 65-131; idem, *On the Reliability of the Old Testament* (Grand Rapids: Eerdmans, 2003); **R. Kletter,** "People Without Burials? The Lack of Iron I Burials in the Central Highlands of Palestine," *IEJ* 52 (2002) 28-48; **E. A. Knauf,** "'Kinneret I' Revisited," in *Saxa Loquentur: Studien zur Archäologie Palästinas/Israels; Festschrift für Volkmar Fritz zum 65. Geburtstag,* ed. C. G. den Hertog, U. Hübner and S. Münger (AOAT 302; Münster: Ugarit-Verlag, 2003) 159-69; **N. P. Lemche,** *Early Israel: Anthropological and Historical Studies on the Israelite Society Before the Monarchy* (VTSup 37; Leiden: E. J. Brill, 1985); idem, *The Israelites in History and Tradition* (Louisville: Westminster/John Knox, 1998); **B. Margalit,** "The Day the Sun Did Not Stand Still: A New Look at Joshua X 8-15," *VT* 42 (1992) 466-91; **P. M. McNutt,** *The Forging of Israel: Iron Technology, Symbolism, and Tradition in Ancient Society* (SWBA 8; JSOTSup 108; Sheffield: Almond, 1990); idem, *Reconstructing the Society of Ancient Israel* (Louisville: Westminster/John Knox, 1999); **A. R. Millard,** "Back to the Iron Bed: Og's or Procrustes,'" in *Congress Volume: Paris, 1992,* ed. J. A. Emerton (VTSup 61; Leiden: E. J. Brill, 1995) 193-203; **P. D. Miller,** *The Divine Warrior in Early Israel* (HSM 5; Cambridge, MA: Harvard University Press, 1973); **E. Neufeld,** "Insects as Warfare Agents in the Ancient Near East (Ex. 23:28; Deut. 7:20; Josh. 24:12; Isa. 7:18-20)," *Or* 49 (1980) 30-57; **K. L. Noll,** "An Alternative Hypothesis for a Historical Exodus Event," *SJOT* (2000) 260-74; **R. Polzin,** *Moses and the Deuteronomist: Deuteronomy, Joshua, Judges* (New York: Seabury, 1980; repr., ISBL; Bloomington: Indiana University Press, 1993); **A. F. Rainey,** "Israel in Merenptah's Inscription and Reliefs," *IEJ* 51 (2001) 57-75; **D. B. Redford,** *Egypt, Canaan, and Israel in Ancient Times* (Princeton, NJ: Princeton University Press, 1992); **G. A. Rendsburg,** "An Additional Note to Two Recent Articles on the Number of People in the Exodus from Egypt and the Large Numbers in Numbers I and XXVI," *VT* 51 (2001) 392-96; idem, "The Date of the Exodus and the Conquest/Settlement: The Case for the 1100's," *VT* 42 (1992) 510-27; **A. Rofé,** "Clan Sagas as a Source in Settlement Traditions," in *"A Wise and Discerning Mind": Essays in Honor of Burke O. Long,* ed. S. Olyan and R. C. Culley (BJS 325; Providence: Brown University Press, 2000) 191-203; idem, "The End of the Book of Joshua According to the Septuagint," *Hen* 4 (1982) 17-36; **J. F. A. Sawyer,** "Joshua 10:12-14 and the Solar Eclipse of 30 September 1131 B.C.," *PEQ* 104 (1972) 139-46; **L. E. Stager,** "Merenptah, Israel and Sea Peoples: New Light on an Old Relief," *ErIsr* 18 (1985) 56*-64*; **M. van der Meer,** *Formation and Reformulation: The Redaction of the Book of Joshua in the Light of the Oldest Textual Witnesses* (VTSup 102; Leiden: E. J. Brill, 2004); **M. Weinfeld,** *The Promise of the Land: The Inheritance of the Land of Canaan by the Israelites* (Taubman Lectures in Jewish Studies 3; Berkeley: University of California Press, 1993); **J. Weinstein,** "The Collapse of the Egyptian Empire in the Southern Levant," in *The Crisis Years: The 12th Century B.C. from Beyond the Danube to the Tigris,* ed. W. Ward and M. S. Joukwsky (Dubuque, IA: Kendall/Hunt, 1992) 142-50; **R. Wilson,** *Genealogy and History in the Biblical World* (YNER 7; New Haven: Yale University Press, 1977); **K. L. Younger,** *Ancient Conquest Accounts: A Study in Ancient Near Eastern and Biblical History Writing* (JSOTSup 98; Sheffield: Sheffield Academic Press, 1990); **Z. Zevit,** *The Religions of Ancient Israel: A Synthesis of Parallactic Approaches* (London: Continuum, 2001).

S. A. Meier

HISTORY OF ISRAEL 2: PREMONARCHIC ISRAEL

This article surveys Israel's history from the period after the conquest to the advent of the monarchy, commonly known in the OT as the period of the *judges. According to a strict reading of the Bible, this period is roughly 350 years, from approximately 1400 to 1050 BCE (cf. Judg 11:29; 1 Kings 6:1). The period is described in Judges, Ruth and the early chapters of 1 Samuel. However, based on archaeological evidence as well as extrabiblical textual evidence, most scholars have collapsed this period to around 1200-1050 BCE (*see* Chronology). Archaeologists call this period Iron Age I.

First we will observe the biblical evidence for the period of the Judges, take an overview of the biblical evidence from Judges, Ruth and 1 Samuel, and evaluate the source material. Then we will evaluate modern theories about the Israelite settlement in this period, investigate the sparse archaeological record, and attempt to draw some tentative conclusions about the historicity and historical plausibility of the biblical narratives.

1. Biblical Evidence for the Period of the Judges
2. Extrabiblical Textual Evidence from Iron Age I
3. Archaeology as a Source for Understanding Israel in Iron Age I
4. Modern Theories about the Israelite Settlement in Iron Age I
5. General Conclusions Based on Biblical, Textual and Archaeological Sources
6. Conclusions

1. Biblical Evidence for the Period of the Judges.

1.1. Overview of the Judges. The book of *Judges is the primary historical source for understanding Israel after the conquest and before the monarchy (for a historical overview of the book see Boling, 3-42; for particular issues, Halpern 1988, 44-82). The English title *Judges* does not fully represent the main characteristics of the book. The judges in question not only have a judicial function but also appear as military leaders. In fact, the Hebrew term for "judges" denotes a function concerning the administration of justice, which is true also in cognate languages to biblical Hebrew (e.g., Akkadian and Ugaritic). Moreover, although the work is composed roughly in chronological order (except for Judg 17—21, which is more thematic in nature), the stories about the judges are not uniform in nature in terms of presentation and theme. In other words, a number of judges are described in detail (often called "major judges"), while others are simply described by their length of office, region and other brief information. These "minor judges" are listed in two sections: Judges 10:2-5 mentions Tola and Jair, while Ibzan, Elon and Abdon are listed in Judges 12:8-15.

Although the biblical text describes the reign of the so-called judges, these descriptions are superimposed with a formulaic and systematic theme. The formula is somewhat simple: the people of Israel sin and move away from the worship of Yahweh, who subsequently delivers them into the hand of a foreign oppressor; after a period of time, the people cry out to Yahweh, who sends them a deliverer (judge) who will rescue them from their oppressors. Thus there is peace in the land during the tenure of the judge. However, upon the judge's death, the people go back to their sinful ways, "doing evil in the sight of Yahweh," and once again they are taken over by a foreign enemy, whether from Moab, Midian or Aram-Naharaim. The writer has taken these premonarchical stories and edited them with this formulaic structure, with the emphasis on the heroic judge and Yahweh's delivering power. Thus the intent of the writer was not to compose a comprehensive history of the period, but rather to magnify the great deeds of Yahweh and his servants.

There are several topics that bear consideration on understanding the nature of this period in Israelite history. The Judges source presents the judges as following each other in sequential order. However, as we noted, the presentation appears somewhat formulaic, since the order may be more geographical, as it betrays a south-north model, at least with the first leaders. Moreover, from the book of Judges it can be seen that there was a lack of political, military and religious centralization in the tribes.

In addition, the judges themselves often are unlikely candidates for heroism, whether they were women (Deborah), seemingly unimportant individuals from unimportant tribes (Gideon) or illegitimate sons (Jepthah). There is also a parochial nature to the leaders, as none appeared to have actually judged "all of Israel" at any one time. They are charismatic leaders, ruling by force of personality. This can be seen with the first judge mentioned, Othniel, a charismatic leader from the southern tribe of Judah who had the "spirit of Yahweh" on him. Similarly, Ehud (from Benjamin, north of Judah) is described as a crafty man who used deceit to kill the *Moabite king Eglon. We are only told a brief note about Shamgar (from *Dan, north and west of Benjamin), who was remembered as a tormentor of the *Philistines. These three judges (in Judg 2—3) are remembered because of their great deeds and their successes. Thus there is no genealogical descent of these leaders—that is, a son or another family member did not succeed them. The only thing that mattered was that they obeyed Yahweh's direction and were militarily successful.

Interestingly, the next judge mentioned is a woman, Deborah (from Ephraim, directly north of Benjamin), who presumably held her power because of her position as a *prophet (Judg 4—5). Compared to most of the other judges, there is a greater amount of information about events during her leadership (although biographical details are minimal; only her husband's name is mentioned). She does not appear to have had the ability to command the armed forces, probably by virtue of the fact that she was a woman, but this is never explicitly stated. However, because of her prophetic position she was able to call forth troops to battle. In fact, it was another woman, Jael, who received the recognition and the glory. Judges 5 is a poem commemorating the great victory of Yahweh and his host against the enemy forces.

The next judge in sequential order was Gideon, who claimed to be from the poorest clan in the tribe of Manasseh (due north of Ephraim), and the least important person in his clan (Judg 6:15). However, since Yahweh was to be with him, he was able to lead Israel in overcoming the bondage inflicted on them by Midian. To show that Yahweh was in control and was the instrument of victory, Gideon is even told to reduce his army to a small size (Judg 7:2-8). The first evidence of dynastic leadership is seen when Gideon's son Abimelech declared himself king in *Shechem for a short time. The writer looked upon this negatively, however. The geographical scheme thus far is clear, as the judges from Othniel to Gideon roughly form a south-north geographic line.

Except for Jephthah, the next judges are minor, at least in their description. Tola and Jair are described in much briefer terms with minimal family history, both described as having judged one after another. Continuing on with the tradition of mediocrity, Jepthah was an illegitimate son and an outcast. He became a judge, it appears, by virtue of the fact that he was victorious over the Ammonites. The next three judges, Ibzan, Elon and Abdon, are once again described with sparse detail. The geographical scheme does not appear to exist for these leaders, as they come from varying tribes in Israel.

Judges 13—16 contains a lengthy narrative concerning Samson, who, although a judge,

fought personal battles with the neighboring *Philistines. These were tantamount to border skirmishes between Samson's tribe (Dan) and Philistia. Once again, the judge here is described in a folkloristic way as a charismatic hero during a period of no centralized authority. Furthermore, Samson is another unlikely hero, as he is somewhat dull in wit, easily tricked by women and makes rash decisions. However, Yahweh again was able to overcome the weaknesses of the leader to fulfill his designs.

The remainder of the book (Judg 17—21) functions somewhat as an appendix, as it does not provide any chronological context. In fact, not only are no judges mentioned, but also there are no local leaders, and the narratives describe anarchy. The only war described is one between all of Israel against one of its own tribes, Benjamin. The book ends with the familiar depressing line "In those days there was no king in Israel; all the people did what was right in their own eyes" (Judg 21:25), implying a promonarchical sentiment. Interestingly, other sections of the book imply an antimonarchical tendency. After having hereditary rule offered to him, Gideon replies to the people that neither he nor his sons would rule, but Yahweh rules over them (Judg 8:23). A similar sentiment is brought out in 1 Samuel 8, where the people ask Samuel for a king, implying a rejection of Yahweh, their king.

Although the book of Ruth provides no chronological information other than it occurred during the "days of the Judges," it does offer information about a seemingly typical Israelite family that has its life centered about village life (for a historical overview of Ruth, see Campbell, 1-45). They are able to move about freely throughout Judah and neighboring Moab. There is no discussion about any larger governmental institution. Furthermore, Israelites intermarry with foreigners in this book, which does not appear to be surprising to the narrator.

The early narratives in 1 Samuel resume the chronological narrative that ended in Judges 16. Eli the priest is the de facto leader at this point, and he is named as a judge only in a formulaic death announcement (1 Sam 4:18). Apparently, Eli's sons succeeded him, possibly implying a hereditary ruling office (at least in the mind of the Samuel source). Although Eli's sons die in battle with the Philistines, Samuel, the next judge, appoints his own sons as judges (1 Sam 8:1-2), much to the dismay of the populace. The people then ask "for a king to govern us, like the nations." It is apparent by this time (we can estimate it to be c. 1050 BCE) that the judge was no longer simply a charismatic leader, but rather a judge because of genealogical legitimacy.

1.2. Observations on the Distinctions of the Major and Minor Judges. Further observations can be made after this brief survey of the judges. The major judges ruled in multiples of twenty years (either twenty or forty years, with the exception of Shamgar, for whom we are given no length of reign, and Jephthah, who reigned precisely six years). Oddly enough, we are given precise numbers for the minor judges (Tola, 23; Jair, 22; Ibzan, 7; Elon, 10; Abdon, 8). Since the structure of the narratives for the so-called minor judges is different, many have argued that they come from a different source than that of the major judges. It is possible that the minor judges were remembered from annalistic lists of names that may have provided facts about their place of origin and length of rule, while the major judges were remembered through the telling of folkloristic stories. However, both types of information (whether folkloristic narrative or annalistic lists) have potential historical value.

2. Extrabiblical Textual Evidence from Iron Age I.

In order to understand this period, the historical narratives in turn must be augmented with other materials, such as other documents from surrounding regions. Few inscriptions, however, have been found in Palestine during Iron Age I (*see* Non-Israelite Written Sources: Syro-Palestinian; Hebrew Inscriptions). Those that have been found shed little if any light on the social and political situation of the period. Many of the inscriptions are written in a very early version of the alphabetic script on bronze arrowheads, identified by the owner's personal name and his father or master. There are also a number of very small inscriptions on potsherds that contain a few letters, seals and personal names. However, there is a potsherd from Izbet Sartah (near Tel Aviv) that contains a crude abecedary (ordering of the Canaanite alphabet from left to right) and appears to be an exercise tablet, full of mistakes. There is also an inscribed text on a pottery bowl from Qubur el-Waladiyah in southern Philistia that has two Canaanite names. It has been interpreted as a dedicatory inscription.

The most famous inscription about Palestine

concerning this period comes from Egypt, the Merneptah Stela (Hasel), a commemorative text dated to the reign of Merneptah of Egypt (c. 1225-1215 BCE). Merneptah claims to have defeated a number of enemies in Syro-Palestine, including the cities of *Ashkelon and *Gezer, the lands of Hatti, *Canaan and Hurru, and the people of Israel. Some have argued that the "people of Israel" suggests a nomadic group that has not become sedentary as of yet. Of course, the biblical sources argue for a fully settled "Israel" in this period. However, one cannot easily rely on a single inscription to make general statements about the nature of Israel in this period.

3. Archaeology as a Source for Understanding Israel in Iron Age I.

As we noted, archaeologists complement the biblical sources by studying the material remains of Syro-Palestine during this period (for recent overviews of this period see Dever; Callaway; Finkelstein) (*see* Archaeology). It has been assumed that there was a somewhat gradual shift from Late Bronze Age Canaanite material culture (c. 1600-1200 BCE) to new "Israelite" settlement patterns in the Iron Age I period (c. 1200-1000 BCE). Scores of new sites are found in the highlands of northern and southern Canaan, and across the Transjordan. More specifically, these new settlements included expanded occupation of the hill country near *Shechem and *Shiloh, in the southern region near and about *Hebron, as well as west of the Sea of Galilee. The largest number of these sites is situated in the regions of Ephraim, Manasseh and even Benjamin, which appears to be consistent with the narratives in Judges. They were smaller occupations than those in the previous period, and unfortified, and most likely were agro-pastoral communities. For the most part these are small, one-period sites that often have been attributed to the settlement of the Israelites. Many of these sites were deserted at the end of the eleventh century BCE. Some of these were not resettled, while others were reinhabited as towns during the monarchy, thus showing a dramatic change in settlement patterns.

Furthermore, many of the fortified Bronze Age cities in Palestine were destroyed, including *Megiddo, Beth-Shean, *Hazor, *Gezer, and *Ashdod. The question is whether or not these destructions are related to each other, or whether they are connected to the biblical narratives concerning the conquest of Canaan. Of course, it is very difficult to connect biblical narratives to archaeological realia, at least without the benefit of texts uncovered from the sites in question. It has been notoriously difficult without written documentation for archaeologists to identify particular ethnic groups with either settlement patterns or distinctive material remains. However, the southern coastal areas exhibit a pottery type found both in southern Greece (Mycenean) and Palestine, and which is described as Philistine bichrome ware. It is evident from Egyptian sources and from the connection with Greece that the Philistines settled this region (*see* Philistines).

A number of factors may have influenced the new settlement patterns. Population increases along the coast, namely, the Sea Peoples, may have caused movement into the highlands. The Arameans from the northeast possibly may have moved into the area at this time. Further, new technological innovations, such as terracing and the increased use of iron, may have made it easier to live in the hill country and Galilee. The fact that Egyptian involvement decreased, along with the numerous ethnic movements, allowed for the possibility of smaller political structures in the region. Thus Palestine in Iron Age I was composed of smaller units, and so the inhabitants resided in villages and towns rather than the larger cities of the Bronze Age.

The material culture of Palestine changed from the Late Bronze to Early Iron Ages. There is still evidence of Egyptian domination during the early part of this period (roughly 1200-1150 BCE), as Canaanite culture persisted and strong Egyptian presence can be seen at key sites such as Beth-Shean, Megiddo, *Lachish and Tel el-Farah. However, by the middle of the twelfth century BCE these sites and others experienced destruction, possibly at the hands of the Sea Peoples or even proto-Israelites. This may correspond with the collapse of Egyptian control in Canaan. Interestingly, Megiddo, Lachish and Beth-Shean were rebuilt shortly after their destruction, all of which retained a Canaanite character to their material remains, as well as a decided Egyptian presence. Megiddo and Beth-Shean, in particular, were important strongholds. Beth-Shean was a well-ordered town with structures built close together, including a major cultic center composed of at least two temples.

Megiddo had a palace and city gate, but no evidence of a city wall. However, all of the sites were destroyed once again by the middle of the twelfth century BCE, corresponding to the collapse of Egyptian domination. The book of Judges (Judg 1:27-35) lists Megiddo, Gezer and Beth-Shean as territories that were not conquered.

Since only a few Iron Age I sites have been excavated, it is no simple matter to describe the *architecture of the region in this period. Most sites were open villages with houses arranged around the perimeter with open areas inside. In some places the houses actually functioned as defenses. The "pillared house" was typical in this period, based on a courtyard divided by a row of pillars. More specifically, these pillared houses had four rooms. The houses were rectangular in shape and surrounded by rooms on three sides, with an entrance on the fourth side that led into an open courtyard. This architectural concept was not necessarily unique to the Israelites, as such houses are found also at Megiddo and in sites in Philistia and the Transjordan. Few fortresses have been found in this period, the exception being one at Har Adir in Upper Galilee. A foundation was also found at Giloh that may have been a base for a tower. Towers are mentioned in Judges at some towns, such as Shechem (Judg 9:46-49), Penuel (Judg 8:17) and Tebez (Judg 9:50-52). Furthermore, many sites exhibit cisterns, silos and agricultural terraces, showing how the inhabitants adapted to the new environmental conditions (Hopkins; Borowski). The pottery in this period is limited to types used for basic subsistence. These include large storage jars, or pithoi, that probably were used as water containers. The most common one is the collared-rim jar, over one meter in height and ovoid in shape, with a collar at the top. It has a widespread use in Iron Age I. As with the four-room house, these are also found at Megiddo and in the Transjordan. It may be concluded that the inhabitants of the central hill country (presumably Israelites) did not have their own pottery tradition and used Canaanite vessels, or at least Canaanite vessel types (see Stager).

3.1. Ethnicity and the Archaeological Record. How can one define *ethnicity from the archaeological record? The settlements and the material culture in the Iron Age I central highlands, for example, have been characterized as a single culture, whether proto-Israelite (Dever) or Israelite (Finkelstein). A number of scholars have argued that the four-room house, the collared-rim jar, and the absence of pig remains in the region show evidence for an exclusively Israelite settlement. However, as we noted, none of these items are exclusive to the highland areas, since four-room houses and collared-rim jars have been found outside the supposed sphere of Israelite influence. Moreover, work done by B. Hesse and P. Wapnish shows that the absence of pig remains is prevalent during much of the Iron Age throughout Canaan. Some of the few Iron Age I sites that were excavated during this period were abandoned, especially in the regions of Manasseh, Ephraim and Judah. However, these abandonments did not bring an end to the material culture. In sum, one cannot be dogmatic about defining specific ethnic groups from archaeological sources (see Sparks; Machinist; Bloch-Smith 1992; 2003).

3.2. Material Remains Derived from Archaeological Sources: Art and Metallurgy. Canaanite miniature art continued to flourish during this period, as there is evidence of Megiddo ivories, as well as ivory works from Tell Miqne and Tell Qasile. There are also a number of cult artifacts from Beth-Shean, Megiddo, Tell Qasile and Ashdod. Nothing has been found that can be determined to be specifically Israelite.

The replacement of bronze with iron was a gradual one, manifesting itself strongly only by the tenth century BCE. In fact, bronze was still used for the casting of weapon and art objects during this period. Artifacts reflect Canaanite traditions of the Late Bronze Age, as well as predictable Cypriot influence (clearly connected to the Sea Peoples). These include double axes, long spearheads and Aegean-type bronze swords.

4. Modern Theories About the Israelite Settlement in Iron Age I.

Scholars who have attempted to interpret the material with the aid of historical, archaeological and sociological analysis have augmented this cursory overview over the past generations. For instance, A. Alt argued for a "peaceful infiltration model," while his student M. Noth theorized that Israel in the premonarchical period was organized as an *amphictyony—a confederation or league of the twelve tribes centered around a sanctuary that was serviced by each tribe for one month of the year. This idea was

based on an analogue from later classical Greek sources. The idea was attractive because Israel was always described as having twelve tribes, even though the names and even the order of the tribes were not always the same in each list. In fact, even if tribes split in two (e.g., Joseph was divided into Ephraim and Manasseh), there were still twelve tribes. However, there has been no archaeological evidence to date for a central shrine during this period. Moreover, the biblical sources do not describe any tribe taking care of a central sanctuary, nor is there evidence of tribes traveling during festivals.

Others (such as Alt and Weippert) have argued that the Israelites in this period were full nomads, comparable to the modern-day Bedouins. B. Halpern (1983) has argued for an "occasional penetration model" (for other theories see Gottwald; Mendenhall; Frick). In other words, an ethnic consciousness and solidarity "dawned" on the tribes, causing a full-blown confederacy to come into being. The most recent consensus, championed by W. G. Dever and I. Finkelstein, argues for the tribes as highland settlers, not as foreign invaders, but those who came from within Canaanite society. The settlement process was gradual, as is shown by the fact that the material cultures of the Late Bronze Age and Iron Age I periods show marked continuities. Both argue for a long-term settlement history and demography characterized by oscillations of periods of nomadization and sedentarization, happening over a period of millennia. However, Dever argues for an indigenous origin of some sort for Israel in Canaan. He characterizes Iron Age I hill country pioneers as agrarian reformers with a new social vision and sees them as early Israelites. There is a gradual move toward urbanization during the Iron Age I period, as well as a steady population growth. Archaeology also gives evidence of the natural emergence of the Israelite state by which tribes and chieftains evolve into states.

5. General Conclusions Based on Biblical, Textual and Archaeological Sources.

5.1. The Nations Surrounding Israel. Many foreign peoples neighboring Israel are mentioned in the biblical text during this period. Inhabiting the southern coastal region were the Philistines (Dothan), centered around five major cities (*Ashdod, *Ashkelon, *Ekron, *Gath and *Gaza), possibly in an amphictyonic league. They evidently were part of the Sea Peoples, who had migrated to the area in the twelfth century BCE. The Philistine contingent of the Sea Peoples apparently had remained in the southern Levant and continued to have a relationship with Egypt. By the end of this period (i.e., the judgeship of Samson) they had become a great threat to Israel. Some Philistine sites have been excavated, including Tell Qasile near Tel Aviv. There, three phases of a temple have been found that show evidence of sacrifices. In addition, an auxiliary temple attached to the main complex has been found, common to Aegean (i.e., Mycenaean) religious architecture, from where the Philistines probably originated. The very small amount of writing found resembles the undeciphered Cypro-Minoan script from a few centuries earlier.

There is even less textual evidence for the *Phoenicians in this period. Although the cities of Tyre, Sidon and Byblos are mentioned in the Late Bronze Age Amarna letters from Egypt, there are no sources from Phoenicia in Iron Age I, and only sparse references in the Assyrian annals of Tiglath-Pileser I (1115-1077 BCE), who lists these cities as giving tribute. The Late New Kingdom Egyptian story of Wenamun shows a Phoenician coast that is independent from Egypt and treats Egyptian merchants badly. Moreover, the ʾAhirom sarcophagus inscription, although somewhat later than this period (c. 1000 BCE), provides evidence of sophisticated Phoenician culture at Byblos during the Iron Age I period. The inscription is above a detailed relief that depicts the king seated on a cherub throne, receiving offerings from dignitaries (for recent translations of West Semitic monumental inscriptions see COS 2.23-46:135-67). At any rate, the area is described by each city (i.e., Sidonians), not by any unified name (Phoenicians), similar to descriptions of Phoenicia in the Bible. However, Phoenician (or better, coastal northern Canaanite) culture flourished in this period. The Phoenician version of Canaanite culture that existed on the coast exhibited bichrome ware pottery (globular flasks and jugs with concentric circles in red and black).

The *Edomites and *Moabites (Bienkowski) and the *Ammonites (Macdonald and Younker) were three major groups that existed in the Transjordan. The biblical writers describe these groups as kingdoms. For example, an Edomite king list is given in Genesis 36:31-

43, and a king of Edom who refused the Israelites passage through his territory is mentioned in Numbers 20:14-21. The Moabites as well are described as having a king during the early periods (Num 21:26). No Ammonite king is mentioned, however, until the time of Jephthah (Judg 11—12), although they were a unified group much earlier (cf. Num 21:25). The Israelites also claimed a close kinship with these three groups, but the relationship with Moab and Ammon is described in a derogatory manner (see Gen 19:30-38).

Documents from the first millennium BCE show that the Transjordanian peoples spoke dialects of Canaanite, and thus were very similar to biblical Hebrew and Phoenician. However, like Israel in the period of the Judges, the material culture of Transjordan in the twelfth and eleventh centuries BCE (Iron Age I) was composed of small settlements that could not have housed significant kingdoms. Thus there does not appear to be any significant level of sociopolitical organization, as there were sparse settlement patterns. Many have argued, therefore, that the isolated biblical statements about kingdoms in these regions in the Bronze and Early Iron Ages were anachronistic. However, if one sees the kings as chieftains, there is no longer an anachronism.

The material culture in the Transjordan region is poorly known in this period. Excavations at Tell es-Saʾidiyeh show a Canaanite-style culture, similar to material at Beth-Shean across the Jordan. In fact, some objects may even show evidence of connections with the Sea Peoples. Tell Deir ʿAlla shows evidence of a seminomadic existence, with evidence of silo pits. Few remains are found in Moab.

5.2. Israelite Religion. Not surprisingly, it is difficult to characterize Israelite religion in this period (see Smith; van der Toorn). The Iron Age I in other Near Eastern regions saw the rise of a national god to prominence. For instance, the Assyrians followed Ashur, the Babylonians Marduk, the Moabites Chemosh, the Ammonites Milcom and the Israelites Yahweh. Interestingly, excavations from this period show that the dead were buried with food, drink, lamps and tools, showing that the living may have been required to care for them, much like customs found in other regions of the ancient Near East. This is all the more interesting because of the biblical taboo against this very thing (Deut 26:14). The *ark of the covenant is the most recognizable religious artifact in Iron Age 1. It often was used in warfare (see 1 Sam 4—7, where the ark was a spoil of war, not unlike Mesopotamian divine images), and there was a belief that Yahweh's presence surrounded the ark. The representation on the ark (the seat with cherubim) is similar to other thrones found at Megiddo and Byblos.

There is sparse and fragmentary evidence for religious activity in this period. The central city of Shiloh has been ruined through erosion and later-period building activities, although there is a Late Bronze Age shrine located there. Further, an "Israelite" shrine has been found at Mount Ebal, north of Shechem, reminiscent of Joshua's altar (cf. Josh 8:30-32). A *"high place" has also been found in the northern Samarian foothills, which brings to mind the biblical high places (e.g., 1 Kings 14:23).

6. Conclusions.

It is a daunting task to combine biblical, textual and archaeological evidence to provide a comprehensive understanding of Israel in the premonarchical period. However, literary and archaeological evidence, although conflicting at certain points, have markers of similarity. The central hill country of Ephraim, Manasseh and Benjamin appears to have been the most populated area, which is in agreement with the book of Judges, as these tribes play the major roles in the narratives. Oddly enough, Judah is only featured with Othniel (Judg 3:7-11) until the later narratives. Furthermore, Israel and Judah are listed separately in 1 Samuel 11:8; 15:4. This either implies an authentic historical situation or an anachronism on the part of the writer living in the period of the divided monarchy.

Israel in the period of the judges is described in the Bible as a segmentary tribal society without a central administration and even a standing army. This appears to be in agreement with archaeological investigations and anthropological research. Of course, extrabiblical textual and archaeological evidence can neither confirm nor deny any of the elements of the biblical narratives. Thus we can describe these narratives as having historical plausibility, but we cannot ascribe to them historical certainty. Archaeological research is also subject to various interpretations. For instance, the destruction layer of a town mentioned in the biblical records could be interpreted as verifying the historicity of the biblical narratives, or it could be interpreted within an entirely different perspective. As we noted, not only is it difficult to pinpoint any biblical event in this period, but also we cannot even be certain which settlements are "Israelite" and which are not. At any rate, the sparse archaeological remains, as well as the few and fragmentary documents from this period, make it difficult to evaluate the historical veracity of the biblical narratives. Thus these narratives ultimately must be evaluated on an internal basis. It is quite apparent that the sources for the premonarchical period are formulaic and employ theologically based interpretations that do not appeal to the historical sensibilities of the modern researcher. Suffice it to say that there are at least "kernels of truth" throughout the sources of Judges, 1 Samuel and Ruth. However, each student of this period must decide how "historical" the sources are. On that matter, there is as yet no consensus.

See also AMPHICTYONY, QUESTION OF; ARCHAEOLOGY, SYRO-PALESTINIAN; ARCHITECTURE; ETHNICITY; HEBREWS; HISTORY OF ISRAEL 1: SETTLEMENT PERIOD; JUDGES; JUDGES, BOOK OF; PHILISTINES.

BIBLIOGRAPHY. A. Alt., *Essays on Old Testament History and Religion* (Oxford: Oxford University Press, 1966); P. Bienkowski, ed., *Early Edom and Moab: The Beginning of the Iron Age in Southern Transjordan* (Sheffield Archaeological Monographs 7; Sheffield: J. R. Collis and National Museums and Galleries on Merseyside, 1992); E. Bloch-Smith, "Israelite Ethnicity in Iron I: Archaeology Preserves What Is Remembered and What Is Forgotten in Israel's History," *JBL* 122 (2003) 401-25; idem, *Judahite Burial Practices and Beliefs about the Dead* (JSOTSup 123; Sheffield: JSOT, 1992); R. Boling, *Judges* (AB 6A; Garden City, NY: Doubleday, 1969); O. Borowski, *Agriculture in Iron Age Israel* (Winona Lake, IN: Eisenbrauns, 1987); J. Callaway, "The Settlement in Canaan: The Period of the Judges," in *Ancient Israel: A Short History from Abraham to the Roman Destruction of the Temple*, ed. H. Shanks (Englewood Cliffs, NJ: Prentice-Hall, 1988) 53-84; E. Campbell Jr., *Ruth* (AB7; Garden City, NY: Doubleday, 1975); W. G. Dever, *Who Were the Israelites and Where Did They Come From?* (Grand Rapids: Eerdmans, 2003); T. Dothan, *The Philistines and Their Material Culture* (New Haven: Yale University Press, 1982); I. Finkelstein, *The Archaeology of the Israelite Settlement* (Jerusalem: Israel Exploration Society, 1988 [1986]); **F. Frick,** *The Formation of the State in Ancient Israel: A Survey of Models and Theories* (SWBA 4; Sheffield: Almond, 1985); **N. Gottwald,** *The Tribes of Yahweh: A Sociology of the Religion of Liberated Israel* (Maryknoll, NY: Orbis, 1979); **B. Halpern,** *The Emergence of Israel in Canaan* (SBLMS 29; Chico, CA: Scholars Press, 1983); idem, *The First Historians: The Hebrew Bible and History* (San Francisco: Harper & Row, 1988); **M. Hasel,** "Israel in the Merneptah Stele," *BASOR* 196 (1994) 45-61; **B. Hesse and P. Wapnish,** "Can Pig Remains Be Used for Ethnic Diagnosis in the Ancient Near East?" in *The Archaeology of Israel: Constructing the Past, Interpreting the Present,* ed N. Silberman and D. Small (JSOTSup 237; Sheffield: Sheffield Academic Press, 1997) 238-70; **D. Hopkins,** *The Highlands of Canaan: Agricultural Life in the Early Iron Age* (SWBA 3; Sheffield: Almond, 1985); **B. Macdonald and R. Younker,** eds., *Ancient Ammon* (SHCANE 17; Leiden: E. J. Brill, 1999); **P. Machinist,** "The Question of the Distinctiveness in Ancient Israel: An Essay," in *Ah, Assyria—: Studies in Assyrian History and Ancient Near Eastern Historiography Presented to Hayim Tadmor,* ed. M. Cogan and I. Ephal (ScrHier 33; Jerusalem: Magnes, 1991) 196-212; **G. Mendenhall,** *The Tenth Generation: The Origins of the Biblical Tradition* (Baltimore: Johns Hopkins University Press, 1973); **M. Noth,** *The Deuteronomistic History* (JSOTSup 15; Sheffield: JSOT, 1981 [1957]); **M. Smith,** *The Early History of God: Yahweh and Other Deities in Ancient Israel* (Grand Rapids: Eerdmans, 2002); **K. L. Sparks,** *Ethnicity and Identity in Ancient Israel* (Winona Lake, IN: Eisenbrauns, 1998); **L. Stager,** "The Archaeology of the Family in Early Israel," *BASOR* 260 (1985) 1-35; **K. van der Toorn,** *Family Religion in Babylonia, Syria, and Israel: Continuity and Change in the Forms of Religious Life* (SHCANE 7; Leiden: E. J. Brill, 1996); **M. Weippert,** *The Settlement of the Israelite Tribes in Palestine: A Critical Survey of Recent Scholarly Debate* (Naperville, IL: Allenson, 1971). M. W. Chavalas

HISTORY OF ISRAEL 3: UNITED MONARCHY

The term *united monarchy* refers to the period of Israelite history that witnessed the paradigm shift in national leadership from that of tribal confederacy to dynastic state. Two defining characteristics distinguishing the Hebrew tribal league during the era of the judges from the Israelite monarchy are usually identified. The first is the supplanting of so-called charismatic leadership (i.e., divinely appointed leaders raised up spontaneously in response to crises) with dynastic succession (i.e., leadership bestowed upon the eldest heir of successive generations within a single ruling family). The second is the move from a more loosely organized alliance of tribes ruled by elders to a more centralized administrative structure based on the model of kingship.

Typically, *Saul's kingship is lumped among the "early attempts" at Hebrew kingship (Hoppe, 560) and then analyzed as the final and most significant of the "first steps" toward monarchy (e.g., Bright, 184-95). The "united monarchy" proper refers to the consolidated Davidic rule over all the tribes of ancient Israel, commencing with *David's installation in Hebron as king over all Israel (2 Sam 5:1-3) and continuing with the reign of his heir and successor, *Solomon (1 Kings 1:38-48; 2:12). Solomon's death and the succession of his son *Rehoboam precipitated the split of the Hebrew united monarchy and spawned the rival divided monarchies of Israel and Judah (as punishment for Solomon's idolatry, according to Ahijah the prophet [1 Kings 11:34-40; 12:12-20]).

1. Recent Scholarship
2. Prelude to Israelite Kingship
3. Historical Overview
4. Ideology of Kingship
5. Assessment of Kingship

1. Recent Scholarship.

1.1. Defining History and Historiography. History is typically defined as the continuum or chronological record of significant events affecting a nation or an institution (and often offering an explanation of their causes). History in the OT refers to the biblical record of the nation of Israel and the institutions of tabernacle/temple and Davidic kingship. R. Alter's (1981, 24-25) application of the category "prose fiction" to the biblical narratives has raised questions about the definition of history in biblical studies. This understanding of biblical narrative as "artefact" emphasizing literary artistry and compositional technique (apart from any correspondence to historical reality) has blurred the ideas of "history-as-event" and "history-as-account" (Kaiser, 2; cf. Howard 2003, 26-29). V. P. Long (1994a,

60) suggests that it is best to recognize that the term *history* is now used in two quite distinct senses both "to refer to the past itself and to interpretive verbal accounts of the past—and to discern in each context which is intended."

Historiography is the selective telling or reporting (in written form) of those historical events shaping and defining a particular nation or institution (usually based on careful appeal to a variety of sources). Historiography in the OT is the selective reporting of the events impacting the nation of Israel and its essential institutions. Long (1994a, 67-69) equates historiography with "representational art" (or referential narrative) constrained by the facts of the past. The reader of biblical historiography must keep in mind (1) the highly selective nature of the reporting in the narratives; (2) the liabilities associated with applying modern and Western literary and ideological templates in the analysis of ancient and Eastern documents; (3) the religious or theological character of the biblical narratives as both "sermon" and "biography" of God (cf. Long 1994a, 30-38; Hill, 30-38).

1.2. Literary Sources. The literary sources for understanding the history of Israel's united monarchy are limited to the Bible itself, essentially 1 Samuel 8—1 Kings 11 (although recent histories of the monarchy tend to rely more on archaeological data and less on biblical texts as sources [see Knoppers 1999, 207-15]). Only three extrabiblical citations or allusions to Kings Saul, David and Solomon or their reigns have been uncovered to date. All three (contested) inscriptions refer to David, and they include the reference to "the house of David" in the Tell-Dan stela fragment, a similar phrase in the Mesha stela, and the expression "the heights of David" in a victory stela of Shishak (or Shoshenq 1 of Egypt) (see Kitchen 2003, 92-93; cf. Provan, Long and Longman, 312 n. 9). The gap in extrabiblical documentation making reference to Israel between the time of the Egyptian Merneptah stela (1209 BCE) and the reference to King Ahab of Israel as an opponent of the Assyrian king Shalmaneser III at Qarqar has caused some scholars to distinguish between a "proto-Israel" and a "historical Israel" (e.g., Dever, as cited in Kitchen 2002, 112). According to K. A. Kitchen (2002, 112), this lack of continuity in the extrabiblical documentation of ancient Israel "does not reside in the history of early Israel itself, but in the failure in witness by external

non-biblical sources, and for very specific reasons." Namely, no pharaoh after Merenptah, save one (Ramesses III [c. 1184-1153]), was involved in Syria-Palestine until the mid-tenth century BCE. Likewise, after Tukulti-Ninurta I of Assyria (c. 1244-1208 BCE), no Assyrian king ventured as far west as the Mediterranean coast until Assurnasirpal II in 882 BCE. Hence, no Egyptian or Assyrian king or chronicler "had clear contact with, or had occasion to say anything about, peoples in Palestine during the 300/350 years between 1200 and 900-860 B.C." (Kitchen 2002, 113).

The books of Samuel and Kings comprise part of the so-called *Deuteronomistic History (Deuteronomy—2 Kings), a grouping of historical books reflecting the literary and theological characteristics of Deuteronomy (see Howard 1993, 77-78). This collection belongs to the larger primary history of the OT (Genesis—Kings), which tells the story of God's faithfulness in the rise and fall of the people of Israel (see Freedman 1991, 5-6, 13-14). Attempts have been made to identify sources within the Samuel—Kings corpus, such as the "succession narrative" (2 Sam 9—20; 1 Kings 1—2) and the "temple construction report" (1 Kings 3—11), which includes the reference to the "annals of Solomon" (an unknown historical source [1 Kings 11:41]) (see Howard 1993, 174). Although widely acclaimed for its literary artistry, the Succession Narrative has been discounted as a historical document in more recent biblical scholarship (see Kaiser, 226-28).

Synoptic parallels are found in 1-2 Chronicles to the reigns of Saul (1 Chron 10), David (1 Chron 11—29) and Solomon (2 Chron 1—9), although the historical value of this later retelling of early Israelite kingship is discounted by critical OT scholarship. Yet more recent biblical scholarship has a growing appreciation for the Chronicler as a historian (see Hill, 28-30). The Chronicler cites the (unknown) records of Samuel the seer, the records of Nathan the prophet and the records of Gad the seer as historical resources for the reign of King David (1 Chron 29:29) (see Hill, 43-45). The Chronicler cites the (unknown) records of Nathan the prophet in the prophecy of Ahijah and the visions of Iddo the seer as historical resources for the reign of King Solomon (2 Chron 9:30) (see Howard 1993, 238-39).

1.3. Nonwritten Material Remains. The archaeological data related to the Israelite united monarchy is meager and provides a sketchy picture of Hebrew kingship at best. Concerning the first Hebrew king, A. Mazar (371) notes that "the time of Saul hardly finds expression in the archaeological record." *Gibeah of Benjamin (identified with Tell el-Ful), Saul's "capital," was strategically located about three miles north of Jerusalem on a main route leading to the city (cf. 1 Sam 11:4; 15:34; 22:6). It is likely that Saul's home in Gibeah was converted into a "palace" of sorts (1 Sam 13:2; 14:16). Excavations at the site yielded the corner of a "modest" or "extensive fortress," depending upon the source consulted (cf. Hoerth, 249; Mazar, 374). Mazar (374) and others tentatively associate the structure with Saul's "palace-fortress," which served as his "headquarters" during this first phase of Israelite kingship.

Mazar (374) goes on to state that "the archaeological evidence concerning David's reign is also poor and ambiguous." David conquered Jebusite *Jerusalem, the "fortress of Zion." Subsequently he established his capital there, renaming it the "city of David" (2 Sam 5:7-9). The move secured a neutral site for the capital city of David's kingdom and a fully operative administrative center (assuming that David merely appropriated the Jebusite bureaucratic machinery already in place [see Mendenhall, 160-63]). The concubines whom David married from Jerusalem (and who had to be left in the palace during Absalom's coup) probably were Jebusite princesses (2 Sam 5:13; cf. 15:16). These marriages likely were part of an alliance with the local Jebusite leaders, since David left the population of the city intact after conquering it (see Bright, 200). Jebusite Jerusalem was located on a prominent ridge, or spur, known as Ophel, between the Kidron Valley on the east and the Tyropean Valley on the west. Excavations uncovered an imposing "stepped structure" that may be a retaining wall of the "fortress of Zion" seized by David (see Mazar, 374-75; Monson, 4-5). The tunnel known as Warren's Shaft, connecting Jebusite Jerusalem with its water supply from the Gihon Spring, is popularly identified as the tunnel or water shaft connection by which David's men entered the city, surprised the Jebusites and captured the city (see Hoerth, 266). Mazar (375) concludes by observing that "the modest archaeological data from the time of David . . . is consistent with the biblical accounts, which do not attribute to him any building operations."

The Bible portrays King Solomon as an energetic builder, crediting him with constructing Yahweh's temple in Jerusalem, an elaborate royal palace known as the Millo (or "supporting terraces" [NIV]), the wall of Jerusalem, the strengthening of fortifications at *Hazor, *Megiddo and *Gezer, and the building of "store cities" and "towns for his chariots" (1 Kings 9:10-19). Solomon's intensive building activity in Jerusalem is attested only indirectly by archaeological data: the design of the temple (see Solomon's Temple) after the pattern of religious architecture of the second millennium BCE in Canaan and northern Syria (see Mazar, 377). The temple ruins of Tell Tainat and ʿAin Dara (in northern Syria) typically are cited as architectural parallels of Solomon's temple (see Monson, 10-21). The motifs of the art forms utilized in the decoration and ornamentation of Yahweh's temple (e.g., gourds, flowers, palm trees, winged cherubim [1 Kings 6:18, 32]) have parallels in Canaanite, Phoenician and Syrian art (see Mazar, 378).

Outside the city of Jerusalem the six monumental or chambered gates discovered in appropriate occupation levels at Hazor, Megiddo and Gezer have been connected to Solomon's building activity (see, e.g., Mazar, 384-87; cf. 1 Kings 9:15), but this identification is now contested (see Monson, 3-4; also Austel, 160-69). If the monumental gates date to the tenth century BCE, then they offer tangible evidence of strategic planning by a centralized administration (see Meyers, 247-52). I. Finkelstein (Finkelstein and Silberman, 141-42), however, challenges the historical connection of these chambered gates to the Israelite united monarchy on the basis of pottery forms, architectural style and carbon dating of wooden roof beam samples from Megiddo. He dates the so-called Solomonic levels of Megiddo, Gezer and Hazor to the early ninth century BCE, "decades after the death of Solomon!" (Finkelstein and Silberman, 141).

Finally, C. Meyers (244-45) speculates that the settlements found in the western Negev were outposts of the early monarchy, "initiated and supported by the state." Mazar (389) posits the same for the Palestine littoral on the basis of the alliances between the *Phoenicians and Israel during the reigns of David and Solomon. Such hypotheses offer plausible explanations for "out-migration" during this time period, but corroboration awaits more substantial and definitive archaeological data.

1.4. Current Approaches and Issues. In their summary of the modern understanding of the study of Israelite history J. H. Hayes and J. M. Miller (64-69) identified four approaches: (1) orthodox or traditional; (2) archaeological; (3) traditio-historical; (4) socioeconomic. W. C. Kaiser (8-15) offers a critique of five approaches, or schools of thought, for the study of the history of Israel: (1) the traditional (or orthodox) school; (2) the Baltimore (or archaeological) school; (3) the Alt/Noth (or traditio-historical) school; (4) the Gottwald (or socioeconomic) school; (5) the non-pan-Israelite tribal confederation schools.

Central to the discussion of methodology is the role of the Bible as a source for the reconstruction of Israelite history. The primary sources for Israelite history commonly cited are Syro-Palestinian archaeology, related fields of ancient Near Eastern studies and the Bible. A number of different "Israels" have emerged in biblical scholarship depending upon the priority accorded the Bible among these historical sources. P. R. Davies (11, 18) identified three "Israels": (1) a "biblical Israel" (i.e., Israel as a literary construct based on the text of the Bible); (2) a "historical Israel" (i.e., the peoples living in Iron Age Palestine known through archaeological discovery and extrabiblical literature); (3) an "ancient Israel" (i.e., the modern historical reconstruction of Israel based on the conflation of data garnered from the study of "biblical Israel" and "historical Israel").

Related to the issue of methodological approaches is the more fundamental question of the reliability of the sources. This is the flashpoint in discussion between the historical maximalists, medialists and minimalists on the value of the Bible as a historical source for the history of Israel (see Howard 2003, 45-49; Bullock, 99-104). The historical maximalist (e.g., Kaiser; Merrill; Provan, Long and Longman) and medialist (e.g., Eichrodt; Meyers) approaches affirm to varying degrees the general trustworthiness of the Bible as a source for Israelite history. The minimalist position is a reductionist approach to the biblical narrative that discounts or flatly rejects the Bible as a credible source for reconstructing Israelite history (e.g., J. M. Miller 1976; Davies; Whitelam).

The medialist approach recognizes that authentic and ancient documentation of Israelite state formation is embedded in the biblical history of Samuel and Kings. The problem is in separating "the legendary embellishments from the record of historical experience" (Meyers, 230). Yet, apart from acknowledging the genre of annals as historically more reliable than prose narrative, little is offered by way of objective control for sorting what is "dubious" from what is "reliable" in the biblical record (see Meyers, 227-30; 252-53). In addition, although the medialist may not doubt the historicity of David and Solomon, the reinterpretation of the pertinent archaeological data prompts Finkelstein (Finkelstein and Silberman, 142) to conclude that "archaeology misdated both 'Davidic' and 'Solomonic' remains by a full century." Such analysis yields a radically altered conception of the Israelite united monarchy, raising considerable doubt about the splendor and extent of the realms of David and Solomon (Finkelstein and Silberman, 142-45).

The maximalist camp rightly recognizes that the ideology of the modern historian as it relates to the nature of the Bible (i.e., as divine revelation or a culturally bound human document) in large measure determines one's position on the reliability of the biblical record (see Provan, Long and Longman, 62-70). Beyond this is the matter of methodology, whether archaeological, historical, literary or ideological in its emphasis (see Kitchen's [2002, 128] list of principles for interpreting historical data from the maximalist viewpoint). This chapter of the study of Israelite history is still being written (see further the discussions in Howard 1998, 40-46; 2003, 25-53; Knoppers 1999, 215-21; Provan, Long and Longman, 3-35).

A second and related question is the exact understanding of the testimony of the available archaeological and historical data concerning the historical character of the early Iron Age (i.e., the twelfth to tenth centuries BCE). According to J. M. Miller (1997, 13-14), the opening centuries of the Iron Age were "a kind of a 'dark age' throughout the ancient world. The Bronze Age empires had collapsed, peoples were on the move, and localized socio-political structures apparently were the order of the day." Most scholars grant that the emergence of a national Israelite state is related to the political absence of the former superpowers of Hatti, Egypt and Assyria in the ancient Near East of the second millennium BCE (e.g., Meyers, 234). Kitchen

(2002, 126-28), however, challenges the notion that the twelfth to tenth centuries BCE were a "dark age" in the ancient world. He has noted that a precise sequence of kings for this time period is extant for both Egypt and Assyria, including records of external wars as well as internal political information (Kitchen 2002, 126). In addition, from Neo-Hittite documents we learn of the series of "mini-empires" that develop and vie for power in the Levant and regions north during this era, including Tabal, Carchemish and Aram-Zobah (Kitchen 2002, 113, 116-23; 2003, 98-107). It is during this "epoch of mini-empires" that a fourth mini-empire emerges: the united monarchy of Israel.

Finally, there are the problems related to the nature and extent of the "kinship" among the tribes of ancient Israel, the demographics of ancient Palestine with respect to the composition and extent of the "Canaanite" population that the Israelite monarchy must "accommodate" in its rule, the issues associated with the competing political and religious ideologies of Yahwism and Baalism in the development of Hebrew kingship, and the ongoing assessment of the viability of the various interpretive theories and socio-anthropological models applied to the data in an attempt to explain the backgrounds and origin of the Israelite monarchy. This is further complicated by the fact that any understanding of the development of kingship in Israel is predicated upon one's interpretation of the biblical accounts of Hebrew settlement in the land of Palestine as presented in the book of Joshua (whether conquest, infiltration, revolt or resettlement) and the organization of the Hebrew tribes during the period of the settlement as described in the book of Judges (whether an *"amphictyony" or some permutation thereof or some other form of tribal confederation).

2. Prelude to Israelite Kingship.

2.1. Kingship Anticipated. The Hebrew monarchy is foreshadowed in several ancient poetic texts of the OT. Among these texts are Jacob's blessing of Judah (Gen 49:9-12), Balaam's fourth oracle (Num 24:15-19) and Hannah's song (1 Sam 2:1-10). According to D. N. Freedman (1980, 118), all three poems date to the eleventh century BCE. Two of the poems anticipate Israelite kingship with the symbol of the "ruler's staff" *(mĕḥōqēq)* and "scepter" *(šēbeṭ)*

(Gen 49:10; Num 24:17), while the third makes reference to Yahweh's "king" *(melek)* and "anointed one" *(mĕšîah)* (1 Sam 2:10). Sometime after Samuel's birth and dedication to Yahweh, a man of God appeared to Eli the priest. He predicted that God would raise up a faithful priest whose family would be priests to his anointed kings forever (1 Sam 2:35). In fact, double citations to an "anointed one" at the beginning and end of the narrative frame the books of Samuel (1 Sam 2:10, 35; 2 Sam 22:51; 23:1). This prompts B. S. Childs (273) to observe, "The focus on God's chosen king, his anointed one, David, appears right at the outset, and reveals the stance from which the whole narrative is being viewed."

Typically, traditionalist scholars include Deuteronomy 17:14-20 in the catalog of OT texts anticipating the Hebrew monarchy (e.g., Howard 1993, 159; Merrill 1994, 263-65). More critical OT scholarship views the passage within the larger framework of the Deuteronomistic History and regards it a later diatribe against Solomonic kingship in light of the overall historical development of the Hebrew monarchy (e.g., P. D. Miller, 147-49; Nelson, 222-25). In either case, Deuteronomy 17:14-20 is valuable as a statement of the "ideals" for Hebrew kingship. The guidelines specify that any candidate selected as king must be a fellow Israelite chosen by God (Deut 17:15), the king may not build up a large stable of horses (against the risk of dependency upon Egypt) (Deut 17:16), the king may not take many wives for himself (against the risk of idolatry) (Deut 17:17a), the king may not amass vast amounts of wealth (Deut 17:17b), and the king must know and obey the law of God (Deut 17:18-19).

Finally, God's covenant with Abraham included the promise of descendants who would be kings (Gen 17:6, 16; 35:11). Again, issues of biblical interpretation arise as those scholars committed to some type of pentateuchal source criticism typically assign Genesis 17 and 35 to the P document and date the texts to the era after the collapse of the Hebrew divided kingdoms (e.g., Fretheim, 457, 584).

2.2. Kingship Demanded. The immediate circumstances precipitating the Hebrew request for a king were Samuel's old age and the appointment of his corrupt sons as judges (1 Sam 8:1-3). The seed bed for distrusting Yahweh's leadership was laid during the period of the judges, an era when a cycle of divinely appointed tribal leaders delivered the Hebrews from the oppression of neighboring peoples (e.g., Ammonites, Moabites). This divine punishment was a result of their moral decay and religious apostasy, but still the Israelites perceived judgeship as an unstable form of governance (cf. the fourfold repetition of the statement juxtaposing the chaos of the period of the judges with the lack of kingship, Judg 17:6; 18:1; 19:1; 21:25). Thus the elders of Israel held council and demanded from Samuel the appointment of a king (1 Sam 8:4-5). Samuel finally relented and granted the Israelites' request for a king, but not before warning the people to beware of the king's treatment of them on three counts: military conscription, forced civil service, taxation (1 Sam 8:9-18) (see Baldwin, 84-87).

The Israelites' penchant for a human king was only reinforced by a series of episodes that revealed their disobedience to the Lord (Judg 2:16-23). The clamor for a Hebrew monarchy began with the people's attempt to install Gideon as a king over them (Judg 8:22-23). It subsequently included Abimelech's grab for power (Judg 9), and eventually it culminated in the fall of Shiloh to the Philistines and the loss of the ark of the covenant (1 Sam 4—5) (see Kaiser, 192-93, 204-7). In the minds of the Israelites God was unable to effectively handle the Philistine threat and provide security for his people. Surely a king could do a better job of protecting Israel (see Bright, 185-86).

Other factors were at work in the process of state formation, however, beyond the pressure of Philistine expansion on Israel's western flank. In addition to the military factor, Meyers (237-43) cites demographic, and techno-environmental factors that led to state formation in early monarchic Israel. Specifically, population growth in the agrarian Hebrew society precipitated "out-migration" in search of more arable land. It also created the need for the centralization of organization to address issues of logistics in the redistribution of commodities no longer manageable by tribal chieftains. Beyond this, the increasing demand for iron implements for agriculture (and warfare) accented the need for a more centralized administrative organization.

3. Historical Overview.
3.1. Chronology. An Israelite *chronology for

eleventh-century BCE Palestine is difficult to reconstruct. Extrabiblical sources for this period of history are scarce, and the biblical record is incomplete. For example, due to textual corruption in transmission, a date formula connected to Saul's reign provides only partial information (1 Sam 13:1). Typically, a forty-year reign for King Saul is established on the basis of the reference to Saul's kingship in Acts 13:21. The only reliable synchronization between ancient Near Eastern and biblical records during this time is the reference to the invasion by Shishak (or Shoshenq I, 945-924 BCE [J. Perny, *CAH* 2.646; Kitchen 1986, 75-76] or 931-910 BCE [Edelman, *ABD* 5.1221-22]) of Judah during the fifth year of Solomon's successor, Rehoboam (1 Kings 14:25-26). This Egyptian incursion into Palestine is dated to 926 or 925 BCE on the basis of temple reliefs at Thebes (or Karnak) and fixes the beginning of Rehoboam's reign around 930 BCE (see Gray, 345-46; Wiseman, 152). Representative chronologies of the Hebrew united monarchy can be compared as in Table 1.

3.2. Hebrew Kingship in the Context of the Ancient Near East. The Hebrew monarchy succeeded partly because of the political vacuum on the international scene during the early centuries of the Iron Age of ancient Near Eastern history. In Egypt the New Kingdom (1570-1085 BCE) had reached its zenith under Ramesses II (1304-1237 BCE). The Twenty-first Dynasty (c. 1070-930 BCE),

Table 1. Representative Chronologies of United Monarchy

Bright:	Saul	1020-1000 (?)
	Ishbosheth	1000-998
	David	1000-961
	Solomon	961-922
Kitchen (2003):	Saul	1042-1010
	Ishbaal	1006-1004
	David	1010-970
	Solomon	971/970-931/930
Merrill (1987):	Saul	1051-1011
	Ishbosheth	1011-1009
	David	1011-971
	Solomon	971-931

beginning the late period of Egyptian history, occupied a time of international decline and internal consolidation for the Egyptian Empire (after repulsing the Sea Peoples in a series of naval battles, but with considerable loss). In Mesopotamia, to the east, the resurgent Assyrian Empire was preoccupied with the Hittites and Babylonians. Toward the end of the second millennium BCE, it appears, the Assyrians were hard-pressed to stave off the aggressive infiltration of the Arameans into their western colonies. To the north, in Asia Minor, the beginning of the Iron Age brought about the fall of the Hittite Empire as a result of the incursion of the Sea Peoples from the Aegean region. One of the tribes of the Sea Peoples, the *Philistines, settled along the southwest coastal plain of Canaan. The name *Palestine* is derived from these Philistine invaders who occupied the coastal region of Canaan from Joppa to Gaza at the beginning of the thirteenth century BCE. Remnants of the Hittite Empire survived in several Neo-Hittite city-states in northern Syria, but these posed little threat to the Israelites. In fact, King Tou (or Toi) of Hamath gave gifts of precious metals to David in recognition of his triumph over Hadadezer of Zobah (a rival of Toi; see 2 Sam 8:9-11). Later, King Solomon brokered the sale of Egyptian horses and chariots to the Hittite kings (2 Kings 10:29) and even married women from among the Hittites (1 Kings 11:1) (on the empires of David and Solomon see Kitchen 2003, 81-158).

As a result of these geopolitical dynamics, the eastern Mediterranean region enjoyed a respite from the massive military campaigns of the international superpowers vying for control of the land bridge of Syro-Palestine. The consequent vacuum of political power permitted numerous small independent states to emerge in the region, including the Ammonites, Arameans, Edomites, Moabites, Philistines, Phoenicians and Israelites. Naturally, the story of the Hebrew united monarchy is intricately connected with the relationship of the Israelites to these neighboring kingdom-states. In fact, it was the Philistine threat that prompted Israel to establish a monarchy. Furthermore, it was the loss of revenue from the satellite states of Ammon, Aram, Edom and Moab during the latter years of King Solomon's reign that contributed to the eventual split of the Hebrew united monarchy, as it necessitated a royal decision either to decrease spending or increase taxes (see 1 Kings 12:3-4, 12-15).

3.3. Geographical Considerations. The Chronicler delineates the ideal borders of national Israel achieved under Kings David and Solomon as stretching from "Lebo-Hamath to the Wadi Egypt" (2 Chron 7:8; cf. 1 Chron 13:5) (*see* Geographical Extent of Israel). The building of the Israelite mini-empire occurred in stages of conquest and annexation over the course of several decades (see Bright, 200-204). The first phase was the consolidation of David's rule over "all Israel" after taking the Jebusite city of Jerusalem and establishing it as his capital (2 Sam 5:1-10). Stage two included the *Ammonite war and the conquest of the southern Transjordan (2 Sam 8:2, 13-14). Phase three included the campaigns in Syria against Aram-Zobah (2 Sam 8:3-7), and phase four saw David subjugate King Tou (or Toi) of Hamath (2 Sam 8:9-10). Kitchen (2002, 114) makes a threefold distinction among the lands controlled by the Israelite united monarchy: (1) the "heartland" or the home territories of Judah and Israel (i.e., the ideal boundaries of tribal Israel from "Dan to Beersheba" [cf. Judg 20:1; 1 Sam 3:20; 2 Sam 3:10]); (2) tributary lands or vassal states (including Edom, Moab, Ammon and Aram); (3) subject-allies (including Geshur, Maacah and Hamath). The (hostile) Philistines to the southeast and the (friendly) Phoenicians from Tyre northward remained independent states (see Bright, 204-5; see also the map of David and Solomon's mini-empire in Kitchen 2002, 115).

3.4. Royal Administration. David's administration included an expanded royal cabinet, as the only officer named in Saul's regime was Abner (the commander of the army [1 Sam 14:50]). Three distinct departments comprised David's royal cabinet: a war office, a priestly office and an administrative office (see Hill, 260-62) (*see* State Officials). Joab, as commander and chief of the army, headed David's war office (2 Sam 8:16), while Abiathar and Zadok served as joint chief priests (2 Sam 8:17). David's administrative office included a recorder (or royal historian), a court secretary, a captain of the royal bodyguard, a "friend" of the king (or personal advisor [2 Sam 15:37]) and David's sons were appointed as priests (NIV: "royal advisers" [2 Sam 8:15-18; cf. 1 Chron 18:14-17]). Later, King Solomon added three posts to the royal cabinet: an official charged with oversight of the twelve district governors, a manager of palace affairs, and an officer over the forced labor gangs (1 Kings

4:1-6) (see the comparative chart delineating the royal officials under David and Solomon in Meyers, 258).

Meyers (257) observes that the double set of military officers (one in command of the Israelite militia and one in charge of the foreign mercenary units, the Cherethites and Pelethites) "reflects the importance of the fundamental source of royal power: the coercive strength of the military." The Succession Narrative illustrates the importance of the military in the transition of power, as the eventual heir to the throne (Solomon) had the support of the Cherethites and Pelethites, the elite royal guard (1 Kings 1:38, 44) (see Ishida 1983, 176-79). Overall, Meyers (259) suggests that "the Israelite monarchy was not a strongly authoritarian regime. . . . Rather it was more a participatory monarchy," given the strong tradition of the elders, with "all the people having a voice in governance" (see 2 Sam 5:3; 19:11-14, 41-43). This partly helps to explain Rehoboam's downfall and the split of the Hebrew united monarchy (see 1 Kings 12:1-5).

4. Ideology of Kingship.
Humanly speaking, Saul was well endowed as Israel's first king, given his family prestige, physical prowess and natural good looks (1 Sam 9:2). In fact, Samuel anointed Saul as a "leader" (*nāgîd*) over Israel (1 Sam 10:1), but the people acclaimed him "king" *(melek)* at the installation ceremony (1 Sam 10:24) (see the discussion in Meyers, 236). The biblical narrative suggests that Saul the farmer moved from the role of a "king on demand" (1 Sam 11:5) to a ruling monarch housed in a centralized court complex attended by royal servants (i.e., his home in Gibeah converted to a "fortress-palace"? [1 Sam 16:18, 21-22; 20:18]). By the time of David and Solomon, Saul's transitional kingship had given way to dynastic rule from a centralized administrative center over a mini-empire.

As Meyers (261) puts it, a king's ability to exercise power "ultimately rested on and was legitimized by a series of symbolic acts, attitudes, icons, and structures connecting the king with deity and human kingship with divine rule" (naturally this created a certain symbiotic relationship between the offices of king and priest; *see* Kings and Kingship). Much of Israelite "royal ideology" was common to the idea of kingship in the ancient Near East (not surprising,

given the initial request of the people to have a king as did the surrounding nations [1 Sam 8:5]) (see Frankfort, 231-76). Symbolic acts connected to the Israelite monarchy included the ritual of the anointing of the king by a "priestly figure" and a public coronation ceremony (1 Sam 9:16, 23-25; 10:1; 16:13; 2 Sam 5:3). Naturally, a royal protocol developed that involved processionals of various sorts (e.g., 1 Sam 15:1; 18:6-7), proper decorum in relationship to the king (e.g., the bringing of gifts upon installation [1 Sam 10:27]), bowing in the king's presence (2 Sam 19:18; 1 Kings 1:23; cf. 2 Sam 15:5) and greeting the king with certain formulaic language (1 Sam 10:24; 1 Kings 1:25, 31, 36). Icons associated with the Israelite united monarchy included monumental buildings such as the Jerusalem temple, sacred objects from Israel's past such as the ark of the covenant (1 Chron 15-16; cf. the Mosaic Nehushtan relic [2 Kings 18:4]), thrones (1 Kings 7:7; 10:18-20), scepters (cf. Gen 49:10; Ps 60:7), crowns (2 Sam 1:10; 12:30; cf. Ps 89:39), royal robes (1 Kings 10:5; 22:10), royal harems (2 Sam 12:8; 1 Kings 11:1-3) and even a tomb complex for the *royal family (1 Kings 2:10; 11:41; 14:31). Finally, the king took on numerous idealized roles as leader of his people, including the idea of "royal adoption" (i.e., the deity adopts the king as his "son" [2 Sam 7:14; cf. Ps 89:26-27]), shepherd of the people (2 Sam 5:2; 7:7), commander and chief of the military (2 Sam 11:1; 12:29), supreme judge of the land (2 Sam 12:1-6; 15:3; 1 Kings 3:16-28), and in some cases more specialized roles (e.g., David as "the poet of Israel" [2 Sam 23:1]; Solomon as "the sage of Israel" [1 Kings 4:29-34]).

The fallout from the shift from theocracy to monarchy in Israel eventually affected Hebrew social structure in numerous ways, including matters of justice, equity, state-sanctioned violence, as well as gender relationships. The rise of the Israelite monarchy disrupted kinship-based social patterns of female-male interdependence that characterized and maintained village life during the settlement of Canaan (*see* Israelite Society). Meyers (268-69) observes that the formal association between males and the wielding of political power in urban settings "inevitably meant the increasing subordination of women." This is seen in the "commodities" approach to securing and controlling the women of the royal harem (2 Sam 16:21-22; 1 Kings 1:1-

4; 3:1; 11:1-8), and more tragically in the personal stories of women such as Bathsheba (2 Sam 11), Tamar (2 Sam 13), and Rizpah and Merab (2 Sam 21) (*see* Women).

5. Assessment of Kingship.

Overall, the people of Israel were the worse off as a result of Saul's reign. Ostensibly, Saul was made king to address the Philistine threat (1 Sam 8:20); yet despite Saul's early military successes (1 Sam 14:47-48), the Philistines controlled more territory at the end of Saul's reign than at his accession (see 1 Sam 31:8). The social fragmentation that characterized the period of the judges was more acute, evidenced in the divided loyalties and hostilities between the "house of Saul" and the "house of David" after Saul's death (2 Sam 2:8-17) (see Kaiser, 220).

David's unique spiritual sensitivities, his capacities for worship, and his familiarity with repentance earned him the epitaph of one whose heart was like that of God (Acts 13:22; cf. 1 Sam 13:14). David's legacy included his role as the architect and general contractor for Yahweh's temple (1 Chron 28—29), and he is credited with the reorganization of the Levitical priests and the creation of the temple liturgy (1 Chron 22—26). David became the model of the "ideal king" for Israel (cf. 2 Kings 18:3; 22:2) and the prototype of the Messiah as the ultimate "shepherd-king" (Jer 33:15; Ezek 34:23-24; 37:24-25; cf. Rev 22:16). David's kingship was not without its dark side, however, as the biblical historians relate (counter to the conventions of ancient Near Eastern historiography) stories of a botched installation ceremony for the *ark of the covenant (2 Sam 6:1-11), adultery and murder (2 Sam 11), incestuous rape (2 Sam 13), an attempted coup (2 Sam 15—18), an unwise census (2 Sam 24), succession intrigue (1 Kings 1) and vindictive deathbed counsel (1 Kings 2:5-9; cf. 2 Sam 23:6-7) associated with David and the his royal family. In each case, the "human wreckage" left in the wake of the event was considerable.

Theologically, Solomon's reign is important because he was, at least initially, a king who knew and obeyed God's *law in keeping with the Mosaic provisions for kingship (Deut 17:18-19) (see Hill, 383). In addition, his *prayer of dedication established Yahweh's temple as a "house of prayer" and emphasized the centrality of prayer for Israel in maintaining covenant relationship with the God of their ancestors (1 Kings 8:30;

2 Chron 6:21) (see Hill, 392). Finally, and most important, his succession to the throne underscored God's faithfulness in keeping his covenant promise to David to establish his dynasty (1 Kings 8:24; 2 Chron 6:15; cf. 2 Sam 7:11-13).

Sadly, the closing years of Solomon's reign were marked by political decline, economic instability and moral decay. Ironically, the king fell prey to the seductions of the foreign women within the royal harem (1 Kings 11:1-3). Overcome by sensuality and materialism, the sage of Israel was unable to avoid the snare about which he had repeatedly warned others (cf. Prov 5:1-14; 7:6-27). The biblical historian attributed the split of Israel's united monarchy to Solomon's sin of idolatry (1 Kings 11:33; perhaps foreshadowed in his worship at the "high places" [1 Kings 3:3]). Tragically, Solomon's gift of wisdom was compromised by his own sin (see Kaiser, 284-85). The united monarchy ended where it began, with the Hebrew tribes in disarray and clamoring for new leadership (1 Kings 12:16). Samuel's warnings about kingship (1 Sam 8:10-18) remained a haunting echo for the Hebrew divided monarchies that were to follow.

See also DAVID; DAVID'S FAMILY; DAVIDIC COVENANT; GEOGRAPHICAL EXTENT OF ISRAEL; HISTORY OF ISRAEL 3: PREMONARCHIC ISRAEL; HISTORY OF ISRAEL 4: DIVISION OF THE MONARCHY; KINGS AND KINGSHIP; SOLOMON; ZION TRADITIONS.

BIBLIOGRAPHY. **R. Alter,** *The Art of Biblical Narrative* (New York: Basic Books, 1981); idem, *The David Story* (New York: Norton, 1999); **H. Austel,** "The United Monarchy: Archaeological and Literary Issues," in *Giving the Sense: Understanding and Using Old Testament Historical Texts,* ed. D. M. Howard and M. A. Grisanti (Grand Rapids: Kregel, 2003) 160-78; **J. G. Baldwin,** *1 & 2 Samuel* (TOTC; Downers Grove, IL: InterVarsity Press, 1988); **B. Birch,** *The Rise of the Israelite Monarchy: The Growth and Development of 1 Samuel 7-15* (SBLDS 27; Missoula, MT: Scholars Press, 1976); **J. Bright,** *A History of Israel* (4th ed.; Louisville: Westminster/John Knox, 2000); **C. H. Bullock,** "History and Theology," in *Giving the Sense: Understanding and Using Old Testament Historical Texts,* ed. D. M. Howard and M. A. Grisanti (Grand Rapids: Kregel, 2003) 97-111; **J. Cerny,** "Egypt: From the Death of Ramesses III to the end of the Twenty-First Dynasty," *CAH* 2.606-57; **B. S. Childs,** *Introduction to the Old Tes-*

tament as Scripture (Philadelphia: Fortress, 1979); **P. R. Davies,** *In Search of 'Ancient Israel'* (JSOTSup 148; Sheffield: JSOT, 1992); **D. V. Edelman,** *King Saul in the Historiography of Judah* (JSOTSup 121; Sheffield: JSOT, 1991); idem, "Saul," *ABD* 5.989-99; **W. Eichrodt,** *Theology of the Old Testament* (2 vols.; Philadelphia: Westminster, 1977); **I. Finkelstein,** "The Emergence of the Monarchy in Israel: The Environmental and Socio-Economic Aspects," *JSOT* 44 (1989) 43-74; **I. Finkelstein and N. Na'aman,** eds., *From Nomadism to Monarchy: Archaeological and Historical Aspects of Early Israel* (Jerusalem: Israel Exploration Society; Washington, DC: Biblical Archaeology Society, 1994); **I. Finkelstein and N. A. Silberman,** *The Bible Unearthed: Archeology's New Vision of Ancient Israel and the Origin of Its Sacred Texts* (New York: Free Press, 2001); **H. Frankfort,** *Kingship and the Gods: A Study of Ancient Near Eastern Religion as the Integration of Society and Nature* (OIE; Chicago: University of Chicago Press, 1978); **D. N. Freedman,** *Pottery, Poetry, and Prophecy: Studies in Early Hebrew Poetry* (Winona Lake: Eisenbrauns, 1980); idem, *The Unity of the Hebrew Bible* (Ann Arbor: University of Michigan Press, 1991); **T. E. Fretheim,** "The Book of Genesis," *NIB* 1.321-673; **F. Frick,** *The Formation of the State in Ancient Israel: A Survey of Models and Theories* (SWBA 4; Sheffield: Almond, 1985); **V. Fritz and P. R. Davies,** eds., *The Origin of the Ancient Israelite States* (JSOTSup 228; Sheffield: Sheffield Academic Press, 1996); **J. Gray,** *I & II Kings* (2d ed.; OTL; Philadelphia: Westminster, 1970); **D. M. Gunn,** *The Fate of King Saul: An Interpretation of a Biblical Story* (JSOTSup 14; Sheffield: JSOT, 1980); idem, *The Story of King David: Genre and Interpretation* (JSOTSup 6; Sheffield: JSOT, 1978); **B. Halpern,** *The Constitution of the Monarchy in Israel* (HSM 25; Chico, CA: Scholars Press, 1981); **V. P. Hamilton,** *Handbook on the Historical Books* (Grand Rapids: Baker, 2001); **L. Handy,** ed., *The Age of Solomon: Scholarship at the Turn of the Millennium* (SHCANE 11; Leiden: E. J. Brill, 1997); **J. H. Hayes and J. M. Miller,** *Israelite and Judean History* (Philadelphia: Westminster, 1977); **A. E. Hill,** *1 & 2 Chronicles* (NIVAC; Grand Rapids: Zondervan, 2003); **A. J. Hoerth,** *Archaeology and the Old Testament* (Grand Rapids: Baker, 1998); **L. J. Hoppe,** "Israel, History of (Monarchic Period)," *ABD* 3.558-67; **D. M. Howard,** *An Introduction to the Old Testament Historical Books* (Chicago: Moody, 1993); idem, *Joshua* (NAC 5; Nashville: Broadman & Holman, 1998); idem,

"History as History: The Search for Meaning," in *Giving the Sense: Understanding and Using Old Testament Historical Texts,* ed. D. M. Howard and M. A. Grisanti (Grand Rapids: Kregel, 2003) 25-53; **V. A. Hurowitz,** *I Have Built You an Exalted House: Temple Building in the Bible in Light of Mesopotamian and Northwest Semitic Writings* (JSOTSup 115; Sheffield: JSOT, 1992); **T. Ishida,** *The Royal Dynasties in Ancient Israel: A Study on the Formation and Development of Royal-Dynastic Ideology* (BZAW 142; Berlin: de Gruyter, 1977); idem, "Solomon," *ABD* 6.105-13; idem, ed., *Studies in the Period of David and Solomon* (Winona Lake, IN: Eisenbrauns, 1983); **W. C. Kaiser,** *A History of Israel* (Nashville: Broadman & Holman, 1998); **G. Keys,** *The Wages of Sin: A Reappraisal of the "Succession Narrative"* (JSOTSup 221; Sheffield: JSOT, 1996); **K. A. Kitchen,** "Assessing the Historical Status of the Israelite United Monarchy," in *Windows into Old Testament History,* ed. V. P. Long, D. W. Baker and G. J. Wenham (Grand Rapids: Eerdmans, 2002) 111-30; idem, *On the Reliability of the Old Testament* (Grand Rapids: Eerdmans, 2003); idem, *The Third Intermediate Period in Egypt, 1100-650 B.C.* (2d ed.; Warminster: Aris & Phillips, 1986); **G. N. Knoppers,** "The Historical Study of the Monarchy: Developments and Detours," in *The Face of Old Testament Studies: A Survey of Contemporary Approaches,* ed. D. W. Baker and B. T. Arnold (Grand Rapids: Baker, 1999) 207-35; idem, "The Vanishing Solomon: The Disappearance of the United Monarchy from Recent Histories of Israel," *JBL* 116 (1997) 19-44; **V. P. Long,** *The Art of Biblical History* (FCI 5; Grand Rapids: Zondervan, 1994a); idem, "How Did Saul Become King? Literary Reading and Historical Reconstruction," in *Faith, Tradition, and History: Old Testament Historiography in Its Near Eastern Context,* ed. A. R. Millard, J. Hoffmeier and D. W. Baker (Winona Lake, IN: Eisenbrauns, 1994b) 271-84; idem, *The Reign and Rejection of King Saul: A Case for Literary and Theological Coherence* (SBLDS 118; Atlanta: Scholars Press, 1989); **A. Mazar,** *Archaeology of the Land of the Bible: 10,000-586 B.C.E.* (New York: Doubleday, 1992); **G. E. Mendenhall,** "The Monarchy," *Int* 29 (1975) 155-70; **E. H. Merrill,** *Deuteronomy* (NAC 4; Nashville: Broadman & Holman, 1994); idem, *Kingdom of Priests: A History of Old Testament Israel* (Grand Rapids: Baker, 1987); **C. Meyers,** "Kinship and Kingship," in *The Oxford History of the Biblical World,* ed. M. D. Coogan (New York: Oxford University Press, 1998) 221-

71; **J. M. Miller,** *The Old Testament and the Historian* (Philadelphia: Westminster, 1976); idem, "Separating the Solomon of History from the Solomon of Legend: Response to Millard," in *The Age of Solomon: Scholarship at the Turn of the Millennium,* ed. L. Handy (SHCANE 11; Leiden: E. J. Brill, 1997) 1-25, 54-56; **P. D. Miller,** *Deuteronomy* (IBC; Louisville: John Knox, 1990); **J. M. Monson,** "The Temple of Solomon: Heart of Jerusalem," in *Zion: City of Our God,* ed. R. S. Hess and G. J. Wenham (Grand Rapids: Eerdmans, 1999) 1-22; **R. D. Nelson,** *Deuteronomy* (OTL; Louisville: Westminster/John Knox, 2002); **F. H. Polak,** "David's Kingship: A Precarious Equilibrium," in *Politics and Theopolitics in the Bible and Postbiblical Literature,* ed. H. G. Reventlow, Y. Hoffman and B. Uffenheimer (JSOTSup 171; Sheffield: JSOT, 1994) 119-47; **R. Polzin,** *Samuel and the Deuteronomist: A Literary Study of the Deuteronomic History* (San Francisco: Harper & Row, 1989); **I. Provan, V. P. Long and T. Longman,** *A Biblical History of Israel* (Louisville: Westminster/John Knox, 2003); **L. Rost,** *The Succession to the Throne of David* (HTIBS 1; Sheffield: Almond, 1982); **M. J. Selman,** *1 Chronicles* (TOTC; Downers Grove, IL: InterVarsity Press, 1994); idem, *2 Chronicles* (TOTC; Downers Grove, IL: InterVarsity Press, 1994); K. W. Whitelam, *The Invention of Israel: The Silencing of Palestinian History* (London: Routledge, 1996); **R. N. Whybray,** *The Succession Narrative: A Study of 2 Samuel 9-20; 1 Kings 1 & 2* (SBT 9; London: SCM, 1968); **D. J. Wiseman,** *1 & 2 Kings* (TOTC; Downers Grove, IL: InterVarsity Press, 1993); **L. J. Wood,** *Israel's United Monarchy* (Grand Rapids: Baker, 1979).   A. E. Hill

HISTORY OF ISRAEL 4: DIVISION OF THE MONARCHY

1 Kings 12:1-19 and 2 Chronicles 10:1-19 report that after the death of *Solomon, his son *Rehoboam went to *Shechem, where all Israel had come to make him king. The Israelites agreed to serve Rehoboam—that is, to accept him as their king—on the condition that he lighten the yoke of service placed on them by his father, Solomon. Rehoboam took three days to consult with his advisors before responding to the people's request. The older men who had counseled Solomon advised Rehoboam to comply with the request in order to cultivate the people's loyal service. Rehoboam, however, ignored their advice in favor of that of his peers, who

proposed that he threaten the people with harsher treatment than they had received under Solomon. At their behest, he replied to the people with a euphemism. The NRSV translates, "My little finger is thicker than my father's loins." But the word "finger" is not in the Hebrew. A better translation might be, "My small member is thicker than my father's loins." Thus claiming greater virility and "machismo" than Solomon, Rehoboam added, "Now, my father placed a heavy yoke upon you, and I will add to your yoke. My father disciplined you with whips, but I will discipline you with scorpions" (1 Kings 12:10-11). Upon receiving Rehoboam's reply, the Israelites responded with an adage of their own: "What portion do we have in David? We have no heritage in the son of Jesse. To your tents, O Israel! Now look to your own house, O David!" (1 Kings 12:16). With that, the Israelites departed, refusing to accept the lordship of Rehoboam or the Davidic dynasty, and the kingdoms of Israel and Judah were permanently divided.

1. Sources
2. Causes of Division
3. Results of Division
4. Conclusions

1. Sources.

The accounts of the division in the books of *Kings and *Chronicles are colored by the interests of their authors. In addition, *textual problems in those accounts render certain details about the event and its causes obscure.

1.1. Theological Explanations. Both Kings and Chronicles focus on theological explanations for the division. Thus for both of them the division was "a turn of affairs brought about by Yahweh" (1 Kings 12:15; 2 Chron 10:15).

In Kings the root cause of the division was Solomon's apostasy, which is described in 1 Kings 11:1-8. Yahweh's response first directly to Solomon (1 Kings 11:9-13) and then to *Jeroboam through the prophet Ahijah (1 Kings 11:29-40) predicted that the kingdom would be torn away from Solomon and awarded to Jeroboam. For David's sake this was delayed until after Solomon's lifetime, and the Davidides were to retain a dominion or fiefdom (a better translation than the more common "lamp") in Jerusalem.

The Chronicler idealizes Solomon and thus cannot blame the division on him. As a result, Chronicles' explanation of the division is more ambiguous than that in Kings. Abijah expresses the Chronicler's view in 2 Chronicles 13:5-7:

> Do you not know that Yahweh the God of Israel gave kingship over Israel to David and his sons in perpetuity as a covenant of salt? But Jeroboam, the son of Nebat, the servant of David's son Solomon rose up and rebelled against his masters. Then vacuous scoundrels gathered around him and strengthened themselves against Rehoboam, son of Solomon, when he was a youth and soft-hearted and not strong enough to resist them.

These verses appear to blame the schism on Jeroboam and his followers, who took advantage of Rehoboam's naïveté. Precisely how this could be so and the division still be "a turn of affairs brought about by Yahweh" is not made clear.

1.2. Religious Apostasy. Both Kings and Chronicles also emphasize the division as the beginning of the northern kingdom's religious apostasy. 1 Kings 12:25-33 describes three heterodox measures instituted by Jeroboam for which he is condemned.

First and foremost, he built royal shrines at *Dan and *Bethel. This was a sin on several levels. It obviously ran counter to the principle of centralization—the idea that Yahweh could be legitimately worshiped only in *Jerusalem—which is a key element of the ideology of the *Deuteronomistic History. Jeroboam also installed golden calves (more precisely, young bulls) at his two shrines, thus violating the prohibition against idols (Ex 20:4-6; Deut 5:8-10). Moreover, it is clear from the phrasing of Jeroboam's invitation in 1 Kings 12:28 ("Here are your gods, O Israel, who brought you up from the land of Egypt") that the Deuteronomistic Historian understands these as shrines to gods (plural) other than Yahweh.

The other two facets of Jeroboam's sin were that he disassociated the priesthood from the tribe of Levi, so that anyone who wanted to do so could become a priest, and that he altered the cultic calendar, appointing a pilgrimage festival on the fifteenth day of the eighth month in contrast to the celebration in Judah of Sukkoth (Tabernacles) on the fifteenth day of the seventh month (Lev 23:33-43). This multifaceted "sin of Jeroboam" became a theme in the book of Kings as every one of Jeroboam's successors "walked in the way of Jeroboam son of Nebat who caused Israel to sin" merely by maintaining the royal shrines of Israel.

Chronicles does not contain a parallel account of Jeroboam's sin, because the Chronicler typically omits material dealing exclusively with Israel, which he regards as illegitimate. But the Chronicler incorporates much the same perspective on Jeroboam in Abijah's speech in 2 Chronicles 13:8-12, albeit without any reference to Jeroboam's change of the religious calendar.

1.3. Judahite Perspective. Both Kings and Chronicles, then, obviously are the products of southern—that is, Judahite—writers, who regard the northern kingdom as rebellious and apostate.

Nevertheless, it is worth observing that the bulk of the united kingdom (ten of twelve tribes) rejected Rehoboam and the Davidic line in favor of Jeroboam. Surely, from their perspective, the northern kingdom was the true continuation of Israel—as suggested in its preservation of the name—and Judah was the splinter state. There are some indications, which are explored below, that Israel and Judah were always distinct and that David and Solomon succeeded in uniting them, somewhat uneasily, for a brief period. The perception in the north, therefore, may have been that the united kingdom was something of a failed experiment, if not a time of subjugation to their southern cousins, and the "division" represented a return to normalcy and self-determination.

The northerners would not have viewed themselves as apostates. The shrines and cultic practices ascribed to Jeroboam were standard features of Israel's religious traditions, and modern critical scholarship has concluded that centralization was a later ideological and political development within Judah, as was the limitation of the *priesthood to Levites (see 3.3 below). There is every indication that the shrines at Dan and Bethel were devoted to the worship of Yahweh. The northern, eighth-century prophets Hosea and Amos did not assume centralization or question the legitimacy of Dan and Bethel as rivals to Jerusalem. Hosea condemned idolatry and worship of other gods as trends within Israel at large, not peculiar to Dan, which he did not even mention, or Bethel. (Hosea characteristically uses a wordplay to refer to Bethel, calling it Beth-aven, "house of wickedness." But it is one among several sites that Hosea condemns; he does not single it out as a royal shrine.) Amos criticized the hypocrisy of worship at Bethel, but not the cultic activity per se (Amos 4:4-5; cf. 5:4-6).

1.4. Role of Jeroboam. A notorious problem presented by the Kings account of the division relates to the role played by Jeroboam.

According to 1 Kings 12:3a, 12 in the Hebrew Bible (MT), Jeroboam returned from Egypt upon Solomon's death and took a leading role in the rebellion against Rehoboam. However, 1 Kings 12:20 indicates that the people became aware of Jeroboam's return only after they had rejected Rehoboam when they summoned him to be their king, so that he had no part in the rebellion itself. The Chronicles version, in line with the Chronicler's standard practice of omitting the material peculiar to the north, has no parallel to 1 Kings 11:40 or 12:20, so that there is no tension within the Chronicles account and no doubt about Jeroboam's leadership role in the schism. It is often asserted, in fact, that the Chronicler added 2 Chronicles 10:2-3a to the story in order to make clear that Jeroboam was primarily responsible for the division, and that the problems in Kings were caused by the later borrowing of these verses into 1 Kings 12:2-3a.

This explanation, however, does not take full stock of the textual evidence, especially that of the LXX of Kings. That evidence is complex: in addition to the variant readings and order of these verses in the Masoretic (Hebrew) Text and the Greek Septuagint (LXX), the latter contains an entire "supplemental" account of Jeroboam (3 Kgdms 12:24a-z), the origin and value of which are debated. Recent treatments of the witnesses (McKenzie 1987; Willis) have argued that the addition of 1 Kings 12:2-3a, which is the source of the tensions in the Kings account, probably was the result of corruption within the textual tradition of Kings, and that in the best reconstruction of the text Jeroboam was summoned to rule Israel only after the division had taken place.

2. Causes of Division.

2.1. Social, Political and Economic Factors. Despite the writer's emphasis on the theological cause of the division, there are clear indications in Kings that there were social, political and economic reasons behind the Israelites' response.

The people's cry for relief from the yoke of hard service obviously alludes to Solomon's conscription of a labor force out of the northern tribes for his building projects (1 Kings 5:13-18;

1 Kings 9:15-22, which claims that Solomon drafted only foreigners for his labor force but did not enslave Israelites, probably is a Deuteronomistic correction to the earlier passage). The labor force actually owed its existence to David, whose cabinet included Adoram as the officer in charge of this force (2 Sam 20:24). This was likely the same Adoniram who was in charge of the labor force under Solomon (1 Kings 4:6) (*see* State Officials) and whom the Israelites stoned to death when Rehoboam sent him to quell the revolt (1 Kings 12:18).

Hand in hand with conscription came *taxation. 1 Kings 4:7-19 details Solomon's redivision of the northern tribes into provinces for purposes of taxation—that is, each province was to supply provisions for the king one month out of the year. The separate "official in the land of Judah" mentioned at the end of 1 Kings 4:19 indicates that Judah was exempted from taxation as from conscription. Solomon's indebtedness, indicated by his attempt to pay Hiram of Tyre by ceding him twenty cities (1 Kings 9:10-14), suggests that the taxes in his realm may have been high, since the debts that they were designed to cover were great. Solomon's economic woes may have contributed to his loss of hegemony over Edom and Aram (1 Kings 11:14-25) and the loss of Israel that followed (1 Kings 11:26-43).

2.2. David's Displacement of Saul. Apart from economic problems, Rehoboam faced resentment caused by historical and political factors surrounding David's displacement of Saul.

Some of this resentment had surfaced in David's own reign; if not in the revolt of Absalom (2 Sam 15—19), then certainly in that of Sheba (2 Sam 20). It was hardly coincidence that Jeroboam came from the tribe of Ephraim, in the heart of what had been Saul's kingdom. Evidence of sectionalism in the account of these revolts (2 Sam 19:11-15) and earlier references to Israel and Judah as separate entities (2 Sam 3:10; 19:43; 1 Kings 1:35) indicate that Israel and Judah were always felt to be distinct in some sense, and that the Davidic-Solomonic period was less a united kingdom than a united rule over a dual kingdom. Again, the perspective of the Israelites was likely quite different from that of the authors of Kings and Chronicles; they saw themselves as a subjugated people, not much different from the *Aramaeans and *Edomites, who revolted against Solomon.

There was already a sense of independence

and unity in the Israelites' ability to band together to compel Rehoboam to journey to Shechem for their ratification of him as their king. Rehoboam's insulation from these signals of brewing discontent only exacerbated their frustration at the insensitivity of the Davidic ruler to their feelings of oppression and their readiness to abandon the Davidides altogether and return to their own traditions. Rehoboam could have done nothing worse on this occasion than send Adoniram, head of the labor force, to try to put down the rebellion. The fact that Rehoboam himself was forced to flee is testimony to his own cluelessness at the level of resentment in Israel stemming from the policies of his father and grandfather. That resentment, which had been latent during Rehoboam's sheltered existence in the palace, now exploded.

2.3. Influence of Yahwistic Prophets. Some scholars have argued, based on the stories in 1 Kings 11:29-39 and 14:1-18, for a further cause of the division in the influence of Yahwistic prophets, especially Ahijah the Shilonite ("from Shiloh"). Some have even found a motive for Ahijah's activism in the alleged suppression by the Davidides of the northern religious institutions associated with the priesthood of Eli at *Shiloh. However, there are problems with this view.

Although 1 Kings 11:29-39 does seem to present Ahijah's oracle as impelling Jeroboam to rebel, the reasons given in the oracle have nothing to do with Shiloh or any northern cultic tradition, but rather focus on Solomon's apostasies. Indeed, the language and ideology of the oracle are Deuteronomistic. The oracle does contain certain inconsistencies, especially concerning the number of tribes under consideration: Ahijah tears his robe into twelve pieces and has Jeroboam take ten of them, saying that one tribe is preserved for David. However, the identity of the twelfth tribe can be explained without resort to another hand, so that the passage may be ascribed to the Deuteronomistic Historian. Thus there probably was not an earlier oracle behind the current one, and if there was, it can no longer be reconstructed.

The passage in 1 Kings 14:1-18 is also the Deuteronomistic Historian's composition as it now stands. It is the first in a series of oracles against the northern royal houses composed by the Deuteronomistic Historian on the basis of older treaty curses involving nonburial. The oracles explain etiologically the succession of "dynasties" in Israel in contrast to the single, Davidic line of rulers in Judah. 1 Kings 14:1-18 also seems to be based on an earlier oracle, but it also may no longer be reconstructable. In any case, the original oracle was a response to Jeroboam's inquiry about Jeroboam's sick son and probably did not forecast the end of his dynasty.

3. Results of Division.
The effects of the division on Israel and Judah were wide-ranging. They are treated here under three categories: political, socioeconomic, religious.

3.1. Lasting Separation. The most obvious political result was, of course, the lasting separation of Israel and Judah as two distinct states.

Israel was the larger of the two in terms of both land holdings and population. Its larger territory afforded it greater and more diverse natural resources and therefore more prosperity; its larger population gave it a more powerful army. The northern kingdom reached its apex politically, militarily and in terms of international prestige during the *Omride dynasty in the ninth century BCE. However, its greater prominence, along with its political instability, contributed to its downfall under the *Assyrians a century later (721 BCE), nearly 150 years before the kingdom of Judah met its demise at the hands of the *Babylonians. In contrast to the single Davidic dynasty enjoyed by Judah, Israel experienced a series of royal houses, some lasting through only two kings, each ending with a bloody coup d'état at the hands of a new military usurper. The reasons for this difference between the Israelite and Judahite monarchies are not entirely clear. The frequently made claim that the conception of kingship in Israel was not dynastic is countered by the repeated attempts throughout its history to found a dynasty.

The relationship between the two states was rocky at first. 1 Kings 14:30 mentions continual war between Jeroboam and Rehoboam, a situation that persisted under their successors (1 Kings 15:6-7, 16, 32). What is probably meant by this constant state of war is the continuing incidence of border skirmishes. The tribe and territory of Benjamin, at the frontier between the two, was caught in the middle and became a frequent battleground; it also appears to have changed hands with some frequency (1 Kings 15:17-22). Apparently, things changed under the

Omrides, and relations became amicable, to judge from stories such as the ones in 1 Kings 22 about cooperative ventures between the kings of Israel and Judah. The stories suggest that this change occurred because of the emergence of a common enemy in *Aram, which even led to a marital union between the Israelite and Judahite royal houses (see 2 Kings 8:27-29), probably in ratification of a treaty.

The division had more immediate consequences relative to other countries in the region. Specifically, the *Egyptian pharaoh Sheshonq (Shishak) evidently saw the schism as an opportunity to reestablish Egyptian hegemony over Palestine. Five years later he led an invasion (1 Kings 14:25-28). Sheshonq's interest in the region had been apparent in his harboring of Hadad the Aramaean and Jeroboam, both of whom were Solomon's enemies (1 Kings 11:19, 40). He may have invaded under the pretense of giving aid to Jeroboam against Rehoboam. Rehoboam's fortresses (2 Chron 11:5-12) may have been built in preparation for this invasion, since these turn out to be predominantly in the Judahite highlands rather than along the frontier with Israel as is sometimes asserted. However, archaeological evidence, including Sheshonq's own victory relief at Karnak, indicates that both Israel and Judah suffered devastation. Only Rehoboam's emptying of the temple and royal treasuries for a sizeable payment to Sheshonq spared Jerusalem.

3.2. Internal Division. In addition to solidifying the political division between north and south, the schism helped to deepen social and economic divisions within each state.

The policies of taxation, forced labor and compulsory military service that were instituted under the Davidides likely continued, although references to them in the biblical materials are harder to find. Taxation certainly would have been required to support the royal institutions of both countries, as well as their building projects and a professional army if such services were not conscripted. The cost of payments like the one to Sheshonq and the later tributes that accompanied subjugation to the Assyrians and Babylonians would have been passed on to the citizens in the form of increased taxes.

The burden of taxation was likely a significant factor in the bifurcation of Israelite society into distinct classes of rich and poor, a situation decried especially by the eighth-century prophet Amos. Similar concerns expressed by *Isaiah (Is 5:8-10) and Micah (Mic 2:1-5) hint that Judah's society may have been equally divided. The account of Amaziah's mustering of an army in 2 Chronicles 25:5, whether historical or not, reflects the practice of military conscription that may have been common in the divided monarchy.

3.3. Cultic Change. The biblical writers, as we have seen, stress the religious consequences of the division in the form of the cultic changes implemented by Jeroboam.

Jeroboam may have found his new kingdom divested of its people's distinctive religious traditions. In particular, the *ark of the covenant appears to have been a northern, especially Ephraimite, cultic symbol of Yahweh's presence, especially in warfare, to judge from the stories about it before the monarchy. David's transfer of the ark to Jerusalem may have been intended as a symbol of his uniting of north and south (2 Sam 6:1-19; 1 Chron 13:1-14; 15:1-28). It soon became a fixture of the Jerusalem cult, especially with its installation in *Solomon's temple (e.g., 1 Kings 8:21; 2 Chron 6:11). This would have left Jeroboam's Israel without any distinct, unifying religious symbol of their own, such that Jeroboam's fear that he might lose subjects to Jerusalem (1 Kings 12:26) may have been well founded.

F. M. Cross (73-75, 279 fn 22) has argued that Jeroboam tried to "out-archaize" David in the shrines at Dan and Bethel by adopting imagery for Yahweh that stemmed from his identification with the Canaanite god El. Whether or not this was the case, it is virtually certain, as scholars have long observed, that Jeroboam's shrines were devoted to Yahweh and not to other gods. Doing otherwise would have alienated the Israelites rather than consolidating them as Jeroboam wished. The images of young bulls were conceived of as pedestals for the presence of Yahweh in the same function as the ark or the cherubim on it. They were not intended by Jeroboam as idols, although they may have come to be worshiped as such in the imaginations of some of Jeroboam's subjects or their heirs.

Jeroboam may have tried to compensate for the absence of a unifying relic by harking back to northern traditions in his establishment of the shrines at Dan and Bethel. These shrines may actually have been older installations refurbished by Jeroboam rather than completely new constructions (on the archaeological evidence for the installation at Dan, see Biran). Jeroboam would have lacked the resources to build "from scratch." Besides, the rebellion emphasized indigenous tribal traditions of the north over against the centralized innovations of Judah and the Davidides. The emphasis on tribal or regional traditions might also explain why there were two royal sanctuaries in Jeroboam's Israel, which was something very unusual in the ancient Near East, where palace and temple typically were conjoined physically and ideologically.

The situation regarding the priesthood put in place by Jeroboam is more complicated. Traditionally, critical scholars have maintained that the Levites were not associated with priesthood until the late monarchy (the time of Deuteronomy, seventh century BCE), and that the limitation of the priesthood to Levites did not occur until after the end of the monarchy, in the exile and later. In this understanding, Jeroboam's appointment of priests from the general population was standard practice at the time, and the Deuteronomistic Historian's accusation that this was sinful is an anachronistic part of his polemic against the north.

F. M. Cross (195-215) has challenged this traditional view, arguing that the Levitical priesthood is ancient and proposing, moreover, that the biblical stories reflect an ancient and prolonged conflict between two Levitical houses: one that claimed Moses as their ancestor ("Mushite"), and one that claimed descent from Aaron. Jeroboam, Cross contends, wished to cultivate the support and traditions of both houses and therefore appointed a Mushite priesthood at Dan and the Aaronites at Bethel. Indeed, this was one of the reasons for the existence of two royal shrines in Israel. The Deuteronomistic Historian's accusation that priests at Jeroboam's shrines were not Levites is simply part of his effort to denigrate the northern cult. Cross believes that Jeroboam, in proclaiming "Behold your gods, O Israel, who brought you up from the land of Egypt" (1 Kings 12:28), was drawing on an older cultic legend that claimed Aaron's authority for the shrine at Bethel that was also polemicized by the Mushites (Ex 32:4). B. Halpern follows Cross in regarding the Levitical priesthood as ancient, but he thinks that the priesthood at both of Jeroboam's shrines was Mushite, albeit from different branches of family.

In the opinion of many scholars the evidence for Cross's proposal is less compelling than that of the traditional critical view for the following reasons. The obviously Deuteronomistic and polemical nature of the story in 1 Kings 12 makes it precarious to try to reconstruct an older tradition being cited by Jeroboam. Cross's analysis of 1 Kings 12:28 also presupposes the priority of Exodus 32:4, which he regards as the work of E(lohist). Yet the simplest explanation of the plural "gods" in Exodus, where Aaron makes only one golden calf, is that this text borrows from 1 Kings 12, where Jeroboam erects two shrines. The writer's claim in 1 Kings 12 that Jeroboam's priesthood was not Levitical (and thus neither Mushite nor Aaronid) remains plausible and would not have been unusual for the time (*see* Priests and Levites).

4. Conclusions.

The Israelite tribes' rejection of Rehoboam as their king and the subsequent division of Israel into two kingdoms both confirmed and concretized long-standing political and religious differences between northern and southern peoples. Ironically, the north's effort at consolidation in opposition to the economic oppression of the Davidides apparently was the beginning of a deep class division in Israel and Judah as both new kingdoms perpetuated the government policies initiated by David and Solomon. Above all, the story of the division illustrates the nature of the historiographical sources in the Bible and the difficulties they present for historical reconstruction. These sources come to us from Judah and reflect a distinctly southern orientation. Whatever materials may have arisen in the north now possess a Judahite veneer and perspective. In addition, their primary concern is theological rather than historical. Social and historical causes and circumstances are not suppressed in the narrative but play a secondary role to the theological explanation of historical traditions. The biblical authors evidently view their task as being that of rendering such explanations (*see* Historiography, Old Testament).

See also HISTORY OF ISRAEL 3: UNITED MONARCHY; JEROBOAM; KINGS AND KINGSHIP; REHOBOAM; SOLOMON.

BIBLIOGRAPHY. **A. Biran,** "Sacred Spaces: Of Standing Stones, High Places and Cult Objects at Tel Dan," *BAR* 24 (1998) 38-45, 70; **F. M. Cross,** *Canaanite Myth and Hebrew Epic: Essays in* *the History of the Religion of Israel* (Cambridge, MA: Harvard University Press, 1973); **B. Halpern,** "Levitic Participation in the Reform Cult of Jeroboam I," *JBL* 95 (1976) 31-42; **L. Hoppe,** "Israel, History of (Monarchic Period)," *ABD* 3.558-67; **J. M. Miller and J. H. Hayes,** *A History of Ancient Israel and Judah* (Philadelphia: Westminster, 1986); **S. L. McKenzie,** "The Source for Jeroboam's Role at Shechem (1 Kgs 11:43-12:3, 12, 20)," *JBL* 106 (1987) 297-300; idem, *The Trouble with Kings: The Composition of the Book of Kings in the Deuteronomistic History* (VTSup 42; Leiden: E. J. Brill, 1991); **M. D. Rehm,** "Levites and Priests," *ABD* 4.297-310; **A. Schenker,** "Jeroboam and the Division of the Kingdom in the Ancient Septuagint: LXX 3 Kingdoms 12:24a-z, MT 1 Kings 11-12; 14 and the Deuteronomistic History," in *Israel Constructs Its History: Deuteronomistic Historiography in Recent Research,* ed. A. de Pury, T. Römer, and J.-D. Macchi (JSOTSup 306; Sheffield: Sheffield Academic Press, 2000); **Z. Talshir,** *The Alternative Story of the Division of the Kingdom (3 Kingdoms 12:24a-z)* (JBS 6; Jerusalem: Simor, 1993); **H. N. Wallace,** "The Oracles Against the Israelite Dynasties in 1 and 2 Kings," *Bib* 67 (1986) 21-40; **T. M. Willis,** "The Text of 1 Kings 11:43-12:3," *CBQ* 53 (1991) 37-44.

S. L. McKenzie

HISTORY OF ISRAEL 5: ASSYRIAN PERIOD

The Assyrian period of Israelite history extends from the mid-ninth century BCE to the late-seventh century BCE. In terms of Assyrian political history, this period extends from the reign of Shalmaneser III (858-824 BCE) to that of Ashur-uballit II (612-609 BCE). In terms of Israel, the period corresponds to the reigns of Omri of Israel (879-869 BCE [all dates for Israel and Judah follow Hayes and Hooker; Egyptian chronology follows Kitchen, *ABD* 2.322-31]) and Jehoshaphat of Judah (877-853 BCE), includes the final destruction of the northern kingdom of Israel (720 BCE), and concludes with the reign of Josiah of Judah (641-610 BCE). This era—a rich period of over two hundred years marked by various phases in the political, socioeconomic and religious fortunes of the divided kingdoms—provides the background for a significant amount of the OT historical narratives and prophetic texts. This article focuses on Assyrian and Israelite/Judean political history in this period, and the primary biblical

data drawn upon is from the OT Historical Books.

1. Preliminary Issues
2. The Emergence of the Neo-Assyrian Empire
3. The Omride Dynasty (879-840 BCE)
4. The Jehu Dynasty (839-748 BCE)
5. The Final Years of Israel (745-720 BCE)
6. The Kingdom of Hezekiah of Judah (727-699 BCE)
7. Judah as an Assyrian Vassal: The Reign of Manasseh (698-644 BCE)
8. The End of the Assyrian Empire: The Reign of Josiah (641-610 BCE)

1. Preliminary Issues.

1.1. Sources. The relevant sources for the Assyrian period of Israelite and Judean history include various biblical texts and extrabiblical data, the latter including epigraphical and archaeological discoveries. In comparison with the earlier periods of the ancestors and the exodus, the Assyrian period has a substantial amount of source material that often permits greater sociopolitical insight and fuller, more certain historical reconstruction. The nature and usefulness of these various sources are, however, a matter of perennial debate among scholars.

1.1.1. Biblical Sources. The OT Historical Books contain two overlapping accounts of Israelite and Judean history in the Assyrian period: 1 Kings 16—2 Kings 23; 2 Chronicles 17—35. The Kings account is often viewed as part of the *Deuteronomistic History, a larger historiographical composition. The case has been made that a first version of this work was put together in the latter part of the Assyrian period, in the reign of *Josiah (Cross, 274-89; Nelson), with other scholars arguing for a still earlier version during the time of *Hezekiah (Campbell, 209; McKenzie, 162; Weinfeld). Regardless of its origins, whether eighth (with subsequent shaping by Josiah in the seventh) or seventh century BCE, it is clear that this complex was supplemented in various ways in the exilic and postexilic periods. The Chronicles account is later than that of Kings, with its earliest roots, perhaps, in the sixth century BCE but probably stemming from later with even later revision and supplementation. The biblical texts themselves claim to rely on earlier sources such as "the Book of the Annals of the Kings of Israel/Judah" (see 2 Kings

15:11; 16:19). Since no documents by these names are extant, their exact nature, scope and contents remain unknown, and some have challenged whether such sources ever existed (Redford, 319-32). At the very least, however, such references reveal the biblical writers' consciousness of their own selectivity in the material presented in the OT.

In addition to the Historical Books, at least some of the oracles of certain writing prophets belong in this period, despite the fact that the final form of their books probably stems from a later time. These texts provide data relevant to Israelite history in the Assyrian period. Specifically, texts from Amos, Hosea, Micah, *Isaiah and *Jeremiah often address situations of the eighth and seventh centuries BCE and can supplement the material in the Historical Books by providing a glimpse of the inner workings of Israelite and Judean politics as well as a more thorough portrait of domestic, social and religious affairs (Miller and Hayes, 224).

1.1.2. Extrabiblical Israelite Sources. Some extrabiblical texts dating to the Assyrian period are available from ancient Israel/Palestine. These are not royal annals such as one finds in Assyria, nor king lists and chronicles such as one finds in Babylonia. Instead, these sources tend to be local and occasional documents such as ostraca, seals and seal impressions, and various *Hebrew inscriptions and letters, many of which are economic in nature. Such items are often important for specific questions but are typically of limited use for wide-scale historical reconstructions.

1.1.3. The Archaeology of Ancient Israel/Palestine. Archaeological remains from Israel and Judah are significant insofar as they provide direct, unmediated evidence. That said, even these sources require interpretation because they are often "silent" in terms of specific people and events. Even so, important archaeological data have come from excavation and occupation evidence at sites such as *Samaria, *Jezreel, *Jerusalem and *Lachish. Sites such as these have provided information pertaining to the date of destruction layers, pottery styles, architecture (city gates, walls, etc.) and domestic artifacts.

1.1.4. Extrabiblical Non-Israelite Sources. Textual and archaeological evidence from outside of Israel abounds for the Assyrian period. The most significant written evidence is the corpus of royal inscriptions from Assyria, Babylonia and Egypt (*see* Non-Israelite Written Sources: Assyrian; Non-Israelite Written Sources: Babylonian). These texts often supplement the Bible by discussing events or dates from a non-Israelite perspective (Cogan 1998, 243). Also critical among the Assyrian texts are the "Eponym Chronicles," or "*limmu*-lists." These lists were produced for the purpose of chronological recording and give a year-by-year account in which each year is named after a key Assyrian official (Akk *limmu* or *līmu[m]*) and mentions some condition or event that transpired that year, or the location of the army at the end of the year. The particular form of these lists seems to have begun with Shalmaneser III (858-824 BCE). The several fragmentary copies of different lists can be used to reconstruct an account covering several hundred years (Hallo, 38).

In addition to the Eponym Chronicles, Assyrian royal annals record the achievements of various kings and display inscriptions report different military accomplishments, often engraved on a stone statue of the victorious ruler. It is in this corpus that a number of specific references to the rulers, events and situations in Israel and Judah during the Assyrian period can be found. These official sources may be supplemented by a wide variety of correspondence from all areas of the Assyrian Empire, including letters, treaties, judicial records, administrative documents and religious texts.

From Babylonia, the main source is the "Babylonian Chronicles," a partial chronological record that gives a year-by-year summary of the king's major military deeds, often with minimal editorial bias (see Grayson 1975). The relevant source material from Egypt is mixed in extent and quality but is often sparse and internally focused, given the uncertain and highly fractious nature of Egyptian politics in this period (Cogan 1998, 244; Spalinger; Kitchen 1986). The states in the immediate vicinity of Israel and Judah also provide some relevant textual sources. The Mesha Inscription, or Moabite Stone (*ANET,* 320; *COS* 2.23:137-38), for example, is a stela set up by Mesha, king of Moab, in the ninth century BCE that refers to Omri. The Tel Dan Inscription (*COS* 2.39:161-62), an *Aramaic text apparently erected by Hazael, king of Aram-Damascus, mentions kings of both "Israel" and the "House of David," though the latter reading has been vigorously debated (see Athas; *COS* 2.39:162 n. 11).

Excavation of non-Israelite sites has also provided information that aids in reconstructing the history of the Assyrian period. The most significant data come from Assyrian locales such as Nineveh (Kuyunjik), Ashur and Dur-Sharrukin (Khorsabad). Evidence of construction, expansion, destruction and rebuilding at such sites gives insight into the development of the Assyrian Empire at various stages. Discovery of the royal texts mentioned above as well as numerous pictorial reliefs has typically occurred during the excavation of these and other key sites.

Finally, for later periods from the mid-eighth century BCE forward, some classical writings provide important information. These include the works of Herodotus, the fifth-century BCE Greek historian, and Josephus, the first-century CE Jewish historian whose work retells the biblical story from creation to the first Jewish revolt against Rome in 66 CE. The historical reliability of these later sources is uncertain and must be evaluated on a case-by-case basis in conjunction with other available evidence (Miller and Hayes, 316).

1.1.5. Nature and Use of Biblical and Extrabiblical Sources. The evaluation and discussion of the available sources has taken new directions and fostered increased debate in contemporary scholarship (Long). How one understands the nature and reliability of the biblical texts, extrabiblical inscriptions and archaeological remains, not to mention the interrelationship of these materials, often dictates the way one reconstructs Israelite history. In terms of the current discussion, it is not an overstatement to say that these issues now constitute the primary area of consideration for the study of Israel's past (see Provan, Long and Longman, 3-104).

Since the 1970s, there has been a growing trend in scholarship to consider the biblical texts as literary and ideological constructs that can be used only cautiously, if at all, as a historical source for ancient Israel (*see* Quest of the Historical Israel). Three primary approaches may be noted:

1. The "maximalist" position: the overall story line of Genesis through 2 Kings is predominantly historically accurate.
2. The "minimalist" position: the OT is largely useless as a historical source for the history of Israel in the Assyrian period but is a literary artifact from the Persian (600-332 BCE) or Hellenistic periods (332-63 BCE).

3. A middle position: portions of the OT, particularly in the Historical Books, preserve some historical information that can be used after careful and critical analysis.

The general tendency has been to date more and more of the material in the OT Historical Books to the exilic and postexilic periods (post-586 BCE), thus placing them in a period at some remove from the events described therein, with the typical, but not necessarily foregone (see Provan, Long and Longman), conclusion following that they are less significant for historical reconstruction than contemporaneous epigraphical and artifactual sources. The biblical texts are clearly a mixture of reportage and interpretation and contain elements (e.g., ancient perspectives and folk traditions) that make them difficult to use as historical sources by modern historiographical standards (see Miller and Hayes, 58-63). But the same holds true for the extrabiblical sources, whether textual, archaeological or artifactual. Complete and total skepticism of the biblical texts as a historical source or, conversely, complete trust in extrabiblical sources is thus unwarranted, and some version of the middle position is the best way forward. Indeed, numerous points of contact between the biblical narratives and extrabiblical data suggest that the biblical texts, although possibly written at a later time, preserve at least some authentic data from the political and social life of ancient Israel in the Assyrian period. Like the later classical sources, however, specific issues and texts must be taken up on a case-by-case basis. Such is the difficult way of history and historiography.

The same is true, as we have already noted, for the extrabiblical sources. Here too debate over the nature and use of sources rages. Scholars have increasingly recognized that these sources cannot be used uncritically, since they are often propagandistic, selective and prone to exaggeration (Grayson 1992, 734; Cogan 1998, 244). Not unlike the biblical texts, then, the Assyrian inscriptions contain gaps of information and are in need of interpretation. They are, in short, no less literary, ideological and theological than the OT texts. Nevertheless, as with the biblical texts, such characteristics do not disqualify them from being used in historical reconstruction, but do indicate that careful attention must be given to their specific genres and purposes first.

The nature and use of the archaeological

sources for the Assyrian period have also come under discussion (*see* Archaeology, Syro-Palestinian). The history of Israel presented in the OT Historical Books and highlighted in the convergences with the extrabiblical inscriptions primarily involves the political history of the state and its kings. Aside from the evidence of city occupation and destruction, however, archaeological data relate primarily not to the political history of kings and governments, but rather to the domestic, everyday life of ancient Israelites. Newer appreciation of this aspect of archaeological research has led to deeper inquiry into topics such as the daily life of *women in ancient Israel and the role of religion in nonofficial and noncultic contexts (e.g., house, family, clan).

These recent developments relating to the evaluation of various source materials demonstrate the importance of method in recent scholarship devoted to reconstructing the history of Israel in the Assyrian period. Given the complexities involved, any reconstruction should make full use of all available biblical and nonbiblical data, particularly looking for points at which various sources converge with regard to specific persons or events. But the historian must neither neglect nor underestimate the literary, theological, even ideological character of the sources at hand.

1.2. Chronology. One of the most complex problems facing the reconstruction of the history of Israel is the *chronology of the Israelite and Judean kings. The problems begin within the OT Historical Books themselves. Two systems of keeping chronology appear: (1) the giving of the total number of years for each king's reign; (2) the synchronization of the kings of the north and south. These two systems do not always match up. Furthermore, there are many textual variations for the chronological figures in the different Hebrew and Greek manuscripts of 1-2 Kings. These observations have led to the conclusion that the chronology in the biblical texts is schematic and theological in nature and cannot be taken at face value (Miller and Hayes, 227). Nevertheless, numerous ways of untangling the biblical chronology and its possible conjunctions with extrabiblical data have been proposed. These proposals include notions of co-regencies between kings, the rounding up or down of total regnal years, and varying calendrical structures (lunar, solar, etc.) and reckonings

(antedating, postdating) for Israel and Judah (see Hayes and Hooker; Thiele; Barnes).

Although no one way of delineating the chronology of the kings of Israel and Judah has achieved consensus, there are some chronological benchmarks that provide a basic framework for the Assyrian period. These include the references in Assyrian inscriptions to the Israelite kings Ahab, Jehu, Joash, Menahem, Pekah and Hoshea, and to the Judean kings Ahaz, Hezekiah and Manasseh, as well as the biblical mention of the Egyptian (Kushite) Pharaoh Tirhaka (Taharqa, 690-664 BCE) and Assyrian kings such as Sennacherib. In each case the Assyrian texts locate the Israelite and Judean kings in the same order and time period as the biblical texts. Thus, although the development of a single, absolute chronology for all facets of the Bible's chronology is probably impossible, a reasonably secure relative chronology of particular kings and events is often attainable in light of the full complement of available evidence.

1.3. The Relationship Between Israel and Judah. One final preliminary issue concerns the relationship between the states of Israel and Judah in the Assyrian period. From the biblical picture one gains the impression that Israel and Judah existed as two wholly separate states after the death of *Solomon (see Bright 227, 269). This separateness is generally seen as the result of different royal and cultic ideologies at local levels and different political and military policies at broader levels. The books of 1-2 Kings solidify this picture of independence by consistently relating the two kingdoms' histories in separate sections, even while providing editorial synchronisms that link them.

A closer look at the biblical and extrabiblical evidence, however, suggests that the political reality of Israel and Judah may have been somewhat different. Even within the OT Historical Books one finds occasional references to the conjoined nature of Israel and Judah and their status vis-à-vis one another (see 1 Kings 15:16-22). Even more pronounced in this regard is the evidence from Assyrian royal inscriptions. Throughout the ninth and eighth centuries BCE, the Assyrian texts refer to several Israelite rulers by name but, with the exception of one inconspicuous reference to Ahaz, never mention a king of Judah until after the destruction of the northern kingdom. This fact alone would indicate that Israel was, at least at times, the major player on the international scene, with Judah a marginal territory whose participation evidently was not noteworthy. According to some scholars, the archaeological data from Judah during the Assyrian period strengthens this impression, insofar as evidence for major regional centers in Judah prior to the late-eighth century BCE is ambiguous (see, e.g., Finkelstein and Silberman, 235).

On the basis of these observations, a few scholars have argued that Judah did not come into existence as a state until late in the Assyrian period (see Davies, 67-70). The full range of biblical and extrabiblical evidence, however, suggests a different explanation. At several key points (some discussed below) the Assyrian and biblical texts suggest that Judah played a secondary, if not subservient, role to the more powerful northern kingdom. Whether that lesser role was official (i.e., as a vassal) or not is not of primary importance. What is clear, regardless, is that from the time of Omri to the fall of Samaria various references to Israel's military composition and geographical constitution indicate that Judah was subsumed under Israel's political shadow. For much of the Assyrian period, then, it does not seem that Israel and Judah existed as completely independent nations—not, at least, from the Assyrian perspective—but rather that Israel occupied the superior role on the world stage and set the political agenda that Judah followed more often than not. At many levels and points, then, Israel and Judah may thus be conceived of as functionally one state with greater and lesser heads (Sasson, 60; cf. Hayes 1988, 23-24). In light of this situation, the following discussion organizes Israel's history in the Assyrian period by the kings of Israel until its destruction in 720 BCE.

2. The Emergence of the Neo-Assyrian Empire.
The Assyrian period of Israel's history began in earnest with the reign of Shalmaneser III (858-824 BCE), but the rise of Assyria was a gradual process, already having begun in the preceding years. The reign of Ashur-uballit (c. 1363-1328 BCE), the first self-proclaimed "King of Assyria," marked the initial appearance of Assyria as a political entity, and the subsequent reigns of Shalmaneser I (c. 1273-1244 BCE), Tukulti-Ninurta I (c. 1243-1207 BCE) and Tiglath-pileser I (c. 1114-1076 BCE) saw the beginnings of an imperial state that was able to expand from Babylonia to the Mediterranean Sea (Grayson 1992, 738-39).

After an intervening phase of decline, the resurgence that resulted in the rise of the "Neo-Assyrian" empire began under Adad-nirari II (909-889 BCE), who took up the practice of annexing conquered territories. Yet it was the Assyrian king Ashur-nasirpal II (883-859 BCE), Shalmaneser III's immediate predecessor, who began Assyria's imperialistic expansion westward, reaching the Mediterranean Sea by 875 BCE and collecting tribute from several cities in Syria-Palestine (Grayson 1992, 741-42). The stage thus was set for Shalmaneser III, who solidified Assyrian power by undertaking annual military campaigns and moving to control territories in northern and southern Syria (see Hallo, 37). It is clear, then, that these later periods were dominated by further developments in Assyrian foreign policy, begun already under Adad-nirari II but taken to deeper levels by rulers such as Ashur-nasirpal II, Shalmaneser III and especially Tiglath-pileser III (745-727 BCE). Among other things, these developments saw a fairly rigid and strictly enforced scheme put in place for dealing with vassals, vassal states and annexed provinces (see Donner, 416-20; cf. Cogan 1993).

3. The Omride Dynasty (879-840 BCE).
3.1. The Reigns of Omri and Ahab.
The biblical account of the reigns of Omri and Ahab appears in 1 Kings 16—2 Kings 8 and in 2 Chronicles 17—20. These texts portray Omri and Ahab as among the worst characters in Israelite history. The extrabiblical data, however, suggest a different evaluation. Indeed, the key issue for considering the history of Israel under the Omrides is the discrepancy between the biblical picture of their reign and the picture gained by historical reconstruction that includes nonbiblical sources (see Matthews, 64).

The biblical texts concerning the Omrides center on the private affairs of the royal family and focus almost exclusively on the issue of religious apostasy and the royal house's propagation of the Baal cult. The only achievements noted for Omri and Ahab are the founding of Samaria (1 Kings 16:24) and various building projects (1 Kings 22:39). The rest of the biblical materials consist mainly of prophetic narratives, including those of *Elijah and *Elisha (see 1 Kings 17—19; 2 Kings 1—2; 4—8).

By contrast, the available extrabiblical evidence suggests that the reigns of Omri and

Ahab witnessed significant developments for Israel in both the domestic and geopolitical realms. Archaeology has shown that during the Omride period impressive cities that functioned as administrative centers were built, and further suggests the emergence of a fully developed territorial state in Israel, defined by sophisticated organization, a standing army and international trade. Artifactual remains at northern sites such as *Samaria, *Megiddo, *Hazor and *Jezreel indicate a major building phase that can be dated to the mid-ninth century BCE (Campbell, 220). Advocates of a "low chronology" for Israelite history have even suggested that several archaeological structures traditionally assigned to the time of Solomon in the tenth century BCE (e.g., the fortifications at Megiddo, Hazor and *Gezer) fit better with the Omride period in the ninth century BCE (see Finkelstein and Silberman, 169-95, 340-44).

In terms of Israel's political history, extrabiblical evidence indicates that Omri and Ahab brought the northern kingdom to international prominence as a significant player on the geopolitical stage. These two kings are the first individuals in Israelite history to be named in ancient Near Eastern texts. In 1 Kings 16 it is said that Omri was an army commander who was proclaimed king by the army when Zimri assassinated Elah. Following his defeat of Zimri, Omri emerged as sole ruler after a period of civil war with Tibni. Thus when Omri came to the throne, he immediately encountered a series of problems that included the need to reestablish order and to end conflict with Judah (see 1 Kings 15:32) (Soggin, 214). Omri seems to have been successful in meeting these tasks and in bringing Israel to prominence over its immediate neighbors. The marriage of Omri's son Ahab to the Phoenician princess Jezebel indicates close relations between Israel and *Phoenicia (1 Kings 16:31), and the later Mesha Inscription retrospectively confirms that Omri established Israelite hegemony over *Moab.

Ahab (868-854 BCE) appears to have continued Israel's ascendancy, begun under Omri. The most important indicator in this regard is Israel's first recorded encounter with the emerging Assyrian Empire, an encounter nowhere mentioned in the OT Historical Books. As Shalmaneser III was leading Assyria's expansion to the west, Assyrian texts note that he met resistance from a coalition of states in southern Syria-Palestine. The Monolith Inscription of Shalmaneser III describes the Assyrian king's battle with this coalition at a place called Qarqar in his sixth regnal year (853-852 BCE) (see Grayson 1996). The Assyrian text claims victory for Shalmaneser III, but one might question this conclusion because he pushes no further west and in subsequent years records more battles with this same coalition. The Monolith Inscription makes clear, however, that the three main leaders of the anti-Assyrian coalition were Adad-idri (i.e., Hadadezer) of Aram-Damascus, *Irḫuleni* of Hamath and Ahab of Israel (written *a-ḫ a-ab-bu KUR sir-ʾi-la-a-a*). Even more revealing is the fact that Ahab is credited on the inscription with having a force of ten thousand soldiers and two thousand chariots, the largest chariot force in the coalition and one that is equal to that of Assyria itself (see Kelle, 641-46).

So, late in the reign of Ahab, Israel appears to have been a major regional power, allied with Damascus in opposition to the Assyrian advance. Ahab also seems to have enjoyed good relations with Osorkon II (874-850 BCE) of Egypt (see Redford, 339-40; Kitchen 1986, 324). Even so, the unusually large size of Ahab's forces at the battle of Qarqar has been a matter of discussion and debate. Perhaps the best explanation is one that also sheds additional light on the nature of the Omride period. Shalmaneser's Monolith Inscription makes no reference to Israel's immediate neighbors Judah, Moab, *Edom, Tyre and Sidon, and some evidence indicates that Omride Israel acted as a dominant partner to many of them. The reference to the marriage of Ahab and Jezebel may suggest a treaty-like relationship with Phoenicia, and then there is the Mesha Inscription's reference to Moabite submission to Omri. With reference to Judah, 1 Kings 22:44 depicts King *Jehoshaphat (877-853 BCE), the contemporary of Omri and Ahab, making peace with Israel; 2 Chronicles 18:3 remembers him as giving unqualified support to Israel; and the Assyrian inscriptions that refer repeatedly to Israel throughout the ninth and eighth centuries BCE are completely silent about Judah.

Such evidence suggests that Omri and Ahab established a small-scale empire in ninth-century Israel that had its capital at Samaria and included the subordinate territories of at least Moab, Edom and Judah (Matthews 65; Miller and Hayes 275; contra Bright 251). Yet when this picture is compared to the biblical traditions, it encounters problems in 1 Kings 20 and 22, which recount stories of Ahab fighting with Aram-Damascus. Not only do these biblical texts omit any reference to the battle of Qarqar, they also identify the king of Damascus as Ben-Hadad not Hadadezer, depict Israel and Aram-Damascus as enemies not partners, and present the Israelite military as weak not strong. Numerous proposals have been made to deal with this discrepancy. For example, one could identify the biblical Ben-Hadad with Hadadezer (as a throne name) and posit that relations between Israel and Aram oscillated during this period (see Bright, 243; Hallo, 39). Other biblical and extrabiblical texts, however, use *Ben-Hadad* as a personal name not a title (1 Kings 15:18; 2 Kings 13:3). Nor does there seem to have been a Syrian king named Ben-Hadad who ruled immediately after Hadadezer (Grayson 1996, 118). Alternatively, many scholars have observed that the references to Ahab in 1 Kings 20 and 22 appear to be secondary (the majority of references are unspecific: "the king of Israel"), and the kings involved in these stories were perhaps originally anonymous (see Soggin, 218). Furthermore, the hostility between Israel and Aram and the relative weakness of Israel in these narratives fit better with what is known of the later Jehu dynasty (cf. 2 Kings 13). Thus we must consider the possibility that these biblical texts actually relate to events that transpired in later years and were editorially or redactionally (but mistakenly) associated with Ahab at a still later point in the compositional history of Kings.

3.2. The Reigns of Ahaziah and Jehoram: The Rise of Aram-Damascus.

After the death of Ahab, Israel's fortunes, and so also those of Judah, began to change for the worse. Shalmaneser III records three more encounters with a western coalition led by Hadadezer of Aram in 849, 848 and 845 BCE. Ahab's successors, Ahaziah and Jehoram, are not named in these inscriptions, but it seems likely that they continued to participate. Even so, they were unable to match the earlier strength of Omri and Ahab. (The issue of whether there were two kings named "Jehoram" or just one is exceedingly complex [see Strange; Miller and Hayes, 280-84; Provan, Long and Longman, 370-71 n. 35].) 2 Kings 1:1 notes that Moab rebelled against Israel after Ahab's death, an event confirmed by the Mesha Inscription, and 2 Kings 8:16-24 says that Edom rebelled

against Judah, which had controlled it, perhaps under Israelite authority (cf. 1 Kings 22:47; 2 Kings 3:9).

Perhaps the most significant development in this period involved the emergence of a new king of Aram-Damascus and, with him, a change in the relationship between Aram and Israel. Sometime during the reign of Jehoram (c. 843 BCE), a king named Hazael usurped the throne in Damascus (see Grayson 1996, 118). Shortly thereafter Hazael seems to have inaugurated a new policy of aggression against his neighbors, particularly against Israel. 2 Kings 8—9 describes Israelite battles with Hazael at Ramoth-gilead that not only resulted in a loss of territory for Israel, but also in the incapacitation of Jehoram.

4. The Jehu Dynasty (839-748 BCE).

4.1. Jehu's Coup.

In the midst of these hostilities between Israel and Aram at Ramoth-Gilead, 2 Kings 8—10 and 2 Chronicles 22 describe *Jehu's coup. Jehu's usurpation of the Israelite throne is presented in the biblical texts as a prophetically sponsored religious revolution. When Jehoram was wounded in battle and taken to Jezreel, Ahaziah of Judah joined him there. Jehu, having been anointed by a prophetic follower of Elisha, struck down both of them in a bloody coup and took the throne in Israel (see Miller and Hayes, 284-85). This sequence of events seems to be reflected in the Tel Dan Inscription, a memorial stela of a ninth-century Aramaean king (probably Hazael), although the fragmentary stela seems to attribute the killing of Jehoram and Ahaziah to the Aramaean king rather than to Jehu, and many of its details and information remain vexing questions for scholars (see Athas).

Jehu's revolution had consequences for Judah as well. When Jehu killed Ahaziah and forty-two Judean princes (cf. 2 Kings 10:14), Athaliah, the daughter of Ahab who had been married to Jehoram of Judah, seized the throne and eliminated the remaining members of Ahaziah's house (2 Kings 11:1). It is significant that the Deuteronomistic Historian neither presents Athaliah's gender negatively nor views her rule as illegitimate in any way (Campbell, 230). Although she was later overthrown and replaced with seven-year-old Joash, Athaliah reigned for seven years in Judah—the only queen to do so in Israelite history.

All of these events took place against the wider geopolitical background of Assyria's continued campaigns to the west. When Shalmaneser III returned to the west in 841 BCE, the situation had changed dramatically. This time, he did not meet a coalition of states, but only Aram-Damascus, led by its new king Hazael. Hazael's aggressive policy toward neighboring states apparently brought an end to the earlier coalition, and he faced Shalmaneser III alone. The Assyrians besieged Damascus in 841 BCE but did not capture the city or remove Hazael from the throne. In the course of the campaign, however, Shalmaneser received tribute from Jehu as well as his submission to Assyria as a vassal (see Shalmaneser III's Black Obelisk [*ANEP*, nos. 351-55]). So, after securing the throne, Jehu voluntarily submitted to Assyrian sovereignty. This event represents a turning point that shaped the course of subsequent Israelite history in the Assyrian period. Jehu's pro-Assyrian policy would be doctrine for nearly a century, and during that time Israel's fortunes would be constantly affected by the struggle for power between Assyria and regional powers such as Aram-Damascus.

With Jehu's accession and bloody purge, the time of relative independence and strength that had existed in the Omride era ended. Moments of such autonomy would be the exception, not the rule, during the rest of the state's history (Miller and Hayes, 289). Jehu's violent actions against Jezebel, Jehoram and Ahaziah, along with his submission to Assyria, certainly strained Israel's relations with its neighbors in Phoenicia, Judah and Aram-Damascus. Still, throughout this period Judah apparently remained a minor partner to the more powerful northern kingdom, which set the course of foreign policy for both kingdoms. The various Assyrian texts of Shalmaneser III that mention Jehu make no reference to Judah or its rulers (see Grayson 1996). Even the Tel Dan Inscription, which most agree refers to the "House of David" and its king, seems to portray Israel and Judah as basically one unit that the Aramaean king dealt with in a single blow.

The course of the dynasty that Jehu initiated divides the subsequent history of the north and south into two parts: (1) a period of weakness under Aramaean oppression in the time of Jehu and Jehoahaz in Israel and Athaliah and Joash in Judah; (2) a period of restoration and prosperity in the wake of Assyrian resurgence in the time of Joash and Jeroboam II in Israel and Amaziah, Uzziah and Jotham in Judah.

4.2. The Dominance of Aram-Damascus: The Reigns of Jehu and Jehoahaz. Significant historical developments took place between 841 and 805 BCE that greatly affected Israel and Judah. These developments were precipitated by Assyrian decline in the last years of Shalmaneser III and the reign of Shamshi-Adad V (823-811 BCE). Neither king campaigned back to Syria after 838-837 BCE, and the Eponym Chronicles note rebellion in Assyria for the last four years of Shalmaneser and the first three years of Shamshi-Adad (Millard 1994, 57). Shamshi-Adad eventually put down the revolt but lost firm control of Babylon and the western area of the empire (Hallo, 41-42).

Foremost among the results of this decline for western regions was Hazael's ability to construct an Aramaean empire that lasted through the reign of his successor (Ben-Hadad), that controlled all of Syria-Palestine, and that subjugated Israel and Judah (see Dion, 199). Several extrabiblical sources attest to Aramaean dominance in the region. The Tel Dan Inscription has already been mentioned, and the Zakkur Stela (*COS* 2.35:155), an Aramaic text erected by the king of Hamath, suggests that Ben-Hadad's influence extended into northern Syria and eastern Anatolia. Hazael's Booty Inscriptions (*COS* 2.40:162-63) refer to the king's crossing of the "river" and may indicate that Hazael even campaigned on the offensive into Assyrian territory north of the Euphrates (see Dion, 201-2; contrast Lipiński, 388-89). Archaeological evidence of destruction at places such as Jezreel also points to Aramaean encroachment into the upper Jordan Valley (Finkelstein and Silberman, 202).

Biblical texts relating to the reigns of Jehoahaz of Israel and Joash and Amaziah of Judah, although tucked away in the middle of the larger prophetic narratives of Elisha, also indicate that Syrian domination reached unparalleled heights at this time. 2 Kings 13:3 states baldly, "The anger of the LORD was kindled against Israel, so that he gave them repeatedly into the hand of King Hazael of Aram, then into the hand of Ben-hadad son of Hazael." 2 Kings 10:32-33 associates Israel's loss of territory in the Transjordan with Hazael's expansion, and 2 Kings 12:17a suggests that Hazael subjugated the *Philistine city of *Gath and virtually all of the land west of the Jordan. Concerning Judah, the only major event noted by the biblical writers for the reign of Joash, successor to Athaliah, is that Hazael threatened Jerusalem and Joash paid him tribute, not unlike a vassal (2 Kings 12:17-18).

Taken as a whole, the available evidence for this period suggests that Hazael did not simply dominate Israel and Judah occasionally but actually established a small empire in Syria-Palestine in the last half of the ninth century BCE. Israel and Judah were apparently vassal states under the control of Aram-Damascus (see Kelle, 649-51; contrast Lipiński, 389-90). If 1 Kings 20:14-15, 24 reflect conditions under the Jehu dynasty, not those under Ahab (see 3.1), then the "governors of the districts" and the "commanders" that replace kings—a system of organization previously unknown in Israel—may indicate that Hazael divided his dominated territories into administrative districts, of which Samaria would have been one.

4.3. The Resurgence of Assyria and Israel: The Reigns of Joash and Jeroboam II. Aramaean dominance came to an end when Assyria experienced a resurgence under the next king, Adad-nirari III (810-783 BCE). Although no full annals for Adad-nirari III have survived, the Eponym Chronicles and other inscriptions indicate that he undertook an extended western campaign beginning around 805 BCE, and there can be little doubt that one of his principal targets was Aram-Damascus. Adad-nirari III's Rimah Stela focuses on Aram-Damascus but also proclaims that the king resubjugated the entire western territory as far as the Mediterranean Sea (*COS* 2.114F:275-76).

These events naturally had consequences for Israel and Judah. Since Israel was aligned as an Assyrian vassal from the time of Jehu's submission in 841 BCE, Assyria's revival meant resurgence for Israel. 2 Kings 13:5 reports that near the end of Jehoahaz's reign the Lord sent Israel a "savior" who rescued them from Syrian oppression; this could be a veiled reference to Adad-nirari III's return to the west. This Assyrian return coincides nicely with 2 Kings 13's description of the subsequent reign of Joash son of Jehoahaz, who was able to recover Israelite territory from Aram and defeat Ben-Hadad three times in battle. The Rimah Stela records the payment of tribute by "Joash the Samarian"—something that apparently took place at some point during the king's western campaign

(see Kelle, 651-53). 2 Kings 14:7 reports that Amaziah of Judah also captured territory in Edom. Additionally, 2 Kings 14:8-14 notes that Amaziah challenged Joash of Israel to a confrontation. This move is odd unless seen as another indication that Israel had long dominated Judah, and Amaziah was attempting to break free from that situation. In response to this challenge Joash captured Amaziah, destroyed part of the wall of Jerusalem, looted the temple, and took Judean prisoners, thereby establishing, if not in fact *reestablishing*, Israelite superiority over Judah (see Provan, Long and Longman, 269; also 374-75 n. 64 on the MT of 2 Kings 14:28: "for Judah *in* Israel").

These events inaugurated a period of national restoration and prosperity in Israel and Judah that would last for nearly fifty years. The bulk of the reigns of Jeroboam II in Israel (788-748 BCE) and Uzziah (785-760 BCE) and Jotham in Judah (759-744 BCE) witnessed this revitalization. True to the religious focus of the Deuteronomistic History, the book of Kings gives only seven verses to Jeroboam II (2 Kings 14:23-29), but even these contain hints of the importance of this period in Israel's history. As long as Assyria maintained a strong presence in the west, its loyal vassals reaped the benefits of renewed stabilization. Thus 2 Kings 14:25 says that Jeroboam II "restored the border of Israel" from Lebo-hamath in northern Syria to the Dead Sea in southern Judah. Likewise, 2 Chronicles 26—27 says that Uzziah of Judah increased the size of his army, captured various surrounding territories, and undertook various building and fortification projects. Although some claims made for Jeroboam and Uzziah are historically unsubstantiated and may be exaggerated (e.g., 2 Kings 14:28; 2 Chron 26:6), the biblical picture of general prosperity accords well with the broader political context in the Assyrian Empire at this time (see Bright, 257). Archaeological discoveries within Israel also testify to increased prosperity in this era. Larger quantities of luxury items, especially ivory inlays, appear in archaeological strata at key eighth-century cities, and the Samarian Ostraca, a collection of ink-inscribed potsherds from eighth-century Samaria, record various shipments of oil and wine into the capital city.

This overall resurgence, however, also carried some negative consequences in the domestic sphere. The prosperity of the time of

Jeroboam II gave rise to an economically strati-fied society characterized by the emergence of an economic elite that controlled land estates meted out by the throne (see Campbell, 234-35). A patrimonial inheritance system had been re-placed by royal land grants that widened the gap between wealthy landowners and dependent tenant farmers. Prophetic books such as Amos and Hosea, particularly in their frequently scathing denunciations of social injustice, pro-vide a glimpse into the various societal implica-tions of this period of "prosperity" (see Dear-man).

5. The Final Years of Israel (745-720 BCE).

5.1. The Syro-Ephraimitic War. The prosperity of the major part of Jeroboam II's reign did not last (see Hayes and Hooker, 53-54; contrast Sog-gin, 229). Following Adad-nirari III, Assyria again went into decline during the reigns of the three subsequent rulers: Shalmaneser IV (782-773 BCE), Ashur-dan III (772-755 BCE) and Ashur-nirari V (754-745 BCE). Although Assyrian texts record military campaigns in the west as late as 773 BCE, Shalmaneser IV was primarily occupied with fighting Urartu in the north, and even these campaigns appear to have been largely defensive in nature. Beginning around 768 BCE, the Eponym Chronicles indicate that Assyria suffered from internal revolt, and cam-paigns to the west radically decreased to the point that half of Ashur-nirari V's reign was spent within the borders of Assyria itself (Hallo, 44).

With Assyrian power waning in the west, Aram-Damascus began to reassert its influence. Both Assyrian and biblical texts introduce Rez-in, the new king of Damascus, as the dominant political force in the area, who attempted to re-establish Hazael's earlier mini-empire in Syria-Palestine. 2 Kings 15:37; 16:5 suggest that Rezin encroached on Israelite territory as early as the final years of Jeroboam II, and the prophetic or-acle against Damascus in Amos 1:3-5, which de-scribes a Syrian invasion of Galilee, may date from this time (c. 750 BCE). Even the Assyrian in-scriptions from this period attribute to Rezin an "extended domain of the house of Hazael" (see Tadmor, 187).

A major event that destabilized matters even more occurred in 745 BCE when Tiglath-pileser III took the throne of Assyria. He immediately undertook a series of campaigns and a program of consolidation and annexation designed to re-establish Assyrian control over the far reaches of the empire (see Tadmor). This Assyrian resur-gence, however, not only caused further insta-bility in the relations between states in the west, but also brought Assyria into conflict with Egypt. The Twenty-fifth (Kushite/Ethiopian) Dynasty was attempting at this time to dominate the Egyptian Delta and to move into southern Syria-Palestine (see Miller and Hayes, 319; Spalinger, 358-59; Kitchen 1986, 358-98). This Egyptian de-velopment likely provided some of the impetus for renewed rebellion in Syria-Palestine.

Thus in the years following 750 BCE, Israel and Judah once again were caught in a mael-strom of opposing forces from Assyria, Egypt and Damascus. Turmoil must have reigned in Samaria over which state to align with and sup-port. 2 Kings 15—17 curtly reports that after the death of Jeroboam II four kings (Zechariah, Shallum, Menahem, Pekahiah) ruled in rapid succession, and three of the four were assassi-nated after only brief reigns (see Miller and Hayes, 315). "Menahem of Samaria" appears in two, and perhaps three, inscriptions of Tiglath-pileser III as offering submission and paying tribute (see Tadmor, 69, 89, 107). These notices coincide well with 2 Kings 15:19-20, which re-ports that Tiglath-pileser ("King Pul") provided military assistance to Menahem, who paid the Assyrian king to help confirm him on the throne. Judah under Jotham (759-744 BCE) and Ahaz (743-728 BCE) was more stable but still suf-fered the effects of Rezin's revitalized Damascus (cf. 2 Kings 15:37).

These events came to a head in the years im-mediately preceding 734 BCE. During this period the tension between the ascendancy of Aram-Damascus and the resurgence of Assyria reached a peak, and the internal political divi-sions within Israel reached their highest level. Although Rezin of Damascus is recorded as pay-ing tribute to Tiglath-pileser as early as 738 BCE (see Tadmor, 55), this action should probably be seen as a nominal tribute designed to buy time, since Assyria was not yet maintaining a sus-tained presence in Syria-Palestine. Throughout these same years Rezin took steps to build a widespread, anti-Assyrian coalition to challenge the resurgent Tiglath-pileser. Pekah of Israel ap-parently played a key part in these develop-ments. Although Assyrian texts place Menahem on the throne in Israel in 738 BCE and Hoshea on the throne by 731 BCE (Tiglath-pileser takes credit for the latter's accession), 2 Kings 15:27 says that Pekah reigned twenty years. Although no clear explanation of this chronological difficulty exists (see Thiele, 129), it is reasonable to conclude that Pekah was already active as a rival king in league with Rezin and his anti-Assyrian movement as early as the time of Jeroboam II. Consider the following items: 2 Kings 15:37 says that both Rezin and Pekah were harassing Judah during the reign of Jotham (759-744 BCE); 2 Kings 15:25 associates Pekah with the Gilead region, where Damascus's control would have potentially been the strongest; Hosea 5:5 may allude to divisions in the north by distinguishing three political entities: Israel, Ephraim, Judah.

Sometime around 734 BCE Pekah, probably with the support of Rezin of Damascus, assassinated Pekahiah, seized the throne in Samaria (cf. 2 Kings 15:25), and moved from rival king to sole ruler. These actions secured the northern kingdom's place among the rebellious states opposing Assyria's resurgence and precipitated a conflict between Damascus, Israel and Judah referred to as the "Syro-Ephraimitic War" (734-731 BCE). The various Assyrian lists of states that paid tribute and that were subjugated during this period suggest that Rezin's anti-Assyrian coalition included Tyre, Ashkelon, Arabia, Gaza and Israel (for a contrary perspective on the nature of this conflict see Tomes; Oded). For the first time in over a century, however, Judah, under King Ahaz, refused to follow the northern kingdom's lead and pursued an independent course.

Some newly published documents might shed light on this development. S. Dalley recently argued that the names of two royal women whose skeletons were recovered from a tomb at Nimrud are Hebrew, and that the two women were Judeans. One of the two, *Yabâ* or *Yapâ* (also called *Banîtu*, "beautiful," in Akkadian), was in fact the chief consort of Tiglath-pileser III. If Dalley is correct about their nationality, these women may have been related to Ahaz (or Hezekiah), and this might explain the pro-Assyrian policies of these two rulers and a number of other factors, including how the *rab šāqeh* could address the citizens of Jerusalem in Hebrew during the siege of Jerusalem, and why Hezekiah was left on the throne at the same time (see 2 Kings 18:26; Dalley, 396-97; and further below). K. L. Younger (2002b) has raised significant philological doubt about the Yahwist-

ic nature of the women's names, however, and so at least that aspect of the matter must remain uncertain for now, even while Dalley's theory remains a tantalizing possibility.

Rezin and Pekah, as indicated by 2 Kings 16:1-18; 2 Chronicles 28:1-25; and Isaiah 7:1-17, besieged Ahaz in Jerusalem in order to replace him with a king (called the "son of Tabeel"; the latter part might be a geographical name [see Hallo, 49]) who would cooperate with the coalition (see Soggin, 239). Although the precise sequence and timing of these events remain unclear (see Irvine, 95-109), Isaiah's promise that Rezin and Pekah's attack would fail proved true (Is 7:7). Tiglath-pileser III campaigned in the west and attacked Philistia in 734-733 BCE. This assault was immediately followed by moves against Arabia and Tyre and the siege and capture of Damascus in 733-731 BCE. 2 Kings 16:8 explains the Assyrian intervention by claiming that Ahaz sent a "bribe" to Tiglath-pileser for help against Aram and Israel. This claim, however, probably should be attributed to the Deuteronomistic History's negative portrayal of Ahaz as an evil king. *Isaiah, often interpreted as highly critical of Ahaz, never mentions such an appeal. Moreover, the Assyrian text that records a payment by Ahaz of Judah *(Ia-ú-ha-zi KUR Ia-ú-da-a-a)* (see Tadmor, 171) presents it as a typical tribute and dates to the time after the Assyrians were already in the area. It also includes the payments of several rulers who are unlikely to have paid tribute in advance (Irvine 107-8; contrast Bright, 274). Whatever the case, by the end of the campaign the Assyrians had not moved against Pekah of Israel. Rather, a rebellion broke out in Israel led by Hoshea sometime around 732 BCE. Samaria was eventually taken, Pekah was deposed, and Hoshea sent tribute to Tiglath-pileser (2 Kings 15:30; cf. Hos 1:10—2:23).

5.2. The Fall of Israel. The northern kingdom of Israel would exist for only one decade after Hoshea's accession to the throne at the close of the Syro-Ephraimitic war. The events and chronology of this final period, however, are extremely complex and remain debated (see Younger 1999; Hayes and Kuan; Naʾaman 1990; Becking). The primary biblical text here is 2 Kings 17:1-6. This text contains several pieces of information that are difficult to correlate: (1) Shalmaneser V campaigned against Hoshea, who submitted and paid tribute (2 Kings 17:3);

(2) Hoshea sent messengers to "King So" of Egypt and withheld tribute from Assyria (2 Kings 17:4); (3) the Assyrian king imprisoned Hoshea (2 Kings 17:4); (4) the Assyrian king invaded all the land, besieged Samaria for three years, and exiled some of the population (2 Kings 17:5-6). The Assyrian texts in turn are unclear concerning which king conquered Samaria and when. Although there are no extant inscriptions of Shalmaneser V, the Babylonian Chronicles attribute a capture of Samaria to him sometime prior to the year 722 BCE (see Grayson 1975, 10, 73; Kelle, 662; contra Younger 1999, 466). Several Assyrian inscriptions of his successor, Sargon II, however, claim that he captured Samaria sometime around 720 BCE (see *COS* 2.118A:293-94; 2.118D:295-96; 2.118E:296-97).

Although a definitive historical reconstruction remains elusive, the following course of events seems plausible. During the beginning years of the reign of Shalmaneser V (726-722 BCE), Hoshea continued to pay tribute to Assyria. Before long, however, Hoshea rebelled and appealed for help to "King So" of Egypt (2 Kings 17:4). No pharaoh by that name is known, and the identity of this king (Osorkon IV [730-715 BCE]?) or place (if it is a geographical name representing "Sais") remains in dispute (see Younger 2002a, 290; Redford, 346-47; Spalinger, 359; Kitchen 1986, 374-75). Regardless, Hoshea's actions were probably part of a larger anti-Assyrian rebellion that centered on Tyre. Josephus (*Ant.* 9.283-284), quoting a source who purportedly relied on Tyre's archives, reports that Shalmaneser V campaigned through Syria-Palestine and besieged Tyre around 725 BCE. If correct, this information might provide the context for the imprisonment of Hoshea mentioned in 2 Kings 17:4 and the capture of Samaria located by the Babylonian Chronicles prior to 722 BCE (cf. 2 Kings 18:9; see Hayes and Kuan). Although Hoshea had been arrested, rebellion continued to foment in Israel over the next three years until the city was taken a second time in what would have been Hoshea's ninth year (722 BCE) (2 Kings 17:6). No extrabiblical texts clearly refer to this particular capture, but most likely it was accomplished by Shalmaneser V. As previously noted, however, the inscriptions of Sargon II record a capture of Samaria as part of his 720 BCE campaign to the west, a capture not explicitly referred to in the OT Historical Books. Sargon's campaign seems to have come in the

wake of another widespread rebellion in Babylonia, Hamath, Gaza and Damascus that broke out during his accession to the throne in 722 BCE (Bright, 276; Younger 2002a, 290-91). These additional references to a capture of Samaria have been explained in numerous ways, including proposals that range from one destruction of Samaria claimed by two different kings, to a double-conquest hypothesis of two destructions, to as many as four separate captures of the capital city (see Younger 1999; Becking).

Whatever the precise course of events, we can be sure that by 720 BCE the northern kingdom of Israel no longer existed as an independent state, but rather was a provincialized territory (called *Samerina*) of the Assyrian Empire. An Assyrian governor assumed control of the area, a significant number of the population were deported, and foreign populations were resettled in their place (2 Kings 17:6, 24). Sargon II claims to have captured 27,280 or 27,290 Israelites, as well as up to two hundred chariots, and there is archaeological confirmation of destruction at cities such as *Tirzah, *Shechem, and Samaria (Campbell, 239). The presence of Israelite exiles in Mesopotamia after 720 BCE is attested also by the appearance of West Semitic personal names in Assyrian texts, but the occasional nature of these references suggests that Israelite ethnic and national identity was lost within a few generations (Cogan 1998, 256).

After the brief record of these climactic events in 2 Kings 17:1-6, the Deuteronomistic History offers an extended commentary that serves as the theological epitaph for the northern kingdom (2 Kings 17:7-18). Israel's historical and geopolitical significance on different occasions throughout its history is counted as insignificant in comparison with its consistent history of apostasy and idolatry against Yahweh, who repeatedly adjured them, "You shall not do this" (2 Kings 17:12).

6. The Kingdom of Hezekiah of Judah (727-699 BCE).

6.1. Expansion Under Assyria (720-714 BCE). Hezekiah came to the throne in Judah at the beginning of the turbulent years that led to the final destruction of the northern kingdom (2 Kings 18:1). It does not appear, however, that Judah became involved in the anti-Assyrian rebellions that marked this period (see Miller and Hayes, 351). The biblical texts are silent about

Hezekiah in this regard. Assyrian records offer a bit more help, however. A building inscription of Sargon II mentions "the land of Judah which is far away" and does not give any indication of rebellious activity (see Younger 2002a, 292). A letter thought to date to about 716 BCE records tribute from Judah along with Egypt, Gaza, Moab and *Ammon (Dalley, 388). Another letter, this one from about 715 BCE, may mention a contingent of Judean troops fighting alongside Assyrian troops in Urartu (Dalley, 388), and Judeans may even be depicted as part of Sennacherib's bodyguard in a relief from his palace in Nineveh (Dalley, 391-92; Hallo, 59). Thus when Assyria began moving rapidly toward the apex of its power near the end of the eighth century BCE, Hezekiah under Judah seems to have played the part of loyal vassal, maybe even erstwhile client (see Dalley; also 1.3 and 5.1 above), to both Sargon and Sennacherib in the newly resubjugated western part of the Assyrian Empire. Such a situation was not destined to last, however.

The primary biblical materials about Hezekiah are 2 Kings 18—20; 2 Chronicles 29—32; Isaiah 36—39. The Chronicles texts provide more details than those in Kings, but both presentations focus on religious reforms such as the removal of *high places, sacred pillars and asherahs. Nonetheless, the period immediately after the fall of the northern kingdom (720-714 BCE) was a time of political ascendancy and expansion for Judah within the Assyrian system. After Sargon II subdued the west in 720 BCE, there were several years of quiet. Perhaps the most significant political development in this period was that Sargon II established a cooperative relationship with the Egyptian rulers in the Delta (against the Ethiopians of the Twenty-fifth Dynasty) and opened trade between Assyria and Egypt (see *COS* 2.118D:296; Kitchen 1986, 375-76; Spalinger, 359). Sargon campaigned through Philistia toward Egypt and appears to have pushed the border of Egypt further south of Gaza to the Wadi el-ʿArish (see Younger 2002a, 312). Significantly, 2 Kings 18:8 says that Hezekiah also expanded Judean territory as far as Gaza. Thus Judah at least bordered the territory that was the primary area of Assyria's expanded trade arrangement. It may even be possible that Sargon II appointed Hezekiah to supervise this vicinity and its activity, as he was one of the few rulers who had remained loyal throughout the

turmoil in Syria-Palestine from 727 to 720 BCE.

In this context the years 720-714 BCE may well represent the height of Judean power. Both domestically and internationally, Judah reaped the benefits of being an important Assyrian vassal charged with administrative responsibilities in the far southwestern corner of the empire. The religious reforms attributed to Hezekiah, which centered on the consolidation of religious and political authority in the capital city, are to be located within this framework. The religious reforms had significant political impact and that may even have been their main *raison d'être* (see Halpern and Hobson, 11-107). Archaeological evidence from Jerusalem and the surrounding country also indicates the emergence of new settlements and the expansion of the capital city to nearly three times its previous size (Cogan 1998, 246; Finkelstein and Silberman, 243). The town lists in Joshua 15 and 19, which are often considered to represent the borders of Judah under Josiah in the seventh century BCE (Naʾaman 1991), may better fit the situation of Assyrian-supported expansion under Hezekiah. He was a vassal of prominent standing within an expanding Assyrian empire, whereas Josiah, as will be shown below, would come to rule a state that had already experienced the might that was Assyria (see Naʾaman 1991, 57-58) and was overshadowed by the resurgent aspirations of Egypt and the imperialistic ambitions of Babylonia. But, again, matters with Hezekiah were destined to change.

6.2. The Ashdod Revolt (714-712 BCE). The ascendancy that Judah experienced in the years following the fall of the north did not last. The biblical texts that describe Hezekiah's reign jump immediately from his accession and reforms to his confrontation with Sennacherib in 701 BCE. Extrabiblical sources, particularly Assyrian inscriptions, reveal another significant course of events that unfolded beginning in 714 BCE and that marked a crucial turning point in Hezekiah's reign.

Sargon II's annals and other inscriptions describe an anti-Assyrian rebellion that broke out in Syria-Palestine in 714 BCE (see *COS* 2.118A:293; 2.118E:296; 2.118F:297). This rebellion was led by Yamani of Ashdod, who had usurped the throne from a pro-Assyrian king appointed by Sargon himself, and included other states such as Philistia, Edom, and Moab (see *ANET,* 287). Assyrian texts claim that the rebels appealed to "*Pir'u* king of *Muṣru*" (probably "Pharaoh, king of Egypt"), most likely the Ethiopian Shabako (716-702 BCE), who had invaded the delta in 715 BCE (Kitchen 1986, 380; Spalinger, 359). The rebels may have also found support in Merodach-baladan, who had seized the throne in Babylon at the death of Shalmaneser V in 722 BCE. Sometime in either 712 or 711 BCE (Sargon's annals and prisms do not match; see Younger 2002a, 313) the Assyrians moved west to put down the Ashdod revolt. There is conflicting Assyrian evidence as to whether Sargon himself led the campaign (see Hallo, 56; cf. Is 20:1). In any event, Yamani fled to Egypt, where the Egyptian king turned him over to Assyria (see *COS* 2.118J:300), and Sargon made Ashdod into a province.

The OT Historical Books are silent concerning the Ashdod revolt. The prophetic narrative in Isaiah 20 explicitly refers to these events but does not state directly that Judah was involved. One of Sargon's texts, however, specifically names Judah as a rebel state that joined with Ashdod (see *ANET*, 287). Indeed, several elements of the biblical presentation of Hezekiah's reign that are placed by Kings and Chronicles in the later context of Sennacherib's invasion in 701 BCE seem to fit better with the earlier Ashdod revolt (see Jenkins). For instance, 2 Kings 18:13 (cf. Is 36:1) links Hezekiah's "fourteenth year" with Sennacherib's invasion in 701 BCE. Some scholars explain this reference by downdating Hezekiah's accession to 715 BCE or proposing that there was a co-regency of Hezekiah with Ahaz, so that the text refers to Hezekiah's fourteenth year of sole rule (see Thiele, 174). But 2 Kings 18:10 places the fall of Samaria in Hoshea's ninth year (722 BCE) and equates it with Hezekiah's "sixth year." Thus his fourteenth year would be 714 BCE, a date that corresponds nicely with the Ashdod revolt. Additionally, both 2 Kings 20 and 2 Chronicles 32 (cf. Is 38) place the story of Hezekiah's life-threatening illness after Sennacherib's invasion in 701 BCE. In this story Hezekiah is promised fifteen additional years of rule (2 Kings 20:6). If these fifteen years are added to Hezekiah's fourteenth year, Hezekiah's reign lasted twenty-nine years, the exact total assigned to him in 2 Kings 18:2. Given the synchronisms with Hoshea's reign, it is unlikely that Hezekiah reigned fifteen years after 701 BCE. Finally, in the context of Hezekiah's illness, the Historical Books place the visit to Judah by envoys from Merodach-baladan, the anti-Assyrian ruler who had seized the throne in Babylon in 722 BCE. Although Merodach-baladan was on the throne again in 705 BCE, in this latter period he was under almost immediate attack by Assyria and would likely not have been free to send messengers abroad (Matthews, 79; contrast Bright, 284).

This combination of evidence indicates Judah's participation in the Ashdod revolt. The Assyrian inscriptions, however, do not name Hezekiah. Given the likely dating of Hezekiah's life-threatening illness to this time, it seems reasonable to conclude that Hezekiah became incapacitated and turned the leadership of the state over to his chief officials, who in turn threw Judah's lot in with Yamani. The prophetic oracle in Isaiah 22 may give a fuller picture as the prophet condemns Shebna, called the "master of the household" (Is 22:15; cf. Jotham in 2 Kings 15:5) (see Goldberg); note also the specific reference to the Ashdod revolt earlier (Is 20:1), which may be related. Yet Sargon's annals refer only to the capture and provincialization of Ashdod and thus give the impression that states such as Judah, Edom and Moab pulled out of the rebellion quickly. Nonetheless, there is good reason to believe that Azekah, a Judean town located on the border of the Shephelah, was attacked. The combination of two fragmentary Assyrian texts (see *COS* 2.119D:304-5), sometimes dated to Sennacherib's later campaign, display several peculiarities in spelling and style suggesting that they come from Sargon II and that the Assyrians seized some Judean territory as a reprisal for participation in the Ashdod revolt (see Galil; Goldberg). Thus Hezekiah remained on the throne but lost the favored status that he had enjoyed and the expanded territory that he had gained.

6.3. Sennacherib's Invasion (701 BCE). In 705 BCE an unexpected turn of events once again upset the political balance of the ancient Near East: Sargon II died on the battlefield in Anatolia, and rebellions broke out throughout the empire. The new Assyrian king, Sennacherib (704-681 BCE), struggled to subdue rebellions in the east throughout his first few years. Consequently, in Syria-Palestine Hezekiah, perhaps indignant following Assyrian reprisals for actions for which he was not responsible, became the ringleader of a revolt that included Sidon, *Ekron and Ashkelon (see *COS* 2.119B:302-3; Gallagher,

255). Assyrian inscriptions even recount how the people of Ekron, wanting to join the rebellion, deposed their pro-Assyrian king, Padi, and turned him over to Hezekiah, who imprisoned him in Jerusalem.

Hezekiah undertook a series of military and political preparations in anticipation of his revolt and Assyria's reaction, some of which have been substantiated by archaeology (Vaughn). These preparations focused on military organization, supply and defense. Hezekiah reorganized and strengthened the army (2 Chron 32:5-6) and built up the walls of Jerusalem (2 Chron 32:5). A small part of a fortification wall that dates to this period, approximately twenty feet thick, has been excavated on the western hill of Jerusalem, and a fortification system with a brick wall has been unearthed at the eighth-century city of Lachish (Finkelstein and Silberman, 255-57). Preparations also involved the completion of the "Siloam Tunnel," a tunnel cut through the rock to bring water into Jerusalem, which bears an inscription that describes the digging process (see Cogan 1998, 250; contrast Dalley). Additionally, numerous storage jars stamped with the seal *lmlk* ("belonging to the king"), found primarily in the southwestern corner of Judah from which Sennacherib's invasion would come, suggest that Hezekiah instituted a system for shipping supplies (Matthews, 82; Vaughn). Even the religious reforms and cultic centralization attributed to Hezekiah may have played a significant part in this political preparation and nationalistic fervor (see the debate in McKay; Cogan 1974; 1993; Spieckermann; Halpern and Hobson, 11-107). The closing of outlying sanctuaries such as *Arad and *Beersheba functioned to make the population more dependent on the central government.

Sennacherib's invasion in 701 BCE is the most well-documented event in Judean history. Numerous biblical and extrabiblical texts, as well as archaeological remains, relate directly to the affair. Consequently, the general course of events is clear (see Gallagher). After subduing rebellions in the east, Sennacherib moved down the Mediterranean coast and captured cities in Phoenicia and Philistia. At this point, Assyrian records indicate that an Egyptian force challenged Sennacherib at Eltekeh but could not defeat him. The Assyrian king then turned his attention to Judah. Sennacherib's inscriptions attest to the massive destruction he inflicted

upon Judean territory. He claims to have captured forty-six fortified cities and exiled 200,150 people (but see De Odorico; Dalley, 394). The Judean city of Lachish suffered the most extensive damage. Archaeological remains indicate a destruction layer there that dates to 701 BCE, and a wall relief in Sennacherib's palace in Nineveh gives a graphic depiction of the battle for the city (Ussishkin).

In spite of the abundant textual and archaeological evidence, the events involved in the final outcome of the invasion, particularly concerning Jerusalem, remain unclear. The biblical account concerning this conclusion in 2 Kings 18—19 (paralleled in 2 Chron 32; Is 36—37) consists of several different traditions that have now been combined (see Gallagher, 145; Childs). The first tradition ("A") appears only in 2 Kings 18:13-16 and says that Hezekiah simply surrendered and paid tribute to Sennacherib. This account matches the Assyrian inscriptions in which Sennacherib claims to have subdued Hezekiah. The second tradition ("B1") is contained in 2 Kings 18:17-19a, 36-37 (cf. Is 36:2—37:9a, 37-38) and says that Sennacherib heard a rumor of an approaching Egyptian force led by Tirhaka (Taharqa), returned home, and was assassinated by his sons. The third tradition ("B2") is found in 2 Kings 19:9b-35 (cf. Is 37:9b-36) and states that an angel killed 185,000 Assyrians in a single night. This third account is often compared to an account from Herodotus (*Hist.* 2.141) that tells of an Assyrian invasion of Egypt that was foiled when a horde of field mice invaded Sennacherib's camp and devoured the quivers, bows and shield handles (see Gallagher, 248-51). Some scholars take these similarities to be a sign that a historical kernel of some sort lies behind these stories (Bright, 301; Gallagher, 245), while others see them simply as evidence of a common folktale (Gonçalves, 483-84; Soggin, 252). Although interpreters often employ the Herodotus material to try to prove or disprove the B2 account, it may well be the product of later Egyptian and Greek adaptations of a Judean tradition (see Strawn). Thus its use in confirming or disconfirming the specifics of the biblical story is complex.

To explain the confusing nature of the biblical and extrabiblical accounts, some scholars propose that Sennacherib campaigned not once, but twice, against Hezekiah. In this view, the first campaign took place in 701 BCE, is reflected in the A tradition, and ended with Hezekiah's surrender. The second campaign was in 688 BCE, is reflected in the B traditions, and ended with Sennacherib's sudden departure from the west and subsequent assassination in 681 BCE (Bright, 298-309). The primary support often given for this hypothesis is that Tirhaka of Ethiopia, whom 2 Kings 19:9 says set out to engage Sennacherib, would have been but a young boy in 701 BCE. Subsequent work on Egyptian chronology, however, has demonstrated that Tirhaka was about twenty years old and perhaps serving as a prince by 701 BCE (Yurco; Millard 1985, 63; Leclant and Yoyotte; cf. Kitchen 1986, 386 n. 823; Redford, 353 n. 163; Spalinger, 360). Moreover, no Assyrian texts mention any campaign to Syria-Palestine in 688 BCE, and archaeological evidence regarding the destruction in 701 BCE indicates that it was of sufficient devastation to obviate any need of further campaigns.

Although the specific details of the conclusion to this affair remain unknown, the evidence suggests that Hezekiah in some way submitted and paid tribute to Assyria. Yet for some reason, Sennacherib relented from the siege without taking Jerusalem and allowed Hezekiah to remain on the throne (see Dalley). Whether this turn of events was due to reports of trouble from elsewhere in the empire (per the B1 account and Akkadian records) or a catastrophic loss of some kind (per the B2 account; cf. Herodotus), both Hezekiah and Judah survived their most direct encounter with Assyrian might. Nonetheless, the land of Judah as a whole was decimated by the invasion. Along with the destroyed cities and exiled people, Sennacherib redistributed parts of Judean territory, putting them into the control of Philistine states such as Ashdod and Ekron (Cogan 1998, 252).

7. Judah as an Assyrian Vassal: The Reign of Manasseh (698-644 BCE).
The reign of Manasseh marked the beginning of a very different period for Judah than that of his father. Manasseh took the throne when he was only twelve years old, and he reigned for fifty-five years, the longest reign of any Judean king. The biblical accounts of his rule in 2 Kings 21 and 2 Chronicles 33, however, primarily theologize about him and portray him as the evil monarch *par excellence* who cannot help but compare poorly with the good kings Hezekiah and Josiah, whose stories frame his. This discrepancy between Manasseh's evil ways and his inordinately long reign is difficult to understand in light of the Deuteronomistic History's operative theological principle: disobedience to Yahweh brings punishment. This, along with its mirror opposite, the premature death of Josiah (see 8 below), are significant exceptions to the Deuteronomistic History's "rule of faith."

The broader historical developments during this period may explain Manasseh's lengthy reign and some of the biblical traditions about him. When Manasseh came to the throne in the years immediately after Sennacherib's invasion, he inherited a Judean state in dire straits. According to Assyrian records, Sennacherib had captured numerous cities, exiled thousands of people, and given away substantial portions of Judean territory (see 6.3 above). Surveys of sites in the Shephelah indicate that 85 percent of the eighth-century settlements were abandoned and not reoccupied in the seventh century BCE (Matthews, 86). Furthermore, during Manasseh's reign the Assyrian Empire reached the height of its power. His rule overlapped some or all of the reigns of Sennacherib, Esarhaddon and Ashurbanipal. Assyrian offensive campaigns to the west were particularly aggressive during this period and were often directed at finally and decisively conquering Egypt. In 679 BCE Esarhaddon marched in a show of force to the border of Egypt and undertook action against Cyprus, Sidon and Tyre (see Miller and Hayes, 366). In 673 BCE he fully invaded Egypt but suffered defeat (*ANET*, 302; Kitchen 1986, 391). In 671 BCE, however, Esarhaddon successfully invaded Egypt, defeated Tirhaka, who was now king, and captured Memphis. Just two years later (669 BCE) Esarhaddon set out again for Egypt to subdue a resurgent Tirhaka, but he fell sick and died en route. His son Ashurbanipal continued the campaign, and by 664 BCE he successfully invaded Egypt, captured Memphis and destroyed Thebes (cf. "No-ammon" [Nah 3:8]; see Kitchen 1986, 394). In the course of these events Manasseh is mentioned only in passing in Assyrian texts as a loyal vassal who provided building materials to Esarhaddon and contributed troops to Ashurbanipal's invasion of Egypt in 668 BCE (*ANET*, 291, 294). Thus the most likely historical explanation of Manasseh's lengthy reign is that he ruled as a loyal Assyrian vassal over a highly marginalized state.

The only biblical story that suggests otherwise is 2 Chronicles 33:10-17. This text states that Manasseh was captured by Assyrian forces, taken in chains to Babylon, humbled himself before the Lord (cf. the apocryphal Prayer of Manasseh), and returned home to institute a series of Yahwistic reforms. The historicity of this tradition is disputed. There were several rebellions in the west during Manasseh's reign, as well as a major rebellion in Babylon by Ashurbanipal's brother in 652-648 BCE, but there is no evidence for Manasseh's involvement in any of these events. This story does not appear in 2 Kings, and as previously noted, Manasseh consistently appears in Assyrian texts as a cooperative vassal. Thus some have concluded that this story reflects only the common motif of a bad king who amends his ways after a trying experience and so is meant to explain how an evil king could enjoy such a long reign (so Miller and Hayes, 376; Matthews, 87; but see Cogan 1998, 254; Bright, 311).

For the OT Historical Books, however, the most important facet of this period of Judean history is religious. The biblical texts demonize Manasseh by telling how he sponsored apostate and idolatrous forms of worship (2 Kings 21:1-9). Scholars hold different positions concerning the reason for these developments. Some interpreters suggest that Assyrian foreign policy included the imposition of Assyrian worship upon vassal states (see Bright, 312; Spieckermann). Others, however, argue the opposite, contending that the available evidence for Assyrian practices does not support such a conclusion (see McKay; Cogan 1974, 1993), at least not unequivocally. There may well have been a difference between annexed territories and vassal states on this matter so that there were exceptions to Assyrian imperial policy (see Donner, 419-20), especially in the west (Cogan 1993). Manasseh's propagation of unorthodox worship (and Ahaz's before him [cf. 2 Kings 16:10-16]), therefore, while probably reflecting Assyrian (and Aramaean) influence, most likely represented a *voluntary* incorporation of Assyrian religious elements that also revived much older religious practices from the time before Hezekiah's reforms. Such rapprochement fits well with some evidence that Judah began to experience a limited economic recovery on the domestic front during the more stable years of Manasseh's rule. Archaeological evidence points to an increase in the population of the Judean highlands and in the agricultural production of the surrounding area (Finkelstein and Silberman, 266).

Manasseh died in 644 BCE, and his son Amon (643-642 BCE) reigned only two years before being assassinated by his own royal officials (2 Kings 21:19-26; 2 Chron 33:21-25). Once again, the biblical texts concentrate on his religious practices that continued those of his father, but the exact circumstances concerning his assassination are unclear. The action may represent an anti-Assyrian move that was precipitated by a broad but short-lived western uprising at the time (see Hayes and Hooker, 82). Whatever the details, a group called "the people of the land," who earlier had assisted in the overthrow of Queen Athaliah, killed the assassins and placed the eight-year-old Josiah on the throne. Many suggestions exist as to the exact nature and makeup of this influential group, but it appears at least to have been one with judicial authority and military strength, perhaps the aristocratic landowners rather than simple farmers or residents of provincial towns outside the capital. One fairly consistent tendency whenever this group appears in the OT Historical Books, however, is that the "people of the land" were a political group whose politics were pro-Assyrian, pro-Davidic and anti-Egyptian. In this case, their action after the death of Amon placed on the throne the last Judean king of any consequence in the Assyrian period.

8. The End of the Assyrian Empire: The Reign of Josiah (641-610 BCE).

When Josiah came to the throne in 641 BCE, the reign of Ashurbanipal was half over, and Assyria had entered a downward spiral from which it would not recover. Beginning already in Ashurbanipal's final years, the Assyrians became increasingly involved with conflicts to the north and were unable to maintain a strong hold on the other parts of the empire (Miller and Hayes, 383). By the mid-620s BCE, Nabopolassar had seized the throne in Babylon and asserted independence from Assyria. The Babylonian Chronicles contain a gap in this period, but when they resume in 616 BCE, Nabopolassar is in complete control of Babylonia and is fighting against Assyria (see Grayson 1975). As Assyria declined, Egypt, an ally of Assyria since early in the reign of Ashurbanipal, benefited the most. During the long reign of Psammetichus I (664-610 BCE), Egypt played an ever-increasing role in the control of Syria-Palestine that filled the void created by Assyrian withdrawal (see Kitchen 1986, 399-408).

Against this background, 2 Kings 22—23 and 2 Chronicles 34—35 depict Josiah as the most righteous king in Judah's history and the one who most closely matches the values of the biblical writers. For this reason, some scholars propose that an edition of the Deuteronomistic History was first produced during his reign. The primary reason for the positive judgment of the biblical writers concerning Josiah is that he is said to have undertaken an extensive religious reform that focused on reversing the apostate practices of Manasseh by centralizing worship in Jerusalem and destroying all outlying sanctuaries. The narratives present this reform as extending even into the territory of the old northern kingdom and resulting in the destruction of sanctuaries at *Bethel and Samaria (2 Kings 23:15-20). Although the accounts in Kings and Chronicles do not correspond exactly (see 2 Kings 23:4-20; cf. 2 Chron 34:3-7), both emphasize that the primary impetus for Josiah's actions was the discovery of a "book of the law" in the temple. The nature and significance of this event, attested only in the biblical narratives, remains debated. Many interpreters identify Josiah's law book with some form of Deuteronomy, but debate continues over whether it was an ancient work that was "found" in the temple, a seventh-century document that was composed then to support Josiah's reform, or some combination thereof. The biblical narratives, at least, emphasize that this law book's concerns for the people's covenant with and exclusive worship of God propelled Josiah's religious actions. Such concerns, especially with cult centralization, are also at work in Deuteronomy (see Deut 12). One should also note that Josiah is the only king to "incarnate" the demands of the Shema in all of Israelite and Judean history (cf. Deut 6:5 with 2 Kings 23:25).

In conjunction with the general historical situation and the special place afforded Josiah by the biblical narratives, many contemporary interpreters consider his reign to be a period of renewed political freedom and territorial expansion, perhaps the greatest period of autonomy that Judah had experienced since the time of David (see Bright, 316; Soggin, 257; Matthews, 78). It is often suggested that, given the decline of Assyria, Josiah was able to annex provincialized territories of the former northern kingdom, including Samaria and Galilee, expand to the south and west, and reestablish Judean rule over the bulk of Syria-Palestine. Extrabiblical evidence that has been marshaled to support this view includes the discovery of Hebrew inscriptions from Mesad Hashavyahu, a small fortress on the Mediterranean coast; the construction of a massive seventh-century fort at the northern city of Megiddo; and the fortification of southern cities such as Arad, Kadesh-Barnea, and Haseva (see Finkelstein and Silberman, 348-49). A more recent study has further suggested that bullae from Josiah's reign indicate that the northern town of Arubbot, just south of Tanaach, was paying taxes to Jerusalem (Matthews, 88).

Although it is true that the final Assyrian kings were powerless to oppose such a Josianic expansion, a closer examination of the evidence, especially concerning the role of Egypt, indicates that it can be interpreted in different ways (Na'aman 1991). There is no clear archaeological evidence to support the claim that Josiah destroyed sanctuaries at Bethel and Samaria or to indicate that the seventh-century fort at Megiddo was built or occupied by Judeans. Inscriptions from the coastal fort at Mesad Hashavyahu indicate the presence of Judeans and Greeks—the latter known to have served in the Egyptian military—and suggest that this outpost may have been Egyptian (Finkelstein and Silberman, 348-53). Indeed, several factors indicate that Egypt under the Twenty-Sixth (Saite) Dynasty came to play the dominant role in Syria-Palestine during this period of Assyrian decline (Redford, 430-69; Na'aman 1991). Extrabiblical texts attest that the Egyptians captured the Philistine city of Ashdod (Herodotus *Hist.* 2.157) and were able to move freely throughout the breadth of Syria-Palestine, which suggests that they were in control of main highways such as the Via Maris. Several artifacts of Egyptian rulers have been discovered as far north as Arvad, and some inscriptions show the forging of treaties between Egypt and Syro-Palestinian states. If this was the case, it suggests that Josiah's was, in fact, *not* a time of autonomy and expansion, but rather that Judah may have been significantly subservient to Egypt throughout most of Josiah's reign (see Na'aman 1991; cf. Miller and Hayes, 383-90), especially its latter portions (Provan, Long and Longman, 276). Although there are no records of Judean vassal payments to Egypt, any such payments would have constituted the normal annual tribute, a payment that is not regularly recorded in either Assyrian or Egyptian texts. Above all, however, Pharaoh Neco II's act of deposing and appointing Judean kings immediately after Josiah's death implies Egyptian control of the royal affairs of Judah, at least from this point forward. Perhaps 2 Kings 23:8 accurately records the true extent of Josiah's territory: from Geba in the north, which was just above Bethel, to Beersheba in the south, to Lachish in the west, a city that apparently was refortified in Josiah's time (see Finkelstein and Silberman, 350-53) (*see* Geographical Extent of Israel).

The events leading to the death of Josiah are unclear, yet they parallel the events that led to the final collapse of the Assyrian Empire. After the death of Ashurbanipal, Assyria quickly succumbed to the combined forces of its enemies. In 614 BCE the Medes captured the city of Ashur and entered an alliance with Nabopolassar of Babylonia. In 612 BCE this new alliance destroyed the Assyrian capital Nineveh and killed the reigning Assyrian monarch. The new Assyrian king, Ashur-uballit II (612-609 BCE), retreated westward with the remnant of his army to Haran. Sometime in 610 BCE the Egyptians, under Pharaoh Neco (Necho) II (610-595 BCE), came to Assyria's aid and engaged the Babylonians and Medes at Haran, but they were forced to withdraw. A year later they counterattacked but were again defeated. Following these battles for Haran, Assyria essentially disappeared from ancient Near Eastern politics.

The OT Historical Books place Josiah's death in the context of these turbulent years. 2 Kings 23:29 states that Pharaoh Neco, while marching up to aid Assyria at Haran, probably in 610 BCE (see Hooker and Hayes), killed Josiah at Megiddo. This statement is exceedingly vague. The account in 2 Chronicles 35:20-24 depicts Josiah as deliberately challenging Neco in battle. The debate over the historical reconstruction here remains unsettled. Many interpreters have favored the Chronicles version and concluded that a powerful Josiah clashed with an invading Egyptian force (see Bright, 324). As previously noted, however, the evidence suggests that Judah may have been subservient to Egyptian control in much of Josiah's reign. Thus perhaps the new pharaoh, Neco II, who had come to the throne earlier in 610 BCE upon the death of Psammetichus I (see Hooker and Hayes), was attempting to secure renewed oaths of loyalty from vassals of the preceding king when he met up with Josiah (see Finkelstein and Silberman, 291). Whatever the case, Josiah, the paradigmatic Deuteronomistic king, dies young and unexpectedly, providing another exception to any simplistic notion of retribution that scholars often find operating in the Deuteronomistic History.

The years 610-609 BCE marked the end of both the reign of Josiah and the vitality of Assyria. After Josiah's death the "people of the land" enthroned Jehoahaz II, who was later deposed by Neco II and replaced with the Egyptian appointee Jehoiakim (2 Kings 23:30-34). Egypt's prominent role in these affairs is a fitting conclusion not only to the reign of Josiah, but also to the entire period of Assyrian dominance. After 609 BCE Assyria would never again play a significant role in the politics of the ancient Near East or in the life of Judah. Until the southern kingdom's end in the exile of 586 BCE, its fate would be intertwined with the two world powers now dominant on the scene: Babylonia and Egypt.

See also ARAM, DAMASCUS AND SYRIA; ASSYRIA, ASSYRIANS; BABYLONIA, BABYLONIANS; CHRONICLES, BOOKS OF; HEZEKIAH; JEHU DYNASTY; JOSIAH; KINGS, BOOKS OF; MANASSEH; OMRI DYNASTY; SAMARIA.

BIBLIOGRAPHY. **G. Athas,** *The Tel Dan Inscription: A Reappraisal and New Interpretation* (JSOT-Sup 360; Sheffield: Sheffield Academic Press, 2003); **W. H. Barnes,** *Studies in the Chronology of the Divided Monarchy of Israel* (HSM 48; Atlanta: Scholars Press, 1991); **B. Becking,** *The Fall of Samaria: An Historical and Archaeological Study* (SHCANE 2; Leiden: E. J. Brill, 1992); **J. Bright,** *A History of Israel* (4th ed.; Louisville: Westminster/John Knox, 2000); **E. Campbell Jr.,** "A Land Divided: Judah and Israel from the Death of Solomon to the Fall of Samaria," in *The Oxford History of the Biblical World,* ed. M. Coogan (Oxford: Oxford University Press, 1998) 206-41; **B. S. Childs,** *Isaiah and the Assyrian Crisis* (SBT 3; London: SCM, 1967); **M. Cogan,** *Imperialism and Religion: Assyria, Judah, and Israel in the Eighth and Seventh Centuries B.C.* (SBLMS 19; Missoula, MT: Scholars Press, 1974); idem, "Into Exile: From the Assyrian Conquest of Israel to the Fall of Babylon," in *The Oxford History of the Biblical World*, ed. M. Coogan (Oxford: Oxford University Press, 1998) 242-75; idem, "Judah under Assyrian Hegemony: A Reexamination of Imperialism and Religion," *JBL* 112 (1993) 403-14; **F. M. Cross**, *Canaanite Myth and Hebrew Epic: Essays in the History of the Religion of Israel* (Cambridge, MA: Harvard University Press, 1973); **S. Dalley**, "Recent Evidence from Assyrian Sources for Judaean History from Uzziah to Manasseh," *JSOT* 28 (2004) 387-401; **P. Davies**, *In Search of 'Ancient Israel'* (JSOTSup 148; Sheffield: Sheffield Academic Press, 1992); **M. De Odorico**, *The Use of Numbers and Quantifications in the Assyrian Royal Inscriptions* (SAAS 3; Helsinki: University of Helsinki, 1995); **J. A. Dearman**, *Property Rights in the Eighth-Century Prophets: The Conflict and Its Background* (SBLDS 106; Atlanta: Scholars Press, 1988); **P. Dion**, *Les Araméens à l'âge du fer: Histoire politique et structurales sociales* (Paris: Gabalda, 1997); **H. Donner**, "The Separate States of Israel and Judah," in *Israelite and Judaean History*, ed. J. H. Hayes and J. M. Miller (London: SCM, 1977) 381-434; **I. Finkelstein and N. Silberman**, *The Bible Unearthed: Archaeology's New Vision of Ancient Israel and the Origin of Its Sacred Texts* (New York: Free Press, 2000); **G. Galil**, "A New Look at the 'Azekah Inscription,'" *RB* 102 (1995) 321-29; **W. Gallagher**, *Sennacherib's Campaign to Judah: New Studies* (SHCANE 18; Leiden: E. J. Brill, 1999); **J. Goldberg**, "Two Assyrian Campaigns against Hezekiah and Later Eighth Century Biblical Chronology," *Bib* 80 (1999) 360-90; **F. J. Gonçalves**, *L'expédition de Sennachérib en Palestine dans la littérature Hébraïque ancienne* (EBib 7; Louvain-la-Neuve: Université catholique de Louvain, Institut orientaliste, 1986); **A. K. Grayson**, *Assyrian and Babylonian Chronicles* (TCS 5; Locust Valley, NY: J. J. Augustin, 1975); idem, *Assyrian Rulers of the Early First Millennium BC II (858-745 BC)* (RIMA 3; Toronto: University of Toronto Press, 1996); idem, "Mesopotamia, History of (Assyria)," *ABD* 4:732-55; **W. W. Hallo**, "From Qarqar to Carchemish: Assyria and Israel in the Light of New Discoveries," *BA* 23 (1960) 34-61; **B. Halpern and D. W. Hobson**, eds., *Law and Ideology in Monarchic Israel* (JSOTSup 124; Sheffield: JSOT, 1991); **J. H. Hayes**, *Amos: The Eighth-Century Prophet; His Times and His Preaching* (Nashville: Abingdon, 1988); **J. H. Hayes and P. K. Hooker**, *A New Chronology for the Kings of Israel and Judah and Its Implications for Biblical History and Literature* (Atlanta: John Knox, 1988); **J. H. Hayes and J. K. Kuan**, "The Final Years of Samaria (730-720 BC)," *Bib* 72 (1991) 153-81; **P. K. Hooker and J. H. Hayes**, "The Year of Josiah's Death: 609 or 610 BCE?" in *The Land That I Will Show You: Essays on the History and Archaeology of the Ancient Near East in Honor of J. Maxwell Miller*, ed. J. A. Dearman and M. P. Graham (JSOTSup 343; Sheffield: Sheffield Academic Press, 2001) 96-103; **S. Irvine**, *Isaiah, Ahaz, and the Syro-Ephraimitic Crisis* (SBLDS 123; Atlanta: Scholars Press, 1990); **A. K. Jenkins**, "Hezekiah's Fourteenth Year: A New Interpretation of 2 Kings xviii 13-xix 37," *VT* 26 (1976): 284-98; **B. Kelle**, "What's in a Name? Neo-Assyrian Designations for the Northern Kingdom and Their Implications for Israelite History and Biblical Interpretation," *JBL* 121 (2002) 639-66; **K. A. Kitchen**, "Egypt, History of (Chronology)," *ABD* 2.322-31; idem, *The Third Intermediate Period in Egypt (1100-650 B.C.)* (2d ed.; Warminster: Aris & Phillips, 1986); **J. Leclant and J. Yoyotte**, "Notes d'histoire et de civilization éthiopiennes," *BIFAO* 51 (1952) 17-27; **E. Lipiński**, *The Aramaeans: Their History, Culture, and Religion* (OLA 100; Leuven: Peeters, 2000); **V. P. Long**, ed., *Israel's Past in Present Research: Essays on Ancient Israelite Historiography* (SBTS 7; Winona Lake, IN: Eisenbrauns, 1999); **V. Matthews**, *A Brief History of Ancient Israel* (Louisville: Westminster/John Knox, 2002); **J. W. McKay**, *Religion in Judah under the Assyrians, 732-609 BC* (SBT 26; Naperville, IL: Allenson, 1973); **S. L. McKenzie**, "Deuteronomistic History," *ABD* 2.160-68; **A. R. Millard**, *The Eponyms of the Assyrian Empire, 910-612 BC* (SAAS 2; Helsinki: Neo-Assyrian Text Corpus Project, 1994); idem, "Sennacherib's Attack on Hezekiah," *TynBul* 36 (1985) 61-77; **J. M. Miller and J. H. Hayes**, *A History of Ancient Israel and Judah* (Philadelphia: Westminster, 1986); **N. Na'aman**, "The Historical Background to the Conquest of Samaria (720 BC)," *Bib* 71 (1990) 206-25; idem, "The Kingdom of Judah under Josiah," *TA* 18 (1991) 3-71; **R. D. Nelson**, *The Double Redaction of the Deuteronomistic History* (JSOTSup 18; Sheffield: JSOT, 1981); **B. Oded**, "The Historical Background of the Syro-Ephraimite War Reconsidered," *CBQ* 34 (1972) 153-65; **W. T. Pitard**, *Ancient Damascus: A Historical Study of the Syrian City-State from Earliest Times until Its Fall to the Assyrians in 732 B.C.E.* (Winona Lake, IN: Eisenbrauns, 1987); **I. Provan, V. P. Long and T. Longman III**, *A Biblical History of Israel* (Louisville: Westminster/John

Knox, 2003); **D. B. Redford,** *Egypt, Canaan, and Israel in Ancient Times* (Princeton, NJ: Princeton University Press, 1992); **J. M. Sasson,** *Hebrew Origins: Historiography, History, Faith of Ancient Israel* (Chuen King Lecture Series 4; Hong Kong: Theology Division, Chung Chi College, Chinese University of Hong Kong, 2002); **C. R. Seitz,** *Theology in Conflict: Reactions to the Exile in the Book of Jeremiah* (BZAW 176; Berlin: de Gruyter, 1989); **J. A. Soggin,** *An Introduction to the History of Israel and Judah* (2d ed.; Valley Forge, PA: Trinity Press International, 1993); **A. Spalinger,** "Egypt, History of (3d Intermediate-Saite Period [Dyn. 21-26])," *ABD* 2.353-64; **H. Spieckermann,** *Juda unter Assur in der Sargonidenzeit* (FRLANT 129; Göttingen: Vandenhoeck & Ruprecht, 1982); **J. Strange,** "Joram, King of Israel and Judah," *VT* 25 (1975) 191-201; **B. A. Strawn,** "Herodotus' *History* 2.141 and the Deliverance of Jerusalem: On Parallels, Sources, and Histories of Ancient Israel," in *Israel's Prophets and Israel's Past: Essays on the Relationship of Prophetic Texts and Israelite History,* ed. B. E. Kelle and M. B. Moore (Library of Hebrew Bible/Old Testament Studies; London & New York: T & T Clark, forthcoming); **H. Tadmor,** *The Inscriptions of Tiglath-pileser III King of Assyria* (Jerusalem: Israel Academy of Sciences and Humanities, 1994); **E. Thiele,** *The Mysterious Numbers of the Hebrew Kings* (rev. ed.; Grand Rapids: Zondervan, 1983); **R. Tomes,** "The Reason for the Syro-Ephraimite War," *JSOT* 59 (1993) 55-71; **D. Ussishkin,** *The Conquest of Lachish by Sennacherib* (Publications of the Institute of Archaeology 6; Tel Aviv: Tel Aviv University, Institute of Archaeology, 1982); **A. G. Vaughn,** *Theology, History, and Archaeology in the Chronicler's Account of Hezekiah* (ABS 4; Atlanta: Scholars Press, 1999); **M. Weinfeld,** *Deuteronomy and the Deuteronomistic School* (Oxford: Clarendon Press, 1972); **S. Yamada,** *The Construction of the Assyrian Empire: A Historical Study of the Inscriptions of Shalmaneser III (859-824 B.C.) Relating to His Campaigns to the West* (CHANE 3; Leiden: E. J. Brill, 2000); **K. L. Younger,** "The Fall of Samaria in Light of Recent Research," *CBQ* 61 (1999) 461-82; idem, "Recent Study on Sargon II, King of Assyria: Implications for Biblical Studies," in *Mesopotamia and the Bible: Comparative Explorations,* ed. M. Chavalas and K. L. Younger (Grand Rapids: Baker, 2002a) 288-329; idem, "Yahweh at Ashkelon and Calah? Yahwistic Names in Neo-Assyrian," *VT* 52 (2002b) 207-18; **F. J. Yurco,** "The Shabaka-Shebitku Coregency

and the Supposed Second Campaign of Sennacherib against Judah: A Critical Assessment," *JBL* 110 (1991) 35-45.

B. E. Kelle and B. A. Strawn

HISTORY OF ISRAEL 6: BABYLONIAN PERIOD

The *Babylonian period in the history of Israel covers the years 609 to 539 BCE. In 610-609 BCE the Babylonian king Nabopolassar and his allies the Medes captured the city of Harran in northern Syria, where the last *Assyrian king, Ashuruballit II, had made an ultimate attempt to save his dying empire from destruction. This opened the Syro-Palestinian corridor to Babylonian armies and bolstered their claim to inherit the hegemonic position formerly held by Assyria. Babylon's pretensions became a reality under the leadership of Nebuchadnezzar II (605-562 BCE), but his successors failed to contain the growing menace posed by the Medes and the Persians. In 539 BCE the *Persian ruler Cyrus II (the Great) put an end to the Neo-Babylonian Empire and sent Nabonidus, the last king of Babylon, into exile. Although the Babylonian period was a short one in the history of Israel, the events associated with it left an indelible imprint on Jewish consciousness. It was the defining moment in the formation of Judaism.

1. Evaluation of Sources
2. Judah on the Eve of Babylonian Intervention
3. Nebuchadnezzar II's Conquest of the Levant (605-586 BCE)
4. Judah Under Babylonian Rule
5. Judean Exiles in Babylonia

1. Evaluation of Sources.

Our main Babylonian source for the period extending from 609 to 539 BCE is the Babylonian Chronicle, which is preserved for the years 626-623 BCE (accession year to third year of Nabopolassar), 616-594 BCE (tenth year of Nabopolassar to eleventh year of Nebuchadnezzar II) and 557-538 BCE (third year of Neriglissar to first year of Cyrus the Great), except for a gap in the year 556 BCE (accession year of Nabonidus). Building inscriptions of the Babylonian kings have survived in large numbers, while economic and administrative documents from Babylonia are known by the thousands. On the Israelite side our main narrative source is the Bible, first and foremost the last chapters of *Kings and *Chronicles. Individual prophetic books are also important. Jeremiah is a primary source for the period leading up to the capture of *Jerusalem and the destruction of the temple, and the situation in Judea after the conquest, while Ezekiel and Second Isaiah are relevant to the situation of the exile community in Babylonia.

Historiographical narratives found in the Bible always reflect the theology of their writers. The same is true of Babylonian sources, but rarely is this emphasized by historians. Neo-Babylonian building inscriptions are essentially religious documents with only occasional references to historical events, but even cuneiform sources that are chronographic in nature or fall within the general category of historiography are colored by theological thinking and must therefore be approached with a critical mind. Only archival (i.e., economic and administrative) texts are unmediated. We have such documents from the kingdom of Judah in the form of ostraca. In spite of their small number, they provide welcome bits of information. Babylonian archival texts, on the other hand, are abundant, and their importance has become now even greater with the recent surfacing of documents that explicitly mention for the first time a community of Judean exiles living in Babylonia.

2. Judah on the Eve of Babylonian Intervention.
During the reign of *Josiah (639-609 BCE) the kingdom of Judah had experienced some kind of revival. This was due mainly to the weakness of Assyria, which was now threatened on all its borders by the Medes, Babylonians and *Egyptians. The reforms of Josiah, which began with the renovation of the temple of Jerusalem in 621 BCE (2 Kings 22:3-7; 2 Chron 34:8-13), signaled the advent of a more assertive policy, which became possible only after the Assyrians withdrew from the region completely following the death of Ashurbanipal (probably 630 BCE). Archaeological surveys and excavations along the eastern border of Judah have confirmed that some sites were reinforced as the result of Josiah's increased control over the area. This would have been impossible at the time of Assyrian overlordship. The kingdom expanded in all directions and even gained control of a small part of the coastal area. Excavations at Mesad Hashavyahu, on the Mediterranean coast just south of Yavneh Yam between Jaffa and *Ashdod, have

revealed the existence of a fortress dating to the end of Iron Age II. The find of a few ostraca that apparently date to the last years of the reign of Josiah indicate that the fortress probably had been built by him and abandoned upon his death in 609 BCE. The ostraca contain no information bearing on the political history of the period. However, the find of a large quantity of Greek pottery in the fort suggests the presence of Greek mercenaries. Such evidence is available also from *Arad slightly later. Greece suffered from overpopulation at that time, and soldiers were forced to sell their services to foreign rulers who sought them because of their superior military technology and equipment. We know that the Egyptian pharaohs employed Greek and Carian mercenaries in that period. The presence of such mercenaries in Judah confirms the increased importance of the kingdom in the last decades of the seventh century BCE.

The total eradication of Assyria at Harran in 609 BCE opened the way for two ambitious rivals: Egypt and Babylon. The main phase of the contest between the two powers was short, lasting from 609 to 605 BCE. In 610-609 BCE the Egyptians had come to the rescue of Ashur-uballit II, the last Assyrian king, presumably with the hope of maintaining a weakened Assyria as buffer zone between Egypt and the rising power of Babylon. This would have allowed Egypt to recover its Levantine empire of the late Bronze Age. The recovery of that empire, which had been a consistent policy of Pharaoh Psammeticus I (664-610 BCE), now seemed within reach. Our main source for the years 610-609 BCE is the Babylonian Chronicle, which tells us that Egyptian armies came to the rescue of Ashur-uballit II in his struggle against the conjugated forces of the Medes and Babylonians. The Bible relates that Pharaoh Neco II, crossing Palestine in 609 BCE on his way to the Euphrates River to meet the king of Assyria, clashed with King Josiah at *Meggido and killed him: "In his days Pharaoh Neco king of Egypt went up to the king of Assyria to the river Euphrates. King Josiah went to meet him; but when Pharaoh Neco met him at Meggido, he killed him" (2 Kings 23:29 NRSV; also 2 Chron 35:20). Josiah probably was trying to prevent the pharaoh from coming to the aid of Assyria, fearing Egypt more than the distant Babylonians. The events are reflected also in a cuneiform letter found in the Babylonian city of Uruk. It probably was sent by the crown prince Nebuchadnezzar to the administrators of the local temple, the Eanna, informing them of his departure to Harran on a military expedition. Egyptian campaigns of 609 BCE along the Mediterranean coast resulted in the destruction of certain sites, notably Arad (Level VII) and Mesad Hashavyahu.

The political history of Judah after Josiah's death at *Meggido was dominated for a few years by Egypt. According to the Bible, while Neco was campaigning in northern Syria, the "people of the land" enthroned Jehoahaz (= Shallum), son of Josiah, as king of Judah (2 Kings 23:30; 2 Chron 36:1). Some have interpreted the fragmentary ostracon 88 from Arad as alluding to Jehoahaz's accession, even claiming that the new king may have been calling for a rebellion against Egypt: "I, I have become king in . . . Strengthen (your) arm and . . . The king of Egypt for . . ." (Smelik, 104-5). Indeed, Jehoahaz ruled for only three months. On his return from Syria, Neco II stopped at Riblah and deposed him and deported him to Egypt, where he died. Then he put on the Judean throne another son of Josiah named Eliakim, whom he renamed Jehoiakim (2 Kings 23:31-34; 2 Chron 36:3-4; Jer 22:10-12).

The Egyptian invasion, the death of Josiah and the removal of Jehoahaz are depicted as traumatic events in Jeremiah 22:10-12 and 2 Chronicles 35:25. Not surprisingly, Jehoiakim adopted a resolutely pro-Egyptian policy. The Bible contains harsh judgments on his oppressive rule and love of luxury, contrasting his policies with the benevolent rule of his father (Jer 22:13-19). His imposition of unfair taxes and subservience to Egypt are denounced in the book of Kings: "Jehoiakim gave the silver and the gold to Pharaoh, but he taxed the land in order to meet Pharaoh's demand for money. He exacted the silver and the gold from the people of the land, from all according to their assessment, to give it to Pharaoh Neco" (2 Kings 23:35 NRSV). If we assume that Jeremiah's negative tone reflects the mood prevailing among the population, serious opposition to his rule seems to have arisen. Prophets and priests who censured the king and his ministers were persecuted and even executed (Jer 26).

3. Nebuchadnezzar II's Conquest of the Levant (605-586 BCE).

Jehoiakim's pro-Egyptian policy may have seemed the only realistic one in the years following the fall of Assyria, but soon the balance of power shifted to Babylon. The watershed occurred in the year 605 BCE when Nebuchadnezzar, still crown prince, defeated the Egyptians at Carchemish. This event is related in the Babylonian Chronicle: "The king of Akkad stayed home, while Nebuchadnezzar, his eldest son and crown prince, mustered [the army of Akkad]. He took his army's lead and marched to Carchemish which is on the bank of the Euphrates. He crossed the river [to encounter the army of Egypt] which was encamped at Carchemish. . . . They did battle together. The army of Egypt retreated before him. He inflicted a [defeat] upon them and finished them off completely" (Babylonian Chronicle 5, obv. lines 1-5 [Grayson, 99]). The battle is also the subject of an oracle against Egypt found in Jeremiah 46:2: "Concerning Egypt, about the army of Pharaoh Neco, king of Egypt, which was by the river Euphrates at Carchemish and which King Nebuchadnezzar of Babylon defeated in the fourth year of King Jehoiakim son of Josiah of Judah" (NRSV). This dazzling victory gave the Babylonians control over the entire Levant down to the border of Egypt.

Nebuchadnezzar did not rest on his laurels at Carchemish. The following year (604 BCE) he campaigned again in the Levant. According to the Babylonian Chronicle, this campaign culminated in the conquest and destruction of the coastal city of *Ashkelon: "He marched to [Ashk]elon and in the month Kislev he captured it, seized its king, plundered [and sac]ked it. He turned the city into a ruin heap" (Babylonian Chronicle 5, obv. lines 18-20 [Grayson, 100]). Excavations at Ashkelon have amply confirmed this account. The city was thoroughly destroyed and not resettled until the Persian period. The "fury of Babylon" continued to devastate the Levantine coast in the following years. There is evidence for massive destruction in Philistine cities such as *Ashdod, *Ekron and Timnah (Tell Batash). Nebuchadnezzar's strategy may have been to create a no-man's-land in order to prevent the Egyptians from regaining the allegiance of these coastal cities.

According to the Babylonian Chronicle, in the year 601 BCE Nebuchadnezzar marched to Egypt and clashed with the pharaoh's army without scoring a victory: "They fought one another in the battlefield and both sides suffered seve-

losses. The king of Akkad and his army turned and [went back] to Babylon" (Babylonian Chronicle 5, rev. line 7 [Grayson, 101]) The following year the Babylonian armies stayed home, but in the year 599 BCE they went back to Syria-Palestine to campaign against the Arab tribes of the desert fringe. Meanwhile, the failed invasion of Egypt in 601 BCE had temporarily weakened Babylonian influence, at least enough to encourage the small Levantine states, including Judah, to rebel against Nebuchadnezzar. The famous Adon letter may well date to that period. Found at Saqqara, near Memphis in Egypt, it is a diplomatic letter in Aramaic sent by Adon, the ruler of one of the several cities named Aphek, to the pharaoh. In the letter, which is fragmentary, Adon pleads for Egyptian help against the Babylonians: "[The troops] of the king of Babylon have come; they have *reached* Aphek, and ... they have taken ... For the lord of kings, the Pharaoh, knows that [your servant] ... to send an army to save me" (Smelik, 123-24).

The situation in Judah at this point is difficult to appraise. Jehoiakim may have chosen to rebel as early as 600 BCE, according to 2 Kings 24:1: "In his days King Nebuchadnezzar of Babylon came up; Jehoiakim became his servant for three years; then he turned and rebelled against him" (NRSV). Then the book of Kings goes on to say that bands of Chaldeans, *Arameans, *Moabites and *Ammonites were sent against him. Clearly, these were advance forays of Babylonian and vassal troops preparing for the massive invasion of 598-597 BCE. Jehoiakim died probably late in the year 598 BCE and was succeeded by his son Jehoiakin, although the exact dates are uncertain. The geopolitical situation at that point can be appraised in part from an inscription of Nebuchadnezzar called the *Hofkalender* ("Court Calendar"). It is dated to his seventh regnal year (598-597 BCE) and commemorates work on the king's south palace in Babylon, stressing that all provinces of the kingdom contributed to the building. A list of provincial officials and vassals follows, including the kings of Ty[re], Gaz[a], Sid[on], Arwa[d], Ashd[od] and two cities whose names cannot be read (*ANET*, 308). This should indicate that Babylonian control over the area by the time of the accession of Jehoiakin was quite firm. According to 2 Kings 24:7, even the Egyptians refrained from intervening: "The king of Egypt did not come again out of his land, for the king of Babylon had tak-en over all that belonged to the king of Egypt from the Wadi of Egypt to the River Euphrates" (NRSV). The stage was set for a successful Babylonian punitive expedition against Judah.

The Judean campaign of Nebuchadnezzar and his first capture of Jerusalem are mentioned in the Babylonian Chronicle for the year 598/597 BCE: "In the month Kislev the king of Akkad mustered his army and marched to Hattu. He encamped against the city of Judah and on the second day of the month Addar he captured the city (and) seized (its) king. A king of his own choice he appointed in the city (and) taking the vast tribute he brought it to Babylon" (Babylonian Chronicle 5, rev. lines 11-13 [Grayson, 102]) About one hundred ostraca were found in the Negev at Tell Arad, identified by most scholars as ancient Arad. They date to various periods of the Judean monarchy. Of particular interest are the eighteen ostraca making up the archive of Eliyashib, commander of the fortress of Arad. They can be dated to the beginning of the year 597 BCE, before the capture of Jerusalem. These ostraca were found in Level VI. Several of them mention deliveries of rations to the Kittim, who undoubtedly were Greek mercenaries employed by the king of Judah. Ostracon 18 is particularly important because it contains the earliest extrabiblical mention of the temple of Yahweh in Jerusalem (*see* Solomon's Temple). Finally, ostracon 24, not belonging to the Eliyashib group, mentions a royal order to control Edomite incursions in the Negev. The *Edomites were allied to the Babylonians and took control of the Negev around the time of the first conquest of Jerusalem. The exact date of this ostracon, however, is uncertain, and could be somewhat later than the time of the first conquest.

Jehoiakin surrendered to the Babylonians without a fight in order to avoid the complete annihilation of Jerusalem. He was led into exile with members of the *royal family and a large portion of the Judean elite, as well as warriors, artisans, priests and even prophets such as Ezekiel. "No one remained, except the poorest people of the land," according to 2 Kings 24:14 (NRSV). The vessels of the temple of Jerusalem were carried off to Babylon with the treasures of the temple and the royal palace. The new king appointed by Nebuchadnezzar was Zedekiah (Mattaniah), Jehoiakin's uncle. Although a Babylonian appointee, he was a legitimate descendant of the house of David. At first, Zedekiah remained subservient to Nebuchadnezzar, but soon Egypt began maneuvering to regain a foothold in the Levant. Zedekiah tried to gather a coalition of neighboring states under his aegis around the year 594 BCE, and open rebellion finally broke out in the year 589/588 BCE.

At this point the Babylonian Chronicle is no longer extant. The second conquest of Jerusalem is known mainly from 2 Kings 25, parts of which are repeated with a number of modifications in Jeremiah 39 and 52. The siege extended over a period of one or two years (588 to 587 or 586 BCE, the year of Jerusalem's capture being uncertain) and resulted in a second deportation of the Judean population and the plunder of the remaining vessels and furnishings of the temple of Jerusalem. More information on the period can be obtained from some twenty ostraca found in the 1930s at the site of Tell ed-Duweir, identified by most scholars as ancient *Lachish. Most of them were found in a room adjoining the main gate of the fortification wall of the city and date to the period just before the destruction of the fortress by the Babylonians during the campaign of 587 BCE. They paint a vivid portrait of the last days of the kingdom of Judah.

Ostracon 3 is the most important one. It mentions that a commander of the Judean army was sent to Egypt ("The commander of the army, Koniah, son of Elnathan, has come down to go to Egypt"), and it refers to a message addressed by a prophet ("As to the letter of Tobiah, the king's servant, addressed to Shallum, son of Yada, from the prophet, saying 'Pay heed!'—your ser[vant] had sent it to my lord" [Smelik, 121-22]). This confirms Jeremiah 37:5, which claims that Egypt, ruled at that time by Pharaoh Apries, initially supported Zedekiah: "Meanwhile, the army of Pharaoh had come out of Egypt; and when the Chaldeans who were besieging Jerusalem heard news of them, they withdrew from Jerusalem" (NRSV). In the end, however, Egyptian military intervention failed to save Judah ("Pharaoh's army, which set out to help you, is going to return to its own land, to Egypt. And the Chaldeans shall return and fight against this city; they shall take it and burn it with fire" [Jer 37:7-8 NRSV; cf. Ezek 30:20-26]). As for the prophet mentioned at the end of the letter, it is tempting to identify him as Jeremiah, who was issuing warnings to his compatriots against blind reliance on Egyptian power. How-

ever, Jeremiah was not the only prophet active in Judah at that time. The letter nonetheless confirms their importance in the political life of Judah on the eve of the Babylonian conquest.

Ostracon 4 is also quite important. The names of the sender and recipient are not mentioned. Jerusalem is referred to as "the city," and the message ends with this statement: "And let him know that we ourselves are watching the smoke-signals from Lachish according to all the signals which my lord gives, for we cannot see Azekah" (Smelik, 125-27). This information strikingly corroborates Jeremiah 34:6-7, which claims that Jerusalem, Lachish and Azekah were the last strongholds of resistance to the Babylonians: "Then the prophet Jeremiah spoke all these words to Zedekiah king of Judah, in Jerusalem, when the army of the king of Babylon was fighting against Jerusalem and against all the cities of Judah that were left, Lachish and Azekah; for these were the only fortified cities of Judah that remained" (NRSV).

The biblical accounts of the capture of Jerusalem give the names of some Babylonian officials. Two of them can be identified from Babylonian sources. Nergal-shareser, mentioned in Jeremiah 39:3, 13 as the Babylonian commander-in-chief, is almost certainly identical with Nergal-shar-usur, who married Nebuchadnezzar's daughter and eventually usurped the throne from his brother-in-law Amel-Marduk (= Evil-Merodach). He reigned from 560 to 556 BCE. Another important Babylonian is Nebuzaradan. He entered Jerusalem with Nergal-shareser after its capture, looted and burned the temple, destroyed the city and organized the deportation to Babylonia, entrusting the remaining population to Gedaliah (2 Kings 25:8-20; Jer 39:9-10; 41:10; 52:12-26). He also freed Jeremiah (Jer 39:11-13; 40:1-5). Later, in 582 BCE, he was put in charge of the third Judean deportation to Babylonia (Jer 52:30). Evidently, he was a very important official and probably is identical with Nabûzēriddin, the highest court official listed in the *Hofkalender* of Nebuchadnezzar with the title *rab nuhatimmu*, which literally means "overseer of the cooks," but in reality referred to a head of the king's household or some kind of prime minister.

4. Judah Under Babylonian Rule.

After the capture of Jerusalem King Zedekiah fled, but he was captured near Jericho and taken to the Babylonian headquarters. His sons were executed in his presence. Then he was blinded and taken captive to Babylon. Jerusalem was extensively though not completely destroyed, clearly with the intent to eliminate it as capital of Judah. The Judean monarchy was abolished, its most prominent representatives now being in exile. Nebuchadnezzar installed a regional administration in Judah with a new capital at *Mizpah (= Tell en-Nasbeh), north of Jerusalem in Benjaminite territory. Nebuchadnezzar's appointee was Gedaliah, son of Ahikam, who belonged to a family of high officials in the kingdom of Judah (2 Kings 25:22; Jer 40:5). Sources for his administration are practically nonexistent. According to Jeremiah 41:1-10, it seems that Gedaliah governed under the surveillance of a Babylonian garrison stationed in Mizpah. His role appears therefore to have been little more than provincial governor under the control of the new imperial administration. The same passage tells us that he was murdered as part of a conspiracy led by a Judean royalist party under the leadership of Ishmael, son of Nethaniah, son of Elishama, a member of the royal family. The date of this conspiracy is unknown. However, Jeremiah 52:30 mentions another Judean deportation to Babylonia in the twenty-third year of Nebuchadnezzar (582/581 BCE), and thus it seems reasonable to assume that it occurred after Gedaliah's murder, which certainly would have been interpreted by the Babylonians as signaling a new rebellion. The account of the plot and its aftermath in Jeremiah 41—43 implies that this was indeed the case.

Recent scholarship on the situation in Judah after the conquest has concentrated largely on the extent to which the land was depopulated. On one side of the debate, there is the traditional view going back to the account of the Chronicler that the Babylonians practiced a systematic policy of destruction and deportation that left Judah a completely desolate area until settlement was allowed to resume in the early Persian period. This view is vindicated by the archaeological evidence of complete destruction at a number of sites, not only in the hills of Judah but also along the coast, Ashkelon being the most conspicuous case. On the other hand, it is obvious that neither Judah nor the surrounding areas were completely depopulated. Even parts of Jerusalem apparently remained inhabited.

Such evidence of continued settlement has induced some to label the traditional opinion as "the myth of the empty land" (Barstad, in Lipschits and Blenkinsopp, 3-20). This, however, is an excessive view. Although ancient traditions may have somewhat exaggerated the extent to which Judah was laid bare, the combined evidence from archaeological and literary sources leaves no doubt as to the greatly reduced state of the country under Babylonian rule (Oded, in Lipschits and Blenkinsopp, 55-74). It also appears that the Babylonians did not seek to exploit Judah systematically in the same way the Assyrians had reorganized their western provinces to benefit the empire economically (Vanderhooft, 104-14). One must also emphasize that contrary to the Assyrians, the Babylonians practiced only one-way deportations, from conquered regions to the center. Therefore it does not seem likely that people from other parts of the empire were settled in Judah, which must have remained demographically depleted under Babylonian rule. Clearly, there was a land to be reorganized and repopulated after the overthrow of the Babylonian regime in 539 BCE. This has led some to posit that Jerusalem and Judah were annexed to the old Assyrian province of Samaria, which would have remained largely intact under the Babylonians. Indeed, there is no evidence for destruction in that region comparable to what happened in Judah in the wake of Nebuchadnezzar's campaigns. However, the evidence for the administrative organization of Palestine under Babylonian rule is almost nonexistent, and therefore no such proposal can as yet be substantiated.

5. Judean Exiles in Babylonia.

The practice of mass deportations had been a mainstay of Assyrian imperialism in the previous centuries, sparing none of the conquered regions. These included the kingdoms of Israel and Judah, which saw many of their inhabitants deported in successive waves to various provinces of the Assyrian Empire. Thus there was already a large contingent of Israelite and Judean exiles in Mesopotamia before the Babylonian period, although we know virtually nothing about them. Eventually they gave rise to the legend of the "Ten Lost Tribes of Israel." Information on the communities exiled to Babylonia as a result of Nebuchadnezzar's campaigns can be gleaned from the Bible and from a growing number of cuneiform documents. Ration lists found in the North Palace in Babylon are the most important source because they mention the name of the exiled Jehoiakin with the title "king of Judah" and enumerate allocations of grain given to him and his five sons while in captivity (Weidner, 925-26; *ANET*, 308). Significantly, Jehoiakin and his family occur among various individuals from the western provinces, notably Byblos, Arwad and Tyre. Even Lydians and Greeks are mentioned. This evidence of relatively good treatment corroborates the biblical account and provides the background for the closing statement of the book of Kings that in the thirty-seventh year of his exile Jehoiakin was released by the Babylonian king Evil-Merodach (= Amel-Marduk), who treated him kindly: "So Jehoiakin put aside his prison clothes. Every day of his life he dined regularly in the king's presence. For his allowance, a regular allowance was given him by the king, a portion every day, as long as he lived" (2 Kings 25:29-30 NRSV).

Another source of information is onomastics. Since the nineteenth century, scholars have studied West Semitic anthroponyms appearing in cuneiform documents from the sixth and fifth centuries BCE with the purpose of finding names of Judean exiles and their descendants. Although a number of names that probably or certainly are Judean have been identified, until recently none of these documents gave any direct information on the life led by the exiles during the Babylonian period. Now, however, a number of cuneiform texts have surfaced that were drafted in two towns named Yahudu and Nashar. Only two of them have been published (Joannès and Lemaire 1999), the rest awaiting full treatment (Pearce). The name of the town Yahudu is identical with the usual designation of Jerusalem in Babylonian historical texts (*al Yahudu*, "city of Judah"). It is significant that the earliest tablet from this group, dated to the thirty-third year of Nebuchadnezzar (572/571 BCE), preserves the orthography *al Yahudaya*, "city of the Judeans," for Yahudu. This strongly suggests that the town had been named after settlers originating in Judah, no doubt a group of exiles. We have a number of parallel examples in cuneiform documents from the sixth century BCE of towns in Babylonia named after Levantine cities, such as Tyre and Sidon. These probably were also settled by deportees from the western provinces of the Babylonian Empire.

Internal evidence from the documents suggests that Yahudu and Nashar were situated in the region of Babylon and Borsippa. This is compatible with Psalm 137, which mentions "the rivers of Babylon" as one of the places where the Judean exiles established residence. This might refer to the network of streams and canals on the Euphrates River near the capital. Most of the texts from Yahudu and Nashar belong to the usual types of legal transactions found in Babylonian archives: promissory notes, receipts for payments, sale and lease documents. The most interesting information comes from the onomastic material. Out of 450 discrete names, no fewer than 122 are West Semitic, and approximately 60 of them contain a possibly Yahwistic element. The majority of these occur in texts from Yahudu, with only a few from Nashar. This indicates that Yahudu was partly settled with individuals of Judean descent.

Another place of settlement for the exiles, according to Ezekiel 1:3; 3:15, was a place called Tel-abib on the Chebar River. The latter has been identified as the Nār-Kabaru ("river Kabaru"), a watercourse in the vicinity of Nippur in central Babylonia mentioned in a handful of cuneiform documents from the sixth and fifth centuries BCE. Documents from Nippur dated to the late fifth century BCE belonging to the archive of the Murashu business family contain a number of West Semitic names that have long been identified as probably Judean. These may have been the descendants of the exiles settled at the Chebar River in the preceding century. The deportees of Judah truly paid heed to the advice of the prophet Jeremiah: "Build houses and live in them; plant gardens and eat what they produce. Take wives and have sons and daughters; take wives for your sons, and give your daughters in marriage, that they may bear sons and daughters; multiply there, and do not decrease" (Jer 29:5-6 NRSV).

Although Babylonia was the most important exile community, there is evidence that Israelites and Judeans had already established residence in Egypt by the time of the capture of Jerusalem. Even the *Arabian peninsula may have become home to Jewish communities toward the end of the Babylonian period, when the Babylonian king Nabonidus (556-539 BCE) conquered northern *Arabia and established residence for ten years in the oasis of Teima. It has been noted that the list of localities that he claims to have captured corresponds exactly to the areas where Jewish communities were attested later, before the rise of Islam. The possibility that Judean exiles followed the Babylonian armies to Arabia might also explain the persistent memory of Nabonidus and his son Belshazzar in the Jewish tradition, notably in the book of Daniel (where Nabonidus is merged with the figure of Nebuchadnezzar) and in the Prayer of Nabonidus from Qumran.

The exile had a profound impact on the culture of ancient Israel. In Babylonia *Aramaic became the main language of the Diaspora. The Aramaic square script was adapted to the *Hebrew language and became what we now know as the Hebrew square script. The exiles abandoned the old Hebrew calendar in favor of the Babylonian one. Many of them even went so far as to take Babylonian names, such as "Zerubbabel" (= Zer-Babili, "seed of Babylon") and "Sheshbazzar" (= Shamash-aba-usur, "O Shamash, protect the father"). The Deuteronomistic interpretation of Jewish history took final shape during the exile, and the Priestly stratum of the Pentateuch also emerged in the milieu of the Diaspora. These authors created the vision of Israel as a unique people bound to its God, the one true God, and laid the ground for the development of Judaism.

See also ASSYRIA, ASSYRIANS; BABYLONIA, BABYLONIANS; HISTORY OF ISRAEL 5: ASSYRIAN PERIOD; HISTORY OF ISRAEL 7: PERSIAN PERIOD; JEREMIAH; NON-ISRAELITE WRITTEN SOURCES: BABYLONIAN.

BIBLIOGRAPHY. **P.-A. Beaulieu,** *The Reign of Nabonidus, King of Babylon, 556-539 B.C.* (YNER 10; New Haven: Yale University Press, 1989); **I. Eph'al,** "Nebuchadnezzar the Warrior: Remarks on his Military Achievements," *IEJ* 53 (2000) 178-91; idem, "The Western Minorities in Babylonia in the 6th-5th Centuries B.C.," *Or* 47 (1978) 74-90; **A. K. Grayson,** *Assyrian and Babylonian Chronicles* (TCS 5; Locust Valley, NY: J. J. Augustin, 1975; repr., Winona Lake, IN: Eisenbrauns, 2000); **F. Joannès and A. Lemaire,** "Trois tablettes cunéiformes à onomastique ouest-sémitique," *Transeuphratène* 17 (1999) 17-34; **A. Lemaire,** *Inscriptions hébraïques: Les ostraca* (LAPO 9; Paris: Cerf, 1977); **O. Lipschits,** *The Fall and Rise of Jerusalem: Jerusalem Under Babylonian Rule* (Winona Lake, IN: Eisenbrauns, 2005); **O. Lipschits and J. Blenkinsopp,** eds., *Judah and the Judeans in the Neo-Babylonian Period* (Winona Lake, IN: Eisenbrauns, 2003); **P. Ma-**

chinist, "Mesopotamian Imperialism and Israelite Religion: A Case Study from the Second Isaiah," in *Symbiosis, Symbolism, and the Power of the Past: Canaan, Ancient Israel, and Their Neighbors from the Late Bronze Age through Roman Palaestina,* ed. W. G. Dever and S. Gitin (Winona Lake, IN: Eisenbrauns, 2003) 237-64; idem, "Palestine, Administration of (Assyro-Babylonian)," *ABD* 5.69-81; **A. Malamat,** "The Twilight of Judah: In the Egyptian-Babylonian Maelstrom," in *Congress Volume: Edinburgh 1974,* ed. G. W. Anderson (VTSup 28; Leiden: E. J. Brill, 1975) 123-45; **L. Pearce,** "New Evidence for Judeans in Babylonia," paper read at the conference "Judah and the Judeans in the Achaemenid Period," University of Heidelberg, July 15-18, 2003, to be published in *Judah and the Judeans in the Persian Period,* ed. M. Oeming and O. Lipschits (Winona Lake, IN: Eisenbrauns, forthcoming); **K. A. D. Smelik,** *Writing from Ancient Israel: A Handbook of Historical and Religious Documents* (Louisville: Westminster/John Knox, 1991); **L. E. Stager,** "Ashkelon and the Archaeology of Destruction: Kislev 604 BCE," *ErIsr* 25 (1996) 61*-72* [= "The Fury of Babylon: Ashkelon and the Archaeology of Destruction," *BAR* 22.1 (1996) 56-69, 76-77]; **E. Stern,** *Archaeology of the Land of the Bible, 2: The Assyrian, Babylonian, and Persian Periods, 732-332 BCE* (New York: Doubleday, 2001); idem, "Israel at the Close of the Monarchy: An Archaeological Survey," *BA* 38 (1975) 26-54; **D. Vanderhooft,** *The Neo-Babylonian Empire and Babylon in the Latter Prophets* (HSM 59; Atlanta: Scholars Press, 1999); **E. F. Weidner,** "Jojachin, König von Juda, in babylonischen Keilschrifttexten," in *Mélanges syriens offerts à Monsieur René Dussaud* (2 vols., paged continuously; Bibliothèque archéologi-que et historique 30; Geuthner: Paris, 1939) 923-35; **E. Yamauchi,** "The Eastern Jewish Diaspora under the Babylonians," in *Mesopotamia and the Bible: Comparative Explorations,* ed. M. W. Chavalas and K. L. Younger Jr. (Grand Rapids: Baker, 2002) 356-77.

P.-A. Beaulieu

HISTORY OF ISRAEL 7: PERSIAN PERIOD

The Persian period in the history of Israel begins in 539 and extends to approximately 330 BCE (*see* Persia, Persians). Little is known of Persian history before 550 BCE, but in the period beginning around 550 the small kingdom of Persia, settled in the region around the ancient city of Susa, began to expand under the able leadership of Cyrus II (the Great). After victories over the Medes and the Lydians, Cyrus turned his attention on the superpower of the day, Babylon, then ruled by Nabonidus (*see* Babylonia, Babylonians). In 539 BCE, Cyrus defeated the armies of Babylon in Opis and soon after entered the capital city. In this way he inherited the vast empire that had been created by the victories of Nabopolassar and Nebuchadnezzar (626-562 BCE.). This territory included Israel, since the northern kingdom was a Babylonian province from the time Nabopolassar had defeated *Assyria, who had earlier incorporated it (722 BCE.) as well as the southern kingdom, Judah. Judah had paid tribute to Babylon from at least 605, but after several rebellions, Nebuchadnezzar felt it necessary to pacify *Jerusalem, destroy much of it, including the temple, and to exile a number of its leading citizens. The focus of the biblical text during the Persian period is on Judah, now considered a Persian province (Yehud).

Alexander the Great brought the Persian period in Judah to a close in approximately 330 BCE. This was the year that, after a series of major defeats at the hand of the Greeks (Granicus [May 334], Issus [November 333] and Gaugamela [October 331]), the last Great King of Persia, Darius III, was assassinated by Bessos, the satrap of Bactria (July 330).

The following historical survey focuses on Persian history only in relationship with Yehud. Thus, attention will mainly be concentrated on the first part of the period, from 539 to approximately 400 BCE, though some minor details occurring during the final decades of the period will also be described.

1. Evaluation of Sources
2. The Cyrus Decree
3. The Early Postexilic Period: Sheshbazzar and Zerubbabel
4. The Later Postexilic Period: Ezra and Nehemiah
5. The Diaspora during the Persian Period
6. The Final Decades of the Persian Period

1. Evaluation of Sources.

1.1. Biblical Texts. Scholars debate over the scope and the historical reliability of the biblical texts that should be associated with the Persian period. While recent scholarship has tended to ascribe the final form of a majority, if not all, of the books of the Hebrew Bible to this period, those that are clearly set in the Persian period include the end (and certainly the final redaction) of *Chronicles, *Ezra-Nehemiah (in reality a single book), Esther, some stories in Daniel (chaps. 6, 9—11), Haggai, Zechariah and Malachi. Some scholars would add significant parts of Isaiah (particularly chaps. 56—66) to this list as well as Joel. Of these, Ezra-Nehemiah offers the single most extensive narrative concerning events in Yehud during the Persian period, while Esther provides a window on a moment in time in the Diaspora.

1.2. Near Eastern Texts. A variety of extrabiblical sources from within the Persian Empire are important to this period. Here focus will be given to those that have been particularly helpful in the reconstruction of the history and society of Judah during this period. They comprise a variety of different types of sources written in the different languages of the Empire (Akkadian, Elamite, Aramaic, Egyptian). Some are written by officials of the central government, others by entities within the satrapies of the empire.

A partial list includes the Babylonian Chronicle, the Cyrus Cylinder, the Behistun Inscription, the Elamite Persepolis tablets, the Murashu archive, the inscription of the Egyptian admiral Udjahorresnet and the Gatadas inscription. Most of these texts will be referenced below, but for a fuller discussion of their nature and contents, see L. L. Grabbe (1992, vol. 1; 2004). These texts have assumed a more significant role in the reconstruction of Persian history in recent work (Briant) since they give an inside picture of events in the empire. However, it would be a mistake to think that these texts are less biased because they were written by insiders (see Provan, Long and Longman, 62-70).

1.3. Greek Sources. Perhaps the most extensive narrative histories of the period come from Greek sources. From the time of Darius I (520-486 BCE) to the very end, Persian interests intersected with the Greek-speaking world in Asia Minor and the mainland. Thus, starting with Herodotus (490-425 BCE, traditionally thought of as the first writer of history), Greeks begin writing about Persian history, customs and institutions. Among the most important historians besides Herodotus, we can mention Thucydides, Xenophon and Ctesias. In this group we can even include the first-century CE Jewish historian Josephus, who wrote about the

Persian period in Greek.

In the past Herodotus was thought to be the most reliable source on the early Persian history because he lived during the period and demonstrated in his writings that he questioned his sources and did not accept them at face value. However, Herodotus, along with all the other Greek writers, is now treated with much more skepticism than previously on the belief that his pro-Greek viewpoint caused him to skew his presentation.

1.4. Archaeological Materials. Besides textual material, researchers also have recourse to the results of archaeological exploration. According to the experts, the Persian period (often called Iron III in archaeological terminology) is difficult to distinguish in the archaeological record of Palestine (see Carter 1999; Stern) (*see* Archaeology, Syro-Palestinian). P. M. McNutt also acknowledges this limitation but cautiously suggests that "the archaeological data we do have do seem to be consistent with some elements in the biblical record" (McNutt, 185). Special notice should be given to the discovery of bullae and cylinder seals (and impressions) that have helped scholars expand the list of known governors of Yehud during the Persian period (Avigad).

2. The Cyrus Decree.

The rise of Persia under Cyrus II is described in general terms in the introductory paragraph of this article. Persian history intersects with Judean history beginning with the defeat of Babylon in 539 BCE.

The Hebrew Bible follows up the report of Cyrus's victory by citing what is commonly known as the Cyrus Decree (2 Chron 36:23; Ezra 1:2-4; cf. also Ezra 6:3-6; 1 Esdr 2:3-7). In this document, Cyrus proclaims that none other than Yahweh, the God of Israel, has commissioned him to allow the people of Judah to return to their land, ending decades of exile instituted by the Babylonians. In addition, he charges the returnees with the task of reconstructing the destroyed temple and even provides them with funds from the royal treasury.

From a Judean perspective Cyrus was a messiah, an anointed deliverer (Is 45:1-7). Documents from the ancient Near East provide a broader perspective. In 1879 H. Rassam uncovered a barrel-shaped cuneiform document that is now in the British Museum and is commonly referred to as the Cyrus Cylinder (*ANET,* 316; *COS* 2.124:314-16). In it Cyrus decreed that the native cults of the Babylonians also were to be restored. Thus, scholars have concluded that the biblical decree directed at the Jewish people is part of an empire-wide program by which the Persians allowed a number, if not all, of the people subjugated by Babylon to return to their lands. This policy was not totally altruistic, however. These people, including Judah, were vassals of the Persians, but the Persians operated with the idea that happy vassals would serve their best interests. A peaceful and supportive Judah, for instance, would make it easier for the armies of Persia to march to one of their most desired destinations for expansion, Egypt (Berquist, 62-63).

However, a minority of scholars (Sacchi, 11) expresses skepticism about the reliability of the Cyrus decrees as recorded in the Bible. Rather than seeing the Akkadian Cyrus Cylinder as supporting the general policy represented in the Decree, P. Sacchi argues that the Cylinder only proves that the policy applies to Babylon. Further, he believes that the wording of the Cyrus Decree in the Bible could only have been written by a Jewish theologian and therefore is fictional.

However, A. Kuhrt has suggested that Cyrus may have enlisted native theologians or diplomats to write local versions of his decree, thus explaining the Babylonian perspective of the Cyrus Cylinder and the Judean perspective of the biblical decree. B. Halpern similarly argues that what we have in Chronicles and Ezra is not the decree itself but a paraphrase and selective rendition of the original Cyrus Decree. No matter what the Persian motivation or the scope of its restoration, the Jewish community living in exile saw the hand of God in this decree.

3. The Early Postexilic Period: Sheshbazzar and Zerubbabel.

The biblical text does not purport to give an exhaustive record of all who returned from the exile and their leaders, but it does focus on the activities of two men who led two different groups back to Judah, namely Sheshbazzar and *Zerubbabel. Sheshbazzar is mentioned first in the narrative of Ezra-Nehemiah and clearly was the first of the two to come back to the land. He was charged by Cyrus to take back with him the temple vessels that were stolen by Nebuchadnezzar (Dan 1) and profaned by Belshazzar (Dan 5). In this context, Sheshbazzar was called the "prince *[nāśî']* of Judah," a title that at one time was thought to link him to the Judean royal family (along with a now denied identification with Shenazzar in 1 Chron 3:18; see Berger), but now is considered simply a way of referring to him as a leader of the community (*NIDOTTE* 3:171-72). Ezra 5 contains a letter written by Tattenai, the governor (so Yamauchi, 156, though Eph'al claims that he is a satrap) of "Across-the-River," and his associates to Darius, the third great king. Darius did not begin to rule until 522 BCE, so this is some time later. Tattenai and his associates have challenged the claim that Cyrus issued a decree to rebuild their temple, so they appealed to Darius, who then checked the royal records kept at Ecbatana. In this letter, Tattenai refers to Sheshbazzar as governor, and thus the first Persian-appointed governor of the province of which we are aware. He also records that Sheshbazzar has already laid the foundation of the temple.

More is known about Zerubbabel from the biblical record. He is mentioned in a genealogy in Chronicles (1 Chron 3:19), Ezra-Nehemiah, Haggai, Zechariah and 1 Esdras. Likely his return was at the head of a later wave than Sheshbazzar's, maybe even as late as the 520s BCE. Zerubbabel is associated with Jeshua/Joshua, the high priest, in Ezra 2 and also in Zechariah. The two are said to have rebuilt the altar and to have reinstituted regular sacrificial ritual. Zerubbabel is also said to have laid the foundation of the temple (Ezra 3:10), surprising because we have observed that Sheshbazzar had already laid the foundation (*see* Postexilic Temple).

In any case, after these initial steps to rebuild the temple, opposition arose to their efforts from a group simply called "the enemies of Judah and Jerusalem" (Ezra 4:1). A vigorous scholarly debate has arisen concerning the identity of these enemies. Some take them to be the descendants of those Judeans who remained in the land during the exile, who came into conflict with the returnees, a group constituted of leaders, who thus may have had a condescending attitude toward the "poor" who had remained. In addition, advocates of this position argue that there may have been conflict over limited land as people returned from Persia (McNutt, 183, 199). However, this theory is unlikely on the basis of what the text itself represents these people as saying. While they are Yahweh worshipers, they also reveal that they only came into Palestine during the reign of Esarhaddon, the king of Assyria who ruled at the end of the eighth and early seventh centuries BCE. The Assyrians moved people around within their empire, and so these people were brought into the northern part of Israel after the Assyrians had deported its former inhabitants. Furthermore, in answer to some of the arguments in favor of seeing the enemies as those who stayed in Judah during the exile, we should point out that archaeology indicates that there was plenty of land to go around (Carter 1995, 440).

Due to the actions of these "enemies," work on the temple languished for a period of time. However, around 520 BCE the prophets Haggai and Zechariah successfully preached that God desired the resumption of the building. Though the builders encountered the above-mentioned challenge of Tattenai and his associates, Darius reconfirmed the commission of Cyrus, and the work on the temple was completed by 515 BCE.

Haggai and Zechariah give us more information about Zerubabbel. He is a descendant of David (see also 1 Chron 3:19) and the Persian-appointed governor of Judah. On the basis of some of the language used of Zerubbabel, it seems a safe conjecture that there was messianic expectation attached to him (Hag 2:20-23, see Japhet and Petersen). However, if this was so, it was short-lived. Zerubbabel mysteriously disappears from the biblical record, giving rise to the scholarly speculation that he was removed from the scene by the Persians, who did not want these expectations to escalate to seditious actions.

4. The Later Postexilic Period: Ezra and Nehemiah.

Our sources do not provide much information about what went on in Palestine during the period between the completion of the temple in 515 BCE and the arrival of Ezra in Jerusalem in 458 BCE. An exception to this is found in Ezra 4:6-23, which H. G. M. Williamson identifies as a long parenthetical statement marked by a "repetitive resumption" that breaks up an account of opposition to temple building during the reign of Darius (Williamson 1985, 57). The parenthetical statement briefly describes an accusation leveled against the Jews during the reign of

Xerxes (486-465 BCE) and a longer report of a successful attempt to stop the reconstruction of Jerusalem of Artaxerxes I (465-424 BCE), though it is not clear when this took place (though it seems logical to think that it was before Nehemiah's work began). The most substantial report of the fifth century concerns Ezra and Nehemiah.

4.1. The Books of Ezra and Nehemiah. The main source for events in Palestine during what we are calling the late postexilic period comes from the books of Ezra and Nehemiah. While Ezra 1—6 concerns events mainly in the period 539-515 BCE, Ezra 7—Nehemiah 13 describe events associated with Ezra and Nehemiah from c. 458 to 430 BCE.

Interestingly, much of Ezra 7 through Nehemiah has the form of an autobiography or memoir. Ezra's memoir is found in Ezra 7—10 and Nehemiah 8, while Nehemiah's encompasses Nehemiah 1—7; 12:27-43; 13:4-31. While some might argue that a memoir heightens confidence in historical reliability, since the writer was a witness to events, D. J. A. Clines, L. L. Grabbe and G. Garbini have each cast doubt on this proposition by either suggesting that autobiographical accounts are likely to be biased or suggesting that the writing is a fictional autobiography. However, Williamson (1995, 257) has shown that Nehemiah's first-person account is generally supported by third-person reports in the book of Nehemiah, which "serves both to support the general historical drift of the narrative and to underscore Nehemiah's own bias from a different direction." Once we accept the basic reliability of the reporting, however, we still must grapple with the fact that the narrative is very selective and episodic. In another place, Williamson points out that "well illuminated are . . . the twelve months of Ezra's work, the building of the wall under Nehemiah and its immediate sequel (say 12 months), and an unchronological account of various reforms some twelve or fifteen years later" (Williamson 1987, 198).

4.2. The Dates of Ezra and Nehemiah. On the surface, the dates for the work of Ezra and Nehemiah appear straightforward. According to Ezra 7:6, Ezra arrived in Jerusalem in the seventh year of Artaxerxes and, according to Nehemiah 2:1, Artaxerxes granted Nehemiah permission to return to Jerusalem in his twentieth year. A complication arises due to the name Artaxerxes, which was a throne name

taken by three kings of Persia:

Artaxerxes I (465-424 BCE)
Artaxerxes II (404-359 BCE)
Artaxerxes III (358-338 BCE)

The date for Nehemiah is relatively uncontested and is set at the twentieth year of Artaxerxes I and thus 445 BCE. Ezra's date is debated, though there is a tendency recently to affirm the traditional date during the same king's reign and thus place his arrival before Nehemiah's in 458 BCE.

However, some scholars contest this traditional dating. For one thing, if Nehemiah arrived after Ezra, why do they not appear in tandem in the narrative more often (some even believe that those passages in which Ezra and Nehemiah appear together are a late editorial manipulation [Neh 8:9; 12:26, 36]). For this and other reasons, they prefer the date 398 BCE, the seventh year of Artaxerxes II. The view that Ezra 7:6 requires a textual emendation to read twenty-seven (thus 438 BCE) or thirty-seven (thus 428 BCE) does not have active defenders. For a defense of the traditional view, see Williamson (1985, xxxix-xliv) and Yamauchi (1990, 253-56).

4.3. Ezra and the Law of God. Ezra was a priest and a teacher of the *law of God (Ezra 7:11). He received permission and support from Artaxerxes to return to Jerusalem in order to teach the law of God. The biblical text takes the position that Artaxerxes allowed this because God moved his heart to do so (Ezra 7:27). Below (see 4.5) we will explore the less altruistic motives that God used to bring the Great King to this point.

The sin that the narrative reports as Ezra's (and also Nehemiah's) most persistent issue is intermarriage. Jewish men were taking foreign wives, and Ezra confronted them in this regard. It is true that the Torah contains no law specifically banning marriage with foreign women. However, going back to the patriarchal narratives, there is the record of animosity toward such unions, particularly with non-Israelites within the land (Gen 24; 28:1-9). Furthermore, in a postexilic context the aversion to such mixed marriages would have been even more keenly felt since the Deuteronomistic History contains stories of events, such as Solomon's marriage to foreign women, that were important contributing causes to the exile in the first place. While some try to hold up the book of Ruth as a counterexample, even as a challenge to the views of Ezra and Nehemiah on this matter, the comparison is not valid since Ruth, in essence, became an Israelite with her declaration to Naomi that "Your people will be my people and your God my God" (Ruth 1:16).

In any case, Ezra's confrontation with these men caused most of them to repent and rid themselves of their foreign wives. Many scholars (Williamson 1985, 129, 279-86) suggest that Ezra's reading of the law recorded in Nehemiah 8 should be historically situated between his arrival in Jerusalem (Ezra 8) and the people's confession (Ezra 9).

4.4. Nehemiah and the Walls of Jerusalem. Though Nehemiah supports many of the values of Ezra, his primary mission was considerably different. He was not a teacher and a priest, but Artaxerxes' cupbearer who became the governor of the province of Judah. The office of cupbearer was not a menial job but one of great importance and intimacy with the king. After receiving a report of the poor condition of Jerusalem, Nehemiah's sad countenance could not be ignored by the king. After finding out the cause of his sadness, Artaxerxes commissioned him to rebuild the walls of Jerusalem.

Nehemiah then traveled to Jerusalem and energetically began his work. However, as with Sheshbazzar and Zerubbabel before him, Nehemiah soon found that he had opposition. The three men specifically mentioned as stirring up trouble for Nehemiah were Tobiah, Sanballat and Geshem. Interestingly, extrabiblical evidence illumines the identity of all three. An Elephantine letter from 410 BCE identifies Sanballat as the "governor of Samaria" (Briant, 587). There are Aramaic inscriptions that indicate that Tobiah was part of a dynasty in the Transjordan; P. Briant (587) speculates he may have been governor of this area. Geshem the Arab is likely the same person as that mentioned on dedication inscriptions found on silver objects at Tell el-Mashuta in Egypt. He is usually taken as leader of the Arab Qedarite kingdom (Yamauchi 1990, 268-70).

Even so, Nehemiah's persistence won the day and the wall was completed. Though this was the focus of his attention, Nehemiah too was concerned about the spiritual well-being of the people. On the day of the dedication of the wall, the book of Moses was read to all the people (Neh 13:1). In Nehemiah 13 Nehemiah prays to God citing all the work that he had done in order to maintain the purity of the people, though

he also expresses his frustration at their continuing sin.

4.5. Persian Self-Interest. As mentioned above, the Bible attributes Persian permission and support for the promulgation of the law and the rebuilding of the wall to God. Even so, God might use secondary causes, and in this case it appears likely that he did. The Persians had a vested interest and what appears to be a coherent foreign policy in acting as they did.

K. Hoglund set the stage for the most recent understanding of the Persian motivation for the work of Ezra and Nehemiah when he placed their work within the broader framework of the military-political events of their day. His reading of the biblical text takes into account archaeological discoveries, such as a distinctive type of fortress built in the middle of the fifth century in Judah, as well as Greek sources on the period. What emerges from his study is that Artaxerxes bolstered Judah in order to have a friendly and reasonably strong ally to protect the border of his empire against the growing threat from Greece and Egypt. Hoglund's thesis has been refined in the work of J. Berquist. The research of Hoglund, Berquist and others makes clear that Judah enjoyed Persian patronage for self-serving motivations, at least during the early part of Artaxerxes' reign.

In addition to this we might introduce the analogy between the relationship of Ezra and Nehemiah with Artaxerxes and an earlier one between an Egyptian named Udjahorresnet and Darius I (Blenkinsopp). Udjahorresnet served the cause of Persia, and Darius supported him in further restoration of certain Egyptian institutions, including the "codification and enforcement of local law codes" (Blenkinsopp, 413).

5. The Diaspora During the Persian Period.
After the Cyrus Decree many Judeans returned to the area around Jerusalem, but not all by far. Many chose to stay in the lands where they had settled during the exile. Thus the Diaspora ("the scattering") came into being. The book of Esther is a narrative set within the Diaspora, and the story is situated during the reign of king Xerxes, who ruled from 486 to 465 BCE.

Many question the historical reliability of the book of Esther. While some, like J. D. Levenson and A. Berlin, admit that it is familiar with a number of authentic Persian customs, they suggest that these points just provide a sense of verisimilitude. In other words, Esther is a history-like story but not an authentic historical work.

Even so, commentators (Jobes) have tried to read the book within the context of the history of the reign of Xerxes. For instance, the banquet thrown in the first chapter is often associated with a huge feast thrown by the king on the eve of an unsuccessful campaign against the Greeks, as mentioned by Herodotus. In addition, the secondary literature has endless debates concerning whether or not the book reflects Persian customs (like the "law of the Medes and Persians" being unalterable) or historical details (there is no record of a Vashti as Xerxes's queen, but there is much about a woman named Amestris).

The debate over the accuracy of the historical details of the Esther narrative will continue into the future. However, the book does open a window on important features of life in the Persian diaspora. For instance, many Jews have integrated into society. Both Mordecai and Esther bear names that are Persian, though Esther also had a Hebrew name (Hadassah, Esther 2:7). At the beginning of the book, Mordecai already has assumed what appears to be a high status in society, and by the end an even higher one. On a darker side, the book also indicates that God's people spread abroad were already the focus of the jealous violence of their enemies.

6. The Final Decades of the Persian Period.
The biblical texts give us a selective view of Judah and the Jews abroad during the Persian period. In particular, the narratives that concern Judah focus on two periods of time: 539-515 BCE, the leadership of Sheshbazzar and Zerubbabel and the rebuilding of the temple; and 458 to about 430 BCE (and this selectively), the leadership of Ezra and Nehemiah, the promulgation of the law and the construction of the city walls. In addition, the book of Esther relates an important incident sometime during the reign of the Persian king Xerxes (486-465 BCE).

The outline of Persian history is fairly well known in the period after the reign of Artaxerxes I until the downfall of the empire at the hands of the Greeks. However, only rarely are there documents or artifacts that relate events in Judah or among the Jewish people of the Diaspora.

6.1. The Jewish Community at Elephantine. One exception comes from the Aramaic documents that describe the activities of a Jewish community on the island of Elephantine, located near the first Cataract of the Nile (*see* Non-Israelite Written Sources: Egyptian Aramaic Papyri). While some Elephantine documents were known earlier, the bulk of them were discovered between 1893 and 1917. The texts include private and official letters, contracts, an important literary text (*The Wisdom of Ahiqar*), as well as an Aramaic copy of the Behistun inscription.

The Jewish community located at Elephantine was a military garrison, and the Jews were mercenaries (Porten). The origin of this community is not known, but they were there before the Persians (under Cambyses) defeated the Egyptians and made it a satrapy of the Persian Empire. The most interesting texts related to Jewish history derive from the decade of 420-410 BCE. It is in this period that we find correspondence between an official named Hananiah, who is relaying instructions from the Great King Darius II and the Egyptian satrap Arasames to the Jews at Elephantine concerning the observance of Passover. The addressee was Jedaniah, known as a religious leader of the community. What is most interesting about this letter is that it confirms a pattern of Persian involvement in the authorization of Jewish religious practices, but precisely what was at issue here (the date, the combination of Passover and Unleavened Bread or the practice of Passover in Egypt, which might be sensitive for obvious reasons) is unclear.

It is some years later, 411 or 410 BCE, that we have another letter, this time from the above-mentioned Jedaniah to Bagohi (Bagoas), the governor of Judah, with the mention also that "we have set the whole matter forth in a letter in our name to Delaiah and Shelemiah, the sons of Sanballat the governor of Samaria." This *Sanballat is likely the opponent of Nehemiah mentioned in Nehemiah 2:10, 19 and confirms the fact that he was governor. In any case, the letter appeals to these two governors for permission to rebuild the temple devoted to Yaho (YHWH) that was destroyed by the Egyptian priests of Khnum with the consent of an official whose name was Vidranga. In this letter they make mention of another letter that they sent concerning the matter of rebuilding to Johanan the high priest (Neh 12:22-23), but this letter has gone unanswered. Interestingly, the finds have also yielded a memorandum of an oral response from the Judean governor and from the son of the Samarian governor to the effect that they gave permission to rebuild the temple. But permission to offer animal sacrifices is conspicuously absent, perhaps indicating a belief that this should be done only in Jerusalem. There is a contract from the Anani archive that indicates that the temple was up and operating by 402 BCE.

6.2. Murder in the Temple. In his *Jewish Antiquities* Josephus mentions that Joannes (Johanan) murdered his brother, the high priest Jesus. He also describes how an official, Bagoas, levied a tax on sacrifices as punishment. Josephus though cannot be trusted in terms of his dating of this event, and it is tempting to date it close to the end of the fifth century since the Elephantine papyri name a high priest Johanan and a governor Bagoas. Williamson (1977) has noted that these are common names and suggests rather that this event took place during the reign of Artaxerxes III, pointing out that we have a coin now with "Yohanan the Priest" from the mid-fourth century. He further draws attention to a Persian military leader named Bagoas from the time of Artaxerxes III (Williamson 1995, 21-22).

See also EZRA; EZRA AND NEHEMIAH, BOOKS OF; HISTORY OF ISRAEL 8: POSTEXILIC COMMUNITY; NEHEMIAH; NON-ISRAELITE WRITTEN SOURCES: EGYPTIAN ARAMAIC PAPYRI; NON-ISRAELITE WRITTEN SOURCES: OLD PERSIAN AND ELAMITE; PERSIA, PERSIANS; POSTEXILIC TEMPLE; SANBALLAT; ZERUBBABEL.

BIBLIOGRAPHY. **N. Avigad,** *Bullae and Seals from a Post-Exilic Judean Archive,* Qedem 4 (Jerusalem: Jerusalem Institute of Archaeology, Hebrew University, 1976); **P.-R. Berger,** "Zu den Namen *ssbsr* und *sn'sr*," *ZAW* 83 (1981) 98-100; **A. Berlin,** *Esther* (Philadelphia: JPS Publishing, 2001); **J. Berquist,** *Judaism in Persia's Shadow: A Social and Historical Approach* (Minneapolis: Fortress, 1995); **J. Blenkinsopp,** "The Mission of Udjahorresnet and Those of Ezra and Nehemiah," *JBL* 106 (1987) 409-21; **P. Briant,** *From Cyrus to Alexander: A History of the Persian Period* (Winona Lake, IN: Eisenbrauns, 2002); **C. E. Carter,** *The Emergence of Yehud in the Persian Period: A Social and Demographic Study* (JSOTSup 294; Sheffield: Sheffield Academic Press, 1999); idem, "Opening Windows onto Biblical Worlds," in *The Face of Old Testament Study,* ed. D. W. Baker and B. T. Arnold (Grand Rapids: Baker, 1995) 421-51; **D. J. A. Clines,** "The Nehemiah Memoir: The Perils of Autobiography," in *What Does Eve Do to Help" and Other Readerly Questions to the Old Testament* (JSOTSup 94; Sheffield: Sheffield Academic Press, 1990); **M. D. Coogan,** *West Semitic Personal Names in the Murasu Documents* (HSM 7; Atlanta: Scholars Press, 1976); **F. M. Cross,** "A Reconstruction of the Judean Restoration," *JBL* 94 (1975) 4-18; **I. Eph'al,** "Syria-Palestine Under Achaemenid Rule," in *CAH*[2] 4:139-64; **T. Eskenazi,** "Current Perspectives on Ezra-Nehemiah and the Persian Period," *Currents in Research: Biblical Studies* 1 (1993) 59-86; **T. C. Eskenazi and K. H. Richards,** eds., *Second Temple Studies, 2: Temple and Community in the Persian Period* (JSOTSup 175; Sheffield: Sheffield Academic Press, 1994); **G. Garbini,** *History and Ideology in Ancient Israel* (New York: Crossroad, 1988); **L. L. Grabbe,** *Judaism from Cyrus to Hadrian* (2 vols.; Minneapolis: Fortress, 1992); idem, *A History of the Jews and Judaism in the Second Temple Period,* Vol. 1: *Yehud: A History of the Persian Province of Judah* (LSTS 47; London: T & T Clark International, 2004); **B. Halpern,** "A Historiographic Commentary on Ezra 1-6: Achronological Narrative and Dual Chronology in Israelite Historiography," in *The Hebrew Bible and Its Interpreters,* ed. W. H. Propp, B. Halpern and D. N. Freedman (BibJS 1; Winona Lake, IN: Eisenbrauns, 1990) 81-142; **K. Hoglund,** *Achaemenid Imperial Administration in Syria-Palestine and the Missions of Ezra and Nehemiah* (SBLDS 125; Atlanta: Scholars Press, 1992); **D. Jansen,** "The 'Mission' of Ezra and the Persian Period Temple Community," *JBL* 119 (2000) 623-46; **S. Japhet,** "Sheshbazzar and Zerubbabel—Against the Background of the Historical and Religious Tendencies of Ezra-Nehemiah," *ZAW* 94 (1982) 66-98; **K. Jobes,** *Esther* (NIVAC; Grand Rapids: Zondervan, 1999); **A. Kuhrt,** "The Cyrus Cylinder and Achaemenid Imperial Policy," *JSOT* 25 (1983) 83-97; **J. D. Levenson,** *Esther* (OTL; Louisville: Westminster John Knox, 1997); **P. M. McNutt,** *Reconstructing the Society of Ancient Israel* (Louisville: Westminster John Knox, 1999); **D. L. Petersen,** "Zerubbabel and Jerusalem Temple Reconstruction," *CBQ* 36 (1974) 366-72; **B. Porten,** *Archives from Elephantine: The Life of an Ancient Jewish Military Colony* (Berkeley and Los Angeles: University of California Press, 1968**); I. Provan, V. P. Long and T. Longman III,** *A Biblical History of Israel* (Louisville: Westminster John Knox, 2003); **P. Sacchi,** *The History of the Second Temple Period* (JSOTSup 285; Sheffield: Sheffield Academic

Press, 2000); **E. Stern,** *Archaeology of the Land of the Bible: The Assyrian, Babylonian, and Persian Periods, 732-332 BCE* (ABRL; New York: Doubleday, 2001); **M. W. Stolper,** *Entrepreneurs and Empire: The Murashu Archives, the Murashu Firm, and Persian Rule in Babylonia* (Uitgaven van het Nederlands Historisch-Archaeologisch Institut te Istanbul 54; Leiden: E. J. Brill, 1985); **J. P. Weinberg,** *The Citizen-Temple Community* (JSOTSup 151; Sheffield: Sheffield Academic Press, 1992); **H. G. M. Williamson,** "The Exile and After: Historical Study," in *The Face of Old Testament Study,* ed. D. W. Baker and B. T. Arnold (Grand Rapids: Baker, 1995) 236-65; idem, *Ezra, Nehemiah* (WBC; Nashville: Thomas Nelson, 1985); idem, "The Governors of Judah under the Persians," *TynBul* 39 (1988) 59-82; idem, "The Historical Value of Josephus' *Jewish Antiquities* XI 2970301," *JTS* 28 (1977) 49-66; idem, "Post-Exilic Historiography," in *The Future of Biblical Studies: The Hebrew Scriptures,* ed. R. E. Friedman and H. G. M. Williamson (Atlanta: Scholars Press, 1987) 189-207; idem, *Studies in Persian Period History and Historiography* (FAT 38; Tübingen: Mohr Siebeck, 2004); **E. Yamauchi,** *Persia and the Bible* (Grand Rapids: Baker, 1990); idem, "The Reverse Order of Ezra/Nehemiah Reconsidered," *Themelios* 5 (1980) 12-13; **R. Zadok,** *The Jews in Babylonia during the Chaldean and Achaemenian Period* (SHJPLI 3; Haifa: University of Haifa Press, 1979).   T. Longman III

HISTORY OF ISRAEL 8: POSTEXILIC COMMUNITY

The period of the postexilic community is commonly seen as beginning with the repatriation of exiled Judeans and their descendants to their homeland under Cyrus the Great's edict of 538 BCE, though historically speaking the picture is decidedly more complex. The period includes the rebuilding of a temple in Jerusalem under the appointed governors Sheshbazzar and then *Zerubbabel, the later governorship of *Nehemiah, the mission of *Ezra and subsequent events that extend into the fourth century.

1. Defining the Postexilic Community
2. Prospects for a History of the Postexilic Community
3. The Period of Temple Reconstruction
4. The Governorship of Nehemiah
5. The Mission of Ezra
6. The Fourth Century BCE

1. Defining the Postexilic Community.

The expression *postexilic community* is commonly used to denote a specific group of Judeans who resided in their homeland during the Achaemenid Persian period (539-333 BCE). While it is recognized that other communities of Judeans were living in Mesopotamia, Elam, Egypt and perhaps elsewhere, the group in view here consisted of Judeans and their descendants, who had been exiled to Babylonia at the demise of the kingdom of Judah in 587 BCE and were repatriated to their homeland beginning with Cyrus the Great's edict of 538 BCE. Their repatriation marks the beginning of the "postexilic" period. Following Ezra-Nehemiah, the experience of exile and return serves to distin-guish members of this community from others living in and around the district of Judah who were foreigners or who were Judeans who never went into exile. The use of the term *community* is an attempt to recognize that in this period Judah was no longer a kingdom, and so the repatriates need to be denoted by some other form of association. Moreover, for many commentators, *community* as a designation is to be preferred to *Judah* because it further seeks to differentiate between the group of repatriates and the Achaemenid Persian district of Judah (Aramaic *Yĕhûd*), all of whose inhabitants might properly be called "Judeans."

This limiting sense of *postexilic community* is problematic, however. As Ezra-Nehemiah itself attests, Judeans who remained in the Babylonian-Elamite diaspora saw themselves as forming a single community with the repatriated exiles in Judah despite their geographical separation (Bedford 2002). Because Judeans in the Babylonian-Elamite diaspora considered the repatriates to be their representatives in the homeland, they too can be construed as members of the postexilic community—the community that has returned to the homeland from exile. There is a further problem: why accept Ezra-Nehemiah's definition of the limits of the community in Judah? It is clear enough from this text that some (many?) repatriated Judeans did not draw a distinction between themselves and Judeans and other local Yahwists who had never gone into exile. For these repatriates and/or their descendants, exile was not a defining characteristic of identity, and so *postexilic* would be a misnomer for them. Perhaps it would be less prejudicial to speak of their understanding of

493

the community as being *postmonarchical* rather than *postexilic*. Similarly, Haggai and Zechariah 1—8 do not evidence a division between repatriates and nonrepatriates at the time of the temple rebuilding, and the community may also include Yahwists from *Samaria (Bedford 2001, 264-85). Furthermore, the books of Chronicles, conventionally dated to the fourth century BCE, emphasize the underlying unity of Judeans with their coreligionists living in *Samaria (Japhet, 325-34). This highlights that contemporary biblical texts display a variety of perspectives as to the identity of the postexilic community.

2. Prospects for a History of the Postexilic Community.

While any history of the postexilic community obviously is predicated on the definition of that expression, academic discussions have focused on the repatriates as the central element of the postexilic community. It is widely agreed that pertinent to an understanding of this community is (1) the relationships within the group of repatriates; (2) the set of relationships between the repatriates and (a) those they found living in and around Judah at their return, (b) Judeans remaining in the Babylonian-Elamite diaspora and (c) the Achaemenid Persian administration. The following sections can comment on but a few aspects of these complex and keenly debated relationships.

It is important to note that currently it is impossible to write a narrative history of Achaemenid Judah or of the Judean community in Judah (however defined). The biblical texts generally dated to this period—Haggai, Zechariah 1—8, Joel, Isaiah 55—66, Malachi, Ezra-Nehemiah, 1-2 Chronicles—do not afford sufficient evidence for the undertaking, and extrabiblical sources (Elephantine papyri, Josephus, epigraphical texts, Achaemenid Persian texts), while adding some important information, do not fill in many of the historical lacunae. Including biblical texts that might arguably be dated to this period—Proverbs 1—9, the Priestly source in the Pentateuch, the whole of the Pentateuch in its final form, some of the psalms, Esther, redactions of preexilic texts, and so on—increases the evidentiary base but also adds to interpretive problems, seen most conspicuously in the parties or social groups that the various texts often are held to represent. The biblical sources ascribed to this period, as well as their relative dating, obviously directly affect the historical reconstruction offered.

A primary problem has been establishing the relationship between the relevant biblical sources, however they are identified. Histories traditionally closely follow Ezra-Nehemiah and seek to relate the other sources to it. Ezra-Nehemiah offers an account of only a few discontinuous events from the period of 538-c. 400 BCE: restoration and temple rebuilding (Ezra 1:1—4:5, 24; 5:1—6:22), covering parts of 538-515 BCE; the halting of the wall reconstruction (Ezra 4:6-23), dated to some time in the fifth century BCE; the missions of *Ezra (Ezra 7—10) and *Nehemiah (Neh 1—13), with Ezra dated to either 458 BCE or 398 BCE (depending on whether he served under Artaxerxes I or II) and Nehemiah dated to 445-432 BCE (Ezra and Nehemiah are contemporaries in Neh 8—10). This is a problematic historical source, not only because of its distinctive view of the limits of the community and the selective nature of the events recounted. As recent studies show, the historical value of Ezra-Nehemiah remains a contentious issue (see Grabbe; cf. Williamson 1985). Following Ezra-Nehemiah, the history of the community often is recounted as a series of conflicts between it and the other groups living in and around Judah, and accounts often include an element of conflict within the community itself over its religious character, direction and leadership (e.g., Hanson, 253-324; Smith, 75-141). Other accounts, while recognizing the role of social conflict, highlight the role of the Achaemenid Persian administration in the history of the community. J. P. Weinberg contends that the central administration established a "citizen-temple community" that was embedded in the district of Judah. Its members, initially all repatriates, had a close connection to the Jerusalem temple that gave them rights to real estate. This community expanded over time to incorporate much of the district of Judah and its population. In this perspective, the history of the postexilic community is the history of the citizen-temple community (*see* Postexilic Temple). Whether social conflict was as endemic to the history of the postexilic community as Ezra-Nehemiah and many historical reconstructions avow, and whether this community was indeed of any particular interest to the Achaemenid Persian administration, are issues that continue to receive critical attention. All discussions attempt to elucidate the shifting and competing understandings of the extent and character of the community evidenced in the contemporary biblical texts as a means of representing postmonarchical Judean self-definition in the homeland.

3. The Period of Temple Reconstruction.

Ostensibly, the purpose of the initial repatriation of Judeans under Sheshbazzar in 538 BCE was to rebuild the temple of Yahweh in Jerusalem (Ezra 1:1-11), but little if anything was done on the project at that time. This inertia was not due to the intervention of Samarians, as Ezra 4:1-5 claims, even accepting that they were unlikely to be supporters. The lack of a legitimate temple rebuilder and concerns over whether this was therefore the divinely appointed time to rebuild curtailed the work. Judah probably had been a semiautonomous district within the larger satrapy Beyond-the-River with the appointment of Sheshbazzar as governor (Ezra 5:14, 16) in the reign of Cyrus. *Zerubbabel was governor from c. 520 BCE, appointed by Darius I. Although Ezra-Nehemiah avers that there were no Judeans left residing in the homeland after the demise of the kingdom of Judah in 587 BCE, the vast majority of scholars view this as tendentious: it serves the author's view that the repatriates and those remaining in the Babylonian-Elamite diaspora were the sole legitimate heirs to the territory, cult and traditions of monarchical Judah. There was a (sizable?) population of Judeans living in and around the homeland that had not gone into exile (Barstad). The common view is that the repatriates formed an enclave within Judah, but even if this were the case, it is unlikely to have been promoted by Sheshbazzar and Zerubbabel, given that they were appointed governors of the whole of Judah, not just as leaders of the repatriates (contra Weinberg, 114). For the early Achaemenid Persian period a strong case can be made that the repatriates did not differentiate themselves from Judeans and other Yahwists whom they found living in and around the homeland, since Haggai and Zechariah 1—8, texts contemporary with the temple rebuilding under Darius I (520-515 BCE), know of no such distinction.

The rebuilding of the temple commenced soon after the arrival of Zerubbabel and Joshua, the high priest, who undertook the work to mark the end of Yahweh's ire, exemplified in the destruction of the kingdom of Judah and the exile, and as a means of integrating the repatriates and Judeans who had remained in Judah (Bedford 2001, 264-99). The ideology supporting the undertaking displays continuity with monarchical-period ideas of the temple and divine *kingship (Bedford 2001, 237-64). This points to the character of the community. It saw itself, through the act of temple rebuilding, as introducing the restoration of Israel. By reestablishing the earthly throne of Yahweh, a return to political and religious normalcy after the destruction of the kingdom of Judah was expected. This included the return of the remainder of the exiles and the eventual reinstatement of indigenous kingship.

4. The Governorship of Nehemiah.

There is a chronological gap of some seventy years in the Ezra-Nehemiah narrative between the completion of the temple and the arrival of Nehemiah as governor, although it is likely that one intervening governor is known from epigraphic evidence (Williamson 1988; also for governors throughout this period). The expectations of Haggai and Zechariah 1—8 were not realized, which may have led to internal debates over the character of the community. Isaiah 55—66 might belong to this period, as it reflects on reasons for the failure while emphasizing inclusiveness. Although in its canonical form Ezra-Nehemiah invites readers to understand the governorship of Nehemiah in the context of the narrow definition of the postexilic community presented in Ezra, recognizing that the Nehemiah Memoir (probably Neh 1—7; 12:31-43; 13:4-31) was originally a separate source permits its distinctive view to appear. This text considers the territorial borders of the district of Judah as important markers of the community's local limits, while recognizing the existence of some Judeans in neighboring Samaria (Neh 4:12). In this sense, Nehemiah's governorship stands in continuity with Zerubbabel's; the postexilic community in the homeland fundamentally coincides with Achaemenid Judah, without distinction between repatriates and those who had remained in the land. Nehemiah does not view the community as a temple-state or a citizen-temple community embedded in the district of Judah (indeed, it is clear that Jerusalem is underpopulated, and the temple is not well supported; Malachi perhaps reflects the latter problem). *Priests figure more prominently among the leadership, alongside others ("elders," "notables," "officials"). The problem with the priestly leadership is that they do not acknowledge Nehemiah's understanding of the limits of the community and have intermarried or have other dealings with the upper classes of Samaria and Ammon. This is held to compromise the community religiously, although a perceived threat to Judean political autonomy is also clearly in view. Distinct religious concerns are held to characterize the community in Nehemiah: the reading of the Torah (shared with Ezra; Neh 7—10), the observance of sabbath, intermarriage, maintenance of the temple and its rituals and personnel (Neh 10; 12:44—13:31). For Nehemiah, the postexilic community had lost its way under local leadership, and so Nehemiah needed to be sent from the Babylonian-Elamite diaspora parent community to redirect it. This emphasizes a major theme in Ezra-Nehemiah of the continuity with and continued connection to this diaspora community as a defining characteristic of the community in Judah (Bedford 2002). Since Judeans in the homeland developed close ties with Samarian Yahwists, building on relationships established between the repatriates and those Judeans who had never been in exile, it is likely that at least some sections of the community in the homeland held a rather different perspective.

5. The Mission of Ezra.

Ezra's mission (Ezra 7—10) reinforces a narrower definition of the postexilic community in comparison with Haggai, Zechariah 1—8 and Nehemiah. Its attention shifts to the distinction between repatriates and "foreigners" living in Judah, over the issue of intermarriage (Ezra 9—10), on the premise that no Judeans remained in the homeland after 587 BCE. Although Ezra 7 claims that Ezra returned with imperial authority to implement his Torah (the exact identity of which remains disputed), it appears from the rest of the narrative that he lacked any direct authority, since he exerts moral suasion over the community (Ezra 9:3—10:6). Political authority continued to reside in the hands of the governor. Here we learn of a group of people within Judah calling themselves "sons of the exile"/ "community of the exile," which seems to be the limited group that Ezra addresses. This should not be pressed to conclude that the repatriates were separatists; indeed, they were integrated with local nonrepatriated Judeans via intermarriage. The book of Ezra is an attempt to reassert the priority of the connection of the Babylonian-Elamite diaspora community to the repatriates, who had been forging links with Judeans and other Yahwists in the homeland. This was viewed as potentially diminishing this diaspora community's connection to the homeland (Bedford 2002). For Ezra, the postexilic community is religious in character: a cultic community focused on the temple and Torah and concerned with purity/contamination from outsiders. The latter is a view that arguably originated in the Babylonian-Elamite diaspora, where the maintenance of group boundaries, done by eschewing intermarriage, helped to preserve the existence of the Judean communities. It is not likely to have been much of an issue for Judeans in the homeland before the arrival of Ezra.

6. The Fourth Century BCE.

Ezra-Nehemiah carries the narrative down to c. 400 BCE (on the late dating of the mission of Ezra). For the fourth century BCE, the books of Chronicles have been read as addressing the problem of relations between Judeans in the homeland and their Samarian coreligionists. These books emphasize the unity of the communities, albeit on Judean terms. By recounting the history of monarchical Israel and Judah, Chronicles seeks to bring north and south together, including "resident aliens," into a single community around the Jerusalem temple (Japhet, 325-51). This emphasis on the temple may denote that among Judeans it had fallen to marginal interest, although it would seem from Josephus's writings and contemporary epigraphical evidence that by the fourth century BCE the high priest had displaced the governor as the political authority in the land, making Judah a temple-state (or at least moving it in that direction) (although see Rooke, 219-37). Chronicles highlights, against Nehemiah, that even if there are political borders currently dividing the two communities, this should not preclude their common religious ties. The Samaritan schism, belonging to a later date, to be sure, proved this hope to be ill-founded.

See also EZRA; EZRA AND NEHEMIAH, BOOKS OF; HISTORY OF ISRAEL 7: PERSIAN PERIOD; NEHEMIAH; PERSIA, PERSIANS; POSTEXILIC TEMPLE; SAMARIA; SANBALLAT; ZERUBBABEL.

BIBLIOGRAPHY. **H. Barstad,** *The Myth of the Empty Land: A Study of the History and Archaeology of Judah During the "Exilic" Period* (Symbolae Osloenses Supplement 28; Oslo: Scandinavian University Press, 1996); **P. R. Bedford,** "Diaspora: Homeland Relations in Ezra-Nehemiah," *VT* 52 (2002) 147-63; idem, *Temple Restoration in Early Achaemenid Judah* (SJSJ 65; Leiden: E. J. Brill, 2001); **L. L. Grabbe,** *Ezra-Nehemiah* (OTR; London: Routledge, 1988); **P. D. Hanson,** *The People Called: The Growth of Community in the Bible* (San Francisco: Harper & Row, 1986); **S. Japhet,** *The Ideology of the Book of Chronicles and Its Place in Biblical Thought* (BEATAJ 9; Frankfurt: Lang, 1989); **D. W. Rooke,** *The Heirs of Zadok: The Role and Development of the High Priesthood in Ancient Israel* (OTM; Oxford: Oxford University Press, 2000); **M. Smith,** *Palestinian Parties and Politics That Shaped the Old Testament* (2d ed.; London: SCM, 1987); **J. P. Weinberg,** *The Citizen-Temple Community* (JSOTSup 151; Sheffield: Sheffield Academic Press, 1992); **H. G. M. Williamson,** *Ezra, Nehemiah* (WBC 16; Waco, TX: Word, 1985); idem, "The Governors of Judah under the Persians," *TynBul* 39 (1988) 59-82.

P. R. Bedford

"HOLY" WARFARE. See ETHICS; WAR AND PEACE.

HONOR AND SHAME

Contemporary social-scientific interpretation employs the anthropological categories of honor and shame to analyze the biblical narratives. However, the use of these categories must take into account the limitations involved in applying contemporary analytical tools to ancient texts or archaeological data. Nevertheless, a careful analysis using current insights from cultural anthropology can enrich our interpretation.

1. The Classic Anthropological Theory
2. The Critique of the Theory
3. The Application of the Theory to the Historical Books

1. The Classic Anthropological Theory.

"Since the beginning of systematic anthropological research in the Mediterranean lands, the terms 'honor' and 'shame' have been used to represent an enormous variety of local social, sexual, economic, and other standards" (Herzfeld 1980, 339). Whereas nineteenth-century researchers often used what is known as the "honor-complex" to describe lower stages of civilization (Giordano, 39), twentieth-century anthropologists employed the notion to identify a "circum-Mediterranean" value system that, since it appears to be homogenous, seems to ignore the traditional division in Muslim and Christian cultures (Giovannini).

The classic definition reads as follows: "Honour is the value of a person in his own eyes, but also in the eyes of society. It is the estimation of his own worth, his claim to pride, but it is also acknowledgement of that claim, his excellence recognised by society, his right to pride" (Pitt-Rivers, 21). As such, honor and shame can be described as reciprocal moral values that represent the integration of an individual into a group (Gilmore, 3). Both reflect the conferral of public esteem on a person and the sensitivity to public opinion on which the person is totally dependent (Pitt-Rivers, 42). Thus they are critical in societies in which all relationships are viewed mainly as dyadic (Peristiany 1965, 10; Campbell 1964, 270). Furthermore, one has to distinguish between "ascribed honor" and "acquired honor"—that is, the honor that is bestowed on a person by birth (or by another person, such as the father) and the "socially recognized claim to worth that a person acquires by excelling over others" (Malina, 33).

Obviously, honor has a hierarchical aspect and is tied to the kinship system. Thus it is hardly surprising that honor and blood are closely related (Campbell 1964, 185). This hierarchy in turn means that only members of (perceived) equal social standing are able to challenge each other's honor.

The description of female honor (generally labeled as shame or [sexual] modesty) was described in male terms, and it has been stressed that the norms for women tend to be formulated more precisely than is the case in the male domain.

It is hardly surprising that honor is neither a gender-specific nor individual phenomenon, but rather at the same time affects the family, kinship group or society. Thus it was possible to talk about the "moral division of labor" (Pitt-Rivers; Malina, 46-48)—that is, that male and female members are responsible for the preservation of their collective honor—and it has rightly been pointed out that the division of honor into male and female realms tends to correspond to the division of roles in the family (Malina, 47).

Shame is the partial or complete loss of honor. This notion applies in general only to men, since honor and shame are parts of the public realm, in which women participate only partially; so men who spend too much time in the house are in danger of losing their honor. Loss of honor is linked to the loss of social status. As is the case with honor, shame always has a public aspect, and has to be displayed to become recognized as such.

In contrast to that, for the female world, shame is a positive value, which is almost exclusively linked to the women's sexuality ("The quality required of women in relation to honour is shame . . . , particularly sexual shame" [Campbell 1964, 287]). It is essential for women to maintain a good reputation. Basically speaking, the good reputation of a female in the eyes of others is evaluated through her display of chaste or modest behavior. If it is the duty of the woman to appear chaste, it is the duty of the man to protect the status of the females in his family. By making men's honor vulnerable through their women, Mediterranean culture gives sex a kind of political significance that it lacks in primitive societies (Pitt-Rivers). Since it is expected of men to display sexual prowess, a certain complication is introduced in the moral division of labor. On the one hand, men are expected to play Don Juan, and on the other hand, it is required of them to protect their women against the intrusion of such Don Juans, since such ability is a major component of reputation and manliness (Bourdieu, 221-25; Campbell 1964, 271).

"Honour and shame are social evaluations and thus participate of the nature of social sanctions . . . Honour and shame are two poles of an evaluation. They are the reflection of the social personality in the mirror of social ideals. What is particular to these evaluations is that they use as standard of measurement the type of personality considered as representative and exemplary of a certain society" (Peristiany 1965, 9-10).

2. The Critique of the Theory.
Since 1980 the theory of a circum-Mediterranean value system based on the notion of honor and shame has been critiqued repeatedly, and several modifications have been proposed (cf. Herzfeld 1980; Giordano; Just, 34-50). As a result, recent anthropological studies based on

fieldwork in the Mediterranean only marginally treat the concept, if paying attention to it at all (see Malaby; Kirtsoglou; Paxson). The starting point for such a reevaluation was the emergence of "self-reflexive" anthropology, noting that the study of the Mediterranean mainly done by Anglo-American anthropologists tends to create an ethnocentric viewpoint that is tainted by several stereotypes that lead to an "archaization" of Mediterranean societies (Giordano, 43; Herzfeld [1984, 451] remarks, "An *ethnography* of the Mediterranean is incomplete without an analysis of the 'Mediterranean' category itself, and that inevitably means that we must include our own familiar forms of discourse in the analysis"). M. Herzfeld (1980; 1984) has put forward several reservations concerning the scholarly construction of the moral values of "honor and shame." His critique of classic anthropological studies of Mediterranean honor has tended to focus on three aspects: (1) linguistic problems, (2) cultural and geographic diversity, (3) stereotypes. Herzfeld has repeatedly called other anthropologists to task for using the concept of "honor" too broadly and ignoring the particular meaning it has in this or that village, in this or that country, in this or that period. For example, honor in one village may consist of self-restraint and resistance to violence and vendetta, whereas in another village honor may be precisely the response to challenge and the seeking of satisfaction (see also Just, 40-45). Therefore, Herzfeld calls for "particularistic ethnographic description." In regard to ethnic and geographical diversity, in the case of the ancient Mediterranean, we have indeed diverse cultures, which need to be treated separately. The broad general assumption of the Mediterranean as a "culture area" with a set of similar, if not identical, values can thus be avoided.

Secondly, L. Abu-Lughod, in her classic 1986 study of North African Bedouins, has shown how poetry can be used to subvert the moral values of a society as well as utilizing language normally reserved for the male sphere (Abu-Lughod, 257). Furthermore, the studies addressing the phenomenon of honor and shame tend to picture women in mainly subordinate and passive roles while at the same time seeming to maintain an actively gendered distinction between the domestic and public areas of social life.

In addition to the aforementioned critique

leveled by anthropologists, biblical scholars have to be aware that they are applying anthropological theory and models conceived during the twentieth century (the problem of "upstreaming") to ancient texts, and also that their "native informants" are generally either literary texts or archaeological artifacts. Therefore, if one wants to interpret a text from the distant past, one has to explain how certain opinions, modes of behavior or social structures functioned in the past. It is necessary that we look at the anthropology of the Mediterranean in terms of two interrelated processes: (1) how anthropologists as authors of written works tended to construct their texts and search for certain characters to describe/characterize the region, and (2) how the people of the Levant themselves construct their identities as authors of their own character. This approach will serve exegetes well, especially since we are not concerned with so-called preliterate societies, but rather with cultures that have a long and complex written history. We always must keep in mind that the texts that we study most likely stem from the elite of the particular society and thus do not necessarily reflect the whole spectrum of the society. In addition to that, social values and concepts do tend to change over time (as they do over geographical distance) and seldom remain monolithic. It is therefore mandatory "that the precise interpretation of moral-value terms requires a clear perception of their linguistic and social context in each community" (Herzfeld 1980, 348).

3. The Application of the Theory to the Historical Books.

The use of social-scientific analysis and models in biblical interpretation is no longer in need of justification, since its application has significantly enriched our understanding of biblical texts (see the rich bibliographies in Malina; Stansell, 74-79; Stone). A detailed study of the phenomenon of honor and shame in the Historical Books of the OT is beyond the scope of this article; thus some guidelines, using a few illustrative examples, must suffice.

Every anthropological analysis of any human value system must start with a collection of data, bearing in mind that not every situation involving an honor-and-shame scenario needs to use explicitly honor-and-shame language; generally, in so-called high-context societies (which most of the ancient societies were) much more is im-

plied than is actually said, since the authors assume that their readers/hearers are "in the know" (see Stone, 134-36). However, this should not be used as an excuse to find honor and shame under every olive tree (Grabbe, 95), and whether honor and shame really are *the* core values of the world of the Hebrew Bible must be determined individually for each set of texts analyzed.

Furthermore, one needs to note that honor (and shame) is, like any other real or ideal commodity in the ancient world, available only in limited supply (i.e., a "limited good" [see Malina, 81-105]; needless to say that honor has rightly been described as the "ultimate limited good"). This is expected in a "peasant society" but also implies that the gain of honor must always come at the expense of somebody else.

Amongst the rich vocabulary, especially the following need to be considered (for a more detailed treatment see Klopfenstein; Stiebert): *kābôd* (*TDOT* 7.22-38), "honor"; *kbd* (*TDOT* 7.13-17), "to be heavy"—that is, "to be honorable" (e.g., Judg 9:9; 13:17; 1 Sam 4:18; 15:30; 1 Chron 4:9); *bôš* (*TDOT* 2.50-60; Klopfenstein 1972: 17-49), "shame" (e.g., 2 Sam 19:6; 2 Kings 2:17; 8:11; 19:26; Ezra 8:22; 9:6); *qlh* II niphal (*TDOT* 13.31-37; Klopfenstein, 184-95), "to be lightly esteemed"—that is, "dishonored" (e.g., 1 Sam 18:23); *klm* niphal and hiphil (Klopfenstein, 109-68), "to be humiliated," "to be put to shame" (e.g., Judg 18:7; 2 Sam 10:5; 1 Chron 19:5).

In addition, G. Stansell has shown that many "personal" encounters during David's rise are governed by challenge and riposte within a system to gain prestige—that is, honor. Furthermore, honor can be gained in battle (2 Kings 14:10) and probably plays a significant role in covenantal relations (see 2 Sam 10:1-6; 19:1-43). Also, it is fruitful to investigate sexual relationships in the light of honor and shame (Stone, 68-133), as well as the attitude of the females (note Prov 11:16: "A gracious woman gets honor . . . " [interestingly, the LXX explicitly introduces the opposition honor and shame into the text by adding "but she who hates virtue is covered with shame" (NRSV, which follows the LXX)].

In taking the criticism leveled against an all-too-broad application of the concept of honor and shame seriously, it is necessary that a detailed *literary* analysis precedes any evaluation of a value system. We have to remind ourselves that the events narrated in the historical books do not necessarily describe actual (historical) events and most likely have been written down many years later. Thus it is highly likely that the texts provide us with insights only into the social world of their authors, and it might be as difficult to argue for continuity over long periods of time as it is over geographical distances.

Also, exegetes have to consider the role of *God for any social analysis of honor and shame (see Campbell 1965). Generally speaking, God (Yahweh) is the ultimate source of honor (he can be called "God of honor," ʾēl hakkābôd [Ps 29:3], or "king of honor," melek hakkābôd [Ps 24:7]) and is thus part of the value system. This is made explicit in 1 Samuel 2:30 when Yahweh says, "For those who honor [kbd] me I will honor, and those who despise [bzh] me shall be treated with contempt [qll]." The verse shows the reciprocal nature of honor: it is entirely appropriate to repay honor bestowed on oneself. At the same time, we need to note that Yahweh is not dependent on any source of honor, and it is hardly surprising that in contrast to other deities, he has no genealogy. Also, Yahweh seems to be aware of the hierarchical structure of honor (kābôd) when he says in Malachi 1:6, "A son honors [kbd] his father, and servants their master. If then I am a father, where is the honor [kābôd] due to me? And if I am a master, where is the respect [môrāʾ] due to me?" Needless to say, it is expected that humans pay the respect due to God. Thus David's answer in 1 Chronicles 17:18, 20 is only fitting: "And what more can David say to you for honoring [lĕkābôd] your servant? . . . There is no one like you, O LORD."

Keeping the caveats against an overly broad and naïve application of the anthropological model of honor and shame in mind, we find that anthropological theory is able to significantly enrich our understanding of the social milieu of the authors of the Historical Books. However, whether it is possible to deduce from these insights how honor and shame functioned in preexilic Israel remains to be seen.

See also ISRAELITE SOCIETY; SOCIAL-SCIENTIFIC APPROACHES.

BIBLIOGRAPHY. L. Abu-Lughod, Veiled Sentiments: Honor and Poetry in a Bedouin Village (Berkeley: University of California Press, 1986); P. Bourdieu, "The Sentiment of Honour in Kabyle Society," in Honour and Shame: The Values of Mediterranean Society, ed. J. G. Peristiany (The Nature of Human Society Series; London: Weidenfeld & Nicolson, 1965) 191-241; J. K. Campbell, "Honour and the Devil," in Honour and Shame: The Values of Mediterranean Society, ed. J. G. Peristiany (The Nature of Human Society Series; London: Weidenfeld & Nicolson, 1965) 141-70; idem, Honour, Family and Patronage: A Study of Institutions and Moral Values in a Greek Mountain Community (Oxford: Oxford University Press, 1964); C. Dohmen, "כבד," TDOT 7.13-17; D. D. Gilmore, ed., Honor and Shame and the Unity of the Mediterranean (Washington, DC: American Anthropological Association Special Publications 22; Washington, DC: American Anthropological Association, 1987); C. Giordano, "Mediterranean Honour Reconsidered: Anthropological Fiction or Actual Action Strategy?" Anthropological Journal on European Cultures 10 (2001) 39-58; M. J. Giovannini, "Female Chastity Codes in the Circum-Mediterranean: Comparative Perspectives," in Honor and Shame and the Unity of the Mediterranean, ed. D. D. Gilmore (American Anthropological Association Special Publications 22; Washington, DC: American Anthropological Association, 1987) 61-74; L. L. Grabbe, "Sup-Urbs or Only Hyp-Urbs? Prophets and Populations in Ancient Israel and Socio-Historical Method," in "Every City Shall Be Forsaken": Urbanism and Prophecy in Ancient Israel and the Near East, ed. L. L. Grabbe and R. D. Haak (JSOTSup 330; Sheffield: Sheffield Academic Press, 2001) 95-123; M. Herzfeld, "Honour and Shame: Problems in the Comparative Analysis of Moral Systems," Man, n.s., 15 (1980) 339-51; idem, "The Horns of the Mediterraneanist Dilemma," American Ethnologist 11 (1984) 439-54; R. Just, "On the Ontological Status of Honour," in An Anthropology of Indirect Communication, ed. J. Hendry and C. W. Watson (ASA Monographs 37; London and New York: Routledge, 2001) 34-50; E. Kirtsoglou, For the Love of Women: Gender, Identity and Same-Sex Relations in a Greek Provincial Town (London: Routledge, 2004); M. A. Klopfenstein, Scham und Schande nach dem Alten Testament: Eine begriffsgeschichtliche Untersuchung zu den hebräischen Wurzeln bôs, klm und hpr (ATANT 62; Zurich: Theologischer Verlag, 1972); T. M. Malaby, Gambling Life: Dealing in Contingency in a Greek City (Urbana, IL: University of Illinois Press, 2003); B. J. Malina, The New Testament World: Insights from Cultural Anthropology (3d ed.; Louisville: Westminster/John

Knox, 2001); **J. Marböck,** "קל ה II," *TDOT* 13.31-37; **H. Paxson,** *Making Modern Mothers: Ethics and Family Planning in Urban Greece* (Berkeley: University of California Press, 2004); **J. G. Peristiany,** ed., *Honour and Shame: The Values of Mediterranean Society* (The Nature of Human Society Series; London: Weidenfeld & Nicolson, 1965); **J. Pitt-Rivers,** "Honour and Social Status," in *Honour and Shame: The Values of Mediterranean Society,* ed. J. G. Peristiany (The Nature of Human Society Series; London: Weidenfeld & Nicolson, 1965) 19-77; **H. Seebass,** "בוש," *TDOT* 2.50-60; **G. Stansell,** "Honor and Shame in the David Narratives," in *Honor and Shame in the World of the Bible,* ed. V. H. Matthews and D. C.

Benjamin (Semeia 68; Atlanta: Scholars Press, 1994) 55-79; **J. Stiebert,** *The Construction of Shame in the Hebrew Bible: The Prophetic Contribution* (JSOTSup 330; Sheffield: Academic Press, 2002); **K. Stone,** *Sex, Honor, and Power in the Deuteronomistic History* (JSOTSup 234; Sheffield: Academic Press, 1996); **M. Weinfeld,** "כבוד," *TDOT* 7.22-38.   A. C. Hagedorn

HOSHEA. *See* HISTORY OF ISRAEL 5: ASSYRIAN PERIOD.

HOUSES. *See* ARCHITECTURE.

HYMNS. *See* POETRY.

I

IBZAN. *See* JUDGES; HISTORY OF ISRAEL 2: PRE-MONARCHIC ISRAEL.

IDEOLOGICAL INTERPRETATION. *See* METHODS OF INTERPRETATION.

INNERBIBLICAL EXEGESIS

Innerbiblical exegesis refers to the citation and interpretation of the Bible within the Bible. The term should be used to refer to the innerbiblical citations within the OT. It also refers to a method of biblical criticism that focuses on the internal exegetical development of the Scriptures as part of the history of biblical interpretation. As such, innerbiblical exegesis is a type of historical criticism that assumes that later texts within the Bible are related formally and exegetically to earlier texts. It should not be understood, however, as merely a form of redaction criticism or tradition history, but rather as an approach to biblical literature that emphasizes an exegetical orientation in ancient Israel that continues into early Jewish and Christian hermeneutical traditions. The most prominent biblical literature for this type of analysis includes the relationship between pentateuchal law codes (e.g., Priestly and Deuteronomic) and the two histories of Israel (i.e., Samuel-Kings and Chronicles).

1. The Study of Innerbiblical Exegesis
2. Techniques in Innerbiblical Exegesis
3. The Deuteronomistic History
4. Chronicles, Ezra and Nehemiah

1. The Study of Innerbiblical Exegesis.

Innerbiblical exegesis as a discrete field of biblical criticism is relatively recent. In the past, biblical criticism had dealt with the exegetical relationships between biblical texts as a part of redaction criticism or tradition history. The scholarly study of innerbiblical exegesis as a discrete methodology begins with N. Sarna's seminal 1963 article "Psalm 89: A Study in Inner Biblical Exegesis." A major development in the study of innerbiblical exegesis was M. Fishbane's monumental *Biblical Interpretation in Ancient Israel,* published in 1985. This work has been followed up, developed and nuanced in the work of Fishbane's students (see Levinson; Sommer; Schniedewind 1999a), as well as in the writings of Israeli scholar Y. Zakovitch. This approach to innerbiblical exegesis is closely tied with the later Jewish hermeneutical tradition (see Fishbane 1985, 2-5; 1998). In the wake of Fishbane's monograph, European scholars have also increasingly discussed *innerbiblische Schriftauslegung,* largely in response to the crisis in traditional literary-critical approaches that have resulted in an ever increasing fragmentation of the biblical text. European scholars, however, tend to view innerbiblical exegesis as a by-product of redaction criticism or tradition history and not usually as an independent approach to biblical literature (see especially Schmid). To simplify the contrast, one might generalize that for European scholars innerbiblical exegesis is an outgrowth of historical criticism beginning with Wellhausen, whereas for American and Israeli scholars innerbiblical exegesis is the beginning of a Jewish hermeneutical tradition that leads into midrash and other forms of Jewish and Christian interpretation of late antiquity. European approaches to *innerbiblische Schriftauslegung* tend to employ it as a method to explain the formation of the text, whereas American approaches tend to see innerbiblical interpretation as a means to understand the historical development of the exegetical process (contrast Schmid with Fishbane 1998).

Fishbane's approach has drawn some criticism. Some scholars have suggested that the approach can rely too heavily on rabbinic models of interpretation (see Kugel 1987). To be sure, Fishbane's approach to innerbiblical interpretation, which has dominated American scholarship, is couched firmly within the Jewish exegetical tradition. Another critique argues that innerbiblical exegesis is still a form of historical criticism and therefore is open to the critiques that newer literary approaches have leveled on the older historical models (see Eslinger). Another approach that may be located under innerbiblical exegesis, if it were to be inclusively defined, is the work of J. Kugel, which essentially deals with the intertextuality and interpretative history of biblical literature, especially the Torah. Whereas Fishbane works consciously within the traditional models of historical criticism, Kugel's monumental *The Bible As It Was*, published in 1997, works within a history-of-interpretation model that moves almost seamlessly between innerbiblical and later Jewish and Christian interpretation.

1.1. The Problem of Terminology. The term *innerbiblical exegesis* seems to have been coined in 1963 by N. Sarna. The implication of *exegesis* is that the text is acknowledging and explicating an earlier text; *innerbiblical* exegesis implies a developing consciousness about the integrity and authority of the written text that is cited. Thus instances where the exegesis is not formally marked should not formally be labeled innerbiblical exegesis; terms such as *interpretation, intertextuality, allusion* and *influence* can point to less direct relationships between texts. Innerbiblical *interpretation* can include the interpretative aspects of the growth of biblical literature, whereas innerbiblical *exegesis* should be reserved for the explicit citation of biblical texts within biblical literature. The importance of innerbiblical interpretation has been increasingly recognized in the work of European scholars, even though this observation essentially serves to understand the redactional development of the canonical text (e.g., contrast Lau with Sommer). A survey of scholarship under the broad category of innerbiblical exegesis shows that the expression sometimes has become a catch-all phrase to discuss a variety of types of interpretation, intertextuality, allusion and influence. These terms— *exegesis, interpretation, intertextuality, allusion* and *influence*—imply quite different relationships between texts (Sommer, 6-31). They also imply very different historical interests and claims.

Intertextuality is also a new literary-critical approach inasmuch as it tends to treat the text as an artifact apart from its author. It too explores the manifold ways that texts can be related to one another, consciously or unconsciously. Intertextuality also implies a signifying system by which any text may be associated with another text apart from a direct historical relationship. For example, Kugel's *In Potiphar's House* has the interesting subtitle *The Interpretative Life of Biblical Texts*. The description of biblical texts as having an "interpretative life" implies a much broader view of the relationship between texts than merely exegetical. Y. Zakovitch, in *"And You Shall Tell Your Son,"* traces the history of a biblical concept, with an interest in understanding a religious idea and relying on methods of innerbiblical interpretation. W. M. Schniedewind, in *Society and the Promise to David*, uses the phrase "innerbiblical discourse" in an attempt to describe the broader phenomenon of interpretation and cultural discourse that is reflected by innerbiblical exegesis.

These approaches still tend to be "text-centric"; that is, they reflect literary theories that begin with the assumption of the text. Recent studies in the field of orality have underscored an oral dimension to ancient literature (*see* Oral Tradition and Written Tradition). Indeed, often there are relationships between texts that cannot be accounted for without acknowledging an oral discourse. One example of this might be the use of 2 Samuel 7—the promise to the Davidic dynasty—in Isaiah 7—11 (*see* Davidic Covenant). In no place in Isaiah 7—11 can we see explicit citation of 2 Samuel 7, yet Isaiah clearly assumes the concept of the Davidic promise. Thus these questions may be asked: Why are no texts cited? Why is there no innerbiblical exegesis in Isaiah 7—11? These questions assume that exegesis is a normal part of the cultural discourse, and indeed exegesis is a typical part of our religious discourse. Yet there is no reason to assume that exegesis would have been part of the religious discourse in the days of *Isaiah of Jerusalem (the late eighth century BCE). The rise of innerbiblical exegesis reflects the rise of the role of the text itself in ancient Judean society. And indeed, the beginnings of a text-centric culture are evident in the Josianic religious reforms precipitated by the discovery of "the scroll of the covenant" (see 2 Kings 22—23). The *Deuteronomistic History, which usually is thought to have been written down originally in the context of the Josianic reforms, evidences this text awareness by using expressions such as "according to that which is written in the Torah of Moses" (see Josh 8:31; 1 Kings 2:3; 2 Kings 14:6; 23:21). Such statements reflect the religious authority of the written text, which also is suggested by the use of the scroll discovered in the temple and read aloud to the people. It is this religious authority of texts that generates innerbiblical and early biblical exegesis.

1.2. The Principle of Theological and Political Attraction. It is important to acknowledge a principle of attraction in innerbiblical interpretation. By "attraction" we refer to the fact that exegesis and interpretation in antiquity were drawn especially to texts that were theologically or politically charged. Texts such as Exodus 19 (the revelation on Sinai), Deuteronomy 12 (the centralization of worship), 2 Kings 17 (the fall of the northern kingdom) and 2 Samuel 7 (the promise to the Davidic dynasty) attracted much more innerbiblical exegesis than did more mundane texts. All texts were not equally ripe for exegetical commentary. For example, when we compare Samuel-Kings with Chronicles, it quickly becomes clear that large portions of the source text (i.e., Samuel-Kings or some early version thereof) were copied (in Chronicles) without any need for interpretation or elaboration. Certain important political or theological issues, however, almost inevitably drew some kind of exegetical development.

The variable attraction to exegesis and commentary is illustrated in a transitional way by the Qumran literature that develops a special genre of exegesis called "pesher" (in Hebrew) for texts that were considered directly God's word (i.e., the prophetic books and the psalms) as opposed to the Pentateuch and the Historical Books. Every word of these prophetic texts was understood by the Qumran community to be God's very word and therefore ripe with meaning. The Pentateuch, in contrast, did not invite this kind of pregnant interpretation at Qumran. To be sure, the Pentateuch became a focus of retelling and rewriting in texts such as *Genesis Apocryphon, Jubilees* and *Reworked Pentateuch* (4Q158). These texts certainly were considered sacred, but they drew a different type of interpretative activity because the Qumran sectarians considered the writings in the Pentateuch and the Historical Books to be of a genre different from prophetic literature. In other words, the extent and nature of innerbiblical and postbiblical exegesis will depend on the theological and political themes of each text as well as the sacred nature of the each text.

Later Jewish and Christian communities developed assumptions about the nature of the text that were different from what was known in biblical antiquity, and they bestowed upon the text an ever increasing sanctity. In Judaism, for example, the Pentateuch became a central focus of interpretation. Whereas Qumran literature wrote pesher on prophetic texts, rabbinic Judaism focused its exegetical energy on the Pentateuch. Rabbinic midrash was devoted to the Torah, in contrast to Qumran pesher. Once the text was infused with a special, even mystical, sanctity, then the sacred text became open to and even drawn to exegesis. Divine meaning could be found in any word of Scripture. To be sure, certain prominent texts were still attractive to exegetes, but the sacred text as a whole could be exegetically mined.

2. Techniques in Innerbiblical Exegesis.
Innerbiblical exegesis employs a variety of techniques for textual citation and interpretation. Innerbiblical exegesis, by its very nature, is not covert. Later interpreters do not hide their dependence and exegetical development of earlier texts, but rather formally mark it.

2.1. Citation Formulas. Biblical literature, particularly in the Historical Books, uses citation formulas to indicate a relationship with other biblical and nonbiblical texts (see Spawn). There are two types of citation formulas: one for canonical texts, and one for noncanonical texts. The typical citation formula used when citing another biblical text is "as it is written" *(kakkātûb)*; alternatively, we find the expression "that which is written" *(hakkātûb)*. The canonical texts can be generically alluded to by a citation formula, as in 1 Kings 2:3, "Keep the charge of the LORD your God, walking in his ways and following his laws, his commandments, his rules, and his admonitions as it is written in the Torah of Moses." More typically we find references to specific biblical texts. Thus in Joshua 8:31 we read, "Moses, the servant of the LORD, had commanded the Israelites—as is written in the scroll of the Torah of Moses—*an altar of unhewn stone upon which no iron had been wielded*" (cf. Deut 27:6; Ex 20:21-22). In 2 Kings 23:21 we read, "The king commanded all the people: Offer the Passover sacrifice to the LORD your God as it is written in this scroll of the covenant" (cf. Ex 12:48; Deut 16:1). In 2 Kings 14:6 King Joash is commended because "he did not put to death the children of the assassins, as it is written in the scroll of the Torah of Moses, where the LORD commanded, *"Parents shall not be put to death for children, nor children be put to death for parents; a person shall be put to death only for his own crime"* (cf. Deut 24:16).

There is a tendency to make an appeal to the authority of the written text precisely when some critical or debated issue is at stake. Although the explicit citations of biblical texts using the expression "as it is written" cited above may seem to be straightforward and involve little exegesis, each asserts the authority of certain textual and exegetical traditions. Joshua 8:31 makes reference to the particular altar law of Deuteronomy 27:6, but the development of the altar law in Deuteronomy is itself the product of some innerbiblical exegesis (see the discussion in Fishbane 1985, 159-62). The textual citation in Joshua 8:31 is generated precisely by the innerbiblical discourse about the altar law. 2 Kings 23:21 commands Israel to observe the Passover "as it is written"; however, exactly how one observed the Passover seems to have been a matter of some debate, or at least of historical development, in ancient Israel. In Exodus 12:9 the Israelites are told not to eat the Passover meat raw or "cooked in any way in water, but roasted over the fire"; in contrast, Deuteronomy 16:7 explicitly commands that the Israelites "shall boil" the Passover meat. In a well-known early harmonization of these traditions, 2 Chronicles 35:13 states that "they boiled the Passover lamb over the fire" (most English translations gloss over this harmonization by translating the Hebrew word *bāšal*, which literally means "to boil," as "to roast"). As Fishbane points out, this harmonization is accomplished by an exegetical blending of the Exodus and Deuteronomy traditions. 2 Kings 23:21 is not explicitly exegetical in its command to "observe the Passover . . . as it is written in the scroll of the covenant." Yet the appeal to "the scroll of the covenant" seems to be explicitly an appeal to the textual tradition of Deuteronomy (as opposed to Exodus). More importantly, the very appeal to a specific textual tradition suggests the awareness of the different

traditions practiced in ancient Israel and later harmonized by the author of Chronicles.

Finally, 2 Kings 14:6 cites that text from Deuteronomy 24:16, which is from "the scroll of the Torah of Moses," that deals with the principle of generational punishment. Yet the principle of generational punishment was part of the divine attributes: Yahweh punishes "the iniquity of parents upon children and children's children, upon the third and fourth generations" (Ex 34:7). Moreover, we witness the punishment of the fathers upon their descendants in many places in the Hebrew Bible (cf. Josh 7:24; 2 Sam 12:11-14; 1 Kings 21:19-29). In accord with Deuteronomy, the prophets Jeremiah and Ezekiel critique this principle of generational punishment (cf. Ezek 18; Jer 31:29-30). Thus the explicit appeal to the written "Torah of Moses" comes precisely in another context where we have extensive innerbiblical discourse about the principle of generational punishment. In sum, there are only a few explicit innerbiblical citations in the Deuteronomistic History, but all occur precisely on issues where there is evidence of a lively innerbiblical discourse. In the Deuteronomistic History the citations themselves are not exegetical. The exegetical currents of these citations are part of the cultural discourse, but they are not included in the historical narrative. This stands in sharp contrast with Chronicles, where exegesis is part of the historical narrative.

Chronicles and *Ezra-Nehemiah also frequently use the expression "as it is written." There are seven occurrences in Chronicles (2 Chron 23:18; 25:4; 30:5, 18; 31:3; 35:12, 26) and six more occurrences in Ezra-Nehemiah (Ezra 3:2, 4; 6:18; Neh 8:15; 10:35, 37). A main point of the citations, especially in Ezra-Nehemiah, seems to stress continuity with the ancient institutions and traditions of preexilic Israel. Chronicles also seems interested to stress the continuity with ancient traditions, even remarking on the failure to continue the ancient traditions: "And they decreed to make a proclamation throughout all Israel, from Beersheba to Dan, that the people should come and keep the Passover to the LORD the God of Israel, at Jerusalem; for they had not been keeping it in great numbers as it is written" (2 Chron 30:5). Of course, the appeal to the written text here is also occasioned by the particular interests of the postexilic community. The book of Ezra, for example, also makes a point about Passover observance (see Ezra 3:6), illustrating that this institution was a particular concern to the postexilic community. The innerbiblical citation formula adds to this ceremony.

Several other expressions that are used in Chronicles in particular indicate the growing awareness and influence of an authoritative text, usually referred to as the Torah (although not necessarily the exact same text as our Pentateuch). In 2 Chronicles 17:9 the priests teach by using "the scroll of the Torah of YHWH." The Chronicler (*see* Chronicler's History) also uses the expressions "according to the commandments of Moses *[kĕmiṣwat mōšeh]*" (e.g., 2 Chron 8:13), "according to the Torah of Moses *[kĕtôrat mōšeh]*" (e.g., 2 Chron 30:16), or "according to the word of YHWH *[kidbar yhwh]*" (1 Chron 15:15; 2 Chron 35:6) to cite Mosaic legislation known in the Pentateuch.

When Chronicles, Ezra and Nehemiah introduce an exegetical component into their textual citation, they employ a different expression: *kammišpāṭ*, usually translated as "according to the ordinance." This expression is well known from the priestly literature, but it is not used there with an exegetical nuance. It may refer to a written statute, but the textual nature of the statute is never explicit in the priestly literature. It is also known from the Deuteronomistic History and the Prophets, but there *mišpāṭ* refers to "tradition" or "custom," as in Ezekiel 5:7, where the prophet accuses Israel of acting "according to the ordinances/customs of the nations *[kĕmišpĕṭê haggôyim]* that are all around you." Similarly, the royal coronation of Joash is performed "according to the custom *[kammišpaṭ]*" (2 Kings 11:14). Chronicles and Ezra-Nehemiah, in contrast, use the phrase *kammišpāṭ* specifically to refer to exegetical interpretations or embellishments of written and authoritative texts (see Schniedewind 1999b, 172-78). Two examples will illustrate this. Nehemiah 8 describes the keeping of the Festival of Tabernacles (Sukkoth). According to Nehemiah 8:18, "And day by day, from the first day to the last day, he read from the book of the law of God. They kept the festival seven days; and on the eighth day there was a solemn assembly, according to the ordinance." There is no explicit pentateuchal prescription that requires the daily reading of the law. This tradition presumably is *kammišpāṭ*, "according to tradition." It has been suggested that the daily reading of the Torah is an exegetical deduction

based on Deuteronomy 31:10-13 (see Fishbane 1985, 112-13). Or, it could simply be a tradition that developed in the observance of Sukkoth. In either case, the use of the expression *kammišpāṭ*, "according to tradition," keys the reader into the embellishment of the pentateuchal law concerning Sukkoth. A well-known example of Chronicles' harmonizing exegesis is in its combination of the Passover prescriptions from Exodus 12:9 and Deuteronomy 16:7 (cited above). It is not coincidental that the Chronicler's exegetical harmonization is described as "according to the tradition" *(kammišpāṭ):* "They boiled the Passover lamb over the fire according to the tradition" (2 Chron 35:13). The use of the expression *kammišpāṭ* shows an awareness that an authoritative text has boundaries. Moreover, this expression allows tradition and custom, with the help of exegesis, to expand the boundaries of the authoritative text.

In Chronicles and Ezra-Nehemiah we witness both the confining nature of the authoritative written text and the liberating possibilities afforded by exegesis. As Socrates poignantly notes in his complaint to Phaedrus, "Written words seem to talk to you as though they were intelligent, but if you ask them anything about what they say, from a desire to be instructed, they go on telling you just the same thing forever" (Plato *Phaedr.* 275d). The advantage of the oral tradition was its flexibility and adaptability. The written text, however, is inflexible. It cannot adapt and address a changing world, except through exegesis. Indications of innerbiblical exegesis are evidence that an authoritative written text had emerged.

2.2. Editorial Marking of Exegetical Comments. Biblical authors use a variety of editorial devices to mark exegetical comments, glosses and insertions. This formal marking of exegetical comments is already evident in an expression such as *kammišpāṭ,* "according to tradition" (see 2.1 above). The use of such editorial devices shows an awareness of the integrity of the text and the exegetical enterprise. The most prominent techniques include deictic particles (e.g., *hwʾ*), the *Wiederaufnahme* ("repetitive resumption") and chiastic citation (also known as Seidel's Law [see below]). These devices are described by Fishbane (1985, 44-65) and Levinson (17-20). It is important to recognize that devices such as the *Wiederaufnahme* are regularly employed as exegetical devices and not merely as narrative markers (contra Long; Spawn, 46). Such devices probably began as rhetorical devices, often of oral discourse, and were taken over and employed as exegetical devices.

Perhaps the most widely used exegetical markers are deictic particles. These include personal pronouns such as *hû'* and *hî'*, "that is/it is," and demonstrative pronouns such as *zeh* and *zō't*, "this (means)." The particle *'et*, usually a direct object marker, is also used to introduce explanatory glosses and can be translated in these contexts as "namely." The simplest type of exegesis is an explanatory note such as we find in Joshua 18:13: "the boundary passed on southward to Luz, to the flank of Luz—*that is, Bethel.*" In this example an editor adds the note that Luz refers to the town that was in the editor's time known as Bethel. The use of deictic particles becomes a regular part of Qumran exegesis, as in this explanation of 2 Samuel 7:10: "[I appointed judges] over my people Israel" [2 Sam 7:10-11a]. "*This* 'house' refers to the house that [they shall build for him] in the last days, as it is written in the book of [Moses]" (4Q174 frag. 1-2 i 2-3).

Another common exegetical technique is known as the *Wiederaufnahme,* a term coined by H. Wiener and developed by C. Kuhl. This translates as "repetitive resumption," which explains the technique: the repetition of a phrase or sentence is used to frame an exegetical or editorial insertion in between the repetition. The technique can be illustrated by comparing a passage from Kings with its expansion in Chronicles. In 1 Kings 14:25-28 we read, "In the fifth year of King Rehoboam, King Shishak of Egypt came up against Jerusalem." 2 Chronicles 12:2-9 repeats this in framing its explanation of why Shishak was allowed to invade the holy city: "In the fifth year of King Rehoboam, King Shishak of Egypt came up against Jerusalem because they had been unfaithful to YHWH" (2 Chron 12:2); "So King Shishak of Egypt came up against Jerusalem" (2 Chron 12:9). Sometimes the *Wiederaufnahme* can be combined with a deictic particle, as in 2 Samuel 7:12-13: "I will raise up your offspring after you, one of your own issue, and *I will establish his kingdom.* It is he that shall build a house for my name, and *I will establish the throne of his kingdom* forever." In this example the expression "I will establish his kingdom" is almost exactly repeated with an exegetical interruption. The interruption, "It is he that shall

build a house for my name," is introduced by a deictic particle (the personal pronoun *hû'*) that explains who will ultimately be allowed to build the temple (for a detailed discussion see Schniedewind 1999a, 83-85).

The exegetical technique known as Seidel's Law uses chiastic citation of the source text in order to elaborate exegetically on the text. The most prominent examples of this technique are in the Prophets (as discussed by Sommer), but one example in the Historical Books is found in 1 Kings 5:5, which chiastically cites 2 Samuel 7:13.

3. The Deuteronomistic History.
The very formation of the Deuteronomistic History might be construed as a case of innerbiblical exegesis because it involves the citation and application of the legal code of Deuteronomy for the interpretation of the history of Israel and Judah. It is well known that the Deuteronomistic History frequently cites or alludes to the laws known from Deuteronomy. The most prominent themes include the centralization law (Deut 12), the prohibition of foreign altars (Deut 16:20-21) and the prophecy-fulfillment theme (Deut 18:21-22). Perhaps even more prominent is 2 Samuel 7, which is recalled throughout 1-2 Kings (see 1 Kings 8:12-61; 9:5; 11:5, 13, 32, 36; 15:4; 2 Kings 2:4; 8:19; 19:34; 20:6). It is also a case of innerbiblical interpretation inasmuch as it involves a redactional development of the Historical Books that entails the interpretation and elaboration of earlier texts without explicitly citing earlier literature.

One topic attracts the most attention for internal exegetical development in the Deuteronomistic History: the status and nature of the promise to David. Other issues that also attract attention can be seen as related to the promise to David. For example, the fall of the northern kingdom attracts several redactional layers (Brettler); of course, the fall of the north is read as legitimating the royal claims of the Davidic kings in Jerusalem. Much attention also surrounds the explanations for the eventual fall of the southern kingdom of Judah—an event that directly challenged the popular view that Yahweh had given David's sons an "eternal throne." We have already noted a case of innerbiblical interpretation within 2 Samuel 7 (2 Sam 7:12-13). Other prominent examples within the Deuteronomistic History include 1 Kings 5:2-5 (where

Solomon explains the dynastic promise to Hiram of Tyre) and 1 Kings 8:12-61 (in Solomon's prayer).

As M. Z. Brettler shows in his analysis of the fall of the northern kingdom told in 2 Kings 17, several editors were eager to have their viewpoints expressed about why the northern kingdom was destroyed as well as why the southern kingdom also would fall. Thus the chapter not only contains at least two explanations of the fall of the northern kingdom, but also includes reflections on the impending destruction of Judah almost a century and a half later. In this case the different interpretations of the fall of the northern kingdom probably should be called redactional layers rather than innerbiblical exegesis. They reflect an innerbiblical discourse about the cause of the destruction of the northern and southern kingdoms, but they do not explicitly cite other biblical texts.

4. Chronicles, Ezra and Nehemiah.

Innerbiblical exegesis reached its climax in postexilic literature as preexilic literature became the sacred canon to the postexilic community. This is well illustrated in Chronicles, Ezra and Nehemiah. To begin with, the use of formal citation formulas such as "as it is written" occurs more frequently in these postexilic historical books than anywhere else in the Hebrew Bible (see 2.1 above). It is well known, for example, that Chronicles follows Samuel-Kings almost verbatim in large sections, and the entire composition of Chronicles has been described as exegetical or relying on a textual hermeneutic (see Willi; Steins; Schniedewind 1999b). Chronicles borrows, however, without citing Samuel-Kings, unless we consider the citation formulas (e.g., "the rest of the acts of Manasseh . . . these are in the Annals of the Kings of Israel" [2 Chron 33:18]) to be references to Samuel-Kings, which is possible. The citation of earlier biblical texts is especially evident in the speeches narrated in Chronicles and Ezra-Nehemiah (see Mason; Schniedewind 1995). In some cases, there is a general appeal to authoritative literature, such as "as it is written in the Torah of Moses," without an explicit citation of the pentateuchal law (e.g., 2 Chron 30:16; Ezra 3:2; Neh 10:34, 36); oftentimes, these appeals do not explicitly seem to line up with a plain reading of the pentateuchal laws, but rather involve an interpretation of the pentateuchal law. Often there are allusions to

other biblical texts, such as the seer Hanani's statement that "the eyes of the LORD range throughout the entire earth" (2 Chron 16:9), which echoes Zechariah 4:10, and Jahaziel's exhortation "to stand and see the salvation of God" (2 Chron 20:17), which recontextualizes Moses' injunction at the Red Sea in Exodus 14:13. These, however, are examples of allusion that belong broadly in the category of innerbiblical interpretation, but not innerbiblical exegesis.

See also HISTORIOGRAPHY, OLD TESTAMENT; METHODS OF INTERPRETATION; NARRATIVE ART OF ISRAEL'S HISTORIANS; ORAL TRADITION AND WRITTEN TRADITION; SOURCES, REFERENCES TO.

BIBLIOGRAPHY. **M. Z. Brettler,** "Ideology, History and Theology in 2 Kings XVII 7-23," *VT* 39 (1989) 268-82; **L. Eslinger,** "Innerbiblical Exegesis and Innerbiblical Allusion: The Question of Category," *VT* 42 (1992) 47-58; **M. Fishbane,** *Biblical Interpretation in Ancient Israel* (Oxford: Clarendon Press, 1985); idem, "Innerbiblical Exegesis: Types and Strategies of Interpretation in Ancient Israel," in *The Garments of the Torah: Essays in Biblical Hermeneutics* (ISBL; Bloomington: Indiana University Press, 1988); idem, "The Hebrew Bible and the Exegetical Tradition," in *Intertextuality in Ugarit and Israel,* ed. J. C. de Moor (Oudtestamentische studiën 40; Leiden: E. J. Brill, 1998) 15-30; **J. L. Kugel,** "The Bible's Earliest Interpreters: Review of Michael Fishbane, *Biblical Interpretation in Ancient Israel,*" *Prooftexts* 7 (1987) 269-83; idem, *In Potiphar's House: The Interpretive Life of Biblical Texts* (San Francisco: Harper & Row, 1990); idem, *The Bible As It Was* (Cambridge, MA: Harvard University Press, 1997); **C. Kuhl,** "Die 'Wiederaufnahme'—ein literarisches Prinzip?" *ZAW* 64 (1952) 1-11; **W. Lau,** *Schriftgelehrte Prophetie in Jes 56—66: Eine Untersuchung zu den literarischen Bezügen in den letzten elf Kapiteln des Jesajabuches* (BZAW 225; Berlin: de Gruyter, 1994); **J. D. Levenson,** "From Temple to Synagogue: 1 Kings 8," in *Traditions in Transformation: Turning Points in Biblical Faith,* ed. B. Halpern and J. D. Levenson (Winona Lake, IN: Eisenbrauns, 1981) 143-66; **B. M. Levinson,** *Deuteronomy and the Hermeneutics of Legal Innovation* (New York and Oxford: Oxford University Press, 1997); **B. O. Long,** "Framing Repetitions in Biblical Historiography," *JBL* 106 (1987) 385-99; **R. A. Mason,** *Preaching the Tradition: Homily and Hermeneutics after the Exile; Based on the 'Addresses' in Chronicles, the Speeches in Ezra and Nehemiah* *and the Post-exilic Prophetic Books* (Cambridge: Cambridge University Press, 1990); **N. Sarna,** "Psalm 89: A Study in Inner Biblical Exegesis," in *Biblical and Other Studies,* ed. A. Altmann (Cambridge, MA: Harvard University Press, 1963) 29-46; **K. Schmid,** "Innerbiblische Schriftauslegung: Aspekte der Forschungsgeschichte," in *Schriftauslegung in der Schrift: Festschrift für Odil Steck zu seinem 65. Geburtstag,* ed. R. Kratz, T. Krüger and K. Schmid (BZAW 300; Berlin and New York: de Gruyter, 2000) 1-22; **W. M. Schniedewind,** *The Word of God in Transition: From Prophet to Exegete in the Second Temple Period* (JSOTSup 197; Sheffield: JSOT, 1995); idem, *Society and the Promise to David: A Reception History of 2 Samuel 7:1-17* (New York and Oxford: Oxford University Press, 1999a); idem, "The Chronicler as an Interpreter of Scripture," in *The Chronicler as Author: Studies in Text and Texture,* ed. M. P. Graham and S. L. McKenzie (JSOTSup 263; Sheffield: Sheffield Academic Press, 1999b) 158-80; **B. Sommer,** *A Prophet Reads Scripture: Allusion in Isaiah 40—66* (Contraversions: Jews and Other Differences; Palo Alto, CA: Stanford University Press, 1998);; **K. Spawn,** *As It Is Written and Other Citation Formulae in the Old Testament: Their Use, Development, Syntax and Significance* (BZAW 311; Berlin and New York: de Gruyter, 2002); **G. Steins,** *Die Chronik als kanonisches Abschlußphänomen: Studien zur Entstehung und Theologie von 1/2 Chronik* (BBB 93; Weinheim: Beltz Athenäum, 1995); **H. Wiener,** *The Composition of Judges II 11 to 1 Kings II 46* (Leipzig: Hinrichs, 1929); **T. Willi,** *Die Chronik als Auslegung: Untersuchungen zur literarischen Gestaltung der historischen Überlieferung Israels* (FRLANT 106; Göttingen: Vandenhoeck & Ruprecht, 1972); **Y. Zakovitch,** *"And You Shall Tell Your Son . . .": The Concept of the Exodus in the Bible* (Jerusalem: Magnes, 1991); idem, *An Introduction to Innerbiblical Interpretation* [Hebrew] (Jerusalem: Ha-Or, 1992).   W. M. Schniedewind

INSET POETRY. *See* POETRY.

INTERTEXTUALITY. *See* METHODS OF INTERPRETATION.

IRON AGE ARCHAEOLOGY. *See* ARCHAEOLOGY, SYRO-PALESTINIAN.

ISAIAH

Of all the prophets whose messages are in the

Latter Prophets (the books of Isaiah through Malachi), Isaiah is unique in participating in a narrative in 1-2 Kings (of the others, there is only an allusion to a word of Jonah in 2 Kings 14:25). In 1-2 Chronicles only Isaiah and *Jeremiah are mentioned, with Isaiah's role being quite different from that in 2 Kings.

    1. "Isaiah ben Amoz the Prophet"—His
        Name in the Text
    2. Isaiah in 2 Kings 18—20
    3. Isaiah in 2 Chronicles

1. "Isaiah ben Amoz the Prophet"—His Name in the Text.

The name of the prophet Isaiah in the MT (Kings, Chronicles and Isaiah) is always *yĕšaʿyāhû,* and in the LXX, *Ēsaias* (apart from 2 Chron 26:22 [see below]). Although other individuals of the same name are in lists in the MT (1 Chron 3:21; 25:3, 15; 26:25; Ezra 8:7, 19; Neh 11:7), the LXX has quite different transliterations, and English versions generally have "Jeshaiah" (but REB: Isaiah).

An unusual feature is the overwhelming use of the prophet's name with patronymic, "Isaiah ben Amoz," with 2 Kings and 2 Chronicles generally adding "the prophet" (2 Kings 19:2, 20; 20:1; 2 Chron 26:22; 32:20, 32; Is 1:1; 2:1; 13:1; 20:2; 37:2, 21; 38:1). The simple "Isaiah (the prophet)" occurs only after an initial long form in that block (2 Kings 19:5, 6; 20:4-19 [8x]; Is 20:3; 37:5, 6; 38:4, 21; 39:3, 5, 8; the only exception being Is 7:3). For other people, patronymics have a narrative function, introducing a new character and/or situating the person sociologically, often with contextual significance (e.g., royal or priestly descent, or kinship links, with names known [Clines]), yet Amoz is unknown elsewhere in the Bible (in rabbinic tradition, brother of King Amaziah [*b. Meg.* 10b; *Lev. Rab.* 6:6]). Perhaps the patronymic became standard to avoid confusion with another, to us unknown, Isaiah. His frequent identification in 2 Kings and 2 Chronicles as "the prophet" aligns him with the succession of prophets who play key roles in both histories (*see* Prophets and Prophecy).

A double peculiarity in 2 Chronicles 26:22 LXX is the absence of the patronymic and the unique transliteration *Iessias.* Given the practice elsewhere in the LXX, this suggests that the translator, probably around 150 BCE, saw reference to a person other than Isaiah ben Amoz, especially since this is the first reference to Isaiah in 2 Chronicles. Possibly, the translator's *Vorlage* did not have the patronymic, and so either the translator assumed a different person or this was the understanding of the tradition shared by the translator. Significantly, there is no textual evidence of later "normalizing" to *Ēsaias*. Perhaps in the Hebrew text tradition the patronymic was subsequently inserted to avoid or correct this interpretation.

2. Isaiah in 2 Kings 18—20.

2.1. Isaiah's Role. In 2 Kings the narrative of the reign of *Hezekiah gives little attention to religious reforms (simply summarized in 2 Kings 18:4 and mentioned in the Assyrian Rabshakeh's taunt in 2 Kings 18:22). The focus is the *Assyrian attacks on Judah and the siege of Jerusalem, with Hezekiah's response to the attacker's arguments (2 Kings 18—19). 2 Kings 20 narrates Hezekiah's illness and the visit of envoys from Babylon.

Isaiah is first mentioned in 2 Kings 19:2 after the taunting in 2 Kings 18:17-37. When Hezekiah sends the officials and senior priests to Isaiah, his response is an oracle, using the standard message formula: "Thus says the LORD" (2 Kings 19:6-7). This provides a striking contrast to the opening words of the Rabshakeh: "Thus says the great king, the king of Assyria" (2 Kings 18:19, 29, 31). Whose words will Hezekiah follow? The oracle begins with "Fear not," a phrase common in prophetic books (19x in Isaiah and Jeremiah), but used as a word of the Lord only here in Samuel-Kings. The defeat of Assyria will come, the Lord promises, because "they have reviled me."

No response of Hezekiah is mentioned. Rather, further messages are delivered to Hezekiah, direct from Sennacherib. This time it is not merely that gods have been impotent against Sennacherib himself, but against all of his predecessors ("the kings of Assyria" [2 Kings 19:11]). Again Hezekiah goes to the temple, this time the narrator giving us the content of his prayer. The narrative of the earlier visit to the temple suggests that Hezekiah had gone mainly to enlist support from the priests, but now he himself is acting in response to Isaiah's first oracle. He affirms Isaiah's oracle, highlighting the Assyrians' "mocking the living God" (2 Kings 19:16), and in his praying for deliverance, the purpose is not Jerusalem's benefit, but "so that all the kingdoms of the earth may know that

you, LORD, are God alone" (2 Kings 19:19).

Now Isaiah takes the initiative in sending further oracles to Hezekiah, again focusing on the mocking and insulting of "the Holy One of Israel" (2 Kings 19:20-31). (This name of God is another feature of the narrative unique in the Historical Books but common to the book of Isaiah [25x], elsewhere only in Jer 50:29; 51:5; Ps 71:22; 78:41; 89:18, and here.) There is heightened description of arrogance and insult, culminating in God's affirmation that he will lead them back to Assyria in the same way that Sennacherib has led captives, with hook and bit (2 Kings 19:21-28).

A new dimension is added in the promise to Hezekiah: Jerusalem will survive and grow (2 Kings 19:29-31), a promise that would be relevant also to exilic readers. In the third oracle the promise of God's defense of the city is made (2 Kings 19:32-34), a promise that seems to contradict the historical reality of a siege. T. R. Hobbs argues, however, that a feature of prophetic style is the use of such language to mean "that the state of affairs that now exists would cease" (Hobbs, 273). This oracle is the first reference in the Hezekiah narrative to Davidic kingship (similar in Isaiah's words to the ill Hezekiah in 2 Kings 20:6). The phrase "for the sake of David (my/his servant)" is a feature of 1-2 Kings, occurring in 1 Kings 11:12, 13, 32, 34; 15:4; 2 Kings 8:19; 19:34; 20:6 (cf. 1 Kings 8:24, 25, 26, 66), but "for my sake" occurs only in these Isaiah oracles and in Isaiah 43:25; 48:11 (2x). In the Hezekiah narrative the concern for God's honor is given prominence in both Isaiah's oracles and Hezekiah's prayer (see further 2.3 below).

Isaiah plays an active role in the narrative of Hezekiah's illness, announcing an initial message, which is modified quickly in response to Hezekiah's prayer (2 Kings 20:1-6). Isaiah is then involved in a healing action, with a fig poultice, and in a dialogue about a sign of healing, the retreat of a shadow on steps (2 Kings 20:7-11; see the commentaries [e.g., Hobbs, 291-94] for various understandings of the sign, depending on the interpretation of Hebrew words).

The final incident gives the dialogue as Isaiah goes to the king, obviously disapproving of Hezekiah's effusive hospitality to Babylonian envoys. Here is a prophetic foreshadowing of the Babylonian exile, concluding with Hezekiah's bland acquiescence (2 Kings 20:12-19).

2.2. Relationship to the Book of Isaiah.

2.2.1. The Text Tradition. Not only is the Hezekiah narrative unique in having Isaiah involved in both words and actions, but also the text is almost identical in Isaiah 36—39. There has been much scholarly debate about the relationship between the two passages. It has been common since W. Gesenius (1831) to view the Isaiah setting as secondary, a view strengthened in the last century with the common acceptance of the separation of First and Second Isaiah. Thus, for instance, R. E. Clements (1980; 1991) argues that Isaiah 36—39 was added as a bridge when the book of Isaiah was formed. Commentaries on Kings or Isaiah of necessity present various arguments.

With a close analysis of the various textual traditions for both blocks, A. Konkel and R. F. Person Jr. (1997; 1999) both argue that it is most likely that each has been based on an earlier text form. This conclusion enhances recognition of the different ways in which the material is used in the two books and gains further support from features of the narrative in each book. Throughout, there is an unusual concentration of instances of the root *bṭḥ*, "trust, have confidence, rely on" (9x in the narrative). In the context of the book of Isaiah the words of the Rabshakeh have added dramatic effect in that they take up earlier words of Isaiah, who has called on king and people to "trust" in God (Is 30:15) and not "rely on" military strength and alliance with Egypt (Is 31:1; 32:9-11, 16-17). This association is not present in Kings, and so there is an aptness of the Isaianic setting. Also relevant in Isaiah are the associations between the Ahaz and Hezekiah narratives (Isa 7—8; 36—39) (Ackroyd 1974; 1982; Seitz).

Outside of the Hezekiah narrative, in all of Genesis-Kings the noun and verb forms of *bṭḥ*, "trust," occur only three times (Deut 28:52; Judg 9:26; 20:36, each with similarities to the Hezekiah situation; this excludes instances of the common adverb "securely, unawares"). Yet it is precisely the feature of Hezekiah's "trust" that is highlighted in the editorial introduction of 2 Kings 18:5 (indeed, in all OT narrative only of Hezekiah is it said that "he trusted in the LORD," with this vocabulary [Knoppers 1992]). This supports Konkel's proposal that the material was prior to Kings but was incorporated in the Former Prophets as fitting the overall theology.

Hezekiah's "relying on the LORD" and the reinforcing oracles of Isaiah concerning the power of God against arrogant oppressors, linked with the warning of exile, were relevant to the exilic community.

2.2.2. Isaiah's Attitude Toward Hezekiah. Often noted is the contrast between Isaiah's positive attitude toward Hezekiah's "trust" in the narrative and the "remorseless critic of the ruling class" (Blenkinsopp, 458) elsewhere in Isaiah—for example, Isaiah 22:8-11, strengthening of defenses, and Isaiah 30:1-18; 31:1-3, turning to Egypt. The contrasts are discussed at length by J. Blenkinsopp (92-95, 458-61), with him concluding that there is "a basic disjunction" between the prophet of Kings/Isaiah 36—39 and the prophet elsewhere in Isaiah. Nevertheless, as we noted previously, the Rabshekah's opening statements relate directly to the content of the prophetic criticism. If such criticisms are known to the writer of the narrative, then the Rabshekah's words force Hezekiah to hear Isaiah's words! At least Hezekiah's actions and the nature of the party that went to Isaiah (2 Kings 19:1-2) point to some response by Hezekiah to an earlier critique of the ruling class. Furthermore, Isaiah's first words in the narrative are not a commendation of "trust," but an exhortation to "not be afraid" (2 Kings 19:6), responding to Sennacherib's arrogance. The fragility of Hezekiah's trust is suggested in the events of 2 Kings 20/Isaiah 39, and so even the narrative includes less than commendatory words of Isaiah.

2.3. The Significance in 2 Kings. A feature of Samuel-Kings is the role of prophets and of the words of prophets that are fulfilled. Upon the downfall of the northern kingdom, the editorial explanation (2 Kings 17:7-40) includes the summary warning that has been given to "Israel and Judah" through prophets, calling for obedience to the word sent through "my servants the prophets" (2 Kings 17:16). The Hezekiah account is the first narrative subsequent to the defeat of the north by Assyria. That the defeat was the result of "neither listening nor doing" is repeated after the introduction to Hezekiah—the question is highlighted: how will Hezekiah respond to the Assyrian threat (2 Kings 18:1-13)? Central to the narrative are the words given by Isaiah and Hezekiah's obedience to the message. The words of Isaiah concerning Assyrian arrogance become Hezekiah's words in the action of prayer, which in turn leads to an even stronger promise of deliverance (2 Kings 19:5-7, 14-34). The link between prayer and prophetic words of deliverance is also seen in the healing in 2 Kings 20:1-11.

The words of Isaiah provide crucial affirmations not previously seen in the message of Kings. Sennacherib is the first king to affirm that Yahweh is impotent even in Jerusalem (earlier the Arameans saw "a god of the hills and not a god of the valleys" [1 Kings 20:23, 28]), and Isaiah becomes the first to proclaim judgment on arrogance (2 Kings 19:5-6, 20-28). He proclaims a promise of a "remnant" that will bear fruit: while in the immediate narrative-time context this relates to the Assyrian attack, in the canonical context of the book as a whole it becomes a sign of hope to exiles. Twice there is affirmation by Isaiah that God's deliverance is an answer to the prayer of trust (2 Kings 19:20; 20:4-5). Isaiah is also the first to announce the coming defeat at the hands of the Babylonians, with Hezekiah's actions being seen as evidence of the nation's leaders again turning to political alliances as a basis for security. Whether in national politics or human illness, Isaiah proclaims a message of the power of the Lord to deliver and to heal. A new basis is also given for hope: not only "for the sake of David my servant," but now "for my sake" is given priority (2 Kings 19:34/Is 37:35; repeated in 2 Kings 20:6). The phrases "for my sake" and "for my name's sake" are seen often in Isaiah and Ezekiel as a basis for hope of deliverance from exile. The reputation of Yahweh among the "kingdoms of the earth" (2 Kings 19:19) is a basis for hope, and those who share the concern for Yahweh's honor, like Hezekiah, are given a promise of deliverance.

Significantly, there is no hint anywhere of Jerusalem being delivered because of the presence of the temple. Although various scholars draw attention to a *"Zion tradition" in the psalms (e.g., Ps 46—48), it is not evident here. R. E. Clements (1980) argues that the idea of inviolability resulted from this deliverance and the subsequent end of the Assyrian Empire, although in all later settings hope is based on trust in Yahweh alone and obeying him, never on the temple. Associated with Zion are promises relating to the *Davidic covenant (2 Sam 7). Significantly, in this narrative, although Isaiah's words include "for the sake of David my servant," the deliverance is linked with Hezekiah's "trust" in Yahweh, seen in prayer that is concerned for Yahweh's honor.

3. Isaiah in 2 Chronicles.

3.1. Isaiah's Role. The name "Isaiah (ben Amoz)" occurs in the MT in 2 Chronicles 26:22; 32:20, 32, the first and last being in citations of the Chronicler's sources. On the other hand, Jeremiah is mentioned in 2 Chronicles 35:25; 36:12, 21, 22, none in citations. In contrast to his active role in 2 Kings 18—20, Isaiah is mentioned only once in the Chronicler's Hezekiah narrative (2 Chron 29—32), being a companion of Hezekiah in prayer, with no details as to the words (2 Chron 32:20).

While elsewhere the Chronicler has made substantive use of material known to us in 1-2 Kings, here the Chronicler has given much more attention to Hezekiah's initiatives in religious reforms (2 Chron 29—31 [i.e., three chapters versus one verse, 2 Kings 18:4]) and briefly describes the response to the Assyrian taunts (2 Chron 32:20-23 [i.e., four verses compared to thirty-seven in 2 Kings 19]). C. T. Begg argues that Isaiah's role is omitted because the Chronicler portrays Hezekiah as a "prophet," emphasizing his initiative throughout, including a number of speeches analogous to prophets elsewhere. W. M. Schniedewind (225), however, points out that a closer analogy is Solomon (also Williamson, 350-51). It is the focus on Hezekiah's fearless leadership that is to the fore. Thus, with Sennacherib's army threatening, Hezekiah makes defense preparations and exhorts the people to rely on God (2 Chron 32:1-8), and in turn Hezekiah shares with Yahweh in the honors (2 Chron 32:22-23). To include Isaiah's role (other than supporting Hezekiah in prayer) would have detracted from the Chronicler's portrayal of Hezekiah.

3.2. Isaiah as Recorder. For the Chronicler, the role of Isaiah is as a recorder of the events. 2 Chronicles 26:22 MT states, "The rest of the matters of Uzziah, from beginning to end, Isaiah ben Amoz the prophet wrote" (for the LXX variant see 1 above). The phrasing relating to records of Hezekiah in 2 Chronicles 32:32 is different: "The rest of the matters of Hezekiah and his loyal [or, 'kind'] deeds, behold, they are written in [b-] the vision of Isaiah ben Amoz the prophet (which is) in [ʿal] the book of the kings of Judah and Israel" (the LXX sees separate sources: "in [en] the prophecy of Isaiah ben Amoz the prophet *and* in [epi] the book of the kings"). Given the place of Ahaz in the book of Isaiah, it is surprising that no similar reference is made in the concluding summary of Ahaz's reign (2 Chron 28:26).

Although it is possible that reference is being made to the canonical book of Isaiah (2 Chron 32:32 uses the same word "vision" as occurs in Isa 1:1), the MT says that the material is "in the book of the kings," and so likely to be different from the prophetic book (so, e.g., Williamson; Dillard). It is also possible that for Hezekiah, the Chronicler shows awareness of Isaiah 36—39 as included in Kings (so Schniedewind, who also argues at length that "the book of the kings of Israel and Judah" refers to the Chronicler's version of Samuel-Kings). It is difficult to see 2 Chronicles 26:22 as referring to the book of Isaiah, since Uzziah appears there only in the title and in referring to his death (Is 1:1; 6:1).

The Chronicler frequently cites "seers" and "prophets" as source material (in addition to Isaiah: 1 Chron 29:29, regarding David: Samuel, Nathan, Gad; 2 Chron 9:29, Solomon: Nathan, Ahijah, Iddo; 2 Chron 12:15, Rehoboam: Shemaiah, Iddo; 2 Chron 13:22, Abijah: Iddo; 2 Chron 20:34, Jehoshaphat: Jehu ben Hanani; 2 Chron 33:19, Manasseh: Hozai [MT] or "the seers" [LXX]). Some suggest that the Isaianic source is fictional, the Chronicler simply citing Isaiah as a prophet who he knew was linked with Uzziah to keep up the pattern. This, however, would not explain the nonmention of Isaiah as a source for the reigns of Jotham and Ahaz (despite the narratives about Ahaz in Is 7; 14:28). Furthermore, the inclusion of "from beginning to end" (a phrase used also for the reigns of David, Jehoshaphat and Josiah) points to access to a larger record, of which Isaiah is said to be the main recorder. For Uzziah, there is no citation of Kings, which, apart from the formulaic beginning and ending, has only one verse, referring to his leprosy and Jotham's co-regency (2 Kings 15:1-6). Rather, 2 Chronicles 26 is a detailed listing of events and accomplishments, which reads as if it comes from written records, plus the event leading to the leprosy.

Although the only explicit evidence is these two verses (2 Chron 26:22; 32:32; and for the former, only the MT refers to "Isaiah ben Amoz"), what we know of Isaiah elsewhere is consistent with the presentation here of Isaiah ben Amoz the prophet as an annalist for the kings.

See also HEZEKIAH; JEREMIAH; PROPHETS AND PROPHECY.

BIBLIOGRAPHY. **P. R. Ackroyd,** "An Interpretation of the Babylonian Exile: A Study of II Kings 20, Isaiah 38—39," *SJT* 27 (1974) 329-52; repr., in P. R. Ackroyd, *Studies in the Religious Tradition of the Old Testament* (London: SCM, 1987) 105-20, 274-78; idem, "Isaiah 36—39: Structure and Function," in *Von Kanaan bis Kerala: Festschrift für Prof. Mag. Dr. Dr. J. P. M. van der Ploeg O.P. zur Vollendung des siebzigsten Lebensjahres am 4. Juli 1979; überreicht von Kollegen, Freunden und Schülern,* ed. W. C. Delsman et al. (AOAT 211; Neukirchen-Vluyn: Neukirchener Verlag, 1982) 3-21; repr., in P. R. Ackroyd, *Studies in the Religious Tradition of the Old Testament* (London: SCM, 1987) 152-71, 282-85; **C. T. Begg,** "The Classical Prophets in the Chronistic History," *BZ* 32 (1988) 100-107; **J. Blenkinsopp,** *Isaiah 1—39* (AB 19; New York: Doubleday, 2000); **R. E. Clements,** *Isaiah and the Deliverance of Jerusalem: A Study of the Interpretation of Prophecy in the Old Testament* (JSOTSup 13; Sheffield: JSOT, 1980); ibid, "The Prophecies of Isaiah to Hezekiah concerning Sennacherib: 2 Kings 19:21-34 // Isaiah 37:22-35," in *Prophetie und geschichtliche Wirklichkeit im Alten Israel: Festschrift für Siegfried Hermann zum 65. Geburtstag,* ed. R. Liwak and S. Wagner (Stuttgart: Kohlhammer, 1991) 65-78; repr., in R. E. Clements, *Old Testament Prophecy: From Oracles to Canon* (Louisville: Westminster/John Knox, 1996) 93-104; **D. J. A. Clines,** "X, X *ben* Y, *ben* Y: Personal Names in Hebrew Narrative Style," *VT* 22 (1972) 266-87; **R. Dillard,** *2 Chronicles* (WBC 15; Waco, TX: Word, 1987); **T. R. Hobbs,** *2 Kings* (WBC 13; Waco, TX: Word, 1985); **G. N. Knoppers,** "'There Was None Like Him': Incomparability in the Books of Kings," *CBQ* 54 (1992) 411-32; **A. Konkel,** "The Sources of the Story of Hezekiah in the Book of Isaiah," *VT* 43 (1993) 462-82; **J. W. Olley,** "'Trust in the Lord': Hezekiah, Kings and Isaiah," *TynBul* 50 (1999) 59-77 idem, "2 Chr. xxvi 22: Isaiah ben Amoz or Isshiah the Prophet?" *VT* 53 (2003) 553-58; **R. F. Person Jr.,** *The Kings-Isaiah and Kings-Jeremiah Recensions* (BZAW 252; Berlin: de Gruyter, 1997); idem, "II Kings 18—20 and Isaiah 36—39: A Text Critical Case Study in the Redaction History of the Book of Isaiah," *ZAW* 111 (1999) 373-79; **W. M. Schniedewind,** *The Word of God in Transition: From Prophet to Exegete in the Second Temple Period* (JSOTSup 197; Sheffield: JSOT, 1995); **C. Seitz,** "Isaiah (Book of)," *ABD* 3.472-88, 501-7; **H. G. M. Williamson,** *1 and 2 Chronicles* (NCB;

Grand Rapids: Eerdmans, 1982).

J. W. Olley

ISHBOSHETH. *See* HISTORY OF ISRAEL 3: UNITED MONARCHY; SAUL AND SAUL'S FAMILY.

ISIN, SECOND DYNASTY OF. *See* BABYLONIA, BABYLONIANS.

ISRAEL
In the Historical Books of the OT, *Israel* is used in four distinct ways. In addition to naming the eponymous ancestor Jacob (renamed Israel in Gen 32; 35 [*see DOTP*, "Israelites"]), these literary traditions represent *Israel* as having been used at various points in Israelite history to name the Israelite nation as a whole (during the time of the tribal league and united monarchy, as reflected in the books of *Joshua, *Judges and 1-2 *Samuel), the northern tribes alone as distinct from Judah (during the time of the divided monarchy, as reflected in the books of 1-2 *Kings), and finally Judah itself as the sole surviving remnant of the former great nation (during the time of the restoration, as reflected in Ezra and Nehemiah). In this last context, at least, it is clear that the designation was not intended to apply to a national entity but rather to a people, restored to ancestral lands in the Persian province of Judah (Yehud). Even in texts representing earlier times it would seem that the ideological concept of Israel as a self-identification was tied more to *ethnicity (a shared cultural/religious and genealogical heritage from a shared ancestor, Jacob/Israel) than to any political/geographical boundaries. The basic kinship-based nature of Israelite society, along with its self-conception of common ancestry, is reflected in the frequent use of kinship language such as "brother" (*'āḥ*) and "sons of" (*běnê*). Even more, as presented by the authors of the Historical Books, the designation applies most appropriately to adherents of the covenant with Yahweh—Abrahamic, Mosaic (Sinaitic, Deuteronomic) or Davidic.

A topic so basic as Israel could be approached from a number of angles: historical, political, social-scientific, theological and so on. In seeking to illuminate the ideological concept of Israel, both in self-understanding (as presented in the biblical text) and in reality, the present article seeks to balance literary, theological and historical analyses of the biblical text as it inter-

sects with the available archaeological data (for a fuller discussion of methodologies see McNutt, chap. 1; Baker and Arnold). From a textual standpoint, W. Brueggemann, in *David's Truth in Israel's Imagination and Memory,* provides an excellent model for understanding the way in which the biblical text presents its truth in various aspects and from various perspectives (individual, tribal, political, theological/religious). The same understanding must guide our search for the nature of Israel more generally. The ideological concept of Israel presented within the Historical Books of the OT (as distinct from the actual national history of Israel) is most evident at its borders and breeches—by the treatment of foreigners, and by the clear signs of persistent disunity that the historical authors sought to overcome. Its overriding referent is the covenant people, descended from Abraham, Isaac and Jacob, and bound in covenant to Yahweh (see *DOTP*, "Israelites"; "Aliens"). Our understanding of the reality of Israel as a sociopolitical entity through the Iron Age must rely heavily on archaeological considerations to counterbalance the ideological agendas of the texts, beginning with the "settlement" period. Although a certain amount of caution is in order (as per Davies's criticisms) in trying to relate these two—the inherited literary conception and the political and cultural realities of Iron Age settlements in the Levant (as reconstructed on the basis of archaeology)—both W. G. Dever and L. E. Stager present compelling evidence that such a correlation is justified. Certainly the archaeology is illuminating for gaining a better understanding of the biblical texts on many points.

1. Diverse Origins: Archaeological and Textual Considerations
2. Israel in the Context of the Conquest
3. The "Pan-Israel" Presentation of the Tribal League in Judges
4. The United Monarchy Conceived as Normative "Golden Age" of Israel
5. Division as Aberration: Josiah Healing Solomon's Rift in Kings
6. The Chronicler's Perspective(s)

1. Diverse Origins: Archaeological and Textual Considerations.
The "minimalist-maximalist" debate currently raging in scholarly circles (see Long; Long, Baker and Wenham; *BAR* 26.2 [March-April

2000]; Zevit) was largely sparked by P. Davies's 1992 book *In Search of "Ancient Israel,"* with Dever taking a leading role on the opposing archaeological front. Although Davies raises important methodological issues for those who would make uncritical use of the ideological literary construct of Israel as presented in the biblical text to create a scholarly reconstruction of "ancient Israel," the extreme skepticism of his conclusions is unwarranted in view of the large body of archaeological and linguistic evidence from the Iron Age that closely correlates in specific details with various biblical texts, as is documented extensively by Dever. Inscriptional evidence from Israel's neighbors also tends to support the existence of such an entity, as well as providing solid confirmation of a modest number of specific rulers and events mentioned in the biblical text, particularly for the Iron Age II period.

The real existence of Israel as a "group of peoples" in the general area of the Levant is attested at the beginning of the Iron Age in the Merneptah Stela (see Dever 2003, 201-8), and new settlements in the hill country appearing just in the wake of the wave of destruction that marks the transition from the Late Bronze Age to Iron Age I in the Levant have been associated with an influx of Israelites around 1200 BCE (see Stager; Miller; Dever calls them "proto-Israelites"). Certainly these settlements represent the culture that does indeed develop later into the Israelite states, well attested in later Neo-Assyrian and Neo-Babylonian sources. Moreover, as demonstrated by Dever, Stager, and King and Stager, the archaeological realia of the Iron Age closely match biblical descriptions in numerous details that would be difficult to duplicate later on. Representative examples include the demonstrated use of specific weights and measures like the *pîm* (1 Sam 13:21), the size of millstones, altar types, leather shields, terracing, settlement patterns and housing compounds reflecting kinship structures, evidence for upper stories and animal stabling in the house. Among other things, Stager demonstrates (contra Albright's theory of nationhood) that tribal kinship structure continued to be the basis of Israelite society throughout the Iron Age, as evidenced by the archaeology of dwellings as well as tombs, reflecting the *bēt 'āb*, with extended family/clan heads having a significant role in governance as the *'am hā'āreṣ*. The Tel Dan Stela, naming the

"house of David" to represent Judah and the "house of Omri" to represent Israel, also reflects this structure. The "house of Israel" is simply the older traditional household defining the people group. Even within this societal rubric the structure was not purely ethnic, however, as adoption and strategic marriage regularly served to overcome outsider status (see Cross 1998; Stager).

Meanwhile, however, archaeological analysis of the earliest settlements also reveals a striking resemblance to standard *Canaanite culture (only poorer, including a more limited repertoire of pottery types, etc.), giving rise to a host of theories presenting alternative explanations for the origin of the Israelites. Ethnic and ideological distinctiveness can be difficult to identify based on cultural remains (Machinist; but see the detailed studies of Miller 2004; 2005). Countering this difficulty, one might justifiably point to things such as the typical lack of painting or other artistic representation on Israelite pottery, or the lack of male figurines (while female figurines are not uncommon), possibly related to an Israelite aniconic tradition either generally or specifically with respect to the (male) deity. Likewise, the striking lack of pig bones at sites identified as Israelite (in distinction from Canaanite or *Philistine sites), despite an abundance of acorns for easy fodder, possibly reflects an Israelite dietary taboo on pork. But given that even the biblical text, despite its clear efforts to present Israel as distinct and unitary, provides abundant evidence for diverse ethnic elements integrated early into Israelite society, it should not be surprising that the early archaeological evidence indicates the same to a certain degree.

Specifically, Exodus 12:38 records that the Israelites, already as they left *Egypt, were a "mixed multitude." If nothing else, Joseph's intermarriage with an Egyptian and the many Egyptian names among the congregation testify to an authorial assumption of a general lack of concern for any kind of ethnic "purity" at that stage. Likewise, from the wilderness period, where the Israelites are said to have spent a full generation as a nomadic population in the Sinai, it is recorded without censure that they were joined by a significant contingent of Midianites, represented as the clan of Moses' Midianite wife and father-in-law (see Judg 1:16, following up on the question raised in Ex 18; Num 10:29-31). Moreover, Deuteronomy 21:10-14 assumes that at the end of most ordinary battles the Israelites will take the young women as wives and merely specifies allowance of a mourning period for them. The Historical Books themselves, although they do contain considerable polemic against intermarriage, also show considerable mixing of populations. Thus, again, it should come as no surprise that the archaeological remains of Israelite settlements show considerable cultural continuity with the preceding Late Bronze Canaanite population, which itself was never a unitary national or ethnic entity but rather a conglomeration of diverse tribal groups, independent city-states and other elements.

Both Dever and Stager seek to explain the apparently diverse origins of the people in the early hill-country settlements, which later developed into the Israelite nation, by combining various popular scholarly theories of Israelite settlement. Somewhat like the *Mayflower* "pilgrim" story for Americans, that diverse population adopted the "exodus" experience of one particular subgroup (Dever [2003] suggests the "House of Joseph," encompassing the tribes of Ephraim, Manasseh and possibly Benjamin) of the society as a foundation story to define their national identity because it resonated strongly with their own diverse stories and supported the values that they held dear. The experience of escaping from the oppression of unjust servitude and the feeling of being outsiders would have closely matched the experience and feelings of impoverished, marginalized Canaanites who had rejected their intolerable social situation on the margins of the great Canaanite city-states and ran off to the hill country to eke out their own poor existence in freedom. These could then have joined up with other elements having common interests and values and shared their local cultural know-how—hence the many close cultural similarities of these hill-country sites with standard Canaanite sites. Other previously nomadic peoples, resonating strongly with (or possibly even contributing to) the forty-year wilderness wandering tradition of the exodus group, could also have joined forces with those groups and settled down among them. The emergence of that diverse group into a more-or-less unified entity, largely forged into loose unity by the outside pressure of territorial competition from the Philistines on their borders, would have been enabled by free intermarriage along with the adoption of a common foundation story, law (conspicuously favoring the poor, op-

pressed and sojourners) and eventually, to some extent at least, Yahwistic religion. Along with the efforts of Dever, Stager and P. McNutt, R. D. Miller (2005) offers a rich spectrum of archaeological evidence and anthropological theory for understanding this early period.

2. Israel in the Context of the Conquest.

In the context of biblical accounts of the conquest we find reluctant incorporation of foreigners juxtaposed with the image of the "faithful foreigner" who is readily and fully integrated into Israelite society. Joshua 9 records a treaty with the Gibeonites (based on a deception and in direct violation of the explicit commands in Ex 34:12, 15-16, which forbid making such treaties alongside warnings against intermarriage), who are then incorporated into Israelite society (albeit reluctantly). Joshua 2 records the sparing of Rahab and her family from Jericho, with Rahab later showing up in the genealogy of *David. Rahab is the most prominent example of the "faithful foreigner" image, represented in the text as exemplifying Israelite ideals better than the Israelites themselves. Jael in Judges 4—5 (of the Kenite clan, noted in Judg 1:16 to be of Midianite descent) provides another. Outside of the Historical Books, Ruth is the next most obvious, where the main point of the book is to prove Ruth's (and therefore David's) worthiness for inclusion in the congregation of Israel despite *Moabite ancestry (combating the blatant prohibition to the contrary in Deut 23:3), based on her exemplary display of covenantal obedience, faithfulness and loyalty.

Meanwhile, Joshua's conquest narrative as a whole also centers on covenant loyalty, appealing to a heritage that is at once ethnic, historical and theological. The challenge issued by *Joshua to the Israelites in the covenant renewal at Shechem in Joshua 23—24 (arguably the climax of the book, intentionally echoed by the confrontation between *Elijah and the prophets of Baal in 1 Kings 18) brings the issue to a head. Joshua's farewell address, like Moses' at the end of Deuteronomy (which sets the tone for the *Deuteronomistic History generally), stresses the need for covenantal loyalty to Yahweh. He warns particularly against making alliances and intermarrying with the survivors of the nations that Yahweh had driven out before them (Josh 23:12). *Israel* is defined in Deuteronomy 33:29 as "a people saved by Yahweh," making the threat of covenant curse in Deuteronomy 32:21 of being made "envious by those who are *not* a people" all the more poignant, along with the threat in Deuteronomy 28:43 of the resident alien rising higher and higher while "you [Israelites]" sink lower and lower. Ultimately, being a part of Israel is a matter of choosing adherence to the covenant. Those choosing not to adhere will ultimately be "cut off" in Israel, in accordance with covenantal law and in fulfillment of the covenantal curses (e.g., Gen 17:14; Ex 12:15-19; 30:33-38; 31:14; Lev 7:20-27; 17:4-14; 20:3-6; 26:38; Num 19:13-20; Deut 4:26-27; cf. Gen 9:11; Josh 7:9; 23:4; Judg 21:6). Also worthy of note in the opening chapters of Joshua is the symbolic inclusion of representatives from each tribe in building a stone memorial at Gilgal, likely to have played a role in periodic Passover celebrations or covenant renewal ceremonies (Josh 3:12; 4:2-9, 20-24). This intentional representation of each tribe anticipates a similarly inclusive treatment in the book of Judges.

3. The "Pan-Israel" Presentation of the Tribal League in Judges.

As shown by A. Malamat, the "Pan-Israel" presentation of the tribal league in Judges is a literary construct that intentionally (if not artificially) includes all tribes and all enemies in order to create a sense of unity and nationhood, even where conflicts were mostly localized in nature (*see* Amphictyony, Question of). But the ideological concept of Israel as a unified entity is present already in the Song of Deborah in Judges 5 (judged by scholarship to be among the oldest texts in the Hebrew Bible) in the violated expectation of solidarity directed toward those tribes that failed in their covenantal obligation to show up in mutual defense. Still, ideology and expectation are not the same as reality, and the civil wars of this tumultuous period generally belie the impression of unity toward which the text strives. One notorious case of reliance on distinctive dialect to sort out "outsider" Israelite tribes as enemies in Judges 12:4-6 clinches the argument.

The book of Judges also notes a considerable number of Canaanite cities, towns and territories that were never conquered, blaming the continuing presence and cultural influence of Canaanites left in the land for the ultimate failure of the tribal league. On the positive side, the Kenite clan is noted in Judges 1:16 as being de-

scendants of Moses' Midianite father-in-law, yet is attributed with defeating the Canaanites under Sisera by the hand of Jael in Judges 4—5, while Samson is famous for his dalliances (and even marriage) with Philistine women.

The Deuteronomistic History also clearly shows an expectation of a higher standard of moral conduct for Israel as over against its neighbors, with the expression "such a thing is not done *in Israel*," echoed most poignantly in Tamar's passionate appeal: "Such a thing should not be done in Israel. Do not do this wicked thing!" (2 Sam 13:12). This moral expectation is made clearest, however, in another breach. The story of the Levite's concubine in Judges 19 deliberately sets up the expectation in Judges 19:11-14 that a Canaanite town, like Sodom and Gomorrah, could not be trusted to honor Israelite hospitality traditions and would not be a safe place to stop for the night. So the closer Canaanite town is passed by in favor of an Israelite town, explicitly because of this expectation of a higher moral standard of conduct in Israel (referring, obviously, not to territorial boundaries but rather to cultural boundaries).

The Benjaminite breach that follows has further significance in the author's depiction of horror at the prospect of having potentially eliminated one of the tribes (Judg 21:2-3, 6, 15-17). This reaction is indicative of the concept of covenantal unity tied to the Abrahamic promise of twelve nations, however artificially construed. This concept of covenantal unity persists despite numerous clues of persistent historical disunity throughout the narrative. By the conclusion of the epic chaos of Judges (signaled as aberrant by the suggestively repeated apologetic refrain "In those days Israel had no king" [Judg 17:6; 18:1; 19:1; 21:25; cf. Deut 12:8]), the reader is well prepared to see the emergence of a unified national entity.

4. The United Monarchy Conceived as Normative "Golden Age" of Israel.

The ideological mark left on the concept of Israel by the united monarchy is really quite astounding, given its chaotic nature and brief duration. According to the Deuteronomistic History, the existence of an Israelite nation as a single, united entity lasted barely seventy-five years—the span of a single lifetime—before it fell apart. And even those few years were fraught with dynastic instability and several civil wars.

What the quick division of the nation (1 Kings 12) after the death of *Solomon reveals is that the unity had always only been tentative at best. This impression is exemplified by repetition of an old saying in poetic form: "What share have we in David, what part in Jesse's son?" (1 Kings 12:16, repeating 2 Sam 20:1). Yet, within the Deuteronomistic perspective, the nation begins as a unity. The split is presented, conversely, as an aberration.

5. Division as Aberration: Josiah Healing Solomon's Rift in Kings.

Among other things, the division of the nation results in conceding the eponymous ancestor's name "Israel" as the national title to the splintering faction. This is something of a surprise from an ideological perspective, as is its generally derogatory popular etymology, as seen in Hosea 12:2-4 (see DOTP, "Israelites," noting Hosea's polemic as a possible catalyst for this development). The division of the nation into northern and southern kingdoms (1 Kings 12), meanwhile, is blamed squarely by the Deuteronomistic Historian on Solomon's multiplication of foreign wives (and foreign alliances) who lead Solomon's heart astray from the covenant (1 Kings 11). In view of the law of the king in Deuteronomy 17:14-20, even Solomon's laudable accomplishments only serve to condemn him the more, beginning with the issue of the wives. Royal marriages often sealed foreign alliances, bringing with them cultural and religious influences that were vehemently condemned in prophetic critique (see Prophets and Prophecy). Alliance with the *Phoenicians provided materials and expertise for the building of the temple. This alliance also contributed to Baal worship in Israel as well as political corruption and turmoil, exemplified notoriously by Jezebel in the north and then by her daughter Athaliah in the south (1 Kings 16:30-33; 21; 2 Kings 9—11). Solomon's typified downfall is thus magnified in Ahab's. The pattern of disastrous alliances is then continued with unreliable *Aram (1 Kings 20), which goads Israel into bullying tactics with Judah (2 Kings 16:5-9), which only pushes Judah deeper into a similarly unreliable alliance with *Assyria, widening the rift first created by Solomon and ultimately resulting in Israel's destruction. Subsequent alliances with *Egypt and *Babylon predictably also turn sour, destroying Judah also in fulfillment of prophetic warnings.

The prophetic voice dominates 1-2 Kings, with the Elijah Cycle forming the heart of the narrative. Its general theme of prophecy and fulfillment continually emphasizes the concept that Yahweh is ultimately in control of all things, whatever appearances may imply. The prophetic message is abundantly clear, epitomized by Elijah's confrontation with the prophets of Baal at the center of this central narrative. Mirroring Joshua's inaugural speech of covenant renewal, a definitive choice is required, a choice to honor the distinct Israelite heritage by covenant loyalty to Yahweh alone. Here, Israel is primarily a covenantal entity. To breech the covenant is to be "cut off" from the true Israel. Judah's experience of the Assyrian crisis under *Hezekiah, meanwhile, serves to underscore the reverse: faithfulness to the covenant will bring God's protection when Israel is threatened, as illustrated by Sennacherib's failed attempt to conquer Jerusalem in 701 BCE (2 Kings 18—19; 2 Chron 29—32; cf. Is 36—37). The vigorous sermons of *Jeremiah against reliance on the temple, however, show the arrogant overconfidence that ensued in the century following Jerusalem's miraculous deliverance. It is further significant that *Josiah, at the culmination of the first edition of the Deuteronomistic History, sought to heal the rift created by Solomon and thus to restore the rightful unity of all-Israel (see Cross 1973; Friedman 1981a; 1981b; Sweeney; Talmon; Cogan and Tadmore). To that effect, Josiah is depicted explicitly as undoing the harms perpetrarted by the syncretistic practices of Solomon, Jeroboam and Manasseh. Josiah's attempt to reunite Israel is exemplified by his inclusion of northern Israelite sites in his sweeping reforms, and possibly also by including Levites and northerners generally in his Passover celebration (2 Kings 23; but more so in 2 Chron 35). J. R. Linville's study on the role of the ideology of Israel in the formation of "social identity" in Kings sees the recovery of this idealized unity as taking place only in the exile (see Linville, 91). Talmon (66-68) argues for a postexilic setting for the distinct anti-syncretistic polemic in Kings, as designed to discredit and reject the nonexiled (particularly mixed northern Israelite/foreign) elements of the postexilic population.

It is one of the legacies of biblical definitions of Israel that the archaeology of Israel in the Neo-Babylonian period has been virtually ignored until recently on the grounds that (from the biblical authors' perspective) Israel was in exile in Babylon during this period, while the *land* of Israel "lay desolate" without them (see the lively debate in Lipschits and Blenkinsopp).

6. The Chronicler's Perspective(s).

By the time of the restoration period, when Chronicles was composed, the deep divisions that had existed during the monarchical period between the northern and southern kingdoms had been largely glossed over and ignored. Not a word does the Chronicler record of all the conflict and civil war under David. The author repeatedly cites the "annals of the kings of *Israel*" as his source, even though clearly the "annals of the kings of *Judah*" (as cited by the Deuteronomist in the Deuteronomistic History) were meant, since the kings of the northern kingdom of Israel are largely ignored by the Chronicler in the *Chronicler's History. Whatever divisions once existed are simply irrelevant, since those cut off by them have long since been swept away, and the remnant incorporated into Judah. It is further interesting that in the context of the restoration, where Judeans comprise the logical referents both in geography and lineage, the Chronicler would choose to appropriate "Israel" as the primary name, when it had been so long associated with the northern faction so roundly criticized for their idolatrous practices by the southern authors of most of the surviving biblical texts. Yet Chronicles goes out of its way to note inclusion of remnants representing various members of the northern tribes in the return and in Israel as reconstituted in the restoration.

H. G. M. Williamson stresses a distinction in attitude toward the concept of Israel found in Chronicles, as one that supports the concept of Pan-Israelism in continuity with earlier books (e.g., stressing David's efforts to include all Israel, and "restoration of Israel's unity" under Hezekiah as well as Josiah [Williamson 1977, 139-40]), and the attitude found in *Ezra-Nehemiah, which is more exclusivist, beginning with its severe anti-Samaritan polemic and general rejection of foreigners (e.g., Ezra 9—10; Neh 10, 13), possibly even extending to nonexiled Israelites (but note also Ezra 6, which does allow assimilation of outsiders). The increased rigidity of cultural boundaries in the construction of social identity in Ezra-Nehemiah is likely to have been the result of a serious threat of cul-

tural assimilation and political oppression. It may also reflect, as Williamson argues, a political rift in the restoration community itself regarding its self-definition and, in particular, treatment of those considering themselves to be Israelites who had not experienced the exile.

See also ARCHAEOLOGY, SYRO-PALESTINIAN; ETHNICITY; GEOGRAPHICAL EXTENT OF ISRAEL; HEBREWS; ISRAELITE SOCIETY; QUEST OF THE HISTORICAL ISRAEL; SOCIAL-SCIENTIFIC APPROACHES; TRIBES OF ISRAEL AND LAND ALLOTMENTS/BORDERS.

BIBLIOGRAPHY. **D. Baker and B. Arnold,** eds., *The Face of Old Testament Studies: A Survey of Contemporary Approaches* (Grand Rapids: Baker, 1999); **W. Brueggemann,** *David's Truth in Israel's Imagination and Memory* (2d ed.; Minneapolis: Fortress, 2002); M. Cogan and H. Tadmor, *II Kings* (AB 11; New York: Doubleday, 1988); **F. M. Cross,** "Kinship and Covenant in Ancient Israel," *From Epic to Canon: History and Literature in Ancient Israel* (Baltimore: Johns Hopkins University Press, 1998) 3-21; idem, "The Themes of the Book of Kings and the Structure of the Deuteronomistic History," in *Canaanite Myth and Hebrew Epic* (Cambridge, MA: Harvard University Press, 1973) 274-89; **P. R. Davies,** *In Search of "Ancient Israel"* (JSOTSup 148; Sheffield: JSOT, 1992); idem, "What Separates a Minimalist from a Maximalist? Not Much," *BAR* 26.2 (2000) 24-27, 72-73; **W. G. Dever,** *What Did the Biblical Writers Know and When Did They Know It? What Archaeology Can Tell Us About the Reality of Ancient Israel* (Grand Rapids: Eerdmans, 2001); idem, *Who Were the Early Israelites and Where Did They Come From?* (Grand Rapids: Eerdmans, 2003); idem, "'Will the Real Israel Please Stand Up?' Archaeology and Israelite Historiography," *BASOR* 298 (1995) 61-80; **R. E. Friedman,** *The Exile and Biblical Narrative: The Formation of the Deuteronomistic and Priestly Works* (Chico, CA: Scholars Press, 1981a); idem, "From Egypt to Egypt: Dtr 1 and Dtr 2," in *Traditions in Transformation: Turning Points in Biblical Faith,* ed. B. Halpern and J. D. Levenson (Winona Lake, IN: Eisenbrauns, 1981b) 167-92; **V. Fritz and P. R. Davies,** eds., *The Origins of the Ancient Israelite States* (JSOTSup 228; Sheffield: Sheffield Academic Press, 1996); **P. D. Hanson,** *The People Called: The Growth of Community in the Bible* (San Francisco: Harper & Row, 1986); **P. J. King and L. E. Stager,** *Life in Biblical Israel* (LAI; Louisville: Westminster/John Knox, 2001); **N. P. Lemche,** *The Israelites in His-*

tory and Tradition (Louisville: Westminster/John Knox, 1998); **J. D. Levenson,** *Sinai and Zion: An Entry into the Jewish Bible* (Minneapolis: Winston, 1985); idem, *Theology of the Program of Restoration of Ezekiel 40-48* (HSM 10; Missoula, MT: Scholars Press, 1976); **J. R. Linville,** *Israel in the Book of Kings: The Past as a Project of Social Identity* (JSOTSup 272; Sheffield: Sheffield Academic Press, 1998); **O. Lipschits and J. Blenkinsopp,** eds., *Judah and the Judeans in the Neo-Babylonian Period* (Winona Lake, IN: Eisenbrauns, 2003); **V. P. Long,** ed., *Israel's Past in Present Research: Essays on Ancient Israelite Historiography* (Winona Lake, IN: Eisen-brauns, 1999); **V. P. Long, D. W. Baker and G. J. Wenham,** eds., *Windows into Old Testament History: Evidence, Argument, and the Crisis of "Biblical Israel"* (Grand Rapids: Eerdmans, 2002); **P. B. Machinist,** "The Question of Distinctiveness in Ancient Israel," in *Essential Papers on Israel and the Ancient Near East,* ed. F. Greenspahn (New York: New York University Press, 1991) 420-42; **A. Malamat,** "Charismatic Leadership in the Book of Judges," in *Magnalia Dei: The Mighty Acts of God,* ed. F. M. Cross, W. E. Lemke and P. D. Miller (Garden City, NY: Doubleday, 1976) 152-68; **P. McNutt,** *Reconstructing the Society of Ancient Israel* (LAI; Louisville: Westminster/John Knox, 1999); **R. D. Miller II,** *Chieftains of the Highland Clans: A History of Israel in the Twelfth and Eleventh Centuries B.C.* (Grand Rapids: Eerdmans, 2005); idem, "Identifying Earliest Israel," *BASOR* 333 (2004) 55-68; **E. T. Mullen Jr.,** *Narrative History and Ethnic Boundaries: The Deuteronomistic Historian and the Creation of Israelite National Identity* (SemeiaSt; Atlanta: Scholars Press, 1993); **H. Shanks et al.,** eds., *The Rise of Ancient Israel: Symposium at the Smithsonian Institution, October 26, 1991, Sponsored by the Resident Associate Program* (Washington, DC: Biblical Archaeology Society, 1992); **L. E. Stager,** "The Archaeology of the Family in Ancient Israel," *BASOR* 260 (1985) 1-35; **M. Sweeney,** "The Critique of Solomon in the Josianic Edition of the Deuteronomistic History," *JBL* 114 (1995) 607-22; **S. Talmon,** "Polemics and Apology in Biblical Historiography— 2 Kings 17:24-41," in *The Creation of Sacred Literature: Composition and Redaction of the Biblical Text,* ed. R. E. Friedman (UCPNES 22; Berkeley: University of California Press, 1981) 57-68; **R. de Vaux,** *The Early History of Israel* (Philadelphia: Westminster, 1978); **M. Weippert,** *The Settlement of the Israelite Tribes in Palestine: A Critical Survey of Recent Scholarly Debate*

(SBT 2/21; Naperville, IL: Allenson, 1971); **H. G. M. Williamson,** *1 and 2 Chronicles* (NCB; Grand Rapids, 1982); idem, *Israel in the Books of Chronicles* (Cambridge: Cambridge University Press, 1977); idem, *Studies in Persian Period History and Historiography* (FAT 38; Tübingen: Mohr Siebeck, 2004); **C. J. H. Wright,** *God's People in God's Land: Family, Land, and Property in the Old Testament* (Grand Rapids: Eerdmans, 1990); **Z. Zevit,** "Three Debates about Bible and Archaeology," *Bib* 83 (2002) 1-27.

R. J. D. Knauth

ISRAELITE SOCIETY

The portrait of Israelite society found in the Historical Books of the Bible shows an emerging and varied culture that evolves out of its household- and clan-based origins into a more complex and more urban-based community. Certainly, the small villages of the central hill country and the Negeb, which were founded in the period 1200-1000 BCE, will continue to contain a large segment of the population, even down to the *Persian period (fifth century BCE). However, the attention of the biblical writers is increasingly drawn to *Jerusalem, *Samaria, *Lachish, *Bethel and *Dan, as well as other cities throughout the two Israelite kingdoms. The international stage that had been dormant after 1200 BCE due to the incursions of the Sea Peoples once again comes alive after 900 BCE with the revival of both *Egypt and *Assyria. As a result, once the Israelite monarchy is firmly established and then the kingdoms of Israel and Judah divide, these people will be faced with the need to make alliances, maintain an army, fortify their walled cities, collect taxes, build roads and other public improvements, and establish a sense of unity that will create an identifiable society. The covenant with Yahweh will serve as one major force in this latter task, although the division of the kingdom and the invasions by foreign nations will place a major strain on established religion—a subject addressed continuously by the prophets.

The task of this article is to describe the various aspects of Israelite society as it is portrayed during the period from the settlement of *Canaan until the return from exile and the reestablishment of the temple-based community in the Persian province of Yehud. Of necessity, this is an abbreviated survey, but major categories such as demographics, the economy, sociopolitical organization and structure, and social and political institutions (family-kinship, marriage customs, gender roles and law) will receive attention.

1. Settlement Period
2. Monarchic Period
3. Exilic and Postexilic Periods

1. Settlement Period.

From the outset, Judges and 1 Samuel portray the Israelite tribes as settled in Canaan and in portions of Transjordan (Gilead), but in a weak condition in relation to their neighbors (*see* History of Israel 1-2). The explanation for this situation is given both in terms of the material culture ("the inhabitants of the plain . . . had chariots of iron" [Judg 1:19]) as well as a theological rationale, which suggests that the Canaanites remained in the land to provide the Israelites with practice in warfare (Judg 3:1-2). What is revealed in the Judges accounts is the rather desperate condition of the Israelite tribes. They lack the weaponry, central leadership and cooperative spirit needed to defeat the *Philistines and other neighboring groups. There is no "Joshua" figure in the book of Judges. The tribes never fully cooperate with any of the judges, nor do they wish to unite into a single nation. Instead, local political enclaves, dominated by village elders, hold control of what land they claim as their territory, and it is during a crisis that they are willing to relinquish their power, temporarily, to a judge (note Jephthah in Judg 11:4-11).

A demographic survey of the village culture of premonarchic Israel would identify it as a segmentary or mixed population loosely tied together by kinship or tribal lineages. They included pastoral nomads, as well as semisedentary and settled farmers who exploited the few resources of the region and functioned symbiotically, each providing products needed by the other (McNutt, 78). Throughout its existence, Israelite society was distinguished by a patrilineal system in which each of its extended families *(bêt ʾābôt)* belonged to a lineage or clan *(mišpāḥâ)* made up of related households. One of the best examples of this patrilineal system and how it worked is found in the story of Gideon. Although he serves as an agent of change, tearing down an altar to Baal in his village (Judg 6:25-32), Gideon does not speak for himself before the offended villagers. Instead, it is his father, Joash, the head of his household, who

serves as spokesman, defending the honor of the family and challenging Baal to take any revenge he might be capable of rather than allow the people to take mob action against Gideon.

Lineages, in which membership and inheritance were based on the father, made up a clan. The clans, which shared defined territory, formed several phratries (kin-based subgroups), which in turn comprised the tribe. Tribal lineages were also, once the Israelites entered Canaan, described as localized, having their own designated territories (Joshua 13—19). The land was "leased" or granted to individual households by Yahweh and passed on from one generation to the next through inheritance customs (note Naboth's insistence on his sons' inheritance rights in 1 Kings 21:3-4). It is unlikely, however, that individuals often were affected by social groups beyond the clan. Everyday life was dominated by interaction with immediate family members and neighbors in their own village or those settlements within a day's walk.

The clan played an extremely important role in the daily life of the Israelites. Each clan's designated territory was further divided into smaller pieces of patrimonial land *(naḥălâ)* assigned to individual households. However, this arrangement actually may have signified that portion of the patrimonial holding which a household had the right to farm and exploit rather than ownership. It was the clan that had ultimate responsibility for keeping the patrimonial holdings intact while allocating its resources and dividing the responsibilities for its productive use among the smaller social units (Bendor, 118; McNutt, 91). Among the institutions designed to ensure this was the "kinsman redeemer" (Ruth 4:1-10), whose responsibility it was to prevent the extinction of a household and a resulting disruption of inheritance rights (Deut 25:5-10).

Marriage functioned as a means of establishing social connections, reinforcing control over land holdings, and providing mutual economic benefit to the families involved. Certainly, intermarriage did occur among clans (exogamy), but most occurred within the clan (endogamy). There was a real advantage in having a spouse who was familiar with local customs and whose social background meant that children would be educated according to the accepted patterns of the village population (Meyers, 36). Endogamous marriage also was based on economic factors, such as the size of the dowry and bride price, but it also took into account land assigned to "orphaned women" (note the daughters of Zelophehad in Num 36:1-12; see van der Toorn, 201). This practice also eliminated much of the concern over choosing an appropriate wife (note Samson's parents in Judg 14:3), since these young women would come from nearby villages (Block, 55). However, it should also be noted that these were arranged marriages, and women had no real say in choosing their marriage partner (Blenkinsopp 1997, 59).

One place to begin an examination of the material culture of the settlement period, Iron I, villages is the ubiquitous four-room house (Stager) (*see* Architecture). This two-storied dwelling had three parallel long rooms, divided by two walls or rows of pillars, and a broad room that ran across one end of the structure (Bunimovitz and Faust, 34). The central room was unroofed, forming a courtyard area where cooking and other home industry tasks could be performed. Having various areas within the structure allowed for the stabling of animals, as well as a workshop and separate sleeping quarters. In addition, there was sufficient space for this nuclear family to separate the sexes to fulfill the demands of ritual purity—for example, when a woman was menstruating (Bunimovitz and Faust, 37). The clustering of these buildings brought the villagers into constant contact with each other, thereby adding to a sense of communal spirit. Coupled with the kin ties between them, this close proximity forged a tightly knit group. While the use of plastered cisterns and terraced hillsides would have facilitated the growth of these village sites, in most cases there is no indication that these farming technologies were invented at this point. Rather, there is clear evidence that both existed elsewhere during the Middle and Late Bronze Ages and were introduced in the hill country as the need to open new fields and boost production arose (Finkelstein 1988, 309).

A way of judging the success of the hill-country villages may be found in their ability to produce agricultural surpluses and thus enhance the diet and the viability of the village population (*see* Agriculture and Animal Husbandry). To expand further upon their success and to protect themselves against ecological disasters such as drought, they engaged in a mixed economy of farming and herding. In addition, to make maximum use of human and technological resources, it seems likely that they developed a system of staggering their planting and harvesting of crops that would provide a continuous supply of food for consumption and local trade (Hopkins 1985, 266).

Once their fields were harvested, community members took their grain to the village threshing floor (Deut 16:13; Job 5:26) (Hopkins 1985, 226). It served as both a communal work space and a gathering place for economic and legal matters. They processed the grain there using a threshing sled to separate the stalks or chaff from the grain (2 Sam 24:22). This was followed by a winnowing and sieving process that eventually resulted in piles of grain arranged around the facility (Ruth 3:3). At that point the threshing floor took on an enhanced social character as a place associated with the future plans of the community, embodied in the distribution of their harvest (Borowski, 59-62).

When harvesting and herding were done, then bills were paid and all debts reconciled. Then negotiation began, with the heads of households establishing covenants to breed and graze their herds, and to obtain grain, as well as additional land and laborers for their crops. The Gezer Almanac, a student text dated to the tenth century BCE, provides graphic evidence of the agricultural calendar. It may be presumed that these work related, festive occasions also provided the setting for the arrangement of marriage contracts, rites of passage for youngsters as they grew into adulthood, and the recounting of the sagas that reinforced their social identity and retold the genealogical history of the community.

Despite the growth evident in the archaeological data from this period, survival in the hill-country villages meant hard work in the fields by both men and women, constant attention to variations in the seasons and an obsession with fertility. Their families had to shoulder the load amidst intermittent drought, insect invasions, and the tragedies associated with childbirth and high infant mortality (King and Stager, 41). Since a good harvest meant the difference between prosperity and poverty, it can be expected that the lessons of the earth and how to make it produce were among the first taught to children. Thus the prophets in a later period will make good use of these agricultural images, knowing that their audience would appreciate metaphors involving vineyards (Is 5:1-7) and summer fruit

(Amos 8:1-2), as well as rapacious merchants who cheated the poor farmers (Amos 8:5-6). It is not surprising to find that the rural villagers maintained their ties to their local communities even when political change provided opportunities for advancement and a move to the new urban centers. For instance, when given the chance to move into the royal household because of his service to King David, Barzillai declined, saying that it was better to "die in my own town, near the graves of my father and my mother" (2 Sam 19:37 NRSV).

Their agricultural surpluses and the attendant growth in population brought the Israelites into direct economic and territorial competition with the Canaanite and Philistine city-states. The farms and herds around the hill country villages eventually became too small to provide the expanding population with an adequate diet. And, according to the biblical account, they were unable to expand into the richer valleys and plains because of the superior military power of their Canaanite neighbors (Josh 17:18; Judg 1:19). As a consequence, some villages developed an interactive relationship with their neighbors on the coastal plain and in Upper Galilee (Stager, 5-11). In this way the territory and the social relationships of the Israelite *bêt 'ābôt* and *mišpāḥâ* are linked to these adjacent areas for mutual military and economic assistance and were normalized by the addition of "brothers" to the lineage's *genealogy (Bendor, 80-82). In addition, hill-country villagers and Canaanite city dwellers peacefully agreed by covenant to exchange certain goods and services, although it can be expected that the Philistines would have had the upper hand (Judg 15:11). This benefited both, but it also gave the villages time to organize into a more cohesive political unit in times of ecological or military emergency.

In other areas, however, the friction between the hill-country villagers and outsiders was immediate and violent. Economic growth, population pressures, political threat and the encroaching settlements all contributed to the Philistines' desire to establish firm control over the Israelite and other hill-country tribes (1 Sam 4:1-11; see Finkelstein 1985, 172-73). It may also explain the story of the migration of the tribe of Dan from close proximity to the Philistine territory to the area north of the Sea of Galilee (compare Josh 19:40-47 and Judg 18).

Social custom and law, as they developed in the village culture, were defined by the extended family and governed by the people's sense of *honor and shame. These social understandings were designed to maintain a spirit of cooperation necessary in such small, unwalled communities of twenty to thirty mud-brick houses with populations of approximately seventy-five to one hundred (McNutt, 66-67). In a situation in which all of the villagers had to rely on the labor and good will of their neighbors, most of whom were kin, the basic values espoused for those who would be honorable included obedience to the covenant with Yahweh, upholding the rights and obligations of their households, and setting an example of hard work and devotion to family (see Mic 6:6-8). Those who had shown themselves to be contributors to the village's economy, and therefore were recognized as honorable, were in turn looked to for advice and became the elders of their village and clan, and they would have been the only "elites" or civil authorities in the village. Shame resulted from antisocial behavior such as lying, stealing, and violations of the religious or civil code (for these basic matters of proper social conduct see the laws in Ex 21:2—23:19). Those branded as dangerous to the life of the village were brought before the gate court, where evidence was presented against them and their fate as members of the community determined (Deut 21:18-21; see Willis, 169-74). Thus Boaz gathered the elders of Bethlehem to confront Naomi's levir to discover whether he would uphold the honor of Elimelech's household and produce an heir for this practically extinct family (Ruth 4:1-6; cf. Deut 25:5-10).

2. Monarchic Period.

The Bible does not report the exact order of events or the precise political climate that contributed to the political transition from village culture to a tribal federation in Israel. It is certain, however, that one unresolved military crisis after another would have provided strong support for the idea of strongman rule, represented by *Saul and later *David (Finkelstein 1989, 63) (*see* History of Israel 3). Continuing clashes with the Philistines reinforced the necessity for a centralized leadership and made it less likely that Saul, once he had been proclaimed chief (1 Sam 11:12-15), could disband the tribes and return his power to the elders (for the various theories on the emergence of the monarchy see

Carter and Meyers). In order to protect their property and their households, the elders had been willing to relinquish a portion of their authority. Perhaps in asking *Samuel to choose a king for them (1 Sam 8:4-5) the elders believed that it would be a temporary solution (Muth, 89). However, the stakes were higher now. A more powerful, central leader had proven to be necessary, and there was no going back, despite concerns over tyranny (1 Sam 8:11-18; 12:13-15).

This is not to say that there would have been a smooth political transition from village elders to chiefs as the leaders of the people. Even chiefs as powerful as Saul and David were subject to the counterbalance created by the elders during those periods when no crisis was evident (1 Sam 10:27; 11:12; 13:10-15; 14:24-46). Regardless of how long a tribe existed, it was always possible that the villages could revolt to demand a new tribe and a new chief or to demand less centralization and a return to the village system (2 Sam 20:1-3; 1 Kings 12:3-4). Nonetheless, statistically the state more often than any other system is the one that replaces the tribe. The expansion and collapse of the tribe carries within it the seeds for the development of states (Flanagan, 313-18). Regional organization was established through alliance, force and economic contacts as tribes were formed (1 Sam 13:2-4). The elders, although they continue to be mentioned in relation to the king and the decision process of government (1 Sam 15:30; 2 Sam 3:17-18; 19:11), clearly are losing their former hold over all matter of issues among the local people.

Although the social institution of the chief was a practical strategy for protecting the villages in early Israel, the people and their leaders were reminded repeatedly that ultimately only Yahweh could feed and protect Israel (1 Sam 12:16-25). For a remarkable period of almost 250 years, the Israelite villages maintained their commitment to a society without monarchs, soldiers and slaves. Then they had to choose between accepting a monarch and becoming a state or facing annihilation altogether. It was a difficult choice with which Israel was never completely satisfied.

While some social institutions and customs from the village culture remain intact despite this transition, the establishment of the more centrally based monarchic culture meant that Israelite society was forced to change. It can be expected that the growth of urban centers such

as Jerusalem and later Samaria meant an increase in total population as well as greater controls being placed on the adjacent villages. Increasingly, the produce of the local villages was funneled into feeding the urban population and providing products that could be exchanged for the luxury items prized by urban elites (McNutt, 158). The time when the village could remain isolated from the world or even regional events was now over. They would benefit from the increase in trade and the introduction of new products, but also they would have to participate in the nation-building activities of the kings, suffer the economic inroads of taxation, and see their labor diverted to military and corvée activities (see Samuel's cautionary statements in 1 Sam 8:11-18 and the clearly defined roles for both genders among the conscripted workers and soldiers).

Following the death of Solomon in the latter part of the tenth century BCE, the division of the kingdoms (see History of Israel 4) led to the weakening of the two nations' defenses, allowing the Egyptian pharaoh Shishak/Shoshenq to campaign freely in Judah and Israel (1 Kings 14:25-26). But Shishak's death a year later curtailed that plan. Instead, it would be the Neo-Assyrians and *Phoenicians who would dominate the political climate in Syria-Palestine for the next three centuries (Gitin, 162-63). During this initial period of the division some adjustments had to be made in Israelite society. To begin with, travel between the two areas would have been more restricted, with King *Jeroboam establishing new royal shrines at Dan and Bethel to discourage pilgrims from returning to Jerusalem for the major religious feasts (1 Kings 12:25-33). The natural resources of the northern kingdom would have aided that area to continue to prosper economically, but the less well-endowed southern kingdom must have experienced real problems and was most likely dominated politically by Israel for much of the next two centuries.

During the first half of the eighth century BCE, Israel and Judah enjoyed a period of economic prosperity and political autonomy unmatched since the establishment of the monarchy. An estimate of the population at the time suggests that in the eighth century BCE 350,000 persons lived in the northern kingdom, while another 110,000 occupied Judah (Broshi and Finkelstein). The growth in population and economic opportunity was facilitated by the defeat of Aram-Damascus by the Assyrian king Adad-narari III in 796 BCE. In eliminating Israel's chief political rival in the region, Assyria gave the smaller states in Syria-Palestine the opportunity to reclaim some lost territory, restore their control over the major trade routes and establish new economic links with Phoenicia.

During this same period the growing population and the increasing demands of the state to increase agricultural production led to the creation of large estates both in the plains and in the hill country (Chaney, 21-23). This move toward a "command economy," driven by the policies of the monarchy, absorbed into itself the decision-making process that previously had existed at the local level by small farmers and village elders (Hopkins 1983, 73-77). Large numbers of destitute, landless households were forced into debt slavery and day labor (Amos 2:8; Yavneh Yam inscription). When households defaulted in repaying their loans, creditors foreclosed on the property and sold the entire household—men, women and children—as slaves (2 Kings 4:1). Legally, creditors were not buying land or selling slaves, but just holding the land as collateral and collecting the wages of its owners as interest until the debt was repaid (Lev 25:35-46; 2 Kings 4:1; Neh 5:1-5). Debt slaves were racially identical with their owners but were distinguished from them by a label of shame. Because they left their own household to work in the household of their creditors, they were labeled "strangers in the land" (Judg 19:16).

Even during this period, however, the population in both Israel and Judah remained 70 percent rural (Knight, 167-72). They continued to marry within their clans, in their own villages or nearby ones, and worship at their local high places. The sabbath and "new moon" festivals would continue to play a significant role in their worship (Is 1:13; Amos 8:5) and as part of the activities required of clan members (1 Sam 20:5-6). The efforts, especially by the kings of Judah, to centralize cultic activity in Jerusalem and eliminate or downplay the importance of local shrines probably had only mixed success (2 Kings 18:4; 23:4-20). It is quite likely, in fact, that the rural population's sense of social identity remained attached to the clan and their patrimonial territory, but the economic demands of the state and the occasional inroads and destructive

force of invading armies must have reminded them of the larger world around them. Thus they were pressed heavily by the urban centers for their products and were forced to pay *taxes to the state and the temple, and their young men were drafted in time of war (1 Kings 20:15). They also were the first to feel the direct effects of invading armies, and it will be their flight to the walled cities that will overtax them during sieges by Syrian, Assyrian and *Babylonian invaders (see 2 Kings 6:24-31). It is no wonder that the rural prophet Micah was so sharp in his condemnation of Jerusalem and Samaria for bringing such disaster on the villages of the land (Mic 1:5-16).

When there was peace the people of the land might marvel at kings who married princesses from other kingdoms (1 Kings 3:1; 16:31), and it is unclear whether they understood how such an alliance might benefit their own country. The marriage customs/practices of royalty had little to do with those of the people as a whole (King and Stager, 38) (*see* Royal Family). For them the old social concerns remained alive and ongoing. Therefore, on the scale of maintaining an ordered existence, it was more important to find the means to care for the destitute widows and orphans (Deut 24:19-20), amicably settle boundary disputes (Deut 19:14), deal with familial disputes over marriage (Deut 22:13-21) or just compensation for injury to animals (Ex 21:33-34). Simply put, having enough to eat took precedence over international affairs (see 2 Kings 4:38-41), and when they became ill, it was the prophet or local priest who was consulted (2 Kings 5:2-3).

What may have tipped the balance, however, within the traditional local means of settling disputes was the increasing role played by a royal court (2 Sam 15:2-4; 1 Kings 4:2-19) and judicial officials appointed by the state (Blenkinsopp 1997, 88) (*see* State Officials). The prophetic indictment of "iniquitous decrees" and "oppressive statutes" (Is 10:1) and the condemnation of judges "who take a bribe" (Amos 5:12; Hos 7:1-3) signal real social and legal changes brought on by the consolidation of power in the central authority. However, these changes in the sociopolitical structure cannot be considered completely bad, since they did bring greater efficiency to resource management and may have dispelled some of the abuses associated with the authoritarian patriarchal system of the *bêt 'āb* (Blenkinsopp 1997, 91).

While the biblical text concerns itself to a great extent with the activities of kings, the bulk of Israelite society continued to maintain their existence on the land, and for the most part they concerned themselves with the everyday aspects of family life and seasonal agricultural necessities. Centralization of authority did infringe upon this pattern of life, but the basic shape of kin-based relationships, the allegiance to family and clan, remained intact. It may be argued that the deportation policies of the Assyrians and Babylonians were a greater shock to the elites and to those tied to the urban centers such as Jerusalem and Samaria. The land was intimately tied to the covenant with Yahweh, and it will be the hope of return that will be chronicled in the songs of the exiles (Ps 137:4-6). For the rural population that was left behind in the wake of the marauding armies, the strength attached to the household and clan remained to hold them together. This surviving portion of the population would become the "people of the land" who would compete in the next period with the returning exiles (Ezra 4:1-5).

3. Exilic and Postexilic Periods.

The exilic community that was formed in Mesopotamia was in great danger of cultural annihilation (*see* History of Israel 6). When the Assyrians destroyed the northern kingdom of Israel in 721 BCE, much of its surviving population was deported (*see* History of Israel 5). While reference to these "Samarians" does occur in the official annals of Sargon II, as well as in Neo-Assyrian economic and legal documents throughout the seventh century BCE (Oded, 94-99), the exact size of this exilic community and its level of organization as a distinct minority group is unknown. Presumably, some of these people assimilated with the surrounding cultures and disappeared from history. Others may well have joined with the new exilic groups as they were brought to Mesopotamia during the late seventh century and throughout the sixth century BCE by the Neo-Babylonians, and formed distinctive communities that survived and held on to their cultural heritage.

The psychological trauma caused by their forced displacement and relocation far from their homeland and in the midst of a strange and intimidating society must have had an effect on many of them. It must have been quite a shock to the people of Judah that they too could be taken "far from the Lord" (Ezek 11:15), a phrase that they had used for the exiles from the northern kingdom. Certainly, the laments found in Psalm 137 and the explicit language of despair over Nebuchadnezzar's triumph in Jeremiah 51:34-35 speak to the fear, despair and hatred generated by the destruction of Jerusalem and the exile. Given the uncertainties of their situation, it is very likely therefore that some would choose to assimilate with their conquerors, accepting the fact that their God had failed them, and disappearing as a distinctive people, while others moved toward a new identity within their understanding of the covenant.

One additional factor in the decision-making process for some of those in the *gôlâ*, or exilic community, was the possibility of opportunities that would allow them to become a part of the economy of their new region (i.e., farmers, herders, fishermen). Less likely was the chance to be appointed to government posts at any level. These positions would have gone to Babylonians, Persians and Medes, with just a small minority from the exiled or expatriate groups (Zadok, 87). Other than the mention of Daniel, Mordecai and Nehemiah in the Bible, there is no clear mention of Judean exiles rising to high office.

A body of economic documents from the Persian period may shed some light on the conditions of the exilic community after 539 BCE. The Murashu documents from Nippur on the alluvial plain of Lower Mesopotamia represent a portion of the correspondence of a major financial concern that made loans and provided business capital. They indicate that a number of Judean families engaged in a range of economic activities and also served as government officials. Opportunities such as this would have drawn some of them into an acceptance of assimilationist accommodations. Approximately 3 percent of the people named in these published texts are Judean in origin (70 out of 2,500). The process of redevelopment, which involved the redeployment of deported peoples in underpopulated or previously devastated areas, served as a key feature of the Babylonian policy's use of exiles (Yamauchi, 243-44). This would have brought new capital into the region, opportunities for employment and economic advancement, which could have benefited these Judean families and given them an additional reason for remaining in the Diaspora.

Those who chose not to assimilate would have to be realistic enough to know that their cultural survival required a complete reformulation of their basic religious and social ideals. This group also would have to find some means of maintaining their identity while accommodating to the reality of their living situation in exile. The solution for them took the form of the "Jewish identity movement." It seems likely that a formal attempt was made at this point to put a greater emphasis on theological matters that previously had been developed during the eighth century BCE. This was coupled with the Holiness Code (Lev 17—26), which placed a greater emphasis on ritual purity and holy living. The key here is to provide a clear sense of the differentiation between what is clean and unclean, pure and impure. Ritual purity, at its heart, involved aspects of personal hygiene (ritual bathing) as well as attention to strict dietary practices. Their endorsement in the Daniel 1—6 stories suggests a formal acceptance by the Jews at least by the time of the postexilic period.

A new emphasis on sabbath worship is the direct result of the destruction of the Jerusalem temple and the shift away from a sacrifice-based cult administered by priests. This weekly celebration is the only holy day in the cultic calendar that could be observed in the exile (Milgrom, 28). Without a central shrine or designated *"high place" in which to worship and make their sacrifices, the exiles and their families would have been most likely to withdraw into private, family-based devotions, including *prayer, recitation of the history of their people, and perhaps the reading or study of written passages from legal or prophetic literature. By commemorating Yahweh's creative act and the injunction to cease work on the sabbath, the exilic community was able to affirm Yahweh as the sole creative force and thereby make an argument for monotheism. The fact that the sabbath provided an opportunity for the parents, who would otherwise be at work, to engage in simple rituals and explain to their children their theology strengthened the cultural foundation of the exilic community.

If circumcision had ceased to be widely practiced during the monarchy period, it was revived in the exile and emphasized as a necessary ritual act of initiation for all Jewish males, involving "more technical than cultic" significance (Zevit,

665). While a precedent is found for this in Genesis 17:9-14 and Exodus 4:24-26, the origin of circumcision is unknown. The emphasis it receives in the royal annals where the Philistines are labeled as the "uncircumcised" may suggest a possible date (Judg 14:3; 1 Sam 17:26; 31:4), but in the exilic and postexilic periods it was the Babylonians and Greeks who did not practice circumcision and thus served as the cultural enemies of the Jews.

One of the greatest dangers to the existence of the exilic community was submersion into the surrounding culture through intermarriage. Endogamy—marriage within a select, defined group—serves as a social response to what may even be described as an instinctive struggle to protect a culture from outside influences. In Israelite society the mother was always the child's first teacher, and if she came from a non-Jewish household, she would present mixed signals that could draw the child away from Judaism. The only other time in which endogamy is emphasized is in the ancestral narratives (Gen 24:3-4; 26:34), and for the same reason: cultural survival. Aside from this emphasis on cultural identity, endogamy makes little economic or political sense. Thus it is not a factor during the monarchy period, and it has to be enforced on the descendants of the returned exiles by the more stringent Diasporic Jews *Ezra and *Nehemiah (Ezra 9:1-4; Neh 13:23-30). It is also likely that the Persian government policy supported this marriage practice as part of its attempt to maintain distinct ethnic units within their provinces (Matthews, 10-11).

A distinction also must be drawn between the Diaspora community that chose to remain in the lands of the exile after 538 BCE and the minority (perhaps 15 percent of the total population) that chose to return to Jerusalem (*see* History of Israel 7-8). The Jewish identity movement and the eventual creation of the synagogue as local community center for prayer and education aided the Jews of the Diaspora in maintaining their cultural identity. Those who returned would, with the help of the Persian government, rebuild the temple and restore a portion of the land to cultivation. Their existence would be governed by the reestablished priestly class and a succession of Persian and Greek administrators over the next three hundred years.

Indications are that the returned exiles quickly expended the funds and resources provided by Cyrus's decree. They also were faced with staunch opposition from both those peoples who had remained in the land during the exile and their neighbors in Samaria and Transjordan (Ezra 4:1-16). This, plus international events occupying the attention of the Persian government, had sidetracked the construction for a generation. In fact, the only event involving the Persian king Darius in the biblical narrative is found in the dispute between the returned exiles, led by their governor *Zerubbabel, and Tattenai, the governor of "the province Beyond the River," involving the rebuilding of the temple in Jerusalem (Ezra 5:1—6:15). According to the biblical account (Ezra 6:2-5), once Darius's bureaucrats had retrieved a copy of Cyrus's original decree and reaffirmed the Persian commitment to support local temples, a royal order was given and funds supplied that quickly led to the completion of the project in 515 BCE. This dependence on Persian assistance is an indication that economic and political conditions at that point were quite tenuous. The returned exiles simply needed what resources they had to build their own houses, plant their fields and make a new start in a land that had to be rehabilitated (Hoglund, 57).

Thus Yehud became a very small part of an empire that was divided by Darius I into twenty provinces or satrapies administered by governors (satraps) appointed by the Persian emperor (Herodotus *Hist.* 3.88-95). Population estimates in Yehud for the early Persian period are about 13,350, and for the later Persian period about 20,650. Jerusalem during this time averaged about 1,500 persons, approximately 20 percent of its size prior to its destruction by Nebuchadnezzar (Carter, 200-201). Like all the political divisions in the empire, their activities would have been monitored through a regular reporting system by the royal bureaucracy based at the imperial capital of Susa. Yehud, as a small administrative unit within a larger province ("the province Beyond the River" [Ezra 7:21]), would have been governed by a local appointee *(pehâ)* and would have had a certain measure of local autonomy to conduct its affairs. Archaeological surveys have demonstrated that the majority of the people in Yehud lived in small, unwalled villages, and only Jerusalem, during the governorship of Nehemiah, was a walled city (Carter, 215).

There is a break in the biblical narrative following the restoration of the Jerusalem temple.

Although this event had been one goal of the returnees (as expressed in Haggai 1:2-11), it could not be more than a visible symbol of their newly restored political condition. Presumably, for the community in Yehud to be successful, its members would have had to continue to develop their social identity and their local economy as one small portion of the Persian Empire. For instance, recent surveys by the Israel Antiquities Authority have discovered many small agricultural installations (wine presses, cisterns, grain storage facilities) that would have served to provision Jerusalem and contributed to the economy of the province (Carter, 250-52). As was the case in the monarchic period, these villages were taxed fairly heavily. They made "in-kind" contributions even after the introduction of coined money, in large part because there would not have been wide distribution of coins and because the system of collecting agricultural products was so long-standing and efficient. Their taxes were used to support the provincial elite (both the temple community and the governor's bureaucracy) and to meet the tribute quota set by the imperial government. That left the average citizen at a subsistence level and did not allow for the creation of a middle class except among those merchants who participated in trade (Carter, 281).

The emphasis that the Persian-appointed Ezra and Nehemiah placed on endogamy as a means of preserving the ethnic identity of the Yehud community suggests that this practice had not been enforced for some time among the returned exiles. This likelihood is more reflective of (1) immigrants who wish to marry into propertied families and thus gain a greater hold on territories that they otherwise might not have possessed, or (2) a community whose demographic factors (lack of females) required them to accept marriage arrangements out of necessity (note the fairly common evidence of intermarriage in the Jewish garrison on the Egyptian island of Elephantine). The first argument is based on the immigrants' desire to "marry up" in order to more quickly make their community viable and welcome in the area (Smith-Christopher, 249-50). Furthermore, it is likely that some of the "foreigners" involved were actually Israelites who had not gone into the exile, and thus had not undergone the "purification" experienced by the exiles.

Another way of looking at this is in terms of

the community's desire to purify itself of "foreign" influences (Eskenazi, 190-91). The constancy of ritual and adherence to the rule of "The Book," advocated by Ezra and Nehemiah, thus would replace the dangers of social evolution and assimilation that were manifested in part by the mixed marriages and the concern over the ability to speak Hebrew (Neh 13:23-24), another "ingredient of national identity" (Blenkinsopp 1988, 363). It would also lead to the redefining of proper marriage partners. Those matches that had been deemed acceptable previously, due to a lack of females among the returnees or some other demographic factor, would, under this new social order, be forbidden.

For such an ideological change to take place, however, it was necessary to draw upon previously held traditions or to create authentic-sounding precedents for social custom. Thus Ezra and Nehemiah's insistence on endogamy is reinforced by the mandate given to the covenantal community to keep itself separate from the "peoples of the land" (Ex 34:12-16; Deut 7:1-11) and by the custom of the ancestors to marry only within their own social group for the first two generations (Gen 24:3-4; 28:1-5). The result is an acceptance of a custom because it is identified as socially and legally valid.

Thus, during the period chronicled in the Latter Prophets, Israelite society took form and evolved from a clan-based village culture into a more complex society dominated by a monarchy. The legal traditions, social customs and familial kinship patterns that marked them have their basis in the agricultural life of the majority of its people. Although archaeology and the biblical text can be used to reconstruct some aspects of this ancient society, it must be understood that much is still unknown and can only be surmised from the data currently at hand. Still, human cultures are enough alike to allow us to say that their lives were determined by the physical environment in which they lived, the needs of family (marriage and inheritance practices), and the outside political and economic influences that forced them to change or accommodate to new situations.

See also CITIES AND VILLAGES; ETHNICITY; ISRAEL; QUEST OF THE HISTORICAL ISRAEL; ROYAL FAMILY; SOCIAL-SCIENTIFIC APPROACHES; STATE OFFICIALS; TRIBES OF ISRAEL AND LAND ALLOTMENT/BORDERS; WOMEN.

BIBLIOGRAPHY. S. Bendor, *The Social Structure of Ancient Israel* (Jerusalem: Simor, 1996); **J. Blenkinsopp**, *Ezra-Nehemiah: A Commentary* (Philadelphia: Westminster, 1988); idem, "The Family in First Temple Israel," in *Families in Ancient Israel*, ed. L. G. Perdue et al. (Louisville: Westminster/John Knox, 1997) 48-103; **D. Block**, "Marriage and Family in Ancient Israel," in *Marriage and Family in the World of the Bible*, ed. K. Campbell (Downers Grove, IL: InterVarsity Press, 2003) 55-143; **O. Borowski**, *Agriculture in Iron Age Israel* (Winona Lake, IN: Eisenbrauns, 1987); **M. Broshi and I. Finkelstein**, "The Population of Palestine in Iron Age II," *BASOR* 287 (1992) 47-60; **S. Bunimovitz and A. Faust**, "Ideology in Stone: Understanding the Four-Room House," *BAR* 28.4 (2002) 32-41, 59-60; **C. E. Carter**, *The Emergence of Yehud in the Persian Period: A Social and Demographic Study* (JSOTSup 294; Sheffield: Sheffield Academic Press, 1999); **C. E. Carter and C. Meyers**, eds., *Community, Identity, and Ideology: Social Science Approaches to the Hebrew Bible* (Winona Lake, IN: Eisenbrauns, 1997); **M. L. Chaney**, "Bitter Bounty: The Dynamics of Political Economy Critiqued by the Eighth-Century Prophets," in *Reformed Faith and Economics*, ed. R. L. Stivers (Lanham, MD: University Press of America, 1989) 15-30; **T. C. Eskenazi**, *In an Age of Prose: A Literary Approach to Ezra-Nehemiah* (SBLMS 36; Atlanta: Scholars Press, 1988); **I. Finkelstein**, "Summary and Conclusions: History of Shiloh from Middle Bronze Age II to Iron Age II," *TA* 2 (1985) 159-77; idem, *The Archaeology of the Israelite Settlement* (Jerusalem: Israel Exploration Society, 1988); idem, "The Emergence of the Monarchy in Israel: The Environmental and Socio-Economic Aspects," *JSOT* 44 (1989) 43-74; **J. W. Flanagan**, "Chiefs in Israel," in *Community, Identity, and Ideology: Social Science Approaches to the Hebrew Bible*, ed. C. E. Carter and C. Meyers (Winona Lake, IN: Eisenbrauns, 1997) 311-34; **S. Gitin**, "Philistia in Transition: The Tenth Century B.C.E. and Beyond," in *Mediterranean Peoples in Transition: Thirteenth to Early Tenth Centuries BCE*, ed. S. Gitin, A. Mazar and E. Stern (Jerusalem: Israel Exploration Society, 1998) 162-83; **K. G. Hoglund**, *Achaemenid Imperial Administration in Syria-Palestine and the Mission of Ezra and Nehemiah* (SBLDS 125; Atlanta: Scholars Press, 1992); **D. C. Hopkins**, "The Dynamics of Agriculture in Monarchical Israel," in *Society of Biblical Literature 1983 Seminar Papers*, ed. K. H. Richards (Chico, CA: Scholars Press, 1983) 177-202; idem, *The Highlands of*

Canaan: Agricultural Life in the Early Iron Age (SWBA 3; Sheffield: Almond Press, 1985); **P. J. King and L. E. Stager,** *Life in Biblical Israel* (Louisville: Westminster/John Knox, 2001); **D. A. Knight,** "Village Law and the Book of the Covenant," in *"A Wise and Discerning Mind": Essays in Honor of Burke O. Long,* ed. S. M. Olyan and R. C. Culley (BJS 325; Providence: Brown University Press, 2000) 163-79; **P. M. McNutt,** *Reconstructing the Society of Ancient Israel* (Louisville: Westminster/John Knox, 1999); **V. H. Matthews,** "The Social Context of Law in the Second Temple Period," *BTB* 28 (1998) 7-15; **C. Meyers,** "The Family in Early Israel," in *Families in Ancient Israel,* ed. L. G. Perdue et al. (Louisville: Westminster/John Knox, 1997) 1-47; **J. Milgrom,** *Leviticus 1— 16* (AB 3; New York: Doubleday, 1991); **R. F. Muth,** "Economic Influences on Early Israel," *JSOT* 75 (1997) 77-92; **B. Oded,** "The Settlements of the Israelite and the Judean Exiles in Mesopotamia in the 8th-6th Centuries B.C.E.," in *Studies in Historical Geography and Biblical Historiography: Presented to Zechariah Kallai,* ed. G. Galil and M. Weinfeld (VTSup 81; Leiden: E. J. Brill, 2000) 91-103; **D. L. Smith-Christopher,** "The Mixed-Marriage Crisis in Ezra 9—10 and Nehemiah 13: A Study of the Sociology of the Post-Exilic Judean Community," in *Second Temple Studies,* 2: *Temple Community in the Persian Period,* ed. T. C. Eskenaszi and K. H. Richards (JSOTSup 175; Sheffield: Sheffield Academic Press, 1994) 243-65; **L. E. Stager,** "The Archaeology of the Family in Ancient Israel," *BASOR* 260 (1985) 1-35; **K. van der Toorn,** *Family Religion in Babylonia, Syria, and Israel: Continuity and Change in the Forms of Religious Life* (SHCANE 7; New York and Leiden: E. J. Brill, 1996); **T. M. Willis,** *The Elders of the City: A Study of the Elders-Laws in Deuteronomy* (SBLMS 55; Atlanta: Society of Biblical Literature, 2001); **E. M. Yamauchi,** *Persia and the Bible* (Grand Rapids: Baker, 1990); **R. Zadok,** "Phoenicians, Philistines, and Moabites in Mesopotamia," *BASOR* 230 (1979) 57-66; **Z. Zevit,** *The Religions of Ancient Israel: A Synthesis of Parallactic Approaches* (New York: Continuum, 2001).

V. H. Matthews

J

JAIR. *See* Judges; History of Israel 2: Pre-monarchic Israel.

JEBUS. *See* Jerusalem.

JEHOAHAZ. *See* History of Israel 5: Assyrian Period.

JEHOIAKIM. *See* History of Israel 6: Babylonian Period.

JEHOIAKIN. *See* History of Israel 6: Babylonian Period.

JEHORAM/JORAM. *See* History of Israel 5: Assyrian Period.

JEHOSHAPHAT

The Hebrew name *Jehoshaphat (yĕhôšāpāṭ)* contains the theophoric element *yĕhô-* and means "YHWH has judged." In the Historical Books the name *Jehoshaphat* designates four different individuals: (1) the son of Ahilud (2 Sam 8:16; 20:24; 1 Kings 4:3; 1 Chron 18:15): a "herald" *(mazkîr)* of high civil rank who served under David and Solomon (see Fox, 110-21, 281, 286, 310); (2) the son of Paruah (1 Kings 4:17): a "prefect" *(niṣṣāb)* over the district of Issachar who served under Solomon (see Fox, 141-49, 287); (3) the son of Nimshi (2 Kings 9:2, 14): the father of King Jehu; (4) the son of King Asa and Azubah: a "good" king over Judah who reigned for twenty-five years in the second quarter of the ninth century BCE (870-846 BCE). The latter was co-regent with Asa for three years, and his first-born son, Jehoram (who reigned 851-843 BCE and was co-regent with Jehoshaphat for four years), succeeded him as king.

This fourth Jehoshaphat is the primary topic for the discussion that follows. After a brief look at the relevant sources, the political history of Jehoshaphat's reign will be considered from the perspectives of foreign and domestic affairs. Finally, the archaeological context of his reign will be explored.

1. Sources
2. Foreign Affairs
3. Domestic Affairs
4. Archaeological Context

1. Sources.
The sources for Jehoshaphat's reign are restricted to the biblical record (1 Kings 22:1-50; 2 Kings 3:1-27; 2 Chron 17:1-21:3). The royal name Jehoshaphat is not mentioned in any extrabiblical documents known to date. The material in Kings is very brief in comparison to that of Chronicles. The Chronicler devotes almost as many words to Jehoshaphat (101 verses) as he does to *Hezekiah (117 verses). While most of the material in Kings refers to Jehoshaphat in the context of contemporaneous northern kings and prophets, the Chronicler demonstrates interest in the divine blessings and retributions associated with Jehoshaphat's piety and political alliances (see Japhet, 743, 756, 782-83, 802; Knoppers 1991).

2. Foreign Affairs.
2.1. Alliance with Ahab. Jehoshaphat's alliances with the northern kingdom began with Ahab (1 Kings 22:1-40; 2 Chron 18:1-19:3). References to the marriage of Ahab's daughter (Athaliah) to Jehoshaphat's son (Jehoram) and to the slaughtering of sheep and cattle are indications that a treaty had been made between the two kingdoms (2 Chron 18:1-2; cf. 1 Kings 22:44). That Jehoshaphat may have been the vassal in this relationship is suggested by the scenario in which he acted as Ahab's substitute in battle.

This is similar to a Hittite treaty from the thirteenth century BCE in which the vassal was required to be ready to die for his suzerain (*COS* 2.18:104).

It was in this treaty context that Ahab asked Jehoshaphat to aid in a military strike to reclaim Ramoth Gilead from the king of *Aram. Jehoshaphat complied, but he insisted on inquiring of a prophet of the Lord. Micaiah son of Imlah was summoned, and he prophesied that Ahab would die in the battle. In response, Ahab entered the battle in disguise, while Jehoshaphat was made to wear royal attire. When the Aramean chariots advanced to kill Jehoshaphat (thinking that he was Ahab), Jehoshaphat suddenly was spared. The reason given for sparing his life is slightly different in the parallel accounts. According to 1 Kings, Jehoshaphat cried out, and the Arameans knew that he was not Ahab (1 Kings 22:32-33)—either because Jehoshaphat told them so or because the Arameans identified his Judean (rather than Israelean) dialect. According to 2 Chronicles, Jehoshaphat cried out in prayer, and the Lord helped him by drawing the Arameans away (2 Chron 18:31). Finally, Ahab did indeed die after "a certain man drew his bow and unknowingly struck the king of Israel between the scale armor and the breastplate" (1 Kings 22:34; 2 Chron 18:33 NRSV). Upon Jehoshaphat's safe return to his palace in Jerusalem, Jehu the seer confronted him and declared that the Lord's wrath was upon Jehoshaphat for helping the "wicked" and "those who hate the LORD" (2 Chron 19:2).

2.2. Alliance with Ahaziah. This event can be dated to c. 852-851 BCE, but the details concerning both the alliance between Jehoshaphat and Ahaziah and the fleet of ships at *Ezion-geber are complicated due to the disparity of the accounts (LXX 3 Kgdms 16:28c-g; 1 Kings 22:47-49; 2 Chron 20:35-37). The account in 1 Kings relates that ships were constructed to retrieve gold from Ophir, that they were destroyed at Ezion-geber, and that Ahaziah desired an alliance for the maritime expedition but Jehoshaphat refused. The Chronicler, on the other hand, begins with the assertions that Jehoshaphat aligned himself with Ahaziah, and that together they built the ships at Ezion-geber to go to Tarshish. The Chronicler then relates that the prophet Eliezer pronounced judgment on Jehoshaphat for making another alliance with the north, and finally, that the ships indeed were wrecked.

2.3. Alliance with Joram. After *Moab reneged on paying a heavy tribute to Israel, Joram decided to invade Moab (2 Kings 1:1; 3:1-27). In order to avoid conflict with the Ammonites or the Arameans, it was necessary to approach Moab from the south. Therefore Joram requested the help of Jehoshaphat. Jehoshaphat in turn mobilized the acting "king" (i.e., "prefect"; cf. 1 Kings 22:48; see Fox, 143) of *Edom. Thus Joram, with the help of Judah and Edom, advanced toward Moab. When their armies and animals began to suffer from dehydration, Jehoshaphat suggested that they inquire of a prophet of the Lord. *Elisha then was summoned, and he prophesied that the Lord would provide water and that Moab would be subdued.

The political circumstances of this account are expounded further in the well-known Mesha stela (*COS* 2.23:137-38). The majority of the extant inscription describes Mesha's dealings with the *Omri dynasty (lines 1-31a), and the final damaged lines concern Mesha's dealings with the Davidic dynasty at Horonaim (lines 31b-34). The synchronization of the Mesha stela with 2 Kings 3 and with 2 Chronicles 20 is difficult on many levels (see Dearman, 196-210).

2.4. Eastern Coalition. The *Moabites, *Ammonites and some of the Meunites from Mount Seir joined forces against Judah (2 Chron 20:1-30). In response, Jehoshaphat and the Judahites sought the Lord's help. Jehoshaphat prayed to the Lord at the temple, and the spirit of the Lord came upon Jahaziel the Levite, who pronounced an oracle of victory. As the Judahite forces approached the coalition, they watched from the wilderness of Tekoa as "the LORD set ambushes" and the enemies destroyed each other (2 Chron 20:22-23). This account shares interesting similarities to the Old Aramaic memorial stela of Zakkur (*COS* 2.35:155), king of Hamath, who also faced a coalition of enemy nations, cried out to his god, and received a similar divine response by means of cultic personnel.

The date of the events in 2 Chronicles 20 is difficult to determine, but an early setting in Jehoshaphat's reign seems likely. References to the "terror of God" being upon Judah's enemies and to Judah enjoying a period of peace both occur at the end of this episode and in a passage describing the early events of Jehoshaphat's reign (2 Chron 17:10; 20:29-30) (see Knoppers

1991, 518). Furthermore, the mention of the "new court" of the temple (2 Chron 20:5) may hint that the repairs made by his father, Asa, were relatively recent (cf. 2 Chron 15:8).

3. Domestic Affairs.

The most noteworthy domestic affair from Jehoshaphat's reign is his so-called judicial reform (2 Chron 17:7-9; 19:4-11). In keeping with the meaning of his name ("YHWH has judged"), Jehoshaphat established a high court in Jerusalem similar to the one that Moses established in the wilderness (Ex 18:13-26; Deut 1:13-18) and to the high court of referral in Deuteronomy 17:6-13 (see also 2 Sam 15:3-4; 1 Chron 23:4; 26:29). Early in his reign Jehoshaphat sent out officials, Levites and priests to teach "the book of the law of the LORD" throughout Judah (2 Chron 17:9). He later appointed judges to serve in the provincial courts of fortified cities and in the high court of Jerusalem (2 Chron 19:4-11). Local cases that were especially difficult or important were referred to the Jerusalem high court. Jurisdiction of the high court was divided between sacred and secular law: the chief priest (Amariah) oversaw "matters of YHWH," while the chief officer (Zebadiah) oversaw "matters of the king." Jehoshaphat's judicial reform has been compared to the Egyptian edict of Haremhab (fourteenth century BCE) and to features of Hittite society, but a case for direct borrowing has not been demonstrated (Albright, 78-80; Fox, 68, 167-68, 172; Weinfeld, 65-88).

4. Archaeological Context.

The archaeological remains from the reign of Jehoshaphat may be sought from what is known about the excavated sites in Judah that feature strata from Iron Age II, and specifically from the second quarter of the ninth century BCE. It is helpful to keep in mind what is known from the biblical record: Jehoshaphat engaged in a number of building projects (2 Chron 17:1-2, 12-13; 21:3; cf. 2 Chron 17:19; 19:5; 21:3), exacted tribute from the Philistines and Arabs (2 Chron 17:11), established a prefect in Edom and controlled the route(s) to Elath (1 Kings 22:47-48; cf. 2 Kings 8:20).

We must begin with the capital city of *Jerusalem. Although 2 Chronicles 19:1 mentions Jehoshaphat's palace, the remains from Stratum XIII (ninth century BCE) are meager at best and provide no light on the reign of Jehoshaphat.

This is likely because the inhabitants of many strata in the city of David built directly on bedrock and thus damaged or destroyed earlier stratigraphy.

*Lachish (Tell ed-Duweir), on the other hand, provides helpful data for Jehoshaphat's reign (Mazar, 427-32). Stratum IV (ninth century BCE) was a well-fortified city that was in use for a relatively long period of time. It featured two rings of fortifications, an outer and inner city gate, and a massive palace-fort ("Palace B").

*Arad Stratum X was a fort with a solid wall and was the longest-lived phase in the life of the fortress. According to the traditional interpretation, this stratum has been assigned to Asa or Jehoshaphat in the ninth century BCE (Aharoni, 245-49; photographs, 28-31; Herzog et al. 1984:4, 8-12). Stratum X was thus thought to be destroyed early during the sole reign of Jehoram—possibly by the *Philistines and Arabs (cf., 2 Chron 21:16-17). Recently, however, Z. Herzog has revised/lowered the chronology of Arad, reassigning Strata XII-IX. Herzog now maintains that Stratum X should be lowered to the mid-eighth century BCE and that Stratum XI represents the time period of Jehoshaphat (Herzog 2002:14, 26, 94).

*Beersheba (Tell es-Seba) Stratum III should also be considered. 2 Chronicles 19:4 mentions Beersheba in connection with Jehoshaphat's reign. Y. Aharoni (244-45) attributes Stratum III's gate, casemate walls, houses, storerooms and palace to the time of Jehoshaphat.

The port of *Ezion-geber (1 Kings 22:48; 2 Chron 20:36) was first identified by N. Glueck with Tell el-Kheleifeh, but now the offshore site of Jezirat Far'on (Coral Island) appears to be a better candidate. Jehoshaphat also would have controlled other forts and caravansaries in the Negev. These would have been strategic sites for purposes of international trade and transaction with south *Arabia (see Aharoni, 245, 249; Mazar, 397, 449-51, 513).

See also HISTORY OF ISRAEL 5: ASSYRIAN PERIOD.

BIBLIOGRAPHY. **Y. Aharoni,** *The Archaeology of the Land of Israel* (Philadelphia: Westminster, 1982); **W. F. Albright,** "The Judicial Reform of Jehoshaphat," in *Alexander Marx: Jubilee Volume on the Occasion of His Seventieth Birthday,* ed. S. Lieberman (New York: Jewish Theological Seminary of America, 1950) 61-82; **J. Blenkinsopp,** "Ahab of Israel and Jehoshaphat of Judah:

The Syro-Palestinian Corridor in the Ninth Century," *CANE* 2.1309-19; **K. Bodner,** "The Locutions of 1 Kings 22:28: A New Proposal," *JBL* 122 (2003) 533-43; **J. A. Dearman,** "Historical Reconstruction and the Mesha Inscription," in *Studies in the Mesha Inscription and Moab,* ed. A. Dearman (ABS 2; Atlanta: Scholars Press, 1989) 155-210; **R. Dillard,** "The Chronicler's Jehoshaphat," *TJ* 7 (1986) 17-22; **N. S. Fox,** *In the Service of the King: Officialdom in Ancient Israel and Judah* (Cincinnati: Hebrew Union College Press, 2000); **Z. Herzog,** "The Fortress Mound at Tel Arad: An Interim Report," *TA* 29 (2002) 3-109; **Z. Herzog et al.,** "The Israelite Fortress at Arad," *BASOR* 254 (1984) 1-34; **S. Japhet,** *I & II Chronicles* (OTL; Louisville: Westminster/John Knox, 1993); **G. N. Knoppers,** "Jerusalem at War in Chronicles," in *Zion, City of Our God,* ed. R. S. Hess and G. H. Wenham (Grand Rapids: Eerdmans, 1999) 57-76; idem, "Reform and Regression: The Chronicler's Presentation of Jehoshaphat," *Bib* 72 (1991) 500-524; **A. Mazar,** *Archaeology of the Land of the Bible, 10,000-586 B.C.E.* (New York: Doubleday, 1990); **K. Strübind,** *Tradition als Interpretation in der Chronik: König Josaphat als Paradigma chronistischer Hermeneutik und Theologie* (BZAW 201; Berlin: de Gruyter, 1991); **M. Weinfeld,** "Judge and Officer in Ancient Israel and in the Ancient Near East," *Israel Oriental Studies* 7 (1977) 65-88; **R. R. Wilson,** "Israel's Judicial System in the Preexilic Period," *JQR* 74 (1983) 229-248.   K. C. Way

JEHU DYNASTY

After Jehu (842-814 BCE) killed Jehoram, the last ruler of the *Omri dynasty, he seized the throne of Israel and was succeeded by four heirs: Jehoahaz (817-800 BCE), Jehoash (800-784 BCE), Jeroboam II (789-748 BCE) and Zechariah (748-747 BCE) (dates from Cogan and Tadmor, 341). The dynasty of Jehu is unique among those of the northern kingdom in many respects. Among Israelite kings of the divided monarchy, Jehu is the only one to receive a righteous evaluation and to be given an unconditional dynastic promise (2 Kings 10:30). Jehoahaz is the only northern king recorded as having a prayer answered (2 Kings 13:4). Generally, northern kings are condemned by *prophets, but three rulers of this dynasty (Jehu, Jehoash and Jeroboam) are supported by prophets. While the northern kingdom's territory gradually decreased from *Jeroboam I until the exile, under Jehoash and

Jeroboam II Israel experienced uncharacteristic military success and expansion. These five Jehuite rulers reigned for nearly a century, more than twice as long as the *Omri dynasty, the second-longest northern dynasty. The biblical material concerning the dynasty is concentrated in the books of Kings (1 Kings 19:16-17; 2 Kings 9—10; 13:1-25; 14:8-29; 15:8-12), but other biblical texts also briefly mention Jehuite rulers (2 Chron 22:7-9; 25:17-24; Hos 1:1, 4; Amos 1:1; 7:9-11). This article first examines Jehu, then Jehuite military engagements, and finally divine support for the dynasty.

1. Jehu: A Righteous Founder
2. Israel's Military Engagements during the Jehu Dynasty
3. Divine Support for the Jehu Dynasty

1. Jehu: A Righteous Founder.

1.1. The Only Righteous Northern King. Whereas the books of *Kings generally portray northern rulers negatively, the portrayal of Jehu is unusually favorable: divinely elected, prophetically anointed and righteously evaluated. The kings of Israel and Judah are evaluated as doing that which is either right or evil in the eyes of Yahweh. Scholars typically attribute these evaluations to a Deuteronomistic redactor because the language reflects a concern similar to that of the book of Deuteronomy (for discussion of Deuteronomistic redaction of the books of Kings see Jones, 28-46, and on the Jehu narrative specifically see Barré, 8-23; Otto, 29-117). Of the northern kings, sixteen are evaluated negatively, two receive no evaluation (Elah and Shallum), and only Jehu is evaluated positively. All of the northern kings who receive Deuteronomistic assessments are criticized for continuing in the sins of Jeroboam I, which involved worship of the golden calves that he had set up at Bethel and Dan (1 Kings 12:28-30). Despite his righteous evaluation, Jehu also is twice described as not turning away from Jeroboam's sins (2 Kings 10:29, 31; cf. 13:2, 6, 11).

1.2. Jehu and David. The ruler who shares the most positive similarities to *David, the ideal ruler of the books of Kings (e.g., 1 Kings 3:3, 6; 9:4; 14:8; 2 Kings 14:3; 16:2), is Jehu. Each of the favorable parallels between these two kings (heroic exploits, prophetic *anointing, divine election, dynastic promise) serves to legitimate their rule, a function that is particularly important for founders of dynasties. In addition to their righteous evaluations, both Jehu and David are military leaders who have heroic exploits attributed to them (e.g., 1 Sam 17:41-51; 2 Kings 9:24, 27; 10:7). The text describes David as killing ten thousand (1 Sam 18:7), and Jehu as orchestrating the deaths of hundreds (2 Kings 10:7, 14, 25).

Both David and Jehu are anointed by prophets at Yahweh's initiative (1 Sam 16:1-13; 1 Kings 19:16; 2 Kings 9:6). *Saul is the only other ruler with a prophetic, divine anointing (1 Sam 10:1). Several scholars argue that most northern and southern kings were anointed (e.g., Mettinger, 185-232; Cogan and Tadmor, 106), but this perspective is not supported by the text, as only six of the forty-two rulers of Israel and Judah are said to be anointed. Additionally, outside of Israel and Judah, royal anointing was rarely practiced in the ancient Near East (see Mettinger, 209).

Apart from Jehu and David, only four other rulers of Israel or Judah are described as divinely elected to rule (Saul, *Solomon, *Jeroboam I, Baasha). In contrast, most Assyrian rulers, despite their status as dynastic successors, still claim divine election in their royal inscriptions because it further validates their royal legitimacy (see Ishida, 6-25).

Jehu and David are two of only four kings to receive dynastic promises from Yahweh (David: 2 Sam 7:16; Solomon: 1 Kings 6:12; Jeroboam I: 1 Kings 11:38; Jehu: 2 Kings 10:30) (*see* Davidic Covenant). However, the promises given to Jehu and David are distinct from those given to Solomon and Jeroboam I because they lack explicit conditional language. Jehu's promise also differs from David's because it limits his dynasty to only four heirs (cf. Esarhaddon's limited dynastic promise [*ANET,* 605d]). E. T. Mullen suggests that the dynastic promise to Jehu provides the only explanation for the later success of his heirs, but he ignores the positive aspects of the narrative regarding the Jehuites (Jehoahaz's prayer, Jehoash's concern for Elisha, Jeroboam's obedience to Jonah's prophecy), which also seem to contribute to their achievements.

1.3. Jehu: Violent Usurper or Zealous Reformer? Jehu is portrayed as an unusually righteous king, but he also orchestrates the slaughters of Jehoram of Israel, Ahaziah of Judah, Jezebel, seventy sons of Ahab, forty-two kin of Ahaziah and many worshipers of Baal. The prophet Hosea appears to condemn Jehu's excessive violence (Hos 1:4), even though much of his

bloodshed seems to have been religiously motivated. The question arises whether Jehu should be understood as a violent usurper who seized the throne on his own initiative or as a zealous reformer who removed the Ahabites from power as an act of obedience. Scholars discuss these tensions within the Jehu narrative.

S. M. Olyan's paradoxical perspective of Jehu as a violent bringer of peace does not easily harmonize with the brutal portrayal of him in the text. Both Jehoram and Jezebel greet Jehu, saying, "Is it peace?" and he promptly responds in the extreme negative by killing them (2 Kings 9:22-24, 31-33).

According to M. S. Moore, the narrative of Jehu's rebellion was written to parody Anat's purge (from the Ugaritic Baal myths [*COS* 1.86:241-74]) in order to ridicule Israel's enemies. However, it is difficult to imagine the connections that Moore suggests (Yahweh as Baal, and Jehu as Anat) being made intentionally within a narrative as virulently anti-Baal as Jehu's (2 Kings 10:18-27).

M. White (45-53) argues that Jehu's rebellion was not popularly supported and was initiated by him alone. However, the perspective of R. Tomes, that Jehu was not motivated by personal ambition, is more reasonable. Jehu's lack of initiative is a major emphasis of the text, since Yahweh, *Elijah, *Elisha, the young prophet and all of his officers take steps to make Jehu king before he begins his rebellion against Jehoram (1 Kings 19:16; 2 Kings 9:1-16).

The text of Kings describes Jehu as violent, but also as obedient to the command of Yahweh. Four times Jehu is said to act in accordance with the word of Yahweh (2 Kings 9:26, 36; 10:11, 17). Jehu's slaughter of the Israelite *royal family is included in his initial commission to extirpate the house of Ahab (2 Kings 9:7-10). However, the killing of the Judean royal family should also be considered part of the judgment against Ahab's house, since Ahaziah of Judah's maternal grandfather was Ahab (2 Kings 8:18, 26). (Ironically, because of the intermarriage between the royal houses of Israel and Judah, a tension is created between the promise of a continuous Davidic dynasty [2 Sam 7:16] and the judgment that all males from Ahab's line should be killed.) The only bloodshed committed by Jehu that does not appear to be divinely mandated is the killing of the worshipers of Baal; nevertheless, this incident is consistent with a broader biblical pattern of violent judgments against idolaters (Num 25:3, 9; Deut 6:14-15; 7:4; 1 Kings 18:40; 2 Kings 23:4, 20). Although Jehu's bloodshed seems excessive, the text portrays him as an obedient zealot.

2. Israel's Military Engagements During the Jehu Dynasty.

2.1. Judah. Outside of the Deuteronomistic formulaic introductions and conclusions, much of the narrative material concerning the Jehu dynasty focuses on military engagements against Judah and *Aram. During the reign of Jehoram, Jehu's predecessor, Judah and Israel appear to be allied because, in addition to the intermarriage, Ahaziah of Judah supported Jehoram in his war against Hazael of Aram (2 Kings 8:28). However, any agreement between the two nations would have been annulled by Jehu's slaughter of the Judean royal family. No mention is made of any Israelite-Judean conflict again until Amaziah of Judah challenges Jehoash of Israel to fight (2 Kings 14:8). Jehoash is reluctant, and he tells an arboreal parable, reminiscent of Jotham (Judg. 9:7-15), in an unsuccessful attempt to discourage Amaziah from his course (2 Kings 14:9-10; cf. Judg 9:7-15). Amaziah persists, and, surprisingly, righteous Amaziah is defeated by unrighteous Jehoash (2 Kings 14:11-14).

2.2. Aram and Assyria. During the dynasty of Omri, Israel and Aram alternated between war (1 Kings 20:1-33; 22:2-36; 2 Kings 6:8-21; 6:24—7:7; 8:28-29) and peace (1 Kings 20:34; 22:1; 2 Kings 6:22-23) (*ANET*, 278d-279a; *COS* 2.113A:261-64, esp. 263), with neither kingdom dominating. However, after Hazael came to power in Damascus (1 Kings 19:15-17; 2 Kings 8:7-15), he led Aram to a series of victories over Israel (*see* Aram, Damascus and Syria).

Immediately before Jehu's coup, an Israelite-Judean alliance waged war against Hazael, and Jehoram was wounded (2 Kings 8:28-29). In his weakened condition Jehoram was easily dispatched by Jehu. Since both Jehu and Hazael wanted to kill Jehoram, an alliance between the two rulers seems probable. The recently discovered Tel Dan Inscription (Biran and Naveh) gives further evidence for a Jehu-Hazael alliance. Although the stela is badly damaged, the author appears to be Aramean (divinely elected by the Aramean god Hadad) and to have killed Jehoram of Israel and Ahaziah of Judah, the two

kings whom Jehu is reported to have killed. Thus the inscription seems to contradict the narrative of Kings. However, the discrepancy between these two texts can be explained by an alliance between Jehu and Hazael (Biran and Naveh, 18; Schniedewind, 83-85). As the senior partner, Hazael would have perceived that Jehu was following his orders in killing Jehoram and Ahaziah. Similarly, the biblical text credits Jehu with the deaths of both kings, even though he gives only the command for the killing of Ahaziah (2 Kings 9:27; 10:4, 11).

Shortly after Jehu seized control of Israel, Shalmaneser III of Assyria defeated Hazael (*ANET*, 280d; *COS* 2.113G:270), and then he forced Jehu to render tribute (*ANET*, 280c; *COS* 2.113C:266-67, esp. 267). Jehu is depicted bowing down and giving tribute on the Black Obelisk of Shalmaneser, the oldest known representation of an Israelite or Judean ruler (c. 830 BCE [*ANEP*, 120-22]). In each of the four Assyrian sources that mention his tribute (see Kelle), Jehu is referred to as a "son of Omri." Whereas T. Schneider argues that Jehu may have actually descended from Omri, N. Na'aman (1998) disagrees and suggests that these Assyrian inscriptions were attempting to give legitimacy to Jehu by listing his royal lineage. Schneider's perspective, however, cannot be ruled out, because commanders of the army, like Jehu, usually were relatives of the king (1 Sam 14:50; 2 Sam 2:8; 8:16; 17:25; 19:13; 1 Chron 2:13-17).

As was typical of agreements between their two nations (e.g., 1 Kings 15:19-20; 20:1-34; 22:1-36; 2 Kings 6:22-24), the Hazael-Jehu alliance did not last long, and during the latter part of the reign of Jehu, Hazael trimmed portions of the Transjordan from Israel (2 Kings 10:32-33). Hazael continued to oppress Israel during the reign of Jehoahaz (2 Kings 13:4), but the text states that Yahweh, in response to the prayer of Jehoahaz, sent Israel an anonymous deliverer to end the oppression.

Scholars make various identifications for this deliverer (Jehoash, Jeroboam II, Elisha [see Cogan and Tadmor, 143]), but the most compelling argument can be made for Adad-nirari III of Assyria (reminiscent of Cyrus [Is 45:1]), who, by his attacks from the north, diverted Aram's attention away from Israel (see Wiseman, 240). Support for an Assyrian-Israelite agreement during this period can be found in an Assyrian source that records Jehoash son of Jehoahaz giving tribute to Adad-nirari (Cogan and Tadmor, 335). Since the Tel Dan Inscription and the five Assyrian texts that mention Jehu and Jehoash all locate the various rulers at approximately the same time as the biblical record, they provide external validation for the historicity of the book of Kings.

When Ben-hadad took over from his father, Hazael, Jehoahaz was able to recover towns from Aram, fulfilling the prophecy of Elisha (2 Kings 13:19, 25). Jehoash's son Jeroboam continued the military success of his father and expanded Israel's borders in accordance with the prophecy of Jonah (see Haran; Na'aman 1993), although the text records few details of his military campaigns (2 Kings 14:25, 28).

2.3. The "King of Israel" in 1 Kings 20 and 22: Jehoahaz, Jehoash or Ahab? A number of scholars argue that the "king of Israel" mentioned in 1 Kings 20 and 22:1-38 refers not to Ahab, but to a later Jehuite king, either Jehoahaz (Miller 1966) or Jehoash (Pitard, 115-25). They base their alternative theory on the anonymous nature of this ruler (only four Ahab references in these verses) and their perception that the events described are more compatible with later Jehuite rulers. Despite these arguments, it is more reasonable to identify this king as Ahab. The Hebrew Bible locates these narratives during his reign and refers to him in these contexts (1 Kings 20:2, 13, 14; 22:20, 39, 40, 41). While Ahab is not mentioned frequently, his ally King *Jehoshaphat of Judah is mentioned thirteen times in 1 Kings 22:1-38, and Jehoshaphat does not overlap with either Jehoahaz or Jehoash. Two additional textual connections are made between this anonymous king and Ahab: he is "resentful and sullen" (1 Kings 20:43; 21:4), and dogs lick up his blood (1 Kings 21:19; 22:38). J. M. Miller (1966, 444) argues that these narratives must be later because Ahab was allied to Aram against Assyria (*ANET*, 278d-279a; *COS* 2.113A:261-64, esp. 263), but an Aram-Israelite alliance is also mentioned in 1 Kings 20:34, and, as noted previously, agreements between these two nations often were short-lived. Since these battle narratives are compatible with Ahab's historical context, the arguments of Miller and Pitard are unpersuasive.

3. Divine Support for the Jehu Dynasty.

3.1. Support for Righteous Jehu. Within the narrative of the Jehu Dynasty, Yahweh plays an active role, occasionally opposing the king (Aram's success against Jehu and Jehoahaz is attributed to Yahweh [2 Kings 10:32; 13:3]), but more frequently displaying unusual support for a northern ruler. Jehu's call to rule Israel and punish the Ahabites originally comes from Yahweh. Yahweh initially commissions Elijah to anoint Jehu, who then is meant to execute judgment (1 Kings 19:16), but curiously Elijah does not accomplish this task. He apparently delegates it to Elisha, who in turn sends one of his prophetic apprentices to anoint and commission Jehu (2 Kings 9:1-10). The original judgment given to Elijah (1 Kings 19:17: "Those who escape the sword of Hazael, Jehu will kill") is expanded in the version spoken to Jehu specifically to target all males of Ahab's dynasty as well as Ahab's wife, Jezebel (2 Kings 9:7). After Jehu fulfills his commission, the text records Yahweh affirming him for his obedience and granting him a dynastic promise. Jehu is the only northern ruler to hear directly from Yahweh.

3.2. Support for Unrighteous Jehoahaz, Jehoash and Jeroboam. While divine support for a righteous ruler such as Jehu is expected, Yahweh, surprisingly, also helps three of Jehu's unrighteous heirs (Jehoahaz, Jehoash, Jeroboam). Despite their negative evaluations, each of these three rulers performs a pious or obedient act, which seems to contribute to their deliverance. Jehoahaz prays, Jehoash displays concern for Elisha and obeys the prophet's detailed commands, and Jeroboam fulfills the prophetic word of Jonah to restore the borders (2 Kings 13:4, 14-18; 14:25). Yahweh then displays compassion toward his people, sees their oppression and acts to deliver these three kings (2 Kings 13:4-5, 23-25; 14:26-27).

In summary, Jehu's dynasty is both unique and paradoxical. It was founded by the only northern ruler with a righteous evaluation, yet he did not turn from Jeroboam's sins. His heirs, despite their evil evaluations, generally are portrayed positively in the narrative. Whereas northern dynasties were highly transitory, the Jehuites experienced royal longevity. Jehu was a military hero, but he gave tribute to Assyria and was defeated by Aram. Yahweh helped Aram against righteous Jehu, but supported Jehu's evil sons Jehoahaz, Jehoash and Jeroboam as they gradually recaptured territory, eventually restoring the borders of the Davidic empire under Jeroboam. The dynasty ended as it began, in a bloody coup, when

Shallum killed the final Jehuite, Zechariah.

See also HISTORY OF ISRAEL 5: ASSYRIAN PERIOD.

BIBLIOGRAPHY. **L. M. Barré,** *The Rhetoric of Political Persuasion: The Narrative Artistry and Political Intentions of 2 Kings 9—11* (CBQMS 20; Washington, DC: Catholic Biblical Association, 1988); **A. Biran and J. Naveh,** "The Tel Dan Inscription: A New Fragment," *IEJ* 45 (1995) 1-18; **M. Cogan and H. Tadmor,** *II Kings* (AB 11; New York: Doubleday, 1988); **M. Haran,** "The Rise and Decline of the Empire of Jeroboam ben Joash," *VT* 17 (1967) 266-97; **T. Ishida,** *The Royal Dynasties in Ancient Israel: A Study on the Formation and Development of Royal Dynastic Ideology* (BZAW 142; Berlin: de Gruyter, 1977); **G. H. Jones,** *1 and 2 Kings* (NCB; London: Marshall, Morgan & Scott, 1984); **B. E. Kelle,** "What's in a Name? Neo-Assyrian Designations for the Northern Kingdom and Their Implications for Israelite History and Biblical Interpretation," *JBL* 121 (2002) 639-66; **T. N. D. Mettinger,** *King and Messiah: The Civil and Sacral Legitimation of the Israelite Kings* (ConBOT 8; Lund: Gleerup, 1976); **J. M. Miller,** "The Elisha Cycle and the Accounts of the Omride Wars," *JBL* 85 (1966) 441-55; idem, "The Rest of the Acts of Jehoahaz: 1 Ki. 20, 22:1-18," *ZAW* 80 (1968) 337-42; **M. S. Moore,** "Jehu's Coronation and the Purge of Israel," *VT* 53 (2003) 97-114; **E. T. Mullen,** "The Royal Dynastic Grant to Jehu and the Structure of the Books of Kings," *JBL* 107 (1988) 193-206; **N. Na'aman,** "Azariah of Judah and Jeroboam II of Israel," *VT* 43 (1993) 227-34; idem, "Jehu Son of Omri: Legitimizing a Loyal Vassal by his Overlord," *IEJ* 48 (1998) 236-38; **S. M. Olyan,** "*Hāšālôm*: Some Literary Considerations of 2 Kings 9," *CBQ* 46 (1984) 652-68; **S. Otto,** *Jehu, Elia, und Elisa: Die Erzählung von der Jehu-Revolution und die Komposition der Elia-Elisa-Erzählungen* (BWANT 152; Stuttgart: Kohlhammer, 2001); **W. Pitard,** *Ancient Damascus: A Historical Study of the Syrian City-State from Earliest Times until Its Fall to the Assyrians in 732 B.C.E.* (Winona Lake, IN: Eisenbrauns, 1987); **T. Schneider,** "Rethinking Jehu," *Bib* 77 (1996) 100-107; **W. M. Schniedewind,** "Tel Dan Stela: New Light on Aramaic and Jehu's Revolt," *BASOR* 302 (1996) 75-90; **R. Tomes,** "'Come and See My Zeal for the Lord': Reading the Jehu Story," in *Narrativity in Biblical and Related Texts,* ed. G. J. Brooke and J.-D. Kaestli (BETL 149; Leuven: Leuven University Press, 2000) 53-67; **M. White,** *The Elijah Legends and Jehu's Coup* (BJS 311; Atlanta: Scholars Press, 1997); **D. J. Wiseman,** *1 & 2 Kings* (TOTC; Downers Grove, IL: InterVarsity Press, 1993).

D. T. Lamb

JEPHTHAH. *See* JUDGES; HISTORY OF ISRAEL 2: PREMONARCHIC ISRAEL.

JEREMIAH

The prophet Jeremiah appears only five times in the OT Historical Books: four times in 2 Chronicles 35—36 and once in Ezra 1. The influence of Jeremiah the prophet as a prominent figure in the last decades of Judah's existence and of the book of Jeremiah as theological interpretation of that period is evident in all five occurrences.

1. Jeremiah in 2 Chronicles
2. Jeremiah in Ezra

1. Jeremiah in 2 Chronicles.

Four references to the prophet Jeremiah bind together the Chronicler's distinctive presentation of Judah's history in the period 609-538 BCE. Terminology from the book of Jeremiah is used to explain God's judgment of conquest and exile.

1.1. 2 Chronicles 35:25. 2 Chronicles 35:25 credits Jeremiah with composing a lament for King *Josiah after his fatal encounter with Pharaoh Neco at Megiddo in 609 BCE. Female and male singers also composed laments that were still performed in the Chronicler's day. According to the Chronicler, these laments were written down, but the collection is not extant.

1.1.1. Jeremiah and Josiah. Jeremiah's activity in 2 Chronicles 35:25 is consistent with the portrayal of the prophet in the book of Jeremiah. According to the book's superscription (Jer 1:1-2), his ministry included the last eighteen years of Josiah's life and reign. The book does not label any of its contents as having been addressed to the circumstances of Josiah's reform or to Josiah himself, nor does it include reports of any encounters between Jeremiah and Josiah. Jeremiah 22:15-16 does cite Josiah as someone who knew the Lord because he did justice and righteousness, especially on behalf of the poor. The book of Jeremiah praises Josiah as a good king in contrast to his successors and despite the failure of his reforms to effect an enduring change within the people's hearts. Jeremiah 22:13-17 compares him explicitly with Jehoiakim. Jeremiah 36 implicitly contrasts Jehoiakim's destruction of the Jeremiah scroll with Josiah's penitent and obedient response to the book of the law (2 Kings 22). Part of the judgment on Jehoiakim is that he is denied proper mourning and burial (Jer 22:18-19; 36:30). Jeremiah's lament for Josiah appropriately contrasts with the silence at Jehoiakim's demise.

2 Chronicles 35:25 reports an ongoing practice of lamenting for King Josiah. This practice continued up to the Chronicler's own time, using the text of Jeremiah's lament. Jeremiah 22:10 apparently forbids the practice shortly after its inception: "Stop weeping for him who is dead [i.e., Josiah]." This admonition is a rhetorical device, however. The grammatical form in Jeremiah 22:10a is not an absolute prohibition against lamenting for Josiah, who was buried in Jerusalem in the tomb of his ancestors. The command is used to draw attention to the much more terrible end of his son and successor, Jehoahaz, who would never return to the land of Judah, even in death.

1.1.2. Dirge and Lament in the Book of Jeremiah. Jeremiah's preaching, as preserved in the book bearing his name, includes lament and dirge forms (e.g., Jer 25:34-38; Jeremiah's "Confessions"). Jeremiah 9:20-22 calls upon the professional women mourners to become tradents of the prophetic word by singing and teaching dirges for the death of Judah and Jerusalem. This association between Jeremiah and the mourners as composer and performers parallels 2 Chronicles 35:25, although the subject of the dirges is different.

1.1.3. Jeremiah's Lament for Josiah. "The laments" mentioned in 2 Chronicles 35:25 are not the biblical book of Lamentations, even though the LXX names Jeremiah as the author of that book. Neither the genre nor the contents of Lamentations fits the designation "lament for Josiah." 2 Samuel 1:17-27 is David's lament for King *Saul and his son Jonathan. It names and describes the deceased, and addresses the mourners and the deceased in the second person. Jeremiah's lament for King Josiah probably would have had similar features, but they are lacking in Lamentations. David's dirge was also taught to the people and written in another book that is not extant (cf. 2 Sam 1:17 and 2 Chron 35:25). The five chapters of Lamentations mourn the later tragedy of the *Babylonian conquest of Jerusalem, and they do not name Josiah.

1.2. 2 Chronicles 36:12. The Chronicler's account of the fall of Judah and Jerusalem is much shorter than the account in 2 Kings and Jeremiah. In 2 Chronicles all four of the last kings are exiled: Jehoahaz to Egypt, and Jehoiakim, Jehoiachin and Zedekiah to Babylon. The final three kings "did evil in the sight of the Lord." 2 Chronicles 36:12 characterizes Zedekiah's evil specifically: "He did not humble himself before the prophet Jeremiah who spoke from the mouth of the Lord." The term "humble oneself" is characteristically used by the Chronicler to indicate the right response to God's word. The famous promise in 2 Chronicles 7:14 lists this verb first. In 2 Chronicles *Rehoboam and the Israelites, *Hezekiah and the inhabitants of Jerusalem, a few people from the tribes of Asher, Manasseh and Zebulon who accept Hezekiah's invitation to celebrate the Passover in Jerusalem, and *Manasseh and Josiah all humble themselves. Amon, however, does not humble himself, and judgment falls. 2 Chronicles 36:12—Zedekiah "did not humble himself before the prophet Jeremiah"—significantly alters this idiom. Nowhere else in 1-2 Chronicles do people humble themselves before anyone but God.

Four narratives report King Zedekiah seeking, hearing and rejecting the word of the Lord through Jeremiah (Jer 21:1-7; 34:1-7; 37:3-10; 38:14-28). He refused to repent and surrender to Babylon as the divine word required (Jer 38:20). All these episodes are set during the final Babylonian siege, but the Chronicler understands them as characteristic of Zedekiah's failure to heed the Lord's prophet throughout his reign. Rebellion against Nebuchadrezzar is the primary example (2 Chron 36:13; Jer 27). Zedekiah's lack of repentance is also representative of the people as a whole (2 Chron 36:15-16; Jer 29:19).

2 Chronicles 36:13-16 summarizes other aspects of Jeremiah's explanation for the Babylonian catastrophe. King and people had "stiffened their necks" and refused to heed the word of the prophetic messengers whom God had "sent persistently" (e.g., Jer 7:25-26; 25:3-4; 32:33). They had "defiled" the Lord's house with "the abominations of the nations" (e.g., Jer 2:7; 7:10, 30; 32:34-35). As elsewhere in Chronicles, the prophetic word interprets history (Schniedewind 1997, 220; 1999, 162).

1.3. 2 Chronicles 36:21. The threat of conquest and exile by the Babylonians is a major theme of the book of Jeremiah (e.g., Jer 7:15;

21:4-7; 25:8-11). 2 Chronicles 36:17-20 reports this catastrophe. According to 2 Chronicles 36:20-21, seventy years of service to Nebuchadrezzar and his sons, prophesied by Jeremiah (Jer 25:11; 27:7; 29:10), were fulfilled at the establishment of *Persian rule. Babylonian hegemony had begun with Nebuchadrezzar's victory at Carchemish in 605 BCE, nearly seven decades before Cyrus conquered Babylon in 539 BCE. The year of Josiah's death, 609 BCE, was exactly seventy years earlier. According to W. Johnstone (260), the Chronicler treats the period following Josiah as a single exilic generation in which all four successor kings and the people were exiled. This generation is the fiftieth in the books' genealogies, and to it Cyrus's edict (2 Chron 36:23) "represents the proclamation of jubilee" (Lev 25:8-12) (Johnstone, 261).

The Chronicler uses Leviticus 26:34-35 to explain the seventy years of desolation as the land's rest, making up for neglected sabbatical years. H. G. M. Williamson (1982, 418) counts approximately 490 years of monarchy, Saul through Zedekiah, in the Chronicler's chronology. This calculation points to different termini for the seventy years. Seven decades after Zedekiah's exile (586 BCE), in 516 BCE, the second temple was completed.

1.4. 2 Chronicles 36:22 (= Ezra 1:1). Isaiah 44:28 and 45:1 mention Cyrus by name, and Isaiah 45:13 promises that "he will build my city and send out my exiles." These references may be the first to come to mind as the words that were fulfilled in the decree issued by Cyrus in his first year. B. Duhm (ix) goes so far as to call 2 Chronicles 36:22-23 (= Ezra 1:1-2) a quotation of Isaiah 44:28, and on this basis he suggests that all of Deutero-Isaiah at one time was attributed to Jeremiah. 2 Chronicles 36:22-23 and Ezra 1:1-2 do not quote Isaiah 44:28. These verses share only two key words, the name "Cyrus" and the verb "build," and a reference to the "house" (2 Chron 36:23; Ezra 1:2) or "temple" (Isa 44:28) of the Lord in Jerusalem. In Jeremiah 51:11 God promises to "stir up the spirit of the kings of the Medes" to destroy Babylon in vengeance for the temple (cf. 2 Chron 36:22; Ezra 1:1: "the Lord stirred up the spirit of King Cyrus"). 2 Chronicles 36:22 and Ezra 1:1 use the fulfillment formula to tie together two aspects of Jeremiah's message of hope, the limit of Babylonian rule and the return of the exiles, with prophecies about Cyrus in Isaiah 40—45 and

the Chronicler's interest in the temple. This restoration of the people and the temple in Jerusalem only begins with Cyrus's proclamation, which functions as a prophecy of salvation (Japhet 2003, 84). It is possible, then, to calculate the seventy years as extending from the temple's destruction in 586 BCE to the completion of the second temple in 516 BCE.

2. Jeremiah in Ezra.
Ezra-Nehemiah is now generally judged to be earlier and by a different author than 1-2 Chronicles. Although Ezra 1:1-3 nearly duplicates 2 Chronicles 36:22-23, Ezra never mentions the seventy years. The repetition of "the Lord stirred up the spirit of . . ." in Ezra 1:1, 5 emphasizes the reference to Jeremiah 51:11 discussed previously (see 1.4 above). In an ironic reversal of earlier conquests (1 Chron 5:26; 2 Chron 21:16), the Lord stirred up a force of returning exiles and King Cyrus, their sponsor, to resettle the city and rebuild the temple. Cyrus also returned the temple vessels plundered by Nebuchadrezzar (Ezra 1:7-11), as promised in Jeremiah 27:22.

See also ISAIAH; PROPHETS AND PROPHECY.

BIBLIOGRAPHY. **J. Applegate,** "Jeremiah and the Seventy Years in the Hebrew Bible: Inner-Biblical Reflections on the Prophet and His Prophecy," in *The Book of Jeremiah and Its Reception,* ed. A. H. W. Curtis and T. Romer (BETL 128; Leuven: Leuven University Press and Peeters, 1997) 91-110; **R. B. Dillard,** *2 Chronicles* (WBC 15; Waco, TX: Word, 1987); **B. Duhm,** *Das Buch Jeremia* (Kurzer Hand-Commentar zum Alten Testament 11; Tübingen und Leipzig: Mohr Siebeck, 1901); **S. Japhet,** *The Ideology of the Book of Chronicles and Its Place in Biblical Thought* (rev. ed.; BEATAJ 9; Frankfurt and New York: Lang, 1997); idem, "Periodization: Between History and Ideology, The Neo-Babylonian Period in Biblical Historiography," in *Judah and the Judeans in the Neo-Babylonian Period,* ed. O. Lipschits and J. Blenkinsopp (Winona Lake, IN: Eisenbrauns, 2003) 75-89; **W. Johnstone,** *1 and 2 Chronicles, 2: 2 Chronicles 10—36: Guilt and Atonement* (JSOTSup 254; Sheffield: Sheffield Academic Press, 1998); **G. Keown, P. Scalise and T. Smothers,** *Jeremiah 26—52* (WBC 27; Dallas: Word, 1995); **W. M. Schniedewind,** "Prophets and Prophecy in the Books of Chronicles," in *The Chronicler as Historian,* ed. M. P. Graham, K. G. Hoglund and S. L. McKenzie (JSOTSup

238; Sheffield: Sheffield Academic Press, 1997) 204-24; idem, "The Chronicler as Interpreter of Scripture," in *The Chronicler as Author: Studies in Text and Texture*, ed. M. P. Graham and S. L. McKenzie (JSOTSup 263; Sheffield: Sheffield Academic Press, 1999) 158-80; **H. G. M. Williamson,** *1 and 2 Chronicles* (NCBC; Grand Rapids, MI: Eerdmans, 1982); idem, *Ezra, Nehemiah* (WBC 16; Waco, TX: Word, 1985).   P. J. Scalise

JERICHO

Jericho, which has been settled for ten thousand years, is one of the oldest continuously inhabited sites on earth. It plays a famous part in the OT story because of its capture and destruction by *Joshua as the first act in the Israelite occupation of *Canaan described in Joshua 5—6. The present article first considers Jericho's place in the geography of Israel and its history in the period of the Historical Books (roughly the Iron Age), and then explains its role in the theology of the Historical Books, with a special focus on Joshua 5—6 and the "devotion to destruction" of city and inhabitants.

1. The Location of Jericho
2. Jericho's History in the Iron Age
3. Jericho in the Historical Books
4. Jericho and Holy War

1. The Location of Jericho.

1.1. An Oasis. Jericho's location is the key to understanding its significance. It is, first, an oasis, also known as "the city of palm trees" (Judg 3:13), located in the Jordan Valley about ten miles northwest of the Dead Sea and eight hundred feet below sea level. The fertility of the place is owed less to the river, which lies some miles to the east, than to the spring ʿAin es-Sultan, which creates an area of lush green in striking contrast to its arid surroundings. It is for this reason that Jericho has been settled since the dawn of history.

1.2. Border City. Jericho is, second, a border location. The deep Jordan Valley and the river itself mark a natural border between east and west. In terms of Israel's tribal divisions (*see* Tribes of Israel and Land Allotments/Borders), Jericho was between north and south, being assigned to Benjamin (Josh 18:21), but close to the northern territory of Ephraim (Josh 16:7). In the late monarchy it appears that Jericho was under the administration of Judah (Holland and Netzer, 737). Thus Jericho was strategically lo-

cated both between east and west, and north and south. It often features in biblical narratives precisely because of its significance as a boundary, not only in the story of its destruction by Joshua but also elsewhere (Judg 3:13; 2 Sam 10:5; 2 Kings 2).

2. Jericho's History in the Iron Age.

2.1. Jericho and the Conquest. The apparent discrepancies between the biblical account of the fall of Jericho and the data uncovered by archaeologists have been a factor in the critical interpretation of the *book of Joshua. The Israelite conquest (where historians accept that there was one) usually is dated to the mid-thirteenth century BCE. This is toward the end of archaeology's Late Bronze period, c. 1550-1200 BCE (Bienkowski, 9), with Iron Age I beginning about 1200 BCE (Iron Age I, 1200-1000 BCE, approximates to the time of the judges, while Iron Age II covers the period of the monarchy, 1000-586 BCE).

2.1.1. Walls in Joshua's Time? It is commonly said that there is no evidence of a walled city in the Late Bronze period—that is, the time when Jericho's walls are said to have fallen down (e.g., Rogerson, 196). J. Garstang, who conducted an excavation in the 1930s, thought that he had found Joshua's walls, but in the 1950s these were redated by K. Kenyon to the Early Bronze, a millennium earlier (Holland and Netzer, 736). The fortifications on the top of the tell are mainly from the Middle Bronze. P. Bienkowski's authoritative account of the archaeology of Jericho in the Late Bronze finds that there were no walls datable to that period (Bienkowski, 124-25). This does not mean, however, that the site was uninhabited. On the contrary, it seems that there was a limited settlement in the period, but that it was small and impoverished by the standards of a Middle Bronze city (Bienkowski, 124-25, 155). K. Kenyon (260-61) put the latest settlement at around 1325 BCE, Bienkowski (156) a little later, at 1275 BCE. Both cited use of tombs and evidence of habitation in a specific area of the tell. Bienkowski's conclusion is based on an extensive study of the pottery evidence. His dating brings the evidence for settlement close to the dating often proposed for Joshua, though he finds no evidence of a destruction in that time (Bienkowski, 156). The rebuilding of the city by Hiel of *Bethel during the reign of Ahab in the ninth century BCE (1

Kings 16:34) falls within this period.

2.1.2. The Archaeological Record and the Biblical Narrative as History. The archaeological record at Jericho, however, is not easy to read. It is possible that the Early and Middle Bronze walls were simply used again by occupants in the Late Bronze (Mazar, 283; Kenyon, 262). It was common for Late Bronze cities not to have their own fortifications (Bienkowski, 124-25; Hess, 137-38). It also has been argued that debris heaped against the Middle Bronze revetment wall could have fallen from a later wall at the top of the tell, now entirely eroded away (Wood; Kenyon, 262). However, this speculation is unnecessary in view of the preceding point.

It follows that the story of Jericho in Joshua's time can hardly be written on the basis of the archaeological record. It would be mistaken either to prejudge the nature of the biblical account on the basis of the archaeology or to force the ambiguous archaeology to fit the biblical picture. The data have led to divergent assessments. A. Mazar maintains that "in this case archaeological evidence does not run directly counter to the biblical tale, as is asserted by some scholars" (Mazar, 283). In contrast, M. D. Coogan (21), citing a lack of pottery from the Late Bronze (in spite of Bienkowski), and the fragmentary nature of the evidence in Iron Age I, thinks that the site was uninhabited from about 1300 to 1000 BCE.

3. Jericho in the Historical Books.

3.1. Jericho in the Book of Joshua. The story of Joshua resumes the narrative, begun in Numbers, of the Israelites' approach to the promised land. Jericho is closely associated there with the plains of Moab and the river Jordan, as the place at the end of the tribes' long wilderness pilgrimage, before they entered Canaan (e.g., Num 22:1; 26:3; 36:13). Deuteronomy too points the reader toward Jericho as the location of entry (Deut 32:49; 34:1). The formula used in Numbers reappears in Joshua in connection with the distribution of the land to the tribes (Josh 13:32; 16:1; 20:8). Thus Jericho is a part of the symbolism that speaks of the transition of the tribes from wilderness refugees to possessors of a land of their own as an inheritance from God.

In the book of Joshua, Jericho continues to have symbolic status, representing the land of Canaan and its opposition to the Israelite advance. It is to Jericho that the spies are directed when they are sent to spy out the land (Josh 2:1), and there the first encounter is made with a Canaanite "king" (Josh 1:3). The miraculous crossing of the Jordan, echoing that of the Red Sea (Ex 15), takes place "opposite Jericho" (Josh 3:16; cf. 4:13, 19). At Jericho, Joshua is met by the mysterious figure who calls himself "the commander of the army of the LORD" (Josh 5:13), who designates the battles to come as a war of Yahweh himself, the God of Israel. The whole movement of the narrative in Joshua 1—5 is toward Jericho, and in due course it is the first city in the land to fall to Israel.

The special importance of the account of its fall in the conception of the book of Joshua is clear. It is woven into the narrative of the crossing of the river (Josh 4:13) and the first occupation of the land (Josh 5); the telling of the way in which it fell most clearly illustrates that it was by the power of God alone (Josh 6); and its harsh treatment becomes a byword for the treatment of other cities that later are subjected to destruction (Josh 10:28, 30). Finally, at the end of his life, Joshua recalls the conquest of the land, and Jericho is the only city expressly named, along with the nations that composed the population of Canaan (Josh 24:11). In the list of the "kings of the land" conquered by the Israelites (Josh 12:7), Jericho stands at the head (Josh 12:9), showing that its significance is, after all, not in itself alone, but that it was foremost in a conquest that affected all of Canaan.

3.1.1. The Account of the Fall of Jericho. The destruction of Jericho, as told in Joshua, is quite different from other conquest accounts, such as *Ai (Josh 8). Its character is both religious and military. In its religious dimension it continues from the miraculous crossing of the river in Joshua 4. The armed men are accompanied by *priests, apparently in the middle of the procession (Josh 6:13), processing with the *ark of the covenant and blowing rams' horns. The number seven also plays an important role in the story (Josh 6:4, 6, 15). The pattern of six days plus one is reminiscent of the chronology of creation (Gen 1:1—2:3). The purpose of the narrative is to show that Yahweh has indeed "given Jericho into the hand of Joshua" (Josh 6:2), according to typical promises in Deuteronomy (Deut 2:31). One strand in scholarship has explained the religious features of the narrative of Josh 3—6 form-critically, as deriving from liturgical enactments of ancient traditions performed at an Israelite sanctuary. H.-J. Kraus proposed that the crossing of the Jordan was memorialized in this way at the sanctuary of *Gilgal. However, this theory remains speculative, and it does not resolve the nature of the relationship between the events and the text.

The military aspect of the action is also clear. Some of the "religious" features are military as well (surrounding the city, blowing horns, marching, shouting and going into battle with the ark; cf. 1 Sam 4:1-4) (Coote, 613). Moreover, Jericho is described initially as under siege (Josh 6:1). And in Joshua 24:11 "the men of Jericho" are said to have fought against Israel. This has been taken as evidence of different traditions underlying the present account (Coogan, 20-21). However, it is best to think of a memory of a military encounter told so as to emphasize God's overriding part in the victory and to portray the victory as an act of worship as well as an act of war. The destruction of Jericho is in fact the OT's parade example of a "holy war" (see 4.1 below).

3.1.2. Jericho Never to Be Rebuilt. Such is the powerful symbolism of Jericho's destruction that it must lie forever as a testimony to God's action on Israel's behalf in giving them the land (Josh 6:26). It is a curiosity that Jericho continues to function as a geographical marker in the distribution of the tribes (Josh 16:1), and indeed that Jericho is listed among the cities allotted to the tribe of Benjamin (Josh 18:21).

3.2. Jericho in Judges to Nehemiah.

3.2.1. Vestiges. In spite of Joshua's curse, there are hints of occupation at Jericho in the time between Joshua and David, in addition to its occurrence in the distribution lists. This is implied by the Moabite king Eglon's capture of "the city of palms" (Judg 3:13), and by the fact that David's shamed envoys to Moab are told to remain there temporarily (2 Sam 10:5). In both incidents Jericho's border location is significant.

3.2.2. Jericho Rebuilt. Nevertheless, 1 Kings records that the city was in fact rebuilt in the reign of Ahab by one Hiel of Bethel (1 Kings 16:34). This passage pointedly echoes Joshua's curse on the city because it reports that Hiel built it at the cost of his eldest and youngest sons—precisely the penalty invoked by the curse. The connection between these two texts is not simple, however. Joshua's curse seems to mean that the person would lose his sons as a punishment. But Hiel appears actually to bring

the terms of the curse upon himself by sacrificing his sons (according to the usual reading of the text), perhaps in a "foundation sacrifice" designed to ward off evil (De Vries, 205). In that case, Hiel's action, while a kind of fulfillment of the curse, is highly ironic. It may comment on the extreme depravity of the kind of religion that leads people to do such things (cf. Deut 12:31), so that they even bring down curses upon themselves without knowing it.

Also in Ahab's time, Jericho plays a role in the story of *Elijah handing over his prophetic authority to *Elisha (2 Kings 2). There are clear echoes of Israel's first entry to the land in this story. The parting of the Jordan, the mention of Gilgal, and the movement in the story between Jericho and Bethel all recall elements in the narrative of Joshua 3—8. The story seems to unite the idea of possession of the land with prophetic authority and the need for loyalty to Yahweh.

3.2.3. Exile and Restoration. Jericho was most fully settled again in the last century before the exile of Judah (i.e., the seventh century BCE), when apparently it was controlled by Judah. In the account of the fall of Judah, King Zedekiah is said to have been captured "in the plains of Jericho" (2 Kings 25:5). And in the restoration of the exiles that began in 539 BCE under the Persian king Cyrus, when people returned "each to his own town" (Ezra 2:1), a number of returnees are mentioned for Jericho (Ezra 2:34 = Neh 7:36). That the occupation persisted is shown by the account of Nehemiah's rebuilding the walls of Jerusalem in the mid-fifth century BCE, where the men of Jericho are numbered among the builders (Neh 3:2).

3.3. The Nature of the Record. The accounts concerning Jericho in the Historical Books have theological and symbolic aspects as well as historical ones. In what sense they are history has to be determined in part by assessing the nature of the biblical materials, and in part from extrabiblical data. Neither kind of evidence permits a clear reconstruction. For example, the report about David's envoys to the Ammonites suggests a tenth-century settlement, though this is not strongly indicated by the archaeological data.

Furthermore, the way in which the record may be judged historical is differently understood. For Coogan, the inclusion of the curse on Hiel (1 Kings 16:34) reflects a Deuteronomistic criticism arising from a secession of Jericho from Judah in Josiah's time. The same interest even motivated the centrality of Jericho in the Joshua narrative (Coogan, 22; Coote, 612). However, Coogan's hypothesis (according to which the traditions of Jericho's destruction originated in the ninth century BCE at the time when it was refortified) depends too much on supposing that the city was desolate until the time of Ahab and Hiel (Coogan [22] makes a concession regarding 2 Sam 10:5). An open-minded view about the relationship between the Joshua narrative and the origins of Israel in Canaan is more appropriate to the material we have.

4. Jericho and Holy War.

4.1. Jericho "Devoted to Destruction." The story of the fall of Jericho is an example of "holy war," the term often used to describe a *war waged by God (or a god). Joshua's war on Canaan was designated a war of God by the "commander of the LORD's army" (Josh 5:14). The central action in a holy war is the "devotion to destruction" (Heb *ḥērem*) of the enemy, where the enemy is not merely subdued but becomes a kind of sacrifice to God, who is waging the war. In Jericho this sentence is carried out more fully than in any other case, with the entire population put to the sword and no booty taken (Josh 6:17-18, 24). The sparing of Rahab is an exception to the blanket condemnation, and commentators debate whether this was a failure on Israel's part to implement the "devotion to destruction" as commanded. R. S. Hess (88-92) thinks that Rahab was spared because in effect she converted to the worship of Yahweh. In contrast, R. Polzin (88) sees the sparing of Rahab as a measure of Israel's wickedness and lack of faith.

4.2. Achan's Family. The story of Jericho's "devotion to destruction" continues in Joshua 7, where the family of Achan is executed for tampering with the devoted things, which in turn contaminated them, and through them potentially Israel. The world of ideas here is that of "holiness," which in OT terms means the sphere that belongs specially to God and that cannot be entered in an unauthorized way by human beings. The same concept underlies that of holy space in the tabernacle and the temple, and in the action of animal sacrifice.

See also HISTORY OF ISRAEL 1: SETTLEMENT PERIOD; JOSHUA.

BIBLIOGRAPHY. **P. Bienkowski,** *Jericho in the Late Bronze Age* (Warminster: Aris & Phillips, 1986); **M. D. Coogan,** "Archaeology and Biblical Studies; The Book of Joshua," in *The Hebrew Bible and Its Interpreters,* ed. W. H. Propp, B. Halpern and D. N. Freedman (BibJS 1; Winona Lake, IN: Eisenbrauns, 1990) 19-32; **R. B. Coote,** "Joshua," *NIB* 2.553-719; **S. J. De Vries,** *1 Kings* (WBC 12; Waco, TX: Word, 1985); **R. S. Hess,** *Joshua* (TOTC; Downers Grove, IL: InterVarsity Press, 1996); **T. A. Holland and E. Netzer,** "Jericho," *ABD* 3.723-39; **K. Kenyon,** *Digging Up Jericho: The Results of the Jericho Excavations, 1952-1956* (London: Benn, 1957); **H.-J. Kraus,** "Gilgal: A Contribution to the History of Worship in Israel," in *Reconsidering Israel and Judah: Recent Studies on the Deuteronomistic History,* ed. G. N. Knoppers and J. G. McConville (SBTS 8; Winona Lake, IN; Eisenbrauns, 2000 [1951]) 163-78; **A. Mazar,** "The Iron Age I," in *The Archaeology of Ancient Israel,* ed. A. Ben-Tor (New Haven; Yale University Press; Tel Aviv: Open University of Israel, 1992) 258-301; **R. Polzin,** *Moses and the Deuteronomist: Deuteronomy, Joshua, Judges* (Literary Study of the Deuteronomic History, Pt. 1; New York: Seabury, 1980); **J. Rogerson,** *The New Atlas of the Bible* (London: Macdonald, 1985); **H. Weippert and M. Weippert,** "Jericho in der Eisenzeit," *ZDPV* 92 (1976) 105-48; **B. G. Wood,** "Did the Israelites Conquer Jericho?" *BAR* 16.2 (1990) 44-58. J. G. McConville

JEROBOAM

Jeroboam was the first king of Israel immediately following the northern rebellion against the house of David in the days of Solomon's son *Rehoboam. He is not to be confused with the later Jeroboam who reigned in the eighth century BCE. His kingship covered the period of approximately 931-910 BCE and is recorded in two sections of the OT Historical Books: 1 Kings 11:26—14:20; 2 Chronicles 10:2—13:20. The name "Jeroboam" is more than likely a defiant variation of the throne name of his rival Rehoboam, and it denotes the meaning "may the people become great," in which he is considered a contender for the people against Rehoboam's oppressions. It appears that as a young man, Jeroboam became a man of some means (1 Kings 11:28). His heritage, however, leaves much doubt in regard to him having any noble origins. His father, an Ephraimite, was Nebat (1 Kings 11:26), whose name is not found elsewhere in the Bible. Controversy surrounds the name of Jeroboam's mother, Zeruah, whose name means "skin disease" or "leper." This name may be a haplographic mistake of "Zeredah," where Jeroboam's family was from (1 Kings 11:26), or it may be a deliberate change from the proper name "Zeruiah" intended to degrade the house of Jeroboam.

It should be noted here that the LXX account of Jeroboam's rise to power and his subsequent rule is quite different from that in the MT. There are a variety of views among scholars as to its historical value and midrashic flavor. However one views the LXX account of Jeroboam, it clearly diverges significantly at points from the MT, such as Jeroboam playing no part in the assembly of the tribes against Rehoboam at Shechem, the events leading to his emergence as king, and Ahijah's denunciatory oracle (for further discussion on the particularities of the LXX account see McKenzie).

To continue with the MT narrative, it shows that as a young man, Jeroboam was placed in charge of the work force of the northern tribes by King *Solomon. The policy of Solomon's son Rehoboam, however, led the northern tribes to rebel and place Jeroboam as a separate king to rule over them. The royal cult that Jeroboam eventually established in the north set the pattern for his successors, who customarily are evaluated as perpetuating his sins (e.g., 1 Kings 16:26). A dynasty was never established following Jeroboam's death, as there had been in the Davidic line (for further discussion of religion under Jeroboam and the division see Toews).

1. Jeroboam's Administration
2. Perspective from 1 Kings
3. Perspective from 2 Chronicles

1. Jeroboam's Administration.
There was early support for Jeroboam's kingship from two *prophets: Ahijah (1 Kings 11:29-39) and Shemaiah (1 Kings 12:21-24). Ahijah's elaborate prophecy over Jeroboam and Shemaiah's counsel for Rehoboam to refrain from war against Jeroboam may have been indicative of widespread public sentiment in favor of Jeroboam. It is suggested that these two prophets stood, as *Samuel had, in the tradition of the old Israelite league. There was general resentment toward Solomon's policies that encroached upon tribal prerogatives, mistreated subjects and fostered foreign cults. Jeroboam's ascension pat-

tern was similar to the earlier *Saul, whose prophetic designation was followed by popular acclaim. To his credit, Jeroboam created a state out of virtually nothing. He had no capital, no military and, most importantly, no religious cult. He placed his first capital at *Shechem (1 Kings 12:25), a central geographic location. Later, he built Penuel in Transjordan, possibly as an alternative capital to Shechem. Eventually, the capital was moved some seven miles northeast of Shechem to *Tirzah, perhaps because, among other reasons, it was more easy to defend. His most significant kingly action certainly was religious. He established an official state cult to rival that of Jerusalem (1 Kings 12:26-33) and all things associated with David, probably to pose as a reformer. He set up two official shrines at opposite ends of his kingdom: *Bethel, with its patriarchal associations, and *Dan, which had a priesthood boasting descent from Moses (Judg 18:30). He also appointed priests for himself, and he instituted an annual feast in the eighth month to rival the feast of the seventh month in Jerusalem (1 Kings 8:2). The schism between his kingdom and the Davidic one was followed by two generations of sporadic sectional warfare, fought to no conclusion and leading to the deterioration and weakening of both states, a condition that was furthered by military blows from Shishak of Egypt on Israel and Judah.

2. Perspective from 1 Kings.
The initial introduction of Jeroboam in the 1 Kings narrative is by no means negative. Solomon's idolatry led to Yahweh raising up "adversaries" against the failed king. This included Hadad the Edomite (1 Kings 11:14) and Rezon the Aramaean (1 Kings 11:23-25). However, Jeroboam is not labeled as one such adversary, but rather is presented as a man of talent and diligence. In particular, 1 Kings 11:28 designates him as a "doer of work" and a "mighty man," probably in a physical and military way. His ultimate failure perhaps may be traced back to self-reliance because of human ability, even as Saul was noted for his physical distinctiveness and yet ended up in tragedy. Ahijah's prophecy (1 Kings 11:29-39) itself has similarities to Saul in the incident of the tearing of Samuel's robe (1 Sam 15:27-31), although Ahijah's tearing of the cloak is a positive for Jeroboam, whereas it was a negative for Saul. The "Joseph" connection at the end of 1 Kings 11:28 is also striking because of

the ensuing language of a new cloak that gets torn in a field, which resonates with the patriarchal narrative (Gen 37:12-36) and may early on set Jeroboam up as a positive, almost Joseph-like character. The point is that the narrative through 1 Kings 11:30 resonates with elements reminiscent of Joseph and Saul that may reflect the early hopes placed on what Jeroboam might become, but also how he might become a failure as Saul had. Nonetheless, a claimant to the throne needed prophetic backing, which Ahijah provided. The fact that the torn material was new creates a more spectacular scene in that the symbolism of tearing away the kingdom from Solomon was a tearing of that which appeared intact and unimpaired, for it was a "new" cloak. It might also denote that a "new" Israel was about to be formed through Jeroboam.

Besides resonances with Joseph and Saul, the most significant parallel is to the *Davidic covenant (2 Sam 7:8-17). The prophecy concerning Jeroboam is indeed amazing in that God promises to build him an "enduring house," similar in extent to that which God built for David (1 Kings 11:38). Yet elements of Deuteronomic protasis and apodosis statements ("if . . . then . . . ") also appear, which may indicate that the eventual failure of Jeroboam is a reflection of the entire nation's Mosaic and Davidic covenant failures. Jeroboam's flight to Egypt immediately following the promise, because of Solomon's aggression, and his eventual return are a common biblical motif, both in earlier Israel's exodus experience (Ex 12:51) and in Jesus' childhood flight and return (Mt 2:13-23). Jeroboam may have had Egyptian backing in his later rise to power. He continues to be a positive figure in the 1 Kings narrative even after his return from Egypt, due to providence (1 Kings 12:15) and Shemaiah's intervention (1 Kings 12:22-24). After this, things turn bad for Jeroboam in the 1 Kings narrative. This is a result of his establishing a cult that conflicts and competes with the Jerusalem cult (1 Kings 12:25-33). His doom is seen in the incident in 1 Kings 13 involving the altar and the man of God, which probably is the inaugural religious sacrifice of Jeroboam's cult, a cult that is immediately rejected and judged, resulting in the crippling of the king's hand. Theologically speaking, there is no patience with Jeroboam, for his idolatry is intolerable as Solomon's was. *David had his own failings, but the promise to his house would remain intact because he was not an idolater as Jeroboam had disappointingly become.

The narrative departs from Jeroboam in 1 Kings 13 to discuss the rather bizarre events revolving around the man of God from Judah, only to return to him to report his failure to repent of his evil even after having witnessed the astounding scene at the Bethel altar (1 Kings 13:33-34). 1 Kings 14:1-20 serves as an inclusio with 1 Kings 11:29-39, in reversal fashion, in that Ahijah's initial favor upon Jeroboam has turned to utter rejection in Ahijah's prophetic announcement of the death of Jeroboam's son Abijah. Jeroboam's disguising of his wife to send her to the prophet Ahijah once again has Saul-like resonances (cf. 1 Sam 28:8). This is going to end badly for Jeroboam, even though his sending of ten loaves with his wife (1 Kings 14:3) may be an attempt to remind the prophet of the ten tribes promised to him (1 Kings 11:31). The judgment from Ahijah is poignant. The Hebrew in 1 Kings 14:10, read literally, says that judgment will befall "him who urinates against a wall" (i.e., every male), and that the house of Jeroboam will be "swept away as dung." The ignoble references to urine and dung are far removed from what was initially intended for the house of Jeroboam. The only fragment of good left to Jeroboam in 1 Kings is that his dead son, Abijah, is mourned and buried (1 Kings 14:18). Another son, Nadab, eventually would reign only two years because he was assassinated by Baasha. A dynasty of Jeroboam is never achieved.

3. Perspective from 2 Chronicles.

The Chronicler's perspective on Jeroboam most likely is built on the narrative found in 1 Kings. As is generally the case with the Chronicler, his concern is with the Judean kings, not the Israelite kings, and so Jeroboam appears in his writings because of his concern with Rehoboam and the house of David. Jeroboam, the knowledge of whom is assumed (2 Chron 10:2), thus serves in an adversarial role in this account to show the consequences of Rehoboam's failure (2 Chron 12:15; 13:2). The narrative thread does not follow him per se, and thus the amount of material devoted to Jeroboam is less in 2 Chronicles than in 1 Kings. One difference between the two accounts is that in the Chronicler's perspective, Jeroboam's idolatry is seen as improving the southern kingdom (2 Chron 11:14-17).

Also, the Chronicler enhances Jeroboam's apostasy in two ways: first, he adds a reference to the goat idols (2 Chron 11:15) not found in 1 Kings, thereby indicating a transgression of Leviticus 17:7; second, he makes explicit Jeroboam's rejection of the Levitical priests (2 Chron 11:14) rather than simply reporting his indiscriminate hiring practices (1 Kings 12:32; 13:33). The Chronicler's account of Jeroboam concludes with him conducting a military battle against the Judean king Abijah (2 Chron 13:1-20), an event that 1 Kings does not mention. Abijah is heroic here, whereas Jeroboam is an assumed failure who is challenged with covenant language (2 Chron 13:4-12). He has met his match in the godly Abijah (2 Chron 13:13-20). That it is Yahweh who is against Jeroboam is clear in that the same term for God "smiting" Jeroboam is used in 2 Chronicles 13:15, 20, even as God gives Jeroboam into the hand of Abijah (2 Chron 13:16).

See also HISTORY OF ISRAEL 4: DIVISION OF THE MONARCHY; REHOBOAM.

BIBLIOGRAPHY. **M. Aberbach and L. Smolar,** "Jeroboam's Rise to Power," *JBL* 88 (1969) 69-72; **J. Bright,** *A History of Israel* (4th ed.; Westminster/John Knox, 2000) 230-40; **M. Cogan,** *1 Kings* (AB 10; New York: Doubleday, 2001); **R. B. Dillard,** *2 Chronicles* (WBC 15; Waco, TX: Word, 1987); **J. Goldingay,** "The Chronicler as Theologian," *BTB* 5 (1975) 102-4; **G. H. Jones,** *1 and 2 Kings,* vol. 1 (NCBC; Grand Rapids: Eerdmans, 1984); **R. W. Klein,** "Once More: 'Jeroboam's Rise to Power,'" *JBL* 92 (1973) 582-84; **M. Kochavi,** "The Identification of Zeredah, Home of Jeroboam, Son of Nebat, King of Israel," *ErIsr* 20 (1989) 198-201; **S. L. McKenzie,** *The Trouble with Kings: The Composition of the Book of Kings in the Deuteronomistic History* (VTSup 42; Leiden: E. J. Brill, 1991); **W. I. Toews,** *Monarchy and Religious Institution in Israel under Jeroboam 1* (SBLMS 47; Atlanta: Scholars Press, 1993); **H. G. M. Williamson,** *1 and 2 Chronicles* (NCBC; Grand Rapids: Eerdmans, 1982)**; D. J. Wiseman,** *1 and 2 Kings* (TOTC; Downers Grove, IL: InterVarsity Press, 1993). J. R. Soza

JERUSALEM

The place name *Jerusalem* appears 660 times in the Hebrew Bible, with more than half of those occurrences in the Historical Books. A minor *Canaanite stronghold in the early biblical period, it becomes the capital of the nascent Israelite state in the tenth century BCE in association with the military activities of *David and the building activities of his successor, *Solomon. By the late eighth century BCE Jerusalem has expanded into a large and important city in the eastern Mediterranean. It is conquered by the *Babylonians in the sixth century BCE. Restored under *Persian rule in the late sixth century, by the fifth century BCE it serves as the center of the minor Persian province of Yehud. As its political and economic role diminishes, its theological and eschatological significance as a holy city intensifies.

1. Background
2. Early History
3. Capital of the United Monarchy
4. Capital of the Southern Kingdom
5. Restoration

1. Background.

1.1. Geography. Jerusalem is situated in the hill country of Palestine on the watershed ridge that separates the Judean hills to the west from the wilderness of Judea to the east. Originally built on a narrow hill (the eastern hill) on the eastern edge of the ridge, it expanded northward during the period of the united monarchy when the earliest settlement was extended to and connected with a small hill to the north (the Temple Mount); and it had spread to the west (the western hill) in the eighth century BCE and later. On average, it is situated 740 m (2,427 ft) above sea level and is 40 km (25 mi) from the Mediterranean coast. The mountainous terrain, with deep valleys (such as the Kidron and the Tyropaean) between the hills, was favorable for defending the original eastern hill; and an ample water supply was available from several springs: the Gihon, on the eastern edge of that hill, produces over one thousand cubic meters of water a day. However, two factors necessary for urban development—accessibility and arable lands—were less favorable. The main international routes in Palestine were north-south arteries. They were connected by interior east-west routes, with the one nearest Jerusalem, for topographical reasons, being slightly north of the city (*see* Roads and Highways). Thus, unlike the major highland sites of the biblical period, Jerusalem was not well situated on a connecting artery. Similarly, the agricultural potential of the land surrounding Jerusalem was limited because of the difficult terrain. It could support a large population, as it did from the eighth to the sixth centuries BCE, only by controlling the agricultural productivity of areas beyond its own hinterlands, which extended 3 to 4 km on the north, west and south (the east being largely unarable wilderness). In other words, the factors that were to make Jerusalem an extraordinarily prominent city involved its historical and religious role as much as, if not more than, its environmental features.

1.2. Sources. Written sources as well as data from archaeological excavations and surveys provide information about the religious, economic, demographic and political history and significance of Jerusalem.

1.2.1. Written Sources. The Historical Books are the major source of information about Jerusalem from the Bronze Age to the Hellenistic period. The place name *Jerusalem* is never mentioned in the Pentateuch, although the term *Salem* (Gen 14:18) may refer to Jerusalem. Unlike the largely theological and eschatological references to Jerusalem in the Prophets and in Psalms, the narratives of the Historical Books recount its conquest, settlement, development, destruction and restoration. Only twice (2 Kings 19:21, 31), in poetic or semipoetic language very close to that of Isaiah, is Jerusalem depicted in imagery rather than in the language of reality.

Until relatively recently the Historical Books were understood to be reliable sources for understanding the events and features that they portray. In the past few decades, however, the traditional assessment of those biblical books as *historiography in the modern sense has led to a more cautious use of biblical data for historical reconstruction. The *Deuteronomistic History (Joshua through 2 Kings), which received its final redaction and editing in the sixth century BCE when the editors knew that the monarchy would form, divide and collapse, provides an editorial spin on the events of the past. Similar didactic processes and theological interests can be observed in the books of Chronicles, Ezra and Nehemiah (*see* Chronicler's History). Doubtless, many of the stories associated with Jerusalem contain legendary or editorial materials, but it is not always easy to recognize them as such. Indeed, the historical narratives so adeptly combine authentic sources with interpretive additions that most readers tend to accept the perspective of the text—about the sacralization and legitimization of a nation and its rulers by the establishment of Jerusalem as political capital and religious center—without recognizing the way it may have distorted or amplified historical reality. The best that modern scholarship can do is to identify and interpret what the text reports, with the understanding that the historical veracity of any given text rarely can be tested.

Less problematic than the biblical text are the few instances in which Jerusalem is mentioned in extrabiblical sources from the ancient Near East. Two of those sources—the Egyptian Execration texts of the early second millennium BCE and the Amarna letters of the fourteenth century BCE—predate the Bible and attest to the existence of a Bronze Age settlement. The third source comes from centuries later, when the annals of the Assyrian ruler Sennacherib mention his attempt to take the city in the early eighth century BCE.

1.2.2. Archaeology. Perhaps no site on earth has been the object of more archaeological research than Jerusalem, despite the enormous problems involved in excavating a city that has been occupied continuously for millennia. Beginning in the mid-nineteenth century, explorers and excavators have endeavored to recover its biblical past. Most of the early work focused on mapping the city, its visible ruins, burial sites and water systems. Perhaps the first "modern" scholar to investigate Jerusalem was the American E. Robinson, who published the results of his first survey in 1841.

Because of the enormous overlay of buildings of the Hellenistic-Roman, Byzantine and later periods, and because most of the area of the ancient city is still inhabited, the kind of extensive field projects that have investigated many other prominent biblical sites have been impossible in Jerusalem. However, the methods developed at other sites for recovering and dating remains of the period of the Hebrew Bible and earlier were eventually brought to Jerusalem by the mid-twentieth century, when the British archaeologist K. Kenyon excavated a broad trench on the edge of the eastern hill from 1961 to 1968. Israeli archaeologist Y. Shiloh then conducted extensive work in the same vicinity from 1978 to 1985. One further project of great significance for the recovery of Iron Age Jerusalem was that of another Israeli, N. Avigad, who excavated from 1969 to 1983 in the center of the Jewish Quarter of the present Old City. Many other, smaller excavation projects and surveys have contributed to our knowledge of the city, and extensive excavations focused on later periods often have provided data concerning earlier ones. In addition, modern construction or road projects invariably reveal unanticipated aspects of the ancient city. And excavations at other sites contribute indirectly to the evaluation of discoveries in Jerusalem.

Because even the major projects have been unable to excavate in the heart of what would have been the royal city, information about specific structures (royal palaces, fortifications, gates, the temple) mentioned in the Bible is virtually unavailable. Thus the wealth of accumulated archaeological information is most useful in helping scholars reconstruct the size and nature of the city in the historical periods that can be correlated with the references to Jerusalem in the Historical Books. Although estimating the size and population of the site is a daunting task that has produced little consensus, the relative change in inhabited area over time is similar in most of the assessments of size and population density. Knowing the extent of Jerusalem in turn makes it possible to postulate what its evolving political and economic role may have been.

1.3. Names. Jerusalem is the name most frequently used to designate the place that served as the capital of the united monarchy, the southern kingdom (Judah) and the province of Yehud. In addition, several other names—city of David, Zion, Jebus, Salem—appear in the Bible and contribute to our knowledge of its history and role.

The name *Jerusalem* is mentioned for the first time in Egyptian Execration texts of the nineteenth-eighteenth centuries BCE, where it appears as *Rušalimum*. It is next mentioned in the diplomatic correspondance recovered from Tell el-Amarna in Egypt; some of those letters, written in Akkadian, were sent to the Egyptian pharaoh by the ruler of *Urušalim*. In addition, it appears as *Ursalimmu* in the Assyrian account of Sennacherib's 701 BCE siege of Jerusalem. Apparently of West Semitic (Canaanite) origin, the Hebrew name *yĕrûšālayim* is believed by most scholars to mean the "foundation of [the god] Shalem," a combination of *yrw,* "to establish," and *šlm,* the name of the Canaanite deity Shalem, who probably was the patron deity of the city. Shalem is known from Ugaritic mythological texts (fourteenth century BCE) as a gracious god.

The name is pronounced as if it has a dual ending, *yĕrûšālayim,* with the letter *yod* inserted before the final consonant. However, it is almost always written without the *yod.* This practice of reading it as if it were spelled differently *(qere perpetuum)* may have arisen under the influence of other place names with similar forms, such as Adorayim. In any case, because the LXX reads *Hierousalēm* (cf. NT *Hierosolyma*), and because biblical texts in Aramaic have *yĕrûšĕlem* (e.g., Ezra 4:8), it seems likely that the original Hebrew name was *yĕrûšālēm,* "Yerushalem" (Tsevat and Ringgren, 348).

Jerusalem is referred to as the city of David more than forty times in the Hebrew Bible, all but one of these occurrences coming in the Historical Books. This designation sometimes refers to the city as a whole and in other places to one sector; just as often it simply is a general term for the oldest part of the city. It first appears in 2 Samuel 5:7 in relation to the establishment of the city as a capital by David, in accordance with the tradition of naming a capital city in relation to its founder or conqueror (cf. *Gibeah of Saul). It also refers to a burial ground in which at least nine of the kings, beginning with David (1 Kings 11:43), were interred. By the late monarchic period, perhaps by the time of its greatest expansion, it is used for the "original" Israelite city (e.g., 2 Chron 32:5).

The origin and meaning of "Zion" as a name for Jerusalem is uncertain. This term appears mainly in the Prophets and in Psalms, often as a designation for the temple, the city, its inhabitants or even all Israel. But it is found six times in the Historical Books, where, except for one poetic reference to "daughter Zion" (2 Kings 19:21), it has a geographical connotation, referring to the stronghold taken by David (e.g., 2 Sam 5:7; 1 Kings 8:1). Because "Mount" sometimes precedes it, its association with a strategically situated pre-Davidic and Davidic settlement seems likely, as does its etymological connection with Arabic terms for "ridge" or perhaps "fortified ridge" (*see* Zion Traditions).

The pre-Israelite name for Jerusalem may have been "Jebus," a term used only four times in the Hebrew Bible, all in the Historical Books. Because this name does not appear in extrabiblical sources, and because it is used parenthetically in Judges (Judg 19:10-11; cf. Josh 18:28) and in 1 Chronicles (1 Chron 11:4, 5), as perhaps a later editorial addition, the historicity of the word as a toponym is in doubt. Rather, it may derive from the gentilic designation of the site's inhabitants in the pre-Israelite period, the Jebusites. These people were considered Canaanites because they lived in the land of *Canaan (see Gen 10:16), but it is likely that they were a non-Semitic people perhaps related to the Hurrians or Hittites.

Although it is not found in the Historical Books, the name "Salem," perhaps a shortened form of "Jerusalem," appears twice in the Hebrew Bible: once as the city of Melchizedek (Gen 14:18), and once in Psalms as a synonym for Zion. Because of Melchizedek's priestly role, the Genesis usage serves to anticipate the priestly presence in later, monarchic Jerusalem.

2. Early History.

Excavations have established that habitation at the site dates back to the late fourth and early third millennia BCE (Chalcolithic and Early Bronze I and II periods); however, even in those Early Bronze periods, which witnessed the growth of urban life in Palestine, the settlements are sparse and nonurban. Not until the early second millennium BCE (Middle Bronze II) are there indications of a sizable settlement—with a three-meter-thick wall, towers to protect the Gihon spring, and the earliest water channel (Siloam channel) bringing water from the spring into the settlement—that perhaps corresponds to the *Rušalimum* named in the Egyptian Execration texts. The very mention of Jerusalem in those texts indicates that it was large enough to be considered a potential threat to Egyptian sovereignty. Yet, occupying about twelve acres, it was hardly more than a walled town in comparison to the extensive urban sites of other parts of the ancient Near East in the Bronze Age.

The same can be said for the Late Bronze Age settlement, for which scattered archaeological remains have been recovered. The evidence of the Amarna letters, as well as several assemblages of material remains (from a tomb and a cistern) that indicate some wealth, attest to the existence of what then would have been a Canaanite settlement by the fourteenth century BCE. However, like other settlements in the highlands of Palestine in this period, Jerusalem was a relatively small and minor part of Egyptian colonial rule, governed by a mayor rather than a king and not as populated or as regionally dominant as contemporary coastal Canaanite settlements, which might be properly called city-states

(Savage and Falconer; Naʾaman, 19-21). Perhaps the material about Adoni-Zedek as ruler of Jerusalem in Joshua 10:1-4 (the first mention of the name "Jerusalem" in the Hebrew Bible) and Adoni-Bezek in Judges 1:7-8, which suggest defeat by the Israelites, were meant to establish the tradition that early Israelites were destined to control this highland center. Adoni-Zedek's name ("My Lord is Zedek/Justice") echoes that of Melchizedek ("My King is Zedek/Justice"), the ruler of Salem (= Jerusalem) in the ancestor narratives of Genesis, and may be relevant to David's establishment of Zadok ("Justice") as a priest in Jerusalem (2 Sam 15:24-29), perhaps in continuity with the sanctity of the site under Jebusite rule.

A somewhat different tradition about early Iron Age Jerusalem appears in Joshua (Josh 15:8; 15:63; 18:28) and Judges (Judg 1:21; 19:10-11), as well as the David narrative (see 1 Sam 5:6-7). These texts claim that Jerusalem was under control of the Jebusites at that time and could not so easily be conquered. That assessment fits with the archaeological data, for the most important discovery dating to pre-Israelite Jerusalem is a monumental structure on the east side of the eastern ridge. Known as the "stepped stone structure," it consists of narrow substructural terraces covered by a superstructural stepped mantle and was constructed to form an enormous artificial mound (originally at least 27 m high and 40 m wide) that most archaeologists consider a platform on which an imposing and impregnable palace or citadel would have been built. This structure, at first thought to be part of the building activities associated with David, now seems best dated to the very end of the Late Bronze Age, from the late thirteenth to early twelfth centuries BCE if not before (Tarler and Cahill, 55; Mazar, Shiloh and Geva, 702-3). Thus it would be an imposing remnant of the citadel of the Jebusites, who apparently dominated Jerusalem for several hundred years at the end of the Bronze Age and beginning of the Iron Age.

3. Capital of the United Monarchy.

One way to measure scriptural interest in Israelite and Judean kings is to note how often they are mentioned in the Historical Books in relationship to the capital. As might be expected, David is at the top of the list, found directly or indirectly in verses naming Jerusalem forty-four times, followed by Solomon (thirty-four times). No other biblical king is mentioned along with Jerusalem more than twenty-five times. The importance of the Israelite polity headed by these two rulers based in Jerusalem is thus reflected in the sustained historiographic attention to them in connection with their capital. Legitimization of the Israelite monarchy is manifest in the narratives of conquest and of monumental building projects of the first two kings of the Davidic dynasty (*see* History of Israel 3: United Monarchy).

3.1. David. No biblical figure is more prominently associated with Jerusalem than King David, and the stronghold from which he is said to have ruled—the city of David—bears his name. The founder of the dynastic state is inextricably and necessarily linked to the establishment of its capital. Because the traditions connecting David and Jerusalem are so powerful, and because the eschatological images of the city and its messianic ruler dominate the prophetic and psalmic literature of the Bible, it is difficult to evaluate the nature of the site in its origins as an Israelite settlement. Jerusalem looms large in the sacred literature of the three monotheistic faiths, making it seem that it must have been grand from the outset. Examining the biblical traditions about the site during the early tenth century BCE—the period of Davidic rule—in conjunction with the archaeological remains gives us a much more realistic idea of its early Israelite history.

According to 2 Samuel, David's initial administrative center is *Hebron, nineteen miles south-southeast of Jerusalem and within the traditional boundaries of the tribe of Judah. David's leadership gradually is extended beyond the southern Judean hills to include northern groups, and eventually the administrative center shifts to Jerusalem after David and his forces overcome the Jebusite inhabitants (2 Sam 5:6-9; 1 Chron 11:4-9). Such a move made good political sense; outside David's own tribal territory, Jebus/Jerusalem would have been neutral and thus could more easily have earned the loyalty of the various lineages comprising early Israel. Following his conquest of Jerusalem, David builds a royal residence with the assistance of Phoenician artisans (2 Sam 5:11). His political activities are accompanied by sacral ones. He brings the *ark of the covenant, the most powerful symbol of Yahweh, the God to whom his rise to power is attributed, to the royal enclave (2 Sam

6:17). He also builds an altar to the LORD on a threshing floor that he purchases from Araunah, a nearby Jebusite farmer (2 Sam 24:18-25), and makes initial preparations for the construction of a temple that would represent God's legitimization of the new polity (1 Chron 22:1-5).

The narratives of the conquest of the Jebusite settlement and establishment of an Israelite one under David contain several specific details that perhaps can be correlated with archaeological data. Although the logistics are not entirely clear, David and his men seem to penetrate the stronghold through an existing water shaft (*ṣinnôr*). The recent redating of one of Jerusalem's water tunnels (*see* Water and Water Systems) to a pre-Davidic period situates the tale about the conquest within a physical reality (Reich and Shukron). The text describing David's building activities mentions "the Millo" (*hammillô*, "the fill"). Scholars dispute the meaning of this term with respect to Jerusalem's topography (the various views are summarized in King, 754). It may anachronistically anticipate the massive fills that were to be brought in for building activities later in the century; alternatively, it may refer to a small hill (Ophel) just north of the eastern hill on which the Jebusite stronghold that became the city of David was located and which "filled" the gap between the eastern hill and the one to the north that eventually would become the Temple Mount. Although excavations have done little to clarify that term, they have shown that some alteration of the stepped stone structure took place at the beginning of the Iron II period, consonant with the establishment of a new political regime.

Topographical issues likewise figure in an analysis of the story of Araunah's threshing floor (*gōren*). The text provides no clues about its location, but it seems to be an unoccupied plot of land and thus probably outside the walls of the city of David. His acquisition of this land for an altar that ultimately would be the site of the temple links David to the central shrine of ancient Israel and also alludes to the fact that the built-up area of his administrative center did not extend much beyond the preceding Jebusite stronghold.

Archaeology has recovered virtually nothing of this earliest Israelite occupation of the site. Some critics therefore dispute the reliability of any of the David narratives, but most understand the confusing archaeological picture as supporting the possibility of an early Iron IIA Israelite occupation (the opposing positions are clearly laid out in Steiner, Cahill and Naʾaman). The reigning assumption is that, because it was conquered but apparently not destroyed, the early tenth-century settlement continued to use existing walls and buildings and that the city of David did not exceed by much that of its Jebusite predecessor. In short, Jerusalem remained a relatively small, fortified town and administrative center with very little residential space. It is difficult to know whether such a modest settlement could have supported the kind of imperial presence in the eastern Mediterranean that the tales of David's exploits suggest, but analogies with Late Bronze Age kingdoms indicate the possibility of such dominion (Naʾaman, 23-24). In any case, the traditions about building activities with political and cultic import are likely the concomitants of a new political entity, symbolized and legitimized by the new ruler's changes and additions to the landscape.

3.2. Solomon. Later in the tenth century BCE, according to the biblical narrative, Solomon undertakes substantial building projects, both political and religious (*see* Solomon's Temple). The northern hill becomes the site of an enormous precinct containing a temple and an adjacent and larger palace, built over a period of close to twenty years (1 Kings 6—7; cf. 2 Chron 2—4). Because the northern hill, or Temple Mount, continues to this day to be a sacred enclosure, archaeology cannot directly testify to the reliability of the biblical accounts of the construction attributed to Solomon. However, this lack of evidence for monumental architecture of the mid-tenth century BCE does not necessarily mean that the biblical materials about Jerusalem in this period are completely unreliable. Indeed, the intensive overbuilding on the Temple Mount would by now have obliterated Iron II remains, and remnants of the temple would not be expected. Moreover, several other kinds of archaeological data are relevant (see Meyers, 248-56).

One is that the Kings narrative refers to other building projects of the tenth century BCE — at *Megiddo, *Hazor and *Gezer—that have been recovered archaeologically. Despite the views of some who see these remains as postdating the tenth century BCE, the establishment of regional administrative centers in that period conforms to what the biblical text suggests. Thus the biblical narratives reflecting similar building activities in Jerusalem cannot be dismissed. The discovery just north of the stepped stone structure of a fragment of a casemate wall—the kind of double wall found at other Israelite cities of the so-called Solomonic period—supports this kind of evidence.

Another kind of evidence pertains to the temple described in the Bible. Although the text does not provide a complete verbal blueprint, it does allow a reasonable reconstruction of its size, materials, use of space and decorative elements. For decades it was supposed that the closest architectural parallel was from Tel Taʿyinat in Syria. The tradition of Phoenician workmanship and materials for the Jerusalem temple, as well as its tripartite ground plan and its situation next to a larger palace, seemed compatible with the Syrian example. However, the Tel Taʿyinat edifice is several centuries later and somewhat different than the purported Jerusalem temple. A much closer parallel is now recognized in the Syrian temple excavated at ʿAin Dara in the 1980s (see Monson). Built at the beginning of the twelfth century BCE, it survives in more or less the same form into the eighth century BCE. It represents an architectural plan that links the earlier Late Bronze Syro-Palestinian temples with subsequent Iron Age ones. Strikingly close to the temple described in 1 Kings, its features make it possible to understand the placement of side chambers and the use of certain construction techniques that hitherto had eluded those studying the biblical depiction. More important, it suggests the authenticity of the architectural description in the Bible, at least with respect to plan and workmanship.

The construction of the temple-palace precinct entailed the extension of Jerusalem toward the north, incorporating Ophel and the northern hill (the Temple Mount) to form a cultic-administrative quarter. This project would have more than doubled the size of the city but would have changed the occupied space (the areas with domestic architecture) very little. Given the complete lack of archaeological evidence for an expansion of the walls of the original eastern hill settlement (and for such evidence the severe limitations on finding remnants of the temple-palace complex do not apply), it is likely that Jerusalem remained a royal administrative center but not yet an urban site with the economic, architectural and demographic features that would characterize a true city.

4. Capital of the Southern Kingdom.

Every king who ruled over the southern kingdom following the death of Solomon and the division of the monarchy is connected to Jerusalem in the formulaic language of the books of Kings and echoed in the books of Chronicles. For each king, even those for whom little else is recounted, the following information is provided: "King PN [proper name] ruled X years in Jerusalem." The dynastic succession is inextricably linked to the royal and religious center established in the tenth century BCE. In the centuries during which the dynasty endured, certainly the topography, size and character of Jerusalem underwent significant changes, some of which are mentioned in the Historical Books, and some of which are visible in the archaeological record. Undoubtedly, many other modifications were neither reported in the text nor recovered in excavations. Nonetheless, perusing the record of the Judean monarchy in relation to archaeological data provides a general notion of the shape and significance of the capital in the rest of the Iron II period.

4.1. Before the Eighth Century BCE. Jerusalem, as capital, was involved in the political struggles of Judah from the moment it was severed from the northern tribes (*see* History of Israel 4: Division of the Monarchy). Much of its military involvement was tantamount to civil war with the northern kingdom, which was larger and had more economic resources than did the southern one. But foreign threats to the capital were also periodically part of the challenges to the small Judean state, beginning in the reign of *Rehoboam (922-931 BCE), who apparently prevented the Egyptian pharaoh Shishak (Shoshenq) from taking Jerusalem as he had taken fortresses to the south. Still, the Historical Books report that the *Egyptians entered Jerusalem and took much of the temple and royal wealth (2 Chron 12:2-3; cf. 1 Kings 14:25-28), and they also describe similar pillage in the mid-ninth century BCE (2 Chron 21:16-17), when the Philistine and Arab attackers of Jerusalem are said to have carried off treasures from the palace of Jehoram (849-842 BCE).

Changes to the city itself seem to be minimal during this period, despite the recurrent military threats. The Chronicler reports the fortifying of towns around Jerusalem (2 Chron 11:5-12) during Rehoboam's reign, Kings mentions similar activities by his grandson Asa (2 Chron 14:6; cf.

1 Kings 15:23), and archaeology suggests that Asa or his son *Jehoshaphat (cf. 2 Chron 17:12) indeed carried out these projects. But nothing is said of such activity in Jerusalem itself during the ninth century BCE. Presumably, Rehoboam and his successors inherited a sufficiently strong fortification system from the David-Solomon era. During the long reign of Jehoash (837-800 BCE), however, the temple and probably the palace too were refurbished (2 Kings 12:6-16). The scanty archaeological remains from the late tenth and the ninth centuries BCE provide indirect testimony to the silence of the biblical accounts with respect to construction work.

4.2. Eighth Century BCE to the Exile. Although the historical narratives portray the tenth century BCE as the period of Jerusalem's maximum greatness, developments in the eighth century BCE are arguably equally significant if not more so. The Chronicler reports the shoring up of Jerusalem's defenses with three towers (2 Chron 26:9-11), along with reorganizing the army, improving its arsenal, and also extending the crown's agricultural resources, all during the reign of Uzziah (Azariah) in the mid-eighth century (783-742 BCE). Similar activities are reported for Uzziah's son Jotham (742-735 BCE), who constructs a new gate to the temple precincts, strengthens the defensive wall in the area of Ophel, and also builds fortresses and new settlements outside the city (2 Kings 15:35; 2 Chron 27:3-4). Such activities are consonant with nationalistic attention to royal power and concomitant economic development, and they may have led to the difficulties that the next monarch, Ahaz (735-715 BCE), faced with the Syrians and that led to Jerusalem's apparent submission to *Assyrian domination (*see* History of Israel 5: Assyrian Period). Ahaz's successor, *Hezekiah (715-687 BCE), reverses those fortunes. The reform attributed to him, briefly mentioned in 2 Kings (2 Kings 18:4, 16, 22) and elaborately recounted in 2 Chronicles (2 Chron 29:1—31:21), represents intersecting political, religious and economic ploys to strengthen Judah in the face of the Assyrian expansion that had led to the conquest of the northern kingdom in 721 BCE. Royal control over the settlements of Judah and perhaps even over some remnants of the northern kingdom apparently brought economic interactions between the capital and the surrounding territories to a new level (2 Chron 31:4-19), although specific changes to Jerusalem are not mentioned except for the repairs made to temple doors (2 Chron 29:3) as part of the cleansing and purification of the sacred precinct.

Archaeological discoveries in Jerusalem and elsewhere in Judah contribute greatly to an assessment of the activities of the monarchs of the eighth century BCE. Although some of these discoveries represent developments that took place throughout the century during which these four kings ruled, most are attributed specifically to the period of Hezekiah. Among the latter are thousands of storage jar handles stamped with the word *lmlk* ("belonging to the king"); some were found in Jerusalem, but most come from sites along Judah's northern and western borders, probably signifying the economic and political control of the crown, especially in areas vulnerable to Assyrian invasion. Other artifacts similarly attest to trade with regional and foreign markets.

The most important discoveries are from Jerusalem itself, and they indicate that in the eighth century BCE the capital reached its zenith and probably remained that way until the Babylonian conquest of 587 BCE. Archaeological work since the 1960s shows that by the end of the eighth century BCE Jerusalem had become a great deal larger, that its defensive system had been extended around the new areas of occupation, and that steps had been taken to assure adequate water supply in the event of siege. The western hill was now occupied with domestic buildings, forming a district known appropriately as the Mishneh, or Second Quarter (2 Kings 22:14; 2 Chron 34:23), and domestic structures spilled down the east side of the eastern hill (Shiloh, 1.28-29). A massive fortification wall, as much as five to seven meters thick in places, surrounded the entire city, including the areas east of the original fortification wall of the eastern hill (Avigad, 46). And the famous channel known as "Hezekiah's Tunnel" was cut in order to divert water from Gihon to the western side of the city. The reasons for these dramatic changes are complex; both an influx of population from the north after the fall of *Samaria to the Assyrians (721 BCE) and an attempt to prevent a similar fate for Judah must have been important factors.

The growing might of Assyria led to the social, economic and political growth of Jerusalem, so that for the first time it truly can be considered an urban center. With a population of at least ten thousand, it was perhaps ten times larger than any other contemporary settlement in Judah. The Assyrian threat, in the form of Sennacherib's invasion of Judah and siege of Jerusalem in 701 BCE, also contributed to the establishment of its importance as a religious center. Miraculously spared destruction at the hand of the Assyrians, who apparently had demolished other Judean sites, Jerusalem would now be understood to have extraordinary and enduring sacral significance. It had become, arguably for the first time in its long history, what geographers call a primate city, in which all political, economic, social and religious functions were centered (Steiner 2001b, 285), even as it succumbed to Assyrian hegemony.

The Chronicler (2 Chron 33:14) attributes additional fortification to Hezekiah's son *Manasseh (687-642 BCE), but no other changes are reported in Chronicles or Kings for the last seven Judean rulers. The weakening of Assyria by the mid-seventh century BCE, however, allowed *Josiah (640-609 BCE) to extend the control of the capital northward into the area of the defunct northern kingdom (2 Kings 23:15-20; 2 Chron 34:6, 33) and refurbish the temple as part of his nationalistic resurgence. Ultimately, after a brief period of Egyptian hegemony, the emerging power of the Babylonians proved too much for the tiny Judean state, whose splendid capital must have seemed a worthy goal. According to both Kings (2 Kings 25:1-21) and Chronicles (2 Chron 36:17-20), Nebuchadnezzar and his forces breached and broke down the fortifications, sacked and burned the temple, destroyed the residential areas, and carried into exile most of those who survived the onslaught (*see* History of Israel 6: Babylonian Period).

5. Restoration.
Whether the people of Jerusalem were killed in battle, escaped to the countryside or went into exile, it now seems certain, as the result of archaeological discoveries, that the city itself was radically reduced in size from its eighth-seventh-century sprawl over both western and eastern hills and the Temple Mount. Fragments of the great wall system may have been left standing, but the occupied city was again no larger than the eastern hill (city of David) and Temple Mount, connected by Ophel. It is unclear how much of Jerusalem remained settled in the immediate aftermath of the conquest, but at the be-

ginning of the Persian period and even with the return of the first of several small groups of exiles, Jerusalem was just a fraction of what it had been before the destruction. Recent estimates differ, but they all acknowledge that the population had shrunk dramatically (e.g., Broshi, 12-13), with recent and more sophisticated methods of demographic analysis suggesting a population of fewer than one thousand inhabitants (Carter, 200-201; cf. Neh 7:4) (see History of Israel 7: Persian Period).

The Achaemenids, in creating the province of Yehud in the Persian I period (538-450 BCE), apparently had no interest in developing Jerusalem as an urban center, in contrast to their development of trade centers along the Phoenician coast (Lipschits). Jerusalem again was a rural community, economically, demographically and politically. Yet Yehud was allowed a measure of local autonomy, with the Persians establishing governors in Jerusalem and granting permission for the temple to be restored (Ezra 1—7). By the Persian II period (450-332 BCE), under the leadership of Nehemiah and with a modest gain in population, some of the walls, gates and towers may have been repaired (Neh 2:17—6:15). Little archaeological material can be correlated with such activity, however, and the narratives, with mention of so many gates—too many for a relatively small settlement—may contain information retrojected from a later period or used to symbolize the modest power of the Persian-appointed governor. In any case, Jerusalem now reaches its maximum Persian-period size of approximately fifteen hundred people (Carter, 201; cf. Neh 11:1). It is still a rather insignificant settlement, although considerably larger than the tiny villages and small towns in the rest of Yehud. As in the tenth century BCE, it occupies the city of David, the Temple Mount and the area in between; the western hill remains in ruins.

Persian-period Jerusalem never regains the demographic, economic or political stature of the preexilic city. Still, with the restoration of the temple and the concomitant reestablishment of its priestly personnel and their judicial/legal and cultic activities, Jerusalem's distinctive place as a religious center, for the Diaspora as well as for Yehud, emerged (see History of Israel 8: Postexilic Community). Jerusalem was willy-nilly freed from the constraints and foibles of being a political capital and economic hub. Despite the resurgence of nationalism in the subsequent Hellenistic and Roman periods, the centrality of its religious role as a "holy city" (Neh 11:1) would thereafter dominate, whether in reality or in eschatological imagination.

See also ARCHAEOLOGY, SYRO-PALESTINIAN; CITIES AND VILLAGES; POSTEXILIC TEMPLE; SAMARIA; SOLOMON'S TEMPLE; WATER AND WATER SYSTEMS; ZION TRADITIONS.

BIBLIOGRAPHY. **N. Avigad,** *Discovering Jerusalem* (Nashville: Nelson, 1983); **D. Bahat with C. T. Rubinstein,** *The Illustrated Atlas of Jerusalem* (New York: Simon & Schuster, 1990); **M. Ben-Dov,** *Historical Atlas of Jerusalem* (New York and London: Continuum, 2002); **M. Broshi,** "Estimating the Population of Ancient Jerusalem," *BAR* 4 (1978) 10-15; **C. Carter,** *The Emergence of Yehud in the Persian Period* (JSOTSup 294; Sheffield: Sheffield Academic Press, 1999); **H. Geva,** ed., *Ancient Jerusalem Revealed* (Jerusalem: Israel Exploration Society, 1994); **I. Kalimi,** "Jerusalem—The Divine City: The Representation of Jerusalem in the Chronicles Compared with Earlier and Later Jewish Compositions," in *The Chronicler as Theologian: Essays in Honor of Ralph W. Klein,* ed. M. P. Graham, S. L. McKenzie and G. N. Knoppers (JSOTSup; London and New York: T & T Clark, 2003) 189-205; **K. Kenyon,** *Digging Up Jerusalem* (London: Benn, 1974); **P. J. King,** "Jerusalem," *ABD* 3.747-66; **O. Lipschits,** "The Achaemenid Imperial Policy and the Status of Jerusalem in the Fifth Century BCE," in *Judah and Judeans in the Achaemenid Period,* ed. M. Oeming and O. Lipschits (Winona Lake, IN: Eisenbrauns, 2005); **B. Mazar, Y. Shiloh and H. Geva,** "Jerusalem: The Early Periods and the First Temple Period," *NEAEHL* 2.698-716; **C. Meyers,** "Kinship and Kingship: The Early Monarchy," in *The Oxford History of the Biblical World,* ed. M. D. Coogan (New York: Oxford University Press, 1998); **J. Monson,** "The New ʿAin Dara Temple: Closest Solomonic Parallel," *BAR* 26 (2000) 20-35, 67; idem, "The Temple of Solomon and the Temple of Ain Dara, Syria," *Qadmoniot* 29 (1996) 33-38; **N. Naʾaman,** "The Contribution of the Amarna Letters to the Debate on Jerusalem's Political Position in the Tenth Century BCE," *BASOR* 304 (1996) 17-28; **R. Reich and E. Shukron,** "Light at the End of the Tunnel," *BAR* 25 (1999) 22-33, 72; **E. Robinson,** *Biblical Researches in Palestine, Mount Sinai, and Arabia Petraea* (3 vols.; Boston: Crocker & Brewster, 1841); **S. H. Savage and S. E. Falconer,**

"Spatial and Statistical Inference of Late Bronze Polities in the Southern Levant," *BASOR* 330 (2003) 31-45; **Y. Shiloh et al.,** *Excavations at the City of David* (6 vols.; Qedem 19, 30, 33, 35, 40, 41; Jerusalem: Institute of Archaeology, Hebrew University of Jerusalem, 1984-2000); **M. Steiner,** *Excavations by Kathleen M. Kenyon in Jerusalem 1961-1967, 3: The Settlement in the Bronze and Iron Ages* (Copenhagen International Series 9; Sheffield: Sheffield Academic Press, 2001a); idem, "Jerusalem in the Tenth and Seventh Centuries BCE: From Administrative Town to Commercial City," in *Studies in the Archaeology of the Iron Age in Israel and Jordan,* ed. A. Mazar (JSOTSup 331; Sheffield: Sheffield Academic Press, 2001b) 280-88; **M. Steiner, J. Cahill and N. Naʾaman,** "David's Jerusalem: Fiction or Reality?" *BAR* 24 (1999) 25-44, 62-63; **D. Tarler and J. M. Cahill,** "David, City of," *ABD* 2.52-67; **M. Tsevat and H. Ringgren,** *"yĕrûšālēm/yĕrûšālayim," TDOT* 6.47-55; **A. G. Vaughn and A. E. Killebrew,** *Jerusalem in Bible and Archaeology: The First Temple Period* (SBLSymS 18; Atlanta: Society of Biblical Literature, 2003). C. Meyers

JEZREEL

Within the OT Historical Books Jezreel is the name of a village in Judah (Josh 15:56; 1 Sam 25:43), the name of a Judean individual (1 Chron 4:3), the name of a wide valley between the Galilee region to the north and the central hill country to the south (Josh 17:16; Judg 6:33), and, most frequently, an Israelite town on the southeast side of the valley, west of Mount Gilboa, in the tribal district of Issachar (Josh 19:18; 1 Kings 18:45, 46; 21:1, 23; 2 Kings 8:29 [cf. 2 Chron 22:6]; 9:10, 15, 16, 17, 30, 36, 37; 10:1, 11). On a few occasions it is not entirely clear which of these latter two is being referred to (1 Sam 29:1, 11; 2 Sam 2:9; 4:4; 1 Kings 4:12). The present article concentrates on the Israelite town.

The ancient site is to be identified with the modern *Zerʿin/Tel Yizreʿel.* The western end of the site was occupied until comparatively recent times, so that excavation was considered unrewarding. In the late 1980s it was discovered, however, that part of the Iron Age settlement extended to the east and so could more easily be excavated. A joint expedition of Tel Aviv University and the British School of Archaeology in Jerusalem undertook seven seasons of work (1990-1996), illuminating the background to

parts of the biblical narrative and not contradicting it in any serious manner.

The name of the town has not yet been found in any ancient source outside the Bible. Evidence from the Amarna letters suggests that the valley once was known as Gina, in which case, though unusual, it is likely to have been later renamed after the town.

1. Biblical Sources
2. Archaeological Evidence
3. Historical Significance

1. Biblical Sources.

1.1. Pre-Omride.

1.1.1. Joshua 19:18. The reference to Jezreel in the context of the tribal inheritance of Issachar (Josh 19:17-23) raises at once the problem of the date of these lists in the second half of the book of Joshua (*see* Tribes of Israel and Land Allotments/Borders). Dates as far apart as the Judges period and the late monarchic period have been suggested for parts of these lists (for a full summary see Williamson 1991), and it is difficult to avoid circular argumentation when comparing the written data with archaeological finds. A regional survey by Z. Gal (94-106), however, has concluded that Israelite settlement of the region of Issachar is unlikely prior to the tenth century BCE, so that the list can hardly predate the united monarchy. Although more recent evidence from Jezreel itself indicating some form of settlement in the Late Bronze Age may necessitate a revision of that conclusion (Ussishkin and Woodhead 1994, 42-43), a date in the tenth century BCE nevertheless probably enjoys a consensus of moderate critical opinion.

1.1.2. 1 Kings 4:12. Such a date would fit well with the evidence of 1 Kings 4:12, where Jezreel appears in a list of Solomon's tax districts. The archival nature of this list is generally accepted, though the value of this conclusion is threatened by the fact that the Hebrew text of the verse is almost certainly corrupt. Nevertheless, the probability remains that the town (and not the valley) of Jezreel is attested here from the Solomonic period.

1.1.3. Other. It is thus of interest to note that the other early references to Jezreel in 1 and 2 Samuel (listed above) are ambiguous, none certainly referring to a town of that name. Mention of the well or fountain in Jezreel in 1 Samuel 29:1, for instance, is almost certainly a reference to the spring in the valley some distance to the northeast of the site (its use is attested since Chalcolithic times), while the mention in 2 Samuel 2:9 seems to refer to a district rather than a town. 2 Samuel 4:4 is the strongest candidate for a town at this early period, but the balance of probability points toward the likelihood of a significant settlement only as part of the policy of regional consolidation during the united monarchy.

1.2. Omride Jezreel.

1.2.1. 2 Kings 9—10. The heaviest concentration of references to Jezreel is in the account of *Jehu's overthrow of the *Omri dynasty, and indeed this is the event with which it was later associated in general memory (cf. Hos 1:4). It is widely agreed that an early and generally reliable source underlies the present Deuteronomistic form of these chapters. They recount how the last king of the Omri dynasty, Joram, was recuperating at Jezreel after being wounded in an encounter with the *Aramaeans and that Ahaziah of Judah was visiting him there (one of a number of indications that relations between the Israelite and Judean royal families were a good deal closer at this time than at first meets the eye). Jehu, the army commander, had both of them assassinated as he approached from the east, and then, on entering the town in triumph, was accosted by Jezebel, Ahab's widow and "queen mother" (2 Kings 10:13). She too was killed, as later were the remaining members of the Omride royal family and the leaders of the Baal cult.

Apart from its signal historical importance, the narrative reveals some small details about the nature of the town. It refers to a tower in terms that suggest that it was a prominent landmark (2 Kings 9:17), presumably on the northern side, possibly at the northeastern corner of the fortifications, given the direction toward which it served as a lookout. 2 Kings 9:31-32 also speaks of a gate structure (cf. 2 Kings 10:8) and near it of some kind of a royal residence with a second story. Finally, if 2 Kings 9:30-37 is taken at face value, the area between the gate and the residence was known as the "portion" of Jezreel (2 Kings 9:10, 36); proposals to emend the text, however slightly, to read either "rampart" or "plot of ground" are unconvincing for various reasons (see Williamson 1991, 82-83, 87).

1.2.2. 1 Kings 21. If Jehu's revolt signals the end of the Omri dynasty, the story of Naboth's vineyard in 1 Kings 21 shows it at the height of its power under Ahab. This narrative vividly portrays a clash of values between traditional Israelite concern for inheritance and land ownership by the common people and the newer power-seeking ambitions of a despotic form of royalty; its outcome upholds the former, even while tacitly conceding the inevitability of the growth of the latter. Nothing that follows can undermine the didactic power of the story and its moral imperatives.

There is an alternative account of Naboth's death in 2 Kings 9:25-26 that cannot be harmonized with 1 Kings 21 and that stands a greater likelihood of being historically closer to the truth. When this consideration is coupled with several stylistic features of the narrative in 1 Kings 21, we probably should conclude that it is a moralistic tale rather than historical reportage. And finally, the clear implications of 1 Kings 21:18, of the fulfillment of the prophecy in 1 Kings 21:19 in 1 Kings 22:37-38, and of the juxtaposition of 1 Kings 20 and 21 are that Naboth's vineyard was in any case considered to be located in *Samaria, not Jezreel at all. The words "in Jezreel" in 1 Kings 21:1 are lacking in the LXX text and probably were added later. These conclusions not only (and most importantly) result in a better understanding of the narrative purpose of the story, but also remove the one bit of supposedly firm textual evidence for Jezreel as the site of a royal palace (insofar as that may be distinguished from a more temporary seasonal residence).

2. Archaeological Evidence.

The only significant archaeological work at Jezreel in the biblical period has been that undertaken in 1990-1996, referred to above. The results are fully summarized in three substantial reports by D. Ussishkin and J. Woodhead (1992; 1994; 1997; each with associated specialist analyses of particular topics). The following summary is based upon these reports without, however, fully documenting each separate statement.

2.1. Pre-Omride Jezreel. No architectural remains earlier than the major building work of Omri and Ahab have been discovered. The evidence of pottery recovered from later fills, however, clearly indicates that the site was inhabited at this earlier phase. It is possible that the earlier settlement was concentrated at the west end of the site, where the excavations have been focused mostly on the later substantial Islamic,

Crusader and Byzantine settlements. The situation is closely analogous with Samaria, where it is also now established that there was some form of settlement before the major building by Omri and Ahab.

2.2. Omride Jezreel. All the evidence we have points clearly in the direction of Omri and Ahab extending and completely redesigning the site. A massive rectangular platform was prepared on the hilltop by leveling down whatever was previously there and by dumping vast quantities of brown soil to raise the lower slopes. The fortifications around this enclosure are now well understood. First, around three sides there was a rock-cut dry moat, about 150 m along the eastern side, 320 m along the southern side, and 200 m or more along the western side (along the northern side the slope falls away steeply into the valley, so presumably it was felt that there was no need for this form of outer defense there). The moat is mostly 8-12 m wide and 5 m deep, though it narrows somewhat in front of the gate on the southern side. Inside this moat was a rampart, secured along its exposed bottom edge by a retaining wall and stretching some 17 m inward toward the main wall, and rising by 2.5-4.5 m. Finally, there was a casemate wall, with substantial square corner towers, each built to a similar design. It has been calculated that the area enclosed by these fortifications was about 45 dunams (11 acres).

Little has been recovered by way of construction within this enclosure. This may have been in part because so much of the building materials later was robbed (see 2.3 below), but even so, some trace would have been expected to remain. More likely, large parts of the enclosure may have been left open for military (and perhaps especially chariot) purposes. It is also possible that parts of the original building plans were never completed. At any rate, no sign of any palatial building is yet known. The gate area was quite damaged; remains of a four-chambered gate are clearly visible, and the excavators tentatively conclude that there is sufficient evidence to postulate that it was in fact six-chambered. But this remains controversial.

The excavations at Jezreel have opened up an important debate about the chronology of Iron Age II, and this has been developed by some into part of the argument against the historicity of the united monarchy. The fundamental point at issue is that some of the pottery associated with the enclosure at Jezreel is similar to some from *Megiddo Level VA-IVB, the stratum that previously had been associated with Solomon and considered to have been destroyed before the period of the Omrides during Shishak's campaign. I. Finkelstein (who provides a recent summary with further references) has used this in particular as a cornerstone in his arguments for a "low chronology" theory of the monarchy period. The debates that this theory have opened up ought to be conducted in exclusively archaeological terms, and no doubt the matter will be resolved at that level by new data and more refined analysis of previous finds. For the time being, it is best to keep an open mind, and to observe that there are various ways of accounting for the data, not all of which by any means necessarily threaten the identification of Solomonic remains at Megiddo or elsewhere (see, for instance, Ussishkin).

2.3. Post-Omride Jezreel. Jezreel ceased to be inhabited, apart from simple squatters, at some point after the fall of the Omride dynasty but still within the Iron Age II period. The circumstances of its abandonment are uncertain. Most of the materials from the site were robbed, although there is evidence of a major fire concentrated in the southeastern tower. Initially, it was suggested that the site was destroyed as part of Jehu's coup. N. Na'aman, however, has argued that the evidence of the burnt tower, together with the find of eight arrowheads, points to its destruction after conflict. He associates this with other evidence for an Aramaean conquest of the northern part of Israel in Jehu's reign and suggests that the destruction was so great that the site could not be rebuilt. H. G. M. Williamson (1996), however, previously had maintained that the evidence should be interpreted as indicating a deliberate anti-Omride policy of abandonment: the robbing of the building materials suggests that the destruction was not violent, a conclusion only reinforced by the highly localized nature of the tower fire, showing what could have been expected throughout the site had that been its fate.

Whatever the truth of the matter, Jezreel was not significantly reinhabited for centuries, and this matches its absence from the biblical record after Jehu's coup. This coincidence of written and material sources in terms of the site's history of settlement is one small pointer toward the general reliability of the relevant written sources, since it is unlikely that the much later historian could have known the situation so exactly by any other means.

3. Historical Significance.
From a historical perspective, it is clearly the massive investment in Jezreel by the Omrides that warrants most comment. Not only does it have several parallels with Samaria, as already noted, but also it is located a mere 15 km from, and hence is within eyeshot of, another major center, Megiddo.

First, in terms of function, Ussishkin has convincingly argued on the basis of the architectural remains that Jezreel served primarily as a military base (note especially the number of chariots that Ahab is reported to have contributed to the anti-Assyrian coalition at Karkar), while Samaria, with its much more refined style and rich remains, is likely to have served as the royal capital. Megiddo, meanwhile, had long been a regional administrative center, and no doubt it continued to play that role alongside the newer Omride foundations. The detail of this will remain uncertain, however, until the current dispute about Megiddo's dating and stratigraphy is resolved.

Besides such functional concerns, however, one should also inquire after the political motivation that lay behind Omri's and Ahab's enterprise. After all, the location of Jezreel is hardly what would have been expected had it been constructed primarily to defend the realm against external aggression, and in theory other centers might equally have been developed to house the military. These observations should be coupled with the recollection that Omri came to power as the result of a military coup that led to several years of civil war (1 Kings 16:21-23), and that the investment in the building of Jezreel far exceeds any functional value. This leads to the suggestion (Williamson 1996) that the building of Jezreel may also have served the purposes of internal social control over a potentially restive population. Such large-scale public works are known to have been used sometimes in antiquity as a means of preventing the population from having the time or resources to organize serious opposition to the regime, and of course the physical sight of Jezreel's fortifications, once completed, would have had the effect of overawing, if not terrorizing, the local population—a favorite device of many rulers until at least as late as the medieval period.

Whether or not this speculation is correct in detail, the conclusion can scarcely be avoided that the fortunes of Jezreel and of the dynasty of Omri seem to have been closely intertwined in both foundation and abandonment.

See also OMRI DYNASTY.

BIBLIOGRAPHY. **I. Finkelstein,** "Omride Architecture," *ZDPV* 116 (2000) 114-38; **Z. Gal,** *Lower Galilee during the Iron Age* (ASORDS 9; Winona Lake, IN: Eisenbrauns, 1992); **N. Na'aman,** "Historical and Literary Notes on the Excavations of Tel Jezreel," *TA* 24 (1997) 122-28; **D. Ussishkin,** "Jezreel, Samaria and Megiddo: Royal Centres of Omri and Ahab," in *Congress Volume: Cambridge, 1995,* ed. J. A. Emerton (VTSup 66; Leiden: E. J. Brill, 1997) 351-64; **D. Ussishkin and J. Woodhead,** "Excavations at Tel Jezreel 1990-1991: Preliminary Report," *TA* 19 (1992) 3-56; idem, "Excavations at Tel Jezreel 1992-1993: Second Preliminary Report," *Levant* 26 (1994) 1-48; idem, "Excavations at Tel Jezreel 1994-1996: Third Preliminary Report," *TA* 24 (1997) 6-72; **H. G. M. Williamson,** "Jezreel in the Biblical Texts," *TA* 18 (1991) 72-92; idem, "Tel Jezreel and the Dynasty of Omri," *PEQ* 128 (1996) 41-51. H. G. M. Williamson

JOASH. *See* HISTORY OF ISRAEL 5: ASSYRIAN PERIOD.

JONATHAN. *See* SAUL AND SAUL'S FAMILY.

JOSHUA
Biblical tradition associates the figure of Joshua closely with Israel's conquest of the land of promise. In the wilderness period Joshua serves as the assistant of Moses. After the death of Moses he leads Israel in a successful conquest of Canaan and then apportions the subjugated land among the tribes (*see* Tribes of Israel and Land Allotments/Borders). Even though Joshua remains obscure as a historical figure, the Historical Books emphasize his theological and national importance by presenting him in a wide variety of significant roles.

1. Joshua in Early Tradition and History
2. Traditional Roles
3. Joshua in the Historical Books
4. Later Developments in the Joshua Tradition

1. Joshua in Early Tradition and History.
1.1. Earliest Traditions. The geographic an-

chor for early traditions about Joshua is the site of his inheritance and burial at Timnath-heres in western Ephraim (Judg 2:9), identified with Khirbet Tibnah, c. 30 km southwest of *Shechem (see Josephus *Ant.* 5.119). In the course of textual transmission Timnath-heres ("Portion of the Sun") was altered to Timnath-serah ("Surplus Portion" [Josh 19:50; 24:30]) to avoid the implication of reverence to a solar deity. Joshua's grave became an object of popular veneration in the Roman period, if not earlier, and supplementary material in the LXX (Josh 21:42 D; 24:31 A) shows that the flint knives of circumcision (Josh 5:2-3) were thought to have been present in his grave. 1 Chronicles 7:20-27 provides Joshua with an Ephraimite genealogy and reports a tradition that a female ancestor, Sheerah, founded Upper and Lower Beth-horon in southwestern Ephraim. Beth-horon was the site of the battle with which Joshua was most closely and distinctively identified, the victory during which the sun "stood still" (Josh 10:10-14). Accordingly, Joshua seems to have originated as a local Ephraimite hero, similar to the military leaders described in Judges.

1.2. Joshua and History. Because the conquest stories reported in Joshua 2—9 focus on the territory of Benjamin, scholars often suggest that Joshua as an Ephraimite represents a somewhat later addition to those narratives, perhaps introduced as a unifying element in the first stage of collecting and writing. Although the book of *Joshua primarily portrays a completely successful conquest by a unified Israel under the sole leadership of Joshua (Josh 11:16, 23; 21:43-45), in other places the book preserves traditions of a disjointed and incomplete conquest performed by individual tribes (Josh 13:1-7, 13; 15:63; 16:10; 17:12-13, 14-18; 23:5, 7; cf. Judg 1:1-36). In fact, whether any sort of violent conquest of the land by Israel ever actually took place is a matter of serious dispute. Many scholars believe that the archaeological evidence does not support the biblical story at this point, but suggests instead that Israel emerged as an indigenous group from within the social and economic structures of Palestine (*see* History of Israel 1: Settlement Period).

2. Traditional Roles.
Traditions preserved in the Pentateuch portray Joshua in a variety of roles: warrior, spy, subordinate associate of Moses and designated suc-

cessor to national leadership. These prepare for the depiction of Joshua in the Historical Books.

2.1. Warrior. In Exodus 17:8-16 Joshua leads Israel to victory against its archetypal enemy, the Amalekites, while Moses provides supernatural aid by keeping his hands aloft on a nearby mountaintop. This victory at Rephidim was memorialized in a written saying and by an altar.

2.2. Spy. Joshua is also presented as a faithful spy with *Caleb, but a critical reading of Numbers 13—14 suggests that he was a latecomer to this role. Caleb appears alone in Numbers 13:30; 14:24 (J), while Joshua appears beside him only in the material scholars attribute to the Priestly writer (Num 14:6, 38). Joshua perhaps was added in order to provide the requisite two witnesses for the loyal spies' testimony. The editorial process by which Joshua perhaps was added to the narrative becomes visible when Moses renames Hoshea, who represents Ephraim in the tribal list of spies in Numbers 13:4-15, as Joshua (Num 13:16). This same tension in the spy tradition is visible between Deuteronomy 1:35-36 (Caleb alone) and Deuteronomy 1:38 (Joshua as well).

2.3. Associate of Moses. Joshua's association with Moses in the Pentateuch anticipates his leadership role "after the death of Moses" (Josh 1:1). He accompanies Moses partway up the mountain of theophany in Exodus 24:13 and remains behind when Moses leaves the tent of divine revelation in Exodus 33:11. The figure of Joshua serves to advance the narrative in Exodus 32:17 and Numbers 11:24-29, where he functions as a foil to the more insightful Moses. Joshua is Moses' "young assistant" (*na'ar* [Ex 33:11]) and "minister" (*mĕšārēt* [Ex 24:13; 33:11; Num 11:28; cf. Deut 1:38]). At the start of the book of Joshua he is still the "minister" of Moses (Josh 1:1), but at the end he achieves the status of "servant of Yahweh" (Josh 24:29).

2.4. Successor to Moses. The Pentateuch portrays Joshua as the divinely appointed successor to Moses. He is commissioned in this role by Moses in Numbers 27:18-23 and by Yahweh in Deuteronomy 31:14-15, 23. Joshua has the spirit and wisdom needed for leadership, and Moses designates him by laying a hand (or hands) on him (Num 27:18; Deut 34:9). He is not on a par with Moses, however, but receives only some of his predecessor's authority and remains subject to the oracular guidance of the priest Eleazar (Num 27:20-21). One indication of this difference in eminence is that Moses achieves an age of 120 years, while Joshua lives to be 110 (Deut 34:7; Josh 24:29).

3. Joshua in the Historical Books.

Joshua appears in the Historical Books in a large number of roles. He functions as a military commander and hero, emulates Moses, models Israel's obedient kings, and obeys and teaches the law of Moses. Joshua is also portrayed as a prophet and as the last of the faithful patriarchs.

3.1. Military Commander. Joshua won battles and secured possession of the land. His very name, *yĕhôšûaʿ* ("Yahweh saves" [cf. Sir 46:1]), points to these victories. In this way Joshua sets the stage for the military deliverers who follow in Judges. There the same verbal root, *yšʿ* ("save, deliver"), is used to characterize the figure of the judge as a *môšîaʿ*, "deliverer" (Judg 3:9, 15)—that is, one who saves the people with Yahweh's help. The descriptions of these victories in the book of Joshua maintain a careful balance between Yahweh's activities in sacral war and the human leadership role of Joshua. Yahweh acts conspicuously by collapsing the wall of *Jericho (Josh 6:20), dropping great stones from heaven (Josh 10:11) or inducing panic in enemy forces (Josh 10:10; cf. 2:11). However, Joshua makes his own contribution by acting independently as a military strategist (Josh 8:3-23; 10:28—11:14). In Joshua 1:1-9 Yahweh gives Joshua his task as commander and promises to be with him (Josh 1:5, 9; 3:7). Throughout the book Joshua receives divine encouragement (Josh 1:6, 7, 9; 8:1; 10:8; 11:6), and in turn he encourages the people of Israel (Josh 10:25; 17:17-18; 18:3; 23:5, 6).

3.2. Leader Like Moses. Joshua is presented as the successor of Moses (Josh 1:5, 17; 3:7), one who emulates the pattern of Moses in several ways. He is respected like Moses (Josh 4:14). Crossing the Jordan recapitulates the Red Sea event (Josh 4:23). Joshua's encounter with the commander of Yahweh's army at Jericho echoes the experience of Moses at the burning bush (Josh 5:13-15; Ex 3:2-5). He repeats Moses' function as intercessor (Josh 7:6-9; Deut 9:25-29). He holds up his sword (a crescent-shaped sword traditionally translated as "javelin") at *Ai to effect victory against the enemy, much as Moses held up his arms at Rephidim (Josh 8:18-23; Ex 17:8-13). Their parallel roles as conquerors and then distributors of promised land are evident when

Joshua 12:1-6; 13:8-33 are read alongside Joshua 12:7-24; 14—19. Moreover, Joshua fulfills what Moses promises or prepares for in regard to Caleb (Deut 1:36; Josh 14:6-15), the daughters of Zelophehad (Num 27:1-11; Josh 17:3-4), the cities of refuge (Deut 4:41-43; 19:1-13; Josh 20:1-9) and the *Levitical cities (Num 35:1-8; Josh 21:1-42).

3.3. Royal Figure. Joshua is also presented as a royal figure, a forerunner for the ideological role played by later kings, and especially for the expansionistic and reforming policies of *Josiah. This resemblance is especially evident when one compares Joshua 1:2-9 to Deuteronomy 17:18-20 and 1 Kings 2:1-4. Other texts that depict Joshua in royal terms are Joshua 1:7; 23:6 (cf. 2 Kings 22:2); Joshua 5:10-12 (cf. 2 Kings 23:21-23); Joshua 8:30-35 (cf. 2 Kings 23:2-3). The author of Chronicles may have modeled the transition from *David to *Solomon on the basis of that from Moses to Joshua.

3.4. One Who Obeys and Teaches the Law. Joshua does not take over Moses' office as lawgiver, but instead consistently points back to the *law that Moses promulgated, highlighting it as the standard for national fidelity (Josh 1:7-8, 13; 4:10; 8:30-35; 11:12-15; 22:2; 23:6). He serves as a teacher of "the book of the law" to the people in Joshua 8:30-35 and confronts them with it again in a concrete way near the end of his life (Josh 24:25-27). Moreover, Joshua himself obeys the command of Moses. Thus, upon crossing the Jordan, he erects stones at Gilgal (Josh 4:8) in approximate conformity with what Moses commanded in Deuteronomy 27:2. He obeys Deuteronomy 11:29-30 and 27:2-13 more precisely in Joshua 8:30-35. He circumcises the new generation with the proper flint knives and celebrates the Passover on the appointed day (Josh 5:2-12; cf. Ex 4:25; 12:18). Nehemiah 8:13-18 also remembers Joshua as the last leader to celebrate the Festival of Booths in accordance with the "words of the law"—that is, with Israel all together as a unified body. His utter annihilation of enemy populations (Josh 6:17-18, 21; 8:26; 10:28-40; 11:11-12, 20, 21) obeys the demands of Deuteronomy 7:1-5; 20:15-18 that they be devoted to destruction. Joshua encouraged careful observance to the law in his two farewell speeches (Josh 23:6-8, 16; 24:14-15), and the obedience he appealed for and modeled in his own life lasted for a generation after his death (Josh 24:31; Judg 2:7, 10).

3.5. Prophet. Joshua sometimes speaks in ways that make him resemble a prophet (cf. Sir 46:1), predicting the future (Josh 6:26; 23:5; cf. 1 Kings 16:34), threatening (Josh 23:12-13, 15-16) and serving as a messenger for the direct communication of Yahweh ("thus says Yahweh" [Josh 7:13; 24:2-13]). The celestial miracle reported in Joshua 10:12-15, when the sun stood still at *Gibeon at the behest of his effective word, is reminiscent of those ascribed to the prophets *Elijah (1 Kings 18:36-39; 2 Kings 1:10, 12) and, especially, *Isaiah (2 Kings 20:8-11). In these verses a poetic couplet addressing sun and moon is attributed to Joshua as a word spoken to Yahweh, resulting in a miraculous extension of daylight that made complete victory possible. Taken in isolation from this context, however, the couplet apparently calls on the heavenly bodies to freeze in shocked amazement over the great victory won by Israel over its enemies. It is said to have been recorded in the Book of Jashar (Josh 10:13), evidently a collection of ancient Israelite *poetry (2 Sam 1:17-27; perhaps 1 Kings 8:12-13 LXX).

3.6. Faithful Patriarch. The Historical Books portray Joshua as an example of faith and obedience who initiates a period of obedience that leads to the secure possession of the land (Josh 21:43-45; 24:31). In a sense, he is the last of the patriarchs. Like Jacob, he built an altar at Shechem (Gen 33:20; Josh 8:30-31) and there demanded that the people put away their foreign gods (Gen 35:2-4; Josh 24:23). His identifiable place of burial within the promised land (Josh 24:30), in contrast to the unknown grave of Moses east of the Jordan (Deut 34:6), is similar to the tombs of the ancestors Sarah and Abraham, Rachel, Leah and Isaac, Jacob and Joseph (Gen 23:19-20; 25:9-10; 35:19, 29; 49:29-32; Josh 24:32). Like those graves, his burial points to Israel's assured ownership of the land.

4. Later Developments in the Joshua Tradition.
Joshua continued to be celebrated as prophet (Sir. 46:1), military hero (Sir 46:1-3, 6; 2 Macc 12:15; Acts 7:45; Josephus *Ant.* 4.165), wonder worker (Sir 46:4-5; Josephus *Ant.* 5.61), intercessor (2 Esdr 7:107) and exemplar of faith (Sir 46:7-8; 1 Macc 2:55). The work discovered at Qumran known as the *Apocryphon of Joshua* (4Q378-379) indicates an ongoing interest in the prophetic role of Joshua, as does 4Q522 (the *Prophecy of Joshua*, or *Work with Place Names*), in which he foretells the building of the Jerusalem temple. Because the names *Joshua* and *Jesus* are identical in Greek *(Iēsous)*, Hebrews 4:8-9 can contrast (by implication) the imperfect rest given by Joshua (cf. Josh 21:44; 22:4) with the ultimate rest to be offered through Jesus. In a similar way, *Barnabas* 12:8-9 sees a foreshadowing of the glory of Jesus in the name and authority given to Joshua. Irenaeus draws a typological parallel between Joshua, who succeeded Moses and showed the way into the promised land, and Jesus, who superseded the Mosaic law and leads Christians to their inheritance (Irenaeus *Frag.* 19; cf. Justin *Dial.* 113, 132). In Jewish tradition Joshua is portrayed as the one who received the Torah from Moses (*m. ʾAbot* 1:1), as the husband of Rahab (*b. Meg.* 14b), and one of three for whom the sun stood still (*b. Taʿan.* 20a). Joshua as spy is referred to by implication in the Qurʾan as one of a pair who encouraged others to faith (Sura 5:23-26).

See also JOSHUA, BOOK OF.

BIBLIOGRAPHY. **M. A. Beck,** "Joshua the Savior," in *Voices from Amsterdam: A Modern Tradition of Reading Biblical Narrative,* ed. M. Kessler (SemeiaSt; Atlanta: Scholars Press, 1994) 145-53; **G. W. Coates,** "The Book of Joshua: Heroic Saga or Conquest Theme?" *JSOT* 38 (1987) 15-32; **L. H. Feldman,** "Josephus's Portrait of Joshua," *HTR* 82 (1989) 351-76; **D. Jericke,** "Josuas Tod und Josuas Grab: Eine redaktionsgeschichtliche Studie," *ZAW* 108 (1996) 347-61; **P. J. Kissling,** *Reliable Characters in the Primary History: Profiles of Moses, Joshua, Elijah, and Elisha* (JSOTSup 224; Sheffield: Sheffield Academic Press, 1996) 69-95; **D. J. McCarthy,** "The Theology of Leadership in Joshua 1—9," *Bib* 52 (1971) 165-75; **R. D. Nelson,** "Josiah in the Book of Joshua," *JBL* 100 (1981) 531-40; **E. Noort,** "Joshua: The History of Reception," in *Past, Present, Future: The Deuteronomistic History and the Prophets,* ed. J. C. de Moor and H. F. Van Rooy (Oudtestamentische Studiën 44; Leiden: E. J. Brill, 2000) 199-215; **J. R. Porter,** "The Succession of Joshua," in *Proclamation and Presence: Old Testament Essays in Honour of Gwynne Henton Davies,* ed. J. I. Durham and J. R. Porter (Macon, GA: Mercer University Press, 1983) 102-32; **C. Schäfer-Lichtenberger,** *Josua und Salomo: Eine Studie zu Autorität und Legitimität des Nachfolgers im Alten Testament* (VTSup 58; Leiden: E. J. Brill, 1995); **H. G. M. Williamson,** "The Accession of Solomon in the Books of Chronicles," *VT* 26 (1976) 351-61. R. D. Nelson

JOSHUA, BOOK OF

Joshua is the sixth book of the OT and functions as a canonical hinge. On the one hand, it brings to completion the main theme of the Pentateuch: Israel's occupation of the *land God promised to the patriarchs; on the other hand, it marks the beginning of a larger narrative, running through 2 Kings, that recounts the history of Israel's life in the land. Befitting its transitional character, Joshua offers various perspectives on the story it sets before the reader, creating a host of exegetical and theological complexities.

In general, the book gives an account of the Israelites' occupation of the land through conquest and settlement under the leadership of *Joshua son of Nun. During the course of the narrative, however, the reader encounters differing points of view on this enterprise. Summaries of Israel's battles in *Canaan, for example, assert that Joshua took all the land of Canaan and struck down all its kings (Josh 10:40-43; 11:16-20; 12:1-24), yet shortly thereafter the reader encounters a proclamation that "a great deal of land remains to be occupied" (Josh 13:1), followed by materials that report failures and trepidation (Josh 15:63; 16:10; 17:12-13, 16-18; 19:47). These in turn are followed by another summary that affirms that Yahweh gave Israel the entire land, granted the people rest from *warfare, and delivered all their enemies into their power (Josh 21:43-45). Along the same lines, strong declarations of obedience to Yahweh and the commands of Moses (Josh 1:16-18; 4:8; 11:15; 24:16-18) clash with portraits of Israelite perfidy and rebelliousness (Josh 7:1-26; 24:19-20), while portrayals of Israelite unity (Josh 1:12-18; 3:14-17; 4:10-13; 8:30-35) conflict with others that depict squabbling and divisions among the people (Josh 17:14-18; 22:10-34).

Vexing historical and theological tensions correspond to those raised by the text itself. The archaeological picture constructed from excavations and surveys throughout the land has raised serious questions about Joshua's account of Israel's occupation, while God's command that Israel engage in the wholesale slaughter of an entire population raises equally troubling theological questions. Thus Joshua is a richly provocative text, presenting many daunting challenges to its interpreters.

1. Structure and Content
2. Compositional Analysis
3. Historical Analysis
4. Literary Analysis

1. Structure and Content.

Joshua falls neatly into four main sections: (1) an introduction comprising a series of speeches (Josh 1:1-18); (2) a collection of materials that relates a swift and comprehensive conquest of the land and its kings (Josh 2:1-12:24); (3) reports and lists associated with Israel's settlement of the land (Josh 13:1-21:45); (4) a sequence of final episodes (Josh 22:1-24:33).

The book begins with an announcement that Moses has died, followed by four speeches that provide a thematic orientation for the following narrative. The first and longest speech, an exhortation from Yahweh to Joshua (Josh 1:2-9), draws together relevant texts from Deuteronomy. Yahweh starts by recapitulating the promise of the land and related assurances of victory (Josh 1:3-5; cf. Deut 11:24-25) and concludes with admonitions that recall the account of Joshua's commissioning as Moses' successor (Josh 1:6-7a, 9; cf. Deut 31:6-8, 23). An intervening admonition to obey "this book of the law," joined with promises of success for doing so, appropriates stock Deuteronomic vocabulary and phrases (Josh 1:7b-8). The next three speeches, consisting of Joshua's command to the officers of the people (Josh 1:10-11); his charge to the tribes of Reuben, Gad and half-Manasseh (Josh 1:12-15); and their expression of allegiance (Josh 1:16-18), recall Deuteronomic texts and vocabulary in a similar fashion (cf. Deut 3:18-22). The use of quotations, stock vocabulary and speeches prompts the reader to view Israel's occupation of the land in terms of the particular perspective and concerns of Deuteronomy (which is virtually all speech).

The next section contains three distinct groupings of material: (1) stories associated with great victories at *Jericho, *Ai and *Gibeon (Josh 2:1-24; 6:1-10:27); (2) an expansive account of the Jordan crossing (Josh 3:1-5:15); (3) an amalgam of battle reports that relate victories over the kings of the south (Josh 10:28-43), the north (Josh 11:1-23) and the entire land (Josh 12:1-24). The first three campaigns in Canaan receive extended treatment and seem to be paradigmatic for all the victories over the peoples of the land. Each confirms Yahweh's promise to deliver the peoples of the land into Israel's power and to allow no one to stand against them

(Deut 7:22-24; Josh 1:5). The walls of Jericho fall at the sound of the trumpet after Yahweh has commanded the Israelites to march around it in ritual procession (Josh 6:15-21). Yahweh also devises a stratagem that enables the Israelites to take Ai (Josh 8:8-29) and throws the five kings at Gibeon into a panic, raining stones on them from heaven and granting Joshua's request to stop the sun (Josh 10:6-14).

Anecdotes precede each of these conquest narratives and provide an individualized counterpoint to the clash of peoples. Before the battle of Jericho Israelite spies are given shelter by a Canaanite prostitute named Rahab and agree to spare her and her family from the fate that will befall the inhabitants of the city (Josh 2:1-24; 6:22-25). Conversely, at Ai the treachery of Achan (an Israelite who has kept plunder devoted to Yahweh) leads to a disastrous defeat, a situation that is reversed only when he and his entire family are executed (Josh 7:1-26). Finally, prior to Joshua's victory over the five kings the Israelites are duped into exempting the entire city of Gibeon from destruction when representatives from the city disguise themselves and claim to be emissaries from a distant town (Josh 9:1-27). The three anecdotes follow a common plot structure that moves from hiding to discovery (with the story of Achan reversing elements of the first and third stories), intimating that all three work together to raise issues of corporate identity.

The account of the Jordan crossing interrupts the Jericho campaign. It infuses the event with ritual and liturgical elements in order to emphasize the sacral meaning of Israel's entry into the land. The priests and the *ark of the covenant assume the foreground as the crossing takes on the character of a solemn procession that is punctuated by the stoppage of the Jordan just as the priests' feet enter the water (Josh 3:1-4:1, 4:10-19). Other ritual elements include the erection of twelve stones (Josh 4:2-5, 8-9), explanations of their meaning for future generations (Josh 4:6-7, 20-24), the circumcision of those who have crossed (Josh 5:2-9), the celebration of Passover (Josh 5:10-12) and a mysterious encounter with the commander of Yahweh's army (Josh 5:13-15).

An overview of Israelite conquests concludes the section, beginning with a formulaic list of the cities and kings that Joshua defeated in the south of Canaan (Josh 10:28-39). The setting then moves to the north with brief reports of a victory over a coalition of kings by the waters of Merom and the subsequent destruction of *Hazor (Josh 11:1-15). Assertions that Joshua defeated all the kings and took the entire land summarize all the campaigns in Canaan (Josh 10:40-43; 11:16-23). A final summary expands the focus of conquest and recapitulates the victories over all the kings both east and west of the Jordan (Josh 12:1-24).

The third section of the book consists of descriptions of Israelite *cities and territory, along with short anecdotes and reports relating the experiences of individual tribes as they settled the land (see Tribes of Israel and Land Allotments/Borders). It begins with a reference to the advanced age of Joshua (signaling a transition from conquest to occupation) and continues with a speech by Yahweh that, as in the opening of the book, describes the land being given to the people and offers assurance of divine aid in taking it (Josh 13:1-7; cf. 1:2-9). In this case, however, the speech emphasizes the land that remains to be occupied—a significant change of perspective from the sweeping claims of the previous chapters.

Descriptions of tribal territories and settlement follow, each with a formulaic introduction and conclusion. The territories of Reuben, Gad and half-Manasseh, tribes that have chosen to settle east of the Jordan, are related first, each beginning with the phrase "Moses gave an inheritance to . . ." and concluding with "this is the inheritance of . . ." (Josh 13:8-33), often with a remark about towns and villages. The text then shifts to the west of the Jordan with a description of the territories of the dominant tribal groups there: Judah (Josh 14:1-15:63) and the Joseph tribes (Josh 16:1-17:18). The formulaic introduction now changes to "the lot was/went out" to intimate the differences between the tribes east and west of the Jordan that will lead to conflict in the final section.

The section related to Judah is noteworthy for presenting a particularly coherent description of tribal boundaries and an extensive city list, within which have been inserted anecdotes associated with *Caleb the tribal leader (Josh 14:6-15; 15:13-19). These anecdotes, which emphasize the energy and initiative of Caleb and his daughter Achsah, implicitly confirm the book's thematic link between faith and success. The two embody the qualities necessary to take the land, and the territory of their tribe exhibits a corresponding completeness. By contrast, the territories of the Joseph tribes receive a confused and fragmented treatment and are capped by an anecdote in which they complain about the Canaanites' iron chariots (Josh 17:14-18).

Joshua's rebuke of the tribes' sluggishness introduces the remaining tribal allotments (Josh 18:1-10). These go on to display a gradual deterioration in description, beginning with the relatively complete account of Benjamin's tribal allotment (Josh 18:11-28) and ending with the report that the Danites lost their allotment completely (Josh 19:48). The allotments are followed in turn by legislation for and identification of cities of refuge and Levitical cities (Josh 20:1—21:42). The section then comes to an end with the kind of sweeping summary statement that concludes the conquest phase, affirming that "Yahweh gave Israel the entire land" (Josh 21:43-45).

Although this summary would seem a fitting end to the book, the narrative continues on through a sequence of endings, each of which offers a sense of closure but also highlights issues that remain to be resolved. The first "ending" occurs when Joshua dismisses the tribes of Reuben, Gad and half-Manasseh and commends them for their faithfulness (Josh 22:1-9). Since the tribes could be released from their obligation only when the land has been completely taken (cf. Josh 1:12-18), the dismissal indicates that the desired ending has been achieved. However, immediately thereafter, the text reports the construction of an altar at the Jordan and an ensuing conflict that almost brings the tribes east and west of the Jordan to war (Josh 22:10-34). The incident, which is resolved only by a delicate compromise, points to serious tribal tensions within the nation as a whole.

Another ending is signaled by notices that Yahweh has given Israel rest from all its enemies and that Joshua is advanced in years (Josh 23:1-3). Joshua then delivers a farewell address that recapitulates many of the themes of the first chapter, warns Israel against intermingling with the peoples of the land, and hints that Israel may vanish from the land because of covenant transgression (Josh 23:4-16). The covenant motif is then picked up in a final, climactic scene in which Joshua leads the assembled leaders and people through a covenant-making ceremony at *Shechem (Josh 24:1-28). The scene opens with a retrospective that demonstrates the grace and

faithfulness of Yahweh (Josh 24:2-13) and then moves to Joshua's charge that the people choose whom they will serve. The ensuing dialogue between Joshua and the people portrays a contrasting unfaithfulness on the part of the people, implicitly through Joshua's charge that they put away the foreign gods among them and explicitly through Joshua's stinging rejoinder that "you cannot serve Yahweh" (Josh 24:14-28). Following this, the book ends as it has begun, with announcements of death, specifically the deaths and burials of Joshua (Josh 24:29-30) and Eleazar (Josh 24:33) and the burial of Joseph's bones at Shechem (Josh 24:32).

Throughout the book the narrator exalts the character of Joshua who, though subordinated to Moses at the beginning (Josh 1:1-2), receives the Mosaic title "servant of Yahweh" at the conclusion (Josh 24:29). Joshua is the only human character to appear throughout the book, and he is presented as an authoritative leader in many ways. The text often notes his meticulous implementation of the commands of God and Moses (e.g., Josh 4:15-17; 11:6, 9, 15). Like Moses, Joshua conveys God's words (Josh 3:9), renders decisions that have permanent impact on the life of the nation (Josh 9:16-27), and gives a farewell speech filled with promises and warnings (Josh 23:1-16). By Yahweh's power Joshua leads Israel to great victories on the battlefield, and miraculous events at the Jordan and Gibeon confirm that Yahweh works powerfully through him (note the narrator's commentary at Josh 4:14; 10:14). Following the subjugation of the land, Joshua oversees the allotment of tribal territories and urges the tribes to take possession of the lands given them. Finally, Joshua also plays the role of covenant mediator, orchestrating a recitation of covenant blessings and curses (Josh 8:30-35) and leading the people in a service of covenant renewal (Josh 24:1-27).

2. Compositional Analysis.

2.1. The Hebrew and Greek Texts of Joshua. Significant differences exist between the Hebrew text of Joshua, based on the Leningrad Codex (c. 1008 CE) and conventionally called the Masoretic Text (MT), and the Septuagint (LXX), a Greek translation of the Hebrew Bible favored by the early church. As a whole, the Greek text is about 4 to 5 percent shorter than the Hebrew text, with notable divergences in Joshua 5; 6; 20 and 24. Study of the Greek text, following the critical edition compiled by M. Margolis, strongly suggests that it derives from an early and different version of the book than that preserved by the Hebrew text, with secondary modifications evident in both editions. The discovery of two fragmentary Hebrew texts at Qumran, designated 4QJosh[a] (portions of Josh 6—10) and 4QJosh[b] (portions of Josh 2—4 and 17) reveal more divergences, while generally (though not always) following the fuller text of the MT (Greenspoon). The results of textual study have demonstrated that both the Hebrew and Greek texts of Joshua have undergone a complex history of transmission and attest to distinctive deviations from an original prototext (Rösel) (*see* Text and Textual Criticism).

2.2. Signs of Editing. Tradition holds that Joshua was composed shortly after the events it recounts. Critical study, however, indicates that the book has undergone a complex process of composition, during which various materials were combined, expanded and edited over the course of time. Signs of this process can be detected throughout the book. First, as noted above, the book presents opposing perspectives on the conquest and occupation of the land (complete vs. partial), often juxtaposing these perspectives at critical junctures. Second, also noted above, the book seems to display a number of different endings: the assertion that Israel took possession of all the land that Yahweh gave them (Josh 21:43-45), the departure of the eastern tribes (Josh 22:1-6), Joshua's farewell address (Josh 23:1-16), the covenant renewal ceremony at Shechem (Josh 24:1-28) and the burial notices (Josh 24:29-33). Third, multiple accounts of the same event and duplicated material suggest the work of different hands. The most notable of these occurs when, at the beginning of the settlement phase, the reader is informed that Joshua "was old and advanced in years" (Josh 13:1), only to be told the same thing after the description of territories has been concluded (Josh 23:1). It is worth noting as well that the text reports that *Hebron was granted to Caleb (14:13-15), but later states that the city was given to the Levites, with Caleb receiving only the fields and pasturelands around it (Josh 21:11-12). Fourth, there are disparities regarding Israel's presence at certain sites. Shechem, for instance, is nowhere listed as one of the cities taken by the Israelites, despite being an urban center of particular significance. Yet the entire

nation gathers at precisely this location to renew the covenant (Josh 8:30-35; 24:1-28), placing the site at the center of Israel's religious and communal life. Fifth, the flow of a textual unit sometimes is interrupted by other material, as if there has been an interpolation of another text. This occurs explicitly with the quotation of Joshua's command to the sun and moon at Gibeon—a bit of poetry that sits somewhat uneasily within its narrative context and that, the reader is informed, has been drawn from the book of Jashar, a mysterious document already in existence when the account was composed (Josh 10:12-14).

The work of an editor is also suggested by summaries, transitional material and commentary, especially when these offer a perspective at variance with the material being commented on. This can be appreciated by comparing the narrator's glowing summary of the occupation (Josh 21:43-45) with another comment, shortly before, that the tribe of Dan did not succeed in taking their allotment (Josh 19:47). Transitional reports concerning the kings of the land provide a mechanism for uniting the stories of conquest while conveying an increasing sense of opposition and danger (Josh 5:1; 9:1-2; 10:1-5; 11:1-5). Commentary explicitly draws attention to itself in the form of many declarations that something or someone remains "to this very day" (Josh 4:9; 5:9; 6:25; 7:26; 8:29; 9:27; 10:27; 15:63; 16:10; cf. 10:14); the comments have the effect of reminding the reader of the gap in time between the events being narrated in the past and the unspecified present in which they are being read.

The activity of editors is nowhere more apparent than in the account of the Jordan crossing (Josh 3:1—4:24). The episode begins with a report that the Israelites left Shittim and camped at the Jordan and is followed by a statement that the officers went through the camp three days later and directed the people to follow the ark of the covenant (Josh 3:1-4). The statement responds to a previous command in which Joshua directed the officers to go through the camp and prepare the people for the crossing (Josh 1:10-11). This fits uneasily, however, with a report that the spies at Jericho spent three days hiding in the hills before reporting back to Joshua (Josh 2:22). Following the chronology of the narrative, the officers' activity thus would seem to have occurred six days, not three, after Joshua's command.

This instance, however, is but the beginning of temporal discontinuity. The crossing of the Jordan is related twice. The first account ends with a report that the priests stood on dry ground in the middle of the Jordan until the entire nation had finished crossing (Josh 3:17). However, the text later returns to the priests in the middle of the Jordan and reports the crossing of the people in haste, with Reuben, Gad and half-Manasseh in the vanguard (Josh 4:10-13). The narrative then relates the miraculous return of waters when the priests exit (Josh 4:15-18).

The reader encounters additional duplicates and incongruities. Joshua issues a command that twelve men be selected from each of the tribes, but the command is disconnected from its context and offers no further instruction (Josh 3:12). However, Yahweh later commands Joshua to select twelve men to take twelve stones from the middle of the Jordan (Josh 4:2-3). The stones, we are told, are deposited in the Israelite encampment (Josh 4:8), but another report states that they were deposited in the middle of the Jordan (Josh 4:9)! Different explanations for the stones also are offered, each with a particular emphasis. The first of these states, in straightforward language, that the stones are to serve as an occasion for telling future generations about the miraculous stoppage of water (Josh 4:6-7). A second takes up the language of the first but invests it with religious imagery, linking the memorial meaning of the stones to the exodus and expanding its significance to all nations (Josh 4:21-24).

Shifting vocabulary and thematic emphases reinforce the sense that multiple perspectives are at play (e.g., "ark of the covenant" [Josh 3:6, 8, 14, 17; 4:9, 15, 18]; "the ark of Yahweh" [Josh 3:13; 4:11]; "the ark of Yahweh your God" [Josh 4:5]; "the ark of the covenant of Yahweh" [Josh 4:7]; "the ark of the covenant of Yahweh your God" [Josh 3:3]; "the ark of the covenant of the Lord of the whole earth" [Josh 3:11]). Various parts of the story seem to emphasize the role of the priests and the sanctity of the ark, the miraculous character and meaning of the stoppage of water, and the exaltation of Joshua as the successor of Moses. To complicate matters even more, much of the duplicate and incongruous material is absent from the Greek version of Joshua.

2.3 Models of Composition. Historical-critical study of Joshua in the nineteenth century linked its composition to that of the Pentateuch and was thereby concerned to identify pentateuchal sources (particularly J and P) as these extended into Joshua. This task was influenced strongly by the notion that the Pentateuch is incomplete apart from Joshua. Thematically, the goal of the pentateuchal narrative—the occupation of the land that God promised—requires the fulfillment that Joshua relates. From this perspective, then, it is better to think in terms of a Hexateuch rather than a Pentateuch. By extension, the textual incongruities in Joshua could therefore be explained by recourse to the same models advanced to explain the composition of Genesis through Deuteronomy. Broadly speaking, this meant that core elements of Joshua 2—11 and 24 could be explained in terms of Yahwistic editing, ritual features in Joshua 3—6 and the meticulous lists of Joshua 13—21 in terms of a Priestly contribution, and the parenetic features of Joshua 1 and 23 in terms of Deuteronomic redaction. No consensus, however, on the identification of traditions and/or the scope of editing could be reached, although the debate remains active (for a detailed discussion see Auld, 1980).

More persuasive have been models that take into account the strong relationship between Joshua and Deuteronomy. Deuteronomy clearly provides both the framework and point of view by which the events of Joshua are rendered. For one thing, the storyline of Joshua presumes and ties up narrative threads from the preceding book, Deuteronomy. The construction of the altar on Mount Ebal, the recording of Moses' commands, and the reading of blessings and curses (Josh 8:30-35) explicitly fulfill a specific charge given by Moses (Deut 11:29-30; 27:1-8). The language and the context of Yahweh's initial speeches to Joshua (Josh 1:1-9) echo the commissioning of Joshua as Moses' successor (Deut 31:1-29). And reports that the Israelites exterminated the inhabitants of the land (Josh 6:21; 8:24-27; 10:40; 11:12, 21) relate the implementation of the Deuteronomic command to do so (Deut 7:1-4).

In addition, Joshua utilizes Deuteronomic motifs to connect events and convey their significance. Joshua follows Deuteronomy's tendency to conceive of things in terms of wholes and integers. Israel acts and is addressed as a unit throughout both books (e.g., Deut. 1:1; 5:1; 11:6; 13:11; Josh 3:17; 5:8; 8:33; 10:43). Obedience to

Yahweh requires observing the entirety of the commands of Moses (e.g., Deut 6:2; 8:1; 10:12-13; 11:13, 22; Josh 1:17-18; 8:35; 11:15). And success entails taking "the entire land" (e.g., Deut 7:1-4; 20:16-18; Josh 10:40-42; 11:16-18, 23; 21:43). More broadly, Joshua explicitly presents Israel as a covenant people in the sense conceived by Deuteronomy and recounts multiple events of covenant renewal (Josh 8:30-35; 24:1-28). Furthermore, the motif of holy war (and of the divine warrior), prominent in Deuteronomy's program for taking the land (Deut 2:30-36; 7:1-4; 9:3; 31:1-6), reverberates through repeated declarations that Yahweh gave the peoples of the land into the power of Israel, who then annihilated them (Josh 6:16; 10:10-11, 42; 11:6).

A number of speeches and summaries offer the most direct evidence that the book has been edited from the perspective of Deuteronomy. Yahweh's initial exhortation to Joshua (Josh 1:2-9) and Joshua's farewell address to Israel (Josh 23:1-16) are dense with the phraseology and themes of Deuteronomy (see Weinfeld 1972). The former quotes, with little modification, Deuteronomy 11:24-25 and 31:6-8, 23, links success with obedience (a key theme of Deuteronomy), and admonishes Joshua to act in accordance with "this book of the law," a phrase that occurs elsewhere in Deuteronomy with reference to itself (Deut 29:21; 30:10; 31:26). The latter contains strong injunctions against intermarriage and apostasy, warning that such will result in Israel's expulsion from the land (cf. Deut 7:3-4; 29:14-29). In a similar fashion, summaries and commentaries throughout the book appropriate the language and concerns of Deuteronomy to offer a perspective on events (Josh 11:16-23; 21:43-45; 22:1-6).

The occurrence of Deuteronomic themes, language and concerns received its most influential explanation by M. Noth, who argued that Joshua constitutes the second segment of a larger work that recounts the story of Israel's life in the land from entry to exile. Noth observed a consistent theological perspective, shaped by Deuteronomic themes and vocabulary, that unites the whole corpus extending from Deuteronomy through 2 Kings. This perspective is expressed through the use of transitional and explanatory notes and compositions, the most extensive of these being speeches delivered by leaders at key junctures in the story (Josh 1:1-8; 23:1-16; 1 Sam 12:1-25; 1 Kings 8:14-33). Noth,

however, could detect little evidence of this editorial perspective in Genesis through Numbers. He therefore surmised that an anonymous editor (Dtr) had assembled materials from a number of sources and forged them into a single work, which he termed the *Deuteronomistic History. The law code in Deuteronomy provided the criteria by which the events of this history were presented and evaluated, and the last episode of the history, the release of Jehoiachin from a Babylonian prison, provided the clue to the time of its composition. Noth therefore concluded that the Deuteronomistic History had been composed during the exile in order to explain the catastrophe that had befallen the nation of Judah.

The main element of Noth's hypothesis, that Deuteronomy through 2 Kings constitutes a unified Deuteronomistic History, has achieved a broad scholarly consensus. The concept of a single editor, however, has not, in the opinion of many, provided a satisfactory explanation for the complexities of the book. The question of the compositional process in Joshua has been addressed in various ways. One model holds that the first edition was Deuteronomistic but was later supplemented by editors connected to the pentateuchal traditions (e.g., Van Seters). Another explains the process in terms of multiple Deuteronomistic editions. On the basis of structural and thematic changes after the death of Josiah, F. M. Cross proposed that the work initially was composed during the reign of Josiah and supplemented during the exile. Following this line, most if not all of Joshua would have been composed to support *Josiah's kingship and reform—a position that has received support from a number of studies that suggest connections between the portrayals of Joshua and Josiah (e.g., Nelson) (see Joshua). Utilizing different criteria, R. Smend proposed that the Deuteronomistic Historian's work (DtrG) was supplemented by a later Deuteronomistic editor who was concerned to stress the necessity of strict obedience to the law (DtrN). In Joshua the work of this editor can be detected through shifts of emphasis in Joshua 1:7-9 and 13:1b-6 and finds its fullest expression in Joshua 23:1-16. Although Smend did not propose a dating scheme for these editions, subsequent studies that derive from his work have extended the editing process from the exile through the postexilic period (for more on this discussion see Boling; Peckham;

Campbell and O'Brien).

At present there exists no agreement on the process by which the book of Joshua came into being, aside from a general acknowledgement that Joshua 2—11; 13—21 and 24 contain ancient source materials. What has emerged strongly from critical scholarship, however, is the recognition that Deuteronomistic theology exerted a formative influence on the way these ancient materials were combined and presented. Thus the issue of the composition of Joshua is inextricably linked to that of the composition of the Pentateuch after all. Although a few commentators maintain an early date for the book's composition (e.g., Woudstra; Howard), there appear nonetheless to be sound reasons for presuming an editorial process that began, at the earliest, in the late monarchy.

3. Historical Analysis.

3.1. Joshua as Historiography. Joshua shapes the events of Israel's past into a narrative reflection on the identity of the people of God. In a fundamental sense it is a foundation narrative—that is, a narrative of origins that provides an explanation of the characteristics and convictions that define the community. Whereas history writing in general reflects on issues of identity, Joshua does so from a richly theological perspective (*see* Historiography, Old Testament). That it does not offer a strictly straightforward account of events can be appreciated by recognizing the many chronological anomalies and multiple points of view that appear throughout the book, many of which we have noted (see 2.2-3 above). Certain segments of the book portray an Israelite invasion that takes the entire land in a blitzkrieg invasion. Yahweh fights for Israel, and the kings of the land cannot muster any effective resistance against the onslaught (e.g., Josh 10:28-42; 11:1-12:24; 21:44). However, other parts of the book reveal that the Canaanites were indeed successful in thwarting Israel's attempt to take the land, and large areas of Canaan remained outside of Israel's control (Josh 13:1-7; 15:63; 16:10; 17:12-13; 19:47). And as the book draws to a close, Joshua affirms that the task remains incomplete but achievable and warns the people against intermingling with the peoples of the land (Josh 23:5-13). The book therefore presents two points of view on how the possession of the land was accomplished: one presents it as a decisive conquest during

Joshua's time, and the other implies a gradual process of settlement and conflict.

Discrepancies are also apparent when one reads Joshua within its larger literary context. The book of *Judges begins with a recapitulation of the conquest that differs significantly from Joshua's. Here the picture is not that of a comprehensive conquest achieved by a united Israel but of localized areas taken and occupied by individual tribes or groups, with varying degrees of success (Judg 1:1-36). Included in the accounts are reports that the tribes did not succeed in driving out populations from cities whose kings Joshua lists as defeated (e.g., *Megiddo, *Gezer, Taanach [compare Judg 1:27-29 and Josh 16:10; 17:12]). In the case of *Jerusalem, the picture is even more complicated. Joshua reports that the king of Jerusalem was defeated and executed at Makkedah (Josh 10:22-26; cf. 12:10) but later reports that the tribe of Judah could not drive out the Jebusites from the city (Josh 15:63). However, Judges begins by stating that Judah and Simeon captured and burned Jerusalem (Judg 1:7), only to report later that the Benjaminites could not drive out the Jebusites who lived in the city (Judg 1:21). That the Canaanites remain a powerful force in the land well after the death of Joshua is demonstrated by the story of King Jabin, who (the text pointedly reports) reigns from Hazor (Judg 4:2). The book of Joshua, however, also mentions a King Jabin, a powerful king of Hazor, which the narrator reports as being "the foremost of all those kingdoms" (Josh 11:10). Joshua goes on to report that the Israelites annihilated the population and burned the city (Josh 11:13-14). If Joshua defeated Jabin and destroyed Hazor, what are we to make of the fact that a powerful king named Jabin is ruling from Hazor early in the period of the judges?

Contemporary scholarship has brought a measure of clarity to these issues. Approaches that focus on the history of traditions have raised the probability that at least some of the source materials incorporated by the Deuteronomistic editors originated and were transmitted at regional sanctuaries. The case for this is particularly strong in Joshua 2—11, which, minus Deuteronomistic editing, exhibits a coherence of content and structure that stands out from the rest of the book in its devotion to detail and imagery. The region approximating the settlement of Benjamin provides the setting for the events in Joshua 2—9, and *Gilgal, an Israelite shrine associated with Benjamin (Judg 3:19; 1 Sam 10:8; 13:4-15), figures prominently in the corpus. The ritual character of many of the episodes in this section (celebration of Passover, circumcision, the procession around Jericho, the lot casting to discover Achan's sacrilege) intimates that the narratives were utilized within the context of worship. The central event—the crossing of the Jordan—makes this especially clear through its emphasis on ritual, priests and the ark of the covenant (Kraus; Wilcoxen). The setting up of memorial stones and commands to explain their meaning to future generations (Josh 4:5-7, 19-24) have a marked liturgical cast and provide an account of the origin of the sanctuary (although an alternative etiology appears in Josh 5:8-9). Connections of other material to Shechem (Josh 24:1-28) and *Shiloh (Josh 18:1-10) suggest a corresponding scenario (see Boling; Butler; Koopmans; Sperling).

Comparative studies that set Joshua within its larger ancient Near Eastern context have also aided in historical analysis. K. L. Younger (1990), for example, has shown that the hyperbolic and totalizing rhetoric of the conquest accounts corresponds to conquest reports in literature throughout the ancient Near East and thus should be understood as conventional language rather than literal report. In addition, the antiquity of much of the material in Joshua is demonstrated by particular elements that manifest affinities with the late second millennium BCE (for illustrations see Hess 1996).

Formal study of the tribal allotments (Josh 13—19) indicates that the unit draws on preexisting collections, although the identity of the primary editor and the point of its incorporation into the book are debated. In this case, many of the materials manifest an administrative rather than cultic origin. Scholars have long observed that the city lists and the descriptions of tribal territories follow different forms and thus probably derive from separate contexts. Both forms must be of great antiquity, and generally they have been dated from the premonarchical to early monarchical periods. The city lists in particular look like the kind of administrative lists that would find their place in a centralized system such as a monarchy. The general area covered by the boundary lists is virtually the same as the borders of David's census and Solomon's districts. Thus they may have assumed roughly their present form during this period (2 Sam 24:4-8; 1 Kings 4:1-19), although there are also good reasons for regarding them as early tribal boundary markers (see Hess 1994). More broadly, an account of the division of territory, after a period of conquest, is known in other ancient literature (Weinfeld 1988).

3.2. Joshua and the Archaeology of Palestine. Early excavations in Palestine were stimulated by an interest in establishing a connection between the archaeological record and biblical events. A connection was made in dramatic fashion by J. Garstang's excavations at Tell es-Sultan (biblical *Jericho) in the 1930s. Garstang found a collapsed wall that he dated to the fifteenth century BCE, and he declared it to be the wall that fell during the Israelite attack. However, subsequent excavations by K. Kenyon, along with more precise methods of dating, revealed that the wall had collapsed a thousand years earlier and, apart from a sparse population in the fourteenth century BCE, the tell remained uninhabited until the ninth century BCE. These results significantly challenged the biblical account of Jericho's fall, as the archaeological record showed that no such city existed during the transition from the Late Bronze Age to the Iron Age (the period commonly assigned to the Israelite conquest). To date, there remains no evidence of anything more than a small settlement (if that) at the site during the Late Bronze Age (see, however, an alternative assessment in Provan, Long and Longman).

A similar situation pertains to the other cities associated with the Israelite conquest. Excavations at el-Jib (biblical *Gibeon) have failed to discover evidence of significant occupation during the period in question, while et-Tell (identified as biblical *Ai) shows evidence of little more than a small village, which did not appear until Iron Age I. A number of other sites show signs of occupation and destruction but offer no clues as to the perpetrators. These include *Hazor, which was destroyed by fire c. 1200 BCE, Megiddo (Tell el-Mutesellim), where a series of destructions are evident, *Lachish (Tell ed-Duweir), where a destruction level has been dated to the mid-twelfth century BCE and thus effectively outside the time frame for the conquest, and *Bethel (Beitin), which is the victim of conquest in Judges 1:22-26 but not specifically in Joshua (cf. Josh 8:17). A variety of situations obtain for other cities reported taken or destroyed, with problems of site identification complicating matters in some cases.

To add to the problems, settlement patterns in the Transjordan clash with the Bible's account of conquests east of the Jordan. There the archaeological record provides no evidence for the existence of the kingdoms of Sihon and Og (Heshbon being uninhabited until the ninth-eighth centuries BCE) or for those of *Moab and *Edom (which do not seem to have been established entities at the time). In sum, then, significant discrepancies exist between the biblical account of the conquest of Canaan and the archaeological record of the region during the transitional period between the Late Bronze Age and the Iron Age. These discrepancies are particularly acute in the case of those sites that play key roles in the account (i.e., Jericho, Ai and Gibeon).

The latter part of the twentieth century saw a shift in archaeological methods and goals, away from the search for monumental remains that would shed light on the biblical text, in favor of a multidisciplinary approach that focused on smaller sites, patterns of settlement and sociological analysis. A series of surveys conducted by Israeli archaeologists in the Shephelah, central highlands and Galilee revealed a sharp rise in population growth in the twelfth century BCE, characterized by the establishment of hundreds of small villages in the regions. The new inhabitants possessed advanced agricultural skills, such as the ability to construct sophisticated hillside terraces for their crops and plastered cisterns to store enough water to sustain life during the dry season. These villagers lived in small, tightly knit communities characterized by a decentralized social structure that probably was held together by kinship ties. Analysis of the material remains contested the conclusion that a new pottery type (the so-called collar rim jar) and house structure (the four-room or pillared house; see Architecture) were signs that these people represented a new ethnic group (i.e., "Israel") as had been previously thought. Rather, the general picture that has emerged demonstrates a strong continuity between these settlers and the Canaanite culture of the Late Bronze Age.

The data gathered by this new archaeological approach, taken together, have been explained in various ways, notably two: (1) distinct structures such as the four-room house and the proliferation of silos indicate a long process or sedentarization in which pastoral nomads eventually established farming communities in the highlands; or (2) the Iron Age I increase in highland villages derived from elements of the old Canaanite population that migrated into the highland regions after the cataclysmic disruptions that devastated the region at the end of the thirteenth century BCE. In any case, the groups that settled the highlands seem to have established a social structure that differed significantly from the hierarchical urban society of the previous era. In other words, archaeological analysis of settlement patterns and material remains strongly suggests that the central areas of what would become the land of Israel were settled mainly by people within the land, rather than from culturally distinct groups from outside the land. From this perspective, Israel "emerged" from indigenous populations in the land—again a vastly different picture than Joshua's account of an invasion (see Dever, *ABD* 3.545-58; Finkelstein).

3.3. Reconstructing History. The gap between the account depicted in Joshua and that rendered by current archaeological analysis raises significant hermeneutical questions. What role does archaeology play in the interpretation of Joshua? Conversely, what role does Joshua play in the interpretation of the archaeological record? Put differently, how should the historian's understanding of Joshua be accommodated to archaeological models, or should it be at all? Does Joshua constitute a reliable source for the interpretation of material remains, and if so, in what way? Archaeologists are concerned to interpret material remains within a broad historical and social context and evaluate the biblical account in terms of its usefulness for interpreting these remains. Biblical scholars, on the other hand, are concerned with the interpretation of the text and value archaeological reconstructions, as these offer useful contextual information. Bringing the two disciplines into dialogue, especially when they present disparate conclusions, is therefore a complex enterprise (see History of Israel 1: Settlement Period).

In the course of the twentieth century, Joshua and archaeology were brought together within one of three interpretive models. The first of these accords priority to the biblical account and posits an Israelite invasion that brought a quick and violent end to the Late

Bronze Age urban culture. This model, which received classic formulation through W. F. Albright, has the strength of respecting the Bible's own claims about Israel's origins but seems to have the least usefulness in explaining patterns of settlement and issues of chronology. A second model explains the origins of Israel in terms of the gradual and peaceful migration of nomadic peoples into previously unoccupied areas of Canaan. This model, initially proposed by A. Alt, has the strength of correlating somewhat with the archaeological record and focuses on aspects of Joshua that reflect more positive connections with Canaanite populations (Rahab, the Gibeonites and Shechem). The model, however, contradicts Joshua's emphasis on Israel's violent origins and has difficulty explaining the agrarian competence of the highland communities. A third model, with variant forms proposed by G. Mendenhall and N. Gottwald, views Israel's origins in terms of conflicts between disenfranchised rural populations and the urban culture centered in the cities of Canaan. This model has the advantage of explaining the apparent continuity between the Iron Age I highland culture and the Late Bronze Age urban culture, while taking into account the element of violence in the biblical text. However, it fails to explain adequately why the biblical record preserves no memory of such a decisive and successful revolution (for a more thorough overview see Younger 1999).

Current archaeological reconstruction, while still influenced by these models, has moved more strongly toward the view that Israel emerged from indigenous elements in Canaan, with a possible influx of external groups. Within this movement, Joshua is accorded varying degrees of usefulness in interpreting the archaeological record. Archaeologists such as I. Finkelstein are skeptical that any reliable historical information can be gleaned from the biblical text and insist rather that archaeological data be interpreted through models that offer a long-term perspective that emphasizes economic, environmental and cultural factors. Others, such as W. Dever (2003), argue that the biblical text constitutes an important interpretive resource if appropriated critically and judiciously.

Along the same lines, biblical scholarship has undertaken a vigorous debate on the historical reliability of Joshua and Judges. Archaeology's picture of small and localized kin-based communities accords well with the "Israel" depicted in Judges, but the continuity between these settlements and the prior urban culture, the agrarian expertise of the settlers, and the lack of occupation at significant sites challenge Joshua's depiction of a united Israel conquering the land.

How, then, is Joshua to be assessed in light of archaeological reconstruction? Responses to this question span a broad continuum and have much to do with presuppositions and starting points. On the one end are a number of biblical scholars who argue that archaeology and social-scientific analysis ought to provide the sole platform for writing the history of Palestine (e.g., Lemche). Joshua, they assert, must be rejected as a reliable source of historical information because it constitutes the reflection of a much later period and is shaped by legend and ideology. On the other end are scholars who assert that Joshua presents a reliable and coherent historical account and attempt to reconcile the archaeological record with the biblical text while harmonizing textual inconsistencies (e.g., Howard).

Both the biblical and archaeological records are complex and resist easy harmonization, and while the discussion of Israel's origins is more contested than ever, it nevertheless has generated important insights. For one thing, the debate on Israel's origins has precipitated a much needed discussion on the convictions, assumptions and methods that inform both biblical and archaeological interpretation. Significant gaps exist in our knowledge and understanding of both the biblical text and the Late Bronze/Iron I transition in Palestine. Filling these gaps and constructing a sense of the whole thus entails making evaluations that unavoidably incorporate one's assumptions, convictions and view of the biblical text. Joshua itself attests to the plasticity of memory and suggests differing perspectives on Israel's origins in the land. Utilizing the biblical text to reconstruct the history of Israel therefore remains a tricky business. Likewise, the accidents of discovery, the possibility of site erosion and misidentification, and challenges to dating schemes caution against overconfidence in what can be ascertained by archaeology. Although advances on both fronts hold promise, the task of correlating Joshua and archaeology probably will always be fraught with a large measure of uncertainty.

4. Literary Analysis.

Literary studies of Joshua focus on how the book may be read as a whole and have taken a cue from the comments of B. Childs, who chided commentators on the book for failing to distinguish between the tasks of biblical interpretation and historical reconstruction. Observing that Joshua has been shaped so as to preserve many tensions, Childs called for a hermeneutical approach that took these tensions seriously rather than seeking to harmonize or minimize them. Drawing on theories of literature developed by M. Bakhtin and B. Ouspensky, R. Polzin addressed these tensions directly and explained them as expressions of two ideological perspectives in dialogue on the issue of interpreting the book of the law (Deuteronomy) and, more generally, the word of God. From Polzin's perspective, Joshua offers a narrative reflection on Deuteronomy that allows opposing voices to speak on the issue of authoritative interpretation of the book. A subordinate voice, which he identifies as that of "authoritarian dogmatism," asserts an inflexible application of the law of Moses. Against this is the voice of "critical traditionalism," which advances the dominant perspective of Deuteronomy and recognizes the need for revision and varying interpretation. These voices can be detected by attention to the ideologies revealed by a close reading of the reporting speech (i.e., narrative) and reported speech (i.e., character's words) within the book. Viewed in this way, the gaps between the commands issued to Israel and Israel's failure to achieve them fully, as well as the gaps between the divine promises and their actual fulfillment, can be seen as a compositional strategy that illustrates the gaps between the divine word and human interpretation. Throughout the book, dual threads that highlight the tensions between divine justice and divine mercy, as well as the confusion of distinctions between citizen and alien, demonstrate that the Israelites are like the peoples of the land: both are unworthy and undeserving of the gift of the land. This strategy, Polzin argues, offered encouragement to the exilic community that had experienced the loss of the land.

Polzin's description of the dialogic character of Joshua constructed a foundation for subsequent literary studies. These have employed a variety of approaches to explore more extensively the tensions between fulfillment/unfulfillment and obedience/disobedience (Gunn), the role of irony in the narrative (Eslinger), and the contesting interplay of plot lines that seek coherence and closure (Hawk 1991). Other readings have focused on the dichotomizing of insiders and outsiders within the book, explaining this element positively in terms of the construction of an ambiguous image of the peoples of the land (Mitchell) and negatively as an assertion of royal power against non-Israelites (Rowlett).

A different direction altogether has been taken by E. T. Mullen Jr., who utilizes sociological analysis of the book to ascertain how the narrative constructs ethnic identity through the appropriation of traditional materials. Viewed in this way, Joshua can be understood as a document that contributes to social cohesion by providing the basis for a shared past. This focus on identity formation defines an important direction for future study of the book.

The three main emphases of Joshua—the possession of the land, obedience to the commands of Moses, annihilation of the peoples of the land—articulate conventional markers of group identity: possession of territory, proper religious practice, ethnic separation. As the plot moves from beginning to end, each of these markers is both affirmed (claims that Israel possessed the entire land, obeyed all the commands of Moses, obliterated all the peoples) and compromised (reports of unoccupied land, disobedience to the commands, remaining peoples), rendering each an unstable element of national identity. As the narrative reaches its conclusion, only the covenant, in which the people choose the God who has chosen them, is left as a defining characteristic of the people (Josh 24:1-27) (see Hawk 2000). Understood in this way, Joshua does not legitimize religious and ethnic violence, but rather undercuts claims of divine sanction for such agendas.

See also DEUTERONOMISTIC HISTORY; HISTORIOGRAPHY, OLD TESTAMENT; HISTORY OF ISRAEL 1: SETTLEMENT PERIOD; JERICHO; JOSHUA; LAND; NARRATIVE ART OF ISRAEL'S HISTORIANS.

BIBLIOGRAPHY. *Commentaries:* R. G. Boling and G. Ernest Wright, *Joshua* (AB 6; Garden City, NY: Doubleday, 1982); T. C. Butler, *Joshua* (WBC 7; Waco, TX: Word, 1983); J. F. D. Creach, *Joshua* (IBC; Louisville: John Knox, 2003); L. D. Hawk, *Joshua* (Berit Olam; Collegeville, MN: Liturgical Press, 2000); R. S. Hess, *Joshua* (TOTC;

Downers Grove, IL: InterVarsity Press, 1996); **D. M. Howard Jr.,** *Joshua* (NAC; Nashville: Broadman & Holman, 1998); **R. D. Nelson,** *Joshua* (OTL; Louisville: Westminster/John Knox, 1997); **M. H. Woudstra,** *The Book of Joshua* (NICOT; Grand Rapids: Eerdmans, 1981). *Studies:* **E. Assis,** " 'How Long Are You Slack to Go to Possess the Land?' (Jos. xviii 3): Ideal and Reality in the Distribution Descriptions in Joshua xiii-xix," *VT* 53 (2003) 1-25; **A. G. Auld,** *Joshua, Moses and the Land: Tetrateuch-Pentateuch-Hexateuch in a Generation since 1938* (Edinburgh: T & T Clark, 1980); idem, *Joshua Retold: Synoptic Perspectives* (OTS; Edinburgh: T & T Clark, 1998); **R. G. Boling,** "Joshua, Book of," *ABD* 3.1002-15; **A. F. Campbell and M. A. O'Brien,** *Unfolding the Deuteronomistic History: Origins, Upgrades, Present Text* (Minneapolis: Fortress, 2000); **B. S. Childs,** *Introduction to the Old Testament as Scripture* (Philadelphia: Fortress, 1979); **F. M. Cross,** "The Themes of the Book of Kings and the Structure of the Deuteronomistic History," in *Canaanite Myth and Hebrew Epic* (Cambridge, MA: Harvard University Press, 1973) 274-89; **W. G. Dever,** "Israel, History of (Archaeology and the 'Conquest')," *ABD* 3.545-58; idem, *Who Were the Israelites and Where Did They Come From?* (Grand Rapids: Eerdmans, 2003); **L. Eslinger,** *Into the Hands of the Living God* (JSOTSup 84; Sheffield: Almond, 1989) 25-54; **I. Finkelstein,** "The Great Transformation: The 'Conquest' of the Highlands Frontiers and the Rise of the Territorial States," in *The Archaeology of Society in the Holy Land,* ed. T. E. Levy (London: Leicester University Press, 1995) 349-65; **I. Finkelstein and N. Silberman,** *The Bible Unearthed: Archaeology's New Vision of Ancient Israel and the Origin of Its Sacred Texts* (New York: Free Press, 2001); **L. J. Greenspoon,** "The Qumran Fragments of Joshua: Which Puzzle Are They Part of and Where Do They Fit?" in *Septuagint, Scrolls and Cognate Writings: Papers Presented to the International Symposium on the Septuagint and Its Relations to the Dead Sea Scrolls and Other Writings, Manchester, 1990,* ed. G. J. Brooke and B. Lindars (SCSS 33; Atlanta: Scholars Press, 1992) 159-204; **D. M. Gunn,** "Joshua and Judges," in *The Literary Guide to the Bible,* ed. R. Alter and F. Kermode (Cambridge, MA: Harvard University Press, 1987) 102-21; **B. Halpern,** "Erasing History: The Minimalist Assault on Ancient Israel," *BRev* 11.6 (1995) 26-37; **L. D. Hawk,** *Every Promise Fulfilled: Contesting Plots in Joshua* (LCBI; Louisville: West-

minster/John Knox, 1991); **R. S. Hess,** "Asking Historical Questions of Joshua 13—19: Recent Discussion Concerning the Date of the Boundary Lists," in *Faith, Tradition, and History: Old Testament Historiography in Its Near Eastern Context,* ed. A. R. Millard, J. K. Hoffmeier and D. W. Baker (Winona Lake, IN: Eisenbrauns, 1994) 191-205; **A. M. Kitz,** "Undivided Inheritance and Lot Casting in the Book of Joshua," *JBL* 119 (2000) 600-618; **W. T. Koopmans,** *Joshua 24 as Poetic Narrative* (JSOTSup 93; Sheffield: JSOT, 1990); **H.-J. Kraus,** "Gilgal: A Contribution to the History of Worship in Israel," in *Reconsidering Israel and Judah: Recent Studies on the Deuteronomistic History,* ed. G. N. Knoppers and J. G. McConville (SBTS 8; Winona Lake, IN: Eisenbrauns, 2000) 163-78; **N. P. Lemche,** *Early Israel: Anthropological and Historical Studies on the Israelite Society before the Monarchy* (VTSup 37; Leiden: E. J. Brill, 1985); **M. L. Margolis,** ed., *The Book of Joshua in Greek* (4 vols.; Paris: Geuthner, 1931-1938); idem, *The Book of Joshua in Greek, Part V: Joshua 19:39—24:33* (Philadelphia: Annenberg Research Institute, 1992); **A. D. H. Mayes,** *The Story of Israel Between Settlement and Exile* (London: SCM, 1983); **G. Mitchell,** *Together in the Land: A Reading of the Book of Joshua* (JSOTSup 134; Sheffield: JSOT, 1993); **E. T. Mullen Jr.,** *Narrative History and Ethnic Boundaries: The Deuteronomistic Historian and the Creation of Israelite National Identity* (SemeiaSt; Atlanta: Scholars Press, 1993); **R. D. Nelson,** "Josiah in the Book of Joshua," *JBL* 100 (1981) 531-40; **M. Noth,** *The Deuteronomistic History* (2d ed.; JSOTSup 15; Sheffield: JSOT, 1991); **B. Peckham,** "The Significance of the Book of Joshua in Noth's Theory of the Deuteronomistic History," in *The History of Israel's Traditions: The Heritage of Martin Noth,* ed. S. L McKenzie and M. P. Graham (JSOTSup 182; Sheffield: Sheffield Academic Press, 1994) 213-34; **R. Polzin,** *Moses and the Deuteronomist: A Literary Study of the Deuteronomic History* (New York: Seabury, 1980); **I. Provan, V. P. Long and T. Longman III,** *A Biblical History of Israel* (Louisville: Westminster/John Knox, 2003); **M. Rösel,** "The Septuagint-Version of the Book of Joshua," *SJOT* 16 (2002) 5-23; **L. Rowlett,** "Inclusion, Exclusion and Marginality in the Book of Joshua," *JSOT* 55 (1992) 15-23; **R. Smend,** "The Law and the Nations," in *Reconsidering Israel and Judah: Recent Studies on the Deuteronomistic History,* ed. G. N. Knoppers and J. G. McConville (SBTS 8; Winona Lake, IN: Eisenbrauns, 2000) 95-110; **S. D. Sperling,** "Joshua 24 Re-examined," in *Reconsidering Israel and Judah: Recent Studies on the Deuteronomistic History,* ed. G. N. Knoppers and J. G. McConville (SBTS 8; Winona Lake, IN: Eisenbrauns, 2000) 240-58; **E. Tov,** "The Growth of the Book of Joshua in the Light of the Evidence of the LXX Translation," in *Studies in the Bible, 1986,* ed. S. Japhet (ScrHier 31; Jerusalem: Magnes, 1986) 321-39; **J. Van Seters,** *In Search of History: Historiography in the Ancient World and the Origins of Biblical History* (New Haven: Yale University Press, 1997); **M. Weinfeld,** *Deuteronomy and the Deuteronomic School* (Oxford: Clarendon Press, 1972); idem, "The Pattern of the Israelite Settlement in Canaan," in *Congress Volume: Jerusalem, 1986,* ed. J. A. Emerton (VTSup 40; Leiden: E. J. Brill, 1988) 270-83; **G. J. Wenham,** "The Deuteronomic Theology of the Book of Joshua," *JBL* 100 (1971) 140-48; **J. A. Wilcoxen,** "Narrative Structure and Cult Legend," in *Transitions in Biblical Scholarship,* ed. J. C. Rylaarsdam (Essays in Divinity 6; Chicago: University of Chicago Press, 1968) 43-70; **K. L. Younger Jr.,** *Ancient Conquest Accounts: A Study in Ancient Near Eastern and Biblical History Writing* (JSOTSup 98; Sheffield: Sheffield Academic Press, 1990); idem, "Early Israel in Recent Biblical Scholarship," in *The Face of Old Testament Studies: A Survey of Contemporary Approaches,* ed. D. W. Baker and B. T. Arnold (Grand Rapids: Baker, 1999) 176-206.

L. D. Hawk

JOSIAH

Josiah son of Amon, was king of Judah c. 640-609 BCE. His mother was Jedidah daughter of Adaiah of Bozkath (located near Lachish in the Judean Shephelah; see Josh 15:39). Josiah came to the throne at the age of eight with the support of "the people of the land" following the assassination of his father, Amon son of *Manasseh, by members of the royal court (see 2 Kings 21:19-26; 2 Chron 33:21-25). He attempted to carry out a major program of religious reform and national restoration as the power of the *Assyrian empire declined. He was killed at *Megiddo by Pharaoh Neco of Egypt, who led his army through the Megiddo pass in a failed attempt to support the remnants of the Assyrian army against the *Babylonians and their allies at Haran. Accounts of Josiah's reign appear in 2 Kings 22:1—23:30; 2 Chronicles 34:1—35:27; 1 Esdras 1:1-33.

1. The Account of Josiah's Reign in the Deuteronomistic History
2. The Account of Josiah's Reign in the Chronicler's History
3. Josiah in Historical Perspective

1. The Account of Josiah's Reign in the Deuteronomistic History.
The account of Josiah's reign in 2 Kings 22:1—23:30 appears in the context of the so-called *Deuteronomistic History (Joshua; Judges; Samuel; Kings), which presents an account of Israel's history from the time of Israel's entry into the land of Israel under *Joshua through the time of the Babylonian exile (Noth 1981). Interpreters argue that the *historiographical perspective of the Deuteronomistic History emphasizes Israel's observance of God's Torah as expressed in the book of Deuteronomy, which serves as the major criterion for assessing Israel's fortunes. Thus the Deuteronomistic History maintains that the Babylonian exile and the earlier destruction of the northern kingdom of Israel by Assyria were prompted by Israel's or Judah's failure to observe Deuteronomic Torah. Indeed, F. M. Cross demonstrates that all of the kings of northern Israel are condemned throughout the Deuteronomistic History for following in the idolatry of northern Israel's first king, *Jeroboam son of Nebat (see 1 Kings 12:1—14:20), who violated Deuteronomy's commands to worship God alone at the site that God would designate (Deut 6:4-25; 12:1-31). Many of the Judean kings also are condemned for violation of Deuteronomy's instructions. Nevertheless, a number of the Judean kings, such as *David, Asa, *Jehoshaphat, *Hezekiah and Josiah, are judged as righteous due to their efforts to observe God's Torah as expressed in Deuteronomy (*see* Law).

Interpreters argue that 2 Kings 22:1—23:30 presents Josiah as one of the most righteous kings of the royal house of David (Cross; Nelson; Sweeney). 2 Kings 22:2 states that Josiah was righteous, much like his ancestor David, who founded the dynastic line: "He did what was right in the eyes of YHWH, and he walked in all the path of David his father; he did not turn to the right or to the left." Asa (1 Kings 15:11) and Hezekiah (2 Kings 18:3) also were praised in this manner. Other kings, such as *Solomon (1 Kings 3:3), Jehoshaphat (1 Kings 22:43), Jehoash (2 Kings 12:2-3), Amaziah (2 Kings 14:3-4),

Azariah/Uzziah (2 Kings 15:3-4) and Jotham (2 Kings 15:34-35), receive qualified praise for acting righteously despite certain lapses. 2 Kings 23:25 goes even further in its praise of Josiah: "Before him there was no king like him, who turned to YHWH with all his heart, with all his soul, and with all his might, according to all the Torah of Moses; nor did any like him arise after him." Such praise is especially significant within the Deuteronomistic History because no other king, not even David, is said to have observed the Torah of Moses so closely. Indeed, the statement draws upon language that describes the ideal king in Deuteronomy's Torah of the king in Deuteronomy 17:14-20 (note especially Deut 17:20) and God's instructions to Joshua in Joshua 1:7-8. Unlike David, who committed adultery with Bathsheba and had her husband, Uriah, killed in a bid to cover up his actions (2 Sam 10—12; cf. 1 Kings 15:5), Josiah is linked to Moses and Joshua.

In keeping with the historiographical perspective of the Deuteronomistic History, the account of Josiah's reign in 2 Kings 22:1—23:30 points to the origins of Josiah's program of religious reform and national restoration in the discovery of "a book of Torah" during the course of the renovation of the Jerusalem temple (*see* Solomon's Temple). The discovery takes place at the time that Josiah commissioned his royal secretary Shaphan to authorize the high priest Hilkiah to disburse funds for the renovation of the temple. Hilkiah reported the discovery of the book of Torah to Shaphan, who in turn read it to the king. Because Josiah's reform calls for the establishment of only one legitimate sanctuary for the worship of God in the land, most interpreters conclude that this book of Torah must be a version of the book of Deuteronomy, which repeatedly emphasizes that God authorizes only one sanctuary for legitimate worship in the land of Israel (contra Ex 20:22-26, which seems to allow for multiple altars). The narrative places this event in the eighteenth year of King Josiah's reign, but it fails to mention that Josiah began to seek God in the eighth year of his reign or that he began to purge Jerusalem of pagan religious installations during the twelfth year of his reign (see 2 Chron 34:3-7). Such a presentation thereby supports the Deuteronomic principles that inform the Deuteronomistic History by emphasizing that the discovery of the book of Torah (i.e., Deuteronomy) motivates Josiah's actions.

The historiographical viewpoint of the Deuteronomistic History is evident also in Josiah's reaction to hearing the words of the book of Torah. Because the king is portrayed as absolutely righteous throughout the narrative, he orders his officers, Hilkiah the priest, Ahikam son of Shaphan, Achbor son of Milcaiah, Shaphan the secretary, and the king's servant Asaiah, to make an oracular inquiry of the prophet Huldah, who resided in the Mishneh quarter of Jerusalem. She reiterates God's earlier decision to destroy Jerusalem, made because of the sins of Josiah's grandfather, Manasseh son of Hezekiah (see 2 Kings 21:10-15), but declares that Josiah will be spared the sight of the demise of Jerusalem because of his righteousness. Her oracular response acknowledges the contention of the Deuteronomistic History that God decided to destroy Jerusalem and the temple as a result of King Manasseh's extensive sins. It also draws upon the portrayal of the death of King Ahab in the Deuteronomistic History (see 1 Kings 21—22). Although Ahab is judged to be one of the worst kings of Israel in the Deuteronomistic History, his repentance upon hearing of his condemnation by the prophet *Elijah for the murder of Naboth of Jezreel and the seizure of his land prompts God to grant Ahab an early death so that he would not have to witness the destruction of his own dynastic house (see 1 Kings 21:17-29). Ironically, Elijah's call for the destruction of the house of Ahab also includes the house of David. Following the marriage of King Jehoram son of Jehoshaphat to Athaliah daughter of Ahab (2 Kings 8:16-18; but see 2 Kings 8:26, which identifies Athaliah as the daughter of Omri), all members of the house of David, beginning with their son Ahaziah, are also descended from the house of *Omri. Although King Jehoiachin son of Jehoiakim of Judah is released from prison by the Babylonian king Evil-merodach at the conclusion of the Kings narrative (2 Kings 25:27-30), no subsequent member of the house of David ever claims the throne in Jerusalem again. In this respect, the fate of the house of David resembles that of the house of Saul: just as Mephibosheth son of Jonathan son of Saul eats at David's table and submits to David's authority as king (2 Sam 9:1-13; 19:24-30), so also Jehoiachin eats at the table of the Babylonian king and never makes any attempt to reassert his royal office.

The account of Josiah's reforms also reflects

Deuteronomistic History's historiography. Josiah's gathering of the people and their leaders at the Jerusalem temple to hear the words of the book of Torah and to renew the covenant in 2 Kings 23:1-3 reflects Joshua's gathering of the people for the same purpose at Shechem (Josh 8:3-35) (Nelson). Indeed, Josiah's stance by the pillar of the temple at this time recalls the stance of King Joash son of Ahaziah at the time of the revolt against Athaliah (2 Kings 11:13-14). The purification of the temple from its pagan vessels, the deposing of the idolatrous priests from throughout the land, the destruction of the *high places in Judah and so on, are all in keeping with Deuteronomy's prohibitions against idolatrous practice and its repeated call for the centralization of worship (see, e.g., Deut 12:2-31). The destruction of various idolatrous facilities associated with Ahaz, Manasseh, Solomon and the other kings of Judah likewise aids in establishing Josiah's unprecedented righteousness in the Deuteronomistic History's portrayal of his reign (2 Kings 23:4-14). Most noteworthy is Josiah's destruction of the *Bethel altar (2 Kings 23:15-20), established by King Jeroboam son of Nebat when the northern kingdom of Israel was formed following its revolt against the house of David (1 Kings 12—13). All of the kings of northern Israel are judged by the Deuteronomistic History to be as wicked as Jeroboam, and his establishment of the worship of the golden calves at Bethel and *Dan serves as the symbol of his apostasy that ultimately prompts the destruction of northern Israel (see 2 Kings 17) (Cross). Finally, Josiah's observance of the Passover festival marks the first time that the holiday was celebrated since the days of Joshua according to the Deuteronomistic History (2 Kings 23:21-23; cf. Josh 5). Altogether, Josiah is the righteous king who rights the wrongs of past kings as expressed throughout the Deuteronomistic History (Sweeney).

The presentation of the early death of Josiah at the hands of Pharaoh Neco of Egypt likewise serves the historiographic agenda of the Deuteronomistic History. The notice in 2 Kings 23:26-27 of God's decision to destroy Judah, Jerusalem and the temple because of the sins of Manasseh precedes the account of Josiah's death at Megiddo in 2 Kings 23:28-30. Josiah emerges as a tragic figure whose righteousness is unable to overcome the sins of his grandfather.

2. The Account of Josiah's Reign in the Chronicler's History.

The account of Josiah's reign in 2 Chronicles 34:1—35:27 appears in the context of the so-called *Chronicler's History in 1-2 Chronicles, which presents an account of Israel's history from the creation of the world through the conclusion of the Babylonian exile when King Cyrus of *Persia issued his decree allowing Jews to return to Jerusalem (Noth 1987). Although the Chronicler's History draws heavily on the Deuteronomistic History, particularly the narratives in Samuel and Kings, it presents a distinctive historiographical and theological perspective (see Williamson). Interpreters argue that the historiographical perspective of the Chronicler's History emphasizes the role of the Jerusalem temple as the holy sanctuary, or center of creation, and the people of Israel as the holy people in the midst of creation. The Chronicler's History thereby gives special emphasis to the holy dimensions of the temple and Israel's life around the temple; for example, it focuses on the structure and construction of the temple, the genealogies and the organization of the Levites, and their functions. It emphasizes the role of the royal house of David, especially because David and Solomon are credited with the building of the temple and the organization of the various Levitical families that would carry out the temple ritual. It presents a highly developed theology of reward and retribution. On the one hand, it emphasizes the need to seek God and to adhere to God's requirements as a measure of holiness in the world; on the other hand, it emphasizes immediate punishment for those who fail to abide by God's expectations or to heed God's prophets and other messengers. Although many dismiss the Chronicler's History for its theological perspectives (Wellhausen), it frequently contains narratives generally regarded as historically reliable (e.g., the account of Hezekiah's fortifications and water channel in 2 Chron 32:1-8, 29-31).

In contrast to Kings, the Chronicler's History presents Josiah as a monarch who rebels against God at *Megiddo and thereby seals his own fate. Indeed, the Chronicler's History presents his grandfather Manasseh in a very different light as well. Whereas the Deuteronomistic History emphasizes that the destruction of Jerusalem was provoked by Manasseh's sins, 2 Chronicles 33:1-20 emphasizes that Manasseh repented of his sins upon being dragged to Babylon in chains to appear before the Assyrian king, and that he returned to Jerusalem, where he proceeded to rebuild the city and to fortify the cities of Judah. Josiah, by contrast, defies the will of God by confronting Pharaoh Neco at Megiddo, and he dies in battle with Neco after failing to listen to Neco's warnings that such confrontation opposes God's will (2 Chron 35:20-27). Because 2 Chronicles 36:15-16 emphasizes that the destruction of Jerusalem took place because the people failed to heed God's messengers and prophets, Josiah therefore earns a measure of culpability for the destruction of Jerusalem in the eyes of the Chronicler. By emphasizing Manasseh's repentance and Josiah's defiance of Neco, the Chronicler's History deals with the theological problems posed by Manasseh's lengthy reign and Josiah's early death—that is, the repentant Manasseh rules for fifty-five years, longer than any other monarch, whereas the defiant Josiah suffers an early death. Indeed, the use of Neco as God's mouthpiece coincides with the use of the Persian monarch Cyrus to announce the end of the Babylonian exile and the rebuilding of the temple at the end of the Chronicler's History (2 Chron 36:22-23).

Other elements of the presentation of Josiah in 2 Chronicles 33:1—35:27 likewise support the historiographical agenda of the Chronicler's History. As noted above, Josiah turns to God in his eighth year and begins to purge Jerusalem and Judah of their pagan installations in his twelfth year. Such a portrayal emphasizes Josiah's auspicious beginnings, and it provides the basis for the contention of the Chronicler's History that the righteous will suffer upon committing wrongdoing and the wicked will receive God's blessing upon repentance (cf. Ezek 18). The discovery of the book of Torah, likely understood by the History to be the entire Pentateuch, in Josiah's eighteenth year once again prompts the king's repentance and his efforts to reform the nation and to restore the covenant. The account of Josiah's reform does not include the extensive actions described in the Deuteronomistic History, but it does emphasize Josiah's reading of the Torah before the people (2 Chron 34:29-30), the renewal of the covenant (2 Chron 34:31-33), and an extensive account of Josiah's efforts to celebrate Passover in Jerusalem, including full accounts of the sacrifices and other rituals together with the role of the Levites (2 Chron 35:1-19).

3. Josiah in Historical Perspective.

The account of Josiah's reign plays an important role in the modern reconstruction of the history of Israel and the development of Israelite religion. Indeed, the account of Josiah's discovery of the book of Torah and its identification with Deuteronomy play a major role in the development of the source theory of the Pentateuch put forward by Wellhausen and his followers. With its emphasis on the centralization of worship together with its emerging emphasis on law and temple ritual, Deuteronomy marks a stage in the development of the very personal and anthropomorphic representations of God put forward in the Wellhausenian conceptualization of the J source and the distant and formalized portrayal of God in the P source. The portrayal of mediators—angels, burning bushes, dreams, etc.—aid in placing the E source between J and D. The firm dating for Josiah's reign in the late seventh century BCE provides the chronological anchor for the D source in the mid-seventh century BCE. J and E were placed before D, respectively, because they were believed to presuppose the Davidic-Solomonic era of the tenth-ninth centuries BCE and the apex of northern Israelite power in the mid-eighth century BCE. P had to be placed afterward in the exilic and postexilic periods of the sixth and fifth centuries BCE.

Historical study of the reign of Josiah emphasizes the decline of the Assyrian Empire in the seventh century BCE (see Kuhrt). Following Assyria's withdrawal from Egypt c. 655 BCE, Assyria found itself increasingly preoccupied with fending off challenges to its rule by Babylonia and its Medean allies. The Babylonian revolt against the Assyrian monarch Assurbanipal led by his brother Shamash-shum-ukin in 652-648 BCE resulted in a bloody conflict that cost Shamash-shum-ukin his life and forced the submission of Babylonia. Because of the Deuteronomistic History's negative assessment of Manasseh, many contend that he remained a loyal ally of the Assyrians during this period. The Chronicler's History's portrayal of Manasseh having been dragged in chains to Babylon to appear before the king of Assyria (presumably Assurbanipal) would support such a contention, although it would suggest that Manasseh remained loyal because he was threatened. But with the death of Assurbanipal at some point during the years 631-627 BCE, and the rise of the

Neo-Babylonian monarch Nabopolassar to the throne in 627 BCE, the revolt that resulted in the fall of Assyria in 609 BCE to the Babylonians and Medes was on.

It is likely no accident that Josiah began his purge of the temple in his twelfth year, c. 628/ 627 BCE. Temple renovation is frequently a signal of claims to political independence because temples symbolize national sovereignty in the ancient world. Josiah's great-grandfather Hezekiah had been allied with the Babylonians in his revolt against the Assyrians in 701 BCE (see especially 2 Kings 20:12-20), and Josiah's attempt to stop Pharaoh Neco of Egypt at Megiddo indicates that he was supporting his Babylonian allies in their efforts to destroy the Assyrian army at Haran. The Babylonian Chronicle indicates that the *Egyptians had attempted to support the Assyrians against the Babylonians as early as 617 BCE, and the pass at Megiddo was the ideal point at which to stop an Egyptian advance into Aram and thereby deprive the Assyrians of Egyptian reinforcements. Although Josiah prevented the Egyptians from arriving in Haran in time to join the Assyrian army's final battle, this move apparently cost him his life. Interpreters are divided, however, on the pretext for Josiah's death. The Chronicler's History indicates that Josiah was killed in battle (2 Chron 35:20-27). The Deuteronomistic History, however, simply states that Neco put Josiah to death (2 Kings 23:29), which has prompted speculation that Neco executed a potentially troublesome vassal (Miller and Hayes). Following his return from Haran, Neco removed the pro-Babylonian Jehoahaz son of Josiah from the Judean throne and replaced him with his pro-Egyptian brother Jehoiakim.

Various attempts have been made to argue that Josiah was able to control a vast empire that encompassed the former territory of northern Israel as well as Philistia and areas of the Transjordan (see Alt). The archaeological evidence, however, is quite ambiguous, since clear evidence of Josiah's expansion beyond the borders of Judah is lacking (Na'aman). Consequently, arguments that the portrayal of Joshua's apportionment of the land in Joshua 13—23 represents the organization of Josiah's kingdom have failed to gain support. Nevertheless, the literary record of Josiah's destruction of the Bethel temple and his advance to Megiddo to meet Neco must be taken seriously. Such actions indicate attempts by Josiah to assert sovereignty over the territory of northern Israel. Nevertheless, Josiah's bid for religious reform and national restoration seems to have died with him, although the image of Josiah appears to underlie attempts to portray the restoration of Israel and the Davidic monarchy in later prophetic literature (e.g., Jer 23:1-8; 33:14-26; Ezek 37:15-28). The image of Josiah may well have influenced expectations concerning the rise of *Zerubbabel son of Shealtiel, the grandson of Jehoiachin, as the restored Davidic king at the time of the rebuilding of the Jerusalem temple in 520-515 BCE (see Hag 2:20-23; cf. Zech 4:1-14; cf. Zech 3:8-10; 6:9-15) and as the future Davidic king in the later protoapocalyptic scenarios of Zechariah 9—14 (see especially Zech 9:9-10; 11:4-14; 12:1-8; 12:10-13; 13:8-9) (for full discussion of the later role of Josiah, see Laato).

See also HISTORY OF ISRAEL 5: ASSYRIAN PERIOD; JOSHUA.

BIBLIOGRAPHY. **A. Alt,** "Judas Gaue unter Josia," in *Kleine Schriften zur Geschichte des Volkes Israel,* vol. 3, ed. M. Noth (Munich: Beck, 1953) 276-88; **F. M. Cross Jr.,** "The Themes of the Books of Kings and the Structure of the Deuteronomistic History," in *Canaanite Myth and Hebrew Epic* (Cambridge, MA: Harvard University Press, 1973) 274-89; **A. Kuhrt,** *The Ancient Near East, c. 3000-330 BC* (2 vols.; Routledge History of the Ancient World; London and New York: Routledge, 1995); **A. Laato,** *Josiah and David Redivivus: The Historical Josiah and the Messianic Expectations of Exilic and Postexilic Times* (ConBOT 33; Stockholm: Almqvist & Wiksell, 1992); **J. M. Miller and J. H. Hayes,** *A History of Ancient Israel and Judah* (Philadelphia: Westminster, 1986); **N. Na'aman,** "The Kingdom of Judah under Josiah," *TA* 18 (1991) 3-71; **R. D. Nelson,** "Josiah in the Book of Joshua," *JBL* 100 (1981) 531-40; **M. Noth,** *The Deuteronomistic History* (JSOTSup 15; Sheffield: JSOT, 1981 [1957]) 1-110; idem, *The Chronicler's History* (JSOTSup 50; Sheffield: JSOT, 1987 [1957]) 110-216; **M. A. Sweeney,** *King Josiah of Judah: The Lost Messiah of Israel* (Oxford and New York: Oxford University Press, 2001); **J. Wellhausen,** *Prolegomena to the History of Israel* (Gloucester, MA: Peter Smith, 1973 [1883]); **H. G. M. Williamson,** *1 and 2 Chronicles* (NCB; Grand Rapids: Eerdmans; London: Marshall, Morgan & Scott, 1982).

M. A. Sweeney

JOTHAM'S PARABLE. *See* LEBANON.

JUDGES

The term *judges* usually refers to named individuals in the book of *Judges: Othniel, Ehud, Shamgar, Barak and Deborah, Gideon (also named Jerubbaal), Tola, Jair, Jephthah, Ibzan, Elon, Abdon, and Samson. The deeds done by these figures are described in Judges 3:7—16:31, and also summarized at Judges 2:10-19, which is part of the introduction to the book. Some would include along with these figures Eli and *Samuel, who feature in 1 Samuel (e.g., Noth, 69-85). However, most references to "the judges" in modern scholarship have in view only the individuals described in the book of Judges. This article follows that convention. The article aims (1) to survey the biblical material relating to Israel's judges, (2) to define the meaning of the terms *judge* and *judged,* (3) to comment on how the individual judges are represented in Judges 3:7—16:31 (the only extensive biblical source), which involves saying something about the book of Judges as a whole, its theological themes and the place of each individual within the larger structure of the book, and (4) to address historical questions raised by the judges accounts.

1. Survey of the Biblical Material
2. Terminology
3. The Accounts in the Book of Judges
4. History and Chronology
5. Conclusion

1. Survey of the Biblical Material.

1.1. The Book of Judges. Detailed accounts of each of the judges are found in Judges 3:7—16:31. Judges 2:6—3:6 provides an overview of the period. The narratives in Judges 1:1—2:5 and Judges 17—21 contribute to the book's characterization of the period and must also be taken into account.

1.2. References in Other Old Testament Books. A number of passages in other OT Historical Books refer to the time of the judges as an identifiable period in Israel's history (Ruth 1:1; 2 Sam 7:7, 11; 2 Kings 23:22; 1 Chron 17:6, 10; Neh 9:27). These books also contain some references to individual judges, of which the most notable is 1 Samuel 12:11.

In the Hebrew text of this passage Samuel, addressing the assembled Israelites, describes God as having sent "Jerubbaal, Bedan, Jephthah and Samuel" to deliver Israel. The name

Bedan is otherwise unattested, and some have also felt it out of place for Samuel to refer to himself in this way. Accordingly, the NRSV translates, "Jerubbaal and Barak, and Jephthah, and Samson," a rendering for which there is some support in the ancient versions (LXX, Syriac, Targum), and which yields four names all attested in Judges, though not exactly in the order in which they appear in Judges. Likely enough, "Barak" is the correct reading. "Bedan" could have arisen through miscopying of "Barak," as the names have the same first consonant, and their second and third consonants are orthographically similar. It is more questionable whether we should replace the MT's "Samuel" with "Samson": in view of his earlier victory over the *Philistines (1 Sam 7), why should Samuel not refer to himself as one of those raised up to deliver Israel? In any case, this brief reference does no more than describe these figures as successful military leaders. It broadly supports but does not supplement the picture in Judges.

The same must be said for other similar references: to Othniel (Josh 15:17; 1 Chron 4:13), to Jerub-Beshet (= Gideon) (2 Sam 11:21), to Elon (Num 26:26), the mention in various texts of the "villages of Jair" (Num 32:41; Deut 3:14; Josh 13:30; 1 Kings 4:13; 1 Chron 2:22). There are references to an "Ehud" at 1 Chronicles 7:10; 8:2, 6, and to a "Tola" at Numbers 26:23, 1 Chronicles 7:1-2. These may well have in view the same individuals as in Judges 3; 10, for the tribal affiliation (Benjamin, Issachar) is the same in each case. But these genealogical texts raise problems of their own (see Japhet, 171, 190-92), and in any case, they provide next to no information beyond the names.

Psalms and the Prophets yield one reference to the period of the judges as a time of idolatry (Ps 106:34-36) and three references to some of the battles fought by the judges (Ps 83:9-12; Is 9:4; 10:26). Interestingly, Gideon's victory over Midian seems to have been particularly remembered in later retellings of Israel's history. These poetic texts, though brief, seem to support the accounts in Judges, thereby again turning our attention back to Judges as the primary source.

2. Terminology.

The use of the term *judges* at Judges 2:10-19 (the introductory summary), and the repeated use of the verb *judged* to describe the actions of many of the figures in Judges (Judg 3:10; 4:4; 10:2, 3; 12:7, 8, 11, 13; 15:20; 16:31) may give the impression of a kind of recognized role or office within Israel, with well-defined functions. But a cursory reading of Judges makes clear that these figures came to leadership by different routes and exercised that leadership in different ways.

The Hebrew words traditionally translated "judge" (*šāpaṭ* [verb], *šôpēṭ* [noun]) include juridical functions within their semantic domain (for the verb see Ex 18:13; Deut 25:1; Judg 4:4-5 [but see 3.2.4 below]; 1 Kings 3:28; for the noun see Ex 2:14; Deut 17:9-12; Josh 8:33; 1 Sam 8:2-3; 2 Sam 15:4). But often they are used in contexts where no such functions are implied, or where political or military leadership is in view (for the verb see Judg 3:10; 15:20; 1 Sam 7:6; 8:5-6; 2 Kings 15:5; Dan 9:12; for the noun see Judg 2:16-19; Amos 2:3; Mic 5:1; Dan 9:12). The verb and the noun seem to reflect a conception according to which exercising leadership and administering justice were seen as overlapping functions. In many cases in Judges the translations "led" or "leader(s)" would give a better sense than "judged" or "judge(s)" because they are less specific and therefore more appropriate to the range of activities in which the figures in Judges actually engage. This is reflected in modern versions (e.g., NIV, NRSV; see also *HALOT* 4.1622-26).

Ehud, Barak and Gideon are not, in fact, described by the term *judge* or said to have "judged" Israel. Barak's role may be seen as an extension of Deborah's: as the verb *judge* is used of her (Judg 4:4), it could on this basis be argued to apply to Barak as well. But this argument does not apply in Ehud's or Gideon's case. Ehud is described as a "savior" (Judg 3:15). In the Gideon account the verb *save* is used of Gideon's actions (Judg 6:14-15; 8:22), as it is of God's (Judg 6:36-37; 7:7); note also the further use of the verb at Judges 6:31; 7:2. Furthermore, Othniel is described as a "savior" who "saved" the Israelites (Judg 3:9), and the verb *save* is also used in connection with Shamgar, Tola, Jephthah and Samson (Judg 3:31; 10:1; 12:2-3; 13:5) in the introductory summary of the judges period (Judg 2:16, 18) and in God's words of rebuke at the beginning of the Jephthah account (Judg 10:12-14). In all these cases the *salvation in question clearly is political—that is, military victory (see *HALOT* 2.448-49, 562). The terms *saved* and *savior,* understood in this sense, are at least as important for understanding the roles of Israel's judges as *judged* and *judge.* They also highlight a key issue in Judges: would the Israelites recognize God as their true savior or not?

3. The Accounts in the Book of Judges.
Literary-critical questions have been much debated in relation to Judges, and we must briefly address them here because they affect our understanding of Israel's judges. Can different strands be detected in particular accounts? Is it correct to argue that those parts of Judges 6—9 that refer to Gideon as "Jerubbaal" derive from a different source from those that refer to him as "Gideon" (see the discussion in Soggin, 103-4)? What of the suggestion that the core of Judges was an earlier "Book of Saviors" consisting essentially of the accounts of Ehud, Deborah/Barak and Gideon/Abimelech, and that the accounts of the other judges are later additions to this core (Mayes, 18-27)? How would this view (one of whose implications is that the use of *judge* [verb and noun] in connection with these figures is a later development) affect our reading of these accounts? B. Halpern (76-103) has suggested that the poetic account of the destruction of Sisera's forces in the Song of Deborah (Judg 5) is largely the source for the prose account in Judges 4, Judges 4 having arisen partly in order to clarify questions raised by the poetic account. Again, this might have implications for our reading of these two chapters.

This article proceeds on the basis that the book of Judges, whatever its sources, is a unified and thoroughly reworked text, and one that cannot be broken down into its constituent sources as easily as traditional literary-critical approaches usually argue. For example, in Judges 6—9 Gideon is generally named "Jerubbaal" in contexts where the author wishes to highlight his role in (at first) attacking Baal worship and (later) causing the people to lapse into idolatry; that is, the name offers increasingly ironical commentary on a particular theme in the narrative and need not be seen as evidence for the presence of two sources. This is not the place to present a detailed case for a unitary reading of Judges, and in what follows I simply assume that such a position is generally defensible (see Satterthwaite and McConville, chap. 4). However,

Table 1. Elements of the Othniel Account

A	(apostasy, v. 7)	The Israelites did what was evil in the LORD's eyes, and they forgot the Lord their God,
B	(other gods, v. 7)	and served the Baals and the Asherahs.
C	(God's anger, v. 8)	And the LORD's anger was kindled against Israel,
D	(enemies, v. 8)	and he sold them into the hand of [enemy X],
E	(subjection, v. 8)	and the Israelites served [enemy X] for [N^1] years.
F	(cry, v. 9)	And the Israelites cried out to the LORD,
G	(judge, v. 9)	and the LORD raised up a savior for the Israelites, and he saved them, [judge Y].
H	(spirit, v. 10)	And the spirit of the LORD came upon him,
I	(deliverance, v. 10)	and he led Israel; he went out to battle, and the LORD gave [enemy X] into his hand;
J	(domination, v. 10)	and his hand prevailed over [enemy X].
K	(peace, v. 11)	And the land had rest [N^2] years.
L	(judge dies, v. 11)	Then [judge Y] died.

we must address the question of the narrative frames in Judges.

3.1. The Narrative Frames. It is customary in analyzing Judges 3:7—16:31 to distinguish between "major" and "minor" judges. Major judges are those figures who are said to have won victories against Israel's enemies: Othniel, Ehud, Deborah/Barak, Gideon, Jephthah and Samson, whose accounts all follow a pattern of sin—punishment—repentance—deliverance. The minor judges are Tola, Jair, Ibzan, Elon and Abdon, whose achievements seem less significant, and whose much briefer accounts (all of them in Judg 10; 12) follow a different pattern. These two recurring patterns I refer to as "major-judge frames" and "minor-judge frames."

3.1.1. The Major-Judge Frames. The frame used in the accounts of the major judges is most easily explained with reference to the first account, that of Othniel (Judg 3:7-11). As we read the longer accounts that follow (Judg 3:12—16:31), it is as though the Othniel account has been broken down into its separate phrases, which then have been turned into a frame (or outline) for the later accounts, with the separate phrases recurring at key points within each of these accounts, particularly the beginnings and endings.

Table 1 shows the Othniel account (Judg 3:7-11) represented as separate "elements," with the specific names and numbers removed.

Table 2 shows how these elements are distributed throughout later accounts, forming a frame for each of them.

The frame is never rigidly applied, for there are frequent variations in the frame elements, particularly in the accounts of Gideon, Jephthah and Samson: elements are omitted, ex-

panded or presented in a different order, and these changes usually are related to features of the accounts in which they occur. This observation calls into question the common tendency to treat the frames as later editorial additions that can be removed, leaving an earlier layer of tradition intact (e.g., Mayes, 19-20). In the following survey of Judges 3:7—16:31 the major-judge frames are treated as an integral part of the accounts in which they occur. The presence of this recuring pattern encourages us to read the individual accounts in relation to each other. (This is a principle underlying many instances of "repetition and variation" in the OT [see Alter, 88-113].) A fact that emerges immediately is that the Othniel account is by far the most simple and straightforward of the major-judge accounts: all the subsequent accounts (with the exception of the vestigial Shamgar account) are longer, more complex and increasingly problematic.

One further point: when the frames refer to *"Israel" or "the Israelites" (elements A, C, E—G, I), they probably do not have all Israel in view; the same applies to the references to "the land" (element K). The accounts usually make clear that the activities of the major judges involved only a few Israelite tribes in each case. It is often said that the frames and the accounts differ on this point, the frames attempting to impose an "all Israel" perspective on the accounts, making it seem as though each judge had brought deliverance for all the tribes, even though the rest of the accounts usually present the judges as no more than local leaders. This is one of the main arguments in the case for seeing the frames as later editorial additions. How-

Table 2. Distribution of Elements Throughout Major-Judge Accounts

	Othniel	Ehud	Deborah and Barak	Gideon	Jephthah	Samson
A apostasy	3:7	3:12	4:1	6:1	10:6	13:1
B other gods	3:7			[6:2-6]	10:6	
C God's anger	3:8				10:7	
D enemies	3:8	3:12	4:2	6:1	10:7	13:1
E subjection (how long)	3:8 8 years	3:13-14 18 years	4:3 20 years	6:2-6 7 years	10:8-9 18 years	13:1 40 years
F cry (God's response)	3:9	3:15	4:3	6:6-10 rebuke	10:10-16 rebuke	
G judge (how chosen)	3:9	3:15	4:6-10 prophecy	6:11-12 angel	11:4-6 elders	13:2-5 angel
H spirit	3:10			6:34	11:29	13:25; 14:6, 19; 15:14
I deliverance	3:10	3:27-29	4:14-16	7:22-25	11:32-33	16:30 [?]
J domination	3:10	3:30	4:23-24	8:28	11:33	
K peace (how long)	3:11: 40 years	3:30: 80 years	5:31: 40 years	8:28: 40 years	[12:7] 6 years; no peace formula	[15:20; 16:31] 20 years; no peace formula
L judge's death	3:11	4:1		8:32	12:7	16:30-31
(other elements)			Song of Deborah	Abimelech narrative		

ever, "Israel" and even "the Israelites" are not the same as "all Israel" (a phrase used only at Judg 8:27; 20:34). Most likely, Judges aims to represent Israel as a political or covenantal unity, so that what happens to a part affects the whole: the frequent references to "Israel" and "the Israelites" are not meant to imply that all Israel was directly involved in all the events narrated but rather to emphasize that these tribes are part of a larger but increasingly fragmented whole (a point that also comes across in the book's prologue and epilogue [Judg 1:1—3:6; 17—21]). The judges were local leaders, not national ones.

3.1.2. The Minor-Judge Frames. The minor-judge accounts also share a clear pattern, as Table 3 shows.

There are variations in these accounts: the first two begin with "X arose after him," the next three with "X judged Israel after him"; the "Further In-

formation" is also slightly varied. However, the presentation is repetitive, and this is particularly evident to the reader because the accounts are short and also clustered into two groups.

M. Noth (69-72) suggested that originally the traditions relating to major and minor judges were separate, and only secondarily were they combined by an editor who noted that Jephthah featured in both sets of traditions. It is true that Judges 12:7, which at present ends the account of Jephthah, does, if taken by itself, read rather like the account of Elon (Judg 12:11-12); that is, the verse may be a vestige of an earlier brief account of Jephthah that was similar in character to those of Tola, Jair and so on. But this reconstruction of the prehistory of Judges, while not impossible, is rather speculative. We will consider below how the accounts of the major and minor judges interact in Judges 10—16.

Table 3. Pattern of Minor-Judge Accounts

	Tola (10:1-2)	Jair (10:3-5)	Ibzan (12:8-10)	Elon (12:11-12)	Abdon (12:13-15)
Succession	Arose after Abimelech to save Israel (10:1)	Arose after him [Jair] (10:3)	Judged Israel after him [Jephthah] (12:8)	Judged Israel after him [Ibzan] (12:11)	Judges Israel after him [Elon] (12:13)
From	Shamir in Ephraim (10:1)	Territory of Gilead (10:3)	Bethlehem in Zebulun (?) (12:8)	Territory of Zebulun (12:11)	Pirathon in Ephraim (12:13)
Further Information	Resided in Shamir (10:1)	30 sons riding on 30 donkeys; 30 towns (10:4)	30 sons, each with a wife; 30 daughters, all married (12:9)	(—)	40 sons and 30 grandsons, riding on 70 donkeys (12:14)
Years as Judge	23 years (10:2)	22 years (10:3)	7 years (12:9)	10 years (12:11)	8 years (12:14)
Death, Burial	Died, buried at Shamir (10:2)	Died, buried at Kamon (10:5)	Died, buried at Bethlehem (12:10)	Died, buried at Aijalon (12:12)	Died, buried at Pirathon (12:15)

3.2. *The Individual Accounts.* This section comments on the accounts of the judges, addressing particular historical issues as appropriate.

3.2.1. Othniel (Judg 3:7-11). Othniel, son of Kenaz, is linked to the tribe of Judah; he is described as a relative of Joshua's heroic contemporary *Caleb (Judg 3:9), and also is associated with one of the more striking conquests in the generation after *Joshua (Josh 15:13-19; Judg 1:9-15). He is said to have been raised up to defeat "Cushan-Rishathaim king of Aram Naharaim" (Judg 3:8), whom K. A. Kitchen (211) justly describes as "the most exotic and distant" of Israel's oppressors in this period. "Cushan-Rishathaim" can be translated "Cushan of double wickedness," and probably it is a pun on a name with a different meaning. Kitchen suggests that Cushan styled himself *resh ʿathaim,* "ruler of Athaim," arguing that Cushan was an Aramaean who established himself as a local leader in Aram Naharaim (= northwestern Mesopotamia), who extended his power southward and briefly exercised control over part of Israel. (The name "Athaim" is not attested elsewhere, but name lists for this part of Mesopotamia at this period are not extant.) The account states neither which tribes were involved nor where and how Othniel defeated him. Are we to understand that Cushan's control briefly extended as far south as the territory of Judah, and that this is how Othniel came to be involved in defeating him? Or did Othniel come to the aid of the northern tribes?

Othniel's account is extremely short and schematic. Some argue that the account is an artificial creation: Othniel is presented as a model of a successful leader, against whom subsequent judges are measured, and the brevity and simplicity of the account are designed to make the point "If only things could have remained this simple!" That is, Othniel functions as a literary paradigm, and the question of historicity hardly arises (Hackett, 134-35; Mayes, 27-28). We should not assume, however, that the traditions available to the narrator were necessarily as skeletal as the present narrative might suggest. Just as plausibly, the narrator could have made the Othniel account more like that of Ehud or Deborah/Barak, but rather chose to present it in an abbreviated, formulaic form, so that its short phrases should be used as "frame elements" in later narratives. The general picture of a local Aramaean leader establishing himself in northwestern Mesopotamia in the late thirteenth to early twelfth century BCE, briefly flourishing and then vanishing is perfectly plausible. As Kitchen (212) notes, Cushan's activities may be compared to those of Hadadezer of Zobah two centuries later (see 2 Sam 8:3-5; 10:6-19).

3.2.2. Ehud (Judg 3:12-30). Ehud, son of Gera, a Benjaminite, is said to have assassinated Eglon, the king of *Moab, who, aided by *Ammonite and Amalekite forces, had occupied the area around *Jericho ("the city of palms") for eighteen years (Judg 3:12-14). Ehud then rallied Israelite forces to drive the Moabites from Israel. Moab became subject to Israel, and an eighty-year peace followed, the longest such period mentioned in Judges. It is not said which tribes responded to Ehud's call; the narrator focuses almost solely on Ehud's bold leadership. One can suppose that at least Benjamin (in whose territory Jericho lay) and Ephraim (where Ehud rallied support [Judg 3:27]) were involved.

The Ehud account has considerable entertainment value (note the element of farce in the description of Eglon's death [Alter, 37-41]). In regard to its role in the structure of Judges, it is longer and more complex than the Othniel account, and Ehud uses more devious means to achieve victory than Othniel apparently did (although, as noted, the narrator gave no details of Othniel's victory), but still, it is basically a success story, with Ehud bravely leading the way to victory.

Eglon, like all the enemy leaders in Judges, is not mentioned outside Judges. The reality of a Moabite kingdom in the early twelfth century BCE has been questioned (Hackett, 153-54). Archaeological finds from Dibon, Heshbon and Medeba at this period are, at present, relatively scanty, but an Egyptian inscription suggests that Dibon at least was settled as early as 1270 BCE. Evidence for an organized Moabite state (large cities, centralization) in this period is lacking, but it is quite conceivable that the leader of a largely pastoral, tribal society would have designated himself as "king" (Kitchen, 195-97).

3.2.3. Shamgar (Judg 3:31). The narrative of Shamgar son of Anath occupies only one verse (he is also mentioned at Judg 5:6). Probably he was a non-Israelite, perhaps a Hurrian, serving in an Egyptian military division named after the *Canaanite goddess Anath. D. Block (172-75) cites an Egyptian inscription from the time of Ramesses III (1198-1166 BCE) and suggests that Shamgar won his victories when this division fought against the Philistines shortly after the arrival of the Sea Peoples in the area. In Judges 3 he is no more than a footnote to the Ehud account, another man whom God used to bring deliverance to Israel with an unorthodox weapon, even though as a non-Israelite, he may not have intended to help Israel.

3.2.4. Barak/Deborah (Judg 4—5). The next account celebrates the achievements of Deborah, wife of Lappidoth, from Ephraim, and Barak, son of Abinoam, from Naphtali (Judg 4:4-6), both of whom led the struggle against "Jabin, king of Canaan, who reigned in Hazor" (Judg 4:2). The prose account of Judges 4 is complemented by the poetic account of Judges 5 (for a helpful discussion of the relationship of the two accounts see Block, 175-84).

Deborah is said to have been "leading [judging] Israel at that time." The NIV translation of the end of Judges 4:5 ("the Israelites came to her to have their disputes decided") suggests that Deborah regularly administered justice, like Samuel at a later period (1 Sam 7:15-17). Block (193-97), however, argues for the translation "the Israelites came up to her for the judgment," this "judgment" being a decision from God in their favor and against their Canaanite oppressors in answer to their cries to God. We may compare Jephthah's description of God as the judge who will decide the dispute between the Israelites and the Ammonites (Judg 11:27). In short, the Israelites come to Deborah for a prophetic word from God, and this fits with the reference to Deborah as a "prophetess" at Judges 4:4 (*see* Prophets and Prophecy). Elsewhere in the chapter, certainly, Deborah's leadership is thoroughly prophetic in character (Judg 4:6-9, 14). In commissioning Barak, Deborah gives the word that the Israelites have been seeking, and from then on Barak takes the lead and defeats Sisera.

Barak is said to have rallied the Israelites to Mount Tabor. From there he attacked Sisera's forces and drove them back to Harosheth Haggoyim, Sisera's base (Judg 4:10, 12-16). "Harosheth Haggoyim" probably means "cultivated land of the Gentiles," and apparently it is identical to the Taanach and Kishon River areas referred to at Judges 5:10-21. The victory seems to have strengthened Israel's hold on northern Canaan (Judg 4:23-24), building on the campaigns of Joshua 11 in a way that Zebulun's and Naphtali's earlier efforts in the same region had failed to do (Judg 1:30, 33). Note that the "King Jabin of Canaan who reigned in Hazor" (Judg 4:3) seems to be a different figure from the "King Jabin of Hazor" of Joshua 11:1. Names frequently recur in royal dynasties (Kitchen, 213).

When Deborah commissions him, Barak demands that she accompany him. Deborah's response implies criticism of Barak, and the outcome is that Sisera is "delivered into the hand of a woman" (Judg 4:9, 22). This is the first occasion in which one of the judges is in some sense criticized. Nonetheless, this account leaves a mainly favorable impression, which is reinforced by the poetic account of Judges 5. This chapter dwells on the themes of Israelite loyalty to God and the defeat of God's enemies. Although some tribes are reproached for not having taken part in the victory over the Canaanites (Judg 5:16-17), the dominant note is of a willing Israelite response to God's call (Judg 5:9-14, 18).

3.2.5. Gideon [Abimelech] (Judg 6:1—9:57). The next enemy said to have afflicted Israel in this period is Midian or, rather, a loose alliance of Midianites, Amalekites and "people of the east" who made periodic destructive raids on the land (Judg 6:2-4). Elsewhere in Judges 6—8 this group is referred to simply as "Midian" (e.g., Judg 6:6, 7, 11, 14 ["the Midianites" in some English translations]). Kitchen (213-14) discusses the link between Midian and the site of Qurayya (northwestern *Arabia), inhabited in the thirteenth and twelfth centuries BCE and thereafter abandoned. As Kitchen notes, the relatively brief time frame within which Midian seems to have flourished is an argument for the antiquity of the traditions underlying Judges 6—8.

Gideon, of the tribe of Manasseh, was raised up to deliver Israel from this enemy. The account of Gideon, along with its sequel, the Abimelech account, mark a turning point in Judges. From Judges 9 on, Israel's fortunes clearly are in decline.

At the beginning of the account elements of the frame are expanded, so as to give the opening a more decidedly negative cast than previously: the narrative dwells on the Midianite oppression for a number of verses (Judg 6:2-6 [element E]), and God, when appealed to, simply denounces the Israelites (Judg 6:6-10 [element F]). Relations between Israel and God have worsened: the judgment is harsher, and salvation is no longer automatically granted. But in spite of his rebuke, God sends his angel to summon Gideon (Judg 6:11-12), who, once persuaded that the summons has come from God (Judg 6:13-24), responds by striking a blow

against Baal and for God and by rallying the tribes of Manasseh, Asher, Zebulun and Naphtali for battle (Judg 6:25-35).

But now Gideon wants reassurances that God will deliver Israel as promised (Judg 6:36-40). Like Barak, but to a greater degree, Gideon tries to impose conditions on God before he will serve him. God grants the signs that Gideon requests, but it becomes clear that Gideon is overly concerned for his own glory as Israel's deliverer: note the repetition of "by my hand" (Judg 6:36, 37).

Judges 7 continues this theme, as God reduces Gideon's army in size for fear that "Israel would only take the credit away from me, saying, 'My own hand has delivered me'" (Judg 7:2). In line with this, the narrator brings out God's role in the victory more than in previous accounts: the Midianite's dream (Judg 7:9-14) suggests an unexpected reversal brought about by God, and in the battle it is God who "sets every man's sword against his fellow and against all the army" (Judg 7:22).

As defeat turns into rout, the battle spreads from the territory of Issachar into that of Manasseh and finally, as Gideon continues the pursuit across the Jordan, into Gilead. When Gideon overtakes and captures the fleeing Midianite leaders, it emerges that he is obsessed with a personal vendetta (Judg 8:18-19): "What about the men you killed at Tabor? . . . They were my brothers." This detail, only revealed late in the narrative, puts much of what has preceded in a new light: Gideon's sole concern has not been God's glory or Israel's deliverance; he also has been avenging a private grievance. There is no reference to God's involvement in any of these events.

For all appearances, however, Gideon has won a great victory, and the Israelites offer him kingship. Gideon refuses in noble-sounding tones: "I will not rule over you, and my son will not rule over you: the LORD will rule over you" (Judg 8:23). But he then undermines God's kingship by constructing an ephod, which emphasizes his personal authority (it is set up in his hometown). Ominously, it is made from earrings captured from the Midianites, an echo of the episode of the golden calf (Ex 32:2-4): like the golden calf, it leads the Israelites into apostasy (Judg 8:24-28). At Gideon's death, idolatry is as deeply rooted in Israel as before, and afterward a syncretistic form of Baal worship returns:

the name *Baal-Berith,* meaning "Baal of the covenant" (Judg 8:33), apparently attempts to blend the religions of Sinai and Canaan (cf. Judg 2:19). Israel has forgotten that it was God who saved them, at least partly because of Gideon's later actions (Judg 8:34).

Ultimately, Gideon's legacy is negative: he has encouraged an idolatrous cult, and he has acted like a king in all but name. His son Abimelech follows these paths to their logical conclusion: he is an idolater whose rise to power is supported by the shrine of Baal-Berith (Judg 9:4), and his life reflects all the worst aspects of monarchy—murderous family intrigues and the destructive and vindictive abuse of power (Judg 9:5, 34-52). It is a relief when he is killed and God's control over events is reasserted (Judg 9:53-57). If we have any doubt as to whether Gideon's leadership was seriously flawed, we have only to look at what happens when his son succeeds him. (For more on this reading of Gideon as a flawed hero at best, a reading quite contrary to many popular expositions of Judg 6—8, see Wenham, 119-27.)

3.2.6. Tola (Judg 10:1-2). Tola, son of Puah, of the tribe of Issachar, the first of the minor judges, is said to have arisen after Abimelech "to deliver Israel" and to have lived in the hill country of Ephraim (Judg 10:1). Apparently, he provided stability within Ephraim after Abimelech's destructive tyranny. We are also told that he led Israel for twenty-three years, and that he was buried at Shamir.

3.2.7. Jair (Judg 10:3-5). No act of salvation is attributed to Jair of Gilead. We learn mainly of his prosperity: his thirty sons, each with his own donkey, and his thirty villages. Note that in the next episode the elders of Gilead appeal to Jephthah rather than to any of Jair's sons when the Ammonites invade—the sons may be wealthy, but they are not warriors.

3.2.8. Jephthah (Judg 10:6—12:7). The account of Jephthah develops themes from the Gideon and Abimelech accounts and traces a further decline within Israel. Like the Gideon account, Jephthah's account begins with an extended description of Israelite idolatry and enemy oppression (Judg 10:6-9). These verses refer to both Philistine and Ammonite oppression, but the rest of the Jephthah account describes only the deliverance from the Ammonites and is set mainly in Transjordan, some distance from the Philistines, so it is like-

ly that the reference to the Philistines is intended to prepare for the account of Samson.

God again condemns the Israelites when they cry for help, this time bluntly telling them, "I will no longer save you" (Judg 10:13). In response the Israelites "put away their foreign gods and worship the LORD." But is this merely a token gesture? The phrase describing God's response is ambiguous (Judg 10:16): either "he could no longer bear to see Israel suffer" (NRSV) or "he grew weary of their efforts to win his favor" (Block, 348-49). Maybe the Israelites are now on their own.

In this crisis the leaders of Gilead approach Jephthah, also a Gileadite, but one whose irregular birth reminds us of Abimelech (Judg 11:1-3). Rather as they have tried to negotiate with God, the elders negotiate with Jephthah, persuade him to be their leader, and swear an oath to this effect at *Mizpah (Judg 11:4-11). But how far is God involved in any of this? For the moment, the narrator offers no comment.

There follows yet another set of negotiations, this time between Jephthah and the Ammonite king (Judg 11:12-28) (on the question of why Jephthah incorrectly identifies the god of the Ammonites as Chemosh rather than Milcom, see Block, 361-62). Only when it becomes clear that battle cannot be avoided does the spirit of the Lord come upon Jephthah; and just at this point, when the narrative has established that God is with him, he attempts to manipulate God with his vow (Judg 11:29-31). The terms of the vow are somewhat ambiguous, but they more likely refer to a human than to an animal: although animals could be kept inside Israelite houses, it would not be natural for Jephthah to speak of an animal coming "out of the doors of my house to greet me" (Judg 11:31). Jephthah has mentioned Chemosh, god of Moab, in his negotiations with the Ammonite king, and now he treats the God of Israel as though, like Chemosh, he accepted human sacrifice (cf. 2 Kings 3:27). Like Gideon, he wants to be sure of victory, but he goes much further than Gideon in his desire to secure it. His daughter falls victim to his terrible vow, which he knows no better than to carry out (Judg 11:34-40).

Negotiation, often in the form of manipulative pleading, is a theme that runs through the entire account of Jephthah. It dominates the exchanges between the Israelites and God (Judg 10:6-16), the Gileadites' approach to Jephthah

(Judg 10:17—11:11), Jephthah's dealings with the Ammonite king (Judg 11:12-28) and finally Jephthah's dealings with God (Judg 11:29-31). Jephthah's painful eagerness to have God on his side echoes the Israelites' plea earlier on (Judg 10:15-16), but he shows no better understanding than they did of what God really requires. The gap between Israel and their God widens in this account, and it is entirely fitting that the Israelites, whose pursuit of foreign gods now seems entrenched, should have a leader who acts in an "outrightly pagan" way (Block, 367).

There is an unpleasant sequel (Judg 12:1-6). As they did with Gideon, the Ephraimites reproach Jephthah for not having summoned them to battle (cf. Judg 8:1-3). Unlike Gideon, and for once abandoning any attempt at negotiation, Jephthah fights with them. Perhaps he is enraged at their criticism, which comes after a victory that caused him great personal loss. And so Jephthah, like Gideon and Abimelech before him, ends up shedding Israelite blood, the defeated Ephraimites being ruthlessly killed as they try to escape. There is no "peace formula" (frame element K) to end Jephthah's account—he has brought no real peace to Israel.

3.2.9. Ibzan (Judg 12:8-10). The series of minor judges resumes with Ibzan of Bethlehem (in either Judah or Zebulun [for the latter see Josh 19:15]). Ibzan is of interest largely because his account, like the earlier account of Jair, forms a contrast with that of Gilead. In this case the contrast is between Jephthah, childless because of his vow, and the many children of Ibzan (Judg 12:8-9).

3.2.10. Elon (Judg 12:11-12). The account of Elon of Zebulun gives no more than his name, tribe, years as leader in Israel and burial place.

3.2.11. Abdon (Judg 12:13-15). The account of Abdon of Ephraim, like that of Jair, adds a few further details that suggest his prosperity.

The accounts of the minor judges are brief and ambiguous (Webb, 160-61). Does the fact that Jair, Ibzan and Abdon were wealthy and had many children indicate that they brought a temporary stability to parts of Israel (hence they were able to raise large families and acquire possessions)? Or are they minor versions of Gideon, leaders whose concerns center on building up their own families and founding a local dynasty (Younger, 278-79)? The accounts could be read either way. No obvious spiritual decline is evident in these accounts; indeed, such concerns scarcely surface. Nonetheless, the minor judges seem to accomplish little. There is a sense of the narrative "treading water" during these short and repetitive accounts. The downward trend begun with Gideon continues through the accounts of Jephthah and Samson, and the minor judges, whose careers lie within this period, hardly interrupt it, with the exception of Tola (Judg 10:1). These figures provide temporary leadership of a sort, but they do not seem to address the fundamental issue of God's relationship with Israel.

3.2.12. Samson (Judg 13:1—16:31). The account of Samson of Dan begins hopefully. An angel tells his mother that he will "begin to deliver Israel from the hands of the Philistines" (Judg 13:5). Later incidents in the chapter seem to confirm God's good intentions (Judg 13:8-23). However, Samson does everything wrong: he is a Nazirite who defiles himself by eating honey from a carcass (Judg 13:4-5; 14:9; cf. Num 6:6), and an Israelite who insists on a Philistine wife (Judg 14:2-3). God's spirit comes upon him repeatedly, yet his behavior, even though it carries out God's aim of stirring up hostility between Israel and the Philistines (Judg 14:4), remains extraordinarily willful. He is led mainly by sexual lust (Judg 16:1-4) and a lethal regard for his own honor (Judg 14:9; 15:3, 7-8, 11), and he seems hardly to concern himself with whether what he does benefits Israel or not. He ends his life with an act of personal revenge that, although hurting the Philistines more than his other actions (Judg 16:28-30), does not remove them as a threat to Israel, as 1 Samuel testifies. Again, there is no "peace formula" to end his account.

Nevertheless, Samson at least has struck some blows for God, and this in spite of the fact that no one else in Israel seems to support him. At one point the Judahites even hand him over to the Philistines with the words "Do you not know that the Philistines are rulers over us?" (Judg 15:11). Samson seems to be the only Israelite who does not acquiesce in this situation.

On another level, however, Samson (the last of Israel's leaders in Judges) is symbolic of Israel in this period: he compromises his holy calling, blunders around, finds himself in difficult situations, is rescued by God, presumes on God (Judg 16:20), and is seemingly deserted by him, but not in the end abandoned. All these things are, at a different level, true of Israel. Possibly some features of Judges 13—16 arise from the narrator's desire to point to this second, symbolic level of meaning—for example, folktale elements such as a barren woman giving birth, the telling of riddles and the use of "magical" strength, which give the narrative a strangely stylized feel. This is a narrative that seems by the manner of its telling to hint that it is not to be taken at face value but rather is a kind of allegory of Israel's position before God.

3.3. Israel's Judges: Themes in the Book of Judges. The preceding section has shown how the accounts of Israel's judges are dominated by the themes of Israel's increasing unfaithfulness and distance from God. On these themes the major-judge accounts and their frames speak with one voice. In assessing Israel's judges, we must bear in mind other unifying themes that also contribute to the characterization of these figures.

3.3.1. God's Spirit and the Judges. God's spirit is said to come upon Othniel, Gideon, Jephthah and Samson to empower these judges for leadership and war (Judg 3:10; 6:34; 11:29; 13:25; 14:6, 19; 15:14); at least, what follows in the narratives of Othniel, Gideon and Jephthah is that they muster armies and fight battles, and in the Samson narrative whenever God's spirit acts on him, the effect, direct or indirect, is to stir up Philistine hostility.

Strikingly, God's spirit does not automatically bring moral transformation: Gideon is self-seeking even after Judges 6:34 (indeed, this aspect of his character emerges clearly only after this point); Jephthah, even more alarmingly, makes his vow immediately after God's spirit comes on him (Judg 11:29-31); Samson's motives are never free from lust and aggression. It is almost as though the coming of God's spirit accentuates what is in these three men's hearts, whether good or bad. Clearly, these texts reflect a complex view of divine-human interaction, one in which human beings are not simply a slate that God's spirit can "wipe clean" (see Younger, 185-87).

3.3.2. Corruption, Fragmentation: Weakness of "Charismatic" Leadership? Israel in these accounts is portrayed as increasingly fragmented and corrupt. The summary in Judges 2:6—3:6, which describes the entire period as one of decline and apostasy, at first does not seem to fit the accounts that follow (Othniel, Ehud, Barak/ Deborah), but it is increasingly validated by the later accounts.

Judges 2:16-19 explicitly links Israel's decline in this period to the character of their leadership: the judges were "charismatic" leaders, endued with power by God's spirit, often able to rally the people against their oppressors and to win striking short-term successes, but unable permanently to change the people's tendency to apostasy. This is more an indictment of the people than of the judges, and one can speculate what might have happened had the people remained faithful to God or been less consistently unfaithful. Considerations of this sort seem to lie behind Armerding's plea that "Judges, far from simply showing the weakness of the various leaders, celebrates the quality of charismatic leadership" (Armerding 174). Armerding has a point. Nonetheless, Judges clearly regards the nondynastic and usually localized leadership of the judges as inadequate to maintain the people's covenant loyalty, and the later judges clearly embody many of the failings of the people as a whole.

Almost by elimination, then, Judges may appear to lead to the conclusion that monarchy (dynastic, nationwide leadership) is the best form of leadership for Israel. Judges 17—21, in which various evils (idolatry, violence, rape, tribal disunity) are ascribed to the lack of a king (Judg 17:6; 18:1; 19:1; 21:25), certainly seems to give that impression. But these chapters, on closer examination, probably are not a blanket endorsement of monarchy (Satterthwaite), and Judges 8—9 spells out the point that some forms of monarchy can be morally and socially destructive. The book of Judges cannot simply be summed up in the slogan "judges bad, kings good" (*see* Kings and Kingship).

4. History and Chronology.

4.1. General Considerations. In working through Judges 3:7—16:31, we have explored particular historical issues, but more general questions remain to be considered. The main historical outlines of the period of the judges are clear (*see* History of Israel 2: Premonarchical Israel). The picture derived from external sources and archaeology, in which Egyptian control in Canaan came to an end in the twelfth century BCE and Philistine power grew during the twelfth and eleventh centuries BCE (see Stager, 113-28), fits with the biblical portrayal. The Philistines are first mentioned in connection with Shamgar (Judg 3:31), but they do not seem to pose a serious threat until the time of Samson (c. 1070 BCE) (on the chronology of this period see 4.2).

The same point emerges if we consider another aspect of the archaeology of the region in this period. The new settlements in the central highlands of Israel, which are such a feature from 1200 BCE on, and which may plausibly be linked with Israel's presence in Canaan (Stager, 97-104; Dever 2003, 91-128, 191-221), start to expand into the Jezreel Plain (the area near *Megiddo) in the eleventh century BCE, with a rise in total population size from an estimated fifty-five thousand to seventy-five thousand (Dever 2001, 110). The picture that emerges from these settlements is of a population with no centralized leadership (for the communities in these new settlements seem to have been egalitarian in character, with all the dwellings being roughly the same size) settling down in the land, growing in numbers over time and extending its boundaries somewhat. In broad terms this all fits with the picture in Judges, which seems to imply an expansion and consolidation of Israelite power in Canaan (see especially Judg 1; 4—5; Judg 1 is negative in tone, but it does suggest that some territorial gains were made).

But how reliable are the accounts of Israel's judges in detail? Scholars frequently attempt to address such questions using the tools of literary criticism, with the aim of disentangling earlier and perhaps genuinely historical traditions from later additions to the text that may have less claim to historical reliability. J. A. Soggin's commentary is a good example of this general approach. But if Judges is a carefully constructed literary unity (the foregoing interpretation has at least suggested how Judges may be read on this basis, though without arguing the case in detail), then it may not be susceptible to the kinds of literary probing and chronological layering favored by conventional literary criticism.

Literary coherence and polish are, of course, not the same as historical reliability. Judges may be a more unified text than has usually been argued, but is it for that reason more credible as history? A recent study by P. D. Guest argues that it is not: the very fact of Judges' literary integrity and artistry suggests that it is basically a literary creation, a piece of theologizing with only a slender basis in history (cf. Brettler, 1-8). J. M. Miller and J. H. Hayes (87-91) find that the schematic presentation of the judges accounts com-

promises them as a historical source: the individual traditions may preserve accurate memories of particular events and of the sociological and religious character of the period, but Judges as a whole cannot provide the basis for a consecutive account of the period.

However, the textual phenomena cited by these scholars—clear structure, literary skill, an obvious theological viewpoint—are perfectly compatible with serious historiographical intent, and the issue of historicity needs to be dealt with on a case-by-case basis. I have attempted to do this at appropriate points above, but one issue remains to be addressed: the chronology of the judges.

4.2. Chronology. In general, the judges seem to be presented in chronological order. Othniel, a figure from the generation after Joshua (Judg 1:11-15), comes first, and Samson, whose opponents, the Philistines, are still a threat in 1 Samuel, comes last. There are other chronological links between the accounts: Shamgar "comes after" Ehud and is described as a contemporary of Jael, hence of Deborah and Barak (Judg 3:31; 5:6); the order Gideon—Abimelech—Tola—Jair is established by links between the accounts (Judg 8:29-32; 10:1, 3), as is the order Jephthah—Ibzan-Elon-Abdon (Judg 12:8, 11, 13).

It might seem that the narrative of Judges 3:7—16:31 requires us to take each of the judges as having led Israel consecutively; that is, the Moabite oppression and Ehud's activity can only have come after the forty years of peace after Othniel's victory (Judg 3:11-15). But the introductory phrase ("the Israelites again did what was evil" [element A]) does not necessarily imply this, and such an interpretation would lead to an impossible conclusion. For if all the figures given in Judges (years of oppression, years the judges led Israel, years of peace achieved by the judges) are treated as consecutive, then the total duration of the events described in Judges is 410 years. If we accept a date of 1000 BCE for the beginning of David's reign over all Israel, which puts the beginning of Eli's leadership of Israel at about 1100 BCE, then the judges period would begin no later than 1510 BCE—impossible even for those who date the conquest to the fifteenth century BCE. But if the judges are seen as a series of local leaders, some of whom overlapped chronologically, then it is possible to telescope the period of the judges drastically (*see* Chronology).

Kitchen (204-10) follows this approach. Accepting the statements in Judges regarding which judge followed which and where each judge was active, Kitchen arrives at a regionally based chronology of the judges period in which, for instance, Othniel, Ehud and Shamgar all secured their victories within the period around 1195-1170 BCE, Deborah and Barak's victory and the forty years' peace that followed overlapped with the eighty years of peace following Ehud's victory (Judg 3:30; 5:31), and Jephthah and Samson were roughly contemporary, both of them active during Eli's leadership. That is to say, different parts of the land experienced peace and conflict at different times.

In this way Kitchen is able to fit all the events of the judges period (and those described in 1 Sam 1—12) into about 160 years, from roughly 1200 to 1042 BCE, a chronology compatible with a thirteenth-century BCE conquest. This approach can accommodate almost all the figures given in Judges. It does, however, entail interpreting the figure of three hundred years given at Judges 11:26 nonliterally, as also the figure of 480 years at 1 Kings 6:1 (on this question see Block, 59-63; Provan, Long and Longman, 162-66.)

A corollary of Kitchen's approach is that Israel in this period almost certainly had many more local leaders than are mentioned in Judges. If so, what did they do? Can their achievements have been any less significant than those of the minor judges? In which case, why were they not also included? Did the writer of Judges simply write about all those for whom he had traditions available, or were there some traditions he did not use (for whatever reason)? These are matters on which we can only speculate.

5. Conclusion.

This article focuses mainly on the accounts of Israel's judges found in the book of Judges, paying particular attention to the issues of literary coherence and historical plausibility. Clearly, many details of the narratives (e.g., the characterization of the individual judges) cannot be independently verified. How many of the details are the result of imaginative re-creation on the narrator's part is hard to say (see, e.g., the discussion of this issue in relation to the Ehud account in Alter, 37-41). In general, however, there is nothing grossly unrealistic in these narratives, except perhaps in the Samson narratives, where, as we noted (see 3.2.12), other factors may be in play.

Among the intertestamental books, Sirach 46:11-12 mentions the judges, "whose hearts did not fall into idolatry and who did not turn away from the Lord" (a charitable description in light of Gideon's and Jephthah's failings). The clearest reference in the NT is Hebrews 11:32-34 where, as part of a survey that also includes "David and Samuel and the prophets," the judges Gideon, Barak, Samson and Jephthah are cited as examples of faith, men who trusted God and were used to bring deliverance. This brief summary is not untrue but clearly it simplifies the more detailed, complex and ambiguous accounts in Judges.

See also HISTORY OF ISRAEL 2: PREMONARCHIC ISRAEL; JUDGES, BOOK OF.

BIBLIOGRAPHY. **R. Alter,** *The Art of Biblical Narrative* (New York: Basic Books, 1981); **C. Armerding,** "Judges," *NDBT* 171-76; **D. I. Block,** *Judges, Ruth* (NAC; Nashville: Broadman & Holman, 1999); **M. Z. Brettler,** *The Book of Judges* (OTR; London: Routledge, 2002); **W. G. Dever,** *What Did the Biblical Writers Know, and When Did They Know It?* (Grand Rapids: Eerdmans, 2001); idem, *Who Were the Early Israelites, and Where Did They Come From?* (Grand Rapids: Eerdmans, 2003); **P. D. Guest,** "Can Judges Survive Without Sources? Challenging the Consensus," *JSOT* 78 (1998) 43-61; **J. A. Hackett,** "'There Was No King in Israel': The Era of the Judges," in *The Oxford History of the Biblical World,* ed. M. D. Coogan (New York: Oxford University Press, 1998) 132-64; **B. Halpern,** *The First Historians: The Hebrew Bible and History* (University Park: Pennsylvania State University Press, 1996); **S. Japhet,** *I & II Chronicles* (OTL; London: SCM, 1993); **K. A. Kitchen,** *On the Reliability of the Old Testament* (Grand Rapids: Eerdmans, 2003); **A. D. H. Mayes,** *Judges* (OTG; Sheffield: JSOT, 1985); **J. M. Miller and J. H. Hayes,** *A History of Ancient Judah and Israel* (Philadelphia: Westminster, 1986) 80-119; **M. Noth,** *The Deuteronomistic History* (2nd ed.; JSOTSup 15; Sheffield: JSOT, 1991 [1943]); **I. W. Provan, V. P. Long and T. Longman III,** *A Biblical History of Israel* (Louisville: Westminster/John Knox, 2003); **P. E. Satterthwaite,** "'No King in Israel': Narrative Criticism and Judges 17-21," *TynBul* 44 (1993) 75-88; **P. E. Satterthwaite and J. G. McConville,** *Exploring the Old Testament,* 4: *The Histories* (London: SPCK; Downers Grove, IL: InterVarsity Press, 2006); **J. A. Soggin,** *Judges* (OTL; London: SCM, 1981); **L. E. Stager,** "Forging an Identity: The Emergence of Ancient Israel," in *The Oxford History of the Biblical World*, ed. M. D. Coogan (New York: Oxford University Press, 1998) 90-131; **B. G. Webb,** *The Book of the Judges: An Integrated Reading* (JSOTSup 46; Sheffield: JSOT, 1987); **G. J. Wenham,** *Story as Torah: Reading the Old Testament Ethically* (Edinburgh: T & T Clark, 2000); **K. L. Younger,** *Judges and Ruth* (NIVAC; Grand Rapids: Zondervan, 2002).

P. E. Satterthwaite

JUDGES, BOOK OF

The book of Judges is the seventh book of the OT. Named for the heroic leaders dominating its central section, it is the second "historical book" in the Christian *canon dating from the Septuagint, but also the second book of the Former Prophets in the Hebrew canon. Judges presents materials relating from the period from the death of *Joshua to shortly before the birth of *Samuel. It envisions Israel as a decentralized society composed of tribes with a mixed level of loyalty to the whole community, exposed to constant threats from surrounding nations, but ultimately also at risk of collapsing from internal deterioration. Over the political and social threats looms the darker concern for Israel's infidelity to its God, Yahweh. The precise significance of these threats, the meaning of Israel's changing community structure, and the role played by its leaders impart to the book a literary diversity deriving both from a process of composition and from the profundity of the issues engaged by the book.

1. Outline of Contents
2. Title and Place in the Canon
3. Materials and Authorship
4. Genre and Composition
5. Theological Themes

1. Outline of Contents.
As the discussion below will show, the book's structure orchestrates diverse material into a coherent literary and theological witness in the final form of the text without flattening the differences among the stories. The outline in Table 1 summarizes the major movement.

2. Title and Place in the Canon.
2.1. Title. The traditional title of Judges in English Bibles derives from the Latin Vulgate title, *Iudices,* translating the Greek *kritai,* which in turn renders the word denoting the leaders fig-

uring in the central unit of the book, the Hebrew *šōpĕṭîm*. This term derives from Judges 2:16-19, but rarely do the individuals in the narratives actually bear this title. Only Yahweh (Judg 11:27) explicitly bears the label *šōpēṭ*. The other occurrences of the root appear in finite

Table 1. Outline of Book of Judges

I. Introductory Overview: The End from the Beginning (1:1—3:6)

   A. Faltering Conquest (1:1—2:5)

   B. Fractured Covenant (2:6—3:4)

   C. Summary Assessment (3:5-6)

II. The Succession of the Judges: Dissolution (3:7—16:31)

   A. Othniel: The Exemplary Judge (3:7-11)

   B. Stage One: Triumph (3:12—5:31)

     1. Ehud the Assassin (3:12-30)

     2. Shamgar: Minor Judge, Major Achievement (3:31)

     3. Deborah the Prophet (4:1—5:31)

   C. Stage Two: Transition (6:1—10:5)

     1. Gideon: Ambiguity Embodied (6:1—8:32)

     2. Abimelech the Usurper (8:33—9:57)

     3. Minor Judges: Order Restored (10:1-5)

   D. Stage Three: Tragedy (10:6—16:31)

     1. Jephthah: A Vow Tragically Kept (10:6—12:7)

     2. Minor Judges: Measure of Mediocrity (12:8-15)

     3. Samson: A Vow Tragically Broken (13:1—16:31)

III. The Finale: A Decadent Community (17:1—21:25)

   A. Inverted War of Conquest (17:1—18:31)

   B. Inverted War of Covenant Justice (19:1—21:25)

verbal forms (Judg 3:10; 10:2, 3; 11:27, 12:7, 11, 13, 14; 15:20; 16:31) and once as the participle (Judg 4:4). For English readers, "judge" seems an imprecise title for the characters featured in Judges. Indeed, the Hebrew term designates much more than its English counterpart (*HALOT*; Mafico). The *šāpaṭ* word family exhibits four overlapping functions. First, the term denotes judicial functions: the hearing of disputes. Since ancient Israelite society was grounded in tribal and clan processes of conflict resolution, any disturbance in the community's *šālôm* required the restoration of proper relationships. Normally the responsibility of the elders, at the higher social levels such as clan and tribe, the term for this restoration of balance appears to have been the verb *šāpaṭ*. The restoration of *šālôm* involves a second nuance of *šāpaṭ*, an executive function: to intervene directly to effect justice (*see* Justice and Righteousness). Yahweh is the quintessential judge in his active intervention and constant rule in history, as is expressed in Jephthah's appeal climaxing his disputation with the king of *Ammon (Judg 11:27). Judges 2:16-19 sees the judges ideally embodying Yahweh's will and saving action. This function, designated the "undifferentiated executive," also lies behind the usage of the cognate in other Semitic languages to denote "ruler, official." Indeed, at Mari the *šāpiṭum* seems to have been a special appointee of the king empowered to conduct missions ranging from arbitration to the conduct of military campaigns (Mafico).

Two extended nuances of *šāpaṭ* appear frequently in the OT as connotations of the senses noted above. First, the acts restoring the community's balance became part of the shared heritage and values of the community, forming traditional precedents leading to the community's affirmation of a code of behavior conducive to the maintenance of community equilibrium. Thus *mišpāṭ* denotes a legal claim, a right, and metaphorically a pattern, plan or habit. In a culture such as Israel's the *šōpēṭ* therefore naturally could be expected to be a guardian of the community ethos, hence the portrayal of the *šōpēṭîm* in Judges as champions of Yahweh's will. Second, these remembered traditional standards of behavior appear not as mere human reflection, but as divine revelation, imparting religiously authoritative status to the body of received traditions and standards. The trajectory of *šāpaṭ* ultimately arrives at the emergence of literary traditions, both narrative and legal, regarded not as fossilized legal or historical ideology, but as authoritative examples of faithful behavior grounded in living community experience. The persons found in the book of Judges do reflect much of the Hebrew term's meaning, and indeed the book as sacred, canonical Scripture

might itself be a powerful embodiment of *mišpāṭ*.

2.2. Place in the Canon. The positions occupied by the book of Judges in the canons of Judaism and Christianity reveal a range of theological functions. Unlike the Christian Bible, which groups the books of Joshua, Judges, 1-2 Samuel and 1-2 Kings together with Ruth, Ezra, Nehemiah, Esther and 1-2 Chronicles as "historical books," the Hebrew Bible classifies Joshua, Judges, 1-2 Samuel and 1-2 Kings as the Former Prophets and follows them immediately with the Latter Prophets: Isaiah, Jeremiah, Ezekiel and Hosea through Malachi (the so-called twelve minor prophets). This canonical categorization intimates a function transcending antiquarian reportage. Prophecy in ancient Israel entailed a divine revelation addressing the concrete sociopolitical issues in Israel's life. At first sight, discerning a prophetic function in Joshua through Kings, especially in Judges, seems difficult. But the Former Prophets pursue relentlessly the theme of Israel's response to Yahweh's word shaping its destiny (see von Rad 1980). The Latter Prophets constitute a unified historical narrative striving not simply to inform, but to confront the reader with a proclamation of the ways of God.

The explicitly theological dimension of Joshua through Kings in general, and Judges in particular, arises directly from the compositional processes that shape the books. Contemporary scholarship almost uniformly sees Joshua through Kings as the work of writers with both historical and theological purposes inspired by the book of Deuteronomy, leading to the term *"Deuteronomistic History" to designate the whole. Several variants of this concept have appeared. M. Noth had argued for a single-historian hypothesis, but the Göttingen school advanced the notion of two or three redactions, all during the exile. English-speaking scholars have inclined toward the model advanced by F. M. Cross and by R. D. Nelson (1981a) and modified by I. Provan, that an optimistic Josianic edition of the books preceded the exilic work, and was in turn preceded by a work celebrating the reign of *Hezekiah. Whatever the model, the book of Judges occupies a crucial role in the story. The present discussion will suggest that the book substantially achieved its final form by the time of Hezekiah and formed the beginning of that stage of the larger narrative.

Scholars have long recognized a connection between the Pentateuch/Torah and the Former Prophets, summarized by terms for the Torah such as *Tetrateuch* or *Hexateuch*. One plausible view sees an early stage of the pentateuchal traditions carrying the narrative from creation to the settlement of the land (the Hexateuch), with the emerging corpus of the Former Prophets starting at the "post-Joshua" context noted in Judges 1 and culminating in the deliverance of Jerusalem from Sennacherib under Hezekiah. On this view, the emerging Torah climaxes with Israel in possession of the promised land, and the nascent Former Prophets likewise climax with the vindication of the Judean monarchy in Jerusalem under Hezekiah. The next major stage would come in the time of Josiah. The placement of the Deuteronomic law at the beginning of the historical narrative identified the law book whose discovery under Josiah climaxes this stage of the history. The conquest traditions in Joshua no longer serve as the end of the hexateuchal narrative, but rather powerfully portray Joshua as the paradigmatic successor to Moses, generating striking similarities between Joshua and Josiah (Nelson 1981b) (*see* Josiah). The emerging Torah then took the form of a "life of Moses" (the Tetrateuch), ending in a text such as Numbers 36:13 (note also the preparation for Moses' death in Num 27:12-23). The rethinking of Judean traditions about the monarchy and sanctuary forced by the destruction of Jerusalem in 587 BCE triggered another revision of the narrative that began with the conquest and culminated not in a glorious deliverance (Hezekiah), nor yet in earnest reform (Josiah), but rather in the catastrophic destruction of the city. A story ending with the loss of the land naturally begins with the winning of the land, so the tradition was divided, with Joshua as the first book of the story of how Israel forfeited Yahweh's gracious gift of the land. Reckoning Deuteronomy with the Torah allowed it to function as an authoritative summation of the whole divine revelation through Moses as well as the keynote for the material to follow in Joshua through Kings, resulting in the classical canonical division.

If this sketch is accurate, then the book of Judges functioned in at least three different contexts. In the "Hezekian" corpus Judges provided the introduction to the story of Israel in the land by highlighting how rapidly Israel fell into religious, military and social crisis, necessitating a new societal structure: the Judean monarchy, seen in its finest hour in the person of Hezekiah. With the Josianic reforms came important contextual shifts in the material. The placement of the Deuteronomic law as the introduction to the Josianic edition of the history reframed Judges. The moral causality highlighted in Judges echoed Deuteronomy's conception of retribution. The emphasis on the paradigmatic status of Joshua and Josiah throws the struggles depicted in the book of Judges into even sharper relief. The opening phrase, "After the death of Joshua," makes explicit the book's concern with succession. Joshua was the appropriate successor to Moses, but who will succeed Joshua (Judg 2:7, 10)? The answer now is not merely "the Davidic king in Jerusalem," but Josiah, the reformer. In both contexts Judges did much more than merely introduce kingship by documenting the need for a new communal structure in Israel. The book's stress on charismatic leaders presented with increasing complexity and decreasing effectiveness (note the absence of "the land had rest" in the stories coming after Gideon), and its analysis of the chaos described in Judges 17—21 (Judg 17:6, 21:25), also provide a kind of inverse job description for the king. By detailing Israel's problem, the writer establishes an agenda for the solution, a pattern for kingship. The exilic edition of the Deuteronomistic History reframed Judges yet again. Rather than ending on the note of vindication, the debacle of 587 BCE causes the stress on Israel's intransigent evil to stand unchanged by the monarchy. Judges' affirmation of the crown can no longer apply directly to any king whom Israel and Judah have known. Either the affirmation must be repudiated as false, raising the question of why the Judeans preserved the book at all after the exile, or the ancient readers projected the hope for a king expressed in Judges forward, still in search of the king implicitly called for by the dark need portrayed by Judges. Only the passing of the centuries could reveal how prophetic that projection would be.

3. Materials and Authorship.

The preceding discussion located the final edition of the book of Judges at the end of a process of compilation and structuring. The book offers the reader several clues about the process by which it came to its present shape. The most vexing dilemma in assessing Judges arises from the need to situate a search for a coherent structure amidst the book's diverse materials. The book possesses a diversity of voices, but how can it be said to project a unified vision?

3.1. The Diversity of the Book of Judges. Neither Jewish nor Christian tradition offers any guidance regarding the authorship of Judges. Readers must discern the origins of the book by investigating its internal features. The most striking feature of the book is its literary diversity. Pioneer critics of the nineteenth century such as G. L. Studer (1835) and E. Bertheau (1845) demonstrated the multilayered character of Judges and developed the essential source-critical data of Judges. The popularity of J. Wellhausen's analysis of the Pentateuch led to a reclassification of some of the data and a reformulation of the conclusions, with the 1883 revision of Bertheau's commentary and the volumes of G. F. Moore and C. F. Burney articulating the consensus. The source-critical analysis itself—that is, the partition of the text—remained largely unchanged for almost a century despite vigorous debate. The consensus identified at least three types of material in the book. Even those who dispute the "documentary" theory still acknowledge these three voices in the book.

First, all identified the critical mass of Judges in the individual narratives featuring the actions of the "major judges." These judges and texts are set out in Table 2.

Table 2. Major Judges and Texts

Othniel	3:7-11
Ehud	3:12-30
Deborah	4:1—5:31
Gideon	6:1—8:32
Jephthah	10:6—12:7
Samson	13:1—16:31

The second kind of material noted by early critics was a set of introductory and concluding formulas employing expressions and ideas also found in Judges 2:11-23 (see Table 3).

These prologues and epilogues frame the narratives so that the crisis of the story results from God's handing over Israel to an enemy because "the Israelites did what was evil in Yahweh's eyes." The oppression drives Israel to "cry out to Yahweh," who then prompts a leader to

arise and defeat the enemy. At the end of the story the epilogues indicate the defeat of the enemy and the duration of the hero's career, and in most cases they note the hero's death. Together with, and echoing the ideological introduction in Judges 2:11-23, the frameworks summarize the entire era depicted in the tradition. By the mid-1800s interpreters agreed that a compiler had gathered these diverse hero stories, composed the introduction, and created the prologues and epilogues to mesh the stories with the conception of the introduction, within which the stories functioned like slides in a slide show. Most importantly, scholars almost universally characterized the language of the introduction and of the frameworks as being derived from and imitative of Deuteronomy. Thus was born the notion of a Deuteronomistic redaction of the judges tradition.

Table 3. Introductory and Concluding Formulas

Prologue	Story	Epilogue
3:7-9a	Othniel, 3:10	3:11
3:12-14	Ehud, 3:15-30a	3:30b
4:1-2	Deborah, 4:3—5:31a	4:23-24; 5:31b
6:1-10	Gideon, 6:11—8:27	8:28-32
10:6-18	Jephthah, 11:1—12:6	12:7
13:1	Samson, 13:1—16:30	15:20; 16:31

Third, interpreters discerned what might simply be called "miscellaneous additions." These materials do not reflect, and at times actually conflict with, the framed deliverer-story pattern. Thus Judges 1:1-36 provides a report of the tribes, from south to north, in their separate efforts to gain control over their territories. Judges 17—18 depicts a Yahwistic but idolatrous shrine, the migration of the Danites, and their subsequent slaughter of the inhabitants of Laish, culminating in the establishment of a sanctuary in *Dan. Judges 19—21 depicts the brutal rape of a Levite's concubine followed by a war of tribal retribution. Judges 17—21 was universally termed "appendices," having no organic connection to the rest of the book. Beyond the fragmentary preface and appendices, interpreters found several other passages in the book that interrupted the framed hero-story pattern. First, the Abimelech story (Judg 8:33-9:57) involved no story of deliverance from a foreign foe by a charismatic hero, but rather depicted divine vengeance on a usurper and tyrant. Second, the so-called minor judge lists in Judges 10:1-5 and 12:8-15 present not spontaneously arising leaders, but an orderly succession of regional leaders. Third, Judges 16 appears composed specifically to balance Judges 14—15 in the light of Judges 13. The repeated conclusion (Judg 15:20; 16:31) offers an example of resumptive repetition, widely recognized as an ancient editorial insertion technique. In addition, Judges 14—15 presents Samson in a positive, even triumphalist, manner, celebrating his trumping of the *Philistines. Judges 14—15 never mentions the vow of Judges 13 as the source of his strength, but instead points to the onslaught of the spirit of Yahweh, coming to a climax with Samson's triumphant prayer for deliverance. Judges 16 presents a negative view of Samson in which the spirit plays no role but the vow is decisive. The chapter ends with a prayer for vengeance whose answer leads to Samson's death. Not only does Judges 16 differ from Judges 14—15, but also it offers a contrapuntal commentary on these chapters. Thus most scholars regard it as entering the tradition, perhaps with Judges 13 as well, after the creation of the framed hero-story collection. Fourth, three passages, Judges 2:1-5; 6:7-10; 10:10-16, offer theological commentary diverging from the frameworks as well as the narratives. Indeed, Judges 6:7-10 is lacking in the Qumran fragment 4QJudg[a], and the MT features an editorial resumptive repetition in Judges 6:6b-7a. These "miscellaneous" passages interrupt the series of framed Deuteronomistic hero stories. Moreover, Judges 1:1—2:5 appears between two literarily interdependent accounts of the death of Joshua (Josh 24:29-33; Judg 2:6-10), likely yet another example of resumptive repetition. Thus exegetes tend to speak of a Deuteronomistically edited deliverer narrative into which these "miscellaneous additions" were clumsily inserted, breaking up the unity of the former work.

We have noted developments in the theory of a Deuteronomistic History (see 2.2 above). Theories of multiple editions of the Deuteronomistic History combined with the assumption that part of Judges is Deuteronomistic introduced confusion into the study of Judges. First, the

original elegance of Noth's vision of a single mind conceiving and executing the Deuteronomistic History slipped away as subsequent analysis perceived multiple Deuteronomistic voices within the book itself. The work of W. Richter became especially important, although his analysis seems overly refined. More importantly, scholars after Noth began to enlarge the concept of Deuteronomistic ideology. No one prior to Noth considered the "miscellaneous additions" to Judges Deuteronomistic, because of the mountain of linguistic, stylistic and content divergences found in these materials. However, a good many scholars in the 1970s to 1990s reclassified these texts as Deuteronomistic (Boling; Peckham; Veijola; Soggin; Gerbrandt; Halpern; Mullen). Clearly, the concern for discerning a unity of vision in the book was asserting itself, even if in an untenable "pan-Deuteronomism."

3.2. Judges as an Authorial Unity. Alongside arguments for a compositional process, a steady minority voice argues for Judges resulting from a largely discrete, unitary authorial act (Cassel; Bachmann; Keil; Bush; Manley; Lilley; Cundall; Gooding; Block). The case for unitary authorship claims a level of structural and thematic coherence in the book of intricate consistency and subtlety, such as a fourteen-layered chiastic structure (Gooding). Such structures are considered beyond the reach of an ancient editor working with preexisting literary materials. Ultimately, these arguments proved as speculative and subjective as the source theories, and they failed to dislodge the argument that the book emerged from a process of compilation involving diverse materials.

The impasse reached by author-oriented interpretations makes a solely reader-referenced analysis of the book tempting. Many recent interpreters claim neither one nor many authors, but assert instead the autonomous reader as a maker of meanings and, indeed, a maker of texts. K. R. R. Gros Louis's 1974 essay offered a new critical reading, and as new literary methods have emerged, new literary analyses have appeared. B. G. Webb's "integrated reading" represents the new critical approach as well. R. Polzin provided a structuralist analysis, while L. Klein employed irony to the point of hermeneutical self-immolation for understanding the inner tensions of the book (see Stone 1991b). Increasingly, rhetorical criticism, with its attendant interest in ideological perspectives, has influenced literary reading. Concern for *women in the book especially has dominated recent literary analysis, as seen in the work of P. Trible and of M. Bal, and in the essays compiled in volumes edited by G. A. Yee and by A. Brenner. J. C. Exum's numerous articles on Judges provide a thorough orientation to this mode of interpretation by a reader of formidable insight. The fruit of this whole tradition of reading appears in the commentary of T. J. Schneider. Few would question that scores of penetrating insights into the text have accompanied these analyses. Still, this question remains: will the abandonment of any author-centered theory of composition facilitate a more integrated approach to a book as diverse as Judges?

3.3. Judges as an Editorial Unity. Interpretation need not remain in a sterile, either-or impasse. Recent research seems to have taken a clue from the suggestive essay by M. Buber to describe the compositional development of Judges in a way that meaningfully accounts for the text in its final form (Stone 1988; Brensinger; O'Connell; Amit; Olson). The method involves a redaction criticism that is acutely aware of how editorial shaping affects the way the finished work is read—that is, it is both diachronic and synchronic (Stone 1997). Y. Amit recharacterizes redaction as a genuine form of literary art, not merely a cut-and-paste operation. Still, one misses the sense of redaction as the transformation of tradition via recontextualization over time, a sense gained from form-critical work for what G. von Rad would have called *Vergegenwärtigung* ("actualization"). From the literary side, the massive and learned study of R. H. O'Connell advances a rhetorical analysis of Judges' present form in constant interaction with proposals for the book's editorial development. Again, we miss the sense of Judges as an inheritance, a tradition received, appropriated and passed on for the next generation. Perhaps the absence of a comprehensive form-critical commentary on Judges has hurt the discipline more than has been imagined. Indeed, it seems impossible to account for the book's literary development as long as interpreters ignore its salient literary qualities.

4. Genre and Composition.

A need remains to determine whether and how the diverse voices in Judges express a coherent compositional vision. Two steps will enable a clearer, richer reading of Judges. First, interpreters should see the final additions to the book as a potentially significant editorial contribution, rather than merely try to prove that the additions are Deuteronomistic. Surely, the insertion of what amounts to 45 percent of the material in the book constitutes a massive recontextualization of the framed deliverance narratives. However, a deeper question also has been missed. In studying material from antiquity, we must always ask, "Why was this material preserved in the first place?" And with Judges, the question is not simply one of preservation but of a persistent reappropriation and recontextualization. Why did this material receive such devoted attention? What was the energy in the tradition that summoned such a response? The peculiar relationship between literature and the community that treasures it normally is captured in the notion of genre. More than merely a literary pattern with a tag, genre gets at the *performative* function that a tradition exercises for its audiences.

All questions of genre in Judges start with the stories about the deliverers. Whatever drove the development of the book of Judges into its final form centered on the role of these remarkable, irascible individuals. Von Rad provided the best lead when he compared the Gideon story with the Succession Narrative and characterized the former as "hero saga." Fortunately, heroic literature is well known from antiquity and has been studied extensively. For the present, we leave aside the approach represented by J. Campbell that sees the hero as a universal human archetype manifested in every religion and literary tradition. More progress will derive from analyzing its features as a type of ancient literature. The ancestral home of such work is the Homeric literature begun by H. M. Chadwick and advanced, in varying ways, by C. H. Whitman, C. M. Bowra and D. A. Miller. Even here, the technical study of the devices and techniques of ancient oral singers need not divert readers from discerning the essential features of heroic literature (Kramer; Gordon; Armerding). The work of G. Steiner, to which we now turn, summarizes this line of analysis in several articles and provides a helpful framework for analyzing Judges.

4.1. The Voice of Remembrance and Celebration. The first voice in the development of Judges was one that simply told the stories of the deliverers, the heroes. The dimensions of the heroic observed in the Homeric materials also mark these narratives. First and foremost, this literature celebrates the exploits of an outstanding individual. Physicality, often virtuosic, becomes the idiom of excellence. Whether handsome or ugly, heroes are never common. The eccentricities of the characters in Judges come immediately to mind. Of course, it is the exploits, the heroic deeds, invariably the violence of these characters that occupy the center of attention, and these deeds are narrated with delicious detail. Steiner describes the mood of heroic literature:

> But one thing is clear; the *Iliad* expresses a specific view of the human condition. . . . The poet revels in the gusto of physical action and in the stylish ferocity of personal combat. He sees life lit by the fires of some central, ineradicable energy. The air seems to vibrate around the heroic personages, and the force of their being electrifies nature. . . . Even insensate objects are kindled by this excess of life. (Steiner 1962, 8)

Such gusto, such remorseless exaltation of the violent, whether by Achilles or in the Song of Deborah, scandalizes the domestic sensibility of later readers. Jael's dispatch of Sisera, whether presented in the ruthless prose of Judges 4 or the brutal poetic economy of Judges 5:24-27, confronts the reader sharply with a vision of life in which honor, valor and a noble death count for more than mere comfort or longevity. Steiner describes this attitude:

> There is joy in it, the joy that burns in the "ancient glittering eyes." . . . There is cruelty . . . and a sheer redness of slaughter. But even in the midst of carnage, life is in full tide and beats forward with a wild gaiety. Homer knows and proclaims that there is that in men which loves war, which is less afraid of the terrors of combat than of the long boredom of the hearth. . . . [The narrator] looks on life with those blank, unswerving eyes which stare out of the helmet slits on early Greek vases. His vision is terrifying in its sobriety, cold as the winter sun. (Steiner 1962, 8-9)

Deborah would agree that those who love Yahweh will "shine like the [winter?] sun in its strength" (Judg 5:31).

4.2. The Voice of Emerging Order. A notable feature of heroic literature is that later generations develop a disquiet with the unreflective exuberance of it. "Heroic ages" typically occur in liminal periods when one social model has collapsed and another is emerging, such as we see precisely in the book of Judges (Whitman; Steiner 1962). The heroic narrator knows already that "a world is passing away, [enemies] . . . are massing on the borders to attack, and there is no lord or hero to rally the defense" (Heaney, xxvii). S. Heaney's words aptly summarize Judges 17 through 1 Samuel 12. Societies must decide what to do with their triumphant warriors and the value system that they embody. And yet, notwithstanding their restless, de-centering energy, can a society simply dispose of its heroes and their inspiring valor? Judges laments the rise of a generation of Israelites who did not know war and thus did not know how Yahweh could act on their behalf (Judg 2:10; 3:1-2).

So the voice of remembrance and celebration could not speak definitively for Israel. Apparently, Israel felt the need to preserve the memory of these persons and their achievements. Therefore, the second voice in Judges may be designated "the moralist." Speaking for a higher level of social organization, the moralist editor preserves intact the dynamism of the hero stories while also channeling and directing it. The literary strategy of the introduction and framework achieves precisely this effect. First, the moralist voice imposes an appearance of regularity on an otherwise diverse group of leaders. The unruliness of the individual is subordinated to a pattern, an "office." Second, this voice speaks with a theological inflection, linking the need for the heroes to Israel's sin. Third, the moralist voice presents the heroes in Judges 2:16-19 as exercising a religious influence. Fourth, the frameworks, with their chronological notices, serialize the hero stories, placing events that probably transpired contemporaneously into a linear series. The effect here is to dole out the heroes one at a time, one per generation, rather than depict Israel crawling with droves of berserkers and Nazirite wild-men. By carefully shaping these frameworks and how they resonate with the preface, the compiler powerfully reshapes the reader's perception of the heroes.

Contrary to conventional interpretation, the narrative thus created does not present a precise, recurring "cycle." First of all, elements appear in the stories that do not appear in the introduction, and vice versa. The introduction tells us that Yahweh "raised up" deliverers, but only Othniel and Ehud are said to be "raised up" by Yahweh. Other means of manifestation appear for subsequent judges, raising the intriguing question of their status. Likewise, the outcry probably does not imply repentance—a point increasingly recognized by commentators. The terminology used is simply the cry of alarm or terror. Additionally, the spirit of Yahweh plays a role in the stories but has no place in the introduction or the frameworks. Ironically, the spirit plays no role in the stories of Ehud and of Deborah, the two most exemplary and effective judges. By contrast, the spirit's involvement with Gideon, Jephthah and Samson raises more questions than it answers, directly preceding Jephathah's vow and Samson's violation of certain provisions of his Nazirite vow. Far from a cycle that mechanically repeats, the text presents a collection of features and formulas that are deployed in telling ways. Their regular recurrence makes the reader look for them, but their variation directs the reader's attention to the larger value structure of the narrative.

Was the moralist a Deuteronomistic editor? With few exceptions (Burney; Greenspahn), most scholars answer in the affirmative. Yet the classic markers of Deuteronomistic theology are lacking. The writer expresses no urge toward the centralization of worship as the result of the land resting, which, by contrast, is a central theme of Deuteronomistic theology. The crucial role of Yahweh, like a conqueror of old, setting up his memorial "name" in a specific, elect place within the land, so prominent in Deuteronomy (S. Richter), is starkly absent from Judges. Nor do we find concern for Yahweh's *torah* as a concrete text, whereas Deuteronomy is the most literarily self-aware book in the Torah. Indeed, Judges shows very little overt or self-conscious concern with the covenant. The term *covenant* appears only four times in the book, and never with its Deuteronomic nuance. Again, Judges displays no sustained interest in *prophecy on the model of Deuteronomy. An unknown prophet speaks in Judges 6:7-10, and Deborah is said simply to be a prophet, but otherwise we miss the correlation of prophecy with fulfillment that is urged by Deuteronomy and is so characteristic of 1-2 Kings. Furthermore, Deuteronomy strongly identifies Levites with priests (*see* Priests and Levites). While Judges 17—18 recognizes a certain preference for Levites as priests, Judges as a whole shows no interest in the exclusive legitimacy of the Levite in the priestly service, nor in the unique priestly vocation of the Levites. Judges 19—21 features a Levite without once implying any cultic functions for him. Again, Judges lacks the supremely distinctive demand of Deuteronomy and its derivatives: to "love" Yahweh. Finally, although Judges 18:30 possibly hints at the destruction of the north in 721 BCE or even the earlier depredations of 732 BCE, the book betrays no sign of the body blow to Hebrew faith of 587 BCE, around which the Deuteronomistic theological writers rallied. These are, admittedly, arguments from absence; nonetheless, the absences here are pregnant. One "presence" in Judges that is alien to Deuteronomy is the role of charismatic leadership. Deuteronomy has all the appearances of a constitutional document (McBride). It envisions an ordered community in which leaders occupy "offices" as extensions of the authority of Moses and signs of the moral government of Yahweh. Nothing in Deuteronomy prepares one for the charismatic, heroic figures of the book of Judges, who lack either institutional precedent or successors.

That said, some features of Judges do prompt an over-the-shoulder look at Deuteronomy. The notion of moral causality found in the frameworks is not exclusive Deuteronomic property, but certainly it is comfortably so. Again, the militant hostility of Deuteronomy toward non-Israelite culture and religion is clearly expressed in the frameworks and introduction, even if often it is lacking in the stories themselves. Likewise, Deuteronomy envisions Israel not mainly as twelve discrete tribes but rather as one large tribe. All Israelites are "kinsfolk," and Deuteronomy ignores the tribal divisions except for its provisions concerning the Levites and the blessing of Moses (*see* Tribes of Israel and Land Allotments/Borders). One of the primary emphases of the moralist voice in Judges is its desire to recontextualize the local heroes so that each now serves the whole nation for a generation. Finally, both Deuteronomy and Judges have a programmatic concern for leadership. The opening question of Judges, "Who shall go up first for us?" (Judg 1:1), and its echo in the book's final story (Judg 20:18), clearly express concern for leadership.

Thus the minority, represented by Burney, seems to be correct. In a penetrating analysis of the introduction and frameworks, Burney showed in detail that their language, style and theological concerns were at best proto-Deuteronomistic, but still not fully so (Burney, xli-l). Somewhat like the conquest traditions in Joshua, the heroic tradition was becoming a past unusable in its unbuffered form (Stone 1991a), and it required transposition into another key in order to serve the community.

4.3. The Voice of the Monarchy. The final stage of the growth of the book of Judges includes the materials, noted previously, designated by most scholars as supplementary. Recent research has argued, however, that "the materials of Judges generally relegated to the final stage of redaction . . . should be seen as part of a deliberate and coherent redactional programme designed to bring the previous form of the Judges into line with the promonarchical and pro-Judahite perspective" (O'Connell, 365-66). The details of the analysis can be summarized by observing how the last additions affect the flow of the book and reshape the heroic tradition.

First, the addition of Judges 1:1—2:5 provides the book with a new introduction. This passage starts with the death of Joshua and then lists the tribes from Judah in the south to Dan (ultimately) in the far north, and the order is clearly from success, through qualified success, through substantial failure, to abject failure, culminating in Yahweh's word of judgment canceling the conquest (Judg 2:1-5). This structure parallels the moralizing introduction (Judg 2:6—3:4), which also starts with Joshua's death, noting the faithfulness and success of one group, here defined generationally rather than geographically, then passing to a series of failures culminating in Yahweh's cancellation of the conquest. Thus the book now has a dual preface, one military, the other theological in emphasis, depicting the dialectical relationship between failure and faithlessness. The important point is the stress placed on the success of Judah in Judges 1, which is paralleled to the faithfulness of the generation surviving Joshua in Judges 2.

Next, the Othniel story (Judg 3:7-11) was seen by W. Richter to contain elements from the stories, from the frameworks and from the introduction, suggesting that the last editor placed it to serve as an exemplary passage, a scorecard, for assessing the rest of the narratives (Olson, 766-68). Othniel is a southern judge, the only one, and represents an ideal pattern. The story also lacks all signs of the heroic tradition, with no circumstantial narrative, only a notice. The Othniel story affords readers an important tool

for analyzing the book. Many interpreters have claimed that the book represents a decline from Othniel to Samson, but typically the decline is seen in terms of standards that are not immanent in the text. But with the Othniel story as the scorecard, comparison of each story with it provides a text-immanent standard for mapping precisely the evaluation of each story.

The comparison yields precisely that decline, though in ways that are unsettling. First, the "doing evil in Yahweh's eyes" is steadily more detailed as the book progresses (Judg 3:7, 12; 4:1; 6:1; 10:6; 13:1). Oddly enough, the formula "the children of Israel *continued* to do evil in Yahweh's eyes" does not occur in Judges 6:1; rather, the text reads only "did evil," as though a new start is in view. Second, the oppressions become more severe, as witnessed either in more circumstantial descriptions (Judg 4:1-3; 6:1-6) or in actual historical severity (Judg 10:7-16; 13:1). Third, the outcry becomes problematic. In the Othniel and Ehud stories (Judg 3:9; 4:3) the outcry of Israel immediately leads to the appearance of the savior. With Gideon, however, the outcry leads not to the rise of a savior, but to a bitter prophetic rebuke upon which the narrative of Gideon's call follows directly (Judg 6:6b-10). Thus the call of Gideon stands under something of a question mark. In the Jephthah story, Israel's outcry leads to Yahweh's refusal to deliver them and his referral of them to the gods that they have chosen (Judg 10:10-14). The enigmatic statement in Judges 10:16b, literally translated "Yahweh's soul became short at Israel's toil," seen in the light of the identical expression used for Samson's yielding to Delilah (Judg 16:16), suggests not reconciliation, but a final break. Thus the career of Jephthah might not reflect Yahweh's direct provision of a savior at all. In the Samson story we find no outcry: Israel falls silent before its offended Lord.

Fourth, the hero stories grow in biographical complexity through the book. Little is said of Ehud or Deborah, but with Gideon a call narrative and a long series of preparatory episodes (Judg 6:11—7:14) lead up to the deliverance story. The Jephthah narrative features a brief biography of Jephthah and a report not of his divine election, but rather of a hard-nosed negotiation with his tribesmen. In the case of Samson, we encounter a full birth narrative (Judg 13:1-24). This increasing biographical complexity correlates with the decline through the series of

Table 4. Declining Outcomes Under Judges

Person or Group	Oppression	Rest/Judge	Reference
Oppression under Cushan-Rishathaim	8		Judg 3:8
Peace under Othniel		40	Judg 3:11
Oppression under Eglon	18		Judg 3:14
Peace with Ehud		80	Judg 3:30
Oppression under Jabin	20		Judg 4:3
Peace after Deborah		40	Judg 5:31
Oppression under Midianites	7		Judg 6:1
Peace with Gideon		40	Judg 8:28
Rule of Abimelech		3	Judg 9:22
Judgeship of Tola		23	Judg 10:2
Judgeship of Jair		22	Judg 10:3
Oppression under Ammonites	18		Judg 10:8
Judgeship of Jephthah		6	Judg 12:7
Judgeship of Ibzan		7	Judg 12:9
Judgeship of Elon		10	Judg 12:11
Judgeship of Abdon		8	Judg 12:14
Oppression under Philistines	40		Judg 13:1
Judgeship of Samson		20	Judg 15:20; 16:31
Totals	111 years	299 years	
Grand Total	410 years		

heroes, generating a subtle critique of the underlying individualism of the heroic tradition. The more we learn of the heroes as individuals, the less we like them. More disturbingly, the spirit of Yahweh becomes more prominent toward the end of the series, suggesting a reservation about this particular manifestation of divine power (Judg 3:10; 6:34; 11:29; 13:25; 14:6, 19; 15:14). Moreover, the text says that the spirit "began to pound" *(wattāḥel . . . lĕpaʿămô)* Samson (Judg 13:25), the latter verb customarily being reserved for descriptions of mental states for nightmares! The critique of the charismatic, though subtle, is pervasive.

Fifth, the outcome of the heroes' activity is less obviously positive. The text notes that "the land had rest" after Othniel, Ehud, Deborah and Gideon (Judg 3:11, 30; 5:31; 8:28), but with Jephthah and Samson a change appears: the text reports only "he judged . . ." (Judg 12:7; 15:20; 16:31). Given the Othniel account as the standard, the absence of the land's resting constitutes a negative judgment on Jephthah and Samson. In addition, the chronological material reinforces this impression. The raw data can be presented thus as in Table 4.

Although many controversies surround the chronology in Judges, its thematic function emerges clearly. In the cases of Othniel, Ehud, Deborah and Gideon, the time of rest is a *multiple* of the years of oppression, but the careers of Jephthah and Samson are fractions. Taken together, these literary moves segment the hero stories into three units: triumphant leaders (Ehud and Deborah), transitional leaders (Gideon and Abimelech), tragic leaders (Jephthah and Samson). The role of the Ephraimites in battle provides a simple indicator of the movement through these three sections. Ehud rallies the Ephraimites to victory at the fords of Jordan (Judg 3:27-29), but Gideon barely avoids conflict with the envious Ephraimites, also at the crossing of Jordan (Judg 7:24—8:3). Jephthah insults them and slaughters a reported forty-two thousand, again, at the fords of Jordan (Judg 12:1-6). The presentation of a decline is captured also by comparing the end of the dual introduction, Judges 3:5-6, with the end of the series of heroes. Judges 3:5-6 states that as a result of the Israelites' apostasy and decline, they intermarry with non-Israelites and "serve their gods." This is precisely what the reader encounters in the story of Samson, who lives for his liaisons with non-Israelite women and who dies in a pagan festival.

The last stage of redaction also saw the introduction of material into the very center of the framed stories: the Abimelech story. In some ways, the story loosely follows the cyclical pattern: Israel sins (Judg 8:33-35), and an oppressor arises and is destroyed (Judg 9:1-57). The story of Abimelech is a devastating critique of usurpers, pretender kings who seize power by violent elimination of the legitimate successors. The question of dynasty also evokes Judges 8:22-27, where Gideon is thought to reject kingship. But a close reading shows that the terminology of kingship *(mlk)* is absent from the story, hence any critique of kingship is diverted. Moreover, Gideon's rejection of hereditary rule leads directly to Israel "playing the harlot" and plunging into apostasy. Thus the Abimelech story injects into the narrative a concern for legitimate dynastic rule as the alternative to "playing the harlot" and experiencing oppressive tyranny. Thus the final editor's work in the center of the book points toward monarchy.

Finally, the "appendices" present the ultimate outcome of rule by the judges. Both narratives in Judges 17—21 present a critique of premonarchical Israel and intimate the superiority of the southern monarchy. Judges 17—18 portrays both the making of an image of Yahweh and an inverted or perverted conquest (Malamat). The overall story also mounts a scathing critique of the northern kingdom monarchy and cult (Noth). Likewise, the scandalous narrative of Judges 19—21 links the horrific events at Gibeah and the consequent intertribal war of retribution with clear allusions to Saul and the northern monarchy (Brettler 1989). Far from being a mere appendix, these admittedly distinct materials have been joined by the editor to the rest of the book by means of several important editorial features. First, the central section's recurring "did what was evil in the eyes of Yahweh" finds an idiomatic parallel with the darker anarchy of "all the people did what was right in their own eyes" (Judg 17:6; 21:25). The construal of the expression in Judges 17:6; 21:25 as anarchic, arrogant self-will is anticipated when Samson rebuffs his parents' objections to his Philistine fiancée by insisting, "She is right *[yšr]* in my eyes" (Judg 14:3). In Judges 17—21 all Israel becomes like Samson. Second, against the central section of the book's presentation of the heroes, Judges 17—21 juxtaposes its own statement about leadership, "There was no

king in Israel" (Judg 17:6; 18:1; 19:1; 21:25), resonating with the dynastic concerns of the Abimelech account. Third, Brettler (1989) has demonstrated an oblique but pervasive anti-Saul/pro-David disposition in Judges 19—21. Fourth, the editor employs the connective "in those days" *(bayyāmîm hāhēm)*. This formula is an editorial device by which a writer presents two blocks of chronologically unrelated material as though they were synchronous, for the purpose of explicit comparison. The comparable Akkadian term *inūmīšu*, "in those days," in its several contracted and dialectal forms came to be employed by neo-Assyrian scribes in the editing of royal annals. As that literary genre developed, the phrase came to be used when the editor inserted sections out of strict chronological sequence in order to juxtapose materials for thematic purposes (Grayson 1980; 1981). Seen in the framework of ancient editorial practice, Judges 17—21 functions as an analysis of the period. Finally, the synchronic chronological notice "in those days" contrasts with the rigorously diachronic chronology of the central section, suggesting an end position or negative climax.

So how does the monarchist voice nuance or reframe the heroic elements of the material? The answer is facilitated by our taking a brief return to the larger heroic tradition, particularly Homer. Homeric scholars have long noted that the *Odyssey* reflects very different values than those of the *Iliad*. The final slaughter of the suitors by Odysseus emphasizes that the tale still moves in the realm of the heroic, but in the *Odyssey* the classical heroic ideals come into question. The most dramatic critique of the heroic ideal occurs when Odysseus encounters the shade of Achilles in the realm of the glorified dead. Achilles, rather than rejoicing in his prominence among the dead due to his heroic exploits, grieves that he died before seeing his son grow into manhood. Odysseus urges Achilles to affirm the classic heroic vision and "grieve no more." In response to this plea Achilles gives a poignant and searching answer:

No winning words about death to me,
  shining Odysseus!
By god, I'd rather slave on earth for another
  man—
Some dirt-poor tenant farmer who scrapes
  to keep alive—

Than rule down here over all the breathless dead

But come, tell me the news about my gallant son. (Homer *Odyssey* 11.487-92)

In a stroke, Achilles repudiates the very essence of the heroic values celebrated in the *Iliad*. Steiner observes,

There is in the Odyssey a critique of the archaic values of the *Iliad* in the light of new energies and perceptions. . . . The *Iliad* has the ruthlessness of the young. . . . Odysseus marks a transition from the simplicities of the heroic to a life of the mind more skeptical, more nervous, more wary of conviction. . . . [H]e looked back to the *Iliad* across a wide distance of the soul—with a nostalgia of smiling doubt. (Steiner 1962, 14)

Steiner's final comment provides an apt characterization also of the final edition of Judges. Where the moralist voice sought, on behalf of the community, to channel and direct the vagrant energies of the heroic tradition, the voice of the monarchist stands for orderly government and domestic tranquility. Such a vision cannot tolerate "all the people doing what is right in their own eyes." The reader, however, venerates the heroic tradition, and the advocate of the monarchy recognizes that such veneration necessitates a demonstration of the ultimate inadequacy of this ideal. The editor achieves this de-centering of the heroic ideal by framing it as something that worked in its own era but ultimately failed and had to be replaced by something else: the Judean, Davidic monarchy. The effect is best seen by juxtaposing the two basic movements of the "main body" of Judges and the "appendices." For the moralist, the problem in Israel is that people "did what was evil in the eyes of Yahweh"; for the monarchist, the problem is "all the people did what was right in their own eyes." For the final editor, there lay beneath Israel's propensity to sin against Yahweh something even deeper: an arrogant anarchism that sets itself up as its own standard for what is right. Similarly, for the moralist voice, the consequence of Israel's evil against Yahweh is oppression by foreign power, but for the final editor, arrogant self-will is capable of destroying Israel just as thoroughly. Indeed, Israel emerges in these last chapters as its own worst enemy. Finally, for the earlier tradition, the heroes appeared as the solution to Israel's leadership need, but the final editor has structured the material to point out how the heroes ultimately failed to enable an orderly community, and now the absence of a king is noted. Perhaps the editor, pondering the moral anarchy of self-will, calls the reader to consider who indeed will deliver Israel from that. In so doing, the writer implicitly states the role of the king. Where is the king who will save Israel from itself?

5. Theological Themes.

Judges provides rich material for theological reflection, though not for the faint of heart. Judges concerns itself with a pivotal matter faced by early Israel: the nature of the community of faith. Should Israel have continued as a confederation of tribes led by charismatic leaders, or was the bold step toward national statehood and kingship indeed the correct move? Readers in the eighth century BCE also debated whether the southern monarchy of a single (Davidic) dynasty was superior to the charismatic approach to kingship taken in the northern kingdom. Was the northern way closer to Israel's ancient ideal and more faithful to the covenant?

The author answers the question by exploring Israel's spiritual fortunes during the period of the tribal confederacy, analyzing Israel's evil and examining two solutions. Clearly, the book views the time of the tribal confederacy as spiritually disastrous. Judges asserts right from its opening chapters the failure of the Hebrews to build faithfully on the achievements of Joshua and the faithful conquest generation. The central section (Judg 3:7—16:31) then depicts their faithlessness as inexorably increasing apostasy: Israel "does what is evil in the eyes of the LORD." Then the final section (Judg 17:1—21:25) probes more deeply, finding the roots of apostasy in an intransigent, imploded self-will by which "all the people did what was right in their own eyes" (Judg 17:6; 21:25). Thus Judges 17—21 climaxes the process of deterioration narrated in Judges 3:7—16:31, but also it provides the Q.E.D. to the thesis advanced in Judges 1:1—3:6. Judges 17—18 resumes the narrative that broke off in Judges 1:34-35 and depicts the only "conquest" of which the Danites were capable, while Judges 19—21 depicts an outrageous breach in the covenant community matching the covenant-breaking in Judges 2:6—3:6.

The book also traces the consequences of Israel's sinfulness. Apostasy brings ever more grave foreign oppressions, but more pervasive as the book unfolds its story is the collapse of the covenant community and the metamorphosis of its sacred traditions from blessings into curses. Tribal discord increases, political crises grow in gravity, Israel's "saviors" become increasingly monstrous (Jephthah) or tragic (Samson). The divine voice becomes increasingly strident in its condemnation (Judg 6:7-10; 10:11-14). Ultimately, even the wind of the spirit seems transformed into a dust devil driving the self-willed Samson over the precipice. In Judges 17—21 Israel's inner collapse comes to the center. The Danites despoil their kin (Judg 17—18) before massacring Laish, and united Israel, exercising "covenant community justice," slaughters more of its own than any foreign foe ever did (Judg 19—21). The external oppressors of Judges 3—16 vanish in Judges 17—21 before an Israel fully capable of destroying itself.

Finally, Judges explores solutions to Israel's woes. In Judges 3—16 the spirit-driven "charismatic" appears ultimately impotent to save Israel. The judges come to represent the very forces threatening Israel. Occasional onrushes of the spirit's power have no impact on the downward spiral, and, in the cases of Jephthah and Samson, even appear to accelerate it. Israel's faithlessness arises from a madness deep in the nation's heart and cannot be dislodged by a tour de force of the spirit. In contrast to the ecstatic-charismatic "power" approach to leadership embodied in the central section of the book, Judges 17—21 insinuates an alternative: kingship. "In those days there was no king in Israel: all the people did what was right in their own eyes." The writer envisions not simply a perpetual, inherited "office" of judge as hoped for by the elders of Israel (Judg 8:21-22), still less a usurper-tyrant such as Abimelech (Judg 9). This king must confront Israel's relentless idolatry, its penchant for self-destruction, and most of all its case-hardened, arrogant self-will. The true task of the king is to save Israel from its most dangerous foe: itself. Israel's destiny depends not on power, but on character. The advocacy of kingship in Judges 17—21 reinforces the glorification of Judah in Judges 1 and offers a fundamental witness to the primacy of the spiritual and moral dimensions of kingship—messiahship—in Israel.

Christian interpretation of Judges of necessity pushes past the OT context of the book and seeks a responsible correlation of the book's themes with the realities proclaimed by the NT.

The presentation of Israel's evil in Judges complements that offered in the NT, which often probes beneath sin as a disobedient act to the underlying sin of willful human arrogance. The NT also depicts sin's consequences both objectively, as bondage to oppressive principalities and powers beyond the person, and subjectively, as moral impotence and disintegration "in the flesh," emphasizing the self-destructive propensity of sinful, godless, self-imploded humanity. Judges portrays a community embodiment of the anguished, frustrated impotence of bondage to sin as Paul describes in Romans 7. Christian theology has classically understood sin as far more than mere juridical or forensic guilt before God; it also has stressed the human predicament of imprisonment in self-will, broken only by the hallowing grace of God. To the extent that Judges depicts the ravages of self-will gone amuck in the community of faith, it portrays that carnality which threatens the very fulfillment of the divine promises.

Unexpectedly, the solution to human depravity proffered in Judges is not the spirit of God. In Judges the occasional *afflatus* of the spirit is itself diverted and perverted as Israel falls under the weight of its own corruption. Instead, the writer calls for an authority to resist each person's doing "what is right in their own eyes." A spirit-impelled Samson is a disaster not for lacking propulsion, but direction. Israel must itself be mastered before its power can redeem. Hence comes the call for a king and the essential OT linkage of kingship with national religious fidelity (*see* Kings and Kingship). Likewise, in the NT the emphasis on the moral and spiritual dimensions of the kingdom of God, with its demand that the disciple of Christ deny self and take up the cross, always informs and fully controls its statements about the believer and the Holy Spirit. Thus the unknown author of Judges would affirm with the NT that charisma, when devoid of character, corrupts.

See also AMPHICTYONY, QUESTION OF; HISTORY OF ISRAEL 2: PREMONARCHIC ISRAEL; JUDGES; NARRATIVE ART OF ISRAEL'S HISTORIANS.

BIBLIOGRAPHY. *Commentaries:* A. G. Auld, *Joshua, Judges, and Ruth* (DSB; Philadelphia: Westminster, 1984); **J. Bachmann,** *Das Buch der Richter: Mit besonderer Rücksicht auf die Geschichte seiner Auslegung und kirchlichen Verwendung* (Berlin: Wiegandt and Grieben, 1868); **D. I. Block,** *Judges, Ruth* (NAC; Broadman & Holman, 2002);

R. Boling, *Judges* (AB 6A; Garden City, NY: Doubleday, 1975); **T. Brensinger,** *Judges* (BCC; Scottsdale, PA: Herald, 1999); **C. F. Burney,** *The Book of Judges, with Introduction and Notes* (2d ed.; London: Rivingtons, 1920); **G. Bush,** *Notes, Critical and Practical, on the Book of Judges, Designed as a General Help to Biblical Reading and Instruction* (New York: Saxton, Pierce, 1844); **P. Cassel,** *The Book of Judges* (New York: Scribner, 1872 [1865]); **A. Cundall,** *Judges* (TOTC; Downers Grove, IL: InterVarsity Press, 1968); **K. F. Keil and F. Delitzsch,** *Joshua, Judges, Ruth* (Edinburgh: T & T Clark, 1865; repr., Grand Rapids: Eerdmans, 1978); **G. F. Moore,** *A Critical and Exegetical Commentary on Judges* (ICC; Edinburgh: T & T Clark, 1895); **D. T. Olson,** "The Book of Judges," *NIB* 2:723-888; **T. J. Schneider,** *Judges* (Berit Olam; Collegeville, MN: Liturgical Press, 2000); **J. A. Soggin,** *Judges* (OTL; Philadelphia: Westminster, 1981); **G. L. Studer,** *Das Buch der Richter grammatisch und historisch erklärt* (Bern: Dalp, 1835). **Studies:** **Y. Amit,** *The Book of Judges: The Art of Editing* (BIS 38; Leiden: E. J. Brill, 1998); **C. Armerding,** "The Heroic Age of Greece and Israel: A Literary-Historical Comparison" (Ph.D. diss., Brandeis University, 1968); **M. Bal,** *Death and Dissymmetry: The Politics of Coherence in the Book of Judges* (Chicago: University of Chicago Press, 1988); **C. M. Bowra,** *Heroic Poetry* (London: Macmillan, 1952); **A. Brenner,** ed., *A Feminist Companion to Judges* (FCB 4; Sheffield: JSOT, 1993); **M. Z. Brettler,** *The Book of Judges* (OTR; New York: Routledge, 2002); idem, "The Book of Judges: Literature as Politics," *JBL* 108 (1989) 395-418; **M. Buber,** "Books of Judges and Book of Judges," in *Kingship of God* (3d ed.; New York: Harper & Row, 1967 [1932]) 66-84; **J. Campbell,** *The Hero with a Thousand Faces* (2d ed.; Bollingen Series 17; Princeton, NJ: Princeton University Press, 1968); **H. M. Chadwick,** *The Heroic Age* (2d ed.; Cambridge Archaeological and Ethnological Series; Cambridge: University Press, 1926); **F. M. Cross,** "The Themes of the Book of Kings and the Structure of the Deuteronomistic History," in *Canaanite Myth and Hebrew Epic* (Cambridge, MA: Harvard University Press, 1973) 274-89; **S. Davidson,** *An Introduction to the Old Testament: Critical, Historical, and Theological* (3 vols.; Edinburgh: Williams & Norgate, 1862-1863); **J. C. Exum,** "The Centre Cannot Hold: Thematic and Textual Instabilities in Judges," *CBQ* 52 (1990) 410-31; **G. E. Gerbrandt,** *Kingship According to the Deuteronomistic History* (SBLDS 87; Atlanta: Scholars Press, 1986); **D. W. Gooding,** "The Composition of the Book of Judges," *ErIsr* 1 (1982) 670-79; **C. Gordon,** *The Common Background of Greek and Hebrew Civilizations* (New York: Norton, 1965); **A. K. Grayson,** "Assyrian Royal Inscriptions: Literary Characteristics," in *Assyrian Royal Inscriptions: New Horizons in Literary, Ideological and Historical Analysis; Papers of Symposium Held in Cetona (Siena), June 26-28, 1980,* ed. F. M. Fales (Orientis antiqui collectio 17; Rome: Istituto per L'Oriente, Centro per le antichità e la storia dell'arte del vicino Oriente, 1981) 35-47; idem, "History and Historians of the Ancient Near East: Assyria and Babylonia," *Or* 49 (1980) 140-94; **F. E. Greenspahn,** "The Theology of the Framework of Judges," *VT* 36 (1986) 385-96; **K. R. R. Gros Louis,** "The Book of Judges," in *Literary Interpretations of Biblical Narratives,* ed. K. R. R. Gros Louis, J. S. Ackerman and T. S. Warshaw (Bible in Literature Courses; Nashville: Abingdon, 1974); **B. Halpern,** *The First Historians: The Hebrew Bible and History* (San Francisco: Harper & Row, 1988) 105-43; **S. Heaney,** *Beowulf: A Verse Translation* (New York: Norton, 2002); **Homer,** *The Odyssey* (New York: Viking, 1996); **L. Klein,** *The Triumph of Irony in the Book of Judges* (JSOTSup 68; Sheffield: JSOT, 1989); **S. N. Kramer,** *History Begins at Sumer* (Garden City, NY: Doubleday, 1959); **J. Lilley,** "A Literary Appreciation of the Book of Judges," *TynBul* 18 (1967) 94-102; **T. L. J. Mafico,** "Judge, Judging," *ABD* 3.1104-6; **A. Malamat,** "The Danite Migration and the Pan-Israelite Exodus-Conquest: A Biblical Narrative Pattern," *Bib* 51 (1970) 1-7; **G. T. Manley,** "The Deuteronomic Redactor in the Book of Judges," *EvQ* 31 (1959) 32-37; **S. D. McBride,** "Polity of the Covenant People: The Book of Deuteronomy," *Int* 41 (1987) 229-44; **D. A. Miller,** *The Epic Hero* (Baltimore: Johns Hopkins University Press, 2000); **E. T. Mullen,** "Judges 1.1-36: The Deuteronomistic Reintroduction of the Book of Judges," *HTR* 77 (1984) 33-54; **R. D. Nelson,** *The Double Redaction of the Deuteronomistic History* (JSOTSup 18; Sheffield: JSOT, 1981a); idem, "Josiah in the Book of Joshua," *JBL* 100 (1981b) 531-40; **M. Noth,** "The Background of Judges 17-18," in *Israel's Prophetic Heritage: Essays in Honor of James Muilenberg,* ed. B. W. Anderson and W. Harrelson (Preacher's Library; London: SCM, 1962) 68-85; **R. H. O'Connell,** *The Rhetoric of the Book of Judges* (VTSup 63; Leiden: E. J. Brill, 1996); **B. Peckham,** *The Composition of the Deuteronomis-*

tic History (HSM 35; Atlanta: Scholars Press, 1985); **R. Polzin,** *Moses and the Deuteronomist: A Literary Study of the Deuteronomic History* (New York: Seabury, 1980); **I. Provan,** *Hezkiah and the Books of Kings: A Contribution to the Debate about the Composition of the Deuteronomistic History* (BZAW 172; Berlin: de Gruyter, 1988); **G. von Rad,** "The Beginnings of Historical Writing in Ancient Israel," in *The Problem of the Hexateuch and Other Essays* (London: SCM, 1966 [1944]) 166-204; idem, "God's Word in History According to the Old Testament," in *God at Work in Israel* (Nashville: Abingdon, 1980 [1941]) 139-59; **S. L. Richter,** *The Deuteronomistic History and the Name Theology* (BZAW 318; Berlin: de Gruyter, 2002); **W. Richter,** *Die Bearbeitungen des "Retterbuches" in der deuteronomistischen Epoche* (BBB 21; Bonn: Hanstein, 1964); idem, *Traditionsgeschichtliche Untersuchungen zum Richterbuch* (BBB 18; Bonn: Hanstein, 1963); **W. Robertson-Smith,** *The Old Testament in the Jewish Church: A Course of Lectures on Biblical Criticism* (2d; New York: Appleton, 1892); **G. Steiner,** *Errata: An Examined Life* (New Haven: Yale University Press, 1997); idem, "Homer and the Scholars," in *Homer: A Collection of Critical Essays,* ed. G. Steiner and R. Fagles (Englewood Cliffs, NJ: Prentice-Hall, 1962) 1-14; **L. G. Stone,** "Ethical and Apologetic Tendencies in the Redaction of the Book of Joshua," *CBQ* 53 (1991a) 25-36; idem, "From Tribal Confederation to Monarchic State: The Editorial Perspective of the Book of Judges" (Ph.D. diss., Yale University, 1988); idem, "On Historical Authenticity, Historical Criticism, and Biblical Authority: Reflections of the Case of the Book of Joshua," *AsTJ* 56 (2002) 83-96; idem, "Redaction Criticism: Whence, Whither, Why? Going Beyond Source and Form Criticism Without Leaving Them Behind," in *A Biblical Itinerary: In Search of Method, Form, and Content; Essays in Honor of George W. Coats,* ed. E. Carpenter (JSOTSup 240; Sheffield: Sheffield Academic Press, 1997) 77-90; idem, review of *The Triumph of Irony in the Book of Judges,* by L. R. Klein, *AsTJ* 46 (1991b) 115-17; **H. Tadmor,** "History and Ideology in the Assyrian Royal Inscriptions," in *Assyrian Royal Inscriptions: New Horizons in Literary, Ideological, and Historical Analysis,* ed. F. Fales (Orientis antiqui collectio 17; Rome: Istituto per L'Oriente, Centro per le Antichità e la storia dell'arte del vincino Oriente, 1981) 13-33; **P. Trible,** *Texts of Terror: Literary-Feminist Readings of Biblical Narratives* (Philadelphia: Fortress, 1984); **T. Veijola,** *Das Königtum in der Beurteilung der deuteronomistischen Historiographie: Eine redaktionsgeschichtliche Untersuchung* (AASF B-198; Helsinki: Suomalainen Tiedeakatemia, 1977) 15-29; **B. G. Webb,** *The Book of Judges: An Integrated Reading* (JSOTSup 46; JSOT, 1987); **M. Weber,** *Ancient Judaism* (New York: Free Press, 1952 [1917-1919]); **C. H. Whitman,** *Homer and the Heroic Tradition* (Cambridge, MA: Harvard University Press, 1958); **G. A. Yee,** ed., *Judges and Method: New Approaches in Biblical Studies* (Minneapolis: Fortress, 1995). L. G. Stone

JUDICIAL OFFICERS. *See* STATE OFFICIALS.

JUSTICE AND RIGHTEOUSNESS

These concepts are prominent in the Historical Books because they are closely connected to government and *kingship. Securing justice and righteousness was perhaps the primary responsibility of the judge or the king in Israel, and any ruler who failed to do so was in serious difficulty (see 2 Kings 21:26; 23:4). However, it is important to point out that in the Historical Books, as in the OT as a whole, these concepts are not precisely congruent with the connotations given to the terms *justice* and *righteousness* in English. There are three primary sets of Hebrew root words involved: *špt*, *ṣdq* and *yšr*. The first, usually translated "just," "justice" or "judge," has to do with order in life and the means of bringing about that order. Both the second and the third have to do with what is "right" in a given situation. Thus a ruler was expected to bring about the right kind of order in his domain. If it could be said of him, as it was of David, that "he did what was just *[mišpāṭ]* and right *[ṣĕdāqâ]* for all his people" (2 Sam 8:15; 1 Chron 8:14), then he was highly successful. In this article righteousness and justice are considered first separately and then together.

    1. Righteousness
    2. Justice
    3. Justice and Righteousness

1. Righteousness.
At the heart of the Israelite conception of behavior is the contrast between that which is "right" and that which is "wrong." For that culture, the modern idea that these concepts might be relative to changing situations or persons would have been unthinkable. The character and will of God had been revealed to Israel, and right was ever

defined as that which conformed to those two factors. This understanding is the same in the Historical Books as it is in the rest of the OT. Nevertheless, it must be noted immediately that the Hebrew writers fully understood that God has not revealed every detail of life, and that it is necessary for persons to make decisions about what seems right to them under the circumstances.

1.1. Right. The preceding point is confirmed by a study of the Hebrew root *yšr,* which has the basic meaning "to be in conformity with, to be right." In both verb and noun forms this root conveys the idea of "what is right in someone's eyes"—that is, "to be pleasing." A vivid example of this occurs in the Historical Books when it is said that Samson found a young Philistine woman "pleasing" and demanded that his parents make arrangements for him to marry her (Judg 14:3, 7). The readers sense that the narrator is leading them to believe that indeed this young woman was not "right," because the question of what was pleasing to God had not been asked. Several of the other verbal usages, while not necessarily raising these overtones, clearly speak of that which the main actor believes best to serve his own self-interests: Saul (1 Sam 18:20), David (1 Sam 18:26) and Absalom (2 Sam 17:4). The noun is used in this same way when it is said that during the judges period "everyone did what was right in their own eyes" (Judg 17:6; 21:25). The remaining occurrences of the verb merely speak of that which "seems like a good idea" (1 Chron 13:4; 2 Chron 30:4).

Apart from the two occurrences of the noun *yāšār* in Judges, almost all other uses of the noun in the Historical Books (twenty-four out of thirty-five) speak of that which was "right in the eyes of the Lord." Most of these are found in the books of Kings and Chronicles (with some being parallels). They normally appear in commendations of kings who are considered on this basis to be "good" kings (e.g., 1 Kings 11:33; 2 Kings 12:2 [2 Chron 24:2]). Several of the remaining usages of the noun imply the same thing: what is right is ultimately determined by what is right in God's estimation. Thus Samuel promises the people that in the fear of the Lord he will teach them "the good and right way" (1 Sam 12:23), and it is said that Hezekiah did what "was good and right and true before Yahweh his God" (2 Chron 31:20). All these occurrences of the root *yšr* tend to confirm the point being made in Proverbs 21:2

that whatever one's own estimation of right may be, the final adjudication belongs to the Lord.

1.2. Righteous, Righteousness. The forms of the root *ṣdq* assume even more directly that "right" is determined by Yahweh alone. The verb occurs only twice (2 Sam 15:4; 1 Kings 8:32 [2 Chron 6:23]). In the first occurrence Absalom implicitly asserts his right to kingship by saying that if he had a chance, he could do right for a wronged person. In the second occurrence Solomon calls upon the Lord in a case when one person has sinned against another to condemn the guilty party and to "justify" the innocent party. The noun form *ṣaddîq,* "righteous one," declares that God is the quintessential such one, doing the right thing consistently, even when his people have done wrong consistently (2 Chron 12:6; Neh 9:8, 33). But that rightness is not only that he brought well-deserved punishment upon them; it is also that he continued to keep his covenant with them when there was absolutely no reason to do so (Ezra 9:15). Such rightness goes far beyond mere legal correctness. This divine character then demands that those who rule in Yahweh's name mirror it (2 Sam 23:3).

The noun *ṣĕdāqâ* occurs fifteen times in the Historical Books. Oddly enough, the alternative masculine form *ṣedeq* does not appear in this portion of the canon even though elsewhere it occurs interchangeably with the feminine form. In most of these fifteen occurrences the emphasis is upon righteous behavior, actions that are right according to some understood norm. This is the way the Lord acts (Judg 5:11; 1 Sam 12:7), and it is the way a king is expected to act (2 Sam 8:15; 22:21, 25; 1 Kings 3:6; 10:9). It reflects conformity to a clear standard, with the result that it can be, and should be, rewarded (1 Sam 26:23; 2 Sam 22:21, 25; 1 Kings 8:32 [2 Chron 6:23]).

Thus it is plain that "righteousness" in the Historical Books is to do that which is right, or correct, or desirable to the Lord. It is not some condition that one possesses in oneself. It is conformity to the absolute standard of the character and wishes of the covenant Lord.

2. Justice.

2.1. Judge. Forms of the root *špṭ* occur 148 times in the Historical Books. Of these, nearly half (seventy-six occurrences) are the noun form *mišpāṭ.* A significant number of the sixty-nine occurrences of the verb form are the participial form *šōpēṭ* (twenty-three occurrences), usually rendered "a judge." This translation tends to confuse many modern readers who do not see the OT *judges operating in the fashion of a modern judicial figure. The confusion is legitimate, for although the OT judges did decide right and wrong when disputes were brought before them (e.g., 2 Sam 15:4; 1 Kings 3:9), their roles were considerably broader than that. Furthermore, the judgments rendered usually were ad hoc rather than, as in our context, by an appeal to some established law code (cf. Solomon's "judgment" concerning the two women claiming the same child [1 Kings 3:28]). In Joshua the judges seem to have been one segment of officialdom. Thus they are included with the "elders," "heads" and "officers" of the people (Josh 8:33; 23:2; 24:1) in official assemblies. The same situation seems to have held true in the kingdom period, when the position of judge is included in listings with "officers," "captains," "governors" and "chiefs of fathers' houses" (1 Chron 23:4; 26:9; 2 Chron 1:2; cf. also 2 Chron 19:5-6; Ezra 10:14).

The inclusion of judges in these lists of officials suggests that their roles may have been somewhat circumscribed. But that is definitely not the case in the book of Judges, where the judge was uniquely appointed by God to deliver Israel from the enemies who had oppressed them (e.g., Judg 2:16, 18; 3:10; 11:27). Typically, these judges were champions who in dependence on God delivered their people out of the wrongful oppression in which they languished. Then, after this act of judgment, they typically would continue to "judge" the people for a period of years. Clearly, while this included hearing disputes and rendering judgments, it also involved overall governing of the land, so that the larger function of the judge was to bring God's order for life to reality in the land. But this position of leadership was not hereditary, and when the judge died, there typically was a hiatus during which the nation would diverge from God's order, and the people soon found themselves back under oppression. Furthermore, the closing chapters of the book of Judges at least imply that even during their lifetimes the judges frequently lacked the requisite authority to enforce their leadership, with the result that "everyone did whatever seemed right to themselves" (Judg 17:6; 18:1; 19:1; 21:25). Among the other nations it was the king who filled the role of judge (1 Sam 8:5), and ultimately the Israelites demanded that they be given a king for this purpose (1 Sam 8:20). A justification for this request was that Samuel's sons whom he had appointed to succeed him as judges proved unequal to the task in that they "accepted bribes and perverted justice" (1 Sam 8:3-5). An illustration of this role of the judge not only to decide what was right in any given circumstance, but also to see that the decision was enforced, is seen when God is called on to "judge" his people by repaying the wicked, bringing on them what they have done (1 Kings 8:32; 2 Chron 6:23). Thus, in the broadest sense, to be a judge in Israel was to have the responsibility of doing everything necessary to bring the divine order into existence, from the smallest dispute between two persons, up to and including the fate of the entire nation.

2.2. Right Order. The Hebrew word *mišpāṭ* expresses the idea of "right, or appropriate, order." The large number of different English terms used to translate the seventy-six occurrences of this word in different translations in the Historical Books is a convincing testimony to the breadth of the concept involved. Some of these are "manner," "custom," "practice," "quota," "plan," "specification," "prescribed way," "ordinance," "law," "regulation," "judgment," "verdict," "justice" and "just cause." This wide array can be summed up under the heading given above: "right order," whether customary or prescribed. Thus the term can be used to describe customary behavior, as is shown by occurrences such as that in Judges 18:7 describing the pattern of life among the Sidonians (see also 2 Kings 1:7; 17:26-27, 33-34), or that in 2 Kings 11:14 telling where the king customarily stood in the temple. One of the more interesting such usages of this term is found in 1 Samuel 8, where Samuel uses it to warn the people of the despotic way in which kings customarily acted (1 Sam 8:9, 11). He said that it was the *mišpāṭ* of kings to act in such ways. But it is more common in the Historical Books, as in the rest of the OT, for the term to refer to a prescribed order. In some cases the idea of prescription is more implicit than explicit. So it is said that the Israelites marched around the city of *Jericho in the same "manner" each day (Josh 6:15). Although they were conforming to the original directions of God (Josh 6:3-4), the point is that they were following the same plan each time. The idea of plan is clearly what is intended in 1 Kings 6:38, where it is said that Solomon finished building the temple "according to all its *mišpāṭ* (NIV: "specifications"; NASB: "plans").

This idea of prescribed order gives rise to a very frequent use of *mišpāṭ* as "regulations" (also "ordinances," "judgments," "laws") (*see* Law). Here the emphasis is upon the fact of prescription. Thus Samuel, after having told the people how kings customarily act (1 Sam 8:9, 11), laid down "regulations" for how the Israelite kings *should* act (1 Sam 10:25). Ultimately, the Israelites believed that it is Yahweh who has laid down the prescriptions for the right order of life (2 Chron 16:12, 14; 19:8), and the term appears in conjunction with the other terms used in the OT to express this idea. These include "statutes," "commandments," testimonies" and "instructions" (see Josh 24:25; 1 Sam 30:25; 2 Sam 22:23; 1 Kings 2:3; 6:12; 8:58; 2 Chron 7:17; 19:10; Ezra 7:10; Neh 1:7; 9:13). Life was to be lived in the light of these prescriptions, but it is clear that "to do *mišpāṭ*" did not so much involve continual appeal to specific prescriptions as it did living a life that generally embodied such a prescribed order. Thus the role of the Israelite king (understood as *šōpēṭ*, "judge") was not so much to enforce specific prescriptions as to see that the kind of order prescribed by Yahweh was maintained in the land (1 Kings 3:11). But that, of course, required that the king be quite familiar with all those prescriptions (2 Sam 22:23; 1 Kings 6:12). Perhaps the greatest irony found in the Historical Books is that Solomon, the man who had asked for wisdom in order to discern *mišpāṭ*, ended up being the king who led Israel away from that divine order (1 Kings 11:33).

When a king or judge made a regulation or acted according to one, English translations frequently say that he "gave judgment" (or "rendered a verdict," or even "did justice"). This is coming closer to the narrower connotations of the English "justice." But even here the broader Hebrew concept of right order must be kept in mind. There is no idea here of abstract "rights" that somehow inhere in the individual. Rather, the issue is, given the revealed character of God the Creator and given his revealed purposes for the order of life in his creation, what is the right thing to do in a given set of circumstances to maintain that order? To be sure, given God's clear valuing of individual persons, persons could expect to be treated rightly. Thus someone's *mišpāṭ* could refer to a "just cause" that the person had (2 Sam 15:4; 1 Kings 8:45, 49, 59; 2 Chron 6:35, 39).

3. Justice and Righteousness.

As we noted at the outset, the duty of the ruler of God's people was "to do justice and righteousness for all his people" (2 Sam 8:15; 1 Kings 10:9). This did not mean to enforce some abstract law code or to ensure the inherent rights of his subjects; rather, it meant to be so in tune with the Author of the universe, his character and his wishes, that his "rightness" and his order for life would be made to prevail in the nation, with the inevitable result that that "good" which is inherent in the creation of the good God will be unleashed upon the earth. These concepts are not unique to Israel, as K. W. Whitelam (44-45) shows. But what is unique is the character of the right order called for in the light of the unique character of the Israelite God.

See also LAW.

BIBLIOGRAPHY. **G. Liedke,** *Gestalt und Bezeichnung alttestamentlicher Rechtssätze: Eine formgeschichtlich-terminologische Studie* (WMANT 39; Neukirchen-Vluyn: Neukirchener Verlag, 1971); **H. Olivier,** "ישׁר," *NIDOTTE* 2.563-68; **J. van der Ploeg,** "šāpāṭ et mišpāṭ," *OtSt* 2 (1943) 144-55; **D. J. Reimer,** "צדק," *NIDOTTE* 3.744-69; **H. H. Schmid,** *Gerechtigkeit als Weltordnung* (Tubingen: Mohr, 1968); **R. Schultz,** "שׁפט," *NIDOTTE* 4.213-20; **M. Weinfeld,** "Justice and Right-eousness—משׁפט וצדקה—the Expression and Its Meaning," in *Justice and Righteousness: Biblical Themes and Their Influence,* ed. H. G. Reventlow and Y. Hoffman (JSOTSup 137; Sheffield: JSOT, 1992) 228-46; **K. W. Whitelam,** "King and Kingship," *ABD* 3.40-48; **D. J. Wiseman,** "Law and Order in Old Testament Times," *VE* 8 (1973) 5-21.

J. N. Oswalt

K

KASSITES. *See* BABYLONIA, BABYLONIANS.

KHIRBET BEIT LEI INSCRIPTIONS. *See* HE-
BREW INSCRIPTIONS.

KHIRBET EL-QOM INSCRIPTION. *See* HE-
BREW INSCRIPTIONS.

KILAMUWA. *See* NON-ISRAELITE WRITTEN SOUR-
CES: SYRO-PALESTINIAN.

KING'S HIGHWAY. *See* ROADS AND HIGHWAYS.

KINGS AND KINGSHIP

In the Bible's view, kingship in Israel was called
into being as a means to *God's ends and not as
an end in itself. Its tragedy is that for most of its
history it was concerned with its own importance
rather than with God and his people. Its redemption lies in the fact that it prepared the way for
the expectation of a king of a different kind: the
Messiah, the king after God's own heart.

The title "king" designates the male sovereign
ruler of an independent state. The term *kingship*
refers to the state, office, authority and dignity of
a king. In the OT, as elsewhere in the ancient
Near East, the term can refer to rulers of states
with varying degrees of size and importance,
ranging from relatively small territories, such as
the city-state of Tyre, to empires like *Egypt, *Assyria and *Babylonia. Royal *women in Israel
were not considered as ruling sovereigns in their
own right but owed what authority or influence
they had to their own initiative (Athaliah) or to
the kings with whom they were associated (Bathsheba) or to both (Jezebel; see Smith).

Israelite kingship did not exist in a vacuum.
As a new development in Israelite political life,
it was influenced by the monarchical systems of
neighboring countries. This is clearly implied in

the account of the people's demand that Samuel
implement the transition to a new political system "like all the other nations" (1 Sam 8:5, 20).
Egypt, Mesopotamia and Canaan had the most
significant influence.

1. Kings and Kingship in the Ancient Near
   East
2. Kings and Kingship in Israel

1. Kings and Kingship in the Ancient Near East.

1.1. Kingship in Egypt. Kingship was the central institution in Egyptian society, and the king
(= pharaoh) had an absolute status as head of
state and representative of the gods, exercising
the divine rule of the cosmos and upholding the
cosmic order that sustained the world and Egypt.
Kingship remained remarkably stable through
Egypt's history (following Baines, 16-53).

Virtually all evidence for kingship that survives comes from elite sources and public documents that are characterized by "decorum,"
notions of politeness and flattery toward the
king. Therefore they often seem to claim capacities for the king that in reality were controversial
or used to be understood metaphorically. For
example, the only human that could be depicted
on temple reliefs as performing the temple cult
was the king. While in reality there were priests
who performed these rites on his behalf, the key
documents portrayed him as sole mediator between the gods and his contemporaries, and
since he was one, while both gods and humans
were many, these documents ascribed him a crucial and uniquely powerful position that eventually came to permeate public consciousness.
The Egyptian understanding of reality envisioned a system of cosmic order (*maʿat*) that sustained a network of relationships between the
gods, the king, the deceased and humanity. All
"natural" phenomena, such as the annual flood-

ing of the Nile River, were integral to this system. The right balance in this cosmic order ensured harmony in the cosmos and happiness for all. This balance, however, was constantly under threat from internal and external enemies. The king's role was to maintain this order by ensuring that the relationships between these constituents remained stable and positive, and since he was the only one who could do so, he acquired a pivotal role. The reliefs and inscriptions that decorate Egyptian temple walls illustrate this. They show the king defeating enemies (thus sustaining Egyptian society) and offering sacrifices to the gods (thus appeasing their just or capricious anger or encouraging their benevolence toward the living and the dead). It is against the perceived threat to the all-sustaining world order that the king's absolute authority and his capacity to judge and punish beyond moral or legal constraints must be understood. Without the king there was no order. Since so much was at stake, any royal action against real or perceived enemies was automatically legitimized.

Another incidence where decorum played an important role is the king's treatment as a limited kind of deity. For example, he could be called the "son" of all the gods and he could refer to them as his "fathers." A number of texts appear to deify the king. Others that portray themselves as royal compositions contain elements of self-deification. Contextual considerations, however, suggest that most of this material was metaphorical or hyperbolic.

1.2. Kingship in Mesopotamia. The complexity of the cuneiform script used in Mesopotamia meant that writing was a skill acquired only by professional scribes, who in turn were employed by the wealthy and the powerful, most notably the king. As in Egypt, then, the surviving documents are positively disposed toward royalty and need to be read in that light.

In the various cultures and throughout the different periods of Mesopotamian history, kings ruled by divine authority and were expected to create a prosperous, well-governed land. A number of significant changes in the concept of kingship can be traced through the region's turbulent history (following Lambert, 54-70).

Sumer, located in the south of the Tigris-Euphrates plain, was organized into city states. Each had its own patron god who was considered the city's supreme ruler. The city god "lived" in the major temple of the city in the form of his statue, alongside other minor gods who inhabited statues in their various temples. The city ruler was considered as the estate manager of the various farms belonging to the gods resident in the city, but his true allegiance belonged to the city's patron god, for whom he was expected to run the city justly and efficiently. Even when a given ruler conquered other cities and thus acquired responsibility for additional gods, priority would be given to his original patron. It is probably against the background of farming that the city rulers acquired the title "Shepherd" as a metaphor for their royal status and function.

New aspects of kingship were introduced by the short-lived dynasty of Akkad. Its founder, Sargon, introduced a more imperial concept, including a newly built capital (Akkad), complete with standing army and a developed palace economy. Naram-Sin, fourth in the dynasty, introduced the concept of divine kingship. The epithet "Shepherd" for the kings fell into disuse.

The decline of the Akkad dynasty led to a period of chaos followed by a return to older Sumerian values under the Third Dynasty of Ur. Nevertheless, the Akkad period had left a permanent imprint on royal conceptions. While kings used the shepherd epithet again, the whole country was now ruled via a central bureaucracy from Ur. This included a tax system that benefited major temples and government administration. Most of the rulers in the Ur III dynasty were deified during their lifetimes and had shrines built, where they received offerings.

This culture soon gave way to the Amorites, nomadic invaders from the West. Originally this resulted in a return to smaller city states, but Hammurabi started what became known as the Babylonian Empire. Kings were not considered as divine any longer, but a radical ideological innovation was introduced: the concept of a divine right to kingship based on the ancestral line.

The Late Babylonian Dynasty (626-539 BCE) emphasized their dependence on the gods and also saw themselves as shepherds. Temple rituals during this period included the public ritual humiliation of the Babylonian king before the patron god Marduk (= Bel) through the high priest at the annual New Year Festivals.

The concept of kingship in Assyria, the empire which coexisted with Babylonia from c. 2000-

612 BCE, differed significantly. First, the king was more dependent on the country's elite, a military aristocracy that could challenge royal supremacy when the interests of the state were at risk. Second, the Assyrian god Ashur was considered the state god rather than merely the god of a particular city. Thus he had a more powerful position in Assyrian religion than the gods of leading Babylonian cities, including Marduk of Babylon. "Theologically, the Assyrian state god was a king, and the human king was his regent" (Lambert, 68). This may explain the assassinations of a number of Assyrian kings. Later evidence suggests that the Assyrians, like their Babylonian neighbors, considered the ancestral line as one of the legitimizing factors in royal succession.

1.3. Kingship in Canaan. During Iron Age I, Canaan and the surrounding territories were dominated by kingdoms ruling over smaller city states like Tyre, Byblos and Damascus. Since these local monarchies in Canaan, Transjordan (kingdoms arose almost simultaneously in Edom, Moab and Ammon) and Syria were much smaller and flourished for much shorter periods of time than the larger empires, less evidence about their nature survives. These kingdoms are geographically close, however, and so they are likely to have influenced Israel. It is therefore both necessary and methodologically justified to use biblical evidence for such influence alongside independent sources to describe monarchical systems current among Israel's neighbors.

The cultural heritage of the important kingdom of Ugarit, which had ceased approximately 130 years before the united monarchy, may well have lived on in those contemporary city kingdoms. Compulsory military conscription, enforced labor for public projects, the duty to provide military equipment, the recruitment of female workers for domestic labor at the royal palace and the confiscation of real estate for the king's use, practices associated with the monarchical system of neigboring peoples by Samuel (1 Sam 8:11-17), were current at Ugarit (Kitchen, 95-96).

Significant impact on the nature of the Israelite monarchy can also be expected from Jerusalem, the new Israelite capital. It had survived as an independent enclave inhabited by indigenous Jebusites until it was conquered by David and established as the royal capital in the early years of his reign (2 Sam 5:5-10). The reference to Melchizedek in Psalm 110:4, "You are a priest forever in the manner of Mechizedek," is to the pre-Israelite Jebusite priest and king mentioned in Genesis 14 and almost certainly reflects historic knowledge of a monarchic system which combined kingship and priesthood. There is also some evidence that belief in the inviolability of Jerusalem/Zion may have been mediated through the integration of the Jebusite cult of Elyon into Yahwism (Day 1998a, 78-79). This extends to the foundation of a temple in the capital as a central national sanctuary with a politically effective unifying function (cf. 1 Kings 12:27). It owes its architecture (threefold structure) to Canaanite precedent (it was built by Phoenician contractors from Tyre, cf. 1 Kings 5; see Kitchen, 122-27). Its location in the capital and its political function to legitimize the dynasty which sponsored it reflects local customs and strategies universally employed by monarchies.

The evidence for other Canaanite practices and attitudes which may have had an influence on the royal ideology in Israel and the organization of the monarchy is circumstantial: (1) At least one text from Ugarit (KTU^2 1.22.II.15-18) suggests that kings were anointed in Canaan (Day 1998a, 80-81); (2) some texts show that kings were considered as gods or sons of the god El (e.g., KTU^2 1.16.I.10-23 and 1.16.II.36-49); (3) two epic texts from Ugarit suggest an idealized image of kingship that included the king's duty to uphold the rights of the poor and vulnerable (KTU^2 1.16.VI.43-50 and 1.17.V.6-8); (4) the designation *(skn)* of a court official known from Canaan is identical with the steward in charge of the royal palace in Jerusalem (Day 1998a, 88-89; see bibliographic references in nn. 40 and 41) (*see* State Officials).

2. Kings and Kingship in Israel.

As in Egypt and Babylonia, most of the surviving documents relating to kingship were penned, archived, transmitted and edited by circles belonging to the royal entourage (priests, scribes, court historians, theologians). So it is surprising that pro-monarchic statements exist side by side with accounts and entire works that are distant, critical of or even hostile to particular kings or the institution as a whole (for references, see 2.2.1). This dynamic tension gives profound insight into the nature of kingship in Israel and the attitudes toward kingship in the historical books of the OT. The following section represents all monarchs in the united and divided kingdoms of Israel and Judah.

2.1. Kings of Israel and Judah. During the period that has sometimes been called the united monarchy, four kings reigned over various parts of Israel. During the divided monarchy twenty kings from various dynasties reigned in the northern kingdom (= Israel). The southern kingdom (= Judah) also had twenty kings, but they were all from the same dynasty, the line of David. In addition, there was one reigning queen, Athaliah, who descended from a northern dynasty.

Table 1, based largely on K. A. Kitchen (8-9), presents an exhaustive list. Foreign rulers described as their respective contemporaries are included in columns 2 and 4. They are listed in chronological order and contemporary monarchs in the twin kingdoms are presented side by side and provided with regnal years or months/days in the case of short reigns. Israelite kings appear in column 1, Judean kings in column 3. The end of a dynasty in Israel or the beginning of a new one is indicated by strings of asterisks. The names of kings also mentioned in nonbiblical records are given in italics. When extrabiblical local Hebrew records are available, this is indicated by "LR" (in brackets if the evidence is contested). The abbreviation AramD stands for Aram of Damascus.

Despite the regular provision of regnal years in the biblical records, establishing an absolute chronology is difficult due to inconsistent methods of recording (accession-year dating vs. non-accession-year dating, different calendar systems; variant recording of coregencies); for informed attempts, see Thiele, Galil and Tetley (cf. also Kitchen, 26-29; Provan, Long and Longman III, 199-202) (*see* Chronology).

For detailed discussions of Saul and Saul's family, David and David's family, the Davidic Covenant, Solomon, Rehoboam, Jeroboam, the Omri dynasty, Jehoshaphat, the Jehu dynasty, Hezekiah, Manasseh, Josiah and Zerubbabel see elsewhere in this volume. The following paragraphs will focus on aspects relating to kingship in general.

2.2. The Reigns of Saul and David. The very existence of a united monarchy has been questioned by a group of scholars sometimes referred to as revisionists (e.g., Whitelam; Davies). A simplified summary of the arguments runs as follows. (1) There is no irrefutable extra-biblical evidence for Israelite kings before Omri, and none for kings of Judah before Ahaziah. The primary sources for present knowledge of a united monarchy are biblical texts. (2) Most of these texts were written during the Persian Period (late sixth century onward), with a strong ideological bias. (3) Archaeological evidence that seemed to reflect cultural shifts and population developments during the time of *Saul, *David and *Solomon has been dated much later by some archaeologists (e.g., Finkelstein). (4) The united monarchy is a literary fiction created by postexilic circles in Jerusalem to provide a cultural and political identity for the newly formed state (Persian province) of Judah (Davies).

At present, however, the balance of the available evidence suggests that Saul, David and Solomon were historical figures. The arguments for this statement may be summarized as follows: (1) Extrabiblical evidence renders numerous details about Saul, David and Solomon mentioned in the biblical texts plausible and credible (Kitchen; Provan, Long and Longman). (2) Although much of the editing of the historical books took place during and after the exile, modern critical methods allow the identification of substantial textual materials and other sources of information from much earlier times (see the essays collected in Day 2004). (3) At the present state of knowledge, the later dating of archaeological data cannot be proven and remains a minority view (see Dever; Kitchen) (*see* Archaeology, Syro-Palentinian). (4) Explanations for the invention of the united monarchy on ideological grounds cannot account for two central features of the relevant texts: (a) the amount of detail, most of which would have been irrelevant for later ideological constructions of the kind suggested by P. R. Davies; (b) the nature of the details—frequently critical of the central characters, disparaging of the monarchical system and disapproving of the nation—would not have lent itself to the purposes suggested by Davies.

The material that deals with Saul, Israel's first king, divides into two parts: the account of Saul's accession to the throne (1 Sam 1—12) and the narrative about his reign (1 Sam 13—31). Two characteristics of this material are conspicuous: (1) the accession account contains pro-monarchical and anti-monarchical materials side by side; (2) the reign narrative, which is dominated by the struggle for supremacy between Saul and his eventual successor David, is surprisingly long and complex.

Table 1. The Kings of Israel

United Monarchy

Saul
22-32 years (estimated) over all of Israel, excluding Judah for last 5 years

Ishbaal (son of Saul)
2 years over northern tribes, excluding Judah
***
David
40 years; 7 years and 6 months over Judah, then over all of Israel

Solomon
40 years

Divided Monarchy

Israel	Foreign Rulers	Judah & Benjamin	Foreign Rulers
Jerob(o)am I 22 years Nadab 2 years	Shishak of Egypt 1 Kings 11:40	Rehoboam 17 years Abijam 3 years	Shishak of Egypt 1 Kings 14:25
*** Baasha 24 years Elah 2 years		Asa 41 years	Benhadad (I) of Aram of Damascus 1 Kings 15:18 (Zerah the Kushite 2 Chron 14:9-13)
*** Zimri 7 days *** *Omri* 12 years (including rival Tibni first 6 years)			
Ahab 22 years	Ethbaal of Sidon 1 Kings 16:31 Benhadad (I/II), AramD AramD 1 Kings 20	Jehoshaphat 25 years	Mesha of Moab 2 Kings 3
Ahaziah I 2 years *J(eh)oram II* 12 years	 Mesha of Moab 2 Kings 3 Hazael, AramD 2 Kings 8:3	Jehoram I 8 years *Ahaziah II* 1 year	 Hazael, AramD 2 Kings 8:28
*** *Jehu* 28 years	Mesha of Moab 2 Kings 3 Hazael, AramD 2 Kings 10:32	Queen Athaliah, first 6 years of Joash's reign J(eh)oash 40 years	Hazael, AramD 2 Kings 12:17-18
Jehoahaz 17 years *Jehoash* 16 years	Hazael AramD 2 Kings 13:22 Benhadad (II/III), AramD 2 Kings 13:24-25	 Amaziah 29 years	
Jeroboam II 41 years Zechariah 6 months ***	(LR)	*Azariah/Uzziah* 52 years *Jotham* 16 years	(LR) Rezin, AramD 2 Kings 15:37 (LR)
Shallum 1 month ***	(LR)		
Menahem 10 years	Pul/Tiglath-Pileser (III) of Assyria 2 Kings 15:19; 1 Chron 5:6, 26	*Ahaz* 16 years	Rezin, AramD 2 Kings 16:5 (LR) Tiglath-pileser (III), Assyria 2 Kings 16:7, 10

Israel	Foreign Rulers	Judah's Benjamin	Foreign Rulers
Pekahiah 2 years			
*** *Pekah* 20 years	Tiglath-Pileser (III), Assyria 2 Kings 15:29		
*** *Hoshea* 9 years	Shalmanezer (V), Assyria 2 Kings 17 So of Egypt 2 Kings 17:4 (LR)	*Hezekiah* 29 years	Shalmanezer (V) Assyria 2 Kings 18:9 (Sargon [II] Isaiah 20; after Ahaz Sennacherib
Fall of Samaria			Assyria 2 Kings 18:13ff. Taharqa, Egypt 2 Kings 19:9 Merodach-Baladan, Babylon 2 Kings 20:12 (x yrs later: Esarhaddon, Assyria 2 Kings 19:37)
		Manasseh 55 years	Assyrian king took him to Babylon 2 Chron 33:11
		Amon 2 years Josiah 31 years Jehoahaz 3 months Jehoiakim 11 years	Necho II, Egypt 2 Kings 23:29 (LR) Necho II, Egypt 2 Kings 23:33ff. Necho II, Egypt 2 Kings 23:33ff. (LR)
			Nebuchadrezzar II, Babylon 2 Kings 24:1
		Jehoiachin 3 months	Nebuchadrezzar II, Babylon 2 Kings 24:1 later Evil-Merodach, Babylon 2 Kings 25:27
		Zedekiah 11 years	Hophra of Egypt Jer 44:30 Nebuchadrezzar II, Babylon 2 Kings 24:10-17 (LR) Baalis king of Ammon Jer 40:14 Fall of Jerusalem

2.2.1. The Tension Between Pro-Monarchical and Anti-Monarchical Materials. The most significant pro-monarchical materials appear in 1 Samuel 9:1—10:16; 11; 13—14, anti-monarchical sentiments come into view in 1 Samuel 7—8; 10:17-27; 12. Scholars have traditionally resolved this tension by splitting statements that reflect these contrasting attitudes into different sources (Wellhausen; Noth). The pro-monarchical statements are thought to be early reflections of what actually happened at the time, while the anti-monarchical statements are thought to reflect the views of the redactor(s) of the *Deuteronomistic History after the monarchy's demise. The fact that they were left in their contradictory state is usually explained by assuming a later editor who added new material with his own view of the

monarchy but who respected the earlier materials he had inherited and left them unchanged. More likely, however, the material accurately reflects a basic tension between attitudes toward monarchy that coexisted side by side—at the time and into the postexilic period (see 2.4). This can be demonstrated by considering the closely intertwined religious and sociopolitical attitudes toward kingship in Israel.

2.2.1.1. Religious Attitudes Toward Kingship: Yahweh as King. There is no consensus over the dating of texts in the Pentateuch, the Historical Books and the Psalms that mention Yahweh as king (Ex 15:18; Num 23:21; Deut 33:5, 26; Judg 8:23; 1 Sam 8:7; 10:19; 12:12; Ps 93:1; 96:10; 97:1; 99:1). Consequently, opinions are divided over the issue whether the concept was adopted in Israel before the monarchy (Whitelam *ABD*). Isaiah 6:5, "my eyes have seen the King, the LORD of hosts," is often considered the earliest record of the designation of Yahweh as king that can be dated with certainty. This text, however, does not invent the tradition; it presumes it (Zenger, followed by Janowski). Furthermore, the belief that the respective national deity was "king" was a universal conviction in the ancient Near East. Irrespective of dating, then, the texts mentioned above almost certainly preserve a pre-monarchic conviction in Israel that Yahweh was king. This had a significant influence on attitudes toward the human monarchy throughout Israel's turbulent history. There are three theological aspects associated with divine kingship: Yahweh as king over the gods, Yahweh as king over Israel, and Yahweh as king over the nations. Yahweh's supremacy over the gods of the nations implies his universal dominion over the whole earth and all nations. This aspect comes to the fore in poetic, prophetic and apocalyptic literature. The first two, however, have strongly influenced attitudes in the historical books toward human kingship in Israel.

1. Yahweh as king over the gods. Statements like Psalm 95:3, "the LORD is a great god and a great king over all gods," show that in principle Israel had an exclusive relationship with Yahweh, but did not deny the existence of other deities (monolatrous henotheism, the belief in many gods, one of which is supreme and receives exclusive worship). Several aspects associated with this belief influenced human kingship in Israel.

a. Kings were seen as divinely equipped military leaders. Belief that Yahweh was superior to the gods of other nations had profound implications for foreign policy. The almost universal conviction that the national deity would support a nation or people in warfare led to the belief that Yahweh could therefore guarantee military victory and prevent economic exploitation by foreigners. The introduction of a divinely sanctioned monarchy was an attempt to institutionalize such military potential.

b. The king was responsible to practice the exclusive worship of Yahweh and to implement and sustain this practice among his people. The historical books and the prophetic literature of the OT show that for much of its history Israel practiced monotheism in principle and polytheism in fact. In the historical books Israel's monarchs are assessed in regular evaluative summaries with regard to their sincerity and effectiveness in pursuing this objective. Those of Hezekiah's and Josiah's reigns in 2 Kings 18:3-6 and 23:25 are positive examples. In the final analysis, however, the demise of successive dynasties in Israel, the fall of Samaria and the fall of Jerusalem are blamed on the failure of successive kings and royal dynasties to fulfill their religious obligations and explained as divine punishment on a disloyal people (cf. 2 Kings 17:7-23 on Israel and 2 Kings 21:1-15 on King Manasseh of Judah; see also 2 Kings 23:26-27).

2. Yahweh as king over Israel also implies ethical obligations. Here the human monarch's role as Yahweh's representative takes on a dual significance.

a. This role assigns the king divine authority (divine right of kings). Its purpose was to enable the establishment and maintenance of social justice, ostensibly by enforcing Yahweh's ethical standards among the people.

b. This role limits royal power by imposing religious and ethical limitations. The law of the king in Deuteronomy 17:14-20 reads like a deliberate attempt to counteract "rights" such as those associated with the "king like all the other nations" described in 1 Samuel 8:11-17. In reality, the first aspect, namely the divine right of kings, dominated Israel's history. Frustration with the social problems caused by monarchic absolutism is reflected throughout the historical books. In the final analysis, the demise of the monarchic enterprise as a whole is blamed also on the failure of successive kings and royal dynasties to fulfill their social obligations and explained as divine punishment on despotic monarchies. It is a sobering thought that such patterns of religious inconsistency and social exploitation have been repeated throughout the history of Christian monarchies, which fashioned themselves on the Davidic paradigm.

In summary, the notion of Yahweh's kingship provides a background for understanding the tensions between pro-monarchical and anti-monarchical materials. The fact that verses which suggest that the institution of a human monarchy was incompatible with Yahweh's kingship (1 Sam 8:7; 10:19; 12:12, 19) were juxtaposed with statements that it was Yahweh himself who instituted the monarchy and chose its first representative (1 Sam 8:7; 12:13) suggests a "sinful-but-still-of-God" view of kingship (Birch, 27). In 1 Samuel 12 the people's desire for a human monarchy is categorized among those sins to which God responded graciously in Israel's history (Camponovo, 87). Yahweh's positive response transformed a human error into a divine opportunity. Monarchy was instituted as a means to God's ends and not as an end in itself.

2.2.1.2. Sociopolitical Attitudes Toward Kingship. There is no consensus over the dating of the exodus and the establishment of Israelites in Canaan (*see* History of Israel 1: Settlement Period). It is clear, however, that kingship was introduced after a people identified as *Israel had been ruled by a series of *judges, local rulers with charismatic authority who combined the functions of military leaders and legal arbitrators. The following paragraphs will sketch sociopolitical aspects that shaped popular opinion and influenced the viewpoints of various interest groups.

1. Dissatisfaction with the internal sociopolitical status quo. Judges, the ad hoc rulers under the old political system, functioned in a climate of political, religious and cultural decentralization. The book of Judges and the opening chapters of 1 Samuel contain many stories describing a situation of moral degeneration and a tendency toward cultural and religious assimilation to Canaanite practices. According to the editors of the book of Judges, these developments were incompatible with Yahwism (see the editorial refrain "In those days there was no king in Israel; all the people did what was right in their own eyes," Judg 17:6; cf. Judg 18:1; 19:1; 20:25). The texts reflect a general frustration among the population with the previous system of judges, which over time had led to moral degeneration, social injustice and political vulnerability. Particular judges had abused their position. Since there was no established system of succession, each vacancy created a power vacuum that had regularly been exploited by Israel's political neighbors. Even exemplary judges like Samuel had not guaranteed the integrity of the office. It was concern over the abusive and exploitative behavior of Samuel's sons—appointed by him as judges who would succeed him—that prompted the decisive step toward monarchy (1 Sam 8:1-5). The priesthood, another institution central to Israelite life, had also been affected (1 Sam 2:12—3:18). Thus the drive toward monarchy was more than a desire to replace specific leaders. The whole system was felt to be in need of revision because the status quo neither gave leaders sufficient authority to maintain

moral order and economic fairness, nor did it provide guidelines that prevented rulers from turning into perpetrators themselves.

2. Radical change in the nature of Israelite society. It was during Samuel's time in office that Israel, for the first time, seems to have enjoyed limited military success over its neighbors. It is becoming increasingly likely that this newfound military prowess was not only due to Samuel's military genius and supernatural divine intervention, but also to population growth in Israel. Archaeological data relevant to this question that are presently becoming available support this impression (Finkelstein and Silbermann). It appears that such growth led to an increased self-confidence that went hand in hand with a desire for cultural self-assertion, economic independence and political autonomy. It is likely that such developments also led to social stratification, and so there was a felt need to defend organized social interests between different strata of Israelite society itself (Gottwald). The biblical texts, however, do not focus on the internal dimensions of social change but highlight the function of kingship vis à vis Israel's geographic neighbors.

3. Economic and political pressure from outside. The Israelite tribes had been under sustained pressure from surrounding people groups. The *Philistines played an important role here (so Alt, whose theory gained wide acceptance; cf. 1 Sam 4:1—8:5, 19-20). Equally important, however, were the *Ammonites (so Na'aman, against Alt). Like other people groups in the region, the Ammonites made the transition from tribal society to nation state at about the same time as Israel. Since the Philistine conquest took place after Saul's victory over the Ammonites (cf. 1 Sam 10:27—11:15 with 13:2—14:46), it seems likely that the initial threat to which the demand for a king as military leader had responded was posed by the Ammonites. Philistine occupation of the hill country, then, was the direct result of the emergence of the Israelite state rather than its primary impetus. A period of political suppression and economic exploitation had created a climate that served as a seed bed for resentment against foreign interference. Consequently, the textual focus is on the protection of Israelite interests against *foreign* exploitation. Once the Israelite monarchy was firmly established, the desire for full political participation on the international plain

came to the fore, and this is celebrated in the accounts of *Solomon's reign and throughout the books of 1 and 2 *Kings.

4. Cultural identity and historic consciousness. Israel had consisted of loosely connected tribes from various backgrounds. What held them together was the collective consciousness of an exodus from Egypt. They defined their identity against a background of economic exploitation, cultural suppression and political repression through monarchical structures in Egypt (Brueggemann), and this caused considerable opposition to a similar political system. Kingship as an institution, however, was not alien to Israel. The "Laws of Officials" (Deut 16:18—18:22; 17:14-20 on the king) provided a constitutional framework that allowed for a monarchic organization without exploitation and suppression (*see DOTP*, Deuteronomy, Book of). While the Deuteronomistic History reached its final form much later, key traditions on which it is based are much older.

In summary, most of these sociopolitical factors recommended a change from charismatic rulers to a monarchical system. Others provoked reservations that are documented in 1 Samuel and, with hindsight, in 1 and 2 Kings. It appears, however, that no serious resistance against the transition to a new system emerged. There was a general consensus that the old system had failed. The institution of kingship, then, was introduced in Israel in an attempt to foster national identity and it functioned socially to fill a religious, moral, economic and political vacuum. Opposition to the monarchy, both at its inception and throughout its troubled history, seems to have focused on the motivation for its introduction (1 Sam 8:6-22) and the manner of its conduct (1 Sam 12:13-15, 24-25) rather than on the institution itself.

2.2.2. The Length and Complexity of Saul's Reign Narrative. Scholars have addressed Saul's role in 1 Samuel in complementary ways. Some see Saul simply as a foil for David (e.g., Noth, Childs, Brueggemann). Others see 1 Samuel 16—2 Samuel 5 (often called the History of David's Rise) as a "royal apology" (*see* Propaganda). Its function was to defend David against charges of complicity in the deaths of key members of Saul's family in order to steal Saul's throne (Rost; see Gordon 1986, 37-41). Such theories tend to downplay the importance of Saul and to emphasize the significance of David. More likely, however, the mate-

rials reflect a postmonarchical perspective that transcends the interests of royal dynasties through a theological stance that integrates human and divine kingship (see 2.4). This can be demonstrated through the complex relationship between Saul and David as well as the stories of other members of the royal households of Israel and Judah.

Just a small part of his accession narrative (1 Samuel 1—12) is actually concerned with Saul in his own right. Saul is not even mentioned until 1 Samuel 9:2, and the narrative about his accession swiftly moves in a three-step process from his "designation" (1 Sam 9:1—10:13) to his "demonstration" (1 Sam 11:1-11) and "confirmation" (1 Sam 11:14-15) in just three chapters (cf. Halpern and Edelmann). In the final analysis, however, Saul's accession does not conclude with his confirmation but with his *rejection* as king (1 Sam 13:4-15; cf. Provan, Long and Longman, 212-14). Just when his reign seemed secure, Samuel announced that Saul's kingdom would pass to another.

2.2.2.1. The Continuing Importance of Saul. The first part of 1 Samuel has given the impression that the narrative "rushes on" to David, that the "tilt of the narrative from the outset is toward David" (Brueggemann 2003, 135). Saul, however, does not fade into the background once Da-vid has appeared on the scene. The narrative about his reign continues for another nineteen chapters (1 Sam 13—31). Even after his definitive rejection in 1 Samuel 15, Saul continues to be treated with considerable sympathy and respect by various main figures—including Samuel and David (1 Sam 31 and 2 Sam 1). Saul is important in his own right, and this is illustrated by a comparison with the parallel section in 1 Chronicles: The Chronicler reduced the coverage of Saul to a single chapter (1 Chron 10). Thus it is not true that Saul "never establishes his own right in the narrative" (Brueggemann 2003, 135). It is an indication of Saul's prominence and appeal in the narrative that recent commentators, including Brueggemann himself, have found much in the books of Samuel to rouse their sympathies for Saul (cf., e.g., Brueggemann 1990, 99-101). The explanation for this surprising phenomenon is given in Saul's status as "the LORD's anointed," most memorably expressed from the lips of David (1 Sam 24:6 [MT 7], 10 [MT 11]; 26:16 and 2 Sam 1:14, 16, 21).

2.2.2.2. The Relative Importance of David. The

swift introduction of David into the story of Saul's reign and the messianic expectations that later came to be associated with the Davidic line have led to an overestimation of David in the history of Jewish and Christian interpretations. This has led to an undervaluing of kings from other families, most notably of Saul, Jeroboam and Jehu. Unease with such romanticizing tendencies has recently caused a backlash in the opposite direction, a trend represented by S. L. McKenzie's and B. Halpern's biographies of David. Their stated aim is to read the biblical accounts about David "against the grain" (McKenzie, 45) and to "contemplate David as his enemies saw him" (Halpern, xv). Thus the readings proposed by McKenzie, however, are in reality *with the grain* of much of the material and Halpern is of course only able to contemplate what David's enemies thought of him through the eyes of the authors and editors of 1 and 2 Samuel, whom many presume to be David's "friends" (cf. Provan, Long and Longman, 215-21). The readings proposed by McKenzie and Halpern were prompted by the biblical materials themselves. David was less important and seen in a less glorified light in the biblical texts than has often been supposed. The texts present a nuanced portrayal of him and inspire trust in the positive as well as the negative aspects of David's career and character.

2.3. The Postmonarchic Perspective of Chronicles. The book which now makes up 1-2 Chronicles was compiled and edited long after the monarchic period. Its attitude toward monarchy in Israel differs significantly from the perspective of the Deuteronomistic History (see 2.4). For this and various other reasons, the book has not received the attention it deserves for the value of its information regarding kingship in Israel. In comparison with the Deuteronomistic History, Chronicles contains much more detailed information about the monarch's role and activities (Japhet, 428-44): (1) political administration, subdivided into civil (esp. 1 Chron 23 to 27), military (considered among the ruler's first priorities) and religious sectors (e.g., 1 Chron 16:4-6, 37-38; 2 Chron 31); (2) construction and public building programs; (3) economic policy and practice; (4) military campaigns. The Chronicler's great skill in describing ceremony and pageantry creates a vivid picture of royal protocol and public religious observance. In particular, his descriptions of the importance of royal

initiative in matters of religion and the monarch's role in the cult has had a lasting influence on the attitudes and practices of Christian monarchies through the ages.

There are three distinctive aspects of the Chronicler's understanding of kingship in Israel (Wil-liamson): (1) it is identified with the kingdom of God (cf., e.g., 1 Chron 28:5; 29:23; 2 Chron 13:8); (2) it is inalienable from the Davidic dynasty (cf. 1 Chron 10:13-14 with 1 Chron 17:13); (3) the promise of continuous Davidic occupancy on the throne becomes the foundation of the monarchic institution and assumes such a central role for understanding Yahweh's relationship with Israel that even the Exodus and Sinai traditions become integrated with it (cf., e.g., 1 Chron 17:7-22 and 2 Chron 6). These three aspects are all the more remarkable because they existed at a time when the monarchic period had long ended. Chronicles expected a restoration of the Davidic dynasty to the throne of Judah. This not only *fostered* an understanding of kingship that eventually led to fully developed concepts of messianism (following Selman; see also 2.4.1); it testifies to a hope in the restoration of the Davidic monarchy so bound up with the realization of the kingdom of God (cf. Japhet, 397, 403) that it actually *presumed* a messianic hope.

2.4. The Postmonarchic Perspective of the Deuteronomistic History. The Deuteronomistic History was compiled and edited after the monarchic period. The historical books are compilations of many sources that have been arranged by later editors. Much of the factual information about the united monarchy and the kingdoms of Israel and Judah, however, is based on reliable data that were contemporary with or close to the actual events (see Kitchen; Provan, Long and Longman III; as well as the articles collected in Day 2004). These editors were not simply compilers of originally independent documents and data, they were gifted theologians who interpreted the history of their people from a comprehensive and theological perspective. For them kingship formed but one episode in the larger plot of Yahweh's providential interaction with his people. What, then, of the tensions between various parts of these composite texts?

Some hint at different attitudes and perspectives that underlay the original sources in their precomposite state. Always, however, the Deuteronomists integrated such tensions and made them their own. They do not indicate editorial errors or the editors' "respect" for their source materials, as if their sources were still in some sense "independent." A good case study is the rise of David. Brueggemann comments: "A theological reading of the 'Rise' is that the narrative evidences the providential intentionality of YHWH who has willed David's exalted rise to power. Just below the surface . . . we may see . . . a series of cunning and ruthless acts of self-advancement on the part of David, acts that are savored and artistically rendered by the narrator who wants us to notice . . . a shamelessly engineered advance, humanly crafted in the guise of divine providence. Thus the narrative rendering has multiple layers of telling that admit of an ironic reading" (Brueggemann 2003, 135). The genius of the narrators lies in the ability to compile and compose a story that not only allows these theological and ironic readings, it actually demands them *in combination*. The Deuteronomists' greatness lies in their ability to prioritize the theological reading while at the same time incorporating an ironic awareness of the opposite and yet complementary attitudes of the story's human protagonists within the divine plan. This betrays a fundamentally ambivalent attitude toward human kingship. The historical books are an account of how divine grace may redeem but not prevent the vagaries of human choice and aberration.

2.4.1. Anointing and the Rise of Messianism. From a Christian perspective, messianism is a set of expectations "focusing on a future royal figure sent by God who will bring salvation to God's people and the world and establish a kingdom characterized by features such as peace and justice" (Rose, 566). Postexilic Judaism shares some of the hopes featured in this definition, but the commonalities should not be pressed too far (Neusner et al.). The two faiths hold in common that the true fulfillment of such hopes is still to come. Where they differ is that Christians are convinced that the Messiah's identity is already known. These more developed concepts of messianism did not arise until after the OT was completed (but see 2.3.1). Its roots, however, lie in the practice of *anointing.

Anointing refers to the religious practice of applying oil to someone in order to consecrate them for a particular task or role, such as priest, prophet or ruler. With kings, the function of such a consecration is to endow them with divine authorization for office, to confer onto them a status of inviolability and to impart them with special powers to accomplish their task (cf., e.g., 1 Sam 10:6-7; 16:13; 24:6 and 10; 1 Kings 1:39). In the OT such persons (always male) can be refered to as *māšîaḥ*, an adjective or a noun with the meaning "anointed" or "anointed one," from which the English word *messiah* is derived. The person to which the word *messiah* refered was normally a contemporary figure, exceptions in the historical books being 1 Samuel 2:10, 35. As the following paragraphs show, these future references and several other subtle editorial strokes prepared for the messianic vision.

2.4.2. The Messianic Function of the Song of Hannah (2 Sam 2:1-10). At first sight the song simply celebrates Hannah's joy over the birth and weaning of her first child. It ends, however, with a reference to Yahweh's "messiah" in poetic parallel with the word *king* (1 Sam 2:10). Thus the prophet mother anticipates her toddler's role as kingmaker long before kingship becomes a main theme in the larger narrative. Through this editorial move the song becomes the "clef sign" for the rest of the book (cf. Gordon 1984, 26). This is the first of only two occasions where the word for messiah refers to a future figure, but it set the tone for later messianic understandings.

2.4.3. The Messianic Function of Dynastic Statements. Scholarship has tended to concentrate on the *Davidic Covenant (cf. 2 Sam 7) as the main source for the development of messianism. After the fall of Jerusalem, the theory goes, messianism arose as an attempt to reconcile theological theory and political reality. The covenant had promised David's line permanent incumbency. Since the divine promise had failed, however, the belief that Yahweh would restore David's descendants to the Jerusalem throne had become a necessity. Messianism became a construct to avoid one of two conclusions—either that Yahweh had abandoned his people for good (emotionally unacceptable) or that Yahweh had broken his promise (theologically unthinkable). In the eyes of the Deuteronomistic editors, however, Yahweh used the promise of dynastic continuity and the curtailment of dynastic aspirations as an important didactic instrument throughout. The following paragraphs will sketch several dynastic statements, the first four with reference to individuals that did not belong to David's line.

1. Divine judgment revoked an apparently unconditional dynastic promise to the house of the priest Eli (1 Sam 2:27-36, esp. vv. 30 and 35). The promise, though not recorded in the Pentateuch or elsewhere, is traced back as far as the installation of Aaron (or Moses) and his descendants into the office of priesthood before the exodus. Prompted by the gross misconduct of Eli's sons, his line lost the priestly office in spite of its perpetual nature. The benefits of the original promise were transferred to a rival family (the reference is most likely to *Zadok's line rather than to Samuel, cf. Gordon 1986, 87-88), with particular reference to a king to be anointed in the (near) future.

2. Divine judgment prevented a scheduled dynastic promise to Saul (1 Sam 13:7-15). The instructions (1 Sam 10:7-8), which Saul had received from Samuel at his anointing, turned out to be a test regarding Saul's suitability for royal office (Provan, Long and Longman, 211-14). Samuel's words in 1 Samuel 13:13-14 indicate that a dynastic promise was to follow the test. In the event, however, the kingdom was transferred to a rival.

3. A conditional and perhaps temporary dynastic promise was squandered by *Jeroboam's apostasy (1 Kings 11:29-39; 12:26—13:10). As with David, Yahweh's prophet introduced Jeroboam to the possibility of kingship in a clandestine way in response to his predecessor's failure (1 Kings 11:29-31). Comparable with David's promise, Jeroboam received a prophetic oracle that contained a conditional dynastic promise: "you shall be king over Israel. If you will listen to all that I command you . . . I will . . . build you an enduring house, as I built for David . . . I will punish the descendants of David, but not forever" (1 Kings 11:37-39). The divine punishment against David's descendants was not to last "forever" (1 Kings 11:39). According to the oracle, however, it was divine judgment that had occasioned Jeroboam's preferment. This may have caused Jeroboam to wonder how perpetual his dynasty was meant to be. Perhaps his kingdom would return to the Davidides once the period of divine punishment had come to an end? It seems likely that Jeroboam erected idols in the form of two golden calves in *Bethel and *Dan precisely to preempt this perceived threat (1 Kings 12:26-30, cf. vv. 31-33). Whether or not it was meant to last, he failed to accept that his promotion to royal status was a means to God's ends

rather than his own. Jeroboam's tragedy lies in his lack of trust in the divine promise. He and his descendants, while on the throne, were to serve God and his people rather than their own interests.

4. Jehu's dynastic promise is limited to four generations (2 Kings 10:30; cf. vv. 31-33). The dynastic promise was a reward for Jehu's single-minded extermination of the house of Ahab. The limitation to four generations was a punishment because Jehu continued with the "sins of Jeroboam."

5. The dynastic statement addressed to Solomon, next in line after David, is conditional (1 Kings 9:1-9). On the basis of the apparently unconditional and perpetual nature of *Nathan's oracle to David and his line, a dynastic statement would appear unnecessary, certainly in the very next generation. At any rate, one would have expected a simple restatement of the dynastic promise in unconditional and perpetual terms. In the event, however, the statement is couched in conditional terms, with the dynasty's survival at stake in every new generation (1 Kings 9:6-9, addressed to Solomon and the people).

In sum, a pattern of dynastic statements emerges where divine promise and threat serve as incentives for officeholders to conduct their business in accordance with the divine will. Promises in all of these, whether conditional and perpetual or not, can and have been revoked and could, at least in theory, be reinstated. It is this hope that fuelled messianic aspirations, combined with a hope in divine mercy to David, who, in this capacity, was not so much an idealized hero, but in his strength and frailty represented all Israel and ultimately all humanity.

See also ANOINTING; CHRONICLES, BOOKS OF; CHRONOLOGY; DAVID; DAVIDIC COVENANT; DAVID'S FAMILY; HEZEKIAH; HISTORY OF ISRAEL 3-6; JEHOSHAPHAT; JEHU DYNASTY; JEROBOAM; JOSIAH; KINGS, BOOKS OF; OMRI DYNASTY; PROPAGANDA; REHOBOAM; ROYAL FAMILY; SAMUEL, BOOKS OF; SAUL AND SAUL'S FAMILY; SOLOMON; STATE OFFICIALS.

BIBLIOGRAPHY. **G. W. Ahlström,** *Royal Administration and National Religion in Ancient Palestine* (SHANE 1; Leiden: Brill, 1982); **A. Alt,** "Die Staatenbildung der Israeliten in Palästina," in *Kleine Schriften zur Geschichte des Volkes Israel II* (Munich: Beck, 1978) 1-33; **J. Baines,** "Ancient Egyptian Kingship: Official Forms, Rhetoric,

Context," in *King and Messiah in Israel and the Ancient Near East*, ed. J. Day (JSOTSup 270; Sheffield: Sheffield Academic Press, 1998) 16-53; **B. Birch,** *The Rise of the Israelite Monarchy: The Growth and Development of 1 Samuel 7—15* (SBLDS 27; Missoula, MT: Scholars Press, 1976); **W. Brueggemann,** *First and Second Samuel* (IntC; Louisville, KY: John Knox Press, 1990); idem, *An Introduction to the Old Testament: The Canon and Christian Imagination* (Louisville, KY: Westminster John Knox Press, 2003); **O. Camponovo,** *Königtum, Königsherrschaft und Reich Gottes in den frühjüdischen Schriften* (OBO 58; Freiburg, CH: Universitätsverlag; Göttingen: Vandenhoeck & Ruprecht, 1984); **B. S. Childs,** *Introduction to the Old Testament as Scripture* (Philadelphia: Fortress, 1979); idem, *Biblical Theology of the Old and New Testaments* (Minneapolis: Fortress, 1992); **P. R. Davies,** *In Search of 'Ancient Israel'* (2d ed.; JSOTSup 148; Sheffield: JSOT Press, 1995); **J. Day,** "The Canaanite Inheritance of the Israelite Monarchy," in *King and Messiah in Israel and the Ancient Near East*, ed. J. Day (JSOTSup 270; Sheffield: Sheffield Academic Press, 1998a) 72-90; idem, ed., *In Search of Pre-Exilic Israel: Proceedings of the Oxford Old Testament Seminar* (JSOTSup 406; London; New York: T & T Clark, 2004); idem, ed., *King and Messiah in Israel and the Ancient Near East: Proceedings of the Oxford Old Testament Seminar* (JSOTsup 270; Sheffield: Sheffield Academic Press, 1998b); **W. G. Dever,** "Histories and Non-Histories of Ancient Israel: The Question of the United Monarchy," in *In Search of Pre-Exilic Israel*, ed. J. Day (2004) 65-94; idem, *What Did the Biblical Writers Know and When Did They Know It?* (Grand Rapids: Eerdmans, 2001; **D. Edelmann,** "Saul's Rescue of Jabesh-Gilead (1 Samuel 11:1-11): Sorting Story from History," *ZAW* 96 (1984) 195-209; **I. Finkelstein,** "The Archaeology of the United Monarchy: An Alternative View," *Levant* 28 (1996) 177-87; **I. Finkelstein and N. A. Silbermann,** *The Bible Unearthed: Archaeology's New Vision of Ancient Israel and the Origin of its Sacred Texts* (New York: The Free Press, 2001); **G. Galil,** *The Chronology of the Kings of Israel and Judah* (Leiden: Brill, 1996); **R. P. Gordon,** *1 & 2 Samuel* (OTG; Sheffield: JSOT Press, 1984); idem, *1 & 2 Samuel: A Commentary* (Exeter: Paternoster, 1986); **N. K. Gottwald,** "The Participation of Free Agrarians in the Introduction of Monarchy to Ancient Israel," *Semeia* 37 (1986) 77-106; **B. Halpern,** *The Constitution of the Monarchy in Israel* (HSM 25; Chico, CA: Scholars Press,

1981); idem, *David's Secret Demons: Messiah, Murderer, Traitor, King* (Grand Rapids: Eerdmans, 2001); **T. Ishida,** *The Royal Dynasties in Ancient Israel: A Study on the Formation and Development of Royal-Dynastic Ideology* (BZAW 142; Berlin: W. de Gruyter, 1977); **B. Janowski,** "Königtum Gottes im Alten Testament," *RGG* 4.1591-93; **S. Japhet,** *The Ideology of the Book of Chronicles and Its Place in Biblical Thought* (BEATAJ 9; Frankfurt: Peter Lang, 1989); **K. A. Kitchen,** *On the Reliability of the Old Testament* (Grand Rapids: Eerdmans, 2003); **W. Lambert,** "Kingship in Ancient Mesopotamia," in *King and Messiah in Israel and the Ancient Near East*, ed. J. Day (JSOTSup 270; Sheffield: Sheffield Academic Press, 1998) 54-70; **G. Lanczkowski,** "Königtum I: Religionsgeschichtlich," *TRE* 19 (1990) 323-27; **P. K. McCarter,** "The Apology of David," *JBL* 90 (1980) 489-504; idem, "Plots True or False: The Succession Narrative as Court Apologetic," *Int* 35 (1981) 355-67; **S. L. McKenzie,** *King David: A Biography* (Oxford: Oxford University Press, 2000); **T. N. D. Mettinger,** *King and Messiah: The Civil and Sacral Legitimation of the Israelite Kings* (ConBOT 8; Lund: Gleerup, 1976); **J. M. Miller and J. Hayes,** *A History of Ancient Israel and Judah* (Philadelphia: Westminster, 1986); **N. Na'aman,** "The Pre-Deuteronomistic Story of King Saul and its Historical Significance," *CBQ* 54 (1992) 638-58; **J. Neusner, W. S. Green and E. Frerichs,** eds., *Judaisms and Their Messiahs at the Turn of the Christian Era* (Cambridge: Cambridge University Press, 1987); **H. M. Niemann,** *Herrschaft, Königtum und Staat: Skizzen zur soziokulturellen Entwicklung im monarchischen Israel* (FAT 6; Tübingen: Mohr/Siebeck, 1993); idem, "Königtum in Israel," *RGG* 4.1593-97; **M. Noth,** *The History of Israel* (New York: Harper & Row, 1960); **I. Provan, V. P. Long and T. Longman III,** *A Biblical History of Israel* (Louisville: Westminster John Knox: 2003); **W. H. Rose,** "Messiah," *DOTP* 565-68; **L. Rost,** *The Succession to the Throne of David* (Sheffield: Almond Press, 1982); **L. Schmidt,** "Königtum II: Altes Testament," *TRE* 19 (1990) 327-33; **M. J. Selman,** "The Kingdom of God in the Old Testament," *TynBul* 40 (1989), 161-183; **C. Smith,** "Queenship in Israel? The Case of Bathsheba, Jezebel and Athaliah," in *King and Messiah in Israel and the Ancient Near East*, ed. J. Day (JSOTsup 270; Sheffield: Sheffield Academic Press, 1998) 142-62; **E. K. Solvang,** *A Woman's Place Is in the House: Royal Women of Judah and Their Involvement in the House of David*

(JSOTSup 349; London: Sheffield Academic Press, 2003); **C. M. Tetley,** *The Reconstructed Chronology of the Divided Kingdom* (Winona Lake, IN: Eisenbrauns, 2005); **E. R. Thiele,** *The Mysterious Numbers of the Hebrew Kings* (3rd ed.; Grand Rapids: Eerdmans: 1986);; **J. Wellhausen,** *Prolegomena to the History of Israel* (Edinburgh: Black, 1885); **K. W. Whitelam,** *The Invention of Ancient Israel: The Silencing of Palestinian History* (London: Routledge, 1996); idem, "King and Kingship," *ABD* 4.40-48 **H. G. M. Williamson,** *1 and 2 Chronicles* (NCB; Grand Rapids: Eerdmans, 1982); **E. Zenger,** "Herrschaft Gottes/Reich Gottes II," *TRE* 15 (1986) 176-89.

K. M. Heim

KINGS, BOOKS OF

The books of Kings are the culmination of the OT's "primary history," which begins with Genesis. Spanning the time from *Solomon to the fall of Judah, they are important for the covenantal history of Israel with God, especially because of their application of "Deuteronomic" theological themes. This article sets the books in their historical context, considers them as narrative, and aims to understand their theology and purpose.

1. Kings in Historical Context
2. Kings in Old Testament Context
3. The Structure of Kings
4. Story and Storytelling in Kings
5. The Theology of Kings
6. The "Audience" of Kings

1. Kings in Historical Context.

1.1. Scope and Transmission. The books of Kings tell the history of the kingdoms of Israel and Judah from the accession of Solomon (970 BCE) to the fall of Judah (587 BCE). Thus they correspond to the "monarchical" period, understood to encompass the united kingdom of Israel, ruled by *David and Solomon, the separate kingdoms of (northern) Israel and Judah, which ended in 722 BCE with the fall of the former to the *Assyrians, and the time of Judah alone (722-587 BCE), extending to the destruction of Judah by the *Babylonian king Nebuchadnezzar. The books are written in retrospect on this long period, from a time in or after 562 BCE, the date of the last recorded incident in them, the release of Judah's king Jehoiachin from prison in exile on the accession of a new Babylonian king, Evil-merodach (Amel-marduk) (2 Kings 25:27-30).

It is probable that the books have been formed from materials and sources that stretch back over the four-hundred-year period that is its subject. Kings itself contains references to annalistic sources ("the Book of the Chronicles of the Kings of Israel" [1 Kings 14:19], "the Book of the Chronicles of the Kings of Judah" [1 Kings 14:29], "the Book of the Acts of Solomon" [1 Kings 11:41]), but nothing of these is known otherwise to history (*see* Sources, References to). Other sources can only be guessed at, but might include prophetic records containing the stories of *Elijah and *Elisha, and perhaps recording the prophetic role in the rise and fall of kings (Cogan 2001, 92-93). If such sources lie behind Kings, they must have been collected and woven together into the work as we have it.

1.2. Authorship of Kings. Any attempt to establish who wrote Kings must ask about the relationship between the exilic end point of the story and the long period that it covers. Modern discussions of authorship typically orient themselves to three main approaches (we will see below how these approaches affect the interpretation of the book). First, in the modern classic on the subject, M. Noth believed that Kings was part of a longer work (Deuteronomy-Kings) written by a single author in the exile. Noth called this work the "Deuteronomistic History" because he found themes in it whose theological foundation was Deuteronomy. Chief among these was Deuteronomy's law confining worship to the place chosen by Yahweh (Deut 12:5), which explains Kings' antipathy to worship at the *high places and its concern to concentrate pure Yahwistic worship in the Jerusalem temple (2 Kings 22—23). Equally important was its emphasis on the Mosaic commandments, Deuteronomy's "commandments, statutes and ordinances" (Deut 5:31; cf. 1 Kings 2:3). Noth believed that the Deuteronomist used sources; others have tried to discern these and say how they were transmitted (e.g., Weippert; Campbell and O'Brien).

The second approach also sees the book as Deuteronomistic but postulates a major edition of it in the time of King *Josiah, supplemented by another in the exile. This idea of a "double redaction" of Kings (Cross, 274-89; Nelson 1981; Knoppers; Sweeney) is based primarily on the lengthy narrative of Josiah's reform of religion (2 Kings 22—23), which portrays that king with great approval as conforming to Mosaic and Davidic models (2 Kings 22:2; 23:25). In the second, exilic edition the triumphal tone is chastened by the new situation. The adjustments made by this second Deuteronomistic hand can be seen in 2 Kings 23:26, which explains that in spite of Josiah's excellence, Judah fell because the sin of *Manasseh, who reigned before him, was so great that Yahweh's anger could not be assuaged. This second edition can also be detected in the body of the book in places such as 1 Kings 9:1-9 (1 Kings 9:1-5, Josianic; 1 Kings 9:6-9, exilic; see Cogan 2001, 297).

In the third influential approach R. Smend postulated several editions, all exilic. His basic *Deuteronomistic History was pro-Davidic, but it then was qualified by a more cautious "nomistic" redactional layer. W. Dietrich refined this by interposing a "prophetic" edition, which was less hospitable to the Davidic heritage.

On any account, the final composition of the book is an exilic (or perhaps postexilic) reflection on a period of political existence that has now ended and has little prospect of revival. The political crisis was at the same time religious, for the self-understanding of Israel and Judah was based on the ancient covenant of Yahweh, God of Israel, and its special form in a covenant with the house of David (2 Sam 7; 23:5). Thus the books of Kings are a document born in severe crisis, a theology wrestling with the meaning of terrible experience, every bit as much as the more plangent book of Lamentations.

1.3. Is Kings "History"? Modern study of Kings often has been taken up with the question to what extent it is "historical." Some judgments on it from this perspective have portrayed it as a theological narrative that should not be judged by the standards of history. Modern writers sometimes find the inclusion of stories of *miraculous events incompatible with a true account of the past, and they speculate on what the "real" history behind the text might have been. However, it is important to make some distinctions here.

Kings is indeed an account of Israel's history, part of its aim being to explain how the situation that it addresses arose out of a series of connected events in the past. Its relationship with history as generally understood can be checked at a number of points against what we know from other sources. For example, visitors to the British Museum in London can see the Black Obelisk of Shalmaneser III, in which "Jehu, son of Omri" (or his envoy) is pictured doing obeisance to the Assyrian king (Cogan and Tadmor, 106-9, 120-21). This places *Jehu in the right historical period, although his payment of tribute to Shalmaneser is not reported in Kings. (The attribution "son of Omri" is curious because Kings tells how Jehu wiped out the house of *Omri; but the Assyrian expression is merely a way of designating the king of Israel.) In Jerusalem it is possible to go through "Hezekiah's tunnel," or the "Siloam tunnel," presumably the tunnel constructed by King *Hezekiah (2 Kings 20:20). The miraculous deliverance of Jerusalem from Sennacherib (2 Kings 2:18-20) often is said to be indirectly supported by that Assyrian king's annals, which imply that he could not take Jerusalem (Cogan, *COS* 2.119B:302-3) (*see* Non-Israelite Written Sources: Assyrian). Archaeology lends color to the biblical story at a number of points, not least in its recovery of *Lachish, reduced first by the Assyrians and then the Babylonians (2 Kings 18:14; cf. Jer 34:7). (On external evidence for the religion of Israel see 5.3.)

These few examples show that Kings' relation to other historical evidence is uneven. Such comparisons show that different historical sources (including the Bible) throw light on history in their distinctive ways, and therefore that records do not always match up neatly. Biblical authors and Assyrian kings have their different interests. The Kings account of the deliverance from Sennacherib could hardly be confirmed or disconfirmed in all its particularity, since the miraculous dimension is not susceptible to that (and Sennacherib would not proclaim it). Kings tells the history of Israel in its own way, with selections and emphases and, indeed, theological purpose. A modern historian probably would pay less attention to Ahab and Elijah than Kings does, and more to Assyria. But that would be another account and another angle. (For more on Kings as history or historiography, see Provan 1995, 6-10.)

2. Kings in Old Testament Context.

2.1. Kings in the Historical Books.

2.1.1. Kings and Samuel. The books of Kings are really a single book (henceforth, the book of Kings, or Kings). The division into two is first seen in the LXX, which numbered Samuel and Kings together as 1-4 Reigns (or Kingdoms).

Samuel and Kings together tell of the rise and fall of monarchy in Israel. The promise to King David that Yahweh would establish his dynastic house "forever" (2 Sam 7:13), and the narrative of David's war with his son Absalom in 2 Samuel 15—20, form the immediate background to the establishment of Solomon as king of Israel, rather than another of David's sons.

2.1.2. Kings in Genesis-Kings. Kings has a wider context, however, in the whole stretch of Genesis to Kings. The story of Israel begins in Genesis with Yahweh's choice of Abraham out of his Mesopotamian background (Gen 11:31-32, cf. Josh 24:2), such that in the exile of Jews to Babylon there is a kind of full circle. Exodus has a blueprint for the tabernacle (Ex 25—31) that is echoed in the instructions for building the temple (1 Kings 6—7). Kings takes from Deuteronomy its law of worship (Deut 12:5), which it sees as an insistence on worship at the Jerusalem temple alone (1 Kings 8:27-30; 2 Kings 21:4), and its exhortations to obey God's "statutes, ordinances and commandments" (1 Kings 6:12 RSV; cf. Deut 5:31).

Finally, the books from Joshua to Kings are known variously as the Historical Books (in the Christian canonical tradition that includes Ruth) and as the Former Prophets, a Jewish designation of the same literature (excluding Ruth). The former term highlights the claim of this long narrative to tell a history; the term "Former Prophets" perceives its kinship with prophecy (the Latter Prophets designating the corpus of prophetic books beginning with Isaiah). Both denotations say important things about Kings, as we will see.

3. The Structure of Kings.

3.1. The Structure of Kings. The book is a carefully structured narrative on both large and small scales. Its subject matter indicates initially a threefold division: 1 Kings 1—11 (Solomon); 1 Kings 12—2 Kings 17 (the two kingdoms); 2 Kings 18—25 (Judah alone). These sections, however, are linked within a unified concept. The first and last sections, for example, echo each other in respect to the themes of kingship and worship. As Solomon reigns over a united Israel, so Josiah briefly and symbolically reclaims the ancestral territory with his incursion into the northern domain (2 Kings 23). In worship, while Solomon's central achievement is to construct the temple, the book ends with the temple's de-

construction at the hands of the Babylonians.

3.1.1. Fulfillment of the Prophetic Word. There are in addition overarching themes or patterns. The first is that of prophetic word and fulfillment. Most striking is the prediction of King Josiah's reform by a prophet in the time of *Jeroboam I, about three hundred years before the event, in which Josiah is expressly named (1 Kings 13:1-3). A connection is thus established between an early event in the period covered by the book and one of its latest and most significant. In this way we are shown how decisive the word of God is in events in history. The story of a shorter-term prophecy fulfillment is designed to confirm this pattern (1 Kings 13:11-32). As a result the whole book, from its account of the beginning of the divided kingdoms to the reform of Josiah, is subject to the expectation of the destruction of the idolatrous system put in place by Jeroboam. Jeroboam's decisive role in bringing about the fall of Israel is also highlighted in a prophecy-fulfillment arc from 1 Kings 11:16 to 2 Kings 17:21-23 (von Rad, 340).

3.1.2. David, Jeroboam and Ahab. A second pattern derives from the interplay between true and false forms of worship. It is a premise of the book that King David was a model of the pious king. David himself charges Solomon to keep Yahweh's commandments as written in "the law of Moses" (1 Kings 2:3). This indeed is a prerequisite of the fulfillment of the dynastic promise (1 Kings 2:4, cf. 2 Sam 7:13). (The present theme, therefore, is connected to the preceding one.) When Solomon turns away from Yahweh, he is contrasted with David (1 Kings 11:4), and when he is told that much of his kingdom will be taken away from him, he is allowed to retain a portion of it "for the sake of David my servant whom I chose, who kept my statutes and my commandments" (1 Kings 11:34; cf. 11:12-13). This recurs as a refrain (1 Kings 14:8; 15:4-5, 11; 2 Kings 8:19; 14:3; 16:2). And the two kings who conducted far-reaching reforms reestablishing the worship of Yahweh—Hezekiah and Josiah—are said to have "walked in all the way of David (their) father" (2 Kings 18:3; 22:2). These two are also said to have kept the laws of Moses (2 Kings 18:6; 23:25), which emphasizes how much they conform to the Davidic pattern.

Running alongside the theme of the Davidic model is the countermodel of Jeroboam. We have noticed the prophecy regarding this first northern king, but he plays a more extensive role in the structure of the book. The sin of Jeroboam is referred to repeatedly in the long middle section, and this becomes one of the springs of tension that points toward resolution in judgment on the north.

Two contrary impulses, then, help structure the book of Kings. The first is apostasy from Yahweh, symbolized by Jeroboam's erection of golden calves in *Bethel and *Dan (1 Kings 12:28-30), which in turn recall the golden calf of Israel's first, archetypal act of idolatry (Ex 32). The second is reform of religion toward Yahweh. This tendency is represented by a number of kings of Judah: Asa (1 Kings 15:11), *Jehoshaphat (1 Kings 22:43), Amaziah (2 Kings 14:3), Azariah/Uzziah (2 Kings 15:3). Their positive appraisal by the author of Kings is expressed formulaically: "He did what was right in the eyes of the LORD." However, the acceptance of these kings is always qualified by a reservation concerning the places of non-Yahwistic worship (the high places), which they did not remove. The reform theme builds to a climax, however, in the accounts of the kings Hezekiah and Josiah, and especially the latter, for these are portrayed as having campaigned ruthlessly against non-Yahwistic worship. The path toward reform seems to have reached its culmination with Josiah, who destroys places of false worship not only in Judah but even in northern territory, which had been lost to Israel since the Assyrian deportations in 722 BCE. It is in this campaign that the prophecy of the unnamed prophet of Judah regarding Bethel (1 Kings 13:2) is expressly fulfilled (2 Kings 23:15-20).

In these latter stages of the book the increasing momentum of reform is matched by an increasing intensity of rebellion against Yahweh in the two most unfaithful kings of Judah: Ahaz (2 Kings 16) and Manasseh (2 Kings 21). There is even a kind of pendulum swing between these opposite forces, each becoming more pronounced (Hoffmann, 154-55).

It will be clear that the two structuring features that we have observed are closely linked: the fulfillment of prophecy and the struggle between two opposing religious forces. They are also spliced with the chronological patterning that alternates the stories of the northern and southern kingdoms. This is because the northern kingdom is portrayed as exercising a malign influence on the south, King Ahab becoming the chief bearer of the incubus of Jeroboam.

Certain kings of Judah are expressly said to have walked in the ways of Ahab: Jehoram (2 Kings 8:18), Ahaziah (2 Kings 8:27), Manasseh (2 Kings 21:3, 13). Ahab indeed has infiltrated the south even through his family. Jehoram, one of Judah's imitators of Ahab, was married to his daughter Athaliah (2 Kings 8:18, 26), and (coincidentally?) he bore the same name as one of Ahab's own sons (Jehoram = Joram), with whom he made common cause in a war against Syria (2 Kings 8:28). Athaliah herself became queen in the aftermath of Jehu's bloody campaign against both tainted royal houses (2 Kings 11), in a culmination of the overwhelming of Judah by the religion and politics of the *Omrides.

This powerful effect of the Omrides on the history told in Kings is attested by further formal considerations. The point about Ahab's influence in his own time is marked by repeated insistent references to "the house of Ahab," especially in 2 Kings 8—9 (note the threefold occurrence in 2 Kings 8:21). And the long cycle of stories about the prophets Elijah and Elisha (1 Kings 17—2 Kings 13), unique in the book, seems to emphasize the danger to Israel and Judah precisely in that period.

3.1.3. The Structure of 1 Kings 1—11. 1 Kings 1—11 is dominated by two features: Solomon's two dreams in which God speaks to him, giving him wisdom and recalling him to obedience (1 Kings 3:4-14; 9:1-9), and the temple building and dedication, which forms a large middle block of this section (1 Kings 5:1—8:66). This narrative symmetry can be extended to the contrast between the opening scenes, in which Solomon's kingdom is established (1 Kings 1—2), and the final chapter, in which the united kingdom bequeathed to his son by David is condemned to be divided, with only a small part left to Solomon's successors in Jerusalem (1 Kings 11). Correspondingly, the faithful Solomon who asks Yahweh for wisdom (1 Kings 3) contrasts with the apostate who marries many foreign wives and worships their gods (1 Kings 11). Thus the structure of 1 Kings 1—11 must represent this transformation of Solomon. Some place this transition at the beginning of 1 Kings 11 (De Vries, xliv-xlv), while others put it earlier (e.g., Parker at 1 Kings 9:1). Some regard the whole of 1 Kings 1—11 as a negative portrait in which the contrasts that we have noted have an ironic character (Eslinger).

3.1.4. The Structure of 1 Kings 12—2 Kings 17.
The long middle section of the book is unified
by its theme of the two kingdoms, Israel (the
northern kingdom) and Judah (the southern).
Their stories are told in parallel, the chronology
of each being given in terms of the other, and of
the regnal years of their respective monarchs.
This interlocking relationship may be seen in
the formulas that introduce and close the accounts of the reigns (e.g., 1 Kings 14:19-20, 21).
As we have seen, the Elijah-Elisha cycle plays a
large part in this section of the book, with its focus on the sin of the house of Ahab. And it
builds toward its climax in the destruction of the
northern kingdom, and the explanation of its
demise in an extended reflection on the failure
of the northern people to hear the *prophets
(2 Kings 17).

3.1.5. The Structure of 2 Kings 18—25. The final section of the book, which deals with Judah
alone, between 722 and 587 BCE, is built around
extremes of reform and apostasy. Part of it (2 Kings
18:1—20:21) occurs again, with variations, in
Isaiah 36:1—39:8.

The account of Hezekiah's reform (2 Kings
18:1-8) is followed, surprisingly, by an extended
treatment of the siege of Jerusalem under the
Assyrian Sennacherib in 701 BCE, in which
Hezekiah first tries to buy off the invader with
tribute raised by raids on the temple treasury
and even on the gold of its fabric (2 Kings 18:13-
16). This does not alleviate the siege, however.
The lengthy account of the siege has long been
attributed to the presence of two or even three
accounts of it (2 Kings 18:13-16; 18:17-19:9a with
19:36-37, and 19:9b-35) (see Hobbs, 246). The
Assyrian attack is finally defeated, by divine intervention, after Hezekiah turns to Yahweh in
prayer (2 Kings 19:14-19). The prophet *Isaiah
enters the story at this point, prophesying the
deliverance that then ensues (2 Kings 19:20-37).
This high point is followed, however, by the all-
time low, the reign of Manasseh, who is expressly likened to Ahab (2 Kings 21:3), and who pursues a rigorous pro-Assyrian policy.

The tide then turns again with Josiah's reform (2 Kings 22:1-23:25). But even this produces no lasting benefit. Rather, the sin of Josiah's
predecessor Manasseh is invoked as overriding,
so that in spite of the great reform, the judgment
on Judah is already fixed (2 Kings 23:26-27). And
the narrative quickly runs to its conclusion in
telling it.

3.1.6. Unity in Kings? This story, as we have
seen (see 1.2 above), has seemed to many to lack
unity, especially because of the dramatic change
in fortunes at its climax. At stake in the debate
about composition, structure and date, however,
is the nature of the book. Is it principally about
hope for the future or about judgment with little
optimism? These theological questions, however, must await some further observations on the
nature of the writing.

4. Story and Storytelling in Kings.
4.1. Character and Plot. Kings is a story with all
the features that go with it. It has characters,
some more roundly drawn than others (Ahab
and Jezebel, for example, stand out more than
most from the stereotypical formulas, and so perhaps Athaliah, Elijah, Jehu). It also has a strong
storyline or plot. This begins with the accession
of a powerful king who builds a temple for the
God of Israel. Solomon's accession declares that
ancient promises have been fulfilled, especially
the promise of rest from enemies, held out since
Moses (Deut 12:9-10), not quite attained under
*Joshua (Josh 13:1; 15:63), and finally won by
David (2 Sam 7:1). The bright new phase, however, goes awry almost from the start, with the powerful king who stands for promise fulfillment
himself becoming the occasion for a new coun-
terpromise: much of the land won by his father
will be lost (1 Kings 11:11-13). What should have
been the story of a united kingdom under God
becomes that of two kingdoms, divided even by
religion and often at war, such that the meaning
of the name of "Israel" is itself called into doubt.
Israel, which had reached such heights in the
kingdom of David and Solomon, finally unravels.
After the northern kingdom is destroyed by the
Assyrian armies (2 Kings 17; 18:9-12), Judah
stands alone. The narrative now springs a surprise, for this late period produces two kings who
are remembered for their reforms: Hezekiah (2
Kings 18—20) and Josiah (2 Kings 22—23). Josiah's reform is documented at length, and he is
portrayed as unparalleled in righteousness (2
Kings 23:25). Surely this should be enough to
save Judah from the same fate that befell Israel.
Yet Josiah suffers an untimely death in war (2
Kings 23:28-30), he is succeeded by a series of
kings who turn Judah away from Yahweh once
again and Judah goes the way of Israel, falling to
Babylon. The story ends with a question against
Israel: Can there be any future now?

4.2. Style and Point of View. The point of view in Kings is related to the question of date and structure. A Josianic edition of the book carries with it a certain point of view: a belief that King Josiah represented a real hope of restoring Judah to peace and prosperity according to the ancient Davidic promise (*see* Davidic Covenant). Seen from this perspective, the book has a clear message: when Judah returns to the true worship of Yahweh in Jerusalem, and turns away from the worship of other gods at sanctuaries up and down the country, and when kings rule according to the commands given through Moses, then the promise of a perpetual, successful Davidic kingdom can come to fruition.

However, this account of the point of view of Kings requires supplementation by another, from a position after the fall of the kingdom, in the Babylonian exile. Now the point of view of the book must be described quite differently. The promise of a perpetual Davidic dynasty has not come to pass. Instead, the people who were given land, king and temple now possesses none of these. And indeed there seems to be little prospect of this situation changing. Kings lacks the visions of a return from exile that alleviate the message of judgment in the two other books with which it is most akin, Deuteronomy and Jeremiah (Deut 30:1-10; Jer 30—33). Instead, it enshrines a more muted hope for the exiles that "their captors would have compassion on them" (1 Kings 8:50). The book ends on an uncertain note, in the midst of exile, with a report of the release of King Jehoiachin from his Babylonian prison (2 Kings 25:27-30), which may be symbolic of a hope of restoration—or it may not. The absence in the end of a clear Davidic hope is all the sharper because the story of the end follows so quickly upon the account of the dynasty's high point in the reform of King Josiah, told with such fanfare in 2 Kings 22—23.

4.2.1. The Voice of the Book of Kings. Where, then, do we find the voice of the book of Kings? Should we be content to discover two quite distinct voices (Josianic and exilic)? The issue raised here faces us acutely with a question of methodology that is unavoidable in modern biblical study: what part should prefinal forms of biblical books play in our interpretation of them? Or to put it in terms of theological interpretation: what kind of authority might be attributed to hypothetical precanonical forms of books? These questions persist even if we are confident that we can determine such precanonical forms.

In my view, the identification of the voice of Kings is inseparable from the point to which it finally leads us: the catastrophe of exile, in shocking dissonance with the expectations engendered by the Davidic promise, recorded first in Samuel (2 Sam 7) and reiterated in Kings (1 Kings 2:2-4; 9:1-9). The "salvation history" is a "judgment history"; the story of Israel, in this account of it (which begins ultimately in Genesis), ends with the invocation of covenantal curse (Deut 28:64-68).

4.2.2. Portrayal of Character and Event. Read in this way, the dissonances of the book become cruxes of its interpretation. The sequel to the superlative Josiah and his deracination of Baal worship in the attribution of Judah's fall to the sins of Manasseh, and then the collapse of leadership from Jehoiakim to Zedekiah, belongs to the effect that the book creates rather than merely being a disappointed appendix. This perspective chimes with our observation about structure, that the final stages of the book are marked by swings from faithfulness to apostasy (see 3.1.2 above). The rapid decline following Josiah is not unexpected when we have already seen that Hezekiah's reform was followed not only by Hezekiah's own erratic behavior, but also by the Ahab-like king Manasseh.

Seen in this way, the account of Josiah's reform (and the deliverance of Jerusalem under Hezekiah) becomes part of a subtle strategy by the author in his project of explaining the character of Israel and Judah and the reasons for the present situation. Assuming that Josiah's measures against non-Yahwistic worship are still in the popular memory in the exile, the author is able to express admiration for the king, and perhaps hope for the future, within an account that nevertheless charts inexorable decline.

In the case of Solomon too (1 Kings 1—11), our observations about structure have already indicated a tension within the portrayal (see 3.1.3 above). The king who prayed to Yahweh for wisdom to rule the people of Israel becomes an apostate, the very model indeed of that which kings should not be, according to the OT's only law of kingship (Deut 17:14-20). So in this case also are we to suppose that there is a simple switch from one kind of portrayal to another? Does Solomon have a good phase followed by a bad one?

As we saw, some regard the whole portrayal of Solomon as critical and ironic. This is because the fabric of the narrative displays some ambiguity in the assessment of the king. This ambiguity is present from the beginning, where the account of the new king's consolidation of his power shows its debt to court intrigue and smacks of undue brutality (1 Kings 1—2). The king's well-known prayer for wisdom to rule (1 Kings 3:3-14) is preceded by the surprising information that he has made a marriage alliance with the Egyptian pharaoh (1 Kings 3:1) and still sacrifices at the high places (3:2)—a practice condemned in Kings (cf. 1 Kings 15:14). In this way Solomon's failure to conform to the Mosaic typology of kingship (Deut 17:16-17), so marked at the end of his story (1 Kings 11), is signaled at the start. The shadow of the pharaoh's daughter hangs over the whole Jerusalem project (see also 1 Kings 9:16).

Even Solomon's great wealth, which appears to proclaim God's favor (1 Kings 3:13; 10), is mingled inextricably with his compromised attitude toward *Egypt in a characterization that puts him in all points at odds with the Deuteronomic king law (1 Kings 10:26-29; Deut 17:14-20).

Our readings of Josiah and Solomon propose a certain "suspicion" of what appears at face value to be said. And yet the promises have always been subject to qualification (as in 1 Kings 3:14), and when the story is read from the perspective of its end, our suspicions are justified. The complex structure of the book of Kings—its twin theme of promise to David and sin of Jeroboam (assigned by Cross [279-85] to the first edition of the Deuteronomistic History), its interconnecting chronologies of the two kingdoms that facilitate the demonstration of the influence of north on south, its highlighting of the clash between prophet and apostate king in the Elijah-Elisha cycle—is designed to prove the failure of kings and people to take the covenantal opportunity offered of old to David.

It follows that story is closely associated here with theology and purpose. The writer whose method we have begun to unearth is unlikely to be offering a triumphalist royal program. Moreover, Kings provides no support for simplistic construals of "Deuteronomic theology," for which it is often held to be a source. Such theology is regularly portrayed as a crude system of rewards and punishments. But Kings, in its treatment of Josiah, expresses eloquently that no such mechanical connection exists. Conversely, Jeroboam II is presented as an evil king, yet in his reign Israel prospered (2 Kings 14:23-27). The success of Jeroboam II—an unavoidable fact for the author—as also his failure to conform to his criteria of rectitude, becomes an occasion for a statement of God's overruling mercy, reminiscent of the deliverance from Egypt (cf. Ex 2:23-25). (For the view that "Deuteronomic," or "Deuteronomistic," theology is not actually found in any biblical texts see Provan 1997, 93-97.)

5. The Theology of Kings.
5.1. Kings as Prophecy.
5.1.1. Prophets in the Narrative. The perception of Kings as prophecy (part of the Former Prophets) is an important balance to the view of it as history. It contains material that also appears in the book of *Isaiah (2 Kings 18:1—20:21 is quite similar to Is 36:1—39:8). A number of prophets, including Isaiah, take important roles in the story: Elijah and Elisha have pride of place, but others include Ahijah, who speaks to Jeroboam (1 Kings 11:29-39), and Huldah, the prophet of Josiah's reform (2 Kings 22:14). Micaiah has a vision of God enthroned, reminiscent of Isaiah's temple vision, and is involved in a theological debate about true and false prophecy (1 Kings 22:1-35). The great conflict on *Carmel takes place between prophets, Elijah and the prophets of Baal, with King Ahab a helpless onlooker, subject to the prophetic word (1 Kings 18:17-20).

Prophets are important figures, not in their own right, but only as bearers of the word of God. Some are unnamed (such as the prophets from Judah and Bethel in 1 Kings 13; see also 1 Kings 20:13, 35). Even Elijah appears abruptly, identified only by reference to his place of origin, which itself requires the narrator's clarifying comment (1 Kings 17:1). Elisha's lineage is scarcely more promising (1 Kings 19:19). Their personal obscurity is a pointer to the real source of authority in the word of God.

Finally, in an important passage, they are grouped as "my servants the prophets," and God declares that prophetic warnings were his regular means of seeking to turn the people back to himself (2 Kings 17:13, 23).

In our observations about the book's structure we saw that God's speech through prophets shows his power to direct events and achieve his purposes. But it also stresses the possibility of a decisive change of mind. Elijah's rhetoric on Mount Carmel is intended precisely to turn people both from outright apostasy and from mere hesitation between two ways (1 Kings 18:21). The possibility of repentance is held out virtually to the end (Wolff).

5.1.2. Prophets, Kings and Power. The theme of the prophetic word as the source of true authority is stated formally in the commission of Elijah, to anoint not only Elisha as his successor, but also Jehu as king of Israel and even Hazael as king of Syria (1 Kings 19:15-16). And it is woven skillfully into the narrative—for example, in Ahab's powerlessness in the matter of Naboth's vineyard (1 Kings 21:4), and in the role of Elisha (and a servant girl!) in the healing of the Syrian commander Naaman (2 Kings 5) (see Ellul, 23-40). The same concept is present in the unlikely victories of the weak over the strong, as in the case of two defeats of the Syrians (1 Kings 20:1-34; 2 Kings 6:23). In the latter instance the vision of heavenly armies vastly outnumbering the foe is a parable on the true balance of power, and also on the ability to see where it lies (2 Kings 6:17). In this analysis, kings are always in the dock before the tribunal of the word of God, which is borne by the prophets.

5.2. God and the Gods in Kings. The worship of other gods is the foremost crime of the kings. Solomon fell into it. And Jeroboam's rejection of the worship of Yahweh in Jerusalem echoes the apostasy of the golden calf, that first breach of the first commandment at the very moment of the forging of the Sinai covenant (cf. Ex 32:8 and 1 Kings 12:28). Jeroboam may have intended his arrangements as a kind of worship of Yahweh (see, e.g., Gnuse, 186-87), since his appeal to the tribes is cast in traditional Israelite terms. But his action is portrayed as idolatrous. And the issue takes shape in Kings as between the worship of Yahweh and of Baal (1 Kings 18), and indeed other gods and goddesses (e.g., Ashtoreth, Chemosh, Milcom [1 Kings 11:33; 2 Kings 23:13]; Asherah, Molech [2 Kings 23:7, 10]). King Ahaz established a Syrian model of worship in the temple (2 Kings 16:10-16). And King Josiah's reformation is conceived as a cleansing of Judah from the worship of other deities (2 Kings 23).

Kings indeed is one of the great apologies for Israel's belief in Yahweh as one, following the Deuteronomic proclamation known as the Shema (Deut 6:4). The confession of God as one appears in 1 Kings 8:60, in Solomon's dedicatory prayer, in one of its strongest forms in the OT. It is at the heart of Elijah's conflict with the prophets of Baal (1 Kings 18:21, 37, 39). And it is the foundation of the miraculous deliverance of Jerusalem from the Assyrians, in that near-climactic story that puts Kings close to the theological territory of the book of Isaiah (2 Kings 19:15). The effect of all this is to show that the God who judges Israel is the same God who made the promise to David "forever" (2 Sam 7:13). His victories over Baal and over the forces (and gods) of Assyria form the background to the exilic audience's present plight. In Kings' affirmations of Yahweh's uniqueness and supreme power lies its hope for the future, as well as a continuing prophetic call to faith and loyalty.

5.3. God and the Gods in Israel's Religion. The nature of the dialogue between mono-Yahwism as we know it from the OT and Canaanite polytheism (*see* Canaanite Gods and Religion) is a function of conceptions of Israel's history. In modern discussion it is widely supposed that premonarchical Israelite and Judahite religion was similar to that of Canaan. Archaeological evidence in the form of inscriptions from Kuntillet-ʾAjrud and Khirbet el-Qom has led a number of scholars to think that Asherah was worshiped by some as Yahweh's consort (Gnuse, 69-73), though the significance of these is disputed (Arnold, 411-13; Smith, 80-114). Modern historical studies go further and propose that Israel was in essence an autochthonous Canaanite people (Gnuse, 58-61). So, is mono-Yahwism the creation of exilic and postexilic theological reflection?

R. K. Gnuse (179-81) adduces texts such as 1 Kings 11:1-8 and 2 Kings 17:29-41 as evidence of polytheistic belief in Israel before the exile. In doing so, he poses an important methodological question. It is clear from a reading of Kings that many in Israel and Judah indulged in polytheistic worship. But does it therefore follow that Yahwism was by nature polytheistic in this early phase, and that biblical monotheism emerged as a result of an evolutionary development? The thesis depends on certain interpretations that may be challenged. For example, does it make sense to suppose that Elijah and Jehu, in promoting the worship of Yahweh against Baal, were unconcerned about the worship of Asherah (Gnuse, 184)? More promising is R. J. Bauckham's recent critique of Gnuse. In Bauckham's view, the OT's monotheism (a term that he accepts with careful qualification) is not an evolutionary culmination, but rather is a matter of perpetual dispute with Canaanite polytheism. This picture fits very well with Kings' concept of a clash of cultures, religion and politics, stretching from Solomon to Josiah and manifested in the polemics of the prophets.

5.4. The Nature of Israel.

5.4.1. Who or What Is Israel? Kings begins with a united Israel under a strong king within maximal borders, proceeds rapidly to a division into two kingdoms, one of which bears the name *Israel*, goes on to chart the disappearance of the latter from history, so that only Judah is left of the Israel that was, and finally relates the loss of all marks of statehood, following a people into exile whose claim to be Israel in any case is in question. The term *Israel* itself, with its various possibilities, invites reflection on its ambiguity (*see* Israel).

The question of who and what constitutes legitimate Israel is involved in the removal of ten tribes from Solomon, in which Jeroboam receives a prophetic commission, parallel to David's own (Ahijah in the role of Nathan), to be "king of Israel" (1 Kings 11:31, 37-38). Does Israel truly continue in the north, therefore? Or is continuance after all in Jerusalem, which with its temple is so important to the vision of true worship in Kings, and which is left to Solomon "for the sake of David my servant whom I chose" (1 Kings 11:34). Each scenario has plausibility, but in fact each is subverted by the development, the north by its apostasy at its inception (1 Kings 12), and the south ultimately by its habit of mimicking the north.

It is northern kings who are dignified with the title "king of Israel." King Ahab again exemplifies the ironies and ambiguities involved in this. In his wars with Syria he is repeatedly designated "the king of Israel" (1 Kings 20:4, 7, 11, 22; and throughout 1 Kings 22). The narrative's preference for this title for Ahab over his name (in 1 Kings 22) in contrast to Jehoshaphat of Judah, who is named regularly, is striking. It seems that attention is being drawn to Ahab's official status, perhaps in an ironic way: can this man match any reasonable claim to bear the title? In addition, his status as king of Israel is juxtaposed jarringly with the mere presence of Jehoshaphat king of Judah. As for the "good" Jehoshaphat, it is equally puzzling that he should make common cause with Ahab.

The duality of Israel, in "Israel" and Judah, poses the question of what constitutes *true* Israel. The ambiguity in the name itself is scarcely accidental. In 2 Kings 17:20, for example, its use in a context that largely concerns the northern kingdom seems to point to an inclusive understanding (with Linville, 209-10, but against Sweeney, 84-85; cf. Provan 1995, 249).

It seems that both kingdoms somehow partake of the status of "Israel" ("two rival microcosms of the collective" [Linville, 23]). On the fall of the north, the mantle devolves upon Judah alone, signaled in the use of the term *nāgîd* ("prince, ruler") for Hezekiah (2 Kings 20:5), a term originally applied to Saul, David and Solomon, and which is used only here for a king of Judah. Judah's privilege is short-lived, of course. The result of this is to pose the question of what might constitute "Israel" in an era after the two "Israels" have come to an end. The use of *nāgîd*, incidentally, helps prepare for the new situation, since it shows that leadership need not be limited to the form of kingship (Linville, 149).

5.4.2. One God and One Israel. If "Israel" is an elusive quantity in Kings, this is strongly at odds with its identity in principle, as the book presents it. The name of Israel is insisted on in close connection with the assertion of Israel's uniqueness as a nation among the nations, in the context of the demonstration on Carmel that Yahweh alone is God. Not only is the supremacy of Yahweh at stake in that confrontation between Elijah and Ahab, but also the true nature of Israel. At the height of the conflict Elijah sets up twelve stones, representing the twelve tribes, and invokes the renaming of Jacob as Israel (1 Kings 18:31, 36; cf. Gen 32:28; 35:10). This status in principle is balanced by Elijah's call to the people to choose. Israel's true identity, it seems, is tied to an acceptance of Yahweh as God (Yahweh is always the "God of Israel," even in the mouth of a king of Judah [2 Kings 19:15]). To ask the question what Israel truly is, is to ask what *kind* of God Yahweh is.

5.4.3. Israel as "Inheritance"; Naboth's Vineyard. The story of Naboth's vineyard reveals most penetratingly the type of society entailed in a choice to serve Yahweh, in sharp contrast to the type of society that Ahab, as a typical ancient

Near Eastern potentate, craves. Naboth refuses to part with "the inheritance of my ancestors" (1 Kings 21:3), and in doing so he invokes a vision of Israel as gift of Yahweh to all the people of Israel, each having an entitlement by virtue of the gift to a possession in the land. The theology of Deuteronomy is writ large here (Deut 4:21; 15:4; Josh 13—22). Israel as land is held in perpetuity by Israel as people, not by decree of a king. Here the "democratic" entailment of Israel's monotheism is as clear as anywhere in the OT, and it stands in sharp contrast to the political tyranny of its polytheistic neighbors.

It is, of course, the hostility evinced by Ahab, under influence of the Phoenician Jezebel, to the very nature of Israel according to Yahwistic tradition that puts in question his true status as "king of Israel."

5.4.4. "Israel" in Exile? What, then, is the entity that eventually goes into exile, shorn of trappings that might qualify it as either "Israel" or "Judah"? This is perhaps the most acute question for the first audience of the book. The clearest answer comes in Solomon's dedicatory prayer, in which he envisages that a disobedient Israel might one day go into exile. In that event, he prays that God would hear their prayer and *maintain their cause* (*mišpāṭ* [1 Kings 8:49])—that is, a legal right that presupposes that their relationship with Yahweh continues. And then they are explicitly equated with "your people, your inheritance, which you brought out of Egypt, from the midst of the iron furnace" (1 Kings 8:51; cf. Deut 4:20). Kings is unlike Deuteronomy and Jeremiah in envisaging a return to land, and so to a form of political life resembling that which had been lost. Here the outward appearance and constitution of the future people is an unresolved question. The book's careful detachment from the historic institutions is strikingly illustrated by the prayer's insistence that God cannot be contained by heaven itself, much less a building (1 Kings 8:27). The true nature of Israel depends not on institutions, not even on possession of land, but on loyalty to Yahweh, and this as manifested in commitments to *justice, as exemplified by the case of Naboth.

6. The "Audience" of Kings.
I have argued that the book of Kings as a whole is addressed to an exilic (or perhaps postexilic) audience. This is based on a study of the style of writing, which undermined triumphalism, and

on the portrayal of Israel, which transcended the particular forms of it recollected in the history. This view does not necessarily invalidate some of the concerns of the theory of several editions of the book. For example, the accounts of Hezekiah and Josiah do affirm the possibility of reconstruction: Hezekiah's humility and prayer, Josiah's repentance and covenant renewal, and indeed Solomon's prayer for wisdom in itself may be taken as models of right behavior. And the power of Yahweh to act for faithful Israel against all the odds is a theme that lies deep in the book. Equally, the tensions explored by the triple-redaction theory (principally between perspectives of unconditional gift and conditionality based on covenant-keeping) are part of the reality conveyed by the text.

The Josianic theory in particular has produced stimulating treatments of parts of the book. An example is P. Dutcher-Walls's analysis of the Athaliah narrative (2 Kings 11—12). Dutcher-Walls finds in this a *propagandistic use of narrative by a member of the royal elite in Josiah's administration, intended to persuade an elite audience, both "supporters of and dissenters from Josiah's reign and policies," of the legitimacy of the king and his dynasty in what she calls Judah's "agrarian monarchy" (Dutcher-Walls, 176). The sociological thesis is supported by an ideological one in which the narrative evinces fundamental commitments to temple and priesthood, covenant, king, and dynasty (Dutcher-Walls, 102-41).

However, the quest for an audience of the book must look finally to the exile or after. Two works illustrate recent trends in interpreting the book from this perspective. The question of the exilic community's crisis of identity informs the analysis by E. T. Mullen. For Mullen, the purpose of Deuteronomy-Kings was "to provide a set of boundaries for the community for which it was produced," and this is based on the premise that ethnic identity is rooted in "shared memories of a common history that binds members together and separates them from others" (Mullen, 14). This was a concern that became sharp after the loss of land, king and temple, and it is this new set of circumstances that demands the framing of the history as an ideological affirmation: an "insistence upon an absolute continuity with the past" (Mullen, 37). The story of Athaliah illustrates the point. Mullen sees it as "a piece of propaganda supporting the concept of the unbroken dynastic line of David in Judah" (Mullen, 32). This is in contrast to Dutcher-Walls, for now it is part of an exilic program designed to persuade a bewildered society that their true nature is defined precisely by the past.

J. R. Linville, like Mullen, is concerned with the identity of Israel after 587 BCE, but is different in important respects. For Linville, the book cannot be dated within the exile, or indeed pinned down to any identifiable group. Furthermore, what he sees as the failure of both kingdoms to fulfill the covenantal demands laid on "Israel" means that the inheritors of the historic traditions now have to discover what it means to be Israel apart from the institutional patterns of yesterday.

This last analysis corresponds to the openness of Kings about the future, visible both in the muted ending of the book and in Solomon's prayer (1 Kings 8 [see 5.4.4 above]). Kings mediates a past full of concrete promises and expectations into a future full of the unknown, but in the care of the one God, the God of Israel. This is what makes it so powerful in its capacity to call readers to a reexamination of what it might mean to be people of God, and in creating readiness for new ways in which this might become reality.

See also CHRONICLES, BOOKS OF; DEUTERONOMISTIC HISTORY; HISTORIOGRAPHY, OLD TESTAMENT; HISTORY OF ISRAEL 3-6; KINGS AND KINGSHIP; NARRATIVE ART OF ISRAEL'S HISTORIANS; PROPHETS AND PROPHECY; SAMUEL, BOOKS OF.

BIBLIOGRAPHY: *Commentaries:* M. **Cogan**, *I Kings* (AB 10; New York: Doubleday, 2001); M. **Cogan and H. Tadmor,** *II Kings* (AB 11; Garden City, NY: Doubleday, 1988); R. L. **Cohn,** *2 Kings* (Berit Olam; Collegeville, MN: Liturgical Press, 2000); S. J. **De Vries,** *1 Kings* (WBC 12; Waco, TX: Word, 1985); R. P. **Gordon,** *1 & 2 Samuel* (OTG; Sheffield: JSOT, 1984); T. R. **Hobbs,** *2 Kings* (WBC 13; Waco, TX: Word, 1985); B. O. **Long,** *1 Kings* (FOTL 9; Grand Rapids: Eerdmans, 1984); idem, *2 Kings* (FOTL 10; Grand Rapids: Eerdmans, 1991); R. D. **Nelson,** *First and Second Kings* (IBC; Atlanta: John Knox, 1987); I. W. **Provan,** *1 and 2 Kings* (NIBC; Peabody, MA: Hendrickson, 1995); idem, *1 and 2 Kings* (OTG; Sheffield: Sheffield Academic Press, 1997); J. **Walsh,** *1 Kings* (Berit Olam; Collegeville, MN: Liturgical Press, 1996). *Studies:* B. T. **Arnold,** "Religion in Ancient Israel," in *The Face of Old Testament Studies,* ed. D. W. Baker and B. T. Arnold (Grand Rapids: Baker; Leicester: Apollos, 1999) 391-420; R. J. **Bauckham,** "Biblical Theology and the Problems of Monotheism," in *Out of Egypt: Biblical Theology and Biblical Interpretation,* ed. C. Bartholomew et al. (SHS 5; Grand Rapids: Zondervan, 2004) 187-232; A. F. **Campbell and M. A. O'Brien,** *Unfolding the Deuteronomistic History: Origins, Upgrades, Present Text* (Minneapolis: Fortress, 2000); M. **Cogan,** "Sennacherib's Siege of Jerusalem," *COS* 2.119B:302-3; F. M. **Cross,** *Canaanite Myth and Hebrew Epic* (Cambridge, MA: Harvard University Press, 1973); W. **Dietrich,** *Prophetie und Geschichte: Eine redaktionsgeschichtliche Untersuchung zum deuteronomistischen Geschichtswerk* (FRLANT 108; Göttingen: Vandenhoeck & Ruprecht, 1972); P. **Dutcher-Walls,** *Narrative Art, Political Rhetoric: The Case of Athaliah and Joash* (JSOTSup 209; Sheffield: Sheffield Academic Press, 1996); J. **Ellul,** *The Politics of God and the Politics of Man* (Grand Rapids: Eerdmans, 1972); L. **Eslinger,** *Into the Hands of the Living God* (JSOTSup 84; Sheffield: Almond, 1989); R. K. **Gnuse,** *No Other Gods: Emergent Monotheism in Israel* (JSOTSup 241; Sheffield: Sheffield Academic Press, 1997); H.-D. **Hoffmann,** *Reform und Reformen: Untersuchungen zu einem Grunthema der deuteronomistischen Geschichtsschreibung* (ATANT 66; Zurich: Theologischer Verlag, 1980); G. N. **Knoppers,** *Two Nations under God: The Deuteronomistic History of Solomon and the Dual Monarchies* (2 vols.; HSM 52, 53; Atlanta: Scholars Press, 1993-1994); J. R. **Linville,** *Israel in the Book of Kings: The Past as a Project of Social Identity* (JSOTSup 272; Sheffield: Sheffield Academic Press, 1998); E. T. **Mullen,** *Narrative History and Ethnic Boundaries: The Deuteronomistic Historian and the Creation of Israelite National Identity* (SemeiaSt; Atlanta: Scholars Press, 1993); R. D. **Nelson,** *The Double Redaction of the Deuteronomistic History* (JSOTSup 18; Sheffield; Sheffield Academic Press, 1981); M. **Noth,** *The Deuteronomistic History* (JSOTSup 15; Sheffield: JSOT, 1981 [1957]); K. I. **Parker,** "Repetition as a Structuring Device in 1 Kings 1—11," *JSOT* 42 (1988) 19-27; G. **von Rad,** *Old Testament Theology,* vol. 1 (Edinburgh: Oliver & Boyd, 1962); R. **Smend,** "The Law and the Nations: A Contribution to Deuteronomistic Tradition History," in *Reconsidering Israel and Judah: Recent Studies on the Deuteronomistic History,* ed. G. N. Knoppers and J. G. McConville (SBTS 8; Winona Lake, IN: Eisenbrauns, 2000 [1971]) 95-110; M. S. **Smith,** *The*

Early History of God: Yahweh and the Other Deities in Ancient Israel (San Francisco; Harper & Row, 1990); **M. A. Sweeney,** *King Josiah of Judah: the Lost Messiah of Israel* (New York: Oxford University Press, 2001); **H. Weippert,** "'Histories' and 'History': Promise and Fulfillment in the Deuteronomistic Historical Work," *Reconsidering Israel and Judah: Recent Studies on the Deuteronomistic History,* ed. G. N. Knoppers and J. G. McConville (SBTS 8; Winona Lake, IN: Eisenbrauns, 2000) 47-61; **H. W. Wolff,** "The Kerygma of the Deuteronomistic Historical Work," in *The Vitality of the Old Testament Traditions,* ed. H. W. Wolff and W. Brueggemann (Atlanta: John Knox, 1975) 83-100, 141-43; repr., in *Reconsidering Israel and Judah: Recent Studies on the Deuteronomistic History,* ed. G. N. Knoppers and J. G. McConville (SBTS 8; Winona Lake, IN: Eisenbrauns, 2000) 62-78.   J. G. McConville

KINSHIP. *See* ISRAELITE SOCIETY.

KUNTILLET ʿAJRUD INSCRIPTIONS. *See* HEBREW INSCRIPTIONS.

L

LACHISH

Lachish was a major Judean city throughout much of the preexilic period. In the postexilic period it lay outside the borders of the province of Judah. It is mentioned twenty times in the Historical Books (and four times in Isaiah, Jeremiah and Micah), of which half are in the book of *Joshua.

The identification of the site is based on only circumstantial evidence, and it has been the subject of dispute in the past. There is now almost universal agreement that it should be identified with the impressive mound known as Tel ed-Duweir, also called Tel Lachish (Davies), and the most recent excavations strengthen the argument considerably. Covering an area of some thirty-one acres in total, it lies in the Shephelah, approximately 30 km southeast of *Ashkelon and roughly double this distance southwest of *Jerusalem, near to one of the main routes from the coastal plain up into the Judean hill country.

The site has been extensively excavated, first by a British expedition (1932-1938) and then by Tel Aviv University under the direction of D. Ussishkin (1973-1994). In addition, a small-scale expedition under Y. Aharoni investigated the so-called Solar Shrine in 1966 and 1968. As far as the period covered by the Historical Books is concerned, the results of the two expeditions are broadly complementary, and the same stratigraphic sequence and enumeration are followed. The region appears to have been settled as early as the Neolithic period, and the site itself was prominent throughout much of the Chalcolithic and Bronze Ages. The present article focuses exclusively on those levels contemporaneous with the Historical Books. The correlation of textual and archaeological evidence is both challenging and illuminating.

1. Biblical Overview

2. Archaeological Evidence and Its Relation to the Textual Sources

1. Biblical Overview.

1.1. Settlement Period. Lachish is referred to eight times in Joshua 10. Its king joined a coalition with four others to attack the Gibeonites, who had made an alliance with the invading Israelites under Joshua. Coming to the aid of the Gibeonites, Joshua comprehensively defeated the coalition, executed the five kings (see also Josh 12:11) and then attacked a number of the southern cities of *Canaan, including Lachish. He laid siege to it, captured it and slaughtered every person in it (Josh 10:31-32). It is not stated that the town itself was destroyed, but clearly it came into Israelite possession, since in Joshua 15:39 it is mentioned as one of the towns in the territory allotted to the tribe of Judah (*see* Tribes of Israel and Land Allotments/Borders).

1.2. Monarchic Period. According to 2 Chronicles 11:9, Lachish was one of the cities that *Rehoboam fortified at the start of his reign in order to serve as a line of defense for his kingdom of Judah, following the secession of the northern tribes of Israel. It is clearly implied that this preceded the invasion by the Egyptian king Shishak (2 Chron 12:1-12), so that Rehoboam's policy appears to have failed in this respect.

Later, Lachish is the site to which King Amaziah fled at the time of a conspiracy against him, and where he was assassinated (2 Kings 14:19; 2 Chron 25:27). This suggests that the city had some kind of royal residence at the beginning of the eighth century BCE.

Finally, at the very end of the same century, Lachish is mentioned as the site where the *Assyrian king Sennacherib made his headquarters during his devastating campaign to crush the revolt of *Hezekiah (2 Kings 18:14, 17; 19:8; 2 Chron 32:9; cf. Is 36:2; 37:8; it is likely that Mic 1:13 also refers to this episode).

The Historical Books do not refer to Lachish in connection with the eventual Babylonian ending of the kingdom of Judah, but a reference in Jeremiah 34:7 does.

1.3. Postexilic Period. Although Lachish lay outside the postexilic province of Judah, it is mentioned in Nehemiah 11:30 as a site of Judean settlement. This puzzle is compounded by the fact that the same applies to several other places mentioned in the list of which it forms a part (Neh 11:25-35). Several explanations have been advanced to try to explain this (for a survey see Williamson 1985, 349-50, 353), including attempts to date the list either much earlier or later than Nehemiah's time. The close dependence of the list on Joshua 15, however, suggests rather that the list may be utopian in nature, not only reflecting an ideal past, but also giving expression to future aspiration.

2. Archaeological Evidence and Its Relation to the Textual Sources.

This section contains an introduction to the main finds at Lachish relevant to the time period of interest here and some reflections on how they relate to the biblical references just described. The discussion is organized according to the main archaeological levels. (For full details of the archaeology of the site see Tufnell; Aharoni; Ussishkin 1978; 1983; 1996; 2004.)

2.1. Level VI. This level relates to the city at the time when Israel first emerged or arrived in Palestine. It was the second Late Bronze Age city on the site, the earlier one being mentioned in an Egyptian source (Papyrus Hermitage 1116A) as well as in several of the Amarna letters. The city of Level VI, prosperous and unwalled, shows evidence of continuing Egyptian influence, which is not surprising in view of the fact that *Egypt remained the imperial power at this time, though clearly the main religious cult was Canaanite. This city was completely destroyed by fire, and the site was abandoned for a period afterward.

The find of greatest importance for our concern is a cache of bronze objects in the gate area underneath the destruction debris. This includes a cartouche of Ramesses III, so that the city could not possibly have been destroyed until sometime during his reign at the earliest, and possibly a little after. This suggests that Lachish was not destroyed until 1160 BCE at the earliest, and this date could easily be lowered to about 1130 BCE, when Egypt finally surrendered control of the Levant.

It is difficult to see how this can be reconciled with theories of a total conquest of the land by Joshua a century or even more before. Although it is true that Joshua 10 does not refer to a destruction of Lachish, it does refer to the slaughter of all its inhabitants and the transfer of settlement to the Israelites; yet no cultural change within Level VI can be detected. Nor does archaeology itself provide any certain evidence as to the identity of those who destroyed the city; it could as easily have been *Philistines as Israelites.

Scholars offer different explanations for this set of data. Some say, for instance, that the narratives of the book of Joshua are of no historical worth whatever, so that the destruction of Level VI has nothing to do with the biblical material. On the other hand, without seeking to explain the evidence away in favor of an exclusively biblically based historical account, we may consider a middle path that in turn has a bearing on how we should read the Joshua account itself. It is clear, not least from the Bible, that it was only over the course of two centuries or more that early Israel took control of the great Canaanite city-states, one of the last being Jerusalem (cf. 2 Sam 5:6-9). Other sites, such as *Megiddo, were also absorbed fairly late in the process. Thus it seems that what is popularly known as "the conquest" was spread out over a much longer period than the book of Joshua at first implies (though see, e.g., Josh 13:1-6; 15:63). The case of Lachish is another example in favor of this conclusion. Its destruction in the twelfth century BCE may have been at the hands of the Israelites as part of this process, or it may have been destroyed initially by the Philistines and then passed into Israelite hands later after a period of abandonment (it is widely agreed that the lists of settlements, including Josh 15, reflect the situation later than the time of Joshua himself; see most recently de Vos). Either way, the conclusion would have to be that the book of Joshua in this, as in other respects, presents the reader with a compressed account, foreshortening a lengthy process into a single event in the interest of demonstrating the might and the goodness of God in providing his people with a land. (By no means would this be the only example in the Bible of chronological compression for theological purposes.) If so, without denying that it has historical material within it, we should read it in this theological light rather than as a historical source pure and simple.

2.2. Level V. After a considerable period when the site was deserted, settlement was renewed at an undetermined date. The site was still unfortified, and most of the remains are of a domestic nature. It is often thought that it dates to the time of the united monarchy, and that it was destroyed by Shishak in 925 BCE. If so, we again have to revise some biblical chronology, this time that of the Chronicler (see 1.2 above). Assuming that his list of fortifications in 2 Chronicles 11:5-12 is historically sound (see Williamson 1982, 240-43), he ascribes the building to the first part of Rehoboam's reign, and the invasion of Shishak follows as judgment for his subsequent faithlessness. But clearly, the city of Rehoboam cannot be represented by Level V (unless, as has sometimes been suggested, Level V had two phases, the later of which, represented by Palace A, might be Rehoboam's palace-fort; however, the data are now differently explained, as discussed below). At the least, therefore, we have to conclude that Rehoboam undertook his building work after and as a response to Shishak's invasion. In fact, however, strong arguments have been advanced for dating the Chronicler's list not to Rehoboam's reign at all, but rather to *Hezekiah's (Na'aman 1986). Clearly this is not certain, and the very uncertainty precludes any facile equation of literary and archaeological strata. Positively, it highlights the nature of the theological typology that is such a marked feature of the Chronicler's style of presentation (*see* Chronicler's History).

2.3. Levels IV and III. These two levels represent Lachish at the height of its power under the Judean monarchy. Although Level IV was destroyed, perhaps by an earthquake, it was rebuilt and developed in Level III without any apparent break in occupation, so that the two may be taken together for our purposes. Although the destruction of Level III can be securely dated now to 701 BCE, the date of the foundation of the earlier Level IV is uncertain. Given the massive development in the status and fortification of the site that this level represents, it is reasonable to see it as part of the early response to the political developments that led to the establishment of Judah as a separate state from Israel. Thus it is theoretically possible that it comes from the time of Rehoboam, regardless of the problems raised by the list in 2 Chronicles 11:5-12 just discussed; but a somewhat later date is equally possible.

The city throughout this time was strongly fortified. The main city wall was some 6 m thick. As a further deterrent against attack and battering rams, this wall was encircled by a glacis that stretched halfway down the slope, where it was supported by an outer revetment wall (formerly mistakenly considered to be a second city wall, and still sometimes depicted as such). Entrance through these fortifications was by a double gate in the southwest corner of the city. A roadway led up the side of the mound, first to an outer gate built as a projecting bastion and then, following a right-angled turn, through a massive six-chambered inner gate.

The center of the site was dominated by the palace-fort. It used to be thought that this developed in three stages through Levels V-III, but the most recent analysis suggests that the first two elements were part of a single construction in Level IV, which then was enlarged in Level III. Behind the palace (the largest single building known so far from ancient Israel) was a huge enclosed open area, suitable for military training and parade purposes, with two blocks of storerooms (and possibly stables; Mic 1:13 associates chariots with Lachish). A monumental stairway went from this parade ground up into the palace itself. Without entering into a full description of the remainder of the site, we may note that this was a major royal and military center, second only to Jerusalem itself.

It was the city of Level III that confronted Sennacherib in his invasion of Judah in 701 BCE. The evidence for the course of his campaign is unusually rich and varied, making it a test case for historical method in relation to ancient Israel and Judah. To the several biblical accounts (see 1.2 above) may be added Sennacherib's own written accounts, the representation in the famous Lachish Reliefs, which depict the attack on and capture of the city, and of course the findings of archaeology in situ (for recent discussions see Gallagher; Grabbe; for the reliefs and their relation to the archaeology of the site see especially Ussishkin 1982). This abundance of material raises several difficult historical issues about the precise course of the campaign and its aftermath, but the situation at Lachish is straightforward.

The reliefs depict the capture of Lachish by means of a siege ramp, and the remains of this have been excavated. Given its size (up to nineteen thousand tons of stone), it represented a considerable investment of effort, and the determination with which the city was defended is apparent from the unexpected discovery of a vast counterramp, to say nothing of the debris of what must have been an exceptionally fierce battle (over 850 arrowheads have been found, as well as the remains of other pieces of armor and weaponry). Following its capture, the city was destroyed in a huge conflagration, evidence for which is widely apparent.

An important consequence of this destruction is that it has finally resolved a long debate about the date and purpose of the so-called *lemelek* store jars. These large vessels, with *lmlk*, "belonging to the king," stamped on the handle, have been found throughout the territory of Judah (*see* Hebrew Inscriptions). Many were found in the destruction in the storerooms inside the gate area at Lachish, indicating both that they come from the period of Hezekiah's preparations for the Assyrian invasion in the closing years of the eighth century BCE, and that in all probability they were associated with the military measures that he took at that time, making provision against the expected siege (see Na'aman 1979; 1986; Vaughn). This well-stratified conclusion has had important consequences for the dating of the pottery sequence of late monarchic Judah (Zimhoni).

2.4. Level II. Lachish lay deserted for some time after this destruction, as is evidenced by the accumulation of silt in the gate area at the lowest part of the mound. Sometime late in the Judean monarchy, however, it was rebuilt, though on a much smaller scale. It is not referred to in the Historical Books (though see Jer 34:7), but it deserves mention here as the context for the famous Lachish Letters (*see* Hebrew Inscriptions). They were discovered in the gate from a period just before the fall of the city to the *Babylonians in 587 BCE.

2.5. Level I. The final period of settlement dates to the *Persian and the early Hellenistic periods. A new, smaller residence was built on the site of the old palace podium, no doubt for the local Persian governor. Probably contemporaneously and in complementary style, the Solar

Shrine was built northeast of the residence, though the nature of its cult, whether Jewish or other, is disputed (see also 1.3 above). For reasons unknown, the end of settlement at Lachish seems to have coincided with the movement of regional governance to Mareshah early in the Hellenistic period.

See also HISTORY OF ISRAEL 1: SETTLEMENT PERIOD; HISTORY OF ISRAEL 5: ASSYRIAN PERIOD.

BIBLIOGRAPHY. **Y. Aharoni**, *Investigations at Lachish: The Sanctuary and the Residency (Lachish V)* (Tel Aviv: Gateway, 1975); **G. I. Davies**, "Tell ed-Duweir = Ancient Lachish: A Response to G. W. Ahlström," *PEQ* 114 (1982) 25-28; **W. R. Gallagher**, *Sennacherib's Campaign to Judah: New Studies* (SHCANE 18; Leiden: E. J. Brill, 1999); **L. L. Grabbe**, ed., *"Like a Bird in a Cage": The Invasion of Sennacherib in 701 BCE* (JSOTSup 363 London: Sheffield Academic Press, 2003); **N. Na'aman**, "Sennacherib's Campaign to Judah and the Date of the *lmlk* Stamps," *VT* 29 (1979) 61-86; idem, "Hezekiah's Fortified Cities and the LMLK Stamps," *BASOR* 261 (1986) 5-21; **O. Tufnell**, *Lachish III: The Iron Age* (London: Oxford University Press, 1953); **D. Ussishkin**, *The Conquest of Lachish by Sennacherib* (Tel Aviv: Institute of Archaeology of Tel Aviv University, 1982); idem, "Excavations at Tel Lachish 1973-1977: Preliminary Report," *TA* 5 (1978) 1-97; idem, "Excavations at Tel Lachish 1978-1983: Second Preliminary Report," *TA* 10 (1983) 97-175; idem, "Excavations and Restoration Work at Tel Lachish 1985-1994: Third Preliminary Report," *TA* 23 (1996) 3-60; idem, *The Renewed Archaeological Excavations at Lachish (1973-1994)* (5 vols.; Tel Aviv: Institute of Archaeology of Tel Aviv University, 2004); **A. G. Vaughn**, *Theology, History, and Archaeology in the Chronicler's Account of Hezekiah* (ABS 4; Atlanta: Scholars Press, 1999); **J. C. de Vos**, *Das Los Judas: Über Entstehung und Ziele der Landbeschreibung in Josua 15* (VTSup 95; Leiden: E. J. Brill, 2003); **H. G. M. Williamson**, *1 and 2 Chronicles* (NCB; Grand Rapids: Eerdmans; London: Marshall, Morgan & Scott, 1982); idem, *Ezra, Nehemiah* (WBC 16; Waco, TX: Word, 1985); **O. Zimhoni**, "Two Ceramic Assemblages from Lachish Levels III and II," *TA* 17 (1990) 3-52. H. G. M. Williamson

LAND

The significance of land for understanding the Historical Books is immediately transparent. It is not only the stage on which most of the narrative is played out, but also a key integrating theological motif. The history of Israel recorded in these books focuses not only on a particular people, but also on the territory that they occupied, forfeited and eventually (albeit partially) recovered. Rather than adopting an atomistic approach—highlighting distinctive land ideologies and possible sociological agendas (see Habel)—this article, while not denying different emphases, reflects a holistic approach to these books that comprise at least two and probably three separate canonical compilations: Joshua-Kings, Chronicles and Ezra-Nehemiah.

1. Land as an Integrating Theological Motif
2. Land as a Fulfillment of the Ancestral Promise
3. Land as a Covenant Obligation
4. Land as an Expression of Divine Punishment
5. Land as an Object of Unrealized Hopes

1. Land as an Integrating Theological Motif.
The importance of land is reflected clearly in the Hebrew text, although not every occurrence of the key terms (*'ereṣ* [533x], *śādeh* [90x], *'ădāmâ* [33x]) in the Historical Books refers to the land of Israel. As elsewhere, *'ădāmâ* mostly refers to soil or arable ground, whereas *śādeh* normally denotes a field or open country. Reflecting a much greater semantic range, *'ereṣ* is used of geopolitical regions (e.g., *Edom, Hamath) or territories (1 Chron 13:2), sometimes carries global or cosmological connotations (clearly in Josh 2:11; 1 Sam 2:8; 1 Kings 4:34; 8:23, 43, 53, 60; 2 Kings 5:15; 19:15, 19; 1 Chron 1:10, 19; 21:16; 2 Chron 2:12; 6:14; 9:22-23; 16:9; 32:19; 36:23; Ezra 1:2; Neh 9:6; cf. Josh 23:14; 1 Kings 2:2), refers simply to the ground (e.g., Judg 6:37-40; 1 Sam 26:8; 2 Sam 2:22; 20:10; 2 Kings 13:18; Neh 8:6), or is employed in a phrase designating the populace in general or a particular sociological group: "the people of the land" (e.g., 2 Kings 11:14; 24:14; Ezra 4:4). However, all three terms (especially *'ereṣ*) are used of the territory associated with Israel and/or Judah for the greater part of their national history, and it is this territorial dimension that is especially significant.

The so-called *Deuteronomistic History traces Israelite history primarily with respect to the land: the book of *Joshua describes how the Israelites possessed the land through Yahweh's assistance; the book of *Judges recounts various encroachments on the land that resulted from Israel's subsequent covenant disloyalty; the books of Samuel highlight how Yahweh established his anointed as the king who brought rest to the land (albeit temporarily); the books of Kings describe the apostasy that eventually led from territorial expansion to exile. However, rather than ending on such a negative note, the historian seems to offer a tiny glimmer of hope; whether or not it alludes to the *Davidic covenant and its messianic promise, the change in Jehoiachin's circumstances (2 Kings 25:27-30) most likely foreshadows the end of exile and restoration to the land (see Murray). Admittedly, this restorative focus is much clearer in the postexilic books; it is the note on which Chronicles ends its "parallel" account of Israelite history, in which land is arguably portrayed as an integral part of Israel's identity (so Japhet, 47). In particular, the Chronicler highlights how full restoration can be achieved by focusing primarily on Jerusalem and *Solomon's temple—both microcosms of the land as a whole. The various stages involved in repatriation and restoration are the primary focus of the ensuing drama in Ezra-Nehemiah, which begins where Chronicles ends, with Cyrus's edict permitting a return to the land. Thus Israel's history is not just about the political fortunes of a people; it is about the experience of that people in relation to a particular place: the land that God had promised to give them.

2. Land as a Fulfillment of the Ancestral Promise.
Obviously, any reflections on the biblical theme of land must begin with the ancestral promise, which in turn must begin with creation (see Brueggemann, 15-16). The territorial dimension of the ancestral promise (Gen 12:1-3, 7) is an important hub throughout the Pentateuch, in which the land motif is linked both to Eden and its associated idea of permanent rest (*see DOTP*, Rest, Peace; Promises, Divine). This is especially so in Deuteronomy, which indisputably provides the immediate literary context and theological agenda for the second part of the primary history in Joshua to Kings. The latter books depict two and possibly three fulfillments of this aspect of the ancestral promise, the first taking place in the settlement era.

2.1. The Settlement Era. While paying careful attention to the text of Joshua should eradicate "flat" readings of the "conquest" that it describes (see Provan, Long and Longman, 148-56; cf. Assis), it remains clear that the promise of land was in some measure realized in the settlement period (cf. Josh 11:23; 21:43-45; 22:4; 23:1). Clearly, what is in view is subjugation rather than full dispossession, as is demonstrated by qualifications elsewhere (e.g., Josh 13:1-2), the juxtaposition of both positive and negative observations in Joshua 23, and the generally more negative picture portrayed in Judges. Nevertheless, while full possession and retention of the land depended on covenant loyalty, the territorial promise made to the patriarchs was at least partially fulfilled under *Joshua. However, as the latter forewarned (Josh 23:12-13), and as Judges so graphically illustrates, Israel's enjoyment of rest in the land was short-lived due to covenant disloyalty. It was not until God's chosen king was installed in Zion that such rest was enjoyed again and more fully.

2.2. The United Monarchy. During the reigns of *David and *Solomon the borders of Israel were extended to those mentioned in Genesis 15:18-21 (cf. 2 Sam 8:1-14; 10; 1 Kings 4:21), and a degree of rest was attained beyond that experienced under the leadership of Joshua (cf. 2 Sam 7:1, 11; 1 Kings 4:24-25; 5:4; 8:56), as is reflected in the construction of the temple during this period (cf. Deut 12:10). Once again, however, the realization of the territorial promise was cut short by covenant disloyalty. Consequently, the division of the territory between the independent states of Israel and Judah after Solomon's demise resulted in diminished borders and various levels of encroachment by surrounding nations.

2.3. The Early Eighth Century BCE. It was not until the early part of the eighth century BCE, some one hundred and fifty years after Solomon's time, that Israel's geographical borders again extended to their ancestral ideal (2 Kings 14:25; cf. 1 Kings 4:25). However, the historian makes it quite clear that this was a temporary divine reprieve for Israel more than an outworking of the ancestral promise. Significantly, the latter is not explicitly mentioned (although presumably it was the theological basis for Jonah's prophecy that Jeroboam's territorial expansionism is said to have fulfilled). In any case, whatever "fulfillment" of the ancestral promise may be seen at this time, covenant disloyalty again ensured that it would not last. Israel, and later

Judah, "moved inexorably toward exile" (Brueggemann, 101), having repeatedly overlooked the fact that the land they occupied constituted not only a divine gift, but also a covenant obligation.

3. Land as a Covenant Obligation.
Like the Pentateuch (especially Deuteronomy), the Historical Books emphasize not only the land's status as Yahweh's gift or inheritance to Israel, but also the covenant responsibilities inextricably bound up with it.

3.1. Israel's Possession and Inheritance. While occasionally referred to, whether in part or in whole, as their *ʾăhuzzâ* ("possession" [e.g., Josh 21:12, 41; 22:4, 19; 2 Chron 31:1; cf. Gen 17:8]), Israel's landholding is more often described as its *naḥălâ* ("inheritance" [e.g., Josh 11:23; Judg 2:6; 20:6; 1 Kings 8:36; 1 Chron 16:18]), a term whose traditional interpretation has been challenged by some (see Habel, 33-35) but defended by others (see Wright, 19 n. 29; Kitz, 601 n. 2). Whatever its precise nuance(s), Israel's *naḥălâ* was "not a *tradable commodity,* but an *inalienable inheritance*" (Brueggemann, 87-88). According to this understanding, Israel had the inalienable right to retain the land, but this—as both biblical and present archaeological evidence suggests (cf. Wright, 56-57)—did not entail the right of permanent sale or transfer. A prime illustration of this is the Naboth incident (1 Kings 21). Such royal confiscation of private landholdings (cf. 1 Sam 8:14), coupled with financial transactions such as those of David (2 Sam 24:24) and *Omri (1 Kings 16:24), most likely explains how the kings of Israel and Judah acquired so much property. Apparently, legislation designed to protect one's rights to a patrimony either proved ineffective (Davies, 358-62) or was largely ignored (cf. 2 Chron 36:21).

3.2. The Title Deeds. Ultimately, however, the land belonged not to Israel or its kings, but to Yahweh (Josh 22:19; 1 Kings 8:36; 2 Chron 6:27; 7:20; cf. Lev 25:23; cf. also 1 Sam 26:19; 2 Sam 20:19; 21:3). This fact is further underlined by its description as a divine gift or inheritance (e.g., Josh 1:2, 11; 21:43; Judg 2:1; 1 Kings 8:36; 1 Chron 16:18; 2 Chron 6:27; 20:11) and the way in which it was distributed among the Israelite tribes by divine lot (cf. Josh 14:2; 18:1-10). A. M. Kitz understands the latter procedure quite differently, arguing that it relates simply to the second aspect of Joshua's delegated function as "estate administrator," a role that neatly corresponds to the book's main twofold division. However, Kitz fails to take adequate cognizance of the book's strong theological overtones (for this and other telling criticisms of Kitz's argument see Hess, 498 n. 11), of which distribution of the land by lot certainly is an aspect.

Yahweh's ownership might also be inferred from the infrequency of the territory's description as "the land of Israel" (used of the entire land only in 1 Sam 13:19; 1 Chron 22:2; 2 Chron 2:17; 34:7), and indirectly implied by its most common epithet, "the land of *Canaan"—which certainly reminds readers that the territory did not belong to Israel originally. In any case, the ultimate ownership of the land is unmistakable. As Yahweh's possession, not only was the land his to distribute, but also his tenancy agreement applied.

3.3. The Tenancy Agreement. Having been given the land, Israel had as its primary responsibility "to possess it" (*yāraš,* "to dispossess, take possession of"; cf. Josh 1:11; 13:1; 18:3; Neh 9:15, 23; the root occurs some eighty times in the Historical Books). Divine assistance clearly was indispensable (cf. Josh 3:10; 8:7; 13:6; 14:12; 23:5, 9; Judg 11:23-24; 2 Chron 20:7; Neh 9:24), but such assistance was assured only as long as Israel submitted to the covenant's requirements (Josh 1:7-10; 23:3-13; Judg 2:20-23; 1 Chron 28:8). In other words, "observance of the law was the condition *sine qua non* for Israel's original occupation of the land and for its continued existence therein" (Davies, 356). According to the Pentateuch, the essential obligation incumbent on Israel was to live as Yahweh's distinct people (Lev 19:2), which entailed, among other things, eschewing Canaanite customs that had polluted the land and evoked their expulsion (Lev 18:24-28; 20:22-26). This latter idea, reflected also in Deuteronomy, apparently is echoed in Kings and Chronicles, where the assimilation of Canaanite practices by Israelites is juxtaposed with ominous reminders of God's punitive response (1 Kings 14:24; 21:26; 2 Kings 16:3; 17:8; 21:2; 2 Chron 28:3; 33:2). Having failed to a large extent in this primary responsibility of ethnic distinctiveness (cf. Josh 13:13; 15:63; 16:10; 17:12; Judg 1:19-33), not surprisingly Israel quickly fell afoul of the underlying rationale: the need to maintain covenant loyalty. Thus with the tenancy agreement broken, it was not long before the consequences for Israel began to be felt.

4. Land as an Expression of Divine Punishment.
Rather than immediate eviction, the judgment visited on the Israelites for their covenant disloyalty was a staged affair. It began with military incursion and economic disaster, but it culminated in expulsion and exile.

4.1. Military Incursion. Since Yahweh's faithfulness (emphasized in Joshua) was not reciprocated by his people (illustrated in Judges), military success quickly gave way to a series of military incursions. Periods in which the land enjoyed "rest" were interspersed with periods in which various parts of the land fell victim to encroachment from and exploitation by Israel's neighbors, before whom Israel apparently was defenseless (cf. Lev 26:17; Deut 28:25-29). This pattern, established in Judges, is largely maintained in the books that follow, with political independence and territorial boundaries being systematically reduced until the threat is not simply temporary subjugation by foreign powers, but loss of the land altogether.

4.2. Economic Disasters. As well as by military incursions, divine displeasure was expressed through economic disaster. Although there are only a few explicit references (e.g., 2 Sam 21:1; 24:13; 2 Kings 8:1), it is clear that Israel's relationship with Yahweh and their experience of the land's fertility (Josh 5:6; although cf. Levine's less positive understanding of "a land flowing with milk and honey") were inextricably connected. Indeed, such economic disaster is a further example of the covenant curses listed in the Pentateuch (cf. Lev 26:19-20; Deut 28:23-24), anticipated both by Solomon in his prayer of temple dedication (1 Kings 8:35-37) and by Yahweh in his response (2 Chron 7:13-14). The most obvious illustration of such a disaster in Israel's history is the drought associated with the prophet *Elijah. Significantly, in the heated exchange between the prophet and the king, each accuses the other of having brought "trouble" on Israel (1 Kings 18:17, 18), a rare term used elsewhere of Achan, whose transgression threatened to curtail the initial conquest (Josh 6:18; 7:25; 1 Chron 2:7), and of *Saul, who is accused by Jonathan of having "troubled the land" (1 Sam 14:29). Clearly, the "trouble" in view by both Ahab and Elijah—the devastating drought in the land—was similarly understood as an expression of divine displeasure. The latter was chiefly due to Israel's idolatry, as the ensuing contest on Mount *Carmel and its immediate aftermath so graphically illustrates.

4.3. Expulsion and Exile. The ultimate example of such covenant curse, again anticipated in the Pentateuch (Lev 26:32-35; Deut 28:63-68) and in the context of the temple's dedication (1 Kings 8:46; 9:1-9; 2 Chron 7:19-22), was physical removal from the land (2 Kings 17:1-23; 25:1-21). Clearly this was something toward which Israel's history had been headed all along (cf. Josh 23:15-16; 1 Kings 14:15; 2 Chron 33:8). Thus the blame for this catastrophe is placed squarely on the shoulders of Yahweh's covenant partners (cf. 1 Kings 13:34; 2 Kings 17:7-23; 18:12; 21:11-15): their history of covenant disloyalty inevitably entailed forfeiture of the land.

While current scholarship debates the extent of the exile and even its historical veracity (for a concise discussion see Smith-Christopher, 45-49; also Provan, Long and Longman III, 278-85), there is overwhelming archaeological evidence to support the biblical portrayal of widespread devastation and depopulation (*see* History of Israel 6-7). It would be a mistake, however, to press either the biblical figures (2 Kings 24:14-17; cf. Jer 52:28-30) or the Chronicler's language (2 Chron 36:20-21) in a literalistic way. Clearly, the land was never entirely empty (2 Kings 25:12; cf. Jer 39:10; 52:16); thus the Chronicler's statement about the land having enjoyed its neglected sabbath rests must be understood as theo-logical hyperbole (cf. Lev 26:32-35).

Whatever its extent, exile was not God's final word. Significantly, both Deuteronomist and Chronicler conclude their respective histories on a more positive note. As the latter observed (2 Chron 36:22-23), the prophetic word had spoken not only of judgment (cf. Jer 25:11) but also of restoration (cf. Jer 29:10-14).

5. Land as an Object of Unrealized Hopes.

The details of the postexilic restoration, subtly presented as a second exodus and conquest, are unfolded chiefly in the books of *Ezra and Nehemiah. Whatever its political motivations and scope (see Provan, Long and Longman III, 286-88), Cyrus's edict (Ezra 1:2-4) permitted the relocation of various people groups to their homelands, and this is clearly interpreted by the biblical authors as the hand of Yahweh (Ezra 1:1; cf. 2 Chron 36:22). From Ezra-Nehemiah we learn that the subsequent repatriation of Israelites was a gradual process (*see* History of Israel

7). The initial group, apparently led by Sheshbazzar, returned around 537 BCE (the total figure, some fifty thousand according to Ezra 2:64-65 and Neh 7:66-67, probably reflects various stages of return between the reigns of Cyrus and Darius, and arguably includes some who had remained in the land). While *Zerubbabel probably returned with this group, he may have arrived with a second wave of exiles at some unspecified time in the late 520s BCE (so Provan, Long and Longman III, 288). In any case, we are explicitly told of at least two further contingents: those who returned with *Ezra (Ezra 7:1-7; 8:1-31), and those who may have accompanied *Nehemiah (Neh 2).

From their response to the activities of their opponents—an amalgam of nonexiled Israelites and other ethnic groups—it would appear that the returnees constituted a minority group in the area formally known as Judah. Moreover, the latter clearly remained a *Persian province ("Yehud")—a fact exploited by those who opposed the reconstruction work being carried out by the Jewish remnant (cf. Ezra 4; Neh 6). Thus, while the Jerusalem temple and the city walls were repaired (symbolically re-establishing Yahweh's kingship in Zion), the restoration achieved fell pitifully short of the grandiose future in the land anticipated by prophets such as Ezekiel and Haggai (cf. Neh 9:30, 36).

The explanation in Ezra-Nehemiah for this conundrum echoes that offered in the past: there was a willingness (on the part of some, at least) to disregard their covenant obligations. In addition to their moral and cultic laxity (cf. Neh 5:7-11; 13:6-11, 15-18), the Israelites, rather than remaining distinct from the nations, were again following the path of assimilation (cf. the anachronistic and theologically loaded description of these "peoples of the lands" in Ezra 9:1-2). As both Ezra and Nehemiah perceived, racial intermarriage (whatever the sociological motivations [see Smith-Christopher, 150-60]) inevitably would lead once more to religious syncretism—hence their concerted efforts to eradicate this practice within the fledgling community lest history repeat itself (cf. Ezra 9—10; Neh 13).

Although there are some indications of territorial "expansion" (cf. Neh 11:30), Ezra-Nehemiah, like both the Deuteronomistic History and Chronicles, ends on a note of hope rather than one of fulfillment. Instead of a return to the glory days of a bygone era, the postexilic community is relatively small, under foreign control, and largely contained in a small fraction of their tribal allotments (as allocated in Joshua), still less the ideal territorial borders mentioned elsewhere (*see* History of Israel 8). The latter ideal and the associated rest remained an unrealized hope in the immediate postexilic era and beyond.

See also CITIES AND VILLAGES; GEOGRAPHICAL EXTENT OF ISRAEL; LEVITICAL CITIES; TRIBES OF ISRAEL AND LAND ALLOTMENT/BORDERS.

BIBLIOGRAPHY. **E. Assis**, " 'How Long are you Slack to Go to Possess the Land' (Jos. XVIII3): Ideal and Reality in the Distribution Descriptions in Joshua XIII-XIX," *VT* 53 (2003) 1-25; **W. Brueggemann**, *The Land: Place as Gift, Promise, and Challenge in Biblical Faith* (2d ed.; Minneapolis: Augsburg Fortress, 2002); **E. W. Davies**, "Land: Its Rights and Privileges," in *The World of Ancient Israel: Sociological, Anthropological and Political Perspectives*, ed. R. E. Clements (Cambridge: Cambridge University Press, 1989) 349-69; **N. C. Habel**, *The Land Is Mine: Six Biblical Land Ideologies* (Minneapolis: Fortress, 1995); **R. S. Hess**, "The Book of Joshua as a Land Grant," *Bib* 83 (2002) 493-506; **S. Japhet**, *I & II Chronicles* (OTL; Louisville: Westminster/John Knox, 1993); **P. Johnston and P. Walker**, eds., *The Land of Promise: Biblical, Theological and Contemporary Perspectives* (Downers Grove, IL: InterVarsity Press; Leicester: Apollos, 2000); **A. M. Kitz**, "Undivided Inheritance and Lot Casting in the Book of Joshua," *JBL* 119 (2000) 601-18; **E. Levine**, "The Land of Milk and Honey," *JSOT* 87 (2000) 43-57; **D. F. Murray**, "Of All the Years of Hope—or Fears? Jehoiachin in Babylon (2 Kings 25:27-30)," *JBL* 120 (2001) 245-65; **I. Provan, V. P. Long and T. Longman III**, *A Biblical History of Israel* (Louisville: Westminster/John Knox, 2003); **D. L. Smith-Christopher**, *A Biblical Theology of Exile* (Minneapolis: Augsburg Fortress, 2002); **G. Strecker**, ed., *Das Land Israel in biblischer Zeit: Jerusalem-Symposium 1981 der Hebräischen Universität und der Georg-August-Universität* (GTA 25; Göttingen: Vandenhoeck & Ruprecht; 1983); **M. Weinfeld**, *The Promise of the Land: The Inheritance of the Land of Canaan by the Israelites* (Taubman Lectures in Jewish Studies; Berkeley: University of California Press, 1993); **C. J. H. Wright**, *God's People in God's Land: Family, Land and Property in the Old Testament* (Exeter: Paternoster, 1990).   P. R. Williamson

LAW

Law plays a very prominent role in the Pentateuch (see Selman), but it also plays an important, if less prominent, role in the OT Historical Books. This article discusses the two major terms for "law" in the Historical Books, the influence of Mosaic law on the Historical Books, and the administration of law from the time of Joshua to the end of the OT period.

1. Terms for "Law" in the Historical Books: *tôrâ* and *dāt*
2. The Influence of Mosaic Law on the Historical Narratives
3. The Administration of Law in the Historical Books

1. Terms for "Law" in the Historical Books: *tôrâ* and *dāt*.
There are many terms for "law" in the Historical Books, including *ḥōq/ḥuqqā* ("statute"), *mišpāṭ* ("judgment, decision") and *miṣwâ* ("commandment"). Only the terms *tôrâ* and *dāt* are treated here.

1.1. tôrâ. The term *torah (tôrâ)*, meaning "law, instruction," is the most important term for "law" in the OT. Of special interest are various "books of the law" mentioned in the Historical Books, and the judicial reforms of *Jehoshaphat.

1.1.1. Torah in the Deuteronomistic History. God exhorts *Joshua to adhere to the law (*torah*) that Moses commanded and to meditate on the book of the law day and night (Josh 1:7-8), an exhortation that Joshua passes along to the Transjordan tribes of Reuben, Gad and half of Manasseh (Josh 22:5), and to all Israel (Josh 23:6). There is reference also to building an altar at Mount Ebal of unhewn stones in accord with instructions in the Mosaic law (Josh 8:30-31), archaeological remains of which may have been found, although the interpretation is disputed (Zertal, 257). On the stones of that altar was inscribed a copy of "the law of Moses," and Joshua read the blessing and the curse written in the law of Moses, and indeed every word of that law, to the people (Josh 8:32-34).

Precisely what this "book of the law" refers to is not immediately obvious. In canonical context, where the book of Joshua appears to be a continuation of the story of the Pentateuch, the book of the law might be thought to refer to all the laws of the Pentateuch, including the book of the covenant written at Sinai (Ex 24:7), or perhaps even the Pentateuch itself, which later Jewish tradition labeled as the Torah. The usual interpretation of critical scholarship, on the other hand, is that it refers to an earlier version of Deuteronomy. In the Pentateuch "the book of the law" is used only of the teachings in Deuteronomy (Deut 28:61; 29:21; 30:10; 31:26). Passages in Joshua that mention the book of the law of Moses also strongly allude to matters found in Deuteronomy: the death of Moses (Josh 1:1-2; Deut 34:1-8), a promise of conquest that closely echoes Deuteronomy (Josh 1:3-5a; Deut 11:24-25a), and God's exhortation for Joshua to have courage, repeating the exhortation that Moses gave Joshua in Deuteronomy at his commissioning (Josh 1:5b-6, 9; Deut 31:7-8, 23). Also drawing from Deuteronomy is the warning not to turn to the right or the left in following the law (Josh 1:7b; 23:6; Deut 5:32; 28:14), the admonition to obey with all one's heart and soul (Josh 22:5; Deut 6:5), and Moses' command to build an altar of stones on Mount Ebal and inscribe on it "all the words of this law" (Josh 8:30-35; Deut 27:1-8), including the blessing and the curse (Josh 8:34; Deut 27:9—28:68). In Deuteronomy 27:8 "all the words of *this* law" that Moses commanded to be put on the Mount Ebal altar stones presumably refers in context to the various laws of Deuteronomy. These many allusions to Deuteronomy fit well with the hypothesis that the book of Joshua is part of the *Deuteronomistic History, a history highly influenced by Deuteronomy. M. Noth (63) thought that Joshua 8:30-35 was directly composed by the Deuteronomist.

Reference to the *torah* of Moses is absent from 1-2 Samuel, but 2 Samuel does refer to a "*torah* of mankind" (2 Sam 7:19) in David's prayer after he receives God's promise of an eternal dynasty. This expression is variously interpreted: "instruction for mankind/people" (ESV, NRSV); "manner/custom of man" (as opposed to that of God) (NASB; BDB); "[This (promise) is] a charter for mankind" (Kaiser, 311-15); or as a question, "[Is this your] usual way of dealing with man?" (NIV). Since the meanings "manner, custom" and "charter" are not well attested for *torah,* and the usual meaning "law, instruction" does not seem apt, some scholars prefer to emend the text after the parallel in 1 Chronicles 17:17, which reads *tôr* (meaning uncertain; perhaps "rank" or "group" or "turn") rather than *tôrat* (cf. RSV, where "future genera-

tions" assumes an emended text, either "the turn *[tôr]* of mankind" or "the generations *[dôrôt]* of mankind").

Jehu of Israel (2 Kings 10:31), and Israel and Judah generally (2 Kings 17:13, 34, 37), are rebuked for not following God's *torah.* Although God would have allowed the people to remain in the land had they followed the *torah,* *Manasseh led them astray (2 Kings 21:8-9; 2 Chron 33:8-9). King Amaziah of Judah, on the other hand, is commended for following Deuteronomy 24:16 ("children are not to be put to death because of their fathers"), as he did not execute the sons of assassins along with the perpetrators themselves (2 Kings 14:6; 2 Chron 25:4).

During the reign of *Josiah, the priest Hilkiah discovered in the house of Yahweh the lost "book of the *torah,*" also called "the book of the covenant" (2 Kings 22:8; 23:2). When Josiah heard the words of this book, he tore his garments in a gesture of grief (2 Kings 22:11) and proceeded to carry out that law by removing mediums and idols from the land (2 Kings 23:24). Indeed, Josiah is said to have followed the *torah* of Moses with all his heart and soul more than any other Israelite king (2 Kings 23:25). Part of his activity involved putting down idolatry and destroying the *high places of Judah and Samaria that Manasseh had allowed, thereby restricting sacrificial worship to Jerusalem (2 Kings 21:3; 23:5-9, 15, 19-20).

J. Wellhausen and his school generally accepted the thesis of W. M. L. deWette's 1805 dissertation (published in 1807) that Josiah's "book of the law" was a version of Deuteronomy and was in fact a pious fraud prepared by Hilkiah or other priests in Jerusalem for political gain. The purpose of Deuteronomy, according to deWette, was to get the king to exalt the Jerusalem priesthood at the expense of the high places by making Jerusalem "the place that Yahweh your God chooses" of which Deuteronomy speaks (Deut 12:5).

Josiah's "book of the law" probably does refer to a version of Deuteronomy, as does the same expression in the Pentateuch and the book of Joshua. It is not so clear, however, that Deuteronomy commanded an immediate end to all altars outside the central sanctuary, as the Wellhausen school believes, nor does it specify the place that God will choose as Jerusalem. The version of Deuteronomy that now exists in fact directed Israel to build an altar of stone at

Mount Ebal on entering the land (Deut 27:1-8) and foresaw that Israel would build other legitimate altars in the land (Deut 16:21). What Deuteronomy 12 does do, however, is predict a future time in which God would centralize sacrificial worship (but not profane slaughter) to the one place that God chooses.

The *Deuteronomistic History reflects a similar tension. It clearly portrays various biblical characters after the time of Moses as constructing or using legitimate altars outside the central sanctuary. These characters include Joshua (Josh 8:30-35, fulfilling Deut 27:1-8), Gideon (Judg 6:24), Manoah (Judg 13:19-20), *Samuel (1 Sam 7:17), *Saul (1 Sam 14:35), *David (2 Sam 24:18-20) and *Elijah (1 Kings 18:30). It also mentions various other altars of Yahweh wrongly torn down by the people (1 Kings 19:10). On the other hand, this history foresees a day when all such altars would be supplanted. In the context of Solomon's using the altar at Gibeon, the text comments, "The people, however, were still sacrificing at the high places, because a temple had not yet been built for the name of Yahweh" (1 Kings 3:2). This text assumes that other altars were permissible at least until the temple was built, but at some point after the construction of the temple they would become obsolete (see High Places). Josiah (c. 621 BCE) then comes along to fulfill the centralization of the cult predicted by Deuteronomy 12 and anticipated by the narrator in 1 Kings 3:2.

1.1.2. Torah in Chronicles. The Chronicler also shows interest in *torah*, although for him the term clearly is broader than in Deuteronomy and includes priestly regulations. He condemns *Rehoboam, who "forsook the *torah* of Yahweh" (2 Chron 12:1). God, speaking to Asa though the prophet Azariah, remarks that Israel had long been "without a teaching priest and without *torah*" (2 Chron 15:3), probably a hendiadys meaning "without a priest giving authoritative instruction," as Weingreen suggests (cited in Williamson 1982, 267). The Chronicler also repeats the book of Kings' evaluations of Amaziah and Manasseh (2 Chron 25:4; 33:8-9 [see 1.1.1]).

The Chronicler commends others for following the law. In portraying positively David's interest in the cult, the Chronicler notes that David had the Zadokite priests offer the regular burnt offerings in accord with "the *torah* of Yahweh" (1 Chron 16:40)—that is, the priestly regulations of the Pentateuch (e.g., Ex 29:38-42; Num

28:3-4). The Chronicler quotes David as admonishing his son *Solomon to "keep the *torah* of Yahweh" (1 Chron 22:12), and Asa directed Judah to "observe the *torah* and the commandments" (2 Chron 14:4). In Solomon's prayer of dedication for the temple the Chronicler modifies 1 Kings 8:25, where the king must "walk before me," with the clarifying paraphrase that the king is to "walk in my *torah*" (2 Chron 6:16). Jehoiada, who after Athaliah's idolatrous reign of terror ran the government until Joash came of age, returned control of the temple to the Levitical priests "as is written in the *torah* of Moses" and "the order of David" (2 Chron 23:18). *Hezekiah is commended for seeking God "in *torah* and commandments" (2 Chron 31:21). Hezekiah's religious reforms included having the festivals celebrated "as is written in the *torah* of Yahweh" (2 Chron 31:3), and having the Levites take their stations "according to the *torah* of Moses" and receive financial support of tithes so that they could devote themselves to "the *torah* of Yahweh" (2 Chron 30:16; 31:4). Josiah's piety "as written in the *torah* of Yahweh" is also commended (2 Chron 35:26).

The Chronicler repeats the account drawn from Kings of the discovery of the Deuteronomic "book of the *torah*" (2 Chron 34:14-19; cf. 2 Kings 22). One variation of wording about the book of the *torah* is worth mentioning. In Kings, Shaphan "read it" (*wyqr'hw* [2 Kings 22:8]), whereas Chronicles says that Shaphan "read in it" (*wyqr' bw* [2 Chron 34:18]). It is possible that the Chronicler rewords the Kings account because the Chronicler intends his audience to apply this language to a broader "book of the law" (i.e., the Pentateuch), not merely the (part of) Deuteronomy to which the Kings account refers (Williamson 1982, 402). On the other hand, R. B. Dillard (281) rightly observes that grammatically, the meaning of the two phrases could be equivalent.

Jehoshaphat is said to have appointed *priests and Levites to teach in the cities of Judah from "the book of the law of Yahweh" (2 Chron 17:8-9), and he reorganized the judiciary, appointing judges from the priests, Levites and heads of families to decide cases involving "bloodshed, *torah* and commandment, statutes and rules" (2 Chron 19:10). Although some consider Jehoshaphat's "book of the law" to consist of royal edicts, evidence is lacking to confirm this hypothesis (Whitelam, 212).

Noting that this whole matter is missing from the parallel in Kings, and in defense of his post-exilic dating of the P source, Wellhausen took the Chronicler's account of Jehoshaphat's judicial reforms as a retrojection of what happened after the exile into the earlier history of Israel, a retrojection that builds on an etiology of Jehoshaphat's name that means "Yahweh judges" (Wellhausen, 191). G. N. Knoppers argues that the Chronicler's account of Jehoshaphat's judicial reforms is based on Deuteronomy 17:8-13, Exodus 18:13-27 and Deuteronomy 1:9-18 rather than on reliable sources. Other scholars are more willing to give the Chronicler the benefit of the doubt (e.g., Dillard, 148; Williamson 1982, 287-88; Whitelam, 185-206), suggesting that although he uses language influenced by texts in the Pentateuch, the Chronicler probably did not simply invent his account but rather is consulting a source that describes a pre-Deuteronomic reform of Israelite legal traditions. W. F. Albright defended the historicity of Jehoshaphat's judicial reforms as similar to those of Haremhab in fourteenth-century BCE Egypt, a reform that also involved priests serving as judges (de Vaux, 1:154).

1.1.3. Torah in Ezra-Nehemiah. Ezra-Nehemiah also refers to *torah*. After the exile *Zerubbabel built an altar on which Jeshua and the priests sacrificed burnt offerings "as is written in the *torah* of Moses" (Ezra 3:2). The narrator remarks that *Ezra was "a scribe skilled in the *torah* of Moses" (also called the "*torah* of Yahweh" and "*torah* of God"), which he studied and taught (Ezra 7:6, 10). Ezra is portrayed as bringing the "book of the *torah*" (Neh 8:1, 3, 5, 8, 18) before an assembly of men and women of Judah at the Western Gate during the days of *Nehemiah (*pace* Williamson [1985, 409 n. 9], who sees "Nehemiah" as a secondary insertion and dates this event to c. 458 BCE). The people listened to his book of the law from early morning to midday, and assistants explained the *torah* and gave the sense (Neh 8:7-8). Rabbinic tradition looked back to Ezra and this event as justifying the use of oral law (rabbinic interpretation) and translation (Aramaic Targumim) alongside the written law.

Ezra's prayer (Ezra 9:6-15) in which he confesses his people's disregard of God's commands influenced Shecaniah to propose that Jews divorce their foreign wives "in accord with the *torah*" (Ezra 10:2-3; cf. Deut 7:1-5). This particular claim is problematic because there is no law requiring a divorce from non-Canaanite foreign spouses: Ruth the *Moabite, ancestor of David, is portrayed very positively in the book of Ruth; Deuteronomy 21:10-14 allows marriage to foreign captive women; and God sided with Moses rather than his bother Aaron and sister Miriam regarding his marriage to a Cushite woman (Num 12:1-9). Some of these wives seem explicitly non-Canaanite (Moabites and Egyptians are mentioned in Ezra 9:1). Moreover, it is doubtful that "the peoples of the land" are actually *Canaanites. Their abominations are said to be "like" those "of the Canaanites" (NIV) and other groups, but they are not actually identified as Canaanites. Canaanites as such may have ceased to exist by this point in history. Thus some conclude that Shecaniah and Ezra misapplied the law out of racist zeal to preserve the "holy seed" (Ezra 9:2) (so Williamson 1985, 159-62).

On the other hand, the biblical narrator gives no hint of disapproval. Given the narrator's previous portrayal of Ezra as an expert in the *torah*, he probably agrees with the actions taken. A more positive reading is possible. The demand to divorce foreign wives "according to the law" probably was understood in terms of principles rather than explicit command. Because the sins of these foreigners were "like" those of the Canaanites, the command not to marry Canaanites could be applied by analogy to intermarriage with such foreigners. Moreover, Shecaniah may also have had in mind Deuteronomy 24:1, where the openly pagan practices of the foreign wives constituted the "unseemly thing/indecency" that justified divorce.

The nature of the *torah* in which Ezra was expert and which he taught the people in Nehemiah 8 is subject to speculation. Scholarly opinions about the contents of Ezra's *torah* have included the following: a collection of legal materials (R. Kittel, G. von Rad, M. Noth, C. Houtman), the Priestly Code P (A. Kuenen, W. O. E. Oesterly, H.-J. Kraus), the Deuteronomic laws (L. Browne, R. Bowman, M. F. Scott, U. Kellermann) and the Pentateuch (J. Wellhausen, E. Sellin, O. Eissfeldt, W. Ruldoph, K. Galling, S. Mowinckel, W. F. Albright, F. M. Cross) (Yamauchi, 256-57). There seems little basis at this late date to limit *torah* to Deuteronomy. Ezra 3:2 uses *torah* in the sense of cultic law. If, as some scholars believe, the

Chronicler also edited Ezra-Nehemiah, then the Chronicler's broader usage that includes cultic law would be expected. Ezra is repeatedly called a priest as well as a teacher of law (Ezra 7:11-12, 21; 10:10, 16; Neh 8:2, 9; 12:26), so he would have had a natural interest in cultic matters. C. Houtman argues that the law book presupposed there does not refer to P, nor to Deuteronomy, nor to our current Pentateuch in whole or part, but rather to some other law book, now lost, analogous to the Qumran *Temple Scroll*, whose laws overlapped with those in the Pentateuch, but which contained some laws that were unique to it (Houtman, 91-115). Against this view, however, it seems doubtful that a book associated with Moses in the postexilic community would have been entirely lost, and the alleged discrepancies that Houtman sees between statements about the law in Ezra-Nehemiah and the laws of the Pentateuch can be explained otherwise (Williamson 1985, xxxviii-xxxix, 288). Wellhausen (408-9, 497) took this "book" as essentially the Pentateuch as we now have it, and indeed suggested that Ezra was its final and principal editor, adding P to the earlier JED document. It is also possible that Ezra brought with him a version of the Pentateuch from Babylonia (Yamauchi, 258). Either way, it is probable that Ezra's law book is in fact related to our current Pentateuch.

1.2. dāt. In Hebrew and *Aramaic portions of Ezra and in Esther the Persian loanword *dāt* occurs in the sense of "law." Of special importance here is the question of precisely what Ezra was authorized to do with *dāt* by the Persian monarch Artaxerxes.

1.2.1. Persian Law as dāt. The noun *dāt* in the singular can be a collective referring to Persian jurisprudence in general (Esther 1:13; 4:16) or to individual decrees of Persian kings whose edicts constituted law (Ezra 8:36; Esther 1:19; 2:8; 3:14-15; 4:3, 8; 8:14; 9:1, 13, 14). Even Ahasuerus's pronouncement that everyone drink freely is considered a *dāt* (Esther 1:8). The plural of *dāt* can refer to the total body of royal edicts and laws in Persia (Esther 1:19; 3:8b) or to a specific group of royal directives such as those that Artaxerxes sent to sanction Ezra's mission (Ezra 8:36).

The story of Esther revolves around the *dāt* issued by Ahasuerus to annihilate the Jews of his empire (Esther 3:9, 14). According to the Bible, a Medo-Persian *dāt* cannot be repealed (Esther 1:19). This has been taken to mean no more than that Persian decrees must be quickly carried out (Clines, 282), but the story of Daniel takes it to mean that a king cannot invalidate his own decrees (Dan 6:8, 12, 15). In Esther, Ahasuerus evidently cannot simply reverse his own decree to annihilate the Jews, but instead must issue a new one allowing the Jews to defend themselves (Esther 8:8, 13). Possible extrabiblical evidence of this quirk in Persian law comes from Diodorus (*Library* 17.30.6), where Darius III, despite his royal powers, is unable to undo the death sentence that he had pronounced on a man whose words had offended him. That text is not clear, however, whether the king's regrets came before or after the man had actually been executed.

1.2.2. dāt *as a Synonym for* tôrâ. Artaxerxes' letter to Ezra in Aramaic authorizes Ezra's mission. There Ezra is called a "scribe of the *dāt* of the God of heaven" (Ezra 7:12, 21). This "God of heaven" is described as "your [Ezra's] God" (Ezra 7:25-26), but it may also have been a title of the Persian celestial god Ahuramazda, who was portrayed as a winged figure and is known to have been worshiped by Darius and Xerxes (Yaumachi, 430-33). Artaxerxes may have identified Yahweh with Ahuramazda. In the Hebrew portion of the book Ezra is similarly labeled as a *scribe skilled in the *torah* of Moses and the *torah* of Yahweh (Ezra 7:6, 10). Thus it seems that in this Aramaic letter *dāt* is a synonym for Hebrew *tôrâ*.

The scope of what Ezra was being authorized to do by Artaxerxes is a subject of debate. The key verses are Ezra 7:25-26, where Ezra is authorized to appoint magistrates and judges who "know the laws [pl. of *dāt*] of your God," to teach the law, and to punish those who disobey the law. This has been understood in several ways (Watts, 1-4; also subsequent essays in that volume): (1) Persia authorized a version of the Pentateuch as the law of Judah (P. Frei); (2) Persia merely authorized Ezra to appoint judges to carry out Persian law with limited influence from Jewish legal traditions (L. Fried); (3) Persia authorized the Pentateuch in a token way as the "official" law of Judah, though with little actual attention to that law's form or content (J. Watts); (4) Persian authorization of Jewish law is fictional rather than historical (L. Grabbe).

One complication in this discussion regarding Ezra's making Jewish law the law of the state has to do with whether Ezra's book of law is in fact the Pentateuch (see 1.1.3). Another complication is that not all the norms of the Pentateuch are "laws" in the sense of norms ever meant to be enforced by the state. A norm such as the Decalogue's "Do not covet" (Ex 20:17; Deut 5:21) is purely a moral precept not easily enforceable by the state. The formulation of certain injunctions lack penalty clauses for noncompliance (e.g., the slave laws of Ex 21:1-11). To make these into "laws" rather than moral admonitions requires the addition of penalty clauses that goes beyond the Pentateuch. Some regulations specify God as enforcer, not the state (e.g., the admonition to treat sojourners, widows and orphans decently [Ex 22:21-24]). For this very reason, even if Ezra had made the Pentateuch in some sense the law of Judah, Nehemiah as governor still would have had to cajole his fellow wealthy Jews not to charge interest to those sacrificing to work on Nehemiah's wall, as he does in Nehemiah 5:6-13. Nehemiah as governor had no legal authority under Mosaic law to stop his fellow aristocrats from taking interest, because the regulations against taking interest from the poor are ones enforced by God rather than by the state (Ex 22:25-27; Lev 25:35-38; Deut 23:19-20). Biblical law covers only a limited number of legal topics, and so the Pentateuch by itself would be inadequate to serve as a complete law code; at most, it could serve as one element of the legal standards of Ezra's day.

2. The Influence of Mosaic Law on the Historical Narratives.

In addition to statements about law associated with the vocabulary of law given above, there are from time to time allusions in the Historical Books to concepts found in pentateuchal laws even where the term *law* is not used. A sampling follows here.

The Historical Books refer to holy days found in the law—for example, sabbaths ([though not until the divided monarchy] 2 Kings 4:23, plus 22x), the Feast of Passover/Unleavened Bread (28x), the Feast of Weeks (2 Chron 8:13) and the Feast of Tabernacles (Judg 21:19 [?]; 1 Kings 8:2; 2 Chron 8:13; Ezra 3:4; Neh 8:14-17). The changing of the date of the Feast of Tabernacles from the seventh to the eighth month is part of the sin of *Jeroboam (1 Kings 12:32-33; cf. Lev 23:34).

Joshua, in accord with the law, circumcised every male (Josh 5:2-9; cf. Gen 17:10-14), removed hung corpses of his enemies before sundown (Josh 10:26-27; cf. Deut 21:22-23), and set up *Levitical cities of refuge (Josh 20:2-9; cf. Num 35:9-15; Deut 4:41-43; 19:1-13). Achan's taking of things "under the ban" brought punishment on Israel, as threatened by the law (Josh 7:12, 20-25; cf. Deut 13:17). Samson's parents are warned that he must not drink wine, shave his head or eat anything ceremonially unclean, per the rules for Nazirites (Judg 13:4-14; cf. Num 6:1-8), although Judges makes no mention of the prohibition of corpse contamination that Samson clearly violates. In Ruth 3—4 the customs surrounding the right of a near relative to redeem and marry Ruth resemble (with some variation) the law of levirate marriage (Deut 25:5-10). Hannah's vow that were she to have a child, no razor would come on his head (1 Sam 1:11) is explained by the law as an application of the Nazirite vow (Num 6:5).

The sons of Samuel, by taking bribes, perverted justice, contrary to the law (1 Sam 8:3; cf. Ex 23:6, 8; Deut 16:19). When David failed to come to eat with Saul's family the fellowship/peace offering associated with the new moon, Saul supposed that David must have been ceremonially unclean (1 Sam 20:26; cf. Num 10:10; Lev 7:20). Saul applied for a time the laws against sorcery and divination (1 Sam 28:9; cf. Ex 22:18; Deut 18:10-14). David was prepared to apply the law requiring fourfold restitution for theft of a sheep (2 Sam 12:6; cf. Ex 22:1). Joab sought asylum at the sanctuary, an option allowed in the law for murderers (1 Kings 2:28-29; cf. Ex 21:13) and perhaps here expanded to include political offenses (Barmash, 15).

Solomon violates the laws against kings taking multiple wives, intermarrying with pagans and committing idolatry (1 Kings 11:1-8; cf. Deut 17:17; Ex 20:3; 34:12-17; Deut 7:1-5). Arguably, "great wrath" came against Israel in 2 Kings 3:27 because Israel had violated the rules of war outside the land (Deut 20:10-20) (see Sprinkle, 285-301). Naboth was falsely accused of violating the law concerning unspecified offenses against God and the ruler (1 Kings 21:10; cf. Ex 22:28). Amaziah obeyed Deuteronomy 24:16 (see 1.1.1). Nehemiah urged fellow aristocrats to follow the laws against usury (Neh 5:10; cf. Ex 22:25; Lev 25:36-37; Deut 23:19).

K. W. Whitelam (218) has argued that in

many of these cases later royal edicts came to be retrojected back into Mosaic law. However, it could just as well be true that royal practice was directly or indirectly influenced by earlier Mosaic law. In principle, the king was not so much to promulgate law as to administer the law of Yahweh (de Vaux, 1:150).

3. The Administration of Law in the Historical Books.
Administration of justice was diverse in the historical narratives, but there does seem to be development over time as to how the law was administered.

Whereas in Genesis it appears that the head of household (the *paterfamilias*) had primary authority (Boecker, 30), by the time of Joshua-Judges this authority was shifting to elders, leaders and *judges (Josh 23:2; 24:1). Although only one "major" judge is described as sitting at court (ironically, a female, Deborah [Judg 4:5]), the "minor" judges of the book of Judges may have served this function. Elders at the city gate served as both witnesses and judges (Ruth 4:1, 11; cf. Deut 21:19-20).

In Deuteronomy priests were to serve as judges, especially for hard cases (Deut 17:8-11; 19:17-18), sometimes administering an oath or a self-curse to help divine the truth (Num 5:19; Ex 22:11). In the Historical Books Samuel serves as both priest, who blesses and conducts sacrifices, and judge (1 Sam 7:15-17; 9:13; 10:8; Ps 99:6). Jehoshaphat's judicial reforms involved the appointment of priests and Levites, along with heads of families, to administer justice (2 Chron 19:8-10). Jeremiah, toward the end of the monarchy, mentions that the job of the priest was closely related to *torah* (Jer 18:18), and Ezra the scribe of the law of God was also a priest (see 1.1.3 and 1.2.2).

After the establishment of the monarchy *kings are portrayed as rendering judicial decisions (see Boecker, 40-49; de Vaux, 1:150-52; Whitelam). In times of war kings such as Saul naturally oversaw martial law over soldiers and civilians (1 Sam 22:6-19). This authority eventually passed to kings in other conditions. Kings thus took the role that once belonged to the judges (1 Sam 8:1, 5). Solomon built the Hall of Justice for the purpose of conducting court (1 Kings 7:7). In principle, administering law so that justice occurred for his people (2 Sam 8:15; 2 Chron 9:8; Ps 45:4; 72:1-2), a king might be

called on to decide an especially difficult case, such as the dispute without witnesses over possession of a child (1 Kings 3:16-28 [Solomon]). Sometimes the king evidently served as a court of appeals, as in the (fictional) case of the wise widow of Tekoa, who asked the king to save her son from her "family" or clan, which intended to execute him for killing his brother (2 Sam 14:4-8) (see Barmash, 11-14). In other cases the king may have had primary jurisdiction from the beginning (2 Kings 6:26-29, a special case during besiegement; possibly also the case of a woman seeking to repossess her house and field in 2 Kings 8:3, and the fictitious case of theft recounted by Nathan to David in 2 Sam 12:1-6) (see Whitelam, 124). It would be impossible for a king to hear all cases and appeals, a fact exploited by Absalom to incite discontent (2 Sam 15:1-6). The innovation of kingship naturally shifted the jurisdiction of some cases from the other judges to kings, and so made the king the highest judicial authority in the land, though it is unclear how and why some cases went to the king while other cases remained in the sphere of lower courts.

In theory, even kings were subordinated to the *torah* of Yahweh (Deut 17:18-20); thus kings were admonished to obey God's commandments (2 Sam 12:14-15; 1 Kings 2:3-4). This is what Solomon expresses a desire to do (1 Kings 8:58). However, David seems not to have been subject to human punishment after committing adultery with Bathsheba and having Uriah, her husband, murdered (2 Sam 12). Ahab, king of Israel (unlike his wife, Jezebel), thought that even he as king was subject to the law of property rights (1 Kings 21:4) (see Barmash, 14). Josiah is portrayed positively as renewing his commitment to obey God's commandments (2 Kings 23:3; 2 Chron 34:31). Saul, on the other hand, is said to have lost his kingship because he failed to keep Yahweh's command (1 Sam 13:14; 15:23), and Solomon's successors lost control of the northern kingdom because he did not follow God's commandments (1 Kings 11:10-11). Moreover, if Solomon's dynasty failed to keep God's commands, it too might prove temporary (1 Chron 28:7).

After the exile it was the law of the Persian king that authorized Ezra to administer the law of God (Ezra 7:26), thus showing the preeminence of Persian law for that state.

See also DEUTERONOMISTIC HISTORY; ETHICS;

EZRA; PRIESTS AND LEVITES; WORD OF GOD.

BIBLIOGRAPHY. **W. F. Albright,** "The Judicial Reforms of Jehoshaphat," in *Alexander Marx: Jubilee Volume on the Occasion of His Seventieth Birthday* [English section] (New York: Jewish Publication Society, 1950) 61-82; **P. Barmash,** "The Narrative Quandary: Cases of Law in Literature," *VT* 54 (2004) 1-16; **H. J. Boecker,** *Law and the Administration of Justice in the Old Testament and the Ancient East* (Minneapolis: Augsburg, 1980); **D. J. A. Clines,** *Ezra, Nehemiah, Esther* (NCB; Grand Rapids: Eerdmans, 1984); **R. B. Dillard,** *2 Chronicles* (WBC 15; Waco, TX: Word, 1987); **C. Houtman,** "Ezra and the Law: Observations on the Supposed Relation between Ezra and the Pentateuch," *OTS* 21 (1981) 91-115; **W. C. Kaiser,** "The Blessing on David: A Charter for Humanity," in *The Law and the Prophets: Old Testament Studies Prepared in Honor of Oswald Thompson Allis,* ed. J. Skilton (Nutley, NJ: Presbyterian and Reformed, 1974) 298-318; **G. N. Knoppers,** "Jehoshaphat's Judiciary and the 'Scroll of Yahweh's Torah,'" *JBL* 113 (1994) 59-80; **M. Noth,** *The Deuteronomistic History* (JSOTSup 15; Sheffield: JSOT, 1991); **M. J. Selman,** "Law," *DOTP* 497-515; **J. M. Sprinkle,** "Deuteronomic 'Just War' (Deut 20:10-20) and 2 Kings 3:27," *ZABR* 5 (2000) 285-301; **R. de Vaux,** *Ancient Israel* (2 vols.; New York: McGraw-Hill, 1965); **J. W. Watts,** ed., *Persia and Torah: The Theory of Imperial Authorization of the Pentateuch* (SBLSymS 17; Atlanta: Society of Biblical Literature, 2001); **J. Wellhausen,** *Prolegomena to the History of Ancient Israel, with a Reprint of the Article "Israel" from the Encyclopedia Britannica* (Gloucester, MA: P. Smith, 1983); **K. W. Whitelam,** *The Just King: Monarchial Judicial Authority in Ancient Israel* (JSOTSup 12; Sheffield: JSOT, 1979); **H. G. M. Williamson,** *1 and 2 Chronicles* (NCB; Grand Rapids: Eerdmans, 1982); idem, *Ezra, Nehemiah* (WBC 16; Waco, TX: Word, 1985); **E. Yamauchi,** *Persia and the Bible* (Grand Rapids: Baker, 1990); **A. Zertal,** "Ebal, Mount," *ABD* 2.255-58.

J. M. Sprinkle

LEBANON

Lebanon often denotes the northernmost border of Israel, but it is also used as a reference to its cedars, which are either symbols of majesty or a costly building material.

1. General Information
2. Lebanon and Israel's Northern Border
3. The Cedars of Lebanon
4. Lebanon—the Remote Country

1. General Information.

Lebanon comes from the Semitic root for "white," probably named so after its snow-covered peaks. It often is used with the definite article, referring to a geographic locality rather than a political entity. It is followed by a determinate demonstrative in Joshua 1:4, translated as "this Lebanon" (RSV).

1.1. Definition. In the Bible *Lebanon* can describe one, two or all of three geographical areas: the mountains close to the Mediterranean coast (Judg 3:3), the parallel mountain range further inland (the Anti-Lebanon) (Josh 3:3), and the fertile Beqa Valley (classical Coele-Syria) situated between the two ranges (Josh 11:17; 12:7). In a few cases (Josh 1:4; 9:1) the LXX, seeking to narrow the geographical area intended, reads *Antilibanos* for wider-definition "Lebanon" used in the MT.

In contrast to the land further inland, the mountain slopes, the adjacent coastland and the southern Beqa Valley have good rainfall, making these areas quite fertile. It follows that the recurring biblical references to Lebanon's forests/cedars, which grew on the western mountain range, often are symbols of fertility. Today, however, due to deforestation (see, e.g., 2 Kings 19:23/Is 37:24; cf. Is 10:34; see *ANET,* 275), only isolated groves are left.

1.2. Historical Context. In ancient times Lebanon was never an independent political entity. Instead, its resources contributed to the wealth of the surrounding states. For example, the *Phoenician coastal cities such as Tyre and Sidon, never parts of Lebanon, benefited economically from its timber (1 Kings 5; *ANET,* 134a).

During the Amarna age (1402-1347 BCE) Lebanon was controlled by the Amurru (the Amorites). Their main center was in the Lebanese mountains, but they also wielded power over a number of cities in the Beqa Valley, and *Hazor holds a prominent place. The kingdom of Amurru was a unique phenomenon in that it was a more extensive kingdom (the capital of which is yet unknown) rather than a city-state (Aharoni, 65-66, 171, 181, 236-39).

At the time of the united monarchy 2 Samuel 8:8 describes how *David took booty from several towns in the southern Beqa Valley. Lebanese territory is further alluded to as part of David's kingdom in 2 Samuel 24:6-7. During the reign of *Solomon the territory began to shrink, but it is not known when Solomon lost control over the Beqa Valley. 1 Kings 9:19/2 Chronicles 8:6 states that Solomon built "in Jerusalem and in Lebanon," but in the Lucianic text and the LXX[B] the word *Lebanon* is missing (Aharoni, 307; Cogan, 303). Later, we read how the area provided timber to the Assyrian kings (2 Kings 19:23).

2. Lebanon and Israel's Northern Border.

In Joshua 1:4; 9:1-2; 11:17; 12:7; 13:5-6; Judges 3:3, *Lebanon* denotes Israel's northern border. Whether these borders reflect an actual period in Israel's history—that is, the kingdom of David and Solomon (cf. 2 Sam 8:3-10; 1 Kings 4:21)—or whether they portray ideal borders is debated (*see* Geographical Extent of Israel).

Joshua 1:4 describes the largest area "from the wilderness and this Lebanon as far as the Great River, the river Euphrates, all the land of the Hittites, and as far the great sea of the sunset [i.e., the Mediterranean]." If the "wilderness" indicates the Negeb and southern Transjordan, then the denoted area includes most of present and ancient Syria—that is, the desert region east of Jordan, between Jericho and the Euphrates. Deuteronomy 11:24 outlines Israel's borders within east-west and south-north limits in nearly identical words: "from the wilderness and Lebanon and *from* the River Euphrates to the western sea." This reading, more acceptable geographically, poses the possibility that Joshua 1:3 is a corrupt reading of Deuteronomy 11:24-25 (Soggin 1972, 26, 29-30).

Joshua 9:1-2 tells how certain kings "across the Jordan, on the mountain and in the Shephelah [the low-lying hills between the coastal plain and the Judean hills] and along the whole coast of the great sea opposite Lebanon [cf. Is 9:1]" went against Joshua (cf. Deut 1:7).

Joshua 11:16-17 outlines the size of Joshua's conquest, while Joshua 12:7 describes Joshua's defeat of the local kings in *Canaan. In both accounts Baal-Gad in "the valley of Lebanon" indicates the northern border of Joshua's conquest. The valley of Lebanon can be identified with the Beqa Valley.

Joshua 13:1-6 lists the areas that Joshua has yet to conquer. Lebanon is mentioned twice. Joshua 13:5 mentions "all the Lebanon in the east, from Baal-Gad below Mount Hermon to Lebo-Hamath" (in the Beqa Valley; cf. 1 Kings

8:65). The *hapax legomenon* expression "all of Lebanon in the east" here must denote the Anti-Lebanon Range. Judges 3:3 describes the same area with "the dwellers of Mount Lebanon, from Mount Baal Hermon until Lebo-Hamath," while Joshua 13:6 has "all the inhabitants of the mountain from the Lebanon until Misrephoth-maim." In the latter two passages, however, Mount Lebanon describes the area between Mount Hermon and Lebo-Hamath—that is, the western mountain range. Israel's extent as envisioned here is smaller than in Joshua 1:3: Joshua 13:1-6 places the northern border in Syria at Lebo-Hamath, while Joshua 1:3 depicts it along the Euphrates. (For the possible locations of Baal-Gad, Misrephoth-maim and Lebo-Hamath see Na'aman, 42-50, 59.)

3. The Cedars of Lebanon.

1 Kings 4:33 tells of Solomon's botanical knowledge, ranging from the cedars of Lebanon to hyssop.

3.1. Parables.

3.1.1. Jotham's Parable (Judg 9:7-15). Jotham tells this parable to the people of *Shechem after the ascent to the throne of his illegitimate half-brother, Abimelech. Joshua 9:15 sums up its message, declaring that Abimelech (the bramble) cannot offer shelter to the people (the cedars), but can only cause their destruction. The situation described in the parable does not correspond completely with that in Shechem. For example, while Abimelech approached the citizens of Shechem, the trees approached the thistle. Hence, some scholars doubt the originality of the parable in its present context (e.g., Soggin 1981, 173-78), while others maintain that a political parable is never created independently of its historical context (Vater Solomon 1985a, 124-25).

3.1.2. Joash's Parable (2 Kings 14:9/2 Chron 25:18). After his victory over the Edomites, Amaziah, king of Judah, desires to meet with Joash, king of Israel, presumably to fight him. Joash, in an attempt to discourage Amaziah, responds with a parable. In this parable Joash portrays Amaziah as a bramble who proposes marriage between his son and the cedar's daughter. Before any reply is made, the wild animals of Lebanon trample the bramble. The parable makes the point that someone who is not strong enough should not think themselves to be more powerful than a superior (Vater Solomon 1985b, 128-29).

3.1.3. Comparison. Both parables are political in their function, and both use the motifs of brambles and cedars, although the Hebrew word for "bramble" differs. The bramble was considered a lowly, useless plant, while the cedar was seen as its antithesis, the epitome of majesty. In both parables the bramble is the focal point, portraying the characters of Abimelech and Amaziah. In contrast, the cedar contributes little to our understanding of either the Shechem citizens or Joash, but merely functions as a contrast to the bramble.

3.2. Building Activities. Lebanon is a rich source of timber, famous especially for its cedars. The cedars are renowned for their beauty and impressive height, and their wood, with its superior quality, was in demand throughout the ancient Near East for construction of ships, buildings and furniture (Cogan, 228). Cedar wood adorned temples and palaces in Egypt (*ANET,* 227a), Sumer (*COS* 2.155:424a, 425b), Babylon (*COS* 2.122B:310a) and Assyria (*ANET,* 276b), and it was used for Baal's palace (*COS* 1.86:261b) in Ugaritic mythology.

3.2.1. The Building of the First and Second Temples (1 Kings 5/2 Chron 2; Ezra 3:7). Cedar wood was used in the first and the second temples. In 1 Kings 5 Solomon commissioned cedar and juniper wood (and algum [2 Chron 2:8]) from Hiram, king of Tyre, in exchange for wheat and olive oil (*see* Solomon's Temple). In addition, Solomon sent Israelites to Lebanon to help cut the trees. The timber then was made into rafts and transported on the water down to Jaffa (2 Chron 2:16).

3.2.2. Palaces. Royal palaces also were built of cedar wood from Lebanon. 2 Chronicles 2:3 tells how David sent for cedars from Hiram to build a palace. Similarly, 1 Kings 7:1-12 states that Solomon had a "house of the forest of the Lebanon." The house itself was a stone building, but its interior decorations, such as columns and beams, were made of cedar wood. Its splendor is further described in 1 Kings 10:17, 21/2 Chronicles 9:16, 20.

4. Lebanon—the Remote Country.
2 Kings 19:23 describes Sennacherib's deforestation of "the far recesses of Lebanon" *(hapax legomenon),* denoting Lebanon as a remote and exotic place. These connotations may also be present in the Epic of Gilgamesh, in which Gilgamesh and his companion Enkidu slay the monster Huwawa in the "cedar forest" (*ANET,* 78-79).

See also GEOGRAPHICAL EXTENT OF ISRAEL.

BIBLIOGRAPHY. **Y. Aharoni,** *The Land of the Bible: A Historical Geography* (rev. ed.; Philadelphia: Westminster, 1979); **M. Cogan,** *I Kings* (AB 10; New York: Doubleday, 2000); **J. K. Kuan,** "Third Kingdoms 5.1 and Israelite-Tyrian Relations during the Reign of Solomon," *JSOT* 46 (1990) 31-46; **N. Naʾaman,** *Borders and Districts in Biblical Historiography: Seven Studies in Biblical Geographical Lists* (Jerusalem Biblical Studies 4; Jerusalem: Simor, 1986) 39-73; **J. A. Soggin,** *Joshua* (OTL; Philadelphia: Westminster, 1972); idem, *Judges* (OTL; Philadelphia: Westminster, 1981); **A. M. Vater Solomon,** "Fable," in *Saga, Legend, Tale, Novella, Fable: Narrative Forms in Old Testament Literature,* ed. G. W. Coats (JSOTSup 35; Sheffield: JSOT, 1985a) 114-25; idem, "Jehoash's Fable of the Thistle and the Cedar," in *Saga, Legend, Tale, Novella, Fable: Narrative Forms in Old Testament Literature,* ed. G. W. Coats (JSOTSup 35; Sheffield: JSOT, 1985b) 126-32; **M. Weippert,** "Libanon," *RlA* 6.641-50.

L.-S. Tiemeyer

LETTERS. *See* WRITING, WRITING MATERIALS AND LITERACY IN THE ANCIENT NEAR EAST.

LEVITES. *See* PRIESTS AND LEVITES.

LEVITICAL CITIES

The Levites (*see* Priests and Levites), charged with a variety of priestly duties, do not receive a land inheritance in *Canaan like the other tribes. For residency they are allotted forty-eight cities dispersed throughout the land. There are two copies of the list of cities assigned to the Levites: Joshua 21 and 1 Chronicles 6:54-81 (MT 1 Chron 6:39-66). In *Joshua the list is part of an appendix to the record of the assignment of the tribal inheritances by Eleazar the high priest, Joshua, and the tribal fathers. After the tribal allotments have been made, the Levites bring a petition before these leaders, requesting that they be assigned towns as Yahweh had instructed Moses (Num 35:1-8). The copy in 1 Chronicles 6 is attached to the genealogies of the Levites (1 Chron 6:1-49 [MT 1 Chron 5:27—6:34]).

    1. The Literary Settings of the Lists of Levitical Cities and the Pentateuchal Background

1. The Literary Settings of the Lists of Levitical Cities and the Pentateuchal Background.

1.1. The List in Joshua 21. In Joshua the assignment of the Levitical cities is closely tied to the preceding allotments of the tribal inheritances (Josh 13—19) and the identification of the six cities of refuge in Joshua 20. The list is headed by the program for the allotment, which is structured on the numerical pattern of four and twelve (Josh 21:4-8). To fit this pattern, the three Levitical families were arranged into four units by assigning two allotments to the family of Kohathites, one for the Aaronites, and one for the rest of the Kohathites. Ideally, each of the twelve tribes was to contribute four towns, making a total of forty-eight towns, and each of the four clans of Levites was to receive twelve cities. Some minor adjustments were made to this pattern. The Aaronites and the Gershonites each received thirteen cities, the Merarites twelve cities, and the rest of the Kohathites ten cities. Another variation concerns the allotments from the tribes; the combined tribe of Judah and Simeon provided nine cities, while Naphtali contributed only three cities.

1.2. The List in 1 Chronicles 6. In Chronicles the order of the catalogue of Levitical cities is structured to parallel the order of the preceding lists pertaining to the Levites except for the inversion of the position of Gershonites and Kohathites (1 Chron 6:1-49 [MT 1 Chron 5:27—6:34]). The list of cities is very similar to the one in Joshua 21 except that the Chronicler sets the list at the time of David and operates from the perspective that the Levites were already living in these towns. Furthermore, the Chronicler omits the introductory programmatic framework and the several tallies. Another noteworthy omission is any reference to the tribe of Dan. This omission may be the result either of textual corruption or the author's recognition that Dan never settled in the Shephelah. The major difference is that the Chronicler lists the cities for the Aaronides (1 Chron 6:54-60 [MT 1 Chron 6:39-45]) before the summary data pertaining to the other families, thereby raising the prominence of the Aaronides. Nevertheless, in the overall perspective of Chronicles the Levites have a major sacral role in the reconstructed postexilic Israelite community. In fact, this list of Levitical cities supports the status of the Levites and legitimates their right to settle in towns throughout the land.

Since the list in 1 Chronicles is so similar to the one in Joshua, either the Chronicler borrowed it from Joshua or both lists are derived from a recension of an official document of the royal court. A. G. Auld, however, argues that Joshua 21 is dependent on 1 Chronicles 6. In his judgment, Joshua 21 is a later effort to improve the role and place of Levites in postexilic Judah. Other interpreters of Chronicles (e.g., De Vries; Williamson; Japhet) have not found the arguments marshaled by Auld sufficient to discard the usual view of the priority of Joshua 21.

1.3. The Program for and Regulations Pertaining to the Levitical Cities as Prescribed in the Pentateuch. Numbers and Deuteronomy stipulate that since the Levites were to serve God, they were not to receive an inheritance of land. Rather, God was their inheritance (Num 18:20; Josh 13:14; cf. Deut 18:1), tangibly expressed in their receiving tithes and portions of the offerings made to God (Num 18:21; Deut 18:1, 3-4; Josh 13:14). For residency they are given the right to own houses in forty-eight towns, dispersed throughout the tribes. They also receive the common or pasture land *(migrāš)* around each town—that is, a square area of five hundred yards surrounding the town walls (Num 35:1-8). Since no land of any consequence was attached to a house in ancient towns, and since there were no cottage industries in ancient villages, it was essential for the Levites' livelihood that they receive the common land for a variety of purposes, especially for grazing their flocks (*see* Agriculture and Animal Husbandry).

Regulations pertaining to the sale of houses belonging to Levites in these cities and of the common land are found in the Jubilee legislation (Lev 25:32-34) (*see DOTP*, Sabbath, Sabbatical Year, Jubilee). The common land around a Levitical town could never be sold. If a Levite sold a house in one of these towns, two provisions accompanied the sale: (1) the original owner could settle the debt at any time and reclaim the house; (2) in the Jubilee Year all Levitical houses returned to their owners, as was the case with any fields in the tribal inheritances. By contrast, houses in walled cities carried a right of redemption for only one year; at the end of that year they became the property of the buyer (Lev 25:29-30).

2. Identification of the Levitical Cities.

Following below are the towns assigned to the families of Levites as recorded in Joshua 21:1-42 and 1 Chronicles 6:54-81 (MT 1 Chron 6:39-66). 1 Chronicles, however, omits six cities, most likely as a result of errors in transmission. Chronicles identifies only two cities as cities of refuge, *Hebron (1 Chron 6:57 [MT 1 Chron 6:42]) and *Shechem (1 Chron 6:67 NIV [MT 1 Chron 6:52]), although another reading understands that all the cities given to the Aaronides and the rest of the Kohathites were cities of refuge. Other variants concern the name of a place or its spellings. In the following list, variations found in 1 Chronicles are recorded in parentheses; if that name is the preferred reading, it is set in italics.

The Aaronides from the Kohathite family received from Judah and Simeon: Kiriath Arba (Hebron), Libnah, Jattir, Eshtemoa, Holon (Hilen), Debir, Ain *(Ashan)*, Juttah (omitted in the MT but present in the LXX[B]), Beth Shemesh; from Benjamin: *Gibeon (omitted possibly due to scribal error), Geba, Anathoth, Almon (Alemeth)—a total of thirteen cities. The other Kohathite clans received from Ephraim: Shechem, *Gezer, Kibzaim (Jokmean), Beth Horon; from Dan: Eltekeh (omitted), Gibbethon (omitted), Aijalon, Gath Rimmon (Chronicles locates the last two sites in Ephraim); from the half-tribe of Manasseh: Taanach (Aner), Gath Rimmon (Bileam, probably *Ibleam* [Kallai]; for Joshua either there was a town in Manasseh with the same name as in Dan or the latter town led to a scribal error here)—a total of ten cities.

The Gershonites were allotted cities from the half-tribe of Manasseh: Golan in Bashan, Be-Eshtarah (Ashtaroth); from Issachar: Kishion (Kedesh), Daberath, Jarmuth (Ramoth), En Gannim (Anem); from Asher: Mishal (Mashal), Abdon, Helkath (Hukok), Rehob; from Naphtali: Kedesh in Galilee, Hammoth Dor (Hammon), Kartan (Kiriathaim)—a total of thirteen cities.

The Merarite family received from Zebulun: Jokneam (omitted), Kartah (Tabor), Dimnah *(Rimmono)*, Nahalal (omitted); from Reuben: Bezer, Jahaz (Jahzah), Kedemoth, Mephaath (this segment is missing in the MT and is supplied from the LXX); from Gad: Ramoth in Gilead, Mahanaim, Heshbon, Jazer—a total of twelve cities.

According to Joshua, six of these towns, three on each side of the Jordan River, also served as cities of refuge (*see DOTP*, Cities of Refuge)—that is, centers of asylum where a person suspected of manslaughter could find refuge from an avenger of blood while that person's responsibility in the death of the avenger's relative was determined (cf. Josh 20:1-9; Num 35:9-34; Deut 4:41-43; 19:1-13). In the list found in Joshua these cities receive prominence by being mentioned first in their respective location, by the identification "a city of refuge for one accused of murder," and by an attached geographical region, except for Bezer (however, in Josh 20:8 Bezer is identified as in the desert on the plateau). The centers of asylum in Cisjordan were Kiriath Arba (Hebron) in the hill country of Judah, Shechem in the hill country of Ephraim, Kedesh in Galilee, and those centers in Transjordan were Golan in Bashan, Ramoth in Gilead, and Bezer. Scripture provides no reasons for these places of asylum also being Levitical towns. It is quite probable that the resident Levites of these towns administrated the law of asylum, both making sure that a fugitive was granted shelter and working for a just trial.

3. Background and Purpose of the Levitical Cities.

Most of the forty-eight towns assigned to the Levites were ordinary towns of various sizes. They were not cult centers. Archaeological discoveries support this observation. Thus the Levites did not have the responsibility of operating small sanctuaries or altars in these towns, as some scholars have proposed. Their primary role was to instruct the local population regarding the covenant, particularly the requirements set forth in the *law, and to encourage the people's faithfulness in serving God (Deut 33:8-11; cf. 2 Chron 15:3). They likely traveled to nearby sanctuaries to assist Aaronide priests with sacrifices and other rituals. Without the Levites dispersed throughout the land, it seems impossible that the general population of Israel would have known the terms of the Sinai covenant. This position finds support in the reference to *Jehoshaphat sponsoring a special mission of princes, Levites and priests to teach God's law throughout Judah (2 Chron 17:7-9). On the other hand, it can easily be imagined that local citizens customarily went to the Levites to receive a decision on a matter of dispute or guidance on the proper way of keeping a law in a specific circumstance.

The Levites played a crucial role in the united monarchy. *David and *Solomon strategically employed them in their programs for making *Jerusalem the center of Yahwistic worship. These kings organized the Levites into groups to serve as choral singers and musicians at the temple (cf. 1 Chron 15:16; 2 Chron 29:25-30). They also settled clans of Levites in strategic cities throughout the land as part of their efforts to strengthen the crown's control. 1 Chronicles records that David and Solomon appointed talented Levites as officials, administrators and record keepers in regard to the service of the Lord and the affairs of the king (1 Chron 26:30-32). These duties no doubt included collecting tithes and other contributions from the local population on behalf of the cult (1 Chron 26:20, 22; 2 Chron 24:5-6; 34:9) and oversight of local matters such as maintenance of records and collection of *taxes for the crown. Other texts indicate that they exercised oversight of royal building projects, especially at the temple (2 Chron 34:12-13). They also functioned as local judges (1 Chron 26:29; 2 Chron 19:8-10). In fact, it is quite possible that several Levitical cities served as local administrative centers. B. Mazar (202), in particular, holds that David appointed Levites to administer the royal estates that he had taken over from Canaanite lords (also Aharoni, 269).

4. Interpretation of the List of Levitical Cities.

4.1. Basic Interpretation. The list in Joshua 21 assumes that Israelite tribes lived on both sides of the Jordan River and that the north and the south were united in covenant with Yahweh. However, the actual Israelite occupation of large portions of many of the tribal allotments as recorded in Joshua and Judges took several decades; thus the Levites could not have occupied many of these cities for some time. Consequently, the presentation of the Levitical cities in Joshua is programmatic, for it assumes that the Levites would not have been able to take up residency in numerous towns assigned them until the respective tribes had gained control of those towns.

Several details in the record of Levitical cities favor the idealistic character of the list in Joshua 21. The towns allocated from Dan presuppose that the Danites would settle in the Shephelah to the west of Benjamin. However, the Danites were unable to control large portions of that area, including Elteke and Gibbethon (Judg 1:34-36). Discouraged, they eventually moved to the northern end of the Huleh Valley (Judg 18). Their move is not reflected in this list, suggesting that its origin preceded that tribe's relocation. Some of these towns did not come under Israelite control until after David's conquests, including Taanach and Ibleam (Bileam) in Manasseh (Judg 1:27), and Rehob in Asher (Judg 1:31). Gezer in Ephraim (Judg 1:29) did not become Israelite until it was given to Solomon by Pharaoh (1 Kings 9:16). Additional support for the early composition of the list is found in the inclusion of the Aaronides as a member of the Kohathite family, for after the construction of the temple in Jerusalem the Aaronides became treated as a distinct group of priests separate from the Levites, a lesser order of priests (cf. 1 Chron 13:2; 2 Chron 11:14; 31:15, 19). This data supports the position that the Levites' occupation of these towns, though never specifically addressed in Scripture, took place over many decades. Whether Levites ever occupied all of the cities in the list at the same time is unknown.

4.2. Critical Interpretations of the List of Levitical Cities. Scholarly interpretations of the list of Levitical towns have varied widely. Dedicated source critics such as J. Wellhausen, along with current historians with a minimalist perspective, dismiss the list as solely the product of imaginative thinking. Two contemporary scholars, J. P. Ross and J. R. Spencer, have written dissertations on the Levitical cities; they take the position that the list of Levitical cities is either a late product of the Priestly school or an adaptation of a town list from the time of the monarchy that the Priestly writer inserted into Joshua 21. Two major reasons support this position: (1) according to present archaeological evidence, only some twenty of the Levitical cities were occupied at the time of the united monarchy; (2) the material about these cities in the Pentateuch and Joshua is embedded in the late Priestly source. Another scholar, E. Ben Zvi, on the basis of a detailed source-critical analysis of both lists of Levitical cities and the various texts pertaining to the cities of asylum, determines that the list was the creation of the postexilic priestly leadership in order to establish the Aaronides as legitimate residents in the areas about Jerusalem and to support their leadership role in Yehud, a Persian province.

Several scholars, nevertheless, have worked on the premise that a sound social-historical tradition underlies the list of Levitical towns. W. F. Albright and Y. Aharoni located the origin of the list at the time of David, for only in that era were all the allotted cities under Israelite control. More recently, C. Hauer, applying a sociological model of analysis to this list of cities, also concludes that the list was part of David's program for establishing a royal ecclesiastical cult. In his judgment, because the Levites were devoted Yahwists and supporters of the crown, David gave them royal endowments throughout the land so that they could promote his extensive cultic and governmental reforms. Their dispersion among the tribes also served to strengthen the central government's authority, especially in areas distant from the capital. Support for this interpretation comes from the surprising scarcity of Levitical towns in two key areas: the region from Jerusalem to Hebron, and the hill country of Ephraim and Manasseh—areas that had been under Israelite control for centuries. B. Mazar modifies the preceding position by assigning the settlement of Levites to the coregency of David and Solomon on the basis of the fact that it would have taken several years for the crown to carry out these Levitical settlements. A small adjustment, advocated by both M. Haran and Z. Kallai, places the settlement of Levites in these towns under Solomon's reign in order to account better for a few details such as the settlement of Gezer, the city that Solomon received as a wedding gift from Pharaoh but that was destroyed shortly after Solomon's death by Pharaoh Shishak and not rebuilt.

R. G. Boling takes a different tack. Drawing heavily on J. Peterson's archaeological study of the Levitical cities along with subsequent archaeological findings, he concludes that the era when the identifiable sites of these cities had the highest percentage of occupancy was the eighth century BCE under the reigns of Uzziah and Jeroboam II. Realizing that it was unlikely that Jeroboam II promoted the widespread settlement of Levites in northern Israel, Boling proposes that the widespread dispersion of the Levites was fostered by an aggressive reform movement designed to establish the teaching of Yahwistic faith throughout the land. This movement was spurred on by eighth-century prophets such as Hosea. Boling's creative proposal, however, is hampered by three factors: (1) the uncertainty of the precise identification of several towns in the list; (2) the inability to identify the tribal identity of the occupants of these towns in the eighth century BCE; (3) the fact that several cities, like those in the Transjordan, were outside Israelite control in the eighth century BCE.

A. Alt, also accepting the list as a historical document, proposed that the settlement of Levites in these towns was part of *Josiah's program to reestablish Davidic control over as much of the promised land as possible. Two prominent facts lead Alt to the position that the list is a reflection of this king's extensive religious reforms that included the relocation of numerous priests: (1) the clustering of Levitical towns in outlying areas; (2) the lack of any such towns in the central and southern hill country (2 Kings 23:8-9, 19-20). A huge obstacle to his proposal is that many of the towns in this list, particularly those north of the Jezreel Valley and those in the Transjordan, never came under Josiah's control.

These multiple interpretations of the Levitical cities show that no scholarly consensus has been reached in regard to the list's origin. A major reason for this impasse lies in the frequently changing fortunes of these towns throughout Israel's history. Levitical occupation of several of these towns lapsed during periods when the central government was weak or even hostile to them, especially in northern Israel. After the nation split into northern Israel and Judah, various religious upheavals produced fluctuating changes in the fortunes of the Levites. In the north *Jeroboam I altered significantly the worship of Yahweh. An important platform of his religious program was the expulsion of Levites from serving as priests (2 Chron 11:13-17). This led many Levites to migrate to Judah, where they labored to make secure the reign of *Rehoboam. Also at the time when the nation divided, several towns in the Transjordan did not remain firmly under Israelite control. On a stela, Mesha, king of *Moab, lists Jahaz, a Levitical town, as one of several towns he regained from the Israelites. It is highly probable that he took control of other Levitical towns in the Transjordan. In addition, the land of Israel suffered incursions of foreign powers, producing changes in the occupancy of specific towns. If Gath Rimmon is Tell el-Jerishe, as B. Mazar believes, it was not rebuilt after being destroyed by Shishak in the ninth century BCE. A similar fate met Mahanaim, a town of great importance to Saul and David, and Gezer. Given the complex history of these Levitical towns during the divided monarchy, the origin of the list of forty-eight Levitical towns must have preceded Israel's loss of control over so many of them.

5. Conclusion.

The witness of the text that the allotment of Levitical cities was made before Israel took occupation of Canaan as described in Joshua 21 fits the data best (Woudstra, 304). That list was programmatic and ideal. From the sparse information available, it appears that David and Solomon implemented the program of Levitical town allotment to promote the people's devotion to Yahweh and to strengthen the central government's rule throughout the land, especially in newly accessed regions. After the division of the kingdom, multiple forces weakened or cut short the Levitical presence in many of the towns on the preserved lists. Nevertheless, it can be easily imagined that reforming kings such as *Hezekiah and Josiah empowered the Levites to reoccupy some of these towns in an effort to reestablish the crown's control over outlying areas, to promote true worship of Yahweh in the countryside, and to win support for the reforms taking place at the Jerusalem sanctuary. It is also possible that Levitical presence in some towns of northern Israel after the nation divided played an important role in the maintenance of Yahwistic faith among portions of that population, such as at the time of Elijah (1 Kings).

See also CITIES AND TOWNS; LAND; PRIESTS AND LEVITES; TRIBES OF ISRAEL AND LAND ALLOTMENTS/BORDERS.

BIBLIOGRAPHY. **Y. Aharoni,** *The Land of the Bible: A Historical Geography* (Philadelphia: Westminster, 1967) 269-73; **W. F. Albright,** "The List of Levitic Cities," in *Louis Ginzberg: Jubilee Volume on the Occasion of His Seventieth Birthday,* ed. S. Lieberman et al. (2 vols.; New York: American Academy for Jewish Research, 1945) 1.49-73; **A. Alt,** "Bemerkungen zu einigen judäischen Ortslisten des Alten Testaments," in *Kleine Schriften zur Geschichte des Volkes Israel* (3 vols.; Munich: Beck, 1959-1963) 2.289-305; idem, "Festungen und Levitenorte im Lande Juda," in *Kleine Schriften zur Geschichte des Volkes Israel* (3 vols.; Munich: Beck, 1959-1963) 2.306-15; **A. G. Auld,** "Cities of Refuge in Israelite Tradition," *JSOT* 10 (1978) 26-40; idem, "The 'Levitical Cities': Texts and History," *ZAW* 91 (1979) 194-206; **E. Ben Zvi,** "The List of Levitical Cities," *JSOT* 54 (1992) 77-106; **R. G. Boling,** "Levitical Cities: Archaeology and Texts," in *Biblical and Related Studies Presented to Samuel Iwry,* ed. A. Kort and S. Morschauser (Winona Lake, IN: Eisenbrauns, 1985) 23-32; **R. G. Boling and G. E. Wright,** *Joshua* (AB 6; Garden City, NY: Doubleday, 1982); **S. J. De Vries,** *1 and 2 Chronicles* (FOTL 11; Grand Rapids: Eerdmans, 1989); **J. Gray,** *Joshua, Judges, Ruth* (NCBC; Grand Rapids: Eerdmans, 1986); **M. Haran,** "Studies in the Account of the Levitical Cities," *JBL* 80 (1961) 45-54, 156-65; idem, *Temples and Temple-service in Ancient Israel: An Inquiry into the Character of Cult Phenomena and the Historical Setting of the Priestly School* (repr., Winona Lake, IN: Eisenbrauns, 1985); **C. Hauer Jr.,** "David and the Levites," *JSOT* 23 (1982) 33-54; **S. Japhet,** *I & II Chronicles* (OTL; Louisville: Westminster/John Knox, 1993); **Z. Kallai,** *Historical Geography of the Bible: The Tribal Territories of Israel* (Jerusalem: Magnes; Leiden: E. J. Brill, 1986) 447-76; **Y. Kaufmann,** *The Biblical Account of the Conquest of Palestine* (Jerusalem: Magnes, 1953) 40-46; **G. N. Knoppers,** *I Chronicles 1—9* (AB 12; New York: Doubleday, 2004); **B. Mazar,** "The Cities of the Priests and the Levites," in *Congress Volume: Oxford, 1959,* ed. G. W. Anderson (VTSup 7; Leiden: E. J. Brill, 1959) 193-205; **J. Milgrom,** *Numbers* (JPSTC; Philadelphia: Jewish Publication Society, 1990); **J. M. Miller,** "Rehoboam's Cities of Defense and the Levitical City List," in *Archaeology and Biblical Interpretation: Essays in Memory of D. Glenn Rose,* ed. L. G. Perdue, L. E. Toombs and G. L. Johnson (Atlanta: John Knox, 1987) 273-86; **J. R. Spencer,** "Levitical Cities," *ABD* 4.310-11; **H. G. M. Williamson,** *1 and 2 Chronicles* (NCBC; Grand Rapids: Eerdmans, 1985); **M. H. Woudstra,** *The Book of Joshua* (NICOT; Grand Rapids: Eerdmans, 1981).   J. E. Hartley

LINGUISTICS

Although no biblical writer was a linguist, there are numerous indications of self-conscious awareness of language in the Historical Books (Weinberg). For example, dialectal differences in pronunciation are used to differentiate social groupings (Judg 12:5-6); the besieged Judean officials in Jerusalem ask the attacking Assyrian commander to address them in *Aramaic rather than in Judean (2 Kings 18:26-28); the influence of Aramaic on the postexilic community prompted the translation (or perhaps, explanation) of pentateuchal readings (Neh 8:8). Since medieval times, the language of the Bible has been studied using philological analysis, which focuses on understanding the language of a specific text. But the application of linguistics to an understanding of the biblical text is a modern phenomenon, as is the science of linguistics itself. This article describes (1) the field of linguistics generally; (2) how linguistics helps to elucidate the form of *Hebrew used in the Historical Books; (3) how linguistics furthers exegesis and interpretation within the Historical Books.

1. Linguistic Analysis
2. Linguistic Approaches to Hebrew
3. Linguistics and Interpretation
4. Conclusions

1. Linguistic Analysis.

Linguistics involves the scientific description or explanation of language phenomena. The discipline of linguistics is vast, with numerous fields of inquiry. Most basically, it encompasses the study of (1) the inventory of human speech sounds (phonetics) and the distinctive sounds that are meaningful within a language (phonology); (2) the grammatical units of language (morphology); (3) the arrangement of words into phrases and clauses (syntax); (4) meaning (semantics); (5) the use of language within the context of speaking (pragmatics). Additional linguistic fields include (1) the use of language in contexts larger than a sentence or single utterance (discourse analysis); (2) the use of language within society (sociolinguistics); (3) the relationship of language to cognition, perception and neurology (cognitive linguistics, psycholinguistics, neurolinguistics); (4) computa-tional models of linguistic processes (computational linguistics). The linguistic study of literature has been less fully developed (see Fabb).

In analyzing a language, a linguist may compare the language to earlier stages of the same language (historical linguistics), to other related languages (comparative linguistics, of which Semitics is the oldest variety), to geographically adjacent languages (contact linguistics), to typologically similar languages (language typology), or to features common to all languages (language universals, universal grammar).

Linguistic theories may be grouped into two main approaches. One approach involves formal (or generative) theories (e.g., Chomsky), which focus on "the formal relationships among grammatical elements independently of any characterization of the semantic and pragmatic properties of those elements" (Newmeyer, 7). A second approach involves functional theories (e.g., Halliday 1994), which focus on the communicative situation as motivating or explaining grammatical structure.

The science of linguistics has much to offer the study of Semitics generally (see the essays in Izre'el) and biblical Hebrew specifically. Recent and notable applications of linguistic theory to the language of the Bible have focused on phonological processes (Idsardi), the Masoretic accents (Dresher) and the verbal forms (Hatav; Cook; Joosten 2002a; 2002b). One important area that thus far has not been resolved involves basic word order and the related notions of topic and focus (for two different approaches see Gross and Shimasaki; see also the review articles by van der Merwe and Holmstedt, respectively). This article, however, examines how linguistics helps to elucidate the form of Hebrew used in the Historical Books and to further exegetical interpretation within those books. Because the Historical Books are essentially narrative stories sprinkled with *genealogies and inserted poems (on some of the shorter poems see O'Connor 1995), narrative is at the center of the following discussion.

2. Linguistic Approaches to Hebrew.

This section examines four areas of linguistics and their contribution to an understanding of the particular forms of Hebrew found in the Historical Books: (1) historical, or diachronic, linguistics; (2) language variation; (3) contact linguistics; (4) linguistic typology.

2.1. Synchronic and Diachronic Perspectives. Modern linguistic study of language began with F. de Saussure (1857-1913). One of Saussure's most important insights was that a language may be viewed either synchronically (as a linguistic system at a particular point in time) or diachronically (by focusing on how features of a language change through time). Saussure believed that, contrary to philological approaches, the synchronic approach should be primary; the diachronic approach should be seen as a series of synchronic analyses. Furthermore, he argued that linguistic forms and structures within a linguistic system should not be explained through recourse to previous forms (their diachronic history), but rather by their place in the language system from a synchronic viewpoint (Saussure, 80-96).

Although most applications of linguistics to biblical Hebrew are synchronic rather than diachronic in orientation, the Historical Books provide an opportunity to examine some features of Hebrew from the diachronic perspective. The Hebrew language found in the Deuteronomistic narratives of Joshua through 2 Kings differs in significant ways from that found in the narratives of Chronicles and Ezra-Nehemiah, though the precise nature of the differences is debated (compare Hurvitz and Ehrensvärd; for details, *see* Hebrew Language). A complicating factor in either a synchronic or diachronic analysis of biblical Hebrew involves scribal redaction and the possibility of scribal updating (a scribe's substitution of later forms when copying an early text) or archaizing (the intentional use of earlier forms). Ultimately, linguists who analyze biblical texts must reckon with a scribally redacted and transmitted text; there is no "direct and precise access to any one synchronic stage of ancient Hebrew" (Barr, 4).

2.2. Language Variation. Language variation is inherently a part of language use on the synchronic level (Saussure, 74-75). Diachronic change, in fact, develops out of synchronic variation (Milroy, cf. Campbell). There are many sources of linguistic variation, but they can be subsumed under two main categories: dialectal variation and superposed variation (Hanks, 219-20; Hoftijzer, 102-4). Dialectal variation is present among subgroups of speakers whose speech is distinguished by geographical, social or demographic factors (e.g., location, class, gender, age). Superposed variation involves varieties of language that are connected with a specific communicational activity. Variation of this sort is a result of the context of use (e.g., letter, legal document, speech to superiors/inferiors, ritual language), register (e.g., oral/literate, formal/informal, prose/poetry) or linguistic environment (e.g., discourse-pragmatics). The central insight is that language varies "both according to who is speaking it and what they are doing as they speak" (Hanks, 220).

Language variation in the Historical Books is both dialectal and superposed. Dialectal variation has been studied extensively in the Deuteronomistic narratives with a view to detecting northern features (i.e., Israelite language as opposed to Judean language; see Rendsburg) within the context of related Canaanite dialects (Garr; Young). Because dialectal variation is tied to the demographics of the speaker, other kinds of dialectal variation are more difficult to detect in the biblical text.

Superposed variation in the Historical Books relates primarily to the context of use or to the linguistic environment. Superposed variation in biblical narrative that has its source in the differences in oral and written registers has been explored by F. H. Polak. He concludes that some portions of biblical narrative exhibit more complex linguistic structures: a greater frequency of subordinate clauses more explicit syntactic constituents in the clause and more complex noun phrases. He considers these dense syntactic features to be indications of literate, scribally produced narrative. Other portions of biblical narrative exhibit greater frequency of pronominal reference and deictics; he considers these features to be indicative of orally produced narrative.

Another example of superposed variation involves the alternation between the two forms of the first-person pronoun (*ʾănî and ʾānōkî*). Although these forms are free variants syntactically and semantically in some of biblical Hebrew, E. J. Revell demonstrates that in the Deuteronomistic narratives the use of the two forms relates to social and pragmatic factors. In speech among humans (i.e., speech not involving the deity) the choice of pronoun is connected to differences in social status, emotional intensity and personal concern of the speaker—factors that Revell subsumes under the heading of "immediacy." The pronoun *ʾănî* is the form that marks immediacy; *ʾānōkî* does not (Revell, 341-49). There is also a diachronic factor in the variation between the two forms; in late narratives (Chronicles and Ezra-Nehemiah) *ʾănî* begins to displace *ʾānōkî* (Polzin, 126-27).

Superposed variation involving discourse-pragmatics, such as this alternation in first-person pronouns, relies on an important linguistic principle: linguistic markedness as reflecting a privative opposition, not an equipollent one. The terms *privative* and *equipollent* have a long history in linguistics, beginning with the Prague School linguists (for a history see Battistella). The terms indicate the nature of the relationship between two items that contrast with one another (O'Connor 2002). In an equipollent opposition, item A and item B are polar opposites. The presence of item A signals the absence of item B; conversely, the presence of item B signals the absence of item A. In a privative opposition, on the other hand, item A and item B are not polar opposites. Instead, item A is "marked," meaning that it is morphologically distinguished and has a special function or nuance. Item B is "unmarked," meaning that it has a wider use and distribution. The presence of item B does not signal the opposite of item A. The Prague School linguists noted that language generally uses privative oppositions, not equipollent ones. The marked form usually occurs less frequently than the unmarked one, has a more limited distribution, and has a specialized pragmatic function. (For another example of discourse-pragmatic markedness see 3.2.3 below.)

2.3. Language Contact. Contact linguistics examines what happens when different languages are in contact with one another (for language contact in the ancient Near East see Kaufman). Language contact often is a cause for linguistic change, either structural (a change in the grammatical structure of a language) or lexical (the borrowing of lexical items) (Winford). In the Historical Books, Aramaic is the main language that comes in contact with Hebrew, especially in the later books written during the time of the *Persian Empire. The question, then, of Aramaic influence on those books is very important (*see* Aramaic Language; Hebrew Language). Less frequently considered, but nonetheless significant, is the contact of Akkadian with Hebrew and the resulting Akkadian loan words (Mankowski).

2.4. Language Typology. Language typology classifies languages (or individual structural components of languages) based on shared formal characteristics (Whaley, 7). With this method, languages that are genetically unrelated and have no geographical proximity can nonetheless be grouped together by shared linguistic features. As a result, typologists can make relatively broad claims concerning the types of language structures that are represented among the world's languages, as well as observations concerning the diachronic development of linguistic features (Comrie).

Language typology helps biblical scholars to view the linguistic features of biblical Hebrew from the perspective of unrelated languages with similar structures. As an example, let us consider that in biblical Hebrew (unlike English) there is no word for "yes." Instead, a positive reply to a yes-no question is expressed as the positive restatement of the question (see Greenstein). In 1 Samuel 23:2 David asks the Lord, "Shall I go up and strike these Philistines?" The Lord's response is "Go up and strike the Philistines and rescue Keilah!" In later forms of Hebrew the particle *kēn* (which in biblical times meant "thus," but not "yes") is used as an equivalent of "yes." How should we interpret the absence of a word for "yes" in the Bible? Does the absence of "yes" in positive answers represent a gap in our knowledge of biblical Hebrew? Should we see God's response in 1 Samuel 23:2 as emphatic or forceful in light of the fact that his answer reiterates the question in its entirety?

A consideration of the question from the viewpoint of language typology provides an explanation of the biblical data. Typologists have classified the ways in which languages express positive responses to yes-no questions into three types (Sadock and Zwicky, 189-91). One type, like English, is a "yes-no answering system," in which a positive particle stands for or accompanies a positive answer, and a negative particle stands for or accompanies a negative answer. A second type is an "agreement-disagreement system," in which the positive particle is used for an answer that agrees with the polarity of the question; a negative particle disagrees with the polarity of the question. For example, in Japanese, to the question "Isn't it hot today?" a reply with the positive particle means, "Yes [I agree with the proposition that it is not hot]." A reply with the negative particle means, "No [I disagree with the proposition—it is not hot]." A third type, like Welsh, is an "echo system." A positive answer repeats the verb of the question with or without additional material; a negative answer uses the negative particle and often repeats the verb of the question.

Of these three types, biblical Hebrew is an echo system in which no special word for "yes" is used. The repetition of some or all of the question in the answer is simply the normal way to express a positive reply and should not be seen as forceful or emphatic. Modern Hebrew, in contrast to biblical Hebrew, has a yes-no answering system (similar to that of English and other European languages), in which *kēn* has become grammaticalized as a positive particle of response.

3. Linguistics and Interpretation.

Linguistic analysis is valuable in a myriad of ways to an understanding of biblical Hebrew as a linguistic system, but not all linguistic analysis has ramifications for exegesis. This section illustrates some of the contributions that linguistics has made to biblical interpretation within the Historical Books.

3.1. Narrative Structure. Discourse analysis is a field of linguistics that has been profitably applied to the narratives of the Historical Books. Although discourse analysis and exegesis are separate enterprises (O'Connor 2002), discourse analysis helps exegetes to understand how biblical narratives are structured, how cohesion and coherence are achieved (for the terms see Halliday and Hasan), and how narratives should be segmented. Of particular interest is the question of how the particular verbal forms and syntactic structures of biblical Hebrew are used in the structuring of narrative.

3.1.1. Foreground-Background. Speakers and writers use language in accord with their communicative purposes. Information that is most relevant will be foregrounded; information that is less relevant or that provides supporting details about the more relevant information will be backgrounded. In narrative discourse the main events of the story are foregrounded—they comprise the backbone or skeleton of the narrative. Backgrounded information provides supplementary material to the main storyline by amplifying or commenting on it (Hopper and Thompson, 280-84).

In biblical narrative, sentences with *wayyiqtol* verb forms (the "*waw*-consecutive imperfect") convey those events that the author/narrative wishes to represent as foregrounded in the narrator. Information that the narrator wishes to background may be initiated by any other verb form or by a verbless sentence (see Longacre, 71-80). We can illustrate the distinction between foreground and background by examining some sentences in 1 Samuel 30.

In 1 Samuel 30:11-12 eight successive events are represented as foregrounded (the *wayyiqtol* verbs are indicated by italics): (1) *they found* an Egyptian man in the countryside; (2) *they took* him to David; (3) *they gave* him bread; (4) *he ate;* (5) *they gave* him water; (6) *they gave* him a piece of pressed fig cake and two pressed raisin cakes; (7) *he ate;* (8) *he regained* his strength. The extensive use of foregrounded material highlights the method by which David's men revived the Egyptian servant. Within the narrative the care that the man received provides implicit motivation for him to help David in return, as depicted in the following verses.

Backgrounded material often is represented by a perfect verb, usually not in initial position within the sentence. This syntactic configuration may be used for various kinds of backgrounded material. In 1 Samuel 30:18 the first sentence is a foregrounded narrative sentence. It depicts David's rescue of all of the individuals who had been kidnapped by the Amalekites ("David rescued *[wayyiqtol]* everyone whom the Amalekites had taken"). The following sentence is backgrounded with a noninitial perfect verb: "and his two wives David *rescued* [perfect]." The second sentence provides further exposition or amplification of the first by focusing on David's personal situation.

A perfect verb may be used to represent events that are possible but do not occur. An event that does not occur is, by definition, not on the storyline and thus is backgrounded. In 1 Samuel 30:2 there are four sentences. The second sentence provides additional information to the first event by informing the reader of what does not occur: "They [the Amalekites] *captured [wayyiqtol]* the women who were in it [the city], both low-born and high-born. They did not *kill* [perfect] anyone. *They carried [wayyiqtol]* them off, *and went [wayyiqtol]* on their way." The narrator explicitly tells the reader that every woman, regardless of social standing, was captured and none was killed.

A perfect verb may also be used for an event that is out of sequence with respect to the main storyline, especially an event that occurs prior to the events on the storyline. In 1 Samuel 30:5 the narrator reiterates that David's two wives were captured—an event that had already been represented in general terms in 1 Samuel 30:2: "And the two wives of David *had been captured* [perfect]—Ahinoam the Jezreelite and Abigail the wife of Nabal the Carmelite." The specific information about David's personal loss is reintroduced at this juncture just before the narrator describes David's internal turmoil about the situation in 1 Samuel 30:6.

In addition, a perfect verb may be used to represent contrastive actions. In 1 Samuel 30:9-10 the narrative describes the progress of David and his six hundred men in pursuing the Amalekites up to the Wadi Besor. There, one group of two hundred stays, too exhausted to continue, while another group of four hundred continues in pursuit. Five sentences depict their split: (1) David and the six hundred men who were with him *went [wayyiqtol]*; (2) *and they came [wayyiqtol]* as far as the Wadi Besor; (3) and the ones who were left *remained* [perfect]; (4) David and four hundred men *pursued [wayyiqtol]*; (5) and two hundred men who were too exhausted to cross the Wadi Besor *remained [wayyiqtol]*. The third sentence (the only backgrounded sentence in these verses) appears to the English reader to be superfluous. In Hebrew, however, the backgrounded sentence alerts the reader to an emerging contrast between two groups of individuals. The differentiation of these two groups is important, because they engage in a bitter dispute at the end of the chapter (1 Sam 30:22-25) over precisely this division. (For a similar contrast between two groups as depicted in foreground-background constructions see 1 Sam 17:1-2; Long, 166-68.)

Habitual actions in the past are another kind of backgrounded information, which are depicted in biblical narrative either by an imperfect verb or by the so-called perfect consecutive (the perfect verb in sentence-initial position, preceded by the conjunction *and*). Habitual actions are not depicted in 1 Samuel 30, but 1 Samuel 1:3-7 provides a good example of habitual events: "and that man *would go up* [perfect consecutive] from his city every year . . . *and he would give* [perfect consecutive] portions to Peninnah . . . but to Hannah *he would give* [imperfect] . . . *and* her rival *would provoke her* [perfect consecutive] . . . *and thus it would go* [imperfect] every year . . . *she would provoke her* [imperfect] . . . and *she would not* eat [imperfect]" (Joosten 2002b, 73).

3.1.2. Participant Reference. Participant reference involves the linguistic means for referring to participants (i.e., the characters) in narrative. This includes, at its most basic level, keeping track of who is doing what in the narrative. More importantly, however, the ways in which participants are referred to can be exploited by

the narrator for the broader purposes of the narrative—for example, to highlight some participants and their actions while downplaying others, to introduce new participants into the narrative, or to contrast the actions of one participant with those of another (Longacre, 139-41).

An analysis of participant reference must begin at the morphological and syntactic level with a catalogue of the linguistic resources that are available for referring to participants. In biblical Hebrew participants may be referred to with a personal name, a descriptive phrase (e.g., a patronymic phrase, a gentilic term, a functional term) either alone or in conjunction with a personal name, or a pronominal element (an independent pronoun or a pronominal affix).

Literary critics have identified three kinds of characters within narrative: full characters, flat characters (or secondary characters) and props (individuals who serve a single role in the narrative) (Berlin). Discourse linguists have applied these distinctions to participant reference (Longacre, 140-41). In 1 Samuel 30 David is quite clearly a full character. He is referred to explicitly with his personal name more often than any other character. Twenty-four times he is the subject of a foregrounded *(wayyiqtol)* sentence, and in all but five instances the personal name is explicitly indicated. The prevalence of the personal name *David* is clearly not simply to indicate who is doing the action; in 1 Samuel 30:18 the personal name is used twice, even though there is no doubt about who is doing the action ("And David rescued everyone whom the Amalekites had taken; and his two wives David rescued"). The redundant repetition of the personal name is one way in which a prominent character is indicated (de Regt). In several places, where the personal name *David* is not repeated, the second sentence continues the action of the previous one, as in 1 Samuel 30:26: "Then David came to Ziklag and he sent from the spoil to the elders of Judah. . . ."

Two participants in the chapter are secondary participants; each assists David in his endeavor to rescue the abducted wives. One is introduced in this pericope as "Abiathar the priest, the son of Ahimelek" (1 Sam 30:7). This lengthy designation by means of personal name, title and patronymic is unusual in biblical narrative; ordinarily, the order is name, patronymic, title. Revell (158, 160, 366-67) argues that the patronymic is used here to confirm that it is the same individual mentioned previously in 1 Samuel 23:6, while the title ("the priest") is used because the participant is acting in an official priestly function within the narrative. The second mention of Abiathar in this verse is entirely redundant in terms of identifying who brings the ephod. However, the narrator again explicitly mentions his name, perhaps to emphasize Abiathar's compliance with David's command.

Another secondary participant is the unnamed Egyptian man who is captured by David's troops. The man identifies himself with respect to his social status: he is a "young man" and a "servant of an Amalekite man" (1 Sam 30:13). The man's name is never mentioned by the narrator, but his importance to the narrative and the fact that he speaks within the narrative (even placing a demand on David) suggest that he is more than a prop.

A number of participants serve as props in the narrative. The Amalekites, referred to with a collective singular gentilic term, are mentioned only in 1 Samuel 30:1. They instigate the crisis that must be resolved in the narrative. David's two wives serve as props who never speak or act. They are mentioned first in 1 Samuel 30:5 with lengthy descriptions specifying their names and other identifying information: the gentilic affiliation in the case of Ahinoam, and the husband's name and gentilic affiliation in the case of Abigail. Compound designations such as these often are used to reintroduce a character that is known from the broader narrative (Revell, 74). The second time they are mentioned in this chapter (1 Sam 30:18), they are referred to only by the descriptive phrase "his [David's] two wives"; only the marital relationship of the women to the main character is mentioned.

A final group of props comprises the men who were part of David's band. They often are explicitly mentioned as acting in concert with David (e.g., "And David and his men entered Ziklag on the third day" [1 Sam 30:1]; see also 1 Sam 30:3, 4), though more often third-person plural affixes on the verbs (1 Sam 30:11, 12, 20) are the sole grammatical information indicating their actions. As noted previously above, when the band splits in two at the Wadi Besor, the two groups are identified by number (the "four hundred" who went with David as opposed to the

"two hundred" who remained behind). When the riffraff from the larger group caused trouble, we have the narrator's evaluation of the complainers: "And each evil and worthless man from the men who had gone with David answered [sg.] and said [pl.] . . ." (1 Sam 30:22). The narrator initially uses a singular verb with the plural subject in order to emphasize the personal and individual concern of the troublemakers (Revell, 250); the subsequent plural verb highlights their mob mentality.

As we have seen, the ways in which participants are referred to within a narrative pericope thus may be used to highlight central characters, to focus on the function that a character plays within the narrative, or to emphasize the relationship that a minor character bears to larger concerns of the narrative.

3.2. Representations of Speech. Biblical narrative makes extensive use of speech. Dialogue often provides the central framework for the plot structure of a story. Reports of speech may also be used to introduce characters, depict their inner thoughts, index social relationships between characters and provide background information to the narrative. A consideration of the ways in which speech is represented and integrated into biblical narrative requires attention to multiple fields of linguistics.

3.2.1. Dialogue. Conversation analysis, a subfield of sociolinguistics, is concerned with describing how speakers create meaning and negotiate communication within dialogue. A central insight of conversation analysis is that dialogue is pragmatically structured into "adjacency pairs," or paired speeches by alternate speakers. The first speech of the adjacency pair is intended to elicit an appropriate and cooperative response by the second speaker. For example, a question by one speaker elicits an appropriate answer to the question by the second speaker; similarly, a command elicits a reply indicating compliance or noncompliance with the command.

The first speech of an adjacency pair may be followed by a variety of appropriate responses, some of which are preferred by the speaker of the first speech, others of which are dispreferred. The second half of an adjacency pair can be classified according to the extent to which it provides a preferred or dispreferred response to the first speaker. For example, if the first half of the adjacency pair represents a request, a preferred response represents a compliance with the request, whereas a dispreferred response represents a refusal.

A complete analysis of biblical dialogue has not been undertaken (see the foundational work in Miller 2003, 233-97, as well as Person on the dialogues in Jonah). However, the analysis of adjacency pairs has been profitably applied to an unusual use of the conjunction *waw* ("and") in biblical Hebrew dialogue. In representations of dialogue in biblical narrative the conjunction *and* may precede speeches in two different pragmatic contexts. In the first context the speech introduced with "and" is connected with an immediately preceding speech by a different speaker; in other words, the speech with *and* occurs in the second pair-part of an adjacency pair. In the second context the speech introduced with "and" is connected to a distant speech within the dialogue that is spoken by the same speaker; ordinarily, the speech with "and" is in the first pair-part. Attention to these features of conversation analysis assists the biblical scholar in an explication of the pragmatic import of *waw* as a discourse marker within conversation.

The first pragmatic context for "and" is illustrated in 1 Kings 2:20-22 in an exchange between Bathsheba and King Solomon:

She said, "I am asking one little request from you. Don't refuse me."

The king said to her, "Ask, my mother, because I won't refuse you."

She said, "Let Abishag the Shunamite be given to Adonijah your brother as a wife."

King Solomon answered and said to his mother, "*And* why are you asking Abishag the Shunamite for Adonijah? Then ask for him the kingdom because he is my elder brother—for him and for Abiathar the priest and for Joab the son of Zeruiah."

In this dialogue there are two adjacency pairs. In the first adjacency pair Bathsheba secures her son's agreement in principle to her unspecified request. In the second adjacency pair Bathsheba makes her request explicit, and Solomon vehemently objects to that request in his speech, beginning with "and." The conjunction is used to mark explicitly a dispreferred response.

The second pragmatic context in which "and" introduces speech is illustrated in Genesis 17:1-16 (here excerpted):

When Abram was ninety-nine years old, the LORD appeared to him and said to him, "I am El Shaddai. Walk before me and be perfect . . ."

Abram fell on his face. God spoke with him, "As for me, behold, my covenant is with you and I will make you the father of many nations."

God said to Abraham, "*And* as for you, you will keep my covenant, you and your descendants after you throughout all generations . . ."

God said to Abraham, "As for Sarai, your wife, you shall not call her Sarai, but Sarah will be her name . . ."

In this passage four consecutive speeches are attributed to God; the third speech begins with "and." In biblical narrative the speech of a single character may be segmented, as here, by more than one quotative frame, the sentence that introduces the speech—for example, "God said to Abraham" (for examples see Gen 47:3-4; Miller 2003, 239-43). The quotative frames serve here to segment God's speech into thematic sections. The first quotation (Gen 17:1-2) introduces the general topic of the conversation: God is making his covenant with Abram. In the second quotation (Gen 17:3-8), God indicates his own responsibilities in the covenant. In the third quotation (Gen 17:9-14), God enumerates Abraham's responsibilities in the covenant; this quotation is the only one introduced with "and." In the fourth quotation (Gen 17:15-16), God enumerates Sarai's responsibilities in the covenant.

What does "and" contribute to God's third quotation? The addition of the conjunction serves to link Abram's responsibilities with the previous quotation that specifies God's responsibilities. God and Abram are the two speech participants in the dialogue; the division of their responsibilities in the covenant is highlighted. The speech in which God lays out the responsibilities of Sarai, who is not a speech-participant, is not introduced with "and" (cf. Gen 9:1-17; see Miller 1999, 180-83).

3.2.2. Polite Language. Polite language is an important part of linguistic pragmatics, the study of the relationship between language and its context of use. In using polite forms, speakers index their understandings of their social relationship(s) to their addressees. Dialogue in the biblical narratives uses three kinds of polite language: morphological indicators of politeness, terms of address and deferential language.

The most important morphological indicator of politeness is the particle *nā'*. A sociolinguistic analysis of the particle *nā'* indicates that it is used in contexts where the speaker wishes to make a request that may threaten the "face" of the hearer (Wilt). The particle is used when the speaker wishes to avoid a bald request, to enhance the relationship with the hearer, or to adapt the relationship with the hearer for the benefit of the speaker. The use (or absence) of the particle relates both to the social relationship between the speech participants and to the rhetorical purposes of the speaker. In essence, the particle is used like "please" and indicates that the speaker is personally involved in the request (Shulman).

Terms of address are noun phrases used to refer to addressees within direct speech (see Miller 2003, 269-71). They may index the relationship of the speech participants with respect to social intimacy or social distance (such as an inferior/superior relationship between speaker and addressee). Terms of address that index social intimacy are derived from familial language. While these terms may be used literally by the speaker to address father (Gen 22:7), mother (1 Kings 2:20), son (1 Sam 2:24), daughter (Judg 11:35), brother (2 Sam 13:12) or sister (2 Sam 13:20), they may also be used metaphorically to index cordial nonfamilial relationships. When the relationship is one of male equals, "my brother(s)" may be used, as in 1 Samuel 30:23, where David addresses his belligerent men as "my brothers," thus emphasizing that he is one of them, rather than his position as their leader, a position seriously in jeopardy at that point (see 1 Sam 30:6, where his men are ready to stone him after the capture of their wives and children). When the relationship is one of a superior to a male inferior, "my son" frequently is used (e.g., Eli addressing Samuel [1 Sam 3:6, 16; 4:16]). When the relationship is one of inferior to male superior, "my father" may be used (e.g., courtiers speaking to their master [2 Kings 5:13]). Speakers use kinship terms metaphorically in order to evoke their personal relationship with their interlocutor(s) as a means of persuasion (Revell, 329-31). Terms of address indicating social distance include "my lord," "the king," "the officer" (2 Kings 9:5), "man of God" (2 Kings

1:9) and "blessed of the LORD" (Gen 24:31). All of these are used by an inferior to a superior; no terms of address are used by a superior in addressing an inferior (Revell, 326-29).

Deferential language refers to language used by an inferior when speaking to a superior that explicitly indexes the social inequalities of their relationship. In biblical Hebrew, deferential language is never required; when it is used, it may be anchored in the viewpoint of the (inferior) speaker or in the viewpoint of the (superior) addressee. When anchored in the viewpoint of the speaker, the phrase "my lord" is used to refer to the (superior) addressee, and first-person pronouns refer to the (inferior) speaker. When anchored in the viewpoint of the addressee, the phrase "your servant" is used to refer to the (inferior) speaker, and second-person pronouns refer to the (superior) speaker. Third-person pronouns may be used for both speaker and addressee in place of first- or second-person pronouns, respectively, when the speaker wishes to use even greater deference through greater distance (Miller 2003, 271-81).

These three strategies may be combined within a single quotation for rhetorical and persuasive effect. In 1 Samuel 29:8 David says to the Philistine king Achish, "But what have *I* done? And what have *you* found in *your servant* since the time that *I* have been with *you* until today that *I* may not go and fight against the enemies of *my lord the king*?" Revell (272, 311) argues that in a social situation such as this that calls for deferential language, first- and second-person pronouns should be considered to mark the immediacy and urgency of the speaker's personal concern. The use of "your servant" (anchored in the viewpoint of Achish) is used to highlight David's claim that he has faithfully served Achish. The use of "my lord the king" (anchored in the viewpoint of David) is used to emphasize David's argument that he is loyal to Achish and considers him, not Saul, to be his king.

By applying sociolinguistic studies of politeness and face-saving strategies to biblical narrative, we are able to understand better the rhetoric of biblical dialogue and the import of characters' speeches. More importantly, we gain insights into the ways in which characters index and negotiate their social relationships through their expression of (or failure to express) politeness.

3.2.3. Integration of Speech into Narrative. Reports of speech are integrated into narrative by means of a quotative frame. The quotative frame is the narrator's indication of the specifics of the speech event—most importantly, who spoke and a characterization of the speech through the choice of a specific speech verb (e.g., "Rachel asked" as opposed to "Rachel demanded"). Sometimes additional information is included in the quotative frame, such as the addressee ("to her mother"), the time ("in the morning") or the speech code ("in Hebrew"). The original locution may also be represented in a variety of ways along a continuum from direct speech (represented as it was putatively originally spoken by the speaker, with the original deixis intact) to indirect speech (represented from the deictic viewpoint of the narrator). In general, biblical Hebrew narrative shows less variety in presenting speech than do narratives in English and other European languages.

In biblical Hebrew direct representations of speech may be integrated into the narrative in three ways, depending upon the syntactic complexity of the quotative frame. In the simplest form a single speech verb is used to characterize the speech from the narrator's viewpoint (e.g., "he answered"). In the second form multiple speech verbs are used to introduce a single speech (e.g., "he answered and he said"); the second verb is always a generic speech verb (usually "say," less frequently "speak"). In the third form the main speech verb is followed by *lēʾmōr*, a frozen infinitival form of the verb "to say" (e.g., "he answered saying").

Indirect representations of speech in biblical Hebrew may be grouped into four types, depending on the degree to which the original locution has been compressed syntactically. In the first type (common in English, less common in biblical Hebrew) the original locution remains a complete sentence and usually is introduced with *kî*, "that" (e.g., "They told Sisera that *Barak the son of Abinoam had gone to Mount Tabor*" [Judg 4:12]). In the second type the original locution has been reduced to an infinitival complement (e.g., "Moses spoke to the Israelites *to perform the passover*" [Num 9:4]). In the third type the original locution has been reduced to a nominal phrase (a noun phrase, a prepositional phrase, or a deictic term) (e.g., "Moses spoke *thus* to the Israelites" [Ex 6:9]). In the fourth type the original locution is completely suppressed and all that remains is a mention that a speech act occurred (e.g., "He [Joseph] kissed all his brothers and wept over them. After that, *his brothers spoke with him*" [Gen 45:15]).

The use of these resources for representing speech within biblical narrative is revealing. Although the overwhelmingly most common way to indicate speech is by the common phrase "and he said," a careful examination reveals that almost any of the forms of direct and indirect speech may be paired with one another in adjacency pairs (Miller 2003, 244-52). What is interesting, however, is that the first half of the adjacency pair ordinarily has more information concerning the specifics of the speech event as well as greater complexity in the quotative frames of direct speech. Furthermore, syntactic complexity (in linguistic terms, "syntactic markedness") within the quotative frame correlates with specifiable pragmatic functions ("pragmatic markedness") within the discourse. The single-verb frame introduces quotations that are unmarked within the discourse. The multiple-verb frame introduces quotations that the narrator marks as particularly salient (or marked) within the dialogue. Direct speeches introduced with the frozen infinitival form *lēʾmōr* are privatively marked with respect to direct speech introduced with a single-verb frame (Miller 2003, 425-27). That is, speeches introduced with *lēʾmōr* are flagged by the narrator as pragmatically marked (O'Connor 2002). These speeches are dialogically extraordinary in some way: for example, the speech has no response; the speaker is a prop in the narrative or a group represented as speaking in unison; the communication takes place across distance; the addressee is unspecified or unidentified; the quotation is semidirect, retold, iterative or hypothetical. By contrast, if *lēʾmōr* is not present, the speech is not marked as either prototypical or nonprototypical.

Biblical Hebrew narrative has some surprising conventions for representing speech. Direct speech, for example, may not be fully direct, in that the narrator may intrude into the speech (e.g., by condensing the speech, as in 1 Sam 18:24). Indirect speech cannot be embedded multiple times within other instances of indirect speech—something that can be done in English (e.g., "He said that she said that I refused"). Instead, direct speech is embedded within direct speech (e.g., 2 Kings 1:6; see Miller 2003, 226-31). Another convention involves the ordinary way of representing a positive response to a command or request. In many cases no overt reply is made to a command (e.g., Ex 4:3), and often the narrator does not indicate that the command was obeyed (e.g., Ex 1:22). The biblical convention is that readers, unless specifically told otherwise, are to assume that a command was obeyed.

We can illustrate several of these features by returning to 1 Samuel 30. Direct speech introduced with a single-verb frame predominates throughout the chapter (eight out of eleven instances). However, the first half of the adjacency pair always contains more information concerning the speech event than the second half. In 1 Samuel 30:13, for example, the first half of the adjacency pair is introduced with the quotative frame "David said to him [the Egyptian man]" (indicating both speaker and addressee), whereas the second half of the adjacency pair is introduced only with the speech verb ("he said") (see also 1 Sam 30:15).

The chapter's only instance of direct speech introduced with a multiple-verb frame occurs in 1 Samuel 30:22, and it follows an initial greeting by David in 1 Samuel 30:21 that is represented with reduced indirect speech ("David asked concerning their welfare"). The vehement (and highly dispreferred) response of the troublemakers in his band is introduced with a multiple-verb frame: "Each evil and worthless man from among the men who had gone with David *answered* and *said*..." The use of a multiple-verb frame (with extensive characterization by the narrator concerning the speakers) is used to highlight this unexpected and tumultuous speech and the crisis that it precipitates.

Direct speech introduced with the frozen infinitival form *lē'mōr* is used in two instances. In 1 Samuel 30:8 the content of David's oracular consultation of the Lord by means of the ephod is introduced with the quotative frame "David inquired of the LORD *saying*." The use of *lē'mōr* in the quotative frame is the narrator's explicit marking that the adjacency pair that follows departs from the ordinary norms of face-to-face conversation (i.e., the quotative frame is marked). (Note that the Lord's reply is introduced simply with "he [the LORD] said to him [David]," even though this speech, like the pre-

vious one, is communicated by oracular means. The quotative frame is unmarked; that is, the narrator provides no explicit indicator concerning whether the speech that follows should be read as pragmatically marked or not.) The other instance of *lē'mōr* occurs in the quotation in 1 Samuel 30:26, which is introduced with the quotative frame "David sent some of the spoils to the elders of Judah as his ally *saying*." We understand from the narrative that the looting takes place repeatedly, as does David's transferal of looted merchandise. Thus the speech is a condensation of many acts of speech, and the narrator flags it as being dialogically unusual through the use of *lē'mōr*.

Indirect speech is used in two instances in the chapter, and in each case the precise content of the original locution is unimportant to the narrative. In 1 Samuel 30:6 indirect speech is used to represent the intentions of his band: "It was exceedingly painful to David because *the people said to kill him.*" In 1 Samuel 30:21 David's greeting to the two hundred men upon returning from recapturing their wives is represented in reduced form, as mentioned above.

Finally, we see in this passage the importance of understanding the convention of biblical narrative to represent the compliance with a command only when it is significant. In 1 Samuel 30:7 David asks Abiathar the priest, the son of Ahimelek, to bring the ephod. The narrator tells us explicitly, "Abiathar brought the ephod to David." David possesses both the ephod and Saul's former priest—his request for divine direction and divine protection will be successful.

By contrast, in 1 Samuel 30:15 the Egyptian man makes a request of David: "Swear to me by God that you will not kill me, or hand me over to my master, and I will take you down." The ensuing narrative depicts only what happens when the Egyptian leads the group to the Amalekites. No mention is made that David did swear to him or that he kept the man safe, but readers are supposed to understand that such was the case. The fate of the unnamed Egyptian, unlike that of David, is not the central concern of the narrative.

4. Conclusions.

Linguistics provides both the theoretical framework(s) and the methodological techniques for better understanding and describing the language of the Historical Books. Importantly, the fruits of linguistic analysis help us to avoid incorrect understandings of the biblical text that might arise from our intuitions as native speakers of languages other than ancient Hebrew.

A number of linguistic fields—most notably syntax, discourse analysis, pragmatics, sociolinguistics, conversation analysis—have significantly advanced our understanding of the structure and interpretation of narratives within the Historical Books. Especially important contributions of linguistics involve an understanding of certain narrative conventions in biblical Hebrew, as well as the differentiation of unmarked and marked constructions and their pragmatic significance.

See also ARAMAIC LANGUAGE; HEBREW LANGUAGE; HERMENEUTICS; INNERBIBLICAL EXEGESIS; METHODS OF INTERPRETATION; NARRATIVE ART OF ISRAEL'S HISTORIANS.

BIBLIOGRAPHY. **J. Barr,** "The Synchronic, the Diachronic and the Historical: A Triangular Relationship?" in *Synchronic or Diachronic? A Debate on Method in Old Testament Exegesis,* ed. J. C. de Moor (OtSt 34; Leiden: E. J. Brill, 1995) 1-14; **E. L. Battistella,** *The Logic of Markedness* (Oxford: Oxford University Press, 1996); **A. Berlin,** *Poetics and Interpretation of Biblical Narrative* (BLS 9; Sheffield: Almond, 1983); **L. Campbell,** *Historical Linguistics: An Introduction* (Cambridge: MIT Press, 1999); **N. Chomsky,** *The Minimalist Program* (Current Studies in Linguistics 28; Cambridge, MA: MIT Press, 1995); **B. Comrie,** *Language Universals and Linguistic Typology* (2d ed.; Chicago: University of Chicago Press, 1989); **J. A. Cook,** "The Hebrew Verb: A Grammaticalization Approach," *ZAH* 14 (2001) 117-43; **L. de Regt,** *Participants in Old Testament Texts and the Translator: Reference Devices and Their Rhetorical Impact* (SSN 39; Assen: Van Gorcum, 1999); **B. E. Dresher,** "The Prosodic Basis of the Tiberian Hebrew System of Accents," *Language* 70 (1994) 1-52; **M. Ehrensvärd,** "Linguistic Dating of Biblical Texts," in *Biblical Hebrew: Studies in Chronology and Typology,* ed. I. Young (JSOTSup 369; London: T & T Clark, 2003) 164-88; **N. Fabb,** *Linguistics and Literature: Language in the Verbal Arts of the World* (Blackwell Textbooks in Linguistics 12; Oxford: Blackwell, 1997); **W. R. Garr,** *Dialect Geography of Syria-Palestine, 1000-586 BCE* (Philadelphia: University of Pennsylvania Press, 1985; repr., Winona Lake, IN: Eisenbrauns, 2004); **E. L. Greenstein,** "The Syntax of Saying 'Yes' in Biblical Hebrew," JANESCU 19 (1989) 51-59; **W. Gross,** *Die Satzteilfolge im Verbalsatz alttestamentlicher Prosa: Untersucht an den Büchern Dtn, Ri und 2 Kön* (FAT 17; Tübingen: Mohr, 1996); **M. A. K. Halliday,** *An Introduction to Functional Grammar* (2d ed.; London: Edward Arnold, 1994); **M. A. K. Halliday and R. Hasan,** *Cohesion in English* (English Languages Series 4; London: Longman, 1976); **W. F. Hanks,** *Language and Communicative Practices* (Critical Essays in Anthropology; Boulder, CO: Westview, 1996); **G. Hatav,** *The Semantics of Aspect and Modality: Evidence from English and Biblical Hebrew* (Studies in Language Companion Series 34; Amsterdam: Benjamins, 1997); **J. Hoftijzer,** "Holistic or Compositional Approach? Linguistic Remarks to the Problem," in *Synchronic or Diachronic? A Debate on Method in Old Testament Exegesis,* ed. J. C. de Moor (OtSt 34; Leiden: E. J. Brill, 1995) 98-114; **R. D. Holmstedt,** "Adjusting our Focus" [review of Shimasaki], *HS* 44 (2003) 203-15; **P. J. Hopper and S. A. Thompson,** "Transitivity in Grammar and Discourse," *Language* 56 (1980) 251-99; **A. Hurvitz,** "Can Biblical Texts Be Dated Linguistically? Chronological Perspectives in the Historical Study of Biblical Hebrew," in *Congress Volume, Oslo 1998,* ed. A. Lemaire and M. Saebø (VTSup 80; Leiden: E. J. Brill, 2000) 143-60; **W. J. Idsardi,** "Tiberian Hebrew Spirantization and Phonological Derivations," *Linguistic Inquiry* 29 (1998) 37-73; **S. Izre'el,** ed., *Semitic Linguistics: The State of the Art at the Turn of the Twenty-First Century* (IOS 20; Winona Lake, IN: Eisenbrauns, 2002); **J. Joosten,** "The Indicative System of the Biblical Hebrew Verb and Its Literary Exploitation," in *Narrative Syntax and the Hebrew Bible: Papers of the Tilburg Conference 1996,* ed. E. van Wolde (BIS 29; Leiden: E. J. Brill, 2002a) 51-71; idem, "Workshop: Meaning and Uses of the Tenses in 1 Samuel 1," in *Narrative Syntax and the Hebrew Bible: Papers of the Tilburg Conference 1996,* ed. E. van Wolde (BIS 29; Leiden: E. J. Brill, 2002b) 72-83; **S. A. Kaufman,** "Languages in Contact: The Ancient Near East," in *Semitic Linguistics: The State of the Art at the Turn of the Twenty-First Century,* ed. S. Izre'el (IOS 20; Winona Lake, IN: Eisenbrauns, 2002) 297-306; **G. A. Long,** *Grammatical Concepts 101 for Biblical Hebrew* (Peabody, MA: Hendrickson, 2002); **R. E. Longacre,** *Joseph, a Story of Divine Providence: A Text Theoretical and Textlinguistic Analysis of Genesis 37 and 39—48* (2d ed.; Winona Lake, IN: Eisenbrauns, 2003); **P. V. Mankowski,** *Akkadian*

Loanwords in Biblical Hebrew (HSS 47; Winona Lake, IN: Eisenbrauns, 2000); **C. L. Miller,** "The Pragmatics of *waw* as a Discourse Marker in Biblical Hebrew Dialogue," *ZAH* 12 (1999) 165-91; idem, *The Representation of Speech in Biblical Hebrew Narrative: A Linguistic Analysis* (2d corrected printing, with afterword; HSM 55; Winona Lake, IN: Eisenbrauns, 2003 [1996]); **J. Milroy,** "On the Social Origins of Language Change," in *Historical Linguistics: Problems and Perspectives,* ed. C. Jones (Longman Linguistics Library; London: Longman, 1993) 215-36; **F. J. Newmeyer,** *Language Form and Language Function* (Language, Speech, and Communication; Cambridge, MA: MIT Press, 1998); **M. O'Connor,** "Discourse Linguistics and the Study of Biblical Hebrew," in *Congress Volume, Basel 2001,* ed. A. Lemaire (VTSup 92; Leiden: E. J. Brill, 2002) 17-42; idem, "War and Rebel Chants in the Former Prophets," in *Fortunate the Eyes That See: Essays in Honor of David Noel Freedman in Celebration of His Seventieth Birthday,* ed. A. B. Beck et al. (Grand Rapids: Eerdmans, 1995) 322-37; **R. F. Person,** *In Conversation with Jonah: Conversation Analysis, Literary Criticism, and the Book of Jonah* (JSOTSup 220; Sheffield: Sheffield Academic Press, 1996); **F. H. Polak,** "The Oral and the Written: Syntax, Stylistics and the Development of Biblical Prose Narrative," JANESCU 26 (1998) 59-105; **R. Polzin,** *Late Biblical Hebrew: Toward an Historical Typology of Biblical Hebrew Prose* (HSM 12; Missoula, MT: Scholars Press, 1976); **G. A. Rendsburg,** *Israelian Hebrew in the Book of Kings* (Occasional Publications of the Department of Near Eastern Studies and the Program of Jewish Studies, Cornell University 5; Bethesda, MD: CDL Press, 2002); **E. J. Revell,** *The Designation of the Individual: Expressive Usage in Biblical Narrative* (CBET 14; Kampen: Kok Pharos, 1996); **J. M. Sadock and A. M. Zwicky,** "Speech Act Distinctions in Syntax," in *Language Typology and Syntactic Description,* 1: *Clause Structure,* ed. T. Shopen (Cambridge: Cambridge University Press, 1985) 155-96; **F. de Saussure,** *Course in General Linguistics,* ed. C. Bally and A. Sechehaye (New York: McGraw-Hill, 1959 [1916]); **K. Shimasaki,** *Focus Structure in Biblical Hebrew: A Study of Word Order and Information Structure* (Bethesda, MD: CDL Press, 2002); **A. Shulman,** "The Particle *nā'* in Biblical Hebrew Prose," *HS* 40 (1999) 57-82; **C. van der Merwe,** "Towards a Better Understanding of Biblical Hebrew Word Order" [review of Gross], JNSL 25 (1999) 277-300; **W. Weinberg,** "Language Consciousness in the Old Testament?" ZAW 92 (1980) 185-204; **L. J. Whaley,** *Introduction to Typology: The Unity and Diversity of Language* (Thousand Oaks, CA: Sage, 1997); **T. Wilt,** A Sociolinguistic Analysis of *nā'*, *VT* 46 (1996) 237-55; **D. Winford,** *An Introduction to Contact Linguistics* (Language in Society; Oxford: Blackwell, 2003); **I. Young,** *Diversity in Pre-exilic Hebrew* (FAT 5; Túbingen: Mohr Siebeck, 1993).

C. L. Miller

LISTS. *See* WRITING, WRITING MATERIALS AND LITERACY IN THE ANCIENT NEAR EAST.

LITERACY. *See* WRITING, WRITING MATERIALS AND LITERACY IN THE ANCIENT NEAR EAST.

LITERARY CRITICISM. *See* METHODS OF INTERPRETATION.

LUZ. *See* BETHEL.

M

MAGIC AND DIVINATION

Interest in magic and divination in the OT has seen a resurgence recently, prompting a reassessment of their place and function within ancient Israelite religion.

At the outset, a study of magic has to contend with a complex situation in which we find condemnation of the phenomena coupled with multiple evidence of the reality of their practice. In some passages magic and divination are viewed positively, while in others they are harshly condemned. Another problem is the terminology: a great many terms are associated with magic and divination, often with different or inconsistent meanings.

Beginning with magic, as the more encompassing concept of the two, we should note that a clear definition has eluded scholars thus far. Traditionally, magic is understood to represent the manipulation and coercion of supernatural powers in order to control events (e.g., in war and politics) or people, for good (e.g., healing) or for harm (e.g., inflicting disease and death). However, this definition derives from a Platonic model that has been passed down over centuries without sufficient critical attention being paid to the presuppositions of that worldview. The distinction that this definition draws between magic and religion, and the implication of a privileged status afforded the latter, are in need of reevaluation. Divination, as a branch or subcategory of magic, is easier to define as "the art of deciphering and interpreting signs in which the future is believed to be read."

This article begins with a brief survey of previous understandings of magic and divination, before looking at the methodology. It then turns to the distinctive character of the Historical Books. Types of magic and divination and their specific terminology are examined, followed by an evaluation of their place and function in the Historical Books and then the drawing of some conclusions, which have implications for the way we understand ancient Israelite religion.

1. A Brief History of Interpretation
2. Methodology
3. The Distinctive Character of the Historical Books
4. Types of Magic and Divination in the Historical Books
5. Place and Function of Magic and Divination in the Historical Books: Interpreting the Evidence
6. Conclusions

1. A Brief History of Interpretation.
From the classics of OT theology comes the notion that magic and divination derive from foreign practices, mainly from Canaan, that such practices are or should be illegal, and that they reflect a worldview in which the magician could coerce the forces of nature. This was understood to be in direct opposition to the cult of Yahweh, the only true master of nature. Debates that centered on the concept of Yahwism and monotheism presented magic and divination as "impure" and "tainted."

More recently scholars have turned to the social sciences for guidance, with leads taken mainly from the fields of sociology and anthropology. Studies of magic have moved from the classic distinction between magic, religion and science, where magic is understood either as a primitive form of religion—a kind of prereligious state belonging to the area of primitive mentality—or as a degeneration of religion. In either case, religion is taken as a yardstick against which to measure intermediation between the human and the divine. This framework, taken from James Frazer's *The Golden*

Bough (first published in 1890, and later expanded), presupposes an evolutionary and, some would say, intellectualist approach, and it has been criticized and refined by E. Evans-Pritchard, M. Eliade (particularly with regard to shamanism), E. Durkheim and, more recently, D. L. O'Keefe and S. Tambiah.

Although it is vital to take seriously the work of anthropologists and sociologists and their call to understand the world of the ancient Israelite in its context, it must be underlined that this task is particularly difficult when applied to societies in the ancient world. In the absence of an ancient Israelite self-definition, a focus on how ancient Israelites understood their place within their world, myth and ritual seems most likely to yield results. The search for a rationale underlying magic considers ideas that ancient Israelites had of their world. If the cosmos was perceived as a complex web of interactions between living beings and forces of nature, then magic would be perceived to be part of the natural order. The new approach has led modern scholarship to regard magic and divination as part of the complex of religious intermediations. This seems to be the more fruitful approach for considering the Historical Books.

2. Methodology.
Two elements need to be taken into consideration when analyzing magic and divination. First, there is an almost unbridgeable distance between our world and that of the ancient Israelites; nonetheless, one possible way to understand their world is to examine their worldview. Second, the narratives themselves yield information about the function of magic in the ancient Israelite society and belief system.

3. The Distinctive Character of the Historical Books.
When assessing the place of magic and divination, we must take into consideration at least two elements. First, the recent reassessment of ancient Israelite history has raised the question of the relationship between the written text and its "real" environment. Since at least the time of M. Noth, there has been a scholarly consensus that the composition of some of the Historical Books has its roots during the troubled times of the exile. As a result, they present not an accurate history (in the modern sense) but rather a theological reflection to explain the sorry state of the

people, whether exiled or remnant.

Second, in view of the complex relationship of the Historical Books to the book of Deuteronomy, a number of questions must be asked. For example, should we read the list in Deuteronomy 18:9-14 as a blueprint from which to understand and assess the stories found in the Historical Books, or should that text be understood as a later development, as an ideological rethinking of a situation? The answer to such questions will determine the framework within which to read magic and divination in the Historical Books. A positive answer to the first part of the question suggests that all expressions of magic and divinatory acts are manifestations of foreign power and thus run counter to the monotheistic faith that the authors were so keen to promote; by contrast, a positive answer to the second part of the question suggests a late establishment of religious boundaries and a tightening of the control of the religious authorities.

4. Types of Magic and Divination in the Historical Books.
1 Samuel 28:6, in which it is said that Saul tries to consult dreams, Urim and prophets, suggests an internal order.

There are many modes of inquiry (typical verbs are *dāraš* and *šāʾal*), magical behavior and practitioners in the Historical Books.

4.1. The Practitioners. There is a broad range of terminology used, including "prophet" *(nābîʾ)*— for example, *Elijah and *Elisha (1 Kings 17—2 Kings 9), Micaiah (1 Kings 22), *Samuel (1 Sam 1—28)—"man of God," "seer" and "priest."

4.1.1. Prophet (nābîʾ). Although the twin figures of Elijah and Elisha have been variously evaluated, there is no doubt of their involvement in magical acts. When the biblical editors want to show that their actions have the strong backing of Yahweh, Elijah and Elisha are consistently shown as tapping into the divine energy through the performance of miracles and acts of magic. There are numerous examples of their magical endeavors: the catastrophic control of weather and its subsequent withdrawal of fertility (1 Kings 17), manifesting primal forces (fire: 1 Kings 18:38; 2 Kings 1:10-14; rain: 1 Kings 18:1), delivering an oracular death sentence on Ahaziah (2 Kings 1:6), healing (2 Kings 5:1-16), inflicting disease (2 Kings 5:25-27; 6:18), resurrecting the dead (1 Kings 17:17-24; 2 Kings 4:1-

37), multiplying food (1 Kings 17:6-16; 2 Kings 4:1-37), using ecstatic techniques (music: 2 Kings 3:15), controlling animals (2 Kings 2:23-24), generally performing acts that are deemed impossible (retrieval of metal axes from the bottom of a lake: 2 Kings 6:5-7; cleansing of poisonous water or food: 2 Kings 2:19-22; 3:16-20; parting of waters with a rolled-up cloak: 2 Kings 2:8, 14).

What is noteworthy in the Historical Books is not so much the prophetic behavior or the performance of miracles as it is the scale of wondrous acts: the acts of the two prophets are larger than life. From a literary perspective, magic clearly is used to reinforce the Deuteronomistic claim to establish prophecy: Elijah and Elisha are set within the literary prophetic framework of the figure of Moses, as both figures are presented as imitating Moses (the "spirit" of Yahweh rests on both of them [1 Kings 17; 19]); they are deeply set within a political and ideological world in which promoting and keeping faith in Yahweh is paramount. This is to be understood within the privileged position given to *prophets and prophecy by the Historical Books. There is no reason for the Deuteronomistic Historian to suppress instances of magic and divination; indeed, they are freely and constructively used to affirm and confirm Yahweh's power and reinforce or establish the institution of prophecy (as against that of the kings).

Both Elijah and Elisha are presented as Moses-like figures whose function is to defend the covenant and maintain the Torah of Yahweh against a people who stubbornly fight his will.

4.1.2. Man of God ('îš [hā]'ĕlōhîm). Elijah and Elisha and others are referred to by the term "man of God" (Judg 13:6; 1 Sam 9:6; 2 Kings 5:20; 6:6-15).

4.1.3. Seer (rōeh *and* ḥōzeh). These terms are used of Samuel in the episode of Kish's donkeys (1 Sam 9:19), Gad inquiring for David (2 Sam 24:11), Heman (1 Chron 25:5) and Jeduthun (2 Chron 35:15).

4.1.4. Priest (kōhēn). *Priests wore an ephod as a means of divination (1 Sam 2:28)—for example, Ahijah (1 Sam 14:3) and Abiathar (1 Sam 23:9-12; 1 Sam 30:7).

4.1.5. Kings. King *David consults the ephod in 1 Samuel 23:9-12; 30:7-8 (see 4.1.4).

4.1.6. Mediums and Spiritists ('ōbôt *and* yiddĕ'ōnî). These terms are used in tandem to designate those who make inquiries of the spirits of the dead, as the woman from Endor, a "medium" (ba'ălat 'ôb), does of the deceased Samuel (1 Sam 28).

4.1.7. Diviners (qōsĕmîm). These appear in tandem with Philistine priests in 1 Samuel 6:2 (cf. Josh 13:22; 1 Sam 15:23; 2 Kings 17:17).

4.2. Modes of Inquiry. Oracular consultations are complex and varied, with many different ways to inquire into the divine will.

4.2.1. The Ephod ('ēpōd). This is an ill-defined object whose modus operandi is obscure but seems to have produced a yes-or-no answer (Judg 8:27; 1 Sam 23:6-11; 30:7-8).

4.2.2. The Lot (gôrāl). The casting of lots is another mode of determining the will of God—for example in narratives concerned with land distribution (Josh 18:6). In some cases the verb *lākad* is used to describe lot casting as the story of Saul's election in 1 Samuel 10:20-21 demonstrates.

4.2.3. The Urim and the Thummim ('ûrîm *and* tummîm). These were part of the priestly garments and could give a yes-or-no answer (1 Sam 14:41; Ezra 2:63; Neh 7:65).

4.2.4. The Ark ('ārôn). The *ark appears to have an oracular function, especially in wartime (Judg 20:27-28; 1 Sam 6; 2 Sam 11:11; 15:25-26).

4.2.5. Necromancy. Necromancy, or divination by means of communication with the spirits of the dead, is prominent in 1 Samuel 28. Although the practice is condemned, clearly it was practiced by some people.

4.2.6. Dreams and Visions. Dreams and visions are ways of communicating with the deity (Solomon: 1 Kings 3:1-15; Samuel: 1 Sam 3). In Judges 7:13-15 a dream received by Gentiles portends an omen of victory for Gideon.

4.2.7. Teraphim (tĕrāpîm.) In Judges 17:5 the teraphim is presented as an Israelite sacred object. Although its use is sometimes condemned (1 Sam 15:23; 2 Kings 23:24), the object was used for divination (2 Kings 23:24).

4.3. Magical Behavior.

Three examples of magical behavior must suffice here: (1) in Joshua 6 the taking of Jericho is engineered through a series of acts that are arguably magicoritualistic in nature, including the circling of the city, the use of the number "seven" and the employment of music; (2) in Judges 6:36-40 Gideon's fleece is used to give a sign in order to make a political decision; (3) 1 Samuel 17:43 exemplifies the common practice of cursing one's enemies in time of war. The story of Saul laying an oath on his troops, preventing them from eating before victory, in 1 Samuel 14:24 presents yet another aspect of cursing.

5. Place and Function of Magic and Divination in the Historical Books: Interpreting the Evidence.

Magic and divination in the Historical Books do not differ radically from the more general picture evoked in the rest of the OT. When instances of magic and divination appear in the Historical Books, they are part of situations of crisis: anxiety in a war situation where the outcome is far from obvious, or a portion of an army is in dire straights, trapped or in a helpless predicament. Magic and divination are prominent in such contexts throughout the entire ancient Near Eastern world of Mesopotamia, Egypt and Ugarit.

Recent research has determined that the assumption that magic and divination are foreign practices is a spurious one. On the contrary, both magic and divination appear at all levels of society: among kings (David consulting Abiathar the priest in 1 Sam 23:6-12), prophets (Elijah and Elisha in 1 Kings 17—2 Kings 9; Micaiah in 1 Kings 22) and private individuals (1 Sam 28).

The examples given in the preceding section demonstrate a great variety of techniques and practitioners: practicing magic and divination is integral to the society. It is often the case in the Historical Books that these techniques are exercised by recognized functionaries on behalf of the group rather than by solitary individuals (as seen, for instance, in postbiblical times).

Within a worldview that takes magic at face value, its primary function through the many oracular consultations performed in the Historical Books seem to be the acquisition of knowledge. A case in point is David's use of divination techniques, mostly associated with situations of political crisis and warfare.

A more rhetorical function, as in the context of the Elijah and Elisha narratives (see 4.1.1), is the Deuteronomistic intention to reinforce the concept of prophecy.

Finally, it could be argued that in the Historical Books the principal function of magic is theological: "inquiring of the Lord," by a variety of means, was common practice. In the debate that argues for the distinctiveness of magic versus religion, the question of the purpose of the

Historical Books is particularly relevant. Israel is not fighting on its own; rather, Yahweh fights on Israel's behalf (e.g., Josh 6). In many examples the use of magic is to show that deeds of war and conquest are impossible without God's intervention, and even the division of land, the basis of ancient Israel's identity, is owed to God's will ("by lot *[gôrāl]*, as the LORD had commanded" [Josh 14:2]). Through its portrayal of "impossible" situations—that is, situations that cannot be resolved by ordinary means—magic is a vehicle to express not so much the general anxiety of the people in times of crisis but rather their dependence on Yahweh.

6. Conclusions.

The debate over foreign magic versus native magic needs qualifying: there is no doubt that magic and divination are indigenous to ancient Israelite society, even if some practices, such as necromancy, may have developed first under Assyrian influence.

Magic and divination were pervasive: they were practiced at all levels of society, from common people (male and female) to priests and kings, for personal or public use. Magic and divination are best understood as part of the ancient Israelite worldview and its belief system. As a consequence, the presentation of the outsider, isolated from the community and coercing the will of the gods, needs to be reassessed.

The ideological conflict over the use and status of magic and divination in ancient Israel should not be minimized, but it is striking that in the Historical Books they are portrayed extensively in many narratives, and they are used by the Deuteronomistic writers to establish claims to prophecy and to reinforce their ideology and control over religious life. Understanding magic and divination broadens our understanding of religious intermediation not only in the Historical Books, but also in the OT in general.

See also CANAANITE GODS AND RELIGION; MIRACLES; SICKNESS AND DISEASE.

BIBLIOGRAPHY. **I. Blythin,** "Magic and Methodology," *Numen* 17 (1970) 45-59; **F. H. Cryer,** *Divination in Ancient Israel and Its Near Eastern Environment: A Socio-historical Investigation* (JSOTSup 142; Sheffield: Sheffield Academic Press, 1994); **E. Durkheim,** *The Elementary Forms of the Religious Life,* ed. M. S. Cladis (Oxford: Oxford University Press: 2001 [1912]); **M. Eliade,** *Shamanism: Archaic Techniques of Ecstasy* (London: Routledge & Kegan Paul, 1964); **E. Evans-Pritchard,** *Witchcraft, Oracles and Magic among the Azande* (Oxford: Clarendon Press, 1937); **O. Garcia de la Fuente,** *La Busqueda de Dios en el Antiguo Testamento* (Madrid: Guadarrama, 1971); **A. Jeffers,** *Magic and Divination in Ancient Palestine and Syria* (SHCANE 8; Leiden: E. J. Brill, 1996); **J. K. Kuemmerlin-McLean,** "Magic, Old Testament," *ABD* 4.468-71; **N. P. Lemche,** *Ancient Israel: A New History of Israelite Society* (BibSem; Sheffield: Sheffield Academic Press, 1988); **D. L. O'Keefe,** *Stolen Lightning: The Social Theory of Magic* (New York: Continuum, 1982); **S. D. Ricks,** "The Magician as Outsider in the Hebrew Bible and the New Testament," in *Ancient Magic and Ritual Power,* ed. M. Meyer and P. Mirecki (RGW 129; Leiden: E. J. Brill, 1995) 131-43; **J. W. Rogerson,** *Anthropology and the Old Testament* (Oxford: Blackwell, 1978); **B. Schmidt,** *Israel's Beneficent Dead: Ancestor Cult and Necromancy in Ancient Israelite Religion and Tradition* (FAT 11; Tübingen: Mohr Siebeck, 1994) 201-20; **S. Tambiah,** *Magic, Science, Religion, and the Scope of Rationality* (Lewis Henry Morgan Lectures, 1984; Cambridge: Cambridge University Press, 1990).

A. Jeffers

MANASSEH

King Manasseh of Judah (698-642 BCE) is known from 2 Kings 21:1-18, which presents him as the ultimate villain, from 2 Chronicles 33:1-20 and the apocryphal "Prayer of Manasseh," which portray him as the paradigmatic penitent, and from Ancient Near Eastern sources, which portray him as the faithful vassal.

> 1. General Information
> 2. The Different Portrayals of Manasseh
> 3. Theological Implications
> 4. Manasseh and the Development of the Deuteronomistic History
> 5. Literary Concerns

1. General Information.

Manasseh was the son of Hezekiah (2 Kings 20:21; 2 Chron 32:1) and Hephzibah (2 Kings 21:1). He began his reign at the age of twelve and reigned in total fifty-five years. His queen was Meshullemeth from the former northern kingdom, and after his death, their son Amon succeeded him on the throne.

Manasseh's young age at the time of his ascent to the throne may imply that he was not the eldest son (Josephus *Ant.* 10.25; *b.Ber.*10a, cf.

2 Kings 18:2). The same impression is given by his name Manasseh: non-Yahwistic names are rare among Judahite monarchs. Thus, it is unlikely that Manasseh was the heir to the throne when he was named (Stavrakopoulou, 116-19, with bibliography). An alternative view is to assume that Manasseh shared the regency with his father for his first ten years (Nelson, 179; Evans, 166).

2. The Different Portrayals of Manasseh.

The character of Manasseh is elusive. The biblical accounts diverge, one portraying him as the epitome of a sinner (2 Kings 21:1-18) and the other as the paradigm of a repenting sinner (2 Chron 33:1-20).

2.1. The Portrayal in 2 Kings 21:1-18.
According to the account in 2 Kings 21, Manasseh reversed the religious reforms carried out by his father. He erected altars to Baal, made a pole to Asherah, built altars to "all the heavenly host" in the Jerusalem temple, and probably also sacrificed his son (Stavrakopoulou, 113), all religious acts that the Deuteronomistic author(s) condemned as alien to the cult of Yahweh (2 Kings 21:2-7a). In addition, Manasseh is accused of shedding innocent blood (2 Kings 21:16).

2.2. The Portrayal According to Neo-Assyrian Inscriptions and Archaeology.
Looking beyond the biblical text, we receive a different picture, that of the faithful vassal. Manasseh is mentioned twice in Neo-Assyrian inscriptions. His name appears among the twenty-two Assyrian vassal kings of the west who were ordered by Esarhaddon to perform work for him, transporting timber and stone from Lebanon to Nineveh for the royal storehouse (*ANET*, 291). Ten years later, during the reign of Assurbanipal, Manasseh is listed as providing troops for the Assyrian campaign to Egypt (*ANET*, 294).

The archaeological evidence from the time of Manasseh's reign points in the same direction. Manasseh inherited a small vassal kingdom suffering the repercussions of Sennacherib's campaign in Judah in 701 BCE. Sennacherib had destroyed large parts of Judah, especially the Shephelah. In contrast, as far as can be deduced from the archaeological data, Judah suffered no great destruction during this period. Instead, we can see examples of a slow recovery and growth. While the settlements in the Shephelah were not rebuilt during Manasseh's reign, the parts of the Judean hills that had been destroyed soon recovered, and its population seems to have expanded, probably owing to the influx of refugees from surrounding areas. In addition, new settlements were built in the Negeb. The archaeological evidence further suggests a restructuring of the economy: with the Shephelah lost, and with it its rich agricultural produce, Manasseh expanded southward (Finkelstein, 169-87).

In view of this data, Manasseh emerges as an astute king of Judah, whose aim was to adopt a policy toward his Neo-Assyrian overlords that best benefited an independent Judah. Given the ascent of the Neo-Assyrian Empire throughout his reign, the prudent course of action was undoubtedly to remain a faithful vassal (Nelson, 178-82; cf. Evans, 166-69). Further, agriculture and trade profited from the lack of war and helped the land of Judah to regain its strength.

2.3. The Portrayal in 2 Chronicles 33:1-20. In contrast to the epitomized sinner of the Deuteronomistic history, the account in 2 Chronicles and the apocryphal lament attributed to Manasseh paint a picture of the penitential sinner: God warns Manasseh and the people of Judah, but they take no heed. As a result, the Assyrians attack Judah and take Manasseh to Babylon in chains (2 Chron 33:11). Manasseh repents, introduces monolatrous worship of Yahweh (2 Chron 33:12-13, 15-17) and fortifies the Jerusalem city wall (2 Chron 33:14).

Did the Chronicler have access to sources in addition to those available to the authors of 2 Kings? Neo-Assyrian sources, for example, may support the Chronicler's claim of an Assyrian attack and of Manasseh's forced journey to Babylon. The Babylonian vassal king Shamash-shum-ukin rebelled against (his half-brother) the Assyrian king Assurbanipal between 651 and 648 BCE. This was the first real Assyrian weakness during Manasseh's reign and consequently an opportunity for Manasseh to rebel. If he did, then this could be the historical event underlying the account in 2 Chronicles 33:11. It would further explain why Manasseh is recorded as having been taken to Babylon rather than to the Neo-Assyrian capital of Nineveh: Assurbanipal would have been in Babylon to quell the rebellion (Evans, 167-68).

Few contemporary scholars, however, accept this theory. The lack of extrabiblical sources supporting an Assyrian attack on Judah at this time, together with the lack of archaeological evidence of any destruction, makes it unlikely that Manasseh did in fact rebel. Further, if Manasseh had been taken to Babylon in chains, it is difficult to account for the silence of this event in the account in 2 Kings, as it would have supported the Deuteronomistic theology of blessing and punishment (Stavrakopoulou, 113-14; cf. Keulen, 220-22).

Looking at the Chronicler's account from a literary point of view, it is possible to regard it as a sermon based on traditional material surrounding Manasseh. A close reading of 2 Chronicles 33:18-19 suggests that the Chronicler inherited the tradition about a prayer of Manasseh, a penitential prayer that focuses on God's infinite mercy and the conviction that repentance is effective. This tradition then became the basis for the Chronicler's reworking of the account in Kings 21 (Schniedewind 1991). This tradition of Manasseh's prayer later took the shape of a specific text, found among the apocryphal books of the OT. In its present form, it is probably a Jewish prayer composed sometime before the destruction of Jerusalem in 70 CE (Charlesworth, 499-500).

3. Theological Implications.
The study of Manasseh involves two theological problems: Manasseh's longevity and Manasseh's part in the fall of Judah in 586 BCE.

3.1. Longevity Versus Death in Battle. Manasseh's long reign and peaceful death stand in stark contrast to his grandson *Josiah's short reign and violent death. This contrast is made acute by the opposite descriptions of Manasseh as the worst of sinners and Josiah as the exemplary advocate for the sole cult of Yahweh, prompting the question, would not the reverse have been more fitting, given the Deuteronomistic theology of rewards of longevity to the pious and vice versa? This problem is partly resolved in the Chronicler's account, which tells of Manasseh's repentance (2 Chron 33:12-13) and hints at Josiah's less than perfect sides (2 Chron 35:22).

3.2. Who Is to Blame for the Fall of Jerusalem? The Chronicler, looking at the history of pre-exilic Judah from a chronological distance, blames the fall of Jerusalem on a cumulative process of turning away from Yahweh. The nation as a whole, including Josiah, contributed to its own fall over an extended period of time: they ignored prophetic warnings, they profaned the temple and they sinned excessively (Halpern, 474-85).

In contrast, the Deuteronomistic Historian blames Manasseh outright for the fall (2 Kings 21:10-15). This is done despite the fact that Manasseh's reign predates the fall of Jerusalem by some fifty-five years and despite Josiah's subsequent religious reforms in accordance with the Law of Yahweh (2 Kings 23:3, 21, 24). The blaming of Manasseh paints a picture of Judah that is irrevocably fallen already at the time of Manasseh, with the result that Josiah's subsequent reforms are rendered pointless. At the same time, when reading the account of Josiah (2 Kings 22:1—23:30), the reader receives the contrary impression that Josiah's reforms have annulled the three chief reasons for God's wrath, including Manasseh's actions (Halpern, 486-89).

What, then, is the rationale behind the account in 2 Kings? One possibility is to see the problem as the reason: the ultimate failure of Josiah's reforms—that they did not seem to have changed the Judahite way of life in any fundamental way (cf. Jeremiah)—and Josiah's untimely death at Megiddo were *the results of* Manasseh's irreversible provocation of Yahweh. Thus, Manasseh caused not only the fall of Jerusalem but also Josiah's impotence to forestall it beyond his own lifetime (Halpern, 492-93).

4. Manasseh and the Development of the Deuteronomistic History.
The account of Manasseh in 2 Kings 21:1-18 is significant for the understanding of the development of the *Deuteronomistic History. Many scholars speak of several editions of the history. A common element of these theories is the idea of one (or more) preexilic edition(s) and one exilic edition. In the particular case of the Manasseh narrative, most scholars regard 2 Kings 21:1-18 as a composite narrative, in part preexilic and in part exilic (Ben Zvi, 355-74; Halpern, 508-14; Eynikel, 233-61), while a few regard it as a unified whole composed by an exilic author (Keulen).

5. Literary Concerns.
In order to fully appreciate the Manasseh narrative of 2 Kings 21, we have to relate to it as an integral part of the entire Deuteronomistic History. Thus we detect that the narrator compares Manasseh with two sets of kings. First, the portrayal of Manasseh is contrasted by the description of the two Judahite kings *Hezekiah and Josiah. Manasseh's restoration of the older sacrificial places and their accompanied worship of deities other than Yahweh are thus consciously placed against the backdrop of Hezekiah's and Josiah's religious reforms favoring monolatrous worship of Yahweh. This polarization serves to categorize the kings of Judah into bad kings and good kings. Second, the narrator compares Manasseh with the two Israelite kings Jeroboam and Ahab. The aim of the first comparison is to portray Manasseh as responsible for the fall of Judah, just as Jeroboam is blamed for the fall of Israel. This comparison of the two events is thus part of a large-scale effort on behalf of the Deuteronomist to picture the fall of the two nations as caused by the kings' worship of foreign deities. Similarly, the aim of the comparison with Ahab is to portray Manasseh as an utterly wicked king and the idolater par excellence (Keulen, 144-60; Schniedewind, 649-61).

See also HISTORY OF ISRAEL 5: ASSYRIAN PERIOD; JOSIAH.

BIBLIOGRAPHY. **E. Ben Zvi,** "The Account of the Reign of Manasseh in II Reg 21.1-18 and the Redactional History of the Book of Kings," *ZAW* 103 (1991) 355-74; **J. H. Charlesworth,** "Manasseh, Prayer of," *ABD* 4:499-500; **E. Eynikel,** "The Portrait of Manasseh and the Deuteronomistic History," in *Deuternomy and Deuteronomic Literature*, ed. M. Vervenne and J. Lust (BETL 133; Leuven: Peeters, 1997) 233-61; **C. D. Evans,** "Judah's Foreign Policy from Hezekiah to Josiah," in *Scripture in Context. Essays on the Comparative Method*, ed. C. D. Evans, W. W. Hallo and J. B. White (PTMS 34; Pittsburgh: Pickwick Press, 1980) 157-78; **I. Finkelstein,** "The Archaeology of the Days of Manasseh," in *Scripture and Other Artifacts: Essays on the Bible and Archaeology in Honor of Philip J. King*, ed. M. D. Coogan, J. C. Exum and L. E. Stager (Louisville: Westminster John Knox, 1994) 169-87; **B. Halpern,** "Why Manasseh is Blamed for the Babylonian Exile: The Evolution of a Biblical Tradition," *VT* 48 (1998) 473-514; **P. S. F. Keulen,** *Manasseh Through the Eyes of the Deuteronomists* (OTS 38; Leiden: E. J. Brill, 1996); **R. Nelson,** "*Realpolitik* in Judah (687-609 B.C.E.)," in *Scripture in Context II: More Essays on the Comparative Method*, ed. W. W. Hallo J. C. Moyer and L. G. Perdue (Winona Lake, IN: Eisenbrauns, 1983) 177-89; **W. M. Schniedewind,** "History and Interpretation: The Religion of Ahab and Manasseh in the Book of Kings," *CBQ*

55 (1993) 649-61; idem, "The Source Citations of Manasseh: King Manasseh in History and Homily," *VT* 41 (1991) 450-61; **F. Stavrakopoulou,** *King Manasseh and Child Sacrifice* (BZAW 338; Berlin: Walter de Gruyter, 2004).

L.-S. Tiemeyer

MARDUK. *See* BABYLONIA, BABYLONIANS.

MASORETIC TEXT. *See* CANON; TEXT AND TEXTUAL CRITICISM.

MEGIDDO

The biblical city of Megiddo is situated on the mound of Tell el-Mutesellim in the Jezreel Valley, on the north side of the Carmel ridge. The center of an important city-state in the second millennium BCE, Megiddo later became a critical strategic and administrative city for the united monarchy under *Solomon and the northern kingdom of Israel that succeeded it. Following the conquest of northern Israel by the *Assyrians in the second half of the eighth century BCE, Megiddo became the capital of the local Assyrian province. Its position near the entrance to the Wadi Ara (Nahal Iron), which serves as the pass through the Carmel range for the Via Maris route from Egypt to Assyria, offers the site great strategic significance, and this was a critical factor during its long occupation from the Neolithic period in the sixth millennium until it was abandoned in the fourth century BCE.

1. Biblical References
2. Excavations
3. Middle Bronze Age (c. 2200-1550 BCE)
4. Late Bronze Age (c. 1550-1135 BCE)
5. Iron Age I (c. 1135-1000 BCE)
6. Iron Age II (c. 1000-732 BCE)
7. From the Assyrian Conquest to the Persian Period (Eighth to Fourth Centuries BCE)

1. Biblical References.
Megiddo is first mentioned in the Bible in Joshua 12:21 as one of the cities conquered by Joshua's army. Subsequently, in Joshua 17:11, the city was allotted to the tribe of Manasseh (1 Chron 7:29), although the *Canaanites were determined to keep living in Megiddo and other towns and were not driven out by the Israelites (Josh 17:12; Judg 1:27). A reference to "Taanach by the waters of Megiddo" in the Song of Deborah in Judges 5:19 probably refers to the river Kishon, which runs near to both sites.

During the reign of Solomon, Megiddo is listed in 1 Kings 4:12 as one of the towns in the administrative district of Baana son of Ahilud, and in 1 Kings 9:15, along with *Hazor and *Gezer, as one the royal cities built up by Solomon. Later, Megiddo is the scene of two famous deaths: Ahaziah, king of Judah, who retired to there to die after being wounded by Jehu during the latter's coup d'état against the house of Omri in Israel (2 Kings 9:27), and *Josiah, king of Judah, who opposed Pharaoh Neco's march to Carchemish to aid Assyria against *Babylon in 609 BCE and was killed in battle at Megiddo (2 Kings 23:29-30; 2 Chron 35:20-24).

A final postexilic reference is found in Zechariah 12:10, where the name occurs as "Megiddon," the form used later in the NT reference to Armageddon (Har-Megiddon) in Revelation 16:16.

2. Excavations.
Megiddo has been the subject of three major excavation projects and several lesser ones. The deep stratigraphy, long sequence and excellent preservation of the site have rendered it critical in the development of the Bronze and Iron Age stratigraphical sequence in Israel, but the archaeological interpretation of the site is also the subject of much controversy.

The first excavation at the tell was directed by G. Schumacher for the Deutscher Palästina-Verein from 1903 to 1905.

From 1925 to 1939 the site was excavated by the Oriental Institute at the University of Chicago. There were three directors—C. Fisher from 1925 to 1927, P. L. O. Guy from 1927 to 1934, G. Loud from 1935 to 1939—when the project was halted due to the outbreak of World War II. This expedition uncovered twenty occupational strata dating from the earliest settlement during the Neolithic period in the sixth millennium to the final abandonment of the mound in the fourth century BCE. The excavations were well published in several volumes that have become foundational in our understanding of Bronze Age and particularly Iron Age stratigraphy, pottery chronology and historical interpretation. However, the mix of directors produced differing interpretations on several key issues, laying the foundations for scholarly disagreement about dating and stratigraphy at the site for years to come.

Between 1960 and 1974 there were several

smaller projects by teams from the Hebrew University in Jerusalem that sought to clarify the results of the Chicago expedition. The most important of these were conducted between 1960 and 1972 by Y. Yadin, who investigated the Iron Age levels in the northeast and west of the mound.

Large-scale excavations were resumed at the site in 1992 by a team headed by I. Finkelstein and D. Ussishkin of Tel Aviv University and B. Halpern of Pennsylvania State University. The renewed excavations were initiated because of Megiddo's foundational role in the archaeology of the region, and because of the ongoing and unresolved controversies that exist about almost every layer and many of the most important architectural features at the site.

3. Middle Bronze Age (c. 2000-1550 BCE).

Following a period of urban decline, the Middle Bronze Age saw the rise of city-states in Canaan, many with close ties to Egypt. Megiddo grew gradually from a small village into a large, well-fortified and prosperous city-state. Prominent features of the Middle Bronze Age town were the city wall, built of mud-bricks on stone foundations, a prominent city gate in the north and a palace near the center of the mound.

Alongside the palace the cultic area, where there had been temples and a large, round, open-air altar in the Early Bronze Age, was transformed into an open paved area characterized by standing stones. Later, in the sixteenth century BCE, a large temple, Building 2048, was constructed in the same area. It was the most prominent building on the mound, built on a raised platform and having dimensions of 21.5 x 16.5 m. The walls were 4 m wide. Similar in design and appearance to its contemporary at *Shechem, Temple 2048 was built with a central axis entrance chamber flanked by two small rooms leading into a long rectangular hall with a shallow niche at the far end. Its many alterations during the five hundred or more years it was in use included raising the floor, converting the two rooms flanking the entrance into massive towers, and replacing the niche in the main hall with a platform. The temple stood at the heart of the city throughout the Late Bronze Age, although it is not clear whether it was finally destroyed with the rest of the city in Stratum VIIA in the twelfth century BCE, which seems likely, or if it continued into the rebuilt elev-

enth-century BCE town of Stratum VI (see 5).

4. Late Bronze Age (c. 1550-1135 BCE).

The sixteenth century BCE witnessed the expulsion of the Asiatic Hyksos kings from Egypt and the subsequent conquest of Canaan by the kings of the Eighteenth Dynasty, which came to power in their place. Tutmoses III (1479-1425 BCE) consolidated Egyptian control over Canaan around 1468 BCE by defeating a confederation of 119 Canaanite cities at Megiddo after their armies fled into the town and capitulated after a seven-month siege. The battle, one of the first great chariot battles in history, is recorded in detail on the walls of the temple of Amun at Karnak. The resulting Egyptian control of Megiddo lasted until the end of the Late Bronze Age.

During the fourteenth century BCE the city was ruled by Biridiya, according to the Amarna letters. Six letters from the king of Megiddo were found at Amarna, and they show that Megiddo was an important political center, ruling over nearby Taanach and having tense relations with other city-states such as Acco and especially Shechem.

The temple continued to dominate the city in the Late Bronze Age, but the location of the palace was moved to the northern edge of the mound, close to the city gate. Four successive palace structures were uncovered there, illustrating the gradual development of the Canaanite palace design. The final phase, dated to the twelfth century BCE, is particularly significant for the hoard of 328 ivories carved in local, Egyptian, Aegean, Assyrian and Hittite styles found in a basement annex.

The city gate at Megiddo, situated near the palace, was a four-chambered gate built with ashlar stones without foundations, and with wooden beams in the masonry to counter the effect of earthquakes. As was common in the Late Bronze Age, there appears to have been no wall around the city, even though the account of Tutmoses' seven-month siege appears to imply some sort of defensive perimeter. The Middle Bronze Age glacis still lay in place outside the line of the former wall, supplemented by the walls of the houses on the edge of the mound.

The city's destruction around 1135 BCE is well dated by two important finds from Level VIIA, the final Late Bronze Age stratum. A cartouche with the name of Ramesses III (1182-1151 BCE) was found in the ivory hoard in the palace, and the copper base of a statuette inscribed with the name of Ramesses VI (1141-1133 BCE) was found buried in a wall in a domestic area in the south of the town. The destruction was massive, with the city being looted and then razed.

5. Iron Age I (c. 1135-1000 BCE).

Following the great destruction of Stratum VIIA, a transitional settlement of poor-quality buildings and storage pits was succeeded by a larger, more impressive town in the eleventh century BCE. Characterized by densely built houses in the south, a palace in the north close to a reduced city gate, the city of Stratum VIA appears to have been a flourishing, prosperous town.

The Canaanite temple that dominated the city in the Bronze Age is thought by many scholars to have continued into the eleventh century BCE, due both to the absence in Stratum VI of any structure on the site of this temple in the excavation report and to the continuation of some of the pottery forms found on the Stratum VIIA temple floor into Stratum VI. On the other hand, the absence of any specifically eleventh-century BCE pottery, and especially the Sea Peoples pottery that is found elsewhere on the site in Stratum VIA, discourages any likelihood that Temple 2048 continued into the eleventh century BCE and supports the conclusion of the excavators that the temple was finally destroyed in Stratum VIIA.

Finds from this level that give an indication of its wealth include jewelry, metal objects and large quantities of painted pottery in the Canaanite tradition. Also found there were large quantities both of collared rim jars and Sea Peoples pottery, suggesting to some scholars the presence in the town of Israelites and Sea Peoples. However, although there may have been a cosmopolitan element to the settlement, Megiddo VIA, along with a similar settlement at Beth Shean a few miles away to the east, appears to represent a temporary resurgence of Canaanite independence in the Jezreel during the eleventh century BCE following the collapse of their culture a century before. This settlement is accurately reflected in Judges 1:27, which notes that although Megiddo was conquered, the Canaanites continued to live there. This revival did not last, however, and the Stratum VIA city was violently destroyed by fire, possibly by *David.

6. Iron Age II (c. 1000-732 BCE).

6.1. Stratum VA/IVB (Tenth Century BCE). A transitory, small, unfortified settlement dated to the first half of the tenth century BCE, the time of David, followed the destruction of the Stratum VIA city, and this in turn was followed by the impressive and controversial city of Stratum VA/IVB, generally attributed to Solomon. This stratum, not properly identified by the Chicago expedition but alluded to in their reports, was clarified by Yadin's exploratory excavations at the site in the 1960s and 1970s, and although his conclusions have become the generally accepted scholarly view, there are some notable alternative interpretations.

According to the traditional view, the Solomonic city was characterized by several impressive public structures, including two palaces, a large domestic building, a large administrative building adjacent to one of the palaces, a six-chamber city gate and its associated city wall, and a postern gate leading to the spring outside the tell.

Two palaces, numbered 6000 in the north of the city and 1723 in the south, illustrate the emergence of a royal Israelite architectural style, characterized by monumental architecture and ashlar masonry in particular (see 1 Kings 7:9-12). The northern palace was built according to a north Syrian design known as *bit hilani,* and the southern palace was built to a similar, if more complicated, plan. The biblical claims of strong *Phoenician influence in Solomon's royal buildings in Jerusalem (1 Kings 5) are reflected in the palaces and other public buildings of Megiddo Stratum VA/IVB. The southern palace was surrounded by a rectangular courtyard with a monumental gate in its north wall. Adjacent to it to the west was a large administrative building, numbered 1482.

6.2. The Question of the "Solomonic" Gate. In the north of the city, above and to the east of the Late Bronze Age Canaanite gate, stood the city gate of Stratum VA/IVB. It had six chambers (four entrances) with two large towers flanking the entrance. A smaller, outer gate and courtyard led to the six-chambered gate. It is similar in design and size to other gates from Hazor and Gezer (1 Kings 9:15), measuring 340 m^2. Like the palaces, it is built entirely of ashlar blocks. The Chicago expedition excavated an offset-inset wall, Wall 325, which they said was contemporary with the six-chambered gate. However, at Hazor and Gezer casemate walls adjoined the gates, and Yadin proposed that a similar wall should also be considered for the Solomonic level at Megiddo. According to Yadin (1972, 147-64), Wall 325 replaced the casemate wall in the next stratum, IVA.

Yadin's interpretation of Stratum VA/IVB has met with much criticism by a number of scholars. Until recently, most of the criticism has centered on the date of the city gate and its associated city wall. Yadin's proposal that there was a casemate wall that preceded the offset-inset wall was questioned, and his placing of the city gate itself in the tenth-century BCE level was rejected by some scholars, including Y. Aharoni (1972), A. Kempinski (91) and D. Ussishkin. Yadin had dated the gate to the earlier stratum, contrary to the Chicago excavators' report, by revising their interpretation of the foundation levels of the gate. Instead of the lower courses of ashlars being foundational, with the surface being higher up, Yadin proposed that the Solomonic gate, like the Late Bronze Age gate below it, had no foundations. It is unlikely, he said, that the builders would have used massive ashlars for the foundations below the floor level. If Yadin is correct, then the gate is earlier than the offset-inset wall, and either there was another wall, a casemate wall as Yadin proposed, or the city had no wall, as was the case in Stratum VI and in the Late Bronze Age.

6.3. I. Finkelstein's Lower Chronology and the "Solomonic" Level at Megiddo. In recent years I. Finkelstein, one of the directors of the renewed excavations, has sought to reinterpret the entire Iron Age pottery sequence in Israel by lowering the Iron Age dates by up to a century. This proposal has enormous implications not only for Megiddo, but also for the entire Iron Age archaeological and historical record.

According to Finkelstein's lower chronology, it is Stratum VI that should be dated to the period of David and Solomon in the tenth century BCE, and Stratum VA/IVB should be dated to the ninth century BCE. There are several elements to Finkelstein's reasoning for his lowering the Iron Age dates at Megiddo in this way. Among them are the presence of other six-chambered gates, such as at *Lachish and *Ashdod, with a similar design to those at Hazor, Megiddo and Gezer that are dated to the ninth and even eighth centuries BCE. Most significantly, Finkelstein argues that the pottery from Megiddo VA/IVB is similar to the pottery from the site of *Jezreel, which is more securely dated to the ninth century BCE.

He also observes that the offset-inset wall runs over the two palaces and therefore postdates them, so if the wall is contemporaneous with the six-chambered gate, then both must be later than the palaces. The latter point has already been dealt with by Yadin's proposal that the gate predates the offset-inset wall, while the former point about the correlation between the pottery of Jezreel and Stratum VA/IVB at Megiddo has been rejected by many scholars as an oversimplification (Mazar; Ben-Tor and Ben-Ami; Halpern, 427-78; Dever). Furthermore, although Finkelstein has claimed that radiocarbon dates from Megiddo support his point of view, new radiocarbon dates from Tel Rehov, a few miles to the east in the Jordan Valley, have offered clear support for the traditional dating (Bruins, van der Plicht and Mazar).

6.4. Religious Dualism in Shrine 2081. In the north of the Stratum VA/IVB city an assemblage of cultic artifacts was found in Locus 2081, a small niche in a courtyard that was part of a larger domestic building situated to the west of the gate area. The assemblage consists of over 120 items, many of which have clear cultic connotations. Among these are two limestone altars, possibly used for burning incense, two limestone offering stands and two stone stelae. Also in the niche was a large number of astragali, several of them worked. The larger altar and offering stand and the smaller altar and offering stand correspond in size to one another, as do the two stelae. It is likely that two deities, male and female, are represented in Shrine 2081, presenting at Megiddo a possible early manifestation of the dualism represented by the worship of Yahweh and his Asherah at Kuntillet ʿAjrud in the early eighth century BCE.

Stratum VA/IVB was destroyed violently by fire, probably by the Egyptian Pharaoh Shishak (Sheshonq), whose campaign in Israel around 925 BCE is described in detail on the walls of the temple of Amun at Karnak and is alluded to in 1 Kings 14:26. Megiddo is one of the cities listed in the Egyptian inscription of the campaign, and a fragment of a stela found at the site with Shishak's cartouche carved on it appears to confirm his presence there.

6.5. Stratum IVA (Ninth and Eighth Centuries BCE). Stratum IVA is generally dated from the ninth century BCE, when the northern kingdom of Israel was ruled by the house of Omri, to the Assyrian conquest in 732 BCE. Megiddo was a fortified military city during this period, surrounded by offset-inset Wall 325. A new four-chambered gate was built over the Solomonic gate. An impressive *water system was constructed in the west, one of several around the country from this period. It consisted of a vertical shaft cut through earlier levels and deep into the bedrock to the level of the spring, which was reached by a horizontal tunnel some 50 m long.

The most impressive of the military structures on the tell were two stable compounds in the north and south of the site. The southern complex was augmented by a large open space that probably served as an exercise yard in front of the stables. Their design was a multifunctional one that occurs frequently in Israelite buildings from the period of the monarchy, each unit consisting of three long rooms divided by pillars. These buildings have been variously interpreted in different contexts as storehouses, barracks and markets, but at Megiddo their identification as stables seems secure due to the presence of tethering holes and mangers in between the pillars. Furthermore, Ahab is known from the annals of the Assyrian king Shalmaneser III to have had two thousand chariots that fought at the Battle of Karkar in 853 BCE. A large grain silo in the center of the city may have been a food storage facility for the horses.

7. From the Assyrian Conquest to the Persian Period (Eighth to Fourth Centuries BCE).

The northern part of the kingdom of Israel was annexed in 732 BCE by the Assyrian king Tiglath Pileser III (known as Pul in 2 Kings 15:19, 29; 1 Chron 5:26) after a violent campaign that included the partial destruction and capture of Megiddo. The region was transformed into the Assyrian province of Magiddu, with Megiddo its new capital. The town was completely rebuilt on a new plan, with Wall 325 being one of the few surviving elements of the Israelite city. A new two-chambered gate was built over its four-chambered predecessor, and many of the new buildings have distinctive Assyrian architectural features.

The Assyrian city, Stratum III, was not destroyed when the Assyrian Empire declined and eventually fell to the Babylonians in the seventh century BCE, but rather evolved into Stratum II. This town, poorly preserved due to its proximity to the surface of the mound, consisted largely of domestic buildings laid out on the same basic city plan as its predecessor, and many of the Assyrian buildings were reused. It was in this city that King Josiah died after his battle with Pharaoh Neco in 609 BCE (2 Kings 23:29-30; 2 Chron 35:20-24).

Few remains survived of the last settlement at Megiddo, Stratum I, which appears to date to the Babylonian and Persian periods from the sixth to the fourth centuries BCE. The mound was abandoned during the fourth century BCE, possibly due to Alexander the Great's conquest of the region in 332 BCE.

See also JEZREEL.

BIBLIOGRAPHY. **Y. Aharoni,** "The Stratification of Israelite Megiddo," *JNES* 31 (1972) 302-11; **P. Beck,** "The Drawings from Hurvat Teiman (Kuntillet ʿAjrud)," *TA* 9 (1982) 3-68; **A. Ben-Tor and D. Ben-Ami,** "Hazor and the Archaeology of the Tenth Century B.C.E.," *IEJ* 48 (1998) 1-37; **H. J. Bruins, J. van der Plicht and A. Mazar,** "14C Dates from Tel Rehov: Iron-Age Chronology, Pharaohs, and Hebrew Kings," *Science* 300 (April 11, 2003) 315-18; **G. I. Davies,** *Megiddo* (Cambridge: Lutterworth, 1986); **W. G. Dever,** "Histories and Non-Histories of Ancient Israel: The Question of the United Monarchy," in *In Search of Pre-Exilic Israel: Proceedings of the Oxford Old Testament Seminar,* ed. J. Day (JSOTSup 406; London: T & T Clark International, 2004) 65-94; **D. L. Esse,** "The Collared Pithos at Megiddo: Ceramic Distribution and Ethnicity," *JNES* 51 (1992) 81-103; **I. Finkelstein,** "The Archaeology of the United Monarchy: An Alternative View," *Levant* 28 (1996) 177-87; idem, "The Stratigraphy and Chronology of Megiddo and Beth-Shan in the 12th-11th Centuries B.C.E.," *TA* 23 (1996) 170-84; **I. Finkelstein and N. A. Silberman,** *The Bible Unearthed: Archaeology's New Vision of Ancient Israel and the Origin of Its Sacred Texts* (New York: Free Press, 2001); **I. Finkelstein, D. Ussishkin and B. Halpern,** eds., *Megiddo III: The 1992-1996 Seasons* (2 vols.; Tel Aviv: Emery and Claire Yass Publications in Archaeology, Institute of Archaeology, Tel Aviv University, 2000); **C. S. Fisher,** *The Excavation of Armageddon* (OIC 4; Chicago: University of Chicago Press, 1929); **P. L. O. Guy,** *New Light from Armageddon* (OIC 9; Chicago: University of Chicago Press, 1934); idem, *Megiddo Tombs* (OIC 33; Chicago: University of Chicago Press, 1938); **B. Halpern,** *David's Secret Demons: Messiah, Murderer, Traitor, King* (Grand Rapids: Eerdmans, 2001); **T. P. Harrison,** "The Battleground: Who Destroyed

Megiddo? Was It David or Shishak?" *BAR* 29.5 (2003) 28-35, 60-64; idem, *Megiddo 3: Final Report on the Stratum VI Excavations* (OIC 127; Chicago: University of Chicago Press, 2004); **A. Kempinski,** *Megiddo: A City-State and Royal Centre in North Israel* (Munich: Beck, 1989); **R. S. Lamon and G. Shipton,** *Megiddo I: Seasons of 1925-34, Strata I-V* (OIC 42; Chicago: University of Chicago Press, 1939); **G. Loud,** *The Megiddo Ivories* (OIC 52; Chicago: University of Chicago Press, 1939); idem, *Megiddo II: Seasons of 1935-39* (OIC 62; Chicago: University of Chicago Press, 1948); **H. G. May,** *Material Remains of the Megiddo Cult* (OIC 26; Chicago: University of Chicago Press, 1935); **A. Mazar,** "Iron Age Chronology: A Reply to I. Finkelstein," *Levant* 29 (1997) 157-67; **G. Schumacher,** *Tell el-Mutesellim I: Fundbericht* (Leipzig: R. Haupt 1908); **D. Ussishkin,** "Megiddo," *OEANE* 3.460-69; **C. Watzinger,** *Tell el-Mutesellim II: Die Funde* (Leipzig: Hinrichs, 1929); **Y. Yadin,** *Hazor, with a Chapter on Israelite Megiddo* (Schweich Lectures; London: Oxford University Press, for the British Academy, 1972); idem, "Megiddo and the Kings of Israel," *BA* 33 (1970) 66-96.   G. Gilmour

MELQUART STELA. *See* ARAM, DAMASCUS AND SYRIA.

MENAHEM. *See* HISTORY OF ISRAEL 5: ASSYRIAN PERIOD.

MERCHANTS. *See* TRADE AND TRAVEL.

MERNEPTAH STELA. *See* ISRAEL.

MESHA INSCRIPTION. *See* DAVID; MOAB, MOABITES; NON-ISRAELITE WRITTEN SOURCES: SYRO-PALESTINIAN.

MESSIANISM. *See* DAVID; KINGS AND KINGSHIP.

METHODS OF INTERPRETATION

Why do we need "methods" for reading the Bible? Although interpretation always begins with expectations and hunches, readers devoted to understanding Scripture recognize the necessity of sharpening interpretive practices and of developing more informed understandings of the Bible itself, its origins and its implications. This article briefly surveys the history of development of biblical interpretation and some of the uses that various interpretive questions have found

in relation to the books of Joshua through Nehemiah.

1. Introduction
2. Traditional Reading
3. Historical-Critical Method
4. Literary Approaches

1. Introduction.
Daniel Patte has distinguished three modes, or levels, of scriptural interpretation. The first, which he calls "ordinary reading," is intuitive and personal, a moment of insight about a passage. Such ordinary reading is operative for scholars and nonscholars, experienced and inexperienced readers alike. The second level of reading is a "self-conscious systematic study of the text and of its features" (Patte, 88) aimed at substantiating or developing what was noted in the first-level, intuitive reading. Disciplined exegetical study is second-level reading. The third level, which Patte criticizes, is the claim that what the reader has found in the text is the only way to read it correctly. It is to assert, "My interpretation has exhausted all possible features of this passage, and no interpretation that disagrees with mine can be valid." The history of biblical interpretation in all its variety demonstrates that no interpretation, nor any interpretive method, can seriously claim such a monopoly on Scripture. At the same time, the Bible yields willingly, perhaps even eagerly, to systematic study along a variety of interpretive lines.

Over two thousand years of biblical interpretation have produced a dizzying array of interpretive methods, deriving from a variety of insights about what biblical literature *is*, and therefore about what it should be read *as*. Although exegetes differ in their emphases and preferences, few exegetical methods are mutually exclusive, and a broad eclecticism reigns. The challenge for many students of the Bible is to keep the exegetical toolbox orderly enough to recognize which tools are useful for which purposes. This can be difficult because so many methods are available, some methods overlap and the same method functions differently depending upon who is using it. A useful schema for mapping exegetical method was offered by M. H. Abrams, who suggested that there are four basic elements involved in any work of art. First, there is the work, or text, itself. Second, there is the work's creator. Third, there is what the text refers to, which Abrams most broadly calls the "universe." Fourth, there is the audience, or readers. Abrams places the "work" in the center of a diagram, with the three other elements arranged around it. He says, "Although any reasonably adequate theory [of interpretation] takes some account of all four elements, almost all theories . . . exhibit a discernible orientation towards one only" (Abrams, 6). Interpretive theories can be roughly categorized as principally oriented toward the text itself, toward the author and author's immediate setting, toward the world to which the text refers, or toward the readers or audience.

Contemporary scholars tend to schematize the history of biblical interpretation into three rough paradigms reflecting the interests of the eras in which they arose. The first of these is variously called "traditional" or "premodern" or "precritical" biblical interpretation, and it encompasses the reading strategies found in Christian and Jewish communities from the beginnings of scriptural interpretation until the eighteenth century. The second, a conglomerate of related methods collectively called "historical criticism," arose around the beginning of the nineteenth century and dominated biblical interpretation until recently. The third is too new to define categorically. Usually it is viewed as a literary paradigm, although its range of interest has been widening over the past two decades. In general, it is characterized by a range of interpretive methods that retain the insights learned by historical-critical scholarship while, like premodern reading, focusing interpretive attention on the canonical (or "final") form of biblical books rather than on the history behind them.

The order and placement of the books Joshua through Nehemiah in the Jewish and Christian *canons shows distinctive understandings. The designation "Historical Books" is a traditional Christian category reflecting the ordering that developed in the Greek Septuagint and the Latin Vulgate Bibles, in which the books narrating events in the life of ancient Israel and Judah were grouped together, along with Ruth and Esther, before the poetic books of Job, Psalms and Proverbs. The Catholic canon also includes the books of Tobit and Judith and sometimes 1-2 Maccabees among the Historical Books.

The Jewish canon, however, probably is more reflective of the books' original groupings and the order of their reception as Scripture. There, *Joshua, *Judges, 1-2 *Samuel and 1-2 *Kings stand in unbroken sequence as the Former Prophets. These are followed immediately by the Latter Prophets: Isaiah, Jeremiah, Ezekiel and the Twelve. Together, the Former and the Latter Prophets comprise the second section of the Jewish Bible, the *Nevi'im*, or Prophets. The remaining books are found in the third division, the *Ketuvim*, or Writings, which begins with Psalms and ends with Ezra, Nehemiah and 1-2 Chronicles, in that order.

These differences in placement and designation clearly affect interpretation. The term "Historical Books" suggests to many readers that the books ought to be understood according to modern genres of history-writing. Such an idea obscures both the differences between ancient and modern *historiography and the generic differences among individual books. Care must be taken to seek clues in the contents of each book to what its theological purposes might be.

2. Traditional Reading.

Until the beginning of the Enlightenment there was widespread agreement that the Bible reflected more or less transparently the events of Israel's history as they occurred. In that sense, biblical interpretation was mimetic, or oriented toward understanding the world reflected in the text. Scripture was not viewed as mere historical record, however, but as divine words speaking through human events rather directly to the concerns of contemporary readers. Although interpreters made little distinction between the text, the world to which it referred, and God as its divine author, for much of traditional interpretive history most interpretation was reader-oriented—that is, its primary aim was to serve the spiritual needs of the community for which it was produced, and especially, to borrow from Cicero's discussion of rhetoric, to teach and to persuade.

Certain problems have prevailed throughout Scripture's history of interpretation. For Jewish interpreters capable both of reading *Hebrew and of perceiving in a relatively direct way the continuity between ancient Israel and the Jewish worshiping community, temporal, geographical and social distance nevertheless presented challenges. For Christian interpreters these challenges multiplied, first because Gentile Christians from earliest times had to read the

OT in translation, and second because as a diverse group with lineages, histories, worship practices and theological assumptions different from those of the OT writers, Christians have had more challenges than have Jews in perceiving direct continuities between ancient Judah and their own communities. Out of the disjunctions perceived between ancient texts and later readers a variety of reading strategies developed to help ferret out the divine message that worshipers expected from Scripture.

Especially in the church's early centuries, reading strategies for connecting the Christian gospel with the story of Israel tended toward a degree of creative license that later was rejected by most interpreters. After the repudiation of Marcion's second-century notion that the OT and its God had nothing to do with Christianity, patristic scholars worked hard to justify the cohesion between their theological understandings and ancient Scripture, tending especially toward a hermeneutic of prediction-fulfillment (in which OT passages were viewed as predictions of Christ or the church), allegory (in which each element of a passage was seen as a symbol for an element in Christian theology), or the milder alternative to both of these, typological interpretation, which did not deny the historical significance of the texts or the events they described, but perceived additional meanings, unforeseen by the original writers, to which these events pointed. Typological exegesis is based on the idea of coherence and repetition of themes in history. Because it affirms both the meaningfulness of events or words in their own time and their reactualized import for subsequent generations, typological interpretation continued to enjoy credibility in preaching and interpretation long after allegorical and prediction-fulfillment hermeneutics became unpopular.

The conviction that Scripture could be read profitably on more than one level at once led both Jews and Christians to theories about literal and homiletical senses of Scripture. Among rabbinical scholars these often were expressed in terms of *peshat* (plain meaning) and *derash* (a more creative development of stories and other information to address readers' legal, ethical or theological concerns). Among Christians various theories of multiple "senses" of Scripture were offered, with distinctions made among, for instance, literal, moral and spiritual interpretations of the same texts.

3. Historical-Critical Method.

In the Middle Ages, in response to a number of factors, including contact with learned Arab classicists, the rise of sects among both Jews and Christians who aspired to read Scripture more literally, the advent of the university as a center of inquiry, and the practice of theological disputations between differing groups, more stress came to be laid on philological and grammatical study of Scripture. Christians had been reading Scripture almost solely in translation. In locations where Jewish-Christian relations allowed, Christian scholars began to study both Hebrew and rabbinic interpretation. By the fifteenth century, with the advent of the printing press and the availability of multiple translations, as well as grammars and lexicons, critical study of the Bible became much easier for Christians.

The Enlightenment brought to Europe an increased appreciation for Scripture as ancient literature written in a very different social world. Critical method in biblical interpretation emerged, especially among Protestants, as an attempt to take the historical dimensions of Scripture seriously by grappling with the problems of factual and historical consistency that had been perceived in them from earliest times. What came to be known as historical-critical method focused attention on the world behind the text, aiming to reconstruct Scripture's origins. Primary modes of historical study include textual criticism (sometimes called "lower criticism") and source, form and redaction criticism (collectively called "higher criticism"). Related to these have been reconstructions of Israelite history and culture with the aid of archaeology and the social sciences.

3.1. Textual Criticism.
Textual criticism (*see* Text and Textual Criticism) is based on the recognition that various ancient manuscripts and translations of the Bible differ with one another, sometimes substantially. Since the original documents penned by biblical writers no longer exist, our only clues to their wording are the copies of copies, the oldest extant manuscripts dating from several centuries after composition. Textual critics seek to reconstruct, on the basis of variant readings, the wording of each verse of the biblical text. As will be seen below, because many biblical books developed over time at the hands of various redactors (editors), and because scribes continued to amend the text as they were copying, the boundary line between

redaction and transmission, and the nature of the "original" manuscript, is a more complex issue than it may at first seem. Still, textual critics operate on the assumptions that each verse of Scripture originally made sense, and that where it appears unintelligible, accidental corruption may have occurred. Sometimes it is fairly easy to reconstruct a passage. For instance, in 1 Samuel 10:21 a phrase that dropped out of the Hebrew text can be reconstructed from the Greek Septuagint. Other times a problem clearly has occurred, but no easy solution is available, such as at 1 Samuel 13:1, in which the Hebrew text says, "Saul was one year old when he began to reign, and he reigned two years over Israel." Here the Septuagint translators, perhaps recognizing a problem they could not solve, omitted the verse entirely. Modern translations cope with this verse in a variety of ways, some guessing and others leaving an ellipsis to indicate the problem.

Textual criticism developed over the course of the nineteenth and twentieth centuries, especially as many hitherto unknown biblical manuscripts came to light, and as archaeologists discovered libraries of clay tablets and monumental inscriptions in the Middle East. Growing success in deciphering these texts and learning to read long-forgotten Semitic languages such as Akkadian and Ugaritic has added greatly to modern knowledge of both Hebrew and the Bible's literary conventions. The single most important development was the discovery of ancient scrolls along the Dead Sea beginning in 1947. These finds have proven a tremendous help in reconstructing difficult passages, especially in the textually problematic books of Samuel.

3.2. Source, Form and Redaction Criticism. These methods originated in somewhat different time periods and from discrete insights about the Bible's history. The three emphases, however, are so deeply interrelated that in practice they are difficult to separate.

3.2.1. Source Criticism. Although the Pentateuch makes no claims about its own authorship, centuries of Jewish and Christian tradition attributed it to Moses. Source criticism of the OT began with attempts to make sense of inconsistencies in facts, names and writing style within the Pentateuch (*see DOTP,* Source Criticism; Pentateuchal Criticism, History of). These inconsistencies came to be accounted for by recognizing

that unlike modern books, many biblical books were assembled over the course of generations by multiple authors.

Throughout the Bible's interpretive history, surprisingly modern questions had been raised about authorship and sources. What was revolutionary in the eighteenth century was the growing freedom to follow these questions where they logically led, unfettered by traditional but finally unsatisfactory assumptions. Early source critics wondered how Moses could have written such a strange and complex document as the Pentateuch, changing style frequently, referring to his own time as if it were already ancient history, adding contradictory facts, writing about himself in the third person, reporting his own death, and commenting that he himself was the humblest man on the face of the earth (Num 12:3). By the end of the nineteenth century these and many other accumulated observations had been forged into the Graf-Wellhausen Documentary Hypothesis, which presented the Pentateuch as four interwoven strands of tradition from various periods from the time of the Israelite monarchy to that of the Persian Empire.

Convictions about the authorship of the Historical Books have not been so firmly embedded in tradition. Frequent internal references to source texts (see, e.g., Josh 10:13; 2 Sam 1:18; 1 Kings 11:41; 1 Chron 9:1) seem to invite inquiry into the books' composition history (*see* Sources, References to). Early attempts to trace pentateuchal strands into Joshua and other books proved unsuccessful, but M. Noth's theory of the Deuteronomistic Historian has, with some refinements, achieved considerable consensus (*see* Deuteronomistic History). According to Noth, a single writer or school used a variety of sources to develop an account of the history of Judah and neighboring Israel from their entrance into the promised land up to the Babylonian exile. This account, closely related to the theology of Deuteronomy and characterized by periodic Deuteronomistic speeches in the mouths of Israel's leaders, was written to make sense of Judah's loss of the land. The most important refinement to Noth's theory was that of F. M. Cross, who suggested a double redaction of the Deuteronomistic History, the first coinciding with King Josiah's evidently Deuteronomic reforms and presenting his reign as the culmination of Israel's national formation, and the second an exilic update accounting for the loss of the land despite Josiah's reforms.

Inquiry into the development of the source texts out of which the Deuteronomistic History was woven has yielded some consensus and much debate. For instance, L. Rost's view of the story of King *David's family in 2 Samuel 9—20 and 1 Kings 1—2 as a continuous narrative by a single author achieved considerable agreement in some respects, especially regarding the differences between this strand and four chapters (2 Sam 21—24) embedded within it. But the narrative evidently has been so skillfully woven into the preceding episodes that there has been little agreement on the point at which this storyline begins. Nor has there been widespread agreement on its original purpose or date.

3.2.2. Form Criticism. Recognition of the variety of materials woven together in the biblical narratives, including not only reports of events, but also poems, songs, sayings, lists, genealogies and formulaic repetitions, began in the late nineteenth century to raise the question of genre. What kinds of writings are these various building blocks? From what social situations do they emerge, and for what reasons? What conventions surround their use? These questions are addressed by form criticism, which analyzes the genres underlying individual passages, and the function of these genres in Israelite society. Although form criticism has not played as prominent a role in the study of the Historical Books as it has in critical work on the Pentateuch, Psalms and Prophets, it certainly has helped scholars ask more precise questions about what the narratives themselves intend to communicate.

For instance, form criticism has clarified the differing viewpoints and purposes in individual narratives of the book of *Judges, which often are striking for their irony and even humor, in contrast to the Deuteronomistic narrative framework that organizes the stories into episodes that repeatedly illustrate a theological point: Israel's recurrent backsliding and punishment, followed by cries for help and divine deliverance. While the fanciful details of some stories, with the judges' varied and often dubious leadership credentials, seem to approach the realm of traditional folk narrative, suggesting that they once circulated independently, they now appear in a narrative framework with a very different agenda. Attention to these formal differences and the purposes that these stories may have

had before their inclusion in the Deuteronomistic storyline helps interpreters make historical sense of the shifts in narrative voice throughout the book of Judges.

3.2.3. Redaction Criticism. Early source critics often sought to uncover and imbue with theological authority the materials that they viewed as original writings from independent sources, untouched by redactional hands. But by the mid-twentieth century interest in the redactors of the biblical texts as creative theologians in their own right arose from the realization that composition and redaction simply could not be viewed as discrete processes. Emerging awareness of ancient writing practices (*see* Writing, Writing Practices and Literacy in the Ancient Near East), in which literary texts such as the Babylonian *Enuma Elish* were continuously subject to the redactional work of their copyists, also helped scholars recognize how thin was the line between composing and editing. The introduction of redaction criticism brought in its wake a renewed interest in the final form of the text as a theological and literary product displaying conventions that do not necessarily correspond to modern sensibilities.

The difference between ancient and modern sensibilities is illustrated by the fact that redactional "seams" often are left in full view of the readers rather than being obscured by more intensive editing. David, for instance, meets Saul for the first time twice, once as a musician recommended for a royal job by Saul's servant (1 Sam 16:14-23), and once again as a young warrior who volunteers to fight Goliath (1 Sam 17:12-58). Some earlier historical critics condescendingly attributed such doublets to the primitiveness of biblical writers, while some biblical inerrantists, also troubled by such phenomena, took pains to explain the difficulties away. More recently it has been suggested that the aesthetics of biblical narrative do not necessarily match modern expectations, and that a skillful interweaving of multiple facets of the story may have been achieved by juxtaposing more than one narrative for the same event (*see* Narrative Art of Israel's Historians).

Recognition of redactors as biblical composers becomes especially salient in the renewed interest in *Chronicles, which had been devalued not only in historical-critical scholarship, but also throughout Jewish and Christian history, largely because of the perception that it rewrites what was considered the more accurate historiography of its parent narrative, Samuel and Kings. But Chronicles' reuse of scriptural material offers a fascinating study in the development of biblical compositions. In recent times Chronicles has been viewed as a theological tour de force with its own inner logic of midrashic harmonization.

3.3. Historical and Cultural Reconstruction. Historical critics have long considered reconstruction of Israel's history a prerequisite for contextualizing biblical texts to understand better their original intents. Indeed, nineteenth-century biblical interpretation benefited from revolutionary insights such as the association of Deuteronomy with King Josiah, and the association of much pentateuchal worship law with the Persian period's second temple rather than Moses' tabernacle. These insights helped account for the evident lack of familiarity in Judges, Samuel and Kings with many pentateuchal laws and narratives, and the keen attention given to them in later books such as Chronicles, Ezra and Nehemiah.

3.3.1. Archaeology. *Archaeology has tremendously affected historical study of the Bible. Until after Napoleon's invasion of Egypt in 1798, European Christians knew little about antiquity or even about the existence of some Near Eastern civilizations buried under the residue of time. With the discovery of ancient Egyptian, Mesopotamian, Canaanite and Israelite cities and artifacts, and the finding and translating of thousands of documents, an impressively detailed reconstruction of the history, culture and literature of regions surrounding Israel emerged. Among the most interesting finds have been stories from Ugarit of Canaanite gods such as El and Baal, both of whom made their way into the Bible (*see* Canaanite Gods and Religion). Such documents, as well as the finding of worship sites and household deities, help scholars make more sense of biblical discussions of heterodox religious practices.

Although archaeological work has given us a much clearer picture of the ancient world, it also has presented unprecedented historical conundrums. Earlier readers were able to take at face value the biblical accounts of persons, wars, conquests and territorial holdings. Archaeological findings not only have failed to confirm some accounts, but also have uncovered contrary evidence. Understandably, the stories of earlier

events, those farthest in time from their actual recording, have been most challenged by the discoveries, while later events, especially from the eighth century BCE on, have found more agreement with the records of neighboring nations and material evidence from Israelite archaeological sites. To cite well-known examples from either end of the Deuteronomistic History, the story of conquest in Joshua remembers *Jericho and *Ai as large Canaanite cities destroyed by the Israelites. But archaeologists have discovered that neither locale was more than a small, unwalled settlement at that time, and no destruction layers correlate with the biblical accounts. These problems, along with other information drawn from both archaeology and biblical interpretation, have given rise to several interesting but as yet contested reconstructions of the origin of Israel in Palestine, reconstructions more congruent with parts of Joshua and Judges that describe partial and gradual occupation of the land (*see* History of Israel 1: Settlement Period). On the other hand, correspondences have been found between narratives in Kings and findings such as inscriptions bearing names of Israelite and non-Israelite personages, and destruction layers of prominent cities of Israel and Judah, especially in the eighth to the sixth centuries BCE. Some evidence is ambiguous; for instance, the account by the Assyrian king Sennacherib of his siege of Jerusalem during *Hezekiah's reign corresponds to that found in 2 Kings 18—19 in its general contours but not in the details, suggesting perhaps some careful wording on both sides regarding an event in which neither side won a decisive victory (*see* History of Israel 5: Assyrian Period).

3.3.2. Social-Scientific Analysis. Contemporary archaeological work has moved more into the realm of cultural reconstruction, attending to settlement patterns, *agricultural methods, technologies and societal structures. Closely related to this effort, and often utilizing its discoveries, is *social-scientific analysis, an approach that has been invoked especially in reconstruction of the emergence of Israel as a nation in Canaan. An early beginning in the study of Israel's origin was that of sociologist M. Weber, who described premonarchic Israel as seminomadic and agricultural groups loosely federated by a common covenant, who could be summoned for military ventures by charismatic leaders. Under Weber's influence, A. Alt theorized that Israel was a nomadic tribe that infiltrated, rather than conquered, the land of Canaan, occupying the highlands and hinterlands before challenging the city-states of Canaan. Nearly forty years later, G. Mendenhall connected the *Hebrews with the troublesome "Habiru" mentioned in the fourteenth-century BCE Amarna letters exchanged between Egypt and its territories in Palestine, and viewed Israel's origins in terms of a "peasant's revolt" of village-dwelling native people against wealthier oppressors living in the cities, a revolt galvanized by the new religion of Yahwism that was brought from the Transjordan by a small band of escapees from Egypt. Enlarging on Mendenhall's ideas, N. Gottwald theorized that the emergence of Israel in the hill country was at least partially due to advances in farming technology, and that Israelite society was based on sociopolitical egalitarianism united by worship of a common god, El. The military power of this group increased as it attracted disaffected peasants from the Canaanite city-states, and Yahwist groups joining them from Egypt provided a religious story of origins. Eventually, as Israel grew more powerful, it was able to wrest control of the land from the Canaanites.

These attempts to address physical evidence as well as the biblical story by using sociological theories have demonstrated some of the possible alternative outlines of Israel's origins, and they have been applauded for valiant efforts to wring understanding from the ambiguous evidence available. No doubt, as reconstructive methods are refined, this line of discussion will continue. At the same time, some scholars deny that enough information exists to construct any reliable story of Israel. This is an area in dispute at present, with some scholars continuing to "maximalize" the relationships between historical events and scriptural historiography, and various "minimalist" theorists placing little faith in the Bible's historical reliability. Most scholars place themselves somewhere between these two extremes, recognizing that all historiography, including the Bible's, involves interpretation from a particular viewpoint, and yet that there is little reason to doubt the basic contours of the story of the monarchies as presented in Kings (*see* Quest of the Historical Israel).

Historical criticism continues to flourish. Whereas early historical critics confidently sought meaning in the reconstructed events lying behind Scripture itself, many contemporary scholars are more reserved about what claims can be made about a world that is millennia away from us. At the same time, recognition of the temporal and cultural differences has increased awareness that anything that can be known about the world of the Bible's origin can help us to understand better the events and themes that the ancient theologians were treating. For instance, C. Meyers's study *Discovering Eve: Ancient Israelite Women in Context* makes use of archaeology and anthropology to reconstruct the lives of ordinary women in the highland villages of premonarchic Israel and to describe their societal and household roles. Her work delineates the subsistence work of families, demonstrating the interdependence of men and women before the monarchy usurped local life, eroding the status of women. The tasks facing families in early Israel, she suggests, included clearing the dry and rocky land for agriculture and producing children to help with the farming tasks and to replenish a population decimated by disease. She offers an interpretation of Genesis 2—3 highlighting the pressing but culturally specific realities reflected in the Eden story.

4. Literary Approaches.
The latter part of the twentieth century saw an explosion of theories and insights about the Bible as written text, and about the writing and reading processes themselves. Apart from social-scientific methods as mentioned above, most new interpretive developments foreground Scripture itself, in the form in which it was stabilized canonically, rather than the history of the community behind the text or the history of the text's composition.

When literary analysis first emerged, many scholars—both those who favored this new movement and those who did not—viewed its interests as inimical to those of historical criticism, since historical work digs past the surface of the text to factors lying behind it, follows the logic of chronology, and revels in breaking the text into component parts, while literary work focuses on the textual surface, follows the logic of narrative, and revels in the text's fullness. But attempts to present historical and literary methods as being fundamentally at odds with each other have proven fallacious because on the one hand, only Scripture's final form is actually available for historical critics to study, and on the other hand, literary criticism depends on some amount of historical spadework in order to comprehend the customs, context and even language of the biblical texts. Although some literary approaches at first tried to dispense with historical contextualization, postmodern and reader-oriented perspectives have reintroduced the intersection between diachronic and synchronic approaches.

4.1. Text-Eminent Perspectives.

4.1.1. Literary Criticism and Narrative Analysis. In the nineteenth and early twentieth centuries "literary criticism" was a synonym for "source criticism." But the former term now is used in a very different way. The current practice owes its origin in large part to a movement called "new criticism," which emerged in the 1940s among interpreters of Western novels and poetry. New criticism, which according to Abrams's scheme (see 1 above) draws attention to the text itself, arose in reaction to an excessively biographical focus on the author as a key to a text's interpretation. New criticism proceeds from the understanding that the meaning of a literary text is best derived from a close reading of the text itself rather than from an inquiry (based, for instance, on personal correspondence) into what the author intended to write. Once written, texts take on a life of their own, and they ought to be interpreted as artifacts, not primarily as communications from an author.

Perhaps because most biblical scholars in the mid-twentieth century were historians and linguists, new criticism had become old by the time it fully entered biblical scholarship in the 1970s. Literary interpretation of the Bible began with the perception that biblical narratives, far from being simple transcriptions of events or primitive folktales, display a surprising literary sophistication that can be better perceived when readers trust the writers' artistic control and seek to infer the conventions of these ancient genres (*see* Narrative Art of Israel's Historians). Although useful relationships may be drawn between, for instance, modern fiction and biblical stories, since both employ character development, dialogue, narrator, time and tempo, and so on, biblical narratives do not necessarily follow the conventions of Western literature. Frequent repetition of words or even whole phrases, long considered a sign of primitiveness, actually seems to signal motifs, similarities and differences among characters' viewpoints, as well as subtle, sometimes ironic distinctions be-

tween the narrator's perspective and those of the characters. Attention to the closely packed details of sustained narratives has yielded both a greater appreciation for Scripture's literary qualities and a greater attention to the import of the biblical stories themselves.

A precursor of literary interpretation among biblical scholars was an essay by E. Auerbach in which he compared the storytelling techniques of a chapter in Homer's *Odyssey* with the near sacrifice of Isaac in Genesis 22. This comparison allowed him to point out the literary sophistication in the Genesis story's sparse and reticent style, which draws readers into the drama of what is said and left unsaid. Not long after, form critic J. Muilenburg's work on Isaiah led him to assert that attention must be paid not only to what is typical in a biblical text, but also to a text's unique expressions. He coined the term "rhetorical criticism" (see 4.1.4 below) as a subdiscipline within form criticism. P. Trible, one of Muilenburg's students, extended his suggestions much further, developing close readings of the literary features of texts. Her *Texts of Terror: Literary-Feminist Readings of Biblical Narratives* retells four stories of violence against women, mostly from Judges and Samuel, using narrative details to uncover critiques of patriarchy within the biblical stories themselves.

The early 1980s saw an explosion of interest in literary analysis of Scripture. R. Alter and A. Berlin sought to describe the conventions of biblical narrative as they could be inferred from close analysis, noting such phenomena as the compactness of narrative descriptions, the development of characters through contrastive actions and speech patterns, and the use of the narrative "eye" as a camera lens focused on what the narrator wished the audience to see. These and other works redirecting critical attention to the biblical texts themselves revealed a rich potential that was quickly and enthusiastically mined by many scholars writing especially about the lengthy narrative complexes in 1-2 Samuel. Important contributors include, among many others, M. Sternberg, C. Exum, J. P. Fokkelman and D. M. Gunn.

4.1.2. Structuralism. Structuralism and structuralist exegesis, like the literary work described above, focuses on the text in isolation from its author and the world that it describes. It seeks embedded structures and systems of relationships of which even the author may be unaware. V. Propp, a Russian folklorist, described thirty-one story elements in fairy tales that occurred in a certain order in every plot. Other structuralist thinkers have taken this further, noting certain recurrent characters in a variety of stories, and the importance of binary oppositions for creating meaning. M. Bal, in her studies of Judges, uses structuralist categories to focus on, among other things, the functions of speaking, seeing and doing, and to attend to who is the subject of these actions and who is the recurring object—for example, in the story of the nameless woman in Judges 19.

4.1.3. Canonical Criticism. Canonical criticism is a theologically oriented approach, and it is associated in one of its forms mostly with B. Childs, and in another form with J. Sanders. Childs takes redaction criticism a step further by interpreting biblical books as they have been placed within a scriptural *canon, in the context of which he claims they should be read. Sanders's approach is more diachronic and descriptive, inquiring into the processes by which the canon came to be shaped, and the theological trajectories that can be detected in the development of scriptural conceptions over time.

4.1.4. Rhetorical Criticism. Scholars disagree on the distinctions between literary criticism and rhetorical criticism, and some, especially those influenced by J. Muilenburg, use the terms interchangeably. A prominent stream of thought, however, connects rhetorical criticism with classical Hellenistic and Roman rhetoric, conceiving of texts not as artifacts on their own, but rather as acts of persuasion directed toward audiences. Less oriented toward aesthetics, rhetorical criticism can be applied to any biblical text of any genre, not just those perceived as artfully crafted. It is pragmatic in nature, inquiring into the intended effects of the language upon its imagined audience. For example, R. Duke uses Aristotle's categories of rhetoric to analyze persuasive strategies in Chronicles (*see* Chronicles, Books of).

4.2. Postmodern and Reader-Oriented Perspectives. Both historical criticism and literary criticism as described above reflect an objectivist view of texts as stable centers of meaning. The latest generation of literary work is characterized by growing awareness of the inescapable role of culturally situated perspective in the writing, reading and interpreting of texts. Just as sci-entific fields have come to see that the presence of the observer affects the outcome of experiments, literary interpreters have come to recognize the role of interpreters not just in the finding of meaning, but also in its making. Divergent readings, then, proceed not necessarily from errors but from differences in the experiences, questions, definitions and assumptions with which various readers approach the same texts. Such observations have given rise to several broadly related critical theories on the writing and reading processes (such as decon-struction-ist and reader-response theories), the dialogical nature of discourse (such as various discussions of intertextuality), the politics of interpretation (such as new historicism and various feminist and ideological critiques), and the ethical responsibilities and commitments involved in biblical interpretation. In addition, studies into the history of scriptural interpretation, presenting how actual readers have interpreted biblical texts, often share reader-oriented insights.

These perspectives tend to overlap considerably, and most scholars working in one area also will appropriate the language and theoretical perspectives of another. They tend to run the gamut of social discourse, often dealing with linguistics, social sciences, history and philosophy. Postmodern theories have developed more as insights and hermeneutical perspectives than as methods.

At the heart of postmodern interpretation is the problem of textual determinacy. Even readers who agree about where meaning ought to reside still read the same texts in variant ways. Few would say (to paraphrase the famous quip about Boehme) that the Bible is like a picnic to which the authors bring the words and the readers the meaning. But clearly there are properties in the Bible and the environment in which it is read that lend themselves to a "surplus of meaning." Difficult questions arise: To what extent does a biblical passage delimit the possibilities for reasonable interpretation? On what grounds are some interpretations more equal than others? Even those who believe in textual determinacy find that no amount of study buys them the definitive meaning—there is always more to say, and someone else will say it. On the other hand, those who have reconciled themselves to, and even revel in, textual indeterminacy continue to produce interpretations as if they still believed that communication worked. The quest for interpretation continues, but in many quarters the search for the final meaning that will close all debate has been abandoned, and the quest is rather for the best local meaning that, with respect for the integrity of both Scripture and interpreters, addresses the religious and intellectual needs of particular people in particular times. Though equipped with more sophisticated tools, we may be returning to an audience-oriented focus reminiscent of some premodern approaches. This issue of textual surplus has spawned several related discussions.

4.2.1. Deconstruction. An offshoot of structuralism, deconstruction describes not what the readers are doing to texts, but rather what texts do before our very eyes—in fact, what the Book of Moses was doing that started the whole enterprise of historical criticism. But whereas source critics sought the causes of Scripture's inconsistencies, deconstructionists are more interested in their effects and implications. D. N. Fewell compares texts to people, whose essence cannot be captured by any characterization, no matter how exhaustive, because they are complex beings, not stereotypes. Deconstruction highlights the features within the text itself (as opposed to the context of the reader) that create a plurality of meanings. By way of example, Fewell analyzes Judges 1:11-15, a brief narration about Caleb and his daughter Achsah that is repeated almost exactly in Joshua 15:16-19. Four recent translations, set side by side, show surprising variety in the names of places and things, the relationships among the characters, the subjects and objects of action, and the speeches of the various participants. After laying all these issues out, Fewell notes that deconstruction does not allow readers to make anything they want of texts, but it does clarify that the same text can have many points, and "deconstruction refuses to allow any one point to prod the others into submission" (Fewell, 141). Study that teases out the complexity of biblical passages and their propensity for frustrating those who aspire to finish their meaning has been called by D. Jobling "friendly deconstruction," releasing the text's own energies.

4.2.2. Reader-Response Criticism. Reader-response critics have claimed convincingly that the social locations of writers and canonizers influenced and delimited their creative choices, and that, similarly, the social locations and inter-

ests of interpreters have influenced and delimited what they see. Insofar as interpreters are situated in societal roles that resemble those of biblical writers, such limitations may not be noticed. Putting on a different lens brings other elements into focus. For example, interpreters who assumed that the book of Judges was primarily historiography, and that history is primarily about rulers and wars, often have overlooked the key roles of a large number of women in that book. Yet a shift in focus shows that women as subjects and objects, especially in terms of violence, constitutes a major theme—in fact, the devolution of women's roles, from Deborah the judge to the nameless raped, murdered and dismembered Levite's concubine, becomes a barometer for the state of Israelite society. Significant insights in biblical interpretation have resulted simply from the sociological changes as the discipline of biblical studies has broadened beyond the purview of white European and American men. Such changes have enabled all scholars to become more cognizant of, and forthright about, their own social location.

4.2.3. Feminist and Other Ideological Analyses. These analyses have more to do with angles of vision than with particular exegetical methods. Feminist scholars, for instance, have employed every kind of exegetical method, from historical criticism to postmodern theory, to focus attention on concerns relevant to women's lives in Scripture and today. Although white women have enjoyed longer access to publication than have other previously underrepresented groups, this is slowly being remedied as more works by black, Asian, Hispanic, and third-world scholars are published. F. Segovia and M. A. Tolbert's edited volumes entitled *Reading from This Place* and R. S. Sugirtharajah's *The Postcolonial Bible* have been especially important in broadening the conversation, as have works by C. H. Felder. R. Weem's *Just a Sister Away* includes a discussion of Jephthah's daughter, and numerous Native American interpreters have highlighted the use of the conquest narratives of Joshua in the treatment of American Indians (see 4.2.6 below).

4.2.4. Intertextuality and Innerbiblical Exegesis. Students of intertextuality and *innerbiblical exegesis have echoed source critics in pointing out that the Bible, far from being a monologue, speaks in many different voices. It may be compared to a town meeting, in which the meaning emerges not in unity of perspectives, nor in the voice of the one who has the last speech, but in the exchange itself. R. Polzin, in his several studies of the Deuteronomistic History, has employed insights on dialogism by Russian literary theorist M. Bakhtin. In *Moses and the Deuteronomist,* Polzin shows the discursive tension resulting from the redactor's monologic use of source material that does not always concur with his own message. This discussion of ancient interpretive issues involved in Moses' reinterpretation in Moab of Sinaitic law, and the Deuteronomist's actualization in exile of Moses' speech, enables Polzin to draw analogies to contemporary tensions between recovering the text's authorial intent and describing its contemporary significance. L. L. Lyke employs an intertextual approach to construct a "thick reading" of the story of King David with the wise woman of Tekoa (2 Sam 14), comparing it with the Cain and Abel story, the theme of "woman with a cause," and other stories of rulers tricked into judging their own cases. Lyke reviews the story verse by verse to show the accumulated impact of these relevant scriptural contexts on the interpretation of this chapter.

Interest in dialogical interpretation of Scripture has encouraged the development of models for navigating such complex interaction. D. Clines and T. Eskenazi have presented a compendium of twenty-seven interpretations of Queen Michal collected from various sources, including encyclopedia entries, sermons, literary studies, commentaries and imaginative retellings. Clines's introductory essay compares and contrasts these treatments and develops a program of comparative interpretation.

4.2.5. New Historicism. New historicism is a recent movement that frustratingly resists definition and theory. This makes it difficult to describe well. It focuses postmodern insights on the problem of recorded history itself. Agreeing with traditional historians that history matters because it shapes current self-perceptions, new historicists also note that since our access to history is primarily through written texts (whether ancient chronicle or modern encyclopedia), it is not objective, but rather is unavoidably situated in the writer's perspective. Histories tell parts of the story while ignoring or distorting other parts, such as histories of the United States that leave gaping holes in the painful stories of various people of color in America. While attention to ideologies evident within Scripture itself has long aided biblical scholars in sorting out sources, new historicism also attends to the role of ideology in contemporary as well as ancient texts. For instance, H. C. Washington has studied the influence of German and Prussian war ideologies on reconstructions of Israelite sacred war traditions among prominent German scholars such as J. Wellhausen, O. Eissfeldt and H. Gunkel, while L. Rowlett has examined the role of Judean politics in Josiah's time in the formation of the book and characterization of Joshua.

4.2.6. History of Biblical Interpretation. Critically reexamined, the history of biblical interpretation has much to teach, both about traditional assumptions to which we may be unwitting heirs, and about clues in the text seen by forebears that may be missed today. S. Haynes has written a comprehensive study of the use of the Genesis stories of Ham, Nimrod and the Tower of Babel in the justification of slavery and segregation in the United States. Appropriations of the conquest narratives to justify war atrocities are not difficult to find, although a thorough study of them is still lacking. S. Niditch's book on war in the Hebrew Bible (see 4.2.7 below) opens with a 1689 sermon by Cotton Mather that poses the Puritans as Israel and the Indians as Amalek, worthy of total destruction. L. Donaldson similarly relates how the massacre of the tribe of Benjamin in Judges 20 was used to justify a Puritan slaughter of Pequot elderly, women and children in 1637. H. Washington describes the citing of Joshua by a district court judge attempting to exonerate William Calley, the platoon leader who massacred civilians in My Lai during the Vietnam War.

Yet the history of interpretation can turn up pleasant surprises as well. J. L. Thompson has studied premodern Jewish and Christian interpretations of Hagar, Jephthah's daughter and the women of Judges 19—21, and he demonstrates that "many struggled with these texts in ways that seem to subordinate their patriarchal instincts to a far more existential concern with issues of justice, humanity, and women's dignity" (Thompson, 6). He suggests that in the contemporary quest to interpret fairly, making assumptions about what early commentators thought without reading them carefully can lead to the very stereotyping that we seek to avoid.

Tracing a passage's history of interpretation also can show how varying interpretive needs have shaped a passage's meaning over time. W. Schniedewind uses reception theory as well as archaeological evidence, social theory, anthropology, psychology and *linguistics to reconstruct the early history of interpretation of the promise to David as found in 2 Samuel 7, in six "moments" from the beginning of the monarchy to the first century CE, showing how this promise was continually reinterpreted to address changing social needs.

4.2.7. Ethics of Biblical Interpretation. Because of the Bible's powerful impact on its hundreds of millions of readers, its interpretation has crucial theological and ethical implications. Interpreters in quest of truth, whether religious or intellectual, should be aware of the Bible's social power and its use for good and ill. A growing recognition that interpretation bears responsibility not just toward Scripture and the norms of scholarship, but also toward the well-being of those affected by our message, has renewed discussion of the ethical dimensions of scriptural interpretation. For instance, D. Patte offers *Ethics in Biblical Interpretation* as a proposal for moving beyond objectivist scholarship that is so focused on factual and methodological purity that it cannot hear others, whether those others are women, minorities or religious conservatives. Although postmodernist theory likewise can lead in unhelpful directions (nihilistic play that reduces scriptural interpretation to absurdity, valiant efforts to find a clever new "ism" to write a book about, even philosophical seasickness and despair), when responsibly invoked, it can open the way for a more self-critical search for ethical selectivity in interpretation. In their introduction to the *Semeia* volume *Bible and the Ethics of Reading,* G. Phillips and D. N. Fewell cite E. Levinas, who argues that ethics is "a radical obligation which precedes and infuses every act of critical thinking" (Phillips and Fewell, 4). Calls to greater awareness of the high stakes involved in reading the Bible have characterized several discussions of the recent past.

S. Niditch's study of war ideologies in the Hebrew Bible is especially relevant to Joshua through Nehemiah. She distinguishes among seven views of war discernible from different parts of Scripture and different moments in Israel's life, concluding with an "ideology of nonparticipation" visible in Chronicles, which combines images available in earlier biblical tradition to begin to form an ideology of peace.

Niditch's nuanced and wide-ranging study forms a framework for exploring the ethical dilemmas and possibilities that Jews and Christians have inherited from Scripture, and the options for faithful response today.

The process of biblical interpretation has been complicated by ever increasing historical and cultural distance and by awareness of the generations of readers who precede us and the multitudinous ways they have interpreted Scripture, not to mention the variegated interpretation occurring around the globe today. As access to information across generations and around the world becomes easier, the discipline of biblical studies shares the dizzying, sometimes daunting effect not of too little knowledge, but of more information than can be assimilated.

Nearly twenty years ago N. Gottwald, perceiving that social-scientific approaches and literary criticism were blowing fresh breezes into biblical scholarship but were out of touch with one another, called for the mutual cooperation of these two disciplines. Expressing a similar sentiment in a different key, D. Jobling suggested that liberationist and deconstructionist analyses could profit by joining forces. Although some interpreters have continued to commend their own method as the superior enterprise that either displaces or contains all others, an increasing number of interpreters have been calling for methodological humility. Hope has been expressed that out of the present ferment a new paradigm will take shape. But at this point, the future is no more than a glow discernible over the horizon.

See also HERMENEUTICS; HISTORIOGRAPHY, OLD TESTAMENT; INNERBIBLICAL EXEGESIS; NARRATIVE ART OF ISRAEL'S HISTORIANS; QUEST OF THE HISTORICAL ISRAEL; SOCIAL-SCIENTIFIC APPROACHES; TEXT AND TEXTUAL CRITICISM.

BIBLIOGRAPHY. **M. H. Abrams,** *The Mirror and the Lamp: Romantic Theory and the Critical Tradition* (Oxford: Oxford University Press, 1953); **A. K. M. Adam,** *What Is Postmodern Biblical Criticism?* (GBSNT; Minneapolis: Fortress, 1995); **R. Alter,** *The Art of Biblical Narrative* (New York: Basic Books, 1981); **E. Auerbach,** *Mimesis: The Representation of Reality in Western Literature* (Princeton, NJ: Princeton University Press, 1953); **M. Bal,** *Death and Dissymmetry: The Politics of Coherence in the Book of Judges* (Chicago: University of Chicago Press, 1988); **J. Barton,** *Reading the Old Testament* (rev. ed.; Louisville: Westminster/John Knox, 1996); **A. Berlin,** *Poetics and Interpretation of*

Biblical Narrative (BLS 9; Sheffield, Almond, 1983); **A. Brenner,** ed., *A Feminist Companion to Samuel and Kings* (FCB 5; Sheffield: Sheffield Academic Press, 1994); **M. J. Buss,** *Biblical Form Criticism in Its Context* (JSOTSup 275; Sheffield: Sheffield Academic Press, 1999); **B. Childs,** *Introduction to the Old Testament as Scripture* (Philadelphia: Fortress, 1979); **D. Clines and T. C. Eskenazi,** *Telling Queen Michal's Story: An Experiment in Comparative Interpretation* (JSOTSup 119; Sheffield: JSOT, 1991); **F. M. Cross,** *Canaanite Myth and Hebrew Epic: Essays in the History of the Religion of Israel* (Cambridge, MA: Harvard University Press, 1973); **L. Donaldson,** *"Postcolonialism and Biblical Reading: An Introduction,"* Semeia 75 (1996) 1-14; **R. Duke,** *The Persuasive Appeal of the Chronicler: A Rhetorical Analysis* (JSOTSup 88; Sheffield: Almond, 1990); **T. C. Eskenazi,** *In an Age of Prose: A Literary Approach to Ezra-Nehemiah* (SBLMS 36; Atlanta: Scholars Press, 1988); **J. C. Exum,** *Tragedy and Biblical Narrative* (Cambridge: Cambridge University Press, 1992); **C. H. Felder,** ed., *Stony the Road We Trod: African American Biblical Interpretation* (Minneapolis: Fortress, 1991); **D. N. Fewell,** "Deconstructive Criticism: Achsah and the (E)Razed City of Writing," in *Judges and Method: New Approaches in Biblical Studies,* ed. G. A. Yee (Minneapolis: Fortress, 1995) 119-45; **J. P. Fokkelman,** *Narrative Art and Poetry in the Books of Samuel* (3 vols.; Assen: Van Gorcum, 1981-1993); **J. L. Gonzalez,** "How the Bible Has Been Interpreted in Christian Tradition," *NIB* 1.83-106; **N. Gottwald,** *The Tribes of Yahweh: A Sociology of the Religion of Liberated Israel, 1250-1050 B.C.E.* (Maryknoll, NY: Orbis, 1979); idem, *The Hebrew Bible: A Socio-Literary Introduction* (Philadelphia: Fortress, 1985); **D. M. Gunn,** *The Story of King David: Genre and Interpretation* (JSOTSup 6; Sheffield: JSOT, 1978); idem, *The Fate of King Saul: An Interpretation of a Biblical Story* (JSOTSup 14; Sheffield: JSOT, 1980); **B. Halpern,** "Settlement of Canaan," *ABD* 5.1120-43; **S. Haynes,** *Noah's Curse: The Biblical Justification of American Slavery* (Oxford: Oxford University Press, 2002); D. Jobling, "Writing the Wrongs of the World: The Deconstruction of the Biblical Text in the Context of Liberation Theologies," *Semeia* 51 (1990) 81-118; **H. D. Lance,** *The Old Testament and the Archaeologist* (Philadelphia: Fortress, 1981); **L. L. Lyke,** *King David and the Wise Woman of Tekoa: The Resonance of Tradition in Parabolic Narrative* (JSOTSup 255; Sheffield: Sheffield Academic Press, 1997); **V. H. Matthews** and **D. C. Benjamin,** *The Social World of Ancient Israel 1250-587 B.C.E.* (Peabody, MA: Hendrickson, 1993); **S. McKenzie and S. Haynes,** eds., *To Each Its Own Meaning: An Introduction to Biblical Criticisms and Their Application* (Westminster/John Knox, 1999); **C. Meyers,** *Discovering Eve: Ancient Israelite Women in Context* (New York: Oxford University Press, 1988); **J. Muilenburg,** "Form Criticism and Beyond," *JBL* 88 (1969) 1-18; **S. N. Niditch,** *War in the Hebrew Bible: A Study in the Ethics of Violence* (New York: Oxford University Press, 1993); **M. Noth,** *The Deuteronomistic History* (JSOTSup 15; Sheffield: JSOT, 1981 [1943]); **D. Patte,** *Ethics of Biblical Interpretation: A Reevaluation* (Louisville: Westminster/John Knox, 1995); **G. A. Phillips and D. N. Fewell,** "Ethics, Bible, Reading As If," *Semeia* 77 (1997) 1-21; **R. Polzin,** *Moses and the Deuteronomist: A Literary Study of the Deuteronomic History* (New York: Seabury, 1980); **L. Rost,** *The Succession to the Throne of David* (HTIBS 1; Sheffield: Almond, 1982); **L. Rowlett,** *Joshua and the Rhetoric of Violence: A New Historicist Analysis* (JSOTSup 226; Sheffield: Sheffield Academic Press, 1996); **J. A. Sanders,** *Torah and Canon* (Philadelphia: Fortress, 1972); **W. M. Schniedewind,** *Society and the Promise to David: The Reception History of 2 Samuel 7:1-17* (Oxford: Oxford University Press, 1999); **F. Segovia and M. Tolbert,** eds., *Reading from This Place* (2 vols.; Minneapolis: Fortress, 1995); **M. A. Signer,** "How the Bible Has Been Interpreted in Jewish Tradition," *NIB* 1.65-82; **M. Sternberg,** *The Poetics of Biblical Narrative* (Bloomington: Indiana University Press, 1985); **R. S. Sugirtharajah,** ed., *The Postcolonial Bible* (The Bible and Postcolonialism 1; Sheffield: Sheffield Academic Press, 1998); **J. L. Thompson,** *Writing the Wrongs: Women of the Old Testament Among Biblical Commentators from Philo Through the Reformation* (Oxford: Oxford University Press, 2001); **E. Tov,** *Textual Criticism of the Hebrew Bible* (Minneapolis: Fortress, 1992); **P. Trible,** *Texts of Terror: Literary-Feminist Readings of Biblical Narratives* (Philadelphia: Fortress, 1984); **H. C. Washington**, "Violence and the Construction of Gender in the Hebrew Bible: A New Historicist Approach," *BibInt* 5 (1997) 324-63; **R. Weems,** *Just a Sister Away* (San Diego, CA: LuraMedia, 1988); **J. Wellhausen,** *Prolegomena to the History of Ancient Israel,* vol. 1 (Cleveland: World, 1957); **G. A. Yee,** ed., *Judges and Method: New Approaches in Biblical Studies* (Minneapolis: Fortress, 1995).

P. K. Tull

MICAIAH BEN IMLAH. *See* PROPHETS AND PROPHECY.

MILITARY OFFICERS. *See* STATE OFFICIALS.

MIRACLES

A discussion of miracles in the Hebrew Bible has to grapple with a number of problems. Y. Zakovitch suggests that it may be an illegitimate pursuit because Hebrew has no word for the English concept "miracle" (Zakovitch, 845). It is arguable that this is no semantic accident but reflects the fact that "in the classical period of Old Testament Literature, what we mean by 'miracle' was unknown" (Ross, 45). This is because the worldview of the ancient Hebrews differed from that which lies behind the modern English concept "miracle," which is expressed in the common dictionary definition of the word: an event inexplicable by natural laws and so ascribed to divine or supernatural action. The significance of recognizing this is that the narrator's worldview plays an important role in the process that lies behind the accounts of events that we have in the OT Historical Books. The way in which "what happened" is recounted depends on how the narrator perceived it, which in turn is colored by the narrator's worldview. Since the accounts in the Historical Books are part of larger literary compositions, we also need to consider another factor that may have affected them: the purposes for which the "miracle stories" are used within the larger story. This article is structured with these considerations in mind.

1. The Hebrew Words Used to Refer to "Miraculous" Events in the Historical Books
2. The Worldview Expressed in the Historical Books
3. The Meaning of the "Miracle Stories" in the Historical Books
4. Miracles and the Modern Worldview
5. Miracles in a Contemporary Theistic Worldview

1. The Hebrew Words Used to Refer to "Miraculous" Events in the Historical Books.
When the Israelites are camped on the east bank of the Jordan preparing to enter Canaan, Joshua says, "Sanctify yourselves, because tomorrow the LORD will do wonders *[niplāʾôt]* among you" (Josh 3:5), referring to the parting of the Jordan. The same word is used by Gideon

to refer to the exodus events when speaking to the angel of the Lord (Judg 6:13). He then asks the angel for a "sign" *(ʾôt)* to authenticate his message (Judg 6:17). This is fire springing from a rock to consume the meal that Gideon had prepared for his visitor. The spontaneous destruction of the altar at Bethel in response to the word of a prophet is called a "sign," but using a different Hebrew word, *môpēt* (1 Kings 13:3). Finally, Elisha's "miracles" are called "great things" *(gĕdōlôt)* (2 Kings 8:4).

1.1. ʾôt. The basic meaning of this word is "mark, sign." It is used of the "banners" that identified individual Israelite tribes (Num 2:2) and of the blood on the door frames that identified the homes of Hebrews (Ex 12:13). The heavenly "lights" are "signs" marking different periods of time (Gen 1:14). In the Historical Books the "sign" often confirms or authenticates a divine or prophetic word (Judg 6:17; 1 Sam 2:34; 10:7, 9; 2 Kings 19:29; 20:9). In two cases (Judg 6:17; 1 Sam 10:7) the "sign" confirms a divine commissioning, as in the case of Moses (Ex 3:12). Joshua describes the acts of God associated with the events from the exodus to the settlement in Canaan as "great signs" (Josh 24:17). Two words in particular are associated with *ʾôt* and bring out its function. One is *zikkārôn* ("memorial"), that which prevents something from being forgotten. The stones taken from the bed of the Jordan are a "sign" in this sense (Josh 4:6-7). The other word is *môpēt* ("wonder," "sign"), which is discussed in 1.2.

1.2. môpēt. This word basically refers to something extraordinary that mediates a message. This might be a person (Ezek 12:6, 11) or an event (1 Kings 13:3, 5). The connotation of that which is extraordinary is indicated by the linking of *môpēt* with *niplāʾôt*, "extraordinary deeds" (1 Chron 16:12; Ps 105:5). The Chronicler's use of *môpēt* in the account of the healing of *Hezekiah (2 Chron 32:24-31), where the parallel passage in Kings (2 Kings 20:1-11) has *ʾôt*, emphasizes the extraordinary nature of the event. In the OT the message conveyed by the *môpēt* is always theological in the sense of being directly or indirectly related to God. An indication of this is the linking of the word with God's "judgments" (1 Chron 16:12; Ps 105:5). Half of the word's thirty-six occurrences in the OT link it with *ʾôt* in the phrase "signs and wonders," which is almost exclusive to Deuteronomy and usually refers to the exodus events. As Nehemiah 9:10 makes clear, the purpose of those "signs and wonders" was to impart knowledge about God ("You made a name for yourself that day"). The aim of this was to bring people to acknowledge that "The LORD is God, there is no other besides him" (Deut 4:35). Like *ʾôt*, *môpēt* can refer to an event that confirms a prophetic word (1 Kings 13:3, 5).

1.3. **niplāʾôt.** This word is the *nipʿal* participle of the verbal root *plʾ*. The verb (usually in the *nipʿal* with the preposition *min*) is used to signify the limited nature of human understanding or ability. It may be a judicial decision that it is "too difficult" for a human judge to make (Deut 17:8) or natural phenomena that are "too amazing" for humans to understand (Prov 30:18-19). The name of the angel of the Lord is "incomprehensible" or "unfathomable" to humans (Judg 13:18). The root is, by contrast, used to express God's activity, in particular God's acts of salvation associated with the exodus. As already noted, Gideon refers to these "extraordinary deeds" (Judg 6:13), as does Nehemiah (Neh 9:17), and Joshua uses the same word to refer to the crossing of the Jordan (Josh 3:5).

1.4. **gĕdōlôt.** This word usually refers to the actions of God, "who does great things beyond understanding and extraordinary deeds without number" (Job 9:10). In Psalm 106:21-22 *niplāʾôt* is used in parallel with *gĕdōlôt*, referring to the exodus events. References to humans saying or doing "great things" usually are negative, indicating pride (Ps 12:3). This, however, is not the case in the reference to Elisha's "great things" (2 Kings 8:4).

2. The Worldview Expressed in the Historical Books.

The preceding word study highlights three aspects of the events to which these words refer as being important for the biblical writers: (1) the events deserve attention because they are in some way "extraordinary" or "amazing"; (2) partly for this reason, they are seen as directly or indirectly acts of God; (3) the events convey a message. This third aspect will be discussed in the next section, with the present section concentrating on the first two.

What a person finds "extraordinary" will depend on his or her prior understanding and experience. It need not be something that is "inexplicable by natural laws," but simply something that is inexplicable by the observer. All the things that excited the amazement of the Israelite sage (Prov 30:18-19) are of that nature. An event, or series of events, can be extraordinary because of the timing involved. Saul's meetings with three different groups of people in sequence, each one a possibly "random" encounter, constitutes a series of "signs" (1 Sam 10:2-7). Other events, like the shadow retreating on the sundial (2 Kings 20:11), might indeed be inexplicable by natural laws. Clearly, what made something a "sign" or "wonder" to the biblical writers was much broader than that by which we today define a "miracle." This cannot be explained simply by asserting that the biblical writers did not have our understanding of "natural law," true though that is. They were aware of regularities in nature, such as the sequence of the seasons and the motions of the heavenly bodies. The fact that the Lord answers Samuel's prayer and sends a thunderstorm at harvest time caused great fear because the people knew that thunderstorms normally did not happen then (1 Sam 12:16-18). Hezekiah was well aware that the sun's shadow normally did not retreat on the sundial (2 Kings 20:10). However, such a departure from the regularity of nature was only one possible cause of the amazement that might lead one to regard an event as a "sign" or "wonder." So, what would lead an ancient Israelite to do that? Y. Zakovitch identifies what he calls "control mechanisms" in the accounts of extraordinary events that indicate that the narrator saw an event as a "miracle," whether or not any of the words that we have examined are used in the account (Zakovitch, 848-49). Not all of his proposed "control mechanisms" are convincing, nor do all of them occur in the Historical Books. The following do seem to be valid:

1. *Prayer.* An event occurring following prayer cannot be taken as merely a coincidence.

2. *Prior Announcement.* This too removes the subsequent event from the realm of coincidence.

3. *Limitation.* The only example of this in the Historical Books is what happened to Gideon's fleece (Judg 6:35-40). It alone was wet with dew when the ground around it was dry, and vice versa.

4. *Paradox.* By this is meant the fact that the event goes against all expectation.

The first two "control mechanisms" are the key ones. The others do not occur on their own in the Historical Books. The importance of prayer and prior announcement (usually a prophetic word) takes us to the heart of the biblical writers' worldview.

Fundamental to the Hebrew understanding of the world was the belief that it is the creation of Yahweh (e.g., Gen 1:1-2:4a; Ps 8; 104; Is 40:28) (*see DOTP,* Creation). Moreover, God continues to hold the world, the events that occur in it and its creatures in being moment by moment. Thus in Amos 5:8 Yahweh is described as the one who created the stars and who continues to turn night into day and day into night, and to cause the rains. In Isaiah 42:5 Yahweh is the one who created the heavens and the earth and the one who gives "breath" and "spirit" to the people living in it. Psalm 104 is a comprehensive statement of this view of Yahweh as creator and sustainer of the world and all that is in it. Having created the world, he sends the rain (Ps 104:13) and causes the plants to grow to provide food for animals and humans (Ps 104:14). He takes away the "breath/spirit" of creatures so that they die, and sends out his "breath/spirit" with the result that they are "created" (Ps 104:29-30). W. Eichrodt observed, "It is hardly going too far to describe this Old Testament view of the maintenance of the world as *creation continua*" (Eichrodt, 2.154). This view might seem to imply that there is no effective distinction between "God" and "nature," but that is not the case. In the OT "nature" is depicted as having a degree of autonomy. It rejoices at the return of the exiles to *Zion (Is 35:1-2). In prophetic "trial speech" oracles it is called upon to be an independent witness of the case between Yahweh and his people (e.g., Is 1:2; Mic 6:1-2). The psalmists frequently call upon nature to praise God (e.g., Ps 69:34). As L. Stadelmann puts it, "The universe seems to have its own life and stands over against Yahweh sufficiently to offer its praises, to act as witness against mankind and to await in awful surrender the day of judgment" (Stadelmann, 7). This relative autonomy of nature means that it could be seen as acting "on its own" to some extent. The Song of Deborah can speak of the "stars" fighting for Israel against Sisera (Judg 5:20), and Joshua directly commands the sun and the moon to stand still (Josh 10:12). It appears that the Hebrews could move easily between the ideas of God acting directly in the world and God acting indirectly through "nature," which has a measure of autonomy. There was no rigid dividing line between these modes of God's activity.

This suggests that a major difference between the Hebrew outlook and the modern Western one is that they thought not in terms of the physical cause of events but in terms of who was the author of events. For them, the world was not primarily a physical structure, but rather a power structure (Ross, 50). The regularities in nature were seen not as the result of the world being a "clockwork mechanism" that runs on its own, but rather as an expression of the faithfulness of the God who created and sustains the world. God sustains the day/night cycle (Gen 1:16-18) and the cycle of the seasons (Gen 8:22). In Psalm 19 the "glory" of God is seen in the regular motion of the sun, and significantly, this is put in juxtaposition with Yahweh as the giver of the moral law. For the Hebrews, the most important aspect of Yahweh's faithfulness was his faithfulness to the covenant with Israel. This was demonstrated when he acted in redemption or judgment. These acts often came in response to the prayers of his people to save them or were linked with prophetic words that announced or explained them. J. L. McKenzie argues that the use of words that express wonder when these acts are referred to in the OT arises not because of the physical phenomena associated with these acts (although sometimes that is a factor), but because of a sense of wonder that Yahweh has done them for his people: "The basis of wonder in the works of judgment and redemption is not the rare or the extraordinary, but the saving will of Yahweh towards His people; Yahweh is never more wonderful than when He appears as the helper and savior of Israel" (McKenzie, 139).

3. The Meaning of the "Miracle Stories" in the Historical Books.

The "miracle stories" in the Historical Books cluster mainly into three groups: (1) the entry into Canaan and the early settlement period (Joshua and Judges); (2) the ark narrative (1 Sam 4:1b—7:1; 2 Sam 6); (3) the *Elijah and *Elisha stories (1 Kings 17—19; 2 Kings 1—6).

3.1. The Entry into Canaan and the Early Settlement Period. The account of the crossing of the Jordan is bracketed by two statements that bring out different aspects of its significance (i.e., its "sign" aspect). In the first (Josh 3:7), Yahweh tells Joshua that it will prove to the Israelites that

Yahweh is with Joshua as he was with Moses, and so exalt him in their eyes. The event itself has some similarity to the crossing of the Reed Sea and authenticates Joshua as Yahweh's chosen successor of Moses as leader of the Israelites. The second statement (Josh 5:1) describes the effect of news of the event on "all the kings of the Amorites . . . and all the kings of the Canaanites." It demonstrated the power of Yahweh and filled them with terror and a sense of hopelessness. These two themes seem to come together in the verse that closes the account of the capture of *Jericho: "So Yahweh was with Joshua, and his reputation was in all the land" (Josh 6:27). Of course, there is also the implicit message that Yahweh is faithful to his people in acting to stop the waters of the Jordan and to bring down the walls of Jericho for them. Yahweh's faithfulness to his covenant partner, Israel, is the main message of the story in Joshua 10:1-15. It is important to note that the battle happens when the Amorite kings besiege Gibeon because they have made a covenant with the Israelites, and the Gibeonites appeal to Joshua for help on the basis of this covenant. In the ensuing battle Yahweh acts in three ways: he throws the Amorites into panic (Josh 10:10), sends a hailstorm that kills more of them than the Israelites kill (Josh 10:11), and causes the sun to stand still to give the Israelites time to complete their victory (Josh 10:13).

The theme of authenticating "signs" continues in the stories in Judges. The angel of the Lord is authenticated by causing fire to spring from a rock to consume a meal that Gideon had prepared (Judg 6:21). The incident of Gideon's fleece (Judg 6:36-40) authenticates the angel's message. Manoah and his wife do not realize who has been speaking to them until they see the angel of the Lord ascend in the flame of their sacrifice (Judg 13:20-21). The major theme of the book of Judges is that of Yahweh acting to deliver his people, despite their sinfulness, when they repent of their sin and cry out for him to save them. Some of the *judges whom Yahweh raises up to deliver them perform deeds that might be called miraculous—for example, Shamgar killing six hundred Philistines with an ox goad, and some of Samson's exploits.

3.2. The Ark Narrative. The extraordinary events that occur while the *ark of the covenant is in Philistine territory lead the Philistines to conclude that the hand of the God of Israel is "heavy upon us and upon Dagon our God" (1 Sam 5:7). They are reminded of the power of the God of Israel shown by the exodus (1 Sam 6:6). That this interpretation of the events is correct is proved by the direction taken by the cart with the ark when it leaves Philistia (1 Sam 6:9-12). The issue of the superiority of Yahweh over Dagon is important because the ark came into Philistine hands when it was brought into battle to try to ensure that Yahweh would save Israel from defeat by them (1 Sam 4:3). The loss of the battle might have shown that the gods of the Philistines were more powerful than Yahweh. Since the subsequent narrative disproves this, it becomes clear that the reason for the loss of the battle was Yahweh's displeasure with Israel, especially Hophni and Phineas, the sons of Eli, who were with the ark (1 Sam 4:4). In further support of this, their death in the battle fulfills an earlier prophecy (1 Sam 2:34). The death of the men of Bethshemesh who looked into the ark is a result of them not respecting the holiness (i.e., otherness) of Yahweh (1 Sam 6:19-20). The same is the case with the death of Uzzah, who touched the ark. Yahweh's otherness means that the ark, which is the symbol of his presence, is not to be treated as if it were an ordinary object.

3.3. The Elijah and Elisha Stories. These stories contain the greatest concentration of "miracles" in the Historical Books. Those in the *Elijah stories all can be related to the central event of the contest with the prophets of Baal on Mount *Carmel. The three stories in 1 Kings 17 authenticate Elijah as a "man of God" commissioned by Yahweh. During the drought Yahweh provides for his servant's physical needs first by the ravens and then through the widow's jar of meal and cruse of oil that never run empty. Elijah's standing with Yahweh is further proved when he is able to revive the widow's son from death. The issue at stake in the contest at Mount Carmel is set out by Elijah at the start of it: "If Yahweh is God, follow him; but if Baal, then follow him" (1 Kings 18:21b). At the end of it the people affirm, "Yahweh, he is God; Yahweh, he is God." The authentication of Elijah is a subtheme. In his prayer Elijah says, "Let it be known this day that you are God in Israel, and that I am your servant, and that I have done all these things at your word" (1 Kings 18:36b). R. Carroll sees "Mosaic" features in Elijah's ministry: "Elijah on Mount Carmel may be viewed as a clear instance of a Mosaic prophet proclaiming the word of Yahweh to the people and mediating the covenant between Yahweh and Israel his people" (Carroll, 410). The other Mosaic features that Carroll notes are the theophany on Horeb (1 Kings 19:8-18; cf. Ex 34:1-10) and the fact that "Moses and Elijah shared unusual retirements from active service" (Carroll, 410) because of the uncertainty about Moses' burial place (Deut 34:5-6) and Elijah's ascension to heaven (2 Kings 2:11).

The Elijah stories clearly form a coherent whole. The coherence of the *Elisha stories is less clear. Some scholars (e.g., Gray, 30) are puzzled by what they see as "trivial" miracle stories that concern the affairs of individuals rather than national affairs, which these scholars seem to think should be the proper concern of a prophet of Elisha's stature. The production and preservation of such stories usually are attributed to "the sons of the prophets" who were motivated by the desire to establish and uphold the reputation of their leader as the worthy successor to Elijah (Gray, 466). The purpose of 2 Kings 2:1-18 clearly is to establish Elisha as Elijah's rightful successor. Some of the other stories show him doing deeds similar to those of Elijah, most notably the ones about the widow's jar of oil (2 Kings 4:1-7) and the raising of the Shunammite's son (2 Kings 4:18-37). These, then, authenticate Elisha as a man of God and an emissary of Yahweh. P. Satterthwaite argues that there is a wider coherence to the Elisha stories. The key to this is the portrayal of Elisha as a "second Joshua" in 2 Kings 2. In this chapter Satterthwaite sees Elisha succeeding Elijah in Transjordan as Joshua did Moses. He then asks whether Elisha's parting of the Jordan near Jericho can be seen as "initiating a second 'conquest' of the land, in which the people's hearts are won back to YHWH, and the quasi-Canaanite worship of the North purged, completing the process begun by Elijah on Mt. Carmel" (Satterthwaite, 8-9). He goes on to argue that the subsequent stories, with their miracles, can be seen as setting Elisha's followers, the nucleus of a restored Israel, over against the northern kingdom as a whole. However, the hope of a restoration of the whole nation was not realized.

4. Miracles and the Modern Worldview.

Modern discussion of miracles has its starting point in David Hume's essay "Of Miracles" (reprinted in Geivett and Habermas, 29-44), pub-

lished in 1748 in section 10 of his larger work *Enquiry Concerning Human Understanding*. The essence of Hume's argument is summed up in this sentence: "A miracle is a violation of the laws of nature; and as a firm and unalterable experience has established these laws, the proof against a miracle, from the very nature of the fact, is as entire as any argument from experience can possibly be imagined" (Geivett and Habermas, 33). Hume went on to argue that the actual testimony to miracles is weak because often the witnesses were poorly educated people and/or people of questionable integrity. Also, there is a general human tendency to exaggerate. Moreover, the alleged miracles generally happened in distant and obscure places. A great deal has been written about Hume's argument, analyzing it, seeking to restate it or to refute it. Here we can only touch briefly on three lines of argument that have flowed from it.

4.1. Miracles Are Impossible. Hume's argument sometimes is interpreted in the "hard" form (Geisler, 27):

1. Miracles are by definition violations of the natural law;

2. Natural laws are unalterably uniform;

3. Therefore, miracles are impossible.

In this form the argument begs the question by simply defining miracles as impossible. Yet that is what people do when they argue that "science" shows that miracles cannot happen. They are appealing not to any empirical evidence against miracles, but rather to an ideological assumption that the world is a closed system of natural causes that are expressed by scientific "laws." This argument fails to appreciate the nature of scientific "laws." They are generalizations based on repeated, testable experience. They are always provisional because they are open to correction and revision in light of new data or further understanding. Thus they cannot be appealed to in order to rule out any unusual event that lies outside their scope. In light of the nature of scientific "laws," it is perfectly in order to argue that "natural law" is the regular, normal pattern of events, and that miracles are "exceptions" to this pattern. The word *violations* is inappropriate in this understanding of natural laws.

4.2. Miracles Are Incredible. Hume's emphasis on the testimony to miracles makes it likely that he intended the argument in a "softer" form about the incredibility of miracles rather than their impossibility (Geisler, 27).

1. A miracle is by definition a rare occurrence;

2. Natural law is by definition a statement of a regular occurrence;

3. The evidence for a regular occurrence is always greater than that for a rare one;

4. Wise persons always base belief on the greater evidence;

5. Therefore, a wise person should never believe in miracles.

C. S. Lewis expressed one line of response to Hume's argument, dealing with his appeal to regular occurrence, or "uniform experience": "Now of course we must agree with Hume that if there is absolutely 'uniform experience' against miracles, if in other words they have never happened, why then they never have. Unfortunately we know the experience against them to be uniform only if we know that all the reports of them are false. And we can know all the reports to be false only if we know already that miracles have never occurred. In fact, we are arguing in a circle" (Lewis, 106). The only way to avoid this vicious circle is to be open to the possibility of miracles. A second objection is that Hume simply counts the evidence, rather than weighing it. The fact that millions of people have died without rising from the dead is taken as conclusive proof against any claim that someone has been raised from the dead. This amounts to relying solely on probability. Yet highly improbable events have happened, such as being dealt a perfect hand at bridge (the odds against this are about 160 billion to 1). The rational response to the claimed occurrence of a very improbable event is to examine the evidence for it and weigh it carefully, not to dismiss it out of hand. Third, Hume's dismissal of witnesses is arbitrary and tendentious. There is no reason to discount the evidence of witnesses simply on the grounds of their level of education, their culture or where they live.

4.4. Miracles Are Unidentifiable. The advances of science mean that now we can understand and do things that previous generations would have regarded as miraculous—for example, fly in airplanes, cure certain diseases. Therefore, it is argued, events that we regard as miracles may turn out to have natural explanations. Indeed, we should assume this and search for such explanations. To do otherwise would stultify science. Thus we should never accept the claim that a particular unusual event is a miracle. Taken in a "hard" form, this argument is really another form of the first one. It assumes Hume's narrow definition of a miracle and that the world is a closed system of natural causes, expressed by scientific "laws." Taken in a "softer" form, the argument is an acceptable warning that if we adopt Hume's definition of a miracle, then the acceptance of a claim that a particular event is a miracle must always be provisional and should not prevent further search for a scientific explanation.

5. Miracles in a Contemporary Theistic Worldview.

A theist cannot accept Hume's narrow definition of "miracle," because accepting it amounts to adopting a semideistic worldview in which God is outside of, and inactive within, his creation except on those rare occasions when he "violates" the laws of nature, which he created, and "intervenes" in the world. A contemporary theist can adopt a nuanced version of the ancient Hebrew worldview. Having created the world as an entity separate from himself, God continually keeps it in being. The "natural laws" that scientists discover are one of God's "normal" ways of working in the world. It is not surprising, therefore, that God sometimes uses these natural laws to produce a "wonder" that becomes a "sign" that says something to his people. The contemporary theist cannot avoid facing the questions that the scientifically inquisitive ask about the possible "natural" explanations of some biblical "wonders." It may be that the stopping of the Jordan and the collapse of the walls of Jericho were the result of seismic activity (see Nur and Cline). That would move them out of Hume's category of "miracle" but leave them as biblical "wonders" because these rare events happened at the time when the Israelites needed them and had been announced in advance. This kind of explanation of a "wonder," which takes both the text and scientific evidence seriously, is different in kind from "rationalizations" such as the suggestion that the "factual basis" of the story of the widow's meal jar and cruse of oil not running out is that her generosity toward Elijah moved the consciences of her wealthier neighbors to meet her needs during the drought (Gray, 381).

A theist cannot accept the assumption that the world is a closed system of natural causes that even God cannot break into. God is free to work in the world in unusual ways. However, the biblical evidence suggests that whenever God does so, there is a reason that is consistent with his purposes for his world and for his people. Thus the theist holds that the ultimate framework for consistency or coherence is to be found not in the material realm that science investigates, but rather in the character and purposes of God, who created that realm. This is why biblical "wonders" are not simply arbitrary events; they are "signs" that say something about God and his purposes.

C. F. D. Moule argues that the only worldview tenable for a consistent theist is that "the only ultimate regularity is to be looked for not within the material realm by itself but in the character of a personal God. It is of his character that the material realm is a manifestation: and what is possible and probable in it is better measured by what is known of the character of God than by what is observed on the much narrower scale of the purely mechanistic" (Moule, 16).

See also MAGIC AND DIVINATION.

BIBLIOGRAPHY. **M. G. Abegg Jr.,** "גדל," *NIDOTTE* 1.823-27; **C. Brown,** *Miracles and the Critical Mind* (Grand Rapids: Eerdmans; Exeter: Paternoster, 1984); **R. P. Carroll,** "The Elijah-Elisha Sagas: Some Remarks on Prophetic Succession in Ancient Israel," *VT* 19 (1969) 400-415; **W. Eichrodt,** *Theology of the Old Testament* (2 vols.; OTL; London: SCM, 1964); **N. L. Geisler,** *Miracles and the Modern Mind* (Grand Rapids: Baker, 1992); **R. D. Geivett and G. R. Habermas,** eds., *In Defense of Miracles* (Downers Grove: InterVarsity Press, 1997); **J. Gray,** *I & II Kings* (2d ed.; OTL; London: SCM, 1970); **P. A. Kruger,** "אות," *NIDOTTE* 1.331-33; idem, "מופת," *NIDOTTE* 2.879-81; idem, "פלא," *NIDOTTE* 3.615-17; **C. S. Lewis,** *Miracles* (London: Fontana, 1966); **S. V. McCasland,** "Signs and Wonders," *JBL* 76 (1957) 149-52; **J. L. McKenzie,** "God and Nature in the Old Testament," *CBQ* 14 (1952) 18-39, 124-45; **C. F. D. Moule,** "Introduction," in *Miracles: Cambridge Studies in Their Philosophy and History,* ed. C. F. D. Moule (London: Mowbray, 1965) 3-17; **A. Nur and E. H. Cline,** "Poseidon's Horses: Plate Tectonics and Earthquake Storms in the Late Bronze Age Aegean and Eastern Mediterranean," *Journal of Archaeology Science* 27 (2000) 43-63; **J. P. Ross,** "Some Notes on Miracle in the Old Testament," in *Miracles: Cambridge Studies in Their Philosophy and History,* ed. C. F. D. Moule

(London: Mowbray, 1965) 43-60; **P. E. Satterthwaite,** "The Elisha Narratives and the Coherence of 2 Kings 2—8," *TynBul* 49 (1998) 1-28; **L. I. J. Stadelmann,** *The Hebrew Conception of the World: A Philological and Literary Study* (AnBib 39; Rome: Pontifical Biblical Institute, 1970); **Y. Zakovitch,** "Miracle (OT)," *ABD* 4.845-56.

E. C. Lucas

MIZPAH

A number of Mizpahs (variant Mizpeh) are known from the Historical Books of the Hebrew Scriptures. This is not surprising, as the root from which the name derived, *sph*, connotes a location with a good view, from which one can keep close watch on activities in the area; it might suitably be rendered "lookout point." Thus it is similar to Hebrew place names derived from a local topographical context, such as the various sites compounded from *Ramah* ("height") or *Gibeah* ("hill") and their variants. However, unlike these more generic topographic terms, *Mizpah* can have a more restricted, military meaning. In Isaiah 21:8, for example, a lookout stands upon his *mispeh*, keeping watch for riders.

1. Identification
2. Approaches to the Study of Mizpah
3. The History and Archaeology of Mizpah of Benjamin
4. Other Mizpa/ehs

1. Identification.

The most important Mizpah of the Bible is that located just north of *Jerusalem in the tribal territory of Benjamin. In the twentieth century there were two leading candidates for Mizpah of Benjamin: Nebi Samwil and Tell en-Naṣbeh. Initially, textual references integrated with general topographic considerations were the only criteria available to judge between the two. In this early period Nebi Samwil was the leading contender for the Mizpah identification, based on its prominent position and the association of the prophet Samuel's name with the tomb at the site (McCown, 23-44). However, archaeological investigations at both sites have tilted the balance sharply toward Tell en-Naṣbeh. Any site that is to be identified with Mizpah must contain material from Iron Age I (c. 1175-950 BCE), and especially from the sixth century BCE, when Mizpah achieved its greatest significance. Nebi Samwil, however, possesses little Iron Age I material but contains substantial Iron Age II (c. 950-586 BCE) remains beginning only with the eighth century BCE, scanty material from the Persian period (c. 586-323 BCE), and more substantial material only after that (Magen and Dadon, 62-65). Its published material remains fail to match up with the history expected of the site based on textual references. On the other hand, Tell en-Naṣbeh, excavated between 1926 and 1935 by W. Badè (Zorn 1997b), does contain material from Iron Age I and impressive remains from Iron Age II, and reaches the peak of its architectural and artifactual development precisely in the sixth to fifth centuries BCE. Finally, those who champion Nebi Samwil have not come up with a satisfying identification for Tell en-Naṣbeh, if it is not Mizpah.

2. Approaches to the Study of Mizpah.

Some scholars approach the study of early textual references to Mizpah in Judges and Samuel with great misgivings (Arnold). They see the prominence of Mizpah in these tales not as a reflection of a real Iron Age I village, but as an attempt by writers working after the fall of Jerusalem in 586 BCE to provide a cultic pedigree for the Mizpah of that era, when, they believe, Mizpah replaced Jerusalem as the religious center of Judah. It is crucial, however, to recognize that this supposed late cultic prominence is based chiefly on only two brief passages, both of which are subject to different interpretations.

The key verse, Jeremiah 41:5, occurs in the context of the coup attempt launched by the Davidic malcontent Ishmael against the Babylonian-appointed administration led by Gedaliah. There it states that "eighty men arrived from Shechem and Shiloh and Samaria, with their beards shaved and their clothes torn, and their bodies gashed, bringing grain offerings and incense to present at the temple of the LORD" (NRSV). The question is where this house of the Lord was located. Some have suggested that these pilgrims were on their way to make their offerings at a newly constructed temple in Mizpah. The argument runs that if Mizpah was the new capital for all of Judah, it should have its own cultic center. The location of a late cultic center at Mizpah is said to gain support from 1 Maccabees 3:46, where Judas and his army gather for prayer and fasting before battle. There it is noted that "Israel formerly had a place of prayer in Mizpah." Finally, supporters

of the exilic cult site at Mizpah note that the Judges-Samuel stories that mention Mizpah also mention cultic activities such as communal gatherings, prayer and fasting that are suggested to be characteristic of the exilic period and later, but not of the Iron Age.

Against these arguments it must first be noted that there is no unambiguous reference to a cult site at Mizpah in the exilic era. Moreover, among all the people associated with Gedaliah's administration, no priests or other cultic personnel are mentioned at all, save for the prophet *Jeremiah (Jer 41:3, 16; 43:5-6). The only postexilic priests attested in contemporary sources are in Jerusalem (Lam 1:4). While the terminology used to describe cultic activities at Mizpah in Judges and Samuel may be late, and there is no guarantee that these are *only* late activities, these may simply be late elaborations of known earlier events for which there were few details. Although *Solomon's temple had been destroyed and ritually contaminated, there is no reason to suppose that surviving cultic personnel did not have the means and rituals necessary to purify the site. If such means did not exist, the site never could have been properly cleansed. Finally, Tell en-Naṣbeh has yielded no evidence in its sixth to fifth century occupation level of a major cult facility. The abundant artifactual remains (figurines, a small incense altar, fragments of cult stands) point to no more than domestic cultic activity, not a major religious center.

3. The History and Archaeology of Mizpah of Benjamin.

3.1. Joshua, Judges, Samuel and Iron Age I (c. 1200-950 BCE). Mizpah first appears as one of fourteen settlements in the tribal allotment of Benjamin north and west of Jerusalem (Josh 18:26) (*see* Tribes of Israel and Land Allotments/Borders). The dates assigned to the composition of the Benjaminite boundaries and settlement lists are varied and range throughout the monarchic period. What is most important to note is that a Benjaminite province/territory is already attested in the bureaucracy established by Solomon (1 Kings 4:18), and certainly some sort of boundary and accompanying list of settlements would have been needed for tax purposes and military enrollments.

Mizpah figures prominently as a gathering point for the Israelite tribes in the stories of the civil war against *Gibeah (Judg 19—21), in the battles against the *Philistines (1 Sam 7:1-14), as one of three stations in the yearly circuit of *Samuel (1 Sam 7:16) and in the election of *Saul (1 Sam 10). There is no need to see here the hand of an exilic or later editor attempting to exalt the position of Mizpah. Mizpah would have been a natural place for forces to assemble for a battle against a Benjaminite town or to face the inroads of the Philistines, who seem to have favored attacks into the central hill country in this general vicinity. No doubt these stories were shaped by later editors for religiopolitical reasons (e.g., the outrage at Gibeah coupled with the assembly at Mizpah is a counterweight to the election of the Gibeahite Saul at Mizpah), but there is little reason to dismiss the basic elements of these tales as completely unhistorical. Of the cultic activities that take place at Mizpah in these stories (swearing oaths, water libations, prayer, fasting, animal sacrifice), oaths and sacrifices have secure contexts in the Iron Age and earlier, the water libation is unique, and fasting for various reasons occurs in a variety of preexilic contexts. That is, most of the activities said to take place at Mizpah do not have to be exilic insertions at all.

Archaeological remains from this period are sparse in Tell en-Naṣbeh Stratum IV and consist primarily of scores of rock-cut cisterns and silos that are typical of Israelite settlement sites in the central hill country (Zorn, *NEAEHL* 3.1098-99). Typical Iron I cooking pots (Wampler, 29, pl. 46:979, 982-983), storage jars (Wampler, 4, pl. 2:16-23, 26-28) and locally produced Philistine bichrome pottery (Wampler, pl. 86) also attest to occupation at this time.

3.2. Kings, Hosea and Iron Age II (c. 950-586 BCE). For a site located on the contentious border between the northern and southern kingdoms, Mizpah is mentioned very seldom during the monarchic era. During the war between Baasha of Israel and Asa of Judah in the early ninth century BCE, Asa was able to seize building materials brought by Baasha in an effort to push his border south to the vicinity of Ramah and use them to counterfortify Mizpah and *Geba on his own northern border (1 Kings 15:22).

A Mizpah is mentioned in Hosea 5:1 in a broad context condemning the priests and rulers of Israel and Judah. It is uncertain if this is Mizpah of Benjamin, Mizpah of Gilead, or another Mizpah. Since the condemnations are aimed in parallel at the two countries, and Tabor

in the north is mentioned in the same verse, it seems more likely that Mizpah of Benjamin in the southern kingdom is meant.

Isaiah 10:27-32 records the route of march of an invader approaching Jerusalem from the north. Instead of taking the main hill country road past Mizpah, the attacker takes the secondary route through the Michmash pass—perhaps a testimony to the toughness of the defenses of Mizpah.

The archeological remains from Tell en-Naṣbeh Stratum III attest to a thriving hill country town. The initial phase of occupation consists of a belt of mostly three-room houses arranged around the periphery of the site, with the broad back rooms of the dwellings forming a sort of casemate wall (*see* Architecture). Facing the entrances were the doorways to other dwellings further up the slope, with additional buildings stepping up beyond these. These were mostly modest structures, averaging no more than 60 m^2 (Zorn, *NEAEHL* 3.1099-1100, 1101; 1997c, 35). No clear remains of monumental public structures were identified. At some point a massive inset-out wall was built around this settlement, but lower down the slope (Zorn 1999). At the northeast corner of the site was an immense inner and outer gate complex (Zorn 1997a). This fortification system likely should be attributed to Asa's building campaign. Just inside this new wall on the south were a band of storage silos, while on the north the intramural space served to draw off water through drains in the city wall. The settlement numbered probably around nine hundred inhabitants (Zorn 1994, 44). Mizpah's importance as a border fortress is also confirmed by the eighty-six royal *lmlk* stamped storage jar handles recovered there (McCown, 156-64, pl. 56:1-14) (*see* Hebrew Inscriptions).

3.3. Jeremiah, Nehemiah and the Babylonian/ Persian Period (c. 586-400 BCE). Mizpah reached its zenith following Nebuchadnezzar's destruction of Jerusalem in 586 BCE, when it was elevated to be the capital of the *Babylonian-appointed administration initially led by Gedaliah. Personnel associated with his administration included Judean and Babylonian soldiers, military officers, royal women, eunuchs and the prophet Jeremiah (Jer 40:6; 41:3, 10, 16; 43:6). Gedaliah also encouraged refugees to return from neighboring lands (Jer 40:7-12). His term of office, however, was cut short when he and many of his followers were assassinated by Ish-mael, a member of the Davidic line, with the connivance of the *Ammonite king (Jer 41:1-3; 2 Kings 25:25). The coup ultimately was foiled by elements loyal to Gedaliah, but the damage had been done, and a number of leading Judeans then fled to Egypt, taking Jeremiah with them (Jer 41:11-17).

The remains from Tell en-Naṣbeh Stratum II dovetail nicely with the textual material (Zorn 2003; 1997c, 31-38, 66; *NEAEHL* 3.1101-2). The previous Iron Age town was systematically lev-eled and replaced by an entirely new architec-tural arrangement. At least six spacious four-room houses (over twice the size of typical Stra-tum III houses) have been identified, along with what may be remains of a Babylonian-style resi-dence, and other structures. The inner gate of the gate complex was demolished to make way for new housing. Jar handles stamped with *m(w)sh*, probably from a royal estate at Mozah, found throughout Benjamin but most promi-nently at Tell en-Naṣbeh, suggest the limited re-source area upon which the postwar admin-istration could draw (Zorn, Yellin and Hayes). Mesopotamian-style coffins (Zorn 1993), a dedi-catory cuneiform inscription (Vanderhooft and Horowitz) and an ostracon bearing a Mesopota-mian name written in Hebrew characters attest to the Babylonian influence at the site (Zorn 2003, 436-37). Finally, the beautiful seal of "Ja'azaniah, the Servant of the King," bearing the image of a rooster in a fighting stance, should be mentioned (McCown, 163, pl. 57:4-5). Found in a tomb reused in the Byzantine peri-od, the owner of this seal may be the officer of the same name mentioned in the texts (2 Kings 25:23; Jer 40:8). The settlement's inhabitants numbered probably around 450 (Zorn 1994, 44).

Mizpah retained some importance down into the fifth century BCE, as attested by Nehemiah 3, where Mizpah is said to have had its own district and two rulers (Neh 3:15, 18), and seems to have been, at least in part, under the special jurisdic-tion of the Persian governor of the Beyond-the-River province. This is well matched by the ar-chaeological remains from Mizpah (Zorn 2003, 443-44). Jar handles marked by Yehud stamp im-pressions show that Mizpah was part of the Judean subprovince (McCown, 164-65, pl. 57:1-3, 13-14, 17-20). Pottery with wedge and circle dec-orations points to trade with *Arabia (Zorn 2001), while Attic wares (McCown, 175-78, pl. 59-

60) and an imitation bronze tetradrachm (Mc-Cown, 174, pl. 102:1) attest to some connections with Greece, at least until the close of the fifth century BCE, when Naṣbeh was destroyed by un-known assailants. This date is confirmed also by the pottery found on the floor of one of the houses (Zorn 2003, 42).

3.4. Maccabees and the Hellenistic and Later Pe-riods. The last reference to Mizpah is in 1 Mac-cabees 3:46, where Jewish forces under Judas gather for religious observances before their battle with the Seleucid army at Emmaus. Miz-pah was chosen because of the earlier cultic as-sociations noted above. Little about the nature of Mizpah in the Hellenistic period can be gained from this brief text. Archaeological re-mains from Stratum I point to an agricultural es-tate. These include a wine press, field tower, two kilns and scattered walls (Zorn, *NEAEHL* 3.1102). Occupation off the main site continued into the Byzantine era, as is attested by the re-mains of a small church and tombs.

4. Other Mizpa/ehs.

4.1. Mizpah in Gilead. In the story of Jacob's flight from Laban in Genesis 31, Laban over-takes Jacob in Gilead. After a parlay, they go their separate ways, but not before setting up sa-cred stones and a pillar as a witness to their agreement. The pillar is named Mizpah (Gen 31:49). This is likely the same Mizpah that fea-tures in the story of Jephthah's war in Gilead against the Ammonites (Judg 10:17; 11:11, 29, 34).

4.2. Mizpah in Harmon. In Joshua 11 Jabin, king of Hazor, gathers together a great coalition to resist the Israelite advance under Joshua. Among these are forces from the land of Miz-pah beneath Mount Hermon (Josh 11:3). After the Israelite victory some of the Canaanite forc-es are chased as far the valley of Mizpah (Josh 11:8).

4.3. Mizpeh in the Shephelah. Among the towns located near *Lachish in the Judean Shephelah was another Mizpeh (Josh 15:38).

4.4. Mizpeh of Moab. During the period of David's flight from Saul, he went to Mizpeh of *Moab and deposited his parents with the king of Moab (1 Sam 22:3).

See also CITIES, TOWNS AND VILLAGES.
BIBLIOGRAPHY. **P. M. Arnold,** "Mizpah," *ABD* 4.879-81; **I. Magen and M. Dadon,** "Nebi Sam-wil," [Hebrew] *Qadmoniot* 118 (1999) 62-77; **T. L.**

McClellan, "Town Planning at Tell en-Naṣbeh," *ZDPV* 100 (1984) 53-69; **C. C. McCown,** *Tell en-Nasbeh Excavated Under the Direction of the Late William Frederic Badè,* 1: *Archaeological and Historical Results* (Berkeley, CA: Palestine Institute of Pacific School of Religion and American Schools of Oriental Research, 1947); **D. Vanderhooft and W. Horowitz,** "The Cuneiform Inscription from Tell en-Naṣbeh: The Demise of an Unknown King," *TA* 29 (2002) 318-27; **J. C. Wampler,** *Tell en-Nasbeh Excavated under the Direction of the Late William Frederic Badè,* 2: *The Pottery* (Berkeley, CA: Palestine Institute of Pacific School of Religion and American Schools of Oriental Research, 1947); **J. R. Zorn,** "Estimating the Population Size of Ancient Settlements: Methods, Problems, Solutions and a Case Study," *BASOR* 295 (1994) 31-48; idem, "An Inner and Outer Gate Complex at Tell en-Nasbeh," *BASOR* 307 (1997a) 53-66; idem, "A Legacy of Publication: William F. Badè and Tell en-Nasbeh," *BAR* 23.4 (1997b) 68-69; idem, "Mesopotamian-style Ceramic 'Bathtub' Coffins from Tell en-Nasbeh," *TA* 20 (1993) 216-24; idem, "Mizpah: Newly Discovered Stratum Reveals Judah's Other Capital," *BAR* 23.5 (1997c) 28-38; idem, "Naṣbeh, Tell en-," *NEAEHL* 3.1098-1102; idem, "A Note on the Date of the 'Great Wall' of Tell en-Naṣbeh: A Rejoinder," *TA* 26 (1999) 146-50; "Tell en-Naṣbeh and the Problem of the Material Culture of the 6th Century," in *Judah and the Judeans in the Neo-Babylonian Period,* ed. O. Lipschits and J. Blenkinsopp (Winona Lake, IN: Eisenbrauns, 2003) 413-47; idem, "Wedge- and Circle-Impressed Pottery: An Arabian Connection," in *Studies in the Archaeology of Israel and Neighboring Lands in Memory of Douglas L. Esse,* ed. S. R. Wolff (SAOC 59; Chicago: Oriental Institute of the University of Chicago; Atlanta: American Schools of Oriental Research, 2001) 689-98; **J. R. Zorn, J. Yellin and J. Hayes,** "The *M(W)H* Stamp Impressions and the Neo-Babylonian Period," *IEJ* 44 (1994) 161-83.

J. R. Zorn

MOAB, MOABITES

Moab is the plateau to the east and northeast of the Dead Sea, the home in the Iron Age of a nation-state of the same name, whose chief deity was Chemosh (Num 21:29). The northern half of the plateau, essentially the area between Madaba and the Arnon River, had several population groups, including parts of the Israelite tribes of

Reuben and Gad and tribal elements of the *Ammonites. This demographic pattern is consistent with the etiological account of Genesis 19:30-38, which indicates that the Moabites were related to the Israelites and the Ammonites through Lot, Abraham's nephew. References to Moab in the Historical Books of the OT largely concern reminders of prior dealings with Israel and/or describe struggles between Moab and Israel or Judah for land and economic control.

1. Moabite-Israelite Relations in the Premonarchical Period
2. Moabite Relations During the Reigns of Saul and David
3. Moabite Relations During the Reign of Solomon
4. Moabite Relations with Israel and Judah During the Divided Monarchy
5. Moabite Relations with the Persian Province of Yehud

1. Moabite-Israelite Relations in the Premonarchical Period.

In the context of a covenant renewal ceremony, Joshua reminds his hearers of the Moabites, whose king Balak had failed in an attempt to gain the upper hand against Israel (Josh 24:8-10). Balak sought to hire Balaam, a well-known seer and diviner, to curse Israel (Num 22—24). References to Balak and/or Balaam for illustrative purposes occur several times in the OT and in later Jewish and Christian literature.

In Judges 11:12-28 Jephthah, one of Israel's *judges, addresses an Ammonite king who had attacked Israel in an attempt to expand his territorial control. Jephthah was from Gilead, a forested area on the hills east of the Jordan River, where Israelites lived among several different population groups. He reminds the king of previous relations between Ammon, Moab and Israel (see Num 20:14-21; 21:21-32; 22-24). Jephthah too cites the story of Balak's fruitless effort to thwart Israel, although in contrast to Joshua 24:9-10, he makes the point that Balak never entered into conflict with Israel.

In the exchange with the Ammonite ruler it is not obvious why Jephthah refers to Moab and to its deity Chemosh. Some interpreters have seen the references as a clumsy or confused effort on the part of an editor in compiling the account (so Moore, 283). A compiler's confusion is possible, but so are other explanations. First, the exchange between Jephthah and the *Ammonite king has diplomatic overtones, as Jephthah seeks to explain the history of the region in terms of past encounters between population groups and the activity of the gods. Moreover, as previously noted, the Transjordanian regions from the Arnon to the Jabbok (Judg 11:22) were inhabited by various Israelite elements as well as by Moabites and Ammonites. Second, it is a common pattern in OT narratives for Moabites and Ammonites to act in concert, even though each state would also seek expansion of its territory (see Judg 3:12-30; 1 Sam 11:1-4).

Judges 3:12-30 records another incursion from Transjordan against Israel, this time a coalition including Ammonites but led by a Moabite king named Eglon, who oppresses the Israelites in the vicinity of the "city of palms" (Jericho or nearby [Deut 34:3; 2 Chron 28:15]). Eglon is assassinated by a left-handed Benjaminite named Ehud, another of Israel's judges, who uses subterfuge to gain private access to the Moabite king. In the transition to monarchy the book of Samuel will refer to the period of Moabite oppression as a time when the Lord "sold" his disobedient people into the hands of enemies (1 Sam 12:9).

2. Moabite Relations During the Reigns of Saul and David.

According to a brief reference, *Saul fought against enemies who surrounded Israel on every side, including Moabites (1 Sam 14:47). Similar remarks are made about *David (2 Sam 8:1-14; 1 Chron 18:1-13), but his relationship with Moab appears more complicated than that of Saul, who essentially followed in the footsteps of the earlier judges and sought to free Israelite elements from foreign control. David, however, when pursued by Saul, entrusted his parents to the care of the king of Moab (1 Sam 22:3-4). The narrator provides no reason for this choice, but a plausible explanation is that David had Moabite ancestors (Ruth 4:13-22; cf. the connection of Judah's descendants with Moab in 1 Chron 4:22) and thus perhaps support among certain Moabite factions. In his later defeat of Moab, David treated the population quite harshly, using measuring lines to set aside a percentage of them for execution (2 Sam 8:2). Again, the narrator provides no reason for either this harshness or the odd means of selection. Perhaps David's actions were a response to an otherwise unnamed horror (see Amos 2:1-3) or to violence

among Moabite factions most opposed to David's influence in Moab.

3. Moabite Relations During the Reign of Solomon.

The harem of *Solomon included at least one Moabite woman, and he granted the Moabite cult special privilege in Jerusalem by constructing a *"high place" for Chemosh on the mountain east of Jerusalem (1 Kings 11:1-8). This illustrates the importance to the Israelite monarchy of diplomatic and other relations with Moab, as well as the defection of Solomon from the exclusive worship of the Lord. The shrine for Chemosh was in use for at least three centuries until *Josiah defiled it as part of his religious reforms (2 Kings 23:13). This theme of Moabite detrimental influence continued in the postexilic period (see 5 below).

4. Moabite Relations with Israel and Judah During the Divided Monarchy.

There are several narrative sources that provide accounts of relations among Moab, Israel and Judah in the ninth century BCE (2 Kings 1:1; 3:4-27; 2 Chron 20:1-30), including a thirty-four line inscription commissioned by the Moabite king Mesha (*COS* 2.1:135-38) that was discovered in 1868 (*see* Non-Israelite Written Sources: Syro-Palestinian). Moab was a vassal of Israel under both *Omri and Ahab. 2 Kings 3:4-27 reports that Moab produced for Israel one hundred thousand lambs and the wool from an equal number of rams, and that after the death of Ahab, Moab rebelled against Israelite hegemony, eventually provoking an invasion of Moab by Israel and Judah (led by kings Jehoram and *Jehoshaphat). Mesha's inscription (lines 4-8) attributes Moab's subjugation to the anger of Chemosh, but it records that after forty years Chemosh had restored control of Madaba to Moab. Lines 10-21 describe armed conflict between Moabites and Israelites at the sites of Ataroth (cf. Josh 16:2), Nebo (cf. Num 32:38; Deut 34:1) and Jahaz (cf. Num 21:23; Josh 13:18; Judg 11:20), with the result that Mesha gained control of the table land between Madaba and the Arnon River. In line 8 the "forty years" of humiliation is described as a point halfway in the reign of Omri's "son[s]" (the Moabite word *bnh* can be read as "his son" or as "his sons"). At the conclusion of the inscription, lines 31-32, comes a reference to Horonaim (Moabite *ḥwrnn*) and possibly a campaign against the "house of David" (= the kingdom of Judah or the Judean king) occupying that city, if *bt [d]wd* is the right textual reconstruction in line 31 (so Lemaire 1994; Rainey). The inscription says nothing (else?) about an attack by Israel and Judah, as narrated in 2 Kings 3, or about an attack on Judah by Moab, acting in concert with Ammon and others, as narrated in 2 Chronicles 20:1-30.

There are chronological and other difficulties in reconstructing the sequence of events from these biblical and Moabite sources, so that scholars vary widely in their reconstructions (Dearman, 157-210; Lemaire 1991; Rainey). One possibility, which assumes a selective interpretation of ninth-century BCE military campaigns on the part of each account, begins with Moab withholding tribute after the death of Ahab. The Mesha inscription provides details of Moab's subsequent recovery from Israel of the plateau north of the Arnon River, a process that likely would have begun with the short reign of Ahaziah but continued into the reign of his successor, Jehoram. Moab attempted to extend its resurgence by joining a coalition from Transjordan that invaded Judah. Perhaps this coalition was aided and abetted by the Arameans (see 2 Chron 20:2) in Damascus, who long sought a greater influence in the region (*see* Aram, Damascus and Syria). The invasion did not succeed, and an Israelite-Judean attack on Moab followed (lines 31-32 of the Mesha Inscription?), inflicting damage on Moab but failing finally to capture or defeat the Moabite king.

There are only scattered references to Moab in the accounts of the divided monarchy after the *Omri dynasty and the reign of the Judean king Jehoshaphat. 2 Chronicles 24:26 reports a Moabite (and Ammonite) conspiracy against the Judean king Joash, and there are occasional reports of marauding bands of Moabites (2 Kings 13:20; 24:2) in both Israel and Judah.

5. Moabite Relations with the Persian Province of Yehud.
Moabite wives were a contributing factor to the problem of syncretism in and around postexilic Jerusalem (Ezra 9:1; Neh 13:23). On the basis of Mosaic instruction (Neh 13:1-4; cf. Deut 23:3-5) that no Moabite or Ammonite be allowed in the Israelite assembly, and in an attempt to reverse the community's dire religious circumstances, Judean men took the drastic step of divorcing their foreign wives.

See also AMMON, AMMONITES; EDOM, EDOMITES.

BIBLIOGRAPHY. **A. Dearman,** ed., *Studies in the Mesha Inscription and Moab* (SBLABS 2; Atlanta: Scholars Press, 1989); **A. Lemaire,** "'House of David' Restored in Moabite Inscription," *BAR* 20.3 (1994) 30-37; idem, "La stèle de Mésha et l'histoire de l'ancien Israël," in *Storia e tradizioni di Israele: Scritti in onore di J. Alberto Soggin,* ed. D. Garrone and F. Israel (Brescia: Paideia, 1991) 143-69; **G. F. Moore,** *Judges* (ICC; New York: Scribner, 1895); **A. F. Rainey,** "'Mesha' and Syntax," in *The Land That I Will Show You: Essays on the History and Archaeology of the Ancient Near East in Honor of J. Maxwell Miller,* ed. J. A. Dearman and M. P. Graham (JSOTSup 343; Sheffield: Sheffield Academic Press, 2001) 287-307.

J. A. Dearman

MOLECH. *See* CANAAN, CANAANITES.

MONARCHY. *See* KINGS AND KINGSHIP.

MOSAIC LAW. *See* LAW.

MOT. *See* CANAANITE GODS AND RELIGION.

MOUNT CARMEL. *See* CARMEL.

MOURNING. *See* DEATH AND AFTERLIFE.

MUNICIPAL ADMINISTRATION. *See* STATE OFFICIALS.

N

NABOPOLASSAR. *See* BABYLONIA, BABYLO-NIANS.

NARRATIVE ART OF ISRAEL'S HISTORIANS

The study of biblical narrative in recent decades has produced new insights that enhance our understanding of the poetics of the historical texts. Careful attention to the techniques employed by the biblical authors, including their allusions, model scenes and rich style, show that these biblical narratives are imbued with an aesthetic that transcends a mere didactic or sermonic objective.

1. The Place of Narrative in Biblical Literature
2. The Historical and Ideological Character of the Narratives
3. The Manner of Writing
4. Different Stories About the Same Event or Period
5. A Purely Original Work, or Rooted in the Surrounding Cultures?
6. Who Composed the Biblical Narrative?
7. Conclusion

1. The Place of Narrative in Biblical Literature.
Narrative occupies an important position in biblical literature, as is reflected in its quantity, structure and content. Quantitatively, about one-third of biblical literature is in the form of narratives, and structurally the stories are the vessels, which carry the significant contents. For example, the stories about the Israelites' wanderings in the wilderness serve as the framework for the laws, while the narrative in the book of Job (Job 1—2; 42:7-17) frames the debate between Job and his companions; even some of the prophetic books conclude with narratives (e.g., Is 36—39; Jer 52). In terms of con-

tent, most of the stories serve one purpose: to tell the history of the people of Israel from the viewpoint of its relations with its God. Because the authors, and later the editors, intended a systematic and chronological description of Israel, the biblical narrative usually is described as *historiography. The book of Genesis devotes only the first eleven chapters to the early history of humanity; then it proceeds to describe, in a detailed and consecutive manner, the development of the relations between God and the Israelites' ancestors. The description starts with Abraham and his offspring, relates their wanderings in Canaan and their migration to Egypt (Gen 11:26—50:26), continues with their emergence as a people in Egypt, their exodus from Egypt, their wanderings in the wilderness and the conquest of Canaan (Exodus through Joshua), then their history in Canaan from the time of the elders and judges to the monarchies of Judah and Israel, concluding with the downfall (Judges through 2 Kings). In addition to this sequence, narratives concerning Israelite history are incorporated in the books of the Latter Prophets and in the final division, the Writings. Some of these stories deal with the period that ends with the downfall (Ruth, Latter Prophets, Chronicles), but from a different viewpoint, and others with the life of the people in exile and the early days of the Second Temple period (Daniel, Esther, Ezra-Nehemiah).

2. The Historical and Ideological Character of the Narratives.
Few of the biblical stories are outright fiction rather than history. The biblical authors preferred to describe events that were supposed to have happened rather than make up imaginary tales. One openly fictional tale is the parable of the poor man's ewe (2 Sam 12:1b-4), which the

prophet Nathan made up to induce King David to admit his compound sin: adultery with Bathsheba and the killing of Uriah. Similarly, the commander of David's army, Joab, seeing that the king longed for his son Absalom, sought to induce him to recall Absalom from his refuge in Geshur, whence he had fled after killing his brother Amnon. Joab got a wise woman of Tekoa to tell the king a fictional personal story, which echoed David's situation with his sons (2 Sam 14:5b-7), and this persuaded the king to send for Absalom. These two stories clearly are presented as fiction, but most of the stories in the Hebrew Bible appear as reports on the real past.

These parables—imaginary tales used as a means of persuasion—show that the biblical authors regarded the narrative as an effective way of communicating messages to their readers, and therefore often used it. They even required their audience to persevere with its use of narrative: "You shall tell your child on that day, 'It is because of what the LORD did for me when I came out of Egypt'" (Ex 13:8). These authors were convinced that if the people were told about God's marvelous deeds and how he delivered them in times of trouble, if they were shown that their destiny was in their own hands and that the past demonstrated that obedience to God was best, whereas rebellion and disobedience led to defeat and exile, then the congregation would keep its part of the covenant and be faithful to God. Thus biblical narratives served their authors as a vehicle for conveying ideological and religious messages, which focused on the belief in the one God and the conception of the universe as subject to his rule.

The choice of the genre of historical narrative was bound up with the formation and nature of the monotheistic faith. This religion distanced itself from its mythological environment and barred its followers from gazing into the deity's close surroundings or observing his relations with his retinue. Thus the only way to know God and his precepts was through the continuing, albeit uneven, connection between him and his people. The past served the biblical authors as a platform for observing and studying God's ways, his management of history, his system of reward and punishment, and the lessons that the people and its leaders must deduce from it all. This required a vast perspective, and

in order to achieve it, the authors painted a historical canvas of hundreds or even thousands of years, which made it possible to perceive the cyclical quality of the time of the judges, or the fulfillment of predictions made decades or centuries earlier, as in the case of the Judahite man of God who foretold, in the reign of Jeroboam I (tenth century BCE [1 Kings 13:2, 31-32]), the rise of Josiah and his reform (seventh century BCE [2 Kings 23:15-18]). In other words, history showed that events were not random, that what might seem random was in fact part of God's plan in response to human behavior. Thus the events in King *Saul's court and kingdom (1 Sam 16—31) were God's response to the king's violation of his commands (1 Sam 13; 15), and the events in King *David's court and kingdom (2 Sam 13—1 Kings 2) were the consequences of David's sins (2 Sam 11—12), and so ultimately was the fate of the kingdoms of Israel and Judah (the books of Kings).

In order to make ideological use of stories from the past, it is necessary to employ a rhetoric that convinces most of the audience of their trustworthiness. Readers of biblical narratives, like readers of any historiography and unlike fiction readers, feel that the text refers to actual people and events. The author took pains to blend in elements that give the story a feel of real history, so that even in miraculous tales, such as the book of Jonah, there are details pinpointing the narrative in a time and place. Jonah is said to be the son of Amittai (Jon 1:1), which links him to the prophet from Gath-hepher, named in 2 Kings 14:25, who was active in the reign of Jeroboam son of Joash of Israel. He also stops in known geographic locations such as Joppa, Tarshish and Nineveh. These physical and temporal links give the story a feel of actuality, while God's repeated miraculous interventions remove it from familiar reality. A reader who is content with the story's meaning and needs no historical foundation for it may conclude that the geography is illusory, like that of the garden of Eden (Gen 2:10-14) or the geographical background of Job and his friends (Job 1—2); by contrast, a reader who needs the historical grounding may cling to such details in the story of Jonah and other miraculous narratives to believe in their authenticity. The authors' efforts to give a historical feel to their narratives shows that they were aware of the rhetorical value of historical writing in creating a sense of trust between the majority of the readers and the text. Readers who are more likely to be persuaded by what seems to be an actual event than by parables with symbolic meaning will be reassured by the references to actual places and times, while for other readers the religious-didactic message is unaffected even if they doubt the supposedly historical allusions. Biblical narratives, then, appeal to both kinds of readers. Yet while most subjects of the biblical narratives are historical rather than fictional, and are intended to persuade the bulk of the readership of their truthfulness, this does not necessarily prove their historicity. That issue must be examined with the tools of the science of history, which is, as we know, fraught with difficulty.

3. The Manner of Writing.

For a narrative to communicate a religious-didactic message without looking like a sermon, it must appeal to the readers and draw them to the subject matter. It must clothe an educational tale, from which lessons are to be drawn, in the garment of a gripping story that stands by itself. Moreover, to appeal to a wide range of readers, including learned ones familiar with scholarly texts, a narrative must use sophisticated poetics that veil some of the object lessons, wield attractive effects, enhance the association between content and form, and create a submerged significance that attracts the learned reader, who is more interested in reading between the lines than in following the explicit plot outline.

The biblical narrative that has come down to us is a written text, even if some parts of it were earlier transmitted orally. Thus we must focus on the written text and the form it was given. The need to appeal to a variety of readers or listeners called for artistic forms that would serve diverse addressees. A brief examination of the elements of the story—plot, characters, narrator, time, style—reveals the way it was done.

3.1. The Plot. The plot is a central element in biblical stories, primarily because it attracts the interest of all the readers. As H. Gunkel puts it, "The old legends subjugate everything to the action. . . . Above all else, the ancient required action from the narrator" (Gunkel, xxxix). And since people's actions reflect their personalities, the biblical plots reveal the character of the figures, while pointing to lessons and implications.

The great block of narrative that ranges from Genesis through Kings is a diachronic account of events that are often explainable by causation. The plot is made up of short stories that revolve around a conflict and lead to a change. Following the sequence, the readers encounter figures from the past, significant events and the effects and changes that they brought about. For example, the account of David's life consists of selected events that show his failings as a human being and king, his recourse to God and his need for the mediation of prophets. Consequently, the stories chosen to depict his reign do little to glorify his achievements, such as his various victories and his consolidation of the kingdom (2 Sam 5—9). On the other hand, much is made of his war against the Ammonites (2 Sam 10—12), in which his failings and sins were exposed, leading to his punishment and the uprisings against him in his kingdom (2 Sam 13—1 Kings 2). The chosen elements of the plot and the associated conflicts illustrate and highlight the issues that concerned the monotheistic faith, such as the place of the king and the exposure of a mortal king's weaknesses and limitations, the role of morality as a judicial criterion, and the hierarchy that set the prophet higher than the king.

A comparison between the story cycles of Abraham and David reveals two different organizations of short tales. The Abraham stories, which depict him in a series of journeys, are not linked causally but are connected by editorial comments on the time and place—for example, "after these things" (Gen 22:1, 20), "at that time" (Gen 21:22), "from there" (Gen 20:1), "now there" (Gen 26:1). Another kind of organization, notably the story cycle of the Davidic succession, is based on cause and effect, whereby almost every story is required for understanding the sequel as a link in the chain that constitutes the long narrative.

3.2. Plots Revolving Around the One God. The emphasis on a single deity meant considering the question of his retinue—whether other figures around him might be mentioned. There was no unanimous decision about it, so some texts do mention other divine entities, such as cherubs (Gen 3:22-24), angels (Gen 18—19) or the sons of God (Gen 6:2, 4; Job 1:6; 2:1; 38:7), but these passages provide little information about them. Moreover, the biblical narrative ruled out the existence of creatures combining the human and the divine: those who were born from the encounter between "the sons of God" and "the daughters of men" (Gen 6:1-4) perished with the deluge. Thus only the human progeny of the sons of Noah survived in this world, so contacts between the divine and the human necessitated linking the upper and lower spheres.

The contacts between the divine and the human form the basis of a number of plots illustrating the interaction of the two spheres. In some of them God himself is involved, acting either directly or by means of divine entities (Gen 1—3; 11:1-9); in others God remains behind the scenes, and events seem to be affected by plausible causes—economic, political, psychological and the like (Gen 37; 39—50). Still other plots are driven by both (i.e., dual causality)—for example, the story of Jeroboam son of Nebat, who rebels against the throne because of the heavy taxes imposed on his tribe, but who also fulfills the role assigned to him by God's emissary the prophet Ahijah the Shilonite (1 Kings 11:26—12:24).

Biblical history shows that when the Israelite nation was in the process of formation, before it settled in Canaan, God and his emissaries often intervened directly (Genesis through Numbers); the interventions gradually decreased after the settlement (Joshua through Judges); with the rise of the monarchy (Samuel through Kings) the interventions became indirect and mediated by the prophets. The development of the plot changed accordingly: when God acted within the events, the plots could deviate from the laws of nature, and there were frequent, almost daily, miracles, as in the story of the exodus from Egypt and the wandering in the wilderness; but when the deity remains distant, behind the scenes, and uses human intermediaries, events develop mostly in accordance with the familiar laws of reality, and it is the narrator or some of the characters who suggest that God is directing the unfolding events. For example, in the story of Joseph, now and then the narrator states that the hero's success resulted from God's intention: "The LORD was with Joseph, and he became a successful man" (Gen 39:2); and Joseph does likewise: "For God sent me before you to preserve life" (Gen 45:5b). Divine intervention is less obvious in sequential stories, but its occurrence is decisive for the entire sequence. For example, in the story of the Davidic succession, God's intervention, in the form of the prophet

Nathan's appearance before the king (2 Sam 12), explains the subsequent events. The election of David and his infusion with the divine spirit, while an evil spirit descended on Saul (1 Sam 16, esp. vv. 13-14), account for everything that followed in Saul's family, including his pursuit of David, culminating in Saul's death in battle (1 Sam 17—31). Even when God is not mentioned at all, as in the book of Esther, there is no doubt about his watchful presence, as Mordecai hints to Esther: "For if you keep silence at such a time as this, relief and deliverance will rise for the Jews from another quarter" (Esther 4:14). The knowledgeable reader knows that "another quarter" is an allusion to divine providence, while the ordinary reader deduces the hand of divine providence from the unexpected denouement and the switch from fear of destruction to "light and gladness, joy and honor" (Esther 8:16). The biblical narratives indicate that even when God does not intervene directly, he watches over human conduct and is responsible for the unfolding of history.

3.3. The Characterization of the Protagonists. The biblical plots revolving around the one God introduce human figures who act on his behalf and are relatively close to the deity. Mostly these are leadership figures such as *prophets, *kings and *priests, who sometimes represent the people's collective being.

The depiction of the human protagonists in the story of the exodus from Egypt shows that closeness to God was a hierarchical principle: "The LORD said to Moses, 'See, I have made you like God to Pharaoh, and your brother Aaron shall be your prophet" (Ex 7:1). The prophet, being closest to God, headed the hierarchy, followed by the king, whether Pharaoh or a king of Israel or Judah. Setting this distance between God and the monarch was highly significant in the monotheistic faith, and it conflicted with the surrounding cultures, in which the kings could be divine.

Moreover, the monotheistic narrative also emphasizes the gulf between the human and the divine by stripping the human figures of heroism in various ways and exposing their dependence on the one God. Samson's powers, for example, depended on the "stirring" of God's spirit (Judg 13:25) or its "rushing on" him (Judg 14:6, 19; 15:14), on his being a Nazirite (Judg 13:5, 16:17-19) and on a direct appeal to God (Judg 16:28-30). Likewise, God's direct intervention and timing convinces Barak that he cannot claim responsibility for the victory on the battlefield (Judg 4:14-16) or even for the death of Sisera (Judg 4:9, 22). God wished to present Gideon as a coward and caused most of the army rallied by him for the battle against the Midianites to be sent home, leaving a fighting force of three hundred men (Judg 7:1-11). Jonathan, son of Saul, was aware that "nothing can hinder the LORD from saving by many or by few" (1 Sam 14:6b). Similarly, the young David, inexperienced and unarmed, believed that he could overcome Goliath, so that "all this assembly may know that the LORD does not save by sword and spear; for the battle is the LORD's and he will give you into our hand" (1 Sam 17:47). These stories present God as the source of all the power and show the human heroes as limited and dependent on God, who sent or chose them.

Distancing the divine from the human reflects the theological principle "Truly, you are a God who hides himself, O God of Israel, the Savior" (Is 45:15), which is especially marked in the Deuteronomistic literature, in which the temple is the abode not of God but only of his name. The more God is hidden from view and the less is known about him, the more may be known about his human emissaries, chosen persons and his people.

This focus on the human is another reason why there are no perfect characters in the biblical narratives. All the protagonists, including kings and prophets, sometimes are depicted as weak. Moses had to strike the rock twice (Num 20:7-12), and even the favorably biased description of David in Chronicles, which leaves out his sins and the revolts against his rule, includes the story about his yielding to Satan and numbering Israel (1 Chron 21:1-17). In this way, the biblical narratives, despite being religious-didactic texts, avoid depicting flat figures or types and develop rounded, complex characters such as Saul and David. This could be achieved only by having God distant and allowing the human protagonists to act out their motives and complexities.

3.4. The Narrator. The biblical narrative often is told by an omniscient narrator who observes the world of the story and knows not just the human characters, but even the mind of God. Yet the narrator does not share his all-encompassing observation with the readers, but only as it suits his intentions, telling the readers, for example, that God repented having created human beings: "And the LORD was sorry that he had made humankind on the earth, and it grieved him to his heart. So the LORD said, 'I will blot out from the earth the human beings'" (Gen 6:5-8). Biblical authors and readers alike assume that the narrator's reports are trustworthy and treat them as the yardstick for the trustworthiness of other figures in the narrative. Yet unlike dry factual histories, the biblical narrative allows for scenes and dialogues reproducing the "original" voices of the characters in the story world, and it is up to the reader to decide which scenes and characters are believable.

The narrator occasionally reveals the chronological gap between the time of telling and that of the described events. This can be seen in explanatory remarks such as "At that time the Canaanites were in the land" (Gen 12:6) and "Formerly in Israel, anyone who went to inquire of God would say . . . for the one who is now called a prophet was formerly called a seer" (1 Sam 9:9). Nor does the narrator hesitate to add judgmental comments of his own, such as the concluding statement of the story about David and Bathsheba, "But the thing that David had done displeased the LORD" (2 Sam 11:27b), or speeches explaining why Israel was exiled (2 Kings 17:7-23). Thus an examination of the narrator's role enables the reader to get to know the world of the authors and their aims.

3.5. The Time. The biblical narrative's treatment of monotheistic history is especially noticeable in its use of time. Biblical stories are short—on average, some twenty-five verses. A story of more than sixty verses, such as that of the marriage of Isaac and Rebekah (Gen 24:1-67), is quite rare, and even the longer ones, such as the story of Joseph or the book of Esther, are made up of short stories.

These short stories make up a historical sequence covering hundreds and even thousands of years. To do this, the authors had to decide which parts to skip and which to develop, while maintaining the continuity. The result was various techniques of abbreviation, such as lists (Gen 5); the use of formulas or phrases that suggest that a long, if undefined, stretch of time has elapsed, such as "Now, a new king arose over Egypt, who did not know Joseph" (Ex 1:8); or specifying the time lapsed, such as "And the land had rest eighty years" (Judg 3:30). Yet when a subject is especially important, the author extends the time of telling. This can be achieved by repetition, as in the description of the tabernacle (Ex 25—31; 35—40), or by incorporating dialogues, as in the story of the purchase of the cave of Machpelah (Gen 23).

Time and space are created and controlled by God (Gen 1:1—2:3), so an implausible passage of time implies divine intervention—for example, the conquest of Jerusalem in Chronicles, where it is described as though it took place in the three days of David's coronation festivities (1 Chron 11—12).

Of special importance are the deviations from the diachronic time sequence that characterize all historical descriptions. Monotheistic history allows for various kinds of prolepsis (i.e., anticipation), mainly in denoting the manifestations of God, his angels or, primarily, his prophets. It does so also by means of dreams and various magical techniques—for example, the consultation with the woman of Endor, who had a familiar spirit (1 Sam 28). Anticipatory comments tell the reader that events are not haphazard, that God is orchestrating them and directing history.

3.6. Functionality. The biblical story is markedly functional, and the various details that it includes are designed to serve the story. This kind of narrative rarely enters into the minds of the protagonists and is sparing in descriptions of figures and places. The functional quality helps keep the story short, so the appearance of a descriptive detail about a figure or a place, or the mind of the protagonist, must be purposeful and contributes to the story or its message. The description of Esau (Gen 25:25) as "red" ('admônî, a play on the name "Edom") and "hairy" (śēʿār, a play on the name "Seir") serves not only to describe the future of "a man of the field" but also to associate him with the history of Edom/Seir and its relationship to Israel. The description of the men of *Gibeah as "a perverse lot" (Judg 19:22) not only informs readers that the men of Gibeah in Benjamin were evil because they violated the code of hospitality, but also indirectly attacks Saul, a son of Gibeah. But even the reader who misses the allusion perceives the sharp criticism of the tribe of Benjamin and the circumstances that led to civil war in Israel.

3.7. Other Rhetorical Means. Despite the functional nature and the brevity of most biblical stories, they are rich in rhetorical devices, which not only enhance the meaning but also serve artistic purposes. Some of these rhetorical devices

are described as follows.

3.7.1. Gaps. The biblical narrative has many gaps, but a closer look at them reveals fresh angles in the story. For example, the gaps in the story of David and Bathsheba (2 Sam 11) expose the marked irony in its telling. As M. Sternberg puts it, "The system of gaps, developed primarily to direct attention to what has not been communicated, becomes the central device whereby the narrator gradually establishes his ironic framework" (Sternberg, 192). In the story of Ehud son of Gera (Judg 3:12-30), the gaps of information in the smooth passage from one scene to the next hint at the hidden hand of God assuring Ehud's success, energize the plot and endow this tale of many stratagems with its distinctive style.

3.7.2. Repetition. Despite their brevity, the narratives are also rich in repetition, possibly due to their oral origin. Unlike orally transmitted stories, however, the written narrative repetitions are not exact but rather are subtly variegated and thus reward close observation. Focusing on the changes can reveal the causes and the needs of the characters, explain the plot, and deepen the meaning of the text. For example, Abraham's servant, sent to bring a wife for Isaac (Gen 24), reflects on his expectations of the meeting with the young woman; then the narrator describes the meeting; later the servant describes it to Laban and Bethuel and also repeats the injunction that Abraham had laid upon him. An analysis of the repetitions, with their many changes adjusted to the changing audience, reveals the author's psychological perception, his delineation of the characters and their discourse, his ironic observation of the developments and his rhetorical gift for speechmaking. Thus the ostensible repetitions actually are a literary device that enriches the biblical narrative and the process of reading.

3.7.3. Declinations of a Hebrew Root or Key Word. Some repetitions take the form of different declinations of a Hebrew root or a key word. This is a sophisticated device used to direct the readers' attention to a central issue in the story. For example, in the story of the binding of Isaac, the repeated use of the word *son* in a number of forms and contexts (Gen 22)— "your son" (2x), "his son" (5x), "my son" (2x)— highlights the enormity of the test from the viewpoints of the tester, the tested and the narrator.

3.7.4. Structures. The storytelling artistry also

is demonstrated in the structures. Some of the stories are constructed on the basis of "three and four," a structure in which the first three parts highlight the difference of the fourth and its impact. An example of this structure is the story of Samson and Delilah (Judg 16:4-21). Delilah failed three times to obtain the secret of Samson's strength, but on the fourth time she succeeded. Other stories are constructed on a crisscross, or chiastic, basis (a-b-b-a or a-b-c-b-a), with parallels between the units of the story centralizing the main issue. The story of Naboth the Jezreelite (1 Kings 21) exemplifies this structure: the false trial in the center (1 Kings 21:11-14) and the parallel elements focus on Ahab, the guilty party.

3.7.5. Story Openings (Expositions) and Endings. Narrative openings and endings to stories also indicate careful planning and choice of vocabulary, syntax and subject matter. For example, the opening of the story of the rape of Tamar by her brother Amnon (2 Sam 13:1-22) clearly indicates that Amnon's love is not disinterested, and the open ending implies that a fateful sequel is yet to come.

3.7.6. Motifs from Other Ancient Near Eastern Cultures, and Internal Biblical Allusions. The use of these motifs and allusions is also highly sophisticated, giving the narrative added depth while emphasizing its ideological uniqueness. The story of the creation in Genesis, for example, which recalls Mesopotamian creation legends, stresses the contrast between the almighty deity and humankind's different place in the world, as well as the distinctive concept of the sabbath and of time, among other things. All these highlight the singular concept of the creation in biblical monotheism.

The story of the concubine in Gibeah (Judg 19), echoing the violated law of hospitality in the story of Sodom and Gomorrah (Gen 19:1-10), clearly is meant to disparage the town of Gibeah and to depict it as worse than "the cities of the Plain" (Gen 19:25, 29). An examination of the reasons for the story's tendency can lead to further insights.

3.8. Conclusion. The study of biblical literature as such is a fairly new development, a field that saw a major breakthrough in the latter half of the twentieth century. Such study continues to produce new insights that enhance the readers' understanding of the poetics and the significance of the narratives.

4. Different Stories About the Same Event or Period.

The book of Chronicles and the books of Samuel and Kings describe the same period and reflect biblical monotheism, yet their histories differ in their depiction of the characters and plots and the role of God in the events, as well as in their use of time and space. This shows that a monotheistic approach need not produce uniform material, because ultimately the time of the composition and the ideological needs dictate the nature of the description.

5. A Purely Original Work, or Rooted in the Surrounding Cultures?

Biblical literature did not spring into being in empty space, and we may well ask to what extent it continued the Canaanite epic. The answer is far from straightforward. On the one hand, the biblical narrative contains motifs, phrases, patterns and characterizations familiar from Ugaritic and Mesopotamian literature; on the other hand, there is no parallel in the literature of the ancient Near East of a written history (as distinct from annals) designed to demonstrate the rule of the divine. That was monotheism's innovation, and it determined the historical character of the biblical narrative.

6. Who Composed the Biblical Narrative?

Since the texts in question were put in writing in the course of some six centuries, from the end of the eighth century to the second century BCE, we may assume that their authors, with their different outlooks, belonged to ideological schools that existed in their days. Some of the stories bear the imprint of a priestly origin and convey priestly messages, while others reflect Deuteronomistic views and messages. Evidently, neither group wrote on behalf of the throne, since their texts often were highly critical of its individual occupants and of the monarchy in general. Most scholars agree that the Deuteronomistic portion of the sequence (from Deuteronomy through Kings) was redacted during the Babylonian exile (sixth century BCE) or a little earlier (the end of the seventh century BCE), and the first four books of the Pentateuch were placed ahead of it some time later, toward the end of the Babylonian exile and the beginning of the Persian period. The various hands that left their imprint on the composite work in the stages of writing or editing also account for its diversity of views even in the unbroken continuity of unfolding history. For example, the book of Genesis allows for a plurality of sacred places of worship (Bethel, Shechem, Hebron and others), while the message of Deuteronomy is that only one place may be sanctified (*see* Deuteronomistic History). And there are many other differences in matters concerning the religion of the one God. We should remember that the events that make up the sequence are meant to express the ideological, polemical and various outlooks of the authors, to reflect the questions that troubled the editors, even their disagreements and their final compromises. The redactors themselves did not hesitate to expose the disputes between the different messages, because they shared the common ideology of monotheism and dealt with the need to understand history and the complexity of the human spirit, which both acts in history and reads about it. Above all, they were aware that for historical writing to influence its readers, it must make use of the rhetorical effects that shape the historical narrative in the Bible.

7. Conclusion.

A study of even a few of the qualities of the biblical narrative reveals that this was historical writing intended above all to teach the biblical religion; yet despite its didactic objective, it is not a string of stereotypical sermons lacking the aesthetic principles that characterize fine literary work. Aesthetic rules, internal and external allusions, model scenes, rich style and more—all these are the authors' tools in addressing even the experienced and sophisticated readership. The result is historical writing that is also fine literature.

See also HERMENEUTICS; HISTORIOGRAPHY, OLD TESTAMENT; INNERBIBLICAL EXEGESIS; METHODS OF INTERPRETATION; WRITING, WRITING MATERIALS AND LITERACY IN THE ANCIENT NEAR EAST.

BIBLIOGRAPHY. **R. Alter,** *The Art of Biblical Narrative* (New York: Basic Books, 1981); **Y. Amit,** *History and Ideology: An Introduction to Historiography in the Hebrew Bible* (BibSem 60; Sheffield: Sheffield Academic Press, 1999); idem, *Reading Biblical Narratives: Literary Criticism and the Hebrew Bible* (Minneapolis: Fortress, 2001); **S. Bar-Efrat,** *Narrative Art in the Bible* (BLS 17; Sheffield: Almond, 1989); **A. Berlin,** "On the Bible as Literature," *Prooftexts* 2 (1982) 323-27; idem, *Poetics and Biblical Interpretation* (BLS 9; Sheffield: Al-

mond, 1983); **H. C. Brichto,** *Toward a Grammar of Biblical Poetics: Tales of the Prophets* (Oxford: Oxford University Press, 1992); **M. Buber,** "Leitwort and Discourse Type," in *Scripture and Translation,* by Martin Buber and Franz Rosenzweig (Bloomington: Indiana University Press, 1994) 143-50; idem, "Leitwort Style in Pentateuch Narrative," in *Scripture and Translation,* by Martin Buber and Franz Rosenzweig (ISBL; Bloomington: Indiana University Press, 1994) 114-28; **J. Even,** *Character in Narrative* [in Hebrew] (Tel Aviv: Sifriyat Po ʿalim, 1980); **C. J. Exum,** *Tragedy and Biblical Narrative: Arrows of the Almighty* (Cambridge: Cambridge University Press, 1992); **J. Fokkelman,** *Reading Biblical Narrative: An Introductory Guide* (Louisville: Westminster/John Knox; Leiderdorp: Deo, 1999); **H. Gunkel,** *Genesis* (MLBS; Macon, GA: Mercer University Press, 1997 [1977]); **D. M. Gunn,** *The Fate of King Saul: An Interpretation of a Biblical Story* (JSOTSup 14; Sheffield: JSOT, 1980); idem, *The Story of King David: Genre and Interpretation* (JSOTSup 6; Sheffield: JSOT, 1978); **D. M. Gunn and D. N. Fewell,** *Narrative in the Hebrew Bible* (OBS: New York and Oxford: Oxford University Press, 1993); **F. Polak,** *Biblical Narrative: Aspects of Art and Design* [in Hebrew] (Jerusalem: Byalik, 1994); **M. Sternberg,** *The Poetics of Biblical Narrative: Ideological Literature and the Drama of Reading* (ILBS; Bloomington: University of Indiana Press, 1985). Y. Amit

NARRATIVE CRITICISM/INTERPRETATION. *See* LINGUISTICS; METHODS OF INTERPRETATION; NARRATIVE ART OF ISRAEL'S HISTORIANS.

NATHAN

The name "Nathan" probably was a popular one in ancient Israel. It occurs in the Chronicler's genealogical data where an otherwise unknown Nathan is the son of Attai and the father of Zabab (1 Chron 2:36). It was the name of *David's son through whom the Gospel of Luke traces the genealogy of Jesus (2 Sam 5:14; Lk 3:31). One of David's most distinguished soldiers, Igal, was the son of Nathan from Zobah, an Aramean state (2 Sam 23:36), while another distinguished soldier, Joel, had a brother named Nathan (1 Chron 11:38). Two sons of another Nathan held senior positions in *Solomon's government: one was a priest, and the other was an overseer of the district officials. No further details are given about their father (1 Kings 4:5).

When *Ezra came to Jerusalem and summoned leaders, they included one called Nathan (Ezra 8:16). Another person named Nathan is listed among those who married foreign women (Ezra 10:39).

The best known Nathan is the *prophet of that name who ministered in the court of King David. The remainder of this article focuses on him and on his ministry.

1. Nathan the Prophet: His Role and Status
2. Nathan and the Dynastic Covenant
3. Nathan Confronts King David
4. Nathan and the Succession

1. Nathan the Prophet: His Role and Status.

Nothing is known about Nathan's pedigree or how he came to work for David. He is referred to as Nathan "the prophet" *(hannābî'),* but unlike his colleague Gad, he is not called a "seer" *(hōzeh* [2 Chron 29:25]). Nathan probably was a court prophet employed by King David, but as R. P. Gordon points out, "Nathan is not to be compared with the kind of fawning time-servers who surrounded Ahab and told him what he wanted to hear" (Gordon, 237) (see 1 Kings 22:6). Nathan played a prominent role in the narratives of Kings and Chronicles as David's confidant and adviser in cultic and family matters (*see* David's Family).

J. F. A. Sawyer observes that the role played by prophets such as Nathan in the royal court is typical of what we find in the literature of Israel's neighbors: "In the Mari texts (eighteenth century BC Syria) there are examples of the king consulting his own prophetic 'adviser,' known as *apilum* 'answerer'" (Sawyer, 20).

Records that Nathan kept of events in the lives of both David and Solomon are referred to by the Chronicler (1 Chron 29:29; 2 Chron 9:29). However, these references probably are not to a separate work written by Nathan, but to records contained within the *Deuteronomistic History (see Williamson, 236-37). The Chronicler also credits Nathan with involvement, together with Gad, in David's musical arrangements for the cult (2 Chron 29:25).

It has been suggested that Nathan was "the leader and the most influential of the persons associated" with a Jebusite and pro-Solomon group in David's court (Jones, 53, 146). There is no conclusive evidence for this in the biblical texts, since Nathan is portrayed not as a man with a political agenda, but as a prophet of Yahweh who receives his messages by divine revelation.

2. Nathan and the Dynastic Covenant.

Nathan's first appearance in the narrative is occasioned by David's desire to build a temple for Yahweh (2 Sam 7; 1 Chron 17). Although Nathan immediately concurs, he returns to David on the next day, explaining that Yahweh has revealed that it is not David who will build the temple for Yahweh, but his son. No indication is given about which son is intended.

G. H. Jones argues that Nathan sought to thwart David's building plans because he was politically motivated and did not want the proposed temple since it would "replace whatever the Jebusites had already built in the city" (Jones, 77). There is no evidence for this in the text, and Nathan's initial acceptance of David's proposal suggests otherwise. Furthermore, there is no suggestion of ambivalence or lack of decisiveness on Nathan's part. He is portrayed as a courageous figure who, having supported the king's proposal, is willing to change his view when he is convinced that it is contrary to Yahweh's will. Initially Nathan spoke, as S. Japhet suggests, in his role as "a counselor who expresses his own thoughts," but having received a vision from God, he speaks as a prophet of Yahweh with a divinely revealed message (Japhet, 328).

Nathan's oracle utilizes the double meaning of the word *house* to produce a wordplay that works just as well in English as in Hebrew. Yahweh informs David that he should not build the house for God, but God would build a house for him (2 Sam 7:11). Nathan's oracle ranks among the most important in the OT. This passage is the initiation of the relationship between the house of David and Yahweh that would be both foundational and programmatic for OT history and theology (*see* Davidic Covenant). This oracle endowed the Davidic dynasty with prophetic approval and divine sanction. Following the demise of that dynasty, it fueled hopes and expectations for the future. Thus Nathan's oracle has been described as "the title deed of the House of David" (Anderson, 123) and as "the seedbed of the messianic hope" (Clements, 56). The oracle fulfills an important function in both the Deuteronomistic History and the work of the Chronicler (*see* Chronicler's History). In the former it fulfills a pivotal role, and it has been described as "the ideological summit of the Deuteronomistic history and the matrix of later messianic expectations" (Anderson, 123). In Chronicles, Nathan's oracle is not so much a turning point as an "organic element" of the work (Japhet, 327).

3. Nathan Confronts King David.

Nathan's daring reprimand of King David is omitted by the Chronicler, but it features prominently in the Deuteronomistic History (2 Sam 12:1-14). Nathan is portrayed as diplomatic but forthright, courteous but uncompromising. His stand against David's unacceptable behavior ranks him among that fearless band of OT prophets, such as Elijah and Amos, who condemned injustice wherever they saw it. The incident also shows the limitations of the Israelite monarch, who was not above the law. Although, as J. Baldwin points out, Nathan "is one of David's subjects," he also is God's mouthpiece and David's judge (Baldwin, 239). David's confession is recognition of his guilt, but at the same time it is an acknowledgment of the authority and standing of Nathan as the prophet of Yahweh.

J. Lindblom draws attention to the striking resemblance between this story and that in 1 Kings 20:35-43, where a prophet deliberately sustains a wound so that he can convincingly play the role of someone who has failed in his duty. Having gained the king's attention, he pronounces Yahweh's guilty verdict on the royal policy. The difference, as Lindblom (53) points out, is that the unknown prophet in Kings employs an enacted parable, whereas Nathan uses a pure parable.

After the death of Bathsheba's first child, as Nathan predicted, Nathan fulfills a supportive and pastoral role by delivering a message of reassurance to David, that in spite of all that had happened, Bathsheba's and David's son Solomon would be known as Jedidiah, which means "loved of the Lord" (2 Sam 12:25). This story shows that Nathan was more than a royal adviser. On the one hand, he was the king's employee, but on the other hand, he represented divine authority and announced both criticism and encouragement in the name of Yahweh.

4. Nathan and the Succession.

Nathan played a major role in the succession of Solomon. He was not among those invited to the premature coronation of Adonijah, and he may have been recognized as sympathetic to Solomon or in favor of Solomon's succession. Alarmed by the news of Adonijah's initiative, Nathan conspired with Bathsheba to gain David's support for Solomon. He enlists Bathsheba's help by pointing out that her life and the life of her son will be in grave danger if Adonijah succeeds David (1 Kings 1:12). Nathan instructed Bathsheba to visit the ailing king and to remind him of his oath that Solomon would succeed him. This mysterious oath is not recorded elsewhere in the narrative, and in Nathan's dynastic oracle the successor of David is not named. Furthermore, when Nathan himself follows up Bathsheba's appeal with one of his own, he does not mention this oath. I. W. Provan (26) suggests that it may have been little more than "pillow-talk" between David and Bathsheba, but M. Cogan (159) suspects that it is a fabrication, while G. H. Jones argues that "Nathan was acting in a very dubious, if not corrupt, manner" (Jones, 53). T. Ishida suggests that Nathan fabricated not only the oath, but also a coup d'état by Adonijah "to furnish a pretext for extracting from David the designation of Sol-omon as his successor" (Ishida, 179). S. J. De Vries, however, argues against such conspiracy theories and points out that "if Nathan and Bathsheba and David were all so clear that David had indeed made such an oath, it should go without saying that it had actually occurred" (De Vries, 10).

Nathan followed Bathsheba into David's presence in a carefully orchestrated plan to alert David to the seriousness of the situation and to shock him into taking action. Together they persuade the ailing monarch to declare that Solomon would succeed him as king. David commanded Nathan the prophet and Zadok the priest to anoint him and to proclaim him king (1 Kings 1:34). Although Nathan's role in delivering the dynastic oracle and in reprimanding David is highly commendable, his role in the conspiracy often is viewed critically. P. K. McCarter refers to him as the "obsequious Nathan of 1 Kings 1, who, bowing and scraping before the king (v. 23) pleads Solomon's case with every courtly indirection and blandishment" (McCarter, 196). However, Nathan's actions must be understood in the context of the tremendous danger that Adonijah would pose for Solomon, Bathsheba and even for himself.

Whether Nathan played a significant role in

Solomon's government is doubtful because there is no indication that Solomon would accept the rebuke of a prophet as his father had done. Nathan could fulfill the role that he played in David's reign only because the monarch was open to guidance and correction. However, the father of two of Solomon's senior officials was called Nathan, and as McCarter (195) suggests, it is possible that their father was Nathan the prophet.

See also DAVID; PROPHETS AND PROPHECY.

BIBLIOGRAPHY. **A. A. Anderson,** *2 Samuel* (WBC 11; Waco, TX: Word, 1989); **J. Baldwin,** *1 & 2 Samuel* (TOTC; Downers Grove, IL: InterVarsity Press, 1988); **R. E. Clements,** *Old Testament Prophecy* (Louisville: Westminster/John Knox, 1996); **M. Cogan,** *1 Kings* (AB 10; New York: Doubleday, 2000); **S. J. De Vries,** *1 Kings* (WBC 12; Waco, TX: Word, 1985); **R. P. Gordon,** *1 & 2 Samuel* (Exeter: Paternoster, 1986); **T. Ishida,** "Solomon's Succession to the Throne of David—A Political Analysis," in *Studies in the Period of David and Solomon and Other Essays,* ed. T. Ishida (Winona Lake, IN: Eisenbrauns; Tokyo: Yamakawa-Shuppansha, 1982) 175-87; **S. Japhet,** *I & II Chronicles* (OTL; London: SCM, 1993); **G. H. Jones,** *The Nathan Narratives* (JSOTSup 80; Sheffield: JSOT, 1990); **J. Lindblom,** *Prophecy in Ancient Israel* (Oxford: Blackwell, 1962); **P. K. McCarter Jr.,** *2 Samuel* (AB 9; New York: Doubleday, 1984); **I. W. Provan,** *1 & 2 Kings* (NIBC; Carlisle: Paternoster, 1995); **J. F. A. Sawyer,** *Prophecy and the Biblical Prophets* (rev. ed.; Oxford: Oxford University Press, 1993); **H. G. M. Williamson,** *1 & 2 Chronicles* (NCBC; Grand Rapids: Eerdmans; London: Marshall, Morgan & Scott, 1982); **D. J. Wiseman,** *1 & 2 Kings* (TOTC; Downers Grove, IL: InterVarsity Press, 1993).

J. McKeown

NATIONAL HIGHWAY. *See* ROADS AND HIGHWAYS.

NEBUCHADNEZZAR II. *See* BABYLONIA, BABYLONIANS; HISTORY OF ISRAEL 6: BABYLONIAN PERIOD.

NECO. *See* EGYPT, EGYPTIANS; HISTORY OF ISRAEL 5: ASSYRIAN PERIOD; JOSIAH.

NEHEMIAH

Known best for the canonical book that bears his name, Nehemiah was a Jewish aristocrat in exile who rose to the status of cupbearer to Artaxerxes I in the Persian royal court at Susa. In response to his own concern for the rebuilding of Jerusalem, he was appointed governor of the Persian province of Yehud (Judah) and arrived in Jerusalem in 445 BCE for his first term, with another term following sometime later. In his autobiography, Nehemiah comes across as a spiritually sensitive and courageous leader, capable of winning the trust of his superiors, inspiring action in others and meeting opposition squarely. His principal achievements were rebuilding the wall of Jerusalem, building a governor's residence and administrative infrastructure, and repopulating the city of Jerusalem. In addition, he administered Torah and sought to rectify social wrongs.

1. Sources
2. Background
3. History
4. Role
5. Character and Achievements

1. Sources.
The earliest evidence for the man Nehemiah, governor of Yehud (the Persian province formerly known as the kingdom of Judah), is the Hebrew canonical book Ezra-Nehemiah (Neh 1—13). The books of Esdras (alpha, beta, gamma) in the LXX appear to be early translated editions of this Hebrew work, beta and gamma following the storyline of the Hebrew Ezra 1—10 and Nehemiah 1—13 respectively, and alpha reproducing 2 Chronicles 35—36; Ezra 1—10; Nehemiah 8:1-13 with extra material at 1 Esdras 3:1—5:6. Of the books of Esdras, then, only Esdras gamma contains information on Nehemiah, and this is nearly identical to the representation in the Hebrew book of Ezra-Nehemiah. Later tradition will either exalt (Sir 49:13; 2 Macc 1:18-36; 2:13; Josephus *Ant.* 11.159-183) or ignore (*2 Bar.* 53—74; Acts 7; Heb 11) him.

This reveals that the evidence for Nehemiah is largely confined to the autobiographical account found in the book of Nehemiah, an account that most likely began as an initial report to the emperor but later was transformed into a text dedicated to Yahweh in order to highlight the achievements of the man Nehemiah (Williamson 1987, 18-19). Such texts, however, need to be treated carefully as a historical source, even if (as we will soon see) many aspects of this account do echo ancient evidence from the early Persian period. It must be remembered that the narrator offers the reader only one perspective on a limited number of events in the tenure of Nehemiah (cf. the more extreme position of Clines).

Other perspectives, however, can be discerned in the book of Nehemiah itself—for example, in those passages that stand apart from the autobiographical account(s). Such passages (Neh 3; 9—11) betray affinity with the accomplishments highlighted in the autobiographical accounts, but in these "the people as a whole under priestly leadership are more prominent" (Williamson 1987, 29). This reminds us that there were others who played a key role during this period, both priestly leadership and the community as a whole (for the contrasting characterization of Ezra and Nehemiah see Eskenazi, 127-54). Furthermore, Nehemiah's account clearly isolates his enemies as external forces who were not part of the province (*Sanballat, Tobiah, Geshem). However, it appears that there were many within the province proper who were not fully supportive of Nehemiah's leadership and were in collusion with the enemies of Nehemiah (Neh 4:12; 6:1-14; 13:1-9, 16, 23, 28, 30) (see van Wyk and Breytenbach). These examples do not necessarily bring into question the pivotal role that Nehemiah played in the events of this period, but they do remind us that we must treat autobiography carefully and seek to corroborate this testimony with other historical evidence from this period.

2. Background.

Although some have linked Nehemiah to the Davidic line (Ginzberg, 4.352; Kellermann, 154-59), there is no firm evidence for this assertion, which was largely based on the reference in Nehemiah 2:3, 5 to *Jerusalem as the city where Nehemiah's ancestors were buried. Such a claim can just as easily be taken as a general declaration of his Jewish background and interest in this city or of his social standing. The text tells us that he was the son of Hacaliah (Neh 1:1; 10:1 [2]) and that one of his brothers was named Hanani (Neh 1:2; 7:2). Nothing is known about Hacaliah, but Nehemiah 1:2 tells us that Hanani recently had returned from Jerusalem and apparently accompanied Nehemiah to the city, where, when the fortifications were complete, he was appointed administrator (Neh 7:2).

3. History.

3.1. Dating Nehemiah. Although there has been considerable debate surrounding the date of Ezra's arrival in Jerusalem (458 BCE or 398 BCE) (*see* Ezra), there is strong consensus that Nehemiah's arrival occurred in the twentieth year of the reign of Artaxerxes I (445 BCE). Nehemiah 13:6 informs us that Nehemiah had returned to Artaxerxes in the thirty-second year of the king (433 BCE) and only "some time later" returned for what is often called his second governorship. The consideration by A. R. W. Green provides the best case for dating Nehemiah's actions to the reign of Artaxerxes II (384 BCE for first arrival, after 372 BCE for return "some time later"), a case built largely on evidence provided by the much later Josephus, even if in the end Green confirms the validity of the earlier date.

Ancient evidence offers only a little assistance for securing the date of Nehemiah's initial arrival in Jerusalem. It is ironic that those who were most discourteous to Nehemiah in his lifetime (his enemies) have provided the most helpful evidence for securing a date for his activities. In a letter written in *Aramaic (408 BCE) Sanballat is recorded as governing Samaria with the assistance of his sons, a scenario that suggests that he was well-advanced in years (see Cowley, nn. 30, 31; cf. Hoglund, 41-43). In the same document Johanan is identified as the high priest, an individual whose father was the high priest in Nehemiah's day (Neh 3:1; 12:22-23). Most importantly, a silver vessel discovered at Tel el-Maskhuta in Egypt and dated to 400 BCE reads, "Qaynu, son of Gashmu, king of Qedar" (a tribe of Arabs), thus placing Geshem (Gashmu), Qaynu's father, earlier in the fifth century BCE (Briant, 587, 977; Eph'al 1982, 192-214). This evidence appears to support the proposal that Nehemiah arrived in Jerusalem in 445 BCE during the reign of Artaxerxes I.

3.2. Context of Yehud and Persia in the Mid-Fifth Century BCE. Nehemiah does not represent the first wave of Jews who returned to the land after permission was granted by the *Persians in 539 BCE. Records of earlier initiatives highlight the leadership of Sheshbazzar (c. 538 BCE) (Ezra 1; 5:13-16), *Zerubbabel (c. 520 BCE) (Ezra 2—6; Hag 1—2; Zech 4) and Ezra (458 BCE) (Ezra 7—10). Nehemiah arrives, however, in the wake of a serious setback in the development of the province of Yehud, a calamity that perhaps is described in the antagonistic letter of Ezra 4:8-23, which records the attempt of Persian officials in the satrapy of Trans-Euphrates (Beyond the River) to sabotage the work of rebuilding the walls of Jerusalem. This is most likely the incident that is reported to Nehemiah by his brother Hanani in Nehemiah 1:3 and that prompted Nehemiah to approach the emperor with his request. That Artaxerxes' suspicion could be so easily aroused against the Jews in the period prior to Nehemiah's arrival is not extraordinary in light of the serious challenge to Artaxerxes' rule represented by the Greek-backed Egyptian revolt of 460 BCE. Archaeological evidence reveals that in the wake of this rebellion the Persian crown constructed fortresses for imperial garrisons throughout the region surrounding the province of Yehud (see Hoglund). Nehemiah's initiative would represent then a final stage of development of the fortification of Persian holdings adjacent to Egypt. Such paranoia over the stability of this southwestern frontier of the empire may also explain the openness of the emperor to send Nehemiah into a province surrounded by powerful governors with dynastic intentions who may pose a serious threat to the crown's interests (see further 4.2.2 and 5.2 on Fried).

4. Role.

4.1. Susa.

4.1.1. Royal City. Although many cities throughout the Persian Empire operated as imperial administrative centers, the cities in the heart of Mesopotamia and Persia, those that had served as capitals of former empires now under Persian hegemony, were favored as royal cities for the emperors: Babylon (Babylonian Empire), Ecbatana (Median Empire) and Susa (Elamite Empire). In addition to these the Persians established their own, at first under Cyrus, Pasargadae, and then later under Darius I (grandfather of Artaxerxes I), Persepolis. The kings moved between these various cities, all enjoying Ecbatana's cool environs during the summer months, some favoring one over the other during the remainder of the year. Darius undertook extensive remodeling of Susa during his reign, establishing its status as a key capital, especially when Persepolis became more of a sanctuary than a capital under Artaxerxes I (Briant, 84-89, 165-70, 573, 971-73). Susa becomes the stage for parts of the story not only of Nehemiah (Neh 1:1) but also of Daniel (Dan

8:2) and Esther (Esther 1:2).

4.1.2. Royal Court. Nehemiah's role within the royal court at Susa is not clearly articulated in the book that bears his name. In the Hebrew text he is called a *mašqeh* ("cupbearer"), while in some Greek manuscripts he is called a *eunouchos* ("eunuch"). This tension is easily rectified by noting that the Greek translation of "cupbearer" is *oinochoos*, which looks and sounds very similar to the word for eunuch (North, *ABD* 4.1068-71). The Hebrew witness should be favored in this case. The level of authority in the Persian royal court is often expressed by the degree of proximity suggested by the person's title. Thus one finds officials with the title "quiver-bearer," "lance-bearer" or, as in Nehemiah 1:11, "cupbearer." The primary role of the cupbearer was to direct the palace department in charge of the king's drinking needs (water, wine). So Xenophon says that the "cupbearers of those kings perform their office with fine airs; they pour in the wine with neatness and then present the goblet conveying it with three fingers, and offer it in such a way as to place it most conveniently in the grasp of the one who is to drink" (Xenophon *Cyr.* 1.3.8; see Briant, 264). Such a person must be trusted by the king and thus could attain status and function beyond bearing the royal cup. So, for instance, a cupbearer in Astyages' Median court controlled who was granted access to the king (Xenophon *Cyr.* 1.3.8; see Briant, 92, 259; cf. Herodotus *Hist.* 3.34). These ancient witnesses show us the plausibility of the scene in Nehemiah 2, as Nehemiah not only has direct access to the king and his queen but also is granted his wish and entrusted with royal authority and resources (see Yamauchi).

4.2. Governor in Jerusalem.

4.2.1. Province of Yehud. Some scholars in the middle part of the twentieth century argued that the territory of the former kingdom of Judah (in Aramaic called Yehud) was part of a province (*mĕdînâh*) controlled from Samaria that only attained independent status as a province under Nehemiah (Alt; Noth). However, 2 Kings and Jeremiah attest to a governor appointed over Yehud by the *Babylonians and ruling from *Mizpah (2 Kings 25:23; Jer 40—41). Ezra 5:14 calls Sheshbazzar a governor, during the reign of Cyrus (cf. Ezra 1), while the prophet Haggai (Hag 1:1, 14; 2:2, 21) refers to Zerubbabel as governor. Nehemiah refers not only to himself as governor but also to a series of governors who preceded him (Neh 5:14-18). The plausibility of Nehemiah's claim has been strengthened by the discovery of jar handles and seals bearing the names of governors in the early Persian period, including Elnathan (whose consort was a woman named Shelomith, strikingly similar to the name of Zerubbabel's daughter [1 Chron 3:19]), Yeho-ezer and Ahzai (Avigad; Meyers; Meyers and Meyers, 14; although see the caution of Williamson 1988, 77 n. 56). This evidence for governors in Yehud strongly suggests that the territory enjoyed provincial status from the outset of Persian rule, if not before, within the satrapy of Trans-Euphrates (capital: Damascus) on par with *Samaria, *Megiddo, *Edom, *Ammon, *Moab, *Arabia, Dor, *Ashdod, Cyprus and *Phoenicia (on the list of provinces see Stern, 80-81; Eph῾al 1998; Briant, 487-90). At least by the time of Nehemiah, if not under him, Yehud was divided into administrative districts *(pelek)*, some of which, if not all, were also subdivided, with each part run by a *śar* (NRSV: "ruler" [Neh 3:9, 12, 14-18]).

4.2.2. Governor of Yehud. Based on the role that Nehemiah plays in the book as well as explicit assertions in the memoir and editorial materials of the book (Neh 5:14-18; 12:26), the dominant view of scholarship has been that Nehemiah served as governor over an independent province within the satrapy of Trans-Euphrates, an area that encompassed all the territory of the former Babylonian Empire that lay across the Euphrates and stretched from Syria in the north to the border of Egypt in the south. The precise definition of the term *tiršātāʾ*, used of Nehemiah on two occasions (Neh 8:9; 10:1 [10:2 MT]), is unknown, even though it appears to be linked to an office of authority in the Persian period (cf. Ezra 2:63; Neh 7:65, 70 [7:69 MT]) and may be equivalent to the ordinary word for governor: *peḥâ* (see Yamauchi). Challenges to Nehemiah's status as governor have been presented, first by R. North, who claimed that Nehemiah's title had been overstated for the sake of honor and that he was nothing more than a building contractor who at times overstepped his responsibilities (North 1971; *ABD* 4.1068-71), and second by J. Weinberg, who described Nehemiah as an administrator of a "citizen-temple community." While North's view has been largely ignored, Weinberg's has exerted considerable influence on scholarship.

Weinberg argued that Jews returning from exile in the early Persian period organized themselves according to a model well established in the Mesopotamian region: the citizen-temple community. These communities, organized according to *bêt-ʾābôt* ("houses of the fathers"), centered around a temple structure that sustained this community both religiously and economically. Weinberg claimed that these Jewish units were sanctioned and encouraged by the Persians and can be discerned in the earliest initiatives of Sheshbazzar, Zerubbabel and, later, Ezra and Nehemiah. Consisting of a combination of temple personnel and property-owning citizenry, these citizen-temple communities (called *puḫru*, similar to Heb *qāhāl*, "assembly") were led by administrators called *šatammu*, who functioned more as facilitators of the assembly than as authoritative leaders. It is this final aspect that undermines Weinberg's claim that Nehemiah served as an administrator because of his close connection with the Persians, his claim of governorship and his proactive form of leadership. Whether such an institution ever existed is the topic of ongoing debate (pro: Blenkinsopp; Janzen; con: Hoglund; Williamson 1999), even if it has highlighted the important role that the temple played in the early Persian period (*see* Postexilic Temple).

Three recent works have highlighted key dynamics of Nehemiah's governorship, one internal and the other two external. First, L. S. Fried's analysis of Nehemiah's negative interactions with powerful political figures in Trans-Euphrates (Sanballat in Samaria, Tobiah in Ammon, Geshem in Arabia, Eliashib in Yehud) notes an important common denominator: each of them represented dynastic families that exerted considerable control over their respective provinces. Fried argues that Nehemiah's initiative is part of an imperial strategy to limit such power, for dynasties represent a challenge to the power of the emperor. Second, J. L. Berquist (112-14) has highlighted the implications of Nehemiah's work for the social dynamics within the province of Yehud. The list of builders of the wall in Nehemiah 3 does reveal the dominance of leaders and priests within the community. It reminds us that such rebuilt cities had the potential to foster an urban elite and separate this elite from the poorer inhabitants in the unprotected countryside. Interestingly, Nehemiah is made aware of the problems created by this wall, and he must initiate reforms to protect the poor

(Neh 5). Third, K. G. Hoglund has offered a new analysis of the historical and political realities of Trans-Euphrates in the mid-fifth century BCE by highlighting the importance of the Athenian-backed Egyptian rebellion of 460 BCE, which led to new initiatives in Yehud, starting with Ezra's mission in 458 BCE and culminating in Nehemiah's refortification of Jerusalem in 445 BCE. This evidence makes plausible the imperial authorization of Nehemiah's mission because it shows how it furthered the imperial agenda. These three scholars help us to see Nehemiah within his social context and remind us of the challenges that he faced as a leader.

5. Character and Achievements.

5.1. Character. The most extensive reflection on Nehemiah's character is found in the autobiographical sections of the book of Nehemiah, where the narrator draws the reader into this character in ways unparalleled in the OT. Obviously, there was more to the character of this man than is presented in these accounts, and it must be admitted that they are presenting Nehemiah in the best possible light, but it is important to take account of this presentation as one key testimony to the character of the man Nehemiah.

The autobiography presents Nehemiah as a leader at work as a mission is birthed in his life through a questioning mind, sensitive heart and prayerful brokenness (Neh 1). His fearlessness is displayed in the risks that he takes first in Susa and then in Jerusalem. He is able to win the permission of those who are over him and ignite the passion of those who were beside him (Neh 2). He faces opposition squarely, whether that opposition was focused on him as an individual leader or on the people corporately, and whether it came from within the community or from outside forces (Neh 4—6). Ultimately, as his initial mission comes to fulfillment, we see a man who is "recommissioned" to new tasks that focus on his spiritual and social legacy. This recommissioning appears to be signaled by the phrase *wayyittēn ʾĕlōhay ʾel-libbî* in Nehemiah 7:5, which echoes the phrase "my God had put in my heart" (*ʾĕlōhay nōtēn ʾel-libbî* [Neh 2:12]), which captures his initial divine commission. This initial commissioning arose out of a deep encounter with God expressed through the powerful penitential *prayer and fasting in Nehemiah 1. Interestingly, this same tone of faith and prayer

can be discerned in the rest of the book, not only in the short prayer dedications scattered throughout (Neh 5:19; 6:14; 13:14, 22, 29, 31) but also in his testimonies of prayer (Neh 2:4; 4:4-5, 9; 6:9) and divine mercy (Neh 2:8, 18, 20; 4:14, 15, 20; 6:16).

5.2. Achievements. As the autobiographical account attests (Neh 5:16), Nehemiah clearly was focused on the rebuilding of the wall (Neh 2—6), which, as we have noted, makes sense in the Persian imperial milieu of the mid-fifth century BCE. However, this appears to be only a portion of his agenda, even if this agenda certainly did not involve the reconstruction of the temple (contra Dequeker 1993; 1997). First, he sought to fortify the city not only by rebuilding the wall but also by constructing a fortress and supplying it with troops. Fried has shown how the reference to both "citadel" and "walls" in Nehemiah 2:8 points to the common vocabulary throughout the Persian Empire for fortresses that housed garrisons composed of cavalry, charioteers, officials, domestic staff and foot soldiers (cf. Neh 2:9). The goals of such fortresses were basically twofold: protection (providing refuge in war) and control (managing and taxing the local population). Second, by mentioning the building of a residence for the governor (Neh 2:8), Nehemiah is suggesting that he is also seeking to build infrastructure to support the administration of the city and province, a goal that is realized in the appointment of his brother Hanani as administrator of Jerusalem, and a loyal friend, Hananiah, as commander of the citadel when the wall is completed (Neh 7:2). Third, Nehemiah also undertakes the repopulation of the city (Neh 7:4-5), a task that he accomplishes by conscripting one out of every ten people to live in Jerusalem (Neh 11:1-4). This move secures a loyal urban elite that would support provincial administration in the future. These first three achievements clearly were designed to provide the physical and political infrastructure for a successful capital and province within the Persian Empire. It is these aspects that appear to be the focus of the section of the book of Nehemiah that most likely formed the original report to the emperor.

However, it is interesting to note the two other areas of achievement that are taken up in the sections of the book of Nehemiah that were added to the original imperial report as it was transformed into a dedicatory inscription, signaled by short prayers such as Nehemiah 5:19; 13:14, 22, 29, 31 (see Williamson 1987, 17-18). One of these achievements is displayed in Nehemiah 5, where Nehemiah credits himself with the adjudication of a serious case of social injustice caused by wealthy Jews who had taken advantage of a drought in the land. It is not too difficult to see that imperial taxation also was a contributing factor to this injustice, as admitted by Nehemiah, who suspended taxation for a period during his rule (Neh 5:14-18). The other is showcased in Nehemiah 13, events that are linked to Nehemiah's second tour of duty as governor of Yehud, where Nehemiah presents himself as an administrator of Torah. Many have noted the close connection between the issues confronted in Nehemiah 13 and those found in the covenant agreement of Nehemiah 10. Although the various issues are related to Torah, we should not miss the importance of their resolution for Nehemiah's political agenda of protection and control.

See also EZRA; EZRA AND NEHEMIAH, BOOKS OF; HISTORY OF ISRAEL 7: PERSIAN PERIOD; HISTORY OF ISRAEL 8: POSTEXILIC COMMUNITY; SANBALLAT; ZERUBBABEL.

BIBLIOGRAPHY. **A. Alt,** "Judas Nachbarn zur Zeit Nehemias," in *Kleine Schriften,* ed. A. Alt and M. Noth (3 vols.; Munich: Beck, 1953-1959), 2.238-45; **N. Avigad,** *Bullae and Seals from a Post-Exilic Judean Archive* (Qedem 4; Jerusalem: Institute of Archaeology, Hebrew University, 1976); **J. L. Berquist,** *Judaism in Persia's Shadow: A Social and Cultural Approach* (Philadelphia: Fortress, 1995); **J. Blenkinsopp,** "Temple and Society in Achaemenid Judah," in *Second Temple Studies, 1: Persian Period,* ed. P. R. Davies (JSOTSup 117; Sheffield: Sheffield Academic Press, 1991); **P. Briant,** *From Cyrus to Alexander: A History of the Persian Empire* (Winona Lake, IN: Eisenbrauns, 2002 [1996]); **D. J. A. Clines,** "The Nehemiah Memoir: The Perils of Autobiography," in *What Does Eve Do to Help? and Other Readerly Questions to the Old Testament,* ed. D. J. A. Clines (JSOTSup 94; Sheffield: JSOT, 1990) 124-61; **A. Cowley,** *Aramaic Papyri of the Fifth Century B.C.* (Oxford: Clarendon Press, 1923); **L. Dequeker,** "Darius the Persian and the Reconstruction of the Jewish Temple in Jerusalem (Ezra 4,23)," in *Ritual and Sacrifice in the Ancient Near East: Proceedings of the International Conference Organized by the Katholieke Universiteit Leuven from the 17th to the 20th of April 1991,* ed. J. Quaegebeur (OLA 55; Leuven: Peeters, 1993) 67-92; idem, "Nehemiah and the Restoration of the Temple After Exile," in *Deuteronomy and Deuteronomic Literature: Festschrift C. H. W. Brekelmans,* ed. M. Vervenne and J. Lust (BETL 133; Leuven: Leuven University Press and Peeters, 1997) 547-67; **I. Eph'al,** *The Ancient Arabs: Nomads on the Borders of the Fertile Crescent, 9th-5th Centuries B.C.* (Jerusalem: Magnes; Leiden: E. J. Brill, 1982); idem, "Changes in Palestine During the Persian Period in Light of Epigraphic Sources," *IEJ* 48 (1998) 106-19; **T. C. Eskenazi,** *In an Age of Prose: A Literary Approach to Ezra-Nehemiah* (SBLMS 36; Atlanta: Scholars Press, 1988); **L. S. Fried,** "The Political Struggle of Fifth-Century Judah," *Transeuphratène* 24 (2002) 61-73; **L. Ginzberg,** *Legends of the Jews* (2d ed.; 7 vols.; Philadelphia: Jewish Publication Society of America, 1947); **A. R. W. Green,** "The Date of Nehemiah: A Reexamination," *AUSS* 28 (1990) 195-209; **K. G. Hoglund,** *Achaemenid Imperial Administration in Syria-Palestine and the Mission of Ezra and Nehemiah* (SBLDS 125; Atlanta: Scholars Press, 1992); **D. Janzen,** *Witch-hunts, Purity and Social Boundaries: The Expulsion of the Foreign Women in Ezra 9—10* (JSOTSup 350; Sheffield: Sheffield Academic Press, 2002); **U. Kellermann,** *Nehemia: Quellen, Überlieferung und Geschichte* (BZAW 102; Berlin: de Gruyter, 1967); **C. L. Meyers and E. M. Meyers,** *Haggai, Zechariah 1—8* (AB 25B; Garden City, NY: Doubleday, 1987); **E. M. Meyers,** "The Shelomith Seal and Aspects of the Judean Restoration: Some Additional Reconsiderations," *ErIsr* 18 (1985): 33*-38*; **R. North,** "Civil Authority in Ezra," in *Studi in onore di Edoardo Volterra,* vol. 6, ed. J. Schacht, M. Liverani and I. Biezunska Malowist (Pubblicazioni della Facoltà di giurisprudenza dell'Università di Roma 45; Milan: Giuffrè, 1971) 377-404; idem, "Nehemiah," *ABD* 4.1068-71; **M. Noth,** *The History of Israel* (2d ed.; New York: Harper & Row, 1960 [1954]); **E. Stern,** "The Persian Empire and the Political and Social History of Palestine in the Persian Period," in *The Cambridge History of Judaism, 1: Introduction: The Persian Period,* ed. W. D. Davies and L. Finkelstein (Cambridge: Cambridge University Press, 1984) 70-87; **W. C. van Wyk and A. P. B. Breytenbach,** "The Nature of the Conflict in Ezra-Nehemiah," *HvTSt* 57 (2001) 1254-63; **J. P. Weinberg,** *The Citizen-Temple Community* (JSOTSup151; Sheffield: Sheffield Academic Press, 1992); **H. G. M. Williamson,** "Exile and After: Historical Study," in *The Face of Old Testa-*

ment Studies: A Survey of Contemporary Approaches, ed. D. W. Baker and B. T. Arnold (Grand Rapids: Baker; Leicester: Apollos, 1999) 236-65; idem, *Ezra and Nehemiah* (OTG; Sheffield: JSOT, 1987); idem, "The Governors of Judah under the Persians," *TynBul* 39 (1988) 59-82; **E. M. Yamauchi,** "Was Nehemiah the Cupbearer a Eunuch?" *ZAW* 92 (1980) 132-42.   M. J. Boda

NEHEMIAH'S SALARY. *See* NON-ISRAELITE WRITTEN SOURCES: OLD PERSIAN AND ELAMITE.

NEO-ASSYRIAN EMPIRE. *See* ASSYRIA, ASSYRIANS; HISTORY OF ISRAEL 5: ASSYRIAN PERIOD.

NEO-BABYLONIAN EMPIRE. *See* BABYLONIA, BABYLONIANS.

NERAB FUNERARY TEXTS. *See* ARAM, DAMASCUS AND SYRIA.

NEW HISTORICISM. *See* METHODS OF INTERPRETATION.

NON-ISRAELITE WRITTEN SOURCES: ASSYRIAN

Assyrian written sources for Israelite history consist of the Assyrian royal inscriptions and Eponym Chronicles. To understand how to use these two sources, it is important to know who wrote them and why and how they did so. To redeploy an old saying, "History is in the eye of the beholder." We must know who the beholders were, their point of view, their reason for an interest in history, the manner in which they chose to express this interest, which events interested them more than others and the nature of the product that they produced.

Thus in this article we will look at who the Assyrian scribes were; their view of the world both within and outside of Assyria, especially Israel; the reason why they were interested in events, past and present, especially as they relate to foreign peoples, once again Israelites in particular; the literary forms that they developed to express their views; why they chose to record some events but not others; and the criteria by which we should assess and use their written records.

    1. Who Were the Assyrian Scribes?
    2. The Assyrian Scribes' View of the World, Especially Israel

    3. The Assyrian Scribes' Interest in the Past
    4. Literary Forms Developed by the Assyrian Scribes to Record Events
    5. The Assyrian Scribes' Criteria for Choosing Events
    6. Reliability of the Assyrian Records

1. Who Were the Assyrian Scribes?

The Assyrian scribes lived in a society that was largely illiterate; even kings, with a few exceptions, could not read or write. This being the case, the scribe possessed a great deal of influence and power. All written materials, from a simple list of the names of workers in a field to highly secret correspondence between the king and his chief officers, required scribes to read and write them. The significance of this fact is clearly shown in the Amarna correspondence, where sometimes at the end of a letter to the pharaoh the scribe adds a note of his own, addressed to his scribal colleague who will be reading aloud the letter to his master, such as "To the scribe of the king, my lord: Thus ʿAbdu-Heba, thy servant. Present eloquent words to the king, my lord,—All the lands of the king, my lord, are lost!" (*ANET,* 488).

There was a hierarchy of scribes, the lowest being those who did such things as compiling lists of laborers and what they were paid, and the highest being the king's chief scribe (*ummânu*). The latter was highly trained, being conversant with the most learned of texts—divinatory, lexical, literary, etc.—and entrusted with state secrets. Lists of *ummânu* accompanied by the name of the king under whom they served were compiled. One study (Pearce, 2272-73) has produced the following statistics: 70 percent of the scribes were administrative, 20 percent were private, and 10 percent were masters of the most profound types of written works: divinatory, lexical, literary, etc.

Most of what we know of scribal training in cuneiform comes not from Assyria but from the early period, especially the Sumerian scribes. The long and intensive training that was the norm in those ancient times must have also been the case with the education of an Assyrian scribe, since they all wrote in cuneiform, the most difficult script in the world after Chinese. Although in Sumerian and Old Babylonian times there were some female scribes, there is no evidence of them in Assyrian civilization.

As to the writing of Assyrian royal inscriptions, which comprise one of the major Assyrian sources for Israelite history, each text was first prepared by a master scribe on clay tablets. When the text was ready, a number of less capable scribes copied it out, often repeatedly, on clay (tablets, cones, prisms and cylinders) or engraved on stone (reliefs, stelae, statues, etc.) and on other materials such as metal (note the bronze gates of Balawat). Scribal writings normally were anonymous, and this is especially true of the Assyrian royal inscriptions. The same royal inscription often was repeated several times, the classic example being the "Standard Inscription" of Ashurnasirpal II (883-859 BCE). To date, more than four hundred copies of this short inscription have been recovered from his palace at Calah. The purpose was to impress the visitor, particularly the foreign dignitary who, like most people of the time, could not read the cuneiform and therefore would not know that this impressively long narration of the king's deeds was simply the same text repeated over and over again. By this method the scribes could capitalize on the illiteracy of the multitude and spare themselves a great deal of extra work thinking up new texts to inscribe. This was particularly useful at high, practically inaccessible places such as Bavian, where even a scribe could not read the inscriptions because of their relative inaccessibility.

There is no direct evidence of how a scribe supported himself, although in some cases a scribe inherited or was given a plot of land. He then could support himself from the harvest, after paying his field workers and, where applicable, taxes on the land to the palace or temple. It stands to reason that the chief scribe of the king received a much larger remuneration than did a scribe employed in keeping records of rations issued to farm workers. Despite the lack of direct evidence to support these assumptions, we do know that the scribes, be they Assyrian, Sumerian or Babylonian, complained not infrequently of being "overworked and underpaid"—a familiar theme even today. To illustrate, note the following quotation from a lengthy complaint made by a royal scribe to the Assyrian king: "I have not been treated in accordance with my deeds . . . if it is befitting that first-ranking scholars and their assistants receive mules, surely I should (at least) be given one donkey" (Parpola 1987, 260-61).

In later Assyrian and *Babylonian times there were scribal "schools" (see Scribes and Schools), in the sense that one speaks today in philosophy of "Kant's School" or "Hegel's School." One of the most important ancient schools was that of Sin-leqe-unninni, the famous compiler of the twelve-tablet version of the Gilgamesh Epic. Sin-leqe-unninni lived about 1300 BCE, but hundreds of years later scribes would proudly state that they had been trained in his tradition. They expressed this by the phrase "(I am a) descendant of Sin-leqe-unninni," which would appear in the colophon of a literary work.

In Neo-Assyrian times there were scribes writing in Akkadian and scribes writing in *Aramaic. Indeed, the first language of many Assyrians in the late period was Aramaic. To illustrate the fact that there were scribes for each of these two languages, one need only look at the Assyrian reliefs on which are portrayed two scribes tallying booty, one scribe holding a clay tablet in his left hand and a reed stylus in his right, and the other scribe holding a roll of papyrus in his left hand and a stylus in his right.

In fact, some Assyrians, whether they were scribes or not, were proficient in more than Akkadian and Aramaic, and translators *(targamannu)* of various languages were available, at least for the king. To take a well-known example, Sennacherib (704-681 BCE) sent an army to lay siege to *Jerusalem with his *tartān* (field marshal), *rab-sārîs* (chief eunuch) and *rab-shākeh* (chief cupbearer). The *rab-shākeh* harangued the people of Jerusalem sitting on the wall to persuade them to surrender without a fight (2 Kings 18). But servants of king *Hezekiah came out of the city and said to the Assyrians (2 Kings 18:26), "Pray, speak to your servants in the Aramaic language, for we understand it; do not speak to us in the language of Judah within the hearing of the people who are on the wall." This proves that the *rab-shākeh*, one of the highest officials in Assyria, could speak Hebrew as well as Aramaic.

The fact that some scribes, among other Assyrians, could speak the various languages of the variety of people within and without the Assyrian empire is important for an understanding of their worldview, for to speak a language fluently, one must have a fundamental knowledge of the culture of the people whose native tongue it is. This point leads directly into the next topic.

2. The Assyrian Scribes' View of the World, Especially Israel.

In the preceding section we learned that some scribes, like some Assyrians in general, could speak languages other than Akkadian and Aramaic. This meant that they had considerable understanding of the people who spoke a particular language. Especially relevant to the subject of this dictionary is that at least one high-ranking Assyrian officer, the *rab-shākeh* (chief cupbearer), could speak ancient Hebrew. Indeed, one wonders if this particular *rab-shākeh*'s ancestors were Hebrew. It certainly is possible, since many Hebrews from *Samaria earlier, under Sargon II (721-705 BCE), had been carried off to Assyria. The same had been done to Aramaeans for over a century before, and men with an Aramaic background had entered and moved up the scale of the Assyrian bureaucracy. Thus when the Assyrian scribes wrote about Israelites in Assyrian royal inscriptions, they, or at least some of them, had a very good understanding of who the Israelites were—their culture, religion, economy, political history, etc.

The Assyrians, including the scribes, were a very religious people—a fact that would not have been surprising in medieval or ancient times, but is not so obvious today in Western secular culture. Therefore, when the scribe records in a royal inscription that the king "by the command of the god Asshur" laid siege to a city, the scribe, the king and all Assyrians believed that the god had indeed issued such a command. Israelites would have had no trouble understanding that, except that they would have substituted for Asshur their own god, Yahweh.

The matter of religion inevitably leads to divination (*see* Magic and Divination). The Assyrians, like the Sumerians and Babylonians, believed that the gods sent messages to humankind to indicate what would happen in the future. To understand these messages, one had to learn how to identify them, read them and deduce what the message was. Did they indicate, for example, that a major disaster such as a flood or foreign invasion would occur? There were numerous ways in which the future could be read, but the most common types were extispicy (examination of a sacrificed animal's entrails) and astrology (the movement of the planets and stars). A huge corpus of texts was compiled dealing with divination, and a diviner had to study this corpus long and seriously before being able to begin making predictions. Kings looked to the royal diviners for indications from the gods as to whether they should undertake a particular campaign or appoint a particular individual to a high office. Thus, returning to our scribe who wrote that the king acted "by the command of the god Asshur," what he means is that the king had received this command by means of divination.

Because of their religion and belief in divination, the Assyrian scribes did not need to record any cause for a given event. The flood, for example, would happen because the gods had decided to inflict it on humankind. An enemy attacked Assyria because the gods wanted that to happen. There is, however, a kind of cause sometimes given for a certain event, particularly if the event was a bad one. This cause could be that someone had offended the gods in some way. An example of this is the concern that Sennacherib had about the fact that the body of his father, Sargon II, was not retrieved from the battlefield for proper burial. Sargon, Sennacherib believed, had committed some sin that had offended the gods. Such an interpretation certainly would have been understood by an Israelite.

Another characteristic of the Assyrians', and particularly the scribes', view of the world is that all phenomena, offices, names of gods, names of plants and so on could and should be arranged in lists. This *Listenwissenschaft* (science of lists) is a fundamental principle of Assyrian thought, and fortunately it has provided us not only with a wealth of words and names, but also with insight into the Assyrian view of the hierarchy of things.

3. The Assyrian Scribes' Interest in the Past.

For many reasons, the Assyrians were abundantly interested in the past. A common motive was the use of the past for propagandistic or didactic purposes. Causes could be furthered and ideas disseminated by means of compositions about former times. The Synchronistic History is a good example of this kind of text. The Synchronistic History contains a series, in chronological order, of descriptions of battles between Assyria and Babylonia that took place in the East Tigris region. Every one of these battles, according to this chronicle, was won by the Assyrians, and the boundary between Assyria and Babylonia was restored after each battle to the status quo.

Now, it is known from other sources that Assyria had lost at least some of these battles, and it is also known that apart from this document there is no reference anywhere to a boundary line between Assyria and Babylonia in the East Tigris region. The purpose of the Synchronistic History is twofold: to show that Assyria never lost a battle against Babylonia, and that there was a recognized boundary between the two powers in the East Tigris region. Careful study shows that the document was written in the reign of Adad-narari III (810-783 BCE), or shortly thereafter, when Assyria was losing ground to the Babylonians in the East Tigris region. Therefore, this is a propagandistic document attempting to show that the situation in the writer's time was illegal and must be reversed.

Chauvinism, excessive national pride, is another factor behind writing history, and this feature is abundantly clear in the Synchronistic History as well as in other texts. Xenophobia, hatred of foreigners and particularly foreign conquerors, evident in the Synchronistic History, is also known from other texts.

Another motive for writing about the past is the "superhero." The Tukulti-Ninurta Epic is a good example. This epic portrays the Assyrian king Tukulti-Ninurta I (1243-1207 BCE) as a kind of superman who embodies all the warlike characteristics of an all-conquering hero championing the Assyrian cause successfully against all enemies, especially, once again, Babylonia.

A practical side to the interest in the past of the Assyrians is abundantly evident in the Assyrian King Lists and the Eponym Lists and Chronicles, the sources relevant to Israelite history, as mentioned before. These lists (see the discussion in 2 above about making lists of everything) were compiled for calendrical reasons. By consulting the Eponym Lists and the Assyrian King Lists, the scribe could discover when an event had taken place.

4. Literary Forms Developed by the Assyrian Scribes to Record Events.

As noted at the beginning of this article, the two Assyrian written sources relevant to Israelite history are the Assyrian royal inscriptions and the Eponym Chronicles. There are various kinds of Assyrian royal inscriptions, and these can be divided conveniently into commemorative inscriptions, labels, dedicatory inscriptions and letters to the god. By far the most numerous are the commemorative inscriptions.

Commemorative inscriptions were written to record the great deeds of the Assyrian king, be it on the battlefield, the hunt or the building sites of palaces and temples. This type of inscription consists of two main genres: the annalistic texts and the display texts. The annalistic texts contain records of the king's successes on the battlefield, and the events are arranged in chronological order. Following the military accounts there is usually a description of a major building project that the text is written to commemorate. The annalistic texts first appear in the Middle Assyrian period, and they are of great help in reconstructing not only the events (such as the siege of Jerusalem), but also their chronological relationship.

Display texts are records of the military and building exploits of the king, but the events are not arranged in chronological order. They present a grand, generalized overview of the king's conquests with no apparent order except that sometimes there is a general geographical arrangement. That is, the display text might begin with a narrative of military victories in the west, such as in Israel or Egypt, then move to the north against, let us say, Urartu, then to the east against the Medes, and finally to the south against Babylonia.

Regarding the labels, these are short inscriptions on objects, such as bricks, recording the name of the king, some of his titles, and his ancestors—in other words, a record of ownership. The dedicatory inscriptions are texts that begin with a dedication to one or more gods, followed by the king's name, titles and names of his ancestors. Thereafter come military and usually, but not always, building events. The building is usually one that is dedicated to the god first mentioned at the beginning of the text. Finally, the letters to the god are represented only by a few, mainly fragmentary, inscriptions, and they are reports to a particular god, such as Asshur, on the deeds, military and building, of the monarch.

The other type of Assyrian document relevant to the history of Israel is the Eponym Lists and Chronicles. The Assyrian calendar was founded on the eponym system. Each year was given the name of an Assyrian official, called a *līmu*. Thus a scribe, at the end of a document, would say *līmu* of PN. Lists of these officials, in chronological order, were prepared so that a scribe would know in what year a particular text was written. Some of these lists add, after the *līmu* name and title, a cryptic entry about what significant event (usually a military campaign) took place that year that involved the king. Such texts are called "eponym chronicles." These lists are the foundation on which the chronology not only of Assyrian history, but also of the whole of the ancient Near East, including Israel, is founded for the first millennium BCE. There are fragments of Eponym Lists before the first millennium BCE, but there is not enough material to reconstruct a complete and consecutive list of the eponyms.

The cornerstone of ancient Near Eastern chronology, the one fact that provides the vital link between the modern calendar and Assyrian (and thus ancient Near Eastern) chronology, is the record in the Eponym Chronicles of a solar eclipse in the eponymy of Bur-Sagale. By comparison with relative chronology of other names and texts, it is well established that this solar eclipse is the one that took place on the morning of June 15, 763 BCE. Thus all the names that are listed in chronological order in the Eponym Lists can be dated according to our calendar. This is one example of the extraordinary value of the Eponym Lists and Chronicles for a study of the whole of the ancient Near East.

Another example of their value with particular relevance to Israelite history is the record in the Eponym Chronicles of the campaign against and conquest of Damascus. The Eponym Chronicle records for the eponym of Mannu-ki-Adad "to Damascus," and this eponym dates to 773 BCE, right in the middle of the reign of Adad-narari III (810-783 BCE). In fact, the capture of Damascus is recorded in royal inscriptions of Adad-narari III, but only the Eponym Chronicle gives us the date.

5. The Assyrian Scribes' Criteria for Choosing Events.

The criteria for choosing events is an area rich with questions but poor with answers. One question relates to the commemorative inscriptions, in particular to the annalistic texts. These purport to be records, in chronological order, of the actions of the king. In other words, whatever the king did was a criterion for the selection of events in these types of texts. But sometimes there are gaps in these texts. Take, for example, Sennacherib's siege of Jerusalem, which was dis-

cussed earlier (see 1 above). In Sennacherib's annals there is first the narrative of the battle of Eltekeh (703 BCE), and then the description of the Assyrian army laying siege to Jerusalem. Immediately after the siege episode the annals jump abruptly to Nineveh, where Sennacherib receives tribute from Hezekiah. What happened to the siege? Was it successful or not? If it was successful, why does Sennacherib not say so in his annals? Furthermore, if it was successful, why did Hezekiah not give the Assyrian king his tribute there and then?

Omission in the Assyrian royal inscriptions was, as we shall see in the next section, one of the ways in which Assyrian scribes dealt with an event that was unfavorable to Assyria. In other words, for some reason the Assyrians abandoned the siege of Jerusalem and returned to Nineveh. The Bible, in fact, says so: "And that night the angel of the Lord went forth, and slew a hundred and eighty-five thousand in the camp of the Assyrians; and when men arose early in the morning, behold, these were all dead bodies. Then Sennacherib king of Assyria departed, and went home, and dwelt at Nineveh" (2 Kings 19:35-36). That was the Bible's version of what happened to the Assyrian siege; the Assyrians simply omitted it because, whatever happened, it was a setback for the Assyrians. Thus deliberate omission of an Assyrian disgrace is one criterion for deciding what an Assyrian scribe would include and what he would not (*see* History of Israel 5: Assyrian Period).

Related to the question of the criteria used for selecting certain events but not others is the manner in which Assyrian royal inscriptions were prepared. In the case of source material available to the authors of royal inscriptions, it is apparent that they had and used Assyrian chronicles, at least in the late Middle Assyrian period. Enough fragments of such chronicles are now known to prove their existence. It is also known that they had booty or tribute lists, and obviously these were used as source material for the lists that appear in the royal inscriptions.

A more difficult problem arises with the assumption that detailed "diaries" of the king's campaigns existed and were used in composing royal inscriptions. The existence of such diaries has not been established as of yet, but two phenomena might suggest that they did exist. One phenomenon is a type of text called "Neo-Assyrian itineraries"; the other has to do with a fluctuation of person in royal inscriptions.

A few Neo-Assyrian documents are known in which is described, in itinerary style, an expedition with distances between stopping points noted. Neither the beginning nor the end of these texts is preserved, and the purpose and occasion of each composition is unknown. But if there are many more of these yet to be discovered, they could well have been a source for Assyrian royal inscriptions. In regard to the fluctuation of person in royal inscriptions, in a few passages in Assyrian royal inscriptions there is an incongruous fluctuation between first and third person. In most cases this fluctuation appears to be the result of a conflation of different sources without any attempt to blend them together in a consistent fashion.

To return to our original question of whether or not there were diaries of campaigns that could be used in the composition of royal inscriptions, the answer must be ambiguous. It is possible that such texts were written, but to date none has been found, and their existence is still questionable. The fact that the Assyrians had writing boards—wooden folding boards with inset wax that could easily be erased and inscribed again—indicates that these boards could be used for quick notation in the field. But so far only one such writing board has been found, at Calah at the bottom of a well. Wooden boards rot in the Mesopotamian climate. Thus we do not know if these boards were used for diaries of campaigns, although they would have been ideally suited to that purpose.

In seeking possible sources for the royal inscriptions, the letters to the god must be considered. The text type is poorly attested, but at least two documents certainly were reports to the god of individual campaigns. But a good deal more material on the letters to the god must be available before definitive statements can be made.

It is manifest that some royal inscriptions were compiled from earlier texts of the same king. The later annalistic texts of Sennacherib, for example, contain abbreviated versions of the earlier campaigns. Sometimes scribes would use inscriptions of preceding monarchs as models. This was particularly the case when a foundation inscription of an earlier king had been discovered during renovation.

6. Reliability of the Assyrian Records.

Assyrian royal inscriptions contain reasonably accurate records of building activities, a fact that is supported by archaeological excavation. They are also a major source of information about official religious cults. The record of military achievements in the Assyrian texts requires special comment because there are fundamental features of which any modern historian of Assyria and its relation with Israel must be aware before attempting to use them as a source.

The difference between annalistic and display texts should be constantly observed because it is obviously essential that the modern scholar know whether the military narration in a given passage is arranged chronologically or not. The matter of recension is another vital question. In the later eras there are frequently several different recensions of the same campaign. Time and again it can be shown that the figures for items such as troops, booty and conquered cities were increased in subsequent recensions of the same narrative during the reign. This is not to say that the earliest account should be accepted at face value. Even the first recension is the result of editing, selecting and conflating various sources.

A careful critical approach to all military narratives in Assyrian royal inscriptions is *de rigueur*. As noted (see 5 above), one danger to watch for is omission. It is well-known that in Assyrian royal inscriptions a serious military setback is never openly admitted. This cardinal principle was ingrained in the Assyrian scribes' thought, and it prevailed in all their work. A simple method of dealing with a setback was to omit it. This was done by Sennacherib's scribes in the narration of the siege of Jerusalem. But insofar as one can tell (and by its nature this is difficult to control), this method was not commonly used.

Another method was to garble the narration in such a way as to confuse the reader and hide the ignominious truth. This device was used by scribes of Sargon II in their treatment of the Assyrian setback at the hands of Merodach-baladan II in 720 BCE. In a collection of annalistic accounts this first humiliating encounter has been woven into an account of a later battle (710 BCE) in which the Assyrians were successful.

Yet another method was blatant falsehood, and when the Assyrian scribes played this theme, they pulled out all the stops. There is the famous case of the battle of Halule (691 BCE). The most reliable account is a brief statement in the Babylonian Chronicles that the Assyrians, under Sennacherib, suffered a defeat and withdrew. But in the account of this same encounter in the annals of Sennacherib, the scribes admit no such thing. On the contrary, they describe Sennacherib's victory and bloodthirsty vengeance on the defeated troops in the longest and most vivid battle description preserved in Assyrian records!

As to the reliability of the Eponym Lists and Chronicles, there is no question of unreliability, except through carelessness, for which there is no proof. The lists had to be accurate because all Assyrian chronology was based on their accuracy. With the Eponym Chronicles, however, the question arises as to why they chose to mention one event, such as the campaign against Damascus by Adad-narari III (see 4 above), rather than another. This question must remain open.

These, then, are the basic considerations that one must bear in mind when using Assyrian royal inscriptions and Eponym Lists and Chronicles as historical sources.

See also ASSYRIA, ASSYRIANS; HISTORIOGRAPHY, OLD TESTAMENT; HISTORY OF ISRAEL 5: ASSYRIAN PERIOD; NON-ISRAELITE WRITTEN SOURCES: BABYLONIAN; SCRIBES AND SCHOOLS; WRITING, WRITING MATERIALS AND LITERACY IN THE ANCIENT NEAR EAST.

BIBLIOGRAPHY. **A. K. Grayson,** *Assyrian and Babylonian Chronicles* (TCS 5; Locust Valley, NY: J. J. Augustin, 1975; repr., Winona Lake, IN: Eisenbrauns, 2000); idem, "Assyria and Babylonia," *Or* 49 (1980) 140-94; idem, "Sources for the Neo-Assyrian Period," *CAH³* 3/1.238-47; **A. K. Grayson et al.,** ed., *The Royal Inscriptions of Mesopotamia: Assyrian Periods* (Toronto: University of Toronto Press, 1987-); **D. D. Luckenbill,** *Ancient Records of Assyria and Babylonia* (2 vols.; Chicago: University of Chicago Press, 1926-1927); **A. Millard,** *The Eponyms of the Assyrian Empire 910-612 BC* (SAAS 2; Helsinki: Helinski University Press, 1994); **A. T. Olmstead,** *Assyrian Historiography* (University of Missouri Studies, Social Science Series 3/1; Columbia: University of Missouri, 1916); **S. Parpola,** "The Forlorn Scholar," in *Language, Literature, and History: Philological and Historical Studies Presented to Erica Reiner,* ed. F. Rochberg-Halton (AOS 67; New Haven: American Oriental Society, 1987) 257-78; idem, "Mesopotamian Scholarship and Royal Ideology," in *State Archives of Assyria* (Helsinki: Helsinki University Press, 1993) 10.xiii-xxvii; **S. Parpola** et al., ed., *State Archives of Assyria* (Helsinki: University of Helsinki Press, 1987-); **L. E. Pearce,** "The Scribes and Scholars of Ancient Mesopotamia," *CANE* 4.2265-78; **J. Van Seters,** *In Search of History: Historiography in the Ancient World and the Origins of Biblical History* (New Haven: Yale University Press, 1983).

A. K. Grayson

NON-ISRAELITE WRITTEN SOURCES: BABYLONIAN

The earliest writing in Mesopotamia goes back to 3200 BCE and is found at the southern Mesopotamian city Uruk (biblical Erech, Arabic Warka). From that point, a stream of records in cuneiform (wedge-shaped) writing was produced that enriches our understanding of ancient history. The historical written sources from *Babylonia investigated in this article go back to those ancient works.

1. Introduction
2. Sources
3. On the Biblical and Babylonian Historical Sources

1. Introduction.

1.1. Survival of Extrabiblical Records: The "Stream of Tradition" and "Cultural Continuity." With regard to these Babylonian sources, the question arises as to how they survived in antiquity so that they eventually could reach us today. This question is addressed by A. L. Oppenheim, who describes how the tradition was transmitted: "First, there is the large number of tablets that belong to what I will call the stream of the tradition—that is, what can loosely be termed the corpus of literary texts maintained, controlled and carefully kept alive by a tradition served by successive generations of learned and well-trained scribes. Second, there is the mass of texts of all descriptions, united by the fact that they were used to record the day-to-day activities of the Babylonians and Assyrians" (Oppenheim 1977, 13). Both types of texts are of value in the investigation of Babylonian historical texts, but the historical materials belonging to the "stream of tradition" provide the framework into which we can fit many important but otherwise isolated facts.

In writing on Mesopotamian historiography, A. K. Grayson speaks of "the cultural continuity from the Sumerians to the Assyrians and Babylonians" as "a vital factor in the genius of Mesopotamian civilization" (Grayson, *ABD* 3.205).

It should be noted that the scribes were most conservative in their transmission of these materials, as is shown by an examination of the textual features of clay tablets.

1.2. Clarification of Terms. By the word *Babylonian*, we refer to one of the two "great cultures" (Grayson, *ABD* 3.205) of ancient Mesopotamia, the other being the *Assyrian. The Babylonian culture and political state flourished in southern Mesopotamia, whereas the Assyrian flourished in the north.

The term *Babylonian* can refer to texts written in Babylonia but with the subject being Assyria, or to texts written elsewhere (e.g., Assyria) but dealing (at least in part) with Babylonian history (cf. the Synchronistic History [see 2.3 below]), or even to texts written in Greek (e.g., texts designed to spell out to foreigners the excellence and antiquity of the native culture, such as in works written by the Babylonian priest Berossus [see 2.3. below]).

The Babylonian sources are most relevant to biblical records in later periods, such as the Neo- and the Late Babylonian periods, although evidence from earlier periods is relevant as well.

Regardless of the period, when citing the native literature, we are discussing the Babylonian branch of the Akkadian language used in Mesopotamia during the second and first millennia BCE. The writing is, in the largest number of examples, a cuneiform script on clay tablets.

2. Sources.

2.1. Organization of the Material. The space allotted for this article does not permit the presentation of a full catalog of texts that might form the basis for an understanding of Babylonian history. Thus I have selected several key documents that I hope will convey an accurate picture.

In this article I am using the widely accepted arrangement of Grayson (e.g., the Religious Chronicle), but we will not investigate questions of primary interest only to the Assyriologist, such as features of the cuneiform script or condition of the tablets.

2.2. The Nature of the Sources. What kind of history writing and sources for a comprehension of history do we find in the Babylonian texts from Mesopotamia? In attempting to answer this question, let us note that the sources are many and variegated.

Here I divide the sources into two parts: (1) chronographic texts, which include "chronicles," "king lists" and "year lists"; (2) nonchronographic sources.

W. W. Hallo has popularized a phrase in current biblical scholarship, "scripture in context," by which he means that biblical texts frequently can be understood best by studying their ancient setting. To paraphrase this, we might say that the chronographic texts offer us the opportunity to see Babylonian history in context. They offer us the best opportunity to compare and contrast genres within Mesopotamia as well as materials from other cultures, such as those found in the Bible.

We begin with the year lists, noting that starting with the Middle Babylonian period (c. 1600 BCE), a custom of dating by regnal year began (see also 2.3 below). Lists of these separate year lists were compiled, which we then could regard as king lists. Often events of more than usual importance were noted in the year lists.

The chronicles are presented by Grayson (1975), with the addition of Walker Chronicle 25 (see also *COS* 1.137:467-68; 1.138:468-70). The king lists are presented by Grayson (*RlA* 6.86-135; see also *COS* 1.134:461-63), and in nonchronographic texts bearing upon Babylonian history, which includes several other genres (see 2.4 below).

2.3. King Lists and Chronicles. Of the seventeen known king lists, many are key sources for Babylonian history, others for Assyrian history, and one, with its text and fragments, for coordinating the information between the two.

We should note that the earliest king lists come from a period before the patriarchs and matriarchs of Israel whose stories are reflected in the book of Genesis. In other words, they come from a time before the history of Israel in the biblical period can be said to have begun.

The king lists and the chronicles have been assigned numbers by Grayson, which have been accepted by modern scholars. For the organization of this material, we are indebted to him. Unless otherwise indicated by quotation, the dates given are those of J. A. Brinkman.

King List 1 is the Larsa King List, covering the southern Mesopotamian city of Larsa from the very end of the third millennium BCE through Hammurapi (1792-1750 BCE) and Samsu-ilūna (1749-1712 BCE).

King List 2 is named after the two southern

Mesopotamian cities Ur and Isin, hence its name, the Ur-Isin King List. It covers the Ur III (2112-2004 BCE) and Isin (2017-1794 BCE) dynasties.

King List 3, also known as King List A, is from Babylon and covers the lengthy period from the first dynasty of Babylon (1894-1595 BCE) to the beginning of the Neo-Babylonian Chaldean dynasty (625 BCE).

King List 4, from Babylon, also known as King List C, gives "the names and regnal years of the first seven kings of the second dynasty of Isin (1157-1069 B.C.)" (Grayson, *RlA* 6.96).

King List 5, known as the "Uruk King List," covers "the period from Kandalūnu (647-627 B.C.) to Darius I (521-486 B.C.) and from . . . Darius III (335-331 B.C.) to Seleucus II (246-226 B.C.)" (Grayson, *RlA* 6.97).

King List 6 covers the Hellenistic period from the time of the conquest of Babylonia by Alexander III ("The Great") (330-323 BCE) to Demetrius II (145-139 BCE).

King List 7, also known as King List B, is from Babylon and records information about the kings of the first dynasty of Babylon (1894-1595 BCE) as well as the names of the kings of the Sealand dynasty.

The last king list that we will deal with in the category of Babylonian king lists is King List 8, the "Ptolemaic Canon," which lists kings from the Neo-Babylonian period and the years that each of them ruled. The list begins with the name of Nabonassar (747-734 BCE) and concludes with the name of Nabonidus (555-539 BCE), the last native dynast to rule before the Achaemenid period.

King Lists 9 through 17 are Assyrian or deal with Assyria and Babylonia, according to texts or fragments at the disposal of modern scholars.

The chronicles summarized and discussed below are all Babylonian historical sources (for more information, see Grayson, *RlA* 6.86-135.).

Chronicles 1-13b are the Babylonian Chronicle Series, which covers the period from Nabû-nāṣir (747-734 BCE) "to at least as late as the second year of Seleucus III (224 B.C.)" (Grayson, *RlA* 6.86). The texts are devoted to political and military matters.

Of special note for the student of biblical history is Chronicle 5, the "Chronicle Concerning the Early Years of Nebuchadnezzar II." This chronicle narrates events up until the tenth year (595 BCE) of Nebuchadnezzar II (604-562 BCE). A point of major interest to the biblical historian is the capture of Jerusalem in 597 BCE, the seventh regnal year of Nebuchadnezzar (see 2 Kings 24:8-17). Jehoiachin, the Judean monarch, was sent into exile from Jerusalem to Babylonia.

Chronicle 14 is the Esarhaddon Chronicle, which recounts events from the reign of that king (667-648 BCE) to "the early part of the reign of Šamaš šuma ukūn (667-648 B.C.)" (Grayson, *RlA* 6.87).

Chronicle 15 is the Šamaš šuma ukūn Chronicle, dealing with the reign of this king and several Babylonian monarchs who ruled in earlier centuries.

Chronicle 16 is the Akītu Chronicle, which describes "interruptions in the Babylonian Akītu festival beginning with Sennacherib's sack of Babylon (689 B.C.) and ending in the accession year of Nabopolassar (626 B.C.)" (Grayson, *RlA* 6.87). These breaks in celebration were momentous because the proper celebration of the Babylonian New Year festival in the temple of Marduk, Esagil, was thought to be critical for the well-being of the nation in the coming year, and any breach in this observance was viewed as having ominous consequences.

Chronicle 17 is the Religious Chronicle, which reports events from the late eleventh to the late tenth centuries BCE. Also concerned with "interruptions in the Babylonian Akītu festival" and, additionally, with "bizarre phenomena" (Grayson, *RlA* 6.87), it apparently focuses on these two events because they are crucial for determining the destinies of human beings. The explanation for the interest in so-called "bizarre phenomena" is that the gods are thought to reveal their will in the appearance of strange and unusual prodigies.

Chronicle 18 is the Dynastic Chronicle, a history of early Babylonia to the eighth century BCE. There is a concern in this chronicle for the final resting place of monarchs. As Grayson notes, "In the Old Testament it is customary to name the burial place of patriarchs, judges and kings" (Grayson 1975, 41). Additional fragments of Chronicle 18 have been published by W. G. Lambert and by I. L. Finkel.

Chronicle 19, the Weidner Chronicle, "concerns a period of time much earlier than that dealt with by the majority of chronicles . . . it is exclusively concerned with the importance of the city Babylon and its patron deity, Marduk, and in particular with the provision of fish for

Marduk's temple, Esagil" (Grayson 1975, 43). B. T. Arnold offers a new translation of this important historical source, explores its historical implications and compares the idea of history in Israel and Mesopotamia (see also 3 below). Arnold (144) sees the Weidner Chronicle as part of the "raw materials" for history writing.

Chronicle 19 is characterized by propaganda, containing counsel admonishing rulers not to neglect Marduk, Esagil and Babylon. In this connection, we may note that in a much later period, that of the last Neo-Babylonian ruler, Nabonidus (556-539 BCE), the priests of Marduk sided with the Achaemenid king Cyrus II (who began ruling in Babylonia in 539 BCE) against Nabonidus, who was their own ruler, precisely because they claimed that Nabonidus had neglected Marduk, Esagil and Babylon.

Chronicle 20 is the Chronicle of Early Kings, covering occurrences from the reign of Sargon I (of Akkad) (2334-2279 BCE) to the reign of Agum III (c. 1450 BCE). As a source, it is considered to be a valuable addition to Babylonian history, but only when checked with or against other sources.

Chronicle 21 is the Synchronistic History, which sketches relationships between Assyria and Babylonia during the period from the sixteenth to the eighth centuries BCE.

Chronicle 22, also known as Chronicle P (after the scholar T. G. Pinches), relates to the Kassite, or Middle Babylonian, period (roughly 1600-1200 BCE) and probably came from the city of Babylon. The reportage is sober and without bombast, thus inspiring confidence in it as a dependable source.

Chronicle 23 is the Chronicle of Market Prices, containing notes of market prices from the beginning of the eighteenth century to perhaps the eighth century BCE.

Chronicle 24 is the Eclectic Chronicle, as the author has used a variety of sources for the history "from some time before the reign of Marduk-šāpik-zēri (1081-1069 B.C.) to a period later than Shalmaneser V (726-722 B.C.)" (Grayson *RlA* 6.89).

Chronicle 25 pertains to "events relating to Babylonia from the reign of Adad-šuma-uṣur (1216-1187 B.C.) to the reign of Adad-apla-iddina (1068-1047 B.C.)." For convenience it may be labeled Chronicle 25 in continuation of Grayson's numbering of the Assyrian and Babylonian chronicles (Walker, 398).

As we noted earlier, Babylonian history was by no means confined to writings in the Akkadian language. The parade example of this is the work of Berossus, a Babylonian priest who lived in the third century BCE. He wrote a "history" of his people in Greek in an attempt to explain the venerable Babylonian culture to the Greek newcomers in the Near East. Berossus's original work is lost, and only fragments survive. The basic premise of Berossus's *Babyloniaca* is that "civilization was the result of divine revelation, not human activity" (Burstein, 7). This is reminiscent, though not identical with, the biblical belief that the world had its origin in the creative will of God, and that the deity revealed himself to humankind.

2.4. The Nonchronographic Sources. Pseudo-autobiographies, contrasted with royal inscriptions, were composed after the king's death. They are also called "narû literature." From such texts we can learn either moral lessons that the author wanted to convey or, by inference, important historical data. However, sifting historical reality from encrusted legend is not always an easy task, as is noted by B. Lewis (107-9). Nevertheless, with judicious usage, much valuable historical information can be learned from material such as birth legends: "One has to be selective in evaluating the Sargon Legend in terms of the type of material considered, and while many of the statements that are offered as facts cannot be accepted at face value, they may derive in some way from actual circumstances" (Lewis, 107).

A second genre of material that provides a valuable source for historical research is prophecy, but not in the sense of that word as used in the Hebrew Bible (*see* Prophets and Prophecy). As Grayson observes, "An Akkadian prophecy is a prose composition consisting in the main of a number of 'predictions' of past events" (cited in Longman, 131). T. Longman notes, "There is but a small transition from a text that *instructs* the next generation about the future to a text that *informs* the next generation about the future" (Longman, 190).

The preferred themes of the historical tradition embodied in epic literature are the exploits of the early kings of Akkad, such as the King of Battle Epic and the Naram-Sin Epic. From a later period we have as an example the Verse Account of Nabonidus. These works give us the opportunity to delve into the political and historical realities of the times and places from which they come.

Royal inscriptions are commissioned by rulers to celebrate their own achievements and have them recorded for posterity. Obviously, such works would contain historical truth, albeit embellished, and thus they form an important component of Babylonian historical writing. They fall into the category of "monumental" inscriptions.

Clearly, there are many other genres that might fall into the category of our present examination from which we might learn. We will take up one of these that otherwise might not occur to us.

Economic and social documents comprise a category sometimes overlooked in the pursuit of historical information. Everyday records may contain invaluable historical facts, as the following example shows. Administrative documents from Babylon consisting of deliveries of oil to people who are receiving rations from the palace contain the name of Jehoiachin, king of Judah. They come from the reign of Nebuchadnezzar II and are read with interest as illustrating 2 Kings 25:27-30. The scholar who first published this material was E. Weidner (translated in Oppenheim 1969).

The custom of dating archival texts by regnal year often can be critical in ascertaining historical fact. When texts dated to particular monarchs are arranged in order, invaluable knowledge is made available to the modern historian as to precisely when a monarch began to rule and when that rule ended. These facts can be placed against biblical data such that often perplexing chronological problems can be resolved.

3. On the Biblical and Babylonian Historical Sources.

In regard to current history writing on the Bible, one hears questions such as "Is the Bible 'historical'?" And if the Bible is historical, "What kind of 'history' does it contain?" Our study of Babylonian historical texts sheds light on these questions, on similarities and on contrasts of the Bible with other literature coming from the ancient Near East (see Dever, 5-6).

B. T. Arnold emphasizes the contrasts between the polytheistic historical writing of the historians of the ancient Near East, on the one hand, and the viewpoint of the "covenant-cen-

tered" historians of ancient Israel, on the other hand: "A conviction that the gods are active in historical events is not the same as a concept of divine self-disclosure or even of an abstract concept of history . . . the similarities between Israel and Mesopotamia are cultural and formal; the differences are ideological and essential" (Arnold, 147-48).

Yet despite these observed differences, as they "rendered an account to themselves of their past," the Babylonian writers, scholars and teachers left us an amazing body of historical material that will continue to shape our own views of what happened in antiquity (see Historiography, Old Testament).

See also ASSYRIA, ASSYRIANS; BABYLONIA, BABYLONIANS; HISTORY OF ISRAEL 6: BABYLONIAN PERIOD; NON-ISRAELITE WRITTEN SOURCES: ASSYRIAN.

BIBLIOGRAPHY. **B. T. Arnold,** "The Weidner Chronicle and the Idea of History in Israel and Mesopotamia," in *Faith, Tradition and History: Old Testament Historiography in Its Near Eastern Context,* ed. A. R. Millard, J. Hoffmeier and D. W. Baker (Winona Lake, IN: Eisenbrauns, 1994) 129-48; **R. Borger,** "§17. Chroniken; §18. Königslisten; §19. Datenlisten und Jahresformeln; §20 Eponymenlisten u.ä.," in *Handbuch der Keilschriftliteratur,* 3: *Inhaltliche Ordnung der sumerischen und akkadischen Texte* (Berlin: de Gruyter, 1975) 36-37; **J. A. Brinkman,** "Appendix: Mesopotamian Chronology of the Historical Period," in *Ancient Mesopotamia: Portrait of a Dead Civilization,* by A. L. Oppenheim (rev. ed., completed by E. Reiner; Chicago: University of Chicago Press, 1977) 335-48; **S. M. Burstein,** *The Babyloniaca of Berossus* (SANE 1, fascicle 5; Malibu, CA: Undena, 1978); **W. G. Dever,** *What Did the Biblical Writers Know and When Did They Know It?* (Grand Rapids: Eerdmans, 2001); **I. L. Finkel,** "Bilingual Chronicle Fragments," *JCS* 32 (1980) 65-80; **A. K. Grayson,** *Assyrian and Babylonian Chronicles* (TCS 5; Locust Valley, NY: J. J. Augustin, 1975); idem, "Königslisten und Chroniken," *RlA* 6.86-135; idem, "Mesopotamian Historiography," *ABD* 3.205-6; **W. W. Hallo,** "The Nabonassar Era and other Epochs in Mesopotamian Chronology and Chronography," in *A Scientific Humanist: Studies in Memory of Abraham Sachs,* ed. E. Leichty, M. deJ. Ellis and P. Gerardi (OPSNKF 9; Philadelphia: Distributed by the Samuel Noah Kramer Fund, The University Museum, 1988) 175-90; **W. W. Hallo and K. L. Younger Jr.,** eds.,

The Context of Scripture (3 vols.; Leiden: E. J. Brill, 1997-2002); **W. G. Lambert,** "A New Fragment from a List of Antediluvian Kings and Marduk's Chariot," in *Symbolae biblicae et Mesopotamicae Francisco Mario Theodoro de Liagre Böhl dedicatae,* ed. M. A. Beek et al. (SFSMD 4; Leiden: E. J. Brill, 1973) 271-80; **B. Lewis,** *The Sargon Legend: A Study of the Akkadian Text and the Tale of the Hero Who Was Exposed at Birth* (ASORDS 4, Cambridge, MA: American Schools of Oriental Research, 1980); **T. Longman III,** *Fictional Akkadian Autobiography: A Generic and Comparative Study* (Winona Lake, IN: Eisenbrauns, 1991); **A. L. Oppenheim,** *Ancient Mesopotamia: Portrait of a Dead Civilization* (rev. ed., completed by E. Reiner; Chicago: University of Chicago Press, 1977); idem, "Babylonian and Assyrian Historical Texts," in *Ancient Near Eastern Texts Relating to the Old Testament,* ed. J. B. Pritchard (Princeton, NJ: Princeton University Press, 1969) 308; **R. A. Parker and W. H. Dubberstein,** *Babylonian Chronology 626 B.C.-A.D. 75* (BUS 19; Providence: Brown University Press, 1956); **M. B. Rowton,** "Chronology: Ancient Western Asia," *CAH²* 1, chap. 6: 193-239; **C. B. F. Walker,** "Babylonian Chronicle 25: A Chronicle of the Kassite and Isin II Dynasties," in *Zikir Sumim: Assyriological Studies Presented to F. R. Kraus on the Occasion of His Seventieth Birthday,* ed. G. van Driel et al. (SFSMD 5; Leiden: E. J. Brill, 1982) 398-417.

D. B. Weisberg

NON-ISRAELITE WRITTEN SOURCES: EGYPTIAN ARAMAIC PAPYRI

The climatic conditions in *Egypt allow for the preservation of fragile material such as papyri to an extent not paralleled in Palestine. Over the past century or more, several collections of *Aramaic papyri from the *Persian (Achaemenid) period have been discovered and published. They shed valuable light on aspects of the language, history and religion of Historical Books in the Bible such as the books of *Ezra and Nehemiah.

1. Survey of the Main Collections
2. Significance for Biblical Studies

1. Survey of the Main Collections.
The main groups of papyri are listed below with details of the standard first or early editions. A very useful translation (into French) and commentary is that of P. Grelot, and a magisterial

new edition of all this material (and more besides) is now found in *TAD,* which certainly should be used for advanced study. Some of the main texts are also included in J. M. Lindenberger and *COS* 3.

1.1. The Elephantine Papyri. The first group of papyri to be discovered came from the island of Elephantine, situated in the Nile River just north of the first cataract opposite ancient Syene (modern Assuan). First published in the early years of the twentieth century, a full collection of all the material as then known was conveniently assembled by A. Cowley in 1923. In 1953 a further collection from the same source was published by E. G. Kraeling.

The majority of these papyri relate to a Jewish military colony that evidently was stationed on the island as part of a border guard for Persian Egypt (Porten 1968). Many of them are of a legal nature—marriage and divorce deeds, conveyances, lawsuits and so on—which give a vivid insight into the way of life of the colony. Some, however, relate more particularly to religious matters, from which we learn that there was a temple dedicated to the Jewish God Yahu (until it was destroyed by local Egyptians). A subscription list indicates, however, that alongside Yahu other deities were venerated, in particular Anath-Yahu, presumably Yahu's consort. Another important, though unfortunately incompletely preserved, papyrus, dated to 419 BCE, seems to give the colonists instruction on the proper observance of the Festival of (Passover and) Unleavened Bread. The prescriptions are very similar to, though not identical with, those now found in the biblical laws.

It is further deserving of mention that fragments of Aramaic versions of the Bisitun inscription (*see* Non-Israelite Written Sources: Old Persian and Elamite) and of the tale of Ahiqar were found among the papyri. The latter is a wisdom text that therefore has little direct relevance for the Historical Books, although it is of interest to note that Ahiqar is called "a wise and ready scribe," using the same term in Aramaic as the Hebrew of Ezra 7:6 *(māhir).*

How these Jews came to be at Elephantine is the subject of considerable speculation. Judged by later standards, their religion clearly was not fully orthodox, and this has been sufficient for some to rule out the initially most obvious solution, that they were the descendants of some who had fled from Judah to Egypt during the period of the Babylonian conquest at the start of the sixth century BCE. (It should be noted, however, that both textual and archaeological evidence now indicates that *Josiah's reform may not have been so successful in eliminating non-Deuteronomic forms of belief and practice as once was thought.) Others, therefore, propose that they must have descended from earlier groups of Judean mercenaries who freely made their way to Egypt, or even that their origins might be sought among refugees from the much earlier Assyrian conquest of the northern kingdom of Israel (although on the face of it this last suggestion is difficult to reconcile with the self-designation by the colonists as "Jews"). All we can say for certain is that they were already well established by the time of the Persian conquest of Egypt under Cambyses in 525 BCE.

1.2. The Arsames Archive. This is a collection of thirteen complete letters, as well as fragments of five or six more, written on leather (thus not strictly papyri). Kept together in a leather bag, they were acquired on the antiquities market with no indication of their exact provenance. They were first published by Driver in 1954.

All the letters are instructions of an official or semi-official nature from the Persian satrap of Egypt, Arsames, or from other high officials to junior administrative officers in Egypt concerning their domain lands. Dating from the last quarter of the fifth century BCE, they indicate that there was frequent unrest in Egypt, especially during the three years or so that Arsames was away from the country attending to his personal estates in Babylon or Persia (cf. Neh 13:6).

1.3. The Hermopolis Papyri. This is a collection of eight letters, written around 500 BCE, from soldiers temporarily stationed in Memphis to their families in Syene (i.e., part of the same military colony described in 1.1 above). For unknown reasons, the letters got only as far as Hermopolis (midway between Memphis in the north of Egypt and Syene in the south), where they were discovered in 1945 but not published until 1966 by two Italian scholars (thus the texts are more conveniently accessible in Gibson, 125-43).

The writers appear to have been members of two Aramaean families. They would have belonged to the garrison stationed on the mainland at Syene, opposite the Jewish colony on the island of Elephantine, and the references to gods and temples differentiate them quite mark-

edly from their Jewish companions. The letters are of a charming personal and domestic nature, and not the least of their importance for us is the clear indication they give of the variety of types of Aramaic that could have been in use within even a very small area.

1.4. The Saqqara Papyri. These 202 pieces of Aramaic papyri were found during excavations at North Saqqara between 1966 and 1973 (Segal). They are very fragmentary for the most part, though a reference to Cambyses supports the evidence from palaeography that they should be dated to the Achaemenid period. Perhaps their chief contribution is to language (they provide further clear evidence of dialectal differences within Imperial, or Achaemenid, Aramaic) and to the understanding of legal and related customs (Williamson 1987).

2. Significance for Biblical Studies.

These papyri have impacted biblical studies in various ways, some more direct than others. The following is a representative sample that includes the main points of scholarly discussion over the years.

2.1. Language. Parts of the book of *Ezra are in *Aramaic, which was the diplomatic language of the Persian Empire. The papyri from Elephantine were the first extensive corpus of Aramaic texts to be discovered that were roughly contemporary with the purported date of the Ezra material, so that not surprisingly there was intense interest in drawing comparisons. Apart from obvious points such as refining lexicographical precision, it was soon observed that in light of this increasing knowledge the Aramaic of Ezra seemed to be earlier than that in Daniel but in some respects later than the Aramaic of the papyri. Scholars differed in the conclusions that they drew from this, some claiming that it pointed toward the inauthenticity of the documents cited, and others more conservatively responding that the differences could be attributed to later scribes updating spelling and the like in light of the way that the language had developed by their time.

With the addition of the more recently published collections to the corpus, however, the situation has become rather more complex. It is now clear that within what was formerly regarded as the monolithic Imperial Aramaic of government and diplomacy there were considerable regional and dialectal variations, so that it would be hasty to judge any particular linguistic feature as completely impossible. Indeed, there are variations even within the small amount of Aramaic included in Ezra (for instance, the spelling of the second- and third-person plural pronominal suffixes -kom/-kon and -hom/-hon). Since the chapters in question include both what purport to be contemporary documents and (possibly considerably) later narrative connections between them, such variety is not unexpected, and it might be explained either as contemporary variant or as later scribal development. On the whole, the newer evidence does not make the case for authenticity stronger, but it makes arguments to the contrary less convincing.

2.2. Epistolography. Since a good deal of the Aramaic material in Ezra is made up of letters and the like, there has been intense study of the general form that letter-writing took in the papyri in order to see the extent to which the conventions used coincide, and these analyses have been increasingly refined as new publications have been added to the data for comparison (see, e.g., Fitzmyer; Alexander; Whitehead; Dion). The general consensus has tended to move in the direction of concluding that these letters, if not authentic, at least accurately reflect the conventions of the period and therefore must derive from it, since the conventions changed markedly in the Hellenistic period.

Recently this conclusion has been strongly challenged, however, by D. Schwiderski in a work that surely is in keeping with the swing of the pendulum in a more skeptical direction regarding the biblical sources for the Persian period in general. At the time of this writing, it is still too soon to judge whether the new analysis will carry conviction.

2.3. History. In 411 BCE the Jewish temple on the island of Elephantine was destroyed by some local Egyptians, and the colonists' petition for protection and permission to rebuild the altar (Cowley, 27; *TAD* 1.62-65; *COS* 3.50:123-25) appears to have gone unanswered. It is not certain whether the petition was addressed to Arsames, the satrap of Egypt, or to Bigvai, the governor in Jerusalem. The former would seem more natural, but we know from Cowley, 30:18, that a petition was also sent to Jerusalem at this time. Either way, two or three years later the colonists wrote again to Bigvai (Cowley, 30; *TAD* 1.68-71; *COS* 3.51:125-30), and from this we

learn of people in Jerusalem who may be fitted with what is known from the book of Nehemiah.

We note first that at the end of the letter it is stated that the colonists had also written "to Delaiah and Shelemiah the sons of Sanballat governor of Samaria." This surely is the *Sanballat who is well known as one of the principal opponents of *Nehemiah (see, e.g., Neh. 2:10, 19). Although it had always been assumed that Sanballat was governor of Samaria (as stated by Josephus), that fact is never explicitly stated in the Bible, whereas this letter confirms it for the first time. He appears still to be alive in 408 BCE, but there is the suggestion that he is elderly, given that his sons seem to be acting on his behalf. This further serves to confirm that Nehemiah's ministry should be dated to the reign of Artaxerxes I (465-425 BCE) rather than the later Artaxerxes II (405-359 BCE). The fact that the colonists wrote to Samaria as well as to Jerusalem and that the reply came from both of them jointly (Cowley, 32; *TAD* 1.76-77; *COS* 3.52:130-31) suggests that relations between the two centers may not always have been as strained as Nehemiah presents it.

In line 18 of the letter the colonists state that previously they had written both to Bigvai (who was governor of Judah [see line 1]) and to Johanan the high priest (perhaps the one mentioned in Neh 12:22-23). This combination of office holders has been linked by many scholars with a story in Josephus (*Ant.* 11.297-301) to the effect that a high priest Jesus was murdered in the temple by his brother Joannes (Greek for "Johanan"), and that Bagoses (= Bigvai) imposed a tax on the daily sacrifices as a punishment. This has then further been used as evidence for a late date for Ezra because of the reference to a possibly contemporary Jehohanan in Ezra 10:6. Alternatively, Bright (391-402) used the same evidence to argue for an intermediary date for Ezra, since he did not think that Ezra could possibly have consorted with a murderer; therefore Ezra must have been later than Nehemiah but earlier than the Josephus incident. None of these arguments should be regarded as more than mere possibilities, however; the names in question are very common at this time, and other possible known individuals could equally well have been referred to by Josephus in the reign of Artaxerxes III (for different opinions on this see Williamson 1977; Schwartz; Grabbe).

Of course, it should not be concluded from

this brief review of direct contacts between the papyri and the biblical texts that this is all that may be derived from the former of historical significance. There is much that they add in other ways to our knowledge of Achaemenid-period Egypt, to the ways of Persian administration and the like, all of which supply additional important background information for the world in which the relevant Historical Books of the OT are set.

2.4. Religious History. It was noted previously that the papyri indicate that preexilic religion may not have been at all as uniform as the biblical sources would lead us to believe. In addition to that, however, there are two specific issues that point to the way in which religion was developing at the later time of the papyri themselves.

First, the petition mentioned in the preceding section apparently received an oral reply, of which Cowley, 32 (*TAD* 1.76-77; *COS* 3.52:130-31), is a brief memorandum. It is of particular interest in that while it permits the colonists to rebuild and offer meal offerings and incense, as they had requested, their further request to offer animal sacrifices is not mentioned, and indeed, according to B. Porten (1979), a reference to this was actually erased from the first draft and written over, indicating that the silence was deliberate. The explanation for this is uncertain. One frequently canvassed possibility is that animal sacrifice was regarded as offensive either to the Egyptians (so that this would be a conciliatory move in order to avoid the original antagonism being renewed) or to the Persians (for whom fire was sacred and would be contaminated by sacrifice), so that this was a diplomatic silence. Alternatively, however, one may consider whether there is a reflection here of Jerusalem hegemony. It appears that the Deuteronomic law of centralization did not yet extend to sanctuaries outside the land of Israel, but as in the case of the offerings at the site of the ruined temple during the exilic period (cf. Jer 41:5, where again meal offerings and incense alone are mentioned) and expectations of the nature of worship outside the land after the exile (cf. Mal 1:11), it may have been felt that animal sacrifice should be offered only at the central sanctuary in Jerusalem. If so, this clearly marks a step along the road toward the eventual exclusive claims of the Jerusalem temple.

Second, mention should be made of the famous so-called Passover Papyrus (Cowley, 21; *TAD* 1.54-55; *COS* 3.46:116-17), which was written a decade or so before the ones just discussed. Important claims about the development of Jewish religion have been based on this papyrus, but it is so badly damaged that caution should be exercised—even the word *Passover* is merely a (very probable) restoration! It appears, however, to record that orders were relayed from the king himself to Arsames and thence via Hananiah to the colonists concerning the date and means of celebration of Passover and Unleavened Bread. Since an earlier ostracon mentions Passover, it is clear that this cannot have been a "first-time order" to keep this festival, so that the question of its precise import remains. Possibilities include the following: (1) This reflects a new custom in which the previously separate festivals of Passover and of Unleavened Bread were combined into one. That these festivals went through such a development is generally accepted on the basis of the evidence of the various biblical law codes, and the situation here would then be comparable with the way that the (late) Chronicler describes the celebrations under Hezekiah in 2 Chronicles 30. (2) On the basis of the way that what survives of the papyrus is phrased, it may be maintained that it is the date of Passover in particular that is being regulated here for the first time. (3) It could be that the aim was to draw the practice of the festival at Elephantine into line with that in Jerusalem. (4) Alternatively, given the possibility that the Egyptians found the celebration of Passover especially offensive, it may simply be a royal affirmation of the rights of the Jews to celebrate nevertheless. However, given that some of the prescriptions that are listed do not conform with either the biblical regulations or what we know of later practice, it is clear that any explanation leaves some matters unresolved. Perhaps the most important observation of all, therefore, is that in principle, at least, the Persian emperor himself is portrayed as micromanaging the religious practices of a small minority people (perhaps in response to some form of petition from them). Thus it usefully illustrates the kind of involvement that we find also in many of the accounts in the books of Ezra and Nehemiah, and to that extent it answers some of the objections that have been leveled against the verisimilitude of these accounts.

See also ARAMAIC LANGUAGE; HISTORY OF ISRAEL 7: PERSIAN PERIOD; HISTORY OF ISRAEL 8:

POSTEXILIC COMMUNITY.
BIBLIOGRAPHY. **P. S. Alexander,** "Remarks on Aramaic Epistolography in the Persian Period," *JSS* 23 (1978) 155-70; **J. Bright,** *A History of Israel* (3d ed.; Philadelphia: Westminster, 1981); **A. Cowley,** *Aramaic Papyri of the Fifth Century B.C.* (Oxford: Clarendon Press, 1923); **P.-E. Dion,** "Les types épistolaires hébréo-araméens jusqu'au temps de Bar-Kokhbah," *RB* 96 (1979) 544-79; **G. R. Driver,** *Aramaic Documents of the Fifth Century B.C.* (Oxford: Clarendon Press, 1954); **J. A. Fitzmyer,** "Some Notes on Aramaic Epistolography," *JBL* 93 (1974) 201-25 (a slightly revised form of this article appears in *A Wandering Aramean: Collected Aramaic Essays* [SBLMS 25; Missoula, MT: Scholars Press, 1979] 183-204, and in *Semeia* 22 [1981] 25-57); **J. C. L. Gibson,** *Textbook of Syrian Semitic Inscriptions, 2: Aramaic Inscriptions* (Oxford: Clarendon Press, 1975); **L. L. Grabbe,** "Who Was the Bagoses of Josephus (Ant. 11.7.1, §§297-301)?" *Transeuphratène* 5 (1992) 49-55; **P. Grelot,** *Documents araméens d'Égypte* (Paris: Cerf, 1972); **E. G. Kraeling,** *The Brooklyn Museum Aramaic Papyri: New Documents of the Fifth Century B.C. from the Jewish Colony at Elephantine* (New Haven: Yale University Press, 1953); **J. M. Lindenberger,** *Ancient Aramaic and Hebrew Letters* (SBLWAW 4; Atlanta: Scholars Press, 1994); **B. Porten,** "Aramaic Papyri and Parchments: A New Look," *BA* 49 (1979) 74-104; idem, *Archives from Elephantine: The Life of an Ancient Jewish Military Colony* (Berkeley and Los Angeles: University of California Press, 1968); **B. Porten and A. Yardeni,** *Textbook of Aramaic Documents from Ancient Egypt* (4 vols.; Jerusalem: Hebrew University, 1986-1999); **D. R. Schwartz,** "On Some Papyri and Josephus' Sources and Chronology for the Persian Period," *JSJ* 21 (1990) 175-99; **D. Schwiderski,** *Handbuch des nordwestsemitischen Briefformulars: Ein Beitrag zur Echtheitsfrage der aramäische Briefe des Esrabusches* (BZAW 295; Berlin: de Gruyter, 2000); **J. B. Segal,** *Aramaic Texts from North Saqqâra, with Some Fragments in Phoenician* (Excavations at North Saqqâra 4; London: Egypt Exploration Society, 1983); **J. D. Whitehead,** "Some Distinctive Features of the Language of the Aramaic Arsames Correspondence," *JNES* 37 (1978) 119-40; **H. G. M. Williamson,** "The Historical Value of Josephus' *Jewish Antiquities* xi.297-301," *JTS* 28 (1977) 49-66 (repr., in *Studies in Persian Period History and Historiography* [FAT 38; Tübingen: Mohr Siebeck, 2004] 74-89); idem, review of *Aramaic Texts from North Saqqâra, with Some Fragments in Phoenician,* by J. B. Segal, *JEA* 73 (1987) 265-69.

H. G. M. Williamson

NON-ISRAELITE WRITTEN SOURCES: OLD PERSIAN AND ELAMITE

Old Persian was the language of the Achaemenid kings as known from the books of *Ezra and *Nehemiah. Relatively little written material survives, but what remains is clearly of importance for the study of these biblical books. Elamite was the main language of the Achaemenid (Persian) bureaucracy, and several thousand tablets have survived from Persepolis, one of the capital cities of the Persian Empire. While not referring to major political events or personages, they shed welcome light on aspects of the imperial administration.

1. Old Persian
2. Elamite

1. Old Persian.
1.1. Language. Old Persian is an Indo-European language, more specifically a member of the Indo-Iranian, or Aryan, family. It was the vernacular of the Achaemenid kings and their court. Already in antiquity it doubtless was one of a number of closely related dialects (such as Avestan), and it has many later descendants down to modern times. A number of loanwords entered biblical *Hebrew and *Aramaic, some of which are recognizable independently from their development through earlier European languages into English—for example, *pardes* (Avestan *pairidaêza,* "enclosure"), "garden, park," in Nehemiah 2:8 (cf. Gk *paradeisos,* paradise).

1.2. Writing. Old Persian is written in a form of cuneiform that is peculiar to itself. With thirty-six main signs (together with a handful of ideograms), it is closer to being alphabetic than the syllabic Akkadian (and so was deciphered first, thus providing vital clues for the decipherment of Akkadian and Elamite). Moreover, it is attested in only a modest number of rock-cut inscriptions and on a few other prestige objects (Dandamaev, 35-36; Cook, 69), not on clay tablets, as might have been expected. Rather, Persian bureaucracy clearly employed Elamite for recording its affairs, and later on, Aramaic.

Thus it plausibly has been proposed that Old Persian was not a literary language at all. Its written form was invented (or at least ordered) by Darius specifically to record his path of accession to the throne in the famous trilingual Bisitun inscription, in which the Elamite text was carved first, with the Old Persian and Akkadian versions following only secondarily. Thereafter, for prestige reasons, Old Persian was imitated on monumental inscriptions on tombs and the like, but it never was used for other forms of writing, whether administrative or literary. It has even been suggested that while the king dictated in Old Persian, the scribe simultaneously recorded in Elamite, and then when reading back to the king or some other recipient of the message, the scribe (or another scribe) retranslated at sight back into Old Persian (Gershevitch).

1.3. Texts. The most convenient collection of Old Persian texts for English-speaking readers remains that of R. G. Kent.

Without question, the most important inscription, and at over four hundred lines by far the longest, is the Bisitun (or Behistun) trilingual (the other two copies being Elamite and Akkadian). It is carved on a virtually inaccessible rock high above the road that runs from Baghdad to Teheran, and it is accompanied by impressive sculptures of Darius, his defeated rebels and over all the representation of the god Ahuramazda. It recalls at length how while Cyrus's successor Cambyses was campaigning in Egypt, a usurper named Gaumata seized the throne by claiming to be Bardiya, Cambyses' brother. He was shown to be a usurper, according to Darius, by the fact that Cambyses himself had already had Bardiya secretly executed. Cambyses died during his return journey from Egypt, whereupon Darius, who claimed to belong to the royal family, gained the support of other leading military commanders to remove the usurper and so to rescue the dynasty. Thereupon a series of rebellions broke out in regions such as Babylon, Media and Armenia, and it was not until the second year of his reign that peace was restored. As well as allusions to all this in the early chapters of the book of Zechariah, the emphasis on the second year of Darius in Ezra 4:24 is doubtless related, as is the suspicious attitude of the governor Tattenai to anything that might portend rebellion in Ezra 5.

The extent to which this narrative may be trusted historically is much debated (see Briant, 119-50). From Darius's point of view, the whole

account looks "too good to be true," as is often the case with such *propaganda. But the more this suspicion is grounded, the more impressive becomes the achievement of the Persian state machinery in disseminating its version of events, for we find that not only were copies of the text distributed throughout the empire and made accessible in different languages, the best-known example of which is the Aramaic version found at Elephantine in southern Egypt (see Greenfield and Porten), but also it clearly is the version of events that became known to the later Greek historian Herodotus. The fact that the Persians could weave such powerful political "spin" needs to be borne in mind when assessing how the Jews reacted to their position within what at the time must have seemed like an almost invincible power.

2. Elamite.

2.1. Language and Writing. The ancient kingdom of Elam, situated to the east of Babylonia and with its capital at Susa, for centuries was involved one way or another with the imperial rivalries of *Assyria and *Babylon. By the start of the Persian, or Achaemenid, period, it had already been partly absorbed into the western empires. At the same time, however, it had succumbed in the east to pressures from the Medes and Persians, and so inevitably passed into the hands of the great Persian king Cyrus at the same time as his absorption of Babylon.

Although the Elamite language has no known affinities (a circumstance that partly accounts for the fact that it remains imperfectly understood in matters of detail), it had a long history of writing, having used different writing systems over the centuries, starting with a simple pictographic system as early as the start of the third millennium BCE (*see* Writing, Writing Materials and Literacy in the Ancient Near East). By the Persian period, however, long contact with the cuneiform system of writing had led to its adoption in a localized form of Akkadian. Thus it is not surprising to find that Elamite scribes provided much of the bureaucracy for the early Persian kings, whose own language, as mentioned above, had no known writing tradition.

2.2. Texts. There are two main groups of texts in the Elamite of the Achaemenid period. First, the Persepolis Fortification Tablets, which comprise the larger of the two groups, date from the thirteenth to the twenty-eighth year of Darius I (509-494 BCE). Over two thousand tablets have been published so far (Hallock 1969; 1978), although well over one thousand more remain unpublished. The majority are accounting texts, detailing payments in kind and rations to a wide variety of people of varying social standing and occupation. The situation with regard to the second group, the Persepolis Treasury Tablets, is similar. At 139, their number is much smaller (for the main publication see Cameron; he published the remainder in a series of later journal articles), and they date from the later period of 492-458 BCE. As far as content is concerned, the chief difference from the Fortification Tablets is that much of the payment is now made in cash rather than kind.

2.3. Biblical Significance. It needs to be recognized that the vast majority of these tablets relate to people and situations close to the heart of the empire with its three capital cities. We should not expect to find here direct references or allusions to any person or event mentioned in the Bible, with its setting in the geographically remote province of Judah. Nevertheless, to the extent that Persian rule was heavily centralized, despite its widespread extent and ethnic diversity, there are aspects of its administrative procedures that are illuminated by these tablets and that are presupposed in some of the biblical accounts (Williamson, 60-63, 212-31). This will apply in particular to those spheres where local officials were dealing directly with their Persian superiors.

2.3.1. Bureaucracy. The overwhelmingly dominant impression given by these tablets is of an almost obsessive concern for bureaucratic exactitude and control (see Hallock 1985; Briant, 434-87). Monthly or daily payments to people of all ranks and even animals are recorded, as are allowances for those on journeys, accounts of which at each way station are reported back to the center. Consolidated accounts are then made up periodically from these individual dockets. Such concerns are echoed in every part of the books of Ezra and Nehemiah, where accounting procedures are belabored and where clearly there is no fear that specific authorization even for comparatively minor matters will be found to have been undocumented (e.g., Ezra 1:8-11; 2:59-63; 4:15, 19; 5:10, 17; 6:1-2; 7:21-22; 8:26-27, 33-34; Neh 2:7-9; 5:14-18).

2.3.2. Travel. These same books also refer to

a number of journeys between Babylon and *Jerusalem, sometimes including the transportation of specified items for the temple or city. The most specific are those of Sheshbazzar (Ezra 1:7-11), *Ezra (Ezra 8) and *Nehemiah (Neh 2), although the implication of several exchanges of letters between the province and the imperial center in Ezra 4—6 is that such travel was a standard feature of official business. The picture that may be built up from the Persepolis tablets is that this is by no means unexpected. We learn of provision made on a daily basis for groups of travelers, both small and large, moving over sometimes considerable distances (for instance, Kandahar, India, Arachosia, Babylon, Sardis and Egypt are mentioned as starting points or destinations). Movement throughout the wide-flung provinces of the empire thus was well regulated and controlled. In addition, we learn of mounted (and no doubt armed) couriers moving swiftly from one station to the next, and also of "elite guides" (lit., "safe-keepers"), while of course the Persian express postal service, having been facilitated by all these arrangements being kept in place, was famed throughout the ancient world (see Herodotus *Hist.* 8.98; Hallock 1985, 606-7). In this context the journeys recorded in the biblical sources are not untoward, even down to the reference to armed guards accompanying them (Neh 2:9).

The leader of each such group evidently carried an authorizing document (variously referred to as either *halmi* or *miyatukkam*), allowing them to draw down rations from the way stations, and although no such document has survived at Persepolis (probably because they were recorded in Aramaic on papyrus or parchment), it is clear that Aramaic Document 6 (Driver) is an example of a similar (in this case private) document. Although not to be directly equated, the authorizing letters mentioned at Ezra 7:21; 8:36 and Nehemiah 2:7, 8-9 no doubt functioned in much the same way.

2.3.3. Support for Local Cults. More controversial is the question whether the Persepolis tablets support the picture in Ezra and Nehemiah of imperial support for the local temple and cult in Jerusalem (*see* Postexilic Temple). Certainly, we find many references to provision being authorized for a considerable number of religious ceremonies and cult officials for a given period of time. At least ten different Persian,

Elamite and Babylonian gods are listed at one point or another. At issue is whether this indicates that the Persians supported foreign cults as a matter of policy (in which case the claimed support for the Jewish cult would not be untoward), or whether the texts speak only of official state cults at the heart of the empire in which part of the offering was made to the Persian god Ahuramazda (Grabbe, 214-15). Although clearly the evidence is indirect and so uncertain at best, it does seem reasonable to conclude that the Persians were prepared to support cults other than that which was exclusively their own on the condition that this acknowledged their own god (and no doubt the legitimacy of Achaemenid rule), and that given the localized nature of the tablets, it is difficult categorically to rule in or out what might have been the case elsewhere. On the Jewish side, the use of the divine title "the God of Heaven" seems to have been a mutually acceptable compromise over the identification of the deity, and Ezra 6:10 also refers to prayers on behalf of the royal family. One further interesting observation in this regard is that the shift in the nature of the support claimed for the Jerusalem cult from provision in kind (Ezra 6:9) to provision of cash for purchase of what was needed in Ezra 7:15-20 fits exactly the chronology of the shift between the Fortification and the Treasury tablets (see 2.2 above).

2.3.4. Nehemiah's Salary. A final topic for which these tablets may be used to set the biblical account into its wider setting concerns Nehemiah's summarizing account of his generosity in not drawing the allowance to which he was entitled (Neh 5:14-18). The reference to "the bread of the governor" fits well with the fact that payment was reckoned in kind, the amount varying according to the status of the recipient. The highest paid official was Parnaka, the chief administrative official under Darius and generally thought to be his uncle. He is recorded as receiving a daily ration of two sheep, ninety quarts of wine and 180 quarts of flour. Given that this far exceeded what any individual or even family could consume, it is clear that it is simply an equivalent of what we would call his salary, and "the bread of the governor" may be regarded similarly.

As attested by the Treasury Tablets, the use of cash had become common for part of such payments by this time. This helps explain the textually obscure verse Nehemiah 5:15, in which Nehemiah criticizes his predecessors for exacting a combination of food and silver from their subjects.

Again, many of the texts record payments of goods not only to the officials, but also on behalf of those working with or under them. Junior officials are referred to as *puhu*, usually rendered "boys," although it is clear that this has nothing to do with age (their rations are often the same as those for an adult male). This is closely comparable with the use of Hebrew *na'ar* (NRSV: "servant") in Nehemiah 5:15, 16, and given their dependence on their superior's salary for their own allowance, it helps to explain the harshness of those who preceded Nehemiah as well as shed light on his own generosity in this regard.

In conclusion, although not all the Elamite texts from Persepolis have been published as of yet, and although many obscurities remain because the language is not fully understood, it is clear that they have much to teach us about the way in which the Persian Empire was administered, and to that extent they may be regarded as an underexploited resource for the illumination of the late Historical Books of the Bible.

See also PERSIA, PERSIANS; HISTORY OF ISRAEL 8: POSTEXILIC PERIOD.

BIBLIOGRAPHY. **P. Briant,** *From Cyrus to Alexander: A History of the Persian Empire,* (Winona Lake, IN: Eisenbrauns, 2002 [1996]); **G. G. Cameron,** *Persepolis Treasury Tablets* (OIP 65; Chicago: University of Chicago Press, 1948); **J. M. Cook,** *The Persian Empire* (London: J. M. Dent, 1983); **M. A. Dandamaev,** *Persien unter den ersten Achämeniden* (BI 8; Wiesbaden: Reichert, 1976); **G. R. Driver,** *Aramaic Documents of the Fifth Century B.C.* (Oxford: Clarendon Press, 1957); **I. Gershevitch,** "The Alloglottography of Old Persian," *Transactions of the Philological Society* (1979) 114-55; **L. L. Grabbe,** *A History of the Jews and Judaism in the Second Temple Period,* 1: *Yehud: A History of the Persian Province of Judah* (LSTS 47; London: T & T Clark International, 2004); **J. C. Greenfield and B. Porten,** *The Bisitun Inscription of Darius the Great: Aramaic Version* (CII, part 1: Inscriptions of Ancient Iran, 5: Aramaic Versions of the Achaemenian Inscriptions, Texts 1; London: Lund Humphries, 1982); **R. T. Hallock,** "The Evidence of the Persepolis Tablets," in *The Cambridge History of Iran,* 2: *The Median and Achaemenian Periods,* ed. I. Gershevitch

(Cambridge: Cambridge University Press, 1985) 588-609; idem, *Persepolis Fortification Tablets* (OIP 92; Chicago: University of Chicago Press, 1969); idem, "Selected Fortification Texts," *Cahiers de la Délégation Archéologique Française en Iran* 8 (1978) 109-36; **R. G. Kent,** *Old Persian: Grammar; Texts; Lexicon* (2d ed.; AOS 33; New Haven: American Oriental Society, 1953); **H. G. M. Williamson,** *Studies in Persian Period History and Historiography* (FAT 38; Tübingen: Mohr Siebeck, 2004).

H. G. M. Williamson

NON-ISRAELITE WRITTEN SOURCES: SYRO-PALESTINIAN

Compared with the documentation from Egypt and Mesopotamia, relatively few indigenous written sources have been recovered from the neighbors of Israel and Judah in Syria-Palestine, and these, with rare exceptions, do not refer to persons or events recounted in the OT Historical Books. Yet the historical experience, culture and literary expression of these neighbors were much closer to those of Israel and Judah than were those of the larger states and empires, and the Syro-Palestinian inscriptions reveal events, conditions, institutions, beliefs and expressions that probably are broadly characteristic of the whole area.

1. Introduction
2. Memorial Inscriptions
3. Dedicatory Inscriptions
4. Epitaphs
5. Treaties
6. Narrative (Prophetic)
7. Correspondence
8. Booty Inscriptions
9. Seals
10. Legal Texts
11. Of Uncertain Genre

1. Introduction.

1.1. Classification of the Inscriptions. Syro-Palestinian inscriptions are written in Northwest Semitic languages and dialects, generally *Aramaic (including an early form known as Samalian, after the site where it was used) and Canaanite (including Phoenician, Ammonite, Moabite and Edomite, as well as *Hebrew [*see* Hebrew Inscriptions]). Most Aramaic inscriptions come from Syria; Phoenician from the coast of Lebanon; Ammonite, Moabite and Edomite from east and south of the Jordan River. Thus the inscriptions may be classified by

language or area (the two overlap considerably, but not entirely), but also by material (stone, papyrus, etc.), by date or by genre. Since genre is the most important category for interpretation, the inscriptions most significant for understanding the literature of the Historical Books and the world that they refer to will be presented here first by genre and then, within each genre, in roughly chronological order.

1.2. Basis of Selection. Most of the inscriptions are short and incomplete, but a few are relatively long, and some almost perfectly preserved. It is the latter two categories that are most revealing, and they are the center of attention in this article.

2. Memorial Inscriptions.

2.1. General Character. In royal memorial inscriptions the king typically introduces himself and then records his military achievements and his completed construction projects, finally invoking curses on anyone damaging the inscription. These inscriptions give the royal court's view of the king's role and accomplishments (versus the view of any opponents or of later chroniclers or historians), are written on stone and usually are prominently displayed. Most are now known by the name of the king who sponsored them.

2.2. Mesha. This Moabite inscription (*COS* 2.23:137-38), sometimes known as "the Moabite stone," was revealed to Western scholars in Diban in 1868. It dates from the later ninth century BCE, and although the bottom portion is missing, it is still the longest inscription known from either side of the Jordan and the most closely related to the history of Israel and the biblical accounts of Israel's relations with its neighbors. It discloses the Moabite king's view of the relations between the monarchies of Israel and *Moab (cf. 2 Sam 8:2; 2 Kings 1:1; 3:4-27). It is uniquely rich in linguistic, literary, historical, military and theological features that have their counterparts in the Historical Books.

After introducing himself, Mesha first reports a series of successful campaigns against Israelite towns in the land of Medeba, which he regarded as his territory. He introduces this narrative by referring to the Israelite king *Omri having taken possession of Medeba. Israel then occupied it until halfway through the time of Omri's "son," which Mesha summarizes as a period of "forty years." Mesha reports that during his own reign his god, Chemosh, returned this territory to Moab. Expressing a political theology shared with many biblical texts, he attributes the enemy's occupation of his territory to Chemosh's anger at the land (cf., e.g., Judg 2:14; 3:8; 2 Kings 13:3), and he credits his own success in defeating the enemy to Chemosh's driving the enemy out (cf. the standard biblical account of Israel's occupation of Canaan). He also campaigned successfully against Atarot, claiming that the people of Gad had lived in that region for ages, but that the king of Israel had rebuilt the city for himself. (In this context, it has been argued, it is likely that the Gadites were not originally Israelites, but had been conquered by the Israelite king.)

Mesha's brief descriptions of his campaigns against Israel are also reminiscent of campaign accounts in the Bible. Comparable are the king's attack against the enemy on the strength of a prophetic oracle, promising *ḥērem*—that is, the destruction of the defeated enemy as an act of devotion to his god, launching a surprise attack at dawn, and dedicating booty to his god. For example, Chemosh tells Mesha, "Go and capture Nebo from Israel," and so Mesha goes by night and attacks Nebo from the crack of dawn until midday, killing everyone in it "because [he] had devoted it to Ashtar-Chemosh." He then took "the vessels of Yahweh and dragged them before Chemosh." Another campaign is introduced with the statement that "the king of Israel had built Jahaz and stayed in it when attacking me, but Chemosh drove him out before me."

Mesha next gives an account of his building activities: walls, gates, towers and a royal palace for the acropolis in Dibon, as well as the rebuilding of other cities in the land. These parallel the activities of Judean and Israelite kings (e.g., those of Baasha and Asa in 1 Kings 15:17-22, as well as those of Solomon in Jerusalem and elsewhere [see 1 Kings 5:13-7:51; 9:15, 17-19]). Particularly notable is his emphasis on the provision of an adequate, accessible water supply in the city (cf. 2 Kings 20:20; 2 Chron 32:30 and the unique account in the Siloam Tunnel inscription). He also refers to using Israelite slaves in one project (Judah's use of conquered people for forced labor is mentioned in 2 Sam 12:31).

In the last, broken part of the inscription Chemosh tells Mesha (again this would have been through a prophetic oracle) to "go down

and attack Horonaim" (northeast of the southern tip of the Dead Sea). According to traces discerned by A. Lemaire, the "House of David," here a term for the southern kingdom, occupied the town at this time—but Bordreuil has since reported a new collation that found no such traces. Mesha reports that he went down, attacked, and captured the town and that (on another plane) "Chemosh returned it in my time."

2.3. Hazael (?). Three fragments found at Tel Dan in the mid-1990s (*COS* 2.39:161-62) and much discussed since then are part of an Aramaic royal inscription probably attributable to Hazael and datable to the later ninth century BCE (although not all commentators accept the original editors' arrangement of the three fragments). Like Mesha's inscription, this material deals with disputed territory. But first the author speaks of his predecessor's death: "My father lay down and went to his fathers" (cf. the formulaic "lay down with his fathers" in Kings and Chronicles). He then claims that "Israel entered the land of my father" (since Hazael is known to the Assyrians and the book of Kings as a usurper, it has been suggested that the word *father* may refer to his patron rather than his progenitor). Next, he writes, Hadad "made me king"—an expression used of a monarch whose legitimacy was not universally recognized (thus also of Zakkur [see 2.5 below]; further of Saul [1 Sam 15:11, 35] and of Solomon [1 Kings 3:7]), and probably implying designation by prophetic oracle (as in the cases of David, Jeroboam I and Jehu). Whereas Hazael claims the authority of Hadad, the stories of *Elisha and *Elijah recognize Yahweh's hand in Hazael's reign (2 Kings 8:13; 1 Kings 19:15). Hazael continues, "Hadad went before me" and enabled the author to reconquer what had been occupied by Israel. The inscription seems to refer to his killing "Jehoram, son of Ahab, king of Israel and Ahaziah, son of Jehoram, king of the House of David," although the names and patronymics of the two kings are largely restored (the "House of David" is quite clear and again would refer to the kingdom of Judah). If the restoration is correct, this account seems to contrast with that in 2 Kings 9. But Hazael may well be boasting of the indirect results of his campaign against Israel—if *Jehu was not serving as a willing tool of Hazael in order to gain the throne of Israel.

2.4. Kilamuwa. Found beside an excavated palace gateway in Zinjirli (east-northeast of the

Gulf of Iskenderun), this inscription (*COS* 2.30:147-48), written in Phoenician, dates from around 825 BCE. The inscription is unusual for its rhetorical style: nicely balanced phrases and rich imagery. Kilamuwa boasts that his accomplishments exceeded those of his predecessors. He then recounts his "hiring" (i.e., making a significant payment or present to) the king of Assyria to drive off another king who was oppressing him (cf. 1 Kings 15:17-22; 2 Kings 16:5-9; 7:6b), and he goes on to claim how as king he treated the oppressed members of his kingdom like a kindly parent and prospered them as never before: "To one I was a father, to another I was a mother, and to another I was a brother. And whoever had not seen the face of a sheep, I made him the owner of a flock . . . and whoever had not seen a tunic from his youth, in my time he was covered with fine linen [cf. what is said of Saul in the lament, similarly hyperbolic, of 2 Sam 1:24] . . . they looked to me as a fatherless child to its mother."

2.5. Zakkur. Found in Afis, southwest of Aleppo, this stela (*COS* 2.35:155), inscribed in Aramaic, dates from around 800 BCE. Within the frame of a dedicatory inscription to the god, Ilu-wer, on the completion of a temple to that god in Afis, Zakkur reproduces a long section of an earlier memorial inscription in which he recounts the siege of his capital city, Hadrach, by a coalition of Aramaean kings headed by Bir-Hadad (biblical form of the name is "Ben-Hadad" [e.g., 2 Kings 13:24]), son of Hazael, "king of Aram" (cf. the coalition of kings under "Ben-Hadad king of Aram" in 1 Kings 20). Zakkur prays to the Lord of the Heavens, who had "made him king," and receives an answer through seers and prophets (cf. 2 Kings 18—19/Is 36—37), in which the deity reiterates that it was he who made Zakkur king. The quoted oracle has phrases almost identical to those found in biblical oracles ("Fear not, for . . . I will stand by you and I will deliver you"). Most of the account of the deliverance from the siege is missing in a gap in the text. Like Mesha, Zakkur goes on to refer to his building activities: fortified cities, temples and the town of Afis, where the inscription was erected. These are followed by curses on anyone who erases the inscription or removes the stela from before Ilu-wer.

2.6. Panamuwa. This inscription (*COS* 2.37:158-60) in Samalian comes from the same site as that of Kilamuwa (see 2.4 above) and

dates from a little before 730 BCE. It concludes in the form of a memorial inscription by Bir-Rakib, but the first part is dedicated to Bir-Rakib's father, Panamuwa, of whom it gives a brief biography, telling more about a king contemporary with those of the two Israelite kingdoms than any other Syro-Palestinian inscription.

Panamuwa survived a coup that involved the killing of his father and his father's "seventy brothers" (cf. Judg 9:1-5). (This recalls the coup of Jehu [2 Kings 10:1-14; 11:1-3].) Panamuwa fled for assistance ("brought a present") to the king of Assyria, who "made him king" and killed the usurper. The inscription goes on to give an unusually full account of the benefits of serving the Assyrian king (this, as well as other features of the inscription, probably is designed to counter anti-Assyrian sentiment in Panamuwa's realm; cf. the pro- and anti-Assyrian and later-Babylonian parties implied in the account in Kings of the history of Israel and Judah in the late eighth to early sixth centuries BCE). Panamuwa's service of the Assyrian king included accompanying him on his campaigns in all directions and participating in the Assyrian king's deportation of eastern populations to the west and vice versa (cf. 2 Kings 17:6, 24). The account of Panamuwa's life concludes with the impact of his death. He died "at the feet of his lord, Tiglath-Pileser" on one of his campaigns and was lamented by the other vassal kings and the whole army. The Assyrian king gave him appropriate rites and erected a monument to him where he had died, taking his body back to Assyria.

2.7. Bir-Rakib. From the same site, this shorter inscription in Aramaic (*COS* 2.38:160-61), dating from later in the reign of Bir-Rakib (c. 730 BCE), is his one complete inscription. In it he boasts of his service among powerful, wealthy kings as a loyal vassal of Tiglath-Pileser, and of his improvement of his ancestral palace, envied by other kings and surpassing that of his ancestors. Clearly, there was competition among the vassals for the suzerain's favor: more than once Bir-Rakib claims that he was more loyal and more strenuous in his service than were his rivals. The theme of outclassing one's predecessors recurs elsewhere in these inscriptions, and it is taken up and used in a novel way by the authors of Kings.

2.8. Azatiwada. This inscription (*COS*

2.31:148-50), from around 700 BCE, exists in two languages (Phoenician and Luwian) and three forms: on a statue of Baal and on stone orthostats and lions at the gates of the city (modern Karatepe, north-northeast of the Gulf of Iskenderun). Azatiwada's precise status is uncertain. He was placed in his position by a king, Awariku, and boasts of supporting the latter, yet he writes of his own accomplishments much as if he himself were a king. He speaks of extending and establishing the borders of the country (cf. 1 Sam 14:47-48; 2 Sam 8:14b-15), of prospering his people, and of building the city where the inscription was found and which was named after him (as was customary in Assyria)—all thanks to Baal. (The author of 1 Kings 16:24 explains the name of the new city, *Samaria, as derived not from that of a king, but from the person who sold the land to the king.)

2.9. Yehawmilk. This Phoenician inscription (*COS* 2.32:151-52), from the later fifth or early fourth century BCE, comes originally from the temple area in Byblos. Yehawmilk recognizes that he was made king by the goddess known as "the Lady, the Mistress of Byblos," and testifies that when he called on her, she responded (see 3 below). He goes on to describe various items of temple furnishings and architecture that he has made for her "here" (biblical references to improvements to the temple made by the kings of Judah do not specify what these are, being more concerned with the financing and administration of the project and the probity of the workers [2 Kings 12:4-15; 22: 3-7, 9]). The king then wishes his goddess's blessing on himself, demands that anyone in the future doing work on these items not remove his name, and invokes the goddess's curse on anyone who does remove his work or his name.

3. Dedicatory Inscriptions.

3.1. General Character. Dedicatory inscriptions characteristically begin with the name of the object being dedicated, followed by a relative clause naming the dedicator and ending with a prayer for blessing. Usually they are dedicated to a deity, either in fulfillment of a vow (a promise of something to a deity in return for an answer to prayer) or in gratitude for or in hopes of divine favor, like several tenth-century Phoenician inscriptions from Byblos (vows and their fulfillment are referred to in Judg 11:30-31, 34-39; 1 Sam 1:11, 20-28; and, as a trick, in 2 Sam 15:7-8).

3.2. Had-Yišʿi. This inscription, the earliest complete Aramaic one of any length (*COS* 2.34:153-54), dating from the mid-to-late ninth century BCE, is atypical, being part of a bilingual, and influenced by the parallel Akkadian, version written on the same statue of the author. The first half reports the setting up of the statue of Had-Yišʿi, king of Guzan, before the god Hadad, who dwells in Guzan (as the Akkadian reads; the Aramaic has adapted the title to the present setting and reads "in Sikan"), whose attributes and benefactions are listed. The purpose of the dedication is spelled out: to assure the king's longevity, the prospering of his dynasty and people, and the efficacy of his prayers. These hopes would be shared by most kings of the time, and often by their people, and are reflected in various places in Kings, especially in the treatment of the reigns of David and Solomon (e.g., 2 Sam 7:8-16; 1 Kings 3:4-14), as well as in psalms going back to the monarchy, such as Psalms 20; 21; 72.

Evidently at a later date, this is copied and supplemented with the second half of the present inscription. Had-Yišʿi now identifies himself as king of Guzan, Sikan and Azran, and the god as lord of Habur—presumably the whole region along the river—dwelling in Sikan (identified with modern Tell Fekheriye, on the western branch of the upper Habur River, where the inscription was found). Claiming that he has improved the statue, he again states the purpose of the inscription, though in different words. Both halves of the inscription end with curses on anyone erasing Had-Yišʿi's name.

3.3. Bir-Hadad. This Aramaic inscription (*COS* 2.33:152-53), found a little north of Aleppo and dating from around 800 BCE, exemplifies a dedicatory inscription erected in fulfillment of a vow: "Stela which Bir-Hadad [biblical Ben-Hadad], son of Attar-hamik . . . , king of Aram, set up for his lord, for Melqart, to whom he had made a vow, and who heard him [lit., his voice]."

3.4. Ekron. In this inscription (*COS* 2.42:164), found at the *Philistine site of *Ekron, a Philistine ruler of around 675 BCE records his dedication of a temple that he has built for an Aegean goddess (reflecting the origins of the Philistines). His name, vocalized as "Achish," is attributed to a king of *Gath in 1 Samuel 21:10-15; 28:1-2; 29; 1 Kings 2:39-40. The concluding prayer asks for blessing, protection and longevity for the king (cf. Yahweh's expectations of Solomon in 1 Kings 3:11, 13-15) and blessing for his land. The dedication referred to in this stone inscription was probably accompanied by much more elaborate rituals and prayers, as were the dedications of the Jerusalem temples described in 1 Kings 8 and Ezra 6:15-17 (which in turn perhaps were memorialized by dedicatory inscriptions in Jerusalem).

The same site has yielded shorter inscriptions with the names of the Semitic deities Baal and Asherah.

4. Epitaphs.

4.1. General Character. Inscriptions on coffins generally name the deceased, refer to his or her location, forbid any disturbance of the tomb (often denying the presence of anything valuable within that might tempt robbers) and curse anyone who does disturb it.

4.2. Nerab. Two Aramaic inscriptions found in Nerab (southeast of Aleppo), dating to around 700 BCE, refer to the burial of two priests of the moon god. In the longer one (*COS* 2.59:184-85) the priest Si'-Gabbar claims that because of his righteousness, his god gave him a good reputation and a long life. He lived to see his descendants of the fourth generation. At the time of his death he could still speak and see well (contrast the more typical condition noted of Eli [1 Sam 4:15] and Ahijah [1 Kings 14:4b]). He asserts that he was laid to rest in his clothes alone, with no silver or bronze.

4.3. Sidon. The Phoenician epitaphs of Eshmunazor (*COS* 2.57:182-83) and his father, Tabnit (*COS* 2.56:181-82), were found in tombs in Sidon. King Eshmunazor (c. 450 BCE) reports in his epitaph that he was both fatherless and, unlike Si'-Gabbar, died prematurely ("I was snatched away when it was not my time"). Evidently, his mother was regent or coruler, as the latter part of the inscription includes a kind of joint memorial inscription reporting their successes. They built temples for Ashtart, Baal and Eshmun, and in return for services rendered they received from "the lord of kings" (the Persian emperor) the lands of Dor and Joppa, including the Plain of Sharon. Here again the importance and the rewards of faithful service to the great king appear.

Eshmunazor's father, Tabnit, identifies himself not only as king of the Sidonians, but first as priest of Ashtoreth. After denying that silver or gold or other riches have been placed with him,

he designates any disturbance of him as "an abomination *[tôʿēbâ]* to Ashtoreth" (the same term is used of condemned foreign practices in 1 Kings 14:24; 2 Kings 16:3; 21:2, 11; Ezra 9:1, 11, 14; and of a foreign deity in 2 Kings 23:13). Both Tabnit and Eshmunazor express the curse that anyone who disturbs the coffin will have no resting place among the "rephaim." (While elsewhere in the Bible this is a general term for the dead, in the Former Prophets and once in Chronicles it is used to refer to a primeval social group and its territory [see especially Josh 12:4; 13:12; 2 Sam 5:18, 22; 23:13; 1 Chron 20:4].)

5. Treaties.

5.1. General Significance. Although copies of parts of several Akkadian treaties issued by the late Assyrian kings have been recovered, including several made with vassals (e.g., King Matiʿ-El of Arpad and king Baal of Tyre), only one treaty in a West Semitic language from the west has come to light. It is clearly of the same general type as those from Assyria, although with several features specific to western culture. Although several Israelite and Judean kings became vassals of Assyria (and later Judean kings became vassals of Babylon), no description of their treaties has been recorded in Scripture, nor has any sample of them been found in excavations in Palestine. Thus this one West Semitic treaty is an invaluable clue to the kind of treaty with which some of the later Israelite and Judean kings would have been familiar.

5.2. Sefire. In 1930 three stelae bearing Aramaic inscriptions (*COS* 2.82:213-17) were found in the village of Sefire, south of Aleppo. They represent parts, and perhaps successive renewals, of a treaty of around the mid-eighth century BCE imposed on Matiʿ-El, king of Arpad (north of Aleppo), by an unknown authority of an unknown location, Bir-Gaʾyah ("son of majesty") of KTK. It has been proposed that these are either names used by Shamshi-ilu, for himself and the local area in which he was the Assyrian governor, or code names for the Assyrian monarch and his country.

5.2.1. The First Stela. The inscription on three sides of the first stela takes the following form. (1) The preamble identifies it as the treaty between these two and their heirs, officers and countries, with the first party being expanded to include the kings of "Upper Aram and Lower Aram." (2) The gods before whom the treaty was

747

concluded are listed. These include the main Assyrian gods, some from Syria (e.g., Hadad of Aleppo, El and Elyon), and cosmic entities such as Heaven and Earth, the Abyss and the Springs, Day and Night. All these are identified as witnesses to the treaty and finally directly appealed to: "open your eyes and see" this treaty. (Hezekiah uses the same phrase in calling on Yahweh to take note of and be prepared to act on the presumptuous words of Sennacherib in 2 Kings 19:16.) (3) A series of conditional curses on Matiᶜ-El are listed (consisting of a violation clause followed by a curse), followed by a list of rites with accompanying curses (e.g., "as this wax is burned by fire, so may Arpad be burned"). (4) When the text reappears on the second side of the stela, it reiterates some of the introduction, this time emphasizing that the treaty is between the gods of the two parties: it is the gods who have concluded it, and the gods will keep it. It also orders that the words of the treaty be spread far and wide. (5) The central stipulations follow. These specify different circumstances and particular actions or inaction by Matiᶜ-El in those circumstances that would constitute violation of the treaty. (6) The third side of the stela has Matiᶜ-El testify that he has written this as a reminder that he and his heirs keep this agreement for their own good. (7) Finally, there are brief blessings, presumably on those who do keep it, and curses on anyone violating it or changing its written text.

5.2.2. The Second and Third Stelae. Only the middle section of writing on the three sides of the second stela has been preserved. Although this is not identical to the text of the first stela, it covers some of the same ground (conditional curses, stipulations and curses on anyone who damages the inscription). It is reasonably presumed that the inscription on (only one side of) the third stela is a part of, or another version of, the same treaty, but here there is no actual reference to the names of the two parties. This inscription consists solely of stipulations. These concern repudiating any plotters against the suzerain and sending back fugitives from him, guaranteeing free passage to his messengers, avenging anyone who might assassinate him and not interfering in any internal conflict over his succession, in agreements between the suzerain and other vassals, or in a disputed territory now claimed by the suzerain. Stipulations such as the first of these obviously would be vio-

lated by Israelite or Judean vassals who plotted with their neighbors or Egypt to throw off the Assyrian or Babylonian yoke. Such violations of vassal treaties brought the wrath of one or the other imperial powers down on Israel and Judah as it would on Arpad and the Aramaean kingdoms.

6. Narrative (Prophetic).

6.1. Overview. Short narrative accounts of the doings of kings appear in some of the memorial inscriptions mentioned above. Apart from these, Syro-Palestinian narrative material is rare. Exceptional is an explicitly religious narrative partially recovered from the fragments of an inscribed plaster wall at the site of Tell Deir ᶜAlla (north of the Jabbok, near its entry into the Jordan).

6.2. Tell Deir ᶜAlla. The reconstructed portions of this wall inscription (*COS* 2.27:140-45), dating from the early eighth century BCE, include a superscription: "The account of [Balaam, son of Be]or, who was a seer of the gods." Thus the main character in what follows is the legendary figure also known from Numbers 22—24. But the other fragments make clear that Balaam is not concerned here with cursing or blessing, as in Numbers, but rather with a vision of the divine assembly (like the prophet Micaiah in 1 Kings 22:19-22). The gods come to him at night, and he sees a vision that they assure him will be fulfilled. When his people see Balaam fasting and weeping and ask him why, he recounts his vision in terms generally reminiscent of biblical poetic prophecies. Prophetic narratives in the Bible similarly envisage a divine visitation and revelation with a dire message for the prophet's audience (e.g., 1 Sam 3; 1 Kings 14:15-16). Unfortunately, the various fragments resist any further construction of a continuous narrative.

7. Correspondence.

Among the very few non-Hebrew letters preserved is one in Aramaic (*COS* 3.54:132-34), from the early sixth century BCE, found in Saqqara in Egypt. It is addressed to the pharaoh from the Philistine king Adon of Ekron. Adon reports the approach of the Babylonian army, now at Aphek (some 40 km north of Ekron), and appeals to the pharaoh not to abandon him but to send troops. Evidently, Adon previously had rebelled against Babylon and become a client of

Egypt, and now he is facing the punitive campaign of the Babylonians and hoping for Egyptian support and protection—the same transfer of allegiance and subsequent vain hope of the Judean kings Jehoiakim and Zedekiah.

8. Booty Inscriptions.

8.1. General Character. Kings regularly took booty from conquered cities. This was variously distributed among the troops as rewards for service, used to supply and adorn the king's capital and court, or dedicated to the deity or deities who had given victory. Evidently, in some cases pieces were inscribed to commemorate the event.

8.2. Hazael. Two bronze pieces of a horse's headgear bearing the same Aramaic inscription (*COS* 2.40:162) have been found as far away as Samos and Eretria in Greece (after a history of transmission that we cannot trace). They read, "What Hadad gave our lord Hazael from Umq in the year our lord crossed the river" (probably the Orontes). Evidently, Hazael originally had plundered them from Umq in a campaign across the Orontes into northwest Syria and taken them back to Damascus, where they were inscribed. Later, when the Assyrians destroyed Damascus, they probably carried them off to Assyria as plunder once more (cf. the gold and bronze objects taken to Jerusalem by David after defeating the Arameans of Damascus and other peoples [2 Sam 8:7-8]; the account of the gold, silver and bronze that the Babylonians took off to Babylon when they destroyed Jerusalem mentions only what was taken from the temple [2 Kings 25:13-17]). Since the inscriptions commemorate a campaign in which the god Hadad had granted Hazael success, Hazael may have placed them in a temple of Hadad, much as David, in recognition of the fact that Yahweh had given him victory everywhere (2 Sam 8:6b), dedicated to Yahweh the precious plunder from his campaigns (2 Sam 8:11-12).

9. Seals.

9.1. General Character. Seals often carry the name of the owner, sometimes with a patronymic, and sometimes with a title or office held by the owner. Since personal names often contain divine names, they may be indications of the religious tradition of the bearer (or, in the case of the patronymic, of his or her father). Names in seals sometimes are identical to names in bibli-

cal books, but that does not necessarily mean that they refer to the same person. Each case has to be considered on its own merits. Two examples follow.

9.2. Specific Names.

9.2.1. Hadadezer. A seal allegedly found in Saqqara in Egypt and with Egyptian motifs in five registers has had one register superinscribed in the Aramaic script of the eighth to seventh centuries BCE with the legend "Belonging to Hadadezer" (*COS* 2.76:202). If authentic, this would be the same name as is used of the king of Aram Zobah in 2 Samuel 8:3-12; 10:15-19; 1 Kings 11:23.

9.2.2. Sanballat. This name appears in the seal impression (*COS* 2.78D:204) on an Aramaic deed of sale among the papyri found in a cave in the Wadi ed-Daliyeh and dating from the mid-fourth century BCE. The impression reads, "Belonging to [ ]iah, son of [San]ballat, governor of Samaria." The name is identical to that of "*Sanballat the Horonite," frequently mentioned in Nehemiah (Neh 2:10, 19; 4:1-7; 6:1-14), and its bearer in the inscription may well be a descendant of the latter.

10. Legal Texts.

The aforementioned papyri from the Wadi ed-Daliyeh are a small collection of legal texts (Gropp, VanderKam and Brady, 3-116) originally composed in the city of Samaria but taken with other valuables by a group fleeing enemies to a remote cave, where their owners apparently died, leaving these documents undisturbed for two millennia. The texts, concerned with loans, marriages and the ownership of property and slaves, disclose some of the legal practices and language of Samaria in the fourth century BCE.

11. Of Uncertain Genre.

11.1. Amman Citadel Inscription. A fragment of an inscription (*COS* 2.24:139) found on the citadel of Amman seems to begin by quoting the Ammonite deity Milcom (cf. 1 Kings 11:5, 33), giving instructions (presumably to a king) for some building and announcing contrasting fates: the death of anyone surrounding the site, and the peaceful stay of the righteous. This is most likely a quotation of a prophetic oracle referring to a temple and to sanctions for appropriate and inappropriate behavior toward it and Milcom.

11.2. Tell Siran. An Ammonite inscription

on a bronze bottle from Tell Siran (*COS* 2.25:139-40) refers to the Ammonite king Amminadab as the "king of the sons of Ammon," the same expression used in the Hebrew of, for example, Judges 11:12, 14, 28; 1 Samuel 12:12; 2 Samuel 10:1. It goes on to list Amminadab's accomplishments—vineyard, gardens, reservoir and cisterns—and to wish him many days and far-off years of gladness and rejoicing, expressing in this way something of the good life that a successful king and his court hoped to enjoy.

See also HEBREW INSCRIPTIONS.

BIBLIOGRAPHY. **Y. Avishur,** *Phoenician Inscriptions and the Bible: Select Inscriptions and Studies in Stylistic and Literary Devices Common to the Phoenician Inscriptions and the Bible* (Jaffa and Tel Aviv: Archaeological Center Publications, 2000); **A. Dearman,** ed., *Studies in the Mesha Inscription and Moab* (SBLABS 2; Atlanta: Scholars Press, 1989); **A. Lemaire and J.-M. Durand,** *Les inscriptions araméennes de Sfiré et l'Assyrie de Shamshi-Ilu* (Geneva: Droz, 1984); **J. C. L. Gibson,** *Textbook of Syrian Semitic Inscriptions,* 2: *Aramaic Inscriptions* (Oxford: Clarendon Press, 1975); idem, *Textbook of Syrian Semitic Inscriptions,* 3: *Phoenician Inscriptions* (Oxford: Clarendon Press, 1982)**; J. A. Fitzmyer,** *The Aramaic Inscriptions of Sefire* (rev. ed.; BibOr 19/A; Rome: Pontifical Biblical Institute, 1995); **D. M. Gropp, J. VanderKam and M. Brady,** eds., *Wadi Daliyeh II and Qumran Miscellanea, Part 2: The Samaria Papyri from Wadi Daliyeh* (DJD 28; Oxford: Clarendon Press, 2001); **J. Hoftijzer and G. van der Kooij,** eds., *The Balaam Text from Deir ʿAlla Re-evaluated: Proceedings of the International Symposium Held at Leiden, 21-24 August 1989* (Leiden: E. J. Brill, 1991); **S. C. Layton,** "Old Aramaic Inscriptions," *BA* 51 (1988) 172-89; **A. Lemaire,** "Prophètes et rois dans les inscriptions ouest-sémitiques (ixe-vi^e siècle av. J.C.)," in *Prophètes et rois: Bible et Proche-Orient,* ed. A. Lemaire (LD; Paris: Cerf, 2001) 85-115; **M. Miller,** "The Moabite Stone as a Memorial Stela," *PEQ* 106 (1974) 9-18; **S. Mittmann,** "Zwei 'Rätsel' der *Mēšaʿ*-Inschrift mit einem Beitrag zur aramäischen Steleninschrift von Dan *(Tell el-Qāḍī)*," *ZDPV* 118 (2002) 33-65; **L. J. Mykytiuk,** *Identifying Biblical Persons in Northwest Semitic Inscriptions of 1200-539 B.C.E.* (SBLAB 12; Atlanta: Society of Biblical Literature, 2004); **S. B. Parker,** "The Composition and Sources of Some Northwest Semitic Royal Inscriptions," *SEL* 16 (1999) 49-62; idem, "Did the Authors of the Books of Kings Make Use of Royal Inscriptions?" *VT* 50 (2000) 357-78; idem, *Stories in Scripture and Inscriptions: Comparative Studies on Narratives in Northwest Semitic Inscriptions and the Hebrew Bible* (Oxford: Oxford University Press, 1997); **J. Tropper,** *Die Inschriften von Zincirli* (ALASP 6; Münster: Ugarit-Verlag, 1993); **D. R. Vance,** "Literary Sources for the History of Palestine and Syria: the Phoenician Inscriptions, Part I," *BA* 57 (1994) 2-19.

S. B. Parker

NUMBERS, LARGE NUMBERS

The presence of enormous numbers in the military accounts of the Historical Books has been considered by some as a serious threat to the veracity of those accounts. How these numbers are explained and interpreted within their cultural and literary milieu is essential to a proper understanding of the theologically conditioned history of Israel offered to us within the pages of Scripture.

    1. Problems with Large Numbers
    2. Interpretation of Large Numbers
    3. Large Numbers as Numerical Hyperbole
    4. Conclusion

1. Problems with Large Numbers.
Although very large numbers are found in the Pentateuch, the Historical Books contain the largest of the numbers to be found in the OT. There are fifty-five examples of numbers exceeding 100,000 in the pages of the OT, forty-two of which are found in the Historical Books. When we compare this latter total with the approximately thirty examples of numbers exceeding 100,000 in other extant ancient Near Eastern historical materials, we recognize that the presence of such numbers in the OT is noteworthy.

Also, the largest numbers within the Historical Books present numerous difficulties in many of the passages. For example, when extrapolated into total population, the census figures of the standing army of Israel named in Numbers 1:46; 2:32 (603,550) and Numbers 26:51 (601,730) suggest a late Bronze Age total for Israel of some 2.5 to 3 million persons. Besides demographic analyses that argue that no people of that size ever populated Palestine in antiquity, we have scriptural evidence of the relative smallness of Israel as they prepare to embark on the conquest of Canaan (Deut 7:1, 7). If indeed Israel was smaller than any of the seven indigenous

Canaanite tribes that they were facing, then Palestine at that time contained 20 million people—a demographic impossibility.

An intrabiblical problem in a passage containing large numbers is found in the account of the numbers of Ephraimites slain at the Jordan for mispronouncing "shibboleth" (Judg 12:6). The number slain (42,000) exceeds the census total for that tribe's militia found in Numbers 1:33 (40,500) and in Numbers 26:37 (32,500). Even allowing for a population increase for the warriors of Ephraim after the conquest to the period of the judges from 32,500 to 42,000 does not alleviate the problem of the enormity of the number of slain.

1 Kings 20:29-30 offers still another account that seems impossible if we accept the large numbers at actual value. The text asserts that after Israel had killed 100,000 Aramean foot soldiers at a nearby battle, 27,000 more fled into Aphek, where a wall collapse apparently killed them all. The remains of a wall of such magnitude are yet to be found. If the numbers offered have some other meaning, the wall may have been much smaller.

Further problems involving large numbers are found in the books of Samuel and Kings when compared to the parallel accounts in Chronicles, since in many cases those numbers differ from one account to another (e.g., 2 Sam 8:4/1 Chron 18:4; 2 Sam 24:9/1 Chron 21:5; 1 Kings 4:26/2 Chron 9:25; 1 Kings 5:15-16/ 2 Chron 2:2, 18; 2 Kings 19:35/2 Chron 32:21). In most of the cases of differing numbers the disagreement can be resolved by textual analysis (Fouts 1992b). A classic conundrum is the differences in the accounts of the census by David given in 2 Samuel 24 and 1 Chronicles 21. The total offered for neither Judah nor Israel stands in agreement between the two passages. Textual analysis does not seem to provide a valid solution to the enormity of the numbers offered, which, like the census of the conquest mentioned above, seem demographically improbable. A solution to this problem must lie elsewhere.

The parallel lists of Ezra 2 and Nehemiah 7, though likewise differing at times in the numbers given, are not problematic in regard to enormous numbers. They are similar to the Samuel-Kings and Chronicles parallels in that the differences in Ezra-Nehemiah may be resolvable primarily through textual analysis.

It is because of problems such as these that the veracity of the accounts sometimes has been called into question. Instead of seeking to understand the numbers as figures of speech or as symbolic, some have derided the passages as unhistorical folktales, thereby claiming to invalidate the historical accuracy of the texts. In the nineteenth century J. W. Colenso was one such scholar who mocked the accounts of Exodus precisely because of the problems manifest in the enormous numbers of the censuses.

2. Interpretation of Large Numbers.

While many have dealt with the problems of enormous numbers by dismissing the veracity of the accounts that contain them, others have sought to understand the processes by which these numbers arose, thereby seeking both to maintain the historical credibility of the texts and to understand the original significance of the numbers themselves.

Attempts to understand the presence of the large numbers are manifold in scope and in variety. Some have sought to reduce the numbers by textual analysis, but in only one case, 1 Samuel 6:19, can the numbers be significantly reduced (Fouts 1992a). Others have sought refuge in interpreting the key Hebrew term ʾelep ("thousand") differently from the number 1,000, yet for the most part the various suggested alternatives lack etymological and syntactical support (see discussion of a popular alternative below). Still others have sought to demonstrate that the large numbers arose from misinterpreting earlier numeral notation systems (Driver 1960; 1964). Other possibilities include factoring the numbers to gain insight, rereading the syntax of numbers to produce smaller amounts, treating the term ʾelep as a determinative, finding meaning by calculating the numerical equivalents of letters and words (gematria), and relating the numbers to Babylonian mathematics (Barnouin). None of these possibilities satisfies all the demands needed for proper understanding of the texts that contain large numbers.

Within biblical scholarship two seemingly competitive views appear to be winning adherents. The first view understands that the key term ʾlp was consistently misread by *scribes as ʾelep ("thousand"), when the vocalization should have been something else, such as ʾallup (modern Heb "colonel"). Thus the largest of the numbers would have arisen when ʾlp as mispronounced was found in the same verse with *ʾlp* when it clearly meant 1,000. The confused scribe simply conflated the two terms, yielding incredibly large numbers in the process. This may be illustrated in the census in Numbers 1, wherein the total given as 603,550 (Num 1:46) should have been read as something like 600 leaders, with 3,550 men, where the term for "leader" and the term for "thousand" would have been indistinguishable in early unpointed consonantal texts. Similarly, another alternative claims that if the vocalization were to remain *ʾelep,* then it was a homonym meaning "clan, troop, squad" or the like. Similar scribal confusion led to similar conflation into the enormous numbers present in the text today. This view, suggested earlier in the last century by W. M. F. Petrie, was developed over the ensuing decades by A. Lucas, R. E. D. Clark, G. E. Mendenhall, J. W. Wenham, J. B. Payne and W. W. Hallo; and most recently by C. J. Humphreys (1998; 2000), D. Merling and G. A. Rendsburg. The view has been criticized by B. E. Scolnic, in part by R. Heinzerling and by D. M. Fouts (2003) because of the implication (and sometimes outright statement) that the incredibly large numbers resulted from consistent mistakes by the Hebrew scribes who misunderstood their own language and literature. Despite the problems inherent in claiming scribal confusion on a consistent basis unparalleled elsewhere in other OT passages, this view continues to garner support.

The second view continuing to gain favor is that the largest numbers in the OT often reflect an ancient Near Eastern literary convention of numerical hyperbole. A variation of this view was suggested recently by R. B. Allen and developed and refined by Fouts (1992b; 1997); E. W. Davies has arrived at similar conclusions. This view allows for the key term *ʾlp* to retain its normally understood meaning of "thousand," thereby obviating the need to appeal to consistent scribal misunderstanding. It has the support of numerous ancient Near Eastern parallels of material of similar genre that exhibit the same numerical hyperbole. It also has the benefit of allowing the texts to continue to bear witness to actual historical events, albeit couched in literary terms intended to convey to the reader the greatness and glory of God.

3. Large Numbers as Numerical Hyperbole.

Within the milieu of the ancient Near East, his-

torical accounts from the earliest times have included royal inscriptions depicting the military victories of various kings. It is well known that many of these accounts include numerical totals of enemies killed, prisoners taken and spoil captured. Although at times these numbers are well within acceptable parameters, at other times the numbers surpass credibility. For example, Sargon of Akkad, who ruled c. 2350 BCE, can claim to have fed 5,400 people daily at his table (Kramer), and his son Rimush (c. 2300 BCE) can claim to have killed or captured 54,000 men in battle (Hirsch; some texts read 54,016; see Gelb and Kienast), a figure conveniently ten times that of his father's well-fed subjects. Shalmaneser I of Assyria (c. 1275-1245 BCE) can claim to have taken 14,400 blinded captives (Grayson 1987), yet his successor Tukulti-Ninurta I (c. 1245-1208 BCE) claims for himself 28,800 captives (Luckenbill), twice the number of Shalmaneser. A later Shalmaneser, the third by that name (c. 859-824 BCE), erected an inscriptional stela that claimed initial totals slain at the battle of Qarqar of 14,000 (Luckenbill), while later stelae commemorating that same victory indicated 20,500, 25,000 and 29,000 killed (Millard). These numbers reflect a common literary convention of purposeful embellishment (numerical hyperbole) for the purpose of glorifying the ruling monarch.

Often in the royal inscriptional accounts figurative language is included in otherwise straight narrative material that also includes these enormous numbers. Shamshi-Adad V (c. 824-811 BCE), after claiming to have killed 13,000 warriors, says that their blood was "like the waters of a stream I caused to run through the square of their city" (Luckenbill). Earlier, another Assyrian, Tiglath-Pileser I (c. 1115-1077 BCE), wrote, "Like a storm demon I piled up the corpses of their warriors . . . I built up mounds with the (corpses of) their men-at-arms on mountain ledges (and) with the blood of their warriors I dyed Mount Hirihu red like red wool" (Grayson 1976).

Similarly, scriptural accounts that include the largest of the numbers often exhibit figurative language in the same context. For instance, 1 Samuel 13:2-7 gives an account of a battle with the Philistines, who had mustered 30,000 chariots, 6,000 horsemen and people "like the sand of the seashore for abundance." 1 Kings 10:26-27 describes Solomon's defenses of 1,400 chariots and 12,000 horsemen; he also made silver like stones in amount and cedars as plentiful as sycamores. 2 Chronicles 12:3 depicts Shishak's Egyptian campaign against Jerusalem with 1,200 chariots, 60,000 horsemen and people "without number." It should not surprise the reader that since God had promised Abraham that his descendants would be "like the stars of heaven" or "the sand of the seashore in number" (examples of literary hyperbole), the numbers offered for the size of Israel's standing army mustered for the conquest would be appropriately large enough (by numerical hyperbole) to fulfill that prophecy.

An appropriate illustration of literary hyperbole juxtaposed with numerical hyperbole may be seen in the admittedly poetic Ugaritic epic of Keret (Kirtu), wherein the hyperbolic terms "peasants beyond number" and an "army beyond counting" are found synonymously parallel with the very large "three-hundred ten-thousands" (Herdner). This example, though not in a narrative format, does demonstrate that the ancient Near Eastern culture did understand the concept of numerical hyperbole.

As another illustration of ancient Near Eastern influence on the literature of the OT, we may cite what Roth has called the "x/x + 1" formula. Because Semitic languages rarely if ever had poetically synonymous words for the cardinal numbers, they would elevate a given number by one (or at times by ten or tenfold) for synonymous parallelism. This convention was widespread among the Semitic literatures, particu-larly in poetry. Thus we find God saying, "For three transgressions of Edom, and for four, I will not hold back its punishment" (Amos 1:11), and Solomon saying, "There are six things that the LORD hates, seven that are an abomination to him" (Prov 6:16). Other examples of this numerical parallelism employing smaller numbers occur in the biblical text (e.g., Job 40:5; Prov 30:15, 18, 21, 24, 29; Ps 90:10). Still another example employing large numbers exists in Scripture: "Saul has slain his thousands, but David has slain his ten thousands" (1 Sam 18:7, 21:11). This text exemplifies how numbers were used even in Israel to glorify their leaders.

4. Conclusion.

It is plausible that the majority of the large numbers of Scripture have been embellished by a factor of ten, one hundred or even a thousand at the discretion of the author using numerical hyperbole within a decimal system. This seems to parallel at least the Sumerian and Middle Assyrian patterns, both of which employed a sexagesimal system, and where the vast majority of their large numbers are easily divided by 6, 60, 600 or 6,000. If numerical hyperbole was employed, and is especially prevalent in the largest numbers of Scripture, then the problems traditionally ascribed to the large numbers can be reconciled easily.

The question arises as to why Israel sacrificed accurate accounting in its historical documents on the altar of literary convention by employing numerical hyperbole in the narrative accounts. The reason appears to be somewhat simple: the nations around them used numerical hyperbole to glorify a given king; the writers of Israel's history did the same to glorify the King of kings (or one of his theocratic rulers). Thus Israel's use of the literary convention of numerical hyperbole may be seen as both polemical and theological, as the most frequent use of the largest numbers anywhere in the ancient Near Eastern corpus of historical inscriptional literature are found in the Bible.

See also CENSUS; HISTORIOGRAPHY, OLD TESTAMENT; NARRATIVE ART OF ISRAEL'S HISTORIANS; NON-ISRAELITE WRITTEN SOURCES.

BIBLIOGRAPHY. **R. B. Allen,** "Numbers," in vol. 2 of *The Expositor's Bible Commentary,* ed. F. E. Gaebelein (Grand Rapids: Zondervan, 1990) 655-1008; **M. Barnouin,** "Remarques sur les tableaux numeriques du livre des Nombres," *RB* 76 (1969) 351-64; **R. E. D. Clark,** "The Large Numbers of the Old Testament—Especially in Connexion with the Exodus," *Journal of the Transactions of the Victoria Institute* 87 (1955) 82-92; **J. W. Colenso,** *The Pentateuch and Book of Joshua Critically Examined* (7 vols.; London: Longman, Green, Longman, Roberts & Green, 1862-1879); **E. W. Davies,** "A Mathemantical Conundrum: The Problem of the Large Numbers in Numbers i and xxvi," *VT* 45 (1995) 449-69; **G. R. Driver,** "Abbreviations in the Massoretic Text," *Textus* 1 (1960) 112-31; idem, "Once Again Abbreviations," *Textus* 4 (1964) 76-94; **D. M. Fouts,** "Added Support for Reading '70 Men' in 1 Samuel vi 19," *VT* 42 (1992a) 394; idem, "A Defense of the Hyperbolic Interpretation of Large Numbers in the Old Testament," *JETS* 40 (1997) 377-

87; idem, "The Incredible Numbers of the Hebrew Kings," in *Giving the Sense: Understanding and Using Old Testament Historical Texts,* ed. D. M. Howard Jr. and M. A. Grisanti (Grand Rapids: Kregel, 2003) 283-99; idem, "The Use of Large Numbers in the Old Testament, with Particular Emphasis on the Use of *ʾelep*" (Th.D. diss.; Dallas Theological Seminary, 1992b); **I. J. Gelb and B. Kienast,** *Die altakkadischen Königsinschriften des dritten Jahrtausends v. Chr.* (FAS 7; Stuttgart: Steiner, 1990); **A. K. Grayson,** *Assyrian Royal Inscriptions,* 2: *From Tiglath-pileser I to Ashur nasir-apli II* (Wiesbaden: Harrassowitz, 1976); idem, *The Royal Inscriptions of Mesopotamia,* 1: *Assyrian Periods, Part 1: Assyrian Rulers of the Third and Second Millennia B.C. (to 1115 B.C.)* (Toronto: University of Toronto Press, 1987); **W. W. Hallo,** *The Book of the People* (BJS 225; Atlanta: Scholar's Press, 1991); **A. Herdner,** *Corpus des tablettes en cunéiforms alphabétiques découvertes à Ras Shamra-Ugarit de 1929 à 1939* (2 vols.; Mission de Ras Shamra 10; Paris: Geuthner, 1963); **R. Heinzerling,** "On the Interpretation of the Census Lists by C. J. Humphreys and G. E. Mendenhall," *VT* 50 (2000) 251; **H. Hirsch,** "Die Inschriften der Könige von Agade," *AfO* 20 (1963) 1-82; **C. J. Humphreys,** "The Number of People in the Exodus from Egypt: Decoding Mathematically the Very Large Numbers in Numbers i and xxvi," *VT* 48 (1998) 196-213; idem, "The Numbers in the Exodus from Egypt: A Further Appraisal," *VT* 50 (2000) 323-28; **S. N. Kramer,** *The Sumerians* (Chicago: University of Chicago Press, 1963); **A. Lucas,** "The Number of Israelites at the Exodus," *PEQ* 76 (1944) 164-68; **D. D. Luckenbill,** *Ancient Records of Assyria and Babylonia,* 1: *Historical Records of Assyria: From the Earliest Times to Sargon* (Chicago: University of Chicago Press, 1926); **G. E. Mendenhall,** "The Census Lists of Numbers 1 and 26," *JBL* 77 (1958) 52-66; **D. Merling,** "Large Numbers at the Time of the Exodus," *NEASB* 44 (1999) 15-27; **A. R. Millard,** "Large Numbers in the Assyrian Royal Inscriptions," in *Ah, Assyria—Studies in Assyrian History and Ancient Near Eastern Historiography Presented to Hayim Tadmor,* ed. M. Cogan and I. Eph'al (ScrHier 33; Jerusalem: Magnes, 1991); **J. B. Payne,** "The Validity of the Numbers in Chronicles," *BSac* 136 (1979) 109-28; **W. M. F. Petrie,** *Egypt and Israel* (rev. ed.; London: Society for Promoting Christian Knowledge, 1931); **G. A. Rendsburg,** "An Additional Note to Two Recent Articles on the Number of People in the Exodus from Egypt and the Large Numbers in Numbers I and XXVI," *VT* 51 (2001) 392-96; **W. M. W. Roth,** "The Numerical Sequence x/x+1 in the Old Testament," *VT* 12 (1962) 300-311; **B. E. Scolnic,** "Theme and Context in Biblical Lists" (Ph.D. diss.; Jewish Theological Seminary of America, 1987); **J. W. Wenham,** "Large Numbers in the Old Testament," *TynBul* 18 (1967) 19-53.

D. M. Fouts

O

OIL. *See* ANOINTING.

OLD PERSIAN SOURCES. *See* NON-ISRAELITE WRITTEN SOURCES: OLD PERSIAN AND ELAMITE.

OLIVES. *See* AGRICULTURE AND ANIMAL HUSBANDRY.

OMRI DYNASTY

Omri was the founder of the first significant dynasty of the northern kingdom of Israel after the division of the monarchy. *Jeroboam I and Baasha had previous dynasties, but each was quickly overthrown by a coup d'etat within two years of the founder's death. Omri's was the first dynasty to achieve significant dynastic succession, lasting at least three generations, and thirty-four to forty-four years (depending on the chronology one follows).

1. Omri
2. Ahab
3. Ahaziah
4. Jehoram (= Joram)
5. Omride Building Projects

1. Omri.

1.1. Omri's Rise to the Throne: The Biblical Data. Omri was the commander of the army under the Israelite king Elah son of Baasha (1 Kings 16:15-16). The army under Omri was encamped at Gibbethon to fight against the Philistines. But Zimri, commander of half the chariot forces, assassinated King Elah in *Tirzah, the capital city, and proclaimed himself king (1 Kings 16:9-10). Zimri also killed all the family of the dynasty of Baasha (1 Kings 16:11-12). When word of this coup d'etat reached Omri, the army there (designated in the text as "all Israel") proclaimed Omri king. Omri and the army then left off the engagement with the Philistines and marched

on Tirzah against Zimri (1 Kings 16:16-17). Whether Omri attacked Zimri, the usurper, out of loyalty to his former king, Elah, or out of ambition and opportunity cannot be determined, but the outcome was clear. Omri's forces laid siege to Tirzah, and the city fell after just seven days. Zimri committed suicide (1 Kings 16:17-20).

At that point a civil war ensued, with Omri and his followers pitted against Tibni son of Ginath and his followers. Tibni is not otherwise identified, but he must have had some prominence in Israel because the biblical text notes that the people were divided: half the people followed Tibni, and half followed Omri. No direct indication of the length and extent of the civil war is given. The text records that Omri prevailed, and Tibni died (1 Kings 16:21-23). However, it is reasonable to assume, based on several chronological references in the Hebrew Bible, that the civil war lasted for four years. Specifically, 1 Kings 16:10, 15 state that in twenty-seventh year of Asa, Zimri began to reign and reigned for seven days. But 1 Kings 16:23 states that in thirty-first year of Asa, Omri began to reign and reigned for twelve years. Finally, 1 Kings 16:28 states that in thirty-eighth year of Asa, Omri died and was succeeded by Ahab. A reconciliation of these chronological references can be made thus:

27th year of Asa: Elah of Israel assassinated
27th year of Asa: Zimri began to reign over Israel, reigned for seven days
27th year of Asa: Zimri committed suicide; Omri and Tibni vie for kingship
31st year of Asa: Omri began to reign, apparently dated after Tibni is dead— four-year civil war
38th year of Asa: Omri died; Ahab began to rule (the twelve-year reign of Omri assumes

his rule from the 27th year of Asa)

In other biblical references Micah clearly recalls Omri's dynasty about 150 years after its demise when he accuses the people of Israel of "keeping the statutes/customs of Omri and the deeds of the house of Ahab" (Mic 6:16). The only other biblical references to Omri are to his descendants as "son, descendant of Omri." In addition, there is a brief statement that Omri purchased a plot of land from a certain Shemer and built a new capital, *Samaria, there (1 Kings 16:24) (see 1.4 below). The Hebrew Bible basically glosses over Omri's reign, but certainly no one can doubt Omri's lasting impact on the northern kingdom, Israel.

1.2. Omri's Background. Omri is virtually unique among Israel's kings in that he has no *genealogy given. Even Tibni, Omri's opponent in the civil war, has a genealogy. The author of 1-2 Kings regularly gives some identification for the kings of Israel, even for usurpers, and even if a limited one. Jeroboam, the first king of Israel, is "son of Nebat, an Ephraimite" (1 Kings 11:26). Baasha, who overthrew Jeroboam's dynasty, is "son of Ahijah of the house of Issachar" (1 Kings 15:27). And Jehu, who overthrew Omri's dynasty, is "son of Jehoshaphat, son of Nimshi" (2 Kings 9:2). (For similar references for the last four dynasties in Israel's last twenty-five years see 2 Kings 15:10, 17, 25, 30.) Only Zimri, who reigned just seven days, and Omri lack identification.

Since Omri has no patronym, no father's house, no family or tribal association given, some scholars have suggested that Omri was not even Israelite (Montgomery and Gehman). For over a century, suggestions have been made that Omri may have been of Arab descent (Layton), a Canaanite (Gray) or a *Phoenician (Kuan). Omri's name may stem from an Arabic root meaning "to live" (Smith 1885) or from an Amorite root, since no Hebrew root for his name is known. More recently it has been suggested that the root is known in Phoenician and Punic (Benz; Kuan).

The suggestion that Omri was a foreigner may be implied by a couple of other factors as well. Many of the professional soldiers in Israel's army from the days of David onward were foreign mercenaries. Among these are Ahimelech the Hittite (1 Sam 26:6), Uriah the Hittite (2 Sam 23:39), Zelek the Ammonite (2 Sam 23:37) and Ittai the Gittite (2 Sam 18:2).

With the close relations established between the Phoenicians and Israel under both David and Solomon, it would not be unexpected to have Phoenician mercenaries in the army of Israel. Additionally, the Hebrew Bible notes the connection between Omri and the Phoenicians based on the marriage he arranged between his son and Jezebel daughter of Ittobaal, king of Tyre. One further Phoenician connection that Omri had was in architecture. The ashlar masonry at Samaria is understood to show Phoenician influence. Others have taken the position that Omri was an Israelite of the tribe of Issachar and from the village of *Jezreel (Napier).

Concerning the civil war between Omri and Tibni, one can suggest that part of the division was between the military forces who supported Omri and proclaimed him king as soon as they heard that Zimri had assassinated Elah, and the people (perhaps a popular assembly) or the elders (representing the people) who supported Tibni (Noth). There is no hard evidence for this apart from the inference in the two passages mentioned above, and the evidence that Tibni has a patronym, indicating that he was an Israelite, while Omri has none. It is equally possible that Omri represented the Canaanite (or non-Israelite) portion of the population, and Tibni represented the Israelite portion (Jones).

1.3. Omri's Foreign Policies. When Omri came to the throne, Israel for nearly fifty years had been involved in almost continuous fighting and border disputes, especially with Judah. In the more recent past, however, the Aramaeans posed the more serious threat. Ben-hadad of Damascus had invaded and occupied Galilee and parts of Transjordan (1 Kings 15:18-21). Omri worked to reduce the external threats. Although Omri had his origin in the military, his strength as a king was in his diplomatic actions. He focused not on military activity, but on developing treaties and alliances and securing the borders through peaceful means. According to 1 Kings 20:34, Omri made concessions to the Aramaeans, perhaps giving some territory to the Aramaeans and allowing them a commercial presence in Samaria (for another possible interpretation of the material see 2.5 below). Most of Omri's alliances, however, were sealed with marriages. The key alliance that Omri established was with the Phoenicians, secured through the marriage of his son Ahab, the crown prince, to the Tyrian princess Jezebel, the daughter of Ittobaal. The second marriage alliance probably also initiated by Omri was between his granddaughter (or daughter) Athaliah (see 1.6 below) and the crown prince of Judah, Jehoram, the son of King *Jehoshaphat. These two alliances greatly reduced external threats and secured the borders of Israel, and also allowed the allocation of significant resources to construction projects.

1.4. Omri's Building Projects—Domestic Policies. Omri and his dynasty are known especially for several building projects, perhaps the most significant ones in the history of the northern kingdom. From the archaeological record, it is difficult to distinguish the remains of Omri's construction from those of later Omrides, so all the Omride building projects are treated more fully following the discussion of each ruler (see 5 below). Here, the discussion focuses on the political and economic rationale for Omri's projects.

Omri began his reign in Tirzah (1 Kings 16:23), the capital of the northern kingdom during Baasha's reign, and then built a new capital, Samaria. At Tirzah, identified as Tell el-Farah north along Wadi Farah about six miles northeast of Shechem, excavators have discovered that the Iron Age strata have a break and gap that match the point when Omri built his new capital. Apparently, he had begun new construction in Tirzah and abruptly stopped. Perhaps Omri began to rebuild Tirzah as his capital during the time of the conflict with Tibni. Once that conflict was resolved, Omri was free to establish his own new capital.

A single verse in the Hebrew Bible states that Omri purchased the hill of Samaria from Shemer for two talents of silver; then he built a fortified city on the hill, and named the city "Samaria," after Shemer, the former owner of the hill (1 Kings 16:24). Certainly, Omri chose the site for its strategic location. It was not the highest hill in the region, but it was well isolated from surrounding higher hills and also had good access through the valley to its west to the major trade and communication routes and the Mediterranean. Samaria remained Israel's capital until the fall of the northern kingdom in 722 BCE, and it remained as a provincial center in the exilic and postexilic periods.

Since Tirzah was located near the head of the Wadi Farah, which led directly down to the Jordan River and to Transjordan beyond, it provided ready access to the east. But Omri faced possible danger from the northeast: the Aramaeans. Also, he was developing closer relations with the Phoenicians to the northwest. Samaria afforded better access to south and northwest, the two directions where Omri arranged political alliances with royal marriages.

After an extensive internal civil war, Omri may have wanted a new capital on a new site with inhabitants he could completely trust. So that he would not have to deal with an existing town and property owners, he purchased the land; it would be crown property, and he could build a fortified city with a royal compound and a population loyal to him alone. Also, this new site would have no previous tribal ties or affiliations; Tirzah, by contrast, had associations with previous kings of Israel, and possibly with the Israelite tribes earlier. In this manner, Samaria paralleled Jerusalem as being a royal possession, and not being in Israelite hands until the time of David.

1.5. Omri from Extrabiblical Sources. Apart from biblical material, Omri is known primarily from the Mesha Stela (*COS* 2.23:137-38; *ANET,* 320-21). According to that stela, Omri oppressed *Moab because Chemosh, Moab's deity, was angry with his land. But in Omri's son's days (or possibly his grandson's days) Mesha was able to regain control of all the Moabite territory. Mesha informs us that Omri had occupied the land of Mehadaba, and that he had built or rebuilt/fortified Ataroth and Jahaz. This indicates that Omri's territory east of the Jordan River extended south to the Arnon tributaries. The Hebrew Bible records that Mesha revolted after the death of Ahab, but it gives little specific information about the earlier subjugation of Moab by Omri. Since Moab had been a vassal of Israel under David (2 Sam 8:2), perhaps the rulers of the northern kingdom were able to maintain control of Moab after the division of the monarchy. Alternatively, Omri himself may have moved more aggressively against Moab once his border disputes with Judah were resolved. The Hebrew Bible indicates that Mesha paid the king of Israel (possibly Omri and then Ahab) one hundred thousand lambs and the wool of one hundred thousand rams annually (2 Kings 3:4). Such a heavy tribute was ample cause for a revolt when the opportune time arrived, during Mesha's reign over Moab.

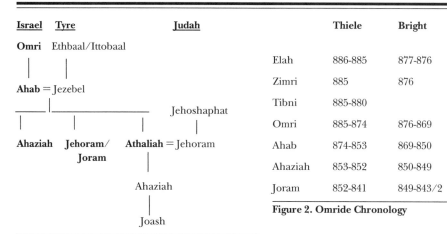

Israel	Tyre	Judah		Thiele	Bright	Hayes & Hooker
			Elah	886-885	877-876	881-880
			Zimri	885	876	880
			Tibni	885-880		
			Omri	885-874	876-869	879-869
			Ahab	874-853	869-850	868-854
			Ahaziah	853-852	850-849	853-852
			Joram	852-841	849-843/2	851-840

Figure 2. Omride Chronology

Figure 1. Omride Family Tree

1.6. Family Tree and Chronology of Omrides.

Omri is known secondarily from a number of Assyrian records that describe the northern kingdom of Israel as Bit Humri ("house/dynasty of Omri"), using that designation until the northern kingdom fell to the Assyrians in 722/721 BCE (see, e.g., COS 2.113F: 269-70; ANET, 281; COS 2.117C: 287-88; ANET, 282-84). This designation follows an Assyrian practice of referring to a region by the name of the ruling dynasty when the Assyrians first had contact with the region.

Figure 1 displays the family tree of the Omrides. Note that although two texts list Athaliah as Omri's daughter (2 Kings 8:26; 2 Chron 22:2), 2 Kings 8:18 lists Athaliah as the daughter of Ahab; note also that *bat* ("daughter") may be translated as "granddaughter," just as *bēn* ("son") may be translated as "grandson" (see, e.g., 2 Sam 19:24; 2 Chron 22:9). Also note that although Omri's dynasty in Israel ended with the death of Jehoram/Joram, his bloodline continued in the Judean dynasty through his granddaughter Athaliah. All later Judean kings continued Omri's bloodline.

Scholars have proposed various chronologies for the Omride dynasty. Figure 2 presents the proposals made by E. R. Thiele, J. Bright, and J. H. Hayes and P. K. Hooker.

2. Ahab.

Ahab was Omri's son and successor. The name "Ahab" is a combination of the Hebrew words for "brother" and "father." It could mean "brother of (the) father"—that is, "just like his father"; alternatively, it could be a theophoric name: "kinsman [brother] of [the Divine] Father." Ahab is most noted for his conflict with Yahwistic prophets, caused in large measure by the influence of Baal religion of his wife, Jezebel. Specifically, he is said to have worshiped Baal (1 Kings 16:31), set up an altar for Baal in the house of Baal that he built in Samaria (1 Kings 16:32), and made an Asherah (1 Kings 16:33). This biblical introduction to Ahab's reign describes him as doing evil in Yahweh's eyes more than all who were before him (1 Kings 16:30).

2.1. Ahab in Biblical Accounts.
There are four major narratives in which Ahab plays a role: (1) 1 Kings 17—18, the contest on Mount *Carmel; (2) 1 Kings 20, the first battle with the Aramaeans; (3) 1 Kings 21, Naboth's vineyard; (4) 1 Kings 22, the second battle with the Aramaeans. Since many historians have questioned the reconstruction of Ahab's reign based on the biblical accounts, especially the account of the battles with the Aramaeans, the present article summarizes the biblical accounts, then considers extrabiblical evidence and finally discusses the differences. It will be noted here that J. Miller suggests that the battle accounts possibly belonged to the time of Jehu's dynasty and later were attributed to the time of Ahab by the Deuteronomistic Historian (Miller and Hayes). He notes the significant disparity between the depiction of Israel as very strong and the king as supporter of Baalism in the Elijah narratives, and Israel as very weak and the king as Yahwistic in the Elisha narratives.

2.1.1. Ahab in the Narrative of the Contest on Mount Carmel.
*Elijah announced to Ahab the beginning of a drought (1 Kings 17:1). Then in the third year of the drought, Elijah presented himself to Ahab and issued the challenge to as-

semble the 450 prophets of Baal and four hundred prophets of Asherah (1 Kings 18:1-19). In that same text it is noted that Jezebel was killing the prophets of Yahweh, but Obadiah, Ahab's steward, hid one hundred prophets (1 Kings 18:3-4). At the conclusion of the contest, after the 450 prophets of Baal had been slaughtered, Elijah announced the end of the drought. Elijah and Ahab returned to Jezreel (1 Kings 18:45-46), where Jezebel threatened Elijah, and Elijah fled (1 Kings 19:1-3). In this narrative Ahab plays only a secondary role, basically responding to Elijah's announcements.

2.1.2. Ahab in the Narrative of the First Battle with the Aramaeans. The Aramaeans, aided by thirty-two kings, besieged Samaria. Ben-hadad, the Aramaean king, asked for all of Ahab's gold and silver, as well as his most beautiful wives and children. Ahab acquiesced to the demand, but Ben-hadad asked for even more. He demanded to be allowed to enter the city, search all the houses and take whatever he desired. At this demand the elders of the city and Ahab balked. Ben-hadad then called for the assault on the city. An unnamed prophet announced victory to Ahab by the hands of the young men of the officials of the provinces of Israel. These very men went out and attacked the Aramaeans, along with an army of seven thousand from Israel, and they defeated the Aramaeans (1 Kings 20:1-21). The prophet then stated that Ben-hadad would return to attack again the following spring. When spring arrived, the Aramaeans came to fight against Israel in the plain at Aphek (they chose the plain because they said that the Israelite gods were gods of hills [hill country], and they would be stronger in the valley/plain). The Aramaeans had a much larger army than did Israel. Again a man of God gave the Israelite king a victory oracle, and again the Aramaeans were defeated. Ben-hadad fled into Aphek. His servants put on sackcloth, went to the king of Israel and pled for his life. Ahab had Ben-hadad brought to him. Ben-hadad offered to restore cities that his father had taken from Israel and to permit Ahab to establish bazaars in Damascus, as Ben-hadad's father had done in Samaria. As a result, Ahab spared him. The prophet then announced the destruction of Ahab's dynasty for sparing the king (*see* Aram, Damascus and Syria).

2.1.3. Ahab in the Narrative of Naboth's Vineyard. The king wanted a piece of property ad-

joining the royal palace, property belonging to an Israelite, Naboth. Apparently, this property was part of Naboth's patrimony, held from the time of the conquest. Naboth could not sell this piece of property outside his father's household or tribe; if a land owner was forced to sell property, the nearest kin had the option to purchase the property to keep it within the family. Jezebel wrote to the elders of Jezreel to carry out a conspiracy against Naboth so that he could be killed, and then the king could obtain the property. Jezebel wrote in Ahab's name and sealed the documents with his seal (1 Kings 21:8). The officials would assume that this was a royal decree. The deed was accomplished, and then word was brought back to Jezebel—although she had written in the king's name and sealed the document with his seal, the officials knew its source! Ahab and Jezebel's crime was exceedingly heinous: they had an innocent man falsely accused, convicted and killed, just to obtain land for a royal vegetable garden. Confronted with his sin, Ahab repented. Thus the final judgment on the house of Ahab-Omri is delayed beyond his lifespan.

There are a number of interesting parallels between this narrative and the narrative of David and Bathsheba in 2 Samuel 11: the king gets what he desires; an innocent man is killed; a prophet confronts the king with a judgment oracle; a death is the judgment for the sin committed; a woman plays a role in the sin (although Jezebel is depicted as far more culpable for the death of Naboth than is Bathsheba for Uriah's death); the king repents; the full force of the judgment falls not on that king, but on others; the misuse of royal power is involved. In Ahab's case, one may contrast the despotic action in which the king (or his surrogate) can exercise royal power to acquire any property he desired with that of the Israelite patrimonial system, in which the land ultimately belonged to Yahweh and was given to each family as an inheritance.

2.1.4. Ahab in the Narrative of the Second Battle with the Aramaeans. An alliance of Israel and Judah led by their respective kings Ahab and Jehoshaphat fought against the Aramaeans. All the prophets gave a positive word about the impending battle, except for Micaiah ben Imlah, who gave a warning word to Ahab about the outcome of the battle. Nevertheless, the two kings engaged the battle. Ahab disguised himself; Jehoshaphat went in his royal clothing. The Aramaeans first attacked Jehoshaphat, thinking that he was Ahab (apparently, Ahab was viewed by the Aramaeans as the chief opponent and leader of the attack). When they realized that he was not Ahab, they stopped pursuing Jehoshaphat. However, Ahab, struck by a stray arrow between the scales of his armor, was fatally wounded. He was brought back to Samaria and buried there.

2.1.5. Summary of Biblical Accounts. In the Mount Carmel and Naboth narratives, Ahab is mentioned by name quite frequently, but the phrase "king of Israel" never appears. By contrast, Ahab is mentioned by name only three times in the narrative of the first battle with the Aramaeans, but "king of Israel" appears twelve times, and three additional times "the king." Ahab is named only once in the second battle with the Aramaeans, and "king of Israel" is found eighteen times, and thirteen times "the king." In the Mount Carmel and Naboth narratives, Elijah the prophet is a key figure who denounces the Canaanite Baalism of Ahab's court and Ahab's (or Jezebel's) Canaanite type of despotism in having Naboth killed and seizing his property. Elijah does not appear in either narrative of the Aramaean battles. In the first narrative of a battle with the Aramaeans, the king is depicted as a Yahwist who consults the elders of the land, who is much weaker than the Aramaeans, who initially receives positive words from the prophets and who almost miraculously defeats the Aramaeans. Then he is denounced by a prophet for sparing the life of the Aramaean king. In the narrative of the second battle with the Aramaeans, both the king of Judah and the king of Israel consult the Yahwistic prophets. Again the king of Israel is depicted as a Yahwist, but one who does not heed the prophetic warning of Micaiah.

2.2. Ahab's Building Projects. The Hebrew Bible relates several statements concerning Ahab as a builder. He erected an altar for Baal in the temple of Baal that he built in Samaria (1 Kings 16:32), and also he made an Asherah (1 Kings 16:33). In addition, in his death notice we are told that he built an ivory house and that he built cities (1 Kings 22:39).

From these two notices and from the archaeological record, it is clear that Ahab continued Omri's significant building projects. Indeed, since Ahab had a longer reign than did his father, and since he, unlike his father, was not troubled by a civil war for the first part of his reign, Ahab probably was responsible for many of the major projects dated to this period.

Since it is quite difficult to distinguish in the archaeological record construction by Ahab from construction by Omri, further discussion of archaeological remains is treated later in a combined manner (see 5 below).

2.3. Ahab's Religious Policies. Ahab receives strong condemnation in 1 Kings for his religious policies. First he is condemned for marrying the Phoenician princess Jezebel (1 Kings 16:31). Clearly, the Phoenicians were Baal worshipers. As a Phoenician princess, Jezebel may have even been a Baal priestess (Yee). Certainly, the Hebrew Bible depicts her as practicing and supporting Baal worship. But even more, Ahab himself served and worshiped Baal (1 Kings 16:31). There is no indication that Ahab completely abandoned Yahweh worship. Indeed, both his sons and his daughter bear Yahwistic names. However, Ahab definitely had syncretistic practices that are soundly condemned by the Hebrew Bible. In addition, he built a temple for Baal and erected an altar for Baal in Samaria, and he made an Asherah (1 Kings 16:32-33). It is the combination of these practices plus his confrontation with Elijah and other Yahwistic prophets that leads to his condemnation by 1 Kings (for discussion of the religion of Israel at this time see Albertz; P. Miller; Day).

2.4. Ahab in Extrabiblical Sources. Ahab is known from the Kurkh Monolith inscription of Shalmaneser III, describing the Battle of Qarqar in 853 BCE (*COS* 2.113A:261-64). In this battle the Assyrians, who were extending their power westward, faced a coalition of smaller kingdoms headed by Hadad-ezer (Adad-idri) of Damascus. This battle marked the first significant encounter between the Assyrians and Israel, although many more would occur in the next century and a quarter leading to the fall of Israel in 722 BCE and the reduction of Judah to vassal status. According to this inscription, Ahab the Israelite brought 2,000 chariots and 10,000 infantry against Shalmaneser, this being the second largest contingent of troops (second only to that of Hadad-ezer) and more chariots than all the other listed ones combined. Ahab is listed third among the allies following Hadad-ezer (Adad-idri), with 1,200 chariots, 1,200 cavalry and 20,000 troops, and Irhuleni of Hamath, with 700 chariots, 700 cavalry and 10,000 troops. This indicates that Ahab was able to muster a significant army and chariot force at that time.

2.5. Differences in Biblical and Extrabiblical Accounts of Ahab. The aforementioned Kurkh Monolith inscription depicts Ahab as having strong military presence in the battle of Qarqar. It also depicts Israel and the Aramaeans (Damascus) as allies, unlike the biblical depiction of the two battles with the Aramaeans. The Hebrew Bible makes no mention of the battle of Qarqar. This omission probably reflects the theological purposes of the author of Kings to depict Ahab in the most negative light possible due to his support of Baalism. In the Kurkh Monolith inscription Israel is quite strong and a leader in the coalition that fought with the Assyrians. But 1 Kings 20 and 22, set at almost the same time, has Israel and Judah together fighting against the Aramaeans, and Israel much weaker than the Aramaeans (at least in 1 Kings 20). Furthermore, there is no reference to Israel's large chariot force in 1 Kings 20; indeed, after an initial defeat in the hill country, the Aramaeans choose to fight in the plain because they believed that Israel's gods were hill country gods (1 Kings 20: 23). For these and other reasons many scholars have assumed that 1 Kings 20 and 22 belong not to Ahab's time, but to the time of Jehu's dynasty; they also assume that the original form of the biblical narrative referred to an unnamed king, with the few references to Ahab being added secondarily by the author of 1 Kings (Jepsen; J. Miller 1966; 1967; Pitard).

3. Ahaziah.

Ahaziah was the son and successor of Ahab. His name is a theophoric one, meaning "Yahweh has grasped/seized [in protection]." He reigned for only two years. Apparently, he fell through a lattice work from an upper floor and died from his injuries. The Hebrew Bible gives no word of any major activities or accomplishments on his part. We do have the brief notice that Moab rebelled after Ahab died. The same note is basically repeated after Ahaziah's death and the succession of his brother Jehoram. Thus it is difficult to assess when Moab actually rebelled. The Mesha Stela seems to imply that it was during the reign of Ahab. In one other note Ahaziah offered to participate in a naval enterprise with Jehoshaphat of Judah, but Jehoshaphat was unwilling (1 Kings 22:47-49). According to Chronicles, such a joint endeavor ended with the ships being wrecked (2 Chron 20:35-37). Ahaziah died with no son, so his brother Jehoram (= Joram) succeeded him (2 Kings 1:17).

4. Jehoram (= Joram).

Jehoram is a theophoric name meaning "Yahweh is elevated/exalted." He was Ahab's second son and succeeded Ahaziah.

4.1. Jehoram/Joram in Biblical Accounts. Jehoram is said to have removed the pillar of Baal that his father had made (2 Kings 3:2). He and Jehoshaphat of Judah led a coalition against Moab after Mesha had rebelled. According to the biblical account, Moab was defeated; Mesha was surrounded in Kir-haresheth. Mesha then sacrificed his eldest son; in response, the Israelites and Judahites withdrew from the battle. During the reign of Jehoram, Ben-hadad, king of the Aramaeans, fought against Israel and besieged Samaria, causing a severe famine in the midst of the city (2 Kings 6:24-25). However, the Aramaeans broke off the siege, and Samaria was spared (2 Kings 7). Following a coup d'etat in Damascus, Jehoram and Ahaziah, king of Judah (and his nephew), fought against Hazael, king of Syria. In the battle Jehoram was wounded (2 Kings 8:28). He returned to Jezreel to recuperate, and Ahaziah, king of Judah, came to visit him there (2 Kings 8:29). At this point Jehu was anointed king by Elisha's messenger and undertook his coup d'etat. Jehu killed Jehoram just outside Jezreel, throwing the corpse on the property that had belonged to Naboth. Ahaziah, king of Judah, was fatally wounded, but he fled in his chariot to Megiddo, where he died. Jehu entered Jezreel; Jezebel, the queen mother, was thrown to her death from her second-story window by her attendants. Jehu then had the seventy sons of Ahab killed in Samaria, along with all the remaining members of Ahab's household and officials (2 Kings 9—10). He then proceeded to kill all the Baal worshipers and destroy the pillar and temple of Baal (2 Kings 10:27). This action brought an end to the Omride dynasty.

4.2. Jehoram/Joram in Extrabiblical Sources. The Tel Dan Aramaic Stela (COS 2.39:161-62), discovered in 1993, speaks of an Aramaean king apparently killing _____ram son of _____, king of Israel, and killing _____iah (son of) _____ of the house of David. Although the names are incomplete, one may confidently restore the name of Jehoram as the king of Israel.

He is the only king of Israel whose name ends in _____ ram. The king of Judah (referred to as the house [= dynasty] of David, as has also been restored in the Mesha Stela) would be Ahaziah.

5. Omride Building Projects.

Archaeological excavations have indicated something of the quality and quantity of construction by Omri and his successor, Ahab. The artisanship of the construction, especially the fine ashlar masonry at Samaria, was of a quality unequaled in the history of the northern kingdom.

5.1. Samaria. Omri began the construction at Samaria probably after four years of civil war with Tibni. The site itself sat astride the summit of a strategic hill, protected by valleys on three sides. The area available near the summit was extended by terraces and retaining walls. The acropolis included the palace and courtyards. It had an inner wall, built probably by Omri, and a much stronger casemate wall, usually attributed to Ahab. The casemate wall was 10 m thick along the north (an outer wall nearly 2 m thick, a 7 m space and an inner wall 1 m thick). Ahab built additional structures on the acropolis and the much stronger casemate wall. Both construction periods use finely dressed ashlar masonry, with walls constructed in a header-stretcher pattern and dry-laid with no mortar. The courses set in trenches below ground level were left with margins and bosses on several sides, but all the visible courses above ground level were dressed smoothly with no margins or bosses. Although the acropolis of Samaria covered only about six acres, the lower city apparently covered about 23-28 acres.

Complementing the ashlar masonry, several volute or proto-ionic/aeolic capitals were discovered on the acropolis. Although not found in situ, these capitals probably sat atop pier walls of the gate or entrance into the palace area.

Numerous fragments of ivory found at Samaria suggest something of the luxury of furnishings to match the ashlar masonry of the exterior. The ivory quite possibly was from ivory paneling in walls and furniture that made up the "house of ivory" referred to in Amos 3:15 and 1 Kings 22:39.

5.2. Jezreel. This site, first mentioned in this period during Ahab's reign, may have been Omri's ancestral home (Olmstead). If so, one would have good reason to assume that he constructed the city. The biblical text does indicate that Jezreel was built by the end of the narrative of Elijah's slaughter of priests of Baal on Mount Carmel (1 Kings 18:46) and further indicates that a palace existed there at the time of Ahab's encounter with Elijah and the Naboth vineyard narrative (1 Kings 21:1). Thus Jezreel must have been built by Omri or early in Ahab's reign.

Archaeological excavation has shown that the eleven-acre site of Jezreel consists of a rectangular fortress with corner towers and a rock-cut moat on three sides and a steep slope on the fourth side. Inside the moat a massive rampart-revetment wall was constructed to produce a larger platform for the fortress. The construction of the site required a tremendous expenditure of labor and resources. The site has only one major construction phase, followed by a period of poorer reuse, perhaps by squatters.

Jezreel has none of the fine ashlar construction found at Samaria. Instead, the construction consists of rough stones and a brick superstructure. Nevertheless, the fortress and moat, with the rampart-revetment walls, are most imposing. It most likely was a major military site, possibly the main headquarters for Ahab's chariot forces. H. G. M. Williamson (1996) proposes that the size and imposing nature of fortifications at Jezreel had propaganda purposes. The site was intended to show the strength and position of the Omride dynasty. It was used as means of social control to impress and intimidate the local population. Williamson suggests that the site was abandoned after Jehu's coup d'etat because it represented the oppressive side of the Omride dynasty. Jehu perhaps made a statement by not reusing the site, but merely leaving it abandoned. N. Na'aman has proposed as an alternative that the site of Jezreel was destroyed by Hazael in a campaign against Israel.

5.3. Other Major Omride Construction Projects. Other cities showing significant construction dated to the Omride dynasty include *Megiddo, *Hazor, and Tel *Dan. I. Finkelstein argues that similar architectural features at such sites and *Gezer show Omride construction and provide evidence for his low chronology, shifting material previously dated to the tenth century BCE into the ninth century BCE. A. Mazar disputes the lower chronology, while arguing for Omride construction, drawing on evidence from strata dated to ninth century BCE by the higher chronology.

5.3.1. Megiddo. Megiddo as a fortified city reached its prime during the reign of Ahab. Although the dates ascribed to the Iron Age strata at Megiddo are debated, I prefer to follow Mazar and date Stratum IVA to Ahab. Thus we have at Megiddo a fortified city with a four-chamber gate and an offset-inset wall, stables and an impressive water tunnel system that remained in use from Ahab's time until the fall of Israel over a century later.

5.3.2. Hazor. Stratum VIII, attributed to the time of Ahab, had fortifications, a water system and a pillared building, originally thought to be stables but now interpreted as a granary. Perhaps the water system was built at a time when the Aramaean threat from the northeast became a reality.

5.3.3. Tel Dan. Stratum III dates probably to the time of Ahab. Belonging to that stratum is a large building with header-stretcher construction known from Samaria, a city wall and a gate complex. Ahab also enlarged the high place of Jeroboam I.

5.4. Summary. The archaeological record from numerous sites in the northern kingdom shows evidence of the massive building projects of the Omrides. Although the evidence does not allow us to determine which king was responsible, it does show the wealth and power of the Omrides. The quality and artisanship establish the Omrides as the northern kingdom's first major dynasty. Although short-lived as a dynasty, the Omrides left a lasting mark on Israel.

See also HISTORY OF ISRAEL 5: ASSYRIAN PERIOD; JEHU DYNASTY; KINGS AND KINGSHIP; SAMARIA.

BIBLIOGRAPHY. **R. Albertz,** *A History of Israelite Religion in the Old Testament Period,* vol. 1 (London: SCM, 1994); **F. L. Benz,** *Personal Names in the Phoenician and Punic Inscriptions: A Catalog, Grammatical Study and Glossary of Elements* (Studia Pohl 8; Rome: Pontifical Biblical Institute, 1972); **J. Bright,** *A History of Israel* (4th ed.; Louisville: Westminster/John Knox, 2000); **J. Day,** *Yahweh and the Gods and Goddesses of Canaan* (JSOTSup 265; Sheffield: Sheffield Academic Press, 2000); **I. Finkelstein,** "Omride Architecture," *ZDPV* 116 (2000) 114-38; **J. Gray,** *I & II Kings* (2d ed.; OTL; Philadelphia: Westminster, 1970); **J. H. Hayes and P. K. Hooker,** *A New Chronology for the Kings of Israel and Judah and Its Implications for Biblical History and Literature* (Atlanta: John Knox, 1988); **A. Jepsen,** "Israel und Damascus," *AfO* 14 (1941- 1945) 153-72; **G. H. Jones,** *1 and 2 Kings* (NCB; Grand Rapids: Eerdmans, 1984); **J. K. Kuan,** "Was Omri a Phoenician?" in *History and Interpretation: Essays in Honour of John H. Hayes,* ed. M. P. Graham, W. P. Brown and J. H. Kuan (JSOTSup 173; Sheffield: Sheffield Academic Press, 1993) 231-44; **S. C. Layton,** *Archaic Features of Canaanite Personal Names in the Hebrew Bible* (HSM 47; Atlanta: Scholars Press, 1990); **A. Mazar,** "Iron Age Chronology: A Reply to I. Finkelstein," *Levant* 29 (1997) 157-67; **J. M. Miller,** "The Elisha Cycle and the Accounts of the Omride Wars," *JBL* 85 (1966) 441-54; idem, "The Fall of the House of Ahab," *VT* 17 (1967) 307-24; **J. M. Miller and J. Hayes,** *A History of Ancient Israel and Judah* (Philadelphia: Westminster, 1986); **P. D. Miller,** *The Religion of Ancient Israel* (Louisville: Westminster/John Knox, 2000); **J. A. Montgomery and H. S. Gehman,** *A Critical and Exegetical Commentary on the Books of Kings* (ICC; New York: Scribner, 1951); **N. Na'aman,** "Historical and Literary Notes on the Excavation of Tel Jezreel," *TA* 24 (1997) 122-28; **A. Nahman,** "Samaria (City)," *NEAHL* 4.1300-1310; **B. D. Napier,** "The Omrides of Jezreel," *VT* 9 (1959) 366-78; **M. Noth,** *Könige* (BKAT; Neukirchen-Vluyn: Neukirchener Verlag, 1964); **A. T. Olmstead,** *History of Palestine and Syria to the Macedonian Conquest* (Grand Rapids: Baker, 1965 [1931]); **D. N. Pienaar,** "The Role of Fortified Cities in the Northern Kingdom during the Reign of the Omride Dynasty," *JNSL* 9 (1981) 151-57; **W. T. Pitard,** *Ancient Damascus: A Historical Study of the Syrian City-state from Earliest Times until Its Fall to the Assyrians in 732 B.C.E.* (Winona Lake, IN: Eisenbrauns, 1987); **W. R. Smith,** *Kinship and Marriage in Early Arabia* (Cambridge: Cambridge University Press, 1885); **W. Thiel,** "Ahab," *ABD* 1.100-104; idem, "Omri," *ABD* 5.17-20; **E. R. Thiele,** *The Mysterious Numbers of the Hebrew Kings* (3d ed.; Grand Rapids: Zondervan, 1983); **S. Timm,** *Die Dynastie Omri: Quellen und Untersuchungen zur Geschichte Israels im 9. Jahrhundert vor Christus* (FRLANT 124; Gottingen: Vandenhoeck & Ruprecht, 1982); **D. Ussishkin,** "Jezreel, Samaria and Megiddo: Royal Centres of Omri and Ahab," in *Congress Volume: Cambridge, 1995,* ed. J. A. Emerton (VTSup 66; Leiden: E. J. Brill, 1997) 351-64; **D. Ussishkin and J. Woodhead,** "Excavations at Tel Jezreel 1990-1991: Preliminary Report" *TA* 19 (1992) 3-56; **H. G. M. Williamson,** "Jezreel in the Biblical Texts," *TA* 18 (1991) 72-92; idem, "Tel Jezreel and the Dynasty of Omri," *PEQ* 128 (1996) 41-51; **G. A. Yee,** "Jezebel," *ABD* 3.848-49.   J. F. Drinkard Jr.

OPHEL. *See* JERUSALEM.

ORAL TRADITION AND WRITTEN TRADITION

Oral tradition and written tradition consider the origins, transmission and formation of the written texts that now exist in the Historical Books. Oral tradition represents narratives and component parts that emerge through storytelling in what some identify as an oral culture. This tradition often appears as themes, motifs and ideas similar to those found in neighboring societies. Written tradition describes the literate aspects of the Historical Books. Their composition may have originated in a written form (or used written sources) or in transcription (with editing) from an originally oral form.

1. Biblical Witness
2. Past Views of Oral Tradition
3. Past Views of Written Tradition
4. Recent Views of Oral Tradition
5. Evaluation in Light of Written Tradition

1. Biblical Witness.

The Historical Books bear witness to both written and oral sources in their composition. Written sources often refer to the book of the law of Moses (Josh 1:8; 8:31, 32, 34; 23:6; 1 Kings 2:3; 2 Kings 14:15; 1 Chron 16:40; 2 Chron 23:18; 25:4; 30:5, 18; 31:3; 35:12; Ezra 3:2, 4; 6:18; Neh 8:14, 15; 10:34, 36; 13:1; note also the book found by Josiah in 2 Kings 22:13, 16; 23:3, 21, 24; 2 Chron 34:21, 24, 31; 35:26). There is also evidence for the consultation of other written sources (*see* Sources, References to): the book of Jashar (Josh 10:13; 2 Sam 1:18); the annals of Solomon (1 Kings 11:41); the annals of the kings of Israel (1 Kings 14:19; 15:31; 16:5, 14, 20, 27; 22:39; 2 Kings 1:18; 10:34; 13:8, 12; 14:28; 15:11, 15, 21, 26, 31; 2 Chron 33:18); the annals of the kings of Judah (1 Kings 14:29; 15:7, 23; 22:45; 2 Kings 8:23; 12:19; 14:18; 15:6, 36; 16:19; 20:20; 21:17, 25; 23:28; 24:5); the records of Samuel the seer, the records of Nathan the prophet and the records of Gad the seer (1 Chron 29:29); the records of Nathan the prophet, the prophecy of Ahijah the Shilonite and the visions of Iddo the seer (2 Chron 9:29); the records of Shemaiah the prophet and of Iddo the seer (2 Chron 12:15); the "midrash" on the prophet Iddo (2 Chron 13:22); the book of the kings of Judah and Israel (2 Chron 16:11; 25:26; 27:7; 28:26; 32:32; reversed to "Israel and Judah" in 2 Chron 35:27; 36:8); the annals of Jehu (2 Chron 20:34); the "midrash" on the book of the kings (2 Chron 24:27); the vision of Isaiah (2 Chron 32:32); the records of the seers (2 Chron 33:19); what is written by David and Solomon (2 Chron 35:4); the laments of Jeremiah (2 Chron 35:25). The act of writing is noted in Judges 8:14 and 1 Kings 21:11; letters are mentioned in Joshua 10:4; Ezra 4:7; Nehemiah 5:5; 6:6; various written records appear in Joshua 18:6; Ezra 6:2; Nehemiah 7:5.

The Historical Books recount oral compositions as well: speeches (e.g., Josh 23; 24), songs (2 Sam 1) and prayers (1 Samuel 2). Nevertheless, explicit testimony occurs in many texts of a written and textual component to the compositions. This awareness increases later in the postexilic period, but it is not absent in the texts purporting to record Israel's early history, both premonarchical and monarchical.

2. Past Views of Oral Tradition.

Modern analysis of the oral traditions behind the biblical text begins with the traditio-historical approach whose genesis lay in the work of H. Gunkel (1862-1932) (see Knight). Although Gunkel worked primarily in Genesis, he developed a method for the identification of oral traditions that had profound significance throughout much of the twentieth century. Tradition was perceived as containing a form and content that were orally received from the previous generation and passed along to the next generation. Tradition was cumulative, and it developed according to the needs of the community. Gunkel was influenced by the ancient Near Eastern mythologies, in his time recently discovered and translated. He believed it possible to identify disconnected elements in the biblical text as foreign, and to trace their origin behind the text. This origin was mythological, and it developed through oral composition until it was written into the biblical text. At that point (or earlier) it may have been demythologized and thereby made acceptable to Israelite monotheism. Among Gunkel's students, A. Alt (1883-1956) applied aspects of this method to historical studies, observing especially the oral nature of the etiologies in Joshua and elsewhere, as used to explain the origin of a name or custom.

Scholars of northern Europe (the Scandinavian or Uppsala School) developed many aspects of oral traditions. In particular they observed the importance of the cult as a creative context for the origin and transmission of oral tradition. Emphasis was placed on psychological aspects of the people and their culture. A characteristic feature to emerge from some of these scholars was the ideology and setting of divine *kingship, the view that the Israelite king was declared divine at his enthronement and at annual commemorations of this event.

Elsewhere, particularly in the English-speaking world, oral tradition was impacted by two events: (1) the research by A. Lord (note also the work of M. Parry) on the oral poetry of Serbo-Croatian bards (applied to Homeric and then other epic poetry); (2) the publication of Ugaritic mythological texts discovered in 1929 and supplemented in the following years (see Kirkpatrick). This material led to the view that lengthy epic poems could be memorized and passed on orally with minimal change in wording. As a result, it was argued that the same could have happened with various portions of Israel's early history. In particular, poems such as Judges 5 represented some of the oldest and most authentic background to Israel's formative history in its land (see Poetry).

3. Past Views of Written Tradition.

For the Historical Books, Noth rejected the application of the pentateuchal documentary hypothesis, with its multiple sources and redactors who wrote with diverse purposes. Instead, he put forward a hypothesis that the entire corpus of *Joshua, *Judges, *Samuel and *Kings was composed as a single literary work in the late seventh and sixth centuries BCE. The author/editor, using earlier written sources, created a work that concurred with contemporary theologies of covenant and monotheism as found in books such as Deuteronomy and Jeremiah. This led to the designation of this corpus among modern scholars as the *Deuteronomistic History. Similar words and phrases suggested linguistic as well as conceptual parallels. The result was a history that sought to explain Israel's ultimate demise (both northern and southern kingdoms, but especially the latter) at the hands of the Assyrians and Babylonians as a result of the growing apostasy of its people and leaders who turned away from their covenantal commitment to the worship of Yahweh alone and pursued other deities. The author of *Chronicles, written perhaps a century later, also composed a theologically interpretive history (see Chronicler's History). However, this work, which began with Adam, emphasized priestly concerns such as might be found in the book of Ezekiel and among the leaders and prophets of the postexilic community in Jerusalem. The Chronicler was thought to have used similar sources as the Deuteronomist, and at times to have accessed the text of the Deuteronomistic History.

In the second half of the twentieth century many scholars followed and developed this hypothesis, often focusing on the number and type of redactions that were made in the composition of the Deuteronomistic History. Some argued for a single redaction at the time of *Josiah (with an exilic addendum) or in the exile. Others suggested redactors working at both periods and thus two significant editions of this history. Still others identified one or more additional and earlier redactors, often concentrating on the time of *Hezekiah as a flourishing period of literary production.

J. Van Seters examined the Historical Books by comparing them to late Babylonian works as well as the accounts of Herodotus and other early Greek "historians." On the basis of his own definition of history writing (which he distinguished from mythology, annals and lists), he concluded that the Historical Books preserve a minimum of reliable preexilic history and were composed in the late exilic period. However, linguistic analysis has suggested the contrary. The texts were composed using a preexilic orthography that can be distinguished from the writing style of the postexilic period (Zevit). Furthermore, an increasing number of forms in the literature of Joshua, Judges, Samuel and Kings can be compared most closely with ancient Near Eastern literature that often is unique to the Bronze and Iron Ages (e.g., conquest accounts, land grants, treaty texts, royal "apologies" for nonhereditary succession, temple construction documents, court annals).

Corresponding to this, literary forms from the Persian period have been identified for books such as *Ezra and *Nehemiah (homeland return decrees, royal and nonroyal letters, ration lists). For Nehemiah, H. G. M. Williamson has noted the apologetic role of his "memoirs" in justifying his tenure in Jerusalem. This has also provided a rationale for the written context of this book. Finally, distinctives of the historiography of Chronicles in the postexilic period may be compared with contemporary Greek historical writing (Hess 1994, 71).

4. Recent Views of Oral Tradition.

S. Niditch has emphasized the importance of the "oral world" as a culture important to the OT and its literature. The preexilic period of ancient Israel as described in the Historical Books occurred in this oral culture. Niditch demonstrates the orality behind the OT literature by the identification of repetition, as in poetry, and by literary forms—for example, narratives of conquest and subsequent enthronement. She contends that there were no libraries in ancient Israel. Archives such as the Jerusalem collection of many papyrus documents served only as a symbol of the legality of the transaction. They were never intended to be opened, as suggested by the bullae that sealed them and alone were preserved long after the papyrus documents were burned or otherwise disintegrated. According to Niditch, the eleventh-century Izbet Sartah abecedary, the tenth-century (?) Gezer calendar, and the ninth-century Moabite stela are, respectively, a magical/symbolic text, a poem, a song. Thus they are either symbols whose content was not meant to be read or transcriptions of basically oral compositions. The extrabiblical evidence for writing in ancient Israel is overstated, and the written seals that do occur were manufactured mainly by professional scribes. For Niditch, Deuteronomy 6:6-9 merely suggests that children were to be brought up in the family business, and that a written text on a doorpost could be used for magical purposes. Only priests were trained to manufacture and write on papyrus and leather. In the view of Niditch, other texts demonstrate a late move toward the writing of tradition, and even then in a largely oral context. Thus 2 Kings 23 requires that the newly found book of the law be read aloud. Nehemiah 8 also requires Ezra to read the law book aloud to the people. Jeremiah 36 demonstrates the memory capacity of an oral culture to recreate the written text after it has been destroyed. The command for the king to copy the law in Deuteronomy 17:18 is best seen as an exaggeration for what probably was only a copy of the Decalogue. Finally, Niditch understands the early sixth-century Lachish ostracon 3, wherein a junior officer claims that he can read and write, as evidence of how unusual literacy was, rather than the contrary.

Additional studies by other scholars have addressed questions of schools and canon formation (see the list in Schniedewind) that may have a bearing on the oral nature of the tradition. However, the so-called minimalist school has little to say to this question, as its proponents regard even the latest biblical "historical books" (e.g., Ezra, Nehemiah, Chronicles) to be largely fictitious literary creations of writers from around the second century BCE. On the other hand, the disappearance of the united monarchy and all earlier history in the Bible from the consideration of some archaeologists (e.g., Finkelstein and Silberman) has resulted in the theoretical role of the editors of Josiah's era being replaced by creative inventors of literate history in the court of the young king. Here as well, the earlier period is not so much preserved in oral tradition as it is largely lost or ignored by the biblical writers of the preexilic "history books."

5. Evaluation in Light of Written Tradition.

The ongoing work of *archaeology in uncovering the habitation and culture of ancient Israel, more intensively excavated than perhaps any other region and period on earth, has added significantly to evidence for writing and reading. Archaeologists have identified archive and scribal rooms adjacent to the palaces of several sites in Palestine (e.g., *Megiddo, *Samaria, *Hazor; for Jerusalem see Jeremiah 36) (see Schniedewind). There are now multiple written texts from every century of the Iron Age, in every major region of the land, occurring in both population centers as well as rural regions (Hess 2002). Given that the chief materials for writing, leather and papyrus, did not survive over the many centuries in the moister climate of inhabited Israel, it is nevertheless clear that a written culture did exist from the beginning in ancient Israel (Millard). Thus the abecedary from the small village of Izbet Sartah is a text to aid in learning the written characters of the alphabet, just as the acrostics in Lamentations and biblical psalms (e.g., Ps 119) aid in learning and are not magical or merely symbolic. The Moabite stela is no more a song or poem than are most of the texts of Judges, Samuel and Kings. They all are prose and share a literary culture. One cannot know whether the texts sealed with the bullae found in Iron Age II Jerusalem were intended to be opened. However, the evidence from other West Semitic cultures (e.g., Alalakh) demonstrates the presence of duplicate legal documents, one for easy consultation and the other permanently sealed unless perhaps a legal dispute required it to be opened. The same could have been true in Jerusalem. Nor is this the only archive in the region. Dating probably from the first half of the eighth century BCE, the sixty-three Samaria ostraca found at the capital of the northern kingdom attest to a writing culture in the administrative apparatus under kings such as Jeroboam II.

Many seals and bullae—there are more than a thousand published from ancient Israel—do not reflect professionally engraved writing, but rather a scratching of the amateurish sort that the owner of the seal might have made. Repetition and literary forms do not presuppose an oral culture any more than they do a written one. The same is true of the ability to memorize lengthy poems and stories, a skill found in both types of culture. The biblical texts, therefore, witness as much to a literate culture as to an oral one in texts such as Deuteronomy 6; 17; 2 Kings 23; Jeremiah 34 (see also the texts cited in §1 above). Of special interest is Judges 8:14, where a youth from Succoth writes. Lachish ostracon 3 attests not only to the ability of one junior officer to write, but also to the presumption by the senior correspondent that such officers were sufficiently literate to correspond with him (*COS* 3.42B:79). In the larger ancient Near Eastern context there is evidence for representatives from various levels of society reading and writing in the Iron Age. Not only would the alphabetic script of Israel make it easier to read and write (those who could read and write their own name and patronym, as found on many seals, likely would know half the alphabet), but also the percentage of items such as seals and bullae with writing on them (often without any iconography) is significantly larger in Israel than in any other contemporary culture.

Oral tradition played an important role in ancient Israel, as one may surmise from the many psalms and poems preserved in the Bible, including those in the Historical Books. However, the capacity for written tradition existed from the beginning of Israel's appearance in Palestine, and the prose texts that dominate this literature attest to its use. Thus the biblical witness, the archaeological evidence (written and nonwritten) and the

similar literary forms from neighboring and contemporary ancient Near Eastern cultures continue to attest to a dominant written tradition behind the Historical Books of the OT.

See also ARAMAIC LANGUAGE; HEBREW INSCRIPTIONS; HEBREW LANGUAGE; NON-ISRAELITE WRITTEN SOURCES; SCRIBES AND SCHOOLS; SOURCES, REFERENCES TO; WRITING, WRITING MATERIALS AND LITERACY IN THE ANCIENT NEAR EAST.

BIBLIOGRAPHY. **I. Finkelstein and N. A. Silberman,** *The Bible Unearthed: Archaeology's New Vision of Ancient Israel and the Origin of Its Sacred Texts* (New York: Free Press, 2001); **R. S. Hess,** "The Genealogies of Genesis 1—11 and Comparative Literature," in *"I Studied Inscriptions from Before the Flood": Ancient Near Eastern, Literary, and Linguistic Approaches to Genesis 1—11,* ed. R. S. Hess and D. T. Tsumura (Winona Lake, IN: Eisenbrauns, 1994) 58-72; idem, "Literacy in Iron Age Israel," in *Windows into Old Testament History: Evidence, Argument, and the Crisis of "Biblical Israel,"* ed. V. P. Long, D. W. Baker and G. J. Wenham (Grand Rapids: Eerdmans, 2002) 82-102; **P. G. Kirkpatrick,** *The Old Testament and Folklore Study* (JSOTSup 62; Sheffield: JSOT, 1988); **D. A. Knight,** *Rediscovering the Traditions of Israel: The Development of the Traditio-historical Research of the Old Testament, with Special Consideration of Scandinavian Contributions* (rev. ed.; SBLDS 9; Atlanta: Scholars Press, 1975); **A. R. Millard,** review of *Oral World and Written Word: Ancient Israelite Literature,* by S. Niditch, *JTS* 49 (1998) 699-705; **S. Niditch,** *Oral World and Written Word: Ancient Israelite Literature* (LAI; Louisville: Westminster/John Knox, 1996); **M. Noth,** *The Deuteronomistic History* (JSOTSup 15; Sheffield: JSOT, 1981 [1957]); **W. M. Schniedewind,** *How the Bible Became a Book* (Cambridge: Cambridge University Press, 2004); idem, "Orality and Literacy in Ancient Israel," *RelSRev* 26 (2000) 327-32; **M. S. Smith,** *The Memoirs of God: History, Memory, and the Experience of the Divine in Ancient Israel* (Minneapolis: Fortress, 2004); **J. Van Seters,** *In Search of History: Historiography in the Ancient World and the Origins of Biblical History* (New Haven: Yale University Press, 1983); **H. G. M. Williamson,** *Ezra, Nehemiah* (WBC 16; Waco, TX: Word, 1985); **Z. Zevit,** "Clio, I Presume," *BASOR* 260 (1985) 71-82. R. S. Hess

OTHNIEL. *See* JUDGES; HISTORY OF ISRAEL 2: PREMONARCHIC ISRAEL.

P

PALACES. *See* ARCHITECTURE.

PANAMUWA. *See* NON-ISRAELITE WRITTEN SOURCES: SYRO-PALESTINIAN.

PEACE. *See* WAR AND PEACE.

PEACEFUL INFILTRATION MODEL. *See* HISTORY OF ISRAEL 1: SETTLEMENT PERIOD.

PEKA. *See* HISTORY OF ISRAEL 5: ASSYRIAN PERIOD.

PEKAHIAH. *See* HISTORY OF ISRAEL 5: ASSYRIAN PERIOD.

PERSIA, PERSIANS

When OT writers mention Persia, they are referring to the Achaemenid Empire, the earliest of the great Iranian empires (c. 550-330 BCE). The name derives from the supposed founder of its ruling dynasty, "Achaemenes," which was also the name of the royal clan (Herodotus *Hist.* 1.125), members of which ruled the empire for over two hundred years. Before its conquest by Alexander of Macedon, it was the largest empire the world had ever seen, spanning the territory from the Hellespont to northern India, including Egypt (most of the time) and extending to central Asia up to the frontiers of modern Kazakhstan. Unlike succeeding periods, no contemporary political entity of even remotely comparable size existed along its frontiers.

    1. Origins
    2. Sources
    3. The Formation of the Empire
    4. Imperial Government and Administration
    5. The King and Royal Ideology

1. Origins.

The Persians themselves were a previously scarcely attested ethnic element in the world of the Middle East. Archaeological and written evidence suggests that until around 600 BCE they consisted of pastoral groups located in the region of modern Fars (de Miroschedji; Sumner 1986; 1994), which at an earlier period had formed part of the important, though poorly known and still surviving, kingdom of Elam (Hansman; Carter and Stolper; Potts). A linguistically related group, the Medes, located further north around the area of modern Ramadan (ancient Ecbatana), appears more prominently in the eighth to sixth centuries BCE, since they had (as a result of their relationship to the Assyrian Empire to the west) begun to coalesce into a state (Brown 1986; 1988) and made some moves toward territorial expansion, which may have embraced the region of Fars (= Persia) and provoked in turn the relatively rapid emergence of a Persian state there. This embryonic political entity subsequently incorporated through conquest the large, highly developed empires and states of western Asia: the great Neo-Babylonian Empire (heir to Assyria), Egypt, Lydia, Elam and Media (see in general *CAH*^{2}, vol. 4; Kuhrt 1995, 656-64). They in turn contributed to the emerging formulation of the Persian imagery of power. This can be seen particularly clearly in royal monuments and iconography (Root 1979) and in some of the elaborations of royalty (Kuhrt 1987), although it should not blind us to important transformations deliberately wrought in the process of adoption and adaptation (see, e.g., Briant 1988a; Kuhrt 1997).

2. Sources.

(See in general Sancisi-Weerdenburg 1987; Sancisi-Weerdenburg and Kuhrt 1987; 1990; Wiese-höfer 1993/1996, BI; Kuhrt 1995, 647-52; Briant 1996, 14-18 = 2002, 5-9.) The sources present particular difficulties, not so much through their scantiness but because they are extremely disparate and exist in a number of different languages and forms. Before excavation and decipherment of scripts the Achaemenid Empire was primarily known through the following sources.

2.1. Classical Writers. The classical writers include especially the Greek historian Herodotus, writing in the fifth century BCE. Since his aim was to celebrate the victories won by Greeks over Persians between 490 and 478 BCE, his valuable information is limited, chronologically, to the early period of the empire. Although Herodotus provides a sense of the broad geographical sweep of the empire, he treats the imperial regions very superficially, apart from Egypt and the northwestern frontier area (i.e., western Turkey), because his focus was the Greco-Persian conflict. Later classical writers, aside from the Alexander historians, exhibit similar geopolitical limitations. Because of the fascination exercised by the wealth and power of the Persian ruler, many of these writers also tend to retail stories of court corruption and intrigue. As a result, the image of the empire to be gleaned from these sources is both partial and sometimes distorted.

2.2. The Old Testament. The OT is the source from which emerged the influential picture of the Persian kings as restorers of the Jerusalem temple and supporters of the Yahweh cult (the books of *Ezra and Nehemiah). A Persian court story, comparable in some respects to the classical tales, is found in the book of Esther.

2.3. Old Persian. The Old Persian script and language was deciphered in the nineteenth century, but since its use was largely limited to monumental royal inscriptions (Kent; Schmitt 1991; 2000) intended to reflect the unchanging majesty of Persian power (the one exception is Darius I's inscription at Behistun), the texts are not directly informative on political changes or administrative structures (see Sancisi-Weerdenburg 1980, chap.1; 1989b/2000; 1999).

2.4. Other Sources. To illuminate this, other sources—Babylonian (*CAH*², vol. 4, chap. 3a; vol. 6, chap. 8b), Egyptian (Posener; *CDAFI*, vol. 4; cf. *CAH*², vol. 4, chap. 3g; vol. 6, chap. 8e; Chauveau), Aramaic (Grelot; Metzger et al. [cf.

Briant 1998]; Segal; Lemaire; Eph'al and Naveh; Porten and Yardeni; Gropp) and Elamite (Cameron; Hallock 1969; 1978) documents—have to be pressed into service, with the Aramaic texts being particularly important. The *Aramaic language had been widely used in the Near East, especially in the Neo-Assyrian Empire (Millard) before the Persian conquest, and therefore it was adopted by the Persians as the most widely-used administrative language (see Greenfield 1985; note also the newly discovered parchments from the Oxus region now in the process of publication, Shaked 2004).

2.5. Archaeology. Archaeologically, the area of the empire has been only spottily covered. Most attention has been paid to the great royal centers of Pasargadae (Stronach; cf. Boucharlat and Benech), Persepolis (Schmidt; Britt Tilia) and Susa (Boucharlat; Harper, Aruz and Tallon, 215-52). But recently more attention has been paid to the Achaemenid levels of long-occupied sites in the conquered territories such as Sardis in Lydia (Mierse; Greenwalt; Dusinberre 1997 and 2003), the Levant and Israel (*Transeuphratène* 1; Stern), and central Asia (Francfort; Briant 1984; Lyonnet; Gardin). One problem is that a number of sites known to have been very important in the period are covered by extensive modern towns, making excavation difficult; this is true of Arbela (modern Erbil in northern Iraq), Damascus and Hamadan (ancient Ecbatana).

3. The Formation of the Empire.

(See in general Kuhrt 1995, 656-67; in detail Briant 1996/2002, chaps. 1-4.) The empire was created through a series of conquests, beginning with Cyrus II ("the Great") of Persia. In 550 BCE he defeated the ruler of the Medes to the north, who had attacked the Persians, probably as part of his drive toward territorial expansion. With this defeat, the territory controlled by the Medes, which probably included the western part of the Iranian plateau, Armenia and Anatolia up to the Lydian frontier, came under Persian domination, and their capital, Ecbatana, with its treasury, fell into Persian hands (Kuhrt 1995, 656-58; Briant 1996, 41-44 = 2002, 31-33). In the 540s BCE Croesus, the Lydian king, came into conflict with his new Persian neighbor, and Cyrus's subsequent victory over him meant that the entire territory from central Anatolia to the Aegean coast was added to his conquests (Kuhrt 1995, 658-59; Briant 1996, 44-48 = 2002, 35-38).

In 539 BCE Cyrus won a major victory over the Babylonian king, and so the Babylonian Empire (including Mesopotamia, Syria, Palestine and the northern ends of the Arabian caravan routes) was incorporated (Kuhrt 1995, 659-60; Briant 1996, 50-55 = 2002, 40-49). It is not known, but seems likely, that the last seven to eight years of his life were spent conquering eastern Iran—certainly by 522 BCE the region was part and parcel of Persia's imperial territory: according to some traditions, he was killed on campaign in central Asia (Briant 1996, 49-50 = 2002, 38-40). Upon his death, the empire stretched from the Egyptian frontier and the Aegean coast to Uzbekistan, and in 526 BCE his son and successor, Cambyses, added Egypt to this already gigantic area (Lloyd; Kuhrt 1995, 661-64; Briant 1996, 61-72 = 2002, 50-61). Persian control here extended to Aswan in the south and was secured through agreements reached with Cyrene, Barca and Libya to the west of Egypt (Herodotus *Hist.* 3.13), and the wealthy Nubian kingdom to the south (Morkot).

The very rapid acquisition of empire created internal problems in Persia, involving a revolt by Cambyses' younger brother Bardiya during the former's absence in Egypt. The serious nature of the internal Persian conflict is strikingly illustrated by the fact that despite being a legitimate son of Cyrus, founder of the empire, Bardiya was quickly assassinated by a small group of Persian nobles, one of whom then acceded to the throne, claiming relationship with Cyrus's family. This was Darius I (522-486 BCE). The turmoil unleashed by these events is known from the massive, in some cases repeated, revolts against his seizure of the throne that took place, particularly on the Iranian plateau, in Babylonia, Armenia and Fars itself (Dandamaev 1976; Kuhrt 1995, 664-67; Briant 1996, 109-35 = 2002, 97-138). They were, however, ruthlessly crushed, and Darius was able to consolidate control in northern central Asia, add the Indus Valley to his realm, and begin to exploit the maritime routes between northern India and the Persian Gulf (Herodotus *Hist.* 4.44). He further strengthened his northwestern frontier by adding Thrace and several Aegean islands to his direct control and creating close links with Macedon in northern Greece (Briant 1996, 154-56 = 2002, 139-46). The attempt by his son Xerxes (486-465 BCE) to consolidate this by adding more of Greece in 480/479 BCE was unsuccessful, al-though the setback for the Persian Empire in this region was, overall, slight (Kuhrt 1995, 670-72; Briant 1996, 545-59, 572-81 = 2002, 528-42, 554-63) and ultimately proved to be temporary.

A sign that the empire achieved its final form under Darius I and Xerxes is that there was no further territorial expansion after their time. It now can be considered to have entered its "mature" phase—a conclusion borne out by the evidence for the tightening up of the administrative structure within this period and the introduction of a more uniform system of taxation (Descat 1985; 1989).

4. Imperial Government and Administration.
(See in general Wiesehöfer 1993/1996, BIV; Kuhrt 1995, 689-701; in detail Briant 1996/2002, chaps. 9-12.)

4.1. Satraps and Subjects. The immense imperial territories were divided into provinces, generally called by the Iranian-derived term *satrapy*. Each province was fairly extensive, and each was governed by a "satrap" (governor) who was virtually always a Persian or Iranian noble and lived in the satrapal capital. In many cases the satrapal center was identical with the old capital of the original political units conquered. Thus in Egypt the satrapal capital was Memphis; in Lydia, Sardis; in Media, Ecbatana; in Mesopotamia, Babylon. But modifications to this older system were also introduced, although not all at the same time, but rather in response to particular circumstances—for example, Hellespontine Phrygia eventually became a separate satrapy with its capital at Daskyleion (Petit, 181-86; Bakir), while either late in Darius I's or during Xerxes' reign the area that had formed the Neo-Babylonian Empire was divided into two new satrapies: "Beyond the River," lying west of the Euphrates and stretching down to the Egyptian frontier; and Babylonia, which comprised the whole of Mesopotamia (Stolper 1989).

The satrapal capital functioned as the administrative center of the governor. Here is where taxes were collected and stored (or sent on), satrapal archives kept, petitions sent, and royal orders and edicts received. Each satrapal capital contained a palace, used by the satrap himself and also maintained for the king on visits (Briant 1988b). Physical evidence of such a palace, decorated in a Persian style, has been found at Babylon (Haerinck; Vallat). Such royal/satrapal residences in the provinces are attested for

Memphis, Daskyleion, Sardis, Babylon, Damascus, Ecbatana and perhaps Samarkand. Each satrapy almost certainly had more than one palatial Persian center, frequently associated with a substantial park/estate, called by the Persian-derived word *paradise* (for a list of *paradeisoi* see Briant 1982b, 451 n. 109). In addition, there were fortified storehouses dotted throughout the provinces (e.g., Grelot, no. 6). In the Persian heartlands (Fars, Elam) were the major royal centers, such as the old city of Susa, which was extensively and lavishly rebuilt for the royal court, and the new, spectacular foundations of Pasargadae and Persepolis.

The satrap himself was, within his satrapy, in control of military affairs, such as general mobilization and the garrisons that served to protect the population as well as maintain order in the province. He also controlled its administrative and financial affairs to ensure the province's continued productivity and profitability. The two concerns were closely linked, as individuals held land grants on which military service and taxes were owed (Stolper 1985; *RlA* 8.205-7).

4.2. Regional Variation. Despite the unification of all these different areas in the person of the Persian king, which creates an impression of uniformity, there were regional diversities in administration and differences in the formulation of dependence and subjection in some regions.

The transhumant populations of the great Zagros mountain chain, for example, were never fully integrated into the central structure. Its productive potential was slight, and topography made military campaigns difficult; in addition, the highly mobile population was hard to pin down. Here the Persians and these scattered mountain dwellers arrived at a modus vivendi. The Persian king regularly presented the local leaders with gifts, which placed the recipients under obligation to help him, and in return, the king was able to draw on their human resources when needed; the tribes helped to secure his routes through the mountains when necessary, and their goodwill reduced the incidence of raids on adjacent settled communities (Briant 1982a, chap. 2).

Arab groups enjoyed another kind of relationship with the central authority. In return for helping to find safe routes through the desert (Herodotus *Hist.* 3.7-9) and organizing the lucrative caravan trade that ran from the southern tip of the peninsula to Palestinian ports, such as Persian controlled Gaza, they paid no tax but instead presented the king with a regular "gift" of incense (Briant 1982a, chap. 3).

Another important frontier group was the Scythians, living in the area beyond the Oxus, whose traditional lifestyle was nomadic; horse-borne warrior elites established and maintained status through booty acquired by raiding. How precisely the Persian authority managed relations with them is unknown, but certainly they supplied warriors to the Persian army, particularly as marines (Dandamaev 1982; Miller, 6-7), which suggests that a reciprocal arrangement had been set up (Briant 1982a, chap. 4). This would have given the Persians potential access to trade routes through central Asia. A carpet in one of the "Scythian Frozen Tombs" of the Altai Mountains, near China, is decorated in a recognizably Achaemenid style reflecting something of this network of relationships (Barber, 199-203).

In the instances cited, climate and environment and ensuing patterns of life determined the solutions found for managing relations with these potentially troublesome groups. Differences in the style of imposition of Persian control in other places indicate specific local factors with which the central authority had to deal.

Egypt, for example, retained its own very characteristic culture, especially in the realm of artistic expression and production, in styles of architecture, and in its belief system, which traditionally assigned a special divine role to the king. As a result, from Cambyses on, Persian kings were hailed as pharaohs, represented as such, and given pharaonic-style formal names and titulary (Posener, 1-87; *CDAFI*, vol. 4). They may even have assumed traditional Egyptian royal dress when acting in Egyptian royal rituals; certainly they are presented in that garb in those contexts (Cruz-Uribe).

In Babylonia too the Persian king acted in accordance with local royal ideology. The king was expected to build and maintain temples and city walls, confirm the protected status of certain cities, ensure that rituals were performed, authorize divine offerings and support (or even take part in) the politically important New Year Festival (Kuhrt 1983; 1987; 1990; 1997). At no point were the essential ingredients for carrying out these crucial rituals dismantled or suppressed by the Persians (Kuhrt and Sherwin-White), but it is very probable that the precise pattern of their enactment and associated royal activities was modified (Kuhrt 1997).

Furthermore, within each satrapy, local conditions varied from place to place not simply because of climate, language and political culture, but because a diversity of political units could all form part of one overall satrapy. Thus in the province "Beyond the River" a place such as *Jerusalem, with the district of Yehud, retained its sacred laws and priestly hierarchy, and it was governed by Jews (Avigad, 30-36); neighboring *Samaria was administered by the local family of *Sanballat (Cross; cf. Leith; Gropp); the *Phoenician cities continued under the control of local rulers (Betlyon; Elayi), while recent evidence suggests that *Ammon, east of the Jordan, also formed a provincial subdivision under a local governor (Herr). So although all these divergent entities were answerable to the Persian satrap in Damascus, internally they lived according to local custom. Similarly, in Turkey there were individual Greek cities variously governed by democratic city councils, oligarchies or city tyrants, and local regional dynasts, attested particularly in Caria, Lycia and Cilicia, yet all these different political units related to the relevant satrap as the overarching authority (see, e.g., Hornblower; CAH^2, vol. 6, chap. 8a; Keen). A similar picture is gradually emerging for the region of Bactria-Sogdia, where the satrap interacted with the local aristocracies of the different communities (Briant 1984; cf. Shaked 2004).

A final instance of the Persian government's flexible approach to ruling their subjects relates to law, although detailed knowledge of Achaemenid legal administration is limited. An interesting hypothesis challenging this view was advanced in 1984 and elaborated in 1996 by P. Frei (Frei and Koch). In his opinion, the Achaemenids developed a specific (and unique) legal instrument for managing their diverse subjects, formulated as a coherent set of statutes (or a "code"), that could be, and was, applied empirewide. The author coined for it the term *Reichsautorisation*, and he used it to try to explain the activities of *Ezra as reported in the OT. Such a code, he argued, is what the author of Ezra has in mind when he speaks of "the law of the king" in contrast to the "law of God" (Ezra 7). This view has attracted a good deal of criticism, as can be gauged from the 2001 volume edited by J. W. Watts, where Frei's thesis is re-presented in English followed by critical discussions.

Two main points undermine Frei's proposition. First, the only evidence that we have for royal law (Old Persian *data-*), namely, the Old Persian royal inscriptions, suggests strongly that it took the form of individual ordinances or decrees issued by the king, never a coherent set of rules or legal digest, as illustrated by this proclamation: "By the favor of Ahuramazda, these are the countries which I seized outside Persia. I ruled over them; they bore me tribute; what was said to them by me, that they did; my law *[data-]* held them firm" (Kent; Schmitt 2000, DNa §3). The second weakness is that in those instances where Frei's thesis can be tested—primarily western Asia Minor and Egypt (Briant 1998; Redford)—the imperial strategy for managing its diverse subjects seems to have hinged on accommodating to local legal norms, as long as these did not undermine the realm's security and smooth functioning. As far as we can judge at present, political expediency and practical considerations appear to have been the guiding principles of the system; there is no indication that an overarching set of rules ever was devised (cf. Briant 2000a; Kuhrt 2001; Rüterswörden; Wiesehöfer 1995).

4.3. Central Control. This variation in patterns of rule should be seen neither as a sign of imperial weakness nor as evidence that the different political units were just loosely joined together and thus constantly liable to fly apart. Rather, the varieties of political relationship and domination should be seen as a positive element that made central government more elastic and sensitive in its response to local needs and conditions while maintaining strong overall control for its own benefit (Briant 1987; Kuhrt 1995, 697-700).

The Persian Empire, it should be noted, lasted over two hundred years, experiencing within that time only one serious loss, Egypt, which had seceded by 400/399 BCE; however, it was regained in 343 BCE, so even its loss proved not to be permanent. Moreover, from Darius I on, the grip of the Achaemenid family on the throne was never broken: despite repeated violent struggles for the succession, its hold of the kingship was never effectively challenged. Aside from the secession of Egypt, and persistently recurring problems in frontier regions, such as the Aegean seaboard and (perhaps) Caspian mountains, all serious revolts from about 480 BCE on, with the exception of Egypt, took place inside the Persian power structure itself and centered on struggles at court for the throne—that is, they did not threaten the structure of the empire, but rather turned on who should dominate it.

Despite local variations in the form of Persian rule, control of the various provinces by the satraps was and remained extremely effective. The rule of exclusively appointing Persians/Iranians to these high positions seems generally to have been the norm, reinforced by Iranians always holding the highest military commands and the most important posts in the provinces. This should not obscure the fact that members of the central authority developed close links with local elites in various areas of the empire, which could lead to the recruiting of members from such groups to powerful governmental positions. The impression at present is that this was exceptional and related to special circumstances (Hornblower; Stolper 1987). Beyond that, there are indications of intermarriage: Persian nobles married women from the families of local dynasts (e.g., Herodotus *Hist.* 5.21; Xenophon *Hell.* 4.1.6-7); local dignitaries or soldiers, who had particularly distinguished themselves, are attested receiving a wife from a high-ranking Persian family (Herodotus *Hist.* 6.41). Particularly interesting is the chance information that the secondary wives of the kings themselves could be non-Persian, and in certain circumstances their sons might succeed to the throne, as in the case of Darius II (Ctesias *FGrH* 688 F15). Thus, although power was carefully restricted to an exclusive group made up of Persian aristocrats, this small group of power holders could, and did, incorporate selected members of the subject populations, so that the governing group established a system of kinship ties and local alliances that reached right into the various dominated groups and helped to root its power at the local level to create an identity of interest.

Lower down on the socioeconomic scale, both local peoples and deportees were allocated land parcels that carried with them the obligation to perform specified military duties when required (Briant 1985). The parcels could be identified according to the kind of service required (Stolper 1985; *RlA* 8.205-7): "bow-land" for archers, "horse-land" for cavaliers, and "chariot-land" presumably relating to chariot drivers and associated requirements. Clearly,

the aim of assigning such "fief-holdings" was to fulfill imperial army requirements. Just as clearly, the surviving sources reveal that after the formative phase, general call-ups were relatively infrequent, and routine needs often were fulfilled by mercenaries, so that at times the obligation associated with the land holding was discharged in the form of a tax. Since the tax probably was payable in silver, a complicated series of arrangements is attested whereby holders of such "fiefs" leased them out to financial firms that managed them for the holders by renting them out, collecting the dues, probably in naturalia, and converting these through sale into silver for tax payments. Although this could be characterized as a deformation of the system, it is clear that it did not break down. Enough evidence survives to show that the names of the original grantees and the expected military service associated with the grant were kept on royal/satrapal registers. Since the grants could not be alienated, when a demand came to supply, say, a cavalier, and the descendant of the grantee was not in a position to carry this out, he supplied and equipped a substitute to perform the service on his behalf (Ebeling; Stolper 1985; van Driel; Briant 1996, 615-17 = 2002, 597-99). Thus there is no reason to suppose that the empire was overly dependent on hired mercenaries and incapable of raising an army throughout its existence when necessary—a fact shown clearly during Alexander's invasion (Kuhrt 1989; Briant 1996, 803-9 = 2002, 783-800).

Much less clear, and still debated, is how the state labor requirements were met. It is possible that conscription for this was organized on the same (or at least similar) basis as army service, and groups of such conscripts were sent to where particular construction projects needed the extra human resources (Uchitel; Briant 1996, 442-52 = 2002, 429-39).

The empire's far-flung territories were connected by a complex road system. Herodotus (*Hist.* 5.52-54; 8.98) describes part of it between Sardis and Susa, but it is known to have been much more extensive, linking all the main centers of the empire and guarded by a series of posting stations that held supplies for travelers of fresh horses, fodder and food. Entitlement to draw on these supplies was obtained by written authorization issued to individuals by the king, members of the court and satraps (Hallock 1969: Q texts; Koch 1986; Graf; Briant 1996, 369-98 =

2002, 357-77). They were extensively used, not simply by the king, royal retinue and army contingents, but also for the speedy communication between king and satrapal authorities and to facilitate the journeys of personal servants of Persian nobles engaged in looking after their landed estates. The clearest illustration is a document issued by the satrap of Egypt, then perhaps in Babylon or Susa, permitting the manager of his Egyptian estates to travel, together with three other servants, to Egypt and draw supplies at posting stations along the way (Whitehead, 64-66).

Landed estates, whose revenues were granted to members of the Persian aristocracy and especially favored people who had performed exceptional services for the king as personal royal gifts, were located throughout the empire (Briant 1985). While some of the highest-ranking owners held such estates in a number of different regions of the empire and thus were perforce absentee landholders, others (including Persians) were fairly firmly settled on their estates with their families. The estates included a fortified dwelling, and it is clear from several accounts that these were permanently guarded by soldiers, and that the estates embraced holders of military fiefs who could be used to fend off attacks or, conversely, levied by the owner in response to larger military threats. Thus the estates within the provinces were another means that served to spread the Persian presence and military control throughout the empire (Xenophon *Anab.* 7.8; Whitehead; Stolper 1985; *RlA* 8.205-7).

The king himself (and members of the royal family) also possessed such estates throughout the empire, carefully laid out and cultivated—the royal *paradeisoi*. Keeping and extending land under production was a prime royal concern to ensure and safeguard an adequate agricultural base and the concomitant creation of state wealth as a result of agricultural productivity. Irrigation projects, both the extension of existing ones and the installation of new ones (Babylonia, Bactria, northern Iran, Egyptian oases [see Briant 2000b; Wuttman]), were particularly fostered by the Persian rulers. The most striking landscape transformation wrought by them is attested in Fars, where it has been established archaeologically that in the four to five hundred years preceding the emergence of the Achaemenid state the area was sparsely settled, with virtually no large urban centers and a pre-

vailing pastoral mode of land exploitation; by the end of the empire the region was construed by historians as a veritable garden of Eden:

> High land, blessed with a healthy climate and full of the fruits appropriate to the season. There were glens heavily wooded and shady cultivated trees of various kinds in parks, also naturally converging glades full of trees of every sort and streams of water, so that travelers lingered with delight in places pleasantly inviting repose. Also there was an abundance of cattle of every kind . . . and in density of population, too, this country far surpassed the other satrapies. (Diodorus Siculus *Bib. Hist.* 19.21 2-4)

The hard reality of this change has been established not only by excavation of the palatial centers of Pasargadae and Persepolis, but also by surveys in the region, which chart the sudden and massive increase of settlements in the Achaemenid period (Sumner 1986).

5. The King and Royal Ideology.

(See in general Kuhrt 1995, 676-789; in detail Wiesehöfer 1993/1996, BII-III; Briant 1996/2002, chaps. 5-8.)

At the apex of the empire stood the king, who regularly proclaimed himself as king of kings and ruler on this earth, but also stressed that he was an Iranian and a Persian, a member of the Achaemenid family, ideally directly descended from his predecessor (*see* Kings and Kingship).

5.1. Succession and Coronation. The king usually chose his successor from among his sons and seems generally to have been expected to choose the eldest. But this was not an unalterable rule; he could, and did, if political considerations so dictated, select a younger son to the position of crown prince (Kent, XPf 27-36). Failing "legitimate" offspring, by which presumably the sons of primary wives are meant, the sons of secondary wives, "bastards," had the next-best claim to succeed, which happened on occasion (Ctesias *FGrH* 688 F15). Conversely, husbands of royal daughters—that is, royal sons-in-law—seem never to have been able to claim the throne, although their offspring could become eligible, failing male royal children. Thus the matrimonial policies of the Achaemenids were carefully guarded, as the marriage of royal daughters to members of the aristocracy could lead to another family laying claim to the throne. This potential threat to the Achaemenid monopoly of power led at times to the practice of endogamy in order to safeguard dynastic integrity (Sancisi-Weerdenburg 1983a).

Table 1. Kings of Persia

Teispes (of Anshan)	c. 650-620
Cyrus I (son)	c. 620-590
Cambyses I (son)	c. 590-559
Cyrus II the Great (son)	559-530
Cambyses II (son)	530-522
Bardiya (Smerdis) (brother)	522
Darius I (son of Hystaspes, grandson of Arsames, descendant of Achaemenes)	522-486
Xerxes (son)	486-465
Artaxerxes I (son)	465-424/423
Darius II (son)	423-405
Artaxerxes II (son)	405-359/358
Artaxerxes III (son)	359/358-338
Artaxerxes IV (Arses, son)	338-336
Darius III (second cousin)	336-330
Alexander of Macedon	330-323

Upon the king's death, an important duty that fell to the legitimate successor was the conveyance of the body in an elaborately decorated hearse to Persepolis for burial in the rock-cut tombs at and near Persepolis, which, from Darius I onward, never varied in their pattern and decoration (Briant 1991). Apart from the empire-wide extinction of the "royal fire," some evidence now shows that regular rituals were performed around the tombs provisioned by the king after burial and a period of public mourning (Henkelman 2003).

The coronation of the king took place in Pasargadae, the royal center laid out by Cyrus. It contained his tomb, built quite unlike the tombs of Darius I and his successors: it was elevated on a series of steep steps, a free-standing, stone-built, gabled building, set in a beautifully laid out park; it was permanently guarded and had special rituals regularly performed around it by *magi* (Persian learned men), who received supplies from the royal treasuries to support the cult (Arrian *Anab.* 6.29.4-7). Here the prospective king went through an initiation ritual: he was dressed in the garments of Cyrus before his rise

to the kingship, ate bitter herbs and drank sour milk (Plutarch *Art.* 3). Although the ritual is not fully understood, it clearly evoked the origins of the dynasty and connected the new king directly with the founder of the empire. Only after this was he adorned with the royal insignia and revealed to the people in his fully crowned, royal glory (Sancisi-Weerdenburg 1983b).

5.2. The Religion of the Achaemenid Rulers. Defining Persian religion in the Achaemenid period is a much discussed issue. It is important to resist the temptation to use Iranian material only attested over six centuries later (such as the Zoroastrian sacred book, the Avesta, and notions about the legendary figure of Zarathustra) to try to read back what beliefs and cultic practices might have been current in the sixth to fourth centuries BCE (Kellens 1991; 2001). The only method that has a chance of shedding some light on the question is to confine any investigation to contemporary evidence, which comes mainly from the Persian imperial centers.

The most important, albeit circumscribed, source is the Persian inscriptions, cast in the form of kingly proclamations. From Darius I's reign onward there are royal statements inscribed on palaces, tombs and cliff faces or deposited in the foundations of buildings. They show that the supreme Persian god was Ahuramazda, with the kings stressing that what they did in war and peace was achieved "with the help of Ahuramazda." Ahuramazda was the prime creator of cosmic and earthly order; through him, with him and as part of his bountiful creation, the Persian monarch ruled "on this earth." This complementarity of god and king may be shown by the image carved on the facades of the Persian royal tombs, where a divine and a royal figure face each other in a reciprocal gesture of greeting and blessing. Ahuramazda and the Persian king together represent right, truth—that is, a cosmic-moral order—hence the empire's inhabitants must remain loyal to the political structure that embodies it. Thus rebellion against the king can be equated with not adhering to Ahuramazda's rule; Darius expresses this clearly when describing a revolt against him: "By them [the rebels] Ahuramazda was not worshiped" (Kent; Schmitt 1991, DB §72). What he meant by this was that the rebels threatened the stability of the god-defined imperial framework and so had to be punished, not that their religious practices were offensive to

775

Table 2. Achaemenid Empire: Chronology of Main Political Events

540	Cyrus II defeats the Medes
540s	Cyrus's conquest of Lydia
539	Cyrus conquers Babylonia
530	Death of Cyrus; accession of his son Cambyses
526/525	Cambyses conquers Egypt
522/521	Revolt of Bardiya, Cambyses' younger brother: assassinated by Darius and six Persian nobles; Darius seizes throne; major series of revolts through large part of empire; at some point after this northern India and Thrace added to empire
499	Ionian revolt begins
490	Battle of Marathon
486	Egypt revolts; death of Darius: succeeded by his son Xerxes
484	Revolts in Babylonia
480/479	Persian invasion of Greece
465	Xerxes assassinated; followed after short period of confusion by his son Artaxerxes I
424	Death of Artaxerxes I; succeeded by his only legitimate son, Xerxes II; Xerxes assassinated by his half brother Sogdianos, who claims throne
423	Sogdianos murdered by his half-brother Darius II, who accedes to throne
405	Darius II dies; his son Artaxerxes II accedes to throne
401	Attempt by the king's younger brother Cyrus to topple him; Cyrus the Younger killed in Battle of Cunaxa
401/400	Egypt secedes
359/358	Artaxerxes II dies; succeeded by Artaxerxes III
343/342	Egypt reconquered
338	Artaxerxes III dies; Arses (= Artaxerxes IV) accedes to throne
336	Arses murdered; Darius III (not a direct descendant) accedes to throne
333	Battle of Issus between Alexander of Macedon and Darius III: Persians defeated
331	Battle of Gaugamela ends in Macedonian victory: Alexander conquers the main royal Persian centers
330	Darius III murdered (?) by two Persian nobles, one of whom proclaims himself king of Persia in eastern Iran and Bactria (= "Artaxerxes V"); Alexander arranges for Darius III's burial and proclaims vengeance on Darius's assassins
330-327	Hard fighting in eastern Iran and central Asia by Alexander
327-325	Alexander rounds off his conquest of the Persian Empire by capturing the formerr Achaemenid-held regions of India
324-323	Alexander returns from India through Persia to Babylonia; dies in Babylon

the Persian ruler. The message is that in order to partake of blessings on this earth and, after death, in heaven, humankind must be loyal to the king, which is elided with reverence for the king's god, Ahuramazda. This is, in essence, also the message delivered by Darius's successor, Xerxes, as commemorated in a set of foundation documents from Persepolis (Kent; Schmitt 2000, XPh §§4-5). Xerxes there elaborates his father's statement (Sancisi-Weerdenburg 1980, chap. 1) by emphasizing the centrality of the royal role in humankind's redemption: the passage from the world of the living to the hereafter is medi-

ated through the person of the king, thus only through fidelity to the Persian monarch and the order that he represents can the individual be saved (Briant 1996/2002, chap. 13.7).

Although Ahuramazda clearly was the supreme deity of the Persian ruler, he was never the sole god. From Darius onward there are repeated references to, for example, "Ahuramazda and the gods" or "Ahuramazda and all the gods." The thousands of Elamite administrative documents from Persepolis (late sixth and earlier fifth centuries BCE) show the central authority repeatedly making generous provisions for a diversity of cults in the Persian homeland, including, alongside Ahuramazda, Elamite and Babylonian gods and, perhaps, divinized local topographical features, such as rivers and mountains. There was no discernible distinction between the provisions made for Persian and non-Persian cults (contra Koch 1977). Indeed, the Elamite god, Humban, receives much larger provisions for cult than Ahuramazda. The royal inscriptions also indicate an evolution over time within Persian religion. In the reign of Artaxerxes II (405-359 BCE) Ahuramazda was associated on occasion with the gods Anahita and Mithra; the latter also figures in an inscription of his successor, Artaxerxes III. What this implies is not clear. A possible hint is provided by a passage from Berossus, the early Hellenistic Babylonian scholar. He seems to say that Artaxerxes II initiated a change by introducing a statue cult of the goddess Anahita in Babylon, and required worship of her by "the Susians, Ecbatanians, Persians and Bactrians," as well as "from Damascus and Sardis" (*FGrH* 680 F11). It is possible that this refers to a royal edict ordering the inhabitants of greater Iran to render cult in this form to the popular Iranian goddess Anahita, whose worship was well established and widespread throughout the region. Simultaneously, the king commanded the establishment of Anahita sanctuaries in the chief satrapal centers of Babylonia, Asia Minor and Syria (Egypt had seceded at this point), where the shrines would serve as a focus for the Persian communities of the imperial diaspora (Briant 1986, 30-31; 1996/2002, chap. 15.8). If this understanding of Berossus is correct, then Artaxerxes' order would have been aimed exclusively at Persians and was intended to strengthen their sense of cohesion and identity as members of the governing elite vis-à-vis their non-Persian subjects.

5.3. The Dynamics of Absolute Power. In several inscriptions and stories surrounding the kings emphasis is placed on their military valor and physical prowess. A king underwent a special education, shared by the sons of the aristocracy: young boys were taken from their parents and subjected to tough training in military and survival skills, as well as being instructed in Persian myths and legends by the *magi* (Strabo *Geogr.* 15.3.18). Learning "to tell the truth" was another aspect of this training, the precise meaning of which is disputed (Sancisi-

Weerdenburg 1993). A possible interpretation is that it related to the concept of loyalty to the king, who himself was empowered to uphold the god-given order because he was conceived as holding the throne as a grant from Ahuramazda (see 5.2 above). This was expressed through total obedience, actively promoting his personal well-being, and guarding him from physical and political dangers. Individuals who had particularly distinguished themselves in this respect could be raised in rank by royal favor, marked by royal "gifts" of a special dress, elaborate ornaments, a horse "that had been ridden by the king" (cf. Esther 6:8-11), sometimes an estate, and particularly through being granted the right of salutation with a royal kiss, which was a mark of high status (Sancisi-Weerdenburg 1989a; Briant 1996, 314-35 = 2002, 302-31). This system of royal rewards resulted in the emergence of a royally created aristocracy that was superimposed on the ranks of the older aristocratic families, effectively limiting their privileges and forcing them to compete with the newer nobility to maintain their position (Kuhrt 1995: 686-89; Briant 1996, 335-50 = 2002, 331-38). All thus became the king's "servants" (Old Persian *bandaka*).

All this demonstrates the absolute power of the king, not subject to legal restrictions, but himself the upholder and embodiment of what was right and just, perhaps encapsulated in the Persian concept of *arta*, commonly translated "truth" (see Kellens 1995). In this role he represented a dignified and vigorous moral force, rewarding the "good" and opposed to all that might threaten this divine order and unleash the forces of moral and political chaos (the "lie" = *drauga* [see, e.g., Kent; Schmitt 1991, DB I §§30-35]). This royal message was expressed visually by the widely diffused image on the central authority's seals, which showed a kingly hero masterfully restraining a rampant wild animal (Root 1991; Garrison and Root), and verbally in the statement of royal virtues found in two exemplars of a royal inscription and composed in the name of two Persian kings (Darius I and Xerxes), ending with an exhortation to communicate it to others:

A great god is Ahuramazda who created this excellent work which one sees; who created happiness for man; who bestowed wisdom and energy upon Darius/Xerxes the king. Says Darius/Xerxes the king: by the favor of

Ahuramazda I am of such a kind that I am a friend to what is right; I am no friend to what is wrong. It is not my wish that the weak has wrong done to him because of the mighty; it is not my wish that the mighty has wrong done to him because of the weak. What is right, that is my wish. I am no friend of the man who is a follower of the Lie. I am not hot-tempered. When I feel anger rising, I keep it under control by my mental [lit., "thinking"] power. I control my impulses firmly. The man who cooperates, him do I reward according to his cooperation. He who does harm, him I punish according to the damage. It is not my wish that a man does harm, it is certainly not my wish that a man if he does harm should go unpunished. What a man says against another man, that does not convince me, until I have heard testimony [?] from both parties. What a man does or performs according to his powers, satisfies me; therewith I am satisfied and it gives me great pleasure and I am very satisfied, and give much to loyal men. I am trained with both hands and feet. As a horseman, I am a good horseman. As a bowman, I am a good bowman, both afoot and on horseback. And the skills which Ahuramazda has bestowed upon me and I have had the strength to use, by the favor of Ahuramazda, what has been done by me, I have done with these skills which Ahuramazda has bestowed upon me. Oh subject, make known vigorously of what sort I am, and of what kind my skill, and of what sort my superiority. Do not let that seem false to you, which your ears have heard. Hear that, which you have been told. Oh subject, do not let that be made [to appear] false to you that has been done by me. Look at that which has been inscribed. Do not disobey the laws. Do not allow anyone to be untrained in obedience. Oh subject, do not force the king to inflict punishment for wrong-doing on the inhabitants of this land. (Kent, DNb; Gharib 1968; cf. Schmitt 2000, DNb, XP1)

Here the king's qualities as a just ruler are the central motif: Ahuramazda has equipped the ruler with the insight and ability to distinguish right from wrong, which enables him to be the guarantor of justice and maintainer of the social order; he can do this because he does not react unthinkingly and is able to control his temper; as a result the king metes out reward and punishment fairly, and only after consider-ation of each case; he judges services rendered according to individual potential and is ever ready to reward loyalty. Following on this ethical image come the physical qualities that give him the sheer bodily strength to campaign, conquer and maintain control; in these too he excels, so that the two aspects confirm the fact that he is fitted to exercise kingship as already affirmed by his god Ahuramazda, to whom he is closely linked because (as this and other inscriptions show) he is part of Ahuramazda's bountiful creation and plan for human happiness. It is, therefore, the duty of all subjects to support and obey the king and spread abroad his excellent qualities. That this text, more than any other, reflects the widely accepted and highest ideals of Persian kingship is shown in three ways: (1) by the fact that the text is written in the names of two different kings—that is, it is not a personal statement but a generic one; (2) by the fact that part of it has been written in Aramaic on a late fifth-century BCE papyrus from the tiny Jewish garrison at Elephantine (Sims-Williams); (3) by the fact that all these qualities, in a different literary form, were attributed by Xenophon to his would-be usurper-hero, Cyrus the Younger: these, according to Xenophon, were the virtues that made Cyrus the most kingly of men and the most fitted to exercise power (Xenophon *Anab.* 1.9). The text conveys powerfully an ideology of legitimate power effectively diffused through the empire.

See also HISTORY OF ISRAEL 7: PERSIAN PERIOD; NON-ISRAELITE WRITTEN SOURCES: OLD PERSIAN AND ELAMITE.

BIBLIOGRAPHY. **N. Avigad,** *Bullae and Seals from a Post-Exilic Judaean Archive* (Qedem 4; Jerusalem: Institute of Archaeology, Hebrew University of Jerusalem, 1976); **T. Bakir,** "Archäologische Beobachtungen über die Residenz in Daskyleion," in *Dans les pas des Dix-Mille: Peuples et pays du Proche-Orient vus par un Grec; Actes de la table ronde internationale, organisée à l'initiative du GRACO, Toulouse, 3-4 février 1995,* ed. P. Briant (Pallas 43; Toulouse: Presses Universitaires de Mirail, 1995) 269-85; **E. J. W. Barber,** *Prehistoric Textiles: The Development of Cloth in the Neolithic and Bronze Ages with Special Reference to the Aegean* (Princeton, NJ: Princeton University Press, 1991); **J. W. Betlyon,** *The Coinage and Mints of Phoenicia: the Pre-Alexandrine Period* (HSM 26; Chico, CA: Scholars Press, 1980); **R. Boucharlat,** "Suse et la Susiane à l'époque achéménide:

Données archéologiques," in *Achaemenid History*, 4: *Centre and Periphery*, ed. H. Sancisi-Weerdenburg and A. Kuhrt (Leiden: Netherlands Institute for the Near East, 1990) 149-75; **R. Boucharlat and C. Benech,** "Organisation et aménagement de l'espace à Pasargades: Reconaissances archéologiques de surface, 1999-2002," *Achaemenid Research on Texts and Archaeology* 001 (2002) (http://www.achemenet.com/ressources/enligne/arta/pdf/2002.001-plg.pdf); **P. Briant,** "Cités et satrapes dans l'empire achéménide: Pixôdaros et Xanthos," *Comptes Rendus de l'Académie des Inscriptions et Belles Lettres* (1998) 305-40; idem, "Dons de terres et de villes: L'Asie Mineure dans le contexte achéménide," *REA* 87 (1985) 53-71; idem, *Etat et pasteurs au Moyen-Orient ancien* (Collection Production pastorale et société; Cambridge: Cambridge University Press; Paris: Maison des Sciences de l'Homme, 1982a); idem, "Ethno-classe dominante et populations soumises dans l'empire achéménide: Le cas d'Egypte," in *Achaemenid History*, 3: *Method and Theory*, ed. A. Kuhrt and H. Sancisi-Weerdenburg (Leiden: Netherlands Institute for the Near East, 1988a) 137-73; idem, *Histoire de l'Empire perse: De Cyrus à Alexandre* (Paris: Fayard [2 vols.; *Achaemenid History*, 10; Leiden: Netherlands Institute for the Near East], 1996); ET: *From Cyrus to Alexander: A History of the Persian Empire* (Winona Lake, IN: Eisenbrauns, 2002 [1996]); idem, "Histoire impériale et histoire régionale: À propos de l'histoire de Juda dans l'empire achéménide," in *Congress Volume: Oslo 1998*, ed. A. Lemaire and M. Sæbø (VTSup 80; Leiden: E. J. Brill, 2000a) 235-45; idem, *L'Asie centrale et les royaumes proche-orientaux du premier millénaire (c. VIIIe-IVe siècles avant notre ère)* (Paris: Éditions Recherche sur les Civilisations, 1984); idem, "Le nomadisme du Grand Roi," *IA* 23 (1988b) 253-73; idem, "Le roi est mort: Vive le roi! Remarques sur les rituels de succession chez les achéménides," in *La religion iranienne à l'époque achéménide: Actes du colloque de Liège, 11 décembre 1987*, ed. J. Kellens (IASup 5; Ghent: Iranica Antiqua, 1991) 2-11; idem, "Polybe X.28 et les qanats: Le témoignage et ses limites," in *Irrigation et drainage dans l'Antiquité: Qanats et canalisations souterraines en Iran, en Égypte et en Grèce,* ed. P. Briant (Persika 2; Paris; Thotm, 2000b) 15-40; idem, "Polythéisme et empire unitaire (Remarques sur la politique religieuse des Achéménides)," in *Les grandes figures religieuses: Fonctionnement pratique et symbolique dans l'antiquité (Besançon 25-26 avril 1984)* (Centre de recherches d'histoire ancienne 68, Paris: Belles Lettres, 1986) 425-43; idem, "Pouvoir central et polycentrisme culturel dans l'empire achéménide," in *Achaemenid History*, 1: *Sources, Structures, Synthesis,* ed. H. Sancisi-Weerdenburg (Leiden: Netherlands Institute for the Near East, 1987) 1-31; idem, *Rois, tributs et paysans: Études sur les formations tributaires au Moyen-Orient ancien* (Annales littéraires de l'Université de Besançon 269; Paris: Belles Lettres, 1982b); **A. Britt Tilia,** *Studies and Restorations at Persepolis and Other Sites in Fars* (2 vols.; Reports and Memoirs 16, 18; Rome: IsMEO, 1972-1978); **S. Brown,** "Median and Secondary State Formation in the Neo-Assyrian Zagros," *Journal of Cuneiform Studies* 38 (1986) 107-19; idem., "The *Medikos Logos* of Herodotus and the Evolution of the Median State," in *Achaemenid History 3: Method and Theory*, ed. A. Kuhrt and H. Sancisi-Weerdenburg (Leiden: Netherlands Institute for the Near East) 71-86; **G. G. Cameron,** *The Persepolis Treasury Tablets* (OIP 65; Chicago: University of Chicago Press, 1948); **E. Carter and M. W. Stolper,** *Elam: Surveys of Political History and Archaeology* (NES 25; Berkeley: University of California Press, 1984); **M. Chauveau,** "Les archives d'un temple des oasis au temps des Perses," *BSFE* 137 (1996) 32-47; **F. Cross,** "The Discovery of the Samaria Papyri," *BA* 26 (1963) 110-24; **E. Cruz-Uribe,** *Hibis Temple Project*, 1: *Translation, Commentary, Discussions and Sign List* (San Antonio, TX: Van Siclen, 1988); **M. A. Dandamaev,** *Persien unter den ersten Achämeniden (6. Jh. v. Chr.)* (Beiträge zur Iranistik 8; Wiesbaden: Reichert, 1976); ibid, "Saka Soldiers on Ships," *IA* 17 (1982) 101-3; **R. Descat,** "Mnésimachos, Hérodote et le système tributaire achéménide," *REA* 87 (1985) 97-112; ibid, "Notes sur la politique tributaire de Darius Ier," in *Le tribut dans l'empire perse: Actes de la table ronde de Paris, 12-13 décembre 1986,* ed. P. Briant and C. Herrenschmidt (Travaux de l'Institut d'études iraniennes de l'Université de la Sorbonne nouvelle 13; Louvain and Paris: Peeters, 1989) 77-93; **G. van Driel,** "The Murašû in Context," *JESHO* 32 (1989) 203-29; **E. R. M. Dusinberre,** *Aspects of Empire in Achaemenid Sardis* (Cambridge: Cambridge University Press, 2003); idem., *Satrapal Sardis: Aspects of Empire in an Achaemenid Capital* (Ph.D. diss; University of Michigan, 1997); **E. Ebeling,** "Die Rüstung eines babylonischen Panzerreiters nach einem Vertrag aus der Zeit Dareios

II," *ZA* 50 (1952) 203-14; **J. Elayi,** *Sidon, cité autonome de l'Empire perse* (Paris: Idéaphane, 1989); **I. Eph'al and J. Naveh,** *Aramaic Ostraca of the Fourth Century BC from Idumaea* (Jerusalem: Magnes, 1996); **H. Francfort,** "Central Asia and Eastern Iran," *CAH*² 4.169-93; **P. Frei and K. Koch,** *Reichsidee und Reichsorganisation im Perserreich* (OBO 55; Freiburg: Universitätsverlag; Göttingen: Vandenhoeck & Ruprecht, 1984; 2d ed., 1996); **J. C. Gardin,** *Prospections archéologiques en Bactriane Orientale (1974-1978), 3: Description des sites et notes de synthèse* (Mémoires de la Mission archéologique française en Asie centrale 9; Paris: Éditions Recherche sur des Civilisations, 1998); **M. Garrison and M. C. Root,** *Seals in the Persepolis Fortification Tablets, 1: Images of Heroic Encounter* (OIP 117; Chicago: University of Chicago Press, 2002); **B. Gharib,** "A Newly Found Inscription of Xerxes," *IA* 8 (1968) 54-69; **D. F. Graf,** "The Persian Royal Road System," in *Achaemenid History, 8: Continuity and Change,* ed. H. Sancisi-Weerdenburg, A. Kuhrt, and M. C. Root (Leiden: Netherlands Institute for the Near East, 1994) 167-89; **J. Greenfield,** "Aramaic in the Achaemenian Empire," in *Cambridge History of Iran, 2: The Median and Achaemenian Periods* (Cambridge: Cambridge University Press, 1985) 698-713; **C. H. Greenwalt,** "Sardis in the Age of Xenophon," in *Dans les pas des Dix-Mille: Peuples et pays du Proche-Orient vus par un Grec; Actes de la table ronde internationale, organisée à l'initiative du GRACO, Toulouse, 3-4 février 1995,* ed. P. Briant (Pallas 43; Toulouse: Presses Universitaires de Mirail, 1995) 125-45; **P. Grelot,** *Documents araméens d'Egypte* (LAPO 5; Paris: Cerf, 1972); **D. Gropp,** *Wadi Daliyeh II: The Samaria Papyri from Wadi Daliyeh* (DJD 28; Oxford: Clarendon Press, 2001); **E. Haerinck,** "Le palais achéménide de Babylone," *IA* 10 (1973) 108-32; **R. T. Hallock,** *The Persepolis Fortification Tablets* (OIP 92; Chicago: University of Chicago Press, 1969); idem., "Selected Fortification Texts," *CDAFI* 8 (1978) 109-36; **J. Hansman,** "Elamites, Achaemenians and Anshan," *Iran* 10 (1972) 101-25; **P. Harper, J. Aruz and F. Tallon,** eds., *The Royal City of Susa* (New York: Metropolitan Museum of Archaeology and Art, 1992); **W. Henkelman,** "An Elamite Memorial: The *Sumar* of Cambyses and Hystaspes," in *Achaemenid History 13: A Persian Perspective: Essays in Memory of Heleen Sancisi-Weerdenburg,* ed. W. Henkelman and A. Kuhrt (Leiden: Netherlands Institute for the Near East, 2003) 101-72; **L. G. Herr,** "Two Stamped Jar Impressions from the Persian Province of Ammon from Tell el-'Umeiri," *Annals of the Department of Antiquities, Jordan,* 36 (1992) 163-66; **S. Hornblower,** *Mausolus* (Oxford: Oxford University Press, 1982); **A. G. Keen,** *Dynastic Lycia: A Political History of the Lycians and Their Relations with Foreign Powers, c. 545-362 BC* (Mnemosyne, bibliotheca classica Batava, Supplementum 178; Leiden: E. J. Brill, 1998); **J. Kellens,** "L'âme entre le cadavre et le paradis," *JA* 283 (1995) 19-56; idem, "Questions préalables," in *La religion iranienne à l'époque achéménide: Actes du colloque de Liège, 11 décembre 1987,* ed. J. Kellens (IASup 5; Ghent: Iranica Antiqua, 1991) 81-86; idem, "Zoroastre dans l'histoire ou dans le mythe? À propos du dernier livre de Gh. Gnoli," *JA* 289 (2001) 171-84; **R. G. Kent,** *Old Persian: Grammar, Texts, Lexicon* (2d ed.; New Haven: American Oriental Society, 1953); **H. Koch,** "Die achämenidische Poststrasse von Persepolis nach Susa," *Archäologische Mitteilungen aus Iran* 19 (1986) 133-47; idem, *Die religiösen Verhältnisse der Dareioszeit* (Wiesbaden: Harrassowitz, 1977); **A. Kuhrt,** "Alexander and Babylon," in *Achaemenid History, 5: The Roots of the European Tradition,* ed. H. Sancisi-Weerdenburg and J. W. Drijvers (Leiden: Netherlands Institute for the Near East, 1990) 121-30; idem, *The Ancient Near East, c. 3000-330 BC* (2 vols.; Routledge History of the Ancient World; London: Routledge, 1995); idem, "Conclusions," in *Le tribut dans l'Empire Perse: Actes de la table ronde de Paris, 12-13 décembre 1986,* ed. P. Briant and C. Herrenschmidt (Travaux de l'Institut d'études iraniennes de l'Université de la Sorbonne nouvelle 13; Louvain and Paris: Peeters, 1989) 217-22; idem, "The Cyrus Cylinder and Achaemenid Imperial Policy," *JSOT* 25 (1983) 83-97; idem, "The Persian Kings and Their Subjects: A Unique Relationship?" *OLZ* 96 (2001) 165-73; idem, "Some Thoughts on P. Briant, *Histoire de l'Empire perse,*" *Topoi,* Supplement 1 (1997) 299-304; idem, "Usurpation, Conquest and Ceremonial: From Babylon to Persia," in *Rituals of Royalty: Power and Ceremonial in Traditional Societies,* ed. D. Cannadine and S. Price (Past and Present; Cambridge: Cambridge University Press, 1987) 20-55; **A. Kuhrt and S. M. Sherwin-White,** "Xerxes' Destruction of Babylonian Temples," in *Achaemenid History, 2: The Greek Sources,* ed. H. Sancisi-Weerdenburg and A. Kuhrt (Leiden: Netherlands Institute for the Near East, 1987) 69-78; **M. Leith,** *Wadi Daliyeh I: The Wadi Daliyeh*

Seal Impressions (DJD 24; Oxford: Clarendon Press, 1997); **A. Lemaire,** *Nouvelles inscriptions araméennes d'Idumée au Musée d'Israël* (Supplément 3 à Transeuphratène; Paris: Gabalda, 1996); **A. B. Lloyd,** "Herodotus on Cambyses: Some Thoughts on Recent Work," in *Achaemenid History, 3: Method and Theory,* ed. A. Kuhrt and H. Sancisi-Weerdenburg (Leiden: Netherlands Institute for the Near East, 1988) 55-66; **B. Lyonnet,** *Prospections archéologiques en Bactriane orientale (1974-1978) sous la direction de J.-C. Gardin, 2: Céramique et peuplement du chalcolithique à la conquête arabe* (Mémoires de la Mission archéologique française en Asie centrale 8; Paris: Boccard, 1997); **H. Metzger** et al., *Fouilles de Xanthos, 6: La stèle trilingue du Letôon* (Institut français d'études anatoliennes; Paris: Klincksieck, 1979); **W. E. Mierse,** "The Persian Period," in *Sardis from Prehistoric to Roman Times,* by G. M. A. Hanfmann et al. (Cambridge, MA: Harvard University Press, 1983) 100-108; **A. Millard,** "Assyrians and Aramaeans," *Iraq* 45 (1983) 101-8; **M. Miller,** *Athens and Persia in the Fifth Century BC: A Study in Cultural Receptivity* (Cambridge: Cambridge University Press, 1997); **P. de Miroschedji,** "La fin du royaume d'Anshan et de Suse et la naissance de l'empire perse," *ZA* 75 (1985) 265-306; **R. Morkot,** "Nubia and Achaemenid Persia: Sources and Problems," in *Achaemenid History, 4: Centre and Periphery,* ed. H. Sancisi-Weerdenburg and A. Kuhrt (Leiden: Netherlands Institute for the Near East, 1990) 321-36; **T. Petit,** *Satrapes et satrapies dans l'empire achéménide de Cyrus le Grand à Xerxès Ier* (Bibliothèque de la Faculté de philosophie et lettres de l'Université de Liège 254; Paris: Belles Lettres, 1990); **B. Porten and A. Yardeni,** *Textbook of Aramaic Documents from Egypt* (4 vols.; Texts and Studies for Students; Jerusalem: Hebrew University, Department of the History of the Jewish People; Winona Lake, IN: Eisenbrauns, 1986-1999); **G. Posener,** *La première domination perse en Égypte* (Bibliothèque d'étude 11; Cairo: Institut français d'archéologie orientale, 1936); **D. T. Potts,** *The Archaeology of Elam: Formation and Transformation of an Ancient Iranian State* (Cambridge World Archaeology; Cambridge: Cambridge University Press, 1999); **D. B. Redford,** "The So-called 'Codification' of Egyptian Law under Darius I," in *Persia and Torah: The Theory of Imperial Authorization of the Pentateuch,* ed. J. W. Watts (SBLSymS 17; Atlanta: Scholars Press, 2001) 135-59; **M. C. Root,** "From the Heart: Powerful Persianisms in the Art of the Western Empire," in *Achaemenid History, 6: Asia Minor and Egypt; Old Cultures in a New Empire,* ed. H. Sancisi-Weerdenburg and A. Kuhrt (Leiden: Netherlands Institute for the Near East, 1991) 1-29; idem, *The King and Kingship in Achaemenid Art: Essays on the Creation of an Iconography of Empire* (Acta Iranica 3/9; Leiden: E. J. Brill, 1979); **U. Rüterswörden,** "Die persische Reichsautorisation der Thora: Fact or Fiction?" *ZABR* 1 (1995) 47-61; **H. Sancisi-Weerdenburg,** ed., *Achaemenid History, 1: Sources, Structures, Synthesis* (Leiden: Netherlands Institute for the Near East, 1987); idem, "Exit Atossa: Images of Women in Greek Historiography on Persia," in *Images of Women in Antiquity,* ed. A. Cameron and A. Kuhrt (London: Croom Helm, 1983a) 20-33; idem, "Gifts in the Persian Empire," in *Le tribut dans l'Empire perse: Actes de la table ronde de Paris, 12-13 décembre 1986,* ed. P. Briant and C. Herrenschmidt (Travaux de l'Institut d'études iraniennes de l'Université de la Sorbonne nouvelle 13; Louvain and Paris: Peeters, 1989a) 77-93; idem, "The Persian Kings and History," in *The Limits of Historiography: Genre and Narrative in Ancient Historical Texts,* ed. C. S. Kraus (Mnemosyne, Bibliotheca Classica Batava, Supplementum 91; Leiden: Brill, 1999) 91-112; idem, "The Personality of Xerxes, King of Kings," in *Archaeologia Iranica et Orientalis: Miscellenea in honorem L. Vanden Berghe,* vol. 1, ed. L. de Meyer and E. Haerinck (Ghent: Peeters, 1989b) 549-61; repr. in *Brill's Companion to Herodotus,* ed. E. J. Bakker, I. J. F. de Jong and H. van Wees (Leiden: E. J. Brill, 2002) 579-90; idem, "Political Concepts in Old Persian Royal Inscriptions," in *Anfänge politischen Denkens in der Antike: Die nahöstlichen Kulturen und die Griechen,* ed. K. Raaflaub and E. Müller-Luckner (Schriften des Historischen Kollegs, Kolloquien 24; Munich: Oldenburg, 1993) 145-63; idem, *Yauna en Persai: Grieken en Perzen in een ander perspectief* (Groningen: Niemeyer, 1980); idem, "Zendan and Ka'bah," in *Kunst, Kultur und Geschichte der Achämenidenzeit,* ed. H. Koch and D. N. Mackenzie (Archäologische Mitteilungen aus Iran 10; Berlin: Reichert, 1983b) 88-92; **H. Sancisi-Weerdenburg and A. Kuhrt,** eds., *Achaemenid History, 2: The Greek Sources* (Leiden: Netherlands Institute for the Near East, 1987); idem, eds., *Achaemenid History, 4: Centre and Periphery* (Leiden: Netherlands Institute for the Near East, 1990); **E. Schmidt,** *Persepolis* (3 vols.; OIP 68-70;

Chicago: University of Chicago Press, 1953-1970); **R. Schmitt,** *The Bisitun Inscriptions of Darius the Great: Old Persian Text* (Corpus inscriptionum iranicarum, part I: Inscriptions of Ancient Iran, vol. 1, texts 1; London: School of Oriental and African Studies, 1991); idem, *The Old Persian Inscriptions of Naqsh-i Rustam and Persepolis* (Corpus inscriptionum iranicarum, part 1: Inscriptions of Ancient Iran, vol. 1, texts 2; London: School of Oriental and African Studies, 2000); **J. B. Segal,** *Aramaic Texts from North Saqqara* (London: Egypt Exploration Society, 1983); **S. Shaked,** *Le satrape de Bactriane et son gouverneur: Documents araméens du IVe s. avant notre ere provenant de Bactriane* (Persika 4; Paris: De Boccard, 2004); **N. Sims-Williams,** "The Final Paragraph of the Tomb-inscription of Darius I (DNb, 50-60): The Old Persian Text in the Light of an Aramaic Version," *BSOAS* 44 (1981) 1-7; **E. Stern,** *The Material Culture of the Land of the Bible in the Persian Period* (Warminster: Aris & Phillips, 1982 [1973]); **M. W. Stolper,** "Belshunu the Satrap," in *Language, Literature and History: Philological and Historical Studies Presented to Erica Reiner,* ed. F. Rochberg-Halton (New Haven: American Oriental Society, 1987) 389-402; idem, *Entrepreneurs and Empire: the Murašû Archives, the Murašû firm and Persian Rule in Babylonia* (Uitgaven van het Nederlands Historisch-Archaeologisch Instituut te Istanbul 54; Leiden and Istanbul: Nederlands Historisch-Archaeologisch Instituut te Istanbul, 1985); idem, "The Governor of Babylon and Across-the-River in 486 BC," *JNES* 48 (1989) 283-305; idem, "Militärkolonisten," *RlA* 8.205-7; **D. Stronach,** *Pasargadae: A Report on the Excavations Conducted by the British Institute of Persian Studies from 1961 to 1963* (Oxford: Oxford University Press, 1978); **W. M. Sumner,** "Achaemenid Settlement in the Persepolis Plain," *AJA* 90 (1986) 3-31; ibid, "Archaeological Measures of Cultural Continuity and the Arrival of the Persians in Fars," in *Achaemenid History,* 8: *Continuity and Change,* ed. H. Sancisi-Weerdenburg, A. Kuhrt and M. C. Root (Leiden: Netherlands Institute for the Near East, 1994) 97-105; *Transeuphratène* 1- (Paris: Gabalda 1989-); **A. Uchitel,** "Foreign Workers in the Fortification Archive," in *Mésopotamie et Elam: Actes de la XXXVIème Rencontre assyriologique internationale, Gand, 10-14 juillet 1989,* ed. L. de Meyer and H. Gasche (MHEOP 1; Ghent: Peeters, 1991) 127-35; **F. Vallat,** "Le palais d'Artaxerxès II à Babylone," *Northern Akkad Project Reports* 2 (1989) 3-6; **J. W. Watts,** ed., *Persia and Torah: The Theory of Imperial Authorization of the Pentateuch* (SBLSymS 17; Atlanta: Scholars Press, 2001); **J. D. Whitehead,** "Early Achaemenid Epistolography: The Arsames Correspondence" (Ph.D. diss.; University of Chicago, 1974)**; J. Wiesehöfer,** *Das antike Persien: Von 550 v. Chr. bis 650 n. Chr.* (Munich: Artemis & Winkler, 1993); ET: *Ancient Persia: From 550 BC to 650 AD* (London: Tauris, 1996 [1993]); idem, "'Reichsgesetz' oder 'Einzelfallgerechtigkeit'? Bemerkungen zu Peter Freis These von der achaimenidischen 'Reichsautorisation,'" *ZABR* 1 (1995) 36-46; **M. Wuttman,** "Les qanats d'Ayn-Manâwîr (oasis de Kharga, Égypte)," in *Irrigation et drainage dans l'Antiquité: Qanats et canalisations souterraines en Iran, en Égypte et en Grèce,* ed. P. Briant (Persika 2; Paris; Thotm, 2000) 110-36.

A. Kuhrt

PERSIAN-PERIOD ARCHAEOLOGY. *See* ARCHAEOLOGY, SYRO-PALESTINIAN.

PESHITTA. *See* TEXT AND TEXTUAL CRITICISM.

PHILISTINES

A people, perhaps of Aegean origin, inhabiting the southwestern coastal strip of Canaan/Israel/Palestine, the Philistines more often than not stood in an adversarial relationship with the Israelites in biblical times. Although the word *philistine* has entered the English language, under the influence of their negative portrayal in the biblical texts, as a term designating an uncultured and uncouth person, recent archaeological activity has indicated that the ancient Philistines were in many respects culturally more advanced than the Israelites when these two peoples first appeared on the historical stage at the beginning of the Iron Age (c. 1200-1150 BCE).

1. The Philistines in the Hebrew Bible
2. The Philistines in Extrabiblical Sources
3. The Archaeology of Philistia
4. Summary

1. The Philistines in the Hebrew Bible.
According to the Hebrew Bible, the Philistines were organized into a confederation of five city-states consisting of the coastal cities of *Ashdod, *Ashkelon and *Gaza, moving north to south, and of the inland cities of *Ekron and *Gath. It is the common scholarly convention

to refer to this coalition of five cities as the Philistine Pentapolis. With the exception of Abimelech, king of (the Philistines in) Gerar (Gen 20:2; 26:1, 8), and of Achish, king of Gath (1 Sam 21:11, 13; 1 Kings 2:39), the Philistine rulers are generally referred to as *sĕrānîm*, which many have related to the Greek word *tyrannos*, "tyrant." If this derivation is correct, then this term, along with a handful of additional words, is an important piece of evidence supporting the theory of the Philistines' origins in the Aegean world.

1.1. "Early" Biblical References to the Philistines. Modern scholarship holds that the Hebrew Bible was not necessarily written in the order in which the books have come down to us. Thus the fact that something is mentioned in one of the earlier books of the Bible does not necessarily indicate that the reference is contemporaneous with the period addressed in the text. Although there are isolated allusions to the Philistines in the books of the Pentateuch (see Gen 10:14; 21:32-34; 26: 1, 6; Ex 13:17), most scholars would regard these references as anachronisms that have crept into the narrative from a much later time period and perspective. It is only when the Historical Books of the Hebrew Bible relate the rise of Israel in its land that references to the Philistines become widespread, which is exactly what one would expect, given the congruence of Israelite historical memory and the findings of archaeology.

1.2. The Philistines in the Samson Cycle. Although Philistia is mentioned briefly as a region not under the control of the Israelites in Joshua 13:2-3 and Judges 3:3, it is only in the later Samson cycle that the Philistines come into their own in the biblical narrative. Previously they had been mentioned among Israel's enemies (Judg 10:6-7), but it is only here that they become the antagonists par excellence of the Israelites.

The book of Judges may be divided into four major units. Following some introductory materials (Judg 1:1-3:4), the stories of the judges (or leaders) who delivered various Israelite tribes from their sin-induced distress are recounted (Judg 3:5-12:15). This is followed by the Samson cycle (Judg 13—16) and a final section in which the crying need of the Israelite tribes for a king is emphasized (Judg 17—21).

Although Samson is reckoned among the judges, the story falls outside of the normal literary pattern of sin-punishment-repentance-deliverance that dominates the stories of the judges. Whereas the other judges act on behalf of the tribes of Israel, Samson seems to be acting on his own, and his problems are occasioned by his impetuous nature and his penchant for Philistine women. Although already dedicated to God before his conception (Judg 13:5), Samson invokes God only just before his death (Judg 16:28). Otherwise, his life is dedicated to the pursuit of pleasure.

In spite or because of his attraction to Philistine women, Samson comes into conflict with the Philistines, engaging them in contests of wits (Judg 14:10-19), burning their crops (Judg 15:4-5), walking off with the city gate of Gaza (Judg 16:3) and killing thousands of them (Judg 15:8, 15; 16:27-30). Some have argued that the character of Samson is related to that of Herakles/Hercules, but others have disputed this contention. Overall, the amusing folktales of the Samson cycle, while conveying a remembrance of a period of conflict between the tribe of Dan and the Philistines, probably cannot be gainfully employed in the reconstruction of a specific period in history. Nonetheless, certain snippets of information do reflect an accurate geographical memory: Timnah, the home of Samson's wife (Judg 14), lay in the Sorek Valley on the border between Israel and Philistia. And certainly Gaza was one of the major Philistine cities.

It is interesting that the only Philistine deity mentioned in this cycle of stories is the supposedly Semitic (but see Singer) deity Dagon (Judg 16:23), whose temple Samson collapses upon himself and the Philistines.

1.3. The Ark of the Covenant Among the Philistines. Another basically self-contained cycle of stories in which the Philistines play a leading, albeit cartoonish, role is the Ark Narrative of 1 Samuel 4:1—7:1 (but see Naʾaman 1992, 654-55). The underlying assumption of this cycle of stories, which interrupts the story of the prophet *Samuel, is that the Israelite tribes and the Philistines were engaged in a continuous conflict. While confronting the Philistines at Ebenezer (1 Sam 4), the Israelites decided to bring out their greatest weapon, the *ark of the covenant, and have God himself lead them to victory. Although the Philistines were frightened of directly confronting this great god in battle, the unexpected happened. The Israelites were defeated; and the ark was captured. Apparently, however, this was only part of God's plan to magnify the power of the ark.

The Philistines brought the ark to the temple of Dagon in Ashdod, where the power of God began to manifest itself against the Philistines and their chief deity. Every morning the priests of Dagon found the statue of their god toppled, and his head and hands removed from his body. In addition, the inhabitants of Ashdod were struck by a plague of tumors (or hemorrhoids). Thus it went wherever the Philistines sent the ark, whether to Gath or Ekron. Finally, they loaded it on a cart drawn by two cows and sent it on its way back to Israel along with golden offerings of mice and tumors/hemorrhoids according to the number of Philistine rulers and cities.

Although this story may be based on an actual capture of the ark by the Philistines, in its current context it serves a symbolic function to underline the power of God and his ark. The Philistines once again are a foil, in this case for the theological message being conveyed, and their god serves as an ineffectual object of ridicule. Once again, it is noteworthy that the only Philistine deity mentioned is a presumably Semitic god.

1.4. The Philistines and the Rise of the Israelite Monarchy. The Philistines finally shed their cartoonish quality in the narratives concerning the rise of kingship in ancient Israel. Indeed, many have felt that the biblical text implies that it was in order to counter a military threat from the Philistines that the people approached Samuel with the request to have him appoint a king to rule over them. However, it has also been argued that the conflict with the Philistines occurred during a later phase of the transition to monarchy (see Na'aman 1992, 652-58).

According to the biblical account, while the Israelites were settled in the central hill country of *Canaan, the Philistines were in the southwestern coastal plain. It was perhaps inevitable that when these two peoples tried to expand their areas of influence, they would come into conflict with one another. Although the Philistines seem to have had the upper hand initially—note how the Israelites had to go to Philistine artisans to have their agricultural tools sharpened (1 Sam 13:19-21)—the Israelite tribes eventually were able to unite around a central

authority figure. Much of the latter part of the reign of *Saul, the first king of Israel, was spent countering the Philistine threat. Although he enjoyed some initial success, Saul ultimately died in battle against the Philistines (1 Sam 31), and his armor was dedicated to the goddess Ashtoreth (Astarte), another Semitic deity, presumably in a temple in Beth-Shean in the Jordan Valley (1 Sam 31:10).

Following Saul's death, it was left to his successor, *David, to establish Israelite dominance over the Philistines. The Hebrew Bible devotes much space to detailing David's variegated relationship with the Philistines. Although what is arguably the most famous and archetypal story about David concerns his defeat of a gigantic Philistine champion named Goliath of Gath, many scholars would consign this account to the David legend. Among other arguments for this assumption is the fact that the Hebrew Bible itself later ascribes the defeat of Goliath to Elhanan, one of David's heroes (2 Sam 21:19) (*see* Goliath). Be that as it may, certain aspects of the Goliath story have been employed to support the theory of an Aegean origin of the Philistines. These include his name, the method of combat between champions to decide the outcome of battle and, most problematically, his armor (see Finkelstein 2002, 142-48).

Although the biblical text refers to skirmishes between the Israelites and the Philistines occasioned by David's assumption of rule over Israel (2 Sam 5:17; 21:15-22; 23:9-17; 1 Chron 11:12-19; 14:8-17; 20:4-8) and seems to relate their ultimate defeat in a linguistically problematic passage (2 Sam 8:1; 1 Chron 18:1), it is David's close relations particularly with the city of Gath that are most worthy of comment. During the time that he was in conflict with Saul, David sought refuge with and became a vassal of Achish, the king of Gath, although the Hebrew Bible claims that David worked against his suzerain's interests (1 Sam 27). Once he ascended the throne, David had among his entourage Obed-edom the Gittite, into whose hands he entrusted the ark of the covenant (2 Sam 6:10-12; 1 Chron 13:12-14; 15:24-25), and Ittai the Gittite, who was one of the few people who remained loyal to David at the time of Absalom's revolt (2 Sam 15:17-22; 18:2). Some have argued that David's private troop consisting of the Cherethites and the Pelethites also has a Philistine connection, although this is disputed by others.

Even though the claim seems to be made that Philistia was incorporated into the kingdom of *Solomon (1 Kings 4:21 [MT 5:1]), this poses problems at both the literary and the historical levels. Whatever one's position on the historicity of a united Israelite kingdom, the Philistines do not appear in the narrative in the same manner as other peoples allegedly incorporated into the Davidic kingdom. The account of the escape of Shimei's slaves from Jerusalem to Gath and their subsequent extradition back to Jerusalem may indicate that Gath and Israel stood in a formal treaty relationship with one another (1 Kings 2:39-41). However, nothing in this brief tale allows any conclusions to be drawn regarding the nature of the relationship. The fact that the Hebrew Bible still has Achish ruling Gath during the reign of Solomon has raised questions about the historical memory encapsulated in this episode.

1.5. The Philistines and Israel/Judah. Following the division of the united monarchy into the rival kingdoms of Israel and Judah, the Philistines play a minor role in the biblical narrative. No longer do they pose an existential threat to the Israelites, despite a number of accounts that hint at some tensions along their mutual borders (e.g., 1 Kings 15:27; 16:15-17). In the worldview of the books of Kings it was possible to cross the border between Israel/Judah and Philistia without any hindrance. In this manner the aforementioned slaves of Shimei escaped to Gath and were brought back, the Shunammite woman was able to spend seven years among the Philistines during a time of drought (2 Kings 8:2-3), and King Ahaziah of Israel was able to send messengers to Ekron to inquire of an oracle of the god Baal (2 Kings 1). This last account is of particular interest because it once again mentions a Semitic deity being worshiped by the Philistines, in this case a manifestation of the Canaanite storm god Baal. The reference to him in the Hebrew text as *baʿal zĕbûb*, "Lord of the Fly/Flies" (from which William Golding derived the name of his renowned novel), is to be understood as an intentional corruption of the epithet "Prince Baal," as it is known from the Ugaritic *zbl bʿl*.

Two incidental comments in 2 Kings indicate that the Aramean king Hazael of Damascus, who ruled over a short-lived empire in the latter part of the ninth century BCE, cam-

paigned against the Philistines and brought at least the northern part of their territory, including the city of Gath, under his control (2 Kings 12:18; 13:22 [according to the Lucianic recension of the LXX]). As indicated later in this article (see 3.2.4 below), this would accord well with the results of recent excavations at the site of Tell eṣ-Ṣafi (Philistine Gath) and with the disappearance of Gath from both biblical (see in particular prophetic oracles against the foreign nations such as Amos 1:6-8; Jer 47) and extrabiblical sources as of the eighth century BCE. Thus it is proper to speak of a Philistine Tetrapolis instead of a Pentapolis in this latter period.

The books of Chronicles appear to supply a number of additional pieces of information, missing in Kings, regarding the fate of the Philistines. Unfortunately, the late date of Chronicles (c. 400 BCE) and its ideological use of the Philistines make it most difficult to weigh the historicity of these accounts. More often than not, the Philistines enter the Chronicler's narrative in order to concretize the Chronicler's theological evaluation of the Judean king being discussed. In this manner, good kings such as Jehoshaphat and Uzziah/Azariah are able to encroach upon Philistine territory (2 Chron 17:10-11; 26:6-7), while bad kings such as Jehoram and Ahaz are in turn victimized by the Philistines (2 Chron 21:16-17; 28:18). This theologically occasioned usage of the Philistines in Chronicles once again poses problems for assessing the historical reliability of the information concerning the Philistines that is peculiar to the Chronicler (see Naʾaman 2003b).

2. The Philistines in Extrabiblical Sources.
Philistia, the Philistines and their various cities and rulers appear in a number of extrabiblical sources, both textual and artistic. For the period of their first appearance on the historical stage, in the twelfth century BCE, these are found mainly in *Egyptian sources, while as of the eighth century BCE, documents from Mesopotamia written in Akkadian are the major sources.

2.1. Egyptian Sources. At the time of the collapse of Late Bronze Age civilization, around 1200-1150 BCE (see Drews), there were a number of groups on the move in the eastern Mediterranean world to whom we, following a designation coined by the Egyptologist Gaston Maspero in

1873 (see Drews, 53-61), give the name *Sea Peoples* (about whom see Sandars). Among these was a group known as the *plst/prst,* or *Peleset,* a term equivalent to "Philistine." They first appear at the time of Pharaoh Ramesses III (c. 1184-1163 BCE), who claims to have defeated them in the fifth year of his reign (see Noort, 56). Most interest, however, centers on inscriptions and reliefs found on the walls of his mortuary temple at Medinet Habu near Thebes dating to his eighth year (*ANET,* 262-63). In the inscriptions Ramesses claims to have repulsed an invasion of Egypt by a large coalition of Sea Peoples, including the Philistines, who previously had overrun the Levant (Amurru). The war was fought both on land and at sea. According to Papyrus Harris I, Ramesses, after his victory, settled the Sea Peoples, whom he had "annihilated," in fortresses (*ANET,* 260-62).

According to a "maximalist" position, the Medinet Habu inscription and Papyrus Harris I can be understood as implying that the eastern Mediterranean was overrun by a wave of Sea Peoples who destroyed the vestiges of Late Bronze Age civilization, only to be halted at the gates of Egypt. Subsequent to the Sea Peoples' defeat, the Egyptians settled at least the Philistines on the southwestern coastal strip of Canaan as mercenaries. A "minimalist" interpretation of the evidence views the conflict in less global and more local terms as a revolt of preexisting Egyptian mercenaries that was given a cosmic interpretation in pharaonic propaganda, as is indicated by the ideological structuring of the scenes around the confines of the Medinet Habu temple (see Cifola). As the proponents of such a position point out, there is nothing in Papyrus Harris I that would imply a settlement of the Philistines anywhere outside of Egypt proper (see Finkelstein 1995, 226-27).

Another dimension is added by the reliefs relating to the inscriptions at Medinet Habu. Here are depicted formulaic representations of Ramesses' defeat of the enemies of Egypt both on land and at sea. The orderly triumph of the Egyptians is contrasted with the chaotic defeat of their enemies. Whatever the historical sequence of events, the reliefs provide us with vivid depictions of the individual Sea Peoples, their ships, armaments, clothes and, in the scenes of the land battle, families (see Sweeney and Yasur-Landau). Characteristic of their ships was a symmetrical shape with a bird-shaped bow and stern

(see Wachsmann, 163-97). For transportation on land they used oxcarts, in which warriors are depicted together with their families. The Philistines can be distinguished from other Sea People warriors by their distinctive "feathered" headdresses.

Subsequent to the time of Ramesses III, the Philistines are mentioned briefly in the Onomasticon of Amenope, dating to about 1100 BCE (T. Dothan, 3-4). In addition, there is the brief funerary inscription of Pedeeset, who may have been an Egyptian official in Philistia or a Philistine serving in Egypt, possibly during the Twenty-second or Twenty-sixth Dynasty (Ehrlich, 65).

2.2. Akkadian Sources. Since Egyptian sources mention the Philistines mainly in the twelfth century BCE, and the Hebrew Bible is concerned with them mainly in narratives revolving around the tenth century BCE, our major textual sources for late Philistine history are found in *Assyrian and *Babylonian inscriptions written in the Akkadian language as of the eighth century BCE.

2.2.1. Before the Assyrian Conquest. As the Neo-Assyrian Empire inexorably expanded westward, it was inevitable that Philistia not only would come into contact with *Assyria but also would fall under its direct political influence. The earliest firm record of Philistia in the Assyrian records comes in the Nimrud Slab Inscription of Adad-nirari III (810-783 BCE), who reached the Mediterranean Sea in 796 BCE and listed the Philistines among the Levantine peoples from whom he received tribute (*ANET,* 281-82). However, it would be another half century before Assyria returned to the area and actually encroached upon Philistine territory under the vigorously expansionist Tiglath-pileser III (744-727 BCE).

2.2.2. Tiglath-pileser III and the Conquest of Philistia. Early in his reign Tiglath-pileser managed to reassert a lost Assyrian hegemony in the northern Levant. Documents from Nimrud, ancient Calah, indicate that a prime motivation of his expansionist policies was the desire to profit from international trade by controlling its distribution hubs. Hence, Nimrud Letter 12, dating to the period before Tiglath-pileser campaigned in the southern Levant, already indicates a desire to control Phoenician trade with Egypt and Philistia.

In a lightning campaign in 734 BCE Tiglath-pileser moved down the Levantine coast and conquered Gaza (*COS* 2.117:284-92). Hanunu, king of Gaza, abandoned his city and fled to Egypt, abandoning Gaza to be plundered by the Assyrians, who established an Assyrian commercial center (*bīt kāri*) nearby, possibly at Tell Ruqeish. In this manner, Tiglath-pileser achieved the twofold aim of establishing an Assyrian beachhead on the border of Egypt, possibly in anticipation of a planned invasion of Egypt, and controlling one of the major commercial centers of the ancient Near East. As a coastal city, Gaza lay both on the sea and on overland routes leading to and from the major markets of Egypt and was the terminus for the lucrative spice trade from the *Arabian Peninsula.

Dating roughly to this time, the Syro-Ephraimite War was fought between the Aramean kingdom of Damascus and Israel on one side and Judah on the other (see Irvine). Although the aim of the war was the formation of a larger anti-Assyrian coalition, scholars are divided about whether the war was fought in anticipation of the Assyrian campaign against Philistia or as a reaction to it. Whichever it was, the Philistines apparently were caught off guard by the Assyrian advance. Hanunu was not treated as an enemy combatant and was allowed to reassume his throne as an Assyrian vassal, which allowed the Assyrians to exploit Gaza's resources with a minimum of administrative upheaval.

It was only the following year that there is evidence of Philistine participation in an anti-Assyrian coalition, when Mitinti of Ashkelon joined the anti-Assyrian resistance movement. Over the next two years Tiglath-pileser moved decisively against the coalition, destroying Damascus and severely truncating Israel. Ashkelon avoided their dire fate through the replacement of Mitinti by a certain Rukibtu, who proved to be a loyal Assyrian vassal (see Ehrlich, 88-104).

2.2.3. Philistia Under the Sargonids. The Neo-Assyrian Empire reached its zenith under Sargon II (720-705 BCE) and his successors, even managing briefly to conquer and control its ancient rival Egypt. Following the death of Shalmaneser V and the conquest of Israel, for which Sargon took credit even though many assume that this took place at the end of his predecessor's reign, a number of revolts broke out among the empire's vassal states, which is a common occurrence during the oftentimes chaotic period following the death of a powerful ruler. In this case, at the beginning of Sargon's

reign Gaza, still ruled by Hanunu, allied itself with its contiguous neighbor Egypt and rose in revolt against the new ruler. The combined force was defeated. Sargon recaptured Gaza and deported Hanunu, whose fate is not related, but on the basis of analogy one can assume that it was not particularly pleasant (*COS* 2.118:293-300).

In 713 BCE Sargon saw fit to depose Azuri, the anti-Assyrian king of Ashdod, and replace him with his younger and more compliant brother Ahimiti. The latter was in turn deposed by the anti-Assyrian party of Ashdod and replaced by a certain Iamani, who attempted to forge a larger anti-Assyrian coalition. In 711 BCE Sargon captured Ashdod, its port Ashdod-Yam (Asdudimmu) and Gath, which by this time had been reduced to a dependency of Ashdod. Ashdod itself was now incorporated into the Assyrian Empire as a province. The city was plundered, and its people were deported and replaced by deportees from other parts of the empire.

Following the death of Sargon in 705 BCE, questions about his succession provided the impetus for a large-scale rebellion against the hated Assyrian overlord. This time the ringleader was *Hezekiah of Judah, supported by Egypt and Philistine Ekron. The people of the latter had deposed their pro-Assyrian king, Padi, and handed him over to Hezekiah. Following the inevitable crushing of the revolt by the new Assyrian ruler, Sennacherib (705-681 BCE), in 701 BCE, most of Hezekiah's territory was apportioned among the Philistine rulers who remained loyal to Assyria: Mitinti of Ashdod, Şilbel of Gaza, and the restored Padi of Ekron. King Şidqia of Ashkelon, who had participated in the rebellion, was also deposed and deported along with his family. Significantly, Sennacherib placed Sharru-lu-dari, son of the pro-Assyrian Rukibtu, on the throne of Ashkelon (*COS* 2.119B-D:302-5).

Following Sennacherib's campaign of 701 BCE, the southern Levant entered a period of relative peace and economic prosperity (see 3.2.3 below) that scholars refer to as the *pax assyriaca*. Indeed, we find the rulers of the Philistine cities of Ashdod (Ahimilki), Ashkelon (Mitinti), Gaza (Şilbel) and Ekron (Ikausu = Achish) as participants in the campaign of Ashurbanipal (669-627 BCE) against Egypt in 667 BCE (*ANET*, 294). This list is significant because it is the only evidence in extrabiblical texts of the Philistine city-states acting in unison, even if that union was forced.

2.2.4. Philistia and the Neo-Babylonian Empire. The Assyrian Empire collapsed relatively quickly following the death of Ashurbanipal. Once again the Philistines were caught between two powers: a seemingly resurgent Egypt to the south and the Neo-Babylonian Empire to the north, the latter of which inherited the mantle of authority from Assyria. Most scholars date the end of Philistine history to their defeat and incorporation into the Babylonian Empire by Nebuchadnezzar II (605-562 BCE) in 604 BCE. An Aramaic letter written on papyrus and found at the Egyptian site of Saqqara records the ineffectual and plaintive plea of King Adon, presumably of Ekron, for help from Egypt against the Babylonian onslaught but Egypt also was unable to assert itself at this time against Babylon (*COS* 3.54:132-34). An administrative document from Babylon mentions the kings of Gaza and Ashdod, now under Babylonian rule, but not their names (*ANET*, 307-8; see Na'aman 2003a, 85 n. 8).

3. The Archaeology of Philistia.
Geographical information in the biblical texts and the continued use of some of the Philistine city names throughout history have enabled us to identify the approximate region of Philistine habitation, although subsequent archaeological findings have refined our knowledge. While the area encompassing the five cities of the Pentapolis formed the Philistine heartland, the outer boundaries of Philistia itself can be fixed at the Wadi el-Arish (the so-called Brook of Egypt) in the south, at the Yarkon River in modern-day Tel-Aviv in the north, at the Mediterranean Sea in the west, and on the western border of the low-lying hills of the Judean Shephelah in the east. Nonetheless, remains of Philistine pottery have been found outside these parameters as far away as the Jordan Valley and coastal sites surrounding the Carmel Range, indicating trade connections throughout ancient Canaan.

3.1. Philistine Pottery. The most common find at archaeological sites in the Holy Land as of the late Neolithic period is pottery, both whole and broken. Since pottery styles and forms change over time, as do the techniques of making it, pottery serves as the primary tool in dating archaeological sites and their layers (strata) relative to one another. Another, and more controversial, use of pottery is as an ethnic identity

marker. Early in the scientific exploration of ancient Canaan a distinctive style of bichrome (two-colored) pottery was identified on geographical and chronological grounds with the Philistines. Further refinements in our understanding allow us to identify three major phases in the pottery associated with Philistine habitation.

3.1.1. Philistine Monochrome Ware. The first phase of Philistine settlement on the southwestern coastal strip of Canaan in the early Iron Age (c. 1200/1150-1000 BCE) is characterized by a style of pottery with a relatively simple brownish- or reddish-black striped decorative scheme. Since the decoration employs only one color at a time, it is referred to as monochrome (one-colored) ware. Its forms and decoration seem to emulate Mycenaean models of the Late Bronze Age (c. 1550-1200 BCE). Hence, it is also known as Mycenaean (= Myc) IIIC:1 ware. Most scholars view the presence of Myc IIIC:1 at a site as evidence of the initial phase of Philistine settlement, which generally is dated to the second quarter of the twelfth century BCE (Dothan and Zukerman; but see Finkelstein 1995 for a dating to the latter part of the twelfth century BCE, which means that in his view there is no connection between the initial settlement of the Philistines in Canaan and the inscriptions of Ramesses III).

3.1.2. Philistine Bichrome Ware. Within about a generation, the monochrome ware had been replaced by a type of light-colored ware characterized by a decorative scheme employing both red and black coloration. Thus this style of pottery is referred to as bichrome ware and is taken to represent the heyday of Philistine material culture. It remained in use from the middle or late twelfth century until the tenth century BCE. Among the decorative motifs are horizontal bands and, higher up on the vessels, bands of metopes including geometric shapes and representations of animals, in particular of birds and fish. T. Dothan, the doyenne of Philistine archaeologists, has identified eighteen distinct shapes in the bichrome repertoire, including shapes derived from Mycenaean, Cypriote, Egyptian and Canaanite prototypes (T. Dothan, 94-218). Although most scholars tend to emphasize the affinities with the Aegean world and use the pottery to indicate the Philistines' ethnic origins there, the facts that the typology includes influences from other areas and that Canaanite pottery traditions continue alongside Philistine styles at most sites associated with the Philistines suggest that the Philistine population included a variegated ethnic mixture.

3.1.3. Late Philistine Ware. The study of Philistine pottery traditions in Iron Age II is still in its infancy. Nonetheless, there are indications that the region of Philistia maintained a distinctive pottery tradition throughout the Iron Age. For Iron Age IIA (tenth and ninth centuries BCE), this ware is characterized by a dark red slip and includes the striped "Ashdod" ware and noticeable Phoenician influence. For Iron IIB-C (eighth and seventh centuries BCE), various regional forms seem to predominate (Ben-Shlomo, Shai and Maeir; Maeir, forthcoming).

3.2. Excavations and Finds in Philistia. Although short and rudimentary excavations were pursued in Philistia already at the very end of the nineteenth century, it is only as of the 1960s that large-scale scientific excavations of Philistine sites were conducted. The following brief discussion highlights some of the knowledge concerning the Philistines that has been gleaned from excavations conducted at the sites of four of the cities of the Philistine Pentapolis (Ashdod, Ashkelon, Ekron, Gath) and from a couple of smaller sites (Tell Qasile, Tel Batash). Because the modern city covers the remains of the ancient city, only sporadic probes have been conducted in Gaza.

3.2.1. Ashdod. Ashdod was the first city of the Pentapolis to be excavated in the modern period. An international team under the direction of M. Dothan (Haifa University) excavated here during the 1960s and 1970s. Results of the excavation indicate that the first phase of Philistine settlement was founded on a thick destruction level from the end of the Late Bronze Age. Although settlement was sparse at first, the city continually expanded during Iron Age I, reaching its fullest extent during Iron Age II, when Ashdod expanded from its acropolis to the lower city (M. Dothan).

In addition to the Myc IIIC:1 ware, which was first identified here, significant finds from Ashdod include an Iron IIA six-chambered monumental gateway of the type often referred to as Solomonic. Its discovery here suggests that a facile ascription of such gateways to Solomon's alleged building activities overstates the case. Also found were various cultic implements, among which are the so-called Musicians Stand,

which is a cultic stand whose fenestrated base includes clay figurines of musicians, and the "Ashdoda" type of seated female figurine. Although the Ashdoda may derive ultimately from Aegean prototypes, there are some significant differences in execution and decoration. Nonetheless, it has often been taken as evidence of the continuation of an Aegean great-goddess cult at Ashdod, a conclusion disputed by some (see Noort, 134-37).

3.2.2. Ashkelon. The excavation of Ashkelon has been ongoing since 1985 under the direction of L. Stager (Harvard University). Here also the presumed arrival of the Philistines is indicated by the introduction of Myc IIIC:1 pottery, which was followed in short order by the classic bichrome ware. An analysis of the faunal remains at Ashkelon indicates that the arrival of the Philistines was accompanied by a change in diet, from one in which sheep and goats provided the main source of meat to one in which pork products were especially prized. Contrary to popular opinion, according to which the Philistines' preferred beverage was beer, the excavators of Ashkelon have documented the importance of wine to their diet and economy. A distinctive style of pinched loom weights indicates a connection with the Aegean world. Meanwhile, the city rapidly expanded to about 150 ha in size and became a major outlet for international trade (Stager).

3.2.3. Ekron. The identification of the seemingly low-lying mound of Tel Miqne (Khirbet al-Muqanna) in the silted-up Sorek Valley with Philistine Ekron became generally accepted soon after the initiation of the joint American-Israeli excavations at the site began in 1981 under the direction of S. Gitin (Albright Institute) and T. Dothan (Hebrew University). However, it was only in the course of the last season of the excavation in 1996 that this identification became indubitable with the find of an inscription mentioning the name of the site in ancient times.

Ekron was a significant Philistine city as of their first appearance in Canaan in the early twelfth century BCE. The city's prime lasted until the early tenth century BCE, when it shrank in size. It is tempting to associate this diminution with pressure from David's Israelite kingdom (or chiefdom), since Ekron lies near the border with Israel/Judah. After some two centuries of decline, Ekron reached its zenith in the seventh century BCE during the *pax assyriaca*, when it became the largest producer of olive oil in the ancient Near East. The presence of a widespread olive oil processing industry at Ekron can have been possible only if one assumes that olive producers from a large area, including Judah, delivered their produce to Ekron. The finding of many horned altars in association with the olive oil industry may perhaps be taken as evidence of an Israelite presence at the site. During the months when there was no olive oil to be processed, the production of textiles employed the oil productions workers (Gitin 1989).

As at Ashkelon, the faunal remains at Ekron indicate a diet distinct from Canaanite patterns (Hesse). Among the most significant finds from the site is a hearth sanctuary dating to Iron Age I, which evidences clear architectural connections with the Aegean world. Among the other Iron Age I cultic objects discovered at Ekron are an iron knife with an ivory handle, a lion-headed drinking cup, the bronze wheels of a type of cult stand known from Cyprus, and incised bovine scapula, which also are derived from Cypriot models. Dating to Iron Age IIB are two dedicatory inscriptions. The first is a short notation dedicating a vessel "to/for Asherat," a well-known Canaanite goddess (see Gitin 1998, 175 and fig. 16). The second is a monumental dedicatory inscription from the wall of a temple erected by Achish son of Padi (both of whom are known from the Assyrian inscriptions) in the early seventh century BCE "for *Ptgyh,* his mistress" (*COS* 2.42:164). The interpretation of the name of the goddess in question is somewhat unclear, although an Aegean origin has been proposed (see Schäfer-Lichtenberger). Nonetheless, it is significant that once again the archaeological evidence, in distinction from the biblical evidence, indicates the prevalence of goddess worship among the Philistines.

3.2.4. Gath. The last of the cities of the Philistine Pentapolis to have been identified with some measure of confidence is the site of Gath at Tell eṣ-Ṣafi, a large mound located some 11 km south of Ekron at the confluence of the Elah Valley and the Coastal Plain. Beginning with a survey season in 1996, a team of excavators under the direction of A. Maeir (Bar Ilan University) has been excavating this site. Contrary to previous assumptions, the Iron Age city at Tell eṣ-Ṣafi was not a town of about 15 ha in size, but rather extended for some 40-50 ha, making it a most formidable city in antiquity. Preliminary re-

sults of the excavations indicate that although there are some traces of the Myc IIIC:1 pottery characteristic of the first phase of Philistine settlement, Gath became truly significant in Iron Age IB, the period characterized by bichrome ware. This seems to be the only period during which both Ekron and Gath were ascendant; otherwise their fates are mirror images of one another. During Iron Age IIA (tenth to eighth centuries BCE), while Ekron was relatively insignificant, Gath enjoyed unprecedented prosperity. Following a massive destruction at the end of the ninth or beginning of the eighth century BCE, Gath lost its status as a major urban center at the very time when Ekron was about to embark on its great urban expansion.

Two of the most significant finds at Gath relate to the mystery of its disappearance from the historical record. First is a major destruction level dating to the period around 800 BCE. Second is a unique siege trench, over 2 km long, surrounding the city on three sides and presumably associated with the destruction level. Preliminary analysis of the material remains combined with the two biblical notices about Hazael's campaign against Gath and Philistia (2 Kings 12:17; 13:22 [according to the Lucianic recension of the LXX]) have led the excavators to posit that it was Hazael who brought an end to Gath's preeminent position in the ancient world (Maeir and Ehrlich; Maeir 2003).

3.2.5. Tell Qasile. Tell Qasile, located in northern Tel-Aviv on the banks of the Yarkon River, is the only major Philistine city to have been founded by the Sea Peoples, presumably as an inland port (Mazar). It was most recently excavated by A. Mazar (Hebrew University). Unfortunately, scholars have no inkling of the city's name in antiquity. Lying on the northern frontier of Philistia, Tell Qasile was a significant Philistine site in the Iron Age I period, but subsequently it seems to have passed into Israelite hands. As a new city founded by the Philistines, it provides many insights into their architectural and urban traditions, which include the widespread usage of the four-room house that had been singled out as an Israelite ethnic marker (*see* Architecture).

Of major significance is a sacred precinct found at the site that went through three phases. The irregular and changing architectural scheme has been related both to Aegean and to Canaanite models. In a public building near the temple a hearth similar to the one at Ekron was discovered, pointing to an Aegean element in the population at Tell Qasile. Among the most significant cultic finds was a gynomorphic vessel, whose breasts served as spouts, once again pointing toward the possible worship of a great goddess in the Aegean mold at the site.

3.2.6. Timnah. Biblical Timnah has been identified at the site of Tel Batash in the Sorek Valley (Kelm and Mazar). As a site located on the border between Israel and Philistia, it changed hands at various times in history and evidences a mixed material culture. In the Late Bronze Age it was Canaanite, in Iron Age I it was Philistine, and as of Iron Age II it was mainly Israelite. In spite of the presence of some distinctively Philistine features, such as bichrome ware and a pyramidal seal depicting a lyre player, the excavators have drawn attention to numerous continuities with Late Bronze Age Canaanite traditions and thus conclude that even during Iron Age I the Philistines simply formed the ruling class, while most of the population remained Canaanite in nature. In many respects, the material culture of Timnah is reflected by that of Beth-Shemesh, slightly to the east in the Sorek Valley. These sites indicate the difficulty of attempting to ascribe ethnic/national identity on the basis of a restrictive view of what constitutes significant ethnic markers.

4. Summary.
The Philistines first appeared in Canaan at the beginning of Iron Age I during the early to mid-twelfth century BCE. Their primary phase of settlement is characterized by monochrome ware, out of which arose the classic Philistine bichrome ware within a generation. After a period of expansion, they appear to have been restricted to the southwestern coastal strip of Canaan, where their subsequent history seems to have been influenced mainly by factors and powers beyond their control. Although the Hebrew Bible more often than not depicts them as a unified entity, there is no extrabiblical evidence to support this portrayal—that is, the Pentapolis appears to be a biblical invention. Indeed, even referring to them as "Philistines" may be oversimplifying a quite complex mixture of both indigenous and immigrant populations. Although it is clear that there was a strong Aegean influence in their material culture and eating habits, for the most part they were acculturated (on the process of accultura-

tion see Stone) to their environment (although their avoidance of circumcision did stand out in the eyes of the biblical authors). As evidence of the former contention, one can cite the presumed retention of their worship of a great goddess and their continued preference for pork products; as evidence of the latter, one can cite the mainly Semitic names of the deities that they worshiped and of their rulers.

See also ASHDOD; ASHKELON; EKRON; GAZA; GATH.

BIBLIOGRAPHY. **D. Ben-Shlomo, I. Shai and A. M. Maeir,** "Late Philistine Decorated Ware ('Ashdod Ware'): Typology, Chronology, and Production Centers," *BASOR* 335 (2004) 1-35; **N. Bierling,** *Giving Goliath His Due: New Archaeological Light on the Philistines* (rev. ed.; Marco Polo Monographs 7; Warren Center, PA: Shangri-La, 2002); **J. F. Brug,** *A Literary and Archaeological Study of the Philistines* (BARIS 265; Oxford: B.A.R., 1985); **B. Cifola,** "Ramses III and the Sea Peoples: A Structural Analysis of the Medinet Habu Inscriptions," *Or* 57 (1988) 275-306; **M. Dothan,** "Ashdod," *NEAEHL* 1.93-102; **T. Dothan,** *The Philistines and Their Material Culture* (New Haven: Yale University Press, 1982); **T. Dothan and M. Dothan,** *People of the Sea: The Search for the Philistines* (New York: Macmillan, 1992); **T. Dothan and A. Zukerman,** "A Preliminary Study of the Mycenean IIIC:1 Pottery Assemblages from Tel Miqne-Ekron and Ashdod," *BASOR* 333 (2004) 1-54; **R. Drews,** *The End of the Bronze Age: Changes in Warfare and the Catastrophe ca. 1200 B.C.* (Princeton, NJ: Princeton University Press, 1993); **C. S. Ehrlich,** *The Philistines in Transition: A History from ca. 1000-730 BCE* (SHCANE 10; Leiden: E. J. Brill, 1996); **I. Finkelstein,** "The Philistines in the Bible: A Late-Monarchic Perspective," *JSOT* 27 (2002) 131-67; idem, "The Settlement of the Philistines in Canaan," *TA* 22 (1995) 213-39; **S. Gitin,** "Philistia in Transition: The Tenth Century BCE and Beyond," in *Mediterranean Peoples in Transition: Thirteenth to Early Tenth Centuries BCE,* ed. S. Gitin, A. Mazar and E. Stern (Jerusalem: Israel Exploration Society, 1998) 162-83; idem, "Tel Miqne-Ekron: A Type-Site for the Inner Coastal Plain in the Iron Age II Period," in *Recent Excavations in Israel: Studies in Iron Age Archaeology,* ed. S. Gitin and W. G. Dever (AASOR 49; Winona Lake, IN: Eisenbrauns, 1989) 23-58; **S. Gitin, A. Mazar and E. Stern,** eds., *Mediterranean Peoples in Transition: Thirteenth to Early Tenth Centu-*

ries BCE (Jerusalem: Israel Exploration Society, 1998); **B. Hesse,** "Animal Use at Tel Miqne-Ekron in the Bronze Age and Iron Age," *BASOR* 264 (1986) 17-27; **S. A. Irvine,** *Isaiah, Ahaz, and the Syro-Ephraimite Crisis* (SBLDS 123; Atlanta: Scholars Press, 1990); **G. L. Kelm and A. Mazar,** eds., *Timnah: A Biblical City in the Sorek Valley* (Winona Lake, IN: Eisenbrauns, 1995); **A. M. Maeir,** "Notes and News: Tell eṣ-Ṣafi/Gath, 1996-2002," *IEJ* 53 (2003) 237-46; idem, "Philisterkeramik," *RlA* (forthcoming); **A. M. Maeir and C. S. Ehrlich,** "Excavating Philistine Gath: Have We Found Goliath's Hometown?" *BAR* 27.6 (2001) 22-31; **D. M. Master,** "Trade and Politics: Ashkelon's Balancing Act in the Seventh Century B.C.E.," *BASOR* 330 (2003) 47-64; **A. Mazar,** *Excavations at Tell Qasile, Part I: The Philistine Sanctuary; Architecture and Cult Objects* (Qedem 12; Jerusalem: Israel Exploration Society, 1980); **N. Na'aman,** "Ekron under the Assyrian and Egyptian Empires," *BASOR* 332 (2003a) 81-91; idem, "In Search of the Reality behind the Account of the Philistine Assault on Ahaz in the Book of Chronicles," *Transeuphratène* 26 (2003b) 47-63; idem, "The Pre-Deuteronomistic Story of King Saul and Its Historical Significance," *CBQ* 54 (1992) 638-58; **E. Noort,** *Die Seevölker in Palästina* (PA 8; Kampen: Kok Pharos, 1994); **E. D. Oren,** ed., *The Sea Peoples and Their World: A Reassessment* (University Museum Monographs 108; University Museum Symposium Series 11; Philadelphia: University of Pennsylvania Museum of Archaeology and Anthropology, 2000); **N. K. Sandars,** *The Sea Peoples: Warriors of the Ancient Mediterranean* (rev. ed.; London: Thames & Hudson, 1985); **C. Schäfer-Lichtenberger,** "The Goddess of Ekron and the Religious-Cultural Background of the Philistines," *IEJ* 50 (2000) 82-91; **I. Singer,** "Towards the Image of Dagon, God of the Philistines," *Syria* 69 (1992) 431-50; **L. E. Stager,** *Ashkelon Discovered: From Canaanites and Philistines to Romans and Moslems* (Washington, DC: Biblical Archaeology Society, 1991); **B. J. Stone,** "The Philistines and Acculturation: Culture Change and Ethnic Continuity in the Iron Age," *BASOR* 298 (1995) 7-35; **D. Sweeney and A. Yasur-Landau,** "Following the Path of the Sea Persons: The Women in the Medinet Habu Reliefs," *TA* 26 (1999) 116-45; **S. Wachsmann,** *Seagoing Ships and Seamanship in the Bronze Age Levant* (College Station: Texas A&M University Press; London: Chatham, 1998).

C. S. Ehrlich

PHOENICIA, PHOENICIANS

The terms *Phoenicia* and *Phoenicians* designate the coastal region north of ancient Israel and the people who inhabited it from the thirteenth century BCE to the first century BCE. The geographic boundaries of Phoenicia are relatively clear. They extended from Mount *Carmel to the Amanus Mountains (Josh 11:8, 19:28; 2 Sam 24:6-7), with the Lebanon and Anti-Lebanon ranges marking its eastern flank (Lipiński 2003). Less clear, however, are the cultural and ethnic identities of the peoples who dwelled in Phoenicia's most prominent city-states (e.g., Arvad, Byblos, Sidon and Tyre). In the Bible each one appears with varying degrees of frequency that correspond to the level of economic, political and theological importance that each held for ancient Israel and the Bible's Judean authors. Thus Arvad and Byblos (Heb *gĕbāl,* "Gebal") receive only parenthetical treatments (Gen 10:18; Josh 13:5; 1 Kings 5:13-18; Ezek 27:8-9), whereas Sidon and Tyre appear prominently. Indeed, the characterizations of Sidon and Tyre, though hardly identical, reflect the Phoenicians' enormous economic, political and religious influence on Israel.

    1. Phoenician Identity
    2. The Historical Context of Israelite-
       Phoenician Relations
    3. Judean Portraits of Phoenician City-states
    4. Judean Polemic and Phoenician Cults

1. Phoenician Identity.

The cultural and ethnic contours of Phoenician identity are something of an enigma (Röllig). Most scholars see the Phoenicians as descendants of the *Canaanite populations who lived in the region before them, but the migrations and international trading activities that punctuate the region's history make this uncertain. Moreover, biblical texts apply the term *Canaanite* to the region later known as Phoenicia (Is 23:11; Obad 20), but also to a number of diverse cultural groups in antiquity (Gen 10:15-20; Judg 1:31-32).

It is ironic that so little is known about the Phoenicians. Already in antiquity they possessed enormous fame for their role in transmitting the alphabetic script to Greek-speaking peoples and for their ubiquitous maritime, mercantile and colonial activities throughout the Mediterranean world. But most of what is known about them comes from non-Phoenician sources (e.g., Assyrian, Babylonian, Egyptian, Greek and Israelite), many of which are tendentious, even polemical, in their characterization of them (Peckham). Thus we can use them only with caution.

Many Phoenician inscriptions have survived, as well as a few letters, but they have yielded only limited information on Phoenician identity (*see* Non-Israelite Written Sources: Syro-Palestinian). An incommensurately larger number of texts must have been composed on papyri or leather, but they have not survived. The extant inscriptions are written in a Semitic language closely related to ancient Hebrew, suggesting some degree of cultural affinity. In fact, there are a great number of parallels between Phoenician inscriptions and Israelite literary texts (Parker; Avishur). Nevertheless, Phoenician inscriptions also demonstrate diversity. Texts from Byblos, for example, are composed in a different dialect and employ a distinct script. Moreover, the Phoenicians' dealings with the Greek world and Anatolia make it likely that those involved in international trade were multilingual.

Etymological research is of limited help in determining Phoenician identity. The origin of the term "Phoenicia" is either Egyptian (*fnḥw*) or Greek (*phoinikē*). The etymology of the Egyptian word is unknown, and that of the Greek word is uncertain (Muhly). The Greek term initially designated a reddish color, perhaps the color of the Phoenicians' hair or skin or the textile dyes for which the traders in this region were internationally renowned. Regardless of the term's etymology, by the first millennium BCE Greek-speaking peoples were applying it generally to the inhabitants of the region.

The archaeological record sheds some light on issues of Phoenician identity, but considered as a totality, it is woefully incomplete. Although excavations have confirmed the region's activity in the large-scale production of reddish-purple dyes, none of the major Phoenician coastal sites has ever been excavated thoroughly below the Roman layer, because many of the most promising excavation sites are presently occupied or lie under protected monuments from later periods. Byblos has yielded information mainly for the Bronze Age (Markoe, 324). Thus the archaeological record produces a composite and fragmentary portrait of Phoenician civilization, one that is particularly weak for the period of the Iron Age (c. 1200-555 BCE). Even with this incomplete portrait, however, it is clear that the term *Phoenician* implies more of a uniform cultural and ethnic identity than was the reality.

Indeed, the people of the region never referred to themselves as Phoenician, but instead identified with the city-states in which they lived (e.g., Tyrians from Tyre, Sidonians from Sidon), much like the Canaanites who lived in the region before them. Assyrian, Babylonian and Israelite texts typically refer to these peoples similarly (e.g., Judg 3:3; 10:11-12; 1 Kings 5:1-14; 11:1, 5; 2 Kings 23:13; 1 Chron 22:4; Ezra 3:7). Even the gods of Phoenicia are distinguished by locale (e.g., Baal of Tyre, Baal of Sidon), and the divine pantheon differs considerably among its city-states. The consistent references to localized personal and divine identities similarly bespeak cultural diversity and complicate the question of whether Phoenicians are direct descendants of the Canaanites.

Phoenician settlements off the mainland pose similar problems for ascertaining Phoenician identity (Moscati). Already by the eighth century BCE the Phoenicians had established trading and industrial colonies in a number of places throughout the Mediterranean world, including Carthage, Cyprus, Sardinia, Sicily, Spain and Utica (the term *Punic* is used to describe these Phoenician cultures, especially after the sixth century BCE). Archaeological excavations carried out at these settlements reveal them to be of a very different character from one another and from those in Syria. A good deal of cultural exchange took place at these locations between Phoenician settlers and the indigenous populations, but since textual and archaeological records are limited, we can only hypothesize to what degree and on what levels such exchange took place. In some cases Phoenician settlers maintained their homeland traditions, especially in matters of religion, hence the discovery of dedicatory inscriptions devoted to the goddess Astarte of Sidon in Spain and Cyprus. Elsewhere, such as at Sidonian settlements in Zinjirli and Karatepe or at the Tyrian city of Carthage, Phoenicians appear to have partially acculturated.

The combined textual and archaeological data thus demonstrate that the term *Phoenician* loosely designates a number of different city-state cultures that lived in relative proximity, and that shared a similar language, as well as an industrious determination for locating new mercantile horizons.

2. The Historical Context of Israelite-Phoenician Relations.

The Phoenicians' mercantile horizons brought their city-states a great deal of wealth, but their wealth naturally made them targets for control by greater Near Eastern powers. Consequently, the history of Phoenicia's city-states is comprised of oscillating periods of autonomy and vassalage, though rarely of economic decline.

Scholars place the start of Phoenician history after the Sea Peoples invasions, when the loss of domination by *Egypt created a power vacuum. Although Ramesses III (c. 1187-1156 BCE) defeated the Sea Peoples, his campaigns ushered in a period of gradual decline for Egypt. No longer capable of maintaining a secure grasp in the Levant, Egypt could not stop its vassals from becoming independent and from reaping the economic benefits that they were once forced to share. Whether Phoenician city-states were willing accomplices in the Sea Peoples' attacks is debated (Bikai), but it is clear that their stability during this turbulent period gave them a greater economic advantage in the ensuing years.

The power vacuum lasted until the reign of the *Assyrian king Tiglath Pileser I (c. 1115-1077 BCE), who marched to Arvad, Sidon and Tyre and demanded tribute. Nevertheless, Assyrian domination was short-lived, and its decline allowed the early Phoenician city-states to flourish and expand their international reach for nearly four hundred years. The decline of Assyrian power also marks the start of Israel's monarchic history, and thus it is during the reigns of *David and *Solomon that the Bible's historical texts first report on Phoenician and Israelite relations.

3. Judean Portraits of Phoenician City-States.

It is only with caution that one can use the Hebrew Bible as a source of information on Phoenician culture and history. This is because the biblical texts were composed primarily from a Judean theological perspective and often are polemical in purpose, and because they were written and edited over a period of several hundred years (Zevit, 439-48). Consequently, they reflect changing political and economic relationships with cities of Phoenician power. Thus, whereas the Phoenician city of Sidon is consistently vilified, Tyre is transformed from a friend and ally of Israel during the period of the united monarchy to an arrogant city of greedy oppor-

tunists after the kingdom is divided.

The different orientations of the two major Phoenician city-states and the contractual relationships that formed because of them account in part for the differences in the way they are characterized in biblical accounts of early Israel and the united monarchy. The twelfth to the tenth centuries BCE mark a transitional period in both Israel and Phoenicia. During this time Israel was transformed from a theocratic and semi-nomadic confederation of twelve tribes to a sedentary monarchic nation with a capital at Jerusalem. The Phoenicians, by contrast, were well underway with their international expansion efforts. Sidon, with some participation from Byblos, began to move north into Anatolia, Cilicia, Aramea and Assyria, and west to Crete, Cyprus, Sardinia, Sicily and Spain. Tyre, on the other hand, expanded its presence primarily in a southern direction into Palestine and North Africa, though Tyrian enclaves are known at Carthage and Cyprus and further north at Carchemish.

3.1. Judean Portraits of Sidon. Sidon is consistently given a negative portrait in the Bible's historical texts. During the time of Joshua and the Judges it appears in a list of Israel's oppressors (Josh 13:2-6; Judg 1:31, 10:11), and as a powerful regional threat (Josh 19:28; Judg 18:28). The worship of Sidonian gods is cited as a partial cause for losses incurred at the hands of *Philistines and *Ammonites. During Solomon's reign Sidonian women are blamed for the introduction of the gods Baal and Astarte into Judah, and thus for turning the king away from worshiping Yahweh (1 Kings 11:1-5). These texts similarly connect the downfall of King Ahab to the princess Jezebel (1 Kings 16:31-33; 2 Kings 23:13), whom the text identifies as a Sidonian, even though her father was also the king of Tyre (Josephus Ant. 8.13.1). Although the Chronicler states that David received timber from both Sidonians and Tyrians when gathering the raw materials for Yahweh's temple (1 Chron 22:3-4), this text was composed during the Persian period and may reflect an anachronistic understanding of Israel's relationship with Phoenician city-states, for both Sidonians and Tyrians were employed in building the second temple (Ezra 3:7).

3.2. Judean Portraits of Tyre. Tyre, on the other hand, is portrayed positively in biblical texts that describe events during the united monarchy. There may be political and economic reasons behind this. During the united monarchy Israel controlled the primary trade routes from Phoenicia to the Red Sea (Kuhrt, 2.408). It thus served Tyre well to maintain good relations with its southern neighbor. Similarly, Tyre's proximity and international reach made it an ideal business partner. Since Jerusalem and Tyre benefited mutually from the relationship, the biblical texts that record the relationship with Tyre do so positively.

Thus Hiram, king of Tyre, is called a friend of David (1 Kings 5:1), and he is credited with assisting the building of David's palace by supplying him with cedar, carpenters and stonemasons (2 Sam 5:11-12; 1 Chron 14:1-2). Solomon similarly enlisted Tyrian artisans when he built the temple of Yahweh, and he supplied Hiram with wheat and oil in exchange for cypress and cedar logs from Lebanon (1 Kings 5:7-11; 2 Chron 2:9). Tyrians supplied the bronze and artisans for constructing the temple's two pillars and sacred vessels (1 Kings 7:13-47; 2 Chron 4:11-17). Solomon relied on Byblos, however, for other timber resources and for its expert masons (1 Kings 5:13-18; Ezek 27:9). The gold, precious stones and *almug*-wood used in the construction of the temple and its liturgical instruments were obtained by way of a joint Tyrian-Israelite expedition to Ophir (1 Kings 9:26-28; 10:11-12; 2 Chron 8:17-18). Joint expeditions to Tarshish also were launched (1 Kings 10:22; 2 Chron 9:21). The historicity of these expeditions, however, remains in question (Lipiński, *CANE* 2.1321-33).

Indeed, the characterization of Tyre during the reigns of David and Solomon is altogether flattering. Biblical texts portray Solomon not simply as an ally of Hiram, but as a quasi-Tyrian king equipped with Phoenician wisdom, wealth and fame (1 Kings 5:1-6; 15:26). The portrayal is underscored by way of literary parallels that draw Solomon and Hiram into close comparison (Peckham, 350-51).

3.3. The Changing Portrait of Tyre in Light of Phoenician History. The positive portrayal of Tyre, however, is gradually replaced with a negative one in biblical texts that detail events after the united monarchy. The change in characterization reflects a deteriorating relationship between Israel and Tyre in the years following the united monarchy.

The early alliance between Tyre and Jerusa-

lem and the latter's emergence as a regional power under David and Solomon did not go unnoticed by Egypt. Five years after Solomon's death, Pharaoh Sheshonq I (c. 945-924 BCE) invaded the Levant (McCarter, 56-57). When he arrived at Jerusalem, King *Rehoboam paid him from the treasures in the royal palace and the temple of Yahweh (1 Kings 14:25-26; 2 Chron 12). The discovery at Byblos of statues of Sheshonq I, Osorqon I (c. 999-959 BCE) and Osorqon II (c. 874-835 BCE), the former two also containing Phoenician inscriptions of the Byblian kings Abibaal and Elibaal (Kitchen, 292-93, 308-9), demonstrates that Egypt and Byblos had resumed trading relations during this period (Pernigotti, 604). In an effort to expand its own influence, Egypt apparently was attempting to strain Judean relations with Phoenicia and Israel. Sheshonq I also had harbored the anti-Solomonic fugitive *Jeroboam (1 Kings 11:40—12:1-3). Whether Byblos or other Phoenician city-states played a role in Sheshonq I's invasion is unknown, but it is possible that the renewed relations between Phoenicia and Egypt contributed to Jerusalem's souring relationship with Tyre.

In the ninth century BCE *Assyria began to show an aggressive interest in Phoenicia's wealth. Heavy tribute was imposed under Assurnasirpal II (c. 883-859 BCE) and Shalmanezer III (c. 858-823 BCE). Tilglath Pileser III (c. 744-727 BCE) later enlarged Assyria's holdings by annexing northern Phoenicia, including Sidon and Arvad, and by installing a network of governors there. Although Tyre remained independent, its autonomy was always in check. Sargon II (c. 721-705 BCE) soon completed the annexation of Phoenicia by suppressing a number of rebellions, fomented at times by Egypt, and ultimately by taking Tyre's holdings on Cyprus.

During the reign of Sennacherib (c. 704-681 BCE) the Phoenician city-states, Sidon chief among them, began to test Assyrian power and withhold their tribute. These acts bore swift and violent repercussions. Once again Phoenicia was brought under Assyrian domination. The period of domination, from the reigns of Tiglath Pileser III to Sennacherib, effectively ended Sidonian supremacy in Phoenicia, but since Tyre retained its independence, it benefited from Sidon's loss and became the leading city in Phoenicia.

Although Tyre was not an Assyrian puppet,

some Judeans must have perceived that the Tyrians were acting as go-betweens in the trade between Assyria and the west, and also with Egypt, and that their continued expansion was the direct result of Assyrian imperial growth (Frankenstein). Thus it is in this context that we see Judean prophets linking Tyre to Sidon and castigating it for its opulence and connection to Assyria (Is 23:1-14, Amos 1:9-10, Hos 9:13 [see also Ps 83:6-9]).

Sidon again asserted its independence during the reign of Esarhaddon (c. 680-669 BCE), but violent punishment was quick in the coming. Sidon was destroyed, its king beheaded and its inhabitants deported. A few years later Egypt successfully incited Tyre to rebel. Esarhaddon assumed direct control over it and restricted its trade in the Mediterranean. He then punished Egypt with an invasion and took Memphis in 671 BCE. Judah too was swept up in the wave of Assyrian control. During the reign of *Manasseh (c. 687-642 BCE) Judah even appears to have supported it (2 Kings 21:16), and archaeological evidence suggests that Judah's economy profited indirectly from Assyrian control of Phoenicia (Elat, 246-47).

In 698 BCE Esarhaddon moved to reconsolidate his power in Egypt, but he died en route. His son Assurbanipal (c. 669-627 BCE) completed the task by taking Thebes in 664 BCE. His intensive focus on Egypt naturally weakened Assyria's grip on Phoenicia. Consequently, Tyre and several other city-states rebelled. Assurbanipal retaliated quickly and put an end to Phoenician autonomy. In Egypt he installed Psametik I (c. 664-610 BCE), intending him to be a tool of Assyrian power, but campaigns in Elam and Babylon prevented him from responding when Psametik I drove out his forces in 653 BCE. Psametik I then established an Egyptian military presence in Phoenicia and Palestine.

For reasons that are unclear, relations between Egypt and Assyria appear to have become friendly during the reign of Psametik I's successor, Necho II (c. 610-595 BCE), who maintained a strong military presence and active trading network in Phoenicia. The close relationship also permitted a joint Egyptian-Phoenician expedition to circumnavigate Africa (Herodotus *Hist.* 4.42). However, Necho II's hold in Phoenicia was ephemeral because he spent much of his efforts unsuccessfully assisting the Assyrians against a growing Babylonian threat (2 Kings 23:29-34; Jer 46:2; 2 Chron 35:20-24; 36:3-4).

By the end of the seventh century BCE the *Babylonians had tipped the balance of power, and under King Nebuchadnezzar II (c. 604-562 BCE) they moved to establish control over Phoenicia (2 Kings 24:7). Tyre and Sidon allied with Philistia and Egypt against him, but their alliance in the face of almost certain annihilation was little more than wishful thinking, as the Judean prophets asserted (Jer 25:22; 27:3, Ezek 32:30). Thus it is on the eve of Babylonian control that attitudes toward Phoenicia, particularly among the prophets, become acutely negative (Jer 47:4-5). Although Nebuchadnezzar II had pressured Tyre and Sidon into assisting the second stage of his attack and eventual destruction of Jerusalem in 586 BCE (2 Kings 24:10—25:21; 2 Chron 36:5-19), the prophets perceived them as willing accomplices eager to remove a competitor and create greater opportunities for profit (Ezek 26—28). Nebuchadnezzar's thirteen-year siege of Tyre (Josephus *Ant.* 10.228; *Ag. Ap.* 1.21), though an ample demonstration of Tyre's own loathing of Babylonian control, was perceived as a divine punishment for its greed (Ezek 26:1-14; 29:18).

When Babylon fell to the *Persians in 539 BCE, Phoenicia again faced a new suzerain. Unlike the Babylonian kings, however, the Persian rulers realized that they stood to benefit if they allowed Phoenician city-states greater autonomy. Persia even bestowed on Tyre the territory between Mount *Carmel and Zarephath, and on Sidon the cities of Jaffa and Dor. Nevertheless, Persia kept close tabs on Phoenicia. Thus Sidon became one of its satrapies and the site of a key military fleet against the Greeks and Egyptians. As a consequence of Persian rule, Phoenician trade and industry again flourished while the Persian Empire grew.

It is in this context that Sidonian and Tyrian merchants were granted the right to conduct business affairs with the Judeans who had returned from exile. In exchange for their timber, they received foodstuffs and oils (Ezra 3:7). The spread of Phoenician interests in the region is evident by the presence of a Tyrian trading enclave in Judea (Neh 13:16). Despite the apparently good commercial relations, Tyre and Sidon still were remembered in Judean prophetic circles as decadent and were even accused of trading Judean slaves abroad (Joel 3:3-8; Zech 9:3-4). Whether the latter claim is based in reality or on a widespread mythmaking cliché among Phoenicia's detractors remains a question (Mazza, 641-43).

4. Judean Polemic and Phoenician Cults.

The changing context of Judean relations with Phoenicia and also with Israel informs biblical polemics against Phoenician forms of religion. In texts that portray events from the time of the united monarchy to the period in which Assyrian hegemony weakened Jerusalemite and Tyrian relations (i.e., from Tiglath-pileser III to Sennacherib), Sidon stands alone among the Phoenician city-states as a target of Yahwist polemic. Indeed, although Solomon's construction of Yahweh's temple adopted Tyrian design (*see* Solomon's Temple), this fact does not appear to have posed any problems for Israelite polemicists. Although many historical factors could be cited as a cause for Israel's schism, biblical texts place the blame squarely on Solomon's tolerance for Sidonian forms of worship (1 Kings 11:1-5; 16:31-33). Anti-Sidonian sentiment and Judean differences with Israel also lie behind the antagonistic accounts of *Elijah and the prophets of Baal (1 Kings 18—19:1-2), King Ahab's Sidonian wife Jezebel (2 Kings 9:30-37), and the brutal eradication of Baal worship by King Jehu (2 Kings 10:18-27).

It is possible that Judeans viewed the religious practices of northern Israel as particularly Sidonian. Archaeological excavations have confirmed the spread of Phoenician cults in northern Israel and beyond after the tenth century BCE (Stern). Nevertheless, it is virtually impossible to delineate artifacts that represent Sidonian as opposed to Tyrian influence, and it is likely that economic and political motives also inform the Judean polemics.

Direct authoritative sources on Phoenician religions are rare, and only a small proportion of Iron Age Phoenician sanctuaries have ever been excavated (Stern). This often makes it impossible to assess the veracity of the biblical characterizations. Some aspects of Phoenician religion do appear to be represented accurately (Zevit, 540). Baal and Astarte (biblical Asherah) were in fact prominent members of the Phoenician pantheon. However, Baal (Phoenician "lord") was a generic title applied to a number of local mountain deities whose identities were not identical, and Astarte was not always Baal's consort. At Sidon Astarte was paired with Eshmun,

at Tyre she was Melqart's wife, but at Carthage Baal-hamon was coupled with Tanit. Such local variations again fit the distinctive cultural portraits of the Phoenician city-states (Ribichini).

Archaeological work also has revealed that at least some Phoenician cults practiced child sacrifice in accordance with what is noted in the Bible (2 Kings 16:3; Jer 7:31; 19:5-6), but most of the evidence comes from non-Levantine sites, especially Carthage (Markoe), which has led some to doubt that the practice ever took place in Israel. Similarly debated is the existence of a god named Molech, to whom some of the Phoenicians are said to have sacrificed these children (Jer 32:35). On the other hand, child sacrifice appears to have been practiced periodically in early Israel (Judg 11:34-40), and there seems to be no reason to doubt the biblical accounts even if they provide a polemical charge (Zevit, 549-53).

Despite the Bible's polemical treatments of Phoenician forms of religion and the ideological differences that they represent, archaeologists have shown that the outward forms of Phoenician cults (e.g., temples, sacrifices, sacred utensils, divine titles, etc. [e.g., 1 Kings 18:1—19:2]) were very similar to those of ancient Judah, Israel, Philistia, Ammon, *Edom and *Moab (Schmitz). For some, these similarities suggest a common Phoenician, and ultimately Canaanite, ancestry (Stern). Our inability to define "Phoenician" identity with precision, however, only complicates the question of influence.

See also CANAANITE GODS AND RELIGION; SOLOMON.

BIBLIOGRAPHY. **Y. Avishur,** *Phoenician Inscriptions and the Bible: Select Inscriptions and Studies in Stylistic and Literary Devices Common to the Phoenician Inscriptions and the Bible* (Tel Aviv-Jaffa: Archaeological Center Publications, 2000); **P. M. Bikai,** "The Phoenicians," in *The Crisis Years: The Twelfth Century B.C. from Beyond the Danube to the Tigris,* ed. W. A. Ward and M. S. Joukowsky (Dubuque, IA: Kendall/Hunt, 1992) 132-41; **M. Elat,** "The Impact of Tribute and Booty on Countries and People within the Assyrian Empire," in *Vorträge gehalten auf der 28. Rencontre assyriologique internationale in Wien, 6-10. Juli 1981,* ed. H. Hirsch and H. Hunger (AfOB 19; Horn: Berger, 1982) 244-51; **S. Frankenstein,** "The Phoenicians in the Far West: A Function of Neo-Assyrian Imperialism," in *Power and Propaganda: A Symposium on Ancient Empires,* ed. M. T. Larsen

(Mesopotamia 7; Copenhagen: Akademisk Forlag, 1979) 263-95; **K. A. Kitchen,** *The Third Intermediate Period in Egypt (1100-650 BC)* (2d ed.; Warminster: Aris & Phillips, 1986); **A. Kuhrt,** *The Ancient Near East, c. 3000-330 BC* (2 vols.; London and New York: Routledge, 1995); **E. Lipiński,** *Itineraria Phoenicia* (OLA 127; Leuven: Peeters, 2003); idem, "The Phoenicians," *CANE* 2.1321-33; **G. Markoe,** "Phoenicians," *OEANE* 4.324-31; **F. Mazza,** "The Phoenicians as Seen by the Ancient World," in *The Phoenicians,* ed. S. Moscati (New York: Rizzoli, 1999 [1988]) 628-53; **P. K. McCarter Jr.,** *Ancient Inscriptions: Voices from the Biblical World* (Washington, DC: Biblical Archaeology Society, 1996); **S. Moscati,** "Substrata and Adstrata," in *The Phoenicians,* ed. S. Moscati (New York: Rizzoli, 1999 [1988]) 580-90; **J. D. Muhly,** "Homer and the Phoenicians," *Berytus* 19 (1970) 19-64; **S. B. Parker,** "The Composition and Sources of Some Northwest Semitic Royal Inscriptions," *SEL* 16 (1999) 49-62; **B. Peckham,** "Phoenicia, History of," *ABD* 5.349-57; **S. Pernigotti,** "Phoenicians and Egyptians," in *The Phoenicians,* ed. S. Moscati (New York: Rizzoli, 1999 [1988]) 591-610; **S. Ribichini,** "Beliefs and Religious Life," in *The Phoenicians,* ed. S. Moscati (New York: Rizzoli, 1999 [1988]) 120-52; **W. Röllig,** "On the Origins of the Phoenicians," *Berytus* 31 (1983) 79-83; **P. C. Schmitz,** "Phoenician Religion," *ABD* 5.357-63; **E. Stern,** "The Phoenician Source of Palestinian Cults at the End of the Iron Age," in *Symbiosis, Symbolism, and the Power of the Past: Canaan, Ancient Israel, and Their Neighbors from the Late Bronze Age through Roman Palaestina; Proceedings of the Centennial Symposium, W. F. Albright Institute of Archaeological Research and American Schools of Oriental Research, Jerusalem, May 29-31, 2000,* ed. W. G. Dever and S. Gitin (Winona Lake, IN: Eisenbrauns, 2003) 309-22; **Z. Zevit,** *The Religions of Ancient Israel: A Synthesis of Parallactic Approaches* (New York: Continuum, 2001).   S. B. Noegel

PILLARED HOUSE. *See* ARCHITECTURE.

PLOTS, NARRATIVE. *See* NARRATIVE ART OF ISRAEL'S HISTORIANS.

POETRY

Songs, hymns and poems are scattered irregularly within the Bible's prose stories. Their appearance has prompted attempts to reconstruct older poetic epics behind the prose accounts, as well as debates over the distinction between Hebrew poetry and prose. Recent research, however, increasingly has focused on comparing their literary and theological roles within their narrative contexts. These studies have emphasized that inset hymns in particular played an early and distinctive role in shaping the Historical Books to function as Scripture.

1. Poetry and Prose
2. Inset Songs
3. Psalms and Scripture

1. Poetry and Prose.

1.1. Hebrew Prose Narrative. A distinctive feature of ancient Hebrew literature is that stories always appear in prose. Unlike Babylonian, Hittite, Ugaritic, Egyptian and Greek cultures, no poetic epic survives from ancient Israel. Instead, prose narrative dominates the Bible's history books. Prose was also used to write stories in Egyptian and Greek cultures, but only in Israel does it seem to have excluded the epic form, at least from the surviving literature.

1.2. Inset Poetry. Prose's monopoly on storytelling did not, however, completely exclude poetry from the Historical Books. The stories occasionally depict characters voicing poetic couplets and singing songs, usually by quoting only excerpts, but sometimes quoting what appear to be the entire pieces. Oracles, vows, boasts, riddles, blessings and curses usually take the form of a few poetic lines—for example, Joshua 6:26; Judges 14:14; 18; 15:16; 1 Samuel 15:22-23, 33; 2 Samuel 20:1; 1 Kings 12:16/2 Chronicles 10:16; 1 Chronicles 12:18. A rare longer oracle appears at 2 Kings 19:21-28. Song excerpts of a few lines or less appear at Joshua 10:12-13; 1 Samuel 18:7; 21:11; 29:5; 2 Samuel 3:33-34; 1 Chronicles 16:41; 2 Chronicles 5:13; 7:3, 6; Ezra 3:11. But the Historical Books also incorporate one complete dirge in 2 Samuel 1:17-27 and five complete hymns: Judges 5:1-31; 1 Samuel 2:1-20; 2 Samuel 22:1-51; 23:1-7; 1 Chronicles 16:8-36.

1.3. Defining Prose and Poetry. Such a list of inset poetry in prose cannot be definitive, however, because of disagreements over how to distinguish the two modes. The distinction between prose and poetry in modern English is far from clear-cut, and ancient Hebrew was no different. Hebrew prose can exhibit poetic tendencies, especially when it employs word plays and parallelism, while poetry can incorporate prose elements as well. Some texts seem to be transitional, using "heightened prose" or "prosaic poetry"—for example, Jotham's parable (Judg 9:7-15), Solomon's boast (1 Kings 8:12-13), the end of Solomon's prayer (2 Chron 6:41-42). The appearance of clearly poetic excerpts in some contexts have led to attempts to read entire stories or books as poetry, such as the Samson stories in Judges 13—16 (Kim). They have also inspired theories of an older epic tradition behind many of the Bible's prose stories (Cross, Damrosch and many others). Evidence for either contention remains ambiguous and elusive. In reaction to this pursuit of poetry within or behind prose, J. L. Kugel has argued that the prose/poetry distinction does not correspond to categories of ancient Hebrew literature at all, which rather mentions genres such as "song," "prayer," "proverb" and so on. Even if one does not follow Kugel in foregoing the category of poetry entirely, analysis of inset poems nevertheless stands on firmer ground if it focuses on texts that are explicitly labeled as a different genre than their contexts.

2. Inset Songs.

2.1. Poetic Fragments.
Excerpts of a few poetic lines usually produce effects on other characters that shape the plots of the stories. So the couplet of a victory song, "Saul has killed his thousands, David his ten thousands" (1 Sam 18:7), stimulates *Saul's jealousy of *David. The narrative of David's rise to power quotes the same lines twice more (1 Sam 21:11; 29:5), and the repetition becomes increasingly ironic as David falls from power in Israel. David provides another example of a song fragment when he sings a dirge to the memory of Abner, four lines of which are quoted in 2 Samuel 3:33-34. This is one of several measures he takes to demonstrate his innocence of Abner's murder. In these and other cases the writers of the Historical Books quote just enough of the poetry for the reactions of other characters to make sense.

A hymn refrain, "(for he is good), his kindness is forever," appears in 1 Chronicles 16:41; 2 Chronicles 5:13; 7:3, 6; Ezra 3:11. Although many translations render it as quotations of characters' speech, the Hebrew text contains no quotation formulas. Instead, it seems that the author(s) of Chronicles and Ezra break with the convention in the rest of biblical literature of restraining the narrator to prose exposition and

here allow the narrator's voice to join the congregation in hymnic praise. This tendency later develops to the extent of having the narrator in 1 Maccabees not only repeat this phrase (1 Macc 4:24), but also voice complete hymns and praise songs in a manner reminiscent of ancient epic style.

2.2. Complete Songs.
David also mourns news of Saul's death with a dirge in 2 Samuel 1:17-27, this time apparently quoted completely. But this song concludes the story of Saul; it has no consequences for the action or speeches that follow, which switch to other issues. David's dirges for Abner and Saul illustrate a wider pattern in Hebrew narratives of using poetic excerpts to advance the plot, but using complete songs for other purposes, including structuring large blocks of narratives, emphasizing religious themes and characterizing the singers (see Watts; Mathys; Weitzman).

2.2.1. Songs and Narrative Structure.
The battle account in Judges 4 concludes with Deborah and Barak singing a victory song (Judg 5:1-31). The placement of this song after the story of the battle is over seems to reflect a literary convention in Israel (cf. Ex 15; Jdt 16) that derived from wider ancient culture. Egyptian battle accounts in particular developed the use of praise hymns to model the appropriate response for readers. The closest parallel to biblical usage is found in the eighth-century Piye stela (COS 2.7:42-51), which after a prose narrative account of the pharaoh's victories concludes with crowds singing praise with a victory hymn (Watts; Weitzman). A distinctive aspect of Israel's appropriation of the victory hymn tradition is the tendency for the singers to be *women (Deborah, Miriam, Judith; also the singers of the couplet about Saul and David). This may account for why Hannah, though giving thanks for the birth of her son (1 Sam 2:1-20), is nevertheless given a victory hymn to sing.

The position of Hannah's psalm does not reflect victory hymn tradition, however. Its expectation of a future king links with the celebration of kingship in David's thanksgiving and last words (2 Sam 22:1-51; 23:1-7) to bracket the books of Samuel with the theme of God's support for King David. The end of Samuel consists of an "appendix" (2 Sam 21—24) centered on two poems that imitate the end of Deuteronomy. Like Moses (Deut 32—33), David ends his career with a retrospective hymn (2 Sam 22:1-51) followed by poetic advice to his successors (2 Sam 23:1-7). Hymns thus mark off the beginning and end of Samuel as distinct from Judges and Kings, and compare its status and that of its main character, David, to Deuteronomy and Moses.

2.2.2. Songs and Religion. The themes of inset hymns typically differ considerably from those of their narrative contexts. David's lament for Saul (2 Sam 1) is a rare secular dirge (see also the fragment in 2 Sam 3) that focuses on the warrior-king's victories for Israel, ignoring entirely the religious critique of Saul in the stories. Hymns, on the other hand, focus on God and so bring to the surrounding stories an emphasis on God's role in events. Theophanies (the forceful appearance of God in nature) play central and distinctive parts in several inset hymns (Judg 5:4-5; 2 Sam 22:8-16; cf. Hab 3:3-15) and so highlight God's power (Mathys). In some contexts (such as Exodus) the theocentric emphasis simply heightens an already strong theme: whereas the stories emphasize God acting through Moses to deliver Israel from Egypt, the Song of the Sea (Ex 15) celebrates God as Israel's one and only warrior, while Moses and the people only sing praise. In other contexts (such as Samuel) the theocentric hymns are in notable contrast to their contexts: whereas the stories of Samuel paint a morally ambiguous portrait of David, the praises of Hannah and David emphasize God's support for the faithful king.

Although the songs have been interpreted as expressing intentionally simplistic and biased views that are relativized by the more nuanced narratives (Noll), the inset hymns seem more likely to have been intended to interpret their contexts religiously. They supply a theological "moral" to the stories that turns artistic literature into religious instruction. In the Historical Books (as elsewhere in the Hebrew Bible) such hymnic instruction emphasizes that God saves Israel (Judg 5:4-5, 20-21; 1 Sam 2:8-10) and that God empowers Israel's institutions (the Davidic monarchy in 1 Sam 2:10; 2 Sam 22:2-4, 21-25, 32-51; 23:2-7; the temple singers in 1 Chron 16) (see Kleinig). The psalms thus serve to introduce or heighten the depiction of God as the central protagonist, no matter whether the surrounding story mentions the deity or not.

2.2.3. Songs and Singers. Quotations in narrative always provide insight into the character of the speakers, so inset songs characterize their singers. That is most obviously the case where the songs contain self-references, as when David describes his own faithfulness to God (2 Sam 22:21-25) or Deborah's song depicts her heroism (Judg 5:7, 12). But the songs also depict their singers as the kind of people who sing such songs, and so serve to shape readers' opinions of their characters. Hannah gives thanks for her answered prayer with a woman's victory song (1 Sam 2:1-10). The song expresses her traditional piety and models it for readers who find themselves in similar situations (so also Is 38:9-20; Dan 2:20-23; the LXX additions to Dan 3; Jdt 16; Lk 1:46-55; and, with an ironic twist in context, Jon 2). Deborah's victory song appears in the more typical context of a battle narrative. Like most inset hymns, this song contrasts thematically with the preceding story, but it does so by emphasizing a woman's point of view on the events. In not only highlighting Deborah as "a mother in Israel" (Judg 5:7) in contrast to the story's characterization of her as prophet, wife and judge (Judg 4:4-5), but also describing Jael's actions with praise and Sisera's mother and her ladies with sarcasm (Judg 5:24-31), women's roles and reactions take center stage in the poem. The Song of Deborah goes beyond characterizing the singer to giving her voice the final say in thematizing the story.

The songs credited to David in 2 Samuel develop the story's depiction of David as a singer and musician (1 Sam 16:14-23). In describing his fidelity to God, however, the songs emphasize most forcefully that David was God's favorite and therefore the model king of Israel. This theme echoes through subsequent Historical Books (see 1 Kings 11:6, 12-13; 2 Kings 18:3; 22:2; and the glorification of David in 1-2 Chronicles), and together with royal psalms and prophecies it stimulated the messianic expectations of Second Temple Judaism and later traditions. The inset hymns thus provide a bridge between the complex David of 2 Samuel and the model king of later traditions, reinterpreting his character for this idealized role.

3. Psalms and Scripture.

3.1. Hymns in Second Temple Judaism. Most inset hymns seem to have found their places rather late in the development of the biblical books, despite the fact that many may themselves be among the oldest texts in the Bible (perhaps Ex 15; Judg 5; Deut 32; Hab 3). The earliest combination of narrative and hymn probably is in Judges 4—5, which could predate these chapters' incorporation into the book of Judges. The hymns that frame 1-2 Samuel, however, seem to have been added to the narratives to frame them as a separate book and shape them for their role as Scripture. Evidence for this includes the way the Samuel appendix (2 Sam 21—24) interrupts the plot, and text-critical disruptions around Hannah's psalm (1 Sam 2:1-10). The Levitical hymn in 1 Chronicles 16 was composed for its place in Chronicles out of pieces from Psalms 105, 96 and 106 and is likely an original part of that book. But its originality there, like the secondary addition of hymns to Samuel (and Exodus, Deuteronomy and Isaiah), indicates that inset hymnody reflects new religious developments in Judaism during the Second Temple period (515 BCE-70 CE).

The composition and recitation of hymns became a highly regarded spiritual practice for educated individuals in this period. That is clear from the placement of appropriate hymns in the mouths of virtuous characters in later Second Temple literature (Judith, Tobit, Luke), including rewritten stories from the Bible (Additions to Daniel, *Pseudo-Philo*, various Targumim) and superscriptions that attribute psalms to various points in David's career (e.g., Ps 3; 34; 51; 54; 56; considerably more appear in the LXX Psalter). The insertion of psalms into the biblical stories both modeled and extended this practice (see Weitzman). They provided biblical warrant for a kind of individual piety that combined the liturgical traditions of the Jerusalem temple with Wisdom literature's emphasis on literacy and learning (Mathys). The Historical Books became acknowledged as Scripture only gradually throughout the Second Temple period. The heightened regard accorded books such as Judges and Samuel as religious texts led to attempts to shape the messages that they carry and the practices that they model. Inset hymns proved very useful for such "canon-conscious shaping" (Sheppard) or "scripturalizing" (Weitzman) of now biblical literature.

3.2. Reading and Singing Scripture. Inset hymns brought to narrative literature more than theological themes and models of piety, however. They brought in musical performance also, specifically the liturgical performances of professional temple musicians (1 Chron 16). By attributing such temple songs to heroes of biblical stories, editors and authors brought corporate liturgy into narrative literature. Biblical scholarship has tended to ignore this effect of the psalms on their contexts, and rather has emphasized the context's effect as individualizing and restricting the psalms' application. But the history of the use of the Bible in ancient Judaism and even Christianity shows that the direction of development tended toward the liturgical use of all genres of Scripture along the model of temple psalmody. Eventually, most if not all the texts—stories and laws as well as poetry and songs—were *sung* as part of corporate worship.

These cantorial practices of Jewish and Christian congregations in late antiquity cannot be traced back to Second Temple times, but inset hymns do come from this period and reflect a first step in the direction of singing biblical texts. Reading in the ancient world was almost always reading aloud, usually to an audience (*see* Writing, Writing Materials and Literacy in the Ancient Near East). The appearance of old and probably well-known hymns in at least Judges and Chronicles, and perhaps in Samuel (also Exodus, Deuteronomy and Habakkuk), can be expected to have elicited audience participation in singing the songs. Their insertion may well have intended such a response and so aimed at adapting the literature for use in public worship. Inset hymnody thus provides the first evidence for the "liturgizing" of the Historical Books for their use in worship as Scripture.

See also NARRATIVE ART OF ISRAEL'S HISTORIANS; PRAYER.

BIBLIOGRAPHY. **F. M. Cross**, "The Epic Traditions of Early Israel: Epic Narrative and the Reconstruction of Early Israelite Institutions," in *The Poet and the Historian*, ed. R. E. Friedman (HSS 26; Atlanta: Scholars Press, 1983) 13-39; **D. Damrosch**, *The Narrative Covenant: Transformations of Genre in the Growth of Biblical Literature* (San Francisco: Harper & Row, 1987); **J. Kim**, *The Structure of the Samson Cycle* (Kampen: Kok Pharos, 1993); **J. W. Kleinig**, *The Lord's Song: The Basis, Function and Significance of Choral Music in Chronicles* (JSOTSup 156; Sheffield: Sheffield Academic Press, 1993); **J. L. Kugel**, *The Idea of Biblical Poetry: Parallelism and Its History* (New Haven: Yale University Press, 1981); **H.-P. Mathys**, *Dichter und Beter: Theologen aus spätalttestamentlichen Zeit* (OBO 132; Freiburg: Universitätsverlag; Göttingen: Vandenhoeck & Ruprecht, 1994); **J. C. de Moor and W. G. E. Watson**, eds., *Verse in*

Ancient Near Eastern Prose (AOAT 42; Neu-kirchen-Vluyn: Neukirchener Verlag, 1993); **K. L. Noll,** *The Faces of David* (JSOTSup 242; Sheffield: Sheffield Academic Press, 1997); **G. T. Sheppard,** *Wisdom as a Hermeneutical Construct: A Study in the Sapientializing of the Old Testament* (BZAW 151; Berlin: de Gruyter, 1980) 145-59; **J. W. Watts,** "Biblical Psalms Outside the Psalter," in *The Book of Psalms: Composition and Reception,* ed. P. W. Flint and P. D. Miller (VTSup 99; Leiden: E. J. Brill, 2005) 288-309; idem, *Psalm and Story: Inset Hymns in Hebrew Narrative* (JSOTSup 139; Sheffield: JSOT, 1992); **S. Weitzman,** *Song and Story in Biblical Narrative: The History of a Literary Convention in Ancient Israel* (ISBL; Bloomington: Indiana University Press, 1997).

J. W. Watts

POSTEXILIC PERIOD. *See* HISTORY OF ISRAEL 7: PERSIAN PERIOD; HISTORY OF ISRAEL 8: POST-EXILIC COMMUNITY.

POSTEXILIC TEMPLE

The first temple (*see* Solomon's Temple), proposed by *David (2 Sam 7:1-3) and constructed by *Solomon (1 Kings 5—6), was destroyed by the Babylonians in 587 BCE at the demise of the kingdom of Judah (2 Kings 25:9, 13-18; Ps 74:3-7). Although the worship of Yahweh continued at least for a time on the site (Jer 41:5), and also continued at *Mizpah, the seat of the Babylonian-appointed Judean governor (Blenkinsopp 1998), the second (postexilic) temple was not rebuilt in *Jerusalem until 520-515 BCE during the reign of the Achaemenid Persian king Darius I. Little is known about the physical attributes of the second temple, except that those who had known the first temple considered its construction to be considerably meaner, which reflects the relative poverty of the postexilic community (Ezra 3:12; Hag 2:3; Ezra 6:2-4 gives the temple's dimensions, but these figures have been corrupted). The first temple served to legitimate the Davidic dynasty and the kingdom that it ruled, since the "house" (temple) of the national deity was built beside the "house" (palace) of the king. That temple was a national shrine superintended by the king, the national deity's viceroy. The postexilic temple was built in a very different political context, under the supervision of the Achaemenid Persian imperial regime and without a Judean king or an independent Judean kingdom. The implications of these

changed circumstances for the roles of Jerusalem temple of Yahweh during the Achaemenid Persian period are commonly discussed in relation to views of the character of the postexilic community (*see* History of Israel 8: Postexilic Community) and the policies of the Achaemenid Persian authorities toward the cults of subjugated peoples. The temple often has been seen as the center of religious, political and economic power in Achaemenid Judah. As a corollary of this, temple personnel, especially the high priest, are considered to have been significant figures in the postexilic community.

A thorough discussion of these issues would necessarily draw on prophetic and other biblical texts dated to the exilic and postexilic periods. However, attention to the central historical texts of the postexilic period—Ezra-Nehemiah and Chronicles—allows for consideration of the main aspects of the debate.

1. Ezra-Nehemiah
2. Chronicles
3. Achaemenid Persian Administration and the Temple

1. Ezra-Nehemiah.

Ezra 1—6 is a narrative recounting the rebuilding of the Jerusalem temple of Yahweh in the reigns of Cyrus the Great and Darius I, following Cyrus's edict of 538 BCE permitting Judeans to return to their homeland for that specific purpose (Ezra 1:1-4). The rebuilding of the temple commonly has been seen as the result of a general, empire-wide Achaemenid Persian policy of benevolence toward the cults of subjugated peoples. There was no such policy, however, and so the rebuilding of the Jerusalem temple must be seen as the result of a specific act of Persian permission to rebuild the shrine of a people that had proven to be rebellious under earlier imperial regimes. The initiative for the rebuilding probably came from Judean exiles in Babylonia who supported Cyrus's takeover of Babylon (Williamson 1985, 11). Cyrus's permission to rebuild was not limited to Judeans in Babylonia (contra Ezra 1:1-6; cf. Ezra 6:2-5), but neither those repatriated under Cyrus (and Cambyses) nor those Judeans already resident in Judah (nonexiles) undertook any work on the temple at Cyrus's decree, since they lacked a legitimate temple builder. The expectation that Cyrus might fill this role (Is 44:28) came to nothing. It is likely that the cult on the temple site was reestablished in the reign of Cyrus (although all the events of Ezra 3 should be dated to the reign of Darius). However, as Haggai 2:15-16 makes clear, no work was actually undertaken on the temple itself at this time. From the perspective of the Achaemenid Persian administration, the Jerusalem temple was a minor shrine that did not command much attention, and so its rebuilding was left in the hands of the local population, who did not take up the work in Cyrus's reign. Furthermore, in the light of Haggai 1:2-4, Judeans were waiting for some sign that the divine ire exemplified by the demise of the kingdom of Judah had in fact abated before rebuilding could commence. Both Haggai and Zechariah (Zech 1:1-17) understand this to be taking place in their day, the second year of the reign of Darius. I would argue that the explanation of Ezra 3:1—4:5 that the rebuilding was thwarted during Cyrus's reign due to the interference of "the peoples of the lands" should be viewed as a later concern retrojected into the period of the early restoration. Ezra 5:11-16, which contends that the Judeans represented their rebuilding efforts as ongoing from the initial repatriation under Cyrus, should similarly be viewed as upholding a later notion that the postexilic community was never anything less than fully committed to the temple's rebuilding and its cult (for an extended argument in support of the foregoing analysis see Bedford 2001, 87-180, 230-64; for an alternative view see Japhet 1991).

The Jerusalem temple of Yahweh was not rebuilt in the reign of Darius as a result of an Achaemenid Persian administrative policy either to establish Judah as a semiautonomous district (contra Meyers and Meyers 1987) or to further the development in the district of a "citizen-temple community" form of polity whose members' close connection with the temple afforded them rights to real estate (contra Weinberg). Both of these views grant significant economic and administrative roles to the Jerusalem temple, but neither can be substantiated on the basis of comparative evidence or by recourse to the actions of the Achaemenid Persians toward subjugated peoples and their cults during this period (Bedford 2001, 185-230). Ezra 5—6 points out that Darius was unaware of any rebuilding edict, and clearly he had not issued one himself, but he was willing to enforce Cyrus's edict once its existence had been confirmed. Furthermore, for this period there is no evidence that the temple served as an economic or political center. Any contention that the high priest must have had an important role in the subprovince sanctioned by the administration is suspect (Rooke, 125-74). Although Zechariah 6:9-15 speaks of the possibility of a diarchy—shared leadership between the governor and high priest—this is unlikely to have eventuated (Goodblatt, 60; Rooke, 146-49). As the book of Nehemiah makes clear for the fifth century BCE, the governor was in charge of affairs within the district of Judah, which also included matters pertaining to the temple.

For Ezra 1—6, the importance of the temple lay primarily in its role as a cultic center. The narrative emphasizes the reinstitution of sacrifices and sacred festivals (Ezra 3:2-6; 6:17, 19-22), the reestablishment of legitimate temple personnel and their roles (Ezra 2:36-65 [esp. 2:59-65]; 3:8-11; 6:18), and the separation of the repatriates from "the peoples of the lands," who, while claiming to be legitimate worshipers of Yahweh, were self-confessed foreigners (Ezra 4:1-3). This highlights Ezra's understanding of the character of the postexilic community: it was a cultic community. This can be contrasted with Haggai and Zechariah 1—8, for whom the symbolic significance of the rebuilt temple lay in its marking the end of the divine ire, the beginning of a new epoch, and, drawing on the monarchical period *Zion ideology and the late monarchical/exilic period "prophecies against the nations," the kingship of Yahweh, who would be reenthroned in his temple. The first two of these points may be reflected in Ezra 1:1, however.

The temple as a cultic center also features in Ezra 7—10, the narrative recounting the mission of Ezra. Although Ezra's mission and role are much discussed, he is described as a priest and scribe (Ezra 7:1-6) who gathers temple personnel from the Babylonian diaspora (Ezra 7:7-8; 8:15-20) to return for service at the Jerusalem temple, and who brings gifts for the temple from Judeans remaining in exile and leading Persian officials, committed to the care of priests and Levites (Ezra 8:24-30). Much of Artaxerxes' rescript (Ezra 7:12-26) is devoted to temple matters: freewill offerings from those in the Babylonian diaspora for the temple in Jerusalem (Ezra 7:15-19); financial support for the temple cult from the central administration (Ezra 7:21-23); tax concessions for temple personnel (Ezra 7:24). Whether the *"law" that Ezra is commissioned to institute in Judah (Ezra 7:14, 26) has any direct bearing on the temple's role is impossible to say. Ezra's blessing of Yahweh in Ezra 7:27 nevertheless affirms that the point of Artaxerxes' rescript is "to glorify the house of Yahweh in Jerusalem." The notion of the cultic community with the temple at its center is reinforced in Ezra 7—10 by Ezra's castigation of priests and others in Ezra 9—10 whose marriage to nonrepatriates is perceived as a threat to the cultic purity of the postexilic community. This reform is to bring those in Judah into line with conceptions of community identity and practices of separatism prevalent among the Babylonian Judean parent community (Bedford 2002). This should not be construed as instituting or reinvigorating a citizen-temple community (contra Weinberg; Blenkinsopp 1991) since patterns of land tenure held to characterize this form of social organization are not attested in Achaemenid Judah (Bedford 2001, 217-30).

The book of Nehemiah recounts the governorship of Nehemiah in Judah covering the period 445 to 432 BCE. The temple barely features in Nehemiah 1—7, the section of the Nehemiah Memoir (probably Neh 1—7; 12:31-43; 13:4-31) dealing with his first period as governor. The narrative focuses on the rebuilding of the city wall of Jerusalem, economic reforms and the intrigues of Nehemiah's political enemies. The temple is mentioned in Nehemiah 6:10-14, perhaps as a place of refuge, but it is clear that although the city is underpopulated, the temple is still functioning. The need for Nehemiah to undertake a synoikism—an enforced movement of peoples into a capital city—to repopulate Jerusalem (Neh 11) undermines claims that a citizen-temple community was operative in Achaemenid Judah, as does Nehemiah 10, a part of a covenant renewal ceremony (Neh 8—10), which makes clear the necessity for radical reforms to the funding of the temple (Nehemiah [re-]institutes the payment of a temple tax, wood offering, firstfruits, Levitical tithes). This episode questions how successful an institution the temple was, given that community funding for it evidently had collapsed. Nehemiah 10 is commonly understood to be a response to the neglect of the temple and its personnel recounted in Nehemiah 13 (Williamson 1985, 331), the latter relating events in the second period of Nehemiah's governorship (also part of the Nehemiah Memoir). Nehemiah 10—13 reinforces

the position of the governor as the official with legal oversight of the temple. It is an institution under his authority; he does not share authority with the high priest, nor does the temple operate as a competing center of political or administrative power within Achaemenid Judah. The fact that nobles and the high priest have family connections with Tobiah the Ammonite and *Sanballat of Samaria (Neh 6:17-19; 13:4, 28), and that Tobiah could be given access to rooms in the temple, means only that certain leading Judeans had an attitude different from Nehemiah's toward relations with those outside the boundaries of the district. The temple's storerooms do not identify the temple as an economic center, since, as Nehemiah 10:38 makes clear, these are to house emoluments for temple personnel. Furthermore, recent attempts to highlight the role of the Jerusalem temple and its personnel as agents in the imperial taxation system (Schaper) and to present Ezra as the equivalent of the senior administrative official in contemporary Babylonian temples (Janzen, 639-41) overstate the administrative and economic roles of the Jerusalem temple in fifth-century Achaemenid Judah (Bedford, forthcoming).

In common with Ezra, in Nehemiah temple and community self-definition are interrelated. The temple is for Judeans only (Nehemiah's view of the community is wider than Ezra's in that it is basically defined by the political boundaries of Judah rather than by being an exile/descendant of an exile), and obligations toward the temple are placed on the community. Thus fulfillment of these obligations marks one as a member of the community.

2. Chronicles.

Community self-definition is also a feature of the books of Chronicles, commonly dated to the fourth century BCE and here assumed to have a different author from Ezra-Nehemiah. Chronicles recounts the history of Israel and Judah, focusing on the monarchical period. The temple and its personnel feature prominently in the narrative. While the temple in view is the first temple, given that the text is written in the late Achaemenid Persian period, it should be expected to reflect understandings of the second temple and its personnel prevalent at that time. The emphasis in Chronicles on the monarchy and its responsibility for building the temple and maintaining its cult and personnel does not reflect a desire for the return of indigenous kingship; rather, it reflects an understanding of the history and identity of the community, for both the preexilic and postexilic periods. As D. Rooke puts it, "The monarchs who are truly David's descendants are the ones who care for the temple, and so a people who rebuild the temple and maintain worship there are likewise David's true descendants" (Rooke, 190). The notion here is that the postexilic community has inherited the role earlier committed by Yahweh to the monarch in respect to the temple: to preserve the symbol of the presence of Yahweh with his people and to conduct the proper forms of worship under the divinely appointed cultic officials. The boundaries of this community for Chronicles are wider than those for either Ezra or Nehemiah. They extend to include the northern kingdom, Israel, represented in the Achaemenid Persian period by Samarians, who are welcomed if they recognize the Jerusalem temple as the only legitimate shrine for the people of Yahweh (Williamson 1991).

Although they differ in particulars, such as the limits of the community, Chronicles, Ezra and Nehemiah agree that the fundamental role of the second temple lies in its legitimization of the postexilic community. This community stands in continuity with monarchical Judah because it is gathered around the restored temple, which serves as the symbol of the divine presence with the people. The community's responsibilities are to rebuild and maintain the temple, and to faithfully worship there.

3. Achaemenid Persian Administration and the Temple.

Does this understanding of the temple expressed in Chronicles, Ezra and Nehemiah exhaust the roles that it played in Achaemenid Judah? As we noted previously, some commentators have contended that the temple also had important administrative and economic roles with the result that the temple priesthood was politically powerful. Their political power may in fact have been minimal (Rooke, 125-239). It can be briefly pointed out that whatever administrative, economic and political roles the temple had, these should not be understood as arising from any Achaemenid Persian administrative policy. Priests were politically significant locally by virtue of their social standing, which is recognized by leading families outside the Judean

community through intermarriage. This status did not result from an explicit administrative position accorded them by the Persians. The temple was neither rebuilt nor supported by the Persians in order to facilitate the administration of Judah. Any economic role for the temple should similarly be seen in local, not empire-wide, terms. If Tobiah was granted rooms in the temple to advance his economic interests in Judah (plausibly suggested by Williamson 1985, 261, 386), this was not the result of any Persian policy. Attempts to view the roles of the Jerusalem temple and its personnel in terms similar to contemporary temples in Babylonia and Asia Minor should be treated with great circumspection (see Bedford, forthcoming).

See also EZRA; EZRA AND NEHEMIAH, BOOKS OF; HISTORY OF ISRAEL 8: POSTEXILIC COMMUNITY; NEHEMIAH; SOLOMON'S TEMPLE.

BIBLIOGRAPHY. **P. R. Bedford,** "Diaspora: Homeland Relations in Ezra-Nehemiah," *VT* 52 (2002) 147-65; idem, "The Economic Role of the Jerusalem Temple in Achaemenid Judah: Comparative Perspectives," in *Sarah Japhet Jubilee Volume,* ed. M. Bar-Asher et al. (Jerusalem: Mosad Bialik, forthcoming); idem, *Temple Restoration in Early Achaemenid Judah* (SJSJ 65; Leiden: Brill, 2001); **J. Blenkinsopp,** "The Judean Priesthood during the Neo-Babylonian and Achaemenid Periods: A Hypothetical Reconstruction," *CBQ* 60 (1998) 25-43; idem, "Temple and Society in Achaemenid Judah," in *Second Temple Studies,* 1: *Persian Period,* ed. P. R. Davies (JSOTSup 117; Sheffield: Sheffield Academic Press, 1991) 22-53; **D. Goodblatt,** *The Monarchic Principle: Studies in Jewish Self-Government in Antiquity* (TSAJ 58; Tübingen: Mohr Siebeck, 1994); **D. Janzen,** "The 'Mission' of Ezra and the Persian-Period Temple Community," *JBL* 119 (2000) 619-43; **S. Japhet,** "The Temple in the Restoration Period: Reality and Ideology," *USQR* 44 (1991) 195-251; **C. L. Meyers and E. M. Meyers,** *Haggai, Zechariah 1—8* (AB 25B; New York: Doubleday, 1987); **J. Schaper,** "The Jerusalem Temple as an Instrument of the Achaemenid Fiscal Administration," *VT* 45 (1995) 528-39; **D. Rooke,** *The Heirs of Zadok: The Role and Development of the High Priesthood in Ancient Israel* (OTM; Oxford: Oxford University Press, 2000); **J. P. Weinberg,** *The Citizen-Temple Community* (SJOTSup 151; Sheffield: Sheffield Academic Press, 1992); **H. G. M. Williamson,** *Ezra, Nehemiah* (WBC 16: Waco, TX: Word, 1985); idem, "The Temple in the Books of

Chronicles," in *Templum Amicitiae: Essays on the Second Temple Presented to Ernst Bammel* (JSNTSup 48; Sheffield: JSOT, 1991) 15-31.

P. R. Bedford

POSTMODERN HERMENEUTIC. *See* HERMENEUTICS; METHODS OF INTERPRETATION.

PRAYER

The book of Psalms has dominated the study of prayer in scholarship on the OT over the past century. However, in recent decades more energy has been expended on the study of non-psalmic prayer, in particular prayers found within the OT Historical Books. This study has revealed a wealth of form, tradition and literature.

1. Defining Prayer
2. Form-Critical Study of Prayer
3. Tradition-Critical Study of Prayer
4. Rhetorical-Critical Study of Prayer
5. Conclusion

1. Defining Prayer.

The preferred starting point for the study of prayer is a clear and concise definition. While some have broadened the definition to include any communication with *God in the second person, recent scholarship has articulated a more limited meaning by identifying prayer as address to God in the second person that is initiated by humans, is intentional in design, introduced by prayer vocabulary (e.g., *hitpallēl*, "to pray"; *qārā᾿ běšēm*, "to call on a name"), but is not conversational (see Balentine; Newman). This being so, there are times when third-person speech is employed and when prayer vocabulary is absent, and yet the composition appears to be a prayer. This is a needed reminder that identifying prayer is often more of an art than a science. Furthermore, the study of prayer is not limited to the identification of prayers in these narrative texts, but also includes texts that speak about the character, theology and impact of prayer.

2. Form-Critical Study of Prayer.

Research on the prayers of the Historical Books was dominated by tools imported from the study of the Psalter, especially form-critical research. Such psalms research was inaugurated in the first half of the last century by the work of H. Gunkel and J. Begrich, and of S. Mow-

inckel, but then was applied to the study of the non-psalmic prayers by scholars such as A. Wendel, L. Krinetzi and H. G. Reventlow (see the review of this earlier phase of research by Balentine). The focus of this scholarship has been on cataloging the formal types and features of prayer, with a subsidiary goal of discerning the oral foundations beneath the compositions that we now find in the OT.

2.1. Narrative Prayers Among Prayers in the Old Testament. Even with the dominance of the study of the Psalter, there were those who argued that there was a distinctive quality to compositions found in the narratives of the Hebrew Bible. C. Westermann (1981, 165-213) argued that prayer evolved from earlier simple prose forms, through the more complex poetic forms of the Psalter, and finally to the extremely complex prayers now found in 1 Kings 8; Ezra 9; Nehemiah 1; 9; this development occurred not only on the stylistic level, but also on the theological level, as can be discerned in the shift from lament to penitence for communal supplication forms. In contrast, M. Greenberg (46) sees no such development, but rather argues that three different types of prayer are evident among the prose prayers and that all three types were used at the same time: patterned prose prayer speech, ritual prayers (psalms), and the totally unconventional and artless prayer. These categories are one way of organizing the various types of prayers in the Historical Books, but one cannot completely abandon the useful categories that arose from the study of the Psalter, especially in light of the fact that early form critics used the narrative books to help fill out the settings of their form-critical categories (e.g., on laments see Gunkel and Begrich).

2.2. Forms of Prayer. Form-critical research on the prayers in the Historical Books has revealed that although prayers in the narrative context contain more prosaic and less poetic elements, the same basic forms are in evidence as those found in the Psalter. P. D. Miller categorizes prayers into prayers for help, prayers of doxology and trust, prayers of confession and penitence, prayers for others, and blessing and curse. The basic categories advanced by W. Brueggemann (1984; 1995) are more helpful because they root the forms more firmly in human experience. Interestingly, it is within the Historical Books, at 1 Chronicles 16:4-6, that one finds justification for the basic types of prayers articulated by Brueggemann as the Chronicler presents David's commission to the Asaphites to "minister before the ark of the Lord, to make petition [prayers of disorientation], to give thanks [prayers of reorientation], and to praise [prayers of orientation] the LORD, the God of Israel" (1 Chron 16:4). This is followed by the account of David committing a psalm to the Asaphites that actually is drawn from three different psalms in the Psalter: Psalms 96:1-13; 105:1-15; 106:1, 47-48—interestingly, each psalm from one of the three categories mentioned above. This diversity of prayer forms can be found throughout the Historical Books.

2.2.1. Prayers of Orientation. Prayers of orientation express praise to God out of a life experience that has reached equilibrium. Although praise is found as a major component in prayers of disorientation throughout the Historical Books, as independent prayers, praise is largely restricted to Chronicles, Ezra and Nehemiah, where the phrase "for he is good, his steadfast love endures forever" is the most common declaration (1 Chron 29:20; 2 Chron 5:13; 7:3; 20:21; 20:26-29; 29:25-30; Ezra 3:10-11; Neh 5:18; described in Neh 8:6). Praise is offered as the nation goes into battle, celebrates successful battle, offers sacrifice, lays the foundation of the temple, and accepts covenant stipulations.

2.2.2. Prayers of Disorientation. Prayers of disorientation, however, assume a radically different setting. They arise from an experience of difficulty in which the supplicant or community is in need of God's rescue, and they often include physical rites such as fasting, sackcloth, ashes, loud wailing and crying, and various postures (lying, sitting, standing). This kind of prayer should be divided into two stages. The first type (stage one) includes those prayers prayed in a period of distress, expressing despair and longing for salvation (Josh 7:6-9; Judg 21:2-4; 1 Kings 17:20-21; described in Judg 2:4; 3:9, 15; 4:3; 6:6; 1 Sam 1:10-18, 27; 8:18; 9:16; Esther 4:1-3). The tone of this type of prayer is noted by the presence of questions such as "why?" and "how long?" The second type (stage two) arises in a similar context, a period of distress; however, it has a radically different tone. In this stage the sense of despair is no longer present, as the supplicant or community has moved either to a sense of confidence that God will save (prayers of trust: Josh 10:12; Judg 12:8; 2 Sam 15:30-31; 1 Kings 3:6-9/2 Chron 1:8-10; 1 Kings 8:22-53/

2 Chron 6:14-42; 1 Kings 8:55-61; 18:36-38; 2 Kings 6:17-20; 19:14-19; 20:2-3; 1 Chron 4:10; 29:10-19; 2 Chron 14:9-11; 20:4-19; Ezra 8:21-23; Neh 5:19; 6:9, 14; 13:14, 22, 29, 30; described in 1 Sam 6:8; 2 Kings 19:4; 1 Chron 5:20; 2 Chron 15:4; Ezra 6:10; Neh 2:4; 4:9) or to a sense of penitence that God will forgive (prayers of penitence: Judg 10:10, 15; 1 Sam 6:6; 12:10; 12:19; 2 Sam 24:10/1 Chron 21:8; 2 Sam 24:17/1 Chron 21:16-17; 2 Chron 30:19; Ezra 9:1—10:1; Neh 1:4-11; 9:5-37; described in Neh 9:1-5; Ezra 10:6; 2 Chron 33:12-13, 19). Related to these forms is the "vow" form, which requests something from God and provides a motivation in a human response following the divine intervention (Judg 11:30; 1 Sam 1:11).

2.2.3. Prayer and Intermediaries. One aspect often connected to contexts of disorientation is the intercessory or intermediary role played by prophets and priests—that is, the practice of "inquiring of God" for direction and help in the midst of disorientation. The Historical Books depict such inquiries through the agency of a *prophet (1 Sam 7:5-9; 8:6; 9:9; 12:17-19; 28:6-7; 1 Kings 13:6; 2 Kings 20:11; 22:20/2 Chron 34:19-28; 32:29) or a *priest (Judg 18:5-6; 20:18-28; 1 Sam 14:36-42; 22:9-15; 28:6-7; 30:7-10). In other instances no intermediary is named, although an intermediary may have been used (Josh 9:14; Judg 1:1; 6:36, 39; 1 Sam 23:1-5; 2 Sam 2:1; 5:17-25/1 Chron 14:8-17; 2 Sam 21:13-14; 1 Kings 3:5-9; 2 Kings 1:16; 2 Chron 18:4). The form of this request appears to have been a question or series of questions (e.g., 1 Sam 23:9-14), although at times the intermediary also had a role to play in seeking God that was more than just relaying a message and that approaches the prayers of disorientation reviewed above. This highlights evidence for a close connection between prophecy and prayer in the Historical Books (1 Sam 15:10; 1 Kings 17:17-24; 18:36-37; 2 Kings 4:32-33; 6:17-20).

2.2.4. Prayers of Reorientation. The condition of disorientation does not endure forever, and when it is resolved and the supplicant experiences salvation, a new form of prayer is employed: the prayer of reorientation—that is, the prayer thanking God for salvation from the distress. Such thanksgiving is found within the Historical Books, although it may also encompass some of the instances cited for the prayers of orientation above (1 Sam 2:1-10; 2 Sam 7:18-29/ 1 Chron 17:16-27; 2 Sam 22:1-51; 1 Kings 3:6-9;

1 Chron 29:14-19; Neh 12:27).

2.2.5. Settings in Life. The forms articulated above have long been discerned within the Psalter, and elaborate theories on *Sitz im Leben* have been developed to provide a context for interpreting the various psalms. All along, however, the narrative literature of the Hebrew Bible stood as a treasure trove to offer appropriate settings for interpreting prayer forms—a point made clear in Gunkel's early study of the forms of the Psalter, where he draws on narrative settings in establishing aspects of his form-critical research (see Gunkel and Begrich).

A poignant example is the prayer form found in Joshua 7, which reveals how disorientation psalms functioned in the life of God's people, especially as they faced major crises of faith and life. Unquestionably, Joshua 7 begins with an instance of disorientation as we see the defeat of the small Israelite force at Ai (Josh 7:1-5). In both action and word Joshua and the elders cry out to God with disorientation stage one (Josh 7:6-9; tearing of clothes, falling face down, placing dust on the heads accompany stage one elsewhere in OT). But God speaks very strongly in response to this expression of prayer, informing Joshua that his prayer is not appropriate at this moment because there is sin in the camp (Josh 7:10-15). Instead, we see that the appropriate communication to God is a confession of sin, which is declared by Achan near the end of the passage (Josh 7:19-21). Joshua 7 is narrative evidence of how the form of prayer is dictated by the setting of the people, but also how the word of Yahweh can change the appropriate form of prayer. The people are at stage one, involved in pure disorientation: blaming God for the predicament. However, they are called to account, and the demand is made that they move from stage one to confession. God speaks into disorientation, and the nature of that speech will set a new direction in the form of prayer.

A second example showing how disorientation psalms functioned in the life of God's people is *Hezekiah's crisis of faith in 2 Kings 18—19. As in Joshua 7, in 2 Kings 18:17-37 we begin with an instance of disorientation precipitated by a military threat, this time by the Assyrian army outside the gates of Jerusalem. Hezekiah's response is to cry out to God using the actions and words of stage one, disorientation (2 Kings 19:1-4; notice again tearing clothes, putting on sackcloth, going into the temple as 1 Kings 8

commanded). God's word breaks in as the prophet speaks a word of confidence (2 Kings 19:5-7), and even though the disorientation heightens (2 Kings 19:8-13), Hezekiah enters the temple again and prays a prayer of trust and confidence (2 Kings 19:14-19). This confident faith is followed by a further prophetic word of salvation (2 Kings 19:20-34) and ultimately by the action of God (2 Kings 19:35-37). Again as in Joshua 7, the voice of God (this time through the prophet) breaks into the midst of a situation of disorientation. However, in contrast to Joshua 7, the word of God is positive, announcing salvation, not offering warning to the people. And this produces a prayer of trust and confidence. This evidence from the narrative tradition of Israel is helpful for understanding a feature in the Psalter that often has been noted by interpreters: there are significant mood swings in psalms of lament, from despair to hope, shifts that were explained either as evidence that the psalmist had returned at a later point to finish the psalms (when the problem had passed) or that a prophetic voice (cult prophet) had spoken a word of encouragement. These narrative contexts reveal the role that the *word of God (i.e., the prophetic word) played in the liturgical life of Israel.

3. Tradition-Critical Study of Prayer.
The various forms of prayer reveal the rootedness of prayer in the experience of the Israelite community. Through these forms the language and practice of prayer were preserved from generation to generation—a feature evident in the narratives of the Historical Books. But prayers also were instrumental in preserving the conceptual traditions of Israel, and as a result they have become mines for the study of tradition history. Such study has been the focus of late on the penitential prayer tradition in the Historical Books, although foreshadowed by the earlier work of G. von Rad, who saw in the prayer of Nehemiah 9 a developed example of what he tagged *das kleine geschichtliche Credo* ("the short historical creed"). This was a form of creedal expression that recited the story of Israel, other examples of which are found in Exodus 15; Deuteronomy 6:20-24; 26:5-9; Joshua 24:2-13; 1 Samuel 12:8; Psalms 78; 105; 106; 136. Here we see how prayer could be a vehicle for the development of tradition history, especially the preservation of the story of Israel. More recently, both J. H. Newman and M. J. Boda have devoted

close attention to this feature in the penitential prayers. Newman highlights ways in which prayers in Second Temple Judaism (including Neh 9) are influenced by Scripture and reveal a strong trend in which "scripture was *prayed*" (Newman, 219). Similarly, Boda focuses on the close relationship between the various penitential prayers (Ezra 9; Neh 1; 9; Dan 9; Ps 106) and the Torah to reveal how these penitential prayers used earlier scriptural tradition as leverage to appeal to God's grace in the present predicament. This kind of study also highlights the innovative character of such prayerful recycling of inscripturated traditions.

4. Rhetorical-Critical Study of Prayer.

The study of form and tradition in prayer is largely focused on the developmental process that lies behind prayers in the Historical Books. However, recent shifts to literary models for interpretation have led to a greater appreciation for the rhetorical value of prayer, in particular the rhetorical significance of prayer to the message of the Historical Books as literature. There is no better place to start than with the short but highly influential study of prose prayer done by M. Greenberg in 1983.

Greenberg goes to great lengths to defend the authenticity of prose prayers now embedded in the narratives of the OT. Based on "analogies in social speech," Greenberg (9) argues that these prayers reflect genuine forms employed by ancient Israel, even if in their present context they are literary creations. Although he appears more concerned with getting behind the embedded character of these prayers in order to defend their authenticity, Greenberg does lay a strong foundation for an interpretive stream that would focus more on the rhetorical role of prayer within narrative literature when he writes, "The specificity of the embedded prayers means that they play a part in the argument of a narrative and its depiction of character" (Greenberg, 17-18), and further, "Study of the narrative art of the Scriptures has something to gain from attention to the embedded prose prayers. Because the embedded prayers are tailored to their circumstances, they can serve to delineate character—as in reality we may believe that, since extemporized prayer gave scope to individuality, a person was revealed by his prayers" (Greenberg, 47).

Although S. E. Balentine points to the earlier work of J. Corvin and of E. Staudt, two dissertations that focused on the Historical Books and on the *Deuteronomistic History respectively, he brought the study of the rhetorical function of prayer in the Historical Books to a new level. His approach was self-described as "synchronic" rather than "diachronic"—that is, investigating how these prayers function in their narrative contexts rather than how they functioned in their original oral context: "I concentrate on prayer as a literary vehicle for providing characterization (of both pray-er and God), for addressing certain themes (e.g., divine justice), and for conveying and promoting certain postures or attitudes (e.g., penitence and contrition) . . . [and am] also concerned to attend to the use of prayer as a means of conveying ideological and theological perspectives, again in relation to both God and human partner" (Balentine, 29). This agenda leads to a far greater illumination of the theological content of these prayers—that is, not only how they characterize God, but also how they characterize humanity in relationship to God.

Others have attempted more limited evaluations of prayers in the narrative contexts of the Historical Books. Weinfeld focused attention on what he called "the liturgical oration" in his work on Deuteronomy and the Deuteronomistic History. These orations take their lead from the book of Deuteronomy, where one finds for the first time the command to recite liturgies. Proclamations of faith in Deuteronomy itself focus on the uniqueness of God and his exclusive sovereignty (Deut 4:32-39; 6:4; 7:9-10; 10:14), but beginning with Deuteronomy 3:23-25 and continuing in the Deuteronomistic History (2 Sam 7:22-24; 1 Kings 8:23; 2 Kings 19:15-19) and Deuteronomistic stratum of Jeremiah (Jer 32:17-23), and ultimately even into the prayers in the books of Daniel, Nehemiah and Chronicles, one finds prayers "opening with the proclamation of the uniqueness of God, and supplemented (especially in the later texts) by the theme of world creation" (Weinfeld, 42). Thus these prayers in the Historical Books play an important role theologically by emphasizing the uniqueness of God as creator and provider, and the uniqueness of Israel as God's elect. Staudt's evaluation of prayer in the Deuteronomistic History concluded that prayers of petition were situated at strategic places in the narrative between crisis and resolution, inhabiting the "hiatus" between

God's promise and action (Staudt, 338; cf. Balentine, 21). In this way, prayer performed a theological function as "the instrument for the participation of the people with their God in the unfolding history of Israel's covenantal relationship" (Staudt, 339; cf. Balentine, 21).

It had long been observed by M. Noth (5-6, 80-81) and O. Plöger, drawing on G. von Rad (267), that the OT Historical Books regularly employed a genre called *die levitische Predigt* (the Levitical Sermon) (see Boda, 6-7). Both Noth and Plöger identified these sermons in the Deuteronomistic History and especially in the *Chronicler's History, noting how the Chronicler used any available opportunity to incorporate such speeches into his account, not only in the form of sermons, but also letters, historical reviews and, particularly important for our purposes, prayers. These observations were exploited in M. A. Throntveit's investigation of royal speeches and prayers in Chronicles, in which he confirmed striking similarities in structure and content between the rhetoric of the two forms (1 Chron 17:16-27; 29:10-19; 2 Chron 6:14-42; 14:11) (Throntveit, 74-75). While both R. L. Braun (xxiv-xv) and R. A. Mason (133-37, 257) explained the similarities between these various "speeches/prayers" as evidence of reliance on contemporary Persian period forms, Throntveit focused on the role that these speeches play in the larger work of the Chronicler. For Throntveit, these prayers (as well as speeches) reveal not only the structural framework of the Chronicler's work, but also the theological message of these books. The prayers often employ historical overviews, thus forging a strong theological link to the past through story. The prayers also often use lament forms or portions of lament forms to focus on the theology that help comes from Yahweh alone, regularly emphasizing this by contrasting the omnipotence of God with the dependence of the people (Throntveit, 74-75, 88).

M. Duggan's work on Nehemiah 9 shows the impact of the prayer form on the rhetoric of Ezra-Nehemiah as a whole. For Duggan, Nehemiah 9 represents "the theological summit" as well as "the spiritual apex" of the Ezra-Nehemiah story (Duggan, 230, 298). Theologically, it claims that the context for interpreting events present to the ancient reader is the larger story that begins with creation. This story is filled with

theology that defines this people by emphasizing God's covenant with faithful Abraham and allegiance to Torah as a present word of God. Spiritually, it suggests that the penitential posture of the leaders Ezra and Nehemiah (Ezra 9; Neh 1) now pervades the community and that this penitential response contrasts the present generation with this past.

These various studies reveal the role that prayer plays rhetorically and, through this, theologically in the Historical Books. As a form of "dramatic narrative," they draw considerable rhetorical attention and become vehicles through which the narrator can communicate key theological emphases in the book.

5. Conclusion.

Whether it is the variety of forms and contexts of prayer, the depth of theological traditions or even the significance of their message to their present literary context, we have seen the vast potential of the study of prayer in the Historical Books. Through these prayers we gain a greater appreciation for the spiritual rhythms of ancient Israel as well as the core theological values that sustained people through the ebb and flow of human experience. Their rootedness in life and effect on literature explains the enduring hold that these prayers have on the imagination of those who study the Historical Books.

See also POETRY.

BIBLIOGRAPHY. **S. E. Balentine,** *Prayer in the Hebrew Bible: The Drama of Divine-Human Dialogue* (OBT; Minneapolis: Fortress, 1993); **M. J. Boda,** *Praying the Tradition: The Origin and Use of Tradition in Nehemiah 9* (BZAW 277; Berlin: de Gruyter, 1999); **R. L. Braun,** *1 Chronicles* (WBC 14; Waco, TX: Word, 1986); **W. Brueggemann,** *The Message of the Psalms: A Theological Commentary* (Minneapolis: Augsburg, 1984); idem, *The Psalms and the Life of Faith* (Minneapolis: Fortress, 1995); **M. Duggan,** *The Covenant Renewal in Ezra-Nehemiah (Neh 7:72b—10:40): An Exegetical, Literary, and Theological Study* (SBLDS 164; Atlanta: Society of Biblical Literature, 2001); **M. Greenberg,** *Biblical Prose Prayer as a Window to the Popular Religion of Ancient Israel* (Los Angeles: University of California Press, 1983); **H. Gunkel and J. Begrich,** *Introduction to Psalms: The Genres of the Religious Lyric of Israel* (Mercer Library of Biblical Studies; Macon, GA: Mercer University Press, 1998 [1933]); **L. Krinetzki,** *Israels Gebet im Alten Testament* (Der Christ in der Welt 6; Aschaffenburg: Pattloch, 1965); **R. A. Mason,** *Preaching the Tradition: Homily and Hermeneutics after the Exile* (Cambridge: Cambridge University Press, 1990); **P. D. Miller,** *They Cried to the Lord: The Form and Theology of Biblical Prayer* (Minneapolis: Fortress, 1995); **S. Mowinckel,** *The Psalms in Israel's Worship* (2 vols. in 1; New York: Abingdon, 1962 [1951]); **J. H. Newman,** *Praying by the Book: The Scripturalization of Prayer in Second Temple Judaism* (SBLEJL 14; Atlanta: Scholars Press, 1999); **M. Noth,** *The Deuteronomistic History* (JSOTSup 15; Sheffield: JSOT Press, 1981 [1957]); **O. Plöger,** "Reden und Gebete im Deuteronomistischen und Chronistischen Geschichtswerk," in *Festschrift für Günther Dehn zum 75. Geburtstag,* ed. W. Schneemelcher (Neukirchen: Kreis Moers, 1957) 35-49; ET, "Speech and Prayer in the Deuteronomistic and the Chronicler's Histories," in *Reconsidering Israel and Judah,* ed. G. N. Knoppers and J. G. McConville (SBTS 8; Winona Lake, IN: Eisenbrauns, 2000) 31-46; **H. G. Reventlow,** *Gebet im Alten Testament* (Stuttgart: Kohlhammer, 1986); **E. Staudt,** "Prayer and the People in the Deuteronomist" (Ph.D. diss.; Vanderbilt University, 1980); **M. A. Throntveit,** *When Kings Speak: Royal Speech and Royal Prayer in Chronicles* (SBLDS 93; Atlanta: Scholars Press, 1987); **G. von Rad,** *The Problem of the Hexateuch and Other Essays* (London: Oliver & Boyd, 1966)**; M. Weinfeld,** *Deuteronomy and the Deuteronomic School* (Oxford: Clarendon Press, 1972); **A. Wendel,** *Das freie Laiengebet im vorexilischen Israel* (Ex oriente lux 5-6; Leipzig: Pfeiffer, 1931); **C. Westermann,** *Elements of Old Testament Theology* (Atlanta: John Knox, 1982); idem, *Praise and Lament in the Psalms* (Atlanta: John Knox, 1981).

M. J. Boda

PRIESTS AND LEVITES

This article is divided into three major sections. First, a concise overview of the appearance of priests and Levites in the Historical Books of the OT is presented. This is followed by a closer look at some of the functions of the religious specialists in different books and contexts. One of the most crucial questions involves the relationship between the literary testimony and its underlying historical reality. Was the division of distinct groups of religious professionals a late development in Israelite religion, or is this division hinted at in early texts? Finally, a synthesis of the historical development of both groups in OT religion is attempted, followed by a concise conclusion.

1. Statistics of Hebrew *kōhēn* and *lēwî* in the Historical Books
2. Functions and Roles of Priests and Levites in the Historical Books
3. Does the Literary Testimony Reflect Historical Reality? Deductions and Reconstruction
4. Conclusion

1. Statistics of Hebrew *kōhēn* and *lēwî* in the Historical Books

The Hebrew terms *kōhēn,* "priest," and/or *lēwî,* "Levite," appear in every historical book of the OT. A look at the internal sequence of these books in the OT and their position in the canon provides some interesting trends (see Table 1).

The religious specialists priests and Levites appear in all the Historical Books. Books describing the earlier premonarchical and early monarchical period (such as Joshua, Judges, 1-2 Samuel, 1-2 Kings) include references to both groups, but they average only a ratio of 3 to 4 percent of verses mentioning either one or both of the two groups in connection to the overall sum of verses of the books. Later postexilic books (e.g., 1-2 Chronicles, Ezra-Nehemiah) show an increased interest, averaging a ratio of between 10 and 11 percent. This quantitative analysis does not necessarily translate into historical realities, since one has to take into account the literary and theological strategies and perspectives of their authors/editors. However, it demonstrates a certain trend, emphasizing the increased importance of religious groups in a changed historical context. Furthermore, it is interesting to note that both priests and Levites are often mentioned together, not only in later texts (e.g., 1 Chron 24:6; 2 Chron 13:9; 19:11; 23:8; 24:11; 34:9; Ezra 8:33; Neh 8:9; 10:39; 13:13) but also in earlier ones (e.g., Josh 3:3; 8:3; 21:1, 4; Judg 17:10, 12, 13; 18:19; 1 Kings 8:4; 12:31). This is significant because it suggests the coexistence of both groups. However, although their exact relationship has been the subject of a great amount of research (Leithart, 18-20; Schaper 2000, 303-8 and passim; Willi; Nurmela, 177-81; Crossley, 184-90; Cody; Grabbe, 52; Blenkinsopp, 92-98), no critical consensus position is in sight.

2. Functions and Roles of Priests and Levites in the Historical Books.

In order to grasp the picture that the biblical

Table 1.

Historical Book	Verses containing terms	Total verses in book	Percentage
Joshua	47	658	7.14%
Judges	20	618	3.23%
1 Samuel	27	811	3.32%
2 Samuel	9	695	1.29%
1 Kings	28	817	3.42%
2 Kings	35	719	4.86%
1 Chronicles	55	943	5.83%
2 Chronicles	93	822	11.31%
Ezra	31	280	11.07%
Nehemiah	63	405	15.55%

writers/editors of these books sketched, no specific reference will be made here to earlier pentateuchal prescriptive instructions dealing with the priesthood of Israel (*see DOTP*, Levi, Levites; Priest, Priesthood). The issue at hand is whether the (predominantly) pentateuchal prescriptive sections and the later descriptive texts found in the Historical Books match up or whether they exclusively contradict each other.

A review of the over four hundred verses containing either *kōhēn* or *lēwî* suggests different specific activities for each group. The Levites generally are in charge of carrying the *ark of the covenant when it has to be moved (Josh 3:3; 8:33; 1 Sam 6:15; 2 Sam 15:24; 1 Chron 13:2; 15:2, 4, 15, 26; 23:26, 27; 2 Chron 5:4; 35:3), although in a few instances the biblical authors do not explicitly refer to the Levites but seem to have utilized the more generic *kōhănîm*, "priests" (e.g., Josh 3:6, 8; 6:6, 12; 1 Kings 8:3). Support for this understanding can be found in the immediate context of the narratives that include specific references to Levites. Joshua 3:3 introduces the group responsible for the moving of the ark as *hakkōhănîm halĕwiyyim*, "the priests, the Levites." The NRSV translates here "levitical priests," while the NIV has "the priests, who are Levites." The remainder of the story refers solely to the "priests" as those responsible for the moving of the ark. A similar phenomenon can be found in 1 Kings 8:3, where the priests are said to have carried the ark during the dedication of the first temple. However, 1 Kings 8:4 details again both groups in the summary statement. In the course of this particular event

an additional specification about the moving of the ark should be considered. 1 Kings 8:6 emphasizes that while generally the Levites are in charge during the regular moving of the ark, priests are to carry the box *ʾel dĕbîr habbayit ʾel qōdeš haqqŏdāšîm*, "into the back chamber of the house [i.e., temple], into the holy of holies" (cf. 2 Chron 5:7). This division seems to be important and should be connected to the concept of grades of holiness, suggesting an intermediate place of the Levites in Israelite religious hierarchy (Jenson, 133).

A similar concept is found in the prescriptive section of 2 Chronicles 29:5, where the Levites are charged by King Hezekiah to sanctify themselves and also the house of Yahweh. Practically, it meant that all *hanniddâ*, "impurity," should be removed from the sanctuary. 2 Chronicles 29:12 contains the descriptive part detailing a list of the involved Levites. However, 2 Chronicles 29:16 provides some important details: while only the priests can go into the *lipnîmâ bêt yhwh*, "the inside of the house of Yahweh" the Levites receive the impure items and carry them outside the city confines. Judging from the textual data, it seems that over time Levites underwent a specialization or some type of division of responsibilities. The picture emerging from the early Historical Books (Joshua, Judges, 1 Samuel, 2 Samuel) suggests that the main job of the Levites was to carry and move the ark. However, once the temple was built and regular worship services were established, there was very seldom the need for moving the ark. The story of David's flight from Jerusalem during the rebellion of Absalom illustrates this point. While David's faithful flee the city, Levites carry out the ark until everybody is safely outside of the city (2 Sam 15:24). Levitical specialization included gate keeping (1 Chron 9:18, 26; 26:17) and guard duty involving martial aspects (2 Chron 23:6, 7; Neh 11:16 [see Spencer, 267-71]), baking (1 Chron 9:31), temple treasure supervision (1 Chron 26:20; 2 Chron 24:5, 6, 11; 31:12, 14; Ezra 8:29, 30, 33), choir and musician duty (1 Chron 9:33; 15:16, 17; 2 Chron 5:12; 7:6; 8:15; 29:25, 30; Neh 12:27), legal functions (2 Chron 19:8) and, increasingly important in a society that becomes more and more centrally administered and supervised, the teaching of the (oral and written) law (2 Chron 17:8; Neh 8:7, 9, 11; 9:4, 5). Under specific circumstances it appears that Levites were more closely involved in the sacrificial offerings. During the reform movement of Hezekiah, and due to the fact that not enough priests had sanctified themselves, Levites are called on to help with the sacrifices (2 Chron 29:34; 30:3, 15). However, an important distinction is made by the Chronicler: the priests do the blood manipulation (zōrĕqîm, "sprinkling") after receiving the sacrificial blood from the hands of the Levites (2 Chron 30:16; 35:11). Under specific circumstances Levites also functioned as supervisors of construction work done on the temple (2 Chron 34:12, 13; Ezra 3:9). Interestingly, the specific task of the reconstruction of the altar after the exile is undertaken by the priests (Ezra 3:2), perhaps due to the functional reason (i.e., the blood manipulation is mainly directed toward the altar) resulting in grades of holiness.

Specialization in priests is less elaborate. Priests focus on sacrifice and blood manipulation (2 Chron 29:22, 24; 30:16; 35:11), specialize in the production of the spice mixture utilized in the Israelite cult (1 Chron 9:30) and blow the trumpets on special occasions (Josh 6:4, 8, 9, 13, 16; 1 Chron 15:24; 16:6; 2 Chron 5:12; 7:6; 13:12, 14; 29:26), which apparently must be distinguished from the general musical accompaniment provided by the Levites in view of the importance of the šôpār, "trumpet," as a typical means of communication in OT times and in later Judaism (Braun, 47-50, 209-18). The purpose of the priestly blowing of the trumpet was either cultic or military. This military aspect of priestly ministry is noteworthy. Their involvement in national war is unmistakable: priests accompany the Israelites in Jericho (Josh 6) and are also present in the wars against the Philistines (1 Sam 14:19, 36). David's guerilla fighters are accompanied by Abiathar, the sole survivor of Saul's attack against the priests of Nob (1 Sam 23:9; 30:7). The close connection between priests and *kings needs to be underlined and seems to be a continuation of the priest's close association with earlier tribal leadership. Priest Eleazar appears with the tribal leader Joshua in the context of the land distribution ceremony (Josh 14:1) or as arbiter in a land dispute (Josh 17:4). Both Zadok and Abiathar work as spies for King David during the rebellion of Absalom (2 Sam 15:35; 17:15).

Sometimes priestly leadership is actively involved in political decisions, as is the case in Adonijah's rebellion, where priest Abiathar sides with the rebel (1 Kings 1:7, 19, 25, 42; 2:22), while Zadok remains faithful to King David (e.g., 1 Kings 1:8, 26, 32, 34).

Priests act on royal directions, as can be seen in the cases of distinct reforms in Israel (2 Chron 17:8; 19:8; 24:5, 6; 29:4; 35:10). Kings appoint priests and establish sanctuaries (1 Kings 12:31, 32; 2 Chron 11:15) and order cult modifications, such as the Assyrian altar that the high priest Uriah built on the instructions of King Ahaz (2 Kings 16:10-16). 2 Chronicles 29:11 provides an interesting perspective on the relationship between royalty and priests and Levites during the reform initiated by King Hezekiah at the end of the eighth century BCE: the king admonishes the religious specialists (2 Chron 29:4 mentions both groups) to "not be negligent," addressing them as bānay, "my sons." Sonship in this context focuses on the hierarchical relationship and dependence. However, this priestly dependence did not always translate into uncritical acceptance of royal orders. 2 Chronicles 26:17 describes how the priest Azariah and eighty priests of Yahweh, who were bĕnê ḥāyil, "men of valor" (lit., "sons of valor"), confront King Uzziah when he wants to burn incense to Yahweh. In the Joash narrative the high priest Jehoiada protects the rightful heir to the throne in the temple and sets up an elaborate counterinsurgency against the usurping Athaliah (2 Chron 22-23). Another priestly activity involves teaching and is parallel to the Levitical teaching ministry (2 Kings 17:27-28; 2 Chron 15:3; 17:8), although it seems to occur less frequently than the Levitical teaching ministry. Priests also bless the community (together with Levites in 2 Chron 30:27) during communal festivals such as Passover.

The Chronicler and Ezra-Nehemiah include a substantial number of priestly *genealogies or lists (e.g., 1 Chron 6:1-80; 9:10-34; 23:1-26; 2 Chron 29:12-14; Ezra 2:36-54; 7:1-5; Neh 7:39-56; 10:1-13; 11:10-23; 12:1-26), emphasizing the importance of impeccable blood relations for the exercising of the priestly and Levitical office. This focus within Israel is important and is to be distinguished from the function of genealogies in Genesis, which must be understood in the context of humanity as a whole (Andersen, 264) (*see DOTP*, Genealogies). As has been demonstrated (Bailey; Andersen; Levin 2001), genealogies are an important organizing factor on the literary level as well as serving to produce a particular view of the past that conformed to present needs (Aufrecht, 223). The Chronicler's positioning of the genealogies of Israel at the beginning defines his concept of *"Israel" both genetically and geographically (Levin 2001, 40). Both the inclusion of two lengthy sections dealing with genealogies of priests and Levites and the highest ratio (in the context of the Historical Books of the OT) of the appearance of the terms *priest* and *Levite* in the book suggest that the subjects of religion, temple and cult were high on the Chronicler's agenda, which may imply a possible connection to the temple (Levin 2003, 243).

In two instances the use of *kōhēn* in the Historical Books seems to be atypical and has resulted in distinct translations. 2 Samuel 8:18 suggests that the sons of David were priests (NJB; NRSV; NIV: "royal advisors"; NKJV: "chief ministers"). The statement seems to have caused problems also in antiquity, as the LXX translates it with *aularchai*, "princes of the court." It has been argued that *kōhănîm* here is a textual corruption of the original *sōkĕnîm*, "stewards" (Wenham 1975, 79-82). The parallel text in 1 Chronicles 18:17 contains a paraphrase suggesting that they were "the chief officials in the service of the king" (NRSV; lit., "the first for the hand of the king"). In support of this interpretation, the actual order of the list of David's officers is also of importance because David's sons do not appear together with the priests Zadok and Abiathar, but rather following the scribe and the head of the personal royal bodyguard.

A similar problem can be found in 1 Kings 4:5, where Zabud, the son of Nathan, is described as a *kōhēn rēʿeh hammelek,* "priest [and] friend of the king." Again, the LXX[B] and the Lucianic recension do not translate *kōhēn* and are

followed by the NJB. The double title is anomalous and could represent a textual conflation (Cogan, 202), although the evidence is not conclusive. The Chronicler does not provide a parallel to this section.

3. Does the Literary Testimony Reflect Historical Reality? Deductions and Reconstruction.

Matching the literary testimony to specific historical reality is not always an easy task. For example, inscriptional references to either *kōhēn* or *lēwî* from Palestine and belonging to Iron Age I/II or the Persian period are extremely scarce. To date, no epigraphical references to "Levites" have been found, while references mentioning *kōhēn* are rather limited and in view of their mostly unprovenanced nature need to be considered critically: the term appears on two unprovenanced seals (Avigad and Sass, 59-60) dated paleographically to the eighth century BCE, one of which refers to "[Ze]karyau, the priest of Dor," suggesting the existence of a Yahwistic sanctuary at Tel Dor (also Davies, 161). It also appears on a silver coin dated to the fourth century BCE and referring to a certain "Yohanan, the priest" (Davies, 255). Dating most probably to the late eighth century BCE, the term appears also on an unprovenanced ivory pomegranate inscription (Lemaire, 236-39; Davies, 118). To be sure, epigraphical material from Palestine is generally rather limited, and no official archive has yet been discovered. However, specific trends can be seen in the biblical texts. It appears that during the last part of the Late Bronze Age and Iron Age I (roughly from 1350-1000 BCE), the biblical texts do not distinguish consistently between priest and Levite. As Joshua 3:3 suggests, priests were Levites, and thus it appears that any reference to a priest involved (at least in the mind of the author/editor) generally is also a reference to Levite. This can be seen clearly in Joshua 18:7, where Levites are connected to the *kĕhunnat yhwh,* "the priesthood of Yahweh," in the context of not receiving ancestral lands. In a tribal society and in the process of settling down, Levites (= sons of Levi) are included in the land distribution and appear mainly in this context in the book of Joshua (Josh 13:14, 33; 14:3, 4; 18:7; 21). Although they do not receive a specific portion of the land, they are allotted some cities and the surrounding grazing lands (e.g., Josh 21:1, 3, 8, 10).

A similar situation can be found in the book

of Judges, where "Levite" first indicates ethnic relations. The picture gleaned from 1-2 Samuel and describing the late eleventh century and early tenth century BCE is similar, although the specific Levitical responsibility of carrying the ark is recognized (1 Sam 6:15; 2 Sam 15:24). This is not introduced as an innovative activity, but rather as a renovation of an earlier tradition (cf. Josh 3:3; 8:33). It seems that the political change from tribal society to more centralized royal administration not only resulted in a social stratification of the society at large, but also in the more distinct religious stratification (priests, Levites, singers, gatekeepers, temple servants) whereby the king functions as the official sponsor of the reorganization. Priestly loyalties are also important in this context, as can be seen in the Nob massacre during Saul's reign (1 Sam 22), as well as in the elevation of Zadok as high priest and the banning of Abiathar by David after the failed coup d'état of Adonijah (1 Kings 2:26-27, 35; 4:2). During this period two possible references to non-Levitical priests are mentioned (2 Sam 8:18; 1 Kings 4:5 [see 2 above]). Religious and political developments are closely interwoven in the period following the end of the united monarchy, as can be seen in the example of Jeroboam I's appointment of *bāmôt* (*"high places") priests who were not of Levitical descent (1 Kings 12:31; 2 Chron 11:15). The same class of priests is installed also at the northern national shrine in Bethel. The comment of the author/editor of 1 Kings is poignant: *wĕheʿĕmîd bĕbêt ʾēl ʾet-kōhănê habbāmôt ʾăšer ʿāśâ*, "and he placed [= installed] in Bethel the *bāmôt* priests that he had made" (1 Kings 12:32). The "making" of priests is connected to the "making" of shrines on high places and the "making" of a new feast calendar (1 Kings 12:31-32; the same Hebrew root is utilized). As a result, there is an exodus of Levitical priests from the northern kingdom toward Judah (2 Chron 11:14; 13:9). This information is not contained in the abbreviated version of 1 Kings 12:31-32, and it should be seen in the light of the Chronicler's particular postexilic *Sitz im Leben*. The focus is on Jerusalem, but Jerusalem in a changed and continually changing world (Japhet, 44).

The construction of the temple (*see* Solomon's Temple) represents a crucial point for Israelite priesthood, both theologically and administratively. With no more foreseeable movements of the ark of the covenant, Levites branch out into distinct specializations connected to the sacred space of the temple and under the patronage of the king. Consequently, the destruction of the first temple also required a redefinition of the priestly (and Levitical) ministry. Instruction seems to have become more important during the postexilic period, and due to the lack of royal leadership, priestly leadership became more important, although the high priestly office never was conceived primarily in terms of civic power (Rooke, 328-29). Priests and Levites always are recorded in different sections (e.g., Ezra 2:36, 40, 61; Neh 7:39, 43; 10:9, 10) with distinct headings. The tripartite division of Israelite religious spectrum (i.e., "lay" Israelite → Levite → priest) is reflected in ritual and legal texts from the Pentateuch (Duke, 647), and this division is also clearly visible in the Chronicler (Nurmela, 174-75). This division should not automatically be understood in terms of confrontation or competition, but rather should be seen in terms of complementation (Knoppers, 59). Priests were serving directly at the altar/temple, while Levites performed duties not directly connected to the sacrificial cult. The regular Israelite was both participant and observer in this ritual drama and represented the lowest grade of holiness in the biblical spectrum.

The reconstruction undertaken so far here has been mainly historical and based on the final text of the Hebrew Bible. Critical scholarship has suggested different reconstructions based predominantly on the traditional dating paradigm argued most forcefully by J. Wellhausen (Rehm, 297-98). Since then, pentateuchal scholarship has continued to further develop Wellhausen's famous JEDP hypothesis, particularly regarding the Priestly source (P). In 1893 A. Klostermann introduced the German term *Heiligkeitsgesetz* (H) as a description of a literary subunit of P involving Leviticus 17—26. In the following decades it was generally accepted that H predated P (Knohl, 2-7). However, more recently the Jewish scholar J. Milgrom (24-28), building on the work of I. Knohl, has suggested a radical change in this paradigm; using linguistic and ideological arguments, he has advanced the view that P antedates H and has situated H at the end of the eighth century BCE. The diachronic study of Biblical Hebrew (Hurvitz) has resulted in similar suggestions, emphasizing the preexilic date of the language of P, which in turn appears to challenge the validity of the overall historical-critical reconstruction of the Pentateuch as a whole. After all, if

P, representing the most complex (and thus late) and developed ritual and religious law system, should be dated to the eighth century BCE (or even earlier), what happened to the original sequence and some of the more important arguments of Wellhausen involving the concept of (religious) evolution from the more primitive to the more complex (*see DOTP*, Leviticus, Book of)? Other aspects of the hypothesis have also been questioned, such as the existence of separate J and E sources, resulting in a combined JE source (van Seters 1994; for more details *see DOTP*, Pentateuchal Criticism, History of; Source Criticism). This brief glimpse of current pentateuchal criticism suggests, as a minimum conclusion, internal fault lines of the traditional hypothesis that raise the question of "how much modification the Documentary Hypothesis can undergo while still maintaining something identifiable as the original hypothesis" (*DOTP*, 804).

It has been argued that the critical presuppositions and foundational ideas of traditional historical criticism are either faulty or in need of updating in light of archaeological or comparative data as well as an improved understanding of ancient literary conventions (*see DOTP*, Historical Criticism, and references there). Practically, this means that if one accepts a postexilic date of P, with its specific regulations for priests and Levites, then a different reconstruction of the history of the Israelite priesthood will result. However, as has been observed elsewhere, pentateuchal criticism appears to be in such a particular state of methodological upheaval, resulting in the questioning of assured results (Wenham 1991; 1999; Houtman; Carr; Rendtorff 1993; 1997; Zenger; Jüngling; Nicholson), that complete dependence on these results would in itself carry the danger of circular reasoning. This is not to suggest that one cannot posit an internal development of Israelite priesthood (in its distinct roles and positions) over the course of hundreds of years. As will be shown below, particularly concerning the functional aspect of priests and Levites, one can observe that changed historical realities (such as the introduction of monarchy, the division of the united monarchy into two separate and mostly competing political and socioreligious entities, the destruction of the temple as the focal point of Israelite religion, the experience of the exile and the required reorientation in the postexilic period) affected and to a certain degree also determined the functions of the involved religious specialists. However, it is doubtful that priestly purity as visible in P (utilizing the terminology of traditional pentateuchal criticism) should directly be translated into the patterns of social organization of Judean society during the Persian period (as suggested by Schaper), particularly when P's *Sitz im Leben* and compositional origin are in doubt.

Another interesting phenomenon that illustrates the complexity (and ambiguity) of the data is the origin of the priestly divisions, as suggested in 1 Chronicles 24:1-19. Placed in the period of David by the Chronicler, the origin of the organizational scheme is difficult to verify. The term *maḥălōqet*, "division, course," appears predominantly in 1-2 Chronicles, with the exception of Joshua 11:23; 12:7; 18:10, where it is used in parallelism to the noun *šēbet*, "tribe," and appears to have been used as a synonymous expression to, or perhaps a subdivision of, the tribal system. In 2 Chronicles the term appears in the context of Solomon's inauguration ritual of the newly built temple structure (2 Chron 5:11), as well as in the context of Joash's coronation (2 Chron 23:8). Later on, it reappears during the reign of Hezekiah in the context of his cult reform (2 Chron 31:2, 15, 16, 17), as well as during the later reform of Josiah prior to the exile (2 Chron 35:4, 10). Although this is not the place to discuss the historical reliability of the Chronicler (*see* Chronicler's History), H. G. M. Williamson's suggestion that this system (whose existence has been validated in external sources for the intertestamental period) originated in the closing years of the Persian period as a response to an imminent social and religious crisis should be considered for a moment. While recognizing that the available sources do not suggest any particular reason for the development of the system of twenty-four subdivisions, Williamson ventures to see its *Sitz im Leben* in the possible exodus of priests from Jerusalem to Shechem and the growing Samaritan community as well as an incident, reported by Josephus (*Ant.* 11.297-301), involving a major disruption of the temple structures and ritual during the governorship of the Persian Bagoas (Williamson, 267-68). In this reconstruction the appearance of the twenty-four priestly divisions in the narratives of David, Solomon, Joash, Hezekiah and Josiah represent only a literary and theological device, legitimizing the later use.

A distinct solution to the issue has been suggested by S. Japhet (423-25), who asserts that an authentic social development is reflected in the list of 1 Chronicles 24, providing a solution to the critical issue of priests returning from exile with only a single (and not even completed) temple functioning in Jerusalem (*see* Postexilic Temple). Japhet (423) seems to date the origins of the administrative organizational structure right at the beginning of the restoration period, which would integrate well with the evidence from Ezra-Nehemiah, where the technical term appears once in connection with Levitical divisions (Neh 11:36). However, there remains one problematic passage, Ezekiel 48:29, which employs the same term with the semantic nuance already found in Joshua (i.e., tribal portions/subdivisions). The close semantic link to tribal divisions may suggest a different solution to the problem: while the term was originally connected to tribal portions during the early history of Israel, its application to priestly and Levitical units may have been a conscious effort by King David to integrate the tribal reality of the early monarchy with the religious system already established earlier. This administrative integration obviously gave its originator (i.e., the king) an important stake in religious leadership, a fact borne out by the later narratives. In this scenario the appearance of the system in the Chronicler should not be understood primarily as a religious innovative response to a changed social context after the exile, but rather should be credited with some historicity. The fact of differing reconstructions should also be cause for caution, particularly when major emphasis is laid on the social context as the sole cause for religious change or innovation, as can be seen in the following examples.

R. Nurmela's (177-81) reconstruction of the role and position of Levitical priesthood posits a conflict between the southern and northern parts of the divided kingdom during the preexilic period that resulted in the Levites' inferior position due to their apostate conduct in the past. However, both the author/editor of Kings and the Chronicler inform their audience that priests too, as well as Levites, moved southward (1 Kings 12:31-32; 2 Chron 11:14; 13:9) as a result of Jeroboam's introduction of new sanctuaries (both local and state sanctuaries) and his installations of religious specialists that were solely dependent on him, regardless of bloodlines or earlier traditions. The suggestion by S. L. Crossley (184-90) that Levites should be understood first in terms of royal servants in the context of a client-patron relationship is intriguing but seems to minimize the clear nexus between temple/sanctuary and Levites. While it is true that Israelite kings appointed and demoted priests, and more especially the leadership positions, they did not seem to interfere directly in the ritual of the temple, an exception being King Ahaz's instruction to the high priest Uriah for the construction of an Assyrian altar type in the temple of Yahweh (2 Kings 16:10-16).

Reviewing the archaeological evidence from Iron Age II Palestine regarding cultic sites, Z. Zevit has pointed out the lack of consistency, lack of replicated architecture or of architectonic features, suggesting significant local variations in shrine or sanctuary design. He assumes that "one of the common threads uniting the disparate sites was a body of cultic know-how shared by various clans of Levites, a guild-caste of specialists in such lore" (Zevit, 656; cf. Schulz, 87-93). Although the final word on some of the supposed cult sites and their specific cultic morphology is not yet spoken (Gilmour), the importance of the religious specialists, connected by kinship bonds, needs to be kept in mind.

The recent suggestion by P. J. Leithart of a comprehensive definition of the priestly and Levitical ministry as "personal attendants to Yahweh in his house" (Leithart, 11-12; cf. Cody, 29), involving aspects such as mediation, protection, guarding, judging and teaching Torah, has some merits inasmuch as it provides a common rationale without necessarily leveling the distinguishing factors between the two groups. However, historical reliability or the reflection of actual historical contexts is only one aspect of biblical texts. They are first and foremost theological texts, without positioning theological versus historical. This theological focus may also explain omissions and some tensions that may exist between the pentateuchal picture of priests and Levites and the one gleaned from the Historical Books. As has been argued by M. Douglas (22) in a study of some of the contentious issues found in Ezra-Nehemiah and their relations to pentateuchal texts, the author/editor of Ezra-Nehemiah had a limited objective and was not trying to write a complete rule book for all aspects of religious law pertaining to priests/Levites in the postexilic period. In other words, historical realities and context determined to a certain degree the representation of religious practices and law. J. G. McConville (87) has sum-

marized the theological focus of the Deuteronomistic Historian (Dtr), traces of which can also
be found in the writings of the later Chronicler:
"For Dtr, priesthood is bigger than the Davidic
synthesis of palace and temple. When it falls
into Babylonian exile, it is the end of a chapter
in its story. But in Dtr's open-ended history,
there is no obituary for priesthood as such."

4. Conclusion.
The biblical picture of priests and Levites in the
Historical Books is complex and multifaceted,
but generally it seems to be in agreement with
pentateuchal legislation. However, an increased
adaptation, and to a certain degree contextualization, of these priestly laws to the historical realities of a later period can be observed. After
the construction of the first temple, Levites specialized in additional areas of priestly ministry.
Age restrictions seemed to have varied (Ezra 3:8:
twenty years; Leviticus—Num 4:3: thirty years),
most probably due to the fact that fewer Levites
seemed to be around after the exile (Neh 7:39,
43). The destruction of the first temple and its
subsequent theological processing changed Israelite religion profoundly. This theological
processing is clearly visible in the work of the
Chronicler and also in the earlier work comprising Joshua to 2 Kings. Both groups should be
considered "personal attendants to Yahweh in
his house," albeit in distinct functions according
to differing grades of holiness.

See also GENEALOGIES; HIGH PLACES; POST-
EXILIC TEMPLE; SOLOMON'S TEMPLE; ZADOK,
ZADOKITES.

BIBLIOGRAPHY. **T. D. Andersen,** "Genealogical Prominence and the Structure of Genesis,"
in *Biblical Hebrew and Discourse Linguistics,* ed.
R. D. Bergen (Dallas: Summer Institute of Linguistics, 1994) 242-66; **W. E. Aufrecht,** "Genealogy and History in Ancient Israel," in *Ascribe to
the Lord: Biblical and Other Studies in Memory of Peter C. Craigie,* ed. L. Eslinger and J. G. Taylor
(JSOTSup 67; Sheffield: JSOT, 1988) 205-35;
N. Avigad and B. Sass, *Corpus of West Semitic
Stamp Seals* (Jerusalem: Israel Academy of Sciences and Humanities; Israel Exploration Society; Institute of Archaeology, Hebrew University
Jerusalem, 1997); **N. A. Bailey,** "Some Literary
and Grammatical Aspects of Genealogies in
Genesis," in *Biblical Hebrew and Discourse Linguis-
tics,* ed. R. D. Bergen (Dallas: Summer Institute
of Linguistics, 1994) 267-82; **J. Blenkinsopp,**
*Sage, Priest, Prophet: Religious and Intellectual
Leadership in Ancient Israel* (LAI; Louisville: West-
minster/John Knox, 1995); **J. Braun,** *Die
Musikkultur Altisraels/Palästinas: Studien zu
archäologischen, schriftlichen und vergleichenden
Quellen* (OBO 164; Freiburg: Universitätsverlag;
Göttingen: Vandenhoeck & Ruprecht, 1999);
D. M. Carr, "Controversy and Convergence in
Recent Studies of the Formation of the Pen-
tateuch," *RelSRev* 23 (1997) 22-31; **A. Cody,** *A
History of Old Testament Priesthood* (AnBib 35;
Rome: Pontifical Biblical Institute, 1969); **M. Cogan,**
1 Kings (AB 10; New York: Doubleday, 2001);
S. L. Crossley, "The Levite as a Royal Servant
during the Israelite Monarchy" (Ph.D. diss;
Southwestern Baptist Theological Seminary,
1989); **G. I. Davies,** *Ancient Hebrew Inscriptions:
Corpus and Concordance* (Cambridge, MA: Cam-
bridge University Press, 1991); **M. Douglas,** "Re-
sponding to Ezra: The Priests and the Foreign
Wives," *BibInt* 10 (2002) 1-23; **R. K. Duke,**
"Priests, Priesthood," *DOTP* 646-55; **G. Gilmour,**
"The Archaeology of Cult in the Ancient Near
East: Methodology and Practice," *OTE* 13 (2000)
283-92; **L. L. Grabbe,** *Priests, Prophets, Diviners,
Sages: A Socio-Historical Study of Religious Special-
ists in Ancient Israel* (Valley Forge, PA: Trinity
Press International, 1995); **C. Houtman,** *Der Pen-
tateuch: Die Geschichte seiner Erforschung neben einer
Auswertung* (CBET 9; Kampen: Kok Pharos,
1994); **A. Hurvitz,** "Once Again: The Linguistic
Profile of the Priestly Material in the Pentateuch
and Its Historical Age; A Response to J. Blenkin-
sopp," *ZAW* 112 (2000) 180-91; **S. Japhet,** *I & II
Chronicles* (OTL; Louisville: Westminster/John
Knox, 1993); **P. P. Jenson,** *Graded Holiness: A Key
to the Priestly Conception of the World* (JSOTSup
106; Sheffield: JSOT, 1992); **H.-W. Jüngling,**
"Das Buch Levitikus in der Forschung seit Karl
Elligers Kommentar aus dem Jahre 1966," in
Levitikus als Buch, ed. H.-J. Fabry and H.-W.
Jüngling (BBB 119; Berlin: Philo, 1999) 1-45;
A. Klostermann, *Der Pentateuch* (Leipzig: A. De-
ichert [Georg Böhme], 1893); **I. Knohl,** *The Sanc-
tuary of Silence: The Priestly Torah and the Holiness
School* (Minneapolis: Fortress, 1995); **G. N.
Knoppers,** "Hierodules, Priests, or Janitors? The
Levites in Chronicles and the History of Israelite
Priesthood," *JBL* 118 (1999) 49-72; **P. J. Leithart,**
"Attendants of Yahweh's House: Priesthood in
the Old Testament," *JSOT* 85 (1999) 3-24; **A. Le-
maire,** "Une Inscription Paléo-Hébraïque sur
Grenade en Ivoire," *RB* 88 (1981) 236-39; **Y. Levin,**

"Understanding Biblical Genealogies," *CurBS* 9 (2001) 11-46; idem, "Who Was the Chronicler's Audience?" *JBL* 122 (2003) 229-45; **J. G. McConville,** "Priesthood in Joshua to Kings," *VT* 49 (1999) 73-87; **J. Milgrom,** *Leviticus 1—16* (AB 3; New York: Doubleday, 1991); **R. D. Nelson,** *Raising Up a Faithful Priest: Community and Priesthood in Biblical Theology* (Louisville: Westminster/ John Knox, 1993); **E. W. Nicholson,** "The Pentateuch in Recent Research: A Time for Caution," in *Congress Volume, Leuven 1989,* ed. J. A. Emerton (VTSup 43; Leiden: E. J. Brill, 1991) 10-21; **R. Nurmela,** *The Levites: Their Emergence as a Second-Class Priesthood* (SFSHJ 193; Atlanta: Scholars Press, 1998); **M. D. Rehm,** "Levites and Priests," *ABD* 4:297-310; **R. Rendtorff,** "Directions in Pentateuchal Studies," *CurBS* 5 (1997) 43-65; idem, "The Paradigm Is Changing: Hopes—and Fears" *BibInt* 1 (1993) 34-53; **D. W. Rooke,** *Zadok's Heirs: The Role and Development of the High Priesthood in Ancient Israel* (OTM; Oxford: Oxford University Press, 2000); **J. Schaper,** *Priester und Leviten im achämenidischen Juda: Studien zur Kult- und Sozialgeschichte Israels in persischer Zeit* (FAT 31; Tübingen: Mohr Siebeck, 2000); idem, "Priestly Purity and Social Organization in Persian Period Judah," *BN* 118 (2003) 51-57; **H. Schulz,** *Leviten im vorstaatlichen Israel und im Mittleren Osten* (Munich: Kaiser, 1987); **J. R. Spencer,** "The Tasks of the Levites: šmr and ṣbʾ," *ZAW* 96 (1984) 267-71; **J. van Seters,** *The Life of Moses: The Yahwist as Historian in Exodus— Numbers* (CBET 10; Louisville: Westminster/ John Knox, 1994); **G. J. Wenham,** "Method in Pentateuchal Source Criticism," *VT* 41 (1991) 84-109; idem, "Pondering the Pentateuch: The Search for a New Paradigm," in *The Face of Old Testament Studies: A Survey of Contemporary Approaches,* ed. D. W. Baker and B. T. Arnold (Grand Rapids: Baker; Leicester: Apollos, 1999) 116-44; idem, "Were David's Sons Priests?" *ZAW* 87 (1975) 79-82; **T. Willi,** "Leviten, Priester und Kult in vorhellenistischer Zeit: Die chronistische Optik in ihrem geschichtlichen Kontext," in *Gemeinde ohne Temple/Community without Temple: Zur Substituierung und Transformation des Jerusalemer Tempels und seines Kults im Alten Testament, antiken Judentums und frühen Christentum,* ed. B. Ego et al. (WUNT 118; Tübingen: Mohr Siebeck, 1999) 75-98; **H. G. M. Williamson,** "The Origins of the Twenty-four Priestly Courses," in *Studies in the Historical Books of the Old Testament,* ed. J. A. Emerton (VTSup 30; Leiden: E. J. Brill, 1979) 251-68; **E. Zenger,** "Das Buch Levitikus als Teiltext der Tora/des Pentateuch: Eine synchrone Lektüre mit diachroner Perspektive," in *Levitikus als Buch,* ed. H.-J. Fabry and H.-W. Jüngling (BBB 119; Berlin: Philo, 1999) 47-83; **Z. Zevit,** *The Religions of Ancient Israel: A Synthesis of Parallactic Approaches* (New York: Continuum, 2001).

G. A. Klingbeil

PRIMARY HISTORY. *See* DEUTERONOMISTIC HISTORY.

PROPAGANDA

In its political sense, propaganda is a systematic effort to conform social opinion to the ideologies or viewpoints of those who hold or seek power. Although the term *propaganda* sometimes is used pejoratively with reference to deliberate falsification, it need not imply wanton carelessness with facts and evidence.

The deliberations in this article concern the role of political propaganda in the early Davidic kingdom, a transitional milieu between the failed regime of *Saul and the rise of *David and *Solomon to power. The primary sources for exploring this issue are, unfortunately, meager by the standards of modern history, including little except the Hebrew books of *Samuel and *Kings. However, the value of these Hebrew sources is enhanced by comparing them to other expressions of royal propaganda from the ancient Near East. In this case, we will consider the role of political propaganda in the reigns of two seventh century Neo-Assyrian kings, Esarhaddon (680-669 BCE) and his son Assurbanipal (668-627 BCE).

1. Political Propaganda in the Ancient Near East: Examples from Neo-Assyria
2. Political Propaganda in Ancient Israel: The Apologies for David and Solomon
3. Conclusions

1. Political Propaganda in the Ancient Near East: Examples from Neo-Assyria.
In ancient *Assyria, as in all transregional states, political policies reflected four fundamental agendas: (1) legitimation of the regime's right to rule, (2) defense of the state's functional integrity, (3) replenishment and expansion of the state's natural and human resources, and (4) orderly transfer of power (Gottwald). Here we will briefly explore three Neo-Assyrian texts that illustrate the role of propaganda in

achieving these political ends.

1.1. "Esarhaddon's Apology": Securing Royal Authority and Succession. Assyrian kings commonly inscribed accounts of their great deeds in foundation deposits (buried in footings of new construction) and in public venues of the palace. The former were for the reading of the gods, while the latter were published to garner support for the administration among its royal courtiers and scholars. When these royal inscriptions are compared to our best reconstructions of actual history, their propagandistic character stands out in relief.

"Esarhaddon's Apology" appears in one section of his historical prism from Nineveh (Nin A [see *ANET*, 289-90]). A central objective of the text was to explain how Esarhaddon came to legitimately possess the throne when he was the youngest of the royal princes. According to the inscription, this unusual turn of events could be traced back to a decision of his father, Sennacherib, who chose the young Esarhaddon as his successor and validated this choice by consulting the gods through divination. Hence, the apology asserted that Esarhaddon's legitimacy rested in both royal and divine election (although, historically speaking, the fact that his mother was the dominant queen certainly helped his ascension). According to the inscription, the royal family at first supported the prince's legitimacy and even took loyalty oaths to that effect, but later they turned on Esarhaddon and slandered him, thus souring his father, Sennacherib, against him. Eventually there ensued an internecine struggle for the throne, and Sennacherib was killed in the fray. Although Esarhaddon claimed in the apology to have remained loyal to Sennacherib during these family hostilities, modern scholars suspect that Esarhaddon actually played a key role in the patricide. At any rate, it is clear enough that Esarhaddon bolstered his legitimacy by averring his own innocence in the coup and by pointing the finger of guilt at his bellicose brothers.

Under what circumstances was this propaganda published? Although it is natural to connect the piece with Esarhaddon's rise to power, we are fairly certain that it was written during his eighth regnal year (673 BCE) to confront two major issues. The first problem was Esarhaddon's decision to forgo the convention of primogeniture by selecting his younger son, Assurbanipal, as successor. It is very easy to see that the story of Esarhaddon's own rise to power, which followed the same path, would have provided ideological support for this choice. The second and perhaps more pressing issue was Esarhaddon's unsuccessful effort to conquer Egypt in the spring of 673 BCE. In Assyrian theology military failure was a chief indicator of divine disapproval and could prompt much talk of conspiracy and rebellion. In response to this threat Esarhaddon's historians composed a new edition of his achievements that accentuated his military might and emphasized the theological importance of keeping sworn oaths to support the king's regime. This idealistic portrayal of the king naturally excluded references to his military setbacks, as was the case in all Neo-Assyrian royal histories.

Archaeologists have discovered twenty copies of Esarhaddon's apology so far; this reflects the profound importance of its propaganda for the survival of his regime.

1.2. "The Sin of Sargon": Religious Reform as Political Propaganda. According to this tale (see Livingstone, 77-79), King Sennacherib of Assyria discovered through divination that his own father, Sargon II, had sinned against the gods by neglecting the cults of *Babylon. Sennacherib responded quickly to this revelation by assuming a new posture of worship and respect toward Babylon and its chief god, Marduk. As the text concludes, Sennacherib encourages his son to continue this pro-Babylonian policy, warning Esarhaddon to persevere through Assyrian resistance and "reconcile the gods of Babylonia with your [Assyrian] gods!"

Although modern scholars at first read this text as a historical report, it turns out that Sennacherib cannot be its historical protagonist, because he was infamous for one great sin: the destruction of Babylon. Assyria's turn toward Babylon should instead be associated with Sennacherib's son Esarhaddon, who worked hard to atone for his father's sins by rebuilding Babylon and restoring its temples. It follows that "The Sin of Sargon" was a fictional work of propaganda sponsored by Esarhaddon, whose goal was to promote the renewal of Babylon's cults in the face of resistance from Assyria's scribal elite (the pro-Assyrian party eventually responded with a fiction of their own, "The Underworld Vision of Kumma" [see Livingstone, 68-76]). The religious dimensions of this reform notwithstanding, a chief motive for the effort was political. Esarhaddon hoped that his actions would garner support in Babylon and so advance his empire's functional integrity in Babylonian regions to the south of Assyria proper. This political move was reinforced at about the same time by the appointment of Esarhaddon's two sons, Assurbanipal and Shamash-shum-ukin, to the thrones of Assyria and Babylon, respectively.

1.3. "Sarbanapal and Sarmuge": The Persistence of Neo-Assyrian Propaganda. This unusual papyrus from Upper Egypt (see *COS* 1.99:309-27) dates to the fourth or third century BCE. It was written in *Aramaic using an Egyptian demotic script and contains a New Year liturgy for Aramaic-speaking exiles in the region, but it also includes, for reasons that are not entirely clear, a tale about two competitors for the royal throne: Sarbanapal and Sarmuge. The tale is introduced by a lament over the ruins of Nineveh (Neo-Assyria's capital), a clue that has helped scholars recognize that Sarbanapal and Sarmuge are none other than Assurbanipal and Shamash-shum-ukin, Esarhaddon's rival sons who contended with each other for their father's throne. A little historical background is in order.

As we have noted, before Esarhaddon died, he divided his realm between his two sons, placing Assurbanipal on the throne in Assyria and Shamash-shum-ukin on the throne of Babylon. Although the division ostensibly was between equals, Assurbanipal covertly assumed control of Babylon, and when Esarhaddon died, he forced Shamah-shum-ukin to take an oath of loyalty and exacted new taxes from the Babylonians. The result was a Babylonian plot to rebel. At first Assurbanipal attempted to foil this plot through various political maneuvers, but when these failed, a full-scale siege of Babylon was ordered. The city eventually fell to Assyria, and Shamash-shum-ukin perished in the conflagration. Assurbanipal then carried many of the survivors back to Assyria as spoil, and he mutilated and flayed the bodies of Babylon's leaders.

Although this historical revue might suggest that Assurbanipal was a villain, our papyrus tells a different story. According to the legend, it was Sarbarnapal, not his father, who had appointed Sarmuge to the Babylonian throne, and the duty given to Sarmuge was not so much to rule Babylon as to insure that tribute was sent back to Assyria. When the ungrateful and devious Sarmuge rebelled against Assyria, Sarbanapal's response was measured and patient, and when war became necessary, he requested that Sar-muge be captured alive. When Sarmuge nonetheless died in the carnage of Babylon's fall, the story tells us that Sarbarnapal lamented the passing of his brother and, on advice from his generals, published this "true" account of the events that transpired. From this we can deduce that the account goes back to Assurbanipal himself, who had it composed to bolster his claim to the Babylonian throne. The original tale was historical insofar as it purported to be an account of actual events, but it was fictional insofar as its composition involved not only an ideological shaping of the story, but also outright fabrications of fact. That the tale became the stuff of popular legend is confirmed by its fascinating history, which began as a semihistorical piece of propaganda in the seventh century BCE and reached Egypt as a third-century Aramaic folktale wrapped in a ritual. The tradition appears in various guises in later Greek and Roman literature, as well as in modern works, such as Byron's tragedy "Sardanapalus" and Delacroix's famous painting "The Death of Sardanapalus." As we can see, the traditions generated by propaganda can be quite resilient.

1.4. Summary: Neo-Assyrian Propaganda. The following features were prominent in the royal propaganda of Neo-Assyrian kings: (1) emphasis was placed on the divine election of the king and on the legitimacy of his claim to the throne; (2) the king was depicted as a great warrior; (3) the king was depicted as religiously pious; (4) the assassinations of competitors in the royal household were covered up by portraying the king as compassionate and measured in his response to those who were killed; (5) presentations of the king's life were uniformly positive, a result that was achieved through the selective use of sources, the careful omission of troublesome facts and the invention of tradition; (6) publication of propaganda was most prominent during periods of threat to the regime's stability—that is, at its inception and during periods of rebellion or succession; (7) propaganda was disseminated to the elite classes through written texts and to the population at large through oral tradition; and (8) because of their earthy and popular appeal, the tales produced by Neo-Assyrian propaganda sometimes persisted in recognizable form until long after they had served the regime's political purposes.

As we will see, all of these features appear in the Hebrew accounts of the early Davidic dynasty.

2. Political Propaganda in Ancient Israel: The Apologies for David and Solomon.

The biblical story of King David is presently nested within the *Deuteronomistic History, a narrative composition that dates several centuries after the times of Saul, David and Solomon. Although this has prompted a few "minimalist" scholars to conclude that there is little of historical value in the biblical accounts of these Israelite kings, most modern scholars believe that the Deuteronomistic History had access to sources that can be traced back to the early monarchy. Perhaps the most important evidence for this conclusion is in fact the propagandistic character of the stories about David and Solomon.

2.1. The Story of David's Rise. The biblical account of the early Davidic dynasty contains two recognizable components: the "Story of David's Rise" (1 Sam 16—2 Sam 6) and the "Succession Narrative" (2 Sam 9—1 Kings 2). We will consider each in turn. The Story of David's Rise established David's legitimacy via the agency of *Samuel, the prophet-judge through whom God elected and then rejected Saul in order to replace him with David (see 1 Sam 13; 15—16). David's divine legitimacy was further reinforced by tales of his military prowess, which included not only a one-on-one triumph over the Philistine giant Goliath but also large-scale victories over enemy nations. When Saul subsequently recognized David as a competitor for his throne, the story's focus shifted to the conflict between them, in which Saul repeatedly attempted to kill David while David responded with kindness and respect for Saul. On several occasions David actually passed up opportunities to eliminate Saul because he viewed his predecessor as "God's anointed." Meanwhile, even Saul's own son and heir apparent, Jonathan, recognized that the future of Israel lay with David. During the unfolding drama, Saul disqualified himself again and again (e.g., 1 Sam 22; 28), while David faithfully spent his military energies righting Saul's previous wrongs (cf. 1 Sam 15; 30). In fact, David's loyalty to Saul endured to the bitter end; he avenged the deaths of Saul and Jonathan by killing an Amalekite who claimed responsibility and responding to their passing with a beautiful poetic elegy (2 Sam 1). David took a similar course of action when Saul's son Ish-Bosheth was assassinated by Rechab and Baanah (2 Sam 4).

The "Story of David's Rise" concludes with a portrait of David's piety as he transfers the holy *ark of the covenant to his newly conquered capital in Jerusalem (2 Sam 6). While we need not question the piety of his action, it appears that more than religion was at stake. The ark apparently was a cult object of northern provenance, suggesting that its relocation to David's capital was a political calculation akin to Esarhaddon's renewal of Babylon's cults. Unfortunately, it is difficult to discern whether most northerners would have appreciated David's religious overture or whether they would have viewed it as the oppressive act of a tyrant.

In this and in other respects, the account of David's rise to power reminds us of Neo-Assyrian propaganda. David is presented as a pious and divinely elected warrior-king who possessed an almost superhuman respect and love for his Israelite enemies. Like Esarhaddon in the death of Sennacherib, David avers that he was far from the scene when Saul, Jonathan and Ish-bosheth perished; like Assurbanipal, he laments the passing of those who challenged his power and authority. These positive images of an innocent David are underscored by juxtaposing them with unflattering portraits of his chief competitors for the throne. Readers are presented with a virtual catalogue of Saul's failures, among them his hot-headed demeanor, which "forced" David into an alliance with Israel's Philistine enemies (1 Sam 21). The trajectory of this propaganda suggests that it was crafted to answer two negative impressions of David held by the ancient audience: he was a murdering usurper and a traitor to the cause. If the Neo-Assyrian evidence is of comparative value here, we can surmise that David was perhaps not as innocent on these two points as the propaganda might suggest. Our perspective on this issue can be further refined by considering the "succession narrative," which follows in 2 Samuel 9—1 Kings 2.

2.2. The Succession Narrative. The title "Succession Narrative" presupposes that a primary theme of 2 Samuel 9—1 Kings 2 was to legitimate Solomon's succession to the throne. Not all scholars would agree with this assessment, but there are good reasons for considering it. The text begins with Solomon's birth and ends with Solomon's rise to the throne, and we cannot read the succession narrative without being struck by its litany of bloody murders, as Solomon's competitors from the house of Saul and from his own household (Amnon, Absolom, Adonijah) were gradually eliminated. Other men complicit with the competitors also met untimely deaths (e.g., Abner, Amasa, Joab). In the murders of these enemies David and Solomon are presented as uniformly innocent, either deeply regretting the deaths or ordering them as a last resort. David's mass killing of Saul's household was necessary to correct Saul's injustice against Gibeon (2 Sam 21), and Solomon's executions of Adonijah, Joab and Shimei came on the heels of their disloyalty to the regime (1 Kings 2). The most sensible explanation for these features is that the narrator wished to avoid the implication of David's and Solomon's roles in the systematic eradication of their regime's political opponents. He offered instead the more positive image of a wise and pious Solomon, the builder of Yahweh's first temple (1 Kings 3—10). Propaganda of this sort must have been an important element in Solomon's effort to secure his hold on Judah and to expand his influence into the "offended" regions of Benjamin and greater Israel. Solomon's thirst for propaganda would have been greater still if, as many scholars believe, his selection as David's successor was an alibi for the assassination of his older brother Adonijah (1 Kings 1-2) (see Halpern; McKenzie).

To sum up, most biblical scholars believe that the story of David's rise and the succession narrative were propagandistic apologies composed to promote the regimes of David and Solomon. The authors of these pro-Davidic traditions shaped their portraits of the two kings by accentuating their best qualities, eliminating negative features from their lives, and highlighting the failures of their opponents. The best evidence for the historical value of these accounts rests precisely in their propaganda, which demands a date close to the events they portray.

2.3. "Court History" or "Succession Narrative"? A number of modern scholars would prefer to call the succession narrative the "Court History," primarily because the text's narrative vortex revolves around David's troublesome conflict with Absalom rather than around Solomon himself. Some of these scholars admit that Solomon's succession is an important theme in our present edition of the court history, but they attribute this effect to later editing of the text by the Deuteronomistic Historian (McKenzie). A few other scholars believe that David comes off so poorly in the court history that it must be a composition written *against* him. On this reading, the appropriate context for such a composition would have been

during the postexilic period, when some factions in Judaism resisted efforts to restore the Davidic monarchy (Van Seters). This last view has in its favor the undeniably negative portrayal of David in the incident with Bathsheba and Uriah (2 Sam 11—12), but this story can also serve as evidence of Solomon's Davidic legitimacy or as a theological explanation for the troubles that marred David's house during Solomon's rise to the throne.

2.4. Davidic Propaganda in the Deuteronomistic History and in Chronicles. If the Deuteronomistic History was composed several centuries after the united monarchy, how did these older accounts of David and Solomon come to reside in this history? One approach, popular in continental scholarship, suggests that the Deuteronomistic Historian himself composed the stories of David and Solomon, using fragmentary traditions from the early monarchy that he generously edited and supplemented according to his own purposes. The chief drawback of this thesis is that it does not adequately explain the profound apologetic shape of the narratives, which best fits a period close to the time of David and Solomon. The more common explanation is that the Deuteronomistic Historian found these stories from the nascent monarchy among his sources and incorporated them, with minor editing, into his history. In this account of the facts, the Deuteronomistic Historian must have found the sources adequate for his theological purposes even in their raw form. This is quite feasible because images of a righteous and successful David, and of a cursed and evil Saul, would have cohered nicely with the Deuteronomistic Historian's retributive theory that blessing was contingent on one's obedience to the Deuteronomic law. Implicit in this assessment of the Deuteronomistic History is that its author took these sources from the early monarchy at face value; little did he know that originally they were the tools of political controversy.

We may posit the following situation. Because early editions of the Deuteronomistic History seem to have promised David an eternal dynasty (so Nelson; Cross; cf. 2 Sam 7), the exile of Israel's king to Babylon in 597 BCE raised new theological questions for Judaism. Editors attempted to answer these questions by proffering a new edition of the history (Deuteronomistic History[2]) that conditioned God's promise on the obedience of David's sons (1 Kings 2:1-12), although Psalm 89 suggests that some Jews found this solution unsatisfying. Several decades later the exile's end prompted the renewal of Judaism's temple cult and a new fervor for restoring the Davidic dynasty. The Hebrew Chronicler spoke to this circumstance by composing a new edition of the story of David and Solomon that expunged from the account every royal fault while recounting in glorious detail the great achievements of their regime (*see* Chronicler's History). Why did the Chronicler require this faultless image of the kings? It is possible that the Chronicler wished to invigorate the movement to restore David's dynasty, but, as is well-known, he was also focused on matters of temple and cult. For this reason it is possible, perhaps even likely, that his interest in David and Solomon was not in their dynasty per se so much as in their roles as the builders of Yahweh's first temple.

3. Conclusions.

It has been proposed that the biblical account of David's rise and reign in the Deuteronomistic History rests mainly on old narrative sources that were composed during the early monarchy as propaganda for David and Solomon. The apologetic nature of this literature is further suggested by comparing it with political propaganda from Neo-Assyria. Ancient authors portrayed their kings as wise, strong, compassionate, pious and successful rulers, and idealized these portraits by omitting more troubling details and by revising or even employing historical fiction. Israel's continuing interest in the monarchy prompted an ongoing reformulation of the Davidic traditions so that they could serve the needs of Jews who lived near the monarchy's end (Deuteronomistic History[1]), during the exile (Deuteronomistic History[2]) and after the exile (Chronicler's History).

See also DAVID; HISTORIOGRAPHY, OLD TESTAMENT; INNERBIBLICAL EXEGESIS; KINGS AND KINGSHIP; NARRATIVE ART OF ISRAEL'S HISTORIANS.

BIBLIOGRAPHY. **F. M. Cross,** *Canaanite Myth and Hebrew Epic* (Cambridge, MA: Harvard University Press, 1973) 274-89; **A. de Pury and T. Römer,** *Die sogenannte Thronfolgegeschichte Davids: Neue Einsichten und Anfragen* (OBO 176; Freiburg: Universitätsverlag; Göttingen: Vandenhoeck & Ruprecht, 2000); **J. Ellul,** *Propaganda: The Formation of Men's Attitudes* (New York: Knopf, 1965); **N. K. Gottwald,** *The Politics of Ancient Israel* (Louisville: Westminster/John Knox, 2001); **B. Halpern,** *David's Secret Demons: Messiah, Murderer, Traitor, King* (Grand Rapids: Eerdmans, 2001); **T. Ishida,** "The Succession Narrative and Esarhaddon's Apology: A Comparison," in *Ah, Assyria . . . : Studies in Assyrian History and Ancient Near Eastern Historiography Presented to Hayim Tadmor,* ed. M. Cogan and I. Eph'al (Jerusalem: Magnes, 1991) 166-73; **M. T. Larsen,** *Power and Propaganda: A Symposium on Ancient Empires* (Mesopotamia 7; Copenhagen: Akademisk Forlage, 1979); **A. Livingstone,** ed., *Court Poetry and Literary Miscellanea* (SAA 3; Helsinki: Helsinki University Press, 1989) 68-79; **R. A. Mason,** *Propaganda and Subversion in the Old Testament* (London: SPCK, 1997); **P. K. McCarter Jr.,** "The Apology of David," *JBL* 99 (1980) 489-504; **S. L. McKenzie,** *King David: A Biography* (Oxford: Oxford University Press, 2000); **R. D. Nelson,** *The Double Redaction of the Deuteronomistic History* (JSOTSup 18; Sheffield: JSOT, 1981); **M. Noth,** *The Deuteronomistic History* (JSOTSup 15; Sheffield: JSOT, 1981 [1957]); **L. Rost,** *Die Überlieferung von der Thronnachfolge Davids* (BWANT 3/6; Stuttgart: Kohlhammer, 1926); **S. Seiler,** *Die Geschichte von der Throngefolge Davids (2 Sam 9-20; 1 Kön 1-2): Untersuchungen zur Literarkritik und Tendenz* (BZAW 267; Berlin: de Gruyter, 1998); **R. C. Steiner,** "The Aramaic Text in Demotic Script: The Liturgy of a New Year's Festival Imported from Bethel to Syene by Exiles from Rash," *JAOS* 111 (1991) 362-63; idem, "Papyrus Amherst 63: A New Source for the Language, Literature, Religion and History of the Arameans," in *Studia Aramaica: New Sources and Approaches,* ed. M. J. Geller et al. (JSSSup 4; Oxford: Oxford University Press, 1995) 199-207; **R. C. Steiner and C. F. Nims,** "Ashurbanipal and Shamash-shum-ukin: A Tale of Two Brothers from the Aramaic Text in Demotic Script," *RB* 92 (1985) 60-81; idem, "You Can't Offer Your Sacrifice and Eat It Too: A Polemical Poem from the Aramaic Text in Demotic Script," *JNES* 43 (1984) 89-114; **H. Tadmor,** "Autobiographical Apology in the Royal Assyrian Literature," in *History, Historiography and Interpretation: Studies in Biblical and Cuneiform Literatures,* ed. H. Tadmor and M. Weinfeld (Jerusalem: Magnes, 1983) 36-57; **H. Tadmor, B. Landsberger and S. Parpola,** "The Sin of Sargon and Sennacherib's Last Will," *SAAB* 2 (1989) 3-51; **J. Van Seters,** *In Search of History: Historiography in the Ancient World and the Origins of Biblical History* (New Haven: Yale University Press, 1983); **K. W. Whitelam,** "The Defense of David," *JSOT* 29 (1984) 61-87; **R. N. Whybray,** *The Succes-*

sion Narrative: A Study of 2 Samuel 9-20 and 1 Kings 1-2 (SBT 9; London: SCM, 1968).

K. L. Sparks

PROPHETIC FORMS OF SPEECH. *See* WORD OF GOD.

PROPHETS AND PROPHECY

Whereas the Christian tradition reserves the label "prophetic" for the last part of its OT canon, Isaiah through Malachi, the second division of the Hebrew Bible, the Prophets *(Nevi'im),* additionally includes the historical writings Joshua, Judges, 1-2 Samuel and 1-2 Kings.

This wider application of the term *prophetic* makes good sense because the Historical Books (which in the Christian tradition also include Chronicles, Ezra and Nehemiah) portray several individuals performing prophetic roles. Indeed, it has been noted that these books "contain phraseology and perspectives that betray the presence of . . . writers/editors who valued highly the work of Israel's prophets" (Petersen 2002, 232).

1. The Identification of a Prophet
2. Israelite Prophecy in Ancient Near Eastern Context
3. Individual Prophets
4. Prophetic Perspectives

1. The Identification of a Prophet.
Like the rest of the OT, the Historical Books employ a variety of terms to refer to things prophetic. The most frequent expression, and also the most difficult to define, is *nābî'*. It usually is seen as being derived from the Akkadian verb *nabû,* "to call, proclaim," but there is no agreement as to whether the term is to be understood actively ("speaker, proclaimer") or passively ("called one"). The term *seer, rō'eh,* by contrast, stresses the prophets' receipt of visions. According to 1 Samuel 9:9, it is the older title for a *nābî'* (see also 2 Kings 17:13). The expression *ḥōzeh* similarly reflects the visionary character of prophecy.

A prophet is also frequently referred to as a "man of God." Prophets so described include Moses (Josh 14:6; 2 Chron 30:16), *Samuel (1 Sam 9), *Elijah (1 Kings 17:18-24; 2 Kings 1:9-13), *Elisha (2 Kings 4—8) and the unnamed man of God in 1 Kings 13.

The application of the title to *David in 2 Chronicles 8:14 and Nehemiah 12:24, 36 suggests that tradition subsequently assigned David a prophetic role. This corresponds with the Chronicler's perception of Heman (1 Chron 25:5), Asaph (2 Chron 29:30) and Jeduthun (2 Chron 35:15) as seers, and it contributes to the Chronicler's tendency to mention prophets, such as Azariah (2 Chron 15:1-7) and Oded (2 Chron 28:9-11), who are otherwise unknown.

2. Israelite Prophecy in Ancient Near Eastern Context.
The phenomenon of prophecy was not restricted to ancient Israel; its neighbors had their own oracular speakers. This is confirmed not only by OT references to non-Yahwistic prophets, but also by a significant number of ancient Near Eastern texts. References to prophets are found throughout Syria-Palestine, in places such as Emar on the Middle Euphrates River, Aram, Ammon, Phoenicia, Anatolia and Mesopotamia. Particularly noteworthy are the second-millennium texts discovered at Mari, as well as the Neo-Assyrian prophetic texts.

Space does not permit a detailed discussion of prophecy in the ancient Near East (see Huffmon; Nissinen 2000; Nissinen et al. 2003), but some comments on the relationship between prophecy in our textual corpus and in Israel's neighboring cultures are in order. One commonality between Israel and Mari is the occurrence of ecstatic prophets (see 1 Sam 10:5; 19:20; 1 Kings 18:26-28), for which Mari, unlike the OT, even has a separate term. Ecstasy has been described as "a fundamental dimension of the encounter with the deity" (Miller, 101), but sometimes it is regarded as a defining feature of Israelite war prophecy that is unattested in Judah (Blenkinsopp, 53-54).

Another similarity is the need for authentication of a prophecy, which at Mari was achieved by checking a prophet's lock of hair. In the Historical Books the problem is illustrated not only by the clash between Elijah and the prophets of Baal (1 Kings 18), but also by Micaiah's confrontation with Ahab's court prophets (1 Kings 22:5-28). This incident, together with *Jeremiah's condemnation of the prophets of peace (Jer 6:13-14; 8:10-11; 28:5-9), suggests that contrary to Mari and the Neo-Assyrian texts where salvation prophecy was the norm, in Israel such oracles were regarded with suspicion, at least by those responsible for our textual corpus.

Since the 1980s there has been a tendency to understand Israel's prophets in terms of their social, religious and political world (Carroll; Culley and Overholt; Kselman; Lang; Petersen 1981; Wilson 1980). This perspective, which draws attention to the formative effect of the prophets' own location, has contributed significantly to our understanding of Israelite prophecy. Nevertheless, P. D. Miller rightly insists that "the word of the prophet to [his] society is rooted firmly in a relationship to the divine effecting a mediation of the divine word to the contemporary community of the prophet" (Miller, 101).

3. Individual Prophets.

Although the OT traces the beginnings of prophecy back to Moses (Deut 18:15-18), prophecy in the strict sense begins with Samuel (see Acts 3:24). Prior to him, Deborah, one of Israel's *judges, is called a "prophetess," *nĕbî᾽â* (Judg 4:4); an anonymous prophet appears in Judges 6:7-10; and there is the unnamed man of God whose condemnation of Eli's priesthood (1 Sam 2:27-36) leads to Samuel's call (1 Sam 3).

3.1. Samuel. *Samuel's role resembles that of Israel's judges (1 Sam 7:15-17; 11:12), but the texts also stress his prophetic function, calling him a prophet (1 Sam 3:20; 2 Chron 35:18), a seer and a man of God (1 Sam 9; 1 Chron 9:22). He is thus a transitional figure representing the succession of the judges by the prophets.

Ministering in the sanctuary at *Shiloh, Samuel is portrayed as a cultic prophet (1 Sam 3:21) who nevertheless could condemn the cult and its personnel. He is also presented as a paradigm of prophetic opposition to kingship (1 Sam 13:8-15; 15:1-31), and he appears to have been in charge of a group of ecstatic prophets (1 Sam 10:5; 19:20). However, this last point depends on understanding the *nip῾al* and *hitpa῾el* forms of the verb *nb᾽* as denoting ecstatic prophecy, which some have questioned, arguing that these verbal forms merely indicate that the people in question acted or behaved like prophets.

3.2. Nathan and Gad. Following the establishment of the monarchy in Israel, we find court prophets, who, like their counterparts in places like Mari, had close links with the royal court. *Nathan, who was consulted by David about the king's plans to build a temple (2 Sam 7:1-17; 1 Chron 17:1-15), is an example of this type of prophet. Yet the links with the royal court did not prevent these prophets from censuring the king, as is illustrated by Nathan's condemnation of David's conduct in the affair with Bathsheba (2 Sam 12:1-25). Nathan's influence at court is

further demonstrated by his critical involvement in the ousting of the royal pretender Adonijah and the institution of *Solomon as David's successor (1 Kings 1:5-53).

Gad, another court seer (2 Sam 24:11; 1 Chron 21:9; 2 Chron 29:25), was associated with David from before his accession to the throne (1 Sam 22:5) until the end of his reign, when he rebuked the king because of his census (2 Sam 24:11-17; 1 Chron 21:9-17).

3.3. From Ahijah to Jehu. From the split of the kingdom after Solomon's death (c. 925 BCE) to the fall of Samaria (722 BCE), references to prophets are effectively restricted to the northern kingdom (Wilson 1995, 90). First, we find Ahijah, who designated *Jeroboam king of the ten tribes of Israel (1 Kings 11:29-39). Jeroboam also enjoyed the prophetic support of Shemaiah, who discouraged *Rehoboam of Judah from warring against the northern kingdom (1 Kings 12:22-24; 2 Chron 11:2-4). Later on, though, Jeroboam was condemned by Ahijah for his religious apostasy (1 Kings 14:1-18).

The ensuing short-lived dynasty of Baasha was similarly condemned by Jehu ben Hanani (1 Kings 16:1-13). Prior to that, 1 Kings 13 recounts a story involving an unnamed man of God and an equally anonymous old prophet. In the first episode (1 Kings 13:1-10) the man of God delivers an oracle against Jeroboam's altar at *Bethel that predicts its defilement by *Josiah almost three hundred years later. Its fulfillment is duly narrated in 2 Kings 23:16. Some regard the story as a *vaticinium ex eventu*, but Wilson (1980, 187-88) has pointed to tensions between the prophecy and Josiah's actions in 2 Kings 23, arguing that 1 Kings 13, which condemns Jeroboam's religious policies of reviving the old shrines at *Dan and Bethel, reflects old traditions.

The second episode (1 Kings 13:11-32), in which an old prophet sets out to establish whether the man of God can recognize a false oracle that goes against his original divine instructions (1 Kings 13:14-19), deals with the issue of false prophecy. The point of the story is that prophets ought to obey their divine instructions even when faced with contradictory oracles.

In 1 Kings 20, an account of two military encounters between Israel and Aram, another unnamed prophet (1 Kings 20:13-14, 22) and an anonymous man of God (1 Kings 20:28) deliver oracles of salvation in order to encourage King Ahab in a time of war; in 1 Kings 20:35-43 a member of the "sons of the prophets" lures Ahab into pronouncing judgment on himself for violations against the prescriptions for holy war.

3.4. Elijah. The most famous prophet apart from the writing prophets (see, e.g., Mal 4:5; Mt 17:1-13; Mk 15:35-36; Jn 1:21, 25; Rom 11:2; Jas 5:17) was active during the reigns of Ahab, Ahaziah and Jehoram, a period when the *Omri dynasty flourished in Israel. Although *Elijah calls himself a prophet only in 1 Kings 18:22 (see also 1 Kings 18:36; 2 Chron 21:12), the narrator instantly highlights his prophetic credentials, stressing that "the word of the LORD came to him" (1 Kings 17:2, 8).

If there is any story in the Historical Books that epitomizes the clash of Israel's religion with the religious practices of its neighbors, it is Elijah's confrontation with the prophets of Baal in 1 Kings 18. Yet the polemic against the veneration of Baal is not confined to this chapter, but rather pervades the Elijah and Elisha stories as a whole (Bronner).

According to the mythological texts from Ras Shamra (c. 1350 BCE), Baal was the god of wind and weather, who dispensed dew, rain and snow and the attendant fertility of the soil. However, having already made it clear in 1 Kings 17:1 that the drought afflicting the country had been foretold by Yahweh's prophet Elijah, the narrator now stresses, in an account redolent with irony (e.g., 1 Kings 18:27), that it is Yahweh, not Baal, who sends the life-giving rain (1 Kings 18:41-46).

Yahweh's superiority over Baal is also emphasized by many of the miracle stories involving Elijah and Elisha, which portray Israel's god as the one who sustains those in need (1 Kings 17:1-7, 8-16; 2 Kings 4:1-7, 38-44), controls human fertility (2 Kings 4:8-17), heals the sick (2 Kings 5) and raises the dead (1 Kings 17:17-24; 2 Kings 4:18-37).

Polemical overtones are also to the fore in 1 Kings 19, where the fleeing Elijah encounters Yahweh at Mount Horeb (1 Kings 19:8), the place where many generations ago Yahweh had appeared to Moses. Like Moses, Elijah encounters wind, earthquake and fire. However, in contrast to the theophany in Exodus 19—20, God was not present in any of these natural elements; instead, he appeared through a "sound of sheer silence" (1 Kings 19:11-12).

This deviation from tradition appears in a different light once we recognize that Baal too was understood to appear through wind, earthquake and fire. While many of the Elijah and Elisha stories emphasize Yahweh's superiority over Baal, 1 Kings 19 thus makes the additional point that Yahweh is also very different from the Canaanite deity.

In the story about Naboth's vineyard (1 Kings 21), Elijah's role resembles that of Nathan when he confronted David after the adultery with Bathsheba. Although Baal worship is not to the fore in this episode, Jezebel's decisive influence and the general context of the Elijah stories suggest that the violation of a family's land holdings (1 Kings 21:3) was understood by the writer as a consequence of the cultural symbiosis of Yahwism and Baalism, which the marriage of Ahab and Jezebel represented.

3.5. Elisha. *Elisha is first introduced in 1 Kings 19:16-21, but the stories about the one who inherited Elijah's prophetic mantle (1 Kings 19:19) are found in 2 Kings 2—13. When, in line with the law that accords the firstborn son a double share of the estate (Deut 21:17), Elisha asks for a double share of Elijah's spirit (2 Kings 2:9-10), his prophetic succession is conceptualized in terms of sonship.

Having been active during the reigns of Jehoram, Jehu, Jehoahaz and Jehoash, Elisha interacted with kings but, like Elijah, he was also particularly involved with Israel's poor (e.g., 2 Kings 4:1-7). He appears as an important political figure who was integrally involved in the revolt that led to Jehoram's assassination and the accession of Jehu (2 Kings 9—10). At the same time, the texts focus on his role as charismatic miracle worker.

Various passages portray Elisha as leader and teacher of a group of prophets known as "sons of the prophets" (2 Kings 2:1-18; 4:1-7, 38-41; 5:22; 6:1-7; 9:1-10). Similar groups appear in 1 Kings 20:35-43 and Amos 7:14, which, together with the mention of the prophets led by Samuel, suggests that they were a recurring phenomenon in the history of Israelite prophecy (cf. Is 8:16). These passages and the references to Ahab's four hundred court prophets in 1 Kings 22:6, 10 also indicate that prophets were not necessarily solitary figures.

3.6. From Micaiah ben Imlah to Huldah. Like Elijah and Elisha, Micaiah found himself in conflict with the Omrides, but his confrontation with Ahab's court prophets also serves as a classic example of interprophetic conflict, which in this case was resolved by the verification or falsification of their predictions (1 Kings 22:5-28; 2 Chron 18:4-27). Another way of interpreting this passage is to see it in terms of the opposition between central and peripheral prophets, for Micaiah is portrayed as someone who had to be brought in from outside (Wilson 1980, 208-12).

Interestingly, the prophetic stories in our textual corpus focus on prophets who did not bequeath us written collections of oracles. Apart from *Isaiah, the only writing prophets to be mentioned are Jonah (2 Kings 14:25), Jeremiah (2 Chron 36:12), Haggai and Zechariah (Ezra 5:1; 6:14). Yet, although we do not possess the written legacies of prophets such as Nathan, Gad and others, the Chronicler suggests that some additional prophetic writings once did exist (1 Chron 29:29; 2 Chron 9:29; 12:15; 13:22; 33:19).

Whereas the book of Isaiah associates Isaiah ben Amoz with the reigns of Uzziah, Jotham, Ahaz and *Hezekiah (Is 1:1; cf. 2 Chron 26:22; 32:32), in 2 Kings he appears only in connection with the resistance to the Assyrians during Hezekiah's reign (2 Kings 18:13—19:37; Is 36—37; also 2 Chron 32:1-23) (see Wilson 1995, 93-94). The remaining passages in 2 Kings recount the oracles that Isaiah delivered to Hezekiah during the king's illness (2 Kings 20:1-11; cf. Is 38) and his prediction of Babylonian exile (2 Kings 20:12-19; cf. Is 39).

The narratives in 2 Kings 18—20 and Isaiah 36—39 consistently refer to Isaiah as a *nābîʾ*, "prophet" (2 Kings 19:2; 20:1, 11, 14; Is 37:2; 38:1; 39:3), although this title seems to have been avoided throughout the rest of the book of Isaiah. Thus Isaiah is presented as the successor of prophets such as Nathan, Elijah and Elisha. Another feature linking him with these earlier prophets is his role as miracle worker (2 Kings 20:7, 10-11; Is 38:7-8, 21).

According to the Historical Books, Huldah is the last prophet before the destruction of Jerusalem, which she foretells in an oracle addressed to Josiah (2 Kings 22:14-20; 2 Chron 34:22-28).

4. Prophetic Perspectives.

Prophecy clearly was a matter of great importance to the writers/editors of the Historical Books. This is evident not only in the amount of space devoted to figures such as Elijah and Elisha, but also in comments stressing that certain events happened "according to the word of the LORD" issued through the prophets. This per-

spective is especially prominent in Kings (1 Kings 14:18; 15:29; 16:12; 17:16; 2 Kings 1:17; 10:17; 14:25; 23:16; 24:2), but comparable statements also appear in 1 Chronicles 11:3 and 2 Chronicles 35:6. When the narrator reflects on the sinfulness and eventual destruction of the northern kingdom, he similarly highlights the prophets' role, noting that "the LORD [had] warned Israel and Judah by every prophet and every seer" (2 Kings 17:13).

Prophets appear at crucial moments in Israel's history, anointing kings (1 Sam 16:13; 1 Kings 19:15), acting as their military advisors (1 Kings 22; 2 Kings 3), but also dethroning some of Israel's rulers (1 Sam 15:28; 1 Kings 14:7-18; 21:19). Indeed, the narrator leaves us with the impression that the prophets were one of Israel's most important oppositional forces (Koch).

Thus D. L. Petersen rightly notes that "much in the former prophets seems to have been influenced by a perspective that took with utmost seriousness the power of the prophets and their words" (Petersen 2002, 233). Attempts to explain this phenomenon either have postulated the incorporation of prophetic sources or records (Campbell; Campbell and O'Brien, 24-33) or have suggested a prophetic redaction of the *Deuteronomistic History, which was responsible for the addition of the prophetic elements (Dietrich).

See also ELIJAH; ELISHA; ISAIAH; JEREMIAH; KINGS AND KINGSHIP; NATHAN; SAMUEL.

BIBLIOGRAPHY. **J. Blenkinsopp**, *A History of Prophecy in Israel* (2nd ed.; Louisville: Westminster/John Knox, 1996); **L. L. Bronner,** *The Stories of Elijah and Elisha as Polemics against Baal Worship* (POS 6; Leiden: E. J. Brill, 1968); **A. F. Campbell,** *Of Prophets and Kings: A Late Ninth Century Document (1 Samuel—2 Kings 10)* (CBQMS 17; Washington, DC: Catholic Biblical Association of America, 1986); **A. F. Campbell and M. A. O'Brien**, *Unfolding the Deuteronomistic History: Origins, Upgrades, Present Text* (Minneapolis: Fortress, 2000); **R. P. Carroll,** "Prophecy and Society," in *The World of Ancient Israel: Sociological, Anthropological, and Political Perspectives; Essays by Members of the Society for Old Testament Study,* ed. R. E. Clements (Cambridge: Cambridge University Press, 1989) 203-25; **R. C. Culley and T. W. Overholt,** eds., *Anthropological Perspectives on Old Testament Prophecy* (Semeia 21; Chico, CA: Scholars Press, 1982); **W. Dietrich,** *Prophetie und Geschichte: Eine redaktionsgeschicht-*

liche Untersuchung zum deuteronomistischen Geschichts-werk (FRLANT 108; Göttingen: Vandenhoeck & Ruprecht, 1972); **H. B. Huffmon,** "Prophecy (ANE)," *ABD* 5.477-82; **K. Koch,** *The Prophets,* 1: *The Assyrian Period* (London: SCM, 1982); **J. S. Kselman,** "The Social World of the Prophets: A Review Article," *RelSRev* 11 (1985) 120-29; **B. Lang,** *Monotheism and the Prophetic Minority: An Essay in Biblical History and Sociology* (SWBA 1; Sheffield: Almond, 1983); **P. D. Miller Jr.,** "The World and Message of the Prophets: Biblical Prophecy in Its Context," in *Old Testament Interpretation: Past, Present, and Future,* ed. J. L. Mays, D. L. Petersen and K. H. Richards (Edinburgh: T & T Clark, 1995) 97-112; **M. Nissinen,** ed., *Prophecy in Its Ancient Near Eastern Context: Mesopotamian, Biblical, and Arabian Perspectives* (SBLSymS 13; Atlanta: Society of Biblical Literature, 2000); **M. Nissinen et al.,** *Prophets and Prophecy in the Ancient Near East* (SBLWAW 12; Atlanta: Society of Biblical Literature, 2003); **D. L. Petersen,** *The Prophetic Literature: An Introduction* (Louisville: Westminster/John Knox, 2002) 226-34; idem, *The Roles of Israel's Prophets* (JSOTSup 17; Sheffield: JSOT, 1981); **A. Rofé,** *The Prophetical Stories: The Narratives about the Prophets in the Hebrew Bible; Their Literary Types and History* (Jerusalem: Magnes, 1988); **I. L. Seeligmann,** "Die Auffassung von der Prophetie in der deuteronomistischen und chronistischen Geschichtsschreibung (mit einem Exkurs über das Buch Jeremia)," in *Congress Volume: Göttingen, 1977,* ed. J. A. Emerton (VTSup 29; Leiden: E. J. Brill, 1978) 254-84; **R. R. Wilson,** "The Former Prophets: Reading the Books of Kings," in *Old Testament Interpretation: Past, Present, and Future,* ed. J. L. Mays, D. L. Petersen and K. H. Richards (Edinburgh: T & T Clark, 1995) 83-96; idem, *Prophecy and Society in Ancient Israel* (Philadelphia: Fortress, 1980).   K. Möller

PSALMS. *See* POETRY.

Q

QUEEN MOTHER. *See* ROYAL FAMILY.

QUEST OF THE HISTORICAL ISRAEL

The phrase "quest of the historical Israel" derives from the well-known "quest of the historical Jesus." Here it refers to a movement of scholarship that emerged in the late eighteenth century and continues in various forms today. It can be used in a broad sense to denote all historical research into ancient Israel—that is, writing the history of Israel; or in a more narrow sense it can describe the question of to what extent it is possible to recover a "historical Israel" as opposed to, for example, the "biblical Israel."

1. Early Quests
2. Modern Quests
3. Future Quests

1. Early Quests.

1.1. German Origins. J. Rogerson (28) argues that W. M. L. de Wette (1780-1849) inaugurated the search for the historical Israel, whereas a century earlier T. K. Cheyne had identified de Wette's elder rival J. G. Eichhorn (1752-1827) as inaugurator. Both de Wette and Eichhorn were German, and indeed it was in German universities that this modern scholarship arose. We may surmise, "In the year 1800, there existed a tradition of critical scholarship [in Germany] in which the investigation of the authorship and sources of Old Testament books was taken for granted, and whose results were readily available. . . . There was also the growth of the modern historical method" (Rogerson, 249).

This latter point is quite important. Coincident with the critical move in biblical scholarship in Germany were new theories of hisoriography. Both trends were accompanied by developing German nationalism. It is a truism

that the historian writes from his or her own situation (Sasson, 8). The historian is not blatantly dependent on the views of his or her time and place, but certainly there are intellectual paradigms present in a given time and place, and also intellectual traditions to which scholars may adhere. Thus J. Sasson, R. A. Oden Jr., and R. Schwartz have noted that nineteenth-century German biblical scholarship was intricately tied with trends in historical theory and ultimately with German unification ideology.

Oden (4-5) argues that this ideology invades historical theory with J. G. Herder (1744-1803). Simply put, there was an underlying paradigm for most of the scholars of the time that assumed an organic analogy for history (Oden, 12): history was a great progressive movement that paralleled the advance of the German people (Oden, 22, 31; Schwartz, 37).

1.1.1. The Rankean Göttingen School. We may discern two subgroups here (Sasson, 8; Oden). There were those scholars who were in the rationalist intellectual tradition of L. von Ranke (1780-1849). In light of Ranke's goal of empirical objectivity—*wie es eigentlich gewesen*—history was to be divorced from philosophy, only those periods for which there were "facts" should be considered, and the pattern of development (on the German analogy) was taken for granted (Sasson, 8). In this group we should place H. G. A. Ewald (1803-1875), a student of Eichhorn at Göttingen (Provan, Long and Longman, 24). Sasson (8-9) considers his work to be a monument to the unification of Germany, in spite of the fact that Ewald actually refused to take the oath of allegiance to the king of Prussia after his native Hanover was annexed, and was dismissed and exiled from Göttingen as a result (Cheyne, 113-15; Rogerson, 92).

With Ewald's student and successor at Göttingen, J. Wellhausen (1844-1918), who took the oath and never was forgiven by Ewald, we are on firmer ground (Smend, 6). Wellhausen's view of history was evolutionary, following a progressive development (Oden, 22). One example should suffice. In his famous *Prolegomena* (1891, 24; 1958, 34-49; 1994, 127-31, 228-45) he describes a sequence of pentateuchal sources that date to times that the Historical Books claim to describe. This sequence of sources sets a sequence for the history of ideas in ancient Israel (Smend, 12), the Historical Books themselves being of minimal value for reconstructing such a history (Bright 1960, 21; Hayes, 37, 41). Wellhausen (1957, 12-13) arrives at the sequence of sources by source criticism, but then he tests the validity of this sequence by seeing if it conforms to the overall progress of history as he expects it to be. Wellhausen expected it, first, to be teleological and coherent like that of Germany (Schwartz, 40), and second, to fit into a Protestant Christian dogmatic system (Bright 1960, 22; Hayes, 55; Rendtorff 1992, 2-3). Following Ranke, he was looking for "facts," and for this reason he thought that oral tradition was not something that the scholar could examine, and so ignored it (Kirkpatrick).

1.1.2. The Burckhardtian Berlin School. The other German intellectual tradition followed the work of Ranke's rival and successor in Berlin, J. Burckhardt (1818-1897). Burckhardt, who had studied under de Wette, opposed Ranke's idealistic objectivity and proposed a reunification of history and philosophy that would explore the evolution of the *Zeitgeisten* of history—the spirits of the times—in a nonchronological way (e.g., Burckhardt's "The State as a Work of Art" in *The Civilization of the Renaissance in Italy*). The underlying analogy was the German *Volksgeist* (Oden, 5-12).

Here the connection to biblical studies is quite direct. H. Gunkel (1862-1932) was a student of Burckhardt, and himself taught at Berlin. Therefore we may place the entire Myth-and-Ritual History-of-Religions movement in this Burckhardtian category (Sasson, 9-10; Oden, 31). This school attempted to trace the evolution of thought along stages analogous to the rest of the ancient Near East (Sasson, 9-10), but this was still the grand Germanic-style progress (Oden, 31). Also following Burckhardt, one did not need Wellhausen's "facts" as much as ideas. Therefore the writers of biblical books

became not authors, but editors of material that could go back to very old oral myths and legends (Rendtorff 1992, 6). Gunkel and others of this school, such as H. Gressmann (1877-1927 [a student of Wellhausen]), who succeeded Gunkel at Berlin, reconstructed the history of the traditions (read *Zeitgeisten?*) regardless of the accuracy of what was contained in these traditions (Gunkel 1964; Kirkpatrick). "Gunkel opened a way of reading Old Testament texts different from Wellhausen's and finally leading in a different direction" (Rendtorff 1992, 8). F. Delitzsch (1813-1890) probably also belongs in this school (Sasson, 9-10).

1.1.3. Turn-of-the-Century German Trends. T. L. Thompson (1992) maintains that it was O. Eissfeldt, a student of both Wellhausen and Gunkel, who first held that Wellhausen's sources and Gunkel's traditions were accurate historically in what they said. Eissfeldt's histories of Israel were little more than summaries of the Bible (Eissfeldt 1914, 38-41; 1947, 12-16). Eissfeldt also represented a return to theological interests, but from an apologetic confessional Christian starting point (Hasel).

A. Alt (1883-1956), himself a student of F. Delitzsch's student R. Kittel, particularly combined Gunkel and Eissfeldt (Thompson 1992). He used Gunkel and Gressmann's "earliest legends" for historical information (Kirkpatrick), which he interpreted in terms of M. Weber's sociology, which was itself in the Rankean rationalist Prussian tradition (Sasson, 8-9). This is not to say that he considered the Hebrew Bible to be a strict historical record, but he was interested in what history lay lurking within its record (Alt), and tradition-history was the means to find it (Bright 1960, 31). Alt was one of the first to use other ancient Near Eastern materials to get at this history (e.g., Alt, 178).

1.2. Scandinavian School. At the same time there was important work outside Germany, particularly in Scandinavia. The Uppsala school, founded upon the work of J. Pedersen (1883-1977), reconstructed Israel's history largely based on source criticism, not unlike Wellhausen (Pedersen, 26-29). S. Mowinckel (1884-1965), however, a student of Gunkel, took the history of myth and folklore as a focus, almost to the disregard of source criticism (Kirkpatrick). The aims of both Mowinckel and the Uppsala school were to examine the diffusion of myth and ritual through uncovering parallel patterns in other cultures (*see* Ringgren). Latter-day scholars in the Uppsala tradition, J. Lindblom and H. Ringgren, have broken with much of this, although the emphasis is still on the cult as creative drama (Ringgren).

1.3. Twentieth-Century German Trends. This did not go unnoticed in Germany. Two of Alt's students in particular incorporated Uppsala ideas into their work: G. von Rad (1901-1971) and M. Noth (1902-1968). Von Rad followed Eissfeldt in his concern for theology, working out a historical, typological, kerygmatic "salvation history," albeit still within an a priori dogmatic system (Hasel). "He used firstly the Form critical method of Hermann Gunkel," taking "up important suggestions from Sigmund Mowinckel" and adapting "the insights of Alt" (Rendtorff 1977, 351, 352, 353). Following Alt, von Rad was more interested in the process of tradition transmission in early Israel than in the result of this transmission (Rendtorff 1977, 355), but in fact he had no "real concern to perfect a method that would be applicable in every instance" (Crenshaw, 33). Von Rad's student R. Rendtorff has completely shed the Documentary Hypothesis (Rendtorff 1992).

Noth followed Alt in his use of Weber, and he parallels both von Rad's interest in salvation history and Gunkel and Mowinckel in their alternatives to source criticism (Bright 1960, 81). "Noth thought bona fide that he worked within the Wellhausian system, simply because he had no alternative way of thinking. What he did had nothing to do with sources and the like, but he felt the need to put his own work in the commonly accepted framework of source criticism" (Rendtorff 1992, 7). This framework is clearly visible in Noth's *History of Israel* (Noth, 141-63). Noth also followed Alt's interest in the biblical record: "History can only be described on the basis of literary traditions, which record events and specify persons and places" (Noth, 42); and Noth presented Alt's whole picture of the history of Israel in biblical times in written form (Rendtorff 1977, 352).

Rendtorff (1992) sees the overarching paradigm as Wellhausian source criticism, although Noth had all but dropped it. Thompson (1992) sees it as Eissfeldtian naïveté regarding the biblical record, although neo-Wellhausians such as R. de Vaux can hardly be accused of such (e.g., de Vaux, 596, 683). Sasson is probably most accurate in saying that the Germanic ideal was the

paradigm. Even with Martin Noth we are still hearing Ranke: "'Israel' was a historical *reality* with its own historical period. . . . The *sequence* of events which constitute the history of Israel . . . has come down to us directly" (Noth, 1 [italics added]). At best, this was merely an ideological underpinning. Things were not always so innocuous, as we may note the case of G. Kittel (1888-1948), a NT scholar and the son of R. Kittel of the Burckhardt school. By 1933 G. Kittel had become a mouthpiece for the Nazis, giving a historical-theological justification for the extermination of the Jews, disguised as biblical scholarship and placed in his most academic works (e.g., *Das Antike Weltjudentum*) (see Albright 1964, 229-37). Such anti-Semitism is as old de Wette (Cheyne, 48), but we must at least credit von Rad for his opposition to the Nazis (Crenshaw).

1.4. Baltimore School. The paradigm also crossed the Atlantic. W. F. Albright's teacher P. Haupt was a student of F. Delitzsch of the Burckhardt school, and with the Albright Baltimore school there was a twist: the analogy became American history (Sasson, 12-14). Without developing this in much detail, one can see the idea of a nation of historically conscious immigrants at work in Albright's work (Sasson, 14), and his interest was in being a "scientific" historian (Albright 1940, 77).

Albright can be seen as the pioneer of the modern quest for the historical Israel. He was the first historian to rely heavily on archaeological and ancient Near Eastern evidence, which became increasingly plentiful during his lifetime (Albright 1968b, 53-57, 193-208, 226-43, 253-77). All histories of Israel written since then owe something to Albright. Yet in many ways Albright's histories of Israel are a throwback to Eissfeldt's; they merely summarize the "uniform biblical tradition" (Albright 1968a, 103), with the miracles removed, for much of Israel's history (e.g., Albright 1964, 24-48, 58-74; 1966, 42-60; 1968a, 95-118, 155-78).

2. Modern Quests.

Modern attempts to write Israel's history fall into five broad categories. The following material draws from I. Finkelstein's (2002, 323-25) list of three categories and W. G. Dever's (2003, x) list of five, but differs from both.

2.1. Maximalist. The first category, into which we must place Albright at the head, is those histories that summarize the Bible (Finkelstein

2002, 323). For in spite of isolated areas of skepticism, these histories draw most of their data directly from the Bible and then present it as history. The paradigmatic history of this nature is that of Albright's student J. Bright (1972, esp. 15-20, 166-76, 234-36, 245-49; cf. Bright 1960, 92), but also R. Albertz (1994, 79-82, 149-50) and G. Mendenhall. Although Mendenhall broke with his teacher Albright on many issues, most notably a radically new understanding of the rise of Israel from indigenous Canaanite origins, his comprehensive histories of Israel draw their data, albeit selectively, directly from the Bible (Mendenhall, 73-100, 153-77). Provan, Long and Longman maintain, "We are almost entirely dependent upon our biblical sources," which "tell the story first and, accepting their perspectives, best," and which deserve the "benefit of the doubt" (Provan, Long and Longman 265, 192, 55).

Sometimes it is possible to break this category down further (Dever 2003, x) into those who hold that the biblical accounts are "probably true," as does P. McNutt (95, 97, 161, 167, 178, 180), and those that merely assume that they are true, as does W. C. Kaiser Jr.

2.2. Qualified Maximalist. The second broad category is a variation of the first. Many scholars who are quite critical on the early history of Israel, and who would fall into even the minimalist category (see 2.3 below) when discussing the twelfth to ninth centuries BCE, nevertheless find "no reason to doubt seriously the reliability" of the Bible for the seventh century BCE and following (Finkelstein and Silberman, 231). This seems to be the case with the later works of A. Soggin (e.g., 1993, 209-32) and G. Garbini (2003, 95), for V. Matthews (58-59, 71) and especially for I. Finkelstein (Finkelstein and Silberman, 23; Finkelstein 2002, 324-25).

N. Gottwald (2001, 2, 25-31) has pointed out that we cannot simply paraphrase the biblical text as a history of Israel. "Most of us seem uncritically, perhaps even unconsciously, to have appropriated the overriding theocratic framework of the biblical writers themselves" (Dever 1992, 197). We cannot write a text-based history, of any period, with the ancient Near East as supplement. "Historians of the 20th century CE who claim to agree with the historians of the 5th century BCE (or, to be precise, with what they consciously or subconsciously reconstruct as the ancient historians' view) may sound rather suspicious to those historians who maintain that there has been some progress in the field of historiographical theory-building within the past 2500 years" (Knauf, 28).

2.3. Minimalist. In the third category, however, we find those who commit the opposite error. As D. N. Freedman wrote some forty years ago, "There is a good deal of scholarly enterprise which seems to proceed from the assumption that the biblical pattern is automatically wrong and that the first principle of operation is to discard it for something else" (Freedman, 313). Among modern historians of ancient Israel is a growing number who hold that whatever the Bible claims is the history of ancient Israel must be wrong (Finkelstein 2002, 324).

2.3.1. Antibiblical. This category has three distinct incarnations. First are those who utilize the Bible but do so in order to generate contrary hypotheses: one should assume that whatever is in the Bible is of "doubtful value as history" (Soggin 1985, 36). N. P. Lemche maintains that "*since* . . . it is from a scholarly point of view highly questionable to maintain anything which even remotely resembles the Old Testament narrative*" (Lemche 1991, 100 [italics added]), a description of Yahwism based on the Hebrew Bible must *consequently* be wrong. Others in this school of thought would be the earlier G. Garbini (1988, 18, 127-33) and the later Lemche (2003, 2).

2.3.2. Extrabiblical. The second subgroup is those who ignore the Bible completely and reconstruct Israel's history solely from archaeological or ancient Near Eastern evidence. This would include P. R. Davies (e.g., 1992, 60-70, 155-61; 2000, 240-41) and the earlier works of T. L. Thompson (e.g., 1992, 215-92, 408-15). It is interesting to note that Thompson was a student of H. Gressmann's student K. Galling; Gressmann was one of the first to disregard the accuracy of the biblical traditions (see 1.1.2 above).

2.3.3. Nihilist. The third subgroup is those who likewise ignore the Bible (Lemche 1985, 377-80; 1988, 45-68) but reconstruct Israel's history with no apparent evidence at all, as in the early histories of Lemche (1988, 88-118, 122-30) and the later Thompson (1999, 155-61, 186-87). One may associate with this group K. Whitelam, who, following Davies, argues that although there is a "historical Palestine" of the Iron Age worth "questing for," it should not be confused with the biblical Israel, "a scholarly construct based upon a misreading of the biblical tradition and divorced from historical reality" (Whitelam, 3).

Surely, however, we cannot allow ourselves to proceed from this assumption—now *against* the text—either (Gottwald 1999, xi). Nor must we agree that "the Old Testament historical narrative should no longer be considered the starting point of the historical investigation" (Lemche 1991, 104). The text does not necessarily have to be the starting point, but if we test our models seriously and equally, surely models can be suggested to us from *any* source—ethnographic analogy, ancient Near Eastern history or even the biblical text (Wright, 346).

2.4. Wellhausian. The fourth category is those few scholars who continue to work firmly within the Wellhausian paradigm (Cross 1973, 79, 84). These historians of Israel rely on writing an intellectual history for the period of the Historical Books based largely on source criticism of the Pentateuch. Examples include early N. Gottwald (1979 [1999], 45-46, 72-75, 150-51) and the collaborative work of J. M. Miller and J. H. Hayes (1986, 90, 94, 97). F. M. Cross, a student of Albright, writes his history of the settlement period from the source criticism of the Pentateuch and archaeology (1973, 198-206; 1998, 63-70), along with an almost Uppsala-like emphasis on oral saga (1998, 22-44).

2.5. Convergence. The final category views the biblical accounts as unproven hypotheses. Unlike the other categories, for this school of thought these hypotheses neither are given the benefit of the doubt or even probability (for any period), nor are they initially suspect. This line of thinking can be understood metaphorically by noting that the biblical text presents one reconstruction of ancient Israel, painting a picture of the world it describes (Matthews, 24). To define this metaphor better, consider a Renaissance painting of the assassination of Julius Caesar. The dress and the architecture may be Renaissance, and there may be elements in the painting that are Romanesque or from other periods between the Roman and Renaissance, which the artist included, knowing that they were "past." This does not mean that Caesar was not assassinated. If a historian studying Roman history, who had explored the issues of Caesar's assassination, were to look at the painting, he or she could pick out details related to the "actual" events, or rather, to the events as that historian had reconstructed them. For subjects such as the history of Rome, of course, such a thing is never done. Historians of ancient Denmark, for example, do not look at Shakespeare's *Hamlet* to see what relates to their own reconstructions. Yet this is exactly what biblical scholars are always doing. Many circumstances have compelled this particular painting, the biblical text's historical-literary epics, to be examined by those dealing with the history of Israel—that is, with what the painting depicts. Although we could easily ignore the painting as irrelevant and write a history of ancient Palestine from other sources (e.g., Finkelstein 1996, 200), we cannot, as P. Machinist observes, "crowd out a focus on the biblical text, without which no historian of ancient Israel and Judah could work" (Machinist, 8). B. O. Long adds, "How would one know where to look for [Israel's] cultural artifacts, or in which chronological period, if not with some minimal and guarded acceptance of the biblical testimony?" (Long 1988, 329). This fifth category of historians, then, confronts the information in the Bible (the "painting") with the results of archaeological excavations in Palestine, or rather with the interpretation of those results (another kind of painting, equally subjective), and finds "anchor points" and areas "broadly congruent" (Gottwald 2001, 163, 169). The point is not merely to compile a list of correspondences between the biblical account and the archaeological evidence, but to enrich the social and political history of Israel that might be written from archaeology and suggest a more intellectual and cultural history not otherwise accessible (Wright, 346).

Into this final category one may place Hayes and Miller (1990, 258-62, 279-84), G. Ahlström (1993, 383-90, 575-76), Gottwald (2001, 24, 198), Matthews (23-38) and especially Dever, who uses such comparisons (2001, 97-243) to "mine 'historical nuggets'" (2001, 101; also 2003, 167-90; 2000, 327, 329). Not only does this final style of quest for the historical Israel prescind from positivistic presuppositions of either extreme, but also it deals seriously with what it is possible to know (note Gottwald 1999, xlvi-xlvii; Matthews, xii-xiii). The latter is crucial to a serious quest for the historical Israel. If a pun on Ranke may be allowed, we must find not *wie es eigentlich gewesen*, but *was wir eigentlich sagen können*.

3. Future Quests.

This category leaves open as many questions as it answers. A thorough exploration of the mechanism by which the biblical "painter" arrived at his history would involve a number of issues: In what period were these relevant portions of the biblical narrative written? Why were they written? Is the biblical writer primarily copyist, novelist or researcher? If novelist or researcher, to what extent were his own rhetorical interests, situation and audience influencing his writing? In that case, what was the nature of the society in which he was writing? If copyist or researcher, how did earlier sources come to be included in his work? What were the societies involved in the composition of such earlier sources? From when, ultimately, did the sources come: from the times that they purport to describe, or from times between then and the author's own? The various works of B. Halpern begin to address these questions. Halpern argues for a genuine historical consciousness and historiographic intentionality at work in the Deuteronomistic Historian and the Chronicler (Halpern 1988). Although the ancient Israelite historians inclined toward bias when interpreting evidence, they seemed to rely on sources for their data rather than on ad hoc concoctions. Halpern acknowledges a premodern theory of causation at work in the historians, but he insists nonetheless that they treated available sources in a trustworthy way and honestly intended to interpret the past without invention or manipulation of the facts. A full evaluation of the means by which these "connections" came about cannot be written without tackling all these issues. Such endeavors will occupy future quests for the historical Israel.

See also HERMENEUTICS; HISTORIOGRAPHY, OLD TESTAMENT; NARRATIVE ART OF ISRAEL'S HISTORIANS.

BIBLIOGRAPHY. G. Ahlström, Ancient Palestine: A Historical Introduction (Minneapolis: Fortress, 2002); idem, The History of Ancient Palestine (Minneapolis: Fortress, 1993); R. Albertz, History of Israelite Religion (2 vols.; OTL; Westminster/John Knox, 1994); W. F. Albright, Archaeology and Religion of Israel: The Ayer Lectures of the Colgate-Rochester Divinity School (5th ed.; Baltimore: Johns Hopkins University Press, 1968a [1942]); idem, Archaeology, Historical Analogy, and Early Biblical Tradition (Rockwell Lectures 6; Baton Rouge: Louisiana State University Press, 1966); idem, From Stone Age to Christianity: Monotheism and the Historical Process (Baltimore: Johns Hopkins University Press, 1940); idem, History, Archaeology, and Christian Humanism (New York: McGraw-Hill, 1964); idem, Yahweh and the Gods of Canaan: A Historical Analysis of Two Contrasting Faiths (Jordan Lectures in Comparative Religion, 1965; Garden City, NY: Doubleday, 1968b); A. Alt, Essays on Old Testament History and Religion (Garden City, NY: Doubleday, 1966 [3 vols.; 1953-1964]); J. Bright, Early Israel in Recent History Writing (SBT 19; London: SCM, 1960); idem, A History of Israel (2d ed.; Philadelphia: Westminster, 1972 [1959]); T. K. Cheyne, Founders of Old Testament Criticism: Biographical, Descriptive, and Critical Studies (London: Methuen, 1893); J. Crenshaw, Gerhard von Rad (Makers of the Modern Theological Mind; Waco, TX: Word, 1978); F. M. Cross, Canaanite Myth and Hebrew Epic: Essays in the History of the Religion of Israel (Cambridge, MA: Harvard University Press, 1973); idem, From Epic to Canon: History and Literature in Ancient Israel (Baltimore: Johns Hopkins University Press, 1998); P. R. Davies, In Search of "Ancient Israel" (JSOTSup 148; Sheffield: Sheffield Academic Press, 1992); idem, "The Intellectual, the Archaeologist, and the Bible," in The Land That I Will Show You: Essays on the History and Archaeology of the Ancient Near East in Honor of J. Maxwell Miller, ed. J. A. Dearman and M. P. Graham (JSOTSup 343; Sheffield: Sheffield Academic Press, 2000) 234-54; W. G. Dever, "Imagining Ancient Israel: Archaeology, Social History, and the Sociology of Knowledge," in Proceedings of the First International Congress on the Archaeology of the Ancient Near East, ed. P. Matthiae et al. (Rome: Università degli studi di Roma "La Sapienza," Dipartimento di scienze storiche, archeologiche e antropologiche dell'antichità, 2000) 323-32; idem, "Unresolved Issues in the Early History of Israel," in The Bible and the Politics of Exegesis, ed. P. Day (Cleveland: Pilgrim Press, 1992) 195-209; idem, What Did the Biblical Writers Know and When Did They Know It? (Grand Rapids: Eerdmans, 2001); idem, Who Were the Early Israelites and Where Did They Come From? (Grand Rapids: Eerdmans, 2003); O. Eissfeldt, Geschichtliches und Übergeschichtliches im Alten Testament (TSK 109/2; Berlin: Evangelische Verlagsanstalt, 1947); idem, Israels Geschichte (Praktische Bibelerklärung 4; Tubingen: Mohr, 1914); I. Finkelstein, "Archaeology and Text in the Third Millennium: A View from the Center," in Congress Volume: Basel, 2001, ed. A. Lemaire (VTSup 92; Leiden: E. J. Brill, 2002) 323-42; idem, "Ethnicity and Origin of the Iron I Settlers in the Highlands of Canaan," *BA* 59 (1996) 198-212; **I. Finkelstein and N. A. Silberman,** *The Bible Unearthed: Archaeology's New Vision of Ancient Israel and the Origin of Its Sacred Texts* (New York: Free Press, 2001); **D. N. Freedman,** "On Method in Biblical Studies: The Old Testament" *Int* 17 (1963) 308-18; **G. Garbini,** *History and Ideology in Ancient Israel* (London: SCM, 1988 [1986]); idem, *Myth and History in the Bible* (JSOTSup 362; Sheffield: Sheffield Academic Press, 2003); **N. K. Gottwald,** *The Politics of Ancient Israel* (LAI; Louisville: Westminster/John Knox, 2001); idem, *The Tribes of Yahweh: A Sociology of the Religion of Liberated Israel, 1250-1050 B.C.E.* (rev. ed.; BibSem 66; Sheffield: Sheffield Academic Press, 1999 [1979]); **H. Gunkel,** *The Legends of Genesis* (rev. ed.; New York: Schocken, 1964 [1901]); **B. Halpern,** *The First Historians: The Hebrew Bible and History* (San Francisco: Harper & Row, 1988); **G. F. Hasel,** *Old Testament Theology: Basic Issues in the Current Debate* (rev. ed.; Grand Rapids: Eerdmans, 1975 [1972]); **J. H. Hayes,** "Wellhausen as a Historian of Israel," in *Julius Wellhausen and His Prolegomena to the History of Israel,* ed. D. A. Knight (Semeia 25; Atlanta: Scholars Press, 1982) 37-60; **J. H. Hayes and J. M. Miller,** eds., *Israelite and Judaean History* (OTL; Philadelphia: Trinity Press International, 1990 [1977]); **W. C. Kaiser Jr.,** *A History of Israel: The Old Testament and Its Times* (Nashville: Broadman & Holman, 2003); **P. Kirkpatrick,** *The Old Testament and Folklore Study* (JSOTSup 62; Sheffield: Sheffield Academic Press, 1988)**; E. A. Knauf,** "From History to Interpretation," in *The Fabric of History: Text, Artifact and Israel's Past,* ed. D. V. Edelman (JSOTSup127; Sheffield: Sheffield Academic Press, 1991) 26-64; **N. P. Lemche,** *Ancient Israel: A New History of Israelite Society* (BibSem 5; Sheffield: JSOT, 1988 [1984]); idem, "The Development of the Israelite Religion in the Light of Recent Studies on the Early History of Israel," in *Congress Volume: Leuven, 1989,* ed. J. A. Emerton (VTSup 43; Leiden: E. J. Brill, 1991) 97-115; idem, *Early Israel: Anthropological and Historical Studies on the Israelite Society before the Monarchy* (VTSup 37; Leiden: E. J. Brill, 1985); idem, *Historical Dictionary of Ancient Israel* (Historical Dictionaries of Ancient Civilizations and Historical Eras 13; Lanham, MD: Scarecrow Press, 2003); **B. O. Long,** review of *The Origin Tradition of Ancient Israel,* vol. 1, by T. L. Thompson, *JBL* 107 (1988) 327-30; **P. Machinist,** review of *History of*

Ancient Israel and Judah, by J. M. Miller and J. H. Hayes, *BAR* 12.6 (1986) 4-8; **V. H. Matthews,** *A Brief History of Ancient Israel* (Louisville: Westminster/John Knox, 2002); **P. McNutt,** *Reconstructing the Society of Ancient Israel* (LAI; Louisville: Westminster/John Knox, 1999); **G. E. Mendenhall,** *Ancient Israel's Faith and History: Introduction to the Bible in Context* (Louisville: Westminster/John Knox, 2001); **J. M. Miller and J. H. Hayes,** *A History of Ancient Israel and Judah* (London: SCM, 1986); **M. Noth,** *The History of Israel* (2d ed.; New York: Harper & Row, 1958); **R. A. Oden Jr.,** *The Bible Without Theology: The Theological Tradition and Alternatives to It* (NVBS 4; San Francisco: Harper & Row, 1987); **J. Pedersen,** *Israel, Its Life and Culture* (Oxford: Oxford University Press, 1964 [1920]); **I. Provan, V. P. Long and T. Longman III,** *A Biblical History of Israel* (Louisville: Westminster/John Knox, 2003); **R. Rendtorff,** "Gerhard von Rad's Contribution to Biblical Studies," in *Proceedings of the Sixth World Congress of Jewish Studies: Held at the Hebrew University of Jerusalem, 13-19 August, 1973, under the Auspices of the Israel Academy of Sciences and Humanities,* vol. 1, ed. A. Shinan (Jerusalem: World Union of Jewish Studies, 1977) 351-56; idem, "The Paradigm Is Changing," *BibInt* [sample issue] (1992) 1-20; **H. Ringgren,** "Scandinavian School," *ABD* 5.1001-2; **J. Rogerson,** *Old Testament Criticism in the Nineteenth Century: England and Germany* (rev. ed.; Minneapolis: Fortress, 1985); **J. Sasson,** "Models for Recreating Israelite History," *JSOT* 21 (1981) 3-24; **R. M. Schwartz,** "Adultery in the House of David," *Semeia* 54 (1991) 35-55; **R. Smend,** "Julius Wellhausen and His *Prolegomena to the History of Israel,*" in *Julius Wellhausen and His Prolegomena to the History of Israel,* ed. D. A. Knight (Semeia 25; Atlanta: Scholars Press, 1982) 1-20; **J. A. Soggin,** *A History of Ancient Israel* (Philadelphia: Westminster, 1985 [1983]); idem, *An Introduction to the History of Israel and Judah* (rev. ed.; Valley Forge, PA: Trinity Press International, 1993); **T. L. Thompson,** *The Early History of the Israelite People* (SHANE 4; Leiden: E. J. Brill, 1992); idem, *The Mythic Past: Biblical Archaeology and the Myth of Israel* (New York: Basic Books, 1999); **R. de Vaux,** *The Early History of Israel* (Philadelphia: Westminster, 1978 [1972]); **J. Wellhausen,** *Israelitische und Judische Geschichte* (9th ed.; Berlin: de Gruyter, 1958 [1894]); idem, *Prolegomena to the History of Ancient Israel* (New York: Meridian, 1957 [1878]); idem, *Prolegomena to the History of Israel* (Scholars Press Reprints and Translations; Atlanta: Scholars Press, 1994 [1878]); idem, *Sketch of the History of Israel and Judah* (3d ed.; London: Adam & Charles Black, 1891 [1881]); **K. Whitelam,** *The Invention of Ancient Israel: The Silencing of Palestinian History* (London: Routledge, 1996); **H. T. Wright,** "Developing Complex Societies in Southwest Asia: Using Archaeological and Historical Evidence," *International Journal of Historical Archaeology* 2 (1998) 343-48.   R. D. Miller II

R

RAHAB. *See* WOMEN.

READER-RESPONSE CRITICISM. *See* METH-
ODS OF INTERPRETATION.

REBUILDING WALLS. *See* EZRA AND NE-
HEMIAH, BOOKS OF; NEHEMIAH.

REDACTION CRITICISM. *See* METHODS OF IN-
TERPRETATION.

REGNAL YEARS. *See* CHRONOLOGY.

REHOBOAM

In the Historical Books Rehoboam is the son of
*Solomon and Naamah the Ammonite, a notewor-
thy queen mother (1 Kings 14:21, 31; on Solomon's wives see 1 Kings 11:1-5). The name "Rehoboam" (Heb *rĕhabĕ ͨ ām*) may derive from either
"the people have become extensive" or "the divine
kinsman has made wide" (*HALOT* 2.1214). The
author of Sirach plays on his name with "broad in
folly and lacking in sense" (Sir 47:23). Rehoboam
succeeded his father on the throne in Jerusalem.
Tragically, his aggression provoked schism by the
northern tribes, and so under Rehoboam the
united kingdom of *David and Solomon was split
with *Jeroboam I (son of Nebat; his name may
also mean "may God increase the nation"). Rehoboam ruled the southern kingdom from 930 to 913
(or by other chronologies, 931 to 914, or 926 to 910
[*see* Chronology]) BCE. 1 Kings 14:21 states that Rehoboam was forty-one years old at inauguration,
and that he reigned for seventeen years (cf.
2 Chron 12:13). The evidence suggests a king who
was preoccupied with political and military consolidation and power.

    1. The Deuteronomist's and the Chronicler's
       Accounts
    2. Rehoboam and Historiography

**1. The Deuteronomist's and the Chronicler's
Accounts.**
The Deuteronomist (1 Kings 12:1-24 [esp. 12:21-
24]; 14:21-31) concentrates on Judah, covenant
fidelity and the Davidic kingdom (see Gray). The
Chronicler (2 Chron 10—12) emphasizes the
priestly (Aaronic) elements of worship in the
southern kingdom, Solomon (cf. the omission of
1 Kings 11 in 2 Chron) and *Hezekiah, periodization and the inclusiveness of the *Davidic
covenant of "all Israel." Consequently, the
works of these two writers show significant variations in their accounts of Rehoboam. For both,
Rehoboam becomes a paradigm for the fundamental success that comes to the leader who follows the Torah and the covenant. Rehoboam
also clearly falls short of the ideal king after the
days of David and Solomon; that is, for the Deuteronomist, the best king appears to be *Josiah,
while for the Chronicler, Hezekiah stands above
the others.

    The Deuteronomist focuses monochromati-
cally on Rehoboam's failure as an instance of
God's revocation of Solomon's kingdom (seen
in the loss of the northern tribes [1 Kings 11:35-
36; 12:15, 24; 15:3-4; 2 Kings 8:18-19]) at the
same time as God's fidelity to the covenant
promise to Judah and David (2 Sam 7). The
Chronicler, on the other hand, has a more nuanced combination of both divine control and
human responsibility.

    The Chronicler, who first presents a positive
account of Rehoboam, uses Rehoboam to reveal
his characteristic hope for restoration following
repentance and fidelity in 2 Chronicles 11:5-23.
Nevertheless, Rehoboam is fundamentally a disobedient king in the estimation of the Chronicler (Williamson). Rehoboam's departure from
the Torah of Yahweh leads to Shishak's discipline (2 Chron 12:1-5), but when repentance is

evident, partial restoration occurs (2 Chron 12:6-8). Furthermore, Jeroboam's splitting of the kingdom appears justified when Rehoboam seems bent on developing the northerners into a corvée. It is evidently the continued rebellion that constitutes the sin of the north. In contrast with H. G. M. Williamson's view that Rehoboam is portrayed by the Chronicler as a victim on the throne, G. Knoppers thinks that the Chronicler finds nothing salutary in Jeroboam. The northerners are rebellious from the outset, but in his interweaving of divine necessity and human responsibility, the Chronicler finds Rehoboam's inexperience susceptible to secession by the wily Jeroboam, who victimizes Rehoboam. It should be observed, however, that the Chronicler does not blame the northerners for the split; their blame is to be found not in their resistance of the corvée, but in their continued disobedience and idolatrous worship. In Rehoboam's arrogant desire to dominate the north we find the human origins of the schism, though we must keep in mind the Chronicler's omission of material critical of Solomon that is found in Kings (Williamson).

1.1. The Division of the Kingdom. Rehoboam's accession begins with an inaugural disaster (see Soggin, 189-94): as his grandfather sought tribal unity at *Hebron (cf. 2 Sam 5:1-3), Rehoboam also travels to *Shechem, a city redolent of covenant history (cf. Josh 24; Deut 11:26-32; 27:1-26), for the coronation (and covenant ceremony?) of "all Israel" (1 Kings 12:1), only to be met by the petition of the recently returned (from exile) Jeroboam I to reduce the *missîm* (labor tax) of Solomon (cf. 1 Kings 5:13-18; 9:15-22). The young king is faced with either the absolutist monarchy of a Solomon or the monarchy of David, and the supposed unity of the tribes reveals itself now as a thin coating over a brooding discontent. This event, in and of itself, is a contemporary commentary on the relationship of the tribes (see Miller and Hayes, 229-31). The position of Benjamin in the secession seems unclear (cf. 1 Kings 12:20 with 12:21).

Rehoboam, preferring the counsel of youth over elders, who clearly have experience on their side, decides (in what is probably a vulgar word play) that his "little finger is thicker than [his] father's loin" (1 Kings 12:10). Rehoboam, with his ego boosted by his council members, decides in favor of an increase in the *missîm*, or corvée, which is a heavy yoke to carry and has

the sting of a scorpion (1 Kings 12:10-11). As S. Japhet observes, in changing imagery from "loins" to "yoke" and "scorpion," Rehoboam for once "displays some discernment" (Japhet, 655). After his messenger Adoram (1 Kings 12:18), perhaps the state supervisor of labor who evokes servitude (cf. 2 Sam 20:24; 1 Kings 4:6), is stoned to death, Rehoboam flees to Jerusalem. Negotiations are stillborn, and the prospects of gaining the wealth of the northern kingdom become a dim memory. It should be observed that the southerners economically needed the resources of the northerners, while the northerners knew the topographical and limited-resource liabilities of the south. It appears that Rehoboam never quite surrendered his dream of unity (1 Kings 14:30).

The followers of Jeroboam I, who had been protected by Shishak (cf. below) in Egypt but who had returned, build on earlier resistance to Davidic kingship. Jeroboam and his associates head for their tents (cf. 2 Sam 20:1) with a familiar cry of rebellion ("We have no portion in David" [1 Kings 12:16]), and the kingdom splits. Priests evidently followed Rehoboam to Jerusalem when Jeroboam I rejected them (2 Chron 11:13-17). This account supports the centralization of worship in Jerusalem as well as true fidelity to Yahweh in the southern kingdom, headed by the true priests. Defections to the south are signs of fidelity. The stability of the southern kingdom, anchored as it was in both temple worship and Davidic kingship, was never achieved in the north, where various dynasties (especially those of *Omri and *Jehu) achieved only modest stability.

Rehoboam's hope to conquer the seceded tribes by force is met by the prophetic warning of Shemaiah to avoid this war because the split is part of Yahweh's plans (1 Kings 12:21-24) under the shadow of the future king Josiah (1 Kings 13:1-32; 2 Kings 23:15-16). The irony is that the prophetic word is not dissimilar to the council of the older men in 1 Kings 12:6-8. The dissolution fulfills the prediction of Ahijah (1 Kings 11:26-40). Thus "politics is not an autonomous zone of life where the working of power has a life of its own" (Brueggemann, 162).

The prophetic warning did not eliminate continual warfare (cf. 2 Chron 13 [Jeroboam and Abijam]; 1 Kings 15:16-22; 2 Chron 16:1-6 [Asa and Baasha]) between the two kingdoms (1 Kings 14:30; 15:6; 2 Chron 12:15). Rehoboam fortified fifteen towns in Judah (including Bethlehem and Hebron) with captains, weapons and food supplies in order to extend his power (2 Chron 11:5-12) (see Miller and Hayes, 239; Na'aman favors a later date for this list). Fortification (of power), or blessing, may be behind the Chronicler's record of Rehoboam's eighteen wives and sixty concubines (2 Chron 11:18-21) as well as his concern that Abijah be his successor (2 Chron 11:22-23).

1.2. Shishak's Invasion. Egypt was safest when the northern peoples of Syria-Palestine were held in check. Judah's sins (idolatry, male prostitution [1 Kings 14:21-24]) lead the Deuteronomist to narrate the account of the Egyptian pharaoh Shishak (first king of the twenty-second Lybian dynasty), who overtakes Judah and plunders the temple of Solomon's fortunes (1 Kings 14:25-28). Rehoboam, clearly a weakened tribal leader who seems to stand helplessly by and observe Shishak's pilfering of the temple, can only muster cheap brass imitations of Solomon's golden armor (1 Kings 14:27), just as he has copied Solomon's idolatries. Worse yet, Rehoboam has to hide the items in a vault for protection. In effect, he boldly locks the door after the thief gets his goods. The Chronicler is more explicit: the invasion of both the fortified cities and Jerusalem is retribution for those sins (2 Chron 12:1-14), but the humility of Judah mollifies the wrath of Yahweh. The promise to David (2 Sam 7) will not be revoked; the throne totters, but remains standing.

2. Rehoboam and Historiography.

2.1. Rehoboam and Shishak. Shishak's invasion of the land is independently attested (*ANET*, 263-64), but the Egyptian account from the temple of Amon at Karnak does not mention the cities in Judah found in the biblical account; instead, the list of over one hundred invaded sites mentions other places (e.g., *Gibeon, *Shechem, *Tirzah, *Megiddo). The Bible does not mention any of the northern kingdom sites listed in the Egyptian account; instead, it focuses on temple robbery.

Some scholars suggest that Rehoboam fortified Judahite locations after Shishak's invasion. Others contend that the archaeological record offers no support of fortifications during the reign of Rehoboam (except Lachish [see Williamson, 240-42]) and argue that the southern "kingdom" at the time of Rehoboam was a small,

rustic collection of villages vastly inferior to their northern neighbors (Finkelstein and Silberman, 229-50). In addition, the archaeological record of religious practice at the time of David and his early successors in Judah reveals little evidence of a uniform monotheistic worship of Yahweh in the temple in Jerusalem from which Rehoboam departed (Niditch). Some scholars, therefore, suggest that Rehoboam's reign and the deflowering of the united kingdom as divine response to religious syncretism is theological rewriting rather than historical description.

2.2. Rehoboam as Paradigmatic History. The carefully selected theological overlays found in the Rehoboam texts—such as evaluating each king on the basis of covenant fidelity, using "Israel" to include both northerners and southerners (especially those faithful to the south), or shifting moral blame from Solomon to Rehoboam, or God's ordering of the division (cf. the "turn of affairs" in 2 Chron 10:15) so that Shemaiah must tell Rehoboam not to fight for the unity of the kingdom, or presenting the Chronicler's paradigm of the fruits of repentance (2 Chron 12:1-12) (see Williamson)—are so integral to the narratives, and (even more) so central to the concerns of the narrators that historians inevitably will be perplexed over precise events, chronological synchrony of two sets of kings, and historical flow (Miller and Hayes, 218-49). The "histories" of 1-2 Kings and 1-2 Chronicles are more fundamentally shaped by theological and political concerns.

In 1 Kings Rehoboam becomes a paradigm of divine fidelity to covenant and Davidic promise in spite of human sinfulness by the one who sits on the throne (1 Kings 14:21-24). He is also the one who triggers the splitting of the kingdom and who permits idolatries and abominable practices in "the city that the LORD had chosen out of all the tribes of Israel to establish his name there" (1 Kings 14:21, 23-24). In particular, under Rehoboam the southern kingdom continues worship at local, idolatrous sanctuaries—an egregious act of sin for the kingdom in whose temple Yahweh dwells—and also engages in the male prostitution cult of fertility (*qādēš* [1 Kings 14:24; cf. Deut 23:18]). Rehoboam's reputation is sealed when his son Abijah is noted for following in the sins of his father (1 Kings 15:3). If some themes remain similar in the two accounts, for the Chronicler, Rehoboam becomes a paradigm of what happens to "all Israel" when repentance occurs (cf. 2 Chron 12:1-12 with 7:14). Thus he becomes a paradigm of hope for repentance for those who will focus on the true worship of God in Jerusalem.

At the larger canonical level the story of Rehoboam fits into several interlocking biblical (and Christian) themes: on the one hand, the Davidic covenant and its promise of an eternal throne, and on the other hand, the hope of a united kingdom and the eventual enthronement of the Messiah on the Davidic throne.

See also HISTORY OF ISRAEL 4: DIVISION OF THE MONARCHY; JEROBOAM.

BIBLIOGRAPHY. **W. Brueggemann,** *1 & 2 Kings* (SHBC; Macon, GA: Smyth & Helwys, 2000); **C. D. Evans,** "Rehoboam," *ABD* 5.661-64; **I. Finkelstein and N. A. Silberman,** *The Bible Unearthed: Archaeology's New Vision of Ancient Israel and the Origin of Its Sacred Texts* (New York: Free Press, 2001); **J. Gray,** *1 & 2 Kings* (OTL; Philadelphia: Westminster, 1963); **S. Japhet,** *I & II Chronicles* (OTL; Louisville: Westminster/John Knox, 1993); **G. Knoppers,** "Rehoboam in Chronicles: Villain or Victim?" *JBL* 109 (1990) 423-40; **J. M. Miller and J. H. Hayes,** *A History of Ancient Israel and Judah* (Philadelphia: Westminster, 1986); **N. Na'aman,** "Hezekiah's Fortified Cities and the *LMLK* Stamps," *BASOR* 261 (1986) 5-21; **S. Niditch,** *Ancient Israelite Religion* (New York: Oxford University Press, 1997); **J. A. Soggin,** *A History of Ancient Israel* (Philadelphia: Westminster, 1984); **H. G. M. Williamson,** *1 and 2 Chronicles* (NCB; Grand Rapids: Eerdmans, 1982).   S. McKnight

RELIGIOUS FUNCTIONARIES. *See* PRIESTS AND LEVITES; STATE OFFICIALS; ZADOK, ZADOKITES.

RETRIBUTION, THEOLOGY OF. *See* CHRONICLER'S HISTORY.

REZIN OF DAMASCUS. *See* ARAM, DAMASCUS AND SYRIA; HISTORY OF ISRAEL 5: ASSYRIAN PERIOD.

RHETORIC, RHETORICAL DEVICES. *See* NARRATIVE ART OF ISRAEL'S HISTORIANS; POETRY; PRAYER.

RHETORICAL CRITICISM. *See* METHODS OF INTERPRETATION.

RIGHTEOUSNESS. *See* JUSTICE AND RIGHTEOUSNESS.

ROADS AND HIGHWAYS

In the ancient world, roads facilitated travel and transportation for governmental messengers and couriers, government officials, traders and merchants, military troops, and residents of the land conducting personal business. Most ancient travel probably was done on foot. Animals used for transportation included donkeys, mules, horses and camels. Roads also accommodated the use of various means of travel, including palanquins, carts, wagons and chariots (*see* Trade and Travel). The following discussion of ancient roads first considers how they were constructed and how they are identified by archaeologists today. Then the major highways of the region are described, followed by descriptions of specific routes mentioned in the OT Historical Books.

    1. Construction of Ancient Roads
    2. Identification of Ancient Roads
    3. Terminology in the Historical Books
    4. Major Highways
    5. Routes Described in the Historical Books

1. Construction of Ancient Roads.
Although examples of paved streets in Israel have been found, open roads were not paved before the Roman period. They were constructed by clearing boulders, brush and other obstacles and then filling in the holes and leveling the surface (Prov 15:19; 22:5; Is 40:3; 57:14; 62:10; Hos 2:6). Maintenance and rebuilding of roads probably occurred in the spring after the winter rains had ended. Governments may have been responsible for this task, but local roads probably were maintained by the local people. Open roads in ancient Israel were two lanes wide (3-4 m) to allow traffic to pass in both directions, but wider and narrower roads probably existed. Pre-Roman roads were not marked with milestones.

2. Identification of Ancient Roads.
Since no maps or detailed literary descriptions of roads in ancient Israel exist, their routes must be surmised by several means: topography, literary references, archaeological evidence and routes of later roads.

    2.1. Topography. Throughout history, roads generally have followed the easiest route of travel. Roads resulted from repetitive movements of humans over the same terrain. Once people discovered a route that provided ease of movement, they tended to use it over and over again. Travelers tended to avoid difficult terrain such as mountains, swamps, rivers, canyons, sand dunes and large bodies of water. Thus an ancient route sometimes can be reconstructed by studying a topographical map.

2.2. Literary References. Ancient writings occasionally name or describe roads of the times. The Bible contains a number of references to roads. For example, Judges 21:19 refers to "the highway that goes up from Bethel to Shechem." The existence and routes of roads mentioned in the Bible sometimes can be corroborated by extrabiblical ancient sources such as Egyptian and Assyrian records.

2.3. Archaeological Evidence. Because ancient roads in Israel were not paved, conclusive archaeological remains are difficult to find. However, the route of a road sometimes left lasting clues in the landscape. Repetitive movement over soil can cause it to compact and form a depression. Ruts and gullies can form from the movement of water over such surfaces (Tsoar and Yekutieli). Ancient routes can be reconstructed also by identifying the location of contemporaneous sites. Adjacent sites likely were connected by a path or road that allowed people to move between them. Thus when several sites were located in a line, one can theorize that they were connected by a road.

2.4. Routes of Later Roads. Roads of later times tend to follow the routes of roads in earlier times. The construction of roads on top of earlier roads can complicate identification of ancient roads. However, later roads can provide helpful clues to the routes of earlier roads. For example, the routes of Roman roads can provide clues to routes of roads in the Iron Age.

3. Terminology in the Historical Books.
The Old Testament uses eight terms for "road": *derek, 'ōraḥ, nātîb/nĕtîbâ, mĕsillâ, maslûl, ma'gāl, šĕbîl, miš'ôl.* The most common word for "road" in the OT, *derek,* occurs 706 times. It does not refer to a specific type of road, but to "any stretch of terrain that may be used as a thoroughfare" (Aitken, 29). The word *'ōraḥ,* a synonym for *derek,* occurs only in poetic passages. The words *nātîb/nĕtîbâ,* which also are found only in poetic passages, usually are translated "path." How-

ever, these appear to be synonymous with *'ōraḥ* and *derek* except that they may focus more on the actual surface of the road. *Mĕsillâ* has the more specific meaning of a constructed highway. *Maslûl,* which likely had the same meaning as the related word *mĕsillâ,* occurs only in Isaiah 35:8. *Ma'gāl,* which does not occur in the Historical Books, is used in poetic passages to refer to a "course of travel." The last two terms are rare words that do not occur in the Historical Books. Overall, the Hebrew terms for roads provide little help in defining distinctions between different types of roads (Dorsey 1991, 211-43; Aitken, 11-33).

In the ancient world, roads often were named according to their destination. The same practice is found in the OT, where *derek* often is used with the name of the city to which it led. Some translators consider *derek* in these constructions to be a preposition that means "in the direction of" or "by way of." The NRSV, for example, translates this construction in the following ways: "the way to the Jordan" (Josh 2:7), "in the direction of the wilderness" (Josh 8:15; Judg 20:42), "by the way of the ascent of Beth-horon" (Josh 10:10), "in the direction of Beth-Shemesh along one highway" (1 Sam 6:12), "toward Ophrah" (1 Sam 13:17), "toward Beth-horon" (1 Sam 13:18), "the way from Shaaraim" (1 Sam 17:52), "the way to the wilderness of Gibeon" (2 Sam 2:24), "by way of the Arabah" (2 Sam 4:7), "the way of the Plain" (2 Sam 18:23), "the way of the wilderness of Edom" (2 Kings 3:8), "in the direction of Beth-haggan" (2 Kings 9:27), "in the direction of the Arabah" (2 Kings 25:4). Other translators think that *derek* is used as a noun in these phrases and that they preserve actual names of roads (Aitken, 29-30; Dorsey 1991, 216-20).

4. Major Highways.
Two major international highways, one that passed through the land of Canaan and the other through Transjordan, followed a north-south route. The direction was required by the terrain and by the location of this land bridge between the populated areas of Mesopotamia and Egypt. A third major highway followed a north-south route through the highlands of Israel.

4.1. The Great Trunk Road. The primary international highway through the land of Canaan connected Egypt with Phoenicia, Syria and Mesopotamia. Historians refer to it as the "Great Trunk Route," the "Coastal Highway," and the "Way of the Sea" or the "Via Maris." The last name, borrowed from Isaiah 9:1, has fallen out of favor because it actually refers to a local route from *Dan to Tyre. The southwestern section of the highway was called the "way of Horus" in Egyptian literature and the "way of the land of the Philistines" in the Bible (Ex 13:17 NRSV).

This highway was populated with major cities. It began at Memphis, in Egypt, and passed by Sile, *Gaza, *Ashkelon, *Ashdod, Jabneel and Aphek. At Aphek, it veered inland to follow along the east side of the Sharon plain and passed by Socoh, Yaham, Gath-padalla and ʿAruna until it entered the Megiddo pass through the *Carmel foothills. At *Megiddo one branch turned northwestward to pass by Jokneam, Acco and Tyre. Another branch turned eastward to pass by Jezreel and Beth-shean. The main route continued northeastward to Mount Moreh, Mount Tabor, Chinnereth, *Hazor, Dan, Damascus, Qatna, Hamath, Ebla and Aleppo. Its distance from Egypt to Damascus was four hundred miles (*see* Aram, Damascus, Syria).

4.2. The National Highway. Another important north-south thoroughfare passed through Israel farther inland from the Great Trunk Road. Scholars refer to it as the "National Highway," the "Ridge Route" or the "Watershed Route." It connected *Beersheba, Debir, *Hebron, Bethlehem, *Jerusalem, *Gibeah, Ramah, *Mizpah, *Bethel, *Shechem, *Samaria, Dothan, Ibleam, Beth-haggan and *Jezreel.

Sections of the National Highway are involved in several accounts in the Historical Books. Judges 19 describes a journey from Bethlehem to Jerusalem to Gibeah. Judges 21:19 refers to a section of the National Highway that passed one to two miles west of *Shiloh and employed the "Ascent of Lubban." Sheba probably used the National Highway when he was being pursued by Joab's army (2 Sam 20:1-22). Benhadad, king of Damascus, used the northern section of the National Highway to conquer the northern cities of Israel (1 Kings 15:20). Tiglathpileser III of Assyria used the same route to conquer northern Israel (2 Kings 15:29). Elisha led a group of blind men along the National Highway from Dothan to Samaria (2 Kings 6:11-23). Ahaziah, king of Judah, fled along this highway from Jezreel south toward Beth-haggan and was shot near Ibleam (2 Kings 9:27). Jehu and his

messengers made several trips between Jezreel and Samaria along this route (2 Kings 10:1-17).

4.3. The King's Highway. The other major international route was located east of the Dead Sea and was called "the King's Highway" (Num 20:17; 21:22). The name probably signified that it was the main road of the region. The King's Highway descended south from the Great Trunk Road at Damascus and passed through Ashtaroth, Ramoth-gilead, Rabbath-ammon, Heshbon, Dibon, Kir-hareseth and Bozrah until it reached Elath on the Gulf of Aqaba, a total distance of around three hundred miles. From there it crossed the wilderness of Paran until it reached Egypt near modern Suez, a distance of around two hundred miles. Syria and Israel battled over this important trade route (2 Kings 10:33). *Edom and Judah fought over the southern portion of the route (2 Kings 16:6). Its northern section from Heshbon to Ashtaroth was called "the road to Bashan" (Num 21:33; Deut 3:1).

5. Routes Described in the Historical Books.

The Historical Books describe a number of routes that were involved in important events in Israel's history. Since journeys on the National Highway have already been described (see 4.2 above), the following section summarizes some of the travels on other roads recorded in the Historical Books.

5.1. Jericho-Bethel Road (Josh 7—8; 2 Kings 2:1-4, 23). The description of the conquest of *Ai suggests that a road led from *Jericho to Ai to Bethel. The discovery of an Iron Age fort along this route confirms its existence. This route may be the "Wilderness Road" mentioned in Joshua 8:15 and Judges 20:42. Also, Elijah and Elisha may have traveled this road (2 Kings 2:1-4, 18-23).

5.2. Gibeon-Makkedah Road (Josh 10:10). Joshua 10:10 describes Joshua's pursuit of the Gibeonites from *Gibeon west "by the way of the ascent of Beth-horon" and then south toward Azekah and Makkedah. South of Aijalon at Eshtaol the road split so that one spur passed south-southwest through Beth-shemesh to Azekah. The other spur continued directly south through Zanoah, Adullam, Keilah and Ashnah to Makkedah. The road continued south from there to Eglon and Beersheba.

5.3. Joshua's Conquest of the Southern Shephelah (Josh 10:25-43). From Makkedah, Joshua's army turned northward to take Libnah (Khirbet el Beida), then southward to conquer *Lachish. King Horam of *Gezer led his army south on the road through *Ekron and *Gath to fight the Israelites, but Joshua's army defeated him. The Israelites then turned southeastward to conquer Eglon (Tell ʿEitun). Then they headed east-northeast to take Hebron and then south on the National Highway to take Debir. They returned to *Gilgal, which would have required traveling north on the National Highway to Jerusalem and then east on the Jerusalem-Jericho Road.

5.4. Gideon's Pursuit of the Midianites (Judg 7:22; 8:4-12). Gideon pursued the fleeing Midianites from Mount Moreh southeastward to the fords of the Jordan located south of Beth-shean. The Midianites may have split into two parties. One crossed the ford at Abel-Meholah (Tell Abu Sus), and the other crossed farther south at the ford of Adam (near Zererah or Zarethan). Gideon may have forded the Jordan at Adam (or just north of there at Tell Abu Sidra) and traveled northeast up the Jabbok River to Succoth and then farther east to Penuel. The remnant of the Midianite army retreated to Karkor, which was located in the Wadi Sirhan, one hundred miles east of the Dead Sea. Gideon caught up with them "by the caravan route east of Nobah and Jogbehah" (Judg 8:11). These two sites probably were located near Amman.

5.5. Samson's Travels to Timnah and Ashkelon (Judg 13:25—14:19). Samson traveled on the road through the Sorek Valley from Zorah and Eshtaol through Beth-shemesh to Timnah (Judg 13:25—14:1). From Timnah he traveled to Ashkelon, probably on a road that led west to Ekron, Yasur and Ashdod and then south to Ashkelon on the coast (Judg 14:19).

5.6. Ophrah Road (Judg 20:45-47; 1 Sam 13:17). 1 Samuel 13:17 refers to a party of Philistines who departed from Michmash and headed toward Ophrah. Rather than turning west on the road toward Bethel, they followed a road that continued north-northeast through Rimmon to Ophrah. This road continued beyond Ophrah to Shiloh. This road may also be described in Judges 20:45-47.

5.7. The Route from Michmash to Beth-horon (1 Sam 13:18). A party of Philistines traveled from Michmash "toward Beth-horon." This party probably passed south to Geba (assuming that 1 Sam 13:16 actually refers to Gibeah and not Geba), west on a road to Ramah and Gibeon,

and then west-northwest to Beth-horon.

5.8. Michmash-Zeboiim Valley (1 Sam 13:18). Another party of Philistines traveled from Michmash "toward the mountain that looks down upon the valley of Zeboiim toward the wilderness" (NRSV). Three Iron Age sites located southeast and east of Michmash indicate the direction of a road that would have led to Jericho. This road formed part of the northern boundary of Benjamin (Josh 16:1-2; 18:12-13). Saul may have used this route when he went up from Gilgal to Michmash (1 Sam 13:15-16).

5.9. Alternative Jerusalem-Bethel Road (1 Sam 14:4-5; 1 Kings 13:9-10). The main route from Jerusalem to Bethel was the National Highway. Another route was located to the east of this road and passed through Anathoth, Geba, Michmash and Ai. A man of God who had traveled from Jerusalem to Bethel probably used this route when he returned (1 Kings 13:10). 1 Samuel 14:4-5 describes part of this route where the valley of Wadi es Suweinit separated Geba from Michmash.

5.10. Bethlehem-Elah Valley Road (1 Sam 17). The Philistines gathered for battle against the Israelites where the Elah Valley enters the Shephelah, near Azekah and Socoh (1 Sam 17:1-2). David traveled back and forth between Bethlehem and the encampment of the Israelites (1 Sam 17:12-20). The road passed west-northwest to the Iron Age site of Khirbet Abhar and then west-southwest to Socoh. The strategic nature of this route is suggested by Rehoboam's reinforcement of Azekah and Socoh (2 Chron 11:7, 9).

5.11. Elah Valley-Rephaim Valley Road (2 Sam 5:17-21). This same route from the Philistine cities into the highlands was used when the Philistines gathered against David in the valley of Rephaim (2 Sam 5:17-21). On this occasion they would have continued northeast from Khirbet Abhar toward Jerusalem rather than turning east toward Bethlehem.

5.12. Gibeon-Gezer Road (2 Sam 5:22-25). 2 Samuel 5:22-25 says that David "struck down the Philistines from Geba all the way to Gezer." "Geba" here may be a corruption of "Gibeon." Since the direct line westward was blocked by David's army, the Philistines headed north to Gibeon and then west on a road that was located south of the Beth-horon ascent. It passed through Chephirah, Aijalon, Gezer and westward to the coast.

5.13. Jerusalem-Jericho Road (2 Sam 10:1-5; 15—17; 19:15-20:3; 2 Kings 25:4-5). Several narratives describe journeys between Jerusalem and Jericho and the fords of Jordan. David used this route when he fled from Absalom (2 Sam 15—17). He "crossed the Wadi Kidron" (2 Sam 15:23 NRSV), ascended the Mount of Olives (2 Sam 15:30), passed by Bahurim (2 Sam 16:5) and continued along the road to the Jordan (2 Sam 16:13-14). This route is described as the road to the Arabah in 2 Samuel 4:7 and 2 Kings 25:4. The Iron Age road probably followed the same route as the later Roman road from Jerusalem to Jericho, which was identified by J. Wilkinson. At some point David crossed one of the fords of the Jordan and may have followed "the way of the Plain" north through Adam, Zarethan and Succoth. When he came to the Jabbok River, he turned eastward and arrived at Mahanaim (2 Sam 17:24).

5.14. The Wilderness of Edom Road (2 Kings 3:8). In 2 Kings 3 Jehoram and Jehoshaphat plan to invade *Moab "by the way of the wilderness of Edom" (NRSV). This road led from *Arad down to the southern end of the Dead Sea.

5.15. The Road from En-Gedi to Edom (2 Chron 20:1-2). This account records the passage of the troops of the Ammonites, Moabites and Meunites "from Edom, from beyond the sea" to En-gedi. A route may have led from En-gedi south to the Lisan and then east across the Lisan to the east side of the Dead Sea. No archaeological evidence supports the existence of a road from En-gedi to the Lisan, but the army may have forded the Lisan during a dry spell and then traveled north. Alternatively, they could have traveled around the southern end of the Dead Sea and then headed north to En-gedi. Another theory is that they crossed the sea on boats and rafts and landed near En-gedi.

5.16. The Road from En-gedi to Tekoa (2 Chron 20:16, 20). The Transjordanian army took "the ascent of Ziz" northwest of En-gedi to advance toward the Judahites at Tekoa. The road from En-gedi to Tekoa is lined with Iron Age sites.

See also CITIES AND VILLAGES; GEOGRAPHICAL EXTENT OF ISRAEL; TRADE AND TRAVEL.

BIBLIOGRAPHY: **Y. Aharoni,** *The Land of the Bible: A Historical Geography* (2d ed.; Philadelphia: Westminster, 1979); **Y. Aharoni et al.,** *The Carta Bible Atlas* (4th ed.; Jerusalem: Carta, 2002); **J. K. Aitken,** "דָּרַךְ," in *Semantics of Ancient Hebrew,* ed. T. Muraoka (Abr-Nahrain Supplement 6; Louvain: Peeters, 1998) 11-37; **B. J. Beitzel,** "Roads and Highways (Pre-Roman)," *ABD* 5.776-82; **D. A. Dorsey,** "Roads," *OEANE* 4.431-34; idem, *The Roads and Highways of Ancient Israel* (Baltimore: John Hopkins University Press, 1991); idem, "Shechem and the Road Network of Central Samaria," *BASOR* 268 (1987) 57-70; **M. Har-El,** *Landscape, Nature and Man in the Bible: Sites and Events in the Old Testament* (Jerusalem: Carta, 2003); **B. MacDonald,** *"East of the Jordan": Territories and Sites of the Hebrew Scriptures* (Boston: American Schools of Oriental Research, 2000); **H. Tsoar and Y. Yekutieli,** "Geomorphological Identification of Ancient Roads and Paths on the Loess of the Northern Negev," *Israel Journal of Earth Sciences* 41 (1993) 209-16; **J. Wilkinson,** "The Way from Jerusalem to Jericho," *BA* 38 (1975) 10-24.

G. L. Linton

ROYAL COURT. *See* STATE OFFICIALS.

ROYAL FAMILY

This article examines the institution of the royal family in Israel and Judah and the roles of its various members as depicted in the Historical Books of the Hebrew Bible.

1. The King
2. Dynasty
3. Wives
4. Concubines
5. Sons
6. Daughters
7. Other Relatives
8. Queen Mother

1. The King.

As far as the biblical record is concerned, the monarch was always male, except for the case of Athaliah (2 Kings 11), who took power following the death of her son Ahaziah in battle. Athaliah is never referred to as either king or queen, although she is described as "reigning" (2 Kings 11:3).

A king *(melek)* in Israel and Judah normally was succeeded at his death by his eldest surviving son (cf. 1 Sam 20:31), although *Solomon is a notable exception, hence the detailed account of the circumstances of his accession to the throne. Young boys who succeeded their fathers as king, such as Joash (2 Kings 11:21) and *Josiah (2 Kings 22:1), may have had regents ruling for them during their minority.

Sometimes a conquering nation replaced the reigning monarch with a son or an uncle (2 Kings 23:34; 24:17). Coups also took place, as when a senior officer assassinated the king and attempted to replace the ruling dynasty with his own family (e.g., 1 Kings 16:8-12).

2. Dynasty.

The Hebrew word *bayit*, "house," is used for the concepts of both "royal family" and "dynasty"—for example, "house of David," "house of Omri." The family of *Saul, as the first king in Israel, is relatively small, with one wife, one concubine, five sons and two daughters recorded (1 Sam 14:49-50; 2 Sam 21:8), compared with Solomon's seven hundred wives and three hundred concubines (1 Kings 11:3 [no doubt the figures are symbolic]).

It was customary to neutralize the preceding dynasty by murdering all the male members (e.g., 2 Kings 10:1-17; 11:1-2). The men of Saul's house died out over a period of time and in various ways, conveniently enough for *David (1 Sam 31:2; 2 Sam 3—4; 21:1-9). David was able to spare Jonathan's crippled son Mephibosheth because his disability meant that he was not a threat to David's rule (2 Sam 9). However, David kept him in Jerusalem, where he could not be the focus of unrest, and David was only too ready to believe that he had aspirations to the throne during Absalom's rebellion (2 Sam 16:1-4). It was also to David's advantage that his wife Michal, Saul's daughter, did not produce grandchildren for Saul (2 Sam 6:20-23).

3. Wives.

In the Historical Books the term *queen (malkâ)* is not used of female royal figures in Israel and Judah, either of Athaliah, who reigned in her own right, or of the king's chief wife or consort (Brenner, 17). In the latter case such women are known only as the king's wife, whether they are anonymous, like the wife of *Jeroboam in 1 Kings 14, or famous in their own right, like Jezebel in 1 Kings 21. The word "queen" is used only of the Queen of Sheba (1 Kings 10:1-13/2 Chron 9:1-9), who appears to have been the sole ruler of her country, with the freedom to visit royalty of other lands accompanied by a large retinue and sumptuous gifts. However, Solomon's numerous wives are referred to as "princesses" (*śārôt* [1 Kings 11:3]), perhaps referring to their own royal parentage.

The role of royal wives was to bear offspring for the king, who usually had married them to form advantageous alliances with other nations or with powerful local families, in order to consolidate his rule (1 Kings 3:1; 16:31; 2 Chron 18:1; 2 Sam 5:13).

A king's wives and concubines were considered an essential part of his royal power, and so for another man to marry his widows or sleep with his concubines was to stake a claim to the throne (2 Sam 12:7-8; 2 Sam 3:6-7; 16:21-22; cf. 1 Kings 2:22). This is relevant to the belief of some that David's wife Ahinoam was originally Saul's wife of the same name (1 Sam 14:50; 25:43, in the light of 2 Sam 12:8) (Levenson and Halpern 513-14). The biblical writer implies that David's marriage to Bathsheba in 2 Samuel 11:27 arose solely out of a desire to legitimate his offspring by her. However, political considerations cannot be excluded, since Bathsheba may have been the granddaughter of Ahithophel, David's counselor, and thus a powerful figure at court until he changed sides in Absalom's rebellion (2 Sam 15:12; 16:23; 23:34) (Bailey 83-101).

A seal dating to the ninth or eighth century BCE is inscribed with the name *yzbl*, "Jezebel" (Avigad). On the other hand, Jezebel is portrayed as using the seal of her husband, Ahab, to engineer the death of Naboth (1 Kings 21:8); this may be to show how she took over and abused the king's royal power. Otherwise, royal wives in Israel and Judah did not wield executive power, although behind the scenes some may have had influence in the political sphere and more openly in religious matters (1 Kings 11:1-8; 16:31-33; 18:13, 19). Since there were queens in some other Near Eastern societies, it is possible that queenship did exist to some degree in Israel and Judah but later was downplayed or denigrated by patriarchal biblical writers, as in the case of Jezebel, and also Athaliah, who ruled alone. It would not have been compatible with the cult of Yahwistic monotheism, its male priesthood and its ties to kingship. Another possible reason for the near absence of female rulers is the emergence of the Israelite monarchy from tribal military leadership.

4. Concubines.

As in the wider population, royal concubines and their offspring had a lower status than did legal wives and sons. In 2 Samuel 15:16 David leaves behind ten concubines to look after his house while he goes into exile, a task unlikely to have been given to a king's wife. Even in premonarchic times, a quasi-royal figure such as Gideon is portrayed as having many children by both wives and concubines, who laid claim to his authority after his death (Judg 8:30—9:2).

The only named royal concubine is Rizpah, daughter of Aiah (2 Sam 3:7). Since a king's ability to rule was associated with his virility, David's servants found a young woman, Abishag the Shunammite, to attend David and share his bed (1 Kings 1:1-4). However, she is not called a concubine, no doubt because David's advanced age and poor physical condition prevented sexual relations between them. Nevertheless, her ambiguous status meant that Adonijah's request to marry her after David's death was interpreted by Solomon as a bid for the throne (1 Kings 2:13-25) (see 3 above).

5. Sons.

There is no special term in Hebrew for the son of a king comparable to English "prince." Some sons may have played a military role like their fathers. Three of Saul's sons fought with him in battle, but as the episode shows, there was a risk of immediate heirs to the throne being killed (1 Sam 31).

The title "son of the king" seems to be based on genealogy. However, a few scholars have argued that because there are examples in the Bible of bearers who lack a patronymic and seem to be involved in administration or security (1 Kings 22.26 = 2 Chron 18:25; Jer 36:26; 38:6; 2 Chron 28:7), the term refers to function rather than lineage, as Near Eastern parallels suggest. Epigraphical evidence may point in the same direction, since owners of seals called "son of the king" are not actually connected with a specific king and may therefore merely be officials. Others interpret the biblical evidence differently, that the sons of the king who are responsible for imprisoning political opponents of the king act not as "police" but as representatives of the judiciary, just as the king is supreme judge (Sacher Fox, 43-48).

David's sons are said to be priests in a brief comment in 2 Samuel 8:18. However, the Chronicler makes them "chief officials in the service of the king" (1 Chron 18:17). This could be because he could not accept the idea of non-Levitical priests. On the other hand, he has no difficulties with David and Solomon exercising quasi-priestly functions (e.g. 1 Chron 21:26; 29:10; 2 Chron 6—7). Another possible explanation is that there was an early corruption of the text in Samuel from *sknym,* "administrators," to *khnym,* "priests." The former word would have been archaic in the Chronicler's day and therefore was paraphrased by him (Wenham). *Rehoboam and *Jehoshaphat apparently delegated some of their own powers to their sons by giving them control of the fortified cities (2 Chron 11:23; 21:3).

Even though most kings had many sons, only one son could ultimately succeed his father, which sometimes made for internal strife (see 4 above).

The king's sons apparently met on festive occasions (2 Sam 13:27-29; 1 Kings 1:9). 2 Samuel 13:7, 20 imply that David's sons had their own households away from the palace.

6. Daughters.

As in the case of the king's sons, there is no specialized Hebrew term corresponding to "princess" for the daughters of Israelite and Judean kings. The singular "daughter of the/a king" is used of Jezebel and Jehosheba (2 Kings 9:34; 11:2 = 2 Chron 22:11), and is also found on one seal and one bulla. The plural appears in Jeremiah 41:10; 43:6; 2 Samuel 13:18.

Kings' daughters could be married off in political alliances or as a reward for the king's officials and to retain their loyalty (1 Kings 4:11,15). David's marriage to Michal, engineered by Saul in order to trap him, according to 1 Samuel 18:17-29, was a strong element in his claim to the kingdom of Saul, hence his desire to have her back after Saul had married her to another man (1 Sam 25:44; 2 Sam 3:13-15). It may be for similar reasons that two of Rehoboam's eighteen wives were descendants of his grandfather David.

One notable figure is Jehosheba, daughter of King Joram of Judah (and according to 2 Chron 22:11-12, wife of the priest Jehoiada), who rescues her nephew Joash from Athaliah and successfully conceals him until he can be proclaimed king (2 Kings 11:2-3).

7. Other Relatives.

From the beginning of the monarchy in Israel, kings appointed their relatives to positions of power. Abner, Saul's paternal cousin, is the commander of his army (1 Sam 14:50-51). Similarly,

Joab, David's nephew by his sister, according to 1 Chronicles 2:16, becomes David's chief of staff. Perhaps this accounts in part for Joab's outspokenness toward David (e.g., 2 Sam 19:5-7; 24:3) (see Schley). Joab's brothers Abishai and Asahel are among David's chief warriors (2 Sam 23:18, 24). In the same vein, Absalom appoints another relative, Amasa, over his own army (2 Sam 17:25). Two of Solomon's sons-in-law were among the twelve officials responsible for victualing the royal household (1 Kings 4:7, 11, 15). Sometimes relatives wielded more general influence at court (2 Sam 13:3; 1 Chron 27:32).

8. Queen Mother.

The royal title that has generated the most discussion in recent years is *gĕbîrâ,* most commonly rendered in English translations as "queen mother." In English, "queen mother" denotes the mother of the reigning monarch. In Hebrew, *gĕbîrâ* evidently is some kind of title related to *gĕberet,* meaning "lady, mistress," but it does not appear to be exactly synonymous with "queen mother." The nature of the role of the *gĕbîrâ* is also hard to define.

We know that *gĕbîrâ* certainly can refer to the mother of the reigning king in at least some of its occurrences. Jeremiah 29:2 and 2 Kings 24:15 refer to the same event, the exile of King Jehoiachin/Jeconiah and his mother, but the passage in Jeremiah refers to the woman as the *gĕbîrâ.* 2 Kings 10:13 speaks of "the sons of the king and the sons of the *gĕbîrâ* " in the context of the northern kingdom; Jeremiah 13:18; 29:2 treat the king and the *gĕbîrâ* as a pair. *Gĕbîrâ* is also the title of Maacah, but it is unclear whether she is Asa's mother or grandmother (1 Kings 15:10-13; in 2 Chron 13:2 "Micaiah" may be an attempt to harmonize the discrepancy with 1 Kings 15:2, where Maacah is said to be Asa's father's mother).

However, although it is common practice for the name of the mother of each king of Judah to be recorded as part of the regnal formula (e.g., 1 Kings 14:21; 15:10; 2 Kings 8:26; 2 Chron 13:2), the title *gĕbîrâ* is not used in such contexts. Yet some scholars assume that the mothers of the kings of Judah automatically bore the title *gĕbîrâ* or had it conferred on them at their sons' accession (Ishida, 156-57, Andreasen, 179-94, Ackerman, 385-401, Ben-Barak, 170-85).

There are only two uses of the title *gĕbîrâ* outside Judah. The reference to the *gĕbîrâ* in 2 Kings 10:13 may be to Jezebel, either in her role as queen mother or possibly as dowager of Ahab. Certainly in 1 Kings 11:19, if we accept the text as it stands, the *gĕbîrâ* mentioned is defined explicitly as Pharaoh's wife Tahpenes. Presumably, the rank of the Egyptian chief consort was seen by Judeans as equivalent to that of their own *gĕbîrâ.*

As for the precise role of the *gĕbîrâ,* it cannot have been an automatic and inalienable rank, since in 1 Kings 15:13 (= 2 Chron 15:15) Asa removes Maacah from the position because of her promotion of the cult of Asherah. On the basis of this passage and some archaeological evidence for Yahweh's association with a female consort Asherah, S. Ackerman has suggested that in Judah the queen mother's role was in the state cult of the heavenly couple. The king would have acted as Yahweh's adopted son, while his mother represented the goddess Asherah, whose worship, Ackerman argues, was a normal part of the Judean royal cult within the temple in Jerusalem. The rank of the *gĕbîrâ* in the chief cult of the realm would have given her the right to determine the royal succession, as she could testify to her son's divine adoption. Ackerman believes that Maacah, Jezebel, Athaliah and Nehushta were also involved in the cult of Asherah.

Some scholars of an older generation, such as Kittel and Molin, saw the title *gĕbîrâ,* "Great Lady," as a relic of a supposed matriarchal period in Palestine. Certainly, a strong cultic role for the queen mother existed in neighboring kingdoms, notably among the Hittites at an earlier date. The difficulty with this idea is the lack of evidence that the term *gĕbîrâ* was ever used of Athaliah or Nehushta, or a number of other royal women who might have been expected to lead such a cult. And who would have taken her place in the state cult and decided the succession if the queen mother predeceased her son?

Other scholars regard the essential role of the *gĕbîrâ* as a political one, providing continuity with the reign of the present king's father. N.-E. Andreasen has suggested that the queen mother was the king's chief counselor, because of the prominence of Bathsheba in 1 Kings 1—2 and the ascription of Proverbs 31:1-9 to "King Lemuel's" mother. However, Bathsheba's activities seem limited to securing the succession for her son Solomon.

A. Brenner (28-32) believes that the title

gĕbîrâ was limited to a few instances where it was conferred on the queen mother acting as regent after the death of her husband or son, or during the minority of her son. Brenner suggests that the title may have been suppressed in the otherwise anomalous case of Athaliah in order to discredit the legitimacy of her reign (cf. Ishida, 155-60).

Another possibility is that the queen mother's influence lay principally in her own ancestry and the terms of her marriage contract, as is argued by K. Spanier in the case of Maacah. She would be chief wife because her family associations gave the Judean king the greatest political and territorial advantages, and so it would be her son who became heir apparent, even if he was not the firstborn of his father. Her son's succession thus would lead to her own promotion to queen mother, with special privileges for the duration of her son's reign. However, Spanier distinguishes the automatic status of queen mother and the role of *gĕbîrâ* as an official court position, implying that the latter had additional cultic responsibilities.

In contrast, Z. Ben-Barak and C. Smith believe that in fact the queen mother had no official political status normally, and the allusions to the influence wielded by the mothers of kings such as Bathsheba and Nehushta reflect strong individual personalities or unusual political circumstances—for instance, when the succession was in question and they could maneuver their own offspring ahead of the firstborn son. The title *gĕbîrâ* was granted to a powerful woman in recognition of that power. The scanty use of the term in biblical sources may reflect either chance, fashion or intention on the part of the writers.

One can only conclude that the office of *gĕbîrâ* undoubtedly entailed a function, but precisely what that was is unclear. Moreover, in the biblical text there are very few women who are explicitly called *gĕbîrâ*, yet much of what has been written on the subject is based on the assumption that royal women such as Bathsheba bore the title and that it meant "queen mother." The paucity of references could be explained in a number of ways. Perhaps other mothers of kings predeceased their sons before they could bear the title. Or it may have been suppressed by the biblical writers because of its links with non-Yahwistic cults. Alternatively, as Smith argues, perhaps only

those royal women who wielded some kind of power and influence were known as *gĕbîrâ*, "Great Lady."

See also DAVID'S FAMILY; JEHU DYNASTY; KINGS AND KINGSHIP; OMRI DYNASTY; SAUL AND SAUL'S FAMILY; STATE OFFICIALS.

BIBLIOGRAPHY. **S. Ackerman,** "The Queen Mother and the Cult in Ancient Israel," *JBL* 112 (1993) 385-401; **N.-E. Andreasen,** "The Role of the Queen Mother in Israelite Society," *CBQ* 45 (1983) 179-94; **N. Avigad,** "The Seal of Jezebel," *IEJ* 14 (1964) 274-76; **R. C. Bailey,** *David in Love and War: The Pursuit of Power in 2 Samuel 10—12* (JSOTSup 75; Sheffield: JSOT, 1990); **Z. Ben-Barak,** "The Status and Right of the *gᵉbîrâ*," in *A Feminist Companion to Samuel and Kings,* ed. A. Brenner (FCB 5; Sheffield: Sheffield Academic Press, 1994) 170-85; **A. Berlin,** "Characterization in Biblical Narrative: David's Wives," *JSOT* 23 (1982) 69-85; repr. in A. Berlin, *Poetics and Interpretation of Biblical Narrative* (BLS 9; Sheffield: Almond, 1983) 23-42; **A. Brenner,** *The Israelite Woman: Social Role and Literary Type in Biblical Narrative* (BibSem 2; Sheffield: JSOT, 1985) 17-32; **T. Ishida,** *The Royal Dynasties in Ancient Israel: A Study on the Formation and Development of Royal-Dynastic Ideology* (BZAW 142; Berlin: de Gruyter, 1977); **J. D. Levenson and B. Halpern,** "The Political Import of David's Marriages," *JBL* 99 (1980) 507-18; **N. Sacher Fox,** *In the Service of the King: Officialdom in Ancient Israel and Judah* (Cincinnati: Hebrew Union College Press, 2000) 43-51; **H. J. Marsman,** *Women in Ugarit and Israel: Their Social and Religious Position in the Context of the Ancient Near East* (OTS 49; Leiden: Brill, 2003); **D. G. Schley,** "Joab and David: Ties of Blood and Power," in *History and Interpretation: Essays in Honour of John H. Hayes,* ed. M. P. Graham, W. P. Brown and J. K. Kuan (JSOTSup 173; Sheffield: Sheffield Academic Press, 1993) 90-105; **C. Smith,** "'Queenship' in Israel? The Cases of Bathsheba, Jezebel and Athaliah," in *King and Messiah in Israel and the Ancient Near East: Proceedings of the Oxford Old Testament Seminar,* ed. J. Day (JSOTSup 270; Sheffield: Sheffield Academic Press, 1998) 142-62; **E. K. Solvang,** *A Woman's Place is in the House: Royal Women of Judah and Their Involvement in the House of David* (JSOTSup 349; Sheffield: Sheffield Academic Press, 2003); **K. Spanier,** "The Queen Mother in the Judaean Royal Court: Maacah—A Case Study," in *A Feminist Companion to Samuel and Kings,* ed A. Brenner (FCB 5; Sheffield:

Sheffield Academic Press, 1994) 186-95; **G. J. Wenham,** "Were David's Sons Priests?" *ZAW* 87 (1975) 79-82.   A. Salvesen

ROYAL LAND GRANT. *See* DAVIDIC COVENANT.

ROYAL MINISTERS. *See* STATE OFFICIALS.

ROYAL MONUMENTS. See WRITING, WRITING MATERIALS AND LITERACY IN THE ANCIENT NEAR EAST.

S

SAGES. **SAGES.** *See* WISDOM.

SALVATION AND DELIVERANCE

In the Historical Books salvation/deliverance most often describes the protection or rescue of an individual, group or nation from others intent on doing them harm. Typically, this deliverance involves the removal or destruction of foreign oppressors. God is the primary agent of deliverance, but often God is portrayed as working with or through a divinely appointed leader. Deliverance often comes in the form of military victories that provide freedom and security to those in distress.

Stories of salvation/deliverance occur with some frequency throughout the Historical Books, with the exception of the books of Ezra and Nehemiah. The theme is particularly prominent in the Judges Cycle (Judg 3—16) and the account of Jerusalem's siege during the reign of King Hezekiah (2 Kings 18—20/2 Chron 32).

1. General Description
2. Vocabulary for Salvation and Deliverance
3. God's Deliverance
4. Deliverance by Humans and Other Gods
5. A Theological Consideration

1. General Description.

1.1. Object of Deliverance. People, individually or collectively, are almost always the object of deliverance. Exceptions to this are rare but include towns *not* rescued (Judg 11:26), a lamb (1 Sam 17:35), territory (1 Sam 7:14), plundered possessions (1 Sam 30:18-19, 22) and a plot of ground containing crops (2 Sam 23:11b-12 [lentils]/1 Chron 11:13-14 [barley]). When people are the beneficiaries of an act of deliverance, the Israelites are the most frequent recipients.

1.2. Threats Requiring Deliverance. In the Historical Books people are most often in need of deliverance from other people. There are no direct references to people being delivered from natural disasters, ferocious animals (except 1 Sam 17:37), agricultural accidents or crumbling buildings, although falling walls do present some problems (Josh 6:20; 1 Kings 20:30). Although these situations were not beyond the scope of God's ability to deliver (see 2 Chron 20:9), examples are lacking in the Historical Books. Likewise, these books do not claim that people are saved from the eternal consequences of their personal sins—a concept foreign to OT writers.

Instead, individuals, such as the two spies sent by Joshua (Josh 2:1-24), are delivered from those who would capture and possibly execute them. Others, such as David, are saved from certain death (see 3.1). Collectively, Israel also faced serious military threats from its closest neighbors (Ammon, Moab, Edom, Philistia, Aram, etc.) and from distant imperial powers (Assyria and Babylon). In addition to needing assistance in battle, the Israelites required deliverance from local raiders who plundered their crops and livestock (Judg 6:3-6; cf. 1 Sam 30:23), and from foreign armies that besieged their cities (2 Kings 6:24; 7:6-7; 18:17; 19:14-19).

In the Historical Books deliverance from these and other enemies often is described with the expression "X delivered Y from the hand of [*miyyad* or, less frequently, *mikkap*] Z." Given the life-threatening dangers that people faced in the ancient world, the absence of a deliverer could have disastrous consequences, as the Danites' brutal massacre of the people of Laish tragically demonstrates (Judg 18:27-28; see also 1 Sam 11:3; 2 Sam 14:6).

2. Vocabulary for Salvation and Deliverance.
A variety of Hebrew words is used to convey the

idea of salvation/deliverance. The most common terms (and some cognates) are discussed here, but the theme is by no means restricted to passages containing these particular terms.

2.1. yāšaʿ and nāṣal. In the Historical Books it is far more common to speak of salvation and deliverance in verbal rather than nominal form. The two most common Hebrew verbs used in this regard are *yāšaʿ* and *nāṣal.* These verbs are close synonyms, and both occur with some frequency. They describe physical assistance rendered by a deliverer (e.g., God, a king, an army) on behalf of a person or persons in danger. Both words connote protecting, assisting and rescuing those threatened with danger. Sometimes the reason they need help is that the danger or threat is more powerful than they are (e.g., 2 Sam 10:11). As noted above, this assistance frequently is of a military nature. The deliverance of one group quite often entails the defeat and destruction of another. Those who experience *yāšaʿ* and *nāṣal* enjoy freedom from oppression and rescue from mortal danger.

2.2. yĕšûʿâ. The substantive *yĕšûʿâ* ("salvation, victory") is used to refer to military deliverance (1 Sam 14:45; 2 Sam 10:11; 2 Chron 20:17), to express Hannah's feeling of vindication (1 Sam 2:1) and to describe God's character (2 Sam 22:51; 1 Chron 16:23).

2.3. tĕšûʿâ. Like the preceding word, *tĕšûʿâ* most often refers to military victory. Sometimes this victory is won by a single individual (Judg 15:18, 2 Sam 23:10); other times an entire army is involved (1 Sam 11:13; 2 Kings 5:1). In both instances the victory is routinely attributed to God.

2.4. Other Terms. Other terms that could be considered include *yešaʿ* ("salvation"), *mālaṭ* ("to save," in Piel), *pādâ* ("to redeem") and *ʿāzar* ("to help, assist").

3. God's Deliverance.

In the Historical Books saving/delivering is one of God's primary activities. God saves Israel from all its troubles (1 Sam 10:19; cf. 1 Sam 14:39; 1 Chron 16:35) and does so repeatedly. This view of God is not unique to the Historical Books, nor does it originate here (see Longman and Reid, 13-47); rather, it is rooted in God's deliverance of Israel from Egypt. This paradigmatic act of salvation is recalled on numerous occasions (e.g., Josh 24:6-7, 17; Judg 6:9; 1 Sam 10:18; 2 Kings 17:36; Neh 9:11-12).

3.1. Recipients. As noted previously, the Israelites are the most common recipients of God's deliverance in the Historical Books. When the Israelites first enter the land of Canaan, God gives them victory over the inhabitants of Jericho and Ai (Josh 6; 8) and helps them defeat a coalition of kings in both the south and the north (Josh 10—11). The book of Joshua also recalls God's deliverance of Israel from the hand of Balaam, a prominent seer hired to curse Israel (Josh 24:10; cf. Num 22—24). In the book of Judges God repeatedly saves Israel from oppressors by raising up *judges to deliver them (Judg 2:16, 18). Although some judges require special assurance that God would use them to deliver Israel (Judg 6:36-37), God uses them to deliver Israel from various enemies (Judg 8:34). Additionally, God saves Israel from the Philistines (1 Sam 7:8-10), the men of Jabesh-Gilead from the eye-gouging Ammonites (1 Sam 11:13), and the inhabitants of Jerusalem from the Assyrian army (2 Kings 20:6; 19:35). God also delivers by protecting a group of exiles returning to Jerusalem with Ezra (Ezra 8:31). These are just a few of the many examples that could be cited as reflecting God's faithfulness to the covenant with Israel (cf. 2 Kings 17:35-39).

The Historical Books also recount instances in which individual Israelites are delivered by God. The spirit-empowered Samson, for example, kills one thousand Philistines with the jawbone of a donkey and attributes his victory *(tĕšûʿâ)* to God (Judg 15:18). God preserves David's life from the deadly hand of Saul on numerous occasions (e.g., 1 Sam 19:11-17; 23:6-14; cf. 2 Sam 12:7; 22:1) and also protects him from other enemies (2 Sam 22:18, 49).

On rare occasions the Historical Books refer to non-Israelites as the recipients of God's deliverance. Through Naaman, the commander of the king of Aram's army, God gives the Aramaeans victory *(tĕšûʿâ)* over Israel (2 Kings 5:1). Likewise, during the reign of King Joash the Israelites are defeated by a much smaller group of Aramaeans (2 Chron 24:24).

3.2. Means. Divine deliverance often is exercised in cooperation with leaders such as judges (Judg 2:16, 18) and *kings (2 Sam 3:18). In these instances the most important factor is God's presence rather than any particular qualifications, or lack thereof, of the human deliverers (see Judg 6:15-16).

God frequently delivers Israel through *war

(e.g., 1 Sam 14:21-23a; 2 Kings 13:17) and is not limited by conventional military means when doing so (1 Sam 17:47). The size of Israel's army does not determine the outcome (1 Sam 14:6), a fact dramatically illustrated in the story of Gideon. God requires Gideon to reduce the army by more than 99 percent in order to make the divine source of Israel's deliverance unmistakably clear (Judg 7:2, 7).

On many occasions God is portrayed as a divine warrior (see von Rad, 41-51). In this role God sometimes marshals the forces of nature to deliver Israel. God throws down hailstones from heaven and causes the sun to stand still in defeating the Amorites (Josh 10:10-14), sends a rainstorm that thwarts Sisera's chariots (Judg 4:15-16; 5:4, 20-21) and uses a thundering voice to throw the Philistines into confusion (1 Sam 7:10).

Sometimes God's assistance was so overwhelming that it rendered Israel's military involvement totally unnecessary. God ended the terrible siege of Samaria by causing the Aramaeans to hear an auditory hallucination that caused them to flee (2 Kings 7:6-7). Similarly, when Judah was threatened during the reign of Jehoshaphat, the people were told that they would not need to fight (2 Chron 20:18). In yet another miraculous deliverance God delivers Jerusalem from the Assyrians by striking down 185,000 soldiers (2 Kings 19:35).

3.3. Reasons. Several factors appear to prompt God's deliverance in the Historical Books. In Joshua, God delivers Israel from the Canaanites because of a previous promise made to Israel's ancestors (Josh 1:3, 6; 21:43-44). In Judges, and elsewhere, God delivers the people in response to a cry for help (e.g., Judg 3:9, 15; 6:6, 14). On one occasion the Israelites beseech Samuel to cry out to God on their behalf so that they might be delivered from the Philistines (1 Sam 7:8-10). Israel was confident that God would hear such cries and respond positively (2 Chron 20:9). God's awareness of Israel's terrible suffering also provides a basis for God's deliverance (1 Sam 9:16; 2 Kings 13:4-5; 14:26-27; cf. Judg 10:16). God's compassion *(nāham)* for the Israelites in their oppression serves as a catalyst for divine deliverance (Judg 2:18; cf. Neh 9:28 *[raham]*). God's willingness to deliver sometimes is dependent on Israel's obedience. Samuel assures them that God will deliver if they commit themselves fully to God (1 Sam 7:3; cf. 1 Sam

12:10-11; 2 Kings 17:37-39). Other times, God's deliverance is said to be an act of self-revelation enabling Israel to "know" God (1 Kings 20:13, 28; cf. 2 Kings 19:19). In the case of the siege of Jerusalem, God claims to deliver the city for God's own sake and for David's (2 Kings 19:34; 20:6).

3.4. Limits. Despite God's graciousness, Israel's recurring sinfulness severely tests the limits of God's willingness to respond. On one occasion God refuses to deliver the Israelites and advises them to let the gods they have chosen deliver them (Judg 10:14). Although eventually God does deliver Israel, it is not entirely clear whether God's decision is based on compassion or irritation (Judg 10:16).

The Historical Books also indicate that God does not deliver on demand. A cry for help does not automatically mean that God will save (2 Sam 22:42). Divine deliverance is not something that can be manufactured. When the Israelites bring the *ark of the covenant into their camp, confident that it would guarantee them a military victory over the Philistines, they are sorely disappointed (1 Sam 4:3, 10-11). God delivers when and how God chooses.

3.5. Results. Divine deliverance granted Israel freedom from oppression, at least temporarily. Numerous passages speak of the land having rest (e.g., Judg 3:11, 30; 5:31b) or of the people having rest from those around them as a result of God's deliverance (Josh 21:44; 2 Chron 32:22). God's repeated acts of deliverance on Israel's behalf were to have inspired the people's allegiance, trust and obedience, encouraging them to trust God rather than any other person or power. Instead, Israel often worshiped false gods, forgetting what God had done for them (Judg 6:7-10; 8:33-34). Israel's failure in this regard is most strikingly illustrated by the people's request for a king (1 Sam 10:18-19).

4. Deliverance by Humans and Other Gods.

4.1. Deliverance by Humans. God is the deliverer par excellence in the Historical Books, but there are passages that emphasize human agents who deliver. Joshua delivers Rahab and her family from death (Josh 6:22-25) and saves the Gibeonites from the Israelites (Josh 9:26) and later from a coalition of five kings (Josh 10:6-11). The Transjordanian tribes are credited with saving the Israelites from God's punishment by giving an acceptable explanation for the altar that they had constructed (Josh 22:31). Individual *judges such as Othniel (Judg 3:9), Ehud (Judg 3:15) and Shamgar (Judg 3:31) rescue Israel from the hands of oppressors. Saul delivers Israel from plunderers (1 Sam 14:48), and his son Jonathan wins a great victory over the Philistines (1 Sam 14:45). David saves Keilah from the Philistines (1 Sam 23:2, 5) and recovers people and possessions taken by the Amalekites in a raid on Ziklag (1 Sam 30:18-19). Female deliverers include Rahab (Josh 2:1- 21), Michal (1 Sam 19:11-17) and Abigail (1 Sam 25:26-35). On two occasions individuals seek deliverance in the form of legal help from a king, though one of these cases is contrived (2 Sam 14:4, 16; 2 Kings 6:26-27). In one memorable episode the foreign king Tiglath-pileser is summoned by King Ahaz of Judah to save (yāšaʿ) the people from the Israelites and the Aramaeans (2 Kings 16:7). It should be noted that although humans can be effective deliverers, they are not always reliable (see Judg 12:2-3), and their ability to deliver sometimes is doubted (1 Sam 10:27; 2 Kings 18:29).

4.2. Deliverance by Other Gods. The gods are not portrayed as effective agents of deliverance (Judg 10:14-16). Samuel warns Israel not to turn to worthless things (tōhû), presumably idols, that cannot save (1 Sam 12:21). The people of Judah are chastised for worshiping Edom's gods, the very gods that were unable to deliver Edom from the Israelites (2 Chron 25:15)! During the siege of Jerusalem the Rabshakeh's brilliantly crafted speech drives home the point that the gods cannot deliver (2 Kings 18:33-35; 19:12). Trying to induce Hezekiah's capitulation, the Rabshakeh points out that none of the gods from other countries have delivered them from the Assyrians and contends that it will not be any different with Israel.

5. A Theological Consideration.
Most readers are encouraged by the stories of salvation and deliverance in this section of the OT, but some find the violence in them, particularly depictions of divine violence, quite troubling (see Craigie, 9-19). As noted earlier, deliverance and destruction often function as two sides of the same coin in the Historical Books, since deliverance for one person or group often means destruction for another. Some regard such activity as a legitimate act of divine justice, believing that those destroyed

were sinners deserving death, while others remain unconvinced. This "salvation through violence" motif is especially problematic for those who wish to use these texts in theologically constructive ways yet reject what W. Wink calls "the myth of redemptive violence" (see Wink, 13-31). For these individuals, many texts considered in this article are quite problematic and need to be handled with care, especially when used for teaching and preaching.

See also JOSHUA, BOOK OF; JUDGES; JUDGES, BOOK OF; WAR AND PEACE.

BIBLIOGRAPHY. **P. C. Craigie,** *The Problem of War in the Old Testament* (Grand Rapids: Eerdmans, 1978); **R. L. Hubbard Jr.,** "יֹשׁע," *NIDOTTE* 2.556-62; idem, "נצל," *NIDOTTE* 3.141-47; **T. Longman III and D. G. Reid,** *God Is a Warrior* (SOTBT; Grand Rapids: Zondervan, 1995); **P. D. Miller Jr.,** "God the Warrior: A Problem in Biblical Interpretation and Apologetics," *Int* 19 (1965) 39-46; **S. Niditch,** *War in the Hebrew Bible: A Study in the Ethics of Violence* (New York: Oxford University Press, 1993); **G. G. O'Collins,** "Salvation," *ABD* 5.907-14; **G. von Rad,** *Holy War in Ancient Israel* (Grand Rapids: Eerdmans, 1991); **J. F. Sawyer,** "יֹשׁע," *TDOT* 6.441-63; **W. Wink,** *Engaging the Powers: Discernment and Resistance in a World of Domination* (Minneapolis: Fortress, 1992). E. A. Seibert

SAMARIA
The region of Samaria, though never explicitly delineated in the Hebrew Bible, included mainly the mountainous territories south of Lower Galilee and the Jezreel Valley (i.e., below the Mount Carmel-Mount Gilboa line), west of the Beth-Shan and Jordan River Valleys, and east of the Sharon and Acco Plains. According to biblical traditions, the southern border fluctuated with the political vicissitudes between north and south (1 Kings 14:30; 15:16-22; 2 Chron 13:19) until King Asa of Jerusalem established it in the area between *Bethel and *Mizpah (Tell en-Naṣbeh), both of which towns served henceforth as border stations (1 Kings 15:16-22). Following other, short-lived centers of royal power in the north (*Shechem, *Tirzah), the site of Samaria (biblical Shomron) became the permanent capital of the northern kingdom early in the reign of King *Omri, around 884 BCE. With the relocation of the capital and the establishment of the new king's authority, the city of Samaria became the permanent political center of Israel.

1. Physical Setting and Salient Features
2. Archaeology
3. Samaria in the Historical Books

1. Physical Setting and Salient Features.
The pre-Omride occupation of the site appears to have involved a small, family-owned villa that produced wine and oil for local use. The only remains from this phase include various non-monumental architectural features (such as a possible beam press, numerous rock cuttings, storage pits, separator vats and cisterns) that either rested immediately on or were set into the rock surface.

When Omri's cosmopolitan royal city replaced this small estate, workers artificially expanded a steep rock scarp that extended around the entire northern, western and probably southern perimeters of the central acropolis area. This salient topographical feature distinguished the raised "central summit" from the lower-lying "peripheral summit." The resultant split-level character of the area inside the city walls provided a rectilinear rock dais of bedrock (roughly 72 m on its western side and 93.5 m on its northern axis) that rose approximately 3.5 m above the surrounding rock. Rather than including common domestic areas, the summit plateau accommodated only the principal housing (main palace), activity areas (a large courtyard east of the palace) and official rooms (along the northern edge of the courtyard and often associated with the "Ivory House" of Ahab) of the royal family and their personal attendants. Various service-oriented buildings, including storage rooms to the west of the palace and possible food preparation areas north of the courtyard, as well as a potential industrial building (an ivory-carving workshop at Samaria?) lay on the lower rock that flanked the elevated royal summit. Although no clear remains of a temple dating to this period have emerged on the summit, a possible shrine (called E 207) existed nearly 900 m east of the royal compound. Excavators have found virtually no trace of a residential or domestic quarter inside the city walls during the Israelite period—quarters such as those seen at *Megiddo and *Hazor. Unlike other royal cities in the northern kingdom, then, the design of Samaria distinguished this city as the true seat of royal administration and power.

Although very few building remains have survived from the Assyrian period, an Assyrian

stela fragment (attributable to Sargon II), fragments from various cuneiform tablets (some representing a letter to Avi-aḥi, the local governor), and significant quantities of Assyrian Palace Ware attest to the use of Samaria as an administrative center during this period. Although again archaeology has recovered little from the subsequent Babylonian period, Jeremiah 41 alludes to the occupation of the city during that time. Samaria continued as an administrative center under Persian occupation in the late sixth and fifth centuries BCE. A deposit .25 m thick of fertile brown soil now covered at least a 45 x 50 m area of the former Israelite courtyard. This presumed garden surrounded the district governor's house and resembles similar features found elsewhere in the Babylonian-Persian empires. A fifth-century Athenian coin, three Sidonian coins from the reign of Abd-astart I (370-358 BCE), fourteen Aramaic ostraca and significant quantities of pottery imported from Aegean centers (e.g., Black- and Red-Figure, White-Ground and Black-Burnished Wares) attest to the solvency of Samaria's economy, which Persia itself apparently underwrote (Ezra 4:14).

Samaria continued to flourish during the Hellenistic period. Yet a series of beautifully constructed round towers (8.5 m in height, 13 to 14.7 m in diameter, and originally misdated to the Israelite occupation) and a subsequent massive defense wall (4 m thick) with square towers also bear witness to the political vicissitudes of a time when the successors of Alexander the Great competed for control over the region. Late in this period the Hasmonean priest John Hyrcanus captured Shechem, burned the Samaritan temple on Mount Gerizim, and launched a three-year siege against Samaria during which he destroyed much of the Fortress Wall and temporarily brought the region under Judean control.

The Roman conquest of Palestine by Pompey in 63 BCE set the stage for the final phase of grandeur at Samaria. The provincial governor Gabinius (57-55 BCE) rebuilt the city walls, created new residential zones, and constructed a forum with an adjoining basilica northeast of the summit. Following an earthquake in 31 BCE, Herod the Great renamed the city Sebaste, a Greek name honoring the emperor Augustus. He commissioned the Augusteum, a summit temple (35 x 24 m) with portico and cella, all situated on a platform whose retaining walls rose 15 m in height. A staircase 21 m wide led from the forecourt up 4.4 m to the temple proper. Another temple and altar dedicated to the goddess Kore, a large stadium (230 x 60 m), a theater and a forum lay on the city's northern and northeastern slopes. Herod also expanded the city's fortifications by building a perimeter wall that stretched for nearly 3 km in circumference and enclosed an area of roughly 160 acres. A main entrance gate flanked by two massive round towers stood west of the city, and a street 12.5 m wide ran along the south side of the acropolis and eventually approached the summit from the east. A thriving bazaar with shops of all kinds lined this columned street.

The grandeur of Samaria faded during the Late Roman and Byzantine periods, and archaeologists have recovered few remains from this time on.

2. Archaeology.

Representing Harvard University, G. Schumacher directed the first official archaeological exploration of Samaria in 1908. G. A. Reisner, along with architect C. Fisher, succeeded Schumacher in 1909 and 1910. The Harvard excavations, which focused on the western half of the summit, revealed much of the Israelite royal palace and, immediately to its west, the so-called Ostraca House, a sizable storeroom complex with dozens of laconic shipping dockets lying on its floors. These inscriptions, which became known as the Samaria Ostraca, record the transfer of various commodities (primarily wine and oil) from outlying villages to the capital city during the reigns of Jehoash and Jeroboam II in the early eighth century BCE (see Hebrew Inscriptions).

A consortium of institutions, mostly from England and Israel, renewed excavations at Samaria from 1932 to 1935. J. W. Crowfoot directed this "Joint Expedition," while K. M. Kenyon supervised all work in the royal quarter and introduced to the project's field methodology new techniques of debris-layer analysis. Kenyon cut a large north-south section across the entire summit east of the earlier excavations by Schumacher and Reisner. Based on the pottery removed from this area, Kenyon attempted to lower the chronology of the stratigraphic history and ceramic traditions at other major Iron Age II sites in Palestine, such as *Megiddo and

*Hazor. Her official report, which did not appear until 1957, offered a new chronological framework against which to understand this period not only at Samaria and in Palestine generally, but also at sites in the Aegean world.

Although the rock surface yielded clear signs of Early Bronze Age I occupation, most of the material remains pointed to Iron Age cultures. The date of the earliest Iron Age settlement, however, became the subject of considerable controversy. Based on 1 Kings 16:24, Kenyon concluded that no Iron Age occupation had occurred at the site prior to the time when Omri purchased the hill from Shemer. From there to the sixth to fifth centuries BCE, she outlined eight major building phases (labeled Periods I-VIII) and assigned Periods I-VI to the time from Omri to the Assyrian capture of Samaria in 722/21 BCE. Further, she believed that new ceramic traditions accompanied each new building phase.

Even prior to Kenyon's official publication of the Samaria pottery and objects, however, R. de Vaux compared the Samaria repertoire with that from Tirzah, where he was excavating, and concluded that the two earliest ceramic phases at Samaria actually predated all Omride building activities and indicated an Iron Age I presence at the site. Although de Vaux's comparisons merely questioned the direct correlation of architectural and ceramic periods, they sparked a long-standing debate regarding both the field methods and historical conclusions espoused by Kenyon at Samaria. G. E. Wright and others, such as W. F. Albright, Y. Aharoni and R. Amiran, quickly drew an official distinction between the ceramic and architectural developments at Samaria and dated the earliest Iron Age pottery to a modest pre-Omride occupation. By the 1990s L. Stager showed that this pre-royal occupation actually reflects the remains of a private family estate belonging to the clan of Shemer, from whom Omri purchased the property.

The debate that swirled around the fieldwork at Samaria resulted mainly from differences in archaeological method and interpretation. Whereas Kenyon assigned dates to discernible floor levels based on the material situated beneath them (sometimes by as much as several depositional layers), Wright and others dated surfaces according to the material found lying directly on them. In reality, each method addresses different aspects of chronology. While Kenyon's system offers the *terminus post quem* (earliest possible date) of a surface's construction, Wright's approach helps ascertain the functional life of the floor—that is, the span of time during which it was actually in use. In chronological terms, then, the latter method relates more to the *terminus ante quem* (latest likely date) for the existence of a specific surface. Recent reevaluations of the Samaria evidence, from both ceramic and stratigraphic perspectives, have confirmed an Iron Age I occupation of the site but have shown (with Kenyon) that this phase lacked any monumental architectural features. Instead, installations either resting on or cut into the rock surface seem to confirm Stager's suggestion that here the Shemer clan maintained a modest family estate that produced oil and wine already during the late premonarchic era. Contrary to Kenyon's principal starting point, the text of 1 Kings 16:24 in no way precludes this conclusion.

Besides these significant adjustments to our understanding of the earliest Iron Age levels at Samaria, a recent reevaluation of the later depositional history of the site has called for a new interpretation of the final phases of Israelite control over the city (see Tappy 2001). In her popular account of the royal cities in ancient Israel, Kenyon again appealed to a single biblical text (2 Kings 17:23-24) in support of the "wholesale transference of populations [that] was basic to Assyrian policy" during the late eighth century BCE. She went on to say that, based on her excavation data from Samaria, "the archaeological record is equally eloquent of the complete destruction of the capital city" (Kenyon, 133). According to Kenyon's final report, the buildings assigned to Period V represent the latest Israelite structures on the north side of the summit. These structures, which include Rooms hk, hq, j, n, among others, should bear the traces of this pervasive Assyrian assault. But close examination of the local stratigraphy and published finds associated with these chambers raises important new questions regarding the nature of the transfer of civil authority from Israelite to Assyrian leadership. In fact, the diverse layers from which excavators removed the purportedly latest Israelite materials can hardly represent a homogeneous matrix or a depositional history centered around a single episode, whether a devastating destruction by military force or a subsequent wholesale leveling for purposes of new construction. Rather, the stratigraphic record reveals a wide array of accumulation types: clean leveling fills; the tumble of rubble-filled matrix; pockets of possible occupational debris; hard-packed floor levels from disparate periods; at least two post-Israelite pit fills; a late foundation trench backfill; and other very late (Hellenistic and Roman) disturbances of earlier surfaces. Many of these deposits represent secondary contexts, a fact that urges discretion when attempting to draw firm historical conclusions based on the pottery assemblages published by the Joint Expedition.

Recent revisions of the published archaeological record, then, indicate that both the Syro-Ephraimite conflict (c. 732 BCE, when Tiglath-pileser III deposed Pekah as Israelite king and installed Hoshea as puppet king) and the events attending the final collapse of Israelite authority in 722/21 BCE (when Shalmaneser V and Sargon II established full Assyrian control over the capital city) transpired with minimal physical destruction to Samaria. Without further fieldwork at Samaria, however, one cannot rely on the official excavation reports alone when establishing or adjusting chronologies at other sites in Israel or the Aegean world.

3. Samaria in the Historical Books.
In the Bible direct references to Samaria first occur in the Historical Books, and the Deuteronomistic History alone (or, more specifically, 1-2 Kings) accounts for 62 percent of all such notices in the OT (72 percent including the Chronicler's history). Overall, the Bible paints a negative historical portrait of the city, the region and the individual kings who ruled there. An ominous chord sounds with the very first mention of Samaria (1 Kings 13:32), which occurs in a context anticipating the ultimate downfall of the capital city and its kingdom. Following this dire pronouncement, the biblical historians focus nearly two-thirds of their references to Samaria on periods of external and internal political turbulence: Samaria's wars with Syria and Judah (1 Kings 16; 20; 22; 2 Kings 6; 13); Jehu's bloody coup (2 Kings 10); a chaotic and rapid succession of five late kings (Zechariah through Pekah [c. 746-732 BCE]), mostly through political assassinations (2 Kings 15); and the final decade of Israelite autonomy over the city under King Hoshea (2 Kings 17), years that ended in capitulation to the Assyrians and the deportation of the Israelites.

857

A significant percentage of the remaining narratives highlight the perceived social and religious atrocities perpetrated by the city's rulers (compare the account of Ahab's behavior toward Naboth in 1 Kings 21 and the complaint against Ahaziah's reliance on Baalzebub, the god of Ekron, in 2 Kings 1) and various periods of economic hardships faced by the kingdom (note the role of famines in 1 Kings 18 and 2 Kings 6). In recounting the history of Samaria, the Bible incorporates only two main prophetic figures from each century of the city's existence: in the ninth century BCE, *Elijah (from the reigns of Ahab through Jehoram [869-843/42 BCE]; note also one episode involving Ahab and Micaiah ben Imlah in 1 Kings 22) and *Elisha (spanning the rules of Jehoram through Jehoahaz [843/42-802 BCE]), and in the eighth century BCE, Amos (during the rule of Jeroboam II [786-746 BCE]) and Hosea (also under Jeroboam II but continuing under Zechariah through Pekahiah [746-736 BCE]). Yet the texts that deal with the kings and capital of the north draw much more heavily on harshly critical prophetic (Elijah) and popular (Elisha) traditions than on available annalistic records. For example, four of the six chapters devoted to King Ahab's reign (1 Kings 16:29—22:40) rely primarily on narratives involving Elijah (1 Kings 17—19; 21) or Micaiah ben Imlah (1 Kings 22). By contrast, Ahab's fleeting moment of popular acclaim and competent leadership appears only in 1 Kings 20:1-34. But even this snatch of narrative receives a sudden and severe critique in a vignette drawn from prophetic traditions (1 Kings 20:35-43).

Furthermore, the compilers often insert disparaging details at key points in their accounts to outweigh rather than simply to counterbalance the presentation of basic facts or positive outcomes for the city. Thus the reader receives an amazingly terse account of the establishment of the royal city by King Omri (1 Kings 16:24), only to learn that both he and his son Ahab were evil and that Ahab constructed a temple and an altar to Baal as well as an Asherah within the new capital (1 Kings 16:25-33). These structures may relate to the so-called E207 Shrine, discovered by the Joint Expedition to Samaria in the 1930s. Similarly, when around the turn of the ninth century BCE Israel faced constant pressure from the Damascene rulers Hazael and Ben-Hadad, "a savior" (perhaps the Assyrian Adad-nirari III) spared the kingdom from the heavy hand of Syria. Yet the biblical narrative points out that both Jehoahaz and Jehoash persisted in ungodly behavior, and that "the Asherah also remained in Samaria" (2 Kings 13:5-11).

It seems clear that the biblical historians meant to compromise the reputation of Samaria by curtailing, perhaps even suppressing, positive aspects of the city or its ruling families. For instance, the writers say little to nothing of Omri's masterful design of the city, or of Ahab's flourish for royal décor (ivory-appointed houses [1 Kings 22:39]), or of significant military victories against Moab (recorded on the Mesha stela) and Assyria (at the Battle of Qarqar in 853 BCE). The tendentious nature of these texts likely stems from the fact that the Historical Books underwent final redaction mainly, if not entirely, in Jerusalemite circles that forever resented the secession of the northern tribes in the late tenth century BCE, near the outset of the reign of *Rehoboam, son of *Solomon (1 Kings 12). Following the north's declaration of independence from the south, twenty kings (including Tibni) ruled over the northern kingdom, initially from political centers at Shechem and Tirzah and then, from the early ninth century BCE on, from the newly established royal city at Shomron (Samaria). But the regional and even international prominence that these rulers brought to the area also rendered its new capital and associated religious centers (e.g., Bethel) the clearest and most dangerous symbols of opposition to the southern kingdom of Judah and its cult at Jerusalem. This deeply rooted north-south schism and the Judahite perspective taken in the final Deuteronomistic History spawned in the OT a critical treatment of the rulers and activities at Samaria.

Nevertheless, extrabiblical texts and archaeology amply demonstrate that the city of Samaria enjoyed an impressive history of accomplishments. The site, located near the center of the northern kingdom of Israel (32°17' N, 35°12' E), provided an ideal spot for Omri to establish a new political capital to succeed Tirzah. Unlike the earlier centers of power, Samaria lay west of the Ephraimite watershed in a position that afforded better access to and control over the main coastal road connecting Egypt, Philistia and Judah with the Jezreel Valley and northern routes to Phoenicia and Damascus. The site's biblical names, Šāmîr (Judg 10:1-2) and somewhat later *Šōměrôn* (e.g., 1 Kings 16:24), likely mean "watch" or "watchman." These appellations derived from the site's earliest recorded private owner, Šemer, whose lineage had maintained a villa on the summit of the hill and had produced oil and wine there. After acquiring the clan-owned property, Omri either chose to retain the old name that Shemer's kin had already assigned to their patrilineal estate, or used an archaic form of the consonantal root of the name *Shemer* to pay adequate respect to the former owners of the hill. In either case, Omri apparently intended the name *Shomron* to garner some legitimacy for the new royal city through its appeal to the earlier history of the site. Through such diplomacy Omri achieved what his son Ahab could not: the transfer of a parcel of land from patrimonial to royal status (contrast Omri's business relationship with Shemer to Ahab's failure with Naboth). Omri's success with Shemer might have stemmed from a shared lineage connection to the tribe of Issachar, with Shemer's genealogical roots possibly tracing to the clan of Shimron. If so, Omri would not represent the only royal figure to hail from that region, since according to 1 Kings 15:27; 16:8, both Baasha and his son Elah also came from "the house of Issachar" (note also the lineage of the earlier judge Tola, who lived at Šāmîr in the hill country of Ephraim [Gen 46:13; Num 26:23; Judg 10:1; 1 Chron 7:1-2]).

By the time Omri established Samaria as the capital of Israel, the overall population of the kingdom had spread west of the Ephraimite watershed, and the political and economic structure of the highland society had become more complex. Numerous settlements of a more uniform character (with virtually no ephemeral campsites as in earlier periods) appeared on the seaward slopes of the northern hill country and survived or thrived there as part of a much larger network of trade. Only a few Iron Age I sites had existed in this area (e.g., Khirbet Kabuba, Khirbet el-Babariya, Khirbet Kusein es-Sahel, Khirbet Qarqaf, Khirbet ed Duweir, west of Samaria), and they all had remained quite small and close to Shemer's family estate. But in the Iron Age II period the western expansion of rural villages left a footprint of settlements that allows the identification of at least eleven lateral and local roadways, which gave the highlands in the Samaria-Shechem area access to the lucrative trade moving along the coastal route. Un-

doubtedly, larger sites along the coastal route became trading stations or clearinghouses for goods and commodities produced by or transported through the matrix of highland villages leading down from Samaria and its associated network of villas, towns and neighboring urban areas.

Thus the new capital center nurtured a symbiotic relationship with settlements in the surrounding countryside. The place names (of at least sixteen separate villages) and clan holdings (representing at least seven separate lineage units) mentioned in the sixty-eight administrative documents known as the Samaria Ostraca indicate that by the early eighth century BCE Samaria lay in the center of a tight constellation of towns and family-owned estates. These estates undoubtedly resembled in character the site of Shamir/Shomron during its pre-royal days, when it belonged to Shemer's family. The surrounding sites, generally located 5-12 km from Samaria, both served the capital city and benefited from interregional trade by offering to passing caravans auxiliary services such as overnight lodging and animal care. In this way, these settlements facilitated trade between the highland centers and the main coastal route. But their close spatial distribution indicates that, despite their small size (100-150 inhabitants per site), not all of these villages represented mere caravan stops. Rather, many of them bolstered their own local economies by producing and trading commodities such as wine and oil (attested in the Samaria Ostraca), much as the Shemer clan had done previously at Samaria.

As this sociopolitical and economic network evolved in the Ephraimite hill country over the course of the ninth and early eighth centuries BCE, even the otherwise critical biblical writers came to view Samaria as the undisputed "head of Ephraim" (Is 7:9) and as the "elder sister" of Jerusalem who claimed authority and influence over numerous "daughters" (outlying villages [see Ezek 16:46, 53, 55, 61; 23:4-5, 33]) belonging to the "land of Samaria," known as the *šědēh Šōměrôn* (Obad 1:19). This political concept resembles that of the "land of Urushalimum" in the Amarna Letters from the Late Bronze Age (cf. also the "domain of the city" in Josh 21:12 and the "country of Edom" in Gen 32:4). Yet while Omri's original choice of Shomron as his new capital both freed him from the baggage of earlier political and military associations and placed his administrative infrastructure in or near a burgeoning network of economic activity, the new orientation toward the open markets of the Mediterranean also brought the entire region of Samaria into greater contact with foreign cultures. King Ahab's politically motivated marriage to the Phoenician princess Jezebel facilitated Samaria's access to the wealth of her homeland but exposed Samaria to the religion and customs of Phoenicia. Under this influence the political leadership of Samaria became increasingly syncretistic and therefore incurred the scorn of Elijah and the orthodox religious establishment generally (1 Kings 17—19). Ironically, world economic developments (especially as they related to Assyrian interests) eventually laid the groundwork for the total collapse of Israelite hegemony over both Samaria and its outlying countryside. By the third quarter of the eighth century BCE, these external pressures combined with great internal upheaval (reflected in multiple political assassinations) to prompt the prophet Micah to employ a satirical reversal of the phrase *śĕdēh Šōmĕrôn* in anticipation of Samaria becoming a "heap of ruins in the open country": *Šōmĕrôn lĕʿî haśśādeh* (Mic 1:6).

Omri's westward shift in the orientation of capital and kingdom did not go unchallenged, however, by political entities situated east of the Ephraimite watershed and the Jordan River Valley. The role assumed by Transjordanian powers in the labyrinth of political intrigues during the ninth and eighth centuries BCE appears more complex and vital to a proper understanding of the history of Samaria than many have recognized. For example, the ultraconservative factions that arose in the mid-to-late ninth century BCE held both religious and political aspirations. With backing from the prophetic leadership and conservative social groups, such as the Rechabites and zealous segments of the military, the populist *Jehu seized the throne of Samaria in 842 BCE (2 Kings 9—10). One significant objective of Jehu's revolt likely involved swinging the power base back to Transjordan. While the initial leaders of Israel arose within the hill country tribe of Ephraim (*Jeroboam I and his son Nadab), an early conspiracy transferred the nascent kingdom's power base to Issachar even while the capital seat itself remained at Tirzah (1 Kings 15:27-29; Baasha and his son Elah). During a brief interregnum, a second coup went awry (Zimri [1 Kings 16:8-20]), and a subsequent

pretender to the throne also failed in his effort (Tibni [1 Kings 16:21-22]). If Omri came from Issachar, as suggested above, then the rise of his dynasty not only held the power base there, but also preserved that tradition for roughly sixty-five of the first eighty-eight years of the nation's overall history. Yet the ruling houses of Issachar controlled the throne in Samaria itself only for the first four decades of the city's royal history (c. 885-842 BCE).

With the violent rise of Jehu, whose ancestral roots may trace to Gilead, a rival from outside Issachar succeeded in breaking that tribe's control over the throne at Samaria and in opening the way to greater political influence from areas to the east. Queen Jezebel even linked Zimri's earlier, failed coup to the designs of Jehu by sarcastically referring to Jehu as "Zimri" (2 Kings 9:31). At any rate, starting with Jehu, every claimant to the throne of Samaria—from the mid-ninth century BCE down to the last, Assyrian-appointed ruler, Hoshea (whose birthplace remains unknown)—seems to have come from a transfluvial area or faction. Ultimately, however, the new seat of power in Transjordan itself proved unstable as competing leaders, such as Shallum, Menahem, his son Pekahiah, and finally Pekah (from roughly 750 to 733 or 731 BCE [2 Kings 15:8-31]), descended into outright anarchy as they contended for the right to rule from Samaria (all but one, Pekahiah, seized the throne by murdering the reigning king).

Yet even in this late eighth-century context the Assyrians continued to call the region of Samaria by the name *Bît Ḫu-um-ri-ia*, "the House(hold) [= Kingdom] of Omri." Even when Jehu orchestrated a dramatic dynastic and power-base shift in the mid-ninth century BCE, the Assyrians preserved the title *ᵐIu-ú-a DUMU ᵐḪu-um-ri-i*, a designation usually translated literally as "Jehu, son of Omri" but better understood as "Jehu, King of *(Bît)-Ḫumri*." Both translations recollect not Jehu's biological father, but the founder of the recognized dynastic or urban power structure. (Similarly, the Mesha Stela forgoes genealogical accuracy by referring to Jehoram as Omri's son rather than as his grandson.) Even until the city of Samaria fell ultimately to Sargon II by 720 BCE, Assyrian scribes sometimes used interchangeably *Bît Ḫu-um-ri-ia* and *Samaria*, much as the contemporary Hebrew prophets themselves employed *Samaria* in reference to both the specific city and the general region.

Eventually, the Assyrians identified virtually the entire Ephraimite hill country with its leading administrative center. In this manner they effectually transformed the highland region into the province of *Sa-me-ri-na-a-a* (Samerina). By the late eighth century BCE the Assryian provinces of Dor, Megiddo and Gilead (cf. Is 9:1) encompassed the Ephraimite hill country on the west, north and east. In 722/21 BCE armies led first by Shalmaneser V and then by Sargon II penetrated the highlands, besieged and occupied the city of Samaria, and prepared to deport large numbers of Israelites and resettle the city primarily with captives from distant Syro-Mesopotamian locations and from southern Arabia (2 Kings 17:24; cf. the Display, Bull, Khorsabad Pavement, and Cylinder Inscriptions of Sargon II). A fragmentary court order from Samaria that bears the Akkadian name *Nergalšallim* and the West Semitic (Israelite?) name *Aya-aḫḫē* seems to suggest a mixed population during this time.

The repopulation and restructuring of Samaria by Assyria, however, did not begin in earnest until around 716 BCE, at least four years after the final subjugation of the city by Sargon II. Immediately after "conquering" Samaria, Sargon turned his attention to punitive campaigns against rebellious cities situated northeast of the Assyrian homeland. Against traditional assumptions, recent close scrutiny of the depositional history of the conquered capital shows the lack of a coherent destruction level that might date to Tiglath-pileser III, Shalmaneser V or Sargon II (see 2 above). Evidently, the Assyrians captured and held Samaria and gradually incorporated it into their overall strategic plan without physically destroying it. If there is any historical credibility to the large number of deportees from Samaria recorded in Assyrian sources (variously listed as 27,280 or 27,290), they surely must have come from the *šĕdēh Šōmĕrôn* ("land of Samaria"), not only from the royal compound atop the capital's summit. Although the southern border of Samerina remained fixed between Bethel and Mizpah (2 Kings 17:28), the province appears ultimately to have subsumed the coastal district of Dor, inasmuch as the Assyrian Eponym List fails to cite a governor of Dor, and a battle itinerary from Esarhaddon's tenth campaign in 671 BCE records Aphek, in the southern Sharon Plain, as belonging to the "land of Samerina."

Neither the Historical Books nor the OT as a whole shows much interest in Samaria after its fall to the Assyrians in the late eighth century BCE or the decline of Assryia itself in the late seventh century BCE. With the waning of Assyrian influence at home and abroad after 633 BCE, Judah's King *Josiah attempted to reannex at least the southern extent of Samerina as far as Bethel (2 Kings 23:4) and perhaps even the entire province (2 Kings 23:29-30/2 Chron 35:20-24). His political and religious reforms included desecrating local shrines in the north and executing their priests (1 Kings 13:1-2; 2 Kings 23:15-20), although he merely closed the *high places of the south and recalled local priests to Jerusalem. Having already anticipated Samaria's decline in 1 Kings 13, the Deuteronomistic History terminates its references to the city with these reports of Josiah's activities.

Subsequent prophetic texts recall the apostasy and just judgment of the northern kingdom and its capital city as a didactic warning for Judah and Jerusalem (Jer 23:13; Ezek 16:46, 51; 23:1-10, 33). Only a few other passages provide further historical details about Samaria. After the fall of Jerusalem to Nebuchadrezzar in 587/586 BCE, the northern boundary of Judah included Gibeon, Mizpah, Bethel and Beeroth. Gedaliah, the Babylonian appointed governor of Judah, established a garrison and district capital at Mizpah (Neh 3:15, 19; Jer 41:1; a secondary capital seems to have existed at Gibeon). Appreciable stores of grain, honey and oil apparently remained available in the region of Samaria as late as the assassination of Gedaliah (Jer 41:4-8). Although these facts may indicate the general value of Samaria to Judah at this time, they do not demonstrate that the Babylonians now officially considered the ravaged south as part of Samaria. Rather, Judah seems to have functioned as an independent province that maintained its own official capital at Jerusalem (Ezra 5:14-16).

That excavators have recovered only meager remains from the Babylonian and Persian periods suggests that the city of Samaria suffered considerable devastation during the period of Babylonian rule. Nevertheless, the city reemerged in the Persian era as the political center of the most important province in the north. But tensions soon escalated between Samaria and Jerusalem, especially around the mid-fifth century BCE. Correspondence between *Sanballat the Horonite (governor of Samaria; Neh 2:10, 19; 13:28), *Nehemiah (governor of Jerusalem) and the Persian court epitomize the strained relations (Ezra 4:10, 17; cf. 1 Esdr 2:16-30). Sanballat, who maintained an army in Samaria, accused the leaders in Jerusalem not only of preparing to rebuild the walls there—an act that Artaxerxes I (464-423 BCE) had sanctioned (Neh 2:1-8)—but also of planning a rebellion, aspiring to elevate Nehemiah as their king, and restoring a pro-kingship prophetic guild in the south (Neh 4; 6). Although the biblical writers recognize the official status of Nehemiah (and his predecessor *Zerubbabel [Hag 1:1]) as governor of Judah (Neh 8:9; 10:1; 12:26), they again slight the northern leadership by omitting acknowledgment of Sanballat's administrative title.

Following the Chronicler's (or some other editor's) comments in the book of Nehemiah, the OT offers no further direct mention of Samaria. Additional details about the city's service as an administrative center during the Persian period, its political vicissitudes during the turbulent Hellenistic period and its grandeur during the Roman period lie beyond the scope of the Historical Books. Since the few (twelve) direct references to Samaria in the NT take no notice of these matters, historical reconstruction of these periods depends on archaeology, the Apocrypha (Judith, 1-2 Maccabees, 1 Esdras) and classical sources (e.g., Josephus).

See also HISTORY OF ISRAEL 5: ASSYRIAN PERIOD; JEHU DYNASTY; OMRI DYNASTY; SANBALLAT; TIRZAH.

BIBLIOGRAPHY. **W. F. Albright,** "Recent Progress in Palestinian Archaeology: Samaria-Sebaste III and Hazor I," *BASOR* 150 (1958) 21-25; **N. Avigad,** "Samaria," *NEAEHL* 4.1000-1010; **B. Becking,** *The Fall of Samaria: An Historical and Archaeological Summary* (SHANE 2; Leiden: E. J. Brill); **J. W. Crowfoot and G. M. Crowfoot,** *Samaria-Sebaste,* 2: *Early Ivories from Samaria* (London: Palestine Exploration Fund, 1938); **J. W. Crowfoot, G. M. Crowfoot and K. M. Kenyon,** *Samaria-Sebaste 3: The Objects from Samaria* (London: Palestine Exploration Fund, 1957); **J. W. Crowfoot, K. M. Kenyon and E. L. Sukenik,** *Samaria-Sebaste 1: The Buildings at Samaria* (London: Palestine Exploration Fund, 1942); **G. Galil,** *The Chronology of the Kings of Israel and Judah* (SHCANE 9; Leiden: E. J. Brill, 1996); idem, "The Last Years of the Kingdom of Israel and the Fall of Samaria," *CBQ* 57 (1995) 52-65; **J. H. Hayes and J. K. Kuan,** "The Final Years of Samaria (730-720 BC)," *Bib* 72 (1991) 153-81; **I. T. Kaufman,** "The Samaria Ostraca: An Early Witness to Hebrew Writing," *BA* 45 (1982) 229-39; **K. M. Kenyon,** *Royal Cities of the Old Testament* (New York: Schocken, 1971); **N. Na'aman,** "The Historical Background to the Conquest of Samaria (720 BC)," *Bib* 71 (1990) 206-25; **A. F. Rainey,** "Toward a Precise Date for the Samaria Ostraca." *BASOR* 272 (1988) 69-74; **G. A. Reisner, C. J. Fisher and D. G. Lyon,** *Harvard Excavations at Samaria, 1908-1910* (2 vols.; HSS; Cambridge, MA: Harvard University Press, 1924); **L. E. Stager,** "Shemer's Estate," *BASOR* 277-278 (1990) 93-107; **H. Tadmor,** "The Campaigns of Sargon II of Assur," *JCS* 12 (1958) 33-40; **R. E. Tappy,** *The Archaeology of Israelite Samaria,* 1: *Early Iron Age through the Ninth Century BCE* (HSS 44; Atlanta: Scholars Press, 1992); idem, *The Archaeology of Israelite Samaria,* 2: *The Eighth Century BCE* (HSS 50; Winona Lake, IN: Eisenbrauns, 2001); idem, "The Final Years of Israelite Samaria: Toward a Dialogue between Texts and Archaeology," in *A Festschrift for Seymour Gitin,* ed. A. Ben-Tor et al. (Jerusalem: W. F. Albright Institute of Archaeological Research and the Israel Exploration Society, 2005); idem, "The Provenance of the Unpublished Ivories from Samaria," in *"I Will Speak the Riddles of Ancient Times" (Ps 78:2b): Archaeological and Historical Studies in Honor of Amihai Mazar on the Occasion of His Sixtieth Birthday,* ed. A. M. Maeir and P. de Miroschedji (Winona Lake, IN: Eisenbrauns, 2005); idem, "Samaria," *OEANE* 4.463-67; idem, "Samaria," *Eerdmans Dictionary of the Bible,* ed. D. N. Freedman, A. B. Beck and A. C. Myers (Grand Rapids: Eerdmans, 2000); **M. C. Tetley,** "The Date of Samaria's Fall as a Reason for Rejecting the Hypothesis of Two Conquests," *CBQ* 64 (2002) 59-77; **R. de Vaux,** "Les fouilles de Tell el-Far'ah, près Naplouse, cinquième campagne," *RB* 62 (1955) 541-89; **G. E. Wright,** "Archaeological Fills and Strata," *BA* 25 (1962) 34-40; idem, "Israelite Samaria and Iron Age Chronology," *BASOR* 155 (1959) 13-29; idem, "Samaria," *BA* 22 (1959) 67-78; **K. L. Younger Jr.,** "The Fall of Samaria in Light of Recent Research," *CBQ* 61 (1999) 461-82; **F. Zayadine,** "Samaria-Sebaste: Clearance and Excavations (October 1965-June 1967)," *ADAJ* 12 (1966) 77-80.   R. E. Tappy

SAMARIA PAPYRI. *See* SANBALLAT.

SAMSON. *See* JUDGES; HISTORY OF ISRAEL 2: PREMONARCHIC ISRAEL.

SAMUEL

Samuel was the prophet and priest who led Israel in the time between the period recorded in the book of Judges and the monarchy. He could be seen as a *judge who became a kingmaker. This article deals with Samuel as a character within the narratives of the Historical Books.

1. Introduction
2. Family Background
3. Early Years
4. Prophet and Judge
5. The Aged Samuel
6. Conclusion

1. Introduction.

It could be argued that Samuel was one of the most successful of Israel's leaders. He came into prominence at a time when Israel was virtually bankrupt spiritually, highly divided politically and struggling economically and militarily. In the latter years of his life, when he handed over power to the newly appointed king *Saul, the people of Israel, although they were still having major military problems with the nations surrounding them, were much more united and seem to have been much more spiritually aware than when Samuel first came on the scene. Samuel's ministry apparently made the concept of a Yahwistic monarchy possible, even if Samuel himself disliked the idea (1 Sam 8:6). The writer of the books of Samuel is aware that Samuel did have faults, but there is no indication that the people were anything but supportive and appreciative of him during the whole of his long period in office. Thus it is interesting that very little detail is provided about the major sections of his ministry.

Outside of 1 Samuel there are a number of references to Samuel, all of which reaffirm this positive picture of Samuel as an exemplary leader. They speak of his Levitical genealogy (1 Chron 6:27-28, 33), his role in appointing officials, making records, carrying out sacrifices and other temple duties (1 Chron 9:22; 11:3; 26:28; 29:29; 2 Chron 35:18; Ps 99:6). Jeremiah (Jer 15:1) places Samuel alongside Moses as a positive example when he records God saying to him, "Even if Moses and Samuel were to stand before me, my heart would not go out to these people." The NT refers to Samuel three times (Acts 3:24; 13:20; Heb 11:32), each time speaking of him as a seminal prophet but giving no further details. However, none of these examples can be described as referring to Samuel in anything more than a passing way.

Almost all that we know of Samuel comes from the thirteen chapters of 1 Samuel that relate to him, but even there Samuel generally is presented very much as part of the supporting cast. 1 Samuel 1—3 speaks of his birth, early childhood and calling, but the focus is on Hannah and Eli as much as, if not more than, on Samuel himself. Only 1 Samuel 3:19-21 and 1 Samuel 7 speak of Samuel's own service before the reader comes to the description of his old age. 1 Samuel 8, 11, 13, 15 and 28 tell of Samuel in relation to Saul, and 1 Samuel 16 and 19 tell of Samuel in relation to *David. 1 Samuel 12 provides a record of Samuel's farewell speech, and 1 Samuel 25:1 refers to his death.

2. Family Background.

1 Samuel 1:1 gives the impression that Elkanah was an Ephraimite, and thus Samuel as well. 1 Chronicles 6, however, lists Elkanah as a Levite, a member of the Kohathite clan. It is quite possible that the account in 1 Samuel speaks of Ephraim as a geographical residence rather than as a tribal identity, but in either case, Samuel clearly was not descended from Aaron and therefore was ineligible for enrollment as a priest. That he did function in a priestly way may indicate either that the rules about priesthood were not applied diligently until after the institution of the temple or that Samuel's adoption into Eli's family was seen at this point as giving him such eligibility. Samuel's parents were deeply spiritual people who took their religious responsibilities very seriously. Hannah may or may not have actually composed the psalm used in thanksgiving for the birth of Samuel, but there is no real reason to doubt that she, and not just the writers of Samuel, chose to use the psalm in this context. Its use in this way reflects both her spiritual understanding and her intelligence.

1 Samuel 1 makes it abundantly clear that regular worship, *prayer, sacrifice and the making and keeping of vows played an important part in the life of this family. However, it is also made clear that the polygamous household was in many ways dysfunctional. The structure of 1 Samuel 1:2 implies that Hannah was the first wife, and that in spite of Elkanah's love for Hannah, Peninnah had been married as a result of Hannah's barrenness. Whether or not this is so,

it is clear that both women were unhappy with their situation; Peninnah's jealous taunting reflects this as much as Hannah's desperate weeping. We are not informed whether the birth of Samuel brought any relief to Peninnah's unhappiness, but there is no doubt about the joy that it brought to Hannah. The family as a whole may have remained somewhat dysfunctional, but there is no indication that Samuel's early years were anything but happy and secure.

3. Early Years.
Samuel remained at home until he was fully weaned. In that context this could mean that he was at the age of five or even older when he was taken to *Shiloh to remain in the service of Eli. Elkanah still traveled with all his family every year to make the annual sacrifice, but Samuel and Hannah remained behind. Hannah seems to have been a fairly determined woman, and clearly she had the primary responsibility for decisions relating to Samuel's upbringing. The thought of leaving a small child to the care of a failing old man such as Eli may cause serious problems for the modern Western mind, but in other cultural contexts it is not unusual for even well-loved children to be brought up by someone other than their parents, and there were always plenty of people around to care for their needs. It seems likely that Samuel would have known from his earliest consciousness that he was destined for God's special service. It is quite possible that he reveled in the thought of his specialness and longed for the time when at last he would be allowed to go to Shiloh with the others. The fact that in later years he continued to use Ramah, the family home, as his base implies that he continued to have good relations with the family. Certainly there is nothing in the text to indicate that he suffered from any particular trauma.

In the middle of a text that speaks of the corruption, immorality and irreligion of Eli's sons, the ineffectiveness of the old priest in dealing with them and the judgment that would come to Eli's house because of this, we read, "Now the boy Samuel continued to grow both in stature and in favor with the LORD and with the people" (1 Sam 2:26). Eli failed dramatically with his own sons, but even in the midst of this corrupt environment he seems to have found a way to protect Samuel's innocence and to inculcate in him a sense of what it means to live as a servant of Yahweh. Even at the stage when Samuel had no personal knowledge of Yahweh he seemed to have had a positive attitude about his work in Yahweh's service. It may be that Samuel had to get up several times every night to help the aged Eli, and that it was not unusual for the old man to forget why he had called, but Samuel apparently responds every time with cheerfulness and patience.

Samuel's first experience of hearing directly from God was not an easy one. It is not difficult to understand his reluctance to return to his beloved master and convey the message of judgment on Eli and his family that had come via the voice in the night. But perhaps for both of them, when the realization came that Samuel's message simply confirmed the warning of impending judgment that the man of God had already given to Eli, there was an encouragement that God was not finished with Israel and would use Samuel to give the nation a new impetus and a new opportunity to hear God's word.

4. Prophet and Judge.
1 Samuel 3:19—4:1 and 7:13-17 provide a general picture of Samuel's nationally recognized ministry as a prophet and a judge, combining political and religious leadership. The towns mentioned in 1 Samuel 7:16 are fairly close together, and some interpreters have suggested that Samuel's itinerant work was much more restricted than is suggested by the phrase "from Dan to Beersheba" (1 Sam 3:20). However, Ramah, Shiloh and Kiriath-jearim are separated from these towns, as is Bethlehem, which Samuel visited later, so it is not unrealistic to see Samuel having widespread influence. The *Philistines were by no means defeated during Samuel's period of leadership, but they were kept at bay, and 1 Samuel 7:2-12 provides one specific illustration of Samuel's activity in encouraging the people to see God as the one who saves, helps and provides for Israel.

5. The Aged Samuel.
5.1. The Institution of the Monarchy. The account in 1 Samuel 8 of the people's request for a king presents a clear picture of the now aging Samuel with his strengths and weaknesses. Samuel obviously felt that their request for a king meant that his attempt, illustrated in 1 Samuel 7, to teach them that Yahweh was the only savior and provider that they needed, had not succeed-

ed. He apparently failed to see that it was his own action in appointing as leaders his sons, who seem to have been just as corrupt as the sons of Eli, that originally stimulated the people's request. He had been a great leader, but his ability to discern God's way forward seems to have begun to be influenced by his own reactions and feelings. He could not keep from taking their request as a personal rejection. The request of the elders may have reflected their failure to trust Yahweh, but their desire for a change of regime is understandable. The fact that they came to Samuel with the request, expecting him to take it forward, is a tribute to his previous work and an indication of their respect for his ability and insight. The fact that Samuel, in spite of his own qualms about what they were asking, was prepared to take it to God, was able to recognize that God was going to grant their request, and therefore was willing to carry it forward is a great tribute to his integrity. His judgment may have been faulty when it came to his own sons, but clearly he still had a lot left to give.

The anointing and eventual appointing of Saul as the first king of Israel provide evidence of Samuel's ongoing abilities. He recognizes that Saul was God's choice. He talks with Saul, challenging and encouraging him, finding a way of giving him the confidence to face what lay ahead (1 Sam 9:15—10:8). He organized the "election" process so that the people as a whole recognized the validity both of the new institution of monarchy and of the newly chosen king (1 Sam 10:17-24). He set up the systems and protocol needed for the new system to be effective (1 Sam 10:25) (see Kings and Kingship).

5.2. Samuel's Farewell Speech. Samuel's address in 1 Samuel 12 reflects something of the tension that he obviously felt over the way the situation had evolved. He wanted to make absolutely certain, and to ensure that everyone else also knew, that unlike Eli and his sons, and possibly unlike his own sons, he had not been removed from office because of some offense. On the contrary, throughout his life he had fulfilled his duties in an exemplary manner. It mattered to him greatly that this point be clarified (1 Sam 12:1-5). He tried to do all he could to ensure that the monarchy had a good chance of succeeding, explaining to all concerned that fearing, serving and obeying God was still the only way to avoid disaster. On the other hand, he wanted it to be very clear that

he himself was not happy about the concept of monarchy in the first place. Samuel's demonstration of the power of God (1 Sam 12:16-18) may have been partially motivated by his desire to show that he was still someone to be reckoned with, someone who had God's ear, but it also had the effect of frightening the people, perhaps to the extent of causing them to abandon the monarchy after all. Samuel clearly did not intend this result, and although the last part of the speech contains the strong encouragement to avoid sin and to maintain righteous behavior, its tone is much more positive. The people would have been left in no doubt that Samuel had not wanted a king, but they also would have been in no doubt that he would continue to support and pray for both nation and king.

5.3. Saul's Condemnation. It is possible that Samuel met with *Saul many times during the early years of his reign, but the two meetings that are recorded (1 Sam 13:1-13; 15:1-35) are negative, and both result in Samuel issuing strong rebukes. It is not absolutely clear whether Saul's first offense was primarily his failure to get on with the task of defeating the Philistines as God had commanded or his breaking of the ritual regulations by carrying out the sacrifice himself. In the second instance, the offense of keeping alive what God specifically commanded to be destroyed is clearer. The first offense resulted in the prediction that Saul's dynasty would not endure. The second was treated more seriously, and Saul is told that he personally had been rejected as king. The only indication that Samuel felt anything other than a sense of righteous indignation when he dealt with Saul in this way is found in 1 Samuel 15:35, where it is poignantly said that Samuel mourned for him. Samuel apparently had taken his mentoring role with the young king seriously, and Saul's failure brought him no joy.

5.4. Samuel and David. The story of the anointing of *David sees a less confident Samuel, afraid of Saul and not finding it quite as easy as he had in his youth to discern God's way forward. However, his desire to serve Yahweh and to follow through with his purposes remains as strong as ever. It is perhaps a further sign of Samuel's failing powers that his only other encounter with David is when David, on his flight from Saul's court, sought out Samuel to bring him up to date with events. Samuel apparently was no longer traveling, but he could still pray and was still involved with prophetic groups.

5.5. Epitaph for Samuel. Samuel's death is recorded briefly in 1 Samuel 25:1. He was no longer the significant player in national life that he once had been, but the contribution that he had made was fully recognized, and all Israel assembled and mourned for him.

We cannot be sure exactly what happened during Saul's visit to the so-called witch of Endor described in 1 Samuel 28. The account is obscure, probably deliberately so, and we have no way of knowing whether this was a trick, the appearance of some kind of evil spirit or an actual visit from the dead Samuel. The message given simply repeats what Saul already knew or feared, and the account adds nothing to our knowledge of the man Samuel.

6. Conclusion.
Samuel—a man who served his God and his country faithfully from the time he came to "know the Lord" as a small child right through the long years of his life; a man who cared deeply both about the one who mentored him and those he mentored; a man who was able, in spite of deep reluctance and pain, to deliver bad news of God's displeasure as well as bring good news of God's choices; a man who, in spite of his blindness concerning his own sons, had great insight and spiritual discernment. Samuel might well be seen as the winner of the award for "best supporting actor" in the OT.

See also HISTORY OF ISRAEL 2: PREMONARCHIC PERIOD; HISTORY OF ISRAEL 3: UNITED MONARCHY; SAMUEL, BOOKS OF.

BIBLIOGRAPHY. **R. Alter,** *The David Story: A Translation with Commentary of 1 and 2 Samuel* (New York: Norton, 1999); **W. Brueggemann,** *First and Second Samuel* (IBC; Louisville: John Knox, 1990); **A. Cook,** "'Fiction' and History in Samuel and Kings," *JSOT* 36 (1986) 27-48; **M. A. Eaton,** *Preaching Through the Bible: 1 Samuel* (Tonbridge: Sovereign World, 1995); **M. J. Evans,** *2 Samuel* (NIBC; Peabody, MA: Hendrickson, 2000); idem, *The Message of Samuel: Personalities, Potential, Politics and Power* (BST; Downers Grove, IL: InterVarsity Press, 2004); **J. Goldingay,** *Men Behaving Badly* (Carlisle: Paternoster, 2000); **R. P. Gordon,** *1 & 2 Samuel* (OTG; Sheffield: JSOT, 1984); **H. W. Hertzberg,** *I & II Samuel* (OTL; London: SCM, 1964); **I. L. Jensen,** *First and Second Samuel* (Chicago: Moody Press, 1995); **R. W. Klein,** *1 Samuel* (WBC 10; Waco,

TX: Word, 1983); **J. C. Laney,** *First and Second Samuel* (Chicago: Moody Press, 1995); **E. Robertson,** "Samuel and Saul," *BJRL* 28 (1944) 175-206; **F. A. Spina,** "Eli's Seat: The Transition from Priest to Prophet in 1 Samuel 1-4," *JSOT* 62 (1994) 67-75.   M. J. Evans

SAMUEL, BOOKS OF

The books of Samuel are comprised of an extended narrative with occasional poetic sections, relating events occurring just prior to and during the early decades of Israel's monarchy. These events include the birth of the monarchy, the reign of Israel's first king, *Saul, and the rise and majority of the reign of *David. The narrative continues that of the two books preceding it in the Jewish canon, *Joshua and *Judges, which together with 1-2 Samuel and *1-2 Kings comprise the Former Prophets. In the Septuagint, 1-2 Samuel are the first and second of the four books of Reigns (or Kingdoms) together with 1-2 Kings. Although the books of Samuel originally were composed as a single literary piece (perhaps as part of a more extended historical work, the *Deuteronomistic History), the Septuagint and Vulgate translators divided them into separate books, a practice followed in the Christian canon.

1. Content and Structure
2. Authorship and Sources
3. Historical Considerations
4. Theological Themes

1. Content and Structure.
The authors and editors of the books of Samuel narrate some of the most compelling and theologically significant episodes of the Bible, usually without interrupting the flow of the narrative to explain overtly the significance of the events (*see* Narrative Art of Israel's Historians). Instead, the historians rely on the sheer power of the story to carry the message forward, a literary technique known as "showing." On rare occasions in the books of Samuel the historians have inserted explicit and authoritative explanations to evaluate motives or qualities of the characters, a technique known as "telling" (e.g., 2 Sam 8:6b) (see Abrams, 23).

The structure of 1-2 Samuel in their present form may be analyzed in five parts: Israel's need for a king (1 Sam 1—7), the reign of Saul (1 Sam 8—15), the rise of David (1 Sam 16—2 Sam 4), the reign of David (2 Sam 5—20) and an epilogue comprised of appendices related to David's reign (2 Sam 21—24). Thus the first unit describes the prelude to the monarchy, while the second its advent and the third its establishment. The fourth unit may be said to narrate the consolidation of the monarchy under David, while the final unit functions as an epilogue to the books generally. Throughout the whole the narrative raises and answers questions about the nature and purpose of Israel's new monarchy: What is the acceptable nature of an Israelite monarchy? Who can serve suitably in this new institution? The first question is addressed primarily in 1 Samuel 1—15 by means of the gripping narratives related to Saul's rise and reign, and especially through the speeches of the prophet Samuel (1 Sam 8 and 12). The second question is addressed throughout both books by means of contrasting Saul and David, who serve as negative and positive prototypes of Israel's kings (Arnold 2003, 32-35).

1.1. Israel's Need for a King (1 Sam 1—7). This unit is devoted to the beginnings of the new Israelite institution of kingship (*see* Kings and Kingship). The opening chapters illustrate the deficiencies of the old tribal confederation centered on priesthood and tabernacle at *Shiloh, and supported by a judges system. The conclusion of the book of Judges describes a period of great instability and uncertainty (Judg 17:6; 21:25). Then 1 Samuel 1—3 legitimizes the prophet Samuel by describing the holy events surrounding his birth and his sensitivity to God's call during childhood. The emphasis on the righteousness of Samuel and his family is heightened by contrasts with Eli and his wicked sons, the priests of the tabernacle at Shiloh. The so-called Ark Narrative of 1 Samuel 4—7 describes the wars between Israel and the *Philistines, and again shows the importance of Samuel's ministry during these years. This was a critical moment in Israel's life because both the religious and the political superstructures had failed, as illustrated first by the Shiloh traditions (1 Sam 1—3) and then by the Ark Narrative (1 Sam 4—7).

The next few chapters trace the fortunes of the *ark of the covenant, from its capture at Ebenezer, its sojourn in Philistia and its eventual return to Kiriath Jearim (1 Sam 4—7). These chapters place Samuel aside temporarily in order to celebrate the power of Yahweh's ark, perhaps Israel's greatest sacred symbol. The full name for the ark appears to have been "the ark of the covenant of Yahweh of hosts, who dwells between the cherubim" (1 Sam 4:4). This epithet for God—Yahweh of hosts—occurs in 1 Samuel 1:3 for the first time in the Bible, and it may reflect an especially close connection to worship at Shiloh. Although the ark eventually is retrieved and the nation repentant, the narrative contains a warning about Israel's deep-rooted problems, which led to the lack of respect and care for the ark in the first place. As the nation's religious failure was made clear by the Elide priesthood at Shiloh, so the political and military failure was illuminated by the Philistine victory at Ebenezer (1 Sam 4:1-11).

1.2. The Reign of Saul (1 Sam 8—15). In addition to the rise of Israelite monarchy generally, this unit narrates the failure of Israel's first king, Saul. 1 Samuel 9—11 functions as a central unit on the accession of Saul, which is framed by ideological speculation in 1 Samuel 8 and 12 on the nature of kingship itself (Long, 183-90). The unit contains both positive and negative attitudes toward the concept of kingship. While the unit may reflect contradictory original sources, the current arrangement uses interchange between the pro- and antimonarchical materials to complement each other: 8:1-22 (negative); 9:1—10:16 (positive); 10:17-27 (negative); 11:1-11 (positive); 11:12—12:25 (negative) (see McCarthy; Childs, 277-78).

After a great victory over the *Ammonites (1 Sam 11), Saul enjoyed modest initial success against the Philistines (1 Sam 13—14). It was for defense against the Philistines that Saul had come to the throne, and for this purpose an Israelite throne existed at all (1 Sam 9:16; 10:5). However, when Saul failed to follow Samuel's instructions regarding the sacrifice before battle, the result was a prophetic rebuke in which Saul was informed that his dynasty would not endure (1 Sam 13:13-14). When Samuel announced that Yahweh had sought out "a man after [God's] own heart" to replace Saul (1 Sam 13:14), he emphasized both Yahweh's freedom in making such a choice and David's character as someone having a certain like-mindedness with Yahweh (Arnold 2003, 199). In an interesting parallel in the Babylonian Chronicle series, Nebuchadnezzar II installs "a king of his own choice [lit., 'heart']," referring to his choice of Zedekiah as vassal ruler in Jerusalem in 597 BCE (Grayson, 102, chronicle 5, lines rev. 11-13).

In 1 Samuel 13 Saul is permitted to continue as king, but it is clear that his line will not continue on the throne in Jerusalem. The great tragedy of that loss becomes apparent when the crown prince, Jonathan, manifests surpassing leadership qualities that would have served him well as Saul's replacement (1 Sam 14). The narrative describes and defends the rejection of Saul by means of analogy between Saul and Jonathan, contrasting the two in order to condemn Saul (Gordon 1984, 57). Saul's war with the Amalekites (1 Sam 15) was divinely initiated, with strict regulations and restrictions. Unfortunately, Saul proved unwilling to accept God's restrictions and suffered prophetic condemnation as a consequence. These three chapters (1 Sam 13—15) narrate Yahweh's rejection of Saul as king of Israel, and as such they serve as a bridge between the justification of kingship as an Israelite institution (1 Sam 8—12) and the rise of David, who is anointed in 1 Samuel 16.

1.3. The Rise of David (1 Sam 16—2 Sam 4). The anointing of David by the prophet Samuel is a turning point in the book (1 Sam 16:1-13), reflecting the final and official rejection of king Saul (1 Sam 15) and the centrality of David from this point forward. At the transitional center of 1 Samuel 16, itself the symmetrical center of 1 Samuel as a whole, David receives the spirit of Yahweh, marking him as Saul's replacement: "the spirit of Yahweh rushed mightily *[ṣālaḥ]* upon David from that day forward" (1 Sam 16:13). In a corresponding note in the next verse, Saul loses the spirit of Yahweh and begins to be tormented by an injurious "evil spirit from Yahweh" (1 Sam 16:14). The rest of 1 Samuel narrates the troubled relationship between Israel's two anointed ones, and this shift of political and spiritual power from Saul to David in 1 Samuel 16:13-14 becomes programmatic for the narrative's depiction of the two.

Saul is now king in name only. He is ineffectual and powerless to provide deliverance from the Philistines, which was the great promise of Israel's new monarchy (1 Sam 9:16). This is nowhere more evident than in the story of David and *Goliath (1 Sam 17), which opens with Israel's army locked in a stalemate with the Philistines in the western foothills. In the face of Goliath's defiance, Saul's paralysis is contrasted with David's fearless determination to defend the honor of Yahweh's name (1 Sam 17:26, 36, 45). David's leadership and victory mobilize the Israelite army, resulting in a great rout of the Philistines (1 Sam 17:52-53), and validate David's anointing (1 Sam 16:1-13), just as Saul's victory over the Ammonites had validated Saul's anointing (1 Sam 11:1-15).

For the last unit of 1 Samuel, David's fortunes are rising while Saul's are declining, at times gradually, at times precipitously. Suddenly, David is perceived as a threat by Saul. The narrative characterizes the two by contrasting the relationship of Saul's family to David with the way Saul himself relates to him. The perduring love of Saul's family for David serves as a foil for Saul's own jealous attitude, which oscillates inexplicably between murderous hatred and gracious tolerance (1 Sam 18—19).

Ultimately, David fears for his life and is forced to flee from Saul, never to return to his royal court (1 Sam 19:18-24). In exile, and permanently estranged from king Saul, David seeks aid from the priest Ahimelech at Nob, the Philistine king Achish and, finally, he seeks refuge in the cave of Adullam (1 Sam 21—22). As David moves further away from the royal power of Saul's court at *Gibeah, he moves deeper into the fringes of Judahite society. Subsequent events related to the Philistine attack on the city of Keilah continue the contrast between Saul and David, who are on opposite trajectories (1 Sam 23). David stumbles on opportunities to kill Saul on two occasions. But the idea of striking the anointed of Yahweh is unthinkable to David, while Saul, on the other hand, is characterized as having an obsession with destroying David (1 Sam 24; 26).

While on the run, David encounters conflict with the wealthy but boorish Nabal, and the latter's noble wife intercedes to prevent a violent conclusion (1 Sam 25). Considerable space is devoted to David's sojourn with the Philistines, among whom he finds protection from Saul while also discreetly warring against potential enemies of Judah (1 Sam 27—31). The continued threat from the Philistines is a reminder that Saul has not functioned as the legitimate anointed one of Israel, evidenced by renewed conflict announced in 1 Samuel 28:4-5.

With imminent battle as the background, Saul visits the necromancer at Endor to conduct a séance, in which he converses with the deceased Samuel (1 Sam 28). In narrating this climactic moment of crisis in Saul's life, the text brings to the surface and makes explicit a contrast between Saul and David that up to this point in 1 Samuel had been employed more subtly: the two men have made important decisions in very different ways. Saul was no longer capable of discerning Yahweh's will through legitimate, authorized means of inquiry (i.e., dreams, lots, prophecy [1 Sam 28:6]), and so he turned to the option of necromancy. On the other hand, David consistently and commendably relied on the prophetic word of Yahweh, as discerned especially through Urim and Thummim (implied by the collocation "inquire of Yahweh/God" to describe David's reliance on the priestly ephod for guidance [see 1 Sam 22:10; 23:2,4; 30:7-8; 2 Sam 2:1; 5:23; similarly, 1 Sam 22:13, 15]). Throughout 1 Samuel, David's reliance on Urim and Thummim prepares for Saul's use of necromancy in 1 Samuel 28:3-19, in order to contrast Israel's two anointed ones specifically by means of the contradictory ways in which they sought guidance (Arnold, 2004).

The next two chapters return to David's life as a mercenary soldier with the Philistines, during which time he exacted revenge against the Amalekites and engaged in covert battles on behalf of various cities of Judah (1 Sam 29—30). David's reliance on the priestly sanctioned Urim in preparation for battle with the Amalekites is a reminder of Saul's failure to accept Yahweh's authority (1 Sam 30:7-8) and demonstrates that David is all that Saul should have been. The Philistine victory at Mount Gilboa, along with the deaths of Saul and Jonathan, merely confirm that Saul had become an illegitimate ruler, since he died at the hands of Israel's greatest enemy, whom he himself had been crowned to subdue (1 Sam 31).

After a report of Saul's death, to which David expresses surprising outrage (2 Sam 1:1-16), the emotional elegy written for Saul and Jonathan reveals David's pain with singular clarity (2 Sam 1:17-27). The remainder of this unit narrates the civil war between the house of Saul in the north and David in Judah, culminating in the death of Saul's son Ish-Bosheth (2 Sam 2—4).

1.4. The Reign of David (2 Sam 5—20). With the end of the rival monarchy in the north, the narrator of the books of Samuel devotes a unit to the consolidation of David's power, beginning with his coronation as king over all Israel (2 Sam 5:1-5) and the formation of a new state through political and religious innovations (2 Sam 5:6—6:23). These innovations included the capture and transformation of *Jerusalem into a new capital city (2 Sam 5:6-10), his construction of a palace (2 Sam 5:11-12), his expulsion of the Philistines from Judah's heartland (2 Sam 5:17-25) and his religious reforms in the new capital city (2 Sam 6:1-23). As a result of these innovations, the images of "King David" and "the city of David/Jerusalem/Zion" became two of the most permanent and powerful images in ancient Israel's ideology (*see* Zion Traditions).

After several chapters of rapid narrative action, 2 Samuel 7 contains speeches almost exclusively. The dialogical nature of the chapter reflects the significance of David and his dynasty in salvation history, past and future. David expresses his intentions to build a temple for Yahweh in 2 Samuel 7:1-3. Nathan the prophet at first confirms David's plan, but later he recants when God reveals an alternate plan during the night (2 Sam 7:4-17). The message of the chapter revolves around a play on "house" *(bayit),* which occurs fifteen times, either with a literal, physical sense (palace or temple), or with a metaphoric denotation (extended family, clan or tribe). Instead of David building a "house" (i.e., temple) for Yahweh, God declares that he will build a "house" for David (2 Sam 7:11 [read "royal dynasty"]), and David's son will in fact build the physical temple (2 Sam 7:13). Moreover, David's line will not end; Yahweh will be a father to David's descendants, and they will be Yahweh's sons (2 Sam 7:13-16). Other passages of the OT designate this relationship between Yahweh and David as a *běrît,* "covenant" (1 Kings 8:23-24; 2 Chron 21:7; Ps 89:1-4, 19-37; cf. 2 Chron 7:18; 13:5; Ps 132:11-18), as does David himself in 2 Samuel 23:5 (*see* Davidic Covenant).

The narrative returns to military concerns in 2 Samuel 8, which is a catalogue of David's successes in the Transjordan and the north (for a recent argument that the source for this chapter was a royal display inscription, see Halpern 2001, 133-226). Once peace is secured for the new kingdom, David turns his attention to the house of Saul in order to show mercy to Mephibosheth, "for Jonathan's sake" (2 Sam 9:1, 7). The Ammonite wars (2 Sam 10—12) become the occasion of David's sin with Bathsheba and murder of Uriah, her husband. Although David has been the ideal king to this point in the books of Samuel, he now appears to be a typical ancient Near Eastern despot, guilty of "taking" that which is not rightfully his, as Samuel warned about despotic rulers (1 Sam 8:11-18) (on "taking," *lāqaḥ*, as a theme word in 2 Sam 11 see Arnold 2003, 527). But even here, David serves as a paradigm of repentance and forgiveness (see 4.3 below).

The extended narrative (2 Sam 13—20) flows from David's sins described in the preceding chapters and the initial judgment pronounced there: "the sword will never depart from your house" (2 Sam 12:10). David's private and intensely personal sin quickly breaks forth in public and violent behavior among his children. Amnon's rape of his half-sister Tamar and its consequences expose the problems and prepare for even more enmity in *David's family (2 Sam 13—14). Absalom's conspiracy involves court intrigue, seditious insurrection, the death of another crown prince and civil war (2 Sam 15—20), and the structure of the book relates all of this in a cause-and-effect continuum to David's sin in the matter of Bathsheba and Uriah.

1.5. Epilogue (2 Sam 21—24). Whereas the preceding units of the books of Samuel created an extended narrative with many literary connections, these final four chapters are a collection of disparate materials with little or no chronological or literary relationship to the whole. These chapters contain a variety of literary types (poetry, annalistic lists, historical narratives), producing a sort of mosaic of David's reign. Most scholars assume a chiastic symmetry in the way the materials are collected (Youngblood, 1051; Arnold 2003, 615-17).

A Yahweh's wrath against Israel (2 Sam
    21:1-14)
  B David's heroes (2 Sam 21:15-22)
    C David's song of praise (2 Sam
      22:1-51)
    C' David's last words (2 Sam 23:1-7)
  B' David's mighty men (2 Sam 23:8-39)
A' Yahweh's wrath against Israel (2 Sam
    24:1-25)

The compiler of the final edition of the books of Samuel saw fit to include these materials as necessary background in order to present a complete portrait of David as the ideal king of Israel.

2. Authorship and Sources.
The authors and editors of 1-2 Samuel are anonymous. The Talmud preserves the rabbinic tradition that these books were written by prophets who lived contemporaneously with the events described: Samuel wrote 1 Samuel 1—24, and Nathan and Gad wrote the rest (*b. B. Bat.* 14b; 15a; cf. 1 Chron 29:29). It is true that much of 1-2 Samuel has been narrated from a decidedly prophetic point of view, which no doubt led to the talmudic speculation.

Biblical scholars have devised a theory over the past six decades to explain the origins and composition of 1-2 Samuel, and it is fair to say that something of a consensus now exists, although the details are much debated. The books of Samuel appear to have been a portion of a longer work tracing Israel's history from Moses to the destruction of Jerusalem by the Babylonians in 587 BCE. This longer history was comprised of Deuteronomy (at least in part), plus Joshua, Judges, 1-2 Samuel and 1-2 Kings—that is, the Former Prophets of the Hebrew canon. These books appear to have presented a theological history of Israel, evaluating Israel's past in light of the covenant relationship established in Deuteronomy and relying on the so-called retribution theology established there. Based on the curses and blessings of Deuteronomy 28, the doctrine of retribution assumes the idea of reward for obedience to the covenant and punishment for disobedience. Such a guiding principle evaluated national and individual successes and failures in terms of the consequences of faithfulness or disobedience to Deuteronomic law. As a result, this extended history is commonly referred to as the *Deuteronomistic History. Although the theory has gone through significant modification through the years, it remains today the best explanation of the origins of these historical books (Knoppers 2000; for representative approaches to the theory see Römer; Römer and de Pury).

Of the books contained in the Deuteronomistic History, 1-2 Samuel have the least amount of editorial and compositional detail that may be considered distinctively "Deuteronomistic" (Römer and de Pury, 123-28). This may be because the historian responsible for 1-2 Samuel appears to have taken large portions of previously existing materials (or "sources") and folded them into his extended treatment. It seems likely that the historian had at least three narrative units available, which had independent histories before their being used to produce the books of Samuel (Halpern 1981, 149-74). The first of these was the Ark Narrative, comprised of 1 Samuel 4:1b—7:1 (and perhaps also 2 Sam 6 [see Miller and Roberts; McCarter 1980-1984, 1.23-26]). The second source likely used by the compiler of 1-2 Samuel was the History of David's Rise, 1 Samuel 16:14—2 Samuel 5:25 (or perhaps continuing through 2 Sam 7 [see Mettinger 1976, 33-47]). The third source was the Court History, otherwise known as the Succession Narrative, 2 Samuel 9—20; 1 Kings 1—2 (Rost; Forshey). At places these sources appear to have been supplemented with other materials (such as the Shiloh traditions in 1 Sam 1—3), serial lists and appendices to comprise the whole. The parameters for these sources, and indeed the independent existence of some of them, have been called into question (for recent views on the parameters, coherence and purposes of the Court History see the essays in de Pury and Römer). Regardless of the origins and extent of individual pieces, it would be a mistake to underestimate the degree of intentionality behind the present arrangement of the books of Samuel and so miss the grander themes in view in the narrative of Saul and David.

It often is assumed that these three original narrative sources—the Ark Narrative, the History of David's Rise, the Court History—constituting the skeletal framework for the books of Samuel were some of the world's earliest and finest works of history. This has especially been said often of the Court History. Likewise, it sometimes has been argued that these pieces were composed soon after the events themselves and were therefore relatively accurate historically. In the last few decades scholars have routinely argued instead that these books are products of the late preexilic, the exilic, or in some cases, the postexilic periods, and that they contain little if anything of historical value. Thus the details of the consensus about these sources has collapsed, even while weaknesses in the arguments for the exilic and postexilic dates for the narrative units of Samuel have been exposed (Knoppers 1999, 212-15).

3. Historical Considerations.
The books of Samuel introduce the reader to numerous people and places over nearly a century of history. As historical books in the Bible, 1-2 Samuel most often are read through the eyes of faith, making them "more than history, not less than history" (Goldingay, 32). That is, the reader is required to consider the historical context of the events described, but understands that those events have a more intrinsic value

than their mere factuality. Thus history is an important instrument of revelation, the means of theologizing favored by Israelite authors, and in most cases those authors assumed that the events they were describing occurred. But these historians were not concerned with writing an exact history, or history in a modern sense. Biblical historiography, in contradistinction to modern history-writing since the Enlightenment, locates the causes of human events in the passions and purposes of Yahweh, the God of Israel (*see* Historiography, Old Testament; Propaganda).

At the same time, it is necessary for contemporary readers to consider the specifics of Israel's historical context. Until recent decades scholars were in general agreement about the particulars of Israel's united monarchy. Although there was no consensus on the premonarchical period and the exodus, let alone the ancestral age, most could agree on the essentials of David's and Solomon's kingdoms. Discussion tended to revolve around the nature of *Israelite society during the early monarchy, and the geographical extent of the kingdom under David and Solomon. However, in the closing decades of the twentieth century this consensus crumbled (Knoppers 1997). Currently, scholars debate whether David and Solomon existed as anything other than legendary figures, or perhaps as fictitious characters created in the Persian or Hellenistic periods. However, an impressive number of factors (e.g., the Tel Dan inscription [*see* Non-Israelite Written Sources: Syro-Palestinian], archaeological evidence related to the occupation levels in Judah and Israel, as well as the biblical narratives) point to David's existence, although the city of Jerusalem was not a large, capital city during the tenth century BCE (*see* Jerusalem). It seems likely that throughout the united monarchy, David and Solomon maintained Jerusalem as a relatively small and neutral capital, intentionally limiting its dominance (Vaughn, 420-21, 428). After the division of the kingdom into Israel and Judah, the need for neutrality was lost, and the city began to experience expansion. It is also possible to view the sudden transformation of *Hazor, *Megiddo, and *Gezer from burnt-out ruin heaps into "roughly comparable complex fortified governmental centers" as evidence for the existence of an efficient military and centrally organized administration powerful enough to effect such transformation (Holladay, 371; on the historicity of the books of Samuel generally, see Halpern 2001).

If we assume the accuracy of the broad outline of events presented in 1-2 Samuel, it remains only to consider the sociopolitical details of this early period of Israel's history, including specifically the transition from a segmented tribal society to statehood. Several scholars have applied anthropological or macrosociological theory to the traditional archaeological and textual data in attempts to explore this transition (Carter, 428-33). Most identify the reigns of Saul and David as "chiefdoms," a type of society that typically preceded in social development a monarchy with centralized power (e.g., Flanagan, 304-18; Miller). It seems more likely that these first appearances of monarchy in ancient Israel involved no such evolutionary development from tribalism to statehood, but rather burst on the scene suddenly as a new Israelite "tribalstate." We now have evidence of other such "tribal kingdoms," in which tribal chiefs retained their patrimonial heritage and identity while assuming the power and administrative structures of a previously existing state (presumably a Canaanite city-state in Israel's case [see Fleming, 47]).

4. Theological Themes.

As integral components of the OT Historical Books, 1-2 Samuel form part of Israel's "witnessing tradition" (Goldingay, 1-86) and invite readers to become part of that tradition. The books of Samuel address questions of the nature and purpose of Israel's monarchy, and they offer the reader explanations of Israel's covenant relationship with Yahweh as king. By presenting contrasting portraits of Israel's first human kings, these books serve a programmatic function for Israel's future perceptions of monarchs, as well as for individuals in God's kingdom.

4.1. Yahweh as King. The idea that God was king in Israel had its origins in the very self-identity of the nation. In theological expressions of Israel's covenant relationship with the Great King, Yahweh, and through explicit references in some of the Pentateuch's early poetry, Yahweh was Israel's king (e.g., Ex 15:18; Num 23:21; Deut 33:5). The concept of covenant became Israel's most important and pervasive relational metaphor to describe the nation's relationship with God, who is thus the Great King, and Israel

the vassal. It should not be surprising, then, that the transition from theocracy to monarchy, which is narrated mostly in 1 Samuel, was a momentous event in the life of ancient Israel, and one that aroused conflicting views of the nature and purpose of monarchy.

As we have noted, the opening seven chapters of 1 Samuel contain reminders of Yahweh's role as king in Israel. The reference to "Yahweh of hosts" in 1 Samuel 1:3 may have been especially associated with the cult at Shiloh, and certainly it became prominent in the later Jerusalem cult, where "Yahweh of hosts" is identified as the "King of glory" (Ps 24:10). In the Ark Narrative the powerful imagery of the *ark of the covenant may best be understood as presenting a visible sign of the presence of Yahweh seated upon a royal throne. The significance of the full name of the ark is that the invisible Yahweh is perceived as a monarch on a throne with sphinxes on either side ("the ark of the covenant of Yahweh of hosts, who is enthroned between the cherubim" [1 Sam 4:4, cf. Ex 25:22]), which corresponds to examples of the iconography of Canaanite and Phoenician royal thrones in which winged sphinxes were used (as on, e.g., the Ahiram sarcophagus [Mettinger 1995, 139; Keel and Uehlinger, 168; Cross, 69]). The idea that the top of the ark served as a royal throne for the invisible Yahweh also became prominent in the Jerusalem cult (Is 37:14-16; Ps 99:1-3), and at times the ark served as Yahweh's footstool or podium (1 Chron 28:2; Ps 99:5; 132:7).

In addition to these indications of Yahweh's royalty, the Ark Narrative generally celebrates God's sovereignty over the Philistines and their deities. Even in the Philistine homeland, and even when they carried the ark to the various Philistine cities in an attempt to rid themselves of Yahweh's power, the Philistines are forced to "give glory" to the God of Israel (1 Sam 6:5). While Israel's own religious and political institutions are failing, the Philistines are learning that Yahweh is indeed king, and that God is capable of protecting Israel from all harm.

4.2. Human King and Messiah. Israel's theological understanding of Yahweh as king was not a concept that could be relinquished easily in the new monarchy. The definition and function of a human monarch came relatively late in Israel's history compared to the roles of priest and judge, and even prophet (*see* Judges; Priests and Levites; Prophets and Prophecy). Israel's old political and religious institutions from the premonarchical period were crumbling, as was clear from the deplorable behavior of the Elide priesthood at Shiloh and the inability of the tribal confederation to provide security in the land. 1 Samuel 1—7 illustrates the deficiencies of the model of a tribal confederation centered around priesthood and tabernacle at Shiloh, and supported by a judges system (*see* Amphictyony, Question of), although the blame for their failure clearly is not Yahweh's. By the time the reader reaches 1 Samuel 12, it becomes obvious to the prophet Samuel, the most ardent adversary of the monarchy, that kingship is necessary and, if rightly constituted, even desirable. Thus much of Samuel's energy in 1 Samuel 8—12 is devoted to constituting the new institution in a way that retains the royalty of Yahweh and defines the role of the human king.

Yahweh governed Israel in the past through certain religious and political institutions (priesthood and tabernacle, with its ark at Shiloh and the network of judges). Paradoxically, these must all be transformed in the new monarchy, yet they must also remain the same. The priesthood will be resuscitated, the tabernacle relocated and rebuilt as a permanent structure to house the ark, and the judges system reconfigured and absorbed by the monarchy. But as symbols of Yahweh's kingship, they will remain. Ultimately, Israel came to define the relationship of the human king to the divine king in a way similar to the *Assyrians and *Babylonians. The real king was the deity, while the human king was only a representative or viceroy. The human king was chosen by the deity to fulfill his wishes in the human kingdom (Roberts, 99). One of the central functions of all Mesopotamian kings was to serve as the primary human link with the gods. All rulers from Hammurapi to Nabonidus claimed that they were called by a great god who had chosen them for the office and who maintained an intimate link with the human king (cf. Ps 2:7, see Saggs, 135-37; Leick, 64; Nemet-Nejat, 217-18).

So initially Saul was given as "leader" or "ruler" *(nāgîd)* over the nation, which connotes that he is the king-designate appointed by Yahweh, and thus emphasizes the primacy of Yahweh's choosing over any public acclaim (1 Sam 9:16). Saul would become "king" *(melek)* only at his public acclamation (1 Sam 10:24), thus preserving *nāgîd* as a theological expression of Israel's monarch as "the one designated by Yahweh" (Hasel, 196-99; McCarter 1980-1984, 1.178-79). Furthermore, the term *nāgîd* may have limited the kingship of Saul by bearing certain traditions stemming from Israel's old tribal confederation, for which *nāgîd* may have referred to the "commander" of the national militia (Cross, 220). Thus the kingship of Saul was defined and circumscribed as a conditional appointment. As long as Saul served under the inspiration of the Spirit of God (1 Sam 10:6, 10), and as long as he avoided violations of the ancient tribal legal traditions, he would serve as Yahweh's vicegerent.

Under David the process of defining the Israelite monarchy continued. His dramatic expulsion of the Philistines from Israel's heartland and transformation of Jerusalem into a new political and religious capital established both the king and his royal city firmly in the psyche of Israel for the rest of biblical history (2 Sam 5:1—6:23). The images of king and city were among the most powerful in ancient Israel's worldview, and the books of Samuel narrate the sociopolitical and religious developments involved in their appearance. In sum, taken together with the Zadokite priesthood (1 Kings 2:26-27), these institutions—Israel's new monarchy, the central worship site, the priesthood—are explicitly tied together in David, Jerusalem and *Zadok. In essence, all the themes relevant to Israel's burgeoning messianism are developed in 1-2 Samuel, some to nearly complete form.

In compiling 1-2 Samuel, the biblical historian consciously attempted to recount the past as a means of lending support and legitimacy to the Israelite monarchy as constituted in the Davidic dynasty. The implication is that Israel's monarchy must always be what the prophet Samuel intended, and the king should always be like David. Thus these narratives are programmatic for Israel's monarchy, and so they argue that Israel's kingdom should have certain defining characteristics. The future perspective of the historian and the inclusion of the narrative in the Jewish and Christian canons transform it from a purely programmatic treatise on what the nature of Israelite kingship ought to be into a theological treatise on the desired character of future kings and of the kingdom generally. The impact of this narrative on the rest of biblical tradition and subsequent traditions in Second Temple Judaism is profound (Halpern 1981, 19-20; Schniedewind, 3, 158-60).

Especially central to this programmatic plan is the covenant between Yahweh and David in 2 Samuel 7. As we have seen, God's promises that David's son would build a temple in Jerusalem and that God would establish a permanent Davidic dynasty were unequivocally taken as a "covenant" in *innerbiblical exegesis, even though the term bĕrît does not appear in 2 Samuel 7 itself (see 2 Sam 23:5; cf. 1 Kings 8:23-24; 2 Chron 21:7; Ps 89:1-4, 19-37). In this sense, the Davidic covenant is a vital link in the singular and organic covenantal trajectory building on Noah, Abraham and Moses in biblical theology, and it becomes programmatic for NT authors when defining Jesus as the "Son of David" (or, relying on 2 Sam 7:14a, as the "Son of God" [cf. Heb 1:5]) (see Arnold 2003, 478-87).

The promise of an ideal son of David to build and lead the nation conflicts with the severe shortcomings of David introduced at 2 Samuel 11 and sustained through 2 Samuel 20. His sin with Bathsheba and his inability to control his family call into question the program detailed by God in 2 Samuel 7. The rejection of King Saul in 1 Samuel highlights the need for a righteous and faithful king and raises the question of whether David himself might be rejected like Saul, making null and void the covenant. The narrative thus suspends a contrastive tension between the Davidic ideal and the reality of David's failures, creating a "deliberately emphasized antinomy" that drives the reader past the pages of 1-2 Samuel for the answers (Satterthwaite, 64-65). Some OT prophetic texts also sustain the tension between the ideal figure of David's son with the realization that few if any of his descendants lived up to that ideal (e.g., Amos 9:11-12; Is 11:1-2; Jer 23:5). The books of Samuel do not resolve the tension fully, but rather set the course for future messianism to evolve by presenting the ideas in germinal form.

As a subtheme related to the nature of Israelite kingship, the books of Samuel also deal with the use and abuse of power. At stake, of course, is the manner in which the human king would use or abuse his God-given power. Will the Israelite king, like other kings both ancient and modern, manipulate and conspire in the process of ruling? Or, rather, would he submit to Yahweh's rulership and acknowledge certain divinely established limits to his power? Samuel warns that an Israelite monarchy could become an unchecked human institution that conscripts Israelite men (and even women!) into military service, confiscates property, and leads ultimately to enslavement, apparently an authentic description of the semifeudal Canaanite political structure as it existed during Iron Age I (1 Sam 8:10-18). The prophetic speech is filled with warnings of "taking" and "serving," which surely adumbrate David's sending to "take" Bathsheba (2 Sam 11:4); and in fact, David's kingship may have had specifically Jebusite influences (Day, 72-90). In general, the books of Samuel present two portraits of Israelite kingship. In the first (Saul), the anointed one failed in his handling of power because he failed to accept Yahweh's authority, which set limits on the new kingship. In the second (David), the anointed one also abused power, but he quickly and earnestly repented and genuinely accepted divinely ordained limits to his power. This theme in 1-2 Samuel is the logical corollary to the definition of Israel's monarchy as a circumscribed and limited office.

4.3. Repentance and Forgiveness. The definition and nature of repentance is an additional theme of 1-2 Samuel, which contributes to the narrative's characterization of Israel's first two monarchs. A close reading of the final form of 1-2 Samuel reveals a pattern in which the three protagonists of the narrative (Samuel, Saul, David) serve to highlight and emphasize the definition and nature of confession and repentance. The macrostructure of 1-2 Samuel creates trajectories for these three main figures that work together to define and illustrate the text's fundamental message. The concept of turning to Yahweh (šûb, "turn back, return") is, of course, central to many of the canonical prophets, particularly Hosea, Joel and Jeremiah (e.g., Hos 14:1-2; Joel 2:12-13; Jer 18:1-12).

First, at a critical juncture in Israel's history, the prophet Samuel seized a moment of tragedy in order to call the nation to repentance. The opening six chapters of 1 Samuel condemn a wicked Elide priesthood at Shiloh and a nation plagued with sin and failure. Samuel then employed terminology characteristic of much of Israelite prophetic preaching in his call for a "return" (šûb) to Yahweh (for linguistic details see Arnold 2003, 130-33). Such genuine repentance is required to restore a right relationship with Yahweh, and it involves at once both a turning away from the sins that have caused the separation and a returning unto God. This return must be "wholehearted," implying there can be no divided loyalties or opinions when one returns to Yahweh. In the case of Samuel's appeal in 1 Samuel 7, repentance involved a repudiation of Israel's allegiance to Canaanite gods of fertility and a renewed commitment to serve Yahweh exclusively. Samuel's message synopsizes the OT prophetic concern for repentance, and it stands like a watchtower over the rest of the books of Samuel.

This first portrait includes not only the sermon that Samuel preached, but also its effects. With Samuel's help, the people of Israel came to understand the nature of wholehearted turning to God as both repudiation of past sins and exclusive devotion to Yahweh. Samuel gathered them at *Mizpah for prayer and fasting, and Israel's corporate confession was succinct and genuine: "We have sinned against the LORD" (1 Sam 7:6). This is the first of three illustrations of confession in 1-2 Samuel, all using the verb "sinned" (ḥāṭāʾ). Samuel's instruction was effective; the Israelites confessed and repented. Yahweh responded at once with victory and peace, where before there had been only conflict and defeat. This first portrait of repentance is paradigmatic for the rest of 1-2 Samuel, defining and illustrating the nature of true confession and repentance.

The second portrait of repentance, Saul, works by way of contrast. As the first example (Samuel at Mizpah) was genuine and effective, the second was insincere and futile. The words and actions of Saul in 1 Samuel 15 were self-serving and self-vindicating. His confession is coerced by the prophet bit by bit, and even then it is disingenuous. He acknowledges wrongdoing instead of repudiating it; Saul regrets his actions because they leave him vulnerable, not because they were self-destructive and wrong. His words of confession are the same as Israel's at Mizpah: "I have sinned" (again using ḥāṭāʾ [1 Sam 15:24; repeated in 1 Sam 15:30]). However, he fails to exemplify the same wholehearted repentance that Israel illustrates. Instead, his words are followed by more words of defensive argumentation, deflection and rationalization. His "I have sinned" was followed by an unfortunate "because"; he sinned because he "was afraid of the people." Saul appears more interested in placating Samuel and the people of Israel than in seeking forgiveness and restoration from Yahweh.

If Samuel's message of repentance (1 Sam 7:2-6) is a watchtower over the rest of 1-2 Samuel, and Israel's confession at Mizpah is a positive example of its effects, then conversely, Saul stands as a benchmark of failure. His confession illustrates precisely the results of resisting Samuel's instruction, and the self-destructive consequences of an unrepentant heart.

The third portrait of repentance is David. Nathan the prophet has replaced the revered Samuel, but his firm "You are the man" confronts David with the same powerful lessons (2 Sam 12:7). And like the Israelites at Mizpah, David has learned well the prophetic lesson of confession and repentance. The terminology we have now come to expect is sincere and genuine. David's "I have sinned" (once again using ḥāṭāʾ [2 Sam 12:13]) is not followed by recrimination or self-vindication. His words stand alone—exposed, naked, vulnerable. David serves as an illustration for the sermon of Samuel in 1 Samuel 7:2-4. Nathan's prophetic pronouncement of forgiveness was just as gripping and profound as the announcement of guilt (2 Sam 12:13b).

4.4. Prophets and Prophecy. As we have seen, Jewish tradition maintains that the books of Samuel were written by prophets (see 2 above), and the importance of the theme of repentance in the books, which is also central to the message of the canonical prophets, is consistent with that tradition. Although we have no substantial evidence of authorship, prophetic or otherwise, the role of prophets and prophecy in 1-2 Samuel clearly is important and may simply reflect the prophetic perspective of the Deuteronomistic Historians responsible for the canonical shape of 1-2 Samuel.

The focus early in the books is, of course, Samuel himself, whose prophetic call may share a literary topos with other divine calls in the OT (1 Sam 3:1-4:1a; cf. Gen 12:1-3; 28:10-22; Ex 3:1—4:20; Josh 1:1-9; Is 6:1-13; 40:6-11; Jer 1:4-10; Ezek 2:1-3:11; Amos 7:14-16). Before Samuel's call, the word of Yahweh was rare, and visions were scarce (1 Sam 3:1), but after his call, Samuel became a trustworthy prophet, whose words became reality (1 Sam 3:19-20). With the rise of the Israelite monarchy it became necessary for Samuel to define the role of prophet, and by implication to model Israelite prophecy for future generations as a ministry of instruction and intercession (1 Sam 12:16-25, esp. vv. 23-25).

Another familiar prophetic theme is sounded when Samuel condemns Saul's appeal to the use of sacrifice to cover his blatant disobedience in the matter of the Amalekites. The nature of sacrifice requires more than the physical act of sacrifice: "To obey is better than sacrifice, and to heed than the fat of rams" (1 Sam 15:22; cf. Is 1:11-17; Jer 7:21-23; Hos 6:6; Mic 6:6-8; Mt 12:7; Mk 12:33; Heb 10:8-9). Indeed, Samuel serves as "kingmaker" in 1 Samuel, anointing both Saul and David, and thereby establishing the prophetic claim to stand over the monarchy as God's appointed overseer (Gordon 1994). The prophetic tone is nowhere more present than in the prediction-fulfillment pattern (so familiar from the books of Kings) employed by the resuscitated prophet in his final condemnation of Saul: "Yahweh has done to you precisely what he spoke through me" (1 Sam 28:17a).

Although there is nothing like a prophetic dynastic succession in Israel, it is clear that Samuel was to serve as model and example for future prophets. Another prophetic figure in 1-2 Samuel is Nathan, who appears in only two chapters but whose influence is powerful nonetheless. In 2 Samuel 7 he is the prophet who announces the Davidic covenant to King David, through which God would graciously bless David and the nation forever. Once again the role of an Israelite prophet in defining and sustaining the monarchy is crucial, as becomes even more apparent in Nathan's second appearance in the narrative. In 2 Samuel 12 it is Nathan who proclaims, "You are the man," exposing David's vile hypocrisy, and it is also Nathan who has the authority to announce just as fervently, "Yahweh has put away your sin" (2 Sam 12:7, 13). Finally, in the concluding images of the books of Samuel, the prophet Gad stands beside David during another moment of crisis, prodding and instructing the king, who at last acquires the very threshing floor upon which Solomon would build the temple, as the Chronicler avers (2 Sam 24; cf. 1 Chron 22:1; 2 Chron 3:1). The prophets of 1-2 Samuel reflect central themes repeated often in Israelite prophetic literature, and they are portrayed as overseeing the establishment and regulation of the Israelite monarchy, as well as the eventual site and building of the future temple (*see* Solomon's Temple). ·

See also DAVID; DAVIDIC COVENANT; DAVID'S FAMILY; GOLIATH; HISTORY OF ISRAEL 2: PRE-MONARCHIC ISRAEL; HISTORY OF ISRAEL 3: UNIT-ED MONARCHY; KINGS AND KINGSHIP; PROPHETS AND PROPHECY; SAMUEL; SAUL AND SAUL'S FAMILY.

BIBLIOGRAPHY. *Commentaries*: **P. R. Ackroyd**, *The First Book of Samuel* (CBC; Cambridge: Cambridge University Press, 1971); idem, *The Second Book of Samuel* (CBC; Cambridge: Cambridge University Press, 1977); **A. A. Anderson**, *2 Samuel* (WBC 11; Waco, TX: Word, 1989); **B. T. Arnold**, *1 and 2 Samuel* (NIVAC; Grand Rapids: Zondervan, 2003); **J. G. Baldwin**, *1 and 2 Samuel: An Introduction and Commentary* (TOTC 8; Downers Grove, IL: InterVarsity Press, 1988); **R. D. Bergen**, *1, 2 Samuel* (NAC 7; Nashville: Broadman & Holman, 1996); **W. Brueggemann**, *First and Second Samuel* (IBC; Louisville: Westminster/John Knox, 1990); **M. J. Evans**, *1 and 2 Samuel* (NIBCOT 6; Peabody, MA: Hendrickson, 2000); **R. P. Gordon**, *1 & 2 Samuel* (OTG; Sheffield: Sheffield Academic Press, 1984); idem, *I & II Samuel: A Commentary* (Grand Rapids: Zondervan, 1988); **H. W. Hertzberg**, *I & II Samuel: A Commentary* (OTL; Philadelphia: Westminster, 1964); **R. W. Klein**, *1 Samuel* (WBC 10; Waco, TX: Word, 1983); **P. K. McCarter Jr.**, *1 & 2 Samuel* (2 vols.; AB 8, 9; New York: Doubleday, 1980-1984); **R. F. Youngblood**, "1, 2 Samuel," in vol. 3 of *The Expositor's Bible Commentary*, ed. F. E. Gaebelein (Grand Rapids: Zondervan, 1992) 551-1104. *Studies*: **M. H. Abrams**, *A Glossary of Literary Terms* (5th ed.; New York: Holt, Rinehart and Winston, 1988); **R. Alter**, *The David Story: A Translation with Commentary of 1 and 2 Samuel* (New York: W. W. North, 1999); **B. T. Arnold**, "Necromancy and Cleromancy in 1 and 2 Samuel," *CBQ* 66 (2004) 199-213; **C. E. Carter**, "Opening Windows onto Biblical Worlds: Applying the Social Sciences to Hebrew Scripture," in *The Face of Old Testament Studies: A Survey of Contemporary Approaches*, ed. D. W. Baker and B. T. Arnold (Grand Rapids: Baker, 1999) 421-33; **B. S. Childs**, *Introduction to the Old Testament as Scripture* (Philadelphia: Fortress, 1979); **F. M. Cross**, *Canaanite Myth and Hebrew Epic: Essays in the History of the Religion of Israel* (Cambridge, MA: Harvard University Press, 1973); **J. Day**, "The Canaanite Inheritance of the Israelite Monarchy," in *King and Messiah in Israel and the Ancient Near East: Proceedings of the Oxford Old Testament Seminar*, ed. J. Day (JSOTSup 270; Sheffield: Sheffield Academic Press, 1998) 72-90; **J. W. Flanagan**, *David's Social Drama: A Hologram of Israel's Early Iron Age* (JSOTSup 73; Sheffield: Almond, 1988); **D. E. Fleming,** "Mari and the Possibilities of Biblical Memory," *RA* 92 (1998) 41-78; **H. O. Forshey,** "Court Narrative (2 Samuel 9—1 Kings 2)," *ABD* 1.1172-79; **J. Goldingay,** *Models for Interpretation of Scripture* (Grand Rapids: Eerdmans, 1995); **R. P. Gordon,** "Who Made the Kingmaker? Reflections on Samuel and the Institution of the Monarchy," in *Faith, Tradition, and History: Old Testament Historiography in Its Near Eastern Context,* ed. A. R. Millard, J. K. Hoffmeier and D. W. Baker (Winona Lake, IN: Eisenbrauns, 1994) 255-69; **A. K. Grayson,** *Assyrian and Babylonian Chronicles* (TCS 5; Winona Lake, IN: Eisenbrauns, 2000); **B. Halpern,** *The Constitution of the Monarchy in Israel* (HSM 25; Chico, CA: Scholars Press, 1981); idem, *David's Secret Demons: Messiah, Murderer, Traitor, King* (Grand Rapids: Eerdmans, 2001); **G. F. Hasel,** "נָגִיד *nāgîd*," *TDOT* 9.187-202; **J. S. Holladay Jr.,** "The Kingdoms of Israel and Judah: Political and Economic Centralization in the Iron IIA-B (ca. 1000-750 B.C.E.)," in *The Archaeology of Society in the Holy Land,* ed. T. E. Levy (London: Leicester University Press, 1995) 368-98; **O. Keel and C. Uehlinger,** *Gods, Goddesses, and Images of God in Ancient Israel* (Minneapolis: Fortress, 1998 [1992]); **G. N. Knoppers,** "The Historical Study of the Monarchy: Developments and Detours," in *The Face of Old Testament Studies: A Survey of Contemporary Approaches,* ed. D. W. Baker and B. T. Arnold (Grand Rapids: Baker, 1999) 207-35; idem, "Is There a Future for the Deuteronomistic History?" in *The Future of the Deuteronomistic History,* ed. T. Römer (BETL 147; Leuven: Leuven University Press, 2000) 119-34; idem, "The Vanishing Solomon: The Disappearance of the United Monarchy from Recent Histories of Ancient Israel," *JBL* 116 (1997) 19-44; **G. Leick,** *The Babylonians: An Introduction* (London: Routledge, 2003); **V. P. Long,** *The Reign and Rejection of King Saul: A Case for Literary and Theological Coherence* (SBLDS 118; Atlanta: Scholars Press, 1989); **P. K. McCarter Jr.,** "Plots, True or False: The Succession Narrative as Court Apologetic," *Int* 35 (1981) 355-67; **D. J. McCarthy,** "The Inauguration of Monarchy in Israel: A Form-Critical Study of 1 Samuel 8—12," *Int* 27 (1973) 401-12; **T. N. D. Mettinger,** *King and Messiah: The Civil and Sacral Legitimation of the Israelite Kings* (ConBOT 8; Lund: Gleerup, 1976); idem, *No Graven Image? Israelite Aniconism in Its Ancient Near Eastern Context* (ConBOT 42; Stockholm: Almqvist & Wiksell, 1995); **P. D. Miller Jr. and J. J. M. Rob-** erts, *The Hand of the Lord: A Reassessment of the "Ark Narrative" of 1 Samuel* (Baltimore: John Hopkins University Press, 1977); **R. D. Miller II,** *Chieftains of the Highland Clans: A History of Israel in the Twelfth and Eleventh Centuries B.C.* (Grand Rapids: Eerdmans, 2005); **K. R. Nemet-Nejat,** *Daily Life in Ancient Mesopotamia* (Westport, CT: Greenwood, 1998 [repr., Peabody, MA: Hendrickson, 2002]); **A. de Pury and T. Römer,** *Die Sogenannte Thronfolgegeschichte Davids: Neue Einsichten und Anfragen* (OBO 176; Freiburg: Universitätsverlag; Göttingen: Vandenhoeck & Ruprecht, 2000); **J. J. M. Roberts,** "Zion in the Theology of the Davidic-Solomonic Empire," in *Studies in the Period of David and Solomon and Other Essays: Papers Read at the International Symposium for Biblical Studies, Tokyo, 5-7 December, 1979,* ed. T. Ishida (Winona Lake, IN: Eisenbrauns, 1982) 93-108; **T. Römer,** ed., *The Future of the Deuteronomistic History* (BETL 147; Leuven: Leuven University Press, 2000); **T. Römer and A. de Pury,** "Deuteronomistic Historiography (DH): History of Research and Debated Issues," in *Israel Constructs Its History: Deuteronomistic Historiography in Recent Research,* ed. A. de Pury, T. Römer and J.-D. Macchi (JSOTSup 306; Sheffield: Sheffield Academic Press, 2000) 24-143; **L. Rost,** *The Succession to the Throne of David* (HTIBS 1; Sheffield: Almond, 1982 [1926]); **H. W. F. Saggs,** *Babylonians* (Peoples of the Past 1; Norman: University of Oklahoma Press, 1995); **P. E. Satterthwaite,** "David in the Books of Samuel: A Messianic Hope?" in *The Lord's Anointed: Interpretation of Old Testament Messianic Texts,* ed. P. E. Satterthwaite, R. S. Hess and G. J. Wenham (Tyndale House Studies; Carlisle: Paternoster; Grand Rapids: Baker, 1995) 41-65; **W. M. Schniedewind,** *Society and the Promise to David: The Reception History of 2 Samuel 7:1-17* (Oxford: Oxford University Press, 1999); **A. G. Vaughn,** "Is Biblical Archaeology Theologically Useful Today? Yes, a Programmatic Proposal," in *Jerusalem in Bible and Archaeology: The First Temple Period,* ed. A. G. Vaughn and A. E. Killebrew (SBLSymS 18; Atlanta: Society of Biblical Literature, 2003) 407-30; **A. G. Vaughn and A. E. Killebrew,** eds., *Jerusalem in Bible and Archaeology: The First Temple Period* (SBLSymS 18; Atlanta: Society of Biblical Literature, 2003).

B. T. Arnold

SANBALLAT

Sanballat, the governor of *Samaria, was a contemporary of *Nehemiah and is described as his most powerful opponent, opposing the rebuilding of the walls of *Jerusalem.

1. General Information
2. Extrabiblical Sources
3. More Than One Sanballat?
4. Sanballat and Nehemiah

1. General Information.

The name *Sanballat* occurs ten times in the OT (Neh 2:10, 19; 4:1 [MT 3:33]; 4:7 [MT 4:1]; 6:1, 2, 5, 12, 14; 13:28), all denoting Nehemiah's main opponent. Sanballat is associated with Tobiah the Ammonite (Neh 2:10, 19; 6:14), Geshem the Arab (Neh 2:19; 6:2) and Noadiah the prophetess (Neh 6:14).

Sanballat's background is uncertain. His name is Akkadian in origin, *Sin-uballit,* meaning "Sin [the Babylonian moon-god] has given life," but this indicates little, given that several people in Judah carried foreign names (e.g., Zerubbabel [Hag 1:1, 12; Ezra 3:2, 8]). Nonetheless, textual and epigraphical evidence suggest that he was a descendant of the settlers who were deported to Samaria after the fall of Samaria in 721 BCE (Josephus *Ant.* 11.302-303; see Zadok, 567-70).

Sanballat is given the epithet "the Horonite" (Neh 2:10, 19; 13:28), which may indicate his birthplace. Most scholars adopt one of two major interpretations. The majority understands the epithet to refer to either Upper or Lower Beth-Horon in Ephraim (cf. Josh 10:10, 11; 1 Chron 7:24; 2 Chron 8:5). In favor of this location is its proximity to the Plain of Ono, where Sanballat proposed to meet Nehemiah (Neh 6:2). Some scholars, however, derive the epithet from Horonaim (Is 15:5; Jer 48:3, 5, 34) in southern Moab (Kellerman, 167). Since an epithet based on the dual form "Horonaim" is likely to have retained the final *mêm,* this interpretation is, on philological grounds, less plausible (Zadok, 570). In favor of it, however, is its Moabite location. Sanballat thus would originate from Transjordan, similarly to his associates Tobiah the Ammonite (Neh 2:10, 19) and Geshem the Arab (Neh 2:19). A Moabite origin of Sanballat, in conjunction with Tobiah's Ammonite heritage, also would shed light on Nehemiah 13:1 and its reference to Deuteronomy 23:3-6 (MT 23:4-7), according to which all Moabites and Ammonites are prohibited from entering the congregation of the Lord (Rowley, 246). However-

er, if this was the author's point, one could rightly ask why Sanballat is not referred to simply as "the Moabite" (Williamson, *ABD* 5.973).

2. Extrabiblical Sources.

2.1. The Elephantine Papyri. The name *Sanballat* is found in the Elephantine papyri, dated to the seventeenth year of the Persian king Darius II (c. 407 BCE). The bearer of this name is referred to as "Sanballat, the governor of Samaria," and as having two sons named "Delaiah" ("the Lord has drawn up, delivered") and "Shelemiah" ("the Lord has requited"), who at this date rule together with their father (*COS* 3.5:130). Given the dating of this papyrus, there is little doubt that this Sanballat is identical to the one mentioned by Nehemiah (dated to the reign of Artaxerxes I).

2.2. The Samaria Papyri. The Samaria papyri, found near Wadi Daliyeh, north of Jericho, include two more references to the name "Sanballat." These texts date probably from the reign of Artaxerxes III (358-339 BCE). First, a bulla contains the Hebrew inscription "to [. . .]iah son of [San]ballat, governor of Samar[ia]" (*COS* 2.78:203-4; Cross 1963, 110-11). Second, an Aramaic fragment of a papyrus contains a reference to "[. . .]uah, son of Sanballat (and) Hanan, the prefect" (Cross 1963, 111).

Given the dating of the papyri to Artaxerxes III's reign, it is difficult, though not impossible, for the Sanballat of the Samaria papyri to be identical with the one mentioned by Nehemiah (c. 445 BCE) and the one mentioned in the Elephantine papyri. In addition, the names of the sons speak against such identification. In the case of the bulla, F. M. Cross tentatively restores the name "Hananiah" in view of the occurrence of a "Hananiah, governor of Samaria" on one of the papyri (Cross 1963, 115). In the case of the papyrus, "[Jesh]ua" or "[Jadd]ua" has been suggested. While the name-ending found on the bulla, "-iah," might fit either "Delaiah" or "Shelemiah," the known sons of Sanballat of the Elephantine papyrus, the ending attested in the papyrus, "-uah," does not.

2.3. Josephus. The Jewish historian Josephus (c. 100 CE) tells us that the high priest Jaddua's son Manasseh marries Nicaso, the daughter of Sanballat (Josephus *Ant.* 11.302-303). The elders of Jerusalem then pressure Manasseh to divorce his wife. Upon his refusal, they expel him from Jerusalem. Manasseh pleads with his father-in-law, who compensates Manasseh's loss of his position in the Jerusalem temple by building the Samarian temple for him.

This narrative is reminiscent of Nehemiah 13:28, where an unnamed young man, the son of (the high priest) Jehoiada, marries an equally anonymous daughter of Sanballat. Nonetheless, the differences caution us against equating the two accounts. First, Jehoiada had a grandson named "Jaddua," but no son with that name is recorded (Neh 12:11). Second, Josephus dates his account to the time of Darius III (335-330 BCE) and Alexander the Great (Josephus *Ant.* 11.304-305). Third, Nehemiah is absent from Josephus's account.

3. More Than One Sanballat?

In view of these extrabiblical sources, several scholars postulate a Sanballat II and a Sanballat III.

3.1. Sanballat II. Cross identifies Sanballat I with the one in the book of Nehemiah (445 BCE). On the basis of the Elephantine papyri, Cross argues that Sanballat's sons Delaiah and Shelemiah took over the governorship around 407 BCE. He further proposes that a son of Delaiah, named "Sanballat II," becomes the next governor. It is his son, named "Hananiah," who appears on the Samarian bulla. Cross's theory is supported by the common practice of papponymy (naming a child after his paternal grandfather) in the Persian and Hellenistic periods (Cross 1963, 120).

3.2. Sanballat III. Josephus's account was long held to be a garbled rendering of Nehemiah 13:28, having no historical value. The turning point came with Cross, who argued that the existence of Sanballat II, unknown from the Bible but supported by the evidence from Elephantine and Samaria, opens the door for yet other hitherto unknown governors bearing the same name. Consequently, he proposes that Josephus's account is, at least in part, historically authentic, telling of an event at the time of Sanballat III during the reigns of Darius III and Alexander the Great (Cross 1966, 202-5). In response to this, several scholars question the historicity of Josephus by showing how his account of the Persian period deviates from what is known from other sources (Williamson 1977, 62-63; cf. Williamson, *ABD* 5.974-75; Grabbe, 236-42.). It also is unlikely that within a few generations two young men of the high priestly family were expelled because of their refusal to divorce a daughter of a governor named "Sanballat" (Rowley, 252, 259-70). Thus there are good reasons to doubt the historicity of Josephus's account. It therefore is preferable to treat Josephus's account as a midrashic expansion of Nehemiah 13:28. The existence of Sanballat III must remain a conjecture until more supporting evidence is found.

4. Sanballat and Nehemiah.

Sanballat's relationship with Nehemiah is described as difficult from its very beginning. Throughout the account Sanballat and his associates make futile attempts to thwart Nehemiah's efforts to rebuild Jerusalem's city walls. They accuse Nehemiah of rebelling against the Persian king (Neh 2:19; cf. 6:7), seek to dishearten those working with Nehemiah (Neh 4:1 [MT 3:33]) and try to create dissent among his followers (Neh 4:7-8 [MT 4:1-2]). As a last resort, they endeavor to harm his reputation (Neh 6:1-13).

Given that we have Nehemiah's account only, our knowledge of the reasons behind this antipathy between Nehemiah and Sanballat is limited. Nonetheless, the extrabiblical evidence suggests that political and commercial considerations played an important part. On the one hand, Nehemiah's account and the Elephantine papyri agree that Sanballat and his associates Tobiah and Geshem wielded significant power. The papyri inform us that Sanballat was "governor of Samaria," a title probably consciously omitted by Nehemiah for the purpose of portraying himself as the only governor. On the other hand, on the basis of the Yahwistic theophoric element "-iah" in his sons' names, Sanballat practiced some form of worship of Yahweh (*COS* 3.5:130). The same can be said for Sanballat's associate Tobiah: although being called an "Ammonite," his Yahwistic name indicates that his parents worshiped the God of Israel. Sanballat's adherence to the cult of Yahweh is further suggested by the support given by Noadiah the prophetess (Neh 5:14). Finally, Sanballat was closely connected by marriage with the family of the high priest Eliashib (Neh 13:28). The picture that emerges from these elements is that of a person affiliated with the cult of Yahweh but opposed to Nehemiah's level of strictness. Furthermore, the fact that the same Eliashib was supportive of Nehemiah in the case of the building of the city wall (Neh 3:1) shows that the high priest did not feel obliged to take sides in the dispute between Sanballat and Nehemiah. In view of these factors, there is reason to believe that Sanballat felt his position in Judah to be threatened. Nehemiah's social reforms threatened to revoke the privileges of the richer strata of the Judahite society (Neh 5). The rebuilding of Jerusalem's wall suggests that Jerusalem enjoyed some status denied to Samaria. Likewise, it appears that Nehemiah enjoyed a special relationship with the imperial court (Hoglund, 224). In addition, Sanballat might have regarded Nehemiah's separatist policies, exemplified by the building of the city wall, as harmful to stability as well as damaging to Jerusalem's trade (Neh 13:16-17) (see Williamson, *ABD* 5.974).

See also EZRA AND NEHEMIAH, BOOKS OF; HISTORY OF ISRAEL 8: POSTEXILIC COMMUNITY.

BIBLIOGRAPHY. **F. M. Cross,** "Aspects of Samaritan and Jewish History in Late Persian and Hellenistic Times," *HTR* 59 (1966) 201-11; idem, "The Discovery of the Samaria Papyri," *BA* 26 (1963) 110-21; idem, "A Reconstruction of the Judean Restoration," *JBL* 94 (1975) 4-18; **L. L. Grabbe,** "Josephus and the Reconstruction of the Judean Restoration," *JBL* 106 (1987) 231-46; **K. G. Hoglund,** *Achaemenid Imperial Administration in Syria-Palestine and the Missions of Ezra and Nehemiah* (SBLDS 125; Atlanta: Scholars Press, 1992); **H. H. Rowley,** "Sanballat and the Samaritan Temple," *BJRL* 38 (1955-1956) 166-98; repr. in idem, *Men of God: Studies in Old Testament History and Prophecy* (London and New York: Nelson, 1963) 246-76; **U. Kellermann,** *Nehemia: Quellen, Überlieferung und Geschichte* (BZAW 102; Berlin: de Gruyter, 1967); **H. G. M. Williamson,** "The Historical Value of Josephus' *Jewish Antiquities* xi.297-301," *JTS* 28 (1977) 49-66; idem, "Sanballat," *ABD* 5.973-75; **R. Zadok,** "Samarian Notes," *BO* 42 (1985) 567-72.

L.-S. Tiemeyer

SAQQARA PAPYRI. *See* NON-ISRAELITE WRITTEN SOURCES: EGYPTIAN ARAMAIC PAPYRI.

SARGON II. *See* ASSYRIA, ASSYRIANS; HISTORY OF ISRAEL 5: ASSYRIAN PERIOD.

SATRAPS. *See* PERSIA, PERSIANS.

SAUL AND SAUL'S FAMILY

Saul (Heb *šāʾûl*, meaning "the one requested"), son of Kish, was the first king of Israel.

1. Sources
2. Family
3. Accession and Rule
4. Military Campaigns
5. Administration System

1. Sources.
The primary source of information about Saul is 1 Samuel 9—31, which forms part of the so-called *Deuteronomistic History (Deuteronomy through 2 Kings). There are two sections of material concerning Saul: the first, 1 Samuel 9—15, deals with his rise to power, his victories, his relationship with *Samuel, and Saul's rejection by Yahweh; the second, 1 Samuel 16—31, deals with Saul's relationship with *David (friendly at first, then hostile) and ends with Saul's death in battle. This second section is mainly concerned with David's accession to the throne and his popularity among the people. The material in 1 Samuel 9—31 is complex, with many apparent contradictions and repetitions; but even though the narrative is generally biased in favor of David, there are hints indicating that Saul was a strong military leader of religious and economic importance (1 Sam 9:1-2; 11; 14:47-48). A short passage in 1 Chronicles 8:33-40; 9:35-44 gives Saul's genealogy.

2. Family.
According to 1 Samuel 9:1, Saul was a member of the Becorath family, possibly one of the oldest families of Benjamin (Gen 46:21; 1 Chron 7:6, 8-9) of the Matri clan (1 Sam 10:21). It is stated that Saul's home was at *Gibeah (1 Sam 10:26), although according to 1 Chronicles 8:29-33 and 1 Chronicles 9:35-39 the Kish family settled in *Gibeon. The mention of *gibbôr ḥayil* (1 Sam 9:1) refers to Kish, Saul's father, and means "a man of wealth" (as in 2 Kings 15:20; Ruth 2:1). Saul's ancestry is traced five generations from his father: Kish, Abiel, Zeror, Bechorath and Aphiah. Abner, Saul's uncle, was the military commander. Saul's wife was Ahinoam, daughter of Ahimaaz, and she bore him three sons: Jonathan, Ishvi (identified with Ishbaal in 1 Chron 8:33; 9:39) and Malchishua; and two daughters, Merab and Michal (1 Sam 14:49). Later, another son, Abinadab, is mentioned (1 Sam 31:2). Merib-baal was Jonathan's son (1 Chron 8:34; 9:40), but he was also called Mephibosheth (2 Sam 4:4; 9:6). Jonathan's grandson

was Micah. According to 2 Samuel 21:8, Rizpah, Saul's concubine, bore two sons: Armoni and another Mephibosheth. Michal (or Merob, see commentaries) bore five children from her second marriage to Adriel (2 Sam 21:8). The Saulide line continued through Jonathan's grandson Micah (1 Chron 8:34-40; 9:40-44).

Jonathan was Saul's eldest son, a commander in Saul's army, and heir to the throne. Jonathan died at the battle of Gilboa alongside his two brothers Malchishua and Abinadab (1 Sam 31:2). Jonathan's son Merib-baal (Mephibosheth) was five years old when Jonathan was killed; he became crippled in an accident after news of Saul's death reached the city. In 2 Samuel 21:1-14 Merib-baal is shown to have escaped execution because of David's love for Jonathan (2 Sam 21:7). Moreover, because he was crippled, Merib-baal could not qualify for religious (see Lev 21:16-24) or military functions, and thus he could not inherit the throne.

Michal was Saul's youngest daughter. She first married David (1 Sam 18:27), then Paltiel (1 Sam 25:44), and eventually returned to David (2 Sam 3:15-16). When Abner transferred his loyalty from Ishbaal to David, the latter's primary condition was that Michal would return to him. Michal remained childless until her death (2 Sam 6:23; but cf. 2 Sam 21:8).

Ishbaal was Saul's youngest and only surviving son, heir to the throne after the battle in which Saul and his three eldest sons were killed. With Abner's support, Ishbaal became a young king over the whole of Saul's kingdom and enjoyed substantial support from the people. When Ishbaal had grown to adulthood, he quarreled with Abner over the latter's attempt to promote his own succession to the throne (2 Sam 3:7-12). Abner's extreme reaction was to switch allegiance to David's side. Ishbaal then was unguarded and soon was assassinated (2 Sam 4:7). The text provides no information about other members of Saul's family, although it does report that two sons of Rizpah and five of Michal were executed (2 Sam 21:8-9).

3. Accession and Rule.

There are three versions of how Saul became king; first, Saul was *anointed secretly at Ramah (1 Sam 9:25—10:1); then he was elected by lot at *Mizpah (1 Sam 10:17-27); and later (1 Sam 11:14-15) he was appointed by the whole people at *Gilgal after the victory over the *Ammonites.

Saul's emergence to kingship in Israel has long been discussed by scholars, and various theories have been proposed. The classic description of Saul's kingship as a continuation of the charismatic leadership known from the book of *Judges is that of A. Alt in 1930. Alt (223-309) saw Saul's rule as transitional between the rule of the *judges of the premonarchical tribal system and a centralized monarchical rule. The change was due to the *Philistines' threat to attempt to expand into the central highlands. It was important that the tribes be united militarily under the existing charismatic office of the judge. The initial aim was to establish a military group to deal with crises when they emerged. However, Saul's election was a permanent one and aimed at dealing with the Philistines' continuing threat. Even though the victory against the Ammonites elevated Saul to kingship, it is still argued that Saul's rule could not have been hereditary, that his leadership was only military, that tribal internal affairs were to continue under the authority of the elders and that Saul was not a true king. Saul's rule has been seen as based more on the tribal system than on the *Canaanite state system—except for Saul's formation of the army, which is seen as a borrowing from the Canaanite system.

A different view of the emergence of monarchy was proposed in the 1980s. Social anthropologists (Frick; Flanagan; Rogerson), in discussing state formation and its stages of development, argued that the Israelites were an association of small chiefdoms, and that in turn the emergence of the Israelite monarchy resulted from the eventual domination of one chiefdom over the others. Thus, as a chief, Saul's political role was close to that of a king, and the competition between Saul and David therefore should be seen as one between two chiefs. This period represents a transitional period within Israel in which society was shifting from "segmented" society to statehood. Two basic models have been established: the "pristine" state and the "secondary" state. J. Flanagan and F. S. Frick suggest that the Israelite monarchy was a secondary state (because of the request made in 1 Sam 8:5). In order to reach such statehood, the Israelites went through an earlier phase of transitional development, when the monarchy emerged. Thus there was no sharp transition from the late stage of chiefdom into the early state, as this modification took time to develop.

A new look at Saul and the monarchy was presented by D. Edelman (1991) and S. Shalom Brooks (2005). Critically using textual, archaeological and anthropological data, these views present Saul as the founder of the Israelite monarchy. Saul united the various groups in the highland region of Samaria and Ephraim, Benjamin, central Transjordan and south Judah to create the new Israelite state under one centralized rule. It was a unity that no later king was able to achieve. Saul was a successful military leader as well; he organized an army and maintained security and stability throughout his reign. Shalom Brooks also argues for a more favorable image of Saul, claiming that the people continued to support the house of Saul even under David and Solomon—support that formed one of the elements which contributed to the schism.

4. Military Campaigns.

One of the most important of Saul's achievements was his military success. He was the first leader to organize a standing army with reserves. His victorious campaigns are reported in 1 Samuel 14:47-48; Saul defeated *Moab, *Ammon, Zoba, the *Philistines and Amalek. Saul's first battle was against the Ammonites (1 Sam 11). Although Saul possessed all the qualities of a king and was initially accepted by the people, he had to prove his military abilities before kingship was consolidated and completely accepted. After that victory, Saul did not disperse his army but concentrated in the central hill country in preparation for the next battle.

The battle of the Michmash Pass (1 Sam 13—14) was initiated by Saul in order to eliminate the Philistines' power from within the hill country, thus uniting the Israelites without the gaps created there by the Philistines' stronghold controlling the pass through Wadi es-Suwenit. Edelman (*ABD* 5.994) suggests that this battle took place early in Saul's reign after his establishment of Gibeon as his capital. However, Shalom Brooks, in examining the text (1 Chron 9:35-44) and archeological data (Demsky), argues that Gibeon was Saul's ancestral home from where he emerged to kingship; only after the battle of Michmash did Saul establish his capital at *Gibeah, which thus carried his name as "Gibeah of Saul." The tactics at Michmash were so successful that they were repeated in modern times (1917) when a brigadier under Allenby's command captured the village of Michmash using exactly the same methods (Gilbert, 183-86).

The battle at the Valley of Elah (also known as Valley of the Terebinith) took place in a location south of and parallel to the Valley of Sorek in the Shephelah of Judah, 14 km southwest of Bethlehem toward Philistia. Although 2 Samuel 21:19 identifies the Israelite champion as Elhanan (cf. 1 Chron 20:5), this victory is attributed to David by the tradition found in 1 Samuel 17 (*see* Goliath). The Valley of Elah had geographical significance; it went through one of the most important routes from the Shephelah to Judah. The purpose of the battle was to gain control over this valley. After the defeat of the Philistine Goliath, Saul pursued the Philistines to *Gath and *Ekron (1 Sam 17:52).

The battle against Amalek (1 Sam 15) occurred a long way south of Saul's kingdom. The Amalekites were nomadic or seminomadic people. Scholars usually locate their region between southwestern Judah and northeastern Egypt. Saul's campaign was motivated by political and economic factors: first, to protect the various groups in the south from Amalekite raids; second, according to I. Finkelstein, this region had much human activity in the Iron Age I period, and the coastal plain under the Philistines was also prosperous. In the central Beersheba basin, the large and rich site of Tel Masos and various other sites in the vicinity of the Negev highland emerged. Tell Masos was once identified with Hormah (Num 21:3; Josh 15:30), but more recently this identification has been rejected. Instead, it is identified with Ir Amalek (1 Sam 15). Finkelstein claims that these human activities resulted in dramatic economic changes in the region. Thus these people shifted from a pastoral livelihood, based on seasonal agriculture, to trade. This shift led to the emergence of an urban center, with its obvious social stratification, one evolving eventually into a state or chiefdom.

The battle of Gilboa (1 Sam 28—31) took place at the foot of Mount Gilboa in the Valley of Jezreel. It was Saul's last battle, and it ended with heavy casualties; a great number of Israelites were killed, including Saul and his three sons. The Valley of Jezreel was of strategic and economic importance. It begins near *Megiddo and continues into the Valley of Beth-Shean, both providing an important section of the "coastal highway" that also led to Damascus. This in turn played a crucial role in trade, as well as in connecting the Israelite groups on either side of the valley.

Edelman (1991, 252) suggests that it was Saul who initiated this battle by encamping at the fountain in *Jezreel, and only then, in response, the Philistines gathered at Aphek. However, Edelman ignores the reference in 1 Samuel 28:1, where it is indicated that the Philistines gathered their army to campaign against Israel. Also, in 1 Samuel 28:5 Saul is clearly described as "very frightened," not as someone who initiated the war, but rather as one who had it imposed on him. Moreover, the conditions of the battle were unusual; until then, all major battles had taken place farther south in the region close to Saul's base. Saul's weaponry was inferior against the sophisticated armor of the Philistines, but it was still effective in keeping them at a distance. The geographical condition of the hill country allowed him to do this, as the Philistines could not use their chariotry there, whereas in the valley the Philistines were sure to have the upper hand.

1 Samuel 30 provides an alibi for David during the battle at Gilboa, but it should be noted that at the time of this battle David was also in treaty with the Philistines and was ready to join the battle in support of them.

5. Administration System.

The administration system under Saul is poorly documented in 1 Samuel. There are only scattered hints that give insight into the organization of the civil, royal and military system. The way in which the Israelite groups were organized prior to the monarchy had inhibited them from establishing a proper army, training soldiers or applying military discipline. This would have required a complex administrative system, which was not present in Israelite society at the time. Before the monarchy, Israelite fighting forces consisted of farmers and shepherds whose livelihood depended on their working the land. Thus they had to support not only themselves, but also their families. In that situation it was difficult to organize and keep an army, much less train one (Eph῾al).

The monarchy changed all that. Saul organized not only a standing army, but also reserves, "and whenever Saul saw a strong man or valiant warrior, he took him into his service" (1 Sam 14:52). The army gradually increased when reserves were called in time of emergency—

for example, for the battle of Gilboa (1 Sam 28:4). It is not clear what the other characteristics of the army were. However, the military and civil services used by Saul, and later by David, were based on an old premonarchical "local" system (Mazar). This is evident in the reigns of Saul, Ishbaal and David, when the highest position after king was that of chief military commander, and only later kings adopted foreign elements into their system. During Saul's and Ishbaal's time, Abner was that commander. In campaigns Abner may have acted as a second in command to the king and as a protector of the interests of the royal family. This is evident after Saul's death when Abner crowned Ishbaal king over Israel (2 Sam 2:8-10).

Special income was needed to maintain the army, the administration and the royal house itself. With respect to the army, it is possible that Saul partly financed the standing army from his own income; Saul came from a wealthy background, which is attested in 1 Samuel 9:1-2. A clue that suggests that heroes were rewarded is found in David's question, "What will be done for the man who kills this Philistine?" (1 Sam 17:26). There are also indications suggesting that soldiers were supported by their own families (e.g., 1 Sam 17:17-18). In addition, mention is made of families paying tribute to the officer in charge of units in which their sons served. An important aspect of income was the booty brought back from campaigns. This booty included not only items of weaponry, but also a wealth of personal items, as well as domestic animals (goats and sheep), which must have represented a substantial income to the soldiers. Another form of income came probably in a form of tributes from vassal groups, such as the inhabitants of Jabesh Gilead, the Ammonites and Amalekites.

Some features of royal administration may be discerned—for example, that the royal house had a feast celebrating the beginning of each month (Malamat). Various members of the royal family were invited to this feast, including Abner and David (1 Sam 20:5, 27). When we hear of David's expected attendance at the feast, he is already Saul's son-in-law. During that feast the king sat on his special seat, probably the "throne chair" (1 Sam 20:25).

There is also a reference to the "servants of Saul" (1 Sam 16:15; 22:7). This group most likely was economically dependent on the king. But the expression "servant of the king" may indicate attachment rather than hierarchy. It could be that the number of servants was directly proportionate to the king's ability to keep them by offering them plots of land and privileges in return for their loyalty and service. 1 Samuel 22:7 hints that they were rewarded with fields and vineyards. Another clue to royal administration can be found in 2 Samuel 9:10 when Ziba, Saul's servant, is called *na'ar,* meaning "servant" or "steward," although in 2 Samuel 13:17 *na'ar* could also indicate a specific office or high rank—that is, superintendent of property. In 2 Samuel 9:10 Ziba's duty is to work in Saul's estate and provide for the family with the produce.

There is an interesting mention of Doeg the Edomite (1 Sam 21:7; 22:9), who is described as "chief of the shepherds," meaning that he was chief of Saul's servants (1 Sam 22:9). It is not clear what his duties were, but Doeg may have been an official responsible for providing supplies for the royal household and supervising a team of servants in the royal house. Doeg's duties might also have involved the complex task of supplying wool, milk, cheese and other food products for feasts and banquets. Doeg's position perhaps reflects the establishment of a loyal relationship between Saul's administrative office and his non-Israelite subjects, and suggests that Saul emerged as a successful king not only among the Israelites, but also among non-Israelite groups.

See also DAVID; GOLIATH; HISTORY OF ISRAEL 3: UNITED MONARCHY; KINGS AND KINGSHIP; SAMUEL, BOOKS OF.

BIBLIOGRAPHY. **A. Alt,** *Essays in Old Testament History and Religion* (Oxford: Blackwell, 1966); **A. Demsky,** "The Genealogy of Gibeon (1 Chronicles 9.35-44): Biblical and Epigraphic Considerations," *BASOR* 202 (1971) 16-23; **D. V. Edelman,** *King Saul in the Historiography of Judah* (JSOTSup 121; Sheffield: JSOT, 1991); idem, "Saul," *ABD* 5.989-99; **I. Eph'al,** "Fighting Techniques and Social Order in Biblical Times," [in Hebrew] הגות במקרא (Tel Aviv: Am-Oved, 1974) 47-59; **I. Finkelstein,** "Arabian Trade and Socio-Political Conditions in the Negev in the Twelfth-Eleventh Centuries B.C.E.," *JNES* 47 (1988) 241-52; **J. Flanagan,** "Chiefs in Israel," *JSOT* 20 (1981) 47-73; **F. S. Frick,** *The Formation of the State in Ancient Israel: A Survey of Models and Theories* (SWBA 4; Sheffield: Almond, 1985); **V. Gilbert,** *The Romance of the Last Crusade: With Allenby to Jerusalem*

(New York and London: Appleton, 1923); **A. Malamat,** *Mari and the Israelite Experience* [in Hebrew] (Jerusalem: Magnes, 1991); **B. Mazar,** *The Early Biblical Period: Historical Studies* (Jerusalem: Israel Exploration Society, 1986); **J. W. Rogerson,** "Was Early Israel a Segmentary Society?" *JSOT* 36 (1986) 17-26; **S. Shalom Brooks,** *Saul and the Monarchy: A New Look* (SOTS; Aldershot: Ashgate, 2005).   S. Shalom Brooks

SCHOOLS. *See* SCRIBES AND SCHOOLS.

SCRIBES AND SCHOOLS
Literacy was rare in the ancient Near East outside of Israel, due to the complex writing systems employed (*see* Writing, Writing Materials and Literacy in the Ancient Near East). The alphabetic system of *Hebrew made literacy at least theoretically more accessible to people there, although the need for professional scribes remained. This article looks at scribes and their training both in Israel and among its neighbors, as well as some implications of scribes and literacy.

1. Scribal Practice in the Ancient Near East
2. Scribal Practice in Israel
3. Scribal Education

1. Scribal Practice in the Ancient Near East.
The most evidence for scribal practice in the ancient Near East comes from Mesopotamia and Egypt. The first written language originated in Mesopotamia, and is attested from as early as the late fourth millennium BCE. It is Sumerian, a non-Semitic language that originally was pictographic or representational in its writing system (Huehnergard, 164). This necessitated many hundreds of discrete signs. When the Semites settled into the area, from about 2400 BCE on, they adapted the Sumerian writing system to represent their own languages, Assyrian and Babylonian, known collectively as Akkadian (Caplice, 170; Lipiński, 53-56). These could use fewer signs because they employed a syllabic writing system to indicate sounds (phonology) rather than concepts. This necessitated one sign per syllable rather than one per word, but still required over five hundred signs. These complex writing systems, written mainly on clay tablets with a reed stylus, required trained scribal personnel who could devote themselves exclusively to their mastery and use (Baker 1994, 66 n. 2). Common folk, and even royalty (see Pearce,

2276-77), could not be expected to write, since their daily tasks, providing for their life needs or performing their official functions, usually did not allow the time to learn such pursuits.

Egypt, where writing developed in the third millennium BCE, combined pictographic and phonological principles in its writing system, which had as many as one thousand signs in the Old Kingdom period (mid-third millennium BCE), shrinking to about 750 signs in the Classical period (second millennium BCE), but growing again significantly during the Ptolemaic period (late first century BCE through early first millennium CE) (Loprieno, 2137-50). While this too was a complicated writing process requiring trained scribes, it is claimed that kings generally were literate (Wente, 2214).

Scribes are evident also in other area cultures that had developed an alphabetic writing system. An example of this is those from Emar on the middle Euphrates during the mid-second millennium BCE (Ikeda) and from coastal Ugarit later in the same century (Rainey).

Scribal training (see 3 below) in Mesopotamia was so time-consuming that scribal practitioners were few in number, and they dedicated themselves mainly to the work of the two major state institutions: palace and temple. Both institutions produced numerous administrative texts, which are well represented among the existent material from the area. These detailed income through offerings, taxes, tariffs, land and animal yields, and distributions through things such as ration lists (see, e.g., *ANET,* 308). The palace also produced other written material in the form of diplomatic and other royal correspondence, legal documents such as law codes, treaties to regulate international relations, omen lists to assist in decision making, socioeconomic texts such as contracts and marriage settlements, and numerous other literary genres. Some kings, such as Ashurbanipal, showed wider interest in areas such as science and literature, exemplified by Ashurbanipal's large library collection (Oppenheim, 15; Black and Tait, 2206; Pearce, 2276-77). Some scribes were not affiliated with either institution and thus were available to the public to produce any of their necessary documentation. On many legal documents, such as contracts, scribes served either as notary or among the witnesses to the text—a source of many of the scribal names known to us (see Visicato).

Scribes were responsible for the physical pro-

duction of all of these texts, as well as for aspects of their ultimate use. For example, in the case of diplomatic correspondence, a messenger delivered the document and presented its contents orally, but a scribe was needed to check the official, written form of the message (Oller, 1468-69).

Many texts ended with a colophon, which included material similar to that found in today's book title pages. This could include the name of the scribe (possibly with his lineage), the writing date of the tablet, the geographical source of the original if the text is a copy, the title of the work (indicated most frequently by an abbreviated first line of the document), the number of tablets in the series, the catch-line or first line of the next tablet in the series, comments on the scribe's care in copying and proofreading, and curses on anyone who defaces or alters the document (Baker 1986). The scribe's self-identification with his work, coupled with his declared care in the entire copying and production process, was significant because he was putting his professional reputation on the line as one who produces work of the highest quality.

Due to their scarcity and the important transactions in which they played a role, scribes had considerable social standing in their community. As secretaries for kings and others of power, scribes could hold considerable personal power of their own. Since they controlled the written material flowing both in and out, they could serve as a royal "chief of staff" and confidant of their employer. They soon had left behind the role of a simple copyist or recorder. Since often they were alone in having direct access to the material in their care, they became interpreters of what appeared to outsiders to be esoteric material. In this they became much like contemporary lawyers. They also assumed administrative functions, such as supervising building and other projects, for both palace and temple (Pearce, 2273-74; Visicato, 234).

2. Scribal Practice in Israel.

Since the written Hebrew language is alphabetic, with only twenty-two letters, it is at least theoretically accessible to more people than was the Akkadian of Mesopotamia or the Egyptian hieroglyphics. Attributions of the ability to write are given to numerous people in the OT, ranging from leaders (e.g., Moses [Ex 24:4]; priests [Num 5:23]; Joshua [Josh 8:32]; tribal leaders

[Josh 18:4]; Samuel [1 Sam 10:25]; David [2 Sam 11:14-15]; Jezebel [1 Kings 21:8]; Jehu [2 Kings 10:1]) to common folk (Judg 8:14; cf. Esther 9:20). There is strong evidence that literacy was wider spread among the Israelites than among its neighbors (Millard 1985; 1995; see DOTP, Writing). Although writing was more accessible in Israel, literacy was not universal, and scribes functioned there as well.

Three Hebrew terms are used of scribes. The most common is sōpēr, "one who enumerates." It occurs over fifty times in the Hebrew Bible. The scribe "writes" in only one OT text, where Shemaiah records the names of priestly officials (1 Chron 24:6), but is also associated with a "pen" (ʿēṭ; Ps 45:1 [MT 45:2]; Jer 8:8). A rarer term derives from the root šṭr, which in Akkadian means "to write" (HALOT 1475-76). Both are used much more frequently to identify government officials. They often are listed with other functionaries, and are not completely synonymous, since the two separate titles identify different people in the same list (2 Chron 26:11; 34:13). Bureaucratic functions that they performed include a military officer in charge of mustering and provisioning troops (Deut 20:5; 2 Kings 21:19; Neh 13:13; 2 Chron 26:11), overseer of laborers (e.g., Ex 5:6), Levitical judicial or temple functionary (1 Chron 23:4; 26:29) and royal secretary (2 Sam 8:17; 20:25; in charge of temple financial revenues [2 Kings 12:11]) (see Fox, 96-110). This is akin to the third term, mazkîr, literally, "one who reminds," a court recorder (2 Sam 8:16; 20:24; 1 Kings 4:3; 2 Kings 18:18, 37; 1 Chron 18:15; 2 Chron 34:8). Since the term is restricted in the Hebrew Bible to lists of personnel, it is difficult to determine with certainty the precise function of this dignitary (see Mettinger; Fox 110-21; see State Officials).

Much discussion has taken place concerning *Ezra, who is called a "scribe" (sōpēr [NIV: "teacher"]) in Ezra 7:6, 11. Some have suggested that by the postexilic period this title designated a high official in the Achaemenid royal court, similar to contemporary American usage in titles such as "secretary of state," or at least one with delegated authority from that court (Schaeder, 39-51; Williamson, 100), though certainty is not possible (Hoglund, 227-28). Association of the term with the Mosaic law (cf. Ezra 7:6) makes the situation more complex. There may well have been an evolution in the understanding of the term. Starting as copyists and transmitters of official documents, there would be a natural extension to scribes becoming viewed as experts on, and thus interpreters of, these documents. The NT indicates numerous cases where scribes were consulted in this interpretational role (e.g., Mt 7:29; 17:10) (see Baker 1994, 76-77). Thus Ezra could have played a dual role under the title scribe: an official representative of the court who was received by his people as one who understood and taught the law (for a detailed discussion of Ezra see Schams, 46-60).

3. Scribal Education.

Since scribes needed extensive training in Mesopotamia and Egypt, scribal schools were established (Mesopotamia: Baker 1994, 66 n. 3; Civil; Visicato, 1 n. 1; Gesche, 1-27; Egypt: Heaton, 101-21; Mettinger, 140-43). The training resembles contemporary apprenticeships, with the novices working under the tutelage of more senior scribes. Numerous "exercise tablets" have been discovered in Mesopotamia, with a discernable distinction between two hands, the learner and the master. These had to cover a wide range of literary genres, since a "graduate scribe" needed skill in matters of accounting, geometry and surveying, legal terminology and protocol, the name and purview of numerous deities, ritual practice, diplomacy, and many more besides, depending on his actual place of employment.

Since copying existent texts was part of their training, scribes became familiar with texts from across the spectrum of genres from earlier generations. Since by its nature a school curriculum is fairly conservative, the basic curricular core would have remained relatively static over the years. This means that many of the curricular texts were accurately preserved over a considerable period of time, as accuracy was one of the elements on which the apprentice was evaluated by his teachers.

Texts were disseminated not only over time, but also over space. Akkadian was, for a period, the lingua franca of the Middle East, serving as the official language for treaties between the Egyptians and the Hittites, for example (ANET, 199-206), even though it would have been the native tongue of neither of the treaty parties, and each would have had copies in their own language. The fourteenth-century BCE Amarna letters between the city-state rulers in Canaan and their protectors in Egypt also were written in Akkadian. Scribes to write and read these documents could have been imported from Mesopotamia, but it is more likely that there were also scribal schools outside of Mesopotamia to handle precisely this kind of demand. There is archaeological evidence for the existence of such schools, which likely followed much the same curriculum as those in the Akkadian homeland, using the same model texts. Some of the curricular texts have been found at remote sites, which could support this claim (Baker 1994, 71).

The existence and nature of scribal education in Israel is debated. Evidence has been adduced from both texts (e.g., Lemaire 1981; *ABD* 2.305-12; Crenshaw; G. R. Davies) and archaeology (Jamieson-Drake). The main cause of the debate is the paucity of information on education in general in Israel, which is the main subject of most studies. There is even less information available on the more limited topic of scribal education. Several texts from the Historical Books have been called on in the discussion. Joshua 18:9 describes several men recording details of a trip through Israel, and Judges 8:13-17 tells of a randomly selected young man able to write. Unfortunately, neither provides any glimpse into how the skills of reading or writing were acquired, and neither mentions anything about scribes as officials. Other texts are called on as oblique references to teachers or tutors (e.g., 2 Kings 10:1, 5; 1 Chron 27:32), but there is no clear evidence that those mentioned are anything more than guardians or attendants of royal children (see *HALOT* 64, "*'mn* II").

An attempt has been made to extrapolate the need for scribes, and thence scribal education, from the scope of public works undertaken and the luxury items available in Judah during the time of the monarchy (Jamieson-Drake). The suggestion is that an analysis of archaeological remains and a study of sociological systems can help determine how many scribes would have been needed to produce and administer all of this. The methodology and suggested results (that there were few scribal schools during the period) have not been well-received, so we are no further along in our understanding.

Since it cannot be gainsaid that a number of Israelites had at least some level of literacy (Millard 1985; 1995; *see DOTP*, Writing), there must

have been some educational process, though not necessarily through a formal, universal educational system. The home was the locus of most education into the skills of everyday life (Lemaire, *ABD* 2.306-7; King and Stager, 43-47; *see DOTP*, Arts and Crafts), and it could also have been the place where elementary literacy was taught. For more formal education, there likely was a more institutionalized process, although since physical evidence for this is lacking, it is determined through logic and analogy with the practice of Israel's neighbors.

A formal training process would increase the professionalism of the students, providing a context in which one could be surer of the accuracy of textual transmission. Although there was some latitude for scribal alteration of the text, there was also great concern that it be transmitted carefully. If this was true for literary texts, where at times in Mesopotamia scribes even preserved the line divisions of the originals that they were copying, one would expect this to be even more the case when scribes were handling the primary religious documents of the people, such as in Israel. A Mesopotamian scribe was at times loath to add something to a damaged text, marking the spot as *ḫūpi*, "broken." A Hebrew parallel has been suggested for the word *ḥuppîm* in Genesis 46:21 (see *HALOT*), although this generally is taken to be a proper name, with no evidence of anything missing from the text. There is, however, evidence that the Israelite scribe preserved the broken text with which he was presented rather than filling in where he knew that there was missing information (cf. 1 Sam 13:1; see Baker 1994, 73). Accuracy of preservation and transmission was more important than reconstruction.

Transmissional accuracy is not alone, however, since, due to the scribe's role as bureaucrat and administrator, we should expect the original facts and calculations to be accurate as well. Mesopotamian wall reliefs show scribes on military campaigns recording booty and casualties. These later were transcribed into the official records of the campaign. Although we have no pictorial representations in Israel to confirm this practice of military scribes, we would assume that scribes accompanied Israel's military maneuvers as well. Thus when figures are recorded in this context of a military muster (e.g., Num 1—2; 1 Sam 14:14; 2 Sam 8:1-14), we should assume their accuracy. Scribes therefore not only performed important administrative functions for their employer, but also performed an important role in transmitting material with diligence through time.

See also NON-ISRAELITE WRITTEN SOURCES; STATE OFFICIALS; WRITING, WRITING MATERIALS AND LITERACY IN THE ANCIENT NEAR EAST.

BIBLIOGRAPHY. **D. W. Baker,** "Biblical Colophons: Gevaryahu and Beyond," in *Studies in the Succession Narrative,* ed. W. C. van Wyk (Old Testament Essays: OTWSA 27, 28; Pretoria: OTWSA, 1986) 29-61; idem, "Scribes as Transmitters of Tradition," in *Faith, Tradition, and History: Old Testament Historiography in Its Near Eastern Context,* ed. A. R. Millard, J. K. Hoffmeier and D. W. Baker (Winona Lake, IN: Eisenbrauns, 1994) 65-78; **J. A. Black and W. J. Tait,** "Archives and Libraries in the Ancient Near East," in *Civilizations of the Ancient Near East,* ed. J. M. Sasson (4 vols.; New York: Scribner, 1995) 4.2197-2209; **R. I. Caplice,** "Akkadian," *ABD* 4.170-73; **M. Civil,** "Education (Mesopotamia)," *ABD* 2.301-5; **J. L. Crenshaw,** "Education in Ancient Israel," *JBL* 104 (1985) 601-15; **G. I. Davies,** "Were There Schools in Ancient Israel?," in *Wisdom in Ancient Israel: Essays in Honour of J. A. Emerton,* ed. J. Day, R. P. Gordon and H. G. M. Williamson (Cambridge: Cambridge University Press, 1995) 199-211; **P. R. Davies,** *Scribes and Schools: The Canonization of the Hebrew Scriptures* (Louisville: Westminster/John Knox, 1998); **N. S. Fox,** *In the Service of the King: Officialdom in Ancient Israel and Judah* (Cincinnati: Hebrew Union College Press, 2001); **P. D. Gesche,** *Schulunterricht in Babylonien im ersten Jahrtausend v. Chr.* (AOAT 275; Münster: Ugarit Verlag, 2000); **E. W. Heaton,** *Solomon's New Men: The Emergence of Ancient Israel as a National State* (New York: Pica, 1974); **K. G. Hoglund,** *Achaemenid Imperial Administration in Syria-Palestine and the Missions of Ezra and Nehemiah* (SBLDS 125; Atlanta: Scholars Press, 1992); **J. Huehnergard,** "Languages: Introductory Survey," *ABD* 4.155-70; **J. Ikeda,** "Scribes at Emar," in *Priests and Officials in the Ancient Near East: Papers of the Second Colloquium on the Ancient Near East—the City and Its Life, Held at the Middle Eastern Culture Center in Japan (Mitaka, Tokyo), March 22-24, 1996,* ed. K. Watanabe (Heidelberg: Winter, 1999) 163-85; **D. W. Jamieson-Drake,** *Scribes and Schools in Monarchic Judah: A Socio-Archeological Approach* (JSOTSup 109; Sheffield: Almond, 1991); **P. J. King and L. E. Stager,** *Life in Biblical Israel* (Louisville: Westminster/John Knox,

2001); **A. Lemaire,** "Education (Ancient Israel)," *ABD* 2.305-12; idem, *Les écoles et la formation de la Bible dans l'ancien Israël* (OBO 39; Fribourg: Éditions Universitaires; Göttingen: Vandenhoeck & Ruprecht, 1981); **E. Lipiński,** *Semitic Languages: Outline of Comparative Grammar* (OLA 80; Leuven: Peeters, 1997); **A. Loprieno,** "Ancient Egyptian and Other Afroasiatic Languages," in *Civilizations of the Ancient Near East,* ed. J. M. Sasson (4 vols.; New York: Scribner, 1995) 4.2135-50; **T. N. D. Mettinger,** *Solomonic State Officials: A Study of the Civil Government Officials of the Israelite Monarchy* (ConBOT 5; Lund: Gleerup, 1971); **A. R. Millard,** "An Assessment of the Evidence of Writing in Ancient Israel," in *Biblical Archaeology Today: Proceedings of the International Congress on Biblical Archaeology, Jerusalem, April 1984,* ed. J. Aviram et al. (Jerusalem: Israel Exploration Society; Israel Academy of Sciences and Humanities, with American Schools of Oriental Research, 1985) 301-12; idem, "The Knowledge of Writing in Iron Age Palestine," *TynBul* 46 (1995) 207-17; **G. H. Oller,** "Messengers and Ambassadors in Ancient Western Asia," in *Civilizations of the Ancient Near East,* ed. J. M. Sasson (4 vols.; New York: Scribner, 1995) 3.1465-73; **A. L. Oppenheim,** *Ancient Mesopotamia: Portrait of a Dead Civilization* (Chicago: University of Chicago Press, 1964); **L. E. Pearce,** "The Scribes and Scholars of Ancient Mesopotamia," in *Civilizations of the Ancient Near East,* ed. J. M. Sasson (4 vols.; New York: Scribner, 1995) 4.2265-78; **A. F. Rainey,** "The Scribe at Ugarit: His Position and Influence," in PIASH 3/4 (Jerusalem: Israel Academy of Sciences and Humanities, 1968) 126-47; **J. Saldarini,** "Scribes," *ABD* 5.1012-16; **H. H. Schaeder,** *Esra der Schreiber* (BHT 5; Tübingen: Mohr, 1930); **C. Schams,** *Jewish Scribes in the Second-Temple Period* (JSOTSup 291; Sheffield: Sheffield Academic Press, 1998); **G. Visicato,** *The Power and the Writing: The Early Scribes of Mesopo-tamia* (Bethesda: CDL, 2000); **E. F. Wente,** "The Scribes of Ancient Egypt," in *Civilizations of the Ancient Near East,* ed. J. M. Sasson (4 vols.; New York: Scribner, 1995) 4.2211-21; **H. G. M. Wil-liamson,** *Ezra, Nehemiah* (WBC 16; Waco, TX: Word, 1985). D. W. Baker

SEALS. *See* NON-ISRAELITE WRITTEN SOURCES: SYRO-PALESTINIAN.

SECONDARY HISTORY. *See* CHRONICLER'S HISTORY; CHRONICLES, BOOKS OF.

SEFIRE STELAE. *See* ARAM, DAMASCUS AND
SYRIA; NON-ISRAELITE WRITTEN SOURCES: SYRO-
PALESTINIAN.

SEIR. *See* EDOM, EDOMITES.

SENNACHERIB. *See* ASSYRIA, ASSYRIANS; HIS-
TORY OF ISRAEL 5: ASSYRIAN PERIOD.

SEPTUAGINT. *See* CANON; TEXT AND TEXTUAL
CRITICISM.

SESHBAZZAR. *See* HISTORY OF ISRAEL 7: PER-
SIAN PERIOD.

SHALLUM. *See* HISTORY OF ISRAEL 5: ASSYRIAN
PERIOD.

SHALMANESER III. *See* ASSYRIA, ASSYRIANS.

SHALMANESER V. *See* ASSYRIA, ASSYRIANS; HIS-
TORY OF ISRAEL 5: ASSYRIAN PERIOD.

SHAME. *See* HONOR AND SHAME.

SHAMGAR. *See* JUDGES.

SHECHEM

The biblical city of Shechem is identified with
the mound at Tell Balatah, situated at the foot of
Mount Gerizim in the heart of the modern city
of Nablus, at the west end of a large crescent-
shaped valley. The center of a major city-state in
the second millennium BCE, Shechem served as
a political and religious center for the Israelite
tribes in the period of the *judges, later declining in importance, particularly after the rise of
nearby *Samaria as the capital of the northern
kingdom of Israel in the period of the divided
monarchy.

1. Excavations
2. Middle Bronze Age (c. 2000-1500 BCE)
3. Late Bronze Age and Iron Age I (c. 1550-
   1000 BCE)
4. Iron Age II (c. 1000-720 BCE)
5. From the Assyrian Occupation to the Hellenistic Period (Seventh to Second Centuries BCE)

1. Excavations.

Shechem has been the subject of two major excavation projects. The first, by an Austro-
German team directed mostly by E. Sellin,

lasted from 1913 to 1934. This was followed
from 1956 to 1973 by the Drew-McCormick Archaeological Expedition, so named after the
two sponsoring institutions, Drew University
and McCormick Theological Seminary. Later
named the Joint Expedition, this American
project was directed jointly by G. E. Wright and
B. W. Anderson.

Together, the American and Austro-German
excavators revealed twenty-four distinct strata at
the tell, ranging from the Chalcolithic to the late
Hellenistic periods—that is, from the fourth millennium to the first century BCE. There were
four major abandonments of the site: (1) the
Early Bronze II and III periods (third millennium BCE); (2) the Late Bronze Age I (mid-
sixteenth to mid-fifteenth centuries BCE); (3)
Iron Ages I and IIA (late twelfth to late eleventh
centuries BCE); (4) the Persian period (fifth to
fourth centuries BCE).

2. Middle Bronze Age (c. 2000-1500 BCE).

After a long period of abandonment of the site
in the third millennium BCE, the Middle Bronze
Age II in the first half of the second millennium
BCE saw Shechem grow from a small unfortified
village in the nineteenth century BCE to a major
fortified town by the sixteenth century BCE. Strategic outposts in the region surrounded the city,
but the majority of the population lived in or
near Shechem itself.

On the acropolis of the tell several distinctive
courtyard buildings from the seventeenth century BCE, probably palaces or temples of the
*Canaanite city-state, were covered over in Mid-
dle Bronze Age IIC to create a large platform,
which served as a foundation for the construction of a massive temple, whose foundations are
still visible on the mound today.

At the same time a large wall, Wall A, was
built on the edge of the mound both as a defensive wall and to retain the large fill covering the
earlier structures. Two gates were set into the
wall, in the northwest and the east of the city.
However, the dominant structure on the mound
was the large temple, dubbed by the excavators
the Migdal, or Fortress Temple. Although it was
built in the sixteenth century BCE, some scholars
have proposed that it was still standing in the
period of the judges, and indeed may have been
the "Tower of Shechem" mentioned in Judges 9
(see 3.3 below).

The foundations of the Fortress Temple measured 26.3 m x 21 m, and its walls were 5.1 m thick. The walls had stone foundations with a mud-brick superstructure. The temple was built with a central axis entrance hall leading between two massive towers into a large main hall divided into three spaces by two rows of pillars. Later in the sixteenth century, the temple was rebuilt on the same foundations to a similar design, and the floor was raised by 0.75 m.

3. Late Bronze Age and Iron Age I (c. 1550-1000 BCE).

3.1. Archaeological Overview. Shechem was destroyed by the *Egyptians at the end of the Middle Bronze Age, in about 1540 BCE, and after a period of abandonment the city slowly recovered, developing into a well-protected city-state capital that dominated much of the central hill country of Canaan. As in the Middle Bronze Age II, several outposts served as part of a protective cordon of settlements around Shechem, guarding access points to the valley.

During the fourteenth century BCE Shechem was ruled by Lab'ayu, a powerful king identified in the Amarna letters. Several letters from other Canaanite rulers to the king of Egypt indicate that Lab'ayu was widely feared; among his many activities, he tried to capture *Megiddo to the northwest, attacked *Gezer to the southwest, and controlled Pella across the Jordan River to the northeast. Excavations revealed a grand city during this period, including fine buildings, a rich assemblage of pottery and multiple high-quality small finds, including two cuneiform tablets and a bronze striding-god figurine. This city was destroyed toward the end of the fourteenth century BCE, but it recovered again in the thirteenth, less prosperous than before, but rebuilt on the same lines.

This city continued unchanged into the early Iron Age, until it was destroyed and abandoned at the end of the twelfth century BCE.

3.2. The Fortress Temple Question. While the Late Bronze Age fortifications were a partial reuse and rebuilding of the walls and gates from the Middle Bronze Age city, the ongoing presence of the Fortress Temple on the acropolis is disputed. Originally discovered and excavated by the Austro-German team, the Fortress Temple was reexcavated by the American expedition, which concluded that it was destroyed at the end of the Middle Bronze Age IIC in the Egyptian destruction, and was covered much later by a granary building dated to the ninth century BCE. Furthermore, the Americans exposed wall fragments below the lines of the granary walls but above the Fortress Temple ruins, indicating to them that there had been an intermediate phase in the Late Bronze Age. This they identified as a rectangular temple, roughly situated over the main hall of the Fortress Temple, but 5 to 6 degrees off line. This Late Bronze temple was on the same lines and had the same orientation as the later granary. Thus, in this interpretation, the massive Fortress Temple of the Middle Bronze Age city was destroyed with the rest of that city in the sixteenth century BCE, and a smaller temple stood in its place in the Amarna age city of Lab'ayu, lasting into the period of the judges. This in turn was destroyed at the end of the twelfth century BCE, and was only replaced in the ninth century BCE by a granary, which was built on the lines of the Late Bronze Age temple (Campbell 2002, 176-81).

Recently, L. Stager has challenged this interpretation, suggesting that the Late Bronze temple never existed (Stager 1999; 2003). Its walls, he states, are simply the foundations of the ninth-century building above it. The difficulties in interpreting the structure stem from the excavation method used by the Austro-German team when they first exposed the temple in the 1920s. They dug trenches along the sides of the building's walls, thereby cutting off the fill inside the temple from the walls and removing all of the stratigraphic associations between the temple's walls, floors, foundation trenches and other features.

According to Stager's theory, then, the Fortress Temple survived the Egyptian destruction at the end of the Middle Bronze Age, served as the city's temple during the Amarna age and the reign of Lab'ayu, and continued to stand at the heart of the city during the period of the judges until it was destroyed along with the rest of the town around 1100 BCE. If so, says Stager, then this building puts in a strong claim to be the Tower of Shechem described in the story of Abimelech in Judges 9. Stager's proposal has gained the tacit approval of members of the American excavation team, including E. F. Campbell (unpublished paper, 2003) and W. Dever (2005, 168-9).

In the large open space in front of the temple, perhaps originally situated on either side of the entrance, were bases for two large standing stones, one of which was recovered. Nearby was a large gray brick altar with white marl curbing. Another altar, dated to the twelfth century BCE, was also found in the forecourt alongside the socket for a third massive standing stone. Now broken but still preserved to a height of 1.45 m, this stone is likely to have originally stood twice as high.

These imposing features indicate that the temple forecourt was an integral part of the temple itself and served as the venue for important ceremonies, as is borne out in the biblical accounts in Judges 9 and Joshua 24.

3.3. Judges 9 and Joshua 24. Judges 9 contains perhaps the most vivid account about Shechem in the Bible. The story of Abimelech's conspiracy contains several references to the temple and its sacred forecourt. In Judges 9:4 the elders of the city of Shechem give Abimelech seventy shekels of silver from the temple of Baal-Berith; in Judges 9:6 Abimelech is crowned by the local lords of Shechem alongside the sacred standing stone in the forecourt of the temple, and by a great sacred terebinth tree that grew there. This sacred terebinth features in the patriarchal narratives as well; it is where Abraham was given the promise of the land by Yahweh (Gen 12:6), and Jacob buried some of his possessions there (Gen 35:4). Finally, at the climax of the tale in Judges 9:46, the people of the city take refuge from Abimelech in the stronghold of the temple of El-Berith, which he then burns to the ground, killing the one thousand people still inside (Judg 9:49).

The account of the renewal of the covenant in Joshua 24 also takes place at Shechem. In Joshua 24:26 the story notes the presence of a large stone, a sacred tree and a sanctuary of Yahweh—elements repeated in Judges 9, binding the two accounts to the same site, the forecourt of the temple at Shechem.

Shechem's dominant position in the central highlands of Canaan and its imposing Fortress Temple and other structures beg the implication that it served as the political and religious center of the region during the Canaanite period. The accounts in Judges 9 and Joshua 24 indicate that the city itself, and the Fortress Temple in particular, were appropriated by the Israelites as a tribal and religious center dedicated to the worship of Yahweh. It is fair to conclude that in the twelfth century BCE Shechem and its temple compound had become the preeminent focus of Israelite religion and tribal identity in this early stage of settlement. Later, following the destruction of Shechem at the end of the twelfth century BCE, the core of Israelite religion and identity moved southward to Shiloh and thence to *Jerusalem, where it remained. In addition to Judges 9 and Joshua 24, other biblical references to Shechem in Joshua 8:30-35, 1 Kings 12, and Deuteronomy 27 indicate the reverence of early Israel for Shechem's role as an important sanctuary and full of patriarchal significance.

4. Iron Age II (c. 1000-720 BCE).

4.1. Archaeological Overview. After the late twelfth-century destruction, the tell lay abandoned for over a century until it was rebuilt on a modest scale during the reign of *Solomon in the tenth century BCE. During this period the temple area appears to have been deliberately deconsecrated and transformed into a grain storage area, with grain silos cut into the building's foundations. This town too ended in destruction, probably at the hands of the Egyptian pharaoh Shishak around 925 BCE.

The city that followed in the late tenth and ninth centuries BCE was larger and better built than its predecessor, reusing the fortification lines of the Middle Bronze Age city. There is evidence of town planning and two-story buildings in the town, which are indications of the revival of the north under *Jeroboam I and the house of *Omri. By the end of the ninth century BCE Shechem had grown into an organized and fortified city. The granary was built in this phase over the remains of the Bronze Age temples. At this time Samaria, some seven miles from Shechem, became the capital of the northern kingdom, and ostraca found there show that supplies of oil and wine were sent there from Shechem.

The city continued to flourish in the eighth century BCE, when Shechem's position at a major junction of the nation's road network enhanced its importance until its destruction by the *Assyrians. Roads led from Shechem northwest to the capital Samaria, north to Tirzah, west to the coast and south to Jerusalem (*see* Roads and Highways).

4.2. House 1727 and the Eighth-Century BCE Destruction of Shechem. One of the domestic units excavated from this period, House 1727, showed several signs of belonging to a well-to-do family in the town (Campbell 1994). Campbell suggests that the house relates effectively to passages in the book of Amos, where the prophet draws comparisons between the rich and the poor and their living conditions (e.g., Amos 5:11). Although the house was built according to the basic four-roomed house design (*see* Architecture), its considerable size, augmented by a large courtyard and several additions and extensions for both animals and people, perhaps related to the accommodation of a growing family, indicates significant status when compared to other parts of the town. The excavators proposed a second and even possibly a third floor, based on the size of the walls and on the presence of split logs used as ceiling beams in the building's destruction debris.

Evidence from the central ground-floor room indicates that the house also served an industrial function. Initially there was an olive-pressing facility in the large central room, but at some stage this was replaced by a furnace for burning limestone to produce calcined lime.

Other downstairs rooms were used for storage of quantities of grain, perhaps items used in the home industries, certainly feed for the animals, and possibly dung as well.

Although this house and its neighbors in Field VII were targeted for destruction by the Assyrians, poorer quality single-story structures of mud-brick on skimpy stone foundations nearby in Field IX show no evidence of massive destruction. Campbell (1994, 48) concludes that there was a selective destruction by the Assyrians, perhaps for more profitable looting, perhaps to punish what he calls "community leaders." The pattern does indicate that even in destruction there was "economic and social diversity" at eighth-century Shechem. These differentiations in wealth and status, though perhaps not great, were observable and effective enough to earn the approbation of the prophet Amos.

5. From the Assyrian Occupation to the Hellenistic Period (Seventh to Second Centuries BCE).

There was a limited occupation of the site in the seventh century BCE during the Assyrian period, and even fewer remains from the Persian period in the sixth century BCE, although the finds, which included a number of Attic black-glazed ware pottery sherds representing vessels imported from the Aegean, suggest that the inhabitants were cosmopolitan and prosperous.

Shechem recovered some prominence in the Hellenistic period when refugees from Samaria rebuilt the town following Alexander the Great's conquest of Samaria in 331 BCE. These new settlers also constructed a massive temple at Tell er-Ras, on top of Mount Gerizim overlooking Tell Balatah. Although the new settlement contained well-built fortifications and houses and lasted through four strata, its survival was compromised by the ongoing strife between the Seleucids and Ptolemies that characterized the third century BCE, and ultimately by the threat posed to the Jerusalem cult by the shrine at Tell er-Ras. When John Hyrcanus reestablished Jewish rule in Jerusalem in the late second century BCE, he attacked and destroyed the Tell er-Ras temple in 126 BCE, and later the city of Shechem itself in 107 BCE. Balatah was never resettled, and it was effectively replaced by the new settlement of Neapolis, established in the first century CE by the Roman emperor Vespasian a short distance away to the west.

See also SAMARIA; SHILOH.

BIBLIOGRAPHY. **R. J. Bull**, "The Excavation of Tell er-Ras on Mt. Gerizim," *BA* 31.2 (1968) 58-72; **E. F. Campbell**, "Archaeological Reflections on Amos's Targets," in *Scripture and Other Artifacts: Essays on the Bible and Archaeology in Honor of Philip J. King*, ed. M. D. Coogan, J. C. Exum and L. E. Stager (Louisville: Westminster/John Knox, 1994) 32-52; idem, "Now How Are Things at Shechem?" McCormick Days Lecture, Chicago, IL, April 28, 2003; idem, *Shechem II: Portrait of a Hill Country Vale; The Shechem Regional Survey* (ASORAR 2; Atlanta: Scholars Press, 1991); idem, *Shechem III: The Stratigraphy and Architecture of Shechem/Tell Balâtah, 1: Text* (ASORAR 6; Boston: American Schools of Oriental Research, 2002); **W. G. Dever**, *Did God Have a Wife? Archaeology and Folk Religion in Ancient Israel* (Grand Rapids: Eerdmans, 2005); **L. E. Stager**, "The Fortress Temple at Shechem and the 'House of El, Lord of the Covenant,'" in *Realia Dei: Essays in Archaeology and Biblical Interpretation in Honor of Edward F. Campbell, Jr. at His Retirement*, ed. P. H. Williams Jr. and T. Hiebert (Atlanta: Scholars Press, 1999) 228-49; idem, "The Shechem Temple: Where Abimelech Massacred a Thousand," *BAR* 29.4 (2003) 26-35, 66-69; **G. E. Wright**, *Shechem: The Biography of a Biblical City* (New York: McGraw-Hill, 1965). G. Gilmour

SHEEP, SHEPHERDING. *See* AGRICULTURE AND ANIMAL HUSBANDRY.

SHESHBAZAR. *See* HISTORY OF ISRAEL 7: PERSIAN PERIOD; HISTORY OF ISRAEL 8: POSTEXILIC COMMUNITY.

SHILOH

Rising to prominence after the destruction of *Shechem in the late twelfth century BCE, and falling from grace in the mid-eleventh century BCE when it was destroyed by the *Philistines, Shiloh played a critical role in the forging of early Israelite identity over a period that lasted only some fifty to seventy-five years. Archaeological excavations there lend support to the biblical accounts of Shiloh's importance in the Early Iron Age, when it served as the location of the tabernacle and the center of the Israelite cult. The site's destruction after the capture of the *ark of the covenant and subsequent abandonment were followed only by a small and nationally unimportant settlement in the eighth century BCE.

1. Biblical References
2. Excavations

1. Biblical References.

Identified with Khirbet Seilun, Shiloh is a well-protected natural hill situated some 2.5 km east of the Jerusalem-Nablus road at the north end of a fertile valley. The ancient town's location is precisely described in Judges 21:19, which states that it was north of *Bethel, east of the highway from Bethel to Shechem, and south of Lebonah.

In 1 Samuel 1 the "house of the LORD," which had been in Shechem (Josh 24:25-26), is now in Shiloh, and an annual festival is situated there (Judg 21:19). The significant characters of Eli and then *Samuel are based there, and the ark was removed from there before being captured by the Philistines at Ebenezer, apparently never to return (1 Sam 4). Although it is not stated explicitly in the biblical text, several passages strongly imply Shiloh's destruction by the Philistines after the capture of the ark (Ps 78:60; Jer 7:12-14; 26:6-9). The site is now heavily eroded, but excavations there have cast light on the nature of the "house of the LORD" and on the date and extent of the Iron Age I destruction of the town.

2. Excavations.

The site was first excavated by a Danish team from 1922 to 1932, when the project was terminated abruptly following the death of the director, H. Kjaer. Publication of the results was consequently delayed, and the final volume on the remains from the Bronze and Iron Ages only appeared in 1969 (Buhl and Holm-Nielsen). A team from Bar Ilan University under the direction of I. Finkelstein conducted renewed excavations at the tell from 1981 to 1984, clarifying and in some cases correcting some of the less certain and more controversial conclusions of the Danish project.

In addition to the erosion of all the remains in the center of the tell, including on the summit, Hellenistic and Roman builders at the site robbed out much of the earlier building material, significantly damaging the remaining Bronze and Iron Age remains. Nevertheless, careful excavation on the slopes of the tell yielded significant results that led to important conclusions about the site's history.

2.1. The Middle Bronze Age. Shiloh was first settled in the eighteenth and seventeenth centuries BCE, during the Middle Bronze Age IIB and IIC. Following an initial unwalled settlement, a city wall up to 5.5 m wide was built around the site, enclosing an area of 1.7 hectares (= 17 dunams = 4 acres). A sloping glacis was built against the wall, which served as a counterweight to the fills inside the wall that overlaid the earliest remains. On the north side of the tell a well-preserved row of rooms built against the inner face of this wall was identified as a group of cellars whose superstructures did not survive, and probably was associated with a shrine further upslope. Objects from this level that suggest the presence of a shrine include cult stands, votive bowls and a bull-shaped zoomorphic vessel. Although no architectural remains of any shrine were found from this period, the circumstantial evidence of the cellar rooms and religious objects, the conceptual similarity to other sites with known cultic significance such as Shechem, the long continuity of religious associations at the site through the subsequent Late Bronze Age into the Iron Age, and the absence of any preserved domestic structures all suggest that Shiloh served in the Middle Bronze Age as a religious center, with a shrine standing somewhere on the summit of the mound (Finkelstein, 375-77). This settlement was destroyed by fire in the sixteenth century BCE.

2.2. The Late Bronze Age.

Following its destruction by fire in the sixteenth century BCE, the site was abandoned, with no settlement and little activity visible in the archaeological remains. One significant corpus of finds, however, suggests that the ruined town continued to serve as a shrine after its destruction and was visited by nomads early in Late Bronze Age I before being abandoned. This was a dump containing offering vessels, bones, ash, sherds and several exotic finds. These may reflect the use of the site by those with a residual memory of the destroyed Middle Bronze IIC shrine.

2.3. Iron Age I.

Following a gap of some two hundred years, Shiloh was resettled in the early Iron Age period, toward the end of the twelfth century BCE. Evidence for the Iron I settlement was found in buildings, silos, installations and work surfaces excavated in several parts of the slopes of the mound. Most impressive was Area C, on the western slope, where both the Danish and the Israeli excavations uncovered a series of pillared buildings built on two levels on the steep slope against the outside face of the Middle Bronze Age city wall, embedded into the glacis. The removal of the glacis to create a foundation for these buildings demonstrates a significant expenditure of effort and suggests that these were more than simply domestic structures downslope from the summit. Indeed, the design and the contents of the two buildings of the complex that were uncovered by both Danish and Israeli excavations indicate that they served a public function rather than a domestic one. The buildings together produced an impressive assemblage of over forty restorable vessels, the vast majority of which were storage jars and cooking pots, suggesting that they served as storerooms. Furthermore, the orientation of the structures also pointed to a potential connection with a larger complex that once stood on the summit.

After the destruction of the pillared buildings, material dumped from above came to rest on the remains. The discarded objects include cult stand fragments, sherds from two possible votive vessels decorated with animal heads, the rim of a cooking pot with a lioness's head in relief, many bones, and the sherds of a cult stand with applied decoration of a leopard attacking a deer.

Although no shrine has been found at Shiloh to support the biblical account in 1 Samuel, enough circumstantial evidence exists for the excavators to propose such an interpretation of the site. The buildings in Area C were auxiliary to a larger building upslope toward the summit. As for the Middle Bronze Age, so too for Iron Age I, no domestic structures were found anywhere at the site by the Danes or the Israelis, and this, together with the evidence from the contents of the dump from upslope on the remains of Area C, suggests that the eroded complex at the center of the mound was a public building with religious significance.

Further evidence for the central importance of Shiloh to the region during its flourishing comes from the surrounding area. The results of surveys conducted in the region show that twenty-six of the Iron I sites surveyed in the region are within 5-6 km of Shiloh—a much higher proportion than *Bethel, for example, which had twelve, or any other site (Finkelstein, 286). Shiloh's rise to prominence as a regional center served as an incentive to the settlement and development of the area around it.

The Iron I settlement at Shiloh was destroyed in the middle of the eleventh century BCE, at around the time of the rise of the united monarchy in Israel. The correlation of the archaeological dates with the biblical descriptions of the loss of the ark to the Philistines at Ebenezer is unavoidable, and even though there is no absolute description of the destruction of the Shiloh sanctuary by the Philistines, it is implied in Psalm 78 and Jeremiah 7. The archaeological evidence shows that the site indeed was destroyed violently by fire at that time, and it lay unsettled for over two hundred years.

2.4. Iron Age II.

A small resettlement of the site in the late eighth century BCE followed the Assyrian conquest of the northern kingdom, but this level produced no significant archaeological remains. The settlement appears not to have been destroyed, but rather gradually abandoned in the seventh century BCE.

See also BETHEL; SHECHEM.

BIBLIOGRAPHY. **M.-L. Buhl and S. Holm-Nielsen,** *Shiloh: Danish Excavations at Tell Sailun, Palestine, in 1926, 1929, 1932 and 1963,* 1: *The Pre-Hellenistic Remains* (Publications of the National Museum, Archaeological-Historical Series 12, Copenhagen: National Museum of Denmark, 1969); **I. Finkelstein,** ed., *Shiloh: The Archaeology of a Biblical Site* (Monograph Series of Tel Aviv University, Sonia and Marco Nadler Institute of Archaeology 10; Tel Aviv: Institute of Archaeology of Tel Aviv University, Publications Section, 1993); **A. Kempinski and I. Finkelstein,** "Shiloh," *NEAEHL* 4.1364-70; **Y. Shiloh,** review of *Shiloh: Danish Excavations at Tell Sailun, Palestine, in 1926, 1929, 1932 and 1963,* 1: *The Pre-Hellenistic Remains,* by M.-L. Buhl and S. Holm-Nielsen, *IEJ* 21 (1971) 67-69.

G. Gilmour

SHISHAK. *See* EGYPT, EGYPTIANS.

SICKNESS AND DISEASE

Sickness and disease were as much a part of biblical life as they are today. The language used to describe those conditions was very different from current medical terminology. However, biblical descriptions and archaeology make it possible to identify some of the diseases that afflicted ancient Israelites. *Paleopathology* is the term given to the study of health and illness using archeological evidence (Jones). The Historical Books of the OT mention some specific sicknesses and diseases, and the present article begins by describing these in terms of current medical understanding. Following that, the article examines how sickness and disease were viewed in ancient Israel and then explores various theological responses elicited by these conditions.

1. Medical Conditions
2. Views of Sickness and Disease
3. Responses to Sickness and Disease
4. Conclusion

1. Medical Conditions.

Determining medical diagnoses for conditions described in ancient literature presents immense problems. In writing their narratives, the authors of the Historical Books did not intend that this issue be the focus of interpretation. Sometimes modern medical ideas are read back into a passage, such as when the hardening of Pharaoh's heart is taken to suggest that he had coronary arteriosclerosis (Sussman, 7). Yet sometimes the description can be specific enough that the condition described can be reliably diagnosed.

One of the more controversial diseases of the OT is what has traditionally been described as "leprosy." The Hebrew term *ṣāra'at* is mentioned several times in the Historical Books (2 Sam 3:29; 2 King 5:1-27; 7:3-8; 15:5-7; 2 Chron 26:19-23). What is regarded as the definitive work on this topic concluded that modern leprosy (or Hansen's disease) cannot be what is meant by this term (Hulse). Instead, it was a chronic, patchy skin condition that peeled and flaked, with underlying redness. This would indicate that *ṣāra'at* probably was a form of psoriasis or skin condition affecting the sebaceous glands. The latter secrete oils around hair follicles, which, when infected, produce greasy scales, itchiness and burning sensations.

Much has been written on the illness that brought Hezekiah to the point of death (2 Kings 20:1-7; 2 Chron 32:24-26; Is 38). 2 Kings 20:7 and Isaiah 38:21 state that Hezekiah had a "boil" *(šĕḥin),* which we may assume was some serious type of abscess. Some have claimed that Hezekiah had bubonic plague, connecting this to previous narrative material and the plague that killed Sennacherib's soldiers (2 Kings 19:35; 2 Chron 32:21). However, the descriptions are too vague to draw clear conclusions. Whatever the nature of the illnesses, the focus is on God's judgment of the Assyrians and his healing of Hezekiah (Rosner, 88).

Similar debate has occurred over other diseases that can only be tentatively described in modern terms. The plague that visited the Philistines at Ashdod (1 Sam 5—6) may have been bubonic plague, especially given the connection with mice, since we now know that rats carry the fleas that spread the infection to humans (Sussman). Saul's behavior has been viewed as arising from a psychiatric condition that manifested itself in spiritual torment (1 Sam 16:14-16), rage (1 Sam 18:10-11) and eventually suicide (1 Sam 31:4). The report of Nabal's heart failure, leading him to become "like a stone" and to his death ten days later (1 Sam 25:37-38), perhaps describes the results of a stroke. With all these descriptions, our diagnoses must remain tentative because the authors' primary intention was not medical, but theological. Thus the theological intent now becomes our focus.

2. Views of Sickness and Disease.

2.1. A Holistic Concept. The Hebrew root word most commonly used in the OT for sickness and disease is *ḥlh,* which carries a broad range of meanings. It can refer to standard medical conditions of ill-health, but also to states of weakness, tiredness and pain. Similarly, the Historical Books of the OT use a Hebrew term for healing *(rp')* that refers to restoration or making whole in a variety of contexts, including healing a sick body (2 Kings 20:5), repairing a broken altar (1 Kings 18:30), restoring infertile land (2 Chron 7:14) and making undrinkable water wholesome again (2 Kings 2:19-22). Thus healing may be needed from various problems, deficiencies or imbalances. Unlike the modern situation, in which sickness sometimes is assumed to have only physical or, possibly, mental origins, the OT concept of sickness allowed that it could also be of moral, spiritual or relational origin.

Sickness and disease therefore were viewed as being interconnected with all aspects of life and health. This underlies the description of Amnon as distraught to the point of illness and visibly haggard because of his lust for his sister Tamar (2 Sam 13:1-4). Although the psychosomatic aspects of illness sometimes have been forgotten by modern medicine, and spiritual aspects rejected, the OT perspective on sickness and disease is multifaceted and holistic. This understanding must be kept in mind when we examine specific instances of sickness and disease in the Historical Books of the OT.

The Hebrew view of sickness and disease was also distinctively different from that held throughout the ancient Near East. The cultures surrounding Israel viewed sickness primarily as demonic in origin. Diagnosing the problem and treating the sickness thus involved various magical practices and rituals believed to combat the activities of demons and evil spirits (*see* Magic and Divination). These included amulets, incantations and various means of divination. Although Mesopotamian cultures had incantation priests *(āšipu)* and physicians *(asû),* in practice both were focused primarily on relieving the sick person through magical means. It is well recognized that the OT records an intense battle for Israel's loyalty between polytheism and Yahweh. "What is not as commonly recognized, however, is that the Scriptures provide evidence that the battle fought over the issue of divine healing was equally pitched" (Brown, 69). This battle forms an important backdrop to any discussion of sickness and disease in the OT.

2.2. Sickness and Disease as Punishment. Arising from the Pentateuch was clear teaching that sickness and disease could be God's punishment on Israel. God declared, "But if you will not listen to me and carry out all these commands, and

if you reject my decrees and abhor my laws and fail to carry out all my commands and so violate my covenant, then I will do this to you: I will bring upon you sudden terror, wasting diseases and fever that will destroy your sight and drain away your life" (Lev 26:14-16 NIV; cf. Deut 29:22-24).

The Historical Books of the OT record many instances of these curses being fulfilled through God's affliction of the unrighteous. Joshua's farewell address reminded Israel of these curses and blessings (Josh 23:15-16; 24:20). David's sin with Bathsheba led to God afflicting his son with an illness that led to death (2 Sam 12:13-15). When King Jeroboam stretched out his hand against the prophet, God shriveled it up, and then God restored it when the king asked for healing (1 Kings 13:4-6). Other cultures also were punished. The Philistines were afflicted with tumors because they had seized the ark of God (1 Sam 5:6-12). Repeatedly throughout these books, sickness, disease and death are sent by God in response to the sins of Israelites and Gentiles.

The sovereign God of Israel was in control of sickness and health. "The Lord brings death and makes alive; he brings down to the grave and raises up" (1 Sam 2:6). When Naaman of *Aram brought his request for healing from "leprosy" to the king of Judah, the king replied, "Am I God? Can I kill and bring back to life?" (2 Kings 5:7). The cultures around ancient Israel saw health and disease arising out of a cosmic battle between good and evil spirits; Israel, however, held that God alone had the power to heal (Ex 15:26). But that power over nature extended to God's ability to inflict sickness and disease on those who transgressed his ways.

2.3. Sickness and Disease as Part of Life. Although the Historical Books record that sickness can be a punishment for evil deeds, and that health can be a reward for righteousness, they do not lend themselves to woodenly applying this principle—although, such application did occur in Israel, as is reflected in the book of Job and later in the Gospels (Lk 13:2, 4; Jn 9:2). Many accounts in the Historical Books note that sickness and death occurred without any hint of censure. Thus Eli became frail and blind as he aged (1 Sam 3:2). Hearing that Israel had been defeated in battle, his sons killed, and the ark of God captured, Eli fell over, broke his neck and died (1 Sam 4:14-18). The passage notes that Eli was an old man and heavy, but it does not suggest that his death was divine judgment. Similarly, his daughter-in-law dies in labor, apparently brought on by her grief, not God. Later we learn that Jonathan's son Mephibosheth was lame in both feet due to an accidental fall (2 Sam 4:4). The misfortune is not blamed on anyone's *sin—not his, nor his father's, nor his caretaker's. It just happened. Similarly, Naomi's husband and two sons are simply reported as having died prematurely, with no mention of God's involvement (Ruth 1:3-5). As David grew old, he became frail and sickly (1 Kings 1:1). Facing death, he told Solomon, "I am about to go the way of all the earth" (1 Kings 2:2). *Elisha, similarly, is not said to be under God's judgment when we are told that he "was suffering from the illness from which he died" (2 Kings 13:14).

Just as sickness, disease and death are not always signs of unrighteousness, so also good health and long life are not always signs of righteousness. The lack of a simple connection between sin and sickness is more fully explored in the books of Job and Ecclesiastes, but its foundation is laid in the narratives of the Historical Books. 2 Kings 13—14 provides examples that defy a simple interpretation of life whereby sickness always represented God's judgment on the sinful. Jehoahaz reigned over Israel for seventeen years, but he "did evil in the eyes of the LORD" (2 Kings 13:2). After years of oppression by the king of Aram, Jehoahaz prayed to God, who then delivered Israel—although, God was motivated by the severity with which Israel was being oppressed (2 Kings 13:4-5). In spite of God's mercy, Jehoahaz and Israel returned to their evil ways, but Jehoahaz reigned on until he went to be with his fathers (2 Kings 13:9). No direct correlation exists between Jehoahaz's righteousness and his health.

In a similar way, Amaziah reigned in Judah for twenty-nine years, doing what was right in the eyes of the Lord (2 Kings 14:1-3). However, he did not remove the high places or eliminate idol worship (2 Kings 14:4). He then foolishly declared war on Israel and was resoundingly defeated, yet he continued to reign, apparently in good health, until he was assassinated (2 Kings 14:19-20). His son Azariah succeeded him and reigned over Judah for fifty-two years, doing what was right in the eyes of the Lord, like his father (2 Kings 15:1-3). He likewise did not eliminate idol worship, yet God afflicted him with "leprosy" (2 Kings 15:4-5). A generally righteous life was not enough to prevent God from afflicting Azariah with illness, and yet the same sin in his father did not lead to sickness. When all these texts are taken into account, a rigid principle of human action leading to divine reaction is not apparent. A summary statement reveals why God acted as he did toward the Israelites: "But the LORD was gracious to them and had compassion and showed concern for them because of his covenant with Abraham, Isaac and Jacob" (2 Kings 13:23). God's grace, faithfulness and mercy led to his actions, not a simple rule of cause and effect. Sometimes, as Jesus later stated explicitly, injury and death result from living in a fallen world and being in the wrong place at the wrong time (Lk 13:1-5).

3. Responses to Sickness and Disease.

3.1. Sickness and Disease Leading to Manifestation of God's Power and Involvement. The authors of the Historical Books sometimes used accounts of sickness and disease to focus the readers' attention on the reasons for the affliction. At other times the focus was more on the responses to the illness. One response was that sickness and disease made possible the manifestation of God's power and attributes and his involvement in people's lives. The miracles performed by *Elijah and Elisha sometimes involved this message.

For example, the worship of Baal in the cultures around Israel was in direct opposition to God. Baal was alleged to be in control of life and death, but God used Elijah in 1 Kings 17 to invalidate this claim and demonstrate that in fact God controls nature. Elijah bursts onto the scene after King Ahab marries a woman from Sidon, an important Phoenician center of Baal worship. Ahab soon promotes Baal worship, and Elijah enters to announce that God will withhold all rain for a few years. After some time in hiding, Elijah travels to Sidon and miraculously demonstrates God's provision of food and oil for a Canaanite woman. Then her son gets sick and dies, and the woman asks Elijah, "What do you have against me, man of God? Did you come to remind me of my sin and kill my son?" (1 Kings 17:18).

Such a question arises naturally from a belief that sin is the source of all sickness. Elijah does not answer her question, but instead wonders to

God, "O LORD my God, have you brought tragedy also upon this widow I am staying with, by causing her son to die?" (1 Kings 17:20). But Elijah's question about the origin of the sickness does not prevent him from praying for healing and taking action by lying on the boy. God answers Elijah's prayer and restores life to the boy, and the woman declares, "Now I know that you are a man of God and that the word of the LORD from your mouth is the truth" (1 Kings 17:24).

Through this story, "Elijah asserts that Canaanite theology is a lie, that Baal is no god at all" (Rice, 141). Sickness provides the necessary setting for this demonstration of God's sovereignty. These miracle stories are based in everyday life, and they show ordinary needs being met miraculously: rain for the crops, food for the hungry, money for the poor, life for the dead. They reveal God's concern for everyday life, and his involvement in life. They should lead to faith and trust in God, and acknowledgment of the truthfulness of God's word, as happened with the widow. Sickness can lead to manifestation of God's glory, as it later did when Jesus gave sight to the blind man, at the same time refuting the idea that sickness is always caused by sin (Jn 9:1-3).

3.2. Sickness and Disease Leading to Baalism. The temptation constantly facing Israel was to turn to Baal and other gods to meet their needs. Sickness and disease sometimes led them in inappropriate directions. The Pentateuch declared that God was Israel's healer (Ex 15:26), but this did not stop the Israelites from sometimes pursuing healing from inappropriate sources. God condemns the pursuit of healing from certain spiritual sources, and the Historical Books describe some notable episodes that demonstrate this.

King Ahaziah fell and injured himself, but then he sent messengers to consult Baal-Zebub, the god of Ekron (2 Kings 1:1-8). Elijah confronted Ahaziah's messengers with a message from God that this injury would prove fatal. The message from the angel of the Lord was clear: "Is it because there is no God in Israel that you are going off to consult Baal-Zebub, the god of Ekron?" (2 Kings 1:3). This incident reflects the inappropriateness of seeking information about health through divination.

King Asa demonstrates more clearly that healing itself can be pursued in inappropriate ways. Asa was a king whose "heart was fully com-

mitted to the LORD all his life" (2 Chron 15:17). However, in his latter years he relied on foreign armies for success, not the Lord. Hanani the seer revealed God's displeasure at this, and in return Asa jailed Hanani and oppressed the people. His feet then become diseased, but Asa was unwilling to turn to God for help. "Though his disease was severe, even in his illness he did not seek help from the LORD, but only from the physicians" (2 Chron 16:12).

This verse has been used to claim that Scripture has a negative view of using medicine and physicians to treat sickness and disease (see 3.3 below). However, the general issue in the context surrounding this incident is where or to whom people turn when in need. Earlier in his reign Asa depended on God for help and relief, as when he said, "LORD, there is no one like you to help the powerless against the mighty. Help us, O LORD our God, for we rely on you" (2 Chron 14:11). Now, however, he rejects God and turns to the physicians. Brown (51) points out that the Hebrew phrase translated as "seek help" in 2 Chronicles 16:12 is used only when referring to religious or oracular situations (see 1 Chron 10:13-14). Immediately after this incident Asa's son is commended because he did not consult the Baals, but rather followed God instead of the practices of Israel (2 Chron 17:3-4). This passage therefore teaches that followers of God should not respond to sickness and disease by pursuing healing based on religious and spiritual sources that are not of God (O'Mathúna and Larimore). Asa's sin was his refusal to rely on the Lord, not his pursuit of medicine.

In contrast, we see other examples of those who were sick and did turn to the Lord. King Hezekiah became sick and was at the point of death (2 Kings 20:1-11; 2 Chron 32:24-26). We are not told why this happened, but only that he prayed to God, who healed him. Hezekiah responded with pride to God's kindness, leading to God's punishment; but then Hezekiah repented, and God relinquished his punishment. Similarly, Jabez prayed that God would keep him safe from harm and free from pain, and God granted his request (1 Chron 4:9-10). When faced with sickness and disease, the appropriate response is to turn to God in prayer that he might bring mercy and possibly even miraculous healing. At the same time, the Historical Books show that healing is not guaranteed, as is clearly demonstrated by the lack of healing for David's son despite much prayer and fasting (2 Sam 12:15-17).

3.3. Sickness and Disease Leading to Use of Medicine. The Historical Books of the OT give little information on the role of medicine in ancient Israel's response to sickness and disease. Other ancient Near Eastern cultures, especially the Egyptians, had large volumes of medical texts. However, as we have already noted, these medical professions were intimately intertwined with the religions of those cultures. Some have taken this historical context, and a questionable interpretation of 2 Chronicles 16:12 (see 3.2 above) to claim that no form of medicine was approved by God. For example, K. Seybold and U. B. Mueller somewhat tentatively speculate that "the Old Testament accounts are one-sidedly biased for the purpose of denigrating medicinal healing practices" (Seybold and Mueller, 23; for other examples see Brown, 48-49).

Yet among the small number of relevant passages, many refer to medicinal practices without any negative comment. When the Israelite soldiers returned their Judean prisoners, they gave them clothing, food, water and healing balm—all presumably good provisions (2 Chron 28:15). As part of Hezekiah's healing from God, Isaiah used a poultice of figs, a common healing remedy (2 Kings 20:7). More generally, the playing of harp music is suggested to help bring relief to Saul (1 Sam 16). The importance of food and water to maintain good health and vigor are noted (1 Sam 30:11-12). Although not part of medicine in its narrowest sense, these practices at least acknowledge the importance of using the broader provisions of God in treating and preventing sickness and disease. They reflect the holistic view of illness and health demonstrated in the Historical Books. Although medicine at that time had few effective treatments to offer, there is no condemnation of using the best that natural (as opposed to spiritual) medicine could offer.

4. Conclusion.
Sickness and disease are viewed in holistic ways in the Historical Books of the OT. Sickness arises as part of the natural, fallen world in which people live, but also it can be sent by God to accomplish his purposes. A variety of responses to sickness and disease can be appropriate, including repentance, prayer and the use of medicine. Not every response is acceptable to

God; in particular, those that neglect God or involve spiritual practices that are not from him are rejected. The rest of the Bible affirms the diverse origins of illness, and also that medical treatment can be acceptable (1 Tim 5:23). However, James turns to one of the central figures of the Historical Books, Elijah, to remind us of the continued importance of pursuing God in the midst of sickness and disease (Jas 5:14-18).

See also MAGIC AND DIVINATION; MIRACLES.

BIBLIOGRAPHY. **D. W. Amundsen,** *Medicine, Society, and Faith in the Ancient and Medieval Worlds* (Baltimore: Johns Hopkins University Press, 1996); **M. L. Brown,** *Israel's Divine Healer* (SOTBT; Grand Rapids: Zondervan, 1995); **E. V. Hulse,** "The Nature of Biblical 'Leprosy' and the Use of Alternative Medical Terms in Modern Translations of the Bible," *PEQ* 107 (1975) 87-105; **R. N. Jones,** "Paleopathology," *ABD* 5.60-69; **M. E. Marty and K. L. Vaux,** eds., *Health/Medicine and the Faith Traditions: An Inquiry into Religion and Medicine* (Philadelphia: Fortress, 1982); **D. O'Mathúna and W. Larimore,** *Alternative Medicine: The Christian Handbook* (Grand Rapids: Zondervan, 2001); **G. Rice,** *Nations Under God: A Commentary on the Book of 1 Kings* (ITC; Grand Rapids: Eerdmans, 1990); **F. Rosner,** *Medicine in the Bible and the Talmud: Selections from Classical Jewish Sources* (augm. ed.; LJLE; Hoboken, NJ: Ktav; New York: Yeshiva University Press, 1995); **K. Seybold and U. B. Mueller,** *Sickness and Healing* (Biblical Encounters; Nashville: Abingdon, 1981 [1978]); **M. Sussman,** "Sickness and Disease," *ABD* 6.6-15.

D. P. O'Mathúna

SIDON. *See* PHOENICIA, PHOENICIANS.

SIGNS. *See* MIRACLES.

SIKAN STATUE. *See* ARAM, DAMASCUS AND SYRIA.

SILOAM CHANNEL. *See* WATER AND WATER SYSTEMS.

SILOAM INSCRIPTION. *See* HEBREW INSCRIPTIONS.

SIN
An exploration of the biblical concept of sin needs to do justice to three interwoven strands: words, metaphors, narrative. The appearance of

one or more terms from the rich vocabulary for "sin" is a clear indication of behavior that is contrary to God's will. Sin often is portrayed metaphorically through reference to common experiences. However, particularly in the Historical Books the primary portrayal of sinful behavior is through the narration of events. Unlike the prophets, the biblical storytellers generally are sparing in their explicit ethical and religious judgments. They prefer to show rather than tell, setting out scene by scene the disastrous effects of sin on individuals, tribes and nations. It is a challenging interpretive task to trace the complex web of influences, motivations and consequences of sinful behavior. In the present article the *Deuteronomistic History (Joshua to 2 Kings), which together with the Pentateuch comprises Israel's primary history (Genesis to 2 Kings), is discussed separately from the later secondary history (Chronicles, Ezra and Nehemiah) (*see* Chronicler's History), although the two share a great deal in common.

  1. The Vocabulary of Sin
  2. Metaphors of Sin
  3. Joshua to 2 Kings
  4. Chronicles, Ezra and Nehemiah
  5. Conclusion

1. The Vocabulary of Sin.

The numerous words in the semantic field for "sin" emphasize the importance of the concept. The following list includes the more significant terms for "sin," although individual nuances tend to be leveled out in summary passages that combine several terms. This often happens when the narrator wishes to emphasize the gravity of the situation (e.g., 2 Kings 17; 2 Chron 29), or when a sinner formally confesses (e.g., 2 Sam 24:17; 2 Chron 6:37). The following sections include references to the cognate verbs as well as the nouns.

1.1. ḥaṭṭāʾt, "Sin." This is the most frequent word for "sin" in the OT. It is used of missing the mark (Judg 20:16), but it is not clear to what extent this is a metaphorical use, and there is no evidence elsewhere that this is a significant metaphorical nuance. Instead, the root is used in general and formal contexts, such as the summary descriptions of the failure of a king (2 Kings 21:16). It is the first term occurring in public confession by notorious sinners (Josh 7:20; 1 Sam 15:24; 2 Sam 12:13).

Sin has a personal orientation. It is sin against someone, whether the Lord (Josh 7:20; 2 Sam 12:13; 1 Kings 8:33) or another person. The assumption is that the parties are in a relationship that has agreed norms of conduct, and sinful behavior violates these. On the human level, a king and his servants have mutual obligations of good treatment and loyal obedience, and a refusal of these is sin (1 Sam 19:4). A vassal king sins by refusing to give tribute to his overlord (2 Kings 18:14). A prophet's duty is to stand between the Lord and his people, and thus the prophet's failure to pray is sin (1 Sam 12:23).

Most often the root refers to sins against the Lord by Israelites, either individually or as a nation. As recounted in the Pentateuch, *Israel is bound to obey the laws of the covenant. These include standards of ethical behavior, but the first commandment (Ex 20:3) and the Shema (Deut 6:4-5) make it a priority for God's people to worship only the Lord. Hence *ḥṭʾ* frequently describes the promotion and worship of idols (1 Kings 16:13) or divination (1 Sam 15:24). In Kings the paradigmatic sin (directly related to the climactic sin of Ex 32) is *Jeroboam's setting up of the two golden calves in *Bethel and *Dan (1 Kings 12:30). The failure to remove them was the ground for the repeated criticism of Jeroboam's successors (1 Kings 16:19; 2 Kings 15:18). Although the *kings bear special responsibility, the people share in the guilt (2 Kings 17:22).

The use of *ḥaṭṭāʾt* to mean "purification offering" appears only in passing in the secondary history (Neh 10:33 [MT 10:34]; 2 Chron 29:21-24).

1.2. rāʿâ, "Evil." The noun is sometimes simply the opposite of "good," with a range of meaning from the neutral ("calamity") to the moral ("evil"). The refrain in *Judges and 1-2 *Kings, "doing evil in the sight of the Lord," emphasizes the ultimate reference point for the narrator's evaluation. Since the Lord's will for Israel's moral and religious behavior is revealed in the *law and freshly applied by the *prophets, the word often describes Israel's failure to hear and obey (2 Kings 17:13). A wise king discerns the difference between good and *evil (2 Sam 24:17), but the historical books demonstrate the endemic sinfulness of Israel's kings, who both reflect the general sinfulness of the people and encourage it through their behavior and laws (2 Kings 21:9). Not even the most godly of kings was able to avoid evil (2 Sam 11:27; cf. 2 Chr 35:21-22).

1.3. ʿāwōn, "Iniquity." The word ʿāwōn does not appear frequently in the Historical Books. It probably is derived from a verb meaning "bend" or "twist," but this nuance is not particularly evident when the root refers to sin. It is a general term covering all kinds of sins that are carried out against persons (2 Kings 7:9) or God (Josh 22:20). It sometimes is difficult to determine whether the word indicates the act of sin (Neh 9:2), the state of sin (guilt; 2 Sam 24:10) or even the consequences of sin (punishment [Gen 4:13]). Often the term is used in formal confession (e.g., 2 Sam 14:9; Ezra 9:6).

1.4. nĕbālâ, "Folly, Outrageous Act." Willful folly is behavior that is wrong from both a pragmatic and a moral or religious perspective (2 Sam 13:12). Achan foolishly attempts to deceive the Lord by hiding spoil (Josh 7:15). Nabal acts according to the meaning of his name ("folly") by spurning the powerful David and doing it in a way that is calculated to offend (1 Sam 25:25). Folly destroys the balanced and ordered relationships that sustain a viable community, and often it is bound up with sinful arrogance (see Wisdom).

1.5. maʿal, "Unfaithful Act." The noun and the verb appear only in *Joshua, *Chronicles and *Ezra-Nehemiah, describing unfaithfulness toward God. The word may be used with specific cultic overtones, as is the case when Achan misappropriates the devoted things (Josh 7:1). *Hezekiah has to purify the temple and sanctify it as a consequence of unfaithfulness (2 Chron 29:6). In the secondary history it is used to describe a variety of moral and religious offenses, emphasizing how this behavior breaks the personal trust required by the Lord (1 Chron 10:13; 2 Chron 36:14). Its ultimate consequence is exile (Neh 1:8).

2. Metaphors of Sin.
It is possible to coordinate many references to sin by attending to foundational metaphors that shape the way people think and live.

2.1. The Journey Metaphor. The sinful deviate from the straight path of obedience and life. Jehu sins by not walking (hlk) in the law of the Lord with his whole heart (2 Kings 10:31), and *David turns aside (swr) in the matter of Uriah (1 Kings 15:5). Jeroboam walks in an evil way and refuses to turn away (šûb) from it (1 Kings 13:33), and others follow his lead (1 Kings 15:34; 2 Kings 17:22). *Manasseh misleads (tʿh) the

people (2 Kings 21:9). To transgress or cross over (ʿbr) is to violate the safe bounds of the commandments (1 Sam 15:24) and the covenant (Josh 7:15) and suffer the consequences of God's judgment.

2.2. The Personal Metaphor. Words drawn from the hostile relations between individuals often express sinful attitudes of individuals or the people to God, who is always the injured party. Eli's sons despise (bzh) the Lord (1 Sam 2:30), and David treats him with contempt (nʾṣ) (2 Sam 12:14). Since the Lord is a king, the people sin by rebelling (pšʿ) against him (1 Kings 8:50). *Samuel gives the people a choice either to hear the word of the Lord or to rebel (mrh) against his "mouth" (1 Sam 12:14). Israel's history shows that the people are more than likely to reject (mʾs) the Lord as their king (1 Sam 8:7).

2.3. The Orientation Metaphor. A person's attitude is reflected through posture and orientation. Just as the repentant return (šûb) to God and orient themselves toward the temple (1 Kings 8:33, 29), so also the rebellious turn their faces away from the Lord's dwelling and turn their backs to him (2 Chron 29:6). Also combining the personal and the spatial is the notion of leave or abandon (ʿzb)—a particular favorite of the secondary history. It is a grave failure of the covenant relationship for Israel to abandon the Lord through spurning his law (1 Kings 18:18; 2 Chron 12:1) and his temple (2 Chron 24:18), and he in turn will abandon them (2 Chron 24:20). Pride is indicated by a root meaning "high," gbh (1 Sam 2:3; 2 Chron 26:16; 32:5-6).

2.4. The Marriage Metaphor. Israel's pursuit of other divinities can be described as prostitution (znh), since marriage assumes an initial commitment (i.e., Sinai) that is then maintained by faithful wholehearted devotion and love (Deut 6:5). Judges describes Israel's whoring after other gods in its opening general summary (Judg 2:17), and then notes specific acts of unfaithfulness (Judg 8:27, 33). *Elijah condemns Jehoram of Judah for seducing (Hiphil of znh) the people (2 Chron 21:11, 13) and announces punishment on him and his family.

3. Joshua to 2 Kings.
3.1. Overview. The opening chapters of Genesis reflect the awareness that all human beings sin and are responsible for their behavior. The Historical Books assume that Israelites have a

responsibility to conform to universal standards of behavior (e.g., 1 Kings 9:10-14). Over and above this the Pentateuch shows how Israel agreed to obey the special requirements of the Lord's covenant with his people. The Historical Books from Joshua to 2 Kings continue both the universal story of sin that begins in Genesis 3 and the specific outworking of the human tendency to sin shown in Israel's failure to keep the covenant law, primarily through idolatry (Ex 20:2; Deut 6:4). Historical criticism has emphasized the close connection between these books and Deuteronomy by calling Deuteronomy to 2 Kings the Deuteronomistic History. However, the death of Moses marks a significant break, and a canonical reading of the primary history needs to recognize both the continuity and the discontinuity with the Pentateuch. The restrained style of the storytellers makes the most sense if they expect readers to bear in mind the fundamental moral and religious requirements of the covenant and the law.

The Historical Books portray a story of sin and judgment on the largest scale. If the Pentateuch tells a reasonably positive story of a journey from landlessness to landedness, the Historical Books reverse the plot, and 2 Kings ends with utter defeat and exile (Brueggemann 2003). The exile of Adam and Eve from Eden as a result of sin is echoed by the larger story of the journey of a sinful nation toward exile. However, this is not a steady decline, but one with many ups and downs. The different stages of Israel's history provide the setting for new forms of sin and disobedience alongside new dispensations of grace and *forgiveness. Furthermore, sin and blame are shared among individuals, families, tribes and nations in an unpredictable way. There are no heroes in the OT, and individuals characteristically display a complex mixture of good and evil as they both respond to and influence others. Despite exceptional men and women of God and the interventions of the prophets, the overall direction of the people of God is toward deepening sin and rebellion. Good kings can do only so much to reform a stiff-necked people (2 Kings 22:16-20). There are more bad kings than good, and the people follow their lead (2 Kings 21:16). Although even under the worst kings there can be a faithful remnant (1 Kings 19:18), this is not enough to avert the coming judgment. The implicit hope evident in the final verses of 2 Kings (25:27-30)

leaves unresolved how the Lord can deal with the depth of the people's sinfulness.

3.2. Joshua. The book of Joshua is largely positive, beginning with accounts of a successful conquest and ending on the high note of the covenant ceremony at *Shechem (Josh 24). However, the emphasis on obedience to the Torah in the first chapter (Josh 1:8, 13) is a foil for the extended account of Israel's first sin when Achan steals some of the devoted things. Although apparently it is Achan alone who covets the spoil (Josh 7:21), the solidarity of individual and nation means that "all Israel" is held responsible (Josh 7:11). His household is implicated along with him, for they must know about the crime (Josh 7:24). Sin, especially at this early stage in the conquest, cannot be tolerated, and only when "all Israel" executes judgment on Achan's household does the Lord turn from his anger (Josh 7:25-26). Achan's confession (Josh 7:21) echoes the temptation narrative (Gen 3:6) as well as the tenth commandment (Ex 20:17), showing how desire for beauty and money can be the beginning of sin and tragedy (cf. 2 Sam 11:2). Joshua's closing exhortation in Joshua 23 further emphasizes the priority of the exclusive covenant between the Lord and his people. The primary temptation to sin is idolatry, and intermarriage is condemned because it will become the gateway for apostasy (Josh 23:13).

3.3. Judges. It is possible that the book of Judges was intended as the negative counterpart to Joshua, although it is anticipated in Joshua 24:19-20, one of the most pessimistic statements of the sinfulness of Israel in the Bible. These verses preface the renewal of the covenant that comes at the climax of Joshua, and they illustrate how pride in success leads to fall. Judges tells the story of an ever descending spiral of sin and folly. At the outset the narrator analyzes the reason for the repeated defeat and repression of the people in his comment that they "did what was evil in the sight of the Lord" (Judg 2:1 [seven times in all]). This is primarily idolatry, and in a growing phrase they are described as worshiping (*'bd*) the Baals (Judg 2:11), the Baals and Asherahs (Judg 3:7), and then seven sets of gods (Judg 10:6). The more extended treatment of the major judges enables a more nuanced exploration of the relation between character and gifts, opportunity and sin. *Faith exists alongside flaws of character and motive that often bring disaster on the leader and others, as can be seen in the consequences of Gideon's making of an ephod (Judg 8:22-27), Jephthah's rash oath (Judg 11:30-31), and Samson's insatiable quest for sex and violence (Judg 14:2; 15:1-8; 16:28-30). The final four dark chapters provide a unique mix of idolatry, violence, folly and tragic irony. The narrator's lament about the lack of a king (Judg 21:25) emphasizes the value of a leader in dealing with evil before it gets out of hand, and here the narrator anticipates the major theme of 1 Samuel.

3.4. 1 Samuel. The Lord calls Samuel in place of the sinful sons of Eli (1 Sam 2:25), although his own sons take bribes and pervert justice (1 Sam 8:3-5). The people's subsequent demand for a king initially is equated with rebellion against the Lord (1 Sam 8:6-8), and Samuel then sets out the capacity of a king to undermine Israel's traditional social structures (1 Sam 8:11-18). However, God in his grace accommodates to Israel's demands (1 Sam 12:19), and *Saul is chosen. Early hints of flaws in character (1 Sam 10:22) soon become disobedience to Samuel (1 Sam 13:8-15) and neglect of his commands (1 Sam 15:9-35). Although Saul expresses some kind of regret (1 Sam 13:12; 15:24), the rest of the book suggests that any dimension of true repentance was undermined by elements of superficiality, deceit and hypocrisy. The account of Saul's deepening sin and madness is a foil for the portrayal of David's godliness and humility. Saul's jealousy of David (1 Sam 17:7-9) leads to attempted murder (1 Sam 18:11) and vindictive pursuit. His paranoia imputes guilt to blameless associates of David and results in the death of innocent priests (1 Sam 22:11-23). Saul's climactic sin is consultation with a medium (1 Sam 28:3-7) in order to raise the spirit of the dead Samuel (1 Sam 28:11-19). The result is not only the death of Saul and his family, but also the defeat of the Israelite army (1 Sam 31). Nor is David unaffected by Saul's deeds, for they complicate his relations with women (1 Sam 25:39-43) and sow seeds that will bear tragic fruit when he becomes king.

3.5. 2 Samuel. The dynastic oracle includes a condition that David's descendants who commit iniquity will be punished (2 Sam 7:14), but the following verses imply that this would not be sufficient to thwart God's purposes for David's house. The multiple dimensions of David's adultery with Bathsheba (2 Sam 11:4) emphasize the fallibility of even Israel's godliest king. The nar-

rator does not explicitly state that David should have been with the troops (2 Sam 11:1), but staying in Jerusalem allows a dangerous amount of leisure and the opportunity for temptation. However, in Israel even the king is not above the law, and Nathan fulfills the prophetic calling to hold the powerful accountable for their sins (2 Sam 12:1-13). The rest of the book shows the personal and political consequences of sin for David, his family and the nation, including incest (2 Sam 13:14), murder (2 Sam 13:28-29) and rebellion (2 Sam 15). David's lament over the death of Absalom (2 Sam 18:33) demonstrates David's inability to reconcile royal duty with his own personal feelings. In 2 Samuel 21—24, an "appendix of deconstruction" (Brueggemann 1988), the book ends ambivalently by describing the Lord's anger against David for taking a *census (2 Sam 24:10). Sin has consequences, even if repentance enables God to be merciful (2 Sam 12:13-14; 24:16-17).

3.6. 1 Kings. *Solomon is portrayed as the greatest of Israel's kings from a political and material point of view, but the author subtly makes it clear that other criteria of evaluation are more important. Solomon's request for wisdom (1 Kings 3:9) is no doubt positive, but it follows an account of a marriage alliance with Egypt. It is the first of many pragmatic political decisions that eventually will incline Solomon to follow other gods (1 Kings 11:2) and provoke divine judgment (1 Kings 11:9-11). His wisdom eventually is used for oppression (1 Kings 12:10-11) and for impressing foreigners (1 Kings 10:1-13). Solomon's behavior contradicts the official theology of his great prayer in 1 Kings 8, in which Solomon acknowledges that the righteous God punishes the guilty (1 Kings 8:32), that all are sinful, and that the ultimate consequence for a sinful nation is exile (1 Kings 8:46). Yet the fundamental assumption of the prayer is that God is merciful. He hears prayer, forgives sin and reverses its consequences. In the disregarding of these promises, Solomon's sin is shown to be all the greater. The immediate consequence of Solomon's sin is a divine word of judgment predicting the split of the kingdom (1 Kings 11:11-12; cf. 11:30-33). This is merely confirmed by *Rehoboam's foolish preference for the advice of his companions over that of the elders (1 Kings 12:6-16). Although the split is approved by God, Jeroboam's attempt to provide religious legitimization for his kingdom through setting up two golden calves compromises the northern kingdom, with ultimately fatal consequences (2 Kings 17:21). The editors regard his action as the paradigm of sin both for Jeroboam's house (1 Kings 13:33) and for later kings (1 Kings 16:19; 22:52; 2 Kings 13:2; 15:28). However, it is acknowledged that individual kings bear varying degrees of guilt for their behavior. David sins in the matter of Uriah (1 Kings 15:5), but the primary criterion for evaluation of the kings of Judah is religious, especially their attitude toward the *high places (1 Kings 15:14). The violation of God's covenantal gift of the *land to families is highlighted in the extended account of Naboth's vineyard (1 Kings 21). The story illustrates the way royal marriages with foreigners could undermine Israel's distinct moral and religious values. Although Elijah announces judgment on Ahab and Jezebel, the story implies that there is a growing disregard of God's covenant, particularly among the wealthier classes. 1 Kings ends with a brief, entirely negative portrayal of Ahaziah (1 Kings 22:51-53).

3.7. 2 Kings. The last book of the Deuteronomistic History portrays the tragic results of the sins of the two kingdoms. The canonical presentation acknowledges the political realities of the day, but traces the root cause of disaster to the interrelated sins of the kings and their people. The reason for the exile of the northern kingdom is set out at length in 2 Kings 17. The primary cause is Israel's wholesale idolatry (2 Kings 17:7-12), although the kings contribute to this (2 Kings 17:8, 22). The sin is enhanced by the people's stubborn refusal to heed the prophets (2 Kings 17:13-14) and by their walking *(hlk)* in the customs and gods of other nations, thus despising *(m's)* the covenant and the laws of the Lord, who saved them from Pharaoh (2 Kings 17:7, 16). The result is divine wrath (2 Kings 17:18), exile and banishment from his presence (2 Kings 17:20). However, there is no direct link between degrees of sin and punishment. Ahab is most evil, but his repentance delays judgment (1 Kings 21:25-29). Israel's final king, Hoshea, does less evil than do other kings, but his political treachery is the final straw and triggers the end of the northern kingdom (2 Kings 17:1-6). Judah is alike in not keeping God's commandments (2 Kings 17:19) but has a somewhat different history. A number of godly kings counter the downward trend, although the narrator implies that the last actions of Hezekiah (2 Kings 20:12-

19) and *Josiah (2 Kings 23:28-30) reflect political and religious folly. However, the accumulated sin of Judah has an inertia that even the radical actions of Josiah in eliminating the high places cannot reverse. In particular, the final punishment of God is traced to the sins committed during the long reign of Manasseh (2 Kings 23:26; 24:3), who is portrayed as an evil antitype of Josiah (cf. 2 Kings 21:3; 23:4). Manasseh not only initiated dramatic syncretistic acts in the temple—the heart of the Lord's presence in the midst of Israel (2 Kings 21:1-9)—but also shed "very much innocent blood" (2 Kings 21:16). Blatant idolatry and institutionalized murder result in a prophetic denunciation that includes a classic statement of the *lex talionis* ("measure for measure"): divine "evil" (in the sense of calamity) is the return for Manasseh's moral and religious evil (2 Kings 21:11-12). Yet the concluding verses imply that sin and punishment will not have the last word (2 Kings 25:27-30).

4. Chronicles, Ezra and Nehemiah.

4.1. Chronicles. In comparison to the Deuteronomistic History, Chronicles has a theology of a more immediate retribution for sin, but this should not be understood mechanically (Kelly). Through selection of existing and addition of new material, and through general summaries (1 Chron 28:8-9; 2 Chron 7:14; 15:2), Chronicles seeks to relate deeds (sin/repentance) closely to consequences (punishment/forgiveness). This reflects an emphasis on God's justice, and it may be directed against those in the restoration community who thought that punishment for their sins could be delayed. Although punishment will follow sin, God's primary desire is for people to repent of their sins and live in obedience to his commandments (2 Chron 24:19). Chronicles' interest in Israel's worship leads to an emphasis on failures to obey the Torah, especially in the speeches (2 Chron 13:8-12) and the accounts of royal sins (2 Chron 21:11; 26:16-21). The notorious passing over of most of the sins of David and all those of Solomon is partly due to a focus on the temple, but it may also be intended to model the ideal eschatological future. The role of Satan in inciting David to take a census of Israel (1 Chron 21:1 [in 2 Sam 24:1 it is the Lord who incites]) is unique in Chronicles and should not be overinterpreted. It may only indicate a nameless adversary and a counterpart to Joab. The guilt of David and others may be reduced by contextual factors, but the primary responsibility of sinners for their actions is inescapable. Sins accumulate and increase God's anger until punishment is inevitable (2 Chron 36:16).

4.2. Ezra. The officials who approach Ezra describe the mixed marriages among the returnees as a case of "faithlessness" (*maʿal* [Ezra 9:2, 4]). Ezra's response is a comprehensive confession of Israel's iniquities and sins, indicating that these marriages are in direct continuity with Israel's past behavior. Although the harsh, exclusive measures adopted raise wider ethical and interpretive issues, Ezra's primary concern is the loss of distinct Israelite identity through idolatry and assimilation, which will provoke the Lord to destroy his disobedient people (Ezra 9:14).

4.3. Nehemiah. A report to Nehemiah of the desperate situation of the returnees from exile results in a wide-ranging confession of the sins of the people, with whom he completely identifies (Neh 1:6-7). His reaction to problems of debt (Neh 5:1-13) exposes the gap that can exist between the letter of the law and the sinful exploitation by the wealthy of powerless social classes. Nehemiah 9 comprises a great confession (Neh 9:6-37) led by Levites on behalf of the people (Neh 9:1-5). The prayer powerfully sets out the tension between Israel's constant sinfulness and the Lord's forgiveness and mercy. Profaning the sabbath (Neh 13:15-22) and mixed marriages (Neh 13:23-27) are further expressions of sin and evil in the covenant community that are in danger of provoking divine wrath and the nation's destruction.

5. Conclusion.
The OT takes sin with utmost seriousness, for the Lord is holy and righteous and calls both humanity and Israel to account. At every level, the consistent pattern is failure, mostly (though not always) through deliberate sinful actions. The normal result of sin is divine judgment, ultimately resulting in death for individuals and families and in exile for the nation. Yet because of God's mercy and long-suffering, there is a space between sin and judgment that opens up other possibilities. The Lord sends prophets to his people, summoning them to repentance, which alone can bring forgiveness and restoration, although the consequences of sin cannot be completely undone. Despite deepening and

recurring sin, the Historical Books refuse to succumb to despair, indicating that Israel should continue to hope in God, who one day will finally deal with sin.

See also ETHICS; EVIL; FORGIVENESS; JUSTICE AND RIGHTEOUSNESS; LAW.

BIBLIOGRAPHY. **W. Brueggemann,** "2 Samuel 21—24: An Appendix of Deconstruction?" *CBQ* 50 (1988) 383-97; idem, *David's Truth in Israel's Imagination and Memory* (2d ed.; Minneapolis: Fortress, 2002); idem, *The Land: Place as Gift, Promise, and Challenge in Biblical Faith* (2d ed.; OBT; Minneapolis: Fortress, 2003); idem, *Theology of the Old Testament: Testimony, Dispute, Advocacy* (Minneapolis: Fortress, 1997); **W. Janzen,** *Old Testament Ethics: A Paradigmatic Approach* (Louisville: Westminster/John Knox, 1994); **B. E. Kelly,** *Retribution and Eschatology in Chronicles* (JSOTSup 211; Sheffield: Sheffield Academic Press, 1996); **R. Knierim,** *Die Hauptbegriffe für Sünde im Alten Testament* (2d ed.; Gütersloh: Mohn, 1967); idem, "On the Contours of Old Testament and Biblical Hamartiology," in *The Task of Old Testament Theology: Substance, Method, and Cases* (Grand Rapids: Eerdmans, 1995) 416-67; **J. G. McConville,** *Grace in the End: A Study in Deuteronomic Theology* (SOTBT; Carlisle: Paternoster, 1993); **M. Sternberg,** *The Poetics of Biblical Narrative: Ideological Literature and the Drama of Reading* (ILBS; Bloomington: Indiana University Press, 1985).   P. Jenson

SO. *See* EGYPT, EGYPTIANS.

SOCIAL-SCIENTIFIC ANALYSIS. *See* METHODS OF INTERPRETATION.

SOCIAL-SCIENTIFIC APPROACHES
Biblical interpretation at its best is comprehensive and inclusive; it seeks to uncover the nuances and ranges of meanings that the ancient hearer and modern reader of the biblical traditions may have seen and heard within them. Much post-Enlightenment biblical interpretation was based in a "humanities" approach that examined the historical, theological and linguistic contexts of texts. The social worlds of the biblical texts and their writers were considered peripheral, and when addressed, scholars tended to restate the biblical writers' viewpoints and analyses of the events they portrayed. This article presents an alternative approach—but one that, appropriately applied, adds significantly to

the insights of more traditional biblical scholarship—one that focuses on the social contexts within and behind the biblical texts.

1. What Is Social-Scientific Criticism?

By the end of the twentieth century social-scientific criticism had emerged as a distinct form of biblical scholarship. The social and behavioral sciences are themselves diverse, including the analyses of many different aspects of human society and culture. Among these are sociology, anthropology, political science, economics, archaeology, as well as psychology and social psychology. However, when scholars refer to social-scientific criticism they generally mean the comprehensive analysis of biblical traditions from the standpoint of sociology and anthropology. With it scholars attempt to provide a set of social contexts for these traditions, using insights gleaned from the studies of societies and groups with similar social, cultural, political, environmental and economic settings. Often, models constructed by social scientists are applied to the biblical texts in order to understand better the world(s) they portray. This comparative approach assumes that while societies and cultures differ in their specific histories, distinct similarities among them may allow scholars to discover patterns and developments that can be applied to contexts separated in time and place.

1.1. The Rise of the Social Sciences. Although Greek, Islamic, Medieval Jewish and even biblical historians engaged in some rudimentary social and cultural analysis (Carter 2001; Wilson, 1984), the social sciences as we know them—distinct academic disciplines—emerged in the late nineteenth century. Interestingly, the figure that many social scientists consider one of the founders of these disciplines was himself a biblical scholar—W. Robertson Smith. Smith was convinced that parallels to biblical cultures could be found among living, tribal cultures in the emerging modern Middle East. He himself traveled to and did field work in Syria-Palestine and sought to apply insights from the Arab and Bedouin cultures back to the biblical texts. This comparative approach, which used the concept of analogical points of contact between ancient and modern examples of societal types, remains one of the basic methods of the social sciences. Many of Smith's conclusions have, over time, been revised and even abandoned, but his interest in and analysis of social contexts and patterns in ancient texts and their modern counterparts proved fertile ground for subsequent study of societies. Among his most influential works were *Kinship and Marriage in Early Arabia* (1885) and *Lectures on the Religion of the Semites: The First Series* (1889). In the latter, Smith explored the importance of sacrifice for both Israelite religion and its social order. In 1991 a long-lost manuscript of Smith's second and third series of lectures on Semitic religion was discovered in the W. Roberston Smith library in Cambridge and subsequently edited by J. Day and published in 1995.

In some respects, the impetus for the social sciences emerged from Enlightenment philosophy, which viewed human cultures, thought and history primarily from a humanistic perspective. The writings of T. Hobbes (1588-1679) and J. Locke (1632-1704) rooted human knowledge in experience and suggested that cultures emerge in different ways based on the interrelationship of environmental settings (or material contexts) and human thought. This meant that instead of a common, universal truth, societies and cultures might follow very different trajectories and emerge with separate and distinct cultural traditions and mores. This was essentially in keeping with the Enlightenment emphasis on human experience rather than divine revelation as the standard for human conduct. As the social sciences emerged and continued to emphasize a comparative approach—seeking to identify common elements of societies where they existed—the concept of the "uniqueness" of ancient *Israel increasingly came under scrutiny.

1.1.1. Sociology. As its name implies, sociology has as its main interest the various elements and structures of human society and the interrelationships among them. In its early stages, sociological analysis focused more on identifying and analyzing broader characteristics of human societies. A. Comte is often considered the founder of the discipline of sociology, though this is in part because of his frequent use of the term (Lenski, Lenski and Nolan). More influential for the early development of the social sciences were the writings of H. Spencer, whose evolutionary perspective came to characterize the study of human culture. Spencer, and early social scientists who followed him, believed that all human societies passed through clearly definable stages, from "savage" to "civilized." German historian F. Tönnies identified two distinct social phases in Western culture, demarcated as a shift from community *(Gemeinschaft)* to society *(Gesellschaft)*, which M. Weber and E. Durkheim applied—though in distinctly different ways—to their study of societies (Mayes). Also influential to later social-scientific analysis was his concept of "ideal types," an idea that M. Weber developed further.

Many of the earliest (and most important) practitioners of this discipline might today be identified as "macrosociologists." This approach to sociology (which also characterizes much anthropological research) typically has a focus that is comparative and crosscultural, historical and macro-organizational. The comparative approach allows scholars to identify elements of societies or cultures that are both similar and unique. The historical focus allows sociologists to identify patterns that may emerge (or diverge) over time within societies with similar social and environmental settings. The macro-organizational interest allows scholars to identify not only the distinct aspects of a society or group but also to analyze the ways in which these elements work together (or against one another) and to evaluate their impact on the society as a whole.

Post-World War II sociology, particularly that of the United States and Europe, has become increasingly concerned with societies and groups on the "micro" level, with the result that the comparative and historical interests have been largely supplanted by a more intense focus on modern groups, practices and social developments. Data for these types of studies are typically gathered from surveys, focus groups and intensive fieldwork on specific groups or trends, and sociology of this type cannot be applied to ancient societies and cultures.

1.1.2. Anthropology. Although it too is concerned with the study of social phenomena, anthropology as a discipline is more broadly concerned with the origins of humanity and human culture. While there are several subdisciplines within anthropology, scholars generally divide the field as a whole into two major categories: physical and cultural anthropology. Physical anthropology is concerned primarily with the origins and evolution of *homo sapiens* from its earlier and divergent hominid ancestors, as well as its place within the hominid family. Cultural anthropologists (the discipline is referred to as "social anthropology" in Europe) are more concerned with the emergence and development of the material and ideological artifacts of human culture. The discipline of archaeology, along with its several subfields, contributes significantly to both physical and cultural anthropology, and is equally important to social-scientific (and historical) criticism of Scripture. Other sub-specialties within the study of anthropology that relate to biblical studies are linguistics, ethnology and ethnography (see below).

1.2. Pivotal Scholars and Approaches. Sometimes referred to as "the triumvirate of the social sciences," M. Weber, E. Durkheim and K. Marx are each linked with a particular "school" or "model" within sociology and anthropology (Malina). Weber is commonly identified with the so-called conflict model, Durkheim is considered the founder of the structural-functional approach, and Marx is identified with a materialist understanding of societies and their institutions.

1.2.1. Weber and the Conflict Tradition. Weber's major contribution to the sociological interpretation of the Hebrew Bible is his work *Ancient Judaism* (1952). Among Weber's observations pertaining to the Historical Books that have been developed by other scholars are the analysis of Israelite social structure based on the ancestral household *(bêt ʾāb)*, the extended family or clan *(mišpāḥâ)* and the tribe *(šēbeṭ)* (Gottwald 1979; Stager); the importance of covenant to Israelite social and religious structure (Cross; Mendenhall 1973); and the identification of "ideal types," such as A. Malamat's identification of the judges as "charismatic leaders" (Malamat). G. Mendenhall's theory of Israel's emergence as a peasant revolt applies a conflict model to Israelite history (Mendenhall 1962), as does B. Lang's analysis of Israelite prophecy and the growth of monotheism (Lang).

Essentially, the conflict model analyzes the types of competition between or among different groups in a society and the tensions that arise within that society as a result. A central question in each of these traditions focuses on the ways in which societies resolve these tensions. In the conflict model, concern is given to the relationships among competing groups, their relationship with the established social order, and their means of establishing and maintaining influence in society and in opposition to groups with competing interests. The conflict tradition generally concludes that social balance is established when one group succeeds in imposing a system of constraints on other social groups.

1.2.2. The Structural-Functional Approach. E. Durkheim is generally considered the originator of this tradition within the social sciences. Rather than focusing primarily on conflict among social groups, this methodology examines the structures and institutions of a society, asking how these component parts and social groups and institutions function within the society. The structural-functional tradition does examine social change, but sees such change as somewhat more measured than does the conflict tradition. Although Durkheim did not specifically write about biblical Israel and its history or social context, his approach has been applied by numerous biblical scholars. French scholar A. Causse used Durkheim's notion of "group mentality" in his analysis of Israelite society and its religious traditions (Causse). He believed that an initial "organic solidarity" characterized earliest Israelite society, but that the family and village-based economy was gradually undermined with the emergence of a centralized monarchy. This in turn gave rise to class distinction, which formed the basis of the prophetic call for the protection of the poor and the establishment of justice. N. Gottwald's influential *Tribes of Yahweh: A Sociology of the Religion of Liberated Israel, 1250-1050 BCE* (1979) draws heavily on the structural-functional approach but is also influenced by a materialist orientation.

1.2.3. Marx and Cultural Materialism. Most early and many contemporary social theorists regard ideas and ideologies as fundamental to social order and development. One might view, for example, the commitment to a covenantal ideal as foundational to the emergent community in ancient Israel and a unifying feature for its "tribal" structure before the establishment of the monarchy. A materialist approach does not deny the power of ideas but sees all elements of human culture, including social structure, customs, art, religion, symbols, etc., as emerging from material contexts. Marx focused on eco-

nomic and material realities and aspects of production, and the ways in which class divisions and social differentiation inevitably lead to social conflict, and often revolution, as the oppressed classes rise up against the elite who are exploiting them. In Marx's view, it is change in the economic or material context (typically referred to as the "base") that leads to shifts in the ideational realm (typically called the "superstructure"). Two additional aspects of Marxist theory that are important for the materialist perspective are the "political economy" and the "mode of production" of a society. The former refers to the interplay between political and economic forces, and the latter to the interrelationship between the "material forces" and "social relations" of a culture's production. Production itself has to do with the use of natural resources, including crops and animal husbandry, as well as the manufacture of tools, weapons and luxury items, for example. It is also concerned with the ways in which economic surplus is created and extracted, and how resources are distributed among the members of a given society.

1.3. Early Applications to Biblical Studies. In his analysis of the use of the social sciences in the study of the Hebrew Bible, F. Frick (2002) divides this form of study into two distinct phases. A first wave is found in the early works of R. Fenton, W. R. Smith, L. Wallis, A. Causse, A. Alt and M. Noth, all of whom developed and applied sociological and anthropological models to their study of the Hebrew Bible (Carter 2001). Noth, for example, applied a comparative methodology to his analysis of Israel in the premonarchic period and identified the "tribal league" as an amphictyony (*see* Amphictyony, Question of). Also part of this first wave would have been studies by R. de Vaux on ancient Israelite religion and society; J. P. E. Pedersen's work, *Israel: Its Life and Culture* (1920, 1934), which was concerned with the role of the covenant and the subsequent development of various sociopolitical institutions within Israel; and G. H. Dalman's *Arbeit und Sitte in Palästina* (8 vols., 1928-42) still provides scholars with useful ethnographic data on agricultural and domestic practices in premodern Palestine, which may serve as parallels for the analysis of Israelite and Judean technologies and practices.

This earliest stage of social-scientific analysis of biblical texts was sometimes marked by a sense of the superiority of both Western (primarily European) civilization and Christianity as a religious tradition that many scholars today find distasteful and parochial. In this respect, the social sciences were children of their age—and both Europe and the United States were engaged in colonial and expansionist political pursuits that found ideological support in a form of cultural imperialism. The West viewed itself as *the* truly civilized society—all non-Western cultures were inferior and in need of Western oversight to help them control their baser, more animal instincts. Further, those practices and beliefs in Western culture that were considered more "primitive" were identified as "vestiges" of earlier cultural impulses that had not yet been purged from the collective human experience. This unilinear, evolutionary schema of societies and cultures has largely been abandoned, though it is common to identify potential trajectories through which cultures and social groups sometimes pass. The emphasis on *possible developments* rather than the assumption that *all* cultures pass through specific identifiable phases keeps social-scientific analysis from becoming either deterministic or positivistic.

1.4. A "Second Wave" of Social-Science Oriented Studies. After these initial forays into social-scientific analysis of biblical texts and cultures, its use by biblical scholars declined sharply and a lengthy hiatus followed, due in part to the rise of the "biblical theology" movement. Programmatic essays by G. Mendenhall in 1962 and N. Gottwald in 1974 were largely responsible for the emergence of the second phase of scholarship that applied the social sciences to Israelite and Judean history and traditions, and Frick himself was an early advocate of this type of study. Full-scale studies by Gottwald in 1979 and R. Wilson in 1980 made more extensive and systematic use of the social sciences and laid the foundation for the growth of social-scientific criticism into an accepted form of biblical scholarship. What began as an emphasis on the origins of earliest Israel and its social structure has expanded to include virtually all aspects of Israelite and Judean society. The contributions of many such studies will be noted throughout the rest of this article.

2. Methodology.

As discussed above, the earliest practitioners of sociology and anthropology examined human culture and societies from both historical and comparative perspectives. It is this emphasis on the "macro" level of societies that is most useful for the study of the social realities behind specific texts of the Hebrew Bible. The processes that underpin such historical and comparative approaches include the collection and study of ethnographic data, the use of analogy, and the development of social and cultural models.

2.1. Ethnography. When a sociologist or anthropologist studies a particular culture, society or element of that culture or society, he typically engages in extended periods of field research. The researcher, often referred to as a "participant observer," collects data through a variety of means. These include interviewing members of a particular social or cultural group, sometimes being assisted in the field by an "informant" (a member of the group being studied), recording events or practices with various media (including sound, videography or still photography), and making site-plans or drawings of important buildings, features or cultural implements. In addition to working with the informant and observing individual or group practices, an ethnographer often checks his interpretations with group members and may use this process of feedback to revise his initial conclusions. Sound methodology demands that an ethnographer carefully plan his fieldwork in order to examine specific aspects of the group or practice he is studying; however, unplanned experiences often lead to discoveries as important as the initial issues or questions that gave rise to the field study.

When the ethnographer returns from the field, she begins the task of interpreting the data she has gathered and drawing conclusions regarding the significance of the events, individuals, and practices and customs she has observed. The interpretive phase of the project may lead to questions that require further study and additional fieldwork. The final ethnographic report of the people or practice she has observed is both descriptive and analytical, and provides readers with a comprehensive and detailed understanding of the group or practice under study. These ethnographic studies are important in their own right—some are reports of cultures that are endangered by first-world development—but in addition may provide scholars with points of comparison with groups with similar structures or practices, or that exist in similar geographic or environmental contexts. This subsequently allows for the development of social models that are drawn from several "cultural cognates" and may be applied to other like groups or practices, both living and dead.

2.2. Emic/Etic and Insider/Outsider Perspectives. In 1967 K. L. Pike developed a framework intended to clarify the nature of observation and interpretation of cultural practices, using terms borrowed from linguistics. He identified the "emic" approach as viewing an event, practices, more, etc. from the "inside" (but sometimes through the researcher's description), and the "etic" approach as the researcher's (the "outsider") analytical or interpretive understanding of that event, practice, symbol or custom. Although Pike did not see the two categories as mutually exclusive, his framework provides a useful reminder that insider observations, descriptions or categories, and outsider interpretations must be tested against one another. The emic/insider witness may come either from the field researcher or from a member of the group under study, while the etic understanding of that witness comes from the researcher's attempt to categorize human culture through an explicitly comparative approach, and to develop broad categories or principles of human behavior. Anthropologist M. Harris suggests that both the emic and etic understandings must be subjected to controls or tests of their validity. In his view, the test of the etic analysis of the insider's emic viewpoint is the ability of the member of the group to recognize or authenticate the interpretation of his or her practice proffered by the field observer. That is, if the insider does not recognize the validity of the description or interpretation, then the particular etic analysis is flawed. Additionally, etic/outsider accounts are useful to the extent that they produce what Harris called "scientifically productive theories about the causes of sociocultural differences" (Harris, 32).

An example of the importance of emic authentication comes from anthropologist M. Douglas's influential study *Purity and Danger* (although she does not use the emic/etic categories). Douglas tells of a group of !Kung Bushmen performing a rain ritual and observed by ethnographers (Douglas). Clouds appeared and rain began falling shortly after the ritual was completed. Later, the anthropologists asked the

Bushmen if they believed their ritual had in fact caused the rain; the Bushmen responded with derisive laughter, for they were under no such illusion regarding a cause-effect relationship between their ritual and the eventual rain. The anthropologist's defective etic assumptions of the nature of the presumed belief of "primitive cultures" in the efficacy of "magic" led to their misunderstanding of both the ritual and its meaning. Only by sharing their analysis of the ritual with the !Kung were the ethnographers able to correct their eventual interpretation, based on the emic perspective of the Bushmen.

2.3. Ethnoarchaeology and Analogy. One of the means used by social scientists in applying their findings from ethnographic research to other cultures, living and ancient, is analogy or analogical reasoning. It is particularly prominent in the subfield of ethnoarchaeology, where archaeologists and ethnographers observe living cultures in order to understand processes and practices, tool manufacture and use, spatial relationships, means of production, site and population density, in the culture's ancient counterpart (Carter *OEANE*). There is considerable debate about the efficacy of identifying and applying such analogs from their current context to a target society in the past, and a number of methodological controls have emerged. Some scholars propose that analogs may only be applied when the observed and target cultures are in similar environmental or geographic contexts, while others are satisfied if broad cultural continuities or similarities are evident. Some would propose the creation of "testable hypotheses" to guide the applications of analogs from one culture to another. Still others complain that analogical reasoning is circular: it assumes a certain level of cultural continuity, and when it finds similarities among cultures from different time aor spatial contexts, it claims to have proven the very continuity it assumes. Effective analogical reasoning, therefore, must concentrate on both continuities and discontinuities that might be equally instructive when creating social reconstructions based on observation of current living cultures.

2.4. Ethnography, Ethnoarchaeology and Biblical Studies. Ethnoarchaeology is of particular use for scholars engaged in the study of the Historical Books of the Hebrew Bible. P. McNutt uses ethnographic and ethnoarchaeological research to examine the emergence of iron technology and its impact on Iron I and Iron II Israel and *Judah (as well as the traditions they produced). Analyzing the relationship of technology to culture and using analogs from African societies, she demonstrates that iron technology sometimes symbolizes relationships in the social and religious sphere. In Israelite society references to the forging of iron symbolize the Israelite enslavement in Egypt, as well as durability, power and Israel's transformation by its deity. Some of the applications of ethnoarchaeology to biblical cultures that are further developed in the article include F. Frick's examination of social and religious developments in the period of transition towards a chiefdom and monarchy (Frick 1979), C. Meyers's analysis of sacrifice and ritual using ethnoarchaeological parallels (Meyers 1995), and C. E. Carter's use of demographic patterns from premodern villages in Syria-Palestine and Mesopotamia to reconstruct the population and social context of Yehud in the Persian period (Carter 1999; 2003).

3. Israelite Origins.

The books of *Joshua and *Judges present different portraits of earliest Israelite history, although the biblical editors have attempted to harmonize these two traditions by using the person of Joshua as a bridge between them. While they differ in scope and sometimes tone, the two traditions share a certain theological orientation and point to some similar social forces. Both assume a covenantal framework providing social and religious order to the newly entered "promised land" (as well as the processes of both entry and settlement) as well as a loose confederation of tribes united by a common commitment to Yahweh and to the broader social entity, Israel. They also demonstrate an aversion to ethnic and religious "other," using a rhetoric of exclusion and ethnic purity to justify the destruction or displacement of the land's original inhabitants and the occupation of Canaan. Both also share a view of Yahweh as a war deity, as well as a conviction that the social change that occurred when Israel emerged came about as a result of external forces (i.e., a new social order came into being when Israel "entered" the land, whether in the form of an invasion from the Transjordan [Joshua] or the more gradual process of settlement among the indigenous population [Judges]). The differences between these textual traditions gave rise to two distinct views

of Israel's emergence. As a result of the renaissance of social-science criticism through the scholarship of Mendenhall and Gottwald, a third theory was developed that attempts to make use of biblical and extrabiblical texts as well as archaeological evidence and social theory.

3.1. External Invasion: Albright's Conquest Theory.

W. F. Albright represented a traditional approach to both archaeology and biblical interpretation. Excavations at Tell Beit Mirsim (which Albright identified with biblical Debir), Beitin (*Bethel), *Lachish and *Hazor, all had destruction layers dating to the end of the Late Bronze Age. Sites such as Tell el-Fûl (*Gibeah of Saul), and Tell Balatah (*Shechem), which the Joshua accounts indicated were not destroyed—and Shechem became an Israelite political and cultic site—showed continuous occupation in the Late Bronze Age and the Iron I period. This, according to Albright, demonstrated the essential "historicity" of the biblical conquest account. Albright was, of course, aware that the archaeological record was negative in the case of *Jericho and *Ai (et-Tell), neither of which seem to exist in the thirteenth century BCE.

More recently, scholars have questioned Albright's interpretation of the data on several grounds. For example, Khirbet Rabud, not Tell Beit Mirsim, is generally accepted as the site of Debir. And further, destruction layers themselves are mute as regards the cause of a site's demise; these sites may have been destroyed by groups other than the Israelites, such as the Sea Peoples.

Archeological data also suggested to Albright that there were ethnic markers of Israelite settlements and technological advances that allowed the fledgling tribes to survive in the hill country that they initially occupied. He considered the four-room house (see Architecture) and the collared-rim storage jars to be distinctly Israelite and evidence of their presence in Palestine, and he believed that iron technology, cisterns lined with plaster and terrace agriculture were new innovations developed by the Israelites to allow them to settle in the inhospitable central hill country, which lacked plentiful water resources available in other parts of Syria-Palestine. Further, he pointed to destruction at the Late Bronze Age site of Hazor in the Galilee region, next to which a small, rustic settlement developed in the Iron I period. Although the conquest theory enjoyed widespread support among Albright's followers through the middle of the twentieth century, several later developments brought its validity into question. Collared-rim storage jars were discovered in the Transjordan and the coastal plain region of Palestine, both considered outside the settlement area of Israel (*see* Geographical Extent of Israel). Albright believed that iron technology was necessary for making tools needed for clearing trees to make arable land to support agriculture, for cutting cisterns into the hill country for the collection of water, and for the forging of iron plow points. However, iron technology is now known to have become widespread only in the end of the Iron I period or the beginning of the Iron II period and was therefore not a factor in the settlement of the central hills or their agricultural development. Both cistern and terrace construction are known to predate the Iron Age and therefore were not introduced by the Israelite population. A. Ben-Tor, who has led extensive recent excavations at Hazor, is one of the few archaeologists who still maintains a conquest explanation of Israelite emergence; conservative biblical scholars tend to accept the biblical traditions, many proposing an early date for the exodus and conquest. The theory, once a majority view, is now distinctly a minority account for Israelite settlement in Palestine.

3.2. External Origins: Alt's Peaceful Infiltration Theory. In contrast to Albright's theory of Israelite origins, which is dependent on the book of Joshua, Alt proposed that the emergence of Israel was a result of a nomadic, tribal group gradually adopting a sedentary lifestyle. This theory is dependent on a romanticized (and now outdated) view of nomadism that considered then contemporary Bedouin and their customs and lifestyle as analogs for the earliest Israelites. The Shasu Bedouin mentioned in Egyptian documents were considered to be a disruptive force in the regions under Egypt's control, and were also seen as potential precursors of the people who came to be identified as Israelites. The Shasu, active in the Transjordan region, where the Israelites are said to have traversed before their occupation of Palestine, were regarded by many scholars as providing a model of this type of sedentarization of nomadic groups. According to Alt's theory, the traditions of the conflict between the various Israelite tribes and their Canaanite "oppressors" in the book of Judges, as well as the Joshua stories of conquest, arose from the tensions typical of nomadic groups and

the agrarian villages among which they were settling. This theory, which was later adopted by Israeli archaeologist I. Finkelstein, found further parallels between Bedouin groups and Israelite origins. Specifically, the Bedouin tents were thought to be the forerunners of Israelite architecture and village planning. The floor plan of the tent itself was considered the pattern for the development of the broad-room (or four-room) house; the oval arrangement of tents with entrances facing a common, public area was considered the origin of a similar arrangement seen in small, unwalled villages in Palestine.

3.3. Internal Origins: The Peasant Revolt Theory. Developed first by Mendenhall, and revised by Gottwald, the peasant revolt theory suggested that the accounts in Joshua and Judges must be combined with extrabiblical textual evidence, new archaeological evidence and social theory in order to provide a coherent account of Israel's emergence in Palestine. One of Mendenhall's major contributions was to raise serious questions about the understanding of nomadism and tribes and tribal cultures that dominated biblical studies (Mendenhall 1962). Both concepts, he argued, were poorly defined by biblical scholars and based upon idealized notions of Bedouin and tribal groups in the premodern Middle East. He proposed that the nomadic traditions within the Hebrew Bible should be understood as a form of "enclosed" or "transhumant" nomadism, in which the groups in question are seasonal nomads rather than continually moving from place to place. Further, he saw the earliest Israelites or Hebrews as related directly to the ʿapiru of the Amarna documents from the fourteenth century BCE (sometimes referred to as the *habiru* or *hapiru*) (see Hebrews). In the Amarna letters and other Mesopotamian texts, the ʿapiru function as "outlaws" responsible for upheaval in the societies in which they were located. Mendenhall believed that they should be considered disaffected peasants who rebelled against or withdrew from the stratified Canaanite city states to the previously underpopulated central hill country, beyond the effective control of their Canaanite overlords. Maintaining an ideology of independence, they united with the group of recently liberated slaves from Egypt. Their common past of oppression and exploitation allowed both groups to unite as one with allegiance to the Israelites' deity Yahweh.

Gottwald further developed Mendenhall's thesis, but from a more materialist perspective, first in a brief article and then in his monumental *Tribes of Yahweh*. In this work Gottwald provided a thorough, though sometimes eclectic (using many different social-scientific models and methods) analysis of Israel's early history and the textual traditions about its emergence. He built as well on his prior work on "domain assumptions," that is, basic perspectives or explanations that biblical scholars used to explain social change (Gottwald 1974). Among these assumptions was that social change, including the emergence of a new group or society within a territory, is always the result of external forces; that is, new groups coming into an area from the outside. These presuppositions also idealize the role of the desert as a "creative force" in the processes of social change and see such change as arbitrary. The two previously reigning theories about Israel's emergence in Canaan shared these assumptions, though in different ways, accepting uncritically the biblical accounts of Israel's entry into the land as the result of non-Canaanite groups coming from the Transjordanian desert. Gottwald argued, as had Mendenhall in effect, that earliest Israel came into existence from within—that is, it was a result of a complex series of related developments in an indigenous population. Both Mendenhall and Gottwald would see the ancient Israelites as, at least in part, *Canaanites. Where they disagree is over the degree to which ideological forces are primary or secondary. Mendenhall believed that the Canaanite and Israelite commitment to Yahwism was the primary factor in its critique of power and its earliest, relatively apolitical social structure. Gottwald would view Yahwism as one of many elements that were important to earliest Israel's social, religious and political development, but not necessarily as its centrally defining element. Further, for Gottwald, Israel's settlement in the central hill country represented a conscious return by the Canaanites who withdrew from (or rebelled against) a system of highly stratified city states to an egalitarian, tribally based social structure—it was in effect a "retribalization" rather than entirely the settlement of a group of already stablished tribes.

4. Social and Political Contexts: From Charismatic Heroes to Monarchy.

The biblical historians present a portrait of pre-monarchic Israel as a group of twelve tribes located in the central hill country of Palestine and the highlands of the transjordan region. Socially, the locus of authority is in the household *(bêt 'āb),* with the extended family *(mišpāḥâ)* and tribe *(šēbeṭ)* adding subsequently more extensive support in this village-based economy. Tribal governance occurred on an ad hoc basis, generally as a response to external threats. This semi-autonomous social structure is depicted as changing to a monarchy as the people of Israel desired a more organized political structure similar to that of their neighboring cultures. If the biblical writers are concerned primarily with Israel's (and later, Judah's) faithfulness to the covenant as the primary means of evaluating their history, how would a social-scientific orientation view these developments?

4.1. The Judges as Charismatic Heroes. Only two of the leaders in Judges and 1 Samuel—Deborah and *Samuel himself—have legal functions, making the designation of these tribal "saviors" as "judges" somewhat curious (*see* Judges). The rest, whether major figures with extensive narratives or minor, barely mentioned judges, are military leaders. Using the theoretical perspective of M. Weber, Malamat proposed that these figures should be seen as charismatic heroes. According to Weber, leaders with a "charismatic" function (not to be equated with an individual's magnetic personality) represent one stage in the social development from a decentralized to an institutionally based form of government. In this process of the "routinization of authority," transitional figures arise in times of crisis to meet specific social needs. The leader's authority is limited both temporally and functionally; it is not hereditary and does not exist in the social group after the charismatic leader has either completed his or her task or dies. In some societies or groups, perhaps under a particularly strong leader or when the social needs warrant, the position becomes "routinized," and in Weber's terms, a "rational" phase of authority, such as monarchy, emerges. The narratives concerning Gideon-Jerubbaal and his son Abimelech (Judg 8—10) may represent an attempt by a charismatic figure to institutionalize or formalize his authority and take on the role of petty king.

4.2. Chiefs and Chiefdoms. Judges, Samuel and Kings all present a somewhat conflicted view of the monarchy. If Jerubbaal declined Israel's request to become king, and Abimelech desired the role, the historians view the emergence of kings and kingdoms as something of a necessary evil. The author/editor of Judges, writing from a period after the establishment of the monarchy, considers the institution as a purveyor of both religious and social order. The editorial comments preceding or succeeding stories of social chaos and religious apostasy indicate that the events occurred when there was no king and everyone did as they pleased (Judg 17:6; 18:1; 19:1; 21:24) (see Judges, Book of). Until recently, most biblical scholars accepted the biblical historians' assessment of the emergence of the monarchy and the identification of *Saul as a king. More recently, scholars have turned to the social sciences for a more nuanced understanding of both the social forces that tend to engender centralized governments and the various social phases that lead toward monarchies.

1 Samuel 8 suggests that Israel's desire for a king came from two related concerns: the fear of social and religious exploitation if Samuel's sons assumed leadership after his death, and the desire to have an institution that functioned in part to regularize its defenses. In contrast to the charismatic leaders, appointed as need arose to liberate Israelite tribes from foreign oppressors, the people desired a king to lead them to battle (1 Sam 8:19-21). At issue, specifically, was the threat of Philistine expansion, which provides the context for the rise of both Saul and *David. Scholars using social-scientific models have proposed an alternative reading of the events leading up to a monarchy and even the designation of both Saul (and perhaps David) as king. Many would see the rise of Israel and its political development in the context of shifts in the Late Bronze Age (c. 1550-1250 BCE) and use the perspective of la longue durée, proposed by F. Braudel, as a heuristic model (Coote and Whitelam; Finkelstein). As Egyptian hegemony in Syria-Palestine declined in the fourteenth and thirteenth centuries BCE, other groups—including the *Philistines—competed for control of resources.

Also contributing to the emergence of a more complex political structure in earliest Israel were the forces of population pressure and agricultural intensification. F. Frick sees these as more important than the Philistine threat, and also views them as providing the impetus for adapting technologies conducive to the environ-

ment in the central hills, such as terrace agriculture, thus increasing the amount of arable land (Frick 1985). One of the results of this agricultural intensification was the development of surplus, which allowed for the emergence of a chiefdom. In this form of political development, one family group emerges as most influential or dominant within a larger social group and the head of that group—the chief, or "big man"—is responsible for providing protection and distributing resources, among other things, in return for receiving or extracting agricultural goods or surplus from other families within the society.

J. Flanagan also suggests that the earliest power structure in "Israel" is best understood as a chiefdom, applying E. Service's model of stages of social development, from a segmentary stage to a chiefdom to a petty monarchy. Flanagan believes that this distinction is maintained by the biblical author/editor, who used the term nāgîd instead of melek (king) to describe Saul and sometimes David. The latter term tended to be used more frequently for monarchs after David. David's kingship is also seen as transitional; the trappings of power and bureaucracy are not fully formed, and in 2 Samuel 24, he is criticized for "numbering Israel," perhaps because a *census would be used as a basis for taxation and the creation of a standing army, both of which were considered a departure from the Israelite ideals that would limit the extent of power of the king.

Recent studies of Israel in the Iron I period suggest that the understanding of chiefdoms must be nuanced. Based in part on the interrelationships among villages in the Iron I period, and in part on sociological theory, C. Meyers points out that chiefdoms exist in simple and complex forms, and that not all chiefdoms are primarily redistributive or uniformly hierarchical in nature. In contrast to Gottwald's analysis of earliest Israelite social structure as "communitarian," having little social differentiation, Meyers prefers the term heterarchy to describe the varying interrelationships of power, hierarchy and status. Hierarchical or stratified structures may exist along with the more "lateral," less hierarchical, or heterarchical forms of social organization. Meyers believes that these types of interrelationships between hierarchical and heterarchical segments of Israelite society may have existed in the premonarchic chiefdom, a protomonarchic phase of development under Saul and perhaps David, and the fully formed monarchy of the subsequent northern and southern kingdoms. She would also apply the concept of heterarchy to describe gender interrelationships in the private, domestic and public spheres of *women's lives in Iron I and Iron II Israel and Judah (Meyers 2002).

4.3. The Monarchy Comes of Age: Solomon and Beyond. According to the biblical writers, it is under *Solomon that the elements characteristic of a Near Eastern monarchy emerge. According to 1 Kings 1—11 and 2 Chronicles 1—9, Solomon was a true "empire builder," though the majority of biblical scholars today believe that the traditions regarding Solomon's wealth and extent of power are exaggerated. Still, major organizational changes occurred under his reign that would have substantial impact in the short and long term. His rise to power was marked by the type of political intrigue common among Israel's neighbors and the kings of the subsequent northern kingdom. His supporters conspired to assure his designation as the approved heir; he solidified his power by eliminating his rivals and settling old scores for his father David.

One of the results of Solomon's rise to power was that the warnings ostensibly issued by Samuel regarding kingship were realized: taxation, conscription and essential "enslavement." If Solomon is to be credited with widespread public works programs, such as the Jerusalem temple (*see* Solomon's Temple) and fortifications at sites like *Megiddo, *Gezer and Hazor (archaeologists continue to debate the dating of remains at the latter sites, with some preferring a ninth century date), these building projects could only be supported through increased taxation, conscription for military service and corvée labor, and an extensive bureaucracy. Not surprisingly, one of the results of the increased economic burden was the rise of rival leaders, such as Jeroboam I, and the secession of the north from the "united monarchy."

4.4. Social Changes During the Monarchy. In order to evaluate the effects of the monarchy on the fabric of life in Israel and Judah, it is necessary first to place these "nation-states" within the context of agrarian societies. G. Lenski, whose work on social stratification and agrarian societies has profoundly influenced biblical scholars in their analysis of both the Hebrew Bible and New Testament (Lenski), has developed a taxonomy of social groups according to their domi-

nant mode of subsistence from their earliest and most simple form—hunter-gatherer societies—to their most complex—the modern information age (Lenski, Lenski and Nolan). Subsistence strategy refers to the means and dominant technologies by which human cultures adapt to their environment. Lenski does not propose that these societies mark distinct phases along a continuum of evolutionary change—that societies will inevitably develop from simple to complex. It is possible, in fact, for cultures of varying levels of complexity and subsistence strategies to exist in close proximity to one another at the same time.

4.4.1. Emergence of Horticultural Societies. Horticulture emerges with the domestication of plants and animals, as societies gradually begin to shift from a hunter-gatherer subsistence mode. One of the characteristics of these groups is the use of the digging stick or hoe to cultivate crops; another is the use of swidden, or slash-and-burn agriculture. This latter strategy prepares land for cultivation through cutting down plants, shrubs and small trees, and subsequently burning them. This in turn provides a layer of nutrient-rich ash to the soil that aids crop cultivation. When the soils no longer support annual growth of crops, the group opens up new arable land through their slash-and-burn technique. Horticultural societies exist on simple and complex levels, and frequently rely on other means of subsistence, such as herding or hunting, to supplement their crops. It is possible that the early Israelites used swidden agriculture as they settled and cultivated the previously underinhabited central hill country, though strictly speaking, theirs was not a horticultural society.

4.4.2. Simple and Complex Agrarian Societies. Many social scientists consider the plow to be one of the most important inventions of the fourth millennium BCE. The plow is more efficient than the digging stick or hoe in allowing farmers to control the growth and spread of weeds and in replenishing the soil's nutrients. The latter in particular allows for plots of land to be used for a longer period of time and supports the cultivation of larger areas of land than do horticultural technologies (Lenski, Lenski and Nolan). Plows were first constructed entirely of wood, including the plow point, but when iron technology became more widespread, iron points were used on plows. This development further increased production, and with it surplus, both of which were necessary for the growth of complex social structures. Religious ideologies were important both for the support of the religious hierarchy and for the emergence of the state, legitimating the extraction of surplus through taxation and sacrifice in ways that simple political ideologies could not sustain.

As production increased, the amounts of tax and tribute received by temple and state authorities allowed these institutions to grow in size and complexity. In addition to the rise of the state, agrarian societies—both simple and complex—tend to see an increase of craft specialization, the growth of stratification, widespread trade and exchange, and the breakdown of traditional lines of authority and influence. Although kinship remains significant in both simple and complex agrarian societies, its importance tends to decline. In its early stages, Israel/Judah was a simple agrarian society, one frequently marked by a mixed-subsistence strategy of agriculture and herding. This mixture would have been somewhat fluid, that is, more prevalent in more marginal areas in which a strictly agricultural subsistence strategy would not have been possible (*see* Agriculture and Animal Husbandry).

4.4.3. Mode(s) of Production and Social Change(s). The initial phases of the Israelite settlement in Canaan were marked by a rustic, subsistence-level economy. Little surplus was available in this village-based, domestic economy in which production of goods was conducted primarily on a local level. In some cases, such as the construction and maintenance of terraces to increase the amount of arable land, or the harvesting and processing of crops, extended families would cooperate.

The rise of the monarchies of Israel and Judah led to what Gottwald calls a "native tributary mode of production" (Gottwald 1992, 84). Land tenure policies favored the elite rather than families, and ancestral lands were wrested from their family's control either through the increase of debt-slavery or through abuses of power, as in the case of Ahab's acquisition of Naboth's vineyard (1 Kings 21). In order to support the growing monarchy, its institutions and bureaucracy, taxation (*see* Taxes, Taxation) increased in the form of extracting resources (surplus) and conscripts to carry out building projects. This extraction of resources and the creation or intensification of a debt cycle resulted in growing class and economic differentia-

tion, the presence of which is confirmed in both biblical texts and the archaeological record. A "foreign tributary mode of production" existed after the destruction of the kingdom of Judah. In effect, it functioned in the same way as that of the monarchy, but over and above the taxes and tribute paid to rich landowners in Yehud, additional taxes were earmarked for the imperial coffers in Persia (Neh 5:1-5) and later in Greece.

5. Institutions and Social Differentiation in Israel and Judah.
In addition to assessing the impact of the monarchy itself, scholars have analyzed a variety of institutions that existed throughout Israelite and Judean history. Also significant for our understanding of the historical books is the function of class and gender distinction.

5.1. Prophecy and Monarchy. Although some of the studies of biblical *prophecy have little impact on the analysis of the historical books, the social context of prophecy is significant. Many scholars, even those writing from a more traditional, literary-historical perspective, have noted the close relationship between prophecy and the monarchy. Since it is written from a prophetic viewpoint, it is not surprising that the Deuteronomistic History highlights the role of prophets in establishing, monitoring and even executing judgment on specific monarchs. Saul, David and Solomon are all designated as kings by prophets, and a prophet similarly is said to offer Yahweh's imprimatur to Jeroboam before he assumes the mantle of leadership as the northern kingdom's first king.

R. Wilson has studied intermediation from a variety of crosscultural parallels and suggests that intermediaries often function to support or subvert social or cultural authority (Wilson 1980). Central prophets are part of the official ruling structure or at least have access and to some extent enjoy the approval of the halls of power. Figures such as Samuel, *Nathan, *Isaiah of Jerusalem and perhaps Huldah, would be examples of central intermediaries. Peripheral prophets are those whose support system is outside of the power structure; their access to power is limited and they frequently either lead protest movements against or directly oppose the monarchy and its policies, as in the case of *Elijah and *Jeremiah. In both cases, the prophets monitor and to some extent seek to impose limits on or regulate the institution of the monarchy.

5.2. Israelite and Judean Religion(s). If the biblical traditions—and many commentators—view the Israelite cultus (both popular and official) in the context of its religious significance, a social-scientific approach would examine both its social and its socioeconomic functions. Sacrifice, for example, was not only a religious obligation to Yahweh, but was a means of extracting surplus from the populace to support the priesthood and the temple economy. In fact, one of the reasons given by Jeroboam for constructing Yahwistic sanctuaries in Dan and Bethel was to keep the economic resources associated with sacrifice from going to the coffers in Jerusalem, which would in turn have supported the Judean royal interests. A second social function of religion is also embedded in this tradition. Jeroboam feared that if the citizens of his newly established kingdom returned to Jerusalem periodically—even if only on the specified "pilgrim festivals"—they might decide to return their allegiance to Judah. Establishing Israelite centers of worship supported the wider social fabric of his kingdom and promoted a cultic/ideological counterpart to the Davidic dynasty, which claimed a covenantal relationship with Yahweh as its foundation. Social scientists have long recognized the way in which religious ideologies are constructed to control or regulate the actions of individuals and groups within a society. In some cases the cultus also functioned to ensure the distribution of resources to those without access to land or unable to grow their own crops.

In an ethnoarchaeological analysis of Hannah's sacrifice (1 Sam 1:21-28), C. Meyers examines the interplay between ritual and environment (Meyers 1995). The specific elements of the sacrifice—the bull, grain and wine—are consistent with a mixed agricultural and animal husbandry subsistence pattern one would find in the foothills of Ephraim. This region is not as well suited for the production of olive oil, which would explain the absence of oil as an element of the sacrifice. Meyers points to a symbiotic relationship between cult and culture, in which the ritual superstructure of early Israelite society is supported by a village-based agrarian and pastoral economy. Also using an ethnoarchaeological approach, but one informed by sociopolitical theory, Frick examines the role of religion in Israel's social development. While many scholars have considered the

religious sphere to be *the* most important element in Israel's identity, Frick contends that it is one of many cultural expressions significant to Israelite self-understanding. Frick also points to the social function of ritual as one that influenced the interrelationships among social and religious systems and structures (Frick 1979).

5.3. Gender Roles in Israel and Judah. One of the results of feminist criticism—much of which is also rooted in the social sciences—has been a more nuanced understanding of women's roles, functions and status in Israelite and Judean society. It had long been held that women had no place in the official cult, owing to the exclusively male priesthood, which was evidently unique to Israel/Judah. All of their neighbors had male and female intermediaries in the form of priests and priestesses, and male and female prophets and sages. Of course, the position (and attendant influence) of queen mother was an integral part of Near Eastern monarchies, including Israel/Judah.

Earliest Hebrew traditions give authority to select women as prophets, including Miriam and Deborah (also a judge), and female prophets are known in later historical contexts, such as Huldah, who functions as both a prophet and legal authority during the reign of Josiah. Women also functioned in official cultic capacities as professional mourners, singers and worship leaders. In addition they were engaged in the production of cultic and ritual clothing and textiles, though these latter roles connote more traditional "female" and domestic duties. Women also functioned as sages and official local and, more rarely, royal advisors, as in the case of the wise woman of Tekoa. Some have also proposed that some of the love poetry, songs and laments in the Hebrew Bible may have been composed by women (Meyers 2000, 9).

When official roles were unavailable to women, they frequently emerged as leaders in what some call "popular" or "folk" religious contexts. These allowed women to enjoy significant levels of authority, the memory of which is retained in traditions that identified women as mediums, "cult prostitutes" and individuals who consulted and manipulated the spirits of the dead, such as the woman of Endor consulted by Saul. As late as the exilic period, Judean women who were part of the diaspora community in Egypt were directly involved in the cult of the "queen of heaven" (perhaps a reference to Asherah). They and their husbands blamed the destruction of Jerusalem and the Judean kingdom not on unfaithfulness to Yahweh, as Jeremiah did, but on their neglect of their female deity (Jer 44:15-30).

6. "Exile" and "Restoration" in Sociological Perspective.

The nature of the exile and restored community in Yehud has become the object of serious study in the past two decades. Although some would prefer the term *deportation* to refer to the movement of the social and political elite from Judah to Babylon in 597 and 587/586 BCE, that there was significant impact on the fabric of life in Judah because of the Babylonian occupation cannot be doubted. The numbers of "deportees" in the first and second waves recorded in the historical materials is open to discussion, and it now appears that the areas in the southern part of Judah were spared much of the devastation that Jerusalem and its environs suffered. Some of the more tendentious texts that chronicle the defeat of Jerusalem and Judah claim that the land was entirely emptied of its inhabitants—either through death or deportation (2 Chron 36:15-21). However, 2 Kings 25 and Jeremiah 39—44 effectively chronicle the beginnings of the diaspora, with communities of Judeans existing in Babylon, Egypt and the former kingdom of Judah.

6.1. The Babylonian Community. Forced deportation of newly subjected peoples was a common strategy in the ancient world. *Assyrian policy with the former kingdom of Israel had been to exchange and intermingle population or ethnic groups. Babylonian policy seemed to allow for ethnic groups to remain together in collectives, evidently thinking that some level of social continuity would allow for more productive labor. Many of the displaced Judeans were settled in agricultural colonies, others apparently were integrated into the institutions intended to support the state in and around the city of Babylon itself. Though there are few, if any, firsthand accounts of the lives of the "exiles" in captivity, it appears that many adjusted readily to their new environment. Judeans took Babylonian names (Sheshbazzar and *Zerubbabel, who figured prominently in the "restoration" community, for example), some became important within the Babylonian commercial sector, as the Murashu documents show, and, when given the opportunity to return to Judah at the beginning of the Persian period, many opted to remain in Babylon.

6.2. Social Adaptations to Displacement. When faced with crises caused by environmental or sociopolitical change, such as the destruction of the monarchy and its institutions and the subsequent population displacement, cultures inevitably find ways to adapt to the new reality. Using a social-scientific methodology, D. Smith has analyzed ethnographic studies of four groups in crisis who adjusted to radical cultural change, and identified specific responses that allowed these groups to cope with their dispossession, marginalization or oppression. Each response may also be seen in the social and psychological responses of the "exilic" and "restoration" communities. In *structural adaptation,* specific changes in the social structure occur, but these have their antecedent in earlier social realities in order to give at least the appearance of continuity. According to Smith, the *bêt ʾābôt* referred to in Ezra-Nehemiah represent a series of real and fictive *genealogies that allowed those "returning" to Judah in the early Persian period to legitimate their claim to ancestral lands. The *bêt ʾābôt* emerged from, or built upon, the traditional social structure of *bêt ʾāb, mišpāḥâ* and *šēbeṭ* of the premonarchic and monarchic periods. A *split in leadership* occurs when a new group of leaders emerges to challenge traditional forms of leadership within a group in crisis. Although both groups are engaged in a form of resistance to the ruling authority, one typically advocates open, perhaps violent resistance, and the other favors what Smith calls "social resistance." He views the conflict between Jeremiah and Hananiah, though set in the late monarchy, as an example of this type of schism in leadership. Other groups develop *new rituals* that *establish social boundaries.* These boundaries and their reinforcing rituals also serve to heighten the distinction between the oppressive, occupying regime and the oppressed community. One may see the process of defining social, ethnic and religious boundaries through concepts of ritual purity under Ezra-Nehemiah as an example of this strategy. Finally, some cultures in crisis develop rich *folk-hero* traditions and literatures, in which the hero is vindicated or rises to prominence despite being marginalized or mistreated by the ruling power. Traditions concerning Joseph, Daniel and the Suffering Servant may have been developed during the exilic period to provide the displaced community a sense of hope for deliverance or vindication. Though Smith does not make this connection, it may be that the biblical story of Esther and the deuterocanonical tradition of Judith also served this purpose in the Persian and perhaps into the Hellenistic periods.

6.3. The Persian Period. Long neglected by biblical scholars as a relatively unimportant, transitional if not "dark age," the social and religious developments of the Persian period are now considered pivotal. Many claim that it is during this period, not the preceding "exilic" period, that much of the editing and composition of many of the books of the Hebrew Bible took place. Shortly after defeating the Babylonians and wresting control of its empire, Cyrus the Great allowed many of the subjects deported during the Neo-Babylonian period to return to their homelands. In some accounts (both biblical and extrabiblical) he permitted and may have even supported the reestablishment of traditional cults. It is in this context that we must view the return of the so-called golah community (*gôlâ*, "exiled") to Judah, known as Yehud, now a province of the Persian imperial structure. Although the biblical lists in Ezra-Nehemiah cannot reflect an entourage of "returnees" at one single time, they do suggest that an external group of Jews came from Babylon and sought to establish themselves as the legitimate socioeconomic, sociopolitical and socioreligious descendants of the preexilic Judeans. They claimed authority over the Judeans who had been left in the land after the fall of Jerusalem, and an extended period of tension, if not conflict, resulted. What is not explicitly stated in the biblical texts from the period is that the political and religious leaders who came to power in Yehud did so as approved agents of the Persian rulers. Their interests, in virtually every social sphere, reflected or respected in some way the interests of the Persian imperial structure. In this way, the Persian and Yehudite policies coincided, so that what occurred in the peripheries of the Persian empire (Yehud) served to support the needs of the core (Berquist).

6.3.1. The Size and Structure of Yehud. In the early twentieth century, Alt proposed that the province of Yehud was under Samarian control until the middle of the fifth century BCE, when Nehemiah was installed as governor of the province with the blessings of the Persian empire. Building upon Alt's proposal, J. Weinberg suggested that there were two distinct communities within Yehud, each with their own ruler. The "golah community" was a type of citizen-temple community, centered around a temple economy, but distinct from those who had remained in the land at the beginning of and subsequent to the exile. Gradually, as the citizen-temple community grew in size and influence, it became the political and religious locus of authority. According to Weinberg's theory, however, the community numbered some 200,000 members by the middle of the fifth century BCE.

Writing in the relative isolation of Latvia in the period of Soviet hegemony, Weinberg was unaware of more recent archaeological discoveries that allow for the reconstruction of governors of Yehud from Zerubbabel through Nehemiah, thus eclipsing Alt's model of Samaritan control of the province and effectively undermining Weinberg's own concept of dual governors.

Also problematic from an archaeological perspective is his proposed population for the province of Yehud. Based on studies of I. Finkelstein and M. Broshi, and A. Ofer, it appears that the population at the end of the Iron II period in the area that later comprised the province of Yehud was approximately 60,000-70,000, far below Weinberg's estimates. Using a similar methodology that combines results from Persian-period excavations and archaeological surveys with population estimation models, Carter has proposed that the population of Yehud ranged between 13,000 in the early stages of the Persian period and about 21,000 from the middle of the fifth century until the end of the Persian period (Carter 1999; 2003). The population of Jerusalem was approximately 1,500 persons during this time. Roughly ninety percent of the inhabitants of Yehud lived in small villages with populations of less than 300. The resulting portrait of Persian-period Yehud is of a relatively small, relatively poor province situated on the periphery of the Persian empire. In fact, its importance to the empire may have been in part its location close to Egypt, which Persia alternately controlled and lost to Greek influence. This location may have been one of the reasons that Jerusalem was fortified in the middle of the fifth century under Nehemiah.

One important question that a small, poor

Yehud raises is the degree to which appropriate structures would have been in place to support the composition or editing of much of the Hebrew Bible. Social-scientific studies of urban centers in agrarian societies suggest that such centers typically account for between three and ten percent of the total population (Lenski 1966). In these urban centers there tends to be a concentration of bureaucratic infrastructure, including specific craft specialization, support for trade and taxation, a scribal class, etc. With a population of about 1500 at any time during the second half of the Persian period, Jerusalem would have accounted for approximately seven percent of the total population of the province, and thus was within the range of such centers. This would suggest that there was sufficient population and infrastructure to account for vigorous literary activity in Jerusalem throughout the Persian period.

6.3.2. Emic and Etic Perspectives Applied to Yehud. It is, of course, impossible to test one's external analysis of Yehudite ideology in the same way that an anthropologist might test his or her etic analysis of a modern social group. However, one may analyze the social and religious perspectives from the Persian period as represented in the biblical texts using the emic and etic framework discussed above.

If we treat traditions in Ezra-Nehemiah, for example, as witnesses to the emic/insider perspectives of Yehud, we might conclude only that the golah community was concerned with ritual and ethnic purity and sought to reestablish older definitions—or perhaps establish new, more strict definitions—of a "true Israel." An emic approach to these biblical texts would see them as promoting a particular understanding of purity, of separation and of "abomination" that the writers believed were divinely sanctioned. An etic understanding would analyze the social function of these categories and the practices implemented by the golah community as an attempt both to define and to regulate membership within the community.

The emic categories of clean and unclean would be interpreted as expressions of the community's need for social and religious order. The emic concept of the "true seed of Israel" would be interpreted from an etic perspective as a concern for establishing social and religious boundaries. And the process call for radical separation—including forced divorce—

would have promoted an ideology of uniqueness both from the Persian authorities and the "people of the land." Seen from an etic point of view, all of these strategies would have been necessary for the survival and perpetuation of the community that was relatively small, vulnerable and to some extent marginalized.

See also AMPHICTYONY, QUESTION OF; ARCHAEOLOGY, SYRO-PALESTINIAN; ETHNICITY; HERMENEUTICS; ISRAELITE SOCIETY; METHODS OF INTERPRETATION.

BIBLIOGRAPHY. **J. Berquist,** *Judaism in Persia's Shadow: A Social and Historical Approach* (Minneapolis: Fortress, 1995); **M. Broshi and I. Finkelstein,** "The Population of Palestine in the Iron Age II," *BASOR* 287 (1992) 47-60; **C. E. Carter,** *The Emergence of Yehud in the Persian Period: A Social and Demographic Study* (Sheffield: Sheffield Academic Press, 1999); idem, "Ethnoarchaeology," *OEANE* 2.280-84; idem, "Social Scientific Approaches," in *The Blackwell Companion to the Hebrew Bible,* ed. L. Purdue (Oxford: Blackwell, 2001) 36-57; idem, "Syria-Palestine in the Persian Period" in *Near Eastern Archaeology: A Reader,* ed. S. Richard (Winona Lake, IN: Eisenbrauns, 2003) 398-412; **A. Causse,** Du groupe ethnique à la communauté religieuse: Le problème sociologique de la religion d'Israël (Études d'histoire et de philosophie religieuses 33; Paris: Alcan, 1937); **R. Coote and K. Whitelam,** "The Emergence of Israel: Social Transformation and State Formation Following the Decline in Late Bronze Age Trade," *Semeia* 37 (1986) 107-47; **F. M. Cross Jr,** *Canaanite Myth and Hebrew Epic: Essays in the History of the Religion of Israel* (Cambridge, MA: Harvard University Press, 1973); **G. Dalman,** *Arbeit und Sitte in Palästina* (8 vols.; Gütersloh: Bertelsmann, 1928-42); **M Douglas,** *Purity and Danger: An Analysis of the Concepts of Pollution and Taboo* (London: Routledge and Kegan Paul, 1966); **I. Finkelstein,** "The Emergence of the Monarchy in Israel: The Environmental and Socio-Economic Aspects," *JSOT* 44 (1989) 43-74; **J. Flanagan,** "Chiefs in Israel," *JSOT* 20 (1981) 47-73; **F. Frick,** *The Formation of the State in Ancient Israel: A Survey of Models and Theories* (SWBA 4; Decatur, GA: Almond, 1985); idem, "Norman Gottwald's *The Tribes of Yahweh* in the Context of 'Second Wave' Social-Scientific Criticism," in *Tracking 'The Tribes of Yahweh': On the Trail of a Classic,* ed. R. Boer (London: Sheffield Academic Press, 2002) 17-34; idem, "Religion and Socio-Political Structure in Early Israel:

An Ethno-Archaeological Approach," in *Society of Biblical Literature, 1979: Seminar Papers*, ed. P. Achtemeier (Missoula, MT: Scholars Press, 1979) 233-53; **N. Gottwald,** "Domain Assumptions and Societal Models in the Study of Pre-Monarchic Israel," VTSup Congress Volume Edinburgh 28 (1974) 89-100; idem, *The Tribes of Yahweh: A Sociology of the Religion of Liberated Israel, 1250-1050 BCE* (Maryknoll, NY: Orbis, 1979); idem, "Sociology of Ancient Israel," *ABD* 6.79-89; **M. Harris,** *Cultural Materialism: The Struggle for a Science of Culture* (New York: Vintage, 1980); **B. Lang,** *Monotheism and the Prophetic Minority: An Essay in Biblical History and Sociology* (SWBA 1; Sheffield: Almond Press, 1983); **G. Lenski,** *Power and Privilege: A Theory of Social Stratification* (New York: McGraw-Hill, 1966); **G. Lenski, J. Lenski and P. Nolan,** *Human Societies: An Introduction to Macrosociology* (6th ed.; New York, McGraw-Hill, 1991); **A. Malamat,** "Charismatic Leadership in the Book of Judges," in *Magnalia Dei—The Mighty Acts of God: Essays on the Bible and Archaeology in Memory of G. Ernest Wright*, ed. F. M. Cross Jr., W. E. Lemke and P. D. Miller Jr. (Garden City, NY: Doubleday, 1973) 152-68; **B. Malina,** "The Social Sciences and Biblical Interpretation," *Int* 37 (1982) 229-42; **A. D. H. Mayes,** *The Old Testament in Sociological Perspective* (London: Pickering, 1989); **P. McNutt,** *The Forging of Israel: Iron Technology, Symbolism, and Tradition in Ancient Society* (SWBA 8; Sheffield: Almond Press, 1990); **G. Mendenhall,** "The Hebrew Conquest of Palestine," *BA* 25 (1962) 152-69; idem, *The Tenth Generation: The Origins of Biblical Tradition* (Baltimore: Johns Hopkins University Press, 1973); **C. Meyers,** "An Ethnoarchaeological Analysis of Hannah's Sacrifice," in *Pomegranates and Golden Bells: Studies in Biblical, Jewish, and Near Eastern Ritual, Law and Literature in Honor of Jacob Milgrom*, ed. D. Wright, D. Freedman and A. Hurvitz (Winona Lake, IN: Eisenbrauns, 1995) 77-91; idem, "The Hebrew Bible," in *Women in Scripture: A Dictionary of Named and Unnamed Women in the Hebrew Bible, the Apocryphal/Deuterocanonical Books, and the New Testament*, ed. C. Meyers, T. Craven and R. Kraemer (Grand Rapids: Eerdmans, 2001) 4-11; idem, "Tribes and Tribulations: Retheorizing Earliest 'Israel,'" in *Tracking 'The Tribes of Yahweh': On the Trail of a Classic*, ed. R. Boer (London: Sheffield Academic Press, 2002) 17-34; **A. Ofer,** "The Highlands of Judah During the Biblical Period," (Ph.D. dissertation, Tel Aviv University, 1993); **K. Pike,** "Etic and Emic Standpoints for the Description of Behavior," in *The Insider/Outsider Problem in the Study of Religion*, ed. R. McCutcheon (London and New York: Cassell) 28-36; **D. Smith,** *The Religion of the Landless: A Sociology of Babylonian Exile* (Bloomington, IN: Meyer Stone, 1989); **W. R. Smith,** *Kinship and Marriage in Early Arabia* (Cambridge: Cambridge University Press, 1885); idem, *Lectures on the Religion of the Semites: First Series, The Fundamental Institutions* (2d. ed.; London: Black, 1894); idem, *Lectures on the Religion of the Semites: Second and Third Series*, ed. J. Day (Sheffield: Sheffield Academic Press, 1995); **L. Stager,** "The Archaeology of the Family," *BASOR* 260 (1985) 1-35; **R. de Vaux,** *Ancient Israel* (2 vols.; New York: McGraw-Hill, 1965); **M. Weber,** *Ancient Judaism* (Glencoe, IL: Free Press, 1952); **R. Wilson,** *Prophecy and Society in Ancient Israel* (Philadelphia: Fortress, 1980); idem, *Sociological Approaches to the Old Testament* (Philadelphia: Fortress, 1984).

C. E. Carter

SOLOMON

The second ruler of the united monarchy in the Davidic dynasty, Solomon is most remembered for his wisdom and the construction of the temple in Jerusalem. Though his reign as described in the book of Kings is commonly viewed today as wrapped in hyperbole, amplified by nostalgic scribes and events after his death (Miller), recent scholarly attempts to discount his existence are unwarranted (a position promoted by Garbini). Solomon's expansive building projects and bureaucratic reorganization resulted in further rebellions against the Judean throne by segments of the Israelite population. The proper religious world of Judah, as it is biblically represented throughout the divided monarchy, is ascribed to his reign.

1. Sources
2. Family
3. State
4. Foreign Relations
5. Religion
6. Wisdom Traditions

1. Sources.

The only early narratives concerning Solomon appear in two related biblical books. 2 Samuel 12:24-25 provides the birth story, his reign is recounted in 1 Kings 1—11, and a parallel and dependent narrative is rendered in 2 Chronicles

1—9. While many theories exist about the possible sources on which both biblical histories are based, accompanied by a great deal of debate about the reliability of cited sources in the narratives themselves, the story of Solomon as told in Kings is heavily literary in character and relatively late in composition. Written at the earliest during the reign of *Hezekiah, the extant narrative is regarded by some as more probably originating in the early Persian period. Clearly, the Kings account has stylized its chronology so that the most devastating aspects of Solomon's reign come at the end of the narration, while the selectively portrayed vignettes of the king emphasize his religious, bureaucratic and judicial qualities. Three lists included in the Kings account of Solomon often are assumed to derive from Solomon's court records (court officials: 1 Kings 4:2-6; district governors: 1 Kings 4:9-19; building projects: 1 Kings 9:15-18); however, none of these lists can be dated so early (Ash). The "Book of the Acts of Solomon," mentioned at the close of the Solomon narrative (1 Kings 11:41), probably existed as a scribal school text from preexilic Jerusalem, but its origins, contents and reliability elude reconstruction (*see* Sources, References to).

Chronicles adapted the narrative of Kings, not least by expunging any untoward behavior from Solomon's life altogether and changing some material to Solomon's advantage (2 Chron 8:1-2). The importance of David and the Levitical priesthood to the author results in the presentation of Solomon as less glorious, and certainly less extravagant, than in Kings. Although arguments have been made for independent sources for the Chronicler's Solomon story, it is not at all clear that the author had any primary documents beyond the Kings account (*see* Chronicler's History; Chronicles, Books of).

*Archaeological materials traditionally have been treated as evidence of Solomon's kingdom (Dever). Among the excavated finds most frequently exploited to prove the existence of a large Solomonic kingdom are the gates at *Gezer, *Hazor and *Megiddo, all having the same basic blueprint; however, recent redating of the gates raises questions about the chronology for the gates, and similar gate designs outside of any possible Solomonic kingdom raise doubts about identifying these gates as particularly Judean. The "four-room house" that is usually described as "Israelite," as well as certain types of pottery, also are used to define the territory of Solomon's reign (*see* Architecture). Recently, "tripartite pillared" buildings have been suggested as border defenses for the united monarchy, although their use and dating remain debated (Blakely). Serious doubts about defining archaeological remains along ethnic and political lines continue to put the most optimistic of these identifications in question. There is clear evidence of a certain amount of cultural continuity throughout much of the Levant in the tenth century BCE; however, there is nothing to show major building programs at Jerusalem, and all indications point to a city of modest means and small importance (Killebrew) (*see* Jerusalem).

Josephus, the Jewish general and historian of the first century CE, retells the history of Judah and Israel, including an extensive section on Solomon. In this he makes use of letters that he was shown at Tyre (*Ag. Ap.* 1.17-18) purporting to be original correspondence between Solomon and Hiram of Tyre in regard to the construction of the temple in Jerusalem and other matters. Many scholars have accepted these documents as original to the tenth century BCE; however, no epistolary materials, except for baked cuneiform tablets, could survive a thousand years on the eastern Mediterranean coast unless sealed in airtight containers. Whatever Josephus saw were not letters written by Solomon and Hiram and should not be used by historians as sources for reconstructing Solomon's reign. The rest of Josephus's history is a creative retelling of the biblical narratives with an eye toward his own political situation in the expanding Roman Empire.

Solomon became a truly legendary figure in later traditions. This is true in Judaism, Christianity and Islam, not to mention the use made of his name in classical pagan magic. Legendary materials concerning him include an enlargement of the size of his kingdom, an expansion of his knowledge of nature, an increase in his economic profits, his complete mastery of magic, and his communication with God. As significant as these stories are in defining the Solomon of memory, they do not represent information about the historical person.

2. Family.

The Bible is quite clear about the parentage of Solomon—so clear that suspicions about his father persist in modern historical studies. His father is reported to be *David, already established on the thrones of both Judah and Israel; his mother is recorded as Bathsheba, daughter of Eliam and wife of Uriah the Hittite, an officer in David's army. David's manner of attaining Bathsheba as a wife is not flattering to the king, as God and Nathan make clear. The narrative of 2 Samuel 12 is careful to show that the child with whom Bathsheba had been pregnant when David is informed of her situation dies. This allows the author to guarantee that the "second child" could not have been sired by her deceased husband, but must be the child of David, who by then had brought her into his house. The very explicitness of this sequence has caused many to doubt the historicity of the story and posit instead that Solomon was the child of Uriah and Bathsheba; indeed, the hypothesis has been expanded to theorize that Solomon was a usurper of the throne from outside David's family altogether (Veijola). Since no outside evidence exists on which to weigh this theory, until such evidence materializes, the parentage of Solomon may be taken to have been David and Bathsheba (*see* David's Family).

According to 2 Samuel 12:24, it was David, not his mother (as with some other biblical sons), who named the infant Solomon; in this way the author demonstrates David's claim as the boy's father. Although it has been argued that the name *Solomon* was a play on the name of David's town, Jerusalem, or a form of the deity name *Shalem,* both are unnecessary hypotheses. A second name is bestowed on the infant by the prophet Nathan, who gave Solomon the name *Jedidiah,* a Yahwistic name suggesting a religious conviction as well as confirming the royal lineage of the child. It has been suggested that one name was a given name, and the other was a throne name, but the biblical texts make no such distinction, and the stories of the reign itself use only "Solomon."

In the biblical records Solomon had no surviving full siblings; no children are attributed to Bathsheba after the birth of Solomon. However, Solomon had several half-brothers and at least one half-sister. The fighting among Amnon and Absalom removed them from the dynastic succession prior to David's death. An older claimant, Adonijah, son of David and Haggith, whose name suggests that he was in fact designated to be the heir apparent, is foiled from taking the throne by a plot hatched by the prophet Nathan

and Solomon's mother, Bathsheba. Solomon enters the plot late in the Kings account.

As for Solomon's immediate family, the book of Kings presents a rather extraordinary portrayal of his consorts. 1 Kings 11:3 insists that included among his "women" were seven hundred princesses and three hundred concubines, while 2 Chronicles reflects no such large numbers of spouses, providing only two: "the daughter of Pharaoh" and Naamah. Since it is the story of the Canaanitization of Solomon in Kings that provides the huge number of foreign wives for Solomon, it is logical to assume that the large numbers are intended to show that Solomon's lust for women led directly to his acceptance of these women's deities (*see* Numbers, Large Numbers). Whereas little concern has been expressed for the wives whom Solomon obtained from Moab, Ammon, Edom, Sidon or the Hittites, vast amounts of ink have flowed about his marriage to the "daughter of Pharaoh." Egypt was not particularly strong in the tenth century BCE, and certainly the most impressive of these Solomonic marriages at that time would have been that to the Sidonian woman. All these marriages appear to have been politically motivated and aimed at demonstrating Solomon's standing among his peers; however, numerous political marriages would have posed an almost impossible diplomatic conundrum. Given that all one thousand women would have had some legal standing and most likely a certain amount of political clout (Solvang), historically speaking, the royal house presented in Kings seems vastly exaggerated, and the smaller house of Chronicles more reasonable.

With Solomon lusting after a thousand women, one would expect a sizable family, but Solomon's recorded children number but three (Schearing). *Rehoboam is the only son recorded for Solomon; his mother was Naamah, an Ammonite, usually assumed to be a princess, based solely on the reference to Solomon's princess consorts. As heir to the throne, Rehoboam displays an astonishing lack of training in the art of statesmanship, which may indicate parents indifferent to the state of the kingdom after their demise, or it may reflect overly doting parents of an only son, whom they spoiled. Taphath and Basemath are the sole daughters ascribed to Solomon; both appear in a list of Solomon's governmental officers. Taphath was married to Ben-abinadab, administrator of Naphath-Dor (1 Kings

4:11). Basemath was married to Ahimaaz, administrator of Naphtali (1 Kings 4:15). Clearly, the daughters helped hold the governing elite together and were employed by Solomon in securing political loyalty (see Royal Family).

3. State.

The Bible describes a Davidic kingdom left to Solomon that included within it *Aram, *Ammon, *Moab and *Edom, with the *Philistine cities virtually vassal territory, in addition to the two minor kingdoms of Judah and Israel. The relationship of Judah with the *Phoenician cities was as one of equals, while *Egypt appears to be in a minor position to the united monarchy. Under Solomon, *Jerusalem, as the royal city with a vast bureaucracy, appears to be a center controlling conquered and occupied outer territories, including the northern state of Israel. The vast kingdom came apart under Solomon as Aram and Edom gained their independence while Israel continued the series of wars already begun with the conflict between Ishbaal and David that continued in revolts by the north to throw off the rule of David (2 Sam 15—20). Solomon's reign is described in terms of kingship in royal succession within a designated family. His own character is presented as the ideal of the ancient Near Eastern ruler: he is chosen by God and accepted by his people, he conducts proper religious ritual, he is wise, he is learned, he is a good judge and a resourceful governor, and he has the admiration of his peers among the contemporary rulers (indeed, is seen by them as their superior). In addition, he has wealth, women and peace for himself. In Kings this all collapses from his overreaching sexual desire and religious pluralism; in Chronicles Solomon remains the perfect ruler to the end of his life.

The geographical extent of the kingdom that Solomon actually ruled is nebulous in the texts and highly debated among scholars. The maximum territory envisioned for his kingdom from the biblical texts is from the Euphrates to the Nile, though few scholars would now accept the Nile as a southern border. Modern maps that extend the northern boundaries of Solomon's reign to the Euphrates can still be found, based on 1 Kings 4:21, but most cartographers place the southern limit of his kingdom at the Wadi el-'Arish. More recent reconstructions have concentrated on the description of the kingdom ex-

tending from *Dan to *Beersheba and consider Solomon's dual rule as king of Judah and Israel to be the extent of his country. H. M. Niemann has pointed out that the Kings narratives reflect an even smaller kingdom, with a reduced Judah around Jerusalem and control of perhaps only the southern third of Israel. Then, for that minority of scholars who maintain that Solomon did not exist, there was no kingdom at all. Many scholars conclude that the narratives concerning Solomon suggest that whatever the extended kingship of David may have been, it was lost before Solomon took the throne, or was lost to Solomon early in his reign. Thus the Kings account, which puts the loss of territory late, after Solomon's worship of foreign deities, is viewed as stylized history (see Geographical Extent of Israel).

The biblical presentation of Solomon's governing structure can be reconstructed from two sources. The first is the list of officers that appears in 1 Kings 4:2-19; the second is the vision related by the stories themselves. The Egyptian origins of the Jerusalem governmental bureaucratic positions, though debated, seem clear. This probably reflects an attempt by Davidic rulers to continue *Canaanite governmental structures from the time of Egyptian control of the area. The royal court included a secretary, the priesthood, an administrator over the royal estate, an army general, a commander of forced labor, and a number of district governors. Whether the lists of these bureaucrats in Kings originated in the time of Solomon or not, the basic formation of any state government in Canaan probably would have included these offices attested in ancient Egyptian documents and among archaeological finds along the eastern Mediterranean (Avishur and Heltzer). If the officers took care of day-to-day activities, it was the king who had the final say on matters political, judicial and religious (see State Officials).

Israel may have voluntarily agreed to take David as its king on a par with Judah, but Solomon treated the northern kingdom as a subjected territory. When Solomon devised his scheme of providing for the royal household and his expanding bureaucracy in Jerusalem, he adapted a method of *taxation that may (or may not) have been used by Egypt: he divided the territory into twelve parts ("tribes") and had each district contribute all the provisions for the royal administration for one month. All twelve political divisions were in Israel; Judah was to derive its bounty from the north. To hold this territory in check, Solomon devised a system with "governors" for each of the twelve "tribes," each directly beholden to the king in Jerusalem with some also related by family ties. Moreover, to keep the populace actively supporting the central monarchy, with its palace and temple complex, and to provide labor for the outlying royal palaces, fortresses and regional governors, several administrators in charge of "corvée" labor were recruited from the areas under subjection. All persons not designated "Israelite" were simply enslaved by the crown (1 Kings 9:20-21). As ideally presented in Kings, all Israelites gladly served Solomon the magnificent (note 1 Kings 4:20-21). In reality, according to the biblical texts, Israel resented David's rule and revolted several times under his reign even before Solomon came to the throne. No doubt there were pockets of revolt even as Solomon came to the throne, but once the forced labor was imposed on the northern populace, full-blown revolution broke out under *Jeroboam, one of Solomon's corvée labor leaders. This revolution Solomon was able to crush, though clearly the Israelites' memory of their harsh treatment at the hands of the dynasty in Jerusalem extended into the reign of Rehoboam, though the division between the two kingdoms may seriously be dated to the later years of Solomon's rule rather than to the stylized beginning of the reign of Rehoboam (a notion buttressed by the revolts in 1 Kings).

The fiscal stability of Solomon's reign rested on *agriculture. The base of this economy was the large number of agricultural workers who tilled small plots of land surrounding villages and who herded large and small livestock in open pasture. If 1 Kings 4:22-23 is an accurate account of the palace's consumption, the king's court took an intolerable toll on the governed (just providing the annual 3,650 oxen, 7,300 beef cattle and 36,500 sheep would have depleted stock swiftly, not to mention the approximately 214,410 bushels of prepared ground grains in season and out). A massive building program and expansion of the military and bureaucratic complexes, as required by the descriptions of Solomon's reign, would have been a huge drain on the small rural states of Israel and Judah. No matter how well the crops may have fared, a for-

ty-year reign with this kind of economic system would have collapsed internally. The Solomon of the Kings narrative enriched his income through *trade, tribute and gifts from impressed wealthy foreign rulers, though how much of this reflects reality and how much serves to enhance Solomon's literary image is unclear. However, the confiscation of all goods and services from the population of Israelite tribes for one month each year to fuel the royal capital also fueled resentment and revolt (Jobling).

4. Foreign Relations.

The united monarchy came into existence during a period of decline in the major powers of the Bronze Age. Small states vied for political power in what had been Egyptian-controlled southwest Asia. Nubia and Libya rose to be the major powers in northeast Africa as Egypt imploded and was overrun. An Arabian kingdom on the Indian Ocean, possibly already crossing the Red Sea into the Horn of Africa, Sheba expanded as a trading power as Egypt's control of the economic life of African and eastern Mediterranean commerce was replaced by minor states in East Africa, Arabia and the Phoenician city states. 1 Kings 9:26-28; 10:11 suggests that Solomon, as a junior partner with Hiram of Tyre, also entered into sea trade for a time.

The eastern Mediterranean *Phoenician cities, especially Sidon, Tyre and Byblos, became the major hub of trade. Expanding into the Mediterranean and beyond with trading colonies and regular trade routes, the Phoenicians brought to their bazaars a wealth of luxury goods from as far away as northern Europe, southern Africa and southern Asia. The production of cedar wood and purple dye from their own resources made these independent cities the cultural center of the tenth century BCE and the logical political allies for a Solomonic court attempting to gain status. In the Bible, Hiram of Tyre plays the major role in Solomon's building campaign and trade negotiations. Although serious questions have been raised concerning the historicity of this relationship, a strong alliance with Tyre in the tenth century BCE would have been the politically, economically and culturally astute course for Solomon to have pursued. It is unquestionable that Tyre would have been the more significant partner in any such alliance.

The *Philistines, concentrated into five central cities with a number of surrounding villages, maintained contact with Cyprus and the Aegean world. Major enemies of Saul and David, the Philistines effectively disappear from the narratives of Solomon, suggesting that peaceful relations had been established in David's time. Archaeologically, it can be seen that the Philistines adapted culturally to the local area, adopting Canaanite, Phoenician and Egyptian traditions. A certain amount of trade and personal interaction certainly transpired along the southwest border of Judah with these peoples to the west.

The former dominating power in the region of Judah and Israel, *Egypt had exhausted itself in the repulsion of the Sea Peoples two centuries before Solomon, and internal squabbles had allowed Libya to overrun Lower Egypt and the Delta. The fighting between Egyptians and Libyans would continue until Sheshonq ultimately overran Egypt and attempted to gain control of Egypt's former Asian territory late in Solomon's reign and early into Rehoboam's rule. Egypt's previous political control of the territory of Judah is evident in the description of Solomon's government, but the political importance for Solomon of Egypt itself would have been minimal, though trade contacts certainly would have been maintained. The notice of a daughter of Pharaoh being married to Solomon is presented as a sign of Solomon's greatness by the authors of Kings and Chronicles, but probably it reflects the devastated state of the Egyptian kings (1 Kings 3:1; 7:8; 9:16, 24; 11:1; 2 Chron 8:11); Siamun would be the most likely father-in-law (Kitchen). The city of *Gezer is reported to have been turned over to Solomon along with the daughter by the Egyptian king (1 Kings 9:16); however, by the tenth century BCE Egypt had lost effective control of the Asian provinces, and only by speculation from the biblical text can Siamun be credited with having held the city at any time. Also, if Egypt was supposed to be Solomon's ally, it is worth noting that Egypt is also depicted as giving refuge and support to Solomon's enemies: to Hadad the Edomite already at the beginning of his reign, and to Jeroboam after his failed rebellion during Solomon's rule (1 Kings 11:17-22, 40).

To the east, Mesopotamia was in a period of near collapse with the Kassite Empire dissolved and the local cities devastated. There is no sign that significant exchange was made at the time of Solomon with *Assyria, just then beginning an attempt to rebuild its own home territory and not yet a major political power. Even less likely is contact with *Babylonia or the gulf cities.

Although the narrative states that Solomon ruled all the territories around Judah and Israel (1 Kings 4:21), it is unlikely that Solomon had effective control of any territory outside of these two kingdoms. Indeed, aside from the attempt to send ships out of Edom (*see* Ezion-geber), the only narrative material recorded concerning the tributary states is that Edom and Aram revolted from Solomon's control. That Solomon was married to an Ammonite tells us, unfortunately, nothing about the relationship between Ammon and Judah.

5. Religion.

So central to the narratives of Solomon is the construction of the temple in Jerusalem (*see* Solomon's Temple) that a description of the religion within the territories of Judah and Israel is warranted. The various permutations of Canaanite religion that composed the Solomonic kingdom derived from Middle Bronze Age traditions (*see* Canaanite Gods and Religion). The highest level of the divine world was envisioned to consist of the divine couple El and Asherah; biblical reports of Yahweh clearly equate the God of Judah and Israel with El, while Asherah is deemed an idol (though biblical and epigraphical evidence suggests that she was still acknowledged as a goddess by some of the populace). A number of secondary deities appear in sections of the biblical texts, so that we know Baal, Shemesh, Yareah, Mot and possibly Anat all had devotees throughout the Judean period. Minor local and specialized deities also appear to have been worshiped by local as well as royal faithful, while the messenger deities (angels) seem to have been accepted by everyone as the normal method of divine communication. That David had not removed the population of Jebusite Jerusalem meant that the old religion would have remained in place into the time of Solomon. Archaeological materials confirm not only the continuation of Canaanite religion, but also the reverence for some Egyptian deities unmentioned in the biblical texts (Hathor and Bes in particular).

What Solomon accomplished by building the temple in Jerusalem, according to the Bible, was to put an end to the worship of other deities, imposing the notion that all divine activities were now to be understood as the work of the single God, Yahweh. Instead of a pantheon, the population was to be loyal only to the God of the royal house of David, a house now embodied in his son Solomon. The temple itself, as described, is a compilation of Syrian, Phoenician and Egyptian motifs (though exactly what temple in Jerusalem is actually described in the texts remains an open debate; some argue that what is described as designed by Solomon is the preexilic temple as remembered by postexilic priests) (*see* Solomon's Temple). The ideal of the temple in the Bible is that it was solely for Yahweh, the unique sanctuary for all Judah and Israel (and Edom and Moab and Ammon, when subjected). Reality, as presented in the book of Kings, is that it also housed worship for other deities, most notably Asherah in some form or another (Bloch-Smith). Although texts of Kings and Chronicles are clear that Yahweh is the only God, and the temple is supposed to be the only legitimate worship site for this deity, this would have been a cultic improbability in the tenth century BCE; indeed, the construction as recounted in Kings describes at most a small palace chapel, not a national shrine (not that these need be separate). In either case, the offerings and tribute to the deity would wind up in the royal hands.

The center of both the Kings and Chronicles portraits of Solomon is the building and dedication of the temple in Jerusalem. The biblical description of the temple reflects a type of sacred sanctuary known from archaeology to be found in Syria-Palestine in the ninth to eighth centuries BCE. The three-room form appeared in chapels connected to palace complexes, which was the case in Jerusalem. This was the king's chapel, and it was part of the royal complex. The designs for the artwork reflect Egyptian motifs with some Phoenician and Phoenicianized-Egyptian artistry. The purpose in building the temple appears to have been to supply the king in Jerusalem a place of worship. That this was historically intended to be the sole place of worship for Judah during the reign of Solomon is unlikely, especially considering the continuing importance of *Gibeon in the narratives (*see* High Places). What the temple did signify was the divine protection of the Davidic rulers as embodied at that time in Solomon. The grand sermon of 1 Kings 8 is a literary construction of the Deuteronomistic author of the book of Kings, and it reflects the theology of a later time.

It is explicitly stated that Solomon worshiped a number of deities (1 Kings 11:6 names Astarte and Milcom), and that this worship was officially established by royal construction of shrines to a large number of these deities (1 Kings 11:7 mentions only Astarte and Milcom but states that he did this for all his foreign wives; 2 Kings 23:13 adds Chemosh). This official polytheistic religion established by Solomon in Jerusalem remained in practice for almost the entire period of the monarchy in Judah (2 Kings 23:13).

6. Wisdom Traditions.
Solomon is portrayed in the Bible as the paradigm of a wise ruler. 1 Kings 3:4-14 presents Solomon's wisdom as a divine gift in response to his request at the Gibeon sanctuary that Yahweh give the new king both an understanding of how to rule the kingdom and a knowledge of "good and evil." The fame of his wisdom is then played out in two manners: first, there are the illustrations of his *wisdom, as in the tale of the court case regarding two women and a baby, which immediately follows the narrative of Solomon receiving his wisdom (1 Kings 3:16-28); second, there are the references to reactions to simply hearing of or being awestruck by his wisdom, as in the story of the Queen of Sheba (1 Kings 10:1-7).

In accumulating vast wealth and many wives, and in ordering the populace to serve the royal family, Solomon comes across as the antithesis of the wise ruler (cf. Deut 17:14-19) and indeed as the embodiment of the evil that *Samuel described as defining kingship (1 Sam 8:11-18). Explicitly, Solomon's wisdom is compromised by lusting after so many women, by his old age, and by his apostasy (1 Kings 11:1-5). This lapse in wisdom is credited with his loss of territory and the rebellion of Jeroboam (1 Kings 11:14-40).

The tradition of Solomon as the fount of Judean wisdom is enhanced by the biblical books attributed to his authorship. The Song of Songs begins by stating that this is Solomon's song (Song 1:1), and he is referred to again near the end (Song 8:11-12). Proverbs repeatedly reports that the sayings, but not the collection, are those of Solomon (Prov 1:1; 10:1; 25:1). Ecclesiastes presents a world-weary vision in the name of the son of David, king in Jerusalem (Eccles 1:1), traditionally acknowledged to be Solomon. Jewish midrash has equated these three books with Solomon's romantic youth, reflective middle age, and pessimistic old age, respectively.

The apocryphal book Wisdom of Solomon, included in some Christian Bibles, is also attributed to Solomon, although an origin in an early first-century CE Egyptian Jewish community is likely. The Solomon appearing in Sirach is honored for wisdom in his youth, keeping Israel at peace and being the wisest person known in the entire world, all of which collapses due to Solomon's desire for women (Sir 47:12-23). The NT knows of a Solomon resplendent in glory (Mt 6:29), though it may be significant that Hebrews 11 does not include Solomon among the ancient faithful. Jewish and Christian authors used Solomon's wisdom and direct conversation with God to compose hymns in his name, as with *Psalms of Solomon* and *Odes of Solomon*. Rabbinic circles, and from them the Hellenistic world, extrapolated outward from comments in 1 Kings 4:29-33 to make Solomon the wisest of all people, knowing all secret knowledge; thus, Solomon's name became a word with magical powers, while his (anachronistic) "Solomonic ring" was seen as a magic amulet of highest potency. Control of all demons (and jinn in Islam) became part of his wisdom, power and kingdom in a number of legendary tales *(Testament of Solomon)*. When early Christian interpreters declared that all biblical texts could be read prophetically, Solomon, through "his" writings, became a major prophet. This tradition became central in the Qu'ran, where Solomon is simultaneously the wisest man who ever lived, the first man to rule the entire world, and a major prophet of Allah. Christian scholars throughout the Middle Ages continued to read Proverbs, Song of Solomon, Ecclesiastes and Wisdom of Solomon as prophetic texts containing insights into their own times.

See also HISTORY OF ISRAEL 3: UNITED MONARCHY; JERUSALEM; KINGS AND KINGSHIP; SOLOMON'S TEMPLE; ROYAL FAMILY; STATE OFFICIALS; WISDOM.

BIBLIOGRAPHY. **G. W. Ahlström,** *The History of Ancient Palestine from the Palaeolithic Period to Alexander's Conquest,* ed. D. Edelman (JSOTSup 146; Sheffield: Sheffield Academic Press, 1993); **P. S. Ash,** "Solomon's District List," *JSOT* 67 (1995) 67-86; **Y. Avishur and M. Heltzer,** *Studies on the Royal Administration in Ancient Israel in the Light of Epigraphic Sources* (Tel Aviv: Archaeological Center Publications, 2000); **J. A. Blakely,** "Reconciling Two Maps: Archaeological Evidence for the Kingdoms of David and Solomon," *BASOR* 327 (2002) 49-54; **E. Bloch-Smith,** "Solomon's Temple: The Politics of Ritual Space," in *Sacred Time, Sacred Place: Archaeology and the Religion of Israel,* ed. B. M. Gittlen (Winona Lake, IN: Eisenbrauns, 2002) 83-94; **W. G. Dever,** "Monumental Architecture in Ancient Israel in the Period of the United Monarchy," in *Studies in the Period of David and Solomon and Other Essays,* ed. T. Ishida (Winona Lake, IN: Eisenbrauns, 1982) 269-306; **G. Garbini,** *History and Ideology in Ancient Israel* (New York: Crossroad, 1988); **E. W. Heaton,** *Solomon's New Men: The Emergence of Ancient Israel as a National State* (Currents in the History of Culture and Ideas; London: Thames & Hudson, 1974); **D. Jobling,** "'Forced Labor': Solomon's Golden Age and the Question of Literary Representation," *Semeia* 54 (1991) 57-76; **A. E. Killebrew,** "Biblical Jerusalem: An Archaeological Assessment," in *Jerusalem in Bible and Archaeology: The First Temple Period,* ed. A. G. Vaughn and A. E. Killebrew (SBLSymS 18; Atlanta: Society of Biblical Literature, 2003) 329-45; **K. A. Kitchen,** *On the Reliability of the Old Testament* (Grand Rapids: Eerdmans, 2003); **G. N. Knoppers,** "The Vanishing Solomon: The Disappearance of the United Monarchy from Recent Histories of Ancient Israel," *JBL* 116 (1997) 19-44; **A. Malamat,** "Aspects of the Foreign Policies of David and Solomon," *JNES* 22 (1963) 1-17; **T. N. D. Mettinger,** *Solomonic State Officials: A Study of the Civil Government Officials of the Israelite Monarchy* (ConBOT 8; Lund: Gleerup, 1971); **A. R. Millard,** "King Solomon in His Ancient Context," in *The Age of Solomon: Scholarship at the Turn of the Millennium,* ed. L. K. Handy (SHCANE 11; Leiden: E. J. Brill, 1997) 30-53; **M. J. Miller,** "Separating the Solomon of History from the Solomon of Legend," in *The Age of Solomon: Scholarship at the Turn of the Millennium,* ed. L. K. Handy (SHCANE 11; Leiden: E. J. Brill, 1997) 1-24; **H. M. Niemann,** "The Socio-Political Shadow Cast by the Biblical Solomon," in *The Age of Solomon: Scholarship at the Turn of the Millennium,* ed. L. K. Handy (SHCANE 11; Leiden: E. J. Brill, 1997) 252-99; **L. S. Schearing,** "A Wealth of Women: Looking Behind, Within, and Beyond Solomon's Story," in *The Age of Solomon: Scholarship at the Turn of the Millennium,* ed. L. K. Handy (SHCANE 11; Leiden: E. J. Brill, 1997) 428-56; **E. K. Solvang,** *A Woman's Place Is in the House: Royal Women of Judah and*

Their Involvement in the House of David (JSOTSup 349; Sheffield: Sheffield Academic Press, 2003); **T. Veijola,** "Solomon: Bathsheba's Firstborn," in *Reconsidering Israel and Judah: Recent Studies on the Deuteronomistic History,* ed. G. N. Knoppers and J. G. McConville (SBTS 8; Winona Lake, IN: Eisen-brauns, 2000) 340-57.   L. K. Handy

SOLOMON'S TEMPLE

Solomon's temple was the embodiment of Israel's religious and national identity. Its setting and design manifested Yahweh's presence, while its splendor provided tangible evidence of his favor. Because it was the dwelling place of Yahweh, the Bible and subsequent traditions represented this edifice as the idealized high point of Israel's history, cultural expression and religious experience. The historical books of the Bible record that the temple was conceived by *David, constructed by *Solomon, frequented by kings and prophets, and destroyed by the Babylonians at the nadir of Israel's history. In those books the temple constitutes a point of reference for Israel's fidelity to Yahweh and a window into its understanding of the cosmos and its place in it.

The temple of Jerusalem is perhaps the most celebrated and thoroughly studied edifice of the ancient Near East. Solomon founded this temple, which is commonly called the "first temple," in 967 BCE (1 Kings 6:1). After his death and the division of the kingdom, the sanctuary served the kingdom of Judah until the Babylonian exile in 586 BCE. *Zerubbabel rebuilt the structure during the return from exile (Ezra 6:14-16) (*see* Postexilic Temple). The Hasmoneans expanded this "second temple," and Herod the Great made massive additions before Jerusalem and the temple fell to the Romans in 70 CE.

Investigation of the "first temple" is hampered by the continuing lack of physical data from the site. The description of the temple in 1 Kings is quite robust, but 200 years of exploration and excavation in Jerusalem have yielded few related artifacts or architectural remains. This has engendered great controversy as to the historical circumstances surrounding the construction of the temple and the nature of the kingdoms of David and Solomon. This lack of data, however, is offset by analogous temples in the textual and archaeological record of surrounding regions. These greatly augment our understanding of temples in this period and add much to what is known today about Solomon's temple.

1. The Temple in the Text
2. The Temple in Its Ancient Near Eastern Context
3. Iconography and Symbolism
4. The Uniqueness of Solomon's Temple
5. The Temple in the Life and History of Ancient Israel

1. The Temple in the Text.

1.1. Geographical and Cosmic Setting. David's move to Jerusalem along with the ark transformed the city into a political and religious center that united Judah in the south with the northern tribes of Israel (2 Sam 5—7). With Solomon's completion of the temple atop Mount Zion, a summit immediately north of the city, it became the archetypal cosmic mountain, the meeting point between heaven and earth, and the dwelling of the national deity (1 Kings 6—8). Jerusalem's geographical setting was well suited for this regal-ritual paradigm that is also attested in neighboring cultures of the ancient Near East. It acquired political centrality through highways emanating from a strategic plateau in the territory of the tribe of Benjamin, a few miles north of the city.

The cosmic significance of the temple was reflected in its grandeur and elevation, positioned above the city on a higher part of the same mountain ridge. This ridge, defined by deep canyons, lay in the midst of a large natural theater in which higher mounts gazed down with envy on Mount Zion, "the joy of the entire world." The lush gardens which surrounded the site were watered by primordial "living water" issuing forth into the valley from the area's sole intermittent spring and an adjacent system of water channels (2 Kings 25:4; Ps 48; 125:1-2). Together these images evoked memories of Eden and Sinai.

1.2. Biblical Sources. The OT records that the temple was constructed in the context of a large-scale building campaign in Jerusalem during the tenth century BCE. To David's royal compound (2 Sam 7:1) Solomon added a pillared hall, new fortifications and several palaces with throne rooms (1 Kings 7:1-12). The primary description of Solomon's temple, found in 1 Kings 6—7, represents one of the most detailed building accounts of the ancient Near East. It provides a meticulous and technical word picture of the temple's architecture along with descriptions of decoration and iconography. The specificity of the account and the obscurity of the vocabulary give the impression that it was based on administrative documents that were contemporary with Solomon's construction efforts.

Other temple-related passages in the historical books include 2 Chronicles 3—4, which largely repeats 1 Kings 6—7, and short reports of minor repairs and additions such as those made by Jehoshaphat (2 Chron 20:5) and Jotham (2 Kings 15:35; 16:10-18). The temple of Solomon figures prominently in other parts of the OT as well. Jeremiah frequented the temple courts (Jer 7; 36; 52), and Ezekiel's vision of a restored temple appears to be derived at least in part from first-hand knowledge of the Jerusalem shrine and its iconography (Ezek 40—43). References in the Psalms to the temple's gates and setting accord well with the picture provided in the historical and prophetic books (Ps 24; 48).

Biblical Hebrew includes several general terms for the Solomonic temple, all of which fall under the classification of "residence" or "dwelling." The most common is *hêkāl*, a term that occurs ninety-three times in the Hebrew Bible and often denotes "palace." Other expressions include *bêt yhwh* ("house of Yahweh," 1 Kings 7:12; 1 Chron 9:11; Neh 6:10), *bêt 'ĕlōhîm* ("house of God," 1 Kings 7:12; 1 Chron 9:11), *miqdāš*, ("holy place," Ps 74:7; Ezek 44:1), *mākôn* ("place," Ps 33:14), *mā'ôn* ("habitation," 2 Chron 36:15; Ps 71:3) and *zĕbul* (1 Kings 8:14; 2 Chron 6:2). This nomenclature stands in stark contrast to the enigmatic and poorly attested words for the architectural features of the temple.

1.3. Temple Design and Materials. The actual floor plan of the temple is easily discernable in the biblical text. According to 1 Kings 6 the temple was built at the center of a large courtyard that was accessible by gates on all sides. The building was oriented to the east and had three divisions, each originally twenty cubits wide. The "porch" (*'ûlām*) was ten cubits long and was reached by a stairway. It was differentiated from the interior of the temple by its large pillars, not by a doorway. The second division was the main hall or *hêkāl*, which was forty cubits long. It was entered through ornate wooden doors of 10-cubit width. The position of the windows and the precise construction of the roof are ambiguous in the biblical account. The third division, the "holy of holies" *(dĕbîr),* most likely constituted a cube with sides of twenty cubits each, but some of its finer details are omitted in the biblical text. The central shrine was enclosed on three sides by multistoried side chambers that enveloped the hall and the holy of holies (1 Kings 6:5).

If the biblical description is taken at face value, the entire building measured 70 by 20 cubits and was 30 cubits high. If the standard royal cubit of 52.5 cm is taken, the width of the main temple was approximately 12 m and its length roughly 40 m. The height of the main structure was approximately 15 m, and the side structure built around the perimeter was at least half that height. The measurements, assuming the cubit is interpreted accurately, make this temple one of the largest ever to be built in the region of Syria and Palestine.

The construction materials and ornamentation of the temple are also relatively easy to ascertain from the biblical accounts. The architects employed finely chiseled, monumental "ashlar" masonry throughout, and the roof was constructed of large beams. The walls and floors were lined with cedar and covered with gold. Cherubs, palmettes, floral patterns and window frames lined the walls of the two interior rooms (1 Kings 6:29; 2 Chron 3:7). The doors to both rooms were also finished with ornate patterns.

Although the biblical record is detailed, several obstacles hinder attempts to reach a precise understanding of the temple using the written sources alone. The first obstacle is the nature of the biblical accounts themselves. They are selective and it seems that they were not intended to provide a complete description of the temple. For reasons unknown to us, the authors chose to leave out many details that may have been included in the official registry of Solomon's court.

A second challenge is that the temple accounts contain many technical terms that occur infrequently in Hebrew and cognate languages. As a result, many of the temple's features eluded clarification until the recent discoveries of architectural parallels in the ancient Near East. What, for example, was the precise nature of the holy of holies? It may have been an elevated room, which would account for its lower height. Or perhaps it housed a small shrine with a lower ceiling, or even part of the original tabernacle itself. Such a design would require secondary, less substantial walls between the two innermost chambers of the temple rather than a large stone wall. This arrangement is hinted at in the biblical text and is known from other temples in the Levant, such as that found at Tell Tayanat in southern Turkey. Many secondary features of the temple are also difficult to understand. The book of 1 Kings describes "blocked" windows, a pentagon-shaped door, cedar panels, floral patterns, palmettes, cedar paneling and lavish gold from floor to ceiling, all of which must still be clarified. The nature of these features must be sought in comparative material from the archaeological record.

1.4. Temple Furnishings. The accessories of the temple, like the interior walls, were overlaid with precious metals so as to reflect the majesty of the temple's divine occupant. These furnishings are listed with their location in the text of 1 Kings 6—7. They are known primarily from biblical texts, although a number of ancient Near Eastern parallels have been found. The courtyard of the temple was the most heavily used part of the sacred precinct and the primary locus of sacrifice (1 Kings 8:64; 2 Chron 7:7). Most ancient Near Eastern temples had basins in their courtyards, and the temple of Solomon was no exception. A large ceremonial basin, described as the "sea" (1 Kings 7:23), was placed in the large outer courtyard of the temple. It was 10 cubits in diameter and was supported by twelve bronze oxen. The water may have been used for oblations or cleaning, but it was likely a symbolic representation of the cosmic waters subdued by Yahweh's divine power, perhaps a vivid reminder of Yahweh's ability to deliver the Israelite tribes at the Red Sea. The outer courtyard also held a large, four-horned altar that was coated with bronze. Ten wheeled carts with basins were stationed at the entrance to the temple (1 Kings 7:27-38). Each was decorated with images of cherubim, lions and trees. Similar mobile basins are known from other sites in the ancient Near East, and it appears that they were used for transporting water or for boiling sacrificial meat (2 Chron 4:6).

Two pillars, Jachin ("he sets up") and Boaz ("in strength"), flanked the temple entrance on the porch (1 Kings 7:15-22). Based on the closest parallels, such as the ʿAin Dara temple, it would appear that they supported the roof of the porch. These 9-m-high, hollow bronze pillars were crowned with capitals comprised of flowery chains, pomegranates and latticework. The pillars have been variously interpreted as scrolls, treaty markers (*maṣṣēbôt*) and symbolic gates into the temple proper.

The main hall of the temple, with its elaborate gold-covered cedar paneling, was lit by ten gold lampstands that corresponded to the ten-wheeled basins in the courtyard (1 Kings 7:49-50). A small incense altar stood at the entrance to the holy of holies (1 Kings 6:20), and a gold-plated table held the twelve unleavened loaves of the "bread of presence" that symbolized Yahweh's covenant with His people.

Inside the holy of holies two massive cherubim stood with wings outstretched over the *ark of the covenant (1 Kings 7:13-14). They were made from olive wood and were plated with gold, each measuring 10 cubits in height and 10 cubits in wingspan. Inside this innermost chamber, the cherubim functioned as Yahweh's throne, and the ark of the covenant, signifying Yahweh's presence in the temple, served as his footstool.

2. The Temple in Its Ancient Near Eastern Context.

2.1. Archaeological Investigation in Jerusalem. Almost two centuries of archaeological investigation in Jerusalem have unfortunately produced no confirmed remnants of the tenth-century temple described in the rich biblical accounts. The one possible exception is a foundation wall identified by L. Ritmeyer on the east side of the temple mount. Although extensive excavations have been conducted in the vicinity of the original temple, archaeological knowledge of the temple mount is limited to the accounts of small probes undertaken by nineteenth-century explorers. The biblical description of the temple is thus inversely proportional to the quantity of relevant archaeological evidence discovered in Jerusalem to date. A complete understanding of the temple therefore must not be sought in the biblical accounts alone but also in the comparative architecture from Israel and surrounding regions.

2.2. Comparative Study of Ancient Near Eastern Temples. Today it is possible to compare the biblical description of Solomon's temple with the physical characteristics of several dozen ancient temples uncovered in neighboring regions. Most of these temples have designs and features that bear a striking resemblance to those of Solomon's temple as reconstructed from the biblical accounts. Moreover, many of these temples belonged to palace-temple complexes in prominent cities within small kingdoms that emerged in the eastern Mediterranean during the first millennium BCE. At Tell Taint in southern Turkey, for example, the small first-millennium BCE temple adjoining the palace seems to have much in common with the design and iconography of Solomon's temple. A staircase leads to its porch, where two pillars flank the entrance into a large hall and to an inner sanctum beyond this hall. There are also numerous second-millennium temples, such as those uncovered at Ebla and Emar, whose layouts are very similar to that of Solomon's temple.

In light of numerous parallels between these temples and the biblical description, Solomon's temple can be placed comfortably within a typology of temples from northern Syria and northern Mesopotamia. It belongs to the "long-room Syrian type," with a rectangular plan, a pillared entrance on the short southern wall, a tripartite division (internal walls), a raised platform or niche opposite the door, and an elevated holy of holies or inner sanctum at the far end. Given the fact that builders exchanged supplies, artisans and raw materials, it should follow that this Syrian tradition of temple building influenced the temples of Phoenicia and Israel (1 Kings 5:13-18). One should not expect architectural uniqueness within the temple built by Solomon.

The ʿAin Dara temple in northern Syria is the most striking parallel to Solomon's temple discovered to date (see figure 1). It is closer in size, date and iconography than any known ancient temple and thus represents a significant new resource for the study of Solomon's temple. Indeed, the ʿAin Dara temple is so well preserved that it offers a physical corollary to the OT's word picture of Solomon's temple. In some cases it may actually clarify the features of the biblical description of the temple.

At ʿAin Dara a large platform supported the superstructure (cf. 1 Kings 6:5-6), and the pillars on the porch were not freestanding (as was previously thought to be the case with Solomon's temple) but instead supported the roof (1 Kings 7:21). The holy of holies in the ʿAin Dara temple was made from a wooden screen built on a platform area. Though it does not represent conclusive evidence, this feature accords with the biblical description of the inner sanctuary (1 Kings 6:20). The so-called side chambers of Solomon's temple have long mystified scholars (1 Kings 6:5). The multistoried hallways that flanked the ʿAin Dara temple on three sides are the first clear example of this enigmatic feature ever to be found. These newly discovered side chambers had doorways on either side of

the temple's front porch, and their multiple stories were reached by "stairs" or "ladders," which have also been unearthed at ʿAin Dara in the form of return staircases (cf. 1 Kings 6:8). These corridors formed an ambulatory that was likely used for storing supplies and wealthy utensils.

Another example of such correlations between artifact and text are the enigmatic windows of Solomon's temple (1 Kings 6:4), now better understood through comparison with Syrian temples. Most commentators translate this term as "latticed windows," based on linguistic study of cognate languages. The interior walls at ʿAin Dara included at least two well preserved window frames, which were carefully cut into the stone. These "decorative windows" have recessed, indented frames on each side, including the top, where they were slightly arched. Horizontal "figure eight-shaped ribbons" filled the upper half of each window. These may represent the window lattice of Solomon's temple as described in 1 Kings 6:4-5. Some of the windows have been carved with side posts, which may represent the opening capability of functional windows. It appears that the "blocked, latticed windows" of Solomon's temple were beautiful decorative stone reliefs such as the ones at ʿAin Dara.

The above examples demonstrate clear correlations between features in Solomon's temple (features hitherto only known from the biblical text) and comparative archaeological examples from elsewhere in the ancient Near East. What was only reconstructed in theory can now actually be seen in artifacts.

3. Iconography and Symbolism.

Solomon's temple and palace complex conformed to a paradigm that was ubiquitous among the second- and first-millennium kingdoms of the ancient Near East. According to this tradition, the national deity resided in a shrine built next to the king's palace on the acropolis of the capital city. This arrangement was the earthly manifestation of a cosmic reality. It included a prominent mountain situated above primordial waters, a heavenly abode for the deity, and an idyllic fertile garden in which the tree of life stood. Otherworldly creatures, such as the cherubim, attended to the needs of the deity and protected the sacred garden. The heavenly and earthly order was preserved—and the purity of Yahweh's original creation sustained—by enacting the temple rituals and safeguarding the authority of the king. The

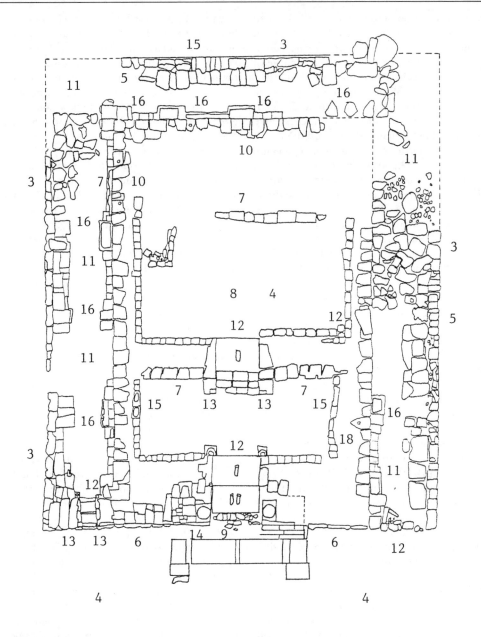

Figure 1. The ʿAin Dara temple and biblical temple terms.

1. Courtyard *(ḥāṣēr)*
2. Foundation *(mô/ûsād)*
3. Terrace platform *(gōbah)*
4. Paved floor *(riṣpâ, ʾereṣ, qarqāʿ)*
5. Exterior wall *(qîr, kōtēl)*
6. Façade wall *(kātēp)*
7. Wall panels *(šĕdērôt)*
8. Hall/Cella *(hêkāl, bayit)*
9. Porch *(ʾûlām)*

10. Holy of holies *(dĕbîr)*
11. Side chamber *(ṣĕlāʿôt, ganzak)*
12. Door *(petaḥ, mĕzûzâ, ḥămišît, sap, miptān)*
13. Pier *(ʾîtôn, ʾayil)*
14. Pillar *(ʿammûd)*
15. Window *(ḥallôn, ḥallônê, šĕqupîm, ʾăṭumîm)*
16. Pilaster and pier *(ʾayil, migrāʿôt)*
17. Upper floor *(ʿălîyyâ, yāṣôʿa)*
18. Staircase *(lûl, maʿălēh)*

Israelite expression of these ideas could be seen in the iconography of Solomon's temple on Mount Zion, in the undulations of the Gihon spring, and in the representation of the tree of life and the cherubim in the art and architecture of Jerusalem. Specifically, for the Israelites the temple of Solomon was a return to Eden. It brought a piece of paradise to the Israelite homeland that permanently anchored Yahweh not to Sinai but to Zion. This concept manifested itself in the gourds, leaves, flowers, fruit and cherubim that decorated the temple, and it animated the ceremonies that took place there. It was an affirmation of the presence, virility and moral supremacy of Yahweh (1 Kings 6:29). In the eyes of the ancient Israelites, therefore, Solomon's temple was an earthly residence for Yahweh, a meeting point between heaven and earth.

This image of primordial purity stood in stark contrast to the tainted world that lay beyond the confines of the temple precinct. These two realms were connected through a series of courtyards and rooms that progressed from the profane on the exterior to the most sacred in the holy of holies, each with its protocol for worship. The wall of the outer courtyard demarcated the temple precinct, and it was in the inner courtyard that most of the rituals took place. Increasing spheres of holiness and opulence characterized the path from the courtyard to the porch, through the main hall (where only *priests could enter), and into the innermost shrine where once a year the high priest came into the presence of Yahweh.

In the Historical Books of the OT, these concepts represent a consistent world order and divine involvement in human affairs that serve as a barometer for Israel's spiritual health and its relationship with Yahweh. Fluctuations in national and personal fidelity to Yahweh are recorded in an orderly manner in these books and more dramatically in the psalms and the prophets. The temple was the setting for much of Yahweh's interaction with his people and the venue of their worship.

4. Uniqueness of Solomon's Temple.

The structure, style and motifs of Solomon's temple are reminiscent of other religious traditions that have been identified in temples and on palace wall reliefs throughout the ancient Near East. Nevertheless, the cultural overlap need not necessarily be considered a wholesale borrowing from the religions of adjacent lands, as many would assume. Rather, Israel's tradition with its temple and texts was expressing itself in the language, art and idioms of its day. Through a process of selective borrowing and innovation, Israel, like other kingdoms, built a unique religious system that combined outside influences and indigenous innovation.

It retained, moreover, a number of significant distinctives. In stark contrast to the iconography of neighboring lands, Israel's central shrine contained no images of the deity or of humans. The layout and design of Israel's temple had much in common with Syrian temples but never included an image of Yahweh. The cherubim, from a different sphere, constituted the throne of God and testified to his superhuman character, while the decoration and use of the temple furnishings told of his creative power and rule over the earth as well as his military victories over the forces of chaos.

5. The Temple in the Life and History of Ancient Israel.

With the transferal of the ark to Jerusalem, Yahweh officially chose Mount Zion as his dwelling (Ps 132:13-14). The place became a conduit of spiritual and political power, and the theology of Zion was born. Some have argued that a previous Jebusite tradition may actually have influenced Israelite religious expression, but this remains only conjecture. In either case, David's successful campaigns demonstrated anew that the God of Israel was also Lord of the entire world. A host of expressions and metaphors could now be used for Zion because it had become a permanent locus of religious activity for the tribes and for the entire kingdom. Although most Israelites never passed beyond the outer court of the temple, the edifice offered a constant reminder of Yahweh's presence among his people. It would have evoked a set of associations hearkening back to Yahweh's revelation on Mount Sinai and the perfect splendor of Eden itself, the place where heaven and earth met.

Kingship, conquest and security were not restricted to the spiritual realm. The palace that adjoined the temple also served as a reminder that the king, God's agent through a special covenant, was on his throne (see Kings and Kingship). If the biblical account is to be taken seriously, then the activity connected to the planning and building of the temple in the days of David and Solomon reflected the times in which they lived. The military conquests, religious imagery and the attempt to move toward cultic centrality, all conform to the paradigm of kingdoms and the institutions of this same period. The international climate of the tenth century BCE suits the biblical account very well indeed, a fact that is further corroborated by the tenth-century architecture and wall reliefs of the ʿAin Dara temple.

In sum, the triad of God, monarch and people intersected in the temple of Solomon. From the moment of its completion, this building and its immediate setting lay at the heart of what may be called a Zion theology (see Zion Traditions). This building complex would remain the tradition's primary vehicle of expression even after it was destroyed. Nowhere is the physical and emotional impact of this theology better expressed than in events recorded in the Historical Books of the OT. Through the vicissitudes of Israelite history this paradigm changed, however, and the Zion theology acquired a life of its own that was independent of the physical temple. It intensified when Jerusalem was spared in the time of Hezekiah, and the tradition was further streamlined with the reforms of Josiah. After the exile of 586 BCE it was invoked once again in order to bring revival and point toward a glorious age to come.

See also ARCHITECTURE; HIGH PLACES; JERUSALEM; POSTEXILIC TEMPLE; PRIESTS AND LEVITES; SOLOMON; ZION TRADITIONS.

BIBLIOGRAPHY. **E. Bloch-Smith,** "'Who is the King of Glory?' Solomon's Temple and Its Symbolism," in *Scripture and Other Artifacts: Essays in Bible and Archaeology in Honor of Philip J. King,* ed. M. Coogan et al. (Louisville: Westminster John Knox, 1995) 18-31; **T. Busink,** *Der Tempel von Jerusalem von Salomo bis Herodes; eine archäologische-historische Studie unter Berücksichtigung des westsemitischen Tempelbaus. I Der Tempel Salomos* (Leiden: E. J. Brill, 1970); **J. Cahill,** "Jerusalem at the Time of the United Monarchy: The Archaeological Evidence," in *Jerusalem in Bible and Archaeology: The First Temple Period,* ed. A. G. Vaughn and A. E. Killebrew (SBLSymS 18; Atlanta: Society of Biblical Literature, 2003) 13-80; **R. J. Clifford,** *The Cosmic Mountain in Canaan and the Old Testament* (HSM 4; Cambridge, MA: Scholars Press, 1971); **W. G. Dever,** *What Did the Biblical Writers Know, and When Did They Know It? What Archaeology Can Tell Us About the Reality of Ancient Israel* (Grand Rapids: Eerdmans, 2001) 144-57; **M. Eliade,** *The Sacred and the Profane: The Nature of Religion* (New York: Harper and Row, 1959); **R. Friedman,** "The Tabernacle in the Temple," *BA* 43 (1980) 241-48; **L. Handy,** "On The Dating and Dates of Solomon's Reign," in *The Age of Solomon,* ed. L. Handy (New York: E. J. Brill, 1997) 96-105; **A. Hurowitz,** *I Have Built You an Exalted House* (JSOTSup 115; Sheffield: JSOT Press, 1992); **O. Keel,** *The Symbolism of the Biblical World* (Winona Lake, IN: Eisenbrauns, 1997); **J. Levenson,** *Sinai and Zion: An Entry into the Jewish Bible* (New York: Harper and Row, 1988); **C. Meyers,** "Jachin and Boaz in Religious and Political Perspective," *CBQ* 45:167-78; **J. Monson,** "The New ʿAin Dara Temple, Closest Solomonic Parallel," *BAR* 26/3 (2000): 20-35; **L. Ritmeyer,** *The Temple and the Rock* (Harrogate: Ritmeyer Archaeological Design, 1997); **L. E. Stager,** "Jerusalem and the Garden of Eden," *ErIsr* 26 (1999) 183-94; **G. E. Wright,** "The Significance of the Temple in the Ancient Near East: III The Temple in Syria-Palestine," *BA* 7 (1944) 65-77. J. Monson

SONGS. *See* POETRY.

SONS, ROYAL. *See* ROYAL FAMILY.

SOURCE CRITICISM. *See* METHODS OF INTERPRETATION.

SOURCES, REFERENCES TO

An examination of the sources that are explicitly referred to in the OT Historical Books (e.g., "the Book of Moses" [Ezra 6:18]; "the Book of the Annals of the Kings of Judah" [2 Kings 16:19]) is noteworthy for at least four reasons. First, the significance of a reference to any source (e.g., the law) is best viewed in the context of how all citations were made in the OT. Second, an exhaustive analysis of these references is instrumental in establishing the purposes of the writers of the Historical Books. Third, this inquiry is closely related to certain scholarly disputes about the use of the *law that have persisted for more than a century: the description of the hermeneutic reflected in the postexilic Historical Books, the contents of the law book of this community, the skill and motivations of the postexilic historiographers as interpreters of the law, as well as individual examples of *innerbiblical exegesis. Fourth, this study advances understanding of an ancient Near Eastern literary convention.

1. Overview of Sources and Citation Devices.
The sources in the OT *historiography include nonlegal repositories such as "the Book of the Kings of Israel and Judah" (e.g., 2 Chron 35:27) and "the Book of the Upright" (e.g., 2 Sam 1:18), as well as legal sources such as "the Book of the Law of Moses" (e.g., 2 Kings 14:6) and "the law" (e.g., Neh 10:34). The sources referred to in the Historical Books are best analyzed according to nonlegal topics (e.g., lamentations, the deeds of kings) and legal topics (e.g., the law) because of the observably different ways that these two subjects were cited. However, as we will see, this classification of the evidence also makes possible the additional observation that after the Babylonian exile certain citation formulas with legal topics were developed from previous forms.

Some of the citation devices used to refer to these sources include: "as it is written" (e.g., Ezra 3:4); "it was found written" (e.g., Neh 13:1); "genealogies—they are written in the Book of the Kings of Israel" (1 Chron 9:1); "according to the ordinance" (e.g., 2 Chron 4:20); and "according to the law" (e.g., Ezra 10:3). After an overview of the devices used to refer to nonlegal topics, we will examine those used with legal referents.

2. Citation Devices with Nonlegal Topics.
In OT historiography a standard four-part citation device is used exclusively to attribute a range of nonlegal topics to some of the aforementioned literary sources. Although the most common referent is "the rest of the deeds of a king," the other nonlegal topics that utilize a form of this citation device include laments (e.g., 2 Chron 35:25), genealogies (e.g., 1 Chron 9:1), prophecies (Jer 25:13) and poetic excerpts from "the Book of the Upright" (e.g., Josh 10:13). This four-part citation device comprises a distinctive syntactic structure: (1) a nominative absolute, variously called *casus pendens* or focus marker by grammars, (2) a particle with a resumptive pronoun, (3) a passive participle of the verb stem "to write," and (4) a literary source.

Among all citation devices, this four-part structure is noteworthy not only because it is used exclusively for nonlegal topics, but also because it possesses a structure that may reflect an ancient literary convention for marking tangential or off-line information in a narrative. An understanding of this latter point requires more than a passing treatment of the syntax of this four-part structure, but a nontechnical treatment, such as is offered here, can refer to part of the evidence: the interchangeability of the second element of this four-part citation device.

The citation devices in 2 Kings 14:18 and 2 Kings 15:11, for example, represent the four parts of this formula and the two versions of second element (italics).

The rest of the deeds of Amaziah, *are they not* written in the Book of the Annals of the Kings of Judah? (2 Kings 14:18)

The rest of the deeds of Zechariah, *behold they are* written in the Book of the Annals of the Kings of Israel. (2 Kings 15:11)

The interchangeability of this second element is observable also in the references to "the Book of the Upright" (see below), as well as in the Chronicler's rewriting of some of the four-part citation devices in his source (e.g., 1 Kings 15:23/2 Chron 16:11; 1 Kings 22:45/2 Chron 20:34). A consideration of the form of this citation device illuminates its function as a focus marker to mark off-line information in a narrative, similar to a footnote by a modern author (Khan, 230-31).

The evidence from the book of Esther is consistent with the use of this device elsewhere, but adds at least one notable observation.

[The deeds of Ahasuerus] are they not written in *the Book of the Annals of the Kings of Media and Persia*? (Esther 10:2)

This attribution to a Persian source (italics) and the distinctive provenance of Esther in general suggest that this putative literary convention may have been used more broadly than the aforementioned Jewish sources imply.

The use of this four-part pattern among a range of nonlegal topics, the interchangeability of the second element, and the provenance of the book of Esther, together with other technical observations, suggest that this four-part citation pattern was a literary convention for marking tangential information in narratives.

Two reformulations of the standard four-part citation pattern are noteworthy. First, either a poetic fragment (Josh 10:12b-13a) or a poetic excerpt (2 Sam 1:19-27) may be attributed to "the Book of the Upright" by a reformulation of this citation device.

> . . . *is this not* written in the Book of the Upright? (Josh 10:13)

> . . . the "Bow," *behold it is* written in the Book of the Upright. (2 Sam 1:18)

In Joshua 10:13 the poetic fragment (Josh 10:12b-13a) is the antecedent of the pronoun (a *neutrum*), while "Bow" in 2 Samuel 1:18 stands as the title of the large poetic excerpt (2 Sam 1:19-27). First Kings 8:53a LXX (1 Kings 8:12-13 MT is transposed after 1 Kings 8:53 LXX) preserves another example of a reformulated four-part device ascribing another poetic referent to "the Book of the Upright." While keeping the basic structure intact, including the interchangeable elements, these reformulated citation devices consistently cite poetic referents instead of nominal phrases (*see* Poetry).

A second reformulation of this four-part device concerns the work of the Chronicler. At three critical junctures (2 Chron 13:22; 24:27; 33:18-19) the Chronicler rewrites the citation devices of his source in order to reinforce his distinctive treatment of the narratives of Abijah, Joash and Manasseh, which are widely recognized to be significant to his purpose.

Not only did the Chronicler triple the amount of space given to Abijah (1 Kings 15:1-8/2 Chron 13:1-14:1), but also, more importantly, he transformed the negative view of this monarch in 1 Kings 15 (e.g., "he committed all the sins that his father did before him; his heart was not true to the LORD his God, like the heart of his father David" [1 Kings 15:3]) into an exemplary Davidic king. According to 2 Chronicles 13:3-21, Abijah was the first king of the divided monarchy to honor God. Specifically, Abijah instructed Jeroboam and all Israel in the true nature of the Davidic covenant and the sons of Aaron (2 Chron 13: 4-12)—themes central to the *Chronicler's History. At 2 Chronicles 13:22 the Chronicler bolsters his treatment of Abijah by rewriting the four-part citation pattern of 1 Kings 15:7a, which includes the rephrasing of the first element (italics) and omission of the second (underlined).

> The rest of the acts of Abijam, *and all that he did,* are they not written in the Book of the Annals of the Kings of Judah? (1 Kings 15:7a)

> The rest of the acts of Abijah, *his behavior and his sayings,* are written in the story of the prophet Iddo. (2 Chron 13:22)

Two observations about the Chronicler's rewriting of this formula are significant for our purposes. First, by the omission of the second element, the Chronicler's new sentence no longer functions as a footnote that signals tangential information. Second, the Chronicler's rewritten phrase (italics) recalls the deeds of Abijah crucial to his distinctive history: Abijah's "behavior" (his fight for the Lord God of Israel [2 Chron 13:13-19]) and "sayings" (his instruction to all Israel [2 Chron 13:4-12]).

The Chronicler's account of Joash in 2 Chronicles 24 represents another considerable rewriting of his source. The Chronicler introduced the account of the deaths of Jehoiada and Zech-ariah (2 Chron 24:15-22) into the narrative of Joash's reign (see 2 Kings 12), together with other changes, in order to portray his rule in two periods: (1) righteous Joash, the defender and repairer of the temple due to the influence of Jehoiada (2 Chron 24:4-14), and (2) Joash, the object of divine judgment (i.e., a Syrian invasion and his assassination [2 Chron 24:23-27]) due to the influence of his apostate princes (2 Chron 24:17-18). In this way, the Chronicler provided a needed explanation regarding the transformation of Joash. That is, by linking his apostasy with the events that followed the death of Jehoiada (see 2 Chron 24:17-22), the priest with whom Joash organized the repair of the temple, the Chronicler steered clear of a possible implication of 2 Kings 12: Joash's work on the temple somehow led to divine judgment ("at that time [the repair of the temple] . . . Hazael set his face to go up to Jerusalem" [2 Kings 12:17]; see Japhet, 840). By portraying his reign according to these two periods, the Chronicler also avoided discouraging his community from emulating righteous Joash and his faithfulness to the temple, an institution that all agree is central to his purpose. Accordingly, in the first element of his rephrased citation formula (underlined) the Chronicler separated Joash's righteous work on the temple (italics) from the evil events of his reign.

> Now the rest of the acts of Joash, and all that he *did,* are they not written in the Book of the Annals of the Kings of Judah. (2 Kings 12:19)

> Accounts of his sons, and of the many ora-cles against him, *and of the rebuilding of the house of God,* behold they are written in the Commentary on the Book of the Kings. (2 Chron 24:27)

No greater rewriting of these four-part formulas is to be observed in Chronicles than that found in 2 Chronicles 33:18-19, which again concludes a narrative pivotal to the Chronicler's purpose.

> Now the rest of the acts of Manasseh, and all that he did, and the sin that he committed, are they not written in the Book of the Annals of the Kings of Judah? (2 Kings 21:17)

> Now the rest of the acts of Manasseh, *and his prayer* to his God, and the words of *the seers* who spoke to him in the name of the LORD the God of Israel, behold, they are in the Annals of the Kings of Israel. *And his prayer,* and how God received his entreaty, and all his sin and his faithlessness, and the sites on which he built high places and set up the Asherim and the images, before he humbled himself, behold, they are written in the Annals of *the Seers.* (2 Chron 33:18-19)

W. M. Schniedewind argues that in 2 Chronicles 33:19 the Chronicler clarified the ambiguities and problems of 2 Chronicles 33:18b, an earlier source fragment, which "troubled him" (Schniedewind, 460). Schniedewind's conclusion partly depends on two unconventional viewpoints: the expression "his God" (*'ĕlōhāyw*) in 2 Chronicles 33:18 does not clearly refer to the Lord God of Israel (i.e., "'his gods,' 'his god' or 'his God' [namely Yahweh]" [Schniedewind, 457]), and the phrase "and his prayer" in 2 Chronicles 33:18b is not a compositional link with Manasseh's prayer in 2 Chronicles 33:13. However, an examination of 2 Chronicles 33:18-19 in the context of an exhaustive analysis of these formulas supports the position that these two verses complement each other and are interrelated by two sets of doublets (italics) as well as an abbreviated citation formula (the third element, the verb stem "to write," is omitted) in 2 Chronicles 33:18. According to the latter perspective, 2 Chronicles 33:18-19 summarizes the Chronicler's extensively reworked narrative of Manasseh, which serves as a type of postexilic and restorationist Israel (Williamson 1982, 389), and his prayer, which is not treated in Kings, is an integral part of this typology.

The Chronicler has skillfully used citation formulas in selected narratives in order to bolster his purposes. Even though he uses the citation formulas in the Abijah, Joash and Manasseh narratives to great effect, the Chronicler typically preserves the basic four-part device of his source elsewhere (e.g., 2 Chron 9:29; 12:15).

In order to properly assess the evidence of citation devices with legal topics, it is also important to observe that these four-part formulas with nonlegal topics are used in OT historiography irrespective of their relation to the postexilic reconstruction era.

3. Citation Devices with Legal Topics.

Citation devices with legal topics use syntactic constructions that are unrelated to those given above. In contrast to the general static use of devices with nonlegal topics, many of the formulas that cite the law in the reconstruction era differ in form and function from those used before this time. Additionally, such differences are generally unaccounted for by the well-documented developments from standard biblical Hebrew to late biblical Hebrew (*see* Hebrew Language). The evidence suggests that certain postexilic citation devices with legal topics reflect a development of the corresponding devices used prior to 539 BCE. As we will see, citation devices with legal topics at times distinguish between the "two hermeneutical horizons" of a reference to the law (what was contained in the law) and its contemporary interpretation (what was regulated from the law). Thus these citation formulas are hermeneutical tools or exegetical devices that facilitated the interpretation and observance of the law.

For more than a century scholars have disagreed about the significance of several of the citation formulas with legal referents (selected examples of this are given below). What may appear to be trivial issues (e.g., the identification of the antecedent of "it" in the citation formula "as it is written in the law") actually have profound ramifications for scholarly assessments of individual examples of innerbiblical exegesis, the description of the hermeneutic reflected in the postexilic literature, the contents of the law book of the postexilic community (are the legal stipulations attributed to their law book contained in our Pentateuch or not?) as well as the skill and motivations of certain postexilic historiographers. These debates have been further compounded by the practice of scholars advocating one view in the debate apart from a treatment of rival interpretations. An examination of citation formulas provides a new perspective from which to reconsider the issues concerned with the law and its interpretation in the reconstruction era.

Since a complete discussion includes a range of technical issues, the development of certain postexilic exegetical devices is best demonstrated by representative examples. The citation devices in 2 Kings 17:34b and Ezra 3:4, for instance, demonstrate some of the features that can be observed between these exegetical devices. Prior to 539 BCE, two or more citation devices normally were used together to attribute a single legal referent to a source. In 2 Kings 17:34b, for example, five citation devices (underlined) are construed together to manage one referent (italics).

> . . . nor *do they act* <u>according to their statutes, according to their ordinances, according to the law</u> or <u>according to the commandment that the LORD ordered</u> the sons of Jacob. (2 Kings 17:34b)

Such compound citation devices are not found among the postexilic formulas. Even when more than one citation device occurs in a single passage from this era (e.g., Ezra 3:4), note how each independent exegetical device (underlined) has its own referent (italics).

> . . . *they celebrated the Festival of Succoth* <u>as it was written</u> [*kakkātûb*], including *the daily burnt offerings* <u>according to the number required by the ordinance</u> for that day. (Ezra 3:4; cf. Num 29)

Furthermore, "as it is written" (*kakkātûb*), an abbreviation of "as it is written in the law," is attested only in the restoration period (Ezra 3:4; Neh 8:15; 2 Chron 30:5, 18). In the postbiblical era *kakkātûb* was shortened to *kk* in the Cairo Geniza text of the *Damascus Document* (see CD 19:1).

Another feature of citation devices with legal referents prior to the restoration era that is represented by 2 Kings 17:34b concerns the verb stem "to do." In contrast to its common use as the referent in citation devices before the reconstruction period (for the verb stem "to do" as a pro-form see Spawn, 68-69), postexilic exegetical devices are customarily construed with detailed referents, as can be seen in Ezra 3:4 (italics).

In the postexilic literature (e.g., Neh 10:34) developed exegetical tools (underlined) are consistently placed beside the referent (italics).

> We—the priests, the Levites, and the people—have cast lots for the wood offering to bring it to the house of our God according to our fathers' house at appointed times annually, *to burn [wood] on the altar of the LORD our God* <u>as it is written in the law.</u> (Neh 10:34; cf. Josh 9:21)

Before the restoration period (e.g., 1 Kings 22:38), a citation device (underlined; a compound construction) was not always positioned next to its referent (italics).

> . . . *the dogs licked up his blood* and the prostitutes bathed themselves <u>according to the word of the LORD which he has spoken.</u> (1 Kings 22:38; cf. 1 Kings 21:19)

In contrast to 1 Kings 22:38, the postexilic historiographers position some of the exegetical devices in ways that make it easier to identify the referent (see 2 Chron 7:17; 35:13, 26; Ezra 3:4b; Neh 10:34, 36). For example, while a disjunctive clause helps the recognition of the referent in Ezra 3:4b, the same syntactic structure in 1 Kings 22:38 ("and the prostitutes bathed themselves") impedes the identification of the clause that is attributed to "the word of the LORD" (cf. 1 Kings 21:19).

In Nehemiah 10:34 the author distinguishes a reference to the law (the italicized phrase in Neh 10:34 is based on Lev 6:12-13) from the creation of procedures (the annual rotation of the wood offering in Neh 10:34a) to satisfy the requirement of the law in the restoration era (Clines, 112; Williamson 1985, 336; 1988, 28). Other scholars read "the wood offering" as the legal requirement attributed to the law book of this community (Fishbane, 213; Shaver, 84, 89, 127). Consequently, they conclude that the law book of Nehemiah's community was different from the Pentateuch of today, which does not contain the requirement for a "wood offering." However, advocates of this latter position must, of course, demonstrate that the abutting phrase is not the legal stipulation in view here. According to an analysis of citation devices, especially the syntax of comparative constructions (for a summary see Spawn, 236-56), the annual rotation of the wood offering should be viewed as the interpretative measures taken by this community to obey the law: to keep a fire burning continuously on the altar (Lev 6:12-13). In the postexilic setting the services of the Gibeonites were no longer available, so new measures—a wood offering—had to be devised to obey the stipulation in Leviticus 6 (see Josh 9:21-27).

Instead of positing another law book for this community, other hypotheses have been floated by scholars. For example, C. C. Torrey (277 n. g), based on Nehemiah 8:14-15 and Nehemiah 10:34, suggested that the writer of Ezra-Nehemiah had a faulty memory of the law book or was otherwise reckless in his citation of it. H. Donner represents a different approach. In his recent study of "as it is written," Donner (231) surprisingly leaves the identification of the referent in Nehemiah 10:34 unresolved (see also Rudolph, 180).

In 2 Chronicles 35:13, "according to the ordinance" clearly distinguishes a reference to the law (Ex 12:8-9) from the steps taken to fulfill it at a later time. That is, 2 Chronicles 35:13a cites the legal requirement that the Passover sacrifice be cooked (underlined), while 2 Chronicles 35:13b depicts the specific measures taken to realize the fulfillment of this stipulation in Josiah's time (italics).

> . . . they [the priests and the Levites] roasted the Passover lamb on the fire, according to the ordinance, *they boiled the holy offerings in pots, in caldrons, and in pans, and carried them quickly to all the people.* (2 Chron 35:13)

The statement of fulfillment is further distinguished from the foregoing material by a conjunction (i.e., *waw*-explicative) in Hebrew (e.g., 2 Chron 7:17).

In 2 Chronicles 30:16a, "according to the law of Moses" refers to the requirement that the recently restored cultic officials assume their duties ("they took their accustomed posts" [NRSV]). In 2 Chronicles 30:16b the separate roles for the *priests and Levites in the cult are stated ("the priests dashed the blood that they received from the hands of the Levites" [NRSV]). The measures of 2 Chronicles 30:16b are not attributed to the law, but merely designate how the requirements of the law in 2 Chronicles 30:16a were satisfied in the time of Hezekiah.

In 2 Chronicles 4:7 the Chronicler uses the form "according to their [the menorahs] ordinance" in such a way—that is, with a suffix—so as to avoid attributing the presence of ten menorahs in the sanctuary to the law.

> He made ten golden lampstands *according to their ordinance,* and set them in the temple, five on the south side and five on the north. (2 Chron 4:7)

In this way, the Chronicler represents conformity to the law to the greatest extent possible (cf. Ex 25; 27).

In the debate surrounding the identification of the referent of "as it is written in the Book of Moses" in Ezra 6:18, a minority view in the discussion (Haag, 396-97; Williamson 1988, 36 n. 2) is supported by the examination of citation formulas.

> Then they set the priests in their divisions and the Levites in their courses for *the service of God at Jerusalem,* as it is written in the book of Moses. (Ezra 6:18 NRSV)

The referent (italics) again is positioned beside the citation device, and thus it is distinguished from the steps taken by the postexilic community (underlined) to satisfy Deuteronomy 12:13-14. The most common alternative interpretation identifies the referent of this citation formula as the appointment of priests and Levites in their various divisions and courses, thereby attributing Ezra 6:18a to "the book of Moses" (e.g., Rudolph, 61; De Vries, 625 n. 22). Since David was viewed as the founder of these divisions (see 1 Chron 23—26), some scholars, based on this alternative interpretation of the citation formula, conclude that the law book of the writer of Ezra-Nehemiah is not the same as the Pentateuch of today (e.g., Houtman, 111; Shaver, 128). This latter interpretation, however, ignores the abutting phrase "the service of God at Jerusalem," an obvious implication of Deuteronomy 12 from the standpoint of the reconstruction era, as the referent of this citation formula (see also the syntax of comparative statements referred to above). Consequently, their characterization of the law book of this community is not established on firm ground. This debate is representative of how the disagreement on the identification of the referent invariably leads to divergent conclusions regarding the law book of this community or its interpretation.

Although they customarily employed positive examples, the postexilic historiographers also warned against the dangers of shoddy exegesis by using negative exegetical devices (e.g., 2 Chron 30:5, 18) or by attributing the undeveloped handling of Scripture ("according to the law" construed with "to do" [Ezra 10:3]; for pro-form see Spawn 2002, 68-69) to Shecaniah, who had just confessed to Ezra of having "broken faith with our God" (Ezra 10:2).

By concentrating citation formulas with legal topics in his final chapters (especially from Hezekiah onward), the Chronicler's History highlights the crucial role of the law in Israel. In Chronicles the further the golden age of the Davidic-Solomonic era recedes into the past, and the nearer Israel's history approaches the disaster of the sixth century BCE, the greater care the Chronicler takes to use these exegetical devices to indicate the proper relationship between Israel and the law. The way forward for his community includes the observance and interpretation of the law.

The postexilic historiographers use these citation devices to cultivate the observance and responsible handling of the law in their day. The impetus for the development of such exegetical tools in the reconstruction era appears to be the vindication of the law in the fall of Jerusalem and the experience of exile. Other issues are best treated in the context of some concluding remarks on all citation devices, to which we now turn.

4. Conclusion.
An examination of the references to sources in the OT indicates a development among citation formulas with legal topics that was not observable among citation devices used for other subject matters. This development concerns both the form and the function of exegetical devices from the reconstruction period and is concentrated in the Historical Books from this era. The development represented in the postexilic exegetical devices given above includes the following features: (1) the use of the abbreviated formula "as it is written," (2) the lack of compound constructions, (3) the consistent positioning of a citation device beside its referent, (4) the marking of two hermeneutical horizons, (5) the use of Hebrew syntax (*waw*-explicative, disjunctive clauses, a suffix) to distinguish these horizons or otherwise clarify the referent, and (6) the use of detailed referents (for a comprehensive summary see Spawn 2002, 241-58).

As we have seen, this study touches upon persistently debated issues connected with Israel's law. The postexilic historiographers were skilled exegetes who were cultivating the observance and responsible interpretation of the law in their communities. Regarding the disputed contents of the law book of the reconstruction era, every regulation attributed to the law of this community is contained in the Pentateuch of today or is otherwise an obvious implication of its contents. Thus there is no need to view the law book of the postexilic community as different from the Pentateuch of today based on the references to the sources noted above.

See also HISTORIOGRAPHY, OLD TESTAMENT; INNERBIBLICAL EXEGESIS; ORAL TRADITION AND WRITTEN TRADITION.

BIBLIOGRAPHY. **D. J. A. Clines,** "Nehemiah 10 as an Example of Early Jewish Biblical Exegesis," *JSOT* 21 (1981) 111-17; **S. J. De Vries,** "Moses and David as Cult Founders in Chronicles," *JBL* 107 (1988) 610-39; **H. Donner,** "'Wie geschrieben steht': Herkunft und Sinn einer Formel," in *Aufsätze zum Alten Testament aus vier Jahrzehnten* (BZAW 224; Berlin: de Gruyter, 1994) 224-38; **M. Fishbane,** *Biblical Interpretation in Ancient Israel* (Oxford: Clarendon Press, 1985); idem, "Inner-Biblical Exegesis," in *Hebrew Bible, Old Testament: The History of Its Interpretation*, 1: *From the Beginnings to the Middle Ages (Until 1300); Part 1: Antiquity,* ed. M. Saebø (Göttingen: Vandenhoeck & Ruprecht, 1996) 33-48; **H. Haag,** "כתב," *TWAT* 4.385-97 [= *TDOT* 7.371-82]; **C. Houtman,** "Ezra and the Law: Observations on the Supposed Relation between Ezra and the Pentateuch," *OTS* 21 (1981) 91-115; **S. Japhet,** *I & II Chronicles* (OTL; Louisville: Westminster/John Knox, 1993); **G. Khan,** *Studies in Semitic Syntax* (London Oriental Series 38; Oxford: Oxford University Press, 1988); **W. Rudolph,** *Esra und Nehemia* (HAT; Tübingen: Mohr, 1949); **W. M. Schniedewind,** "The Source Citations of Manasseh: King Manasseh in History and Homily," *VT* 41 (1991) 450-61; **J. R. Shaver,** *Torah and the Chronicler's History Work: An Inquiry into the Chronicler's References to Laws, Festivals, and Cultic Institutions in Relationship to Pentateuchal Legislation* (BJS 196; Atlanta: Scholars Press, 1989); **K. L. Spawn,** *"As It Is Written" and Other Citation Formulae in the Old Testament: Their Use, Development, Syntax, and Significance* (BZAW 311; Berlin: de Gruyter, 2002); **C. C. Torrey,** *Ezra Studies* (Chicago: Chicago University Press, 1910); **H. G. M. Williamson,** *1 and 2 Chronicles* (NCB; London: Marshall, Morgan & Scott, 1982); idem, *Ezra, Nehemiah* (WBC 16; Waco, TX: Word, 1985); idem, "History," in *It Is Written: Scripture Citing Scripture,* ed. D. A. Carson and H. G. M. Williamson (Cambridge: Cambridge University Press, 1988) 25-38. K. L. Spawn

STATE OFFICIALS
Regardless of the territorial size of the kingdom, the stability of a king's throne depended on the efficiency and loyalty of his circle of officials and functionaries (civil, military, religious). The purpose of this article is to examine the bureaucratic organization of the Israelite monarchies based on extant sources, primarily the Historical Books of the Hebrew Bible and the epigraphical material from archaeological excavations. Al-

though the corpus of evidence on Israelite officialdom is generally fragmentary, the study of official titles and their ancient Near Eastern analogues helps to reconstruct a tentative picture of the Israelite bureaucracy and its operation. In addition, sociological studies on state formation in antiquity clarify the process that *Israelite society underwent as it evolved over time into a complex stratified system headed by a king(s)—first as a kingdom of politically unified clans, and later as two separate political entities: Israel in the north and Judah in the south.

1. Methods for Reconstructing Israelite Officialdom
2. The Royal Ministers at Court
3. The Municipal Administration
4. Foreign Influence on the Israelite State Organization

1. Methods for Reconstructing Israelite Officialdom.

1.1. Biblical Sources. The historical reliability of biblical sources presents a constant challenge to scholars attempting to reconstruct aspects of Israelite history. A reconstruction of the Israelite administrative organization, including the monarchy and its state officials, also relies heavily on data gleaned from biblical texts (to some extent these are supplemented by epigraphical material from archaeological excavations). Although most scholars accept information on the Israelite bureaucracy from the books of *Samuel and *Kings as generally historical (with additional material from Isaiah, Jeremiah, Ezekiel and Amos), many of these same scholars deem data from the books of *Chronicles to be untrustworthy. The latter is usually dismissed as tendentious and chronologically too far removed from the events of the First Temple period. Yet despite these problems, the Chronistic writings contain material not found in the Deuteronomistic records that seems credible, especially since data on officialdom and the state organization rarely conceal ideological motives. Furthermore, since all of the books of the Bible express the ideologies and agendas of their writers, each one needs to be evaluated for its historical accuracy. A text's historicity may also be evaluated based on its genre. For example, lists of royal officials (e.g., 2 Sam 8:16-18; 20:23-26; 1 Kings 4:1-19) seem to derive from royal archives. References to annal-type documents—the "Book of the Chronicles of the Kings of Israel" (1 Kings 14:19 and seventeen other references), the "Book

of the Chronicles of the Kings of Judah" (1 Kings 14:29 and fourteen other references), the "Book of the Acts of Solomon" (1 Kings 11:41)—suggest access to original sources. In contrast, certain narratives that allegedly recount historical events clearly depict idealizations of reality, such as the extensive territory of the Davidic-Solomonic empire (e.g., 1 Kings 4:21) or Solomon's widespread fame (e.g., 1 Kings 4:29-34). Unfortunately, aside from the lists of monarchic officials for the united kingdom, much of the biblical data on state officials are extremely fragmentary, and their context often fails to elucidate the functions of the officials mentioned.

1.2. Ancient Near Eastern Sources. Since the discovery and decipherment in the nineteenth century of cuneiform texts from Mesopotamia and hieroglyphic texts from Egypt, scholars have enthusiastically utilized these sources to understand Israelite culture in its ancient Near Eastern context. This method, known as the comparative approach, relies on the assumption that various cultural parallels existed between the Near Eastern cultures and ancient Israel. Needless to say, conclusions drawn from comparisons between the biblical material and the vast collections of extrabiblical data have led to some hasty conclusions regarding similarities between Israel and its neighbors in the area of literature, law, ritual and sociopolitical organization. For decades, direct borrowing was presumed for components of Israelite administration as well. R. de Vaux and T. N. D. Mettinger, for example, posited that Israelite officialdom was modeled heavily after the Egyptian system, as evidenced by comparable offices and titles of several ministers of state. More recent works caution against assumptions of borrowing, arguing rather for phenomenological analogies (Fox; Layton). Since Israel and Judah were organized under a monarchical system, their bureaucratic organization resembled those of other monarchies in the region, albeit on a smaller scale. Nevertheless, comparative sources from Egypt, Mesopotamia and the Levantine states are essential in studies on Israelite officialdom to elucidate the fragmentary material on the subject in biblical texts and *Hebrew inscriptions.

1.3. Archaeological Evidence. Archaeological excavations in the Levant, in particular in Israel and Jordan, have yielded numerous finds inscribed with paleo-Hebrew script. This epigraphical corpus, dating from the ninth to early sixth centuries BCE, consists primarily of seals, seal impressions (bullae and jar handles), ostraca (inscribed pottery sherds) and marked weights. A few monumental inscriptions, such as the Siloam Tunnel inscription, the Tel Dan stela, and the Mesha stela, have also been recovered. Seals, bullae, inscribed jars and ostraca often are connected to bureaucratic practices in the Israelite kingdoms and those of Transjordan (*Ammon, *Moab, *Edom), as many officials and other functionaries in central and regional administrations possessed seals incised with their name and/or title. Ostraca, which functioned as ancient scrap paper, were used to write short notes—for example, receipts for provisions and orders for their distribution at military outposts. Thus, the epigraphical material, no matter how brief the text, is extremely useful in the reconstruction of Israelite officialdom and the state organization. Yet scholars must exercise caution in drawing conclusions based on these finds. One difficulty is associating names found in inscriptions with persons named in biblical texts. Criteria for such associations must be based on more data than simply a single name and an approximate date for the object. Additional useful information includes a title and/or patronymic. A more serious obstacle to utilizing epigraphical finds is that a large percentage derives from the antiquities market rather than controlled archaeological excavations. Those items from illicit excavations lack provenance and, consequently, exact dating. Many others are believed to be forgeries. In recent decades forgeries have become so sophisticated that objects from the antiquities market often cannot be authenticated. Any conclusions drawn from this material must remain tentative until methods for authentication are perfected (Fox, 23-42).

2. The Royal Ministers at Court.

Officials of varying status, including high-ranking ministers, were essential components of the Israelite states. The majority of Hebrew official titles are found in the OT Historical Books, especially Samuel, Kings and Chronicles (a few appear in the Torah and the Prophets). Most titles, comparable to those of other ancient Near Eastern states, belong to the period of the Israelite monarchies—the unified kingdom of Israel (tenth century BCE) and the divided kingdoms of

Israel (late tenth to late eighth centuries BCE) and Judah (late tenth to early sixth century BCE).

2.1. The Development of a Bureaucracy in Israel. The process of state formation in Israel beginning in the latter half of the eleventh century BCE inaugurated a bureaucratic system initially headed by a chief or petty king. *Saul, the first so-called *melek* ("king") of Israel, appointed family members to positions of power, especially as military leaders (see 2.3 below). A more sophisticated administrative apparatus was put in place by *David when he moved his court from *Hebron to *Jerusalem, the capital named for him: *ʿir dāwīd* ("city of David"). Solomon's list of officials shows further expansion based on a more complex centralized governmental system. The term *śārîm*, used in the Solomonic list to introduce the hierarchy of appointees (1 Kings 4:2), refers to civil, military and religious personnel (often the term denotes only military positions). Individual titles in the list further define specific positions.

Biblical evidence indicates that families of officials are attested for the united kingdom as well as the divided kingdom. Certain professions, in particular those of scribe and priest, seem to have been hereditary due to the nature of the office. Others were distributed among the members of several elite families. According to a recent study, in *Samaria, and probably in Jerusalem as well, these families of officials, along with the royal family, controlled the means of production: the laborers (Jaruzelska, 160-96). Scholars generally adduce familial relationships of officials based on the same patronymic, as in the case of Azariah and Zabud, the former being King Solomon's minister over the prefects and the latter being the "king's friend," who are sons of Nathan (1 Kings 4:5). In this case, as in others, it is uncertain, however, whether the same patronymic necessarily refers to one person or to two unrelated individuals (two Nathans). More secure data are available in connection with several prominent court families in Judah in the reigns of *Josiah, Jehoiakim and Zedekiah. Names of royal officials that predominate from the mid-seventh to early sixth centuries BCE belong to the families of Shaphan, Neriah, Hilkiah and Achbor. In a number of cases, their patronymics include a grandfather's name, implying that they descended from a long line of dignitaries (2 Kings 22:3; 25:22; Jer 32:12; 36:11; 51:59). Scholars usually assume that since the circle of Israelite officials was relatively small, a name plus a patronymic is sufficient to verify a person's identity if the chronology corresponds. Many of these families of officials resided at court, and their children, future royal functionaries, grew up with royal princes (*yĕlādîm* [1 Kings 12]). Similar customs are attested from Egyptian and Mesopotamian royal courts; the assumption was that sons of officials raised with the princes would become loyal ministers of the future king.

2.2. Civil Officials and Courtiers of the Early Monarchy. The Bible first mentions civil officials in connection with the reign of David (for military, judicial and religious appointees see 2.3 and 2.4 below). Saul's officials are simply designated by a generic title, *ʿăbādîm* ("servants"), which does not identify their function, although apparently they comprised the king's entourage. Specific officials of Saul and his son Ishbosheth included only military officers and a priest. In contrast, David installed a number of civil officials and courtiers at his court in Jerusalem. 2 Samuel lists four civil officials by name and title: *mazkîr* ("herald"), Jehoshaphat son of Ahilud (2 Sam 8:16); *sôpēr* ("scribe"), Seraiah (2 Sam 8:17); *yôʿēṣ hammelek* ("royal advisor"), Ahitophel the Gilonite (2 Sam 15:12); and *ʿal ham mas* ("overseer of corvée"), Adoram son of Abda (2 Sam 20:24). The appointment of these officials indicates that David used bureaucrats (unrelated to him) in his kingdom for various tasks: to assemble the populace and issue royal proclamations, to keep records, to advise him on policies and other matters, and to organize and enforce corvée labor obligations—a form of *taxation widely practiced in the Syro-Palestinian world. Scholars are basically in agreement on the definitions of most official titles, but a few are still debated. For example, some scholars define *mazkîr* as "recorder" or "archivist," while others, who assume that the roles of recording were subsumed in the position of the scribe, define *mazkîr* as "herald." The latter interpretation is more convincing for several reasons, in particular because a designation for "herald" is attested in most ancient Near Eastern bureaucracies (Akkadian *nāgiru;* Egyptian *whmw;* Ugaritic *yṣḥ*). Additional titles of courtiers in the Chronicler's lengthy list of David's men include a tutor for the royal princes, Jehiel son of Hachmoni (1 Chron 27:32), and a *rēʿeh hammelek* ("companion" of the king), Hushite the Archite (1 Chron 27:33). The role of the latter is understood as "companion," based on etymology and narrative depictions in which this courtier acts as a confidant of the king. The title *rēʿeh* appears again in the Solomonic list of royal appointees (1 Kings 4:5; cf. Gen 26:26); similar titles are attested from the Egyptian (*rḥ nswt*), Babylonian and Assyrian courts (*ibru*). The Chronicler also lists twelve stewards in charge over the treasuries of the royal estates; their laborers; and the vineyards, orchards, cattle, camels, asses and flocks of the king (1 Chron 27:25-31). Some scholars question the antiquity of the Chronicler's list, claiming that it is a much later retrojection into the tenth century BCE; others, however, consider it authentic, especially in light of the steward's personal names, which were common in the preexilic period (Japhet, 478).

The biblical list of officials from Solomon's reign reflects an expanded bureaucratic organization for both the central government and the regional administration (1 Kings 4:2-19). Solomon added a second scribe to his cabinet: Elihoreph and Ahijah, the sons of his father's scribe Shisha (1 Kings 4:3). He also appointed an *ʿal habbayit* (royal house minister), Ahishar (1 Kings 4:6). The exact nature of the latter's position is still debated by scholars who question whether this minister's purview encompassed the palace complex alone or extended over royal estates statewide. Biblical texts situate the home office of the royal house minister in capital cities, yet it is likely that his authority extended to royal property elsewhere in a supervisory capacity. It must be realized that in Israel, as in other Near Eastern kingdoms, the jurisdiction of officials could cross administrative divisions. Titles semantically related to *ʾăšer ʿal habbayit* are attested in Ugaritic (*ʿl bt*), Akkadian (*ša muḫḫi ekalli; rab ekalli*) and Egyptian (*mr pr wr*). Solomon also appointed an *ʿal hannīṣṣābîm* ("chief prefect") and twelve district prefects to administer his newly organized twelve-district kingdom. The chief prefect oversaw the twelve regional prefects, who were charged with taxation responsibilities in their respective districts (see 3.1 below).

2.3. Military and Judicial Officers of the Early Monarchy. Titles of military officers are of the earliest attested in the biblical record. Apparently, every political structure, no matter how simply organized, required military leaders to secure it. The so-called *judges in the premonarchical period functioned as generals or ruled jointly with them, as in the case of Deborah and Barak (Judg 4). Saul, the first anointed king of Israel, relied heavily on his military officers: his uncle Abner son of Ner, *śar haṣṣābāʾ* ("army commander" [1 Sam 14:50]); Doeg the Edomite, *ʾabbîr hārōʿîm* ("strongman" [1 Sam 21:8]); and later David as *śar-ʾālep* ("chief of thousands" [1 Sam 18:13]). Likewise, when David ascended the throne, he appointed his nephew Joab, the son of his sister Zeruiah, as army commander. Loyalty was of utmost importance for the army commander, and often relatives were trusted more than nonrelations. Other military officers are mentioned in conjunction with David's reign: Benaiah son of Jehoiada, commander of the Cherethite and Pelethite mercenary forces (2 Sam 8:18); and Abishai, *rōš haššelōšîm* ("commander of troops of thirty"), another nephew (2 Sam 23:18-19). Solomon later promoted Benaiah to army commander (1 Kings 4:4), after assassinating Joab for supporting his rival to the throne, his brother Adoniah. Other chief officers are listed in Chronicles according to military clans and divisions (1 Chron 27:2-22).

The judicial system in Israel traditionally was within the purview of local elders (*see DOTP,* Leadership, Elders). According to Deuteronomy, Moses chose *šōpĕṭîm* ("judges") from among his officers (Deut 1:15-16; 16:19-20). Judges were stationed at city gates, the meeting and market places of fortified settlements. Biblical evidence is unclear as to when and where judges became appointees of the central government. David is one of only two kings whom the Bible credits with appointing judges (that datum derives from a tendentious note of the Chronicler stating that David selected six thousand officers and justices from Levitical families [1 Chron 23:4; 26:29]). In reality, the king was chief justice of the land, and as such, he was obligated to provide additional judges to hear cases. In fact, when David's son Absalom petitioned the populace to follow him in rebellion against his father, he promised to hear the people's legal pleas, a task that David apparently ignored (2 Sam 15:3-4). Based on judicial practices of Israel's neighbors, it seems that the legal system was jointly in the hands of government judges and local elders.

2.4. Religious Functionaries of the Early Monarchy. According to the Bible, *priests played key roles in the life of the Israelites from premonarchical times. Before the formation of the monarchy, with its hierarchical organization, a powerful leader could exercise multiple functions, including that of cult officiant. *Samuel, for example, served as military commander, judge, prophet and priest. When he anointed Saul as king, he retained his role as priest, although Saul also kept a descendant of the house of Eli as his *kōhēn* ("priest"): Ahijah son of Ahitub (1 Sam 14:3). Three priests are named in conjunction with David's reign; two of them are associated with important but competing priestly families: Abiathar son of Ahimelek, David's pre-Jerusalem priest, and *Zadok son of Ahitub (perhaps a brother of Ahijah, Saul's priest), the prominent priest of David's Jerusalem-based monarchy. Zadok, Abiathar, and the third, Ira the Jairite (a non-Levite), are mentioned in a list of David's officials (2 Sam 20:23-26). Priestly roles consisted of all cult-related matters, including determining auspicious times for battle (e.g., Abiathar [1 Sam 30:7]). The Chronicler, whose ideology dictates that all priests must descend from the tribe of Levi, altered a record in Samuel that lists David's sons as priests (cf. 2 Sam 8:18; 1 Chron 18:17); he also added various Levite functionaries to David's staff (1 Chron 15:5-10, 22; 26:29-32). When Solomon became king, he retained Zadok and his descendants as priests but banished Abiathar and his house for backing the bid of his brother Adonijah for the throne. Especially in the monarchical period it is evident that priests, like military officers, were the extended arms of the central government serving at the Jerusalem temple and at other cult sites. The distribution and location of shrines at administrative centers, even in small fortresses (e.g., *Arad in the Negev), suggests close ties between civil, military and religious personnel. According to G. W. Åhlström (44-74), these agents of the monarchy were stationed at *Levitical cities.

2.5. Civil Officials in Israel and Judah. The Bible does not preserve lists of officials for either Israel or Judah after the dissolution of Solomon's kingdom (c. 925 BCE). For the period of the divided kingdom, biblical data on state officials are attested only within the context of narratives. Not surprisingly, many of the titles known from the Davidic and Solomonic lists of officials reappear. Importantly, archaeological evidence from the lands of Israel and Transjordan in the form of stamp seals, bullae, ostraca and a few short lapidary inscriptions (spanning the eighth to sixth centuries BCE) confirms the use of these titles for the period in question. The composition of the bureaucracy of the kingdoms of Israel and Judah appears similar to that of the Davidic-Solomonic era, but the hierarchical organization indicates certain shifts. Generally, delineating a hierarchy within the civil administration is problematic due to a lack of explicit evidence in either the biblical or the epigraphical material. Nevertheless, fragmentary data consisting of groups of three or more officials mentioned together in a certain order point to the position of the *ʾăšer ʿal habbayit* (*nĕgîd habbayit* in Chronicles) as the highest office (no evidence exists for a vizier-like Israelite minister). This minister is always attested in biblical accounts in connection with the king or a capital city (e.g., 1 Kings 16:9; 18:5; 2 Kings 18:18). Centered in the palace complex of the capital, the jurisdiction of the royal house minister probably extended to royal property statewide, although those estates would have been managed by subordinate local officials. In Judah, at least, this minister's realm also encompassed diplomatic missions (e.g., Eliakim [2 Kings 18—19]). A second top-level official was the *sôpēr hammelek* ("court scribe"), who is to be differentiated from other scribes who operated in the temple, military and municipal administrations. This scribe no doubt handled the royal correspondence in addition to overseeing (and carrying out) basic accounting and record-keeping tasks essential to every administration. The Bible actually mentions other functions of the scribe, such as control over the temple treasury (2 Kings 12:11) and diplomatic missions (Shebna [2 Kings 18-19]). Both the titles *ʾăšer ʿal habbayit* and *sôpēr* are attested on seals and seal impressions of the eighth to seventh centuries BCE. A third high-level official was the *mazkîr* ("herald"). Although the Bible mentions this title only in conjunction with the kingdom of Judah, it is highly probable that the office existed in Israel as well. Biblical texts record the *mazkîr*'s functions in a military-diplomatic capacity (Joah son of Asaph [2 Kings 18—19]) and secondarily as a financial officer (Joah son of Joahaz [2 Chron 34:8-13]). The herald consistently appears side by side with the scribe in accounts of specific events, implying that the two worked closely together, the former as spokesperson for the king, and the latter as recorder. Although the title *mazkîr* is as yet unattested in epigraphical sources from Israel, a Moabite seal with that title is extant. Another high-ranking officer, known from the united monar-

chy, *ʿal hammas* ("chief of corvée"), is unattested for Israel and Judah after the schism. Northerners, who revolted during the reign of Solomon's son *Rehoboam, murdered the king's corvée minister Adoram (1 Kings 12:18), who served under David and Solomon. It is highly doubtful, however, that this key office and its functions ceased to exist; in fact, tax obligations in the form of labor are known from several Judean records (2 Kings 15:20; Jer 22:13; the letter from Mesad Hashavyahu), and generally they were common in the region. Other titles attested for the Davidic-Solomonic period that disappear from the biblical record include *yôʿēṣ hammelek* ("royal advisor"), *rēʿeh hammelek* ("king's companion"), and *ʿal hanniṣṣābîm* and *niṣṣābîm* ("chief prefect" and "prefects"). Some of the roles of this last group may have dissolved with the fall of the unified monarchy, although de Vaux (210) suggests that the positions of the *śārê hammĕdînôt* ("district officers") in Israel were comparable to those of the *niṣṣābîm* (1 Kings 20:14-20). Of the other offices, that of royal advisor probably also continued in one form or another. A title that appears in Israel but not in Judah is *mišnēh hammelek* (2 Chron 28:7). Although defined as "second to the king," based on the root *šny*, this office holder seems to have been a minor official, but one considered a trusted courtier and perhaps a personal escort of the king (cf. Jonathan vis-à-vis David [1 Sam 23:17]). Three other titles belong to household functionaries who served in the palace complex: *sārîs*, *sōkēn* and *naʿar*. The *sārîs*, whose title translates as "eunuch," functioned primarily as a palace attendant for various members of the royal family. Possibly, these attendants were foreign eunuchs imported to serve in the inner palace. Similar roles can be attributed to the *sōkenet* (a female attendant [1 Kings 1:2]). The use of the masculine form of that title, *sōkēn* (Is 22:15), may reflect Isaiah's deprecation of the title bearer who held the high office of *ʾăšer ʿal habbayit* (the wide range of usage for the term *sōkēn* in Semitic cultures leaves the issue unresolved). The designation *naʿar* (fem., *naʿărāh*) also encompassed a range of positions, from handmaiden and squire to steward of a royal estate (Ziba [2 Sam 9:9-11]; *Eliakim naʿar Yokin* on a *lmlk* jar-handle seal impression).

In addition to function-related titles, four titles denote status relationships either ascribed to individuals by virtue of genealogy or acquired through membership in a special court circle. The two most widely attested, both in biblical and epigraphical records, are *bēn hammelek* ("son of the king") and *ʿebed hammelek* ("servant of the king"). The first, *bēn hammelek*, is an epithet reserved for members of the royal family, either a son or close relative of the king. Seals incised with this title as well as biblical personages so entitled suggest that Israelite princes, like those of Egypt and Mesopotamia, regularly served in the state administration (2 Chron 28:7; Jer 36:26). Some office holders with function-related titles seem to have belonged to this category too. A few scholars maintain that the title *bēn hammelek* was also honorific, thereby bestowed on nonroyalty. Not a single case exists, however, that identifies an Israelite commoner as a *bēn* [or *bat*] *hammelek*. The second status-related title, *ʿebed hammelek*, is a generic designation for any royal minister regardless of the particular office. Thus all the king's men—those of highest rank to lowest status—were labeled *ʿăbādîm* ("servants") vis-à-vis the ruler. The title *ʿebed hammelek* or *ʿebed RN* (a specific royal name), found in biblical accounts and on seals, was no doubt borne by high officials of the king. Two other status-related titles are *zĕqēnîm* ("elders") and *yĕlādîm* ("children"), the latter appearing only opposite the former. Besides denoting the traditional clan elders, *zĕqēnîm* also signifies senior ranking within the bureaucracy. Like *ʿebed*, the designation *zĕqēnîm* (always plural) is not role specific; rather, it refers to a group of senior palace functionaries, such as the group that Rehoboam consulted (1 Kings 12). The term *yĕlādîm* in the latter narrative may be a technical term for junior functionaries of the king, although in that case used pejoratively. The Bible specifies that as children, these officials were raised in the palace household with Rehoboam, then a young prince (a comparable epithet, *ḥrd n kȝp*, is attested from the pharaonic court).

2.6. Military and Judicial Officials in Israel and Judah.

Military leaders continued to play key roles in the kingdoms of Israel and Judah after the division of the monarchy. Names of officers of varying status are mentioned in the biblical text, especially by the Chronicler: army commanders (*śar ṣābāʾ* [1 Kings 16:16]), chariot commanders (*śar maḥăṣît hārekeb* [1 Kings 16:9]) and commanders of divisions of thousands and divisions of hundreds (2 Chron 17:14-18; 23:1).

An army scribe is mentioned by name (Jeiel [2 Chron 26:11]); others no doubt filled this key post. Two officers entitled *šālîš* (third man on the chariot, the armor bearer) are named in the context of historical narratives (2 Kings 9:25; 15:25). Several military officers from Israel are notorious as usurpers of the throne. Omri, a *śar ṣābāʾ* (early ninth century BCE), overthrew King Ela (1 Kings 16:16). Zimri, commander of half the chariotry, was a challenger of Omri whose coup failed (1 Kings 16:9). Pekah, another *šālîš*, overthrew King Pekahiah (latter eighth century BCE [2 Kings 15:25]). Many officers served as regional commanders (see 3.1 below). The title *naʿar*, mentioned with civil officials, also appears in military contexts where it refers to squire, runner (pl., *rāṣîm*) or armor bearer (*nōśēh kēlîm*) of an army officer (the *rāṣîm* often were members of the royal guard [1 Kings 14:27-28; 2 Kings 10:25]).

Only the Chronicler provides additional information about judicial officials in the period of the divided kingdom. According to 2 Chronicles 19:5-11, King *Jehoshaphat assigned judges to the cities of his kingdom and established a high court in Jerusalem composed of lay judges and priests to deal with difficult cases. Such a move would have placed the high court under the watchful eye of the monarchy and, in particular, the king as chief justice (e.g., Jotham [2 Kings 15:5]). Most cases, however, were tried by local judicial systems (see 3.1 below).

2.7. Religious Functionaries in Israel and Judah.

The influential role of priests continued during the divided monarchy. The Chronicler's record indicates that King Jehoshaphat appointed priests and Levites to serve on the high court in Jerusalem under the leadership of the high priest Amariah (2 Chron 19:11). Other high priests are mentioned in conjunction with the acts of specific kings (e.g., 2 Chron 26:20; 31:10; 2 Kings 22:3-14; 25:18). It seems that the power of individual priests and their influence at court depended on circumstances of the time. Most notable is the (high?) priest Jehoiada, who was instrumental in deposing the non-Davidide Athaliah from the throne of Judah, anointing the child-king Joash in her place, and subsequently instituting cult reforms in the temple (2 Kings 11—12). Athaliah, a worshiper of Canaanite deities, had installed a priest of Baal in Jerusalem (Mattan [2 Kings 11:18]). Two centuries later, in the reign of the reforming king Josiah, the high priest Hilkiah also conducted major cult alterations in the temple (2 Kings 23:4). At the time the northern kingdom was established in Israel, *Jeroboam I instituted the practice of appointing non-Levitical priests. Amaziah, the priest at the Bethel shrine during the ministry of Amos, was such a royal appointee (of Jeroboam II). In Judah (according to the Deuteronomistic historian), legitimate priests continued to be descendants of the house of Zadok.

3. The Municipal Administration.

3.1. Civil, Judicial and Military Officials. Municipal administrators also were part of the state organization. The highest city official was the *śar hāʿîr* (or *ʾăšer ʿal hāʿîr*), the governor, whose jurisdiction extended to the regions surrounding the city (cf. the twelve district prefects of Solomon's reign). The title *śar hāʿîr* is attached to governors of Samaria and Jerusalem, the capitals of Israel and Judah, but lesser urban centers and small fortresses were governed by this class of official as well. For example, a *śar* administered the fortress of Mesad Hashavyahu, and the fortress of Arad was governed by an officer named Eliashib, although his title is unattested in the Arad correspondence. It is unclear whether the latter two officials belonged to the category of civil or military; possibly these divisions overlapped in smaller settlements. Examples of princes appointed as municipal officials outside the capital are known from the reign of Jehoshaphat (2 Chron 21:1-3). Clearly, governors of royal descent were commissioned by the crown, but whether all such officials were directly appointed by the king is uncertain. The roles of these officials varied. Amon, the governor of Samaria in the reign of Ahab, was charged with the incarceration of dissidents (1 Kings 22:26); Maaseiah, the *śar* of Jerusalem under King Josiah, administered the funds for the temple's repairs (2 Chron 34:8). A number of ostraca from Arad indicate that Eliashib controlled the distribution of the fort's provisions. The letter from Mesad Hashavyahu designates the *śar* as magistrate; his role as judge fits the theory that government-appointed judges operated statewide; often they cooperated with the local elders in the legal process. The titles of two lesser local officials attested in the Bible include *šōʿărîm* ("gatekeepers"), guards and messengers stationed at city gates (2 Sam 18:26; 2 Kings 7:10-11), and *šōṭrîm,* policing agents (possibly record keepers if the title is defined based on etymology: Akk *štr* [2 Chron 26:11]). The ever growing corpus of epigraphical finds (seals, seal impressions and ostraca) with personal names but lacking official titles suggests that many more administrators belonged to local government than can be identified with certainty (e.g., Samaria Ostraca; *lmlk* impressed handles; City of David archive [see Fox, 204-49]).

3.2. The Central Authority and the Periphery. Information about the network that connected the central authority to local governments is available mainly from the kingdom of Judah for the late eighth-seventh centuries BCE, albeit in bits and pieces. Administrative records from cities and towns removed from the seat of the monarchy in Jerusalem, such as *Lachish, *Beersheba, Arad and Mesad Hashavyahu, have been recovered in archaeological excavations at those sites. Large storage jars marked with *lmlk* and rosette impressions, symbols of the crown, reflect the intricate network established by certain kings (e.g., *Hezekiah and *Josiah) for the distribution of goods. Personal names impressed on a percentage of the *lmlk* jars may reflect a system of compensation for state officials during their tenure of office (cf. the Samaria Ostraca, which probably record products sent from lands granted by the king to officials at court).

4. Foreign Influence on the Israelite State Organization.

Recent studies on Israelite state officials have questioned earlier assumptions that the Israelite monarchies and their bureaucracies were modeled after those of neighboring states. The infrequent occurrence of unquestionably foreign terms *(sōkēn and sārîs)* and features in the Israelite state organization preclude tracing it to any single foreign prototype or even a combination of prototypes. Evidence pointing to foreign inspiration, whether Egyptian, Canaanite or Mesopotamian, needs to be viewed in its proper perspective. For example, the use of Egyptian hieratic numerals and other symbols in Hebrew administrative documents and the resemblance of certain Egyptian official titles to Israelite ones (e.g., Heb *yĕlādîm* and Egyp *ḥrd n k3p*) can be attributed to indirect transmission mediated via local Canaanite institutions that were influenced by Egypt hundreds of years before the formation of any Israelite state (note especially the corvée system and its overseers). Most official positions in the Israelite bureaucracies are endemic to a monarchical system of the period and would have developed in Israel independently as the monarchy evolved into a more complex administrative organization. For example, the high office of the ʾ*ăšer ʿal habbayit*, the royal house minister, is attested in Egyptian, Levantine and Mesopotamian bureaucracies. In each case, linguistically, the title is nearly an exact translation of the Hebrew title. Clearly, the main purview of this important minister was similar. In contrast, the title *mazkîr* ("herald") shows semantic distinctions in Akkadian, Ugaritic, Egyptian and Hebrew, which may be the result of independent development with somewhat different emphases on the functions of the office. Notably, a number of Israelite official titles have Moabite, Ammonite and Edomite analogues (Fox, table B). It seems that the Transjordanian states had monarchical systems in the ninth to sixth centuries BCE similar to those of Israel and Judah. Yet despite these similarities, it is important to account for distinctions in individual systems and even for variations during the reigns of different kings. Although the titles of the ministers of state generally were stable, individual personalities of office holders and historical circumstances influenced the extent of their power and the range of their responsibilities.

See also KINGS AND KINGSHIP; ROYAL FAMILY; SCRIBES AND SCHOOLS.

BIBLIOGRAPHY. **G. W. Åhlström,** *Royal Administration and National Religion in Ancient Palestine* (SHANE 1; Leiden: E. J. Brill, 1982); **N. Avigad and B. Sass,** *Corpus of West Semitic Stamp Seals* (Jerusalem: Israel Academy of Sciences and Humanities; Israel Exploration Society; Hebrew University of Jerusalem Institute of Archaeology, 1997); **Y. Avishur and M. Heltzer,** *Studies on the Royal Administration in Ancient Israel in Light of Epigraphic Sources* (Tel Aviv-Jaffa: Archaeological Center Publication, 2000); **M. Cogan,** *I Kings* (AB 10; New York: Doubleday, 2001); **M. Cogan and H. Tadmor,** *II Kings* (AB 11; Garden City, NY: Doubleday, 1988); **I. Finkelstein,** "The Emergence of the Monarchy in Israel: The Environmental and Socio-Economic Aspects," *JSOT* 44 (1989) 43-74; **N. S. Fox,** *In the Service of the King: Officialdom in Ancient Israel and Judah* (Cincinnati: Hebrew Union College Press, 2000); **F. S. Frick,** *The Formation of the State in Ancient Israel: A Survey of Models and Theories* (SWBA 4; Sheffield: Almond, 1985); **M. Heltzer,** *The Internal Organization of the Kingdom of Ugarit: Royal Service-System, Taxes, Royal Economy, Army, and Administration* (Wiesbaden: Reichart, 1982); **S. Japhet,** *I & II Chronicles* (OTL; Louisville: Westminster/John Knox, 1993); **I. Jaruzelska,** *Amos and the Officialdom in the Kingdom of Israel: The Socio-Economic Position of the Officials in the Light of the Biblical, Epigraphic and Archaeological Evidence* (Seria Socjologia 25; Poznań: Adam Mickiewicz University, 1998); **S. C. Layton,** "The Steward in Ancient Israel: A Study of Hebrew (ʾ*šer) ʿl habbāyit* in Its Near Eastern Setting," *JBL* 109 (1990) 633-49; **P. K. McCarter Jr.,** *I Samuel* (AB 8; Garden City, NY: Doubleday, 1980); idem, *II Samuel* (AB9; Garden City, NY: Doubleday, 1984); **P. McNutt,** *Reconstructing the Society of Ancient Israel* (LAI; Louisville: Westminster/John Knox, 1999); **T. N. D. Mettinger,** *Solomonic State Officials: A Study of the Civil Government Officials of the Israelite Monarchy* (ConBOT 5; Lund: Gleerup, 1971); **J. Pécirková,** "The Administrative Organization of the Neo-Assyrian Empire," *ArOr* 45 (1977) 211-28; **D. Redford,** *Egypt, Canaan, and Israel in Ancient Times* (Princeton, NJ: Princeton University Press, 1992); **H. Reviv,** *The Society in the Kingdoms of Israel and Judah* [in Hebrew] (Jerusalem: Bialik Institute, 1993); **U. Rüterswörden,** *Die Beamten der israelitischen Königszeit: Eine Studie zu śr und vergleichbaren Begriffen* (BWANT 117; Stuttgart: Kohlhammer, 1985); **R. de Vaux,** *Ancient Israel,* 1: *Social Institutions* (New York: McGraw-Hill, 1961).

N. S. Fox

STRUCTURALISM. *See* METHODS OF INTERPRETATION.

SUSA. *See* NEHEMIAH.

SYNCHRONISTIC HISTORY. *See* NON-ISRAELITE WRITTEN SOURCES: ASSYRIAN.

SYRIA. See ARAM, DAMASCUS AND SYRIA.

SYRO-EPHRAIMITIC WAR. *See* HISTORY OF ISRAEL 5: ASSYRIAN PERIOD.

T, U, V

TARGUMS. *See* TEXT AND TEXTUAL CRITICISM.

TATENAI. *See* HISTORY OF ISRAEL 7: PERSIAN PERIOD.

TAXES, TAXATION

Taxes may be defined as that which is due to a state authority under a quota or recognized contract. Taxation describes the system used to satisfy this requirement. Taxes are a form of debt that is owed and to be paid at stipulated times. In the ancient world the "creditor" for this "debt" would be the royal house and the administration it represented. However, throughout history intermediaries have functioned as tax collectors. This could become complex, as in cases where estate owners obtained what they owed from the serfs and slaves who worked their lands, or in situations where taxes were collected by quasi-independent businesses or "banks" designated to gather the taxes from the people. Thus the distinction between taxes and debts cannot be drawn sharply.

1. Historical and Cultural Background
2. Ancient Israel

1. Historical and Cultural Background.

The royal house might be only a part of those making demands with regard to taxes. In many ancient Near Eastern contexts, such as Palestine during the Egyptian New Kingdom, taxes were gathered for the benefit of temples. In other cases, local royalty was responsible to pay additional obligations to imperial conquerors whose demands the regional rulers passed on to their populations. This was true among the Canaanite city-state rulers during the Egyptian New Kingdom rule (c. 1550-1150 BCE), and recurred in subsequent centuries with various oppressors during the period of the judges (c. 1200-1050

BCE), the Aramean incursions of the early monarchy, the Neo-Assyrian control of the northern kingdom of Israel (c. 734-722 BCE) and its successor Assyrian colonies as well as the control of the southern kingdom of Judah (c. 734-625 BCE), the Neo-Babylonian rule of Judah (c. 605-539 BCE), and the Persian period, when Judea was part of the larger empire (c. 539-330 BCE). At such points taxes become similar to tribute, and indeed it is difficult to distinguish them.

Throughout history taxes have taken several forms, including objects such as agricultural produce, coinage or weighted metal, and some form of labor rendered by individuals for a period of time. Despite the presence of large archives from ancient Near Eastern palaces, with an abundance of administrative textual data (indeed, the overwhelming majority of texts in cuneiform archives are administrative, often amounting to 80 percent or more of the archive), few if any of these tablets record the sort of information that one might expect to clarify a taxation procedure. Instead, many fall into categories of debt contracts, receipts, inventories and census lists. Nevertheless, these texts and interpretive models provide useful background for understanding taxation in ancient Israel.

The agricultural produce commonly demanded for payment was barley. As the food of most people, this formed the basis for numeration, debt interest and, we may presume, tax rates to be paid. Silver was the metal used with greatest frequency to pay debts. In earlier times it was weighed. During the Persian period stamped coinage was introduced. The basic unit, a shekel of silver, bought one ration of barley. Assuming two meals per day, that created about sixty rations of barley per month. Sixty shekels came to equal one mina of silver. From this it is apparent why Mesopotamian interest rates (and perhaps tax rates) were set at an ideal figure of one shekel per month (= twelve per annum) for each mina—that is, 20 percent per year. In reality, many debts, private and royal, easily approached 50 and even 100 percent. The figures set in ancient Near Eastern law collections and edicts do not reflect historical reality, as represented in the administrative documents (Hudson and Van de Mieroop).

Labor was constantly in demand by the wealthy and especially by royalty. In addition to service in palaces, great houses and temples, there was a need for agricultural work on lands already owned by the highest classes of society, and for other projects, such as the construction of defenses and the erection of royal buildings and storehouses. Texts from the second millennium west Semitic archives of Emar, Alalakh, Ugarit, Mari, Ekalte and elsewhere include lists of names sometimes associated with towns or groups of people. Some of these reflect labor gangs (corvée) called up for service. Texts from Alalakh suggest that they could work close at home, at the palace or even in another land (Hess 2002). They could be compensated for their time and labor. A fourteenth-century Amarna letter, EA 365, describes how the ruler of Megiddo brought a corvée to cultivate fields in the Jezreel Valley at Shunem. The term used there, *massu*, anticipates the Hebrew *mas*, "corvée (workers)." The ruler complains that no other servants of pharaoh are bringing their corvée. Compare the prophecy in Genesis 49:15 about the tribe of Issachar, that this tribe, settled in the Jezreel Valley, would become a corvée (see Rainey).

Generally, *land was inalienable (Snell). However, the evidence suggests that it could be transferred to the creditor if specified in a debt contract where the debtor forfeited repayment. It could also be transferred to the king, either in cases where he gave the land for limited use or in cases of treason, where the property transferred to the royal domain. There is reason to suspect that many loan contracts, with huge interest rates, had as their objective not the repayment of the loan, but rather the acquisition of labor and especially of the land holdings of poorer and unfortunate inheritors of small plots of land. Wealthy land owners, and most of all the royal house, as chief creditor, could thus acquire land for themselves. This meant that they required more labor to work the land, and

they would achieve this by further "loans" or taxes on those who needed the credit in order to survive on their land. This created a spiraling increase of wealth among a few and of debt servitude and loss of land among the many.

In order to counteract such debt and loss of land, rulers instituted a kind of reverse taxation. This was the Mesopotamian *mīšarum*, or *andurarum*, a proclamation of release from debt servitude and loss of land (for many, the only source of wealth production). Proclaimed at the beginning of a new king's reign and at certain periods later in the reign, it provided for a release of debt and thus a return of many individuals who could function as a tax base for the king, as well as a key source of human power for military service. For Israel, Leviticus suggests that this would be applied in the *děrôr,* the release proclaimed in the Jubilee Year every fifty years (Lev 25). In the ancient Near East this safety valve began as early as the twenty-fifth century BCE and continued with hints of its occurrences into the Neo-Babylonian period, and perhaps later. In ancient Israel, however, it is not clear when or if this practice was ever used. Jeremiah 34 may suggest that something like a release took place during the Babylonian siege of Jerusalem; however, King Zedekiah revoked it when the siege was lifted.

2. Ancient Israel.

There is little in Joshua and Judges to suggest a tax in substance. However, the texts state that the corvée (Heb *mas*) was used by the Israelites against some Canaanites (Josh 17:13; Judg 1:28), especially those in *Gezer, Galilee and the hill country west and north of Benjamin (Josh 16:10; Judg 1:30, 33, 35). Insofar as the remains of early Iron Age village settlements in the central hill country of Palestine represent Israel, the widespread absence of massive defenses and other architectural structures characteristic of centralized authority supports both the portrayal of Israel's population as primarily subsisting in village life and the absence of royal taxation among the people in the book of Judges.

The "way of the king" *(mišpaṭ hammelek)* in 1 Samuel 8:11-18 describes the perception of royal life, pictured at the threshold of Israel's kingship. The first type of taxation portrayed is a corvée for male (charioteers, administrators, agriculturalists, weapons manufacturers) and female (perfumers, cooks) members of Israelite society. This text also conceives of the appropriation of fields that specialize in export crops, such as vineyards and olive groves. The best of the beasts of burden as well as one-tenth of the flocks and of the produce of the fields would be taxed. The picture portrayed, one that may have been fulfilled as early as the united monarchy, is an authentic reflection of taxation in the Bronze Age cities of the West Semitic world as attested in their archives (e.g., Ugarit, Alalakh, Emar).

The first king of Israel, *Saul, is nowhere portrayed as taxing the nation. Nevertheless, he promises to the household of the warrior who will stand against Goliath an exemption from taxes (1 Sam 17:25). The text includes the Hebrew term *ḥopšî*, whose antecedents at Alalakh and Ugarit describe free-born individuals exempt from certain royal obligations.

In the biblical discussion of the administration of King *David there appears a reference to Adoniram, who was in charge of the corvée in Israel. The texts suggest that David's building projects and other ventures required this form of taxation on Israel. Presumably, the same Adoniram appears in the *Solomon narratives of the construction of the temple with the same position (1 Kings 4:6; 5:14). However, his efforts for the sovereigns earned him hatred among those who were so taxed, which must have included Israelite citizens as well as the former Canaanites (2 Chron 8:8). When Solomon's son sought to increase the corvée burden on the people (perhaps not only in opposition to their request, but also in violation of the historical Semitic precedents of a ruler proclaiming remission of debt and forced labor upon accession to the throne), he sent Adoniram to enforce his wishes among the northern tribes. However, they stoned him (1 Kings 12:18; 2 Chron 10:18), thereby rejecting Rehoboam's royal authority.

1 Kings 4:7-19 provides a Solomonic administrative list of governors and their provinces who supplied the food for the royal court and the fodder for the war horses. This list represents the closest biblical example of administrative lists from Ugarit and Alalakh, and it suggests a similar tax structure, in which different parts of the kingdom were responsible for monthly provisions throughout the year. This list betrays no signs of distortion or editorial interference. All the apparent anomalies in its structure have parallels in the Bronze Age cuneiform administrative texts (Hess 1997). Taxations of labor groups (1 Kings 5:13-15; 2 Chron 2:2, 18) included a corvée (Heb *mas*) of 30,000 sent to Lebanon for cedar timber in groups of 10,000 each month. In addition, there were 70,000 carriers and 80,000 stonecutters who formed another type of corvée labor (Heb *sabbāl*) administered by a force of 3,600. This latter group, perhaps drawn from a labor pool distinct from the Israelites who formed the *mas* corvée, were under the direction of *Jeroboam (1 Kings 11:28). In contrast to the hated leader of the citizen labor gangs, Jeroboam was respected by the Israelites to the point where he became the first ruler of the northern kingdom. These labor gangs were responsible for the many fortifications in Jerusalem and other cities of the kingdom, as well as for the temple, the palaces and the other government buildings in the capital. Thus the united monarchy by the time of Solomon had established a system of taxation that included both the produce of the country as well as the corvée. In addition to receiving much gold annually (666 talents), Solomon received money from merchants, the princes of his land and Arabian kings (1 Kings 10:14-15).

There are hints that kings of the divided monarchy continued practices of tax collection (Holladay; Fox). An emergency corvée of all Judeans was used by Asa to rebuild defenses in Benjamin at Geba and Mizpah and so to prevent King Baasha of Israel from another assault on the southern kingdom (1 Kings 15:22). *Jehoshaphat would receive "gifts" (Heb *minḥâ*) from his subjects and tribute (Heb *maśśā'*) of silver and flocks of goats and rams from Philistines and Arabs (2 Chron 17:5, 11). During the reign of Joash, his attempt to repair the temple included money (Heb *kesep*) that had been gathered in a census, as well as other funds from temple vows and contributions (2 Kings 12:4). That all this was given to the priests may suggest their involvement in the process of collecting such taxes.

Later kings were involved in the collection of taxes to pay tribute to international conquerors. Thus King Menahem of Israel taxed all the free citizens of wealth fifty shekels of silver to pay King Tiglath-pileser III of Assyria (2 Kings 15:20). Pharaoh Neco of Egypt levied a tribute on King Jehoiakim (c. 609 BCE) that required an assessment (Heb root ʿrk) of the Judeans and a tax that they had to pay (2 Kings 23:33-35).

Several other biblical and extrabiblical texts from the time of the monarchy may touch on issues of taxation. The first, from the northern kingdom of the ninth century BCE, is the usurpation of Naboth's patrimony through the perjury of false witnesses arranged by Jezebel so that her husband, King Ahab, could acquire this special vineyard (1 Kings 21). Although this may reflect the practice of the Canaanite city-states (Jezebel's Tyrian heritage), where the king had greater ownership rights over the land, it clearly violated early Israel's understanding of the inalienable nature of the land grants to its citizens (Lev 27). Israel's wealthy class continued this practice of land acquisition and impoverishment of the poorer citizenry through taxation/loan systems that produced debt servitude similar to other ancient Near Eastern nations. The apparent absence of any release (e.g., děrôr) led to the prophetic critique in the eighth century BCE (Amos 2:6-7; 5:10-12; 8:4-6; Mic 2:1-2, 9; Is 3:13-15; 5:8). The sixty-three Samaria ostraca from the capital of the northern kingdom in the first half of the eighth century BCE most likely represent shipments to the crown and the wealthy class resident at the capital from both royal and private estates (rather than some sort of tax receipts).

More than 1,700 lmlk ("belonging to the king") seal impressions on jars dating to the end of the eighth century BCE and the time of King *Hezekiah have been found in sites throughout the Judean kingdom (Vaughn). These are likely evidence for storage and distribution of a liquid commodity (wine or oil) as part of a major administrative build-up in the years prior to the Assyrian invasion of 701 BCE. Such a build-up reflected a period of economic expansion second to none and compared by biblical writers using language resembling that applied to Solomon (2 Chron 32:27-30). This storage suggests a taxation that prepared the nation for the devastation by Sennacherib. Its results of provision during the crisis served at least some of the population of Judah in a way that the policy of Assyrian capitulation, followed by King *Manasseh in the seventh century BCE, did not. His taxation would have left the country to be used by the Assyrian Empire as it

saw fit. A brief respite from tribute during the reign of King *Josiah was followed by alternative tribute owed, first to Egypt and then to Babylon in the final decades of the nation's "independence."

An ostracon whose paleography and names may date it from either the time of Joash or Josiah (640-609 BCE) provides insight into the combined royal and religious authority used in the taxation process (Bordreuil, Israel and Pardee). Although dubbed a forgery by some, its authenticity has largely been accepted. The whole is translated, "As ʿAshayu the king has commanded you to give by the hand of Zakaryahu silver of Tarshish for the house of Yahweh: 3 shekels." The name ʿAshayu is widely understood as a form of the name Josiah, although it could also be Joash. Zakaryahu may be the man of 2 Chronicles 24:20 who was murdered by his uncle Joash, or the Levite of 2 Chronicles 35:8 who was in charge of the temple during the reign of Josiah, or someone else. Most interesting is the figure from the time of Josiah who might have been responsible for collecting funds during the temple's renovation. What is clear is that taxation was carried on under royal authority and that the collection center to which the money went was the temple in Jerusalem.

Cyrus allowed the Judeans to return from exile. The Greek historians describe gifts that were given from the provinces to the Persian emperor in the first decades of his administration (Briant). Judea, as a province, would have sent its share. With the advent of Darius (c. 520 BCE) there appears to have begun a more systematic taxation program that increased with time. In the mid-fifth century BCE the enemies of Judah and opponents of the reconstruction of its walls suggest that such a fortification would foment rebellion and an end to the payment of taxes (Ezra 4:13). The term royal taxes (middat hammelek) as well as poll taxes and land taxes are mentioned in the Ezra passage as examples of Persian impositions on their subjects. The reforms of *Nehemiah, whatever imperial interests they may have reflected, balanced tax demands by the Persians for both the defenses of Jerusalem and its garrison with demands by the governor for relief from interest on the tax payments made by the local population (Neh 5:1-19) (Hoglund).

Although sporadic, and at times buried in sources that need to be examined critically, from Israel's earliest memories through to the postexilic period the evidence suggests the ongoing practice of taxation. The earlier evidence demonstrates similarities with what is known of the Bronze Age system of taxation. However, preexilic texts also indicate the emergence of a distinctive system of taxation during the monarchy. Nevertheless, the influence of imperial taxation began with the Assyrians and became the dominant concern of the citizens of Judah during the Babylonian and Persian periods.

See also CENSUS; KINGS AND KINGSHIP; LAND; STATE OFFICIALS.

BIBLIOGRAPHY. **Y. Aharoni,** *The Land of the Bible: A Historical Geography* (2d ed.; Philadelphia: Westminster, 1979 [1962]); **P. Bordreuil, F. Israel and D. Pardee,** "King's Command and Widow's Plea: Two New Hebrew Ostraca of the Biblical Period," *NEA* 61 (1998) 2-32; **P. Briant,** *From Cyrus to Alexander: A History of the Persian Empire* (Winona Lake, IN: Eisenbrauns, 2002 [1996]); **N. S. Fox,** *In the Service of the King: Officialdom in Ancient Israel and Judah* (HUCM 23; Cincinnati: Hebrew Union College Press, 2000), esp. 136-41; **R. S. Hess,** "The Bible and Alalakh," in *Mesopotamia and the Bible: Comparative Explorations,* ed. M. W. Chavalas and K. L. Younger Jr. (Grand Rapids: Baker, 2002) 209-21; idem, "The Form and Structure of the Solomonic District List in 1 Kings 4:7-19," in *Crossing Boundaries and Linking Horizons: Studies in Honor of Michael C. Astour,* ed. G. D. Young, M. W. Chavalas and R. E. Averbeck (Bethesda, MD: CDL, 1997) 279-92; **K. G. Hoglund,** *Achaemenid Imperial Administration in Syria-Palestine and the Missions of Ezra and Nehemiah* (SBLDS 125; Atlanta: Scholars Press, 1992); **J. S. Holladay Jr.,** "The Kingdoms of Israel and Judah: Political and Economic Centralization in the Iron IIA-B," in *The Archaeology of Society in the Holy Land,* ed. T. E. Levy (New York: Facts on File, 1995) 368-98; **M. Hudson and M. Van de Mieroop,** eds., *Debt and Economic Renewal in the Ancient Near East* (Institute for the Study of Long-term Economic Trends and the International Scholars Conference on Ancient Near Eastern Economies 3; Bethesda, MD: CDL, 2002); **A. F. Rainey,** "Compulsory Labor Gangs in Ancient Israel," *IEJ* 20 (1970) 191-202; **D. C. Snell,** "Taxes and Taxation," *ABD* 6.338-40; **A. G. Vaughn,** *Theology, History, and Archaeology in the Chronicler's Account of Hezekiah* (ABS 4; Atlanta: Scholars Press, 1999). R. S. Hess

TEL DAN STELA. *See* ARAM, DAMASCUS AND SYRIA; DAVID; ISRAEL; NON-ISRAELITE WRITTEN SOURCES: SYRO-PALESTINIAN.

TELL EL-FUL. *See* GIBEAH, GEBA.

TELL EL-KHEFEILEH. *See* EZION-GEBER.

TELL EN-NAṢBEH. *See* MIZPAH.

TELL QASILE. *See* PHILISTINES.

TELL SIRAN INSCRIPTION. *See* NON-ISRAELITE WRITTEN SOURCES: SYRO-PALESTINIAN.

TEMPLE MOUNT. *See* JERUSALEM.

TEXT AND TEXTUAL CRITICISM

In discussions of textual criticism, the word *text* has a precise technical sense and refers to the exact wording of the surviving manuscripts (handwritten copies) of an ancient literary composition (or group of compositions). *Textual criticism,* on the other hand, can be described as the scholarly discipline that seeks to trace the history of the transmission of the text of a given work as it was repeatedly hand-copied by ancient and medieval scribes, and to recover, as much as possible, an authoritative starting point ("the original text") for the translation and interpretation of the work in question. In the case of the Historical Books of the OT (as of the Hebrew Bible as a whole), this goal is accomplished primarily by comparing the surviving Hebrew manuscripts, and by examining the extant ancient versions (that is, translations done in antiquity) with a view to determining the Hebrew texts on which they are based. (It needs to be noted that *criticism* in this context refers simply to scholarly analysis, and does not imply being "critical" in the sense of giving a negative evaluation.) The present article will first give a brief overview of the textual evidence (manuscripts and versions) that is currently available for the Historical Books in general. Second, it will mention the main theories currently being proposed to account for the textual diversity that the manuscripts and versions reflect. Third, it will focus on the textual history of the six primary literary units comprising the Historical Books, noting any distinctive features that scholars have discovered. Finally, by way of illustrating the business of textual criticism in the Historical

Books, it will give a few examples of significant textual variants in these books and how they can be explained.

1. Textual Evidence Bearing on the Historical Books in General
2. Theories to Account for the Diversity
3. The Textual Evidence Bearing on the Historical Books in Particular
4. Illustrative Examples

1. Textual Evidence Bearing on the Historical Books in General.
There are essentially two kinds of evidence that allow biblical scholars to trace the history of the biblical text and to recover an authoritative "original text." (It should be noted that the concept of an "original text" is disputed, and—as used here—does not necessarily rule out the existence of earlier forms of that text.) These two kinds of evidence consist of the following two broad categories of "witnesses to the text": manuscripts and ancient versions.

1.1. Manuscripts. The most direct and reliable witnesses are the surviving Hebrew manuscripts themselves. These are all handwritten copies (usually on parchment or papyrus) that were produced by ancient or medieval scribes hundreds of years after the original texts were first written.

1.1.1. The Masoretic Text (MT). This is the standardized Hebrew text which was produced by Jewish scholars known as "Masoretes" ("transmitters") in the centuries preceding CE 800 and which continues to be the fundamental point of departure for all study of the Hebrew Bible today. A major innovation in this form of the text is the introduction of vowel signs as well as other kinds of careful textual annotation. The MT includes the entire OT and is extant today in some 6,000 copies, the oldest dating to about the year CE 1000. Although these copies of the MT do show some slight variations, they are collectively a miracle of textual uniformity. For centuries this form of the text was virtually identified, by both Jews and Christians, with the original text of the Hebrew Bible.

1.1.2. The Dead Sea Scrolls. The mid-twentieth century discovery of the Dead Sea Scrolls has revolutionized the study of the text of the OT, since they included many biblical manuscripts that were more than a thousand years older than the earliest extant copies of the MT. Furthermore, although some of these biblical manuscripts proved to represent a form of the consonantal text (dubbed Proto-Masoretic), which was very close to the MT, there were others that departed significantly from it. In fact, the net effect of the discovery of the Dead Sea Scrolls was the realization that around the turn of the era the Hebrew Bible was current in many different textual forms. However, there was also some evidence that the Proto-Masoretic text already enjoyed something of a privileged status at this time.

1.2. Ancient Versions. In the nature of the case, translations can only serve as indirect witnesses to the biblical text, since they must first be translated back into a hypothetical Hebrew original before they can be compared with the evidence of the Hebrew manuscripts. Nevertheless, the ancient versions do provide valuable evidence, since they frequently testify to a Hebrew parent text (or *Vorlage*) that is much older—and therefore closer in time to the original text—than any of the extant Hebrew manuscripts. The most important ancient versions are the following:

1.2.1. The Septuagint (LXX). By far the oldest—and therefore potentially the most valuable—of the ancient versions is the ancient Greek translation known as the Septuagint (from the Latin *septuaginta*, meaning "seventy"). Strictly speaking, the Septuagint refers to the Greek translation of the Pentateuch, which was produced in Egypt in the third century BCE, allegedly by seventy (or seventy-two) translators. However, the term was later expanded to include the Greek version of the remaining books of the Hebrew Bible as well as a number of other Jewish religious texts later dubbed "the Apocrypha." The Historical Books were among the former and were done by various translators during the second century BCE. They reflect different translation styles and levels of competence. A comparison with the MT shows that the parent text of the Septuagint frequently appears to diverge from the MT. However, the degree of divergence is often difficult to establish, since some of the Greek translators may have taken liberties with the Hebrew text from which they were working. A further complication in dealing with the Septuagint is that the original translation (called the Old Greek) underwent a series of revisions, or "recensions" (often reflecting an attempt to conform the Greek more closely to a Hebrew text similar to the MT), which are part of the later textual history of the Septuagint. Consequently, that history is very complex, especially since it in turn became the basis of a series of "daughter translations," notably the Latin version (*Vetus Latina*), which was used in the Latin-speaking churches. It needs to be remembered that during the first three centuries of the Christian church the Septuagint was the accepted form of the OT and was considered inspired by many.

1.2.2. The Minor Greek Versions. This term refers especially to the three translations associated in antiquity with Theodotion, Aquila and Symmachus, all of whom lived in the second century CE, although it has recently become apparent that elements of Theodotion's translation go back to a rendering done in the first century BCE (the so-called *kaige*-Theodotion). Unfortunately, these versions have only survived in fragmentary form. However, enough has been preserved to indicate that their Hebrew parent text appears to be close to the MT.

1.2.3. The Targums. These are *Aramaic renderings of most of the books of the Hebrew Bible, in many cases representing as much an interpretative paraphrase as a strict translation. They appear to have been oral in origin and to have been written down at a later date. They date from before the turn of the era to the early middle ages. There are multiple Targums to the Pentateuch, but only one for most of the Historical Books, namely Targum Jonathan to the Prophets. It is difficult to date but was considered authoritative by the fourth century CE. Its parent text appears to be close to the MT. There is no Targum to Ezra-Nehemiah, which belongs to the third division (the Writings) of the Hebrew Bible, not the second (the Prophets). There is, however, a separate Targum to Chronicles, which also belongs to the Writings. Because of the tendency of the Targums to expand on the text, it is not always possible to discern the Hebrew that they are translating, but in stretches of text where that possibility does exist, the original Hebrew appears to be close to the MT.

1.2.4. The Peshitta. This is the standard Syriac version of the Bible. The OT translation appears to have begun in the second century CE, and most of it to have been completed in the third. However, it is probable that the Historical Books of *Chronicles and Ezra-Nehemiah were not translated until some time after the third century. Scholars debate whether the translators of the Peshitta were Jewish or Christian, and it may be that they were Jewish converts to Chris-

tianity (so Weitzman). The text of the Peshitta appears to have undergone considerable evolution, but for most of the OT its earliest stages seem to reflect a text that is virtually identical with the MT.

1.2.5. The Vulgate. Unlike the other ancient versions, this Latin translation can be dated with some precision (390-405 CE) and can be ascribed to a known translator (the church father Jerome). It is based on a Hebrew text that is very close to the MT.

2. Theories to Account for the Diversity.

Although most of the ancient versions, going back as early as *kaige*-Theodotion in the first century BCE, appear to reflect a Hebrew text that is very close to the MT, both the earliest form of the Septuagint and the biblical manuscripts of the Dead Sea Scrolls give evidence of considerable textual diversity in the centuries preceding CE 100. How can we account for this diversity? Four prominent contemporary biblical scholars give different answers to this question (Wolters, 21-23).

2.1. F. M. Cross Jr. Cross adopted from his teacher W. Albright the "local texts theory," according to which the Hebrew manuscripts of the OT can be correlated with three geographical areas: Egypt, Palestine and Babylon. The textual traditions that originated in these areas roughly correspond with the parent texts underlying the Septuagint, the Samaritan Pentateuch and the MT, respectively (Cross). For the Historical Books this means that the Egyptian and Babylonian textual traditions need to be distinguished.

2.2. S. Talmon. Talmon correlates the textual diversity not with geographical location but with religious affiliation. One textual tradition (the Septuagint) was preserved by the Christian church, another (the MT) by rabbinic Judaism and a third (the Samaritan Pentateuch) by the Samaritan sect. However, it is likely that other religious groups, now defunct, would have been the bearers of yet other textual traditions (Talmon). Only the first two mentioned are represented in the Historical Books.

2.3. E. Tov. In addition to the three text types distinguished by Cross and Talmon, Tov recognizes two others: one characterized by the distinct "Qumran orthography," which is widely represented among the biblical Dead Sea Scrolls, and another that he calls "unaligned" (that is, not clearly identified with any of the other four) (Tov, 114-17).

2.4. E. Ulrich. Carrying the differentiation of text types even further, Ulrich argues that a simple threefold or fivefold scheme cannot do justice to the great diversity of the OT text around the turn of the era. Instead, he sees a succession of "literary editions" of individual books (or parts of books) as temporary stages of the overall evolution of the biblical text toward its canonical form. Each literary edition was produced by a creative editor who was responding to a new religious situation, and each such edition could be called the "base text" with respect to subsequent scribal modifications (Ulrich).

3. The Textual Evidence Bearing on the Historical Books in Particular.

For each of the six textual units of the Historical Books there are specific features of the textual evidence that need to be taken into account by the exegete of these books. As a rough-and-ready index of the reliability of the MT as assessed in contemporary textual scholarship, the discussion of each of the six units will include a reference to the first volume of the series *Critique textuel de l'Ancien Testament* (*CTAT-1*), edited by D. Barthélemy under the auspices of the United Bible Societies. This volume records the discussions and conclusions of a panel of six leading scholars with respect to the main proposals that have been made to depart from the MT. It should be noted that the emendations they discuss include changes in Masoretic vocalization (the vowel signs added by the Masoretes).

3.1. Joshua. The main text-critical issue in Joshua is the relationship of the MT to the Old Greek, which appears to reflect a Hebrew parent text that is significantly different, especially in chapters 5, 6, 20 and 24. In fact, some scholars have concluded that the Old Greek represents the first of two "literary strata" of the book of Joshua, while the second stratum is represented by MT and the other ancient versions (including later recensions of the Septuagint) (Tov, 327-32). Scholars disagree on which of the two text types represents the most valuable tradition. However, even those who generally prefer the MT usually adopt at least some readings from the Old Greek, for example the list of eleven towns in Judah after Joshua 15:59, or the *Levitical cities of Reuben in Joshua 21:36-37. One of the most significant finds among the Dead Sea Scrolls are

two fragmentary manuscripts of Joshua that appear to belong to the same text type as that underlying the Old Greek. *CTAT-1* discusses ninety-four places where changes to the MT of Joshua (656 verses) have been proposed, and it accepts emendations in thirty-three of them, many on the basis of the Old Greek. This works out to an average of one accepted emendation for every 19.9 verses (*see* Joshua, Book of).

3.2. Judges. The Dead Sea Scrolls include some tantalizing scraps of the Hebrew text of Judges (mainly of chapter 9), but they are too fragmentary to base any firm textual conclusions on them. Putting these aside, the chief textual problem is the relationship between the two distinct versions of the Septuagint of Judges, usually designated A and B. They are so different that the Rahlfs edition of the Septuagint prints both of them alongside each other. Some scholars have concluded that they represent separate and independent translations of the Hebrew text, while others see the one as a thoroughgoing revision of the other on the basis of a developing Hebrew *Vorlage*. Thus W. R. Bodine argues that the B text corresponds to the Theodotionic recension of the Septuagint, and the A text is close to its later Hexaplaric recension. *CTAT-1* discusses 86 places where changes to the MT of Judges (618 verses) have been proposed, and it accepts emendations in 12 of them, yielding an average of one accepted emendation for every 51.5 verses (*see* Judges, Book of).

3.3. 1 and 2 Samuel. It is generally conceded that the Hebrew text of Samuel has been poorly preserved. The MT has evidence of many copying errors, especially examples of haplography (scribal omissions triggered by repeated sequences of letters, usually at the ends of words). With the help of the ancient versions, especially the Septuagint, nineteenth-century scholars like J. Wellhausen and S. R. Driver succeeded in repairing a good deal of the damage. Although other scholars were critical of their efforts, especially their reliance on the Septuagint, they were largely vindicated in the twentieth century when the Dead Sea Scrolls turned out to contain a number of fragmentary Hebrew manuscripts that supported the Septuagint readings in Samuel (4QSam[a], 4QSam[b], and 4QSam[c]). These were manuscripts that could be dated to before the turn of the era—in fact, in the case of 4QSam[b], to the mid-third century BCE. (A more refined analysis [McCarter 1980, 7-10] showed that the Qumran Samuel manuscripts corresponded most closely to a particular phase in the development of the Septuagint text: not to the original Old Greek of the second century BCE—largely preserved in the Codex Vaticanus—nor to the Lucianic recension of the fourth century CE but to a "proto-Lucianic" stage in between.) Because of the discovery of these early Samuel manuscripts, exegetes and translators today are much more prone to emend the MT of Samuel than they were before. In the words of P. K. McCarter, whose commentary on the books of Samuel first included all of the relevant Qumran evidence, "It is no longer possible to defend a textual reconstruction that relies exclusively on the MT or turns to the versions only when the MT is unintelligible" (McCarter 1980, 8). At the same time, it is necessary to guard against a kind of eclectic atomism, which picks and chooses readings from either the MT or the presumed *Vorlage* of (one stage of) the Septuagint without regard to the internal coherence of the distinctive readings of each. Thus it is possible to show that the Old Greek and the MT of 1 Samuel 1 each have their own integrity, which is lost if either text is emended in an ad hoc fashion (Walters). *CTAT-1* discusses 308 places where changes to the MT of 1 and 2 Samuel (1506 verses) have been proposed, and it accepts emendations in sixty-nine of them, yielding an average of one accepted emendation for every 21.8 verses (*see* Samuel, Books of).

3.4. 1 and 2 Kings. Although there are some fragmentary Hebrew manuscripts of Kings among the Dead Sea Scrolls, they are of little text-critical value. The small scraps that have survived generally support the MT. On the other hand, the Septuagint of Kings (known as 3 and 4 Reigns) differs fairly dramatically from the MT in certain respects. Thus there are a number of "miscellanies" (small anthologies of passages drawn from various parts of Scripture) inserted into the text at various points, whole blocks of text are transposed (e.g., 1 Kings 20—21), and an entire system of chronology is introduced that is at variance with that contained in the MT. It is widely agreed, however, that these changes do not represent an independent Hebrew textual tradition. Instead, they are in all likelihood innovations introduced within the Greek textual tradition itself. When these innovations are discounted, the underlying Hebrew text appears to be quite close to the MT. *CTAT-1* discusses 174

places where changes to the MT of 1 and 2 Kings (1536 verses) have been proposed, and it accepts emendations in nineteen of them, yielding an average of one accepted emendation for every 80.8 verses (*see* Kings, Books of).

3.5. 1 and 2 Chronicles. With one exception (4QChr), there is almost nothing in the Dead Sea Scrolls that is relevant to the text of Chronicles, and even the exception is so minimal that it is of almost no text-critical value. With respect to the ancient versions, in the case of Chronicles it is not the Septuagint but the Peshitta that presents the textual critic with special problems. The Septuagint appears here to be a quite literal rendering of a Hebrew *Vorlage* that closely approximates the MT. As for the Peshitta, although in the rest of the OT it generally reflects (at least in its earliest witnesses) a Hebrew parent text that is close to the MT, this is not the case in Chronicles. Here the Peshitta often diverges widely from the MT. However, this divergence should not be taken as evidence of an alternative Hebrew textual tradition in this case but rather as an indication that the Peshitta translator was working from a defective Hebrew manuscript of Chronicles that in many places was illegible, forcing the translator to either omit illegible bits of the text or to use his imagination in reconstructing partially legible passages (Weitzman, 112-21). Although the Hebrew text of Chronicles is generally well preserved, there is an exception for the proper names that appear in such abundance in the *genealogies and lists of personnel. They have often been transmitted in quite a garbled form because their context does not have the delimiting effect of an argument or story. Another special problem in Chronicles is its relation to its sources, which presumably included Samuel and Kings. The latter cannot, without further ado, be used to correct parallel passages in Chronicles, since the Chronicler often deliberately diverges from his sources. *CTAT-1* discusses 205 places where changes to the MT of 1 and 2 Chronicles (1763 verses) have been proposed, and it accepts emendations in thirty of them, yielding an average of one accepted emendation for every 58.8 verses (*see* Chronicles, Books of).

3.6. Ezra-Nehemiah. These books are unusual in that they have no Targum. On the other hand, the Greek translation in the Septuagint is supplemented by 1 Esdras, which is an alternative version of parts of Ezra-Nehemiah, but with significant omissions, additions and displacements. The relationship between these Greek versions and the Hebrew-Aramaic text of the canonical books is complicated and debated. Nevertheless, there are places where the Semitic text of the MT can be corrected on the basis of the Greek. The matter has been further complicated by the discovery of three fragments of the Hebrew and Aramaic texts of Ezra (4QEzra) at Qumran. *CTAT-1* discusses ninety-nine places where changes to the MT of Ezra-Nehemiah (684 verses) have been proposed, and it accepts emendations in fifteen of them, yielding an average of one accepted emendation for every 45.6 verses (*see* Ezra and Nehemiah, Books of).

4. Illustrative Examples.

4.1. 1 Samuel 10:1. This verse reads as follows in the NRSV (italics added): "Samuel took a vial of oil and poured it on his head, and kissed him; he said, 'The LORD has anointed you ruler over *his people Israel. You shall reign over the people of the LORD and you will save them from the hand of their enemies all around. Now this shall be the sign to you that the LORD has anointed you ruler over* his heritage.'" The italicized words do not occur in the MT, but they are found in the Septuagint. It is possible that the words were originally found in the Hebrew as well but that an early scribe, when copying this passage from a Hebrew manuscript, inadvertently skipped from the first occurrence of "the LORD has anointed you ruler over" to the second, thus omitting the italicized section (an example of haplography or parablepsis). This mistake was then copied by other scribes, and eventually all copies of the Hebrew text had the shortened version of this verse. However, the committee of *CTAT-1* believes that it is more likely that what we have here is not an omission from the MT, but an expansion in the Septuagint, and can be safely disregarded in translations. So too the NIV.

4.2. 1 Samuel 10:27—11:1. Again, these verses read as follows in the NRSV (italics added): "But some worthless fellows said, 'How can this man [Saul] save us?' They despised him and brought him no present. But he held his peace. *Now Nahash, king of the Ammonites, had been grievously oppressing the Gadites and the Reubenites. He would gouge out the right eye of each of them and would not grant Israel a deliverer. No one was left of the Israelites across the Jordan whose right eye Nahash, king of the Ammonites, had not gouged out. But there were*

seven thousand men who had escaped from the Ammonites and had entered Jabesh-gilead." In this case the italicized words were added not because they are found in one or more of the ancient versions but because they actually occur in one of the Qumran Samuel manuscripts (4QSam^a)—a manuscript that is about one thousand years older than any existing copy of the MT, and thus has a claim to be taken seriously. Moreover, the Jewish historian Josephus also tells the story reflected in the italicized words. Once again, however, the authors of *CTAT-1* were not persuaded that these words are an original part of the Hebrew text. Similarly, the translators of the NIV do not include them.

4.3. 2 Samuel 21:19. A rendering of the MT of this verse reads as follows: "Then there was another battle with the Philistines at Gob; and Elhanan son of Jaare-oregim, the Bethlehemite, killed Goliath the Gittite, the shaft of whose spear was like a weaver's beam" (NRSV). This is an astonishing statement, since the well-known story of *David and *Goliath in 1 Samuel 17 (originally part of the same biblical book as 2 Samuel) states that it was David, not Elhanan, who killed Goliath the Gittite. The puzzle is solved, however, when we compare 1 Chronicles 20:5, which is clearly a parallel passage. There we read the following (italics added): "Again there was war with the Philistines; and Elhanan son of Jair killed *Lahmi the brother of* Goliath the Gittite, the shaft of whose spear was like a weaver's beam" (NRSV). On that reading David was still the slayer of Goliath, and Elhanan killed Goliath's brother. Of the two parallel passages about Elhanan, the one in 2 Samuel and the other in 1 Chronicles, it appears that the former has suffered some textual corruption: the word for "weavers" *(oregim)* has become part of Elhanan's father's name, "Lahmi the brother" has become "the Bethlehemite," a confusion that is understandable in light of the underlying Hebrew (*'tlḥmy'ḥy* becomes *bythlḥmy*). It is perhaps surprising that neither the NRSV nor the NIV correct our text in light of its parallel, especially since this was already done by the KJV, which says in 2 Sam 21:19 that "Elhanan the sonne of Iaare-Oregim a Bethlehemite, slewe *the brother of* Goliath the Gittite," with a note referring to the parallel passage. Here *CTAT-1* does admit an emendation of the MT, although it does not allow the restoration of the word for "brother."

In the nature of the case, these three illustrative examples (as indeed the entire foregoing discussion) have highlighted the variation that can be observed in the textual transmission of the Historical Books of the Hebrew Bible. However, it needs to be stressed that the relative uniformity of the witnesses to the biblical text is far greater than its variety, and that the great mass of textual variants is trivial as regards the literary, historical or religious significance of the stories these books tell. In the great majority of cases the textual discrepancies that loom so large under the textual critic's microscope are like the brush strokes of an impressionistic painting, which blend unobtrusively into the work of art when viewed from an appropriate distance.

See also CANON; HEBREW LANGUAGE; INNER-BIBLICAL EXEGESIS; METHODS OF INTERPRETATION; WRITING, WRITING MATERIALS AND LITERACY IN THE ANCIENT NEAR EAST.

BIBLIOGRAPHY. **D. Barthélemy**, *Critique textuelle de l'Ancien Testament. 1. Josué, Juges, Ruth, Samuel, Rois, Chroniques, Esdras, Néhémie, Esther. Rapport final du Comité pour l'analyse textuelle de l'Ancien Testament hébreu institué par l'Alliance Biblique Universelle* (OBO 50/1; Fribourg/Suisse: Éditions Universitaires, and Göttingen: Vandenhoeck & Ruprecht, 1982); **W. R. Bodine**, *The Greek Text of Judges* (Chico CA: Scholars Press, 1980); **F. M. Cross Jr.**, "The Evolution of a Theory of Local Texts" in *Qumran and the History of the Biblical Text*, ed. F. M. Cross and S. Talmon (Cambridge, MA: Harvard University Press, 1975) 306-20; **S. R. Driver**, *Notes on the Hebrew Text and the Topography of the Books of Samuel* (Oxford: Clarendon Press, 1913 [1890]); **P. K. McCarter**, *I Samuel* (AB; Garden City, NY: Doubleday, 1980); idem, *Textual Criticism: Recovering the Text of the Hebrew Bible* (Philadelphia: Fortress Press, 1986); **S. Talmon**, "The Textual Study of the Bible—A New Outlook," in *Qumran and the History of the Biblical Text*, ed. F. M. Cross and S. Talmon (Cambridge, MA: Harvard University Press, 1975) 321-400; **E. Tov**, *Textual Criticism of the Hebrew Bible* (Minneapolis: Fortress/Assen: Van Gorcum, 1992); **E. Ulrich**, "Multiple Literary Editions: Reflections Toward a Theory of the History of the Biblical Text," in *Current Research and Technological Developments on the Dead Sea Scrolls: Conference on the Texts from the Judaean Desert, Jerusalem, 30 April 1995*, ed. D. W. Parry and S. D. Ricks (STDJ 20; Leiden: Brill, 1996) 78-105; **S. D. Walters**, "Hannah and Anna: The Greek and Hebrew Texts of 1 Samuel 1," *JBL* 107 (1988) 385-412; **M. P. Weitzman**, *The Syriac Version of The Old Testament: An Introduction* (University of Cambridge Oriental Publications 56; Cambridge: Cambridge University Press, 1999); **J. Wellhausen**, *Der Text der Bücher Samuelis Untersucht* (Göttingen: Vandenhoeck und Ruprecht, 1871); **A. Wolters**, "The Text of the Old Testament," in *The Face of Old Testament Studies. A Survey of Contemporary Approaches*, ed. D. W. Baker, B. T. Arnold (Grand Rapids: Baker Books, 1999) 19-37; **E. Würthwein**, *The Text of the Old Testament: An Introduction to the Biblia Hebraica* (2d ed.; Grand Rapids: Eerdmans, 1995).

A. Wolters

THOUSANDS. *See* NUMBERS, LARGE NUMBERS.

TIGLATH-PILESER III. *See* ASSYRIA, ASSYRIANS; HISTORY OF ISRAEL 5: ASSYRIAN PERIOD.

TIMNAH. *See* PHILISTINES.

TIRHAKAH. *See* EGYPT, EGYPTIANS.

TIRZAH

Tirzah was originally a *Canaanite city in the northern territory of Israel. It was the capital of the northern kingdom from the time of *Jeroboam I until the reign of *Omri, who moved the capital to *Samaria.

1. Meaning
2. Witness of the Biblical Materials
3. Location
4. Excavations

1. Meaning.

Originally a female name, *tirṣâ*, from the root I *rṣh*, can be interpreted as "pleasant" or "beauty." This probably is the context of the usage in Song of Songs 6:4, where the beauty of (the city?) Tirzah is praised and compared to the beauty of Jerusalem.

2. Witness of the Biblical Materials.

The earliest mention of Tirzah is in Joshua 12:24, in the context of the kings defeated by Joshua. It is possible that the city came under the dominion of the tribe of Manasseh, which can be deduced from the story of the daughters of Zelophehad (Num 26:33; 36:11; Josh 17:3), one of whom is named Tirzah.

Although originally establishing the capital of Israel in *Shechem (1 Kings 12:25), Jeroboam

I subsequently moved it to Penuel (Peniel) in Transjordan and finally to Tirzah, where it remained until the reign of Omri (1 Kings 16:23-24). Some have argued that all three locations were used simultaneously, thus providing different advantages to the king by enabling him to move freely between them as the need arose to oversee various building and military projects (Donner, 387).

However, at a certain stage the capital clearly is in Tirzah. This seems to be the case in 1 Kings 14:17, which describes Jeroboam's wife visiting Ahijah the prophet and returning home to Tirzah (the LXX, in the equivalent location, 3 Kgdms 12:24n, reads *sarira,* most likely a textual error, via the exchange of similarly looking radicals, for *šĕredâ,* and thus changes the location to Jeroboam's birthplace [1 Kings 11:26 MT = 3 Kgdms 12:24b LXX]). It is apparent from the text, therefore, that the seat of power in the early divided monarchy's northern kingdom was in Tirzah. The reasons for the move from the other two locations are not very clear; possible reasons might include a mixture of safety concerns (Tirzah was located further away in the hills) and a strategy similar to that employed by David (establishing his capital in the newly conquered non-Israelite, and so politically unbiased, Jebusite stronghold of *Jerusalem).

The next act in the history of the city is in connection with the rule of Baasha. The biblical record informs us that Baasha killed Jeroboam's son and successor Nadab and reigned in Tirzah for twenty-four years (1 Kings 15:33). After Baasha's death, his son Elah reigned for two years (1 Kings 16:8), only to be replaced by one of his own officials, Zimri, a commander of half of Elah's chariots. When the army was laying siege to the Philistine city of Gibbethon (1 Kings 16:15), Zimri seized the opportunity and murdered Elah while he was involved in a drinking bout in the house of the royal majordomo, Arza, after which he set himself as king in Elah's place and proceeded to kill off his family and friends, "the house of Baasha" (1 Kings 16:9-11). Zimri, however, did not enjoy his kingship for long. After only seven days Omri, the commander of Elah's troops (thus a higher-ranking officer than Zimri), was chosen to succeed Elah by the army, and he broke up the military advances and besieged Tirzah (1 Kings 16:17). Seeing that his fate was sealed, Zimri sought refuge in the city's inner citadel and committed suicide by burning down the palace over himself (1 Kings 16:18). Omri then shifted the capital from Tirzah to his new city, *Samaria (1 Kings 16:23-24).

The last biblical reference to Tirzah is in 2 Kings 15. Again it is in connection with a rebellion. This time it is Menahem son of Gadi, quite possibly a military commander in Tirzah, who conspired against Shallum and deprived him of crown and life (2 Kings 15:14-16).

3. Location.

After the disintegration of the northern kingdom, Tirzah's location became unknown. Different suggestions have been made as to the site. So, for example, E. Robinson identified it on linguistic grounds with Tulluza, some 6 km (4 mi) north of Shechem. Another suggestion was Teyasir, the ruined fortress north of Shechem. W. F. Albright, however, dismissed both identifications as lacking any archaeological support. In turn, basing his arguments on the strategic rationale, Albright proposed that the city likely was located northeast of Shechem, to protect the area from attacks of Aramaeans (from the north) and *Ammonites (from the east), yet would need to have been located centrally enough to control attacks from *Philistines and *Phoenicians as well (from the west). The Samaritan Ostraca provided additional information; they include the names of some clans of Samaria. Among them are Noah and Hegla, the sisters of Tirzah (Josh 17:3). Although Tirzah is not mentioned, Albright assumed that her territory would have to have been in close proximity. Eliminating other possibilities, Albright concluded that, owing to the lack of other feasible archaeological sites in the area, Tirzah has to be associated with Tell el-Farʿah North, 11 km (7 mi) northeast of Shechem, on the Nablus-Tubas road.

R. de Vaux, assisted by A. M. Stève, conducted nine seasons of excavations of the site between 1946 and 1960. Although no written evidence providing a clear indication of the place's identity was discovered at the site, most scholars today accept Tell el-Farʿah North as the site of ancient Tirzah.

4. Excavations.

De Vaux discovered remains going back to the Chalcolithic period, mostly red-burnished pottery and a sanctuary surrounded by a large public place, the city wall and fortified two-entry city gates from the Early Bronze Age, suggesting that it was an important town at the time. W. G. Dever (142) argues that the stratum in question, VIIa, fits rather well into a later period, and sees it as Solomon's district administrative center.

The finds from the Middle and Late Bronze Ages hint at a less influential role. Just inside the city walls was a basin, which de Vaux took to be of ritual significance.

The Iron Age revealed several important features. Period VIIc, defined as the early ninth century BCE, has an unfinished building, probably intended as a palace, as some of its features resemble the palace at Samaria. Also in this period the libation basin carved out of one stone was used. On the basin stood the *maṣṣēbāh*, making the square area a cultic place, a type of "gate shrine." This finds a possible echo in 2 Kings 23:8, where *Josiah is credited with breaking down the "high places of the gates." Moreover, a number of female figurines were found in the vicinity, signifying the likelihood of an Asherah cult in the town. The excavations of the period include a complex of public buildings that seem never to have been finished. The site's unused building materials, partly dressed stone and the lack of ruins lead to the opinion that it was abandoned at a certain point that de Vaux identifies as the reconstruction project aborted when Omri transferred the capital to Samaria.

The next period, VIId, between the ninth and eighth centuries BCE, shows another season of prosperity in Tirzah, although no longer in the function of capital. The finds include an impressive palace, the cellars of which housed a considerable amount of pottery, including storage jars and large terracotta "bathtubs." The layout of the city reveals large public buildings, probably the administrative headquarters, and sizeable four-room houses separated from the less impressive housing of the poor by a partition wall. The identification of the large houses with the patrician class (see de Vaux 1952; 1955; *NEAEHL* 2.433; Chambon 1984; *NEAEHL* 2.439-40) suggests that this kind of purposeful separation of the rich from the poor during the reign of Jeroboam II accords well with the picture painted by the eighth-century prophets (Amos 5:11; Hos 8:14; Is 9:8-10). T. L. McClellan (86), however, questions the validity of the claim and suggests that the poorer buildings belong to the older stratum, which had a different quality of construction.

In the following period, VIIe, seventh to fifth centuries BCE, the city gradually lost its prominence and splendor, signs of which can be seen in the partitioning of the palace and the use of the formerly cultically important basin as a feeding trough. Eventually, after serving as an Assyrian garrison (or colony), the site was abandoned, and although some signs of use can be traced to the Roman and Hellenistic period, it was over time completely deserted.

See also JEROBOAM; OMRI DYNASTY; SAMARIA.

BIBLIOGRAPHY. **W. F. Albright,** "The Site of Tirzah and the Topography of Western Manasseh," *JPOS* 11 (1931) 241-51; **A. Chambon,** "Farʿah, Tell el- (North): Late Bronze Age to the Roman Period," *NEAEHL* 2.439-40; idem, *Tell el-Fârʿah I: L'age de Fer* (Memoire 31; Paris: Éditions Recherche sur les Civilisations, 1984); **W. G. Dever,** *What Did the Biblical Writers Know and When Did They Know It?* (Grand Rapids: Eerdmans, 2001); **H. Donner,** "The Separate States of Israel and Judah," in *Israelite and Judean History,* ed. J. H. Hayes and J. M. Miller (OTL; Philadelphia: Westminster, 1977) 381-434; **T. L. McClellan,** review of *Tell el-Farʿah I,* by A. Chambon, *BASOR* 267 (1987) 84-86; **E. Robinson,** *Later Biblical Researches in Palestine and in the Adjacent Regions* (Boston: Crocker & Brewster, 1856); **R. de Vaux,** "Farʿah, Tell el- (North): Identification and History," *NEAEHL* 2.433; idem, "La Quatrième de Fouilles a Tell el-Farʿah, près Naplouse," *RB* 59 (1952) 551-83; idem, "Les Fouilles de Tell el-Farʿah, près Naplouse," *RB* 62 (1955) 541-89. A. Turkanik

TOBIAH. See EZRA AND NEHEMAIH, BOOKS OF.

TOLA. See JUDGES; HISTORY OF ISRAEL 2: PRE-MONARCHIC ISRAEL.

TORAH. See LAW.

TOWNS. See CITIES AND VILLAGES.

TRADE AND TRAVEL

Moving goods means moving people. There were numerous motives for travel in the ancient world, but one of the more prominent reasons was trade. Interestingly, two of the Hebrew terms that describe economic activity in the OT, *sôḥēr* and *rôkēl,* are both translated as "merchant, trader," and derive from verbs that denote movement and, more specifically, travel:

shr, "go around, travel," and *rkl*, "go from one to another for trade" (see Sweet, *ISBE* 1.750; see also, e.g., 1 Kings 10:15, 28; 2 Chron 1:16; 9:14; Neh 3:31, 32; 13:20). This article unites the two concepts and focuses on their extent and relationship during the period that corresponds to the Historical Books of the OT.

    1. Importance and Extent of Trade
       and Travel
    2. Trade
    3. Travel

1. Importance and Extent of Trade and Travel.
According to economic theorists, trade has a significant influence in the diffusion of civilization, as can be observed in the Assyrian colonization of the Anatolian plateau through trade at the beginning of the second millennium BCE (Leemans, 3; Holladay 2001, 183-88). However, apart from a few examples of extensive international trade like this one, the scale of economic activity in the ancient Near East was dependent on the demands of the local markets. What was not being produced by the private households or the local communities had to be supplied by trade, which in turn also promoted travel. Thus the extent of trade in the ancient Near East was conditioned by the necessity of the markets: distributive or local trade responded to the requirements of the consumers and consisted of articles that were not produced nearby, whereas long-distance trade involved moving goods from one country to another (Leemans, 2). However, economic records show that most goods were created locally, even mostly within the private household, which functioned as a self-subsisting economic unit (King and Stager, 192), and that long-distance trade was more limited in terms of volume of goods (Snell, *ABD* 6.625; see also Snell 1997). Nevertheless, both types depended on the existence of markets and their accessibility. Long-distance trade was connected to king and palace, as can be seen in the international horse-trade during *Solomon's reign whereby Israel served as an agent between Egypt and Anatolia (1 Kings 10:28-29) (see Snell *ABD* 6.628). Although Israel was located on the seacoast, maritime trade did not play an important role throughout the history of ancient Israel, except for Solomon's Red Sea fleet and his *Phoenician sea-trade relations (1 Kings 9:26) (see King and Stager, 183), when trade ex-

tended as far as Ophir, possibly in southeastern Arabia (1 Kings 9:28).

2. Trade.
K. Polanyi sees three different models of economic behavior in ancient societies: reciprocity, redistribution and exchange. Probably all three were functioning alongside each other, and any one of them could take precedence in different sectors of society (see Holladay 1995). Where a local community produced more than was necessary for its own subsistence, as in the case of some wine-producing villages in the Judean hill country, other communities entered into an exchange system with them, while larger cities such as Hebron, Jerusalem and Shechem served as marketplaces and turntables for produce on a larger scale (King and Stager, 192).

2.1. Markets. During Solomon's reign these "storage cities" (1 Kings 9:19) referred to a network of royal warehouses all over Israel and Lebanon that controlled the international commerce between Egypt, the Arabian peninsula in the south, and Syria, Anatolia and Mesopotamia in the north (King and Stager, 194). However, the most important markets were still the small local ones, and trading usually took place near the city gate, which served as the center of economic activity with sufficient space for the bazaar, a collection of booths lining the street on both sides. The excavations at Ashkelon show that the Hebrew term *ḥûṣôt* should be understood as referring to the "bazaar" or "marketplace," not to "streets," as it is usually translated (Stager, 65; cf. 2 Sam 1:20; 1 Kings 20:34 RSV). These markets usually were located inside the gate, but some did stand outside the gate, as can be seen in the ninth-century BCE structures excavated outside the city gate of Dan, which have been identified by A. Biran (25-29) as the marketplace of the city.

2.2. Products. In ancient Israel's agro-pastoral economy, the products that were traded locally on the markets included dairy products (milk, cheese, butter, etc.), livestock (oxen, sheep, goats, etc.) and agricultural produce (grains, olives, olive oil, grapes, beans, almonds, dried fruit, etc.). Israel also exported goods such as cereals, honey, olive oil, wood, salt, textiles and limestone. According to 1 Kings 5:10-11, Israel traded wheat and olive oil with Phoenicia in exchange for cedars and cypress. Other imports included metals from the Sinai peninsula (silver, copper, lead, iron, etc.), aromatics from Arabia (1 Kings 9:28; 2 Chron 8:18; 9:9), horses and chariots from Egypt and Anatolia (1 Kings 10:28-29), and linen and ivory from Egypt (Ezek 27:7) (see King and Stager, 194).

2.3. Currency. The exchange of goods through bartering was a common mode of economic activity in ancient Israel, as can be seen in the trade of commodities between Solomon and Hiram (1 Kings 5:1-12). This continued even after monetary currencies were introduced, which did not happen until the middle of the first millennium BCE, when Israel became an administrative unit within the Medo-Persian Empire (Snell, *ABD* 6.625). When taxes were levied during the monarchical and postexilic periods, payment usually was exacted in natural commodities (1 Sam 8:14-17; 1 Kings 4:7, 22-23; Neh 10:32-39). King Mesha of Moab paid an annual tribute to the king of Israel in lambs and wool (2 Kings 3:4). Nevertheless, commodities that could be counted and measured were also assigned a corresponding value in silver, usually in the form of broken pieces of silver *(Hacksilber),* an ingot or, from postexilic times onward, minted coins. The Hebrew term *kesep,* "silver," is used synonymously in the OT for money and was used to buy, for example, land (2 Sam 24:24; 1 Kings 16:24), livestock (Ezra 7:17), timber and stone (2 Kings 12:11), or food supplies (2 Kings 6:25). Silver was used at all social levels, as is indicated by the story of Saul's servant who had with him a quarter-shekel of silver while his master had no money on him (1 Sam 9:8). Nevertheless, there is little silver found in archaeological excavations preceding Hellenistic levels, indicating that the use of money in Israel for economic activity was rather limited in scope (see Sweet, *ISBE* 1.563-64).

A number of texts, especially in the prophetic literature of the OT, indicate an ambiguous attitude toward trade because it often was associated with dishonesty and fraudulence (e.g., Amos 8:5).

3. Travel.

The central geographical location of Israel in the Levant made it an important thoroughfare for merchants, messengers, soldiers, and other travelers. Bordered by the desert in the east and the Mediterranean in the west, at places stretching no more than 60 km across, Israel created a bottleneck that connected Egypt with Syria, Anatolia and Mesopotamia. During part of Israel's history this proved to be a blessing, as during Solomon's reign for example, but also a curse at other times when foreign powers recognized the military and strategic economic value of such a privileged geography (Cline, 360; King and Stager, 176).

3.1. Roads. According to D. A. Dorsey (1991, 2), "As yet no archaeological remains of an open road datable to the Iron Age have been uncovered in Israel." Only with the arrival of the Roman Empire were roads paved and constructed to last. Nevertheless, a complex system of *roads and highways that traversed ancient Israel during the Iron Age can be reconstructed on the basis of: (1) geographical and topographical determinism (e.g., a road following the natural course of a valley); (2) literary sources from the OT and the intertestamental period; (3) archaeological remains of city streets and gateways that can provide some ideas about corresponding open roads; (4) later archaeological remains of roads (e.g., Roman milestones) (Beitzel, *ABD* 5.776; cf. Dorsey 1991, 2). The most important routes that ran in a north-south direction through Israel were the Way of the Sea *(derek hayyām* [Is 9:1]), or Way of the Land of the Philistines *(derek ʾereṣ pĕlištîm* [Ex 13:17]), and the King's Highway *(derek hammelek* [Num 20:17]), the former being part of the Great Trunk Road, an international road system that connected Egypt with Mesopotamia. This coastal highway, known in Egyptian sources as the Way of Horus *(ANET,* 21), led from Memphis in the Nile Delta through *Gaza along the Mediterranean coast, turning inland at the Carmel Range across the Jezreel Plain at Megiddo toward the Sea of Galilee, continuing north to *Hazor and Damascus, where it joined up with the King's Highway, which started at the Gulf of Aqaba and traversed the whole of the Transjordanian Plateau. A third north-south route crossed the central highlands connecting *Shechem, *Bethel, *Jerusalem, Bethlehem, *Hebron and *Beersheba, as is attested in Judges 21:19, where the Hebrew term *mĕsillâ* is used, which refers to a highway that has been reinforced by grading and removing stones or other obstacles (Dorsey 1991, 228-33; see also Judg 20:31; 1 Sam 6:12; 2 Kings 18:17). During Solomon's reign these international roads were subjected to taxes and import duties that contributed to the wealth of the kingdom (King and

Stager, 194). Important east-west roads included the route from Joppa on the Mediterranean, through Jerusalem, down to *Jericho, and across the Jordan River, up to Rabbah of *Ammon, where it connected with the King's Highway (2 Sam 10:1-5; 2 Kings 5:4; Josh 10:10). From Gaza a road went eastward through Beersheba to Bozrah, the Edomite capital (Josh 15:3). Further north there was an important road leading from Acco southeast to Megiddo, further east to Beth-shan, and across the Jordan Valley to Ramoth-gilead (Dorsey 1991, 157-207). Traveling along these roads was a difficult enterprise, and among the hazards were deteriorating road surfaces, bandits, foul weather and wild beasts. Samson encountered a young lion along the Sorek Valley road between Zorah and Timnah (Judg 14:5-6), and *Elijah advised Ahab to return speedily from Mount *Carmel to *Jezreel because oncoming rains would make the road impassable for his chariot (1 Kings 18:44). Numerous ancient travelogues report the danger of robbery (Judg 5:6-7; cf. ANET, 477-78), so that traveling usually was undertaken in caravans, which could be as large as 100-200 donkeys (Beitzel, ABD 6.646), as the account of the visit of the Queen of Sheba indicates (1 Kings 10:2).

There is a marked increase in travel and transport from the Persian period onwards. An improved and maintained road system connected the various parts of the empire that even included the construction of bridges, such as the one mentioned by Herodotus across the Halys River in Asia Minor (Thiele, 200). There was a royal postal system with way stations, usually spaced at intervals of 16-24 km, where messengers could change horses and thus cross the empire from Persepolis to Sardis in nine days, covering a remarkable distance of about 2,500 km (Dorsey, ISBE 4.896; cf. Herodotus Hist. 8.98). The usage of bĕnê rekeš, "colt," in Ostracon 6.1 from Arad indicates that there was even some kind of express-mail service available and sheds some light on the biblical usage of the technical term in Esther 8:10, 14 (Klingbeil 1995, 302; see also Esther 3:13). All this forms a backdrop for Ezra's and Nehemiah's repeated lengthy journeys from the eastern part of the empire to Jerusalem (Ezra 7:9; 8:31-32; Neh 2:9-11).

3.2. Means of Transport. Aside from walking (Judg 16:1-3; 2 Sam 15:30; 1 Kings 18:46), the most common mode of overland travel in an-

cient Israel during the monarchy was by donkey (ḥămôr [Judg 1:14; 1 Sam 25:20; 2 Sam 17:23]) for common people, and by mule (pered) or hinny (pirdâ) for royalty as an important indicator of their social status. The king's sons were provided with mules (2 Sam 13:29), and during his coronation, Solomon was put on David's own hinny (1 Kings 1:33, 38, 44). Being hybrids, mules had to be imported to Israel, and they represented a luxury item without any long-term productive value, yet they were the ideal vehicle for the rugged Palestinian terrain (see Klingbeil 2003, 413-24).

Camels were another alternative for the ancient traveler, but they were used predominantly for long-distance and international trade. The Black Obelisk of Shalmaneser III (late ninth century BCE) reports two-humped camels as tribute from Sua the Gilzanean and from Egypt; on the Lachish Reliefs from Senacherib's palace in Nineveh (eighth century BCE) a fully packed camel appears. In 1 Chronicles 12:40 it is mentioned that during David's coronation, mules and camels were transporting foods in order to emphasize the importance of the event (Klingbeil 2003, 416). Returning from exile, the Israelites brought with them camels, and on a list of animals in Ezra 2:66-67 this pack animal appears third, behind horses and mules and before donkeys (see also 1 Sam 15:3; 1 Kings 10:2; 2 Kings 8:9).

Horses were used mainly for military purposes during the Iron Age, but they also played an important role in King Solomon's economic enterprises. The horse had been introduced into Palestine from Mesopotamia during the second millennium BCE, and in the tenth century BCE it was used for the chariotry of the Israelite army (1 Kings 10:26). Monumental buildings dating from the tenth/ninth century BCE excavated at Megiddo have been identified as barracks, storehouses or bazaars, but recent evidence such as teeth marks in the feeding troughs points to their original designation as stables for about 450 horses (King and Stager, 188-89). Chariots were an important strategic element in warfare, especially in the plains and valleys during numerous conflicts with the Philistines (2 Sam 8:4).

The distance that could be covered traveling along the roads of ancient Israel depended on the mode of travel, but normally it averaged 27-37 km per day. Mules and camels could travel about 40-48 km per day, and a horse-drawn chariot about 45 km. Professional armies could march about 32 km per day, as is indicated by the Assyrian army taking a little more than two months to cover the distance from Nineveh to Lachish in 701 BCE (King and Stager, 186). Marching from Jerusalem to Kirhareseth, the capital of Moab, was a journey of seven days (1 Kings 3:5-10), covering about 185 km. Ezra traveled with a caravan from the Babylonian border to Jerusalem in about three and a half months (Ezra 8:31; 7:9), making it a slow journey of about 1,450 km in one hundred days.

Hospitality was a sacred duty and a key factor for traveling through ancient Israel and beyond; it was received and had to be given to the sojourner based on the understanding of kinship (cf. Lev 19:33-34; Judg 3:15; Ps 23:5-6; Is 58:6-7). The Phoenician widow of Zarephath shared her bread with Elijah despite her scarce provisions (1 Kings 17:10-11). Eating with others had ritual overtones, and spending the night in someone's tent or house created a social and moral bond between the participants (Gen 19), while the refusal of hospitality was met with punishment (1 Sam 25:11).

3.3. Motives for Travel. There were times in Israel when travel came to a near standstill (Judg 5:6), but under less pressing circumstances there were enough reasons for traveling. As we have noted, economic activity was one of the more prominent motives for traveling, but beyond that and often combined with it, there were a number of other reasons: (1) military travel, involving the movement of troops and armies, which seems to have occurred almost on a yearly routine basis (2 Sam 11:1); (2) messengers who delivered communications to political allies (2 Sam 2:5), military commanders (2 Sam 11:19) and others; (3) government officials visiting foreign dignitaries (2 Sam 10:2), collecting *taxes or conducting a *census (2 Kings 15:20; 2 Sam 24:1), obtaining provisions for the king's household (1 Kings 4:27) and conducting other business; (4) travel for religious purposes, involving visits to a cultic center or attending religious festivals (1 Sam 1:3-7; 2 Kings 10:18-21); (5) travel for political purposes, including the large-scale deportations of ethnic groups throughout the ancient Near East, as in the case of the Assyrian and Babylonian exiles (see Dorsey, ISBE 4.891-92; Beitzel, ABD 6.648).

People also traveled for courtship (Judg 14:5-7), to search for employment (Judg 17:7-10), to attend a wedding banquet (Judg 14:8-10) or a funeral (1 Sam 25:1), or for any of the other innumerable reasons for which we still leave the familiar in search for new places and horizons.

See also AGRICULTURE AND ANIMAL HUSBANDRY; CITIES AND VILLAGES; ROADS AND HIGHWAYS.

BIBLIOGRAPHY. **B. J. Beitzel,** "Roads and Highways (Pre-Roman)," *ABD* 5.776-82; idem, "Travel and Communication (OT World)," *ABD* 6.644-48; **A. Biran,** "The ḥûṣôt of Dan," in *Frank Moore Cross Volume,* ed. B. Levine et al. (Eretz-Israel 26; Jerusalem: Israel Exploration Society, 1999) 25-29; **L. Casson,** *Ships and Seamanship in the Ancient World* (2d ed.; Baltimore: Johns Hopkins University Press, 1995); idem, *Travel in the Ancient World* (2d ed.; Baltimore: Johns Hopkins University Press, 1994); **E. H. Cline,** "Trade and Exchange in the Levant," in *Near Eastern Archaeology: A Reader,* ed. S. Richard (Winona Lake, IN: Eisenbrauns, 2003), 360-66; **D. A. Dorsey,** *The Roads and Highways of Ancient Israel* (ASOR Library of Biblical and Near Eastern Archaeology; Baltimore: Johns Hopkins University Press, 1991); idem, "Travel," *ISBE* 4.891-97; **M. Elat,** *Economic Relations in the Lands of the Bible, c. 1000-539 B.C.* [in Hebrew] (Jerusalem: Bialik, 1977); idem, "The Iron Export from Uzal (Ezekiel 27:19)," *VT* 33 (1983) 323-30; **J. S. Holladay Jr.,** "The Kingdoms of Israel and Judah: Political and Economic Centralization in the Iron IIA-B (ca. 1000-750 BCE)," in *The Archaeology of Society in the Holy Land,* ed. T. E. Levy (London: Leicester University Press, 1995) 368-98; idem, "Toward a New Paradigmatic Understanding of Long-Distance Trade in the Ancient Near East: From the Middle Bronze II to Early Iron II—A Sketch," in *The World of the Aramaeans: Biblical Studies in Honour of Paul-Eugène Dion,* vol. 2, ed. P. M. Michèle Daviau, J. W. Wevers and M. Weigl (JSOTSup 325; Sheffield: Sheffield Academic Press, 2001) 136-98; **Y. Ikeda,** "Solomon's Trade in Horses and Chariots in Its International Setting," in *Studies in the Period of David and Solomon and Other Essays,* ed. T. Ishida (Winona Lake, IN: Eisenbrauns, 1982); **P. J. King and L. E. Stager,** *Life in Biblical Israel* (LAI; Louisville: Westminster/John Knox, 2001); **G. A. Klingbeil,** "רכשׁ and Esther 8,10.14: A Semantic Note," *ZAW* 107 (1995) 301-3; idem, "Methods and Daily Life: Understanding the Use of Animals in Daily Life in a Multi-disciplinary Framework," in *Life and Culture in the Ancient Near East,* ed. R. E. Averbeck, M. W. Chavalas and D. B. Weisberg (Bethesda, MD: CDL Press, 2003) 401-33; **W. F. Leemans,** "The Importance of Trade: Some Introductory Remarks," in *Trade in the Ancient Near East: Papers Presented to the XXIII Rencontre assyriologique internationale, University of Birmingham, 5-9 July, 1976,* ed. J. D. Hawkins (London: British School of Archaeology in Iraq, 1977) 1-10; **K. Polanyi,** *The Livelihood of Man,* ed. H. W. Pearson (Studies in Social Discontinuity; New York: Academic Press, 1977); **D. C. Snell,** *Life in the Ancient Near East, 3100-332 BCE* (New Haven: Yale University Press, 1997); idem, "Trade and Commerce (ANE)," *ABD* 6.625-29; **L. E. Stager,** "Ashkelon and the Archaeology of Destruction: Kislev 604 B.C.E.," in *Joseph Aviram Volume,* ed. A. Biran et al. (Eretz-Israel 25; Jerusalem: Israel Exploration Society, 1996) 61-74; **R. F. G. Sweet,** "Buying," *ISBE* 1.562-65; idem, "Commerce," *ISBE* 1.748-51; **E. R. Thiele,** "Roads," *ISBE* 4.199-203. M. G. Klingbeil

TRANSPORTATION. *See* TRADE AND TRAVEL.

TRAVEL. *See* TRADE AND TRAVEL.

TRIBES OF ISRAEL AND LAND ALLOTMENTS/BORDERS

The definition of the tribes of *Israel is an anthropological question that concerns the biblical concept of tribe and the groups that are so designated as part of Israel. Land allotments/ borders considers three areas of concern: (1) the covenant nature of the gift of *land as an inheritance; (2) the forms of literature used to describe the allotments in Joshua 13—21 and their geographical definition; (3) the relationship of these territories to the larger entity of the land of *Canaan.

1. The Tribes of Israel
2. The Covenant and the Allotments
3. The Literary Forms of the Allotments
4. The Tribal Territories
5. Tribal Territories and Canaan

1. The Tribes of Israel.
From its earliest historical memories, the nation of Israel was defined by its composition in tribes. Despite internal challenges, such as the "redistricting" of the Solomonic age (1 Kings 4), and external threats, such as the division of the kingdom and the deportations of its members, the tribal structure remained a constituent part of Israel's constitution as a nation into the post-

exilic period (Ezra 6:17). So essential an element were the tribes to Israel's self-identity that the nation identified itself by tribal names—for example, the southern kingdom of Judah (e.g., 1 Kings 12:32) and the northern kingdom of Ephraim and Manasseh (e.g., 2 Chron 30:1).

1.1. An Israelite Tribe. Although the concept of a tribe differs in various cultures, it is incorrect that the biblical idea of an Israelite tribe was amorphous with little more than a unified center. Instead, the tribe was understood as a kinship-based patrimonial group whose descendants claimed relationship with one another through marriage and bloodlines that they traced back through the (usually) male relatives to one of twelve ancestral figures, the sons of Jacob/Israel (Schloen, 113-15, 135-83). As the patriarchal stories of Genesis suggest, tribal reality was modeled on the nuclear family and the extended family (Heb *bêt 'āb*) that was composed of the oldest male and his wife and children, as well as daughters-in-law, unmarried daughters, grandchildren and other dependents. This self-sufficient unit lived together in a single house or adjacent houses. A village of such families constituted a clan (Heb *mišpāhâ*), and these were clustered in a region that formed a tribe (Heb *šēbeṭ*). The biblical and extrabiblical evidence suggests that a clan might have at least a dozen nuclear families and half as many extended families at any one time. In the early period this could amount to about 150 people, with perhaps 7,500 in a tribe. The structure of the family was extended to the clan and to the tribe, so that each level had its elders who represented the tribal interests, and each member of the society had an identity defined by family ties. Thus the tribe functioned as an extended family (*see* Israelite Society).

1.2. The Identity of the Tribes of Israel. The twelve tribes of Israel, understood as the twelve sons of Jacob/Israel, are deeply embedded in the oldest stories of the family (Gen 29—35) and continue throughout the nation's history. Although there are diverse ways of expressing this relationship, the tribal composition of Israel is never otherwise understood. Although Joseph is a son of Jacob, his two sons Ephraim and Manasseh normally are mentioned as separate tribes (Gen 48; Num 1) and are so treated in the land allotments (Josh 16—17). This results in thirteen tribes. In the composition of the *Deuteronomistic and *Chronicler's Histories, however, not all tribes receive equal mention. While the tribes of Judah, Ephraim and Naphtali occur in all the Historical Books, others do not. Some, such as Benjamin (last mentioned in 1 Kings 15:22), Manasseh (2 Kings 10:33) and Issachar (1 Kings 15:27) disappear in the Deuteronomistic History but remain in the Chronicler's account and sometimes in Ezra and Nehemiah. Others disappear midway through the narratives of both historical traditions: Reuben (last mentioned in 2 Kings 10:33; 1 Chron 12:37) and Gad (2 Kings 10:33; 1 Chron 12:37). The tribes of Simeon, Dan, Zebulun and Asher are nowhere mentioned in Samuel, Kings, Ezra or Nehemiah. Levi is not found in Judges, Samuel, Kings or 2 Chronicles.

The only text in the Historical Books where the names of all twelve tribes appear is in the allotment of Joshua 13—21. In the roster of the tribes in Judges 5:14-18 the tribal names of Reuben, Dan, Benjamin, Ephraim, Issachar, Naphtali and Zebulun are mentioned. Makir (Judg 5:14) and Gilead (Judg 5:17) also are mentioned, but they are not separate Israelite tribes. Makir and Gilead are clans of Manasseh identified with groups that settled east of the Jordan (Num 32:39; Deut 3:15; Josh 13:31; 17:1, 3), unlike other elements in Manasseh who settled to the west.

2. The Covenant and the Allotments.
The tribes are identified not only by bloodlines but also by the land given to them in the allotments, as recorded in the book of *Joshua. This land constituted God's blessing on his people that formed his covenant relationship with them (see DOTP, Covenant). The land, already promised to the patriarch Abram (Gen 12:7) and reaffirmed throughout the Pentateuch, is again given to the generation of Israel that will enter and take possession of it (Josh 1:3-5). In the view of Deuteronomy and the Deuteronomistic History, this gift was given to the people of God as long as they remained faithful to the covenant. If they turned away from the covenant, God would revoke his gift and thrust them out of the land (Deut 28; Josh 1:5-9; 23:9-13; 24:16-20; 2 Kings 17:7-41; 23:26-27).

The tribal allotments of Joshua were set in the context of God's relationship with his people. That was defined by a covenant, something that was reaffirmed in the text both before and after the giving of the land (cf. Josh 8:30-35;

24:1-28). Comparison with land grants among West Semitic peoples reveals that they also were set within a treaty context. Most illustrative is the eighteenth-century BCE gift of Alalakh and other places to a leader who assisted his overlord in a battle (AT 456). This and other texts (cf. the treaty between Ugarit and Mukish/Alalakh) demonstrate boundary descriptions and other forms with a document not unlike a biblical covenant, where the history leading to the land grant is reviewed, legal stipulations are placed upon the vassal (cf. Israel as God's covenantal vassal) in return for the land, a ceremony involving the killing of an animal seals the agreement, and deities are invoked to bear witness to the event and the solemn agreement (Hess 1994b). Thus the allotments form part of a covenant between Israel and their God, just as neighboring second-millennium BCE West Semitic land grants and boundary descriptions were contained within a treaty/covenant document (Hess 2002).

3. The Literary Forms of the Allotments.
There are three types of allotment texts within the allotments of Joshua 13—21 (Alt): boundary descriptions, town lists, territory lists. For most tribes west of the Jordan we find boundary lists. However, these may be mixed with town lists that do not describe boundaries but include significant population centers within the tribal land. Finally, territory lists occur for the tribes east of the Jordan River. These may merely enumerate regions within a tribe such as Reuben or Gad, or they may serve as boundary descriptions of the totality of the geography defined by the tribe. As the ancient Near Eastern parallels and forms suggest, the boundary lists are among the earliest parts of this document, reaching back to the second millennium BCE.

The town lists may also be compared with second-millennium BCE town lists from Ugarit and Alalakh (and now from Hazor [Hess 1996; 2001]). Although there is no exact parallel to the form of these lists, they suggest an administrative source that may have been used for government and juridical purposes. If so, and if the demography of Israel changed with the appearance of new towns, then these lists must have changed to reflect a reality at the end of the northern and southern kingdoms' history (Hess, ISBE 4.907-13). Nevertheless, the comparisons that do exist with second-millennium

BCE archives and the careful form in which town lists fit within the outlined tribal boundaries suggest an origin not distant from the boundaries themselves (Kallai; Hess, *ISBE* 4.907-13; 1996).

4. The Tribal Territories.
For the tribes west of the Jordan, their boundaries are identical to the eastern, southern and western borders of Canaan (Aharoni). For the most part, the northern border of Judah is identical to the southern border of Benjamin. The identification of specific sites in the descriptions of Joshua 13—21 often is disputed (Hess 1996; Na'aman; Aharoni; Kallai).

4.1. Transjordanian Tribes. Joshua 13:8-14 summarizes the allotment of the tribal lands east of the Jordan Valley. Details of Reuben (Josh 13:15-23), Gad (Josh 13:24-28) and the half-tribe of Manasseh follow (Josh 13:29-31). The southern boundary for all these allotments was the Arnon River, with *Moab to the south and Reuben to the north. The northern border may have lain north of the Yarmuk in the Bashan (the modern Golan Heights). Reuben's inheritance description includes a territorial description (Josh 13:16) and a town list (Josh 13:17-20). Gad also contains a regional list (Josh 13:25) and a town list (Josh 13:26-27a). The forested area of Gilead from the region north of where the Jordan River meets the Dead Sea to the Jabbok River comprised the central territory of Gad. The apparent inclusion of Levitical towns from Manasseh and Reuben in Gad's territory (Josh 21:38-39) may suggest expansion of the tribe. The Transjordanian Manasseh list includes two regions (Gilead and Bashan) and a list of four sites (Josh 13:29-31).

4.2. Southern Tribes. Judah and Benjamin have the most extensive boundary descriptions and town lists. Judah's boundary description begins in the south and proceeds in counterclockwise direction (Josh 15:1-12). The same is true of Benjamin (Josh 18:11-20), though its description begins with its northern border. The districts of Judah include the southern (Josh 15:21-32); three in the Shephelah, or western low hill country related to earlier city-states of Adullam, Lachish and Kegila (Josh 15:33-36, 37-41, 42-44); the Mediterranean region (Josh 15:45-47), which some maintain was occupied at a later period; three districts in the southern

mountain region surrounding Debir, *Hebron and Maon (Josh 15:48-51, 52-54, 55-57); a district around Beth-zur to the north (Josh 15:58-59); an abbreviated town list (Josh 15:60); and a district eastward to the Dead Sea (Josh 15:61-62) that seems to have been settled in the eighth and seventh centuries BCE. In addition, the LXX adds a district with the town of Bethlehem (omitted in the MT) and surrounding villages in Joshua 15:61a. Such a district would bring the number of Judean districts to twelve. Benjamin preserves town lists comprising two districts, one to the east (Josh 18:21-24) and one to the west (Josh 18:25-28). This is related to the Judean lists, and part or all of these lists are thought to have comprised a separate Judean town list at some point (especially if the western list of Josh 15:45-47 was added only later). Dan, with no boundary description, also had a town list that could be divided into eastern (Josh 19:42-44) and western districts (Josh 19:45-48). The boundaries for Judah and Ephraim exclude any separate territory for Dan. Thus some would locate Dan's lists in the Ekron district of Judah (Josh 15:45-47) (see, e.g., Alt; Aharoni), before its movement to the north (Judg 18:11). Simeon, preserving only a town list (Josh 19:1-9), may relate to Judah's southern (esp. Josh 15:26-32) and central Shephelah districts (Josh 15:42). According to 1 Chronicles 4:31-33, Simeon had five towns; however, the Joshua texts list more, perhaps added as settlement grew.

4.3. Joseph Tribes. Situated between Benjamin to the south and the Jezreel Valley and Galilee to the north, Ephraim and its northern neighbor Manasseh occupied the central hill country where both the biblical texts (Joshua, Judges, Samuel; cf. Josh 17:14-18) and the archaeological settlement evidence from the twelfth century BCE suggest that the Israelite tribes first settled (Hess 1994a). The southern boundary appears first (Josh 16:1-3), and the western, northern and eastern boundaries occur in Joshua 17:10. Ephraim's southern boundary (Josh 16:5-6a) is followed by the boundary between the two Joseph tribes (Josh 16:6b-8). Manasseh's northern and southern boundaries (Josh 17:7-10) are followed by the only town list (Josh 17:11) that appears to comprise towns located outside the tribal borders, primarily in Issachar to the north. For the allotment east of the Jordan to Makir, warrior clans of Manasseh, see 4.1 above (Josh 13:29-31; 17:1).

4.4. Northern Tribes. Issachar is described by a town list (Josh 19:17-23) that places its territory in the eastern Lower Galilee, the eastern Jezreel Valley and the Beth-Shean Valley. Settlement does not appear to have occurred before the tenth century BCE. Its vulnerable location in the Jezreel Valley and the name *Issachar* (derived from *śkr*, "hire, take into paid service") suggest its susceptibility to servitude by the regional Canaanite cities.

Naphtali, with its boundary description (Josh 19:33-34) and town list (Josh 19:35-38), comprises much of the Upper Galilee as well as the Huleh Valley to the east. If the location of Kadesh is related to Barak's home (Judg 4:11), then it is probably in the south, where chariot warfare was possible (Aharoni; Naʾaman). Then the nearby oak of Zaanannim (Judg 4:11) should be located in the south and so should the rest of the border description of Joshua 19:33. The origin of this list should precede the Davidic incorporation of Ijon and Abel-beth-maacah into Israel, as these are not mentioned in Joshua.

Zebulun's description (Josh 19:10-16) contains a boundary description that outlines the western half of Lower Galilee, north of the Jezreel Valley and including the Beit Netophah Valley (Battof Depression), the richest part of the Galilee in terms of soil and agriculture. The description begins in the south and moves east until it turns north. Joshua 19:15 indicates a count of twelve towns, but fewer than that are mentioned. The western boundary would include Asher's eastern boundary.

Asher has a boundary description that begins in the south and turns north along the eastern border (Josh 19:24-28) and then returns south along the western coastal line (Josh 19:29-30). At least some of this region apparently was settled during the monarchy, since part of this region may have been ceded to Hiram by Solomon in payment for his services (1 Kings 9:11-12).

4.5. Levitical Towns. Having received no land for their inheritance, the tribe of Levi was assigned forty-eight towns scattered throughout the other tribes (Josh 21:41) (*see* Levitical Cities). Joshua 21 lists forty-four towns, with the remaining four perhaps found in Reuben's allotment as described in 1 Chronicles 6:63,

where the list of Levitical towns is repeated. Increasing archaeological evidence supports an eighth- or seventh-century BCE date for the Israelite habitation of many of these towns. Yet some form of this must have been envisioned from the covenant ceremony of Joshua 24 and its vision of a nation taught (by the Levites?) to worship God.

5. Tribal Territories and Canaan.

The Egyptian concept of Canaan in the Late Bronze Age (as found in Egyptian itinerary lists and thirteen occurrences in the fourteenth-century BCE Amarna correspondence) matched the early biblical descriptions of the land and equated it with the land God promised to Israel (e.g., Num 34:1-12) (Aharoni; Hess 1994a; 1998). Canaan north of the Galilee was neither assigned to nor occupied by Israel's tribes. In southern Canaan the Jordan River and the Dead Sea defined its eastern border. Thus the Transjordanian tribes were not in the land of promise. However, the tribal territories west of the Jordan included all of southern Canaan—that is, despite the incomplete occupation of the land by Israel (Josh 13:2-6; Judg 1), the idealized tribal boundaries were intended to be contiguous and thus to cover the entire land. Although no rationale for the particular divisions of the tribal territories is given, at least in some cases these divisions are an inheritance of the Late Bronze city-states in the land. Thus they describe geopolitical realities that delineate natural divisions within the land.

Some scholars, arguing for a Hellenistic date for the invention of the biblical conception of the borders of Canaan and of the Israelite tribal system, contend that it was a fiction created to provide an identity for the Judeans of the Hellenistic period and to justify the political goals of groups such as the Maccabees (Lemche; Thompson, esp. 353-423). However, this contention must be weighed against the correlation between the second-millennium BCE inscriptional evidence (Egyptian itineraries, Amarna texts, Alalakh texts) and archaeological evidence of the settlement of peoples in the hill country during the twelfth century BCE.

See also AMPHICTYONY, QUESTION OF; GEOGRAPHICAL EXTENT OF ISRAEL; ISRAELITE SOCIETY; LAND.

BIBLIOGRAPHY. **Y. Aharoni,** *The Land of the Bible: A Historical Geography* (2d ed.; Philadelphia:

Westminster, 1979 [1962]); **A. Alt,** "The Settlement of the Israelites in Palestine," in *Essays on Old Testament History and Religion* (BibSem 9; Sheffield: Sheffield Academic, 1989 [1953-1964]) 133-69; **R. S. Hess,** "Asking Historical Questions of Joshua 13—19—Recent Discussion Concerning the Date of the Boundary Lists," in *Faith, Tradition, and History: Old Testament Historiography in Its Near Eastern Context,* ed. A. R. Millard, J. K. Hoffmeier and D. W. Baker (Winona Lake, IN: Eisenbrauns, 1994a) 191-205; idem, "The Book of Joshua as a Land Grant," *Biblica 83* (2002) 493-506; idem, *Joshua* (TOTC; Downers Grove, IL: InterVarsity Press, 1996); idem, "Late Bronze Age and Biblical Boundary Descriptions of the West Semitic World," in *Ugarit and the Bible: Proceedings of the International Symposium on Ugarit and the Bible; Manchester, September 1992,* ed. G. J. Brooke, A. H. W. Curtis and J. F. Healey (UBL 11; Münster: Ugarit-Verlag, 1994b) 123-38; idem, "Occurrences of Canaan in Late Bronze Age Archives of the West Semitic World," in *Past Links: Studies in the Languages and Cultures of the Ancient Near East,* ed. S. Izre'el, I. Singer and R. Zadok (IOS 18; Winona Lake, IN: Eisenbrauns, 1998) 365-72; idem, "Tribes, Territories of," *ISBE* 4.907-13; idem, "Typology of a Late Bronze Age Administrative Document from Hazor," UF 33 (2001) 237-43; idem, "A Typology of West Semitic Place Name Lists with Special Reference to Joshua 13—21," BA 59.3 (1996) 160-70; **Z. Kallai,** *Historical Geography of the Bible: The Tribal Territories of Israel* (Jerusalem: Magnes; Leiden: Brill, 1986); **N. P. Lemche,** *The Canaanites and Their Land: The Tradition of the Canaanites* (JSOTSup 110; Sheffield: JSOT, 1991); **N. Na'aman,** *Borders and Districts in Biblical Historiography: Seven Studies in Biblical Historiography* (JBS 4; Jerusalem: Simor, 1986); **J. D. Schloen,** *The House of the Father as Fact and Symbol: Patrimonialism in Ugarit and the Ancient Near East* (SAHL 2; Winona Lake, IN: Eisenbrauns, 2001); **T. L. Thompson,** *Early History of the Israelite People from the Written and Archaeological Sources* (SHANE 4; Leiden: E. J. Brill, 1992).

R. S. Hess

TRIBUTE. See TAXES, TAXATION.

TUKULTI-NINURTA EPIC. See NON-ISRAELITE WRITTEN SOURCES: ASSYRIAN.

TWELVE TRIBES. See AMPHICTYONY, QUESTION OF; TRIBES OF ISRAEL AND LAND ALLOTMENTS/ BORDERS.

TYRE. See PHOENICIA, PHOENICIANS.

UGARIT, UGARITIC. See CANAAN, CANAANITES; CANAANITE GODS AND RELIGION.

UZZIAH. See HISTORY OF ISRAEL 5: ASSYRIAN PERIOD.

VINE, VINEYARD. See AGRICULTURE AND ANIMAL HUSBANDRY.

W, X, Y

WAR AND PEACE

The OT Historical Books give war a great deal of attention, at times in an apparently detached fashion. Peace, on the other hand, receives little attention. This article examines literary, historical, social and religious aspects of this phenomenon.

1. Literary Overview
2. Historical Matters
3. Social Matters
4. Morality in Warfare
5. A Time for Peace
6. Conclusion

1. Literary Overview.

In this article the *Deuteronomistic History (Joshua through 2 Kings) is understood as having been written in the early exile. It is a narrative attempt to understand the loss of the land. The books of Chronicles were written after the exile and address the resettlement and the reconstruction of Israel as a religious community. The books of Ezra and Nehemiah are a small collection, separate from that of the Chronicler, providing insights into the political and social struggles of the community after the exile.

1.1. Joshua. The book of Joshua presents a systematic occupation of *Canaan from the successful crossing of the Jordan River (Josh 1—5), to the conquest of the south-central region of the land (Josh 6:1-27; 7:1—8:29), and the claiming of the central regions (Josh 8:30-35). This section concludes with the covenant with *Gibeon (Josh 9:3-27).

The conquest of the south and west region (Josh 10:1-43) is prompted by the attack on the new allies by local rulers (Josh 10:1-15). Makkedah (Josh 10:28), Libnah, *Lachish (Josh 10:29-32), Hormah (Josh 10:33), Eglon (Josh 10:34-35), *Hebron and Debir (Josh 10:36-39)

are put to the sword. *Gilgal remains Joshua's base camp (Josh 10:15, 40-43).

Control of the northern country results from the clash of the hill dwellers of Galilee and the city dwellers of *Hazor (Josh 11:1-15). A summary of the conquest (Josh 11:21—12:24) and the equitable division of the land (Josh 13:1—22:34) form the climax to the story of the conquest. The covenant at *Shechem (Josh 24:1-28), the death and burial of Joshua (Josh 24:29-31) and the burial of the bones of Joseph (Josh 24:32-33) complete the story of the exodus.

1.2. Judges. The opening of the book of Judges (Judg 1:1-36) differs in detail from the story in Joshua. A pattern of disobedience, occupation and oppression, and deliverance is quickly established in Judges 3:7-31. The subsequent story becomes increasingly violent. Two defensive conflicts (Judg 4:1—5:31; 6:1—8:35) are followed by intertribal wars (Judg 9:1-57; 10:1—12:7). Tribal unity becomes fragile (see Judg 15:9-17). The disobedient migration of the tribe of Dan (Judg 17:6—18:20) ends with the massacre of the innocent inhabitants of Laish (Judg 18:21-31). The concluding chapters retell the horrific story of the betrayal of hospitality and the murder of an innocent woman by the inhabitants of *Gibeah (Judg 19:1-30). The book ends with a bloody civil war (Judg 20:1—21:12) and the rescue of the remnant of Benjamin (Judg 21:13-23).

1.3. 1 and 2 Samuel. The books of Samuel recount the transition from the *judges to the rule of *Saul and *David. In the political and historical context of the ancient Near East, the inevitable result is warfare. Only brief respites from violence follow.

1.3.1. 1 Samuel. After relating the birth and calling of Samuel (1 Sam 1—3), 1 Samuel moves directly into stories of warfare (1 Sam 4:1-2), with the *Philistines defeating Israel and taking possession of the *ark of the covenant (1 Sam 4:4-22). There is a call for a strong central military leadership (1 Sam 8:5, 20), and Saul is appointed (1 Sam 10:1).

Saul's first activity involves warfare (1 Sam 11) at Jabesh Gilead. His reign is characterized by war with the Philistines (1 Sam 13—14). After Saul's rejection (1 Sam 15), David emerges as the new hero (1 Sam 16—17), and he does what Saul could not do: defeat the Philistines. David's subsequent rise to prominence is based on his reputation as a successful soldier.

David's early life was as a mercenary of the Philistines (1 Sam 20—30), and he builds his reputation as a successful fighter. Saul's reign ends as it began, with warfare, as he and his son Jonathan die in battle at Gilboa (1 Sam 31). The monarchy is born in conflict and war.

1.3.2. 2 Samuel. In 2 Samuel 2, David consolidates power in Hebron. A "long war" (2 Sam 3:1) continues between Judah and Israel until the Israelites are defeated (2 Sam 2:12-28). The violence continues with David's capture of Jerusalem (2 Sam 5) and his wars against the Philistines (2 Sam 5:17-25; 8:1), *Moab (2 Sam 8:2), Hadadezer of Rehob (2 Sam 8:3-5), *Aram (2 Sam 8:6-8), Hamath (2 Sam 8:9-12) and Edom (2 Sam 8:13-14). By 2 Samuel 15—18, Israel has a staff commander of a standing army.

War with *Ammon (2 Sam 10) is followed by civil wars (2 Sam 16—19; 20). The final catalog of David's military achievements (2 Sam 21:15-22) is followed by a warrior's psalm (2 Sam 22; cf. Ps 18), a muster of David's officers (2 Sam 23:8-39) and an attempt at a military census (2 Sam 24).

1.4. 1 and 2 Kings.

1.4.1. 1 Kings. 1 Kings covers the period in Israel and Judah's history from the death of David (1 Kings 1—2) until the death of Ahab (1 Kings 22:37). *Solomon comes to power after civil war (1 Kings 2:19-25). Shimei's rebellion is suppressed (1 Kings 2:28-35), and Solomon's policies and reorganization of his administration (1 Kings 4) give rise to internal protest (1 Kings 11:14, 23).

The reign of *Rehoboam (1 Kings 12—14) endures Shishak's invasion as well as continued threat from outside (1 Kings 14:25-28). Rehoboam's attempt at invasion of the north is aborted (1 Kings 12:21-24). Asa's reign (1 Kings 15:9-24) involves war with the Israel and deals with

former enemies (1 Kings 15:16-21). Nadab of Israel is assassinated by Baasha during a war with the Philistines (1 Kings 15:23-31). This is followed by a succession of conflicts until the rise of Omri with the death of Elah at the hands of Zimri, and Zimri's death at the hands of Omri (1 Kings 16:8-20). Ahab's reign concludes with wars against Aram (1 Kings 20) and an alliance with *Jehoshaphat against Ramoth-gilead (1 Kings 22:1-36).

1.4.2. 2 Kings. The opening chapters of 2 Kings contain a violent clash of powers (2 Kings 1:9-16), the departure of *Elijah accompanied by the war cry "The chariots of Israel and its horsemen!" (2 Kings 2:12), and the Israelite version of the war with Moab (2 Kings 3). After 2 Kings 5 there is tension between Israel and Aram, then open warfare (2 Kings 6—7). The activities of *Elisha in 2 Kings 8—9 lead to more warfare into the reign of Jehu, Elisha's protégé. During Jehu's reign Israel suffers decline (2 Kings 10:32-36).

Later, Hazael continues his attacks upon Israel (2 Kings 12:17-18), and Jehoash is assassinated by his own servants (2 Kings 12:20-21). Eventually Israel's army is reduced to a pitiful few (2 Kings 13:1-7). There is some respite for Israel after Hazael's death (2 Kings 13:24-25). A brief war with Judah (2 Kings 14:8-14) and territorial gains under Jeroboam II in the north are followed by a series of coups d'état (2 Kings 15:8-16). In 2 Kings 15:17-22 the Assyrian king Pul (Tiglath Pileser III) annexes the northern half of the nation (2 Kings 15:29-31). There is a brief respite for Israel (2 Kings 16:5-20), but soon the whole of Israel and its capital, *Samaria, have fallen to an invasion of the *Assyrians (2 Kings 17:1-6).

*Hezekiah (2 Kings 18—20) is under pressure from Assyria, and 2 Kings 18:13—19:37 depicts the heavy toll of an Assyrian invasion. By the reign of *Josiah, *Egypt has become involved, and in a futile war with that country's leader, Neco, Josiah is killed in battle at *Megiddo (2 Kings 23:29-30). By the end of the book *Babylon, the new world presence, has dominated Judah, then attacked and ransacked its main cities, including the capital, *Jerusalem.

1.5. 1 and 2 Chronicles.

1.5.1. 1 Chronicles. In the opening census (1 Chron 1—9) the men of Reuben, Gad and the half-tribe of Manasseh are soldiers (1 Chron 5:18), as are the other half-tribe of Manasseh (1 Chron 5:23-24). The descendants of Issachar (1 Chron 7:1-5), Benjamin (1 Chron 7:7, 9, 11), Asher (1 Chron 7:40) and Ulam of the Gibeonites (1 Chron 8:40) are trained in warfare and skilled in the handling of weapons.

In 1 Chronicles 12 David attracts numerous ambidextrous archers from Benjamin (1 Chron 12:1-7) as well as spearmen from Gad (1 Chron 12:8-15), an officer corps from the kin of Saul in Benjamin (1 Chron 12:16-18), and Manassites, deserters from Saul's army (1 Chron 12:19-22; cf. 1 Sam 27:6; 30:1, 14, 26). The meeting of tribal representatives in 1 Chronicles 12:23-37 is that of a military muster.

In 1 Chronicles 13—14 the Hebron assembly appoints David king with the approval of the military leaders (cf. 2 Sam 5:1-2). The taking of Jerusalem continues the conquest (1 Chron 8:22-36; cf. Ps 105:1-15; 96; 106:1, 47-48). In the Chronicler's version of the "covenant with David" (1 Chron 17) the gift of rest is replaced with the subjugation of enemies (1 Chron 17:10; cf. 2 Sam 7:11). The same language of subjugation is used in the following chapters (1 Chron 18:1/ 2 Sam 8:1).

In 1 Chronicles 27 David's military status is emphasized. The structure of the Davidic administration is based on a census condemned earlier (1 Chron 27:24). David's organization is a staff of twelve hereditary military commanders, each with a division of twenty-four thousand men (1 Chron 27:1-15). The foundation of this administration is exploited later by Rehoboam (2 Chron 11—12).

1.5.2. 2 Chronicles. The interest in military details is continued in the second book (2 Chron 1:2; cf. 1 Kings 3:3-5.). Such detail is added to the reign of Rehoboam (2 Chron 10—12; cf. 1 Kings 12—14); the war between Abijah and Jeroboam (2 Chron 13; cf. 1 Kings 15:1-8); the defeat of Zerah the Ethiopian (2 Chron 14:9-13); the reign of Asa (2 Chron 15); the war with Israel and the appeal to Ben-hadad of Aram and the subsequent war with Baasha of Israel (2 Chron 16); the account of Jehoshaphat's reign (2 Chron 17:2, 12-19). 2 Chronicles 20 includes a long and stylized account of the battle against the Moabites (cf. 1 Kings 22). It is only at the end that the narratives of 2 Chronicles and 1 Kings coincide (2 Chron 20:31-37; cf. 1 Kings 22:41-47).

Comparison of the reign of Jehoram (2 Chron 21), with its addition of the Philistine invasion, the reign of Amaziah (2 Chron 25), the reign of Azariah (Uzziah) (2 Chron 26), the reigns of Jotham (2 Chron 27:1-9), Ahaz (2 Chron 28:1-27) and Hezekiah (2 Chron 29—32) with the parallels in the Deuteronomic History show the military emphases of the Chronicler's additions. This continues into the reign of Josiah (2 Chron 34—35; esp. 2 Chron 35:20-24). In a manner similar to that of the Deuteronomist, the Chronicler insists that the military defeats are to be seen as punishments for apostasy and abandonment of Yahweh.

1.6. Ezra and Nehemiah. Ezra and Nehemiah tell of no wars. During his journey to Judah, *Ezra was delivered "from the hand of the enemy and from ambushes by the way" (Ezra 8:31). His concern is the establishment of a Torah-based community, free from the "pollution" of intermarriage. At no time does he appeal to a military enforcement of these ideals.

Similarly, Nehemiah's references to things military are few. *Nehemiah is accompanied on his journey to Judah by "officers of the army and cavalry" (Neh 2:9) for protection. In the face of opposition of *Sanballat and "the army of Samaria" (Neh 4:2), Nehemiah establishes a civil guard to watch over the building sites at night (Neh 4:9). Armed men are also stationed "according to their families with their swords, spears and bows" (Neh 4:13) in strategic places on the walls. In the census (Neh 7:6-73) there is no mention of soldiers.

However, both Ezra and Nehemiah look upon military victory as blessing (Neh 9:9-11, 22-25), and upon defeat, invasion, and deportation as signs of God's displeasure and judgment (Neh 9:27-28).

1.7. Summary. The Historical Books tell a story of a nation whose early political history was shaped by war. Its subsequent history is played out against the background of conflict, death and battle.

National survival in violent times, the need for a share of limited resources, the competitive, agonistic context of the ancient Near East are valid reasons for this violence. However, the form of the literary discourse has shifted. The metaphor of a paradise lost to be regained later (the Genesis story) is now replaced by the meta-narrative of a struggle against hostile forces to acquire something promised but not yet possessed. It is the story of a people emerging from crisis, from a period "when chaos poses its most potent threat" (Rowlett, 11). At such times, people "tend to foster narratives of identity,"

(Rowlett, 11), and such narratives expound their past and hopes for their future. Times of "social drama" are times for the creation of new paradigms of behavior in which the participants find meaning and new structure to life. In the story Israel told at a time of exile there is the constant sound of war. It is a struggle that, at this stage, they have lost. Yet they have also been provided with a new beginning. War per se receives no condemnation in this literature. Certain wars might be deemed silly or unnecessary (1 Kings 12:21-24; 2 Kings 14:8-14), but such activity is not seen as necessarily wrong.

War was a common feature of life in the ancient Near East and the world of the OT (Raaflaub and Rosenstein, 1). Pillaging raids (2 Kings 13:20), intertribal conflict (Judg 19—20) and full-scale invasions (2 Kings 15:29) were expectations of life lived in a context of limited resources of unpredictable supply. States of war were without formal declaration and consisted of prolonged periods of conflict, raiding, skirmishing, besieging, pillaging and fighting. During times of militarization (2 Sam 8:15-18; 1 Kings 4:1-6) (Hobbs 1988) the effects would be widespread.

Because of the predominant character of warfare, it is important to understand the nature and technical character of the activity and its social impact. Since religion provided motivation for warfare and then sustained warriors and kings at war, it is equally important to understand the role of religious thought and ideology in this activity and the way in which this activity and its remembrance shape the character of the host society, its ideals and its values. Finally, it is important to ask after visions of or hopes for peace. If they are present, how are they achieved, and what is the nature of the peace achieved?

2. Historical Matters.

2.1. Organization. In the time of the judges military organization was minimal, reflecting the loose social organization of Israel. The Chronicler's vision of reorganization is reminiscent of this period (see also Num 1). By the middle of the monarchic period there is a sophisticated military culture, organized along the lines of many other states of the ancient Near East. This was begun in the reign of Saul (1 Sam 14:47-52), was continued by David (2 Sam 8:15) and built upon by his successors.

At the head of the army was the "commander in chief" (2 Sam 8:15; 1 Kings 2:35). The "mighty men" of David (2 Sam 23:8-39) formed the basis of an early military staff. The common military organization was a division of the army into "thousands" (1 Sam 8:12), "hundreds" (1 Sam 22:7; 2 Kings 11:19) and "fifties" (1 Sam 8:12). The term *yād* ("hand") (2 Kings 11:7) signified a squad of five men. The infantry—swordsmen, spearmen, archers (1 Chron 5:18) and slingers (2 Kings 3:25)—were so organized.

Cavalry were rare in the Israelite and Judean armies, and despite reference to "the chariots of Israel and its horsemen" (2 Kings 2:12; 13:14), there is little literary or archaeological evidence for them. Shalmaneser's record of the Battle of Qarqar (853 BCE) mentions only chariots and foot soldiers in Ahab's army (*ANET*, 279).

Chariotry fought in *zĕmādîm*, "squadrons" (2 Kings 9:25). The size of this force during periods of the monarchy often was small (2 Kings 13:7). Chariots are unsuited to siege warfare, and they had limited use primarily as transport or as psychological weapons (Jer 47:3).

Specialized troops, such as engineers and a commissary department, were essential. Siege engines and machines of war (2 Chron 26:15) needed skilled military engineers (2 Kings 24:16).

Supplies were necessary to conduct a campaign (2 Sam 11:1; 2 Kings 3:4-13). Reference to Saul's "baggage master" (1 Sam 17:22) suggests a rudimentary commissary (see also the Arad letters).

Military architects were responsible for fortresses, garrison outposts, scattered throughout Israel/Judah and along its borders. The army was managed from Jerusalem with skilled scribes and record keepers (2 Kings 25:19).

Specialized mercenary units were used. In the united monarchy Benaiah has command of "Kerethites" and "Pelethites" (2 Sam 8:18), names associated with the Philistines. One of David's generals was from *Gath (1 Sam 15:19-22). In the Arad letters the recipients of supplies—the troops manning the outer perimeter of forts—were "Kittim," the Hebrew word commonly used for Greeks.

The overall divisions of the army depended on the territory under the control of the king and on the human resources at his disposal. David's grandson Rehoboam divided the country into manageable military districts (2 Chron 11:5-12).

2.2. Leadership. A society's core values, born and nurtured in the collective experiences, are reflected in its leaders. In the restrictive context of an agrarian society, in which resources are limited and often unpredictable, notions of protection and provision dominate. Saul is not a romantic "antihero," a symbol of the triumph of the individual spirit over a cruel world, but rather an ultimate failure of the ideal ruler. With the exception of Josiah (2 Kings 23:28-30), the Historical Books judge all such defeats as punishment for wrongdoing.

The early leader is the local hero, well-known by the men he leads. In the monarchy the military skills of the king are valued, and those who hold command under him are also prized for their success in battle. In the postexilic period, as depicted in the books of Chronicles, there is a reversion to the older, tribal ideal. By implication, leaders of the armies of ancient Israel/Judah are trusted, skilled and trained in war, successful, and able to offer provisions and security to the people (1 Sam 7:14; 2 Sam 7:1) and rewards to their loyal followers (1 Sam 22:7). But above all of this is the ideal of the leader who is pious and whose faithfulness in practicing and maintaining the worship of Yahweh is consistent (Hobbs 1989, 89-108).

It is also these qualities and characteristics that are sought in God. God is a provider of goodness and blessing, a "refuge," a "help in times of trouble," a "rock" and "stronghold," a "deliverer from enemies," one who "trains hands for war" and is proudly depicted as a warrior par excellence. All of this is fully expounded in the psalm of David (Ps 18) reproduced in 2 Samuel 22.

2.3. Weapons. Military dynasties such as ancient Israel and Judah were heavily dependent upon a strong military presence to enact their political will. Organized military institutions are consumers of large amounts of raw materials and produce.

2.3.1. Types. Weaponry included javelins, spears (2 Sam 2:23), slings (2 Chron 26:14) and bows (1 Chron 12:2), which use muscle power or elasticity. Shock weapons consisted of the mace, a club, hand-held javelin (2 Sam 18:14) and sword. The evidence for this latter group is both archaeological and documentary. The ax is not found in the OT as a weapon of war. Protective armor and clothing such as shields, helmets and body armor were important (1 Sam 17:38-40;

1 Kings 22:34). Mobility on the battlefield was dependent upon chariots (1 Kings 22:34) or, for the ordinary soldier, legs and feet.

2.3.2. Manufacture and Acquisition. Materials needed were suitable wood for bows, arrows, spear and javelin shafts, chariot frames and wheels, shields, wagons, camping equipment, such as tent frames; metals such as bronze (copper and tin) and iron for blades, points, fittings, armor, helmets; oils for lubrication of wheels, preservation of weapons; bindings of leather or rope for chariots, sandals, belts, quivers, scabbards; cloth and leather for uniforms, cloaks, and tents.

Serious problems of supply were constant throughout the ancient Near East. Lack of direct archaeological evidence for manufacture of such tools of war is compensated for by reference to royal factories in 1 Samuel 8:10-18. Another method of supply of weaponry was confiscation from a defeated enemy (1 Kings 14:26-27).

2.4. Strategy and Tactics.

2.4.1. Strategy. The campaign of *Joshua provides all the elements of good military strategy: good use of terrain, wise deployment of forces and a long-term plan of action. All of this is based on an intimate knowledge of the terrain and on the command of an organized and disciplined army, which are conditions more suited to the centralized bureaucratic control of the monarchy. The memory, preservation and repetition of these stories suggests that they assumed the status of a strategic handbook. Military strategy during the monarchy displays similar use of terrain (e.g., 2 Kings 3).

2.4.2. Tactics. The Historical Books contain depictions of all of the forms of battle tactics known in the ancient world. The siege (2 Kings 6:24—7:20) was a messy and terrible form of warfare (Kern, 9-85). In the pitched battle, ranks of soldiers were drawn up in order (1 Sam 4:1-2, 10; 2 Sam 8:1-6; 2 Kings 14:11-14). Its purpose was to defeat the enemy's army in the field before plundering their cities. It was in every sense a "clash of arms" that ended when one side broke and fled (2 Sam 22:35-43). A few battles were deliberately fought against uneven odds (Judg 7), and there are sufficient illustrations from the history of warfare to suggest that a successful outcome against superior numbers is feasible. Stealth was used on occasion (1 Sam 14:1-15; 2 Sam 5:6-10). Related to this is the lure into an ambush (Josh 8:4-23). Some confrontations involve miraculous deliverance by God (Josh 5—7; 10:1-14; 2 Kings 19:35-37). The model is that of the deliverance at the Sea of Reeds (Ex 14). Although modern historiography does not regard divine intervention as a suitable historical cause, remembrance of battles in this way was common in ancient Near Eastern warfare (Rowlett, 49-70). However, in the OT it provides no automatic guarantee of future victory.

3. Social Matters.

The social effects of militarization and warfare were deep (Hobbs 1988; Raaflaub and Rosenstein). The supply of material and human resources exacted a high price from the populace (1 Sam 8:1-10).

3.1. Recruiting and Terms of Service. Recruiting led to displacement of the young village men and their families. The early army was raised by tribal muster, and men served for a short period of time. During the period of the monarchy the organization of the army became more complex with the establishment of a conscripted standing army (2 Sam 24) (*see* Census). Soldiers joined at age twenty (Num 1:3), with few responsibilities (Deut 20:1-9), and then trained in military skills (1 Chron 12:1-15). "Study of war" (Mic 4:3) was part of the soldier's experience. Such displacement and possible early death had wide effects on the traditional social structures, such as inheritance and the care of widows and orphans.

3.2. Political and Ideological Shifts. It is possible that the notion of group membership shifts from covenant partner to a form of citizenship in which disobedience to Yahweh is now replaced with treason against the king and his person (2 Kings 9:23). Internal social control becomes essential (2 Chron 11:5-12). Externally, the state must negotiate with or fight neighboring states for access to resources (1 Kings 20:7, 34).

Culturally, poetic images of Yahweh become laden with military characteristics (2 Sam 22:15, 32-43). The heroic stories remembered are those of the military hero, and the accompanying songs, such as "Saul has slain his thousands, but David his tens of thousands!" (1 Sam 18:7; 21:11), transform ancient notions of honor.

3.3. Religion and Warfare. In the Historical Books religion rarely functions as a deterrent to warfare. Exceptions are the prophetic intervention to stop Rehoboam (1 Kings 12:21-24) and the lonely voice of Micaiah ben Imlah (1 Kings

22:5-28). However, Joshua receives a divine word in prophetic form that gives him assurance of military success (Josh 1:2-7); Elisha becomes involved, for religious reasons, in two cases of "regime change" (2 Kings 8:7-15; 9:1-13); *Isaiah the prophet offers divine assurance of the safety of the city of Jerusalem and the defeat of the Assyrian enemy (2 Kings 19:20-37).

In the Historical Books religion functions mainly as a support for the current regime, especially in its warlike activity against enemies. Samuel's insistence on the total destruction ("ban" [see 4.1 below]) of the Amalekites (1 Sam 15:1-35) is an example of this support. The supposition that divine help is needed before battle (1 Kings 22) is a constant. Religion was part of the broader social and political structure. Modern ideas of a separate religious structure and ideology, of the inherent wrongness of warfare, and of an automatic opposition to warfare from the religious institutions and personnel are foreign to this ancient world. To the modern mind, the notion that religion be used in support of warfare is somehow indecent, but such sensitivities do not fit the context of the Historical Books.

The "imagined communities" of ancient Israel/Judah were clients of a patron deity, allied together in a covenant. The primary value of this bond was loyalty. Honor was mutual, and it was achieved by the exploits of either partner. The goal of this relationship and its resultant institutions was to maintain the notion of the divine and cosmic order upon which the relationship is predicated. The main threat to this relationship is the incursion of chaos and disorder in the form of cosmic and earthly powers such as dangerous enemies. All social, political and religious activities are outside the sphere of ethics and morality as we understand them today (i.e., as a matter of private conscience or choice); rather, they are for the maintenance of cosmic order (by force) (Judg 5:31), the sustenance of the deity and people (through war booty and tribute) (2 Sam 8:1-8), and the subjection of the enemies of divine order (by warfare) (2 Sam 22:44-51). Within this perception of the world, warfare is valued as an obligation, a religious duty.

4. Morality in Warfare.

In his classic book *On War*, Carl von Clausewitz offers a definition of morality or "moral powers": "the talents of the commander, the virtue of the army and national feeling." He uses the terms descriptively of abstract notions born of the age in which he lived. Normally, when the modern Christian considers the morality of the OT presentation of warfare, the thought is of a more prescriptive notion of morality. It is important to ask, then, What motivates the activity of warfare in the Historical Books?

First is the desire to protect and preserve the covenant gift of God, the land, and the people on it. This is common in the defensive battles and skirmishes of the earlier period (Judg 4; 5; 7) and in the final defensive battles of the Judean monarchy (2 Kings 24—25). Within this view, loss of land is regarded as a sign of unfaithfulness and punishment (2 Kings 10:32-36). Second is obedience to the command of God to a national leader (1 Sam 15; cf. Deut 20:10-18). Failure to obey completely is also a sign of unfaithfulness and is punished.

At the heart of warfare is the battle, either pitched in an open field or by siege. Fighting is conducted to its limits. The purpose of battle is to destroy an enemy, seen as a pollutant, and the level of killing is excessive to modern sensitivities. Israel/Judah fell victim to enemy aggression on numerous occasions (e.g., 1 Sam 4:10), but the two nations were willing participants in the most brutal and excessive forms of combat. The behavior of armies in these cases is taken for granted and never criticized or modified in the Historical Books.

4.1. The Ban. Of great interest and concern to the modern reader is the practice of the "ban": the complete annihilation of an enemy, his army, his women, children and livestock, and the destruction of his cities and towns (Deut 20:10-18; Josh 8:24-29; 1 Sam 15:3). The problems raised by this practice are enormous. In ancient times there were no rules of warfare that protected the victims. Victims were taken along with their possessions and regarded as fair gain. In Deuteronomy it is clear that Israelite practice of the ban was to avoid pollution. In the book of Joshua the motivation for the ban is to test the obedience of the people (Mitchell, 51-82). In either case, the ban represents "a controversial and dangerous ideology" (Niditch 1993a, 68). Neither of these ancient motivations solves the moral dilemma of the modern Christian reader, for whom there are broader theological issues that come into play when considering these

records. These issues include the nature of God as revealed in Jesus, and the example set by Jesus for his followers.

4.2. "Thou Shalt Not Kill." At first glance, the commandment "Thou shalt not kill" (Deut 5:17) appears to be an anomaly, but in ancient Israel a distinction was made between various kinds of killing. Laws distinguish between intentional killing (Num 35:16-21) and unintentional killing (Num 35:22-28). At times, the status of the victim plays a role in the judgment of the crime (Ex 21:20-21). Other terms are "to put to death," restricted to the activity of God (Deut 32:39); "to cut off from the people" (Ex 30:33), a pruning metaphor to indicate a social, if not a physical, death. In warfare, killing was circumscribed by its own sets of rules and conventions. Death in battle was given a different status than death in peacetime (2 Sam 3:22-30; 1 Kings 2:5). Other vocabulary is used. "To slay with the [edge of the] sword" usually is restricted to permitted wartime actions (Josh 6:21; 8:24). The precise term used in the commandment in Deuteronomy 5:17, *rāṣaḥ*, is restricted to actions against a member of the covenant community. It is murder, and the term is not used of the slaying of an enemy in battle (Josh 20:3, 5, 6; Judg 20:4; 1 Kings 21:19; 2 Kings 6:32).

5. A Time for Peace.

5.1. Observations on the Language of "Peace." The Historical Books are a collection of literature filled with the memory of warfare. It is important to inquire about its perspective(s) on peace. Three important points are to be made. First, there is an almost complete absence of the grand prophetic or psalmic visions of peace and prosperity. Second, it is unhelpful to inject into ancient literature the categories of modern psychology. It is anachronistic to suggest that the term *šlm* and its cognates have much to do with an inner sense of well-being. Third, there is little indication in the distribution of the vocabulary as to how this state is achieved. The verbal root and its cognates, often associated with "peace," are used in Historical Books in the following ways.

There are mundane uses of the term. A form of the verbal root indicates something completed (1 Kings 6:7; 7:51; 9:25; Neh 6:15). An adjective is used of the dedicated heart (i.e., the will) (1 Kings 8:61; 11:4; 15:3, 14; 2 Kings 20:3). The verb can be used in the sense of paying back a debt or an insult, restoring an upset social balance (Judg 1:7; 2 Sam 3:39; 2 Kings 4:7; 9:26), or restoring something lost or stolen (2 Sam 12:6). The noun is used as a greeting (Judg 6:23; 19:20; 21:13; 1 Sam 16:4, 5; 20:7, 21; 25:6; 2 Sam 18:28, 29; 1 Kings 2:13; 5:12; 2 Kings 4:23; 9:18, 22). The plural noun signifies peace offerings (Josh 8:31; 22:23; 1 Sam 10:8; 11:15; 2 Sam 6:17; 24:25; 1 Kings 3:15; 9:25; 1 Chron 16:1; 2 Chron 31:2).

The term is used in connection with warfare as a time of the cessation of hostilities (Josh 9:15; 2 Sam 10:19; 1 Kings 22:44 [MT 22:45]) and the making of peace, or the prolonged absence of fighting (Judg 4:17; 1 Sam 7:14; 2 Sam 17:3).

In Ezra-Nehemiah the term is used for the completion of the wall of Jerusalem (Neh 6:15), and Ezra cautions the people against making peace with their immediate neighbors (Ezra 9:12).

5.2. Achieving Peace. The means of achieving "rest" from enemies or war (Josh 14:15; 21:44; 22:4; Judg 3:11; 5:31; 2 Sam 7:1; 1 Kings 5:4; 1 Chron 22:9; 23:25; 2 Chron 20:30) is not always peaceful. Often it is predicated on warfare, siege and conquest (Judg 4:23). Note the violent conditions narrated in 2 Samuel 3:1—4:12; 5:6-10, 17-25 preceding the report that David received rest from his enemies in 2 Samuel 7:1. This peace often is accompanied by the subjugation of Israel's neighbors (2 Sam 8:1-14) and the occupation of their land. 2 Samuel 22 (cf. Ps 18) is set in the context of "deliverance from the hand of all [David's] enemies, and from the hand of Saul" (2 Sam 22:1). It is a true "warrior psalm," which glories in battlefield prowess and the violent humiliation of an enemy.

The story told in the Historical Books is that of conflict, victory or defeat. The metanarrative that shapes their perspective on the world is that victory equals blessing; the achievement of victory is through obedience. Defeat equals divine displeasure and judgment; the cause of defeat is disobedience and betrayal of the covenant patron.

5.2.1. The Deuteronomist. For the Deuteronomist, the explanation for the defeat of Israel (2 Kings 17) and Judah (2 Kings 24—25) is the tendency to forsake Yahweh and to refuse to listen to the prophets who had warned them (2 Kings 17:12-18). It is possible that the Deuteronomist's presentation of monarchy is ironic. The dangers of the initial request for a king "to fight our battles for us" (1 Sam 8:20) have been realized in the failed attempt to govern the people and to survive in the international scene by military means. Where prophetic characters appear, they reject the notion that blessing comes from the exercise of military power (2 Kings 19:20-34; cf. Ps 44:4-10).

Does the Deuteronomist present a vision of hope and peace? This question is widely debated in OT scholarship. The date of the initial edition (Josianic or postexilic) and the relationship of the book of Jeremiah to this corpus figure in this debate. The note of hope among the faithful exiles that some scholars have found (Hobbs 1985, 368-69) still persuades. However, this expression of hope states little as to how that hope is to be realized. In the Deuteronomistic History the exiled king is still seen as living, which suggests that the renewed community would be a form of monarchy. An intriguing possibility is that the story of Elisha and Naaman (2 Kings 5) is a "counterhistorical" anecdote, subverting the usual power plays of the grand story and offering a glimpse at an alternative way for nations to live together. However, this is only a glimpse.

5.2.2. The Chronicler. Prophets figure less in the Chronicler's story, but he has established a rhythm of military fortune dependent upon obedience, similar to the book of Judges. The establishment of the Davidic monarchy is a military act, and subsequently much space is devoted to military leaders and activities (see 2 Chron 29:3-10; 33:10-13; 36:17 and their parallels). The Chronicler's conclusion holds out a vision of hope of deliverance through the direct intervention of the Persian king Cyrus (2 Chron 36:23).

Some see this vision anticipating the Christian vision of Jew and Gentile meeting together in Christ (Dillard, 302-3). In the broader canonical context of the passage this has possibilities, but the dominant role for the military throughout the Chronicler's story suggests that the renewed community will be built along military lines, with a military organization of men equipped for war, trained and skilled in the handling of certain weapons. As with 2 Kings 5, it is also possible that Jabez (1 Chron 4:9-10) subverts the normal acquisition of land through violence. Ezra and Nehemiah, however, are not kindly disposed to Gentiles (Ezra 10:44; Neh 13:23-27).

6. Conclusion.

There are several ways of understanding the violent history portrayed in the Historical Books.

None of these understandings is complete in itself or exclusive of the others. First, this history may be read as a grand cautionary tale advising readers to avoid the pitfalls of the past that relied too much on military might. Second, it may be read as a grand, ironic narrative of tragedy: power corrupts and destroys. Third, it may be read as a nostalgic memory of the past and an expression of longing for an ancient time of glory. All of these are possible.

Taken in isolation, the Historical Books' discourse is depressing, and it is relieved by very little in the way of peace, perhaps somewhat by contrary stories such as those of Naaman or Jabez. It is on the broader landscape of the entire biblical canon that the story must be read. These narratives of violence must be brought into the dialogue with the prophetic and psalmic visions of peace and with the life and ministry of Jesus of Nazareth.

See also ETHICS; KINGS AND KINGSHIP; SALVATION AND DELIVERANCE.

BIBLIOGRAPHY. **S. Anglim et al.,** *Fighting Techniques of the Ancient World, 3000 BC-AD 500: Equipment, Combat, Skills and Tactics* (New York: Thomas Dunne Books, 2002); **P. C. Craigie,** *The Problem of War in the Old Testament* (Grand Rapids: Eerdmans, 1978); **D. Dawson,** *The First Armies* (Cassell's History of Warfare; London: Cassell, 2001); **R. B. Dillard,** *2 Chronicles* (WBC 15; Waco, TX: Word, 1987); **R. Gabriel and K. Metz,** *From Sumer to Rome: The Military Capabilities of Ancient Armies* (Westport, CT: Greenwood, 1991); **V. D. Hanson,** *The Western Way of War: Infantry Battle in Classical Greece* (New York: Knopf, 1989); **T. R. Hobbs,** *2 Kings* (WBC 13; Waco, TX: Word, 1985); idem, "An Experiment in Militarism," in *Ascribe to the Lord: Biblical and Other Studies in Memory of Peter Campbell Craigie,* ed. L. E. Eslinger and G. Taylor (JSOTSup 67; Sheffield: JSOT, 1988) 457-80; idem, *A Time for War: A Study of Warfare in the Old Testament* (Wilmington, DE: Michael Glazier, 1989); **P. B. Kern,** *Ancient Siege Warfare* (Bloomington: Indiana University Press, 1999); **M. Lind,** *Yahweh Is a Warrior: The Theology of Warfare in Ancient Israel* (Scottdale, PA: Herald Press, 1980); **P. D. Miller Jr.,** *The Divine Warrior in Early Israel* (HSM 5; Cambridge, MA: Harvard University Press, 1973); **G. Mitchell,** *Together in the Land: A Reading of the Book of Joshua* (JSOTSup 134; Sheffield: JSOT, 1993); **S. Niditch,** *War in the Hebrew Bible: A Study in the Ethics of Violence* (Oxford: Oxford University Press, 1993a); idem, "War, Women and Defilement in Numbers," in *Women, War and Metaphor: Language and Society in the Study of the Hebrew Bible,* ed. C. Camp and C. Fontaine (Semeia 61; Atlanta: Scholars Press, 1993b) 39-57; **K. Raaflaub and N. Rosenstein,** eds., *War and Society in the Ancient and Medieval Worlds: Asia, the Mediterranean, Europe, and Mesoamerica* (Center for Hellenic Studies Colloquia 3; Cambridge, MA: Harvard University Press, 1999); **G. von Rad,** *Holy War in Ancient Israel* (Grand Rapids: Eerdmans, 1991); **L. Rowlett,** *Joshua and the Rhetoric of Violence: A New Historicist Analysis* (JSOTSup 226; Sheffield: JSOT, 1996).

T. R. Hobbs

WARREN'S SHAFT. *See* WATER AND WATER SYSTEMS.

WATER AND WATER SYSTEMS

Water is essential for sustaining the life of plants and animals, including humans. One of the determinants for human habitation is the availability of water sources for human and animal consumption and for agricultural pursuits. Climatic and ecological conditions in Palestine dictate heavy reliance on precipitation. In addition to precipitation (rain, dew, snow), the amount of which is regionally determined, the most sought-after water sources are perennial, including springs, brooks, streams, rivers and lakes. Availability of water determines the location and nature of human settlements, as is demonstrated by the Stone Age settlement near the Yarmuk, the Neolithic settlements by the spring at Jericho or near the spring of Ain Ghazal. When water sources are absent but the need for a settlement is present, humans find ways to adapt to prevailing conditions by digging wells and pools, hewing cisterns, designing catchment and distribution systems, and building aqueducts and other systems such as tunnels and canals for transporting water from one place to another.

1. Israelite Water Use
2. Water Systems in Ancient Palestine
3. Water Systems—Typology and Dating

1. Israelite Water Use.

Israelite settlement, which originated in the hill country, was enabled mostly because of the Israelites' mastery of hewing cisterns and plastering them. Israelite hamlets and villages throughout the hill country flourished during the Iron Age because of their ability to collect rainwater and store it, and in turn to use it efficiently when needed. Israelite settlement in arid zones such as the Negev was possible because of the Israelites' skills in diverting and collecting runoff water that was used for agriculture as well as for human and animal consumption.

2. Water Systems in Ancient Palestine.

The need for water in the urban setting was already extant in pre-Israelite periods, and it produced several water systems. With the rise of the monarchy and the development of urban life among the Israelites, new systems had to be designed to sustain the growing population in the cities, especially in times of war. Cities such as *Jerusalem, *Gibeon and *Megiddo, which were built near perennial springs, could use these sources openly in times of peace. However, during periods of hostilities, these sources had to be protected from being captured by the attacking enemies while providing water to the besieged inhabitants. To this end, under the supervision of the central government, systems were designed and built to enclose the open water sources and divert the water into the city or to provide the citizens with an intramural water source by tapping the water table inside the city. As we will see, some of these systems are alluded to in the Bible.

3. Water Systems—Typology and Dating.

In addition to open collection pools and enclosed hewn cisterns, several types of water systems were developed (Cole; Shiloh, 289-92). These include systems that reach a water source through a tunnel; some combine a shaft and a tunnel; a few allow access from the outside and through a tunnel. Other systems depend on the collection of runoff water and the manual transport of water from a source to a holding tank.

3.1. Jerusalem. Throughout its history, Jerusalem had several water systems, most of which centered on the Gihon Spring, located at the bottom of the eastern slope, which was the only perennial water source of Jerusalem and was the reason for the city's location.

3.1.1. Warren's Shaft. Since its discovery by Charles Warren in 1867, it was theorized that Warren's Shaft was the ṣinnôr, the water shaft, through which David's men under the leadership of Joab penetrated Jerusalem and con-

quered it (2 Sam 5:8; also 1 Chron 11:6). Recent archaeological work strongly suggests that Warren's Shaft, which was a natural phenomenon, was never used for drawing water, and its existence was unknown until the eighth century BCE. Thus the reference to the ṣinnôr must have been to another water system constructed in Middle Bronze Age II (eighteenth-seventeenth centuries BCE) that included a spring-fed pool and a guard tower made of cyclopean masonry (Reich and Shukron).

3.1.2. The Siloam Channel. Two water systems dated to the Iron Age, known as the Siloam Channel and Hezekiah's Tunnel, are also fed by the Gihon Spring. The Siloam Channel, possibly alluded to in Isaiah 8:6, is about 400 m long and carries water partially in a rock-hewn and stone-covered channel to reservoirs and garden plots in the Kidron Valley. The channel has window-like openings; it has been suggested that they were used to divert water for irrigation and for collecting runoff water. The system lies outside the fortifications, and its vulnerability suggests peacetime usage (Shiloh, 285).

3.1.3. Hezekiah's Tunnel. The system known as Hezekiah's Tunnel, 533 m in length, carries the water of the Gihon Spring to a pool on the west side of the hill. It is the most sophisticated because of its method of construction. The winding tunnel was hewn from both ends simultaneously, and the two teams managed to meet each other in the middle. This moment was commemorated in an inscription discovered in 1880 that reads in part, "While [the stonecutters were] still [striking with] the axe, each man toward his fellow, . . . [there was heard] the voice of a man calling to his fellow, as there was a *zdh* in the rock" (Borowski, 105). The word *zdh* is translated by most scholars as "crack, fissure," and is used by some to explain the way the stonecutters achieved their feat of meeting by following the natural fissure, which must have run from the spring all the way to the pool. The construction of the tunnel is attributed to *Hezekiah, following two biblical references describing how he diverted the water of the Gihon in preparation for his revolt against Sennacherib in 701 BCE: "And the rest of Hezekiah's deeds and his great exploits including building the pool and the channel and bringing water into the city, they are indeed written in the chronicles of the kings of Judah" (2 Kings 20:20; see also 2 Chron 32:30). Paleographically, the inscription dates to the eighth century BCE, the time of Hezekiah's reign.

3.2. Hazor. The water system at *Hazor is similar in principle to the one at *Gezer (see 3.4 below), since both tap into the groundwater below the site rather than reach a perennial water source outside the confines of the site. The system at Hazor included an entrance structure, a vertical shaft with a descending staircase along its walls, a stepped sloping tunnel and a water chamber. The nature of the system made it safe for the local inhabitants. The excavators dated its construction to the ninth century BCE, and its demise to the destruction of Hazor in 732 BCE (Yadin, 233-47; Ben-Tor and Bonfil, 239-46).

3.3. Megiddo. During the time of the Israelite monarchy, Megiddo had two water systems, both connected with the northern spring ʿAin el-Qubi, located in a cave.

3.3.1. The Gallery (Locus 629). Gallery 629 is a narrow passageway connecting the inside of the city to the spring. It was built of ashlar and rubble masonry. Although the excavators originally dated it to the twelfth century BCE, it has been redated to the tenth century BCE and related to the Solomonic city (Lamon, 10-12; Davies, 92-93; Shiloh, 276). This system was in use during peaceful times and went out of use with the construction of the city wall (Locus 325).

3.3.2. The Shaft and Tunnel. The shaft (Locus 925) and tunnel (Locus 1000) are the heart of the water system at Megiddo. They connect the inner part of the city with the water source located outside the walls. In principle, this system is highly reminiscent of those at Hazor and Gezer; however, it went through several modifications (Lamon, 12-23; Shiloh, 276-78). Entrance to the system from the outside through the water source was prevented by a massive wall (Lamon, 23-26). The excavators dated the construction of the system to the twelfth century BCE, but it was redated to the ninth century BCE, to the time of Ahab and his major construction efforts. The system went out of use after the destruction of the site by the Assyrians in the eighth century BCE.

3.4. Gezer. The Gezer water system was excavated by R. A. S. Macalister at the beginning of the twentieth century (Macalister, 1.256-65; 3, plate LII). The system, which is quite similar to the one at Hazor, includes an entrance area, a stepped tunnel, and a water chamber (Shiloh, 281). Unlike in Jerusalem, Megiddo and Gibeon, the builders of the Gezer system reached the water table below the site rather than incorporating an outside water source. The excavator dated the system to what he termed the Second Semitic period (equivalent to what we now call Middle Bronze Age II); however, Y. Yadin and Y. Shiloh date it to the beginning of the tenth century BCE because of the similarities to the Hazor system, which is securely dated (Shiloh, 281).

3.5. Gibeon. The ancient site of Gibeon had two water systems, both excavated by J. B. Pritchard in 1956-1957 (Pritchard 1961; 1962, 53-78; Shiloh, 282-83).

3.5.1. The Tunnel. The entrance to this system is inside the city; it led to a stepped tunnel with a water chamber at its bottom. A feeder channel carried the water from an underground spring (ʿAin el-Balad) to the water chamber. The water chamber could also be entered from the outside; however, when needed, this entrance could be blocked and concealed to protect the water source. The plan of the tunnel suggests that it was constructed after the pool (see 3.5.2 below) was already in place, and Pritchard (1962, 63) dates this system to about the tenth century BCE. It went out of use probably after the conquest of the site by Nebuchadnezzar in 598 or 586 BCE, or even earlier during Sennacherib's campaign in Judah in 701 BCE (Pritchard 1962, 71).

3.5.2. The Pool. An earlier system is that of the pool and stairway located just inside the city wall and adjacent to the entrance to the tunnel system. The system is made of a stone-hewn circular pool with an inside staircase and a parapet leading into a water chamber at the same level of the water source of the tunnel and at a distance of about 5 m from the spring (Shiloh, 283). There are biblical references connecting Gibeon and the Gibeonites to water (Josh 9:21, 23, 26; Jer 41:12). One particular reference in 2 Samuel might be to the pool and stairway system when it mentions the "Pool of Gibeon" as the site of a military encounter between Joab and Abner and their soldiers: "And Abner son of Ner with the servants of Ish-Bosheth son of Saul came from Mahanayim to Gibeon. And Joab son of Zeruyah and David's servants went out [of Hebron] and met them at the pool of Gibeon; and they sat at the pool, one group on one side and the other on the other side" (2 Sam 2:12-13).

3.6. Beersheba. In monarchical times *Beersheba had two water sources, a well and a reservoir (Herzog).

3.6.1. The Well. The well is located outside the gate and was used during Iron Age II by the inhabitants and travelers in times of peace. The upper part, about 5 m, was dug in the conglomerate layers and was lined with dressed stones. The rest of the well, to a depth of over 69 m, was hewn from the limestone rock. The well remained in use during the Hellenistic period and went out of use probably in the Herodian period as the result of an earthquake.

3.6.2. The Reservoir. To secure water for the inhabitants in times of war, a very elaborate water system was constructed when Beersheba was built as a fortified town in the tenth century BCE. This system continued to serve, with major modifications, until the fall of the city at the end of the eighth century BCE. The heart of the system is a complex of five plastered holding tanks roughly arranged in the shape of the letter *H* with an elongated horizontal bar. The entrance into the system was gained through a deep rectangular shaft, the walls of which were supported with stone walls, with a spiraling staircase leading down into the reservoir through a narrow tunnel-like entrance. The reservoir, which had the original capacity of 700 cubic m, was fed through an elaborate system of channels, control chambers and silting sumps, with runoff water rushing down Wadi Hebron. When the site was resettled in the Persian and Hellenistic periods, the nature of the system changed, and part of it was reconditioned to become a cistern for the collection of rainwater.

3.7. Beth-Shemesh. The water system at Beth-Shemesh is located inside by the city gate. The plastered cruciform reservoir, that could hold 7,700 cubic ft of water, is entered through a stepped corridor leading from the gate area into the western wing. The system was fed by channels with runoff water, which could be drawn also through a narrow shaft in the ceiling (Bunimovitz and Lederman). According to the excavators, the system was constructed in the tenth century BCE and went out of use in the seventh century BCE.

3.8. Arad. The water system in the fortress of *Arad was in use in the ninth to sixth centuries BCE. It was made of a rock-hewn feeder channel and at least three oval plastered holding tanks, of which only one has survived. The channel entered the citadel under the defense wall from the west, and to protect the site from enemy penetration through the channel, it was constructed narrowly. Unlike all the other systems previously mentioned, the Arad system had to be filled manually from an outside source, which probably was the well located at the bottom of the hill on top of which stood the fortress (Shiloh, 288; Amiran et al., 210-19).

3.9. Other Systems. Many other sites contain the remains of Iron Age water systems similar to the ones described above, some of which are *Lachish (Shiloh, 287), Kadesh Barnea (Shiloh, 289), Ible'am (Shiloh, 283) and Tell es-Sa'idiyeh (Shiloh, 289). Some water systems are alluded to in ancient records such as the Bible, where several pools in Jerusalem (e.g., 2 Kings 18:17 = Is 36:2), *Hebron (2 Sam 4:12), *Samaria (1 Kings 22:38) and other places are mentioned, and the Mesha (Moabite) inscription (Smelik), which mentions the construction of cisterns in Qarhoh.

See also AGRICULTURE AND ANIMAL HUSBANDRY; CITIES AND VILLAGES; JERUSALEM.

BIBLIOGRAPHY. **R. Amiran et al.,** *Arad* [in Hebrew] (Tel Aviv: Hakkibutz Hameuchad; Israel Exploration Society; Israel Antiquities Authority, 1997); **A. Ben-Tor and R. Bonfil,** eds., *Hazor V: An Account of the Fifth Season of Excavation, 1968* (Jerusalem: Israel Exploration Society and Hebrew University of Jerusalem, 1997); **O. Borowski,** *Daily Life in Biblical Times* (SBLABS 5; Atlanta: Society of Biblical Literature, 2003); **S. Bunimovitz and Z. Lederman,** "Beth-Shemesh: Culture Conflict on Judah's Frontier," *BAR* 23.1 (1997) 43-49, 75-77; **D. Cole,** "How Water Tunnels Worked," *BAR* 6.2 (1980) 8-29; **G. I. Davies,** *Megiddo* (Cities of the Biblical World; Cambridge: Lutterworth, 1986); **Z. E. Herzog,** "Water Supply at Tel Beersheba in the 1st Millennium BCE," in *Cura Aquarum in Israel: In Memoriam Dr. Ya'akov Eren; Proceedings of the 11th International Conference on the History of Water Management and Hydraulic Engineering in the Mediterranean Region, Israel, 7-12 May 2001,* ed. C. Ohlig, Y. Peleg and T. Tsuk (Schriften der Deutschen Wasserhistorischen Gesellschaft 1; Sieburg: Deutschen Wasserhistorischen Gesellschaft, 2002) 15-22. **R. S. Lamon,** *The Megiddo Water System* (University of Chicago Oriental Institute Publications 22; Chicago: University of Chicago Press, 1935); **R. A. S. Macalister,** *The Excavation of Gezer, 1902-1905 and 1907-1909* (3 vols.; London: Murray, 1912); **J. B. Pritchard,** *Gibeon, Where the Sun Stood Still: The Discovery of the Biblical City* (Princeton,

NJ: Princeton University Press, 1962); idem, *The Water System of Gibeon* (Museum Monographs; Philadelphia: University Museum, University of Pennsylvania, 1961); **R. Reich and E. Shukron,** "Light at the End of the Tunnel," *BAR* 25.1 (1999) 22-33, 72; **Y. Shiloh,** "Underground Water Systems in the Land of Israel in the Iron Age," in *The Architecture of Ancient Israel: From the Prehistoric to the Persian Periods,* ed. A. Kempinski and R. Reich (Jerusalem: Israel Exploration Society, 1992) 275-93; **K. A. D. Smelik,** "The Inscription of King Mesha," *COS* 2.23:137-38; **Y. Yadin,** *Hazor: Rediscovery of a Great Citadel of the Bible* (New York: Random House, 1975).

O. Borowski

WEAPONS. *See* WAR AND PEACE.

WELLS. *See* WATER AND WATER SYSTEMS.

WHEAT. *See* AGRICULTURE AND ANIMAL HUSBANDRY.

WISDOM

Six questions help clarify the role of wisdom in the Historical Books of the OT. First, what was the nature of wisdom? Second, who were the practitioners of wisdom? Third, how were they trained? Fourth, on what occasions was wisdom employed? Fifth, what did wisdom contrast? Sixth, was wisdom responsible for authoring the Historical Books?

1. Nature of Wisdom
2. Practitioners of Wisdom
3. Training for Sages
4. Occasions for Wisdom
5. Wisdom in Contrast
6. Wisdom Tradition as Author of the Historical Books
7. Conclusion

1. Nature of Wisdom.

Wisdom words (including *ḥokmâ* ["wisdom"], *bînâ* [insight], *ʿēṣâ* ["counsel"], *ʿormâ* ["prudence"] and *ṭaʿam* ["discernment"]), together with wisdom events (episodes where proverbs, fables, parables, counsel or dramatic ruse are used for persuasion) lead to the following general definition of wisdom: *counsel leading to successful action* (see Whybray 1974, 10). Ethical edges remain intentionally blurred in this definition, consistent with the range of wisdom found in the Historical Books. A course of ac-

tion that was embraced by one because of its effectiveness may have been despised by another as abhorrent. Sapiential resources servicing both aims went by the title *wisdom.* As suggested below, this tension may account for a trend found in certain passages of the Hebrew Bible—a trend toward marginalizing wisdom deemed ethically deficient while enshrining wisdom perceived to be consonant with piety.

2. Practitioners of Wisdom.

As a rule, the Historical Books are concerned with national figures and events of state. Thus our picture of wisdom is limited largely to leaders, whether served by sages or acting as sages themselves.

2.1. Sages Serving Leaders. In times of deliberation and crisis, leaders interacted with sages. Some served the court in an appointed role, while others operated independently.

2.1.1. Appointed Sages. Some invited sages gave only cameo appearances, such as the wise woman of Tekoa, recruited by Joab to persuade David to rescind Absalom's exile (2 Sam 14:1-21). Other invited sages filled long-term roles as royal counselors. A brief account from the reign of Amaziah illuminates their privileges at court. After defeating the Edomites, Amaziah turned to worship their ineffective gods. When a nameless prophet dared to question such folly, Amaziah retorted, "Have we made you king's counselor? Stop! Why should you be executed?" (2 Chron 25:16a). Evidently, only someone invested as royal counselor might dare oppose the king so blatantly and still wish to keep his head. Note the wisdom language in the prophet's reply, as if to underscore his claim as a source of wisdom, court-sanctioned or not: "I *know* that God has *determined* ["taken counsel," from *yâṣâ*] to destroy you because you have done this, and paid no attention to my *counsel*" (2 Chron 25:16b).

Administration lists preserve the names of royal counselors appointed to serve David and Solomon, suggesting that their contribution to state deliberations was highly regarded (uncle Jonathan, Ahithophel and Hushai ["king's friend"] under David in 1 Chron 27:32-33, and priest Zabud ["king's friend"] under Solomon in 1 Kings 4:5). Whether such individuals termed *wise* or *royal counselor* belonged to a social group responsible for a wisdom tradition is unclear (pro: Brueggemann; Murphy, 102; con: Blenkinsopp 1995, 39; Weeks, 90-91; Whybray 1990; pro, with reservations: Crenshaw 1998b, 21; Grabbe 1995a, 162-63, 175-76).

2.1.2. Independent Sages. The aforementioned sages offered their services at a leader's invitation. In times of crisis, however, others were known to interject advice unsolicited. After the defeat of Absalom, Joab besieged the entire town of Abel Beth-Maacah because it sheltered rebel leader Sheba with his troops. As a battering ram began thundering against city walls, an unnamed wise woman took the initiative to negotiate with Joab from atop those walls. She secured the city's peace in exchange for the head of rebel forces (2 Sam 20:14-22) (see the favorable observations by Camp [14-29] concerning the sort of wisdom employed by the women of Abel and Tekoa, contrasted by Ackerman [56]). Sages such as this unnamed woman evidence wisdom operating outside the court.

In addition to their individual episodes, the wise persons around David may serve a cumulative purpose. By appearing wiser than the aging king, they portray David as declining in wisdom, thereby showcasing the wisdom of Solomon all the more (Provan, 167-69).

2.2. Leaders as Sages. In addition to sages who serv leaders, several leaders themselves demonstrated wisdom skills, often in speech. During the period of the *judges, Gideon's son Jotham emerged from hiding as sole survivor after Abimelech's fratricidal bloodbath. From the safety of nearby Mount Gerizim, Jotham shouted an extended fable to the lords of Shechem, hoping to dissuade them from embracing so vicious a leader as his half-brother. His tale likened Abimelech to a mean bramble ruling over a noble forest. Jotham concluded with a metaphoric forest-fire curse, a curse that came true with incendiary accuracy (Judg 9).

When Ben-Hadad of Aram threatened to decimate Samaria, King Ahab sought to deter him with one succinct proverb. Envisioning a soldier getting outfitted for battle, he retorted, "One who dons should not boast as one who doffs" (1 Kings 20:11). Ben-Hadad disregarded the warning, to his detriment. Foreign kings Zeba and Zalmunna likewise employed a proverb in their futile attempt to escape execution (Judg 8:21).

Twin roles of leader and sage combined preeminently in the person of King Solomon. His pursuit and practice of wisdom dominate

1 Kings 3—4 and set the tone for the remainder of his reign. Authorship ascriptions within Proverbs concur with his reputation for large numbers of wise sayings, although scholars differ concerning how fully to associate Solomon with wisdom, from a historical point of view (see Scott, 9). His ability to render just verdicts demonstrated his sapiential skill (1 Kings 3:28). Even the monumental temple-building (*see* Solomon's Temple) activity may have been regarded as a corollary of Solomon's wisdom (1 Kings 5:7, 12; cf. Prov 9:1, where architecture appears at home in a wisdom setting [Gordon, 99-101]). His reputation for wisdom grew to international proportions before his reign suffered decay due to his failure to abide by the Torah (Spina, 27-28).

3. Training for Sages.
Since schools for grooming sages and scribes are attested in Mesopotamia (both temple-based and palace-based) and in Egypt (palace-based), the question of their establishment in Syria-Palestine has been raised. Ugarit (Syria) offers reliable evidence, but in Israel indications are limited to (1) a cuneiform tablet uncovered in Shechem sent by a teacher to his pupil's parents; (2) the designation of Hachmoni as entrusted "with the king's sons" ([tutor?] 1 Chron 27:32); (3) the suggestive town name Kiriath-Sepher ("book-town"); (4) epigraphical evidence demonstrating a knowledge of writing (see discussion in Crenshaw 1998a, 85-113; Grabbe 1995a, 171-74; G. I. Davies, 209-10; P. R. Davies, 87).

4. Occasions for Wisdom.
In the Historical Books wisdom serves primarily to persuade (except Samson's riddle—a case of entertainment gone awry [Judg 14:12-18]). Three occasions account for most instances of sapiential persuasion: to deter hostility, to expose error, to aid deliberation.

4.1. To Deter Hostility. Wisdom was most frequently called on to defuse immanent anger. In the first two examples given below, the wise were at a disadvantage and sought peace by claiming innocence. Fugitive David employed an historic proverb to quell Saul's wrath. With the saying "It is from the *wicked* that wickedness issues," he declared that he was harmless to Saul, and so begged him to quit the manhunt (1 Sam 24:13). Some years later the wise woman of besieged Abel Beth-Maacah took a similar tack. Pointing out that her town had gained fame for defusing differences, she urged Joab not to overreact by destroying the entire city (2 Sam 20:14-22) (see 2.1.2 above).

Gideon and Abigail similarly argued from a position of disadvantage, though not by claiming innocence. Rather than denying an alleged offense, they resorted to flattery, thereby persuading opponents to rise above petty revenge. Gideon cloaked his compliments in an agricultural proverb (Judg 8:2). The discerning (ṭāʿam [1 Sam 25:33]) Abigail praised David, then wielded a wordplay dismissing her husband, Nabal, as a fool (nĕbālâ [1 Sam 25:25]).

In contrast to these four examples, it was from a position of advantage (real or presumed) that Ahab and Jehoash employed wisdom to deter hostility. Their tactic amounted to verbal volleys aimed to deflate the threats of cocky opponents (Ahab: 1 Kings 20:11; Jehoash: 2 Kings 14:9-10).

4.2. To Expose Error. As well as deterring hostility, wisdom served to expose error. Jotham hoped that a fable would convince Shechemite lords of their error in following Abimelech (Judg 9) (see 2.2 above). Joab summoned the wise woman of Tekoa so that David would commute Absalom's exile (2 Sam 14:1-24) (on the use of dramatic deception for persuasion see Camp, 21).

It was by exposing deceit that Solomon's wisdom first was validated. Through ruse he discerned the true identity of imposter and authentic mother alike (1 Kings 3:16-28).

At times, prophets exposed error by employing forms associated with wisdom. Nathan unfolded a parable to expose David's guilt in the Bathsheba incident (2 Sam 12:1-7). Later, an unnamed prophet would use dramatic ruse to uncover Ahab's misguided mercy toward Ben-Hadad (1 Kings 20:37-43).

4.3. To Aid Deliberation. A third occasion for wisdom concerned aiding deliberation. Absalom was unsure how best to attack his fleeing father, so he consulted advisers Ahithophel and Hushai. When their counsel conflicted, the rebel king broke the deadlock in Hushai's favor (2 Sam 16:20—17:14). Years later, King Rehoboam would seek advice of elders and peers to craft domestic policy. To his demise, he rejected the former and embraced the latter (1 Kings 12:1-15).

5. Wisdom in Contrast.

The hues of wisdom grow clearer when viewed in contrast to three categories: power, ethics, spirituality.

5.1. Wisdom and Power. As we have noted, it was to avert hostility that wisdom most often appears in the Historical Books (see 4.1 above). Whereas Proverbs verbally denounced hotheadedness, in the Historical Books wisdom practitioners actually engaged angry adversaries. Abigail shrewdly soothed David's offended pride, the wise woman of Abel Beth-Maacah deftly dismantled Joab's siege, and with a proverb the fugitive David shook Saul to his senses. Wisdom thus comprised an ancient form of power, a form capable of binding brute force.

5.2. Wisdom and Ethics. One might assume that wisdom and ethical behavior were minted from the same ingot, so that any behavior termed "wise" in the OT likewise would be ethical. Yet such was not always the case. At times, wisdom's cleverness deteriorated into the devious. Two types of deviousness deserve observation. The first involved solid strategy to advance evil ends; the second featured inferior strategy to advance good ends. Wisdom, as biblically conceived, was wide enough to encompass both.

Solid strategy for evil ends occurs in the following two wisdom samples. First, Jonadab (author of Amnon's Tamar-trapping trick) was enthusiastically labeled "very wise" despite the ghastly goal achieved by his counsel (ḥākām mĕʾōd, nuanced by the NRSV to read "very crafty" [2 Sam 13:3]). Second, during the rebellion that followed soon after, turncoat advisor Ahithophel proposed to Absalom a solid military strategy that, if implemented, likely would have led to the death of David. Although the writer of Samuel clearly objects to the rebellion, Ahithophel's advice was evaluated according to its ability to achieve successful action (i.e., military victory), not according to its ethical merit. Even unto his self-inflicted death, Ahithophel retained a reputation for impeccable wisdom (2 Sam 16:23) (on the wisdom of Jonadab and Ahithophel see McCarter).

Inferior strategy that brings good ends appears in the accounts of Hushai and Micaiah. Within the Absalom scenario described above, Hushai the spy cleverly countered Ahithophel's formidable counsel with a plan that actually was inferior. If adopted, Hushai's plan would buy defensive time for exiled David. Though devious, Hushai's strategy aimed for a good end: David's restoration. Absalom fell for the ruse, which resulted in his demise (2 Sam 16:15—17:14).

In a prophetic story laced with wisdom elements, the prophet Micaiah disclosed to King Ahab a divine council where deception was chosen as the best strategy to lure the doomed ruler into his final battle. God would cause false prophets to issue flattering, misleading oracles, leading to military disaster (1 Kings 22:19-23). Ahab emerged the consummate fool because even after discovering his divine opponent's strategy, he determined to blunder ahead, trusting lying oracles. Through their misleading advice good resulted: the king's wicked rule came to an end. In the cases of Hushai and Micaiah, wisdom used deceptive means to produce noble ends (cf. the Gibeonites' "prudent" (ʿormâ) strategy in Josh 9:3-27).

What may be concluded regarding wisdom and ethics? First, if we experience concern when biblical writers describe shady counsel as "wise," such concern may indicate a need to expand our concept of what the ancients meant by "wisdom" rather than a need to shift our ethical center. Alternatively, this very tension may warrant reading some attributions of "wise" as ironic (Whybray 1974, 90). Second, the accounts of Hushai and Micaiah suggest that devious wisdom employed against the devious wicked may constitute a derivative of retribution—a principle so highly esteemed by sages ("To the perverse you give a twisted response" [Ps 18:26b]). Third, the fact that skill in wisdom may be used for evil ends should sound a caution. One must continually beware of wisdom's abuse, for "wisdom as a means of achieving goals has rarely been able to evaluate the goal itself. With no control other than the limitations of technology and power, the possible almost automatically becomes the imperative" (Mendenhall, 331).

5.3. Wisdom and Spirituality. Spirituality comprises a third category contrasting wisdom. Since one might seek advice from sage as well as from *prophet or *priest, their roles overlapped (Grabbe 1995b, 60). At times, reason might be pitted against revelation. Three principles stemming from this tension may be discerned in the Historical Books: (1) *God is the ultimate source of wisdom; (2) to rely on human wisdom independent of divine direction may prove disastrous; (3) God is able to upset any wisdom that opposes him.

First, from a survey of wisdom-related materi-

al in the Historical Books, it is the stories surrounding Solomon's wisdom that emerge towering above the rest, both in length and concentration of the wisdom theme (1 Kings 3:1-28; 4:29-34; 10:1-13, with parallels in Chronicles). This suggests that a central concept found in these stories carried special significance for the ancient audience: God is the ultimate source of wisdom.

Second, to rely on human wisdom independent of divine direction may prove disastrous. After following divine strategy in the campaign against Jericho, *Joshua followed his own strategy against Ai. His intelligence was insufficient, however, leading to initial defeat (Josh 7). It was not until he consulted with God that Israel was able to correct hidden rebellion and resume a pattern of military victory. Not long after, a delegation of Gibeonites arrived, claiming to have come from a far country. They supported their claim with contrived evidence—a strategy of crafty resourcefulness (ʿormâ [Josh 9:4]). Joshua and the Israelite elders swallowed their tale of stale bread and so were tricked into a treaty. Quickly the biblical writer points out their failure to consult God, relying instead solely on human insight (Josh 9:14).

Another example of the contrast between reliance on divine direction versus human wisdom arises from a comparison of *David and *Solomon. David's early life was marked by frequent consultations with God (1 Sam 23:9-12; 30:7-8, 2 Sam 2:1; 5:19). In contrast, Solomon was portrayed as seldom seeking out God, and that he did so only early in his reign (when requesting wisdom and when dedicating the temple). Perhaps peaceful conditions created less need for divine oracles. Or perhaps revelation fell prey to presumptuous reliance on reason. The latter seems more likely, for in an arresting use of wisdom language, God warned of a reversal of Israelite fortunes. If the nation failed to follow him closely, the land once famous for its proverb-writing king eventually would itself become a proverb, a taunt on the lips of passersby (1 Kings 9:7). In the end, Solomon did drift from God so that adversaries were raised up against him (1 Kings 11:14, 23) (see Parker, 89; Provan, 172). The centrality of this tension—reason versus revelation—may have given rise to the sage's rather remarkable admission that one must "trust in the LORD with your whole mind [lēb], and do not rely on your own insight [bînâ]" (Prov 3:5).

Third, God is able to upset wisdom that opposes him. Like the accounts of Solomon's early reign, the Absalom material is similarly thick with wisdom themes (e.g., Jonadab's scheme, the use of ruse by Absalom and the Tekoa woman, and Hushai's contest with Ahithophel). Consider in particular the Ahithophel/Hushai contest. The remark that Ahithophel's advice was esteemed on par with a divine oracle suggests that this was nothing less than a showdown between reason and revelation (2 Sam 16:23). Unbeknownst to him, Ahithophel's case was lost before the opening argument. Although it contained inferior advice, the spy Hushai's counsel of delay won the day because God had already determined to overthrow Absalom (2 Sam 17:14). Evidently foreseeing David's return and his own inevitable demise, Ahithophel excused himself from Absalom's council, methodically (sagelike?) arranged his affairs and tragically ended his life. One can only wonder whether this episode contributed to the observation, "No wisdom, no insight, no counsel can withstand the LORD" (Prov 21:30).

6. Wisdom Tradition as Author of the Historical Books.

Some have proposed that the Historical Books (or portions known as the Succession Narrative, such as 2 Sam 19—20; 1 Kings 1—11) should be viewed as the product of a wisdom tradition, leading to their tentative classification as Wisdom Literature. Accounts of wise persons, an interest in human experience, together with attentiveness to choice-and-consequence patterns, have contributed to this classification (Blenkinsopp 1993; Gordon; Lemaire). A wisdom source has similarly been proposed for *Ezra, based on his role as scribe (Blenkinsopp 1993, 24; Grabbe 1995a, 158, 163). Caution should be exercised, however, lest wisdom themes be too quickly equated with wisdom authorship (Sheppard, 3-4; Crenshaw 1976; 1998b, 29-30).

7. Conclusion.

The Historical Books provide a vital portrayal of wisdom. These accounts show that wisdom sometimes operated as expediency, apart from ethical concern. Yet they take care to establish that in the final analysis this powerful force stems from and answers to divine authority. As valuable as wisdom is, to presume on its effectiveness apart from divine direction is the height of folly.

See also LAW; SCRIBES AND SCHOOLS; SOLOMON; STATE OFFICIALS.

BIBLIOGRAPHY. **J. S. Ackerman,** "Knowing Good and Evil: A Literary Analysis of the Court History in 2 Samuel 9—20 and 1 Kings 1—2," *JBL* 109 (1990) 41-64; **J. Blenkinsopp,** *Sage, Priest, Prophet: Religious and Intellectual Leadership in Ancient Israel* (LAI; Louisville: Westminster/John Knox, 1995); idem, "Wisdom in the Chronicler's Work," in *In Search of Wisdom: Essays in Memory of John G. Gammie,* ed. L. G. Perdue, B. B. Scott and W. J. Wiseman (Louisville: Westminster/John Knox, 1993) 19-30; **W. A. Brueggemann,** "The Social Significance of Solomon as a Patron of Wisdom," in *The Sage in Israel and the Ancient Near East,* ed. J. G. Gammie and L. G. Perdue (Winona Lake, IN: Eisenbrauns, 1990) 117-32; **C. V. Camp,** "The Wise Women of 2 Samuel: A Role Model for Women in Early Israel?" *CBQ* 43 (1981) 14-29; **J. L. Crenshaw,** *Education in Ancient Israel: Across the Deadening Silence* (ABRL; New York: Doubleday, 1998a); idem, "Method in Determining Wisdom Influence upon 'Historical' Literature," in *Studies in Ancient Israelite Wisdom,* ed. J. Crenshaw (New York: Ktav, 1976) 481-94; idem, *Old Testament Wisdom: An Introduction* (rev. ed.; Louisville: Westminster/John Knox, 1998b); **G. I. Davies,** "Were There Schools in Ancient Israel?" in *Wisdom in Ancient Israel: Essays in Honour of J. A. Emerton,* ed. J. Day (Cambridge: Cambridge University Press, 1995) 199-211; **P. R. Davies,** *Scribes and Schools: The Canonization of the Hebrew Scriptures* (LAI; Louisville: Westminster/John Knox, 1998); **R. P. Gordon,** "A House Divided," in *Wisdom in Ancient Israel: Essays in Honour of J. A. Emerton,* ed. J. Day (Cambridge: Cambridge University Press, 1995) 94-105; **L. L. Grabbe,** *Priests, Prophets, Diviners, Sages: A Socio-Historical Study of Religious Specialists in Ancient Israel* (Valley Forge, PA: Trinity Press International, 1995a); idem, "Prophets, Priests, Diviners and Sages in Ancient Israel," in *Of Prophets' Visions and the Wisdom of the Sages: Essays in Honour of R. Norman Whybray on His Seventieth Birthday,* ed. H. A. McKay and D. J. A. Clines (JSOTSup 162; Sheffield: JSOT, 1995b) 43-62; **A. Lemaire,** "Wisdom in Solomonic Historiography," in *Wisdom in Ancient Israel: Essays in Honour of J. A. Emerton,* ed. J. Day (Cambridge: Cambridge University Press, 1995) 106-18; **P. K. McCarter Jr.,** "The Sage in the Deuteronomistic History," in *The Sage in Israel and the Ancient Near*

East, ed. J. G. Gammie and L. G. Perdue (Winona Lake, IN: Eisenbrauns, 1990) 289-93; **G. E. Mendenhall,** "The Shady Side of Wisdom: The Date and Purpose of Genesis 3," in *A Light unto My Path: Old Testament Studies in Honor of Jacob M. Myers,* ed. H. N. Bream, R. D. Heim and C. A. Moore (GTS 4; Philadelphia: Temple University Press, 1974) 319-34; **R. E. Murphy,** *The Tree of Life: An Exploration of Biblical Wisdom Literature* (3d ed.; Grand Rapids: Eerdmans, 2002); **K. I. Parker,** "Solomon as Philosopher King: The Nexus of Law and Wisdom in 1 Kings 1—11," *JSOT* 53 (1993) 75-91; **I. W. Provan,** "On 'Seeing' the Trees while Missing the Forest: The Wisdom of Characters and Readers in 2 Samuel and 1 Kings," in *In Search of True Wisdom: Essays in Old Testament Interpretation in Honour of Ronald E. Clements,* ed. E. Ball (JSOTSup 300; Sheffield: Sheffield Academic Press, 1999) 153-73; **R. B. Y. Scott,** *Proverbs, Ecclesiastes* (2d ed.; AB 18; New York: Doubleday, 1985); **G. T. Sheppard,** *Wisdom as a Hermeneutical Construct: A Study in the Sapientializing of the Old Testament* (BZAW 151; Berlin and New York: de Gruyter, 1980); **F. A. Spina,** "In but Not of the World: The Confluence of Wisdom and Torah in the Solomon Story (1 Kings 1—11)," *AsTJ* 56 (2001) 17-30; **S. Weeks,** *Early Israelite Wisdom* (Oxford: Clarendon Press, 1994); **R. N. Whybray,** *The Intellectual Tradition in the Old Testament* (BZAW 135; Berlin and New York: de Gruyter, 1974); idem, "The Sage in the Israelite Royal Court," in *The Sage in Israel and the Ancient Near East,* ed. J. G. Gammie and L. G. Perdue (Winona Lake, IN: Eisenbrauns, 1990) 133-39.

P. B. Overland

WIVES, ROYAL. *See* ROYAL FAMILY.

WOMEN

Women often are seen, and indeed see themselves, as peripheral within the OT records. The account is presumed to be about and for men, with women referred to only when such reference directly affects the main story about men. The existence of Bible dictionaries that contain an article on women but no corresponding article on men could be seen as confirming that impression. However, an examination of the material in the texts themselves is necessary before it is possible to judge whether or not such a view is justified. If it is not, then such articles about women may be seen as providing a necessary corrective.

Of the 249 chapters between Joshua and Nehemiah (excluding the book of Ruth, which will be looked at in another volume), 118, almost half, contain a direct reference of some kind to women or to a woman. This does not include any general references to families, households or to the nation as a whole. When we consider the number of chapters that consist solely of military records or of descriptions of temple furnishings, it appears that women might not be quite so invisible as first appears. That said, more than half of the chapters that refer to women do so only in passing or by naming women as relatives of significant men. There are only about forty-one women (with five appearing in two separate accounts) who might be said to have a part to play in the drama of Israel's written history recorded within these books, and many of those have only "walk-on" or "one-line" parts. It is worth noting that of those forty-one, thirty-one are found in the books of Samuel and Kings, and only five of these reappear in the books of Chronicles, which cover largely the same historical period. This provides further evidence of the Chronicler's emphasis and interest in systems and structures and the more significant focus on relationship in Samuel and Kings. It also shows the danger of trying to make generalizing statements about this section of Scripture as a whole. The remaining ten women of whom anything significant is said are found in Joshua (two) and Judges (eight). Ezra and Nehemiah mention several women in passing, but none in any way that provides information on their individual characters. It is likely that the Chronicler and those responsible for the writing of Ezra and Nehemiah may be linked. It probably is not an exaggeration to say that the writers of these books show little direct interest in the characters or concerns of women, but it appears, even at first glance, that the same could not be said of the writers of Joshua to 2 Kings, books often collectively known as the *Deuteronomistic History because of their strong connections in vocabulary and in theological approach with the book of Deuteronomy.

    1. Women as Characters in the Narrative
    2. Passing References to Women, and
        Women Identified but Not Described
    3. Conclusion

1. Women as Characters in the Narrative.
    1.1. In Joshua. The two women in Joshua who

could in any sense be seen as characters in their own right are Rahab (Josh 2:1-24; 6:22-25) and Caleb's daughter (Josh 15:16-19).

Rahab is a Canaanite woman from Jericho who supported two spies sent into the town by Joshua before Israel invaded the land. She is described as a prostitute, but within this story she is portrayed more as a landlady, and it is possible that the word used to describe her, *zōnâ*, could be translated or interpreted as "innkeeper." She is clearly pictured as an independent businesswoman of intelligence and initiative. Her words and actions in hiding the spies and in deceiving the Jericho government officials indicate both political awareness and a great deal of courage. She believed that the fall of Jericho was inevitable and was willing to throw her lot in with Israel in spite of the immediate danger. However, this is not depicted simply as a matter of political expediency. The writers make explicit her spiritual insight relating to the power of Yahweh, as she says, "The LORD your God is God in heaven above and earth below" (Josh 2:11). This understanding apparently developed into a genuine commitment, as certainly she was incorporated into the Israelite community (Josh 6:25). In the NT, Hebrews and James both speak of her, mentioning her faith and righteousness (Heb 11:31; Jas 2:25). Matthew includes her in the genealogy of Jesus as an ancestor of David—in fact, as the mother of Boaz, himself a good man with a strong faith (Mt 1:5). The fact that Rahab was a woman apparently made no difference to the spies' willingness to trust her or in Joshua's sense of responsibility toward her—that is, she is seen in her own right as a competent partner in the bargain made.

Caleb's daughter is also portrayed, although very briefly, as a woman of initiative who was able to influence her husband and her father. Apparently, she had already been given land by her father as her share in his property, and later she received highly desirable property with access to water (Josh 15:19). There is no indication of any problem with land being given to a woman, although it may, of course, have been seen then as part of her husband's property. The specific reference to Caleb's daughter in the genealogies of 1 Chronicles (1 Chron 2:49) is perhaps an indication that her place in the earlier accounts has been noted.

There is another woman who is worth mentioning, not because of her presence in the book of Joshua, but because of her absence. In Joshua 7 we read the account of Achan's theft of plunder that had been "devoted" to Yahweh and should have been destroyed. As a result of this crime, Achan, the gold and silver that he had looted and stashed in his tent, and "his sons and daughters, his cattle, donkeys and sheep, his tent and all that he had" (Josh 7:24) were destroyed. The missing woman is Achan's wife. It may be, of course, that she is seen as part of his property and therefore assumed to have been destroyed as well. However, the specific mention of sons and daughters, rather than a general reference to the entire household, makes this less likely. Was Achan a widower, or was his wife somehow exonerated and excluded from punishment? We have no way of knowing.

1.2. In Judges. Joshua's reference to Caleb's daughter Achsah is repeated word for word in Judges 1:12-15. Apart from her, there are eight women who could be described as being of note in Judges. The first and perhaps most significant of these is Deborah, "a prophetess, the wife of Lappidoth," who "was leading Israel at that time" (Judg 4:4). She is the only female judge, but her capacity to act in that role is unquestioned, and her leadership of Israel is described (Judg 4—5) in exactly the same terms as that of the male judges. We are told of her expertise in settling disputes (Judg 4:5), and the Israelites seem to have had no problem in taking such advice from a woman. Unlike most of her male counterparts, she did not lead the army, but nevertheless it is made explicit that she was the one who planned strategy and provided motivation (Judg 4:6, 8). Deborah herself was not a soldier; however, success in the campaign that she organized against Sisera, the commander of a Canaanite army, was ensured by another woman, Jael, who did take what could be seen as military action. Jael was married to Heber, a Kenite descended from Moses' in-laws. She may or may not have been an Israelite, but certainly she allied herself to the Israelite cause, and after luring Sisera to take shelter in her home, she killed him by plunging a tent peg into his brain. It is interesting that Jael, rather than being condemned for unfeminine behavior, is presented as a hero (Judg 5:24-27).

On the other hand, the third notable woman in Judges, Jephthah's daughter (Judg 11:28-40), is pictured more as a victim than a hero. As often happens with narratives in the Deuteronomistic History, the account of Jephthah's vow and its consequences is recorded without explicit comment, and readers are left to draw their own conclusions. Nevertheless, the impression is strongly given that something here is not as it should be, and definitely there are conclusions to be drawn. Whether or not Jephthah's vow to destroy whatever came to meet him was appropriate, and whether or not he should have interpreted it in the way he did, are questions to be answered elsewhere, but however misguided Jephthah may have been, we can be sure about his commitment to Yahweh and his integrity. We can be sure also that Jephthah's daughter was precious to him, and that keeping his vow was a great sacrifice. Her loss was not an insignificant handing over of property. The text makes it clear that the loss of a potentially fruitful life for this young girl was not inconsequential, either to herself or to the whole community; it was something to be mourned.

The fact that Manoah's wife, who became the mother of Samson, is not named in the account in Judges 13 probably is significant in view of the way the story unfolds. It is quite apparent that for Manoah, and almost certainly for the whole society in which they lived, the understanding of women and the testimony of women were not rated very highly. However, it is also apparent that this perspective was not shared by the angel of Yahweh. The angel comes to bring the good news to this childless woman that she is "going to conceive and have a son" (Judg 13:3). Both she and her son are to take up the Nazirite vow, she temporarily, he permanently. She recognizes the awesomeness of the encounter and the inappropriateness of questioning the visitor. She shares the news with her husband, whose response is to pray that the visitor might return so that he could be sure about what was going to happen. The angel does come back, again appearing before the woman alone. When she eventually brings her husband to meet the angel, the angel simply tells Manoah that his wife has already been told everything that is necessary. The woman's spiritual insight in not asking for the angel's name is confirmed when Manoah, with less discernment, does ask and is given short shrift. When eventually it dawns on Manoah that they really have been visited by God, he fears for his life, and it is his wife who, again with more spiritual discernment, sensibly recognizes that if God was going

to kill them, he would not have brought them the message in the first place. The story of Manoah's wife stands as a clear refutation of any impression that the society, contemporary or future, might have that women were intrinsically incapable or, indeed, less capable than men of hearing from God, understanding God's ways or speaking for God.

The next two women who have a speaking part in the account are Samson's Philistine first wife (Judg 14:1-20) and his Philistine lover Delilah (Judg 16:4-22). We learn that women from among Israel's enemies are no more to be seen as inconsequential than are Israelite women, like Samson's mother. They are as capable as their male counterparts of bringing trouble to Israel, and although this probably is more a reflection of Samson personally than of any more general principle, both these women proved more than capable of manipulating Samson into revealing confidential information.

The final two noteworthy female characters in Judges are Israelite women involved in situations reflecting the extent of the syncretism and the complete corruption of this nation, which was meant to be the people of Yahweh living under his covenant. Micah's mother (Judg 17:1-4) shows nothing of the spiritual discernment possessed by Manoah's wife. When her son, upon hearing her place a curse on whoever stole her silver, confesses to the theft, she blesses him in Yahweh's name, dedicates the silver to Yahweh and, presumably in an attempt to keep her son on the straight and narrow, decides that the appropriate thing to do is to turn it into an idol and give it back to him. It is clear that although many of the references to women in Judges are positive, women too were involved in the irreligion of their time.

The Levite's concubine (Judg 19:1-30) appears to have had the status of a wife. Her unfaithfulness (Judg 19:2) seems to have been her leaving him to return to her parents rather than any illicit sexual liaison. Again the events are recorded with little editorial comment, but the description of her subsequent treatment when eventually she does return with her husband leaves the reader unsurprised that she left in the first place. The story depicts a society in which women are seen as being present solely for the benefit of men and expendable if that is to the advantage of men. The woman's death was a loss to the man, and that was recognized by the whole nation as unacceptable and needing to be avenged; that she was raped and abused apparently was seen as largely irrelevant to the main issue of his loss. The only light in this dreadful story as far as women are concerned is that the account appears to have been recorded as an example of the depths to which the nation had sunk. In other words, the writers at least recognize that this was not how things were meant to be.

1.3. In 1 Samuel. The thirty or so female characters who play some active part in the story of Israel's monarchy recorded in Samuel and Kings are characterized only by their variety. They are poor and rich, wise and foolish, good and bad, young and old, married and unmarried, Israelite and non-Israelite, believer and nonbeliever, hero and victim. There are queens and other royals, women of national significance politically and spiritually, and women who apparently are of no importance at all. Each of them adds to our understanding of how society viewed women and of how that view might not be seen as adequately reflecting reality or the perspective of Yahweh.

Significantly, the story of the power struggles that characterized the history of Israel as men wrestled for control of the tribes and nations is introduced, in terms of both narrative and theology, by the story of a woman with no power at all: the barren Hannah. In Hannah we are presented with a woman of spiritual insight who, in spite of her despair at her own circumstances, is convinced that God is in control and is willing to listen and respond to her outpourings. She is a woman of integrity and of capability. She is able to make vows and is willing to keep them. In reflecting on her own circumstances, she comes to understand that God can turn upside down the values of the world, and that human power struggles are largely irrelevant when viewed in the light of God's control. It cannot be an irrelevance that the prayer in 1 Samuel 2, which provides the theological introduction to the whole of the royal history, is placed in the mouth of this woman. Peninnah, Elkanah's wife, does not appear personally in the account, but she is significant in her role as Hannah's "rival" (1 Sam 1:6), the thorn in her flesh. There is no explicit criticism of polygamy within the OT, but this story, like so many others—not least those within *David's family—where unhappy results of polygamous marriages are de-

scribed, certainly provides a critique.

At the end of 1 Samuel 4 the death of the unnamed wife of Eli's corrupt son Phineas is recorded. Upon hearing the news of the death of her father-in-law and her husband—one wonders if the order here is significant, and she felt more keenly the loss of the kindly old Eli—she went into labor and died soon after her son was born. However, what seems to have been most on her mind as she names the newborn baby boy was the capture within battle of the ark of God: "She named the boy Ichabod . . . saying, 'The glory has departed from Israel, for the ark of God has been captured'" (1 Sam 4:21-22). Given the context just after the account of Hannah's faith and the corruption of Eli's sons, it is possible that the writer is again drawing attention to the fact that spiritual awareness still existed in Israel, not least among the women.

The next significant women within 1 Samuel are Saul's daughters Merab and Michal, who come into the picture in 1 Samuel 18, but it is worth noting the mention of the young women who helped Saul to find *Samuel (1 Sam 9:11-13). We do not know their names or even how many of them there were. They were insignificant servant girls, seemingly not important enough to be invited to the festival, although perhaps the water that they were fetching was for the feast. Nevertheless, they were aware of what was going on, and they were more than happy to give directions to the visitors. It is hard to see what relevance this little story has within the overall account of the history of Israel, but perhaps it is emphasizing that big stories are made up of little incidents, and the history of Israel is as much about servant girls collecting water as it is about the anointing of kings.

Merab and Michal might be seen as much more significant than the anonymous servant girls. They were, after all, the daughters of the king, women of consequence and status. However, within the text both are presented primarily as pawns in the power games played by their father and his rivals. Merab does not have a speaking part; however, we learn that she was offered as a marriage partner to *David as a spur to encourage him to fight against the Philistines and hence be killed but that actually she was given to someone else (1 Sam 18:17-19). It is not absolutely clear whether this was because David spurned the opportunity or because Saul reneged on the bargain, but it is clear that Merab's own views seem to have been completely irrelevant to all concerned. Many years later Merab again suffered when five of her sons were executed as part of another bargain made between men (2 Sam 21:8)—that the problems arising in Israel at that time were the result of mistreatment by Saul of the protected Gibeonites was pointed out by the Lord, but the solution was decided upon in diplomatic negotiation in which it is very clear that the mothers of the seven descendants of Saul who were to be executed played no part. It is obvious that the thought that the women involved might be consulted in circumstances such as these never occurred to the male players, but it seems that the biblical writers are pointing out, at least to alert readers, that there are questions to be asked about this kind of society.

We have more details about the life and character of Merab's sister Michal, but she too is portrayed as being seen by both Saul and David as a tool to be used for their benefit regardless of her own feelings. We know, however, that she did have feelings, as the narrator notes that she loved David (1 Sam 18:20, 28)—the only time in the OT that a woman is actually described as loving a man. Saul saw her love as a further opportunity to manipulate and destroy David. David seems to have seen it as an opportunity to further his own position; there is no indication that he actually reciprocated Michal's feelings. So Michal and David were married (1 Sam 18:27). Michal demonstrated her love for David when she took his side against her father and risked her own life to help him escape (1 Sam 19:11-17). Apparently, David left her behind without a single thought. There is no indication that in the time that followed he made any attempt to see her again or thought anything about her until years later when it seemed that his connection with her might again be politically convenient for him. In the meantime, Michal had married again, to Paltiel, who clearly did love her (1 Sam 25:44; 2 Sam 3:16), but David apparently decided that his rights, and perhaps the need to win over the northern tribes by continuing his association with Saul's family, were more important than the feelings or desires of Michal or, indeed, of Paltiel. Once again the text is quite aware of how the society worked in relation to women, and once again there is the sense that questions of the appropriateness or rightness of those workings are being deliberately prompted in the mind of the reader. There is no doubt that when Michal appears in the text for the last time (2 Sam 6), she is bitter and unable to appreciate David's exuberant worship of God when the ark is brought up to Jerusalem. She can only feel resentment that the royal dignity, which perhaps is all that she feels she has left, has, in her view, been set aside. The writer certainly is critical of what Michal has become, but perhaps there is also a hint of understanding and even sympathy for how she got there.

David's second wife, Ahinoam of Jezreel, is mentioned only in passing, but the circumstances in which he met and married his third wife, Abigail, are described in detail in 1 Samuel 25. The writer speaks of her as "intelligent and beautiful" (1 Sam 25:3), but it is the former trait that is emphasized in the story. She is depicted as a natural leader who is trusted by the employees of her boorish first husband and assumed to be capable of dealing with difficult situations. She is both politically aware and spiritually astute, and she has a remarkable understanding of human nature, or at least of the way that David's mind works. It seems that she is a woman of faith. She certainly realizes that David is most likely to be won over by theological arguments, and she clearly understands how such arguments work. She was confident of David's ultimate success (1 Sam 25:31), and she asks that when his success comes, she will not be forgotten. It is possible that David married Abigail in payment for a perceived debt or in order to protect her from possible opposition from Saulide militants after she undermined Nabal's opposition to David. In any case, it is not surprising that David wanted such an enterprising and gifted woman as a member of his own court.

The last woman to appear in 1 Samuel is the female medium consulted by Saul before his final battle, a woman popularly known as "the witch of Endor." We cannot be sure whether she was a spiritist or a charlatan, but in neither case could she be described as a woman who trusted in Yahweh. She is clearly presented by the writer as a villain rather than a hero, and yet, like many of the women already described, she is also pictured as an intelligent and competent person who, like Abigail, understood very well how men react. Women are in no sense idealized in the text, nor are they excused from blame by their gender. They are as responsible as men for their own actions and as capable as men of disobeying Yahweh's commands.

1.4. In 2 Samuel. The picture of women as competent and responsible, capable of both good and evil, of hurting and of being hurt, continues in 2 Samuel and indeed throughout the books of Kings. The references to Michal in 2 Samuel 3 and 6 have already been noted. In 2 Samuel 4 there is a brief but noteworthy mention of the actions of Mephibosheth's nurse. When the news of Israel's defeat and the death of both Saul and Jonathan came through, she felt that it was necessary to take the young child Mephibosheth and flee the country, presumably to protect him from the widespread destruction of previous royal connections that tended to happen when regimes changed. She certainly kept the young boy safe so that when, many, many years later, David suddenly remembered his promise to look after Jonathan's family, Mephibosheth was still there in Lo Debar (2 Sam 9). However, it also seems that in her haste, she was the one responsible for Mephibosheth's disability.

The next major female role in the story is that of Bathsheba (2 Sam 11—12). She was the wife of Uriah, a well-known and respected soldier in David's army (2 Sam 23:29), and the daughter of Eliam and probably therefore the granddaughter of David's friend and adviser Athithophel (2 Sam 23:34). One day she was at home, bathing after her menstrual period (2 Sam 11:2, 4), when David sent guards to fetch her. He then slept with her, and she returned home. The text focuses on David and his blameworthy behavior, and there is no way of knowing whether Bathsheba was a willing or a reluctant partner to the offense, or whether she even knew that her bathing had been watched. David saw, wanted and took. Bathsheba's desires seem to have been irrelevant, and perhaps for that reason are not recorded. There is no indication whatsoever that this was a great love story or anything more than a one-off satisfaction of David's lust. From David's point of view, it was simply unfortunate that she conceived, and the best solution all round was to convince Uriah that he was the father. When Uriah's integrity prevented this from happening, he was removed from the picture so that David could marry Bathsheba, and other trouble or damage to David's reputation could be avoided. We are told that Bathsheba mourned for Uriah, and there is no indication that this was anything other than

genuine. Whether she had any choice in the subsequent marriage is also unclear. After the death of her first child and the subsequent birth of *Solomon, we hear nothing more of Bathsheba until the very end of David's reign. At that point she collaborates with Nathan in ensuring that Solomon is made the next king. In 1 Kings 1—2 Bathsheba comes across as somewhat scheming and manipulative. However, whether this is an indication that she was always so and probably deliberately flaunted herself before David years before or whether the way she had been treated made her somewhat cynical cannot be determined. Bathsheba is in many ways the most ambiguous of all the female characters in Samuel and Kings.

There is no such ambiguity in the story of Tamar. She is David's beautiful, good-hearted, obedient, righteous daughter who is totally destroyed by her family. Amnon, her half-brother, following his father's example, sees, wants and takes. Tamar is brutally raped and equally brutally discarded, left unmarriageable and desolate. Her father was furious but took no action. This is a devastating story, a terrible reflection of the society and the way in which women often were viewed as objects whose major function is to satisfy the lusts of men rather than as people with feelings, desires and rights of their own. The only light in so dark a story is that it is a denunciation. The writer portrays with great insight the enormity of the offense and the pain and desolation of the woman scorned. She may have been of no account to her half-brother and of little account to her father, but the way the story is written conveys the strong impression that she was by no means insignificant to the writer and, by inference, certainly not so to God.

As in many societies, the attitude toward women of this society was not consistent or logical. Although in general women were not highly respected, it was recognized that there were women who were intelligent and gifted, worthy of being consulted and able to show initiative and take the lead in various situations—women with the reputation of being wise. Two such women are found in 2 Samuel. In 2 Samuel 14 Joab seeks out a "wise woman" from Tekoa to use as part of his subterfuge to persuade David to bring Absalom back home. She not only was a gifted actress but also was able to grasp the situation quickly and easily and to speak on her own initiative, taking Joab's suggested plot and then responding to events as they occurred. In 2 Samuel 20 the "wise woman" from Abel Beth Maacah worked out a strategy to save her town and persuaded both the attacking troops and the town authorities to go along with it. The two women in 2 Samuel 17—the female servant who was chosen to carry the message for David's couriers out of Jerusalem and the farmer's wife who protects the couriers from Absalom's men—have no such reputation for wisdom but nevertheless show remarkable bravery and intelligence. It is interesting that we are told about the servant girl even though in the end her service apparently was not required. It seems likely that she was chosen because she was brave and capable, but also because, ironically, as a woman she would not have been suspected of being so. It is hard to believe that the writer here is unaware of that irony. Similarly, it does not seem to have occurred to Absalom's men that Bahurim's wife might have either the capacity or the daring to deceive them.

Like Tamar, the final female character in 2 Samuel, Rizpah, is a tragic figure who apparently has no control over her own destiny. She is a former consort of Saul whose two sons, alongside the five sons of Merab, were executed by David at the request of the Gibeonites to make some kind of amends for the crimes committed by Saul against them. The reader is left to judge whether David's action, which was not in itself demanded by the law, was appropriate, but Rizpah's agony and the way in which she protected the bodies of her sons are recorded in detail. It is interesting that her action, which in itself stemmed from her powerlessness to affect the course of events, stimulated David into providing a proper burial not only for her sons, but also for Saul and his other descendants.

We also should note here a woman who never actually appears in the story but is mentioned in passing eighteen times in Samuel and Kings and a further eight times in Chronicles: Zeruiah, David's sister and the mother of the three warriors Joab, Abishai and Asahel. These men are constantly referred to as sons of Zeruiah rather than by their father's name, and although we are given no details, the implication is that she was highly influential in their lives and perhaps was the cause of both their undoubted skills and the trouble that David had with them.

1.5. In 1 Kings. We have already noted Bathsheba's reappearance at the beginning of 1 Kings,

when she conspires with Nathan to ensure that David confirms Solomon as the new king. There is no sign of any meaningful relationship between Bathsheba and David at this time. David, now quite old and probably incapable of sexual activity, is cared for by Abishag, a young Shunammite girl brought in to act as a human hot-water bottle for him. Abishag epitomizes the view of women as property. Discussions take place about her, but she plays no part in them. She is desired by Adonijah, Solomon's ousted half-brother, and he asks Bathsheba to persuade Solomon to let him have her. We are told nothing of Abishag's feeling in the matter. Adonijah's request leads to his death, and we have no further information about what happened to Abishag. The ambiguity surrounding Bathsheba continues here. Adonijah is convinced that she has influence with Solomon, and indeed Solomon agrees to grant her request, whatever it might be. Yet the request apparently is denied. Did Bathsheba indeed speak out on Adonijah's behalf but was not in fact as influential with Solomon as everyone assumed? Or did she really intend Solomon to act as he did and therefore speak in such a way as to ensure Adonijah's death? Again we simply do not know, but it is clear that whatever happened at an earlier stage, Bathsheba here is an actor in her own right, not merely a pawn in the hands of others.

On the other hand, Pharaoh's daughter, like Abishag, is more a part of the scenery than a character in the play (1 Kings 7:8; 9:24; 11:1). She very probably was married to Solomon out of political expediency, and all we know of her is that she had a palace built for her. Whether this was actually for her benefit or rather for Solomon to display his trophy wife is unclear. Like the women of Israel, foreign women can be pictured either as significant players or as part of the furnishings, and the Queen of Sheba, who enters the story in 1 Kings 10, certainly is the former. She is intelligent, wealthy, powerful, and she has an inquiring mind. She is a significant leader of a parallel nation who treats Solomon with respect and is equally well treated by him. The fact that she is a woman appears to have been irrelevant in these circumstances; certainly no comment is made indicating that there was anything anomalous about her position. Whether her lavish praise of Solomon's wisdom was ingenuous or part of her diplomatic repertoire is unclear. But in any case, she was granted "all she desired and asked for" (1 Kings 10:13) before she returned home. It seems likely that the writer has included her story primarily to emphasize Solomon's wealth and wisdom, but it is possible also that the issue of Solomon's susceptibility to flattery is being raised.

Jeroboam's wife was sent to ask the prophet Ahijah about her son's health (1 Kings 14:1-17), but none of her words are recorded. In contrast, the widow from Zarephath who played host to *Elijah speaks several times. It is interesting that this foreign woman is portrayed most positively in 1 Kings. She was generous, willing to share what little she had and apparently trusting Elijah's God both before she had seen his largesse and after the healing of her son (1 Kings 17:13-15, 24). In the NT her role is affirmed by Jesus himself (Lk 4:26). Jezebel, probably the most evil woman mentioned in the Historical Books (with the possible exception of Athaliah), also is a foreigner, a Sidonian princess (1 Kings 16:31; 18—19; 21). She was a powerful character who controlled and manipulated her husband, Ahab, as well as his government. She was greedy, violent and totally lacking in moral sense. She assumed that to be the ruler of a nation meant to be above the law. She sought to eradicate Yahwism in Israel, perhaps because she sensed that its influence was bound to limit her own power. Even Elijah feared her. It is not surprising that her death was as violent and ugly as the life she lived (2 Kings 9). The writers make it very clear that God will not tolerate such behavior in Israel, either from men or from women, and they castigate Ahab for his weak acquiescence to Jezebel's anti-Yahwist approach. However, Jezebel's actions and her influence over Ahab are condemned simply because they were evil; there is no suggestion that it was wrong for her as a woman to exert influence, good or bad, on Ahab.

1.6. In 2 Kings. The story in 2 Kings 2 of the unnamed prophet's wife probably is there to illustrate *Elisha's miraculous powers, but it tells of a woman who seeks and receives help from God. The Shunamite woman whose story follows (2 Kings 4:8-37) also is unnamed, but we know much more about her. She, like several of the women considered here so far, is portrayed as more dynamic and more spiritually aware than her husband. She takes the lead both in providing accommodation for Elisha, seen by her as "a holy man of God" (2 Kings 4:9), and in dealing with the emergency that arises with her son's illness. She saw the unanticipated birth of her son as a gift from God and assumed that God, through Elisha, would heal him. She is determined and insists that Elisha himself, not just his servant, accompany her back to the farm. It is probable that her husband had died by the time the family came back from Philistia, where, following Elisha's suggestion to the wife, they had spent the seven years of famine (2 Kings 8:1-6), but certainly it is the woman herself who takes the initiative in seeking the return of her land.

Naaman's wife is mentioned only briefly, but it is her ease of communication with both the young Israelite captive girl who served her and her husband that laid the foundation for his healing from leprosy and his coming to faith in Yahweh (2 Kings 5).

2 Kings 11 gives the account of the power-hungry and violent queen Athaliah. After the death of her son Ahaziah, she murdered all the possible heirs. The details are sparse, but one can speculate that she was the power behind the throne in Ahaziah's reign and was unwilling to surrender that influence. It is uncertain how many of those killed were her own descendants, but Joash, Ahaziah's son, clearly was among those destined for death. Joash was saved only by the bravery and wit of his aunt Jehosheba, who kept him hidden for six years. Athaliah ruled as queen for the whole of that time until the priest Jehoiada staged a coup and proclaimed Joash king. Athaliah's reign clearly was unpopular, and "all the people of the land rejoiced" (2 Kings 11:20) at her death. However, the main reason given for opposition to her is her support for Baal worship (2 Kings 11:17-18), and again there is no discussion of any difficulty about a woman being in charge. The Chronicler notes that Jehosheba (Jehoshabeath) was "the wife of the priest Jehoiada" (2 Chron 22:11), but interestingly, there is no mention of this in Kings.

The last noteworthy woman in 2 Kings is, although mentioned only in 2 Kings 22, one of the book's most significant characters. Huldah was the prophet who supplied God's response when in the course of Josiah's restoration of the temple the book of the law was found. We are given detailed information about her identity. She was "the wife of Shallum son of Tikvah, son of Harhas, keeper of the wardrobe; she resided in Jerusalem in the Second Quarter" (2 Kings 22:14). Why she, rather than Jeremiah or any other prophet who was present at the time, was seen as the appropriate person to speak for God in these circumstances is not made clear. In any case, Josiah's senior government officials clearly assumed that she was the person to ask, and her prophecy comes across with as much authority and theological perception as does any other. Again the fact of her being a woman is not seen as in any sense anomalous or deserving of comment or explanation.

1.7. In 1-2 Chronicles, Ezra and Nehemiah. Michal is the only woman who receives anything more than a cursory mention in 1 Chronicles, and we are told absolutely nothing about her except that 1 Chronicles 15:29, when describing the ark being brought into Jerusalem, repeats 2 Samuel 6:16 telling of Michal's reaction to David's dancing. Even the follow up to this, given in 2 Samuel 6:20-23, is omitted by the Chronicler. In 2 Chronicles the Queen of Sheba (2 Chron 9:1-12), Athaliah (2 Chron 22—23), Jehosheba (2 Chron 22:11-12) and Huldah (34:19-28) all appear again as actual characters within the story. 2 Chronicles 9:1-12 repeats the record of the Queen of Sheba's visit in 1 Kings 10:1-13 virtually word for word (see comment in 1.5 above). A significant difference from the Kings account is that Chronicles, although it speaks of Pharaoh's daughter as Solomon's wife, makes no mention of the vast number of other wives and concubines reported in 1 Kings 11, nor of Solomon's encouragement of and participation in the idolatrous practices of these women. Thus it seems that the Chronicler, unlike the writer of Kings, is deliberately presenting Solomon in a positive light. So although the text of 1 Kings is repeated, it is less likely that the writer is conscious of any irony or intends any implicit criticism of Solomon in the mention of the fact that the Queen of Sheba goes away with everything she came for. The account of Athaliah's reign also closely parallels that of Kings, although, as previously noted, we learn a little more of Jehosheba's background in Chronicles, and the account there gives more details of how the priest Jehoiada organized the rebellion. As in Kings, the account strongly criticizes Athaliah but does not suggest that her being a woman plays any part in the inappropriateness of her rule. The account of the visit to Huldah and of

her prophecy has some slight differences in wording from that in Kings, but the content is the same. Again there is no indication given that there was anything unusual, inappropriate or worthy of comment in a woman prophet being consulted in this way.

As already noted, although there are a number of what might be seen as significant references to women arising within general discussions in Ezra and Nehemiah—for example, in the condemnations of mixed marriages found in Ezra 9—10 and Nehemiah 13—there are no occasions where a woman could legitimately be described as a character within the narrative.

2. Passing References to Women, and Women Identified but Not Described.
Apart from the characters discussed above, the vast majority of references to women in Samuel, Kings and Chronicles are to the wives and, in particular, the mothers of kings. We are told the names of the mothers of all except three of the kings of Judah. The missing three are David, Jehoram and Ahaz. Surprisingly, none of the mothers of the kings of Israel are named, although we assume that Jezebel was the mother of Ahab's sons Ahaziah and Jehoram (= Joram), who were his two immediate successors. Since all the accounts are written from a perspective of the southern kingdom, with every Israelite automatically being classified as evil, and since Jehoram of Judah and Ahaz also are classified as evil, the implication could be that the naming of the mother implies a positive influence on her son. However, the omission of David's mother and the naming of Manasseh's mother, Hephzibah, and Amon's mother, Meshullemeth, probably counteracts that view. Outside of these references to the wives and mothers of kings, references to women are largely incidental. Joshua 1:14 records that the wives of the men from the eastern tribes were permitted to remain at home while the men went to fight in the west. Judges 12:8 comments that Ibzan's thirty daughters were married outside his clan, and Judges 16:27 reports that when Samson destroyed the temple of Dagon, it was "crowded with men and women." 1 Samuel 8:16 warns the Israelites that if they appoint a king, he will take for his own use their "male and female servants"; in 1 Samuel 15:3 Saul is told to destroy all the Amalekites, "men and women, children and infants"; in 1 Samuel 21:5 David persuades Ahimelech the priest

to give him holy bread by telling him that "women have been kept from" himself and the men who supposedly were with him. When David went raiding from Ziklag, "he did not leave a man or a woman alive" (1 Sam 27:11), and when the Amalekites raided Ziklag, they captured all the women and children related to David's troops (1 Sam 30:1-2).

In 2 Samuel the women of both Israel and Philistia are referred to in David's lament for Saul (2 Sam 1:19-27), and when the ark was brought into Jerusalem, celebratory bread and cakes were given to everyone in the crowd, "both men and women" (2 Sam 6:19). In 1-2 Kings virtually the only other reference to women is 2 Kings 17:17, where in the midst of the condemnation of the corruption in the northern kingdom it is said that the people "sacrificed their sons and daughters in the fire." In the information about genealogies and temple structures in 1 Chronicles there are occasional references to women, such as those to Caleb's wives and concubines in 1 Chronicles 2; Jabez's mother, who "gave birth to him in pain" (1 Chron 4:9); Eleazer's daughters, who married their cousins because their father had no sons and (1 Chron 23:22); and the three daughters of Heman the singer (1 Chron 25:5). Like 2 Samuel, 1 Chronicles reports that bread and cakes were given to "each Israelite man and woman" who was rejoicing at the entry of the ark into Jerusalem (1 Chron 16:3). In 2 Chronicles 15:16 it is noted that "King Asa also deposed his grandmother Maacah [Absalom's daughter and Rehoboam's wife] from her position as queen mother, because she had made a repulsive Asherah pole," indicating that the behavior of women was seen as significant and that they were held accountable. 2 Chronicles 20:13 records that both men and women were present at the prayer assembly called by King Jehoshaphat, and 2 Chronicles 28:10 states that after an encounter with the prophet Oded, the northern army sent home "the men and women of Judah and Jerusalem" whom they had captured and intended to make slaves. In 2 Chronicles 29:9 Hezekiah cites Judah's unfaithfulness to Yahweh as the reason why their "sons and daughters and . . . wives are in captivity," and 2 Chronicles 31:18 organizes the distribution of resources to the families of faithful priests and Levites, including their wives and daughters.

In the list of returned exiles in Ezra 2 we learn that when the daughter of Barzillai married, her husband took her father's name, and that there were both men and women among the slaves and the singers. In the discussion of intermarriage with their pagan neighbors (Ezra 9—10) involving the sons and daughters of Israelites, both men and women joined in repentant weeping. The fact that more attention is paid to the sons marrying foreign women may be an indication that women were seen as more significant than men in passing on religious ideas and in teaching culture. *Nehemiah also speaks of female slaves and singers (Neh 7:67) and of problems resulting from mixed marriages (Neh 13:23-27). In addition, Nehemiah tells of the participation of Shallum's daughters in the building of the wall (Neh 3:12) and of the outcry from "the men and their wives" against the usury that was exacerbating famine conditions (Neh 5:1). It is also made explicit that the various ceremonies of law reading, confession and covenant sealing described in Nehemiah 8—10 involved all the Israelites, women as well as men.

3. Conclusion.

The culture of Israel over the several hundred years from the time of Joshua through to the time of Nehemiah certainly was a strongly masculine-dominated one. In general, women were seen as peripheral—sometimes, possibly very often, important in relationship or indeed in their own right, but nevertheless peripheral to the society as a whole. It also seems clear that the biblical writers such as the Chronicler were men of their own time, men who shared the common assumptions of their society and therefore thought to include women only if there was some particular reason to do so. Having said that, it is clear that women are by no means missing in these accounts, and the writers of the Deuteronomistic History do regularly present a clear picture of the life, interests, thoughts and feelings of women and could be seen as critiquing and even criticizing the society and culture that they describe, particularly in terms of its attitudes toward women.

See also ISRAELITE SOCIETY.

BIBLIOGRAPHY. **A. Bach,** *Women, Seduction and Betrayal in Biblical Narrative* (Cambridge: Cambridge University Press, 1997); idem, ed., *Women in the Hebrew Bible: A Reader* (London: Routledge, 1999); **M. Bal,** *Lethal Love: Feminist Literary Readings of Biblical Love Stories* (ISBL;

Bloomington: Indiana University Press, 1987); **P. A. Bird,** "Images of Women in the Old Testament," in *The Bible and Human Liberation: Political and Social Hermeneutics,* ed. N. K. Gottwald (Maryknoll, NY: Orbis, 1983) 52-288; idem, *Missing Persons and Mistaken Identities: Women and Gender in Ancient Israel* (Minneapolis: Fortress, 1997); **P. A. Bird, K. D. Sakenfeld and S. H. Ringe,** eds., *Reading the Bible as Women: Perspectives from Africa, Asia and Latin America* (Semeia 78; Atlanta: Scholars Press, 1997); **B. Bow,** "Sisterhood? Women's Relationships with Women in the Hebrew Bible," in *Life and Culture in the Ancient Near East,* ed. R. E. Averbeck, M. W. Chavalas and D. B. Weisberg (Bethesda, MD: CDL Press, 2003) 205-15; **A. Brenner,** ed., *A Feminist Companion to Judges* (FCB 4; Sheffield: Sheffield Academic Press, 1999); idem, ed., *A Feminist Companion to Samuel and Kings* (FCB 5; Sheffield: Sheffield Academic Press, 1994); **T. C. Eskenazi,** "Out from the Shadows: Biblical Women in the Postexilic Era," *JSOT* 54 (1992) 25-43; **M. J. Evans,** *Woman in the Bible* (2d ed., Carlisle: Paternoster, 1998); **C. Exum,** *Fragmented Women: Feminist (Sub)versions of Biblical Narrative* (JSOTSup 163; Sheffield: Sheffield Academic Press, 1993); **J. Hackett,** "Women's Studies and the Hebrew Bible," in *The Future of Biblical Studies: The Hebrew Scriptures,* ed. R. E. Friedman and H. G. M. Williamson (SemeiaSt; Atlanta: Scholars Press, 1987) 141-64; **C. C. Kroeger and M. J. Evans,** eds., *The IVP Women's Bible Commentary* (Downers Grove, IL: InterVarsity Press, 2002); **C. L. Meyers,** *Discovering Eve: Ancient Israelite Women in Context* (New York: Oxford University Press, 1988), idem, "Everyday Life in Biblical Israel: Women's Social Networks," in *Life and Culture in the Ancient Near East,* ed. R. E. Averbeck, M. W. Chavalas and D. B. Weisberg (Bethesda, MD: CDL Press, 2003) 185-204; **J. H. Otwell,** *And Sarah Laughed: The Status of Women in the Old Testament* (Philadelphia: Westminster, 1977); **K. Van der Toorn,** *From Her Cradle to Her Grave: The Role of Religion in the Life of the Israelite and the Babylonian Woman* (BibSem 23; Sheffield: Sheffield Academic Press, 1994). M. J. Evans

WONDERS. *See* MIRACLES.

WORD OF GOD

The concept "word of God" is important throughout the Bible, particularly in prophetic texts, where often it has connotations related to the self-revelation of God to humans. In the OT Historical Books several terms and collocations are so used and are considered here.

1. Specific Terms and Expressions
2. Prophetic Forms of Speech in the Historical Books
3. The "Word of God" in History

1. Specific Terms and Expressions.
The Historical Books contain a variety of terms and phrases related to this topic.

1.1. dābār in "Word of God/Yahweh." Although *dābār* is one of the most common Hebrew terms for "word," quite frequently it is translated as "matter," "thing," "affair" and a variety of other common words. Often, *dābār* can describe any word written or spoken between humans. However, this term is commonly used to depict communication from God to humanity. Mention of the "word(s) of God/Yahweh" most often describes a particular message from God to God's people. In the whole OT the phrase "word of Yahweh" is used nearly 250 times. Roughly half of these occurrences are found in the Historical Books. In an overwhelming majority of cases the phrase of choice is "the word of Yahweh" (*dĕbar yhwh*) rather than "the word of God" (*dĕbar ʾĕlōhîm*). In either case, the phrase represents a subjective genitive in which Yahweh/God (the genitive) is the subject of the act of speech implied by "word" (the construct noun). Thus God actively communicates the contents of particular messages to human recipients.

The Historical Books typically do not depict God speaking to humans directly. Instead, God uses *prophets to convey a message for the people. Thus the prophet plays an important role in bringing God's word to humanity. When God speaks through a prophet in this manner, the word of God appears in various formulaic statements that identify the words as expressly God's words rather than the prophet's words. Perhaps with the aid of such prophetic formulas the hearers of the word of God had little hesitancy assigning the words to God rather than to the bearer of God's word. In 1 Kings 12:20-24, for example, when Jeroboam and Israel separated from Judah, it was the word of Yahweh given by Shemaiah, the man of God, that persuaded Rehoboam and Judah not to rise up against the people of Israel (1 Kings 12:22).

However, the phrase "the word of Yahweh" does not always introduce a specific prophetic speech from God to God's people. The phrase may also describe prophetic speech in general. In the days when young Samuel served under Eli in Shiloh, the "word of Yahweh" was "rare" *(yāqār),* and visions were not common (1 Sam 3:1). The biblical writer here emphasizes the lack of communication from God to Israel during that time, due to vacancies in the prophetic office. In the case of 2 Chronicles 19:11, the phrase *dĕbar yhwh* might best be translated as "matter(s) concerning Yahweh" rather than as a specific word or message from Yahweh; a parallel construction is present in the same verse: *dĕbar hammelek* ("matter[s] concerning the king"). In this example the context seems to suggest matters in general about or concerning Yahweh rather than a particular message from Yahweh.

1.1.1. "The Word of Yahweh Came to . . ." Frequently, the prophetic task is initiated by the phrase "the word of Yahweh" coupled with a form of the verb *hāyâ* ("come to pass, happen, occur"), and thus often is translated as "the word of Yahweh came to X." It occurs once without the verb with apparently the same connotation (1 Kings 19:9). This collocation functions as a means of ordaining the messenger for a particular prophetic task. In such cases, the word of Yahweh "comes" to the prophet with instructions for the message to be given. For example, after Nathan the prophet gives David initial approval to build a house for Yahweh, the word of Yahweh "came" *(hāyâ)* to Nathan that night with specific instructions to the contrary (2 Sam 7:4-5). To say that the word of Yahweh "came to" an individual suggests that "the word became an active reality in the life of the prophet from a source other than the prophet's own mind" (Fretheim). In some way, the phrase "the word of Yahweh came to X" functions to recruit the prophet to deliver the word of Yahweh. Of course, this phrase can be found in many of the prophetic books, sometimes as a superscription at the beginning of the book (cf. Ezek 1:3; Jon 1:1; Hag 1:1; Zech 1:1).

At times, this collocation hints at a personification of the word of God. For example, one reads of the word of God involved in activities such as running swiftly (Ps 147:15), creating the heavens (Ps 33:6) and falling on Israel (Is 9:8 [MT 9:7]). Some have suggested, then, that the word of God became hypostatized, which is to say that the idea of "the word of Yahweh/God"

developed into an entity separate from God, or even a separate deity (Grether; Ringgren). The development of such a hypostasis of the word of God "witnesses . . . to the experience of the Word as a living and present reality, the effects of which men could discern from day to day, and in them be confronted by the operation of the living God himself" (Eichrodt, 2.77). However, there is good reason to question whether this process in general is hypostatization at all, or merely an expression of the tendency to personify abstractions: "Human emotions and activities are objectified and considered autonomous just as often as divine attributes: evil, perversity, anxiety, hope, wrath, goodness, faithfulness, etc." (Gerleman, 332). Discussions concerning potential hypostases have taken place with regard to other related concepts such as the name of Yahweh, and caution has been expressed recently regarding these attempts (Mettinger; Richter).

1.1.2. "Hear the Word of Yahweh." Four times in the Historical Books one finds the formula "hear the word of Yahweh." The formula always uses an imperative form of the verb *šāmaʿ,* "hear, listen, obey." While it is far more prevalent in the writings of the prophets (twenty-nine times; especially Isaiah, Jeremiah, Ezekiel), this phrase seems to introduce a message from Yahweh with much the same force as the oft-cited "thus says Yahweh . . ." (see 2 below). In fact, in one case (2 Kings 7:1) this formula is conjoined with the "thus says Yahweh" formula following immediately after it.

1.1.3. "Word of Yahweh" Commanded. In some cases, the phrase "word of Yahweh" appears to describe the words of Yahweh in the role of a command or instruction (e.g., 2 Sam 12:9; 1 Kings 20:35; 2 Kings 7:16; 1 Chron 10:13; 15:15; 2 Chron 34:21; 35:6). Although the Ten Commandments are "ten words" (cf. Exod 34:28; Deut 4:13; 10:4), one cannot be certain that the "word of Yahweh" ever refers to the Decalogue itself.

1.1.4. "Word of God." Compared with "the word of Yahweh," the phrase "the word of God" *(dĕbar [hā]ʾĕlōhîm)* occurs infrequently in the Historical Books (Judg 3:20; 1 Sam 9:27; 2 Sam 16:23; 1 Kings 12:22; 1 Chron 17:3; 25:5; 26:32; Ezra 9:4). The Chronicler's account in 1 Chronicles 17:3 is paralleled in 2 Samuel 7:4, which uses the phrase "word of Yahweh" rather than "word of God." In addition, not every occurrence of *dĕbar (hā)ʾĕlōhîm* should be translated as "the word of God." As in the aforementioned case of *dĕbar yhwh* in 2 Chronicles 19:11, likewise *dĕbar (hā)ʾĕlōhîm* in 1 Chronicles 26:32 should be translated as "the matters concerning God," particularly in light of the parallel phrase "the matters concerning the king" within the same verse.

1.2. ʾēmer/ʾimrâ. Outside the Historical Books, the nouns *ʾēmer* and *ʾimrâ* are used frequently to describe God's word. Since both words are formed from the root *ʾmr* ("speak, say"), these nouns often are understood to describe the spoken word. Of fifty-five occurrences in the OT, *ʾēmer* is found forty-five times in Job, Psalms and Proverbs. By way of comparison, this word occurs only twice in the Historical Books (Josh 24:27; Judg 5:29). Even though Joshua 24:27 is the only example that uses *ʾēmer* within the context of God's word, it refers generally to "all the words of Yahweh" rather than a specific message of God.

The term *ʾimrâ* is used in a similar fashion. Of its thirty-seven occurrences in the OT, nineteen are found in Psalm 119. The single occurrence of this word in the Historical Books is found in David's Song in 2 Samuel 22:31, which is paralleled in Psalm 18:31. In those occurrences the word is used to form the phrase "the word of Yahweh."

1.3. nĕʾūm. The word *nĕʾūm* often can be translated "utterance," "declaration" or "oracle" and is almost always used within the context of prophetic speech. It is often supposed, therefore, that this word functions in a technical way to identify prophetic oracles and other expressions (*HALOT* 2.657-58). Of 375 occurrences in the OT, *nĕʾūm* is found only nine times in the Historical Books. As one might expect, the vast majority of occurrences can be found in the Prophetic Books. Except for one occasion (2 Sam 23:1), this word is used in the Historical Books in much the same way as the majority of occurrences in the Prophetic Books. It appears in the utterance formula *nĕʾūm yhwh* ("declares Yahweh"), identifying Yahweh as the source of the prophetic utterance. Found at the beginning, middle or end of a prophetic utterance, *nĕʾūm* seems to serve as a periodic reminder to listeners that an utterance is indeed coming from Yahweh rather than the prophet.

1.4. millâ. The word *millâ* may also convey the meaning "word." Of thirty-eight occurrences in the OT, it is found thirty-four times in the

book of Job. However, in those cases it usually describes human words rather than divine words. Once in the Historical Books (2 Sam 23:2) this term refers to the word of Yahweh. The context of that passage is similar to a prophetic speech (cf. the phrase *nĕʾūm dāwīd*, "utterance of David," in 2 Sam 23:1).

1.5. Prophetic Formulas Involving the "Word of God." As we have seen, the word of God spoken by prophets often is introduced by a formula that identifies the text as a prophetic speech, and that identifies God as the source of those words. Perhaps the most common formula in the Historical Books is the phrase *kōh ʾāmar yhwh*, "thus says Yahweh." While over half of the 293 OT occurrences are found in the book of Jeremiah, this phrase is found fifty-six times in the Historical Books. Like other prophetic formulas, this phrase functions primarily to identify the message as Yahweh's words rather than the prophet's. The prophet is sent by Yahweh to deliver the divine message to the intended recipient(s). This concept of a messenger being sent as a mediator with a divine word can be seen in other ancient Near Eastern cultures as well. The Mari texts, for example, contain a number of prophetic oracles, which also involve a prophet being sent to convey a divine message, usually to a king. The Mari archives deal mostly with royal affairs, so naturally most of the prophetic oracles are directed toward the king. Like numerous examples in the OT, these oracles often are introduced with the formula "thus says DN [divine name]" (Malamat 1987; for the Mari texts see Roberts; Nissinen).

2. Prophetic Forms of Speech in the Historical Books.

These parallels with the ancient Near East led form critics in the twentieth century to identify a primary form of the prophetic judgment-speech as a messenger's speech with two parts: the reason (or accusation) and the announcement of judgment (Westermann 1991a, 86-87). The messenger formula "thus says Yahweh" plays a central role in the investigation of speech forms in the OT. Westermann in particular identified three major kinds of speech in the Prophetic Books of the OT: (1) accounts (historical narratives), (2) prophetic speeches, (3) utterances from humans to God (lament and praise) (Westermann 1991a, 90-91). The second type, the prophetic speech, is the most common form in the written prophets, and it can be found in the Historical Books as well. This category is further divided into judgment speeches directed against individuals ("JI") and those directed against a nation ("JN") (Westermann 1991a, 129-68, 169-209).

The form of the JI consists of three basic parts: (1) an introduction, which often involves a summons to "hear," commonly expressed in the formula "hear the word of Yahweh"; (2) an accusation, usually a simple declaratory statement in the second person, indicating the accusation against the offender; (3) an announcement of judgment that would come upon the recipient. The announcement of judgment is almost always preceded by "therefore" *(lākēn)* or the formula "therefore thus says Yahweh" *(lākēn kōh ʾāmar yhwh)*. The clause "thus says Yahweh" *(kōh ʾāmar yhwh)* generally introduces the speech as a whole, while "therefore thus says Yahweh" *(lākēn kōh ʾāmar yhwh)* introduces the announcement portion of the JI (Westermann 1991a, 149). In its early form the announcement of judgment contained a simple statement of the punishment that would come to pass upon the recipient of the judgment speech (Westermann 1991a, 149-50). Often the announcement of a sign *(ʾôt)* accompanied the announcement of judgment. This functioned to attest to the announcement of judgment in the event that the judgment would not appear until many years later (Westermann 1991a, 158-59).

Later the JI was adapted and expanded into the judgment speech against a nation, JN (Westermann 1991a, 169-76). Since the recipient of the accusation was a nation or a portion of a nation rather than an individual, generally there were a greater number of transgressions involved. The accusation was expanded to contain usually two parts: a general accusation followed by a more developed concrete indictment. The announcement of judgment also usually has two parts: a speech from God in the first person, indicating intended action against the recipients, then the announcement itself in the third person. Like the announcement in the JI, the JN announcement commonly begins with the introductory "therefore" or "therefore thus says Yahweh."

These forms of prophetic speech use the concept "word of God" and appear frequently in the Historical Books. In 1 Kings 21, for example, Elijah announces judgment against King Ahab, who along with his wife, Jezebel, killed Naboth in or-der to seize his vineyard. The introduction of the JI (part 1) describes the commissioning of Elijah to impart the message: "Then the word of Yahweh came to Elijah the Tishbite, saying . . ." (1 Kings 21:17). The accusation (part 2) is presented in the second person as a question in 1 Kings 21:19 ("Have you killed, and also taken possession?"), followed by a declaratory statement in the next verse ("Because you have sold yourself to do what is evil in the eyes of Yahweh . . ."). Finally, the announcement of judgment (part 3) is given in the following verses: "I will bring disaster on you . . ." (1 Kings 21:21-24).

While the concept "word of God" denotes the divinely commissioned speech of prophets in those Historical Books comprising the *Deuteronomistic History, a significant shift occurs in the way the concept is used among the temple priests and scribes of the Persian period. In the books of Chronicles "word of Yahweh" is used instead as one of a handful of expressions for citing Mosaic law (1 Chron 15:15; 2 Chron 35:6). Other expressions are "as it is written" (e.g., 2 Chron 23:18; occasionally in Ezra-Nehemiah as well [e.g., Ezra 3:2]), "according to the commandments of Moses" (e.g., 2 Chron 8:13) and "according to the Torah of Moses" (e.g., 2 Chron 30:16). Thus a significant shift is discernible within the Historical Books from "word of Yahweh/God" as a technical term for prophetic revelation to a description of the law of Moses, which is essentially a new authoritative source (Schniedewind, 130-38). The Chronicler and his audience appear to have accepted the writings of the prophets as authoritative religious texts (Williamson, 242-43), and in the process the concept "word of God" has been transformed in the books of Chronicles into a means of citing sacred, authoritative Scripture more generally.

3. The "Word of God" in History.
The creative activity of the word of God in history has been investigated as an all-encompassing "theology of history" in the Deuteronomistic History (von Rad, 1.334-47; and on the way this relates to the books of prophecy [von Rad, 2.80-98]). Thus the Deuteronomistic Historian used prophetic announcements of the word of God and their corresponding fulfillments as a means of creating an inner rhythm in the story of Israel, proving also the central role of the word of God in driving that story forward (1 Kings 13:5, 26; 14:18; 15:29; 16:12, 34; 17:16; 22:38; 2 Kings

1:17; 2:22; 4:44; 5:14; 7:16; 10:17; 14:25; 23:16; 24:2; similarly, 1 Chron 11:3). A delay in the fulfillment of a prophetic word, such as in the two-hundred-year history of the condemned northern Israel, may be explained as resulting from the grace of Yahweh, who responded to the slightest good even in Israel's kings (1 Kings 21:29; 2 Kings 10:30; 13:23; 15:12). The Historical Books emphasize not only God's word of judgment acting in Israel's history, but also prophetic words of salvation, specifically in Nathan's oracle to David (2 Sam 7). Solomon's prayer of dedication for the new temple recalls the Davidic covenant and succinctly expresses this Deuteronomistic account of history: "You promised with your mouth and have this day fulfilled with your hand" (1 Kings 8:24). G. von Rad concludes that the Deuteronomistic Historian was not interested in writing a secular history or a history of the faith and religion of Israel: "His concern was rather with the problem of how the word of Jahweh functioned in history. This word operates in two ways: as law it operates destructively, and as gospel it works as salvation" (von Rad, 1.343-44). This is truly a "salvation history" in that it presents a course of history brought to a prescribed fulfillment by a creative and active "word of God," which is decisive for the life and death of Israel.

See also LAW; PROPHETS AND PROPHECY.

BIBLIOGRAPHY. **W. Eichrodt,** *Theology of the Old Testament* (2 vols.; OTL; Philadelphia: Westminster, 1961-1967); **T. Fretheim,** "Word of God," *ABD* 6.962; **G. Gerleman,** "דָּבָר *dābār* word," *TLOT* 1.332; **O. Grether,** *Name und Wort Gottes im Alten Testament* (BZAW 64; Giessen: Töpelmann, 1934); **A. Malamat,** "A Forerunner of Biblical Prophecy: The Mari Documents," in *Ancient Israelite Religion: Essays in Honor of Frank Moore Cross,* ed. P. D. Miller Jr., P. D. Hanson and S. D. McBride (Philadelphia: Fortress, 1987) 33-52; **T. N. D. Mettinger,** *The Dethronement of Sabaoth: Studies in the Shem and Kabod Theologies* (ConBOT 18; Lund: Gleerup, 1982); **M. Nissinen,** *Prophets and Prophecy in The Ancient Near East* (SBLWAW 12; Atlanta: Society of Biblical Literature, 2003); **S. L. Richter,** *The Deuteronomistic History and the Name Theology:* lešakkēn šᵉmô šām *in the Bible and the Ancient Near East* (BZAW 318; Berlin: de Gruyter, 2002); **H. Ringgren,** *Word and Wisdom: Studies in the Hypostatization of Divine Qualities and Functions in the Ancient Near East* (Lund: H. Ohlssons, 1947); **J. J. M.**

Roberts, "The Mari Prophetic Texts in Transliteration and English Translation," in *The Bible and the Ancient Near East: Collected Essays* (Winona Lake, IN: Eisenbrauns, 2002) 157-253; **W. M. Schniedewind,** *The Word of God in Transition: From Prophet to Exegete in the Second Temple Period* (JSOTSup 197; Sheffield: Sheffield Academic Press, 1995); **G. von Rad,** *Old Testament Theology* (2 vols.; New York: Harper, 1962-1965); **C. Westermann,** *Basic Forms of Prophetic Speech* (Louisville: Westminster/John Knox, 1991a); idem, *Prophetic Oracles of Salvation in the Old Testament* (Louisville: Westminster/John Know, 1991b); **H. G. M. Williamson,** *Studies in Persian Period History and Historiography* (FAT 38; Tübingen: Mohr Siebeck, 2004). B. T. Arnold and P. Cook

WRITING, WRITING MATERIALS AND LITERACY IN THE ANCIENT NEAR EAST

The Historical Books report reading and writing as unexceptional activities, from the "book of the law" in Joshua 1:8 to "the book of the annals of the kings of Media and Persia" in Esther 10:2. Their testimony has to be set beside the epigraphical evidence to create a larger picture.

1. Uses of Writing in the Historical Books
2. Writing Materials
3. Evidence of Writing in the ancient Near East c. 1200 to 300 BCE
4. Literacy in the ancient Near East c. 1200 to 300 BCE
5. Writing and Literacy—Correlating Biblical and Archaeological Evidence

1. Uses of Writing in the Historical Books.

1.1. Books—Compilations of Narrative History, Law, Poetry, Prophecy Intended for Future Audiences. Throughout Kings and Chronicles there are references to *sources where additional information can be found—for example, "the books of the chronicles of the kings of Israel" and "of Judah" (e.g., 1 Kings 14:19, 29). More specific are "the book of the chronicles of Solomon" (1 Kings 11:14) and several in Chronicles: "the book of Samuel," "of Nathan," "of Shemaiah," "of Jehu" (1 Chron 29:29; 2 Chron 9:29; 12:15; 20:34), "the sayings of the seers" (2 Chron 33; 19), "the book of the kings of Israel and Judah" (2 Chron 16:11). Isaiah recorded events of Uzziah's reign (2 Chron 26:22). Joshua 10:13 and 2 Samuel 1:18 mention a "book of Jashar," apparently containing poems, and Jeremiah composed laments written in a book so named (2 Chron 35:25). "The book of the law" or "the book of the law of Moses" is the authority for Israel's conduct from Joshua 1:8 to Nehemiah 13:1, the whole, or part of it, being found neglected in the temple during Josiah's reign (2 Kings 22:8-21; also termed "the book of the covenant" [2 Kings 23]). Samuel wrote a "book of kingship" (1 Sam 10:25), and directions for the Levites were attributed to David (2 Chron 35:4).

1.2. Registers—Lists of Persons or Places Recorded for Future Reference. After Israel's entry into the promised land, Joshua commissioned a survey of the territory so that it could be shared between the tribes (Josh 18:3-10). In Chronicles, Ezra and Nehemiah, a specific Hebrew verb is used for enrolling people in a genealogy (*hityaḥēś* [e.g., 1 Chron 4:33; 5:1; Ezra 2:62; Neh 7:5, 64]).

1.3. Letters—Messages Sent from One Person or Group to Another, Usually with Immediate Relevance. Letters passed between kings (2 Kings 5:5; 19:14 [cf. 2 Chron 32:17]; 20:12), between kings and officials (2 Sam 11:14; 2 Kings 10:1, 2, 6), or in the king's name bearing his seal (1 Kings 21:8-12; Esther 3:12; 8:8, 10), and from the king to the people (2 Chron 30:1). According to 2 Chronicles 21:12, the prophet Elijah wrote a letter to Jehoram, king of Judah. Ezra presents several letters in *Aramaic that passed between the Jews of Jerusalem, their opponents and the Persian kings. The note of the men of Succoth written by a *naʿar*, someone who was not an independent citizen, also deserves mention (Judg 8:14).

1.4. Royal Monuments for Display to the Contemporary and Later Public; Royal Decrees. There is no mention of royal inscriptions or even epitaphs—Absalom's monument was not necessarily inscribed (2 Sam 18:18). The only written monument reported is the stones erected at Mount Ebal bearing the terms of the covenant (Josh 8:32). Cyrus's proclamation permitting the rebuilding of the temple was written (2 Chron 36:22 = Ezra 1:1), as were the decrees of Xerxes in the book of Esther. The production of those decrees "in the script of each province and the language of each people" (Esther 3:12; 8:9) is reflected in Darius I's Bisitun inscription rendered on the cliff in Old Persian, Elamite and Babylonian and at Elephantine in Aramaic, and in the Xanthos stela displaying texts in Greek, Lycian and Aramaic.

2. Writing Materials.

The Babylonians and the Assyrians usually wrote their cuneiform script on tablets of clay, which could be held in the hand; larger ones were laid on boards while being inscribed. Cuneiform tablets normally were dried in the sun; baking in a potter's kiln was reserved for special cases. Cuneiform tablets can survive in perfect condition, but often have suffered damage through tumbling from shelves or being crushed by falling masonry, exposed to weather, or discarded in antiquity. By contrast, papyrus, the common writing material of Egypt for documents and texts of all sorts, exported to the Levant and also to Mesopotamia, only survives where it has been dehydrated or, rarely, carbonized. Consequently, papyrus documents are not found in most areas of occupation in either region. Where such documents have perished, testimony to their former existence may be gained from the clay bullae that once sealed them and preserve imprints of the papyrus fibers on their backs. In Egypt from at least the mid-second millennium BCE onward, leather rolls were prepared that could be inscribed, and then the ink could be washed off so that they could be reused. Leather rolls probably were in use across the Fertile Crescent too, although they are not mentioned specifically until the sixth century BCE. Another writing material was the waxed tablet, which consisted of a wooden panel with a border like a picture frame, the lower surface coated with wax, on which the message was scratched. Like the leather roll, this could be reused, simply by smoothing the wax surface. Such tablets were current from Babylonia to Egypt from at least 2000 BCE onward and were used for many tasks, from accountancy to school exercises to the copying of extensive literary compositions. The wood usually has perished, like the papyrus, although a few pieces have been found in Assyria, where King Sargon also had deluxe examples in ivory. Lastly, among the writing materials in daily use come potsherds, which were the scrap paper of antiquity, although, like papyrus and leather, they were suitable only for scripts that could be written with pen and ink, not for cuneiform. Often the potsherds—ostraca—survive where papyrus or leather perish.

Royal inscriptions and notices intended to last were cut in stone. When they have been buried untouched, they often survive in good condition, but where they have been exposed to the weather and human interference, they may be in poor condition; they may have been broken for use as building blocks or smashed by conquerors. A common practice in Egypt was to plaster stone surfaces and then write on them in ink—that, according to Deuteronomy 27:4, 8, was how the stones that Joshua set up at Shechem were to be treated (Josh 8:32), although as they were exposed to the weather, the plaster would not last long (cf. the Tell Deir ʿAlla plaster inscription [see 3.2.3]). Occasionally, owners' names or dedications were engraved on metal and other materials.

Although thousands of Babylonian cuneiform tablets and Egyptian inscriptions survive, it should be remembered that they are only a very small proportion of the documents originally written; most were discarded once they had served their purposes. The same was true in Israel and adjacent countries; the scores of ostraca that are available present only ephemeral texts.

3. Evidence of Writing in the Ancient Near East c. 1200 to 300 BCE.
Archaeological discoveries over the past 150 years have supplied a great deal of evidence of writing, but those discoveries are haphazard in time and place; nowhere does a complete range of all texts written survive. (For texts mentioned here in §3 see *COS;* Gibson; Renz and Röllig.)

3.1. Writing in the Ancient Near East Before the Time of the Historical Books. Assyria, Babylonia and Egypt had two-thousand-year-old writing systems that scribes applied for any form of recording, from placing names of persons on possessions to proclaiming royal triumphs on stone monuments, with many mundane administrative tasks in between. These two scripts had been used throughout the second millennium BCE in the Levant, the Babylonian writing and language serving as the international medium, as seen in the Amarna letters. The cuneiform script was readily adapted for writing various languages—for example, Hurrian and Hittite. The Egyptian, however, remained bound to its own language, but was written by Egyptian officials in Canaan and sometimes for local princes, notably at Byblos early in the millennium. With the end of the Late Bronze Age, these two an-

cient scripts fell out of use in the Levant, together with other, less widespread systems such as the cuneiform alphabet of Ugarit, reappearing only at times of Egyptian or Assyro-Babylonian domination (e.g., Shishak's stela at Megiddo; Assyrian stelae and cuneiform tablets at Samaria and other sites).

During the Late Bronze Age the Canaanite linear alphabet developed and took root, presenting the newly established tribal kingdoms of the early Iron Age with a simple twenty-two letter writing system, so they had no need to create new systems. Although few examples of that script from the Late Bronze Age survive, most writing having been done on perishable materials, they are sufficient to allow the deduction that writing was practiced for many purposes, including the writing of literature (Millard 1998).

3.2. Writing in the Levant in the Period Covered by the Historical Books.

3.2.1. The Period of Joshua and Judges (Twelfth and Eleventh Centuries BCE). Brief texts alone survive from early Iron Age I, the two centuries of upheaval c. 1200 to 1000 BCE. Most numerous are over fifty bronze arrowheads engraved with personal names, perhaps of squadron commanders, possibly intended to be deposited as votive gifts at shrines with prayer before battle or thanksgiving afterward. Apart from a group said to have been found near Bethlehem, these arrowheads appear to come from Lebanon or Syria. A few personal names are also found incised on pottery at sites in the Holy Land and at Byblos. A potsherd excavated in a storage pit by a house of the early twelfth century BCE at Izbet Sartah on the western edge of the Ephraimite hills was lightly incised with the letters of the alphabet several times over, apparently by someone learning his ABCs. At Byblos a bronze blade carries an imperfectly understood inscription of six lines, considered a dedication, dated in the eleventh century BCE. (For these texts see Sass.)

3.2.2. The Period of the United Monarchy (Tenth Century BCE). From the tenth century BCE and from Byblos come the first surviving examples of the alphabet used for continuous sentences. The sarcophagus made for King Ahirom by his son Ittobaal is judged the earliest, followed by dedications to the goddess of Byblos by several kings, two of them placing their inscriptions on statues inscribed for the pharaohs Sheshonq (c.

945-925 BCE [the Shishak of 1 Kings 14:25]) and his son Osorkon (c. 924-889 BCE), most likely during their lifetimes. At *Gezer was found a small stone tablet (the "Gezer Calendar" [11.1 x 7.2 cm]) bearing seven lines of incised words listing the tasks of the farmer during the months of the year. The script and language suggest a date late in the tenth century BCE. A very small number of names scratched on pots are the only other texts from this time.

3.2.3. The Period of the Divided Monarchy (Ninth Century BCE). Accidents of survival and discovery have resulted in the recovery of major stone monuments from this century that are significant for understanding the Historical Books. From within Israel comes the Tel Dan stela, fragments of an Aramaic victory monument celebrating the defeat of Israel and Judah possibly by Ben-Hadad or Hazael of Damascus. At Dhiban in Moab the famous Moabite Stone was brought to light in 1868. It commemorates the triumph of Mesha of Moab (2 Kings 3:4-5) over Israelite towns north of his territory around 840 BCE (cf. Num 32:34-38). There are Ammonite inscriptions from Amman and Aramaic ones from sites in Syria, the most important being the bilingual Assyrian and Aramaic dedication and curses on a life-size statue found at Tell Fekheriyeh on the Khabur River opposite Gozan. Late in the century, King Kilamuwa's successes were summarized in Phoenician on a stela at Zinjirli in southern Turkey. Besides these displays of royal pride, there is only one other text of any length and that is on a different material. In the ruins of a building, identified as a shrine, at Tell Deir ʿAlla in the Jordan Valley, destroyed around 800 BCE, lay pieces of wall plaster on which an account had been written in ink of visions that the prophet Balaam son of Beor saw. The inscription, in a local Aramaic dialect, has introductory phrases in red ink, the rest in black, following Egyptian practice, and is set out like a column of a scroll. Far to the south on a hilltop on the road from Gaza to the Gulf of Aqaba lie the ruins of a caravanserai, Kuntillet-ʿAjrud. Travelers left graffiti in *Hebrew and Phoenician on the plastered walls and on two large jars. They exhibit someone's ability to write out the letters of the alphabet in order, blessings in the name of Yahweh of Samaria and his Asherah, of Yahweh of Teman and his Asherah, and parts of a poem that refer to Baal. There are also personal names on pottery and stone vessels and a

dedication of a stone basin to Yahweh. The whole collection is dated to around 800 BCE. In Judah, Stratum XI at Arad yielded a few sherds with traces of personal names written in ink. Across the Near East the letters of the alphabet began to be used on decorative bricks and on ivory carvings (as at Samaria) to ensure that the constituent parts were assembled in the proper order.

3.2.4. The Period of the Divided Monarchy (Eighth Century BCE). Inscriptions on stone from this century include the Aramaic victory stela of Zakkur, king of Hamath, the three Aramaic stelae from Sefire setting the terms of the treaty between a king of Arpad and his suzerain, and a series of Aramaic monuments of kings of Samʾal (Zinjirli) in southern Turkey. In Cilicia too, at Karatepe, stands the Phoenician inscription recording the achievements of Azitawad, with its counterpart in Hittite hieroglyphs, while another bilingual Phoenician-Hittite inscription of Azitawad's suzerain, Urikku, was uncovered near Adana (Tekoglu and Lemaire). Excavations at Samaria found a morsel of a Hebrew stela, while in Jerusalem the famous Siloam Tunnel inscription and the notices on tombs at Silwan belong to the end of this century. A greater variety of writing now occurs: in every area owners' names and dedications are incised on metal objects, seals engraved with their owners' names and patronyms or professions appear, with bullae bearing imprints of seals (including those of Kings Ahab and Hezekiah) and jar handles stamped with royal and personal seals. Ostraca and graffiti become more numerous, notably the 102 ostraca from Samaria (c. 775 BCE), several from Arad, and graffiti in tombs at Khirbet el-Qom near Hebron. The site of Gibeon yielded dozens of jar handles scratched with the name of the place and a particular vineyard from the end of the century.

3.2.5. The Period of Judah Alone (Seventh Century BCE). Assyria's control of most of the region ended many local dynasties, reducing the production of royal monuments in the West Semitic tongues. On the coast, King Akhayus of *Ekron dedicated an inscribed slab in a temple, and in Ammon, King Amminadab had a record of his works engraved on a small bronze bottle. Assyria's control brought the spread of Aramaic to become the lingua franca (see 2 Kings 18:26), and that is exemplified by an Aramaic ostracon from Ashur conveying a message from an official in

Babylonia to the Assyrian king around 650 BCE, by cuneiform tablets with Aramaic annotations, and by Aramaic legal deeds found in Upper Mesopotamia, inscribed on clay tablets when papyrus was lacking and often containing translations of Assyrian legal formulas. The use of papyrus and leather in Mesopotamia led to stamp seals replacing the traditional cylinder seals, sometimes bearing their owners' names engraved in Aramaic. A rare survivor, a papyrus from Saqqara in Egypt, preserves part of a letter in Aramaic from Adon, apparently king of Ekron, seeking military help from the pharaoh against the Babylonians, at the end of the century. Two powerful priests in northern Syria had their gravestones inscribed in Aramaic early in the century. In Judah some ostraca and graffiti survive from the first half of the century, and more from the second half, from sites scattered across the country. As well as weights engraved with their denominations, hundreds of Hebrew seals and bullae belonging to these years are now known. Most of these once sealed papyrus documents, but only one papyrus has been found, dehydrated in a cave in Wadi Murabba'at near the Dead Sea. It was used twice, first for a letter, and then, inverted, for a list of names and amounts of grain.

3.2.6. The End of Judah and the Exilic Period (Sixth Century BCE). Distinguishing Hebrew inscriptions of the late seventh century BCE from those of the early sixth is difficult in the absence of dates, nor does palaeography allow certain distinction between inscriptions made before and after the fall of Jerusalem. From the last two decades of Judah's existence have been discovered the bulk of the ostraca from Arad, the "Lachish Letters," and other ostraca and graffiti from Jerusalem, Mesad Hashavyahu, Tell esh-Shari'a and other sites. Seals and bullae continued to be produced.

3.2.7. The Persian Period (Sixth to Fourth Centuries BCE). Aramaic, which had become widely used under the Neo-Babylonian rule, became the administrative language of the Persian Empire from the Indus to the Aegean. Seal-stones, both cylinders and stamps, carry their owners' names in Aramaic letters, and cuneiform tablets sometimes had Aramaic annotations scratched or written in ink on them. There are memorials inscribed in Aramaic on stone, especially in Turkey (see Gibson, vol. 2), but more and more writing was done on perishable materials and thus

rarely has survived. Arid areas of Egypt have yielded documents on papyrus and leather. The well-known fifth-century Aramaic papyri from Elephantine, at Egypt's southern frontier, illustrate the documentation of family affairs, administration within a small community, and the religious concerns of a Jewish population far from their homeland. They include correspondence with authorities outside Egypt (see Porten; COS 3.46-53:116-32). In a bag in Egypt were found letters written on leather, sent by the Persian governor Arsham, then living in Babylon (in Porten and Yardeni, vol. 1). Also from Elephantine come the earliest examples of book-rolls with West Semitic texts, the Aramaic version of Darius I's Bisitun inscription, the Wisdom of Ahiqar and other fragments (in Porten and Yardeni, vol. 3). Another literary composition was written on the wall of a tomb in Egypt, as if on a roll, but is too badly damaged to offer much connected sense (Lemaire 1995). Hundreds of ostraca have been unearthed in the area of Idumea, written in Aramaic. Although brief, they give information about the economy and the local Persian administration in the fifth and fourth centuries BCE (Eph'al and Naveh; Lemaire 1996; 2002). On the coast of the Levant people continued to use Phoenician, and a few inscriptions on stone survive.

4. Literacy in the Ancient Near East c. 1200 to 300 BCE.

Levels of literacy in ancient societies are impossible to measure; estimates may be made, but they will be largely speculative because differing needs will have produced different results in varying cultures and situations. Observable uses of writing and the distribution of written texts are indicative, with due consideration to the accidents of survival and discovery.

4.1. Writing and Literacy in Mesopotamia and Egypt. Assyro-Babylonian and Egyptian cultures continued despite the upheavals at the end of the Late Bronze Age, although there were fluctuations in power. *Scribes copied traditional literary texts (e.g., Gilgamesh, Sinuhe), created new works—epics and wisdom literature, hymns and prayers, rituals—and wrote the praises and achievements of kings, their diplomatic correspondence, and treaty texts. Wherever there were royal officials, there were scribes to ensure that *taxes and tribute were paid regularly, recorded and stored. They produced the documents that administration and law required. The fact that texts survive in greater numbers from the end of a period of occupation results in an uneven representation of scribal activity through the period, yet it is clear that established practices continued until the end of the Persian Empire. Changes in language and style naturally occurred, but the scribes were conservative, following stereotyped patterns in literary and legal phraseology. Assyrian royal inscriptions display basically the same religious and political attitudes expressed in virtually the same terms from around 1200 to 600 BCE. Schools for scribes almost certainly did not exist in the form of regular classes; rather, pupils would attach themselves to a practicing scribe and learn from him, much as disciples learned from Jewish rabbis. Where areas of domestic occupation have been cleared in Mesopotamian towns they reveal owners keeping their business archives and some storing books, including schoolbooks, in their homes, beside other houses without written texts (see Pedersén). This proves that writing and thus reading were not restricted to temples, palaces and administrative offices, and it implies that there was a wider knowledge of the existence of writing among the population. Again, in any kingdom that collected taxes and where any shrines expected regular offerings, writing is likely to have been evident.

4.2. Writing and Literacy Among Israel's Neighbors. In areas where the Canaanite-Phoenician alphabet was in use the epigraphical evidence is far less. As we noted, the documents are either monumental inscriptions or seal-stones, ostraca and graffiti (see 3.2). Records of legal and administrative activities, letters and literary works are absent, except for the Balaam text from Tell Deir ʿAlla (see 3.2.3). Nevertheless, the presence of narratives (e.g., the Moabite Stone) and extensive treaty requirements, enforced by curses (Sefire), shows abilities to compose and write such texts, and the less elevated documents show the application of writing in daily life. Greek and Latin sources point to the existence of Phoenician literature now lost (Krings).

4.3. Writing and Literacy in Iron Age Israel. The epigraphical remains from Israel portray a situation where most writing was done for administrative purposes, on ostraca, accompanied by royal and official seals stamped on jars and bullae. It is important to recognize that these ostraca are found widely distributed across the country, mainly, although not exclusively, in Judah. They are present in the capitals, Samaria and Jerusalem, in government centers, Lachish and Arad, but also in remote frontier forts (Horvat ʿUza, Tel ʿIra) (see Millard 1985). Evidently, there was someone at each site who could read these records, even if they were not written there. The large number of seals and bullae bearing only the names of their owners and their patronyms or titles also implies an ability to read the tiny script whenever there was need to identify the seals. Hebrew graffiti in tombs (Khirbet el-Qom, Khirbet Beit Lei) and other places, and personal names on pots also indicate a readiness to write, again over a wide area. The clay bullae with imprints of papyrus fibers on their backs prove the existence of many longer texts, now perished, comparable to those found in Egypt. The few formal notices engraved on stone found at Samaria (a tiny piece of a stela) and Jerusalem (Siloam Tunnel, Silwan Tombs, two fragments of inscribed stone) suggest that writing was displayed for public reading. The Gezer Calendar and a few examples of letters of the alphabet written in order may be remnants of scribal exercises. More advanced exercises may be seen in an ostracon from Arad (no. 88) that appears to bear part of a royal inscription, and in a piece of a bowl from Horvat ʿUza that bears thirteen lines of what seems to be part of a prophetic oracle. Other traces of literary writing appear at the remote caravanserai Kuntillet ʿAjrud on the road from Gaza to Ezion-geber. From the end of the monarchy come two silver amulets buried in a tomb on the edge of the Hinnom Valley (Ketef Hinnom), engraved with blessings closely similar to Numbers 6:24-26.

5. Writing and Literacy—Correlating Biblical and Archaeological Evidence.

5.1. Writing. Writing in the Historical Books is associated with the elite, from Joshua to Mordecai, with kings and their officials, with prophets and priests. They wrote and sent letters, or read books and sealed agreements (e.g., Josh 18:3-9; 2 Sam 11:14; 2 Chron 26:22; Neh 9:38; Esther 3:15). There is no mention of royal inscriptions; the only written monument reported is the plastered stones erected at Mount Ebal (see 1.4 and 2). At the same time, it is assumed the law was contained in a book (Josh 24:26), and it was read to the people on various occasions (2 Kings 23:2; 2 Chron 17:9; Neh 8). In these books little is said about the life of ordinary people, so nothing about the mundane role of writing appears in them.

The absence of such writings from the archaeological sites of the Holy Land has led to conclusions that there was no literature there before the Assyrian conquest of Samaria, or hardly any literacy at all (Thompson, 391; Blenkinsopp, 41). Support is found in the argument that writing developed only where there was a certain level of state organization that Israel and Judah did not reach until the eighth century BCE at the earliest (Jamieson-Drake), but that is falsified by the overall circumstances of writing in the ancient Near East and specifically by the existence of major ninth-century texts such as the Moabite Stone, for Moab was no more developed than Israel at that time. The predominance of ostraca among Hebrew inscriptions has caused one scholar to suppose that all documents were brief and ephemeral (Warner), yet the wider context of writing in the ancient Near East demonstrates the normality of the archaeological situation in Israel and Judah. In Egypt records of diplomacy and administration are extant only on the rare occasions when the papyri have been carried from the damp Nile Valley to a dry place. Had the Assyrians and Babylonians written on perishable materials, little would be known of their societies or culture; the monuments on stone both there and in Egypt give a very partial picture. That is the position evident in most of the Levant, where little survives except stone monuments. The West Semitic monuments were written for the elite and attest a level of literacy already developed in the ninth century BCE to celebrate royal prowess and piety and to record other texts (see 4.1.2). Aramaic, Phoenician and Transjordanian seals from the eighth century BCE onward indicate a need to identify individuals, presumably officials and wealthy citizens. Ostraca and graffiti, mainly from the Transjordanian kingdoms, show writing employed for the whole range of recording. To imply that the Hebrew kingdoms were different from their neighbors, adjacent or more distant, because no royal inscriptions, lengthy documents or extensive literary works have been discovered, is to treat ancient Israel without paying attention to its ancient context and the problems of survival. There is nothing to suggest that Isra-

el had a lesser need for writing than did its neighbors; in fact, the number of extant Hebrew inscriptions is far greater than those of its neighbors. It is noteworthy that even in Assyria very few clay tablets are available from the ninth century BCE, although that was a time of major military expansion and building works by the kings Ashurnasirpal and Shalmaneser III, which undoubtedly generated much documentation (see Millard 1995).

Most writing was done by professional scribes who had a monopoly where complicated systems were used that demanded specialized training. The cuneiform script was restricted in its application by the need to impress the signs on a plastic surface; it was rarely painted or scratched on hard surfaces, although it was engraved on metal and stone for display. Egyptian hieroglyphs and their cursive hieratic and demotic forms were easily painted or scratched on almost any surface, hard or soft. The numbers of scribes in either society is difficult to estimate and varied in time and place, but it never rose above a small fraction of the populace. Some served in palaces and temples, while others worked for the wealthy, for merchants and businessmen, writing letters, accounts and legal deeds.

The Canaanite-Phoenician alphabet of twenty-two letters certainly was simpler to learn and could be applied to any surface. That does not necessarily imply a wider use of writing than the other scripts; the extent of writing will have depended on the needs of society. However, the distribution of Hebrew ostraca and graffiti in particular indicates that there were people reading and writing far from the major centers (see 4.2). All the Hebrew ostraca deal with administrative or military matters, with the two exceptions previously noted (see 4.2).

There is a common view that writing in the biblical world was confined to temples and palaces, to religious cult and royal administration. The distribution of ancient texts disproves that. As we observed, even if the Hebrew seals and ostraca are the instruments or products of administration, they are so widespread as to indicate that readers and probably writers were to be found as commonly. Most people would have been unable to write, perhaps slightly more could read, but all could be aware of writing as a means of recording information about them for good or ill (e.g., taxes) and of documents and books as sources of authority.

5.2. Literacy and Orality. Writing began as an *aide-mémoire,* and that continued to be its primary function throughout the period when, no doubt, most transactions were completed orally and traditions were memorized. Yet epic poems that were sung or recited at religious festivals (e.g., the Babylonian Creation Epic, the Ugaritic Baal myths) and probably on other occasions (the Epic of Gilgamesh) were also kept in writing. Rituals and incantations were written so that they would be correctly recited in order to ensure their efficacy; letters—written messages—ensured correct communication, whether the contents were memorized by the messengers or not. Monumental inscriptions conveyed messages of power and authority to contemporary and future audiences and assumed that some would want to read them. Legal deeds supplied independent testimonies in case contracts were contested, and names on seals served to identify and authenticate. In most of these cases the compositions probably were created orally and then written—a process seen in 2 Kings 19:9-14. Across the times covered by the Historical Books, written and oral existed side by side, the authority residing in the written texts that could be consulted as needed (see Millard 1997; 1999).

The references to writing in the Historical Books conform well with what is known from other ancient texts and from epigraphical remains about uses of writing in the period that they cover.

See also HEBREW INSCRIPTIONS; NON-ISRAELITE WRITTEN SOURCES; ORAL TRADITION AND WRITTEN TRADITION; SCRIBES AND SCHOOLS.

BIBLIOGRAPHY. **J. Blenkinsopp,** "The Social Roles of the Prophets in Early Achaemenid Judah," *JSOT* 93 (2001) 39-58; **I. Eph'al and J. Naveh,** *Aramaic Ostraca of the Fourth Century BC from Idumaea* (Jerusalem: Magnes, 1996); **J. C. L. Gibson,** *Textbook of Syrian Semitic Inscriptions* (3 vols.; Oxford: Clarendon Press, 1971-1982); **D. W. Jamieson-Drake,** *Scribes and Schools in Monarchic Judah: A Socio-Archaeological Approach* (JSOTSup 109; Sheffield: Sheffield Academic Press, 1991); **V. Krings,** "La littérature phénicienne et punique," in *La Civilisation phénicienne et punique: Manuel de recherche,* ed. V. Krings (HO 1/20; Leiden: E. J. Brill, 1995) 31-38; **A. Lemaire,** "Les inscriptions araméennes de Cheikh Fadl (Egypte)," in *Studia Aramaica: New Sources and New Approaches; Papers Delivered at the London Conference of the Institute of Jewish Studies, University College London, 26th-28th June 1991,* ed. M. J. Geller, J. C. Greenfield and M. P. Weitzman (JSSSup 4; Oxford: Oxford University Press, 1995) 77-132; idem, *Nouvelles inscriptions araméennes d'Idumée au Musée d'Israël* (Transeuphratène Supplément 3; Paris: Gabalda, 1996); idem, *Nouvelles inscriptions araméennes d'Idumée, Tome II* (Transeuphratène Supplément 9; Paris: Gabalda, 2002); **A. R. Millard,** "An Assessment of the Evidence for Writing in Ancient Israel," in *Biblical Archaeology Today: Proceedings of the International Congress on Biblical Archaeology, Jerusalem, April 1984,* ed. A. Biran (Jerusalem: Israel Exploration Society, 1985) 301-12; idem, "The Knowledge of Writing in Iron Age Palestine," *TynBul* 46 (1995) 207-17; idem, review of *Oral World and Written Word: Orality and Literacy in Ancient Israel,* by S. Niditch, *JTS* 49 (1998) 699-705; idem, "Books in the Late Bronze Age in the Levant," in *Past Links: Studies in the Languages and Cultures of the Ancient Near East; Essays in Honour of Anson Rainey,* ed. S. Izre'el, I. Singer and R. Zadok (IOS 18; Winona Lake, IN: Eisenbrauns, 1998) 171-81; idem, "Oral Proclamation and Written Record: Spreading and Preserving Information in Ancient Israel," in *Michael: Historical, Epigraphical and Biblical Studies in Honor of Prof. Michael Heltzer,* ed. Y. Avishur and R. Deutsch (Tel Aviv-Jaffa: Archaeological Center Publications, 1999) 237-41; **O. Pedersén,** *Archives and Libraries in the Ancient Near East 1500-300 B.C.* (Bethesda, MD: CDL, 1998) 129-213; **B. Porten,** *Archives from Elephantine: The Life of an Ancient Jewish Military Colony* (Berkeley: University of California Press, 1968); **B. Porten and A. Yardeni,** *Textbook of Aramaic Documents from Ancient Egypt; Newly Copied, Edited and Translated into Hebrew and English* (4 vols.; Jerusalem: Hebrew University, Department of the History of the Jewish People, 1986-1999); **J. Renz and W. Röllig,** *Handbuch der Althebräischen Epigraphik* (3 vols. in 4; Darmstadt: Wissenschaftliche Buchgesellschaft, 1995-2003); **B. Sass,** *The Genesis of the Alphabet and Its Development in the Second Millennium B.C.* (ÄAT 13; Wiesbaden: Harrassowitz, 1988); **R. Tekoglu and A. Lemaire,** "La bilingue royale Louvito-Phénicienne de Çineköy," *Compte rendus de l'Académie des Inscriptions et Belles Lettres* (July-October 2000) 961-1007; **T. L. Thompson,** *Early History of the Israelite People from the Written and Archaeological Sources* (SHANE 4; Leiden: E. J. Brill, 1992); **S. Warner,** "The Alphabet: An

Innovation and Its Diffusion," *VT* 30 (1980) 81-90. A. R. Millard

WRITTEN TRADITION. *See* ORAL TRADITION AND WRITTEN TRADITION.

XERXES. *See* EZRA AND NEHEMIAH, BOOKS OF; PERSIA, PERSIANS.

YAHWEH. *See* GOD.

YEHAWMILK. *See* NON-ISRAELITE WRITTEN SOURCES: SYRO-PALESTIAN.

YEHUD. *See* EZRA; HISTORY OF ISRAEL 7: PERSIAN PERIOD; HISTORY OF ISRAEL 8: POSTEXILIC COMMUNITY; NEHEMIAH.

Z

ZADOK, ZADOKITES

The figure of Zadok is probably best known to many English speakers through G. F. Handel's 1727 coronation anthem *Zadok the Priest,* the opening line of which is based on the narrative of 1 Kings 1:38-40 and proclaims, "Zadok the priest and Nathan the prophet anointed Solomon king." In fact, knowing that Zadok is a priest who is associated with the anointing of Solomon is to know quite a large proportion of the available information about this mysterious figure, whose origins, exact function and ultimate fate are obscure, but whose influence lived on in the claims of the later Jerusalem high priests to be his descendants. This article examines the relevant issues in three parts.

1. Zadok's Origins
2. Zadok in the Biblical Sources
3. Zadokites

1. Zadok's Origins.

1.1. Who Was Zadok? Zadok is presented in the books of 2 Samuel, 1 Kings and 1 Chronicles as a priest who is a member of the royal administration during the reign of *David and the early part of the reign of *Solomon. However, the picture of Zadok in Chronicles differs significantly from that in Samuel-Kings, and one of the ways in which this is evident is in each work's treatment of Zadok's origins.

The attempt to establish who Zadok was and where he came from has exercised scholars for well over a century because the biblical text contains several conflicting sets of information about him. Zadok is first mentioned in the text at 2 Samuel 8:17, in what appears to be a list of David's officials for his new kingdom, as a priest who is the son of Ahitub. Prior to this, an Ahitub who is descended from Eli the priest of *Shiloh has appeared in 1 Samuel 14:3; thus the implica-

tion of calling Zadok "son of Ahitub" is that he is a member of the ancient priestly family from Shiloh (cf. 1 Sam 1:3, 9). But this association is called into question by the fact that in 2 Samuel 8:17 Zadok is said to have a priestly colleague named Ahimelech son of Abiathar. This piece of information conflicts with other material in Samuel that shows Zadok's priestly colleague as a man named Abiathar (2 Sam 15:35; 20:25), who is the son of Ahimelech (1 Sam 23:6; 30:7) and the grandson of Ahitub (1 Sam 22:20). The natural conclusion from this is that the genealogical material in 2 Samuel 8:17 is garbled, and that instead of reading "Zadok the son of Ahitub and Ahimelech the son of Abiathar were priests," it should read "Zadok and Abiathar the son of Ahimelech the son of Ahitub were priests."

Another difficulty with accepting the description of Zadok as the son of Ahitub and therefore as a descendant of Eli is that it is inconsistent with the narrative development in Samuel and Kings. In 1 Samuel 2:27-36 it is prophesied that Eli's family will be ousted from the priesthood, and another priest, this one faithful, will replace them. This prophecy is seen as being fulfilled when in 1 Kings 2:26-27 Solomon expels Abiathar from his position as priest, leaving Zadok as the sole royal priest. But if Zadok too is a descendant of Ahitub, and therefore of Eli, then the expulsion of Abiathar cannot be the fulfillment of the prophecy, despite the writer's clear statement that it is (1 Kings 2:27).

Neither is the information in Chronicles about Zadok any more helpful for establishing Zadok's true identity. In 1 Chronicles 6:8 he is listed in a *genealogy of priests that ultimately goes back to Levi, the ancestor of the tribe that was acknowledged from earliest times as priests. However, this too is suspect for a number of reasons. First, according to this genealogy, Zadok son of Ahitub is a descendant not of Eli but of Aaron, who in Exodus is shown as the brother of Moses and the first high priest. But since the name *Ahitub* for Zadok's father seems to have been derived mistakenly from the Elide genealogies of 1 Samuel, neither the identity of Ahitub as Zadok's father nor Ahitub's inclusion in an Aaronide genealogy can be taken as representing historical fact. Of course, it might be argued that Zadok's father Ahitub was a different Ahitub from the Elide Ahitub, and that the author of Chronicles may be right to show him as a descendant of Aaron. But this depends on the name of Zadok's father being derived from a source other than the Elide genealogies of 1 Samuel, which in the context is most unlikely. Second, the sequence of names Amariah-Ahitub-Zadok occurs twice in the genealogy of 1 Chronicles 6 (1 Chron 6:7-8; 6:11-12), which suggests that there has been a certain amount of schematization in the way that the genealogies were composed. Third, the names of the chief priests who appear in the subsequent narrative of Chronicles, and indeed in the narrative of 1 and 2 Kings, differ significantly from those who appear in the genealogy. This once again suggests that the genealogies are not primarily intended to be vehicles of accurate historical information.

The effect of these observations is that Zadok is left with no undisputed credentials for his important priestly position. So who was he, and why did David appoint him? Two main answers to this question have been proposed.

1.2. Zadok the Jebusite? The longest-running theory about who Zadok was and why David appointed him suggests that Zadok had been a priest among the Jebusites, the people who lived in *Jerusalem before David conquered the city (cf. Josh 15:63; Judg 1:21; 2 Sam 5:6), and that after the conquest David retained Zadok as priest in the new administration as a way of appeasing the resident Jebusite population. This certainly would account for Zadok's lack of convincing priestly credentials in the biblical text, and for his close association with Jerusalem. It might also explain why in 1 Kings 1, Zadok supports Solomon rather than Adonijah to succeed David, since Solomon was born in Jerusalem and may have been of mixed blood through his mother, Bathsheba. However, critics of the theory point out that it is highly speculative and lacks

direct evidence. It also raises the question of how likely it is that David would have appointed a pagan priest to high office in his avowedly Yahwistic administration.

1.3. Zadok the Israelite? In response to the perceived inadequacies of the Jebusite hypothesis, some scholars have maintained that Zadok was in fact a member of an Israelite priestly group that claimed descent from Aaron the brother of Moses. F. M. Cross argued that Zadok was David's priest from *Hebron, a center of residence in Judah for Aaronide priests and the place where David was first anointed king. Appointing Zadok the Aaronide alongside Abiathar the Elide meant that the priesthoods from both the south and the north of the kingdom were represented in the new administration. Another scholar who argues for Zadok being an Israelite is S. M. Olyan, who interprets 1 Chronicles 12:27-28 to mean that Zadok was the son of the Aaronide Jehoiada, and therefore of Israelite priestly descent. However, neither of these arguments rests on any more substantial ground than the Jebusite hypothesis. Certainly, portraying Zadok as an Israelite removes the difficulty of having a pagan priest in a top position in a Yahwistic kingdom; but it also raises the question of why there is so much conflicting genealogical information about Zadok if he was indeed of known indigenous priestly origins. The lack of consistent genealogy is, however, quite understandable if Zadok was of foreign origin, as is the attempt to validate him by giving him Israelite priestly forebears.

2. Zadok in the Biblical Sources.

2.1. General. Apart from probable passing references in the books of Ezra and Nehemiah, Zadok appears only in the books of 2 Samuel, 1 Kings and 1 Chronicles. Critical scholarship of Samuel-Kings and Chronicles is in general agreement that the books of Chronicles are a later version of the narrative of Samuel-Kings, with a particular theological slant that reflects the concerns of the period in which, and the author(s) by whom, Chronicles was produced. Hence, the treatment of Zadok in each set of documents is examined here separately in order to understand the theological nuances of each one.

2.2. Zadok in the Books of Samuel and Kings. Zadok's main characteristics in Samuel-Kings are his connection with Jerusalem and his loyalty to David. Following his introduction in 2 Samuel 8:17 as a priest in David's Jerusalem-based administration, Zadok appears as a guardian of the *ark of the covenant and a loyal supporter of David during Absalom's rebellion against David (2 Samuel 15), and as David's emissary for peace to the elders of Judah after the rebellion (2 Sam 19:11-15). Finally, Zadok supports Solomon as David's successor instead of Solomon's elder brother Adonijah, and he anoints Solomon, in line with David's wishes (1 Kings 1—2). Although Solomon initially appoints Zadok as his priest in place of Abiathar (1 Kings 2:35), Zadok is not shown as being active during the reign of Solomon. Indeed, both Zadok and Abiathar are said to have been priests for Solomon (1 Kings 4:4), but this probably should be disregarded in favor of the statement in 1 Kings 4:2 that Azariah the son of Zadok was Solomon's priest.

In a narrative that often has been regarded as an apology for the Davidic dynasty, therefore, Zadok is always on "the right side": he supports both David, God's chosen king, and Solomon, who is David's chosen successor. Indeed, Zadok is shown in Samuel-Kings more as a loyal party member than as a highly religious priest. The narrative's main concern is to establish the Davidic dynasty, and in this context Zadok and the Davidic monarchy validate each other.

2.3. Zadok in the Books of Chronicles. By comparison with Samuel and Kings, the portrait of Zadok in the books of Chronicles is much more theologically loaded, reflecting a heightened anxiety about correct cultic procedures that emerged during the postexilic period, and conforming to the three-tiered hierarchical structure of priesthood that appears in other biblical material of the same era. To begin with, Zadok is incorporated into the genealogies of 1 Chronicles 1—9 as part of the high priestly line that descends from Aaron and his elder son Eleazar (1 Chron 6:8, 53). This therefore makes him a full-blooded Israelite who is a member of the most exclusive division of priests in Israel. This identity as an Israelite priest is then underlined by showing Zadok among the numbers of armed troops from all the tribes who come to David in Hebron to make him king (1 Chron 12:23-40). Zadok, together with twenty-two commanders from his father's house, is listed as the third of three elements in the Levite contingent (the other two are Levites and Aaronides

[1 Chron 12:26-28]), thereby once again associating him with the official priestly tribe. Moreover, it is notable that Zadok's contingent is the only one in the whole list that consists entirely of commanders, thereby implying that Zadok and his family are of high-class stock. Thus this picture of Zadok reflects the one already given in the priestly genealogy, where Zadok's line, consisting of high priests, is a branch of the Aaronide clan, which in turn is a branch of the Levite tribe (1 Chron 6:1-15).

Three chapters later, David summons Zadok and Abiathar "the priests" along with the Levites in order to move the ark of the covenant from the house of Obed-Edom to Jerusalem (1 Chron 15:11). Zadok's presence is part of a ritually acceptable procedure of transferring the ark, by contrast with the previous disastrous attempt to bring it into the city (1 Chron 13:1-14; cf. 1 Chron 15:13-14). Then, once the ark has been transferred, Zadok and his fellow priests are appointed to minister before the tabernacle at the shrine at *Gibeon (1 Chron 16:39-40). Hence, by the time Zadok appears in the list of David's officials as a priest (1 Chron 18:16), in a notice that repeats the distorted genealogies of 2 Samuel 8:17, his identity has already been established not only as an Israelite who is loyal to David, but also as a high-caste priest of sufficient cultic acceptability to be involved with both the ark of the covenant and the tabernacle. Thus he is eminently qualified to be one of the chief priests of the new kingdom.

Another significant feature of Zadok's portrayal in Chronicles is his connection with the temple. Although Solomon builds the temple after David has died, it is David who makes all the preparations for it before his death (see Solomon's Temple). Part of these preparations is to organize the priests and Levites by lot into divisions for carrying out their duties, and Zadok and Ahimelech the son of Abiathar (*sic*) are said to assist David in doing this (1 Chron 24:3, 6, 31). This episode is interesting for several reasons. First, it is quite different from Samuel-Kings, where nothing is done about the temple building or organization until Solomon's reign, after Zadok has disappeared from the scene. Second, it epitomizes how the inconsistent genealogical information from Samuel-Kings about Zadok and the priest(s) who served alongside him is regularized in Chronicles: Zadok is taken as the son of an Aaronide Ahitub (1 Chron 6:8), and no other Ahitub appears in the narrative; the priest Abiathar appears alongside Zadok only once (1 Chron 15:11), and he is given no genealogy; the notice of 1 Chronicles 18:16, borrowed from 2 Samuel 8:17, is taken at face value to indicate that Abiathar was succeeded as Zadok's associate by his son Ahimelech; and thereafter, when a priest accompanies Zadok, it is Ahimelech the son of Abiathar (1 Chron 24:3, 6, 31). Finally, it emphasizes once again Zadok's position as the most exalted priest in the kingdom: he is a son of Eleazar, Aaron's elder son from whom the high priestly line descends, and as such he is senior to Ahimelech, who is a son of Ithamar, Aaron's younger son (1 Chron 24:3). This same emphasis on Zadok's seniority comes in 1 Chronicles 27:17, where he is named as the chief officer over the Aaronides, who are a subgroup of the Levites.

Zadok's final appearance comes in 1 Chronicles 29:22, where he is anointed priest at the same time that Solomon is confirmed as David's successor, in the presence of the nation. Despite his anointing, Zadok does not appear at all in the subsequent description of Solomon's reign in 2 Chronicles 1—9, and it seems that as in Samuel-Kings, his effective period of service is limited to David's reign.

In Chronicles, therefore, as in Samuel-Kings, Zadok is characterized by loyalty to David and an association with Jerusalem. However, the significance of these characteristics has been changed by the addition of extra ones: Zadok now also appears as an Aaronide priest who is at the top of the ritual hierarchy and is involved with the preparations for the temple. Hence, instead of Zadok and the monarchy validating each other, as is the case in Samuel-Kings, in Chronicles Zadok and the Jerusalem priesthood validate each other. Zadok's exalted position in the priestly hierarchy, his anticipatory involvement with the temple, and his anointing probably reflect the self-understanding of those (high) priests in Jerusalem who claimed descent from Zadok at the time when Chronicles was written, several hundred years after Zadok's death.

2.4. Zadok in the Books of Ezra and Nehemiah. Although there is no narrative material about Zadok outside Samuel-Kings and Chronicles, possible passing references to him occur in the books of Ezra (Ezra 7:2) and Nehemiah (Neh 11:11). In each case, the reference occurs in a genealogical list that is related to the list of high priests in 1 Chronicles 6:1-15 but does not correspond exactly to it. The lists in Ezra and Nehemiah are intended to validate the high priestly credentials of specific individuals: in Ezra it is *Ezra himself who is validated, while in Nehemiah it is a priest named Seraiah. However, it is interesting to note that while these genealogies both include the name *Zadok* (which presumably refers to David's priest and not the later Zadok of 1 Chron 6:12), they go back several generations before Zadok. Ezra's genealogy goes right back to Aaron, the "head priest" (Ezra 7:5), while Seraiah's genealogy goes back two generations before Zadok to the unknown Ahitub (Neh 11:11). Thus it seems that for all his importance, Zadok could not function as a validating figure in his own right, and that descent from Zadok was significant only when Zadok himself was located within a wider and more fundamental context of Israelite priestly descent.

3. Zadokites.

The term *Zadokite* refers to a group of priests associated with the Jerusalem temple who claimed to be descended from Zadok. Although it is possible that the Jerusalem priests regarded themselves from early on as descendants of Zadok, the "sons of Zadok" as a group do not appear in the OT before the exile, and there is no mention of them at all in the Historical Books. None of the Jerusalem priests in the books of Kings except Zadok's son Azariah (1 Kings 4:2) are said to be descendants of Zadok; and even in the postexilic books of Chronicles, with their concern to accommodate history to contemporary orthodoxy, the only chief priest described as being of the house of Zadok is King *Hezekiah's priest Azariah (2 Chron 31:10)—a description that probably is a theological statement about the nature of Hezekiah's reign as a second Davidic era. Despite their absence from the Historical Books, by the time of the book of Ezekiel in the exilic period the Zadokites apparently had become a distinct group of priests who claimed the exclusive right to serve in the temple (cf. Ezek 40:46; 43:19; 44:15; 48:11), although this is the only place in the OT where the "sons of Zadok" are mentioned specifically. The precise history of subsequent developments in the priesthood is obscure, and reconstructions of the Zadokites' position consist largely of inferences drawn from other texts about priests and priesthood in the light of the material in Ezekiel. However, the genealogy in 1 Chronicles 6:1-15 indicates that in postexilic times the high priesthood of the Jerusalem temple came to be linked with descent from Zadok. Zechariah 3 implies that this development may have begun in earnest in the last decades of the sixth century BCE with Joshua son of Jehozadak, whose patronym probably indicates Zadokite descent.

See also GENEALOGIES; PRIESTS AND LEVITES; SOLOMON'S TEMPLE.

BIBLIOGRAPHY. **J. R. Bartlett,** "Zadok and His Successors at Jerusalem," *JTS* 19 (1968) 1-18; **A. Cody,** *A History of Old Testament Priesthood* (AnBib 35; Rome: Pontifical Biblical Institute, 1969); **F. M. Cross,** "The Priestly Houses of Early Israel," in *Canaanite Myth and Hebrew Epic: Essays in the History of the Religion of Israel* (Cambridge, MA: Harvard University Press, 1973) 195-215; **C. E. Hauer,** "Who Was Zadok?" *JBL* 82 (1963) 89-94; **R. Nurmela,** *The Levites: Their Emergence as a Second-Class Priesthood* (SFSHJ 193; Atlanta: Scholars Press, 1998); **S. M. Olyan,** "Zadok's Origins and the Tribal Politics of David," *JBL* 101 (1982) 177-93; **G. W. Ramsey,** "Zadok," *ABD* 6.1034-36; **D. W. Rooke,** *Zadok's Heirs: The Role and Development of the High Priesthood in Ancient Israel* (Oxford: Oxford University Press, 2000); **H. H. Rowley,** "Zadok and Nehustan," *JBL* 58 (1939) 113-41; **J. Schaper,** *Priester und Leviten im achämenidischen Juda: Studien zur Kult- und Sozialgeschichte Israels in persischer Zeit* (FAT 31; Tübingen: Mohr Siebeck, 2000).   D. W. Rooke

ZAKKUR MEMORIAL STELA. *See* ARAM, DAMASCUS AND SYRIA; NON-ISRAELITE WRITTEN SOURCES: SYRO-PALESTINIAN.

ZECHARIAH. *See* EZRA AND NEHEMIAH, BOOKS OF.

ZEDEKIAH. *See* HISTORY OF ISRAEL 6: BABYLONIAN PERIOD.

ZERUBBABEL

Zerubbabel, descendant of one of the last Davidic kings of Judah, returned from the exile to Yehud, where he became governor of this province of the *Persian Empire. He was one of the leaders of the project of rebuilding the temple in Jerusalem in the second half of the sixth century BCE.

1. Name and Origins
2. Public Life

1. Name and Origins.

1.1. Background in the Exile. Zerubbabel is a Babylonian name that means "seed, offspring of Babylon" *(zēr bābili)*. Zerubbabel's presence at the head of the list of returned exiles (Ezra 2:2 = Neh 7:7) suggests that he was born in exile and later in his life returned to Judah/Yehud after the edict of Cyrus allowed the Judean exiles to return to their homeland and rebuild the temple with financial support from the Persian authorities (Ezra 1:1-4; 6:3-5, 8-10). These returnees came in groups, starting from 538 BCE, but it is not completely clear whether Zerubbabel belonged with one of the earliest groups (the position adopted in the present article) or whether he came a number of years later (e.g., c. 520 BCE).

1.2. Zerubbabel's Father. Zerubbabel is identified as the son of Shealtiel in Ezra 3:2, 8; 5:2; Nehemiah 12:1 (cf. Hag 1:1, 12, 14; 2:2, 23), whereas the genealogy in 1 Chronicles 3:19 lists Zerubbabel as a son of Pedaiah, a younger brother of Shealtiel (1 Chron 3:17). This problem usually is resolved by assuming that Pedaiah was the adoptive father of Zerubbabel, or that Shealtiel died childless and that Pedaiah married the widow of his brother and had a son with her; this son, in accordance with the law of levirate marriage (Deut 25:5-10), was legally considered to be a son of Shealtiel.

1.3. Davidic Ancestry. Zerubbabel was a grandson of Jehoiachin (1 Chron 3:17), one of the last kings of Judah, who had been deported into exile by Nebuchadnezzar in 597 BCE and replaced as king by his uncle Mattaniah/Zedekiah. Interestingly, this Davidic ancestry is not highlighted whatsoever in the books in which Zerubbabel figures most prominently: Ezra, Nehemiah, Haggai, Zechariah. Even on those occasions where the name of Zerubbabel's father is mentioned, no explicit mention is made of the fact that his father was a son of Jehoiachin, and so the fact that they were descendants of King *David is not exploited in any noticeable way.

1.4. Sheshbazzar and Zerubbabel. Zerubbabel sometimes has been identified with Sheshbazzar, who is called a "prince of Yehud" in Ezra 1:8, but this is difficult to maintain for a number of reasons. First, the word used for "prince" does not necessarily imply royalty. Second, the identification of Sheshbazzar and Zerubbabel suggests a situation in which a Jewish person has two Babylonian names without a Hebrew name being mentioned, which, though not impossible, is highly exceptional. Third, although some of the activities of Sheshbazzar and Zerubbabel are quite similar, the two seem to be clearly distinguished in Ezra 5:14, where Sheshbazzar is a distant figure while Zerubbabel is personally involved in the exchange with Tattenai (Ezra 5:2).

2. Public Life.

2.1. Zerubbabel the Governor.
In the book of the prophet Haggai, Zerubbabel has the title governor (pehâ). The same title is used in Ezra-Nehemiah in the narrative and in quoted documents for individual governors such as Sheshbazzar (Ezra 5:14), Tattenai ("governor of the province of Beyond the River") (Ezra 5:3, 6; 6:6, 13) and Nehemiah (Neh 5:14, 15, 18; 12:26). In striking contrast, Zerubbabel's name is never accompanied by the title governor in either Ezra or Nehemiah. On the other hand, there is an unnamed "governor of the Yehudites" who can be identified as Zerubbabel in Ezra 6:7 (in a letter; the authenticity of the words is debated), and there is another unnamed "governor" in Ezra 2:63 (in narrative; in this case the word used is tiršātā), which refers to either Sheshbazzar or Zerubbabel.

Ezra-Nehemiah describe Zerubbabel as a leader of the people: at a number of occasions he is mentioned with other leaders (in the list of returnees [Ezra 2:2 = Neh 7:7; cf. Neh 12:1]; at the occasion of the building of the altar [Ezra 3:2], the laying of the foundations of the temple [Ezra 3:8], the conflict with the adversaries [Ezra 4:3], the resumption of the temple building project [Ezra 5:2]); in all but one of these cases (Ezra 3:2) Zerubbabel is the first leader to be mentioned. If Zerubbabel can be identified with one of the unnamed governors of Ezra 2:63 and Ezra 6:7 (or both), then this can be included as more evidence of his leader position.

These data, combined with the evidence from the book of Haggai, allow for the conclusion that Zerubbabel indeed was a "governor," which raises the question of why he never has this title in Ezra-Nehemiah. An answer to this question must take into account the fact that the situation with respect to Joshua the high priest is in many ways similar: in Ezra-Nehemiah Joshua

the son of Jehozadak is never referred to as "high priest," though one can conclude on the basis of Haggai (Hag 1:12, 14; 2:2, 4) and Zechariah (Zech 3:1, 8; 6:12) that he in fact was high priest. The absence of the titles of Zerubbabel and Joshua has been shown (Japhet, 81-86) to be part of the perspective of the narrator, who wanted to convey the message that not just the leaders but the people as a whole were participating in the rebuilding of the temple and of society (the presence of long lists with names of ordinary people in Ezra-Nehemiah is also part of this perspective).

As governor, Zerubbabel was the civil leader of Yehud, already by that time a separate province (and not a subprovince under the jurisdiction of Samaria, as has long been thought [on this issue see Williamson, 83-84]) within the satrapy of Beyond the River. A great number of scholars have concluded that Zerubbabel and Joshua the high priest shared political power in a construction called "diarchy." This very popular thesis has, in recent research, been shown to be unfounded. There is no historical evidence that at this phase of the Persian Empire (or any later phase) the high priest exercised political power (Rooke, 238-39), and the frequently quoted passages from the prophet Zechariah (Zech 4:14; 6:9-15) do not support the thesis either (Rose, 66-68, 200-206).

2.2. Zerubbabel and the Davidic Monarchy.
Some have thought that Zerubbabel was not just appointed as governor, but as vassal king (e.g., Lemaire, 52-56). This is highly unlikely, however, in light of the policy of the Babylonians and the Persians toward the area (Meinhold, 199-200; Naʾaman, 37-44). Also, if Zerubbabel had indeed been appointed as king, then one has to conclude that not only Ezra-Nehemiah but also Haggai and Zechariah have concealed this continuation of the Davidic monarchy, which would be extremely strange (see Kings and Kingship).

A less radical alternative to this theory is much more widespread; according to this proposal, prophets such as Haggai and Zechariah had aspirations for the restoration of the monarchy and promoted Zerubbabel for the position of king, but eventually nothing came out of this. This also has been questioned recently, particularly because kingship is most likely not an issue in the Zerubbabel oracle in Haggai 2:20-23 (the designation "servant" is not reserved for kings, and as both the vocabulary and the details of the imagery make clear, the "seal" imagery is used not for the transfer of authority, but to communicate the concept of special care and protection [Rose, 209-12, 218-43]), and the Zemah figure in Zechariah 3:8; 6:12 (often called "the Branch") should not be identified with Zerubbabel (the name *Zemah*, linking back to the messianic prophecy in Jer 23:5-6, the presence of several emphasis markers in Zech 6:12-13, and the consistent future reference of the oracle make him a messianic figure [Rose, 124-41]).

2.3. Zerubbabel and the Building of the Temple. In the decree in which he permitted Judean exiles to return to their homeland, Cyrus had also made arrangements for the building of the temple in Jerusalem (Ezra 1:2-4), which included financial support from the Persian authorities (Ezra 6:3-5, 8-10). Zerubbabel plays a major role in the rebuilding of the temple (*see* Postexilic Temple). He is mentioned at the occasion of rebuilding the altar recorded in Ezra 3:2, and (possibly a number of years) later at the occasion of the laying of the foundation (Ezra 3:8). The building activities were delayed for different reasons, including opposition from the "people of the land" (Ezra 4:4; those who did not belong to the returned community) who were not (allowed to be) involved in the project (Ezra 4—6), and a lack of concern from the returned exiles (Hag 1). The project gets a new impetus in the year 520 BCE when the prophets Haggai and Zechariah challenge the people to increase their efforts (Ezra 5:1-5; Hag 1), which eventually results in the completion of the temple in 515 BCE (Ezra 6:14-18).

Even when he is mentioned in his role as temple builder, Zerubbabel figures without a title (Ezra 5:2), leaving room for the conclusion that Cyrus, not he, represents the royal authority behind the temple building project (cf. Ezra 5:11-12; 6:14). Remarkably (but apparently in line with the perspective of the narrator of the book of Ezra), Zerubbabel is not mentioned at the occasion of the dedication of the temple (Ezra 6:14-18; cf. Zechariah's prophecy [Zech 4:9] that Zerubbabel, as the one who started the project, would also finish it) after its completion in 515 BCE.

2.4. Zerubbabel's Absence. The absence of Zerubbabel in the narrative of the temple dedication and in all historical narrative from that moment onward has given rise to much specula-

tion concerning what may have happened to him. Some have speculated that the Persians decided that they needed to take action against him when he became the object (cooperating or not) of messianic aspirations of the prophets Haggai and Zechariah, and so they removed him from his office. We have already noted the questionable nature of the interpretation of certain prophecies in Haggai and Zechariah. Apart from that, the removal thesis also fails to explain that not only Zerubbabel, but also Joshua the high priest, is not mentioned in the dedication narrative. There is also no evidence for an intervention or change of policy toward the Jews on the side of the Persians or of an interruption of the building of the temple at this stage.

It is not unusual in biblical historiography that the narrative falls silent on a certain character; this may be no more than an indication that the narrator had concerns other than those of later readers. That Zerubbabel and Joshua are not mentioned on the occasion of the dedication of the temple can be explained within the aforementioned perspective of the narrator of Ezra-Nehemiah (see 2.1).

2.5. Zerubbabel's Daughter. The discovery some decades ago ("in the Jerusalem region," the site of discovery and its circumstances are unknown [Avigad, 1, 11-13, 31-32]) of a seal with the inscription "Belonging to Shelomith, servant of Elnathan, the gover[nor]" sometimes has been considered as providing further evidence against the idea that Zerubbabel was removed from his office by force, but the evidence is inconclusive. In 1 Chronicles 3:19 we find the following note on the descendants of Zerubbabel: "the sons of Zerubbabel: Meshullam and Hananiah, and Shelomith was their sister"—that is, Zerubbabel's daughter has the same name as the woman mentioned on the seal. The designation "servant" (*'āmâ*) in contexts like these could be used for either a woman of unfree status married to a free man, or as a title of some official in the service of a king or other person in a ruling capacity (Kessler, 504-5).

Thus there are two alternative explanations that seem to exclude one another: either Shelomith was a woman of unfree status, married to Elnathan, or she was an official of some status in the administration of the governor. In the first scenario the identification with the daughter of Zerubbabel becomes problematic, assuming that she was a free woman. In the civil-servant scenario (one has to assume that there were women in such positions), the possibility of the identification with Zerubbabel's daughter remains a possibility (for those willing to accept the somewhat problematic dating of this and related seals), but in that case one cannot maintain that Elnathan was a son-in-law of Zerubbabel or that the office of governor in this way stayed in the family.

2.6. Later Traditions. In the apocryphal book 1 Esdras, a Greek reworking of Ezra-Nehemiah, Zerubbabel's role is enlarged. He is explicitly identified as being "of the house of David" (1 Esdr 5:5), and he features in the story of the bodyguards (1 Esdr 3—4 [followed by Josephus in *Ant.* 11]), in which he wins a wisdom contest at the court of Darius and then is given permission to go to Jerusalem and rebuild the temple. In Sirach 49:11-12, Zerubbabel is honored with Joshua for their role in the rebuilding of the temple. In the NT, Zerubbabel is included in the genealogy of Jesus in Matthew 1:12-13 and Luke 3:27.

See also EZRA; EZRA AND NEHEMIAH, BOOKS OF; HISTORY OF ISRAEL 8: POSTEXILIC COMMUNITY; NEHEMIAH; POSTEXILIC TEMPLE.

BIBLIOGRAPHY. **N. Avigad,** *Bullae and Seals from a Post-Exilic Judean Archive* (Qedem 4; Jerusalem: Institute of Archaeology, Hebrew University, 1976); **S. Japhet,** "Sheshbazzar and Zerubbabel—Against the Background of the Historical and Religious Tendencies of Ezra-Nehemiah, I," *ZAW* 94 (1982) 66-98; **R. Kessler,** "Die Sklavin als Ehefrau: Zur Stellung der ʾāmāh," *VT* 52 (2002) 501-12; **A. Lemaire,** "Zorobabel et la Judée á la lumière l'epigraphie (fin du VIᵉ s. av. J.-C.)," *RB* 103 (1996) 48-57; **A. Meinhold,** "Serubbabel, der Tempel und die Provinz Jehud," in *Steine, Bilder, Texte: Historische Evidenz ausserbiblischer und biblischer Quellen,* ed. C. Hardmeier (ABG 5; Leipzig: Evangelische Verlagsanstalt, 2001) 193-217; **N. Naʾaman,** "Royal Vassals or Governors? On the Status of Sheshbazzar and Zerubbabel in the Persian Empire," *Hen* 22 (2000) 35-44; **D. W. Rooke,** *Zadok's Heirs: The Role and Development of the High Priesthood in Ancient Israel* (OTM; Oxford: Oxford University Press, 2000); **W. H. Rose,** *Zemah and Zerubbabel: Messianic Expectations in the Early Postexilic Period* (JSOTSup 304; Sheffield: Sheffield Academic Press, 2000); **H. G. M. Williamson,** "Persian Administration," *ABD* 5.81-86.

W. H. Rose

ZION TRADITIONS

In the Historical Books the Zion traditions are the theology and traditions concerning the rule of Yahweh on earth by means of the election of (1) the house of *David, the dynasty through whom he would rule, and (2) Zion/Jerusalem, the place from which he would rule.

The Zion traditions in the Historical Books represent one strand of the Zion traditions in the OT and concern how Yahweh exercised his kingship over all creation through a human (Davidic) king in Zion/Jerusalem (Roberts 2003, 165). Although it was not the case in other parts of the OT, the Zion traditions in the Historical Books understand the Davidic traditions and Zion traditions as being inextricably bound together. Yahweh's promise to preserve David's household is bound up with his promise to preserve Zion/Jerusalem, David's capital city. Yahweh's choice of David leads to his choice of Zion as his dwelling place, the place of his royal throne.

The Zion traditions concerning David and Zion/Jerusalem emerged midstream in the history of Israel in the context of already established Mosaic (Deuteronomic) traditions, which were reticent about kingship (Deut 17:14-20) and about a permanent earthly dwelling place for Yahweh (Deut 12). Not only did a particular king (David) and a specific place for Yahweh's habitation (Zion/Jerusalem) emerge, but also the traditions associated with them almost came to overshadow the Mosaic tradition for a time, persisting and strengthening even after Israel went into exile, an event that one would have expected to undermine these traditions.

1. Terminology
2. The Theology of Zion in the Historical Books—David and Zion
3. Development of the Zion Traditions in the Historical Books
4. Zion and the Future
5. Conclusion

1. Terminology.

1.1. Tradition. *Tradition,* in its general sense, refers to valued stories that are preserved and passed on by one generation in a community to the next. The traditioning process involves the reinterpretation and application of those stories by the succeeding generations to their own, new situation. In this way, traditions both reflect and shape the identity of the community that is preserving and applying them. Over time, traditions develop and change because the situations and community preserving and interpreting them change. Traditions, then, are both preserved stories/narratives and the interpretation (application) of those stories.

The plural *traditions* is used because there were competing traditions existing alongside each other in the same historical moment and because each of the various traditions developed over time.

The terms *tradition* and *theology* sometimes are used interchangeably; thus *Zion tradition* sometimes is used interchangeably with *Zion theology*. However, *tradition* and *theology* have different connotations: *tradition* accents how interpretation (application) changed over time, whereas *theology* focuses on a systematic understanding of the overall usage of a concept, without needing to account for its development over time.

1.2. Zion versus Jerusalem. The biblical text seems to indicate that *Zion* was the name of the *Canaanite fortress, and that Jebus, the Canaanite city in which the fortress Zion was located, was the last remaining Canaanite holdout in the promised land. Perhaps the name at one time referred to the mountain ridge on which the fortress was built. In the Historical Books Zion was almost exclusively referred to as "the city of David," which in later periods pinpointed a section of *Jerusalem after Jerusalem had expanded beyond the original confines of David's city. Only in 2 Kings 19 (a prophecy by Isaiah) is "Mount Zion" mentioned, and there in parallel with Jerusalem (2 Kings 19:21).

In contrast to the prophetic literature and the psalms, the Historical Books seem to avoid using the name *Zion*. When Zion is mentioned (only six times), usually it is qualified as "Zion, the city of David." The six mentions of Zion in the Historical Books are the account of David's conquest of the Jebusite fortress of Zion in 2 Samuel 5:7 (paralleled in 1 Chron 11:5), the introduction to the account of Solomon's dedication of the temple in 1 Kings 8:1 (paralleled in 2 Chron 5:2), and the account of Isaiah's prophecy against Sennacherib, king of Assyria, in 2 Kings 19:21, 31. Everywhere else in the Historical Books "city of David" is used when referring to that section of Jerusalem that historically had been Zion.

However, because the prophetic literature and the psalms contemporary with the writing of the Historical Books used Zion almost interchangeably with Jerusalem, it has become customary to speak of a "Zion tradition" in the Historical Books at any point at which the text reflected upon the theological significance of Jerusalem (Zion, the city of David). It might technically be more accurate to speak of "Jerusalem traditions" in the Historical Books.

1.3. Zion Traditions. In contemporary scholarship the concept of the Zion traditions has been primarily based on and developed from studies in the prophetic literature and the psalms, not from studies in the Historical Books. The Zion traditions outside the Historical Books have different contours from those within the Historical Books, which stressed the close association of the choosing of David and his dynasty with the choosing of Zion/Jerusalem as the place of Yahweh's dwelling.

2. The Theology of Zion in the Historical Books—David and Zion.

In this section the Zion traditions are examined from the perspective of the final shape of the tradition (i.e., a theological perspective). In the following section the development of the Zion traditions through time (i.e., tradition proper) is described.

Unlike the prophetic literature and the psalms, where Davidic traditions and Zion traditions often were treated independently of one another, the Historical Books almost always tied the Zion traditions to broader Davidic traditions (Roberts 2003, 165). Theologically there were three primary emphases: the (connected) election of David and Zion, Yahweh's presence in the city of David (Zion), and Yahweh's covenant with David (which included Zion).

2.1. The Election of Zion ("Jerusalem, which Yahweh has chosen"). Yahweh's election of Zion as his dwelling place had its basis in Deuteronomy 12: "But you are to seek the place the LORD your God will choose from among all your tribes to put his Name there for his dwelling. To that place you must go" (Deut 12:5; cf. Deut 12:11, 14, 21, 26). The place and the tribe were not named, but Yahweh would do the choosing, and he would choose a location within a tribe in Israel.

Yahweh, acting through his chosen king (David), completed the conquest by capturing Zion. Again, through David's agency of bringing the *ark of the covenant into Zion, Yahweh took up residency in Zion/Jerusalem. When Yahweh subsequently made a covenant with David, it included a promise about a house of Yahweh in Jerusalem as well. Yahweh's election of Zion was inextricably bound up with his election of David. And election was permanent, both for David's descendants (2 Sam 7:13-16; 1 Chron 17:12-14) and for Zion/Jerusalem (2 Chron 33:4).

Scholars disagree whether the Historical Books should be understood simply as a human, politically motivated apologetic for David's kingship and Zion's centrality, or as a theological argument for Yahweh's exercise of sovereign kingship in selecting David and Zion/Jerusalem (Roberts 1973).

2.2. The Presence of Yahweh in Zion ("A place for Yahweh's name to dwell"). Although Yahweh initially resisted David's purpose to build Yahweh a permanent resting place (2 Sam 7:5-7), Yahweh later did inhabit the temple (1 Kings 8:10-11; 2 Chron 7:1-2) and, by extension, Zion/Jerusalem, the site of the temple.

Whether Yahweh actually dwelt in Zion/Jerusalem has been debated. Pointing to the language of "a place for his name to dwell," L. J. Hoppe (44) has argued that "it is God's name rather than the Deity itself that was to be found in Jerusalem." In contrast, T. N. D. Mettinger (1-13) has argued that "the name" was the presence of Yahweh, which coheres with the other language and imagery of the Solomonic prayer. Yahweh, *the king,* was present on earth in the temple in Jerusalem and ruled from there (*see* Deuteronomistic Theology).

Solomon's prayer dedicating the temple could be cited in support of both positions. On the one hand, Solomon variously and repeatedly reminded Yahweh that "you have put your name there" (1 Kings 8:16-20, 29, 48; 2 Chron 6:5-10, 20; cf. 2 Sam 7:13), and the prayer also contains the imagery of "may your eyes be open toward this temple" (2 Chron 6:20) and "hear from heaven, your dwelling place" (1 Kings 8:30, 39, 43, 49; 2 Chron 6:21, 30, 33, 39). These statements create an impression of Yahweh dwelling elsewhere, not in the temple. On the other hand, Solomon introduced his prayer by saying to Yahweh that he had "built a magnificent temple for you, a place for you to dwell forever" (1 Kings 8:13; 2 Chron 6:1-2). He invited Yahweh and his ark to come to their "resting place" (2 Chron 6:41). The glory of the Lord (certainly a sign of his presence) did indeed come, such

that the priests had to leave the temple precincts (1 Kings 8:11; 2 Chron 5:14, 7:1-2).

Yahweh's presence made the environs of the temple (Zion/Jerusalem) holy. Moreover, the presence of the sovereign Lord of the universe made Zion/Jerusalem an invincible place. The miraculous deliverance of Zion/Jerusalem in Hezekiah's day underscored the inviolability of Zion (2 Kings 18:13—19:37; 2 Chron 32:1-23). Finally, Yahweh's presence made Zion/Jerusalem the one place of worship, the place toward which Israel must pray. Worship at the shrines in the northern kingdom of Israel as well as at the *high places in the southern kingdom of Judah was condemned because Yahweh was not there; he was in Zion/Jerusalem.

This raises a question, addressed in the next section: If Yahweh was present there, how could Zion/Jerusalem fall, the temple be destroyed, and Israel and its king go into exile?

2.3. Covenant ("For the sake of David and Jerusalem"). Yahweh made a covenant with David, his chosen servant, that David would perpetually have descendants on the throne (2 Sam 7), by implication in Jerusalem (*see* Davidic Covenant). Solomon, in his prayer at the dedication of the temple, understood that Yahweh's covenant promises to David extended to Zion/Jerusalem as well (1 Kings 8:26-30; 2 Chron 6:17-21). In the judgment on David's house that split the kingdom in two, Yahweh acted "for the sake of David and for the sake of Jerusalem," and thus the covenant with David had become also a covenant with Zion/Jerusalem (e.g., 1 Kings 11:13, 32).

Even after the schism between the two kingdoms the covenant connection between David and Zion/Jerusalem persisted. All David's royal descendants reigned in Jerusalem (e.g., 1 Kings 2:11; 11:42; 14:21; 15:2, 10; 2 Chron 12:13; 13:2; 20:31; 21:5). The criteria for the place of their burial seems to have been their faithfulness to the covenant: covenant obedience led to burial in the city of David (e.g., *Jehoshaphat [1 Kings 22:50; 2 Chron 21:1]), while covenant disobedience resulted in burial elsewhere (e.g., *Manasseh [2 Kings 21:18; 2 Chron 33:20]).

Covenant cut two ways. It required faithfulness both from Yahweh and from his covenant people. Yahweh was faithful and dwelt in Zion/Jerusalem, remaining there and even delivering Zion/Jerusalem and its king when they were obedient and repentant (e.g., 2 Kings 18—19; 2 Chron 32:1-23). "For David's sake" (i.e., Yahweh's covenant with David) he spared Jerusalem/Judah (2 Kings 8:19; 19:33-34; 20:6). Thus Yahweh, by not removing David's descendants, preserved Jerusalem and Judah (McKenzie, 68).

Israel, however, was not faithful. The sin of generation after generation of covenant-breaking kings and people built up to intolerable levels, demanding divine judgment in fulfillment of the covenant stipulations. Finally the people were exiled for their covenant unfaithfulness, and Jerusalem, as "covenant partner," was destroyed.

Even though the king and his people broke the covenant and Yahweh razed Jerusalem by means of the Babylonians, Yahweh remained faithful to his covenant and restored his people to Zion/Jerusalem through the providential means of Cyrus (2 Chron 36:22-23). Covenant—Yahweh's faithfulness to his covenant with David (and Jerusalem)—was the explanation for his restoration of Jerusalem and bringing his people back to Jerusalem.

3. Development of the Zion Traditions in the Historical Books.

In the preceding section the theological themes associated with Zion in the Historical Books were described; in this section the focus is on the development of the tradition through time. Teasing out all the threads of the historical development is difficult, but there are clear distinctions and developments between the exilic books (Joshua through Kings—the so-called *Deuteronomistic History) and the postexilic books (Chronicles, Ezra and Nehemiah).

The Historical Books presented the Zion traditions as emerging in the midst of already established Mosaic traditions that grew out of the book of Deuteronomy. The theology of the Historical Books assumed Yahweh's kingship and measured Israel by its faithfulness (or lack of faithfulness) to the law (Deuteronomy). As king, Yahweh oversaw everything concerning Israel's welfare, including raising up leadership at need. Nondynastic *judges were the chosen mode of leadership. When Israel asked for a king like the nations have (Deut 17:14), Yahweh would be the one to choose a king for Israel—that is, a human king to govern under his own ultimate kingship—and that king, Deuteronomy 17 specifies, should be an Israelite who read and meditated on Torah rather than one who amassed wealth and made alliances as the Canaanite

kings did. In a parallel development, Yahweh's presence (with the ark) had no permanent location during the first centuries after Israel's conquest of the land. The ark (and therefore Yahweh's presence) was found in various locations at different times during that period. But it was always Yahweh's prerogative, according to Deuteronomy 12, to select the place for his name to dwell. The place would not be chosen, and the worship was not to be performed, in the manner of the Canaanites. In light of Deuteronomy 12, 2 Samuel 7:5-7 is understood to mean that the idea of having a fixed place of worship may have had Canaanite overtones (McConville, 29-30) and therefore was problematic. "Centralized" worship was to be before Yahweh's presence, yes, but not in a fixed location.

Yet the Zion tradition that developed, thrived and persisted included a fixed place of worship and kings who looked more like their Canaanite neighbors than like the king described in Deuteronomy 17. Not only did Zion traditions emerge in Israel, but also they seemed to eclipse the former Mosaic traditions (e.g., Zion supplanted Sinai as the mountain of the Lord, and a human king seemed to supplant the divine king [1 Sam 8:7-9]). Finally, the Zion traditions persisted, if possible, more strongly after the fall of Jerusalem than before, where a restored Zion came to embody hope for the future of Israel. "If God is king, then the establishment of a human king is at least superfluous and probably idolatrous. And so how did it happen that the religion came to focus increasingly upon a royal dynasty and a state sanctuary, the house of David and the house of YHWH on Mount Zion?" (Levenson, 97).

The Historical Books as well as the prophetic literature and the psalms were written after David and Zion, and the theology associated with them had become a central piece of Israel's religion, yet they treated the Zion traditions very differently. The prophetic literature and the psalms took Yahweh's presence in, and election of, Zion/Jerusalem as givens, and they were comfortable celebrating that fact by praising Yahweh's choice of Zion using elements from Canaanite mythology (e.g., Zion, like the Canaanite Mount Zaphon, was praised as the highest of the mountains).

The Zion traditions in the Historical Books flowed out of the strongly anti-Canaanite theology of Deuteronomy. The Historical Books wrestled with the tension between the stipulations of Deuteronomy 12 and 17 and the Canaanite overtones that kingship and worship in Israel seemed to have taken on (1 Sam 8). Due to the Canaanite origin and association of the name *Zion*, the anti-Canaanite theology of Deuteronomy perhaps explains why the name *Zion* was avoided in the Historical Books.

The Historical Books were shaped by their commitment to guard Yahweh's position as king of Israel by arguing that Yahweh was the one who chose David, and through David he chose Jerusalem.

3.1. Significant Events Before David. Little or nothing can be inferred from Joshua about Yahweh's reign through David and Zion (although Josh 22 does address the importance of worshiping Yahweh in the place of his choosing). The book of Judges put the tribe of Judah (David's tribe) in the foreground, particularly with respect to the taking of Zion/Jerusalem (Judg 1:8; contrast 1:21), which pointed to David, who finally took Zion/Jerusalem and brought it permanently under Israelite dominion.

3.2. Foundational Events in the Reign of David. Zion traditions emerged and developed based on three key events recounted in sequence from the beginning of David's reign: David's capture of Zion/Jerusalem (2 Sam 5:6-10; 1 Chron 11:4-9); his bringing the ark of the covenant to Zion, the city of David (2 Sam 6; 1 Chron 13; 15—16); his desire to build a temple for Yahweh (2 Sam 7; 1 Chron 17). A fourth signal event, from much later in David's life, was his purchase of the site for the temple (2 Sam 24; 1 Chron 21).

3.2.1. David's Capture of Zion (2 Sam 5:6-10; 1 Chron 11:4-9). In the biblical narrative Zion was the final Canaanite holdout in the promised land. With its fall, the conquest of Canaan begun by Joshua was completed. Having chosen David to act on his behalf, Yahweh took Zion and completed the conquest. In the same stroke, David and Zion were bound inextricably together. David made Zion the capital of his kingdom; Zion "took his name" and became known, in the Historical Books, as "the city of David" (2 Sam 5:7, 9; 1 Chron 11:5, 7).

3.2.2. David's Bringing the Ark of Covenant Up to the City of David (2 Sam 6; 1 Chron 13). By saying that David brought the ark of the covenant up to "the city of David" (as opposed to using the name *Jerusalem* [see 2 Sam 6:12]), the Historical Books accented Yahweh's presence coming into

David's city and therefore the connection between the choice of David and the choice of the city for Yahweh's presence (2 Sam 6; 1 Chron 13; 15:1—16:6). With this action, the city of David (Zion/Jerusalem) became the religious capital as well as David's political capital.

3.2.3. David's Desire to Build Yahweh a Temple (Covenant with David) (2 Sam 7; 1 Chron 17). Having achieved rest from his enemies, and therefore having achieved rest for all Israel, David desired to give Yahweh rest as well, so David purposed to build a temple in which Yahweh could dwell. In response to David's desire, Yahweh instead made a covenant with David, a covenant that promised a perpetual dynasty for David and that a temple would be built, but by David's son, not by David himself. Moreover, Yahweh's response to David questioned David's desire to build a permanent house for Yahweh (2 Sam 7:6-7; 1 Chron 17:5-6; cf. 1 Kings 8:27; 2 Chron 6:18). Yahweh's response pointed to the Deuteronomic concern against worshiping Yahweh by imitating the manner of Canaanite worship in fixed places (Deut 12:4, 30-31 in context).

3.2.4. David's Purchase of the Site for the Temple (2 Sam 24:16-25; 1 Chron 21:15—22:1). Although David did not build the temple for Yahweh's name (presence), he prepared for it in every way: he purchased the land for its site (2 Sam 24:16-25; 1 Chron 21:15—22:1), provided many of the materials (1 Chron 22:2-4), encouraged his son Solomon about building the temple (1 Chron 22:5-19; 28:1-10), organized the Levites and priests for worship (1 Chron 23—24), and provided the plans for the design and building of the temple (1 Chron 28:11-21). The tradition linking David to the temple (Yahweh's presence in Zion/Jerusalem) grew from the account of temple preparations in Samuel and Kings to the greatly expanded account of temple preparations in Chronicles.

3.2.5. Solomon's Prayer. Solomon's actions took place after David's reign, but in light of the covenant with David that his son would build the temple and of the close connection in Chronicles' account between David and Solomon's building of the temple (1 Chron 13—29), they are appropriately treated as actions of David. Solomon's prayer and related actions at the dedication of the completed temple (1 Kings 8; 2 Chron 6—7) were central to the Zion traditions—prayers of repentance toward the temple (the place of Yahweh's presence in Zion/Jerusalem) would lead to forgiveness and deliverance. Zion/Jerusalem became the focus of hope on earth for Israel because it was the place where heaven touched earth, where Yahweh, who lived in heaven, also dwelt on earth (*see* Solomon's Temple).

Comparing Solomon's prayer in Kings (exilic) and Chronicles (postexilic) shows an increasing focus on Jerusalem's preeminence. Where 1 Kings 8:16 had "Since the day I brought my people Israel out of Egypt, I have not chosen a city in any tribe of Israel to have a temple built for my Name to be there, but I have chosen David to rule my people Israel," 2 Chronicles 6:5-6 inserted "nor have I chosen anyone to be the leader over my people Israel. But now I have chosen Jerusalem for my Name to be there" prior to "I have chosen David to rule my people Israel." The net effect was to put Jerusalem ahead of David. But Chronicles had not forgotten David, as is evidenced by the addition of a unique closing to the prayer in Chronicles: "Now arise, O LORD God, and come to your resting place, you and the ark of your might. May your priests, LORD God, be clothed with salvation, may your saints rejoice in your goodness. O LORD God, do not reject your anointed one. Remember the great love promised to David your servant" (2 Chron 6:41-42). In a postexilic context the implication of this additional closing text was twofold: first, Solomon's call for God to come to his resting place was transformed into a postexilic plea for Yahweh to return to the temple in Jerusalem; second, Solomon's reminder to God of his promise to David was recast as a postexilic plea to raise up a descendant of David to rule.

3.3. Significant Events and Developments after David.

3.3.1. Schism of the Kingdom (1 Kings 11— 2 Kings 17; 2 Chron 10—32). In the Historical Books David and the Zion traditions remained interconnected throughout the post-Davidic era. When Yahweh judged *Rehoboam and Solomon and formed the northern kingdom of Israel with ten tribes taken away from the descendants of David (1 Kings 11:11-36), he left one tribe to David's descendants for the sake of his covenant with David and with Jerusalem (1 Kings 11:11-13, 31-36).

In a political-religious move, *Jeroboam, the first king of the northern kingdom, made shrines in *Bethel and *Dan to prevent his sub-jects from returning to Jerusalem for worship (1 Kings 12:26-29). This became the defining sin of the northern kingdom. All the following kings in the north were judged for failing to remove those shrines and to return to worship at Jerusalem (e.g., 1 Kings 15:34). The southern kings, descendants of David, in Judah were judged according to several things, particularly whether or not they removed high places of worship and focused worship in Jerusalem (e.g., 1 Kings 22:42-43; 2 Kings 18:3-4). Universally, David's descendants reigned in Zion/Jerusalem and, according to their relative covenant faithfulness, were buried in the city of David or not.

3.3.2. Miraculous Deliverance from the Siege of Sennacherib (2 Kings 18:13—19:37; 2 Chron 32:1-23). The signal event in the period between the schism of the kingdoms and the exile of Israel was the miraculous deliverance of Zion/Jerusalem from the hand of the Assyrian king Sennacherib (2 Kings 18:13—19:37; 2 Chron 32:1-23) during Hezekiah's reign. This reinforced the popular belief that Zion/Jerusalem was inviolable because Yahweh's name dwelt there.

3.3.3. Hezekiah and Josiah: Reformer Kings. *Hezekiah (2 Kings 18—20; 2 Chron 29—32) and *Josiah (2 Kings 22:1—23:30; 2 Chron 34—35) were the two descendants of David who were noted for "walking in the ways of David." They carried out reforms that included a stress on worshiping in Zion/Jerusalem only, and their repentance and faithfulness to the Davidic covenant benefited Zion/Jerusalem by delaying Yahweh's judgment.

3.3.4. Exile. In spite of Zion/Jerusalem's apparent invincibility that stemmed from Yahweh's presence there, Zion/Jerusalem fell to the Babylonians because of the covenant disobedience of its inhabitants. The books of Kings, written during the exile, recounted Zion/Jerusalem's final days in rapid-fire fashion, relying on earlier arguments about covenant unfaithfulness to explain this disaster (2 Kings 24). The books of Chronicles, written after the exile, saw the exile in a more positive light—the land enjoyed its neglected sabbath rests (2 Chron 36:21)—and ended on the note of hope generated by Cyrus's decree to rebuild Jerusalem, thus demonstrating once again Yahweh's ultimate kingship and covenant faithfulness.

3.3.5. Restoration of Jerusalem. Yahweh remained faithful to his promise to Zion/Jerusalem and to David and restored his people to

Jerusalem. The accounts of the restoration of Jerusalem and the temple in Ezra-Nehemiah demonstrated confidence in Yahweh's covenant faithfulness, shown in the rebuilding of Jerusalem and the temple (*see* Postexilic Temple).

4. Zion and the Future.
Against the backdrop of a hopeful, eschatological future as articulated in the prophetic and psalmic Zion traditions, the Historical Books of Ezra and Nehemiah gave a much more sober-minded picture of the future. There was no indication of Yahweh's glory (presence) having returned to the temple (Zion/Jerusalem), and there was virtually no mention of David and his descendants, nor a restoration of a Davidic descendant. There was still a concern about corruption (e.g., marriage to foreign wives [Ezra 9—10; Neh 9—10]; Tobiah [Neh 6:17-19; 13:4-5]), but there was a tacit hope in Yahweh's covenant faithfulness, shown in his restoration of the people along with the rebuilding of Jerusalem and the temple (Neh 9).

5. Conclusion.
Bound together with David and his descendants, Zion/Jerusalem in the Historical Books became a central focus of Israel's theological reflection. It emerged and overcame the established tradition of Deuteronomic theology, became dominant and persisted, even in the face of the catastrophe of the exile. The Zion traditions in the Historical Books represented the growing tradition and defense of Yahweh's universal rule in Zion through David and his descendants.

See also DAVID; DAVIDIC COVENANT; JERUSALEM; KINGS AND KINGSHIP; POSTEXILIC TEMPLE; SOLOMON'S TEMPLE.

BIBLIOGRAPHY. **J. H. Hayes,** "The Tradition of Zion's Inviolability," *JBL* 82 (1963) 419-26; **R. S. Hess and G. J. Wenham,** eds., *Zion, City of Our God* (Grand Rapids: Eerdmans, 1999); **L. J. Hoppe,** *The Holy City: Jerusalem in the Theology of the Old Testament* (Collegeville, MN: Liturgical Press, 2000); **G. N. Knoppers,** "'The City Yhwh Has Chosen': The Chronicler's Promotion of Jerusalem in Light of Recent Archaeology," in *Jerusalem in Bible and Archaeology: The First Temple Period,* ed. A. G. Vaughn and A. E. Killebrew (SBLSymS 18; Atlanta: Society of Biblical Literature, 2003) 307-26; **J. D. Levenson,** *Sinai and Zion: An Entry into the Jewish Bible* (San Francisco: HarperCollins, 1985); **J. G. McConville,** "Jerusalem in the Old Testament," in *Jerusalem Past and Present in the Purposes of God,* ed. P. W. Walker (Grand Rapids: Baker, 1994) 21-52; **S. L. McKenzie,** *Covenant* (St. Louis: Chalice Press, 2000); **T. N. D. Mettinger,** *In Search of God: The Meaning and Message of the Everlasting Names* (Philadelphia: Fortress, 1988); **B. C. Ollenberger,** *Zion the City of the Great King: A Theological Symbol of the Jerusalem Cult* (JSOTSup 41; Sheffield: Sheffield Academic Press, 1987); **J. J. M. Roberts,** "Davidic Origin of the Zion Tradition," *JBL* 92 (1973) 329-44; idem, "Solomon's Jerusalem and the Zion Tradition," in *Jerusalem in Bible and Archaeology: The First Temple Period,* ed. A. G. Vaughn and A. E. Killebrew (SBLSymS 18; Atlanta: Society of Biblical Literature, 2003) 163-70; **A. G. Vaughn and A. E. Killebrew,** eds., *Jerusalem in Bible and Archaeology: The First Temple Period* (SBLSymS 18; Atlanta: Society of Biblical Literature, 2003); **M. Weinfeld,** "Zion and Jerusalem as Religious and Political Capital: Ideology and Utopia," in *The Poet and the Historian: Essays in Literary and Historical Biblical Criticism,* ed. R. E. Friedman (HSS 26; Chico, CA: Scholars Press, 1983) 75-115.   J. A. Groves

Archaeological Periods

The following are generally recognized dates for archaeological periods pertaining to the ancient Near East, though variations will be found among articles within the *DOTHB*.

Neolithic	8500-4500 BCE
Chalcolithic	4500-3500 BCE
Early Bronze	3500-2250 BCE
Early Bronze I	3500-3100 BCE
Early Bronze II	3100-2650 BCE
Early Bronze III	2650-2250 BCE
Early Bronze IV/Middle Bronze	2250-1925 BCE
Middle Bronze II	1925-1550 BCE
Middle Bronze IIA	1925-1700 BCE
Middle Bronze IIB	1700-1600 BCE
Middle Bronze IIC	1600-1550 BCE
Late Bronze	1550-1200 BCE
Late Bronze I	1550-1400 BCE
Late Bronze IIA	1400-1300 BCE
Late Bronze IIB	1300-1200 BCE
Iron Age	1200-586 BCE
Iron I	1200-1000 BCE
Iron IIA	1000-900 BCE
Iron IIB	900-700 BCE
Iron IIC	700-586 BCE
Neo-Babylonian	586-539 BCE
Persian	539-332 BCE
Hellenistic	332-53 BCE

Palestine

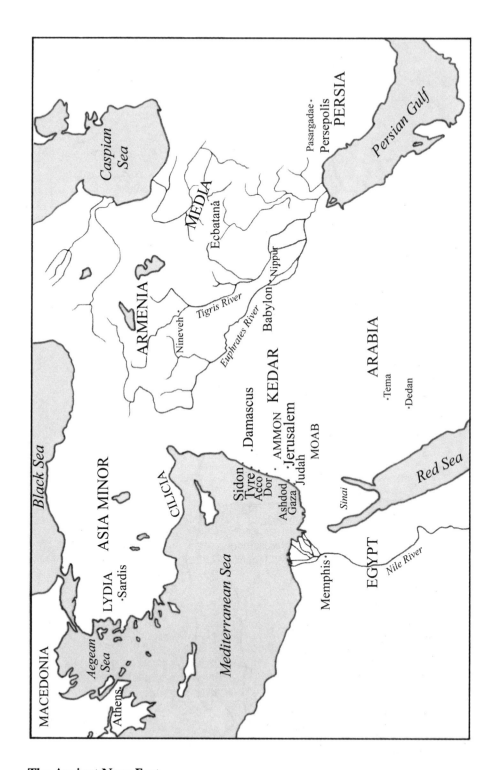

The Ancient Near East

154-56, 159, 161, 164, 167, 171-74, 176, 179, 181, 183-84, 188, 194, 197-218, 222-25, 228-30, 232-33, 238, 242, 245, 247, 260, 262-65, 267, 270-71, 273-74, 287, 289, 297-302, 304, 306-8, 312, 314, 320-22, 324, 331-35, 337, 340-48, 350-59, 367-68, 384, 387-88, 390-93, 395-96, 403, 408-9, 415, 423-24, 442-57, 475, 488, 499-501, 503, 507, 509-10, 512-14, 516, 518-19, 523-24, 531, 533-35, 539, 543, 545-47, 549-56, 561, 570, 575-77, 579, 590-91, 602, 606-7, 612-14, 618-23, 625-27, 629-31, 633, 640, 644-46, 648-53, 655-57, 660-63, 665, 667, 669, 672-73, 679-82, 686, 692-94, 699, 704-7, 709-13, 715-18, 744, 746, 749, 751, 753, 756-57, 759, 762, 764, 784, 789, 794-95, 799-802, 805, 807, 812-14, 817, 819, 822-27, 838-40, 844-54, 863, 865-77, 880-83, 886, 896-98, 901, 903-5, 914-16, 922-29, 934-35, 937, 940-41, 943-46, 952, 959, 961, 965-66, 972-77, 979, 981-82, 984-88, 990, 992-95, 997-98, 1000-1001, 1003-4, 1012-16, 1019-25

Davidic Covenant, 35, 159, 205-9, 352, 355, 503, 620, 628, 716, 869, 1021

Davidic dynasty, 36, 202, 207-11, 270, 392, 423-24, 452, 455, 504, 532, 535, 551, 619, 628, 716, 802, 821, 823, 874, 917, 921, 1014

Dead Sea Scrolls, 144-45, 150, 286, 355, 371, 574, 955-58, 960

death, 6, 13, 35, 44-45, 94-95, 99-101, 111, 127-28, 130-31, 139, 143, 152, 164, 177, 181, 183-85, 187, 200-202, 204, 210, 215-18, 225, 238, 241, 243, 247, 250-51, 254, 256-57, 272-73, 286, 293, 299-300, 307, 320-21, 323-25, 331, 335, 346, 352, 354, 364, 373, 391-92, 408, 410, 421, 424, 435-36, 442, 444, 450, 452, 454, 461, 464, 467, 471, 473-74, 476, 479-80, 505, 513, 518, 524, 539-40, 545-46, 553, 557, 559-61, 565, 568-69, 576-79, 583, 585-86, 592, 594-96, 598, 600, 602, 627, 644, 647, 654, 656, 670-71, 674-76, 685, 698, 706-7, 711-12, 717, 733, 744-45, 747, 749, 755, 757-61, 770, 775-76, 783-84, 787-88, 795, 799, 822, 826, 839, 845-47, 849, 851, 853-54, 863, 866, 869-70, 880-81, 883, 893, 895-98, 902-3, 905, 914, 918, 921, 923, 929, 937, 961, 972-74, 977-78, 986, 991-92, 994-96, 1003, 1014-15

Debir, 120-22, 190, 247, 336, 399, 654, 843-44, 911, 969, 972

Deborah, 27, 29-30, 34, 116, 182, 319, 347, 360, 421, 435-36, 580-86, 589-92, 595, 598-601, 649, 691, 799-800, 826, 913, 917, 990

Decalog, 89, 263-64, 351, 648, 766, 1000

deconstruction, 399-400, 625, 691, 903

Dedan, 36, 38-39, 292, 312

Deir 'Alla, 73, 340, 440, 1006

deliverance, 127, 273, 298, 304, 320, 323-24, 338, 346, 370, 410, 412, 421, 510, 512, 518, 537, 582-83, 585-87, 591, 594, 596-97, 600, 624, 627-30, 686, 711, 745, 851-54, 868, 919, 972, 977, 979, 1021, 1024

Deuteronomistic History, 88, 90-91, 146, 159-60, 162, 164, 171-72, 176, 218-29, 250, 253-55, 258, 266, 271, 300, 337, 384, 392-98, 403, 406-9, 413, 417, 425, 443, 446, 453, 458, 473, 476-77, 489, 502, 505-7, 516-17, 519-20, 544, 547-48, 562, 568, 574-79, 591, 594, 596, 605-6, 615, 618-19, 623-24, 629, 633-34, 639, 642-43, 645, 650, 674, 676, 685-87, 692, 715-17, 765, 767, 809-10, 822-24, 828, 858, 861, 866, 870, 877, 880, 900, 902, 916, 929, 968, 972, 979, 998, 1022

Dhiban, 74, 1006

Diaspora, 290, 295, 485-86, 490-91, 497, 527, 555, 805

Dibon, 585, 744, 843

diseases, 2, 257, 545, 670-71, 688, 700, 895-99

divided monarchy, 39, 43, 72, 155, 202, 221, 253, 441, 456, 534, 613, 648, 657, 707, 921, 947

divination, 103, 128-29, 137-38, 218, 648, 670-73, 726, 820, 896, 898, 900

divine kingship, 142, 351, 611, 616, 618

division of the monarchy, 755, 757, 947

divorce, 646, 735, 878-79, 920

dogs, 15-16, 78, 96, 120, 356, 374, 423, 537, 939

donkeys, 3, 8-9, 11-13, 15, 182, 291, 383, 422, 584, 587, 672, 725, 841, 852, 965, 990

Dor, 76-78, 93, 150-51, 189, 286, 336, 654, 721, 747, 796, 814, 861, 923

dynasty, 35, 43, 47, 99-100, 106-9, 111, 139, 173, 198, 203-4, 207-10, 249, 251, 256, 304, 308, 310, 322-23, 353-54, 364, 423, 450, 455, 465-66, 490, 503, 532, 534-37, 545-46, 553, 557-59, 588, 602-3, 611-13, 621, 628, 632, 644, 649, 707, 716, 732, 740, 746, 755-59, 761-63, 768, 775, 823, 826, 840, 846, 860, 865, 867, 869, 873, 925, 1014, 1019-20, 1022-23

Early Bronze Age, 4, 8, 22, 40, 80, 82, 95, 127, 189, 198, 333, 361, 390, 678, 856, 961

Ebla, 13, 126-27, 380, 843, 932

Ecbatana, 488, 720, 768-71

Eden, 639, 688, 709, 774, 902, 929, 934-35

Edom, Edomites, 2, 11, 19, 36, 39-41, 65, 69, 73-74, 87, 94, 120, 123-24, 156, 183, 201, 204-5, 231-36, 242, 268-69, 275-76, 285,

291, 308, 320-21, 323-24, 326, 339, 373, 380-81, 392, 440-41, 448, 454, 463-64, 466, 470-71, 481, 532-33, 545, 571, 612, 639, 651, 713, 721, 743, 753, 797, 842-43, 845, 851, 854, 859, 884, 923-24, 926-27, 943, 945, 949, 965, 973, 984, 1014

Eglon, 24, 145, 182, 435, 543, 585, 601, 706, 843-44, 967

Egypt, Egyptians, 19, 23-24, 28, 34, 39, 41, 52-54, 56, 60, 64-65, 67, 69-70, 72-73, 93, 95-96, 98-102, 111-13, 121, 123, 125, 129, 141, 165, 178, 181-85, 187-88, 190, 192-93, 205, 231-33, 235-46, 248, 260, 268-69, 275-76, 282, 285-86, 289-92, 297, 299-300, 306, 308-9, 316, 318-19, 321-22, 325-28, 335, 338-39, 345-47, 349-51, 353, 360-61, 373, 386-89, 391, 406, 418-19, 421, 425, 427-31, 433-34, 437, 440, 443, 445-48, 450-51, 453-54, 457, 459, 463, 467, 469-82, 484, 487, 490-91, 493, 507, 511, 515, 518-20, 539, 545-46, 549, 553, 575, 577-79, 610-12, 614-15, 618, 629, 632-33, 636, 646, 652, 673-74, 677-78, 687-88, 704, 708-9, 711-12, 719-21, 727, 735-41, 743, 748-49, 754, 768-74, 776-77, 781-82, 786-88, 794-96, 798, 800, 820-21, 839-40, 842-43, 852, 858, 882, 884-86, 888, 890, 899, 903, 911-12, 917-19, 923-26, 942, 947, 949, 952-53, 955-56, 963-965, 973, 985, 1004-5, 1007-10, 1024

Ehud, 24, 145, 182, 421, 426, 435, 580-85, 589-92, 595, 598-601, 706, 713, 854

Ekron, 16, 70-72, 76, 94-96, 101, 188-89, 203, 245-48, 250-51, 305-6, 308-9, 319, 339, 426, 432, 439, 471-73, 480, 746, 748, 782, 784-85, 787-92, 844, 858, 882, 898, 969, 1006-7

El, 9, 18, 22, 75, 118, 126-30, 133-36, 138-40, 142, 243, 339-43, 390-91, 456, 612, 664, 687-88, 748, 845, 891-92, 926

Elah, 93, 121, 186, 247-48, 251, 305-6, 463, 534, 614, 755-56, 758, 790, 844, 859-60, 882, 961, 973

Elam, Elamites, 97-98, 289, 486, 493-96, 720, 735, 738-42, 769, 776-77, 780, 1004

Elath, 232, 235, 274-76, 324, 533, 843

Elephantine, 53, 141, 278, 285, 287, 291, 326, 342, 490-92, 494, 528, 735-40, 778, 878-79, 1004, 1007, 1010

Elephantine papyri, 278, 287, 492, 494, 878-79

Elhanan, 356-57, 784, 882, 959

Eli, 91, 94, 182, 216, 263, 265, 299, 436, 446, 455, 580, 590-91, 621, 665, 698, 747, 826, 863-67, 893, 896, 901, 903, 945, 992, 1000, 1012-13

Eliashib Archive, 372

Elijah, 5-7, 34, 114, 139-40, 146, 151-53, 217, 247-58, 260, 300,

322, 335-37, 346, 348, 355, 423, 462, 516, 518, 535, 537-38, 543, 562, 576, 623-24, 626-27, 629-31, 641, 645, 657, 671-73, 697-701, 717, 744, 758-60, 762, 797, 825-28, 843, 858, 860, 897-99, 901, 904, 916, 965-66, 973, 996, 1002, 1004

Elisha, 5-6, 15-16, 34, 46, 52, 116, 152, 217, 249-58, 303, 322-23, 335-36, 346, 348, 355, 423, 462, 464-65, 532, 535-38, 543, 562, 623, 626-27, 629-30, 671-73, 695-99, 701, 744, 758, 761, 763, 825, 827-28, 843, 858, 897, 973, 977, 979, 996

Elohim, 168, 330, 376

Elon, 182, 421, 435-37, 580, 582-84, 588, 590, 601

Elyon, 129-30, 340, 342, 355, 612, 748

Emar, 127, 219, 825, 885, 888, 932, 951-52

emic, 268-69, 910, 920

empty land, 75, 285, 483

En-Gedi, 75-76, 845

Enlil, 99, 108-9

Enuma Elish, 109, 112-13, 130, 686

Ephraim, Ephraimites, 26, 64, 70, 87, 114, 117-18, 173, 182, 208, 269, 271, 276, 311-12, 316, 323-24, 330, 383, 427, 436-37, 439, 441, 454, 456, 468, 477-78, 516, 541, 544, 560, 584-85, 587-88, 601, 654-56, 751, 756, 787, 792, 857-61, 863, 878, 882, 917, 967-69, 1005

Esarhaddon, 25, 101-2, 105, 111, 233, 248, 285, 309, 325, 473, 488, 535, 615, 674, 732, 796, 819-22, 824, 861

Esdras, 59, 145, 147, 158, 161, 277-78, 284, 288, 292-93, 295, 488, 575, 718, 862, 958, 960, 1019

Eshnunna, 107

Esther, 19, 142, 164, 179, 185, 187, 283, 286, 294, 337, 384, 418, 486, 490-92, 494, 593, 647, 650, 683, 708, 711-12, 720, 769, 777, 807, 886, 919, 936, 960, 965-66, 1003-4, 1008

ethics, 249, 259-67, 274, 616, 684, 690, 693, 778, 900, 905, 977, 986-88

ethnicity, 63-65, 73, 112, 268-71, 390, 432, 438, 514

ethnoarchaeology, 910-11

ethnography, 498, 907

etic, 268-69, 910, 920

etiologies, 22, 116, 155, 403, 420-21, 570, 646, 705, 764

Euphrates River, 36, 38, 42-44, 48, 51, 53, 97, 99-100, 107, 110, 123, 184, 244-45, 309, 316-17, 321, 326, 465, 479-81, 484, 611, 651, 720-22, 770, 825, 885, 924

evil, 8, 56, 58, 104, 109, 171, 182, 207, 252, 272-74, 283, 293, 347, 351, 367, 371, 424, 435, 468, 473-74, 534, 537, 539, 543, 546, 582, 590, 594-95, 600, 602-4, 629, 663, 667, 711, 713, 758, 823, 858, 866, 868, 896-97, 900-905, 914, 927,

Articles
Index